REA's Books Are The B[...]

(a sample of the <u>hundreds of letters</u> REA receives e[...])

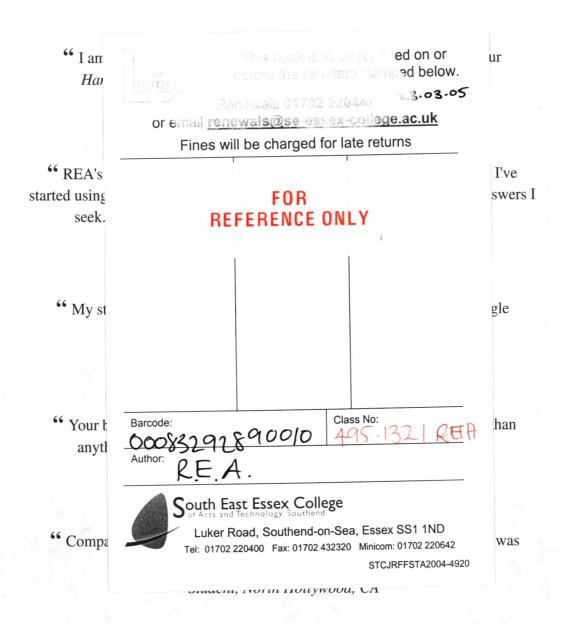

" I am [...] ur Han[...]

" REA's [...] I've started using [...] swers I seek.

" My st[...] gle

" Your b[...] han anyth[...]

" Compa[...] was

Student, North Hollywood, CA

" Your book was responsible for my success on the exam, which helped me get into the college of my choice... I will look for REA the next time I need help. "

Student, Chesterfield, MO

(continued from front page)

" Just a short note to say thanks for the great support your book gave me in helping me pass the test... I'm on my way to a B.S. degree because of you! "
Student, Orlando, FL

" I just wanted to thank you for helping me get a great score on the AP U.S. History exam... Thank you for making great test preps! "
Student, Los Angeles, CA

" Your *Fundamentals of Engineering Exam* book was the absolute best preparation I could have had for the exam, and it is one of the major reasons I did so well and passed the FE on my first try. "
Student, Sweetwater, TN

" I used your book to prepare for the test and found that the advice and the sample tests were highly relevant... Without using any other material, I earned very high scores and will be going to the graduate school of my choice. "
Student, New Orleans, LA

" What I found in your book was a wealth of information sufficient to shore up my basic skills in math and verbal... The section on analytical ability was excellent. The practice tests were challenging and the answer explanations most helpful. It certainly is the *Best Test Prep for the GRE*! "
Student, Pullman, WA

" I really appreciate the help from your excellent book. Please keep up the great work. "

(more on previous page)

Research & Education Association

CHINESE DICTIONARY

Words, Phrases & Expressions

CHINESE   ENGLISH
ENGLISH   CHINESE

**Staff of Research & Education Association,
Carl Fuchs, Language Program Director**

 这本書很好

Research & Education Association
Dr. M. Fogiel, Director
61 Ethel Road West
Piscataway, New Jersey 08854

REA'S CHINESE DICTIONARY
WORDS, PHRASES & EXPRESSIONS

Printed in the United States of America

Library of Congress Control Number 2002114235

International Standard Book Number 0-87891-454-4

Research & Education Association
61 Ethel Road West
Piscataway, New Jersey 08854

CONTENTS

Gazebo, Huaching Hot Springs

Romanization Systems:

Pinyin, Wade-Giles, Yale

The following charts provide a comparison of only the most basic structural elements of three major romanization systems and are intended to assist students in dealing with a wider range of published materials on China and Chinese. They do not, therefore, include detailed explications of the orthography of each system. Keep in mind that all are attempts to fit Chinese sounds into a Western alphabet and thus are approximations. See the "Sounds" section in this book's Introduction for advice on proper pronunciation.

A Note on the Systems

Pinyin, dating from the mid-20th century, is based on a Russian transliteration system and on the conventional method of transliterating Russian. Hence, the existence of such graphs as "x" which is actually the Cyrillic letter used for the palatal spirant involved. "C," in Slavic languages that use the Latin alphabet, represents "ts." The use of the voiced consonant graphs for unaspirated consonants also corresponds to the Russian usage.

Wade-Giles, the oldest of the systems (introduced in 1859), has undergone several modifications in its long history. Some of its seeming peculiarities reflect the fact that it was originally intended to provide a bridge between various versions of Mandarin. It is, however, linguistically more accurate than either pinyin or Yale in using only the graphs for unvoiced consonants (Mandarin has only five voiced consonants: m, l, n, r, ng) and indicating aspiration by means of an apostrophe. Tones in Wade-Giles are represented by superscript numbers. This system is not nearly as common as it once was, but is still found in many books.

Yale is strictly a pedagogical system. However, having been designed specifically for American English speakers (Yale University created it for military pilots), it is the most intuitive system for those used to American pronunciation. It is actually linguistically more logical than pinyin. Incidentally, it is the Western system most widely used in the Republic of China (Taiwan) for teaching Chinese to foreigners. Yale is the system used in this book.

Initial Consonants

Pinyin	Labial	Labio-Dental	Dental	Alveolar	Palatal	Post-velar
Stops	b p		d t			g k
Spirants		f	s	sh	x	h
Affricates			c z	zh ch	j q	
Laterals			l	r	l[1]	
Nasals	m		n		n[1]	ng

[1]Always followed by *i* or *u*

W-G	Labial	Labio-Dental	Dental	Alveolar	Palatal	Post-velar
Stops	p p'		t t'			k k'
Spirants		f	s	sh	hs	h
Affricates			ts ts'	ch ch'	ch[1] ch'[1]	
Laterals			l	j	l	
Nasals	m		n		n	ng

[1]Always followed by *i* or *u*

Yale	Labial	Labio-Dental	Dental	Alveolar	Palatal	Post-velar
Stops	b p		d t			g k
Spirants		f	s	sh	sy	h
Affricates			ts dz	j ch	j[1] ch[1]	
Laterals			l	r	l[1]	
Nasals	m		n		n[1]	ng

[1]Always followed by *y* or *i*

Vocalic Consonants

Pinyin	Wade-Giles	Yale
zi	tzu	dz
ci	tz'u	ts
si	szu/ssu	sz
shi	shih	shr
zhi	chih	jr
chi	ch'ih	chr
ri	jih	r

The Finals

Pinyin	W—G	Yale
a	a	a
o	o	o
e	eh (after *y*/*i*) o (elsewhere)	e
ai	ai	ai
ei	ei	ei
ao	ao	au
ou	ou	ou
an	an	an
en	en	en
ang	ang	ang
ong	ung	ung
r	erh	r
yi[1]	i	yi
y[2]	y	y
you/iu[3]	yu/iu	you
yan/ian[3]	yen/ien	yan
w/u[3]	w/u[3]	w

[1]When a complete word.
[2]at the beginning of a syllable.
[3]At the beginning of a syllable and after an initial consonant respectively.

Archway with Great Wall, Badali

PART I

INTRODUCTION

A. GENERAL

This dictionary of the Chinese National Language (gwó-'ywǔ) is designed primarily for the use of speakers of English who have acquired some familiarity with spoken Chinese but who are not yet completely fluent in that language, and especially for those in that category who are in contact with native speakers of Chinese. At about this point the learner is able to paraphrase many things which he cannot yet express precisely as a native speaker would; but by directing such paraphrases towards a native speaker he can often elicit the normal Chinese expression, and thereby add it to his vocabulary. However, in this process there are difficulties and pitfalls; sometimes it is difficult to achieve understanding through paraphrase, and sometimes one thinks that understanding has been achieved when actually the information acquired is not the information wanted. It is as an aid in avoiding such pitfalls and difficulties that the present work should have its best use.

Although this dictionary is fairly large, there are relatively few lexical items treated in it: about 2,500 on the English-Chinese side, and about twice that number on the other side. The treatment accorded these items, however, is often fairly exhaustive. It is not possible, in the correlation of English and Chinese, to be both concise and accurate. For example, the English word "break" can be, and is, used in a large variety of situations; in Chinese one has to take account of a great many details in each particular situation in order to use the Chinese expression that a native speaker would use. Thus, "to break" as of a long slender brittle thing is one term, "to break" as of a box or other hollow object is another, "to break" as of a pane of glass is another; "to break" simply into two or a small number of fragments is one, "to break" into tiny pieces is another; "to break" something in any one of these ways by striking it calls for a special expression, "to break" something by dropping it calls for another; and so on. To list the English word "break" and give as its equivalent any *one* of these Chinese expressions, or even any relatively small handful of them, would be like equating

English "thing" and the Chinese word which means "box"; a box is a thing, but so are a large number of entities which are not boxes.

As a result, consulting this work will generally call for a certain amount of diligence and study; this requirement will be greater for initial consultations than for subsequent ones, when the pattern has been learned. In the process of finding out about some single item, it will often happen that other information is picked up incidentally. The acceptance of such incidentally acquired information will aid in achieving the goal: fluency in the language.

Since the number of English words treated is so small, it will often happen that a particular word is not found. If the word not found is the name of a concrete object, then eliciting the desired information directly from a native speaker is relatively easy. Otherwise, there are usually alternative ways of expressing the idea in English, and one or more of these alternative ways should be looked for.

In general, simple colloquial ways of saying things should be searched for rather than rare or literary ways. Thus, look for "worn out" or "worn down" rather than "dilapidated"; for "house" or "home" rather than "residence"; "die" rather than "decease"; "cooking" rather than "cuisine"; and so on.

Do not expect Chinese words ever to have quite the same ranges of meaning as English words. The case of "break", cited above, is extreme; but there is almost always some difference. "Accident" is a noun in English; Chinese sentences about the same thing use a verbal expression. There is no word at all equivalent to our "berry"; the Chinese have terms for specific berries, a general word for "fruit", and an even more general word for "fruits-and-nuts", but no term which covers just berries and nothing else. Such differences run all through the vocabulary. As much as possible, learn in terms of the ranges of meaning of *Chinese* words without worrying about what the English equivalents would be—do this even when consulting the English-Chinese side. As much as possible, learn words in terms of the sample sentences given on both sides, or in simple cases make up sentences for yourself; for anything less than a sentence is an artificial, though convenient, abstraction from what is involved when we speak.

The remainder of this introduction is an integral part of the dictionary, and should be consulted whenever necessary. The writing system used throughout the dictionary is explained in Section B; certain regional variations in pronunciation to which the user may have to accustom his ear are mentioned in Section C; important changes of sound are dealt with in Section D; the structure of Chinese sentences is treated in Section E, which also serves as an essential aid in understanding entries on the Chinese-English side; characters are dealt with briefly in Section F.

B. SOUNDS

1. Symbols Used

In this dictionary the sounds of Chinese are written with the following letters and other symbols:

Representing *consonant sounds:* b ch d dz f g h j k l m n ng p r sh t ts w y yw.

Representing *vowel sounds:* a e o i u r z.

Representing *tones:* accent marks put over a letter, as follows: first tone ā, second tone á, third tone ǎ, fourth tone à.

Representing *stress* (or *loudness* or *prominence*): a raised tick (') placed before a syllable.

Representing *point of syllable division:* a hyphen (-) or a space between syllables.

Commas (,), periods (.), question marks (?), and exclamation marks (!) are used as in English.

No capital letters are used.

In the interest of economy, some of the above letters or groups of letters, or other symbols, are used to represent more than one sound, but only when (1) the sounds are similar and (2) they occur only in mutually exclusive environments, so that the conditions under which a single symbol represents one or another sound can be clearly defined.

The system used here is only one of many possible choices, and is not necessarily the best for all purposes; but as a help in learning Chinese it has proved somewhat more effective than the Wade-Giles system, heretofore very widely in use. Because of the widespread use of the latter system, each syllable which differs in Wade-Giles transcription from the present system is listed in proper alphabetical order in the Chinese-English side of the dictionary with a cross reference to the equivalent transcription in the present system.

2. Consonants at the Beginning of a Syllable

In the following, the first column lists a symbol, the second column the conditions under which that symbol represents the sound described in the third column, and the fourth column gives examples. The order is as follows: f l m n r s w y p t k b d g ts dz ch j sh h ng yw; this order is used because it puts the most familiar sounds first and groups together those which represent similar difficulties.

Symbol	Conditions	Description	Examples
f	everywhere.	as in English *fan.*	fàn "food".
l	everywhere.	as in English *law.*	lā "to pull".
m	everywhere.	as in English *man.*	màn "slow".
n	everywhere.	as in English *Nan.*	nán "difficult".
r	everywhere.	as in English *run.*	rén "person".

(There is some variation in the pronunciation of this sound among Chinese; but any variety of English initial r except a Scotch "burr" or "trill" sounds perfectly acceptable to Chinese ears.)

s	everywhere.	as in English *sand.*	sān "three".
w	everywhere.	as in English *way.*	wèy "because of".
y	everywhere.	as in English *yeah.*	yě "also".

(But note that yw is treated as a special symbol.)

p	everywhere.	as in English *pin,* but with a stronger puff of breath.	pàw "cannon".

2

B. SOUNDS

Symbol	Conditions	Description	Examples
t	everywhere.	as in English *tin*, but with a stronger puff of breath.	tàw "suit of".
k	everywhere.	as in English *kin*, but with a stronger puff of breath.	kàw "to rely on"

(The puff of breath or "aspiration" which follows the first consonant of the English words *pin*, *tin*, *kin*, can be tested by holding a small slip of very light-weight paper before the lips as the words are spoken. The paper will flutter slightly just as the first consonant ends. For the Chinese sounds written with the same letters, the paper should flutter considerably more.)

Symbol	Conditions	Description	Examples
b	everywhere.	as in English *bin*, but without voicing; or as English *p* in *pin*, but without any puff of breath.	bàw "newspaper".
d	everywhere.	as in English *din*, but without voicing; or as English *t* in *tin*, but without any puff of breath.	dàw "to".
g	everywhere.	as in English *get*, but without voicing; or as English *k* in *kin*, but without any puff of breath.	gàw "report".

(There are three ways to acquire these sounds: (1) Practice with the slip of paper as suggested above, and try to say the words so that the paper does not flutter at all. (2) Hold your hands over your ears and say the words *bin, din, get;* you will hear a buzz that begins with the initial consonant and continues throughout in the case of *bin* and *din*, until the final *-t* in the case of *get*. Then try to say the words so that the buzz does not begin until *after* the initial consonant. (3) Say the words *spin, stick, skin,* with the slip of paper, and notice that it does not flutter. Take the initial *s-* away and try to say the *p, t,* and *k* in just the same way, without causing the paper to flutter.)

Symbol	Conditions	Description	Examples
ts	everywhere.	like the *ts h* of English *it's hot* with the initial *i* left off.	tsăw "grass".
dz	everywhere	like the *ts* of English *hats off* with the initial *ha* left off.	dzăw "early".

(Pretend you're a phonograph record, with the expressions *it's hot* and *hats off* recorded on it; put the needle down just past the place where the *i* of *it's hot* or the *ha* of *hat's off* is recorded. The difference between ts and dz is comparable to the difference between p and b, t and d, or k and g as described earlier.)

Symbol	Conditions	Description	Examples
ch	(1) before i, y, or yw.	much as in English *cheat*, but with the tip of the tongue held down behind the lower front teeth.	chì "air". chyán "money".
	(2) elsewhere.	a cross between *true* and *choose*—as though we said *chrue* instead of *true*.	chū "exit". chá "tea".
j	(1) before i, y, or yw.	like Chinese ch in the same conditions, except with no puff of breath.	jì "remember". jyāw "teach".
	(2) elsewhere.	like Chinese ch in the same conditions, except with no puff of breath.	jū "pig" já "brake".

(The most important thing in pronouncing correctly ch and j *not* before i, y, or yw, is to draw the tip of the tongue back and up to the roof of the mouth; avoid scrupulously making a sound like the English *ch* in *chase* or *chair*, or *j* in *jack* or *jump*, which are made with the tongue much farther forward in the mouth.)

3

Symbol	Conditions	Description	Examples
sh	(1) before i, y, or yw.	much as in English *sheet*, but with the tip of the tongue held down behind the lower front teeth.	shī "west". shyǎw "small".
	(2) elsewhere.	a cross between the *sh* of *shoe* and the *shr* of *shrew*, with the tongue drawn well back and up.	shū "book". shǎw "few".
h	everywhere.	either like the English *h* in *hand* or with friction at the back of the mouth, as in German *ach*.	hǎw "OK". hú "lake".

(Most speakers of Chinese vary between these two; either is acceptable, but to use always the English *h* sound may make your pronunciation occasionally unpleasant to Chinese ears.)

ng	everywhere (occurs only when the preceding syllable ends in *ng*).	like the *ng* of *singer* (*not* like the *ng* of *finger*!)	bù-'shíng-nga! "It won't do!"

(Be particularly careful with this sound if you find that you pronounce the English words *singer* and *finger* alike; in this case you may have the right sound in both words, or the wrong sound in both.)

yw	everywhere.	the sounds of *y* as in *yes* and *w* as in *won't* pronounced at the same time.	ywè "month".

(The tongue is in the position for *y*, but the lips are rounded as for *w*. Sometimes the *y*-part of the sound starts just slightly before the lips are rounded, but often the two are simultaneous.)

3. Groups of Consonants at the Beginning of a Syllable

Groups of consonants at the beginning of a syllable consist of one of the consonants described above other than y, w, or yw, followed by y, w, or yw. Each consonant of the group then represents the same sound that it stands for when not in such a group. Examples: fwó "Buddha"; lyǎn "face"; myàn "surface"; nwǎn "warm"; swàn "calculate"; pwò "to break"; tyān "day"; dwèn "pause"; chyán "money"; chwán "boat"; chywán "all"; shywé "to learn".

4. Consonants at the End of a Syllable

The following consonants and groups of consonants occur at the ends of syllables: m, n, ng, r, w, y, wr, ngr.

m	everywhere.	like English *m* in *ham*.	wǒm "we". nǐm "you". tām "they".
n	(1) except as mentioned under (2).	like English *n* in *can*.	wén "smell". tán "converse".
	(2) when the next syllable begins with y.	the tongue does not quite reach the roof of the mouth, and the preceding vowel is slightly nasalized.	'tán-yi-tán "converse a bit".

4

Symbol	Conditions	Description	Examples
ng	everywhere.	like English *ng* in *sing* or *singer* (*not* like the *ng* in *finger*!)	táng "candy, sugar". háng "trade". húng "red".

(As with ng at the beginning of a syllable, be particularly careful if you find that you pronounce the *ng* of *singer* and *finger* alike, because in that case the one sound you use may be right or it may be wrong.)

r	everywhere.	like the *r* in *bar, fur*.	wár "to play". fèr "portion of".

(In many varieties of English, *r*'s after a vowel are not pronounced. Whatever variety of English you speak, be sure to pronounce the r in Chinese; but don't trill or roll it; make an English *r*-sound, not a French or German *r*-sound.)

w	everywhere.	like English *w* in *how, wow, know.*	năw "brains". gĕw "dog".

(In English writing *aw* is used not for an *a*-sound followed by the *w* -sound—except in the speech of some people from the southern part of the United States. But Chinese aw consists of a as described in subsection 5 below followed by w as described here.)

y	everywhere.	like English *y* in *they*.	năy "milk". gĕy "give".

(Similarly, English *ay* doesn't stand for an *a*-sound plus the *y*-sound, but Chinese ay has the Chinese a as described in subsection 5 followed by y as described here.)

wr	everywhere.	w and r as described above, but sometimes pronounced at the same time instead of one after the other, or sometimes with the r-sound first.	gĕwr "small dog".

(Producing both sounds at once is possible, since the w consists of rounding the lips, r consists of curling the tongue back—different parts of the speech apparatus are used.)

ngr	everywhere.	the back of the tongue does not reach the roof of the mouth for the ng; the vowel is strongly nasalized; r as described above.	héngr "horizontal stroke".

5. Vowels

The vowels (and two vowel groups) are a, e, o, ee, oe, i, u, r, z. Only a and e begin a syllable; the others always have a consonant before them. a is made with the lower jaw well down and the mouth wide open; e, ee, o, and oe are made with the lower jaw partly down and the mouth partly open; i, u, r, and z are made with the lower jaw not down at all, and the lips close together.

a	(1) except as detailed below.	like the English *a* of *father* or *ma.*	mă "horse". hăw "OK". hăy "seas".
	(2) between y and n.	like the English *a* of *hand*.	yān "smoke". dyàn "electricity".
	(3) between yw and n.	like the English *a* of *bat*, but variable; some speakers make it like (1), some like (2).	ywàn "court". chywán "altogether".
	(4) between w and ng.	like (1) or like the English *o* of *long*.	hwăng "nervous".

5

Symbol	Conditions	Description	Examples
e	(1) except as specified below.	about like English *u* in *but* or *huh*.	hē "to drink". chē "cart". hĕn "very".

(When final in the syllable, this sound often begins with the back of the tongue drawn back and up towards the roof of the mouth, like the *oo* of *book* without the lips rounded; but it then glides from this to the sound described above.)

	(2) after **y** or **yw**, final in the syllable.	like the English *e* of *met* or *eah* or *yeah*.	yĕ "also". ywè "month".
	(3) between **w** and **y** or vice versa; or between **w** and **n**.	very short, and often nearer the *oo* of *book* or the *i* of *pick*, depending on whether it is followed by **w** or by **y**.	dwèy "right". dyēw "lose". dwèn "pause". wèy "because of". yèw "again".
	(4) before **w** and not after **y**.	as in (1) or a bit farther back.	gĕw "dog".
ee	everywhere.	the first **e** is as above, depending on the preceding sound; the second as (1) above.	héer "box".
o	everywhere.	about like the English *aw* of *law*.	wŏ "I". wŏm "we".
oe	everywhere.	o gliding into the first variety of e described above.	wōer "nest".
i	(1) final in the syllable.	like the English *ee* of *see*.	mǐ "rice grain".
	(2) not final in the syllable.	like the English *i* of *pin*.	mín "people".

(Consonants before **i** are often pronounced with a little y-glide after them, as though one said **myín** instead of **mín**.)

u	(1) final and not after **yw**.	like the English *oo* of *moon*.	wŭ "five". shū "book".
	(2) followed by a consonant and not after **yw**.	like the English *oo* of *book*.	húng "red".
	(3) after **yw**.	like the *oo* of *moon* and the *ee* of *see* pronounced simultaneously.	ywŭ "rain". ywùn "to ship".

(The tongue is in the *ee*-position, and the lips are rounded as for *oo*. This is the same position as described already for the consonant sound written **yw**.)

z	everywhere.	like the *oo* of *look* pronounced without rounding the lips; the throat is tense and the back of the tongue is held down tightly.	dż "word". tsż "jab". sż "four".

(This sound occurs only after the consonants **dz**, **ts**, and **s**. With the consonant **dz** and the vowel *z*, only one *z* is written.)

r	everywhere.	like the middle-western American English *ir* of *shirt* or *ur* of *hurt, fur*.	r̀ "sun". chr̄ "to eat". jŕ "straight". shr̀ "is".

(This sound occurs only after the consonants **r**, **ch**, **j**, and **sh**. With the consonant **r** and the vowel *r*, only one *r* is written.)

6. Tones

A syllable uttered in isolation has one of four tonal contours or *tones*. In longer expressions, the individual syllables may have one of a larger number of contours, all related to that one of just four which the same syllable has in isolation; or they may have no definite tonal contour at all. These last are called *toneless* syllables, and are written without any tone mark.

The distinctiveness of the tonal contours described below depends on the loudness or prominence of the syllable in question: more distinct when louder, less distinct when softer.

Symbol	Conditions	Description	Examples
⁻(ā)	everywhere.	high, level, sometimes cut off sharply at the end.	gāw "high". tsā "to scrape".
´(á)	everywhere.	relatively high, rising, with increasing loudness; often cut off sharply at end.	rén "person". báw "thin". ná "take". tsúng "from".
(ǎ)	(1) stressed at end of a phrase (before pause).	low in pitch, rising at the end, and gradually less loud.	mǎ "horse", kǔ "bitter". yěw "there is". hǎw "OK".
	(2) before another syllable with third tone (ˇ).	mid-low, rising, sometimes not distinguishable from second tone (´).	wǒ 'yěw "I have". hǎy-'kěw "seaport". (the first syllables in each case).
	(3) otherwise.	low, with no rise.	yěw-'rén "there are people". mǎ-'chē "horse cart".
`(à)	(1) stressed.	falling from high to mid-low or low.	rè "hot". hàw "number".
	(2) unstressed.	falling, but often only slightly, and from whatever level is reached by the preceding syllable; if none, from mid-high.	'shàng-shyàw "colonel". kàn-bu-'jyàn "can't see".
(no symbol)	everywhere.	short, middle pitch.	tā-de "his". rén-de "people's". wǒ-de "mine". hwày-de "bad ones". de-hwà "in case".

7. Syllables and Stress

Stress means the relative degree of loudness or prominence of syllables when they are joined together. In the English sentence *I saw her yesterday*, *saw* and *yes-* are louder than the other syllables. The equivalent feature of Chinese is here written with a raised tick (') at the beginning of a syllable: wǒ 'dzwó-tyan 'kàn-jyan ta-le. "I saw her yesterday."

Stress is important in Chinese, but in many cases it is variable. The word shàng-'shyàw "colonel" is literally "upper field-officer"; it is pronounced as indicated, with stress on the second part, normally, or when identifying a person as an "upper field-officer" rather than as an

"upper general-officer" (shàng-'jyàng) or "upper company-officer" (shàng-'wèy); but it is pronounced as 'shàng-shyàw when one identifies a person as a colonel rather than as a "middle field-officer" ('jūng-shyàw "lieutenant colonel") or "lower field-officer" ('shàw-shyàw "major").

Generally speaking, the syllables of Chinese are kept quite distinct even in rapid speech. But in some cases two successive syllables are coalesced: 'shém-me "what?" is most often pronounced 'shéme or even shém. When such coalescence takes place, the resulting unit, even if it contains two vowels separated by a consonant as in the case of shéme, is a single syllable-like unit in that it bears a single tone the contour of which is distributed throughout, and is, as a whole, stressed or unstressed. Other examples: 'dzán-men "we" is usually dzám; 'wǒ-men, 'nǐ-men, 'tā-men "we, you, they" are

very often wǒm, nǐm, tām; 'jè-me "thus" is more often 'jème, jèm, or dzèm; 'jè-li "here" is in Peiping and vicinity usually jèr (with a change of l to r); 'jè-yī "this one" is often, or usually, jèy—so commonly that jèy has come to be used instead of jè in such forms as 'jèy-yī "this one", jèy-'lyǎng-ge "these two", and so on.

C. REGIONAL DIFFERENCES

The present dictionary operates in terms of the so-called "Chinese National Language" (gwó-'ywǔ), and in terms of the speech of Peiping, on which the National Language is primarily based. This variety of Chinese is mutually intelligible with all the dialects spoken in the northwest, northeast, and southwest, but in the southeastern provinces along the seacoast, up as far as Shanghai, only Chinese who have specially studied the National Language understand and speak it, their own dialects being widely divergent from those of the balance of the country and from each other. The dialect of Canton, for example, that of Shanghai, and that of Peiping differ from one another as greatly as do the German of Berlin, the Dutch of The Hague, and the English of London.

Although the dialect differences among the many millions of Chinese in the northwest, northeast, and southwest are not great enough to cause *native speakers* thereof any serious trouble in communicating with one another, the foreigner who learns one particular dialect as an adult has a considerably more difficult time attuning his ears to the others. Since the necessity for doing so may frequently arise, the present section lists some of the chief differences in pronunciation that will be found.

1. The element -r (see entry -r in Chinese-English side and Section D of the Introduction) is fairly widespread (*e.g.*, Peiping, Nanking, Chungking, Chengtu); in Hangchow the same element is found but with different pronunciation (-l instead of -r); in Hueichou the equivalent element is -n; in some places it is -z. But it is not always added to the same elements: the verb wár "to play", for example, is restricted pretty much to Peiping. Where -r or an equivalent is not used so often, nouns which in Peiping end in -r will often (but not always) add -dz—itself found in Peiping as an alternate for -r as well as in nouns with which -r is not used.

2. The sounds written in this dictionary by ch, j, and sh *not* before i, y, or yw are, in the northeastern provinces and in some parts of Hupeh, Hunan, and Szechwan, not kept distinct from ts, dz, and s in the same position. Thus sǎw "to sweep" and shǎw "small" will in those places both be pronounced as sǎw; sż "four" and shř "is, are" will both be sż. Chinese from some parts of the southeast whose native dialect is completely mutually unintelligible with gwó-'ywǔ often speak gwó-'ywǔ as a language acquired in school or as adults, with this same feature.

3. In some areas ch, j, and sh before i, y, or yw are replaced completely by ts, dz, and s; in some areas (a few in the northwest) both sounds are found before i, y, and yw, the ch-j-sh series in some words, the ts-dz-s series in others.

4. In many areas final -n and -ng are pronounced without full contact of the tongue (tip or back) against the roof of the mouth, and with nasalization of the preceding vowel. In some areas -an is so pronounced but -ang keeps the -ng as a distinct sound; in some areas both of these have a nasal vowel and no nasal consonant, the nasal vowels having, however, different tongue positions. In some areas even the nasalization is gone, so that -an rhymes completely with -a. No data are at present available for a full statement.

5. The syllables ywe, jywe, chywe, shywe, nywe, lywe (with any tone) are represented in Hupeh, Hunan, Yünnan, Szechwan, and a few other places by two series of syllables: that just listed, and a series yo, jyo, chyo, shyo, nyo, lyo (the letters here representing the individual sounds ascribed to them in Section B). Roughly four-fifths of the elements which in Peiping have the pronunciations first listed fall into the second series in the areas where both series are found.

6. In some districts of Hupeh, Hunan, and Szechwan, and along the lower Yangtze, syllable-initial n- and l- are confused, so that such words as nán "difficult" and lán "basket" would both begin indifferently with n- or with l-.

7. In most of Szechwan, hu is replaced by fu; in some of Szechwan and some districts of Hupeh and Hunan there is not only this replacement but also the replacement of any syllable-initial hw- by f-: thus fa instead of hwa, fey instead of hwey, and so on.

8. Along the Yangtze, initial l- and r- are in some districts confused; this confusion is found occasionally elsewhere, but is not common.

9. In Hupeh, Hunan, and Szechwan, and in small areas elsewhere, ng is usually prefixed to words which in Peiping begin with a or e: ngè instead of è "to be hungry."

10. In some districts of Honan, Hupeh, and Hunan, and in southern Szechwan along the Yangtze valley, there is a fifth tone distinct from the four tones of Peiping. The fifth tone has different characteristics in different places: in Nanking it is high and short, cut off abruptly when final in the phrase. Syllables which in these dialects have the fifth tone are merged variously in other tone classes in dialects which have only four.

11. In Szechwan and elsewhere in the southwest there are four tones as in Peiping, but with quite different characteristics. The first tone is high and level as in Peiping; but the second is low and level; the third is high and falling; and the fourth is low and rising. With some exceptions, elements having the Peiping first tone in Peiping have the Szechwan first tone in Szechwan, and so on, so that it is essentially a matter of simple substitution, orally or aurally, to interpret something said in one tonal system in terms of the other.

D. CHANGES OF SOUND

1. *Occasional Changes.* Some elements in Chinese vary in pronunciation without any correlated change in meaning. The most frequent case of this is that of an element which in certain compounds or contexts loses its tone: bù-'hǎw "not good", with bù "not"; but 'hǎw-bu-hǎw "is it good?" with bu toneless. Cases of this kind are properly indicated in the body of the dictionary and in the subsequent sections of the Introduction.

Some elements occur in all possible contexts with either of two tones, or even sometimes with any of three tones. When the alternate forms would be separated by considerable unrelated material in the Chinese-English side of the dictionary, both are given with a cross reference to the one under which information is given.

More rarely, elements vary freely in other respects than tone. Such cases are handled as in the case of free tone variations.

2. *Regular Changes.* The element -r or -er (see entry in form *-er) differs from most constituent elements of expressions in Chinese in that it is joined onto the previous syllable as part of that same syllable, instead of constituting a syllable in itself. The merging of a syllable with suffixed -r or -er calls for certain systematic changes in the vowels and consonants of the original first syllable; the tone is not affected. The following table shows what changes are made:

Syllables ending in:	When adding -r become:	Example:
-a	-ar	hwā : hwār
		hwāer
-an	-ar	hwān : hwār
-ay	-ar	hwáy : hwár
-aw	-awr	hàw : hàwr
-ang	-angr	háng : hángr

Syllables ending in:	When adding -r become:	Example:
-e	-er, -eer	gè : gèer or gèr
		hé : héer or hér

(Speakers differ in the latter usage. With the first and second tones the writing with two e's has generally been used; with the third and fourth tones the writing with one e has generally been used.)

-o	-oer, -or, -er	wǒ : wǒer, wǒr
		wò : wòr, wòer

(Speakers differ here also; all the writings have been used on occasion.)

-en	-er	gēn : gēr
-ey	-er	swèy : swèr
-ew	-ewr	gěw : gěwr
-eng	-engr	héng : héngr
-i	yer	dī : dyer
(yi)	(yer)	(yì : yèr)
-in	-yer	jìn : jyèr
(yin)	(yer)	(yìn : yěr)
-ing	-yengr	bìng : byěngr
(ying)	(yengr)	
-u	-ur	shù : shùr
-ung	-ungr	húng : húngr
-z (sz, dz, tsz)	-er	sž : sēr
		dž : dzèr
		tsž : tsèr
-r (r, shr, chr, jr)	-er	ř : rèr
		shř : shèr
		chř : chěr
		jř : jér

E. FORMATION OF SENTENCES

GUIDE TO THE CHINESE–ENGLISH SIDE

1. General Comments: The Forms of Entries

The *smallest meaningful elements* which are put together to form sentences in Chinese (or any other language) are called *morphemes.*

Structure of Chinese Morphemes. Most morphemes in Chinese consist of a single syllable, and most syllables constitute a single morpheme: rén "person"; bīng "soldier"; shyǎw "small"; dà "large"; hěn "very, quite"; jwā "to grasp or scratch with the fingers". A few Chinese morphemes consist of less than a syllable: hwàr "picture" consists of hwà "to depict" plus -r (no precise meaning save that the form ending in it is not likely to be a verb). A few, on the other hand, consist of more than one syllable: 'bwō-li "glass"; jī-lu-gā-'lár "in every nook and cranny."

Types of Morphemes. Some Chinese morphemes have a relatively independent status, being used on occasion as a whole sentence or as a major constituent of a sentence; all the morphemes cited above are examples. Others occur only in certain types of combinations with other elements. For example, jǎng "person in charge of through official or military appointment" is never used all alone, but is added freely to designations of governmental bodies or military units: páy-'iǎng "platoon leader" and the like. These morphemes are termed *bound;* the type mentioned earlier are termed *free.* The distinction is not sharp, but is very useful. Some bound morphemes are of sufficient importance to merit listing as separate entries in the body of the dictionary; they are there marked with an asterisk (*) to indicate their bondage.

Lexical Units. Some combinations of morphemes have meanings which are simply the sum of the meanings of the constituent elements, whether the latter be free or bound. páy-'jǎng "platoon leader" is an example. Other combinations are used conventionally, as wholes, with meanings which are *more* than simply the sum of the meanings of the parts: chr̄ "to eat" and kǔ "bitter", but chr̄-'kǔ "to suffer".

Each morpheme, and each combination of morphemes with such specialized meaning, constitutes a *lexical unit*, in the sense of an expression which must be learned as a whole. The items given as entries on the Chinese-English side of this dictionary are lexical units in this sense.

Form of Entries. About each lexical unit there are two types of information which must be acquired: (1) its meaning (in terms of English) and (2) the ways in which it is used alone, or in combination with other lexical units, to form whole sentences.

Information of type (1) is given for each lexical unit where it is entered alphabetically.

Information of type (2) is given for each lexical unit where it is entered alphabetically, in those cases in which such information applies only to that specific lexical unit. There are, however, large numbers of lexical units which operate in closely similar ways in the formation of sentences, so that statements about this can be made once for all of them.

To make this possible, most entries in the Chinese-English side are followed by a *code symbol*, in the following fashion:

gūng-'mín (*Npers*) citizen.

The code symbol *Npers* refers the user to the appropriate subsection of Section 6 of this part of the Introduction, in which a series of statements which apply to all entries so coded are made. The code symbols themselves have been designed to be somewhat suggestive, as an aid to memory: thus the *N* in *Npers* suggests *noun*, and the *pers* suggests *personal*, so that the whole symbol suggests *personal noun*, a term used in the introductory section (and occasionally in entries) to refer to lexical units of this type. It has not been possible, however, to make the code symbol this obvious in all cases.

The expressions (not code symbols) "literary", "a bit literary", and "literary quotation", which will be found sprinkled among the entries, are explained in Section F of the Introduction.

The following sections consist first (Subsections 2–5) of general statements about the structure of Chinese sentences which cannot be allocated specifically to one or another code symbol, and then (Subsection 6) of an alphabetical listing of the code symbols with the relevant statements made for each.

2. Sentence Elements

A Chinese sentence consists of a *nucleus*, either standing alone or surrounded by one or more *particles*, *nominal referents*, *adverbial modifiers*, and *linking elements*. A whole sentence may itself participate in a larger sentence; for this see the discussion in Subsection 5, and that in Subsection 6 under the code symbols A (8, 9, and 10), H (2), and Vsent.

The nucleus may be *nominal*, *adjectival*, or *verbal*. For sentences with nominal nucleus see Subsection 3; for those with adjectival nucleus see the discussion under the code symbol *A;* for those with verbal nucleus see the discussion under the code symbols I, IN, RC, RC1, RC2, RC3, RC4, V, V2, VN1, VN2, VN3, Vpred, and Vsent.

Particles are given as entries and their use in sentences is described there; see particularly le, gwo, je, de, and, closely related, the adverbs bū and méy.

Nominal referents are non-nuclear nominal expressions standing in any of various relations to the nucleus and to each other. The formation of nominal expressions is dealt with under the code symbols Dem, Demord, M (and the various symbols beginning with M), N (and the various symbols beginning with N), Num, Preord, and Pron.

Nominal referents are either *marked*, meaning that they follow a *coverb* (K) which indicates their function in the sentence, or *unmarked*, which means that there is no such coverb and that the function in the sentence depends on position relative to the nuclear element and on what type of nuclear element is involved. A combination of coverb and nominal expression may also be said to function as an *adverbial modifier* in the sentence.

Nominal expressions are also either *definite* or *indefinite* in form. A *Nunique* is definite; any nominal expression consisting of, or beginning with, a Dem, Demord, or Pron is definite; all *ordinal expressions* (see Preord) are definite; all other nominal expressions are indefinite. With certain nuclei (I, RC1) the positions in which certain nominal referents may occur depends on their definiteness or indefiniteness.

10

Nominal referents which are in all cases unmarked, or which are only marked in some cases, include the following:

1. *Actor* (with *A, I, RC1, RC2, RC3, V, V2, Vpred,* or *Vsent* as nucleus) specifying the thing or person characterized, or the thing or person which performs the action indicated by the verb. Thus **wǒ** "I" is actor in the following sentences:

> **wǒ yěw yì-dyǎr-'è.** "I'm a bit hungry."
>
> **wǒ méy-'dàw-gwo jūng-gwo.** "I've never been to China."

2. *Agent* (with nuclear *I, RC2, RC4*) specifying a person (rarely a thing) which *causes* an action. In the following sentences **wǒ** and **nǐ** "you" are agents:

> **nǐ 'wèy-shéme méy-láy-'shìn?** "How come you haven't written?" (*literally* "How come you haven't caused letters to come?")
>
> **wǒ bǎ-'jǐr 'sz-chéng lyǎng-'bàr.** "I tore the paper in two."

3. *Undergoer* (with nuclear *I*) specifying a person or thing which experiences, suffers, or undergoes the action of an actor. In the following sentence **wǒ** is undergoer:

> **wǒ 'lyéw-le hěn-dwō-de-'shyě.** "I lost a lot of blood." (*literally* "I experienced a lot of blood flowing out.")

4. *Goal* (with *RC2, RC4, V, V2*) specifying an object (thing or person) towards which the action indicated by the nucleus of the sentence is directed, and which is altered in position or structure by that action. In the following sentence **'jàng-peng** "tents" is goal:

> **'fēng bǎ 'jàng-peng gwā-'dǎw-le.** "The wind blew the tents down."
>
> **'jàng-peng jyàw-'fēng gěy gwā-'dǎw-le.** "The tents were blown down by the wind."

5. *Percept* (with *RC2, V*) specifying a person or thing towards which the action indicated by the nucleus of the sentence is directed, but which is *not* altered in position or structure by that action. In the following sentence **tā** "he" is percept:

> **wǒ háy méy-'kàn-jyan ta-ne.** "I haven't seen him yet."

6. *Recipient* (*V2* especially, *RC4*, and general; see under entry **gěy**) specifying a person (not a thing) who receives something or for whose benefit or detriment the action specified by the nucleus occurs. In the following sentence **wo** is recipient:

> **chǐng-ni bǎ nèy-bǎ-'fǔ-dz 'dì-gey wo.** "Please pass that ax over to me."

7. *Terminus* (with *RC3, RC4, V*) specifying a time or place arrived at by an action, or a state resulting from an action. In the following sentences the nominal expressions at the ends of the sentences are termini:

> **nǐ 'shéme-shŕ-hew ké-yi 'dàw-jèr?** "When can you get here?"
>
> **bǎ-'bǐng bāy-chéng lyǎng-'kwàr.** "Break the cake into two pieces."

There are a few types of usually unmarked nominal referents for which no names have been devised; these are dealt with at relevant points in Subsection 6.

Adverbial modifiers include *adverbs* (*H*); adjectives used adverbially (*A*, paragraphs 11, 12); nominal expressions which specify places or times (see section entitled *Time and Place Expressions* below); and combinations of coverb (*K*) with following nominal expression.

Linking elements are *conjunctions* (*J*).

3. Sentences with Nominal Nuclei

A nominal sentence consists of two nominal expressions which are equated, or the equation between which is denied. The second nominal expression is the nucleus; the first is often left out and understood from context. The equating may be indicated by **shŕ** "is, are, am" before the nucleus, or by nothing at all; but if the identification is denied, the nucleus is always preceded by some marking verb form, often **bú-shr** "isn't, aren't, am not". Examples:

> **wǒ shŕ nǐ-de-'péng-yew.** "I'm your friend."
>
> **tā shŕ měy-gwo-'bīng.** "He's an American soldier."
>
> **wǒ 'bú-shr 'jūng-gwo-rén.** "I'm not a Chinese."
>
> **'bú-shr 'jūng-gwo-rén.** "(Someone we're talking about) isn't a Chinese."

No verb at all in the affirmative is customary in cases in which the second nominal expression is some expression of quantity or measure:

> **tā 'jīn-nyan 'jǐ-swèy-le?** "He this year how many years-of-age?" *means* "How old is he this year?"
>
> **shyàn-dzày 'shéme-shŕ-hew?** *or* **shyàn-dzày 'jǐ-dyǎn-jūng?** "What time is it now?"
>
> **tā-de-tǐ-'jùng yì-bǎy-'èr-shr-'bàng.** "Her weight a hundred and twenty pounds." *means* "She weighs a hundred and twenty."
>
> **'jèy-shyē-jī-'dzěr ('měy-) yì-dá 'wǔ-máw-chyán.** *or* **'jèy-shyē-jī-'dzěr 'wǔ-máw-chyán yì-'dá.** "These eggs are fifty cents per dozen."

4. Time and Place Expressions

Time and place expressions are nominal expressions which refer to places or to points or periods of time. The formation of time and place expressions shows some irregularity, so that relevant entries are given in fairly full shape. For the formation of time expressions see *Ntime, Mtime, MdistT, Msemel;* for the formation of place expressions see *Nplace* and *Mpos.* The discussion at *Demord* is also relevant for time expressions.

1. *Time-When Expressions.* A time-when expression indicates the point of time at which an action occurred or will occur or is occurring, as in answer to a question phrased with "when?". "Point of time" is to be taken relatively; a day is a point of time on the scale of weeks or months, an hour on the scale of days, and so on.

A time-when expression in a sentence comes initially or after an initial nominal referent:

'jīn-nyán tā 'jǐ-swèy-le? *or* tā 'jīn-nyán 'jǐ-swèy-le? "How old is he this year?"

tsúng 'bā-dyǎn-jūng dàw 'shŕ-dyǎn-jūng 'bù-shywǔ 'chū-chywù. "It's not permitted to leave the premises between eight and ten."

wǒ 'dàw-nèr de-shŕ-hew, tā háy méy-chŕ-'wán dzǎw-'fàn-ne. "When I got there, he hadn't finished breakfast yet."

A short time-when expression, as in the first example, is more apt to come after an initial unmarked nominal referent (when there is any unmarked nominal referent before the verb). A longer one, as in the second sentence or the third, will precede the first unmarked nominal referent if there is any such.

2. *Duration and Frequency.* A time expression specifying how long some activity lasts (in terms of *elapsed time*, not in terms of starting-point and endpoint), or specifying *frequency*, comes at the end of the sentence:

wǒ-men dzày chúng-'chìng jù-le sān-'nyán-le. "We've lived in Chungking for three years."

wǒ 'dzwó-tyan 'kàn-jyan ta 'sān-tsž. "I saw him three times yesterday."

3. *Temporal Terminus.* A time expression may come after a *V* or an *RC3* (possibly, but rarely, an *RC4*) in the function of a nominal referent of the type termed a *terminus*—specifying point of time *until which* or *beyond which* some activity is carried on:

wǒ-men yì-'tyān tsúng 'dzǎw-chen 'máng-dàw 'wǎn-shang. "We're busy the whole day, from morning to evening."

4. *Location.* Sentences which serve to locate things use place expressions in one of the following ways; the second three are practically equivalent and the first of those three is most common:

'yān dzày 'jwō-dz-shang. "The cigarettes are on the table." (*We are interested in the cigarettes; the sentence tells where they are to be found.*)

'jwō-dz-shang yěw-'yān. "There are cigarettes on the table." (*We are interested in the table; the sentence gives us some information about it.*)

yěw-'yān dzày 'jwō-dz-shang. (*ditto*)

dzày 'jwō-dz-shang yěw-'yān. (*ditto*)

5. *Place at Which.* A specification of the place at which (in which, on which, etc.) something occurs is given by the coverb dzày before the place expression, or by a place expression following an *RC* which has dzày as postverb:

nǐ dzày-'nǎr dzwò-'shŕ? "Where do you work?"

tā 'dzwò-dzày 'něy-bǎ-'yǐ-dz-shang láy-je? "Which chair has he been sitting in?"

6. *Place from Which.* A specification of the place from which, past or through which, or the direction from which, an activity occurs is given by the coverb tsúng followed by a place expression:

tā tsúng 'měy-gwo láy-de. "He's from the United States."

tā tsúng 'wū-dz-li 'pǎw-chū-láy-le. "He came running out of the house."

7. *Place to Which.* A specification of direction *in* which or place or direction *towards* which is given with the coverb shyàng or wàng:

shyàng-'dzwǒ dzěw. "Go to the left."

A specification of place *to* which is given by using a place expression as terminus after an appropriate *V* or *RC3* or *RC4:*

nǐ 'shéme-shŕ-hew ké-yi 'dàw-jèr? "When can you get here?"

A specification of place *beyond* which is given with the coverb gwò, the verb gwò, or an *RC3* or *RC4* with gwò as postverb:

jèy-ge-'hé dzám dzěme 'gwò-ne? "How can we get across this river?"

8. Finer shades of meaning in expressions of location, attained in English by a variety of prepositions and compound prepositions (*on, on top of, onto the top of, from the top of,* etc.) are attained in Chinese by combining the small available number of coverbs (verbs, postverbs) with a larger number of relative place expressions suffixed to a nominal expression. Thus with tsúng "from", dzày "at", and dàw "to", the relative place expressions 'lǐ-tew (lǐ, li) "inside", 'shàng-tew (shàng, shang) "topside", and the two nouns 'jwō-dz "table", 'wū-dz "room", such shades as the following are attainable:

tsúng 'jwŏ-dz-shàng "from on top of the table"

dzày 'jwŏ-dz-shang "on top of the table"

dàw 'jwŏ-dz-shang "onto the table"

tsúng 'wū-dz-li "from inside the room"

dzày 'wū-dz-li "in the room"

dàw 'wū-dz-li "into the room"

5. Questions and Requests

Questions in Chinese are of two kinds: *alternative questions* and *question-word questions*.

ALTERNATIVE QUESTIONS

An alternative question is a sentence which posits two or more alternative possibilities; the answer is given by stating which of the possibilities is the case. When there are two possibilities given, specifically whether a particular thing is the case or is not the case ("Is this or isn't this a book?"), Chinese cannot phrase an answer simply in terms of "yes" or "no," since there are no general words for "yes" and "no" in the language; the phrasing of the answer has to depend on the specific words used in the question.

Alternative questions are formed in the following ways:

1. *Repetition of a verb or adjective with* **bū** (*or* **méy**) *between.* Examples:

 nǐ 'shr̀-bu-shr̀ 'jūng-gwo-'bīng? "You are-not-are Chinese soldier?" *means* "Are you a Chinese soldier?" *Aff. A.:* 'shr̀. "Am." *means* "Yes." *Neg. A.:* 'bú-shr̀. "Not am." *means* "No."

nǐ 'chywù-bu-chywù? "You go-not-go?" *means* "Are you going?" *Aff. A.:* (wǒ) 'chywù. "Yes, I'm going." *Neg. A.:* (wǒ) 'bú-chywù. "No, I'm not going."

nèy-bĕn-'shū 'hăw-bu-hăw? "That book good-not-good?" *means* "How's that book?" *Aff. A.:* 'hăw. "OK." *or* hĕn 'hăw. "Quite good." *etc.* *Neg. A.:* 'bù-hăw. "Bad." *or* bù-hĕn 'hăw. "Not very good." *etc.*

tā 'yĕw-méy-yew 'yān? "He has-not-has cigarettes?" *means* "Has he any cigarettes?" *Aff. A.:* 'yĕw. "Yes." *Neg. A.:* 'méy-yĕw. "No."

yĕw-'méy-yew bǐ-'jèy-ge-hăw-de-'yān? "Are there any cigarettes better than these (available)?" *Aff. A.:* 'yĕw. "Yes." *Neg. A.:* 'méy-yĕw. "No."

Notice that with all verbs and adjectives save yĕw "to have; there is, there are" the negative element inserted is bū (toneless: bu); with yĕw the negative element inserted is méy.

The affirmative and negative answers to the questions are phrased with the verb or adjective which occurred in the question; in the first example, shr̀ "is, equals", in the question and therefore in the answers; in the second example, chywù "to go"; in the third, hăw "to be OK"; in the last two, yĕw. More elaborate answers are possible, and are often more polite. Thus to any of the above questions the answer might be (wǒ) bù-'jr̆-dàw "I don't know"; to the last, one might say shyàn-dzày 'méy-yew "not right now"; to the second, one might say wǒ shyăng 'bú-chywù "I don't think I'm going" or "I guess I won't go"; and so on. These longer answers are generally better to use, in order to avoid misunderstanding or bad feeling because of unintended impoliteness. Note, however, that even in the longer answers, with the one exception of the "I don't know" answer, the verb or adjective of the question forms the nucleus of what is said.

Answers to other types of alternative questions are in the main similar to the answers to this type; further comment is given only where they are different.

2. *Addition of* **bū** (*or* **méy**) *plus verb or adjective at the end of the sentence.* Examples:

nǐ shr̀ jūng-gwo-'bīng bú-shr̀? "You are Chinese soldier not-are?" *means* "Are you a Chinese soldier?" *Answers as to type 1.*

tā yĕw-'yān méy-yew? "He has cigarettes not-has?" *means* "Has he any cigarettes?"

yĕw bǐ-jèy-ge-'hăw-de-yān méy-yew? "There are cigarettes better than these not are?" *means* "Are there any cigarettes better than these?"

3. *Addition of* **méy-yew** *to a sentence containing* -le. Examples:

nǐ 'kàn-jyàn(-le) ta méy-yew? "Have you seen him?" *Aff. A.:* 'kàn-jyàn-le. "I have." *Neg. A.:* 'méy-kàn-jyan. *or* 'méy-yew. "I haven't."

chr̆-le dzăw-'fàn méy-yew? "Have you had breakfast?" *Aff. A.:* 'chr̆-le. "Yes." *or* 'chr̆-gwo-le. "Yes, I've had my breakfast." *or* 'yǐ-jing 'chr̆-gwo-le. "I've already eaten." *Neg. A.:* 'méy-chr̆. *or* 'méy-yew.' "No." *or* háy-'méy-chr̆-ne. *or* háy-'méy-ne. "Not yet."

If a sentence contains le after the verb or at the end, this and 4 below are the only ways of making an alternative question of it. With RC, as in the first example, the le is sometimes omitted. This and 4 below are also the methods of making alternative questions when the sentence contains gwo, either in addition to le or in place of it.

The affirmative answer must contain the verb of the sentence itself. The negative answer, however, may consist of 'méy-yew alone or modified as indicated in the second example above.

4. *Addition of* -ma. This is the most generally applicable way of making alternative questions and is usable in place of any of the three ways so far given

-ma means simply "Is this statement so or not?" Examples:

nǐ shr̀ 'jūng-gwo-bīng-ma? "Are you a Chinese soldier?"

nǐ 'chywù-ma? "Are you going?"

nèy-běn-'shū 'hǎw-ma? "Is that book good?"

tā yěw-'yān-ma? "Has he any cigarettes?"

yěw bǐ-jèy-ge-'hǎw-de-yān-ma? "Are there any cigarettes better than these?"

nǐ 'kàn-jyàn ta-le-ma? "Have you seen him?"

chǐ-le dzǎw-'fàn-le-ma? "Have you had breakfast?"

The answers are as in 1, 2, and 3. If -ma is replaceable by **'méy-yew**, as in the last two cases, then a negative answer may consist of **'méy-yew** or its modifications, as in 3.

5. *Longer Alternatives.* — *a.* An alternative (agreement-disagreement type) question is made with an *RC* in potential form either by method 4 or by putting both the potential forms into the sentence:

nèy-gēr-'jù-dz nǐ 'kàn-de-jyàn 'kàn-bu-jyàn? "That post you can-see can't-see?" *means* "Can you see that post?" *Aff. A.:* **kàn-de-'jyàn.** "I can." *Neg. A.:* **kàn-bu-'jyàn.** "I can't."

A long answer might take the form **kàn-de-'jyàn, kě-shr kàn-bu-'chīng-chu** "I can see it (*i.e.*, my eyes are all right), but I can't make out clearly what it is (*i.e.*, because of dust or fog)."

b. Alternatives not of the agreement-disagreement type, but of multiple-choice identification, are made by repeating, with modifications, longer expressions:

nǐ-de-'péng-yew shr̀ 'nán-de shr̀ 'nywǔ-de? "Your friend is male is female?" *means* "Is your friend a man or a woman?" *Answers:* **shr̀-'nán-de.** "A man." *etc.*

Ordinarily no word is included for the "or" expressed in English. Sometimes, however, such a word is included, usually **'háy-shr**, sometimes **'hwò-shr** or **'hwò-je shr̀**:

jè-ge hé-dz-lǐ-tew shr̀ 'píng-dz (háy-)shr̀ 'wǎn háy-shr 'gwō? "What's in this box? Is it bottles or bowls or plates?" *Answer in the form* **shr̀ 'píng-dz.** "It's bottles."

The same pattern is sometimes used for the agreement-disagreement type of alternative question:

tā 'shr̀-bīng 'bú-shr bīng-nga? "Well, is he a soldier or isn't he?"

tā shr̀ 'láy-ne háy-shr 'bù-láy-ne? "Well, is he coming or isn't he?"

nǐ shr̀ 'yàw-wa háy-shr 'bú-yàw-ne? "Well, are you going to take it or aren't you?"

6. *Questions with Negative Emphasis.* Similar to 4 but differing in emphasis are questions ending in -ma but with the verb preceded by **bū** or **méy**:

tā bú-shr nǐ-de-'péng-yew-ma? "Isn't he your friend?"

7. *Expressions with Postposed Alternative Questions.* A simple statement or suggestion may be followed, sometimes with intervening pause, by an interrogative comment of the forms **'dwèy-bu-dwèy** or **'dwèy-ma** "is that right?" or **bú-'dwèy-ma** "isn't that right?":

wǒ-men gēn-ta 'chywù, 'hǎw-bu-hǎw? "We'll go with him, OK?"

wǒ dzày-'jèr 'děng ta, 'ké-yi-bu-ké-yi? "I'll wait here for him, may I?"

wǒ bǎ jèy-ge ná-'dzěw, 'shíng-ma? "I'll take this along with me, all right?"

In such cases the questioning part is the postposed phrase, not the main part of the sentence, and so the answer is phrased with the verb or adjective used there:

'hǎw. "OK."

'ké-yi. "Sure you may."

bù-'shíng. "No, you may not."

QUESTION-WORD QUESTIONS

A number of words in Chinese have the dual function of being *N*, *Pron*, *A*, etc., and of at the same time indicating either (1) that the sentence is a question, or (2) indefiniteness. Here only the question use is relevant. Such questions cannot be answered by expressing agreement or disagreement, or by indicating which alternative is the case; they call for more explicit information of some kind (as to an English question such as "Who is he?"). These *question-words* do not have some special position in the sentence, as their equivalents in English do ("why?" always begins the sentence in English), but come rather in the normal position for an *N*, a *Pron*, and so on, depending on what they are.

1. *Questions about Identity.* **shwéy** or **shéy** means "who?"; **nǎ** or **něy** means "which?"; **shém-me** or **shéme** means "what?":

tā shr̀-'shéy? "Who's he?"

wǒ děy gēn-'shéy shwō-'hwà? "Who must I speak with?"

'jèy-ge-dūng-shi shr̀-'shéy-de? "Whose is this?"

nǐ 'něy-tyān ké-yi 'dàw-jèr? "Which day can you get here?"

'něy-yí-ge-'wǎn shr̀ dzwèy-'gwèy-de? "Which bowl is most expensive?"

'jè-shr̀ shéme? "What's this?"

2. *Questions about Place.* This is properly a subdivision of 1, since the forms used are **'nǎ-li** (shortened to **nǎr**) "where?"; **shéme-'dì-fang** "what place?, where?";

'něy-ge-dì-fang "which place?"; and various specific combinations involving nǎ or shéme:

> nǐ dàw-'nǎr chywù? "Where are you going?"
> hwǒ-chē-'jàn dzày-'nǎr? "Where's the railroad station?"

3. *Questions about Time,* This also is properly a subdivision of 1; the most often used expression is shéme-'shŕ-hew "what time?, when?"; but all sorts of specific combinations such as 'něy-tyān "what day?" are possible:

> tā 'shéme-shŕ-hew 'dàw-de? "What time did he get here?"

4. *Questions about Manner.* In addition to combinations such as shéme-'fá-dz "what method?, what plan?", which fall logically under 1, there is also the form 'dzěm-me or dzěme "how?":

> dàw hwǒ-chē-'jàn chywù dzěme 'dzěw-wa? "How do I go to get to the station?"
> tā 'dzěme néng bàn-de-'hǎw-ne? "How can he do it right?"

5. *Questions about Kind.* 'dzěme-yàng means "of what kind?, in what condition?"; 'shéme-yàng is similar:

> tā 'jīn-tyan dzěme-'yàng-le? "How is he today?" (*Asked, for example, of someone known to have been ill.*)

6. *Questions about Quantity.* jǐ means "how many?" when the answer is expected to be relatively small—say not more than ten or twelve; 'dwō-shaw means "how many?" when a larger answer is expected or when there is no particular expectation:

> tā yěw 'jǐ-ge-háy-dz-le? "How many children has he?"
> jèy-ge-gūng-'chǎng yùng-je 'dwō-shǎw-rén? "How many people does this factory employ?"

dwō (rarely dwō-shaw) precedes an *A* in similar questions:

> nèy-ge-'fáng-dz yěw 'dwō-dà? "How big is that house?"

7. *Questions about Reason.* 'wèy-shéme is "why?"; dzěme "how?" is sometimes used where English would have "why?":

> nǐ 'wèy-shéme 'láy-de dzěme-'wǎn-ne? "Why are you so late?"

> nǐ 'dzěme 'láy-de dzème-'wǎn-ne? "How come you're so late?"

8. *Answers to Question-Word Questions.* The answers to question-word questions, in Chinese as in English, are full sentences (even though sometimes very short) giving the information requested, and do not necessarily turn on the phrasing of the question.

For slight variations in emphasis of questions of both types (alternative and question-word), see the entries ne and a.

REQUESTS

There is no special sentence set-up for making requests (orders, commands, suggestions) in Chinese. A request may simply be a sentence specifying what the person spoken to is to do:

> bǎ nèy-bǎ-'yǐ-dz 'dì-gey wo. "Pass me that chair."

The actor, nǐ "you", may perfectly well be expressed:

> nǐ bǎ nèy-bǎ-'yǐ-dz 'dì-gey wo. (*ditto*).

These requests, with or without nǐ, are pretty brusque, in Chinese as in English. Politeness equivalent to the prefixing of "please" in English is achieved in Chinese by prefixing chǐng "to request, to invite":

> chǐng(-ni) bǎ nèy-bǎ-'yǐ-dz 'dì-gey wo. "Please pass me that chair."

Request sentences often add -ba, but -ba is not confined to requests and orders, having rather a general meaning of "I think it must be so":

> 'dzěw-ba! "Scram!"
> wǒ-men 'dzěw-ba! "Let's get going!"
> bú-'dwèy-ba! "That can't be right!" *or* "I don't think that can be right!"

The degree of brusqueness of such sentences depends considerably on the tone of voice in which they are said.

Negative requests, or *prohibitions,* have all of the variations outlined above (with or without chǐng or -ba); but, instead of prefixing a negative adverb to the nucleus, one precedes it with 'bú-yàw or byé "don't":

> chǐng-ni byé 'dzěw. "Please don't go."
> 'byé dzěw. "Don't go!" (*brusque*) *or* "Please don't go."
> byé 'dzěw-ba! "No! Don't go!" (*fairly polite*).

Here also the degree of politeness depends a great deal more on the circumstances and the tone of voice than on the actual words chosen.

6. Alphabetical Listing of Code Symbols with Explanation and Comment

A = Adjectives

1. Adjectives are used as attributives before nouns or containing measures (*Mcont*). An adjective or adjectival expression of more than one syllable generally adds de:

> 'hǎw-rén "good people"
> shīn-'yī-fu "new clothes"
> dà-'shŕ-tew "a big stone"
> yí-'dà-wǎn-'fàn "a big bowl of rice"
> hǎw-'kàn-de-'nywǔ-rén "good-looking women"

2. When an adjective functions as nucleus of a sentence, it may be preceded by a nominal referent (*actor*) which specifies the person or thing characterized. Usually one or more adverbs or particles surround the adjective to indicate that the characterization is relative, not absolute. On occasion the actor is omitted:

jèy-jāng-'jwō-dz hěn 'dà. "That table is quite big."

wǒ jywé-je 'tày dà. "I think (it) is too big."

3. With an adjective as sentence nucleus, a second nominal referent, marked by bǐ "as compared with" or lí "as measured from", may follow the actor:

'jèy-jāng-jwō-dz bǐ 'nèy-jāng-jwō-dz 'dà. "This table is bigger than that one."

'jèy-ge-dì-fangr lí hwǒ-chē-'jàn bù-'ywǎn. "This place isn't far from the railroad station."

4. If a second nominal referent marked by bǐ (not by lí) is present, a third nominal referent may be placed *after* the adjective, stating the amount of difference:

'nǐ bǐ-'tā 'gāw sān-'tswèn. "You're three inches taller than he."

'wǒ bǐ-'tā 'dà shɍ-'swèy. "I'm ten years older than he."

'jèy-ge bǐ 'nèy-ge 'hǎw yì-dyǎr. "This is a little better than that."

5. If there is no second nominal referent, the same type of third nominal referent after the adjective indicates desirable or undesirable *excess*:

jèy-kwày-'bǎn-dz 'cháng-le sān-'tswèn. "This board is three inches too long."

'tyān-chi 'rè-le yì-dyǎr. "The weather has gotten a bit warmer."

6. The verb yěw "to have, there is, there are" followed by an expression of quantity and an adjective indicates measurement:

jèy-jāng-'jwō-dz yěw 'lyèw-chɍ-cháng. "This table is six feet long."

wǒ yěw yì-dyǎr-'rè. "I'm a bit warm."

'jù-dz yěw yì-'rén-gāw. "The post is the height of man."

wǒ-nèy-pǐ-mǎ méy-yew 'nǐ-nèy-pǐ 'kwày. "My horse doesn't have the speed of yours."

'jèy-ge-léw yěw 'dwō gāw? "How high is this building?"

7. The verb shɍ "is, equals" followed by an adjective plus de indicates assignment of the actor to a *class* of, say, "large" things or "small" things, rather than a comparative judgment of size:

tā-chwān-de-'yī-fu shɍ 'húng-de. "The dress she's wearing is a red one."

'nèy-jāng-jwō-dz 'bú-shr dǐng-'dà-de. "That table isn't one of our largest ones."

8. A few adjectives, or expressions built on them, precede or follow entire sentences as comments on them:

'dzwèy hǎw 'shǎw chɍ. "It would be best to eat only a little."

wǒ 'gēn-ni 'chywù, 'hǎw-bu-hǎw? "I'll go with you. OK?"

'jème-je hǎw. "Doing it this way will be all right."

wǒ shyǎng 'tā dzwò nèy-jyàn-'shɍ-ching hěn 'hǎw. "I think he'd do that job quite well." or "I think it would be quite OK for him to do that job."

9. After a sentence ending in a verb or adjective, another adjective or adjective expression may occur as a further characterization of the action or state already detailed; in this case the original sentence often, but not always, adds de. The last example in par. 8 is a case of this when taken in the first sense given. The last example below has two such final commenting adjectives, each a comment on all that precedes it:

tā 'dzěw-de hěn 'kwày. "He's walking very fast." or "He walks very fast." or "He walked very fast."

chǐng 'shwō 'màn-yi-dyǎr. "Please speak a bit more slowly."

wǒ-de-'shyé 'tsā-de 'lyàng le 'dwō. "My shoes are much better polished."

10. When the same sort of postposed commenting adjective expression is added to a sentence in which the verb is not in final position, the verb is often repeated again, with de added, directly before the final adjective expression:

tā dzwò 'jèy-jyàn-shɍ-ching dzwò-de hěn 'hǎw. "He did that job quite well." or "He's doing that job quite well."

11. Some adjectives and adjective expressions, mainly monosyllabic adjectives or expressions based thereon, are used immediately before other adjectives, or before adverbs, or before verbs, in the function of adverbial modifiers to the latter:

hǎw 'jyěw méy-'jyàn! "Good long-time haven't seen!"="Haven't seen you in a long time."

'bú-dà hǎw. "Not too terribly good."

chǐng 'màn-yi-dyǎr shwō. "Please speak more slowly."

12. *a.* Monosyllabic adjectives are doubled, the second repetition having first tone regardless of the tone of the underlying simple adjective, and suffix final de to form *intensives:* some speakers consistently use the second tone rather than the first on the second syllable; some speakers often add the element -r to the second syllable, according to the rules of combination for -r given in Section D. Thus:

16

hēy "black": hēy-'hēy-de "very black"

hwáng "yellow": hwáng-'hwāng-de "very yellow"

hǎw "OK": háw-'hāw(r)-de "very, very fine"

kwày "fast": kwày-'kwāy-de *or* kwày-'kwār-de "very fast"

b. Many two-syllable adjectives form a similar intensive by doubling each syllable independently, with no tone changes, and adding **de:**

'rúng-yì "easy": 'rúng-rung-yì-'yì-de "extremely easy"

c. Such intensives are not full-fledged adjectives; they are used as attributive adjectives (*Aattr*) and as adverbs (*H*).

13. Many adjectives serve as main verbs (*mainV*) or as postverbs (*postV*) in resultative compounds (*RC*). *RC* with an adjective as main verb are usually of types one or three; those with an adjective as postverb are of type two:

'ān-jìng-shyà-chywù (*RC1*) "to calm down" ('ān-jìng "calm")

'máng-dàw (*RC3*) "to be busy until" (a time limit) (máng "busy")

nùng-'hwày-le (*RC2*) "to spoil" *something* (hwày "spoiled, bad, out of fix, out of order")

Aattr = Attributive Adjectives

1. Attributive adjectives are used as attributives before nouns:

'nán-rén "male person", "man"

'nywǔ-rén "female person", "woman"

2. The verb shr̀ "is, equals" followed by an attributive adjective plus **de** indicates assignment of the actor to a class of objects which share the characteristic denoted by the attributive adjective:

ni-de-'péng-yew shr̀ 'nán-de shr̀ 'nywǔ-de? "Is your friend male or female?"

Dem = Demonstratives

Demonstratives function as, or participate in, nominal expressions in the ways outlined below. Nominal expressions beginning in a demonstrative are *definite*.

1. The demonstratives jè(y) "this, this here, here" and nèy, nà "that, that there, there" constitute complete nominal expressions, but only at or near the beginning of a sentence:

'jè-shr̀ wǒ-de-'péng-yew. "This is my friend."

2. A demonstrative followed by a measure (*M*) constitutes a nominal expression: 'jèy-ge "this"; 'nèy-tyān "that day".

chú-le 'jèy-ge dēw hěn hǎw. "Except for this one they're all quite OK."

3. A demonstrative followed by a measure and a noun constitutes a nominal expression: jèy-wǎn-'fàn "this bowl of rice".

'jèy-pǐ-mǎ bǐ 'nèy-pǐ-mǎ 'kwày. "This horse is faster than that one."

4. A demonstrative followed by a numeral and a measure constitutes a nominal expression: 'jèy-jǐ-tyān "these few days" (meaning "these past few days").

'něy-yí-ge dēw 'ké-yi. "Any one of them will do."

5. A demonstrative followed by a numeral, a measure, and a noun constitutes a nominal expression: jèy-'yí-ge-rén "this one person".

jèy-'lyǎng-ge-nywǔ-rén 'dēw-shr̀ wǒ-de-'péng-yew "These two women are both my friends."

Demord = Ordinal Demonstratives

Ordinal demonstratives participate in nominal expressions as outlined below. Nominal expressions beginning in an ordinal demonstrative are *definite*.

1. An ordinal demonstrative followed by a measure (*M*), almost always an *MdistT*, *Msemel*, or *Mtime*, constitutes a nominal expression:

'jīn-tyān "this day", "today"

'dzwó-tyān "yesterday"

'shyà-tsz̀ "next time"

2. An ordinal demonstrative followed by an *Ntime* constitutes a nominal expression:

'shàng-lǐ-bày "last week"

3. An ordinal demonstrative followed by a numeral and a measure (as in par. 1) constitutes a nominal expression:

shyà-'lyǎng-tsz̀ "the next two times"

There are limitations on all of the above, and full examples are given at relevant entries.

H = Adverbs

1. Adverbs are used directly before an adjectival or verbal nucleus of a sentence, or separated therefrom only by another adverb or adverbial expression, as adverbial modifiers to the nucleus:

(wǒ) hěn 'hǎw, shyè-shye. "I'm quite well, thanks."

'lyǎng-ge 'dēw ké-yi. "The two collectively are possible."="Both are all right."

màn-'mār-de dzěw. "Go very slowly." (*With intensive form from adjective* màn "slow"; *see Section A, par. 12.*)

2. After a sentence ending in a verb or adjective, certain adverbs (mainly those longer than one syllable) may occur as a further characterization of the action

or state already detailed; in this case the sentence to which the addition is made often, but not always, adds **de**.

> **'nà hăw-de 'hĕn.** "That's extremely fine."
>
> **'nà hăw 'jí-le.** "That's very, very fine." (*jí is confined to this usage.*)

I = Intransitive Verbs

1. Intransitive verbs, or expressions built on them, are used as attributives to nouns, always with **de** added save in special cases listed as entries:

> **'láy-le-de-rén** "the ones who have come"
>
> **'yĭ-jing-'láy-le-de-rén** "the ones who have already come"

2. With an intransitive verb as nucleus of a sentence, a nominal referent in the function of *actor* may be included; an actor placed after the verb is *indefinite* and must be indefinite in form; an actor placed before the verb is *definite* regardless of its form:

> **'láy-le hĕn-dwō-de-'bīng.** "A lot of soldiers came."
>
> **tā kwày 'láy-le.** "He'll be coming soon."

With compound *I* of two or more syllables (not *RC*), only a preposed actor is used:

> **míng-tyan-'wăn-shang dà-dzŭng-'tŭng yàw yăn-'shwō.** "Tomorrow night the president is going to make a speech."

A preposed actor, if not definite in form, can be rendered indefinite by prefixing **yĕw** "there's ... which":

> **yĕw-'rén yăn-'shwō láy-je.** "(*At the meeting*) there was someone who made a speech."

3. With an indefinite actor after the intransitive verb, another nominal referent is sometimes placed before the verb, designating the *causal agent:*

> **nĭ 'wèy-shéme méy-láy-'shìn?** "Why haven't you (seen to it that) some letters came?"="Why haven't you written?"
>
> **nĭ jù-'dzwĕy-ba!** "You (cause to) stop the mouth!"="Shut up!"

The agent may be understood from context:

> **jù-'dzwĕy-ba!** "Shut up!"
>
> **'dzày láy wăn-'fàn!** "Bring another bowl of rice!"

The above construction is relatively limited; normally to use an intransitive verb causatively one uses a resultative compound with the intransitive verb in question as second member (postverb); see *RC2*.

4. With an actor before or after the intransitive verb, another nominal referent is sometimes placed at the beginning of the sentence, designating the *undergoer* of the stated experience:

> **wŏ 'lyéw-le hĕn-dwō-'shyĕ.** "I've lost a lot of blood." (**lyéw** "to flow", **shyĕ** "blood".)

> **wŏ-de-'yī-fu 'dyàw-le yí-ge-'kèw-dz.** "My clothes there dropped off a button."="I lost a button off my clothes."
>
> **wŏ 'shyĕ (wàng-wày) 'lyéw-de hĕn 'kwày.** "I was losing blood fast."

5. Some intransitive verbs occur with a designation of place after them; an actor, if any is specified, precedes the verb:

> **tsúng 'chyán-tyan 'chĭ, wŏm 'dzĕw-le hĕn-dwō-'lù.** "Since the day before yesterday we've walked a lot of road."="We've done a lot of walking since the day before yesterday."

6. Intransitive verbs occur as main verbs (*mainV*) or as postverbs (*postV*) in resultative compounds (*RC*). *RC* with an intransitive verb as main verb are of types one or three (sometimes, with the verb used causatively, of type two or four); those with an intransitive verb as postverb are of type one or two:

> **'dzĕw-láy** (*RC1*) "to come walking" (*both parts I*)
>
> **'dzĕw-dàw** (*RC3*) "to walk to" (*a place*)
>
> **dă-'lyè-le** (*RC2*) "to break by striking" (**lyè** *I* "to crack")

IN = Intransitive Verb and Noun

IN are lexical units consisting of an intransitive verb and a noun standing in the relation of *actor* to the verb. The special meaning of the unit is retained even if the parts are separated by other words or if the actor is made definite and thereby precedes the verb; on occasion an agent or an undergoer is added before the group. Thus **shyà-'ywŭ** "to rain":

> **shyà yí-jèn-'ywŭ** "to rain once"
>
> **'ywŭ 'shyà-de hĕn 'dà.** "The rain is coming down hard."

For full treatment of the possibilities see *I*.

J = Conjunction

A conjunction is placed either at the beginning of the sentence or, if a nominal referent precedes the nucleus, immediately after that nominal referent:

> **rè-shr nĭ 'shyăng ...** "If you think ..."
>
> **nĭ rè-shr 'shyăng ...** (*ditto*)

Some conjunctions consist of an element (often an *H*) plus **shr** "is, are". Of these, some function also as combination of adverb (*H*) and verb **shr**:

> **bú-shr 'tā jyèw-shr 'nĭ.** "If it isn't he then it's you."

K = Coverbs

Coverbs serve to mark nominal referents in a sentence, either (1) connecting the following nominal referent to a preceding one, or (2) indicating the relation of the following nominal referent to all the rest of the sentence. Thus:

> **wŏ hé-'nĭ** "you and I"

wǒ-men gēn yín-'háng jyè-'chyán. "We borrow money from (*literally* with) the bank."

In case (2), the coverb, together with the nominal referent it precedes and marks, functions adverbially in the sentence, coming always before the nuclear word.

l; lc = láy; láy *or* chywù

The symbols *l* or *lc* given in the coding of a verb (*I*, *V* *RC*) indicate that when that verb is used as the nucleus of a sentence, **láy** (in the first case), or **láy** or **chywù** (in the second), are added later. The details of meaning are given at the entry **láy**.

Furthermore, if in a particular sentence no other words intervene between an *I* or *V* which calls for final **láy** or **chywù** and that final element, the group is an *RC* of type one or two.

M = Measure

A measure is a noun-like form which is used on occasion immediately after a numeral or demonstrative. An *autonomous* measure (*MgroupA, MpersA, Mauton, Mmeas, Mpos, Mtime, MdistT, MdistS*) carries a full meaning when not followed by a noun; thus **yì-'shěng** "a province". An *auxiliary* measure (*Mclass, Mcont, Mgroup, Mpart, Munit*) used without a following noun carries specific meaning only in the light of the context; thus **yí-'kwày** is "a hunk" of anything which might come in hunks, including "dollars" because **yí-kwày-'chyán** "one hunk money" means "one dollar".

Measures are used in nominal forms as follows:

1. Numeral followed by measure:
   sān-'shěng "three provinces"
   sż-'lǐ "four miles"
   'yí-ge "one"

2. Numeral followed by measure followed by noun:
   yí-ge-'rén "a person"

3. A measure plus a noun:
   ge-'rén "a person"
This is equivalent to the same preceded by numeral **yī** "one, a, an" and occurs only when the whole expression is preceded directly by a *V, I, RC,* or *K* (verbs and coverbs), or by *A* or *H*.

4. A demonstrative or an ordinal demonstrative followed by a measure:
   'jèy-ge "this"
   'jīn-tyān "today"

5. A demonstrative plus a measure plus a noun:
   'jèy-ge-rén "this person"

6. A demonstrative plus a numeral plus a measure:
   'jèy-yí-ge "this one"

7. A demonstrative plus a numeral plus a measure plus a noun:
   'jèy-yí-ge-rén "this one person"

mainV = Main Verb

The first of the two constituents of an *RC* is called the main verb. When in the discussion of a form the phrase "*As mainV:*" occurs, it indicates that the following subentries are, or that the following sentences include, resultative compounds with the head entry functioning as a main verb. If the head entry is an *A* or *I*, the *RC* are of type one or three (save for a few cases in which an *I* is used causatively as *mainV* in an *RC2* or *RC4*); if the head entry is a *V*, the *RC* are of type two or four.

Mauton = Autonomous Measures (See also M)

A random group of noun-like words meaning mainly, but not entirely, geographical and political areas, function as measures rather than as nouns, and are coded in this way. They are autonomous measures, but have no other special characteristics. For example:

   lyǎng-'gwó "two countries"
   sān-'shěng "three provinces"

Mclass = Classifying Measures (See also M)

Classifying measures are auxiliary measures, with meanings such as "kind of, grade of, class of": **sān-jǔng-'fǔ-dz** "three kinds of axes", with *Mclass* **jǔng**. They are special in that almost any noun may be preceded by a classifying measure, there being various limitations in the use of other types of measures with the different types of nouns.

Mcont = Containing Measures (See also M)

A containing measure is an auxiliary measure, designating some containerful of the substance named by the noun:

   yì-wǎn-'fàn "a bowl of rice"

MdistS = Spatially Distributive Measures (See also M)

MdistT = Temporally Distributive Measures (See also M)

When a distributive measure is used with a numeral larger than one, it indicates that the things or events specified are at different and discrete *places* (spatial) or that they occurred at different and discrete *times* (temporal). Thus **'sān-chù-'chyǎng-àn** "three cases of robbery" at different places, perhaps at the same time or during the same night; **'sān-tsż-'chyǎng-àn** "three cases of robbery" at different times, perhaps at the same house or store.

Temporally distributive measures are used:

1. After a verb, or a verb and any postposed noun referent, as an indication of *frequency*:

> wǒ 'dzwó-tyan 'kàn-jyàn ta 'sān-tsz̀. "I saw him three times yesterday."

2. Between a verb (*V* or *I*) and a nominal referent:

> 'dǎ yí-tsz̀-ᴗchyéwr "play ball once"
>
> 'shyà-le sān-jèn-'ywǔ. "There were three spells of rain."

3. More rarely, before a group of *V* and noun or of *I* and noun, the latter group being thereby nominalized:

> 'nèy-tsz̀-chū-'snr̀ "that accident" (chū-'shr̀ "to have an accident")

Mgroup = Grouping Measures (See also M)

Grouping measures are used with appropriate nouns (mainly personal nouns and mass nouns) to indicate groups of some kind:

> yì-chywún-'rén "a group of people"
>
> yì-chywún-'ywú "a school of fish"

Occasionally a grouping measure is used with a collective noun:

> yí-tàw-jwō-'yǐ "a matching set of tables and chairs"

MgroupA = Autonomous Grouping Measures (See also M)

Autonomous grouping measures are also used, with full meaning, without any following noun:

> yì-lyáⁿ 'bīng "a company (*military unit*) of soldiers"
>
> yì-'lyán "a company, troop, battery"

Mmeas = Measures of Weight, Length, Area, Etc. (See also M)

These are used:

1. Before a noun:

> sān-jīn-'táng "three catties of sugar"

2. Preceded by yěw and followed by an adjective:

> 'jèy-kwày-'bīng yěw 'sān-jīn-'jùng. "This piece of ice has three catties heavy."="This piece of ice weighs three pounds."

3. After adjectives:

> 'jèy-kwày-'bīng 'jùng sān-'jìn. "This piece of ice weighs three catties too much."

Or,

> 'jèy-kwày-'bīng bǐ 'nèy-kwày-'bīng 'jùng sān-'jìn. "This piece of ice is three catties heavier than that piece."

Mpart = Partitive Measures (See also M)

A partitive measure indicates a part or portion of something named by a unit noun or mass noun; except for dyǎr "a little bit of", partitive measures with mass nouns are not distinguishable from individualizing measures with mass nouns, and are not specially designated. Thus:

> yì-tséng-'léw "one floor of a building"
>
> dyǎr (or dyǎn) "a little, a bit", the most general partitive measure, is used in the patterns given above for *Mmeas*.

MpersA = Autonomous Personal Measures (See also M)

A few elements also used in other ways are sometimes used as measures specifying various kinds of people. In a hospital, thus, nèy-'chwáng, literally "that bed" (chwáng being otherwise a noun), may be said to mean "that bed's patient, the patient assigned to that bed".

Mpos = Measures of Position and Shape (See also M)

Mpos participate in *expressions of place* as follows:

1. Preceded by a numeral occasionally, more often by a demonstrative:

> 'jè-li (usually reduced to jèr) "here"
>
> 'lyǎng-byar "both sides"

2. Preceded by a nominal expression, most often lǐ "space inside" and shàng "space on top of or above", but occasionally others:

> 'wū-dz-lǐ "in the room"
>
> 'jwō-dz-shang "on the table"

3. Type 1 in turn preceded by a nominal expression:

> 'jwō-dz-de-'lyǎng-byar "both sides of the table"
>
> 'wǒ-jèr "here where I am"

Msemel = Semelfactive Measures (See also M)

A semelfactive measure indicates *single action*, though not necessarily instantaneous action. Semelfactive measures follow verbs; the numeral is usually yī "one".

1. After a verb of striking, hitting, kicking, and the like, a term specifying the instrument with which the blow is delivered functions as a semelfactive measure meaning "a blow with" that instrument:

> 'dǎ-ta yì-'chywán. "Strike him a blow with the fist."
>
> 'tī-ta yì-'jyǎw. "Kick him once with the foot."

2. After some verbs one or another measure occurs with no meaning except that described above for all semelfactive measures:

'gàw-sung wo yì-'shēngr *literally* "Tell me a little noise *meaning* "(Just) let me know."

'dǎ-ta yi shyàr. "Hit him once."

3. After a one-syllable verb (*V*) the same morpheme is repeated as semelfactive measure; only yī "one" is possible before it:

tā 'shyang-le yì-shyǎng. "He thought for a minute."

chǐng-ni 'tīng-yi-tīng. "Listen to me for a minute."

wǒm 'tán yì-tán-'hwà-ba. "Let's talk a bit."

Mtime = Measures of Time (See also M)

Measures of time are autonomous measures which specify periods of time: **tyān** "day", **nyán** "year". Thus:

'jèy-jǐ-tyān "these few days"

'lyǎng-nyán "two years"

Munit = Unit Measures (See also M)

A unit measure is used with a personal noun, non-personal unit noun, or (some of them) with a non-personal mass noun; as indicated at entries, some of them are used with time nouns or place nouns.

The *Munit* used with personal nouns have specific connotations as outlined under *Npers*.

An *Munit* used with a non-personal unit noun adds no meaning to the unit noun itself except when some choice is possible: thus **yì-bǎ-'yǐ-dz** "one chair" and **yì-jāng-'yǐ-dz** "one chair" differ in that the *Munit* **bǎ** used in the first case emphasizes the fact that the chair has a back by which it can be picked up and carried around, whereas the *Munit* **jāng** used in the second case stresses rather the flat sitting surface of the chair (see entries **bǎ** and **jāng**).

An *Munit* used with a mass noun has *individualizing* function, specifying some quantity or portion of the mass in terms of which it can be counted or measured; see under *Nmass*.

N = Nouns

A *noun* is a noun-like form which is not counted by prefixing numerals directly; instead, a *measure* is inserted between the numeral and the noun: **rén** "person, people", but **'sān-ge-rén** "three people", with inserted measure **ge**. Chinese nouns undergo no changes of form comparable to English *man*, *men*, *man's*, *men's*.

At noun entries the measure or measures used with the noun (unless this follows automatically from the type of noun) are indicated directly after the code symbol. Whether or not the choice of measure helps to determine the meaning can be determined (if this information is not also given) by looking up the measures.

Nouns participate in nominal expressions as follows:

1. A noun alone:

bīng "soldier(s)"

'shŕ-tew "stone(s)

'shŕ-ching "affair(s), matter(s)"

lǐ-'bày "week(s)"

chéng "(walled) city"

2. A noun preceded by another noun or by a nominal expression:

jywūn-'gwān "army officer"

chyán-'pyàw-dz "money ticket"="bill" (paper money)

'yí-kwày-chyán-de-chyán-'pyàw-dz "one-dollar bill"

jèy-ge-'tswēn-dz-li-tew "this village's inside"="in this village" (final noun **'li-tew** "inside")

3. A noun preceded by an adjective or adjective expression, or by a verb or verb expression:

'dà-rén "adult person, adult people"="adults"

gān-'dì "dry land'

gān-le-de-'dì "dried land"

dzwèy-'hèw-de-shèng-'lì "final victory"

'rúng-yì-dzwò-de-'shŕ "easy-to-do work" = "work that is easy to do"

dǎ-dž-'jī "strike-letter machine"="typewriter"

mày-'shū-de-rén "sell-book person"="bookseller"

4. A numeral plus a measure plus a noun:

yí-ge-'rén "a person"

'sān-ge-rén "three people"

'lyǎng-kwày-chyán "two dollars"

5. A measure plus a noun:

ge-'rén "a person"

This is equivalent to the above with yī "a, an, one" as numeral, and occurs as an alternate to the latter only after a verb (*V, I, RC, K*) or *A* or *H*.

6. A demonstrative plus a measure plus a noun:

'jèy-ge-rén "this person"

jèy-wǎn-'fàn "this bowl of rice"

7. A demonstrative plus a numeral plus a measure plus a noun:

'jèy-yí-ge-rén "this one person"

8. Any of the last four types (4–7) with an adjective or adjective expression, or verb or verb expression, inserted before the noun; any of them with an adjective inserted before a containing measure (*Mcont*):

yì-wǎn-hěn-hǎw-'chŕ-de-'fàn "a bowl of very good rice"

yí-'dà-wǎn-'fàn "a big bowl of rice"

Nabstr = Abstract Nouns (See also N)

Abstract nouns do not enter into constructions with measures except with a classifying measure, usually **jŭng** "kind of, class of, type of":

'nèy-jŭng-nyán-'líng "that kind-of age"="such an age as that"

Ncoll = Collective Nouns (See also N)

A collective noun refers to several discrete things (or people) taken as a unified group. They do not enter into constructions with measures save occasionally with a classifying measure (**jŭng** "kind of, class of, sort of"), or (with certain ones only) a grouping measure:

'jèy-jŭng-fù-'mŭ "this kind-of parents"="such parents as these"

yí-tàw-jwō-'yǐ "a matching set of tables and chairs"

When a collective noun precedes a verb in a sentence, a summarizing adverb such as **dēw** or **chywán** "all, both, altogether, all in all" is usually placed directly before the verb:

wǒ-de-'fù-mǔ 'dēw bú-'dzày-le. "My parents are both dead."

Nmass = Mass Nouns (See also N)

Mass nouns refer to substances which come in a continuous mass:

shwěy "water"

'shŕ-tew "stóne"

dyàn-'shyàn "wire"

dì "land"

yán "salt"

chyán "money"

Unit measures used with mass nouns specify some quantity, piece, extension, size-and-shape, of the substance in question. In some cases measures are listed for a mass noun where it is entered in the dictionary; for others the measure that is most apt to be used follows from the type of substance in question. The following list will be useful:

1. With *Nmass* designating solids of indefinite extent in three dimensions (stone, iron, wood, glass), most commonly *Munit* **kwày** "irregular piece or hunk of".

2. With *Nmass* designating solids of indefinite extent primarily in two dimensions (paper, cloth): **kwày** as above; **jāng** "sheet of"; sometimes **tyáw** "slip or strip of".

3. With *Nmass* designating solids of indefinite extent primarily in one dimension (rope, string, thread, wire): **tyáw** for an indefinitely long piece; **gēn** or **gēr** for a short piece; sometimes **kwěn** "a bundle of" (*e.g., sticks*).

4. With *Nmass* designating masses composed of tiny solid particles (sand, sugar, salt): **lì** or **lyèr** "a grain of"; or by weight or containerful (*Mmeas, Mcont*).

5. With *Nmass* designating liquids: **dī** or **dyēr** "a drop of"; or by containerful.

6. With *Nmass* designating surfaces or extents (*as* surfaces, not solids; thus land, fields): **kwày** for an indefinite area of, **pyàn** for "an extent of, an expanse of"; or by precise measurement of area (*Mmeas*).

7. *Nmass* designating things which are in a state neither solid nor liquid (jellies, greases, salves, viscous liquids, paraffin, mud) are made to fall within the classifications of solid or liquid. One *Munit*, however, emphasizes this intermediate state: **tān** "a gooey, sticky mess of in the process of melting and spreading out":

yì-tān-chèw-'yéw "a gob of tar melting and spreading out"

But if such a substance is bought and sold, it is often measured by weight or containerful (*Mmeas, Mcont*).

Npers = Personal Nouns (See also N)

Personal nouns refer to people or kinds of people (but not collectively, in which case the noun is an *Ncoll*, nor by specific personal name, in which case the noun is an *Nunique*).

In construction with measures, personal nouns occur with the *Munit* **ge**, which carries no meaning at all save to indicate that the individuals are being enumerated *as* individuals; with the *Munit* **wèy**, which indicates the same thing plus a degree of politeness; and with the *Munit* **kěw**, when one is concerned with economics or with census.

The *NumG* (**shŕ** "ten", and so on) function as grouping measures with personal nouns, but not with any other type of noun: either **yì-bǎy-'rén** "one hundred people" or **yì-bǎy-ge-'rén** "one hundred unit people" for "a hundred people", but, with a different type of noun, only **yì-bǎy-ge-'wǎn** for "a hundred bowls".

Npers form collective nouns (*Ncoll*) by adding -men: **'peng-yew** "friend(s)"; **'péng-yew-men** "friends collectively", as, for example, all the friends of a certain person.

NpersT = Personal Nouns Used as Titles (See also N)

These share all the features outlined above for *Npers*, and, in addition, are used as titles. A form used as a title follows the person's name:

'jāng-shyān-sheng "Mr. Jāng"

'lǐ-jǔ-shí "Chairman Lǐ"

Nplace = Place Nouns (See also N)

Place nouns are not often used with measures; when the contrary is true this is specified at the entry and full details are given.

Place nouns participate in *place expressions* as follows:

1. Place noun alone:

'lǐ-tew "inside" (of something not mentioned but understood)

2. Place noun preceded by a designation of the object relative to which the place is located:

'wū-dz-lǐ-tew "room's inside"="inside the room"

In some cases a place noun has a single short form and one or more longer forms; *e.g.:* **lǐ** (or **li**) "inside"; longer forms **'lǐ-tew, 'lǐ-tewr, 'lǐ-byan, 'lǐ-byar, 'lǐ-myan, 'lǐ-myar**. When this is the case, the short form is used principally after coverbs of direction (**shyàng-'lǐ** "towards the inside"), the longer forms elsewhere.

Ntime = Time Nouns (See also N)

A time noun designates a time, absolute or relative, or a period of time. Measures for time nouns, when any are used, are designated at the entries.

A nominal expression ending in a time noun is a *time expression*.

NumG = Group Numerals

NumU = Unit Numerals

Unit numerals are the morphemes for "one" through "nine" and **jǐ** "a few; how many?"; group numerals are the morphemes for "ten", "hundred", "thousand", and "ten thousand". Numeral expressions consist of one of these or of expressions compounded from them as follows:

1. Multiples of the group numerals are formed by prefixing the proper unit numerals:

'èr-shŕ "twenty", and so on.

For "ten" one says simply **shŕ**; but for "hundred", "thousand", and "ten thousand" one says:

yì-'bǎy "one hundred"

yì-'chyān "one thousand"

yí-'wàn "one ten thousand"

If "ten" forms the last part of a larger numerical expression, one says **yì-'shŕ**; thus:

yì-'bǎy-yì-'shŕ "one hundred and ten"

2. Numbers larger than ten thousand are expressed in multiples of **wàn** "ten thousand", instead of in multiples of a thousand as in English:

'shŕ-wàn "a hundred thousand", and so on.

3. Compound numbers up to 9,999 are formed the same in Chinese as in English, save that Chinese is regular for the 'teen's and the 'ty's:

shŕ-'sān "thirteen"

sān-shr-'sż "thirty-four"

Compound numbers beyond 10,000 are the same save for the comment made in point 2.

4. *One or more* successive zeros, other than in final position, are expressed by the term **líng** used *once:*

yì-'bǎy-líng-'yī "a hundred and one"

yì-'chyān-líng-'yī "a thousand and one"

5. Either standing alone, or at the end of a compound number in the digits position, two successive unit numerals indicate *approximate number:*

sż-'wǔ "about four or five"

6. **jǐ** replaces a unit numeral in the digits position to indicate approximateness:

èr-shr-'jǐ "twenty-odd"

7. An alternative way of expressing compound numbers, particularly in giving dates in the Western calendar or in reading off figures in Arabic notation, is to read off digit by digit, using **líng** once for *each* zero and **dyǎn** for a decimal point:

'yī 'jyěw-'sż-'sż-'nyán "the year 1944"

'sān-'sż-'wǔ-'dyǎn-'chī-'bā-'jyěw "345.789"

8. There are two words for "two": **èr** and **lyǎng**, used as follows:

a. Only **èr** is used in compound numbers, except that **bǎy** "hundred" and the two larger group numerals may be preceded by either to indicate "two hundred" and the like.

b. Only **èr** is used in *ordinal* expressions (see *Preord*).

c. **lyǎng** is otherwise used for just "two" (not "two hundred and *two*" and the like) with most measures. A few measures permit either **lyǎng** or **èr** for just "two"; one requires **èr**. When **èr** is permitted or required under these circumstances by a particular measure, that fact is indicated at the entry.

Numeral expressions participate in nominal expressions as follows:

1. Alone. This is confined almost entirely to mathematical statements such as:

'lyèw jyā-'lyèw dé shŕ-'èr. "Six plus six is twelve."

2. A numeral plus a measure:

sān-'shěng "three provinces"

3. A numeral plus a measure plus a noun:

yí-ge-'rén "a person"

4. A demonstrative plus a numeral plus a measure:

'jèy-yí-ge "this one"

5. A demonstrative plus a numeral plus a measure plus a noun:

jèy-'yí-ge-rén "this one person"

Nunique = Unique Nouns (See also N)

Unique nouns refer to things of which there is only one: proper names of people and places, and a few words such as **tyān** "sky, heaven". Unique nouns, as such, are not used in construction with measures. But since two people or two places may have the same proper name, that name is sometimes used as an ordinary personal noun or unit noun to state just that fact:

> **yěw 'lyǎng-ge-chúng-'chìng.** "There are two Chung-kings." (if there were)

This is not done with a single-syllable surname of a person. There the fact has to be stated in a different way:

> **yěw 'lyǎng-ge-shìng-'jǎng-de-rén.** "There are two people named Jǎng."

This second method is possible with all unique nouns. A unique noun is a *definite* nominal expression.

Nunit = Unit Nouns (See also N)

Unit nouns refer to discrete objects other than people (dog, cow, horse, bowl, cup, book, and the like). The unit measure or unit measures used with each unit noun are indicated at the entry, since there is not much chance of predicting accurately what measure will be used. However, the use of a particular unit measure with a particular unit noun often refers to some characteristic feature of the thing named by the noun: thus tools and instruments which one grasps in the hand for use (scissors, knives, rakes, fans) often take the *Munit* **bǎ**, which turns on just this feature of the objects named by the nouns.

NunitC = Unit Nouns Used as Containing Measures

(See also N)

An *NunitC* shares the characteristics outlined above for *Nunit*; in addition, being the name of an object which might on occasion function as a container for something else, it functions as an *Mcont*. Thus **yí-ge-'wǎn** "a bowl", with **wǎn** as a noun and the measure **ge**, but **yì-wǎn-'fàn** "a bowl of rice", with **wǎn** as a containing measure and the noun **fàn**.

postV = Postverbs

The second of the two constituents of an *RC* is called a *postverb*. When in the discussion of a form the phrase "As *postV:*" occurs, it indicates that the following subentries are, or that the following sentences include, resultative compounds with the head entry functioning as a postverb. If the head entry is an *A* or *I*, the *RC* are of type one or two; if the head entry is a *V*, the *RC* are of type three or four.

Preord = Ordinal Prefix

An ordinal prefix is an element prefixed to an expression containing a numeral to give it *ordinal* meaning ("first", "second", and so on). There are only a few *Preord;* the chief one is **dì-**. An ordinal prefix enters into nominal expressions as follows:

1. *Preord* plus numeral (rare):

   > **dì-'yī** "in the first place, point one"

2. *Preord* plus numeral plus measure:

   > **dì-'chī-shr-chī-'shr̄** "the seventy-seventh division"

3. *Preord* plus numeral plus measure plus noun:

   > **'téw-yí-ge-rén** "the first person" (of those in a line, for example)
   >
   > **'téw-lyǎng-ge-rén** "the first two people"

If a particular thing is regularly numbered ordinally, the ordinal prefix is often omitted; thus with numbered streets in a city:

> **'sān-jyē** "third street"

A number of nouns (of which **jyē** "street" is one) require no measure in this case, functioning themselves as measures *only* in such ordinal constructions.

Ordinal expressions are *definite*.

Pron = Pronouns

Pronouns are the words for "I, you, he", etc., and for "who". Nominal expressions beginning in a pronoun are *definite*. Pronouns participate in nominal expressions as follows:

1. A pronoun alone:

   > **wǒ** "I, me"

2. A pronoun (with or without added **de**) plus almost any nominal expression not itself consisting of, or starting with, a pronoun:

   > **wǒ-de-'chyán** "my money"
   >
   > **wǒ-'shěw-li** "in my hand"

de is used in this case always with **shwéy** or **shéy** "who"; it is optionally omitted with the others before terms designating body parts or relatives:

> **wǒ-'shěw** "my hand"
>
> **wǒ-'fù-chin** "my father"

RC = Resultative Compounds

Resultative compounds are verb compounds having the following special characteristics:

1. Of the two negative adverbs, **bū** "don't, doesn't, won't" and **méy** "haven't, hasn't, didn't", only the latter is used before an *RC* with any degree of freedom. **bū** is sometimes used in the meaning of "purposely not" do such-and-such:

   > **ni 'bú-dzwò-'wán bù-gěy-'chyán.** "If you purposely fail to finish the job you won't get any money."

2. Most *RC* have a *simple form* and two *potential forms*, made by inserting **de** and **bu**, respectively, between the main verb and the postverb of the simple form:

dǎ-'hwày "strike something so that it breaks"

Potential forms:

dǎ-de-'hwày "be able to break by striking"
dǎ-bu-'hwày "be unable to break by striking"

The simple form describes a situation in which the action designated by the main verb results in the action or state designated by the postverb; the potential forms specify that the action or state specified by the postverb can, or cannot, be brought about by the action designated by the main verb.

Exceptions: RC with postverb **dzày** "in, at, on" or **gěy** "to, for" (a person) have no potential forms; a few others also have no potential forms, and this is indicated for these few others at the entries. Some *RC* have *only* the potential forms; this is indicated by citing the *RC* with **bu** inserted and defining accordingly. This **bu** is ignored in alphabetization. In some cases where both simple and potential forms exist, there is some unexpected change of meaning; in such cases both are given with their meanings.

RC1 = Resultative Compounds, Type One

An *RC1* has an *I* or *A* as main verb and another *I* or *A* as postverb.

1. *In simple form.* An *RC1* as nucleus of a sentence may be accompanied by a nominal referent in the function of *actor;* an actor placed after the *RC1* is *indefinite* and must be indefinite in form; an actor placed before the verb is *definite* regardless of its form:

'pǎw-láy-le hěn-'dwō-de-jǐng-'chá. "A lot of policemen came running up."

nèy-ge-'rén jyèw 'pǎw-láy-le. "The man at once came running up."

A preposed actor not definite in form can be rendered indefinite by prefixing **yěw:**

.yěw hěn-'dwō-de-jǐng-'chá 'pǎw-láy-le. "A lot of policemen came running up."

2. *In potential forms.* An actor is used as with the simple form, but the actor is always definite, before the verb:

wǒ 'jàn-bu-chǐ-'láy. "I can't stand up."

RC2 = Resultative Compounds, Type Two

An *RC2* has a *V* as main verb and an *I* or *A* as postverb. There are two subtypes:

1. *Subtype One.* These are causatives to the underlying *I* or *A* used as postverbs: **húng** (*A*) "red":

nùng-'húng "to make red"
tú-'húng "to paint red"

The possible combinations are endless; only a sampling of those most apt to be heard are given at entries.

a. Subtype One in Simple Form. As sentence nucleus, an *RC2* of subtype one may take two nominal referents: an *agent* and a *goal*. The agent precedes the *RC2;* the goal is most frequently placed between the agent and the verb, marked by preposed coverb **bǎ**, but may on occasion be placed either first in the sentence, for emphasis, or after the *RC2* (the last being the most rare):

tā bǎ nèy-ge-'wǎn dǎ-'swèy-le. "He broke that bowl."

'nèy-ge-wǎn tā háy méy-dǎ-'swèy. "(But) he hasn't broken *that* bowl yet."

The relative emphasis on agent and goal may be reversed by beginning the sentence with the latter and marking the former with preposed coverb **jyàw** or **bèy:**

'jàng-peng jyàw-'fēng gwā-'dǎw-le. "The tents were blown down by the wind."

It is quite generally the custom to use *RC2* of subtype two in simple form only with added **le** or with preposed **méy.**

b. Subtype One in Potential Forms. Both agent and goal precede the verb; the goal is apt to come first, in emphatic position, and the agent is often omitted:

'jèy-ge-wǎn nǐ dǎ-bu-'swèy. "You can't break *this* bowl."

2. *Subtype Two.* The remainder of *RC2* fall in this subtype; the main verb, rather than the postverb, is the component of chief importance, the postverb often indicating only successful completion:

kàn "to look at"
'kàn-jyàn "to see"

a. Subtype Two in Simple Form. As sentence nucleus, this subtype calls for an *actor* and a *percept* rather than an agent and a goal; the percept is limited to emphatic position at the beginning of the sentence or to position after the verb:

wǒ háy méy-'kàn-jyàn ta. "I haven't seen him yet."

tā-de-'péng-yew wǒ háy méy-'kàn-jyàn. "His friend, though, I haven't yet seen."

b. Subtype Two in Potential Forms. The positions for actor and percept are as with the simple form:

'dǐ-shyà-nèy-ge-'dz̀ wǒ kàn-bu-'jyàn. "I can't see the character below it."

wǒ kàn-bu-'jyàn 'dǐ-shyà-nèy-ge-'dz̀. "It's the character below it that I can't see."

RC3 = Resultative Compounds, Type Three

RC3 have an *I* (rarely an *A*) as main verb, and a *V* (one of a relatively small number) as postverb.

1. *In Simple Form.* Two nominal referents occur; an *actor*, before the *RC3*, and a *terminus* after the *RC3*. The terminus designates a place, point, position, or time which is *reached* (dàw, dzày), or *passed* or *exceeded* (gwò), or a resulting *state* (chéng):

ᵗā 'păw-dàw 'fáng-dz-li chywù-le. "He ran into the house."

tā 'păw-gwò 'jyē láy-le. "He ran across the street."

wǒ-men yì-'tyān tsúng 'dzăw-chen máng-dàw 'wǎn-shang. "We're busy all day from morning to night."

2. *In Potential Forms.* These are relatively rare. The terminus may come in initial emphatic position:

'jèy-tyáw-hé nǐ 'fù-bu-gwò-'chywù. "You can't swim across this river."

RC4 = Resultative Compounds, Type Four

RC4 have a *V* as main verb and another *V* (one of a limited set) as postverb. Those with gěy as postverb are treated separately.

1. *In Simple Form.* There are potentially three nominal referents: agent, goal, and terminus. The agent and goal come before the *RC4*, the terminus after. The arrangement before the verb may be either *agent* bǎ *goal* or *goal* jyàw (or bèy) *agent*. The terminus indicates a place, point, or position *reached* or *passed*, or resulting *state*:

chǐng-ni bǎ-'yān ná-dàw 'jèr-lay. "Please bring the cigarettes over here."

'jàng-peng jyàw-'fēng 'gwā-dàw hé-'nèy-byar chywù-le. "The tents were blown to the other side of the river by the wind."

With agent omitted:

'jàng-peng dēw gěy gwā-dàw hé-'nèy-byar chywù-lě. "The tents were all blown to the other side of the river."

The goal is not omitted, nor is the terminus. With terminus indicating a resulting state:

bǎ tyě-'sẓ 'wān-chéng yí-ge-'chywār. "Bend the wire into a circle."

2. *In Potential Forms.* These are rare with *RC4;* the nominal referents are as with the simple form:

'nèy-ge-dūng-shi tā 'ná-bu-dàw nèr jyèw hwèy 'hwày-de. "That thing is apt to break before he can get it there."

3. *With Postverb* gěy *in Simple Form.* The nominal referents are agent, goal, and recipient: the recipient follows the *RC4;* the agent comes before the *RC4;* the goal comes either at the beginning for emphasis, after bǎ directly before the *RC4,* or after the recipient:

chǐng-ni bǎ-'yān dì-gey wo. "Please pass me the cigarettes."

tā 'jyè-gey wo yí-kwày-'chyán. "He loaned me a dollar."

V = Transitive Verbs

With a *V* as nucleus of a sentence, the nominal referents include an *actor* (omitted on occasion) and a *goal*, a *percept*, or a *terminus* (only one of these three). The goal or percept may likewise be omitted on occasion. The actor precedes the verb. With actor only:

'wǒ kāy. "I'll drive."

tā háy méy-'dàw-ne. "He hasn't arrived yet."

With actor understood (as in answering a question "Where is he?"):

háy méy-'dàw. "Hasn't gotten here yet."

A *percept* designates a person, object, or situation towards which the action denoted by the verb is directed, but which is not, as the result of that action, altered in position or structure. The percept is placed either at the beginning of the sentence (for emphasis) or after the verb:

kàn 'nèy-ge-rén. "Take a look at that fellow."

tā 'cháng-cháng shyăng-'nǐ. "He's always thinking about you."

'tā wǒ 'jyàn-gwo, tā-'tày-tay wǒ háy méy-'jyàn-gwo. "I've met him, but I haven't yet met his wife."

A *goal* designates a person, object, or situation on which the action denoted by the verb operates and which that action alters in position or structure. A goal is placed in either of the positions in which a percept is placed, or is placed directly before the verb with preposed bǎ.

chǐng-ni bǎ jèy-bǎ-'fǔ-dz 'dž-shì 'kàn-yi-kàn, 'dzày shwō. "Please wait until you've examined this axe carefully."

Here the verb is kàn "to look at" as in the first example of percept; but here the meaning is that the thing looked at is to be handled, turned around, manipulated, and so forth, in the process.

A *terminus* designates arrived-at point or resultant state. A terminus is normally after the *V:*

tā 'shéme-shŕ-hew ké-yi 'dàw-jèr? "When can he get here?"

tā háy méy-chéng-'dīng-ne. "He hasn't become an adult yet."

The *V* which are used with a terminus are generally those which are used as postverbs in *RC3* and *RC4,* calling there also for a terminus.

V2 = Transitive Verbs Followed by Two Nominal Forms

A *V2* is preceded by an actor (sometimes omitted) and followed by two nominal referents: *recipient* and *goal:*

tā 'gěy-le wo 'yí-kwày-chyán. "He gave me a dollar."

tā 'sùng-le wo yì-tyáw-'tǎn-dz. "He sent me a blanket." (*as a gift*)

The goal may come in emphatic position at the beginning of the sentence:

'nèy-tyáw-'tǎn-dz wǒ 'bù-néng 'gěy-ni. "I can't let you have that particular blanket."

VN1 = Verb-Noun Combination, Type One

A *VN1* is a combination of verb and goal (or percept or terminus; one cannot distinguish them) which is "frozen"—having special meaning not predictable from the meaning of the verb and the noun, and not freely separable (compare *VN2*). Thus dzěw-bèy-'ywùn "to pass through a period of ill luck, to get bad breaks":

tā shyàn-dzày dzěw bèy-'ywùn-ne. "He's meeting up with a good deal of bad luck right now."

A *VN1*, as it functions in a sentence (since it takes only an actor, containing within itself any other possible nominal referent), works like either an *I* or an *A*. Unless there is clear indication at an entry that a particular *VN1* works like an *A*, it is to be taken as working like an *I*.

VN2 = Verb-Noun Combination, Type Two

A *VN2* is a combination of verb and goal (or percept or terminus) which has a meaning not predictable from the meanings of the parts, but the parts of which can be separated, or even come in reverse order in the sentence, without losing that special meaning. Thus dzwo-'shèw is "to celebrate the birthday of an older person":

tā 'jīn-nyan dzwò 'wǔ-shr-wǔ-'swèy-de-'shèw. "He celebrates his fifty-fifth birthday this year."

VN3 = Verb-Noun Combination, Type Three

A *VN3* operates as does a *VN2*, but in addition may function as a noun with the meaning "N which has been V'ed". Thus chǎw-'fàn is "to fry rice" or "fried rice".

Vpred = Verbs Used Before a Nuclear Verb

A *Vpred* is placed before another verb (*V, I, RC;* rarely *A*); the second verb is the nucleus, and the various nominal referents are arranged accordingly:

wǒ hěn 'ywàn-yi chywù. "I'm quite anxious to go."

wǒ děy 'dzěw-le. "I've got to leave now."

wǒ yàw chī̌-'fàn. "I'm going to eat."

Vsent = Verbs Followed by an Entire Sentence

A *Vsent* is preceded by an actor (unless actor is understood from context), and is followed by an entire sentence with its own nucleus, its own actor, etc.:

wǒ 'chǐng-ni chī̌-'fàn. "I'm inviting you to dinner."

shéy jyàw-ni 'chywù-de? "Who told you to go?"

tā shwō tā bú-'ywàn-yi chywu. "He said he doesn't want to go."

F. CHARACTERS

1. Since this is a dictionary of *spoken* Chinese, no effort has been made to see that the Chinese-English side includes the characters which are most apt to occur in any particular variety of written Chinese. However, each entry in the Chinese-English side is preceded by the characters with which the particular form is normally written, and the characters which so occur are listed in the Character Index which follows the Chinese-English side.

2. Chinese characters represent an essentially different type of writing system from the systems of western European languages and of English. The unit symbols of the latter are *letters;* a letter represents a recurrent *sound* of the spoken language, and by stringing letters out in the same order in which the sounds occur in an utterance, that utterance is portrayed. Chinese characters, in contrast to this, represent not *sounds* but *morphemes* of the spoken language (see Section E, Subsection 1). Since any utterance consists of a string of morphemes, the proper characters strung out in the proper order can similarly portray the utterance. Such a system obviously requires a much larger number of unit symbols, since any language has a larger number of morphemes than it has sounds.

The above statement has to be modified slightly: a single Chinese character is used to represent either a morpheme or a syllable, whichever is smaller. Thus to the morpheme bīng "soldier", which is also one syllable, corresponds a single character; to the morpheme bīng "ice" (a different morpheme from that for soldier although it sounds the same) corresponds another single character; to the morpheme 'bwō-li "glass", which is two syllables, corresponds a sequence of two characters, one representing each of the syllables of the morpheme; and to the syllable hwàr "picture", which is two morphemes, hwà "to depict" plus a fused element -r, corresponds a sequence of two characters, one representing each morpheme.

It is also true that sometimes the same character is used to write things which strike one as being quite unrelated in meaning, not by any stretch of the imagination cases of a single morpheme. Thus the same character is used to write the morpheme dūng "east" and the first syllable of the two-syllable morpheme 'dūng-shi "thing". Chinese writing is no more capricious in this, however, than is English writing in using the same letter or combination of letters for distinct sounds (*th* for the distinct sounds of *thin* and *this*, for example).

3. Characters are by no means completely distinct from each other in form. Many characters representing morphemes with similar meanings have smaller visual parts in common; many characters representing morphemes with identical or similar sound have smaller visual parts in common. These interrelationships on a level lower than that of characters as wholes, however, do not parallel in any systematic way similar relationships between the morphemes represented.

The Chinese have made use of these partial similarities to the eye for one important purpose: the establishment of some order in which characters can be listed, comparable to arbitrary alphabetical order in English and other alphabetical writing systems. The most common of these is as follows: Each character consists of a recurrent partial called a *radical*, and various added figures. The radicals, 214 in number, are arranged in groups depending on the number of strokes used in drawing them, and, within each group, in an arbitrarily fixed sequence. Each character is then grouped under the radical which it contains, and a character calling for a larger number of strokes *in addition* to those used for the radical follows one which calls for a smaller number of strokes *in addition* to the radical. Where this number of added strokes is the same for several characters, the order is once again arbitrary, but usually follows that found in a certain very large dictionary of characters published in the eighteenth century. Whether this established order is followed in such cases or not, the group of characters whose ordering would have to be determined on such an arbitrary principle is generally so small that for purposes of finding a particular one any order is satisfactory.

In the Character Index of this dictionary the characters which occur in the Chinese-English side are ordered in this way. After each is given the pronunciation, or pronunciations, of the morpheme (or morphemes) which that character is used to represent. Since the body of the Chinese-English side is alphabetized according to pronunciation, this serves as a convenient means of cross reference.

4. The specific nature of the Chinese writing system has led to the development of a number of specialized *literary styles*, involving sequences of morphemes which do not occur in the spoken language itself, morphemes used with shades of meaning they do not have in the spoken language, or even morphemes no longer used in the spoken language. Some of the typical phrases of one or another literary style, however, are often quoted in ordinary speech, particularly, but not exclusively, by educated Chinese. Some of these are important enough to require inclusion in the present dictionary, small though it is.

Entries on the Chinese-English side marked *literary quotation* are expressions of this kind, borrowed from the literary (written) language but apt to be quoted.

Entries marked *a bit literary* are expressions not necessarily used by a speaker of Chinese as literary quotations in the above sense, but still likely to be heard mainly from the lips of an educated Chinese.

Entries marked *literary* are expressions, or morphemes, not ordinarily occurring in speech at all, save sometimes in designations of official government agencies and the like.

PART II

CHINESE–ENGLISH

NOTES ON THE USE OF THE CHINESE-ENGLISH SIDE

Alphabetical Order. *Single syllables* are arranged in straight alphabetical order. Syllables differing only in tone are arranged in the following manner: **ju** (no tone), **jū, jú, jǔ, jù.**

Entries containing more than one syllable are arranged under those of one syllable, or in comparable order when the single-syllable entry is lacking. Thus **jǔ-'yì** *precedes* **jù-'dzwò** because **jǔ** precedes **jù.**

The forms **bū** "not" and **yī** "one" are ignored in the alphabetization save in a few cases where those forms themselves are of prime importance. Thus **kàn-bu-'jyàn** would be alphabetized as though the second syllable were not there.

Characters. The characters for an entry *precede* the entry.

Typefaces. Chinese material is in **boldface**. English equivalents and definitions are in lightface. Explanation and comment are in *italics*.

Code Symbols. The italicized abbreviations in parentheses after most entries and some subentries are code symbols referring to Section E, Subsection 6, of the Introduction.

Asterisk. An asterisk (*) before an entry indicates that it is a *bound morpheme* (see Section E, Subsection 1, of the Introduction).

Degree Sign. The degree sign (°) is used in Chinese or English sentences as follows: "He isn't °coming here any more. *or* °going to come here again." Here the degree sign indicates that both "He isn't coming here any more." and "He isn't going to come here again." are acceptable versions.

A

阿，呵（呀，哇，哪，啊）

a (*or* **ya, wa, na, nga,** *beginning in the same consonant with which the preceding syllable ends*) *sentence-final element showing surprise, hesitation, or politeness.* ‖**tā 'dzěme bù-'láy-ya?** How is it he doesn't get here? ‖**'tyān 'dzěme háy bú-'lyàng-nga?** How come it isn't light yet? ‖**'wèy-shéme-ya?** Why? *or* How come? ‖**lǎw-'lwó-a!** *or* **lǎw-'lwó-ya!** Hey there, Lwó old pal! ‖**shř 'jèy-ge-a?** This one? ‖**'nèy-jyàn-shř-ching-nga, wǒ 'jywé-de bù-hǎw-'bàn.** As for that matter now, I feel it's going to be tough to handle. ‖**'nèy-ge-rén-na! hm!** That fellow! Huh! (*What the devil can he do?*)

ai *Wade Romanization for* **ay.**

按

ān (*V*) to install. **ān dyàn-'hwà** to install a telephone; *etc.*

安

***ān** (*A*) peaceful, restful, at ease. *Limited to negative use:* **bù-'ān** restless, uneasy, *itself used mainly in certain fixed groups:* **'lyáng-shīn bù-'ān** have an uneasy conscience; **dzwò-'lì bù-'ān** be worried, uneasy; **chīn-'shř bù-'ān** be so worried that one can't eat or sleep well.

鞍

***ān, 'ān-dz** (*Nunit,* **ge, fù**) saddle (*for any animal*).

安慶

ān-'chìng (*Nunique*) Anking, *another name for* **hwéy-'níng** Huai-ning (*capital city of Anhwei province*).

安葬

ān-'dzàng (*V*) to make ceremonial burial arrangements and bury (*formal term, or used for greater politeness for the act of burial itself*). ‖**tā hwéy jyā-'shyāng-chywu gěy tā-'fù-chin ān-'dzàng.** He returned to the ancestral home to arrange the funeral of his father.

安徽

ān-'hwēy (*Nunique*) Anhwei *province*.

安靜

ān-'jìng (*A*) quiet, peaceful, calm, silent. (*Opposites* **chǎw, fán, bù-'ān, nàw, 'rè-nàw.**) ‖**jèy-yí-'dày hěn ān-'jìng.** This district is very quiet. ‖**dà-'jyā shwèy-'jyàw-le, 'chǐng nǐ-men ˙ān-jìng-dyǎr.** Everyone's gone to bed; please be quiet. ‖**'chǐng nǐ-men ān-jìng (yí-)shyàr, wǒ tīng-bu-'jyàn.** Please calm down for a moment; I can't hear.

'ān-jìng-shya-chywù to calm down, quiet down. ‖fēng yǐ 'tíng, 'làng jyew màn-'mār-de 'ān-jìng-shyà-chywu-le. When the wind stopped, the sea gradually calmed down.

安置

'ān-jr̀ (V) arrange *things*, put *things* in their proper places; arrange employment for *someone*. ‖nǐ bǎ-ta 'ān-jr̀-dzày 'něr-le? Where (*in what section, department*) did you put him to work? ‖wǒ bǎ jèy-shyē-'dūng-shi ān-jr̀-'hǎw-le jyew ''láy. I'll be coming as soon as I get these things arranged. ‖'ān-jr̀ yí-ge-'jyā bú-shr 'rúng-yì-de. It isn't easy to get a family settled (*of someone moving his family from one establishment to another*).

安南

ān-'nán (*Nunique*) Annam (Indo-China).

安排

'ān-pay (V) arrange *matters satisfactorily;* arrange *things physically, putting them in certain places*. ‖'jèy-ge-shr̀-ching bù-hǎw 'ān-pay. This matter isn't easy to arrange. ‖tā 'mǎy-le hěn-dwō-de-'jyā-jywu, kě-shr bù-'jr̀-dàw dzěme ān-pay 'hǎw. He bought a lot of furniture, but he doesn't know °what to do with it. or °where to put it for best effect.

安培

'ān-péy (M; *or Nunit*, ge) ampere.

安慰

'ān-wèy (V) comfort *someone*. ‖chú-le tā-de-'nywǔ-ér, 'méy-yew rén néng 'ān-wèy ta. No one but his daughter could comfort him.

    (*Nabstr*) source of pleasure, satisfaction. ‖tā-de-'gūng-dzwo-de-chéng-'gūng jyew-shr tā-de-ān-'wèy. The success of his work is his only source of satisfaction.

安陽

ān-'yáng (*Nunique*) An-yang (*city in Honan province*).

按

àn *see* èn.

岸

àn (M) bank, shore, coast, (*of a body of water*). ‖'làng-tew dǎ-dzay 'àn-shang, hěn hǎw 'kàn. The waves beating against the shore are very beautiful.

    dūng-'àn east shore, *etc.;* hé-'àn river bank. ‖tsúng 'shī-àn dàw 'dūng-àn yěw dwō-'ywǎn? How far is it from the west bank to the east bank (*across water*)? or How far is it from the West Coast to the East Coast (*across land*)?

    shàng-'àn to land (*as from a sea voyage*).

按

*àn (K) by the ... (*period of time*). àn-'chī at regular intervals; àn 'jūng-dyǎr by the hour, hourly; àn-'ywè by the month; àn-'shr̀ or àn-je 'shr̀-hew on schedule, on time; àn-'nyán annually, by the year. ‖'jèy-jǔng-kān-'wù 'háy-shr àn-'chī chū-'bǎn. This type of publication is still put out regularly. ‖jèr-de-'shīn-shwěy shr̀ àn-'ywè 'gěy-ma? Do they pay by the month here? ‖hwǒ-'chē àn-'shr̀ 'kāy-le. The train left on schedule.

暗

àn (A) dark, *but not totally lacking light* (*of a color, room, the sky, etc.*). (*Opposites* lyàng, gwāng, *literary* *míng; for colors* chyǎn, dàn.) *Used as postV with same meaning:* ‖bǎ jèy-jyān-'wū-dz nùng-'àn yì-dyǎr. Make this room a little darker.

案

*àn, 'àn-dz (*Nunit*, ge, jyàn, jwāng) case *at law*, bill *in a legislative meeting*, act *of a legislative body*. ‖'něy-ge-fǎ-'tíng bàn jèy-ge-'àn-dz-ne? What court is handling this case?

暗淡

àn-'dàn (A) dim (*of light*), cold, distant (*of human feelings*). (*Opposites* lyàng, 'hwēy-hwáng; *for feelings* 'rè-shīn.)

按照

'àn-jàw or 'àn-je (K) according to. ‖'àn-jàw nǐ-swǒ-'shwō-de, nàme 'jèy-ge jyew 'dwèy-le. According to what you said, then, this is right. ‖nǐ àn-je tā-'gàw-su-ni-'shwō-de chywù 'dzwò, jyew 'bú-hwèy 'tswò. You do whatever he told you, and you can't go wrong.

暗中

'àn-jūng (H) in darkness, secretly. ‖tā 'àn-jūng dǎw-'gwěy. He's secretly upsetting your plans. ‖tā 'àn-jūng 'bāng nǐ-de-'máng. He's helping you without your knowing it.

暗扣，暗鈕

àn-'kèwr (*Nunit*, ge) hook-and-eye fastener.

暗室

àn-'shr̀ (*Nunit*, jyān) photographic darkroom; (*in literary expressions*) a dark place *where no one can see you*. ‖bù-'chī 'àn-shr̀. Don't cheat (even) in a dark place.

案由

àn-'yéw (*Nunit*, ge, jyàn) summary *of the purpose or subject of a communication*, summation *of a case at law*. With M dwàn, section of such a summary. ‖jèy-ge-àn-'yéw 'jì-de hěn 'shyáng-shi. This summation was recorded in great detail.

ao *Wade Romanization for* **aw.**

二
àr *see* èr.

熬
áw (*I*) to work hard and long *under none too pleasant circumstances.* ‖tā-de-'gūng-fu wán-'chywán shŕ 'áw-chū-lay-de. His skill (*or* achievement) is the result of much hard and long work. ‖tā dzwó-'wǎn-shang 'áw-le yí-'yè, méy-shwèy-'jyàw. He kept at it all last night, without any sleep.

(*V*) to cook for a long time. áw-'yàw to brew medicine; áw-'jēw to brew congee (*which requires long boiling*). ‖'jèy-ge-yàw děy 'dwō 'áw yì-hwěr. This medicine must be boiled a while longer.

熬爛
áw-'làn (*RC2*) to boil *something* to shreds.

熬刑
áw-'shíng (*VN2*) to bear torture.

澳大利亞
'àw-dà-lì-'yǎ (*Nunique*) Australia.

奧國
'àw-gwo (*Nunique*) Austria.

澳洲
àw-'jēw (*Nunique*) Australia (*the continent*).

澳門
àw-'mén (*Nunique*) Macao (*city in Kwangtung province*).

挨，捱
āy *or* áy (*V*) *followed by a verb, not a noun* to receive, get. ‖tā āy-'mà-le. He got a scolding (mà to scold). *Similarly* āy-'fá get punished; āy-'kēng get cheated; āy-'shwō get called down; āy-'shwā get fired *or* turned down.

Frequently the second verb is preceded by a Num-M group such as yí-dwèn. ‖tā 'āy-le yí-dwèn-'shwō. He got a calling down. *but* ‖tā āy-'shwō-le. He got called down.

挨班
āy-'bār (*VN1*) to take turns. āy-je-'bār-de (*H*) taking turns, each in his turn. ‖tām āy-je-'bār-de 'gwò-lay gēn-ta lā-'shěw. They came each in turn to shake hands with her.

埃及
'āy-jī (-gwó) (*Nunique*) Egypt.

挨家
*āy-'jyār (*VN1*) to go from door to door. āy-'jyār-de, āy-je-'jyār-de (*H*) going from door to door. ‖shywún-'jǐng āy-'jyār-de 'chá. The policemen searched from house to house.

挨肩
āy-'jyār (*H*) close together, crowded. *Limited to a few combinations:* āy-'jyār tsā-'bèy be crowded close together *physically, literally* crowded and rubbing backs (*as in a crowd of people*); āy-'jyār-de-'dì-shyung brothers born close together (*say within a year*).

挨門
āy-'mér (*H*) going from door to door. ‖tā āy-'mér-de wèn 'rén-jyā 'yàw-bu-yàw. He goes from door to door asking people if they want some.

挨次
āy-'tsż (*H*) one by one, in turn, each in his turn.

捱
áy *see* āy.

矮
ǎy (*A*) short, not tall. (*Opposite* gāw.)

哎，嗳
‖ày! Hello! (*telephone*).

愛
ày (*V*) to love *or* like *a person, a place, a thing*; (*Vpred*) to like *to do something*, be fond of *doing something*; (*Vsent*) to like for *someone to do something*. ‖nǐ háy 'y-ta-ma? Do you still love her? ‖wǒ hěn 'ày jèy-ge-'dì-fang. I'm very fond of this place. ‖wǒ bú-'ày chī 'jèy-ge. I don't like eating this. ‖tā ày shwō-'hwà. He likes to talk.

礙
ày (*V*) to bother, disturb; *as mainV*: ày-bu-'jáw to bother, disturb, hinder *someone in his work.* ‖'nèy-ge-dūng-shi ày-bu-'jáw wo. That (thing) isn't in my way.

ày-'yǎn (*A*) to trouble the eye. ‖'nèy-ge-dūng-shi gē-nèr hěn ày-'yǎn. That thing doesn't look right to me there.

ày-'shŕ to matter, be of concern. ‖'bú-ày nǐ-'shŕ. It doesn't concern you.

愛情
'ày-chíng (*Nabstr*) love, feeling of love *or* affection. ‖tā-men-de-'ày-chíng hěn 'chwén-jyé. Their love is very pure.

愛爾蘭
'ày-ěr-lán (*Nunique*) Ireland.

愛國
ày-'gwó (*VN2, A*) to love one's country; to be patriotic.

璦琿

ày-'hwēn (*Nunique*) Ai-hun (*city in Heilungkiang province*).

愛人

'ày-rén (*Npers*) lover, beloved, sweetheart. ‖tā 'tyān-tyān 'děng tā-'ày-rén-de-'shìn. Each day she waits for a letter from her sweetheart.

愛上

'ày-shàng (*RC2*) to fall in love (with). ‖tā 'ày-shang-le nèy-ge-'gū-nyang. He fell in love with that girl.

愛惜

ày-'shī (*V*) to be sparing in the use of *a thing;* to love protectingly *a person*.

礙事

ày-'shr̀ (*VN1*) to be in the way, be an impediment, be a source of disturbance. ‖nèy-ge-'jwō-dz bǎy-'nàr jēn ày-'shr̀. That table is really in people's way there. ‖'bú-ày-'shr̀. It doesn't matter (*said of anything*).

B

吧，罷

ba *sentence-final element which makes the sentence into a request or suggestion (see Section E §5 of Introduction) or indicating that the statement is a conclusion the speaker is just reaching from the evidence at hand.* ‖jè-shr 'tā-de-ba. This seems to be his (*rather than someone else's*). ‖jè 'bú-shr tā-de-ba. This doesn't seem to be his. ‖'jèy-jyàn-shr̀ yīng-gay 'tā dzwò-ba. I guess he ought to be the one to take care of that matter.

八

bā (*NumU*) eight.

巴掌

'bā-jang (*Nunit, ge; Msemel*) palm of the hand. **dǎ-rén yì-'bā-jang** to give someone a blow with the palm.

巴結

'bā-jye (*V*) to flatter, to bribe *someone with some ulterior motive*. ‖tā hěn hwèy 'bā-jye (rén). He knows how to flatter people.

疤瘌

'bā-la (*Nunit, ge*) scar, pockmark (*except from smallpox, which is* **'má-dz**). *The scar must be a depression in the surface, or wrinkles, never a ridge or bump.*

巴黎

bā-'lí (*Nunique*) Paris.

巴拿馬

bā-na-'mǎ(-gwó) (*Nunique*) Panama.

巴西

bā-'shī(-gwó) (*Nunique*) Brazil.

拔

bá (*V*) to pull *something* up *or* out, to extract *something rooted somewhere*. **bá-'yá** to pull teeth; **bá-'yíng** to break camp (*pulling out the tent pegs and poles*); **bá-'máw** to weigh anchor.

    As mainV: **'bá-chū-lay** extract out; **'bá-shyà-lay** extract downwards (*as a tooth*); **bá-'shé** to fracture *something hard and easily broken* by pulling it out from its rooting; *etc.* ‖bǎ nèy-'lyǎng-kē-'shù dēw gěy 'bá-le. Pull those two trees out by the roots. *or* Uproot those two trees.

把

bǎ (*Munit*) *with Nunit naming things which have handles or parts grasped by the hand in using; e.g.*, **'jyǎn-dz** (*scissors*); **'shàn-dz** (*hand fan*); **'tyáw-chu** (*broom*); **'fǔ-dz** (*ax*); **sǎn** (*umbrella*); **'yàw-shr** (*key*); **'yǐ-dz** (*chair*).

把

bǎ(r) (*Mgroup*) handful of, bunch of, *with Nunit or Nmass naming particularly things often sold in bunches on the market; e.g.*, **mǐ** (*rice grain*); **tsǎw** (*grass*); **hwā(r)** (*flowers*); **tsày** (*vegetables*); **'lwó-be** (*turnips*).

把柄

'bǎ-bǐng (*Nunit, ge*) shortcomings, defects (*of a person, particularly when they are the basis of criticism*). ‖tā 'jwā-jù wǒ-de-'bǎ-bǐng gěy shwō-'kāy-le. He seized upon my shortcomings and revealed them.

把持

bǎ-'chŕ (*V*) to monopolize, control *through use of undue influence*. ‖tā 'yí-ge-rén bǎ jèy-jyàn-'shr̀-chíng bǎ-'chŕ-je. He is monopolizing that matter (*remark in criticism*).

把舵

bǎ-'dwò (*VN2*) to steer, to handle the rudder, (*boat only*).

靶子

'bǎ-dz (*Nunit, ge*) target (*for target practice*).

把手
'bǎ-shěw (*Nunit*, ge, gěr, tyáw) arms *of a chair*, railing, banister; anything grasped with the palm down (*not hung from*) for support.
(*Nabstr*) yěw 'bǎ-shěw to be certain, to be sure of things, to be secure.

把守
'bǎ-shěw (*V*) to guard. ‖yěw lyǎng-ge-'bīng 'bǎ-shěw chéng-'mén. There are two soldiers guarding the city gate.

把戲
bǎ-'shì (*N*) tricks of magic; practical jokes; acts of skill.
wár (*or* dǎ *or* shwǎ) bǎ-'shì to pull practical jokes, to play tricks.

把兄（把）弟
bǎ-'shyūng(-bǎ)-'dì (*Ncoll*) sworn brothers (*people who aren't brothers by blood but assume a comparable relationship*).

把握
'bǎ-wò (*Nabstr*): yěw 'bǎ-wò to be certain, to be sure of things, to be secure. ‖tā-'nèy-ge-rén hěn yěw 'bǎ-wò. That man is very sure of himself (*not said in criticism*). ‖nǐ dwèy-ta yěw shéme-'bǎ-wò-ma? Are you sure about him? (*that he's going to keep his promise, etc.*).

霸，覇
bà (*A*) obstinate, unreasonable, dominating, (*in one's rights or desires*). (*V*) to rule by might (*mainly literary*). ‖tā-'nèy-ge-rén jēn 'bà. He's really dominating.
(*Npers*) ‖tā shr̀ jèy-ge-'dì-fang-de-yí-ge-'bà. He's one of the local big shots (*member of the gentry who oppresses and dominates*).

霸道
'bà-dàw (*A*) unreasonable, ornery. (*Opposite* jyǎng-'lǐ.) ‖tā-'jèy-ge-rén hěn 'bà-dàw, nǐ gēn-ta 'shwō méy-'yùng. That guy is very unreasonable, there's no use arguing with him.

罷工
bà-'gūng (*VN2*) to go on strike.

霸佔
bà-'jàn (*V*) to control *a territory or a position or property* exclusively and by might; to infringe on. ‖tā bà-'jàn rén-jyā-de-tsáy-'chǎn. He's infringing on the property rights of others. ‖'yí-ge-rén bà-'jàn yí-ge-'dìfangr. Each man controls one territory exclusively.

罷課
bà-'kè (*VN2*) to go on strike (*of students; usually for political reasons*).

罷了
'bà-lyǎw that's all; merely that; be finished, done. *Confined to following kind of use:* ‖nǐ yàw-shr bù-shwō-'hwà yě jyèw 'bà-lyǎw. If you'll keep quiet (about it) it'll be a closed incident. ‖nǐ yàw bú-'dzwò, jyèw 'bà-lyǎw. OK, if you don't want to do it, we'll just forget about it.

罷免
bà-'myǎn (*V*) to remove from office. ‖tā bèy rén-'mín gěy bà-'myǎn-le. He was removed from office by the (will of the) people.

罷市
bà-'shr̀ (*VN2*) to shut up businesses *in protest against governmental authorities.*

搬
bān (*V*) move *or* transport *something heavy or complex*. As *mainV*: bān-dàw transport *something to a place, etc.* bān-'jyā (*VN2*) to move *in the sense of changing one's residence.* ‖'jèy-ge-dūng-shi tày 'chén, tā bān-bu-'dùng. This thing is too heavy; she can't lift it.

般
bān (*Mclass*) *with Npers; after Dem* this (that) special type of; *after NumU* yī the average; *in latter case requires* de *except before* rén. yì-'bān-rén the average person; yì-bān-de-'shywé-sheng the average student; jèy-bān-'shywé-sheng this special type of student.

班
bān (*MgroupA*) squad (*military*).

班
bān (*MgroupA*) class (*of students*); cast *or* troupe (*of actors*). ‖tā yěw 'gwǎng-dūng-'kěw-yīn, kě-shr jèy-yì-'bān-de-'shywé-sheng dēw 'dǔng-de tā-de-'hwà. He has a Cantonese accent, but all the students in the class understand him.
(*MdistT*) yì-bān-'shìn a collection of mail. ‖'mèy-yì-tyān yěw jǐ-bān-'shìn? How many times is the mail collected per day?

瘢
bān (*Nunit*, ge) scar, pockmark, (*except from smallpox, which is* 'má-dz). *Literary; usual colloquial form is* 'bā-la.
jǎng-'bān (*VN2*) to have a scar.

斑
bān (*Nunit*, ge) spot, growth, mark, *on a living surface, on the skin, a leaf, a piece of meat, or fur of a garment.*

'shēng-láy-de yěw-'bān to have skin markings at birth. ‖nǐ néng bǎ jèy-shyē-'bān tsā-'dyàw-ma? Can you remove these spots? (or are they really bān).

jǎng-'bān (VN2) to break out *with pimples or any rash from any disease.*

斑點

bān-'dyǎn (Nunit, ge) spots (*on a surface*), flaws (*in something like jade; ingrown or acquired, removable or not*). ‖'bàw-'shēn-shang-de-bān-'dyǎn (shř) shř-bu-'dyàw-de. The leopard cannot change his spots.

班子

'bān-dz (Nuntt, ge) (1) company of actors, *same as* shì-'bān-dz, shì-'bār. ‖jèy-yí-ge-'bān-dz hěn 'shèw 'rén-de-hwān-'yíng. This company of actors was cordially welcomed by the community.

(2) An establishment for prostitution.

班長

bān-'jǎng (Npers) squad leader (*military*).

板，版

*bǎn, 'bǎn-dz (Nunit, kwày, ge) board, (*of wood or similar-shaped object of any substance*). shŕ-'bǎn stone slab; tyě-'bǎn sheet *or* bar *or* plate of iron; hēy-'bǎn a blackboard.

板凳

bǎn-'dèng (Nunit, ge, jāng) any chair or stool without a back. cháng-bǎn-'dèng (M also tyáw) bench (*without a back*).

半

bàn half. (1) *Used as a numeral when saying* half *of something:* 'bàn-tyān half a day (*also figuratively* a long time); bàn-'děw half a peck; bàn-'nyán half a year; bàn-ge-'ywè half a month.

(2) *When* half *of something is added to one or more wholes of that thing, the number of wholes is specified by a numeral before the measure, and* bàn *follows the measure:* yì-tyān-'bàn a day and a half; yí-ge-bàn-'ywè a month and a half; 'lyǎng-jīn-bàn-'táng two and a half catties of sugar; 'lyǎng-dyǎn-'bàn(-jūng) two thirty (*time*).

(3) *Used as measure, only after* yī (*one*): yí-'bàn-de-rén half of the men. ‖jèy-shyē-'rén-li yí-'bàn shř 'shǎ-dz. Half of these men are dupes.

(4) yí-'bàr *may work like* yí-'bàn *or may work as an* H: yí-'bàr twēy-'tsź yí-'bàr 'jyèw half refusing and half coming closer (*said of a woman who is half willing*).

(5) yì-dwō-'bàr most of them, the majority. ‖'nèy-shyē-rén-li yì-dwō-'bàr shř 'shǎ-dz. The majority of those people are dupes.

拌

bàn (V) to mix *solid or powdery ingredients; mainly as* mainV *in compounds:* bàn-dzay yí-'kwàr mix things together. ‖bǎ-jyàng hé-'myàn 'bàn-dzay yí-'kwǎr. Mix the sauce and the noodles together.

bàn-'ywún (RC2) to mix evenly, mix until distributed evenly.

辦

bàn (V) to arrange *some matter,* manage, control *matters, affairs, work such as office work.* bàn 'àn-dz to handle a case at law (*said of the clerks or lawyer, not of judge*); bàn-'shř to manage *or* arrange affairs, matters of business; bàn-'gūng to work in an office *or* do similar work elsewhere.

As mainV: bàn-'dàw to work at and accomplish, to complete, *after exerting the necessary energy;* bàn-'hǎw finish *some job satisfactorily, etc.*

絆

bàn (V) to trip. ‖tā 'bàn-le wǒ yí-shyà. He tripped me. ‖'shyǎw-shīn-dyǎr byé 'bàn-je. Be careful, don't trip over.

As mainV: bàn-'dǎw to trip someone so that he falls; bàn-'tǎng-shya to trip someone so that he falls on his back. ‖tā jyàw nèy-tyáw-'shéng-dz bàn-'tǎng-shya-le. He was tripped by that rope and fell down.

半輩子

bàn-'bèy-dz (Ntime) half of one's life, middle age.

半球

bàn-'chyéw (Nunit, ge) hemisphere. shī-'bàn-chyéw western hemisphere, dūng-'bàn-chyéw eastern hemisphere.

半島

bàn-'dǎw (Nunit, ge) peninsula.

半道

bàn-'dàw (Nplace) halfway *or* part way (*to somewhere*). ‖nèy-lyàng-'chē dzěw-dàw bàn-'dàwr 'hwày-le. The car broke down along the way.

拌嘴

bàn-'dzwěy (VN2) to quarrel, argue, *noisily.*

辦罪

bàn-'dzwèy (VN2) to punish. bàn tā-de-'dzwèy to take care of his crime, to punish him.

辦法

'bàn-fǎ (Nunit, ge) method, plan, solution, way of handling a problem. ‖'ywán-dzé méy-'tswǒ, kě-shr 'bàn-fa bú-'dwèy. The theory is all right, but the practical methods are wrong.

半瘋

bàn-'fēngr (Npers) half-wit. ‖tā-shwō-'hwà-de-yàng-dz yěw dyǎr-bàn-'fēngr. The way he talks shows a bit of the half-wit in him.

辦公費

bàn-gūng-'fèy (*N*) expense allowance *in addition to salary*.

辦公室

bàn-gūng-'shř (*Nunit*, **jyān**) office, office room.

半規

bàn-'gwēy (*Nunit*, **ge**) semicircle.

半徑

bàn-'jìng (*Nunit*, **ge**) radius of a circle.

半中腰

bàn-jūng-'yāw (*Nplace*) middle part of something long. **'léw-de-bàn-jūng-'yāw** halfway to the top of the building; **chyān-'bǐ-de-bàn-jūng-'yāw** the middle of the pencil.

半價

bàn-'jyà (*N*) half-price, half *of some previously understood* price. ‖**wǒ 'swàn-ni 'bàn-jyà 'hǎw-le.** OK, I'll charge you half the price.

半空中

bàn-kūng-'jūng (*Nplace*) mid-air. ‖**fēy-'jī dzày bàn-kūng-'jūng jáw-chi 'hwǒ láy-le.** The plane burst into flames in mid-air

伴郎

bàn-'láng (*Npers*) best man (*at a wedding*).

辦理

bàn-'lǐ (*V*) to manage, *usually some temporary project such as a wedding, rather than a continuing enterprise. Compare* **gwǎn-'lǐ.**

半路

bàn-'lù (*Nplace*) halfway *or* part way *to somewhere,* (*on a trip*). ‖**jèy-pǐ-'mǎ dzěw-daw bàn-'lù jyèw bù-'dzěw-le.** This horse went halfway and then refused to budge.

伴侶

bàn-'lywǔ (*Npers*) companion. ‖**tā shř wǒ-yí-ge-lywǔ-'shíng-de-bàn-'lywǔ.** He's one of my traveling companions.

半身像

bàn-shēn-'shyàng (*Nunit*, **ge**) bust (*statue*); (*with M* **jāng**) picture of someone from the waist up.

辦事的

bàn-'shř-de (*Npers*) clerk *of a commercial concern.*

辦事員

bàn-shř-'ywán (*Npers*) official employee. (*One step higher than a purely clerical worker.*)

半數

bàn-'shù (*N*) half *of some already understood amount or quantity.* ‖**nǐ 'gěy-le ta bàn-'shù jyèw 'gèw-le.** If you'd paid him (only) half as much, it would have been enough.

半天

bàn-'tyān (*Ntime*) (*literally*) half a day; (*figuratively*) a long time. ‖**tā 'děng-le bàn-'tyān, tā tsáy 'chū-lay.** After she'd waited a long time he finally came out.

半夜

bàn-'yè (*Ntime*) midnight.

幫，帮

bāng (*V*, *Vsent*) to help *someone who can't do much for himself.* ‖**wǒ 'bāng-ta 'dzwò.** I'll help him do it.
　(*V2*) to give *someone money as a help without much hope of having it returned.*
　'bāng-ta yí-jywù-'hwà. Put in a good word for him.

幫

bāng(r) (*Mgroup*) *with Npers:* **yì-bāng-'rén** group of people; **yì-'bāng-de-rén** people of a single group (*political, business, professional, etc., with the meaning of Mclass*).
　*bāng(r) side of something. **shyé-'bāngr** side of a shoe; **chwán-'bāng(r)** the sides of a boat.

幫工的

bāng-'gūng-de (*Npers*) helper.

幫助

'bāng-jù (*V*, *Vsent*) help, assist, *someone.* ‖**tā 'bāng-jù wo bàn nèy-jyàn-'shř.** He helped me take care of that matter.

幫忙

bāng-'máng (*VN2*) to help, give assistance, *to someone very busy at something, or working hard at something.* ‖**wǒ láy 'bāng nǐ-de-'máng.** I'll come and help you out.

幫忙的

bāng-'máng(r)-de (*Npers*) helper, assistant, (*at physical or routine work, like special help hired during the rush season at a store*); special assistant (*under special conditions*).

幫手

'bāng-shěw (*Npers*) helper, assistant.

榜

bǎng (*Nunit*, **jāng**) list of names (*especially of those who have passed an examination in a school, or, formerly, of successful candidates for governmental appointments*). ‖**'bǎng-shang yěw nǐ-de-'míng-dz-ma?** Is your name on the list?
　(*Literary*) bulletin.

35

綁

băng (*V*) to fasten *or* tie up *a thing, like a package (not to wrap it, but to make the package secure) or a person, such as a prisoner;* to kidnap. *As mainV:* **'băng-shàng** *or* **'băng-chǐ-lay** tie up; **'băng-jǐn** tie tightly; **băng-'dzěw** *or* **'băng-chywù** kidnap; **băng-dzày** tie *something* to. ‖**ching-ni bǎ jèy-ge-'bāw gěy-wo 'băng-shàng.** Please tie up this package for me. ‖**tām bǎ nèy-ge-'dzéy 'băng-dzay 'shù-shang-le.** They tied the thief to a tree. ‖**bǎ-ta 'băng-chi-lay!** Tie him up! ‖**nèy-ge-'kwò-rén jyàw-rén băng-'dzěw-le.** That rich man has been kidnapped.

膀子

'băng-dz (*Nunit,* ge) upper arm, *from the elbow through the shoulder and shoulderblade; same body part of an ape.*

Wing *of a chicken or other bird, especially as cut into small pieces for eating.*

綁票

băng-'pyàwr (*VN1*) to kidnap *someone.* ‖**nèy-ge-'kwò-rén-de-'háy-dz jyàw-rén băng-'pyàwr-le.** That rich man's son was kidnapped.

綁票匪

băng-pyàwr-'fěy (*Npers*) kidnapper.

榜樣

'băng-yàng (*N*) an example, *a person who is imitated or who might be.* ‖**byé 'shyáw-ta, tā 'bú-shr yí-ge-hǎw-'băng-yàng.** Don't take after him, he isn't a good example.

磅

bàng (*Mmeas*) pound (*weight*).
(*Nunit,* ge) fairly large scale *that weighs things in terms of the English system (pounds, ounces, etc.).* **gwò-'bàng** (*VN1*) be weighed.

棒

*bàng, 'bàng-dz (*Nunit,* gēn) club, bat, stick, *like a policeman's stick, always of that shape, usually of wood, and often used for striking.*

棒球

bàng-'chyéw(r) (*Nunit,* ge) a baseball; (*N.* tsż, *etc.*) baseball (*the game*). ‖**wǒ 'dǎ-le yí-'shyà-wǔ-de-'bàng-chyéw.** I've been playing baseball all afternoon.

棒子

'bàng-dz (*N*) corn (Indian corn, maize). (*with M* lì) one grain; (*M* ge) one ear; (*M* kē) one plant of.

棒子麵

bàng-dz-'myàr (*Nmass*) cornmeal (*made from maize, Indian corn*).

蚌埠

bàng-'fǔ (*Nunique*) Pang-fou *or* Pengpu (*city in Anhwei province*).

班

bār (*N,* tsż *and other MdistT*) a turn, a turn of duty. ‖**jīn-tyan-'wǎn-shang shř 'shéy-de-'bār?** Whose turn is it tonight?
jř-'bār (*VN2*) to stand one's turn of duty, be on duty for an assigned period; **āy-'bār** to take turns, take one's turn; **ā̠ -je-'bār-de** taking turns.

把

bàr (*Nunit,* ge) handle *of a small object such as a knife, pot, kettle, cup, broom, etc. (not for lifting and carrying a heavy object, nor for opening and closing something).* **dāw-'bàr** knife handle; **hú-'bàr** pot handle; *etc.*

皰, 疱

bāw (*Nunit,* ge) a boil, a protruding bump, a swelling.
pèng yí-ge-'bāw (*VN2*) to strike oneself on something and cause a swelling; **jǎng-'bāw** (*VN2*) to develop (a case of) boils; **'jǎng yí-ge-'dà-bāw** to have a big bump swell out, to become swollen.

炮, 炰

bāw (*V*) to broil *with little or no fat.*
bāw yáng-'rèw (*VN3*) broiled lamb with onions and soya sauce and little water *cooked in a very heavy frying pan.* (*Other VN with* **bāw** *are also VN3.*)

包

bāw (*V*) to contract *for services in exchange for regular payments.* **bāw-'fàn** (*VN3*) to board, take meals; **bāw-'chē** (*VN3*) to rent a car *and make regular payments for its use.*

包

bāw (*V*) to wrap *something, covering it completely;* to cover completely *as in metal plating. As mainV:* **'bāw-shàng** *or* **'bāw-chǐ-láy** wrap up; **'bāw-dzay** wrap *something* in.
bāw-'jǐn to gild *something;* **bāw-'yín** to silverplate *something.*

包

bāw(r) (*Mcont*) package of, bundle of, packet of, *anything.* **yì-bāw-'yī-fu** bag of laundry; **yì-bāw-'myán-hwā** bale of cotton.

包辦

bāw-'bàn (*V*) to take care of *some job* without help (from) or interference (by others). ‖**'swǒ-yěw-de-'shř tā-'yí-ge-rén bāw-'bàn-le.** He did the whole job himself. ‖**nèy-dyǎr-'tsày ni-'yì-rér bāw-'bàn-ba.** That food is all for you (to eat).

包子

'bāw-dz (*Nunit*, **ge**) small loaves (*about roll-sized*) of steamed bread with a stuffing of meat, sweets *or* vegetables; (*with or without yeast*).

包袱

'bāw-fu (*Nunit*, **ge**) bundle *wrapped in cloth*.

包工

bāw-'gūng (*VN2*) to contract for work.
    (*N*) contracting system, *the system of using a contractor for work.*

包管

bāw-'gwǎn (*V*) to guarantee *something*, to guarantee *someone something* (*particularly* I guarantee you). ‖wǒ bāw-'gwǎn ni tā yí-'dìng bù-'hwéy-láy-le. I promise you that he's not coming back. ‖wǒ bāw-'gwǎn dzwò-de hěn 'hǎw. I guarantee that it'll be done quite well.

包裹

bāw-'gwǒ (*Nunit*, **iyàn**, **ge**) parcel, package.

包含

bāw-'hán (*V*) to include, to contain, to consist of. ‖jèy-kwày-'shŕ-tew-li bāw-hán tyě hé-'měng. This piece of stone contains iron and manganese.

包括

'bāw-kwò (*V*) to include, *as a package includes several things; or abstractly.* 'bāw-kwò-dzày be included in. ‖'fàn-chyán gēn 'fáng-chyán dēw 'bāw-kwò-dzay 'nèy. Board and rent are both included (*i.e., in the amount named*).

包廂

bāw-'shyāng (*Nunit*, **ge**) box *in a theater.* bāw-shyāng-'wèy-dz box seats.

包頭

'bāw-téw (*Nunique*) Pao-t'ou (*city in Suiyüan province*).

包圍

bāw-'wéy (*V*) to seize; to surround. ‖jèy-ge-'chéng bèy wǒ-men-de-'bīng bāw-'wéy-le. This city has been surrounded by our troops.

薄

báw (*A*) thin *in dimension;* weak *of human relationships.* (*Opposites* hèw *in both meanings;* shēn *for second only.*) ‖jèy-jāng-'jŕ tày 'báw, bù-néng 'lyǎng-myàn 'yùng. This paper is too thin to be used on both sides.
    Used as postV; ‖bǎ jèy-ge-'rèw chyē-'báw yì-dyǎr. Slice the meat a little thinner.

薄情

'báw-chíng (*or* 'bwó-chíng; *A*) characterized by weakness of sentiment. ‖tā hěn 'báw-chíng. *or* tā-de-'chíng hěn 'báw. He's not very ardent (in his love).

雹子

'báw-dz (*Nunit*, **ge**; *usually works like Nmass*) hail (*precipitation*). shyà 'báw-dz (*IN*) to hail. ‖'báw-dz yí dàw-'dì jyèw 'hwà-le. The hail melted as soon as it reached the ground.

飽

bǎw (*A*) enough, plenty, sufficient, (*especially of eating*). ‖wǒ 'chŕ tày 'bǎw-le, bù-néng 'dzày chŕ-le. I've eaten too much, I can't eat any more.
    Used as postV only with chŕ eat. ‖'fàn bú-'gèw, wǒ méy-chŕ-'bǎw. There isn't enough food; I'm not full.

保

bǎw (*V*, *Vsent*) to go bail for, give bond for, be guarantor for, *a person;* bail *someone out of jail.* ‖wǒ 'bǎw-ni, 'hǎw-bu-hǎw? I'll go bail for you, OK? ‖wǒ 'bǎw-ni 'chū-lay. I'll bail you out. ‖wǒ 'bǎw-ni, jèy-ge-'yánse bú-'twèy. I guarantee that this color won't run.
    As mainV: bǎw-bu-'jù *or* bǎw-bu-'dìng to be unable to protect or guarantee.

寶貝

bǎw-'bèy (*N*, **ge**) any small and very valuable thing. *Various M used depending on what the valuable thing is, as in following example.* ‖jèy-kwày-'shŕ-tew shŕ yi-kwày-bǎw-'bèy. This stone is a priceless thing.

保持

bǎw-'chŕ (*V*) to maintain, keep unaltered. ‖wǒ 'háy bǎw-'chŕ 'ywán-láy-de-'tày-du. I still maintain my original attitude.

保全

bǎw-'chywán (*RC2*) to preserve *something* intact.

保定

bǎw-'dìng (*Nunique*) Paoting, *another name for* chīng-'ywàn Ch'ing-yüan (*city in Hopeh province*).

保管

bǎw-'gwǎn (*V*) to hold in trust, take care of (*legally*). ‖tā-'fù-chin-de-tsáy-'chǎn dēw gwēy yí-ge-'shìn-twō-gūng-'sz bǎw-'gwǎn. His father's property was held (*for him*) by a trust company.

保管處

bǎw-gwǎn-'chù (*Nunit*, **ge**, **chù**, **swǒ**) place for keeping things (*officially*). dǎng-'àn-bǎw-gwǎn-'chù archives.

寶貴

băw-'gwèy (*A*) valuable, precious, rare.

保護

băw-'hù (*V*) defend, protect, guard, (*physically, like a bodyguard*). ‖tā yěw 'lyăng-ge-'bīng 'băw-hù ta. He has two soldiers guarding him.

保障

băw-'jàng (*V*) to safeguard; (*Nunit*, **ge**) a safeguard. rén-'mín-de-băw-'jàng safeguards for the people (*such as a Bill of Rights*).

保證

băw-'jèng (*V*) to go bond for, guarantee, vouch for, *a person.*

保證人

băw-jèng-'rén (*Npers*) guarantor.

寶雞

băw-'jī (*Nunique*) Pao-chi *or* Paoki (*city in Shensi province*).

保重

băw-'jùng (*VN1*) be careful (*of one's physical condition*). ‖'yì-rén chū-'wày yàw băw-'jùng-shye. When you go out alone, take good care of yourself.

堡壘

băw-'lěy (*Nunit*, **ge, dzwò**) fort, fortress.

保留

băw-'lyéw (*V*) to hold in reserve, reserve. ‖chǐng-ni gěy-wo băw-'lyéw jèy-ge-'dzwò-wey. Please hold this seat for me (*said to an usher or the like, not to someone sitting by you*).

飽滿

băw-'măn (*A*) full (*as a face*). ‖tā-de-'lyăn 'jăng-de hěn băw-'măn. She's grown quite full in the face.

保母

băw-'mǔ (*Npers*) nurse (*for a child*).

飽暖

băw-'nwăn (*A*) well-fed and warm. ‖yí-ge-'rén dzày băw-'nwăn-de-shŕ-hew hwèy 'wàng-le 'byé-rén-de-'jī-han. When one is well-fed and warm he is apt to forget the hunger and cold of others.

保山

băw-'shān (*Nunique*) Pao-shan (*city in Yünnan province*).

保守

băw-'shěw (*V*) to protect, defend, conserve, **preserve.**

保壽險

băw 'shèw-shyăn (*VN2*) to get (*or* have) life insurance.

寶石

băw-'shŕ (*Nunit*, **kwày, ge**; *Nmass*, **kwày**) precious stone, gem; precious stone-like substance *of mineral extraction, such as jade.*

保險

băw-'shyăn (*VN2*) to insure, get insurance. ‖tā-de-'chē băw-'shyăn-le méy-yew? Has his car been insured? ‖wǒ băw-'shyăn, 'jèy-ge-'yán-se bú-'twèy. I guarantee that this color won't run.

保險櫃

băw-shyăn-'gwèy (*Nunit*, **ge**) safe (*for valuables*).

保險箱

băw-shyăn-'shyāng (*Nunit*, **ge**) safe (*for valuables*).

保存

băw-'tswén (*V*) to keep safely, preserve *something* in a safe place, *with someone as a guard*. ‖tā băw-'tswén-le 'sān-shyāng-de-gǔ-'dǔng. He has three boxes of antiquities stored safely away.

抱

bàw (*V*) to hold, carry, bring, take, *in the folded arms as one carries a baby. As mainV:* 'bàw-jù to hold fast in the arms; *etc.* ‖nèy-ge-băw-'mǔ 'bàw-je yí-ge-shyǎw-'hár. The nurse is carrying a baby in her arms.

報

bàw (*Nunit*, **jāng**; **fèr** for one issue) newspaper.
    In compounds report, message. **dyàn-'bàw** telegram (*literally* electric message).

暴

bàw (*A*) violent, fierce, (*of weather or temperament*). **bàw-'fēng** violent wind; **bàw-'ywǔ** violent rain; **bàw-fēng-'ywǔ** violent storm. ‖tā 'pí-chi hěn 'bàw. He has a violent temper.

報酬

'baw-chéw (*VN1*) to give compensation, payment, reward. ‖wǒ 'gěy-ni dzwò jèy-jyàn-'shŕ, nǐ gěy-wo 'dwō-shaw-'bàw-chéw? If I do this for you what compensation will you give me?

報仇

bàw-'chéw (*VN1*) to take revenge, get revenge. ‖tā kàn tā-de-'chéw-rén yí-bù-yí-'bù-de 'dzěw-jìn-le, tā shyăng bàw-'chéw-de-shŕ-hew 'kwày-le. As he saw his enemy approaching step by step, he felt that the time for revenge was at hand.

抱歉
bàw-'chyàn (A) to feel sorry *because of some fault (term used in apologetic expression)*. ‖shàng-lǐ-'bày wǒ bù-néng 'láy hěn bàw-'chyàn. I must apologize for not having been able to come last week.

報答
'bàw-dá (V) to repay *someone for a favor or kindness*.

報到
bàw-'dàw (VN1) to report arrival, to report upon arrival, report presence, sign in. ‖lǐ-bày-'yī wǒ děy 'gǎn-hwéy-chywù bàw-'dàw. I have to hurry back on Monday and sign in.

暴躁
'bàw-dzàw (A) hot-tempered.

爆發
bàw-'fā (I) to develop suddenly and violently. ‖tā-de-'bìng bàw-'fā-le. His illness struck suddenly.

報復
bàw-'fú (V) to retaliate for insult or injury.

報告
bàw-'gàw (V) to report *something*. ‖wú-shyàn-'dyàn 'měy-yí-ge-'jūng-téw bàw-'gàw 'yí-tsz̀-shīn-'wén. The news is reported over the radio once each hour.

報館
bàw-'gwǎn (Nunit, jyā) newspaper publishing company.

報賬
bàw-'jàng (VN2) to make out an expense account.

報紙
bàw-'jř (Nunit, jāng; fèr one copy) newspaper.

爆裂
bàw-'lyè (I) to crack with a cracking sound; to explode, *as a volcano*.

報名
bàw-'míng (VN1) to enroll *(in a school, for membership in some society, for an examination, etc.)*. ‖'nèy-ge-shywé-'shyàw bàw-'míng-de-shěw-'shywù dzěme-'yàng? What's the procedure for enrolling at that school?

抱不平
bàw-bu-'píng (A) indignant. ‖wǒ kàn 'nèy-jǔng-shř-ching, wǒ 'shīn-lǐ-tew bàw-bu-'píng. When I see a thing like that I feel indignant.

報喜
bàw-'shǐ (VN2) to report good tidings, bring good news *(especially of the arrival of a child)*

報稅
bàw-'shwèy (VN1) to declare goods for duty. ‖nǐ 'yěw-méy-yew yīng-gay-bàw-'shwèy-de(-dūng-shi)? Have you anything to declare?

報攤
bàw-'tār (Nunit, ge) newsstand.

報應
'bàw-yìng (Nunit, ge) one's just deserts; *mostly used in* dé 'bàw-yìng get one's just deserts *(from heaven, fate)*.

抱怨
'bàw-ywàn (V) to hold a grudge *against someone*. ‖'dž-jǐ bǎ 'shř-ching dzwò-'hwày-le, kě-shr bàw-ywan 'byé-rén. He himself muffed the job, but he holds a grudge against others *(for it)*.

擘
bāy (V) to break *something* by twisting in the hands. *As mainV:* ‖bǎ jèy-kwày-'bǐng 'bāy(-chéng) lyǎng-'bàr. Break this cake into two pieces. ‖nǐ 'néng-bu-néng bǎ jèy-ge-'gàr gěy-wo 'bāy-kay? Can you break open this cover for me?

白
báy (A) white, light. *(Opposite* hēy.*)*
    (H) gratis, for nothing, in vain. báy 'sùng to give *something as a gift;* báy 'lay to come in vain.

白字
báy-'dž (Nunit, ge) a character *(in writing Chinese) used in place of another which represents the same or similar pronunciation; (comparable to a misspelled word in English)*.

白話
báy-'hwà (Nmass; jywù) colloquial language, *and written Chinese in which an effort is made to conform to colloquial usage, (in contrast to* wén-'hwà *or* wén-'lǐ *written Chinese in literary style)*.

白金
báy-'jin (Nmass) platinum.

白種人
'báy-jǔng(-rén) (Npers) (members of the) Caucasian *or* White race.

白濁
báy-'jwó *or* báy-'jwò (Nabstr) gonorrhea.

白蘭地
báy-lán-'dì (Nmass) brandy.

白毛
báy-'máw(r) (*Nmass*) mold, mildew. **'jǎng yì-tséng-báy-'máw** to mold, to mildew.

白事
báy-'shr̀ (*Nunit, tsz̀*) funeral.
　　bàn báy-'shr̀ make arrangements for and manage a funeral.

白菜
báy-'tsày (*Nunit, téw, kē*) celery-cabbage (*a Chinese vegetable similar to cabbage*).

百
bǎy (*NumG*) hundred.

擺
bǎy (*V*) arrange *things* in a display. **'pù-dz méy-kāy-'mér yǐ-'chyán 'dūng-shi dēw bǎy-'hǎw-le.** Before the store opens they arrange everything for proper display.

擺渡
'bǎy-dù (*Nunit, ge, jr̆*) very simple boat used for ferrying a stream.

百貨公司
bǎy-hwò-gūng-'sz̄ (*Nunit, jyā*) department store, (*literally* hundred goods industry).

百科全書
bǎy-kē-chywán-'shū (*N; bù, tàw, for the set of volumes*) encyclopedia.

百靈廟
bǎy-líng-'myàw (*Nunique*) Pai-ling-miao (*city in Suiyüan province*).

百姓
bǎy-'shìng (*also* **lǎw-bǎy-'shìng**) (*Ncoll*) the people. **jèy-ge-'jèng-fu yěw lǎw-bǎy-'shìng dzwò hèw-'dwèn.** This government has the whole-hearted support of the people.

敗
bày (*I*) be defeated *in a battle or war or fistfight, etc.* **shéy 'bày-le?** Who lost? *Otherwise mainly in compounds.*

拜
bày (*V*) to worship *a deity;* to kneel before *a person.* **bày-'fwó** to worship, do homage to, *a Buddha;* **bày-'shén** to worship a god; **bày dzǔ-'shyān** to worship (*one's*) ancestors. **tā shyàng tā-'mǔ-chin bày-le yí-'bày.** He knelt down for a moment before his mother. **hwéy-'bày** (*VN1*) to return a formal call.

拜訪
bày-'fǎng (*V*) to make a formal call *on somebody.* **tā chywù bày-'fǎng tā-de-'péng-yew.** He's gone to pay a call on his friend.

敗仗
bày-'jàng (*N, tsz̀*) a losing battle. **dǎ bày-'jàng** fight a losing battle.

敗類
bày-'lèy (*Npers, ge*) a black sheep *in a group of people.*

拜年
bày-'nyán (*VN1*) to make a call on New Year's Day and give good wishes (*a custom in China, particularly among relatives*). **bày-'nyán!** Happy New Year!

拜託
'bày-twō! *or* **'bày-twō 'bày-twō!** Please!

本
běn *or* **běr** (*Munit, Mpart*) binding, binder. *With Chinese books, bound in a series of small fascicles,* **yì-běn-'shū** *is one fascicle of a book; with western-style binding, it is one book. Used with various terms for books, magazines, and other bound things.* **yì-běn-báy-'jr̆** booklet or pad of white paper.

本錢
'běn-chyán (*Nmass*) capital, money invested.

本地
běn-dì (*Aattr*) native, indigenous *to a particular area.* **běn-'dì(-de)-rén** the natives *of some particular area.* **běn-'dì-de-fēng-'sú** indigenous customs, local customs.

本子
'běn-dz, běr (*Nunit, ge*) bound volume, *either blank for the keeping of notes or, like a telephone book, containing data of public interest but not of scholarly importance.*

本分
běn-'fèn (*N*) one's duty, responsibility. **dū-'dzé 'jèng-fǔ shr̀ rén-'mín-de-běn-'fèn.** It is the responsibility of the people themselves to keep a watchful eye on the government.

本家
běn-'jyā (*Npers*) member of the same clan, person having the same surname. **tā shr̀ nǐ-de-běn-'jyā.** He's your clansman. *or* He has your surname.

本來
běn-'láy (*J*) originally, at first; in the first place, to start with. **běn-'láy wǒ bù-'jr̆-daw, 'hèw-láy tā 'gàw-su wo, tsáy 'jr̆-daw.** I didn't know it at first; later on (when

he told me) I learned of it for the first time. ‖tā 'běn-láy jyèw méy-'shwō! In the first place, he didn't even say it!

本領

běn-'lǐng (*Nabstr*) ability. ‖'jèy-ge-rén-de-běn-'lǐng hěn 'dà. He's a very capable man.

本人

'**běn-rén** oneself, in person (*follows designation of someone*). ‖tā-'běn-rén bù-jř-'dàw. He himself doesn't know. ‖wǒ-'běn-rén bù-néng 'chywù, wǒ pày yí-ge-dày-'byǎw. I can't go in person, I'll send a representative.

笨

bèn (*A*) stupid, dumb. (*Opposite* **líng, 'tsūng-ming, 'jī-ling, gwěy**.)

崩, 迸

bēng (*I*) to break open with a great deal of noise (*as of a dam or dike under water pressure*). 'shān 'bèng-le have an avalanche, landslide, (*literally* mountain breaks open). ‖kāy-'shwěy, dàw-dzay bwō-li-'běy-lǐ-tew, yí-'shyà-dz, 'běy-dz jyèw 'bēng-le. Put hot water in a glass and it bursts immediately.

綳, 繃, 絣

*****bēng** (*mainV*) in '**bēng-shàng, bēng-'jǐn, 'bēng-chi-lay** to tighten *a suspended thread or rope or wire;* to stretch tightly *a cloth or paper covering over an opening*. ‖bǎ 'shéng-dz bēng-'jǐn-le. Stretch the rope tightly. ‖'gūng-shàng-de-'shyán-dz 'bēng-de hěn 'jǐn. The string on the bow is stretched quite taut.

繃帶

bēng-'dày (*Nunit*, tyáw, jywǎn) bandage.

甭

béng *abbreviated form of* '**bú-yùng** (*Vpred*) there's no use, there's no need to. ‖jèy-ge-'hwèy shyàn-dzày chywǔ-'shyāw-le, ni béng 'láy-le. Now that the party's been cancelled, there's no need for you to come.

蹦, 迸

bèng (*I*) to jump up and down *usually in one place*. ‖nèy-pi-'mǎ 'bèng-de hěn 'gāw. That horse jumped very high.

As mainV: '**bèng-dàw** (*Ic*) to jump *from someplace to someplace:* '**bèng-gwò** (*Ic*) to jump across, over, *something. In each case a relatively high jump with effort, in contrast to* **tyàw** *which is an ordinary jump, not necessarily with effort, not necessarily high.*

Used as H in one case: **bèng(r) 'tswèy** extremely brittle.

本

běr *see* **běn, 'běn-dz.**

碑

bēy (*Nunit*, ge) monument, gravestone, memorial, memorial tablet, *usually with material specified:* **shŕ-'bēy** stone monument.

背

bēy (*V*) to carry *something* on the back; (*figuratively*) to be weighed down *by debts, etc.* ‖nèy-ge-'nywǔ-rén 'bēy-je yí-ge-shyǎw-'hár. That woman is carrying a baby on her back. ‖wǒ 'bēy-le hěn-dwō-de-'jày. I'm weighed down with debts.

As mainV: '**bēy-dàw** carry on the back to someplace, *etc.*

杯, 盃

bēy(-dz) (*NunitC*) cup, glass. **bēy** *is more often used as Mcont*, '**bēy-dz** *as Nunit.*

背包

bēy-'bāw(r) (*Nunit*, ge) pack carried on the back.

背帶

bēy-'dày (*Nunit*, tyáw) suspenders.

北

běy (*Nplace*) north. *See* **dūng** east.

北海

běy-'hǎy (*Nunique*) Pei-hai *or* Pakhoi (*city in Kwangtung province*).

北極的地方

běy-'jí-de(-dì-fang) (*Nplace*) The Arctic.

北京

běy-'jīng (*Nunique*) Peking, *older name for* **běy-'píng** Pei-p'ing (*city in Hopeh province*).

北平

běy-'píng (*Nunique*) Pei-p'ing *or* Peking (*city in Hopeh province*).

被

bèy (*K*) by (*an agent*), at the hand of. ‖wǒ-men-de-'mǎy-may bèy-ta gěy 'hwèy-le. Our business was ruined by him. ‖jàng-peng bèy-'fēng gwā-'pǎw-le. The tents were overturned by the wind.

背

bèy (*V*) to memorize *something*. **bèy-'shū** to learn the content of books by heart. *The RC2* '**bèy-shyà-láy** *is used more often than the simple verb:* ‖wǒ bù-néng bǎ jèy-shěw-'shŕ 'bèy-shyà-lay. I can't memorize this poem.

備

bèy (*V*) to prepare *an animal* for carrying something on its back. **bèy-'mǎ** to saddle a horse; **bèy-'ān** to saddle, put the saddle on.

背
bèy (*Nunit*, **ge**) back (*part of body, excluding the lower part and waist*). **bèy, bèr** back *of a chair, knife, etc.*

背
bèy (*A*) deaf; *said of* **'ěr-dwo** ear (*not of a person*). ‖**tā 'ěr-dwo yěw yì-dyǎr-'bèy.** He's a little deaf.

輩子
'bèy-dz (*Ntime*) lifetime. ‖**tā 'máng-le yí-'bèy-dz, kě-shr sž-'hèw tsáy chéng-'míng.** He labored all his life, but only achieved fame after his death.

被告
'bèy-gàw (*Npers*) the accused, the defendant (*legal*).

背後
bèy-'hèw (*Nplace*) behind a person. ‖**tā jyèw 'jàn-dzay ni-de-bèy-'hèw.** He's standing right there behind you.

背着
'bèy-je (*K, occasionally V*) going (*or* to go) contrary to, going against *conscience, advice;* behind *someone's* back *in the figurative sense.* ‖**tā bèy-je 'lyáng-shīn dzwò-'shr̀.** He's doing this against his conscience. ‖**tā 'bèy-je ni 'yèw shwō yí-yàngr-de-'hwà.** He talks differently behind your back.

背景
bèy-'jǐng (*Nabstr*) background (*in a picture; of a person*).

背面
bèy-'myàr (*Nplace*) reverse side, back, (*off anything flat*), reverse face, other face, other side. ‖**jèy-kwày-'bù 'jèng-myàr shr̀ 'húng-de, kě-shr 'bèy-myàr shr̀ 'hwáng-de.** The right side of this material is red, but the reverse side is yellow.

背時，悖時
bèy-'shŕ (*VN1*) *literally* against the times, *meaning* forced away from current tendencies, unlucky. ‖**wǒ shyǎng tā yěw yì-dyǎr-bèy-'shŕ.** I think he's having a bit of bad luck.
　　bèy-'shŕ-de-shŕ-hew an unfavorable period *in a person's life, when he has to be careful or he will suffer unfortunate consequences.*

逼
bī (*V*) to force, compel, urge, put the pressure on, *but not actual physical compulsion; as mainV it may be actual physical pressure:* **bī-'jìn** to close in (on), *as in military operations.* ‖**ni byé 'bī-wo, wǒ dz̀-'rán hwèy 'dzwò.** Don't put the pressure on me; I'll do it of my own accord. ‖**tā-men yì-fēn-jūng-yì-fēn-'jūng-de bī-'jìn-le.** Minute by minute they closed in.

鼻
*bí, 'bí-dz (*Nunit*, **ge**) nose.

鼻青眼腫
bí-'chīng yǎn-'jǔng (*literary quotation*) to have a black eye (*literally* to have black nose and swollen eyes). ‖**tā bí-chīng-yǎn-'jǔng-de.** He has a black eye. ‖**tā 'bèy-rén 'dǎ-de bí-'chīng yǎn-'jǔng.** Someone's given him a black eye.

鼻涕
'bí-ti (*Nmass*) waste matter in the nose. **shǐng 'bí-ti** to blow the nose.

筆
bǐ (*Munit*) *individualizes financial items in terms of accounts kept separately.* **yì-bǐ-'chyán** a fund (*or* amount) of money reserved for a particular purpose, *with separate accounting;* **yì-bǐ-'jàng** an account, *for one transaction with one customer;* **yì-bǐ-'jìn-shyàng** *or* **yì-bǐ-shēw-'rù** one source of income.

筆
bǐ (*Nunit*, **gwǎn, jř, gēn**) writing-brush, pen, pencil.

比
bǐ (*V*) to point *or* aim. ‖**shyàng 'gāw-yi-dyǎr 'bǐ.** Aim a little higher. ‖**tā yǔng-'shěw bǐ-je tā-de-'lyǎn.** He's pointing at his (*someone else's*) face (with his hand). ‖**tā yùng-'shěw 'shyàng-'dūng 'bǐ-yi-bǐ.** He pointed east (with his hand).

比
bǐ (*V*) to compare (*K*) compared with, than; (*mainV*) compare. ‖**tā bǐ-ni 'gāw.** He's taller than you. ‖**'jèy-lyǎng-ge 'dzěme néng 'bǐ-ne?** How could these two (*possibly*) be compared? ‖**'bǐ-chi-lay, 'jèy-ge háy bù-'rú 'nèy-ge-ne.** Comparing them, this isn't even as good as that one (*neither is very good*).
　　bǐ-bu-'shàng (*RC2*) can't be compared.

比方
'bǐ-fang (*Nunit*, **ge**) an example (*in speaking*). ‖**'bǐ-fang shwō** .... for example, ...

筆記
bǐ-'jì (*Nunit*, **dwàn**) memorandum, notation, notes, *taken at a lecture or the like. Many Chinese literary works are* **bǐ-'jì**; *that is, fragmentary thoughts put down from time to time by some scholar or philosopher or statesman.*

比較
bǐ-'jyàw *or* **bǐ-'jyǎw** (*V*) to compare; (*H*) relatively. ‖**ni bǐ-jyàw-bǐ-'jyàw, jyèw 'jř-daw něy 'hǎw něy 'hwày.** Just compare them, you'll find out which is good and which is bad (*a retail clerk would use such a sentence*

42

often). ‖'lyǎng-ge dēw 'bù-hǎw, kě-shr jèy-ge bǐ-'jyàw 'hǎw-yi-dyǎr. Neither one of them is much good, but, (if you ask me), this is relatively a bit better.

比利時
'bǐ-lì-shŕ (short form 'bǐ-gwo) (Nunique) Belgium.

比賽
bǐ-'sày (V) to compete in. ‖wǒ-men bǐ-'sày wǎng-'chyéwr. Let's play a game of tennis i.e., let's keep a record of the score and see who comes out on top. (Nunit, tsž) game, competition, as a football game, etc. ‖lǐ-bày-'lyèw-de-bǐ-'sày chywǔ-'shyāw-le. Saturday's game has been called off.

彼此
bǐ-'tsž (H) among or between themselves, yourselves, ourselves. ‖'rú-gwo bǐ-'tsž 'míng-bay, 'shéme-shr̀ dēw hǎw 'bàn. Things will be much easier to manage if there is mutual understanding.

必
bì (Vpred) must, to have to. Used in the negative (bú-'bì not have to, not be necessary to, not be obliged to); for affirmative one uses a reinforced combination: bì-'děy must, to have to; bì-snywū-'děy be absolutely obliged to; bì-'yàw ought to, should. ‖'měy-yí-ge-rén bì-'děy àn-'shŕ 'dàw. Everyone must be here on time. ‖shyàn-'dzày ni bú-'bì 'láy-le. There's no longer any need for you to come. ‖ni bú-'bì shyàn-'dzày 'láy. There'll be no need for you to come until later. ‖ni 'shr̀-bu-shr bì-shywū-'děy 'chywù? Do you absolutely have to go? ‖bì-'yàw-de-shŕ-hew wǒ dzày 'dzwò. I'll do it at the time that it becomes necessary.

箆
bì (V) to comb; particularly bì-'téw to comb the hair (literally the head) with long strokes for a long time with a very fine-toothed comb in order to clean it.

閉
bì (V) to close (almost exclusively of eyes and mouth). bì-'yǎn, 'bì-shang 'yǎn-jing to close the eyes, figuratively to refuse to see something or to die; bì-'kěw to close the mouth, have nothing to say.

壁
*bì (Nunit, shàn) wall (literary).

箆子
'bì-dz (Nunit, bǎ, ge) comb with very fine teeth on both sides of a central spine.

畢節
bì-'jyé (Nunique) Pi-chieh (city in Kweichow province).

秘魯
bì-'lǔ(-gwó) (Nunique) Peru.

秘密
'bì-mì (A; Nunit, ge) secret. ‖jèy-jyàn-shr̀ hěn 'bì-mì. This matter is quite secret. ‖jèy-shr̀ 'jywūn-shr̀-'bì-mì. This is a military secret.
    'bì-mì-gūng-'wén secret document.

避免
bì-'myǎn (V) to avoid, circumvent, difficulties, trouble. ‖tā dzwò 'jèy-ge yīn-wey yàw bì-'myǎn hěn-dwō-'má-fan. He's doing this in order to avoid a lot of trouble.

必須
bì-'shywū (V) to need, require. ‖gày 'fáng-dz, 'mù-tew shr̀ bì-'shywū-de. For building a house one needs wood. ‖yàw 'hwó-je bì-'shywū chr̀-'fàn. You've got to eat to live.

畢業
bì-'yè (VN2) to graduate, be graduated, (from school).

濱江
bīn-'jyāng (Nunique) Pin-chiang or Harbin (city in Kirin province).

冰
bīng (Nmass, kwày) ice.

冰
*bīng (mainV) to freeze by applying ice or putting on ice, 'bīng-shàng to freeze, rarely 'bīng-chi-láy. ‖bǎ 'gwǒ-dz gěy 'bīng-shang. Put the fruit on ice to freeze it. ‖chǐng-ni bǎ jèy-bēy-'shwěy 'dzày 'bīng-yi-bīng, yīn-wey bú-'gèw 'lyáng-de. Please put this glass of water on ice again for a while; it isn't cold enough yet.

兵
bīng (Npers) soldier; member of any of the armed forces.

兵器
bīng-'chì (Nunit, jyàn, ge) weapons.

兵器庫
bīng-chì-'kù (Nunit, ge, swǒ) arsenal (for storage), armory.

兵船
bīng-'chwán (Nunit, jř, tyáw) warship.

兵工廠
bīng-gūng-'chǎng (Nunit, ge) arsenal (for production, not storage, of armament).

兵士
bīng-'shr̀ (Ncoll) enlisted personnel.

兵營
bīng-'yíng (Nunit, dzwò) barracks.

餅

bǐng (*Nmass; kwày*) any kind of *relatively* hard cake-like product *made from dough by baking, frying, or steaming; sweet, salty, sour, hot, or tasteless. In compounds used as we use* cake; *e.g.,* ywú-'bǐng fish-cakes.

餅乾

bǐng-'gān (*Nunit,* kwày, ge) cookies and biscuits (*in British and American senses*).

病

bìng (*A*) ill (*opposite* hǎw); (*N*) illness, sickness, disease, yěw-'bìng to be ill; bìng 'hǎw-le to have recovered from an illness; 'bìng-rén sick person, hospital patient. ‖tā-de-'lyǎn fā-'báy, kǔng-'pà yěw-'bìng. His face looks pale; I'm afraid he's sick.

並，并

bìng (*H; used only with* bù *or* méy) really, definitely, certainly. ‖wǒ 'jywé-de 'nèy-ge-dūng-shi 'bìng bù-'hǎw. I don't think it's at all good. ‖nèy-ge 'bìng bù-'má-fan. (Contrary to expectations,) it's no bother at all.

病車

bìng-'chē (*Nunit,* lyàng) ambulance; hospital-car.

不

bù (bù *before fourth tone and toneless syllables;* bù *before first, second, and third tone syllables, and optionally instead of* bù *in isolation*). (*H*) don't, doesn't, won't. *The verb* shř to be *is negated only with* bù; *the verb* yěw *to have, there is, there are is never negated with* bù, *nor are RC; contrast* méy *haven't, hasn't, didn't. Lexical units containing* bù *are alphabetized as though the* bù *were not present; thus for* bú-'gwò *see under* gwò.

捕

bǔ (*V*) arrest, apprehend. *As mainV:* bǔ-'dzěw arrest and take away (*to jail*). ‖shywún-'jǐng 'bǔ-le 'yí-ge-táw-'fàn. The police caught one of the escaped prisoners.

補

bǔ (*V*) to mend, patch, repair *clothing, a tire,* to fill *a tooth; i.e., to affix a piece to something where that something has an undesirable hole or gap. As mainV:* 'bǔ-chi-láy, 'bǔ-shàng, *etc.* ‖tā-de-'yá 'yǐ-jing 'bǔ-chi-lay-le. He's already had his tooth filled. ‖tā bǎ pwò-'wà-dz gěy 'bǔ-shang-le. She darned the (torn *or* worn) stockings.

步

bù (*Mauton*) a pace, a step; *in compounds also* infantry. ‖tā 'dzěw-de 'kwày; tā-de-'bù hěn 'dà. He walks fast because he takes long steps.

布

bù (*Nmass,* kwày) cloth, other than wool. ‖'bù méy-yew yáng-'máw 'nwǎn-he. Cotton (*cloth*) isn't as warm as wool (*cloth*).

簿

*****bù, 'bù-dz** (*Nunit,* běn) notebook, ledger.

步鎗

bù-'chyāng (*Nunit,* jř) infantry rifle.

不足掛齒

bù-dzú gwà-'chř (*literary quotation; VN1*) not worth mentioning (*in politely shrugging off proffered thanks*). ‖'jèy-ge bù-dzú gwà-'chř. Oh, that's not worth mentioning; forget it.

步法

bù-'fǎ (*N*) a step, type of step (*as in dancing*).

部下

bù-'shyà(-de-rén) (*N*) subordinates *in governmental or military organization.* ‖tā-bù-'shyà-de-rén dēw 'dàw-le. All his subordinates are present. ‖tā-de-bù-'shyà dzàw-'fǎn-le. His subordinates revolted.

撥

bwō (*V*) (1) to adjust the position *of something laterally with the end of a finger or of a pointed object. As mainV:* 'bwō-dàw move *something thus to a position;* bwō-'kwày set *a clock* faster *or* ahead. ‖chǐng-ni bǎ-'jūng bwō-'kwày-yì-dyǎr. Please set the clock ahead a bit. ‖bǎ-'jūng 'bwō-dàw 'shř-dyǎn-yí-'kè. Set the clock for ten fifteen. ‖ni bǎ nèy-ge-'gàr gěy 'bwō-kay-le gěy-wo 'kàn-yi-kàn. Push the lid aside and let me take a look.

(2) To make a financial readjustment *or a transfer of funds (as when A owes B and B owes C, so A pays C). As mainV:* 'bwō-gěy give *someone something* in financial readjustment. ‖wǒ jyàw-ta 'bwō-gey ni nèy-ge-'kwǎn. I'll have him transfer the money to you (*as per arrangement*).

渤海

bwō-'hǎy (*Nunique*) Gulf of Chihli.

舶來品

bwō-láy-'pǐn (*Nmass;* ge an item or kind of) imported goods.

玻璃

'bwō-li (*Nmass*) glass (*the substance*).

鄱陽湖

bwō-yáng-'hú (*Nunique*) Po-yang Lake.

駮，駁

bwó (*V*) to argue with *a person;* (*mainV*) bwó-'dǎw to argue *someone* down; **'bwó-hwéy-chywù** to give the clinching argument which stops one's opponent. ‖tā bǎ-ta gěy bwó-'dǎw-le. He defeated him in the argument. ‖ni byé 'bwó-wo. Don't give me any argument. ‖wǒ shr̀ bwó-bu-'dǎw-de. You can't argue me down.

伯

*bwó (Npers) father's older brother. See Appendix A.

薄

bwó see báw; in some cases both pronunciations are used; in others bwó is a reading pronunciation only.

博

bwó (A) variegated, of all kinds; wide (of knowledge). ‖tā-de-'shywé-wen hěn 'bwó. His learning is very broad.

脖子

'bwó-dz (Nunit, ge) neck. ‖tā-de-'bwó-dz-shang 'jǎng-le yí-ge-'jr̆. He had a mole on his neck.
    mwó 'bwó-dz to cut one's throat.

博物館

bwó-wù-'gwǎn (Nunit, dzwò, ge) museum.

栢林

bwò-'lín (Nunique) Berlin.

編

byān (V) to braid, plait. byān-'shí to plait mats; byān 'byàn-dz to braid hair, etc. Also mainV: ‖tā bǎ-'tsǎw byān-chéng yì-lǐng-'shí. She plaited the straw into a mat.

編

byān (V; mainV) edit, compile. 'byān-chū-láy compile or edit for publishing; byān-'hàw (VN1) compile in an ordered set of classes, such as alphabetical or numerical. ‖tā shyàn-'dzày jèng dzày 'byān yì-jǔng-'bàw. He's editing a newspaper now. ‖'nèy-běn-shū 'yǐ-jing 'byān-chu-lay-le. The editing of the book is done.

邊

byān or byār (Mpos) side, edge, border. With Dem and Num: 'nèy-byar that side, yonder; 'lyǎng-byān both sides, two sides, etc. 'dūng-byan east side, edge, etc. with other direction words; 'hǎy-byar shore, beach; 'hé-byar side of a river, etc. ‖'jūng-gwo·'běy-byār-de-tǔ-'dì jùng 'mày-dz hǎw. The soil of northern China is good for growing wheat. ‖bǎ nèy-lyǎng-bǎ-'yǐ-dz gē-dzay 'jwō-dz-de-'lyǎng-byār. Put these two chairs one on each side of the table.

編輯

'byān-jì (Npers) editor.

邊境

byān-'jìng (Nplace) border area of a country.

邊界

byān-'jyè (Nunit, tyáw) border between two countries or states or provinces (the actual line, not the area).

扁

byǎn (A) flat, in the sense of without protruding spots, or in the sense of vertical dimension being markedly less than the horizontal dimensions. ‖tā-de-'lyǎn 'jǎng-de yèw 'byǎn yèw 'kwān. His face is both flat and wide. ‖jèy-ge-'shyár bú-shr 'fāng-de, shr̀ 'byǎn-de. This box isn't cubical, it's shallow.

變

byàn (I) to change, alter. ‖nǐ 'dzěw-le yǐ-'hèw jywú-'shr̀ chywán 'byàn-le. After you left the situation changed completely. Used causatively: ‖tā byàn-le 'yàng-dz. He's changed his attitude (appearance, nature).
    As mainV: 'byàn-chéng change into; byàn-'báy turn pale; byàn-'swān turn sour, spoil, etc. ‖tā 'hú-rán 'byàn-chéng yí-ge-hěn-rè-'shīn-de-hwèy-'ywán. Suddenly he became a very enthusiastic member. ‖tā 'pà-de 'lyǎn dēw byàn-'báy-le. He was frightened and he turned pale.

辯

byàn (I) to argue about something logically, to try to give rational reasons for something. ‖tā méy-'lǐ bù-néng 'dzày 'byàn-le. Having no valid reason, he can't argve further. ‖ni béng 'byàn! There's no use in your trying to rationalize about it.

遍, 徧

byàn or byàr (Msemel) one time, once (twice, etc.) through. ‖gěy-wo 'chàng yí-byàn. Sing it through for me once.
    byàn used alone after a verb means throughout, everywhere. ‖'nèy-běn-shū wǒ jǎw-'byàn-le jǎw-bu-'jáw. I looked everywhere for that book and couldn't find it.

便道

byàn-'dàw (Nunit, tyáw) sidewalk.

變動

'byàn-dùng (V) to change, alter.
    (Nunit, ge) a change. ‖nǐ-de-'jì-hwà yěw shéme-'byàn-dùng-ma? Has there been any change in your plans?

辯護

byàn-'hù (V) to give the case for the defense, (particularly legal) ‖tā 'chǐng yí-ge-lywù-'shr̄ tì-ta byàn-'hù. He asked a lawyer to take his case.

辯論

byàn-'lwèn (*V*) to argue about, discuss, *something.*
byàn-'lwèn yí-ge-jǔ-'jǎng to discuss an ethical principle *held by someone.* ‖'**nèy-tsž-byàn-'lwèn shř 'shéy 'yíng-le?** Who won the argument that time?

變形蟲

byàn-shíng-'chúng (*Nunit,* ge) amoeba.

錶，表

byǎw (*Nunit,* ge) watch (*timepiece*).
   In compounds also chart, table, blank, dial, form, *something with indicators or elements arranged in a pattern which is read, which shows something.*
   (*V*) to manifest, show, *emotion and the like.*

表

*****byǎw** (*Npers*) cousin who is not father's brother's child. *See Appendix A.*

表情

byǎw-'chíng (*VN1*) to display emotion, show emotion, (*particularly by facial expression*).
   (*N*) display of emotion. ‖**nǐ 'kàn tā-'lyǎn-shang-de-byǎw-'chíng nǐ jyèw 'jř-daw tā 'shīn-li nán-'gwò.** When you look at the expression on his face, you can tell that he's suffering.

表格

byǎw-'gé (*Nunit,* jāng) blank, form (*to be filled out*).

表決

byǎw-'jywé (*VN1*) to reach a decision *by voting.* ‖'**jèy-jyàn-shř yīng-dang téw-'pyàw byǎw-'jywé.** This matter must be voted on in order to reach a decision.

表示

byǎw-'shř (*V*) to show, express, make clear. ‖**nǐ 'yīng-dang byǎw-'shř nǐ-de-'tày-dù.** You should make your attitude clear.

表現

byǎw-'shyàn (*V*) to express *one's reaction, feelings,* by facial expression or behavior, or verbally. *Also mainV:* ‖**tā shwō nèy-jywù-'hwà byǎw-'shyàn-chu-lay tā bù-'gāw-shìng.** His saying that, shows that he isn't happy. ‖**tā bù-'gāw-shìng-de-'yàng-dz byǎw-'shyàn-dzay 'lyǎn-shang.** His unhappiness shows on his face.

表同情

byǎw túng-chíng (*VN1*) to show one's sympathy, to be sympathetic. ‖**tā gēn 'chyúng-rén byǎw 'túng-shíng.** She has sympathy for the poor.

表演

byǎw-'yǎn (*V*) to give a demonstration of *a trick, an experiment, etc;* to act out, perform. ‖**jèy-ge-yǎn-'ywán byǎw-'yǎn-de hěn 'hǎw.** This actor is very good. ‖**tā dzày nèy-ge-shř-yàn-'shř-li byǎw-'yǎn nèy-ge-'fāng-fǎ gěy wǒ-men 'kàn.** He demonstrated that method in the laboratory for us.

憋，閉

byē (*V*) to hold in, restrain, confine, *air or a person.* ‖**tā 'byē-le yì-kěw-'chì jyèw 'fù-gwò-chywu-le.** He held his breath and swam across.
   As mainV: **byē-bu-'jù** to be unable to hold in, be unable to restrain. ‖**tā byē-bu-'jù, jyèw dà-'shyàw-le.** He couldn't restrain himself, and burst into loud laughter. ‖**nǐ bù-néng 'lǎw bǎ shyáw-'hár byē-dzay 'jyā-lǐ-tew.** You can't confine your children to the house all the time.

別

byé (*Aattr*) others, other (*not the others or another*). '**byé-rén** other people, others; **byé-'dì-fang** other places; *except in the two combinations just given and a very few others* **byé-** *adds* **-de.** ‖**jèy-ge bú-shr 'nǐ-de, shř 'byé-rén-de.** This is 't yours, it's someone else's. **tā gēn 'byé-de dēw bù-yí-yàng.** He's not like anyone else. ‖**tā dàw byé(-de)-'dì-fang chywù-le.** He's gone somewhere else. ‖'**byé-de-'nywǔ-rén dēw bù-'chwān 'nèy-yàng-de-'yī-fu; 'nǐ 'wèy-shéme 'pyān-yàw 'chwān?** Other women don't wear such clothes; why do you insist on wearing them?

別

byé (*V*) to pin *something,* fasten *something* with a pin. *As mainV:* '**byé-shàng** or '**byé-chǐ-lay** pin *something* up; **byé-dzay yí-'kwàr** pin *things* together; *etc.* ‖**bǎ jèy-lyǎng-kwày-'bù 'byé-dzay yí-'kwàr.** Pin these two pieces of cloth together.

別

byé *abbreviated form of* '**bú-yàw** (*Vsent*) don't (*giving prohibitions*). ‖**nǐ byé dzwò-'shēng; tīng-ta 'jyǎng.** Don't make any noise; listen to him talk.

憋忸，別忸

'**byè-nyew** (*A*) upset, disturbed, uncomfortable, *physically or mentally.* ‖'**gūng-rén chwān-le 'shywē-dz 'jywé-de hěn 'byè-nyew.** When a workman wears boots (*instead of sandals or going barefoot*) he feels quite uncomfortable.
   byè-bye-nyew-'nyèw-de most upsetting. ‖**nèy-ge-rén-de-'yàng-dz byè-bye-nyew-'nyèw-de.** That man's manner °makes one feel uncomfortable. *or* °upsets one a little.

C

cha *Wade Romanization for* ja.

ch'a *Wade Romanization for* cha.

插
chā (*V*) to insert *something in a depression, or between two other things with part of the thing inserted still sticking out.* ‖tā-de-'jyě-jye bǎ-'hwār chā-dzay 'píng-dz-lǐ-tew-le. His sister put the flowers in the vase.

叉子
'chā-dz, chār (*Nunit*, ge) an X-mark.
    hwà (*or* dǎ) yí-ge-'chā-dz draw an X, make an X.

查, 察
chá (*V*) to investigate, inspect. *As mainV:* chá-'chīng to investigate thoroughly; chá-'míng to make clear through an investigation; 'chá-chū-lay to discover, find out about. ‖shywún-'jǐng bǎ jèy-ge-'dì-fang dēw chá-'chīng-le. The police have investigated this place thoroughly. ‖fēy bǎ jèy-jyàn-'shŕ-ching chá-'míng-le bù-'kě. We've got to clarify that matter. ‖dyàn-hwà-de-hàw-'mǎr 'chá-chu-lay(-le) méy-yew? Did you find out the telephone number?
    chá ge-shwěy-'lwò shŕ-'chū (*literary*) to clear up *something*, get to the bottom of *something.*

茶
chá (*Nmass*) tea *in general, or in liquid form ready to drink.*

茶杯
chá-'bēy (*NunitC*, ge) teacup.

茶點
chá-'dyǎn (*Ncoll*) refreshments (*literally* tea and cakes).

茶房
'chá-fang (*Npers*) waiter *in a hotel or ship dining room.*

察哈爾
chá-hā-'ěr (*Nunique*) Chahar province.

茶壺
chá-'hú (*NunitC*) teakettle; teapot.

茶會
chá-'hwèy (*Nunit*, ge) tea party.

查賬
chá-'jàng (*VN2*) to audit; to investigate accounts *when they don't balance properly.* ‖jīn-nyan-de-'jàng 'chá-gwò-le, méy-'tswèr. This year's accounts have been audited, and there were no errors.
    chá-'jàng-de auditor.

査稅
chá-'shwèy (*VN2*) to make a customs inspection.
    chá-'shwèy-de customs inspector.

茶碗
chá-'wǎn (*Nunit*, ge) teacup.

茶舞會
chá-wǔ(-'hwèy) (*Nunit*, ge) tea dance.

茶葉
chá-'yè (*Nunit*, ge) tea leaf; (*Nmass*) tea *in dried-leaf state ready to brew.*

岔
*chà (*mainV*) to split. 'chà-kāy to interrupt. ‖tām-shwō-'hwà bèy-'nǐ gěy 'chà-kay-le. You interrupted their conversation.
    'chà-jìn-chywu to break into *a conversation.* ‖tām shwō-'hwà de-shŕ-hew tā 'chà-jin-chywu-le. He broke in while they were talking.
    'chà-chū-lay to branch out (*as a tree trunk*). ‖jèy-kē-'shù-gēr-'dì-shya 'chà-chu yí-ge-'jēr-lay. This tree has a branch right at the ground.

岔道
chà-'dàw (*Nunit*, tyáw) branch road. ‖'jèr yěw 'lyǎng-tyáw-chà-'dàw, tā bù-'jŕ-daw dzěw 'něy-tyáw. There are two branch roads here; he doesn't know which one to take.

chai *Wade Romanization for* jay.

ch'ai *Wade Romanization for* chay.

chan *Wade Romanization for* jan.

ch'an *Wade Romanization for* chan.

攙
chān (*V*) to help *someone*, support *someone* by holding *him* at the elbow, hand, or arm. ‖gwò-'chyáw de-shŕ-hew nǐ 'chān-chan ta. Help him while he's crossing the bridge.

纏
chán (*V*) to roll up (*as a string*). *As mainV:* 'chán-chi-láy *or* 'chán-shang same as above; 'chán-dzày to roll up *string, etc.* around *something; etc.*

產, 產業
*chǎn, chǎn-'yè (*Nabstr*) property. ‖tā-'swǒ-yěw de-chǎn-'yè dēw shŕ tā-fù-'mǔ-'lyéw-gey-ta-de. He inherited all his property from his parents.

chang *Wade Romanization for* **jang.**

ch'ang *Wade Romanization for* **chang.**

噇, 嚐
cháng (*V*) to taste, try, sample. ‖tā shyān 'cháng-cháng kěw-'wèy. She samples its flavor first. *As mainV:* ‖nǐ cháng-de-chū-lay shr̀ shéme-'wèr-ma? Can you tell what flavor it is?

長
cháng (*A*) long. (*Opposite* **dwǎn.**)

常
cháng *or* **'cháng-cháng** (*H*) often, usually, always. ‖tā 'cháng-cháng kāy-'chē dàw-'nàr-chywu, kě-shr 'yěw-shŕ-hew 'dzěw-je chywù. He usually drives there, but sometimes he walks. ‖wǒ 'cháng-cháng dǎ wǎng-'chyéw. I often play tennis.

場
cháng, chǎng (*MdistT*) a spell of, period of. bìng a period of illness; dà-'kū a crying spell; shì a performance of plays; hwǒ-'dzāy a fire (disaster); shwěy-'dzāy a flood; chyéw a ball game; mèng a dreaming spell; ywǔ a period of rain; 'gwān-sz a lawsuit (*in a particular court*); fū-'chī a period of marriage to a certain person.
     dzwò yì-cháng-'gwān to serve a term as an official; **dāng yì-cháng-'bīng** to serve a period of enlistment as a soldier; **'kū yì-'cháng** to cry for a while.

長安
cháng-'ān (*Nunique*) Ch'ang-an (*capital of Shensi province*).

長城
cháng-'chéng (*Nunique*) the Great Wall.

長崎
cháng-'chí (*Nunique*) Nagasaki (*Japan*).

長蟲
'cháng-chung (*Nunit*, **tyáw**) snake.

長春
cháng-'chwēn (*Nunique*) Ch'ang-ch'un (*capital of Kirin province*).

常德
cháng-'dé (*Nunique*) Ch'ang-tè *or* Changteh (*city in Hunan province*).

長度
cháng-'dù (*Nabstr*) length.

長江
cháng-'jyāng (*Nunique*) The Yangtze River.

長久
cháng 'jyěw (*A*) for a long time. ‖jèy-ge-'bǐ ké-yi 'yùng-de hěn cháng 'jyěw. This pen can be used for a long time.

長溜
cháng-'lyèw (*Mgroup*) long line. ‖yěw yì-cháng-'lyèw-de-rén 'děng-je mǎy-'pyàw. There's a long line of people waiting to buy tickets.

長沙
cháng-'shā (*Nunique*) Ch'ang-sha (*capital of Hunan province*).

嘗試
cháng-'shr̀ (*V*) to try, taste, *used also of things other than foods.* ‖jyàw-ta cháng-'shr̀ cháng-'shr̀, tā jyěw 'jŕ-daw-le. Let him get a taste of it (*e.g., a job*), then he'll know (that he doesn't want to keep the job).

長途
*****cháng-'tú** long-distance, *only before nouns.* 'cháng-tú-chì-'chē long-distance (*inter-city*) bus; 'cháng-tú-dyàn-'hwà long-distance phone call; 'cháng-tú-lywǔ-'shíng long trip.

場
chǎng *see* **cháng.**

場
*****chǎng** (*N*) open space in which some activity is carried on. fēy-jī-'chǎng airfield; dzú-chyéw-'chǎng football field; mù-'chǎng pasture land.
     'chǎng-dz (*Nunit*, **ge**) *or* **chyéw-'chǎng** ball court, ball field.

厰, 廠
*****chǎng, 'chǎng-dz** open space enclosed by a wall or a line of trees or a fence. kūng-'chǎng open court; dà-'chǎng large court; dà-kūng-'chǎng large open court; gūng-'chǎng factory; tíng-chē-'chǎng auto parking area. ‖nèy-ge-'fáng-dz-'chyán-tew yěw yí-ge-dà-kūng-'chǎng. There's a wide court in front of that house.

敞着
'chǎng-je (*I*) to be open, leave open, *book, door, etc.* ‖tyān 'lěng, byé 'chǎng-je 'mén. It's cold, don't leave the door open.

唱
chàng (*V*) to sing (*must be followed by an object*). *As mainV:* ‖tā yì-'jŕ 'chàng-shàng-chywu chàng-daw hěn-'gāw-de-yīn. He sang a scale up to a very high note.

唱歌
chàng-'gē(er) (*VN2*) to sing a song *that has words.*

唱戲

chàng-'shì (*VN2*) to play (sing) a part in Chinese drama, or in any drama involving singing.
    chàng-'shì-de actor (*or* actress) in such drama.

chao *Wade Romanization for* **jaw.**

ch'ao *Wade Romanization for* **chaw.**

碴兒

chár (*Nunit*, **ge**) a mistake, a fault.
    yěw-'chár to have faults.

抄

chāw (*V*) to copy, to imitate. ‖**tā 'chāw 'byé-ren-de-'fá-dz.** He's imitating someone else's method. *As mainV:* ‖**wǒ shyǎng nǐ ké-yi bǎ jèy-'dwàn 'chāw-shyà-lay.** I think you might copy that passage down.
    chāw-'shū (*VN2*) to plagiarize, to lift passages without indicating the source.

超過

chāw-gwò (*RC3*) to go above, exceed, go past *some understood point.* ‖**jèy-ge-'shù-mu 'yǐ-jing 'chāw-gwò nǐ-shywū-'yàw-de-le.** This amount is already in excess of what you need. ‖**jèy-ge-shù-mu 'yǐ-jing 'chāw-gwò 'nèy-ge-shù-mu-de-lyǎng-'bèy.** This amount is already more than twice that amount.

鈔票

chāw-'pyàw (*Nunit*, **jāng**) banknote.

潮

cháw (*A*) damp, slightly wet.

潮

cháw (*N*) the tide(s). **cháw 'shàng-láy** *or* **'cháw 'láy** the tide comes in (*or* up); **'cháw 'twèy** *or* **'cháw 'twèy-chywù** *or* **'cháw 'shyà-chywù** the tide goes down (*or* out). **dzǎw-'cháw** morning tide; **wǎn-'cháw** evening tide. ‖**'ywè yī 'shàng-lay 'cháw jyèw 'láy-le.** The tide comes in as soon as the moon rises.

朝

cháw (*V*) to face towards. ‖**jèy-dzwò-'léw shr cháw-'běy-de.** This building faces north. ‖**tā 'cháw-je-ta 'shyàw.** He smiled at her. ‖**bǎ 'jèy-kwày-'tsáy-lyàw-de-'myàr cháw-'wày.** Turn this material (*cloth*) right side out.

朝

***cháw** (*N*) dynasty.

吵

chǎw (*A*) to be noisy, disturbing. ‖**jèy-tyáw-'jyē hěn 'chǎw.** This street is very noisy (*unfavorable comment;* **'rè-nàw** *would mean* bustling *but not necessarily unpleasingly so*). *As mainV:* **chǎw-'shǐng** to wake *someone* up by being noisy.

(I) to quarrel. **'chǎw-chǐ-láy** to start to quarrel. ‖**'shwō-je 'shwō-je, tā-men 'chǎw-chi-lay-le.** They talked and talked until, they got themselves into a quarrel.

炒

chǎw (*V*) to fry in oil over a very hot fire, stirring constantly. **chǎw-'fàn** (*VN3*) fried rice; **chǎw-'myàn** (*VN3*) fried noodles.

吵嘴

chǎw-'dzwěy (*VN1*) to quarrel noisily.

拆

chāy (*V*) to take *something* apart intentionally, disassemble. **chāy-'shìn** to open mail; to open someone else's mail. *As mainV:* **'chāy-kāy** to take apart; **chāy-'hwày** to ruin *something* unintentionally while taking it apart; *etc.* ‖**dí-'bīng háy méy-gwò-'hé, wǒm jyèw bǎ-'chyáw gěy 'chāy-le.** Before the enemy soldiers crossed the river we took the bridge down. ‖**tā bǎ nèy-ge-'bāw 'chāy-kay-le.** He opened the package.

差事

'chāy-shr (*Nunit*, **ge**) job (*way of making a living*); mission (*task of going somewhere to accomplish something*); assignment of work.

柴

cháy (*Nmass*, **kwày**) firewood. **dǎ-'cháy** to fetch firewood.
    hwǒ-'cháy (*Nmass*, **kwày**) firewood; (*Nunit*, **gēn, gēr**) a match.

che *Wade Romanization for* **je.**

ch'e *Wade Romanization for* **che.**

車

chē (*Nunit*, **lyàng**) car, cart, train-car, *or any wheeled vehicle.* **yí-lyè(-hwǒ)-'chē** railroad (*or* subway) train.

車錢

'chē-chyán (*Nmass*) fare *for a rickshaw, cart, taxi, bus ride.*

車帶

chē-'dày (*Nunit*, **tyáw, ge**) tire (*for a vehicle*). **yí-fù-chē-'dày** set of tires.

車房

chē-'fáng (*Nunit*, **swǒ, jyān, ge**) garage (*for storage, not servicing; part of one's own house*).

車夫

'chē-fu (*Npers*) driver (*of a bus*), engineer (*locomotive*); chauffeur; cart-driver.

車站

chē-'jàn (*Nunit*, **ge**) railway station, bus stop.

車軸
chē-'jéw(r) (*Nunit,* tyáw, gēn) axle.

車輛
chē-'lyàng (*Ncoll*) vehicles, vehicular traffic.

車馬
chē-'mǎ (*Ncoll*) traffic. ‖**shywún-'jǐng jř-'hwēy 'jyē-shang-de-chē-'mǎ.** The policeman is directing the traffic on the street.

車頭
chē-'téw (*Nunit,* lyàng) locomotive.

扯
chě (*V*) **to tear** with the hands, *paper, cloth, and such materials, or meat, etc. As mainV:* **'chě-kāy** tear open, **tear apart; chě-'swèy** to tear into pieces; **'chě-chéng** to tear into *two pieces, three pieces, etc.* ‖**tā bǎ-'shìn 'chě-le.** He tore the letter up.

扯着脖子
chě-je 'bwó-dz (*H*) loudly (*literally* tearing the throat). ‖**tā chě-je 'bwó-dz 'rǎng yì-'shyěw.** He screamed at the top of his voice all night long.

撤
chè (*V*) to withdraw, pull back *troops, people;* to recall *a diplomat, etc.;* to clear away *dishes after eating. As mainV:* **chè-'twèy** or **'chè-chū-chywù** to withdraw, (*of troops*); **chè-hwéy-chywù** to withdraw *troops,* or to back *a train or vehicle because of an obstruction blocking its progress.* ‖**tā-men-de-jywūn-'dwèy 'yǐ-jing chè-'twèy-le.** Their troops have already withdrawn. ‖**jywūn-'dwèy 'yǐ-jing tsúng nèy-ge-'chéng 'chè-chu-chywu-le.** The troops have already withdrawn from that city. ‖**tā bǎ nà-shyē-'jř-ywán dēw gěy 'chè-hwéy-chywu-le.** He ordered all those employees back to headquarters.

徹底
chè-'dǐ (*H*) thoroughly. ‖**nǐ bǎ-ta chè-'dǐ-de 'yán-jyèw yí-shyà.** Make a thorough study of it.

chen *Wade Romanization for* jen.

ch'en *Wade Romanization for* chen.

摻
chēn (*V*) to pull! *something soft* with the hand, *adjusting its position or shape.* (*See also* lā *and* bá.)
   As mainV: **'chēn-chū-lay** pull *something* out; **chēn-'jř** to pull straight; **chēn-'píng** to pull smooth; *etc.* ‖**bǎ nèy-jāng-'jř 'chēn-chu-lay.** Pull that piece of paper out' (*from the stack in which it is piled*). ‖**chǐng-nǐ bǎ jèy-ge-'dān-dz chēn-'jř-le.** Please pull that sheet straight.

晨
*chén morning; **'dzǎw-chen** (*Ntime*) is the usual term. ***chén** *occurs in a few compounds; certain morning papers call themselves a* **chén-'bàw** *instead of* **dzǎw-'bàw,** *though the latter is the general term.*

沉
chén (*I*) to sink (*in liquid*). *As mainV:* **'chén-shyà-chywù** or **'chén-dàw** to sink to *the bottom.* ‖**'chwán 'chén-le.** or **'chwán 'chén-shyà-chywu-le.** The boat sank.

沉底
chén-'dǐ, chén-'dyěr (*IN*) to sink to the bottom. ‖**'táng dēw chén-'dyěr-le.** The sugar sank to the bottom.

陳列
chén-'lyè (*V*) to display, exhibit, *formally (as in a showcase or museum).* ‖**'chwāng-hu-lǐ-tew chén-'lyè-le hěn-dwō-'hwò.** There are a lot of goods displayed in the window.

陳列所
chén-lyè-'swǒ (*Nunit,* ge) museum *for some special type of collection.*

沉悶
'chén-mèn (*A*) depressing, dull, uninteresting, lonely, depressed. ‖**jèy-ge-dì-fang hěn 'chén-mèn.** This place is very depressing. ‖**wǒ hěn 'chén-mèn.** I'm quite depressed.

陳述
chén-'shù (*V*) to give a detailed oral report, report orally in detail. ‖**tā dàw tā-de-'shàng-sž-'chyán-tew-chywù chén-'shù.** He's going before his boss to make a report. *Often justifying or explaining something that shouldn't have happened.*

塵土
chén-'tǔ (*Nmass*) dirt, dust. ‖**mǎn-'chù dēw-shr chén-'tǔ.** There was dust everywhere.

趁
chèn (*V*) avail oneself of *an opportunity, a convenience, someone's absence or presence, etc.* **chèn-je 'jī-hwey** taking an opportunity. ‖**tā chèn-je 'jī-hwey jyèw 'dzěw-le.** He took the opportunity to leave. ‖**wǒ 'chèn nǐ 'dzày-jèr de shŕ-hew 'gàw-su nǐ.** I'll take advantage of your being here to tell you; (instead of having to write you about it).
   chèn-'byàn or **chèn-'byàr** (*H*) at one's convenience. ‖**nǐ chèn-'byàn 'dày-lay.** Bring it along at your convenience.

襯
chèn (*V*) to wear *underneath,* wear *inner garments.* ‖**nǐ 'lǐ-tew yàw-shr chèn yí-jyàn-'hèw-yī-fu, 'dà-yī jyèw bú-tày 'dà-le.** If you'll wear a heavy dress underneath, your coat won't be too loose.

稱
chèn (*A*) to harmonize, (*of colors, of tones*); to be matched, (*of husband and wife, etc.*). ‖**jèy-lyǎng-ge-'yán-sè bú-'chèn.** These two colors don't harmonize.

稱
chèn (*V*) to be worth *so-much money* (*of an estate or person*). ‖**tā-'jèy-ge-rén shyàn-dzày 'chèn yì-bǎy-'wàn.** He's worth a million dollars right now.

襯衫
chèn-'shān (*Nunit,* **jyàn**) shirt.

襯衣
chèn-'yī (*Nunit,* **jyàn**) underclothing, any inner garment.

cheng *Wade Romanization for* **jeng.**

ch'eng *Wade Romanization for* **cheng.**

稱霸
chēng-'bà (*VN1*) to acquire power *or* control *over some territory* through exercise of power, *not through legal right.* ‖**tā bǎ 'byé-rén-de-'dì-fang dēw 'jàn-le, 'dz̀-jí chēng-'bà.** He occupied the territory of others by force and made himself the ruler.

稱呼
'chēng-hu (*V*) to address *someone with a certain title or kinship term.* ‖**wǒm 'dzěme 'chēng-hu ta?** How shall we address him? ‖**wǒm 'chēng-hu ta 'shyān-sheng 'dwèy-de.** We ought to call him Mister.

盛
chéng (*V*) to contain *or* hold *some quantity;* (*said of any container*). ‖**jèy-ge-'píng-dz néng 'chéng dwō-shaw-'shwěy?** How much water will this bottle hold?
   As mainV: **'chéng-chǐ-lay** to fill *a container;* **chéng-'mǎn** to be filled, full; **'chéng-jìn(-chywu)** to put *something* into *a container until it is full.*

成
chéng (*I*) to be OK, to do, to be satisfactory, *only in such expressions as:* **'chéng-bu-chéng?** *or* **'chéng-ma?** Will it do? *or* Is it all right? *or* Is it satisfactory? ‖**'nèy ge bù-'chéng.** It won't do. ‖**'nèy-ge 'chéng.** That one's all right.
   (*V*) to accomplish, finish satisfactorily, *only in certain VN combinations, listed as separate entries.*
   As postV: **'bǎy-chéng** break *something* into *so-many pieces;* **'wān-chéng** to bend *something* into *a circle, a hook, etc.;* **'byàn-chéng** to change *something* into; **'dzwò-chéng** to accomplish *work,* finish *a job.* ‖**'jèy-jyàn shr̀ 'dzwò-chéng-le dzày dzwò 'nèy-ge.** When this job is done, then do the other. ‖**bǎ jèy-kwày-'bǐng bǎy-chéng sān-'kwàr.** Break this cake into three pieces.

乘
chéng (*K*) times, multiplied by. ‖**'èr chéng-'sz̀ dé-'bā.** Two times four gives eight. ‖**ná-'èr chéng-'sz̀ jyèw dé-'bā.** Take two and multiply by four and you get eight. ‖**'èr chéng-'sz̀ 'děng-ywú 'bā.** Two times four equals eight. ‖**'èr chéng-'sz̀ chéng-'lyèw dé sz̀-shr-'bā.** Two times four times six is forty-eight.

城
chéng (*Nunit,* **dzwò, ge**) city with a wall, city; *in some combinations* wall.
   chéng-'lǐ downtown, uptown, in town; **chéng-'wày** in the suburbs, in the outskirts.
   cháng-'chéng the Great Wall.

呈報
chéng-'bàw (*VN1*) to submit a report *formally to a superior.*

成本
chéng-'běn (*Nabstr*) cost of production. ‖**jèy-ge-'jyà-chyan 'bú-swàn 'gwèy, yīn-wey chéng-'běn 'gāw.** The price isn't high when you realize that the cost of production is what it is.

成本的
chéng-'běn-de, chéng-'běr-de bound into pads or fascicles. **chéng-'běr-de-'shū** bound books; **chéng-'běr-de-'pyàw** a book of tickets.

城牆
chéng-'chyáng (*Nunit,* **dzwò, shàn, myàn**) city wall.

承德
chéng-'dé (*Nunique*) Ch'eng-te (*capital of Jehol province*).

成丁
chéng-'dīng (*VN1*) become an adult, come of age (*legal*).

成都
'chéng-dū (*Nunique*) Ch'eng-tu (*capital of Szechwan province*).

程度
chéng-'dù (*Nabstr*) degree, standard, quality, (*of anything*). ‖**tā-de-gwó-'wén-chéng-'dù hěn 'hǎw.** His Chinese is very good.

成分
'chéng-fèn (*N*) part, percentag proportion; *limited to sentences like the followin* ‖**jèy-jǔng-'jyèw-lǐ-tew yěw 'dwō-shaw-'chéng-fèn-de-hwó-'jyěw?** What proportion of alcohol is there in this liquor? ‖**'chéng-fèn hěn °'dwō.** *or* °'**gāw.** The proportion is very high.

‖'jèy-jǔng-'jyěw-lǐ-tew-de-hwǒ-'jyěw 'chéng-fèn hěn 'dwō. In this kind of liquor the proportion of alcohol is quite high.

成功
chéng-'gūng (VN2) to complete a task successfully.

成績
chéng-'jì (Nunit, ge) record of attainment ‖tā-dzwò-'shr̀-de-chéng-'jì hěn 'hǎw. His working record is very good.

成就
chéng-'jyèw (VN1) to bring to satisfactory completion. ‖'jèy-jyàn-shr̀ shr̀ yéw-tā-nǔ-'lì ér chéng-'jyèw-de. This matter was brought to satisfactory completion by dint of his efforts.

誠懇
chéng-'kěn (A) sincere.

城門
chéng-'mén (Nunit, ge) city gate.

承認
chéng-'rèn (V, Vsent) to admit, confess. ‖tā bù-chéng-'rèn tā dzwò-le 'nèy-ge. He doesn't admit that he did that (not necessarily of something wrong).

成心
chéng-'shīn (H) on purpose, intentionally. ‖tā chéng-'shīn 'dzwò jèy-ge. He did it on purpose.

誠實
'chéng-shr (A) honest.

城市
chéng-'shr̀ (Nunit, ge) city in contrast to country. ‖chéng-'shr̀-de-kūng-'chì bù-rú 'shyāng-shyà-de 'hǎw. City air isn't as good as country air.
    'chéng-shr̀-'shēng-hwó (Nabstr) city life, life in cities.

懲罰
chěng-'fá (V) to punish; to inflict a penalty, prison sentence, fine, on someone. shèw chěng-'fá be punished. ‖'fàn-le wěy-dzàw-'dzwèy, tā 'yīng-gay shèw chěng-'fá. Having committed a forgery, he must be punished.

抽
chēw to draw something relatively small out from a much larger object in which it fits loosely, as a drawer from a desk; to inhale. As mainV: 'chēw-chū (lc) to draw out; 'chēw-dàw (lc) to draw something out to a position; 'chēw-kāy to open by drawing out, to draw something away from something else. chēw-'yān to smoke. ‖bǎ 'chēw-ti 'chēw-chū-lay. Pull the drawer (completely) out.

抽屜
'chēw-ti (Nunit, ge) drawer.

籌
chéw (V) to raise money, funds. ‖tā tì-wo 'chéw-le 'sān-wàn-kwày-'chyán. He raised thirty thousand dollars for me.

仇，讎
*chéw (N) hatred, a grudge, a score to settle; limited to bàw-'chéw to get revenge; yěw-'chéw to have a score to settle with someone; and compounds like 'chéw-rén enemies, people who have grudges against each other; chéw-'hèn hatred and desire for revenge. ‖'jèy-lyǎng-'dǎng-de-chéw-'hèn hěn 'shēn. Between these two (politica¹) parties there exists deep hatred.

愁
chéw (A) worried, concerned, anxious.

籌備
chéw-'bèy (V, Vsent) to make preparations in advance for some meeting or project or official undertaking. ‖tā-men shyàn-'dzày chéw-'bèy kāy yí-ge-hwān-yíng-'hwèy. They're making preparations for a welcoming party.

醜
chěw (A) ugly. (Opposite měy.)

臭
chèw (A) to smell bad. (Opposite shyāng.) ‖'jèy-jǔng-yān-de-'wèr yěw dyǎr-'chèw. This kind of tobacco has something of a bad odor.

chi Wade Romanization for ji.

ch'i Wade Romanization for chi.

七
chī (NumU) seven.

棲
chī (I) to alight and rest (of a bird; figuratively of wandering people). (Fairly literary.) 'chī-dzày alight on. ‖'nyáwr 'chī-dzay 'shù-shang. The bird lit on the tree. ‖'yěw-de-rén 'méy-yew dì-fang chī-'shēn. There are people who have no place to settle down.

沏
chī (V) to prepare something by pouring hot water on it. chī-'chá to brew tea by pouring hot water on the tea leaves.

期
chī (MdistT) issue of. yì-chī-dzá-'jr̀ one issue of a magazine.
    Class in a school. dì-'sān-chī bì-'yè to graduate as one of the third class graduated at a particular school.

*chĭ (*N*) period of time. àn-'chī (*H*) at regular intervals, *as in paying;* dàw-'chī to reach the end of some assigned period; gwò-'chī to become overdue; mǎn-'chī to reach the terminal point, (*as of a lease*); shĭng-'chī (*Ntime,* ge) week.

bù-'chī ér 'ywù (*literary*) to meet *someone* accidentally, without appointment. ‖nèy-tyān wǒ 'pèng-jyan ta 'jēn-shř bù-'chī ér 'ywù. When I met him that day it was really by accident.

漆

chī (*V*) to paint, apply paint to, varnish, *something.* ‖wǒ děy 'chī jèy-jāng-'jwǒ-dz. I must paint this table.

As mainV: 'chī-shàng to put on *a coat of paint.* ‖wǒ bǎ jèy-jāng-'jwǒ-dz 'chī-shang yí-dàw-'chī. I'll put a coat of paint on this table.

(*Nmass*) paint. yí-dàw-'chī or yì-tséng-'chī a coat of paint; húng-'chī red paint, *etc.*

妻

'chī-dz (*Npers*) wife. *See Appendix A.*

欺負

'chī-fu (*V*) to persecute, bully; get the better of, take advantage of *someone.* ‖tā lǎw 'chī-fu rén. He's always bullying people.

膝蓋

chī-'gày or chī-'gàr (*Nunit,* ge) kneecap.

騎

chí (*V*) to sit astride. chí-'mǎ to ride horseback; chí dž-shíng-'chē to ride a bicycle; chí-'chyáng to straddle a fence (*literally and figuratively as in English*).

(*K*) to travel by means of *a vehicle which one straddles* (*compare* dzwò).

As mainV: 'chí-dzày to sit astride; 'chí-shàng to sit down, astride; 'chí-bu-shàng-'chywù to be unable to mount (*because the horse is too high, not through weakness, etc.*).

(*N*) cavalry. chí-'bīng cavalry troops.

奇

chí (*H*) strangely, wonderfully, exceptionally. *Limited to use before some adjectives, particularly:* chí 'gwày exceptionally queer, out of the ordinary; chí 're (*literary but used*) exceptionally hot; chí 'hán (*newspaper usage*) exceptionally cold.

棋

chí (*N*) chess. shyà-'chí (*VN2*) to play chess or checkers; shyà yì-pán-'chí to play one game of chess or checkers.

chí-'pán (*Nunit,* ge) chessboard or checkerboard; chí-'dzěr (*Nunit,* ge) chessman or checker.

旗

'chí(-dz) (*Nunit,* ge) flag. dz *is not used when referring to national, or other similar flags.* gwó-'chí national flag; shyàw-'chí school flag.

shēng-'chí to hoist the flag; jvàng-'chí *or* shyà-'chí to bring down the flag; gwà-'chí to hang a flag (*on a wall, for example*); dǎ-'chí to hold *or* carry a flag.

祈求

'chí-chyéw (*V*) to beg, pray to. ‖tā 'chí-chyéw shàng-'dì. He prays to God.

(*Nabstr*) ‖tā-de-'chí-chyéw 'yǐ-jing dé-daw 'yīng-shywǔ-le. His prayers have been answered, (by a promise of fulfillment).

齊全

chí-'chywán (*A*) complete, not lacking any part, entire. ‖jyā-jywù dēw chí-'chywán-le. The furniture is complete; (*i.e., all the necessary pieces have been obtained*).

As postV: 'ywù-bèy-chí-'chywán to prepare *something* completely, get *it* completely ready; 'mǎy-chí-'chywán to buy everything necessary. ‖dūng-shi háy méy-'mǎy-chí-'chywán-ne. We haven't yet bought everything that has to be bought.

其中之

*'chí-jūng-jř *plus a numeral,* one (two, three, *etc.*) among others. ‖yěw hěn-'dwō-de-hǎw-'shū; 'nèy-běn jyèw-shr chí-jūng-jř-'yī. There are a lot of good books; that's one of them.

杞人憂天

'chí-rén-yēw-'tyān (*literary*) (one who) worries needlessly. ‖tā 'jyǎn-jř shr 'chí-rén-yēw-'tyān. He really is a needless worrier. ‖byé 'chí-rén-yēw-'tyān-le. Don't worry needlessly.

其實

chí-'shř (*J*) really, in fact. ‖tā hǎw 'shyàng 'jř-daw hěn-dwō-de-'shř, chí-'shř-a. He seems to know a lot, but actually ... (*no need to say anything further*). ‖chí-'shř wǒ méy-'dàw-gwo nèr. Actually I've never been there.

其他

chí-'tā (*Pron*) the rest, the others. ‖tā méy-'láy, chí-'tā 'dēw láy-le. He hasn't come; all the others have. ‖'jèy-ge-fǎ-dz 'ké-yi; chí-'tā-de dēw bù-'shíng. This plan will work; none of the others will. ‖jř yěw tā-'yí-ge-rén 'dwèy; chí-'tā-de-rén dēw bú-'dwèy. He's the only one who's right; all the others are wrong.

其次

chí-'tsż (*H*) next. ‖tā 'yǐ-jing 'jìn-chywù-le, chí-'tsż jyèw-shr 'ní-le. He's already gone in; you're next.

Next in quality. ‖chí-'tsż shř 'nèy-běn-shū. That book is the next best.

其餘的

chí-'ywú-de (*Aattr*) the rest, the remaining ones, the others. ‖wǒ 'jř yàw 'jèy-běn-shū, chí-'ywú-de(-shū) dēw gěy-ni. I want only this book; the rest are for you.

乞丐
chí-**'gày** (*Npers*) (*literary*) beggar.

氣
chì (*Nmass*) air, atmosphere, gas. yěw-**'chì** (*of a person or of the nose* **'bí-dz**) to be breathing, still be alive; **'byē yì-kěw-'chì** to hold one's breath; **yì-kěw-'chì** (*H*) in one gulp, in one holding of the breath. ‖jèy-bēy-**'jyěw tày 'dwō, nǐ byé 'yì-kěw-chì hē-'wán.** This glass of wine is too much for you to drink in one gulp.

氣
chì (*A*) angry; (*particularly*) chì **'jí-le** *or* hěn **'chì** *or* chì-de **'hěn** extremely angry.
　(*Nabstr*) anger, bad temper, *most often in* ‖tā-de-**'chì hěn 'dà.** He's very quick-tempered. *or also* He has great potentialities (*for getting things done*).

汽車
chì-**'chē** (*Nunit*, **lyàng**) automobile.

汽車站
chì-chē-**'jàn** (*Nunit*, **ge**) bus stop.

汽船
chì-**'chwán** (*Nunit*, **jř**) steamship.

氣球
chì-**'chyéw** (*Nunit*, **ge**) balloon.

汽鍋
chì-**'gwō** (*Nunit*, **ge**) steam boiler.

氣候
'chì-hew (*Nabstr*) climate.

契紙
chì-**'jř** (*Nunit*, **jāng**) written contract *or* agreement.

氣象臺
chì-shyàng-**'táy** (*Nunit*, **ge, chù**) meteorological station.

氣味
'chì-wer (*Nabstr*) bad odor. ‖**'wū-dz-li yěw dyǎr-'chì-wer.** There's a bit of a bad smell in the room.

氣油
chì-**'yéw** (*Nmass*) gasoline.

chia *Wade Romanization for* **jya.**

ch'ia *Wade Romanization for* **chya.**

chiang *Wade Romanization for* **jyang.**

ch'iang *Wade Romanization for* **chyang.**

chiao *Wade Romanization for* **jyaw.**

ch'iao *Wade Romanization for* **chyaw.**

chieh *Wade Romanization for* **jye.**

ch'ieh *Wade Romanization for* **chye.**

chien *Wade Romanization for* **jyan.**

ch'ien *Wade Romanization for* **chyan.**

chih *Wade Romanization for* **jr.**

ch'ih *Wade Romanization for* **chr.**

chin *Wade Romanization for* **jin.**

ch'in *Wade Romanization for* **chin.**

親
chīn (*V*) to kiss; *usually* **'chīn-chin** *or* **'chīn yí-shyàr.** ‖jyàw-wo **'chīn yí-shyàr.** Let me give you a kiss (*to a child*).
　chīn-**'dzwěy** *or* chīn-**'dzwěr** (*VN1*) to kiss.

親，親屬
*chīn, chīn-**'shǔ** (*Ncoll*) relatives. *Prefixed to a kinship term denotes closest degree of connection; thus* chīn-**'gē-ge** *means* one's own older brother, *whereas* **'gē-ge** *may mean* older male cousin; *similarly* chīn-**'bwō-bwo** one's father's older brother, *contrasting with* **'bwō-bwo** *alone which may mean* one's father's older male cousin; *etc.*
　See also Appendix A.

親愛
chīn-**'ày** (*A*) to be very much in love. ‖tām-**'lyǎ hěn chīn-'ày.** Those two are very much in love.
　(wǒ-de-)chīn-**'ày-de** (my) sweetheart (*term of endearment in addressing the person*).

親戚
'chīn-chi (*Ncoll*) relatives; (*Nabstr*) relation. ‖wǒ-men-**'lyǎ 'méy-yew 'chīn-chi.** We're not related.

親自
'chīn-dž (*H*) oneself. ‖bú-'yàw-jǐn, wǒ yàw **'chīn-dž chywù 'dzwò.** Never mind, I'll do it myself (*particularly of someone not sending a servant or subordinate on an errand*).

親熱
chīn-**'rè** (*A*) very close, affectionate, (*of friends, relatives, lovers*). ‖tām-**'lyǎ hěn chīn-'rè.** Those two are very close.

親身
'chīn-shēn (*H*) oneself. ‖bú-'yàw-jǐn, wǒ yàw **'chīn-shēn chywù 'dzwò.** Never mind; I'll do it myself (*particularly of someone not sending a servant or subordinate on an errand*).

琴

chín (*Nunit*, **jāng, ge, jyà**) musical instrument with strings; *usually specified, as* **gāng-'chín** (*Nunit*, **jyà**) piano.

勤

chín (*A*) diligent, steady, industrious. (*Opposite* **lǎn** lazy.) ‖**tā dzwò-'shr̀(dzwò-de) hěn 'chín.** He works very industriously.

秦朝

'chín-cháw (*Nunique*) Chin dynasty (*255–206 B.C.*).

秦皇島

chín-hwáng-'dǎw (*Nunique*) Ch'in-huang-tao (*city in Hopeh province*).

勤謹

'chín-jǐn (*A*) industrious, diligent, steady.

榛椒

chín-'jyāw (*Nunit;* **ge; kē** one plant) pepper (*the plant or vegetable, not the granulated form*).

芹菜

chín-'tsày (*Nunit;* **gēr** a stalk of, **bǎr** a bunch of, **kē** one plant) celery.

寝室

chín-'shř (**chín-'shŕ** *or* **chín-'shř**) (*Nunit*, **jyan**) bedroom.

ching *Wade Romanization for* **jing.**

ch'ing *Wade Romanization for* **ching.**

青

chīng (*A*) green, blue, the color of fresh things, young, fresh, natural, natural-colored.

    Black *of clothing, leather, materials of which things are made,* hair. ‖**tā-de-'téw-fa hěn 'chīng.** Her hair is quite black.

    yí-kwày-'chīng bruise, blackened spot on the skin.

輕

chīng (*A*) light (*in weight*). (*Opposite* **jùng.**) **bù-chīng** heavy; *or* serious, bad *as if an illness, an accident, a wound.*

清

***ching** (*V*) to clean, purge, clear up; *only in* **chīng-'dǎng** (*VN1*) to purge a political party of undesirable elements; *and in* **chīng-'jàng** (*VN2*) to clear up accounts, clear off an account.

清

chīng (*A*) clear, (*as of water, the atmosphere*). (*Opposite* **dzwó** muddy.)

    As postV: **chá-'chīng** to investigate thoroughly, investigate and clear up; **kàn-'chīng** to see clearly; **tīng-'chīng** to hear clearly.

shwō-bu-'chīng be unable to speak clearly (*because of bad articulation, too much hurry, lack of ordered thinking; etc.*).

清朝

'chīng-cháw (*Nunique*) The Ch'ing *or* Manchu dynasty (*1644–1912 A.D.*).

清楚

'chīng-chu (*A*) clear, intelligible, understandable, in good order. *As postV:* **shwō-'chīng-chu** to speak clearly; **kàn-'chīng-chu** to see clearly; **shēw-shr-'chīng-chu** to straighten *things* out *until they're right.* ‖**dyàn-'hwà-de-'shēng-yin bù-'chīng-chu.** This is a bad phone connection. ‖**jyáw 'dūng-shi de-shŕ-hew, shwō-'hwà shwō-bu-'chīng-chu.** You can't talk clearly while chewing.

青島

chīng-'dǎw (*Nunique*) Ch'ing-tao (*city in Shantung province*).

青海

chīng-'hǎy (*Nunique*) Tsinghai *province.*

青海

chīng-'hǎy (*Nunique*) Ching Hai Lake (*also called* Lake Kokonor).

青腫

chīng-'jǔng (*A*) black and blue. **dǎ-de yí-'lyèw-de-chīng-'jǔng** beat *someone* until *he is* black and blue.

    yèw 'chīng yèw 'jǔng to be black and swollen.

清理

'chīng-lǐ (*V*) to clean up, settle, clear up, straighten out. ‖**bǎ 'jwǒ-dz-shang-de-'dūng-shi gěy-wo 'chīng-li-chīng-li.** Straighten out the things on top of this table for me.

傾盆大雨

chīng-'pén-dà-'ywǔ (*N*) very heavy downpour of rain. ‖**'nèy-yí-jèn-'ywǔ-a, 'jēn-shr chīng-'pén-dà-'ywǔ.** That was certainly a terrific downpour.

清醒

'chīng-shǐng (*A*) alert, clear-thinking. ‖**tā 'nǎw-dz hěn 'chīng-shǐng.** He's quite alert.

    'chīng-shǐng-de-téw-'nǎw clear head, clear thinking mind.

輕視

'chīng-shř (*V*) to look down on; to ignore.

傾向

chīng-'shyàng (*V*) to be leaning toward, *but not on.* ‖**jèy-ge-'chyáng yěw dyǎr-'wāy, chīng-'shyàng 'dzwǒ-byar.** This wall isn't quite upright, it leans a little to the left.

Often figuratively: to incline politically, (*of public opinion and the like*).

傾斜度

chǐng-shyé-'dù (*Nabstr*) grade of a slope (*that is, angle from the horizontal*).

靑菜

chǐng-'tsày (*Nmass;* bǎr bunch of) fresh vegetables.

淸苑

chǐng-'ywàn (*Nunique*) Ch'ing-yüan (*city in Hopeh province*).

晴

chíng (*A*) clear *of the sky, weather.* chíng-'tyān clear weather. ‖shyàn-'dzày (tyān) 'chíng-le. It's cleared up now (*the sky*).

情

chíng (*Nabstr*) sentiment, feeling, affection. yěw-'chíng to be sentimental about each other; byǎw-'chíng (*VN1*) to express *or* show one's feelings. ‖nèy-jǔng-de-'chíng hěn 'rúng-yì gǎn-'dùng rén. It's very easy to arouse that type of feeling in people.

情感

chíng-'gǎn (*Nabstr*) affection, love.

情人

'chíng-rén (*Npers*) sweetheart.

情形

'chíng-shing (*Nabstr*) situation. ‖jīn-tyan dà-'jywú-de-'chíng-shing bù-'hǎw. The political situation today isn't good.

情緒

chíng-'shywù (*Nabstr*) feelings, moods.

情願

chíng-'ywàn (*Vpred*) to prefer to *do one thing rather than others when none of them is very satisfactory.* ‖'lyǎng-běn-'shū dēw bù-'hǎw, kě-shr wǒ chíng-'ywàn yàw 'jèy-ge. Neither book is any good, but I prefer this one.

晴雨表

chíng-ywǔ-'byǎw (*Nunit,* ge) barometer.

請

chǐng (*Vsent*) request, invite, ask, *someone to do something;* please. ‖tā 'chǐng-wo dàw tā-'jyā-chywu chr̄-'fàn. He's invited me to dinner at his house. ‖chǐng 'dzày shwǒ (yí-byàn). Please repeat.

頃

chǐng (*Mmeas*) *a unit of area. See Appendix B*

請安

chǐng-'ān (*VN1*) to wish *someone* best regards (*of subordinates to a superior or of younger to older*). ‖wǒ gěy-nín chǐng-'ān. My best wishes to you, sir. (*Literally* I wish you peace.)

請求

chǐng-'chyéw (*V*) to request *formally from the proper authorities.* ‖nǐ-chǐng-'chyéw-de-'shr̀ bàn-bu-'dàw. What you've requested can't be arranged. (*Nunit,* ge) formal request.

請求書

chǐng-chyéw-'shū (*Nunit,* jyàn, jāng; fēng *if in an envelope*) application, request (*official document*).

請坐

‖chǐng-'dzwò. Please sit down. Have a seat.

請教

chǐng-'jyàw *begins a request for information from a stranger;* please tell (me). ‖chǐng-'jyàw, dàw-'nàr-chywu dzěme 'dzěw? Excuse me; can you tell me how to get to that place?

請客

chǐng-'kè (*VN2*) to invite guests *for some social function, formal or informal;* to foot the bill *when several people go somewhere together.* ‖shéy chǐng-'kè? Who's paying? ‖shéy yě 'méy-chǐng-'shéy; 'dz̀-jǐ fù 'dz̀-jǐ-de-'chyán. Nobody's inviting anybody; we're going Dutch.

請示

chǐng-'shr̀ (*VN1*) to ask for instructions, ask what one should do. ‖jèy-ge wǒ-men děy chǐng-'shr̀, tsáy néng 'bàn. We've got to get this checked (*by someone*) before we do it.

請帖

chǐng-'tyē (*Nunit,* jāng, fèr) *written* invitation *for attendance at something.*

請問

chǐng-'wèn *begins a request for information from a stranger;* please, may I ask (you). ‖chǐng-'wèn, 'jīn-líng-'dà-shywé dzày-'nǎr? Excuse me, can you tell me where I'll find Nanking University?

慶賀

'chìng-hè (*V*) offer congratulations to *someone, or on the occasion of something.* ‖wǒ 'chìng-hè nǐ-de-chéng-'gūng. I congratulate you on your success.

慶祝

'chìng-jù (*V*) celebrate *something.* ‖'jīn-tyan wǒm 'jywù-jí-dzày yí-'kwàr láy 'chìng-jù shwāng-shŕ-'jyé. We are gathered here today to celebrate the Double Tenth (*Oct. 10, the Chinese national holiday*).

慶祝會
chìng-jù-'hwèy (*Nunit,* **ge**) a party *in celebration.*

親家
'chìng-jya (*Npers*) one's children's husbands' or wives' parents. ‖**tā shr̀ wǒ-de-'chìng-jya.** He's my child's spouse's father. ‖**tā shr̀ wǒ-de-chìng-jya-'tày-tay.** He's my child's spouse's mother.

chiu *Wade Romanization for* **jyew.**

ch'iu *Wade Romanization for* **chyew.**

chiung *Wade Romanization for* **jyung.**

ch'iung *Wade Romanization for* **chyung.**

cho *Wade Romanization for* **jwo.**

ch'o *Wade Romanization for* **chwo.**

chou *Wade Romanization for* **jew.**

ch'ou *Wade Romanization for* **chew.**

吃，喫
chr̄ (*V*) to eat *a solid food, a viscous liquid food;* to take *pills, solid medicines.* (*Compare* **hē** to drink.) **chr̄-'yān** to smoke (*rare; most people say* **chēw-'yān**); **chr̄-'fàn** to eat, have dinner, have a meal; **chr̄-'chá** to partake of refreshments including tea (*literally* to eat tea).
　　To undergo, to suffer *in certain fixed combinations entered separately.*
　　*chr̄ (*N*) food. **lěng-'chr̄** cold food.

吃穿
chr̄-'chwān (*Ncoll*) food and clothing.

吃飯鈴
chr̄-fàn-'lyéngr (*Nunit,* **ge**) dinner bell.

吃彊
chr̄-'jyāng (*VN1*) take a dare.

吃苦
chr̄ 'kǔ(-tew) (*VN2*) to suffer, to endure sufferings, (*literally* to eat bitterness).

吃虧
chr̄-'kwēy (*VN2*) to take a loss; to get a beating, to get your fingers burned (*figurative*), *all unnecessarily.* **chr̄ ge-dà-'kwēy** to get thoroughly rooked.

吃力
chr̄-'lì (*A*) to be strenuous, to require strength. ‖**'jèy-jyàn-'shr̀-ching 'dzwò shr̀ 'ké-yi dzwò, kě-shr tày chr̄-'lì-le.** That thing can be done if needs be, but it requires tremendous effort.

吃剩下的
chr̄-'shèng-shya-de (*Nmass*) leftovers, remains *of a meal;* **chr̄-'shèng-shya-de-'fàn** *or* **chr̄-'shèng-shya-de-'tsày** *or* **chr̄-'shèng-shya-de-'dūng-shi** left-over food.

吃醋
chr̄-'tsù (*VN2*) to be jealous, (*literally* to eat vinegar).

遲
chŕ (*H*) late, past the proper time. *Only completely colloquial in* **chŕ 'dàw** to arrive late; *elsewhere* **wǎn** *is more used:* **dzěw 'wǎn-le** *rather than* **dzěw 'chŕ-le** to have left late.
　　In compounds to delay.

遲緩
chŕ-'hwǎn (*A, rather literary*) to be late, remiss, behind schedule.

尺
chř (*Mmeas.* **·ər** *or* **lyǎng**) foot (*unit of length*). *See Appendix B.*

尺寸
chř-'tswèn (*N*) size in linear measurements, *of something small enough to be measured in feet and inches.* ‖**'jèy-jāng-jwō-dz shr̀ shéme-chř-'tswèn?** What size is this table? ‖**'jèy-tàw-yī-fu-de-chř-'tswèn bǐ 'nèy-tàw-de 'dà.** This suit is of a larger size than that one.

赤楊樹
chř-yáng(-'shù) (*Nunit,* **kē**) alder tree (*variety of birch*); **chř-yáng-'mù** (*Nmass*) wood from that tree.

chu *Wade Romanization for* **ju.**

ch'u *Wade Romanization for* **chu.**

chü *Wade Romanization for* **jywu.**

ch'ü *Wade Romanization for* **chywu.**

齣
chū (*MdistT*) performance. **yì-chū-'shì** one performance of a play.

出
chū (*I, lc*) to come out, go out; to appear (*of a publication*); to come up (*of the sun, moon, etc., or of plants appearing above the ground as they grow*). ‖**'tày-yang háy méy-'chū-lay.** The sun hasn't come up yet. ‖**'bàw háy méy-'chū-lay-ne.** The papers aren't out yet.
　　(*Used causatively*) to produce crops, *said of land;* (*and many specific meanings with specific nouns, listed separately*). ‖**'jèy-dày-dì-fang chū hwā-'shēng.** This region produces peanuts.

As *postV*, *with final lc, with same meaning as above; with almost any verb of motion:* 'ná-chū-láy take *something* out; 'dzěw-chū-láy walk out, go out; *or of other type of verb:* 'shwō-chū-lay speak out, speak up; shyě-bu-'chū-lay to be unable to express oneself in writing.

初
chū (*Preord*) first, of the first group; *followed by the numerals from one to ten to form designations for the first ten days of the month in the lunar calendar.*

(*H*) for the first time, *literary except in* chū 'shywé to be learning for the first time; *and in* chū-'dàw-de *something or someone* newly arrived, *or the first to* arrive. ‖tā sh̀ yí-ge-'chū-shywé-tán-'chín-de(-rén). He's a beginner at playing the piano.

出版
chū-'bǎn (*IN*) be published, come off the press.

出產
chū-'chǎn (*IN*) to produce *agricultural or manufactured goods.*

(*Nabstr*) production, output.

出場
chū-'chǎng (*IN*) to come on stage (*of an actor*); to perform (*in a play, game, party, political rally, etc.*).

出岔
chū-'chàr (*IN*) to go astray, to go amiss, to have unexpected consequences (*usually : ad*). ‖jīn-tyan tā-shwō-de-'hwà 'yèw chū-'chàr-le. What he said has made trouble again today.

出差費
chū-chāy-'fèy (*Nmass*) expense allowance *while on an official trip.*

出錢
chū-'chyán (*IN*) to contribute money.

出子兒
chū-'dzěr (*IN*) to make a move in a board game; chū yí-ge-'dzěr to move one piece.

出租
chū-'dzū (*A*) for rent; *also the sign put on a place for rent.* ‖jèy-ge-'fáng-dz chū-'dzū. This house is for rent

出發
chū-'fā (*I*) to leave, to set out, to go. ‖wǒ-men míng-tyan-'dzǎw-chen tsǔng-'jèr chū-'fā. We set out from here tomorrow.

出範圍
chū 'fàn-wey (*I|N*) to be beyond *someone's* jurisdiction; to be outside of *one's* proper field of activity; to be irrelevant. ‖nèy-ge-shr̀ chū-le ni-de-'fàn-wéy-le. That matter is out of your field.

出鋒頭
chū 'fēng-tèw (*I*) to show off, boast, always seek to be in a prominent position; *or* to be in the lead in activities *with no feeling of reprobation.* ‖shyàn-'dzày shr̀ tā chū 'fēng-tew de-shŕ-hew. He's in his heyday right now. *or* He's at the peak of his career.

出汗
chū-'hàn (*IN*) to sweat.

出乎意外
'chū-hu-yì-'wày (*A*) beyond all expectation. ‖tā 'jīn-tyan néng 'láy jēn 'chū-hu-yì-'wày. That he should be able to come today is really beyond all expectation.

出貨
chū-'hwò (*IN*) to produce goods, merchandise, manufactured things.

出疹子
chū 'jěn-dz (*IN*) to break out in a rash.

出主意
chū 'jú-yì (*IN*) to (produce a) scheme, to plan, figure out a plan.

出口
chū-'kěw (*IN*) to be exported; (*Nabstr*) exporting. chū-kěw-'mǎy-may exporting business; 'chū-kěw-'rù-kěw import-export business, importing and exporting.

出力
chū-'lì (*IN*) to exert effort, contribute strength, *to some enterprise.*

出馬
chū-'mǎ (*I*) to do something oneself *instead of having a subordinate do it.* Usually *preceded by* H 'chīn-dz *or* 'chīn-shēn oneself, in person, *the complete expression having the same meaning as that given above.*

出毛病
chū 'máw-bìng (*IN*) to be out of control, to have something go wrong. ‖tā-de-'chē chū-le 'máw-bìng-le. His car is out of control. *or* His car is out of order (*not necessarily unusable*).

出賣
chū-'mày (*A*) for sale; *also the sign put on something for sale.*

(*V*) to sell out, betray *someone who has trusted you.*

出門
chū-'mén, chū-'mér (*IN*) to go out *of a door;* (*figuratively to go away from one's own village, house, or country; to travel*). ‖tā 'chū-le jèy-ge-'mér jyèw 'wàng-le. He forgot as soon as he got out the door. ‖tā yì-

'nyán-yĭ-chyán jyèw chū-'mér-le. He went away (from home) a year ago.

    chū-'mén-dz (IN) (of a girl) to marry and leave home (for her husband's home).

出門證
chū-mén-'jèng (Nunit, jāng) pass, permit, *permitting exit, and often permitting entry also.*

出名
chū-'míng (IN) to be well known. ‖jèy-běn-'shū hěn chū-'míng. This book is very well known.

出面
chū-'myàn (IN) to attend, to turn up at, *a function.*

出牌
chū-'páy (IN) to play out a card *or* a mah-jong piece; dǎ (or chū) yì-jāng-'páy play one card.

出入
chū-'rù (Ncoll) expenditures and income; (*particularly*) chū-'rù shyāng-'dĭ *or* chū-'rù shyāng-'fú the income and expenditures cover each other, are balanced; chū-'rù bù-'fú income and expenditures are not balanced (*meaning the expenditure is greater*). ‖'jèy-ge-ywè 'swéy-rán 'yùng-de-chyán hěn 'dwō, kě-shr chū-'rù shyāng-'dĭ-le. Although we spent a lot this month, our income will still cover it.

出身
chū-'shēn (Nabstr) origin, birth, source *of a person.* ‖tā-de-chū-'shēn hěn 'dī. He's of quite humble birth.

出聲
chū-'shēngr (IN) to utter a sound. ‖nĭ byé chū-'shēngr! Don't utter a sound!

出售
chū-'shèw (V) to sell, to sell out, (*a business, land, etc*). ‖tā bǎ-'chē chū-'shèw-le. He sold his car. ‖tā-de-'pù-dz chū-'shèw-le. His business has been sold out.

出席
chū-'shí (IN) to attend a meeting (*formal*).

出事
chū-'shr̀ (IN) to have an accident, to have something go amiss. ‖'nèy-tsż-chū-'shr̀ hěn wéy-'shyǎn. That accident was very serious.

出險
chū-'shyàn (I) to appear, come into view. ‖'shwěy-myàr 'hū-rán chū-'shyàn-le yí-ge-chyán-shwěy-'tǐng. Suddenly, on the surface of the water, there appeared a submarine.

    In compounds: chū-'shyàn-dzày to appear at *a place.*

出血
chū-'shyě (IN) to bleed (*as from the gums, witnout any gushing out of blood*).

出庭
chū-'tíng (IN) to appear in court (*of lawyer, judge, plaintiff, defendant*).

出錯
chū-'tswèr (IN) to make mistakes.

出外
chū-'wày (IN) to travel far from home.

出演
chū-'yǎn (I) to appear in a play.

出怨言
chū 'ywàn-yán (IN, *fairly literary*) to complain, utter complaining words.

除
chú (K) dividing, divided into *in mathematical sense.* ‖'èr chú-'sż dé-'èr. Two into four gives two. *Notice carefully that the divisor comes before* chú, *the dividend after it.* ‖'sān chú-'shf °chú-bu-'jìn. *or* °bù-néng dé 'jěng-shùr. Three won't go into ten evenly. *or* Three into ten doesn't give an integral number. ‖bǎ 'jèy-yì-háng-de-'shùr píng-'jywūn 'chú-yi-chú. Average this column of figures.

鋤, 鋤頭
chú(-dz), chúr, 'chú-tew (Nunit, bǎ) hoe.

除
chú(-le) (K) except for. ‖cḷ·ú-le 'tā 'méy-rén hwèy shwō jèy-jǔng-'hwà. There's no one but he who can say such things.

    chú ... yĭ-'wày except for *such-and-such,* in addition to *such-and-such;* chú-le ... lìng-'wày beyond *such-and-such,* even more than *such-and-such;* 'chú-tsż-yĭ-'wày besides this, in addition to this. ‖'chú-tsż-yĭ-'wày 'háy yěw 'sān-jyān-'shr̀-ching yàw 'jì-jù-le. In addition to this there are three more things which you must remember. ‖chú-'tā yĭ-'wày 'háy yěw 'sān-ge-rén. There are three others besides him.

除去
'chú-chywù (RC2) not count, take away, eliminate. ‖bǎ nèy-'lyǎng-ge-rén 'chú-chywù. Don't count those two men.

除掉
chú-'dyàw (V) abolish, eliminate, take out. ‖bǎ 'jèy-yí-dwàn chú-'dyàw. Eliminate that passage (*from a document or book*).

厨子
'chú-dz (*Npers*) cook, chef. (*Called this to his face only by his employers.*)

厨房
chú-'fáng (*Nunit, jyān, ge*) kitchen.

除非
chú-'fēy (*J*) unless. ‖chú-'fēy nǐ 'láy, wǒ bú-'chywù. I won't go unless you come.

储存箱
chú-tswén-'shyāng (*Nunit, ge*) bin, built-in storage place.

處罰
chǔ-'fá (*V*) to impose punishment (*said of a judge, etc.*).

處治
chǔ-'jř (*V*) to deal with, arrange, govern, control, *a situation, especially a difficult one.*

處置
chǔ-'jř (*V*) to manage, arrange properly, superintend *the physical arrangements of an establishment;* to use corrective measures on, correct *a person who is misbehaving (but not a criminal);* get even with someone *for a minor offense against you.*

處不來
chǔ-bu-'láy (*RC1*) be unable to get along *with someone.* ‖wǒ gēn-ta chǔ-bu-'láy. I can't get along with him. ‖wǒ-men-'lyǎ bǐ-'tsž chǔ-bu-'láy. We two don't get along.

處女
chǔ-'nywǔ (*Npers*) virgin. lǎw-chǔ-'nywǔ old maid.

處世
chǔ-'shř (*VN1*) to get along *in the world, especially with other people.* chǔ-'shř-de-'fāng-fa way of getting along with one's fellow man. ‖yěw jīng-'yàn-le yì-'hèw tsáy 'jř-dàw dzěme chǔ-'shř. It takes experience to know how to get along in the world.

處
chù (*MdistS*) specifies localization. a 'dì-fang (*place, spot, locality*); a 'jáy-dz (*establishment including house, garden, etc.*); a 'mǎy-mày (*business at one address*); an 'àn-dz (*law case at one place*); a chyǎng-'àn (*case of robbery at one place*); lyǎng-chù-chyǎng-'àn (*two cases of robbery at two different places*).

   *chù (*Nunit, ge*) (1) office, commission, board *which functions at a particular location or in a particular area,* or repository *with its supervising board or commission:* bǎw-gwǎn-'chù repository (*governmental*). (2) point, feature. hǎw-'chù good points, good features; hwày-'chù bad points, bad features, drawbacks.

處處
'chù-chù (*H*) everywhere. ‖nèy-ge-'rén 'chù-chù pèng 'dīng-dz. Wherever that man goes he beats his head against a blank wall.

處州
chù-'jēw (*Nunique*) Chuchow, *another name for* lì-'shwey Li-shui (*city in Chekiang province*).

畜類
'chù-lèy (*N*) animal, *as contrasted with man in Buddhist theory; is an insult when applied to people.*

畜生
'chù-sheng (*Nunit, ge*) animals *excluding humans, and excluding lower forms of the animal kingdom such as snakes, fish, insects, and even birds;* (*an insult to a person*).

chua *Wade Romanization for* **jwa**.

ch'ua *Wade Romanization for* **chwa**.

chuai *Wade Romanization for* **jway**.

ch'uai *Wade Romanization for* **chway**.

chuan *Wade Romanization for* **jwan**.

ch'uan *Wade Romanization for* **chwan**.

chüan *Wade Romanization for* **jywan**.

ch'üan *Wade Romanization for* **chywan**.

chuang *Wade Romanization for* **jwang**.

ch'uang *Wade Romanization for* **chwang**

chüeh *Wade Romanization for* **jywe**.

ch'üeh *Wade Romanization for* **chywe**.

chui *Wade Romanization for* **jwey**.

ch'ui *Wade Romanization for* **chwey**.

chun *Wade Romanization for* **jwen**.

ch'un *Wade Romanization for* **chwen**.

chün *Wade Romanization for* **jywun**.

ch'ün *Wade Romanization for* **chywun**.

chung *Wade Romanization for* **jung**.

ch'ung *Wade Romanization for* **chung**.

沖，冲

chūng (*V*) to wash, (*as water washes things, not to clean something with water*); to rinse. *As mainV:* **chūng-'dzěw** wash something away; **chūng-daw 'àn-shang** wash *something* ashore, run aground. ‖**'ywǔ bǎ 'chyáng-shang-de-'tǔ dēw 'chūng-shyà-lay-le.** The rain washed the dirt off the wall. ‖**dà-'làng bǎ-'chwán chūng-dàw 'àn-shang chywù-le.** The big waves °washed the ship ashore. *or* °drove the ship aground. ‖**nèy-shyē-'jyā-jywù yīng-gay 'dzày yùng-'shwěy 'chūng yí-byàr.** Those utensils must be rinsed out again.

衝

chūng (*I*) to crash *or* dash ahead *pushing obstacles aside.* *As mainV:* **'chūng-jìn** (*lc*) dash *or* crash in; ‖**tā bǎ-'mén dǎ-'pwò-le, 'chūng-jìn-chywù-le.** He broke the door open and dashed in. ‖**yěw húng-'dēng de-shŕ-hew tā kāy-je 'chē 'chūng-gwò-chywù-le.** While the light was red he drove his car (crashing) across (*the intersecting street*). (*Compare English:* He crashed the light.)

充足

'chūng-dzú (*A*) sufficient. ‖**tā-'ywù-bèy-de-'fàn hěn 'chūng-dzú.** The food she'd prepared was quite sufficient.

充分

chūng-'fèn (*A*) sufficient, adequate. ‖**yí-ge-gwó-'jyā yīng-gay yěw chūng-'fèn-de-jywūn-'bèy.** A country must have adequate armament.

充滿

chūng-'mǎn (*V*) to be filled with (*water, sand, remorse, satisfaction, etc.*). ‖**jèy-jyān-'wū-dz chūng-'mǎn-le 'yān.** This room is filled with smoke. ‖**tā-de-'lyǎn-shang chūng-'mǎn-le 'gāw-shìng-de-'yàng-dz.** His face was covered with an expression of good spirits.

蟲

'chúng(-dz), **chúngr** (*Nunit,* tyáw) *any elongated* worm, bug, insect; (*Nunit,* ge) *any* bug, insect, spider *which is not long and thin.*

崇拜

chúng-'bày (*V*) to worship, think very highly of *a person or a deity.* ‖**tā chúng-'bày 'gùng-chǎn-jǔ-'yì.** He esteems highly the principles of communism. ‖**tām chúng-'bày tā-men-de-lǐng-'shyèw.** They worship their leader.

重慶

chúng-'chìng (*Nunique*) Ch'ung-ch'ing *or* Chungking (*city in Szechwan province*).

重（重新）

chúng(-'shīn) (*H*) over again, once again. ‖**'jèy-ge-dż 'tswò-le, yàw chúng**(-'shīn) **'shyě.** This character is wrong, you'll have to write it again.

衝

chùng (*V*) to face *in a direction, of a building or window, etc.* ‖**jèy-jyān-'wū-dz chùng-'lǐ**(-de). This room faces in (*towards the courtyard*).

   (*K*) facing *a direction, of anything.* ‖**tā chùng-'nán jàn-je.** He's standing facing south.

衝

chùng (*A*) bright, strong (*of a light, fire*); brave (*of a person, deed*). ‖**jèy-ge-'hwǒ hěn 'chùng.** This fire is very bright.

衝盹兒

chùng-'dzwěr (*VN1*) to nod from sleepiness.

船

chwán (*Nunit,* jř, tyáw) ship, boat.

傳

chwán (*V*) to spread *something by written or spoken word.* *As mainV:* **'chwán-chū** (*lc*) spread out, spread far and wide; **'chwán-dàw** (*lc*) spread to *some place.* ‖**bǎ hǎw-'shyāw-shi 'chwán-dàw gè-'chù.** Pass the good word around.

傳遍

chwán-'byàn (*V*) to be told everywhere, spread far and wide (*of news, etc.*). ‖**jèy-ge-'shyāw-shi chwán-'byàn-le gè-'chù.** This news has been spread everywhere.

船橋

chwán-'chyáw (*Nunit,* ge) bridge (*on a ship*).

傳道

chwán-'dàw (*VN1*) to spread a doctrine, proselytize, *particularly of missionaries.*

   chwán-'dàw-de (*Npers*) missionary.

傳給

'chwán-gěy (*V*) to will, bequeath, pass on. ‖**tā bǎ-'fáng-dz 'chwán-gěy-le tā-de-'ér-dz.** He left the house to his son.

船長

chwán-'jǎng (*NpersT*) captain *of a ship.*

船主

chwán-'jǔ (*Npers*) master, owner, *of a ship.*

傳教

chwán-'jyàw (*VN1*) to do missionary work, spread a faith.

61

傳教士

chwán-jyàw-'shř (*Npers*) missionary.

傳令

chwán-'lìng (*VN1*) to issue orders (*official; military*). ‖**tā chwán-'lìng jyàw-rén bǎ nèy-ge-'dzéy gěy 'děy-jù.** He ordered them to catch that thief.

傳令兵

chwán-lìng-'bīng (*Npers*) messenger, *a soldier who carries orders.*

傳染

chwán-'rǎn (*V*) to infect *with a disease, bad habit, etc.* ‖**tā-de-'bìng hwèy chwán-'rǎn rén.** ⁄ His disease may spread to others.

傳說

chwán-'shwō (*I*) to spread rumors; speculate. ‖**jywù rén chwán-'shwō, tā yǐ-jing 'sž-le.** According to what people say, he's already dead.

船頭

chwán-'téw (*Nunit*, ge) bow, prow, *of a ship.*

船尾

chwán-'wěy (*Nunit*, ge) stern *of a ship.*

船位

chwán-'wèy (*Nunit*, ge) accommodation for passage on a ship (*cabin, bunk, etc.*).
     dìng chwán-'wèy to book boat passage.

喘

chwǎn (*V*) to breathe quickly or heavily. **chwǎn-'chì, chwǎn-'chyér** (*VN2*) to catch one's breath; **chwǎn (yì-)kěw-'chyèr** to relax for a minute, catch one's breath; **'chwǎn-bu-chū 'chyèr-lay** be out of breath; **'chwǎn-gwò yì-kěw-'chyèr-lay** to rest *after being very busy or financially pressed,* to come up for air

喘病

'chwǎn-bìng (*Nabsir;* **chǎng** an attack of) asthma.

串

chwàn, chwàr (*Mgroup*) string of; *with* **'yàw-shr** bunch of keys; **'jū-dz** string of pearls; **ywú** string of fish; **chyán** string of coins (*of the Chinese type, with a hole in the middle; formerly a unit of currency*); **'shř-dz, 'dzǎw-dz, là-'jyāw** string of persimmons, dates, peppers (*respectively*), *hung up to dry;* **nyàn-'jū** rosary (*Christian or Buddhist*).

串通

chwàn-'tūng (*I*) to band together, to be in league with someone. ‖**'yùng-rén gēn-'dzéy chwàn-'tūng-le bǎ 'dūng-shi tēw-'dzěw-le.** The servant and the thief worked together in the robbery.

瘡

chwāng (*Nunit*, ge) boil, festered sore.
     jǎng-'chwāng to develop a festered sore, boil.

窗，窗戶

*chwāng, 'chwāng-hu (*Nunit*, ge, myàn) window.

窗戶簾

chwāng-hu-'lyán(-dz), chwāng-hu-'lyár (*Nunit*, ge; **dwèy** *for* a pair) window shade, window curtain.

床，牀

chwáng (*Nunit*, jyà) bed.
     (*Munit*) *with* **'dān-dz** bedsheet; **'tǎn-dz** blanket; **'rù-dz** mattress; **'bèy-wō** blanket rolled up and tucked in at the sides *so that someone can slip into it to sleep.*

床罩

chwáng-'jàw(r) (*Nunit*, ge) bedspread.

闖，撞

chwǎng *or* **chwàng** (*V*) to rush into *or* toward, crash into *or* toward. *As mainV:* **'chwàng-shàng** to crash together; **'chwàng-gwò** (*lc*) to dash toward and against; **chwàng-'dǎw** to run down, knock down as one rushes along; **chwàng-'jìn** (*lc*) to burst into (*a room, a person*). ‖**tā chì 'jí-le, 'chwàng-jìn 'wū-dz-li chywù-le.** He got very angry and burst into the room.

創造

chwǎng-'dzàw (*V*) to originate, to develop, to make for the first time, *usually of some material object.* ‖**'shéy chwǎng-'dzàw-de jèy-ge-'mwó-shíng?** Who originated this model? (*of typewriter, boat, etc.*).

創作

chwǎng-'dzwò (*V*) to devise, create *particularly ideas, plans, etc.* ‖**jèy-ge-jì-hwa shř shéy jwǎng-'dzwò-de?** Who devised this plan?

創牌子

chwǎng 'páy-dz (*VN2*) to build up a business from scratch.

闖，撞

chwàng *see* **chwǎng.**

揣

chwāy (*V*) to carry *something* in a pocket, or in one's clothes near the chest. *As mainV:* **'chwāy-dàw** (*lc*) carry *something thus to a place;* **chwāy-'dzěw** to walk away with *something;* *with special meaning* **'chwāy-shàng-chywu** to pull something up, adjust (*for example, a skirt, underwear*). ‖**tā bǎ-'chyán dēw chwāy-dzay 'dēwr-li-tew.** He put all the money in his pocket.

春，春天

*chwēn, 'chwēn-tyan (*Ntime*) spring (*the season*).

純
chwén (*A*) pure, unadulterated *of a thing*. ‖**jèy-jyàn-'yī-fu shř chwén-'sž-de.** This clothing is pure silk.

純潔
'chwén-jyé (*A*) innocent, unsophisticated. ‖**'chwén-jyé-de-rén 'shīn-lǐ-tew méy-yew 'hwày-de-gwěy-'jì.** An innocent person has no dirty tricks in his mind.

純粹
chwén-'tswèy (*A*) pure, unadulterated; typical. ‖**jèy-ge-'hwò hěn chwén-'tswèy.** This merchandise is the genuine article. ‖**tā shř ge-chwén-'tswèy-de-'yīng-gwo-'shēn-shř-'pày.** He's typical of the English gentleman.

吹
chwēy (*V*) to blow, blow on *something*, to let air blow on, ventilate; **chwēy-'byér** blow a whistle. *As mainV:* **chwēy-'dǎw** to blow down; **chwēy-'lyáng** to cool *something* by blowing on *it*; **chwēy-'myè** to blow out *a light*; **chwēy-'pǎw** to blow *something* away; **'chwēy-chǐ-láy** to blow up (*e.g., a bubble* pàwr). ‖**tā-de-'màw-dz jyàw-'fēng gěy chwēy-'pǎw-le.** His hat was blown away by the wind.

吹火筒
chwēy-hwǒ-'tǔng (*Nunit,* gēr) blowtorch.

鎚，錘
'chwéy-dz (*Nunit,* bǎ) hammer.

垂頭喪氣
'chwéy-téw-sàng-'chì (*literary quotation*) be very depressed, (*literally* hang one's head with no spirit). ‖**tā 'jīn-tyan bù-'gāw-shìng, 'chwéy-téw-sàng-'chì-de.** He's unhappy today; way down in the dumps.

戳
chwō (*V*) to jab *several times with a long object like a rifle, pencil, cigarette; piercing the thing jabbed against or not.* **chwō yí-ge-dùng** to pierce a hole. *As mainV:* **'chwō-kāy** to cause an opening by piercing; **'chwō-jìn-chywu** to jab *something* in; **chwō-'tūng** to jab *something* through *to the other side;* **chwō-'shyā** to blind *by piercing the eye.* ‖**tā yùng chyān-'bǐ bǎ-'jř chwō yí-ge-'dùng.** He jabbed a hole in the paper with his pencil.

掐
chyā (*V*) to pinch *between two fingernails, or between one fingernail and a finger,* and to pull out *the thing thus grasped. As mainV:* **'chyā-chū-lay** pull out; **'chyā-shyà-lay** pull up, out, down, *etc.;* **chyā-'hwār** to pick flowers. ‖**tā bǎ tā-de-'rèw 'chyā-shyà yí-'kwày.** He pulled out a pinch of his flesh.

Since the Chinese frequently count on their fingers by placing the thumbnail against the twelve joints in the other fingers, **chyā-'jř** *means* to count. ‖**chyā-'jř 'swàn-yi-swàn 'háy yěw 'jǐ-tyān?** Count it out; how many days are there left?

卡
chyǎ (*V*) to catch *as an obstruction, catches a moving object.* **'chyǎ-jù** catch and stop; **chyǎ-dzày** to catch in on, at. ‖**tā chř-'ywú de-shř-hew, 'tsž 'chyǎ-dzay 'sǎng-dz-li-le.** While he was eating fish a bone caught in his throat. ‖**tā shyà-'chē de-shř-hew, tā-de-'yī-fu jyàw-'mén 'chyǎ-jù-le.** When he was getting out of the car, his clothes caught on the door.

卡子
'chyǎ-dz (*Nunit,* ge) bridge (*for teeth*); clasp, fastener (*in clothing*); clip (*for paper*).

卡針
chyǎ-'jēr (*Nunit,* gēr, ge) bobby pin.

千
chyān (*NumG*) thousand.

鉛
chyān (*Nmass*) lead; graphite.

簽
chyān (*V*) to sign (*official*); **chyān-'míng;** (*very formal*), **chyān-'dž** sign one's name; **chyān 'tyáw-ywè** to sign a treaty.

鉛筆
chyān-'bǐ (*Nunit,* gēn, gēr, jř) lead pencil.

千鈞一髮
'chyān-jywūn-yì-'fǎ (*literary quotation*) tremendous danger, very critical situation (*literally* thirty thousand catties (on) one hair). ‖**'jèng-shr 'chyān jywūn-yì-'fǎ-de-shř-hew, tā 'táw-le.** At that extremely critical point he left.

潛水艇
chyān-shwěy-'tǐng (*Nunit,* jř, ge) submarine.

千萬
chyān-'wàn (*H*) by all means, without fail. ‖**nǐ chyān-'wàn děy 'láy.** You must come without fail.

錢
chyán (*Nmass*) money. *With M* **kwày** *or* (*formal and literary*) **ywán,** a dollar; *with M* **máw** a dime *or* ten cents; *with M* **fēn** a cent; **yí-ge-shyáw-'chyár** a small coin; *with M* **bǐ** an amount *or* fund of money; *with M* **fèr** an allotment of funds from a larger amount.

Preceded by a nominal expression or a verbal expression used nominally, means cost of, price of, expense of; *thus:* **'dzū-chyan,** rent; **'jyèw-chyan** tip, (*literally* money for liquor); **'dyàn-chyan** cost of lighting; **'shwěy-chyan** cost of water (*as in a house*); *etc.* **'běn-chyán** capital; **'lì-chyán** profit *or* interest.

péy-chyán to lose money; jwàn-'chyán *or* jèng-'chyán to make money; gěy-'chyán to pay; jyè-'chyán to borrow money; hwàn-'chyán to change bills; hwán-'chyán to repay money; yùng-'chyán to spend money; fèy-'chyán to waste money.

chyán-'bāw purse; chyán-'gwèy money box.

前

chyán (*Nplace*) ahead, in front, *freely only after K; otherwise one uses a longer form such as* chyán-byan, 'chyán-byar, 'chyán-myan, 'chyán-myar, 'chyán-tew.

Before a noun: front-, future-, *as* chyán-'twěy front legs; chyán-'tú the road ahead, prospects for the future.

After an expression of time (also yǐ-'chyán) *ago, as* 'sān-nyán-chyán three years ago.

Similarly before some expressions of time, the past. 'chyán-jǐ-tyān the past few days; 'chyán-tyan day before yesterday; 'chyán-nyan year before last.

錢

chyán (*Mmeas*) mace (*measure of weight*). *See Appendix B.*

錢包

chyán-'bāw(r) (*Nunit*, ge) money pouch, money bag.

前程遠大

'chyán-chéng ywǎn-'dà (*literary quotation*) the future looks promising.

錢櫃

chyán-'gwèy(-dz) (*Nunit*, ge) money box, coffer.

前後

chyán-'hèw (*H*) including the front part and the back part; including the early and the late. ‖jèy-ge-'léw-li chyán-'hèw yěw 'wǔ-shr-jyān-'wū-dz. Including the front part and the back part, this building has fifty rooms. ‖jīn-tyan-de-'chá-hwèy chyán-'hèw láy-le 'wǔ-shr-ge-rén. The tea party which was held today was attended by fifty people, including the early and the late comers.

前進

‖chyán-'jìn! Forward! Advance! (*military, or metaphorically from the military use*).

錢夾子

chyán-'jyā-dz (*Nunit*, ge) billfold.

前門

chyán-'mén (*Nplace*) front door, gate.

錢票

chyán-'pyàw(-dz), chyán-'pyàwr (*Nunit*, jāng) bills (*money, not something to be paid*). yì-jāng-'wǔ-kwày-chyán-de-'pyàw-dz five-dollar bill.

前任

chyán-'rèn(-de-rén) (*Npers*) predecessor *in office.* ‖tā shř wǒ-de-chyán-'rèn. He was my predecessor in office.

chyán-'rèn-de-jǔ-'shí the former chairman.

錢匣

chyán-'shyá(r), chyán-'shyá-dz (*Nunit*, ge) money box.

前線

chyán-'shyàn (*Nunit*, ge) front line, front (*military*).

錢箱

chyán-'shyāng(r), chyán-'shyāng-dz (*Nunit*, ge) money box.

前提，前題

chyán-'tí (*Nunit*, ge) logical premise.

前途

chyán-'tú (*Nabstr*) prospects for the future; (*literally*) the road ahead. ‖chyán-'tú yěw-'wàng. (*Literary quotation*) The future looks promising.

淺

chyǎn (*A*) light *in shade;* shallow *of water, a container, a person, a person's knowledge.*

chyǎn-'hwáng-(sè) light yellow, blond.

欠

chyàn (*V2*) to owe *someone something, especially money.* chyàn-'jày to owe a debt, to be in debt; chyàn 'rén-chíng to owe a debt *in the sense of owing a person thanks or a return for favors done.* ‖wǒ 'chyàn-ta hěn-dwō-'chyán. I owe him a lot of money.

(*V*) to deserve to be ... ‖tā jyèw chyàn 'dǎ. He deserves to be spanked. or He ought to be spanked.

(*K*) to lack, be short, *in giving time.* ‖chyàn 'wǔ-fēn (dàw) 'sž-dyǎn. It's five to four.

鎗，槍

chyāng (*Nunit*, jř, gēn, bǎ; gǎn *for long ones only*) small arms, *especially* rifle.

(*Msemel*) a shot; fàng yì-'chyāng to fire a shot.

搶

chyāng(-je) (*K*) against, up-, *wind:* chyāng(-je) 'fēng upwind, against the wind. ‖jèy-jř-'chwán chyāng-je 'fēng 'dzěw. The ship's going against the wind.

鎗把

chyāng-'bà(r) (*Nunit*, bǎ, ge) rifle butt, pistol butt.

鎗彈

chyāng-'dàn (*Nunit*, ge, lì) rifle or other small arms bullet.

腔調
chyāng-'dyàw(r) (*Nabstr*) (foreign, special) accent. ‖tā shwō-'jūng-gwo-hwà dày 'měy-gwo-chyāng-'dyàw(r). He has an American accent when speaking Chinese.

鎗子
chyāng-'dzěr (*Nunit*, ge, lì) bullet *for rifle or other small arms.*

鎗法
'chyāng-fǎ (*Nabstr*) technique with firearms, shooting technique.

鎗管
chyāng-'gwǎr (*Nunit*, gēn, tyáw) barrel *of rifle or other small arms.*

鎗砲
chyāng-'pàw (*Ncoll*) weapons of war.

鎗響
chyāng-'shyǎng (*Nunit*, shēng) rifle crack, pistol shot, (*the noise made*).

鎗械
'chyāng-shyè (*Ncoll*) firearms, weapons.

牆
chyáng (*Nunit*, myàn) wall. chéng-'chyáng city wall. 'chyáng-shang means either on top of a wall, or on the face of a wall.
　　gwà-dzay 'chyáng-shang to hang from the wall; jàn-dzay 'chyáng-shang to stand on a wall.

強，彊
chyáng (*A*) strong, powerful; preferable. ‖'jèy-lyǎng-ge-dūng-shi 'jèy-ge 'bǐ-jyàw 'chyáng-yi-dyar. Of these two things this is relatively a little better.
　　chyáng-'gwó (*Nunit*, ge) a power, a powerful country.

強辯
chyáng-'byàn, chyǎng-'byàn (*V*) to argue about *dogmatically or obstinately.* ‖tā chyáng-'byàn jèy-ge-'wèntí. He's arguing this question dogmatically.

牆櫃
chyáng-'gwèy(-dz) (*Nunit*, ge) closet.

牆紙
chyáng-'jǐ (*Nmass*) wallpaper.

牆爐
chyáng-'lú(-dz) (*Nunit*, ge) fireplace (*built into a wall*).

強詞奪理
chyáng-tsź dwó-'lǐ (*or* chyǎng-...) (*literary quotation*) to play with words, argue dogmatically, argue sophistically.

搶
chyǎng (*V*) to rob, take something away by force ‖wǒ bèy 'chyǎng-le. I've been robbed.
　　'chyǎng-je (*H*) in competition, racing. ‖tā 'chyǎng-je shyàng-'chyán 'pǎw-le. He raced ahead.
　　As mainV: 'chyǎng-chywù-le or chyǎng-'dzěw-le to be robbed and taken away (*of a thing*). ‖tā-de-'shēng-yì bèy 'byé-rén 'chyǎng-chywù-le He was forced out of business.

搶案
chyǎng-'àn (*Nunit*, tsź, chù, ge) case of robbery.

敲
chyāw (*V*) to beat, tap, strike, with a stick. chyāw-'gǔ to beat a drum; 'chyāw-rén yí-'gwèn-dz to strike someone a blow with a stick.
　　As mainV: 'chyāw-kāy to beat open with a stick, chyāw-'hwày to break by beating with a stick; etc. ‖tā bǎ-'mén 'chyāw-kāy-le. He beat the door open with a stick.

敲
chyāw (*V*) to cheat *someone by asking a higher price because you know that person has plenty of money;* to work a racket on *someone in this way.* ‖wǒ bèy tā-men 'chyāw-le 'yì-bǐ-chyán. They cheated me out of a large sum of money.
　　chyāw jú-'gàng (*VN1*) to work a racket on *someone, as above.* ‖tā 'chyāw-le wǒ yí-ge-jú-'gàng. He rooked me.
　　chyāw-shàng (*RC2*) with same meaning.

橋
chyáw (*Nunit*, ge, dzwò) bridge (*over a river, etc.*).

瞧
chyáw (*V*) glance at, have a look at. 'chyáw-chyaw take a look. As mainV: 'chyáw-jyàn to catch sight of, find, come across. ‖wǒ 'chyáw-jyan ta dzày jyē-'nèy-byan dzěw. I caught sight of him across the street. ‖'chyáw-je bú-'tswò. Just glancing at it it looks OK. ‖'chyáw-je-dyǎr byé 'jyàw-ta 'pǎw-le. Look out, don't let him get away. ‖wǒ chyáw-je 'bàn-ba. I'll see what I can do.

僑民
chyáw-'mín (*Npers*) citizen living outside his country.

巧招，巧着
chyǎw-'jāwr (*Nunit*, ge) clever trick. shř yí-ge-chyǎw-'jāwr to play a clever trick (on him 'dwèy-ta or 'gēn-ta). May imply being indirect, pulling wires, doing things behind the scenes; all with a tone of criticism.

巧妙

chyăw-'myàw (*A*) ingenious (*of a person*); clever (*of something done*).

俏皮話

chyàw-pí-'hwà(r) (*Nmass; jywù*) unpleasantly witty talk *which tends, indirectly, to hurt others.*

切

chyē (*V*) to cut with a sawing motion *with a knife or other utensil, but not with a saw.*
    As mainV: **'chyē-chéng** cut into *so many slices, pieces, etc.;* **chyē-'swèy** to cut to pieces. ‖**bǎ jèy-ge-'bǐng chyē-chéng shŕ-'èr-kwày.** ˏCut this cake into twelve pieces.

切

chyè (*M; always with NumU* **yī**) all *of several things.* ‖**yí-'chyè-de-rén dēw 'láy-le.** Everybody came. ‖**yí-'chyè-de-'bǐng dēw 'hwày-le.** ˙All the cakes are ruined.

竊

*chyè *literary equivalent of* **tēw** to steal.

秋

*chyēw, 'chyēw-tyan (*Ntime*) autumn, fall.

秋季

chyēw-'jì (*Ntime*) autumn (*season*); autumn term *at school.* ‖**chyēw-'jì kāy-'shywé de-shŕ-hew tā méy 'hwéy-lay.** When school opened in the fall he didn't come back.

求

chyéw (*V*) to ask, beg. **chyéw-'rén** to ask for help. ‖**wǒ 'chyéw-ni 'tì-wo yǎn-'shwō.** I beg you to give my speech for me.

球

chyéw (*Nunit*, **ge**) ball, sphere.
    chyéw(r) (*Nunit*, **ge**) ball (*for games*); ball game. **dǎ-** (*or* **wár-**)**'chyéw(r)** to play ball *or* to play with a ball; **sày-'chyéw(r)** to play a ball game.

球棒

chyéw-'bàng (*Nunit*, **gēn**) baseball bat.

囚犯

chyéw-'fàn (*Nper*) prisoner (*in jail*).

球手

chyéw-'shěw (*Npers*) ballplayer; (*specifically*) batter (*baseball*).

球員

chyéw-'ywán (*Npers*) ballplayer.

窮

chyúng (*A*) poor, destitute. **'chyúng-rén** poor people. ‖**tā 'chyúng-de méy-'fàn chř.** He's so poor he can't keep body and soul together.

瓊山

chyúng-'shān (*Nunique*) Ch'iung-shan *or* Kiungchow (*city on Hai-nan Island*).

圈

*chywān (*V*) form a circle with *something. As mainV:* **'chywān-chi-lay** to encircle; **'chywān-chū-lay** to mark with a circle (*to make a passage stand out from the rest of the text*); **'chywān-shang** encircle and enclose *something,* (*as with a fence*). ‖**yùng 'shéng-dz bǎ 'jèy-ge-jī-'jyǎwr gěy 'chywān-chi-lay.** Circle this space (corner) in with a rope.

圈

'chywān(-dz), chywār (*Nunit*, **ge**) circle, loop. **chywān, chywār** (*M*) a round, a circuit. **hwà yí-ge-'chywār** draw a circle; **ràw-je 'fáng-dz dzěw yì-'chywār** walk once around the house; **dǎ yì-chywār-'páy** play one round of cards. ‖**yùng 'shéng-dz dzày 'ràw yì-'chywār.** Loop the rope around again.

全

chywán (*H*) altogether, completely; *before nouns and measures:* all of, the entire, the whole of. **chywán-'shēn** the whole body (*human or animal*); **'chywán-shén** (*H*) with all one's attention, effort, energies, spirit; **chywán-shŕ-'jyè** the whole world; **chywán-'tǐ** (*H*) in a body, all together; **chywán-'bù** the whole undivided quantity (*of work, jobs, plans, etc.*). ‖**chŕwán-shŕ-'jyè-de-rén dēw yí-'yàng.** People are the same everywhere.

權，權力

*chywán, chywán-'lì (*Nunit*, **ge**) rights, duties, powers *given by law or tradition.* ‖**wǒ yěw chywán-'lì shwō wǒ swǒ-yàw-shwō-de-'hwà.** I have the right to say anything I want to say.
    yěw-'chywán (*A*) to have authority, be in authority.

拳，拳頭

*chywán, 'chywán-tew (*Nunit*, **ge**) fist.
    chywán (*Msemel*) blow with the fist. ‖**dǎ-ta yì-'chywán.** Strike him a blow with the fist.
    dǎ-'chywán (*VN1*) to box.

泉，泉源

*chywán, 'chywán-ywán (*Nunit*, **ge**) spring (*for water*).
    chywán-'shwěy (*Nmass*) spring water.

權柄

'chywán-bǐng (*Nunit*, **ge**) lawful power, authority, moral right. ‖**nǐ 'méy-yew jèy ge-'chywán-bǐng shwō jèy-ge-'hwà.** You have no right to say that (*shows strong disapproval*).

66

全都
'chywán-dēw (H) all, altogether, completely; both. (Stronger than chywán or dēw alone.) ‖nèy-shyē-shū 'chywán-dēw 'hwày-le. Those books are completely ruined.

泉州
chywán-'jēw (Nunique) Chüanchow, another name for jìn-'jyāng Chin-chiang (city in Fukien province).

拳術
chywán-'shù (Nabstr) the art of unarmed self defense.

勸
chywàn (Vsent) to persuade, urge someone to do something. ‖tā 'chywàn-wo kàn 'tā-shyě-de-'shū. He urged me to read the book he'd written (not necessarily successful urging).
    As mainV: 'chywàn-jù to calm someone down; 'chywàn-gwò-lay to bring someone around (to your way of thinking).

勸捐
chywàn-'jywān (VN1) to solicit donations.

缺
chywē (V) to lack, be without. ‖wǒ 'chywē-le 'jǐ-kwày-chyán. I'm a few dollars short (some of what I had is missing).

缺點
chywē-'dyǎn (Nunit, ge) limitation, drawback, shortcoming. ‖'jèy-běn-shū yěw jǐ-ge-chywē-'dyǎn. This book has several shortcomings.

缺乏
'chywē-fá (V) to have an inadequate supply of, to lack (formal and serious). ‖'dé-gwo 'chywē-fá ywán-'lyàw. Germany has an inadequate supply of raw materials.

缺少
'chywē-shǎw (V) to lack something needed. ‖wǒ 'chywē-shǎw yí-ge-'rén bāng wǒ-de-'máng. I'm short of help.

缺席
chywē-'shí (VN1) to fail to attend a meeting (very formal).

瘸
chywé (I) to be lame. chywé-'twěy (IN) to have one leg shorter than the other. ‖wǒ chywé-'twěy-le. I'm lame.
    'chywé-dz (Npers) lame person.

確信
chywè-'shìn (Vsent) to believe firmly that. ‖wǒ chywè-'shìn tā 'shwō-gwo jèy-jywù-'hwà. I firmly believe that he said that.

確實
chywè-'shŕ (A) correct, true, accurate of news, etc. ‖jèy-ge-'shyāw-shi hěn chywè-'shŕ. This news is quite accurate.

chywen Romanization found in Spoken Chinese, Basic Course (EM 506, 507), for syllables spelled chywun in this dictionary.

屈服
chywū-'fú (I) to submit to, to bend to someone's will, to obey unwillingly. ‖tā shyàng tā-de-'dí-rén chywū-'fú-le. He bowed to the will of his enemies.

曲江
chywū-'jyāng (Nunique) Ch'ü-chɪ ng (city in Kwangtung province).

曲解
chywū-'jyě (V, literary) to misinterpret what someone means.

趨勢
chywū-'shř (Nabstr) tendency. ‖shyàn-'dzày shř-'jyè-shang yěw 'lyǎng-jǔng-chywū-'shř. There are two tendencies in the world today.

衢縣
chywū-'shyàn (Nunique) Ch'ü-hsien or Chüchow (city in Chekiang province).

取
chywǔ (V) take out, withdraw, something left somewhere for safe-keeping or repairs, as money from a bank, or one's hat from a checkroom. As mainV: 'chywǔ-chū (lc) emphasis on taking out; 'chywǔ-hwéy (lc) emphasis on taking back out; chywǔ-'chyán withdraw money.
    chywǔ-'shìn to collect mail.
    chywǔ-'shyě to let blood.

娶
chywǔ (V) to marry (of a man); chywǔ 'chǐ-dz or chywǎ 'tày-tay, or chywǔ 'shí-fu take a wife: chywǔ 'yí-tày-tay to take a concubine.

取得
'chywǔ-dé (V) to gain people's confidence, respect, etc. ‖tā 'chywǔ-dé rén-'mín-'dwèy-ywu-tā-de-'shìn-yǎng. He commands people's respect and admiration.

取燈
chywǔ-'dēngr (Nunit, gēn, gēr) match for lighting fires; (local Peiping).

曲子
'chywǔ-dz, chywǔr (Nunit, dwàr, ge) songs (with words). One usually says gēer nowadays, but chywǔ-dz, chywǔr is heard, more often of quite informal songs; not national anthems, hymns, etc.

取消
chywǔ-'shyaw (*V*) to cancel, call off *a game, an appointment*, to kill *legislation*. ‖lǐ-bày-'èr-ge-bǐ-'sày chywǔ-'shyāw-le. Tuesday's game has been called off.

取笑
chywu-'shyàw (*V*) to make fun of, tease (*slightly literary*).

去
chywu (*I*) to go, *indicating motion not towards the speaker or the speaker's point of reference.*
    (1) *When followed by another verb:* to go in order to *do something.* ‖děy chywù chř-'fàn. I've got to go eat.
    (2) *When preceded by other verbs, serves simply to indicate direction of motion.* ‖tā pǎw-daw 'nàr chywù-le. He ran over to that place.
    (3) *Used as a postverb with same sense:* ‖wǒ chū-bu-'chywù. I can't get out.
    (4) *In functions one and two at the same time:* ‖tā dàw fàn-'gwǎr chywù chř-'fàn-le. He went to the restaurant to eat.
    See **láy** *for details on functions two and three.*

去掉
chywù-'dyàw (*RC3*) to ge rid of, clean out, get out. ‖nǐ bǎ 'nèy-jǐ-jywù-'hwà chywù-'dyàw. Take these sentences out (*of a document*).

去年
'chywù-nyan (*Ntime*) last year.

去世
chywù-'shr̀ (*VN1*) to die, to depart this world. (*Polite and literary.*)

羣
chywún (*Mgroup*) naturally and physically close group of. *With Npers:* rén group of people; **'gūng-rén** gang of workers; *with names of animals:* **láng** pack of wolves; **ywú** school of fish; **nyǎw**(r) flock of birds; **yáng** flock of sheep; **é** flock of geese; **nyéw** herd of cattle; *others:* **shù** clump of trees; **fēy-'jī** group of planes in formation, in a cluster; **chwán** group of boats.

裙
*chywún, 'chywún-dz (*Nunit, tyáw*) skirt; *always a separate garment hanging from the waist in China.*

羣起而攻之
'chywún-chǐ-ěr-'gūng-jr (*literary quotation*) to bear down on, gang up on, attack in a body. ‖dà-'jyā dēw dwèy-ywu tā 'chywún-chǐ-ěr-'gūng-jr. Everybody ganged up on him.

裙帶
chywún-'dày (*Nunit, tyáw*) skirt belt.

D

搭
dā (*V*) to lift *something* up into place; to bridge over the space between two things with; to erect *a structure;* to go aboard. **dā yí-ge-'jyà-dz** to erect a scaffolding; **dā yí-ge-'chyáw** to build a bridge; **dā-'chwán** to go aboard ship; **dā-'chē** to board a train *or* car.
    As mainV: **'dā-chǐ-láy** to lift *something* up; **dā-'dzěw-le** to lift up and take away; **'dā-shàng** to bridge a gap, to add even more of *something.*

答碴
dā-'chár (*VN1*) to interrupt, cut in, *when people are talking,* to answer.

不搭調
bù-dā-'dyàwr (*VN1*) to be flat (*in singing*).

搭伙, 搭夥
dā-'hwěr (*VN1*) to get together, collaborate. ‖tām-'lyǎ dā-'hwěr dzwò 'mǎy-may. They went into a business partnership.

搭窩
dā-'wō (*VN2*) to build a nest (*of a bird*).

答應
'dā-yìng *see* **'dá-yìng.**

打
dá (*MgroupA*) dozen. **yì-'dá-de-'wà-dz** a dozen (pairs) of socks.

答
*dá (*V*) to answer.
    As mainV: **dá-bu-'shàng, dá-bu-'chū, dǎ-bu-'chū-láy** to be unable to answer. ‖tā 'wèn de-shŕ-hew wǒ yì-'shŕ dá-bu-'shàng. I couldn't answer his question offhand.

答案
dá-'àn (*Nunit, ge*) answer *to a problem, mathematical or otherwise, always in writing.*

達到
'dá-dàw (*RC3*) to reach *a goal.* ‖wǒ 'fēy 'dá-dàw 'mù-dì bù-'kě. I must reach my goal. *or* I must achieve my purpose (*quite formal*).

答覆
'dá-fù (*V*) to make a formal (*written*) answer to *someone.* ‖nǐ 'dá-fù tā-le méy-yew? Have you answered him yet? (*Implies that the request was for something difficult and the reply is one declining to conform to it.*) ‖nǐ 'jŕ-dàw dzěme 'dá-fù-ma? Do you know how to answer that?

答聲
dá-'shēngr (*VN1*) to reply, to answer *when asked a question; used only in negative.* ‖tā méy-dá-'shēngr. He made no reply.

答數
dá-'shù(r) (*Nunit*, **ge**) answer, solution, *to a mathematical problem.*

答應
'dá-yìng *or* **'dǎ-yìng** (*V*) to answer affirmatively, to indicate acceptance of *an invitation, a request, etc.* ‖nǐ 'dá-yìng ta 'chywù-le-ma? Have you told him you'd go?

打
dǎ (*V*) to strike, to hit.

　　As mainV: **dǎ-'lyè-le** to crack by striking; **dǎ-'pwò-le** to break *something* to pieces by striking; *etc.*

　　In specific combinations with certain goals, **dǎ** *is used with a number of other meanings; the most important of the combinations are entered separately. The principal special meanings are:* to obtain *some ordinary necessity of rural life* by the customary method; *thus* to buy *wine, vinegar, oil;* to gather *firewood;* to draw *water* from a well; to play *games of various kinds;* to play *a card;* to play *a musical instrument which is struck or plucked;* to strike with *something;* to fire *a gun;* to send *messages;* to pack, make up, prepare, fix up; to use, to carry, *e.g., an umbrella.*

　　As mainV, the meanings likewise depend on context, with great freedom of formation; only those with specialized meanings are given as entries. Thus **'dǎ-shàng-láy** *in the following two sentences:* ‖'dí-rén 'dǎ-shàng-lay. The enemy is advancing towards us. ‖tā bǎ-'ywú 'dǎ-shàng-lay-le. He brought in the fish.

打
dǎ (*K*) by, by way of (*route*). ‖nǐ dǎ 'ná-yì-tyáw-'jyē láy-de? By which street did you come?

打扮
'dǎ-ban *or* **'dá-ban** (*V*) to get dressed; to make up (*cosmetics*); clean up and get ready; to make up *for going on the stage.* ‖nèy-ge-'nywǔ-rén 'dǎ-ban-de hěn hǎw-'kàn. That woman makes (herself) up quite attractively.

打包
dǎ-'bāw (*VN2*) to wrap, to unwrap, *a package.*

打敗
dǎ-'bày (*RC2*) to defeat *in battle.* ‖tā bǎ 'dí-rén gěy dǎ-'bày-le. He defeated his enemy. ‖tā bèy 'dí-rén gěy dǎ-'bày-le. He was defeated by his enemy.

打個叉
dǎ ge-'chār (*VN2*) to make an X, draw an X-mark.

打柴
dǎ-'cháy (*VN2*) to gather firewood, get firewood.

打旗
dǎ-'chí (*VN2*) to carry a flag aloft (*of a person*).

打旗號
dǎ chí-'hàw (*VN2*) to send flag signals, semaphore signals.

打起來
'dǎ-chǐ-láy (*RC2*) to blow up *a tire;* to bundle up *a package;* to break out (*of war*); *other meanings depending on context (see* **dǎ**).

打氣
dǎ-'chì, dǎ-'chyèr (*VN2*) to pump air into *something, such as a tire.* **dǎ-'dzù-le 'chì** to inflate *a tire.*

打出去
dǎ-'chū-chywù (*RC2*) to strike *something* and cause *it* to go out *of someplace.*

打鎗
dǎ-'chyāng (*VN2*) to fire *a rifle or other small arm.*

打球
dǎ-'chyéw(r) (*VN2*) to play a ball game, to play ball.

打拳
dǎ-'chywán (*VN1*) to box (*pugilism*).

打定
dǎ-'dìng (*RC2*) to settle; *particularly* **dǎ-'dìng jú-'yì** make up one's mind, decide, reach a decision.

打賭
dǎ-'dǔ (*VN2*) to bet, to place a bet.

打盹
dǎ (ge-)'dwěr (*VN2*) to take a nap.

打點
dǎ-'dyǎn (*VN1*) to strike the hour (*of a clock*).

打電報
dǎ dyàn-'bàw (*VN2*) to send a telegram.

打電話
dǎ dyàn-'hwà (*VN2*) to make a phone call.

打字
dǎ-'dz̀ (*VN2*) to typewrite.

打字機
dǎ-dz̀-'jī (*Nunit*, **ge, jyà**) typewriter.

69

打字員
dǎ-dz̀-'ywán (*Npers*) typist.

打子兒
dà- dzὲr (*VN2*) to gather (*edible*) seeds; to go to seed (*of a flower, or of a woman meaning* grow old); to play caroms, hit a carom *with the finger.*

打發
dǎ-fā (*V*) to send for, order, *a boy, a servant to come and do something.* ‖wǒ 'dǎ-fā yí-ge-'yùng-rén dā 'shyāng-dz. I've sent for a servant to carry the bags.

打膈兒
dǎ-'géer (*VN2*) to hiccup.

打鼓
dǎ-'gǔ (*VN2*) to beat a drum.

打官話
dǎ gwān-'hwà (*VN1*) to boast and give excuses like a politician.

打官司
dǎ 'gwān-sz (*VN1*) to go to law *about something.*

打光棍
dǎ 'gwāng-gwèr (*VN1*) to lead a single life, be a bachelor.

打號
dǎ-'hàw (*VN2*) to send (flag) signals.

打回電
dǎ hwéy-'dyàn (*VN2*) to return a telephone call, call back; to send a return telegram.

打仗
dǎ-'jàng (*VN2*) to fight, be at war.

打折扣
dǎ jé-'hew (*VN2*) to give a discount.

打擊
'dǎ-jī (*Nunit*, ge) mental blow, shock. ‖'nèy-jyàn-shr̀ gey-ta yí-ge-hěn-'dà-de-'dǎ-jī. That affair gave him a great shock.
    'shèw yí-ge-'dǎ-jī to receive a mental blow.

打鐘
dǎ-'jūng (*VN2*) to ring a large bell by striking *it.*

打架
dǎ-'jyà (*VN1*) to argue violently, coming to blows.

打箭爐
dǎ-jyàn-'lú (*Nunique*) Tatsienlu, *another name for* kāng-'dìng Kang-ting (*capital of Sikang province*).

打醬油
dǎ 'jyàng-yéw (*VN2*) to buy soya sauce.

打攪
dǎ-'jyǎw (*V*) to disturb *someone, someone's thoughts; used in polite phrases.* ‖'jīn-tyan 'dǎ-jyǎw-'dǎ-jyǎw hěn dwèy-bu-'chǐ. Very sorry to have disturbed you today.

打酒
dǎ-'jyěw (*VN2*) to buy wine.

打開
'dǎ-kāy (*RC2*) to open by striking; to open *something that opens on hinges, like a trunk, trapdoor, etc.*

打捆
dǎ-'kwěn, dǎ-'kwěr (*VN2*) to put *bedding or other such material* up into bundles.

打來回
dǎ láy-'hwér (*VN2*) to make a round trip. ‖wǒ dàw běy-'píng dǎ ge-láy-'hwér. I made a trip to Peiping and back.
    To send back *something purchased and found unsatisfactory.*

打雷
dǎ-'léy (*VN1*) to thunder.

打鈴
dǎ-'líng, dǎ-'lyéngr (*VN2*) to ring a small bell by striking *it.*

打鑼
dǎ-'lwó (*VN2*) to strike a gong.

打獵
dǎ-'lyè (*VN1*) to go hunting.
    dǎ-'lyè-de hunter.

打門
dǎ-'mén (*VN1*) to knock at a door.

打砲
dǎ-'pàw (*VN2*) to fire a large-caliber weapon, a cannon.

打拍子
dǎ 'pāy-dz (*VN1*) to beat time, keep time.

打牌
dǎ-'páy (*VN2*) to play cards or mah-jong (*any game involving cards or pieces*).

打個平手
dǎ ge-píng-'shěw (*VN2*) to come to a draw (*in any combat*).

打舖蓋

dǎ 'pū-gay (*VN2*) to make up a bedding-roll.

打破

dǎ-'pwò (*RC2*) to smash *something to pieces* by striking *it*.

    dǎ-'pwò 'jì-lù to break the record (*in some sport*).

打票

dǎ-'pyàw (*VN2*) to buy tickets; *especially* **dǎ chē-'pyàw** buy railroad *or* bus tickets.

打入

dǎ-'rù (*RC2*) to branch out *into another line of business*, force your way into *another line*. ‖**jèy-ge-dyàn-'chì-gūng-'sž yě dǎ-'rù-le gāng-'tyě-gūng-'yè.** This (electric) company has gone into steel too.

打傘

dǎ-'sǎn (*VN2*) to use *or* carry an umbrella.

打掃

dǎ-'sǎw *or* **'dǎ-sew** *or* **dá-sew** (*V*) to clean up. **'dǎ-sǎw 'wū-dz** to clean house (*including the figurative meaning as in English*).

打閃

dǎ-'shǎn (*VN1*) to lighten (*of lightning in the sky*).

打勝

dǎ-'shèng (*VN2*) to win a victory *in battle*.

打手勢

dǎ 'shěw-shr (*VN2*) to send hand signals; to gesture.

打行李

dǎ 'shíng-li (*VN2*) to pack up *one's* baggage.

打行李票

dǎ shíng-li-'pyàw (*VN2*) to check baggage (*getting the receipt*).

打輸

dǎ-'shū (*VN1*) to be defeated *in fight, game, argument*.

打水

dǎ-'shwěy (*VN2*) to fetch water from a well.

打算

'dǎ-swàn (*V*) to calculate, ngure out, plan. ‖**wǒm 'dǎ-swàn-'dǎ-swàn 'míng-tyan-de-'shr.** Let's plan tomorrow's work.

打算盤

dǎ 'swàn-pan (*VN2*) to calculate with an abacùs.

打聽

'dǎ-tīng (*V*) to inquire about (*train schedules and the like*). ‖**wǒ 'pay yí-ge-'rén dàw-'nèr chywù 'dǎ-tīng**

tā-de-'chíng-shing. I sent someone there to ask about his state of affairs (*health, business conditions, etc.*).

打醋

dǎ-'tsù (*VN2*) to buy vinegar.

打眼

dǎ-'yǎr (*VN2*) to bore a hole, drill a hole.

打油

dǎ-'yéw (*VN2*) to buy oil.

打魚

dǎ-'ywú (*VN2*) to go fishing (*with a net, not ◆ pole*).

    dǎ-'ywú-de fisherman.

大

dà (*A*) big, large; adult; important; main, chief. **dà-'chwán** big ship; **'dà-rén** adult; **dà-'gwān** important official; **dà-'lù** main road. (*Opposite in all these meanings, shyǎw.*)

    (*H*) greatly, to a great extent, loudly. **dà 'kū** to weep loudly (*as a baby*); **bú-'dàhǎw** not too terribly good; **dà 'chàng-chi-lay** to sing loudly.

大

dà (*Nunit, ge*) small coin, *no longer used, but still referred to in such expressions as:* ‖**yí-ge-'dà yě 'méy-yew** (*local Peiping*). I haven't a cent, or I'm dead broke.

大車

dà-(bǎn)-'chē (*Nunit, lyàng*) large two-wheeled cart, *animal-drawn, with no built-on cover.*

大前年

dà-'chyán-nyan (*Ntime*) year before year before last.

大前天

dà-'chyán-tyan (*Ntime*) day before day before yesterday.

大豆

dà-'dèw (*Nunit, ge*) soya beans.

大隊

dà-'dwèy (*MgroupA*) group, *in Air Forces organization; unit of this size in certain special military organizations other than the Army itself.*

    dà-dwèy-'jǎng group commander; commanding officer of any such group.

大多數

dà-dwō-'shù(r) (*Nabstr*) majority, largest number. **dà-dwō-'shù-de-'pyàw** the majority of the votes.

大總統

dà-dzǔng-'tǔng (*NpersT*) president (*of a country*).

大方
'dà-fang (A) generous, dignified. ‖tā-'jèy-ge-rén hěn 'dà-fang. He's quite generous. ‖nèy-ge-'yán-sè hěn 'dà-fang. That color is quite dignified.

大綱
dà-'gāng (Nunit, ge) outline (written).

大高個
dà-gāw-'gèr(-de-rén) (Npers) big tall man.

大概
dà-'gày (J) probably, in all probability. ‖dà-'gày tā bù-'láy. In all probability he's not coming.

大褂
dà-'gwàr (Nunit, jyàn) Chinese smock or coverall.

大後年
dà-'hèw-nyan (Ntime) year after year after next.

大後天
dà-'hèw-tyan (Ntime) day after day after tomorrow.

大話
dà-'hwà (N) big talk, boasting.
     shwō dà-'hwà to boast, to talk big.

大茴香
dà-hwéy-'shyāng (Nmass) anise (the spice).

大會
dà-'hwèy (Nunit, ge) general meeting, assembly.
     kāy dà-'hwèy to hold a general meeting; to participate in a general meeting.

大丈夫
dà-'jàng-fu (Npers) hero, great man.

大致
dà-jr̀ (J) in the main, generally. ‖dà-'jr̀ rén dēw 'shǐ-hwan tīng hǎw-'hwà. Generally, people like to hear nice things.

大衆
dà-'jùng (Ncoll) the people, the masses.
     dà-'jùng-de-'yì-sz the opinion of the people.

大家
dà-'jyā (Nunique) everybody. ‖dà-'jyā jyèw 'shyàw-le. Everybody burst out laughing.

大家夥
dà-(jyā-)'hwěr (H) all together, all in one group. ‖wǒm dà-'hwěr chywán 'chywù-ba. Let's all go together (local Peiping).

大局
dà-'jywú (Nabstr) the general political and military situation.

大理
dà-'lǐ (Nunique) Ta-li (city in Yünnan province).

大量
dà-'lyàng (A plus N) great capacity, great ability to endure; broadmindedness. dà-'lyàng-de-rén a man of great capacity for anything, from liquor to generosity; dà-'lyàng-chū-'chǎn large-scale production; dà-'lyàng bàn-'hwò to acquire goods on a large scale or to take inventory on a large scale. With parts separated and reversed in order: ‖jèy-ge-'rén 'lyàng hěn 'dà. This man has a great capacity.

大麥
dà-'mày(-dz) (Nmass) barley (grain).

大拇指
'dà-me-jǐ, 'dàm-jǐ (Nunit, ge) thumb.

大名
dà-'míng (N) your name in polite sentences. ‖nín dà-'míng dzěme 'chēng-hu? May I ask your name?

大人
'dà-rén (Npers) adults, grown-ups.

大人物
dà-rén-'wù (Npers) personage, important person.

大聲
dà-shēng(r) (H) aloud; loudly. ‖chǐng 'dà-shēng-dyǎr 'shwō. Please speak a little louder.

大師傅
'dà-shř-fu (NpersT) cook, chef, used in addressing him politely.

大使
dà-'shř (NpersT) ambassador.

大事記
dà-shr̀-'jì (Nunit, běn) chronology (written).

大小
'dà-shyǎw (Nabstr) size. ‖'dà-shyǎw hé-'shr̀. The size is right. ‖lwén-'dày-de-'dà-shyǎw 'chéng-le. The size of the tire is OK.

大學生
dà-shywé-'shēng (Npers) college student.

大學校
dà-shywé(-'shyàw) (Nunit, ge) university, college.

大體
dà-'tǐ (Nabstr) essence, essential content, structure, outline of an argument, essay, situation. ‖jèy-ge-'shr̀-ching-de-dà-'tǐ 'yǐ-jing chéng-'gūng-le. The main outline of this proposition has already been carried into effect.

大廳
dà-'tīng (Nunit, jyān, ge) living room, parlor, in a fairly extensive house.

大餐間
dà-'tsān-jyān (Nunit, ge, jyān) dining salon on board ship.

大同
dà-'túng (Nunique) Ta-t'ung (city in Shansi province).

大言不慚
'dà-yán-bù-'tsán (literary quotation) to brag without reserve, (literally big talk without shame). ‖tā shwō nèy-jywù-'hwà 'jēn-shr 'dà-yán-bù-'tsán. When he said that he was certainly bragging unashamedly.

大衣
dà-'yī (Nunit; jyàn) overcoat, topcoat.

大約
dà-'ywē (J) probably, most likely. ‖yàw-shr bú-'shyà-ywǔ, tā dà-'ywē 'láy. If it doesn't rain he'll probably be here.

單
dān (H) only, not more than. ‖wǒ 'dān dzwò 'jèy-jyàn-shr̀. I'm only going to do this.
    Before nouns single, alone. dān-'rén one person alone; dān-rén-'chwáng single bed; dān-rén-de-'wū-dz single room.

擔, 担
dān (V) to carry on a pole supported on the shoulder, or on a pole supported at each end on the shoulders of several men. As mainV: 'dān-dàw to carry something in this way to a place; 'dān-chǐ (l) lift and carry thus, 'dān-'píng to balance the pole and burden by putting equal amounts in front and in back of the shoulder; etc.
    dān is used also metaphorically as in English: shoulder a responsibility, etc. (examples are given as separate entries).

單
*dān, 'dān-dz, 'dār (Nunit, jāng; tyáwr if on a strip of paper) list; bill (to be paid). tsày-'dān menu (M also ge); míng-'dān list of names; etc.
    'dān-dz (Nunit, tyáw, chwáng) bed sheets.

擔保
dān-'bǎw (V) to guarantee, go bond for the performance and behavior of someone or something. ‖jèy-ge-'byǎw wǒ dān-'bǎw yì-'nyán. I guarantee this watch for a year. ‖jèy-ge-'rén, wǒ 'tì-ni dān-'bǎw. I'll guarantee you that this man is OK.

擔承
dān-'chéng (V) to take the blame. dān-'chéng...dzwèy-'míng to take the blame implied by such-and-such a designation of fault or crime. ‖wǒ bù-néng dān-'chéng jèy-ge-dzwèy-'míng. I can't stand being accused of such a thing as that.

單獨
'dān-dú (J) alone, all alone; isolated. ‖wǒ 'dān-dú 'yí-ge-rén 'láy-le. I came all alone (stronger than simply wǒ 'yí-ge-rén 'láy-le which means almost the same).

擔負
'dān-fù (V) to bear responsibility, a burden (particularly financial). ‖'jèy-ge gwēy 'nǐ 'dān-fù. This is your responsibility.

躭擱
'dān-ge (I) to tarry, delay. ‖tā dzày-'nàr 'dān-ge-le lyǎng-'jūng-tew chywù yéw-'shān. He stopped over there a couple of hours to make a trip in the hills.

丹麥
dān-'mày(-gwó) (Nunique) Denmark.

擔任
dān-'rèn (V) assume, take on, shoulder responsibility for some duty, affair. ‖tā bù-néng dān-'rèn jème-'dwō-de-'gūng-dzwò. He can't be responsible for so much work.

擔心, 躭心
dān-'shin (A) to be worried, to have a burden on one's heart. ‖wǒ hěn 'tì-ni dān-'shin. I'm very much worried about you.

單數
'dān-shùr (Nunit, ge) odd number (1, 3, 5, 7, etc.).

躭課
'dān-wù (V) to waste time. ‖tā jēn 'dān-wù 'shŕ-hew. He really wastes time. ‖wǒ 'dān-wù-le nǐ-men-de-'shŕ-hew jēn dwèy-bu-'chǐ. I'm very sorry to have wasted your time.

撢
dǎn (V) to dust off with a dust cloth or feather duster. 'dǎn-dz (Nunit, bǎ) duster (cloth or feather).

As mainV: dǎn-'gān-jìng dust *something* clean. ‖bǎ jèy-jāng-'jwǒ-dz yùng 'dǎn-dz dǎn-'gān-jìng. Dust this table clean with a dust rag.

膽

'dǎn(-dz), 'dǎr (*Nabstr*) degree of bravery or cowardice. ‖tā 'dǎn-dz 'dà. He has great courage. ‖tā 'dǎr 'shyǎw. He's quite a coward.

蛋

dàn (*Nunit,* ge) egg, *usually with type specified.* jī-'dàn chicken egg.

淡

dàn (*A*) light (*of wine*), weak (*of tea*), thin (*of a liquid*). (*Opposite* núng thick, strong, heavy.) Mild, unsalty (*of food*). (*Opposite* shyán salty.) Light, pale (*of a color*). (*Opposite* shēn, àn dark.)

擔，石

dàn (*Mmeas*) picul (*measure of weight*). *See Appendix B.*

蛋白

dàn-'báy (*Nmass*) egg white.

彈

'dàn-dz, dàr (*Nunit,* ge, lì) bullet, ammunition, *for small arms;* marbles (*children's playthings,*); *in compounds,* other small round things.

彈子兒

dàn-'dzěr (*Nunit,* ge, lì) bullet.

淡而無味

'dàn-ér-wú-'wèy (*literary quotation*) tasteless, insipid, (*of food, a picture, book, etc.*); dull, uninteresting, (*of a person*). ‖'jèy-ge-rén 'dàn-ér-wú-'wèy. He's quite dull and ordinary.

但凡

'dàn-fan (*or* 'dàn-fen) (*J*) if at all possible. ‖'dàn-fan néng 'chywù de-'hwà, wǒ jyèw 'chywù. If it's at all possible, I'll go.

蛋黃

dàn-'hwáng(r) (*Nmass*) egg yolk.

但是

'dàn-shr (*J*) but. ‖wǒ 'tīng shr 'tīng-jyàn-le, dàn-shr wǒ bú-'shìn. I heard it, but I don't believe it.

彈藥

dàn-'yàw (*Nmass*) ammunition.

當

dāng (*V*) to serve as, become. dāng-'bīng serve as (*or* be) a soldier. *With other nouns naming offices or functions, either* dāng *or* dzwò *is used:* dāng-'gwān *or*

dzwò-'gwān, *more often the latter:* serve as an official.

'dāng-shàng (*RC2*) become *with same range of meaning as above.*

(*V or K*) take as. ‖tā bǎ 'jèy-jyàn-shr̀-chin dāng 'shyàw-hwar (shwō). He took the matter as a joke. *or* He spoke of it as a joke (*though it was serious*).

當

dāng (*K*) at *a time in the past;* in compounds at *a place.* ‖dāng nǐ 'láy de-shŕ-hew 'bú-shr nàme-yàng. But when you came here it wasn't that way at all. ‖dāng nǐ dzày-'jèr de-shŕ-hew 'bú-shr nàme-yàng. But while you were here it wasn't that way at all.

當場

dāng-'chang (*H*) (right) at a certain place in the presence of people; in public; *rare in colloquial use.* ‖tā dāng-'chǎng jyèw 'bèy-rén 'kàn-chu-lay-le tā-de-'tswèr. Right at that spot his mistakes were revealed.

當初

dāng-'chū (*H*) formerly.

當前

dāng-'chyán (*used before nouns*) before us *in the figurative sense.* dāng-'chyán-de-'wèn-tǐ the problem before us.

當地

dāng-'dì (*before nouns*) of a locality, district; local. dāng-'dì-de-'gwān the local magistrate.

當中

dāng-'jūng (*Nplace*) the center of, middle of. ‖tā dzày wǒ-men-dāng-'jūng dzwò jyǎng-'hé-de-rén. He will serve as mediator between us. ‖'hé-de-dāng-'jūng 'shwěy 'lyéw-de hěn 'kwày. The current is swift in the middle of the river.

當局

dāng-'jywú (*Ncoll*) governmental officials *now in office;* the present administration *of the government.*

當 .... 面

dāng...'myàn(-shang) to *someone's* face, in front of *someone.* ‖dāng tā-de-'myàn 'shwō ta yí-dwèn. Give him a good scolding right to his face.

當然

dāng-'rán (*J*) naturally, of course. ‖tā dāng-'rán bù-jŕ-'dàw-le. Of course he doesn't know. ‖dāng-'rán-de-le! Naturally! Of course!

當心

dāng-'shīn (*A*) careful. ‖dāng-'shīn-dyǎr, byé 'shwāy-je. Be careful, don't fall.

Bridge, Summer Palace, Beijing

Carved fence, Summer Palace, Beijing

(*V*) be careful of, watch out for *a person*, be on guard against *a person*. ‖nǐ dǎng-'shĭn-je tā. Watch out for him.

當時
dǎng-'shŕ (*H*) (right) then, at that (very) moment. ‖tā jyàw chì-'chē 'pèng-le, dǎng-'shŕ jyèw 'sž-le. He was struck by a car and died immediately.

當選
dǎng-'shywǎn (*I*) to be elected.

黨
dǎng (*Nunit*, ge) political party; *now usually taken to mean the* gwó-mín-'dǎng Chinese National People's Party.

(*Nunit*, ge; *or Mgroup*) gang, group.

擋
dǎng (*V*) to obstruct *someone's* passage, to obstruct the passage *of water, light, etc. As mainV:* 'dǎng-shàng *or* 'dǎng-chǐ-láy to close up *a passage.* ‖jèy-tyáw-'lù dēw 'dǎng-shàng-le. This road is blocked.

*dǎng (*N*) an obstruction, block. lú-'dǎng insulation *against heat around a fireplace.*

檔案
dǎng-'àn (*Nunit*, jyàn) archives; *with the M one document kept among archives.*

檔案室
dǎng-àn-'shŕ (*Nunit*, jyān) room for keeping archives, archive.

黨國要人
'dǎng-gwó-'yàw-rén (*Npers*) important person of party and country. *Since most members of the government are also members of the* gwó-mín-'dǎng, *high officials are often referred to by this term.*

黨徒
dǎng-'tú (*Npers*) member of a party, gang, group, *with common purpose; (implies disapproval).*

黨務
'dǎng-wù (*Nunit*, jyàn) (political) party matter, affair.

黨員
dǎng-'ywán (*Npers*) party member; *particularly* member of the gwó-mín-'dǎng.

當
dàng (*V*) to take *or* use *something* as. ‖wǒ bǎ nèy-běn-'shū dàng 'wǒ-de-le. I've been using this book as though it were mine. ‖tā bǎ 'byé-rén-de-shyǎw-'hár dàng tā-'dž-jǐ-de 'kàn-dày. He treats other people's children as though they were his own (*comment of approval*).

當成
'dàng-chéng (*V*) to assume *that something is something.* ‖wǒ 'bǎ-ta 'dàng-chéng 'hǎw-rén-le. I assumed that he was a good guy (*but he wasn't*).

當作
'dàng-dzwò (*V*) to consider *something as being such-and-such.* ‖wǒ 'bǎ-ta 'dàng-dzwò 'hǎw-rén-le. I considered him to be a good guy (*but he wasn't*).

當一回事
dàng (yì-)hwéy-'shŕ (*VN2*) to take *something* as a serious matter, to take *something* seriously. ‖tā 'shwō-ni yí-'dwèn, byé 'bǎ-ta dàng yì-hwéy-'shŕ. He gave you a scolding, but don't take it seriously.

刀
'dāw(-dz), dāwr (*Nunit*, bǎ) knife *with only one edge sharp unless the contrary is specifically mentioned.* 'lyǎng-rèn-de-'dāw two edged knife.

dǎ-(*or* 'chyē- *or* kǎn-)rén yì-dāw to strike (*or* cut *or* chop down on) someone with one blow of a knife.

刀把
dāw-'bàr (*Nunit*, ge) knife handle.

刀背
dāw-'bèr (*Nunit*, ge) the unsharpened back side of a knife.

刀尖
dāw-'jyār (*Nunit*, ge) point of a knife.

刀口
dāw-'kěw (*Nunit*, ge, *but rare with M*) sharp edge of a knife.

刀片
dāw-'pyàn, dāw-'pyàr (*Nunit*, ge) knife blade; razor blade.

刀翼
dāw-'yì (*Nunit*, pyàr, ge) propeller blade; electric fan blade.

島
dǎw (*Nunit*, ge) island.

倒
dǎw (*I*) to turn upside down, *or* turn *something* over on its side.

Of a business, to fail, close. ‖tā-de-'pù-dz 'dǎw-le. His store has failed.

As mainV: 'dǎw-shyà to fall down (*as of a wall, a pole*); 'dǎw-chū-chywù to sell out *a business*; 'dǎw-gěy to sell *a business* to someone.

Used as postV with any mainV specifying causal action involved. ‖dyàn-shyàn-'gān-dz jyàw-'fēng gwā-'dăw-le. ·The telephone pole was blown over by the wind.

倒閉

dăw-'bì (*I*) to close, fail, *of a store, business.* ‖nèy-ge-pù-dz 'yĭ-jing dăw-'bì-le. That store has already failed.

禱告

dăw-'gàw (*V*) to pray to *a deity, heaven.* ‖tā dăw-'gàw 'tyān chyéw-'ywŭ. He prayed for rain.

倒換

dăw-'hwàn (*V*) to exchange, change, *places.* ‖wŏ-men-'lyă dăw-'hwàn 'dzwèr. Let's change seats (with each other).

倒換班

dăw-'hwàn 'bār (*VN2*) to change shifts.

倒閘

dăw-'já (*VN2*) to shift gears (*in a car or truck*).

搗亂

dăw-'lwàn (*VN1*) make trouble, cause a disturbance.

搗麻煩

dăw 'má-fan (*VN2*) to stir up trouble. ‖nĭ 'cháng-cháng gēn-ta dăw 'má-fan. You're always stirring up trouble with him.

倒霉

dăw-'méy (*or* 'dăw-le 'méy-le) (*A*) out of luck, unfortunate. (*Opposite* dzĕw-'ywùn lucky, fortunate.)

倒手

dăw-'shĕw (*VN2*) to change hands, (*of a business, etc.*).

導演

dăw-'yăn (*V*) to direct *a play, a demonstration, movie.*

導遊

dăw-'yéw (*VN1*) to conduct a tour, *for sightseeing, etc.*

導員

dăw-'ywán (*Npers*) director *of plays;* conductor *of an orchestra.*

道

dàw ('*Nunit*, tyáw) road; course, way, (*of life*). ‖jèy-tyáw-'dàw 'dzĕw-je bù-'píng. This road is quite rough to walk on. *or* This way of life is not smooth going, not easy.

'dàwr (*Nunit*, tyáw) band, strip, streak, line, course, way. ‖jèy-ge shr̀ dày-'dàwr-de-'jr̆. This is ruled paper (*i.e., paper that carries lines*).

道

dàw (*MdistT*) one course of tsày (*food*), or of a specific dish; one round of jyĕw (*drinks*); one levying of shwèy (*taxes, customs, duties, imposts*).

(*Munit*) one mén (*door*); or with any word naming a long narrow feature of terrain along which one theoretically could walk: hé (*river*), jàn-'háw (*trench*), já (*dam*), bà or dī (*dike*), tí (*reef*); a range of shān (*hills, mountains*).

(*Mpart*) a coat of yéw (*paint; with either* dàw *or* dàwr). (*M*) a beam of gwāng(-'shyàn) (*light*).

到

dàw (*V, lc*) to go to. ‖dàw-'jèr-lay. Come here! (*literally* to here come).

(*I*) to arrive; *therefore, with* -le, to be present. ‖tā háy-méy-'dàw. He hasn't arrived yet. ‖'dàw! Here! (*answering roll-call*).

(*V*) to arrive at *a place.* ‖wŏ méy-'dàw-gwo 'jūng-gwo. I've never been to China (*literally* I've never arrived at China). ‖nĭ 'shéme-shŕ-hew 'dàw-de? When did you arrive?

(*K*) until *a time,* at *a time.* ‖dàw 'nèy-ge-shŕ-hew nĭ 'tsáy gāy 'dzĕw. You don't have to leave until then. ‖tsúng shyàn-'dzày dàw míng-tyan-'wăn-shang nĭ bù-néng 'lí-kay jèr. From now until tomorrow evening you can't leave here. ‖chà 'wŭ-fēn (bú-)dàw 'wŭ-dyăn. It's five minutes to five.

As postV: forms (1) *RC which must be followed by a designation of the place to which the action goes, and by final* láy *or* chywù. 'dzĕw-dàw (*lc*) walk to, go to *a place;* 'păw-dàw (*lc*) run to, move fast to *a place;* 'ná-dàw (*lc*) take *something to a place.*

(2) *Without final* láy *or* chywù, *similar meaning with no implication of actual change of location.* 'kàn-dàw to read to *a certain page, a certain chapter;* 'shwō-dàw to speak to *a certain point in some organized statement;* 'jyè-dàw to borrow as much as *some amount of money.*

(3) *Without final* láy *or* chywù, *meaning to be so-and-so or do so-and-so until a certain time.* ‖wŏm tsúng 'dzăw-chen yì-'jŕ 'máng-dàw 'wăn-shang. We're busy straight through from morning to evening.

倒

dàw (*H*) contrary to expectation. ‖'wŏ bú-'rèn-shr ta, 'tā dàw 'rèn-shr ta! Even I don't know her, and yet he does!

倒

dàw (*I*) to be inverted, turned upside down; *mainly as postV.* ‖nèy-jāng-'hwàr gwà-'dàw-le. That picture is hung upside down. ‖tā bù-shŕ-'dz, bă-'bàw kàn-'dàw-le. He's illiterate; he looks at the newspaper upside down.

Used causatively: dàw-'chē *or* kāy-'dàw 'chē back a car, drive a car backwards.

Also used figuratively of people who try to revert to earlier ways of doing things.

倒

dàw (*V*·) to pour. **dàw-'chá** to pour tea, *etc.*

    As mainV: **'dàw-dzày** to pour *something* into *or* onto; **'dàw-chū-láy** to pour *something* out of *some container, etc.* ‖**byé bǎ-'shwěy dàw-dzay 'jwǒ-dz-shang.** Don't pour the water on the table.

稻

*dàw (*Ncoll*) rice *growing in a field.*

到案

dàw-'àn (*VN1*) to appear in court, *of plaintiff or defendant.*

道邊

'dàw-byār (*Nplace*) edge of the road; sidewalk. (*Rare in China.*)

到場

dàw-'chǎng (*VN1*) to turn up at a place *where something is happening.* ‖**kāy-'hwèy de-shŕ-hew tā méy-dàw-'chǎng.** He didn't turn up for the meeting.

到期

dàw-'chī (*VN1*) to reach a prearranged date, to become due. ‖**jèy-běn-'shū 'yı-jing dàw-'chī-le, gǎy 'hwán-le.** This book is already due; it's got to be returned.

到處

'dàw-chù (*Nplace*) everywhere. ‖**tā 'dàw-chù shywān-'chwán.** He's spreading propaganda everywhere.

道歉

dàw-'chyàn (*VN1*) to extend apologies, to apologize. ‖**wǒ gěy-ta dàw-'chyàn-le.** I apologized to him.

道德

dàw-'dé (*Nabstr*) feeling for ethical propriety. ‖**tā-'nèy-ge-rén hěn yěw dàw-'dé.** He has a well-developed sense of ethics.

到底

dàw-'dǐ (*H*) fundamentally, at bottom, after all. ‖**tā dàw-'dǐ shŕ tsúng-'nǎr láy-de?** Well, where is he from (originally), anyhow?

道理

'dàw-lǐ (*Nunit, ge*) moral purpose; ethical and logical reason *underlying someone's behavior.* ‖**'jèy-jywù-hwà hěn yěw 'dàw-lǐ.** That expression (*of opinion, etc.*) is quite justifiable. ‖**tā-dẓwò-de-'shŕ méy 'dàw-lǐ, hěn 'nán jyàw-rén 'pèy-fu.** His acts are not reasonable; it's difficult for people to have any respect for him.

道路

'dàw-lù (*Nunit, tyáw*) roadway; road.

到了兒

dàw-'lyǎw(r) (*H*) finally; to the end (*particularly*) **tsúng-'téwr dàw-'lyǎwr** from beginning to end.

到了末了兒

dàw-le mwò-'lyǎwr (*J*) finally, at last. ‖**dàw-le mwò-'lyǎwr tā 'dzěw-le.** Finally he left. or When everything was over he left. ‖**dàw-le mwò-'lyǎwr tā dzěw-le.** But when it came to a real test, he scrammed (*despite his previous boasting of bravery*).

到任

dàw-'rèn (*VN1*) to take office *after appointment or election.*

倒吸一口氣

'dàw-shī (yì-)kěw-'chì (*VN2*) (*figuratively*) to hold one's breath *at a critical moment.*

道喜

dàw-'shǐ (*VN1*) to congratulate. ‖**wǒ gěy-ta dàw-'shǐ.** I congratulated him.

倒是

'dàw-shr (*H*) sure, indeed, yes of course, *implying a following* 'but,' 'and yet,' *which is usually expressed.* ‖**'hǎw, dàw-shr 'hǎw, 'bú-gwò...** That's well enough, but then... ‖**wǒm chywù kàn dyàn-'yěngr dàw-shr 'ké-yi, 'bú-gwo wǒ bú-'ywàn-yi.** We could go to a movie, but I don't want to.

道謝

dàw-'shyè (*VN1*) to extend thanks, express thanks, *often when declining something.*

到頭

dàw-'téwr (*VN1*) to reach the end *of anything. Often with* **dàw** *as postV:* ‖**tā háy méy-dzěw-daw 'téwr-ne.** He hasn't walked to the end yet.

稻草

dàw-'tsǎw (*Nunit, gēr, gēn*) rice straw.

待

dǎy (*I*) to stay temporarily. *Does not extend to the idea of living at a place, as does* **jù.** ‖**wǒ dǎy-'jèr hǎw-le.** I'd better stay here.

    As mainV: **'dǎy-dzày** to stay at, remain at; **'dǎy-shyà-chywù** to start staying, settle down. ‖**wǒ jyèw dzày-'jèr 'dǎy-shyà-chywù-le.** I'm going to stay right here.

    'dǎy (yì-)hwěr (*H*) presently, by and by; take your time, don't hurry, wait a minute (*local Peiping*).

歹

dǎy (*A*) morally bad, reprehensible, perverse (*of people only*). (*Opposite* **hǎw.**) ‖**'tày-yang jàw 'hǎw-rén, yě**

jàw **'dǎy-rén.** The sun shines on good men and bad man alike. **‖tā bù-'jř-dàw hǎw-'dǎy.** He doesn't know good from evil.

逮

dǎy (or **děy, dēy,** *both local Peiping*) to arrest, catch, *a thief, a fugitive*. *As mainV:* **'dǎy-chi-láy** *same as above;* **'dǎy-jù** to catch and hold; **'dǎy-'dzěw** to arrest and take away *(i.e., to jail)*. **‖byé 'jyàw-rén 'dǎy-je!** Don't get caught! **‖'děy-ta! sž-'hwó bù-'gwǎn!** Get him dead or alive!

戴

dày (*V*) to put on *clothes or ornaments, including head-gear, necktie, collar, gloves, glasses, earrings, etc., but not coats, trousers, underwear, shoes, socks, dresses, skirts, or belts* (*see* **chwān**). *As mainV:* **'dày-shàng** or **'dày-chi-láy** *with same meaning*.

待

dày (*V*) to treat, deal with, *people; usually has adjectival predicate following to show the nature of the treatment.* **‖tā 'dày-rén hěn 'hǎw.** He treats people very well.

帶

dày (*V, lc; K*) to go with; to lead, to take, bring. **‖nǐ 'dày-wo chywù, 'hǎw-bu-hǎw?** Will you take me there?

    As mainV: **'dày-dàw** (*lc*) take *something to a place;* **'dày-hwéy** (*lc*) take *something* back to *a place;* **dày-'dzěw** take *something* away, *etc.* **‖bǎ jèy-běn-'shū dày-hwéy 'jyā-chywù.** Take this book back home.

    dày-'hwàr (*VN2*) to bring word, bring news.

帶

dày (*V*) to carry, be accompanied by (*in a general sense*). **dày-'jyā-jywù-de-'fáng-dz** furnished house; **dày-'dàw-de-'jř** ruled paper; **dày-dzǎw-'fang-de-'wū-dz** room with bath; **dày-'shyár-de-'táng** candy in boxes. **‖tā shwō-'hwà dày 'gwǎng-dūng-'kěw-yīn.** When he speaks, he has a Cantonese accent.

代

dày (*Mgroup*) a generation of. **‖nèy-yí-dày-de-'rén** that generation of people. **‖tām-'jyā-lǐ-tew yěw 'sž-dày(-de-rén).** There are four generations in that family. (*Note use of* **de.**)

帶

*dày, 'dày-dz (*Nunit,* **gēn, gēr, tyáw, tyáwr**) strap, ribbon, belt.

    dày (*Munit*) belt of, section of, region of, *some kind of terrain.* **yí-dày-shù-'lín-dz** wooded region; **'jèy-yí-dày-de-'dì-fangr** this section; **chū-'myán-hwa-de-yí-dày-de-'dì-fangr** cotton belt.

袋

'dày(-dz), dàr (*NunitC,* **ge**) sack, bag, *of cloth or paper.* • *As M,* **dày** *is also used with* **yān** *to mean* a smoke (*i.e., the period of smoking that one gets from a single pipeful of tobacco*).

代表

dày-'byǎw (*V*) to represent officially, be a representative for *someone.* **‖'jyǎng-fū-rén 'dày-byǎw 'jūng-gwo(-rén) dàw 'měy-gwo láy.** Madame Chiang comes to the United States as a representative °of China. *or* °of the Chinese people.

帶大

dày-'dà (*RC2*) to bring up, raise *children.*

大夫

'dày-fu (*NpersT*) (medical) doctor.

帶勁

dày-'jìn (*A*) powerful, strong. **‖tā 'nèy-jywù-hwà hěn dày-'jìn.** That remark of his carried great weight. **‖tā dzwò nèy-jyàn-'shř hěn dày-'jìn.** He did that job very eagerly, with gusto, and with great interest.

代價

dày-'jyà (*Nunit,* **ge**) sacrifice, cost (*figurative*). **‖yùng 'jàn-jēng-de-'fāng-fa láy 'jyě-jywé 'jàn-jēng dày-'jyà 'shř hěn 'dà.** The use of war to end war calls for great sacrifice.

帶扣

dày-'kèw(r) (*Nunit,* **ge**) belt buckle.

代理

dày-'lǐ (*V*) to be in charge of *temporarily.* **‖tā tì 'jāng-shyān-sheng dày-'lǐ gūng-'sž-de-'shř-ching.** He's taking charge of the company's affairs for Mr. Jāng.

代數

dày-'shū (*VN2*) to stand for a figure *in algebra.* **‖X dày yí-ge-'shù.** X represents a number.

    (*Nabstr*) algebra.

代替

'dày-tì (*V*) to represent, speak for, substitute for *someone.* **‖yàw-shr nǐ yěw-'bìng, wǒ yèw 'dày-tì ni chywù.** If you're sick, I'll go in your place.

待遇

'dày-ywù (*Nabstr*) wages, salary, treatment *in general, given employees by employers.* **‖'nàr-de-shèr 'dày-ywu dzěme-'yàng?** How are you treated there?

的

de (*reading form* **dì**) (1) *Placed between a group of elements which modify a nominal form and that nominal form:* **hěn-hǎw-'kàn-de-'nywǔ-rén** a very good looking woman; **dzwèy-'hèw-de-shèng-'lì** final victory; **tā-shwō-de-'hwà** what he says; **mày-'shū-de-rén** bookseller; **yì-'wū-dz-de-rén** a whole roomful of people.

(2) *In some such groups, the nominal form which might follow the* **de** *is omitted, so that the* **de** *forms a derived noun from the group to which it is added:* **mày-'shū-de** bookseller; **lā-'chē-de** rickshaw-puller; **dzwèy-'hǎw-de** the best of all; **dǐng-'dà-de** the oldest.

(3) *Added to an adjective expression used as nucleus in a sentence, with* **shr̀** *prefixed to the nucleus, expresses classification:* ‖**jèy-běr-shū shr̀ dzwèy-'hǎw-de.** This book is one of the best. ‖**dǐng-'dà-de-háy-dz shr̀ 'nán-de.** The oldest child is a boy. ‖**'tā-chān-de-'shyé shr̀ 'hwáng-de.** The shoes HE has on are brown.

(4) *Similarly added to an RC in potential form:* ‖**bǐ-'jèy-ge-hǎw-de-'wū-dz shr̀ jǎw-bu-'jáw-de.** Rooms better than these just aren't to be found.

(5) *Added to a V or I, indicates occurrence in past time with emphasis on the specific time of the occurrence rather than on the occurrence itself:* ‖**nǐ 'shéme-shŕ-hew 'dàw-de?** When did you get there? ‖**tā 'chywù-nyan dàw-de 'jūng-gwo.** He got to China last year. ‖**wǒ-men 'bā-dyǎn-jūng chr̄-de 'fàn.** We ate dinner at eight o'clock. *In some such sentences, however, the emphasis on specific time of occurrence is lost, being shifted rather to the specific place or other specific feature other than the occurrence or action itself:* ‖**tā tsúng 'měy-gwo láy-de.** He comes from the United States.

(6) *Doubled intensive forms of A and H (see under A and H in Section E of Introduction) add* **de:** **hǎw-'hǎwr-de** very very good; **yí-ge-'yí-ge-de** one by one.

(7) **de** *is often inserted between a sentence and a postposed comment; if the sentence-nucleus is a verb, the verb is often repeated:* ‖**tā 'dzěw-de hěn 'kwày.** He walks very fast. ‖**tā dzwò nèy-jyàn-'shr̀-ching dzwò-de hěn 'hǎw.** He did that job very well indeed. (*Compare* ‖**'tā dzwò nèy-jyàn-'shr̀-ching hěn 'hǎw.** He would be a good man to have to do that job.)

(8) *Similar to the last is a construction in which the elements following* **de** *indicate a resultant state:* ‖**jèy-jǐ-'shyé 'pwò-de bù-néng 'chwān.** This shoe is worn out to such an extent that you can't wear it. ‖**tā 'sàw-de méy-lyǎr jyàn-'rén-le.** He's so ashamed that he can't face people.

Specific cases in which **de** *is regularly used, or regularly omitted when use might be expected, are given at relevant points in the dictionary.*

的話
de-hwà *placed at the end of conditional expressions, with or without a J such as* **'rè-shr** *or* **'yàw-shr** *if.* ‖**(rè-shr or̂ yàw-shr or 'rú-gwo) tā 'láy de-hwà, wǒ jyèw 'chywù.** If he comes I'm going to go. ‖**tā láy de-hwà, dzěme 'bàn-ne?** If HE comes what in the world will we do?

的時候
de-'shŕ-hew *see* **shŕ-hew.**

得
dé (*V*) to attain, obtain, get, achieve. **'dé-'bìng** to take sick; **dé jùng-shāng-'fēng** to catch the flu; **dé-'shèng** to win victory. ‖**'èr chéng-'èr dé-'sz̀.** Two times two gives four.

More often as main V: **'de-dàw** to achieve, attain, arrive at *the answer;* **dé-bu-'jáw** to be unable to find *the answer,* achieve, attain.

(*I*) to be ready, finished, completed. ‖**'fàn 'dé-le.** Dinner's ready.

As post V: **chr̄-'dé-le** finish eating; **dzwò-'dé-le** finish working; accomplish one's task; *etc., freely with any main V:* ‖**'jèy-jyàn-shr̀ nǐ 'dzwò-bu-dé.** You can't do this job.

得
dé (*Vpred*) *in negative, slightly literary,* **bu-'dé** one ought not, one had better not *do so-and-so; but freely colloquial as* **bù-'dé bū-** can do nothing but *so-and-so.* ‖**bù-'dé swéy-'yì lwàn 'dzěw.** You oughtn't just go wherever you want to. ‖**wǒ bù-'dé bú-'chywù.** I can do nothing but go. ‖**'dé-le-ba! byé 'shwō-le!** Quit it! That's enough! Don't say anything more!

得當
dé-'dàng (*A*) proper, right. ‖**tā shwō-'hwà hěn dé-'dàng.** He speaks quite properly (*in the sense of saying the right things*).

得分
dé-'fēr (*VN2*) to make points, make a score, *in playing a game;* to get a certain grade *in a course in school.* ‖**tā dì-'lǐ dé-daw 'dwō-shaw-fēr?** What grade did he make in geography?

德國
'dé-gwo (*Nunique*) Germany.

得獎
dé-'jyǎng (*VN2*) to win a prize, earn a reward, get a medal.

不得了
bù-dé-'lyǎw (*A*) extreme; terrible; without limit. ‖**jèy-jyàn-'shr̀-ching 'jēn bù-dé-'lyǎw.** This matter is really terrible, I can't imagine what we can possibly do about it. ‖**tā shr̀ yí-ge-bù-dé-'lyǎw-de-rén-'wù.** He's really a great man. ‖**tā 'shì-hwan-de bù-dé-'lyǎw.** His happiness knew no bounds.

德縣
dé-'shyàn (*Nunique*) Te-hsien *or* Tehchow (*city in Shantung province*).

得意
dé-'yì (*A*) successful, prosperous. ‖**tā shyàn-'dzày shr̀ hěn-dé-'yì-de-shŕ-hew.** He's really in a period of success now.

得意忘形

dé-'yì-wàng-'shíng (*literary quotation*) to have attained prosperity and thereby have become careless (of one's moral obligations).

頓 (?)

dèn (*V*) to pull on in sudden tugs, (*as a rope*). *As mainV:* dèn-'dwàn-le to break into segments by pulling in sudden tugs; 'dèn-shyà-láy to pull *something* down with sudden tugs. ‖nǐ 'dèn-yi-dèn ⟨ èy-ge-'shéng-dz. Pull on that rope a couple of times (*local Peiping*).

燈

dēng (*Nunit*, dzǎn; *sometimes* ge) lamp, light *in the sense of an artificial source of illumination.*

dēng-'dǐ-shya under a lamp, in lamplight, in artificial light. ‖jèy-ge-'yán-se, 'dēng-dǐ-shya 'kàn, hěn 'měy. This color is very beautiful under the light.

登

dēng (*V*) to press down with the foot, step on. dēng-'bǎr to press down a foot-pedal.

As mainV: 'dēng-dzày to step onto, step up onto; 'dēng-shàng-chywu to step up on. ‖nǐ dēng-dzay 'yǐ-dz-shàng-tew bǎ-'dēng 'dyǎn-shàng. Step up on the chair and light the lamp.

登

dēng (*V*) to publish; to cause to be published; to publish something in. dēng-'bàw publish something in a newspaper; dēng gwàng-'gàw to put an ad in a paper.

As mainV: dēng-dzày to publish *something* in *a particular place, paper;* 'dēng-chū-lay to publish. ‖nèy-yí-dwàr-shīn-'wén yi-jīng 'dēng-chū-lay-le. That bit of news has already been published in the papers.

登場

dēng-'chǎng (*VN1*) to go on stage (*of an actor*).

燈罩

dēng-'jàwr (*Nunit*, ge) lampshade.

登記

dēng-'jì (*I*) to register, check in. ‖nǐ dēng-'jì-le méy-yew? Have you registered yet? (*for a hotel, for voting; not for courses in school*).

燈泡兒

dēng-'pàwr (*Nunit*, ge) light bulb.

燈塔

dēng-⟨ ⟩ (*Nunit*, ge, dzwò) lighthouse.

燈油

dēng-'yéw (*Nmass*) oil *for lamps.*

等

děng (*V*, *Vsent*) to wait, wait until, wait for. 'děng-(yì-)děng, 'děng (yì-)hwěr wait a moment, wait a bit, wait a while. ‖děng tā 'hwéy-lay (de-shŕ-hew) dzày 'shwō. Wait until he comes back.

As mainV: 'děng-dàw wait until *a time.*

等

děng (*Mclass*) class of, degree of, grade of. 'shàng-děng-(de-) first class, best possible *anything, as:* 'shàng-děng-'tsāng first-class cabin (*also called* 'yì-děng-'tsāng *or* 'téw-děng-'tsāng).

等等

'děng-děng(-de) and so forth. 'jwō-dz, 'yǐ-dz, shū-'jwō, 'děng-děng(-de-dūng-shi) tables, chairs, desks, and so forth.

戥子

'děng-dz (*Nunit*, ge) small balance for weighing gold, jewels, medicine, letters, *etc.*

戥桿

děng-'gǎr (*Nunit*, ge) horizontal beam of a balance *or* scales *from which the trays hang.*

等級

děng-'jí (*Nunit*, ge) rank *in an official hierarchy.* ‖jywūn-'dwèy-li fēn 'dwō-shaw-děng-'jí? How many ranks are there in the army?

等於

'děng-ywú (*V*) be equal to *in the mathematical sense;* be equal *or* similar to *in general.* ‖'èr jyā-'sż 'děng-ywú 'lyèw. Two plus four equals six. ‖nǐ shwō 'jèy-jywù hwà 'děng-ywú méy-'shwō. You might as well not have said anything; (the desired result didn't follow your speaking). ‖'děng-ywú 'líng. It all adds up to nothing.

瞪

dèng (*V*) to stare at *with eyes wide open.* 'dèng-rén yì-'yǎn to give someone a black look; gēn-rén dèng-'yǎn to be angry with somebody, to be quarreling with somebody; dèng-je 'yǎn(-jing) having eyes wide open.

凳子, 櫈子

'dèng-dz (*Nunit*, ge) stool, *backless and armless* chair. cháng-'dèng-dz bench.

兜

dēw (*V*) to carry *something* in a pocket made *by turning up the lower part of a long gown in front, or formed with a handkerchief, apron, etc.* *As mainV:* 'dēw-dàw carry *something* to a place in this *way;* 'dēw-chǐ-láy pick *something* up *this way;* dēw-'dzěw to pick up and carry away *this way; etc.* ‖tā bǎ 'shèng-shya-de-dūng-shi chywán dēw-'dzěw-le. She gathered up what was left over and carried it off in her gown.

都
dēw (*or* **dū**) (*H*) both, all, altogether; *summarizes and adds up the items specified before it.* ‖wǒ-'fù-mǔ dēw bú-'dzày-le. My parents are both dead. ‖bǎ jwō-'yǐ dēw tsā-'gān-jìng-le. Wipe clean all the furniture. ‖wǒm 'dēw yàw 'chywù. We're all going. ‖wǒm dēw bú-'chywù. None of us are going. ‖wǒm bù-'dēw chywù. We're not all going (*some of us may*). ‖'shéme dēw 'hǎw. Everything is all right. ‖'shéme dēw bù-'hǎw. Nothing is all right. ‖tā 'shéme dēw 'jŕ-dàw. He knows everything. ‖tā 'shéme \dēw bù-'jŕ-dàw. He doesn't know anything. ‖lyán 'jèy-ge tā dēw 'jŕ-dàw. He knows everything, even this.

兜
dēw(r) (*Nunit*, **ge**) pocket (*in clothing*).

斗
děw (*Mcont, Mmeas*) a dry measure. *See Appendix B.* (*NunitC*) wooden container with square sides. **yān-'děw** pīpe (*smoking*).

陡
děw (*A*) steep, *as a hillside.* (*Opposite* **píng**.)

抖擻
'děw-lew (*V*) to shake *something* in the hand *by moving the hand and forearm rapidly back and forth horizontally, as in shaking clothes out.*
    As *mainV*: **'děw-lew-chū-lay** to expose *something hidden* by this action; (*also figuratively, as in English* a shake-up).

逗, 鬭, 鬥
dèw (*V*) to tease, make fun of (*with no bad intentions*). **dèw-'shyàwr, dèw-je 'wár** make fun, tease. ‖tā gēn-ta dèw-je 'wár. He's teasing him; playing with him.

豆
*dèw, 'dèw-dz, dèwr (*Nunit*, **ge**) beans.

豆腐
'dèw-fu (*Nmass*) bean-curd, *made from soya beans ground into powder.*

豆角
dèw-'jyǎwr (*Nunit*, **gēr**) string beans.

逗留
'dèw-lyéw (*I*) to stop, stay. ‖tā 'dèw-lyéw-le lyǎng-'tyān. He stayed over for two days (*somewhat literary*).

逮
děy *see* **day**.

逮
děy *see* **dǎy**.

得
děy (*Vpred*) to have to, must, need to. *Not used in negative except in:* **bù-'děy bū-** to have no alternative but *to do so-and-so.* *Stronger groups:* **bì-'děy, bì-shywū-'děy, děy-'yàw.**

低
dī (*A*) low *physically, in rank, of a pitch.* (*Opposite* **gāw** high.)
    (*V*) to lower; **dī-'téw(r)** *or* **'dī-yi-dī** to duck.

滴
dī (*Mpart*) drop *of any liquid.* **yì-dī-'shwěy** drop of water.
    (*I*) to drip, *especially as mainV:* **'dī-shyà-láy** to drip down, *etc.* ‖'ywǔ tsúng 'fáng-shang 'dī-shyà-láy-le. The rain dripped down from the roof of the house.

提防
'dī-fang (*V*) to be on the alert *against*, to be on guard *against.* ‖ni 'yīng-gay děy 'dī-fang-je ta. You must be on the alert against him.

提溜
'dī-lyew *or* **'dī-le** (*V*) to carry *something* in the hand *with the arm hanging down the side of the body.* As *mainV:* **'dī-le-chī-láy** to pick *something* up *in that way;* **'dī-le-dàw** to carry *something* this way to a place; **dī-le-'dzěw** to pick up and take away. *In these compounds and similar ones* **'dī-le** *may reduce to* **dī**. ‖tā bǎ 'shyāng-dz dī-le-'dzěw-le. He picked up the suitcase and carried it off.

敵
*dí *only before nouns and certain measures;* enemy. **'dí-rén** (*Npers*) an enemy (*person*); **dí-'jywūn** (*N*) the enemy army; **dí-gwó** (*Nunit*, **ge**) an enemy (*country*).

的確
dí-'chywè (*H*) surely, certainly, really. ‖tā dí-'chywè bú-'rèn-shr wo. He really doesn't know me. *or* I assure you he doesn't know me.

迪化
dí-'hwà (*Nunique*) Ti-hua (*capital of Sinkiang province*).

嫡系
dí-'shì (*Npers*) direct descendant. ‖tā-men shŕ 'kǔng-dž-de-dí-'shì. They're direct descendants of Confucius.

抵
*dǐ (*V*) *used in negative:* **bù-'dǐ** not to be as good as. ‖'jèy-ge háy bù-'dǐ 'nèy-ge. This is not even as good as that.

dǐ *as mainV:* **dǐ-bu-'jù, dǐ-bu-'gwò** to be unable to resist, stop, fight back, *an attack, etc., because of inferiority;* to be incomparable with *something, because of inferiority.*

底

dǐ, dyěr (*Nunit,* ge) bottom part of anything; *thing usually specified.* **.běy-'dyěr** bottom of a cup; **shyāng-'dyěr** bottom of a box, *etc.* ‖**běy-dz-'dyěr-shang yěw chá-'yè.** There are some tea leaves in the bottom of the cup.

底稿

dǐ-'gǎwr (*Nunit,* ge) rough draft, general idea *on which a document or talk will be built by amplification.*

抵抗

dǐ-'kàng (*V*) to resist, fight back against. ‖**tā shwō-'nǐ, nǐ 'wèy-shéme bù-dǐ-'kàng(-ta)?** He is speaking (ill) of you, why don't you strike back?

底片

dǐ-'pyàn (*Nunit,* jāng) photographic negative.

底細

dǐ-'shì (*Ncoll*) background details. ‖**tā-de-dǐ-'shì nǐ 'jř-dàw-bù-jř-'dàw?** Do you know the details of his background? (*implying always that something about them has been concealed*).

底下

'dǐ-shyà (*Nplace*) space beneath *anything;* the part which follows (*in reading something*); lower range *in rank, etc.* ‖**jwō-dz-'dǐ-shya yěw-'tǔ.** There's dust under the table. ‖**'dǐ-shyà 'háy yěw shéme?** What comes next? (*when something is being read or told*). ‖**háy yěw 'shéy dzày nǐ-'dǐ-shya dzwò-'shř?** Who else is there working under you?

底下人

'dǐ-shyà-rén (*Npers*) servant.

抵押

dǐ-'yā (*I*) to give something as security; (*Nabstr*) security. ‖**nǐ 'ná shéme-'dūng-shi dǐ-'yā?** What are you going to give as security? ‖**wǒ ná 'jèy-ge dāng dǐ-'yā.** I'll use this as security.
dǐ-yā-'pǐn items pledged as security.

地

dì (*Nplace*) ground, earth, land-surface of the earth. **'dì-shang** on the ground, on the floor; **'dì-shyà** *may mean* under the earth, *or, by contrast with* **'tyān-shang** in the sky, *it often means* on the ground; **dzày 'dì-li dzwò-'gūng** to work in the fields.
(*Nmass*) land. **jèy-kwày-'dì** this piece of land; **yì-lǐ-'dì** a mile (*literally* a mile of land).

第

*dì (*Preord*) *prefixed to numerical expressions to make them ordinal:* **dì-'yì-tséng-léw** the first floor; **dì-'sān-ge-rén** the third man; *etc.*
dì-'yī (*J*) in the first place, to start with, point one.

弟

*dì (*Npers*) younger brother *or* male cousin. *See Appendix A.*

遞

*dì (*V*) hand over, pass *something* by hand; *in* **'dì-yi-dì** pass *something* along *by hand; and in compounds like* **'dì-gěy** pass *something* to *a person;* **'dì-gwò-láy** hand *something* over; **'dì-shàng-chywù** pass *something* up to a superior, submit *something.* ‖**wǒ gèw-bu-'jáw, chǐng-ni gěy-wo 'dì-yi-dì.** I can't reach it, will you pass it to me?

地板

dì-'bàn (*Nmass*) floor. **jèy-kwày-dì-'bǎn** this portion of the floor, part of the floor.

地產

dì-'chǎn (*Nmass*) property *in land,* real property.

地球

dì-'chyéw (*Nunit,* ge) the earth, the globe; bowling ball. **dǎ dì-'chyéw** to bowl, go bowling.

地道

dì-'dàw (*Nunit,* tyáw, ge) tunnel.

地道車

dì-dàw-'chē (*Nunit,* lyàng) subway train, subway car. (*M* lyè *to specify the whole train*).

地帶

'dì-dày (*Nunit,* ge) district, region.

地點

dì-'dyǎn (*Nunit,* ge, chù) a place, an address, location of a place, site. ‖**shywé-'shyàw-de-dì-'dyǎn shř-'nǎr?** Where is the site of the school? (*if the school hasn't yet been built*). *or* Where will I find the school?

地方

'dì-fang(r) (*Nplace,* ge, chù) place, locality, region; point *or* situation. ‖**tā dàw shéme-'dì-fang chywù-le?** Where's he gone to? ‖**nǐ 'jèy-ge-dì-fangr shyě 'tswò-le.** You wrote something wrong here. ‖**'jèy-ge-dì-fang nǐ bù-néng yùng 'nèy-ge-dž.** You can't use that word at this point (*i.e., in this situation, under these conditions*).
dì-fang-'jèng-fǔ local government; **dì-fang-'gwān** local authorities; *etc.*

帝國

'dì-gwó (*Nunit,* ge) an empire.

地震
dì-'jèn (*Nunit*, tsż) earthquake.

　　dì-'jèn fā-'shēng occurrence of an earthquake, there's an earthquake.

地軸
dì-'jéw (*Nunique*) axis of the earth.

地基
dì-'jī (*Nunit*, ge, dzwò) foundation *for some structure*.

地址
dì-'jŕ (*Nunit*, ge, chù) an address (*location*).

地主
dì-'jǔ (*Npers*) landlord, land owner.

地角
dì-'jyǎw (*Nunit*, ge) cape (*of land into water*).

地理
dì-'lǐ(-sì)wé) (*Nabstr*) (the study of) geography.

地名
dì-'míng, dì-'myéngr (*Nunit*, ge) address (*name or designation of a place*).

地平線
dì-píng-'shyàn (*Nunit*, ge, tyáw) horizon *when on land*.

地心吸力
dì-'shīn-shī-'lì (*Nabstr*) the force of gravity.

地下車
dì-shya-'chē (*Nunit*, lyàng) subway car, subway train (*M lyè specifies the latter*).

地線
dì-'shvàn (*Nunit*, tyáw, gēn) ground wire (*radio*).

地毯
dì-'tǎn (*Nunit*, ge) carpet.

地圖
dì-'tú (*Nunit*, jāng) map.

地位
'dì-wèy (*Nunit*, ge) position, job; social position.

地窨子
dì-'yìn-dz (*Nunit*, ge, tséng) basement, cellar.

釘
dǐng (V) to drive *a small pointed thing* into a surface *by hammering on it*; to drive *a nail*; to bite *as a mosquito bites*; to fasten *with nails*.

　　As mainV: 'dǐng-dàw (*lc*) to drive *a nail* into; 'dǐng-jìn (*lc*) to drive *a nail* in; 'dǐng-jù to nail fast; dǐng-'jǐn to nail tight.

　　'dǐng-chǐ-láy to fasten together *not necessarily with nails*, to bind *books*; dǐng-'shū to bind books; dǐng-'jǎng to nail on a horseshoe.

釘
dǐng (V) keep an eye out for, keep an eye on. ‖nǐ 'dǐng-je tā; byé jyàw-ta 'pǎw-le. Keep an eye on him; don't let him get away. ‖dǐng-je-dyǎr. Keep alert! Be careful!

釘子
'dǐng-dz (*Nunit*, ge, gēr) nails (*for fastening*).

丁香
'dǐng-shyāng (*Nunit*, dwèr) lilac (*flower*).

　　dǐng-shyāng-'shù (*Nunit*, kē) lilac bush.

頂
dǐng (V) to push the head against; to carry on the head. dǐng-je 'fēng upwind (*i.e., with head into the wind*); ‖tā 'téw-shang 'dǐng-je yí-ge-'lán-dz 'dzéw-gwo-chywu. She walked by carrying a basket on her head. dǐng yí-'jýwù to talk back, argue, challenge.

　　As mainV: dǐng-'dzéw to force someone to leave (*figurative*); dǐng-'dǎw to knock over, down; dǐng-'hwéy-chýwu to force someone to retreat (*physically or in an argument*).

頂
dǐng (*Munit*) *for headgear of any kind and for* jyàw-dz sedan chair. yì-dǐng-'màw-dz a hat.

頂
dǐng or tǐng (H) very much, most, extreme. ‖dǐng 'hǎw! OK! Darn good!

　　dǐng 'ày to like *something* very much; dǐng 'dwǒ at most. ‖dǐng-'dà-de shŕ ge-shyǎw-nywǔ-'hár. The oldest is a little girl.

頂(兒)
*dǐng, *dyěngr (*Nunit*, ge) top part *of something*. fáng-'dǐng roof; shān-'dǐng mountain cap; màw-'dyěngr topknot on a cap, *etc*.

頂樓
dǐng-'léw(r) (*Nunit*, jyān) attic.

頂棚
dǐng-'péng (*Nunit*, ge) ceiling (*usually refers to a ceiling made of paper*).

頂屋
dǐng-'wū (*Nunit*, jyān) attic.

訂，定
dìng (V) to arrange for, contract for, settle, subscribe to, reserve, book. dìng chwán-'wèy to book passage

on a boat; **dìng-'dzwèr** to reserve seats; **dìng 'hé-tung** to conclude a contract; **dìng-'pyàw** to book tickets; **dìng-'jyàr** to fix prices (*eliminating the necessity of bargaining*); **dìng-'bàw** to subscribe to a newspaper; **dìng ge-'ř-dz** to fix the day (*for some event*).

定舶
dìng-'bwò (*VN1*) to cast anchor (*somewhat literary*).

定舶處
dìng-bwò-'chù (*Nunit*, **ge**, **chù**) berth, slip (*for a ship*).

定錢
'dìng-chyán (*Nmass*) money on deposit.

定罪
dìng-'dzwèy (*VN2*) to pass sentence *in court*.

定做
dìng-'dzwò (*V*) to arrange to have made, to order made, to have made to order. **dìng-'dzwò-de-'yī-fu** tailor-made clothing.

定規
dìng-'gwēy, **'dìng-gwey** (*V*) to select and decide on *a date, a person* (*among several applicants*), *a place, a thing*.

訂婚
dìng-'hwēn (*VN2*) to get engaged (to be married).

都
dū *see* **dēw**.

嘟嚕
'dū-lu (*Mgroup*) a bunch or cluster of *something, joined together but in random arrangement, particularly of things joined together at one end but hanging loose at the other.* A cluster *or* bunch of **'pú-taw** (*grapes*); a bunch of **'yàw-shr** (*keys*); a bunch of **'hwār** (*flowers on a single main stem*); a string of **ywú(r)** (*fish*).

嘟囔
'dū-nang, **'dū-neng** (*V*) to complain, murmur, grumble, *about something.*

毒
dú (*A*) poisonous, deadly, cruel; dangerously hot *of sunshine.*
    (*Nmass*) poisonous substance; **fú-'dú** take poison.
    (*MainV*) **dú-'sž** to poison *someone* to death.

獨
*****dú** (*H*) alone; *only in a few combinations.* **dú 'chàng** to sing alone, sing a solo; **dú 'dzèw** to play a solo.

毒氣
dú-'chì (*Nmass*) poison gas.

獨自
dú-'dž (*H*) alone, independently, by oneself. ‖**tā dú-'dž 'yí-ge-rén dzày-'nàr 'dzěw**. He's walking around there all by himself.

獨立
dú-'lì (*I*) independent. ‖**fù-'nywǔ jīng'jì dú-'lì**. Women are economically independent.
    dú-lì-'gwó an independent country.

獨山
dú-'shān (*Nunique*) Tu-shan *or* Tuhshan (*city in Kweichow province*).

毒蛇
dú-'shé (*Nunit*, **tyáw**) poisonous reptile.

獨身
dú-'shēn (*Aattr*) unmarried. **dú-shēn-'nán-dz** bachelor; **dú-shēn-'nywǔ-dz** unmarried woman.

讀書
dú-'shū (*VN2*) to study books; to study. (*Fairly literary; ordinary term is* **nyàn-'shū**.)

毒水
dú-'shwěy, **dú-'shwěr** (*Nmass*) liquid poison, poison dissolved in water.

獨裁政治
dú-tsáy-'jèng-jř (*Nabstr*) the philosophy or theory of autocracy.

獨裁政體
dú-tsáy-jèng-'tǐ (*Nunit*, **ge**) autocratic government, autocracy.

毒瓦斯
dú-wǎ-'sž (*Nmass*) poison gas.

毒藥
dú-'yàw (*Nmass*) poison, poisonous drug.

堵
dǔ (*V*) to block *a road, traffic, any passageway or conduit.* As mainV: **'dǔ-shàng**, **'dǔ-chǐ-lay** to block up, be blocked, obstructed, stuck. ‖**wǒ-'sǎng-dz 'dǔ-de hěn**. My throat is all clogged up. ‖**wǒ-'bí-dz 'dǔ-de hěn**. My nose is all clogged up. ‖**bǎ nèy-tyáw-'lù 'dǔ-shang**. Block that road. ‖**bǎ nèy-ge-'mén 'dú-chǐ-lay**. Block the door.
    dǔ-'dzwěy (*IN*) to be quiet, keep one's mouth shut, (*from depression or because of being defeated in an argument*).

賭

dǔ (*Nunit*, ge) bet, wager.

　　dǎ (yí-ge-)'dǔ to make a bet. ‖dzám 'dǔ-dyǎr shéme. Let's make a bet . . . . *or* I'll bet you that . . . .

塔

dǔ (*Munit*) *with* chyáng wall.

鍍

dù (*V*) to gild, to plate.　yùng-'jīn dù 'shěw-shr plate the jewelry with gold; dù-'jīn-de gold-plated; dù-'yín-de silver-plated.

　　dù yì-tséng-'jīn to apply one layer of gold plate.

渡

dù (*V*) to ferry across; dù-'hé (*VN2*) to ferry across a river.　'dù-gwò (*lc*) to ferry across; dù-'dzěw to ferry away; 'dù-dàw (*lc*) to ferry to *a place* (*somewhat literary*).

度

dù (*Mmeas*) degree, *for anything measured in degrees.* 'sz̀-shr-wǔ-'dù(-de)-'jyǎwr a forty-five degree angle.

　　In N compounds, the first member specifying the quality measured: wēn-'dù temperature; shr̄-'dù humidity; wān-'dù curvature; sù-'dù *or* shù-'dù speed; gāw-'dù altitude; *etc.* ‖jīn-tyan wēn-'dù 'bā-shr-dù. Today's temperature is eighty degrees.

渡船

dù-'chwán (*Nunit*, jr̄) ferryboat.

肚子

'dù-dz (*Nunit*, ge) stomach; belly.

度數

'dù-shù (*Mmeas*) degree (*same as* dù *alone*).

東

dūng (*Nplace*) east. dūng *is to the other directions in Chinese as* north *is to the others in English; when boxing the compass one says* 'dūng 'nán 'shī 'běy east, south, west, north. East *and* west *come first in the compound direction expressions:* dūng-'nán southeast; shī-'nán southwest; shī-'běy northwest; dūng-'běy northeast.

　　The simple direction words are used (1) *after a V or K of motion:* ‖shyàng-'dūng dzěw. Go east. *or* Go to the east. ‖jèy-tyáw-tyě-'lù shr̀ tsúng-'dūng-dàw-'shī-de. This railroad runs east and west.

　　(2) *Before nominal expressions:* dūng-'mén the east gate (*especially of a city*); dūng-'chyáng east wall (*of a small enclosure*).

　　Elsewhere the simple direction words are replaced by longer forms: dūng-'bù eastern region *or* part; 'dūng-byan *or* 'dūng-byar eastern side. ‖tā tsúng 'měy-gwo-'dūng-bù láy-de. He comes from the eastern part of the United States.

China has no dūng-'bù *or* shī-'bù, *such words being used primarily when pointing to regions on a map; but one does speak of the* 'běy-fāng north *and the* 'nán-fāng south *of China:* ‖tā shr̀ 'běy-fang-rén. He's a southerner. *Otherwise there are idiomatic combinations for giving locality in terms of a direction from a landmark, especially a city:* ‖tā tsúng jīng-'dūng láy-de. He's from east of Peiping (jīng-'dūng *literally* capital's east). *Some of the provinces have names of this kind:* shān-'dūng mountain's east; shān-'shī mountain's west; shǎn-'shī Shan-plateau's west; hú-'nán lake's south; hú-'běy lake's north; *etc.*

冬（冬天）

*dūng, 'dūng-tyan (*Ntime*) winter.

東海

dūng-'hǎy (*Nunique*) The East China Sea.

東海

dūng-'hǎy (*Nunique*) Tung-hai (*city in Kiangsu province*).

東京

dūng-'jīng (*Nunique*) Tokyo.

東家

'dūng-jya (*Npers*) owner, host. ‖jèy-ge-'fáng-dz-de-'dūng-jya shr̀-'shéy? Who's the owner of this house?

東西

'dūng-shi (*Nunit*, ge, jyàn) thing. 'dūng-shi *is always something material, that can be touched, tasted, seen, heard; the word for* thing *in the immaterial sense* (matter, affair) *is* shr̀. *Calling a person a* 'dūng-shi *is an insult, but saying that a person isn't a* 'dūng-shi *is worse.*

懂

dǔng (*V*) to understand, comprehend. ‖wǒ-'shwō-de nǐ 'dǔng-bu-dǔng? Do you understand what I said?

　　As postV: tīng-'dǔng to listen to and understand; kàn-'dǔng to look at (*or* read) and understand, *etc.* ‖wǒ tīng-bu-'dǔng nǐ-de-'hwà. I don't understand what you're saying.

懂事

dǔng-'shr̀ (*A*) to have an understanding of things in general. ‖tā-'nèy-ge-rén hěn dǔng-'shr̀. That man has lots of common sense.

　　dǔng-'shr̀-de-rén a practical person.

董事

'dǔng-shr̀ (*Npers*) member of a board *of directors or trustees.*

董事會

dǔng-shr̀-'hwèy (*Nunit*, ge) board of trustees, trustees.

洞

dùng (*Nunit*, ge) hole, cavity, burrow, cave. **dùng-'kěw** (*Nunit*, ge) mouth of a cave; **dùngr** a small hole, small cavity.

    dǎ yí-ge-'dùng(r) to drill a hole; **wā yí-ge-'dùng(r)** to dig a hole.

凍

dùng (*I*) to freeze; **'dùng-je-le** to have caught a cold. *As mainV:* **dùng-'lyè** to freeze and burst *or*, (*of skin*) to freeze and crack open; **'dùng-shàng** to freeze over *of a river, etc.;* **dùng-'bīng** to freeze into ice.

動

dùng (*I*) to move *only in the sense of to stop being at rest. As postV:* **dzěw-bu-'dùng** to be unable to walk; **lā-'dùng(-le)** to set something into motion by pulling at it; *etc.* ‖**byé 'dùng!** Don't touch! (*that is, don't disturb it*), *or* Don't move!

    dùng yí-ge-'dzěr to move a piece in some board game; *also used causatively in some other cases.*

    Note **'dùng-bu-dùng** *in the following use.* ‖**nèy-ge-shyǎw-'hár 'dùng-bu-dùng jyèw 'kū.** That child cries at the drop of a hat (*i.e., the moment you make any motion at all*).

動作

dùng-'dzwò (*Nabstr*) exercise, calisthenics.

動感情

dùng 'gǎn-chíng (*VN1*) to stir up one's own emotions, become aroused. ‖**tā-'jèy-ge-rén yǎn-'shwō de-shŕ-hew hěn 'rúng-yì dùng 'gǎn-chíng.** When that fellow makes a speech he lets his emotions run away with him.

動機

dùng-'jī (*Nunit*, ge) reason, motive. ‖**tā-de-dùng-'jī hěn 'hǎw.** His motives are good.

動脈

dùng-'mày (*Nunit*, tyáw) artery (*blood*).

動人

dùng-'rén (*A*) arousing, exciting, moving, *to sympathy or admiration.* ‖**tā-de-yǎn-'jyǎng hěn dùng-'rén.** His speech was very moving.

動身

dùng-'shēn (*VN1*) to start to go, *of someone going on a long trip.* ‖**tā dùng-'shēn-le méy-yew?** Has he left yet?

動手

dùng-'shěw (*VN2*) to move one's hand, *either* to strike someone; *or figuratively* in order to get some job going.

    dùng-chi 'shěw-lay-le to have started to fight, to have come to blows.

動手術

dùng shěw-'shù (*VN2*) to undergo a surgical operation.

動彈

'dùng-tan *or* **'dùng-ten** (*I*) to be moving, to move, be in motion, *only in the sense of not being at rest.* ‖**nǐ byé 'dùng-ten; wǒ bǎ nèy-ge-mì-'fēng tsúng nǐ-'bwó-dz-shang 'děy-shya-lay.** Don't move; I'll catch that bee (that's on your neck).

洞庭湖

dùng-tíng-'hú (*Nunique*) The Tung-t'ing Lake.

動物

'dùng-wu (*Nunit*, ge, jǔng, téw, jř, tyáw, *etc.*) animal; member of the animal kingdom.

動物園

dùng-wu-'ywán (*Nunit*, ge) zoo.

動武

dùng-'wǔ (*VN1*) to use force (*not military*) to come to blows, resort to violence.

動議

dùng-'yì (*VN1*) to make a motion (*in a meeting*).

端

dwān (*V*) to carry with hand *or hands* stretched out, *as one carries a tray in front of oneself. As mainV:* **'dwān-dàw** (*lc*) carry *something thus to a place;* **'dwān-chǐ-láy** pick up *in this way;* **'dwān-shàng** (*lc*) to bring on *food carried this way,* serve food.

端莊

dwān-'jwāng (*A*) dignified (*of a woman only*).

端架子

dwān 'jyà-dz (*VN1*) to make an unnatural and dramatic gesture *with hand, face, or whole body; figuratively also, as when someone turns down an invitation to dinner.*

短

dwǎn (*A*) short (*opposite* **cháng** long); *in extent or duration.*

    Also as in this sentence: ‖**wǒ 'dwǎn-le 'yí-kwày-chyán.** I'm short a dollar.

短處

dwǎn-'chù (*Nunit*, ge) shortcoming, fault, defect, (*especially of a person*).

短褲

dwǎn-'kù (*Nunit*, tyáw) shorts, trunks (*outside garment*).

短篇

dwǎn-'pyǎn (*Aattr*) short (*of a story, document, editorial, etc.*).　yí-ge-dwǎn-'pyǎn(-de)-'gù-shr a short story; dwǎn-pyǎn-'gù-shr or dwǎn-pyǎn-shyǎw-'shwō short story (*as a special type of writing, not just a story that happens to be short*).

斷

dwàn (*I*) to break into segments, *of something long*. *As postV* bǎy-'dwàn to break *something long* into segments *by grasping the ends and applying pressure up or down.*

緞

*dwàn, 'dwàn-dz (*Nmass*) satin cloth.

段

dwàn, dwàr (*Mpart*) segment *of something that has length more than width and thickness; or of some continuous event.* A stretch of lù (*road*), a paragraph or short portion of shīn-'wén (*the news*), hwà (*a story or recounting of something*); a measure or movement or portion of yīn-'ywè (*music*).

斷定

dwàn-'dìng (*Vsent*) to decide. ‖nǐ 'dzěme néng-gèw dwàn-'dìng tā-'dzwò-de bú-'dwèy-ne? How could you decide that he hadn't done it right?

斷崖

dwàn-'yá(y) (*Nunit*, ge) bluff, cliff, precipice. (*Somewhat literary.*)

頓, 撉

dwēn (*I*) to jolt, shake several times, bounce up and down. 'dwēn yí-shyà(r) shake once. ‖chí-'mǎ de-shŕ-hew 'dwēn-de 'lì-hày. When riding a horse you bounce up and down quite violently. ‖wǒm 'dwēn-le yí-'shyà-dz. We got a jolt (*physical*).

噸

dwēn or **dwèn** ton. *See Appendix B.*

燉

dwèn (*V*) to cook by placing in water over a slow fire. báy 'dwèn or chīng 'dwèn to do this with little or no soya sauce; húng 'dwèn to do this with a good deal of soya sauce; dwèn-'jī(-'rèw, *etc.*) (*VN3*) chicken (*or meat, etc.*) cooked this way.

頓

dwèn (*MdistT*) a short spell, a pause for. yí-dwèn-'fàn a meal.

āy yí-dwèn-... *with a V in the blank to be* ...*-ed for a spell:* āy yí-dwèn-'shwō to get a calling down; *etc.*

Used after verbs: 'shwō-ta yí-'dwèn or bǎ-ta 'shwō yí-'dwèn give him a talking to; 'nàw-le yí-'dwèn to cause a disturbance for a while.

鈍

dwèn (*A*) dull, dulled, *of a knife blade, etc.* (*Opposite* kwày.)

堆

dwēy (*V*) to heap up, pile up. ‖bǎ-'shū dēw gěy 'dwēy-nèr. Pile the books up there.

As mainV: dwēy-'mǎn pile up, load up *until the space covered is full.* ‖dwēy-'mǎn-le 'nǎr-nǎr dēw-shr 'shū. There were piles of books all over, filling the whole place up.

堆

dwēy, dwēr (*Mgroup*) pile of, heap of. Bank of shywě (*snow*); crowd of rén (*people*); stack of tsǎw (*hay, straw*); etc.

對, 兌

dwèy (*V*) to dilute with. dwèy-'shwěy to dilute with water, add water; dwèy-'jyěw to add some wine, dilute with wine.

As mainV: 'dwèy-dzày to put *the diluting liquid* into *the diluted mixture.* ‖dwèy-'shwěy dwèy-dzay 'yàw-li. Dilute the medicine with water.

對

dwèy (*A*) correct, right (*opposite* tswò wrong, mistaken). ‖wǒ 'shwō-de 'dwèy-bu-dwèy? Have I said the right thing? or Did I speak correctly? ‖'jèy-jyàn-shr wǒ °'dzwò-de bú-'dwèy. or °méy-dzwò 'dwèy. I did that thing wrong.

對

dwèy (*V*) to set *a clock or watch* to the right time. dwèy-'jūng, dwèy-'byǎw to check, correct, proof-read. ‖chǐng-ni gěy-wo 'dwèy-yí-dwèy wǒ 'shyě-de-wen-jāng. Please proof-read this article (I wrote) for me. ‖chǐng-ni gěy-wo 'dwèy-yi-dwèy 'shù-mu. Please check these figures for me.

對

dwèy (*K*) to a person, only in such expressions as: ‖wǒ dwèy-ta 'shwō...I said to him... ‖wǒ dwèy-ta hěn 'hǎw. I've been very good to him.

'dwèy-je facing. ‖wǒ 'dwèy-je tā 'dzwò-je. I'm sitting facing him. ‖tā-de-'chwāng-hu dwèy-je 'chyáng. His window faces a wall.

Note such forms as lyǎn-dwèy-'lyǎn or myàn-dwèy-'myàn face-to-face.

隊

dwèy (*Mgroup*) organized group of, team of, *people of some special kind.* A body of bīng (*soldiers in formation*); a team of chyéw-'ywán (*ball-players*).

yīn-ywè-'dwèy a band (*music*).

對

dwèy, dwèr (*Mgroup*) pair of *things which are not identical, but matching more or less as mirror-images do.*

A set of 'shwàng-sheng (*twins*); a pair of dž-'mèy *sisters*); a pair of bā (*eights in poker*).

對半兒
dwèy-'bàr (*VN1*) to go halves, each pay his own, go Dutch, (*only of two people*).

對不起
dwèy-bu-'chǐ (*RC2*) to be unable to face *someone* as an equal. *Used as a polite expression of apology*, I beg pardon, excuse me, *etc.; when one has made a slight social error, or when one must leave a group, etc.*

對待
'dwèy-dày (*V*) to treat, deal with *people; usually with a following expression of manner of treatment.* ‖tā 'dwèy-dày wǒ-men hěn 'hǎw. He treated us very well.

對敵
dwèy-'dí (*Npers*) opponent, opposing force, enemy. ‖tā shr̀ wǒ-de-yí-ge-dwèy-'dí. He's one of my opponents.

對抵
dwèy-'dǐ (*I*) to offset each other, balance each other (*of two things; e.g., accounts, etc.*) ‖jèy-lyǎng-jywù-'hwà dwèy-'dǐ-le. These two statements cancel each other out.

對方
'dwèy-fāng (*Npers*) the opposing party, opponent; the other party. wǒ-men-de-'dwèy-fāng our opponent(s), the other side (*in a game for example*).

對付
'dwèy-fù (*A*) satisfactory *though not perfect.* ‖tā 'dzwò-de jèy-jyàn-'shr̀-ching hěn 'dwèy-fu. He did an adequate enough job of it.

(*V*) to meet *a situation* successfully, to deal with *a person who constitutes a problem* successfully. ‖wǒ bù-jr̄-'dàw dzěme 'dwèy-fu ta. I don't know how to handle him.

過兒
dwèy-'gwèr (*Aattr*) across the street, the river, the road, *etc.* ‖dwèy-'gwèr-de-'fáng-dz dzwó-tyan-'wǎn-shang jáw-le 'hwǒ-le. The house across the street caught fire last night.

兌換
dwèy-'hwàn (*V*) to change *money* (*give smaller denominations for larger, or vice versa*). ‖wǒ gěy-ni dwèy-'hwàn 'wǔ-kwày-chyán. I'll give you change for five.

隊長
dwèy-'jǎng (*Npers*) captain, leader, person in charge *of some team, group, unit of people.*

對不住
dwèy-bu-'jù (*RC2*) to be unable to face *someone* as an equal. *Used as a polite expression of apology, when one has made an accidental slight social error or when one must leave a group, etc.*

對勁兒
dwèy-'jyèr (*VN1*) to be matched, equal, well fit together. ‖tām-'lyǎ hěn dwèy-'jyèr. Those two get along very well together. ‖tām-'lyǎ bú-dwèy-'jyèr. Those two don't get along well together. ‖wǒ shyàn-'dzày yěw yì-dyǎr-bú-dwèy-'jyèr. I'm not feeling up to par right now. ‖tā yí-'kàn, nèy-ge-'chíng-shing bú-dwèy-'jyèr, tā jyèw 'pǎw-le. He saw immediately that the situation was unfavorable, so he escaped.

對門
dwèy-'mén, dwèy-'mér (*Nplace*) the building *or* house across the street from this one.

對面
dwèy-'myàn, dwèy-'myàr (*Nplace*) the building *or* space facing this one *across the street, river, road, etc.;* the other side *of anything.* ‖tā 'jèng dzwò wǒ-de-dwèy-'myàr. He sat directly opposite me (*and facing me; thus across a table, but not across an aisle*).

對手
dwèy-'shěw (*Npers*) (1) rival, competitor, (2) one's match, one's equal *at something.* ‖tā 'bú-shr wǒ-de-dwèy-'shěw. He's no match for me.

兌現
dwèy-snyàn (*VN1*) to cash (*a check*), redeem (*a bond, etc.*). ‖jèy-jāng-'pyàw-dz 'néng-bu-néng dwèy-'shyàn? Is this bill redeemable? (*e.g., of a banknote put out by bank that may have failed since*).

對題
dwèy-'tí (*VN1*) to be to the point; *more often used in negative.* ‖ni-'shwō-de bú-'dwèy-'tí. You didn't stick to the point in your remarks.

隊員
dwèy-'ywán (*Npers*) members of a team, group, unit.

對於
'dwèy-ywu (*K*) concerning, as to. ‖wǒ dwèy-ywu 'nèy-jyàn-shr̀-ching 'méy shéme kě-'shwō-de. I have nothing to say about that matter.

多
dwō (*A*) much, many. ‖yěw hěn-dwō-de-'tswèr. There are a lot of errors. ‖'tswò-de-dì-fang bú-tày 'dwō. There aren't so very many errors.

(*H*) *before A* how much so?, to what extent?, *or, with stress*, how much so! ‖'nèy-dzwò-léw yěw dwō-'gāw? How high is that building? ‖'nèy-dzwò-léw 'dwō-gāw-a! How high that building is!

(H) before verbal expression more, some more. ‖**nĭ yīng-gay 'dwō 'chĭ-yì-dyăr.** You ought to eat a little more.

Added to an expression of quantity or number to mean more than *that amount:* **sān-shr-dwō-'nyán** more than thirty years; **sān-shr-'dwō-ge-rén** more than thirty people.

多半
dwō-'bàn *(J)* probably. ‖**dwō-'bàn tā bù-'láy.** He's probably not coming.

    dwō-'bàn-de most of. **dwō-'bàn-de-rén** most of the men.

一多半兒
yì-'dwō-bàr *(N)* most of *something.* ‖**nèy-běn-'shū-de-yì-'dwō-bàr tā dēw bù-'dŭng.** He doesn't understand the greater part of that book. ‖**jèy-shyē-'rén-li yì-'dwō-bàr dēw bú-'ywàn-yi 'dzěw.** Most of these people aren't at all willing to go.

多喒
'dwō-dzěn *(Ntime)* when, at what time? ‖**nĭ 'dwō-dzěn ké-yi 'láy?** When can you come? *(local Peiping).*

多嘴
dwō-'dzwěy *(A)* be talkative; be inclined to indulge in gossip.

多會兒
'dwō-hwer *(Ntime)* when, at what time? ‖**nĭ 'dwō-hwer chĭ-'fàn?** When do you eat? *(local Peiping).*

多麼
'dwō-me *(H) used like* **dwō** *as H before A and some verbal expressions.* ‖**'nèy-dzwò-léw (yěw) dwō-me 'gāw?** How high is that building? ‖**'nèy-dzwò-léw 'dwō-me gāw-a!** How high that building is! ‖**tā 'dwō-me 'àyta!** Gee! How he loves her! ‖**tā 'dwō-me ày chĭ-'fàn!** Gee! How he loves to eat!

多少
'dwō-shǎw how much? how many? *when the answer is expected to be larger than about ten, or when there is no definite expectation (compare* **jĭ**). ‖**'dwō-shaw-chyán?** How much? ‖**dzwò 'jèy-jyàn-shr̆ děy yùng 'dwō-shaw-shr̆-hew?** How long will it take to do this job? *(Literally* To do this job must use how much time?*)*

    dwŏr *occurs as an abbreviation of* **dwō-shaw** *in some expressions:* ‖**dwŏr-'chyán?** How much?

多數
'dwō-shùr *(N)* the majority of *any group.* ‖**jèy-shyē-'rén-li 'dwō-shùr ....** The majority of these men ....

多謝
‖**dwō-'shyè!** Many thanks!

哆索
'dwō-swo *(A)* to quiver, shake, shiver, tremble. ‖**tā-'shěw jr̆ 'dwō-swo.** His hand is always trembling. ‖**tā-**

'shěw yěw yì-dyăr-'dwō-swo. His hand is trembling a little. ‖**tā 'lěng-de jr̆ 'dwō-swo.** He's shivering from the cold. ‖**tā shwō-'hwà dwō-dwo-swo-'swō-de.** His voice trembled as he talked.

奪
dwó *(V)* to take away, deprive someone of *something.* *(A sneak-thief doesn't* **dwó**; *it implies open maneuvering.)* ‖**tā bǎ wǒ-de-'dì-wèy dwó-le.** He deprived me of my job.

    As mainV: **dwó-'dzěw** *or* **'dwó-chywù** to take away.

躲
dwǒ *(V)* to avoid *a person, situation, danger;* to escape, hide from, withdraw from, *such things.* **dwǒ-'ywŭ** to take cover from the rain. ‖**wǒ shàng-'nàr chywù 'dwǒ (yì-)dwěr 'ywŭ.** I went there to avoid the rain. ‖**tā 'dwǒ-ta.** He avoids her.

    As mainV: **'dwǒ-kāy** to withdraw, to draw back out of the way; **'dwǒ-chĭ-láy** to take cover, to hide. ‖**'dwǒ-kay 'dwǒ-kay!** Make way!

朵
dwǒ, dwěr *(Munit)* a **hwār** *(flower), or with the term for any specific kind of flower.*

躲避
dwǒ-'bì *(V)* to avoid, sidestep, *a person, trouble, worry, etc.*

舵輪
dwò-'lwér *(Nunit,* ge) steering wheel.

顛
***dyān** *(V)* to move up and down. **'dyān-dyan** to estimate *the weight of something by holding it in the palm, face up, and moving the hand up and down. As mainV:* **'dyān-chĭ-láy** to jolt up and down. ‖**chē 'kāy-de 'kwày de-shŕ-hew wǒm jyèw 'dyān-chi-lay-le.** When the car went fast we were jolted up and down.

點
dyăn *(V)* to count off, itemize. *Usually* **dyăn 'míng(-dz)** *(VN2)* call a roll, read names off a list; **dyăn-'chyán** *(VN2)* to count off, check through, financial items on a bill or in an account book. *As mainV:* **'dyăn-chū-lay** to check *the things counted* off as one reads *them, in order to keep one's place or to keep the record straight;* **'dyăn-dàw** to call a roll up to *the name of a particular person.* ‖**tā 'dyăn-dàw 'nĭ de-shŕ-hew nĭ bú-'dzày-jèr.** When he reached you in calling the roll you weren't here.

典
dyăn *(V)* to mortgage *(of the bank, not the owner).* **'dyăn-gey** to mortgage for *the owner;* **'dyăn-chū-chywù** to be mortgaged. ‖**wǒ bǎ jèy-swǒ-'fáng-dz 'dyăn-chū-chywù-le.** I've mortgaged my house.

點

dyǎn (V) to ignite, apply a match to, kindle. dyǎn-'hwǒ to light a fire; dyǎn-'dēng to light a lamp; etc. As mainV: 'dyǎn-shàng to light; 'dyǎn-jáw to get lit, or set fire to. ‖yì-'dyǎn jyèw 'jáw. It ignites the moment you touch the flame to it.
(Figuratively) quick-tempered.

點

dyǎn, dyǎr (Mpart) a little bit of, a drop of, small piece of, a little of anything at all. 'kwày-yi-dyǎr a little faster; 'hǎw-yi-dyǎr a little better; 'cháng(-le) yì-dyǎr a little too long; etc., after adjectives.
yěw yì-dyǎr-'kwày it's a bit fast(er); yěw yì-dyǎr-'rè it's rather hot; etc., after yěw and before an adjective.
Form dyǎn only, with N jūng, hour, o'clock. 'sān-dyǎn-jūng three o'clock.

點

dyǎn, dyǎr (Nunit, ge) dot, period, decimal point. dyǎn yí-ge-'dyǎr to write a period.
(Figuratively) point in an argument or discussion.
dyǎr only, raindrop. dyàw-'dyǎr (IN) to rain when it is just starting and only a few drops are felt.

典故

dyǎn-'gù (Nunit, ge) the story of something (real, true); the story of someone's life; the story behind something.

點心

'dyǎn-shǐn (Nmass) pastry, cakes, and the like, of the kind used for casual refreshment, afternoon teas, between-meal snacks.

點頭

dyǎn-'téw(r) (VN1) to nod one's head (indicating yes).

店

dyàn (Nunit, ge, jyān) store, shop; usually in compounds. dzá-hwò-'dyàn general store; fàn-'dyàn hotel (Western type); etc.

電

dyàn (Nmass) electricity. jyē-'dyàn to connect an electric circuit, connect the circuits in a house to the power line. (Used mainly in compounds.)

墊

dyàn (V) to put padding under, in order to soften or raise. 'dyàn-je 'shwèy to pad a surface before sleeping on it. ‖ywàn-dz-lǐ-tew 'dì-shang tày 'cháw, 'dyàn-je dyǎr-'dūng-shi dzwò-je-ba.' The ground in the garden is too wet; put something under you when you sit down.

dyàn-'dàwr, dyàn-dyàn 'dàwr (figuratively) to smooth the way.

墊 (子)

*dyàn, 'dyàn-dz, dyàr (Nunit, ge) pad, cushion. yǐ(-dz)-'dyàn cushion on a chair; shyé-'dyàr pad in a shoe or doormat.

電報

dyàn-'bàw (Nunit, ge, fēng in an envelope, jāng written on paper) telegram. dǎ dyàn-'bàw send a telegram; shēw dyàn-'bàw or jyē dyàn-'bàw receive a telegram; fān dyàn-'bàw to code or decode a telegram (substituting number groups for the characters).

電報機

dyàn-bàw-'jī (Nunit, ge) telegraph apparatus.

電報局

dyàn-bàw-'jywú (Nunit, jyā, ge) telegraph office, either a place where telegrams can be sent and received, or a business office.
dyàn-bàw-jywú-'jǎng director of a telegraph office (government official).

電波

dyàn-'bwō (Nabstr) radio beam, radio waves.

電表

dyàn-'byǎw (Nunit, ge) electric current meter; electric clock.

電車

dyàn-'chē (Nunit, lyàng) electric car, (particularly) streetcar.
dyàn-chē-'jàn streetcar stop.

電氣

dyàn-'chì (Nmass) electric power.

電池

dyàn-'chǐ (Nunit, ge, jyé) battery (electric).

電燈

dyàn-'dēng (Nunit, dzǎn, ge) electric lamp, electric light.

電燈泡

dyàn-dēng-'pàwr (Nunit, ge) electric light bulb.

墊子

'dyàn-dz (Nunit, ge) pad put on something to soften it when you sit down.

電話

dyàn-'hwà (Nunit, ge) telephone; telephone message. dǎ dyàn-'hwà, tūng dyàn-'hwà to make a phone call; jyē dyàn-'hwà to answer the phone, receive a call.

電話格子
dyàn-hwà-'gé-dz (*Nunit*, ge) telephone booth.

電話機
dyàn-hwà-'jī. (*Nunit*, ge, jyà) telephone, telephonic apparatus.

電話局
dyàn-hwà-'jywú (*Nunit*, jyā, ge) telephone exchange, telephone office.

電話綫
dyàn-hwà-'shyàn (*Nmass*) telephone lines, telephone wires.

惦記
'dyàn-jì (*V*) be concerned about, be anxious about.

電烙鐵
dyàn-'làw-tye (*Nunit*, ge) electric iron (*for clothes*).

電鈴
dyàn-'líng, dyàn-'lyéngr (*Nunit*, ge) electric bell.
    'èn dyàn-'lyéngr to ring a bell by pressing a button.

電碼
dyàn-'mǎr (*Nunit*, ge) telegraph *or* radio code; the code signal for a single letter *or* word. **fān dyàn-'mǎr** to encode *or* decode.

電門
dyàn-'mén (*Nunit*, ge) electric switch. **kāy dyàn-'mén** close a switch (*turn it on*); **gwān dyàn-'mén** open a switch (*turn it off*).

電瓶
dyàn-'píng (*Nunit*, ge) battery (*electric*). **gān-dyàn-'píng** dry cell.

電綫
dyàn-'shyàn (*Nmass*, tyáw, gēn) electric wire, wire.

電燙
dyàn-'tàng (*V*) to *permanently* wave. **dyàn-'tàng 'téw-fa** to get a permanent wave.

電梯
dyàn-'tī (*Nunit*, ge) elevator (*electric*).

電影
dyàn-'yǐng, dyàn-'yěngr (*Nunit*, ge) a movie.
    With M jywǎn, jywǎr, reel of movie film.

電影院
dyàn-yǐng-'ywàn (*Nunit*, jyā) movie theater.

店員
dyàn-'ywán (*Npers*) clerk.

叼
dyāw (*V*) to hold between the teeth, *as a pipe*; to hold in a beak. ‖**nyǎwr dyāw-je yí-kwày-'rèw.** The bird has a piece of meat in his beak.

彫
dyāw (*V*) to sculpture, to sculpt. **dyāw-'hwǎr** to sculpt flowers.

彫刻
dyāw-'kè (*Nabstr*) the art *of* sculpture.
    dyāw-'kè-de-dūng-shi a sculptured thing, a thing made by sculpturing.

彫刻家
dyāw-kè-'jyā (*Npers*) sculptor.

釣
dyàw (*V*) to pull *something* upwards *on a string or rope*.
    dyàw-'ywú to fish *with hook and line*.
    As mainV: **'dyàw-shàng** (*lc*) to catch *the fish* on the hook and pull it up; **'dyàw-chǐ-lay** *emphasizes the pulling up*.

調
dyàw (*V*, *lc*) to transfer *someone* to *a place*. ‖**bǎ-ta gěy dyàw-'nǎr chywù-le?** Where was he transferred to?
    As mainV: **'dyàw-dàw** (*lc*) transfer *someone* to *a place*; **dyàw-'dzěw** transfer *someone* away; **'dyàw-hwéy** (*lc*) to transfer *someone* back to *a place*.

吊
dyàw (*I*) to hang loosely from a pivoting point *like a pendulum*.
    'dyàw-sž (*RC2*) to kill by hanging, to hang.

掉
dyàw (*I*) to fall, drop, fall off, drop off; (*causatively*) to lose *something that falls from the clothing, etc.* As *mainV:* **'dyàw-shyà** (*lc*) to drop down; **'dyàw-chū** (*lc*) to fall out of *something* (*a plane for example*); **'dyàw-dzày** to fall onto *or* into; **dyàw 'dì-shya** to fall *or* drop to the ground. ‖**wǒ-de-'yī-fu dyàw-le yí-ge-'kèw-dz.** I lost a button off my clothes.
    As postV: **dǎ-'dyàw** to cause *something* to fall by striking *it*; **yáw-'dyàw** to cause *something* to fall by shaking *it; etc.*
    Contrast **dyàw** *with* **dǎw**: *a branch of a tree may* **dyàw** *to the ground; the whole tree would* **dǎw** *to the ground, and could only* **dyàw** *over a cliff on which it was growing.*

調查
dyàw-'chá (*V*) to investigate, check up on. ‖**dyàw-'chá jèy-ge-'shř-ching.** Investigate this matter.

掉點
dyàw-'dyǎr (*IN*) to drizzle *before a rain*.

調（子，兒）
'dyàw-dz, dyàwr (*Nunit*, ge) melody, tune.

掉片了
dyàw-'pyàr-le (*IN*) to peel off (*of paint*).

吊喪
dyàw-'sāng (*VN1*) to attend a funeral

爹
dyē (*Npers*) papa, daddy.

碟（子，兒）
'dyé-dz, 'dyéer (*Nunit* ge; fù, tàw a set of) plates (*for serving food*).

蝶形領帶
'dyé-shíng-lǐng-'dày (*Nunit* ge, tyáw) a bow tie.

地兒
dyèr (*Nabstr*) background *of a pattern* (*in printed cloth, for example*).

丟
dyēw (*V*) to lose; to discard, cast aside. *As mainV*: 'dyēw-chū-chywù to throw away; 'dyēw-dzày to lose *something* at *a place*; dyēw-'dzěw to throw away; 'dyēw-dàw (*lc*) to lose *something* at *a place*, to discard *something* at *a place*; 'dyēw-shyà-chywù to throw down, discard. ‖wǒ 'dyēw-le yí-kwày-'chyán. I lost a dollar. ‖bǎ 'jyèw-'yī-fu 'dyēw-chū-chywu. Throw out the old clothes. ‖bǎ 'nèy-jyàn-shr̀-ching dyēw-'kāy-le. Put that matter out of your mind.

丟臉
dyēw-'lyǎn (*VN1*) to behave in a way that causes loss of face; to lose face; to behave disgracefully, misbehave.

丟人
dyēw-'rén (*VN1*) to behave in a way that causes loss of face; to behave compromisingly, disgracefully. ‖byé gěy-wo dyēw-'rén-le. Don't misbehave.

子
*dz *element added to other elements to form nouns. Thus*: shì drama, 'shì-dz actor; shwā to brush, 'shwā-dz comb; *etc.*

資格
'dz̄-ge (*Nabstr*) qualifications *for anything*. ‖'nǐ yěw 'dz̄-ge. You have the qualifications. ‖tā bú-'gèw dz̄-ge. He's not sufficiently qualified.

姿勢
'dz̄-shr̀ (*Nabstr*) form *at a sport*, bodily posture, stance (*as when playing some athletic game*); gait.

滋味
'dz̄-wèr (*Nabstr*) taste, sensation, *produced by some food or by some act*. ‖'dz̄-wèr bú-'dà hǎw 'shèw. The taste of it wasn't too good. *or* (*figuratively and literally*) It left a bad taste in my mouth.

紫
dz̀ (*A*) purple.

子彈
dz̀-'dàn (*Nunit*, ge', kē, lì) bullet; cartridge; live shell.

仔細
dz̀-'shì (*A*) careful, meticulous.

自
*dz̀ self (dz̀-'jǐ); from; (*both meanings literary*).

字
dz̀, dzèr (*Nunit*, ge) character (*unit symbol of the Chinese writing system*); a type for one character (*printing*).

自稱自讚
dz̀-'chēng-dz̀-'dzàn (*literary quotation*) to boast, brag. ‖tā 'cháng-cháng dz̀ 'chēng dz̀ 'dzàn. He's always blowing his own horn.

自大
dz̀-'dà (*A*) conceited.

自動機
dz̀-dùng-'jī (*Nunit*, jyà, ge) self-operating motor.

自動手鎗
'dz̀-dùng-shěw-'chyāng (*Nunit*, bǎ) automatic pistol.

字典
dz̀-'dyǎn (*Nunit*, běn, běr) dictionary of Chinese characters which gives no expressions of several characters.

自己
'dz̀-jǐ (*H*) oneself. ‖wǒ-'dz̀-jǐ bú-'chywù. I myself am not going. ‖wǒ bú-'dz̀-jǐ 'chywù. I'm not going alone. *Used nominally*: ‖tā 'dz̀-jǐ gēn 'dz̀-jǐ shwō-'hwà. He's talking to himself.

自個，自己個
dz̀-(jǐ-)'gěr (*H*) by oneself, alone; oneself. tā-'dz̀-jǐ-gěr-de-dǎ-dz̀-'jǐ his own typewriter (*not someone else's*). ‖ràng-wo 'dz̀-gěr láy-ba. Let me do it myself; (don't do it for me).

字紙簍
dz̀-jř-'lěw(r) (*Nunit*, ge) wastebasket.

自主（的）
dz̀-'jǔ(-de) (*Aattr*) of one's own free will; free *from interference*. ‖tām jyē-'hwēn shr̀ dz̀-'jǔ-de. Their marriage was of their own free will.

92

自傳
dz̀-'jwàn (*Nunit*, běn) autobiography.

字據
dz̀-'jywù (*Nunit*, jāng) note (*signed when borrowing money*)

自來水
dz̀-láy-'shwěy (*Nmass*) tap water, running water.

自來水筆
dz̀-láy-shwěy-'bǐ (*Nunit*, gwǎn, jǐ) fountain pen.

自立
dz̀-'lì (*I*) economically independent.

字母
dz̀-'mǔ(r) (*Nunit*, ge) alphabet.

自然
dz̀-'rán (*A*) natural, free-and-easy, free from artifice; (*H*) naturally, as a matter of course. ‖tā hěn 'dz̀-rán. He's quite natural. ‖tā méy-'nyàn-gwo yīng-'wén, dz̀-'rán bú-'hwèy kàn yīng-wén-'bàw. He hasn't studied English, so naturally he can't read English newspapers.
    'dz̀-dz-rán-'rán-de natural, free-and-easy; suave.

自然律
dz̀-rán-'lywù (*Nunit*, ge) a natural law (*e.g., gravitation, the second law of thermodynamics, etc.*).

自殺
dz̀-'shā (*I*) to commit suicide.

自行車
dz̀-shíng-'chē (*Nunit*, lyàng) bicycle.
    chí (dz̀-shíng-)'chē to ride a bicycle.

自食其力
'dz̀-shf̣-chí-'lì (*literary quotation*) self-reliant, self-supporting, independent. ‖tā bú-'kàw-rén, tā néng 'dz̀-shf̣-chí-'lì. He doesn't depend on others; he's °self-supporting *or* °self-reliant.

自始至終
dz̀-'shf̣ jǐ-'jūng (*H*) (*literary quotation*) from beginning to end (*of some period of time*). ‖tā dz̀-'shf̣ jǐ-'jūng méy-'mán-ywèn-gwo. From beginning to end, he hasn't complained.

自相矛盾
dz̀-shyāng máw-'dwèn (*literary quotation*) to argue inconsistently, disproving one's own points.

字體
dz̀-'tǐ (*Nunit*, ge) type-face, type-style; style of handwriting.

自從
dz̀-'tsúng (*K*) ever since. ‖dz̀-'tsúng dǎ-'jàng yǐ-'hèw wǒ jyèw bù-chēw-'yān-le. Ever since the war started I haven't been smoking.

自由
dz̀-'yéw (*A*) be free, have liberty. ‖tā dzày-'jyā 'yì-dyǎr yě bú-dz̀-'yéw. He enjoys no freedom at his home.   (*Nabstr*) freedom. 'měy-yí-ge-ày-dz̀-'yéw-de-rén every lover of liberty.

自圓其說
'dz̀-ywán-chí-'shwō (*literary quotation*) be capable of carrying one's arguments to logically valid conclusions. ‖byé-rén 'swèy-rán bù-'jywé-de tā 'dwèy, 'kě-shr tā hěn 'hwèy 'dz̀-ywán-chí-'shwō. Although other people don't think so, he's very capable of reaching his conclusions logically.

自願效勞
'dz̀-ywàn shyàw-'láw (*I*) to volunteer for service.

硪
dzá (*V*) to strike *something* a sharp blow, usually from above. dzá 'gēn-jī to build a foundation, *literally for a building, or figuratively for a career, friendship, etc. As mainV:* dzá-'pwò to break *something* into pieces by striking *it* a sharp blow; dzá-'hwày *or* dzá-'sǎn, *etc.*, 'dzá-shyà-chywù to strike from above; 'dzá-shàng-chywu to strike from below, (*as a nail on the ceiling*); dzá-'jìn-chywù to drive in, (*as a nail*); *etc.*

雜
dzá (*A*) variegated; of all kinds. ‖jèy-shyē-'shr̀-ching hěn 'dzá. These matters are all different. ‖tā shr̀ dzwò °dzá-'shr̀-de. *or* °dzá-'hwó-de. He does all sorts of odd jobs to make his living.

雜貨
dzá-'hwò (*Ncoll*) groceries. dzá-hwò-'pù, dzá-hwò-'dyàn grocery store, general store.

雜誌
dzá-'jř (*Nunit*, běn, běr) magazine, periodical.

雜亂
dzá-'lwàn (*A*) confused, mixed up; noisy. ‖dzày shr̀-'chǎng-li hěn dzá-'lwàn. The market-place is full of noise and confusion.

咱們
'dzán-men *or* dzám (*Pron*) we, us, *in informal use and indicating specifically that the person spoken to is included.* ‖'dzám chř-'fàn-ba. Let's (*and you too*) eat.

攢
dzǎn (*V*) to collect, save. dzǎn-'chyán to save money, *accumulating a bit at a time;* dzǎn yéw-'pyàw to col-

lect stamps. *As mainV:* **'dzăn-chǐ-láy** *or* **'dzăn-shàng** to save up, to collect together.

盏

dzăn (*Munit*) one **dēng** (*lamp*); one cup of **jyěw** (*wine*)

讚成

'dzăn-chéng (*V*) to approve of, support, be for, accept, prefer, advocate *someone. someone's conduct. a proposal, an opinion.* ‖**ni-de-'hwà wǒ bú-'dzàn-chéng.** I can't approve of what you say.

讚助

dzàn-'jù (*V*) to give backing to, to support *a person, a plan, a principle.*

暫時

'dzàn-shŕ *see* **'jàn-shŕ.**

髒

dzāng (*A*) dirty. ‖**shyǎw-'hár-de-'shěw hěn 'dzāng.** The child's hands are dirty.

葬

dzàng (*V*) to bury. **hǎy 'dzàng** to bury at sea; **hwǒ 'dzàng** to cremate.

藏青

dzàng-'chīng (*Aattr*) navy blue, dark blue.

葬禮

dzàng-'lǐ (*Nunit, tsz*) burial ceremony.

糟

dzāw (*A*) awry, confused, messed up, (*of situations, projects, plans, etc.*). *As postV:* **dzwò-'dzāw** to get *something* messed up in working at *it:* **nàw-'dzāw** to fuss with *something* and get *it* messed up; *etc.* (*very general*). ‖**'dzāw-le!** Shucks! It didn't work! *or* Shucks! Something's gone wrong! ‖**tā-de-'hwà shwō-'dzāw-le.** His talking ruined the situation.

遭

dzāw(r) (*Msemel*) times. ‖**ni ràw-je jèy-ge-'tswēn-dz pǎw yì-'dzāw.** Run once around the village.

糟糕

dzāw-'gāw (*A*) confused, messed up, completely spoiled; *much like* **dzāw.**

糟蹋

'dzāw-ta (*V*) to ruin, undermine, waste. ‖**ni byé bǎ nèy-shyē-'tsày dēw 'dzāw-ta-le.** Don't waste all that food. ‖**tā 'dz̀-jǐ 'dzāw-ta 'dz̀-jǐ-de-'shēn-tǐ.** He's ruining his health.

遭遇

'dzāw-ywu (*V*) to experience, meet with, undergo, (*some unpleasant happening*). (*Nunit, ge*) one's experiences, lot in life, fate. ‖**tā-de-'dzāw-ywù hěn kě-'lyán.** His lot in life is quite pitiful.

鑿

dzáw (*V*) to chip small pieces out, to chip a piece off, *of something with a chisel, or hammer and chisel. As mainV:* **dzáw-shyà-lay** to chisel *pieces* off; **'dzáw-chū-lay,** to chisel, *e.g., some image,* out of *wood, stone, etc.;* **dzáw-'hwày** to spoil, break, *by chiseling; etc.* ‖**nèy-ge-dyāw-kè-'jyā, 'dzáw-le yí-ge-shŕ-'shyàng.** The sculptor chiseled a statue.

澡

***dzǎw** (*Nunit, ge*) bath. **shǐ-'dzǎw** (*VN2*) to take a bath.

早

dzǎw (*H*) early, earlier. ‖**ni 'láy-de hěn 'dzǎw.** You've come quite early. ‖**děy 'dzǎw-dyǎr 'dzěw.** I must go a little early (*or* earlier). ‖**'dzǎw-a!** Good morning! (*Southern*).

棗

***dzǎw, 'dzǎw-dz, dzǎwr** (*Nunit, ge*) date (*the fruit*). **dzǎw-'gāw** (*Nmass*) date cake.

早(晨)

***dzǎw, 'dzǎw-chen** (*Ntime*) morning, A.M. **dzǎw-'chē** morning train, early train; **dzǎw-'bàw** morning paper; **dzǎw-'fàn** breakfast.

早點

dzǎw-'dyǎn (*Nunit, dwèn*) breakfast.

澡房

dzǎw-'fáng (*or* **shǐ-dzǎw-'fáng**) (*Nunit, jyān, ge*) bathroom.

早年

'dzǎw-nyán (*Ntime*) one's early life, in one's early life. ‖**tā 'dzǎw-nyán (de-shŕ-hew) jyèw dàw 'wày-gwo chywù-le.** He went abroad in his early years.

澡盆

dzǎw-'pén (*or* **shǐ-dzǎw-'pén**) (*NunitC, ge*) bathtub.

早日

'dzǎw-r̀ (*Ntime*) at some early date. ‖**ni 'dzǎw-r̀ 'hwéy-lay!** Come back soon! (*implying in the near future, but not the next few days*).

早上

'dzǎw-shang (*Ntime*) morning, A.M.

澡堂

dzăw-'táng (*Nunit*, **jyā**, **swǒ**) (public) bathhouse. (*Also called* **shĭ-dzăw-'táng**.) **nywŭ-dzăw-'táng** public bathhouse for women; *unless so specified it is for men only.*

早餐

dzăw-'tsān (*Nunit*, **dwèn**) breakfast.

早晚

dzăw-'wăn (*H*) sooner or later. ‖tā dzăw-'wăn hwèy 'jŕ-dàw-de. He'll find out sooner or later.

造

dzàw (*V*) to make *on a large scale;* to build *a house, a ship, etc.;* to make up *rumor or gossip;* to give rise to, occasion, cause. ‖'fáng-dz dēw dzàw-'wán-le. The house is all built. ‖nèy-jŕ-'chwán 'dzàw-le 'sān-ge-ywè tsáy dzàw-'wán-le. It took three months to build that ship. ‖tā gěy rén-'mín dzàw 'shìng-fú. He's doing this for the welfare of the people. ‖'nèy-jyàn-shŕ-ching shŕ tā-'dz̀-ji-'dzàw-de. He created that story out of his imaginaticn.

躁

dzàw (*A*) cranky, sour, quick-tempered. ‖tā 'pí-chi hěn 'dzàw. He's very sour-tempered. *or* He's very quick-tempered.

造反

dzàw-'făn (*VN1*) to mutiny, rebel, overthrow authority (*usually of political rebellion*). ‖shwěy-'shěw dzàw-'făn-le. The sailors mutinied.

造孽

dzàw-'nyè (*VN2*) to commit a sin; to suffer from one's wrongdoings.

宰

dzǎy (*V*) to slaughter *an animal (as a sacrifice or for eating).* ‖'kè-rén nème-'dwō, dzǎy-le 'sān-jŕ-'jī 'háy bú-gèw 'chŕ. There are so many guests that even if you killed three chickens it wouldn't be enough.

崽

***dzǎy**, **'dzǎy-dz** (*Nunit*, **ge**) the young (*of animals*). **jū-'dzǎy(-dz)** shoats, piglets, *also used in the South as an epithet in insulting people;* **nyéw-'dzǎy(-dz)** calves; etc.

再

dzày (*H*) again, once again. ‖chǐng 'dzày shwō. Please repeat. ‖wǒ 'dzày yàw yì-gēr-yáng-hwěr (*with stress on* dzày). I want another match. ‖wǒ 'dzày yàw yì-gēr-yáng-'hwěr (*with stress on* yáng-hwěr). Then also I want a match. *or* I want a match too. ‖tā 'dzày láy wǒ ɟyèw 'dzěw. If he comes again I'm leaving. ‖tā 'méy-dzày láy. He hasn't come again (since the first

time). ‖tā 'bú-dzày láy-le. He won't come again. ‖tā 'dzày bù-láy-le. He won't ever come again. ‖tā 'dzày méy-láy. He never came another time.

在

dzày (*V*) to be at, in, on. ‖'yān dzày 'jwō-dz-shang. The cigarettes are on the table.

(*K*) at, in, on *a place*, at *a time*. ‖dzày 'jwō-dz-shang yěw-'yān. There are cigarettes on the table. ‖wǒm dzày-'jèr tán-'hwà-ne. We're having a conversation here. ‖dzày 'sān-dyǎn-jūng-yǐ-'chyán tā háy bù-jŕ-'dàw-ne. Before three o'clock (*literally* before three o'clock) he still didn't know.

(*PostV*) *forms RC3 and RC4 which have no potential forms; the RC is followed by a designation of place at or to which*, or by **yí-'kwàr** together: **dzwò-dzày 'jèr** sit here; **jàn-dzay 'jwō-dz-shang** stand on the table; **bǎ-ta gē-dzày 'jwō-dz-shang** put it on the table; **hé-dzày yí-'kwàr** put together, pool; **lyéw-dzay yí-'kwàr** flow together, merge.

(*I*) to be alive. ‖wǒ-'mŭ-chin háy 'dzày-ne, kě-shr wǒ-'fù-chin bú-'dzày-le. My mother is still alive, but my father is dead.

(*Vpred*) *like English* is, are, am *followed by a verb plus* -ing *to indicate continuing activity:* ‖tā dzày chŕ dzǎw-'fàn-ne. He's having his breakfast. ‖wǒ chywù 'kàn-ta de-shŕ-hew, tā jèng dzày chŕ dzǎw-'fàn-ne. When I went to see him he was just eating his breakfast.

載

dzày (*V*) to carry, hold, *mainly freight but also people* (*of a vehicle, boat, or other means of transport*). ‖jèy-lyàng-'chē néng 'dzày dwō-shaw-'hwò? How much freight will this car carry? ‖jèy-lyàng-'chē dēw dzày-'mǎn-le. This car is packed full. ‖jèy-lyàng-'chē bǎ jèy-shyē-'dūng-shi 'dzày-daw 'nèy-ge-chéng-li chywu. This car will transport these things to that city.

在乎

'dzày-hu (*I*, *V*, *Vsent*) to be concerned (about), to care (about). ‖wǒ bú-'dzày-hu nǐ 'láy-bu-láy. I don't care whether you come or not.

載重 (汽) 車

dzày-jùng-(chì-)'chē (*Nunit*, **lyàng**) motor truck, lorry.

載重量

dzày-jùng-'lyàng (*Nabstr*) maximum load *for a bridge*, maximum pay load *for a vehicle, etc.*

再三再四的

dzày-'sān-dzày-'sz̀-de (*H*) repeatedly, again and again. ‖wǒ dzày-'sān-dzày-'sz̀-de gēn-ta 'shwō láy-je. I've told him (so) again and again.

在意

dzày-'yì (*VN1*) to mind; to be careful. ‖tā-shwō-de-'hwà nǐ byé dzày-'yì. Dont mind what he says. ‖chǐng-ni dwèy-ywu nèy-jyàn-'shr̀-ching dzày-'yì-yì-dyǎr. Please be a bit careful about that 'hing. *or* Please pay some attention to that matter.

責，責任

*dzé, dzé-'rèn (*Nunit*, ge) responsibility, duty. fù-'dzé to shoulder the responsibility. ‖jèy-ge-'kàn-hu-de-dzé-'rèn shr̀ kàn-hu 'bìng-rén. This nurse's responsibility is to care for the patient.

責備

dzé-'bèy (*V*) to reprimand, scold, rebuke.

摘要

dzé-'yàw (*VN1*) to make a brief summary of the important points. ‖ching-ni bǎ jèy-pyàn-'cháng-'wén-jāng gěy-wo dzé-'yàw. Please make a brief summary of that (long) essay for me.

則巳

dzé-'yǐ unless; *confined to* bū- . . . dzé-'yǐ not *do so-and-so* at all unless it is done completely and well. ‖tā bù-'shywé dzé-'yǐ, yì 'shywé yí-'dìng jyèw bǐ 'rén(-jya) 'hǎw. He refuses to learn at all unless (if he does study) he can surpass everyone else. ‖tā bù-'míng dzé-'yǐ, yì 'míng jīng-'rén. (*Literary*) He says nothing at all usually, but when he does speak he attracts people's attention by his ability.

怎麼

dzěm *see* 'dzěm-me.

怎麼

'dzěm-me, 'dzěme, dzěm (*H*) how, in what way, like what, to what extent? ‖dàw hwǒ-chē-'jàn chywù dzěme 'dzěw? How do you get to the station?

    'dzěme-je doing it how? ‖dzwò jèy-jyàn-'shr̀-ching nǐ shyǎng 'dzěme-je tsáy 'hǎw? How do you think this job could be done satisfactorily?

    Before nominal forms in a few cases: ‖dàw-'dǐ shr̀ 'dzěm-yì-hwéy-'shr̀? After all, what sort of affair is it?

這麼

dzèm(e) *see* 'jè-me.

怎麼

'dzěme *see* 'dzěm-me.

怎麼樣

dzěme-'yàng(r), dzěm-'yàng(r) how?, what kind of?, what way? ‖tā shyàn-dzày dzěme-'yàng? How is he now?

    dzěme-'yàng(r)-de *before nouns:* ‖'dzěme-yàngr-de-'tsày? What kind of food?

增，增加

*dzēng, dzēng-'jyā (*V*) to add (*personnel, extra workers*); to be increased (*as of a salary*). ‖nǐ-'nàr dzēng-'jyā-le 'dwō-shaw-rén? How many (new) people did

you add at your place? ‖tā-de-shīn-'shwěy dzēng-'jyā-le. His salary was increased. ‖tā-de-shīn-'shwěy dzēng-'jyā-le yí-'bèv. His salary was doubled.

增光

dzēng-'gwāng (*VN2*) to be a credit to (*something*); to contribute to *something's* reputation. ‖tā tì gwó-'jyā dzēng-'gwāng. He was a credit to his country. *or* He added to his country's glory.

掙扎

'dzēng-jā (*I*) to struggle, fight. ‖tā wèy-le 'shēng-hwó 'dzēng-jā hěn 'jyěw. He's been struggling for his living for a long time.

贈

dzèng (*V2*) (*somewhat literary*) to give *someone something* as a free gift. ‖wǒ 'dzèng-ni yì-gwǎn-'bǐ. I'm giving you a pen.

    dzèng-'chywàn complimentary ticket.

子兒

dzěr (*Nunit*, ge) (1) a small coin made of copper. yěw-'dzěr be rich.

    (2) A piece for a board game. chí-'dzěr chess man, checker.

    (3) (*Nmass;* lì) seeds, eggs. hwā-'dzěr flower seeds; jī-'dzěr chicken eggs; ywú-'dzěr fish roe.

字兒

dzèr (*N*) heads (*of a coin*). ‖yàw-shr 'dzèr wǒ 'chywù. If it's heads I'll go. (Tails *is* mèr.)

走

dzěw (*I*) to leave, depart.

    (*I, lc*) to come, go, *especially if on foot.* 'dzěw-je °láy (*or* °chywù) to come (go) walking, come (go) on foot.

    (*I.*) *Used with locative goal:* dzěw-'lù, dzěw-'dàw(r) to walk; dzěw shwěy-'lù to go by water; 'dzěw-(yi-) dzěw take a walk; dzěw yì-'chywān, dzěw yì-'chywār to take a walk around, go in a circuit.

    As mainV: 'dzěw-chū (*lc*) to come out, walk out; to come forward. 'dzěw-dàw (*lc*) to go (*particularly on foot*) to a place; dzěw-bu-'dùng to be unable to walk, (*as of an old man*); dzěw-'dyēw-le to get lost (*of someone else, not of oneself*); 'dzěw-gwò (*lc*) to walk by, go by; to walk across, over *something like a street or a frozen river;* 'dzěw-jìn (*lc*) to walk or go in; 'dzěw-kāy to leave, to get away.

    As postV: gwā-'dzěw-le to blow *something* away (*of the wind*); lā-'dzěw-le to drag *something* away; etc.

    (*V*) to move (*in a board game*). dzěw yí-ge-'dzěr to move a piece. ‖shr̀-'shéy 'dzěw? Whose move is it?

走背運

dzěw 'bèy-ywùn (*VN1*) to get bad breaks, be unlucky, be in an unlucky period of one's life.

走江湖的(人)
dzěw-jyāng-'hú-de(-rén) (*Npers*) acrobat.

走邪路
dzěw shyé-'lù (*VN1*) to take the wrong road (*in c moral sense*).

走頭無路
dzěw-'téw wú-'lù (*literary quotation*) to come to the end of the road and have no further path to follow.

走運
dzěw-'ywùn (*VN1*) to get the breaks, be lucky, be in a lucky period of one's life. **dzěw hǎw-'ywùn** *or* **dzěw húng-'ywùn** *same as above but stronger.*

揍
dzěw (*V*) to hit, strike, sock. ‖**'dzěw-ta yí-dwèn.** Sock him one. ‖**'dzěw-ta yì-'chywán.** Give him a sock with your fist.
    As mainV: **dzèw-'shāng-le** to strike and wound.

皺
dzèw (*A*) wrinkled (*any surface*). (*Opposite* **píng** smooth.)

奏
dzèw (*V*) to play *a musical instrument*, play *music*. **dzèw shíng-jywūn-'gēer** to play a march.

賊
dzéy (*Npers*) a thief. (*One who steals silently, sneakingly*.)

租
dzū (*V*) to rent. **dzū 'fáng-dz** to rent a house; *etc.* (*said of the person contracting to take the thing rented, not the owner*). ‖**dzū 'dūng-shi de-shŕ-hew děy àn-'chī fù 'dzū-chyán.** When you rent something you have to make regular payments.
    dzū-gěy to rent *something to someone.*
    chū-'dzū to be for rent.

足
dzú (*A*) enough, sufficient, ample (*more limited than* **gèw**). ‖**nǐ hē 'dzú-le-ma?** Did you have enough to drink? ‖**tā shwèy 'dzú-le.** He's had enough sleep.

族
dzú (*Mgroup*) race, racial strain, clan. (*China has* **hàn** the Chinese proper, **mǎn** Manchus, **méng** Mongols, **hwéy** Mohammedans, **dzàng** Tibetans.) ‖**tām shŕ yì-'dzú-de-rén.** They are of a single racial strain.
    mín-'dzú the people of a nation.

足稱
dzú-'chèn (*V*) to be worth *so much money*. ‖**tā dzú-'chèn yì-bǎy-'wàn.** He's worth a million dollars (*said of a (legal) person, or of property*).

足球
dzú-'chyéw(r) (*Nunit*, **ge**) soccer ball; (*Nunit*, **tsž**) soccer.
    'měy-gwo-dzú-'chyew(r) American football.

足夠
dzú-'gèw (*A*) sufficient, ample. ‖**jèy-shyē-chyán wèy-'wǒ dzú-'gèw-le.** That money is quite enough for me.

不足爲恥
bù-dzú wéy-'chř (*literary quotation; VN1*) to be too slight to be ashamed of. ‖**nèy-ge bù-dzú wéy-'chř.** Don't worry about it; it isn't anything you need be ashamed of; it's nothing.

阻
dzǔ (*V*) to stop, impede, block, prevent. ‖**tā-dzěw-de-'lù 'bèy-rén gěy 'dzǔ-le.** His path was blocked by someone (*literally or figuratively*).

組
dzǔ (*Mpart*) section of an organization. *In compounds* **kwày-jì-'dzǔ** comptroller section; **wén-shū-'dzǔ** secretarial section; *etc.* ‖**jèy-ge-gūng-'sž fēn lyèw-'dzǔ. dì-'yì-dzǔ shŕ ....** This company is organized in six sections. The first section is ....

阻礙
dzǔ-'ày (*V*) to prevent *someone's* progress, serve as a barrier. ‖**nèy-kwày-'shŕ-tew dzày-'nàr dzěw-'ày wǒ-men, chǐng-ni gěy 'nwó-kay.** That stone (there) is blocking our way; please push it aside.

祖國
dzǔ-'gwó (*Nunit*, **ge**) mother country, fatherland, the land of one's ancestors.

組織
dzǔ-'jŕ (*V*) to organize, form, *some committee, club, business, etc.* (*Nabstr; Nunit*, **ge**) organization; an organization, (political) machine. ‖**tā-men-de-'lì-lyàng hěn 'dà, yīn-wey tām (shŕ) yěw-'dzǔ-jŕ(-de).** They're very powerful because they're organized.

阻止
dzǔ-'jř (*V*) to stop, block, prevent. ‖**tā yàw 'láy, 'hèw-láy bèy-'rén gěy dzǔ-'jř-le.** He was going to come, but then someone stopped him.

棕色
*****dzūng, dzūng-'sè, dzūng-'shǎr** (*N*) dark brown color (*the green tint is often predominant in a shade termed thus*). **dzūng-'sè-de-'lyàw-dz** dark-brown (cloth) material. ‖**tā-'chwān-de-'yī-fu shŕ dzūng-'shǎr-de.** He's wearing dark-brown clothes.

97

蹤跡

dzǔng-'jì (*Nunit*, ge) clue, trace. ‖shyàn-'dzày, wǒm jǎw-bu-'jáw tā-de-dzǔng-'jì. By now it's too late for us to pick up his trail.

宗教

dzǔng-'jyàw (*Nunit*, ge) religion, religious denomination. ‖yěw rén 'shwō, kǔng-'jyàw bú-shr dzǔng-'jyàw. There are some who say that Confucianism isn't a religion.

棕樹

dzǔng-'shù (*Nunit*, kē) palm tree.

總

dzǔng (*H*) always; without exception; without alternative; altogether. ‖yí-ge-rén 'dzǔng děy chř-'fàn. A man has to eat (*there's no choice in the matter*). ‖nèy-ge-shyǎw-'hár 'dzǔng(-shr) bù-tīng-'hwà. That child is always disobedient. ‖'rén 'dzǔng yàw 'sž-de, bú-gwò dzǎw-'wǎn-de-'wèn-tí. All men must die; be it sooner or later. ‖tā-de-'tsáy-chǎn 'dzǔng yěw yì-bǎy-'wàn-dzwǒ-'yèw. His property (in all) amounts to about a million dollars. ‖bǎ yì-nyán-de-'jàng gěy-wo dzǔng 'swàn yí-shyàr. Sum up the whole year's accounts for me.

總而言之

'dzǔng-ér-'yán-jř (*J*) in short, in brief, in a word. ‖'dzǔng-ér-'yán-jř-a, wǒ bù-jř-'dàw. In short, I just don't know.

總管子

dzǔng-'gwǎn-dz (*Nunit*, tyáw) main conduit. shwěy-dzǔng-'gwǎn-dz water main; méy-'chì-dzǔng-'gwǎn-dz gas main.

總之

dzǔng-'jř (*J*) in short, in brief. ‖dzǔng-'jř-a, tām dēw bú-'dzàn-chéng. In short, none of them agree.

總開關

dzǔng-kāy-'gwān (*Nunit*, ge) master switch.

總理

dzǔng-'lǐ (*NpersT*) prime minister, premier, (*of a government*).

總數

dzǔng-'shù(r) (*Nunit*, ge) the total amount. ‖bǎ jèy-shyē-'shù-mu dēw 'jyā-chi-lay 'dé yí-ge-dzǔng-'shùr. Add these numbers together and get the total.

總統

dzǔng-'tǔng (*or* dà-dzǔng-'tǔng) (*NpersT*) president (*of a government*).

　　fù-dzǔng-'tǔng vice president.

縱

dzùng (*V*) to spoil *a child, a subordinate*. *As mainV:* dzùng-'hwày to spoil.

鑽

dzwān (*V*) to drill *a hole*. dzwān 'kū-lung to sneak into, scurry into; dzwān bèy-'wōer to go to bed. *As mainV:* 'dzwān-gwò-chywù to drill through *or* pass through; 'dzwān-chū-láy to come out of *a tunnel* (*as a train*), *or a burrow* (*as some animal or worm*); dzwān-'tūng-le to drill a hole through. ‖nèy-ge-'fàn-rén bǎ-'chyáng dzwān-'tūng-le, jyèw 'táw-le. That prisoner bored a hole through the wall and escaped.

攢

dzwàn (*V*) to hold *something* in the clenched fist. *As mainV:* dzwàn-'jǐn-le to hold *something* tightly in the clenched fist; to tighten *by turning in the clenched fist;* dzwàn-'sūng-le to loosen *in the same way;* dzwàn-'shěw to hold *someone's* hand tightly.

鑽

'dzwàn(-dz) (*Nunit*, bǎ, ge) brace and bit, awl, drill.

鑽石

dzwàn-'shŕ (*Nunit*, ge) diamond (*jewel*).

尊

*dzwēn (*Npers*). See Appendix A.

尊稱

'dzwēn-chēng (*V2*) to address *someone as such-and-such.* ‖tā 'dzwēn-chēng ni dzwò 'shyān-sheng. He addresses you as his teacher.
　　(*Nunit*, ge) title, term used in addressing someone. ‖tā-de-'dzwēn-chēng shŕ 'shéme? How should he be addressed? (*as mister, teacher, etc.*)

尊敬

dzwēn-'jìng (*V*) to have respect for *a person.* ‖wǒ dzwēn-'jìng 'nèy-ge-rén. *or* wo dwèy-ywu 'nèy-ge-rén hěn dzwēn-'jìng. I have a lot of respect for that man.

遵守

'dzwēn-shěw (*V*) to obey, observe, follow, hold fast to *rules, principles, etc.*

遵義

dzwēn-'yì (*Nunique*) Tsun-i *or* Tsunyi (*city in Kweichow province*).

座兒

dzwèr (*Nunit*, ge) seat, place to sit (*e.g., in a restaurant it may be a table*); the base, support, bottom *of something.* yǐ-dz-'dzwèr the seat of a chair; píng-dz-de-'dzwèr the base of a vase; shyàng-'dzwèr the base of a statue.

98

堆

dzwēy, dzwēr (*Mgroup*) a pile of, heap of, group of. A crowded group of **rén** (*people*); a heap of **méy** (*coal*); a pile of **cháy** (*firewood*), etc.

嘴

dzwěy (*Nunit*, **ge, jāng**) mouth (*of person or animal*), bill (*of bird*). ‖'**jèy-jywù-hwà 'jyèw dzày wǒ-'dzwěy-byār, wǒ 'wàng-le.** That phrase was right on the tip of my tongue (*literally* edge of my mouth), and then I went and forgot it.

     *dzwěr mouth of objects. **píng-'dzwěr** mouth of a bottle; *etc.*

嘴巴

dzwěy-'bà(-dz) (*Nunit*, **ge**) cheeks.   '**dzwěy-ba** (*Msemel*) a slap on the cheek. '**dǎ-rén yí(-ge)-'dzwěy-ba** give someone a slap on the cheek.

嘴唇

dzwěy-'chwén (*Nunit*, **pyàr**) the lips. **shàng-dzwěy-'chwén** upper lip; **shyà-dzwěy-'chwén** lower lip.

最

dzwèy (*H*) *used exclusively before A and H:* most; (*sometimes*) very. **dzwèy 'hǎw** best; **dzwèy 'hwày** worst; **dzwèy 'kwày** fastest; *etc.;* **dzwèy-'hèw-de-shèng-'lì** final victory.

    '**dzwèy hǎw bú-gwò** ... at most, certainly does not exceed *such-and-such,* or at most, cannot be more than *such-and-such,* or it would be best not to exceed *such-and-such.* ‖'**dzwèy hǎw 'bú-gwò 'sān-kwày-chyán.** It would be best not to pay more than three dollars.

醉

dzwèy (*A*) drunk. '**dzwèy-sž-le** to be dead drunk.

罪

dzwèy (*Nunit*, **ge**) sin, crime (*legal, moral, religious*). **fàn-'dzwèy** to commit a crime, be guilty of a sin; **shú-'dzwèy** to atone for sin, *or* to pay the penalty for a crime; **hwěy-'dzwèy** to repent one's sins, *or* to regret one's crimes.

醉鬼

dzwèy-'gwěy (*Npers*) drunk, drunkard.

罪名

'**dzwèy-míng** (*Nabstr*) type of crime, class of offense (*literally* crime name; *e.g., first degree murder, second degree murder,* etc.) ‖**tā 'fàn-le shéme-'dzwèy-míng?** What crime did he commit?

捉

dzwō (*V*) to arrest, catch, (*fugitives, animals*). *As mainV:* '**dzwō-jù** catch and stop; '**dzwō-chū-láy** catch and pull out *of hiding;* **dzwō-'dzěw** arrest and take

away. ‖**wǒ 'dzwō-jù-le yì-jř-'nyǎwr.** I caught a bird. ‖**wǒ 'dzwō-ju tā-de-dwǎn-'chù.** I seized on his shortcomings.

琢磨，捉摸

dzwó-me (*V*) to think *something* over, cogitate about. *As mainV:* '**dzwo-me-chi-láy** to start turning *something* over in your mind; '**dzwó-me-chū-lay** to figure *something* out. ‖**wǒ 'shyān děy 'dzwó-me yí-shyà-dz, dzày 'shwō.** I've got to think about it a bit first before I say anything. ‖**nèy-jyàn-shř wǒ háy méy-'dzwó-me-chu-lay.** I haven't figured that thing out yet; (I don't understand it yet).

昨天，昨兒(個)

'**dzwó-tyan, dzwóer(-ge)** (*Ntime*) yesterday.

左

dzwǒ (*Nplace*) left, left side. (*Longer forms* '**dzwǒ-byan,** '**dzwǒ-byar.**) ‖**shyàng-'dzwǒ dzěw.** Go to the left. ‖**jèy-ge-'pù-dz dzày jèy-tyáw-'jyē-de-'dzwǒ-byan.** This store is on the left side of the street.

    Before nouns: **dzwǒ-'yǎn** left eye; **dzwǒ-'snéw** left hand; **dzwǒ-'jyǎw** left foot; *etc.*

左傾

dzwǒ-'chīng (*A*) radical, leftist. (*Opposite* **yèw-'chīng** conservative.) ‖**tā-de-'sž-shyǎng yěw yì-dyǎr-dzwǒ-'chīng.** His ideas are a bit leftist, a bit radical.

左近

dzwǒ-'jìn (*Nplace*) the vicinity, nearby. ‖**wǒ jyèw 'jù-dzay hwǒ-chē-'jàn-dzwǒ-'jìn.** I live right near the station.

左右

dzwǒ-'yèw (*after numerical expressions, or H*) more or less, approximately. ‖**wǒ yěw yì-'bǎy-kwày-chyán dzwǒ-yèw.** I have about a hundred dollars.

    dzwǒ-'yèw wéy-'nán to be in a tight spot.   '**dzwǒ-yí-tsž-'yèw-yí-tsž-de** time and time again.

作，做

dzwò (*V*) (1) *with a personal goal, sometimes with an impersonal goal:* to serve as, function as, be. **dzwò-'gwān** to be an official *or* officer. ‖**wǒm ná jèy-ge-'shyāng-dz dzwò 'yǐ-dz yùng.** We'll use that box as a chair.

    (2) *Usually when the goal is impersonal:* to do, work, make, produce. **dzwò-'shř** to work; **dzwò-'gūng** to work, *but usually only of physical labor;* **dzwò-'fàn** to prepare food, to cook; **dzwò 'mǎy-may** to engage in business; **dzwò-'mèng** to dream; **dzwò li-'bày** to engage in worship, to go to church.

    As mainV: '**dzwò-chéng** to serve as, function as; to make. **dzwò-bu-'chǐ** to be unable to afford doing *such-and-such;* '**dzwò-chi-láy** to start to do *or* make *something;* to build up *a business;* '**dzwò-chū-chywù** to-build up *a business;* **'dzwò-chū-láy** to work *something* out; to assume *an air or manner;* **'dzwò-dàw** to attain *such-and-such a goal* by working; **dzwò-'hǎw** to finish making *or* doing; **dzwò-'hwày** to spoil *or* ruin *what one is working at;* **'dzwò-shyà-chywù** to keep on working. ‖**'dzwò-dzwo 'shř-shr.** Take a try at it.

座
dzwò (*MdistS*) one **fáng-dz** (*house*), a **shān** (*mountain*), a **chéng** (*city*), a **léw** (*building*), a **myàw** (*temple*), a **tǎ** (*pagoda*), and *in general for such large things that occupy sites and are not movable; for most such things one or more other measures are used too.*

坐
dzwò (*I*) to sit. ‖**chǐng 'dzwò.** Have a seat. ‖**wǒ dzày 'tā-nèr 'dzwò-le yì-hwěr.** I visited him at his place for a while (*literally* I sat for a while at his place).

Used with specification of place: ‖**wǒ dzwò-'jèr hǎw.** It's OK, I'll sit here. *Most frequently with the name of some vehicle, providing that vehicle is one in which one could sit while riding:* **dzwò-'chē chywù** to go by car, train, *etc.;* **dzwò fēy-'jī chywù** to go by plane; **dzwò-'chwán chywù** to go by boat (*but: not with* bicycle *or* horse *since one does not* **dzwò** sit *on them, but* **chí** straddles *them*); **dzwò-dzwo 'chwán** go for a sail.

As mainV: **'dzwò-dzày** to sit in, on, at, *a place.* **'dzwò-shàng** to sit down on something; **'dzwò-shyà (-chywù)** to sit down.

作對
dzwò-'dwèy, dzwò-dwèr (*VNí*) to oppose, be against. ‖**tā gēn-wo dzwò-'dwèy.** He's against me.

作活
dzwò-'hwó(er) (*VN1*) to do sewing, carpentry, bricklaying.

dzwò-'hwóer-de (*Npers*) girl hired to do sewing; carpenter; bricklayer.

作整壽
dzwò jěng-'shèw (*VN2*) to celebrate the 40th, 50th, 60th, *etc.,* birthday.

作家
'dzwò-jyā (*Npers*) writer, author.

作假
dzwò-'jyǎ (*VN1*) to pretend; to falsify, forge. ‖**yí-ge-'rén tày 'kè-chi de-shř-hew, 'rén shyǎng tā shř dzwò-'jyǎ.** If a man is too polite people think he's pretending.

座客
dzwò-'kè (*Npers*) passengers (*on a train, boat, etc.*).

作客
dzwò-'kè (*VN1*) (1) to be a guest at a party, to go to a party, attend a party. (2) To go abroad (*and be a guest of the foreign country*).

坐臘
dzwò-'là (*I*) to be on the spot (*a bit vulgar; literally* to sit on a candle).

坐牢
dzwò-'láw (*I*) to be in prison.

作品
dzwò-'pǐn (*Nunit,* **ge, běn, jāng, pyān**) works of art, *including books, essays, paintings, sculpture, musical works.*

作壽
dzwò-'shèw (*VN2*) to celebrate the birthday of an older person. **dzwò 'wǔ-shr-wǔ-swèy-de-'shèw** to celebrate the fifty-fifth birthday.

作爲罷論
dzwò-wéy-bà-'lwèn (*V*) to retract and forget about, take back. ‖**bǎ jèy-jyàn-'shř-ching dzwò-wéy-bà-'lwèn-ba.** I take it back; let's forget about that thing.

座位
'dzwò-wèy (*Nunit,* **ge**) seat, place to sit (*in church, streetcar, theater, etc.*).

作用
'dzwò-yùng (*Nunit,* **ge**) motive, underlying purpose. ‖**tā shwō nèy-jywù-'hwà yěw shéme-'dzwò-yùng méy-yew?** Is there any purpose behind what he said?

E

俄羅斯
*****ē, *****é, *****è; **è-lwó-'sž; 'è-gwo** (*Nunique*) Russia. **sū-'ē** Soviet Russia.

鵝
é (*Nunit,* **jř**) goose.

蛾 (子)
*****é, 'é-dz** (*Nunit,* **ge**) moths *of all kinds* (*not butterflies*).

鵝黃
é-'hwáng (*A*) light yellow, canary yellow.

餓

è (A) hungry. ‖wǒ 'è-le. I'm hungry. ‖wǒ yèw yì-dyǎr-'è. I'm a bit hungry.

惡

*è (A) bad. 'è-rén bad man, evil man (somewhat literary).

惡貫滿盈

'è-gwàn-mǎn-'yíng (literary quotation) to accumulate all sorts of evil in one's deeds. ‖dzǔng 'yěw-yì-tyān tā 'è-gwàn-mǎn-'yíng 'bèy-rén 'dǎy-le. There will come a day when all his evil deeds will lead to his arrest.

鱷魚

è-'ywú (Nunit, tyáw) alligator, crocodile.

按

èn (or àn) (V) to press with the finger or palm. èn-'lyéngr to ring a bell by pressing a button; èn 'lǎ-ba to blow a horn by pressing a button; èn dyàn-'mén to turn a light on (or off) by pressing the switch.
　　As mainV: èn-'hwày to break by pressing; 'èn-shàng to press down as a thumbtack; 'èn-dzày to press something on, at, against; etc. ‖tā bǎ-ta 'èn-dzay nèr dǎ yí-'dwèn. He held him down (there) and struck him.

兒

*-er see *-r.

而

*ér (H) (literary) and, and yet, also, but, nevertheless; like, as. Occurs in a number of the literary quotations used in everyday speech, but not freely introduced into new sentences, e.g. bù-'chī ér-'ywù to have no appointment and yet to meet, meet someone accidentally.

兒 (子)

*ér, 'ér-dz (Npers) son; in compounds child. See Appendix A.

兒童福利

ér-túng-fú-'lì (Nabstr) child welfare.

而已

ér-'yǐ that's all (at end of sentence). In the following examples; note that bú-gwò only, not more than, usually precedes. ‖tā bú-'gwò shr̀ yí-ge-'shywé-sheng ér-'yǐ. He's just a student, that's all. ‖wǒ yǐ-'wéy nǐ 'jř-daw hěn-'dwō; nǐ 'jř jř-dàw 'jèy-ge ér-'yǐ. I thought you knew a lot of things; but you only know this, that's all.

耳 (朵)

*ěr, 'ěr-dwo (Nunit, ge, jř) ear (on head).

而且

ěr-'chyě or ér-'chyè (J) but also. Introducing a second phrase; the first is often introduced with bú-'dàn not only. ‖nǐ bú-'dàn hwèy shwō 'yīng-gwo-hwà, ér-'chyě néng shwō 'è-gwo-hwà. Not only can you speak English, but you can also speak Russian.

耳環

ěr-'hwán (Nunit, ge, jř; fù or 'jwèy-dz a pair of) ear-rings.

耳旁風

ěr-páng-'fēng (N) hot air, nothing, something of no importance or meaning. ‖tā bǎ tā-'mǔ-chin-de-'hwà 'dǎng-dzwò ěr-páng-'fēng. He treated his mother's words as so much hot air.

二

èr or àr (NumU) two.

erh Wade Romanization for er and ar.

歐 (洲)

*ēw, 'ēw-jēw (Nunique) the continent of Europe. 'ēw-shř-de European style.

偶而

ěw-'ěr (H) once in a while, occasionally; by chance.

偶然

ěw-'rán (J) by chance, by accident.

藕色

'ěw-sè, 'ěw-shǎr (Nabstr) lavender-colored, light purple.

F

發

fā (or fá; both pronunciations are used in any situation) (V) to send out, send forth, issue forth; to pay out, distribute, give out. fā-'chyán to pay out money, and similarly with any term for money in any form; fā-'shwěy to flood, be flooded; fā-'shìn to send out mail,

or to mail; fā-'páy to deal out cards; fā-'bīng to send out troops.
　　As mainV: 'fā-chǐ-láy to rise (as dough); 'fā-chū (lc) to send out; 'fā-shyà (lc) to hand down, distribute, from a higher echelon to lower ones, of orders, publications, etc.
　　After fā is used any adjective which describes a physical state, color, or taste; the meaning is: to be-

come..., to turn...; *also sometimes with terms for mental states:* fā-'báy to turn pale, white, light, (*as of a face or the sky*); fā-'húng to turn red; fā-'lyàng to become bright, shiny; fā-'lěng to become cold (*and shiver*); fā-'rè to be feverish, to get hot; fā-'swān to turn sour; *or* (*of a part of the body*) to get sore; fā-'chéw to get worried; fā-'lǎn to get lazy, feel lazy; fā-'nù (*literary*) to get angry; fā-'kwáng to go crazy; fā-'hwēn to grow faint, feel dizzy.

發表
fā-'byǎw (*I*) to appear, be published, be made public; (*V*) to issue, make known, make public. ‖wǒ-'shyě-de-wén-'jāng 'yǐ-jing dzày 'bàw-shang fā-'byǎw-le. The article I wrote has already appeared in the paper.

發愁
fā-'chéw (*VN1*) to worry, be concerned. ‖wǒ 'jēn tì-ni fā-'chéw. I'm really worried about you.

發怵
fā-'chù (*A*) afraid, timid, to lack courage.

發球
fā-'chyéw(r) (*VN2*) to serve (*as in tennis*).

發怯
fā-'chywè (*A*) afraid, timid, lack courage.

發達
fā-'dá (*A*) prosperous.

發抖
fā-'děw (*I*) to quiver, shake.

發動機
fā-dùng-'jī (*Nunit,* jyà, ge) motor, engine.

發火
fā-'hwǒ, fā-'hwěr (*A*) hot, peppery; hot-tempered. ‖tā 'tīng-wán jèy-jywù-'hwà jyèw fā-'hwěr-le. When he heard that his temper flared up.

發展
fā-'jǎn (*V*) to develop, work out; expand. ‖tā fā-'jǎn-le yì-jǔng-de-gūng-'yè. He worked out a line of industry (*for himself*). ‖'jūng-gwo 'jàn-hèw yīng-gay fā-'jǎn gūng-'yè. After the war China must develop and expand her industry.

發覺
fā-'jywé (*V*) to discover, uncover *a plot,* to realize *something unpleasant not theretofore recognized.* ‖nǐ-de-'jì-hwà dēw bèy nǐ-de-'chéw-rén fā-'jywé-le. Your plan was discovered by your enemies.

法碼
fā-'mǎr (*Nunit,* ge) a weight *used on a scale.*

發明
fā-'míng (*V*) to invent. ‖fēy-'jī shr̀-'shéy fā-'míng-de? Who invented the airplane?

發麯
fā-'myàn (*VN2*) to cause *flour made into dough* to rise *by putting yeast in it.*
(*N*) raised dough. fā-myàn-'bǐng kind of cake made with yeast.

發脾氣
fā 'pí-chi (*VN1*) to lose *one's* temper.

發燒
fā-'shāw (*I*) to have a fever.

發生
fā-'shēng (*I*) to happen, take place, occur, arise; come into the picture. ‖jīn-tyan yěw yí-jyàn-'shr̀-ching fā-'shēng-le. Something came up today.
fā-'shēng hwǒ-'jǐng a fire breaks out, a fire occurs, there is a fire (*one which burns something down*).

發生作用
'fā-shēng-dzwó-'yùng (*literary quotation*) to take effect (*of medicine, etc.*).

發生疑問
'fā-shēng-yí-'wèn (*sometimes* yí-'wèn fā-'shēng-le) (*literary quotation*) a doubt arises, a problem arises; something comes up requiring further consideration. ‖jèy-jyàn-shr̀-ching běn-'láy wǒ yǐ-'wéy chywán 'dwèy-le; shyàn-'dzày 'yèw 'fa-shēng-yí-'wèn-le. Originally I thought this matter was all straight; but now there's some question about it again.

發生意外
'fā-shēng-'yì-'wày (*literary quotation*) an accident happens, something unexpected and unlooked-for occurs.

發行
fā-'shíng (*V*) to put *money, goods, etc.,* into circulation. ‖jèy-ge-'pyàw-dz shr̀ 'něy-ge-yín-'háng fā-'shíng-de? What bank issued this note?

發現
fā-'shyàn (*V*) to discover; (*I*) to appear. ‖Columbus fā-'shyàn-le 'měy-jēw. Columbus discovered America. ‖wǒ 'dyēw-de nèy-běn-'shū dzày 'jwǒ-shang fā-'shyàn-le. I lost that book, and it turned up on the table.

發財
fā-'tsáy (*VN2*) to make a fortune, amass a fortune.

罰

fá (*V*) to punish. ‖**tā-'nèy-ge-rén bù-chéng-'tsáy, yīn-wey 'shyǎw de-shŕ-hew fù-'mǔ bù-kěn 'fá-ta.** He's a good-for-nothing because when he was small his parents weren't willing to punish him.
   Legally: punish by fine or imprisonment.

法子，法兒

'fá-dz, fár (*Nunit, ge*) a way, method, plan, means of doing something. **shyǎng-'fár** to think of a way *of doing something,* try to think of a way *of doing something,* to try *to do something.* ‖**méy(-yew) 'fá-dz.** It can't be done. ‖**nǐ yùng shéme-'fá-dz bǎ nèy-ge-'mér 'kāy-kay-de?** How did you get that door open?

乏味

fá-'wèy (*A*) to be dull, uninteresting (*literary*).

發言

fā-'yán (*VN1*) to speak (*formally*). **fā-yán-'rén** spokesman.

發言權

fā-yán-'chywán (*Nabstr*) the right to express one's opinions.

發源（地）

ı̣a-ywán(-'dì) (*Nunit, ge*) origin, source. ‖**jèy-tyáw-'hé-de-fā-ywán-'dì dzày sz̀-'chwān.** The source of this river is in Szechwan.

乏

fá (*A*) to be tired (**lèy** *is more often used*).

罰金

fá-'jīn (*Nmass; bǐ*) fine (*legal punishment*).

罰款

fá-'kwǎn (*N*) to impose a fine in punishment (*legal*).

法

***fǎ** (*Nunit, jyàn, tyáw; ge*) law, act, bill. **lì-'fǎ** to enact a law; **túng-gūng-'fǎ** the child labor act; **láw-gūng-'fǎ** labor laws, *etc.*
   Added to a verb means way of . . . : **'bàn-fǎ** (*or* **'bàn-fa**) way, method, means of operating, managing; **'fāng-fǎ** (*or* **'fāng-fa;** *similarly with all such compounds*) plan for doing something; **'kàn-fǎ** point of view, way of looking at things. *Sometimes has this meaning when added to nouns:* **'chyǎng-fǎ** technique with firearms, shooting form.

法國

***fǎ, *fà; 'fǎ-gwo, 'fà-gwo** (*Nunique*) France.

法案

fǎ-'àn (*Nunit, ge*) bill, law. ‖**nèy-ge-fǎ-'àn háy méy-'tūng-gwò.** That bill hasn't been passed yet.

法官

fǎ-'gwān (*Npers*) judge (*in court*).

法律

fǎ-'lywù (*Nunit, tyáw, ge*) law (*on the statute books*).

法庭

fǎ-'tíng (*Nunit, chù, ge*) court of law; courtroom.

法院

fǎ-'ywàn (*Nunit, chù, ge*) court of law.

法國

'fà-gwo (*Nunique*) France.

翻

fān (*I*) to turn upside down, be inverted (*also causatively*). *In causative sense:* to look for *by turning everything upside down and looking under it;* to turn over *pages, looking for something in the book.*
   As postV: **pèng-'fān** to overturn *by colliding;* **dǎ-'fān** to overturn *especially by striking; etc.*
   As mainV: **'fān-gwò** (*lc*) to turn over; **'fān-shàng** (*lc*) to turn *the other side of something* up; **'fān-chū-lay** to turn *something* inside out; *also metaphorically in searching for something.* ‖**chwán bèy-'fēng gěy gwā-'fān-le.** The wind overturned the boat. ‖**bǎ nèy-ge-kǎ-'pyàr 'fān-shàng-lay.** Turn that card face up.

帆

fān (*Nunit, ge, shàn*) sail (*of cloth, on a boat*). **fān-'chwán** (*Nunit, jř, tyáw*) sailboat.
   gwà-'fān to spread sail; **yáng-'fān** to set the sails; **shyà-'fān** to strike sail.

番

fān (*Mgroup*) a series of **hwà** (*words*), sentences, forming a speech (*informal*); a **yǎn-'jyǎng** (*lecture*); *etc. with other nouns for talk and speech.* ‖**tā shwō-le jǐ-fān-'hwà.** He gave several talks.

一帆風順

yì-'fān fēng-'shwèn (*literary quotation*) to have all one's sails in the wind; to be lucky.
   Used as a farewell remark: Bon voyage!

番薯

fān-'shǔ (*Nunit, ge, tyáw*) potato.

翻譯

'fān-yì (*V*) to translate, interpret, (**fān** *is sometimes used instead of* **'fān-yì** *for* translate). *As mainV:* **'fān-yì-chū-lay** to translate *when it is from the not generally known language into the one known.* ‖**wǒ bù-'dǔng tā shwō shéme-'hwà; chǐng-ni gěy-wo 'fān(-yì).** I don't understand what he's saying; please translate for me.

fān dyàn-'măr to encode *or* decode; *particularly in telegraphy, where characters are transmitted as numbers.*

fān-yì-'ywán interpreter.

煩

fán (*A*) fed up, bored; worried, disturbed. ‖**wǒ 'shīn-lǐ-tew hěn 'fán.** I'm very disturbed.

(*V*) (*somewhat literary*) to disturb *someone;* bore *someone.* ‖**nǐ byé law 'fán-ta.** Don't always be bothering him.

fán-'shr̆ boring matters, bothersome matters, troublesome affairs.

凡

***fán** (*before nouns*) all, every, each. ‖**'fán-rén dēw chr̆-'fàn.** All men eat.

'**fán-shr̆** all *those who are,* all *that which is.* ‖**'fán-shr̆ shyăw-'hár dēw bù-'shywǔ 'jìn-lay.** All (*those who are*) children are forbidden to enter.

(*Both somewhat literary, but* '**fán-shr̆** *is more often used colloquially.*)

煩悶

fán-'mèn (*A*) dull, uninteresting. ‖**jīn-tyan-de-'shyāw-shi hěn fán-'mèn.** Today's news is quite dull.

To be grieved. ‖**wǒ 'shīn-lǐ-tew hěn fán-'mèn.** I'm very sad.

反

făn (*I*) to rebel, to riot; (*of children, etc.*) to behave boisterously, make lots of noise. ‖**tā-de-jywūn-'dwèy 'făn-le.** His troops rebelled.

As mainV: '**făn-dàw** to reach *a place* in a rebellion which is spreading. ‖**jywūn-'dwèy háy méy-'făn-dàw 'jèy-ge-chéng.** The rebellion of the troops hasn't yet reached this city.

反倒

făn-'dàw (*J.*) and yet, *showing contrast with what has gone before.* ‖**wǒ méy-dă-'nǐ, nǐ făn-'dàw dă-le 'wǒ-le.** I dïdn't strike you, and yet you've struck me!

反對

făn-'dwèy (*V*) to oppose, be opposed to. ‖**wǒ făn-'dwèy nǐ shwō 'nèy-jywù-hwà.** I'm opposed to your saying THAT. ‖**wǒ făn-'dwèy 'nǐ shwō nèy-jywù-hwà.** I'm opposed to YOUR saying that.

反個兒

făn-'gèr (*VN2*) to turn *something* inside out (*or* upside down). ‖**bă nèy-ge-'bǐng făn yí-ge-'gèr dzày 'já-yi-já.** Turn that (*fish*) cake over and fry it some more.

反攻

făn-'gūng (*VN1*) to launch a counteroffensive. (*Nunit,* **tsz̆**) counteroffensive, counterattack.

反正

făn-'jèng (*J*) anyway, anyhow, by any means. ‖**făn-'jèng wǒ bù-néng 'chywù; nǐ byé 'shwō-le.** I can't go anyway, so stop talking about it.

反之

'**făn-jr̆** (*J*) (*literary*) on the contrary. ‖**'nǐ shwō shr̆-'báy; 'făn-jr̆ 'tā shwō shr̆-'hēy.** You say it's white; on the contrary, he says it's black.

反抗

făn-'kàng (*V*) to resist (*an enemy, higher authority, power*). (*Nabstr*) resistance.

反目

făn-'mù (*VN1*) to quarrel, have a spat (*particularly of husband and wife*).

反面

'**făn-myàn,** '**făn-myàr** (*Nplace*) the reverse, wrong side of, *any flat thing that has two faces, one of them being the* right *face.* ‖**nǐ 'yě ké-yi dzày 'jr̆-de-făn-myàr 'shyě.** You can write on the reverse side of the paper too. ‖**tā 'cháng-cháng shwō 'făn-myàr-de-'hwà.** He always says the opposite from what he means.

反手

făn-'shěw (*VN1*) to strike back, counterattack (*in hand-to-hand combat*).

反應

făn-'yìng (*VN1*) to react, respond. ‖**wǒ 'dă-ta de-shŕ-hew tā méy-făn-'yìng.** When I struck him he didn't react.

(*Nabstr*) ‖**jèy-ge-'jēn 'dă-shyà-chywù; yěw shéme-făn-'yìng méy-yew?** Has there been any reaction to the injection?

飯

fàn (*Nmass*) rice; (*also* **báy-'fàn**) plain white boiled rice, cooked rice; *with M* **dwèn** meal.

In many contexts simply means food. **chr̆-'fàn** (*VN2*) to eat. **wăn-'fàn** evening meal; **dzăw-'fàn** breakfast; **wǔ-'fàn** noon meal; '**fàn-chyán** payment for food, for meals.

犯

fàn (*V*) to violate, transgress against. **fàn-'dzwèy** to commit a crime; **fàn-'fă** to break the law; **fàn-'gwēy** to violate regulations; **fàn-'tswèr** to make a mistake. *In compounds:* an offense. '**chū-fàn** the first offense.

飯車

fàn-'chē (*Nunit,* **lyàng**) dining car (*on a train*).

飯店

fàn-'dyàn (*Nunit,* **jyān, jyā, swǒ**) hotel *of the Western type with meals optional.* Compare **lywǔ-'gwăn.**

飯館子（兒）

fàn-'gwǎn-dz, fàn-'gwǎr (*Nunit*, jyā, jyān, ge) restaurant.

犯人

'fàn-rén (*Npers*) prisoner (*criminal*).

犯人室

fàn-rén-'shr̆ (*Nunit*, jyān) cell (*in a jail*).

犯不上

fàn-bu-'shàng (*RC2*) not be worthwhile. ‖wǒ fàn-bu-'shàng yùng 'shŕ-kwày-chyán mǎy 'nèy-yì-běr-shū. It isn't worthwhile for me to spend ten dollars for that book.

飯廳

fàn-'tīng (*Nunit*, jyān, ge) dining room.

飯菜

fàn-'tsày (*Ncoll*) food, things eaten at a meal. ‖'tām-nàr-de-fàn-'tsày 'hǎw-bu-hǎw? How's the food over there?

飯碗

fàn-'wǎn (*NunitC*, ge) rice bowl.
    A person's job, way of making a living. ‖tā 'dyēw-le tā-de-fàn-'wǎn. *or* tā 'dzá-le tā-de-fàn-'wǎn. He lost his job (*literally* He broke his rice bowl).

範圍

fàn-'wéy (*Nabstr*) sphere, sphere of influence or authority, compass, scope. ‖tā gwǎn-bu-'jáw, yīn-wey bú-dzày tā-fàn-'wéy-jr̆-'shyà. He can't do anything, because it's out of his jurisdiction.

方

fāng (*Aattr*) square (*shape*). **fāng-'jwō-dz** square table. *Prefixed to Mmeas to form square measures. See Appendix B.*
    (*Mauton*) side of a dispute, contending party, *especially at law.* **shwāng-'fāng** both parties, both sides; **'yì-fāng** one side; *etc.*
    *fāng (*Nplace*) part, territory. **nán-'fāng** southern part (*e.g., of a country*); *similarly with other direction words and their compounds.*

方便

'fāng-byàn (*A*) convenient, handy.

方子

'fāng-dz (*Nunit*, jāng) prescription. **kāy 'fāng-dz** to write a prescription.

方法

'fāng-fa (*Nunit*, ge) method, way of doing something.

方針

fāng-'jēn (*Nunit*, ge) aim, purpose, policy, direction one is going in (*figuratively*). ‖jèy-ge-gūng-'sz̄-de-fāng-'jēn bú-'dàn-shr jwàn-'chyán, yě yàw tí-'gāw rén-'mín-'shēng-hwó-de-byāw-'jwěn. The policy (*purpose, aim*) of this company isn't merely to make a profit, but also to raise the standard of living of the people.

方塊

fāng-'kwày, fāng-'kwàr (*Aattr*) square-shaped. *In cards:* (*Nunit*, ge) diamonds.

方面

'fāng-myàn (*Mpos*) side *of anything;* (*figuratively*) *of a question, discussion.* ‖měy-yí-ge-'wèn-tí yěw 'lyǎng-'fāng-myàn. There are two sides to every question.

防

fáng (*V*) to be on the lookout against (*or* for), to be prepared against, alert against. **fáng-'shwěy** to guard against flood; **fáng-'lwàn** to guard against disorder. ‖ni byé fáng-'wǒ, yīng-gay fáng-'dzéy. Don't be watching ME so carefully; guard against the thieves.

房（子）

*fáng, 'fáng-dz (*Nunit*, swǒ, dzwò, jyān) house. *In compounds sometimes room, building.* **fáng-'dzū** house rent; **'fáng-chyán** room rent, house rent; **fáng-'mén, fáng-'mér** door to a room; **fáng-'kè** roomer, paying house guest; **fáng-'jǔr** landlord, house owner; **fáng-'dǐng** roof.

妨礙

fáng-'ày (*V*) to block, prevent *someone from doing something.* ‖tā dzwò 'jèy-jyàn-shr̆-ching áng-'ày wo. His doing that will hinder me.

防備

fáng-'bèy (*V*) prepare (against), be on guard (against). ‖ni děy fáng-'bèy-je-dyǎr 'tā. You must be a bit on guard against him.

房產

fáng-'chǎn (*Nmass*) property (*houses and buildings only*).

防毒劑

fáng-dú-'jì (*Nmass*) antiseptics.

防護

fáng-'hù (*V*) to protect, guard from danger. ‖ni-de-dzé-'rèn shr̆ fáng-'hù 'jèy-yí-dày-de-'dì-fang, byé 'bèy-rén 'jàn-le. Your responsibility is to defend this region, and not let anyone occupy it.

防止

fáng-'jǐ (V) to stop, check, terminate. ‖wǒm bì-'děy fáng-'jǐ chwán-rǎn-'bìng. We must check (the spread of) contagious diseases.

房間

fáng-'jyān (Nunit, jyān, ge) room. In a hotel one has a fáng-'jyān, not a 'wū-dz, which is another term for room.

防空洞

fáng-kūng-'dùng (Nunit, ge, chù) air-raid shelter.

防空室

fáng-kūng-'shr̀ (or -'shǐ) (Nunit, jyān, swǒ, ge) air-raid shelter under a building, in a basement.

房樑

fáng-'lyáng (Nunit, gēn, gēr) horizontal beam in the structure of a house.

防線

fáng-'shyàn (Nunit, tyáw, dàw) line of defense (military).

房艙

fáng-'tsāng (Nunit, jyān, ge) cabin (on a ship). A large cabin for many passengers paying small fares is tǔng-'tsāng.

防禦

fáng-'ywù (V) to guard against an enemy.

倣

fǎng (V) to imitate, copy. ‖tā-chwān-de-'yī-fu shr̀ fǎng 'měy-gwo-de-'yàng-dz 'dzwò-de. The dress she's wearing is modeled on an American style.

彷彿

'fǎng-fù (Vpred) to appear to be, seem to be, (often with shr̀-de later in the sentence). ‖tā 'fǎng-fù bú-'ywàn-yì 'dzěw (shr̀-de). He doesn't seem to want to go.

倣效

fǎng-'shyàw (V) to imitate, pattern on, model on, a fashion, a standard, etc. ‖byě fǎng-'shyàw wo! Don't imitate me.

放

fàng (V) to release, let go of, let go, set free. fàng-'chyāng to fire a rifle; fàng-'pàw to fire a gun; fàng-'shwěy to turn on the water (at a tap); fàng-'shēng dà 'rǎng to let out a loud yell (literally to release the voice and yell loudly); fàng-'dzéy to release a thief.

To put something at a place; to put an ingredient into food. fàng-'yán to put some salt in. bǎ nèy-ge-'dūng-shi fàng-'nàr. Put that thing there.

As mainV: 'fàng-chǐ-láy to store things away; 'fàng-chū-chywù to release, to let out, or (of a weapon) to go off; 'fàng-gwò (lc) to permit someone to pass across a boundary; 'fàng-hwéy (lc) to put something back, or to let someone go back (as to one's base); 'fàng-jìn (lc) to put something into something; 'fàng-shyà (sometimes lc) to put something down; 'fàng-dzày to put something at, or on a place; fàng-dzay yí-'kwàr to put things together; fàng-dzay yì-'byār set something aside.

As mainV, with an A as postV, means to make, to render. fàng-'dà to enlarge; fàng-'kwān to broaden; fàng-'píng to put something down flat instead of lopsided; fàng-'sūng to loosen a belt, etc.

放棄

fàng-'chì (V) to abandon, give up, renounce, discard. ‖nǐ byé fàng-'chì nǐ-'dz̀-jǐ-de-chywán-'lì. Don't renounce your rights.

放假

fàng-'jyà (VN2) to release someone for a vacation; to have a vacation.

放浪

'fàng-làng (A) loose (morally); playboyish.

放盤

'fàng-pán (VN1) to have a special sale with reduced prices.

放砲

fàng-'pàw (VN2) to fire a gun (large-caliber weapon); (figuratively) to go boom, to burst (as a tire).

放心

fàng-'shīn (A) to rest easy, be assured. ‖wǒ bú-fàng-'shīn. I'm anxious about it; concerned about it.

放血

fàng-'shyě (VN2) to let blood (medically).

放學

fàng-'shywé (VN1) to let school out.

fei Wade Romanization for fey.

分

fēn (V) to divide, separate, distinguish, share; to be divided into, contain, include parts, be composed of. ‖wǒ bǎ nèy-kwày-'bǐng fēn lyǎng-'kwàr. I'll divide this cake into two pieces. ‖měy-gwo fēn sz̀-shr-'bā-'shěng. The United States is composed of forty-eight states. ‖wǒ-men fēn-'byār sày-'chyéw-ba. Let's choose sides (literally divide up into sides) and play ball.

As mainV: **'fēn-chéng** to divide into, be divided into *so many parts, pieces, etc.*; **fēn-'chīng** or **fēn-'chīng-chu** or **'fēn-chū-lay** to distinguish *which is which*; **'fēn-chū-chywu** to branch out, share, distribute, issue; **'fēn-gěy** share *something* with *somebody*; **'fēn-kāy** to separate, keep apart.

分
fēn (*Mpart*), **yì-fēn-'jūng** a minute; **yì-fēn-'chyán** a cent, a penny.

    (*Mmeas*) one-tenth **tswèn** (*inch*); one one-hundredth of a **lyǎng** (*tael*).

    Used in giving fractions and percentages: **'X-fēn-jr-'Y** is *Y* Xths, (*where Y and X are numbers*); **'èr-fēn-jr-'yī** one half; **'měy-gwo-'rén-kěw-de-'shf-fēn-jr-'bā** eight-tenths of the American population; **'bǎy-fēn-jr-'èr-shf** twenty percent.

    'shf-fēn 'hǎw perfect (*literally* ten parts good).

    See Appendix B.

分
fēn (*Mmeas*). *See Appendix B.*

分
*fēn before nouns branch-. **fēn-'chū** branch office *of something the main office of which ends in* ***chū**; *the following similarly:* **fēn-'gwǎn** branch-gwǎn (*library, museum, etc.*); **fēn-'háng** branch bank, branch store; **fēn-'hàw** branch store; **fēn-'jywú** branch-jywú (*post office, police station, telephone office, telegraph office, etc.*); **fēn-'shyàw** branch school; **fēn-'hwèy** branch organization; *etc.*

分辨
fēn-'byàn (*V*) to distinguish between (*in thinking or talking*). ‖**děy fēn-'byàn nèy-lyǎng-ge-'yì-sz.** You've got to distinguish between those two ideas.

    As mainV: **fēn-'byàn-chū-lay** to tell the difference between.

    fēn-'byàn shr-'fēy to tell right from wrong.

分別
fēn-'byé (*V*) to distinguish between. ‖**tā bù-'néng fēn-'byé 'húng gēn-'lywù.** He can't distinguish between red and green.

    As mainV: **fēn-'byé-chū-lay** to tell the difference between.

    (*H*) separately, distinctly.

分岔
fēn-'chàr (*VN2*) to fork (*as of a road*); to branch out, (*as a road and a branch road*). ‖**nèy-tyáw-'lù-fēn-sān-ge-'chàr-de-dì-fang yīng-gay 'lì yí-ge-'páy-dz.** There ought to be a signpost there where the road forks into three branches.

分期
fēn-'chī (*H*) in installments. **fēn-'chī fù-'kwǎn** (*a bit literary*) or **fēn-'chī gěy-'chyán** to pay installments.

分道
fēn-'dàw(r) (*VN2*) (*literally and figuratively*) to take different roads. ‖**tsúng-'jèr chǐ, wǒm děy fēn-'dàwr dzěw.** From here on we have to take different roads.

吩咐
'fēn-fù (*V*) to give instruction *or* instructions to. ‖**tā chū-'mér de-shf-hew tā-'fù-chin 'fēn-fu ta yàw 'shyǎw-shīn.** When he left home his father instructed him to be careful.

分毫
fēn-'háw (*H*) to the tiniest possible extent; *usually with* **bū-** to mean not at all, not even to the slightest extent. ‖**wǒ fēn-'háw dēw bù-'jr-'dàw.** I don't know even the slightest thing about it.

    'fēn-háw bù-'chā to be exactly the same, completely identical.

分居
fēn-'jywū (*VN1*) to separate (*of a married couple*). ‖**tām yǐ-jing fēn-'jywū hěn 'jyěw-le.** They've been separated for a long time.

分配
'fēn-pèy (*V*) to allocate *something* among several people. ‖**nǐ 'gěy tā-men 'fēn-pèy 'shr-ching 'dzwò.** Allocate this matter among them (for them to take care of).

分手
fēn-'shěw (*VN1*) to part, say good-by.

分數
'fēn-shù(r) (*Nunit, ge*) a grade *in school*; a score *in a game*. ‖**dà-'kǎw-de-'fēn-shù hěn 'yàw-jǐn.** The grade in the final exam is very important.

分說
fēn-'shwō (*V*) to explain, state one's case about. *Limited in use to the following type of situation:* ‖**tā méy-yew 'jī-hwèy fēn-'shwō nèy-ge-'shr-shr-de-jēn-'shyàng.** He was given no chance to explain the real situation.

汾陽
fēn-'yáng (*Nunique*) Fen-yang (*city in Shansi province*).

坟
fén (*Nunit, ge*) grave, tomb.

坟地
fén-'dì (*Nunit, kway, pyàn, ge*) graveyard.

粉
fén (*Nmass*) powder (*any kind, including face powder but not gunpowder*).

粉 (紅)

fĕn (*Aattr*), fĕn-'húng (*A*) pink.

粉碎

fĕn-'swèy (*N*) tiny bits, very fine particles. 'swèy-chéng fĕn(-'swèy) to shatter into very tiny pieces, to disintegrate; fĕn-'shēn swèy-'gŭ (*literary*) to sacrifice oneself to the point of physical collapse for the good of some cause.

糞

fĕn (*Nmass*) manure, excreta. mǎ-'fèn horse manure; nyéw-'fèn cattle manure; rén-fèn human excreta.
     fèn-'fū (*Npers*) person who collects human excretions for fertilizer.

分, 份

fèn, fèr (*Munit*) one issue, number, edition, (*of something published periodically*). yí-fèr-'bàw one issue of a newspaper.
     (*Mpart*) part, portion. ‖wǒm bǎ jèy-shyē-'chyán 'fēn-chéng sān-'fèr. We'll divide this money into three °parts. *or* °shares.

奮鬥

fèn-'dèw (*I*) to struggle *in competition*. wéy gwó-'jyā-de-'chyán-tú yùng-'lì fèn-'dèw to struggle mightily for the future of one's country.

分, 份

'fèn-dž (*Nunit, ge*) faction, element, group, *within an organization*. ‖yí-ge-'jèng-fŭ-'lǐ-tew něy-'dǎng-de-'fèn-dž dēw 'yěw. In one government there are all kinds of elements.

分量

'fèn-lyàng (*Nabstr*) weight (*like* 'jùng-lyàng *but on a smaller scale*). ‖nèy-ge-'dzwàn-shŕ yěw dwō-shaw-'fèn-lyàng? How much does that diamond weigh?

封

fēng (*V*) to seal. fēng-'mén to seal a door; fēng 'shyāng-dz to seal a box.
     To block *a passage*. fēng-'lù to block a road; fēng-'hé to close off a river (*as ice does in winter*).
     As mainV: 'fēng-chǐ-láy *or* 'fēng-shàng to seal up; fēng-'jǐn-le to seal tightly; fēng-dzay yí-'kwàr to seal *things* together.

封

fēng (*Munit*) one shìn (*letter in an envelope*); one dyàn-'bàw (*telegram in an envelope*); *etc. for other communications which come in sealed envelopes.*

風

fēng (*N*) wind; *with M* jèn storm. gwā-'fēng (*IN*) to be windy; chǐ-'fēng (*IN*) the wind rises; fēng °shī-le *or* °'píng-le the wind dies down; fēng-'kěwr a draft;

fēng-'làng storm at sea (*literally* wind and waves); fēng-'ywǔ storm (*literally* wind and rain); fēng-'chwēy-ywǔ-'dǎ-de weatherbeaten. ‖jīn-nyan gwā-'fēng-de-r̀-dz bù-'dwō. There haven't been many windy days this year. ‖fēng 'dà-de bǎ-rén dēw °chwēy-'dǎw-le *or* °gwā-'dǎw-le. The wind is so strong that it topples you over.

瘋

fēng (*A*) insane. ‖tā yěw yì-dyǎr-'fēng. He's a little off.
     bàn-'fēngr (*Npers*) half-wit (*in calling names*).
     fēng-'gěw mad dog (*literally or in calling names*).

蜂

fēng (*Nunit, ge*) stinging insects; bees, wasps, hornets. mì-'fēng (honey) bee.

風潮

fēng-'cháw (*N*) wind and tide, the movement of wind and tide; (*figuratively*) unrest, agitation, ferment of ideas. ‖gūng-rén nàw fēng-'cháw. The workers are arising (*getting active politically, organizing, educating themselves, tending to strike, etc.*). ‖fēng-'cháw 'gwò-chywu. The period of unrest has passed by.

丰度

fēng-'dù (*Nabstr*) well-behaved *or* well-bred manner, conduct, appearance (*a bit literary*).

豐富

'fēng-fu (*A*) abundant, rich. ‖nèy-ge-dì-fang-de-ywán-'lyàw hěn 'fēng-fu. That territory is abundant in material resources.

風景

'fēng-jing (*Nabstr*) scenery, view. ‖'shān-de-'fēng-jing hěn hǎw 'kàn. Mountain scenery is beautiful.

蜂蜜

fēng-'mì (*Nmass*) (bee's) honey.

瘋人院

fēng-rén-'ywàn (*Nunit, swǒ, ge*) insane asylum, mental hospital.

風箱

fēng-'shyāng (*Nunit, ge*) bellows.

風俗

'fēng-su, fēng-'sú (*Nabstr*) customs, practices, usages. 'fēng-su-shì-'gwàn custom and tradition. ‖'gè-chù-de-'fēng-su bù-yí-'yàng. Every place has its own customs.

丰采

fēng-'tsǎy (*Nabstr*) (*a bit literary*) virile appearance, striking features.

風土人情

'fēng-tǔ-rén-'chíng (*Nabstr*) local manners and customs. ‖wǒ gāng 'dàw-jèr; 'fēng-tǔ-rén-'chíng dēw bù-'shéw-shí. I've just arrived here; I'm totally unfamiliar with the local customs.

封條

fēng-'tyáw(r) (*Nunit*, jāng) seal *on an envelope, door, svitcase, etc.*

蜂窩

fēng-'wō(er) (*Nunit*, ge) beehive, hornet's nest, wasp's nest. mì-fēng-'wō(er) beehive.

風雨無阻

fēng-'ywǔ-wú-'dzǔ (*literary quotation*) come hell or high water, rain or shine.

縫

féng (*V*) to sew, *usually* by hand. *As mainV:* 'féng-shàng to sew up, sew on; 'féng-chǐ-lay to sew up; 'féng-dzay yí-'kwàr to sew *things* together; *etc.*

縫

fèng(r) (*Nunit*, tyáw) crack, split; seam; part (*in hair*). ‖'bwō-li 'lyè-le yì-tyáw-'fèngr. The glass cracked.

奉承

'fèng-cheng (*V*) to praise, try to please *someone* with good words (*often with an ulterior motive*).

奉到

'fèng-dàw (*V*) to receive (*like* 'shèw-dàw *but a bit more formal, polite, and literary*).

奉贈

fèng-'dzèng (*V2*) to give free, offer free (*a bit literary*). ‖'jèy-běn-shū shř wǒ fèng-'dzèng ni-de. This book is a free gift from me to you.

奉令

fèng-'lìng (*H*) by order, under orders, by order of *so-and-so* (*official*). ‖wǒ fèng-'lìng láy-'jèr 'kàn-ni. I came here to see you under orders. ‖wǒ fèng tā-de-'lìng dzwò jèy-jyàn-'shř. I did this under orders from him.

奉命

fèng-'mìng (*H*) unaer orders, by order of *someone* (*official or unofficial*).

分兒

fēr (*Mauton*) point *in scoring in a game;* grade *in school.* ‖wǒ-men 'yǐ-jing yěw sān-'fēr-le. We've already made three points. ‖ni jèy-mén-'gūng-ke dé-le dwō-shaw-'fēr? What grade did you get in this course?

浮

féw (*or* fú) (*I*) to float *on the surface of a liquid.* *As mainV:* 'féw-dzày to float on (*particularly* 'shàng-byan the surface); 'féw-chǐ-láy to float up to the surface; 'féw-dàw to float to *a place.*

(*A*) for people, (*figuratively*): ‖'nèy-ge-rén hěn 'féw. That man isn't stable, he floats around from one thing to another.

浮標

féw-'byāw (*Nunit*, ge) buoy.

否決

féw-'jywé-le didn't pass, was voted down (*of a bill, a motion*).

否認

féw-'rèn (*Vsent*) to deny. ‖tā féw-'rèn jèy-jyàn-'shř-ching shř 'tā-dzwò-de. He denies that he did this thing.

非

fēy (*H*) not, isn't, aren't. *Literary except in the following use:* 'fēy *or* 'fēy-děy *followed by verb or verb expression, optionally followed by* bù-'kě *or* bù-'shíng, *meaning* absolutely must, without fail must. ‖wǒ 'fēy(-děy) chywù. *or* wǒ 'fēy(-děy) chywù bù-'kě. *or* wǒ 'fēy(-děy) chywù bù-'shíng. I've absolutely got to go. *or* It just wouldn't do for me not to go. *An alternative is to replace* děy *by* yàw *in all the above.*

飛

fēy (*I*) to fly. *As mainV:* 'fēy-dàw (*lc*) to fly to *a place;* 'fēy-gwò (*lc*) to fly past, fly over; 'fēy-shyà (*lc*) to fly down; 'fēy-chǐ-láy *or* 'fēy-shàng (*lc*) to fly up; fēy yí-ge-'chywār to fly in a circle, fly around, circle, (*as a plane about to land*).

(*H*) very fast. *Limited to:* fēy 'kwày very fast; fēy 'pǎw to run very fast.

菲（洲）

*fēy, 'fēy-jēw (*Nunique*) (the continent of) Africa.

非常

fēy-'cháng (*H*) extremely, extraordinarily. ‖jīn-tyan tā fēy-'cháng(-de) gāw-'shìng. He's extraordinarily light-hearted today.

飛禽

fēy-'chín (*Nunit*, jř, ge) birds that can fly.

飛機

fēy-'jī (*Nunit*, jyà) airplane. fēy-jī-'téw *or* fēy-jī-chyán-'bù bow of a plane; fēy-jī-'shìn air mail.

飛機場

fēy-jī-'chǎng (*Nunit*, ge) airport, airfield.

飛機母艦
fēy-jī-mǔ-'jyàn (*Nunit, jī̆, tyáw, ge*) aircraft carrier.

菲律濱
fēy-lywù-'bīn (*Nunique*) The Philippines.

飛舞
fēy-'wǔ (*I*) to wave. flap (*as of a flag*)

飛揚
fēy-'yáng (*I*) to fly around (*as dust in the air*). *As mainV:* **fēy-'yáng-chi-lay** to spray upwards and fly around (*as dust blown by the wind*).

肥皂
féy-'dzàw (*Nm... , ...ap.*

肥
féy (*A*) fat (*of an animal*); loose (*of clothing*); rich, fertile (*of soil, land*).

匪
fěy (*A*) fast (*as in fast company*), fast and loose; just on the borderline of respectability, or a little outside it. ‖**tā-shwō-'hwà-de-yàng-dz hěn 'fěy.** His manner of talking is not quite respectable (*too much profanity, obscenity, and talk of improper things, showing lack of moral responsibility*).

    fěy-'chì the air, appearance, of being this way. ‖**tā 'fěy-li-fěy-'chì-de.** He has the air of being not too refined (*but one can't tell for sure from his behavior alone*).

    'fěy-rén a morally reprehensible person. *In compounds may have stronger meaning:* **tú-'fěy** bandits.

廢
fèy (*V*) to waste, expend uselessly. **fèy-'chyán** to waste money; **fèy-'hwà** idle talk, hot air, nonsense; **fèy-'jř** waste paper; **'fèy-wù** trash, useless things.

費
fèy (*V*) to expend, pay out; to require the expenditure of.

    fèy-'chyán (*VN2*) to pay out money; (*A*) to be expensive.

    fèy-'shīn, (*A*) to use one's mind, expend one's mental energy, go to trouble; to be troublesome, call for the expenditure of energy or thought.

    fèy-'lì or **fèy-'jìn** (*VN1, A*) to use energy, effort; to be strenuous.

肺
fèy (*Nunit, ge*) lungs.

肺病
fèy-'bìng (*Nabstr*) tuberculosis.

肺炎
fèy-'yán (*Nabstr*) pneumonia.

費用
'fèy-yùng (*Nabstr*) expenses, expenditures.

fo *Wade Romanization for* **fwo.**

fou *Wade Romanization for* **few.**

夫
*****fū** (*Npers*) person who does *something*. **'chē-fu** car driver; **'hwǒ-fu** fireman (*locomotive*); **'dà-shř-fu** chef (*polite term of address*); **chīng-'dàw-fū** street-cleaner; *etc.*

夫
*****fū** (*Npers*) uncle by marriage to father's or mother's sister. *See Appendix A.*

敷
fū *or* **fú** (*V*) to cover *financially*; to smear, cover *by smearing* (*so...ewhat literary*). ‖**rù bù-fū-'chū.** The income doe...n't cover the expenses. ‖**jèy-ge-'yàw shř wày-'fú-de.** This medicine is to be applied externally.

孵蛋
fū-'dàn (*VN2*) to set (on eggs). ‖**jī dzày fū-'dàn.** The hen is setting.

夫婦
'fū-fù (*Ncoll*) man and wife.

夫人
'fū-rén (*NpersT*) madame (*polite term of address for the wife of an important man*).

孵窩
fū-'wō (*VN1*) to set (*of a hen*).

浮
fú *see* **féw.**

扶
fú (*V*) to lean the hand on *table, wall, someone else. As mainV:* **'fú-dzay** to lean on (*as above*); **'fú-chi-lay** to help *someone* up with the hands; *etc.* ‖**tā fú-je léw-'tī shyà-'léw.** He came downstairs leaning on the bannister (*literally* leaning on the stairsteps).

服
fú (*I*) to be convinced. *As postV:* **nùng-'fú** to convince; **shwō-'fú** to convince by talking, by using words; **dǎ-'fú** to convince by beating, *etc.*

    (*V*) *in the special group* **fú 'shwěy-tǔ** to acclimatize oneself, adapt oneself to a climate; *and in* **fú-'yàw** (*VN2*) to take (liquid) medicine *or* **fú-'dú** (*VN2*) to take poison.

福（氣）
fú(-chì) (Nabstr) blessings, happiness, good fortune, prosperity. yěw-'fú(-chì) to be lucky, have good fortune. ‖nèy-ge-rén hěn yěw 'fú-chì. He's very lucky.

伏兵
fú-'bīng (Npers) sniper.

沸點
fú-'dyǎn (Nunit, ge) boiling point.

福州
fú-'jēw (Nunique) Foochow, another name for mǐn-'héw Min-hou (capital city of Fukien province).

福建
fú-'jyàn (Nunique) Fukien province.

俘虜
fú-'lěw, fú-'lǔ, fú-'lwǒ (V) to capture an enemy, an enemy's fighting equipment (anything movable).
(Npers) captive, prisoner.

扶手
'fú-shew (Nunit, ge) arms of a chair; rails of a bridge; bannister of a staircase; etc.; place to support oneself by one's hand.

服侍
'fú-shr (V) to wait on, serve.

拂曉
fú-'shyǎw (Ntime) daybreak, sunrise, very early morning (literary).

服從
fú-'tsúng (V) to obey. ‖nǐ děy fú-'tsúng wo. You must obey me.

複翼飛機
'fú-yì-fēy-'jī (Nunit, jyà) biplane.

腐
fǔ (I) to get spoiled, soured, rotten. ‖'rèw yǐ-jing 'fǔ-le. The meat is already spoiled.
The process may be desirable; 'dèw-fu bean-curd.

斧
fú(-dz) (Nunit, bǎ) ax, hatchet.

腐敗
fǔ-'bày (A) corrupt, ineffective, inefficient, spoiled, decadent, old and useless (of people or institutions).

複雜
fǔ-'dzá (A) complicated, intricate. ‖tā-shwō-de-'hwà hěn fǔ-'dzá. What he says is very intricate and hard to follow.

腐化
fǔ-'hwà (A) rendered ineffective, inefficient, corrupt, spoiled, decadent, old, worn-out (of a person or institution). fǔ-'hwà(-de)-fèn-'dž a corrupting element or faction.

府上
'fǔ-shàng (N) home, residence, in asking someone politely where he lives. The answer contains shè-'shyà humble home.
'wáng-fǔ the honorable Wáng residence.

膚施
fǔ-'shř (Nunique) Fu-shih (city in Shensi province).

負
fù (V) to assume, shoulder, bear, responsibility, blame, debts, tasks, etc. (a bit literary). fù 'dzé(-rèn) to shoulder a responsibility; fù-'jùng to bear a heavy burden; fù-'dàn to bear a burden.

負
*fù prefixed to numbers: minus, in the sense of negative number, not of subtraction. fù-'sān minus three. ‖jèng-'sž jyā fù-'sān dé (jèng-)'yī. Plus four plus minus three gives (plus) one.
fù-'hàw (Nunit, ge) the minus sign.

付
fù (V) to pay (money that is due). fù-'chyán to make a payment; fù-'jàng to pay a bill; fù-'kwǎn to hand over money; fù-'shwèy(-chyán) to pay taxes; 'fù-le Paid (written on bill).
As ma.nV: fù-'chǐng to pay in full, clear up a debt.

赴
fù (V) to attend. fù-'yàn attend a party, feast (a bit literary); fù-'hwèy attend a meeting.

附
fù (V) (often 'fù-yěw, 'fù-je) to be accompanied by, to have enclosed with it (in the case of a letter). ‖tā-de-'shìn-li 'fù-le yì-jāng-jř-'pyàw. His letter was accompanied by a check.

付
fù (Mgroup) a deck of páy (cards); a set of ten pairs of 'kwày-dz (chopsticks); a set of jwǒ-'yǐ (furniture); a pair of 'jwó-dz (bracelets); a pair of yǎn-'jyèngr (glasses); a set of wǎn-'dyéer (dishes); etc.; a set of something which comes in some conventional set, the units of which need not be identical or matching, but are of similar design and meant to be used together.

浮
*fù (I) to swim, fù-'shwěy to swim (in the water). As mainV: 'fù-dàw (lc) to swim to a place; 'fù-gwò (lc) to swim by, to swim across; etc.

副
*fù *before nouns* vice-. **fù-dzǔng-'tǔng** vice president (*of a government*). *Likewise prefixed to the term for the person in charge of an organization to form the term for his chief assistant:* **fù-jīng-'lǐ** assistant manager; **fù-jywú-'jǎng** assistant chief of an establishment (called a **jywú**); **fù-jǔ-'shí** vice chairman; *etc.*

父
*fù (*Npers*) father, grandfather, uncle. *See Appendix A.*

付表決
fù byǎw-'jywé (*VN1*) to vote (*in a meeting, in formal parliamentary procedure*).

付齊
fù-'chí (*V*) to pay in full. ‖**wǒ-de-'jàng dēw fù-'chí-le.** My bill has been paid in full.

婦道
fù-'dàw (*Nabstr*) the proper moral path for women, womanly virtues.

副官
fù-'gwān (*NpersT*) adjutant; aide-de-camp.

復活節
fù-hwó-'jyé (*N*) Easter. ‖**fù-hwó-'jyé-de-shŕ-hew 'nywǔrén dēw chwān shīn-'yī-fu, dày shīn-'màw-dz.** At Easter time women all put on new clothes and new hats.
    gwò fù-hwó-'jyé *or* **'chìng-ju fù-hwó-'jyé** to celebrate Easter.

附近
fù-'jìn (*Nplace*) vicinity, neighborhood, surrounding area. ‖**jèy-ge-'léw-fù-'jìn yěw yí-ge-'pù-dz ké-yi 'mǎy 'nèy-jǔng-dūng-shi.** There's a store near this building where you can buy that sort of thing.

附錄
fù-'lù (*Nunit*, **ge**) appendix (*of a book*). **fù-'lù dì-'sān** Appendix III.

婦女
fù-'nywǔ (*Ncoll*) womankind.

浮水衣
fù-shwěy-'yī (*Nunit*, **jyàn; tàw** *if in more than one piece*) swimming suit.

賦閑
fù-'shyán (*VN2*) to be out of a job. ‖**tā fù-'shyán-le sān-'nyán-le.** *or* **'tā fù-le sān-nyán-'shyán-le.** He's been out of work for three years.

蝴蝶
fù-'tyěr (*Nunit*, **ge**) butterfly.

副業
fù-'yè (*Nunit*, **ge**) sideline, secondary business, avocation.

附議
fù-'yì (*V*) to second *a motion.* ‖**wǒ fù-'yì tā-de-tí-'yì.** I second his motion.

復原
fù-'ywán (*I*) to recover, get better. ‖**tā-de-'bìng 'yǐ-jing fù-'ywán-le.** His illness is already gone away.

富於
'fù-ywú (*V*) to be rich in. ‖**jèy-ge-gwó-'jyā 'fù-ywú 'méy.** This country is rich in coal.
    'fù-ywú 'gǎn-chíng to be highly emotional.

富裕
'fù-ywù (*Aattr*) extra, to spare. ‖**nǐ 'yěw-méy-yew 'fù-ywù-de-'chyán?** Have you any money to spare?

佛
*fwó (*also* **fú**) (*Nunique*) Buddha. **bày-'fwó** to worship a Buddha; **fwó-'jyàw** Buddhism; **fwó-'shyàng** (*Nunit*, **dzwò, dzwēn, ge**) a Buddha, an image of Buddha; **nyàn-'fwó** to repeat the name of Buddha as a kind of prayer.

G

疙疸
'gā-da (*Nunit*, **ge**) a knot *in string or in wood;* a boil *on the skin.* **jǎng yí-ge-'gā-da** to grow a boil; **jì yí-ge-'gā-da** to tie a knot.
    lǎw-'gā-da (*colloquial*) the youngest child of a family.

疙里疙疸的
gā-li-gā-'dā(-de) (*A*) not smooth (*of a surface; of speaking; of the unfinished side of porcelain, etc*).

乾
gān (*A*) dry. (*Opposite* **shŕ** damp.) *As postV:* **tsā-'gān** to wipe dry; *etc.* *As mainV:* **'gān-chéng** to dry

into.   gǎn-cheng 'kwàr to dry into lumps, (*as of mud*).

乾杯
gǎn-'běy! Bottoms up! (*a toast; literally* Dry the cup!).

乾等
gǎn 'děng (*I*) to wait, mark time, *with nothing to do while waiting*.

杆子
'gǎn-dz (*Nunit*, gēr, jř) rod, stick.

乾燥無味
'gǎn-dzàw-wú-'wèy (*literary quotation*) (*A*) dry, dull, tasteless, boring.

乾果
gǎn-'gwǒ(-dz), gǎn-'gwěr (*Nunit*, ge) nuts and dried fruits. *In China there are special* gǎn-gwǒ-'pù *nut-and-dried-fruit stores, which sometimes sell a few other things.*

甘蔗
'gǎn-je (*Nunit*, gēr) sugar cane.

乾淨
'gǎn-jìng (*A*) clean. *As postV:* tsā-'gǎn-jìng to wipe clean, etc.

乾冷
gǎn-'lěng (*A*) biting cold, dry and cold *but not snowing*.

乾洗
gǎn-'shǐ (*V*) to dry-clean.

甘心
gǎn-'shīn (*A*) willing, content; (*H*) willingly, contentedly. ‖jèy-jyàn-shř-ching shř tā-'dž-jǐ gǎn-'shīn 'dzwò-de. He did it himself willingly (*of some unpleasant task*).

甘肅
'gǎn-su (*Nunique*) Kansu *province*.

乾草
gǎn-'tsǎw (*Nmass*) hay.

乾脆
gǎn-'tswèy (*A*) direct, unequivocal. ‖tā-shwō-de-'hwà hěn gǎn-'tswèy. He speaks very directly, right to the point.

橄欖
gán-'lǎn (*Nunit*, ge) olives.

趕
gǎn (*V*) to drive.   gǎn-'chē to drive a cart or vehicle *pulled by an animal*; gǎn-'mǎ to drive a horse; gǎn-'jū to drive pigs (*herding them to a barn or to the field, etc.*).   (*V*) to hurry and catch (*or make a train, etc.*); to hurry and overtake (*a person, etc., literally or figuratively*). *As mainV:* gǎn-'dàw to arrive in time (*to make a train, etc.*); gǎn-'dyàw to drive *something* out, get rid of; 'gǎn-gwò to catch up with and pass; gǎn-'jìn to drive *an animal, a person* into (*a stable, a house, etc.*); gǎn-'hwéy (*lc*) to hurry back, drive back; 'gǎn-kāy to break up (*a conspiracy, etc.*); gǎn-'sàn to scatter (*a group*); 'gǎn-shàng (*lc*) to catch up with (*literally or figuratively*).
'gǎn-je (*H*) working hurriedly, against time.

敢
gǎn (*Vpred*) to dare to, venture to. ‖wǒ gǎn 'shwō tā 'bú-shr ge-'hǎw-rén. I'll venture to say he's NOT a good man. ‖bù-gǎn 'dāng! (*polite phrase in negative answer to a compliment or complimentary question*): I couldn't dare to claim that!

擀
gǎn (*V*) to roll out (*dough only;* gǎn-'myàn, gǎn-'pyér). *As mainV:* gǎn-'píng to roll smooth and flat; gǎn-'dà to roll until it's bigger (*covers a bigger area*); gǎn-'báw to roll thin; *etc.*

桿
gǎn (*Munit*) a chyāng (*rifle*).

感情
'gǎn-chíng (*Nuostr*) influence, emotion, affection, sentiment. ‖tā gēn-ni yěw shéme-'gǎn-chíng? What influence has he with you?

感到
'gǎn-dàw (*RCS; potential forms not used*) to have reached *the same conclusion, opinion, feeling*. ‖wǒ yě gǎn-dàw tā shř 'jème-yàngr. I've also come to feel that he's like that.

感動
gǎn-'dùng (*V*) to move the emotions of, to be persuasive to, *people*. ‖tā-de-yǎn-'jyǎng hěn gǎn-'dùng rén. His speech was very convincing.

感激
gǎn-'jí (*V*) to feel grateful to.

感激不盡
‖gǎn-'jí bú-'jìn! I'm eternally grateful!

趕緊
'gǎn-jǐn (*H*) in a hurry, hurriedly, immediately. ‖jèy-jyàn-shř-ching nǐ děy 'gǎn-jǐn 'dzwò. Take care of this in a hurry.

感覺

gǎn-'jywé (*Vsent*) to feel *that*. ‖wǒ gǎn-'jywé tā dwèy-wǒ hěn 'hǎw. I feel that he's been very good to me. (*Nabstr*) feeling, opinion.

趕快

gǎn-'kwày (*H*) quickly, as soon as possible.

擀麪棍(杖)

gǎn-myàn-'gwèr (*or* -'jàng) (*Nunit*, ge, gēr) rolling pin.

感謝

gǎn-'shyè (*V*) to feel grateful to. ‖wǒ hěn gǎn-'shyè ta. I feel very grateful to him.

幹

*gàn *before nouns* main, principal. gàn-'shyàn (*Nunit*, tyáw) main road, trunk line; main conduit; gàn-'lù (*Nunit*, tyáw) main railroad line.

幹

gàn (*V*) to do. gàn-'shr̀ to do things, work; bú-'gàn-le to quit work, quit, stop doing something, give up some matter, decide not to do something.

　　As mainV: 'gàn-chū-lay to produce, come out with *something completed and contrary to expectations.* ‖tā 'gàn-chū-láy-le yí-jyàn-'hǎw-'shr̀. He's really produced a good piece of work there (*often sarcastic*).

　　gēn-rén 'gàn-shàng to quarrel with somebody, argue against someone.

贛州

gàn-'jēw (*Nunique*) Kanchow, *another name for* gàn-'shyàn Kan-hsien (*city in Kiangsi province*).

幹麼

gàn-'má *or* gàn 'shéme (*H*) how come?, what for? ‖nǐ gàn-'má dzwò 'jèy-ge? What are you doing this for? ‖gàn-'má bú-fàng-'shīn-ne? Why don't you just take it easy? ‖gàn-'má? *or* gàn 'shéme? (*As sentence*) How come? *or* What for? *or* What are you trying to do?

幹甚麼

gàn 'shéme *see* gàn-'má.

贛縣

gàn-'shyàn (*Nunique*) Kan-hsien (*city in Kiangsi province*).

鋼

gāng (*Nmass*) steel. gāng-'tyě iron and steel; gāng-'bǎn steel plates; gāng-'sz̄ steel wire.

剛

gāng (*H*) *with temporal meaning:* just now, just recently, just lately, just a moment ago, *but not right this minute of speaking. Otherwise:* just *what would* be expected; only such-and-such, less than would be expected. ‖tā gāng 'láy. He's just arrived. ‖tā gāng 'láy-de. He's a newcomer, a beginner. ‖tā 'gāng yàw gēn-ni 'shwō. He' just about to tell you (*i.e., he's just, a moment a⸱ ⸱, reached the point of being about to tell you*). ‖gāng 'hǎw! Just right!

　　Before expressions of quantity: gāng 'wǔ-jīn just (exactly) five catties *or* only five catties (*when more were expected*).

鋼筆

gāng-'bǐ (*Nunit*, gwǎn, jī̀, gēr) metal pen (*of any kind for writing*).

鋼琴

gāng-'chín (*Nunit*, jyà, ge) piano.
　　gāng-chín-'jyā (*Npers*) pianist.

剛剛

gāng-'gāng (*H*) *same as* gāng, ‖wǒ gāng-'gāng 'kàn jyan ta. I just now saw him.

鋼盔

gāng-'kwēy (*Nunit*, dǐng, ge) helmet (*of metal*)

肛門

gāng-'mén (*Nunit*, ge) anus.

剛纔

gāng-'tsáy (*H*) just this minute, just a minute ago, (*indicating a point in time just before the time of speaking*). ‖gāng-'tsáy gēn-ni shwō-'hwà de nèy-ge-rén shr̀-'shéy? Who was that man who was just talking with you?

港

*gǎng (*Nunit*, ge) harbor. hǎy-'gǎng port, bay, *or* harbor *on the seacoast;* gǎng-'kěw *same meaning, or* harbor entrance.

乾兒

*gār (*N*) something made by drying something. píng-gwo-'gār (*Nmass*, ge, kwày) dried apples; nyéw-rèw-'gār (*Nmass*) dried beef; myàn-bāw-'gār (*Nmass*) dry bread; bǐng-'gār (*Nmass*) biscuit, cookies, crackers.

高

gāw (*A*) high, tall, *literally and figuratively, as in English, of a pitch or note, of prices, etc.* (*Opposites* ǎy short, dī low.)

　　gāw-'ǎy (*Nabstr*) height. ‖jèy-lyǎng-ge-'dūng-shi-de-gāw-'ǎy chà-bu-'dwō. These two things are almost the same height.

　　gāw-'dù (*Nabstr*) altitude. ‖fēy-'jī fēy-daw shéme-gāw-'dù? To what altitude does this plane fly?

糕
gāw(r) (*Nmass*) cake (*relatively soft texture as compared to* **bǐng**). dzǎw-'gāwr date cake; jī-dàn-'gāw egg cake.

高出
'gāw-chū (*A*) higher than *by so much*. ‖'jèy-dzwò-léw bǐ nèy-shàn-'chyáng 'gāw-chū yí-'jàng. This building is ten feet higher than that wall.

高等
gāw-'děng (*A*) high-class, high quality; (*of people, residential districts, stores, etc.*).

高爾夫
gāw-ěr-'fū (*N*) golf. dǎ (yí-'tsż-) gāw-ěr-'fū play (a game of) golf.

高麗
gāw-'lì (*Nunique*) Korea.

高明
gāw-'míng (*A*) good, efficient, intelligent. ‖nǐ-jèy-ge-'fádz hěn gāw-'míng. Your method is excellent.

高聲
'gāw-shēng (*H*) loudly, very loudly. ‖tā 'gāw-shēng shwō-'hwà. He's talking very loudly (*particularly under circumstances where one is supposed to be quiet, as in a library*).

高興
gāw-'shìng (*A*) good-spirited, happy, high-spirited, cheerful.

鎬（借用）
gǎw (*Nunit*, bǎ) pick (*tool*).

稿（子）
'gǎw(-dz) (*Nunit*, pyān) a draft *of an article, essay, speech. The last draft of a speech before actual oral delivery is still a* **gǎw**; *any handwritten draft of something to be published is a* **gǎw**; *the published form is not.*

皋蘭
gǎw-'lán (*Nunique*) Kao-lan (*capital of Kansu province*).

告
gàw (*V*) to sue, make an accusation (*at court*) about *someone*.
     ywán-'gàw-rén plaintiff; bèy-'gàw-rén defendant.

告奮勇
gàw fèn-'yǔng (*VN1*) to volunteer to *do something*. ‖tā-'dž-jǐ gàw fèn-'yǔng 'jyā-rù jywūn-'dwèy. He volunteered to join the army.

告假
gàw-'jyà (*VN2*) to ask for leave, vacation, time off. ‖wǒ shyàng-ni gàw lyǎng-tyān-'jyà. I'm asking you for two days off.

告饒
gàw-'ráw (*VN1*) to ask forgiveness, pardon. ‖tā láy-'jèr shyàng-ni gàw-'ráw. He's come here to ask your forgiveness (*to forestall impending punishment or revenge*).

告示
'gàw-shr (*Nunit*, jāng, ge) notice, sign, bulletin *posted in a public place*.

告訴
'gàw-su or **'gàw-sung** (*V*) to tell, inform *someone of something, someone how to do something.* 'gàw-sung yì-'shēng(r) let someone know, tell once, just tell, just mention. ‖rú-gwo tā 'láy de-hwà chǐng-ni 'gàw-sung wo yì-'shēngr. If he comes please let me know.

該
gāy (*Vpred*) need to, have to, must, be necessary to. ‖shyàn-'dzày wǒ gāy 'dzěw-le. I've got to go now. *or* I ought to go now. ‖shyàn-dzày gāy-'shéy? Whose turn is it now?
     gāy-'gǎy-de-dì-fang places (*in something written, etc.*) where changes must be made.
     (*V*) to owe *money*. gāy-'chyán to owe money. ‖nǐ ké-yi 'gāy-je. You can owe it (*and pay it later; used mainly in Peiping; the more general term is* **chyàn**).

改
gǎy (*V*) to change, alter, revise, correct. ‖wǒ bǎ jèy-jywù-'hwà gěy 'gǎy-le. I've changed this sentence.
     As mainV: 'gǎy-gwò-lay to change for the better. ‖tā-de-'pí-chi háy méy-'gǎy-gwò-lay. His temper hasn't improved any.
     gǎy jú-'yì to change one's mind.

改變
gǎy-'byàn (*V*) to change *something (suddenly)*. ‖tā gǎy-'byàn tā-de-fāng-'jēn. He changed his policies.

改組
gǎy-'dzǔ (*V*) to reorganize, change the structure, arrangement, pattern of. gǎy-'dzǔ 'jèng-fǔ to reorganize a government.

改過自新
'gǎy-gwò-dž-'shīn (*literary quotation*) to turn over a new leaf, reform oneself, make a new start.

改進
gǎy-'jìn (*V*) to change for the better, improve. ‖tā-de-'sž-shyǎng gǎy-'jìn-le hěn 'dwō. He's greatly im-

proved his ways of thinking (*e.g., from very conservative to very progressive*).

(*Nabstr*) improvements, progressive features.

改良
gǎy-'lyáng (*V*) to improve, alter *something* for the better.

改選
gǎy-'shywǎn (*VN2*) to vote *in a periodically recurring election*. **měy-sz̀-'nyán °gǎy yí-tsz̀-'shywǎn** *or* **°gǎy-'shywǎn yí-'tsz̀** to vote once every four years.

蓋
gày (*V*) to cover. *As mainV:* **'gày-shàng** *or* **'gày-chǐ-láy** to cover up; **'gày-gwò-chywù** (*figuratively*) to conceal *or* hide *something.*

To build. **gày 'fáng-dz** to build a house; **gày-'léw** to put up a building. *As mainV:* **'gày-chǐ-láy** to raise *a building, a house.*

概
gày (*M*) limited to use after **yī**, *meaning* every, all. ‖**bù-néng yí-'gày ér-'lwèn.** You can't generalize.

蓋
'gày(-dz), gàr (*Nunit*, **ge**) cover, cap, top *for some container* (*the container is usually specified*). **chá-hú-'gàr** teakettle lid; **shyāng-dz-'gàr** suitcase lid; **píng-dz-'gàr** bottle cap

個，个
ge (*reading-form* **gè**) (*Munit*) *used for any Npers, and for many Nunit; Nunit which use* **ge** *are so marked. In the combinations* **jèy-ge** *and* **nèy-ge** *is often used with any noun whatsoever, the meanings being simply* this *and* that, *pointing something out without enumerating number or quantity or kind.*

'gè-ge *before almost any noun* every, each and every (*equivalent to* **'měy-ge** *or* **měy** *plus other measures*).

擱
gē (*V*) to put, place at *a place*. **gē-'nàr** put it there. ‖**jèy-shyē-'dūng-shi dzěme 'gē?** Where shall I put these things?

Put *something* in. **gē dyǎr-'yán** put a little salt in. ‖**nǐ bǎ nèy-ge-tí-'yì gē yì-'byār-ba.** Set that suggestion aside (*for the time being*).

As mainV: **'gē-hwéy** (*lc*) put *something* back (*where it came from*); **gē-'kāy** to lay *something* aside; **'gē-shya** put *something* down; (*figuratively*) drop *something*, suspend *a project, etc.*; **'gē-dzày** to put *something* at, on, in; **gē-bu-'shyà** to be unable to hold, contain *something* (*said of a container, support, etc.*).

哥
*gē (*Npers*) older brother *or* male cousin. *See Appendix A.*

歌
gē(er) (*Nunit*, **ge**) a song (*with words*). **chàng-'gēer** to sing a song; *or* (*Nunit*, **shěw**) a song.

胳臂
'gē-be (*or* **'gē-bwo, 'gē-bey**) (*Nunit*, **jř, ge**) arm (*human or ape*).

胳臂肘
gē-be-'jěw(r) (*Nunit*, **ge, jř**) elbow.

疙疸
'gē-de (*Nunit*, **ge**) a spot of a rash. **jǎng 'gē-de** to develop a rash. **húng-'gē-de** a red rash.

鴿子
'gē-dz (*Nunit*, **jř, ge**) pigeon.

擱在心上
gē-dzay 'shīn-shang (*VN1*) to keep *something unpleasant* in one's mind; feel unhappy about *something;* be unable to get *something unpleasant* off one's mind. ‖**nǐ byé bǎ tā-nèy-jywù-'hwà gē-dzay 'shīn-shang.** Don't let what he said weigh on your mind.

胳肢窩
'gē-je-wō (*Nunit*, **ge**) armpit.

磕膝瓣（借用）
gē-le-'bàr (*Nunit*, **ge**) knee.

疙里疙疸的
'gē-li-gē-'dā-de *same as* **'gā-li-gā-'dā-de.**

歌譜
gē(er)-'pǔ (*Nunit*, **běn, běr, jāng**) music written down, score.

歌舞
gē-'wǔ (*N*) song and dance. **gē-wǔ-'shì** *or* **gē-wǔ-'jywù** a song-and-dance show.

割
gé (*V*) to cut off, into (*particularly something that protrudes above a surface, like a boil or like growing plants*); to harvest *grain, etc.* **gé-'tsǎw** to cut grass; **gé-'mày** harvest wheat.

As mainV: **'gé-chū-lay** to cut *something* out (*including surgical operation*); **'gé-shyà-lay** to cut *something* off; **'gé-kāy** to cut *something* open. ‖**bǎ-'bāw gěy 'gé-kay, jyàw 'néng 'lyéw-chu-lay.** Cut open the boil and let the pus flow out.

隔
gé (*K*); **'gé-yì-tyān** skipping one day; **'gé-jǐ-tyān** skipping a few days; **'gé-jǐ-ge-'mér** passing by a few

houses (*before going to another door*). ‖**nǐ 'gé-yì-tyān dzày 'chywù.** Skip one day and then go. ‖**ta gé-yì-tyān chywù yí-'tsź.** He goes there every other day.

格子
'gé-dz (*Nunit, ge, jyà*) shelf. **shū-'gé-dz** bookshelves; **wǎn-'gé-dz** shelf for dishes.

格子, 格兒
'gé-dz, géer (*Nunit, jāng*) a lined box on a form to be filled out (*one for name, one for age, etc.*). *Also similar-shaped designs:* **gé-dz-'bù** checkered cloth, cloth with a checkered design.

蛤蜊蚌
gé-li-'bèng(-dz), gé-li-'bèngr (*Nunit, ge*) sea shells.

蛤蜊殼
gé-li-'chyàw (*Nunit, ge*) sea shells.

格外
gé-'wày (*H*) extra-, especially. **gé-'wày(-de) hǎw** extra good; **gé-'wày 'tsūng-míng** especially intelligent, extraordinarily intelligent.

隔
gè (*V*) to press and rub against, (*as a stone in one's shoe*). *As mainV:* **gè-'hwày** to rub and injure; **gè-'téng** to press and rub against and cause to hurt; *etc.* ‖**jèy-tyáw-'lù bù-'píng, bǎ wǒ-de-chì-chē-pí-'dày gè-'pwò-le.** This road isn't smooth; it's made a hole in the tire.

各
gè *before measures* each, every. **gè-'chù** every place, everyplace, everywhere; **gè-'jǔng-de** every kind of· **'gè-jǔng-gè-'yàng(r)-de** all kinds of; **'gè-shr̀-gè-'yàng(r)-de** various kinds of, all varieties of.

In some cases used before a noun instead of a measure: **gè-'dì(-fang)** everywhere; **'gè-rén** each person. **'gè-ge** each, every. *Used directly before nouns:* **gè-ge-'rén** every person, each person.

個子, 個 (兒)
'gè-dz, gèr (*V*) size *for people; rarely, for things of relatively small size.* ‖**tā-'nèy-ge-rén-de-'gèr hěn 'dà.** He's quite a large man. ‖**tā-'nèy-ge-rén-de-'gèr hěn 'gāw.** He's quite a tall man.

nèy-ge-dà-'gèr that tall fellow; **'dà-gèr-de-'wǎn** large-size bowl; **'shyǎw-gèr-de-'wǎn** small-size bowl. *Note stress:* **dà-'gèr** *is* a large *or* tall fellow; **'dà-gèr-de** *is* large-size(d).

個人
'gè-rén (*Aattr*) personal, private. ‖**jèy-jyàn-shr̀-ching shr̀ 'wǒ-'gè-rén-de-shr̀-ching.** This matter is my personal affair.

個性
'gè-shìng (*Nabstr*) personal nature, personality. ‖**tā-de-'ge-shìng hěn 'chyáng.** He has a strong personality (*hard to change his mind; good or bad comment*).

跟
gēn (*V, lc*) to go with, come with; to go along with *someone in the sense of being in agreement with him.* (*K*) with, and. **'shū gēn-'jř** books and paper; **'dyàn gēn-'shwěy** electricity and water; *etc.*

Sometimes used where English would have a different preposition: **gēn yín-'háng jyè-'chyán** to borrow money from a bank.

Reinforced with **je** *means* following. ‖**wǒ 'gēn-je ni 'dzěw.** I'll walk behind you, I'll follow you. *Also relative to time:* **gēn-je dì-'èr-tyān** the next day following that.

Used in stating that two things are equal or not equal: ‖**nǐ gēn-'tā yí-'yàng 'hǎw.** You and he are equally good. ‖**tā 'dzěme néng gēn-ni 'bǐ?** How could he be compared to you?

gēn . . . shr̀-de to be just the same as. ‖**tā-dzěw-'dàw-de-'yàng-dz gēn tā-'fù-chin shr̀-de.** He walks just like his father. ‖**nèy-ge-'rén gēn tā-de-'mǔ-chin shr̀-de.** That man is like his mother.

As mainV: **'gēn-shàng** to keep up with, keep pace with *in walking or figuratively.* **'gēn-dàw** (*lc*) to follow *someone or* accompany *someone to a place.*

根
gēn, gēr (*Nunit, ge*) root of a plant, root (*figuratively*) *as in* **'è-gēn** *or* **'hwày-gēn** the root of evil.

Foundation. **bǎ-'gēn dzá-'hǎw-le** build the foundation well.

根 (兒)
gēn, gēr (*Munit*) for relatively small, long and thin things. A blade of **tsǎw** (*grass*), a **máw(r)** (*hair*), a **gwèr** (*rod, pole*), a **'jù-dz** (*post or pillar fixed vertically*), a **yān** (*cigarette*), a **yáng-'hwǒ** (*match*), a stalk of **chín-'tsày** (*celery*).

根本
'gēn-běn (*H*) as a basic point, first of all. ‖**wǒ 'gēn-běn méy-'chywù.** (*All your accusations are wrong, because,*) as a basic point, I didn't even go (*there*). ‖**'gēn-běn tā 'shwō-de hěn 'màn.** (*You're wrong in blaming him when you can't understand what he says, because,*) after all he really does speak quite slowly. ‖**'gēn-běn tā 'shwō-de hěn 'kwày.** (*Well, it's natural enough that you don't understand him;*) after all he does speak very fast.

'gēn-běn-(de-)'wèn-tí fundamental problems, underlying problems, root problems.

跟前
'gēn-chyán, 'gēn-chyár (*Nplace*) the area right in front of anything (*literally and figuratively*). ‖**mén-de-'gēn-chyár yěw yì-kē-'shù.** There's a tree right in

front of the door. ‖jyèw dzày nǐ-de-'gēn-chyár, nǐ kàn-bu-'jyàn. It's right in front of your nose and you can't see it.

跟斗，跟頭

'gēn-dew (*Nunit*, ge) a fall head foremost. dǎ 'gēn-dew *or* shwāy 'gēn-dew to fall head foremost; bàn yí-ge-'gēn-dew to stumble and fall head foremost; fān 'gēn-dew to turn a somersault.

根基

'gēn-ji (*Nunit*, ge) foundation (*literally and figuratively*). dǎ 'gēn-ji to build a foundation. ‖tā-de-'yīng-wén shwō-de hěn 'hǎw, yīn-wey 'dǎ-le 'wǔ-nyán-de-'gēn-ji. He speaks English very well, since he spent five years acquiring a fundamental knowledge of it.

根據

'gēn-jywù (*K*) basing on ... as reason and evidence. (*Nabstr*) basis, evidence. ‖nǐ 'gēn-jywù 'shéme shwō jèy-jywù-'hwà? What basis have you for such a statement? ‖shwō jèy-jywù-'hwà nǐ yěw 'gēn-jywù méy-yew? Have you any evidence for such a statement?

根據地

'gēn-jywù-'dì (*Nunit*, chù, ge) military base. 'hǎy-jywūn-gēn-jywù-'dì naval base.

艮（借用）

gén (*A*) funny, humorous, productive of enjoyable laughter. ‖'jèy-jywù-hwà hěn 'gén. That's a very funny remark. ‖nèy-ge-shyǎw-'hár hěn 'gén. That child is very funny.

耕

gēng (*V*) to plow. gēng-'dì to plow the soil; gēng-'tyán to plow a field.

更正

gēng-'jèng (*V*) to set right, correct. *In a Chinese newspaper* gēng-'jèng *is the heading equivalent to the English* Correction, *for a note correcting an error made in a previous issue.*

更

gèng (*H*) even ... -er, still ... -er, *used in comparing a new thing mentioned with one or more already discussed.* ‖tā hěn 'hǎw, (kě-shr) 'nǐ bǐ-ta gèng 'hǎw. He's very good; (*but*) you're even better. ‖tā 'chyán-tyan yěw-'bìng, 'dzwó-tyan 'hǎw-le yì-dyǎr, 'jīn-tyan 'gèng 'hǎw(-yi-dyǎr). He was sick day before yesterday, better yesterday, and today (a little) better again.

    With gèng *the comparison is between something that is good (or bad, etc.) and something else that is also good, but not so much so.*

鈎，勾

gēw (*V*) to carry *something* on a hook-shaped holder, *or* on a joint of the finger, *or* at the elbow, bent into a hook. *As mainV also:* to mark with a hook-shaped mark, *as when checking items in an account.* 'gēw-chǐ-lay to lift *something* on a hook (*as above*); 'gēw-shàng to fasten a hook onto *something*; 'gēw-chū-lay to pull *something* out (*as from under the bed*) with a hook, *or,* to mark *items* with a check; 'gēw-dàw (*l*) to pull *something* to a place (*usually* here) on a hook; *etc.*

    To cancel, forget about (*literally* write off) *an account, a bill, debt.* ‖bǎ nèy-bǐ-'jàng 'gēw-le. Write off that account, forget about it (*we won't try to collect it*).

溝

gēw (*Nunit*, tyáw, dàw) a ditch. shwěy-'gēw water ditch; yīn-'gēw a covered ditch (*not a tunnel, but a ditch dug from above and then covered at the top*). *This term is used for the most usual kind of ditch for sewage disposal.*

鈎子，鈎兒

'gēw-dz, gēwr (*Nunit*, ge) hook; hook-shaped mark; hook-shaped stroke in writing Chinese characters. ywu-'gēwr fishhook.

狗

gěw (*Nunit*, jī, tyáw, ge) dog. gūng-'gěw (male) dog; mǔ-'gěw bitch.

夠，彀

gèw (*A*) sufficient, enough. gèw ... (-de) enough to. ‖'fàn bú-gèw 'chr(-de). There isn't enough food to eat. (*H*) ‖jèy-ge-'chá bú-gèw 'rè. This tea isn't hot enough. ‖'gèw-ma? Enough? ‖'gèw-le. Enough, OK no more. ‖jèy-jyàn-shr-ching 'jēn-shr gèw-'shèw-de-le. That job is really plenty to take (*meaning it's almost too much to endure*).

夠

gèw (*V*) to reach. ‖nǐ byé 'máng; děng wǒ 'gèw nèy-běn-'shū. Don't be in a hurry; wait for me to reach out and get the book (*for you*).

    Mostly as mainV: 'gèw-jáw to reach to *something*; gèw-bu-'jáw to be unable to reach *something* (*both also figuratively*). gèw-bu-'shàng not be qualified for, not be able to reach the status or level required to do *such-and-such* (*used in polite refusals which show modesty*). ‖wǒ gèw-bu-'shàng shwō 'nèy-ge. I'm not qualified to say.

構成

'gèw-chéng (*RC3*) to constitute, form, make up. ‖jèy-shyē-'swǒ-yěw-de-ywán-'yīn 'gèw-chéng jèy-ge-jywú-'myàn. All these reasons go together to constitute this situation.

給

gěy (*V2*) to give. ‖**tā gěy-wo 'wŭ-kwày-chyán.** He's giving me five dollars.

(*K*) for the sake of, for the benefit of, for, *marking the recipient.* ‖**chǐng 'gěy wŏ-men 'jyè-shaw.°** Please introduce us.

(*Vsent*) give *someone* the chance to do, let *someone* do something (*same as* ràng). ‖**chǐng-ni gěy 'wŏ-men dzwò jèy-jyàn-'shř-ching.** Please let us take care of this matter. *or* Please·také care of this matter for us (*in the latter case* gěy *is K, not Vsent*).

(*H*) (1) for someone's sake, *indicating a recipient not explicitly mentioned.* ‖**chǐng gěy 'jyè-shaw.** Please introduce (*us*).

(2) *Indicating that someone or something undergoes the action, particularly in sentences of the following type:* ‖**'shù jyàw-'fēng (gěy) gwā-'dăw-le.** The trees were blown down by the wind.

gěy-'chyán to pay; **gěy-'jyà(r)** to make an offer (*in bargaining*).

(*PostV*) *forms RC4 which have no potential forms:* **'dì-gěy** pass *someone* something; **'jyè-gěy** lend *someone* something; *etc.*

箍

gū (*V*) to tie *a metal strip, wire, etc.* around *something.* ‖**bă nèy-ge-'shyāng-dz gū yì-chywār-tyě-'tyáw.** Tie a metal strip once around this box.

As mainV: **'gū-chǐ-lay** to tie up; **'gū-shàng** tie up, tie together; **gū-'jǐn** tie tightly; *etc.*

姑

***gū** (*Npers*) father's sister. *See Appendix A.*

菩朵

'gū-du (*Nunit, ge*) (flower) bud.

穀子

'gū-dz *see* **'gŭ-dz.**

孤兒

gū-'ér (*Npers*) orphan.

孤兒院

gū-ér-'ywàn (*Nunit, ge, swǒ*) orphan asylum.

孤寂

'gū-ji (*A*) lonely (*a bit literary*). ‖**jèy-ge-'dì-fang hěn 'gū-ji.** This place is very lonely. ‖**tā 'jywé-de hěn 'gū-ji.** He feels very lonely. (*Not said directly of a person, only of a person's feelings.*)

穀轆

'gū-lu (*V*) to roll *something* along. *As mainV:* **'gū-lu-gwò** (*lc*) to roll *something* over (*from one place to another*); **'gū-lu-dàw** (*lc*) to roll *something* to a place; *etc.*

(*I*) to growl, *as the stomach;* to make a noise *of this kind.*

(*Nunit, ge*) a wheel. **chē-'gū-lu** ·cart wheel.

沽名釣譽

gū-'míng dyàw-'ywù (*literary quotation*) (*A*) to be self-centered; to fish for compliments, try to acquire a good reputation, try to build oneself up.

姑娘

'gū-nyang (*NpersT*) (1) any unmarried girl; (2) young unmarried girl, young lady (*showing respect*). *Used mainly in the North:* **'shyáw-jye** *is more widespread.*

孤身

'gū-shēn (*N*) one person alone (*a bit literary*). ‖**tā-shř 'gū-shēn.** He's a bachelor. *or* He's a lone traveller. *or* He lives alone.

  'gū-shēn-de-nán-'dž bachelor; **'gū-shēn-de-nywŭ-'dž** unmarried woman.

(*H*) ‖**nǐ-'yí-ge-rén 'gū-shēn(-de) 'chū-chywu, yàw 'shyăw-shīn.** When you go out all by yourself, you must be careful.

骨

***gú, 'gú-tew** *see* ***gŭ, 'gŭ-tew.**

鼓

gŭ (*Nunit, ge*) drum. **dă-'gŭ** to beat a drum.

凸

gŭ (*A*) bulging, protruding, swollen. ‖**tā-de-năw-'mén-dz hěn 'gŭ.** His forehead is quite protruding.

As mainV: **'gŭ-chǐ-lay** (*RC1*) to bulge out, start to protrude, develop a bulge, *in an upward direction;* **'gŭ-chū** (*lc*) (*RC1*) with same meaning, but in any direction. ‖**dàn-'gāw 'jēng-de 'gŭ-chǐ-lay-le.** The cake rose as it steamed.

古

gŭ (*A*) ancient, dating from way back. ‖**jèy-ge-'chéng hěn 'gŭ-le.** This city is very old.

  'gŭ-rén the ancients (*people*): *or, politely,* people who have died. ‖**tā 'yǐ-jing chéng -'gŭ-rén-le.** He's already passed on.

估

gŭ (*V*) to appraise, estimate   **gŭ-'jyà** to estimate the value *or* price. ‖**'gŭ-yi-gŭ jèy-běn-'shū jǐ 'dwǒ-shaw-chyán.** Estimate how much this book is worth.

As mainV: **gŭ-'dwèy** to estimate correctly, **gŭ-'tswò** to estimate wrongly

股（子）

gŭ(-dz) (*Munit*) *with* wèr, an odor, a smell (*usually bad*); a column of yān (*smoke*); a (rising) column of chì (*air, steam*); a strand of **'téw-fa** (*hair*), shéngr (*rope*). shyàn (*string*).

骨
*gǔ, *gú, 'gǔ-tew, 'gú-tew (*Nunit*, ge, gĕr; *Nmass*, kwày) bone. *A whole bone in the body or taken out of the body, calls for M* ge *or* gĕr; *a piece of bone calls for M* kwày. **gē-be-'gǔ(-tew)** arm bones, etc. **gǔ-'rèw** *literally* bones and flesh, *used as English uses* flesh and blood *for one's immediate relatives.*

古巴(國)
gǔ-'bā(-gwó) (*Nunique*) Cuba.

股東
gǔ-'dūng (*Npers*) part owner of the capital of an enterprise; stockholder.

古董
gǔ-'dǔng (*Nunit*, ge) an old thing, an antique (old, rare, and valuable). *Sarcastically of a person:* ‖tā shř ge-lǎw-gǔ-'dǔng. He's way out of date, he's behind the times.

鼓動
gǔ-'dùng (*RC2*) to stir up, arouse. **gǔ-'dùng rén dzàw-'fǎn** to stir up people so that they revolt.

股子
'gǔ-dz (*Nmass;* fèn, fèr) share, interest (*not profit on money, but part control and participation in an enterprise*). ‖jèy-ge-'mǎy-may-de-'gǔ-dz 'chywán-shr tā-'yí-ge-rén-de. He controls all the interest in that enterprise.

股份
gǔ-'fèn (*Nmass*) shares of stock.

古怪
gǔ-'gwày (*A*) mysterious, strange.

鼓掌
gǔ-'jǎng (*VN2*) to clap, applaud. ‖tām 'gǔ-le hǎw-jǐ-'tsż-de-'jǎng. They applauded many times.

古跡
'gǔ-jì (*Nunit*, ge) something still remaining from ancient times, *as* ruins of old temples and buildings and cities and the like (*not small portable things, and not ideas and customs*).

估計
gǔ-'jì (*V, Vsent*) to estimate and plan. ‖wǒ gǔ-'jì, dzwò 'jèy-ge-'mǎy-may dĕy yùng yí-'wàn-kwày-chyán. I figure that running this business will require ten thousand dollars.

骨節炎
gǔ-jyé-'yán (*Nabstr*) arthritis.

鼓勵
gǔ-'lì (*V*) to encourage; (*Vsent*) to encourage *people to do something.* ‖gǔ-'lì ta dzwò hǎw-shr̀. Encourage him to do good things.

股票
gǔ-'pyàw (*Nunit*, jāng, fèn *or* fèr) stocks, shares. ‖tā gāng 'mǎy-le 'yì-bǎy-kwày-chyán-de-nèy-ge-gūng-'sż-de-gǔ-'pyàw. He's just purchased a hundred dollars' worth of shares in that company.

古玩
gǔ-'wán (*Nunit*, ge) an antique. **gǔ-wán-'pù** an antique store (*where antiques are sold*).

僱
gù (*V*) to employ, hire. **gù-'chē** hire a car, a taxi, a rickshaw; **gù 'gūng-rén** to hire a workman.
 As mainV: **gù-bu-'dàw** *or* **gù-bu-'jáw** be unable to hire.
 gù-'ywán employees.

顧
gù (*V*) to think of, be considerate of, take into consideration. ‖nǐ byé 'dān gù 'dż-jǐ. Don't think just of yourself.
 As mainV: **'gù-dàw** to reckon with, have respect for. ‖'yě dĕy 'gù-dàw 'byé-rén-de-yì-'jyàn. You must take other peoples' opinions into account too.

故去
gù-'chywù (*RC1; potential forms not used*) to die (*a bit literary*).

固定
gù-'dìng (*A*) fixed, constant, permanent, continuing. ‖jèy-ge-'shř-ching shr̀ gù-'dìng-de, bú-shr lín-'shŕ-de. This job is permanent, not temporary.

固執
gù-'jŕ (*A*) stubborn, obstinate (*critical remark*).

故事
'gù-shr (*Nunit*, ge, dwàn, pyān) story. ‖nǐ gĕy-wo shwō yí-ge-'gù-shr. Tell me a story.

故意
gù-'yì (*H*) on purpose. ‖tā gù-'yì láy-de. He came on purpose.

工
gūng (*Nabstr*) work (*done by humans*). **dzwò-'gūng** to work, *tending to refer to physical rather than mental labor.* **gūng hé-'lyàw** labor and material, *as that necessary to build or manufacture something.* **'gūng-rén** (*Npers*) workman. **'gūng-chyán** wages.

120

攻

gūng (V) to attack. gūng-'chéng to attack a city. *As mainV:* **'gūng-dàw** to reach *a place* in an attack; **'gūng-gwò** to break past *a place, a line of defense,* in an attack.

供

gūng (V2, Vsent) to supply *someone with something;* to give *someone* financial aid *to do something.* ‖wǒ **'gūng-ta** 'lyáng-shr. I'm supplying him with food. ‖wǒ **'gūng-ta** nyàn-'shū. I'm paying his school expenses.
    As mainV: **'gūng-gěy** *same meanings as above;* **'gūng-ji** *same but also* Nabstr supplies.
    These are the expressions used formally, as in supplying an army with equipment, but are also used in less formal circumstances.

公

gūng (Aattr) (1) public. ‖**'jèy-jyàn-shr shr 'gūng-de, bú-shr 'sz-de.** This matter is public, not private.
    (2) Male *of animals.* (*Opposite* **mǔ** female.) **gūng-'nyéw** bull.
    (3) *Prefixed to Chinese measures of length, weight, etc., forms the terms for the equivalent units of the Metric System:* **gūng-'lǐ** (Mmeas) kilometer; **gūng-'chr** (Mmeas) meter, *etc. See Appendix B.*

弓

gūng (Nunit, **jāng, ge**) bow (*weapon*). **gūng-'jyàn** (Ncoll, **fù, tàw**) bow and arrows. **kāy-'gūng** *or* **lā-'gūng** to draw a bow.

公

*****gūng** (Npers) father-in-law. *See Appendix A.*

公

*****gūng** *prefixed to* Mmeas *to form units of the Metric System. See Appendix B.*

公安

gūng-'ān (Nabstr) public safety.

公安局

gūng-ān-'jywú (Nunit, **ge, chù**) police station.

工廠

gūng-'chǎng (Nunit, **jyā, ge**) factory.

工程

'gūng-chéng (Nunit, **ge**) a construction enterprise *for bridge, building, ship, etc.* ‖**jèy-ge-'gūng-chéng hěn 'dà.** This is a big building job.
    gūng-chéng(-'shywé) (Nabstr) engineering; the study *or* science of engineering (*civil, mechanical, etc.*).

工程師

gūng-chéng-'shr (Npers) an engineer (*civil, mechanical, etc.*).

供出來

'gūng-chū-lay (RC2) to disclose, reveal, confess (*in court*). ‖**tā bǎ tā-hwǒ-'bàr-de-'míng-dz dēw 'gūng-chu-lay-le.** He revealed the names of all his accomplices.

公道

'gūng-dàw (A) impartial, fair, moderate. ‖**'jyà-chyán hěn 'gūng-dàw.** The prices are quite reasonable. ‖**wǒm 'shwō yí-jywù-'gǔng-dàw-'hwà.** Let's speak more fairly. (*For example, of someone who has been condemned unjustly, but by a powerful party so that taking his part calls for courage.*)

工資

gūng-'dz (Nmass, **fèn, fèr**) wages. *New expression, used mainly for factory wages, or in discussing wage problems.*

工作

'gūng-dzwo (Nabstr) work (*done by humans*).

工夫，功夫

'gūng-fu (Nabstr) (1) leisure time, free time. ‖**nǐ yěw 'gūng-fu méy-yew?** Have you a moment to spare?.
    (2) Time, period *or* span of time. ‖**'lyǎng-dyǎn-jūng-de-'gūng-fu ké-yi dzwò hěn-dwō-de-'shr.** You can get a lot done in two hours' time.
    (3) Time and energy spent on some task. **shyà 'gūng-fu** to spend time at a task. ‖**dzwò 'jèy-jyàn-shr-ching fēy-děy shyà 'gūng-fu tsáy 'chéng-ne.** You've got to spend time and energy to get this task done right.
    (4) *The result of time and energy spent in learning something:* skill. ‖**'jèy-ge-dz hěn yěw 'gūng-fu.** These characters show a great deal of skill at writing.
    gūng-fu-'dz *means* calligraphy acquired by practice *and therefore inferior to good handwriting which has come about without effort, through native ability.*

公共

gūng-'gùng (Aattr) public, not private. **gūng-gùng-chì-'chē** bus (*intra-city*); **'gūng-gùng-'wèy-shēng-wěy-ywán-'hwèy** public health commission.

工合

gūng-'hé *abbreviated form of* **'gūng-yè-hé-dzwò-'shè** Industrial Cooperative Society.

工會

gūng-'hwèy (Nunit, **ge**) labor union.

公債

gūng-'jày (Nabstr) public debt. **fā gūng-'jày** to issue government bonds; (Nunit, **jāng**) *or* **gūng-jày-'pyàw** (Nunit, **jāng**) government bonds.

公正
gūng-'jèng (*A*) equitable, impartial. ‖**jèy-ge-fǎ-'gwān hěn gūng-'jèng.** The judge is impartial.

攻擊
'gūng-ji (*V*) to attack, *military or just by words or actions.* **'kǎy-shř 'gūng-ji** to start to attack. ‖**bàw-'jř-shang shyàn-'dzày 'gūng-ji jèy-ge-'shīn-shř-'jǎng.** The papers are now attacking the new mayor.

恭敬
'gūng-jìng (*V*) to respect, admire *someone* for ability, nobility, age, position.
    gūng-gung-jìng-'jìng-de (*H*) very respectfully, very reverently.

工具
gūng-'jywù (*Nunit*, ge) tools, machinery, means of production; *also figuratively, as money, human speech, etc.* ‖**'chyán shř jyāw-'yì-de-gūng-'jywù.** Money is the medium of transacting business. ‖**yùng tā-de-rwò-'dyǎn dāng gūng-'jywù 'gūng-ji ta.** Use his weak points as a means of attacking him.

公開
gūng-'kāy (*V*) to make public. ‖**bǎ jèy-jyàn-'shř-ching gěy gūng-'kāy-le.** Make this matter public.
    gūng-'kāy-de-'shř-ching publicly known matter.

功課
gūng-'kè (*Nunit*, ge, mér) course, class in a particular subject, subject of instruction. ‖**wǒ 'tyāw-le lyǎng-'mér-gūng-'kè.** I chose two courses.

公款
gūng-'kwǎn (*Nmass*) public monies, treasury funds. *With M* **bǐ** an item of the public monies *with separate accounting.*

功勞
'gūng-láw (*Nunit*, ge) credit for something done. ‖**jèy-ge-'gūng-láw yīng-gay shř 'tā-de.** The credit should be his.

公路
gūng-'lù (*Nunit*, tyáw) highway.

公民
gūng-'mín (*Npers*) citizen.

公平
'gūng-píng (*A*) fair, just. ‖**jèy-ge-fǎ-'gwān-pàn-de-'àn-dz hěn 'gūng-píng.** The judge's decision was quite fair.

恭喜
gūng-shǐ (*V*) to congratulate *someone.* ‖**nín dzày-'nǎr gūng-'shǐ?** *is a polite way of asking someone where*

he works; literally Where is it that you do such successful work that I must offer you congratulations for it?

弓形
'gūng-shíng (*Aattr*) bow-shaped, arch-shaped. **'gūng-shíng**(-de) **-'mén** an arched doorway *or* gate.

公使
gūng-'shř (*NpersT*) minister (*diplomatic*).

公事
gūng-'shř (*Nunit*, jyàn) official, public business, *in contrast to* **sz-'shř** personal *or* private matters. **bàn gūng-'shř** to conduct official business.
    A document pertaining to official business *or* public affairs.

公事房
gūng-shř-'fáng (*Nunit*, jyān) an office (*place of work*).

供獻
gùng-'shyàn (*V2*) to offer *someone something.* ‖**wǒ gùng-'shyàn-le ta yí-ge-'jì-hwa.** I offered him a plan. *One does not politely mention oneself as recipient, except in joking.*
    (*Nunit*, ge) contribution, offering. ‖**nǐ yěw shéme-gūng-'shyàn méy-yew?** Have you any contribution to make? (*e.g., money, services, an article for publication, etc.*).

公司
gūng-'sz (*Nunit*, jyā, ge) company, corporation.

工頭
gūng-'téw(r) (*NpersT*) foreman.

公文
gūng-'wén (*Nunit*, jyàn, pyān, jāng) an official document.

公務員
gūng-wù-'ywán (*Npers*) civil service employee, government employee.

工業
gūng-'yè (*Nabstr*) business and industry. **gūng-yè-jūng-'shīn** an industrial center.

工業合作社
'gūng-yè-hé-dzwò-'shè (*Nunit*, ge) an Industrial Cooperative Society. (*Abbreviated to* **gūng-'hé.**)

工藝
'gūng-yì (*Nabstr*) industrial arts, technology, ·(*e.g., weaving and other hand skills*).

公園
gūng-'ywán (*Nunit*, ge, chù) (public) park.

公寓

gǔng-'ywù (*Nunit,* swǒ, jyā) residence hotel. ‖wǒ jù-dzay gǔng-'ywù-lǐ-tew. I'm staying in a gǔng-ywù.

拱

gǔng (*V*) to push with the shoulder(s) or head.
    As mainV: 'gǔng-kāy to push open (*as a door*); gǔng-'jìn (*lc*) push one's way in; 'gǔng-dàw (*lc*) to push to *a place; etc.* ‖'nyéw bǎ-'mén 'gǔng-kāy-le. The ox pushed the door open.

共產黨

gùng-'chǎn-dǎng (*Nunique*) Communist party; (*Npers,* ge) a member of the Communist party. 'gùng-chǎn-jǔ-'yì the Communist principles, Communism.

共總

gùng-'dzǔng (*J*) altogether, all in all. ‖gùng-'dzǔng wǒm yěw 'dwō-shaw-rén? How many of us are there altogether?

共和

gùng-'hé *before nouns* republican. gùng-hé-'gwó (*Nunit,* ge) republic; gùng-hé-jr̀-'dù republican governmental system; gùng-hé-'jèng-fǔ republican government.
    (*The American Republican Party is called* gùng-hé-'dǎng.)

瓜

gwā (*Nunit,* ge) melon. shī-'gwā watermelon (*literally* western melon); 'tyán-gwā melon like the honeydew, but with much thinner skin.

刮

gwā (*I*) to blow (*of the wind*). gwā-'fēng (*IN*) to be windy. *As mainV works as V as well as I:* 'gwā-chǐ-láy (*RC1, RC2*) to blow up (*of a storm*), or to blow *something* up (*as wind blowing up the dust*); gwā-'dwàn (*RC2*) to blow on and break off short (*as the wind breaks off a tree branch*); 'gwā-gwò-chywù (*RC1*) to blow over (*of a storm*), (*RC4*) to blow *something* past or across *something;* gwā-'pǎw (*RC2*) to blow *something* away; *etc.* ‖dyàn-'gān jyàw-'fēng gwā-'shé-le. The telephone pole was snapped in two by the wind.

刮

gwā (*V*) to scrape *with a sharp-edged thing.* gwā-'lyǎn to shave. *As mainV:* 'gwā-shyà-chywu to scrape off, rub off; gwā-'pwò to cut the surface of *the thing being scraped,* cut oneself *while shaving; etc.* ‖bǎ dzāng-'dūng-shi 'gwā-shyà-lay. Scrape the dirt off.

刮臉刀

gwā-lyǎn-'dāw(r) (*Nunit,* bǎ, ge) razor. gwā-lyǎn-dāw-'pyàr (*Nunit,* pyàr, ge) razor blade.

刮

gwǎ (*V*) to hack at *with a sharp-edged tool. As mainV:* 'gwǎ-shyà(-lay) to hack *a piece* off; gwǎ-'hwày to spoil *something* by hacking at it; *etc.* ‖tā bǎ shù-'jěr gěy gwǎ-'dwàn-le. He hacked the branch of the tree until it fell.

絓

gwǎ (*or* gwā) (*V*) to catch, *as a projection catches one's clothes or two cars catch each other's fenders. Mainly as mainV:* 'gwǎ-shàng to catch; gwǎ-'jù to catch and stop; 'gwǎ-dzày to catch on *or* at; gwǎ-'dǎw to catch and cause to fall down; *etc.* ‖tā 'pǎw de-shŕ-hew 'yī-fu gwǎ-dzay shù-'jěr-shang. When he was running, his clothes caught on a branch of a tree.

掛

gwà (*V*) to support *something* so that it hangs (*as from a strap*) ; to hang *something. As mainV:* 'gwà-shang *or* 'gwà-chǐ-láy to hang *something* up, *or* to hang up (*in phoning*) ; 'gwà-dzày to hang *something* at *a place.* ‖bǎ-'hwàr gwà-dzay 'chyáng-shang. Hang the pictures on the wall.

褂子, 褂 (兒)

'gwà-dz, gwàr (*Nunit,* jyàn) Chinese gown, short or long, with no lining.

掛號

gwà-'hàw (*VN1*) to register (*as mail*), (*literally* to hang up a number). ‖jèy-fēng-'shìn yīng-gay gwà-'hàw. This letter should be registered.

掛牌子

gwà 'páy-dz (*VN2*) to hang out one's shingle. gwà 'dày-fú-de-'páy-dz to go into practice as a doctor; gwà lywù-'shŕ-de-'páy-dz *same for* a lawyer.

關

gwān (*Nunit,* ge) a pass, defile, or gate *which is one of the few possible routes between two territories so that it can be defended, or so that it is a logical place for customs houses and the like.* (shān-)gwān-'kěw a mountain pass *of this kind;* gwò-'gwān to pass through a pass; hǎy-'gwān customs house; gwān-'shwèy customs, import taxes.

關

gwān (*I*) to be closed, *and causatively* (*V*) to close. gwān-'mén (*VN2*) to close a door; close (*as a store in the evening*) ; gwān-'dēng (*VN2*) to turn off an (electric) light (*compare* gwān dyàn-'mén to turn off an electric switch, to open a circuit); gwān 'lú-dz (*VN2*) to turn off a (*gas or electric*) stove.
    As mainV: 'gwān-shàng to close, turn off, *as above;* gwān-'jǐn to close tightly, seal tight; 'gwān-chǐ-láy to close up, *or* lock up *a person, a culprit; etc.*

官
gwăn, gwăr (Npers) official; officer. dzwò-'gwăn or dăng-'gwăn to serve as an official or officer, be an official or officer. jywūn-'gwăn Army officer.

官俸
gwăn-'fèng (Nmass, fěn, fèr) salary of a government worker.

官服
'gwăn-fú (Nunit, jyàn; tăw for whole suit of) officer's uniform.

關照
'gwăn-jàw (V) to speak to, consult, report to; to take care of, look after. ‖ni 'dzěw de-shŕ-hew chǐng-ni 'gwăn-jaw wǒ yì-shēngr. When you're ready to go, consult with me a bit. ‖wǒ-de-'ér-dz dzày-'nàr dzwò-'shr̀; chǐng-ni 'gwăn-jàw-gwan-jaw. My son is working there; please look after him a bit.

關緊要
gwăn jǐn-'yàw (VN1, literary) shr̀ gwăn-jǐn-'yàw-de is of great importance; bù-gwăn jǐn-'yàw-de is of no importance, is unimportant.

觀衆
gwăn-'jùng (Ncoll) a (watching) audience. ‖gwăn-'jùng 'hū-rán dēw 'shyàw-chi-lay-le. The whole audience suddenly burst out laughing.

官價
gwăn-'jyà (Nunit, ge) prices fixed by the government or by local authorities; particularly maximum prices, ceiling prices.

關監
gwăn-'jyăn (VN2) to imprison. ‖tā 'yǐ-jing 'gwăn-le 'lyăng-nyán-de-'jyăn-le. He's already been in prison for two years.

關鍵
gwăn-'jyàn (Nunit, ge) key factor in a situation. ‖'dzěme-yàng dzàw fēy-'jī shr̀ dǎ-'jàng-hěn-'dà-de-yí-ge-gwăn-'jyàn. The technique of building planes is a very important factor in fighting a war.

觀看
gwăn-'kàn (V) to watch as a spectator, passive observer, or audience (a bit literary).

關老爺
'gwăn-lăw-yé or 'lăw-yé (Nunique) a deity worshipped in many parts of China; a hero of the Three Kingdoms period canonized as the God of War. lăw-yé-'myàw a temple for the worship of this deity. bày (gwăn-)'lăw-yé to worship this deity.

關係
'gwăn-shì (Nabstr) relation, connection; relevance. ‖méy-yew 'gwăn-shi. (I) have no relation or connection (with him). or, It doesn't matter (it's unrelated to the matter at hand). ‖jèy-ge yěw hěn-'dà-de-'gwăn-shi. This °has a great deal of relevance, or °is of major importance.

關心
gwăn-'shīn (A) concerned. ‖wǒ dwèy 'nèy-jyàn-shr̀-ching hěn gwăn-'shīn. I'm quite concerned about that matter. (V) to be concerned about. ‖wǒ hěn gwăn-'shīn nǐ. I'm quite concerned about you.

官銜
'gwăn-shyán (Nunit, ge; jǔng, jí) official title. ‖tā-de-'gwăn-shyán shr̀-'shéme? What's his official title? (In English one would often simply say: What is he in the government? or What's his position in the government?).

關餉
gwăn-'shyăng (VN2) to give out pay (originally military). ‖jīn-tyan gwăn-'shyăng-le. Today was payday. ‖jywūn-'dwèy 'shéme-shŕ-hew gwăn-'shyăng? When do they pay in the army?

官司
'gwăn-sz (Nunit, ge) lawsuit. dǎ 'gwăn-sz to sue.

關痛癢
gwăn tùng-'yăng (VN1); bù-gwăn tùng-'yăng-de is of no importance, pay no attention to it. ‖tā chū-le 'shr̀-le, 'byé-rén jywé-de hăw 'shyàng bù-gwăn tùng-'yăng shr̀-de. He had an accident, but other people feel that it seems to be of no concern at all.

關於
'gwăn-ywú (K) concerning, with respect to. ‖gwăn-ywu 'jèy-jyàn-shr̀-ching wǒ 'méy shéme-'yì-jyàn. I have no opinion about that matter.

管
gwăn (V) to manage, control, govern (very general). As mainV: gwăn-'jù(-le) to get something under control; gwăn-'jáw to be directly in charge of; gwăn-bu-'dàw to be unable to control.

    shǔ ... 'gwăn to be in someone's jurisdiction or control. shǔ nǐ-'gwăn it's your responsibility, in your jurisdiction.

    gwăn (Vpred) to be in charge of doing such-and-such. ‖tā gwăn shyě-'shìn. He's in charge of correspondence.

    (K) In addressing ‖tā gwăn-wo jyàw 'gē-ge. He addresses me as brother.

    bù-'gwăn (K) regardless of. ‖bù-'gwăn nǐ 'shwō shéme, wǒ yí-'dìng 'chywù. Regardless of what you

124

say, I'm certainly going (anyway). or ‖bù-'gwǎn dzěme-'yàng, wǒ yí-'dìng 'chywù. No matter now, I'm going. (That is, I'm certainly going, however it has to be managed.) ‖tā jř gù 'dž-ji, bù-gwǎn 'byé-ren. He is concerned only about himself, with no regard for others. ‖'béng gwǎn-ta! Don't mind him! ‖wǒ bù-'gwǎn-ni-le. I'll have no more to do with you. ‖'jèy-jyàn-shř-ching nǐ gwǎn-bu-'jáw. This is none of your affair. ‖jèy-ge-'já gwǎn-bu-'jù jèy-ge-'wén-dz-le. This brake won't control the wheel any more.

管
gwǎn (Munit) a **bǐ** (pen), writing instrument; and for any kind of writing instrument which includes **bǐ**: a **chyǎn-'bǐ** (pencil), a **máy-'bǐ** (writing-brush), etc.

管 (子, 兒)
*gwǎn, 'gwǎn-dz, gwǎr (Nmass, tyáw, ge) tube, pipe, conduit. **shwěy-'gwǎn(-dz)** water pipes; **chì-'gwǎn** windpipe (in throat); **méy-chì-'gwǎn** gas pipes, gas mains.

管保
gwǎn-'bǎw (V) to guarantee. ‖wǒ gwǎn-'bǎw jèy-ge-'dūng-shi ké-yi yùng 'sān-nyán. I guarantee that this can be used for three years.

管閘
gwǎn-'já (VN2) to be in charge of the brakes. **gwǎn-'já-de** (Npers) brakeman (on a train)

管賬
gwǎn-'jàng (VN2) to keep accounts. **gwǎn-'jàng-de** (Npers) bookkeeper.

管家
gwǎn-'jyā (VN1) to keep house. **gwǎn-'jyā-de** (Npers) butler; housekeeper.

管理
gwǎn-'lǐ (V) to be in charge of, take care of and manage things, affairs (quite formal). **gwǎn-'lǐ-rén** (Npers) person in charge of a hotel, a factory, etc. (not governmental).

管事
gwǎn-'shř (VN2) to be in charge of the affairs of some business or office. **gwǎn-'shř-de** (Npers) person in charge, manager.

管轄
gwǎn-'shyá (V) to govern a village, district, etc.; to be in charge of a government installation, office, department. ‖jèy-ge-'tswēn-dz shř-'shéy gwǎn-'shyá? Under whose jurisdiction is this village?

慣
gwàn (I) to be accustomed to something. ‖wǒ dwèy-ywu jèy-jyàn-'shř-ching 'yǐ-jing 'tīng-de hěn 'gwàn-le. I've already gotten quite accustomed to hearing about that matter.

    (V) Particularly as mainV in **gwàn-'hwày** to spoil a child. ‖wǒ bǎ-ta gwàn-'hwày-le. I've spoiled him. As postV: **shwèy-'gwàn** be accustomed to sleeping (in a certain place, for example); **chř-'gwàn** be accustomed to eating (such-and-such food); etc. ‖wǒ chř-'gwàn-le wày-gwo-'fàn. I'm quite accustomed to eating foreign food. ‖wǒ shwèy-bu-'gwàn jèy-ge-'chwáng. I'm not accustomed to sleeping in this bed.

灌
gwàn (V) to pour something in. ‖ná jèy-ge-'píng-dz chywù gwàn dyǎr-'shwěy-lay. Take this bottle and get some water. ‖gwàn 'bàn-píng-dz-de-nyéw-'nǎy. Fill half a bottle with milk.

    As mainV: **gwàn-'mǎn** to pour full. ‖bǎ jèy-ge-'píng-dz gwàn-'mǎn-le nyéw-'nǎy. Fill this bottle full of milk.

罐子
'gwàn-dz (NunitC, ge) jug, jar; canister (high and relatively narrow, with or without handle and lip; but no wider at bottom than at top). **shwěy-'gwàn-dz** water pitcher.

灌溉
gwàn-'gǎy (V) to irrigate, water a garden. **gwàn-'gày mǐ-'tyán** to irrigate a rice field, flood a rice field.

罐頭
'gwàn-tew, gwàr (Mcont) can of (canned) food. **yí-gwàr-nyéw-rèw-'gàr** can of dried beef. **'gwàn-tew** (Nmass) canned food. **chř 'gwàn-tew** to eat canned food; **jwāng 'gwàn-tew** to can food.

光
gwāng (I) to have no clothes on all or part of the body. **gwāng-je 'jí-nyang** stripped to the waist.

    (Nabstr) light (not a source, but the light itself). ‖jèy-ge-'gwāng hěn 'chyáng. This light is very strong. **'gwāng-shywé** science of optics.

    As postV: finished, completed; general with any V as mainV: ‖'tsày yǐ-jing chř-'gwāng-le. The food's all eaten up.

    (H) only one thing, not others: ‖nǐ 'gwāng yěw 'jèy-ge-'běn-lǐng bù-'shíng. It isn't enough for you just to have this one kind of ability.

光滑
'gwāng-hwa (A) smooth. ‖shyǎw-'hár-de-'pí-fu hěn 'gwāng-hwa. A baby's skin is very smooth.

光棍
gwāng-'gwèr (Npers) bachelor; hoodlum, rascal.

光榮
'gwǎng-rúng (*A*) glorious, (*as of a heroic action*). (*Nunit*, **ge**) glory, thing to be proud of. **yí-ge-gwó-'jyā-de-'gwǎng-rúng** an achievement of *or* event in the history of a nation of which one is proud.

光線
gwǎng-'shyàn (*Nunit*, **dàw**, **tyáw**) beam of light, ray of light.

光陰
'gwǎng-yīn (*Nabstr*) time, time available. ‖**nǐ yīng-dāng 'jǐ-daw dzěme 'yùng nǐ-de-'gwǎng-yīn.** You must know how to use your time.

廣
gwǎng (*A*) extensive, wide. ‖**tā-de-'jǐ-shr hěn 'gwǎng.** His knowledge is very broad.

廣播
gwǎng-'bwó (*or* **gwǎng-'bwò**) (*V*) to broadcast (*radio*). **gwǎng-'bwó shīn-'wén** to broadcast the news.
    As mainV: **gwǎng-'bwó-dàw** (*lc*) to broadcast to a place; **gwǎng-'bwó-chū-lay** to broadcast *something*.

廣東
gwǎng-'dūng (*Nunique*) Kwangtung *province*.

廣告
gwǎng-'gàw (*Nunit*, **ge**) advertisement. **chū gwǎng-'gàw** to send out advertising matter; **dēng gwǎng-'gàw** to have an advertisement put into *a paper or magazine, etc.*
    tyē gwǎng-'gàw to post a bill.

廣告牌
gwǎng-gàw-'páy, **gwǎng-gàw-'pár** (*Nunit*, **shàn**, **myàn**, **ge**) billboard.

廣州
gwǎng-'jēw (*Nunique*) Kuang-chou *or* Canton (*capital of Kwangtung province*).

廣州灣
gwǎng-jēw-'wān (*Nunique*) Kuang-chou Wan *or* Kwang-chowwan (*bay in Kwangtung province*).

廣西
gwǎng-'shī (*Nunique*) Kwangsi *province*.

廣義的
gwǎng-'yì-de (*H*) in general. ‖**gwǎng-'yì-de shwō, 'bāw-hán hěn-dwō-de-'yì-sz.** Generally speaking, it includes many ideas (*i.e.*, permits of many interpretations). (*The opposite of* **gwàng-'yì-de** *is* **shyá-'yì-de** specifically.)

逛
gwàng (*V*) to sightsee, make a tour and look at *scenery, sights, etc.* ‖**wǒm ¯hywù 'gwàng-yi-gwàng-ba.** Let's go sightseeing.
    gwàng *means also* to visit prostitutes.

摑打
'gwāy-da (*V*) to beat *with a flat surface*, spank *or* pat (*not as punishment*). ‖**tā dzày tā-jyān-'bǎr-shang 'gwāy-da-gwāy-da.** He patted him on the shoulder.

拐
gwǎy (*I*) to turn. **gwǎy-'wār** *or* **gwǎy-'jyǎw(r)**to turn a corner; **gwǎy-jyǎwr-de-dì-fangr** a corner (*as in a street or road*).
    As mainV: **'gwǎy-gwò** (*lc*) to turn around; **gwǎy-'jìn** (*lc*) to turn into *a street;* **'gwǎy-chū** (*lc*) to turn out from (*e.g., a street*) ; *etc.*
    Figuratively: ‖**jèy-ge-rén-de-'nǎw-dz bù-gwǎy-'wār.** This man has °a one-track mind. *or* °a stubborn mind.
    'gwǎy-gwò 'shēn-lay to turn around (turn one's body around).

拐
gwǎy (*V*) to decoy, kidnap, swindle (*implies absence of violence; by persuasion*). *As mainV:* **gwǎy-'dzěw** to kidnap and carry off. ‖**tām bǎ jèy-ge-shyǎw-'hár gwǎy-'dzěw-le.** They decoyed the child and ran off with him.

拐子
'gwǎy-dz (*Npers*) person who limps; abductor.

拐棍
gwǎy-'gwèr (*Nunit*, **jǐ**, **gēn**, **gēr**, **ge**) walking stick, cane.

怪
gwày (*V*) to blame. ‖**byé 'gwày-ta.** Don't blame him (*said under fairly trivial circumstances; not serious*).
    (*A*) queer. ‖**'jèy-ge-rén hěn 'gwày.** This guy is quite queer.
    (*H*) rather. ‖**jèy-ge-'dūng-shi gwày bú-'tswò-de.** This thing is rather good (*showing surprised concession*).

怪物
'gwày-wu (*Nunit*, **ge**) strange being; queer bird (*of people*).

滾
gwěn (*I and causative*) to roll. *When this term describes the motion of a person it is a very ill-mannered equivalent of* **dzěw**.

As main V: 'gwěn-gwò (*lc*) to roll over (*as a ball*); gwěn-dàw (*lc*) to roll to *a place;* 'gwěn-chū (*lc*) to roll out; 'gwěn-jìn (*lc*) to roll in; *etc.*

‖'gwěn-kay! Scram! Make way! Get out of my way! ‖gwěn 'dàn! Roll away, you egg! (*even stronger insult*).

gwěn (*H*) *before a few V and A:* gwěn 'rè terribly hot, boiling hot; gwěn 'kāy to boil violently.

棍子，棍兒

'gwèn(-dz), gwèr (*N unit*, gēr, tyáw, ge) rod, stick, pole, cane. (*M semel*) blow with a stick. ‖dǎ-ta yí-'gwèn-dz. Give him a blow with the stick.

歸

gwēy (*V*) to pertain to, belong to. ‖'jèy-ge gwēy-'nǐ. This belongs to you. (*As in distributing property to the survivors on the death of the former owner, or in assigning jobs to various subordinates.*)

gwēy ... 'gwǎn, is *so-and-so's* to take care of; gwēy ... 'dzwò is *so-and-so's* to do; gwēy ... 'yǎng is *so-and-so's* to raise, care for (*as an adopted child, or when people are divorced*); *etc.*

gwēy (*lc*) to put *things* in *their* proper places, tidy *things* up; 'gwēy-jr-gwēy-jr to set *things* in order, tidy *things* up; gwēy-'lèy (*VN1*) to classify *things;* *as main V:* 'gwēy-dzày to put *things* at a place; *etc.*

歸了包堆

gwēy-le bāw-'dzwēy (*J*) putting it all together (*after itemizing various expenditures*). ‖gwēy-le bāw-'dzwēy wǒ 'chū-le shŕ-'wǔ-kwày-chyán. So all in all I spent only fifteen dollars.

規定

gwēy-'dìng (*V, Vpred, Vsent*) to decide, reach a decision about. (*Nabstr*) decision. fǎ-'lywù-gwēy-'dìng legal decisions, legal regulations, laws.

規則

'gwēy-dzé (*N unit*, ge) prescribed procedure. ‖dzěme yùng jèy-ge-jī-chi yīng-gay yěw yí-'dìng-de-'gwēy-dzé. There have to be definite rules for operating this machinery.

歸罪

gwēy-'dzwèy (*VN2*) to give blame, blame. ‖'jèy-jyàn-shŕ-ching nǐ bù-néng gwēy-'dzwèy ywú-'tā. You can't blame him for this affair. ‖'yīng-gay gwēy shwéy-de-'dzwèy? Who's to blame?

歸功

gwēy-'gūng (*VN2*) to give credit. ‖'jèy-ge yīng-gay gwēy-'gūng gěy-'nǐ. Credit for this °must be given to you. *or* °is due you. ‖'jèy-tsž-de-shèng-'jàng yīng-gay gwēy tā-de-'gūng. This time the victory should be accredited to him.

歸化城

gwēy-hwà-'chéng (*N unique*) Kweihwacheng, *another name for* gwēy-'swéy Kuei-sui (*capital of Suiyüan province*).

規矩

'gwēy-jywu (*A*) observant of the rules. ‖nǐ 'gwēy-jywu yì-dyǎr. Stick to the rules a bit more (*don't be so inconsiderate of what society says one should do*). ‖tā-'nèy-ge-rén dǐng 'gwēy-jywu-de. He's extremely careful to behave as one should.

(*N unit*, ge) rules and regulations (*not legal, but those imposed by tradition or those of a private establishment*).

gwēy-gwey-jywu-'jywū-de (*H*) respectfully, reverently; very frankly, plainly.

規模

'gwēy-mwó (*Nabstr*) scope, scale. ‖nèy-ge-dzǔ-'jŕ-de 'gwēy-mwó hěn 'dà. That organization is quite extensive.

歸綏

gwēy-'swéy (*N unique*) Kuei-sui (*capital of Suiyüan province*).

軌

gwēy (*N unit*, tyáw) (wheel) track; rail. chē-'gwěy wheel track, rut; tyě-lù-'gwěy railroad rail; gwěy-'dàw railed way, railway (*the actual track*).

鬼

gwěy (*N unit*, ge) ghost, spirit, devil. (*Not primarily spirit of the dead, which is technically hwén, or in Christianity 'líng-hwén soul.*)

鬼計

gwěy-'jì (*N unit*, ge) clever trick; bad trick. wár gwěy-'jì *or* shŕ gwěy-'jì to pull a trick; yùng gwěy-'jì to use a trick *to accomplish some end.*

鬼計多端

gwěy-'jì dwō-'dwān (*literary quotation*) be tricky, wily, clever, full of tricks and short-cuts. (*Said of a person; is either a compliment or a warning to avoid the person; depending on context.*)

鬼臉

gwěy-'lyǎn, gwěy-'lyǎr (*N unit*, ge) grimace, funny facial expression. dzwò gwěy-'lyǎr to make faces.

貴

gwèy (*A*) expensive. (*Opposite jyàn cheap, reasonable.*) *In certain fixed groups,* honorable, *forming polite ways of asking for information.* ‖gwèy-'shìng? What is your honorable name? ‖gwèy-'gwó? From what honorable country do you come? ‖gwèy-'chù? From

what honorable locality do you come? ‖gwèy-'shěng?
From what honorable province do you come?

The answers to all these replace gwèy *by* bì humble.

櫃

'gwèy(-dz) (*Nunit*, jyà, ge) counter; bureau; cabinet; wardrobe; show case, display case. shū-'gwèy(-dz) bookćase, book cabinet; chyán-'gwèy old-style cabinet for money; wǎn-'gwèy china cabinet; bwō-li-'gwèy glass case in a store for displaying goods; yī-'gwèy clothes wardrobe.

貴族

gwèy-'dzú (*Nunit*, jyǎ, ge) family of high social position; family of the nobility.

貴州

gwèy-'jēw (*Nunique*) Kweichow *province*.

貴筑

gwèy-'jú (*Nunique*) Kuei-chu (*capital of Kweichow province*)

貴重

'gwèy-jùng (*A*) precious, valuable.

桂林

gwèy-'lín (*Nunique*) Kuei-lin *or* Kueilin (*capital of Kwangsi province*).

櫃臺

gwèy-'táy, gwèy-'tár (*Nunit*, ge) counter, desk *in a hotel or store*.

　gwèy-'táy-shang-de-'rén desk clerk, *or* waiter behind a counter *in a restaurant*.

貴陽

gwèy-'yáng (*Nunique*) Kweiyang, *another name for* gwèy-'jú Kuei-chu (*capital of Kweichow province*).

鍋

gwō (*NunitC*, ge) pot, kettle. gwō-'bǐng a kind of thick bread baked in a gwō *with almost no oil*.
　gwō-'yān-dz (*Nmass*) soot.
　gwō-pén-wǎn-'dzàn (*Ncoll*, tàw) dishes and kitchen utensils.

蟈 蟈

'gwō-gwo, 'gwō-gwèr (*Nunit*, ge) large green cricket.

國

gwó (*Mauton*) country, nation, state. 'jūng-gwo China; 'fà-gwo France; 'měy-gwo the United States; *etc.*; lyán-hé-'gwó United Nations.

國旗

gwó-'chí (*Nunit*, myàn, ge) national flag.

國都

gwó-'dū (*Nunique*) capital of a country. 'měy-gwo-de-gwó-'dū the capital of the United States.

國防

gwó-'fáng (*Nabstr*) national defense.

國會

gwó-'hwèy (*Nunique*) Congress; Parliament; Diet. gwó-hwèy-yì-'ywán member of Congress. lyǎng-'ywàn-de-gwó-'hwèy a bicameral legislature.

國際

gwó-jì-'gwǎn-shì (*Aattr*) international. gwó-jì-'gwǎn-shì international relations; gwó-jì-túng-'méng Allies.

國家

gwó-'jyā (*Nunit*, ge) country, nation.

國界

gwó-'jyè (*Nunit*, tyáw) border between countries, national boundary. gwò gwó-'jyè to cross a national boundary; hwà gwó-'jyè to draw a boundary line; dìng gwó-'jyè to agree on, settle, *a boundary line*.

國聯

gwó-'lyán (*Nunique*) League of Nations (*full form* 'gwó-jì-lyán-méng-'hwèy).

國民

gwó-'mín (*Npers*) citizen of a country.

國民黨

gwó-mín-'dǎng (*Nunique*) the (Chinese) Nationalist Party, Kuomintang.

國術

gwó-'shù (*Nabstr*) art of self-defense, boxing, wrestling, jiu-jitsu, judo, *etc.*

國王

gwó-'wáng (*Npers*) king.

國務

gwó-'wù (*Nunit*, jyàn) national affairs.

國務部

gwó-wù-'bù (*Nunique*) State Department (*U. S.*).

裹

gwǒ (*V*) to bind *or* tie something around, without covering completely; to put a string *or* strap around. *As mainV:* 'gwǒ-chǐ-láy *or* 'gwǒ-shàng to bind up, to tie up. ‖yùng bēng-'dày bǎ tā-de-'gē-be 'gwǒ-chi-lay. Bandage his arm.

果，菓，

*gwǒ, 'gwǒ-dz, gwèr (*Nunit*, ge) nuts; fruit. shwěy-'gwǒ fruit; gān-'gwǒ nuts *or* dried fruit; gwǒ-'shù fruit trees, nut trees.

菓子醬

gwǒ-dz-'jyàng (*Nmass*) preserved fruit, preserves.

菓（木）樹

gwǒ-(mù-)'shù (*Nunit*, kē) fruit and nut trees.

菓園(子)

gwǒ-'ywán(-dz) (*Nunit*, ge) orchard, grove of fruit or nut trees.

過

gwò (*V*) to pass by, cross, get to a place beyond, exceed. gwò-'hé to cross a river; gwò-'shān to get past some mountains; gwò-'jyē to cross a street.

   'bú-gwò shř does not exceed being, isn't more than. ‖tā 'bú-gwò shř yí-ge-'shywé-sheng. He's only a student.

   With temporal meaning: gwò-'yè to pass the night, spend the night (*at some place, or doing something*); 'gwò (yì-)hwěr (*H*) wait a minute, wait a while; gwò-'shyà spend the summer; *etc.*

   With a further extension of meaning: gwò-'shŕ to have become out of date, old-fashioned, old; gwò-'nyán to celebrate the new year; gwò 'shēng-r to celebrate a birthday; gwò 'ř-dz to live, make a living.

   (*I, lc*) to pass by, go past. ‖hěn-dwō-'ř-dz 'gwò-chywù-le. Many days passed by. ‖tā tsúng wǒ-'shēn-byar 'gwò-chywù-le. He just passed by me.

   To come over, go over. ‖gwò-lay 'kàn-yi-kàn. Come over and take a look.

   Used as postV forming RC1 and RC2: 'dzěw-gwò (*lc*) to walk past, walk by; 'pǎw-gwò (*lc*) to run past, run by; *etc.*

   (*V, lc*) to go over, across, come over, across *a river, street, etc.* ‖wǒm 'dzěme néng-gew gwò-'hé-ne? How can we get across the river?

   Used as postV forming RC3 and RC4: 'dzěw-gwò (*lc*) to walk across; *etc.* ‖hé-'shwěy 'dùng de-shŕ-hew ké-yi 'dzěw-gwo 'hé-chywu. When the river is frozen you can walk over it.

   In its transitive meaning also used as K: gwò-'hé dàw-'nàr chywu cross the river and go to that place.

   As mainV: gwò-bu-'chywù be unable to go across, or, to make trouble for (gēn) *someone*; gwò-bu-'gwàn be unable to adapt oneself to *physical circumstances of life.*

   Before some words for periods or points of time, forming Ntime or H: gwò-'wǔ afternoon; 'gwò-tyan some later day; 'gwò-nyan next year.

過

gwò (*I, lc*) to pass by, go by.

   'gwò-láy(-de)-rén person who has had personal experience *at something being discussed.*

   'gwò-chywù *euphemism for* to die; *also* to get out of date, become old-fashioned, pass out of style, out of the picture.

過

gwò (*Nunit*, ge) mistake. ‖wǒ 'méy-yew 'gwò. I haven't made any mistakes.

不過

bú-'gwò (*J*) although, but, though, even so. ‖bú-'gwò wǒ bú-'dà ywàn-yi 'chywù. But I'm not too anxious to go.

過

*gwò *added to verbs: without* méy, *in a question, is like saying in English* did you ever . . .: *or* have you ever . . .; *with* méy, *in a statement, is like saying in English* I've never . . .; *or* I didn't ever . . . . ‖nǐ 'nyàn-gwo néy-běn-'shū-ma? Have you ever read that book? ‖wǒ méy-'dàw-gwo 'jūng-gwo. I've never been to China. ‖wǒ 'nyàn-gwo-le néy-běn-'shū, 'nyàn-le sān-'tsž-le. I HAVE read that book, I've read it three times.

   In some cases is almost equivalent to le, *though* le *may be added too:* ‖nǐ chř-gwo dzǎw-'fàn méy-yew? Have you had breakfast yet?

過磅

gwò-'bàng (*VN1*) to weigh in, be weighed in (*of heavy things; of plane passengers; in a physical examination; of a prize-fighter or jockey*).

過期

gwò-'chī (*VN1*) to pass the due date, become overdue (*as of a book from a library*).

過道

gwò-'dàwr (*Nunit*, tyáw, ge) aisle; passageway; corridor.

過繼

'gwò-jì (*V*) to adopt (*a related child*). 'gwò-jì-gěy be adopted by (*a relative*).

過重

gwò-'jùng (*VN1*) to become overweight.

過慮

gwò-'lywù (*I*) to worry overmuch.

過敏

gwò-'mǐn (*A*) too sensitive, oversensitive. ‖tā-shén-'jing gwò-'mǐn. He's too sensitive.

H

哈爾濱

hā-ěr-'bīn (*Nunique*) Harbin, *another name for* **bīn-'jyāng** Pin-chiang (*city in Kirin province*).

哈喇

'hā-la (*A*) rancid (*of oily things only, or of their odor*).

哈邋子

hā-'lá-dz (*Nmass*) saliva *drooling out.* **lyéw hā-'lá-dz** to drool, (*figuratively*) to have one's mouth water *because one sees something good to eat, or something one would like.*

哈密

hā-'mì (*Nunique*) Ha-mi (*city in Sinkiang province*).

蛤蟆

'há-ma (*Nunit*, **ge**) frog.

hai *Wade Romanization for* **hay.**

含

hán (*V*) to hold in the mouth (*not like a pipe, which is partly outside the mouth*).
    To conceal, hide, keep secret *a motive, a plan:* **'nǐ jèy-jywù-'hwà-lǐ-tew hán-je shéme-'yì-sz?** What's the hidden meaning in what you say?

邋

hán, 'hán-shr *see* **háy, 'háy-shr.**

寒暑表

hán-shǔ-'byǎw (*Nunit*, **gēr**, **ge**) thermometer.

涵義

hán-'yì (*VN1*) to conceal the real meaning, *giving a clue by saying something that on the surface seems to mean something else.* (*Nunit*, **ge**) a concealed meaning or idea, an implication. ‖**tā-de-'hwà yěw shéme-hán-'yì?** What's the meaning (hidden) behind what he said?

喊

hǎn (*V*) to cry out, call out. ‖**tā-'hǎn jyèw-'mìng.** He hollered for help.
    hǎn-'jyèw (*VN1*) to call for help.
    As mainV: **'hǎn-chū-lay** to call out; **'hǎn-chǐ-lay** to (start to) scream.

旱

*hàn (*I*) to dry up *from lack of rain* ‖**tyān 'hàn-le.** There's a drought. ‖**jèy-ge-'dì-fang dà 'hàn.** This locality is suffering from a severe drought.

漢朝

'hàn-cháw (*Nunique*) The Han dynasty (*206 B.C.–220 A.D.*). *This dynasty was quite prosperous, so that China is still sometimes referred to with the term* ***hàn**; *thus* **hàn-'dz** Chinese characters.

漢中

hàn-'jūng (*Nunique*) Hanchung, *another name for* **nán-'jèng** Nan-cheng (*city in Shensi province*).

漢口

hàn-'kěw (*Nunique*) Han-k'ou *or* Hankow (*city in Hupeh province*).

漢水

hàn-'shwěy (*Nunique*) The Han Shui (*river*).

行

háng (*Mgroup*) line of, row of, column of. **yì-háng-'jù-dz** row of pillars; **yì-háng-de-'rén** line of people. *Also* line *of text in a book*, line *of a poem;* line *of business, of study, etc.*
    (*Nunit*, **ge**) *in last sense above;* also an office, branch or branch office of some *business:* **dzǔng-'háng** main office; **fēn-'háng** branch office; **yín-'háng** bank; **yáng-'háng** foreign company doing business in China.
    dzày-'háng *or* **nèy-'háng** (*VN2*) to be in a certain business, *thus* to know what one is talking about when discussing it; **wày-'háng** (*VN1*) *opposite of the last;* **'běn-háng** our establishment *in business speech or signs,* or our line of business; **háng-'hwà** trade talk, shop talk.

航

háng (*V*) to navigate (in). **háng-'hǎy** to navigate the seas; **háng-'kūng** to navigate in the sky.
    (*Nabstr*) navigation.

航程

háng-'chéng (*VN1*) to navigate along a nautical route. (*Nabstr*) navigation.
    háng-chéng-r-'jì ship's log.

杭州

háng-'jēw (*Nunique*) Hangchow, *another name for* **háng-'shyàn** Hang-hsien (*city in Chekiang province*).

杭州灣

háng-jēw-'wǎn (*Nunique*) Hang-chou Bay.

航空母艦

háng-kūng-mǔ-'jyàn (*Nunit*, **jř**, **tyáw**, **ge**) aircraft carrier.

航空信

háng-kūng-'shìn (*Nunit*, **fēng**) air mail letter.

航行

'háng-shíng (*I*) to travel by water. ‖**wǒ 'háng-shíng gwò dì-jūng-'hǎy.** I crossed the Mediterranean by boat.

行市

'háng-shr (*Nunit*, **ge**) current price, exchange rate; market. ‖**'jèy-jǔng-hwò méy 'háng-shr.** There's no market for this line of goods.

杭縣

háng-'shyàn (*Nunique*) Hang-hsien (*city in Chekiang province*).

航線

háng-'shyàn (*Nunit*, **tyáw**) shipping route, trade route (*sea or air*).

hao *Wade Romanization for* **haw.**

毫

háw (*Mmeas*). *See Appendix B.* (*H*) *reinforces* **bū**, not even the least little bit so, *in certain set phrases; or reinforces* **wú** *similarly:* **'háw bú-gù-'jì** be extremely thoughtless; **háw wú-yí-'wèn** beyond the shadow of a doubt.

好

hǎw (*A*) good, OK, satisfactory (*opposite* **hwày**); morally good (*opposite* **dǎy**); well, in good health (*opposite* **bìng**); strong (*opposite* **rwò**). ‖**'hǎw, wǒm jyèw 'chywù-ba.** OK, so we'll go. ‖**wǒ 'gēn-ni chywù, °'hǎw-ma? *or* °'hǎw-bu-hǎw?** I'll go with you then; will that be OK? ‖**'hǎw(-ba).** OK.

May be followed by a V: **hǎw-'chr** good to eat; **hǎw-'kàn** good to look at, good-looking, attractive; **hǎw-'tīng** good to listen to, beautiful; **hǎw shwō-'hwàr** good-natured to talk to, pleasant to converse with; **hǎw-'shyàw** funny.

(*H*) *before adjectives or adverbs: an intensive.* ‖**hǎw jyéw méy-'jyàn!** Long time no see! ‖**hǎw 'rúng-yi.** Very easy. ‖**'hǎw 'rúng-yi!** *sarcastically* Really easy yet! (*meaning* very difficult).

(*H*) *before a verb:* **hǎw 'shyàng** it seems very much as though . . . .

Before quantity words: **hǎw-'dwō(-de)** many, quite a number of. **hǎw-'jǐ** (*plus M*) *or* **hǎw-'shyē** quite a few.

(*J*) *only in second part of sentence.* So that, in order to. ‖**wǒ dàw-nèr 'chywù hǎw jyàw-ta 'shǐ-hwǎn.** I went there to please him.

(*N*) in **wèy** . . .(-de) **hǎw** for so-and-so's good. **wèy nǐ-de-'hǎw** for your good.

好處

'hǎw-chù (*Nunit*, **ge**) good points; advantages.

好歹

hǎw-'dǎy (*Nabstr*) good and evil. ‖**tā bù-'jǐ-daw hǎw-'dǎy.** He can't tell good from evil.

好點

hǎw-'dyǎn (*Nunit*. **ge**) good points; advantages.

好法兒

'hǎw-far (*or* **'hǎw-fer**) ‖**dzěme 'hǎw-fer?** How come you say he's so hot? Give the evidence; tell us what good points he has.

好漢

hǎw-'hàn (*Npers*) courageous person (*male only*).

好壞

hǎw-'hwày (*Nabstr*) quality. ‖**'jèy-jǔng-hwò-de-hǎw-'hwày hěn nán-'shwō.** It's very hard to determine the quality of this type of thing.

好 傢 伙

‖**hǎw-'jyā-hwo!** Boy oh boy! (*what a night!; and the like*).

好玄了

‖**hǎw 'shywán-le!** That was a close call!

好意

hǎw-'yì (*Nunit*, **ge**) good intention. ‖**nèy-shr wǒ-de-hǎw-'yì.** That was meant well on my part (if it went wrong, I'm sorry).

不好意思

bù-hǎw-'yì-sz (*A*) embarrassed; ashamed; shy.

號

hàw (*M*) day of the month. **'shǐ-ywè 'yí-hàw** the first of October; **hàw(r)**, **'hàw-shu** (*M*) number *when things are numbered ordinally; e.g.,* number of a house on a street; shoe size or dress size, *etc.;* prisoner number *such-and-such.*

hàw (*Nunit*, **ge**) a firm or store *located at such-and-such a place on a particular street.* **běn-'hàw** this firm *or* this store *or* our establishment, *in polite and formal reference to one's own business.*

好

hàw (*Vpred*) to like to, enjoy . . .-ing, desire to. ‖**tā hàw kàn-'shì, chēw-'yān, hē-'jyéw, shwō 'dà-hwà.** The things he always wants to do and gets a kick out of are seeing plays, smoking, drinking, and boasting.

耗子

'hàw-dz (*Nunit*, **ge**) mouse *or* rat. **'dà-hàw-dz** rat; **'shyǎw-hàw-dz** mouse.

號碼

hàw-'mǎr (*N unit. ge*) number *assigned for identification; e.g., telephone* number, *a motor's serial* number.

還

háy (*H*) (1) still (*reference to time*). ‖**tā háy méy-'láy.** He still hasn't come. ‖**tā 'háy bù-láy!** He's still not coming! ‖**tā háy bú-yàw 'láy.** He still doesn't want to come. *or* He still isn't going to come. ‖**tā 'háy láy-ne.** He still comes (*every once in a while*). *or* He's still going to come (*don't get impatient*).

(2) Still more, still further, again, more. ‖**tā 'háy yàw chř yì-wǎn-'fàn.** He's going to eat (still) another bowl of rice. ‖**'jèy-běn-shū bǐ 'nèy-běn háy 'hǎw.** This book is (still) better than that (*but both are good; see also* **gèng**). ‖**'jèy-ge 'háy swàn 'hǎw.** This still counts as good (*though it's only fair relative to some others*). ‖**'háy yěw yí-ge.** There's still another.

孩子，孩兒

'háy-dz, hár (*N pers*) child. **shyǎw-'hár** baby; **nán-'háy-dz** (small) boy; **nywǔ-'háy-dz** (small) girl.

害怕

háy-'pà (*V*) to be afraid of, fear.
(*I*) to be afraid, be frightened.

還有呢

‖**'háy yěw-ne?** Well, what's next? (*when someone interrupts a story abruptly*). ‖**'háy yěw-ne.** And that isn't all, either!

海

hǎy (*N abstr*) the sea. **hǎy-'àn** seashore, seacoast; **hǎy-àn-'shyàn** coastline; **'hǎy-byār** beach, shore; **hǎy-'dǐ** sea bottom; **hǎy-'jàn** a sea battle; **hǎy-'lǐ** (*M meas*) nautical mile; **hǎy-'myàn** sea level; **hǎy-'shwěy** sea water.

hǎy-'dzàng (*V*) to bury at sea.

海鷗

hǎy-'ēw (*N unit,* **jř, ge**) sea gull

海港

hǎy-'gǎng (*N unit,* **ge**) harbor.

海狗

hǎy-'gěw (*N unit,* **jř, tyáw, ge**) seal (*sea animal*).

海關

hǎy-'gwān (*N unit,* **ge**) custom house.

海州

hǎy-'jēw (*N unique*) Haichow, *another name for* **dūng-'hǎy** Tung-hai (*city in Kiangsu province*).

海軍

hǎy-'jywūn (*N unique*) Navy. **'hǎy-jywūn-jywūn-'gwān** Naval officer. **'hǎy-jywūn-shàw-'wèy** ensign (*officer*); *etc., with other terms of rank.*

海口

hǎy-'kěw (*N unique*) Hai-k'ou *or* Hoikow (*city on Hainan Island*).

海口

hǎy-'kěw (*N unit,* **ge**) seaport.

海拉爾

hǎy-lā-'ěr (*N unique*) Hu-lun *or* Hailar (*city in Heilungkiang province*).

海南島

hǎy-nán-'dǎw (*N unique*) Hai-nan Island.

海參崴

hǎy-sēn-'wèy, hǎy-shēn-'wèy (*N unique*) Vladivostok.

海灣

hǎy-'wān (*N unit,* **ge**) bay (*on the seashore*).

海牙

hǎy-'yá (*N unique*) The Hague.

害

hày (*V*) to injure *a person in any way whatsoever* (*physically, financially or by undermining his reputation*).
hày rén-'mìng to take a person's life (*either by force or by indirect methods*).
To get, catch *a disease.* **hày-'bìng** to get sick.

害羣之馬

hày-chywún-jr-'mǎ (*literary quotation*) the black sheep of a group, the bad apple in the barrel. ‖**tā shř ge-hày-chywún-jr-'mǎ.** He's the bad apple in the barrel.

害怕

hày-'pà *see* **háy-'pà.**

害臊

hày-'sàw (*A*) feel ashamed; be shy. ‖**tā hěn hày-'sàw.** He's very shy.

害羞

hày-'shyēw (*A*) feel ashamed; be shy.

喝

hē (*V*) to drink *a liquid, including a liquid food such as soup;* to take *liquid medicine* (*compare* **chř** to eat).

喝醉

hē-'dzwèy (*RC1*) to get drunk.

合

hé (*V*) to be in accord with *or* in agreement with; to put *things* together, merge, pool; to close up *a box, a suitcase*. **hé 'pāy-dz** *or* **hé yīn-ywè** to keep time with the music. ‖**jèy-ge-'tsày bù-'hé wǒ-de-kěw-'wèy.** This food doesn't suit my taste.

 As mainV: **'hé-chì-láy** *or* **'hé-shàng** to close *a box, suitcase, book* (*anything with a lid or cover on a hinge*); **hé-bu-'dàw** can't be equivalent to as much as (*in equating currencies*); **hé-bu-'láy** can't get along together (*of people*); **'hé-shyà-chywù** to put *a cover down* on *something*; **hé-dzày yí-'kwàr** to cooperate, work together, pool resources, merge. ‖**jèy-jāng-'pyàw-dz shyàn-dzày hé 'jūng-gwo-chyán 'hé-de-dàw 'sān-bǎy-kwày-chyán-ma?** Could I get as much as three hundred dollars in Chinese money for this bill now?

 (*H*) together, cooperatively. *Limited to a few cases:* **hé 'dzwò** to work together; **hé 'chàng** to sing in chorus; **hé 'dzèw** to play (*musical instruments*) in ensemble.

合

hé (*Mmeas*) a unit of capacity. *See Appendix B.*

和

hé (*K*) with, and. **wǒ hé-'nǐ** you and I.

河

hé (*Nunit*, **tyáw, dàw**) river. **hé-'àn** *or* **hé-'byār** river bank; **hé-'shwěy** river water; **hwáng-'hé** the Yellow River.

盒 (子, 兒)

***hé, 'hé-dz, 'héer** (*NunitC*, **ge**) (small) box. **hé** (*Mcont*) (small) box full. **hé-dz-'gàr** (*Nunit*, **ge**) box top.

河壩

hé-'bà (*Nunit*, **ge**) river dam.

荷包 (兒)

'hé-bāwr (*NunitC*, **ge**) small bag for money *made of soft cloth, with a drawstring near the top.*

河北

hé-'běy (*Nunique*) Hopeh *province.*

合併

hé-'bìng (*V*) merge, unite. ‖**hé-'bìng jèy-'lyǎng-ge-jī-'gwān ké-yi shěng-'chyán.** Merging these two organizations would save money.

和氣

'hé-chì (*A*) agreeable, easy to get along with, congenial (*of a person or his manner*).

河道

hé-'dàw (*Nunit*, **tyáw**) course of a river, river bed. **'gān-le-de-hé-'dàw** dry river bed.

河堤

·**hé-'dī** (*or* **hé-'tí**) (*Nunit*, **dàw, ge**) dike along a river.

合法

hé-'fǎ (*A*) legal, according to law. ‖**yùng hé-'fǎ-de-shěw-'shywù.** Use legal methods.

合肥

hé-'féy (*Nunique*) Ho-fei (*city in Anhwei province*).

合格

hé-'gé(er) (*VN2*) to meet the qualifications, be eligible, be competent.

河溝

hé-'gēw(r) (*Nunit*, **tyáw**) small brook, stream.

合股

hé-'gǔ (*VN2*) to pool capital. **hé-'gǔ-de-'mǎy-may** joint-stock company.

合乎

'hé-hu (*V*) to suit. ‖**'jèy-jyàn-shr̀-ching 'hé-hu nǐ-de-'yì-sz-ma?** Does this suit your taste?

和緩

hé-'hwǎn (*I*) to relax, ease up, lose tension, (*of a situation, etc.*); to calm down (*as of a river when it has flowed past rapids to a place where it flows more gently*). *Used causatively:* ‖**tā-de-'hwà hé-'hwǎn-le 'jin-jāng-de-'kūng-chi.** His words eased the tension in the air.

荷花

hé-'hwār (*Nunit*, **děwr**) kind of water lily.

合夥

hé-'hwǒ, hé-'hwěr (*VN1*) to work together, cooperate, collaborate. ‖**wǒm hé-'hwěr dzwò jèy-jyàn-'shr̀.** Let's get together and do that job.

 hé-'hwǒ-de-'mǎy-may a business operated by (two or more) partners.

河口

hé-'kěw(r) (*Nunit*, **ge**) mouth of a river.

荷蘭 (國)

hé-'lán(-gwó) (*Nunique*) Holland.

河流

hé-'lyéw (*Nunit*, **tyáw, dàw**) river.

和美

hé-'měy (*A*) close knit, harmonious, *especially of a family group.*

河南

hé-'nán (*Nunique*) Honan *province.*

133

和平

hé-'píng (*Nabstr*) peace (*opposite of war*). **dǎ-'jàng 'wèy-de-shř chyéw hé-'píng** to fight a war in order to achieve peace.

楬色(兒)

'hé-sè, 'hé-shǎr (*Nabstr*) dark brown.

和尙

'hé-shang (*Npers*) monk (*Buddhist*).

合式

hé-'shř (*VN1*) to fit (*as of clothes*): to be suitable; to be fitting, suitable; to be congenial, (*of people*). **wǒ-chwǎn-de-'shyé bù-hé-'shř; tày 'jǐn.** The shoes I'm wearing don't fit; they're too tight. **nèy-ge-rén gēn wǒ-men bù-hé-'shř.** That man isn't congenial. *or* That man doesn't fit into our group.

合算

hé-'swàn (*I*) be worth it. **mǎy jèy-ge-'dūng-shi bù-hé-'swàn.** It isn't worthwhile to buy that thing. *or* It doesn't pay to buy that thing.

核桃

'hé-taw (*or* 'hé-tew) (*Nunit, ge*) walnuts.

河堤

hé-'tí *see* hé-'dī.

合同

'hé-túng (*Nunit, jāng, ge*) contract. **chyān** (*or* lì) '**hé-túng** to sign a contract; **chywǔ-'shyāw yí-ge-'hé-tung** to terminate a contract.

賀

hè (*V*) to congratulate (*a bit literary*). **wǒ 'hè-ni.** I (must) congratulate you.

    hè-'nyán (*VN1*) to extend greetings *or* good wishes for the new year. **hè-'shř** (*VN1*) to extend greetings *or* good wishes.

和乔

'hè-le, 'hwò-leng (*V*) to stir *something: Often repeated:* **nǐ 'hè-le-hè-le nèy-bēy-kā-'fēy.** Stir that cup of coffee.

    As main V: **hè-le-'hwày** to ruin by stirring, **hè-le-'hwà** to cause to dissolve by stirring.

hei *Wade Romanization for* hey.

含

hén *see* hán.

痕跡

'hén-jì (*Nunit, ge*) trace, stain, mark, clue. **jēng-'tàn 'jǎw-bu-jáw 'hén-jì.** The detective can't find any clues. **nǐ-de-'yī-fu-shang yěw yí-kwày-'yéw-de-'hén-jì.** There's a spot of grease on your clothes.

很

hěn (*H*) quite, very. **hěn 'hǎw** quite good, quite OK; **hěn 'dwō** quite a lot; **hěn shyǎng 'chywù** very much want to go.

    Stronger when used after the adjective (affirmative only): **nèy-jyàn-shř hǎw-de 'hěn.** That's excellent. **'tā dzěw-de 'kwày-de 'hěn.** He's walking very fast.

狠

hěn (*A*) mean, cruel, unkind. **tā jēn 'hěn.** He's really cruel. **tā 'dày-rén jēn 'hěn.** He really treats people cruelly.

狠心

hěn-'shīn (*A*) cruel-hearted, cold-blooded. **tā 'shīn hěn 'hěn.** He's very °cold-blooded. *or* °cruel-hearted.

恨

hèn (*V*) to hate *a person or a thing. Used as Vpred only before* bù-néng: **wǒ 'hèn bù-néng shyàn-'dzày jyèw 'chywù.** I hate not being able to go right now (I wish very much that I could).

很，慌

heng *in final position after A plus* de, *alternative form of* hěn *very much so.* **tā 'lèy-de heng.** *or* **tā 'lèy-de hěn.** He's very tired.

哼

hēng (*V*) to make a noise without saying a word, to say "hm". **tā 'hēng-le yì-shēng.** He hmed.

橫

héng (*Aattr*) horizontal. **héng-'shyàn** horizontal line. **bǎ jèy-ge-'gwèn-dz 'héng-je 'bǎy-je.** Put this pole in a horizontal position.

橫濱

héng-'bīn (*Nunique*) Yokohama.

橫棍(兒)

héng-'gwèn, hén-'gwèr (*Nunit, gēr*) horizontal pole; rung (*of a ladder*).

橫豎

héng-'shù (*J*) anyway, no matter what the case may be (*a bit literary*). **wǒ yě bù-'shwō-le, héng-'shù nǐ bù-'dǔng.** I'm not going to say anything more, you wouldn't understand anyway.

衡陽

héng-'yáng (*Nunique*) Heng-yang (*city in Hunan province*).

橫
hèng (*A*) rude, fierce, *and showing this in one's facial expression and manner.*
  hèng 'sž to die a violent death.

猴
'héw(-dz), **héwr** (*Nunit,* **ge**) monkey.

猴筋(兒)
héw-'jīn, **héw-'jyēr** (*Nunit,* **gēr, ge**) rubber band.

吼
hěw (*I*) to howl, growl, whine (*animal or wind; figuratively of a person, especially a wife*). **'hěw yì-shēngr** to howl a howl.

吼聲
hěw-'shēng (*Nunit,* **ge**) roar (*as of a lion; literary*).

厚
hèw (*A*) thick (*in dimension*) (*opposite* **báw**); kind-hearted (*of a person*); heavy (*of clothing*); warm and personal (*of human relations*).

候
hèw (*V*) to wait (for). ‖**'hèw yì-'hwěr.** Wait a while.
  'hèw-hèw to send one's best regards and inquiry as to the health of *someone* to *him*. ‖**chǐng-ni gěy-wo 'hèw-hew ta.** Please give him my best.

後
hèw (*Nplace*) behind, in back. *Freely only after K; otherwise one uses a longer form such as* **'hèw-byan, 'hèw-byar, 'hèw-myan, 'hèw-myar, 'hèw-tew.**
  Before a noun: hind-. **hèw-'twěy** hind legs; **hèw-'dēng** tail light.
  After an expression of time (also **yǐ-'hèw**) from now, in the future. (*Opposite* **yǐ-'chyán** ago.) **'sān-nyán-yǐ-'hèw** three years from now *or* three years later, after three years. *Similarly before some expressions of time:* **'hèw-tyan** day after tomorrow; **'hèw-nyan** year after next.
  (*H*) later on (*in contrast to* **shyān** first). ‖**shyān 'dàw-de shyān 'chř, 'hèw dàw-de 'méy-yew-de chř.** First come first served; those who come later on won't get anything.

後半天
'hèw-bàn-tyān, **'hèw-bàn-tyār** (*Ntime*) afternoon, P.M.

後半夜
'hèw-bàn-yè (*Ntime*) very late at night (just before daybreak).

候補
hèw-'bǔ (*V*) to be waiting to take *an office when the outgoing holder leaves it.* **hèw-bǔ-'rén** candidate *for an elective or appointive position.*

後起之秀
'hèw-chǐ-jr-'shyèw (*Npers*) (*literary quotation*) bright and promising young man.

後坐力
hèw-dzwò-'lì (*Nabstr*) recoil, kick, (*as of a gun*).

後跟
hèw-'gēn, **hèw-'gēr** (*Nunit,* **ge**) heel. **jyǎw-hèw-'gēr** heel of foot; **shyé-hèw-'ger** heel of a shoe.

後悔
hèw-'hwěy (*A*) regret, remorse (*after something has been done*).

後來
'hèw-'lay (*Ntime*) afterwards, after *what has already been said took place or has taken place.*

後晌
hèw-'shǎng or **'hèw-shang** (*Ntime*) afternoon, P.M.

後生
hèw-'shēng (*Npers*) youngster (*i.e., someone younger than you are*).

候選
hèw-'shywǎn (*VN1*) to be a candidate for election. **hèw-shywǎn-'rén** candidate for an elective office.

後臺
hèw-'tǎy (*Nplace*) backstage; (*figuratively*) behind the scenes, (*as a political boss*).

後裔
'hèw-yì (*Npers*) descendant.

黑
hēy (*A*) black; dark. (*Opposites* **báy, lyàng.**) **hēy-myàn-'bāw** black bread *or* brown bread; **hēy-'bǎn** blackboard; **hēy-'yè-li** (*Ntime*) (dark) night time. ‖**'tyān háy méy-'hēy-ne.** It (the sky) isn't dark yet.

黑暗
hēy-'àn (*Aattr*) dark, unenlightened; *as in* **hēy-àn-shŕ-'dày** the Dark Ages, the Middle Ages.

黑龍江
hēy-lúng-'jyāng (*Nunique*) Heilungkiang *province.*

黑下
'hēy-shye (*Ntime*) night time. ‖**děng 'hēy-shye dzà, 'shwō.** Let's wait till night time.

ho *one Wade Romanization for* **he**, *which is also used.*

hou *Wade Romanization for* **hew.**

135

hsi *Wade Romanization for* shi.

hsia *Wade Romanization for* shya.

hsiang *Wade Romanization for* shyang.

hsiao *Wade Romanization for* shyaw.

hsieh *Wade Romanization for* shye.

hsien *Wade Romanization for* shyan.

hsin *Wade Romanization for* shin.

hsing *Wade Romanization for* shing.

hsiu *Wade Romanization for* shyew.

hsiung *Wade Romanization for* shyung.

hsü *Wade Romanization for* shywu.

hsüan *Wade Romanization for* shywan.

hsüeh *Wade Romanization for* shywe.

hsün *Wade Romanization for* shywun.

呼呼的
'hū-hū(-de) (*H*) snoring. ‖tā 'hū-hū-de shwèy-'jáw-le. He went to sleep snoring. (*i.e.*, He slept soundly.)

忽略
'hū-lywè (*V*) to disregard, neglect, be forgetful of. ‖tā 'hū-lywè-le nèy-jyàn-'shr̀-ching. He neglected that matter.
(*A*) forgetful, careless.

忽然
'hū-rán(-jyān) (*J*) suddenly, all of a sudden.

呼吸
'hū-shī (*I*) to breathe; (*V*) to breathe in. ‖tā 'hū-shī(-le) 'shīn-shyān-de-'kūng-chì. He breathed in the fresh air. ‖dày-fu jyàw-ta 'hū-shī. The doctor told him to take a breath.

湖
hú (*Nunit*, ge, pyàn) lake.

壺
hú (*NunitC*, bǎ, ge) kettle with spout and lid, *smaller at the top than at the bottom.*

弧
hú (*Nunit*, ge) arch; (*mathematical*) arc.

胡
hú (*H*) blindly, without knowing how, *or* in a bungling way *either purposely or not.* hú 'jr̄-shr̀ to go around giving confusing and improper orders; hú 'nàw to create a disturbance: hú 'shwō to talk nonsense.

糊
hú (*V*) to paper. hú-'chyáng to paper a wall; hú 'wū-dz to paper (*the walls and ceiling of*) a room.

煳
hú (*I*) to smoulder. ‖fàn 'hú-le. The rice is burning (*that is, not with flames, but just turning brown*).
   As *mainV*: tàng-'hú-le to scorch *clothes* when ironing; *etc.*

斛
hú (*Mmeas*) a unit of capacity. *See Appendix B.*

湖北
hú-'běy (*Nunique*) Hupeh *province.*

糊塗
'hú-du (*A*) stupid, muddled, mixed-up, addle-brained. ‖tā ràw 'hú-du-le. He's all mixed up.

鬍子
'hú-dz (*Nmass*) facial hair, beard. jǎng 'hú-dz to grow a beard.

湖州
hú-'jēw (*Nunique*) Huchow, *another name for* wú-'shīng Wu-hsing (*city in Chekiang province*).

胡椒
hú-'jyāw (*Nmass*) black pepper seeds. hú-jyāw-'myàr black pepper (*powdered*).

胡來
'hú-láy (*A*) irresponsible, untrustworthy, non-conformist; *against the principles of society, or* against the principles of the person who addresses someone else thus.

糊裡糊塗
'hú-li-hú-'dū (*A*) be all mixed up. (*Same as* hěn 'hú-du *or* ràw 'hú-du.)

狐狸
'hú-li (*Nunit*, ge) fox.

胡擼
'hú-lu (*V*) to brush, touch *or* feel *with a brushing motion*, with the hand, (*as in stroking a cat*). As *mainV*: hú-lu-'gǎn-jìng to brush clean (*as crumbs from a table*); hú-lu-'dzěw to brush away; 'hú-lu-shyà-chywu to brush off and down; hú-lu-'jìn-lay to brush in towards oneself, *as cards from a table.*

葫蘆
'hú-lu(r) (*Nunit, ge*) gourd.

胡亂
hú-'lwàn (*H*) aimlessly, purposely, in a hurry without any care to details: *Also separated with a verb repeated after each:* **hú 'pà lwàn 'pà** to be afraid for no reason whatsoever. ‖**jèy-jyàn-shr̀ shr̀ 'hú-dzwò-lwàn-'dzwò-de.** This job was done all wrong, without any proper planning or thinking at all.

胡蘿蔔
hú-'lwó-be (*Nunit, gēr*) carrot.

湖南
hú-'nán (*Nunique*) Hunan *province.*

狐朋狗黨
hú-'péng gěw-'dǎng (*literary quotation*) birds of a feather flock together (*referring to people one doesn't approve of*).

胡說霸道
'hú-shwō-bā-'dàw (*I*) to talk utter nonsense, say all sorts of things that have no connection with anything at hand; to brag, boast.

胡思亂想
'hú-sz-lwàn-'shyǎng (*literary quotation*) (*I*) to imagine all sorts of things, dream up all sorts of impossible things.

胡同
hú-'tùng(r) (*Nunit, tyáw*) alleys (*in Peiping*).

護
hù (*V*) to protect, look after; to favor *one side of a fight or argument.* **hù-'bīng** guard, sentry.

護照
hù-'jàw (*Nunit, jāng, ge, běr*) passport.

護士
'hù-shr (*NpersT*) nurse (*for sick people, not for a child*).

互相
hù-'shyāng (*H*) each other, one another. **hù-'shyāng bāng-'máng** to help each other, give mutual assistance.

hua *Wade Romanization for* **hwa.**

huai *Wade Romanization for* **hway.**

huan *Wade Romanization for* **hwan.**

huang *Wade Romanization for* **hwang.**

hui *Wade Romanization for* **hwey.**

hun *Wade Romanization for* **hwen.**

烘
hūng (*V*) to roast on a spit *over a flame. Forms VN3 with names of things roasted:* **hūng-'jī** to roast chicken; roast chicken.
　　Also to warm up over *or* near to a flame: **bǎ-'shǒu 'hūng-yi-hūng** warm up one's hands.
　　hūng-'hūng-de *as an intensive after a few A:* **'rè hūng-'hūng-de** steaming hot (*of the air in a room, etc.*); **'lwàn hūng-'hūng-de** very noisy and crowded; **'máw hūng-'hūng-de** very hairy; **'chòu hūng-'hūng-de** very evil-smelling.

轟，閧
hūng (*V*) to drive *or* chase *ahead of oneself by moving the hands and arms, extended to the sides and partly downwards, back and forth, (as one chases chickens; sometimes to produce the same effect by other means). As mainV:* **'hūng-chū** (*lc*) to drive out; **hūng-'dzǒu** to drive away; **hūng-'pǎw** *same but faster;* **'hūng-kǎy** *or* **hūng-'sàn** to scatter; *etc.* ‖**tā bǎ-'jī dēw hūng-'pǎw-le.** He drove the chickens away.

轟炸
hūng-'jà (*V*) to bomb from a plane.

轟炸機
hūng-jà-'jī (*Nunit, jyà*) bomber.

紅
húng (*A*) red. **húng-'táng** brown sugar; **húng-'jwǎn** red brick (*building brick which is red*); **húng-'shǐn** hearts (*at cards; also called* **húng-'táwr** red peaches).
　　(*Of people*) popular, loved, respected, much trusted. **húng-'yǎn** red eyes. ‖**tā yǎn-'húng-le.** *or* **tā 'húng-le 'yǎn-le.** He got jealous (greedy, covetous).

紅利
húng-'lì (*Nmass, fèr*) bonus, dividend.

紅人（兒）
'húng-rén, 'húng-rér (*Npers*) a person favored and coddled by someone in an influential position.

紅十字會
húng-shŕ-dz-'hwèy (*Nunique*) International Red Cross.

洪水
húng-'shwěy (*Nmass, pyàn*) flood.

紅銅
húng-'túng (*Nmass*) copper.

哄
hǔng (*V*) to amuse, entertain *a child;* to pet *or* baby *an adult,* treat *an adult* like a child; (*Vsent*) to coax

137

someone to do something. As mainV: **hǔng-'hǎw** to calm down, (as a crying baby). **hǔng-'háy-dz-de** (baby) nurse, nursemaid.

huo Wade Romanization for **hwo.**

化, 花

hwā (V) to spend, expend. **hwā-'chyán** to spend or expend money. As mainV: **'hwā-chū-lay** expend; **hwā-'gwāng** spend all, spend away.

花

hwā (A) blurred, not clear. ‖**yǎn-jing 'hwā-le.** My eyes are blurred (from old age or from the light). or I am far-sighted (opposite of near-sighted, but only if from old age, presbyopia).

  Also loud of a color.

花 (兒)

hwā(r) (Nunit, dwǒ, dwěr) flower. In compounds also arranged in a pattern, (as flowers often are). **hwā-'ywán** flower garden, occasionally just garden; **hwā-'píng** flower vase; **hwā-'pér** flower pot; **hwā-'gū-du** (or more literary **hwā-'léy**) bud.

  hwā-'yàng(r) pattern, design; scheme, plan, plot. **hwā-'bù** cloth printed with a design; **hwā-'yī-fu** print dress.

花旗

hwā-chí-'gwó (Nunique) the United States (expression mostly used in central and southeastern China).

  hwā-chí-yín-'háng The National City Bank of New York.

花子, 化子

'hwā-dz or **jyàw-'hwā-dz** (Npers) beggar.

化費

'hwā-fèy (V) to expend; (Nmass) expenses, expenditures. (A bit formal.)

花卷兒

hwā-'jywǎr (Nunit, ge) steamed bread in one of many shapes, about the size of a roll or bun.

華盛頓

hwā-shēng-'dwèn (Nunique) Washington (city unless otherwise specified).

花臺, 花(兒)臺兒

hwā-'táy, hwā(r)-'tár (Nunit, dzwò) flower bed.

劃

hwá (I) to figure out, make calculations, (usually about money). ‖**nǐ 'hwá-yi-hwá 'kàn-kàn hé-'swàn-bu-hé-'swàn.** Figure out a bit whether it's worth it or not.

  As mainV: **hwá-bu-'láy** not be worthwhile. ‖**yùng jème-'dwō-chyán mǎy 'jèy-ge-dūng-shi hwá-bu-'láy.** It isn't worthwhile to spend that much money for this.

劃

hwá (V) to scrape, scratch; to rake (with a rake). **hwá yí-'shyàr** to scratch once (particularly with a fingernail).

  As mainV: **hwá-'dzěw** to scrape something off, away; **hwá-chū** (l) to carve out some figure; on a surface. ‖**bǎ jèy-ge-'dz hwá-le 'chywù.** Scratch out this character (i.e., eliminate it).

划

hwá (V) to row. **hwá-'chwán** to row a boat. As mainV: **'hwá-gwò-lay** to row across, etc.

  'hwá-dz (Nunit, ge, jǐ) rowboat.

滑

hwá (I) to slip along, slide. **hwá-'bīng** to skate on ice. As mainV: **hwá-'dǎw** to slip and fall.

  (A) slippery, smooth; also figuratively of a person.

滑稽

'hwá-ji (A) funny, humorous.

滑頭

'hwá-téw (A) slippery, wily, not too sincere, clever, tricky, unreliable, (all of a person); also in a good sense, clever.

話

hwà (Nmass) speech, language. **yì-jǔng-'hwà** one language; **yí-jywù-'hwà** a sentence, saying, remark, comment, phrase, clause; **yì-pyān-'hwà** a larger amount of talk than **yí-jywù-'hwà**, about some specific subject.

  shwō-'hwà to speak; **shwō jūng-gwo-'hwà** to speak Chinese; **tīng-'hwà** to hear speech and accept it; to obey, be obedient.

畫

hwà (V) to draw, paint, depict. **hwà-'tú** to draw a map. **hwàr** (Nunit, jāng) picture (painted, not photographed). **hwà-'hwàr** to draw a picture, paint a picture.

  As mainV: **'hwà-chū-lay** to sketch out, trace (just with the finger or a pointer, or actually making a mark); to mark as a passage in a book; to finish painting or drawing. **'hwà-shyà-lay** to note down something observed; to mark as a passage in a book.

化

hwà (I) to change from solid to liquid, or from liquid to gas; in some compounds: physical change in general. **hwà-'chì** to turn to gas; **hwà-chéng 'shwěy** to turn to water (of ice). ‖**'bīng jèng dzày 'hwà-ne.** The ice is just melting.

  As mainV: **'hwà-chéng** to melt into, evaporate into (such-and-such a resulting substance); **hwà-'kāy** to melt and break up (as of ice in a river).

  'hwà-shywé chemistry.

畫報
hwà-'bàw (*Nunit*, běr, fèr, jāng) illustrated magazine, picture maga_ine.

畫筆
hwà-'bǐ (*Nunit*, gwǎn, jř) artist's brush.

化裝
hwà-'jwāng (*V*) to make up and dress oneself (*as for the stage*). ‖tā hwà-'jwāng yí-ge-'nán-rén. She's making up for the role of a man.
    Also to apply make-up (*powder, rouge, etc.*); hwà-jwāng-'pǐn toilet articles (*usually for a woman*) *or* make-up (*stage*); hwà-jwāng-'shř dressing room (*theater*).

畫家
hwà-'jyā (*Npers*) artist, painter.

畫品
hwà-'pǐn (*Nunit*, jāng) painting.

化學作用
'hwà-shywé-dzwó-'yùng *or* 'hwà-shywé-dzwò-'yùng (*Nabstr*) chemical action.

化學家
hwà-shywé-'jyā (*Npers*) scientist who specializes in chemistry, chemist.

化學藥品
'hwà-shywé-yàw-'pǐn (*Nabstr*) chemical substances, chemicals.

化爲泡影
hwà-'wéy-pàw-'yǐng (*literary quotation*) to go up in smoke, be all washed up, (*as of one's plans, dreams, hopes*).

化驗
'hwà-yàn *or* hwà-'yàn (*V*) to subject *something* to chemical analysis.

化學師
hwà-yàn-'shř (*Npers*) chemist.

化緣
hwà-'ywán (*VN1*) to beg for alms (*of Buddhist monks only*).

歡喜
'hwān-shǐ (*V*) to like *someone*, enjoy the company of *someone*; (*Vpred*) to be fond of *doing something*. ‖tā hěn 'hwān-shǐ kàn dyàn-'yěngr. He's very fond of movies.

歡實
'hwān-shr (*A*) active, lively.

歡迎
'hwān-yíng (*V*) to welcome *someone* ‖'hwān-yíng! Welcome!
    hwān-yíng-'hwèy (*Nunit*, ge) party held to welcome someone, reception.

還
hwán (*V2*) to pay back, repay *somebody with something*. ‖wǒ děy 'hwán-ni nèy-běn-'shū. I must return that book to you.
    hwán-'chyán to repay money; hwán-'jàng to pay a bill, debt, account. *As mainV:* 'hwán-gěy to return something to *a person;* hwán-'chǐng to pay off *one's debts*, clear up *one's debts*.
    hwán-'jyà(r) to haggle about prices, bargain.

還
hwán *reading form of* háy.

環境
hwán-'jìng (*Nabstr*) environment, circumstances. hwán-'jìng-jr-'shyà under *such-and-such* circumstances ‖dzày 'jèy-jǔng-hwán-'jìng-jr-'shyà nǐ 'bù-néng shwō jèy-jywù-'hwà. You can't say this in these circumstances (*you'll hurt someone's feelings, or get yourself hurt*).

緩過來
'hwǎn-gwò-láy (*RC1*) to come to slowly, *after a faint or dizzy spell, etc.;* to return slowly to normal (*as of frozen feet*). hwǎn-'shǐng-gwò-láy *same as first meaning of above.*

換
hwàn (*V*) to change, convert. hwàn-'chyán to get money *for a check or draft or receipt;* hwàn yí-kwèy-'chyán to change a dollar; hwàn shyàn-'chyán to get cash *for a check or note, etc;* 'hwàn-hwàn kūng-'chì to change the air (*as in a room*); hwàn 'yī-fu to change one's clothes.
    As mainV: hwàn-bu-'chū (chyán) (*l*) be unable to get money for. ‖jèy-ge-'hwò hwàn-bu-chū 'chyán-lay. You can't get any money for these goods. ‖jèy-ge-jř-'pyàw hwàn-bu-chū 'chyán-lay. This check will bounce.

患難
'hwàn-nàn (*Nunit*, ge) misfortune, calamity in one's life. dzày 'hwàn-nàn de-shŕ-hew in time of misfortune; 'hwàn-nàn-de-'péng-yew friend in need.

幻想
'hwàn-shyǎng (*V*) to imagine, fancy, dream in vain of; (*Vpred*) to imagine, fancy, dream in vain of *doing so-and-so;* (*Vsent*) to imagine, fancy, dream in vain that. ‖byé 'hwàn-shyǎng nà-shyē-bù-kě-'néng-de-shř-ching. Don't dream about such impossible things.

慌

hwang *in final position after A plus* **de**, *alternative form of* **hěn** *very much so.* ‖**tā 'lèy-de hwang.** *or* **tā 'lèy-de hěn.** He's very tired.

慌

hwāng (*A*) nervous, excited, frightened, startled (*only of people*). ‖**byé 'hwāng!** Keep calm! ‖**tā hwāng-'hwāng-de 'pǎw-le.** He was startled and ran away.

荒

hwāng (*A*) waste and desolate, (*of places, land*). **hwāng-'dì** untilled and desolate land. **'hwāng-lyáng** cold, lonely and desolate (*of places, land; opposite of* **'rè-nàw**).

荒廢

hwāng-'fèy (*H plus V*) to spend in vain. **hwāng-'fèy °'shŕ-hew,** *or* **°'gūng-fu** to waste one's time; **hwāng-fèy 'chyán** to waste money.

荒謬

hwāng-'nyèw *or* **hwāng-'myàw** (*A*) irrational, absurd. ‖**tā dzwò jèy-jyàn-'shŕ hěn hwāng-'nyèw.** It was utterly absurd for him to do this.

黃

hwáng (*A*) yellow. *Many things which are called* brown *in English are covered by this term:* **hwáng-'shyé** yellow shoes. **'hwáng-sè** *or* **'hwáng-shǎr** (*Nabstr*) yellow, brown.

簧

***hwáng** (*Nunit*, **gēr**, **ge**) *usually* **'tán-hwáng** (elastic) coiled spring.

黃膽病

hwáng(-dǎn)-'bìng (*Nabstr*) jaundice.

黃豆

hwáng-'dèw (*Nunit*, **ge**, **lì**) soya beans.

皇帝

hwáng-'dì (*Npers*) an emperor. **'yīng-gwo-hwáng-'dì** the King of England.

皇宮

hwáng-'gūng (*Nunit*, **dzwò**) palace, residence of an emperor.

黃海

hwáng-'hǎy (*Nunique*) The Yellow Sea.

黃河

hwáng-'hé (*Nunique*) The Yellow River.

皇后

hwáng-'hèw (*Npers*) queen, empress.

黃熱病

hwáng-rè-'bìng (*Nabstr*) yellow fever.

皇上

'hwáng-shàng (*Nunique*) the emperor (*used by people in speaking of their own emperor, with respect*).

黃銅

hwáng-'túng (*Nmass*) brass.

黃油

hwáng-'yéw (*Nmass*) butter.

謊

hwǎng (*Nunit*, **ge**) a lie. **shwō-'hwǎng** *or* **sā-'hwǎng** tell lies; **hwǎng-'hwà** false words, lies.

晃眼

hwǎng-'yǎn (*VN1*) to dazzle the eyes, glare. ‖**nèy-ge-'gwāng hwǎng-'yǎn hwǎng-de hěn 'lì-hày.** That light is very dazzling.

愰(悠)

'hwàng(-yew) (*I*) to wobble around as if in unstable equilibrium; to loaf and lay around and do bunk fatigue. **'hwàng-hwang-yew-yēw-de** (*H*) wobbling *or* mentally uncertain. ‖**nèy-jŕ-'shyàng 'hwàng-hwang-yew-'yēw-de 'dzěw-gwò-láy-le.** The elephant walked along swaying from side to side.

懷

***hwáy** (*N*) the bosom, the chest; (*particularly*) **'hwáy-li** in one's bosom, in one's arm next to the chest.

(*V*) to carry, (*as a pregnant woman her unborn child*); or, (*said of* **shīn** the heart): have in the heart, the heart contains *evil thoughts, etc.* (*a bit literary, but quite generally used*).

踝子骨

hwáy-dz-'gǔ (*Nunit*, **ge**) anklebone.

淮河

hwáy-'hé (*Nunique*) The Huai Ho (*river*).

懷寧

hwáy-'níng (*Nunique*) Huai-ning (*capital city of Anhwei province*).

懷疑

'hwáy-yí (*V*) to be doubtful of, suspicious of; (*A*) doubtful, suspicious. ‖**wǒ 'hwáy-yí tā-de-'tày-du.** I'm suspicious of his attitude.

壞

hwày (*A*) bad (*opposite of* **hǎw**). (*I*) **'hwày-le,** *and as post V,* spoiled, gone bad, gotten out of order, out of commission, broken, rendered useless, *etc.* **hwày-'fàn** poor food; **'hwày-le-de-'fàn** spoiled food; **hwày-'dàn**

bad egg (person); 'hwày-le-de-'dàn a bad egg, an egg gone bad; hwày-'lù poor road, rough road; hwày-'hwà remarks that shouldn't be made; hwày-'tyār nasty weather; hwày-'twěy lame or broken leg.

As postV: dǎ-'hwày to render useless by striking; shwō-'hwày to bungle in one's speech, *spoiling the purpose, such as an agreement one is trying to reach; etc.*

壞處
'hwày-chu (Nunit, ge) bad points, bad features, drawbacks, shortcomings, *in some thing or some person.*

昏
hwēn (A) dizzy. ‖wǒ 'jywé-de 'téw hěn 'hwēn. My head feels quite dizzy.

As mainV: 'hwēn-gwò-chywù to faint; hwēn-·dǎw to get dizzy and fall, *or*, to faint.

婚禮
hwēn-'lǐ (Nunit, tsż) wedding, wedding ceremony. jywǔ-'shíng hwēn-'lǐ to hold a wedding.

婚姻
hwēn-'yīn (Nabstr) marriage. ‖tā-men-de-hwēn-'yīn hěn mǎn-'yì. Their marriage is very satisfactory.

婚約
hwēn-'ywē (Nunit, ge, tsż) engagement (to be married).

混
hwén (A) mixed-up, irrational. ‖jèy-ge-'rén jēn 'hwén. He's really mixed up.

    hwén-'dàn a fool (very strong epithet).

混
hwèn (I) to engage in aimless and uninteresting activity. ‖wǒ 'hwèn-le yì-tyān. I fooled around all day without accomplishing anything (from the speaker's own point of view).

    hwèn-'chyán to engage in something for the sake of getting some funds, *without having any real interest in it.*

混，渾
hwèn, hwén (I) to be mixed together, mixed up, confused.

As mainV: 'hwèn-dzày (yì-'chǐ or yí-'kwàr) to mix *things* together, mix in with *fast company,* confuse *things in one's mind.* ‖tā gēn nèy-yì-'bāng-de-wú-'lày 'hwèn-dzay yí-'kwàr. He's mixing in with a fast bunch.

會兒
hwěr (Mtime) short while; *only with* yī, nèy, jèy. 'děng yì-hwěr wait a while, wait a bit; 'nèy-hwěr at that

moment, at that time, at that juncture. ‖'jèng dzày 'nèy-hwěr tā 'dzěw-jìn-lay-le. Just at that very moment he walked in.

灰
hwēy (A) grayish, dull colored.

灰
hwēy, hwēr (Nmass) ashes. yān-'hwēy cigarette ashes *or* ashes from a chimney (carried in the smoke); méy-'hwēy coal ashes.

    hwēy-'shīn (∧) be disheartened, disillusioned, (*literally* with heart turned to ashes).

恢復
'hwēy-fu (V) to recover, get back, be reinstated in; (I) to return to normal, recover health. ‖tā 'hwēy-fu-le tā-de-'shř-ching. He's been reinstated in his job.

恢復邦交
'hwēy-fu bāng-'jyāw (VN1) to return to the normal state of international relations. ‖dǎ-wán 'jàng yǐ-'hèw, lyǎng-ge-gwó-'jyā yèw 'hwēy-fu bāng-'jyāw-le. After the war the two countries resumed normal relations.

徽號
'hwēy-hàw (Nunit, ge) symbol (in the same very general sense as the English word).

徽章
hwēy-'jāng (Nunit, ge) button with an inscription worn to indicate belief or membership; an identification badge.

灰鼠
hwēy-'shǔ (Nunit, ge) squirrel (gray only).

詼諧
'hwēy-shyè (A) humorous; inclined to make jokes, (of a person).

回
hwéy (I, lc) to return. 'hwéy-lay to come back; 'hwéy-chywu to go back. (V, lc) to return to; hwéy-'jyā lay to come back home; hwéy-'jyā chywu to go back home.

As mainV: hwéy-dàw (lc) to return to a place. *As postV*: 'dzěw-hwéy (lc) to walk back; 'pǎw-hwéy (lc) to run back; *etc., with verbs of motion.*

    (V) (I used causatively) to return *something*, cause *something* to return. hwéy dyàn-'hwà to call back (phone); hwéy dyàn-'bàw to send an answering telegram, etc. Also as in hwéy-'chín to play through one's piano lesson *after practicing it (as for the teacher).*

    As postV in this sense is often like English back. 'dǎ-hwéy-láy to send back (a message); 'jǎw-hwéy-láy to give back (change, money), *or* get back *something lost;* 'sùng-hwéy-láy to send back; 'fàng-hwéy (lc) to put *something* back *where it was.*

    'hwéy-rén yì-shēng (V2 *with any personal reference instead of* rén) to announce a guest.

hwéy (K) hwéy-'hwà shwō to say in reply.

In nominal compounds answering, return. hwéy-'dyàn an answering telephone call *or* telegram; hwéy-'shìn an answering letter, return letter.

回

hwéy (*Msemel and MdistT*) time, occasion, occurrence, -ce (*once, twice, etc.*); chapter *in a piece of fiction, novel*. yì-hwéy-bǐ-'sày game, competition (*one playing or holding of a game or competition*); yì-hwéy-'shř a matter. ‖tā 'kàn-gwo wo yì-'hwéy. He did see me once. ‖wǒ 'dzwò-gwo yì-'hwéy. I've done it once. ‖wǒ 'dzwò-gwo 'sān-hwéy. I've done it three times. ‖jè-shr dì-'yì-hwéy wǒ 'dàw-jèr. This is the first time I've been here.

'shàng-hwéy last time; 'shvà-hwéy next time.

回答

'hwéy-dā *or* 'hwéy-dá (V) to reply to, answer *someone;* (*Vsent*) to answer that. ‖nǐ yīng-gay 'hwéy-dā ta. You must answer him. ‖tā 'hwéy-dā-le tā-de-'péng-yew bù-néng 'láy. He answered that his friend couldn't come.

回想

hwéy-'shyǎng (V) to think back, look back. ‖tā hwéy-'shyǎng tā-'tsúng-chyán-de-'shř-ching. He recalled his past.

As mainV: hwéy-'shyǎng-dàw to think back to, look back to, be reminded of. ‖tā hwéy-'shyǎng-dàw tā-'shyǎw-de-shŕ-hew. He was recalling his childhood.

回頭

hwéy-téw (J) a little later, just a minute. ‖'hwéy-téw dzày 'shwō. We can talk in just a minute. ‖hwéy-téw 'jyàn! So long! (*if expecting another meeting very soon*).

回憶

hwéy-'yì (V) to think back, look back, recall; *slightly more literary equivalent of* hwéy-'shyǎng.

(*Nunit,* ge) memory, recollection.

毀

hwěy (I) be ruined, destroyed, torn to pieces, wrecked; (*also causatively*). ‖byé bǎ nèy-běn-'shū 'hwěy-le. Don't destroy that book.

As postV: jà-'hwěy to ruin by bombing; dǎ-'hwěy to ruin by striking; *etc.*

悔

*hwěy (A) to feel regret, remorse. (*Particularly* hèw-'hwěy.) ‖wǒ hěn hèw-'hwěy. *or* wǒ hèw-'hwěy-de hěn. I feel great remorse. *or* I feel very sorry.

(*Vsent*): ‖wǒ hèw-'hwěy· nèy-tsz méy-'chywù. I'm sorry I didn't go that time (*said only of something that the speaker himself has done or failed to do*).

毀謗

hwěy-'bàng (V) to attack viciously *a person, an institution*, (*with words, not physically*).

毀滅

hwěy-'myè (V) to destroy utterly. ‖'dí-rén bǎ-'chéng dēw hwěy-'myè-le. The enemy totally destroyed the city.

匯

hwèy (V) to send *money in a form other than coins and bills.* hwèy-'kwǎn to transmit funds *thus. Also* hwèy (*lc*). *As mainV:* hwèy-dàw (*lc*) to send *money thus to a place; etc.*

會

hwèy (*Vpred*) to be able to *through having learned how.* ‖nǐ hwèy shwō yīng-gwo-'hwà-ma? Do you speak English?

Also to be inclined to *or* apt to *or* desirous of *because one has acquired a habit.* ‖wǒ bú-'hwèy chēw-'yān. I don't smoke.

Means also to be apt to *or* liable to under stated conditions (*also of things as well as people*). ‖rè-shr nǐ 'dǎ-ta, tā hwèy shēng-'chì(-de). If you hit him he's liable to get mad. *In these conditions -de is often added at the end.*

Followed by an adjective or adjective expression, often with de *added,* to be able to be *or* become *or* get. ‖tā bú-hwèy 'hǎw(-de). He can't get well.

會

*hwèy (*Nunit,* ge) meeting, conference, association, club, committee, *etc.* (*temporary or permanent*); a fair; *except in a few special combinations always is specified by preceding words.* wěy-ywán-'hwèy commission, committee; hwān-yíng-'hwèy party given to welcome someone, reception; chá-'hwèy tea party; ján-lǎng-'hwèy an exhibit, *etc.*

hwèy-'bàw organization's publication; hwèy-'chǎng place of a meeting; hwèy-'fèy dues; hwèy-'ywán members of an organization.

kāy-'hwèy to hold a meeting *or* to open a meeting; chywù kāy-'hwèy to go to a meeting; bì-'hwèy to close a meeting; sàn-'hwèy to break up at a party.

匯兌

hwèy-'dwèy (*Nabstr*) transmission of money or funds from one place to another. ‖dǎ-'jàng de-shŕ-hew hwèy-'dwèy hěn 'nán. In war time it's very difficult to transmit money from one place to another.

匯合，會合

hwèy-'hé (I) to come together, (*as of two rivers*). ‖yěw lyǎng-tyáw-'hé dzày chúng-'chìng-nèy-ge-dì-fangr hwèy-'hé. There are two rivers that flow together at Chungking.

會戰

hwèy-'jàn (*VN1*) to join battle. ‖'lyǎng-jywūn dzày-'nàr hwèy-'jàn. The two sides joined battle there.

會章

hwèy-'jāng (*Nunit*, ge) (1) insignia showing membership in, or contribution of funds to, *some organization;* the emblem of *an organization.*
(2) Constitution of *an organization.* gwēy-'dìng hwèy-'jāng to establish a constitution.

賄賂

'hwèy-lu (*V*) to bribe.

匯率

hwèy-'lywù (*Nabstr*) rate of exchange. ‖shyàn-'dzày jūng-'měy-de-hwèy-'lywù shř 'dwō-shaw? What's the current rate of exchange of Chinese and American money?

匯票

hwèy-'pyàw (*Nunit*, jāng) draft, money order. (*Not a check, which is* jř-'pyàw.) kāy hwèy-'pyàw to write a draft; mǎy hwèy-'pyàw to buy a draft *or* money order.

會意

hwèy-'yì (*VN1*) to catch on, understand. ‖nǐ 'kan-ta yì-'yǎn, tā jyèw hwèy-'yì-le. Give him the eye; he'll catch on (*to what you want him to do*).

會議

hwèy-'yì (*VN1*) to confer, hold a conference. (*Nunit*, ge) conference.

豁

hwō (*I*) to crack open, split and separate. hwō 'kěw-dz (*VN2*) to crack into a crack. *As mainV:* hwō-'kāy to split open. *As postV:* sž-'hwō to tear, producing a crack or split in the thing torn. *In all cases implies that the split goes only partly across the surface, so that the areas on either side are still joined at one or both ends of the split.*

活

hwó (*A*) alive, living; (*of a thing*) to be movable *or* removable; loose (*of a part that should be fixed*). ‖rén 'hwó-je děy chř-'fàn. While a man is alive he must eat. ‖nèy-ge-lwó-sz-'dyēngr yěw yì-dyǎr 'hwó-le. That screw has come loose a little.
As mainV: hwó-bu-'lyǎw be unable to live (*as of a sick man or because of inadequate income or physical or mental conditions of life, often not literally true*). 'hwó-gwò-lay to come to (*from a faint*).
(*H*) *only in* hwó 'máy to bury alive; hwó 'děy to capture alive.
hwó(er) (*N*) *in* dzwò-'hwó(er) to make one's living by a manual job (*especially sewing*).

活動

'hwó-dùng (*A*) loose but not detached (*as of a tooth*); active politically *or* socially. ‖wǒ-de-'yá 'hwó-dùng-le. My tooth is loose. ‖jèy-ge-'rén hěn 'hwó-dùng. He's very active in political life. ‖shyàn-dzày gùng-chǎn-'dǎng bù-hěn 'hwó-dùng. Right now the communist party isn't very active.
(*V*) to pull wires in order to get *a job.* ‖tā 'hwó-dùng yí-jyàn-'shř-ching. He's pulling wires to get himself a job.

活該

‖hwó-'gāy! *or* nǐ hwó-'gāy! It serves you right! You deserved it!

活潑

'hwó-pwo (*A*) lively, active, (*as of a baby*).

火

hwǒ (*Nunit*, ge) fire. jáw-'hwǒ *or* chǐ-'hwǒ to catch fire, break out into flames; lúng-'hwǒ to build a fire; myè 'hwǒ to extinguish a fire; tūng-'hwǒ to stir up a fire *with a poker;* chwēy-'hwǒ to blow on a fire; shān-'hwǒ to fan a fire.
hwǒ-'twěy (*Nunit*, ge) ham; hwǒ-'shyǎn fire insurance; hwǒ-'mén *or* hwǒ-'mér knob to turn on the gas of a gas stove, *or* on a radiator to turn the heat on or off.
hwěr to get angry, flare up. ‖tā jyèw-'hwěr-le. He flared up.

伙, 夥

'hwǒ(-dz), hwěr (*Mgroup*) group of rén (*people*), *or with other Npers.* ‖tām shř yì-'hwěr-de. They belong to the same clique (group, set). *Thus may imply people who hang around together or join together for some common purpose.*
dà-'hwěr (*Mgroup*) big crowd, big group. dā-'hwěr H) cooperating, working together.
shyǎw 'hwěr, shyǎw-'hwǒ-dz (*Npers*) strong young man.

伙伴

hwǒ-'bàr (*Npers*) partner, working companion, comrade (*business or otherwise*).

火車

hwǒ-'chē (*Nunit*) train *or* train car; with M lyàng *specifically the latter, with M* lyè *specifically the former.* hwǒ-chē-'jàn (*Nunit*, ge) railroad station; hwǒ-chē-'dàw (*Nunit*, tyáw) railroad track; hwǒ-chē-'téw (*Nunit*, ge) locomotive.

火災

hwǒ-'dzāy (*Nunit*, tsž, cháng) fire, *destructive and on a very large scale, as the burning of a city.*

伙計, 夥計

'hwǒ-ji (*Npers*) waiter, clerk, *in a store, restaurant,*

火警
ıwǒ-'jǐng (*Nunit*, tsz, cháng, chù, chī) fire (*destructive, as a building burning*)..

火酒
ıwǒ-'jyěw (*Nmass*) alcohol (*ethyl*).

火苗
ıwǒ-'myáw(-dz), hwǒ-'myáwr (*Nunit*, ge) (a tongue of) flame.

火奴魯魯
hwǒ-nú-lú-'lǔ (*Nunique*) Honolulu.

火山
hwǒ-'shān (*Nunit*, ge, dzwò) volcano.

火星
hwǒ-'shīng (*Nunit*, ge) sparks.
　　(*Nunique*) Mars (*the planet*).

和
hwò (*V*) to mix *ingredients, as in cooking*.. hwò-'myàn to mix ingredients into dough.

貨
hwò (*Nunit*, ge) pieces of goods, freight, commodities, items of merchandise.. hwò-'chē (*Nunit*, lyàng) freight car; hwò-'chwán (*Nunit*, jř, tyáw) freight ship, freighter.
　　báy-'hwò merchandise made of silver; hwáng-'hwò merchandise made of gold.
　　ywùn-'hwò to ship goods; chū-'hwò to produce goods (*of a certain place or territory, or of a factory*).

禍
hwò (*Nunit*, ge) calamity, catastrophe. chwǎng-'hwò to bring about a calamity; chū-'hwò a calamity happens.

禍根
hwò-'gēn (*Nunit*, ge) root of trouble, source of evil. ‖'nèy-ge shř yí-ge-hwò-'gēn. That's a source of trouble (*usually a person who later on is apt to give rise to trouble*).

或者
'hwò-je (*J*) perhaps, *or* or perhaps. ‖wǒ 'hwò-je bù-néng 'dzěw. I may not be able to go. ‖hwò-je 'nǐ shwō hwò-je 'wǒ shwō, méy shéme-'fēn-bye. Maybe you'll speak, maybe I will; it doesn't make any difference. ‖(*K*) 'nǐ, hwò-je 'wǒ, méy shéme-'fēn-bye. Maybe you, maybe me, it doesn't matter.

禍首
hwò-'shěw (*Npers*) ringleader of a group that makes trouble for others.

或是
'hwò-shr (*J*) or, otherwise; (*used twice*) either... or .... ‖hwò-shr 'nǐ dzwò, hwò-shr 'wǒ dzwò. Either you do it or I will (*it doesn't matter*).

或許
'hwò-shywǔ (*J*) perhaps, maybe, possibly.

貨物
'hwò-wù (*Nunit*, ge) commodities, merchandise, *in economic discussion rather than business or retailing talk*.

I

i *Wade Romanization for* yi.

J

扎
jā (*V*) to jab *with any thin pointed thing*. jā 'ěr-dwo to grate on one's ears (*literally, to pierce the earlobe*). *As main V:* 'jā-gwò (*lc*) to pierce; jā-'hwày to spoil by jabbing; 'jā-shyà-chywù to jab downwards; *etc.* ‖tā yùng tsž-'dāw bǎ dí-'bīng jā-'sž-le. He jabbed his bayonet through (the enemy soldier) and killed him.

煠，炸
já (*V*) to fry *in a thin layer of fat on a flat surface*, (*as eggs*). já-chwēn-'jywǎr (*VN3*) (fried) egg rolls.

閘，牐
já (*Nunit*, dàw, ge) dam; watergate; canal lock.
　　dì-'yí-ge-já low gear; dì-'èr-ge-já middle gear; *etc.* hwàn-'já *or* bān-'já to shift gears; bān-daw dì-'yí-ge-já to shift into first.

炸
jà (*V*) to break *by applying pressure from inside*, to cause to explode; to bomb. *As main V:* jà-'lyè to cause to burst by applying inner pressure or by bombing; jà-'hwày to destroy *similarly:* jà-'swèy to blow to

bits; *etc;* jà-chéng to bomb *or* burst to the state of *such-and-such.*

　'jà-de fěn-'swèy blown to smithereens.

乍

jà (*H*) *in stating a time* suddenly for the first time. ‖jà yí-'kàn, nèy-ge-'dūng-shi bú-'tswò. Just taking one look, this thing isn't bad (*but it will prove so later. Without* jà *this would mean* At first sight it seemed not bad *not implying necessarily that it turned out otherwise.*) ‖jà (yí-)'kàn, nèy-ge-'dūng-shi jyèw bú-tswò. At very first sight the thing was clearly not bad (*and that impression turned out to be correct*). jà (yì-)'tīng at very first hearing *is used similarly.*

詐

jà (*V2*) to cheat, defraud, swindle. ‖tā 'jà-le wo 'wǔ-kwày-chyán ('dzěw-le). He cheated me out of five bucks (and absconded with it). *As mainV:* 'jà-chywù to abscond with, take away by cheating; jà-'dzěw *or* jà-'pǎw to abscond with.

　To pretend. jà 'sž to play dead, feign death; jà 'bìng to malinger, feign sickness.

炸彈

jà-'dàn (*Nunit,* ge) a bomb.

jan *Wade Romanization for* ran.

粘

jān (*V*) to paste, glue, make *things* stick together. *As mainV:* 'jān-shàng to paste *things* together; 'jān-dzày to paste *something* on *something;* 'jān-chǐ-láy to paste together in one place, (*as pictures in an album*); *etc.* ‖bǎ jèy-ge-bù-'gàw jān-dzay 'chyáng-shang Paste this notice on the wall.

　jān *is used generally, but more often for small things put together;* tyē *is better for putting something relatively small on something much larger.*

氈,毡

*jān, 'jān-dz (*Nmass*) felt (*material*). jān-'màw felt hat.

粘帖兒

jān-'tyěr (*VN2*) to post a bill.

贍養費

jān-yǎng-'fèy (*Nmass,* fèn, fèr) allowance; alimony. (*Formal term but not solely legal.*)

展

jǎn (*I*) to open outwards, to spread outwards, (*as a bud into a flower*); (*V*) to spread *wings* (*a bit literary*). *As mainV* jǎn-kāy (*RCI*): ‖'gū-du 'jǎn-kāy-le. The buds have opened.

撣布

jǎn-'bù (*Nunit,* kwày, tyáw) dustcloth, dustrag.

展期

jǎn-'chī (*VN2*), jǎn yì-'chī to postpone the date; to put off for one (*or* two, *etc.*) set period, one semester, one quarter, *etc.* ‖jèy-ge-jēw-'kān shyàn-dzày bù-néng chū-'bǎn, děy 'jǎn yì-'chī. This journal can't appear this week, it has been necessary to postpone (*publication*) for a week.

展覽

jǎn-'lǎn (*V*) to display, exhibit, spread out in display. jǎn-'lǎn hwà-'pǐn to exhibit paintings, to hold an exhibition of paintings. jǎn-lǎn-'hwèy an exhibition.

戰

*jàn (*N*) battle; war. dà-'jàn a (great) war; jàn-'chē tank (*vehicle*): jàn-'hèw after the war; jàn-'shŕ war time; dzày jàn-'shŕ in wartime, during the war; jàn-'háw trench; jàn-'shř war affairs, matters of fighting; 'jàn-shř-hwò-'shěw a leading war criminal.

佔

jàn (*V*) to occupy, seize (and occupy) by force, *property or territory, or someone's wife, etc.*

　gěy-rén jàn 'dì-fangr to reserve (*or* keep) a place for someone (*as in a restaurant, where those who have arrived hold a seat for someone who is coming late*).

　jàn rén-de-'shŕ-hew to waste someone else's time, make demands on someone else's time.

　jàn …-(de) 'pyán-yì take unfair advantage of *someone.*

站

jàn (*I*) to stand. ‖nǐ jàn-'nàr, wǒ jàn-'jèr. You stand there, I'll stand here.

　As mainV: 'jàn-chǐ-láy to stand up; 'jàn-dzày to stand at, on, in; 'jàn-jù to stop, stand still; jàn-'mǎn to stand around filling up an entire space (*as a room*); jàn-'wěn to stand steadily, keep one's balance while standing.

　(*I*) to stand *as in line;* jàn-'gǎng (*VN1*) to stand guard, stand watch, jàn-'gǎng-de (*Npers*) policeman

　In compounds: a stand, stop, stopping place. hwǒ-chē-'jàn railroad station; dyàn-chē-'jàn streetcar stop; chē-'jàn stop for any vehicle that follows a regular route.

戰敗

jàn-'bày (*V*) to defeat *someone in battle or war.* ‖shŕ-'shéy jàn-'bày-le? Who lost?

戰爭

jàn-'jēng (*Nunit,* tsż, cháng, chù) a war.

戰艦

jàn-'jyàn (*Nunit,* tyáw, jŕ) battleship.

145

戰局

jàn-'jywú (*Nabstr*) military situation.

戰況

jàn-'kwàng (*Nabstr*) military situation, military developments.

戰利品

jàn-lì-'pǐn (*Nunit*, **ge**) booty, something captured.

佔領

jàn-'lǐng (*V*) to seize and occupy *someone else's place, property*.

戰略

jàn-'lywè (*Nabstr*) military strategy.

戰勝

jàn-'shèng (*V*) to be the victor over *someone*, to defeat *someone, in war or battle*. ‖shr̀-'shéy jàn-'shèng-le? Who won?

暫時

'jàn-shŕ *or* 'dzàn-shŕ (*J*) for the time being, for the present.

站臺

jàn-'táy (*Nunit*, **ge**) platform (*as at a railway station*).

佔優勢

jàn-yēw-shr̀ (*VN2*) to gain an advantage, to gain the upper hand. ‖wǒ-men gēn 'tā-men 'dǎ, jàn 'yēw-shr̀. We are at an advantage in fighting them.

jang *Wade Romanization for* **rang.**

章

jāng (*Munit; often ordinal*) chapter (*of a book*). yì-jāng-'shū chapter of a book; jèy-běn-'shū-de-dì-'yì-jāng the first chapter of this book.

張

jāng (*Munit*) *for all sorts of things which have flat but not too extensive surfaces, or for thin flat objects:* a 'jwō-dz (*table*); a 'yǐ-dz (*chair*); a shyàng-'pyàr (*photograph*); a hwàr (*picture, painting*); a tú (*diagram*); a dì'tú (*map*); a jŕ-'pyàw (*check*); a piece of jŕ (*paper*).

    Also a dzwěy (*mouth*) (*said of one who likes to gossip or who is talkative*).

張

jāng (*V*) to open, *in certain specific contexts*. jāng-'gūng to draw a bow; jāng-'shěw to open the hand; jāng-'sǎn to open an umbrella; jāng-'dzwěy to open the mouth *and talk, (or sometimes) and eat. As mainV:* 'jāng-kāy *or,* jāng-chǐ-láy to open up (*in same contexts*).

章程

'jāng-chéng (*Nunit*, **ge**) regulation, rule. yì-běn-'jāng-chéng rule book, book of regulations, *for students at a university, employees of a bank, etc.* (*Not regulations for customers, as bank rules for depositors, which is* 'gwēy-dzé.)

彰德

jāng-'dé (*Nunique*) Changteh, *another name for* ān-'yáng An-yang (*city in Honan province*).

漳州

jāng-'jēw (*Nunique*) Changchow, *another name for* lúng-'chī Lung-ch'i (*city in Fukien province*).

張家口

jāng-jyā-'kěw (*Nunique*) Chang-chia-k'ou, *another name for* wàn-'chywán Wan-ch'üan *or* Kalgan (*capital of Chahar province*).

長

jǎng (*I*) to grow. ‖tā 'jǎng-de hǎw 'shyàng tā-'fù-chin. He resembles his father very much (*literally* The way he has grown is such that he is similar to his father). ‖tā 'jǎng-de hěn hǎw 'kàn. He's good looking.

    As mainV: 'jǎng-chǐ-láy to rise (*as of water*), to grow up (*as of grass*); 'jǎng-chū-láy to grow out of something, develop (*as grass out of the earth*); 'jǎng-chéng to grow into (*as small trees into a forest*); jǎng-'dà to grow up (*as a person or animal*); jǎng-'gāw to grow tall; 'jǎng-gwò to grow or rise or develop past *some point or mark, as water rising above the banks of the river*; jǎng-'hǎw to heal.

    Also used causatively (*V*): to develop, to suffer the growth of; to raise, increase. jǎng-'chwāng to have boils develop on one's skin; jǎng húng-'bān to develop a red rash; jǎng 'hú-dz to grow a beard; jǎng-'shyèw to rust; jǎng-'jǎr to develop soft, dark, rotting spots, (*of an apple*); jǎng-'jyàr to advance prices, raise prices; jǎng-'chúng to get wormy.

掌

*jǎng (*Nunit*, **ge**) flat surface of the hand or foot. shěw-'jǎng palm of the hand; jyǎw-'jǎng sole of the foot.

    'dǎ-rén yì-'jǎng (*with Msemel*) slap someone.

掌

jǎng (*V*) to keep, control, manage. jǎng-'shr̀ to manage affairs (*in a business, in an office*).

    jǎng-'shr̀-de a person with functions much like those of a chief clerk. jǎng-'yìn to be custodian of seals (*in older times*).

    jǎng-'chwán to operate a boat. jǎng-'dwò to control the rudder.

146

長
*jăng (Npers) person in charge (of whatever is designated by what precedes) especially by virtue of governmental or military appointment or election. lyán-'jăng company (troop, battery,) commander; páy-'jăng platoon leader; hwèy-'jăng head of any (governmental) organization (called a hwèy); bù-'jăng minister (head of a ministry of government); chwán-'jăng captain of a ship (Navy or Merchant Marine); jăng-'gwān a superior officer or official.

掌權
jăng-'chywán (VN1) to be in authority, exercise authority.

掌櫃
jăng-'gwèy. (VN1) manage a store, shop. jăng-'gwéy-de shopkeeper, boss.

長勁
jăng-'jìn (VN1) to grow strong (of a person).

長進
'jăng-jìn (RC1) to make progress, improve (work, something one is learning, etc.).

漲
jàng (V) to stretch on a framework (as a shoe on a shoetree). ‖wŏ-de-'shyé tày 'shyăw-le, nǐ gěy-wo 'jàng-yi-jàng. My shoes are too small, stretch them for me.
As postV: hē-'jàng to drink until the stomach is bloated. ‖wŏ (hē-)'shwěy hē tày-'dwō-le, hē-'jàng-le. I drank too much water, my stomach is too full.

仗
jàng (Mauton; Nunit, tsż, hwéy) battle, war, fighting, almost exclusively with dă. dă-'jàng to fight, to wage war, have a battle; dă-chi 'jàng láy-le to start fighting a war; dă yí-'jàng or dǎ yí-tsż-'jàng or dǎ yì-hwéy-'jàng to fight one battle.

賬
jàng (Nunit, ge; bǐ) account, bill. kāy-'jàng to write out a bill (to be paid), issue a bill; swàn-'jàng to work out accounts, figure out accounts, (or figuratively) to settle accounts, get even. ‖shyě-dzay tā-de-'jàng-shang. Put it on his bill. or Charge it to his account.

仗
jàng(-je) (V) to depend on. ‖jèy-jyàn-'shr̀-ching chywán 'jàng-je ni(-le). This matter depends entirely on you (you have the sole responsibility).

丈
jàng(r) (Mmeas) a unit of length. See Appendix B.

賬單
jàng-'dān, jàng-'dār (Nunit, jāng) bill (presented for payment).

丈夫
'jàng-fu (Npers) husband. See Appendix A.

丈母
jàng-'mŭ (Npers) mother-in-law. See Appendix A.

賬目
'jàng-mù (Nmass) financial accounts.

帳蓬，帳棚
'jàng-peng (Nunit, ge) tent. dā 'jàng-peng to put up a tent; chāy 'jàng-peng to take down a tent.

jao Wade Romanization for raw.

滓
jăr (Nunit, ge) soft dark rotting spot on the skin of a piece of fruit. jăng-'jăr to develop such spots.

招
jāw (I) to confess in court; jāw-'dzwèy (VN1) to confess one's guilt in court. As mainV: 'jāw-chū-lay (RC2) to disclose something, confess something in court.

招
jāw (V, Vsent) to invite, bring on; to invite someone to do something; gather, attract people to a place for some purpose. jāw-'dzār to invite catastrophe, be dangerous, be bad luck; jāw-rén 'láy invite people to come, or attract people together as a salesman on the street getting a crowd around him; jāw-'bīng to draft soldiers, raise an army; jāw-'shěw to beckon with the hand, asking someone to come (Chinese do this with the palm down).

著
jāw(r) (Mauton; Nunit, ge) a clever method, plan. yùng yì-'jāwr use (or using) a clever method to do something. ‖wŏm shyăng yí-ge-'jāwr bă-ta 'pyàn-chū-lay. We'll think of some trick to get the better of him and get him to come out.

招待
jāw-'dày (V) to entertain, be hospitable to; to usher. ‖wŏ 'chǐng-ta jāw-'dày ni. I'll ask him to take care of you (a host speaking to a guest).
nywŭ-jāw-'dày waitress (in a restaurant).

招待室
jāw-dày-'shr̀ (Nunit, jyān, ge) waiting room, reception room.

招待所

jăw-dày-'swǒ (*Nunit*, *ge*) Reception House (*an expression found in the names of fancy or would-be fancy hotels*)

招待員

jăw-dày-'ywán (*Npers*) an usher.

着地

jăw-'dì (*VN1*) to touch the ground. ‖jèy-bă-'yĭ-dz tày 'gāw, 'dzwò-je jèr 'jyǎw bù-néng jăw-'dì. This chair is too high; sitting here your feet can't touch the ground.

招呼

'jāw-hu (*V*) to beckon to, wave to, make some gesticulation or gesture to *someone*, (*as a greeting*).

    To take care of, look after, help orient, *someone just arrived at a strange place*.

着急

jăw-'jí *or* jáw-'jí (*VN2*) to get worried, get excited. jăw yí-jèn-'jí be worried for a spell.

招領處

jăw-lĭng-'chù (*Nunit*, *ge*) lost-and-found department (*place, not column in a paper*).

着凉

jāw-'lyáng *or* jáw-'lyáng (*VN1*) to catch cold.

着上

'jāw-shàng (*RC2*) to catch, contract, (*a disease*).

着手

jāw-'shěw (*VN1*) to get to work, start to work (*literally to put a hand to something*)

招貼

jăw-'tyē (*V*) to post *a bill, an advertisement*. jăw-'tyē gwǎng-'gàw to post an advertisement (*on a bulletin board, wall, in a window, etc.*).

招搖

'jāw-yáw (*I*) to show off. ‖tā hěn 'shĭ-hwan 'jāw-yáw. He likes to show off.

着

jáw (*I*) to catch fire; jáw-'hwǒ (*VN2*) to catch fire. jáw-chi 'hwǒ láy to catch fire, burst into flame; jáw-'wán-le be burned completely, burned out, burned down; yì 'dyǎn jyèw 'jáw to get angry easily; to catch fire easily.

    As postV, has less specific meaning: to succeed in, be able; to establish contact. jăw-'jáw to hunt for and find; 'mǎy-jáw to try to buy and succeed; jăw-bu-'jáw

be unable to find; măy-bu-'jáw be unable to buy (*because something is not for sale, not for lack of funds*); 'shwèy-jáw go to sleep.

着急

jáw-'jí *see* jăw-'jí.

着凉

jáw-'lyáng *see* jāw-'lyáng

找

jǎw (*V*) to look for, ask for, seek, hunt for, try to get in touch with. jǎw-'chár to find fault; jǎw tā-de-'chár to find fault with him. 'jǎw-je 'kān to shop around, look around, *hunting something or looking at random in a store.* ‖dǎ dyàn-'hwà 'jǎw-ta. Try to get him on the phone. ‖jǎw-ta láy. Get him here. ‖jǎw-ta chywù. Go find him.

    gěy-rén jǎw 'má-fan make trouble for someone, bother someone (*often unintentionally*). *As mainV*: 'jǎw-jáw to look for and find; 'jǎw-chū-láy to discover *something or someone who is in hiding* (*intentionally or unintentionally*); 'jǎw-dàw to call *people* to *a place*; 'jǎw-dàw yí-'kwàr to call *people* together; 'jǎw-hwéy-láy to recover, regain, take back. 'jǎw-hwéy-lay-de-'chyán change, money given in change.

照

jàw (*V*) to shine on, to be reflected from. jàw 'jìng-dz to look in a mirror. *As mainV*: jàw-'shĭng (*the sun*) wakes *someone* up by shining *on him;* 'jàw-dzày to shine on.

照

jàw (*K*) according to. jàw-'yàngr exactly according to pattern, exactly the same as the model; jàw-'cháng to be the same as usual; jàw jèy-ge-'yàng-dz in this situation, according to this situation. ‖tā jàw-'yàngr 'yì-dyǎr yě méy-'gǎy. He hasn't made any change at all in it.

照顧

'jàw-gu (*V*) to take care of (*a person*), to mind (*a child*), to look after, maintain (*a thing, a person*); to patronize (*a particular store*). 'jàw-gu-de hěn jēw-'dàw to show every consideration, take excellent care of. ‖'jàw-gu-jàw-gu wǒ-de-'háy-dz. Take good care of my child (*as in a letter to relatives or friends with whom the child is staying*).

照管

jàw-'gwǎn (*V*) to take charge of, run, operate. (*Same as gwǎn alone.*)

照例

jàw-'lì (*I or H*) follow tradition, behave according to custom; according to custom, tradition.

Circular doorway, Huaching Hot Springs

Dancers in Royal Costume

照料

'jàw-lyàw (V) to take care of, to care for, (*child, sick person, baggage, etc.*). ‖**tā tì tā-de-'fù-chin 'jàw-lyàw jyā-'tíng.** He's taking care of the family for his father.

照相 (片兒)

jàw shyàng (-'pyàr) (VN2) to take pictures, have one's picture taken. **'jàw-shyà-lay** (RC2) to take one or more pictures of *something*.

照相機

jàw-shyàng-'jī (Nunit, ge) camera.

摘

jāy (V) to pluck off; to take off *or* down. **jāy 'màw-dz** take off a hat; **jāy-'hwār** to pick flowers; **jāy-'máw** to pluck out feathers (*as when preparing a fowl for cooking*).

As mainV: **'jāy-shyà-lay** take off, pluck off (and down); **'jāy-kāy** to unravel *or* untangle (*a knotted string*); **jāy-'shé** to pluck *flowers* breaking *the stems;* etc.

宅

'jáy(-dz) (Nunit, ge) residence. (*Also* **jù-'jáy.**) *Homes in Peiping are often marked with a sign bearing two characters: the surname and* **jáy**: *thus* **lǐ-'jáy** the Lǐ residence.

窄

jǎy (A) narrow. (*Opposite* **kwān** broad.) (*Of people*) narrow-minded.

債

jày (Nunit, bǐ, ge) loan (*almost exclusively money*) **jyè-'jày** to borrow; **hwán-'jày** to return; **fàng-'jày** to grant a loan, extend a loan; **yàw-'jày** to request the return of the money borrowed.

jày-'jǔ (Npers) creditor.

je *Wade romanization for* **re.**

着

je added to V, I, K, A, to indicate that the action or state is in process continually during the moment of speaking or the moment referred to. ‖**tā-men 'dwèy-je dzwò-je.** They were (*or* are) sitting facing each other. ‖**byé 'nème gwāng 'kàn-je rén bù-shwō-'hwà!** Don't just stare at people like that without saying anything! ‖**'tyān háy 'hēy-je-ne.** It's still dark (*in the morning*).

For contrast with **le,** *see* **le.**

遮

jē (V) to conceal, hide, cover up; to shade *a light*. *As mainV:* **'jē-jù** to conceal from sight; **jē-chǐ-lay** *or*

'jē-shàng to cover up; *etc.* ‖**'ywe-ıyang bèy 'ywúntsay 'jē-le.** The moon was hidden by the clouds. ‖**'rén chwān 'yī-fu jē 'shēn-ti.** People wear clothes and conceal their bodies.

摺

jé (V) to plait *cloth*, to fold accordion-like. *Particularly* **'jé-chǐ-lay** (RC2) to fold up accordion-like. ‖**bǎ dì-'tú 'jé-chǐ-lay.** Fold up the map.

轍

jé (Nunit, tyáw, dàw, háng, lyèw) track left by a wheel; **chē-'jé** tracks left by a car.

摺子

'jé-dz (Nunit, ge) bankbook, account book; (*one Chinese type is a long thin sheet of paper folded together accordion-like and slipped into a stiff cover*). ‖**wǒ-de-'jé-dz dēw. shyě-'mǎn-le.** My account book is all filled up.

lì ge-'jé-dz to open an account; **chywǔ-'shyāw 'jé-dz** to close an account. **jèy-ge-'jé-dz dzwò-'fèy-le.** This account has been invalidated.

哲學

'jé-shywé (Nabstr) philosophy.

這

jè, .jèy (Dem) this, this here, here. *Used alone with very indefinite meaning at beginning of sentence.* ‖**'jè-shř wǒ-de-'tày-tay.** This is my wife. *or* Here is my wife. *Followed by a measure (with or without a noun)* this, these; **'jè-ge** *or* **'jèy-ge** *when the object is only specified by context:* ‖**'jèy-ge wǒ shyǎng bù-'hǎw.** I don't think this is any good. *Otherwise:* **'jèy-tyān** this day *that I'm speaking of;* **jèy-ge-'rén** this man; *etc.;* **'jèy-shyē** these *with a Nunit,* this quantity of *with other nouns:* **'jèy-shyē-rén** these men.

Followed by a numeral, then by measure (and noun): **jèy-yí-ge-'rén** this one man; **jèy-'sān-ge-rén** these three men.

jè, jèy, *and other longer forms built thereon, contrast with the parallel forms involving* **nà, nèy,** *much as do English* this *and* that; *but neither is used like English* this *in* This is my idea *or* here *in* Here is a simpler way to do it, *where* this *and* here *point towards something not yet said. Thus* ‖**'jè-shř ge-hǎw-'fá-dz.** *means* This (*something already said*) is a good method. *not* Here is a good method.

浙江

jè-'jyāng (Nunique) Chekiang *province.*

這裏, 這兒

'jè-li *same as* **jèr,** *which is more often.*

這麼

'jè-me, 'jème, jèm, dzème, 'dzèm (*H*) so, thus, in this way, like this, to this extent: jème-'dwǒ-de-shū this many books; dzèm 'kwày so fast (that . . .).

　　'jème-je doing it thus. ‖'jème-je bǐ 'nème-je 'hǎw. Doing it this way is better than doing it that way.

　　Before nominal forms in a few cases: 'jème-yì-hwéy-'shr̀ such a matter as this.

這(麼)樣(兒)

'jè(me)-yàng(r) (*H*) this way. 'jème-yàng-de (*before nouns*) this kind of, such . . . as this.

這麼

jèm(e) *see* 'jè-me.

jen *Wade Romanization for* ren.

真

jēn (*H*) really, truly. ‖'tyān-chi 'jēn gèw 'lěng-de! It's really cold enough! ‖'jēn-de-ma? Really? ‖'jēn-de-ya! Really!

　　(*Aattr*) true. ‖shwō jēn-'hwà! Tell the truth! ‖tā-'shwǒ-de bú-shr̀ 'jēn-de. What he says isn't true. 'jēn-shr̀ (*H.*) *same meaning.*

針

jēn (*Nunit,* gēr, ge, tyáw) pin; *in compounds:* pointer, hand. byǎw-'jēn hand on a watch, *or* pointer on a dial; dà-'jēn minute hand; shyǎw-'jēn hour hand.

　　dǎ-'jēn to inoculate; 'dǎ-ta yì-'jēn to give him one injection.

真個的

‖jēn-'gé-de! Really! Ain't it the truth! (*expression of sympathy to a person who's telling you his troubles or difficulties*).

　　‖No fooling! That's the straight goods!

真正

jēn-'jèng (*Aattr*) real, genuine, true. ‖'jè-shr̀ jēn-'jèng-de-è-ywú-'pí. This is genuine alligator skin.

真空

jēn-'kūng (*Aattr*) void of air, evacuated, containing a vacuum.

真空管

jēn-kūng-'gwǎn, jēn-kūng-'gwǎr (*Nunit,* ge) vacuum tube, radio tube.

真理

jēn-'lǐ (*Nabstr*) truth. jǎw jen-'lǐ to search for the truth (*as of a philosopher*)

針線活

jēn-shyàn-'hwó (*Nunit,* ge, jyàn) needlework, sewing. dzwò jēn-shyàn-'hwó to sew.

真相

jēn-'shyàng (*Nabstr*) the truth, the real situation, the true picture. dyàw-'chá jēn-'shyàng to investigate and try to ascertain the true picture (*as of a detective*).

枕

jěn (*V*) to rest one's head on, at. *As mainV:* 'jěn-dzày to rest one's head on, at *a place.*

　　'jěn-tew (*Nunit,* ge) pillow. ‖tā jěn-je 'jěn-tew 'shwèy. He's sleeping with his head resting on a pillow.

疹子

'jěn-dz (*Nmass*) measles-spots. chū 'jěn(-dz) to have the measles.

賑

jèn (*V*) to give relief. jèn-'dzāy to give relief in time of catastrophe, flood, famine, fire.

　　(*N*) fàng-'jèn to give alms, give to charity (*of government, Red Cross, as a matter of necessity, not purely voluntary charity; and on a large scale*).

鎮

jèn (*Nunit,* ge) trading center, market. (*In the country*) a centrally located village which serves as a trading center; (*in the city*) a marketing district.

陣

jèn (*MdistT*) a short (and sudden) spell of: ywǔ (*rain*), fēng (*wind*), fēng-'ywǔ (*storm*). A short (and sudden) blast of *some sound:* a burst of gǔ-'jǎng (*applause*), a burst of pàw-'shēng *or* chyāng-'shēng (*gunfire*). ‖tā 'bìng-le yí-'jèn(-dz). He was sick for a spell (*indefinitely long period*). ‖tā 'pǎw-le yí-'jèn(-dz). He ran a ways.

　　yí-jèn-yí-'jèn-de spasmodic, in fits and starts.

陣地

'jèn-dì (*Nunit,* ge) position in battle array, area or point in battle formation.

鎮定

jèn-'dìng (*A*) calm, settled; (*V*) to settle, calm down, cause to get settled down. jèn-'dìng rén-'shīn to calm people('s hearts) down.

振作

jèn-'dzwò (*V*) to pluck up *one's spirits, courage.* jèn-'dzwò 'jīng-shén to pluck up one's spirits. *As mainV:* jèn-'dzwò-chi-lay *same meaning.* ‖nǐ shyǎng 'fá-dz bǎ tā-de-'jīng-shén jèn-'dzwò-chi-lay. Try to cheer him up.

鎮靜

jèn-jìng (*A*) calm, steady, cool and collected (*of a person*).

150

鎮江

jèn-'jyāng (*Nunique*) Chen-chiang *or* Chinkiang (*capital of Kiangsu province*).

鎮南關

jèn-nán-'gwān (*Nunique*) Chen-nan-kuan (*city in Kwangsi province*)

陣亡

jèn-'wáng (*I*) to die in battle, to die in line of duty. ‖**tā jèn-'wáng-le.** He died in action.

jeng *Wade Romanization for* **reng.**

睜

jēng (*V*) to open (*only eyes*). **jēng-'yǎn** to open one's eyes; *as mainV:* **'jēng-kay 'yǎn-jing** open one's eyes. (*Figuratively*) to realize *or* be willing to see *something one hasn't been willing to see before;* (*as in English*).

蒸

jēng (*V*) to cook by steaming. **jēng-'fàn** (*VN3*) steamed rice.   **jēng-'chì** (*Nmass*) steam.

爭

jēng (*V*) to fight for, to contest the control of. ‖**wǒ gēn-ta 'jēng nèy-ge-'dūng-shi.** We're quarreling about which one of us gets that (thing).

徵兵

jēng-'bīng (*VN2*) to draft soldiers, to induct soldiers.   **jēng-bīng-'jywú** draft board.

爭辯

jēng-'byàn (*V*) to argue about. ‖**tām jēng-'byàn nèy-ge-'wèn-tí.** They're arguing about that problem.

爭氣

jēng-'chì (*VN2, A*) to strive to attain socially correct reputation and power. ‖**nèy-ge-rén bù-jēng-'chì.** He doesn't do what's expected of a person.

蒸氣鍋

jēng-chì-'gwō (*Nunit, ge*) boiler, steam generator.

徵求

jēng-'chyéw (*V*) to advertise for, look for, *workers, helpers, employment, etc.* (*not necessarily for someone who is going to be paid*): to look for, seek to get, *a place to live, someone to agree with you, etc.*

掙扎

'jēng-jā (*I*) to struggle under adverse circumstances. ‖**tā dzày 'hwàn-nàn-'lǐ-tew 'jēng-jā.** He's working under difficulties.

爭論

jēng-'lwèn (*V, I*) to argue hotly. ‖**tām jēng-'lwèn shéme-'wèn-tí?** What are they arguing about?

徵聘

jēng-'pìn (*V*) to advertise *for workers, help.*

整

jěng (*Aattr, particularly before Ntime or Mtime*) **all; entire, whole. jěng-'tyān** all day, (*figuratively*) always; **jěng-'yè** all night; **jěng-'nyán** all year; the year round.

     (*Before numerals, or H*) exactly, precisely. **jěng-'sān-ge** exactly three (*as expected*). ‖**wǒ 'jěng yěw 'sān-ge.** It's just exactly three that I have (*how lucky! since that's how many you want*).

     jěng-'jēng(r), **jěng-'jēng**(r) (*H*) just exactly, just right.

     (*Before nouns, as Aattr*) **jěng-'shīn** total salary; **jěng-'shùr** an even number.

整

*jěng (*V*) to straighten out, put in good order (*physically*).

整齊

jěng-'chí (*A*) neat, in order.

整頓

jěng-'dwèn (*V*) to arrange, to straighten out *matters, affairs.*

整個兒(的)

jěng-'gèr(-de) all, the whole of *used before nouns which take M ge and a few others.* **jěng-'gèr-de-'fáng-dz** the whole house; **jěng-'gèr-de-rén** the whole person. ‖**jěng-'gèr-de-rén dēw 'shī-le.** He was wet all over.

整理

'jěng-lǐ (*V*) to straighten out, arrange, put in order *things physically, or matters, affairs.* ‖**wǒ 'jěng-lǐ 'jwō-dz-shang-de-'dūng-shi.** I'm straightening out the things on the table.

     As mainV: **'jěng-lǐ-chū-lay** straighten out; **'jěng-lǐ-chǐ-lay** straighten up.

掙

jèng (*V*) to earn, take in, have as income. **jèng-'chyán** to earn money by working. *As mainV:* **'jèng-jìn-lay** *with same meaning.*

證

jèng (*V*) to bear witness about, prove, solve. ‖**chǐng-ni gěy-wo bǎ jèy-ge-'wèn-tí 'jèng-yi-jèng.** Please solve this problem for me.

正

jèng (*H*) just, exactly, precisely. (1) (*With reference to time*) ‖**tā jèng dzày chī-'fàn**(-ne). He's just now eating. ‖tā jèng yàw chř-'fàn(-ne). He's just on the point of eating. ‖nǐ 'láy-de 'jèng shř 'shŕ-hew. You came just at the right time.

(2) (With reference to space) ‖'chwāng-hu jèng 'dwèy-je tā-de-'mér. The window is right opposite his doorway.

(3) (Otherwise) ‖wǒ-de-'shyé 'jèng hé-'shř. My shoes fit just right. ‖'nǐ-shwō-de gēn 'tā-shwō-de 'jèng shyāng-'fǎn. What you say and what he says are directly contrary. ‖wǒ-de-'chē gēn 'tā-de-chē jèng 'jwàng-shang. My car and his had a (direct) head-on collision. ‖jèy-jyàn-'yī-fu tā 'chwān-je jèng 'hǎw(r). That dress fits her just right. ‖nǐ 'láy-de jèng 'hǎw(r). You've come just at the right moment.

(Aattr, before nouns) due, true, exact, correct. jèng-'nán due south, etc., with other direction words; 'jèng-myàr the right side of something that has a right side and a wrong side, like printed cloth; jèng-'lù the right road.

dzěw jèng-'lù to follow the right road; (figuratively) to do the right things in life.

正

*jèng prefixed to numbers: plus, in the sense of positive number. not of addition. ‖fù-'sān jyā jèng-'sż dé (jèng-)'yī. Minus three plus (plus) four gives (plus) one.

jèng-'hàw (Nunit, ge) the plus sign.

政（府）

*jèng, 'jèng-fǔ (Nunit, ge) government. 'jūng-yāng-'jèng-fǔ central (national) government; shěng-'jèng-fǔ state or provincial government; 'dì-fang-'jèng-fǔ local government.

正常

'jèng-cháng (A) normal. ‖tā-de-'jīng-shén hěn 'jèng-cháng. His mind is quite normal.

掙錢

jèng-'chyán (VN2) to earn money.

正確

'jèng-chywè (A) accurate, true. ‖jèy-ge-'shyāw-shi hěn 'jèng-chywe. This news is quite accurate.

正當

'jèng-dang (A) upright, honest. ‖jèy-ge-'rén yùng 'jèng-dang-de-'fāng-fa jwàn-'chyán. He uses honest methods to make money.

政黨

jèng-'dǎng (Nunit, ge) political party.

證婚

jèng-'hwēn (VN2) to witness a wedding; officiate at a wedding; perform a wedding ceremony.

鄭州

jèng-'jēw (Nunique) Chengchow, another name for jèng-'shyàn Cheng-hsien (city in Honan province).

正經

jèng-'jīng (A) serious, serious-minded. ‖tā hěn jèng-'jīng-de shwǒ .... He said, with a serious expression, ...

政治

'jèng-jř (Nabstr) politics in the general sense. jeng-jř-'shywé political science; 'jèng-jř-bèy-'jīng the political background of some event or decision, etc; 'jèng-jř-'wèn-tí political problems, political questions; jèng-jř-'jyā statesman; 'jèng-jř-twán-'tǐ political body.

政界

jèng-'jyè (Nunique) political circles, government circles. ‖tā dzày jèng-'jyè hěn yěw-'míng. He's quite well known in government circles.

證據

'jèng-jywù (Nunit, ge) point of evidence, item of evidence. ‖nǐ 'shwō nèy-jywù-'hwà yěw shéme-'jèng-jywù méy-yew? Have you any evidence to back up that statement?

正楷

jèng-'kǎy (Nabstr) style of written characters like that which is printed clear to the eye.

政客

jèng-'kè (Npers) politician (bad sense).

證明

jèng-'míng (Vsent) to prove that, bear witness that. ‖nǐ 'jèng-míng-jèng-míng tā 'nèy-tyān méy-'láy. Prove that he didn't come that day.

證（明）書

jèng(-'míng)-'shū (Nunit, jāng) certificate.

正片

jèng-'pyān(-dz) (Nunit, ge) feature picture, main feature.

證人

'jèng-rén (Npers) witness (in court or to a document).

正式

jèng-shř (A) official, formal. 'jèng-shř-de shēng-'míng-le has been officially proclaimed.

鄭縣

jèng-'shyàn (Nunique) Cheng-hsien (city in Honan province).

正題
jèng-'tí (*Nunit*, ge) subject of discussion, the thing being talked about.
    bú-shr 'jèng-'tí is beside the point, irrelevant.

政體
jèng-'tǐ (*Nabstr*) system of government. gùng-hé-jèng-'tǐ republican form of government; *etc.*

政策
jèng-'tsè (*Nabstr*) policies; *political, economic, commercial, legal, social, financial.*

這兒
jèr (*place expression*) this place, here. ‖dàw wǒ-'jèr láy. Come here to me. ‖tā shéme-'shŕ-hew ké-yi 'dàw-jèr? When can he get here? ‖jèr-de-'fàn bù-'hǎw. The food here is no good.
    'jèr-jyèw *or* 'jàr-jyèw (*same characters*)·(*H*) right now, right this minute. ‖'jèr-jyèw 'dzěw-ba! Get out of here this minute!

這兒那兒的
jèr-'nàr-de (*Nplace*) high and low, here and there. ‖jèr-'nàr-de wǒ dēw jǎw-'dàw-le, dēw 'méy-yew. I've hunted high and low but they aren't anywhere.

州
jēw (*Nunit*, ge) an older administrative unit between the shyàn (*district*) and the shěng (*province*) in the hierarchy; *often used for* state of the U. S. jēw-'jǎng governor *of a* jēw; governor *of a state.*

周朝
'jēw-cháw (*Nunique*) The Chou dynasty (*1122–256 B.C.*).

周到
jēw-'dàw (*A*) thorough, taking everything into account. ‖tā jāw-'dày rén hěn jēw-'dàw. He entertains his guests with thorough hospitality. ‖tā 'shyǎng-de hěn jēw-'dàw. He thinks things through thoroughly and completely.

週轉不靈
'jēw-jwǎn-bù-'líng (*literary quotation*) to be difficult of access (*as money, resources*); to be hard to move (*as a part of a machine, or a part of the body*).

周密
jēw-'mì (*A*) careful, alert, carefully worked-out with attention to detail. ‖jèy-ge-'dì-fang-de-jǐng-'wèy hěn jēw-'mì. The defenses of this position are worked out in great detail.

週末
jēw-'mwò (*Ntime*, ge) weekend. 'shàng-yí-ge-jēw-'mwò last weekend; 'bèn-jēw-'mwò this weekend.

週圍
'jēw-wéy (*Nplace*) (the territory *or* area) around the circumference of, around the perimeter of. ‖'hú-de-'jēw-wéy dēw-shŕ 'shān. There are hills all around the lake. ‖'hú-de-'jēw-wéy yěw 'dwō-shaw-'lǐ? How many miles is it around the lake?

軸
*jéw (*N*) axle, axis. chē-'jéw axle of the wheels on a car or cart.
    jéw(r) (*Munit*) a spool of shyàn (*thread*).

軸心
jéw-'shīn (*Nunique*) Axis (*political: Germany and Japan*).

皺眉
jèw-'méy (*VN2*) to frown, to wrinkle the eyebrows. jèw yí-'shyà-dz-'méy to frown once.

鷄
jī (*Nunit*, jǐ) chicken. gūng-'jī rooster; mǔ-'jī hen. jī-'rèw chicken *as eaten*, chicken meat; jī-'dàn (chicken) eggs; jī-'fángr henhouse, chicken coop; jī-'máw chicken feathers.

基本
'jī-běn (*Nabstr*) fundamentals. 'jī-běn-de-'wèn-tí a fundamental question.

機器
'jī-chì (*Nunit*, jyà) machine, piece of machinery.

機器匠
jī-chì-'jyàng (*Npers*) mechanic.

基礎
'jī-chǔ (*Nunit*, ge, dzwò) foundation, base, (*for a building, statue, pillar, etc.*). *Sometimes figuratively as in* 'tsáy-jèng-'jī-chǔ financial foundation, resources, backing.

鷄蛋青(兒)
jī-dàn-'chīng, jī-dàn-'chyēngr (*Nmass*) egg white, albumen (*of chicken egg*).

鷄蛋黃兒
jī-dàn-'hwáng(r) (*Nunit*, ge) egg yolk (*of chicken egg*).

基督
'jī-dū (*Nunique*) Christ.

基督徒
jī-dū-'tú (*Npers*) a Christian.

鷄子兒
jī-dzěr (*Nunit*, ge) chicken eggs.

機關
'jī-gwān (*Nunit, ge*) (1) an office, agency, bureau, institution (*governmental or private*).
(2) The controlling *or* key mechanism in some mechanical device.

機關鎗
jī-gwān-'chyāng (*Nunit, jī, găn, ge*) machine gun.

饑寒
jī-'hán (*Nabstr*) hunger and cold (*literary*). *Separated and used as adjectives:* ‖tā shyàn-dzày yèw 'jī yèw 'hán. He's both hungry and cold now.

機會
'jī-hwèy (*Nunit, ge*) an opportunity, chance. ‖wǒ méy-yew 'jī-hwèy 'kàn-jyàn ni. I have no chance to see you. *or* (At present) there's no chance of my seeing you.

炭(幾)乎
'jī-(jī-)hu (*J*) almost, all but. ‖'jī-hu méy-bǎ-wo 'shyà-'sž. It all but frightened me to death.

機件
jī-'jyàn (*Nunit, jyàn, ge*) machine parts.

機械
jī-'jyè (*Nunit, jyàn, ge*) mechanical tool, instrument (*ruler, T-square, compass, wrench, screwdriver, slide-rule, etc.*).
Device, small machine.

犄角
'jī-jyaw (*Nunit, jī; dwèy or* shwāng *for a pair of*) horns (*of an animal*).
jī-'jyǎw(r) (*Nplace, ge*) corner (*of a table, a city square, etc.*).

犄裡角落
'jī-li-gā-'lár (*Nplace*) everywhere, from top to bottom, high and low. ‖wǒ 'jī-li-gā-'lár dēw jǎw-'dàw-le. I've hunted high and low. ‖wǒ 'jī-li-gā-'lár dēw shyǎng-'dàw-le. I've racked my brains.

機師
jī-'shŕ (*Npers*) chauffeur, locomotive engineer, plane pilot.

擊退
jī-'twèy (*RC2*) to beat back (*an enemy*). *Slightly literary; the thoroughly colloquial equivalent is* dǎ-'twèy.

極
jí (*H*) extremely. jí 'hǎw extremely good; jí 'hwày extremely bad. *More often used after A, with* -le

added: hǎw 'jí-le, hwày 'jí-le, *etc.; this way of expression is stronger.*
běy-'jí(-de-dì-fang) the north polar regions, the Arctic; *similarly for* Antarctic.

集
jí (*Nunit, ge*) rural market place. dzày 'jí-shang at the fair; găn-'jí to go to the market.

即
jí (*H*) immediately, right away; *slightly literary equivalent of* jyèw.

急
jí (*A*) excited, angry, upset; urgent, hasty. ‖tā jyèw 'jí-le. He flared up with anger. *or* He became furious.

級
jí (*Mmeas*) rank, grade. ‖tā bǐ-wo gāw yì-'jí. He's one rank higher than I.
'jyē-jí (*Nunit, ge*) rank, grade.

吉安
jí-'ān (*Nunique*) Chi-an *or* Kian (*city in Kiangsi province*).

極端
'jí-dwān (*Nabstr*) an extreme. dzěw 'jí-dwān to go to extremes; shwō 'jí-dwān-de-'hwà to make extreme statements. 'jí-dwān-jǔ-'yì extreme principles, overly radical *or* overly conservative principles.

極點
jí-'dyǎn (*Nplace, ge*) an extreme point, farthest point. ‖'nèy-ge-dūng-shi hǎw-dàw jí-'dyǎn-le. (*Figuratively*) That thing is good to the greatest possible degree.

急瘋
jí-'fēng-le (*A*) to have become extremely upset *or* worried, to have become crazy with worry.

及格
jí-'gé *see* jì-'gé.

脊骨
jí-'gǔ (*Nunit, tyáw*) backbone.

吉利
'jí-lì (*A*) lucky, auspicious. ‖bù-'jí-lì-de-'ŕ-dz an unlucky day, inauspicious day.

極力
jí-'lì (*VN1*) to try hard; (*Vpred*) to try hard to. ‖jí-'lì dzwò nèy-jyàn-'shŕ-ching. Try hard to do that job.

吉林
'jí-lín (*Nunique*) Kirin *province*.

激烈
jí-'lyè (A) violent, radical. ‖tā shwō-'hwà hěn jí-'lyè. He speaks very violently.

急流
jí-'lyéw (Nunit, ge) rapids in a stream.

脊梁
'jí-nyang (Nunit, ge) upper part of the back of the body.

急性
jí-'shìng (A) quick, hasty, of hasty disposition. (Opposite màn-'shìng.) ‖jèy-ge-rén hěn jí-'shìng. He has a hasty disposition.
     Of a disease, quick-acting, acute. ‖jèy-ge shř jí-'shìng-de-'bìng. This is a quick-acting disease (he'll either recover quickly or die quickly).
     jí-'shìng-dz (Npers) quick-tempered person.

急於
'jí-ywú (H) eagerly, anxiously. ‖tā 'jí-ywú yàw 'dzěw. He's very eager to go.

幾
jǐ (NumU) a few; or, how many? (expecting an answer of only a few, often less than ten). Can be added to NumG as other NumU are: 'èr-shr-'jǐ twenty-some, twenty-odd. ‖'jǐ-dyǎn-jūng? What time is it?
     'jǐ-ge-'dzèr a few words (literally and figuratively as in English).

擠
jǐ (A) crowded, pressed together. ‖'jyē-shang hěn 'jǐ. The street is crowded.
     (V) to crowd, jostle, press, squeeze. ‖tā 'jǐ-wo. He pushed me, he crowded me.
     jǐ-'nǎy or jǐ nyéw-'nǎy to milk a cow (literally squeeze milk).
     bǎ-rén 'jǐ-de méy-'lùr-le (figuratively) crowd someone into a corner, get someone up a tree.
     As mainV: jǐ-'byǎn to squeeze flat, compress; 'jǐ-chū (lc) to squeeze out, burst out (as things from a tightly packed trunk); 'jǐ-dàw (lc) to squeeze something to a place (as in packing a trunk); jǐ-dzay (yí-'kwar) to squeeze together, to bunch together; 'jǐ-gwò (lc) to squeeze through a door, a crowd, across a street; 'jǐ-jìn (lc) to squeeze into a place; jǐ-'mǎn to be squeezed full, to pack in a hall, a room until it is full; jǐ-'sž to crush to death. ‖'jyē-shang-de-rén dēw 'jǐ-láy jǐ-'chywù-de. The people in the street were milling around in crowds.

給
jǐ alternant literary pronunciation of gěy, used in some combinations.

濟南
jǐ-'nán (Nunique) Tsinan, another name for lì-'chéng Li-ch'eng (capital of Shantung province).

濟寧
jǐ-'níng (Nunique) Chi-ning or Tsining (city in Shantung province).

幾時
jí-'shŕ (H) at what time?, when?, what date?

給養
jǐ-'yǎng (Nmass) supplies, provisions.

記
jì (V) to remember, to keep in mind; to make a written record of, to note down. ‖wǒ 'jì-je nèy-jyàn-'shř. I'm keeping that in mind. ‖nǐ 'jì-yi-jì tā-shwō-de-'hwà. Remember (or Make a note of) what he says.
     jì-'jàng to keep books (financial), to put something on an account, to charge it; jì 'jūng-dyǎr to record the time (of arrival, of departure).
     As mainV: 'jì-dzày to make a notation or a written record of something on (or in) a place; 'jì-jù to fasten in the memory, fix in the memory; 'jì-shyà (-lay) to keep track of, write down, remember.

季
jì (Mtime) season of the year. yí-jì-yí-'jì-de season by season, season after season. ‖yì-'nyán yěw sž-'jì. A year has four seasons.
     A school term (also shywé-'jì). chyēw-'jì fall term; chwēn-'jì spring term; jì-'kǎw term-final examination. 'shyà-jì summer season, etc.

寄
jì (V) to transmit, (particularly) to mail. jì-'shìn to mail letters. As mainV: jì (lc); 'jì-dàw (lc) to mail something to a place; etc.

繫
jì (V) to tie. jì 'shéng-dz to tie a rope, to put on a tie or a belt; jì yí-ge-lǐng-'dày to put on a necktie; jì yí-ge-'bǎwr to tie up a package, to button up; jì yí-ge-'kèw to button a button or to tie a knot.
     As mainV: 'jì-shang to tie up, button up, to put on a belt, a tie; jì-'jǐn to tighten; jì-'hǎw to tie securely; jì-'sūng yì-dyǎr to tie more loosely, to loosen up a bit.

繼承
jì-'chéng (V) to inherit, fall heir to. ‖tā jì-'chéng-le tā-'fù-chin-de-chǎn-'yè. He inherited his father's property.

記得
'jì-de (V, Vpred) to remember, to remember to, (to keep in mind, not to recall) ‖wǒ háy 'jì-de ta. I still remember him. ‖wǒ jì-de 'chywu. I kept it in mind that I had to go.

嫉妒

'jì-dù (A) be jealous; (V) be jealous of. ‖tā dwèy-ywu ta hěn 'jì-dù. or tā hěn 'jì-dù ta. He's very jealous of him.

及格

jì-'gé or jí-'gé (VN1) to qualify, pass an exam.

記號

'jì-hàw(r) (Nunit, gè) sign, mark, notation made to serve as a reminder. dzwò ge-'jì-hàwr to make a notation which will serve as a reminder. ‖wén-az dēw shr̀ yi-jǔng-'jì-hàwr, 'mù-dì shr̀ 'jyàw-rén 'jì-je rén-shwō-de-'hwà. Writing is all a kind of mnemonic device, the aim being to remind people of what someone has said.

計畫

'jì-hwà (V, Vpred) to figure out, to plan. ‖'jì-hwa-jì-hwa dzěme 'dzwò. Let's plan what to do.
(Nunit, ge) plan, proposal, plan of action.

記者

jì-'jě (Npers) reporter. shīn-wén-jì-'jě news reporter.

寂靜

jì-'jìng (A) quiet (a bit literary). ‖'jèy-ge-dì-fang hěn jì-'jìng. This place is very quiet (free from noise, not necessarily free from disturbances).

忌口

jì-'kěw (VN1) to be limited in one's diet. ‖tā shyàn-dzày jì-'kěw, bù-néng chr̄ 'shyán-de. He's on a diet now; he can't eat anything salty.

記錄

'jì-lu (V) to make a formal written record of, take minutes of. 'jì-lu kāy-'hwèy-de-shr̀-ching take minutes of a meeting. As mainV: 'jì-lu-shyà-lay with same meaning.
(Nmass) minutes, records. shyě 'jì-lu to take down notes, minutes. ‖'jì-lu 'shyě-de hěn 'chīng-chu. The minutes are written very clearly.

記念，紀念

jì-nyàn (V) to remember with feeling, to celebrate the memory of. ‖wǒ 'jì-nyàn ta. I remember him for his good qualities.
jì-nyàn-'bēy memorial column; jì-nyàn-'tsè(-dz) album for people to sign their names in on special occasions, sometimes adding a bit of verse, or album for photographs of special occasions, family album.

既然

'jì-rán (J) because, since, on account of, for the reason that. ‖'jì-rán tā 'yǐ-jing 'dzěw-le, wǒm yě béng 'shwō-le. Since he's already gone there's no point in talking about it.

寂然無聲

'jì-rán-wú-'shēng (literary quotation) very quiet, silent, (of a place).

記性

'jì-shìng (Nabstr) memory, ability to remember. ‖'nèy-ge-rén 'jì-shing bù-'hǎw. He has a poor memory.

技術

'jì-shu (Nabstr) technique, skill.

繼續

'jì-shywù (Vpred) to continue doing so-and-so, to continue to. ‖wǒ jyèw 'jì-shywù-shwō-'hwà. I'm going to go right on talking. As mainV: 'jì-shywù-shyà-chywu to continue, go on; jì-shywù-bu-'shyà-chywu be unable to continue.

計算

'jì-swàn (Vsent) to figure out, to calculate. ‖nǐ 'jì-swàn-jì-swan děy yùng 'dwō-shaw-chyán. Figure out how much money it will take.

計算機

jì-swàn-'jī (Nunit, jyà, ge) adding machine; cash register.

祭壇

jì-'tf̃ (Nunit, ge) altar.

紀元

jì-ywán, jì-ywán-'chyán (Ntime) B.C., before Christ. jì-ywán-'hèw (Ntime) A.D., Anno Domini, after Christ. jì-ywán-'chyán 'yī-'jyěw-'sž-'wǔ-'nyán the year 1945 B.C.

jih Wade Romanization for r.

筋

jīn (Nunit, tyáw) tendon; nerve; vein.

斤

jīn (Mmeas) catty (measure of weight). See Appendix B.

今

*jīn (Demord) this, for certain periods of time. 'jīn-tyan or 'jīn-r̀ or jyēr(-ge) today; 'jīn-nyan this year; tsúng-'jīn yǐ-'hèw from now on; jīn-'shr̀ (a bit literary) the world of today (same as shyàn-'dzày-de-shr̀-'jyè).

金

*jīn (N) metal. wǔ-'jīn the five metals (jīn gold, yín silver, túng copper, tyě iron, shí tin); wǔ-jīn-'háng store something like a hardware store.

金

jīn(-dz) (*Nmass*) gold. jīn-'chyán gold money or *just* money. jīn-'yè-dz gold leaf.

金本位

jīn-běn-'wèy (*Nabstr*) the gold standard (*financial*).

金鋼鑽

jīn-gāng-'dzwàr (*Nunit*, ge, lì) diamond (*cut*).

金鋼石

jīn-gāng-'shŕ (*Nmass*) diamond (*uncut, rough*). (*Nunit*, ge, lì) diamond (*cut*).

金華

jīn-'hwá (*Nunique*) Chin-hua or Kinhwa (*city in Che-kiang province*).

金鷄納霜

jīn-jī-'nà(-shwāng) (*Nmass*) quinine; (*with* shwāng) sulphate of quinine in powdered form.

禁住

'jīn-jù (*RC2*) to hold, bear, carry *weight, so much weight, so many people, so much baggage.* ‖jèy-ge-'shéng-dz jīn-de-'jù jīn-bu-'jù? Will this rope hold up under the weight?

jīn-bu-'jù be unable to afford, be unable to take it, stand it. ‖wǒ jīn-bu-'jù tā 'dǎ. I can't stand his beating me. ‖wǒ jīn-bu-'jù-le, jyèw shyàw-le. I couldn't restrain myself, so I burst out laughing.

晉江

jìn-'jyāng (*Nunique*) Chin-chiang (*city in Fukien province*).

筋疲力盡

jīn-'pí-lì-'jìn (*literary quotation*) to be completely exhausted physically.

金屬

jīn-'shǔ (*Nabstr*) metals. ‖'yín shŕ yì-jǔng-jīn-'shǔ. Silver is a metal.

經用

jīng-'yùng (*A*) durable, lasting, (*of a commodity, apparatus*). ‖gāng-'bǐ bǐ 'máw-bǐ jīn-'yùng. A fountain pen is more durable than a writing brush.

緊

jǐn (*A*) tight; urgent; close, near. ‖wǒ-de-'shyé tày 'jǐn. My shoes are too tight. *Used causatively:* 'jǐn-yì-jǐn to tighten; *but more often as postV:* nùng-'jǐn to tighten; jì-'jǐn to tie tightly; gwǒ-'jǐn to wrap around tightly; *etc.*

Before nouns: jǐn-'dyěngr-shang on the very top; jǐn-'chyán-byar at the very front; jǐn-'hèw-myar at the extreme rear; *as well as usual meanings given above.*

As H: jǐn 'gēn-je following closely (upon) (*time or space*).

錦標

jǐn-'byāw (*Nunit*, ge) prize, award. *Originally a small banner given as a mark of honor; now any award.* dé jǐn-'byāw to win a prize, to win the championship.

緊張

jǐn-'jāng (*A*) nervous, tense, excited, exciting, (*of a person's manner or of a situation*).

緊急

jǐn-'jí (*A*) urgent, critical, crucial, (*of a situation*).

緊急救護

jǐn-'jí-jyèw-'hù (*Nabstr*) first aid.

謹慎

jǐn-'shèn (*A*) to be careful, take heed, be on guard.

盡

jìn (*postV*) use up, exhaust. ‖'hwà dēw shwō-'jìn-le. Everything has been said. ‖'yān dēw chēw-'jìn-le. The cigarettes have all been smoked. ‖'tsày dēw chŕ-'jìn-le. The food's all eaten up. ‖'lù dēw dzěw-'jìn-le. (*Figuratively*) I'm at the end of the road. (I've tried every possible way and I can't find the answer.)

進

jìn (*V or I, lc*) to enter, go in, come in. jìn-'jàn to come into the station (*of a train*); jìn-'chéng to go downtown; jìn shywé-'shyàw to enter a school, to start going to a particular school; *etc. As mainV:* 'jìn-dàw (*lc*) to enter.

As postV: 'dzěw-jìn (*lc*) to walk in or go in; 'pǎw-jìn (*lc*) to run in; 'ná-jìn (*lc*) to take *something* in; *etc.* ‖chyán-'jìn! Forward! (*military*).

近

jìn (*A*) near, close, closeby; recent. ‖wǒ-dzwò-'shŕ-de-dì-fang lí-'jèr hěn-'jìn. The place where I work is quite close to here.

jìn-'r lately, in the last few days (*quite flexible*); 'jìn-lay (*Ntime*) recently; 'jìn-lay-de-'shŕ-ching recent events.

勁（兒）

jìn, jyèr (*Nmass*) energy, strength, power. yung-'jìn to strive, use effort. ‖nǐ-de-'jìn bú-'gèw. You aren't strong enough.

進步

jìn-'bù (*I*) to advance, increase, make progress. (*Nabstr*) progress, advances. ‖tā nyàn yīng-'wén jìn-'bù-de hěn 'kwày. He's making rapid progress in learning English.

157

進攻
jìn-'gūng (V) to advance and attack *a position (in fighting)*.

進展
jìn-'jǎn (I) to make progress; (*Nabstr*) progress. ‖gūng-yè-jìn-'jǎn hěn 'kwày. Industrial progress is rapid.

禁止
jìn-'jǐ (*literary*) it is forbidden to. ‖jìn-'jǐ chēw-'yān. Smoking is prohibited. ‖jìn-'jǐ rù-'nèy. No Admission. ‖jìn-'jǐ jān-'tyē. Post no bills.
    jìn *alone in a few combinations:* jìn-'jyěw prohibit (the sale, manufacture, and consumption of) liquor.

進口
jìn-'kěw (VN2) to enter port; jìn hǎy-'kěw to enter port; to be imported; jìn-kěw-'hwò imported goods.
    jìn-'kěwr (*Nunit*, ge) an entrance, an approach (*as to a bridge; also* rù-'kěw(r)).

進款
jìn-'kwǎn (*Nmass;* fèn, fèr, bǐ) income.

盡力
jìn-'lì (VN2) to try one's best. ‖jìn wǒ-de-'lì-lyang. I'll try my best.
    jìn-je 'lì (H) trying one's best, to the utmost of one's ability; jìn rén-'lì to do what is humanly possible.

盡量
jìn-'lyàng(r) (H) to full capacity. jìn-'lyàng-de 'chǐ to eat to full capacity; jìn-'lyàng-de 'dzwò to do one's utmost.

進深
'jìn-shēn (*Nmass*) depth. shì-'táy-de-'jìn-shēn the depth of 'a stage; 'fáng-dz-de-'jìn-shēr. depth of a house *measured from the door to the opposite side*.

進行
jìn-'shíng (V) to go ahead with, make headway with *some matter*.

進行曲
jìn-shíng-'chywǔ (or -chywū) (*Nunit*, dwàr, pyān) a march (*piece of music*). dzèw jìn-shíng-'chywǔ to play a march.

禁食
jìn-'shí (VN1) to fast (*a bit literary; Biblical*).

近於
'jìn-ywú (H) tending to, approaching, close to. ‖nǐ-shwō-de-'hwà yěw yì-dyǎr-'jìn-ywú-'kūng-shyǎng-le. What you say is a bit on the imaginative side.

驚
jīng (I) to be frightened, skittish, (*of a horse*). ‖mǎ 'jīng-le. The horse was frightened.

精
*jīng (H) skillfully; *confined to a few combinations*. jīng 'jwāng to bind (*books*) skillfully; jīng 'dzàw to manufacture skillfully; jīng 'shywǎn to select carefully; jīng 'jǐ to make with care, skillfully.

經
*jīng (*Nplace*) longitude. 'shī-jīng west longitude; 'dūng-jīng east longitude; 'dūng-jīng yì-bǎy-yì-shí-'bā-'dù 118 degrees east longitude.
    Also classic books; religious canons. wǔ-jīng the Five Canons of Confucius.

經(過)
'jīng(-gwò) to pass by, pass through, go by. 'jīng-le hǎw-jǐ-dàw-'shěw-le. It's passed through a number of hands. *Otherwise gwò is usually used:* ‖tsúng 'yǎ-jēw dàw 'ēw-jēw jīng-gwo húng-'hǎy. Going from Asia to Europe you pass through the Red Sea. ‖wǒ bú-'ywàn-yi jīng-'gwò nèy-swǒ-'fáng-dz. I don't want to go past that house. ‖wǒ jīng-'gwò hěn-dwō-de-'hwàn-nàn. I've been through a lot of difficulties.

驚動
jīng-'dùng (V) to disturb, arouse *a person or situation*. ‖tā shwèy-'jyàw-ne, byé jīng-'dùng ta. He's sleeping, don't arouse him.

經費
jīng-'fèy (*Nmass*, bǐ, fèn, fèr) expenses, money needed. yéw-'lì-de-jīng-'fèy money needed for travel.

驚慌
jīng-'hwāng (A) to be alarmed, excited, frightened. ‖tā hěn jīng-'hwāng-le. He got very excited.

經濟
jīng-jì (*Nabstr*) economics. jīng-jì-'shywé the study of economics; dzày jīng-'jì-shang economically, from the economic point of view; jīng-'jì dž-'lì *or* jīng-'jì dú-'lì to be economically independent.

經理
jīng-'lǐ (V) to manage (*an establishment*), to handle, take care of (*a matter*). ‖tā jīng-'lǐ jèy-jwāng-'shì-ching. He's handling this matter (*quite formal*).
    (*Npers*) manager (*of a hotel, bank, etc.*).

經歷
jīng-'lì (V) to experience, go through. ‖tā jīng-'lì-gwo hěn 'dwō-wéy-'shyǎn. He's been through a lot of danger.

經商
jīng-'shāng (*VN1*) to be engaged in business, in commerce, in trade. **jīng-'shāng-de** business man.

精神
'jīng-shen (*Nabstr*) spirits, feelings, mental outlook. ‖**'jīn-tyan nǐ-de-'jīng-shen hěn 'tùng-kwày.** You're in very good spirits today.

經售
jīng-'shèw (*V*) to have for sale, carry in stock. ‖**tām jīng-'shèw nèy-jǔng-'hwò.** They carry that merchandise.

津貼
jīng-'tyē (*Nmass;* **bǐ**) pension, subsidy, financial aid *given to supplement other resources.*

驚訝
'jīng-yà (*A*) to be surprised. ‖**'tīng-jyan jèy-jywù-'hwà, tā hěn 'jīng-yà.** He was very surprised to hear that.

經驗
jīng-'yàn (*V*) to experience. ‖**tā jīng-'yàn-gwo jèy-jyàn-'shr̀-ching.** He's been through this matter. *or* He's experienced this thing.

     (*Nunit,* **ge**) experience. ‖**tā dwèy-ywu 'nèy-jyàn-shr̀-ching yěw yí-ge-hěn-'kǔ-de-jīng-'yàn.** He had a very bitter experience in connection with that matter.

經營
jīng-'yíng (*V*) to carry on *or* to build up *a business.* As *mainV:* **jīng-'yíng-chǐ-lay** to build up *a business.* ‖**tā dzày 'nán-měy-jēw jīng-'yíng-chi-lay shù-'jyāw-'mǎy-may.** He's building up the rubber industry in South America.

井
jīng (*Nunit,* **yǎn, kěw, ge**) well (*for water*). **jīng-'shwěy** well water; **shwěy-'jīng** well for water; **yán-'jīng** salt well.

景
jīng (*Nmass,* **dwàn**) period in one's life. **hǎw-'jīng** *or* **shwèn-'jīng** lucky *or* fortunate *or* prosperous period; **hwày-'jīng** *or* **nì-'jīng** *the opposite meaning;* **wǎn-'jīng** the late period in one's life, the autumn of one's life.   *Also used for* season: **'shyà-jīng tyār** summertime, etc.

警報
jīng-'bàw (*Nunit,* **ge**) a danger signal, an alarm. **fā jīng-'bàw** to send out a danger signal.

警備
jīng-'bèy (*V*) to guard, to garrison, *a place when an emergency threatens.* ‖**jèy-ge-dì-fang dēw jīng-'bèy-hǎw-le.** This district is well guarded.

警察
jīng-'chá (*Npers*) policeman. **jīng-chá-'jǎng** chief of police; **jīng-chá-'jywú** police headquarters, station; **jīng-chá-'tīng** police bureau; **jīng-chá-dāng-'jywú** police authorities.

警告
jīng-'gàw (*V*) to warn, caution (*not as formal or serious as* **jīng-'jyè**).

景緻
'jīng-jr (*Nabstr*) beautiful or picturesque scenery. ‖**kàn nàr-de-'jīng-jr.** Look at that beautiful scenery! (*always in the landscape*).

警戒
jīng-'jye (*V*) to warn, caution. ‖**jīng-'jyè ta, shyà-'tsz̀ bú-yàw 'dzày dzwò jèy-jyàn-'shr̀.** Caution him not to do the same thing next time.

警鈴
jīng-'líng (*Nunit,* **ge**) alarm bell. ‖**jīng-'líng 'shyǎng-le.** The alarm bell has sounded.

警醒
jīng-'shǐng (*A*) vigilant, wide awake. ‖**swéy-rán hěn 'wǎn-le, kě-shr tā hěn jīng-'shǐng.** Although it's late, he's quite wide awake.

景象
jīng-'shyàng (*Nabstr*) the actual situation, the atmosphere, climate of affairs. ‖**jīng-'shyàng hěn 'tsǎn.** The situation is pitiful.

竟
jìng (*H*) always, everywhere. **jìng 'shyǎng** to think only of, to dwell on. **jìng shyā-'mēng** to be always guessing blindly, hit-or-miss. ‖**hwǒ-chē-'jàn-li jìng-shr̀ 'bīng.** The station was full of soldiers everywhere

敬
jìng (*V2*) to offer *someone something;* (*particularly*) **jìng-'rén bēy-'jyěw** to offer someone a toast, to drink a toast to someone. ‖**jè shr̀ fàn-'gwǎr 'jìng-de.** This is on the house (*a restaurant owner speaking*).

     (*V*) to respect, to worship. **jìng-'shén** to worship God, to worship a god.

靜
jìng (*A*) calm, quiet, peaceful, (*of a place, of waves, of people*). ‖**fēng 'píng 'làng 'jìng.** The wind is down and the waves are calm.

     (*H*) **jìng 'hèw** to wait quietly and patiently.

淨
jìng (*H*) only, solely. **ni jìng chr̄-'rèw bù-'shíng.** It doesn't do for you just to eat meat.

(*Aattr*) net. jìng-'lì net profit; jìng-'lyàng net weight, payload.

淨

jìng (*V*) to clean and dress *a chicken, etc.* jìng-'jī to dress a chicken.

鏡

'jìng(-dz) (*Nunit*, myàn, ge) mirror. *In compounds* mirror *or* lens. yǎn-'jìng *or* yǎn-'jyèngr glasses, spectacles.

敬啓

jìng-'chǐ *ending for a letter, equal to* respectfully yours. jìng-chǐ-'jě *at the beginning of a letter, equal to* dear sir, dear sirs. (*Both quite formal.*)

競爭

jìng-'jēng (*V, Vsent*) to be in competition, to compete. ‖tām-'lyǎ jìng-'jēng kàn shéy 'pǎw-de 'kwày. Those two are competing to see who can run faster.

敬重

jìng-'jùng (*V*) to respect *a person.*

境況

jìng-'kwàng (*Nabstr*) situation, circumstances. ‖jìng-'kwàng màn-'mār-de jwǎn-'hǎw-le. The situation is slowly changing for the better.

鏡框

jìng-'kwàngr (*Nunit*, ge) picture frame.

敬禮

jìng-'lǐ (*Nabstr*) salutation, formal gesture of greeting, salute. shyàng-'rén shíng jìng-'lǐ to make a formal gesture of greeting to someone.

競選

jìng-'shywǎn (*V*) to compete in an election for, to run for the office of. ‖tā jìng-'shywǎn dzǔng-'tǔng. He's running for president.

鏡頭

jìng-'téw (*Nunit*, ge) lens.

jo *Wade Romanization for* rę.

jou *Wade Romanization for* rew.

支

jř (*V*) to open, put up, (*a tent or umbrella*). jř-'sǎn put up an umbrella; jř-'péng to put up a tent. *As mainV:* 'jř-shàng *or* 'jř-chǐ-láy *with same meaning.* *Also* to open *a window* outwards and support *it with a rod to keep it open.*

支

jř (*V*) to get *money, pay.* jř-'shīn to get paid; jř-'chyán to get money, get money due one.

隻

jř (*Munit*) *for boats, birds, paired things, some animals, and for relatively small long inflexible objects.* One chwán (*boat*); one nyǎw (*bird*); one 'yǎ-dz (*duck*); one shěw (*hand*); one shyé (*shoe*); one yān (*cigarette*); one chyān-'b' (*pencil*); one mǔ-'jī (*hen*); one head of nyéw (*cattle*).

汁(兒)

*jř, *jér (*Nmass*) juice, sap. jywú-dz-'jř orange juice; píng-gwo-'jř apple juice; fēng-shù-'jř sap of the maple tree.

枝(兒)

*jř, *jér (*Nunit*, jř, gér) branch, limb, (*as of a tree*). shù-'jř tree limb.
    (*Munit*) a detachment of bīng (*soldiers*); a stem of hwār (*flowers*); a stick of jú-'gār (*dry bamboo*).
    Also as Munit with noun compounds containing it: yì-jř-shù-'jř a tree limb.

之

*jř *literary equivalent of* de *in its function of indicating that what precedes modifies or is attributive to what follows; occurs in some colloquial expressions.* 'X-fēn-jř-'Y (*mathematical*) Y Xths, *e.g.*, 'shř-fēn-jř-'yī one-tenth. ... jř-'jyān between, among ..., mutual among ...; ... jř-'wày outside of ..., in addition to ..., beyond ...; *similarly with* jř-'nèy, jř-'jūng, jř-'shyà, jř-'dwō *for which see the element after* jř.

知(道)

*jř, 'jř-dàw (*V, Vsent*) to know, know how, know that. *In negative is stressed either* bù-'jř-dàw *or* bù-jř-'dàw. ‖wǒ bù-jř-'dàw tā 'shéme-shř-hew 'láy. I don't know when he's coming. ‖wǒ bù-jř-'dàw dzěme 'dzwò. I don't know how to do it.
    'jř(-daw) hǎw-'dǎy to know right from wrong; jř 'shyēw-chř *or* jř-'chř to have a sense of shame, to know when one should be ashamed, to avoid doing things for which one would feel ashamed.

芝加哥

jř-jyā-'gē (*Nunique*) Chicago.

支棱

'jř-lèng (*V*) to prick up *one's ears.* 'gěw 'jř-lèng 'ěr-dwo. The dog pricks up his ears.

支路

jř-'lù (*Nunit*, tyáw) branch road, by-road.

支流

jř-'lyéw (*Nunit*, tyáw) branch river, tributary.

支票

jr̄-'pyàw (*Nunit,* **jāng**) check (*for money, not in a restaurant*). **kāy jr̄-'pyàw** to write a check.

知心

jr̄-'shīn (*or* **jr̄-dàw 'shīn**) (*VN2*) to know a friend very well, very intimately (*literally* know *his* heart); to understand people.
     jr̄-'shīn (*Npers*) bosom friend.

知識

'jr̄-shr (*Nabstr*) knowledge, education *especially that derived from experience.* ‖**rén-de-'jr̄-shr yěw-'shyàn.** Human knowledge is limited.

支使

'jr̄-shr (*V*) to order *people* around. ‖**tā 'cháng-cháng 'jr̄-shr rén.** He's always bossing people (and he himself sits there taking it easy). ·

直

jr̄ (*A*) straight; honest and upright (*of a person*); (*sometimes*) perpendicular. **jr̄-'shyàn** a straight line *or* a perpendicular line.
     (*H*) continuously, all along. **jr̄ dàw shyàn-'dzày** all along right up to the present; **jr̄ 'tsèng** to rub continuously (*as a tight heel on a shoe rubs the foot*); **jr̄ 'wèn** to inquire continuously.
     yì-'jr̄ (*H*) straight ahead, straight through. **yì-'jr̄ 'dzěw** walk straight ahead; **yì-'jr̄ dàw shyàn-'dzày** straight through to the present.

值

jr̄ (*A*) of value; inexpensive, at a bargain. ‖**'nèy-ge-dūng-shi hěn 'jr̄.** That thing is quite inexpensive.
     (*V*) to be worth *so much.* ‖**'nèy-ge-dūng-shi jr̄ 'wǔ-kwày-chyán.** That thing is worth five dollars.
     jr̄-'chyán to be valuable. **jr̄-'chyán-de-dūng-shi** a valuable thing, a thing worth money. (**'jr̄-de** *is used like* **jr̄** *in the above ways.*)
     In a number of set expressions, some a bit literary: **jr̄-bu-'dàng 'mǎy** isn't a very good buy; **bù-'jr̄-de yì-'tīng** not worth listening to; **bù-'jr̄-de yí-'kàn** not worth looking at; **bù-'jr̄-de yí-'mà** not worth scolding, beneath contempt; **bù-'jr̄ yí-'gù** (*literary*) beneath notice.

侄，侄

·'jr̄ (*Npers*) brother's child. *See Appendix A.*

值班

jr̄-'bān (*VN1*) to take one's turn at duty, to be on duty, to be on call. ‖**'jyēr shr̀-'shéy jr̄-'bān?** Who's on duty today?

直骨籠通

'jr̄-gu-lūng-tūng (*A*) having straight lines with no frills or fringes, *as a dress* (*unfavorable comment*).

‖**tā-chwān-de-'yī-fu 'jr̄-gu-lūng-tūng-de.** She wears dresses with very severe lines.

執照

jr̄-'jàw (*Nunit,* **jāng**) official license *or* certificate. **lǐng jr̄-'jàw** apply for a license. **kāy-chē-jr̄-'jàw** driving license; **jyē-hwēn-jr̄-'jàw** marriage license.

直接

'jr̄-jyē (*H; Aattr*) direct, immediate, face-to-face. ‖**wǒmen 'jr̄-jyē 'jyāw-shè.** We talked things over face-to-face. *or* We carried on direct negotiations.

執行

'jr̄-shíng (*V*) to put into effect, to put into action, (*a matter, a law, a proposal*). ‖**jèy-ge-fǎ-'lywù 'yǐ-jing 'jr̄-shíng-le.** This law has already gone into effect.
     'jr̄-shíng-de-rén an executive.

執事先生

'jr̄-shr̀-shyān-sheng *in a business letter, as a heading about half-way in between* Dear Sir *and* To Whom it May Concern, *indicating politeness when the exact name of the person addressed is not known.*

植物

'jr̄-wu (*Nabstr*) plant life, items of the vegetable kingdom. **jr̄-wu-'ywán** botanical gardens; **jr̄-wù-'shywé** botany.

職務

jr̄-'wù (*Nabstr*) a duty, responsibility, business, function. ‖**tā yěw jr̄-'wù méy-yew?** Has he been assigned any duties? ‖**shyàn-'dzày nèy-ge-jywūn-'gwān méy-yew jr̄-'wù.** At the moment that officer has no assignment.

職業

jr̄-'yè (*Nunit,* **ge**) profession, occupation, job. ‖**(dzwò) 'dày-fu shr̀ yì-jǔng-jr̄-'yè.** A doctor is (a member of) a profession.

職員

jr̄-'ywán (*Npers*) member of the staff of any large institution (*school, big office, etc.*). ·

紙

jř (*Nmass;* **jāng** a sheet of) paper. **jř-'bēy-dz** paper cups; **jř-'páy** playing cards; **jř-'shyāng-dz** cardboard box; **jř-'tyáwr** slip of paper; **jř-'yān** cigarettes (*literally* paper smoke).

止

jř (*V*) to stop the flow of *something*. **jř-'shyě** to staunch bleeding, stop bleeding; **jř-'téng** to relieve pain.
     As mainV: **'jř-jù** same as above. **bǎ hé-'lyéw 'jř-jù-le** to stop the flow of a river, dam a river. ‖**bǎ tā-de-'hwà 'jř-jù-le.** Stop his talking, make him keep quiet (*as by arguing him down, or by shushing him*).

只，祗

jř (*H*) only, just, exclusively. ‖**tā jř shyǎng nǐ-'yí-ge-rén.** He's thinking only of you. ‖**'dēng dēw 'hēy-le, wǒ-men jř 'hǎw shwèy-'jyàw.** The lights are all out, there's nothing for us to do but go to sleep.

　　jř 'yàw if only. ‖**yí-ge-'rén yì-'tyān jř 'yàw chř 'sān-dwèn-'fàn jyèw 'gèw-le.** If a man eats just three meals a day it's enough.

指

jř (*V*) to point, point out, indicate, show. **jř-'lù** to point the way, show the way. ‖**chǐng 'jř-yi-jř.** Please point.

　　'jř(-je) (*V2, Vsent*) to rely on *someone or something* for. ‖**tā 'jř-je tā-de-'běn-ling chř-'fàn.** He's relying on his capacity to eat.

　　'jř-je . . . shwō to be indicating *something* in one's speech, be speaking of *something* (*often not clearly*): ‖**nǐ 'jř-je 'shéme shwō?** Just what do you mean? What are you hinting at?

　　As mainV: **'jř-chū-láy** to show, point out.

指（頭）

*jř, 'jř-tew or 'jř-tew (*Nunit*, ge) finger. **shěw-'jř-tew** finger, **dà-shěw-'jř** or **dà-me-'jř** thumb; **jyǎw-'jř-tew** toe; **dà-jyǎw-'jř-tew** big toe. **shŕ-'jř** index finger; **jūng-'jř** middle finger; **wú-míng-'jř** fourth finger (*literally* nameless finger) **shyǎw-'jř(-tew)** little finger.

指導

jř-'dǎw (*V*) to advise, serve as advisor to; to conduct *a musical organization.* **jř-'dǎw 'shywé-sheng** to advise students, direct students *where to go to register, etc.* **jř-'dǎw yīn-ywè-'dwèy** to conduct an orchestra. **jř-dǎw-'ywán** (*musical*) conductor; advisor *for students.*

指不定

jř-bu-'dìng it's uncertain, it's not definite. ‖**jř-bu-'dìng dzěme-'yàng-le.** It's not certain what's going to happen (*but it will probably be bad*).

指點

'jř-dyǎn (*V, Vsent*) to explain something to *someone,* teach *someone how to do something by actual demonstration.* ‖**nǐ 'jř-dyǎn ta dzěme 'dzwò.** You show him how to do it.

指摘

'jř-dzé (*V*) to point out *the faults of someone,* find fault with *someone.* ‖**tā ày jř-'dzé byé-ren(-de-'tswo).** He likes to find fault with others.

指揮

'jř-hwēy (*V*) to direct, order. **jř-'hwēy chē-'mǎ** to direct traffic; **jř-'hwēy jywūn-'dwèy** to command an army. (*Vsent*) ‖**tā dzày-'nàr jř-'hwēy rén dzwò 'shř-ching.**

He was there to direct people doing things (*like a foreman or person in charge of a ceremony*).

指揮官

jř-hwēy-'gwān (*Npers*) an officer in command.

指明

jř-'míng (*V*) to point out clearly, explain, demonstrate. ‖**nǐ bǎ nǐ-de-'yì-sz dēw 'shyě-chū-lay, jř-'míng-gey ta 'kàn.** Put down your idea and explain it for him.

指南針

jř-nán-'jēn (*Nunit*, ge) compass (*for orientation*).

指示

'jř-shř (*V*) to give instructions to, instruct. (*Nunit*, ge) an instruction *how to do something.*

止於此

jř ywú-'tsz (*VN1*) to come to an end here (*literary*). ‖**jř ywú-'tsz-le-ma?** Is that all you've got to say? Is that the best you can do? ‖**tā jyèw jř ywú-'tsz-le-ma?** Has he reached the limit of what he's able to do? Is this his best? (*derogatory comment*).

制

jř (*V*) to regulate, govern, restrain. ‖**tā shyǎng-'tár 'jř-ta.** He tried to restrain him. *As mainV:* **'jr-jù** to succeed in restraining; **jř-bu-'jù** to be unable to restrain *someone.* ‖**jèy-ge-rén (wǒ) jř-bu-'jù.** This fellow is uncontrollable.

至

jř (*H*) most. **jř-'dwō** at most, at the outside; **jř-'wǎn** at the latest; **jř-'shǎw** at least, at the very least; **jř-'dzǎw** at the earliest; **jř-'gāw** at the very tallest. ‖**wǒ jř-'wǎn bú-hwèy gwò 'bā-dyǎn láy.** At the very latest it mustn't be later than eight o'clock when I get here.

治

jř (*V*) to treat, doctor, cure *an illness.* **jř-'bìng** to treat an illness. *As mainV:* **jř-'hǎw** to cure *an illness,* to be cured.

質

*jř (*N*) element. **tyě-'jř** iron as an element; **túng-'jř** copper as an element; *etc.*

志（向）

'jř(-shyang) (*Nabstr*) purpose, aim, ambition. ‖**tā-de-'jř-shyang hěn 'dà.** His ambition is very great.

制度

'jř-dù (*Nunit*, ge) system *of government, of education, of farming, of economic organization, etc.* **'jīng-jì-'jř-dù** economic system.

制動器
jr̀-dùng-'chì (Nunit, ge) brake on a wheel (not the brake lever).

製造
jr̀-'dzàw (V) to manufacture, make. jr̀-dzàw-'fǎ method of manufacture; jr̀-dzàw-'pǐn manufactured goods; jr̀-dzàw-'chǎng factory.

制服
jr̀-'fú (RC2) to control, subjugate with force or by persuasion. ‖tā bǎ-ta jr̀-'fú-le. He subjugated him. (Nunit, tàw) a (military or other) uniform.

致敬
jr̀-'jìng (VN1) to show respect, make a gesture of respect, salute. ‖tā shyàng gwó-'chí jr̀-'jìng. He saluted the flag.

置之不理
'jr̀-jr-bu-'lǐ (literary quotation) to ignore, dispose of summarily, pigeonhole. ‖wǒ 'gàw-sung ta hǎw-jǐ-'hwéy, tā dēw 'jr̀-jr-bu-'lǐ. I warned him several times, but he just ignored my warnings.

智利(國)
jr̀-'lì(-gwó) (Nunique) Chile.

秩序
'jr̀-shywù (Nabstr) degree of order or disorder. ‖'hwèy-táng-de-'jr̀-shywù hěn 'hǎw. Everything was in order and well arranged in the meeting place.

製藥
jr̀-'yàw (VN2) to compound medicines, mix prescriptions and dispense them.

志願
'jr̀-ywàn (Nunit, ge) wish, desire, purpose.

志願書
jr̀-ywàn-'shū (Nunit, jāng, ge) signed pledge, signed agreement to participate and share in profits and losses, to obey the rules, etc.

至於
'jr̀-ywu (K) as to, with reference to, with regard to. ‖'jr̀-ywu 'nèy-ge wǒ 'méy shéme 'shwō-de. I have nothing to say about that.

ju Wade Romanization for ru.

豬
jū (Nunit, ge, jr̄) pig, hog. 'mǔ-jū sow; 'gūng-jū boar; jū-'rèw pork.

珠 (子)
'jū(-dz) (Nunit, ge, kē) pearl; bead. yí-'chwàr-'jū-dz string of beads. In compounds: a small bead-like thing. yǎn-'jū pupil of the eye; hàn-'jū bead of sweat; lèy-'jū teardrop.

珠江
jū-'jyāng (Nunique) The Pearl River.

豬圈
jū-'jywàn (Nunit, ge) pig pen.

諸事不宜
'jū-shr̀ bù-'yí (literary quotation) everything is unpropitious. Said by superstitious people on a day when the stars are unfavorable. ‖'dzwó-tyan 'jū-shr̀ bù-'yí. Yesterday was unpropitious.

諸事如意
'jū-shr̀ rú-'yì (literary quotation) everything as you would wish it. ‖'jù-ni 'jū-shr̀ rú-'yì! Best wishes to you!

諸位
‖jū-'wèy! Gentlemen! or Ladies and gentlemen! (Form of address in speaking to a group of people formally.) ‖jū-'wèy-'shyān-sheng, 'tày-tay, 'shyáw-jye! Ladies and gentlemen!

豬油
jū-'yéw (Nmass) lard.

竹 (子)
'jú(-dz) (Nmass; kē, gēr) bamboo. yì-kē-'jú(-dz) or yì-kē-jú-'shù bamboo tree.

主意
jú-'yì (Nabstr) determination, will-power, clarity of plan combined with determination. ‖tā gěy-ni chū jú-'yì. He's going to make a suggestion to you based on his understanding of the situation. ‖nǐ byé lǎw gǎy jú-'yì. Don't always be changing your mind.

煮
jǔ (V) to boil. Forms VN3: jǔ-'rèw boiled meat; jǔ-'fàn boiled rice. As mainV: jǔ-'gān to boil dry; 'jǔ-shàng to put on to boil; jǔ-'shéw to boil until well-cooked or well-done.

主
*jǔ (Npers) owner of, person in authority of. jyā-'jǔ master of the house; mǎy-'jǔ purchaser; màay-'jǔ the seller, in stating the terms of a contract; dì-'jǔ land owner; tsáy-'jǔ propertied person; jày-'jǔ creditor; chwán-'jǔ captain of a ship.

主筆
jǔ-'bǐ (Npers) editor-in-chief (*the one who writes the editorials*).

主持
jǔ-'chŕ (V) to be in authority about, have charge of, direct, manage (*official, formal*). ‖shŕ-'shéy jǔ-'chŕ? Who's in charge?

主前
'jǔ-chyán (Ntime) B.C. (*among Christians*). 'jǔ-chyán 'èr-bǎy-nyán two hundred B.C.

主顧
'jǔ-gù (Npers) customer in a store.

主管
jǔ-'gwǎn (V) have charge of, direct, manage. jǔ-'gwǎn-rén-'ywán director.

主後
'jǔ-hèw (Ntime) A.D. (*among Christians*). 'jǔ-hèw 'èr-bǎy-nyán two hundred A.D.

主婚
jǔ-'hwēn (VN1) to give away the bride at a wedding. jǔ-'hwēn-rén person who gives the bride away.

主張
jǔ-'jāng (V) to advocate, propose and support, favor, *a proposal, motion, plan.* (Nunit, ge) proposal, thing advocated.

主講
jǔ-'jyǎng (I) to give the main speech, be the chief speaker *at some function.*

主角
jǔ-'jyǎw (Npers) principal character in a play *or* story.

主角
jǔ-'jywé (Npers) principal character in a play *or* story.

主人
'jǔ-rén (Npers) host; landlord. nywǔ-'jǔ-rén hostess; landlady.

主任
jǔ-'rèn (NpersT) director *of a section of a governmental or other institution.*

主席
jǔ-'shí (NpersT) chairman. *Used as title for Chiang Kai-shek because he was the chairman of the highest body in the Nationalist Government.*

主使
jǔ-'shř (V) to instigate, bring about from behind the scenes, *some unfortunate occurrence.*

主修
jǔ-'shyēw (V) to specialize in, major in *a subject in school.* jǔ-'shyēw lì-'shř to major in history.

主要
jǔ-'yàw (A) essential, of essential importance, main, chief. jǔ-'yàw-'yì-sz the main idea; jǔ-'yàw-de-'jèng-rén chief witness at a trial.

主義
jǔ-'yì (Nunit, ge) doctrine, principle, ism. gùng-chǎn-jǔ-'yì communism.
sān-mín-jǔ-'yì (*literary*) the three principles of the people (of Sun Yat-sen): mín-'dzú-jǔ-'yì the principle of nationalism; mín-'chywán-jǔ-'yì the principle of people's rights; mín-'shēng-jǔ-'yì the principle of people's livelihood.

祝
jù (V2) to wish *someone something; used in formulas like* ‖jù-ni 'jū-shř rú-'yì. I wish you the best. *or* I wish you luck.

鑄
jù (V) to make with *or* of metal, cast *metal.* jù-'chyán to coin money (*coins, not bills*); jù-'tyě to cast iron; jù jīn-'shyàng to cast a gold statue; jù jīn-'rén to cast a gold statue of a person.

註
jù (V) to write down, note down, make notes. *As mainV:* 'jù-shàng *or* 'jù-shyà-lay *with same meaning.*

住
jù (I) to stop, stay, live. *Sometimes causatively:* ‖jù-'dzwěy-ba! Shut up! *With designation of place after it:* ‖wǒ jù-'jèr hǎw. I'll just stay here. *or* I'd rather stay here.
As mainV: 'jù-dàw to stay until *a time;* 'jù-dzày to stay at, live at, stop at *a place;* jù-dzay yí-'kwàr to stay together; 'jù-shyà to settle down, stop wandering around.
As postV: 'jàn-jù to come to a halt; 'lyéw jù to detain, hold back; kàw-bu-'jù not be reliable; 'ná-jù to catch and hold onto, (*as a ball*), 'rén bu-'jù to be unable to tolerate *someone;* shěw-bu-'jù to be unable to defend; jīn-bu-'jù to be unable to bear *a pain;* 'tíng-jù to come to a halt, (*as of a car*).

築
jù (V) to build (*somewhat literary*). jù-'chéng to build a city wall; jù-'tí to build a dike; jù-'já to build a dam; jù-'chyáw to build a bridge; jù-'lù to build a highway.

蛀
jù (*V*) to eat (*of moths or other insects eating cloth*). ‖**wǒ-de-pí-dà-'yī dēw jyàw-'chúng gěy 'jù-le.** My fur coat has been eaten by moths.

柱(子)
'jù(-dz) (*Nunit*, gēr, ge) post, pillar (*always perpendicular*). **fáng-'jù** an upright beam in a house; **láng-'jù(-dz)** porch pillar.

著作
'jù-dzwò (*Nmass;* běn, pyān, jāng) literary work, (*as book, article, paper, etc.*).

住戶
'jù-hù (*Nunit*, ge, jyā) group of people living under a single roof *or* in a single house. ‖**jèy-tyáw-'jyē yěw 'wǔ-shr-jyā-'jù-hù.** There are fifty families (*or* homes) on this street.

住紮
jù-'já (*V*) to be quartered at *a place,* (*of soldiers or an army*).

著者
jù-'jě (*Npers*) writer, author (*literary*).

住址
jù-'jř (*Nunit*, ge, chù) address (*of a person*). ‖**nǐ-de-jù-'jř shr̀** (*or* dzày)-'nǎr? What's your address?

注重
jù-'jùng (*V*) to emphasize, stress. **nǐ 'gàw-sung wo yīng-gay jù-'jùng 'něy-yì-dyǎn.** Tell me which point I should emphasize.

助理
jù-'lǐ (*Npers*) an assistant (*as to a manager*).

著名
jù-'míng (*A*) famous, well-known, (*of a thing or person*). ‖**jèy-jāng-'hwàr hěn jù-'míng.** That picture is very famous.

助手
'jù-shěw (*Npers*) an assistant (*as to a doctor doing an operation, a lawyer at a trial*).

助學金
jù-shywé-'jīn (*Nmass*, bǐ, fèn, fèr, shyàng) money granted to assist one in studying, *not as any special honor as most scholarships or fellowships are.*

註冊
jù-'tsè (*VN1*) to register *in a school, in a governmental organization as for the draft, etc.* (*not in a hotel or hospital*). **jù-tsè-'bù(-dz)** register, roster (*book*).

注意
jù-'yì (*V*) to pay attention, focus the attention. ‖**chǐng-ni jù-'yì nèy-ge-'rén.** Please watch that man. *or* Please pay attention to that man (*observe what he tries to do*).
     As mainV: **jù-'yì-dàw** to pay attention to the point of, notice until *or* up to. ‖**wǒ méy-jù-'yì-daw 'nèy-ge.** I hadn't noticed that yet.

juan *Wade Romanization for* **rwan.**

jui *Wade Romanization for* **rwey.**

jun *Wade Romanization for* **rwen.**

jung *Wade Romanization for* **rung.**

鐘
jūng (*Nunit*, ge, kěw) large bell; clock. *With M* **dyǎn** (*hour or o'clock*); *with M* **kè** (*quarter-hour*); *with M* **fēn** (*minute*); *with M* **myǎw** (*second*): **lyǎng-dyǎn-'bàn(-jūng)** two thirty; **lyǎng-dyǎn-yí-'kè(-jūng)** two-fifteen; *etc.*
     'jūng-dyǎn, 'jūng-dyǎr, 'jūng-tew (*Ntime*, ge) an hour (*period of time*). ‖**yí-ge-'jūng-dyǎr 'dwō-shaw-chyán?** How much per hour?
     àn-je 'jūng-dyan on schedule.
     jūng-'léw bell tower, carrillon.

中
*****jūng** (*Demord*) *designates the middle or intermediate of three levels or stages or classifications or grades.* **jūng-'jyàng** General *or* Admiral of the middle rank; **jūng-'shyàw** Lieutenant Colonel *or* Commander; **jūng-'wèy** First Lieutenant *or* Lieutenant j. g.; **jūng-'shr̀** sergeant (*intermediate of three ranks of non-coms*); **jūng-'dwèy** squadron (*Air Forces*), *equivalent unit in certain military-like but non-Army organizations such as the police:* **jūng-'bù** middle part *or* region; **jūng-děng(-de)** average, intermediate in grade.

中(國)
*****jūng, 'jūng-gwo** (*Nunique*) China (*originally middle kingdom*). **jūng-'měy** Chinese and American; **jūng-'shī** Chinese and Western; **jūng-'wén** Chinese (written) language (*sometimes said for the spoken language*).

鍾情
jūng-'chíng (*V*) to fall in love with *a person* (*a bit literary*). **yí 'jyàn jūng-'chíng** to fall in love at first sight.

忠告
jūng-'gàw (*Vsent*) to advise, counsel *someone to do something.* (*Nabstr*) advice, counsel.

165

中古
jūng-'gǔ (Ntime) the Middle Ages (of European history).

中間（兒）
jūng-'jyān, jūng-'jyàr (Nplace) space between, among; space at the center of. dzày jèy-lyǎng-jāng-'jwō-dz(-de)-jūng-'jyàr between these two tables; dzày jèy-jāng-'jwō-dz(-de)-jūng-'jyàr in the middle of this table. ‖dzày lyǎng-ge-chéw-'dí-de jūng-'jyàr hěn 'nán dzwò-'rén. It's hard to get along when one is caught between two enemies.

中心
jūng-'shīn (Nplace) center. jūng-shīn-'dyǎn center of a circle (or figuratively). ‖Kansas City dzày 'měy-gwo-de-jūng-'shīn. Kansas City is located in the heart of the United States. ‖Kansas City shr̀ 'měy-gwo-de-jūng-shīn-'dyǎn. Kansas City is the central point of the United States.

中午
'jūng-wǔ (Ntime) noon.

中央
jūng-'yāng (Nplace) center, middle part. 'hé-de-jūng-'yāng the center of the river.
    Central; pertaining to the central government. jūng-yāng-'jèng-fǔ the Central Government (of China); jūng-yāng-yín-'háng the Central Bank of China; jūng-'yāng-'jèng-jr̀-wěy-ywán-'hwèy Central Political Council.

中用
'jūng-yùng (A) useful, (of a person, plan, procedure).

腫
jǔng (I) to swell up. ‖tā-de-'yǎn-jing 'jǔng-de hěn 'dà. His eye is all swollen up.
    As mainV: 'jǔng-chī-láy with same meaning; jǔng-'dà to swell up big; etc.
    'jǔng-shāng swollen wound.

種
jǔng (Mclass) kind of. Used with any noun at all. yì-jǔng-'rén kind of people; yì-jǔng-'jèng-fǔ kind of government; etc.
    'hwáng-jǔng-rén people of the Yellow race; etc., with other color words.

種（兒，子）
jǔng(r), 'jǔng-dz (Nmass; lì) seeds. shyà 'jǔng-dz to plant seeds.

種族
jǔng-'dzú (Nunit, ge) race (of people).

中
jùng (I) to hit the bull's-eye, hit the target. As postV: dǎ-'jùng with same meaning; shè-'jùng with same meaning, with a gun. ‖'jùng-le! A hit! ‖méy-'jùng! A miss! (V) ‖wǒ 'jùng-le dì-'èr-tyáw-'shyàn. I got a two (i.e., a hit in the number two zone of the target).

重
jùng (A) heavy; serious, weighty, important. ‖nèy-běn-'shū yěw lyǎng-bàng-'jùng. This book weighs two pounds.
    jyā-'jùng to put on weight; to emphasize. gwò-'jùng to become overweight.

種
jùng (V) to plant, grow, raise agricultural produce; to till the soil, the land. jùng-'dì to till the soil, farm; jùng-'dì-de farmer; jùng-'dèwr to plant beans; jùng-'tsày to plant vegetables; etc. jùng 'jwāng-jya to farm; jùng-'jwāng-jyà-de farmer. As mainV: 'jùng-shàng or 'jùng-shyà-chywù to plant.

種（牛）痘
jùng (nyéw-)'dèwr (VN2) to vaccinate. jùng 'lyǎng-hwéy-nyéw-'dèwr to vaccinate twice (perhaps a year apart); jùng 'lyǎng-tsz̀-nyéw-'dèwr to vaccinate twice (perhaps a day or so apart); jùng 'lyǎng-ge-nyéw-'dèwr to vaccinate twice (maybe at the same time).

中毒
jùng-'dú (VN2) to be poisoned.

中風
jùng-'fēng (I) to have a paralytic stroke. ‖tā jùng-'fēng-le 'chà-yi-dyǎr 'sz̀-le. He had a stroke and almost died.

種禍
jùng-'hwò (VN1) to sow the seeds of calamity or misfortune, do something that will lead to disaster. A longer fixed phrase for the same is jùng-'shyà-le hwò-'gēn.

重量
'jùng-lyàng (Nmass) weight. ‖jèy-ge-'dūng-shi-de-'jùng-lyàng shr̀ 'dwō-shàw? How much does this thing weigh?

重傷風
jùng-shāng-'fēng (Nabstr) influenza. dé jùng-shāng-'fēng to catch the flu.

重視
'jùng-shr̀ (V) to have a high regard for a subordinate, for a younger person, or for some matter.

重要
jùng-'yàw (A) important.

重音
jùng-'yīn (Nabstr) stress, accent, emphasis. ‖nèy-jywù-'hwà-de-jùng-'yīn dzày-'nǎr? Where should this sentence be stressed?

抓
jwā (V) (1) to scratch. jwā-'téw to scratch one's head, etc.‖'māw 'jwā-le wo yí-'shyàr. The cat scratched me. (2) To grasp in the hand. jwā-'dzéy to nab a thief. As mainV: 'jwā-chǐ-láy to pick up, or to arrest or nab a person; jwā-'dzěw to arrest someone; 'jwā-jù to hold something firmly in the hand.

抓鬮
jwā-'jyēw (VN1) to draw lots.

專
jwān (H) only and exclusively. ‖wǒ 'jwān kàn 'nèy-běn-shū. I read this book exclusively. (Stronger than jǐ, and implying by one's own choice.)

磚
jwān (Nunit, kwày) bricks. jwān-'dàw brick road; jwān-'fáng brick house.
    pū-'jwān to pave with bricks; chì-'jwān or mǎ-'jwān to build with bricks.

專制
jwān-'jr̀ (A) despotic. jwān-jr̀-'jèng-tǐ an autocracy.

專門
jwān-'mén, jwān-'mér (VN2) to specialize. jwān 'nǎ-yì-mér? specialize in what?
    jwān-'mén-de specialist; jwān-'mén-de-'dày-fu specialist (doctor); 'kwèng-yè-jwān-'mén-de specialist in mining.

專門家
jwān(-mén)-'jyā (Npers) specialist.

轉
jwǎn (I and causative) to make a partial turn (less than 360 degrees); to transfer, forward, transmit. jwǎn-'shēn to turn around (of a person); jwǎn-'lyǎr to turn away from (literally or figuratively); jwǎn-'fēng (IN) the wind changes direction, or (figuratively) conditions are improving; jwǎn-'shìn to forward mail.
    As mainV: 'jwǎn-dàw (lc) to forward mail to a place; 'jwǎn-gwò (lc) to turn around, e.g., jwǎn-gwò 'shēn-lay to turn around facing the speaker, jwǎn-gwò 'shēn-chywu to turn around facing away from the speaker; 'jwǎn-hwéy (lc) to turn back, double back.

轉變
jwǎn-'byàn (V) to change (as one's attitude). jwǎn-byàn 'tày-du to change one's attitude..

轉機
jwǎn-'jī (I) to take a turn for the better.

轉運
jwǎn-'ywùn (V) to ship, convey goods. As mainV: jwǎn-'ywùn-dàw (lc) to ship to a place.
    jwǎn-'ywùn-'gūng-sz̄ express company, moving company.

轉
jwàn (I and causative) to turn (especially of a full 360-degree circuit). jwàn-'wār to turn a corner (at an angle), or to go in a circle; jwàn-'lyǎr like jwàn-'lyǎr; 'jwàn-yi-jwàn to turn around (as in screwing on a cap). As mainV: 'jwàn-gwò (lc) to turn oneself around; 'jwàn-dàw (lc) to turn to a place, a point, a degree.
    'jwàn-láy jwàn-'chywù to mill around (as a crowd).

賺
jwàn (V) to earn, make money. jwàn-'chyán to make money; jwàn-'lì to make a profit.
    As mainV: 'jwàn-gwò with same meaning. jwàn-gwò 'lì to make a profit; 'jwàn-hwéy-lay to recover financially.

傳記
jwàn-'jì (Nunit, běn, pyān) a biography.

裝
jwāng (V) to pack, load something; to pack into or on a container or holder; to carry, hold, (of a container). jwāng-'chyāng to load a gun; jwāng 'gwàn-tew to pack in cans, to can; jwāng 'héer-li to put into boxes; jwāng-'hwò to pack merchandise; 'chē(-li) 'jwāng hěn-dwō-de-'hwò the car holds a lot of goods.
    As mainV: 'jwāng-dàw, 'jwāng-dzày to load something into or on; 'jwāng-shàng to load on; jwāng-'mǎn to pack full; jwāng-'hǎw be finished packing; 'jwāng-shyà to load up; jwāng-bu-'shyà won't hold so much.
    The thing loaded may be anything. bǎ-'jyěw jwāng-dzay 'píng-dz-li put liquor up in bottles.

裝
jwāng (V) to imitate, make up like, act the role of; to affect the manners and appearance of, disguise oneself as. ‖tā 'jwāng dzǔng-'tǔng. He disguised himself as the president. ‖jūng-gwo-'shì-li-tew yěw hěn-dwō-'nán-de jwāng 'nywǔ-de. In Chinese plays many male actors play female parts.
    jwāng 'sz̄ to feign death; jwāng 'bìng to feign illness, malinger.

椿
jwǎng (Mclass) a line of 'mǎy-may (business) ; (Munit) a fairly large-scale 'shr̀(-ching) (affair, matter, enterprise). (Nunit, ge) post, stake, pile.

裝訂
jwǎng-'dǐng (V) to bind books.

莊子
'jwǎng-dz (Nunit, ge) small rural farming settlement of a few families; a farmstead.

庄稼，莊家
'jwǎng-jya (Nunit, ge) a farm; (Nabstr) crops. 'jwǎng-jya-rén (or -rér) farmers, peasants.

裝模作樣
jwǎng-'mwó dzwò-'yàng (I) to assume airs, to put on airs, to be haughty, to pretend to sophistication.

裝飾
'jwǎng-shr̀ (V) to decorate, dress up, put a display (in a store window for example) ; to make up, use cosmetics and dress. ‖nèy-ge-'nywǔ-rén 'jwǎng-shr-de hěn 'lì-hay. That woman makes up very heavily.

莊嚴
'jwǎng-yán (A) serious, formal, stern, imposing. ‖tā-de-'tày-du hěn 'jwǎng-yán. His manner is dignified and imposing.

壯
jwàng (A) strong, healthy. ‖tā 'jǎng-de hěn 'jwàng. He's very healtay.

撞
jwàng (V) to run into, dash into, collide with. jwàng-'rén to hit someone (as when driving a car) ; jwàng-'chē to have a collision.
   As mainV: jwàng-'hwày to collide with and crack up; jwàng-'dǎw te overturn by running into.

拽
jwày (V) to pull something, the person pulling being at rest. As mainV: 'jwày-dàw (lc) to pull something to a place; etc.

准
jwěn (Vsent) permit someone to do something, allow, let (quite formal). ‖'jwěn-ta 'jìn-lay. Let him come in.
   As mainV: 'jwěn-gěy give permission to someone.

準
jwěn (A) accurate, (of schedules, times, timepieces, predictions). ‖nǐ-de-'byǎw 'dzěw-de 'jwěn-bu-jwěn? Does your watch run accurately?

準備
jwěn-'bèy (Vpred) to get ready to, prepare to, to inten to. As mainV: jwěn-bèy-'hǎw to be ready. ‖tā jwěn-'bèy 'dzěw. He's preparing to leave. or He's planning to leave. ‖tā jwěn-bèy-'hǎw-le jyèw yàw 'dzěw. He's all ready and is going right away.

準確
jwěn-'chywè (A) accurate, exact, precise. ‖tā 'shwō-de hěn jwěn-'chywè(-de). He speaks very accurately. ‖'shyāw-shi hěn jwěn-'chywè(-de). The news is quite accurate.

準得
jwěn-'děy (Vpred) must certainly. ‖nǐ chr̄-'wán nèy-ge-'gwā jwěn-děy 'bìng. If you eat that melon up you'll certainly get sick.

準時
jwěn-'shŕ (H) on time, on schedule. ‖'chē jwěn-'shŕ 'dàw-de. The train arrived on time.

准許
jwěn-'shywǔ (Vsent) permit, allow someone to do something. (Same as jwěn alone.)

追
jwēy (V) to chase after, pursue, catch up with (literally or figuratively). As mainV: 'jwēy-shàng catch up with, overtake; jwēy-'dzěw to chase away. ‖tā shywé 'yīng-wén shywé-de hěn 'hǎw; wǒ shyǎng bǎ-ta 'jwēy-shang. He's learning English very well; I want to catch up with him.

錐子
'jwēy-dz (Nunit, ge) awl.

追究
jwēy-'jyēw (V) to inquire, look into, investigate, dig into. ‖wǒ-men yàw jwēy-'jyēw tā dzěme 'sž-de. We'll look into the circumstances of his death.

墜子
jwèy-dz (Nunit, jr̆; fù for a set) earrings.

墜入情網
'jwèy-rù chíng-'wǎng (VN1) to fall very deeply in love (literary).

墜胎
jwèy-'tāy (VN1) to have an abortion, miscarriage. (N) abortion, miscarriage.

桌(子，兒)
*jwō, 'jwō-dz, jwōer (Nunit, jāng) table. jwō-'yǐ (Ncoll; fù) chairs and tables, furniture; jwō-'twěy, jwō-'twěr, jwō-dz-'twěy table legs; jwō-'myàr top of a table; jwō-'bù (Nunit, kwày) tablecloth; shū-'jwō desk; fàn-'jwō dining table.

鐲子
'jwó-dz (*Nunit*, ge, jī; fù *for* a set) bracelet.

夾
jyā (*V*) to carry, hold, between the upper arm and body, *or between two flat surfaces pressed together* (*as between the palms or between the pages of a book*); to sandwich *something between other things*. **'jyā-dz** (*Nunit*, ge) a folder; other holders of that kind.

As main V: **'jyā-dzày** to carry thus at or in a particular holder. **jyā-dzay 'shū-li** to carry in a book; **jyā-dzay 'shěw-li** to carry between the palms; **'jyā-chǐ-láy** to file away (*as a document*), to get hold of *something in this way;* **'jyā-shàng** to pin down, fasten down *thus;* **jyā-dzày jūng-'jyān** to be caught between things, to be involved.

家
jyā (*Nunit*, ge) home, family. **hwéy-'jyā** (*with or without lc*) go home, come home, go back home, come back home. ‖**tā-'jyā-li yěw 'dwō-shaw-rén?** How many are there °in his household? *or* °in his family?

(*Mgroup*) household, *in taking census and the like:* ‖**jèy-ge-'tswēn-dz-li yí-'gùng yěw 'sān-shr-jyā.** Altogether there are thirty households °in that village. *In kinship terms:* **lǎw-'jyār** (my) parents (*quite colloquial and informal*); **jyā-'jǎng** head *or* heads of a family (*oldest males*).

See also Appendix A.

佳
jyā (*A*) good (*literary*, hǎw). **'jyā-rén** beautiful gïrl (*also literary*).

家
jyā (*Munit*) for stores, business establishment. A **'pù-dz** (*store*), a **gūng-'sz** (*department store*), *etc.*

家
***jyā** (*Npers*) one who specializes as a technical expert *in such-and-such.* **jwān-mén-'jyā** a specialist; **kē-shywé-'jyā** a scientist; **lì-shř-'jyā** historian.

加
jyā (*V*) to add, increase, raise. **jyā-'chyán** to get a raise; **jyā-'shīn** to get a raise in salary; **jyā-'yán** to add (more) salt; **jyā-'yéw** to increase the gasoline intake, step on the gas, (*figuratively*) work harder.

Often used with an A instead of a N after it: **jyā-'jùng** to add weight, emphasize, stress, to put on weight; **jyā-'chyáng** to become stronger; **jyā-'jǐn** to speed up, to increase efforts; **'jyā (yì-)dyǎr-'shyǎw-shīn** to be a little more careful.

As main V: **'jyā-chǐ-láy** add up, add together; **'jyā-dzày** add to; **jyā-dzay yí-'kwàr** add together; **'jyā-dàw** add to; **'jyā-shàng** add up.

'**èr jyā-'èr dé-'sż.** Two and two is four.

家產
jyā-'chǎn (*Nmass*) family property, estate.

家當
'jyā-dangr (*Nunit*, ge) items of family belongings, substance, fortune.

家賊
jyā-'dzéy (*Npers*) a thief in the house, one who pulls an inside job. ‖**jyā-'dzéy nán 'fáng.** It's hard to defend against a thief in the house.

加足
jyā-'dzú (*RC2, potential forms not used*) to store up *or* acquire sufficiently. ‖**'chì-yéw děy jyā-'dzú-le.** We must be sure to have enough gasoline.

咖啡
jyā-'fēy (*Nmass*) coffee.

傢伙
'jyā-hwo (*Nunit*, ge)· tools, implements, utensils. **hwày-'jyā-hwo** bad implement *or* **méy-'yùng-de-'jyā-hwo** useless tool *is said of a person to mean* hopeless *or* useless creature.

傢具
'jyā-jywù (*Nunit*, jyàn) furniture.

嘉陵江
jyā-líng-'jyāng (*Nunique*) The Kaling River.

加侖
jyā-'lwén (*Mmeas*) gallon.

加拿大
jyā-ná-'dà (*Nunique*) Canada.

加入
jyā-'rù (*V*) to enter into, join, start to participate in. **jyā-'rù jywù-lwò-'bù** to join a club.

嘉興
jyā-'shīng (*Nunique*) Chia-hsing *or* Kashing (*city in Chekiang province*).

家世
'jyā-shr̀ (*Nabstr*) family, ancestry. ‖**tā-de-'jyā-shr̀ hěn 'dī.** He's of humble birth.

家鄉
jyā-'shyāng (*Nplace*) ancestral home (*region or city, not house*).

加速板
jyā-sù-'bǎn (*Nunit*, ge, kwày) accelerator pedal in a car.

家庭

'jyā-tíng   (*Nunit, ge*)   family.   jyā-tíng-'shēng-hwó family life, domestic existence; jyā-tíng-lǐ-'bày religious worship *or* ceremony carried on within the family.

家務 (事)

'jyā-wu *or* jyā-wù-'shř (*Nabstr*) family matters, family affairs.

假

jyǎ (*A*) false, counterfeit, artificial.   jyǎ-'yá false teeth. ‖tā shwō jyǎ-'hwà. He's lying.

     (*H*) falsely. ‖tā jyǎ 'shyàw-le. He smiled a false smile (pretending friendship where there was none).

假裝

jyǎ-'jwāng (*Vpred*) to pretend to, to do *such-and-such* falsely, deceptively. ‖tā jyǎ-'jwāng 'ày-ta. He pretended to love her.

假冒爲善

jyǎ-màw-wéy-'shàn (*literary quotation*) hypocritical. ‖tā shř jyǎ-màw-wéy-'shàn-de-rén. He's a hypocrite.

假意

jyǎ-'yǐ-de (*H*) falsely, deceptively, in order to deceive people. ‖tā jyǎ-'yì-de shwō . . . He said, deceively, ...

價

jyà (*Nunit, ge*) a price.   gěy-'jyà to name a price; hwán-'jyà to bargain, to haggle (*of the purchaser*); jyàw-'jyà to name a price (*of the seller*); 'jyà-chyán the price, the amount asked for *or* paid.

嫁

jyà (*I*) to get married (*of a girl*). As mainV: 'jyà-gěy to marry *a husband*, or to give *a girl* in marriage. ‖tā 'yǐ-jing 'jyà-le. She's already married. ‖tā yàw 'jyà-gey ta. She's going to marry him. ‖tā-'fù-chin bǎ-ta 'jyà-gey nèy-ge-'rén. Her father is giving her in marriage to that man.

嫁

jyà (*V*) to shift *blame, etc.*   jyà-'hwò gěy-ta shift the blame to him.

架

jyà (*Munit*) a fēy-'jī (*airplane*) and for most other N ending in jī; a pair of wàng-ywǎn-'jìng (*field glasses*); a shū-'jyà (*bookshelf*); *etc.*

架

jyà (*V*) to support, as on a framework or scaffolding, or with the hands and arms; to hold *thus*.

     As *mainV*: 'jyà-chi-lay to prop up; jyà-'dzěw to force *someone* to go by grabbing him and pushing him along; 'jyà-shàng to prop up; 'jyà-dzày to prop something up on *or* at. ‖bǎ 'hwày-le-de-'jwō-dz yùng-'jwǎn 'jyà-chi-lay. Prop the (broken) table up with bricks. ‖bǎ dzwèy-'gwěy jyà-'dzěw-le. The drunkard was taken away.

假

jyà (*Nmass*) vacation period.   fàng-'jyà to have a vacation; fàng yì-tyān-'jyà to have a day off; gàw-'jyà to ask for time off, to ask for leave.

架

*jyà, 'jyà-dz, *jyàr (*Nunit, ge*) (1) a shelf, a scaffolding.   shū-'jyà bookshelf; hwā-'jyà a shelf for flowers; yī-'jyà frame for hanging clothes; pú-taw-'jyà grape arbor.

     (2) Pride, dignity.   dā 'jyà-dz *or* bǎy 'jyà-dz to build up *or* maintain one's dignity too much.

假期

jyà-'chī, jyà-'chí (*Ntime*) holiday season.   dzày jyà-'chī-de-shŕ-hew dàw hǎy-'byār chywù to go to the shore for the holiday *or* during the holidays.

價格

jyà-'gé (*Nabstr*) price-range. ‖nǐ 'mày-de shř shéme-jyà-'gé-de-'hwò? What's the price-range of the goods you sell?

價值

'jyà-jr (*Nabstr*) value (*monetary, or, figuratively*). ‖tā-de-'hwà méy 'jyà-jr. What he says is of no value.

價牌

jyà-'pár (*Nunit, ge*) price tag.

駕駛員

jyà-shř-'ywán (*Npers*) pilot (*plane or boat*).

價條

jyà-'tyáwr (*Nunit, ge*) a price tag.

尖

jyān (*A*) sharp (*of a point, not of an edge*).   As *postV*: mwó-'jyān to grind (*metal*) to a sharp point; shyēw-'jyān to sharpen *a pencil, etc.* ‖tā-de-'dzwěy hěn 'jyān. He has a sharp tongue (*literally* mouth) *or* He has protruding lips.

煎

jyān (*V*) to fry on a greased surface without mixing or stirring.   *Forms VN3:* jyān-jī-'dzěr fried eggs, *etc.*

間

jyān (*Munit*) one.   One 'wū-dz (*room*); one 'fáng-dz (*room*).   'fáng-jyān hotel room, quarters.

奸

jyān (A) crafty, cunning, villainous, false (of a person).
jyān-'shyàw (I) to smile craftily, treacherously.

肩 [膞（兒）]

jyān (literary), **jyān-'băng(r)** (colloquial) (Nunit, **ge**)
the shoulder (including the shoulder-blade area).

堅持

jyān-'chŕ (A) be insistent, hold to one's own idea. (V)
to hold to, maintain unaltered. ‖**tā jyān-'chŕ tā-'dz̆-jĭ-de-'yì-jyàn.** He held persistently to his own ideas.
‖**tā jyān-'chŕ dàw-'dĭ.** He stuck to his own idea to the
end. or He held fast to the end.
    jyān-'chŕ bú-'ràng to take a firm stand and stick to
it stubbornly.

堅強

jyān-'chyáng (A) strong in character, persistent. ‖**wŏm-de-dà-dzŭng-'tŭng-de-'yì-jŕ hěn jyān-'chyáng.** Our
president has a very strong and stable will.

監督

jyān-'dū (V) to supervise (people, workers). (Npers)
supervisor; **shywé-sheng-jyān-'dū** supervisor of students.

間諜

jyān-'dyé (Npers) spy.

堅固

jyān-'gù (A) stable, strong. ‖**'jwō-dz bù-jyān-'gù.** The
table isn't stable.

監禁

jyān-'jìn (V) to imprison. ‖**jyān-'jìn ta.** Put him in
prison.
    As mainV: **jyān-'jìn-chĭ-láy** with same meaning;
jyān-'jìn-dzày to imprison someone in a place.

堅決

jyān-'jywé (A) to have one's mind firmly made up. ‖**ta-de-'tày-du hěn jyān-'jywé.** His attitude is completely
fixed.

監牢獄

jyān-láw-'ywù (or **jyān-'láw, jyān-'ywù, láw-'ywù**)
(Nunit, **ge**) prison, jail.

艱難

jyān-'nán (A) difficult to take care of, difficult to control,
hard to master (of a matter).

奸淫，姦淫

jyān-'yín (Nabstr) adultery, fornication. **gēn ... fàn**
(or **tūng**) **jyān-'yín** to commit adultery with.

檢

jyăn (V) to pick up with the hand; to choose, select.
jyăn 'yí-ge to choose one.
    As mainV: **'jyăn-chĭ-láy** to pick up; **'jyăn-chū-láy**
to pick out. ‖**jèy-ge-'dūng-shi shŕ 'jyăn-de.** This thing
was picked up (having been lost by someone). ‖**nèy-ge-'bīng tì nèy-ge-hăw-'kàn-de-'gū-nyang jyăn shěw-'jywàr.** That soldier picked up the good-looking girl's
handkerchief. or That soldier picked out a handker-
chief for that good-looking girl.

減

jyăn (V) to reduce, decrease. **jyăn-'shīn** to get a cut in
salary, to cut salaries. As mainV: **'jyăn-chywù** take
away (decrease by so much); **jyăn-'shăw** or **'jyăn-shyà**
to decrease, lessen.
    jyăn-'jyà (VN2) to reduce prices or to hold a sale,
or (N) a sale. **'dà-jyăn-'jyà** Big Sale.
    (K) minus. ‖**'sż jyăn-'èr dé-'èr.** Four minus two is
two. ‖**'èr jyăn-'sż dé 'fù-èr.** Two minus four is minus
two.

剪

jyăn (V) to clip, cut with scissors; **jyăn-'tsàw** to cut the
grass, mow the lawn. As mainV: **'jyăn-kāy** to cut
apart; **jyăn-'dwàn** to cut into segments; **'jyăn-chéng**
to cut into pieces, etc.
    'jyăn-dz (Nunit, **bă**) scissors.

鹼

jyăn (Nmass) lye. **yí-kwày-'jyăn** a cake of prepared lye
for washing.
    In compounds alkaline.

檢查

jyăn-'chá (V) to inspect, check up, examine. ‖**shwèy-'gwān-de-rén jyăn-'chá 'shyāng-dz.** The customs officials examine the baggage.

簡單

jyăn-'dān (A) simple (of a method, plan, idea).

簡章

jyăn-'jāng (Nunit, **fèr, běn, jāng**) a school bulletin (booklet, posted notice, etc.).

簡直

jyăn-'jŕ (H) simply, just. **nĭ jyăn-'jŕ bù-jŕ-'dàw.** (In
other words) you just don't know.

減價

jyăn-'jyà (VN1) to reduce prices, hold a bargain sale.
‖**shyàn-dzày 'dà jyăn-'jyà.** Big Sale on Now.

簡捷了當

jyăn-'jyé lyăw-'dàng (literary quotation) direct, frank,
to the point.

儉樸
jyǎn-'pǔ (A) thrifty in one's ways, given to a simple life.

儉省
jyǎn-'shěng (A) thrifty (complimentary comment). (I) be thrifty. ‖nǐ-de-'chyán jyǎn-'shěng-je yùng. Be thrifty with your money.

檢驗
jyǎn-'yàn (V) test (technically). jyǎn-'yàn yàw-'pǐn to test medicines (try them out on guinea pigs, analyze them chemically).

檢閱
jyǎn-'ywè (V) to review troops.

賤
jyàn (A) cheap; low, mean, humble, low-class (derogatory). jyàn-'jyà chū-'mày for sale at a low price, for sale cheap. ‖jèy-ge-dūng-shi hěn 'jyàn. This thing is °of poor quality. or °quite low priced. ‖jèy-ge-'jyà-chyán hěn 'jyàn. The price is quite reasonable.

濺
jyàn (V2) to splash. jyàn-wo yì-'shēn splashed me all over; jyàn-wo yì-'twěy splashed my leg. ‖chē 'dzěw-gwò-chywu de-shŕ-hew 'jyàn-wo yì-shēn-'ní. When the car drove by it splashed me all over with mud.
    As mainV: jyàn-'dzāng to splash and dirty.

箭
jyàn (Nunit, gēn, jŕ) arrow. shè-'jyàn shoot an arrow; gūng-'jyàn bow and arrow.

建
jyàn (V) to found, establish, set up. jyàn shywé-'shyàw to found a school; jyàn-'gwó to found a nation.

見
jyàn (V) to meet, talk with, see, consult, interview, have contact with. jyàn-'myàn to meet (face-to-face).
    Followed by A: to seem, appear; jyàn 'hǎw to seem better, appear to be well; jyàn 'lǎw to look old, look older than one's real age; jyàn 'shīn to refinish, remodel, make something look like new.
    As mainV: 'jyàn-jáw to succeed in meeting, interviewing, talking to; jyàn-bu-'jáw to be unable to get in and interview or to see someone hard to get to.
    As postV, with mainV of perception: 'kàn-jyàn to see; 'tīng-jyàn to hear; 'wén-jyàn to smell; 'pèng-jyàn, 'ywù-jyàn to meet accidentally, etc.

艦
*jyàn (Nunit, jŕ, tyáw) ship (particularly in naval terms). jyàn-'chyáw bridge of a battleship; jyàn-'dwèy fleet; jyàn-'jǎng captain of a ship, skipper;

jàn-'jyàn battleship; háng-kūng-mǔ-'jyàn aircraft carrier.

件
jyàn (Munit) a 'shŕ(-ching) (affair, matter of business, matter) and with any word which has more or less the same type of abstract meaning. An article of 'yī-fu (clothing) and for many words for specific garments; an article of 'jyā-jywù (furniture; but not for specific pieces of furniture); a piece of 'shíng-li (baggage) and for specific words for things carried; a wén-'jyǎn (document).

鍵子
'jyàn-dz (Nunit, ge) a key (on a typewriter or piano).

見方
jyàn-'fāng square. 'sż-lǐ-jyàn-'fāng four miles square (sixteen square miles); 'èr-lǐ-jyàn-'fāng two miles square (four square miles). ‖'jèy-yí-kwày-'dì shŕ 'wǔ-lǐ-jyàn-'fāng. This piece of land is five miles square.

建築
'jyàn-jù, jyàn-'jú (V) to build, make. 'jyàn-jù 'fáng-dz, 'chyáw, 'lù to build houses, bridges, roads.

建築師
jyàn-jù-'shŕ (Npers) architect.

漸漸的
jyàn-'jyàn-de (H) gradually. ‖tā jyàn-'jyàn-de bǎ-'bìng yǎng-'hǎw-le. He gradually got over his illness.

見解
'jyàn-jyě (Nunit, ge) opinion, view. ‖tā-de-'jyàn-jye hěn 'gāw. He's very wise (that is, his viewpoint is high because of a wealth of experience). ‖jèy-ge-rén hěn yěw 'jyàn-jye. He has good judgment.

健康
'jyàn-kāng (A) healthy.

建設
jyàn-'shè (V) to establish firmly, found, develop. jyàn-'shè shywé-'shyàw to found a school; jyàn-'shè gwó-'jyā to build up a nation industrially or economically.

薦信
jyàn-'shìn (Nunit, fēng) a letter of introduction, of recommendation.

建議
jyàn-'yì (V, Ksent) to suggest, propose; to suggest that, propose that. (Nunit, ge) proposal, suggestion.

將
jyāng (H) only, barely, just. ‖jè-shyē-'chyán 'jyāng(-jyāng) 'gèw. This money will just barely be enough.

漿
jyāng (V) to starch; **jyāng 'yī-fu** to starch clothing.

江都
jyāng-'dū (Nunique) Chiang-tu (city in Kiangsu province).

僵局
'jyāng-jywú (Nunit, ge) atmosphere of (social) tension, the "ice" that one breaks; deadlock, impasse. ‖**shyǎng-'fár 'jyě-le jèy-ge-'jyāng-jywú.** Try to break the deadlock.

將來
'jyāng-láy (Ntime) from now on, hereafter, in the future; later. ‖**nǐ 'jyāng-láy jyèw 'jř-dàw-le.** You'll know it later. ‖**'jyāng-láy-de-'shř-ching mey-yew rén 'jř-dàw.** No one can foretell the future.

韁繩
'jyāng-shéng (Nunit, tyáw) reins. **lā 'jyāng-shéng** to pull on the reins.

江西
jyāng-'shī (Nunique) Kiangsi province.

江蘇
jyāng-'sū (Nunique) Kiangsu province.

講
jyǎng (V) to explain, expound upon. ‖**chǐng-ni bǎ jèy-ge-'wèn-tí 'dzày 'jyǎng-yi-jyǎng.** Please explain the problem again.

As mainV: **'jyǎng-dàw** to reach a point, a conclusion *in an exposition or debate;* **jyǎng-'tūng** to convince, reason with and convince; **jyǎng-'hwà** to speak; **jyǎng-'lǐ** to argue logically, appeal to reason; **jyǎng-'jyà(r)** to bargain, haggle.

jyǎng-'ywán (Npers) a speaker (one who gives a formal talk).

獎
jyǎng (Nunit, ge) reward, prize; **dé-'jyǎng** win a prize, earn a reward.

講和
jyǎng-'hé (VN1) to negotiate peace, make peace; put out a peace feeler.

獎章
jyǎng-'jāng (Nunit, ge) a medal or insigne given as a reward; medal of honor.

獎金
jyǎng-'jīn (Nmass, fèn, fèr, bǐ) a monetary reward, prize.

講究
'jyǎng-jyēw (A) to be meticulous, particular; (V) to be meticulous or particular about. ‖**tā-'nèy-ge-rén hěn 'jyǎng-jyēw °'yī-fu** or °'**chwān.** He's very meticulous about °his clothes or °what he wears.
(V) to care a great deal about, to take care in.

獎勵
jyǎng-'lì (V, Vsent) to give someone a reward as an encouragement for further work.

獎品
jyǎng-'pǐn (Nunit, ge) a prize. **dé ivǎng-'pǐn** to win a prize.

獎學金
jyǎng-shywé-'jīn (Nmass, fèn, fèr, bǐ) scholarship, fellowship.

講廳
jyǎng-'tīng (Nunit, jyān) a lecture hall.

講演
jyǎng-'yǎn (V) to give a speech about, to talk formally on a subject. (Nunit, pyān, tsž) a speech.

降
jyàng (I) to descend, fall, drop, go down. *Figuratively:* **jyàng-'bān** to flunk and stay in the same year's work another year.
As mainV: **'jyàng-dàw** to fall to (e.g., **'dì-shang** the earth); **'jyàng-shyà** to descend. ‖**fēy-jī 'jyàng-shyà-lay-le.** The plane landed. or The plane fell.

將
***jyàng** (Npers) officer of general or admiral rank. **jyàng-'gwān** general or admiral; **shàw-'jyàng** lowest rank, **jūng-'jyàng** middle rank; **shàng-'jyàng** top rank.

強
jyàng (A) to be stubborn, hard to convince.

漿子, 漿糊
'jyàng-dz or **'jyàng-hú** (Nmass) paste (adhesive).

強嘴
jyàng-'dzwěy (VN1) to shoot off one's mouth, to talk back, argue, complain; to be stubborn.

降落
jyàng-'lwò (I) to descend, come down; land (of a plane). **jyàng-lwò-'chǎng** landing field for planes or gliders, parachute landing area.
jyàng-lwò-'sǎn parachute.

醬油
jyàng-'yéw (Nmass) soya bean sauce.

教
yāw (*V*) to teach *a person or a subject*. (*V2*) to teach *someone something*. **jyāw-'shū** to teach. *As mainV:* **'jyāw-gěy** to teach *someone* (*how to do something*).

跤
jyāw (*Msemel*) a fall, a tumble. **'shwāy-le yì-jyāw** to take a tumble.

交
jyāw (*V2*) to hand over, turn over, deliver, commit, *something to someone*. **jyāw-ni 'sz̀-kwày-chyán** turn four dollars over to you. *As mainV:* **'jyāw-gěy** *with same meaning;* **'jyāw-gěy ... 'gwǎn** to turn *something* over to *such-and-such a person* to take care of, to put *something* in *someone's* care; **'jyāw-chū-lay** to hand out; **'jyāw-jìn** (*lc*) to turn *something* in.
   jyāw-'chyán to make payments; **jyāw 'péng-yew** to make friends; **jyāw hwèy-'fèy** to pay dues.

焦
jyāw (*I*) to shrivel up and turn color through burning; to burn (*as of food*). ‖**fàn 'jyāw-le!** The rice is burning!
   As postV: **shāw-'jyāw-le** to boil and accidentally burn; *similarly with other mainV for methods of cooking.*

澆
jyāw (*V*) to water *flowers, land*. *As mainV:* **jyāw-'shř-le** *with same meaning.*

驕傲
jyāw(-'àw) (*A*) proud, conceited, snooty.

交情
'jyāw-chíng (*Nabstr*) friendship. **yěw 'jyāw-chíng** be friendly, be friends.

交換
jyāw-'hwàn (*V*) to trade, exchange, barter. **jyāw-'hwàn 'míng-pyàn** to exchange greeting cards; **jyāw-'hwàn fú-'lǔ** to exchange prisoners.

交戰
jyāw-'jàn (*VN1*) to join battle, start to fight. **jyāw-jàn-'gwó** belligerent countries (*international law*).

交界
jyāw-'jyè (*VN1*) to meet at a border. **lyǎng-'gwó jyāw-'jyè-de-dì-fang** the place where two countries come together, frontier.

膠卷
jyāw-'jywǎr (*Nunit*, ge, jywǎn, jywǎr) a reel of film.

膠水
jyāw-'shwěr (*Nmass*) glue, mucilage, gum.

交響樂
jyāw-shyǎng-'ywè (*Nunit*, dwàn, dwàr) a symphony (*composition*).

交通
jyāw-'tūng (*Nabstr*) communication and transportation; traffic. **jyāw-'tūng-de-'gwēy-jywu** traffic rules. **jyāw-tūng-'bù** Ministry of Communication. **jyāw-tūng-yín-'háng** The Bank of Communication (*one of the Chinese government banks*).

交易
jyāw-'yì (*V*) to exchange. **jyāw-'yì gǔ-'pyàw** to deal in stocks; **jyāw-'yì gūng-'jày** to deal in government bonds.
   jyāw-yì-'swǒ the stock exchange.

嚼
jyáw (*V*) to chew. *As mainV:* **jyáw-'swèy** to chew up thoroughly; **jyáw-'dùng** to chew up; **jyáw-bu-'dùng** to be unable to chew (*because of toughness*).
   'jyáw-dz (*Nunit*, ge; fù) bit (*for a horse*).

腳
jyǎw (*Nunit*, jř) foot. **jyǎw-'jř-tew** toe; **dà-jyǎw-'jř-tew** big toe.

繳
jyǎw (*V*) to turn in *something due*; **jyǎw-'chyán** to turn in a fee, money due; **jyǎw-'jywàn** to turn in an examination paper. *As mainV:* **'jyǎw-jìn** (*lc*) *same meaning;* **'jyǎw-shàng** (*lc*) to submit.

攪
jyǎw (*V*) to stir, stir up. **bǎ-'fàn 'jyǎw-yi-jyǎw** stir the rice a bit.
   To disturb, annoy, arouse *people*.
   As mainV: **'jyǎw-chǐ-láy** to stir up; **jyǎw-'lwàn** stir up, mix up; **jyǎw-'shǐng** to awaken *someone* by disturbing him. ‖**'dǎ-jyǎw dǎ-jyǎw!** (*a polite phrase*) Sorry to have disturbed you. *or* Forgive me for taking your time.

鉸
jyǎw (*V*) to cut (*as with scissors, a lawnmower, a scythe*); **jyǎw-'tsǎw** to cut the grass. *As mainV:* **'jyǎw-kāy** cut apart, cut loose; **'jyǎw-shyà-lay** to cut down; **jyǎw-'dwàn** to cut into segments; **'jyǎw-chéng** to cut into *so many pieces; etc.*

角
jyǎw(r) (*Mpos*) an angle, corner. **'jwǒ-dz-de-sz̀-'jyǎwr** the four corners of the table; **yí-ge-'sān-jyǎwr(-shíng)** a triangle (*geometry*); **dì-'jyǎw(r)** a point of land (*jutting into water*) *or* (*figuratively*) the ends of the earth, far far away; **sān-shr-wǔ-'dù-de-'jyǎwr** a thirty-five degree angle.
   (*Nunit*, ge) a horn *on an animal;* **nyéw-'jyǎw** a cow's horns.

較比
jyǎw-'bǐ (K; H) as compared with; relatively. *Same as* 'bǐ-jyàw *and* bǐ.

脚步
jyǎw-'bù(r) (Nunit, ge, bù) a footstep, pace, step. jyǎw-bùr-'shēng-yīn the sound of footsteps.

校對
jyǎw-'dwèy see jyàw-'dwèy.

脚墊
jyǎw-'dyàn(-dz), jyǎw-'dyàr (Nunit, ge) a doormat.

脚骨
jyǎw-'gǔ (Nunit, ge) a foot bone.

脚行
jyǎw-'háng (Npers) porter at a station, redcap.

脚後跟
jyǎw-'hèw-gēn (Nunit, ge) heel of the foot.

狡猾
jyǎw-'hwá (A) cunning, wily, clever.

脚掌
jyǎw-'jǎng(r) (Nunit, ge) sole of the foot. jyǎw-'jǎng (tày) 'píng have flat feet, fallen arches.

脚鷄眼
jyǎw-'jī-yǎn (Nunit, ge) corn (on the foot). jǎng jyǎw-'jī-yǎn to have corns grow.

脚尖
jyǎw-'jyār (Nunit, ge) toe of the foot (not the separate toes).

脚色
jyǎw-'sè (Npers) a person playing a part, role; a figure. ‖tā shr̀ yí-ge-hěn-'yàw-jǐn-de-jyǎw-'sè. He's a very important figure. or He plays a very important part.

繳械
jyǎw-'shyè (VN1) to surrender one's weapons (having been defeated).

脚踏車
jyǎw-tà-'chē (Nunit, lyàng) bicycle. chí jyǎw-tà-'chē to ride a bicycle.

脚腕(子，兒)
jyǎw-'wàn(-dz), jyǎw-'wàr (Nunit, ge) ankle.

脚歪
jyǎw 'wǎy (N and I) sprain or turn one's ankle. ‖wǒ jyǎw 'wǎy-le. or wǒ 'wǎy-le 'jyǎw. I turned my ankle.

脚印兒
jyǎw-'yèr (Nunit, ge) footprint.

呌，叫
jyàw (V) to be called, named, termed. ‖'jèy-ge-dūng-shi jyàw 'shéme? What's this thing called? ‖'jūng-gwó-hwà 'jèy-ge jyàw 'shéme? What's this called in Chinese?

(Vsent) to call on, select, beg, elect, appoint, require, force, someone to do something; to demand that, ask that, insist that someone do something. ‖wǒ-men jyàw-ta dzwò 'shū-ji. We selected him to be secretary. ‖shr̀-'shéy jyàw-ni 'láy-de? Who told you to come?

(V) to order. jyàw-'méy to order coal; jyàw-'tsày to order dishes in a restaurant; jyàw wǎn-'fàn to order dinner; jyàw-'chē call a cab; with special meaning jyàw dyàn-'hwà make a phone call; jyàw-'dzwèr to draw a crowd (as of a particular program).

As mainV, may have any of the above meanings: 'jyàw-chǐ-lay to yell out loud, scream; 'jyàw-chū-lay to yell out, speak out (not be able to keep quiet because of joy or sorrow, etc.) or to call someone out; jyàw-'dzěw to call someone away, to be called away; jyàw-'shǐng to awaken someone by calling him; jyàw-'tūng to put through a phone call; jyàw-bu-'tūng can't get through.

(Vsent) to cause someone to do something: jyàw-rén nán-'gwò makes people feel sorry; jyàw-rén jàw-'lyáng causes colds, gives rise to colds; jyàw-rén 'hú-dù confuses people.

(K) marks agent: ‖'shù jyàw-'fēng (gěy) gwā-'dǎw-le. The tree was blown over by the wind. ‖tā jyàw-rén 'dǎ-le. He got beaten up by somebody.

教
jyàw (V) same as jyāw to teach, but most often used in the following combinations: jyàw-'shywé to teach school; jyàw-'kè to give lessons, teach school.

窨
jyàw (Nunit, ge) underground storage place or cell. dì-'jyàw same meaning.

教
*jyàw (Nunit, ge) doctrine, teaching, religious faith. fwó-'jyàw Buddhism; jī-dū-'jyàw Protestantism; tyān-jǔ-'jyàw Catholicism; dàw-'jyàw Taoism; dzūng-'jyàw (Nunit, ge) a religion; jǔ-'jyàw (Npers) bishop; etc.; jyàw-'táng (Nunit, ge) a church (religious building or meeting place). In other compounds often has the meaning teaching rather than religious teaching.

校對
'jyàw-dwèy (V) to proofread. ‖jèy-pyān-de-wén-'jāng shr̀-'shéy 'jyàw-dwèy-de? Who proofread this article?

校正
'jyàw-jèng (*V*) to make corrections in, correct. ‖**chǐng-ni gěy-wo 'jyàw-jèng wǒ-de-'tswèr.** Please correct my errors.

叫化子
jyàw-'hwā-dz (*Npers*) a beggar.

叫喚
'jyàw-hwan (*I*) to cry out, scream.

教課書
jyàw-kè-'shū (*Nunit, běn*) textbook.

教授
jyàw-'shèw (*Npers*) a professor.

教士
'jyàw-shr̀ (*Npers*) an evangelist, teacher of religion.

教訓
'jyàw-shywùn (*V*) to give moral instruction to; to scold, admonish. (*Nunit, ge*) a moral lesson; **dé yí-ge-'jyàw-shywùn** to learn a lesson (*from some experience*).

教員
jyàw-'ywán (*Npers*) a teacher, school teacher.

教育
'jyàw-ywù (*Nabstr*) education. **chéng-rén-'jyàw-ywù** adult education.

街
jyē (*Nunit, tyáw, dàw*) street. (*Mord*): **sān-'jyē** Third Street; **jyē-'kěw(r)** entrance to a street; street intersection; **shǐn-jyē-'kěw(r)** New Street—*often a designation for a fairly old street because it was new when it got the name.*

結
jyē (*V*) to enter into a contract, conclude a contract. **jyē-'hwēn** (*VN2*) to get married; **jyē-'méng** (*VN2*) to make an alliance, enter into an alliance.
　　Also to develop, grow, *in these combinations*: **jyē-'dzěr** to go to seed (*of a flower*); **jyē-'gwǒ** to bear fruit (*of a plant*); **jyē 'gū-du** to develop buds, to bud; **jyē-'wǎng** to make a web *or* net (*as of a spider*); **jyē-'shè** to form an association, a club.

間
jyē (*K*) skipping certain specified members of a series. ‖**nǐ 'jyē yì-tyān 'láy yì-hwéy.** Come every other day. ‖**nǐ 'jyē lyǎng-tyān 'láy yì-hwéy.** Come every third day. ‖**'jyē jǐ-tyān dzày 'shwō.** Wait a few days and then we'll talk about it. ‖**nǐ 'jyē yí-ge-dz̀ 'shyě yí-ge-dz̀.** Write down every other character.

接
jyē (*V*) to receive *guests, mail, etc.;* to catch *a ball;* to meet *someone coming from elsewhere, as at the station.* **jyē 'kè-rén** to meet *or* receive guests; **jyē-'chyéwr** to catch a ball; **jyē-'chē** to meet the train (*in order to meet someone coming on it*); **dàw hwǒ-chē-'jàn chyẁù jyē-'rén** go to the station to meet someone. *With special meaning* **jyē dyàn-'hwà** to answer the phone.
　　As mainV also means to connect. **'jyē-dàw** to receive (*as mail*), *or* to connect *something* to *something;* **'jyē-gwò** (*lc*) to accept *something* and take it over (*literally or figuratively*); **jyē-jìn** (*lc*) to usher in, to receive and conduct *a guest* in; **jyē-jù** to catch and hold, succeed in catching (*as a ball*); **jyē-shang** to connect *things* together, tie, join *things* together; **jyē-bu-'shàng** can't get in touch, can't establish contact.
　　'jyē-je (*H*) continuing, going on, *or* tying in where one left off when interrupted. ‖**tām 'jyē-je tán-'hwà.** They continued to talk. ‖**děng yì-hwěr tā 'jyē-je shwō ....** A little later he picked up the thread again and said ....

接班
jyē-'bān (*VN2*) to take a turn. ‖**shyàn-dzày shr̀-'tā jyē-'bān.** Now it's his turn.

接辦
jyē-'bàn (*V*) to take over the management *or* conduct of an office, a business matter, etc.

接待
jyē-'dày (*V*) to receive *guests* (*in the sense of greeting them upon arrival and entertaining them*). ‖**'kè-rén láy de shŕ-hew 'méy-yew rén jyē-'dày tā-men.** When the guests arrived there was no one there to receive them.

街坊
'jyē-fang (*Npers*) neighbor on the same street.

結果
jyē-'gwǒ, jyé-'gwǒ (*Nunit, ge*) a solution, an answer *to a problem;* outcome, final score *of a game or contest.* ‖**jèy-ge-'wèn-tí-ya, méy jyē-'gwǒ.** Now for this problem, there's just no answer. ‖**bǐ-'sày-de-jyē-'gwǒ bú-'tswò.** The outcome of the game was OK.
　　(*V*) to put an end to. ‖**tā jyē-'gwǒ-le 'nèy-ge-rén.** He got rid of that fellow (*either fired him, or broke off relations with him, or gave him his walking papers, or killed him*).

階級
'jyē-ji (*Nunit, ge*) class; rank (*military*). **'nèy-ge-jyē-ji-de-rén** that class of people, social class. ‖**nèy-ge-jywūn-'gwān shr̀ shéme-'jyē-ji?** What rank is that officer?

接濟
jyē-'jì (V2) to supply *someone with something*. jyē-'jì jywūn-'dwèy jywūn-'hwǒ to supply the army with arms.
    (*Nmass*) supplies.

接近
jyē-'jìn (A) to be close, *physically or figuratively*. ‖jèy-lyǎng-ge-'dì-fang hěn jyē-'jìn. These two places are very close together.

接見
jyē-'jyàn (V) to receive *a visitor, an interviewer, more or less formally*. ‖tā méy 'gūng-fu jyē-'jyàn ni. He's too busy to see you.

結論
jyē-'lwèn (*Nunit*, ge) conclusion, decision. ‖nǐm 'dé-le shéme-jyē-'lwèn-le? What conclusion have you reached?

接收
'jyē-shèw (V) to receive, take over, *something sent or transferred*.

接受
'jyē-shèw (V) to accept (*as a gift from someone, or a compliment, a kind word, a recommendation, an opinion, a suggestion*). ‖wǒ 'jyē-shèw nǐ-dè-'yì-jyàn. I accept your suggestion.

結實
'jyē-shr (A) solid, strong, durable, well-built (*of a thing or a person*).

接棧生
jyē-shyàn-'shēng (*Npers*) central (*telephone operator*).

結束
'jyē-sù, 'jyé-sù (V) to conclude, bring to an end, *an activity, a matter of business*; to close up *an office and its activities*. ‖jèy-ge-dì-fang dàw 'lyèw-ywè jyèw 'jyé-sù-le. This place is going to close down in June (*of a government office or the like*).

接吻
jyē-'wěn (VN2) to kiss. ‖tā gēn-ta jyē jǐ-ge-'wěn. He kissed her several times.

截
jyé (V) to cut *or* cut apart *something having length*, to separate, cut off. *Mainly as mainV:* 'jyé-jù *or* jyé-'jǐ to cut *someone* off, (*as traffic cuts a person off from chasing someone else*); jyé-'dwàn to cut into segments, cut off a segment of. ‖wǒ shwō-'hwà de-shŕ-hew tā bǎ-wo 'jyé-jù-le. While I was talking he cut me off, interrupted me, made me stop.

節
jyé (*Nunit*, ge) festival. gwò-'jyé to celebrate a festival; wǔ-ywè-'jyé the May festival.

截
jyé (*Mauton*) segment, portion, *of something long*. yì-'jyé-de-'cháng-chung a segment of a snake; yì-'jyé-yì-'jyé-de segment by segment. ‖jèy-ge-'hwā-wén shŕ yì-'jyé-yì-'jyé-de. The pattern is a repeating one (*figure repeated at regular intervals*).

刦
jyé (V) to rob, plunder; jyé-'dàwr-de highway robber.

結果
jyé-'gwǒ *see* jyē-'gwǒ.

竭力
jyé-'lì (*Vpred*) to try hard to, endeavour to. ‖tā jyé-'lì nyàn-'shū. He tried hard to study. *or* He studied hard.
    jyé-'lì-de (H) hard, with effort. ‖tā jyé-'lì-de 'pǎw. He ran hard.

節略
jyé-'lywè (*Nunit*, pyān, dwàn, dwàr, jāng, ge) summary; memorandum (*diplomatic*). shyě yí-dwàr-jyé-'lywè to write *or* prepare a summary.

節目
'jyé-mù (*Nunit*, ge) program *or* schedule (*as at a theater*). jyé-mù-'dān (*Nunit*, jāng) playbill, printed (written) listing of scheduled events.

解
jyě (V) to relieve tension, to loosen, to release. jyě-'mèr to relieve loneliness, to entertain, amuse; jyě-'kě to relieve thirst; jyě-'è to relieve hunger; jyě lǐng-'dày to untie a necktie.
    As mainV: 'jyě-kāy to untie *a knot, a necktie, etc.*: jyě-'sūng to loosen *a knot, a necktie, etc.*: jyě-'sàn to disperse, scatter; to dissolve *a parliament*: jyě-'fàng to emáncipate.

姊
*jyě (*Npers*) older sister *or* female cousin. *See Appendix A*.

解除
jyě-'chú (V) to get rid of, eliminate (*formal*). jyě-'chú tyáw-'ywē to terminate a treaty; jyě-'chú jywūn-'bèy to disarm.
    jyě-chú-jǐng-'bàw the all-clear signal (*air raid*).

解凍
jyě-'dùng (I) to melt *ice*. ‖hé jyě-'dùng-le. The (*ice on the*) river has melted.

節子
'jyě-dz or jyē-dz (*Nunit*, ge) knot in wood: shù-'jyě-dz, mù-'jyě-dz knot in a tree, in wood.

結子
'jyě-dz or jyēer (*Nunit*, ge) knot *in cord or rope;* dǎ ge-jyēer tie a knot.

解決
jyě-'jywé (*V*) to solve *a problem.* ‖rǐ 'ké-yi-bu-ké-yi jyě-'jywé jèy-ge-'wèn-tí? Can you solve this problem? jyě-'jywé-de-'fāng-fa method of solution. ‖wǒ 'bǎ-ta gěy jyě-'jywé-le. I got rid of him. *or* I solved the problem he represented for us. *or* I killed him.

解剖
jyě-'pěw (*VN1*) to dissect a human body, (*particularly*) a cadaver. jyě-pěw-'shywé anatomy.

解手（兒）
jyě-'shěw(r) (*VN1*) to urinate (*often used euphemism*).

解釋
'jyě-shr̀ (*V*) to explain. ‖nǐ 'jyě-shr̀-jyě-shr jèy-jywù-'hwà. Explain this sentence. ‖chǐng-ni 'jyě-shr 'wèy-shéme dzwò 'nèy-jyàn-shr̀? Can you explain why you did that?

借
jyè (*V*) to borrow. jyè-'chyán to borrow money; gēn yín-'háng jyè-'chyán to borrow money at the bank; jyè-'jày to borrow money; jyè 'kwǎn to borrow large sums of money (*as a country might*); jyè-'shū borrow a book; gēn tú-shū-'gwǎn jyè-'shū borrow books from a library.
  As mainV: 'jyè-lay to borrow *also* 'jyè-chywù *and* jyè-'dzěw. jyè-'chū-chywu to lend out; 'jyè-gěy (*with two objects*) to lend *someone something.*

藉着
'jyè-je (*K*) by means of, making use of. ‖wǒ-men jyè-je nèy-ge-'chyáw gwò-le 'hé. We crossed the river by using the bridge. ‖jyè-je hěn-dwō-de-'bīng wǒm 'tsáy néng dǎ-'shèng. We can only win by using a great many soldiers.

界
*jyè (*Nunit*, tyáw) boundary, limit. gwó-'jyè border of a country; shěng-'jyè border of a province or state; jyè-'shyàn (*Nunit*, tyáw) a boundary line.
  gwò-'jyè to cross a boundary.

間壁兒
jyè-'byǎr (*Nplace*) next door. jyè-'byǎr-nèy-ge-'fáng-dz the house next door; jyè-'byǎr-de-rén next door neighbors.

借字
jyè-'dzèr (*Nunit*, jāng) promissory note, an I.O.U.

戒指
'jyè-jr (*Nunit*, ge) (finger) ring.

介紹
'jyè-shaw (*V2*) to introduce. ‖wǒ 'jyè-shaw ni yí-ge-'péng-yew. *or* wǒ gěy-ni 'jyè-shaw yí-ge-'péng-yew. I'll introduce someone to you who will be your friend. ‖wǒ 'gěy ni-men 'jyè-shaw. I'll introduce you. ‖chǐng gěy 'jyè-shaw. Please introduce us.
  jyè-shaw-'rén one who introduces; jyè-shaw-'shìn a letter of introduction.

介意
jyè-'yì (*VN1*) to feel offended, be hurt; to pay attention. ‖byé jyè-'yì. Don't take offense. ‖'nèy-jyàn-shr̀-ching 'bú-yàw jyè-'yì. Pay no attention to that matter.

借約
jyè-'ywē (*Nunit*, jāng) note kept by creditor, an I.O.U

今兒（個）
'jyēr(-ge) (*Ntime*) *same as* 'jīn-tyan today.

揪
jyēw (*V*) to seize with the hand, (*as when taking someone by the scruff of the neck*). *AsmainV:* 'jyēw-jù or jyēw-shàng to seize *thus* and bring to a halt, *or* to seize firmly. ‖tā jyēw-je 'shéng-dz bù-sā-'shěw. He held tightly to the rope and wouldn't let go. ‖tā 'jyēw-jù tā-de-'lǐng-dz 'twēy-ta. He seized him by the collar and shook him.

究竟
jyēw-'jìng or jyèw-'jìng (*J*) after all, in the end, finally. jyèw-'jìng tā 'wèy-shéme bù-néng 'láy? After all, what is the real reason he can't come? (*literaw*).

九
jyěw (*NumU*) nine.

酒
jyěw (*Nmass*) liquor, wine, any kind of alcoholic beverage. jyěw-'chì liquor breath, smell of liquor.

久
jyěw (*A, H*) long (*of time*); for a long time. hǎw jyěw méy-'jyàn! Long time no see! ‖nǐ láy-'jèr hěn 'jyěw-le-ba! Have you been here for quite a time? ‖wǒ-men bù-'jyěw jyèw yàw 'dzěw-le. We'll be going before long now.

酒館
jyěw-'gwǎn(-dz), jyěw-'gwǎr (*Nunit*, jyǎ, ge) bar (*for drinks*).

酒精

jyěw-'jīng (*Nmass*) alcohol (*ethyl, grain*).

九江

jyěw-'jyāng (*Nunique*) Chiu-chiang or Kiukiang (*city in Kiangsi province*).

九龍

jyěw-'lúng (*Nunique*) Kowloon (*city in Kwangtung province*).

就

jyèw (*H*) (1) then, immediately then, *often introducing statement of consequence after a condition containing* yī once, as soon as. ‖wǒ yī 'dàw, tā jyèw 'dzěw-le. As soon as I arrived he left. ‖'fàn jyèw 'dé-le. Dinner will be ready right away.

(2) *In a statement of result, after a condition with* rè-shr *or* yàw-shr, *where the condition and the result are in contrast:* ‖nǐ yàw 'dǎ-ta, tā jyèw 'chì-le. If you hit him he's going to get mad.

With (1) *compare* tsáy *then and only then, no sooner, not otherwise; with* (2) *compare* yě, *used when the result is parallel to the condition* (*i.e.,* If you go I'll go too).

(3) Just, exclusively, nothing but. ‖jèy-ge-'háy-dz 'jyèw chyàn 'dǎ-le. This kid's got to get a beating; that's all there is to it.

救

jyèw (*V*) to save, deliver, rescue, aid. ‖jyèw-'mìng! Help! save (my) life! ‖jyèw tā-de-'mìng. Save his life.

jyèw-'hwǒ to extinguish a fire, a conflagration.

As main V: 'jyèw-chū-lay rescue *someone*: 'jyèw-chǐ-láy rescue someone *from a river, etc.;* 'jyèw-gwò-lay to bring someone back to life, revive (*as from a faint*).

舊

jyèw (*A*) old *usually of a thing, but* 'jyèw-rén an old employee. 'jyèw-nyán the past year, last year.

舅

*jyèw (*Npers*) mother's brother. *See Appendix A.*

就地

jyèw-'dì (*Nplace*) right on the spot, right there, at that very place and time. ‖nǐ háy-shr jyèw-'dì chywǔ-'tsáy-ba. Just get your material (*or* personnel) right here locally.

救護

'jyèw-hù (*V*) to save and protect; to salvage. 'jyèw-hù shāng-'bīng to bring in the wounded (soldiers).

jyèw-hù-'ywán a lifeguard; jyèw-hù-'dwèy ambulance corps; jyèw-hù-'chē ambulance.

救火車

jyèw-hwǒ-'chē (*Nunit*, lyàng) fire engine.

救濟

'jyèw-jì (*V*) to extend relief to, relieve the distress of; jyèw-ji 'chyúng-rén to help the poor (*with money or food*).

救濟會

jyèw-jì-'hwèy (*Nunit*, ge) a relief society or benevolent society. ‖húng-shŕ-dz-'hwèy shr̀ yì-jǔng-de-jyèw-ì-'hwèy. The Red Cross is a kind of relief society.

舊金山

jyèw-jīn-'shān (*Nunique*) San Francisco.

究竟

jyèw-'jìng *see* jyēw-'jìng.

就職

jyèw-'jŕ (*VN2*) to take up a post, a position, assume a function. ‖tā láy-'jèr jyèw shéme-'jŕ? What's his job going to be here?

救生船

jyèw-shēng-'chwán (*Nunit*, jī, tyáw, ge) lifeboat.

救生帶

jyèw-shēng-'dày (*Nunit*, ge) life belt.

就是

'jyèw-shr (*J*) (1) indeed is, is definitely. ‖'jèy-běn-shū jyèw-shr 'wǒ-shyě-de. This is the book I wrote. *Compare* ‖'jèy-běn-shū shr̀ 'wǒ-shyě-de. This is a book I wrote. *or* I wrote this book.

(2) Even if. jyèw-shr 'dzèm-je even if this is so. ‖'jyèw-shr nǐ 'láy, wǒ yě bú-'chywù. Even if you come, I won't go.

(3) 'bú-shr ... 'jyèw-shr ... if it isn't *this* then it's *that,* either ... or .... ‖bú-shr 'tā-dzwò-de jyèw-shr 'nǐ-dzwò-de. Either he did it or you did.

(4) Regardless. ‖wǒ 'jyèw-shr bú-'chywù! I'm just not going, that's all there is to it!

就事情

jyèw 'shr̀(-ching) (*VN2*) to take on a job, to take a post, assume a duty.

就許

'jyèw-shywǔ (*J*) maybe, perhaps, probably (*more probably than* 'yě-shywǔ *which indicates hesitation*).

窘

jyǔng (*A*) hard up, poor, embarrassing. ‖tā 'jīng-jì hěn 'jyǔng. He's hard up economically. ‖jèy-ge-'chíng-shíng hěn 'jyǔng. This situation is very embarrassing.

圈

jywān (*V*) to imprison, fence in, confine. *As mainV:* **'jywān-chǐ-láy** *or* **'jywān-shàng** *with same meaning;* **'jywān-dzày** to confine, *etc.*, *at a place:* **jywān-dzay yí-'kwàr** imprison together, fence in together.

捐

jywān (*V2*) to give, donate, will, contribute *something to someone.*

    (*V*) **jywān-'chyán** to donate money *or* to raise money by subscription or donations.

    Most often as mainV: **'jywān-gěy** *with same meaning.* **‖tā bǎ tā-de-tsáy-'chǎn-de-yí-'bàr jywān-gey húng-shí-dz-'hwèy.** He willed half his property to the Red Cross.

卷

jywǎn (*V*) to roll up, *as a rug or other flat flexible thing.* *As mainV:* **'jywǎn-chǐ-láy** *with same meaning:* **'jywǎn-chū-láy** to roll up with *a specified side* outward. (*Opposites:* to unroll, *as a scroll, is* **'dǎ-kāy**; to unroll *or* pull down, *as a rolled screen, is* **'fàng-shyà-lay** *or* **'lā-shyà-lay.**)

卷 (兒)

jywǎn, jywǎr (*Munit*) a roll of, reel of. **yì-jywǎr-dyàn-'yǐng** a reel of movie film; **yì-jywǎr-'hwàr** a rolled-up scroll painting; **yì-jywǎr-de-'shéng-dz** a reel of rope; **jyāw-'jywǎr** picture film in rolled form.

卷子

'jywǎn-dz (*Nunit*, **jāng**, **ge**) an examination paper. **jyāw 'jywàn(-dz)** to turn in one's examination papers (*of student*); **shyě 'jywàn-dz** to take a written examination; **fā 'jywàn-dz** to pass out examination papers (*before the examination, or after correction*).

撅

jywē (*V*) to break *something long* by grasping at the ends and applying bending pressure. (*Compare* **bāy**, *which need not be applied to a long object.*) *As mainV:* **jywē-'shé** *with same meaning:* **'jywē-chéng (lyǎng-'dwàr)** to break (*thus*) into (two segments).

撅嘴

jywē-'dzwěy (*VN1*) to purse the lips. **jywē-je 'dzwěy** with pursed lips, pursing the lips.

蹶過去

'jywē-gwò-chywù (*I*) to faint and fall over.

掘

jywé (*V*) to dig (*especially by pushing some implement straight down and then flipping or forcing the dirt out; compare* **páw**, **wā**). **jywé-'jǐng** to dig a well. *As mainV:* **'jywé-kāy** *with same meaning.*

決

jywé (*H*) unquestionably, really, completely, definitely, *before statements of possibility.* **‖tā 'jywé hwèy shwō hěn-'hǎw-de-jūng-gwo-'hwà.** He really can speak excellent Chinese. **‖jywé kàn-bu-'jyàn.** It's completely impossible to see it.

    Usually before **bū** *or* **méy:** **‖tā 'jywé bù-'dzěw.** He's definitely not going.

    Occasionally otherwise: **‖tā jywé 'dzěw.** He's definitely going (*but* **yí-'dìng** *is commoner in this case*).

覺

jywé: **'jywé-je** (*Vpred, Vsent*) to be feeling (that). **‖wǒ 'jywé-je bù-hǎw-'yì-sz.** I feel ashamed. **'wǒ 'yěw yì-dyǎr-'jywé-je tā bù-'hwáy hǎw-'yì.** I'm coming to feel that he's not playing entirely square with us.

    As mainV: **'jywé-chū-lay** to discover that *such-and-such is the case.*

絕版

jywé-'bǎn (*VN1*) to go out of print (*a book*).

覺得

'jywe-de (*Vsent*) to consider that, feel that, be of the opinion that, suspect that. **‖wǒ bù-'jywé-de nèy-ge 'pyán-yì.** I don't call that cheap.

    (*Vpred*) to feel *with adjective following.* **‖wǒ 'jywé-de hěn 'hǎw.** I feel fine. **‖wǒ 'jywé-de 'shēn-dz hěn 'hǎw.** *or* **wǒ 'shēn-dz 'jywé-de hěn 'hǎw.** I feel fine (*specifically physically*).

    (*V*) **‖wǒ bù-'jywé-de 'jèy-yàngr.** I'm not of that opinion. *or* I don't feel that that's so.

決定

jywé-'dìng (*RC2*) to decide, to settle definitely, (*a plan or a problem*). **‖tā bù-néng jywé-'dìng dzěme 'dzwò.** He can't decide what to do.

決斷

jywé-'dwàn (*Nabstr*) ability to make quick and definite decisions. **‖'jèy-ge-rén hěn yěw jywé-'dwàn.** He has great ability to make good decisions quickly.

絕對

jywé-'dwèy (*H*) (*intensified* **jywé** unquestionably) beyond any doubt whatsoever.

覺乎

'jywé-hu *same as* **'jywé-je** (see under **jywé**).

絕交

jywé-'jyāw (*VN1*) to break off with *someone.* **‖wǒ gēn-ta jywé-'jyāw-le.** I've broken off with him.

絕裂

jywé-'lyè (*I*) to break off with *someone.* **‖wǒ gēn-ta jywé-'lyè-le.** I've broken off with him.

决赛

jywé-'sày (*VN1*) to hold *or* participate in the final competition *or* contest, *after a series of preliminaries.* (*Nabstr*) final competition; final heat of a race.

决心

jywé-'shīn (*Vpred*) to make up one's mind definitely, decide to, resolve to. ‖**tā méy-jywé-'shīn 'hwéy-lay.** He hasn't decided to come back.

    shyà jywé-'shīn (*VN1*) used *similarly.*

    jywé-'shīn-de (*A, H*) resolute, determined; resolutely.

爵位

jywé-'wèy (*Nunit, ge*) title. **yěw jywé-'wèy** to be titled, have a title, be of the nobility or royalty. **yěw shéme-jywé-'wèy?** has what title?

jywen *Romanization found in Spoken Chinese, Basic Course (EM 506, 507), for syllables spelled* **jywun** *in this dictionary.*

菊花（兒）

jywū-'hwā(r) *or* **jywú-'hwā(r)** (*Nunit, dwǒ, dwěr*) chrysanthemum.

居民

jywū-'mín (*Npers*) inhabitant, resident. **jèy-ge-'chéng-de-jywū-'mín** the residents of this city (*formal term*).

拘泥

'jywū-nì (*V*) to be petty or formalistic about, to be inclined to stick to all the little regulations about. ‖**tā jìng 'jywū-nì 'shyǎw-de-'shr̀-ching.** He's always so darned formal about every little thing.

居然

'jywū-rán (*J*) contrary to expectations, *and therefore* surprisingly. ‖**'jywū-rán nèy-ge-'hwày-rén hwèy byàn-'hǎw-le!** Isn't it strange that bad egg should be able to turn over a new leaf! ‖**tā 'jywū-rán fǎn-'dwèy 'jèng-fǔ!** He really is daring to oppose the government!

拘束

'jywū-su (*A*) to feel ill at ease because of the requirements of formality. ‖**byé 'jywū-su!** Make yourself at home. *or* Feel at your ease.

局

*****jywú** (*Nunit, ge*) government and other offices of various kinds. **yéw-jèng-'jywú** post office; **dyàn-bàw-'jywú** telegraph office; **dyàn-hwà-'jywú** a telephone central (*the place*) *or* business office; **gūng-ān-'jywú** police station; **fēn-'jywú** a branch office; **jywú-'jǎng** person in charge of such an office.

橘（子）

*****jywú, 'jywú-dz** (*Nunit, ge*) orange; tangerine. **jywú (-dz)-'jr̄** orange juice; **jywú(-dz)-'pí** orange rind;

jywú-hwáng-'sè, jywú-hwáng-'shǎr orange color; **jywú-'hwáng** (*A*) orange (*color*).

菊花

jywú-'hwā(r) *see* **jywū-'hwā(r).**

局势

'jywú-shr̀ (*Nabstr*) situation, outlook, prospects. ‖**shyàn-dzày jàn-jēng-'jywú-shr̀ hěn 'hǎw.** Right now the military situation is good.

举

jywǔ (*V*) to hold *or* lift overhead with one or both hands (*but not on the flat of the hand like a tray*). **jywǔ-'shěw** to raise the hand(s) overhead, to hold the hand up. ‖**nǐ-men-'dzàn-chéng-de-rén dēw chǐng jywǔ-'shěw.** All those in favor raise their hands.

    As mainV: **'jywǔ-chǐ-láy** *with same meaning.* **'jywǔ-chū-láy** pick out and specify (*figuratively, as of ideas*).

一举成名

yì-'jywǔ chéng-'míng (*literary quotation*) to become famous all of a sudden, attain fame overnight.

举动

jywǔ-'dùng (*Nabstr*) action, conduct, behavior. ‖**tā-de-jywǔ-'dùng hěn chí-'gwày.** His behavior is very strange.

举行

jywǔ-'shíng (*V*) to hold *ceremonies.* ‖**tām dzày lǐ-bày-táng jywǔ-'shíng hwēn-'lǐ.** They held the wedding in the church.

锯

jywù (*V*) to saw. *As mainV:* **'jywù-kāy** to saw apart; **'jywù-chéng** to saw into *two, etc.;* **'jywù-shyà-lay** to cut down, saw down; **jywù-'dǎw** to cut down, saw down (*as a tree*).

    'jywù(-dz) (*Nunit, ge*) a saw. **jywù-'chěr** (*Nunit, ge*) a sawtooth.

句

jywù (*Munit*) *with* **hwà,** sentence, expression, clause, phrase, statement; a **shr̄** (*poem*).

    'jywù-dz (*Nunit, ge, jywù*) a sentence, *etc.* ‖**wǒ gěy-ni jǐ-jywù-jūng-'gàw(-de-'hwà).** I'll give you a bit of advice.

据

jywù (*K*) according to. **jywù wǒ 'kàn** as I see it, . . .; **jywù 'tā shwō** according to what he says, ...

具

jywù (*Munit*) *for bodies:* **yí-jywù-sz̄-'shr̄** a corpse.

聚

jywù (*I*) to gather together. ‖wǒ-men ꞏjywù-yi-jywù. Let's get together.

    As mainV: 'jywù-dzày ('yí-'kwàr *or* yì-'chǐ) gather (together), gather *people* (together); 'jywù-dàw to gather at (to) *a place.*

颶風

jywù-'fēng (*Nunit*, jèn) hurricane.   gwā jywù-'fēng to have a hurricane.

聚會

jywù-'hwèy (*VN2*) to gather together for a meeting; to attend a meeting. ‖wǒm 'jywù-hwèy-jywù-hwèy-ba. Let's have a get-together.

聚精會神

jywù-'jīng hwèy-'shén(-de) (*literary quotation*) to concentrate one's attention; with attention concentrated.

拒絕

jywù-'jywé (*V*) reject, refuse; (*Vpred*) to refuse to. ‖'jèng-fǔ jywù-'jywé tā-de-'chíng-chyéw. The government rejected his petition. ‖tā jywù-'jywé 'dá-fu. He refused to answer.

聚樂部

jywù-lè-'bù *or* **jywù-lwò-'bù** (*Nunit*, ge, chù) a club (*for amusement; a place, not an organization without a place of meeting*).

距離

jywù-'lí (*N*) distance *between two points.* ‖jèy-lyǎng-ge-'dì-fang jywù-'lí shŕ-'lǐ. These two places are ten miles apart.

劇烈

jywù-'lyè (*A*) violent. ‖pàw-'shēng hěn jywù-'lyè. The noise of the gun was very violent.

具體

jywù-'tǐ (*A*) concrete (not abstract). (*H*) concretely. ‖jywù-'tǐ 'shwō-lay, . . . speaking quite concretely, ...

均

jywūn (*H*) equally, *of a division.* 'fēn-de hěn 'jywūn divided equally; jywūn 'fēn to divide equally.

軍

jywūn (*N, Mord*) army; an army as part of the whole army, *as* dí-'sān-jywūn the third army; jywūn-'dwèy the army as an organization in the field. ‖jywūn-'dwèy 'kāy-dàw chyán-'shyàn chywù-le. The army has been sent to the front.

    'jywūn-rén military personnel (*officer and enlisted*); jywūn-'hwǒ ammunition *or* firearms and ammunition; jywūn-'gwān army officer.

軍器

jywūn-'chì (*Nunit*, ge, jyàn) military weapons.

軍器庫

jywūn-chì-'kù (*Nunit*, ge) an arsenal, armory (*for storage*).

君子

jywūn-'dž (*Npers*) wise and virtuous man (*literary*).

軍政部

jywūn-jèng-'bù (*Nunique*) Ministry of War (*China*).

軍事

jywūn-'shŕ (*Nunit*, jyàn) military affairs, military business.

均勢

jywūn-'shr̀ (*Nabstr*) balance of power (*in international politics*).

軍事行動

'jywūn-shŕ-shíng-'dùng (*Nabstr*) military operations.

君士坦丁堡

jywūn-shŕ-tǎn-dīng-'bǎw (*Nunique*) Istanbul (Constantinople).

軍需品

jywūn-'shywū(-pǐn) (*Ncoll*) military equipment, matériel, supplies.

軍樂隊

jywūn-ywè-'dwèy (*Nunit*, ge) military band (*music*).

K

ka *Wade Romanization for* **ga.**

k'a *Wade Romanization for* **ka.**

措擦

'kā-cha (*V*) to scrape with a sharp tool (*as in removing encrusted dirt or paint*). *As mainV:* 'kā-cha-shyà (*lc*) to scrape *something* off.

咖啡

kā-'fēy (*Nmass*) coffee (*also* jyā-'fēy).

卡車

kǎ-'chē (*Nunit*, lyàng) truck, motor truck.

卡片（兒）

kǎ-'pyàn, kǎ-'pyàr (*Nunit*, jāng) visiting card; index card; *any* card (*except playing card*).

kai *Wade Romanization for* gay.

Wade Romanization for kay.

kan *Wade Romanization for* gan.

k'an *Wade Romanization for* kan.

看

kān (*V*) to guard, watch over, take care of. ‖chǐng-ni gěy-wo kān(-je) 'shíng-li. Please watch my baggage for me.
    kān-dēng-'tǎ-de(-rén) lighthouse-keeper.

刊

*kān issue, edition; *confined to constructions like the following:* ywè-'kān (*Aattr*) monthly, *as* 'ywè-kān-de-dzá-'jr a monthly magazine; ji-'kān (*Aattr*) quarterly (*in the same way*); nyán-'kān annual; 'èr-ywè-kān the February issue *or* edition. ‖jèy-ge-dzá-'jr-de-'èr-ywè-kān háy méy-chū-'bǎn. The February issue of this magazine hasn't appeared yet.

看護

'kān-hu *or* 'kàn-hu (*Npers*) a nurse (*for sick people, not babies*). kān-hu-'jǎng head nurse, superintendent of nurses.

看守所

kān-shěw-'swǒ (*Nunit*, ge) jail, prison (*for detention before trial, not for imprisonment as punishment*).

看財奴

kān-tsáy-'nú (*Npers*) miser.

砍

kǎn (*V*) to chop. kǎn-'téw to decapitate; kǎn-'shù *or* kǎn-'mù to cut down trees for lumber. *As mainV:* kǎn-'dǎw *or* kǎn-'dyàw to chop down; kǎn-'dwàn to chop into segments; 'kǎn-chéng to cut into *so many* pieces.

砍肩兒

kǎn-'jyār (*Nunit*, jyàn) sleeveless upper garment; vest. shyǎw-kǎn-'jyār undershirt.

看

kàn (*V*) to examine, appraise; to watch, look at, attend and observe; to see, visit *a person;* (*figuratively*) to see *matters from a particular point of view*, to feel about *matters;* to look to *someone for support or help,* to rely on; to read silently. kàn-'bìng to examine an illness (*as a doctor does*); kàn dyàn-'yěngr to attend movies; kàn-'shì to attend a play; jywù wǒ 'kàn as I see it; kàn-'bàw to read a newspaper; kàn-kan 'pù-dz to mind a store; kàn-kan shyǎw-'hár to mind a baby. ‖wǒ děy chywù 'kàn-ta. I must go see him. ‖wǒm děw kàn-je 'nǐ-le. We all depend on you now. ‖bǎ jèy-ge-'dūng-shi 'kàn-yi-kàn. Examine this thing. ‖'kàn-je (yì-dyǎr) nèy-ge-'hwǒ. Be careful of the fire. ‖bǎ jèy-ge-'dūng-shi 'kàn yí-byàr. Examine this thing. *or* Look this thing over. *or* Read this thing over. ‖kàn-'yàngr hǎw shyàng bú-'tswò. Just taking a superficial look it seems to be OK. ‖kàn nèy-ge-'yàng-dz kǔng-'pà bù-'shíng-le. Looking at it from that point of view I'm afraid it won't do. ‖'kàn-je hǎw shyàng bù-'hǎw. It doesn't look too good (*though it really is*).

    As mainV: kàn-bu-'chǐ to be unable to respect *someone,* to look down on *someone;* kàn-'chǐng *or* kàn-'chǐng-chu to see clearly *despite fog,* or *figuratively;* 'kàn-chū-lay to come to see, to discover, realize, to get *what someone is driving at;* kàn-'chwān to see through, see beyond; 'kàn-dàw to read as far as *a certain page* (kàn-de-'dàw to see, grasp, understand *a point, but be unable to put it into effect*); kàn-'dǔng to read and understand, *or* see and understand; 'kàn-jyàn to see, to have seen (*with the eye*); kàn-'tswò to see wrong, to read *something* wrong.

    'kàn-fǎ (*Nabstr*) point-of-view, judgment, decision, interpretation. ‖'nǐ-de-'kàn-fǎ dzěme-'yàng? How do you see it? *or* What do you make of it?

看遍

kàn-'byàn (*VN1*) to look everywhere, search thoroughly. ‖shéme-'dì-fang dēw kàn-'byàn-le. They looked everywhere.

看護

'kàn-hu *see* 'kān-hu.

kang *Wade Romanization for* gang.

k'ang *Wade Romanization for* kang.

糠

kāng (*Nmass*) chaff, bran, husks. mǐ-'kāng rice chaff; mày-'kāng wheat chaff.

康定

kăng-'dìng (*Nunique* Kang-ting (*capital of Sikang province*).

康健

kăng-'jyàn (*A*) to be healthy, in good health.

扛

káng (*V*) to carry on the shoulder, neck, or upper part of the back. **káng-'chyáng** to bear arms.

　As mainV: **káng-bu-'dùng** be unable to carry *thus*; **'káng-chǐ-lay** to lift on the shoulder, *etc.*; **káng-'píng** to balance on the shoulder; *etc.* (*May also apply to something slung between the shoulders of two or more men.*)

抗

kàng (*V*) to resist. **kàng-'dí** to resist the enemy; **kàng-'jywǎn** to resist taxation.

抗告

kàng-'gàw (*V*) to contest *a court decision*, to appeal from *a court decision*. **tā bù-'fú fǎ-'tíng-de-pàn-'dwàn, 'yèw kàng-'gàw.** He doesn't acquiesce in the court's decision, but is going to appeal again.

　kàng-gàw-'rén appellant.

kao *Wade Romanization for* **gaw**.

k'ao *Wade Romanization for* **kaw**.

烤

kăw (*V*) to roast in a pan, oven, or on a spit. *Forms VN3:* **kăw-'yā-dz** roast duck; **kăw myàn-'bāw** toasted bread, *or* to toast bread, *or* to bake bread. **'kăw-kaw 'hwǒ** to warm oneself by the fire. *As mainV:* **kăw-'sž** to roast to death (*used figuratively by a person in a very hot and dry place, particularly when sitting by the fire*).

考

kăw (*I*) to take an examination; (*V*) to give an examination to, to examine (*for knowledge*). **wǒ shyàn-dzày chywù 'kăw.** I'm going for an exam. **wǒ 'kăw-kăw ni.** Let me question you.

　kăw-'tí (*Nunit,* wèn) subject of examination; examination question.

考查

kăw-'chá (*V*) to survey *land*, go prospecting for *minerals, etc.*, to investigate archeologically (*ruins, etc.*). **kăw-'chá dì-'shř** to survey the lay of the land; **kăw-'chá jīn-'kwàng** to prospect for gold. *Also:* to investigate *commercial possibilities, international disputes.*

考古

kăw-'gǔ (*VN1*) to perform archeological explorations; **kăw-gǔ-'shywé** archeology; **kăw-gǔ-'jyā** archeologist

考卷

kăw-'jywàn, kăw-'jywàr (*Nunit,* jāng) an examination paper. **jīn-tyan jyàw-'ywán fā kăw-'jywàn.** Today the teacher returned the exam papers.

考慮

kăw-'lywu (*V*) to take *some proposition* under advisement, consider, think over. **ràng-wo kăw-'lywù-kăw-'lywù.** Let me think it over a bit.

考試

kăw-'shř (*I*) to have an examination, take *or* hold an examination (*of information*). **wǒ gěy tā-men kăw-'shř.** I'm holding an exam for them.

　kăw-'shř-wěy-ywán-'hwèy a board of examiners (*as in a school*).

靠

kàw (*V*) to lean on, depend on; to border on, be located by; to veer *in a direction*. *Often* **'kàw-je** *or* K. **tā kàw-je 'chyáng 'jàn-je.** He's standing leaning against the wall. **wǒ-de-'fáng-dz kàw-je hǎy-'byǎr.** My house is by the seashore. **kàw-je 'dzwǒ-byar 'kǎy.** Veer to the left (*speaking to a car driver*). **tā jyèw 'kàw-je yí-ge-'nǐ.** He's relying only on you.

　As mainV: **'kàw-dzày** to lean *something* against, at, on *a place*; **kàw-bu-'jù** to be unreliable, untrustworthy. **bǎ 'tī-dz kàw-dzay 'chyáng-shang.** Lean the ladder against the wall. **tā kàw-je 'hwǒ kàw-de tày 'jìn-le.** He's too close to the fire.

開

kāy (*I*, *causative, and* V) (1) *central meaning:* to open, come open, come apart (*in the sense of something moving away from something else, or of things moving away from each other*). **kāy-'mén** to open a door; **kāy-'hwār** to blossom (*flowers open*); **kāy-'kěw** to open the mouth *and* speak, to say something, *or* to burst (*as of a dam, or a river through its banks*); **kāy-'chwán** to leave (*of a boat*), *or* to cast off; **hwǒ-'chē 'kāy** the train leaves.

　(2) *From use with vehicles* (*V*) to operate *a self-propelled vehicle*, to drive. **kāy-'chē** to drive a car. **'wǒ kāy** I'll drive.

　(3) To break open (*of a surface, as of ground being tilled for the first time, or of a mine being opened*). **kāy-'hwāng** to cultivate land for the first time, break virgin soil; **kāy-'kwàng** to open *or* exploit a mine.

　(4) *Similarly with a liquid:* **shwěy 'kāy-le** the water is boiling; **kāy-'shwěy** (*VN3*) boiling water.

　(5) To open, (*of a route or conduit*). **kāy dyàn-'mén** to turn on an electric switch; *from this* **kāy-'dēng** to turn on a light.

　(6) To open *or* start a ceremony, an activity, *or* to initiate *a custom*. **kāy ... dyǎn-'lǐ** to inaugurate a ceremony; **kāy-'lǐ** to initiate a custom.

(7) From **kāy-'mén** to open a door, *thus* to open for business. **kāy 'pù-dz** to open and operate a shop (*similarly with any enterprise*).

(8) *Related to (5):* to open fire with. **kāy-'chyāng** to open fire with a rifle; **kāy-'pàw** to open fire with a cannon *or* large-caliber weapon; **kāy-'hwǒ** to open fire; **kāy jǐ-'chyāng** to fire a few shots.

(9) To write *a prescription, a bill, a check, etc.* (*thus opening the route by which someone can obtain money or medicines*). **kāy-'jàng** to send a bill, to write a bill; **kāy jř-'pyàw** to write a check; **kāy yàw-'fāngr** to write a prescription.

(10) To violate *a prohibition, particularly religious.* **kāy-'lì** (*ambiguous; see 6*) to violate a custom; **kāy-'jāy** to break a prohibition against eating meat (*especially of monks that have taken such a vow*). *Not all the specific meanings of* **kāy** *are covered in the above, and some expressions combine several of them: entries listed separately are only important examples, by no means exhaustive.*

As main V: may have any of the above meanings, depending on context: **'kāy-chū** (*lc*) to drive out, to write out, to open out; **kāy-'dà-lè** to open wide, to turn on loud (*as of a radio*); **'kāy-dàw** (*lc*) to drive to *a place,* to send *a check, etc.,* to; **kāy-'dzěw-le** to drive away; **'kāy-gěy** to make *a check* out to *someone;* **'kāy-gwò** (*lc*) to drive past; to drive ahead of (*literally or figuratively*), to outdo, outdistance, outrun; **'kāy-jìn** (*lc*) to drive into *a place;* **kāy-'kwày-le** to drive fast; **kāy-'tswò-le** to drive off one's course, lose one's way when driving. *All these translations are partial: other meanings and other combinations exist, but are easily recognized.*

As post V: only the central meaning; forms RC1 and RC2: **'kāy-kāy** to open; **'dzěw-kāy** to walk *or* go away; **'lí-kāy** to leave *a place;* **'dǎ-kāy** to open *a suitcase* (*or something else with a hinged lid*); **'sàn-kāy** to disperse *a crowd; etc.*

開拔

kāy-'bá (*V*) to dispatch *an army;* **kāy-'bá jywūn-'dwèy** to dispatch an army. *As main V:* ‖**'bīng kāy-'bá-dàw chyán-'shyàn chywù-le.** Troops have been dispatched to the front.

開場

kāy-'cháng *or* **kāy-'chǎng** (*VN1*) to start a performance. ‖**'shì kāy-'chǎng-le.** The play has begun. *Also, specifically,* to open a gambling establishment; to start to gamble.

開車執照

kāy-'chē-jŕ-'jàw (*Nunit,* **jāng**) driver's license.

開除

kāy-'chú (*V*) to expel, kick out, *a student;* discharge *a soldier* (*dishonorably or without honor*). **kāy-'chú dǎng-'jí** to expel from a political party.

開刀

kāy-'dāw (*VN2*) to ~operate, have an operation. **kāy lyǎng-tsɀ-'dāw** to operate twice, have two operations (*surgical*).

開放

kāy-'fàng (*V*) to open *or* release *something* to the public. ‖**'jīn-tyan nèy-ge-gūng-'ywán kāy-'fàng.** Today that park is open to the public. **mén-'hù kāy-'fàng jǔ-'yì** the open door policy.

開封

kāy-'fēng (*Nunique*) K'ai-feng (*capital of Honan province*).

開關

kāy-'gwān (*Nunit,* **ge**) an electric switch.

開會

kāy-'hwèy (*VN2*) to open a meeting, hold a meeting. **chywù kāy-'hwèy** go to a meeting (*or a party, a reception, etc.*).

開支

kāy-'jř (*V*) to expend. ‖**nǐ 'jīn-tyan kāy-'jř-le 'dwǒ-shaw-chyán?** How much did you spend today? (*Nmass,* **fèr, bǐ**) expenditures.

開礦權

kāy-kwàng-'chywán (*Nabstr*) prospector's rights.

開審

kāy-'shěn (*V*) to open a *court* inquiry.

開心

kāy-'shīn (*VN2*) to feel happy. **gēn-rén kāy-'shīn** (*or* **ná, jàw** *instead of* **gēn**) to amuse oneself at the expense of someone.

開消

kāy-'shyāw (*V*) to expend, pass out *money.* (*Nmass,* **fèr, bǐ**) expenditures.

開頭

kāy-'téw(r) (*H*) at the beginning, at first. ‖**kāy-'téwr-de-shŕ-hew nǐ shwō 'nà-yàngr; shyàn-'dzày nǐ vèw shwō 'jè-yàngr.** At first you said that, but how you say this.

開庭

kāy-'tíng (*VN1*) to open a court session.

開玩笑

kāy 'wán-shyàw (*VN2*) to crack a joke. **kāy tā-de-'wán-shyàw** to make fun of him.

開演

kāy-'yăn (*I*) to begin a performance. ‖**'shì kāy-'yăn-le.** The play has begun.

開夜車

kāy yè-'chē (*VN1*) to burn the midnight oil, work very hard at studying late at night, cram all night (*literally to drive the night train*).

ke *Wade Romanization for* ge.

k'e *Wade Romanization for* ke.

棵

kē (*Munit*) a plant. **yì-kē-'shù** a tree; **yì-kē-'tsày** a vegetable (*the whole plant as it grows*); **yì-kē-dàw-'tsăw** one rice-plant (*similarly with any term for something that grows in the soil when one entire plant is meant*).

磕

kē (*V*) to fall against *or* strike a projection; *or* to strike some object against some surface (*as when knocking ashes out of a pipe*). ‖**bă yān-'děw 'kē-yi-kē.** Knock the ashes out of the pipe.

As mainV: **'kē-dzày** to knock against. **kē-dzày tày-'jyēer-shang-le** to knock against the edge of a step; **bă 'kē-chi-'gày kē-dzay táy-'jyēer-shang-le** to knock one's shin against the edge of a step; **'kē-shyà-lay** *or* **'kě-chū-lay** to knock *ashes* out; **kē-'swèy-le** to strike *thus* and break to pieces; *etc.*

科

kē (*Mauton*) a branch of service. ‖**nǐ shr̀ 'nǎ-yí-'kē-de?** What branch of service are you in?

In compounds also a branch of a section of a ministry in the government; a branch of learning, a science. **kē-'shywé** science; **kē-shywé-'jyā** scientist; **bù-'kē** infantry; **pàw-'kē** artillery; **chí-'kē** cavalry; *etc.*

磕膝蓋

kē-chi-'gày (*Nanit*, ge) the front part of the knee, kneecap.

咳嗽

ké-sew (**'ké-su**, **'ké-se**) (*I*) to cough. ‖**tā 'ké-sew lyăng-'shēngr.** He coughed a couple of times.

(*Nabstr*) a cough. ‖**tā yěw 'ké-sew méy-yew?** Does he have a cough? (*doctor making a diagnosis*).

可身 (兒)

ké-shēn, ké-'shēr (*VN1, A*) to fit in at the waist, to be tailored to fit the lines of the body. ‖**'yī-fu bù-ké-'shēr.** The dress is formless (*or* loose *or* severe).

可以

'ké-yi *see* ***kě, 'kě-yǐ.**

渴

kě (*A*) be thirsty. ‖**wǒ 'kě-le.** I'm thirsty. ‖**wǒ yěw yì-dyăr-'kě.** I'm a bit thirsty (*not said without* yì-dyăr).

可 (是)

kě (*H*) **'kě-shr** (*J*) but: **kě** *shows surprise, contrast, or emphasis,* **'kě-shr** *is general.* ‖**kě bú-'shr̀-ma!** Ain't it the truth! ‖**kě bù-'shíng!** But that just won't do now! ‖**'nèy kě jēn 'hwày!** Gee, but that's really bad! ‖**kě 'lyăw-bu-dé!** Oh dear! Gosh! But it can't be so! ‖**wǒ hěn 'shǐ-hwān 'chywù, 'kě-shr bù-'néng chywù.** I'm anxious to go, but I can't.

可

*kě *prefixed to V* (*occasionally I*) *forms A with much the meaning of English* -able, -ible. **ke-'shyàw** laughable, worth laughing at; **kě-'kàn** readable, worth reading; **kě-'pà** reliable; **kě-'pà** alarming, productive of fear; **kě-'táw-de-'lù** avenue of escape, escape route; **kě-'tyāw** choosable, capable of being chosen; **'méy shémᵉ kě-'tyāw-de** to have no choice (*because all are goᴄ.,, or all are bad*); **kě-'wár** amusing, diverting, relaxing.

Note: **'kě-bu-kě 'shyàw** worth laughing at or not? etc.

A number of these formations have a V not used alone; these are listed separately.

可 (以)

*kě (*rare*), **'kě-yǐ, 'ké-yi** (*Vpred*) may, can (*usually but not always of a human agent*). ‖**nǐ ké-yi 'dzěw-le.** You may go. *or* You can go. ‖**wǒ dzày-'jèr 'děng-ta, 'ké-yi-bu-ké-yi?** Is it all right for me to wait for him here? ‖**'nèr-de-fàn ké-yi 'chr̄.** The food there is OK. ‖**wǒ-men kàn dyàn-'yěngr-chywu dàw-shr 'ké-yi.** It's all right for us to go to the movies (*but other things are not OK*). ‖**tā-nèy-ge-'bìng (shr̀) ké-yi-'hǎw-de.** His illness is not fatal; he may get better.

可別

kě-'byé (*intensified* byé don't) don't under any circumstances. ‖**kě-'byé 'nème-yàngr!** Under no circumstances do that!

可著

'kě-je (*K*) within the confines of, according to the size *or* capacity of. ‖**'kě-je jèy-ge-'wū-dz-de-'dà-shyǎw dzwò dì-'tǎn.** Make a rug to fit this room. ‖**kě-je 'jyǎw dzwò-'shyé.** Make shoes to fit the feet. ‖**'kě-je 'téw dzwò 'màw-dz.** Make the hat (to) fit the head.

Figuratively to be stiff, inflexible, to stick to ordinary daily routine; *or* to be neither stingy nor extravagant.

可憐

kě-'lyán (*A*) pitiful, pitiable. ‖**kě-lyán-'jyèr-de!** Poor fellow!

可慮
kě-'lywù (A) productive of worry, worrisome (*of a situation or matter*).

可能
kě-'néng (A) be possible. ‖dàw-'nàr chywù shr̀ kě-'néng-de. It's possible to go there (*but better not to*).
  kě-'néng dǎw-shr kě-'néng it's possible all right, *but then* ... (*used formally or by students*).

可能性
kě-néng-'shìng (Nabstr) chance, possibility. ‖'méy-yew kě-néng-'shìng. There's not the slightest possibility (*used formally or by students*).

可惜
kě-'shī (A) to be a shame, too bad, regrettable.

可許
'kě-shywǔ (Vpred) it is allowable now *or* at last for so-and-so to do so-and-so. ‖wǒ-men 'kě-shywǔ dzwò 'nèy-ge-le! At last we may do that! (*Official.*)

可畏
kě-'wèy (A) be frightening; be worthy of being feared. *Of a young person;* be promising (*in the sense that he is going to become a competitor to be feared*). ‖nèy-ge-hèw-'shēng hěn kě-'wèy. That youngster is very promising.

刻
kè, kē (V) to carve, engrave. kè tú-'jāng to carve personal seals (*a specialized art in China*); kè-'dz̀ to carve characters; kè-'hwār to engrave designs.
  As mainV: 'kè-dzày to carve on, engrave on *a surface.* 'kè-shang to carve, engrave. ‖bǎ tā-de-'míng-dz 'kè-shàng. Carve his name.

刻
kè (Munit) yí-kè-'jūng a quarter of an hour. sǎn-dyǎn-yí-'kè three-fifteen (*o'clock*).

課(程)
kè(-'chéng) (Nunit, mér, ge) a course in school. ‖nǐ 'jīn-nyan nyàn-le shéme-kè-'chéng? What courses are you taking this year? ‖wǒ nyàn 'sān-mér-'kè. I'm taking three courses.

客(人)
kè(-rén) (Npers) a guest. kè-'chē passenger car (*railroad*); kè-'dyàn an inn, small hotel; kè-'tīng living room, parlor. *As M:* yí-kè-'fàn one guest's food.

刻(薄)
kè, 'kè-bwo, 'kè-be (A) mean, sarcastic (*of a person*). ‖jèy-ge-rén hěn 'kè-be. He's mean (*he likes to say*

and do things that make people unhappy, he likes to find fault).
  shwō kè-be-'hwà to make biting remarks, remarks criticizing others.

客氣
'kè-chi (A) polite, courteous, ceremonious. bú-'kè-chi *or* bú-yàw 'kè-chi *or* byé 'kè-chi *polite phrase suggesting* make yourself at home, that's perfectly all right; *often as answer to* dwèy-bu-'chǐ excuse me, pardon me.
  kè-chi-'jyèr polite manner; 'jyǎ-kè-chi-'jyèr an air of false politeness.

kei *Wade Romanization for* gey.

k'ei *Wade Romanization for* key.

ken *Wade Romanization for* gen.

k'en *Wade Romanization for* ken.

啃
kěn (V) to bite into *as in* kěn 'píng-gwo to bite into an apple; to gnaw at *as in* 'gěw kěn 'gǔ-tew a dog gnaws at a bone.
  As mainV: kěn-'swèy-le to chew into pieces; kěn-bu-'dùng to be unable to bite into *or* gnaw at. *Always implies that part of the thing bitten remains outside the mouth, and that it takes some force to bite into it.*

肯
kěn (Vpred) to be willing to, to promise to; *negative* to refuse to. ‖tā bù-'kěn twèy-'ràng. He won't budge from his position, he won't give in. ‖tā hěn 'kěn 'bāng-ju rén. He's (*always*) willing and glad to help people. ‖'jèy-ge-dūng-shi nǐ kěn 'chū 'dwō-shaw-chyán 'mǎy? Well, how much would you pay for this thing? (*said in bargaining*).

keng *Wade Romanization for* geng.

k'eng *Wade Romanization for* keng.

坑
kēng (V) to injure, cheat, or entrap *someone.* ‖wǒ jyàw-rén gěy 'kēng-le. I've been had. *or* I've been taken for a ride. *or* I've been cheated.

傾家蕩產
kēng-'jyā dàng-'chǎn (*or* chīng-...) (*literary quotation*) to lose everything, lose family and fortune, be ruined completely.

坑

kēng(r) (*Nunit*, **ge**) a shallow hole *or* pit *in the ground, on a level flat surface.* **'gěw páw-'kēng** dogs dig holes; **'gūng-rén wā-'kēng** workmen dig holes.

摳

kěw (*A*) to be stingy, tight, tight-fisted.

    kěw-'shū (*VN1*) to cram, bone, study hard in order to pass an examination *without necessarily learning anything that will be remembered thereafter.* ‖**tā-nèy-ge-rén jyèw-shr kěw-'shū, méy-yew 'jēn-shywé-'wèn.** That guy just crams for his exams, he has no real knowledge.

口口糖

'kěw-kcw-táng (*or* **kéw-** *or* **'kěw-** *or* **'kèw-**) (*Nmass*) chocolate; chocolate candy.

口

***kěw** (*N*) mouth; *for the part of the body, human or animal, the usual indepel.*)nt *word is* **dzwěy**; **kěw** *occurs in many compounds, often with a meaning of a mouth-like part of something other than a human or animal body.* **hé-'kěw** river mouth; **hàn-'kěw** the city Hankow (mouth *of* the Han river); **mén-'kěw(r)** doorway, entryway, entrance, vestibule, exit; **shāng-'kěw** the opening of a wound; **rù-'kěw, chū-'kěw** entrance, exit, *or* import *and* export; **hày-'kěw** a seaport.

    'kěw-dz a tear, cut, hole, rip, wound, burst, opening *in cloth, skin, the bank of a river, etc.;* (*M*) a person, *in enumerating them, as* ‖**ni-'jyā-li yěw ji-'kěw-dz?** How many people are there in your family?

    lyǎng-'kěw-dz a married couple.

    kěw-'tyáw tongue (*meat*); **kěw-'shwěy** saliva; **shù-'kěw** to wash out the mouth.

    kěw (*Munit*) (1) *for Npers when the emphasis is on taking census:* **lyǎng-bǎy-kěw-'rén** two hundred people; **rén-'kěw** population. (2) a mouthful of. **yì-kěw-'fàn** a mouthful of food. (3) *for certain objects that have a mouthlike opening:* **yì-kěw-'jūng** a (*bell-shaped*) bell. (4) a bite (*as when an insect bites*). **'yǎw yì-kěw** to bite once, bite one bite (*mosquito, insect, dog*).

口

kěw (*H*) by word of mouth. ‖**jèy-ge-'gù-shr shr kěw 'chwán-de.** This legend was passed down by word of mouth. ‖**kěw 'shwō wú-'píng.** Verbal agreement is not evidence (*formal; used on documents*).

口氣

'kěw-chì (*Nabstr*) expression, attitude; implication *or* connotation *of words.* ‖**wǒ kàn tā-'kěw-chì bù-'hǎw, jyèw méy-'shwō-le.** I recognized that he wasn't favorably inclined, so I kept quiet. ‖**nèy-ge-dz-de-'kěw-chì hěn 'tsū, ni byé 'yùng.** That word has rude connotations, don't use it.

口輕

kěw-'chīng (*A*) to be lightly seasoned, not have much salt.

口淡

kěw-'dàn (*A*) to be lightly seasoned, not have much (*or* enough) salt.

口袋

'kěw-dày (*NunitC*, **ge**) a soft bag, a pocket.

口供

'kěw-gùng (*Nunit*, **pyān, jāng**) statement, confession, deposition. **jāw 'kěw-gùng** to give a deposition orally; **shyě 'kěw-gùng** to write a deposition.

口重

kěw-'jùng (*A*) to be heavily seasoned, have lots of salt.

口頭

'kěw-téw(r) (*H*) orally, by word of mouth. **'kěw-téw-chǐng-'chyéw** an oral request; **'kěw-téw jyāw-'dày** to pass on *or* transmit by word of mouth; **'kěw-téw bày-'twō** to ask a favor orally.

口吻

kěw-'wěn (*Nabstr*) manner of speaking, manner of expression, implication *or* connotation of *or* atmosphere surrounding what one says. ‖**wǒ tīng tā-de-kěw-'wěn yěw yì-dyǎr-chí-'gwày.** I noticed that his manner of speaking was a bit strange.

口胃

kěw-'wèy (*Nabstr*) taste, preference for one type of food or another. ‖**jèy-ge-'tsày bù-'hé tā-de-kěw-'wèy.** This food doesn't suit his taste.

口音

'kěw-yīn (*Nabstr*) manner of pronouncing, accent. ‖**tā shwō-'hwà dày yì-dyǎr-'nán-fāng-de-'kěw-yīn.** He speaks with a bit of a southern accent.

叩

kèw (*V*) to knock at. **kèw-'mén** to knock at a door (*literary*).

扣

kèw (*V*) (1) to detain, arrest, hold *people or things. As mainV:* **'kèw-chi-láy** *or* **'kèw-jù** *or* **'kèw-shyà** *with same meaning.*

    (2) To discount, take off. **'kèw yí-kwày-'chyan** to knock a dollar off the price. *As mainV:* **'kèw-shyà** *with same meaning.*

    (3) To button up. **kèw 'lǐng-dz** to button one's collar. *As mainV:* **'kèw-shàng** *or* **'kèw-chi-láy** *with same meaning;* **kèw-'jǐn-le** to button tightly.

扣

kèw (*V*) to invert, turn upside down, *something that has a right side and a wrong side.* **kèw-'wǎn** to turn a bowl upside down. *As mainV:* **'kèw-shàng** to cover *something* up; **'kèw-dzày** to cover *something* under a container. ‖**nǐ yùng nèy-ge-'dyé-dz bǎ nèy-wǎn-'tsày 'kèw-shang.** Cover the bowl of food with that plate. ‖**bǎ 'há-ma kèw-dzay 'wǎn-dǐ-shya.** Turn that bowl upside down over the frog. ‖**wǒ-'shěw kèw-jė 'bǐ.** My hand is palm downwards covering the pen.

扣 （子，兒）

'kèw(-dz), kèwr (*Nunit*, ge) a knot *in a string;* a button (*Chinese style is a large knot at the end of a short string which passes through a loop at the end of another*) **'dǎ yí-ge-'kèw(r)** to tie a knot; to make a (*Chinese-style*) button.

扣門兒

kèw-'mér (*Nunit*, ge) a loop *in a string;* a buttonhole (*Chinese style is a loop at the end of a short string through which a knot at the end of another is passed*). **'dǎ yí-ge-kèw-'mér** to tie a loop; to make a (*Chinese-style*) buttonhole.

扣襻（子，兒）

kèw-'pàn-dz, kèw-'pàr (*Nunit*, ge) a button; a knot. (*See* **kèw**.)

ko *Wade Romanization for* **ge.**

k'o *Wade Romanization for* **ke.**

kou *Wade Romanization for* **gew.**

k'ou *Wade Romanization for* **kew.**

ku *Wade Romanization for* **gu.**

k'u *Wade Romanization for* **ku.**

哭

kū (*I*) to cry (*as a baby*). *As mainV:* **'kū-chǐ-láy** to burst out crying. ‖**shyǎw-'hár dzày 'kū-ne.** The baby is crying.

窟

'kū-lung (*Nunit*, ge) a hole, cavity, cave. **yá-'kū-lung** a tooth cavity. (**'kū-lung** *is not usually used for a hole being dug in the ground.*) ‖**'dzéy dzày chyáng-'gēr wā yí-ge-'kū-lung.** The thief dug a hole through the base of the wall.

苦

kǔ (*A*) bitter to the taste; bitter, hard, difficult, (*of experience or life*). **kǔ-'gwā** a variety of bitter melon,

yellowish and elongated; **kǔ-'gūng** hard labor; **kǔ-'shř** bitter experiences, difficult matters.

    (*H*) **kǔ 'shyàw** to smile or laugh bitterly; **kǔ 'gàn** to work hard, strive hard.

    N in: **chř-'kǔ** (*VN2*) to suffer bitterly.

苦處

'kǔ-chù (*Nunit*, ge) handicap, source of suffering emotional trouble. ‖**tā yěw hěn-dwō-de-'kǔ-chù.** He has many difficulties or hardships.

褲 （子）

*kù, 'kù-dz (*Nunit*, tyáw) pants, trousers. **kù(-yāw)-'dày** or **kù(-yāw)-'dàr** (*Nunit*, tyáw) trousers belt; **kù-'twěr** (or **kù-'twěy**) (*Nunit*, jř, ge) trousers leg.

褲岔兒

kù-'chǎr (*Nunit*, tyáw, ge) shorts (*outer garment or underclothing*).

褲

kù-'dāng (*Nunit*, ge) seat of the trousers.

褲脚

kù-'jyǎw(r) (*Nunit*, ge) edge of trousers leg; cuff.

庫倫

kù-'lwén (*Nunique*) Ulan Bator or Urga (*capital of Outer Mongolia*).

kua *Wade Romanization for* **gwa.**

k'ua *Wade Romanization for* **kwa.**

kuai *Wade Romanization for* **gway.**

k'uai *Wade Romanization for* **kway.**

kuan *Wade Romanization for* **gwan.**

k'uan *Wade Romanization for* **kwan.**

kuang *Wade Romanization for* **gwang.**

k'uang *Wade Romanization for* **kwang.**

kuei *Wade Romanization for* **gwey.**

k'uei *Wade Romanization for* **kwey.**

kun *Wade Romanization for* **gwen.**

k'un *Wade Romanization for* **kwen.**

kung *Wade Romanization for* **gung.**

k'ung *Wade Romanization for* **kung.**

空

kūng (*A*) empty, open, unoccupied, hollow, in vain. **kūng-'wèy-dz** an unoccupied seat; **kūng-'fáng** an unoccupied room, a vacancy; **tā shĕw kūng-'fáng** she lives alone (*as a widow*); **kūng-'dì** unused *or* unoccupied land; **kūng-shīn-'chyéw** *or* **'lǐ-tew-shr̄-'kūng-de-'chyéw** a hollow ball; **snwō kūng-'hwà** to speak empty words, meaningless words, talk aimlessly.

(*H*) **kūng 'shyǎng** to dream, to wish for in vain, to let one's mind wander.

kūng 'shyà-hew rén to try in vain to frighten people, to make idle threats.

As *postV*: **pū-'kūng-le** to catch at (*a fly*) and miss, to visit *someone* and find them not at home.

空

***kūng** pertaining to the air *or* skies; **kūng-'chì** (*Nmass*) air, atmosphere. ‖**wū-dz-li-de-kūng-chì bú-dà 'hǎw.** The air in the room isn't very good.

kūng-'jywūn air force.

空前（的）

kūng-'chyán(-de) (*Aattr*) unprecedented. **kūng-'chyán-de-'shr̄-ching** a matter without any precedent. ‖**jèy-jèn-dà-'ywǔ shr̄ kūng-'chyán-de.** This rain is unprecedented. *or* I never saw the likes of this rainstorm.

箜中

'kūng-jung (*Nunit*, ge) top (*toy*). **jwàn 'kūng-jung** to spin a top; *but* **dĕw 'kūng-jùng** *for the kind that is mounted on a string and is spun on the string.*

空曠

kūng-'kwàng (*A*) open, sparsely occupied *or* populated, not crowded. **kūng-kwàng-de-'dì** open country. ‖**jèy-dày-'shyāng-shya hĕn kūng-'kwàng.** This territory is quite open (*means not only free of crowds and people but also free of too many trees and the like*).

空襲

kūng-'shǐ, **kūng-'shí** (*Nunit*, tsż) air raid. **'kūng-shí-jǐng-'bàw** air raid alarm.

孔子

kǔng-'dž (*Nunique*) Confucius. **kǔng(-dž)-'jyàw** the teachings of Confucius, Confucianism.

恐怕

kǔng-'pà (*Vpred*, *Vsent*) to fear that, be afraid that (*not implying emotional fear*). ‖**kǔng-'pà yàw shyà-'ywǔ.** I'm afraid it's going to rain.

空

kùng (*I*) to be emptied, vacated (*compare* **kūng** empty, *not necessarily implying previous fullness*). **kùng-'wèy-dz** a vacated seat; **kùng-'fáng** a vacated room.

空場

kùng-'chǎng(r) (*Nunit*, ge) an open space, square, vacant lot, commons. ‖**chéng-'li-tew yĕw ge-kùng-'chǎngr.** There's an open square in the city.

控告

kùng-'gàw (*I*) to accuse *in court*, to sue *someone*. **bèy-kùng-'gàw-de-rén** the accused; **kùng-'gàw-rén** the appellant, the accuser.

控制

'kùng-jr̄ (*V*) to control. **'kùng-jr̄ 'mǎ** to control a horse, get a horse under control.

As *mainV*: **kùng-jr̄-bu-'jù** be out of control (*as a machine or horse*).

空兒

kùngr (*Nmass*) free time. ‖**nǐ yĕw-'kùngr méy-yew?** Have you a spare moment?

kuo *Wade Romanization for* **gwo.**

k'uo *Wade Romanization for* **kwo.**

誇獎

'kwā(-jyǎng) (*V*) to praise, flatter *a subordinate, a younger person, a student.* ‖**tā lǎw 'kwā-jyǎng ta.** He's always praising him.

As *mainV*: **kwā-'hwày-le** to spoil by too much praise.

胯

kwà (*V*) to carry with a strap, to support by linking arms *or* at the elbow. **kwà-je 'gē-be dzĕw** to go arm-in-arm; **kwà-je yí-ge-'lán-dz** to carry a basket over the arm.

As *mainV*: **kwà-'dzĕw-le** to carry away; **'kwà-chǐ-láy** *or* **'kwà-shàng** to pick up; **'kwà-dzày ('gē-be-shàng)** to put on (the arm) for carrying; *etc.*

寬

kwān (*A*) wide, broad (*opposed to* **jǎy** *narrow*). ‖**jèy-ge-'jyē yĕw 'èr-jàng-'kwān.** This street is twenty feet wide.

寬大

kwān-'dà (*A*) broad-minded, tolerant *of opposing beliefs.*

寬厚

kwān-'hèw (*A*) generous, kind. (*Opposite* **'kè-bwo.**)

寬容

kwān-'rúng (*A*) tolerant, big about things. (*V*) to tolerate *someone despite his offenses.*

款

'kwǎn(-dz) (*Nmass*; bǐ, fèr) money, funds. **chywǔ-'kwǎn** to obtain money *as at a bank*; **jyè-'kwǎn** borrow money, obtain credit; **fàng-'kwǎn** to extend credit.

筐 (子，兒)

'kwăng(-dz), kwăngr (*NunitC*, ge) basket (*often differs from what would be called* 'lán-dz *in that it is purely utilitarian; usually without handle rising over top*).

狂

kwáng (*A*) violent, furious; crazy, proud, conceited (*of a person*). kwáng-'fēng a violent storm, a blizzard. (*H*) foolishly and loudly. kwáng 'shyàw to laugh loudly and hysterically.

礦

kwàng (*Nunit*, ge, chù) a mine. kwàng-'yè the mining industry; yín-'kwàng, méy-'kwàng, *etc.*, silver mine, coal mine, *etc.* ‖jèy-ge-'kwàng 'chū-de bù-'dwō. This mine doesn't produce much.

kāy-'kwàng to open up *or* operate a mine.

曠

kwàng (*I*) to leave work without permission, take French leave. kwàng-'gūng *with same meaning;* kwàng-'jŕ *an official* leaves his post without permission; kwàng-'shywé to skip school; kwàng-'kè to skip class.

框 (子，兒)

*kwàng, 'kwàng-dz, kwàngr (*Nunit*, ge) frame, casement, framework. mén-'kwàng door frame; chwāng-hu-'kwàng window casement; jìng-'kwàng picture frame.

礦穴

kwàng-'shywè (*Nunit*, ge) mineral deposit, pocket.

塊 (兒)

kwàr (*Mauton*) *used after* (*postV*) dzày *or* chéng: ‖tām 'dzwò-dzày yí-'kwàr. They sat together. ‖wǒm bă-wǒ-men-de-'chyán 'hé-dzay yí-'kwàr. Let's pool our capital. ‖bă-'bǐng 'bāy-chéng lyăng-'kwàr. Break the cake in two.

Occasionally after other postV: ‖tām dzěw-daw yí-'kwàr. They met as they were walking. ‖'lyăng-tyáw-'hé lyéw-daw yí-'kwàr-le. The two rivers flow together.

快

kwày (*A*) fast, rapid, quick; sharp (*of an edge*). kwày-'chē express train. ‖wǒ-'byăw tày 'kwày-le. My watch is (too) fast. ‖jèy-bă-'dāw bù-hěn 'kwày. This knife isn't very sharp. ‖tā-'năw-dz hěn 'kwày. He's very smart (*student talk*).

(*H*) quickly, in just a minute now. ‖kwày 'wán-le almost done. ‖'fàn kwày 'dé-le. *or* 'fàn kwày yàw 'dé-le. Dinner's almost ready. ‖wǒm kwày 'dàw-nèr-le. We're almost there.

塊

kwày (*Munit*) hunk, odd-shaped piece, piece, brick, cake of. A loaf of myàn-'bāw (*bread*); a piece of rèw (*meat*); a cake of 'yí-dz (*soap*); a băw-'shŕ (*precious stone*); a hunk of 'shŕ-tew (*rock, stone*); a piece of dì (*land*); a tyán (*field*); *etc.* With chyán (*money*), a dollar; yí-kwày(-'chyán)-de-'pyàw-dz a one-dollar bill.

筷子

'kwày-dz (*Nunit*, jŕ; shwāng *for* pair of; fù *for* a set of) chopsticks.

會計

'kwày-jì (*Npers*) a bookkeeper *or* accountant. kwày-jì-'shŕ an expert accountant; kwày-jì-'ywán junior accountant.

快樂

'kwày-lwò *or* 'kwày-lè (*A*) happy, high-spirited. ‖shèw-'shāng-de-rén háy 'kwày-lè. The wounded men were still in good spirits.

快慢

kwày-'màn . (*Nabstr*) speed. ‖nèy-ge-'dyàn-mén gwăn kwày-'màn-de. That switch controls the speed.

昆虫

kwēn-'chúng(r) (*Nunit*, ge) insect.

坤角 (兒)

kwēn-'jywé(er) (*Npers*) an actress in old-style Chinese drama.

昆明

kwēn-'míng (*Nunique*) K'un-ming (*capital of Yünnan province*).

捆

kwěn (*V*) to tie, bind. *As mainV:* 'kwěn-dzày to tie *something or someone* to *or* at *a place;* kwěn-'jǐn-le to tie tightly; 'kwěn-chǐ-láy *or* 'kwěn-shàng to tie up; *etc.* ‖bă-ta kwěn-dzay 'shù-shang. Tie him to a tree. ‖bă tā-men-'lyă kwěn-dzay yí-'kwàr. Tie the two of them together. ‖bă tā-de-'shěw kwěn-dzày 'hèw-myan. Tie his hands behind his back. ‖bă jèy-ge-'shíng-li kwěn-'jǐn-le. Tie the baggage tightly.

捆 (兒)

kwěn, kwěr (*Munit*) a tied-up bunch of, a spool of, a tied-up bundle of. yì-kwěn-dàw-'tsăw a tied-up sheaf of rice straw; yì-kwěn-dzāng-'yī-fu a bundle of dirty clothes; yì-kwěr-'shyàn a spool of thread; yì-kwěr-dyàn-'shyàn a spool of wire.

困

kwèn (*A*) be sleepy; (*I*) to sleep. *As mainV:* 'kwèn-dzày to sleep at *a place;* to be stranded at *a place.*

191

困難

'kwèn-nan (*A*) difficult. ǁ**jèy-jyàn-'shr̀-ching hěn 'kwèn-nan.** This matter is very difficult.

(*Nunit*, **ge**) a difficulty, a trouble. ǁ**tā hǎw 'shyàng yěw shéme-'kwèn-nan, 'shwō-bu-chū-'láy.** He seems to have some trouble that he can't tell about.

盔

kwēy *or* **kwéy** (*Nunit*, **dǐng, ge**) a helmet; (*particularly*) **gāng-'kwēy** a steel hélmet.

虧

kwēy (*A*, *V*) to be ungrateful (to). **kwēy-'shīn-de-rén** an ungrateful person. ǁ**tā cháng-cháng 'kwēy-le rén.** He's always ungrateful to people.

盔甲

kwēy-'jyǎ *or* **kwéy-'jyǎ** (*Ncoll*; **tàw, fù**) armor, helmet and mail.

虧空

kwēy-kùng (*A*) to be in debt. ǁ**tā 'kwēy-kùng-le 'lyèw-bǎy-kwày-chyán.** He's in debt to the tune of six hundred dollars.

傀儡

kwěy-'lěy (*Nunit*, **ge**) a puppet (*as in a Punch and Judy show*); *figuratively as in English:* **kwěy-lěy-'jèng-fǔ** a puppet government.

濶，闊

kwò (*A*) rich, wealthy (*opposite* **chyúng**); broad, wide, spacious, extensive (*opposite* **jǎy, shyǎw**).

擴充

kwò-'chūng (*V*) to extend, enlarge (*as a business*).

擴大

kwò-'dà (*V*) to enlarge, widen (*as a road*). **kwò-dà-'chì** amplifier (*electric*).

擴張

kwò-'jāng (*V*) to extend, enlarge, expand, amplify (*as a business, an organization, a factory, military activities, a war, etc.*). *As mainV:* ǁ**jàn-'shr̀ kwò-'jāng-dàw 'yìn-du-le.** The war has spread to India.

L

拉

lā (*V*) to pull. **lā-'chē** pull a rickshaw; **lā 'tí-chín** play a violin (*pull the bow*); **lā-'byéer** blow a whistle; **lā-'lyéngr** ring a bell *by pulling a rope or string*; **lā-'shěw** to shake hands (*literally* to pull hands); **lā-'shř** to move the bowels.

As mainV: **lā-bu-'dùng** to be unable to pull *something* (*because it is too heavy or the like*); **lā-'jǐn-le** to pull tight *or* to pull taut (*as a rope or a stocking*); **lā-'jìn** (*lc*) to pull *someone* into, to get *someone* involved *in something;* **'lā-jù-le** to hang onto *something* (*such as a strap*) tightly; **'lā-shyà-lay** to pull down (*as a curtain or window blind*); (*figuratively*) to pull *someone* down from *a position of fame;* **'lā-kāy** to pull apart, to pull open; **lā-'jìn-hu** to draw closer to *someone,* become friendly with *someone* (*always with an ulterior motive*); *etc.*

ǁ**lā-'chē-de bǎ-ta lā-daw mén-'kěwr.** The rickshawman took him right to the door. ǁ**bǎ 'yǐ-dz 'lā-gwò-lay.** Pull up a chair. ǁ**dyàw-'ywú-de bǎ-'wǎng 'lā-shàng-lay-le.** The fisherman pulled in his nets. ǁ**tā bǎ nyéw-'jyěr lā-'cháng-le.** He stretched the rubber band out.

拉賬

lā-'jàng (*VN2*) to run into debt, get deeper and deeper into debt.

拉圾

lā-'jī (*Nmass*) rubbish, garbage.

拉圾堆

lā-jī-'dwēy (*Nunit*, **ge**) rubbish heap.

拉圾桶

lā-jī-'tǔng (*Nunit*, **ge**) ashcan, garbage can.

拉鍊（兒）

lā-'lyàn, lā-lyàr (*Nunit*, **tyáw**) zipper.

拉薩

lā-'sā (*Nunique*) Lhasa (*capital of Tibet*).

剌

lá (*V*) to cut *something fairly big with a knife,* cut into, slash, *without any chopping or hacking motion* (*not with foods; often unintentionally*). **'lá-le chywù** to cut out, cancel out, cross out. ǁ**bǎ jèy-shyē-'dz̀ 'lá-le chywù.** Cross out these characters.

As mainV: **'lá-shyà** (*lc*) cut off, slash off, down, (*as a finger*); **'lá-chū** (*lc*) to cut out (*as an appendix*); **lá-'pwò-le** to cut *the skin, for example,* so that a break *in the skin* results; **lá-'sž-le** to die from an error in a surgical operation. ǁ**tā-de-'shěw lá-'pwò-le.** He cut his hand.

喇叭

'lǎ-ba (*Nunit* ge) bugle, trumpet. **lǎ-ba-'shěw** a bugler. **chwēy 'lǎ-ba** to blow a trumpet, play a trumpet.

蠟

là (*Nunit*, **jř**, **gér**) a candle. **là-'táy**, **là-'tár** candlestick. **dyǎn-'là** to light a candle; **bǎ-'là chwēy-'myè-le** *or* **chwēy-'là** blow a candle out; **bǎ-'là nyē-'myè-le** to pinch a candle out between the fingers; **là 'myè-le** the candle went out.

辣

là (*A*) to be hot, heavily seasoned, peppery; (*V*) to be hot to *the tongue*, to burn *the tongue*. ‖**jèy-ge-là-'jyāw hěn 'là**, **'là-le wǒ-de-'shé-tew**. This pepper is very hot, it burned my tongue.

邋

****là** (*V*) to leave behind, pass, outdistance. ‖**wǒ 'là-le wǒ-de-'shū**. I left my book behind (I'll be back for it). *More often as mainV:* **'là-dzày** to leave *something* at *a place*. ‖**wǒ bǎ chyán-'bāw là-dzay 'jyā-li-le**. I left my pocketbook at home.
    'là-shyà ᴖ leave *someone* behind. ‖**bǎ-ta 'là-shyà-le**. (We) left him behind (unintentionally). ‖**byé jyàw tā-men bǎ-ni 'là-shya**. Don't let them outdistance *or* surpass you (*literally or figuratively, of any type of competitive activity*).

辣椒

là-'jyāw (*Nunit*, ge; kē) a pepper. **là-jyāw-'myàr** ground-up seeds of peppers.

lai *Wade Romanization for* **lay**.

攔

lán (*V*) to stop, cut off, isolate, hold back. *As mainV:* **'lán-chǐ-lay** isolate, cut off, enclose; **'lán-chū-chywù** to fence out, shut out; **'lán-hwéy** (*lc*) to fence off, fend off, hold back, restrain; **'lán-jù** to hold back, restrain and bring to a stop. ‖**já bǎ-'shwěy 'lán-jù-le**. The dam holds the flood back. ‖**byé 'bǎ-wo 'lán-jìn-chywu**. Don't fence me in. ‖**yí-'bù-fen-'dí-rén-de-'bīng bèy wǒ-men 'lán-chǐ-lay-le**. We isolated and cut off one section of the enemy troops.

欄

lán (*Mauton*) columns or pages in a newspaper devoted to a particular function. **shè-hwèy-'lán** society page; **gwǎng-gàw-'lán** classified ad section; **jèng-jř-'lán** political news columns; **gwó-jì-shīn-wén-'lán** section of international and foreign news. ‖**'jèy-yì-lán shř-'shéy fù-'dzé?** Who's in charge of this column?

籃（子）

lán (*Mcont*); **'lán-dz** (*NunitC*, ge) basket (*utilitarian or decorative, always with a handle curved over the top*). **yì-lán(-dz)-'píng-gwo** a basket of apples.

藍［色（兒）］

lán (*A*) **'lán-sè**, **'lán-shǎr** (*Nabstr*) blue; blue color.

籃球（兒）

lán-'chyéw(r) (*Nunit*, tsž) basketball (*the game*); (*Nunit*, ge) a basketball. **dǎ yì-hwéy-lán-'chyéw** play some basketball.

欄杆

'lán-gān (*Nunit*, lyèw, háng) a low wooden fence around something.

蘭州

lán-'jēw (*Nunique*). Lanchow, *another name for* **gǎw-'lán** Kao-lan (*capital of Kansu province*).

襤褸

lán-'lywǔ (*A*) shabby, unkempt. (*Literary.*)

藍圖

lán-'tú (*Nunit*, jāng) a blueprint.

懶

lǎn (*A*) to be lazy.

攬

lǎn (*V*) to be greedy for. **lǎn-'chywán** (*VN*, *A*) to be greedy for power, to grasp for power; **lǎn-'shř dzwò** to monopolize work, want to do everything oneself. *Used mainly in these specific combinations.*

懶散

'lǎn-sàn (*A*) careless, carefree, negligent, sloppy. ‖**tā shéme-'shř dēw bú-jù-'yì, yěw yì-dyǎr-lǎn-sàn**. He never concentrates his attention on anything, he's a bit diffuse and sloppy.

爛

làn (*A*) to be rotting, to have infected spots on the surface (*of foods, plants*); soft, tender (*as from cooking*). ‖**'píng-gwo dēw 'làn-le**. The apples are all spoiled. ‖**rèw yǐ-jing 'làn-le**. The meat is already tender. ‖**tā-'shěw-'pwò-de-dì-fang 'làn-le**. The wound on his hand is festering.
    As postV: **dǎ-'làn-le** to beat to a pulp; **jǎng-'làn-le** to become festered; **gē-'làn-le** to keep *apples, etc.* so long that they rot; **jǔ-'làn-le** to boil until tender; **kǎw-'làn-le** to roast until tender; *etc.*

亂

làn *see* **lwàn**.

狼

láng (*Nunit*, jř, ge) wolf.

廊

'láng-dz (*Nunit*, tyáw, ge) corridor; veranda, porch.
dzěw-'láng corridor.

浪

'làng(-tew) (*Nunit*, ge) waves (*in the sea*). ‖'yí-ge-
'làng-tew 'dǎ-gwò-lay. One wave beat (*the shore*).
‖'làng 'jìng-le. The sea is quiet. ‖'làng ywè láy ywè
'dà. The sea is getting rough.

浪費

làng-'fèy (*V*) to waste *time, money, energy.*

浪漫

'làng-màn (*A*) carefree, unconventional; romantic, flirta-
tious, girl-crazy *or* boy-crazy.

lao *Wade Romanization for* law.

勞步勞步

‖láw-'bù-láw-bù! Thanks for having come to see us
(*said to guests as they leave*).

勞工

láw-'gūng (*Npers*) a member of the working class; láw-
gūng-'wèn-tí labor problems; láw-gūng-lì-'fǎ labor
legislation.

老虎

'láw-hu (*Nunit*, jr, ge) tiger.

勞駕

láw-'jyà; láw-'jyà-láw-jyà Thanks! (*for a favor done or
one that one hopes will be done: Peiping*). ‖láw-'jyà bǎ-
'táng dì-gey wo. Please pass the sugar (*literally
Thanks for passing me the sugar; said before it is
passed*).

老

lǎw (*A*) old; (*of meat*) tough. 'lǎw-rén an old-timer,
an old employee; lǎw-shř-de old-fashioned, old-style.
‖jèy-'shř-nyán láy, tā byàn hěn 'lǎw-le. He's aged
a lot in the last ten years.
    (*H*) *indicating customary action. sometimes also
annoyance to the speaker:* always. ‖tā 'lǎw 'jù-dzay
nàr. He's always lived there.
    tā 'lǎw-shř 'nàme-yàngr. He's always doing that
sort of thing. ‖wǒ 'lǎw méy-chywù 'kàn-ta-le. I haven't
gone to see her for a long time. ‖jèy-ge-dì-fang lǎw
shyà-'ywǔ. It's always raining here.
    (*H*) *with specific other H:* lǎw 'dzǎw a long time
ago; lǎw 'ywǎn a long way away, far away.

老板

'lǎw-bǎn (*NpersT*) the owner of a store; *sometimes applied to* a famous (old-style) actor.

老百姓

lǎw-bǎy-'shìng (*Npers*) common man, man in the street.

老媽子

lǎw-'mā-dz (*Npers*) a maid, married female servant
(*Peiping*).

老年人

'lǎw-nyán-rén (*Npers*) an old person, an aged person.

老手

lǎw-'shěw (*Npers*) an old hand *at anything.* 'jūng-gwo-
lǎw-'shěw an old China hand (*translation of the English*).

老實

'lǎw-shr (*A*) stolid (*with emphasis on honesty or on
being not very bright, or both*).

老師

lǎw-'shř (*NpersT*) a teacher, tutor.

老頭（兒，子）

lǎw-'tewr, lǎw-'téw-dz (*Npers*) the Boss, the Old Man;
sometimes an older husband or father.

老天爺

lǎw-tyān-'yė (*Nunique*) a god (*in general parlance; not
the specific Buddhist, Taoist, Mohammedan, or Christian term*). ‖lǎw-tyān-'yé! Oh Lord!

老爺

'lǎw-yé (*NpersT*) *term of address for a person of high
rank, and for a judge.* ‖'lǎw-yé! Your Honor!
    See also gwān-'lǎw-yé, **yé, and Appendix A.*

老爺兒

lǎw-'yéer (*Nunique*) the sun (*Peiping*).

老玉米

lǎw-'ywù-mi (*Nmass*) corn, maize.

落

làw (lwò, lè) (*I*) to descend, come down, alight, (*of birds,
planes, curtain at a theater*); to set (*of sun, moon*);
to recede (*of tide, flood*).
    Causatively: làw-'jyà to mark down prices; 'làw ge-
hǎw-'myéngr to depart (*an office, this world*) leaving
a good name behind one (*or leaving nothing but a
good name, with no other reward*).
    As mainV: 'làw-shyà (*lc*) *with same meaning.* ‖lǎw-
'yéer 'làw-shyà-chywu-le. The sun has set. ‖fēy-'jī

làw-dzày 'chăng-shang. The plane has landed. ‖**'làng 'làw-shyà-chywù-le.** The waves have receded. ‖**dí-rén-de-dì-'tú 'làw-dzày wǒ-men-'shěw-lǐ-tew-le.** The enemy's maps have fallen into our hands.

烙

làw (V) to iron *clothes, etc.* **làw 'yī-fu** to iron clothes; to cook on a flat surface *as one cooks pancakes,* with a little grease.

    làw-'bǐng (VN3) a kind of thin, salty, pancake-like bread *cooked this way.*

    As mainV: **làw-'píng-le** to iron flat, smooth. **'làw yí-ge-'yèr** to iron a crease *into pants, etc.*

烙鐵

'làw-tye (Nunit, bǎ, ge) an iron, flatiron.

來

láy (I) to come (*indicates merely motion towards the speaker or his point of reference, thus the element of meaning common to English* come *and* bring, *in contrast to that common to* go *and* take). ‖**nǐ 'shéme-shŕ-hew láy?** When are you going to come?

    Causatively: ‖**'dzày láy wǎn-'fàn.** Bring another bowl of rice (*o a waiter*). ‖**nǐ 'wèy-shéme bù-láy-'shìn?** Why don't you send any letters? (*This latter only possible in this type of sentence: the former is common for serving anything at a table.*)

    As mainV: **láy-bu-'jí** be unable to come, be unable to finish *something.*

    As postV; forms RC1 and RC2; the inclusion of lc or l after the entry of an I or V indicates that such RC1 or RC2 exist: **'ná-láy** to bring; **'dzěw-láy** to walk this way, towards here; **'pǎw-láy** to run towards here; *etc.*

    As sentence-final element; the inclusion of lc after the entry of an I, V, or RC indicates that either **láy** *or* **chywù** *comes at the end of the sentence; l indicates that* **láy** *so occurs:* **dzwò-'chē láy** to come by car; **hwéy-'jyā láy** to return home, coming in this direction; **dàw-'jèr láy** come here; **'pǎw-gwò-láy** to run over this way; **pǎw-gwò 'chyáw-lay** to run this way over the bridge; **'jàn-chǐ-láy** to stand up (*after* **chǐ** *the* **láy** *is required but carries little if any meaning of its own*).

    Special expressions: **gēn-rén láy-'wǎng** to have relationship with people, mix in with someone, get acquainted and carry on some kind of relationship, business or social.

    àn 'jè-yàng láy shwō, . . . under these conditions, . . .; granted that this is true, ...

    'láy-hwéy (H) back and forth. **'láy-hwéy 'pǎw** to run back and forth; **láy-hwéy-'pyàw** a round-trip ticket; **'láy-láy-hwéy-'hwéy-de** (H) back and forth and back and forth repeatedly; **'láy-hwéy(-de) 'nyàn** to read and reread, read again and again.

    'dzày láy yí-tsż 'kàn-kàn. Try it once again.

來函

'láy-hán (Nunit, fēng) your letter, an incoming letter. (*Literary.*)

來著

láy-je *sentence-final element:* to have just been doing *whatever is expressed by what goes before:* ‖**nǐ 'shwō shéme láy-je?** What were you just saying? ‖**wǒ 'jìn-lay de-shŕ-hew tā 'jàn-dzày nèr láy-je.** When I came in he was standing there and had been standing there for a while. *When a specific past time is given, it implies activity continuing at that time; when no time is specified, it means activity that has now ceased but was in process just a minute ago.*

來歷

láy-'lì (Nabstr) background, past history *of a person.* ‖**tā-'jèy-ge-rén 'méy-yew láy-'lì.** This fellow has no background or experience worth mentioning. ‖**méy-yew-láy-'lì de-hwà, hěn 'nán jǎw-'shŕ.** If you have no experience or background it's hard to get any work. ‖**tā-de-láy-'lì bù-'míng.** His background is dubious.

來頭

'láy-téw (Nabstr) background, past history, family, connections, (*of a person*). ‖**tā 'láy-téw dà-de 'hěn.** He has a glorious past. *or* He has plenty of power backing him up. ‖**'jèy-ge-rén méy shéme-'láy-téw.** He has no background to speak of.

來往

láy-'wǎng (Nabstr) social intercourse, comings and goings. ‖**wǒ gēn-ta méy-yew láy-'wǎng.** His path and mine don't often cross.

來源

'láy-ywán (Nunit, ge) source, place of origin. ‖**shwèy-'shēw-de-'láy-ywán 'méy-yew-le.** The sources of revenue are all gone. ‖**jèy-ge-'sż-shyǎng-de-'láy-ywán shŕ yéw kǔng-'dž-de-'shywé-shwō láy-de.** This idea stems originally from the teachings of Confucius.

賴

lày (V) to blame *someone:* to deny *what one has done.* ‖**nǐ dzwò-'hwày-le byé 'lày-wo.** If you do it wrong don't blame me. ‖**tā jìng lày ('byé-)rén.** He's always passing the buck.

了

le (*reading-pronunciation* **lyǎw**). *The marker of completed action.* (1) *With an active predicate; that is, with a V, I, or an RC not in potential form; specifies that the action has already taken place:* ‖**tā 'chū-chywù-le.** He's gone out. *or* He went out. ‖**tā pǎw-daw 'nàr chywù-le.** He ran over there. ‖**'fáng-chyán, 'fàn-chyán, dēw 'yǐ-jing 'gěy-le.** Your room and meals are already paid for. ‖**yí-'chyán-de-'jyèw-fáng-dz jà-'hwày-le.** The old houses that were there formerly have all been bombed to pieces. ‖tā gěy-ni shēw-'tyáw-le-ma? Did he give you a receipt? ‖'jǐ-tyān shì-'wán-le? How many days will it take before they have all been washed? (*here* le *indicates completion before a certain future time*). ‖wǒ 'shŕ-le yì-gwǎn-dž-láy-shwěy-'bǐ. I found a fountain pen. ‖wǒ 'dzwó-tyan-'wǎn-shang kàn-le 'lyǎng-ge-dyàn-'yěngr. I saw two movies last night.

(2) *With an active predicate*, le *comes immediately after the verb or at the end of the sentence (except for* -ma, -ne, méy-yew, *etc.). With the last example above compare:* ‖wǒ 'dzwó-tyan-'wǎn-shang kàn dyàn-'yěngr-le. I went to the movies last night. *Compare also the following pairs:* ‖wǒ 'dzwó-tyan nyàn-le 'sān-běn-shū. I read three books yesterday. ‖wǒ 'dzwó-tyan nyàn-'shū-le. I studied yesterday. ‖wǒ 'dzwó-tyan chŕ-le hěn-dwō-'fàn. I ate a lot of food yesterday. ‖nǐ chŕ-'fàn-le méy-yew? Have you eaten? *Position at end of sentence emphasizes the whole event; position after the verb emphasizes what follows, not the action expressed by the verb.*

(3) RC1 *and* RC2 *with an adjective as postV often require* le, *unless* méy *precedes:* ‖bǎ-'shěw tsā-'gān-le. Wipe your hands (until they have become) dry.

(4) *With a stative predicate; that is,* A, *or* RC *in potential form, or many* Vpred, *or some* A *also used as* V *when so used, or* yěw *or* méy *(before a noun); indicates that the state in question has already started to exist and is therefore in existence at the moment of speaking or point of time reference:* ‖tā 'yǐ-jing 'hǎw-le. He's already recovered now. ‖wǒ bù-'téw-téng-le. My headache has stopped. ‖'nèy-ge-rén 'yǐ-jing yěw-'chyán-le. That man is (already) rich. ‖wǒ 'méy-yew chyán-le. I'm out of money. ‖wǒm děy 'dzěw-le. We must go. (*Literally* We have reached the state of having to 'go.) ‖jèy-ge-'dì wǒ sǎw-bu-'gān-jìng-le. This floor's gotten so I can't clean it up. *or* I've gotten to a state where I can't clean up this floor.

(5) *With a noun predicate the meaning is similar to the last:* ‖tā 'jīn-nyan jǐ-'swèy-le? How old is he (*literally* has he become) this year? ‖tā 'jīn-nyan 'lyèw-swèy-le. He's six this year. ‖shŕ-dyǎn-'bàn-le. It's ten-thirty.

(6) *When a verb is followed by an expression of duration or frequency*, le *is used only after the verb, or there and also after the expression of duration or frequency:* ‖wǒ-men dzày chúng-'chìng jù-le 'sān-nyán. We stayed in Chungking three years. ‖wǒ-men dzày chúng-'chìng jù-le 'sān-nyán-le. We've been in Chungking for three years now.

(7) *In stating a time or condition under which something happens*, le *contrasts with* je: ‖wǒm 'chŕ-le 'fàn jyèw kàn-'shū. After we've eaten we'll study. ‖wǒm chŕ-je 'fàn bú-kàn-'shū. We don't study while eating.

(8) le *contrasts with* de; le *emphasizes the thing done*, de *emphasizes the time at which done:* ‖tā dàw-'nǎr chywù-le? tā kàn tā-'mǔ-chin chywù-le. Where did she go? She went to see her mother. ‖'shéme-shŕ-hew chywù-de? 'chyán-tyan chywù-de. When did she go? She went the day before yesterday. ‖tā chywù-nyan dàw 'jūng-gwo chywù-le. He went to China last year (*emphasis on* China). *but* ‖tā 'chywù-nyan dàw jūng-gwo chywù-de. It was last year that he went to China (*emphasis on* last year).

(9) *For contrast with* gwo *see* gwo.

(10) *Compare the following:* gān-'dì dry land: 'gān-le-de-'dì dried land, land that has dried off; 'hǎw-rén a good guy *or* a healthy guy: 'hǎw-le-de-'rén one who has recovered from illness. *Similar contrast with or without* -le-de *between any adjective used before a noun and the noun; the* de *is automatic when the element before the noun becomes longer than one syllable.*

郎當，襤褸
'lē-te (A) dirty, filthy, untidy.

落
lè *see* làw; lè *is literary pronunciation.*

樂
lè *or* lwò (A) happy. ‖tā hěn 'lè. He's happy and smiling.

樂觀
lè-'gwān (A) optimistic.

lei *Wade Romanization for* ley.

冷
lěng (A) cold (*opposite* rè); cold, unenthusiastic, unfriendly (*of people or figuratively of the atmosphere*).   (H) coldly (*figurative sense*). ‖tā lěng 'shyàw-le. He laughed coldly, sarcastically. ‖wǒ 'lěng-dàw 'gǔ-tew-li chywù-le. I'm chilled to the bone.

冷清
lěng-'chīng (A) lonely, isolated. ‖jèy-ge-'dì-fang hěn lěng-'chīng. This place is very lonely.

冷淡
lěng-'dàn (A) be cold, indifferent; (V) be cold and indifferent towards *someone*. ‖tā dwèy-wo hěn lěng-'dàn. He's very cold to me.

冷孤丁的
lěng-gu-'dyēngr-de (H) suddenly, unexpectedly, without warning, out of the blue.

冷藏室
lěng-tsáng-'shř (N unit, jyān) a cold-storage room.

樓

léw (*Nunit*, **dzwò, ge**) a building of two or more stories. **dì-'sān-tséng-léw** the third floor of the building; **yí-dzwò-'sān-tséng-de-léw** a three-story building.

    shàng-'léw *or* **dàw léw-'shàng-chywu** go upstairs; **shyà-'léw** *or* **dàw léw-'shyà-chywu** go downstairs.

樓房

'léw-fáng (*Nunit*. **dzwò, ge**) a building of two or more stories, *when necessary to contrast with* **'píng-fáng** building of one story.

樓梯

léw-'tī (*Nunit*, **dwàr, jyéer**) a flight of stairs. **dzěw léw-'tī** walk on stairs; **shàng léw-'tī** walk upstairs; **shyà léw-'tī** walk downstairs.

    yì-tséng-léw-'tī a flight connecting two successive floors; **yí-dèng-léw-'tī** a single step of a flight.

簍（子，兒）

'lěw(-dz), lěwr (*Nunit*. **ge**) round basket of bamboo or other plant material, with or without a handle.

漏

lèw (*I*) to leak. **lèw-'shwěy** water leaks; **fáng-'dǐng lèw-'shwěy** the roof is leaking.

    As mainV: **'lèw-chū** (*le*) to leak out; **'lèw-shyà-chywù** to leak down.

    As postV: **jǔ-'lèw-le** to burn a hole in the container while cooking so that the contents leak out; **dǎ-'lèw-le** to strike a container and cause a leak; *etc.* ‖**shyà-'ywǔ de-shŕ-hew 'fáng-dz 'lèw-le.** When it rains the house leaks. ‖**tā bǎ-'gwō gěy dǎ-'lèw-le.** He knocked a hole in the kettle and the contents leaked out.

漏

lèw (*V*) to leave out. ‖**tā 'lèw-le yí-ge-'dz.** He left out a character (*in writing something*).

    As postV: **shwō-'lèw-le** to let *something* slip out when it shouldn't be said. ‖**tā shwō-'hwà shwō-'lèw-le.** He slipped up when talking and let something out that he shouldn't have said.

露

lèw *or* **lù** (*the latter more literary*) to expose to view, reveal, uncover. **lèw-'myàr** to show one's face; to show up, be present, be present in person; **lèw-'lyǎn** to attain popularity by demonstrating some special skill, to command admiration.

    As mainV: **lèw-chū-lay** to disclose; uncover. ‖**swǒ-yěw-de-'bì-mì dēw 'lèw-chū-lay-le.** All the secrets were disclosed. ‖**shwèy-'jyàw de-shŕ-hew bǎ-'lyǎn lèw-dzay 'wày-myan.** Sleep with your head uncovered. ‖**tā-chwān-de-'yī-fu 'gē-be lèw-je bàn-'jyé.** The dress she's wearing leaves the lower arms uncovered.

露頭角

lèw (*or* **lù**) **téw-'jyǎw** (*VNI. A*) to stand head and shoulders above others (*literally* head and horns), to be outstanding. ‖**nèy-ge-yǎn-'ywán hěn lèw téw-'jyǎw.** That actor is really outstanding.

雷

léy (*Nunit*. **shēng**) thunder. **dǎ-'léy** to thunder; **bèy-'léy 'dǎ-le** be struck by thunder (*that is,* by lightning); **dǎ yì-shēng-'léy** to thunder once; **gēn 'léy 'pī-le yí-'yàng** be thunderstruck (*figurative, always by something unexpected and terrible*).

類

lèy (*Mclass*) kind of. ‖**tām dēw-shr yí-'lèy-de-rén.** They're all the same kind of person (*they all think alike, have the same habits, or the same social status*).

    lyǎng-lèy-de-'shŕ-ching two classifications of business, matters, affairs.

    fēn-'lèy to classify, file according to kind, separate. ‖**shū fēn lyǎng-'lèy.** There are two kinds of books.

    rén-'lèy human kind, **chù-'lèy** animal kind (*terms contrasted in Buddhist theory*): **ywú-'lèy** fish, **nyǎw-'lèy** feathered creatures.

淚

lèy (*Nmass*) (*often* **yǎn-'lèy** *literally* eye tears) tears. ‖**tā mǎn-'lyǎn dēw-shr 'lèy.** His face was covered with tears. ‖**tā yǎn-'lèy 'lyéw-chū-lay-le.** His tears flowed.

累

lèy (*A*) to be tired, exhausted. **lèy** *or* **'lèy-rén** be tiring, exhausting (*of work, tasks*). ‖**wǒ 'lèy-de pá-bu-'dùng.** I'm so tired I can't even crawl, *or* I'm so tired I can't move.

    As mainV: **lèy-'hwày-le** to wear oneself out; **lèy-'sž-le** to be tired to death (*figuratively*). ‖**wǒ 'jyàn-jŕ lèy 'pā-shyà-le.** I'm so tired I can hardly stand (*literally* I'm about to fall flat on my face).

類似

'lèy-sž (*A*) to be similar; (*V*) to be similar to; (*Nabstr*) similarity, resemblance.

離

lí (*K*) from (*in giving distances*). ‖**gūng-shŕ-'fáng lí wǒ-'jù-de-dì-fang bù-'ywǎn.** The office isn't far from where I live. ‖**hwǒ-chē-'jàn lí fàn-'dyàn yěw sān-'lǐ.** The railroad station is three miles from the hotel. **'lí-je** *in* ‖**hwǒ-chē-'jàn gēn fàn-'dyàn lí-je hěn-'ywǎn.** The railroad station and the hotel are quite far apart.

    (*V*) to leave. **lí-'àn** to pull away from the shore; **bù-lí dzwǒ-'yèw** is always hanging around nearby; **lí-'hwēn** to be divorced; **lí-'tí** to get off the subject; **lí-le 'tí-le** be beside the point.

犂

lí (*Nunit;* bǎ) a plow.

蓠 , 厘

lí (*Mmeas*). *See Appendix B.*

離笆

'lí-ba (*Nunit,* myàn, shàn, lyèw) fence (*bamboo or other wood*). jú-'lí a bamboo fence. ‖yán-je 'lù yěw 'lí-ba. There's a fence alongside the road.

離奇

lí-'chí (*VN1, A*) strange; (*H*) strangely. ‖tā-de-'shíng-wey hěn lí-'chí. His behavior is quite strange.

離間

lí-'jyàn (*V*) to cause a rift between, drive a wedge between *two friends, etc.*

離開

'lí-kāy (*RC2*) to go away, leave, separate from. ‖jèy-ge-'chwán 'yǐ-jing 'lí-kay mǎ-'téw-le. This ship has already left the pier. ‖wǒ děy 'lí-kay jèr. I've got to get out of here.

理

lǐ (*V*) to set in order, straighten out. ‖bǎ 'shyāng-dz 'lǐ-yi-lǐ. Put (the things in) the suitcase in order. ‖gěy-wo lǐ-'shū. Straighten out my books for me.

    As mainV: lǐ-'chīng-chu straighten out and clear up; lǐ-'hwày-le get things messed up while trying to straighten them out; *etc.*

    lǐ-'fǎ to cut hair, to get a haircut; lǐ-fǎ-'gwǎn barber shop; lǐ-fǎ-'jyàng barber.

理

lǐ (*V*) to address, say hello to, speak to, hail, *someone.* 'shéy yě bu-lǐ-'shéy-le. We're not talking to each other. *or* We're not on speaking terms.

理

lǐ (*Nabstr*) logic, reason. yěw-'lǐ to be reasonable, logical. ‖tā-shwō-de-'hwà hěn yěw-'lǐ; shr̀-'nǐ 'méy-lǐ. What he said was quite logical; it's you who are in the wrong.

裏

lǐ (li) (*Nplace*) inside.

    Used after K of direction and motion, as wǎng-'lǐ towards the inside, inwards; *otherwise an extended form is used:* 'lǐ-tew(r), 'lǐ-myan, 'lǐ-byan, 'lǐ-myar, 'lǐ-byar.

    All are added to N; li *then is usually toneless:* 'fáng-dz-li in the house; 'wū-dz-li in a room; *but* chéng-'lǐ downtown.

里

lǐ (*Mmeas*) Chinese mile; *usually about one-third of an English mile, but not constant throughout China.* lyǎng-lǐ-'lù *or* èr-lǐ-'lù a two-mile stretch of road, a distance of two miles. ‖'shàng-shān yì-'bǎy-'lǐ, 'shyà-shān 'bā-shr-'lǐ. It's a hundred lǐ to the top of the mountain, and eighty lǐ back. (*This is often said in the Chinese countryside where it is the habit to estimate distances in terms of time consumed in travel even though they are expressed in a unit of distance.*)

禮

*lǐ (*Nunit;* tsz̀; jyàn, ge) ceremony, rite. shíng-'lǐ to perform a ceremony *or* to participate in a ceremony; hwēn-'lǐ wedding; sāng-'lǐ ceremony of mourning; dzàng-'lǐ funeral; jywūn-'lǐ military courtesy, etiquette; jř-'lǐ to know how to behave, to know etiquette; sùng-'lǐ to send a gift; shēw-'lǐ to receive *or* accept a gift; hwán-'lǐ to give a gift in return.

禮拜

lǐ-'bày (*Nabstr*) act of worshipping. dzwò lǐ-'bày to worship, go to church (*Christian term*); lǐ-bày-'táng (*Nunit,* ge) a church (*building, place*).

    (*Ntime,* ge) a week; běn-, shyà-, shàng-lǐ-'bày this-, next-, last week; lǐ-bày-'yī, -'èr, . . . -'lyèw Monday, Tuesday, . . . Saturday; lǐ-bày-'tyān *or* lǐ-bày-'r̀ Sunday; 'shyà-lǐ-bày-'sān Wednesday of next week.

禮服

lǐ-'fú (*Nunit,* jyàn; tàw) formal attire. chwān lǐ-'fú to wear formal attire; dà-lǐ-'fú very formal attire.

理會

lǐ-'hwèy (*V*) to notice; to understand, comprehend. ‖wǒ méy-lǐ-'hwèy nèy-jyàn-'shr̀-ching. I didn't notice that. *or* I didn't understand that, I didn't take that in.

理智

lǐ-'jr̀ (*Nabstr*) reason, intellect, intellectual capacities, head *versus heart.* ‖tā hěn yěw lǐ-'jr̀. He's really intelligent. ‖tā-de-lǐ-'jr̀ 'gwǎn-jù tā-de-'gǎn-chíng. His head rules his emotions.

禮節

lǐ-'jyé (*Nabstr*) manners, customs. ‖chywù jyàn 'hwáng-dì yěw shéme-lǐ-'jyé méy-yew? Is there any (*special*) courtesy (*to be observed*) when presented at court?

理科

lǐ-'kē (*Nabstr;* mér) general science (*as a course of study in secondary schools*).

禮貌

'lǐ-màw (*Nabstr*) etiquette, manners. ‖jèy-ge-rén hěn yěw 'lǐ-màw. He has excellent manners.

理想

lǐ-'shyǎng (*Aattr*) ideal. ‖'jèy-běn-shū shŕ wǒ-(de-)lǐ-'shyǎng(-de). This book is my ideal.

理學士

lǐ-'shywé-shr (*Npers*) bachelor of science. ‖tā yěw yí-ge-'lǐ-shywé-shr-de-shywé-'wèy. He has the degree of bachelor of science.

理所當然

'lǐ-swǒ-dāng-'rán (*J*) of course, as a matter of course.

禮堂

lǐ-'táng (*Nunit*, ge) hall *or* auditorium.

禮物

'lǐ-wu (*Nunit*, jyàn, ge, fèr) a gift. sùng 'lǐ-wu send a gift, give a gift.

理由

lǐ-'yéw (*Nunit*) a reason *for doing something.* ‖wǒ jŕ yěw 'yí-ge-lǐ-'yéw. I have only one reason.

利

lì (*Nabstr*) advantage, profit, interest; yěw-'lì to be favorable, be of advantage. sān-fēh-'lì three-percent interest.

立

lì (*V*) to stand *something* up; to set up, establish, put into effect, enact. lì-'fǎ (*VN3*) to enact laws; lì ge-'jé-dz to open an account (*literally* account-book); li yì-jāng-'dż-jywù draw up a contract, deed, mortgage, *etc.*

    As mainV: 'lì-chǐ-láy to stand something up on end; lì-'jèng to stand upright (lì-'jèng! Attention! *to soldiers*); bǎ chí-'gān 'lì-chi-lay. Set up the flagpole. ‖'shywé-sheng kàn-jyan 'shyān-sheng láy-le, jyèw 'lì-chi-lay-le. When the students saw the teachers coming, they sprang to their feet.

粒

lì (*Nunit*) a grain of, speck of *something hard.* yí-lì (-de)-'shā-dz a grain of sand; yí-lì(-de)-là-jyāw-'dzěr a grain of pepper; yí-lì-'mǐ a grain of rice; *etc.*

曆, 歷

*lì (*N*) calendar, calendar system. lì-'fǎ a calendar system; yīn-lì the lunar calendar; yáng-lì the solar calendar; shī-'lì the Western (Christian) calendar; jyèw-'lì *or* shyà-'lì the old calendar *Chinese, lunar; now replaced officially*); lì-'shū an almanac.

立場

lì-'chǎng (*Nunit*, ge) standpoint, viewpoint, point of view. ‖tā 'jàn-je gwó-mín-'dǎng-de-lì-'chǎng-shang láy shwō-'hwà. He speaks from the Kuomintang point of view.

歷城

lì-'chéng (*Nunique*) Li-ch'eng (*capital of Shantung province*).

利錢

'lì-chyán (*Nmass*) interest *on investment.* dé 'lì-chyán *or* shēw, ná, chř, jwàn 'lì-chyán to draw interest; chū 'lì-chyan, gěy 'lì-chyan, fù 'lì-chyan to pay interest.

栗子

'lì-dz (*Nunit*, ge) a chestnut.

利害

'lì-hày (*A*) severe, serious, injurious; powerful, extreme. ‖tā 'bìng-de hěn 'lì-hay. He's seriously ill. ‖'fēng 'gwā-de hěn 'lì-hay. The wind is blowing furiously. ‖tā-de-'dzwěy hěn 'lì-hay. He has a critical (*or* sharp *or* sarcastic) tongue.

力戰

lì-'jàn (*V*) to fight bitterly against. ‖wǒm 'lì-jàn 'dí-rén. We fought the enemy bitterly, with all our strength.

立刻

lì-'kè (*J*) immediately, at once. ‖tā lì-'kè jyèw 'pǎw-le. He scrammed immediately.

歷落

'lì-lew, 'lì-le (*A*) clear-cut, distinct, neat and complete. ‖tā dzwò-'shř hěn 'lì-le. He works very neatly. ‖tā shwō-'hwà hěn 'lì-le. He speaks very distinctly. ‖nèy-ge-lǎw-'tày-tay twěy-'jyǎwr 'dàw hěn 'lì-lew. She's surprisingly spry on her feet for an old lady.

力量

'lì-lyang (*Nabstr*) force, power, authority. hěn yěw 'lì-lyang very powerful, very effective.

例如

lì-'rú (*literary*) for example (*referring to events as precedents*).

立時

'lì-shŕ (*J*) at once, immediately. ‖tā 'lì-shŕ jyèw 'pǎw-le. He scrammed immediately.

歷史

lì-'shř (*Nabstr*) history; jūng-gwo-lì-'shř Chinese history, the history of China; lì-shř-'shywé the study of history, the science of history; lì-shř-'jyā a historian.

麗水

lì-'shwěy (*Nunique*) Li-shui (*city in Chekiang province*).

利物浦

lì-wù-'pǔ (*Nunique*) Liverpool (*England*).

利益

'lì-yì (*Nunit*, ge) an advantage, point in favor. ‖nǐ 'nème-yàng 'dzwò, dwèy nǐ-'dž-jǐ 'méy shéme-'lì-yì. There's no advantage for you in doing that.

利用

'lì-yùng (*V*) to take advantage of, make use of. 'lì-yung shf-'jyān to make use of available time, not let it go to waste. ‖byé 'lì-yùng wo. Don't take advantage of me; don't cheat me.

利於

'lì-ywú (*V*) to be favorable to.

lia *Wade Romanization for* lya.

liang *Wade Romanization for* lyang.

liao *Wade Romanization for* lyaw.

lieh *Wade Romanization for* lye.

lien *Wade Romanization for* lyan.

鱗

lín (*Nunit*, ge) (fish) scales; ywú-'lín fish scales.

臨

lín (*V*) to be located near to and facing. lín-'jyē faces the street; lín-'hú faces the lake, is on (by) the lake; lín-'hé is on (by) the river. ‖'fáng-dz-lín-'jyē-de-yí-'myàr yěw 'lyǎng-ge-'chwāng-hu. The side of the house that faces the street has two windows in it.

臨川

lín-'chwān (*Nunique*) Lin-ch'uan or Linchwan (*city in Kiangsi province*).

臨海

lín-'hǎy (*Nunique*) Lin-hai (*city in Chekiang province*).

鄰居

lín-'jywū (*Npers*) next-door neighbor.

臨了

lín-'lyǎw(r) (*Ntime*) almost at the end of *some period of time*, the eleventh hour. ‖tā dzày kāy-'hwèy-de-lín-'lyǎwr tsáy 'láy. He didn't arrive until almost the end of the meeting.

臨沂

lín-'yì (*Nunique*) Lin-i or Linyi (*city in Shantung province*).

臨榆

lín-'ywú (*Nunique*) Lin-yü (*city in Hopeh province*).

吝嗇

'lìn-sè (*A*) to be stingy, tight. ‖tā hěn 'lìn-sè. He's very stingy.

零

líng (*Nunit*, ge) zero. yí-ge-'líng or yí-ge-'líng-dž a zero. (*Used in forming numerals; see NumU, NumG.*)

    Since items counted after líng *are smaller portions than those counted before it* (*e.g.,* yì-'bǎy-líng-'sān one hundred and three), líng *is used before nouns to mean* partial, fragmentary. 'líng-chyán small change; líng-'pyàw small-denomination bills; líng-'gūng part-time work.

    (*H*) líng 'mày to sell bulk *rather than in packages,* individually *rather than in sets.*

靈

líng (*A*) alert, quick, accurate; in good working order. ‖wǒ-de-'chē bù-'líng-le. My car's out of order. ‖tā shwō-'hwà shwō-de hěn 'líng. He speaks very cleverly. (*It may mean that what he says usually comes true.*)

    (*Nunit*, ge) coffin. ‖'sž-rén-de-'líng háy dzày-'jèr. The dead man's coffin is still here.

鈴

líng, lyéngr (*Nunit*, ge) a small bell. èn-'lyéngr ring a bell by pushing a button; lā-'lyéngr ring a bell by pulling a string (*occasionally by pushing a button*); dǎ-'lyéngr ring a bell by striking it; yáw-'lyéngr ring a bell by swinging it back and forth; mén-'lyéngr doorbell; fàn-'lyéngr dinner bell. ‖lyéngr 'shyǎng-le. The bell is sounding.

    A large bell is jūng.

零七八碎

líng-chī-bā-'swèy (*Aattr*) random, odds and ends of. líng-chī-bā-'swèy-de-dūng-shi odds and ends, random bits, miscellaneous things.

鈴鐺

'líng-dang (*Nunit*, ge) bell. *See also* líng.

零度

líng-'dù zero degrees. líng-'shyà sān-shr-'dù or líng-'dù-yǐ-'shyà sān-shr-'dù thirty degrees below zero; líng-'shàng sān-shr-'dù or líng-'dù-yǐ-'shàng sān-shr-'dù thirty degrees above zero. ‖'wēn-dù dzày líng-'dù. The temperature is (at) zero.

靈分

'líng-fèn (*A*) skillful.

靈魂

'líng-hwén (*Nunit*, ge) soul (*Christian term*).

靈機一動

líng-'jī yí-'dùng (*literary quotation*) as a sudden inspiration, as a sudden idea. ‖tā líng-'jī yí-'dùng jyèw 'pǎw-le. Realizing all of a sudden what was about to happen, he scrammed.

零件

íng-'jyàn, líng-'jyàr (*Nunit, ge*) parts, spare parts, accessories. ‖jèy-ge-'jyà-chyan bú-'swàn líng-'jyàr dzày-'nèy. This price doesn't include accessories.

翎毛，翎兒

íng-'máw, lyéngr (*Nunit, gēr*) a feather, colored and attractive like a peacock's. ‖'màw-dz-shang dày yì-gēr-'lyéngr. There's a feather in the hat.

零星

líng-'shīng (*Aattr*) partial, fragmentary, in small parts. líng-shīng-wù-'pǐn merchandise which comes in small units (*needles, pins, thimbles, etc.*).

零吃

'líng-shŕ (*Nmass*) snacks, tidbits fit for between-meal eating. ‖tā 'shì-hwan chŕ-'líng-shŕ. He likes to nibble on tidbits.

領

líng (*V*) to lead, guide, show the way (*physically, of a route*). ‖shŕ-'shéy 'líng-je nǐ-men 'jìn-lay? Who guided you in? *or* Who ushered you in?
    líng-'lù (*VN1*) to lead the way; líng-'lù-de(-rén) a guide.
    As mainV: líng-'dàw (*lc*) to conduct *someone* to a *place;* líng-'dzěw-le to usher away; *etc.*

領

líng (*V*) to get, receive, lay claim to. líng-'chyán to collect money (*pay or otherwise*); líng hù-'jàw to get passports.

領

*líng, 'líng-dz (*Nunit, tyáw*) collar (*separate piece or separate garment*). chèn-shān-'líng-dz shirt collar; líng-'kěwr neck of a dress or any other garment; líng-'jāng collar insignia (*military, etc.*).

領導

líng-'dǎw (*V*) to lead, direct, guide. ‖'shyān-sheng líng-'dǎw 'shywé-sheng. A teacher guides his students. ‖shŕ-'shéy líng-'dǎw nǐ-men dàw-'nàr chywù-de? Who showed you the way to get there?

領帶

líng-'dày (*Nunit, tyáw*) necktie. jì líng-'dày to tie a necktie; jyě líng-'dày to untie a necktie.

領粥

líng-'jēw (*VN1*) to receive relief (*originally in the form of congee or porridge jēw, now in any form, but not money*). líng-'jēw-de-rén people on the breadline.

領教

líng-'jyàw (*VN1*) to receive instruction, be taught (*a bit literary*).

領結

líng-'jyéer (*Nunit, ge*) the bow of a bow tie. dǎ ge-líng-'jyéer to tie a bow in a tie.

領袖

líng-'shyèw (*Npers*) a leader. ‖líng-'shyèw-de-tsáy-'néng shŕ tyān-'shēng-de. The ability to be a leader is innate (*not learned*).

領頭

líng-'téwr (*VN1*) start something, set a pattern. ‖tā líng-'téwr dzwò jèy-jyàn-'shŕ-ching! He started it! ‖'yí-ge-rén líng-'téwr, dà-'jyā dēw 'gēn-je 'dzwò-le. One man started it, and everybody followed suit.

令

lìng (*Nunit, ge, dàw*) an order, edict, regulation. fā-'lìng to issue an order; shyà-'lìng to hand down an order; jyē-'lìng to receive an order.

另

lìng (*Preord*) different, other, *mainly before* yī. 'lìng-yí-jyàn-'shŕ still another matter (*not the one we have been speaking of*); 'lìng-yì-jǔng-rén another kind of person, still another kind of person (*other than the kinds that have been mentioned*). ‖tā-'dz̀-jǐ méy-'láy; tā pày 'lìng-yí-ge-rén láy-le. He didn't come in person; he sent someone else.
    (*H*) again, *in addition to previous occurrences*. 'lìng 'sùng yí-jyàr-lay send one more, send another. ‖tā 'lìng gěy-le wo yì-bǎy-kwày-chyán. He gave me another hundred dollars.

令

*lìng *prefixed to certain kinship terms when speaking to someone about a member of his family.* **See Appendix A.**

另外

lìng-'wày (*Nplace*) outside of, besides, beyond, in addition to. ‖chú-le 'jèy-sān-kwày-chyán lìng-'wày 'háy yěw 'shŕ-kwày-chyán. In addition to this three dollars, there's also another ten. ‖tā líng-wo dàw lìng-'wày-yí-ge-dì-fang chywù 'kàn. He conducted me to yet another place for me to look at. ‖lìng-'wày 'háy yěw yí-ge-'kè-rén. There's still another guest.

liu *Wade Romanization for* lyew.

lo *Wade Romanization for* lwo.

lou *Wade Romanization for* lew.

lü *Wade Romanization for* lywu.

爐（子）

*lú, 'lú-dz (Nunit, ge) stove, furnace. hwǒ-'lú *with same meaning;* bì-'lú fireplace in a wall.

蘆梗兒

lú-'gěngr (Nunit, gér) reed, cane (*stems of certain water plants used for making things*).

廬州

lú-'jēw (Nunique) Luchow, *another name for* hé-'féy (*city in Anhwei province*).

蘆筍

lú-'swěn (Nunit, gér) asparagus.

蘆草

lú-'tsǎw (Nunit, ge) rushes, bulrushes.

鱸魚

lú-'ywú (Nunit, tyáw) bass (*fish*).

硵精

lǔ-'jīng (Nmass) spirits of ammonia (*often called* yǎ-mwó-ni-'yǎ).

鹿

lù (Nunit, jř) deer.

路

lù (Nunit, tyáw) a road, a route, a way. lù-'shyàn route; dzěw-'lù to go, walk, progress, take a walk, make a trip; 'lù-shang on the way; bàn-'lù-shang halfway (*more or less*); lù-'kěw(r) street corner, end of a street, entrance to a street; yěw èr-lǐ-'lù ywǎn is two miles away.

(*Mord*) *numbering busses or trains by the routes they follow:* ‖dzwò 'èr-lù-chē jyèw 'ké-yi-le. Take the number two bus (*or* streetcar) and you'll be all right.

In street names: 'běy-mén 'èr-lù Second Street from the North Gate; *etc.*

陸

*lù (N) land. dà-'lù (N) mainland *as opposed to* dǎw islands; lù-'dì (N) land *as opposed to sea;* ywǎn-'ywār-de 'kàn-jyàn lù-'dì to sight land from afar.

*lù pertaining to the Army, *in contrast to the Navy* (*hǎy) *and Air Force* (*kūng). lù-'jywūn the Army.

路程

lù-'chéng (Nunit, ge) a route, a journey. ‖nǐ dzěw shéme-lù-'chéng? Which route are you following?

路過

lù-'gwò (V) to go past, go by. ‖wǒ lù-'gwò nèy-jyān-'pù-dz. I went past that store.

露天

lù-'tyān (*sometimes* lèw-'tyān) (Nplace) open air. ‖tām dzày lù-'tyān-de-dì-fang jàw-'shyàng. They're taking pictures at an open-air spot.

lù-tyān-de-'lyáng-táy an open-air platform (*no roof*).

露營

lù-'yíng (VN1) to camp out, to bivouac.

luan *Wade Romanization for* lwan.

lüan *Wade Romanization for* lywan.

lüeh *Wade Romanization for* lyv

lun *Wade Romanization for* lwen.

聾（子）

lúng (A) deaf. 'lúng-dz (Npers) a deaf person.

攏

lúng (V) to build up a fire (lúng-'hwǒ); to put into a fire as fuel. lúng-'lú to build a fire in a stove. *As mainV:* 'lúng-chǐ-láy *or* 'lúng-shàng build up a fire. ‖dǎ-'cháy lúng-'hwǒ. Get some firewood for a fire.

攏

lúng, lǔng (V) to gather in together (*as with the arms spread out and brought together*). lǔng-'chywán to grasp power; lǔng-'àn to draw close to shore (*of a boat*).

As mainV: 'lǔng-dzày (yí-'kwàr) to gather (together); lǔng-dàw (lc) to gather things to a place; 'lǔng-chǐ-láy gather up. ‖bǎ swǒ-yěw-de-'shū děw 'lǔng-dzày yí-'kwàr. Gather all the books up together. ‖bǎ dàw-'tsǎw lǔng-chéng yì-'kwěr. Gather the rice-straw into sheaves.

龍溪

lúng-'chī (Nunique) Lung-ch'i (*city in Fukien province*).

攏總

lúng-'dzǔng, lǔng-'dzǔng (H) altogether. ‖bǎ jèy-jǐ-ge-'shù-mu lǔng-'dzǔng 'hé-dzày yí-'kwàr, yěw 'dwō-shǎw? Add all those figures together and how much is it?

隆重

lúng-'jùng (A) formal (of a celebration, meeting, ceremony); impressive.

龍江

lúng-'jyāng (Nunique) Lung-chiang or Tsitsihar (capital of Heilungkiang province).

龍鬚菜

lúng-shywū-'tsày (Nunit, gēr) asparagus.

絡頭

'lúng-tew (Nunit, ge) bridle. mǎ-'lúng-tew bridle for a horse. 'shàng(-shang) 'lúng-tew to put a bridle on.

龍頭

'lúng-tew (Nunit, ge) a spigot, tap, faucet. shwěy-'lúng-tew water faucet; méy-chì-'lúng-tew gas cock.

攏

lǔng (V) to comb; lǔng-'téw comb one's hair (literally head).

    'lǔng-dz (Nunit, bǎ) a comb.

    As mainV: lǔng-'jŕ-le to comb hair out straight; lǔng-'lwàn-le to comb into a tangle; lǔng-'rwǎn-le to comb until soft.

亂

lwàn (A) to be confused, in disorder, mixed-up, helter-skelter; in trouble. ‖'shū hěn 'lwàn. The books are all in confusion. ‖tā-shwō-de-'hwà hěn 'lwàn. What he's saying is all mixed up (it can't be understood).

    (H) lwàn 'yáw to shake something irregularly; lwàn 'màw to burst upwards irregularly (as sparks from a chimney).

    'lwàn-dz (Nunit, ge) a state of confusion or trouble. chū yí-ge-'lwàn-dz to reach a state of confusion; nàw yí-ge-'lwàn-dz to cause a disturbance.

    As postV: shwō-'lwàn-le to cause trouble or confusion by what one says; shyě-'lwàn-le to cause trouble by writing; etc.

亂七八糟

lwàn-chi-ba-'dzāw (A) to be helter-skelter, at sixes and sevens, all in confusion. ‖tā-de-'wū-dz lwàn-chi-ba-'dzāw. His room was all in confusion.

亂堆

lwàn-'dwēy (Nunit, ge) a pile of waste material, a pile of junk, a pile of stuff, a junk-pile. wǒ tsúng lwàn-'dwēy-lǐ-tew bǎ 'jyè-jr jǎw-'jáw-le. I found my (lost) ring in a junk-pile.

亂紙

lwàn-'jŕ or làn-'jŕ (Nmass) waste paper. lwàn-jŕ-'lěwr waste paper basket.

亂亂騰騰的

'lwàn-lwàn-teng-'tēng-de (Aattr) in a commotion, all in confusion (as of a crowd).

淋

lwén (V) to shower down on. ‖'ywǔ 'lwén-ta-le. The rain showered down on him.

    As mainV: lwén-'shŕ-le to shower down on and (make) wet; lwén-'tèw-le to get wet through. ‖'ywǔ bǎ-ta lwén-'shŕ-le. The rain got him wet. ‖yì-'shēn dēw lwén-'tèw-le. He got wet through.

輪

*lwén (I) to rotate, take turns. As mainV: lwén-dàw 'ni-le it's your turn.

    'lwén-je ('bār) take turns; (H) taking turns, in rotation.

輪 (子)

*lwén, 'lwén-dz (Nunit, ge) a wheel. bǎ-'lwén steering wheel; lwén-'dày a wheel belt, a machine belt; a tire.

    lwén-'chwán a steamship; lwén-'dù a steam ferry (both from the old side-wheel type of boat, but term still used).

倫敦

lwén-'dwēn (Nunique) London.

輪流

lwén-'lyéw (I) to take turns; (H) taking turns. ‖wǒmen lwén-'lyéw dàw yī-'ywàn chywù 'kàn-ta. We'll take turns going to the hospital to see him.

論

lwèn (V) to discuss. lwèn yí-jyàn-'shŕ-ching to discuss a matter. As mainV: ‖wǒm háy méy-'lwèn-dàw nèy-jyàn-shŕ-ching. We haven't reached any discussion of that matter yet. ‖bú-'lwèn. It doesn't matter. ‖bú-'lwèn něy-ge, dēw 'ké-yi. It doesn't matter which one, any is OK. ‖'dǎy-ta! sž-'hwó bú-'lwèn! Catch him! Dead or alive doesn't matter! (or Catch him dead or alive!)

論

lwèn (K) by some unit of weight, measure, etc.: lwèn-'bàng by the pound; lwèn-'shyár by the box; lwèn-'gèr by the piece, individually. ‖jèy-ge-'gwǒ-dz shŕ lwèn-'gèr mày, bú-shr lwèn-'jīn. This fruit is sold by the individual piece, not by the catty.

騾子

'lwó-dz (Nunit, téw, ge; rarely pǐ) mule. lwó(-dz)-'chē a mule cart; jywūn-yùng-'lwó an army mule.

螺口

lwó-'kěw (Nunit, ge) a screw-top; a bottle-top that screws on. bǎ lwó-'kěw gěy jwàn-'kāy-le unscrew the top; bǎ lwó-'kěw gěy 'jwàn-shàng-le screw on the top.

羅馬尼亞（國）

lwó-ma-ni-'yǎ(-gwó) (*N unique*) Rumania.

羅馬

lwó-'mǎ (*N unique*) Rome. lwó-mǎ-'dż Latin letters, the Latin alphabet; Romanized writing *of Chinese*.

羅盤

'lwó-pán (*N unit*, ge) a compass (*for direction*).

螺絲

'lwó-sz (*N unit*, ge) a screw, bolt; a sea-shell *of this shape*. ‖bǎ 'lwó-sz gěy 'jwàn-jìn-chywù. Screw the screw in. ‖bǎ 'lwó-sz gěy 'jwàn-chū-lay. Screw the screw out.

螺絲釘（兒）

lwó-sz-'dīng, lwó-sz-'dyēngr (*N unit*, ge) a screw, bolt.

樂

lwò *see* lè.

洛

lwò *see* làw.

擺

*'lwò (*V*) to pile up neatly. *As mainV*: 'lwò-chǐ-la 'lwò-shàng; 'lwò-dzay (yí-'kwàr) to pile up (together, ‖bǎ-'shū gěy 'lwò-chǐ-lay. Pile the books up one on top of another.

    lwèr (*Mgroup*) a neat pile of. yí-lwèr-'shū a neat pile of books (*one column*); yí-lwèr-de-myàn-'bāw a neat pile of (*slices of*) bread (*piled one on top of another*); yí-lwèr-de-'páy a deck of cards *or* one trick (*in a card game*).

落後

lwò-'hèw *or* lè-'hèw (*VN1, A*) to leave behind, forge ahead of; (*figuratively*) to become passé. ‖tā-de-'sž-shyǎng hěn lwò-'hèw. His ideas are way behind the times.

駱駝

'lwò-two (*N unit*, jř) a camel. lwò-two-'dwèy a camel caravan.

落伍

lwò-'wǔ *or* lè-'wǔ (*VN1, A*) to be unable to catch up with, to be left behind; (*figuratively*) to be out of date.

洛陽

lwò-'yáng (*N unique*) Lo-yang (*city in Honan province*).

倆

lyǎ (*NumU*) two, both. *Confined to a few expressions as the following:* wǒ-men-'lyǎ(-rén) we two; nǐ-men-'lyǎ(-rén); tā-men-'lyǎ(-rén) you two, they two;

dzám-'lyǎ(-rén) we two; *any of these with* rér *for* rén: 'lyǎ-rén, 'lyǎ-rér two people. ‖yí-ge-rén 'lyǎ-rér méy-'gwān-shi. One person or two, it doesn't matter.

    lyǎ-'shěw both hands; lyǎ-'ěr-dwo both ears; lyǎ-'yǎn-jing both eyes; *and so on with paired body parts;* lyǎ-'mér both doors; *and other paired things.*

    Note that lyǎ *is* lyǎng *plus a measure: thus* 'lyǎ-rén *equals* 'lyǎng-ge-rén; *the shorter form is highly colloquial and mainly Peiping speech.*

連

*lyán (*V*) to join, connect. ‖jèy-'lyǎng-tyáw-'jyē 'lyán-je. These two streets are connected.

    As mainV: 'lyán-chǐ-lay to join, connect; 'lyán-dzày (yí-'kwàr) to connect *things* (together); 'lyán-shàng to join, connect. ‖tā-lyǎng-ge-'méy-maw 'lyán-shang-le. His eyebrows join at the middle. ‖bǎ jèy-'lyǎng-tyáw-'shéng-dz lyán-dzay yí-'kwàr. Join these two pieces of rope together.

連

lyán (*K*) even including, even; *followed by H* yě *or* dēw. ‖lyán-'tā dēw 'chywù-le. They all went, even he. ‖lyán-'tā yě 'chywù-le. Even he went along too (*no real difference in meaning from preceding*). ‖lyán-'tā wǒ dēw (*or* yě) bú-'rèn-shr. I don't even know him. *or* I don't know any of them, not even him.

    Sometimes followed by V instead of N: lyán-'lǐ dēw bù-'lǐ not even say hello *to someone.*

連

lyán (*MgroupA*) company, troop, battery (*military*). yì-lyán-de-'pàw-bīng a battery of artillery soldiers; lyán-'jǎng company commander, *etc.;* lyán-'fù deputy commander of a company, etc.

簾（子，兒）

*lyán, 'lyán-dz, lyár (*N unit*, ge) curtain, drape. chwāng-hu-'lyán, chwāng-hu-'lyár window curtains; mén-'lyán, mén-'lyár door curtains; jú-'lyán-dz flexible curtain made of strips of bamboo.

聯合

lyán-'hé (*V*) to join with, form a federation *or* unity with. ‖'méy-gwo gēn 'jūng-gwo lyán-'hé. *or* 'méy-gwo lyán-'hé 'jūng-gwo. America and China are allied. *or* America is allied with China.

    As mainV: lyán-'hé-chǐ-lay *with same meaning.*

    lyán-hé-'gwó (*N unit*, ge) an ally; *collectively* the United Nations.

連蒙帶虎

lyán-'mēng-dày-'hǔ-de (*H*) under false pretenses, by guile. ‖tā lyán-'mēng-dày-'hǔ-de jyèw bǎ-ta dày-'dzěw-le. He enticed her away under false pretenses.

聯盟

lyán-'méng (I) to be allied, have good political relations. ‖'jūng-gwo gēn 'měy-gwo lyán-'méng. China and the United States are allied.

    As mainV: lyán-'méng-chǐ-lay to become allied.

    lyán-méng-'gwó (Nunit, ge) an ally; collectively the Allies (World War I); gwó-jì-lyán-'méng League of Nations (abbreviated as gwó-'lyán).

聯系，連系

'lyán-shì (Nunit, ge) a relation, interconnection. ‖jèy-lyǎng-jyàn-'shř méy-yew 'lyán-shì. These two matters are unrelated.

連續

lyán-'shywù (I) to carry on again after an interruption. ‖'jīn-tyan-de-yǎn-'jyǎng 'míng-tyan dzày lyán-'shywù. Today's lecture will be continued tomorrow.

    As mainV: lyán-'shywù-shyà-chywù with same meaning.

    (H) one after another, in a stream. ‖tām lyán-'shywù-de wǎng-'shǐ dzěw. They moved westward incessantly, in a continuous stream (as of a migration).

斂

lyǎn (V) collect, pull together physically by spreading the fingers out and pulling them together thus drawing scattered matches or other small objects to a single point; or any method which involves this same type of motion, actually or by analogy. lyǎn-'chyán to accumulate and hoard money. ‖bǎ nǐ-de-'jīng-shen 'lyǎn-yi-lyǎn. Collect your wits. or Pull yourself together (intellectually, not emotionally). ‖bǎ 'dūng-shi 'lyǎn-ba 'lyǎn-ba, gāy 'dzěw-le. Get your things together; we've got to go.

    As mainV: 'lyǎn-dzày (yí-'kwàr) to gather things (together); 'lyǎn-chǐ-láy gather things up; 'lyǎn-dàw gather things in to a place. ‖bǎ jè-shyē-'jř dēw 'lyǎn-dzày. nèy-ge-'shyāng-dz-li. Gather up these papers and put them in this box.

臉

lyǎn (Nunit, ge) face. shǐ-'lyǎn to wash the face; (shǐ-)lyǎn-'pén washbasin; lyǎn-'pí the skin of the face; 'lyǎn-pí 'hèw to have thick skin on the face (meaning to be a heel, a rat); 'lyǎn-shang·r) on the face; superficially, appearances. ‖'lyǎn-shang bù-hǎw-'kàn. It doesn't look right (to do such a thing).

    'lyǎn 'chén-shyà-chywù-le to have one's face fall, to become gloomy.

    lyǎn (Nabstr) "face", reputation for conformity with the accepted rules of society, conventions, etiquette, etc. (not a matter of right and wrong).

    dyēw-'lyǎn (VN1, A) of an action, "face"-losing; bú-yàw 'lyǎn to have no dignity, no sense of social fitness, not to care whether you have a reputation for social correctness or not (very strong adverse com-

ment); méy-yew 'lyǎn to be in disrepute, to have lost "face". ‖tā 'méy-yew 'lyǎn 'dzày shwō-le. He didn't have the brass to apply again. This term requires careful handling, and it is well not to use such expressions until one has observed their use extensively.

臉蛋兒

lyǎn-'dàr (Nunìt, ge) cheek.

練

lyàn (V, Vpred) to practice (on, with), to practice doing something, to learn how to do something. lyàn-'chín to practice a musical instrument called a chín (usually piano); lyàn-'chyāng or lyàn kāy-'chyāng to practice (firing a) rifle; lyàn-'tsāw to drill (military).

    (V) to cause to practice, to drill someone. lyàn-'bīng to drill troops.

    As mainV: lyàn-'hǎw-le to learn well.

鍊圈 (子)

lyàn-'chywān(-dz), lyàn-'chywār (Nunit, ge) a link (in a chain).

鍊 (子，兒)

'lyàn-dz, lyàr (Nunit tyáw, ge) a chain.

    lyàn, lyàr (Mgroup) a chain of, string of. yí-lyàn-'jū-dz a string of pearls; yì-chywār-'lyàn-dz a circular chain, a circle of links joined together.

練習

'lyàn-shí (V, Vpred) to practice, learn how to (nearly equivalent to lyàn alone) ‖tā 'lyàn-shi shyě-'dz. He's practising at writing characters.

    'lyàn-shí (Nmass) exercise, drill. lyàn-shí-'bù book of exercises. ‖'měy-yí-'kè-de-'hèw-tew yěw yí-dwàr-'lyàn-shí. There's a section of exercises at the end of each chapter.

量

lyáng (V) to measure, measure out. ‖ná 'bēy-dz lyáng-'shwěy. Take the cup and measure out the water. ‖lyáng 'sān-wǎn-de-'myàn. Measure out three bowls (English cups) of flour. ‖bǎ jèy-ge-'táng 'lyáng-yi-lyáng. Measure this sugar. ‖nǐ 'lyáng-yi-lyáng nǐ yěw dwō-'jùng. Find out how much you weigh.

涼

lyáng (A) cool. (Opposite 'nwǎn-he.) jāw-'lyáng to catch cold.

樑

lyáng (Nunit, tyáw, gēr) horizontal beam in a building, usually wooden lyáng-'mù horizontal beam of wood; 'fáng-lyáng ceiling beam; 'chyáw-lyáng bridge beam. 'bí-lyáng the bridge of the nose.

不良

bù-'lyáng (A) bad, not right, (of digestion). ‖wǒ-shyāw-'hwà bù-'lyáng. I have indigestion.

量杯

lyáng-'bēy (*NunitC*) a measuring cup.

涼快

'lyáng-kwày (*A*) cool, *when coolness is desired;* cool and comfortable. ‖**'jīn-tyan 'tyān-chi hěn 'lyáng-kway.** It's quite cool and comfortable today. (*Compare* **'jīn-tyan 'tyān-chi 'yěw yì-dyǎr-'lyáng.** It's a bit chilly today.)

良心

'lyáng-shīn (*Nabstr; occasionally Nunit,* **ge**) conscience. ‖**tā hěn yěw 'lyáng-shīn.** He's very conscientious. *also* He's very grateful, *or* kind, *or* loyal. ‖**tā 'lyáng-shīn fā-'shyàn-le.** He's realized that he was in the wrong, and is repenting. ‖**tā 'lyáng-shin yěw-'kwèy.** He's conscience-stricken. ‖**dzám píng 'lyáng-shīn shwō.** Let's speak of this frankly and openly, according to our real beliefs.

粮食

'lyáng-shr (*Nmass*) foodstuffs, edibles, provisions.

涼臺

'lyáng-táy (*Nunit,* **ge**) porch, veranda (*outside a house in the open air*).

兩

lyǎng (*NumU*) two.

兩

lyǎng (*Mmeas;* **èr** *for* two) tael (*measure of weight*). *See Appendix B.*

晾

lyàng (*V*) to expose to the air; to dry, to cool *by this process.* **lyàng 'yī-fu** to hang clothes up to dry. ‖**bǎ nèy-ge-'tāng 'lyàng-yi-lyàng.** Let this soup cool off.

    As mainV: **lyàng-'gān-le** to dry *something this way;* **lyàng-'lyáng-le** to cool *something this way;* **'lyàng-chǐ-lay** to hang *something* up for an airing; **'lyàng-dzày** to hang *something* at a place for an airing.

亮

lyàng (*A*) bright, light. (*Opposite* **àn** *sometimes* **hēy.**) ‖**'tyān yǐ-jing 'lyàng-le.** It's already light (*in the morning*). ‖**'tyān háy 'lyàng-je-ne.** It's still light (*in the evening*). ‖**dyàn-'dēng 'jàw-de hěn 'lyàng.** The electric light is shining brightly. ‖**'bwō-li 'tsā-de jēn 'lyàng.** The glass has been polished until it sparkles.

輛

lyàng (*Munit*) one **chē** car, cart (*any kind*)

量

***lyàng** (*Nabstr*) capacity, quantity of. **'jùng-lyàng** weight; **'rúng-lyàng** volume, cubic capacity; **jyěw-'lyàng** capacity for liquor or wine (*of a person*).

諒解

'lyàng-jyě (*V*) to excuse *someone for having done something.* ‖**wǒ ké-yi 'lyàng-jyě ni.** I can understand and excuse you (*for that*).

    (*Nabstr*) understanding. ‖**'yīng-gwo dzwò nèy-jyàn-'shr dé-dàw 'è-gwo-de-'lyàng-jyě.** England is doing that with the understanding of Russia.

量入爲出

lyàng-'rù wéy-'chū (*literary quotation*) to live within one's income.

聊

lyáw (*V*) to chat about, discuss casually, to chew the rag about, *lengthily and to not much purpose.* ‖**tām-'!yǎ-rér 'lyáw-chi-láy-le.** The two of them got to talking. ‖**nǐm dzày lyáw 'shéme?** What are you folks jawing about?

了解

lyáw-'jyě (*V*) to understand *someone* as to his motives, and to excuse *his* shortcomings because of the understanding. ‖**wǒ lyáw-'jyě tā-de-'nán-chù.** I understand his difficulties (*so I can't judge him too harshly*).

遼甯

lyáw-'níng (*Nunique*) Liaoning *province.*

了

lyǎw (*postV; always in potential form*) *used with practically any V, I, or A as mainV:* be possible to carry *something* through. ‖**tā 'sž-bu-lyǎw.** He won't die though (*of a sick person*). ‖**nème-'dwō-de-fàn wǒ chř-bu-'lyǎw.** I can't possibly eat up so much food. ‖**wǒ-de-'byǎw hwày-bu-'lyǎw.** My watch is a very good one, it can't possibly get out of order. ‖**'dí-rén tày 'chyáng, wǒm dǎ-bu-'lyǎw.** The enemy is too strong, we can't fight him. ‖**'tāng tày 'rè, wǒ hē-bu-'lyǎw.** The soup is too hot, I can't eat it (*literally* can't drink it).

    lyǎw *in the following two expressions:* ‖**'lyǎw-le-ba!** Enough! Let's quit it. *or* Let's put an end to this.

    'lyǎw-bu-dé extreme, extraordinary: **lyǎw-bu-'dé-de-fàn-'dyàn** an extraordinary hotel. ‖**'jèy-ge-rén jēn 'lyǎw-bu-de.** He's really an extraordinary guy. ‖**yěw 'shéme-lyǎw-bu-dé-de?** It doesn't matter too much, don't worry about it. *or* What the devil do you see in it (*or* him) of such importance? Why are you giving such praise?

料 (子，兒)

'lyàw(-dz), lyàwr (*Nmass;* **kwày**) material, materials, raw materials for making or building something. **gūng-'lyàw** labor and material (*economic term*); **gūng-lyàw-'fèy** *or* **gūng-'lyàw-chyán** cost of labor and material.

尥 蹶子
lyàw 'jywě-dz (VN2) to kick backwards (as an animal). ‖'mǎ 'lyàw yì-hwéy-'jywě-dz. The horse gave a kick backwards. *Compare* tī.

料理
'lyàw-lǐ (V) to arrange *matters, affairs.* ‖'jèy-jyàn-shr̀-ching shr̀-'shéy 'lyàw-lǐ? Who's going to take care of that matter? (*Especially of a wedding, funeral, meeting, banquet, etc.*)

列
lyè (V) to arrange, classify, file *data.* lyè-'byǎw to make a chart with certain data. *As mainV:* 'lyè-dzày arrange *data* at; 'lyè-chéng arrange *data* into *such-and-such a form.* ‖bǎ jè-shyē-'shù-mu lyè-cheng lyǎng-'háng. Arrange these figures in two columns. ‖jīn-tyan-de-'tsày-míng dēw lyè-dzay 'dān-dz-shang-le. Today's bill of fare is all displayed on the menu.

列
lyè (Mgroup) a (hwǒ-)'chē train (*a string of* hwǒ-'chē *train-cars tied together*).

裂
lyè (I) to crack open, break by cracking, *usually with the thing broken not completely separated into two or more pieces. As postV:* dǎ-'lyè-le to crack by striking; *etc.* ‖wǒ-'shěw-shang 'lyè yí-ge-'kěw-dz. My hand is chapped. ‖'gwǎn-dz (gěy) jàng-'lyè-le. The pipe has burst a crack (from internal pressure).

烈
lyè (A) fierce, violent. lyè-'hwǒ a blazing fire. ‖'hwǒ 'shāw-de hěn 'lyè. The fire is burning furiously. ‖'jèy-ge-rén 'pí-chi hěn 'lyè. He has a violent temper.

列強
lyè-'chyáng (Ncoll) the great powers, the powerful countries of the world. lyè-'chyáng-jr-'yī one of the great powers.

趔趄
'lyè-chye (I) to lose one's balance. ‖tā yí 'lyè-chye jyèw 'shwāy-le. He lost his balance and fell down.

烈士
lyè-'shr̀ (Npers) a martyred patriot.

裡兒
lyěr (*occasionally* lǐ) (Nunit, ge) lining (*as of a coat*). dà-yī-'lyěr lining of a coat; shàng yí-ge-'lyěr to put in (*or* sew in) a lining; bǎ-'lyěr 'chāy-shyà-lay to rip out a lining, to remove a lining. ‖'shyèw-dz-de-'lyěr 'pwò-le. The lining of the sleeve is torn.

The wrong side of material (cloth) that has a right and a wrong side. ‖jèy-kwày-'bù-de-'lyěr méy-'hwār. The wrong side of the cloth has no design in it (*is plain; the right side has a printed figure*).

溜
lyēw (I) to slip, slide along. lyēw-'bīng to skate on ice, go ice-skating.
  As mainV: 'lyēw-shyà (lc) to slide down, coast down, glide down. 'lyēw-chū-chywù to slip away quietly. ‖'chē tsúng 'shān-shang màn-'mār-de 'lyēw-shyà-chywù-le. The car coasted slowly down the hill.

溜邊
lyēw-'byār (Nplace) along the edge, along the rim. ‖tā dzày 'hú-de-lyēw-'byār 'jàn-je. He's standing by the edge of the lake.

溜邊溜沿
'lyēw-byār-lyēw-'yàr (H) even with the rim, full to the brim. ‖'wǎn 'mǎn-de 'lyēw-byār-lyēw-'yàr-de. The bowl is full to the brim.

遛達
'lyēw-da (I) to take a stroll. ‖wǒm 'lyēw-da-lyēw-da-ba. Let's take a stroll.
  As mainV: 'lyēw-da-dàw (lc) to take a stroll to *a place; etc.*

流
lyéw (I) to flow (*of a liquid*). lyéw-'shyě (IN) to have blood flow, to lose blood, to bleed; lyéw-'shwěy (IN) to have water flow out. ‖'gwǎn-dz lyéw-'shwěy. Water is flowing from the pipe.
  As mainV: 'lyéw-chū (lc) to flow out; 'lyéw-jìn (lc) *or* 'lyéw-dàw (lc) to flow to *a place*; 'lyéw-shyà (lc) to flow down, flow downstream, float downstream. ‖'shyě tsúng 'shāng-kěw 'lyéw-chu-lay. Blood flowed from the wound. ‖dà-'mù-tew tsúng 'shàng-lyéw 'lyéw-shyà-lay-le. A big log floated down from upstream.
  'shàng-lyéw, 'shyà-lyéw (Nplace) upstream, downstream; 'shàng-lyéw-rén, 'shyà-lyéw-rén upper class people, lower class people.

留
lyéw (V) to keep, reserve, hold on to; to leave behind, to keep behind, to detain. lyéw-'hwà to leave word; lyéw 'shr̀-hew reserve some time *for some particular purpose.*
  lyéw-'jǔng(r) (VN2) to leave a seed, *hence* to have children, have young, breed (*not polite with reference to humans*).
  lyéw-'shén take care, be careful, keep your head. ‖lyéw-'shén 'jyǎw-di-shya! Watch your step!
  lyéw-'yì pay attention; lyéw 'hú-dz to grow a beard.
  As mainV: 'lyéw-dzày to retain *someone or something* at *a place*; 'lyéw-dàw to keep *something* until *a time;*

'lyéw-gĕy to will *something to somebody*, to keep *something for someone;* **'lyéw-shyà** to leave *something behind, when in motion or when dying, or to* 'hold, reserve.

‖**gĕy-wo 'lyéw-shyà yí-ge-'dzwò-wèy.** Hold a seat for me. ‖**tā dzwò-'gūng dzwò-de 'hăw, bă-ta 'lyéw-dzày jèr.** He's a good worker, let's keep him here. **'tā-'fù-chin 'sž de-shŕ-hew jř gĕy-ta 'lyéw ge-hăw-'myéngr.** When his father died he left him nothing but a good name. ‖**bă-'kè 'lyéw-dzày jèr.** Let's keep the guest here, let's have our guest stay here. ‖**lyéw-ta 'jù-shya.** Ask him to stay overnight.

瘤
'lyéw(-dz) (*Nunit,* **ge**) a tumor. **jăng 'lyéw-dz** to grow a tumor, develop a tumor.

溜
lyéw(r) *see* **lyĕw(r).**

留傳
lyéw-'chwán (*V*) to hold on to and pass down to one's heirs. ‖**tā-de-'jì-shu lyéw-'chwán tā-de-'dž-swēn.** His technical skill was passed on to his descendants.

流露
lyéw-'lù (*V*) to show, express (*as a facial expression shows one's feelings*). *As mainV:* **lyéw-'lù-chū-lay** *with same meaning.* ‖**tā-de-'yì-sz dēw dzày tā-byăw-'chíng-'lĭ-tew lyéw-'lù-chu-lay.** His facial expression reveals what's in his mind.

流行
lyéw-'shíng (*I*) to spread (*as a disease*), to become prevalent; (*A*) to be prevalent. **lyéw-shíng-'bɪng** an epidemic disease.

流行性感冒
lyéw-shíng-shìng găn-'màw (*Nabstr*) epidemic influenza.

流水賬
lyéw-shwĕy-'jàng (*Nunit,* **bĭ**) current account.

流域
lyéw-'ywù (*N*) river basin; *usually specified, as:* **hwáng-'hé-lyéw-'ywù** the Yellow River river basin.

溜
lyéw(r), lyéw(r), lyèw(r) (*Munit*) braid, queue. **yì-'lyĕwr-de-'tew-fa** a braid of hair; **yì-lyĕwr-de-'byàn-dz** a queue.

   lyèw (*Mgroup*) a line of, column of, row of. **yí-lyèw-de-'fáng-dz** a row of houses; **yí-lyèw-de-mă-'yĭ** a column of ants.

六
lyèw (*NumU*) six.

遛
lyèw (*V*) to walk. **lyèw-'gĕw** to walk a dog; **lyèw-'mă** to take a horse for walk.

   (*I*) take a walk. **gēn nywŭ-'péng-yew 'lyèw-yi-lyèw** to take a walk with one's girl; **lyèw-'wār** or **lyèw-lyew 'wār** go for a walk.

   As mainV: **'lyèw-dàw** (*lc*) to stroll to *a place,* to take *a horse* to *a place* (*not riding it*).

溜
lyèw(r) *see* **lyĕw(r).**

鎦子
'lyèw-dz (*Nunit,* **ge**) finger ring.

驢 (子)
'lywú(-dz) (*Nunit,* **téw, jř**) donkey.

理，縷
lywŭ (*V*) to tidy up, straighten out. *As mainV:* **'lywŭ-chĭ-lay** or **lywŭ-'hăw-le** *with same meaning;* **'lywŭ-dzày yí-'kwàr** to arrange things together. ‖**wŏ bă 'shyāng-dz dēw lywŭ-'hăw-le.** I've straightened out everything in the suitcases (*as when packing for a trip*).

縷
lywŭ (*Munit*) a curl of **yān** smoke (*as from a chimney; somewhat literary*). A strand of **sž** silk; a strand of **shyàn** thread (*both not literary*).

旅館
lywŭ-'gwăn (*Nunit,* **ge, jyăn**) a hotel.

履歷
lywŭ-'lì (*Nunit,* **jāng**) a record of attainments and qualifications. ‖**tā-de-lywŭ-'lì hěn 'cháng.** He has a long list of attainments and qualifications.

旅行
lywŭ-'shíng (*I*) to travel, take a trip. ‖**wŏ-men 'shyà-tyan dàw-'năr chywù lywŭ-'shíng?** Where shall we go this summer?

   lywŭ-shíng-'shè a travel bureau; **lywŭ-shíng-'jèng** a permit to travel; **lywŭ-shíng-jř-'pyàw** traveller's checks.

呂宋
lywŭ-'sùng (*Nunique*) Luzon *or* The Philippines. (*Nunit,* **jř, gér**) cigars, *which were imported into China from the Philippines in earlier days, then being called* **lywŭ-sùng-'yān.**

屢次
lywŭ-'tsż (*H*) many times, each of many times. ‖**wo lywŭ-'tsż 'gàw-su ni, nĭ lywŭ-'tsż bù-'tīng.** I tell you over and over again, and you never listen.

綠 [色（兒）]

lywù (A) 'lywù-sè, 'lywù-shǎr (Nabstr) green; green color.

律

*lywù (N) law. fǎ-'lywù (or lywù-'fǎ) the law. lywù-'shr̄ (Npers) lawyer.

M

嗎

ma sentence-final element showing that the sentence is a question, but adding no other special tone; see Section E §5 of Introduction.

媽

mā (NpersT) mamma. ‖wǒ-de-'mā-ya! Oh my mamma! (expression of extreme distress when in dire need).

Title for a married woman servant: 'jàw-mā if her name is Jàw. lǎw-'mā-dz (Npers) a married woman servant.

摩索

'mā-se (V) to smooth out with the hand something that is wrinkled; to rub out, massage (as the stomach when it hurts). As mainV: mā-se-'píng-le with same meaning. ‖méy-yew 'làw-tyě, yùng-'shěw 'mā-se-mā-se 'hǎw-le. There's no iron, so smooth it out with your hand.

麻袋

má-'dày(-dz) (NunitC, ge) burlap bag.

麻煩

'má-fàn (A) troublesome, annoying. ‖jèy-ge-'fá-dz hěn 'má-fàn. This procedure is very annoying and difficult. ‖bìng bù-'má-fàn. No trouble at all! (polite answer to an apology for having troubled you or taken your time).

(V) to bother, cause trouble for, disturb. ‖nǐ byé 'má-fàn rén. Don't bother people (with your petty troubles).

麻藥

má-'yàw (Nmass) anaesthetic. gěy-ta dǎ má-'yàw give him an anaesthetic by injection; gěy-ta shàng má-'yàw the same but by external application; jyàw-ta 'wén-wén má-'yàw have him inhale the anaesthetic.

碼

mǎ (Mmeas) yard; in Chinese measurement about two chř (feet) plus seven tswèn (inches).

馬

mǎ (Nunit, pǐ) horse. mǎ-'ān-dz saddle for a horse; mǎ-'chē horse-drawn carriage; mǎ-'pì horse's buttocks; mǎ-'pyàw receipt on a bet at a race track; mǎ-'shì(-bān) a circus, with horses and other animals.

'mǎ-shàng or mǎ-'shàng on horseback thus immediately, post-haste, quickly.

mǎ-'lù (Nunit, tyáw; Mord) a highway; an avenue.

碼

mǎ (V) to pile up neatly on top of each other. mǎ-'shū to pile up books; mǎ-'páy to pile up mah-jong pieces into the "wall", the building of which precedes the play; mǎ-'jwān to pile up bricks as when making a wall; mǎ-'chyáng to build a wall thus.

As mainV: 'mǎ-shàng-le or 'mǎ-chǐ-láy to build up thus; 'mǎ-chéng to build up into a resulting shape. ‖bǎ swǒ-yěw-de-'jwān 'mǎ-chéng yí-ge-'chyáng. Take all the bricks and build a wall.

馬來，馬來亞

mǎ-láy, mǎ-láy-'yǎ (Nunique) Malaya. mǎ-láy-bàn-'dǎw Malay Peninsula.

馬力

mǎ-'lì (Mmeas) horsepower.

馬尼剌

mǎ-ní-'lā (Nunique) Manila.

馬趴

'mǎ-pā (Nunit, ge) used in 'shwāy yí-ge-'mǎ-pā to fall flat on one's face.

碼頭

mǎ-'téw (Nunit, ge) dock, pier.

螞蟻

mǎ-'yǐ, mǎ-'yì (Nunit, ge) ant.

罵

mà (V) to cuss out, call someone names. 'mà-ta yí-'dwèn to cuss him out, give him a good scolding; āy yí-dwèn 'mà to get a cussing out, a scolding. ‖tā 'mà-ta shr̀ yí-ge-'fēn-dz. He cussed him out, calling him a nitwit.

罵街

mà-'jyē (I) to cuss, swear, scold, just in general, not at anyone. ‖tā dzày-'nàr mà-'jyē. He's just cussing out the world.

mai Wade Romanization for may.

饅頭

'mán-tew (Nunit, ge) small roll-shaped loaf of steamed bread raised with yeast.

埋怨

'mán-ywàn (V) to blame, hold responsible *for something that could have been avoided.* ‖tā-'ér-dz 'sž-le, tā 'mán-ywàn 'dày-fu. His son died, and he held the doctor responsible.

滿

mǎn (A) full. ‖jèy-ge-'bēy-dz-de-'shwěy hěn 'mǎn. This cup is full of water. (*Notice that in Chinese it is the water which one says is full.*)

'mǎn-shr̀ (V) to be full of, everywhere, crowded around. ‖jèy-ge-'bēy-dz 'mǎn-shr̀ 'shwěy. This cup is completely full of water. ‖hwǒ-chē-'jàn-li 'mǎn-shr̀ 'bīng. The station is swarming with soldiers. ‖'jyē-shang 'mǎn-shr̀ 'rén. The streets are full of people.

mǎn *before a noun.* mǎn-'chéng the whole town; mǎn-'chù everywhere; mǎn-'wū(-dz) the whole room. ‖mǎn-'wū-dz-de-rén dēw 'jàn-chǐ-láy-le. Everyone in the (whole) room stood up.

As postV: dàw-'mǎn-le to pour something full; dzwò-'mǎn-le have all seats taken; *etc.*

滿足

mǎn-'dzú (V) to satisfy, meet the demands of. ‖wǒ děy shyǎng 'fá-dz mǎn-'dzú wǒ-de-ywú-'wàng. I must figure out some way to satisfy my desires.

滿意

mǎn-'yì (A) satisfied. (V) to be satisfied about. ‖wǒ bù-mǎn-'yì jèy-ge-'rén. I'm not satisfied about this fellow. *or* I'm disturbed about this fellow.

慢

màn (A) slow. màn-'chē a slow train, *or* a local train; màn-'hwǒ a slow fire. ‖nǐ 'dzěw-de hěn 'màn. You're walking very slowly. ‖wǒ-de-'byǎw 'màn-le. My watch is slow.

màn-'mān-de *or* màn-'mār-de *or* màr-'mār-de very slow, very dull, very slowly.

As mainV: 'màn-shyà-láy to slow down, check speed (*translation from English;* 'màn-le *would be more typical Chinese*).

漫

*màn (I) to become too full *of some liquid.* As mainV:* 'màn-gwò (lc) to overflow; 'màn-jìn (lc) to overflow into, (*as water when a boat ships water*); 'màn-dàw (lc) to overflow to. ‖'shwěy 'màn-dàw 'nǎr-nǎr dēw 'shr̀. The water has flooded over everything everywhere. ‖hé-'shwěy màn-gwo 'chyáw chywù-le. The water in the river has risen over the bridge. ‖'shwěy 'màn-jìn 'chwán láy-le. The boat has shipped water.

慢走慢走

‖'màn dzěw màn dzěw! *polite phrase, said to a friend when he has been visiting you and is leaving:* Watch your step! *or* Be careful! *or* Don't let anything happen to you! (*Literally* Go slow go slow!)

蔓延

màn-'yán (I) to spread out, diffuse, (*as of a disease, of famine, of other bad things*). *As mainV:* màn-'yán-dàw (lc) spread out to; *etc.* ‖shwěy-'dzāy màn-'yán-dàw 'wǔ-shěng. The flood spread to five provinces.

忙

máng (A) busy, in a hurry. bāng-'máng (VN2) to give *someone* help. ‖nǐ 'máng shéme? What's the hurry? Where's the fire?

máng-'shr̀ pressing business, rush job.

盲

*máng blind. 'máng-rén blind person; sè-'máng (Aattr) color blind. (*See* shyā.)

盲腸

'máng-cháng (Nunit, ge) appendix (*in body*). gé 'máng-cháng *or* lá 'máng-cháng to remove the appendix. máng-cháng-'yán appendicitis.

mao *Wade Rŏmanization for* maw.

貓

māw (Nunit, jr̆, téw) cat. 'gūng-māw tom cat; 'mǔ-māw female cat. māw-'lèy the cat family (*including tigers, lions, etc.*).

摸

māw, mwō (V) to reach *or* grope for; *also figuratively. As mainV:* 'māw-jáw to reach out for, grope for, and succeed in grasping; māw-bu-'chīng to be unable to make head *or* tail of *something.* ‖tā-de-'yì-sz wǒ māw-bu-'chīng. I can't make head or tail of what he means.

毛

máw (Nunit) *with* chyán money, a dime, ten cents.

錨

máw (Nunit, ge) an anchor. pāw-'máw *or* shyà-'máw to cast anchor; chǐ-'máw to weigh anchor.

毛

máw(r) (Nunit, gēr) body hair, fur, feathers; wool. máw-'tǎn(-dz) wool blankets; máw-'yī wool sweater; máw-'bǐ writing brush; máw-'jīn towel with fuzzy surface; máw-'shyàn wool thread, yarn.

毛病

'máw-bìng (Nunit, ge) bad habit; defect; trouble; slight illness (*but not too serious*). ‖tā shwō-'hwà yěw yí-ge-'máw-bìng. He has a bit of an impediment in his speech.

茅房

'máw-fáng (*Nunit*, ge) toilet, outhouse.

毛腰

máw-'yāw (*V.N1*) to bend at the waist; be bent at the waist (*as with age*).

冒

màw (*V*) to brave, dare, face blindly. màw-'shyǎn (*VN1*, *A*) to run risks, take risks *or* to be risky, dangerous, bold, adventurous; màw-je 'ywǔ despite the rain, in the teeth of the rain, through rain; màw-je 'dí-rén-de-pàw-'hwǒ braving and facing and going ahead in spite of the enemy's gunfire.

帽

*màw, 'màw-dz (*Nunit*, dǐng) hat, cap, headgear. byàn-'màwr cap with a visor.

冒

*màw (*I*) to emerge, come out into the open. màw-'yān (*IN*) to be smoking (*as of a chimney or a stove*). *As mainV:* ǁ'yān 'màw-chū-láy-le. The smoke's coming out.

冒失

'màw-shr (*A*) thoughtless, without consideration, inconsiderate. ǁtā hěn 'màw-shr-de pǎw-'jìn rén-jyā-'wū-dz-li chywù-le. He ran into someone's house abruptly without any consideration at all. ǁ'màw-màw-shr-'shr̄-de: nǐ byé 'màw-màw-shr-'shr̄-de jyèw chywù dzwò jèy-jyàn-'shr̀. Don't just go ahead blindly and take the job without thinking it over first.

埋

máy (*V*) to bury, conceal. *As mainV:* 'máy-dzày to bury at *a place, a time*. máy-'téw kǔ 'gàn to bury one's head (*in one's work*) and work hard, *thus* to work silently, hard, and long, without publicity. ǁ'gěw bǎ 'gú-tew máy-dzay 'dì-shya. The dog took the bone and buried it in the ground. ǁ'dí-rén 'máy-le hěn-dwǒ-de-'dì-léy. The enemy planted a lot of land mines.

埋没

máy-'mwò *or* máy-'mù (*V*) to set aside *one's real ability* in order to do a job much below one's level. *As mainV:* máy-'mwò-dzày to suppress one's real ability in *some sort of superficial work.* ǁbyé 'jyàw-ta máy-'mù-le tā-de-'tyān-tsáy. Don't let him waste his genius in routine work.

買

mǎy (*V*) to purchase, buy. ǁ'jèy-běn-'shū 'mǎy-de hěn 'jŕ. This book was worth buying.

As mainV: 'mǎy-gwò-lay to buy out, buy over, (*as someone else's establishment or someone else's share in an enterprise*); 'mǎy-jáw to succeed in buying; mǎy-bu-'jáw can't be found for sale; mǎy-'tūng to buy *or* bribe *a person.*

mǎy (*lc*): chǐng mǎy dyǎr-'chá-yè láy please buy some tea and bring it here; 'mǎy-chywù *similarly.*

買賣

'mǎy-may (*Nunit*, ge) business, business establishment; business, trade. dzwò 'mǎy-may to be in business. 'mǎy-may-rén *or* dzwò-'mǎy-may-de merchant. ǁtā-de-'mǎy-may shyàn-dzày 'hǎw-bu-hǎw? How's business with him these days?

賣

mày (*V*) to sell. mày-'shū-de bookseller; mày-'chē-de automobile dealer; *etc.* mày 'jyàn-hwǒ to sell things cheap, have a bargain sale. ǁjèy-ge-'dūng-shi mày 'dwō-shaw-chyán? What do you sell this for?

As mainV: 'mày-chū-chywù to sell out; mày-bu-'chū to be unable to sell *because there is no market.* mày-hwò-'ywán salesman.

麥（子）

mày *or* mwò (*Nunit*, tyáw) blood vessel. dùng-'mày artery; jìng-'mày vein; shyǎw-'mày capillary. hàw-'mày to feel the pulse, take the pulse.

脈

*mày, 'mày-dz (*Nunit*, kē; *Nmass*) wheat. mày-'tyán wheat field. mày-'jyěw liquor made from wheat (*brewed, not distilled*). jùng 'mày-dz to plant wheat.

賣力氣

mày 'lì-chi (*VN1*) to work very hard, expend one's effort. ǁtā hěn mày-'lì-chi-de bàn nèy-jyàn-'shr̀. He worked very hard at taking care of that matter.

賣命

mày-'mìng (*VN1*) to work so hard that (*figuratively*) one sells one's life. ǁtā bù-néng gěy-ni mày-'mìng-de dzwò. He can't kill himself working for you (*you mustn't expect him to*).

麥穗兒

mày-'swèr (*Nunit*, gēr, swèr) ear of wheat.

賣藝

mày-'yì (*VN1*) to sell one's skill, *particularly at acrobatics and kindred forms of entertainment.* mày-'yì-de(-rén) an acrobat, street-corner musician, *etc.*

mei *Wade Romanization for* mey.

們

*men (*reading form* mén) *added to Npers forms Ncoll:* 'péng-yew-men friends (*all the friends of a certain person, taken collectively*); 'háy-dz-men children (*all those of one family, village, or other natural group, taken collectively*); *etc.*

Added to Pron forms the plurals, often with reduction to a single syllable: **wǒ** I, me : **'wǒ-men** *or* **wǒm** we, us; **'dzán-men** *or* **dzám** we, us, you and I; **nǐ** you : **'nǐ-men** *or* **nǐm** you folks; **tā** he, him, she, her : **'tā-men** *or* **tām** they, them.

悶

mēn (*A*) stifling, lacking good ventilation; (*of a person*) full of ideas but not inclined to talk. ‖**jèy-ge-'wū-dz hěn 'mēn.** This room is stifling. ‖**jèy-ge-'rén hěn 'mēn.** He inhibits himself, he doesn't express his ideas though he has them.

V, as mainV: **mēn-'sž-le** to suffocate to death; **'mēn-chǐ-láy** *or* **'mēn-shàng** to render airtight, seal off. ‖**bǎ-'hwǒ 'mēn-shàng.** Extinguish the fire (*as by covering it with ashes*).

See also **mèn.**

門

mén, mér (*Nunit,* **shàn, ge**) door. *With M* **shàn** *specifies the part that closes, otherwise* a doorway, gate, entrance, exit. *Figuratively* the entrance to some accomplishment, the hang *or* knack of doing something, the right way to do something. **mén-'kěwr** (*Nunit,* **ge**) doorway; **mén-'kwàng** door frame; **mén-'lyéngr** doorbell; **mén-'pyàw** tickets *to be collected at a door in order to get in;* **mén-'shwān-dz** bolt on a door.

門（兒）

mén, mér (*Mauton*) specialty, special line of endeavor. ‖**tā shywé 'něy-yì-mér?** What line is he learning?

yì-mén-gūng-'kè one subject *or* specialized field of instruction *or* study.

yì-mér-'chīn-chi a blood *or* marital relationship. ‖**wǒ gēn-ta yěw yì-mér-'chīn-chi.** We're related.

門插棍

mén-'chā-gwèr (*Nunit,* **gēr, ge**) sliding bolt on a door.

門戶

mén-'hù (*Nunit,* **ge**) gateway (*figurative*). ‖**jyèw-jīn-'shān shř 'měy-gwo-shī-'àn-de-mén-'hù.** San Francisco is America's gateway in the west.

悶

mèn (*A*) lonely, depressed. **mèn-de 'hěn** *or* **'mèn-de-hwang** to feel very lonely and depressed, have the blues. ‖**jèy-ge-'dì-fang hěn 'mèn.** This place is very lonely and depressing. *As mainV works like* **mēn;** *but* **mèn** *also occurs in the following:* **'mèn-jù-le** to argue *someone* down so that *he* can't offer any reply. ‖**'jèy-tsž bǎ-ta 'mèn-jù-le, tā kě méy-'hwà shwō-le.** This time I argued him down so that he really had nothing he could say.

燜

mèn (*V*) to cook in a closed container by steaming. *Forms VN3:* **mèn-'rèw** meat cooked thus.

蒙自

méng-'dž (*Nunique*) Meng-tzu *or* Mengtsz (*city in Yünnan province*).

蒙古

méng-'gǔ (*Nunique*) Mongolia.

猛烈

měng-'lyè (*A*) fierce, violent, potent, powerful, (*as of a wild animal, a medicine, a disease*).

猛然

měng-'rán(-jyān) (*J*) suddenly, violently, unexpectedly.

夢

mèng (*Nunit,* **ge**) dream. **dzwò yí-ge-'mèng** to have a dream.

Used adverbially: **mèng-'shyǎng** to fancy, dream, imagine (*not when actually asleep*); **mèng-'shǐng** to wake up from one's dreams.

Also used as V to dream of, dream that. *As mainV:* **'mèng-jyàn** to dream of, dream that *something happens.* ‖**tā dzwò-'mèng hwéy-'jyā-le.** He dreamed that he had gone back home. ‖**tā 'mèng-jyàn tā-'jyā-li-de-rén.** He dreamed of the folks back home. ‖**nǐ gwǎn-bu-'jù wǒ-de-'mèng-shyǎng.** You can't stop me from dreaming.

謎兒

mèr (*Nunit,* **ge**) riddle. **shwō yí-ge-'mèr** to tell a riddle; **tsāy yí-ge-'mèr** to solve *or* guess a riddle.

Reverse of a coin, tails (*opposite* **dzèr**).

謀

méw (*V*) to plan *or* scheme *or* plot to get *or* accomplish *some end.* **méw-'shř** to try to plan how to get a job (*by contacting the right people*); **méw-'shēng** to make a living when it's hard to make a living, eke out an existence; **méw-'shā** to plot murder (*legal term*). (*All a bit literary.*)

謀殺未遂

méw-'shā wèy-'swéy (*literary quotation; legal term*) to attempt murder and fail.

某

měw *a term which is used to replace each syllable in the name of some person whose name one does not wish to mention.* ‖**wǒ shyǎng měw-měw-'měw-de-'yì-sz hěn 'bù-hǎw.** I think that so-and-so's idea is very bad (*when so-and-so is a person whose name has three syllables*). **'měw-rén** that certain person, you know who I mean.

沒

méy (1) *the negative adverb for* **yěw: yěw-'chyán** there is some money : **méy-yew 'chyán** there isn't any money.

(2) *A replacement for* **méy-yew** *before a nominal expression:* **méy-'chyán** there isn't any money. *For these two uses see* **yěw.**

(3) *Negative adverb for any verb, forming the negative equivalent of the expression with* **-le:** ‖**wǒ 'yǐ-jing bìng 'hǎw-le.** I've already gotten over my illness. : ‖**wǒ bìng háy méy 'hǎw-ne.** I haven't gotten over my illness yet. **méy** *and* **-le** *do not both occur in the same sentence except when* **méy** *is in function* 1 *or* 2: ‖**wǒ méy(-yew) 'chyán-le.** I'm out of money. *For this function of* **méy** *see* **-le.** *In some contexts the presence or absence of* **méy** *makes no difference in meaning from the English point of view:* ‖**tā 'chà-yi-dyar 'sž-le.** *or* **tā 'chà-yi-dyar méy-'sž.** He almost died. *The first is, literally,* He missed dying by a little; *the second is, literally,* He missed it only by a little, but didn't die.

煤

méy (*Nmass;* **kwày**) coal. **méy-'chyéw(r)** ball-shaped pieces of powdered coal held together by dampening it and then drying it out, *used for stoves in China.* **méy-'lú** coal stove.

梅

méy (*Nunit,* **ge**) plum *or* prune. **gān-'méy** dried plums or prunes. **méy-'hwār** flowers of the plum or prune tree; clubs (*at cards*).

眉 (毛)

'méy(-maw) (*Nunit,* **dàw**) an eyebrow. *With M* **gēr** one hair from (*or* in) the eyebrow.

煤氣

méy-'chì (*Nmass*) coal gas, cooking gas. **méy-chì-'lú-dz** gas stove, gas range.

玫瑰

méy-'gwèy (*Nunit,* **kē**) rose bush. **méy-gwèy(-'hwār)** (*Nunit,* **dwǒr**) rose.

玫瑰紫

méy-gwèy-'dž (*Nabstr*) color between rose and purple; *about the same as* magenta.

眉開眼笑

méy-'kāy yǎn-'shyàw (*literary quotation*) to beam with joy.

每

měy (*Dem*) each, every.

美

měy (*A*) beautiful, good, fine, artistic; (*sarcastically*) proud, too elated to be considered proper according to Chinese custom, too obviously happy. ‖**byé tày 'měy-le.** Don't show your happiness too much.

美 (國)

*měy, 'měy-gwo (*Nunique*) the United States; America. **'měy-jēw** the American continent; **běy-'měy-jēw** North America; **nán-'měy-jēw** South America. **jūng-'měy** China and the United States. **měy-'jīn** American money.

美點

měy-'dyǎn (*Nunit,* **ge**) feature of beauty. ‖**tā-jèy-ge-rén-de-'lyǎn yěw yí-ge-měy-'dyǎn.** His face has a kind of beauty (*or has it under some circumstances, as when he has a certain expression on it*).

美滿

měy-'mǎn (*A*) happy and contented. ‖**tā-de-hwēn-'yīn hěn měy-'mǎn.** His married life is very happy and satisfactory.

美髯公

měy-rán-'gūng (*Npers*) person who has a beautiful long beard. *Calling a person this is an allusion to the first person so termed, a general and hero of the Three Kingdoms period in the third century A.D.*

美容館

měy-rúng-'gwǎn (*Nunit,* **jyā, ge, jyān**) beauty parlor.

美術

měy-'shù (*Nabstr*) art in general. **měy-shù-'jyā** artist; **měy-shù-'gwǎn** art gallery.

美意

měy-'yì (*Nunit,* **ge**) kind thought, kindness. ‖**nǐ byé 'wù-hwèy ta, jè-shř tā-de-měy-'yì.** Don't misunderstand him; this was (*intended as*) a kindness on his part.

妹

*mèy (*Npers*) younger sister *or* female cousin. *See Appendix A.*

迷

mí (*V*) to be very fond of. ‖**tā hěn 'mí nèy-ge-'dūng-shi.** He's crazy about that thing.
    mí-'lù to lose one's way. ‖**tā mí-'lù-le.** He's lost his way.
    As mainV: **'mí-shàng** to become very fond of, crazy about; **'mí-jù** to fascinate, enchant. ‖**tā bǎ-ta mí-'jù-le.** She cast her spell over him. ‖**tā 'mí-shàng-le dyàn-'yěngr-míng-'shīng.** She's nuts about movie stars.

米

mǐ (*Nmass*) rice grain. **dàw-'mǐ** *with same meaning.* **mǐ-'fàn** cooked rice ready to eat.

蜜

mì (*Nmass*) honey. **mì-'fēng** (*Nunit,* **ge**) bee; **mì-fēng-'wō** (*Nunit,* **ge**) beehive.

密

mì (A) thick, dense. ‖rén-'kěw hěn 'mì. The population is very dense.

密 (秘), (密秘)

*mì, 'mì-mì (A) secret, concealed. ‖jèy-jyàn-'shr̀-ching hěn 'mì-mì. This matter is most secret.

蜜餞

mì-'jyàn (Aattr) preserved (i.e., fruit). mì-'jyàn-de-'píng-gwo preserved apples.

密碼

mì-'mǎr (Nunit, ge) code, cipher. fān mì-'mǎr to encode or decode.

秘書

mì-'shū (Npers) secretary.

miao Wade Romanization for myaw.

mieh Wade Romanization for mye.

mien Wade Romanization for myan.

民

*mín (N) people, races, populace. 'rén-mín (Ncoll) the people; gwó-'mín (Npers) citizen.

民法

mín-'fǎ (Nmass; tyáw) civil law (versus criminal law). 'mín-fǎ-de-'yí-shr̀ civil ceremony, civil procedure.

民主 (的)

mín-'jǔ(-de) (Aattr) democratic. mín-jǔ-jǔ-'yì democracy (the theory, the principle); mín-jǔ-'dǎng democratic party (used for the American Democratic Party).

民衆

mín-'jùng (Nmass) the people. ‖yīng-gay dzwēn-'jùng mín-'jùng-de-'yì-sz. The will of the people must be respected.

閩侯

mǐn-'héw (Nunique) Min-hou (capital city of Fukien province).

閩江

mǐn-'jyāng (Nunique) The Min Chiang (river).

名 (兒)

míng, myéngr (Nabstr) name, fame, reputation. hěn yěw-'míng to be quite famous.
    *míng, 'míng-dz (Nunit, ge) name; title (as of a book). ‖jèy-ge-dūng-shi jyàw shéme(-'míng-dz)? What's this thing called?

shìng-'míng name and surname of a person; míng-'dān, míng-'dār list of names.

明

*míng (Demord) next after the present one, with a few periods of time: 'míng-tyan' tomorrow, short forms 'myéngr, 'myéngr-ge, myér, myér-ge; 'míng-nyan next year.

明白

'míng-bay (A) clear, understandable, intelligible; clear about something, understanding, quick to grasp meanings. ‖jèy-jyàn-shr̀-ching hěn 'míng-bay. This matter is quite clear. ‖tā-'nèy-ge-rén hěn 'míng-bay. He's quite quick at getting what you mean, he understands things quickly and judges them well. ‖wǒ 'háy-shr bú-'dà 'míng-bay. I'm still not clear about it (explain it some more).

明朝

'míng-cháw (Nunique) The Ming dynasty (1368–1644 A.D.).

明瞭

míng-'lyǎw (V, Vsent) to understand (a bit literary). ‖wǒ bù-míng-'lyǎw nǐ-de-'yì-sz. I don't understand what you mean.

名滿天下

'míng mǎn tyān-'shyà (literary quotation) become or be world-famous, internationally famous. ‖tā 'míng mǎn tyān-'shyà. He is known all over the world. or He has a world-wide reputation.

明媚

míng-'mèy (A) lovely (of weather or scenery).

名聲

'míng-shēng (Nabstr) reputation of a person or an institution.

明顯

míng-'shyǎn (A) obvious, clear. ‖tā-de-'tày-du 'yǐ-jing hěn míng-'shyǎn-le. His attitude has become quite obvious (he no longer attempts to conceal it).

名望

'míng-wàng (Nabstr) good reputation, mainly of a person.

名義

míng-'yì (Nunit, ge) an official title. ‖wǒ 'chywù-nàr dzwò-'shr̀ tām gěy-wo shéme-míng-'yì? If I go to work there what title will I get?

名譽

míng-'ywù (Nabstr) reputation or notoriety (of a person).

命
mìng (*Nunit, tyáw, ge*) a life; fate, destiny. ‖jyèw-'mìng! Help! Save my life! ‖tā-de-'mìng hěn 'hǎw. His destiny bodes good.
    mìng-'hǎw-de-rén *or* hǎw-'mìng-de-rén people blessed with good fortune.

命令
'mìng-lìng (*Nunit, ge*) an order. fā 'mìng-lìng to send out orders, issue orders; shyà 'mìng-lìng to send down orders (*to subordinates*) ; 'fú-tsúng 'mìng-lìng to obey orders; tīng 'mìng-lìng to be obedient to orders.

命運
'mìng-ywùn (*Nabstr*) fate, destiny. ‖byé 'jìng kàw 'mìng-ywùn. Don't rely too much on destiny.

mo *Wade Romanization for* mwo.

mou *Wade Romanization for* mew.

模（子）
'mú(-dz) *or* 'mwó(-dz) (*Nunit, ge*) mold, die. ‖'jèy-lyǎng-kwày-'bǐng yí-'yàng; tsúng 'yí-ge-mú-dz 'chū-lay-de. These two cakes are the same; they were made in the same (cake-)mold.

畝
mǔ (*Mmeas*) a unit of area. *See Appendix B.*

母
*mǔ (*N*) mother; grandmother; aunt; (*see Appendix A*). mǔ-'dž mother and child.
    *mǔ (*Aattr*) female *of animals.* mǔ-'māw female cat; mǔ-'shr̄-dz lioness; mǔ-'jī hen; mǔ-'jū sow; *etc.*

幕
mù (*Mauton*) act *or* scene of a play. dì-'yí-mù *or* dì-'yí-mù-shì *or* dì-'yí-mù-de-'shì *or* 'shì-de-dì-'yí-mù the first act of the play.
    (*Nunit, ge*) the curtain. ‖'mù háy méy-'làw-shyà-láy-ne. The curtain hasn't come down yet.
    yān-'mù smoke screen.

募
mù (*V*) to raise, collect *money*, solicit *funds*, raise *troops.* mù-'kwǎn to solicit and collect funds; mù-'bīng to raise troops.

墓
*mù (*N*) tomb (*full form* fén-'mù) (*Nunit, ge*). mù-'bēy (*Nunit, ge*) gravestone, headstone.

木
*mù, 'mù-tew (*Nmass*) wood. mù-tew-'shyá-dz *or* mù-'shyá wooden box; mù-tew-'fáng-dz *or* mù-'fáng wooden house; mù-'shū wooden comb.

mù-'chǎng-dz (*Nunit,* jyā, jyān) lumber yard; mù-tew-'bǎn-dz *or* mù-'bǎn, mù-'bǎr wooden board.

目標
mù-'byāw (*Nunit, ge*) target, objective, aim, purpose; a target *in target practice.* ‖tā 'jèng jùng-le nèy-ge-mù-'byāw. He hit square in the center of the target.

目前
'mù-chyán (*J*) for the time being, at present.

目的
'mù-dì *or* 'mù-dí (*Nunit, ge*) an objective, purpose, aim, goal. ‖tā 'méy shéme-'mù-dí. He has no particular purpose.
    mù-dí-'dì (*Nplace, ge*) a destination (*not always-localized*). ‖nèy-ge-'chéng shr̄ wǒ-men-de-mù-dí-'dì. That city is our objective (*military*).

木匠
'mù-jyang (*Npers*) carpenter.

募捐
mù-'jywān (*VN1*) to take up a collection, raise funds through voluntary contribution. 'mù-jywān-tyàw-wǔ-'hwèy benefit dance; 'mù-jywān-yéw-yì-'hwèy benefit entertainment; 'mù-jywān-ywùn-'dùng campaign to raise funds through contribution.

目錄
'mù-lu (*Nunit, ge*) table of contents. ‖'mù-lu(-shang) bù-shyáng-'shì. The table of contents isn't very detailed.

木料
'mù-lyàw, mù-'lyàw (*Nmass*) lumber, wood supply for building.

牧師
'mù-shr (*Npers*) minister, preacher, pastor (*Christian*).

木紋（兒）
mù-'wén, mù-'wér (*Nabstr*) grain (in wood). ‖byé 'shwèn-je mù-'wér 'chyē, 'héng-je chyē. Don't cut it with the grain, cut against the grain.

摸
mwō, māw (*V*) to touch, feel, rub *in order to get the feel of;* to grope at. ‖nǐ 'mwō-yi-mwō kàn nèy-jāng-'jř 'píng-bu-píng. Feel that paper and see if it is smooth or not.
    mwō-je 'mér-le to have been feeling out the way, the method; to get the feel of some technique, method. *As mainV:* 'mwō-jáw-le to have found *the method,* to have reached *something for which one has been grasping or groping;* mwō-'chīng-le to have gotten *something* clearly, have gotten the hang of *something.* ‖wǒ bàn-'tyān mwō-bu-chīng tā shr̄ shéme-'yì-sz. For a long time I couldn't grasp his idea.

模
*mwó *see also* *mú.

磨
mwó (*sometimes* mwò) (*V*) *usually* 'mwó-mwo to sharpen *an edge* (*as on a grindstone*), to mill *grain*. mwó-'myàn to mill wheát flour; mwó-mwo 'dāw to sharpen a knife; mwó-'mwò to rub an inkstick in water in order to make liquid ink for writing. *As mainV:* mwó-'jyán-le *or* mwó-'kwày-le to grind sharp; 'mwó-chéng ('fěn) to grind into (powder); *etc.*

模範
mwó-'fàn (*Nunit, ge*; *Npers*) model, example, model to be followed, good model. ‖tā shr̀ wǒ-men-de-mwó-'fàn. He's our model. ‖tā-de-'shíng-wéy shr̀ wǒ-men-de-mwó-'fàn. His behavior is the example which we follow.

     mwó-'fàn-shywé-'shyàw model school, an ideal school; mwó-'fàn-jyān-'ywù model prison.

蘑菇
'mwó-gu (*Nunit, kē, ge*) mushroom. (*A*) fussy (*student talk*).

模形
'mwó-shíng (*Nunit, ge*) scale model in three dimensions.

抹
mwǒ (*V*) to rub over; to smear with. mwǒ 'jwō-dz to wipe off a table (*us with a rag*); mwǒ hwáng-'yéw to spread on butter; chr̄-wán-le 'fàn bǎ-'dzwěy 'mwǒ-yi-mwǒ to wipe the mouth after eating; mwǒ yǎn-'lèy to wipe away tears.

     As mainV: 'mwǒ-dzày to spread on *a place*; 'mwǒ-chywù to wipe *something* away; 'mwǒ-shàng to spread *something* on; mwǒ-'píng-le to rub smooth *or* to spread on evenly; *etc.* ‖tā 'lyǎn-shang 'mwǒ-shang-le yi·tséng-'fěn. She put a coat of powder on her face. ‖tā-de-'shyèw-dz bǎ 'jwō-dz-shang-de-'tǔ dēw mwǒ-'chywù-le. His sleeve wiped off all the dust on the table.

墨
mwò (*Nunit, kwày*) Chìnese inkstick. mwó-'mwò *or* yán-'mwò to rub an inkstick in water to make liquid ink for writing. mwò-'shwěy *or* mwò-'shwěr liquid ink, ink.

末
mwò (*Preord*) the last of a series. 'mwò-yí-ge the last one; 'mwò-yí-ge-'rén the last person; 'mwò-yí-'yè-shang on the last page.

     mwò-'lyǎwr (*Preord*) used as above, *or Ntime* at last, finally. ‖dàw-le mwò-'lyǎwr tā tsáy 'míng-bay. Only at the very last did he catch on.

     mwò (*Demord*) *in* mwò-'tsz̀ the last time, final time.

磨
*mwò *see* mwó. *In the following forms* *mwò *is usual:* mwò-'chǎng, *or* mwò-'fáng *or* 'mwò-fang (*Nunit, jyān, jyǎ, ge*) mill (*place where grain is ground*).

脈
mwò *see* mày.

莫非
mwò-'féy (*J*) (*literary*) it couldn't be other than, it couldn't be otherwise than that.

莫明其妙
mwò-'míng chí-'myàw (*literary quotation*) to be completely at sea, completely baffled.

墨西哥
mwò-shī-'gē (*short form* 'mwò-gwo) Mexico.

莫斯科
mwò-sz-'kē (*Nunique*) Moscow.

棉(花)
*myán, 'myán-hwa (*Nmass*) cotton. myán-(hwa-)'shyàn cotton thread; myán-'bù cotton cloth; myán-shyàn-'wà-dz cotton stockings; myán-bù-'yī-fu cotton clothing.

免
myǎn (*V*) to avoid, circumvent, get rid of, dismiss. ‖'bǎ-ta gěy 'myǎn-le. Get rid of him (*an employee*). ‖myǎn-bu-'lyǎw-le. It can't be avoided, we'll have to face it.

     myǎn-'jí (*VN2*) to kick *someone* out of a position, job.

     myǎn-'fèy (*VN2*) to avoid expense.

勉強
myǎn-'chyǎng (*Vsent*) to urge, compel, force *someone*, *often against his will or ability, to do something.* ‖kàn-hu myǎn-'chyǎng nèy-ge-'bìng-rén chr̄-'yàw. The nurse forced the patient to take his medicine. ‖nǐ bú-'ywàn-yi 'chr̄ byé myǎn-'chyǎng-je chr̄. If you don't want to eat it don't force yourself (to).

緬甸
myǎn-'dyàn (*Nunique*) Burma.

面
myàn (*Munit for things with flat surfaces or faces:* a chí (*flag*); a 'jìng-dz (*mirror*); a chyáng (*wall*). (*Maton* page of a book, newspaper, *etc.*

     (*pos*) side, face. 'shyá-dz-de-yí-'myàn one side of the box; 'fáng-dz-de-'jèy-myàn this side of the house.

     (*Added to certain Nplace and Mplace to form longer forms*): 'lǐ-myàn, 'lǐ-myàr inside; 'wày-myàn, 'wày-myàr outside; 'chyán-myan front side; 'hèw-myan rear side; **'shàng-myàn** upper surface; **'shyà-myan** under surface; **'dwèy-myàn**, **'dwèy-myàr** facing side, opposite side.

(*Nplace*) surface. **'myàn-shang**, **'myàr-shang** on the surface.

麵

myàn (*Nmass*) wheat flour; noodles.' **myàn-'fěn** wheat flour.

myàr anything in powdered form. **yàw-'myàr** powdered medicine; **hú-jyāw-'myàr** powdered (granulated) pepper.

myàn-'kěw-dàr flour sack. ,

面（子）

'myàn(-dz) (*Nunit*, ge) face (*of a person*). **myàn-'chyán** right in front of *someone;* **dzày wǒ-de-myàn-'chyán** right in front of me. **myàn-'sè** or **myàn-'shǎr** facial coloring (*momentary or relatively permanent*).

'myàn-dz social standing, prestige. **gù 'myàn-dz** (*A*) to be concerned about one's dignity and social standing, be careful of it; **'myàn-dz-shang bù-hǎw-'kàn** doesn't look proper, isn't properly in conformity with social rules; **méy(-yew) 'myàn-dz** not to have any social connection, *with each other;* or to have lost prestige.

Compare **lyǎn**.

麵包

myàn-'bāw (*Nmass;* **kwày, pyàn**) Western-style bread. **myàn-bāw-'fáng** bakery where Western-style bread and cake is sold.

面部

'myàn-bù (*N;* **no measures used**) face (*human*). ‖**tā 'myàn-bù shèw-'shāng.** He was wounded in the face.

麵糊

myàn-'hú (*Nmass*) batter, relatively thin dough, *made with wheat flour.*

面積

myàn-'jí (*Nabstr*) area, surface area. ‖**jèy-ge-'dì-fang-de-'myàn-jí hěn 'dà.** This place covers a big area.

面目

'myàn-mù (*Nunit*, ge) appearance; nature. **běn-'láy-de-'myàn-mù** original appearance *or* original nature (*of someone*); **jēn-'myàn-mù** real nature (*of someone*). ‖**tā shēng-'chì de-shŕ-hewr, bǎ tā-de-jēn-'myàn-mù dēw 'shyǎn-chū-láy-le.** When he got angry he was revealed in his true colors.

描

myáw (*V*) to (re)trace *a figure, a stroke, in writing or drawing,* slowly and carefully, in order to improve its appearance. **'dzày myáw yí-ge-'dž** to retrace a character, writing over the lines already drawn.

myáw-'dž to trace characters, *as when a child learning to write places a thin sheet of paper over a character and copies it with his brush.*

瞄

myáw (*V*) to aim. **myáw-'chyāng** to aim a gun. *As mainV:* **myáw-'jwěn-le** to aim correctly.

瞄準

myáw-'jwěn (*RC2*) to aim *a gun.*

描寫

myáw-'shyě (*V*) to describe in detail, realistically. ‖**wǒ děy gěy-ni myáw-'shyě tā-de-'dùng-dzwò.** I must describe his motions for you.

秒

myǎw (*Mmeas*) *with* **jūng**, a second (one-sixtieth of a minute).

媌條

'myǎw-tyǎw (*A*) slender (*of a person*), graceful. (*A bit literary.*)

廟

myàw (*Nunit*, dzwò) temple. **fwó-'myàw** Buddhist temple; **dàw-'myàw** Taoist temple; **kǔng(-dž)-'myàw** temple of Confucius; **tày-'myàw** temple for ancestorworship.

滅

myè (*I*) to go out, be extinguished. **myè-'dēng** the lights go off; **dēng 'myè-le** the lights are off; **'hwǒ 'myè-le** the fire is out.

Causatively: to destroy utterly, annihilate.

As postV: **nùng-'myè-le** to extinguish, put out; **chwēy-'myè-le** to blow out; **gwā-'myè-le** to blow out (*by the wind*)*;* **dǎ-'myè-le** to annihilate in war *or* combat; **nyǎn-'myè-le** turn off *electric light* by turning a switch.

滅亡

myè-'wáng (*V*) to bring about the ruin or annihilation of *a country.* **'dž chywǔ myè-'wáng** (*literary quotation*) to bring about one's own downfall.

217

N

哪

na *see* **a.**

拿

ná (*V*, *lc*) to grasp, pick up, carry, bring, take; (1) in the hand, or something light enough to be lifted in one or both hands without effort, or (2) by any means whatsoever (*compare terms with only a specific meaning, e.g., under CARRY on English-Chinese side*).

ná-'dzéy to nab a thief; ná-'chywán to take authority; ná-ta gēn-ni 'bǐ take him, now, and compare him with you; ná-ta kǎy-'shīn make fun of him.

As mainV: 'ná-chū (*lc*) to take out; 'ná-dàw (*lc*) to take to *a place;* ná-'dìng-le (jǔ-'yì) to make up (one's mind), reach (a decision); ná-'dyàw to pick off (*as fruit from a tree*), take down (*as a picture from a wall*); 'ná-dzày to hold at *or* in *a* place (*e.g.*, 'shěw-li in one's hand); ná-'dzěw-le to take away; 'ná-hwéy (*lc*) to take back; 'ná-jù-le to catch hold of and stop (*as a ball flying through the air*); 'ná-kāy to take *something* away, remove, clear out; *etc.*

ná-'shěw 'jř-(yi-)jř to point with the hand.

ná-shěw(-de) *before nouns* particularly good, skilled, specialized, *as:* ná-shěw-'tsày the specialty of the house (*a restaurant*), an especially fine dish.

那

nǎ, něy (*Dem*) which?, which one?, which, which one, *of two or more.*

那裡

'nǎ-li *same as* **nǎr** *which is more frequently used.*

那

nà, nèy (*Dem*) that, that there, there. *Use parallels use of* jè, jèy; *see the latter for details.* ‖'nà nǎr 'shíng-nga! That won't do!

(*J*) (*always at beginning of sentence; same as* 'nà-me) then, in that case, if that is so. ‖'nà, wǒm jyèw bù-néng 'chywù. In that case we just can't go.

納

*nà (*V*) to hand in, turn in. nà-'shwèy to pay taxes; nà hwèy-'fèy to pay dues in an organization.

nà-'tsǎy to send presents to a bridegroom (*from the bride's family*).

那裡

'nà-li *same as* **'nàr**, *which is more often used.*

那麼

'nà-me, 'nàme, 'nème (*H*) so, thus, in that way, like that, to that extent. *Parallels* 'jè-me; *see the latter for details.*

(*J*) (*always at beginning of sentence*) then, in that case, if that is so. ‖'nà-me, wǒm jyèw bù-néng 'chywù. In that case we just can't go.

nai *Wade Romanization for* **nay.**

那麼

'nàme *see* **'nà-me.**

那（麼）樣（兒）

'nà(me)-yàng(r) (*H*) that way; *parallels* 'jè(me)-yàng(r).

男

nán (*Aattr*) male (of humans); the character is used on the door of a men's room: MEN. nán-'hár, nán-'háy-dz male children, boys; 'nán-rén men; nán-'dž a man; 'nán-tsè-'swǒ toilet for men, men's room.

南

nán (*Nplace*) south. *See* **dūng** east.

難

nán (*A*) difficult, hard. (*Opposite* 'rúng-yì.) *Used with following V:* nán-'tīng difficult *or* unpleasant to listen to, unpleasant to the ear, discordant; nán-'kàn *similarly for the eye,* repulsive, ugly; nán-'bàn hard to manage; nán-'shèw *or* nán-'gwò hard to bear, *or* (*of a person who suffers from something hard to bear*): be blue, feel blue, feel unhappy, suffer; *in these combinations* nán *is also the opposite of* **hǎw.**

nán-'gwān difficulty, impasse, source of trouble; nán-'tí a knotty problem, difficult question to answer. ‖dzwò-'rén hěn 'nán. It's hard to act as a human being should.

南昌

nán-'chāng (*Nunique*) Nan-ch'ang (*capital of Kiangsi province*).

難道

nán-'dàw (*J*) it's hard to believe that, it's hard to accept *such-and-such* as a fact. ‖nán-'dàw lyán 'jèy-ge nǐ dēw bú-'hwèy-ma? Am I supposed to believe that you don't even know how to do this? ‖nǐ shř yí-ge-'běy-píng-rén; nán-'dàw lyán tyān-'tán dēw méy-'chywù-gwo-ma? You're from Peiping; do you mean to say that you haven't even gone to the Altar of Heaven? (*a famous place in Peiping*).

男子漢

nán-dž-'hàn (*Npers*) a real man, *with no feminine or effeminate characteristics.*

218

難怪
nán-'gwày (*J*) it would be hard to wonder that . . ., no wonder . . . . ‖**nán-'gwày tā 'shyàw-chū-lay-le.** No wonder he burst out laughing.

南海
nán-'hǎy (*Nunique*) The South China Sea.

南鄭
nán-'jèng (*Nunique*) Nan-cheng (*city in Shensi province*).

南極的（地方）
nán-'jí-de(-dì-fang) (*Nplace*) the Antarctic.

南京
nán-'jīng (*Nunique*) Nan-ching *or* Nanking (*city in Kiangsu province*).

男男女女
'nán-nán-nywǔ-'nywǔ everybody *when there are many*. ‖**'nán-nán-nywǔ-'nywǔ dēw 'láy-le.** Everybody came.

南寧
nán-'níng (*Nunique*) Nanning, *another name for* **yūng-'níng** Yung-ning (*city in Kwangsi province*).

難爲情
'nán-wéy-chíng (*A*) embarrassing, embarrassed. ‖**tā 'jywé-de hěn 'nán-wéy-chíng.** He felt very embarrassed.

南洋
nán-'yáng (*Nunique*) The South Seas. **nán-'yáng-chywún-'dǎw** South Sea Islands.

囊
náng (*NunitC*, **ge**) bag; *somewhat literary; colloquial expression is* **kěw-'dày.**

暖
*năng *see* ***nwăn.**

nao *Wade Romanization for* **naw.**

那兒
năr (*place expression*) where?, which place? (*of two or more places*). ‖**nín 'năr?** Where are you calling from? (*on telephone*). ‖**'năr dēw 'jǎw-le.** I looked everywhere.

那兒
nàr, nèr (*place expression*) that place, there. *Use parallels that of* **jèr,** *which can be consulted for details.*

撓
náw (*V*) to scratch. **náw-'téw** to scratch the head.

惱
năw (*A*) angry; (*V*) to be angry at *someone*. (*A bit literary.*)

腦（子）
'năw(-dz) (*Nunit*, **ge**) brain. *Used figuratively as in English:* ‖**jèy-ge-'rén méy 'năw-dz.** He's got no brains. **dà-'năw** cerebrum; **shyǎw-'năw** cerebellum; **năw-'mén-dz, năw-'měr** forehead.

腦袋
'năw-day (*Nunit*, **ge**) the head (*of the body*). *Figuratively:* ‖**nǐ yěw jǐ-ge-'năw-day!** How dare you! The nerve! (*literally* How many heads have you anyway!) ‖**wǒ 'năw-day 'téng.** I have a headache.

腦筋
'năw-jīn (*Nabstr*) brains, intelligence *or* its absence. ‖**jèy-ge-rén 'năw-jīn hěn 'líng-mín.** He's very alert and sharp.

鬧
nàw (*A*) noisy, disorderly; (*V*) to annoy, disturb; to be annoyed *or* troubled *or* disturbed by. **nàw-'yá** to have a toothache; **nàw 'dù-dz** to have a stomach ache. **nàw-'tyār** to have bad weather, unseasonable weather; **nàw-'gwěy** to be haunted by ghosts (*of a place*), or to play some sort of a trick, pull a stunt, a practical joke; **nàw-'shèr** to get into trouble, cause trouble.

    As mainV: **'nàw-chǐ-láy** to start to fight, get into a scrap; **'nàw-chū (lay)** to stir up, cause; **'nàw-chu 'shǐ-láy** *or* **nàw-chu 'lwàn-dz-lay** to cause trouble; **nàw-chu 'shyàw-hwa-lay** to cause laughter and invite gossip; **nàw-'dà-le** to stir up a lot *of trouble;* **'nàw-gwò-chywù** to blow over, *of trouble, an incident;* **nàw-'shǐng-le** to wake *someone* up by creating a disturbance. ‖**jèy-ge-'dì-fang-de-shwěy-'dzǎy ywè 'nàw ywè 'lì-hay.** The flood here is getting more and more serious.

鬧鐘
nàw-'jūng (*Nunit*, **ge**) alarm clock. ‖**nàw-'jūng 'shyǎng-le.** The alarm clock has started to ring. ‖**bǎ nàw-'jūng 'bwō-dàw 'bā-dyǎn ('shyǎng).** Set the alarm for eight.

奶
*năy (*Npers*) paternal grandmother. *See Appendix A.*

奶
năy (*Nmass*) milk. **nyéw-'năy** cow's milk. **năy-'bǐng** cheese; **năy-'yéw** cream.

奶罩
năy-'jàwr (*Nunit*, **ge, tyáw**) a brassiere.

耐
*này (V) to endure patiently.   này-'fán *or* này-'fár *or* này shīn-'fár to endure suffering *or* annoyance patiently, be patient.   *As mainV:* này-bu-'jù to be unable to endure *pain, etc.*

呢
ne *sentence-final element showing surprise, annoyance, hesitation, or, (with preceding* háy *or* dzày *before the nucleus)* action in process at the moment of speaking. ‖tā yěw 'dwō-shaw-péng-yew-ne? How many friends HAS he, anyway? ‖wǒ-men dàw-'nǎr chywù-ne? So where the devil SHALL we go then? ‖jīn-tyan wǒm dzày-'jèr jù-ne háy-shr dàw-'nàr chywù-ne? Well, shall we stay here today or go over there? ‖'dzěme-ne? How? *or* Why? ‖'shéme-ne? What? ‖'nǎ-yí-ge-ne? Which one? ‖tā háy méy-'láy-ne. He STILL hasn't come. ‖'tyān háy 'hēy-je-ne. It's still dark outside. ‖tā 'jèng dzày chř-'fàn-ne. He's just eating right this minute.

nei *Wade Romanization for* **ney.**

那麼
'nème *see* **'nà-me.**

能
néng (Vpred) can, be able, be possible to.   néng-káng-'chyāng-de-rén men able to bear arms; néng-dzwò-'shr-de-rén capable people, people able to work. ‖bù-néng-dzwò-de-'shr byé 'yīng-chywú rén 'dzwò. Don't promise to do work you can't do. ‖jèy-gwǎn-'bǐ háy néng 'yùng. This pen can still be used. ‖jèy-pyān-wén-'jāng néng mày 'dwō-shaw-chyán? How much could I sell this essay for?

膿
néng *see* **núng.**

能幹
'néng-gàn (A) capable, able.

能够
néng-'gèw (Vpred) can, be able, be possible to; *same as* néng *alone.*

能力
néng-'lì (Nabstr) ability. ‖tā-de-néng-'lì hěn 'dà, *or* tā yěw hěn-'dà-de-néng-'lì. He's a person of great ability.

能耐
'néng-nay (Nabstr) ability; *same as* néng-'lì.

弄
nèng *see* **nùng.**

淳
nèng (A) muddy.

那兒
něr *see* **nǎr.**

那兒
nèr *see* **nàr.**

那
něy *see* **nǎ.**

那
nèy *see* **nà.**

内
*nèy within, inside, interior.   yǐ-'nèy within a *certain time or space:* 'lyǎng-dyǎn-jūng-yǐ-'nèy within two hours (*presumably starting from now*).   jǐ-'nèy *same as above, or* within *certain limits of time:* tsúng 'lyǎng-dyǎn dàw 'sz̀-dyǎn jǐ-'nèy sometime between two and four o'clock.

内容
'nèy-rúng (Nabstr) contents, body *of a speech,* substance, content, central points *of something.* ‖tā-yǎn-'shwō-de-'nèy-rúng hěn 'chūng-shŕ. The content of his speech was substantial stuff.

啊
nga *see* **a.**

泥
ní (Nmass) mud.

你
nǐ (Pron) you, *when speaking to one person.* 'nǐ-men, nǐm you, *when speaking to more than one person.* ‖nǐ 'hǎw. Hello (*informal greeting*).

匿
nì (V) to hide, conceal; *literary equivalent of* **tsáng.**

膩
nì (A) bored, fed up; boring, dull.   (V) to bore, be dull to. ‖jèy-jyàn-'shr-ching hěn 'nì-rén. That's terribly boring.   *As mainV:* nì-'sž-le to be bored to death.   *As postV:* dzwò-'nì-le to work at something until completely tired of it; chř-'nì-le to eat *something* until you're sick and tired of it.

逆
*nì (K) against.   nì-'shwěy against the current, (*literally or figuratively*).

niang *Wade Romanization for* **nyang.**

niao *Wade Romanization for* **nyaw.**

nieh *Wade Romanization for* **nye.**

nien *Wade Romanization for* **nyan.**

你們
nǐm *same as* **nǐ-men** (*see* **nǐ**).

您
nín (*Pron*) you, *when speaking to one person only, and being polite, as to strangers, superiors, and the like. For two or more persons one says simply* **nǐ-men, nǐm.**

凝
níng, nìng (*I*) to freeze, shrink and become solid from cold, become set, to cake. *As mainV:* **'níng-shàng** *or* **níng-'jù-le** *with same meaning;* **'níng-dzày** (**yí-'kwàr**) to freeze (together); **'níng-chéng** to freeze into *such-and-such a' shape.* ‖**nèy-yi-běy-de-'shwěy níng-chéng bīng-'kwàr-le.** That cup of water has frozen into a hunk of ice.

捊
níng *see* **nìng.**

寧波
níng-'bwō (*Nunique*) Ningpo, *another name for* **yín-'shyàn** Yin-hsien (*city in Chekiang province*).

寧國
níng-'gwō (*Nunique*) Ningkwo, *another name for* **shywán-'chéng** Hsüan-ch'eng (*city in Anhwei province*).

檸檬
'níng-méng (*Nunit*, **ge**) lemon.

寧夏
níng-'shyà (*Nunique*) Ning-hsia (*capital of Ningsia province*).

寧夏
níng-'shyà (*Nunique*) Ningsia *province.*

寧願
níng-'ywàn (*Vpred*) to prefer an inferior thing to another. ‖**wǒ níng-'ywàn yàw 'jèy-ge, bú-yàw 'nèy-ge.** I'd just as soon have this rather than that (*even though ordinarily one would choose the latter*). ‖**wǒ níng-'ywàn bù-chī-'fàn yě bù-chī 'nèy-ge.** I'd rather not eat at all than eat that.

捊
nǐng *or* **níng** (*V*) to twist, turn around and around (*as a screw*). ‖**bǎ nèy-kwày-shī-de-'bù 'nǐng-yi-nìng.** Wring out that wet cloth.
   As mainV: **'nǐng-shyà-láy** *or* **'nǐng-kāy** to unscrew; **'nǐng-shàng** to screw on; **'nǐng-jìn-chywù** to screw in; **nǐng-'sūng-le** to loosen by screwing; **nǐng-'jǐn-le** to tighten by screwing; **nǐng-'gān-le** to wring dry; *etc.*

凝
nìng *see* **níng.**

niu *Wade Romanization for* **nyew.**

no *Wade Romanization for* **nwo.**

nou *Wade Romanization for* **new.**

nü *Wade Romanization for* **nywu.**

奴隸
nú-'lì (*Npers*) slave. **dzwò nú-'lì** to be a slave.

努力
nǔ-'lì (*VN2*) to exert efforts, strive hard, work hard. ‖**tā hěn-nǔ-'lì-de dzwò-'shì.** He worked extremely hard.

怒
nù (*A*) angry (*literary*). ‖**tā dà-'nù.** He became very angry.

nuan *Wade Romanization for* **nwan.**

nüeh *Wade Romanization for* **nywe.**

nun *Wade Romanization for* **nwen.**

濃
núng (*A*) strong, heavily flavored, (*of a liquid; opposite* **dàn**); thick, viscous, (*of a liquid; opposite* **shī**). ‖**yàw áw-'yè, děy hē núng-'núng-de-kā-'fēy.** If you want to burn the midnight oil, you've got to drink some very strong black coffee.

膿
núng *or* **néng** (*Nmass*) pus, matter in a sore. **lyéw-'núng** (*IN*) to have pus running out *or* leaking out. ‖**tā-de-shāng-'kěw lyéw-'núng-ne.** His wound is infected and pus is leaking out.

農
*núng agriculture, farming. **'núng-rén** farmer; **núng-'chǎng** farm; **'núng-shywé** the science of agriculture; **núng-'yè** farming as a way of life, an enterprise; **núng-'jyè** farmers as a class, farming circles.

農夫
núng-'fū (*Npers*) farmer.

濃厚
núng-'hèw (*A*) thick, viscous, (*of a liquid; opposite* shi).

農村
núng-'tswēn (*Nunit*, ge) rural community, small village surrounded by farms. (*Nplace*) farm and village, rural territory *in contrast to urban districts*. núng-'tswēn-de-'shēng-hwó rural life.

弄
nùng, nèng (*V*) arrange, take care of, see to, tend to, handle, treat, (*in very general sense*). ‖nǐ nùng 'jèy-ge, wǒ nùng 'nèy-ge. You see to this, I'll see to that.

Most normally used as mainV with any postV of changing state or location, with general causal meaning, not specifying the precise method by which the change is brought about, only indicating that a causal agent is involved.

Thus with myè (*I*) to go out, be extinguished, *one has* gwā-'myè-le to blow out (*by the wind*); dǎ-'myè-le to annihilate or destroy in battle, but nùng-'myè-le *simply* to put out, to extinguish, annihilate, destroy, *with method not indicated.*

Similarly with hwày (*I*) to be out of order, out of commission, useless, broken, *one has* dǎ-'hwày-le to break by striking; dzá-'hwày-le to break with a sharp tap; yà-'hwày-le to break by pressing down from above, *all specifying the method by which the breaking is brought about*, but nùng-'hwày-le to break something, *with method not indicated.*

暖 (和)
*nwǎn, *nwǎng, *nǎng, 'nwǎn-he, 'nwǎng-he, 'nǎng-he (*A*) warm. (*Opposite* lyáng cool.) *As mainV:* 'nwǎn-he-gwò-là'y, *or* 'nwǎn-he-chǐ-láy to warm up, get warm.

暖氣管子
nwǎn-chì-'gwǎn(-dz) (*Nunit*, ge) radiator (*for steam heat*).

暖氣爐 (子)
nwǎn-chì-'lú(-dz) (*Nunit*, ge) radiator (*for steam heat*).

暖水壺
nwǎn-shwěy-'hú (*Nunit*, ge) thermos jug.

暖
*nwǎng *see* *nwǎn.

那威 (國)
nwō-'wēy(-gwó) (*Nunique*) Norway.

挪
nwó (*V*) to change *position, place*. nwó 'dì-fangr to change position, *on small or large scale*; nwó 'yǐ-dz to move a chair to a different position and location. nwó-'wōer to change one's position *or* job: ‖wǒ shyàn-dzày bù-néng nwó-'wōer. I can't make any change now, I've got to stay here.

As mainV: 'nwó-kāy to remove, get rid of *something*; 'nwó-shàng-chywù to move *something* to a higher place; nwó-shang 'léw to move one's family upstairs, *i.e.*, to a new apartment; 'nwó-dàw (lc) to move to *a place; etc.*

年
nyán (*Mtime*) year. 'jīn-nyan this year; 'chywù-nyan last year; 'míng-nyan next year.

nyán-'chīng (*A*) young; nyán-'lǎw (*Aattr*) old; 'chīng-nyán (*Npers*) young people; chīng-nyán-'hwèy the Y.M.C.A.; nywǔ-chīng-nyán-'hwèy the Y.W.C.A.

黏
nyán (*A*) sticky.

年份
'nyán-fèn (*Ntime*, ge) fiscal year. (*Mord*): dì-'yì-nyán-fèn-de-'shīn-shwěy the salary budget *or* expenditure for the first year.

年級
'nyán-jí (*Mtime*) grade in school. (dì-)'yì-nyán-ji freshman year; (dì-)'èr-nyán-ji sophomore year; *etc.*

年紀
'nyán-jì (*Nabstr*) age given in years. ‖tā 'dwō dà 'nyán-jì? How old is he?

年鑑
nyán-'jyàn (*Nunit*, běn) yearbook, annual report.

年齡
'nyán-líng (*Nabstr*) age, *as in an expression like* 'shìng-byé hé 'nyán-líng sex and age.

年歲
nyán-'shwèy *see* nyán-'swèy.

年歲
nyán-'swèy (*Ntime*, ge) years of age. ‖tā-de-nyán-'swèy shr̀ 'dwō-shaw? How old is he? (*The answer uses* swèy.)

A year; the year's harvest. ‖'jīn-nyan-de-nyán-'swèy hěn 'hǎw. Had a good harvest this year.

年頭
nyán-'téw(r) (*Ntime*, ge) crop season, business year. ‖'jèy-ge-nyán-téwr bù-'hǎw. Business was bad this year. *or* Crops were bad this year.

Detail, Beijing Palace

Elephant Statue, Countryside

念

nyàn (*V*) to read out loud. **nyàn-'shū** to study (*from the old method of studying by reading a book out loud*); *from this,* **nyàn** *is used as V meaning* to study. ‖**tā dzày 'měy-gwo 'nyàn-le 'sān-nyán-'shū.** He studied for three years in America. ‖**jèy-ge-dẓ dzěme 'nyàn?** How do you read this character? ‖**jèy-ge-dẓ nyàn "'chū".** This character is read "chū".

As mainV: **'nyàn-chū-lay** to read *something* out (**nyàn-chu 'shēngr-lay** to read out loud); **'nyàn-chǐ-lay** to start to read; to read out loud; to start to study. *To read silently, and not for learning purposes, is* **kàn.**

念頭

'nyàn-tew (*Nunit,* ge) idea, thought. **gǎy 'nyàn-tew jwǎn 'nyàn-tew** to change one's mind.

娘

*nyáng (*Npers*) mother, mama; mother-in-law. *See Appendix A.*

鳥

nyǎw(r) (*Nunit,* jr̄, ge) birds. **nyǎw(r)-'lèy** birds as a class of beings; **nyǎw-'shèw** beasts and birds.

揑

nyē (*V*) to grasp tightly (lift, carry, take, bring) between the thumb and one or more of the fingers, *but not between the fingernails; similarly* with tweezers or clothespin. **nyē-je 'bí-dz** (*H*) holding one's nose, *thus* against one's will.

As mainV: **'nyē-chǐ-láy** to pick up *thus*; **nyē-'jǐn-le** to grasp *thus* tightly; **'nyē-shàng** to pick up *thus* and hold; **'nyē-dàw** (*lc*) to carry *something* held *thus* to a place; *etc.*

揑

nyē (*Munit*) pinch of. **yì-nyē-'yán** pinch of salt.

揑造

nyē-'dzàw (*V*) to make up *rumors, stories, etc.* ‖**nèy-ge-yáw-'yán shr̀-'tā nyē-'dzàw-de.** He made that story up out of whole cloth.

孽

nyè (*Nunit,* ge) sin. **dzàw yí-ge-'nyè** *or* **dzwò yí-ge-'nyè** to commit a sin.

紐約

nyēw-'ywē *or* **nyěw-'ywē** (*Nunique*) New York (City). **nyēw-ywē-'chéng** *specifies the city definitely;* **nyēw-ywē-'shěng** New York State.

牛

nyéw (*Nunit,* téw, jr̄) cow, bull, ox, cattle. **shwěy-'nyéw** water buffalo; **nyéw-'rèw** beef; **nyéw-'nǎy** cow's milk; (**nyéw-**)**nǎy-'bǐng** cheese; **nyéw-'yéw** butter; **nyéw-'chē** ox cart.

牛排

nyéw-'páy (*Nmass;* kwày) beefsteak.

紐西蘭

nyéw-shì-'lán (*Nunique*) New Zealand.

扭

nyěw (*V*) to turn *or* twist round and round. *Usually as mainV:* ‖**bǎ 'lyǎng-gēr-tyě-'sẓ 'nyěw-dzày yí-'kwàr.** Twist these two wires together. **'nyěw-chǐ-láy** *same meaning,* or to tangle, get into a fight.

'nyěw-gwò (*lc*) to turn *something* around. **'nyěw-gwò 'téwr-lay** turn the head towards the speaker; **'nyěw-gwò 'shēn-chywù** turn one's body away, turn one's back to someone.

yì-nyěw-yì-'nyěw-de wobbling from side to side, *as a fat woman walking in high heels which can hardly support her weight.*

紐（子）

*nyěw, **'nyěw-dz** (*Nunit,* ge) button. *Chinese button is a knot on the end of a short piece of string, which fits through a small loop on the end of another piece* **nyěw-'kèwr,** **nyěw-'pàr** *with same meaning.*

女

nywǔ (*Aattr*) female (*of humans*); *the character is used on the door of a women's retiring room:* WOMEN. **nywǔ-'hár** *or* **nywǔ-'háy-dz** female children, girls; **'nywǔ-rén** women; **'nywǔ-dẓ** a woman; **nywǔ-'shì-dz** *or* **nywǔ-yǎn-'ywán** actress (*the former term not always complimentary*). **nywǔ-jāw-'dày** waitress, usherette (*not always polite*); **nywǔ-'jǔ-rén** hostess.

女士

nywǔ-'shr̀ (*NpersT*) a miss, young lady (*same as* **'shyǎw jye**).

O

o *Wade Romanization for* **e.**

ou *Wade Romanization for* **ew.**

P

pa *Wade Romanization for* **ba.**

p'a *Wade Romanization for* **pa.**

趴
pā (*I*) to fall with face down. *Usually as main V:* **'pā-shyà** (*often lc*) to fall face down, fall on hands and knees, sink down with face down; **'pā-dzày** to fall face down on *or* at *a place, e.g.,* **'pā-dzày 'dì-shang** to drop to the earth with face down.

爬
pá (*I*) to climb *or* crawl on hands and knees. **pá-'chyáng** to climb up a wall. *As main V:* **'pá-chi-láy** *or* **'pá-shàng** to climb up; **'pá-shyà-chywù** to climb down; **pá-'dzěw** to crawl away; **'pá-dàw** (*lc*) to crawl to *a place.* ‖**tā tsúng 'fáng-shang 'pá-shyà-lay-le.** He's climbing down the side of the house. ‖**pú-taw-'shù pá-shang 'jyà-dz.** The grapevine is creeping up the trellis.

怕
pà (*V*) to be afraid of; (*Vpred*) to be afraid to; (*Vsent*) to be afraid that. ‖**byé 'pà!** Don't be afraid! ‖**wǒ bú-'pà-ta.** I'm not afraid of him. ‖**wǒ bú-pà 'dzěw.** I'm not afraid to go.

pai *Wade Romanization for* **bay.**

p'ai *Wade Romanization for* **pay.**

pan *Wade Romanization for* **ban.**

p'an *Wade Romanization for* **pan.**

盤
pán (*V*) to coil *something* around. ‖**bǎ 'shéng-dz 'pán-yi-pán.** Coil the rope.

    As main V: **'pán-dzày** to coil *something* around *something*, be coiled around *something*; **'pán-chi-láy** to coil up, (*like a snake*); **'pán-chéng** to coil *something* into *a design, a shape; etc.* ‖**bǎ 'shéng-dz 'pán-dzày 'gwèn-dz-shang.** Coil the rope around the stick. ‖**tā bǎ tyě-'sž pán-cheng yí-ge-'chywǎr.** He coiled the wire into a loop. ‖**cháng-chung 'pán-chi-lay-le.** The snake coiled itself up.

盤 (子, 兒)
*pán, 'pán-dz, pár (*NunitC, ge*) plate, tray, flat dish. **chí-'pán** chessboard; **'swàn-pan** abacus.

    (*MdistT*) game of. **yì-pán-'chí** game of chess.

番禺
pán-'ywù (*Nunique*) P'an-yü *another name for* **gwǎng-'jēw** Kuang-chou *or* Canton (*capital of Kwangtung province*).

盼
pàn (*V, Vsent*) to wait expectantly for, expect *someone to do something.* ‖**wǒ pàn nǐ 'dzǎw-yì-dyǎr 'hwéy-lay.** I'll expect you to come back a little earlier. ‖**wǒ jèng 'pàn-je ta-ne.** I'm expecting him any minute now.

判斷
pàn (*V*) to announce *a decision* in court. **pàn 'àn-dz** to announce the settlement of a case, pass sentence. ‖**fǎ-'gwān háy méy-'pàn-ne.** The judge hasn't announced the decision yet.

判
pàn-'dwàn (*V, Vsent, Vpred*) to reach *a decision* in court, (*like* **pàn-'jywé**)*; or* to ascertain. ‖**tām pàn-'dwàn jèy-ge-'dūng-shi shř-'tā 'tēw-de.** They ascertained that the thing had been stolen by him.

判斷力
pàn-dwàn-'lì (*Nabstr*) ability to make judgments. ‖**tā-'nèy-ge-rén méy pàn-dwàn-'lì.** He has no ability to make judgments.

判決
pàn-'jywé (*V, Vpred*) to reach *a decision* in court. ‖**fǎ-'gwān pàn-'jywé fá-ta yì-'bǎy-kwày-chyán.** The judge fixed a fine of one hundred dollars on him.

盼望
'pàn-wàng (*V, Vsent*) to wait expectantly for, expect *someone to do something; same as* **pàn** *but with more of an element of hoping for what is to happen.*

    (*Nabstr*) hope. ‖**méy-yew 'pàn-wàng.** There's no hope.

pang *Wade Romanization for* **bang.**

p'ang *Wade Romanization for* **pang.**

旁
páng (*Auttr*) other, others; side. *Only before nouns:* **'páng-rén** other people; **'páng-de-'gěw** other dogs; **'páng-de** others; **páng-'mér** side door.

    'páng-byan, 'páng-byar (*Nplace*) vicinity, neighborhood. **jwō-dz-'páng-byar** around the table, near the table, in the vicinity of the table.

    (*H*) as a spectator, from the sidelines. **páng 'tīng** to sit in on *a conference, a meeting*, listen without participating; **páng 'gwān** to look at as a spectator; *limited to these combinations and a few others.*

膀胱
'páng-hwang (*Nunit*, ge) bladder (*in the body*).

鎊
păng (*V*) to plow. **păng-'dì** to plow land; **păng-'tyán** to plow a field. *As mainV:* **'păng-chū-láy-le** to plow *something up, out.* *Chinese plowing does not generally turn the soil, and thus is more comparable to English harrowing.*

胖
pàng (*A*) fat (*of people; opposite* **shèw**). *As mainV:* **'pàng-chĭ-lay** to get fat.

pao *Wade Romanization for* **baw.**

p'ao *Wade Romanization for* **paw.**

抛
paw-'máw (*VN2*) to cast anchor.

刨
páw (*V*) to dig *as a dog digs, with a scooping motion backwards that throws the soil out.* ‖**'gĕw páw-'kēng.** The dog is digging a shallow hole.
   As mainV: **'páw-chĭ-lay** or **'páw-chū-lay** to dig *something up;* **páw-'dzĕw-le** to dig up and remove (*as a tree*); **'páw-shyà-chywù** to dig deeper and deeper.
   páw-'gēr to dig out a root; (*figuratively*) to get to the bottom of something. ‖**byé páw-'gēr-le.** Don't be so nosy.
   (*K*) minus. ‖**'shŕ páw(-le)-'sān 'háy-yew 'chĭ.** Ten minus three leaves seven.

跑
păw (*I, lc*) to run, move fast. *As mainV, same combinations as for* **dzĕw** *to walk.*
   As postV: **gwā-'păw-le** to blow away (*of the wind*); **chwēy-'păw-le** to blow away; **dă-'păw-le** to drive away, beat away; **găn-'păw-le** to drive away; *etc.*

跑道
păw-'dàw (*Nunit*, tyáw) racecourse.

跑馬場
păw-mă-'chăng (*Nunit*, ge) racetrack (*for horse racing*).

跑堂的
păw-'tángr-de (*Npers*) waiter.

礮
pàw (*Nunit*, dzwēn, ge) large-caliber weapons; *in combinations also* artillery. **pàw-'hwŏ** gunfire; **pàw-'shēng** sound of guns; **pàw-'shù** artillery technique; **'pàw-shywé** science of artillery; **'pàw-bīng** artillery soldiers, troops; **pàw-'kē** artillery *as a branch of service.* **kāy-'pàw** to open fire with large-caliber weapons; **fàng-'pàw** to fire a large-caliber weapon.

泡
'pàw(-dz), pàwr (*Nunit,* ge) bubble. **yí-dz-'pàwr** soa bubble; **shwěy-'pàwr** water bubble *or* blister; **(dyàn-dēng-'pàwr** or **dyàn-'pàwr** electric light bulb.

砲仗
'pàw-jang (*Nunit,* ge) firecracker. **yí-gwà-'pàw jang** string of firecrackers.

礮壘
pàw-'lěy (*Nunit,* dzwò, ge) fort.

礮臺
pàw-'táy (*Nunit,* ge) gun platform; fort.

拍
pāy (*V*) to slap *or* pat *with the flat of the hand or with a flat paddle.* **pāy-'shĕw** to clap hands, applaud. ‖**byé 'pāy mă-'pì-le!** Stop that apple polishing. (*Literally refers to urging on the other fellow's horse unnecessarily.*)
   As mainV: **pāy-'píng-le** to pat something smooth; **pāy-'dyàw-le** to make something fall by patting it; *etc.*

拍子
'pāy-dz (*Nunit,* ge) (1) racket, paddle. **chyéw-'pāy-dz** tennis *or* pingpong racket.
   (2) Time. **dă 'pāy-dz** to beat time, keep time; **àn-je 'pāy-dz tyàw-'wŭ** to dance in proper time.

拍掌
pāy-'jăng (*VN1*) to applaud.

拍賣
pāy-'mày (*V*) to sell at auction. ‖**'jèy-ge-dūng-shi pāy-'mày-le 'wŭ-kwày-chyán.** This thing was auctioned off at five dollars.
   As mainV: **pāy-'mày-chū-chywu** to auction off.

排
páy (*V*) to set up in a row, a column, an ordered sequence, a schedule. **páy-'shū** line up the books; **páy jyé-'mù** to arrange a schedule of events, program; **bīng páy-'dwèy** the soldiers fall into formation. *As mainV:* **'páy-shàng** to line up; **'páy-chéng** to set up into *an arrangement.* ‖**bă 'yĭ-dz 'páy-chéng lyăng-'háng.** Arrange these chairs in two rows.

牌
páy (*Nunit,* jāng) cards *or* playing pieces for a game. **jŕ-'páy** playing cards; **gŭ-'páy** dominoes; **má-'jyàng-'páy** mah jong pieces; **dă-'páy** or **wár-'páy** to play cards *or* dominoes *or* mah jong.
   'páy-dz, pér (*Nunit,* ge) metal plate (*as a license tag*); label giving brand *or* make; brand; trade-mark;

check from a checkroom; tag (*as a dog tag*) ; **gěw-'pár dog tag** (*for a dog, not the soldier's identification tag*) ; **shíng-li-'pár** baggage check. ‖**jèy-ge-'chá shɿ̀ shéme-'pár-de?** What brand of tea is this?

排

páy (*Mgroup*) row of.   **'téw-yì-páy-'yǐ-dz** the first (front) row of seats.
    (*MgroupA*) platoon.

排版

páy-'bǎn (*VN1*) to set type.

排字

páy-'dẓ (*VN2*) to set type.   **páy lyǎng-háng-de-'dẓ** to set two columns of characters.

排列

páy-'lyè (*VN1*) to arrange in a line *or* column; to arrange as an exhibit.

排演

páy-'yǎn (*VN1*) to work out the staging of a play.

派

pày (*Vsent*) to appoint, select *someone to do something.* ‖**pày-ta dzwò nèy-jyàn-'shɿ̀-ching.** Appoint him to do that job. ‖**pày-ta dàw-'nàr-chywu.** Send him there.

派

pày (*Mgroup*) a faction, party, group with common feeling and purpose. ‖**tām-'lyǎ shɿ̀ yí-'pày-de.** Those two belong to the same group.
    *pày (Nunit, ge): **fǎn-dwèy-'pày** the opposing party; **hwáy-yí-'pày** sceptics (*as a class*) ; **lè-tyān-'pày** optimists (*as a class*) ; **'měw-měw-'pày** the faction favoring Mr. X.

pei *Wade Romanization for* **bey.**

p'ei *Wade Romanization for* **pey.**

pen *Wade Romanization for* **ben.**

p'en *Wade Romanization for* **pen.**

噴

pēn (*V*) to sprinkle, cause to spurt.   **pēn-'shwěy** to spurt water, sprinkle water. *As mainV:* **'pēn-chū-lay** to spurt out. *Implies forcing the liquid through a narrow opening.*

噴頭

'pēn-téw (*Nunit, ge*) nozzle *or* spray, *as on a hose or for a shower bath.* ‖**bǎ 'pēn-téw 'kāy-kay.** Turn on the shower.

盆

'pén(-dz), pér (*NunitC, ge*) tub *or* basin. **(shǐ-)dzǎw-'pén** bathtub; **(shǐ-)lyǎn-'pén** washbasin.

peng *Wade Romanization for* **beng.**

p'eng *Wade Romanization for* **peng.**

烹

pēng (*V*) to simmer in a pan with sauce after searing. *Forms VN3:* **pēng-'ywù** fish so cooked.

烹調

'pēng-tyáw (*Nabstr*) cooking. **'pēng-tyáw-shywé** science of cooking (*as in a home economics course*).

棚（子，兒）

'péng(-dz), péngr (*Nunit, ge*) awning.

朋友

'péng-yew (*Npers*) friend.

捧

pěng (*V*) to carry, lift, take, hold, bring, in the palms of the two hands with the edges pressed together; (*figuratively*) to support, rally for, praise *someone.* **pěng 'shì-dz** to organize fans behind an actor. ‖**tā 'pěng-ta 'pěng-de hěn 'lì-hay.** He supported him strongly.
    As mainV: **'pěng-chǐ-láy** *or* **'pěng-shàng** to lift up (*as specified above*) : *etc.* ‖**tā 'shěw bǎ-'hwār 'pěng-chǐ-lay-le.** He picked up the flowers in his hands.

捧

pěng (*Munit*) double handful of.   **yì-pěng-'mǐ** double handful of rice grain.

挕

pèng (*V*) to run into, bump into. *As mainV:* **'pèng-dàw** (*lc*) *with same meaning,* or to come up against, meet with; **pèng-'hwày-le** to bump into and break; **pèng-'dǎw-le** to bump into and overturn; **'pèng-shàng** to run into (*each other*) ; **'pèng-jyàn** to meet *someone* by accident; **'pèng-shyà-lay** to knock something down; *etc.* ‖**lyǎng-lyàng-hwǒ-'chē 'pèng-shang-le.** The two trains collided. ‖**tā bǎ nèy-ge-'dēng pèng-'dǎw-le.** He knocked over the lamp.
    'pèng-yi-pèng 'ywùn-chi take a chance, try one's luck.

挕巧

pèng-'chyǎwr (*H*) by chance, by accident. ‖**wǒ jīn-tyan pèng-'chyǎwr 'mǎy yì-bǎ-'sǎn; yùng-'jáw-le.** I just happened to buy an umbrella today; and I've sure been using it.

披

pĕy (V) to wrap someone (or an animal) around with *something*. As mainV: 'pĕy-shàng *with same meaning; etc.* ‖tā 'pĕy-le yí-ge-'dĕw-peng. He put on a cape. ‖yùng yí-ge-'tăn-dz gĕy shyăw-'hár 'pĕy-shang. Wrap a blanket around the baby.

陪

péy (V) to accompany; to be with and entertain. péy-'kè to entertain a guest; (Npers) guest who is not the guest of honor.

(K) accompanying, being with. péy-ta 'dzwò-yi-dzwò sit with him for a while; péy-ta 'chywù go along with him and keep him company.

賠

péy (V) to lose *money in business*. péy-'chyán to lose money; péy-'bĕr to lose one's capital; péy-je 'bĕr 'mày to sell below cost.

(V2) to pay out *money to someone* (as recompense). ‖nĭ dĕy 'péy-ta 'wŭ-kwày-chyán. You've got to pay him five dollars.

賠償

péy-'cháng (V) to pay, repay, pay back. péy-'cháng swĕn-'shr̀ to pay indemnity for damage.

陪襯

péy-'chèn (V) to complement, add to, enhance; to use *something* as a complement, enhancement. ‖jèy-ge-dì-'tăn ké-yi péy-'chèn jèy-ge-'chwāng-hu-lyár. This rug would match the window curtains nicely and bring out their beauty. ‖jèy-ge-'yī-fu dzày péy-'chèn yí-ge-húng-'lĭ-dz. Put a red lining in this dress to enhance its looks.

As mainV: péy-'chèn-chi-lay *with same meaning*.

賠罪

péy-'dzwèy (VN1) to apologize. ‖nĭ shyàng-ta péy-'dzwèy. Apologize to him.

培上

'péy-shàng (RC2) to bank *a fire*. ‖bă-'hwŏ gĕy 'péy-shang. Bank the fire.

陪審

péy-'shĕn (V) to assist in trying *a case*.
péy-shĕn-'ywán jury member; jury.

配

pèy (V) to match, go with, complement. ‖tām-'lyă bú-'pèy. Those two (*e.g., a prospective bride and groom*) don't match each other. ‖'lywù-de pèy 'húng-de. Green matches red.

As mainV: 'pèy-shang *with same meaning*.

佩服

'pèy-fu (V) to respect, admire (*ability, not appearance*). ‖wŏ hĕn 'pèy-fu ta. I respect him very much.

配合

pèy-'hé (A) go well together (*of colors or personalities*). ‖jèy-'lyăng-ge-'yán-sè hĕn pèy-'hé. These two colors go very well together.

(V) to match, put together in a pleasing way. ‖tā 'jŕ-daw dzĕme pèy-'hé 'yán-sè. He knows how to blend colors.

配角兒

pèy-'jywéer (Npers) subsidiary actors, supporting actors.

pi *Wade Romanization for* **bi**.

p'i *Wade Romanization for* **pi**.

批

pī (V) to write down one's opinion of. ‖chĭng-ni bă jèy-ge-wén-'jyàn gĕy 'pī-yi-pī. Please take a look at this document and note down your opinion.

As mainV: 'pī-shàng *with same meaning*; 'pī-chū-lay to write one's opinion on *a document* and send *it* out (*of a superior looking over a subordinate's work*).

批

pī (Munit) a batch of, quantity of. yì-pī-'hwò a batch of merchandise; yì-pī(-de)-'lyàw-dz a batch of material.

批發

pī-'fā (Aattr) wholesale. pī-fā-'dyàn wholesale house; pī-'fā-'shāng(-rén) wholesale merchant.

批准

'pī-jwĕn (V) to indicate approval of in writing (*of higher authority*). ‖nĭ-men-swŏ-'chyéw-de-'shŕ-ching yi-jing 'pī-jwĕn-le. What you asked for has been OK'd.

批評

'pī-ping (V) to criticize *someone, something*.

皮

pí (Nmass; kwày) skin (human); 'pí(-dz) (Nmass; kwày) leather, fur, animal skin, fruit skin; pí *in combinations sometimes* rubber. pí-'gwăn-dz rubber hose; pí-'hwò leather goods; pí-'jyā-dz billfold *or* pocketbook of leather; pí-'bāw leather billfold, leather case; pí-'shyé leather shoes; pí-'dày leather belt (*clothing or machine*), *or* tire; pí-dà-'yī fur coat. ‖wŏ-'shĕw-de-pí 'pwò-le yí-kwày. The skin of my hand was broken in one place. ‖shyēw 'píng-gwo-'pí. Peel the apple.

皮包骨

pí-bāw-'gǔ (A) all skin and bones. ‖tā-'nèy-ge-rén 'shèw-de pí-bāw-'gǔ. He's so thin he's nothing but skin and bone.

脾氣

'pí-chi (Nabstr) temperament. ‖tā 'pí-chi hěn 'hǎw. He has a good temperament. ‖tā-fā 'pí-chi-le. He got mad. or He lost his temper.

疲乏

'pí-fá (A) tired.

啤酒

pí-'jyěw (Nmass) beer.

枇杷桶

pí-pa-'tǔng (NunitC, ge) large bulging barrel.

皮筒子

pí-'tǔng-dz (Nunit, ge, jyàn) pelt; piece of fur (not yet made into a garment).

脾胃

pí-'wèy (Nunit) taste, artistic taste. ‖jèy-ge-'dūng-shi bù-'hé tā-de-pí-'wèy. This thing doesn't suit his taste. More generally: ‖'dzème-yàng-'shwō-fa bù-'hé wǒ-de-pí-'wèy. It doesn't please me to have it said that way.

匹

pǐ (Munit) for mǎ horse; occasionally 'lwó-dz mule; a bolt of bù (cloth).

劈柴

pí-'cháy (VN3) to split kindling; kindling.

屁 (股，戶)

*pì, 'pì-gu, 'pì-hu (Nunit, ge) the buttocks, the rear.

piao Wade Romanization for byaw.

p'iao Wade Romanization for pyaw.

pieh Wade Romanization for bye.

p'ieh Wade Romanization for pye.

pien Wade Romanization for byan.

p'ien Wade Romanization for pyan.

pin Wade Romanization for bin.

p'in Wade Romanization for pin.

拼

pīn (I) to engage in battle to the death. ‖wǒ gēn-ni 'pīn-le. I'll fight you until one or the other of us is dead.
    pīn-'mìng (VN1) same as above, or to risk one's life in combat.
    pīn(-je) 'mìng (figuratively) very hard, as though one's life depended on it. ‖wǒm pīn-je 'mìng dzwò jèy-jyàn-'shr̀. We must work our heads off at this job.

拼

pīn (V) to spell out. pīn-'dz̀ to write words out in letters (in contrast to the use of characters); pīn-'yīn to represent speech-sounds in writing; pīn-yīn-'dz̀ an alphabetical writing system.
    As mainV: pīn-'tswò-le to misspell.

貧窮

pín-'chyúng (A) poor, poverty-ridden.

貧寒

'pín-hán (A) poor, penurious (literary).

貧民

pín-'mín (Npers) poor people.

品

*pǐn (N) goods, stuff. dzwò-'pǐn (Nunit, ge) painting or other product of one's skill for sale; hwò-'pǐn (Nunit, ge) article of merchandise.

品行

'pǐn-shíng (Nabstr) character, behavior, conduct.

ping Wade Romanization for bing.

p'ing Wade Romanization for ping.

平

píng (A) level, smooth; peaceful; equal, balanced; leveled out; common. ‖'dì hěn 'píng. The ground is quite smooth.
    'píng-shŕ time of peace or ordinary times.
    As postV: nùng-'píng-le to smooth out; lā-'píng-le to pull smooth (as bedcovers); etc.

憑

píng (K) according to. píng 'lyáng-shīn according to one's conscience, dictated by conscience; píng tā-'shwō-de according to what he said.

瓶 (子，兒)

'píng(-dz), pyéngr (NunitC, ge) bottle, jar, usually with small neck, bigger at bottom than at top. píng-'kěw(r), pyéngr-'kěw(r) mouth of a bottle; píng-dz-'gàr bottle cap. yì-píng-nyéw-'nǎy bottle of milk; yì-pyéngr-mwò-'shwěr bottle of ink; hwā-'pyéngr flower vase.

平安

píng-ˈān (*A*) peaceful, at peace, safe, restful, secure. ‖yí-ˈlù píng-ˈān! Bon voyage! ‖tā ˈshīn-li hěn píng-ˈān. He's very serene.

平常

ˈpíng-cháng (*A*) normal. **ˈpíng-cháng-de-shŕ-hew** normal times; **ˈpíng-cháng-de-rén** ordinary people.

平等

píng-ˈděng (*Aattr*) legally equal. dž-ˈyéwˇ píng-ˈděng liberty and equality. ‖rén ˈdēw-shr píng-ˈděng-de. All men are equal. ‖wǒ-men yīng-gay dé-daw píng-ˈděng-de-ˈdày-ywu. We must attain °a state in which we are all treated equally. *or* °a state of economic equality.

平分

píng-ˈfēn (*V*) to divide equally.

蘋菓

ˈpíng-gwo (*Nunit*, ge) apple.

平衡

píng-ˈhéng (*A*; *postV*) balanced, in .equilibrium. ‖bǎ jèy-ge-ˈtyǎn-píng nùng-píng-ˈhéng-le. Get this scale balanced.

平均

píng-ˈjywūn (*H*) averaging up, averaging out, equally. ‖bǎ jèy-kwày-ˈbǐng gěy tā-men píng-ˈjywūn ˈfēn-yi-fēn. Divide this cake up equally among them.   **píng-jywūn-ˈshù** the average (*number*).

評論

píng-ˈlwèn (*V*) to discuss critically. **píng-ˈlwèn-ˈjyā** critic, commentator. **píng-ˈlwèn** (*Nunit*, pyān) editorial; commentator's *or* critic's piece in a publication.

評判

píng-ˈpàn (*V*, *Vsent*) to referee, umpire. ‖tā gwǎn píng-ˈpàn shéy ˈyíng. His job is to decide who wins.   **píng-pàn-ˈywán** (*Npers*) referee, umpire.

憑什麼

ˈpíng-shéme (*H*) based on what?, why?, for what reason? ‖tā ˈpíng-shéme lǎwˈ jŕ-shr rén-ne? What right has he got to be so bossy?   **ˈwèy-shéme** why? *calls merely for explanation*; **ˈpíng-shéme** why? *calls for justification.*

平穩

píng-ˈwěn (*A*) regular, steady, smooth, normal. ‖ˈchē džěw-de hěn píng-ˈwěn. The car is riding quite smoothly.

po *Wade Romanization for* **bwo.**

p'o *Wade Romanization for* **pwo.**

p'ou *Wade Romanization for* **pew.**

pu *Wade Romanization for* **bu.**

p'u *Wade Romanization for* **pu.**

撲通

pu-ˈdūng, pu-ˈtūng *imitative of the sound produced when something falls into water without splashing violently, especially if the sound is echoed back and forth as from the walls of a well.* ‖tā pu-ˈtūng-de-yì-ˈshēng ˈtyàw-shyà ˈshwěy chywù-le. He dived into the water with a sort of resounding swoosh.

撲

pū (*I*) to rear up on the hind legs and grab with tne forepaws, *or* to leap at and claw, (*of an animal*); (*V*) *to do this to something or somebody.* ‖ˈláw-hu pū-ˈrén. The tiger sprang and clawed at the man.   **yì-ˈpū pū-ˈkūng-le.** to make a grab and get nothing, (*also figuratively*).   *As mainV:* **pū-ˈdǎw-le** to claw at and cause to fall down; *etc.*

鋪

pū (*V*) to spread something out over. **pū-ˈchwáng** to make a bed; **pū ˈjwǒ-dz** to cover a table (*as with a tablecloth*). *As mainV:* **ˈpū-dzày** to spread *something* out at *a place;* **ˈpū-shàng** to put on flat, spread out. ‖bǎ dì-ˈtǎn pū-dzay ˈdì-shang. Spread the rug over the floor. ‖mǎ-ˈlù-shang ˈpū-shang yì-ˈtséng-yáng-ˈhwēy. The avenue is paved with (a layer of) concrete.

瀑布

pū-ˈbù (*Nunit*, ge) waterfall.

鋪蓋

ˈpū-gay (*Nmass*, fèr, tàw) bedding (mattress and blankets). dǎ ˈpū-gay to roll up a bedding roll *or* to undo a bedding roll; **pū-gay-ˈjywǎr** (*Nunit*, ge) bedding roll.

僕人

ˈpú-rén (*Npers*) servant.

菩薩

ˈpú-sa (*Nunique*) Buddha; (*Nunit*, ge, dzwēn) a (statue *or* image of) Buddha; (*Npers*, wèy) a living Buddha (*reincarnation*).

葡萄

ˈpú-taw (*Nunit*, ge) grapes. yì-dū-lu-ˈpú-taw bunch of grapes; **pú-taw-ˈshù** grapevine; **pú-taw-ˈgār** raisins.

葡萄牙（國）

pú-taw-'ʽí(-gwó) (*Nunique*) Portugal.

譜（子，兒）

*pǔ, 'pǔ-dz, pǔr (*Nunit*, **běn, ge**) volume, book, (*of music unless otherwise specified*). **gē-'pǔ** book of songs; **chín-'pǔ** book of music for a stringed instrument.

shŕ-'pǔ manual of cookery; **jyā-'pǔ** genealogical register.

(*Nabstr*) standard, plan of organization. ‖**tā shwō-'hwà yì-'dyǎr-de-'pǔr dēw 'méy-yew.** He speaks without any logical consistency.

普遍

pǔ-'byàn (*A*) general, prevailing. ‖**'jyàw-ywù 'háy bú-'gèw pǔ-'byàn-ne.** Education isn't yet sufficiently widespread.

樸素

pǔ-'sù (*A*) having simple tastes. ‖**tā-'nèy-ge-rén-de-'yī-fu hěn pǔ-'sù.** He has very simple tastes in clothing.

普通

pǔ-'tūng (*A*) common, ordinary. ‖**tā bú-'gwò shŕ yí-ge-pǔ-'tūng-de-rén.** He's just a run-of-the-mill fellow. ‖**'jèy-ge-fāng-fǎ bú-shŕ pǔ-'tūng-de.** This method is not commonly used.

舖（子）

*pù, 'pù-dz (*Nunit*, **jyā, jyān, ge**) store, shop. **shyé-'pù** shoe store; **fàn-'pù** small food store, *or* restaurant; **rèw-'pù** butcher shop.

潑

pwō (*V*) to empty *a liquid* from a container with a throwing motion. **pwō-'shwěy** to throw water out. *As mainV:* **pwō-'shŕ-le** to throw water *onto*, water *a lawn;* **'pwō-chū-chywù** to throw out, spill out. ‖**bǎ nèy-pén-'shwěy, pwō-dzay 'hèw-mér-wày.** Empty that basin of water out the back door.

坡（兒）

pwō(er) (*Nunit*, **ge**) slope. ‖**jèy-ge-'pwōer hěn 'shyé.** This slope is quite steep. ‖**'lù-shang yěw yí-ge-shyǎw-'pwōer.** There's a slight slope in the road.

婆

*pwó (*Npers*) maternal grandmother; mother-in-law. *See Appendix A.*

破

pwò (*A*) broken down, torn up; (*I*) to break, tear, tear up. *Used causatively:* **pwò 'shŕ-kwày-chyán-de-'pyàw-dz** to break a ten dollar bill (*figuratively*)*;* **pwò-'tǔ** to break ground, open the ground, (*as for building or burying*). ‖**wǒ 'shěw-shang-de-'pí 'pwò-le sān-'kwày.** The skin on my hand was broken in three places.

As postV: **dǎ-'pwò-le** to strike and break; **shwāy-'pwò-le** to fall and break; *etc.*

破產

pwò-'chǎn (*VN1*) to go bankrupt.

破釜沉舟

pwò-'fǔ-chén-'jēw (*literary quotation*) burning one's bridges behind one.

破舊

pwò-'jyèw (*A*) old and broken-down, old and shabby. **pwò-'jyèw bù-'kān-le** to be old and broken-down past the point of use.

破爛

'pwò-làn (*A*) shabby, worn out. **'pwò-làn bù-kān-le** to be worn out past the point of use. ‖**tā-'chwān-de-dà-'yī hěn 'pwò-làn.** The coat he was wearing was very shabby.

篇（兒）

pyān, pyār (*Munit*) for formal speeches or for writings: **yì-pyān-wén-'jāng** an article; **yì-pyān-sh‚ǎw-'jwàn** a biography; **yì-pyān-shyǎw-'shwōer** a novel; **yì-pyān-yǎn-'jyǎng** a speech; **yí-'dà-pyān-de-'hwà** a would-be conversational item which unnecessarily approaches the length and authority of a lecture, a lot of hot air.

片（子）

*pyān, *pyàn, 'pyān-dz, 'pyàn-dz (*Nunit*, **ge**) reel (*film*)*;* phonograph record. **dyàn-yǐng-'pyān** movie reel; **shīn-wén-'pyàn-dz** newsreel; **lyéw-shēng-'pyàn** phonograph record.

偏見

pyān-'jyàn (*Nunit*, **ge**) prejudiced point of view, prejudice. ‖**tā dwèy-ywu 'nèy-jyàn-shŕ-chíng yěw ‿yān-'jyàn.** He's prejudiced about that.

便宜

'pyán-yì (*A*) cheap in price (*not necessarily in quality*). **jàn ...-de 'pyán-yì** take advantage of *somebody.* ‖**tā hěn 'shǐ-hwān jàn rén-'jyā-de 'pyán-yì.** He likes to take advantage of people.

片

*pyàn *see* ***pyān.**

騙

pyàn (*V2*) to cheat *someone* out of *something.* ‖**tā 'pyàn le wo hěn-'dwō-de-chyán.** He cheated me out of a lot of money. ‖**tā 'pyàn-wo.** He cheated me. *or* He fooled me. ‖**jèy-ge-'pù-dz jıng pyàn-'chyán.** This store always swindles you out of your money.

片

pyàn, pyàr (*Munit*) a flat piece *or* expanse of. **yí-pyàn-kǎ-'pyàn** a card; **yí-pyàn-'shwěy** an expanse of water *or* a flood; **yí-pyàn-tsǎw-'dì** an expanse of grassland; **yí-pyàn-'rèw** a slice of meat; **yí-pyàn-myàn-'bāw** a slice of bread.

飄

pyāw (*I*) to wave to and fro *in the breeze;* to be wafted to and fro *on the surface of a body of water.* As *mainV:* **'pyāw-shyà-lay** to be wafted *or* borne down; **'pyāw-shàng-chywù-le** to be wafted *or* carried upwards; **pyāw-'dzěw-le** to be wafted *or* carried away; *etc.*

漂

pyāw (*I*) to be wafted to and fro on the surface of body of water. *As mainV: like preceding entry, but with the limitation of meaning here indicated.*

飄蕩

pyāw-'dàng (*I*) to wave in the breeze (*literary*).

飄舞

pyāw-'wǔ (*I*) to dance in the breeze, (*as a flag; a bit literary*).

飄揚

pyāw-'yáng (*I*) to flap in the breeze (*a bit literary*).

瞟

pyǎw (*V2*) to cast *a glance.* **'pyǎw-rén yì-'yǎn** to cast an approving glance at someone, wink at someone.

票

pyàw (*Nunit.* **jāng**) ticket, stamp, ration stamp, bill (*banknote*)*;* vote. **'pyàw-dz** (*Nunit,* **jāng**) bill (*banknote*). **chē-'pyàw** railroad, streetcar, *or* bus ticket; **mén-'pyàw** ticket for admission; **yéw-'pyàw** postage stamp; **shywǎn-jywǔ-'pyàw** ballot; **pyàw-'jyà** ticket price; **pyàw-'jyā-dz** wallet, billfold; **téw-'pyàw** to cast a vote.

漂亮

'pyàw-lyang (*A*) neat and attractive.

撇

pyē, pyě (*V*) to cast *something* away with a backhand motion. *As mainV:* **'pyē-shyà** to discard *something or* desert *somebody;* **'pyě-chū-lay** to cast out, throw out; **pyě-'dzěw-le** to throw away; **pyē-'hwày-le** to break *something* by throwing it *thus; etc.* ‖**tā bǎ nèy-kwày-'shŕ-tew tsúng 'chwāng-hu-li-tew 'pyě-chū-lay.** He threw the stone out the window.

R

兒

***-r, *-er** element added to other elements primarily to form nouns. This element becomes an integral part of the preceding syllable, by rules given in Introduction Section D; thus: **hwā** or **hwār** flowers; **hwà** to depict, **hwàr** picture; **dà-'dāw** big knife, **shyǎw-'dāwr** small knife; etc.

日

***ŕ** sun; day. **'ŕ-tew** (*Nunique*) sun. **'ŕ-dz** (*Ntime*) or **ŕ** (*Mtime*) day (*24 hours*). **ŕ-'gwāng** sunlight; **ŕ-li** during the day; **ŕ-'yè** day and night; **'ŕ-dz bù-'dwō** not many days; **ŕ-'jyěw** a long time; **'ŕ-cháng** daily; **ŕ-'yùng-de** used every day, needed every day.

日本

ŕ-'běn (*Nunique*) Japan.

日內瓦

ŕ-nèy-'wǎ (*Nunique*) Geneva (*Switzerland*).

不然

bù-'rán (*J*) otherwise (*a bit literary*). ‖**wǒ děy 'dzǎw-dyǎr chywù, bù-'rán wǒ jyèw 'gǎn-bu-shàng 'chē-le.** I've got to leave a bit early, otherwise I won't be able to make the train.

然而

rán-'ér (*J*) but, and yet (*a bit literary*). ‖**wǒ bù-'shǐ-hwān nèy-ge-'fāng-fa, rán-'ér méy-yew 'byé-de-fá-dz.** I don't like that method, and yet there's no alternative.

然後

rán-'hèw (*J*) afterwards. ‖**nǐ ràng-wo shwō-'wán-le, rán-'hèw nǐ dzày 'shwō.** Wait till I'm done talking, then you can have your say.

染

rǎn (*V*) to dye. **rǎn 'yī-fu** to dye clothing. *As mainV:* ‖**bǎ jèy-jyàn-'yī-fu 'rǎn-chéng 'hwáng-sé.** Dye these clothes yellow.

嚷

***rang** (*I*) *usually* **'rang-rang** to brawl, argue noisily. As *mainV:* **'rang-rang-chū-lay** to blab out *a secret.*

嚷

rǎng (*I; V*) to call out, cry out, shout. ‖**tā 'rǎng-jyèw-'mìng-nga!** He shouted out "Help!"
    As mainV: **'rǎng-chǐ-láy** *or* **'rǎng-chū-lay** to raise one's voice, shout out.

讓

ràng (*V*) to give in to *a person.* **ràng-'lù** to make way.
As *mainV:* **'ràng-gěy** to turn *something* over to *someone;* **'ràng-kāy** to give way, make room; **'ràng-chū yí-ge-'dì-fang** to make room; **'ràng-chū** to let out *material, a dress.*
(*Vsent*) to permit *someone to do something.* ‖**ràng-wo 'chywù.** Let me go. ‖**ràng-ta gēn-wo 'chywù.** Let him go with me. ‖**ràng-'wǒ-ba!** Let me (pay)! or This is on me.
(*K*) *like* jyàw, *marks agent, but sometimes implying less forceful causality:* ‖**'yī-fu ràng 'r̀-tew shày-'gān-le.** The clothes dried in the sun. ‖**ràng dú-'chì dú-'sž-le.** He was gassed to death.

饒

ráw (*V*) to forgive, excuse *a person.*

饒恕

ráw-'shù (*V*) to forgive, excuse *a person.*

繞, 遶

ràw, răw (*V*) to move in a circle *around.* **'ràw-je dzěw** to take a detour, go roundabout; **ràw-'wār** to take a detour *or* to beat around the bush; **ràw yì-'dzāwr** to go around in a circle; **'ràw yí-shyàr** to make one circuit around something; **ràw 'hú-du** to be all balled up and confused. ‖**ràw-je 'tswēn-dz chywán-shr̀ 'shù.** There's woods all around the village. ‖**wǒ-men děy 'ràw-je jey-ge-'tswēn-dz dzěw.** We'll have to detour around the village.
As *mainV:* **'ràw-gwò** (*le*) to pass around; **'ràw-chǐ-láy** to coil up *a rope.*

惹

rě (*V*) to cause, give rise to, invite. **rě shr̀-'fēy** to invite trouble; **rě 'léw-dze** *or* **rě-'hwò** to have a collision *or similar serious trouble.* As *mainV:* **'rě-chū** (**shèr, hwò, 'léw-dze,** *etc.*)**-lay** *with same meaning.* ‖**wǒ bù-'gǎn 'rě-ta.** I don't dare provoke him.

熱

rè (*A*) hot. (*Opposite* lěng cold.) (*V*) to warm up *food; for causative meaning otherwise one uses* rè *as postV, e.g.,* **nùng-'rè** to heat *something;* **mwó-'rè-le** to make hot through friction.
rè-'tyār hot weather.

熱情

'rè-chíng (*A*) enthusiastic, zealous; sentimental; *in human relationships.*

若非

rè-'fēy, rwò-'fēy (*J*) unless, if not (*literary*).

熱河

rè-'hé (*Nunique*) Jehol *province.*

熱烈

'rè-lyè (*A*) red hot, burning hot.

熱鬧

'rè-nàw (*A*) noisy and bustling (*as a market place*).

熱心

rè-'shīn (*A*) enthusiastic.

若是

'rè-shr̀, 'rwò-shr̀ (*J*) if, in case. ‖**'rè-shr̀ tā-'láy (de-hwà), wǒ jyèw 'chywù.** If he comes, I'll go.

熱水鍋

rè-shwěy-'gwō (*Nunit,* **ge**) hot water tank.

人

rén (*Npers*) person, people; someone. **'nán-rén** man; **'nywǔ-rén** woman; **'rén-rén** everybody. **'lyǎ-rér** two people; **'sā-rér** three people; **'wǔ-rér-de-'dzwèr** seats for five.
'rén-téwr person, people (*unflattering term*).
rén-'dwēr a crowd, press of people. **rén-'lèy** man, mankind (*contrasted with animal in Buddist theory*); **rén-'kěw** population (*statistics, economics*); **rén-'shù** number of people (*statistics*); **rén-'mín** people of a country (*political*); **rén-'ywán** personnel (*business, governmental*); **'rén-shēng** human life (*philosophical*); **'rén-wù** a character, personage (*historical, political*).
rén-'shān-rén-'hǎy-de (*H*) with people crowding all around, high and low, milling around.
'rén-shr̀ human affairs, personnel affairs.
rén-'gūng manpower, labor (*economic; goes with* ywán-'lyàw materials, dz-'běn capital). **'rén-jya** people; others, other people.

忍

rěn(-de) (*Vpred*) to bear, endure. ‖**'mǔ-chin bù-'rěn-de dǎ shyǎw-'hár.** The mother can't bear having her child beaten. As *mainV:* **rěn-bu-'jù** to be unable to stand *something.* ‖**tā rěn-bu-'jù, 'kū-le.** She couldn't bear it, and started crying.

忍耐

rěn-'này (*A*) patient, long-suffering. (*V*) to be patient *or* long-suffering about. ‖**tā bù-néng rěn-'này nèy-ge-'kǔ.** He can't bear that suffering.
rěn-này-'lì (*Nabstr*) intestinal fortitude, ability to remain patient in the face of difficulties and suffering.

忍受

rěn-'shèw (*I, V*) to endure. ‖**tā hěn néng rěn-'shèw nèy-jǔng-de-'hwán-jing.** He's quite able to bear up under such circumstances.

任

rèn (*V*) to hold *an office;* to be responsible for *a task, an assignment of work.* ‖**tā dzày-'nàr rèn mì-'shū-de-**

jf-'wù. He's responsible for the secretarial work there.

    'rèn-wù (*Nunit*, ge) responsibility, duty.

認
rèn (*V*) to know, understand, recognize, admit, confess. rèn-'rén to recognize people (*as of a very young child*); rèn-'jàng to acknowledge one's debt; rèn-'dzwèy to confess to a crime or fault; rèn-'tswèr to recognize and admit one's mistakes.

    As mainV: 'rèn-chū-lay to recognize, realize, find out, discover; rèn-'chīng-le to recognize clearly; rèn-'tswò-le to recognize mistakenly as: rèn-'tswò rén-le to mistake somebody for somebody else, *or to* misinterpret a person when first meeting him.

任何
'rèn-hé (*Aattr*) any whatsoever. 'rèn-hé-'shŕ-hew any time at all. ‖'rèn-hé-rén dēw 'jŕ-dàw dzěme 'dzwò. Anybody knows how to do that.

認眞
rèn-'jēn (*A*) serious. ‖tā hěn rèn-'jēn. He's serious about this. ‖tā (dzwò-'rén) hěn rèn-'jēn. He's quite a serious person.

認可
rèn-'kě (*I*) to indicate approval. ‖děy 'jīng(-gwò) 'tā rèn-'kě, wǒ-men tsáy néng 'dzwò jèy-jyàn-'shŕ. We've got to submit it for his approval before we can do this.

任命
'rèn-mìng (*V, Vsent*) to appoint *an official;* to appoint *someone to hold an office, at a particular level in the Chinese administrative hierarchy.* ‖'rèn-mìng tā chywù 'gwǎn-lǐ nèy-ge-chywū-'ywù. Appoint him to take charge of that district.

認識
'rèn-shr (*V*) to know, be acquainted with. ‖wǒ bú-'rèn-shr ta. I don't know him. ‖wǒ bú-'rèn-shr jèy-ge-'dz. I don't recognize this character.

認輸
rèn-'shū (*VN1*) to admit defeat, give up.

認爲
'rèn-wéy (*Vsent*) to take *something to be something*, to admit *or* acknowledge *or* feel *that something is so.* ‖wǒ 'rèn-wéy jèy-ge-'wèn-tí 'yīng-gay 'dzème-yàng jyě-'jywé. I feel that this problem should be solved in this way.

扔
rēng (*V*) to throw. rēng-'chyéw to throw a ball (rēng-'chyéw-de pitcher *in baseball*); rēng yí-ge-'chyán to toss a coin.

    To throw away. ‖bǎ nèy-běn-'shū 'rēng-le; wǒ bú-'yàw-le. Throw that book out; I don't want it.

    As mainV: 'rēng-shyà to throw out, discard, leave behind, throw down; 'rēng-chū-chywù throw out; rēng-'dyàw to throw out, discard, throw away; *etc.*

仍舊
réng-'jyèw (*J*) still, remaining. ‖tā réng-'jyèw méy-'gǎy. He still hasn't changed any.

仍然
'réng-rán (*J*) still, continuing. ‖tā 'réng-rán bù-tīng nǐ-de-'hwà. He's still not heeding you.

刃
rèr (*N*) cutting edge. dāw-'rèr knife edge. mwó-'rèr to sharpen the cutting edge; kāy-'rèr to put an edge on a tool (*for the first time*). ‖'rèr yǐ-jing 'dwèn-le. The edge is already blunted.

柔
réw (*A*) soft, pleasing, (*of a color or of sound*).
    réw (*Nunit*, ge) flat (*symbol in music*).

柔和
réw-'hé (*A*) soft, agreeable, gentle, pleasing, (*of a person or personality*).

柔弱
réw-'rwò (*A*) weak, *of a personality, or of a person's voice or expression, revealing his personality.* ‖tā-shwō-'hwà-de-'shēng-yīn hěn réw-'rwò. He speaks with a weak voice.

肉
rèw (*Nmass*) flesh; meat. shyě-'rèw flesh and blood. ɥyéw-'rèw beef; jū-'rèw pork; jī-'rèw chicken; *etc.* rèw-'pù butcher shop. (nyéw-)rèw-'páy beefsteak.

如
*rú (*K*) as, thus (*literary*, if). rú-'tsž (*H*) so, like this, thus; rú-'shyà as follows, given below (*in text*); *since Chinese texts are written from top to bottom and right to left,* the form rú-'dzwǒ as given to the left, as follows, *is also used.* rú-'shàng as given above; rú-'yèw as given to the right (*in preceding text*).

如果
'rú-gwo (*J*) if, in case.

如何
‖rú-'hé? *more literary equivalent of* dzěme-'yàng? How's it going? *or* How about it?

如今
rú-'jīn (*Ntime*) nowadays, these days, at present (*a bit literary*).

如意
rú-'yì (*A*) propitious, according to one's wishes (*a bit literary*).

乳房
rǔ-'fáng (*Nunit*, ge) breasts.

入
*rù (*V*) *more literary equivalent of* **jìn** enter.   **rù-'kěw** entrance; **rù-'shywé** to enter school, matriculate; **rù-'tǔ** to enter the earth, *thus* to bury, be buried, burial.

入不敷出
rù bù-fú 'chū (*literary quotation*) income doesn't cover expenditures: to be unable to make ends meet.

褥套
rù-'tàw (*NunitC*, ge) flat bag of cloth with two pockets opening towards the center, closed by rolling it up; used particularly for bedding in former times.

入伍
rù-'wǔ (*VN1*) to enlist in the armed services.

鎔解
rúng-'jyě (*I*) to melt; fuse, (*of a metal*). ‖**'tyě dzày 'lú-dz-lǐ-tew rúng-'jyě**. The iron is melting in the furnace.
     rúng- molten; **rúng-'tyě** molten iron; **rúng-'shí** molten lead.

溶解
rúng-'jyě (*I*) to dissolve. ‖**'táng dzày kā-'fēy-lǐ-tew rúng-'jyě-le**. The sugar has melted in the coffee.

容量
rúng-'lyàng (*Nabstr*) volume, cubic content, capacity. ‖**nèy-ge-'píng-dz-de-rúng-'lyàng 'dwō-shaw?** What's the capacity of that bottle?

榮幸
rúng-'shìng (*A*) honored; *used in polite expressions.* ‖**wǒ-men hěn rúng-'shìng 'jīn-tyan yěw 'jāng-shyān-sheng láy-'jèr gěy wǒ-men yǎn-'jyǎng**. We are much honored to have Mr. Jāng come to speak to us.

容不下
rúng-bu-'shyà (*RC2*) be unable to hold, be too small to hold. ‖**jèy-jyān-'wū-dz rúng-de-'shyà 'shŕ-ge-rén**. This room can hold ten people.

容易
'rúng-yì (*sometimes* **'yúng-yì**) (*A*) easy.   *Used with following V:* **rúng-yi-'dzwò** easy to do; **rúng-yi-'shwō** easy to say; *etc.*

用
rùng *see* **yùng** (*pronunciation* **rùng** *is found mainly in Peiping and Tientsin among speakers who vary between the two*).

軟
rwǎn (*A*) soft, yielding, *to the touch;* weak (*of a person or a person's appearance*).   (*Opposite* **yìng**.)

軟和
'rwǎn-he (*A*) soft, yielding, *to the touch.*

軟弱
rwǎn-'rwò (*A*) weak and flabby. (*of a person, physically*); weak, timid, (*of a person's character*).

閏
*rwèn intercalary, intercalated.   **'rwèn-ywè** the intercalary month of the year *by the lunar calendar.*

瑞典 (國)
rwèy-'dyǎn(-gwó) (*Nunique*) Sweden.

瑞士
rwèy-'shŕ(-gwó) (*Nunique*) Switzerland.

弱
rwò (*A*) faint, weak. ‖**tā 'shēn-tǐ hěn 'rwò**. His health is weak. ‖**wǒ 'jywé-de yěw yì-dyǎr-'rwò**. I feel a bit faint. ‖**jèy-ge-'gwāng hěn 'rwò**. The light is very dim.   **rwò-'gwó** weak nations.

若非
rwò-'fēy *see* **re-'fēy**.

若是
'rwò-shr *see* **'rè-shr**.

S

撒
sā (*V*) to let go of *something*, release *something particularly from the hand*, cast *something* from one.   **sā-'shěw** to open the hand and let something go; **sā-'gē-dz** to release a (carrier) pigeon from the hand; **sā-'wǎng** to cast a net (*fishing*); **sā-'hwǎng** to tell lies; **ná . . . sā-'chì** to take it out on *someone;* **sā-'yě** (*VN1, A*) to get fresh; to get wild.
     As mainV: **'sā-chū-chywù** to pass out *leaflets or the like,* cast *something* outwards, release *something.* ‖**fēy-'jī sā chwán-'dān**. The plane is scattering leaflets. ‖**tā bù-'kěn sā-'shěw**. He refused to let go. *or* (*figuratively*) He refused to let go of his °job *or* °personnel. *etc.*

三
sā (*NumU*) three. *Confined to a few expressions as the following:* **wǒ-men-'sā(-rén)** we three; **nǐ-men-'sā(-rén)** you three; **tā-men-'sā-rén** they three; **dzám-'sā(-rén)** we three; *any of these with* **rér** *for* **rén.**

  'sā-rén, 'sā-rér three people: **'sā-rér 'lyǎ-rér méy-'gwān-shi** two or three people, it doesn't matter.

  Note that **sā** *equals* **sān** *plus a measure in the above expressions; informal (mainly Peiping)* **'sā-rén** *is the same as more formal* **'sān-ge-rén.**

灑
sǎ (*I*) to spill. *Used causatively to* sprinkle, scatter, *as in* **sǎ-'shwěy** to sprinkle water. *As mainV:* **'sǎ-dzày** to spill on; **'sǎ-chū-láy** to spill out; **'sǎ-shyà-láy** to spill down; *etc.* ‖**'chá chywán sǎ-dzay tā-'shēn-shàng-le.** The tea spilled all over her. ‖**'shyá-dz dǎ-'dǎw-le, 'yán dēw 'sǎ-chū-láy-le.** The box was knocked over and all the salt spilled out.

sai *Wade Romanization for* **say.**

三
sān (*NumU*) three.

三角 (兒，形)
'sān-jyǎw(r), sān-jyǎw-'shíng (*Nunit*, **ge**) triangle. **(sān-)děng-'byān(-de)-'sān-jyǎw-shíng** equilateral triangle; **'èr-děng-'byān(-de)-'sān-jyǎw-shíng** isosceles triangle; **'bù-děng-'byān(-de)-'sān-jyǎw-shíng** scalene triangle; **'jř-jyǎw-'sān-jyǎw-shíng** right triangle; **'sān-jyǎwr-lyàn-'ày** triangular love affair.

傘
sǎn (*Nunit*, **bǎ**) umbrella, parasol. **ywǔ-'sǎn** umbrella; **yǎng-'sǎn** western-style umbrella.

散
sǎn (*I*) to come apart, fall to pieces, (*of something that is assembled from parts*). *As postV:* **dǎ-'sǎn-le** to cause to fall to pieces by striking; **chwēy-'sǎn-le** to cause to fall to pieces by blowing; *etc. As mainV:* **'sǎn-kāy** to fall open. ‖**tā yí 'dzwò-shyà-chywù, bǎ-'chwáng dzwò-'sǎn-le.** The minute he sat down on the bed it fell apart.

散
sàn (*I and causative*) to disperse, break up, scatter, adjourn. **sàn-'bù** or **'sàn-yi-sàn 'bù** to take a stroll (*literally* to scatter one's steps at random). ‖**'hwèy yǐ-jing 'sàn-le.** The meeting's been adjourned.

  As mainV: **'sàn-kāy** to break up (*as a mob, etc.*); **'sàn-dzày** to be scattered to *a place; etc.*

  As postV: **hūng-'sàn-le** to cause to disperse, drive in various directions; **dǎ-'sàn-le** to drive away *a group* in various directions, by striking; *etc.* ‖**tā bǎ 'shù-shang-de-'nyǎwr dēw dǎ-'sàn-le.** He beat the birds out of the trees. ‖**'yéw-tày-rén bèy-'bī-pwò 'sàn-dàw shr̀-'jyè-gè-'chù.** The Jews have been scattered by persecution to the four corners of the earth.

嗓 (子)
*sǎng, sǎng-dz (*Nunit*, **ge**) throat (*inside*); voice. ‖**wǒ 'sǎng-dz 'téng.** I have a sore throat. ‖**tā 'sǎng-dz 'yǎ-le.** His voice is hoarse.

sao *Wade Romanization for* **saw.**

掃
sǎw (*V*) to sweep. *As mainV:* **sǎw-'gān-jìng-le** to sweep *something* clean.

掃興
sǎw-'shìng (*A*) disappointed, disillusioned. ‖**tā 'jywé-de hěn sǎw-'shìng.** He feels very dispirited.

臊
sàw (*I*) to become ashamed. ‖**tā 'sàw-le.** or **tā hày-'sàw-le.** He's ashamed. (*Local Peiping.*)

掃箒
'sàw-shu (*Nunit*, **bǎ**) broom.

塞
sāy or **sēy** (*V*) to slip something forcibly into a narrow slot or opening. *As mainV:* **'sāy-jìn-chywù** *with same meaning;* **'sāy-dzày** to slip *something* into *a place;* **sāy-'jìn-le** to insert tightly. ‖**bǎ jèy-ge-'píng-dz-'sāy-dz sāy-'jǐn-le.** Put the bottle stopper in tightly. ‖**bǎ 'myán-hwa gēn-'yàw 'sēy-jìn 'ěr-dwo-li-tew chywù.** Pack the cotton and medicine into his ear.

腮幫子
sāy-'bāng-dz (*Nunit*, **ge**) part of the cheek below the cheekbone.

塞子
'sāy-dz (*Nunit*, **ge**) stopper, cork, for sink, bottle, *etc.*

賽
sày (*I*) to compete; (*V*) to compete in. **sày-'chyéwr** (*VN3*) to compete in a ball game, *or* a ball game; **sày-'mǎ** (*VN3*) to race horses, *or* a horse race; **sày-'chwán** (*VN3*) to race boats, *or* a boat race; **sày-'pǎw** (*VN3*) to race on foot, *or* a foot race.

  As mainV: **sày-bu-'gwò** to be unable to compete successfully with, be unable to beat. ‖**wǒ shyǎng nǐ yí-'dìng sày-bu-'gwò wo.** I don't think you can possibly beat me. ‖**wǒ-men láy 'sày-sày wǎng-'chyéwr.** Let's have some tennis. ‖**shyàn-dzày jìn-'jř sày-'mǎ.** Horse-racing is forbidden now.

色 (兒)
*sè or ***shǎy** or ***shǎr** (*N*) color. *Names of specific colors end often in* ***sè** *or* ***shǎr,** *less often in* ***shǎy.**

色帶
sè-'dày (*Nunit*, tyáw) spectrum.

色彩
'sè-tsǎy (*Nabstr*) coloring (*as of opinions*). ‖tā-'jèy-ge-rén dày dyǎr-'sè-tsǎy. That fellow's opinions are a bit colored (*meaning he's communistically inclined*).

搜
sēw (*V*) to search out, search for. ‖shywún-'jǐng āy-'jyǎr-de sēw-le. The police searched from door to door. *As mainV:* 'sēw-jáw to search for and find; 'sēw-chū-láy to search out.

餿
sēw (*A*) turned, sour, (*of watery or oily foods*).

搜集
'sēw-jí *or* 'sēw-jì (*V*) to search out and collect. 'sēw-jí yéw-'pyàw to collect stamps.

搜尋
sēw-'shywún (*V*) to search for and get.

塞
sēy *see* sāy.

殺
shā (*V*) to kill, *most often* to murder (*a person*). *As mainV:* shā-'sž-le *with same meaning*. shā-rén-'dzwèy (*N*) the crime of murder.

紗
shā (*Nmass*) gauze, wire screening, open-mesh *or* sheer cloth. tyě-'shā wire screening; shā-chwāng (*Nunit*, shàn) window screen.

沙 (子)
'shā(-dz) (*Nmass*) sand. shā-'dì sandy soil; shā-'jř sandpaper; shā-'náng *or* shā-'dày sand bag; shā-'tǔ sandy dirt, sand; shā-tǔ-'dwēy *or* shā-tǔ-'dwēr sand dunes; shā-'táng granulated sugar.

沙發 (椅)
shā-'fā(-yǐ) (*Nunit* ge, jāng) sofa.

沙市
shā-'shř (*Nunique*) Sha-shih *or* Shasi (*city in Hupeh province*).

沙灘
'shā-tān (*Nunit*, pyàn, ge) beach.

傻
shǎ (*A*) silly, foolish; feeble-minded. 'shǎ-dz (*Npers*) fool; idiot.

shai *Wade Romanization for* shay.

搧
shān (*V*) to fan. shān-'hwǒ to fan a fire. ‖yùng 'shàn-dz gěy-wo 'shān-shān. Fan me a bit with that fan. *As mainV:* shān-'myè-le to fan out *a fire*; shān-'jáw-le to fan up *a fire*; shān-'dǎw-le to overturn *something* by fanning; *etc.*

山
shān (*Nunit*, dzwò) mountain, hill. gāw-'shān mountain; shyǎw-'shān hill; shàng-'shān to climb a mountain; shyà-'shān to climb down a mountain; shān-'dì hilly *or* mountainous country; shān-'mày mountain range; shān-'dǐng *or* shān-'dyěngr mountain top; shān-'jyār mountain peak; shān-'gēr *or* shān-'jyǎw(r) foot of a mountain; shān-'gǔ (*literary*) *or* shān-'gēw(r) valley; shān-'kěw(-dz) *or* shān-'kěwr mountain pass; shān-'pwō(er) slope of a hill; shān-'yáng goat; shān-'wū blackbird.

删
shān (*mainV*) skip, leave out, take out, delete.

山東
shān-'dūng (*Nunique*) Shantung *province*.

山海關
shān-hǎy-'gwān (*Nunique*) Shanhaikwan, *another name for* lín-'ywú Lin-yü (*city in Hopeh province*)

山西
shān-'shī (*Nunique*) Shansi *province*.

汕頭
shān-'téw (*Nunique*) Shan-t'ou *or* Swatow (*city in Kwangtung province*).

山藥
'shān-yàw (*Nunit*, ge) yams.

閃
shǎn (*I*) to flash. ‖jèy-ge-'gwāng yì 'shǎn jyèw 'gwò-chywù-le. That light flashed once and went out. (*N*) lightning. dǎ-'shǎn (*VN2*) to lighten.

閃光
shǎn-'gwāng (*VN1*) to flash, sparkle, flicker.

陝西
shǎn-'shī (*Nunique*) Shensi *province*.

善
shàn (*A*) good-hearted. ‖tā 'shīn hěn 'shàn. He's a good-hearted fellow.

扇子
'shàn-dz (*Nunit*, bǎ) fan. dyàn-'shàn electric fan. shàn (*Munit*) panel *or* leaf of. yí-shàn-'mén door

(not doorway); yí-shàn-'chwāng-hu window (solid piece, not the space it fits); yí-shàn-'chyáng wall.

膳費
shàn-'fèy (N mass, fèr) cost of food, board.

善終
shàn-'jūng (I) to die a natural death (a bit literary).

傷
shāng (V) to be injurious to, be bad for; to wound. shāng-'wèy be bad for the stomach; shāng-'shīn be injurious to the heart, or (A) unhappy, hurt. ‖dzwò 'jèy-jyàn-shr̀-ching shāng-bu-'lyǎw rén. Doing that can't hurt anyone. ‖dzày 'shāng-de-dì-fang shàng yì-dyǎr-'yàw. Put a little medicine on the wounded place. (N) in shèw-'shāng be wounded; shāng-'kěw (N unit, ge) open face of a wound.

商
*shāng (N) business, commerce, trade. shāng-'jyā or 'shāng-rén business man, merchant; shāng-'jyè commercial world, commercial circles; shāng-'hwèy chamber of commerce; shāng-'pǐn merchandise; shāng-'chwán merchant ship; shāng-'kē business (as a course in school).

傷風
shāng-'fēng (VN1) to catch cold; (N abstr) a cold. ‖tā yěw yì-dyǎr-shāng-'fēng. He has a light cold. ‖tā shāng-'fēng shāng-de hěn 'lì-hay. He caught a bad cold.
jùng-shāng-'fēng (N abstr) influenza.

商量
'shāng-lyang (V) to discuss and plan. ‖wǒ děy gēn-ta 'shāng-lyang-shāng-lyang nèy-jyàn-'shr̀-ching. I've got to talk that matter over with him.

商業
shāng-'yè (N abstr) commerce and trade as a field of enterprise. shāng-yè-'chywū business district (of a city); 'shāng-yè-shywé-'shyàw business school; 'shāng-yè-jwàng-'kwàng business conditions.

賞
shǎng (V2) to reward someone (usually of lower rank) with something. ‖tā bǎ wǒ-'dyēw-de-pí-'bāw 'sùng-hwéy-láy-le, wǒ 'shǎng-ta 'wǔ-kwày-chyán. He returned the pocketbook I had lost and I gave him five dollars reward.

賞識
'shǎng-shr̀ (V) to be appreciative of someone lower in rank. ‖tā hěn 'shǎng-shr̀ tā-de-'dzwò-pǐn. He was very appreciative of her paintings.

晌午
'shǎng-wǔ (N time) noon.

上
shàng (N place) upper area, space above, top; surface, face; longer forms 'shàng-byan, 'shàng-byar, 'shàng-myan, 'shàng-myar, 'shàng-tew(r). Alone: ‖shyàng-shàng 'lā. Pull upwards. After nouns: ‖'yān dzày 'jwō-dz-shang. The cigarettes are on the table. ‖'hwàr dzày 'chyáng-shang. The pictures are on the wall. ‖nèy-dzwò-'léw-de-'shàng-byar yěw yí-ge-'jīn-dyěngr On top of that building there's a golden dome.

yi-'shàng in the foregoing; after a noun above, more than. ‖yǐ-'shàng-shwō-de-'hwà wǒ dēw méy-'tīng-jyàn. I haven't heard what's been said up to now. ‖'wǔ-kwày-chyán-yǐ-'shàng-de-dūng-shi tā mǎy-bu-'chǐ. He can't afford to buy anything above five dollars.

(D emord) first and foremost; or last month, week, etc.: 'shàng-děng-de top grade; shàng-'tsz̀ last time; shàng-lyǎng-'tsz̀ last two times; 'shàng-yi-'bān the class just before this one; shàng-'ywè last month; shàng-lǐ-'bày last week; shàng-lǐ-bày-'yī Monday of last week.

*shàng in compounds 'as first member, upper, former. shàng-'ywù or shàng-'wèy captain (Army) or lieutenant senior grade (Navy); shàng-'shyàw colonel (Army) or captain (Navy); shàng-'jyàng general or admiral of the topmost of the three ranks in the Chinese system; shàng-'pù upper berth; shàng-'yī coat, jacket, blouse; shàng-yì-'ywàn upper house, senate; 'shàng(-bàn)-shēn upper part of the body, bust; 'shàng-lyéw upper part of the course of a river; 'shàng-lyéw-shè-'hwèy upper 'strata of society; shàng-'wǔ or 'shàng-bàn-tyàr morning, A.M.; shàng-'hǎy Shanghai (literally upper sea).

上
'shàng(-láy) (RC1) to come up (of a person mounting stairs or taking an elevator, of clouds, of moon and sun, of tides, of water rising, etc.). 'shàng-chywù (RC2) to go up (stairs, go aboard, get onto a vehicle, of an airplane climbing, etc.).

shàng (V, often lc) to go to, get onto, mount higher on or in. shàng-'jyē to go to the street, meaning to go to the business section of town; shàng-'chwáng to go to bed; shàng-'chē to board a train or car; shàng-'chwán to board a ship; shàng fēy-'jī to board a plane; shàng-'chǎng to go on stage; shàng-'àn to land (of boat, not plane); shàng-'shywé to go to school; shàng-'bān or shàng-'kè to go to class or to work; shàng-'tsāw to go to drill (military or just physical exercises); shàng-'shr̀ to go to market; shàng-'rèn to take an office; shàng-'léw to go upstairs; shàng léw-'tī to climb stairs; shàng 'tī-dz to climb a ladder; shàng-'gēw to take the hook, to bite (of fish or figuratively); shàng 'swèy-shu or shàng 'nyán-ji to get along in years, to get old.

(V) to cause to be put on or applied, apply, put on impose. shàng-'yàw to apply medicine externally;

shàng-'yéw to apply oil, to oil *a machine;* shàng yì-tséng-'yéw *or* shàng yí-dàw-'yéw to apply a coat of paint *or* varnish; shàng-'tsày to serve a course of food; shàng-'tāng to serve the soup (*etc., with various courses*) : shàng-'shwèy to impose taxes; shàng-'shyán to tighten a spring; shàng-'jūng to wind a clock; shàng-'byǎw to wind a watch; shàng-'bǎr to be boarded up, to board up (*a store at night*).

shàng (*postV, lc*) *forms RC of all four types, adding to the mainV the meaning of* motion upwards *or* motion upwards onto something. 'pá-shàng (*lc*) to climb up; 'dzěw-shàng (*lc*) to walk up; 'lā-shàng (*lc*) to pull up; 'bǎy-shàng (*lc*) to lay out *things on a shelf or the like* in a display; *etc.*

shàng (*postV*) *forms RC of all four types, adding to the mainV the meaning of* coming together, closing up. 'gwān-shàng to close; 'bì-shàng to close *the eyes;* 'gày-shàng to cover *something* up; 'hé-shàng to close down *a lid,* close up *a suitcase; etc.*

尚且
'shàng-chyě (*H*) even (*literary*), still, yet. ‖'tā 'shàng-chyě bù-jř-'dàw, nǐ gèng béng 'shwō-le. Even HE doesn't know it, to say nothing of you.

上當
shàng-'dàng (*VN2*) to be gypped. ‖tā shàng-le nèy-ge-rén-de-'dàng. He was gypped by the other fellow. ‖jèy-ge-'dūng-shi wǒ 'mǎy shàng-'dàng-le. I was gypped when I bought this.

上帝
shàng-'dì (*Nunique*) God (*Protestant term*).

上海
shàng-'hǎy (*Nunique*) Shang-hai *or* Shanghai (*city in Kiangsu province*).

上下
shàng-'shyà more or less, approximately; *used after an expression of quantity.* ‖wǒ yàw 'wǔ-kwày-chyán-shàng-'shyà-yì-'mǎ-de-'bù. I want some cloth that costs about five dollars a yard. ‖yì-'shř yěw yí-'wàn-rén shàng-'shyà. A division has about ten thousand men.

上訴
shàng-'sù (*VN1*) to make an appeal (*legal*).

上算
shàng-'swàn (*A*) worthwhile, worth it. ‖nǐ shwō nèy-jywù-'hwà bú-shàng-'swàn. It isn't worth the risk involved for you to say that.

上司
'shàng-sz (*Npers*) boss, supervisor (*unofficial*)

尚未
shàng-'wèy (*H*) not yet (*a bit literary*). shàng-'wèy chéng-'nyán is still under age.

shao *Wade Romanization for* shaw.

燒
shāw (*V*) to burn; to cook by boiling or simmering. shāw yí-ge-'kū-lung to burn a hole; shāw-'hwǒ yùng ... use *such-and-such* to build a fire; shāw-'ywú (*VN3*) fish *so* cooked (húng-shāw-'ywú *is more often said,* húng red *because of the color*).

As *mainV:* shāw-'hwày-le to spoil by burning; to burn out; to have a short circuit; 'shāw-chǐ-láy to start burning; 'shāw-shàng to start *something* cooking, to put *something* on to cook; shāw gwāng-le *or* shāw-'wán-le to burn up *or* to burn down; shāw-'hwěy-le to burn to ruins; 'shāw-chéng ('hwēr) to burn to ashes; shāw-'shàng-le to wound by burning.

shāw (N) heat. yěw-'shāw have a temperature (*of a sick person*) : fa-'shāw to have a fever.

稍微
shāw-'wēy (*H*) just a little. ‖nǐ shāw-'wēy 'tsā-yi-tsā jyèw 'shíng-le. Just rub off a little of it. *or* Just rub it off a little.

杓 (子)
'sháw(-dz), sháwr (*NunitC, bǎ, ge*) spoon.

韶州
sháw-'jēw (*Nunique*) Shiuchow, *another name for* chywǔ-'jyāng Ch'ü-chiang (*city in Kwangtung province*).

少
shǎw (*A*) few, little, scarce. ‖'hǎw-rén hěn 'shǎw. Good men are scarce. ‖wǒ-de-'chyán hěn-'shǎw. I only have a little money.

(*H*) less, not so much, seldom. ‖'dzwèy hǎw 'shǎw chř yì-dyǎr. It would be best to eat a little less. ‖shǎw 'yàw yì-dyǎr! Don't want so much! *or* Don't ask for so much! ‖'shǎw gwǎn shyán-'shř! Pay less attention to other people's business! ‖tā shyàn-dzày hěn 'shǎw shàng-'nàr chywù. He doesn't go there very often nowadays.

少
shàw in compounds, junior, subsidiary. shàw-'wèy *or* shàw-'ywù second lieutenant, ensign; shàw-'shyàw major, lieutenant commander; shàw-'jyàng general *or* admiral of the lowest of the three ranks *in the Chinese system.*

哨兒
shàw(r) (*Nunit, ge*) whistle. chwēy-'shàw(r) to blow a whistle *or* to whistle.

少年
'shàw-nyán (*Npers*) young people. 'shàw-nyán lǎw-'chéng (*literary quotation*) be young but mature.

稍息，少息
‖'shàw-shi! At ease! Rest!

紹興

shàw-'shīng (*Nunique*) Shai-hsing *or* Shaohing (*city in Chekiang province*).

篩

shāy (*V*) to sift; to pan.   shāy 'shā-dz to sift sand; shāy 'jīn-dz to pan gold; shāy-'mǐ to sift rice grains. 'shāy-dz (*Nunit, ge*) sieve, strainer.

色（兒）

*shǎy *or* *shǎr *see* *sè.

晒，曬

shày (*V*) to shine on (*of the sun*) ; to expose to the sun. *As mainV:* shày-'húng-le to be sunburned; shày-'hēy-le to be very sunburned; shày-'gān-le to dry by exposing to the sun; shày-'shǐng-le to shine on and wake up (*of the sun*). ‖'sān-tyān dǎ-'ywú 'lyǎng-tyān shày-'wǎng. *Literally* He fishes three days and dries his nets for two. *But figuratively* He works a while and then rests a long time. ‖shǐ-wán-le 'yī-fu, bǎ 'yī-fu dēw 'shày-shang. When the clothes are all washed hang them up in the sun.

晒臺

shày-'táy (*Nunit, ge*) sun porch.

賒

shē (*V*) to buy *or* sell on credit. ‖wǒ-men-'jèr shr̀ 'shyan-chyán-jyāw-'yì, bù-shē-'jàng-de. We're on a cash and carry basis here, no credit is extended. ‖wǒ 'shē-gěy ni 'dwō-shaw-chyán? How much credit have I extended to you?

奢望

shē-'wàng '(*V*) to expect *too much* (*a bit literary*). ‖byé shē-'wàng (tày-'dwō-le). Don't expect too much.

蛇

shé (*Nunit, tyáw*) snake.

折

shé (*I*) to break crosswise (*of something long and brittle*). *As postV:* dǎ-'shé-le to break something crosswise by striking; *etc.* ‖tā 'shwāy-le, bǎ-'twěy shwāy-'shé-le. He fell and broke his leg.

舌頭

'shé-tew (*Nunit, ge*) tongue.   shé-tew-'màw(r) visor cap.

捨

shě (*V*) to give *something* away (*as alms; a bit literary*). 'shě-de to be able to stand (giving). ‖'shě-de-ma? Can you stand it? ‖tā bù-'shě-de chyán 'mǎy tày-'gwèy-de-dūng-shi. He can't bear to spend money for anything too expensive.
As mainV: shě-bu-'kāy to be unable to part with.

設

shè (*V*) to establish, found. ‖tām dzày-'nàr yèw shè-le yí-ge-'fēn-háng. They're establishing a branch there too.

社

*shè (*Nunit, ge*) society, group, organization.   lywǔ-shíng-'shè travel bureau; 'gūng-yè-hé-dzwò-'shè Industrial Cooperative Societies.
     shè-'hwèy (*Nabstr*) society (*sociological sense*). shè-'hwèy-'wèn-tí social problems.

舍

'shè *prefixed to certain kinship terms when speaking to an outsider about a member of one's own family. See Appendix A.*

設備

shè-'bèy (*V*) work out, plan.
     (*Nabstr*) furnishings and conveniences. ‖jèy-swǒ-'fáng-dz yěw 'shīn-shr̀-de-shè-'bèy. This house has modern conveniences and furnishings.

設法

shè-'fǎ (*VN1*) to think of some way *to do something*. ‖chǐng-ni shè-'fǎ gěy-wo 'jyè yì-'bǎy-kwày-chyán. Please think of some way to borrow a hundred dollars for me.

設計

'shè-jì (*V*) to design *buildings, gardens, etc.;* (*Nabstr*) design. ‖jèy-swǒ-'fáng-dz shr̀-'shéy 'shè-jì-de? Who designed this house?

社交

shè-'jyāw (*Nabstr*) participation in social activities. ‖tā-de-shè-'jyāw hěn 'gwǎng. He's very active socially.

社評

shè-'píng (*Nunit, pyān*) editorial.

舍下

shè-'shyà my humble hut; *used in polite answer to a polite question about where you live.* ‖nín 'fǔ-shang? shè-'shyà dzày běy-'píng. Where is your honorable mansion? My humble hut is in Peiping.

什麼，甚麼

'shém-me *or* 'shéme (*reading pronunciation* 'shén-mwò *or* 'shr̀-mwò) *alone or before nominal expressions:* what?, which?, some. ‖nǐ 'shéme-shr̀-hew 'láy-de? What time did you come? ‖nǐ 'chī-de shéme-'fàn? What did you have to eat? ‖nǐ yěw shéme-'fāng-fa bàn jèy-jyàn-'shr̀-ching-ma? Do you have some way of taking care of this? ‖jèy-ge-dì-fang 'shyà-tyan 'rè-dàw shéme-chéng-'dù? How hot does it get in the summer here? ‖tā-de-'yīng-wén 'shywé-dàw shéme-chéng-'dù-le? How much English has he learned?

'shéme-de (H) in some way, in any way; some kind, any kind. ‖nǐ yàw shéme-'yàng-de-'jyěw? 'shéme-de dēw 'chéng. What kind of wine do you want? Any kind is all right.

shéme-'yàngr what kind of, any kind of, some kind of; what way, some way. ‖tā dày shéme-'yàngr-de-'màw-dz? What kind of hat is he wearing?

深

shēn (A) deep (of a hole, water, shade of a color, knowledge); high (of a cliff if one is at the top; opposite chyǎn shallow, light in shade, low). shēn-hwáng deep yellow. ‖shēn-'shēn-de hú-'shī yí-shyà. Take a deep breath.

伸

shēn (I) to stretch out, extend. Causatively: shēn-'shěw to reach out the hand; shēn 'shé-tew to stick out the tongue. As mainV: 'shēn-dàw to extend to a place; 'shēn-chū-láy to extend out from something; etc. ‖tā shyà yí-'tyàw, 'shyà-de jf shēn 'shé-tew. He was so frightened that he stuck out his tongue (the facial expression of fright is so described in Chinese). ‖'mǎtéw shēn-dàw shwěy-jūng-'jyàr (chywù). The dock reaches out into the water. ‖'téw byé 'shēn-dàw chwāng-hu-'wày-tew chywù. Don't stick your head out the window.

身

'shēn(-dz) (Nunit, ge) body. ‖tā 'shēn-dz hěn 'pàng. He's very fat.

'shēn-shang on one's body, or bodily state, health. ‖tā 'shēn-shang méy-'chyán. He has no money with him.

'shēn-byār on one's body, on one, with one, beside someone. ‖tā tsúng wǒ-'shēn-byar 'dzěw-gwò-chywu. He walked past me.

yì-'shēn the whole body. ‖tā yì-'shēn chywán 'shī-le. He got wet all over. ‖tā 'jyàn-le yì-shēn-'ní. He got splashed all over with mud.

shēr (Mgroup) suit of. yì-shēr-'yī-shang suit of clothing consisting of an upper and a lower garment.

申斥

'shēn-chr (V) to call down a subordinate. ‖tā 'shēn-chr ta yí-dwèn, He called him down. ‖tā shěw-le yí-dwèn-'shēn-chr. He got a calling down.

身段

shēn-'dwàn, shēn-'dwàr (Nabstr) bodily shape, figure. ‖tā shēn-'dwàr 'jǎng-de hěn hǎw-'kàn. She has a swell figure.

森林

shēn-'lín or sēn-'lín (N) forest, woods. ‖tā dzày shēn-'lín-lǐ-tew mí-'lù-le. He got lost in the woods.

身量

shēn-'lyàng (Nabstr) height of a person. ‖tā shēn-'lyàng jǎng-de hěn 'gāw. He's grown quite tall.

身體

'shēn-tǐ (Nabstr) health, bodily condition. ‖tā 'shēn-tǐ hěn 'jwàng. He's in very good health.

神

shén (Nunit, ge) deity, high-ranking spirit. shén-'gwěy fairy, sprite; shén-'fù (NpersT) priest, Catholic father.

In compounds shén often refers to human behavior or a human spirit. ‖'shén bù-'jr, 'gwěy bù-'shyǎw (literary quotation). Heaven only knows! (Literally The deities don't know and the spirits don't know.)

神氣

'shén-chì (A) successful and happy about it; conceited, act big. ‖tā shyàn-'dzày jēn 'shén-chì. He's really successful and contented now. ‖nǐ 'kàn tā dwō-me 'shén-chì! (Favorable, but with a feeling of sour grapes.) See how successful he is! (Or unfavorable and sarcastic.) Look how big he's acting!

(Nabstr) appearance, carriage, bearing, looks, manner, air. ‖tā-'shén-chì bú-'dwèy. He's acting suspiciously.

神戶

shén-'hù (Nunique) Kobe (Japan).

神經

shén-'jīng (Nunit, tyáw) nerves literally and figuratively. shén-'jīng bù-'ān be nervous; shén-'jīng gwò-'mǐn be too sensitive; shén-'jīng shf-'cháng be unbalanced, abnormal.

神色

shén-'sè (Nabstr) expression, countenance, looks. ‖tā-de-shén-'sè bú-'dwèy. He doesn't seem quite normal.

審

shěn (V) to try a person (in court); to try a case. ‖fǎ-'gwān dzày fǎ-'tíng shěn-'àn. The judge is in court trying cases.

嬸

*shěn (Npers) father's younger brother's wife. See Appendix A.

審察

shěn-'chá (V) to investigate and look into a situation, a case; (said of a jury, but not of a judge). shěn-'chá-de-jyé-'gwǒ conclusions from an investigation; verdict.

审判
shěn-'pàn (*V*) to try *a person or a case* (*formal legal term*). **shěn-pàn-'gwān** judge.

审問
shěn-'wèn (*V*) to cross-examine *or* question *someone*.

瀋陽
shěn-'yáng (*Nunique*) Shen-yang *or* Mukden (*capital of Liaoning province*).

生
shēng (*A*) raw, new, young, fresh, strange, alien; (*of a phrase or sentence*) meaningful but not ordinarily said. **shēng-'tsày** raw vegetables; **'shēng-rén** stranger, newcomer. ‖**'nèy-jywù-hwà yěw yì-dyǎr-'shēng.** I know what you mean but we don't usually say it that way.

升
shēng (*I*) to rise; (*causatively*) to raise, hoist, promote. ‖**chì-'chyéw 'shēng-chi-láy-le.** The balloon rose. ‖**tām dzày-'nàr shēng-'chí.** They're hoisting the flag. ‖**tā 'shēng-le gūng-'téwr.** He's been promoted to foreman. ‖**tā hēng-le lyǎng-'jí.** He's been advanced two grades.

生
shēng (*V*) to bear *a child;* to give rise to, produce, make. **shēng-'hwǒ** to make a fire; **shēng 'háy-dz** to bear a child; **shēng-'chǎn** to produce agricultural products *or* to give birth; **shēng-'rén** to be born (*in asking for a birthday date*); **shēng-'chì** to get angry (*literally* to produce gas); **shēng-'shř** to make trouble; **shēng-'bìng** to get sick.
   As mainV: **'shēng-dzày** to be born at *a place or time;* **'shēng-shyà-láy** to be born. ‖**tā yì 'shēng-shyà-lay tā-'mǔ-chin jyèw 'sž-le.** His mother died when he was born.

升
shēng (*Mmeas*) *a unit of capacity. See Appendix B.*

聲
shēng (*Mauton*) sound, noise, tone; tone of a Chinese syllable. **'yì-shēng** first tone (ˉ); **'èr-shēng** second tone (ˊ), *etc.*
   In compounds: **'pàw-shēng** noise of cannon fire; **'jūng-shēng** sound of a bell; *etc.*
   shēngr (*Msemel*) a bit, *in* **'gàw-sung wo yì-shēngr** *or* **'jyàw-wo yì-shēngr** give me a bit of notice.

甥
*****shēng** (*Npers*) sister's child. *See Appendix A.*

生成的
shēng-'chéng-de (*H*) from birth. ‖**tā shēng-'chéng-de jyèw nème-'lǎn.** He was born lazy.

生活
'shēng-hwó (*Nabstr*) existence, living conditions. ‖**tā-shyàn-'dzày-de-'shēng-hwó hěn 'kǔ.** His life is very hard right now.
   shēng-hwó-'fèy living expenses.

牲口
'shēng-kew (*Nunit*, téw, ge, pǐ, jř, *depending on kind*) domestic animals (*excluding cat and dog*). **yǎng 'shēng-kew** to raise animals.

生力軍
shēng-'lì-'jywūn (*Nmass*) fresh troops.

聲明
shēng-'míng (*I. Vsent*) to declare, proclaim, assert that. ‖**tā yǐ-jing shēng-'míng tā méy-'dzwò-gwo nèy-jyàn-'shř-ching.** He's already asserted that he didn't do it.

生命
shēng-'mìng (*Nunit*, ge) life.

生日
'shēng-ř (*Nunit*, ge) birthday.

聲望
shēng-'wàng (*Nabstr*) fame, prestige.

生物
shēng-'wù (*Nabstr*) living things. **shēng-wù-'shywé** biology.

生意
shēng-'yì (*Nunit*, ge) way of making a living; business. ‖**tā dzwò shéme-shēng-'yì?** How does he make his living? ‖**shēng-'yì 'hǎw-bu-hǎw?** How's business?

聲音
'shēng-yīn (*Nunit*, ge) noise, sound; voice. ‖**jèy-ge-dǎ-dž-'jī-de-'shēng-yīn tày 'dà.** That typewriter makes too much noise.

繩（子，兒）
'shéng-dz, shéngr (*Nmass*, tyáw) rope, twine, coarse string.

省
shěng (*V*) to save, accumulate by using less. **shěng-'chyán** to accumulate money by spending less; **shěng 'shř-hew** to save time; **shěng 'lì(-lyàng)** to conserve one's strength. *As mainV:* **'shěng-shyà-lay** *same meaning.*

省
shěng (*Mauton*) province of China; *sometimes* state *of the U. S.* **shěng-'jǎng** governor; **shěng-jǔ-'shí** chairman of a provincial government.

省得
shěng-de (*J*) lest, in order to prevent *someone from doing something.* ‖**shyàn-dzày 'dzǎn yì-dyǎr-'chyán, shěng-de yi- hèw méy-chyán 'yùng.** Save some money now so you won't be broke later on.

盛
shèng *H*) in abundance, all around; *only of flowers blooming.* ‖**'ḥwār 'kāy-de hěn 'shèng.** The flowers are blooming all around.

剩
shèng (*V*) to have left, still have. ‖**wǒ ̇háy 'shèng 'wǔ-kwày-chyán.** I still have five dollars left. ‖**'byé-rén dēw 'dzěw-le, jyèw 'shèng-le 'nǐ-le.** Everyone else has gone, there's only you left.

   As mainV: **'shèng-shyà** to be left over. ‖**shèng-shya-de-'fàn dēw dàw-le.** The food that was left over was all thrown out.

勝
***shèng, shèng-'lì** (*Nabstr*) victory. **dé-'shèng** or **dé-daw shèng-'lì** to win victory. **shèng-'jàng** (*Nunit,* ge, tsż) victorious battle.

   ***shèng** (*postV*) be victorious. **dǎ-'shèng-le** to fight and win. ‖**jèy-tsż-'jàng dǎ-'shèng-le yǐ-'hèw, 'shī-wàng 'dzày méy-yew jàn-'jēng.** When this war is won, we hope there won't ever be another.

聖誕
shèng-'dàn (*Nunique*) Christmas. **shèng-dàn-'jyé** (*Nunique*) Christmas festival.

聖經
shèng-'jīng (*Nunit,* běn) Bible.

聖賢
shèng-'shyán (*NpersT*) Saint.

聖壇
shèng-'tán (*Nunit,* ge) altar.

收
shēw (*V*) to receive, accept, collect. **shēw-'pyàw** to collect tickets; **shēw jŕ-'pyàw** to accept *or* honor a check.

   As mainV: **'shēw-chǐ-láy** to gather up and put away; **shēw-'dàw** to receive; **'shēw-shyà(-láy)** to accept, receive and keep. ‖**nǐ shēw-'dàw wǒ-de-'shìn-le-ma?** Have you received my letter? ‖**wǒ bǎ tā-de-'lǐ-wu 'shēw-shyà-le.** I accepted his gift.

收成
'shēw-chéng (*Nabstr*) harvest. ‖**'jīn-nyán-de-'shēw-chéng bú-tày 'hǎw.** This year's harvest wasn't too good.

收工
shēw-'gūng (*VN1*) to put away one's work and quit for the day.

收獲
'shēw-hwò (*VN1*) to harvest crops; (*figuratively*) to get some results. (*Nabstr*) crops; results. ‖**tā 'kǔ gàn-le yì-'cháng, kě-shr méy-yew shéme-'shēw-hwo.** He worked very hard for a while, but he has no results to show for it.

收入
'shēw-rù (*V*) to take in *money.* ‖**nǐ 'jèy-ge-ywè 'shēw-rù 'dwō-shaw-chyán?** How much did you take in this month?

   (*Nmass,* bǐ, fèr) income.

收生
shēw-'shēng (*VN1*) to act as midwife. **shēw-'shēng-de** midwife.

收拾
'shēw-shr (*V*) to clean up and straighten out, tidy up. ‖**nǐ bǎ jèy-ge-'wū-dz 'shēw-shr-shēw-shr.** Straighten up this room.

收攤（兒）
shēw-'tān, shēw-'tār (*VN1*) to quit work, knock off (*at the end of the day*).

收藏
shēw-'tsáng (*V*) to gather up *valuable things* and store *them* away. *As mainV:* **shēw-'tsáng-dzày** to store *things* at *a place; etc.* ‖**tā-'jyā shēw-'tsáng-le hěn-dwō-de-'shū.** His family has accumulated a fine library.

收条
shēw-'tyáw (*Nunit,* jāng) receipt.

收音機
shēw-yīn-'jī (*Nunit,* jyà, ge) receiving set (*radio*); receiver (*telephone*).

熟
shéw or **shú** (*A*) ripe; be well acquainted with someone; be cooked, done. **'shéw-rén** acquaintance. ‖**'gwǒ-dz háy méy-'shéw-ne.** The fruit isn't ripe yet. ‖**wǒ gēn-ta hěn 'shéw.** I know him very well. *or* He and I know each other very well. ‖**'fàn kwày 'shéw-le.** The rice will be done soon.

   As posV: **jǎng-shéw-le** to ripen; **jǔ-'shéw-le** to boil until cooked; *etc.*

熟練的
shéw-'lyàn-de or **shú-'lyàn-de** (*A*) skilled, expert.

熟智
'shéw-shì or **'shú-shì** (A) familiar *with a process, a matter.* ‖tā bàn nèy-jyàn-'shr-ching, bàn-de hěn 'shéw-shì. He knows all the tricks of the trade involved in handling that matter.

守
shěw (V) to defend, guard; to keep *a secret, a promise;* to stick to *a rule, a principle.* shěw 'mì-mì or shěw 'bì-mì to keep a secret; shěw shŕ-'kè to keep to the time appointed, be punctual. ‖'dí-rén nème-'chyáng, wǒ-men dzěme 'shěw jèy-ge-'chéng? How can we defend this city when the enemy is so strong?

手
shěw (Nunit, jŕ, ge) hand. **'shěw-byān** or **'shěw-byār** (Nplace) place easily reached by the hand. ‖nǐ 'shěw-byān yěw-'chyán-ma? Have you any money handy?
In compounds also hand *in the sense of worker:* jù-'shěw assistants; shwěy-'shěw sailors, crew (*not Navy*).
(*Mgroup*) a hand of. yì-shěw-'páy a hand of cards.

首都
shěw-'dū (Nunit, ge) capital city of a country.

手段
shěw-'dwàn (Nabstr) method, means, steps to be taken. ‖jèy-ge-'rén hěn yěw shěw-'dwàn 'dwèy-fù jèy-jyàn-'shr-ching. He knows very well what steps to take in handling this matter. ‖'jèy-ge-rén hěn 'shí-hwan yùng shěw-'dwàn. He likes very much to use indirect methods to get what he wants.

手電燈
shěw-dyàn-'dēng (Nunit, ge) flashlight.

手工
shěw-'gūng (Nabstr) handicraft. shěw-gūng 'yè handicraft industries.

手巾
'shěw-jīn (Nunit, tyáw) towel. shǐ-ľyǎn-'shěw-jīn face towel; shǐ-dzǎw-'shěw-jīn bath towel.

手指頭
shěw-'jŕ-tew (Nunit, gēr, ge) finger. cà-shěw-'jŕ-tew thumb.

手紙
shěw-'jŕ (Nmass, jāng, jywǎr *for* a roll) toilet paper.

守秩序
shěw 'jŕ-shywu (VN1) to keep order, observe regulations. ‖'chǐng ni-men shew 'jì-shywu! Please keep order!

手絹
shěw-'jywàr (Nunit, tyáw, ge) handkerchief.

手鐲子
shěw-'lyèw-dz (Nunit, ge) finger ring.

守信
shěw-'shìn (VN1) to keep one's promises, to keep faith (*a bit literary*).

守時刻
shěw shŕ-'kè (VN1, A) to be on time; punctual.

首飾
'shěw-shŕ (Nunit, ge) ornament, piece of jewelry. ‖tā 'dày-le hěn-dwō-de 'shěw-shr. She wears a lot of jewelry.

手術
'shěw-shù (Nunit, ge) surgical operation. dùng 'shěw-shù to perform an operation *or* undergo an operation.

手續
shěw-'shywu (Nabstr) procedure, series of actions *or* processes (*not legal*). ‖jyè-'chyán-de-shěw-'shywù hěn 'máa-fan. The red tape you have to go through to borrow money is very annoying.
shěw-shywù-'fèy service fee, contractor's fee.

手套
shěw-'tàw (Nunit, jŕ; fù *for* a pair of) gloves. dày shěw-'tàw to wear gloves.

手提箱
shěw-tí-'shyāng (Nunit, jyàn, ge) hand luggage.

守衞
shěw-'wèy (V) to stand guard over, defend.

手藝
'shěw-yì (Nabstr) skill at working with the hands. ‖'jèy-ge-rén hěn yěw 'shěw-yì. He's very skillful with his hands.

受
shèw (V) to receive *something without one's own volition and without necessarily wanting to accept it;* to be the recipient *or* target *or* object of; to bear, endure. shèw-'dzwèy to have a bitter experience.
Often with a V or A used nominally as goal: shèw-'rè to suffer from the heat; shèw-'kǔ to have a bitter experience; shèw-'pyàn to get cheated; shèw 'gūng-jī be the object of an attack *in a newspaper or a speech;* shèw-'hày to be attacked *physically or otherwise,* be the victim of damages inflicted; shèw 'hwèy-lu to receive a bribe; shèw-'shāng to get wounded. ‖nǐ jème 'gūng-ji ta, wǒ 'kàn tā shèw-bu-'lyǎw. If you attack him this way I don't think he'll be able to take it.

瘦

shèw (*A*) thin, lean, slender, (*of person or animal, or of meat*). **shèw-gāw-'tyáwr** tall thin person.

獸

***shèw** (*Nunit*, **ge**) animal. **yě-'shèw** wild animal; **dzěw-'shèw** beasts (*contrasted to birds and fish*); **shèw-'lèy** members of the animal kingdom; **shèw-'yī** veterinarian; **shèw-yī-'ywàn** veterinary hospital.

受報應

shèw 'bàw-yìng (*VN1*) to get one's just deserts.

受屈

shèw-'chywū (*VN1*) to receive unjust treatment, be the object of persecution *or* injustice.

受歡迎

shèw 'hwān-yíng (*VN1*) to be received warmly *or* with appreciation. ‖**tā-de-yǎn-'jyǎng hěn shèw 'hwān-yíng.** His lecture was very favorably received.

受累

shèw-'lèy (*VN1*) to be troubled, be bothered. ‖**dwèy-bu-'chǐ jyàw-'nín shèw-'lèy.** Excuse me for disturbing you (*polite phrase used in thanking someone for a favor done*).

壽險

shèw-'shyǎn (*Nmass*) life-insurance. **bǎw shèw-'shyǎn** to insure one's life, get life-insurance.

受刺激

shèw 'tsż-jī (*VN1*) to have one's feelings hurt.

受委屈

shèw wěy-'chywū (*VN1*) get a raw deal.

誰

shéy *see* **shwéy.**

稀

shī (*A*) thin, watery (*of liquids*); sheer (*of cloth*); thin (*of hair*).

西

shī (*Nplace*) west. *See also* **dūng** east. *In compounds*, Western (*non-oriental*): **shī-'shr̀-de** Western style; **shī-'lì** the western (*Christian*) calendar; **dà-shī-'yáng** Atlantic Ocean; **'shī-yáng** Western countries.

吸

shī (*V*) to inhale. **hū-'shī** to exhale and inhale. **shī yì-kěw-'chì** take a breath; **shī-'yān** to smoke *tobacco*; (*a bit literary*). *As mainV*: **'shī-jìn-chywù** to breathe in.

錫

shī (*Nmass*) tin.

熄

shī *or* **shí** (*V*) to extinguish. **shí-'dēng** to put out lights; **shí-'hwǒ** to put out a fire. **shí-dēng-'hàw** taps (*bugle call*).

西安

shī-'ān (*Nunique*) Sian, *another name for* **cháng-'ān** Ch'ang-an (*capital of Shensi province*).

西班牙 (國)

shī-ban-'yá(**-gwó**) (*Nunique*) Spain.

西伯利亞

shī-bwo-lì-'yǎ, shī-be-lì-'yǎ (*Nunique*) Siberia.

西藏

shī-'dzàng (*Nunique*) Tibet.

西紅柿

shī-húng-'shr̀ (*Nunit*, **ge**) tomato.

西江

shī-'jyāng (*Nunique*) The West River.

西康

shī-'kāng (*Nunique*) Sikang *province*.

希臘 (國)

shī-'là(**-gwó**) (*Nunique*) Greece.

吸墨紙

shī-mwò-'jř (*Nunit*, **jāng**) blotter.

西寧

shī-'níng (*Nunique*) Hsi-ning *or* Sining (*capital of Tsinghai province*).

稀少

shī-'shǎw (*A*) sparse (*of population, of trees in a particular terrain*), few and far-between (*in space, not time*).

犧牲

'shī-shēng (*V*) to sacrifice. ‖**tā 'shī-shēng tā-de-'shìng-mìng.** He sacrificed his life.

吸收

shī-'shēw (*V*) to absorb (*as a surface absorbs liquid*). ‖**jèy-jǔng-tsáy-'lyàw shī-'shēw 'shwěy-ma?** Does this material absorb water?

希望

'shī-wàng (*Vpred*) to hope, desire, *or* plan to *do something*; (*Vsent*) to hope, desire, *or* plan that *something will happen*. ‖**wǒ 'shī-wàng néng 'láy.** I hope I'll be able to come. ‖wǒ 'shī-wàng tā néng 'láy. I hope he'll be able to·come.

(Nabstr) hope. ‖wǒ dwèy-ywu 'tā yěw hěn-'dà-de-'shī-wàng. I have great hopes for him.

吸引力

shǐ-yǐn-'lì (Nabstr) power of attraction (of a magnet, a personality, etc.). ‖tā-de-shǐ-yǐn-'lì hěn 'dà. He has a magnetic personality.

席

shí (Nunit, jāng, lǐng) mat. Formerly one sat on mats when eating; thus shí (MpersA) the guest scheduled to sit on a certain mat: ‖nèy-shí háy méy-'dàw. That guest hasn't arrived yet. Also from this, jyěw-'shí wine and mats, means a feast: chǐ jyěw-'shí to eat a feast.

jī-'shí or byān-'shí to weave mats.

熄

shí see shī.

媳婦（兒）

*shí-fu or *shí-fer. See Appendix A.

習慣

shí-'gwàn (Vpred) to be used to doing something. ‖tā hěn shí-'gwàn dzwò jèy-jyàn-'shr̀-ching. He's quite accustomed to doing this work.

(Nabstr) habit; custom, tradition. ‖tā 'yǎng-chéng yì-jǔng-shí-'gwàn, měy-tyan-'wǎn-shang hěn 'wǎn 'shwèy. He's gotten into the habit of going to bed late every night.

洗

shǐ (V) to wash. shǐ-'shěw to wash one's hands; shǐ-'lyǎn to wash one's face; shǐ-'dzǎw to take a bath; shǐ-'téw to shampoo or to get a shampoo; shǐ 'yī-fu or shǐ 'yī-shang to wash clothes; shǐ-'shyàng to develop films. shǐ-shěw-'fáng wash room with no bathtub; shǐ-dzǎw-'jyān or shǐ-dzǎw-'fáng bathroom with a bathtub; shǐ-dzǎw-'bù or shǐ-dzǎw-'jīn bath towel; shǐ-dzǎw-'pén bathtub; shǐ-dzǎw-'yī bathrobe; shǐ-téw-'shwěy liquid shampoo soap; shǐ-'yī-fu-de laundryman; shǐ-'yī-shang-'fáng laundry (place).

As mainV: 'shǐ-chū-láy to develop films, or, to wash out.

喜歡

'shǐ-hwan (A) feel happy; (V) to like; (Vpred) to desire to, like to. ‖wǒ hěn 'shǐ-hwan. I feel very happy. ‖wǒ bù-'shǐ-hwan ta. I don't like him. ‖wǒ bù-'shǐ-hwan dzwò nèy-jyàn-'shr̀. I don't want to do that.

喜劇

shǐ-'jywù (Nunit, ge, chǎng) comedy, play with a happy ending; (figuratively) comic behavior.

喜事

shǐ-'shr̀ (Nunit, jyàn) happy affair, happy occasion. ‖tā-'jyā-li yěw shǐ-'shr̀. There's a happy occasion (wedding, birth, etc.) happening in his family.

細

shì (A) fine, thin, slender; detailed; minute; fine-grained; smooth. ‖tā-de-'pí-fu 'jěng-de hěn 'shì. Her skin is very smooth. ‖jèy-jǔng-'shyàn hěn 'shì. This type of thread is very fine. ‖tā-de-'shīn hěn 'shì. He gives great attention to detail.

戲

shì (Nunit, chū, chǎng) play, operetta, drama. jīng-'shì Chinese drama in the Peiping style; jyèw-'shì or dà-'shì old-style Chinese drama; shīn-'shì modern drama. chàng-'shì to sing a role in a drama; yǎn-'shì to put on or stage or perform a play; tīng-'shì or kàn-'shì to attend a play. shì-'ywán(-dz) theater (for plays only); 'shì-dz actor (informal term, not too respectable); shì-'dān-dz or shì-'dǎr theater bill; playbill; shì-'táy stage; shì-'píng drama review.

系

*shì (Nunit, ge) department of instruction. hwà-shywé-'shì chemistry department; etc.

細情

shì-'chíng (Ncoll) details, particulars. ‖'shì-chíng wǒ bù-jī-'dàw. I don't know the details of it.

細則

shì-'dzé (Nunit, tyáw) by-laws.

戲法兒

shì-'fǎr (Nunit, ge) magician's tricks. byàn shì-'fǎr to do tricks.

戲劇

shì-'jywù (Nmass; bù, běr) drama in written form.

細茵

shì-'jywùn (Nunit; ge, but only rarely used) bacteria.

細目

shì-'mù (Ncoll) details, particulars.

系統

'shì-tǔng (Nunit, ge) system, organization worked out in detail. ‖tā shwō-'hwà méy-yew 'shì-tǔng. He speaks in a random fashion.

shih Wade Romanization for shr.

心

shīn (Nunit, ge) heart, mind. Used in many expressions concerning emotion, belief, mood, and the like:

‖wǒ 'shīn-li shyǎng jèy-jyàn-'shř-ching shř 'tā-dzwò-de, kě-shr wǒ méy-shwō-'hwà. I thought to myself (*literally* in the mind) that he must have been the one who did it, but I didn't say anything. ‖tā 'shīn tày 'rwǎn. He's too kind-hearted. ‖tā 'shīn hěn 'hǎw. He's good-hearted. ‖tā bǎ wǒ-de-'shīn shwō-hwó-'dùng-le. He has led me to doubt my former opinion. ‖nǐ byé fā-'chéw-le, 'shīn fàng 'kwān yì-dyǎr. Don't worry, set your mind at ease. ‖tā 'shīn-li yěw-'bìng. He must have a guilty conscience.

With literal meaning heart: ‖tā 'shīn yěw-'bìng. He has heart disease.

新

shīn (*A*) new, recent, modern. 'shīn-rén newcomer, new employee, bride *or* bridegroom; shīn-'láng bridegroom; shīn-'nyáng-dz bride; shīn-'shř-de new style, modern. (*H*) newly, recently, just. 'shīn-láy-de-'rén newcomer; shīn-shyà-de-'shywě new-fallen snow (*only if some snow remains from an earlier fall*); shīn-'dìng-de-shf-jyān-'byǎw newly arranged schedule (*as of trains*).

心病

shīn-'bìng (*Nabstr*) heart disease; troubled conscience.

心情

shīn-'chíng (*Nabstr*) mood. shỳan-dzày tā shīn-'chíng bù-'hǎw. He's in a bad mood right now.

心地

shīn-'dì (*Nplace*) bottom of one's heart (*figuratively*). ‖nèy-ge-rén(-de) shīn-'dì hěn 'hǎw. Fundamentally he's a good guy.

心臟

shīn-'dzàng (*Nunique*) heart (*biological*).

薪金

shīn-'jīn (*Nmass*) salary.

新嘉坡

shīn-jyā-'pwō (*Nunique*) Singapore.

新疆

shīn-'jyāng (*Nunique*) Sinkiang *province*.

辛苦

shīn-'kǔ (*A*) tired out, weary, fatigued. 'shīn-shin-ku-'kǔ-de jwàn-'chyán to make one's living (*literally* to earn money) through long hours of tiring work.

欣賞

shīn-shǎng (*V*) to admire, enjoy. ‖wǒ hěn 'shīn-shǎng jèy-ge-dì-fang-de-'fēng-jǐng. I enjoy the scenery here a great deal.

新西蘭

shīn-shī-'lán (*Nunique*) New Zealand.

心事

'shīn-shř (*Nunit*, ge) something weighing on one's mind. `tā 'jīn-tyan hǎw 'shyàng yěw 'shīn-shř shř-de. He seems to have something on his mind today.

薪水

'shīn-shwěy (*Nmass*, fèr) salary.

新鮮

'shīn-shyan (*A*) fresh *vegetables, air;* refreshingly and attractively new *style, pattern, etc.;* new and strange *idea.* ‖nǐ-jèy-jywù-'hwà jēn 'shīn-shyan. That remark of yours really strikes me as odd.

新鄉

shīn-'shyāng (*Nunique*) Hsin-hsiang *or* Sinsiang (*city in Honan province*).

心思

'shīn-sz (*Nabstr*) something weighing on one's mind.

新聞

'shīn-wén (*Nunit*, ge, pyān) news. 'shīn-wén-jì-'jě reporter *or* correspondent; shīn-wén-'bàw News *in the names of certain newspapers only, e.g.,* chúng-'chìng-shīn-wén-'bàw The Chungking News.

心願

shīn-'ywàn (*Nunit*, ge) desire, wish. ‖tā-de-shīn-'ywàn méy-'cháng. His wishes didn't come true.

信

shìn (*V*) to believe, believe in. ‖tā-shwō-de-'hwà wǒ dēw bú-'shìn. I don't believe a word she said. ‖nǐ 'shìn ta-ma? *or* nǐ 'shìn tā-de-'hwà-ma? Do you believe him? ‖tā bú-'shìn 'gwěy. She doesn't believe in ghosts.

信

shìn (*Nunit*, jāng; fēng *if in an envelope*) letter, mail. ‖yì-'tyān sùng °'lyǎng-hwéy-'shìn. *or* °'lyǎng-tsž-'shìn. The mail is delivered twice a day.
shìn-'shyāng mailbox; shìn-'fēng(r) envelope.
shyèr (*Nunit*, ge) short message, *oral or written.* ‖tā yěw-'shyèr-ma? Is there any news from him?

信件

shìn-'jyàn (*Nmass*) mail. ‖jyér 'láy-le hěn-dwō-de-shìn-'jyàn. There was a lot of mail today.

信任

'shìn-rèn (*V*) to trust *a person, a source of information.* ‖wǒ hěn 'shìn-rèn ta. I have a lot of confidence in him.

信陽

shìn-'yáng (*Nunique*) Hsin-yang *or* Sinyang (*city in Honan province*).

信仰
'shìn-yăng (*Nabstr*) belief, faith. ‖wǒ dwèy-ywu tā-de-'hwà méy-yew shéme-'shìn-yăng. I have no faith in what he says.

信用
'shìn-yuńg (*Nabstr*) trustworthiness. ‖jèy-ge-'rén hěn yěw 'shìn-yùng. He's very trustworthy.

星（星）
shīng(-shing) (*Nunit*, ge) star.

星期
shīng-'chī (*Ntime*, ge) week. běn-shīng-'chī thıs week; shàng-shīng-'chī last week; shyà-shīng-'chī next week. shīng-chī-'r̀ or shīng-chī-'tyān (*sometimes just* shīng-'chī) Sunday; shīng-chī-'yī, -'èr, -'sān, *etc.* Monday, Tuesday, Wednesday, *etc.* shīng-chī-'mwò or shīng-chī-'wěy weekend.

興奮
shīng-'fèn, shìng-'fèn (*A*) excited and happy.

興寧
ₕhīng-'níng (*Nunique*) Hsing-ning or Hingning (*city in Kwangtung province*).

行
shíng (*I*) to do, be OK, be satisfactory, work, be permitted, be feasible. ‖wǒ shyǎng bù-'shíng. I don't think that'll do. ‖'nà jyèw bù-'shíng(-le). That won't work. ‖wǒ gēn-ni 'chywù, 'shíng-bu-shíng? Would it be all right for me to go with you?
    (*A*) *with similar meaning.* ‖'jèy-ge-rén hěn 'shíng. He's quite capable.
    Literary and in compounds: (*I*) to travel, go; (*V*) to perform, do.

形
*shíng (*Nunit*, ge) shape, figure. sān-jyǎwr-'shíng three-cornered figure, triangle; *etc.*

行車表
shíng-chē-'byǎw (*Nunit*, jāng, běr) tımetable (*for trains or buses*).

行竊
shíng-'chyè (*V*) to steal (*more literary equivalent of* tēw).

行動
shíng-'dùng (*Nabstr*) conduct, behavior. ‖nǐ yàw jù-'yì tā-de-shíng-'dùng. You'd better have an eye on his conduct.

行蹤
shíng-'dzūng (*Nabstr*) trail left by one traveling. ‖wǒ bù-jr̄-'dàw tā-de-shíng-'dzūng. I have no idea where he is.
    shíng-'dzūng bú-'dìng (*a bit literary*) to be always on the move; to be a vagrant.

行好
shíng-'hǎw (*VN1*) to perform good deeds. *Usually used in asking for charity or other such help:* ‖nín 'shíng-shing 'hǎw-ba! *equivalent to anything from* Brother, can you spare a dime? *to* Will you do your part in furthering this charitable enterprise?

行政
shíng-'jèng (*Aattr; before N only*) executive. shíng-jèng-'ywàn the Executive Ywàn (*branch of Chinese Central Government*); shíng-jèng-jī-'gwān executive organization; shíng-jèng-'chywū administrative district; shíng-jèng-rén-'ywán executive personnel.

行軍囊
shíng-jywūn-'náng (*NunitC*, ge) barracks bag.

行李
'shíng-li (*Nunit*, jyàn) luggage, baggage. shíng-li-'chē baggage car; shíng-li-'fáng baggage room; shíng-li-'pyàw baggage check. dǎ 'shíng-li to pack one's baggage.

行禮
shíng-'li (*VN2*) to perform the proper acts of courtesy. shíng jywūn-'li to salute (*with hand, rifle, etc.*).

行人
'shíng-rén (*Npers*) traveler. túng-'shíng-de-rén fellow-travelers.

形容
'shíng-rùng (*V*) to describe. *As mainV:* 'shíng-rúng-bu-'chū-lay to be unable to describe. ‖jyǎn-'jŕ 'shíng-rúng-bu-chū-'láy-de nème hǎw-'kàn. Really nothing can describe how beautiful it is.

形勢
shíng-'shr̀ (*Nabstr*) appearance or condition of things; topography. shíng-shr̀-'tú topographical map.

行爲
'shìng-wey (*Nabstr*) conduct. ‖jèy-ge-rén-de-'shíng-wéy bú-'jèng. His conduct isn't proper.

行醫
shíng-'yī (*VN1*) to practice medicine.

行營
'shíng-yíng (*Nunit*, ge) field headquarters (*military*).

醒

shǐng (*I*) to wake up. ‖'shǐng-yi-shǐng! *or* 'shǐng-yi-shyěngr! Wake up!

    As mainV: 'shǐng-gwò-láy to come to *from a faint.*

    As postV: nàw-'shǐng-le to wake *someone* up by making noise; jyàw-'shǐng-le to wake *someone* up by calling; *etc.*

擤

*shǐng (*V*) to blow *the nose.* shǐng 'bí-dz *or* shǐng 'bí-ti to blow the nose.

姓

shìng (*Nunit, ge*) surname. ‖jūng-gwo-'míng-dz 'shyān shyě-'shìng. In a Chinese name you write the surname first.

    shìng-'míng (*Nunit, ge*) name and surname, full name.

    shìng (*V*) to have as surname. ‖tā shìng-'jāng. His name is Jāng. ‖gwèy-'shìng? What is your honorable name? (*polite way of asking for identification*). ‖bì-shìng 'jāng. My humble name is Jāng (*the polite way to answer*).

性（子，兒）

'shìng(-dz), shyèngr (*Nabstr*) nature, character, quality, disposition. ‖tā-'shìng hěn 'jí. *or* tā 'shyèngr 'jí. He's very impatient. ‖jèy-ge-'yàw 'shìng hěn 'lì-hay. This medicine is very potent.

杏（子，兒）

'shìng(-dz), shyèngr (*Nunit, ge*) apricot. shìng-'shù apricot tree; shìng-'hwáng(-sè) apricot-yellow color.

性別

shìng-'byé (*Nabstr*) sex, *in such contexts as* shìng-'byé hé 'nyán-líng sex and age.

性情

'shìng-ching (*Nabstr*) disposition. ‖tā-de-'shìng-ching hěn 'hǎw. He has a good disposition.

興趣

'shìng-chywu (*Nabstr*) interest. ‖wǒ dwèy-ywu 'nèy-jyàn-shř-ching 'méy-yew shéme-'shìng-chywu. I have no interest in that matter.

興奮

shìng-'fèn *see* shīng-'fèn.

性格

shìng-'gé (*Nabstr*) character *of a person.* ‖tā-de-shìng-'gé hěn 'chyáng. He has great strength of character.

性質

'shìng-jr (*Nabstr*) property, nature, attribute. ‖chīng-'chì dēw yěw shéme-'yàngr-de-'shìng-jr? What are the properties of hydrogen?

杏仁（兒）

shìng-'rén, shìng-'rér (*Nunit, ge*) almond.

幸運

'shìng-ywùn (*A*) lucky.

shou *Wade Romanization for* shew.

濕

shř (*A*) wet, damp. shř-'dù humidity.

詩

shř (*Nunit, shěw*) poem. shř-'jyā *or* 'shř-rén poet.

師

shř (*MgroupA*) division (*military*). shř-'jǎng divisional commander.

失，失敗

*shř, shř-'bày (*I*) to fail, be defeated. *The following entries now listed under* shŕ *are properly pronounced with first tone:* shř-'bày, shř-'cháng, shř-'dyàw, shř-'dzú, shř-'dzūng, shř-'lǐ, shř-'shěw, shř-'shìn, shř-'wàng, shř-'yè, shř-'ywē.

獅子

'shř-dz (*Nunit, jř, téw, ge*) lion. sž-shr-'sž-jř-'sž-'shř-'shř-dz forty-four dead stone lions (*a tongue-twister*).

詩集

'shř-jí (*Nunit, bù, běn*) collected poetical works of one poet.

施手術

shř sněw-'shù (*VN2*) to perform a surgical operation.

詩選

shř-'shywǎn (*Nunit, bù, běn*) anthology of verse.

十

shŕ (*NumG*) ten.

實

shŕ (*Aattr*) true, real. ‖tā-shwō-de shř 'shŕ-hwà. What he says is true.

拾

shŕ (*V*) to pick *something* up. *As mainV:* 'shŕ-chǐ-láy *with same meaning.* ‖wǒ 'dzwó-tyan dzày 'jyē-shang 'shŕ-le yí-ge-'shŕ-kwày-chyán-de-'pyàw-dz. I picked up a ten-dollar bill in the street yesterday.

石

shŕ (*Mmeas*) a unit of capacity. *See Appendix B.*

食

*shŕ (*V*) to eat; (*N*) food (*both literary*). shŕ-'táng dining room; shŕ-'wù provisions, provender, food supplies.

式
*shŕ *see* *shr̆.

時 (候)
*shŕ, 'shŕ-hew (*Ntime,* ge) time. ‖'nèy-ge-shŕ-hew 'chē 'kāy-de. At that time the train left. *or* That was when the train left. ‖'nèy-ge-shŕ-hew 'chē 'kāy-le. At that time the train had already left. ‖nĭ 'shéme-shŕ-hew 'dàw-de? When did you arrive? ‖dĕy yùng 'dwō-shaw-shŕ-hew? How long will it take?

    de-'shŕ-hew *after any expression means* when *doing so-and-so, or while* doing so-and-so. ‖(dzày) wŏ-men shwō-'hwà de-shŕ-hew tā 'láy-le. While we were talking he arrived. ‖wŏ-men shwō-'hwà de-shŕ-hew tā 'láy-de. It was while we were talking that he came.

石 (頭)
*shŕ, 'shŕ-tew (*Nmass*) stone, rock. shŕ-'mă stone (*statues of*) horses.

失敗
shŕ-'bày (*I*) to fail, be defeated. ‖tā-de-'mǎy-may shŕ-'bày-le. His business failed.

石碑
shŕ-'bēy (*Nunit,* ge) stone monument with an inscription.

時常
'shŕ-cháng (*H*) quite often. ‖tā 'shŕ-cháng láy wŏ-men-'jèr. He quite often comes to our place.

失常
shŕ-'cháng (*VN1*) to deviate from normal. ‖tā-de-shén-'jīng shŕ-'cháng-le. He's not in his right mind.

時代
shŕ-'dày (*Ntime,* ge) age, era. jūng-gŭ-shŕ-'dày the Middle Ages.
    shŕ-dày-dzá-'jr̆ Time Magazine.

拾掇
'shŕ-dew (*V*) to repair; to straighten out. ‖bǎ 'shyāng-dz 'shŕ-dew-shŕ-dew. Straighten out (*the things in*) this box. *or* Fix this box. ‖wŏm 'yīng-gay bǎ dyàn-'hwà 'shŕ-dew-shŕ-dew. We must have the phone fixed.

失掉
shŕ-'dyàw (*V*) to lose *one's balance, confidence, etc.* ‖wŏ dwèy-ywu tā shŕ-'dyàw-le 'shìn-rèn. I've lost confidence in him.

十字
shŕ-'dz̆ (*Nunit,* ge) figure in the shape of the character shŕ (*ten*); cross or intersection. shŕ-dz̆-lù-'kĕwr road intersection, *usually at right angles;* (*figuratively*) at the crossroads, in an open or public place. ‖'hwà yí-ge-shŕ-'dz̆. Make an X-mark.

識字
shŕ-'dz̆ (*VN1*) to be literate.

十字架
shŕ-dz-'jyà (*Nunit,* ge) cross; (*particularly*) Cross, crucifix.

實在
shŕ-'dzày (*H, A*) really; real, genuine, honest. ‖tā shŕ-'dzày shwō-le jèy-jywù-'hwà. He really said this. ‖tā-'jèy-ge-rén hĕn shŕ-'dzày. He's a real, genuine, honest fellow. ‖shŕ-'dzày-de-'chíng-shíng dàw-'dĭ shr̆ shéme-'yàng? After all, what is the real situation?

失足
shŕ-'dzú (*VN1*) to make a moral *or* ethical misstep, *intentionally or not* (*literary*).

失蹤
shŕ-'dzūng (*I*) to disappear without a trace. ‖tā 'hū-rán shŕ-'dzūng-le. Suddenly he disappeared completely from view.

石膏
shŕ-'gāw (*Nmass*) plaster, plaster of Paris. shŕ-gāw-'mú-dz plaster cast.

實際
shŕ-'jì (*A*) practical, actual, factual. ‖wŏ-men shyàn-dzày 'shyǎng-yi-shyǎng shŕ-'jì-de-shr̆-ching. Let's think of practical things for a while now.
    shŕ-'jì-shang (*J*) as a matter of fact, in fact. ‖shŕ-'jì-shang tā shr̆ yí-ge-'hăw-rén, jyèw-shr tā shwō-'hwà bù-hăw-'tīng. As a matter of fact he's a nice fellow, although he does talk harshly.

石家莊
shŕ-jyā-'jwāng (*Nunique*) Shih-chia-chuang (*city in Hopeh province*).

時間
shŕ-'jyān (*Ntime,* ge) period of time. dìng shŕ-'jyān to make an appointment. shŕ-'jyān-'byăw timetable; shŕ-'jyān-dì-'dyăn scheduled time and place for any sort of entertainment.

時局
shŕ-'jywú (*Nabstr*) current (*political and military*) affairs. shŕ-'jywú-de-'chíng-shíng current (*military and political*) events or situation.

失禮
shŕ-'lĭ (*A*) having bad manners. ‖dwèy-bu-'chĭ, shŕ-'lĭ-shŕ-lĭ. Forgive me, my manners are very bad (*polite apology*).

實力

shŕ-'lì (Nabstr) strength, power, authority. ‖bú-yàw shwō kūng-'hwà, wǒ-men yàw yěw shŕ-'lì. Don't just mouth empty words; we've got to have real power.

時髦

shŕ-'máw(r) (A) fashionable, stylish, *especially of clothes*.

石棉

shŕ-'myán (Nmass) asbestos.

石腦油

shŕ-nǎw-'yéw (Nmass) asphalt.

時評

shŕ-'píng (Nunit, pyān) editorial.

失守

shŕ-'shěw (VN1) to fall, be captured. ‖dzwó-tyan-'wǎn-shang nèy-ge-'chéng shŕ-'shěw-le, bèy 'dí-rén jàn-'ling-le. That city fell to the enemy last night.

失信

shŕ-'shìn (VN1) to break one's word (*a bit literary*).

時興

shŕ-'shīng (A) fashionable, stylish, in fashion. ‖dzày yī-jyěw-èr-'bā de-shŕ-hew, má-'jyàng dzày 'měy-gwo hěn shŕ-'shīng. Mah jong was quite the rage in the U. S. in 1928.

實行

shŕ-'shíng (V) to put into effect. ‖nǐ 'shéme-shŕ-hew shŕ-'shíng nǐ-de-'jì-hwà? When are you going to put your plans into effect?
 shŕ-shíng-'jyā man of action.

時時

'shŕ-shŕ (H) from time to time. ‖yí-'dìng 'shŕ-shŕ dēw yěw byàn-'hwà. There are bound to be changes from time to time.

時事

shŕ-'shř (Nabstr) current events. shŕ-'shř-'shīn-wén news of current events.

實現

shŕ-'shyàn (I) to come true. ‖tā-de-'hwà dēw shŕ-'shyàn-le. Everything he said came true.

失望

shŕ-'wàng (A) disappointed.

失業

shŕ-'yè (VN1) to lose one's job. shŕ-'yè-'wèn-tí the problem of unemployment.

實用

shŕ-'yùng (A) practical. ‖nǐ-de-'jì-hwà shyǎn-dzày bù-shŕ-'yùng. Your plan isn't practical at present.

時運

shŕ-'ywùn (Nabstr) luck, fortune. ‖tā shŕ-'ywùn hǎw. He's lucky.

失約

shŕ-'ywē (VN1) to break one's promises (*a bit literary*).

使

shř (V) to use (*a bit more literary than* yùng). ‖nǐ 'néng-bu-néng 'jyè-gey wo nǐ-de-dǎ-dz̀-'jī 'shř-yi-shř? Could you lend me your typewriter to use a while?

屎

shř (Nmass) excrement. lā-'shř to defecate.

史

*shř (N) history. lì-'shř history *in general*; sẕ-shyǎng-'shř history of human thought; jīng-jì-'shř economic history; (lì-)shŕ-'shywé the study of history.
 yěw-'shř-yǐ-'láy (*literary quotation*) ever since the beginning of history, as far back as there are any records.

室

*shř *see* *shř.

使喚

'shř-hwan (V) make use of. ‖nǐ 'hwèy-bu-hwèy 'shř-hwan 'kwày-dz? Can you use chopsticks?
 Direct *the activities of servants*. ‖tā hěn 'hwèy 'shř-hwan rén. He's good at directing his servants' work.
 'shř-hwan-rén (Npers) servant.

使壞

shř-'hwày (VN1) to play dirty tricks. ‖tā gěy-wo shř-'hwày. He played a dirty trick on me.

使勁

shř-'jìn (VN2) to use effort, try hard. ‖nǐ bǎ-'mén shř-'jìn 'twēy-yi-twēy. Give the door a hard push. ‖wǒ bù-néng 'dzày shř-'jìn-le. I can't use any more effort at it (*or it'll break, or because I'm tired out*).

始終

shř-'jūng (J) all the time, from beginning to end *of some period of time* without pause. ‖tā 'jìn-láy yǐ-'hèw shř-'jūng méy-'shwō yí-jywù-'hwà. He hasn't said a word (all the time) since he came in.

使命

shř-'mìng (Nunit, ge) mission, assignment.

是

shr̀ (*similar to V but with special characteristics described here*) is, are, equals, is definitely. **shr̀** *is negated by preceding* **bū-**, *never by preceding* **méy**; *a literary equivalent of* **bú-shr**, *colloquial in some combinations, is* **fěy**. *Although a V,* **shr̀** *has the peculiarity (except when not followed by anything in the same sentence) of functioning not as the nucleus of a sentence, rather of emphasizing a following nuclear or sometimes non-nuclear expression.*

(1) *Followed by a nominal nucleus:* ‖**wǒ shr̀ měy-gwo-'bīng.** I'm an American soldier. (*See Section E §3 of Introduction for omission of* **shr̀** *in some such sentences.*)

(2) *Followed by a nominalized adjectival nucleus:* ‖**tā-chwān-de-'shyé shr̀ 'hwáng-de.** The shoes he has on are brown.

(3) *Followed by a nominalized verbal nucleus (V or I plus* **de**), *is often dropped in affirmative:* ‖**tā (shr̀) tsúng 'měy-gwo láy-de.** He comes from the United States. **shr̀** *is kept in the negative:* ‖**tā bú-shr tsúng 'měy-gwo láy-de.** He isn't from the United States.

(4) *Stressed and followed by an ordinary verbal or adjectival nucleus:* ‖**fàn-'dyàn 'shr̀ dzày 'yèw-byan.** The hotel really is to the right. ‖'**jèy-ge-rén 'shr̀ 'jí-ling.** He's really clever.

(5) *Similar to the last is an idiomatic type of introductory comment of the form A* **shr̀** *A:* ‖'**hǎw shr̀ 'hǎw, kě-shr wǒ bù-'shǐ-hwan.** Sure it's good, but I just don't like it. ‖'**dwèy shr̀ 'dwèy, bú-gwo tā bú-'shìn.** Certainly it's true, but just the same he doesn't believe it.

(6) *The forms* '**shr̀.** *or* '**shr̀-le.** *or* '**shr̀-de.** *are about the equivalent of English Yes. or True enough. or So it is., indicating agreement with a statement made by someone else; the form* '**bú-shr.** *is the comparable negative.* ‖**tā 'láy-le hěn 'jyěw-le-ba.** '**shr̀-de.** He's been here a long time now. Yes, so he has.

(7) *When* **shr̀** *is put before a nominal form in the earlier part of a sentence,* **de** *usually comes later:* ‖**shr̀-'tā bú-ywàn-yi 'dzěw-de.** It's HE who won't go. ‖**shr̀-'shéy 'gàw-su ni-de?** Who was it who told you so? ‖**shr̀ 'jèy-běr-shū 'shwō-de.** It's THIS book that says so.

試

shr̀ (*I*) to try; *usually* '**shr̀-yi-shr̀** *or* '**shr̀ yí-shyàr** to take a try. ‖**wǒ bù-jī-'dàw 'hǎw-bu-hǎw, kě-shr wǒ shyǎng 'shr̀-yi-shr̀.** I don't know whether it's any good or not, but I'm going to have a try at it. ‖**gěy-wo nèy-shwāng-'shyé 'shr̀-yi-shr̀ 'kàn.** Give me that pair of shoes to try (on).

(*Vpred*) to try to. ‖**ni 'shr̀ yùng 'jèy-ge 'kàn-yi-kàn.** Try using this and see how it goes.

市

shr̀ (1) (*Nunit,* **ge**) market place. ‖**tā shàng-'shr̀-le.** He's gone to market. ‖'**shr̀-shang méy-'tsày.** There are no vegetables on the market.

(2) (*Nunit,* **ge**) municipality (*one type of city from the governmental point of view*). **shr̀-'jǎng** mayor of a municipality.

(3) *Prefixed to certain Mmeas designates units of the Market Standard system of weights and measures. Thus* **shr̀-'mǔ** (*Mmeas*) the Market Standard **mǔ**, about .1644 acre. *See Appendix B.*

市

*****shr̀ *prefixed to Mmeas to form units of the Market Standard System. See Appendix B.*

士

*****shr̀ (*Npers*) (1) scholar. **shr̀-núng-gūng-'shāng** scholars, farmers, workers, and merchants (*four classes of earlier society*); '**bwó-shr̀** holder of the Ph.D. degree.

(2) Non-commissioned officer. **shyà-'shr̀** corporal; **jūng-'shr̀** sergeant; **shàng-'shr̀** first sergeant (*there are only these three grades and the terms do not equate perfectly*); **shr̀-'bīng** *or* **bīng-'shr̀** enlisted personnel.

式

*****shr̀ *or* *shŕ model, style, pattern, fashion; *full forms* '**yàng-shr̀** *or* **shŕ-'yàng** (*Nabstr*). **shīn-'shr̀-de** modern; **lǎw-'shr̀-de** old-fashioned; **shī-'shr̀-de** western-style.

室

*****shr̀ (*or* *shŕ) (*Nunit,* **jyān**) room. **kè-'shr̀** living room; **wò-'shr̀** bedroom; **àn-'shr̀** darkroom.

事

'**shr̀(-ching)**, **shèr** (*Nunit,* **jyàn**) matter, affair, business, things, (*in the abstract sense*). **dzwò-'shr̀** to do things, work; **chū-'shr̀** to depart from normal; to have an accident.

視察

shr̀-'chá (*V*) to inspect, *of a government agent.* **shr̀-chá-'ywán** inspector.

市場

shr̀-'chǎng (*Nunit,* **ge**) market place.

世傳

shr̀-'chwán (*V*) to hand down from generation to generation. *Mostly used as follows:* ‖**jèy-jǔng-de-'yì-shu shr̀ tām-'jyā shr̀-'chwán-de.** That artistic skill has been passed down from generation to generation in their family.

市區

shr̀-'chywū (*Nunit*, dày, ge) business district of a city.

似的

shr̀-de *put after an expression usually beginning with* (hǎw) 'shyàng; *to seem like, seem as though.* ‖tā hǎw 'shyàng tā-'fù-chin shr̀-de, ày chēw-'yān. He's very much like his father in being fond of smoking. ‖tā hǎw shyàng bú-'ywàn-yi 'láy shr̀-de. It seems very much as though he doesn't want to come. ‖tā (hǎw 'shyàng) 'fēng-le shr̀-de. Seems like he's gone insane.

釋放

shr̀-'fàng (*V*) to release *a prisoner.*

是非

shr̀-'fēy (*Nabstr*) right and wrong. ‖tā bù-'dǔng shr̀-'fēy. *or* tā bù-'míng shr̀-'fēy. He can't tell right from wrong.

世故人情

'shr̀-gù-rén-'chíng (*Nabstr*) practical experience, worldly experience, knowledge of the ways of the world. ‖tā hěn 'jī-dàw 'shr̀-gù-rěn-'chíng. He's quite worldly wise.

侍候

'shr̀-hèw *same meaning as* 'tsz̀-hèw to wait on, serve *someone.*

似乎

'shr̀-hu (*Vpred*) to seem, look like. ‖tā 'shr̀-hu hěn gāw-'shìng. He seems very happy.

事件

'shr̀-jyàn (*Nunit*, ge) affair, matter, incident. ‖kǔng-'pà 'yèw yěw shéme-'shr̀-jyàn fā-'shēng-le. I'm afraid something else is going to happen now.

世界

shr̀-'jyè (*Nunique*) the world. ‖shr̀-'jyè-shàng 'méy-yew 'nàme-yàngr-de-rén. There's no one like that in the world.

　'shr̀-jyè-dà-'jàn world war, war on world scale.

勢力

'shr̀-lì (*Nabstr*) position, power, influence. ‖tā yěw hěn-'dà-de-'shr̀-lì. He has a great deal of influence.

勢利

'shr̀-li (*A*) characterized by a tendency to flatter those above him and despise those below him.

試手

shr̀-'shěw (1) (*VN1*) to try out a new employee.
　　(2) (*VN1*) to try one's hand at something. ‖tā

gāng 'láy, děy shr̀-'shěw shr̀ 'jī-tyān. He's just gotten here, he'll have to try his hand at it a few days.

事實

shr̀-'shŕ (*Nunit*, ge) facts. ‖tā-shwō-de-'hwà gēn shr̀-'shŕ bù-'fù. What he said doesn't correspond to the facts.

試驗

'shr̀-yàn (*Nunit*, ge) laboratory experiment. dzwò 'shr̀-yàn to perform an experiment.

事業

'shr̀-yè (*Nabstr*) enterprise, career.

書

shū (*Nunit*, běn, běr) book. *When a Chinese book is bound in several fascicles,* yì-běr-'shū *means* one fascicle of a book. shū-'běr (*Nunit*, ge) volume; shū-'pù *or* shū-'dyàn bookstore; shū-'jyŵú *or* shū-'gwǎn publishing house which also retails books; shū-'bāw briefcase *or* small case for carrying books; shū-'jyà(-dz) open bookcase; shū-'gwèy(-dz) closed bookcase; shū-'gé-dz bookshelf; shū-'jyā-dz book end; shū-'jwō desk; shū-'píng book review.

梳

shū (*V*) to comb. shū-'téw *or* shū 'téw-fa to comb one's hair. 'shū-dz (*Nunit*, bǎ) comb.

輸

shū (*V*) to lose *money, in gambling, a game, etc.* ‖wǒ 'shū-le 'lyǎng-kwày-chyán. I lost a couple of dollars. ‖shr̀-'shéy 'shū-le? Who's losing? *or* Who's losing it?
　As mainV: 'shū-gěy to lose to *someone.* ‖wǒ 'shū-gey tā yì-pán-'chí. I lost a game of chess to him.

叔

*shū (*Npers*) father's younger brother. *See Appendix A.*

舒服

'shū-fu (*A*) comfortable.

書記

'shū-jì (*Npers*) clerk, secretary.

梳粧

shū-'jwāng (*I*) to fix up (*of a woman at a mirror*). shū-jwāng-'táy dresser (*furniture*).

書家

shū-'jyā (*Npers*) calligrapher.

書面

shū-'myàn (*Aattr*) in writing. shū-'myàn-'dá-fú written answer.

252

疏遠

shū-'ywǎn (A) be out of contact. ‖gēn-ta shū-'ywǎn yì-
dyǎr. Don't get mixed up with him too much.

熟

*shú see *shéw.

贖罪

shú-'dzwèy (VN2) to pay a fine and so avoid other punishment for a crime.

熟識

'shú-shr̀ (A) be well acquainted. ‖wǒ gēn-ta bú-'dà hěn
'shú-shr̀. I'm not too well acquainted with him.

數

shǔ (V) to count, count up. ‖nǐ 'shǔ-yi-shǔ yěw 'dwō-
shaw-rén. Count up how many people there are. ‖bǎ
jèy-shyē-'chyán 'shǔ-yi-shǔ. Count this money up.

署

*shǔ (Nunit, ge) board, commission. wèy-shēng-'shǔ
Board of Public Health; etc.

屬...管

shǔ ... 'gwǎn (V) to belong to, be under the control of.
‖hǎy-nán-'dǎw shǔ 'jūng-gwo 'gwǎn. The island of
Hainan belongs to China. (gwǎn may be replaced by
other verbs meaning control, take care of, particularly
gwǎn-'shyá.)
     shǔ-'dì possessed or controlled territory; shǔ-'ywán
subordinate personnel.

暑假

shǔ-'jyà (Nunit, ge) summer vacation. fàng shǔ-'jyà
to take a summer vacation.

屬於

shǔ-'ywú (V) to belong to, be under the control of.
‖táy-'wān 'tsúng-chyán shǔ-'ywú 'jūng-gwo ('gwǎn).
Taiwan formerly belonged to China.

樹

shù (Nunit, kē) tree. shù-'gàn or shù-'shēn tree trunk;
shù-'gǎr bough; shù-'chà-dz tree branches that fork
off from the trunk; shù-'jr̄(-dz) smaller branches;
shù-'jēr twigs; shù-'pí tree bark; shù-'gēn or shù-'gēr
tree roots; shù-'jyār treetops; shù-'lín-dz woods,
forest. yǐng-táw-'shù cherry tree; etc. with other
designations of different varieties.

豎

shù (V) set up on end, vertically. ‖bǎ nèy-gēr-'gwèn-dz
'shù-je 'kàw-dzay 'chyáng-shang. Lean that pole
upright against the wall.
     As mainV: 'shù-chi-láy to stand something up on
end in a vertical position. ‖bǎ nèy-ge-chí-'gān-dz 'shù-
chi-lay. Fix the flagpole in an upright position.

術

*shù (N) science, art, technique. pàw-'shù artillery
technique; 'yì-shù painting or drawing technique,
sculpture, etc.

數

shù(r) (Nunit, ge) number, figure. ‖nǐ 'dé-de shéme-
'shùr? What figure do you get? (in calculating).
     shù-'dž or shù-'mǎr digits, written numbers; shù-
'shywé mathematics.

速度

shù-'dù or sù-'dù (Nabstr) speed. 'měy-yì-dyǎn-jūng-
'sž-shr-lǐ-de-shù-'dù forty miles per hour.

樹立

shù-'lì (V) to build up, establish. ‖wǒm láy shù-'lì yí-
ge-'hǎw-'jī-chǔ-ba. Let's get a firm basis established.

數目

'shù-mu (Nunit, ge) number, amount, quantity, (particularly of money). ‖'jèy-ge-shù-mǔ 'háy bú-'gěw.
That amount still isn't enough.

shua Wade Romanization for shwa.

shuai Wade Romanization for shway.

shuan Wade Romanization for shwan.

shuang Wade Romanization for shwang.

shui Wade Romanization for shwey.

shun Wade Romanization for shwen.

shuo Wade Romanization for shwo.

刷

shwā (V) to brush, brush off, use a brush on, apply with
a brush; to brush someone off, jilt. shwā-'yá to brush
one's teeth; shwā-'téw to brush one's hair; shwā-'yéw
to apply paint with a brush; shwā yì-tāng-'kè to cut
a class. ‖wǒ āy 'shwā-le. I got brushed off (figuratively).
     As mainV: shwā-'gān-jìng to brush clean; 'shwā-
shyà-chywù to brush dust or dirt off. ‖bǎ 'jwō-dz 'yǐ-
dz dēw shwā-'shin-le. Paint the tables and chairs up
and make them look like new.

刷子

'shwā-dz (Nunit, bǎ) brush.

耍

shwǎ (V) to play. shwǎ-'chyéwr to play ball or to
play catch; shwǎ 'hwā-téw or shwǎ 'hwār-téw to play
tricks (on someone); shwǎ-'dāw to juggle swords;
shwǎ-'chyán to gamble.

栓

hwān (*V*) to **fasten** *something to something else.* As *mainV:* **'shwān-chǐ-láy** or **'shwān-shang** to fasten up, tie up, (*as a boat to a dock*); **'shwān-jù-le** to fasten so as to prevent motion; **'shwān-dzày** to fasten *something to something.* ‖**bǎ mǎ-'shéng-dz gěy shwān-'jīn-le.** Tie the hitching rope tightly. ‖**bǎ-'chwán shwān-dzay mǎ-'téw-páng-'byār.** Fasten the boat to the dock.

栓子

'shwān-dz (*Nunit,* **ge**) bolt. **mén-'shwān-dz** bolt on a door; **mù-'shwān-dz** wooden bolt.

雙

shwāng (*Mgroup*) **pair of,** *for things that come in pairs, usually those for which the Munit* **jī** *is used.* **yì-shwāng-'shyé** pair of shoes; **yì-shwāng-'wà-dz** pair of stockings; **yì-shwāng-'kwày-dz** pair of chopsticks; *etc.* In compounds, *double.* **shwāng-'dǎ** doubles (*tennis, etc.*); **shwāng-'gwěy** double track (*railroad*); **'shwāng-shùr** even number; **'shwāng-rén-fáng-'jyān** double room.

霜

shwāng (*Nmass*) **frost.** **shyà-'shwāng** to frost (*weather*). **táng-'shwāng** sweet covering, frosting, (*as on pastry*); **shř-'shwāng** dried persimmons with a sugar coating.

爽

shwǎng (*A*) **frank, open, outspoken** (*favorable comment; literary*).

爽快

shwǎng-'kwày (*A*) **outspoken, direct, free from hesitation** (*favorable comment*). **shwǎng-shwang-kwày-'kwày-de** (*H*) quickly, without hesitating, straight from the shoulder.

爽目

shwǎng-'mù (*A*) **pleasant to the eye** (*a bit literary*).

雙生

'shwàng-sheng (*or* **shwāng-'shēng**) (*Ncoll;* **dwèy** pair of) **twins.**

摔

shwāy (*I*) **to fall** (*of a person*); (*V*) **to throw** *something down.* **shwāy ge-mǎ-'pā** to fall flat on one's face; **shwāy ge-pì-hu-'dwěr** to fall flat on one's seat. As *mainV:* **shwāy-'hwěy-le** to ruin *something* by throwing *it* down; **shwāy-'shāng-le** to fall and hurt oneself; *etc.* ‖**tā bǎ-'twěy shwāy-'shé-le.** He fell and broke his leg.

衰弱

shwāy-'rwò (*A*) **physically weak, in poor health.**

摔，甩

shwǎy (*V*) **to brush** *or* **knock to one side** (*literally or figuratively*); **to forsake, jilt, let down.** As *mainV:* **'shwǎy-shyà-chywù** to throw down; **'shwǎy-chū-láy** to throw out; *etc.* ‖**tā bǎ-ta 'shwǎy-ćàw yì-'byār chywù-le.** He brushed her aside. *or* He jilted her. ‖**tā bǎ tā-'shěw-shang-de-'chúng-dz 'shwǎy-shya-chywù-le.** He shook the bug off his hand.

順

shwèn (*A*) **going smoothly, prosperous.** ‖**tā-de-'mǎy-mày 'dzwò-de hěn 'shwèn.** His business is going smoothly and prosperously.

(*K*) **with** *wind or current,* **in accordance with** *an opinion or idea,* **along** *a route.* ‖**'chwán shwèn-'shwěy 'dzěw, dzěw-de hěn 'kwày.** The boat goes quite fast when it's going with the current. ‖**shwèn tā-de-'yì-sz dzwò-ba!** Let's act in accordance with his ideas. ‖**yí-'lù shwèn-'fēng!** Good luck on your trip! (*Literally* May you be with the wind throughout the journey.) ‖**'chwán shwèn-je 'àn 'dzěw-je.** The boat is going along the shore.

順利

shwèn-'lì (*A*) **prosperous, doing well.**

順從

'shwèn-tsúng (*V*) **to be unquestioningly obedient to.**

順眼

shwèn-'yǎn (*A*) **appealing** *or* **pleasant to the eye.** ‖**shīn-'yàng-dz-li, 'yěw-de 'kàn-je shwèn-'yǎn, yěw-de kàn-je bú-shwèn-'yǎn.** Some of the new styles are appealing to the eye, some of them aren't.

誰

shwéy *or* **shéy** (*Pron*) **who?, who, whoever, someone.** ‖**shéy 'láy-le?** Who's come? ‖**shéy-de-'màw-dz?** Whose hat is this? ‖**tā shwō-'shéy-ne?** Who's he talking about? ‖**tā gēn-shéy shwō-'hwà?** Who's he talking °to *or* °with? ‖**tā-shwō-de-'hwà shéy dēw bù-'dǔng.** Nobody understands what he's saying. ‖**bú-'lwèn shéy 'láy, wǒ dēw bù-'hwān-yíng.** No matter who comes I won't have any welcome for him.

水

shwěy (*Nmass*) **water; shwěy, shwěr** *in compounds* **liquid, juice, water.** **mwò-'shwěy** *or* **mwò-'shwěr** ink; **jywú-dz-'shwěy** *or* **jywú-dz-'shwěr** orange juice. **shwěy-'pàw(r)** watery blister *or* water bubble; **shwěy-pén** water basin (*container; similarly with other containers*); **shwěy-'nyéw** water buffalo *or* snail; **shwěy-'ní** cement or concrete (*literally* watery mud); **shwěy-'gwǒ** fruit; **shwěy-'dzāy** flood; **shwěy-'chē** water wheel; **shwěy-'shěw** sailor *or* collectively crew (*not Navy*); **shwěy-'bīng** sailor (*Navy*).

水份
shwĕy-'fèn (*Nabstr*) water content *of anything.* ‖jèy-ge-'gwŏ-dz shwĕy-'fèn hĕn 'dwō. This fruit (or nut) is very juicy.

水坑
shwĕy-'kēng (*Nunit, ge*) pool of stagnant, muddy water.

水平尺
shwĕy-píng-'chř (*Nunit, gēr*) level (*surveying instrument*).

水獺
shwĕy-'tà (*Nunit, ge*) otter.

水彩畫
shwĕy-tsăy-'hwàr (*Nunit, jāng*) pictures painted in water colors.

水土
shwĕy-'tŭ (*Nabstr*) climate and soil conditions. ‖'nèy-ge-dì-fang-de-shwĕy-'tŭ gēn-wo bù-hé-'shř. The climate there doesn't agree with me.

水銀
shwĕy-'yín (*Nmass*) mercury (*metal*).

水源
shwĕy-'ywán (*Nunit, ge*) source of a river.

稅
shwèy (*Nabstr*) taxes, customs, duties, imposts. chēw-'shwèy to levy a tax; shàng-'shwèy *or* nà-'shwèy to pay a tax or duty. yí-dàw-'shwèy one levying *or* payment of a tax; shwèy-'shēw tax receipts.

睡
shwèy (*A*) be asleep; (*I*) to go to sleep. shwèy-'yī night clothes. *As mainV:* shwèy-'jáw to get to sleep.

睡覺
shwèy-'jyàw (*VN2*) to sleep for a period and then wake up. shwèy yì-shyăw-'jyàw to take a nap; shwèy wŭ-'jyàw to take a nap just after noon, to siesta.

說說
shwèy-'shwō (*I*) to go around proselytizing for a belief, or trying to persuade influential people to back you up in your side of an argument (*a bit literary*).

說
shwō (*V, Vpred*) to say, speak. shwō-'hwà to speak, talk; shwō jūng-gwo-'hwà to speak Chinese; shwō-rén yí-dwèn to give someone a talking-to; shwō dà-'hwà to talk big, boast; shwō shyā-'hwà *or* shwō hwăng-'hwà to tell lies; shwō shyán-'hwà to say

things about someone that ought to remain unsaid; 'tì-ta shwō lyăng-jywù-'hwà put in a good word for someone. ‖wŏ gĕy-ni 'shwō-shwo jèy-jyàn-'shř-ching. Let me explain the matter to you. ‖ni bù-néng 'shwō-le bú-'swàn. You mustn't back out after giving your word. ‖wŏ gēn-ni shwō-je 'wár. I'm just kidding you. ‖tā shwō tā méy-'dàw-gwo nèr. He says he's never been there.

As mainV: 'shwō-chĭ-láy to bring up *a subject* in talking; 'shwō-chū-lay to speak out, *or* to disclose *something which had been kept a secret;* shwō-bu-chū-'láy be unable to speak; shwō-'fú to persuade *someone* that one is right; shwō-'hăw-le to reach an agreement in talking; shwō-'jáw-le to say just the right thing, *or* to guess just the right thing; shwō-'míng-le to explain *something;* shwō-'míng-bay-le to talk *something* out and get it clarified; shwō-'pwò-le to disclose *something,* let the cat out of the bag.

說法
'shwō-fă(r) (*Nunit, ge*) line of reasoning, chain of points in an argument. ‖ni-'nème-yàngr-de-'shwō-făr bù-néng bă-ta shwō-'fú-le. The line of reasoning you're using there will never convince him.

說不來
'shwō-bu-láy (*RC1*) to be out of sympathy and therefore unable to discuss things fruitfully. ‖wŏ gēn-ta hĕn 'shwō-de-láy. He and I really get along very well with each other.

說明書
shwō-mír̄ ̄ū. (*Nunit, bĕn*) book of explanations; technical manual of operation, maintenance, and overhaul *accompanying a machine or apparatus.*

瞎
shyā (*Aattr, I*) blind; go blind. shyā(-le)-'yăn-de-rén *or* 'shyā-dz (*Npers*) blind man. ‖tā 'shyā-le yì-jř-'yăn. *or* tā yì-jř-'yăn 'shyā-le. He's blind in one eye.

Figuratively shwō shyā-'hwà to tell lies; *or with* shyā *as H,* shyā 'shwō to speak falsely; shyā 'byān to fabricate *a story.*

匣 (子，兒)
'shyá(-dz), shyár (*NunitC, ge*) small box.

狹義的
shyá-'yì-de (*Aattr*) narrowly interpreted. ‖jèy-ge-dìng-'yì yĕw lyăng-jŭng-'jyĕ-shwō-'fāng-fă: 'shyá-yì-de gēn 'gwăng-yì-de. This definition can be interpreted in two ways: narrowly and broadly.

下
shyà (*Nplace*) lower area, space below, bottom; *longer forms* 'shyà-byan, 'shyà-byar, 'shyà-myan, 'shyà-myar, 'shyà-tew(r). *Alone:* ‖shyàng-'shyà 'lā. Pull down-

wards. *After nouns, only longer forms:* ‖nèy-ge-'dĕng-dz dzày jwŏ-dz-'shyà-byar. The stool is under the table.

yi-'shyà in what comes later; *after a noun* below, *less than:* ‖tā-yi-'shyà-shwō-de-'hwà wŏ dĕw méy-jù-'yì. I didn't pay any attention to what he said after that. ‖'wŭ-kwày-chyán-yi-'shyà-de-dūng-shi tā bù-'măy. She doesn't want to buy anything that costs less than five dollars.

(Demord) lower grade; *or* next *month, week, etc.:* 'shyà-dĕng-de lower grade, lower class; shyà-'tsž next time; shyà-'lyăng-'tsž next two times; 'shyà-yí-'bān the class just after this one; 'shyà-'ywè next month; shyà-li-'bày next week; shyà-li-bày-'yī Monday of next week.

shyà in compounds as first member, lower, later: shyà-'shŕ corporal *(lowest of three grades of non-commissioned officer in the Chinese Army)*; shyà-'pù lower berth; shyà-'yī lower garments *(trousers, skirts)*; shyà-yì-'ywàn lower house, House of Commons, House of Representatives; 'shyà-(bàn)-shēn lower part of the body; shyà-'lyéw lower part of the course of a river; 'shyà-lyéw-shè-'hwèy lower strata of society; shyà-'jàn the next station *(railway)*; shyà-'wŭ *or* 'shyà-bàn-tyār afternoon, P.M.; shyà-bàn-'yè part of the night after midnight.

下

shyà *(I, lc)* to come down; to go down; to come downstairs; to get off a vehicle. shyà-'ywŭ *(IN)* to rain; shyà-'shywĕ *(IN)* to snow; shyà-'shwāng to frost; shyà 'báw-dz to hail.

(V, sometimes lc) to come down from along, *or* by means of; to dismount from a vehicle. shyà-'chwáng to get (down) out of bed; shyà-'chē to get off a train *or* car; shyà fēy-'jī to get off a plane; shyà-'chăng to leave a stage, go off stage, *or (figuratively)* to leave political life; shyà-'shywé to leave school; shyà-'bān *or* shyà-'kè to leave class *or* work; shyà-'gūng to leave work, go off duty; shyà-'rèn to leave office; shyà-'léw to come downstairs; shyà léw-'tī to climb down stairs; shyà 'tī-dz to climb down a ladder; shyà-'shān to climb down a mountain; shyà-'pwŏer to come down a slope.

(V) to descend to, come down to. shyà-'shwĕy to be launched *(of a ship; literally* to descend to the water); shyà-'dì to get up and walk after being bedridden *(literally* to descend to the ground); shyà-'shyāng *(lc)* to go (down) to the country *(as on vacation)*

(V) to cause someone *or* something to descend into: shyà-'dzàng to bury *or* to get buried; shyà-'ywù *or* shyà-'jyān *or* shyà jyān-'ywù to imprison.

(V) to cause to descend. shyà-'jŭngr to sow seed; shyà-'dàn to lay an egg; shyà-'yàw to put medicine in; shyà dú-'yàw to put poison in; shyà-'lìng *or* shyà 'mìng-lìng to pass down orders *to one's inferiors or* to issue an order; shyà dwàn-'ywù to pass judgment or

to make a decisive statement; shyà-'shĕw to take action *in order to accomplish something (literally* to lower the hand).

(mainV) forms RC of types 1 and 2, adding to the mainV the meaning of motion downwards. 'dzwò-shyà to sit down; 'tăng-shyà to lie down *on one's back;* 'pā-shyà to lie down *on one's face;* 'gē-shyà to put *something.* down; 'rēng-shyà to throw *something* down; *etc.*

(mainV, lc) forms RC of all four types, adding to the mainV the meaning of motion downwards *or* motion downwards onto something; *also figurative:* 'pá-shyà *(lc)* to climb down; 'dzĕw-shyà *(lc)* to walk down; 'lā-shyà *(lc)* to pull down; 'ān-jìng-shyà-chywù to calm down; *etc.*

下

shyà *(V)* to play *a board game.* shyà yì-pán-'chí to play a game of chess *(literally* to play a board of chess).

嚇

shyà *(V)* to startle *or* frighten. ‖tā 'shyà-le wŏ yí-'tyàw. He startled me and made me jump.

As mainV: shyà-'hwày-le to frighten seriously; shyà-'sž-le to frighten to death.

夏(天)

*shyà, 'shyà-tyan *(Ntime)* summer.

下

shyà(r) *(Msemel)* time, times; *used mainly after an I of motion or a V of striking, handling, etc., but also after other nuclei.* 'ràw yí-shyàr to make one circuit; 'dzĕw yí-shyàr to take a walk; 'dă-ta yí-shyàr strike him one blow. 'shyà-dz *(Msemel)* similarly, but also *as follows (with* yī *only):* ‖yí-'shyà-dz tā jyèw 'hwēn-gwò-chywù-le. Quick as a flash he fell back in a faint.

下巴頦

shyà-ba-'kēer *(Nunit,* ge) chin.

夏布

shyà-'bù *(Nmass)* linen cloth.

下工夫

shyà 'gūng-fu *(VN2)* to work hard, study hard, use time and energy at some task. shyà kŭ-'gūng to work extremely hard at something.

廈門

shyà-'mén *(Nunique) another name for* sž-'míng Ssuming *or* Amoy *(city in Fukien province).*

夏威夷

shyà-wā-'yí *(Nunique)* Hawaii.

先

shyān (H) first, earlier (*contrasted with* hèw then, next, later). **nǐ 'shyān chywù, wǒ swéy-'hèw jyèw 'láy.** You go first, I'll come later on. ‖**'shyān gàn-'shr̀, hèw 'wár.** Business before pleasure. ‖**'shyān dàw chúng-'chìng, 'hèw dàw běy-'píng.** We'll go to Chungking first, then on to Peiping.

鮮

shyān (A) fresh. **shyān-'rèw** fresh meat; **shyān-'hwār** fresh flowers.

暹羅

shyān-'lwó (Nunique) Siam (Thailand).

鮮明

shyān-'míng (A) bright, fresh and clear (*as of a color*).

先生

'shyān-sheng (NpersT) mister, sir, gentleman, teacher, husband. **'wáng-shyān-sheng** Mr. Wáng; **'nèy-wèy-'shyān-sheng** that gentleman *or* that teacher; **wǒ-de-'shyān-sheng** my teacher *or* my husband. ‖**shyān-sheng 'hǎw?** How are you, Sir?

鮮豔

shyān-'yàn (A) fresh and beautiful (*as of flowers, colors*)

鹹

shyán (A) salty. **shyán-'ywú** salt fish; **shyán-'rèw** salt pork.

閒

shyán (A) idle, unoccupied. *Often characterizes that which idle hands find to do:* **shyán-'shr̀** other people's business; **shyán-'hwà** gossip. **shyár** (Nmass) idle time, leisure. ‖**méy-'shyár.** I've been busy all the time.

弦

shyán (Nunit. gēr) stretched string *or* wire; flat *or* coiled spring. **chín-'shyán** the string of a musical instrument; **byǎw-'shyán** watch spring; **jūng-'shyán** clock spring.

    shàng-'shyán to wind up a coiled spring, to wind a watch *or* clock; **bǎ-'shyán jwàn-'jǐn-le** to tighten the string of a musical instrument.

險

shyǎn (A) dangerous, risky. **shyǎn-'lù** dangerous road. ‖**dzwò 'nèy-ge hěn 'shyǎn.** It's risky to do that.

顯

shyǎn (A) noticeable. ‖**'dzāng-de-nèy-'kwày hěn 'shyǎn.** That spot of dirt is very noticeable.

    'shyǎn-chū-láy to reveal, make clear. ‖**nǐ-de-'hwà-**

li-tew 'shyǎn-chū-láy nǐ 'shīn-lǐ bù-gāw-'shìng. Your words show that you don't feel happy.

顯白

'shyǎn-bey (V) to show off *something;* (Vsent) to demonstrate that. ‖**tā 'shyǎn-bey tā yěw-'chyán.** He makes it apparent that he has plenty of money (*uncomplimentary*).

顯明

shyǎn-'míng (A) obvious. ‖**tā hěn shyǎn-'míng-de 'ày-ta.** It's obvious that he likes her.

顯微鏡

shyǎn-wéy-'jìn (Nunit, ge) microscope.

縣

shyàn (Mauton) administrative district within a province, *about like a county.* **shyàn-'jǎng** district magistrate.

線，綫

shyàn (Nmass, tyáw) thread; wire; line. **tyě-'shyàn** iron wire; **sz̄-'shyàn** silk thread; **chyán-'shyàn** front line, front (*military*)!

    (Munit) ray of. **yí-shyàn-'gwāng** a ray of light; **yí-shyan-'shī-wàng** a ray of hope.

陷

shyàn (I) to sink down (*as into mud*). *As mainV:* **'shyàn-shyà-chywù** to sink, settle (*as of the ground*); **'shyàn-dàw (chywù)** to sink into mud, *etc.* ‖**lyǎng-'jyǎw 'shyàn-dàw 'ní-lǐ-tew chywù-le.** Both feet sank into the mud.

    (I) to fall (*as of a city*) to the enemy.

獻

*shyàn (V) to offer, contribute. **shyàn-'jīn** to contribute money. *As mainV:* **'shyàn-gěy** to contribute *or* offer *something to a superior.*

限 (制)

'shyàn(-jr̀) (Vsent) to impose *some limitation.* ‖**wǒ 'shyàn-jr ta yì-'tyān yùng 'sān-kwày-chyán.** I restricted him to spending not more than three dollars each day.

    bù-'kě shyàn-'lyàng (*literary quotation*) to be without limit, be unlimited. ‖**tā-de-'chyán-tú bù-'kě shyàn-'lyàng.** There's no limit to what he may accomplish.

現在

shyàn-'dzày (J) now, at the present, for the present.

    *shyàn (Aattr) at hand, present. **shyàn-'dày** modern times; **shyàn-'kwǎn** cash *contrasted with credit;* **shyàn-'chyán** cash on hand, ready money; **shyàn-'chyán jyāw-'yì** to carry on business on a cash basis; **shyàn-'shyàng** phenomenon, that which is observed as it occurs.

    shyàn-'yěw-de (Aattr) now available, now at hand.

鮮華
'shyàn-hwo (A) bright and pleasing (of colors).

綫索
'shyàn-swǒ (Nunit, ge) trace, clue, trail. ‖jèy-ge-'àn-dz 'yǐ-jing yěw 'shyàn-swǒ-le. There are already some clues in this case.

香
shyāng (A) fragrant. shyāng-'shwěr perfume; shyāng-'yān cigarette (literally fragrant smoke).

鑲
shyāng (V) to fix or mount something in a setting. shyāng-'yá to fill a tooth; shyāng jyǎ-'yá to fit someone with false teeth; shyāng 'jyè-jr to set a precious stone into a ring. ‖yùng nèy-kē-'jū-dz shyāng 'jyè-jr. Make a ring using that pearl. ‖bǎ jèy-ge-'shyá-dz 'shyāng yí-'dàw-jīn-'byār. Put a gold rim on this box.

箱
*shyāng, 'shyāng-dz (NunitC, ge) relatively large box, case, suitcase, trunk. shěw-tí-'shyāng suitcase.

鄉 (下)
*shyāng, 'shyāng-shyà (Nplace) country (contrasted with city). 'shyāng-shyà-rén country people; shyāng-'tswēn country village, village. shyà-'shyāng or dàw 'shyāng-shya chywù or (a bit literary) dàw shyāng-'jyān chywù to go to the country.

相差
shyāng-'chà (A) differ. ‖jèy-lyǎng-ge-'shù-mu shyāng-'chà bù-dwō. The two figures aren't very different. or The difference between the two figures isn't great.

相襯
shyāng-'chèn (A) in symmetry, match (as of colors); a good match (of a couple).

相當
shyāng-'dāng (A) suitable. ‖tā yěw yí-ge-shyāng-'dāng-de-'shr̀-ching dzwò. His job is just right for him. (H) fairly. ‖'jèy-ge-dūng-shi shyāng-'dāng bú-'tswò. This thing's fairly good.

相等
shyāng-'děng (VN1) to be identical, equal, congruent. ‖jèy-lyǎng-ge-'sān-jyǎwr-shíng shyāng-'dǎng. These two triangles are congruent.

相對
shyāng-'dwèy (Aattr) relative (contrasted with absolute). shyāng-dwèy-'lwèn the theory of relativity.

相反
shyāng-'fǎn (VN1) to be opposites. ‖jèy-'lyǎng-ge-'dūng-shi jèng shyāng-'fǎn. These two things are just the opposites of each other.

廂房
'shyāng-fáng (Nunit, jyān) rooms separated from the main house of a compound. sān-jyān-'shyāng-fáng a three-room unit separated from the main house of a compound.

相仿
shyāng-'fǎng (A) similar but not identical.

相符
shyāng-'fú (VN1) not coincide with, not agree with. ‖tā-shwō-de-'hwà gēn-shr̀-'shŕ bù-shyāng-'fú. What he says doesn't fit the facts.

相干
shyāng-'gān (VN1) be related, have something to do with. ‖tā-dzwò-de-'shr̀ gēn-'nǐ bù-shyāng-'gān. What he does doesn't concern you. ‖jèy-shr̀ bù-shyāng-'gān-de-'shr̀-ching. That's an irrelevant matter.

香港
shyāng-'gǎng (Nunique) Hongkong (city in Kwangtung province).

相合
shyāng-'hé (VN1) to have an affinity, be in agreement.

相近
shyāng-'jìn (A) closely similar, closely related in characteristics.

香蕉
shyāng-'jyāw (Nunit, gēr, tyáw) banana.

相配
shyāng-'pèy (A) be a good match (of a couple); be in symmetry or harmony. ‖tām-'lyǎ-rér hěn shyāng-'pèy. Those two make a fine match.

相信
shyāng-'shìn (V) to believe, trust. ‖wǒ shyāng-'shìn nǐ-de-'hwà. I trust what you say.

湘潭
shyāng-'tán (Nunique) Hsiang-t'an or Siangtan (city in Hunan province).

相同
shyāng-'túng (A) similar, almost identical.

詳細 (的)
'shyáng-shì(-de) (H) carefully, with care to details. ‖tā-de-bàw-'gàw 'shyě-de hěn 'shyáng-shì. His report was written very meticulously.

想

shyǎng (*I, V, Vpred, Vsent*) to think; to think *or* want *or* plan to *do so-and-so.* ‖tā 'shyǎng-le °yì-shyǎng. *or* °yì-'hwěr. He thought for a minute. ‖tā 'cháng-cháng shyǎng-'nı. He's always thinking of you. ‖tā 'cháng-cháng shyǎng dàw-'nàr chywù. He's always wanted to go there. ‖wǒ 'shyǎng tā yǐ-jing 'chř-le dzǎw-'fàn-le. I think he has already eaten breakfast.

As mainV: 'shyǎng-chǐ-láy to recall, call to mind, think up; 'shyǎng-chū-láy think out, plan out, work out *a plan;* 'shyǎng-dàw to think of a number of things, up to and including *such-and-such;* 'shyǎng-kāy to get something out of one's mind; shyǎng-bu-'kāy be unable to get something out of one's mind. ‖wǒ 'shyǎng-le bàn-'tyān, tsáy 'shyǎng-chǐ-lay tā shř-'shéy. I thought a long time before I could remember who he is. ‖tā 'shyǎng-le bàn-'tyān, tsáy 'shyǎng-chū-láy-le yí-ge-hǎw-'fá-dz. He thought for a long time before he could work out a good method. ‖wǒ háy méy-'shyǎng-dàw 'nèy-ge-wèn-tí-ne. I hadn't turned my thoughts to that problem yet. ‖byé shēng-'chì, shyǎng-'kāy-je dyǎr. Don't get angry; just relax and let those things leave your mind.

響

shyǎng (*I*) to sound, *of something struck or scratched or pulled, etç.* ‖lǎ-ba 'shyǎng-le. The horn sounded.

As postV: chwēy-'shyǎng-le to cause to sound by blowing; lā-'shyǎng-le to cause to sound by pulling; *etc.* ‖'jèy-ge-lyéngr 'hwày-le, èn-bu-'shyǎng-le. The bell's broken; you can push the button but it doesn't sound.

*shyǎng(r) (Nunit, shēng) sound made by something. chyāng-'shyǎng rifle-crack; lwó-'shyǎng sound of a gong.

嚮導（的）

shyǎng-'dǎw(-de) (*Npers*) guide (*person; a bit literary*).

想法（兒，子）

shyǎng-'fár, shyǎng 'fá-dz (*VN2*) to think of a way *to do something,* try *to do something.* ‖nèy-ge-shyǎw-'hár shyǎng-'fár-de 'nàw. That child is just hunting for ways to make a nuisance of himself. ‖chǐng-ni shyǎng 'fá-dz bǎ 'chwāng-hu 'kāy-kay. Try to think of some way to open the window. *or* Try to open the window.

想盡

shyǎng-'jìn (*V*) to think of all *the possibilities.* ‖tā shyǎng-'jìn 'fāng-fǎ tǎw tā-de-'shǐ-hwan. He tried in every way possible to please him.

想家

shyǎng-'jyā (*VN1, A*) to be homesick.

響亮

shyǎng-'lyàng (*A*) loud and clear (*of a sound*).

享受

shyǎng-'shèw (*I*) to enjoy oneself; (*V*) to enjoy *some kind of existence;* (*Nabstr*) enjoyment, pleasure, comfort. ‖tā hěn 'hwèy shyǎng-'shèw. He knows how to enjoy himself. ‖tā 'jř-daw dzěme shyǎng-'shèw wù-'jř-de-'shēng-hwó. He knows how to enjoy material comforts.

想像

'shyǎng-shyàng (*V*) to imagine. ‖nǐ ké-yi 'shyǎng-shyàng 'nèy-ge-shŕ-hew-de-'chíng-shíng. You can just imagine the state of affairs at that time. ‖jèy-jyàn-'shř-ching `jēn-shř 'shyǎng-shyàng-bu-'dàw-de. You really just can't imagine what it's like.

想要

shyǎng-'yàw (*V, Vpred*) to want (to) and be planning more or less vaguely (to). ‖tā 'cháng-cháng shyǎng-'yàw dàw 'měy-gwo chywù. He's always been trying to plan a trip to the United States.

象

shyàng (*Nunit, jř, ge*) elephant. shyàng-'yá ivory.

巷

shyàng (*Nunit, tyáw*) alley, small side street.

向

shyàng (*K*) towards (*of motion*); facing, facing towards, (*when at rest*). ‖shyàng-'chyán dzěw. Go forward. ‖shyàng-'yèw jwǎn. Turn to the right. ‖tā shyàng-je nèy-ge-'fáng-dz 'jàn-je. He's standing facing that house.

(*V*) to favor, be in favor of. ‖tā lǎw 'shyàng-je ta. He's always taken her part.

像

shyàng (*V, Vsent*) to resemble, seem like; to seem as though. shř-de *is often added later in the sentence.* ‖tā shyàng 'fēng-le shř-de. He would appear to be crazy. ‖tā hěn 'shyàng tā-'fù-chin(-shř-de). He very much resembles his father.

shyàng 'yàng-dz to be in good shape, be in good form. ‖nǐ 'dày-de jèy-ge-'màw-dz hěn shyàng 'yàng-dz. That hat looks very nice on you.

項

shyàng (*Munit*) article *or* section *of a formal document;* an item *or* matter of 'shř-ching (*business*). yí-shyàng-yí-'shyàng-de item by item.

像，相

*shyàng (*N*) image, statue. fwó-'shyàng (*Nunit, dzwēn, ge*) a statue of Buddha, *or, with* ge, *also* a picture of Buddha; túng-'shyàng a statue of bronze *or*

brass *or* copper; **shŕ-'shyàng** a stone statue; **bàn-shēn-'shyàng** a bust *or* a picture which shows someone from the waist up.

    jàw-'shyàng to take pictures; **shǐ-'shyàng** to develop films; **shyàng-'pyàn** *or* **shyàng-'pyàr** (*Nunit*, **jāng**) photographs.

向來
'shyàng-láy (*J*) always and customarily up to now. ‖**tā 'shyàng-láy bú-'ày chŕ 'tyán-de.** He's never liked to eat sweet things.

相貌
'shyàng-màw (*Nabstr*) looks (*of a person*). ‖**tā-de-'shyàng-màw jǎng-de hěn 'hǎw.** She's very good-looking.

橡皮
'shyàng-pí (*Nmass*) rubber; eraser. **shyàng-pí-'shù** rubber tree. **shyàng-pí-'gāw** adhesive tape; **shyàng-pí-'chywār** rubber band (*literally* little rubber circle).

橡實
shyàng-'shù (*Nunit*, **kē**) oak.

削
shyāw (*V*) to peel with a knife *something on which the skin sticks tightly, as an apple.*

消愁
shyāw-'chéw (*VN2*) to get rid of one's worries, drown one's sorrows (*a bit literary*).

消遣
shyāw-'chyǎn (*VN1*) to spend time pleasurably (*as with a hobby*). ‖**dzwèy-'jìn tā dzwò shéme-'shŕ-ching shyāw-'chyǎn?** What's he been doing lately in his spare time?

消毒藥
shyāw-dú-'yàw (*Nmass*) disinfectant.

消防隊
shyāw-fáng-'dwèy (*Nunit*, **ge**) troop of fire fighters, fire brigade.

消化
'shyāw-hwa (*I*) to be digested. ‖**wǒ-chŕ-de-'dūng-shi yěw yì-dyǎr bù-'shyāw-hwa.** Something I ate isn't being digested right. ‖**wǒ 'shyāw-hwa bù-'lyáng.** I have indigestion.

    shyāw-hwa-'lì (*Nabstr*) digestion. ‖**'jèy-jǔng-yàw 'dzēng-jyā nǐ-de-shyāw-hwa-'lì.** This medicine will improve your digestion.

消貨，銷貨
shyāw-'hwò (*VN2*) to sell goods; to sell; to engage in selling. **shyāw-'hwò-de-'jì-lù** *or* **shyāw-hwò-'dān** sales record.

銷路
shyāw-'lù (*Nunit*, **ge**) market *or* demand *for some product.* ‖**jèy-ge-'hwò-de-shyāw-'lù shyàn-dzày bù-'hǎw.** There isn't a very good market for this commodity right now.

消磨時間
shyāw-'mwó shŕ-'jyān (*VN2*) to kill time.

消滅
shyāw-'myè (*VN2*) to annihilate, eliminate, get rid of completely, *living things or their characteristics such as power.* ‖**wǒ-men shyǎng 'fá-dz shyāw-'myè 'dí-rén-de-'shŕ-lì.** We're trying to find a way to extirpate the power of the enemy.

消息
'shyāw-shì (*Nabstr*) news about something one is already interested in, information, advices, communiques. ‖**tā 'dzěw-le yi-'hèw, háw-wú-'shyāw-shì.** Since he left, there hasn't been a bit of news from him.

逍遙
shyāw-'yáw (*A*) free, unrestricted. ‖**tā shyàn-dzày 'jywé-de hěn shyāw-'yáw.** He feels quite free from restrictions now.

    (*V*) *in* **shyāw-'yáw fǎ-'wày** to escape the clutches of the law, *or* to escape punishment.

學
shyáw *see* **shywé.**

小姐
'shyáw-jye, 'shyǎw-jye (*NpersT*) young lady, Miss; *polite term for* daughter *of person spoken to or about.*

小
shyǎw (*A*) small; young. *When before a N or a Mcont, the N or Mcont often adds* **-r**. **shyǎw-'hár** (small) child; **shyǎw-nán-'hár** (small) boy; **shyǎw-'gěw(r)** puppy, *and similarly with the young of other animals;* **shyǎw-'jŕ-tew** little finger; **shyǎw-'shŕ** *or* **shyǎw-'shèr** small matter, unimportant matter; **shyǎw-'yì-sz** small kindness *or* favor *or* consideration; **shyǎw-'chyár** small coins, pennies; **shyǎw-'bàwr** a small-format newspaper specializing in tabloid news; **shyǎw-'chēer** (small) cart; **'shyǎw-rén** small-minded and mean person; **shyǎw-'dàw(r)** *or* **shyǎw-'lù(r)** side road *or* shortcut; **shyǎw-'fēng(r)** breeze; **shyǎw-'kwàr** (*M*) small bit of; (**shwèy**) **yì-shyǎw-'jyàw** (take) a short nap; **'shyǎw-de-dì-fang** details. ‖**tā 'shyǎw(-de)-shŕ-hew dzày 'jūng-gwo jù.** He lived in China when he was small.

shyăw (H) in shyăw 'yùng to undervalue or belittle an employee; shyăw 'kàn to consider someone as beneath you, or to belittle someone; 'shyăw jìn-chywù to take in clothing, make some item of clothing smaller, or, (generally) to make something smaller.

As postV: nùng-'shyăw-le to make smaller; jyăw-'shyăw-le to make something smaller by cutting; yā-'shyăw-le to make something smaller by pressing; etc.

小的
shyăw-der (Nunit, ge) little things, incidentals, details; small children; the young of animals.

小費
shyăw-'fèy (Nunit, ge) tip, (for waiter, etc.).

小傳
shyăw-'jwàn (Nunit, ge, běn) biography.

小聲
'shyăw-shēng (H) in a low voice, in a whisper. ‖chǐng 'shyăw-shēng shwǒ. Please keep your voice lower.

小心
'shyăw-shīn (A) careful. ‖'shyăw-shīn-yì-dyăr byé 'shwāy-je. Be a bit careful, don't fall down.
(V) be careful of. ‖'shyăw-shīn hwǒ-'jù. Be careful of the fire.

小時
'shyăw-shŕ (Mtime) hour. ‖wǒ tsúng běy-'píng dàw 'tyān-jīn dzwò-'chē dzwò-le 'sān-shyăw-shŕ. It took me three hours to get from Peiping to Tientsin.

小數點
shyăw-shùr-'dyăr (Nunit, ge) decimal point.

小說
shyăw-'shwōer (Nunit, bù, běr) novel.

小偷
shyăw-'tēwr (Npers) sneak thief.

小條
shyăw-'tyáwr (Nunit, ge) note. ‖'lyéw yí-ge-shyăw-'tyáwr. Leave a note.

笑
shyàw (I. V) to smile or laugh; to smile or laugh at. 'dà shyàw to laugh (at). ‖tā 'cháng-cháng 'shyàw 'rén-jya-de-'tswèr. He's always laughing at people's mistakes. ‖tā 'dà 'shyàw-chī-láy-le. He burst out laughing. ‖yěw shéme-kě-'shyàw-de? What is there to laugh at? (straight question or sarcastic).

效
*shyàw effect, result. yěw-'shyàw (A) effective. ‖'jèy-jǔng-yàw hěn yěw-'shyàw. This medicine is very effective.

校
*shyàw (N) school; full form shywé-'shyàw. shyàw-'dǔng trustee of a school; shyàw-'jăng school principal or superintendent, or college president; shyàw-'ywán school grounds or campus.

校（官）
*shyàw, shyàw-'gwān (Npers) fielα officers (Army); equivalent ranks in Navy. shàw-'shyàw major (Army), lieutenant commander (Navy); jūng-'shyàw lieutenant colonel (Army), commander (Navy); shàng-'shyàw colonel (Army), captain (Navy).

效法
shyàw-'fǎ (V) to imitate, pattern oneself after. ‖wǒm yīng-gay shyàw-'fǎ 'tā-de-băng-'yàng. We must follow his example.

效果
'shyàw-gwǒ (Nunit, ge) results, effects, of any cause. ‖nǐ shwō jèy-jywù-'hwà, bú-'hwèy yěw shéme-'shyàw-gwǒ. What you said won't have any result.

笑話
'shyàw-hwa (V) to laugh at. 'shyàw-hwar (Nunit, ge) joke.

效勞
shyàw-'láw (VN1) to offer one's services, volunteer to help (a bit literary).

效率
'shyàw-lywù (Nabstr) degree of efficiency. shíng-'jèng-'shyàw-lywu efficiency in administration.

笑容
'shyàw-rúng (Nunit, ge) smiling face. ‖tā 'lyăn-shang yì-'dyăr-de-'shyàw-rúng dēw 'méy-yew. His face is completely sober, serious, and strict. ‖tā 'lyăn-shang dày-je 'shyàw-rúng. He was wearing a smile.

些
shyē (Mgroup) used only with Dem jèy, nèy, něy: 'jèy-shyē these or this quantity of; 'nèy-shyē those or that quantity of; 'něy-shyē which ones or which quantity of; with any following noun.
After A or H, a bit more . . . : 'pyán-yì-shye a bit cheaper; 'kwày-shye a bit faster; etc.
In certain combinations with A before N: 'hăw-shyē-rén quite a few people; 'hăw-shyē-'r̀-dz quite a few days.

261

歇

shyē (I) to rest. 'shyē-yi-shyē or 'shyē yì-hwěr take a rest. (V) in such cases as shyē-'jyà to take a vacation; shyē-'bār to rest from one's work or to have some time off work (particularly when different people work and rest in rotation). ‖tā dzày-'nàr 'shyē-le lyǎng-'jūng-tew yèw 'dzěw-le. He rested there a couple of hours and then went on. ‖wǒm 'shyē-shye 'chwǎn-chwan 'chyěr-ba. Let's rest a minute and catch our breath.

鞋

shyé (Nunit, jr; shwāng for a pair) shoes. bù-'shyé cloth shoes (the usual Chinese type); pí-'shyé leather shoes; shyé-'pù shoestore; shyé-'dàr shoelaces; shyé-'dyěr shoe soles; shyé-'myàr shoe uppers; shyé-'yéw shoe polish; shyé-'dyàr pad in a shoe.

斜

shyé (A) aslant, neither perpendicular nor parallel to a reference line or surface. ‖nèy-ge-'jù-dz yěw yì-dyǎr-'shyé. That pillar isn't quite vertical. ‖nèy-ge-fáng-'lyáng yěw yì-dyǎr-'shyé. That house beam isn't quite horizontal. ‖tā-dzěw-de-'lù yěw yì-dyǎr-shyé. (figuratively) He doesn't quite stick to the straight and narrow. ‖jèy-ge-'rén yěw yì-dyǎr-'shyé. That fellow is just a bit crooked.

    shyé-'yǎr cross-eyes.

    shyé-'dù angle of inclination.

    (V) in ‖tā shyé-je 'shēn-dz 'jǐ-gwò-chywù-le. He turned his body sideways and edged through.

寫

shyě (V) to write. shyě-'dž to write (characters); shyě-'shìn to write letters; shyě-'jàng to enter something on an account, charge something. shyě-dž-'jǐ writing paper; shyě-dž-'jwǒ(er) or shyě-dž-'táy writing desk.

    As mainV: 'shyě-chū-láy to write something out; 'shyě-gěy to write to or for someone; 'shyě-shyà-láy to write something down; 'shyě-dzày to write something on something. ‖wǒ 'nǎw-dz 'hwēn-le, 'shyě-bu-chū-'láy. I get so confused I can't get down what I want to say.

血

shyě (or shywě; reading pronunciation shywè) (Nmass) blood. In the combinations listed the form of this element most commonly used in each combination is given. shyě-'sž or shyě-'sēr capillaries visible through the skin, or blood found in phlegm or other discharge; shyě-'shíng (Nabstr) blood type; shywě-'yā blood pressure (called gāw high or dī low); shywě-'rèw flesh and blood (literally only). lyéw-'shyě (IN) to lose blood (as from a wound); chū-'shyě (IN) to lose blood (as from the gums, without an obvious wound); fàng-'shyě to let blood; jywān-'shyě to donate blood.

寫作

shyě-'dzwò (I) to engage in writing. ‖tā 'cháng-cháng shyě-'dzwò. He's always at his writing.

    (Nabstr) writing, literary creation. ‖wǒ 'cháng-cháng dzày 'bàw-shang 'kàn-jyan tā-de-shyě-'dzwò. I'm always seeing his stuff in the paper.

卸

shyè (V) to unload the things on a vehicle. shyè-'hwò to unload things; shyè-'chē to unhitch draft animals from a cart.

    As mainV: 'shyè-shyà (lc) with same meaning; 'shyè-kāy to remove things from a vehicle. ‖chē 'tíng-dzay nàr wǒ-men lì-'kè jyèw děy bǎ-'hwò 'shyè-shya-lay. When the car stops there, we've got to get the stuff unloaded right away.

謝

*shyè (V) to thank. ‖'shyè-shye. Thanks. ‖dwō-'shyè. Many thanks. ‖shyè-'tyān shyè-'dì! Thank heaven! (literally thank heaven and thank earth).

懈怠

'shyè-dày (A) listless. ‖tā dzwò 'shr-ching hěn 'shyè-dày. He does his work very listlessly.

洩漏

shyè-'lèw (V) to disclose something, intentionally or unintentionally. ‖shr-'shéy shyè-'lèw nèy-ge-'shyāw-shi? Who let that out?

    As mainV: 'shyè-lèw-chū (lc) with same meaning. ‖'shr-ching 'shyè-lèw-chu-chywù-le. The thing has leaked out.

修

shyēw (V) to sharpen a point. shyēw-'bǐ to sharpen a pencil; shyēw shěw-jí-'gàr to pare the fingernails; shyēw jyǎw-jí-'gàr or shyēw-'jyǎw to pare the toenails. As mainV: shyēw-'jyān-le to sharpen to a point by cutting or paring with a sharp tool. ‖bǎ gwèn-dz shyēw-'jyān-le. Sharpen the end of the stick to a point.

修（理）

*shyēw, 'shyēw-li (V) to repair, rebuild; sometimes to build. shyēw(-li) 'chē to repair a car; shyēw 'fáng-dz to build a house (a bit literary); 'shyēw-li-shyēw-li 'fáng-dz to repair or rebuild a house; shyēw-'byǎw to repair a watch; shyēw pǐn-'shíng to regulate one's conduct.

休（息）

*shyēw, 'shyēw-shi (I) to rest. shyēw-'jyà (VN1) to take a vacation or furlough. ‖shyàn-dzày 'shyēw-shi 'shŕ-fēn-jūng. Now we can rest for ten minutes. or Now there will be a ten minute intermission.

修補
shyēw-'bǔ (V) to repair by darning or patching. ‖bĕn-'háng shyēw-'bǔ 'wén-'dày. We fix flats.

修改
shyēw-'gǎy (V) to revise. ‖jèy-pyān-wén-'jāng dĕy dĕng 'shyēw-gǎy yǐ-'hèw tsáy néng fā-'byǎw. This article has got to be revised before it can be published.

修正法
shyēw-jèng-'fǎ (Nunit, tyáw) amendment (law).

修鞋舖
shyēw-shyé-'pù (Nunit, jyān, jyā, ge) snoe repair shop.

宿
shyĕw (Mtime) night. 'lyǎng-tyān yì-'shyĕw two days and a night.

銹
shyèw (I) to rust. (Nmass) rust. jǎng-'shyèw to get rusted. ‖'jèy-ge-dì-fang hĕn 'cháw; tyĕ 'sz dēw jǎng-'shyèw-le. This is a very damp place; all the wire gets rusted.

袖（子）
shyèw, 'shyèw-dz (Nunit, jř) sleeve. shyèw-'kĕwr cuff of a sleeve.
   shyèw-'shĕw (VN1) to put one's hand in one's sleeves with arms folded; (figuratirely) shyèw-'shĕw páng-'gwān to look on as a passive observer.

兇
shyūng (A) fierce, violent, fearful, (of a person, fire, animal).

凶
shyūng (Aattr; before N only) unlucky, bad, evil, dark, cruel, unfortunate. shyūng-'shř sad affairs (deaths, funerals, etc.); shyūng-'ř(-dz) black days; shyūng-'nyán years of unhappiness.

兄
*shyūng (Npers) older brother. See Appendix A.

凶宅
shyūng-'jáy (Nunit, swǒ) haunted house.

胸口
'shyūng-kĕw(r) (Nunit, ge) the space between the lungs; center of the chest. ‖tā 'shyūng-kĕw 'téng. His chest is sore.

胸脯兒
shyūng-'pú(r) (Nunit, ge) chest, breast. jī-'shyūng-púr(-de-) 'rèw meat from a chicken breast.

匈牙利（國）
shyūng-yá-'lì(-gwó) (Nunique) Hungary.

熊
shyúng (Nunit, jř, ge) bear. gĕw-'shyúng the Tibetan bear; 'rén-shyúng small brown bear.

宣布
shywān-'bù (V, Vsent) to announce formally (that). ‖jīn-tyan dà-'hwèy yǐ-jing shywān-'bù 'bì-mù. Today the conference has already announced its adjournment.

宣城
shywān-'chéng (Nunique) Hsüan-ch'eng (city in Anhwei province).

宣傳
shywān-'chwán (V) to spread propaganda about. ‖jèy-ge-bàw-'gwǎn 'wán-chywán tì nèy-ge-jèng-'dǎng shywān-'chwán. This newspaper devotes itself completely to propagandizing for that political party.

宣戰
shywān-'jàn (VN1) to declare war. ‖'jūng-gwo dwèy (or shyàng) ř-'bĕn shywān-'jàn-le. China declared war on Japan.

宣判
shywān-'pàn (V) to pass sentence (judge in court). ‖fǎ-'gwān shywān-'pàn sž-'shíng. The judge passed the sentence of death.

懸，玄，險
shywán (A) very dangerous. ‖chē dzĕw-daw nèy-tyǎw-jǎy-'lù, hǎw 'shywán-le. It's really dangerous when the car goes along that narrow road.
   (I) to be hanging; be left undecided, unsettled.

選
shywǎn (V) to choose, select, elect, vote for. ‖nǐ shywǎn-'shéy? Who are you voting for? ‖jèy-'lyǎng-ge-dūng-shi nǐ shywǎn 'yí-ge-ba. Take your choice of these two things.
   'shywǎn-shàng to elect someone to office. ‖shř-'shéy bèy shywǎn-'shàng-le? Who got elected?
   (N) in compounds: jìng-'shywǎn political campaign; dà-'shywǎn election for the highest elected officials in a country.

選擇
shywǎn-'dzé (V) to choose, select.

選舉
shywǎn-'jywǔ (I) to hold an election; (V) to vote for; (Nunit, tsż) an election. shywǎn-jywǔ-'chywán the right to vote.

選任
shywǎn-ˈrèn (*V*) to choose by election. ‖**ˈměy-gwo-dà-dzǔng-ˈtǔng shr̀ shywǎn-ˈrèn(-de).** The presidency of the United States is an elective office.

In China this is the topmost of several ways of choosing officials.

靴子
ˈshywē-dz (*Nunit*, **jr̄**; **shwāng** *for* a pair) boots.

學
shywé (*or* **shyáw**) to study, learn; to imitate. *In compounds* (*N*) school; learning. **shywé-ˈshyàw** school; **ˈdà-shywé** *or* **dà-shywé-ˈshyàw** college *or* university; **ˈjūng-shywé** *or* **jūng-shywé-ˈshyàw** middle school *or* high school; **ˈshyǎw-shywé** *or* **shyǎw-shywé-ˈshyàw** primary school; **ˈshywé-sheng** student; **dà-shywé-ˈshēng** college student; **jūng-shywé-ˈshēng** high school student; **shyǎw-shywé-ˈshēng** grade school student; **shywé-ˈchī** school term *or* semester; **shywé-ˈnyán** school year; **shywé-ˈfēr** academic credits; **shywé-ˈywàn** college (*as a part of a University*); **shywé-ˈhwèy** learned society. **shàng-ˈshywé** go to school; **shyà-ˈshywé** leave school *or* get out of school (*at the end of the day*).

Added to names of subjects, is like English -ology, *the science of . . .:* **ˈshēng-wù-shywé** the science of living things, biology; **ˈhwà-shywé** the science of changes, chemistry; *etc.*

As mainV: **shywé-ˈhwèy-le** to learn how, catch on. ‖**tā ˈshywé-de hěn ˈkwày.** He learns very fast. ‖**tā shyàn-dzày shywé ˈswàn-shywé.** He's studying mathematics now. ‖**tā dzěme ˈshywé dēw shywě-bu-ˈhwèy.** No matter how hard he studies he can't learn.

尋(摸)
ˈshywé-me (*V*) to wander around looking for *something* (*as in window-shopping*). *As mainV:* **shywé-me-ˈjáwle** to look for *something this way* and find *it*. ‖**wǒ dàw shyǎw-ˈshèr-shang gěy-ni ˈshywé-me-shywé-me yěw-ˈméy-yew ni-ˈyàw-de-dūng-shi.** I'll have a look around in the market to see if I can find the things you want.

學問
shywé-ˈwèn (*Nabstr*) learning, knowledge. ‖**tā-de-shywé-ˈwèn hěn ˈbwó.** He's a person of very wide learning.

學位
shywé-ˈwèy (*Nunit*, **ge**) academic degree. ‖**tā yěw ˈyí-ge-shywé-ˈwèy.** He has one degree.

血
shywě *see* **shyě**.

雪
shywě (*Nmass*) snow. **shyà-ˈshywě** (*IN*) to snow. **yì-dwēy(-de)-ˈshywě** snowbank.

雪花膏
shywě-hwār-ˈgāw (*Nmass*) cold cream *or* vanishin cream.

血統
shywě-ˈtǔng (*Nunit*, **ge**) blood relationship. ‖**tām-ˈlyǎ °(shr̀) ˈyí-ge-shywě-ˈtǔng.** *or* °**yěw shywě-tǔng-ˈgwān-shi.** Those two are blood relatives.

血
shywè *see* **shyě**.

shywen *Romanization found in* Spoken Chinese, Basic Course (*EM 506, 507*), *for syllables spelled* **shywun** *in this dictionary.*

需(要)
****shywū**, **shywū-ˈyàw** (*V, Vpred, Vsent*) to need, require; to need to. ‖**wǒm ˈshywū-yàw hěn-dwō-de-jywūn-ˈhwǒ.** We need plenty of firearms. ‖**wǒ (ˈshywū-)yàw ˈmíng-tyan ˈkàn-ni.** I must see you tomorrow. ‖**ni (shywū-)ˈyàw wǒ ˈmíng-tyan ˈláy-ma?** Do you need me to come tomorrow?

In compounds, **shywū** *is* (*N*) needs, requirements. **jywūn-ˈshywū** military needs.

虛心
shywū-ˈshīn (*A*) open-minded, open to reason, reasonable, (*of a person*).

徐州
shywú-ˈjēw (*Nunique*) Süchow, *another name for* **túng-ˈshān** T'ung-shan (*city in Kiangsu province*).

許
shywǔ (*Vpred*) to be permitted to, be permissible to; *most often in negative* **bù-ˈshywǔ** it is not permitted to. ‖**bù-shywǔ chēw-ˈyān.** Smoking is forbidden.

shywǔ *is sometimes an abbreviation of* **ˈyě-shywǔ** perhaps, particularly in **shywǔ ˈhwèy** may perhaps *or* perhaps may *do so-and-so.*

(*H*) **shywǔ-ˈdwō** *before nouns* a great many: **shywǔ-dwō-ˈr̀-dz** a great many days; *etc.* **ˈshywǔ-shywu-dwō-ˈdwō-de** a very great many indeed. **shywǔ-ˈjyěw yǐ-ˈchyán** a long time ago.

許可
shywǔ-ˈkě (*Nabstr*) permission. ‖**ni ˈdé-le ˈshéy-de-shywǔ-ˈkě dzwò jèy-jyàn-ˈshr̀-ching?** Whose permission did you get to do this?

許可證
shywǔ-kě-ˈjèng (*Nunit*, **jāng**) permit, license.

婿
****shywù.** *See Appendix A.*

熏

shywŭn (*V*) to smoke, cure; to suffocate *someone*. **shywŭn-'rèw** (*VN3*) smoked meat; *etc.* ‖**jèy-ge-chèw-'wèr jēn shywŭn-'rén**. This bad smell really suffocates you.

    As mainV: **shywŭn-'sž-le** to kill *or* die from suffocation in smoke.

勳章

shywŭn-'jāng (*Nunit,* **ge**) decoration, medal, award for any kind of merit.

循

shywún (*K*) going with, following along. ‖**shywún-je jèy-tyáw-'lù dzěw, nǐ jyèw 'dàw-le**. Follow this road and you'll get there. ‖**shywún-je 'tsž-shywu dzěw**. Advance one after another.

尋

***shywún** (*V*) to search for; *literary, but often found in the expression* **shywún-'rén** *newspaper heading like* missing people (*literally* hunting for people).

巡警

shywún-'jĭng (*Npers*) policeman. **shywún-jĭng-'jywú** police station.

訓話

shywùn-'hwà (*VN2*) to make a speech *to subordinates.* ‖**lyán-'jǎng shyàng tā-de-bù-'shyà shywùn-'hwà**. The company commander made a speech to those under him.

訓練

shywùn-'lyàn (*V*) to train *or* to discipline *students, troops, subordinates, animals.*

so *Wade Romanization for* **swo.**

sou *Wade Romanization for* **sew**

ssu *Wade Romanization for* **sz.**

蘇俄

sū-'è (*Nunique*) Soviet Russia.

蘇格蘭

sū-ge-'lán (*Nunique*) Scotland.

蘇州

sū-'jēw (*Nunique*) Soochow, *another name for* **wú-'shyàn** Wu-hsien (*city in Kiangsu province*).

蘇聯

sū-'lyán (*Nunique*) The Soviet Union.

俗 (氣)

'sú(-chì) (*A*) unrefined in one's tastes. ‖**tā-'néy-ge-rén-chwān-de-'yī-fu dēw hěn 'sú-chì**. That fellow's clothes are all in bad taste.

速

***sù** *see* ***shù.**

素

sù (*A*) simple, plain, (*of taste, dress, food*). **sù-'sè** *or* **sù-'shǎr** quiet colors, pastel shades. **sù-'tsày** simple fare, *containing no meat;* **chř-'sù-de-rén** vegetarian.

suan *Wade Romanization for* **swan.**

sui *Wade Romanization for* **swey.**

sun *Wade Romanization for* **swen.**

鬆

sūng (*A*) loose, not tight (*opposite* **jĭn**); puffy, light, (*of a cake*). ‖**shyé-'dàr 'sūng-le**. My shoestrings are loose.

    As postV: **nùng-'sūng-le** to loosen; **jwàn-'sūng-le** to unscrew; *etc.*

松 (樹)

sūng(-'shù) (*Nunit,* **kē**) pine tree. **sūng-'mù** pine wood.

松鼠

sūng-'shǔ(r) (*Nunit,* **ge**) squirrel.

鬆

súng (*A*) cowardly (*extremely impolite, almost profanity*).

送

sùng (*V2*) to send *someone something,* present *someone* with *something.* ‖**tā 'sùng-wo yì-bāw-yān-'yè**. He sent me a package of tobacco.

    (*V*) to see *someone* off on a trip (*compare* **jyē**). ‖**wǒ dàw hwǒ-chē-'jàn chywù 'sùng-ni**. I'll go to the station and see you off.

    (*V, lc*) to go with, take. ‖**wǒ 'sùng-ni chywù**. I'll take you there.

    As mainV: **'sùng-gěy** send *or* give *something* to *someone;* **'sùng-dàw** (*lc*) send *something* to *a place; etc.* ‖**nǐ yàw bù-'shǐ-hwan jyèw 'sùng-hwey-lay**. If you don't like them send them back.

送殯

sùng-'bìn (*VN1*) to attend a funeral and follow the coffin. **gěy-ta sùng-'bìn** attend his funeral.

送別

sùng-'byé (*VN1*) to see *someone* off on a trip; *more literary equivalent of* **sùng-'shíng.**

宋朝

'sùng-cháw (*Nunique*) The Sung dynasty (*960–1279 A.D.*).

送行

sùng-'shíng (*VN1*) to see *someone* off on a trip. ‖wǒ-men gěy-ta sùng-'shíng-ba. Let's see him off.

酸

swān (*A*) tired, sore. ‖wǒ 'shěw hěn 'swān. My hand is tired.

酸

swān (*A*) sour (*tasting*). swān-'tsày pickled vegetables, sour pickles (*not just cucumber pickles*).

算

swàn (*V*) to calculate, figure out. swàn-jàng to figure out an account, settle an account; swàn-'chyán to charge money for something.

    Special expressions: ‖'swàn-le-ba! Let's let it go. *or* Let's count it as all figured out and settled. ‖(jyèw) 'swàn-le-ba. Let's call it a day. *or* OK, that price will do (*in bargaining*). *or simply* OK, I agree. ‖jyèw swàn 'wǔ-kwày-chyán-ba. Let's say five dollars.

    (*V*) *followed by an adjective expression* to count as being *so-and-so*. ‖'jè bú-'swàn hěn 'hǎw. This can't really be counted as too good.

    'swàn-shr (*V*) be figured as, be classed as. ‖'jè-shyē-dūng-shi swàn-shr 'shéy-de? Who do you figure this stuff belongs to? *or followed by an adjective:* ‖jè jyèw swàn-shr 'hǎw-de-ma! Is this supposed to be good? (*implying disapproval*).

    As main V: 'swàn-chū-láy to figure out *the answer to a problem;* 'swàn-chi-láy to figure *everything* up together; 'swàn-dzày to figure something onto (*some-one's account, for example*). ‖nǐ bǎ jè-shyē-'jàng dēw 'swàn-dzày wǒ-de-'jàng-shang. Put all this on my account.

蒜

swàn (*Nunit,* kē, ge) garlic.

算數

swàn-'shù (*Nabstr*) arithmetic.

蒜頭疙疸

swàn-tew 'gā-da (*Nunit,* ge) Chinese-style button (*see* 'kèw-dz).

孫

*swēn (*Npers*) grandchild. *See Appendix A.*

損

swěn (*A*) cruel, unkind.

損害

swěn-'hày (*Nabstr*) damage.

穗（兒）

swèr (*Nunit,* ge) braid, tassel. lyán-dz-'swèr tassels on a curtain; sz̄-swèr silk braid, silk tassel.

尿脬

swéy-'pāw (*Nunit,* ge) bladder (*part of body*).

隨

swéy (*K*) following. ‖wǒ swéy-ni 'chywù. I'll follow you. ‖wǒ 'swéy-je nǐ 'shwō. I'll say whatever you say. ‖nǐ bǎ nèy-ge-'dūng-shi swéy-'shēn 'dày-chywù. Take that thing along with you.

隨便

swéy-'byàn (*H, J*) as you wish, however you like. swéy tā(-de-)'byàn however he likes. ‖chǐng swéy-'byàn. (*Polite phrase*) Please make yourself at home. ‖swéy-'byàn shéme dēw 'ké-yi. Any way you like is all right.

隧道

swéy-'dàw (*Nunit,* tyáw) tunnel.

隨和

'swéy-he (*A*) agreeable, easy to get along with.

雖然

swéy-'rán (*J*) although. ‖swéy-'rán tā 'méy-chǐng-'wǒ, wǒ yě yàw 'chywù. Although he hasn't asked me, I'm going just the same. ‖swéy-'rán shyà-'ywǔ, kě-shr wǒ yě yàw 'chū-chywù. Even though it's raining, I'm going to go out.

隨時

'swéy-shŕ (*J*) at any time desired. ‖nǐ 'swéy-shŕ dēw ké-yi 'láy. You can come any time you like.

隨意

swéy-'yì as you wish, however you like (*used like* swéy-'byàn).

隨員

swéy-'ywán (*NpersT*) attaché (*lowest diplomatic rank*).

綏遠

swéy-'ywǎn (*Nunique*) Suiyüan *province*.

歲

swèy (*Mtime*) year of age. ‖nǐ-de-'háy-dz 'jīn-nyan jǐ-'swèy-le? How old is your child this year? (swèy *gives age in calendar years of life: a child born on the last day of a year is two* swèy *old the next day.*)

    'swèy-shù(r) (*Nabstr*) age. ‖'jèy-ge-rén °'swèy-shùr dwō 'dà? *or* °dwō 'dà 'swèy-shùr? What's his age? ‖tā 'swèy-shu hěn 'dà. He's well along in years.

碎

swèy (*I*) to break into pieces. **swèy-'bīng** cracked ice. ‖**bǐng-'gān dēw 'swèy-le.** The biscuits had crumbled to bits.

    As postV: **dǎ-'swèy-le** to break *something* to pieces by striking; **yã-'swèy-le** to break *something* to pieces by pressing; *etc.*

    (*A*) in small pieces. ‖**jèy-ge-'dūng-shi 'shwāy-de hěn 'swèy.** This is broken up into quite small pieces.

    (*N*) *in compounds:* **fěn-'swèy** pieces so fine as to resemble powder; **swèy-'kwàr** broken bits.

縮

swō (*I*) to shrink. ‖**jèy-shyē-'yī-fu 'shǐ-le yǐ-'hèw jyèw 'swō-le.** When the clothes had been washed they shrank.

    As mainV: **'swō-jìn-chywù** to shrink back, *or* to hold back *something one is about to say;* **swō-'dwǎn-le** to shrink in length, shorten. ‖**jèy-jyàn-'yī-fu swō-'dwǎn-le.** This dress has shrunk (*in length*).

鎖

swǒ (*V*) to lock, secure. **swǒ-'mén** to lock a door. *As mainV:* **'swǒ-shàng** *or* **'swǒ-chǐ-láy** to lock up, chain up, secure. ‖**bǎ-'gěw 'swǒ-chi-lay.** Chain the dog.

    (*Nunit*, ge) lock. ‖**jèy-ge-'yàw-shr gēn jèy-ge-'swǒ bú-'dwèy.** This key doesn't fit this lock.

所

swǒ (*Munit*) *for* **'fáng-dz** house. (*N*) *in compounds:* (1) small building, *as* **tsè-'swǒ** *or* **byàn-'swǒ** toilet, outhouse. (2) place, office, bureau, *as* **'shr̀-wù-'swǒ** business office.

所

swǒ that which . . . (*occupies the position of an H, directly before a verb; a bit literary*). ‖**wǒ-men swǒ-'tswén-de-'hwò dēw 'hwày-le.** The things we stored away are all spoiled. ‖**nǐ swǒ-'tīng-jyàn-de-'hwǎ dēw-shr̀ 'jyǎ-de.** What you heard was all completely false. ‖**wǒ swǒ-'dzwò-de-'shr̀ dēw-shr̀ 'nán-de.** The work I've done was all difficult.

    swǒ *before a verb is a literary equivalent of resultative de after a verb:* ‖**tā tēw 'dūng-shi wèy-'chyúng swǒ-'bī** *is literary for colloquial* **tā méy-yew-'chyán, 'bī-de tēw 'dūng-shi.** Being poor, he was forced to steal.

所僅有的

swǒ-jǐn-'yěw-de (*Aattr*) unique, only one of its kind (*literary*). ‖**jèy-jǔng-de-rén-'tsáy shr̀ shyàn-'dzày swǒ-jǐn-'yěw-de.** This type of person is unique nowadays.

索桑敦

swǒ-sāng-'dwēn (*Nunique*) Southampton (*England*).

所有 (的)

'swǒ-yěw(-de) *before nouns:* all, every. ‖**'swǒ-yěw-de-rén dēw 'dzěw-le.** Everyone's gone. ‖**tā 'swǒ-yěw-de-'dì-fang dēw 'dàw-gwo.** He's been everywhere.

所有人

'swǒ-yěw-rén (*Npers*) owner (*legal*).

所有物

swǒ-yěw-'wù (*Nabstr*) property, belongings (*legal*).

所以

'swǒ-yǐ, 'swó-yǐ, 'swó-yi (*J*) therefore, so. ‖**dzwó-tyan shyà-'ywǔ, swǒ-yǐ 'lěng-le.** It rained yesterday, so it's cold.

撕

sž (*V*) to tear, rip. *As mainV:* **sž-'pwò-le** to break by tearing; **sž-'hwày-le** to ruin by tearing; *etc.* ‖**bǎ jèy-'pyār 'sž-shyà-lay.** Tear out this page.

絲

sž (*Nmass*) silk. **sž-'pǐn** silk goods; **jr̄-'sž** to weave silk; **sž-'dày** silk ribbon. *In some compounds,* thread, strand. **tyě-'sž** iron wire; **túng-'sž** copper wire.

    sēr (*Munit*) strand. **yì-sēr-'téw-fa** a strand of hair; **yì-sēr-yì-'sēr-de** strand by strand. *In compounds:* **shyě-'sēr** capillary; **bù-'sēr** a raveled thread from cloth.

絲

sž (*Mmeas*). *See Appendix B.*

私，私人

*****sž, sž-'rén** (*Aattr*) private, unofficial; *in compounds also* hidden, secret. **sž-'shr̀** private *or* personal affairs.

司機(的，生)

sž-'jī(-de), sž-jī-'shēng (*Npers*) operator *of a vehicle, machine, switchboard, etc.*

司令

sž-'lìng (*NpersT*) commander *of some military unit.* **sž-lìng-'bù** headquarters.

思明

sž-'míng (*Nunique*) Ssu-ming *or* Amoy (*city in Fukien province*).

私生子

sž-shēng-'dž (*Npers*) child born out of wedlock.

私下 (裏)

sž-'shyà(-li) (*H*) in private, in secret. ‖**tā sž-'shyà-li 'hwèy-lù ta.** He bribed him secretly.

267

思想

sž-'shyǎng (*Nabstr*) thought, way of thinking, mentality, ideas. ‖tā-de-sž-'shyǎng hěn dzwǒ-'chīng. He's quite radical-minded.

斯文

'sž-wén (*A*) gentle, scholarlike. (*Opposite* tsū-'yě rough, rude.) 'sž-sz-wen-'wén-de very mildly and gently.

死

sž (*A*) dead. 'sž-rén dead person; (*figuratively*) sž-'hú-tùngr blind alley. ‖jèy-ge-rén-de-'shīn-yǎr hěn 'sž. (*Figuratively*) He has a one-track mind.

As *postV*: dǎ-'sž-le to kill by striking; bìng-'sž-le to die of illness; è-'sž-le to die of hunger, *or* (*figuratively*) to be very hungry; *etc.*, *often with figurative intensive meaning.*

死疙疸的

sž-ge-'tángr-de *or* sž-ge-'dár-de (*Aattr*) solid (*not hollow*).

死刑

sž-'shíng (*Nabstr*) capital punishment. 'pàn-rén sž-'shíng to sentence someone to death.

死尸

sž-'shr̄ (*Nunit*, ge, jywù) corpse.

死於非命

'sž-ywú-fēy-'mìng (*literary quotation*) to die an unnatural and terrible death.

四

sž (*NumU*) four.

sž(-jēw)-'wéy (*Nplace*) in every direction, all around *something;* sž-'chù (*Nplace*) everywhere; sž-'myàr (*Nplace*) all four sides of, all sides of, all around.

四川

sž-'chwān (*Nunique*) Szechwan *province.*

伺候

'sž-hew *see* 'tsž-hew.

似乎

'sž-hū (*Vpred*) to seem to. ‖tā 'sž-hu bù-jř̄-'dàw. He doesn't seem to know.

szu *Wade Romanization for* sz.

T

ta *Wade Romanization for* 'da.

t'a *Wade Romanization for* ta.

他

tā (*Pron*) he, him, she, her. tā-men *or* tām they, them. tā *is occasionally used to refer to things instead of people, but only after a K or V:* ‖bǎ-ta 'ná-lay 'yùng-yi-yùng. Get it and use it. (*This usage is derived from an attempt to translate the English it into Chinese; it is not normal Chinese.*)

塌

tā (*I*) to collapse, cave in, fall to pieces. ‖jèy-ge-'fáng-dz 'tā-le. The house has caved in.

As *mainV*: 'tā-shyà-chywù-le to collapse; tā-'hwày-le to collapse and be ruined.

As *postV*: dǎ-'tā-le to strike and cause collapse; jà-'tā-le to bomb and cause collapse; *etc.*

塔

tǎ (*Nunit*, dzwò) tower, pagoda. dēng-'tǎ lighthouse. tǎ-'dyěngr *or* tǎ-'jyār top of a tower.

踏

tà (*V*) to step on, tramp on. tà-'shywě to walk on snow; tà-'ywè to walk on moonlit ground; tà-'chīng to walk on green grass. (*All a bit literary.*) jyǎw-tà-'chē bicycle.

tai *Wade Romanization for* day.

t'ai *Wade Romanization for* tay.

他們

tām *same as* tā-men (*see* tā).

tan *Wade Romanization for* dan.

t'an *Wade Romanization for* tan.

貪

tān (*A*) avaricious, grasping. ‖tā-'nèy-ge-rén hěn 'tān. He's a greedy and avaricious fellow.

tān-'chr̄ gluttonous.

攤

tān (*V*) to spread *things* out, (*as for a display*). As *mainV*: 'tān-kǎy *with same meaning* 'tān-dzày to spread *things* out at *a place; etc.* ‖bǎ-'shū dēw 'tān-dzày 'jwō-dz-shang. Spread the books out on the table.

灘
tān (*Munit*) *for substances in a blob which is passing from solid to liquid state and smearing and flattening out in the process.* yì-tān-'ní blob of mud.

攤
'tān(-dz), tār (*NunitC,* ge) display counter *usually rough and improvised.*

貪贓
tān-'dzāng (*VN1*) to take bribes.

談
tán (*V*) to converse about, talk, chew the rag. tán-'hwà *or* 'tán-yi-tán, *or* 'tán yì-tán-'hwà to converse; tán-'tyār to chat, gossip. *As mainV:* ‖wǒm háy méy-'tán-dàw 'nèy-ge-wèn-tí. We haven't reached that subject yet.

彈
tán (*V*) to play *a stringed instrument* by plucking, strumming, or striking a keyboard. tán-'chín to play a stringed instrument *in this way;* tán gāng-'chín play a piano.
To flick at something with the finger. tán-'chyéwr to shoot a marble; tán 'myán-hwa to bow cotton and make it fluffy (*cotton is fluffed by placing it around a taut string and plucking the string*).

彈簧
tán-'hwáng (*Nunit,* gēr, ge) coil, coiled spring.

談論
tán-'lwèn (*V*) to discuss formally.

談判
tán-'pàn (*V*) to confer about, negotiate. ‖'lyǎng-gwó dzày tán-'pàn dzěme 'dìng nèy-ge-shāng-'ywē. The two countries are conferring about the establishment of a commercial treaty.

彈性
'tán-shìng (*Naostr*) elasticity. ‖'gāng yěw hěn-'dà-de-'tán-shìng. Steel is extremely elastic.

檀香山
tán-shyāng-'shān (*Nunique*) Honolulu.

彈壓
tán-'yā (*V*) to quiet, quell, *as of troops in times of crisis* (*official term*).

毯子
*tǎn, 'tǎn-dz (*Nunit,* tyáw, ge) blanket. dì-'tǎn carpet.

坦白
tǎn-'báy (*A*) frank, candid.

探出
'tàn-chū (*RC2,* lc) to lean out. ‖tā tsúng 'chwāng-hu tàn-chu 'téw-lay 'kàn-yi-kàn. He leaned (his head) out of the window to take a look.

探險
tàn-'shyǎn (*VN1*) to seek adventure, go in search of adventure.

探詢處
tàn-shywùn-'chù (*Nunit,* ge) information desk; *the characters are used as a sign equivalent to English* INFORMATION.

tang *Wade Romanization for* dang.

t'ang *Wade Romanization for* tang.

湯
tāng (*Nmass*) soup. jī-'tāng chicken soup; jī-tāng-'myàn chicken soup with noodles; *etc.*

糖
táng (*Nmass*) sugar, candy. báy-'táng (white) sugar; húng-'táng brown (red) sugar.

堂
*táng (*N*) hall, room. kè-'táng classroom; dzǎw-'táng public bathhouse; shŕ-'táng dining room (*in a hotel, etc., not a private house*); jyǎng-'táng lecture hall.
(*Munit*) yì-táng-'kè class *to be attended at a particular time and place.*

堂
*táng (*Npers*). *See Appendix A.*

唐朝
'táng-cháw (*Nunique*) The T'ang dynasty (618–907 A.D.). *This dynasty was quite prosperous, so that China is still sometimes referred to with the term* *táng.

塘沽
táng-'gū (*Nunique*) T'ang-ku (*city in Hopeh province*).

躺
tǎng (*I*) to lie down (*not with face down*). *As mainV:* 'tǎng-shyà *with same meaning* 'tǎng-dzày to lie at *or* on *a place.*

躺椅
tǎng-'yǐ (*Nunit,* bǎ, jāng, ge) sofa or settee, *with back or arms or both, long enough to lie down on.*

燙
tàng (*A*) very hot, burning hot (*of an object, not the weather*).

(V) to iron, to burn. **tàng 'yī-fu** to iron clothes; **tàng-'téw** to curl one's hair with a hot curling iron; **tàng-'shěw** to burn one's hand.

As mainV: **tàng-'hú-le** to scorch *clothes* when ironing; **tàng-'téng-le** to burn till it hurts.

遏

tàng (*Msemel*) one trip to somewhere. ‖**wǒ dàw-nèr 'chywù-gwo yí-tàng.** I've made a trip there. ‖**měy-yì-dyǎn-'jūng yěw yí-tàng-'chē.** There's a train for that place every hour.

tao *Wade Romanization for* **daw.**

t'ao *Wade Romanization for* **taw.**

掏

tāw (V) to grope through the contents of a container you can't see into, trying to find. **tāw-'chyán** look for one's money; (*figuratively*) to foot the bill. *As mainV:* **'tāw-chū-lay** to fish for, find, and take out; **tāw-'dzěw-le** to fish for, find, and take away; **tāw-bu-'jáw** to be unable to find when hunting thus; **'tāw-dàw** to hunt for *up to a certain place; etc.* ‖**nǐ chǐng-'kè, wǒ tāw-'chyán.** You invite the guests; I'll pay the bill. ‖**wǒ yì tāw 'kěw-dàr, chyán 'méy-le.** When I felt in my pocket, the money was gone.

逃

táw (I) to escape; (V) to escape from. **táw-'ywù** to escape from jail. ‖**yěw ge-'dzéy 'táw-le.** A thief has escaped.

táw-'fàn (*Npers*) escaped criminal, escaped prisoner.

As mainV: **táw-'pǎw-le** to run away; **táw-'dzěw-le** to get away; **'táw-chū** (*lc*) to escape from; *etc.*

桃 (子，兒)

'táw(-dz), táwr (*Nunit, ge*) peaches. **táw-'hwār** peach blossoms; **táw-'shù** peach tree. **táw-'sè** or **táw-'shǎr** peach-colored; (*figuratively*) romantic, pertaining to affairs of the heart. **táw-sè-'shīn-wén** tabloid-style news about women and love.

逃難

táw-'nàn (*VN1*) to leave a troubled place. **táw-'nàn-de** refugees.

淘汰

táw-'tày (V) to weed out, eliminate by slow natural process. ‖**méy-'yùng-de-rén dēw bèy táw-'tày-le.** Useless people get weeded out.

逃役

táw-'yì (*VN1*) to evade a draft *or* levy.

討

tǎw (V) to beg for, ask for, get. **tǎw-'fàn-de** a beggar; **tǎw 'tày-tay** to get a wife. *With V as object:* **tǎw-'dǎ** to be asking for a beating; **tǎw-'mà** to invite a

scolding through one's actions. ‖**tǎw-'jày bǐ jywàn-'kwǎn háy 'nán.** It's even harder to ask for the return of a loan than it is to solicit a free contribution.

討論

tǎw-'lwèn (V) to discuss formally.

討厭

tǎw-'yàn (A) annoying, distasteful, unpleasant, boring, disgusting. (V) to dislike, be bored by, be disgusted by. **tǎw-yàn 'tèw-le** be thoroughly disgusting.

套

tàw (V) to put on a cover, *usually flexible, which leaves part of the thing covered exposed. As mainV:* **'tàw-shàng** *with same meaning* **'tàw-chǐ-láy** to cover up *thus;* **'tàw-jìn-chywù** to put *something* in such a cover; **'tàw-dzày** to put something in *a cover which covers it this way.* ‖**dzwò yí-ge-'kěw-dày bǎ 'shyāng-dz 'tàw-chi-lay.** Make a bag to put around the suitcase. ‖**'tàw-shàng yí-jyàn-dà-'gwàr.** Slip the smock on. ‖**tyār hěn 'lěng, dzày 'tàw-shang yí-jyàn-'yī-fu.** It's cold; better put on something else over what you're wearing.

tàw-'shyé (*Nunit, jř; a pair of* **shwāng**) galoshes, rubbers, overshoes.

套

tàw (*Mgroup*) set of, suit of, *things which come customarily in a set, but which are not exact duplicates of each other* (*compare* **fù**). Suit of **'yī-fu** (*clothing*); set of **wǎn-'dyéer** (*dishes of various sizes and shapes which match in design*); suite of **'jyā-jywu** (*furniture*); a set of matching **jwō-'yǐ** (*tables and chairs*).

苔

*****tāy** (N) coating of something. **shé-'tāy** coating on the tongue; **'shé-tew yěw-'tāy** the tongue is coated. **chīng-'tāy** green moss, (*as on a stone*).

擡

táy (V) to lift, carry, take, bring, *when done by two or more people, and when the thing transported is lifted completely off the ground;* to lift *a body-part. As mainV:* **'táy-chǐ-láy** to pick up, raise *something* up; **'táy-shàng-láy** to carry *something* upwards (*e.g., upstairs*); **'táy-dàw** (*lc*) to carry to *a place;* **táy-'gāw** to lift high, (*often figuratively as of prices or self-esteem*). ‖**bǎ 'bìng-rén táy-daw yī-'ywàn chywù.** Carry the sick man to the hospital. ‖**'sž-ge-rén táy 'jyàw-dz.** Four men carry a sedan-chair. ‖**táy-'téw 'kàn-kan.** Lift your head and take a look.

臺 (子)

'táy(-dz) (*Nunit, dzwò, ge*) platform, stage, raised boxing ring, *etc.* **shì-'táy** stage; **jàn-'táy** platform at a station; **yǎn-jyǎng-'táy** speaker's platform; **shū-jwāng-'táy** dresser (*furniture*); **tyān-wén-'táy** astronomical observatory; **wú-shyàn-dyàn-'táy** radio station; **'lyáng-táy** porch; **pàw-'táy** gun platform.

     táy-'chyéw billiard ball, billiards; **táy-'jyē**(er) steps at the entrance of a building *or elsewhere in the open* (*not usually made of wood*); **táy-'bù** table linen.

     shàng-'táy to mount a platform (stage, etc.), (*figuratively*) to come into the public eye; **shyà-'táy** to descend from a platform, (*figuratively*) to leave a high public position.

撑槓
táy-'gàng (*VN2*) to lift a pole, (*of two or more people*); (*figuratively*) (*VN1*) to argue.

台州
táy-'jēw (*Nunique*) Taichow, *another name for* **lín-'hǎy** Lin-hai (*city in Chekiang province*).

台山
táy-'shān (*Nunique*) Toisan, *another name for* **shìng-'níng** Hsing-ning *or* Hingning (*city in Kwangtung province*).

臺灣
táy-'wān (*Nunique*) Taiwan.

臺灣海峽
táy-wān-hǎy-'shyá (*Nunique*) Straits of Taiwan.

太
'ày (*H*) too; *sometimes just* very. ‖**tày 'gwèy, wǒ mǎy-bu-'chǐ.** It's too expensive, I can't afford to buy it. ‖**nǐ 'dzěw-de tày 'kwày yì-dyǎr.** You're walking a bit too fast. ‖**bú-'tày yí-'yàng.** They're not too similar. ‖**tày bù-yí-'yàng**(-le). They're far too different from each other. ‖**tā 'tày yěw-'chyán-le.** He's too darned rich. ‖**byé děng tày 'jyěw-le dzày 'láy.** Don't wait too long before you come again. ‖**tày fèy-'lì.** It takes too much effort.

態度
'tày-dù (*Nabstr*) attitude, manner, air, seeming. ‖**tā-de-'tày-du hū-'rán 'gǎy-le.** His attitude suddenly changed.

泰國
'tày-gwó (*Nunique*) Thailand.

太平
'tày-píng (*Nabstr*) peace. **tày-píng-'nyán** years of peace, time of peace. **tày-píng-'yáng** (*Nunique*) the Pacific Ocean.

太太
'tày-tay (*NpersT*) Mrs., madam, lady, (*for married woman only*)

太陽
'tày-yang (*Nunique*) the sun. **tày-yang 'chū-lay** the sun comes up; **tày-yang 'shyà-chywu** the sun goes down; **tày-yang-'gwāng** sunlight; **tày-yang-'dyèr** sunny spot, sunny place.

太原
tày-'ywán (*Nunique*) Taiyuan, *another name for* **yáng-'chywū** Yang-ch'ü (*capital of Snansi province*).

te *Wade Romanization for* **de.**

t'e *Wade Romanization for* **te.**

特別
tè-'byé (*Aattr, H*) special, particular, distinctive, especially, particularly. ‖**'jīn-tyan 'tyān-chi tè-'byé 'hǎw.** It's a particularly nice day today. ‖**jè-shr̀ tè-'byé-'kwày**(-de)-'**chē.** (*With* de:) This is an especially fast train. (*Without* de:) This is an express train. ‖**tā shr̀ yí-ge-tè-'byé-de-rén.** He's an uncommon sort of person (*either complimentary or uncomplimentary comment*).

特殊
tè-'chú, tè-'shū (*Aattr*) especially good. exceptional; specific. ‖**'jèy-ge-'chíng-shing shr̀ tè-'chú-de.** This situation is exceptional. *Almost exclusively of abstract situations; compare* **tè-'byé.**

特派
tè-'pày (*Vsent*) to appoint *someone especially to do something.* ‖**dà-dzǔng-'tǔng tè-'pày-le yí-ge-'rén chywù 'jǎw-ta.** The president appointed someone especially to go look for him.

特任
tè-'rèn (*Vsent, V*) to appoint, *when appointment is made by a chief executive and his government.* ‖**dà-'shr̀-de-'dì-wèy shr̀ tè-'rèn-de.** An ambassadorship is an appointive office.

特性
'tè-shìng (*Nabstr*) special traits, characteristics. ‖**tā-'nèy-ge-rén yěw yì-jǔng-'tè-shìng.** He has an idiosyncrasy.

特殊
tè-'shū *see* **tè-'chú.**

特為
tè-'wèy (*K*) especially for the benefit of, especially for something. ‖**wǒ tè-'wèy jèy-jyàn-'shr̀-ching 'láy-de.** I came especially for this.

tei *Wade Romanization for* **dey.**

t'ei *Wade Romanization for* **tey**.

teng *Wade Romanization for* **deng**.

t'eng *Wade Romanization for* **teng**.

膡
tēng (*V*) to steam; to apply steam to *for cooking or re-heating.* **tēng 'bāw-dz** (*VN2*) to steam Chinese dumplings.

痛，疼
téng (*A*) hurt, ache, be sore. ‖**wǒ-'dù-dz (jywé-de) yěw yì-dyǎr-'téng.** My stomach hurts a little.
    Preceded by a noun naming a body-part, forms a compound adjectival expression: ‖**wǒ 'téw-téng.** I have a headache. ‖**wǒ bù-'téw-téng-le.** My headache has stopped.
    téw-téng-'yàw headache medicine.
    (*V*) to be very fond of *a close relation.* ‖**tā hěn 'téng tā-'ér-dz.** He's very fond of his son.

騰
téng (*V*) to empty; clear out of. **téng 'wū-dz** to clear a room; **téng-'fáng** to move out of a house. *As mainV:* **'téng-chū-lay** to clear out, empty. ‖**bǎ 'shyāng-dz-lǐ-tew-de-'dūng-shi 'téng-chu-lay.** Empty out the things in the suitcase.
    téng-shyà 'shŕ-hew to make time *for something.*

騰衝
téng-'chūng (*Nunique*) T'eng-ch'ung (*city in Yünnan province*).

騰越
téng-'ywè (*Nunique*) T'eng-yüeh, *another name for* T'eng-ch'ung (*city in Yünnan province*).

偷
tēw (*V*) to steal *quietly. As mainV:* **tēw-'dzěw-le** to steal and go away with. ‖**tā-de-'chyán dēw jyàw-'dzéy tēw-'dzěw-le.** His money was all stolen by a thief.
    (*H*) on the sly. ‖**shyǎw-'māwr tēw chŕ-'rèw.** The kitten stole and ate the meat. ‖**tā tēw-'tēw-de 'chū-chywù-le.** He sneaked out.

偷工減料
tēw-'gūng jyǎn-'lyàw to do shoddy work, *with insufficient labor and material (said of one who contracts to manage a job).*

偷懶
tēw-'lǎn (*I*) to goldbrick, loaf on the job. ‖**tā lǎw tēw-'lǎn.** He's always loafing on the job.

頭
téw (*Nunit*, ge) head (*of body*). **'téw-fa** (*Nunit* gěr) hair on the head; **téw(-fa)-'jěr** (*Nunit*, gěr) hairpins; **téw-'nǎw** (*Nunit*, ge) brain (*in body*); (*Nabstr*) brains, intelligence.

頭
téw (*Munit*) head of (*for some domestic animals; some vegetables*); stalk of (*for certain vegetables*). A head of nyéw (*cattle*); a head of yáng (*sheep*); a stalk of báy-'tsày (*celery-cabbage*); a head of yáng-báy-'tsày (*cabbage, lettuce*); a stalk of swàn (*garlic*).

頭
téw (*Preord*) the first. **tew-yí-'tsż** the first time; **'téw-yí-ge-rén** the first person, the first person in line; **téw-lyǎng-'tsż** the first two times; *etc.*
    Without yī: **téw-'děng** first class; **téw-děng-'chē** first class railway compartment, first class on the railroad.
    Before a noun: **téw-'jyǎng** first prize; **'téw-rén** *or* **'téwr** (*Nunique*) the boss, the head man.

頭（兒）
téw(r) (*Mpos*) front end, head. **jyē-'téwr** end of a street; **ywè-'téwr** beginning of the month, first part of a month; **tsúng-'téwr dàw-'lyǎwr** from beginning to end, from start to finish.
    Added to other place words to make the longer forms: **'chyán-tew(r)** front, front side, front end; **'hèw-tew(r)** back, back side, back end; **'shàng-tew(r)** upper part; **'shyà-tew(r)** lower part; **'wày-tew(r)** outside; **'lǐ-tew(r)** inside.

投標
téw-'byāw (*VN2*) to enter a bid for a contract.

投資
téw-'dż (*VN1*) to invest money. ‖**wǒ-men téw-'dż bàn gūng-'chǎng-ba.** Let's invest our money and start a factory.

頭裏
'téw-le (*Nplace*) place in front of, (*in a line*). **dzày-wǒm-'téw-le-de-rén** the people ahead of us.

投票
téw-'pyàw (*VN2*) to cast a vote.

投宿
téw-'sù (*VN1*) to stay for the night (*literary*).

透
tèw ʻ(*H*) thoroughly, completely; *confined to position after A.* **tǎw-yàn 'tèw-le** thoroughly disgusting; **má-fan 'tèw-le** exceedingly troublesome; *etc.*

透氣（兒）

tèw-'chì, tèw-'chyèr (*IN*) air passes through, air penetrates. ‖wǒm 'chū-chywù 'tèw-tew 'chì. Let's go out for a breath of air. ‖bǎ 'tǎn-dz gē-dzay 'wày-myan tèw-tew 'chyèr. Put the blankets out to air.

透風

tèw-'fēng (*IN*) breeze passes through. ‖jèy-ge-mén-'fēngr tèw-'fēng. The wind is leaking through the seams of the door.

透光

tèw-'gwāng (*IN*) light penetrates, light escapes, light passes through. ‖nèy-ge-'chwāng-hu tèw-'gwāng. The window admits light. *or* There's a light showing at that window. ‖jèy-ge-shyàng-'shyá-dz tèw-'gwāng, bù-néng 'yùng-le. That camera has sprung a light leak, you can't use it.

ti *Wade Romanization for* di.

t'i *Wade Romanization for* ti.

剔

tī (*V*) to remove undesired portions from something *with the finger or an instrument.* tī-'yá to pick the teeth; tī. 'gú-tew to remove bones *from meat. As mainV:* 'tī-chū (*lc*) *or* tī-'dzěw-le *with same meaning.* ‖yùng shyǎw-'dāwr bǎ hé-tew-'rèw 'tī-chu-lay. Pick the meat out of the walnuts with a small knife.

踢

tī (*V*) to kick. 'tī-rén yì-'jyǎw give someone a kick. *As mainV:* 'tī-chū-chywù kick *someone* out.

梯（子）

*tī, 'tī-dz (*Nunit,* ge) ladder. léw-'tī stairs in a building; dyàn-'tī (electric) elevator.

堤，隄

tí (*Nunit,* tyáw, dàw) dike, dam. hé-'tí river embankment.

題

tí (*V*) to inscribe. tí jǐ-ge-'dz̀ to put down a few words of comment. tí-'shř *or* tí-'jywù *or* tí-'tsź to jot down original verse.

提

tí (*V*) to carry, lift, bring, take, *in the hand with the arm held down along the side of the body; (figuratively)* to bring up *a subject, or* to make *a proposal, or* to give *the name of someone* as a nomination. ‖tā 'tí-je yí-ge-'lán-dz. He was carrying a basket. ‖wǒm bǎ jèy-jyàn-'shř 'tí-yi-tí. Let's bring up this matter for a bit of discussion.

As mainV: 'tí-chǐ-lay to pick up *an object, or* to bring up *a subject;* 'tí-chū-lay to carry *an object* out, *or* to bring out *a point;* tí-chu shū-'sùng file a claim; 'tí-dàw (*lc*) to carry *an object* to *a place, or* to reach *a particular subject* in the course of discussion; tí-'dzěw-ie to carry away; tí-'gāw-le to raise. ‖tām shyàng 'jèng-fǔ 'tí-chu kàng-'yì. They entered a protest against the government. ‖bǎ 'shyāng-dz tí-daw chē-'jàn chywu. Carry the suitcase to the station.

提案

tí-'àn (*Nunit,* ge) proposal, motion, (*in a formal meeting*)

提包

tí-'bāw (*Nunit,* ge) small suitcase, handbag, briefcase.

提琴

tí-'chín (*Nunit,* ge) violin. lā tí-'chín to play a violin.

提前

tí-'chyán (*V, Vpred*) to move a scheduled event to a time earlier than that originally planned. ‖wǒm děy tí-'chyán kāy-'hwèy. We've got to start the meeting earlier than we'd planned. ‖kāy-'hwèy děy tí-'chyán sān-'tyān. We've got to start the meeting three days early.

提早

tí-'dzǎw (*V, Vpred*) same as tí-'chyán; *if amount of time is specified* tí-'chyán *is preferable.*

提貨單

tí-hwò-'dān (*Nunit,* jāng) bill of lading.

題目

'tí-mu (*Nunit,* ge) theme, subject, topic, problem; heading (*as of a chapter or paragraph*). chū 'tí-mu to state a problem (*as in giving an exam*).

提箱

tí-'shyāng (*Nunit,* ge) suitcase, *same as* shěw-tí-'shyāng.

提議

tí-'yì (*VN3*) to make a motion *in a formal meeting;* a motion. ‖wǒ tí-'yì sàn-'hwèy. I move to adjourn.

體格

tǐ-'gé (*Nabstr*) physique, posture. 'tǐ-gé-jyǎn-'chá physical examination; jyǎn-'chá tǐ-'gé to give a physical examination.

體重

tǐ-'jùng (*Nabstr*) body weight. ‖tā-de-tǐ-'jùng yì-bǎy-er-shr-'bàng. She weighs a hundred and twenty.

體諒
tǐ-'lyàng (A.) be sympathetic, considerate. ‖tā dwèy-ni hěn tǐ-'lyàng. He's very considerate of you. (V) to be sympathetic towards, considerate of. ‖tā hěn tǐ-'lyàng ni. He's very considerate of you.

體面
'tǐ-myàn (A) graceful. ‖tā 'jǎng-de hěn 'tǐ-myàn. She's quite graceful. ‖tā-men-de-hwēn-'li 'bàn-de hěn 'tǐ-myàn. Their wedding ceremony was gracefully done and in good taste.

體裁
tǐ-'tsáy (Nabstr) style, fashion, pattern, format, usually having to do with writing or formal speaking.

體統
'tǐ-tǔng (Nabstr) dignity. méy-yew 'tǐ-tǔng be undignified.

體無完膚
'tǐ-wú-wán-'fū (literary quotation) picked to pieces, completely destroyed. ‖tā bǎ-ta 'mà-de 'tǐ-wú-wán-'fū. He cussed him out until there was nothing left of him.

體育
tǐ-'ywù (Nabstr) physical education; athletic sports.

剃
tì (V) to shave. tì-'téw to give or get a haircut, of the old-fashioned Chinese type which involved some shaving of the head. tì-'téw-de barber; tì-téw-'dyàn barber shop; both featuring the old-fashioned method. (Compare lǐ-'fǎ, gwā-'lyǎn.)

替
tì (K) as a substitute for, on behalf of (a person); sometimes like gěy for the benefit of (a person). ‖wǒ tì-ni 'chywù. I'll go in your place.

替工
'tì-gūng (Npers) substitute. ‖tā 'dzěw-le, jǎw yí-ge-'tì-gung. He's gone, so find a substitute for him.

tiao Wade Romanization for dyaw.

t'iao Wade Romanization for tyaw.

tieh Wade Romanization for dye.

t'ieh Wade Romanization for tye.

tien Wade Romanization for dyan.

t'ien Wade Romanization for tyan.

ting Wade Romanization for ding.

t'ing Wade Romanization for ting.

聽
tīng (V, Vsent) to listen to; to hear. tīng-'shì to attend the Chinese theater; tīng-'hwà to heed what someone says, obey; tīng 'mìng-lìng to obey orders. ‖wǒ 'shwō-shwō ni 'tīng-tīng. I'll talk; you listen a bit.
As mainV: tīng-'chīng-chu to listen and hear clearly or to catch a name, etc; 'tīng-chū-lay to make out what is heard; tīng-'dǔng-le to listen and understand; 'tīng-jyàn to hear; tīng-bu-'jyàn to be unable to hear, or to be deaf; tīng-'yàn-le to hear something over and over again until one is tired of hearing.

廳
*tīng (Nunit, ge) station, bureau, agency (fairly large); hall. jǐng-chá-'tīng police station or headquarters.

聽差的
tīng-'chāy(-de) (Npers) porter, doorman, male servant.

聽衆
tīng-'jùng (Ncoll) audience (always a listening audience).

聽說
'tīng-shwō (Vsent) to hear it said that, to hear tell that. ‖wǒ 'tīng-shwō ni 'bìng-le. I heard you were sick.

停
tíng (I) to stop. ‖chǐng-ni °'tíng-yi-tíng. or °'tíng yí-shyàr. or °'tíng yì-hwěr. Stop a minute. or Wait a minute.
Used causatively: tíng-'chē to stop a car, park a car; tíng-'gūng to stop work; tíng-'kè to stop having class; tíng-'jàn to stop war, have an armistice.
As mainV: 'tíng-shyà-lay to come to a stop (of something in motion, more often of a car or plane than of a stationary machine); 'tíng-jù to stop (of car or plane, of a machine, of a procedure or ceremony); 'tíng-dzày to stop at a place.
As postV: dzěw-'tíng-le (no potential forms) to stop going, of a clock, watch, machine, or to stop walking; etc. (not too common).

停戰書
tíng-jàn-'shū (Nunit. jāng, fèr) armistice (signed document).

停止
tíng-'jǐ (Vpred) to stop doing something. ‖tā tíng-'jǐ shwō-'hwà. He stopped talking.

頂
tǐng see dǐng.

tiu *Wade Romanization for* **dyew.**

to *Wade Romanization for* **dwo.**

t'o *Wade Romanization for* **two.**

tou *Wade Romanization for* **dew.**

t'ou *Wade Romanization for* **tew.**

tsa *Wade Romanization for* **dza.**

ts'a *Wade Romanization for* **tsa.**

擦
tsā (*V*) to scrape, rub, clean, polish, (*as with a cloth*). **tsā-ˈshyé** polish shoes; **tsā-ˈlyǎn** to wipe the face; **tsā-ˈshěw** to wipe the hands; **tsā ˈyǎn-jr** to put on rouge; **tsā-ˈshāng** to graze the skin and cause an abrasion.

As mainV: **ˈtsā-chywù** *or* **tsā-ˈdzěw-le** to wipe away; **ˈtsā-shyà-chywù** wipe off; **ˈtsā-gwò-chywù** to brush past; **tsā-ˈgān-le** to wipe dry; **tsā-ˈgān-jìng-le** to wipe clean. ‖**yùng ˈshěw-jīn bǎ-ˈlyǎn tsā-ˈgān-le.** Wipe your face dry with the towel. ‖**bǎ nèy-dī-ˈyéw ˈtsā-chyà-chywù.** Wipe that spot of oil off.

擦洗
tsā-ˈshǐ (*V*) to clean by rubbing *with water and a rag.*

tsai *Wade Romanization for* **dzay.**

ts'ai *Wade Romanization for* **tsay.**

tsan *Wade Romanization for* **dzan.**

ts'an *Wade Romanization for* **tsan.**

參觀
tsān-ˈgwān (*I*) make an informal tour of inspection.

餐巾
tsān-ˈjīn (*Nunit, tyáw, kwày*) cloth napkin *used at a dinner table.*

參加
tsān-ˈjyā (*V*) to participate in. **tsān-ˈjyā bǐ-ˈsày** to take part in a game *or* competition.

參考
tsān-ˈkǎw (*V*) to consult *books, documents,* as references.

參謀
ˈtsān-méw (*NpersT*) staff officer. **tsān-méw-ˈjǎng** chief of staff.

(*I*) to serve in an advisory capacity, give advice. ‖**wǒ ˈtì-ní ˈtsān-mew.** I'll advise you.

蠶
tsán (*Nunit, tyáw, ge*) silkworm.

蠶豆
tsán-ˈdèw (*Nunit, ge*) lima beans.

殘廢
tsán-ˈfèy (*Aattr*) minus a body-part, crippled, blinded, partly incapacitated.

慘
tsǎn (*A*) miserable, wretched, unhappy; productive of misery. (*H*) terribly, miserably. ‖**shā-rén shr̀ yí-jyàn-ˈtsǎn-shr̀.** To kill a man is a terrible thing. ‖**wǒ ˈjywé-de hěn ˈtsǎn.** I feel terrible (about it).

tsang *Wade Romanization for* **dzang.**

ts'ang *Wade Romanization for* **tsang.**

倉
tsāng (*Nunit, ge*) storage place on a farm, shed, barn. **tsāng-ˈfáng** (*Nunit, swǒ, jyān*) barn, granary. **tsāng-ˈkù** (*Nunit, ge*) place of storage (*not restricted to farm*).

艙
tsāng (*Nunit, ge*) cabin (*on ship*). **ˈtéw-děng-tsāng** first class cabin; **ˈèr-děng-tsāng** second class cabin; **ˈsān-děng-tsāng** third class accommodations, *the same as* **ˈtǔng-tsāng** steerage; **tsāng-ˈmyàr** deck above cabins in the open.

蒼梧
ˈtsāng-ˈwú (*Nunique*) Ts'ang-wu (*city in Kwangsi province*).

蒼蠅
ˈtsāng-ying (*Nunit, ge*) fly (*insect*).

藏
tsáng (*V*) to hide; to set aside in a secure place. **tsáng-ˈshū** to collect books; **tsáng-shū-ˈjyā** book collector. *As mainV:* **ˈtsáng-chǐ-láy** to hide *things* away; **ˈtsáng-dzày** to hide *something* at *a place; etc.* ‖**shyǎw-ˈhá bǎ ˈpíng-gwo tsáng-dzay bèy-ˈhèw.** The child hid the apples behind him. ‖**tā-ˈjèy-ge-rén ˈtsáng-bu-jù ˈhwà.** This guy can't keep a secret.

tsao *Wade Romanization for* **dzaw.**

ts'ao *Wade Romanization for* **tsaw.**

操場
tsāw-ˈchǎng (*Nunit, ge*) drill field (*military*).

操縱
tsāw-ˈdzùng (*V*) to dominate, control, manipulate. ‖**tā tsāw-ˈdzùng jīn-ˈrúng.** He controls the currency.

操練

tsăw-'lyàn (*VN1*) to drill (*military*).

操心

tsāw-'shīn (*A*) worried, care-worn; careful, painstaking.

草

tsăw (*Nunit; gĕr* blade of; *pyàn* field of) grass. gān-'tsăw hay; tsăw-'dì lawn, meadow, pasture land; tsăw-'chăng pasture; tsăw-'mù grass and trees, vegetation, plants; tsăw-'màw straw hat.

　　tsăw-'dz̀ running-hand characters; tsăw-'găw(r) rough written draft.

猜

tsāy (*Vsent*) to guess that. ‖wŏ 'tsāy tā bù-néng 'láy. My guess is that he can't come. *As mainV:* tsāy-bu-'chū(-!ay) be unable to figure out *or* guess. ‖wŏ tsāy-bu-'chū tā shr̀-'shéy. I can't figure out who he is.

　　tsāy-'shyăng (*Vsent*) to guess that, to conjecture that.

才, 纔

tsáy (*H*) then and only then. (*Contrast* jyèw.) ‖wŏ 'jīn-nyán tsáy dàw 'mĕy-gwo 'láy-de. I just came to the U. S. this year. ‖wŏ-men dĕng tā 'dàw-le yī-'hèw, tsáy chr̄-'fàn. We didn't eat until he arrived. ‖nĭ 'gēn-ta chywù tsáy 'hăw. The only thing for you to do is go with him.

　　‖tsáy-'bù-ne! Not at all!

裁

tsáy (*V*) to cut with scissors. tsáy 'yī-fu to cut cloth in making clothes. *Figuratively* tsáy-'rén to fire someone.

財產

tsáy-'chăn (*Nmass; fèr*) assets; wealth and property.

財閥

'tsáy-fá (*Npers*) tycoon, financial big shot.

裁縫

'tsáy-feng (*Npers*) tailor.

才幹

tsáy-'gàn (*Nabstr*) ability, gift, talent. ‖tā hĕn yĕw tsáy-'gàn. He's very gifted.

才剛, 纔剛

tsáy-'gāng *same as* gāng-'tsáy.

裁料

tsáy-'lyàw(r) (*Nmass*) source material *for preparing a report;* material *for building a house, etc.;* material *for sewing.*

裁判

tsáy-'pàn (*V*) to act as referee in *some matter; primarily legal, but also for games.* tsáy-pàn-'gwān judge, official who serves as arbitrator; tsáy-pàn-'ywán referee, umpire, arbitrator.

踹

tsăy (*V*) to step on. ‖wŏ 'tsăy-le nĭ-·jyăw-le-ma? Did I step on your foot?

　　As mainV: 'tsăy-shyà-chywù to step downwards, press downwards with the foot; 'tsăy-dzày to step on *or* at. ‖wŏ 'lyăng-ge-'jyăw tsăy-dzay 'bīng-shang. I stepped on the ice with both feet.

探

*tsăy (*V*) to pluck, choose, collect. tsăy-'hwār to pluck flowers; tsăy-'mì to gather honey (*said of bees, not beekeepers*).

探取

tsăy-'chywŭ (*V*) to assume *an attitude;* to adopt *a form of government, a scheme of operation.* ‖'jūng-gwo-de-'kwàng-yè shyàn-dzày tsăy-'chywŭ 'shī-yàng-de-'fāng-fă. The mining industry in China is adopting western methods.

探訪

tsăy-'făng (*V*) to collect news, information, (*as a reporter does); almost always in* tsăy-'făng 'shīn-wén to gather news.

探納

tsăy-'nà (*V*) to accept *a proposal, point of view; said particularly of someone in authority accepting and approving a suggestion made by a subordinate.*

探用

tsăy-'yùng (*V*) to adopt and put into use. ‖nĭ tsăy-'yùng shéme-'fāng-fa? What method have you adopted?

菜

tsày (*Nmass*) food other than staple foods, *eaten for taste and interest or variety.* yí-dàw-'tsày a course *of a meal ·* yì-wăn-'tsày a dish (*in the sense of one of the types of food served at a meal*); jyàw-'tsày *or* dyăn-'tsày to order *in a restaurant;* tsày-'dān(-dz) *or* tsày-'dār menu; tsày-'tān(-dz) *or* tsày-'tār booth, stall, *or* stand in a market.

　　In some combinations refers exclusively to the vegetable subdivision of the above. tsày-'ywán(-dz) vegetable garden.

tse *Wade Romanization for* **dze.**

ts'e *Wade Romanization for* **tse.**

册

tsè (*Mauton*) volume of a book. **dì-yí-'tsè** volume one; **yěw-'lyǎng-tsè-de-'shū** a book in two volumes.

    'tsè-dz (*Nunit*, **běr**, **ge**) pamphlet; register; list in booklet form; album.

厠所

tsè-'swǒ (*Nunit*, **jyān**, **ge**) toilet.

tsen *Wade Romanization for* **dzen.**

ts'en *Wade Romanization for* **tsen.**

tseng *Wade Romanization for* **dzeng.**

ts'eng *Wade Romanization for* **tseng.**

噌 (斥)

tsēng (*V*) to scold. **'tsēng-ta yí-dwèn** give him a scolding. **'āy yí-dwèn-'tsēngr** to get a scolding.

層

tséng (*Munit*, *Mpart*) layer of, coat of. A layer of **ní** (*mud*); a coat of **yéw** (*paint*); a shelf of a **'jyà-dz** (*cabinet*); a floor of a **léw** (*building*); a deck of a **tsāng** (*cabin*), *thus* a deck of a ship.

    dì-'yì-tséng-léw the first floor of a building; **yí-dzwò-'sān-tséng(-léw)-de-'léw** a building of three stories.

    chyān-tséng-'gāw thousand layer cake, a cake with many layers.

曾經

tséng-'jīng (*H*) at some time before the present. ‖**wǒ tséng-'jīng 'kàn-gwo ta.** I've already seen him. *or* I saw him. *or* I've seen him. ‖**wǒ tséng-'jīng chywù 'kàn-gwo ta yí-'tsż.** I've been to see him once. *or* I went to see him once. *Notice that* **tséng-'jīng** *is used only in the affirmative, and that the verb is always followed by* **-gwo.** *With this construction the emphasis is on the fact that the thing has been experienced; with* **'yì-jing** *it would be rather on the fact that the experience is now over.*

蹭

tsèng (*V*) to graze, rub, scrape against. ‖**fēy-'jī tsèng-je shù-'jyār 'fēy-gwò-chywù-le.** The plane flew by, grazing the treetops.

    As mainV: **'tsèng-gwò-chywù** to graze by, brush by; **'tsèng-shàng** to graze by *something wet.* (*such as paint*) and get some of it on you. ‖**tā-de-'yī-shang 'tsèng(-shàng)-le yí-kwày-'yéw.** He brushed against the grease and got a spot on his clothes.

湊

tsèw (*V*) collect, gather together. ‖**wǒ-men 'tsèw-le 'wǔ-kwày-chyán.** Between us we got up a fund of five dollars.

tsèw yí-'kwàr *or* (*with RC*) **tsèw-dzày yí-'kwàr** *or* **tsèw-dàw yí-'kwàr** gather *things or people* together *or* band *them* together *or* get *them* into one place *or* get *them* into a team; **tsèw-'dwèr** to pair off.

    As mainV: **'tsèw-shàng** to gather up more; **'tsèw-chū-lay** to get together and contribute money for a fund. ‖**wǒm-dà-'jyā hé-dzày yì-'chǐ; 'tsèw-shàng shŕ-'èr-ge-rén jyèw 'gèw-le.** Let's all get together; if we can get twelve of us that will be enough.

湊合

'tsèw-he, 'tsèw-hu, 'tsèw-hwo (*H*) getting along with materials or situations inferior to those desired. ‖**chǐng-ni 'tsèw-he-tsèw-he jù-dzay 'jèr-ba.** Try to be contented with staying here for now.

    tsèw-he-'shŕ patchwork that serves in place of a thorough job; *as a sentence means more or less* Don't compliment us too much; we're just putting things together as best we can for the emergency; in time we may be able to do a really good job, but not right now.

tso *Wade Romanization for* **dzwo.**

ts'o *Wade Romanization for* **tswo.**

tsou *Wade Romanization for* **dzew.**

ts'ou *Wade Romanization for* **tsew.**

tsu *Wade Romanization for* **dzu.**

ts'u *Wade Romanization for* **tsu.**

粗

tsū (*A*) rough, roughly built; rough-surfaced; rough, vulgar (*of a person*).

粗野

tsū-'yě (*A*) coarse and vulgar, unrefined, (*of a person*).

tsuan *Wade Romanization for* **dzwan.**

ts'uan *Wade Romanization for* **tswan.**

tsui *Wade Romanization for* **dzwey.**

ts'ui *Wade Romanization for* **tswey.**

tsun *Wade Romanization for* **dzwen.**

ts'un *Wade Romanization for* **tswen.**

tsung *Wade Romanization for* **dzung.**

ts'ung *Wade Romanization for* **tsung.**

葱

tsūng (*Nunit*, **kē**, **gēr**) green onion. yáng-'tsūng the round (western-type) onion. tsūng-hwār-'bǐng kind of fried cake with onion in it.

聰明

'tsūng-ming (*A*) clever, intelligent, smart, bright, brilliant.

從

tsúng (*K*) *marks point in time or space from which, or from the direction of which, or through and past which, motion or development takes place:* (1) *place from which:* ‖tā tsúng 'měy-gwo láy-de. He's from the United States.

(2) *Direction from which:* ‖jèy-tyáw-tyě-'lù tsúng-'dūng dàw-'shī. This railroad goes from east to west.

(3) *Place through or past which:* ‖tām tsúng 'chyáw-dǐ-shya 'gwò-láy-de. They came under the bridge.

(4) *Time from which:* tsúng 'lyǎng-dyǎn dàw 'sz̀-dyǎn from two o'clock to four o'clock.

(5) *(Figuratively)* tsúng 'dà-tǐ-shang 'kàn looking at it from a general viewpoint.

(6) *These set phrases are related to 4 and 5:* tsúng-'téwr dàw-'lyǎwr *or* tsúng-'téwr dàw-'wěy *or* tsúng-'téwr dàw 'mwò-lyǎwr from beginning to end; tsúng 'chǐ-téwr *or* tsúng 'chǐ-chū from the beginning and continually thereafter down to now.

(7) tsúng . . . 'chǐ starting with . . . *or* start from . . ., *is usually temporal, but not always:* ‖tsúng-'téwr chǐ ('kàn). Start (reading) from the beginning. ‖tsúng 'míng-tyan 'chǐ, bù-'shywǔ dzày-'jèr chēw-'yān. Beginning tomorrow there'll be no smoking here.

(8) tsúng-'jūng from inside from behind the scenes, (*usually figurative*) ; from among them.

(9) *Distinguish between* tsúng *and* lí, *the latter meaning* from *in stating distances, not motions.*

從

tsúng (*V*) to obey, follow obediently (*a bit literary*). ‖byé 'máng tsúng. Don't just obey someone else blindly.

從前

tsúng-'chyán (*J*) formerly (*in contrast to now*). ‖tsúng-'chyán nǐ 'nème shwō, shyàn-dzày nǐ 'jème shwō. You used to say that, now you say this.

從來

tsúng-'láy (*J*) customarily in the past. ‖tā 'tsúng-láy jyèw méy-hǎw-'hāwr-de nyàn-'shū. He's never been accustomed to studying very hard. ‖tā tsúng-'láy jyèw jù-'jèr. He's always lived here.

從事

tsúng-'shr̀ (*V*) to devote oneself wholeheartedly and exclusively to. tsúng-'shr̀ gé-'mìng to throw oneself heart and soul into the cause of the revolution.

躥

tswān (*I*) to make a leap or spurt. *Usually as mainV:* 'tswān-shàng-chywù to leap or spurt upwards; 'tswān-gwò-chywù to leap up and over *or* across. ‖chyáng-'dzěr tsúng tā-de-'shēn-shang 'tswān-gwò-chywù-le. The bullet went through his body. ‖shyǎw-'māwr 'tswān-shang 'shù-le. The cat sprang up into the tree.

村

*tswēn, 'tswēn-dz, tswēr (*Nunit*, ge) village, rural settlement. tswēn-'jǎng village chief, village head man. tswēn-'jwāng (*Nunit*, ge) the houses comprising a village.

存

tswén (*V*) to deposit *money*, check *baggage, clothes*; to store *something*. *As mainV:* 'tswén-chǐ-láy to store away, *etc.*; 'tswén-dzày to store *something* at *a place*, *or*, to continue to exist, continue to be alive. ‖bǎ wǒ-men-de-'chyán tswén-dzay yín-'háng-lǐ-tew. Deposit our money in the bank. ‖tā bǎ tā-de-bǎw-'gwèy-de-dūng-shi dēw 'tswén-chi-lay-le. She stored away all her valuables.

寸

tswèn (*Mmeas*) a unit of length. See Appendix B.

催

tswēy (*V*) to drive on, urge on *always literal, of motion*. ‖nǐ byé 'tswēy-wo! Don't rush me!

As mainV: tswēy-'dzěw-le to rush *someone* away; *etc.*

唾

tswèy (*V*) to spit. tswèy-'tán to spit up phlegm; tswèy 'tù-mwo to spit out saliva. *As mainV:* 'tswèy-chu-lay to spit *something* out.

搓

tswō (*V*) to rub *with a twisting motion of the hand*. tswō-'shěw to rub the hands together, *as in washing them*; yùng-'yéw tswō-'bèy to rub oil into the back with the hands; tswō-'myàn to knead dough; tswō-'shyàn to twist cotton *by hand* into a thread. *As mainV:* tswō-chéng (yí-ge-'tyáwr) to rub and twist into (a long strip); 'tswō-dzày to rub something on something.

錯

tswò (*A*) be wrong, make mistakes. tswò-'lù wrong road; tswò-'jyě misinterpretation, wrong explanation;

tswò-'shř *or* 'tswò-chù *or* tswò-'wù *or* tswèr mistakes. ‖'jèy-jyàn-shř-ching shř 'nǐ dzwò 'tswò-le. It was you who did this thing wrong.

As mainV: ‖wǒ bǎ 'jī-hwèy "tswò-gwò-chywù-le. I missed my opportunity.

辭
tsź (*V*) to quit, resign. tsź-'jŕ *or* tsź-'shř to resign one's job, quit one's job.

詞
tsź (*Nunit,* shěw) Chinese verse of a certain style. tyán-'tsź to compose such verses. *In the tsź style not only the number of syllables (characters), but also the sequence of tones in each line and in each group of lines, is fixed.*

磁（器）
tsź (*Nmass*) porcelain. tsź-'chì (*Nunit,* jyàn, ge) porcelain ware, china.

慈
tsź (*A*) motherly, kind, sympathetic (*literary*).

辭呈
'tsź-chéng (*Nunit,* jāng) resignation (*document*). ‖tā bǎ 'tsź-chéng 'dì-shang-chywù-le. He handed in his resignation.

慈善
'tsź-'shàn (*A*) charitable, inclined to charity. tsź-'shàn-jī-'gwān charitable organization.

辭行
tsź-'shíng (*I*) to say goodbye *to someone staying behind.* ‖wǒ dàw-'nàr chywù gēn-ta tsź-'shíng. I'm going over there to say goodbye to him.

磁實
'tsź-shr (*A*) solid, firm, strong. (*of things*).

辭謝
tsź-'shyè (*I*) to decline with thanks.

此
tsž (literary) this; here. ‖tsž-'lù bù-'tūng. This road is closed.

The following combinations are not literary: tsž-'hèw (*J*) from now on, after this; tsž-'wày (*J*) besides this, in addition to this.

次
tsž (*Preord*) the next. *Limited: most common in* 'tsž-(yì-)děng-de next lower in quality *or* next to the highest in quality *or* of poor quality.

(*A*) inferior. ‖jèy-ge-tsáy-'lyàw hěn 'tsž. This material is quite inferior in quality.

次
tsž (*Msemel*) time, occurrence.

(1) *As designation of frequency after verb:* ‖wǒ 'dzwó-tyān chywù 'kàn-ta sān-'tsž, tā dēw bú-dzày-'jyā. I went to see him three times yesterday, but he wasn't home.

(2) *As designation of frequency after verb and before noun:* dǎ yí-tsž-dyàn-'hwà to telephone once; dǎ yí-tsž-'chyéw play ball once; kàn 'sān-tsž-dyàn-'yěngr go to the movies three times.

(3) *Similarly before verb plus noun, nominalizing the whole expression:* 'nèy-tsž-chū-'shř an accident (*literally* that occurrence have an accident).

With Demord: 'shàng-tsž, shàng-'lyǎng-tsž last time, last two times; 'shyà-tsž, 'shyà-lyǎng-tsž next time, next two times.

刺（兒）
tsž, tsèr (*Nunit,* gēr) splinter, sliver; fishbone. ywú-'tsž fishbone; mù-'tsèr wood splinter.

tsž (V) to stab. tsž-'dāw bayonet; tsž-'kè an assassin.

tsž-'yǎn (*VN1, A*) stabs the eyes, *thus* sharp, harsh, bright (*of a color or light*); tsž 'ěr-dwo (*VN1, A*) stabs the ears, *thus* harsh, blaring (*of a sound*); tsž-'gǔ (*VN1, A*) stabs through the bones, *thus* biting (*of cold or of hate; a bit literary*).

賜給
'tsž-gěy (*RC4*) to grant *someone something* (*literary*).

伺候
'tsž-hèw *or* 'sž-hèw (*or* 'shř-hèw) to wait on, serve people (*as in a restaurant*). ‖'wèy-shéme méy-yew 'chá-fang 'tsž-hew wǒ-men-ne? How come there isn't any waiter here to serve us?

次序
'tsž-shywù (*Nabstr*) scheduled order of events, proper order, proper procedure. àn 'tsž-shywù in proper sequence, in order.

tu *Wade Romanization for* du.

t'u *Wade Romanization for* tu.

脫落
tū-lu (1) (*V*) to drag on. ‖'yī-fu tày 'cháng-le, tū-lu 'dì-shang-le. The dress is too long; it's dragging on the floor.

(2) (*I*) to fray. ‖yī-fu-'byār 'tū-lu-le. The edge of the dress is fraying.

(3) tū-lu 'dzwěy (*VN1*) to make a slip while speaking. ‖tā 'shwō tū-lu 'dzwěy-le. He made a slip.

(4) (*I*) to lose one's grip. ‖wǒ 'jwày tū-lu (shěw)-le, 'shwāy-shyà-chywù-le. I lost my grip and fell down.

圖

tú (*Nunit*, **jāng**) chart, map, diagram, picture, illustration. **hwà-'tú** to draw a map, diagram, chart. **dì-'tú** map; **tú-'shū** maps, books, documents; **tú-shū-'gwǎn** library.

塗

*tú (*V*) to etch in, shade in. *Used as mainV:* **'tú-chéng** to paint *something* into *something:* **bǎ báy-de-'dž 'tú-chéng 'hēy-dž** paint the white characters black; **tú-'hēy-le** (**tú-'húng-le,** *etc.*) to paint *something* black (red, *etc.*)**;** **'tú-shàng** to fill in *an outline with some color:* **tú-shang mwò-'shwěr** to ink in; **'tú-chywù** or **tú-'dzěw** to ink out, to paint out, *some part of something which isn't wanted in the final picture;* **tú-'yín** to paint a silver color.

圖案

tú-'àn (*Nunit*, **jāng**) drawings, designs, plans, *usually made with straight sharp lines.* **tú-àn-'hwàr** design drawing, *as a type of art distinct from pictorial drawing.*

徒步

tú-'bù (*H*) on foot (*a bit literary*). **tú-'bù lywǔ-'shíng** to make a journey on foot.

屠夫

tú-'fū (*Npers*) butcher (*a bit literary*).

屠戶

tú-'hù (*Npers*) butcher (*a bit literary*).

圖章

tú-'jāng (*Nunit*, **ge**) personal seal. **dǎ tú-'jāng** to stamp one's personal seal on *a document.*

徒刑

tú-'shíng (*N*) prison term. **yì-nyán-tú-'shíng** prison term of one year. **'pàn-ta 'wǔ-nyán-tú-'shíng-de-'dzwèy** impose a five year prison sentence on him.

土

tǔ (*Nmass*) earth, dirt, soil, clay.

  tǔ-'rǎng soil *agriculturally speaking:* ‖**jèr-de-tǔ-'rǎng-chū-de-dàw-'mi bù-hěn 'hǎw.** The soil around here doesn't produce very good or very much rice.

  tǔ-'dèwr (*Nunit*, **ge**) potatoes; **tǔ-'dàw** or **tǔ-'lù** dirt road.

  In some combinations means of a certain rural locality: **'tǔ-rén** rustics, natives; **tǔ-'yīn** rural or rustic accent; **tǔ-'fěy** bandits.

吐

tǔ, tù (*V*) to spew forth, spit out, vomit out (*almost always from the mouth*). *As mainV:* **'tǔ-dzày** to spit *something* out at *a place;* etc. ‖**tā bǎ-'tsž 'tǔ-chū-lay-le.** He spat out the fish bones.

土耳其（圖）

tǔ-ěr-'chí(-gwó) (*Nunique*) Turkey.

吐痰

tǔ-'tán (*VN2*) to cough up phlegm.

兔（子，兒）

'tù(-dz), tùr (*Nunit*, **ge, jř**) rabbit.

吐沫

'tù-mey, 'tù-me, 'tù-mwo, 'twò-mey, 'twò-me, 'twò-mwo (*Nmass*) saliva. **tswèy** (or **tù** or **tǔ**) **'tù-mey** to spit.

突然

tù-rán (*J*) very suddenly and unexpectedly.

tuan *Wade Romanization for* **dwan.**

t'uan *Wade Romanization for* **twan.**

tui *Wade Romanization for* **dwey.**

t'ui *Wade Romanization for* **twey.**

tun *Wade Romanization for* **dwen.**

t'un *Wade Romanization for* **twen.**

tung *Wade Romanization for* **dung.**

t'ung *Wade Romanization for* **tung.**

通

tūng (*I*) to pass through. *Usually with agent or undergoer:* **tūng-'chē** to be open to traffic, *or* be accessible by train; **tūng-'shìn** to correspond by mail; **tūng 'shyāw-shi** to keep in touch, be reached by communications; **tūng dyàn-'hwà** to put through a phone call, make a phone call; **tūng-'chì** or **tūng-'fēng** to permit the passage of air, to leak air. ‖**jèy-tyáw-'lù 'tūng-le.** This road is open to traffic. ‖**nèy-ge-'tswēn-dz tūng hwǒ-'chē-ma?** Is that village reached by the railroad?

  'tūng-dàw (*RC3*) to reach to, extend to. ‖**hwǒ-'chē tūng-daw nèy-ge-'tswēn-dz-ma?** Does the railroad get to the village?

  'tūng-gwò (*RC3*) to reach past, go through. ‖**hwǒ-'chē 'tūng-gwò nèy-ge-'tswēn-dz.** The railroad goes through and beyond the village. *Or.* to be passed, *of a proposition voted on in a meeting.* ‖**nèy-ge-yì-'àn 'tūng-gwò-le shyà-yī-'ywàn.** That bill has been passed by Congress.

  As postV: **nyàn-'tūng-le** to study and understand thoroughly.

通

tūng (*A*) versed in the Chinese classics; well-read *in some other language if so specified.* ǁ**jèy-ge-'rén 'yīng-wén hěn 'tūng.** He's well-read in English literature.

通告

tūng-'gàw (*V*) to announce. ǁ**tūng-·gàw dà-'jyā 'bā-dyǎn-jūng (yàw) kāy-'hwèy.** Announce to everybody that the meeting will be at eight o'clock.

    (*Nunit,* **jāng, ge**) announcement, bulletin, notice. **fā tūng-'gàw** to send out announcements; **tyē tūng-'gàw** to post a notice.

通知

'tūng-jr̄ (*V*) to inform, let know, notify. ǁ**nǐ 'shéme-shŕ-hew dzěw, 'tūng-jr wo yì-shēngr.** Let me know when you go.

    (*Nunit,* **ge**) notice. **fā 'tūng-jr̄** send out notices.

通票

tūng-'pyàw (*Nunit,* **jāng**) through ticket.

通信處

tūng-shìn-'chù (*Nunit,* **ge**) mailing address.

通行

tūng-'shíng (*A*) open to traffic (*as of a road, pass, frontier*); current and accepted (*as of currency*). ǁ**nèy-ge-jyāw-'jyè-de-dì-fang yèw tūng-'shíng-le.** That boundary point is open to traffic. ǁ**má-'jyàng dzày 'jūng-gwo hěn tūng-'shíng.** Mah-jong is quite fashionable in China.

通行證

tūng-shíng-'jèng (*Nunit,* **jāng**) pass (*permit to enter or exit*).

通通的，統統的

tūng-'tūng-de (*H*) thoroughly, completely. ǁ**tā tūng-'tūng-de dēw ná-'dzěw-le.** He took away absolutely everything.

同

túng (*K*) with, and (*same as* **hé, gēn**). **bù-'túng** (*A*) not the same, different. ǁ**wǒ-de-'yì-jyàn gēn 'nǐ-de bù-'túng.** Our ideas aren't the same. (**túng** *is not used as an A.*)

    yì-'túng (*H*) together, in a single group. ǁ**wǒm yì-'túng 'chywù-ba.** Let's go there together.

銅

túng (*Nmass*) brass; *also generic term for the various copper alloys.* **túng-'bǎn** (*Nunit,* **kwày, pyàn**) copper plate *or* (*Nunit,* **ge**) a copper (*small coin*); **túng-'byār** copper lining; **túng-'sz̄** *or* **túng-'sēr** copper wire;

túng-'shyàng bronze statue; **túng-'dzěr** a copper (*small coin*).

同

****túng** *plus a term designating a group, plus or minus* **de**, *specifies* co-members of the group. **túng-'dǎng(-de)** members of a single political party or faction, co-workers, comrades; **túng-'yè(-de)** colleagues in a profession; **túng-'lèy(-de)** birds of a feather (*good or bad*); **túng-'shywé(-de)** fellow students, classmates; **túng-'bān(-de)** classmates.

同病相憐

túng-'bìng shyāng-'lyán (*literary quotation*) to have sympathy for other people's difficulties because you have the same difficulties yourself; to be in the same boat.

同情

'túng-chíng (*A*) sympathetic; (*V*) be sympathetic to. **gēn ... byǎw 'túng-chíng** to show sympathy for *so-and-so.* ǁ**wǒ 'túng-chíng ni.** I'm on your side. *or* I feel for you.

童子軍

túng-dž-'jywūn (*Npers*) boy scout.

童工

túng-'gūng (*Nabstr*) child labor. **túng-gūng-'fǎ** Child Labor Law.

潼關

túng-'gwān (*Nunique*) T'ung-kuan *or* Tungkwan (*city in Shensi province*).

同盟國

túng-méng-'gwó (*Nunit,* **ge**) ally; allied countries.

同謀犯

túng-méw-'fàn (*Npers*) accomplice, partner in crime.

同人

'túng-rén (*Ncoll*) equals, *one's* peers, *one's* colleagues.

銅山

túng-'shān (*Nunique*) T'ung-shan (*city in Kiangsu province*).

同時

túng-'shŕ (*H*) at the same time. ǁ**tām-'lyǎ túng-'shŕ 'láy-de.** The two of them arrived at the same time. (*J*) and yet, but at the same time. ǁ**nǐ bù-'shǐ-hwan nèy-ge-'rén, kě-shr túng-'shŕ ni yèw shwō tā hěn 'hǎw!** You don't like that fellow, and yet (at the same time) you say he's OK!

同樣

túng-'yàng (*A*) same. ǁ**jèy-shyē-·shū dēw-shr túng-'yàng-de.** These books are all the same.

同意
túng-'yì (A) to be of one mind, agree.

通
tǔng (V) to poke at, poke into, *with a rod-shaped object.* yùng 'gwèn-dz tǔng-'hwǒ poke the fire with a
stick; yùng-'gwèn-dz tǔng yí-ge-'kū-lùng poke open a
hole with a stick. ‖tā yùng shěw-'jř-tew tǔng-wo yí-
shyàr. He poked me with his fingers.
    As mainV: 'tǔng-jìn-chywu to poke in;. 'tǔng-chū-
chywù to poke out; *etc.*

桶 , 筒 , (子 , 兒)
'tǔng(-dz), tǔngr (NunitC, ge) barrel, keg, drum, tank.
yì-'tǔng-dz-'pí-jyěw barrel of beer.

統計
tǔng-'jì (Nabstr) statistics. tǔng-jì-'shywé statistical
theory, statistics *as a science.*

統制
'tǔng-jř (V) to control, dominate, *politically, socially,
economically.* ‖yéw-jèng-'jywú, dyàn-hwà-'jywú, tyě-
lù-'jywú, 'děng-děng, yéw 'jèng-fǔ 'tǔng-jř. The post
office, the telephone system, the railroad system, etc.,
are all controlled by the government.

統一
tǔng-'yī (V) to unite. tǔng-'yī 'jūng-gwo to unite
China. tǔng-'yī ywǔ-'yán to bring about uniformity
of speech, *eliminating dialect differences.*

痛
tùng (A) hurt, ache, have a pain; *used like téng in this
sense only.*

痛苦
tùng-'kǔ (A) suffering, in pain, *(rather mental than
physical).* ‖tā ‘dyěw-le 'shř yǐ-'hèw, tā 'jywé-de hěn
'tùng-kǔ. Since he lost his job he's felt pretty low.

痛快
'tùng-kwày (A) comfortable, refreshed, happy; frank,
outspoken. tùng-tung-kwày-'kwār-de wár yì-'wǎn-
shang to make a night of it, throw cares to the wind
and celebrate all evening.

團體
twán-'tǐ (Nunit, ge) group, organization, united body.
'chīng-nyán-twán-'tǐ young people's organization.

推
twēy (V) to push; to push *someone into prominence,* to
elect, to select; to push *responsibility away,* to shirk,

to evade; to push *a clipper or lawnmower,* to clip, to
mow. twēy-'chē to push a car along; twēy-'tā dzwò
jǔ-'shí elect him chairman; twēy 'dzé-rèn to shirk
duty; twēy-'tsǎw to cut the grass with a lawnmower;
twēy-'téw to clip the hair.
    *As mainV: combinations may have meanings stem-
ming from any of the above, only some of them being
given here:* 'twēy-dàw (lc) push *something to a place;*
twēy-'dùng get something moving by pushing it, *or*
get oneself moving, get going, get a move on; 'twēy-
gěy shift *blame onto someone;* 'twēy-jìn (lc) to push
something into a place; etc. ‖tā bǎ 'shíng-li 'twēy-jìn
chē-'jàn chywù-le. He pushed the luggage (*on a cart*)
into the station. ‖bǎ 'chwāng-hu twēy-'kāy. Push the
window open. ‖shyàng-'shàng twēy. Push upwards.
‖byé bǎ 'dzé-rèn 'twēy-gey 'tā. Don't pass the buck
to him.

推戴
twēy-'dày (Vsent) to support, back, be in favor of so-
and-so to do something. ‖rén-'ɪ.ín twēy-'dày tā dzwò
dzǔng-'tǔng. The people were in favor of having
him as president.

推子
'twēy-dz (Nunit, ge, bǎ) clippers (*barber's*).

推廣
twēy-'gwǎng (V) to expand *business (a bit literary).*

推銷
twēy-'shyāw (V) to promote the sales of. twēy-shyāw-
'ywán salesman.

推測
twēy-'tsè (Vsent) to predict that; (V) to predict *a situation.*

推諉
twēy-'wěy (I) to make excuses; (Vsent) to make excuses for the fact that. ‖tā twēy-'wěy bù-kěn 'láy.
He made excuses for not coming.

腿 (兒)
twěy, twěr (Nunit, tyáw) legs. jwō-'twěy or jwō-'twěr
table legs; *etc.*
    twěy-'jyǎwr 'lì-le have legs and feet in good work-
ing order, to get around well (*of an old person*).

退
twèy (I) to withdraw, retire, move back, give way, retreat. twèy-'sè, twèy-'shǎr (IN) the color fades;
runs. ‖yī-fu dēw twèy-'shǎr-le. The color has all faded
in the dress. *As mainV:* 'twèy-chū (lc) to back out,

withdraw; **'twèy-jìn** (*lc*) to back in; **'twèy-shyà-chywù** to back down; **'twèy-hwéy** (*lc*) to go back backwards, *or* to reject and return *goods not wanted; etc.* ‖**tā bă-·chē tsúng chē-'fáng-li 'twèy-chu-lay-le.** He backed his car out of the garage. ‖**jèy-ge-jywūn-'dwèy tsúng hé-'àn twèy-'dzěw-le.** The troops retreated from the river bank. ‖**nǐ bù-'shǐ-hwan ta, nǐ jyèw 'twèy-hwéy-chywu.** If you don't like it, send it back.

退讓
twèy-'ràng (*I*) to give in courteously. ‖**nǐ bù-néng 'lǎw twèy-'ràng.** You can't ALWAYS be giving in.

脫
twō (*I*) come off (*of something that covers a surface; usually with agent or undergoer*). **twō 'yī-fu** to take off clothing; **twō 'màw(-dz)** to take off one's hat; *similarly with any garment that covers part of the surface* (*thus not a belt*); **twō 'téw-fa** to lose hair; **twō-'pí** to shed a skin.
     As mainV: **'twō-shyà** (*lc*) to take off *a garment, etc.* ‖**'cháng-chung twō-'pí-le.** The snake shed its skin. ‖**tā-de-'téw-fa 'twō-le.** His hair is falling out. ‖**bă nǐ-de-dà-'yī 'twō-shyà-lay.** Take off your coat.

拖
twō (*I*) to drag along (*on the ground, or, in time*). ‖**jèy-jyàn-'shř-ching yèw 'twō-le 'lyǎng-tyān.** This matter has been delayed again a couple of days. *As mainV:* ‖**tā-de-cháng-'chywún-dz 'twō-dzay 'dì-shya.** Her long skirt is dragging on the floor.

託，托
twō (*V*) to lift, hold, carry, on the palm *or* palms held in front of one and upward; (*V, Vsent*) *figuratively* to ask for *a favor. As mainV:* **'twō-dàw** (*lc*) to carry *thus* to *a place;* **'twō-chǐ-lay** to lift *something* up *thus; etc.* ‖**nèy-ge-'hwǒ-ji bă 'pán-dz 'twō-jìn-chywu-le.** The waiter carried the tray in. ‖**wǒ 'twō-ta 'jàw-yìng wǒ-de-'dì-di.** I entreated him to care for my little brother.

托付
'twō-fu (*V, Vsent*) to entrust *someone* with *something or* with *doing something.*

託福
‖**'twō-fú!** (*or said twice*) I'm fine, thanks! (*Very polite and high-toned answer to a greeting, implying that one is well because of the benign influence of the person spoken to.*)

脫離
twō-'lí (*V*) to break off from, break away from, break off. ‖**wǒ gēn tā-men twō-'lí 'gwān-shì.** I'm breaking relations with them. ‖**wǒ 'dzwó-tyan gāng twō-'lí-le 'wéy-shyǎn.** I just got out of danger yesterday.

拖延下去
twō-'yán-shyà-chywu (*RC2*) to delay, put off. ‖**jàw 'jè-yàngr-twō-'yán-shyà-chywu, kǔng-'pà dzwò-bu-'wán-le.** With this kind of procrastination I'm afraid we'll never get the job done.

馱
twó (*V*) to carry on the back (*of an animal, not a human*). *As mainV:* **'twó-dàw** (*lc*) to carry to *a place; etc.* ‖**nèy-téw-'lywú twó-le lyǎng-'kwāng-de-'tsày.** The donkey has two baskets of vegetables on his back. ‖**yùng-'lywú bă-'tsày twó-daw 'shř-shang.** Take the vegetables to market on the donkey's back.

妥
twǒ (*postV*) satisfactory, OK. **bàn-'twǒ-le** to manage *something* successfully; **shyǎng-'twǒ-le** to think about and reach a satisfactory decision about; *etc.* ‖**nǐ 'yàw bù-bāng-'máng, jèy-jyàn-'shř-ching bàn-bu-'twǒ.** If you don't help, this thing can't be done right.

妥當
twǒ-'dàng (*A*) reliable and correct, (*of organization, person, affairs*). ‖**jèy-jyàn-'shř-ching 'bàn-de hěn twǒ-'dàng.** This matter has been taken care of quite accurately and reliably.

妥靠的
twǒ-'kàw-de (*A*) reliable, dependable, (*of a person*).

吐沫
'twò-mey, 'twò-me, 'twò-mwo *see* **'tù-mey.**

添
tyān (*V*) to obtain additional *personnel, money, funds, office space, etc.* ‖**wǒm jèr 'háy děy tyān-'rén.** We still have to get some more people here.

天
tyān (1) (*Nunique*) sky, heaven. **'tyān-shya** *or* **tyān-'dǐ-shya** everywhere under heaven, everywhere; **shàng-'tyān** to go to heaven; **'fēy-shang 'tyān (chywù)** to fly up *into the sky.* ‖**'tyān jř-daw!** Heaven only knows!
     (2) *Used in stating temperature or conditions of light in the sky; see* **'tyān-chì.**
     (3) (*Mtime*) day. **'jīn-tyan** today; **'dzwó-tyan** yesterday; **'míng-tyan** tomorrow; **'nèy-tyan** that day; **'sān-tyan** three days; **'tyān-tyan** *or* **'měy-tyān** every day, each day.

天邊
tyān-'byăr (*Nplace*) horizon; far-away place. ‖**tā 'dzěw-dàw tyān-'byăr chywù-le.** He's gone far away. *or* He's gone to the ends of the earth.

天氣，天兒
'tyān-chì, tyār (*Nabstr*) weather. *In stating tempera- ture, either of these or just* tyān *is used:* ‖'tyān-chì (*or* 'tyār *or* 'tyān) hěn 'lěng. It's quite cold. *Stating ap- proval or disapproval of the weather, or describing it in other such terms, also, any of the three forms is used:* ‖'tyān-chì hěn 'hǎw. It's nice weather. ‖'tyān hěn 'hǎw. It's a nice day. *Stating conditions of light in the sky, only* tyān *is used:* ‖tyān kwày 'hēy-le. It's getting dark.

天旱
tyān 'hàn (*N plus A*) there is a drought. ‖tyān 'dà hàn. There's a serious drought. ‖tyān 'hàn-le bàn-'nyán-le. There's been a drought for six months. ‖'jèy-ge-dì- fang (tyān) 'hàn. There's a drought here.

天眞
tyān-'jēn (*A*) natural, unaffected, (*of a person or his behavior*).

天津
'tyān-jīng (*Nunique*) T'ien-ching *or* Tientsin (*city in Hopeh province*)..

天井
tyān-'jǐng (*Nunit, ge*) courtyard in a compound.

天主
'tyān-'jǔ (*Nunique*) God (*Catholic term*). tyān-jǔ-'jyàw the Catholic Church; tyān-jǔ-(jyàw-)'táng a Catholic church (building).

天藍 [色（兒）]
tyān-'lán (*A*); tyān-lán-'sè, tyān-lán-'shǎr (*Nabstr*) sky blue.

天秤
tyān-'píng (*Nunit, ge*) balance, scales, *with two trays hanging from a beam.*

天然
tyān-'rán (*A*) natural, untouched, not artificial. tyān- 'rán-de-fēng-'jǐng beauties of nature.

天生
tyān-'shēng (*Aattr*) inborn, natural.

天使
tyān-'shř (*Npers*) angel (*Christian term*).

天線
tyān-'shyàn (*Nunit, tyáw, gēr*) aerial, antenna.

天才
'tyān-tsáy (*Nabstr*) genius, talent. ‖tā yěw 'tyān-tsáy. He has talent.

天文
'tyān-wén (*Nabstr*) astronomy. 'tyān-wén-shywé the science of astronomy.

塡
tyán (*V*) to fill in and close up *a ditch, a gap;* to fill out *a form;* to stuff *a duck for slaughter. As mainV:* 'tyán-jìn-chywu *with same meaning;* tyán-'mǎn-le to fill full; 'tyán-shang *or* 'tyán-chi-lay to fill up and close. ‖bǎ nèy-ge-'gōw 'tyán-chi-lay. Fill in that ditch. ‖bǎ-'byǎw gěy 'tyán-shang. Fill in this form.

田
tyán (*Nmass; kwày*) field, cultivated land (*not garden, orchard*). 'mày-tyán wheat field; 'dàw-tyán *or* shwěy- 'tyán rice paddy; tyán-'dì fields, farm land.

甜
tyán (*A*) sweet to the taste. tyán-'tsày beets. ‖wǔ- 'wèy, jyèw-shr 'tyán, 'swān, 'kǔ, 'là, 'shyán. There are five tastes: sweet, sour, bitter, peppery, and salty.

挑
tyāw (*V*) to choose, select, pick out. tyāw-'byār choose sides; tyāw-'tswèr *or* tyāw-'yǎn to find fault, pick out errors. *As mainV:* 'tyāw-chū-lay *with same meaning.* ‖nǐ 'tyāw nǐ-'shǐ-hwan-de-'shū 'nyàn. Choose what- ever book you'd like to read.

挑
tyāw (*V*) to pick up, carry, take, bring, *on a pole sup- ported on the shoulder or slung from the shoulders of two people.* 'tyāw-dz (*Nunit, ge*) carrying pole with baskets hung from the two ends; tyāw-'tyāwr-de(-rén) (*Npers*) peddler who carries his goods thus. *As mainV:* tyāw-'píng-le to balance on the shoulder; tyāw- 'dzěw-le to carry something off *thus;* 'tyāw-chi-lay to lift up *thus; etc.* ‖tā 'tyāw-le 'lyǎng-kwāng-de-báy- 'tsày shàng-'shř chywù 'mày. He was carrying two baskets of celery cabbage on a pole slung over his shoulder, taking them to market to sell.

挑剔
'tyāw-tì (*A*) choosy, particular; (*V*) find fault with *someone.*

條
tyáw (*Munit*) *for things with extension primarily in one direction:* a length of 'shéng-dz (*rope*); a twěy (*leg*); a length of 'gwǎn-dz (*pipe*); a 'chúng-dz (*worm*); a 'kù-dz (*pair of trousers*); a 'dày-dz (*belt*); a shěw- 'jywàr (*handkerchief*); a tyě-'lù (*railroad*); a jyē (*street*); a 'dàw(r) *or* 'lù (*road*); a 'hú-tùngr (*alley or lane*).

An article or section of a legal document. fǎ-'àn- dì-'yì-tyáw article one of the law.

'tyáw-tyáw yěw-'lǐ taken section by section it makes sense, *therefore* logical, well reasoned out.

條（子，兒）

'tyáw(-dz), tyáwr (*Nunit, ge*) (1) brief note, short message.
    (2) Band, stripe, strip, line, *as in decoration*.

調羹

tyáw-'gēng (*Nunit, bǎ*) spoon.

條件

tyáw-'jyàn (*Nunit, ge*) terms, conditions, (*as for a surrender or an agreement*).

條款

tyáw-'kwǎn (*Nunit, tyáw*) article in a treaty *or other document*.

笤箒

'tyáw-shu (*Nunit, bǎ*) broom.

調停

'tyáw-tíng (*V*) to act as an intermediary in the settlement of *difficulties*. ‖pày-ta chywù 'tyáw-tíng láw-'dž-'jyēw-fen-de-'shr̀-ching. Appoint him to arbitrate the labor dispute.

條約

tyáw-'ywē (*Nunit, ge*) treaty.

挑撥

tyǎw-'bwó (*V*) to carry tales back and forth between two parties and thus break up their friendship. ‖tām-'lyǎng-ge-rén bèy-rén tyǎw-'bwó, dǎ-chi 'jyà-lay-le. Those two were split up by someone and have started to quarrel.

挑撥是非

tyǎw-'bwó shr̀-'fēy (*I*) to come between people and set them against each other.

跳

tyàw (*I*) to jump; (*of the heart*) to beat. tyàw-'hé to commit suicide by jumping in the river. *As mainV*: 'tyàw-chì-lay to jump up; to bounce; 'tyàw-dàw (*lc*) to jump to; 'tyàw-gwò (*lc*) to jump over, across; 'tyàw-shàng (*lc*) to jump up, jump on; 'tyàw-hwéy (*lc*) to jump back, bounce back. ‖yí 'tyàw, tyàw-gwo 'hé-lay-le. He jumped across the river in one bound.

跳板

tyàw-'bǎn (*Nunit, kwày*) diving board; gangplank.

跳舞

tyàw-'wǔ (*I*) to dance. tyàw-wǔ-'hwèy a dance; tyàw-wǔ-'tīng ballroom; tyàw-wǔ-'chǎng dance hall, cabaret.

貼

tyē (*V*) to stick to, paste something onto. tyē-'tí stick to the subject, be relevant. *As mainV*: 'tyē-dàw *or* 'tyē-dzày make *something* stick to *something*. ‖bǎ bù-'gàw tyē-dzay 'chyáng-shang. Post the announcement on the wall. ‖tā tyē-je 'chyáng 'jàn-je. He's standing close to the wall.

帖（子，兒）

'tyē(-dz), 'tyě(-dz), tyěr (*Nunit, jāng*) announcement card, invitation card; label (*on a box, etc.*).

鐵

tyě (*Nmass*) iron. 'tyě-jyang blacksmith; tyě-'kwàng iron mine; tyě-'sz *or* tyě-'sēr *or* tyě-'shyàn iron wire; tyě-sz-'wǎng wire fence; tyě-'shā iron wire screen; tyě-'shéng-dz iron cable; tyě-'tyáw iron band, iron rod. 'tyě-de-'shr̀-shŕ the real facts in the case, as solid and immovable as iron.

鐵板

tyě-'bǎn (*Nmass, kwày*) sheet iron.

鐵軌

tyě-'gwěy (*Nunit, tyáw*) iron rail, railroad rail.

鐵甲

tyě-'jyǎ (*Nmass; fù, tàw* a complement of) armor, armor plate.

鐵架（子）

tyě-'jyà(-dz) (*Nunit, ge; fù, dwèy for* a set of) andirons.

鐵路

tyě-'lù (*Nunit, tyáw*) railroad. tyě-lù-'jywú railroad administrative office *or* railroad bureau (*part of government in China*).

tzu *Wade Romanization for* dz.

tz'u *Wade Romanization for* tsz.

W

哇
wā see a.

哇
wā (*I*) to vomit. **'wā yì-shēng** to make the sound of vomiting suddenly. *As mainV:* **'wā-chū-lay** to vomit forth.

挖
wā (*V*) to dig *something* up, excavate *something*, gouge *something* out. **wā 'ěr-dwo** to clean out one's ears; **wā-'yǎn** to gouge out the eyes; **wā-'kwàng** to excavate for a mine. *As mainV:* **'wā-chū-láy** to scoop out; **'wā-shyà-chywù** to dig deeper and deeper.

呱
wā, wà (*I*) to wail, sob, (*as a child*). **wā-'wā-de 'kū** to weep with wailing sounds; **'wā-de yì-shēng 'kū-chū-lay-le** to burst out with wailing and weeping.

瓦
wǎ (*Nmass*) earthenware material, clay; (*Nunit*, pyàr, kwày) tiles. **wǎ-'fáng** house with a tile roof; **wǎ-'pér** earthenware basin.
'wǎ-jyang specialist in laying tile.

襪 (子)
'wà(-dz) (*Nunit*, jř; shwǎng a pair of) stockings; socks.

wai *Wade Romanization for* **way.**

彎
wān (*A*) bent, curved; (*I*) to bend. **wān-'yāw** to bend at the waist, *thus* to bend over.
As mainV: **wān-chéng** to bend *something* into a shape, or to a *so-many-degree angle*; **'wān-gwò** (*lc*) to bend *something* over; **'wān-shàng-láy** to bend up; *etc.* ‖**tā bǎ shù-'gǎr gěy 'wān-shyà-chywù-le.** He bent the tree limb down to the ground.
As postV: **nùng-'wān-le** to cause *something* to bend; **dǎ-'wān-le** to strike *something* and cause *it* to bend; *etc.*
wār (*Nunit*, ge) a turning around, a circuit, a circle; a wave in the hair. **gwǎy-'wār** to turn a corner.

完
wàn (*A*) finished, done, completed. ‖**dēw 'wán-le.** Everything's done.
Most often as postV, very freely: **chř-'wán-le** to have finished eating; **dzwò-'wán-le 'shř** to finish one's work; *etc.*

丸子
'wán(-dz) (*Nunit*, ge) pill. **yàw-'wán** *or* **wán-'yàw** medicine in pill form.

玩
wán, wár (*V*) to amuse oneself with, play with (*Peiping almost always* **wár**). **wár-'chyéw** to play ball; **wár-'páy** to play cards; **wár 'nywǔ-rén** to flirt with a woman. ‖**dēw wár-'wán-le.** We've done everything we can to entertain ourselves. *or* (*figuratively*) It's all gone. *or* It's all destroyed.

完滿
wán-'mǎn (*A*) come to a very satisfactory conclusion. ‖**jèy-jyàn-'shř-ching 'bàn-de hěn wán-'mǎn.** The matter has been finished in an entirely satisfactory way.

碗
wǎn (*NunitC*, ge) bowl, cup. **chá-'wǎn** teacup; **fàn-'wǎn** rice bowl.

晚
wǎn (*A, H*) late. **wǎn-'fàn** evening meal; **wǎn-'bàw** evening paper; **'wǎn-shàng** evening. ‖**wǒ kǔng-'pà yàw 'wǎn-.-dyǎr 'dàw.** I'm afraid I'm going to get there a little late. ‖**tyān 'wǎn-le.** It's getting late.

萬
wàn (*NumG*) ten thousand; (*Aattr*) *only before nominal expressions* a very great many. **wàn-'lǐ-cháng-'chéng** The Great Wall.

萬全
wàn-'chywán (*Nunique*). Wan-ch'üan *or* Kalgan (*capital of Chahar province*).

萬縣
wàn-'shyàn (*Nunique*) Wan-hsien (*city in Szechwan province*).

往往
'wǎng-wǎng (*J*) generally apt to, usually apt to, often *or* frequently so. ‖**tā 'wǎng-wǎng dzwò tswò-'shř.** He's usually inclined to make mistakes. ‖**tā 'wǎng-wǎng dzwò tswò-'chē.** He often takes the wrong train.

望
wàng (*Vsent*) to hope that, expect that. ‖**wǒ wàng nǐ 'láy.** I expect you to come.

286

往 (望)

wàng (*less often* **wǎng**) (*K*) towards, in the direction of. **wàng-'yèw 'dzěw** go to the right; **wàng-'dzwǒ 'jwǎn** turn to the left; **wàng-'hèw 'nwó** put forward, put off until later; **wàng 'hǎw-le dzwò** do better, operate in a way that makes for improvement; **wàng-'lǐ 'shēw** take in, call in, (*as a bond issue*); **wàng-'shyà 'dzwò** (**-chywù**) to keep on working.

忘 (記)

'wàng-(jì) (*I; V; Vpred; Vsent*) to forget; to forget to; to forget that. ‖**wǒ bǎ nèy-jyàn-'shr̄-ching dēw gěy 'wàng-le.** I forgot all about that matter. ‖**wǒ wàng-le 'chywù-le.** I forgot to go. ‖**wǒ 'wàng-le tā yàw 'láy.** I forgot that he was coming. ‖**'nèy-jyàn-shr̄-ching wǒ dzǔng wàng-bu-'lyǎw.** I can't forget that matter. *or* I can't get that matter out of my mind.

忘其所以

'wàng chí swǒ-'yǐ-le (*literary quotation*) to forget oneself, forget one's station in life; *either for a person who behaves above his station or for a person who is inconsiderate of circumstances or acts too happy.*

忘恩負義

wàng-'ēn fù-'yì (*literary quotation*) to be ungrateful.

妄想

'wàng-shyǎng (*I*) to indulge in vain hopes, expect for too much. ‖**tā 'jēn shr̄ 'wàng-shyǎng.** He's really dreaming now.

望遠鏡

wàng-ywǎn-'jìng (*Nunit,* ge, jyà) field glasses, telescope.

歪

wāy (*A*) not straight, not squared off, not flush, not vertical, leaning to one side, askew. ‖**fēy-'jī wàng-'yèw wāy-le.** The plane was banking to the right. ‖**wǒ 'shēn-dz yì 'wāy, jyèw 'shwāy-shyà-chywù-le.** As soon as I leaned to one side, I lost my balance and fell. *As postV:* **gē-'wāy-le** to place *something* askew; **bǎy-'wāy-le** to arrange *things* in a lopsided pattern; *etc.* ‖**jèy-ge-'dz̀ shyě-'wāy-le.** This character's been written °at a slant. *or* °out of line with the rest.

歪

wǎy (*V*) to twist *or* turn (*as an ankle*). ‖**wǒ bǎ-'jyǎw 'wǎy-le.** *or* **wǒ wǎy-le 'jyǎw-le.** I turned my ankle.

外

wày (*Nplace*) outside, space outside of, outside of expectations. *Extended forms* **'wày-byan, 'wày-byar, 'wày-myan, 'wày-myar, 'wày-tew. chú** (*or* **dzày**) ... **yǐ-'wày** in addition to ..., besides .... ‖**wǒm dàw chéng-'wày chywù chí-'mǎ-ba.** Let's go out of the

city and go horseback riding. ‖**chú-'tā yǐ-'wày 'méy-yew 'byé-rén néng 'dzwò.** There's no one except him who can do it.

In compounds **wày** *may mean* external, alien, foreign. **wày-'yī** *or* **wày-'tàw(r)** overcoat; **wày-'byǎw** external appearance (*as of a person*); **'wày-rén** outsider; **'wày-gwo** foreign country; **'wày-gwo-rén** foreigner; **wày-'jyǎw** foreign affairs, diplomacy; **wày-jyǎw-'bù** Ministry of Foreign Affairs; **wày-'jyǎw-jèng-'tsè** foreign policy; **wày-'yáng** (*Nplace*) overseas, abroad; **wày-'chyáw** resident aliens.

(*H*) externally: **wày 'yùng** use externally (*as medicine*).

wei *Wade Romanization for* **wey.**

溫度

wēn-'dù (*Nabstr*) temperature. ‖**jīn-tyan-de-wēn-'dù dàw bā-shr̄-'dù-le.** The temperature today has gone up to eighty degrees.

溫哥華

wēn-gē-'hwá (*Nunique*) Vancouver (*Canada*).

溫和

'wēn-hé (*A*) mild, warm, tepid, (*of weather, water*); gentle, mild, (*of a person*).

溫州

wēn-'jēw (*Nunique*) Wenchow, *another name for* **yǔng-'jyā** Yung-chia (*city in Chekiang province*).

溫習

'wēn-shi (*V*) to brush up on, review. ‖**wǒ děy 'wēn-shi 'shū, ywù-bey 'kǎw.** I've got to brush up to get ready for the exam.

瘟疫

wēn-'yì (*Nabstr*) plague (*disease*).

聞

wén (*V*) to smell, sniff at. *As mainV:* **'wén-ɹyàn** to smell; **'wén-chū-lay** detect by smelling. ‖**jèy-ge-'wū-dz-lǐ-tew yěw méy-'chì, nǐ 'wén-jyàn-le méy-yew?** There's gas in this room; do you smell it?

In compounds **wén** *may also mean* hear: **shīn-'wén** news.

文

wćn, wér (*Nmass,* pyān) essay, article, writing; literature. **dzwò yì-pyān-'wér** to write an essay. **wén-'dz** writing system; **wén-'hwà** literary language; **wén-'fǎ** rhetoric, formal rules of composition; **'wén-shywé** the study of literature and composition, the liberal arts (*versus science*); **wén-'kē** the liberal arts curriculum; **wén-shywé-'ywàn** liberal arts division of a college; **wén-'jāng** (*Nunit,* pyān) article, essay; **wén-'jyàn** documents, papers.

'jūng-wén Chinese language and literature; 'yīng-wén English language and literature; etc., *sometimes used for* jūng-gwo-'hwà, *etc.*

蚊 (子)
*wén, 'wén-dz (*Nunit,* ge) mosquito.

文不對題
'wén bú-dwèy-'tí (*literary quotation*) to be off the subject, miss the point in what you say *or* write.

文火
wén-'hwǒ (*Nabstr*) slow fire, *for cooking.*

蚊帳
⌐én-'jàng (*Nunit,* ge) mosquito net.

文選
wén-'shywǎn (*Nunit,* bù, běn) prose anthology.

文學士
wén-'shywé-shr (*Npers*) bachelor of arts. ‖tā yěw yí-ge-'wén-shywé-shr̀-de-shywé-'wèy. He has the degree of bachelor of arts.

文雅
wén-'yǎ (*A*) well educated, well bred, and gentle, (*of a person*).

文藝
wén-'yì (*Nabstr*) liberal arts, (*including such things as drama, music, etc.*).

穩
wěn (*A*) steady, smooth, even-tempered, (*as of a vehicle, a person*). ‖jèy-ge-'dūng-shi fàng-dzay 'jèy-ge-dì-fang bù-'wěn. Putting that thing here won't make it secure. ‖chē 'kāy-de hěn 'wěn. The car is going along smoothly and steadily.
As mainV: wěn-'jù-le to put *something* on a firm basis, *or* to trap *someone* by pretending friendship.
As postV: jàn-'wěn-le to stand still and firm; dzwò-'wěn-le to sit firmly; *etc.*

吻
*wěn lips. jyē-'wěn to kiss.

穩當
'wěn-dang (*A*) secure, safe, firm. ‖tā-de-'hwà shwō-de hěn 'wěn-dang. What he said holds together well and is not apt to invite criticism.
'wěn-wěn-dāng-'dǎngr-de very safely, very securely.

穩固
wěn-'gù (*A*) firm, stable. ‖jèy-ge-'gēn-jī 'dǎ-de hěn wěn-'gù. The foundation (*physical, financial, of human relationships, etc.*) has been built very firmly.

問
wèn (*V*) to ask, inquire about, investigate. ‖chǐng-'wèn? I beg your pardon, but might I ask you for some information? ‖wèn-ta dzěme 'dzěw. Ask him how we should go. ‖wǒ děy 'wèn-yi-wèn dzěme 'dzěw. I've got to inquire how to go.
wèn-'àn to try a case *in court,* (*said of the judge*).
shyàng-ta wèn-'hǎw *or* wèn-ta 'hǎw give *someone's* regards to him.
As mainV: wèn-bu-'jáw to be unable to find anyone from whom to get required information, *or* to have no business asking about something.

問安
wèn-'ān (*VN1*) extend greetings *to someone older or to a superior,* (*a bit literary*).

問候
wèn-'hèw (*V*) to give regards to, greet. ‖chǐng-ni gěy-wo °'wèn-hew-wèn-hew ta. *or* °shyàng-ta 'wèn-hew-wèn-hew. Give him my best.

問詢處
wèn-shywùn-'chù (*Nunit,* ge) information desk.

問題
'wèn-tí (*Nunit,* ge) problem, question, subject. ‖'háy yěw yí-ge-'wèn-tí. There's still another question (*for us to take up*). ‖'dzěme-yàng jyě-'jywé jèy-ge-'wèn-tí? How can we solve this problem?

威風
'wēy-fēng (*Nabstr*) air of superiority. ‖tā hěn yěw 'wēy-fēng. He acts very uppish. ‖tā 'wēy-fēng hěn 'dà. *Either favorable:* He has the appearance of authority *or unfavorable:* He's terribly snobbish.

微風 (兒)
wēy-'fēng(r) (*N*) breeze, light wind.

威海衛
wēy-hǎy-'wèy (*Nunique*) Wei-hai-wei (*city in Shantung province*).

微生虫
wēy-shēng-'chúng (*Nunit,* ge) bacteria.

微生物
wēy-shēng-'wù (*Nunit,* ge) bacteria.

圍
wéy (*V*) to wrap around; to surround; to enclose. ‖'wéy-je jèy-ge-'tswēn-dz dēw-shr̀ 'shù. The village is surrounded by trees. ‖tā 'wéy-le yì-tyáw-wéy-'jīn. He put a scarf around (*his neck*).
As mainV: 'wéy-dzày to wrap *something* around *something;* 'wéy-chǐ-láy to enclose completely, fence in

completely; *etc.* ‖**dí-rén bǎ-'chéng 'wéy-chi-lay-le.** The enemy encircled the city.

圍脖兒
wéy-'bwóer, (*Nunit*, **ge**) bib; scarf.

維持
'wéy-chŕ (*V*) to maintain, keep up, hold together. **'wéy-chŕ 'myàn-dz** to keep up appearances, maintain dignity; **'wéy-chŕ 'jŕ-shywù** to keep order; **'wéy-chŕ 'shēng-hwó** to stay alive, get along, manage to keep on living.

爲恥
wéy-'chŕ (*VN1*) be ashamed (*literary*). ‖**wǒ yǐ 'jèy-ge wéy-'chŕ.** I'm ashamed of this.

圍牆
wéy-'chyáng (*Nunit*, **dzwò**) wall enclosing *something*.

圍裙
wéy-'chywún (*Nunit*, **tyáw**, **ge**) apron.

圍嘴
wéy-'dzwěr (*Nunit*, **ge**) bib.

違反
wéy-'fǎn contrary to, against. ‖**ní dzwò 'jèy-jyàn-shŕ shŕ wéy-'fǎn fǎ-'lywù.** Your doing that is against the law.

圍巾
wéy-'jīn (*Nunit*, **tyáw**) shawl, scarf.

爲職業
wéy jŕ-'yè (*VN1*) make *something* one's profession (*literary*). ‖**tā yǐ dzwò lywù-'shŕ wéy jŕ-'yè.** He's a lawyer by profession.

爲難
wéy-'nán (*A*) to be in a difficult position, face troubles.

爲人
wéy-'rén (*VN1*) to behave properly (*socially*); to play the proper role in human affairs. ‖**tā wéy-'rén hěn 'hǎw.** He plays his part in the world very well.

爲生
wéy-'shēng (*VN1*) to make a living (*literary*). ‖**tā kāy-'chē wéy-'shēng.** He drives a taxi for his living.

危險
wéy-'shyǎn (*A*) dangerous, critical. **wéy-shyǎn-'shìng** quality of being dangerous. ‖**wéy-shyǎn-'shìng hěn 'dà.** The possibility of danger is very great.

    wéy-shyǎn-'chī period of danger. **wéy** *alone is literary, but one says* **wéy-'jí-de-shŕ-hew** critical times.

濰縣
wéy-'shyàn (*Nunique*) Wei-hsien (*city in Shantung province*)

維也納
wéy-yě-'nà (*Nunique*) Vienna.

唯一的
wéy-'yī-de (*Aattr*) exclusive, only, sole. ‖**jè shŕ wéy-'yī-de.** This is the only one.

緯
***wěy** (*Nplace*) latitude. **'běy-wěy** north latitude; **'nán-wěy** south latitude. **'běy-wěy 'sž-shr-'dù** 40 degrees north latitude.

    wěy-'shyàn (*Nunit*, **tyáw**) parallel of latitude.

委
wěy(-rèn) (*Vsent*) to appoint *someone to do something* in an executive capacity; *the appointee is at a certain level in the Chinese governmental hierarchy.* **wěy-'ywán** committee member *so appointed;* **wěy-ywán-'hwèy** committee, commission *of this level.*

尾巴
'wěy-ba (*Nunit*, **tyáw**) tail. **mǎ-'wěy(-ba)** horse's tail; *etc.*

委屈
'wěy-chywū (*A*) wronged, feel grievances. ‖**tā 'jywé-de hěn 'wěy-chywū.** He feels that he's been dealt with unjustly. ‖**tā 'shèw-le 'wěy-chywū.** He got a raw deal.

胃
wèy (*Nunit*, **ge**) stomach.

位
wèy (*Munit*) replaces **ge** *for people when being polite:* **jèy-wèy-'shyān-sheng** this gentleman, *where he* **wèy**, *as much as the polite title* **shyān-sheng**, *carries the tone of courtesy.*

喂，餵
wèy (*V, Vsent*) to feed (*a child, an animal*). **wèy-'nǎy** to give a child the breast. ‖**děy wèy-'mǎ chŕ-'tsǎw.** I must feed the horses.

    As main V: **wèy-'bǎw-le** to force-feed, to stuff.

爲
wèy (*K*) for the sake of, for the benefit of *a person.* **wèy-'tā 'tè-byé 'pyàw-lyang** is especially attractive for her, is especially becoming to her (*as of some color or dress*).

    Because of *in the following two cases:* **'wèy-shéme** why?, how come?, because of what?; **'wèy-de-shŕ**

(J) the reason is that, because of the fact that. ‖'rén chr̄-'fàn 'wèy-de-shr̀ yàw 'hwó-je. People eat because they want to live.

未
wèy *literary equivalent of* méy *before verbs:* wèy-'jyǎn for méy-'jyǎn hasn't decreased, hasn't receded.

味
*wèy taste, flavor; *full form:* kěw-'wèy. wèr (Nabstr) taste, flavor, smell; bad odor. ‖jèy-ge-'tsày shr̀ shéme-'wèr? What does this food taste of? ‖jèy-ge-'dūng-shi yěw-'wèr-le. This stuff has gone bad and smells.

位（子）
*wèy, 'wèy-dz (Nunit, ge) seat, position, situation. dzwò-'wèy place to sit, seat, (as in a theater); shywé-'wèy scholastic degree; kè-'wèy guest's seat; shén-'wèy an ancestral shrine or memorial tablet. ‖chǐng-ni gěy-wo 'dìng yí-ge-'wèy-dz. Please get a seat for me.

未必盡然
wèy-bì-'jìn-rán (literary quotation) (H) not necessarily, not inevitably. *As a whole sentence:* But it isn't necessarily so. *or* But it isn't inevitably true.

衛兵
wèy-'bīng (Npers) guard, sentry (military).

未婚妻
wèy-hwēn-'chī (Npers) fiancee.

位置
'wèy-jr (Nunit, ge) position. ‖tā shyàn-'dzày yěw shéme-'wèy-jr? What position does he hold now?

胃口
'wèy-kěw (Nabstr) appetite. ‖'jīn-tyan wǒ méy-yew 'wèy-kěw. I have no appetite today. ‖'jīn-tyan wǒ 'wèy-kěw bù-'hǎw. My appetite's bad today. ‖jèy-ge-'dūng-shi bú-'dwèy tā-de-'wèy-kěw. This isn't to his taste (literally or figuratively).

未遂罪
wèy-swéy-'dzwèy (Nunit, ge) an attempted crime that doesn't succeed (legal).

窩
wõ(er) (Nunit, ge) nest, burrow, hive. dā-'wõ to build a nest. (M) yì-'wõer-de-nyǎw one family of birds (in one nest).

    bèy-'wõer a blanket rolled up and tucked in at the sides so that someone can slip into it to sleep.

    ṇwó-'wõer to move: ‖ni byé nwó-'wõer! Don't budge, just stay still where you are!

我
wǒ (Pron) I, me. wǒ-men or wǒm we, us.

臥
*wò to recline, sleep. wò-'chē sleeping car; wò-'pù berth (in sleeping car); wò-'shr̀ bedroom.

我們
wǒm *same as* wǒ-men (see wǒ).

屋
'wū(-dz), wūr (Nunit, jyān) room (in house, etc.). ‖tā dzày 'wū-dz-li-tew. He's in the room. (Said often where English would say He's in the house.)   wū-'dǐng roof.

烏魯木齊
wū-lǔ-mù-'chí (Nunique) Urumchi, another name for dí-'hwà Ti-hua (capital of Sinkiang province).

侮辱，污辱
'wū-rǔ or wǔ-rù (V) to insult someone.

巫術
wū-'shù (Nabstr) witchcraft, magic (a bit literary).

烏鴉
'wū-yā (Nunit, ge) crow.

烏煙瘴氣
wū-'yān-jàng-'chì(-de) (literary quotation) clouded with black dirty smoke literally, or figuratively black, unpleasant, low, and crooked, as the atmosphere surrounding a bunch of scoundrels.

無
*wú without, not; literary, sometimes equivalent to colloquial bū or méy. Important fixed expressions follow as separate entries.

勿
*wú, *wù (H) don't. Literary; found on signs such as wú-'dùng don't touch; wú 'gāw-shēng tán-'hwà don't speak out loud (SILENCE).

無期徒期
wú-'chī-tú-'shíng (Nabstr) life imprisonment.

無罪
wú-'dzwèy (Aattr) guiltless, innocent.

無法無天
wú-'fǎ-wú-'tyān (literary quotation) to be completely lawless and immoral.

無關
wú-'gwān (V) doesn't concern. ‖wú-'gwān nǐ-de-'shr̀. It doesn't concern you. Alternative form bù-'gwān.

蕪湖
wú-'hú (Nunique) Wu-hu (city in Anhwei province).

梧州
wú-'jēw (*Nunique*) Wuchow, *another name for* **tsāng-'wú** Ts'ang-wu (*city in Kwangsi province*).

無精打采
wú-'jīng-dǎ-'tsǎy-de (*literary quotation*) blue, in low spirits.

無賴
wú-'làỳ (*A*) lacking moral standards, rascally, unprincipled, worthless. **wú-'làỳ-de-rén** fast company.

無論
wú-'lwèn no matter. **wú-'lwèn 'shéme** no matter what; **wú-'lwèn rú-'hé** no matter what, in any case, in spite of anything and everything.
(*J*) ‖**wú-'lwèn nǐ dzěme 'shwō wǒ dēw bú-'shìn.** No matter what you say, I just won't believe it.
Alternative form **bú-'lwèn.**

無聊
wú-'lyáw (*A*) bored, uninterested; uninteresting, dry, dull.

無任.....之至
wú-'rèn . . . jǐ-'jǐ exceedingly. ‖**wú-'rèn 'hwān-yíng jǐ-'jǐ.** You are exceedingly welcome (*to someone who is coming on a visit*). ‖**wú-'rèn 'rúng-shìng jǐ-'jǐ.** I am extremely honored (*as in making a formal introduction*).

吳興
wú-'shǐng (*Nunique*) Wu-hsing (*city in Chekiang province*)

無數次
wú-shù-'tsż countless times. ‖**wǒ 'yǐ-jing 'chywù-gwo wú-shù-'tsż-le.** I've (already) been there time and time again.

吳縣
wú-'shyàn (*Nunique*) Wu-hsien *another name for* **'sū-jew** Soochow (*city in Kiangsu province*).

無線電
wú-shyàn-'dyàn (*Nunit,* ge, jyà) radío. **wú-shyàn-dyàn-'táy** radio station; **wú-shyàn-dyàn-'bàw** radiogram.

無效
wú-'shyàw (*VN1*) not be in effect, fail to attain a result. ‖**tsúng 'sż-ywè-yí-'ṙ 'chǐ, jèy-ge-fǎ-'lywù chywán-'gwěy wú-'shyàw.** Starting April first, this law will be ineffective.
Alternate form **méy-yew 'shyàw-lì.**

無所謂
wú-swǒ-'wèy (*A*) be of no importance, make no difference, not matter.

無從 (說起)
wú-'tsúng, wù-'tsúng (*Vpred*) not know how to begin doing or telling something. ‖**wǒ wú-'tsúng shwō-'chǐ.** I don't know how to begin my story.

無謂
wú-'wèy (*Aattr*) aimless, pointless, dull, uninteresting. **wú-'wèy-de-shṙ-ching** nonsense.

無疑的
wú-'yí-de, wù-'yí-de (*J*) certainly, definitely, without doubt.

無意 (的，中)
wú-'yì-de, wú-yì-'jūng (*H*) unintentionally, not on purpose.

無影無蹤
wú-'yǐng-wú-'dzūng (*I*) disappeared without a trace.

五
wǔ (*NumU*) five.

握
wǔ (*V*) to cover, conceal, (*especially with the hand*). As *mainV:* **'wǔ-chǐ-láy** or **'wǔ-shàng** to cover up. ‖**tā yùng-'shěw wǔ 'ěr-dwo.** He covered his ears with his hands. ‖**tā yùng-'shěw bǎ-'lyǎn 'wǔ-chi-lay-le.** She hid her face in her hands. ‖**byé bǎ shyǎw-'hár 'wǔ-je-le.** Don't cover the child too much (*in bed*). *or* Don't dress the child too warmly.

舞
wǔ (*Nabstr*) style of dancing. **tyàw-'wǔ** to dance. ‖**nǐ-'tyàw-de shṙ shéme-'wǔ?** What kind of a dance are you doing?

午
*****wǔ** noon; *full forms* **'shàng-wǔ** or **jūng-'wǔ.** **'shàng-wǔ** or **wǔ-'chyán** morning, A.M.; **'shyà-wǔ** or **wǔ-'hèw** afternoon, P.M.; **wǔ-'fàn** noon meal. **wǔ-'yè** (*literary*) midnight.

武昌
wǔ-'chāng (*Nunique*) Wu-ch'ang (*capital of Hupeh province*).

武器
wǔ-'chì (*Nabstr*) weapons, arms.

武官
wǔ-'gwān (*NpersT*) military attaché.

武裝
wǔ-'jwāng (*I*) to take up arms. As *mainV:* ‖**tām chywán wǔ-'jwāng-chi-lay-le.** They've all taken up arms.
wǔ-'jwāng-hé-'píng armed peace.

武術

wǔ-'shù (*Nabstr*) art or technique of fighting, *with weapons or with fists.*

誤

wù (*V*) to fail to make, to miss. **wù-'chē** to miss a train; **wù-'dyǎn** to be behind schedule; **wù-'hwèy** to misunderstand; **wù-'jùng** to miss the desired target and hit *something or someone* accidentally.

霧

wù (*Nmass*) fog. **shyà-'wù** (*IN*) a blanket of fog descends. ‖**wù hěn 'dà, wǒ kàn-bu-'chū-lay.** The fog is too thick, I can't see through it. ‖**'r̄-tew yí 'shàng-lay, 'wù jyèw 'sàn-le.** As soon as the sun came up the fog disappeared.

無

wù- *see combinations beginning with* **wú-**.

物

*****wù** (*N*) thing, goods, commodities; living things. **'dùng-wù** member of the animal kingdom; **'jŕ-wù** member of the vegetable kingdom; **'kwàng-wù** something in the mineral kingdom. **'rén-wù** personage. **wù-'jǔ** the owner of something (*legal*); **wù-'jyà** prices of commodities; **wù-'pǐn** commodities.

務必

wù-'bì (*Vpred*) to have to. ‖**wù-'bì shyǎw-'shīn.** You have to be careful. (*A bit literary.*)

物產

-wù-'chǎn (*Nmass*) material resources. **tyān-rán-wù-'chǎn** natural resources.

物證

wù-'jèng (*Nunit*, **jyàn**, **ge**) material evidence (*legal*).

物質

'wù-jŕ (*Nmass*) material, substance, stuff. **'wù-jŕ(-de)-shyǎng-'shèw** material comforts.

物理

wù-'lǐ (*Nabstr*) physics. **wù-lǐ-'shywé** the science of physics; **wù-li-shywé-'jyā** physicist.

物從其類

'wù-tsúng-chí-'lèy (*literary quotation*) birds of a feather flock together.

物以類聚

'wù-yǐ-'lèy-jywù (*literary quotation*) birds of a feather flock together.

Y

呀

ya *see* **a.**

壓，押

yā (*V*) to press down, pin down. *As mainV:* **yā-'hwày-le** to break by pressing down on; **yā-'dǎw-le** to upset by pressing down, *or,* (*figuratively*) to take *someone* down a peg; **yā-'tā-le** to press down on *something hollow* and cause *it* to collapse; **'yā-dzày** be pressed down in the middle of, buried in the middle of *a pile of papers,* (*as of the particular document you want*); **yā-shyà-chywù** to weigh down on *something.* ‖**nèy-ge-bàw-'dùng bèy shywún-'jǐng 'yā-shyà-chywù-le.** The riot was quelled by the police.

押，壓

yā (*V*) to table *a written proposal:* to mortgage. *As mainV:* **'yā-chǐ-láy** to table, set aside; **'yā-chū-chywù** to mortgage. ‖**nèy-ge-tí-'yì 'yā-chǐ-láy-le.** The proposal was set aside for the time being. ‖**wǒ bǎ 'fáng-dz 'yā-chu-chywù-le.** I mortgaged my house.

鴨

'yā(-dz) (*Nunit*, **jŕ**, **ge**) duck.

牙

yá (*Nunit*, **ge**) tooth. **yá-'yī(-sheng)** *or* **yá-'dày-fu** dentist; **shyàng-'yá** ivory. ‖**wǒ yěw yì-dyǎr 'yá-téng.** I have a bit of a toothache.
    yá-'shǎr ivory (*color*).

芽（兒）

*****yá, yár** (*Nunit*, **gēr**) sprout, seedling. **dèw-'yár** bean sprouts; **tsày-'yár** seedlings of any vegetables; **yá-'tsày** sprouts used as food (*usually bean sprouts*); **fā-'yár** to put forth a shoot (*of a seed*).

啞

yǎ (*A*) low, quiet, (*of a voice*). ‖**tā-de-'shēng-yīn 'yǎ-le.** His voice dropped down.

雅氣

yà (-'chì) (*A*) in good taste, (*of a color, decoration, person*).

啞吧

'yǎ-ba (*Npers*) mute (*person who can't speak*).

阿根庭（國）

yǎ-gēn-'tíng(-gwo) (*Nunique*) Argentina.

壓，軋

yà (*V*) to crush, roll over and press down, crush with a lateral motion. ‖**chē 'yà-ŕén-le.** The car's run over someone.

　　As mainV: **yà-'píng-le** to roll *something* smooth, (*as a pavement*); **yà-'swèy-le** to crush *stone* into small pieces; **yà-'hwày-le** to crush and break.

壓根兒

yà-'gēr (*J*) from the very beginning.

yai *Wade Romanization for* **yay.**

煙

yān(*N mass*) smoke. **yān(-'jywǎr)** (*N unit*, **gēn, gēr, jǐ**) cigarette; **chēw-'yān** to smoke; **'yān-tǔng** chimney; **yān-'hwēy** soot *or* tobacco ashes; **yān-'hwǒ** fireworks; **yān-'tsǎw** tobacco (*as raw material*); **yān-'yè(-dz)** tobacco leaf; **yān-'héer** cigarette case; **yān-'děw(r)** pipe (*smoking*); **yān-'téw(r)** cigarette butt; **yān(-hwēy)-'pár** *or* **yān(-hwēy)-'dyéer** ash tray.

淹

yān (*I*) to drown, *not necessarily to death;* to be flooded, submerged. *As mainV*: **yān-'sž-le** to drown to death; **yān-'hwày-le** to be spoiled by being submerged. ‖**jèy-ge-'fáng-dz chywán bèy-'shwěy yān-'hwày-le.** The house was totally ruined by the flood.

醃

yān (*V*) to corn *beef*, to salt *pork*, to pickle *vegetables with salt rather than vinegar*. **yān-'rèw** (*VN3*) kind of Chinese salt pork.

臙脂

'yān-jr (*N mass*) rouge. **tsā 'yān-jr** to apply rouge.

煙臺

yān-'táy (*N unique*) Yen-t'ai *or* Chefoo (*city in Shantung province*).

沿

yán (*V*) to have along the edge *or* side. ‖**jèy-jyàn-'yī-fu 'yán-le** Jyang-dàw-'byǎr. This dress has two lines of trimming along the edges.

　　(*K*) extending along, bordering. ‖**yán-'lù yěw hěn-'dwō-de-'táw-hwār.** There were a lot of peach blossoms along the edge of the road.

　　'yán-je (*K*) skirting, passing along. ‖**'chwán yán-je 'àn dzěw-de.** The boat was skirting the shore.

嚴

yán (*A*) harsh, cruel, strict. ‖**tā-'fù-chin hěn 'yán.** His father is quite strict.

鹽

yán (*N mass*) salt.

延

***yán** (*mainV*) to prolong. **yán-'cháng** to prolong, extend, take more time; **'yán-shyà-chywù** to delay, move a deadline to a later date. ‖**dàw 'shŕ-hew wán-bu-'lyǎw, yèw děy yán-'cháng lyǎng-ge-'ywè.** If we can't get it done by the time set, we'll have to prolong our work on it for a couple of months.

嚴格的

'yán-gé-de (*H*) severely, rigorously, in a narrow sense; being very choosy. ‖**'yán-gé-de 'shwō-chi-láy, jèy-ge jyèw bù-néng 'yùng.** If you want to be very rigorous about it, you can't use this.

嚴禁

yán-'jìn (*V pred*) it is strictly forbidden to (*quite official*). ‖**yán-'jìn yān-'tsǎw rù-'kěw.** It is strictly forbidden to import tobacco.

嚴重

yán-'jùng (*A*) serious (*as a situation, an illness*).

研究

'yán-jyēw, 'yán-jyèw (*V*) to make a special and thorough investigation *or* study of. **yán-jyèw-'gūng-dzwò** research work. ‖**wǒ děy 'yán-jyēw yí-shyàr dzày 'shwō.** I'll have to go into it a bit before I say anything.

言論自由

yán-'lwèn dz-'yéw (*N abstr*) freedom of speech.

顏料

yán-'lyàw (*N mass*) pigment, paint (*for painting pictures*), dye (*for dyeing clothes*).

顏色

'yán-sè, 'yán-shǎr (*N unit*, **ge**) color.

言語

'yán-ywǔ *or* **'ywán-yi** (*I*) to make remarks, say something. ‖**tā méy-'yán-ywǔ.** He didn't say a word.

眼

yǎn (*M unit*) *for* **jǐng** (*a well*).

演

yǎn (*V*) to perform in, put on, demonstrate in. **yǎn-'shì** to act in a play, put on a play; **yǎn dyàn-'yěngr** to act in the movies. **yǎn-'ywán** actor.

掩

***yǎn** (*mainV*) to cover, hide *something* from view, from danger, *etc.* **'yǎn-chǐ-láy** *or* **'yǎn-shàng** to hide *something* away; **'yǎn-jù** to cover up. ‖**tā bǎ tā-dz-jǐ-de-'tswèr 'yǎn-chi-lay-le.** He covered up his faults. ‖**tā bǎ nèy-ge-'kěwr 'yǎn-jù-le.** He closed *up* the crack.

眼（睛）

yǎn(-jing) (*Nunit,* jř, ge) eyes. 'yèw-yǎn right eye; 'dzwǒ-yǎn left eye; jēng-'yǎn *or* 'jēng-kāy 'yǎn-jing to open the eyes (*literally or figuratively*); bì-'yǎn *or* 'bì-shàng 'yǎn-jing *or* hé-'yǎn *or* 'hé-shàng 'yǎn-jing to close the eyes (*literally or figuratively*); yǎn-'jū(r) eyeball..

演變

yǎn-'byàn (*I*) to develop, unfold. ‖wǒm 'kàn jèy-ge-'chíng-shíng dzěme yǎn-'byàn. We'll watch and see how this affair develops.
    (*Nabstr*) development. 'lì-shř-de-yǎn-'byàn the unfolding of history.

眼光

yǎn-'gwāng (*Nabstr*) eyesight, vision (*literally or figuratively*); insight, good judgment; point of view. ‖tā hěn yěw yǎn-'gwāng. He has real insight. ‖tsúng 'tā-men-de-yǎn-'gwāng láy 'kàn, jèy-ge shř 'hǎw-de. Look at it from their point of view; it isn't so bad.

掩護

yǎn-'hù (*V*) to serve as a protective cover for. ‖fēy-'jī yǎn-'hù nèy-ge-'chwán. The planes convoyed the ship.

眼花了

yǎn 'hwā-le (*I*) to have one's eyes blur, to see double; to suffer from presbyopia *or* farsightedness. ‖wǒ yǎn 'hwā-le. My eyes are getting bad. *or* My eyes are blurring.

眼鏡（兒）

yǎn-'jìng, yǎn-'jyèngr (*Nunit,* fù) eyeglasses, glasses.

演講

yǎn-'jyǎng (*I*) make a speech.

眼淚

yǎn-'lèy (*Nmass*) tears (*from eye*). lyéw yǎn-'lèy to shed tears.

眼皮（兒）

yǎn-'pí, yǎn-'pyér (*Nunit,* ge) eyelid. 'shàng-yǎn-pí upper lid; 'shyà-'yǎn-pí lower lid.

演習

yǎn-'shí (*V, Vpred*) to rehearse, practice. (*Nabstr*) rehearsal, practice. ‖jīn-tyan-'wǎn-shang yěw 'kūng-shí-yǎn-'shí. This evening there will be a practice air raid. ‖méy-kāy-'mù yǐ-chyán, wǒ-men shyān yǎn-'shí yí-'tsž. Before the play opens we'll have a rehearsal.

掩飾

'yǎn-shř (*V*) to conceal *something by speaking.* ‖tā yùng-'hwà 'yǎn-shř tā-de-'tswò. He covered up his errors by his talk.

演說

yǎn-'shwǒ (*I*) to make a speech.

雁

yàn (*Nunit,* jř, ge) wild goose; *often differentiated from* swallows *by saying* dà-'yàn *for the* wild goose.

驗

yàn (*V*) to test, check up on. yàn-'shyě to test the blood *or* to have a blood test; yàn-'fèy to test the lungs. ‖'měy-yì-nyán děy 'yàn yí-tsž shēn-'tǐ. Each year you must have a physical checkup.

燕（子，兒）

'yàn(-dz), yàr (*Nunit,* ge) swallow (*bird*).

延安

yán-'ān (*Nunique*) Yenan, *another name for* fǔ-'shř Fushih (*city in Shensi province*).

宴會

yàn-'hwèy (*N*) dinner party. kāy yàn-'hwèy to hold *or* attend a dinner party.

秧

yāng (*Nunit,* gēr) young rice plants, *also specified as* dàw-'yāng. *In compounds* (*also* 'yāng-dz, yāngr, yār) young plants, sprouts, shoots. chā-'yāng(r) to plant seedlings; 'sūng-yāng pine tree seedlings; 'sāng-yāng mulberry seedlings.

陽

yáng (*Nabstr*) the principle of light in Taoist theory, good, maleness, positivity; *contrasted with* yīn.

揚

yáng (*V*) to raise *head, hand, arm, voice, eyebrows, flag, sail, dust. As mainV:* 'yáng-chǐ-láy *with same meaning.* ‖yáng-chi 'téw-lay. Raise your head (*when it is down, not raise it to look at something very high*).
    yáng-'méy tù-'chì (*literary quotation*) to emerge suddenly from obscurity (*literally to raise the eyebrows and exhale*).

洋

yáng (*Nunit,* ge) ocean. 'dà-yáng (*Nunit,* ge; *Mauton*) ocean. hǎy-'yáng oceans and seas; tày-píng-'yáng (*Nunique*) Pacific Ocean; dà-shī-'yáng Atlantic Ocean; běy-bīng-'yáng Arctic Ocean; nán-bīng-'yáng Antarctic Ocean; yìn-du-'yáng Indian Ocean.
    In compounds yáng *often means* from beyond the ocean, *thus* foreign. yáng-'chē rickshaw (*from Japan*); yáng-'hwǒ matches; yáng-'háng foreign firm doing business in China; yáng-'dyǎn-shīn western-style pastry; yáng-'là western-style candles; yáng-'sǎn umbrella; yáng-'chyán gold or silver dollar, Chinese or foreign; yáng-'táy balcony, porch. 'dūng-yáng Japan; 'shī-yáng the West.

羊
yáng (*Nunit, jř, téw, ge*) sheep.   **yáng-'rèw** mutton, lamb; **yáng-'máw** wool.

陽曲
yáng-'chywū (*Nunique*) Yang-ch'ü *another name for* **'tày-ywán** Taiywan (*capital of Shansi province*).

洋灰
yáng-'hwēy (*Nmass*) cement, concrete.   **yáng-hwēy-'dàw** concrete road.

揚州
yáng-'jēw (*Nunique*) Yangchow, *another name for* **jyāng-'dū** Chiang-tu (*city in Kiangsu province*).

楊梅
yáng-'méy (*Nunit, ge*) strawberries.

癢
yǎng (*A*) itch, tickle. *With a noun preceding designating the body-part which itches, forms an adjectival expression:* **'shěw-yǎng** *or* **shěw-'yǎng-yang** to have one's hand itch, *etc.* ‖**wǒ 'shěw-yǎng-yang.** My hand itches.

養
yǎng (*V*) to bear *a child;* to raise *children, flowers;* to keep *or* husband *domestic animals;* to raise and support *a family;* to give *a wound, or one's voice, etc.* a chance to recuperate; (*I*) to rest, recuperate, convalesce. **yǎng shyǎw-'hár** to bear a child; **yǎng-'hwār** to raise flowers; **yǎng-'jī** to raise chickens; **yǎng-'nyéw** to keep cows; **yǎng-'jyā** to raise and support a family; **yǎng-'bìng** to convalesce from an illness; **yǎng-'lǎw** to take care of one's old age.
As mainV: **yǎng-'dà** to rear *a child*, raise *animals* to maturity; **yǎng-'chéng** to develop *a bad habit, etc.* ‖**'dày-fu 'gàw-sung wo děy 'yǎng jǐ-tyān tsáy néng 'hǎw.** The doctor told me I'd have to rest a few days to get well. ‖**tā-'mǔ-chin 'shīn-shin-ku-'kǔ-de bǎ shyǎw-'hár yǎng-'dà-le.** His mother raised her child under the greatest hardships. ‖**tā shyàn-'dzày yǎng-'chéng-le yì-jǔng-'hwày-de-shī-'gwàn.** He's developing a bad habit now.

養氣
yǎng-'chì (*Nmass*) oxygen.

養活
'yǎng-hwó (*V*) to feed *or* support *people.* ‖**tā 'yǎng-hwó yì-'jyā-de-rén.** He's feeding a whole household of people.

樣
yàng (*Mclass*) kind of, way of, method of. **'jème-yàng(r)** *or* **'jè-yàng(r)** this kind of, such; **'nàme-yàng(r)** *or* **'nà-yàng(r)** that kind of, such; **'dzěme-yàng(r)** what kind of. ‖**jèr yěw 'sān-yàngr(-de)-'tsày.** There are three dishes available (*kinds of food*).
yí-'yàng (*A*) be the same.
'yàng-dz (*Nunit, ge*) model, pattern, type, kind; way, appearance. ‖**'hwàn yí-ge-'yàng-dz 'dzwò.** Change your way of doing this. ‖**tā-jǎng-de-'yàng-dz hěn hǎw-'kàn.** He's very good looking.

樣品
yàng-'pǐn (*Nunit, ge*) sample. ‖**nǐ 'shyān gěy-wo sùng yí-ge-'yàng-pǐn 'kàn-yi-kàn.** Send us a sample to look at first.

樣式
'yàng-shr (*Nabstr*) style, pattern, model. ‖**nǐ 'shǐ-hwān shéme-'yàng-shr-de-'shyé?** What style of shoes do you like?

yao *Wade Romanization for* **yaw.**

秧兒
yār *see* **yāng.**

腰
yāw (*V*) to weigh *something*, to weigh out *some quantity of something.* ‖**bǎ jèy-ge-'bāwr 'yāw-yi-yāw 'kàn-kàn yěw dwō-'jùng.** Weigh this package and see how much it is. ‖**chǐng gěy-wo'yāw yì-jīn-'myàn.** Weigh me out a catty of flour.

腰
yāw (*N*) waist. **wān-'yāw** to bend the waist, to lean over. ‖**wǒ 'yāw-téng.** *or* **wǒ 'yāw-swān.** (The back of) my waist hurts.
yāw-'shēn waist of a dress; **yāw-'dày** belt at the waist. ‖**jèy-jyàn-'yī-fu 'yāw-jūng-jyār 'dà-yì-dyǎr.** This dress is a little big around the waist.

要求
'yāw-chyéw (*V, Vsent*) to demand; to demand that.

搖
yáw (*V*) to shake back and forth. **yáw-'téwr** to shake the head (*meaning no as in English*); **yáw-'chwán** to row a boat; **yáw-'lyéngr** to ring a bell *held in the hand and moved back and forth;* **yáw-'shěw** to wave the hand to left and right in front of the body (*meaning sometimes* don't); **yáw-'lár** cradle.
As mainV: **yáw-'dùng** to cause to move by shaking back and forth; **yáw-'hwày-le** to cause to break *or* to ruin by shaking back and forth; **yáw-'jáw-le** to rock to sleep; *etc.*

謠傳
'yáw-chwán (*V, Vsent*) to spread as a rumor; rumor has it that. ‖**'yáw-chwán tā bù-'láy-le.** Rumor has it that he's not going to come.

(*Nunit,* **ge**) unconfirmed rumor. ‖**jèy-ge bú-'gwò shr̀ (yí-ge-)'yáw-chwán, bù-'kě 'jìn shìn.** This is only a rumor; you can't accept it unreservedly.

搖幌

'yáw-hwàng (*V*) to wave back and forth laterally; *sometimes same as* **yáw** to shake back and forth laterally. ‖**'shyàng dzày-'nàr 'yáw-hwàng 'bí-dz.** The elephant was over there waving his trunk back and forth.

As mainV: **'yáw-hwàng-chǐ-láy** to start to roll *or* shake *or* heave, back and forth; **yáw-hwàng-'hwày-le** to break by shaking *or* waving back and forth; *etc.*

謠言

yáw-'yán (*Nunit,* **ge**) rumor. ‖**tā lǎw dzàw yáw-'yán.** He's always spreading rumors.

咬

yǎw (*V*) to bite, to bite into. **yǎw-'yá** to clench one's teeth, (*figuratively*) to decide resolutely *to do something despite all difficulties.*

As mainV: **'yǎw-shyà-láy** to bite off *a piece of something.* ‖**tā jyàw 'gè-dz 'yǎw-le hǎw-jǐ-'kěw.** He was bitten in several places by fleas.

要

yàw (*V*) to want, need, beg for, seek to get. **yàw-'jyàr** to require *a certain* price, charge *so much;* **yàw-'mìng** to require one's life, (*figuratively*) to be terrible, awful, *or* (*literally*) to want to take someone's life, be out for someone's scalp; **yàw-'fàn** to beg for food; **yàw-'fàn-de** beggar. ‖**wén-'gwān bú-yàw 'chyán.** Officials mustn't covet money (*old saying*). ‖**tā yàw 'shwěy hē.** He wants some water.

要

yàw (*Vpred*) to be going to; to need to; to want to. ‖**hwǒ-'chē 'kwày yàw 'láy-le.** The train'll be here in a minute. ‖**wǒ yěw yí-jyàn-'shr̀ yàw 'gàw-sung ní.** There's something I want to tell you. ‖**tsúng běy-'píng dàw shàng-'hǎy yàw 'jīng-gwò 'tyān-jīng.** Going from Peiping to Shanghai you will pass through Tientsin. ‖**wǒ yàw 'shyǎng-yi-shyǎng dàw-nǎr 'chywù.** I want to think a bit about where I'm going.

藥

yàw (*Nmass*) medicine. **chr̄-'yàw** to take solid medicine; **hē-'yàw** to take liquid medicine; **fú-'yàw** to take *any* medicine (*somewhat literary*); **jr̀-'yàw** *or* **pèy-'yàw** to make *or* prepare medicine; **jwā-'yàw** to get Chinese herbal medicine from a druggist; **tsǎy-'yàw** to collect medicinal herbs; **yàw-'my n-hwa** medicinal cotton; **yàw-'fáng** druggist's shop, pharmacy; **yàw-'pù** old-style Chinese store dealing in medicinal herbs; **yàw-'kù** place for storing drugs (*as in a hospital*).

In some compounds **yàw** *has an extended meaning:* **hwǒ-'yàw** gunpowder and explosives.

要

'yàw(-shr) (*J*) if, in case. *Form* **yàw** *is always placed after the actor, if any is present, and often takes* **de-hwà** *at the end of the condition.* ‖**yàw-shr nǐ tày 'chén (de-hwà), jyèw děy děng 'shyà-yí-tsz̀-de-fēy-'jī dzěw.** (**'yàw-shr** *could also follow* **nǐ**) If you weigh too much you'll have to wait for the next plane. ‖**nǐ yàw dzěw de-'hwà wǒ 'gēn-ni chywù.** If you go I'll go with you. ‖**nèy-yí-tsz̀ yàw-shr tā 'dzày-jèr, wǒm yí-'dìng dǎ-'páy-le.** If he'd been here that time we would have played cards.

The **shr̀** *of* **yàw-shr** *sometimes means* is: ‖**yàw-shr 'wǒ, wǒ jyèw ywàn-yi 'chywù.** If it were I, I'd be glad to go. ‖**wǒ yàw-shr 'ní (de-hwà). . . .** If I were you . . . .

要強

yàw-'chyáng (*A*) ambitious.

要不然

'yàw-bu-rán (*J*) otherwise. ‖**háy hǎw 'dzǎw-yì-dyǎr 'láy-le 'yàw-bu-rán wǒ-men gǎn-bu-shàng 'chē-le.** It's just as well we got here a bit early, otherwise we would have missed the train.

要不是

'yàw-bu-shr̀ (*J*) if not. ‖**'jīn-tyan 'yàw-bu-shr nǐ 'láy de-hwà, wǒ jyèw méy 'fá-dz-le.** If you hadn't come today, I would have been stuck.

瘧子

'yàw-dz (*Nabstr*) malaria. **fā 'yàw-dz** to contract malaria.

要緊

'yàw-jǐn (*A*) important, of importance. ‖**bú-'yàw-jǐn.** It isn't important. *or* Never mind. *or* OK, don't bother, *etc.*

yàw *stands for* **'yàw-jǐn** *in some compounds* (*a bit literary*): **'yàw-rén** important people, (*particularly*) **'dǎng-gwó-'yàw-rén** important personages of party (*Kuomintang*) and country.

鑰匙

'yàw-shr (*Nunit,* **bǎ**) keys (*to locks*).

椰子

'yē-dz (*Nunit,* **ge**) coconut. **yē-'shù** coconut tree.

爺

*yé (*Npers*) male parent *or* grandparent. *See Appendix A.*

野

yě (*A*) wild, untamed, uncivilized, uncultivated. **yě-'shèw** wild animal; **yě-'rén** primitives (*American Indians, etc.*) *or* an uncultured person; **yě-'dì** wild country, uncultivated land; **yě-'tsǎw** wild growth, weeds, jungle; **yě-'yā-dz** wild duck, pheasant.

Gateway Mosque, Moslem Sector

Gateway with iron pots, Beijing

也

yě (*H*) also, too; so. ‖**yàw-shı nı 'chywù, wǒ yě 'chywù.** If you go, I'll go too. ‖**yě 'jyèw-shr jèy-'yí-ge-dì-fang ké-yi 'chywù.** So this is the only place we can go. ‖**yě chà-bu-'dwō-le.** It was a close shave too. ‖**tā lyán 'jèy-ge yě bù-'dǔng.** He doesn't understand anything, not even this.

也許

'yě-shywǔ, 'yé-shywǔ (*J*) maybe, perhaps. ‖**wǒ 'yě-shywǔ láy.** I may come. ‖**'yě-shywu tā bù-'jř-dàw.** Maybe he doesn't know.

耶穌

'yě-sū (*Nunique*) Jesus.   **yě-sū-'jyàw** Protestant Christianity.   **yě-sū-jyàw-'táng** Protestant Church.

野餐

yě-'tsān (*Nunit*, **ge**) picnic meal.   **chř yě-'tsān** to have a picnic.

頁

yè (*Mauton*) page (*of a book, newspaper, etc.*).   **dì-'yí-yè** page one.

夜

yè (*Mtime*) night.   **'lyǎng-tyān yí-'yè** two days and one night; **'sān-ř 'sān-yè** three days and three nights; **jěng-'yè** *or* **yí-'yè** all night; **'yè-lí** *or* **hēy-'yè-li** at night, during the night time.

    yè-'dzéy *or* **yè-'dàw** burglar (*at night*); **yè-'hú** chamber pot; **yè-'māw-dz** owl (*literally* night cat; *sign of bad luck, not of wisdom*); **yè-'chǎng** late show, midnight show; **bàn-'yè** midnight; **yè-'bān-de** on the night shift; **yè-'bān-de-'hù-shr** night nurse.

葉

'yè(-dz), yèr (*Nunit*, **ge**) leaf (*of plant*).   **yān-'yè** tobacco leaf; **shù-'yè** tree leaf.

    (*Munit*) *for a small boat:* **yí-'yè-byān-'jēw** a (little leaf of a) small boat (*poetic and literary*).

yeh *Wade Romanization for* **ye.**

yen *Wade Romanization for* **yan.**

悠（鞦）

yēw (*I*) to swing. *As mainV:* **'yēw-gwò-lay 'yēw-gwò-chywu** to swing back and forth, swing to and fro.

鞦韆

'yēw-chyar (*Nunit*, **ge, jyà**) swing.   **dǎ 'yēw-chyar** to swing on a swing.

油

yéw (*Nmass*) oil, grease.   **chì-'yéw** gasoline; **hwáng-'yéw** *or* **nyéw-'yéw** butter; **yì-tséng-'yéw** film of oil

or coat of paint.   **yéw-'hwàr** oil painting; **yéw-'nì** grease; **yéw-'tyán** oil field; **yéw-'yè** the oil business; **yéw-yán-'dyàn** general country store (*literally* oil salt store); **yéw-'dēng** oil lamp.

油

yéw (*V*) to paint *a house, furniture, etc.* ‖**wǒ-men 'yèw děy 'yéw-yew 'fáng-dz-le.** We've got to paint the house again. ‖**'fáng-dz yǐ-jing yéw-'hǎw-le.** The paint job on the house is already done.

由

yéw (*K*) from *a place*, by way of *a place, a route*. ‖**nǐ yéw 'něy-tyáw-'lù láy-de?** By which road did you come?

    According to *someone's desires or ideas*. ‖**tā yéw-je 'shyèngr nàw.** He makes trouble as the fancy strikes him. ‖**yéw-je 'tā-de-yì-sz dzwò 'hǎw-le.** Go ahead and do it according to his ideas.

    (*Vsent*) to let *someone do something* according to his own preference. ‖**yéw-ta 'dzwò-ba.** Let him do it as he sees fit.

    bù-yéw-'fēn-shwō-de (*H*) without any chance to explain, railroading, fórcing.

郵

*****yéw** mail, posts.   **yéw-'jèng** postal administration; **yéw(-jèng)-'jywú** post office; **yéw-jèng-'dzǔng-jywú** main post office; **yéw-jèng-'fēn-jywú** branch post office; **yéw(-jèng)-'chē** mail truck *or* railway post office; **yéw-'pyàw** postage stamps; **yéw-'fèy** postage, postal fee; **yéw-'bāw** package sent by mail.

郵差

yéw-'chāy (*Npers*) mailman.

油漆

yéw-'chī (*Nmass*) paint, lacquer, varnish. ‖**yéw-'chī wèy-'gān.** (*Sign*) WET PAINT (*literally* paint hasn't dried).

尤其

'yéw-chí (*K*) and especially. ‖**tām dēw 'hwày, 'yéw-chí 'tā.** They're all bad, especially he.

    'yéw-chí-shř (*J*) above all. ‖**'yéw-chí-shr děy jwěn-'shŕ 'dàw.** Above all, remember to be on time.

郵件

yéw-'jyàn (*Nabstr*) the mails; postal matter. ‖**yéw-'chāy láy 'shēw yéw-'jyàn.** The mailman comes to collect the mail.

游客

yéw-'kè (*Npers*) tourist, excursionist (*a bit literary*).

遊廊

yéw-'láng (*Nunit*, **ge, tyáw**) porch.

游歷
yéw-'lì (*V*) to make a trip to *a far place*, (*as of a tourist*) ; (*I*) to travel, tour.

遊戲
yéw-'shì (*I*) to play, have a party. ‖**tā-men dzày-nàr yéw-'shì.** They're having a good time there.

(*Nabstr*) game, play, entertainment, amusement. ‖**jīn-tyan-'wǎn-shang yěw yéw-'shì.** There's an entertainment tonight.

游行
yéw-'shíng (*I*) to have a parade, hold a parade; to travel from place to place. ‖**tām jywǔ-je dà-'chí dzày 'jyē-shang yéw-'shíng.** They hoisted a big flag and paraded through the streets.

猶疑
yéw-'yí (*A*) hesitant. ‖**wǒ dwèy-ywu jèy-jyàn-'shř-ching yěw yì-dyǎr yéw-'yí, bù-'jř-daw 'dzěme dzwò 'hǎw.** I'm rather hesitant about this matter, I don't know what it would be better to do. ‖**byé yéw-'yí bú-'dìng.** Don't be hesitant and undecided, make up your mind.

游藝
yéw-'yì (*Nabstr*) program of entertainment. **yéw-yì-'hwèy** meeting for entertainment (*as in a school*) ; exhibition of work done *by students*.

游泳
yéw-'yǔng (*I*) to swim. **yéw-yǔng-'yī** bathing suit; **yéw-yǔng-bì-'sày** swimming match.

游泳池
yéw-yǔng-'chŕ (*Nunit*, **ge**) swimming pool.

游園會
yéw-ywán-'hwèy (*Nunit*, **ge**, **tsž**) garden party.

有
yěw (*similar to V but with special characteristics described here*) to exist, to be, there is, there are, to have, to be characterized by. **yěw** *is made negative by preceding* **méy**, *never by preceding* **bū**; *a literary equivalent of* **méy-yew** (*colloquial in some combinations*) *is* **wú.**

(1) *Preceded by a possessor and followed by a designation of thing possessed:* ‖**nǐ yěw jǐ-ge-'háy-dz?** How many children have you?

(2) *Preceded by a designation of place and followed by a designation of thing located, temporarily or permanently:* ‖**wū-dz-li yěw 'jwō-dz.** There are tables in the room. ‖**tyān-shang yěw 'shīng-shing.** There are stars in the sky.

(3) *Similarly with the designation of place preceded by* **dzày**: ‖**dzày 'jwō-dz-shang yěw-'yān.** There are

cigarettes on the table. *This emphasizes more the location, contrasting it with other possible locations.*

(4) *More rarely, the same with the parts reversed:* ‖**yěw-'yān dzày-'jwō-dz-shang.** There are cigarettes on the table. (*Same emphasis as last.*)

(5) *A combination of the first and second above, with possessor and location both specified:* ‖**wǒ 'jyā-li yěw bù-'shǎw-de-'shū.** I have quite a few books at home.

(6) *Followed by a nominal form,* **yěw** *expresses merely existence:* there is, there are. ‖**yěw-méy-yew 'yān?** *or* **yěw-'yān méy-yew?** Are there any cigarettes? ‖**yěw-'méy-yew bǐ-'jèy-ge-'hǎw-de-'yān?** Are there any cigarettes better than these? *or* Can you get any better cigarettes than these?

(7) *Similar to the last, is the same with the nominal form followed by a V:* ‖**'méy-yew 'fàn chř.** There's no food to eat.

(8) *When* **yěw** *stands before a nominal form at or near the beginning of a sentence in which some other verb is the nucleus, it marks the nominal form as indefinite:* ‖**yěw-rén 'shwō** .... There are people who say .... ‖**'yěw-yì-tyān** .... Once upon a time .... ‖**yěw jř-'shř-dz tsúng dùng-wu-'ywán 'pǎw-chu-láy-le.** There's a lion which has escaped from the zoo.

(9) **yěw-de** *before a noun likewise marks it as indefinite:* some. ‖**'yěw-de-shŕ-hew tā-dzwò-de 'dwèy, 'yěw-de-shŕ-hew tā-dzwò-de bú-'dwèy.** Sometimes he does right, sometimes he does wrong. ‖**'yěw-de-rén 'láy, 'yěw-de-rén bù-'láy.** Some of them are coming, some of them aren't.

(10) **yěw-de** *itself is used, without a following noun, to mean* some: ‖**nèy-shyē-'shū-li 'yěw-de 'hǎw, 'yěw-de bù-'hǎw.** Of those books, some are good, some are bad.

(11) **yěw-de** *before a V may mean* to have something to do, *whatever the V specifies to:* **yěw-de 'chř** have something to eat, *and the like. Special is:* ‖**yěw-de 'shř.** Yes, a great many of them are. (*As in answering a question like* Are many of them Mohammedans?)

(12) **'swǒ-yěw-de** *is used like* **yěw-de** *to mean* all of: ‖**swǒ-yěw-de-'kè-rén dēw 'dzěw-le.** All the guests have left.

(13) **yěw** *is followed by an expression of measurement, often consisting of numeral plus measure plus adjective:* ‖**'jèy-kwày-'bǎn-dz yěw sān-chř-'cháng.** This board is three feet long. ‖**wǒ 'dàw-gwo nèr 'yǐ-jing yěw sān-'tsž-le.** I've already been there three times.

(14) **yěw** *is followed by many nominal expressions* (*sometimes V or I used as nominal in this position*), *the whole functioning like an A:* **yěw-'chyán** be rich (*literally* have money); **yěw-'yùng** be useful (**yùng** *basically a V* to use). *Many of these are given as subentries under the second part.*

298

友善

yĕw-'shàn (*A*) friendly. **yĕw-'shàn-de-'tày-du** friendly manner.

又

yèw (*H*) again, in turn; *indicating the same action or characterization repeated, or another action or characterization, of the same actor.* ‖tā 'yèw láy-le! Here he comes again! ‖tā 'shyān dàw 'mĕy-gwo, hèw-lay 'yèw chywù 'ēw-jēw-le. First he came to the United States, then later on he went on to Europe.

    yèw . . . yèw . . . both *this* and *that, where this and that are actions or descriptions:* ‖wǒ 'yèw kě yèw 'è. I'm hungry and thirsty. ‖tā yèw 'shwō yèw 'shyàw. He talked and laughed. ‖tā-de-yăn-'shwō yèw 'cháng yèw 'chèw. His speech was both long and dull.

右

yèw (*Nplace*) right, right side; *longer forms* 'yèw-byaṇ *or* 'yèw-byar. ‖shyàng-'yèw dzěw. Go to the right. ‖jèy-ge-'pù-dz dzày jèy-tyáw-'jyē-de-'yèw-byan. This store is on the right side of the street. *Before nouns:* **yèw-'yăn** right eye; **yèw-'shěw** right hand; **yèw-'jyăw** right foot; *etc.*

右傾

'yèw-chīng (*A*) leaning to the right (politically).

幼稚

'yèw-jr (*A*) childish, immature.

一

yī (**yí** *before a syllable with fourth tone or no tone;* **yì** *before a syllable with first, second, or third tone;* **yī** *at the end of an expression or when in a series of digits read off one by one*).

    (1) (*NumŬ*) one; *with less stress* a, an. *Directly after a V, A, I, K, the unstressed* yī *meaning* a, an *is often dropped:* ‖tā shř **yí-ge-'rén** *or* tā shř ge-'rén. He's a person.

    (2) *Before nouns or measures,* all, all of, the whole of. **yì-'tyān** all day; **yí-'lù**(-shang) the whole way, throughout the journey; **yì-'shēng** all one's life; **yí-'yè-li** all night long; **yì-'shēn** one's whole body. *A noun may follow:* **yì-shēn-'ní** one's whole body covered with ⸱ud; **yì-'wū-dz-de-rén** the whole room packed with people.

    (3) (*H*) once, as soon as, *usually with* jyèw *in ext part of sentence.* ‖yí 'kàn jyèw 'jŕ-dàw. As s⸳⸳n as he looked he immediately knew. *or* At one glance he knew. ‖yì 'wāy jyèw 'shwāy-le. As soon as he leaned over he immediately fell. *or* He no sooner leaned over than he fell.

    yí 'kàn, *literally* at one glance, *is generalized to mean* immediately, very quickly, *even when no looking is involved.*

醫

*yī medicine, medical. **'yī-sheng** (*NpersT*) doctor; **'yī-shywé** medicine (*as a science*); **yī-'shù** curing technique, applied medicine; **yī-'ywàn** hospital; **yī-'kē** medical course *in a school.* **jūng-'yī** Chinese herbal doctor; **shī-'yī** doctor trained in western medical science; **jywūn-'yī** army doctor; **shèw-'yī** veterinarian; **yá-'yī**(-sheng) dentist.

衣 (服，裳)

*yī, 'yī-fu, 'yī-shang (*Nmass*) clothes. **yí-jyàn-'yī-shang** article of clothing; **yí-tàw-'yī-shang** suit of clothing (*for male or female*); **yī-'gwèy**(-dz) clothes cabinet, wardrobe. **dà-'yī** overcoat; **shàng-'yī** coat, blouse, jacket; **lǐ-'yī** inner garment; **ywǔ-'yī** raincoat; **fú-shwěy-'yī** *or* **yéw-yǔng-'yī** swimming suit; **shwèy-'yī** night clothes.

依照

'yī-jàw (*K*) according to. **'yī-jàw nǐ-de-'hwà** according to what you say.

埃及 (國)

'yī-jí(-gwó) (*Nunique*) Egypt.

一

yí *see* yī.

姨

*yí (*Npers*) mother's sister. *See Appendix A.*

宜昌

yí-'chāng (*Nunique*) I-ch'ang (*city in Hupeh province*).

儀器

yí-'chì (*Nunit*, ge, bǎ, gēr, tyáwr, kwày, *depending on shape;* fù a set) instruments, small tools, *like drafting tools, surgical instruments, etc.*

益處

'yí-chù (*Nunit*, ge) benefit, advantage. ‖jèy-jǔng-de-'jŕ-fǎ dwèy-ywu wǒ-de-'bìng 'méy shéme-'yí-chù. This treatment isn't doing me any good.

遺傳

yí-'chwán (*V*) to pass *something* down in a family, *biologically.* *As mainV:* **yí-'chwán-gěy** to pass something (*i.e., a disease*) down to *one's child.*

一切

yí-'chyè (*Aattr*) all of. ‖tā bǎ yí-'chyè-de-dūng-shi dēw ná-'dzěw-le. He took everything away. ‖yí-'chyè-de-'shř tā dēw bù-'gwǎn. He won't have anything to do with the whole business

一定

yí-'dǐng (*H*) certainly, without fail. ‖tā yí-'dìng gēn ni 'chywù. He's definitely going to go with you.

(*A*) certain. ‖bù-yí-'dìng. That's not certain. *or* Not necessarily.

胰子
'yí-dz (*Nmass; kwày cake of*) soap. yí-dz-'fěn soap powder; yí-dz-'pyàr soap flakes.

一共
yí-'gùng (*J*) altogether, all in all. ‖wǒ-men yí-'gùng yěw 'dwō-shaw-rén? How many of us are there altogether? ‖yí-'gùng 'dwō-shaw-chyán? How much (money) in all? ‖yí-'gùng shr̀ 'wǔ-kwày-'èr-máw-'wǔ. Altogether five twenty-five.

疑惑
'yí-hwo (*Vsent*) to suspect that. ‖wǒ 'yí-hwo tā méy-'dzwò nèy-jyàn-'shr̀. I suspect that he didn't do it. *or* I doubt that he did it.

yěw yì-dyǎr-'yí-hwo to be a bit uncertain, have one's doubts.

一致
yí-'jr̀ (*H*) all in the same way, all in agreement. ‖dà-'jyā yí-'jr̀ 'tūng-gwò nèy-ge-fǎ-'àn. Everybody approved that bill, *or* The bill passed unanimously.

(*A*) the same, in agreement. ‖tā-men-de-'yì-jyàn bù-yí-'jr̀. Their ideas are not in agreement.

遺囑
'yí-jú (*Nunit, ge; jāng if written*) last will and testament.

一律
yí-'lywù (*Aattr*) uniform, all the same. ‖jèr-de-shīn-'shwěy dēw-shr̀ yí-'lywù-de. The pay here is uniform.

疑心
yí-'shīn (*V, Vsent*) to suspect, be doubtful about, suspect that. ‖wǒ yí-'shīn shr̀-'tā tēw-de. I suspect that it's he who took it.

遺失
'yí-shŕ (*I*) to get lost (*of a thing*). (*A bit literary.*) yí-shŕ-'wù missing articles; yí-shŕ-'wù-rèn-lǐng-'chù lost and found department.

儀式
'yí-shr̀ (*Nabstr*) ceremonial proceedings. jyē-'hwēn-de-'yí-shr̀ kind of marriage ceremony; tyān-jǔ-'jyàw-de-'yí-shr̀ Catholic ceremony; *etc.*

遺書
yí-'shū (*Nunit, jāng, pyān*) last will and testament (*written*).

一向
yí-'shyàng (*H*) always in the past, uniformly in the past. ‖tā yí-'shyàng 'lǎw-shr̀ bú-ày shwō-'hwà. He's never been very talkative.

疑問
yí-'wèn (*Nunit, ge*) doubt, question. ‖wǒ 'háy yěw yí-ge-yí-'wèn-ne. I still have a question.

一樣
yí-'yàng (*A*) the same. ‖tām-'lyǎ bù-yí-'yàng. Those two are different. ‖tām-'lyǎ yěw yì-dyǎr-bù-yí-'yàng. Those two aren't quite the same.

(*H*) to the same degree, the same extent, in the same way. ‖wǒ-de-'mǎ gēn 'nǐ-de-mǎ yí-'yàng 'kwày. My horse is just as fast as yours. ‖'wǒ-de-mǎ gēn 'nǐ-de-mǎ bù-yí-'yàng 'kwày. My horse and yours aren't equally fast.

椅 (子)
*yǐ, 'yǐ-dz (*Nunit, bǎ, jāng*) chair. *yǐ *includes any object designed to be sat on which has back or arms or both.* shā-fā(-'yǐ) sofa.

尾巴
'yǐ-ba (*Nunit, gēr, tyáw*) tail (*of animal*).

以前
yǐ-'chyán (*J*) formerly, at an earlier time. ‖yǐ-'chyán wǒ-men 'jù-gwo nàr. We did live there once.

Preceded by expression of time: ago. 'sān-nyán-yǐ-'chyán three years ago *or* three years earlier.

Preceded by a sentence: before *doing such-and-such.* ‖wǒ chr̄-'fàn yǐ-'chyán děy shǐ-'shěw. Before I eat dinner I've got to wash my hands.

以 .... 而論
yǐ- . . . ér-'lwèn (*a bit literary*) as far as *so-and-so* is concerned; *so-and-so is* wǒ, nǐ, *or* tā. ‖yǐ-'tā ér-'lwèn, tā-de-'dž-ge jyèw bú-'gèw. As for him now, his qualifications just aren't adequate.

以防
yǐ-'fáng (*V*) to defend against (*a bit literary*). ‖wǒm yàw 'ywù-bèy yǐ-'fáng bú-'tsè. We ought to prepare to defend ourselves against the unexpected.

yǐ-'fáng-wàn-'yī (*H*) just in case, just as protection against the small chance of something happening.

以後
yǐ-'hèw (*J*) afterwards, later on. ‖wǒ-men yǐ-'hèw yàw dàw-'nàr chyù dzwò-'shr̀. We're going to go there to work later. ‖yǐ-'hèw wǒ-men jyèw dàw-'nàr chyù dzwò-'shr̀-le. Later on we went there to work.

Preceded by expression of time: later by so much time. 'sān-nyán-yǐ-'hèw three years later *or* three years from now.

Preceded by a sentence: after *doing such-and-such.* ‖wǒm chr̄-'fàn yǐ-'hèw jyèw chyù dàw-'nàr chyù kàn-'shì. After we eat dinner we're going to a show.

已經

'yǐ-jing (*H*) already. le *or* gwo *occurs later in the sentence.* ‖wǒ yǐ-jing 'jyàn-gwo ta-le. I've already met him. ‖wǒ yǐ-jing °chř-le dzǎw-'fàn-le. *or* °'chř-gwo dzǎw-'fàn(-le). I've already had breakfast. ‖wǒ yǐ-jing 'kàn-jyan ṭa-le. I've already seen him.

以來

yǐ-'láy *after a sentence:* since *doing such-and-such.* ‖wǒ dàw 'měy-gwo yǐ-'láy méy-'kàn-gwo dyàn-'yěngr. Since I got to America I haven't seen a single movie. *A bit literary;* yǐ-'hèw *would be used more colloquially.*

已然

yǐ-'rán (*J*) since, already, *referring primarily to changes of state rather than to events, otherwise like* 'yǐ-jing. ‖tā yǐ-'rán 'jè-yàngr-le, nǐ bú-yùng 'dzày shwō-le. Since he's already like this, there's no use your saying anything more.

以為

yǐ-'wéy (*Vsent*) to have it as one's opinion that. ‖'wǒ yǐ-'wéy tā bù-'láy, (kě-shr tā jēn 'láy-le). I didn't think he was going to come, (but he did turn up).

yǐ . . . wéy use *such-and-such* as, take *such-and-such* to be, consider *such-and-such* to be. ‖nǐ yǐ 'shéme wéy 'gēn-jywù shwō nèy-jywù-'hwà? What basis do you have for that statement? (*More literary*): ‖yǐ 'dzěw wéy 'myàw. It's better to go.

yǐ mày-'bàw wéy 'shēng depend on selling papers for a living.

一

yì *see* yī.

議案

yì-'àn (*Nunit, ge*) motion *in parliamentary procedure,* bill *in a legislative body.*

義（大利國）

yì-dà-'lì(-gwó) (*short form* 'yì-gwó) (*Nunique*) Italy.

沂州

yì-'jēw (*Nunique*) Ichow, *another name for* lín-'yì Lin-i *or* Linyi (*city in Shantung province*).

意志

'yì-jř (*Nabstr*) will, will power. ‖jèy-ge-rén-de-'yì-jř hěn 'jyān-chyáng. He has a strong will.

一直

yì-'jŕ (*H*) straight, straight through, straight ahead, directly. ‖yì-'jŕ dzěw. Go straight ahead. ‖tā tsúng běy-'píng yì-'jŕ fēy-daw chúng-'chìng chywù-le. He flew straight from Peiping to Chungking. ‖wǒm tsúng 'dzǎw-chen yì-'jŕ 'máng-dàw 'wǎn-shang. We're busy from morning straight through to evening. ‖tā yì-'jŕ jyéw 'jŕ-dàw nèy-ge-'wèn-tí-de-dá-'àn. He knew the answer to the problem all the time.

意見

'yì-jyan (*Nunit, ge*) opinion, point of view. ‖wǒm-'lyǎ-rén-de-'yì-jyan bù-'hé. We two don't seem to agree.

議決

yì-'jywé (*V*) to reach *a decision* through discussion.   yì-jywé-'àn act *or* resolution of a governing body.

議論

'yì-lwèn (*V*) to talk about, discuss. ‖tām dēw 'yì-lwèn jèy-jyàn-'shř-ching. They were all talking about it.

意料

'yì-lyàw (*Vsent*) to expect that. ‖wǒ 'yì-lyàw tā bú-hwèy 'láy. I'd anticipate that he won't be able to come.

As mainV: 'yì-lyàw-bu-'dàw be unable to foresee something.

(*Nabstr*) expectations. ‖jèy-jyàn-'shř-ching 'chū hu wǒ-de-'yì-lyàw-jŕ-'wày. That matter is beyond m expectations.

一時

yì-'shŕ (*Ntime*) right now, right at the moment. ‖wǒ yì-'shŕ 'shyǎng-bu-chř-'láy. I can't think of it right at the moment. ‖wǒm 'shyān 'jù-jèr yì-'shŕ, yì-'hèw dzày 'shwō. We'll stay here for the moment, later on we'll see what we can do.

藝術

'yì-shù (*Nabstr*) art.   yì-shù-'jyā artist; yì-shù-'pin (*Nunit, jyàn*) work of art.

意思

'yì-sz (*Nabstr*) idea, opinion; meaning. yěw 'yì-sz interesting, meaningful. ‖'wǒ-de-yì-sz shř 'jè-me yàngr . . . . My idea is as follows . . . . ‖nǐ dàw-'dǐ shř shéme-'yì-sz? What do you mean by that anyhow? ‖jèy-ge-dz-de-'yì-sz shř shéme? What does this character mean?

意外

yì-'wày (*Nabstr*) something impossible to anticipate, something unanticipated. chū yì-'wày-de-shř to have an accident; to have something unexpected happen.

義務

'yì-wu (*Nunit, ge*) duty. yì-wu-'shì benefit performance of a drama; yì-wu-'shīn loyalty to duty; yì-wu(-jŕ)-'ywán officer of a society who works for no pay. ‖wǒ shyàn-dzày jř jìn 'yì-wu. I'm just doing my duty.

意義
'yì-yì (Nabstr) significance, meaning, purpose. ‖'jèy-jyàn-shr̀-ching hěn méy 'yì-yì. This matter isn't worth bothering about.

議員
yì-'ywán (Npers) representative in a governing body, senator, representative, member of parliament.

因
yīn (K) because of (a bit literary). yīn-'bìng chǐng-'jyà to ask for a few days off because of illness. yīn-'tsž (J) because of this, hence, therefore. ‖yīn-'tsž tā bú-'ywàn-yì. Hence his unwillingness. (Literary; colloquial expressions would use 'swǒ-yi instead of yīn-'tsž.)

陰
yīn (A) dark, overcast, cloudy. As mainV: 'yīn-shàng-láy-le to cloud over.
    yīn-'tyān to get cloudy. ‖jīn-tyan yīn-'tyān-le. It's gotten cloudy today.
    (Nabstr) the principle of darkness in Taoist theory: evil, femaleness, negativity, contrasted with yáng.

音
*yīn (N) sound. kěw-'yīn manner of speech, accent; 'shēng-yīn sound, noise, sound of a voice, enunciation, diction; gwǎng-dūng-'yīn Cantonese accent; shàng-hǎy-'yīn Shanghai accent; etc., with source specified.
    'yīn-shywé acoustics (science).

殷勤
'yīn-chín (A) courteous, polite, attentive.

音符
'yīn-fú (Nunit, ge) musical note (written).

陰涼
yīn-'lyáng (A) cool and shady.

因爲
'yīn-wèy (J) because

音樂
yīn-'ywè (Nmass) music. dzèw yīn-'ywè to play music (on an instrument); yīn-ywè-'dwèy band, orchestra; yīn-ywè-'hwèy concert; yīn-ywè-'jyā musician (composer or instrumental performer, not singer).

銀（子）
yín(-dz) (Nmass) silver. yín-'chì silver goods, silverware; yín-'bēy silver cup, loving cup; yín-'háng bank (for money); yín-háng-'jyā banker.

銀本位
yín-běn-'wèy (Nabstr) the silver standard (financial)

鄞縣
yín-'shyàn (Nunique) Yin-hsien (city in Chekiang province).

引
yǐn (V) to draw a crowd, attract people. yǐn-'rén jù-'yì to attract (people's) attention; yǐn rén-de-'hwà to call attention to what someone has said, quote someone; yǐn-'lù to lead the way; yǐn-'lù-de a guide. As mainV: 'yǐn-chī-láy to arouse people's attention; 'yǐn-gwò (lc) to conduct water, gas, etc. (as through a pipe). ‖tā-shwō-de-'hwà hěn yǐn-rén 'shyàw. What he said got a laugh. ‖'shwěy shr̀ tsúng jèy-gēr-'gwǎn-dz 'yǐn-jìn-láy-de. The water comes in through this pipe.

飲料
yǐn-'lyàw (Nmass) stuff to drink. yǐn-lyàw-'shwěy drinking water.

隱藏
yǐn-'tsáng (V) to conceal something; more literary equivalent of tsáng.

隱痛
yǐn-'tùng (Nabstr) co. cealed suffering; dull pain. ‖tā yěw yí-ge-yǐn-'tùng. He's suffering from something he can't tell anybody about.

印
yìn (V) to make an impression on a surface by pressing something on it. yìn-'shwā (V) to print; yìn-shwā-'swǒ print shop; yìn-shwā-'pǐn printed matter; yìn-'shū to print books; yìn-'bàw to print newspapers; yìn-'hwār to stamp on a design, as in yìn-hwār-de-mýan-'bù or yìn-hwā-'bù printed cottons. 'yìn-chū-láy to get something printed. ‖'jèy-yì-pyār 'yìn-de hěn 'hwày. This page was badly printed.

印（子，兒）
'yìn(-dz), yèr (Nunit, ge) mark or trace left by something pressing on something. jyǎw-'yèr footprint; shěw-'yèr handprint or fingerprint; jǐ-tew-'yèr fingerprint.
    yìn (Nunit, ge) seal (emblem).

印地安人
yìn-di-'ān-rén (Npers) American Indian.

印度（國）
'yìn-du(-gwó) (Nunique) India. 'yìn-du-rén Indian (from India only).

飲馬
yìn-'mǎ (VN2) to water a horse (a bit literary).

印象
yìn-'shyàng (*Nunit*, ge) impression *of someone.* ‖wǒ jř 'jyàn-gwo ta yí-'tsz̀, kě-shr wǒ dwèy-ywu-ta-de-'yìn-shyàng hěn 'hǎw. I've only seen him once, but I have a good impression of him.

英（國）
*yīng, 'yīng-gwo (*Nunique*) England. yīng-'wén English language and literature; yīng-gwo-'hwà English language; 'yīng-gwo-rén Englishman.

yīng *is prefixed to Mmeas to indicate units of the English system of weights and measures:* yīng-'lǐ mile; yīng-'chř English foot; yīng-'tswèn English inch; yīng-'mǔ acre; yīng(-jīn)-'bàng British pound (*money*). *See Appendix B.*

應當
'yīng-dāng (*Vpred*) should, ought to.

應該
'yīng-gāy (*Vpred*) should, ought to.

英名
'yīng-míng (*Nunit*, ge) name and reputation of a hero. ‖tā-de-'yīng-míng chwán-'byàn-le shr̀-'jyè. His fame spread throughout the world.

英雄
'yīng-shyung (*Npers*) hero.

應用
yīng-'yùng (*V*) actually use, put in practice. ‖jèy-ge-'fāng-fǎ ké-yi yīng-'yùng. This method °can really be used in practice. *or* °is really practicable.

yīng-yùng-'pǐn necessary materials and tools; 'měy-tyān-yīng-yùng-'pǐn everyday necessities.

營
yíng (*MgroupA*) battalion.

營
yíng (*Nunit*, dzwò, ge) encampment. dā-'yíng to establish camp; bá-'yíng to strike camp.

'bīng-yíng barracks (*military*); jí-jūng-'yíng concentration camp.

迎
yíng (*V*) to face and approach. yíng-'kè to welcome guests, receive visitors; yíng-'nyán to look forward to the new year; yíng-'dí to encounter an enemy.

As mainV: 'yíng-shàng-lay to come up to *someone,* approach *someone.*

yíng-je (*K*) facing. yíng-je 'fēng facing the wind.

贏
yíng (*V*) to win *money, a contest, etc.* ‖bǐ-'sày shéy 'yíng-le? Who won the game? ‖shéy 'yíng? Who's ahead?

營幕
yíng-'mù (*Nunit*, dzwò, ge) tent.

營盤
yíng-'pán (*Nunit*, dzwò, ge) encampment, barracks.

營業
yíng-'yè (*VN2*) to run a business.

影（子，兒）
'yǐng(-dz), yěngr (*Nunit*, ge) shadow. dyàn-'yǐng movies.

yǐng-'yìn (*V*) to photostat, reproduce photographically.

影響
yǐng-'shyǎng (*V*) to influence. ‖jèy-jyàn-shr̀-ching yǐng-'shyǎng wo hěn 'dà. This matter has influenced me a great deal.

(*N*) influence, effect. ‖tā gěy-wo-de-yǐng-'shyǎng hěn 'dà. His influence on me has been very great.

硬
yìng (*A*) hard, stiff, inflexible, unyielding, solid, powerful. (*H*) unyieldingly, insistently, inflexibly. ‖tā 'yìng shwō tā 'láy-gwo-le. He claimed insistently that he had come.

應酬
'yìng-chew (*V*) discharge one's social responsibilities towards *someone.* ‖wǒ děy 'yìng-chew-yìng-chew ta. I must discharge my social debt to him.

(*Nunit*, ge) social responsibilities, engagements.

應付
'yìng-fu (*V*) to deal with, cope with *people, situations;* to manage to pay *bills, etc.* ‖nǐ shyǎng 'fá-dz gěy-wo 'yìng-fu-yìng-fu jèy-shyē-'jày-jǔ. Please figure out some way of dealing with all these creditors of mine.

應驗
yìng-'yàn (*V*) to bear out *a prediction,* fulfill *a prophecy,* answer *a prayer.* ‖tā-swǒ-shwō-de-'hwà yìng-'yàn le. What he said came true. ‖'jèy-ge jyèw-shr yìng-'yàn tā-de-'hwà. This bears out what he said.

yu *Wade Romanization for* yew.

yü *Wade Romanization for* ywu.

yüan *Wade Romanization for* ywan.

yüeh *Wade Romanization for* ywe.

yün *Wade Romanization for* ywun.

擁護

'yūng-hù or 'yǔng-hù (V, Vsent) to support, back up someone; to back up someone in doing something. ‖tā 'yūng-hu wo dzwò shěng-'jǎng. He backed me for governor.

邕寧

yūng-'níng (Nunique) Yung-ning (city in, Kwangsi province).

庸人

'yūng-rén (Npers) foolish people (a bit literary). ‖'yūng-rén dz̀-'rǎw. Foolish people make trouble for themselves (literary quotation).

容易

'yúng-yì see 'rúng-yì.

永（遠）

*yǔng, yǔng-'ywǎn (H) always from now on. ‖ní yǔng-'ywǎn 'jì-jù 'àn-shŕ 'dàw. Hereafter remember to be on time.

　　yǔng is confined to yǔng bū-, especially yǔng bú-'dzày never again. ‖wǒ yǔng bú-'dzày dzwò nèy-jyàn-'shř-le. Never again will I do that.

永昌

yǔng-'chāng (Nunique) Yungchang, another name for bǎw-'shān Pao-shan (city in Yünnan province).

勇敢

yǔng-'gǎn (A) brave.

擁

'yùng-hù see 'yūng-hù.

永嘉

yǔng-'jyā (Nunique) Yung-chia (city in Chekiang province).

用

yùng (V) make use of, use, utilize. ‖ní ké-yi yùng wǒ-de-yáng-'sǎn. You can use my umbrella. ‖ná nèy-ge-chyǎn-'bǐ 'yùng-yi-yùng 'hǎw-le. Well, you can use that pencil; that'd be all right. ‖ní ké-yi ná bàw-'jř dāng-'sǎn 'yùng. You can use a newspaper as an umbrella.

　　yěw-'yùng (VN2) to be useful. ‖nèy-ge-'sǎn 'pwò-le, méy-'yùng-le. That umbrella's broken, you can't use it.

　　bú-'yùng or 'yùng-bù-yùng (Vpred) there's no need to . . ., is there any need to . . .: ‖'yùng-bu-yùng dzwò 'nèy-ge? Is there any need to do that?

　　(K) using, making use of, with an instrument or means. ‖tā yùng yá-'shwā-dz shwā-le 'yá. He brushed his teeth with a toothbrush. ‖jèy-ge-tí-'shyāng shŕ yùng-'pí dzwò-de. This suitcase is made of leather.

‖yùng-'chwán bǎ jywūn-'hwǒ ywùn-dàw 'nàr. Ship the munitions there by boat. ‖yùng-'hwěy bǎ-hwǒ 'péy-shàng. Bank the fire with ashes. ‖yùng-le yì-dyǎr-'gūng-fu tsáy ké-yi dzwò-'wán. You can only finish the job by using more time and energy.

　　As mainV: yùng-bu-'jáw there's no need to; 'yùng-shàng to take advantage of. ‖wǒ-men-de-ywán-'lyàw dēw yùng-'wán-le. Our materials are all used up. ‖nǐ yùng-bu-'jáw shēng-'chì. There's no need for you to get angry.

用處

'yùng-chù (Nunit, ge) useful feature. ‖jèy-běn-'shū yì-'dyǎr-yùng-chu dēw 'méy-yew. This book has no useful features at all.

用功

yùng-'gūng (A) studious, hard-working.

用盡

yùng-'jìn (RC2) to use up, use all of. ‖wǒ yùng-'jìn wǒ-de-'lì-lyàng bāng tā-de-'máng. I used all my powers to help him.

用人

'yùng-rén (Npers) servant.

用心

yùng-'shīn (VN1, A, H) be careful, use one's brains, be diligent. ‖tā shyě-'dz̀ hěn yùng-'shīn. He writes very carefully.

用刑

yùng-'shíng (VN2) to use torture; to give the third degree. ‖yùng 'kǔ-shíng jyàw-ta-jāw-'rèn. They tortured him cruelly to make him confess.

用意

yùng-'yì (Nunit, ge) purpose, intention, underlying and sometimes concealed intention.

冤

ywān (V) to cheat, trick, deceive, fool. ‖wǒ bù-'ywān-ni! I wouldn't fool you! or I'm not kidding! ‖tā bǎ-wo ywān 'kǔ-le. He cheated me badly. ‖wǒ jēn 'ywān! I really got rooked!

　　'ywān-chyán overpayment, money one is cheated out of. ‖byé-hwā 'ywān-chyán! Don't pay too much!

圓

ywán (.1) round, circular, spherical. ‖'ywè 'ywán-le. The moon is full.

　　(Munit) with N chyán dollar (a bit literary)

員

*ywán (Npers) personnel, member. rén-'ywán personnel; yì-'ywán delegate; hwèy-'ywán member of an association or club; wěy-'ywán committee or commission member.

園 (子)

*ywán, 'ywán-dz (*Nunit*, ge) garden, orchard. tsày-'ywán(-dz) vegetable garden; hwā-'ywán-dz, or hwā-'ywár flower garden; gwǒ-'ywán-dz orchard or nut grove.

原版

ywán-'bǎn (*Nunique*) original copy, original edition of some book or document.

元朝

'ywán-cháw (*Nunique*) The Yüan or Mongol dynasty (1206–1368 A.D.).

圓圈

ywán-'chywār (*Nunit*, ge) circle.

園丁

ywán-'dīng (*Npers*) gardener.

原子

ywán-'dž (*Nunit*, ge) atom. 'tàn-chì-ywán-'dž carbon atom.

原故

'ywán-gu (*Nunit*, ge) reason. ‖tā bù-néng 'láy yěw 'lyǎng-ge-'ywán-gu. He has two reasons why he can't come.

圓規

ywán-'gwēy (*Nunit*, ge) compasses (for drawing circles).

圓滑

'ywán-hwá (*A*) smooth; overly tactful.

原價

ywán-'jyà(r) (*Nunique*) original cost, original price (economic, but not very definite).

原來

ywán-'láy (*H*) originally. ‖ywán-'láy shǐ-'nǐ-ya! Oh! it was you all the time!
ywán-'láy-de-'fāng-fǎ the method used at the beginning.

原路

ywán-'lù (*Nunique*) the same route already followed. ‖tā tsúng ywán-'lù 'hwéy-chywù-le. He went back by the same route.

原諒

ywán-'lyàng (*V*) to forgive a person his offenses.

原料

ywán-'lyàw (*Nmass*) raw materials.

圓滿

ywán-'mǎn (*A*) satisfactory, favorable, happy. ‖tā-de-hwēn-'yīn hěn ywán-'mǎn. His marriage is quite happy.

原始

ywán-'shǐ before nouns primitive, of early times, of the earliest times. ywán-'shǐ(-de)-shǐ-'dày prehistoric times; ywán-'shǐ(-de)-rén prehistoric man.

原文

'ywán-wén (*Nunique*) the words actually used by a person being quoted. ‖'ywán-wén bú-shr 'jème-yàngr 'shyě-de. The original didn't read that way.

原因

ywán-'yīn (*Nunit*, ge) reason, cause (not purpose).

遠

ywǎn (*A*) far away, distant. ywǎn-'dūng the Far East.
Notice the use of K lí *with A* ywǎn *in the following sentences:* ‖'jèr lí, chē-'jàn bù-'ywǎn. It's not far from here to the station. or This place isn't far from the station. ‖'jèr lí chē-'jàn yěw 'èr-lǐ 'ywǎn. This place is two miles from the station. ‖nǐ 'lí-ta 'ywǎn-je dyǎr. Stay a little distance away from him.
(*H*) by far, far and away (a bit literary). ‖'jèy-ge 'ywǎn bǐ 'byé-de 'hǎw. This is far and away better than all the others. ‖tā 'ywǎn bù-'rú-ni. He's far inferior to you.

怨

ywàn (*V*) to complain or grumble against someone or about something. ‖nǐ byé 'ywàn 'byé-rén, dēw-s'.r nǐ-'dž-jǐ-'dzwò-de. Don't grumble against others, it's all your own fault.
'ywàn-yán (*N*) complaining words; chū 'ywàn-yán to grumble and complain.

院 (子)

*ywàn, 'ywàn-dz (*Nunit*, ge) court, yard, courtyard; in compounds also hall, large meeting place, or official body; one of the five independent branches of the Chinese government. fǎ-'ywàn court of law; dyàn-yǐng-'ywàn movie theater. shíng-jèng-'ywàn Executive Ywàn; lì-fǎ-'ywàn Legislative Ywàn; sž-fǎ-'ywàn Judicial Ywàn; kǎw-shì-'ywàn Examination Ywàn; jyān-chá-'ywàn Control Ywàn.

願意

'ywàn-yì (*Vpred*) be willing to, like to. ‖tā hěn 'ywàn-yì dzwò jèy-jyàn-'shǐ-ching. He's quite willing to do this job. or He'd like very much to do this job.
ywàn alone is used with the same meaning on a literary level.

約

ywē (*Vsent*) to reach an agreement with *someone to do something*. ‖**wǒ 'ywē-ni chū-chywu chř-'fàn.** I'd like to arrange to take you out to dinner.
　　ywē-'ḥwèy (*Nunit, ge*) appointment, date.

月

'wè (*Ntime, ge*) month; (*Mtime*) month of the year. **'yí-ywè** or (*lunar calendar*) **'jēng-ywè** January; **'èr-ywè, 'sān-ywè,** etc. February, March, etc.: **shŕ-'èr-ywè** or (*lunar calendar*) **'là-ywè** December; **'rwèn-ywè** intercalary month *by the lunar calendar*.
　　'běn-ywè this month; **'shàng-ywè** last month; **'shyà-ywè** next month.
　　ywè-'téw early part of the month; **ywè-'wěy** or **ywè-'dǐ** end of the month.
　　ywè-'dà a month of thirty days; **ywè-'shyǎw** a month of twenty-nine days; *both in the lunar calendar.*
　　In some compounds (and alone in the literary language) moon.

越

ywè (*H*) used *twice:* the more . . . the more . . . . ‖**'ywú 'dǎ-de ywè 'dwō ywè 'hǎw.** The more fish caught the better. ‖**ywè 'dwō ywè méy-'yùng.** The more there are the more useless it is.
　　ywè 'láy ywè . . . , more and more . . . . **ywè 'láy ywè 'hǎw** better and better. ‖**tā 'bìng-de ywè 'láy ywè 'lì-hay.** His illness is getting worse and worse.

樂

*****ywè** (*N*) music. **yīn-'ywè** music. **ywè-'dwèy** orchestra or band; **ywè-'chì** (*Nunit, ge*) musical instrument; **ywè-'pǔ** (*Nunit, běr*) score.

月份牌

ywè-fēn-'pár (*Nunit, ge*) calendar (*chart, not system*).

岳州

ywè-'jēw (*Nunique*) Yüeh-yang *or* Yochow (*city in Hunan province*).

月亮

'ywè-lyang (*Nunique*) moon. ‖**'ywè-lyang 'shàng-lay-le.** The moon's (come) up. ‖**'ywè-lyang 'chū-lay-le.** The moon's (come) up. *or* The moon's (come) out (*from behind the clouds*).

越獄

ywè-'ywù (*VN1*) make a jail break (*a bit literary*).

ywen *Romanization found in Spoken Chinese, Basic Course (EM 506, 507), for syllables spelled* **ywun** *in this dictionary.*

魚，漁

ywú (*Nunit, tyáw, ge*) fish. **ywú-'wǎng** fishnet; **ywú-'gēw**(r) fishhook; **ywú-'gār** fishing rod; **ywú-'shŕ** bait

or fish food; **ywú-'tsż** fishbone; **ywú-'bǐng** *or* **ywú-'byěngr** fish cakes.
　　dǎ-'ywú *or* **dǎy-'ywú** *or* **děy-'ywú** to fish *or* to catch fish, *particularly with a net;* **dyàw-'ywú** to fish *or* to catch fish *with a line.*

於

ywú (*K*) for, towards, with reference to (*a bit literary*). ‖**ywú-'tā yěw-'lì.** It's good for him. *or* It's in his favor. ‖**ywú-'tā °bú-'lì.** *or* °**méy-'lì.** It's of no advantage to him.
　　ywú-'shīn wú-'kwèy be unashamed (*literary*).

娛樂

ywú-'lè (*less often* **ywú-'lwò**) (*Nabstr*) amusement, recreation. ‖**'wǎn-shang yěw shéme-ywú-'lè-ma?** Is there any recreation (*scheduled for*) this evening?
　　ywú-lè-'chǎng place of amusement.

輿論

ywú-'lwèn (*Nabstr*) public opinion. ‖**ywú-'lwèn 'gūng-ji ta hěn 'lì-hay.** Public opinion condemns him vigorously.

雨

ywǔ (*Nmass*) rain. **shyà-'ywǔ** (*IN*) to rain; **shyà 'sān-jèn-'ywǔ** to rain three times; **fēng-'ywǔ** storm. **ywǔ-'sǎn** umbrella; **ywǔ-'shwěy** rain water; **sān-'tswèn-de-ywǔ-'shwěy** three inches of rain(fall); **ywǔ-'yī** raincoat.
　　‖**ywǔ 'gwò tyān 'chīng.** (*Literary quotation*) After the rain the sky is blue.

與

ywǔ (*K*) for, with, towards, concerning (*a bit literary*). ‖**wǒ 'ywǔ-ni yì-túng 'chywù.** I'll go with you.
　　X-ywǔ-Y-jr-'bǐ in the proportion of X to Y: **'sān-ywǔ-'yī-jr-'bǐ** in the ratio of three to one. ‖**nèy-ge-shywé-'shyàw-de-'nywǔ-shywé-sheng gēn 'nán-shywé-sheng 'bǐ, 'děng-ywú 'èr-ywǔ-'yī-jr-'bǐ.** The women students in that school outnumber the men students two to one.

語

*****ywǔ** (*N*) speech, words, spoken language. **gwó-'ywǔ** the Chinese national language; **ywǔ-'yán** speech; **ywǔ-yán-'shywé** the study of spoken language, linguistic science; **ywǔ-yán-shywé-jyǎ** linguistic scientist.

遇

ywù (*V*) to come up against, meet with. **ywù-'shyǎn** to meet with danger, have an accident; **ywù-'nàn** to meet with tragedy, get killed; **ywù-'tsż** to meet with an assassin (*whether he succeeds in assassinating you or not*).
　　As mainV: **'ywù-jyàn** to meet *someone.* ‖**tā dzày 'jyē-shang ywù-jyan tā-'fù-chin-le.** He met his father on the street.

獄
*ywù (*N*) prison, jail.

預備
'ywù-bèy (*V*) to prepare, get ready. (*Vpred*) to prepare to, get ready to. ‖**wǒm 'ywù-bèy ˌdzěw.** We're getting ready to go. *As mainV:* **'ywù-bèy-chū-láy** get *things* out and get *them* ready, *as clothing gotten out of drawers and closets and packed for a trip.*
    'ywù-bèy-jīng-'bàw preparatory signal (*air raid alarm*).

預防
ywù-'fáng (*V*) to take preventative measures against. **ywù-'fáng shīng-húng-'rè** to take preventative measures against scarlet fever.
    dǎ ywù-fáng-'jěn give *or* get an immunizing inoculation.

預計
ywù-'jì (*Vsent*) to anticipate that, plan to. ‖**wǒ-men ywù-'jì wǒ-men-de-'gūng-dzwò wǔ-'ywè-lǐ-tew ké-yi 'wán.** We figure that our work can be finished in May.

愉快
'ywù-kwày (*A*) pleasant, comfortable. ‖**tā 'jīn-tyan 'jīng-shén ˌjywé-de hěn 'ywù-kwày.** He feels quite happy today.

預料
ywù-'lyàw (*Vsent*) to predict *that something will happen. As mainV:* **ywù-'lyàw-dàw** to predict *something.* ‖**'jèy-jyàn-shř-ching wǒ 'dzǎw jyèw ywù-lyàw-'dàw-le.** I predicted this matter long ago.

玉門
ywù-'mén (*Nunique*) Yü-men (*city in Kansu province*).

玉米
'ywù-mi (*Nmass*) corn, maize. **ywù-mi-'bàngr** (*Nunit, ge*) ear of corn.

浴室
ywù-'shř (*Nunit, jyān*) bathroom (*a bit literary*).

預先
ywù-'shyān (*H*) in advance, beforehand. ‖**wǒ děy ywù-'shyān 'gàw-sung ni, ...** I must tell you in advance, . .

預算
ywù-'swàn (*Vsent*) to make advance plans *or* calculations. ‖**wǒ ywù-'swàn wǒ 'wǔ-tyān-jr-'nèy yí-'dìng néng 'dàw-nèr.** I figured out that I would certainly be able to get there within five days.
    ywù-swàn-'shū (*Nunit,* **jāng, běn, fèr**) budget (*on paper*).

育嬰堂
ywù-yīng-'táng (*Nunit, ge*) foundling's home.

暈
ywūn *or* **ywùn** (*A*) faint, dizzy. ‖**wǒ téw 'ywūn-ĺe.** My head feels faint.
    As mainV: **'ywūn-gwò-chywù** to faint.
    As postV: **shwō-'ywún-le** to get *a person* all confused by talking to *him;* **nàw-'ywún-le** to upset *someone.*

勻
ywún (*A*) balanced, even, evenly distributed. ‖**'yán-sè 'hwà-de hěn 'ywún.** The color is spread on very evenly.
    As postV: **fēn-'ywún-le** to divide evenly; **bàn-'ywún-le** to mix in evenly, *as salt stirred into soup.* ‖**ni bǎ jèy-kwày-'bǐng gěy fēn-'ywún-le yì-'rén yí-'kwày.** Divide this cake evenly, one piece to a person.

勻
*ywún (*mainV*) in **'ywún-shyà-láy** *or* **'ywún-chū-ˌláy** (*RC2*) to leave over *time, money, effort, place.* ‖**'ywún-shyà yì-dyǎr-'shř-hew(-lay) gēn-wo 'tán-yi-tán.** Leave a little time to talk with me.

雲彩
'ywún(-tsay) (*Nmass*) clouds. **yí-'pyàn-de-'ywún-tsay** an expanse of clouds; **'báy-ywún** white clouds; **'hēy-ywún** black clouds *or* storm clouds *or* rain clouds.

雲南
ywún-'nán (*Nunique*) Yünnan *province.*

暈
ywùn *see* **ywūn**.

熨
ywùn (*V*) to press *or* iron *clothes. As mainV:* **ywùn-'hù-le** to scorch *clothes* when pressing *them.*

運
ywùn (*V, lc*) to ship, transport, convey, *goods, produce, etc.* **ywùn-'hwò** to ship goods. *As mainV:* **ywùn-'dzěw** to ship *something* away; **'ywùn-dàw** (*lc*) to ship *something* to *a place;* **'ywùn-jìn** (*lc*) to ship *something* in; *etc.*

運氣
'ywùn-chì (*Nabstr*) luck, *good or bad; but* **tā yěw 'ywùn-chì** he's lucky, *meaning good luck as in English.*

熨斗
'ywùn-dew (*Nunit,* **bǎ, ge**) flatiron, iron (*old-fashioned style*).

運動

'ywùn-dùng (*I*) to exercise *physically;* (*Nabstr*) exercise, sports; movements.   **shywé-sheng-'ywùn-dùng** *or* **shywé-sheng ywùn-'dùng** student movement; **ywùn-dùng-'ywán** athlete; **ywùn-dùng-'yī** sports clothes; **ywùn-dùng-'chǎng** playground, athletic field.

(*V*) to work on *someone,* try to bring *someone to do what you want him to.* ‖**wǒ děy 'ywùn-dùng-ywùn-dung ta, chǐng-ta bāng-'máng.**   I've got to work on him and get him to help.

運河

ywùn-thé (*Nunique*) The Grand Canal.

運輸

ywùn-'shū (*Nabstr*) transportation, shipping. ‖**dǎ-'jàng-de-shŕ-hew ywùn-'shū hěn 'nán.**   In war time transportation is quite difficult.

CHARACTER INDEX

NOTE

The following index covers (1) all those characters which appear *alone* or *as the first character of an expression of several characters* in the Chinese-English side of the dictionary; (2) all those characters which are virtually interchangeable with one of those covered by (1).

The arrangement is in five columns. In the first column appears a number in decimal form. The part of the number before the decimal point indicates the *radical number*, and the part after the decimal point indicates the *number of added strokes*. In the second column appears the character itself. In the third column appears the pronunciation (or pronunciations) of that character; in transcription. This serves as a cross reference to the proper entry or entries in the Chinese-English side, where the arrangement is alphabetical by transcription. The fourth and fifth columns are usually blank, but when there are other characters virtually interchangeable with the one being listed, they appear in the fifth column, and the proper index number is listed in the fourth column. An exception to this method of cross reference is made when two virtually interchangeable characters occur one immediately below the other; in this case there is a brace after the second column and the pronunciation or pronunciations of the two are given but once.

1.	一	yī, yí, yì.	33.9.	壹	4.4.	乍	jà.		
1.1.	丁	dīng, dìng.			4.4.	乏	fá.		
1.1.	七	chī.	75.5.	柒	4.7.	乖	gwày.		
1.2.	丈	jàng.			4.9.	乘	chéng.		
1.2.	下	shyà.			(5.)	乙			
1.2.	三	sān, sā.	28.6.	叁	5.1.	九	jyěw.	96.3.	玖
1.2.	上	shàng.			5.2.	乞	chǐ.		
1.2.	万	wan.	140.9.	萬	5.2.	也	yě.		
1.3.	不	bū, bú, bù.			5.7.	乳	rǔ.		
1.4.	世	shr̀.			5.10.	乾	gān.		
1.5.	丢	dyēw.			5.12.	亂	làn, lwàn.		
1.7.	並	bìng.	51.5, 117.5.	并 立	(6.)	亅			
					6.1.	了	le, lyǎw.		
(2.)	丨				6.7.	事	shr̀.		
2.2.	个	gè.	9.8, 118.8.	個 箇	7.	二	èr.	56.2, 154.5.	弍 貳
2.3.	中	jūng, jùng.			7.2.	互	hù.		
2.3.	丰	fēng.			7.2.	井	jǐng.		
2.6.	串	chwàn.			7.2.	五	wǔ.		
(3.)	丶				7.5.	些	shyē.		
3.2.	丸	wán.			(8.)	亠			
3.3.	丹	dān.			8.4.	交	jyāw.		
3.4.	主	jú, jǔ.			8.6.	享	shyǎng.		
(4.)	丿				8.7.	亮	lyàng.		
4.2.	久	jyěw.			9.	人	rén.		
4.3.	之	jr̄.			9.2.	仇	chéw.		

9.2.	仍	réng.	
9.2.	介	jyè.	
9.2.	今	jīn.	
9.2.	什	shém (*in* 'shém-me, shéme).	
9.3.	仗	jàng.	
9.3.	付	fù.	
9.3.	以	yǐ.	
9.3.	令	lìng.	
9.3.	他	tā.	
9.3.	仝	túng.	30.3. 同
9.3.	仔	dž.	
9.4.	份	fèn.	
9.4.	仿	fǎng.	9.8. 做
9.4.	伏	fú.	
9.4.	休	shyēw.	
9.4.	伙	hwǒ.	36.11. 夥
9.4.	任	rèn.	
9.4.	件	jyàn.	
9.5.	佔	jàn.	
9.5.	住	jù.	
9.5.	佛	fwó.	
9.5.	估	gǔ.	
9.5.	你	nǐ.	
9.5.	伴	bàn.	
9.5.	伯	bwó.	
9.5.	伸	shēn.	
9.5.	似	sž, shř.	
9.5.	伺	sž, tsž.	
9.5.	低	dī.	
9.5.	作	dzwò.	
9.5.	位	wèy.	
9.6.	依	yī.	
9.6.	佳	jyā.	
9.6.	供	gūng.	
9.6.	來	láy.	
9.6.	例	lì.	
9.6.	佩	pèy.	
9.6.	使	shř.	
9.7.	俘	fú.	
9.7.	俄	ē, é, è.	
9.7.	保	bǎw.	
9.7.	便	pyán, byàn.	
9.7.	信	shìn.	
9.7.	俗	sú.	
9.7.	俏	chyàw.	
9.7.	侮	wū.	
9.8.	值	jŕ.	
9.8.	倣	fǎng.	
9.8.	候	hèw.	
9.8.	個	ge, gè.	2.2, 118.8 个 筒
9.8.	倆	lyǎ.	
9.8.	們	men.	
9.8.	倫	lwén.	
9.8.	修	shyēw.	
9.8.	倉	tsāng.	
9.8.	借	jyè.	
9.9.	假	jyǎ, jyà.	
9.9.	健	jyàn.	
9.9.	偶	ěw.	
9.9.	偪	bī.	162.9. 逼
9.9.	偏	pyān.	
9.9.	偷	tēw.	
9.9.	停	tíng.	
9.10.	傢	jyā.	
9.10.	傀	kwěy.	
9.10.	備	bèy.	
9.10.	傘	sǎn.	
9.11.	債	jày.	
9.11.	傳	chwán, jwàn.	
9.11.	傾	chīng, kēng.	
9.11.	傷	shāng.	
9.11.	催	tswěy.	
9.12.	僑	chyáw.	
9.12.	僱	gù.	
9.12.	僕	pú, pǔ.	
9.12.	像	shyàng.	
9.13.	儀	yí.	
9.13.	價	jyà.	
9.13.	儬	jyǎng.	
9.13.	儉	jyǎn.	
9.13.	儆	jǐng.	149.13. 警
9.13.	傻	shǎ.	
9.16.	儲	chú.	
(10.)	几		
10.2.	元	ywán.	
10.3.	充	chūng.	

10.3.	兄	shyūng.			
10.4.	兜	shyūng.			
10.4.	光	gwāng.			
10.4.	先	shyān.			
10.5.	兔	myǎn.			
10.5.	兔	tù.	10.6.		兔
10.5.	兌	dwèy.			
10.6.	兒	ér.			
10.6.	兔	tù.	10.5.		兔
11.	入	rù.			
11.2.	內	nèy.			
11.4.	全	chywán.			
11.6.	兩	lyǎng.			
12.	八	bā.	64.7.		捌
12.2.	公	gūng.			
12.2.	六	lyèw.			
12.4.	共	gùng.			
12.5.	兵	bīng.			
12.6.	其	chí.			
12.6.	具	jywù.			
12.6.	典	dyǎn.			
(13.)	冂				
13.3.	册	tsè.			
13.7.	冒	màw.			
(14.)	冖				
14.8.	冤	ywān.			
14.12.	寫	shyě.			
(15.)	冫				
15.3.	冬	dūng.			
15.4.	冲	chūng.	85.4.		沖
15.4.	決	jywé.	85.4.		決
15.4.	冰	bīng.			
15.5.	冷	lěng.			
15.8.	准	jwěn.			
15.8.	凍	dùng.			
15.9.	湊	tsèw.	85.9.		湊
15.14.	凝	níng, nìng.			
(16.)	几				
16.1.	凡	fán.			
16.12.	凳	dèng.	75.14.		橙
(17.)	凵				
17.2.	凶	shyūng.			
17.3.	出	chū.			
(18.)	刀				

18.1.	刃	rèn.			
18.2.	分	fēn.			
18.2.	切	chyē.			
18.3.	刊	kān.			
18.4.	划	hwá.			
18.4.	列	lyè.			
18.5.	初	chū.			
18.5.	利	lì.			
18.5.	判	pàn.			
18.5.	刨	páw.			
18.5.	別	byé.			
18.5.	删	shān.			
18.6.	制	jr̀.			
18.6.	刻	kè.			
18.6.	刮	gwā.			
18.6.	剌	lá.			
18.6.	刷	shwā.			
18.7.	刺	tsz̀.			
18.7.	削	shyāw.			
18.7.	剃	tì.			
18.7.	則	dzé.			
18.7.	前	chyán.			
18.8.	剛	gāng.			
18.8.	剔	tī.			
18.9.	副	fù.			
18.9.	刮	gwǎ.			
18.9.	剩	shèng.	154.10.		賸
18.9.	剪	jyǎn.	124.9.		翦
18.10.	創	chwǎng.			
18.10.	割	gé.			
18.12.	劃	hwá.			
18.13.	劇	jywù.			
18.13.	劈	pǐ, pī.			
19.	力	lì.			
19.3.	加	jyā.			
19.3.	功	gūng.			
19.5.	助	jù.			
19.5.	努	nǔ.			
19.7.	勁	jìn.			
19.7.	勉	myǎn.			
19.7.	勇	yǔng.			
19.8.	務	wù.			
19.9.	動	dùng.			
19.10.	勛	shywūn.	19.14.		勳

19.10.	勞	láw.		
19.10.	勝	shèng.		
19.11.	勤	chín.		
19.11.	募	mù.		
19.11.	勢	shr̀.		
19.14.	勳	shywūn.	19.10.	勛
19.18.	勸	chywàn.		
(20.)	勹			
20.2.	勾	gēw.		
20.2.	勿	wú, wù.		
20.2.	匀	ywún.		
20.3.	包	bāw.		
20.4.	匈	shyūng.		
(21.)	匕			
21.2.	化	hwā.		
21.3.	北	běy.		
(22.)	匚			
22.5.	匣	shyá.		
22.8.	匪	fěy.		
22.11.	匯	hwėy.		
(23.)	匸			
23.2.	匹	pǐ.		
23.9.	匿	nì.		
24.	十	shŕ.	64.6.	拾
24.1.	千	chyān.		
24.2.	升	shēng.		
24.2.	午	wǔ.		
24.3.	半	bàn.		
24.7.	南	nán.		
24.10	博	bwó.		
(25.)	卜			
25.3.	卡	chyǎ, kǎ.		
(26.)	卩			
26.4.	印	yìn.		
26.4.	危	wéy.		
26.6.	卷	jywǎn, jywàn.		
26.6.	卸	shyè.		
26.7.	卽	jí, jì.		
(27.)	厂			
27.7.	厚	hèw.		
27.8.	原	ywán.		
27.9.	厠	tsè.	53.9.	廁
27.10.	廈	shyà.	53.10.	廈
27.12.	廠	chǎng.		

(28.)	厶			
28.3.	去	chywù.		
28.6.	叄	sān.	1.2.	三
28.9.	參	tsēn.		
29.	又	yèw.		
29.1.	叉	chā.		
29.2.	反	fǎn.		
29.2.	及	jí.		
29.2.	収	shēw.	66.2.	收
29.2.	友	yěw.		
29.6.	受	shèw.		
29.6.	叔	shū.		
29.6.	取	chywǔ.		
29.16.	叢	tsúng.		
30.	口	kěw.		
30.2.	只	jř.		
30.2.	叩	kèw.		
30.2.	可	kě.		
30.2.	古	gǔ.		
30.2.	句	jywù.		
30.2.	另	lìng.		
30.2.	史	shř.		
30.2.	司	sz̄.		
30.2.	台	táy.	133.8.	臺
30.2.	叨	dyāw.		
30.2.	右	yèw.		
30.2.	叫	jyàw.		
30.3.	向	shyàng.		
30.3.	合	hé.		
30.3.	吉	jí.		
30.3.	吃	chř.		
30.3.	各	gè.		
30.3.	名	míng.		
30.3.	吊	dyàw.		
30.3.	吐	tǔ, tù, twò.		
30.3.	同	túng.	9.3.	仝
30.4.	吵	chǎw.		
30.4.	呈	chéng.		
30.4.	吹	chwēy.		
30.4.	吩	fēn.		
30.4.	否	fěw.		
30.4.	含	hén, hán.		
30.4.	吼	hěw, hèw.		
30.4.	吸	shī.		

30.4.	告	gàw.		30.8.	啞	yǎ.
30.4.	叫	jyàw.		30.8.	問	wèn.
30.4.	君	jywūn.		30.8.	唯	wéy.
30.4.	吝	lìn		30.9.	喘	chwǎn.
30.4.	呂	lywǔ.		30.9.	喊	hǎn.
30.4.	吧	ba.		30.9.	喜	shǐ.
30.4.	吻	wěn.		30.9.	喝	hē.
30.4.	吳	wú.		30.9.	喫	chr̄.	30.3.	吃
30.4.	呀	a, wa, ya, na, nga.		30.9.	喇	lǎ.
				30.9.	善	shàn.
30.4.	听	tīng.	128.16.	聽	30.9.	喂	wèy.	184.8.	餧
30.5.	周	jēw.		30.10.	嗎	ma.
30.5.	呼	hū.		30.10.	嗓	sǎng.
30.5.	和	hé, hwò.		30.10.	嗄	a, wa, ya, na, nga.	30.4.	呀
30.5.	命	mìng.				
30.5.	呢	ne.		30.11.	嘗	cháng.
30.5.	呱	wā, wà.		30.11.	嘉	jyā.
30.5.	味	wèy.		30.12.	嘟	dū.
30.5.	咖	jyā, kā.		30.12.	噉	jywē.
30.6.	响	shyǎng.	180.13.	響	30.12.	嘴	dzwěy.
30.6.	哈	hā.		30.13.	噸	dwēn, dwèn.
30.6.	哄	hǔng.		30.13.	嗳	ày.
30.6.	咳	ké.	76.6.	欬	30.13.	噴	pēn.
30.6.	品	pǐn.		30.14.	嚇	shyà.
30.6.	咱	dzán.		30.16.	嚮	shyǎng.
30.6.	哇	wā.		30.17.	嚷	rǎng, rǎng.
30.6.	咬	yǎw.		30.17.	嚴	yán.
30.6.	哆	dwō.		30.18.	嚼	jyáw.
30.7.	哲	jé.		30.19.	囊	náng.
30.7.	哼	hēng.		(31.)	口	
30.7.	哥	gē.		31.2.	囚	chyéw.
30.7.	哭	kū.		31.2.	四	sz̀.	129.7.	肆
30.7.	哪	ne, na.		31.3.	回	hwéy.
30.7.	哦	a, wa, ya, na, nga.		31.3.	因	yīn.
				31.4.	困	kwèn.
30.7.	哨	shàw.		31.5.	固	gù.
30.7.	唐	táng.		31.8.	圈	chywān, jywān.
30.7.	員	ywán.		31.8.	國	gwó.
30.7.	唱	chàng.		31.9.	圍	wéy.
30.8.	啤	pí.		31.10.	圓	ywán.
30.8.	啊	a, wa, ya, na, nga.		31.10.	園	ywán.
				31.11.	圖	tú.
30.8.	商	shāng.		31.11.	團	twán.
30.8.	啐	tswèy.		32.	土	tǔ.

44.9.	屬	shǔ.	44.18.		屬
44.9.	屠	tú.			
44.11.	屢	lywǔ.			
44.12.	履	lywǔ.			
44.12.	層	tsēng.			
44.18.	屬	shǔ.	44.9		屬
46.	山	shān.			
46.4.	岔	chà.			
46.5.	岸	àn.			
46.5.	岳	ywè.			
46.8.	崇	chúng.			
46.8.	崩	bēng.			
46.9.	崴	dzǎy.			
46.19.	巔	dyān.			
(47.)	川				
47.3.	州	jēw.			
47.4.	巡	shywún.			
48.	工	gūng.			
48.2.	左	dzwǒ.			
48.2.	巧	chyǎw.			
48.4.	巫	wū.			
48.6.	差	chāy, chà.			
49.	已	yǐ.			
49.1.	巴	bā.			
49.6.	巷	shyàng.			
(50.)	巾				
50.2.	市	shr̀.			
50.2.	布	bù.			
50.3.	帆	fān.			
50.4.	帋	jr̀.	120.4.		紙
50.4.	希	shī.			
50.5.	帖	tyē.			
50.6.	帝	dì.			
50.7.	帮	bāng.	50.9, 50.14.		幇幫
50.7.	師	shr̄.			
50.7.	席	shí.			
50.8.	帳	jàng.			
50.8.	常	cháng.			
50.9.	帽	màw.			
50.9.	幇	bāng.	50.7, 50.14.		邦幫
50.11.	幕	mù.			
50.14.	幫	bāng.	50.7, 50.9.		邦幇
(51.)	干				
51.2.	平	píng.			
51.3.	年	nyán.			
51.5.	并	bìng.	1.7, 117.5.		並竝
51.5.	幸	shìng.			
51.10.	幹	gàn.			
52.	幺	yāw.			
52.1.	幻	hwàn.			
52.2.	幼	yèw.			
52.9.	幾	jī, jǐ.			
(53.)	广				
53.4.	床	chwáng.	90.4.		牀
53.5.	府	fǔ.			
53.5.	底	dǐ.			
53.5.	店	dyàn.			
53.6.	度	dù.			
53.7.	庫	kù.			
53.7.	座	dzwè.			
53.8.	康	kāng.			
53.8.	庸	yūng.			
53.9.	廂	shyāng.			
53.9.	廁	tsè.	27.9.		厠
53.10.	廈	shyà.	27.10.		厦
53.10.	廊	láng.			
53.12.	廠	chǎng.	27.12.		厰
53.12.	廚	chú.			
53.12.	廢	fèy.			
53.12.	廣	gwǎng.			
53.12.	廟	myàw.			
53.16.	廬	lú.			
53.22.	廳	tīng.			
(54.)	廴				
54.5.	延	yán, yàn.			
54.5.	廸	dí.			
54.6.	建	jyàn.			
(55.)	廾				
55.4.	弄	nèng, nùng.			
(56.)	弋				
56.2.	弍	èr.	7, 154.5.		二貳
56.3.	弐	shŕ, shr̀.			
57.	弓	gūng.			

57.1.	帚	dyàw.	30.3.	吊	
57.1.	引	yǐn.			
57.4.	弟	dì.			
57.5.	弦	shyán.			
57.5.	弧	hú.			
57.7.	弱	rwò.			
57.8.	張	jāng.			
57.8.	強	chyáng, jyàng.	57.13.	彊	
57.10.	彀	gèw.			
57.12.	彈	tán.			
57.13.	彊	chyáng, jyàng.	57.8.	強	
57.19.	彎	wǎn.			
(59.)	彡				
59.4.	形	shíng.			
59.8.	彫	dyāw.	172.8.	雕	
59.11.	彰	jāng.			
59.12.	影	yǐng.			
(60.)	彳				
60.4.	彷	fǎng.	190.4.	髣	
60.5.	彼	bǐ.			
60.5.	往	wǎng, wàng.			
60.6.	很	hěn, heng.			
60.6.	後	hèw.			
60.6.	律	lywù.			
60.7.	徐	shywú.			
60.7.	徒	tú.			
60.8.	得	dé, děy.			
60.8.	從	tsúng.			
60.9.	復	fú, fù.			
60.9.	徧	byàn.	162.9.	遍	
60.9.	循	shywún.			
60.10.	微	wēy.			
60.12.	徵	jēng.			
60.12.	德	dé.			
60.14.	徽	hwēy.			
61.	心	shīn.			
61.1.	必	bì.			
61.3.	志	jr̀.			
61.3.	忍	rěn.			
61.3.	忌	jì.			
61.3.	忙	máng.			
61.3.	忘	wàng.			

61.4.	忠	jūng.			
61.4.	忽	hū.			
61.4.	快	kwày.			
61.4.	念	nyàn.			
61.5.	急	jí.			
61.5.	怪	gwày.	61.6.	恠	
61.5.	怒	nù.			
61.5.	怕	pà.			
61.5.	性	shìng.			
61.5.	思	sz̄.			
61.5.	怎	dzěm (in dzěm-me, dzěme).			
61.5.	怨	ywàn.			
61.6.	恨	hèn.			
61.6.	恐	kǔng.			
61.6.	恭	gūng.			
61.6.	恠	gwày.	61.5.	怪	
61.6.	恢	hwēy.			
61.7.	患	hwàn.			
61.7.	悔	hwěy.			
61.7.	您	nín.			
61.8.	悶	mēn, mèn.	61.14.	懣	
61.8.	惦	dyàn.			
61.8.	情	chíng.			
61.8.	惡	ě.			
61.9.	意	yì.			
61.9.	惹	rě.			
61.9.	感	gǎn.			
61.9.	惱	nàw.			
61.9.	愛	ày.			
61.9.	想	shyǎng.			
61.9.	愁	chéw.			
61.9.	愉	ywù.			
61.10.	慌	hwāng, hwang.			
61.10.	愰	hwàng.			
61.10.	態	tày.			
61.10.	慈	tsź.			
61.11.	慶	chìng.			
61.11.	慢	màn.			
61.11.	慘	tsǎn.			
61.11.	慣	gwàn.			
61.12.	憿	} byè, byē.			
61.12.	憨				
61.12.	憑	píng.			
61.13.	懈	shyè.			

317

61.13.	懂	dǔng.			
61.13	應	yīng, yìng.			
61.13	懆	dzàw.			
61.14.	懣	mēn, mèn.	61.8.	悶	
61.15.	懲	chěng.			
61.16.	懸	shywán.			
61.16.	懷	hwáy.			
61.16.	懶	lǎn.			
(62.)	戈				
62.3.	戒	jyè.			
62.3.	成	chéng.			
62.3.	我	wǒ.			
62.4.	或	hwò.			
62.9.	戥	děng.			
62.10.	截	jyé.			
62.12.	戰	jàn.			
62.13.	戲	shì.			
62.14.	戳	chwō.			
62.14.	戴	dày.			
(63.)	戶				
63.4.	房	fáng.			
63.4.	所	swǒ.			
63.5.	扁	byǎn.			
63.6.	扇	shàn.			
64.	手	shěw.			
64.1.	才	tsáy.			
64.1.	扎	jā.			
64.2.	扔	rēng.			
64.2.	扑	pū.	64.12.	撲	
64.2.	打	dǎ.			
64.3.	扛	káng.			
64.3.	托	twō.			
64.3.	扣	kèw.			
64.4.	抓	jwā.			
64.4.	找	jǎw.			
64.4.	抄	chāw.			
64.4.	折	shé.			
64.4.	扯	chě.			
64.4.	承	chéng.			
64.4.	扶	fú.			
64.4.	抗	kàng.			
64.4.	技	jì.			
64.4.	抛	pāw.			
64.4	把	bǎ.			
64.4.	批	pī.			
64.4.	抖	děw.			
64.4.	投	téw.			
64.5.	招	jāw.			
64.5.	抽	chēw.			
64.5.	拂	fú.			
64.5.	拘	jywū.			
64.5.	拒	jywù.			
64.5.	拐	gwǎy.			
64.5.	拉	lā.			
64.5.	抹	mwǒ.			
64.5.	拏	ná.	64.6.	拿	
64.5.	拔	bá.			
64.5.	拜	bày.			
64.5.	拌	bàn.			
64.5.	抱	bàw.			
64.5.	披	pēy, péy.			
64.5.	拍	pāy.			
64.5.	抬	táy.	64.14.	擡	
64.5.	抵	dǐ.			
64.5.	拖	twō.			
64.5.	拆	chāy.			
64.5.	押	yā.			
64.6.	拒	jǐ.			
64.6.	拽	jwāy, jwày.			
64.6.	拳	chywán.			
64.6.	挂	gwà.			
64.6.	拿	ná.	64.5.	拏	
64.6.	按	àn, èn.			
64.6.	拾	shf.	24.	十	
64.6.	拴	shwān.			
64.6.	挑	tyāw, tyǎw.			
64.6.	挖	wā.			
64.7.	挨	āy, áy.			
64.7.	振	jèn.			
64.7.	挫	dzwō.			
64.7.	捐	jywān.			
64.7.	捆	kwěn.			
64.7.	挪	nwó.			
64.7.	捌	bā.	12.	八	
64.7.	捕	bǔ.			
64.7.	捅	tǔng.			
64.8.	捵	chēn.			

318

75.1.	未	wèy.		
75.2.	朴	pǔ.		
75.2.	朵	dwǒ.		
75.2.	机	jī.	75.12.	樸
75.3.	构	sháw.	75.12.	機
75.3.	杏	shìng.		
75.3.	杆	gān.		
75.3.	村	tswēn.		
75.3.	杷	chǐ.		
75.4.	枕	jěn.		
75.4.	枝	jī.		
75.4.	板	bǎn.		
75.4.	枇	pí.		
75.4.	杯	bēy.	108.4.	盃
75.4.	松	sūng.		
75.4.	東	dūng.		
75.4.	杭	háng.		
75.5.	查	chá.		
75.5.	柴	cháy.		
75.5.	柱	jù.		
75.5.	染	rǎn.		
75.5.	柔	réw.		
75.5.	架	jyà.		
75.5.	某	měw.		
75.5.	柏	bwó.		
75.5.	柒	chǐ.	1.1.	七
75.6.	核	hé.		
75.6.	根	gēn.		
75.6.	校	jyǎw, jyàw, shyàw.		
75.6.	格	gé.		
75.6.	框	kwàng.		
75.6.	桂	gwèy.		
75.6.	栗	lì.		
75.6.	案	àn.		
75.6.	栢	bwò.		
75.6.	栖	chǐ.	75.8.	棲
75.6.	桃	táw.		
75.6.	桌	jwō.	75.8.	棹
75.7.	桿	gǎn.		
75.7.	梅	méy.		
75.7.	梳	shū.		
75.7.	梯	tī.		
75.7.	條	tyáw.		

75.7.	桶	tǔng.		
75.7.	梧	wú.		
75.8.	棹	jwō.		
75.8.	植	jí.		
75.8.	椅	yǐ.		
75.8.	棋	chí.		
75.8.	極	jí.		
75.8.	棍	gwèn.		
75.8.	棉	myán.		
75.8.	棒	bàng.		
75.8.	棚	péng.		
75.8.	森	shēn.		
75.8.	棲	chǐ.	75.6.	栖
75.8.	棵	kē.		
75.8.	棗	dzǎw.		
75.8.	棕	dzūng.		
75.8.	椀	wǎn.	112.8.	碗
75.9.	楊	yáng.		
75.9.	椰	yē.		
75.10.	榛	chín.		
75.10.	構	gèw.		
75.10.	榜	bǎng.		
75.10.	榮	rúng.		
75.11.	椿	jwāng.		
75.11.	概	gày.		
75.11.	樓	léw.		
75.11.	樂	lè, lwò, ywè.		
75.11.	模	mú, mwó.		
75.11.	樣	yàng.		
75.11.	樑	lyáng.		
75.12.	橫	héng.		
75.12.	橄	gán.		
75.12.	機	jī.	75.2.	机
75.12.	橡	shyàng.		
75.12.	橘	chyáw.		
75.12.	橘	jywú.		
75.12.	樸	pǔ.	75.2.	朴
75.12.	樹	shù.		
75.13.	檢	jyǎn.		
75.13.	檀	tán.		
75.14.	櫃	gwèy.		
75.14.	櫈	dèng.	16.12.	凳
75.14.	檸	níng.		
75.18.	權	chywán.		

85.8.	涵	hán.	85.11.	演	yǎn.
85.8.	混	hwén, hwèn.	85.11.	漳	jāng.
85.8.	淚	lèy.	85.12.	潮	cháw.
85.8.	涼	lyáng.	85.12.	澈	chè.
85.8.	淋	lwén.	85.12.	澆	jyāw.
85.8.	深	shēn.	85.12.	潘	} chyān.
85.8.	淘	táw.	85.12.	潛	
85.8.	添	tyān.	85.12.	潑	pwō.
85.8.	淺	chyǎn.	85.12.	潼	túng.
85.8.	淨	jìng.	85.13.	激	jí.
85.8.	清	chīng.	85.13.	澳	àw.
85.8.	淹	yān.	85.13.	濃	núng.
85.8.	淮	hwáy.	85.13.	澡	dzǎw.
85.9.	渣	jǎ.	85.14.	濶	kwò.
85.9.	湖	hú.	85.14.	濘	nìng, nèng.
85.9.	港	gǎng.	85.14.	濱	bīn.
85.9.	減	jyǎn.	85.14.	濕	shř. 85.10. 湿
85.9.	渴	kě.	85.14.	濰	wéy.
85.9.	渤	bwō.	85.14.	濟	jǐ.
85.9.	湯	tāng.	85.15.	瀑	pū.
85.9.	渡	dù.	85.15.	瀋	shěn.
85.9.	湊	tsèw. 15.9. 凑	85.15.	濺	jyàn.
85.9.	溫	wēn.	85.18.	灌	gwàn.
85.9.	游	yéw.	85.19.	灑	sǎ. 85.6. 洒
85.9.	湘	shyāng.	85.19.	灘	tān.
85.10.	準	jwěn.	86.	火	hwǒ.
85.10.	滑	hwá.	86.2.	灰	hwēy.
85.10.	溝	gēw.	86.4.	炒	chǎw.
85.10.	溜	lyèw.	86.5.	炸	já.
85.10.	滅	myè.	86.5.	点	dyǎn. 203.5. 點
85.10.	湿	shř. 85.14 濕	86.6.	烘	hūng.
85.10.	滋	dz.	86.6.	烤	kǎw.
85.10.	溶	rúng.	86.6.	烈	lyè.
85.11.	漲	jàng.	86.6.	烙	làw.
85.11.	漢	hàn.	86.6.	烏	wū.
85.11.	滾	gwěn.	86.6.	烟	yān. 86.9. 煙
85.11.	漏	lèw.	86.7.	烹	pēng.
85.11.	滿	mǎn.	86.8.	然	rán.
85.11.	漫	màn.	86.8.	無	wú, wù.
85.11.	漂	pyāw, pyàw.	86.9.	照	jàw.
85.11.	滴	dī.	86.9.	煮	} jǔ.
85.11.	漿	jyāng, jyàng.	86.9.	煑	
85.11.	漸	jyàn.	86.9.	煩	fán.
85.11.	漆	chī.			

86.9.	湖	hú.		
86.9.	暖	nwǎn.	72.9.	暖
86.9.	煤	méy.		
86.9.	煎	jyān.		
86.9.	煙	yān.	86.6.	烟
86.10.	熊	shyúng.		
86.10.	熄	shī, shí.		
86.11.	熱	} rè.		
86.11.	熱			
86.11.	熬	áw.		
86.11.	熟	shéw, shú.		
86.11.	熨	ywùn.		
86.12.	燒	shāw.		
86.12.	燙	tàng.		
86.12.	燈	dēng.		
86.12.	燉	ḍwèn.		
86.12.	燋	jyāw.		
86.12.	燕	yàn.		
86.12.	燜	mèn.		
86.13.	營	yíng.		
86.14.	熏	shywūn.		
86.15.	爆	bāw, bàw.		
86.16.	爐	lúng, lǔng.		
86.16.	爐	lú.		
86.17.	爛	làn.		
(87.)	爪爬	pá.		
87.4.	爭	jēng.		
87.8.	爲	wéy, wèy.		
87.14.	爵	jywé.		
88.	父	fù.		
88.6.	爹	dyē.		
88.9.	爺	yé.		
(89.)	爻			
89.7.	爽	shwǎng.		
(90.)	爿			
90.4.	牀	chwáng.	53.4.	床
90.13.	牆	chyáng.		
91.	片	pyān, pyàn.		
91.8.	牌	páy.		
92.	牙	yá.		
(93.)	牛			
93.4.	牧	mù.		
93.4.	物	wù.		
93.5.	牲	shēng.		

93.6.	特	tè.		
93.7.	犂	lí.	93.8.	犛
93.8.	犄	jī.		
93.8.	犁	lí.	93.7.	犁
93.16.	犧	shī.		
(94.)	犬			
94.2.	犯	fàn.		
94.4.	狂	kwáng.		
94.5.	狐	hú.		
94.5.	狗	gěw.		
94.6.	狠	hěn.		
94.6.	狡	jyǎw.		
94.7.	狹	shyá.		
94.7.	狼	láng.		
94.8.	猛	měng.		
94.8.	猜	tsāy.		
94.9.	猪	jū, dž.	152.9.	豬
94.9.	猴	héw.		
94.9.	猫	māw.	153.9.	貓
94.9.	猶	yéw.		
94.10.	獅	shř.		
94.11.	獄	ywù.		
94.13.	獨	dú.		
94.15.	獸	shèw.		
96.	玉	ywù.		
96.3.	玖	jyěw.	5.1.	九
96.4.	玫	} méy.		
96.4.	玫			
96.4.	玩	wán.		
96.4.	玻	bwō.		
96.6.	珠	jū.		
96.6.	班	bān.		
96.7.	現	shyàn.		
96.7.	球	chyéw.		
96.7.	理	lǐ, lywǔ.		
96.8.	琢	dzwó.		
96.8.	琴	chín.		
96.9.	瑞	rwèy.		
96.13.	環	hwán.		
96.13.	瑷	ày.		
96.15.	瓊	chyúng.		
97.	瓜	gwā.		
98.	瓦	wǎ.		
98.6.	瓶	píng.		

Ref	Char	Pron.	X-ref	X-char
109.10.	瞎	shyā.		
109.11.	瞟	pyǎw.		
109.12.	瞪	dèng.		
109.12.	瞧	chyáw.		
(111.)	矢			
111.3.	知	jr̄.		
111.7.	短	dwǎn.		
111.8.	矮	ǎy.		
112.	石	shŕ.		
112.4.	砍	kǎn.		
112.5.	砲	pàw.	112.16.	礮
112.5.	破	pwò.		
112.5.	砸	dzá.		
112.6.	研	yán.		
112.7.	硬	yìng.		
112.8.	碑	bēy.		
112.8.	碎	swèy.		
112.8.	碗	wǎn.	75.8, 108.5.	椀 盌
112.9.	碰	pèng.		
112.9.	碟	dyé.		
112.10.	磕	kē.		
112.10.	碼	mǎ.		
112.10.	磅	bàng.		
112.10.	確	chywè.		
112.10.	磁	tsź.		
112.11.	磚	jwān.		
112.11.	磨	mwó.		
112.13.	礪	lǔ.		
112.14.	礙	ày.		
112.15.	礦	kwàng.		
112.16.	礮	pàw.	112.5.	砲
(113.)	示			
113.3.	社	shè.		
113.4.	祈	chí.		
113.5.	祇	jř.		
113.5.	祝	jù.		
113.5.	祕	bì, mì.	115.5.	秘
113.5.	神	shén.		
113.5.	祖	dzǔ.		
113.6.	票	pyàw.		
113.6.	祭	jì.		
113.8.	禁	jīn, jìn.		
113.9.	福	fú.		
113.9.	禍	hwò.		
113.13.	禮	lǐ.		
(115.)	禾			
115.2.	私	sź.		
115.4.	科	kē.		
115.4.	秒	myǎw.		
115.4.	秋	chyēw.		
115.5.	秩	jŕ.		
115.5.	秘	bì, mì.	113.5.	祕
115.5.	秦	chín.		
115.5.	租	dzū.		
115.5.	秧	yāng.		
115.7.	稀	shī.		
115.7.	程	chéng.		
115.7.	稍	shāw, shywē.		
115.7.	稅	shwèy.		
115.9.	稱	chèn, chēng.		
115.9.	種	jǔng, jùng.		
115.10.	稟	} gǎw.		
115.10.	稿			
115.11.	糠	kāng.	119.11.	糠
115.14.	穩	wěn.		
(116.)	穴			
116.2.	究	jyēw, jyèw.		
116.3.	空	kūng, kùng.		
116.4.	突	tū, tù.		
116.5.	窄	jǎy.		
116.6.	窓	} chwǎng.		
116.7.	窗			
116.7.	窖	jyàw.		
116.7.	窘	jyǔng.		
116.8.	窟	kū.		
116.9.	窩	wō.		
116.10.	窮	chyúng.		
116.17.	竊	chyè.		
117.	立	lì.		
117.5.	站	jàn.		
117.5.	竝	bìng.	1.7, 51.5.	並 幷
117.6.	章	jāng.		
117.6.	竟	jìng.		
117.7.	童	túng.		
117.8.	豎	shù.	151.8.	豎
117.9.	竭	jyé.		

No.	Char	Reading		Cross-ref	Char
130.9.	腮	sāy.		181.9.	顋
130.9.	腰	yāw.			
130.10.	腿	twěy.			
130.10.	膀	bǎng, páng.			
130.11.	膚	fū.			
130.11.	膠	jyāw.			
130.11.	膝	chī.			
130.12.	膩	nì.			
130.12.	膳	shàn.			
130.13.	臉	lyǎn.			
130.13.	膿	néng, núng.			
130.13.	臊	sàw.			
130.16.	臟	yān.		130.6.	胭
(131.)	臣				
131.2.	臥	wò.			
131.11.	臨	lín.			
132.	自	dž.			
132.4.	臭	chèw.			
133.	至	jr̀.			
133.4.	致	jr̀.			
133.8.	臺	táy.		30.2.	台
(134.)	臼				
134.4.	舀	wǎy.			
134.7.	舅	jyèw.			
134.7.	與	ywǔ.			
134.9.	興	shīng, shìng.			
134.11.	舉	jywǔ.			
134.12.	舊	jyèw.			
135.	舌	shé.			
135.2.	舍	shè.			
135.6.	舒	shū.			
(136.)	舛				
136.8.	舞	wǔ.			
(137.)	舟				
137.4.	航	háng.			
137.4.	般	bān.			
137.5.	船	chwán.			
137.5.	舶	bwō.			
137.5.	舵	dwò.			
137.10.	艙	tsāng.			
137.14.	艦	jyàn.			
(138.)	艮				
138.1.	良	lyáng.			
139.	色	shǎy, sè.			

No.	Char	Reading		Cross-ref	Char
(140.)	艸				
140.4.	芝	jr̄.			
140.4.	花	hwā.			
140.4.	芹	chín.			
140.4.	芽	yá.			
140.5.	若	rè.			
140.5.	苦	kǔ.			
140.5.	茅	máw.			
140.5.	苗	myǎw.			
140.5.	苔	tāy.			
140.5.	英	yīng.			
140.6.	茶	chá.			
140.6.	荒	hwāng.			
140.6.	草	tsǎw.			
140.7.	莊	jwāng.			
140.7.	荷	hé.			
140.7.	莫	mwò.			
140.8.	菲	fēy.			
140.8.	華	hwā, hwá.			
140.8.	菊	jywū, jywú.			
140.8.	菓	gwǒ.			
140.8.	菩	pú.			
140.8.	菜	tsày.			
140.9.	著	jù.			
140.9.	葫	hú.			
140.9.	落	làw, lè, lwò.			
140.9.	葡	pú.			
140.9.	葬	dzàng.		32.10.	墓
140.9.	蔥	tsūng.			
140.9.	萬	wàn.		1.2.	万
140.9.	葉	yè.			
140.10.	蒸	jēng.			
140.10.	蓋	gày.			
140.10.	蒙	méng.			
140.10.	蒜	swàn.			
140.10.	蒼	tsāng.			
140.10.	蓇	gū.			
140.11.	蔓	màn.			
140.12.	蕪	wú.			
140.13.	薄	báw.			
140.13.	薪	shīn.			
140.14.	藍	lán.			
140.14.	藏	dzàng, tsáng.			
140.14.	藉	jyè.			

140.15.	藝	yì.		145.5.	袖	shyèw.
140.15.	藕	ěw.		145.6.	裂	lyè.
140.15.	藥	yàw.		145.6.	裁	tsáy.
140.16.	蘼	mwó.		145.7.	裝	jwāng.
140.16.	蘆	lú.		145.7.	裙	chywún.
140.16.	蘇	sū.		145.7.	裡	lǐ.
140.16.	蘋	píng.		145.7.	裏	
140.17.	蘭	lán.		145.7.	補	bǔ.
(141.)	虍			145.8.	製	jr̀.
141.5.	處	chǔ, chù.		145.8.	褂	gwà.
141.6.	虛	shywū.		145.8.	裹	gwǒ.
141.7.	號	hàw.		145.8.	褓	byǎw.
141.11.	虧	kwēy.		145.9.	複	fú.
142.	虫	chúng.		145.9.	褐	hé.
142.4.	蚌	bàng.		145.10.	褥	rù.
142.4.	蚊	wén.		145.10.	褲	kù.
142.5.	蛀	jù.		145.10.	襤	lē.
142.5.	蛇	shé.		145.14.	襤	lán.
142.6.	蛤	gé, há.		145.15.	襪	wà.
142.7.	蜂	fēng.		145.16.	襯	chèn.
142.7.	蛾	é.		146.	西	shī.
142.8.	蜡	là.		146.3.	要	yàw, yāw.
142.8.	蜜	mì.		146.12.	覆	fú.
142.9.	蝴	fú, hú.		147.	見	jyàn.
142.9.	蝶	dyê, dyè.		147.4.	規	gwēy.
142.10.	螞	mǎ, má.		147.5.	視	shr̀.
142.11.	螺	lwó.		147.9.	親	chīn, chìng.
142.12.	蟲	chúng.		147.13.	覺	jywé.
142.15.	蠟	là.		147.18.	觀	gwān.
142.18.	蠶	tsán.		148.	角	jyǎw.
143.	血	shyě, shywe, shywè.		148.6.	解	jyě.
				149.	言	yán.
144.	行	háng, shíng.		149.2.	計	jì.
144.5.	術	shù.		149.2.	訂	dìng.
144.6.	街	jyē.		149.3.	訓	shywùn.
144.9.	衝	chūng, chùng.		149.3.	記	jì.
144.9.	衛	wèy.	144.10. 衞	149.3.	討	tǎw.
144.10.	衡	héng.		149.3.	託	twō.
144.10.	衞	wèy.	144.9. 衛	149.4.	許	shywǔ.
144.18.	衢	chywū.		149.4.	設	shè.
145.	衣	yī.		149.5.	詐	jà.
145.3.	表	byǎw.		149.5.	註	jù.
145.4.	衰	shwāy.		149.5.	評	píng.
145.5.	被	bèy.		149.5.	詞	tsź.

154.17.	贛	gàn.		
155.	赤	chr̄.		
156.	走	dzěw.		
156.2.	赴	fù.		
156.3.	赶	gǎn.	156.7.	趕
156.5.	趁	chèn.		
156.5.	超	chāw.		
156.5.	越	ywè.		
156.7.	趕	gǎn.	156.3.	赶
156.10.	趨	chywū.		
157.	足	dzú.		
157.2.	趴	pā.		
157.5.	距	jywù.		
157.5.	跑	pǎw.		
157.6.	跤	jyāw.		
157.6.	跟	gēn.		
157.6.	路	lù.		
157.6.	跳	tyàw.		
157.8.	踝	hwáy.		
157.8.	踏	tà.		
157.8.	踢	tī.		
157.11.	蹤	dzūng.		
157.12.	蹶	jywě.		
157.12.	蹭	tsèng.		
157.18.	躦	tswān.		
158.	身	shēn.		
158.6.	躲	dwǒ.		
158.8.	躺	tǎng.		
159.	車	chē.		
159.2.	軍	jywūn.		
159.2.	軌	gwěy.		
159.4.	軟	rwǎn.		
159.5.	軸	jéw.		
159.6.	較	jyǎw, jyàw.		
159.6.	載	dzày.		
159.7.	輕	chīng.		
159.8.	輛	lyàng.		
159.8.	輪	lwén.		
159.8.	輩	bèy.		
159.9.	輸	shū.		
159.10.	輿	ywú.		
159.11.	轉	jwàn, jwǎn.		
159.12.	轍	jé, jě.		
159.14.	轟	hūng.		

160.	辛	shīn.		
160.7.	辣	là.		
160.9.	辦	bàn.		
160.12.	辭	tsź.		
160.14.	辯	byàn.		
(161.)	辰			
161.6.	農	núng.		
(162.)	辵			
162.4.	近	jìn.		
162.4.	迎	yíng.		
162.6.	追	jwēy.		
162.6.	逆	nì.		
162.6.	迷	mí.		
162.6.	迸	bèng.		
162.6.	送	sùng.		
162.6.	逃	táw.		
162.6.	退	twèy.		
162.7.	這	jè, jèy.		
162.7.	逛	gwàng.		
162.7.	連	lyán.		
162.7.	逍	shyāw.		
162.7.	速	sù.		
162.7.	逗	dèw.		
162.7.	透	tèw.		
162.7.	通	tūng, tǔng.		
162.7.	造	dzàw.		
162.8.	週	jēw.		
162.8.	逮	děy.		
162.8.	進	jìn.		
162.9.	過	gwò.		
162.9.	遍	byàn.	60.9.	徧
162.9.	逼	bī.	9.9.	偪
162.9.	違	wéy.		
162.9.	遇	ywù.		
162.9.	運	ywùn.		
162.10.	遛	lyèw.		
162.10.	遞	dì.		
162.10.	遠	ywǎn.		
162.11.	遮	jē.		
162.11.	遲	chŕ.		
162.11.	遭	dzāw.		
162.12.	遺	yí.		
162.12.	遷	shyān.		

162.12.	遶	ràw.	120.12.		繞
162.12.	遼	lyáw.			
162.12.	選	shywǎn.			
162.12.	遵	dzwēn.			
162.13.	還	háy, hwán.			
162.13.	避	bì.			
162.15.	邋	là.			
162.15.	邊	byān.			
(163.)	邑				
163.3.	邕	yūng.			
163.4.	那	nǎ, nà, něy, nèy.			
163.8.	部	hù.			
163.8.	郵	yéw.			
163.9.	都	dēw, dū.			
163.10.	鄉	shyāng.			
163.12.	鄭	jèng.			
163.12.	鄰	lín.			
163.12.	鄱	bwó.			
163.12.	鄞	yín.			
(164.)	酉				
164.3.	配	pèy.			
164.3.	酒	jyěw.			
164.7.	酸	swān.			
164.8.	醉	dzwèy.			
164.8.	醃	yān.			
164.9.	醒	shǐng.			
164.10.	醜	chěw.			
164.11.	醫	yī.			
164.11.	醬	jyàng.			
(165.)	釆				
165.13.	釋	shr̀.			
166.	里	lǐ.			
166.2.	厘	lí.	166.11.		釐
166.2.	重	chúng, jùng.			
166.4.	野	yě.			
166.5.	量	lyáng.			
166.11.	釐	lí.	166.2.		厘
167.	金	jīn.			
167.2.	針	jēn.	167.9.		鍼
167.2.	釘	dīng.			
167.3.	釣	dyàw.			
167.4.	鈔	chāw.			
167.4.	鈎	gēw.			
167.4.	鈍	dwèn.			
167.5.	鉤	gēw.			
167.5.	鈴	líng.			
167.5.	鉄	tyě.	167.13.		鐵
167.5.	鉛	chyān.			
167.6.	鉸	jyǎw.			
167.6.	銅	túng.			
167.6.	銀	yín.			
167.7.	鋤	chú.			
167.7.	銷	shyāw.			
167.7.	鋪	pū.			
167.7.	銹	shyèw.			
167.8.	錐	jwēy.			
167.8.	錘	chwéy.			
167.8.	鋼	gāng.			
167.8.	錦	jǐn.			
167.8.	錮	gù.			
167.8.	錫	shī.			
167.8.	錢	chyán.			
167.8.	錯	tswò.			
167.9.	鍼	jēn.	167.2.		針
167.9.	錨	máw.			
167.9.	鍵	jyàn.			
167.9.	鍋	gwō.			
167.9.	鍊	lyàn.			
167.9.	鍍	dù.			
167.10.	鎮	jèn.			
167.10.	鎊	pǎng.			
167.10.	鎖	swǒ.			
167.10.	鎗	chyāng.			
167.10.	鎔	rúng.			
167.10.	鎦	lyèw.			
167.10.	鎬	gǎw.			
167.11.	鏡	jìng.			
167.12.	鐘	jūng.			
167.13.	鐯	jwó.			
167.13.	鐵	tyě.	167.5.		鉄
167.14.	鑄	jù.			
167.17.	鑲	shyāng.			
167.17.	鑰	yàw.			
167.19.	鑽	dzwān, dzwàn.			
167.20.	鑿	dzáw.			
168.	長	cháng, jǎng.			
169.	門	mén.			
169.2.	閃	shǎn.			

169.3.	閉	bì.		
169.4.	閒	shyán.		
169.4.	閏	rwèn.		
169.4.	開	kāy.		
169.4.	間	jyān, jyē, jyè.		
169.5.	閘	já.		
169.5.	鬧	nàw.		
169.6.	閔	mǐn.		
169.10.	闖	chwàng.		
169.11.	關	gwān.		
(170.)	阜			
170.4.	防	fáng.		
170.5.	阻	dzǔ.		
170.5.	附	fù.		
170.5.	阿	à.		
170.6.	限	shyàn.		
170.6.	降	jyàng.		
170.7.	陣	jèn.		
170.7.	除	chú.		
170.7.	陝	shǎn.		
170.7.	陡	děw.		
170.7.	院	ywàn.		
170.8.	陳	chén.		
170.8.	陷	shyàn.		
170.8.	陸	lù.		
170.8.	陪	péy.		
170.8.	陰	yīn.		
170.9.	隊	dwèy.		
170.9.	階	jyē.		
170.9.	隆	lúng.		
170.9.	隄	tí.		
170.9.	陽	yáng.		
170.10.	隔	gé.		
170.13.	險	shyǎn.		
170.13.	隨	swéy.		
170.13.	隧	swéy.		
170.14.	隱	yǐn.		
(172.)	隹			
172.2.	隻	jr̄.		
172.4.	雇	gù.		
172.4.	集	jí.		
172.4.	雅	yǎ.		
172.4.	雁	yàn.	196.4.	鴈
172.8.	雕	dyāw.	59.8.	彫
172.9.	雖	swéy.		
172.10.	雞	jī.	196.10.	鷄
172.10.	雙	shwāng, shwàng		
172.10.	雜	dzá.		
172.11.	離	lí.		
172.11.	難	nán.		
173.	雨	ywǔ.		
173.3.	雪	shywě.		
173.4.	雲	ywún.		
173.5.	雷	léy.		
173.5.	零	líng.		
173.5.	雹	báw.		
173.5.	電	dyàn.		
173.6.	需	shywū.		
173.9.	霜	shwāng.		
173.11.	霧	wù.		
173.12.	露	lèw, lù.		
173.13.	霸	bà.		
173.16.	靈	líng.		
174.	青	chīng.		
174.8.	靜	jìng.		
175.	非	fēy.		
175.7.	靠	kàw.		
176.	面	myàn.		
(177.)	革			
177.4.	靴	shywē.		
177.6.	鞋	shyé.		
177.6.	鞍	ān.		
177.9.	鞦	chyēw, yēw.		
177.13.	韁	jyāng.		
180.	音	yīn.		
180.5.	韶	sháw.		
180.13.	響	shyǎng.	30.6.	响
181.	頁	yè.		
181.2.	頃	chǐng.		
181.2.	頂	dǐng, tǐng.		
181.3.	項	shyàng.		
181.3.	順	shwèn.		
181.4.	頓	dwèn.		
181.4.	預	ywù.		
181.5.	領	lǐng.		
181.7.	頭	téw.		
181.9.	顋	sāy.	130.9.	腮
181.9.	題	tí.		

181.9.	顏	yán.			
181.10.	類	lèy.			
181.10.	願	ywàn.			
181.12.	顧	gù.			
181.14.	顯	shyǎn.			
182.	風	fēng.			
182.6.	颶	jywù.			
182.11.	飄	pyāw.			
183.	飛	fēy.			
184.	食	shŕ.			
184.2.	飢	jī.	184.12.	饑	
184.4.	飯	fàn.			
184.4.	飲	yǐn.			
184.5.	飽	bǎw.			
184.6.	餅	bǐng.			
184.6.	養	yǎng.			
184.7.	餓	è.			
184.7.	餐	tsān.			
184.8.	餒	wèy.	30.9.	喂	
184.10.	餻	gāw.	119.10.	糕	
184.10.	餿	sēw.			
184.11.	饅	mán.			
184.12.	饒	ráw.			
184.12.	饑	jī.	184.2.	飢	
185.	首	shěw.			
186.	香	shyāng.			
187.	馬	mǎ.			
187.3.	馱	twó.			
187.4.	駁	bwó.			
187.4.	馱	twó.			
187.5.	駕	jyà.			
187.6.	駱	lwò.			
187.8.	騎	chí.			
187.9.	騙	pyàn.			
187.10.	騰	tēng, téng.			
187.11.	驟	lwó.			
187.12.	驕	jyāw.			
187.13.	驚	jīng.			
187.13.	驗	yàn.			
187.16.	驢	lywú.			
188.	骨	gú.			
188.13.	體	tǐ.			
188.13.	髒	dzāng.			
189.	高	gāw.			

(190.)	髟				
190.4.	髣	fǎng.	60.4.	彷	
190.8.	鬆	sūng, sùng.			
190.9.	鬍	hú.			
191.	鬥	dèw.			
191.5.	鬧	nàw.	169.5.	鬧	
191.6.	鬨	hūng.			
191.10.	鬭	dèw.			
191.14.	鬮				
194.	鬼	gwěy.			
195.	魚	ywú.			
195.6.	鮮	shyān, shyàn.			
195.12.	鱗	lín.			
195.16.	鱸	lú.			
195.16.	鱷	è.			
196.	鳥	nyǎw.			
196.4.	鴈	yàn.	172.4.	雁	
196.5.	鴨	yǎ.			
196.6.	鴿	gē.			
196.7.	鵝	é.			
196.10.	雞	jī.	172.10.	雞	
(197.)	鹵				
197.9.	鹹	shyán.			
197.10.	鹺	jyǎn.			
197.13.	鹼				
198.	鹿	lù.			
198.8.	麗	lì.			
199.	麥	màry.			
199.4.	麴	myàn.			
199.9.	麵				
200.	麻	mā, má.			
200.3.	麼	mā.			
201.	黃	hwáng.			
(202.)	黍				
202.5.	黏	nyán.			
203.	黑	hēy.			
203.5.	點	dyǎn.	86.5.	点	
207.	鼓	gǔ.	107.9.	皷	
207.	鼓				
209.	鼻	bí.			
210.	齊	chí.			
(211.)	齒				
211.5.	齣	chū.			
212.	龍	lúng.			

PART IV

ENGLISH–CHINESE

NOTES ON THE USE OF THE ENGLISH–CHINESE SIDE

Alphabetical Order. The alphabetical order is absolute. Main entries consisting of two words are alphabetized as though the letters formed a single word with no intervening space; e.g., CAN, CANDY, and CAN OPENER would follow each other in that order.

Typefaces. English material is in **boldface**. Chinese definitions and equivalents are in lightface. Explanation and comment are in *italics*.

Degree Sign. The degree sign (°) is used in either Chinese or English sentences in the following manner: "He isn't °coming here any more. *or* °going to come here again." Here the degree sign indicates that both "He isn't coming here any more." and "He isn't going to come here again." are acceptable versions.

A

A (AN). *Where English has* **a** *or* **an** *before a noun specifying merely an indefinite example of the item named by the noun, Chinese has sometimes the unmodified noun, sometimes the noun preceded by* yī *plus a measure; after a verb, the measure alone may replace the* yī-*plus-measure combination.* ‖**Is there a shoe store near here?** (jèr-)'fù-jìn yěw shyé-'pù-ma? ‖**That's a female cat.** nà-shř 'mǔ-māw. ‖**This is a book.** jè-shř 'shū. ‖**A lion is heavier than a lioness.** 'gūng-shř-dz bǐ 'mǔ-shř-dz 'jùng. ‖**Have you an envelope?** (nǐ) 'yěw-méy-yew (yí-ge-)shìn-'fēngr? ‖**Give me a book to read.** gěy-wo yì-běr-'shū kàn. ‖**She bought a female cat.** tā 'mǎy-le yì-jř-'mǔ-māw. ‖**A Mohammedan may have four wives.** yí-ge-'hwéy-hwey kě-yi chywǔ 'sż-ge-tày-tay. ‖**A lion escaped from the zoo.** yěw yì-jř-'shř-dz tsúng dùng-wu-'ywán 'pǎw-chu-lay-le. ‖**He's a good man.** tā-shř ge-'hǎw-rén.

(Each, per) shown by order of sentence elements, sometimes with **each** měy *plus a measure.* ‖**These eggs are fifty cents a dozen.** *is expressed as* **These eggs are fifty cents one dozen.** jèy-shyē-jī-'dzěr shř 'wǔ-máw-chyán yì-'dá. *or as* **These eggs each dozen fifty cents.** jèy-shyē-jī-'dzěr 'měy-yì-dá 'wǔ-máw-chyán. ‖**These books are three for a dollar.** jèy-shyē-'shū °shř 'yí-kwày-chyán 'sān-běr. *or* °měy-'sān-běr 'yí-kwày-chyán.

ABDOMEN. 'dù-dz.

ABLE. **Be able to.** ké-yi, néng; shíng, -de-lyǎw, -bu-lyǎw. *(See also* CAN.*)* ‖**Will you be able to come?** nǐ néng 'láy-ma? ‖**He may be able to come.** tā 'yé-shywu ké-yi (*or* néng) 'láy. ‖**He won't be able to do that.** 'nèy-jyàn-shř tā bàn-bu-'lyǎw. ‖**I won't be able to come anyway.** fǎn-jèng wǒ láy-bu-'lyǎw. *or* fǎn-jèng wǒ

bù-néng-'láy. ‖**Do you think he'll be able to do that?** nǐ 'jywé-de °tā bàn nèy-jyàn-'shř 'shíng-ma? *or* °tā néng 'bàn nèy-jyàn-'shř-ma? *or* °'nèy-jyàn-shř tā bàn-de-'lyǎw-ma?

Able (*competent*) néng dzwò-'shř, néng-gan, yěw 'běn-shr, yěw 'néng-na, yěw gàn-tsáy. ‖**He's a very able assistant.** tā shř ge-hěn-'néng-gan-de-'jù-shew. ‖**We need three hundred able men immediately.** wǒm 'jí-kè yàw yùng 'sān-bǎy-ge-néng-dzwò-'shř-de-rén.

ABOUT. (*Concerning*) gwān-ywu, jyáng. ‖**This book is about international relations.** jèy-běn-'shū 'jyǎng-de shř gwó-jì-'gwān-shì. ‖**He's writing a book about Napoleon.** tā 'jèng dzày 'shyě yì-běn-°jyǎng-(*or* °gwān-ywu-)ná-pwò-'lwèn-de-shū.

(*Almost*) 'chà-bu-dwō, 'chà-bu-dwō jyèw, jyèw, kwày. ‖**Dinner is about ready.** 'fàn jyèw 'dé(-le). ‖**The time is about up.** 'shř-hew 'chà-bu-dwō °jyèw (*or* °kwày) 'dàw-le. *or* 'kwày dàw 'shř-hewr-le.

(*Approximately*) 'chà-bu-dwō, chyán-'hèw, dzwǒ-'yèw, shàng-'shyà. ‖**He was about five miles from home.** 'tā lí-'jyā chà-bu-dwō 'wǔ-lǐ-dì. ‖**This place is about fifty li from the city.** 'jèy-ge-'dì-fang lí-'chéng yěw 'wǔ-shr-lǐ dzwǒ-'yèw.

Be about to 'jèng yàw, 'kwày yàw. ‖**The train is about to leave.** hwǒ-'chē 'kwày yàw 'kāy-le.

ABOVE. (*Spatially*) dzày (*or* dàw *or* tsúng) ...°-shang, °'shàng-byan, °'shàng-byar, °'shàng-myan, °'shàng-myar, °'shàng-tew. ‖**The plane is flying above the clouds.** fēy-'jī dzày 'ywún-tsay-'shàng-byan 'fēy.

(*Numerically*) yǐ-'shàng. ‖**He's above forty.** tā-de-'nyán-jì dzày 'sż-shř-yǐ-'shàng.

(*In the foregoing*) yǐ-'shàng, 'chyán-myan. ‖**What's mentioned above isn't correct.** 'chyán-myan swǒ-'shwō-de bú-'dwèy.

Be *so far* above lí ... yěw 'gāw. ‖How far above sea level are we? wǒm-'jèr lí hǎy-'myàn yěw dwō-'gāw?

To rise above 'gāw-chū. ‖We're eight thousand feet above sea level now. wǒm shyàn-dzày 'gāw-chu hǎy-'myàn 'bā-chyān-'chǐ.

Above all 'yéw-chí-shr. ‖Above all, remember to be on time. 'yéw-chí-shr yàw 'jì-jù-le shěw shǐ-'kè.

The following sentences are quite differently expressed in Chinese. ‖He's above average height. *is expressed as* He is taller than the average man. tā bǐ yì-'bān-rén 'gāw. ‖He's above doing anything like that. *is expressed as* He doesn't attempt to do such things as that. tā bú-'jǐ-ywu dzwò 'nà-yàng-de-shì. *or as* He isn't capable of doing such things as that. tā(-shì) bú-'hwèy dzwò 'nà-yàng-de-'shì-de. ‖He can't keep his head above water. *literally is* tā dzày 'shwěy-li bù-néng bǎ-'téw 'lěw-dzày shwěy-'shàng-byar. *but figuratively is expressed as* He can do nothing but go under. tā bù-'néng bú-jyè-'jày. ‖He's above suspicion. *is expressed as* He's completely reliable. tā-shì háw-'wú kě-'yí-de.

See also BEYOND.

ABSENT. chywē-shí. ‖Three members were absent because of illness. yěw 'sān-wèy-hwèy-'ywán yīn-'bìng 'chywē-shí.

(*Often expressed as* not arrive) bú-'dàw. ‖He's absent today. tā 'jyēr méy-'dàw.

ACCELERATOR. (*On automobile*) jyā-sù-'bǎn; (*on machine gun*) jyā-sù-'dž.

ACCENT. jùng-yīn. ‖Where's the accent in this English word? jèy-ge-'yīng-wén-'dž-de-'jùng-yīn dzày-'nǎr? (*With source specified*) kěw-yīn, ...-yīn. ‖He speaks English with a Russian accent. tā shwō 'yīng-wén dày 'è-gwo-'kěw-yīn. ‖He speaks with a Cantonese accent. tā shwō-'hwà dày 'gwǎng-dūng-yīn.

To accent jyā-jùng. ‖Accent the first word of this sentence. 'jèy-jywù-hwà-de-'téw-yí-ge-dž jyā-'jùng.

Be accented shwō-de 'jùng-shye. ‖The first word of this sentence should be accented. 'jèy-jywù-hwà-de-'téw-yí-ge-dž 'yīng-dang shwō-de 'jùng-shye.

ACCEPT. 'jyē-shèw, shēw, 'shēw-shyà. ‖Germany accepted the Allied terms. 'dé-gwo 'jyē-shèw-le lyán-hé-'gwó-de-'tyáw-jyàn. ‖Has the school accepted you as a student? shywé-'shyàw 'shēw-le nǐ-le-ma? ‖He accepted the money I gave him. tā 'shēw-shya-le wǒ-'gěy-ta-de-'chyán. ‖Do you accept American money? *is expressed as* Does this place use American money? 'jèy-ge-dì-fang yùng 'měy-gwo-chyán-'pyàw-ma? ‖Have you accepted the invitation? *is expressed as* Have you agreed to go? nǐ 'dā-yíng 'chywù-le-ma? ‖Will you accept this position? *is expressed as* Would you like to do this work? nǐ 'ywàn-yi dzwò jèy-ge-'shì-ma?

ACCIDENT. Have an accident chū-'shì; (*literary*) 'fā-shēng yì-'wày. ‖In case of accident, notify the manager. 'rú-gwo 'fā-shēng yì-'wày, tūng-jr 'gwǎn-lǐ-rén.

By accident (*without appointment*) bù-'chī. ‖We met them by accident. wǒm túng-tam bù-'chī ěr-'ywù.

Automobile accident, *and other accidents, are usually expressed more specifically.* Hit someone jwàng-'rén; run into something *or* cause damage rě-'hwò, rě 'lěw-dz; have one's car overturn fān-'chē; have a collision jwàng 'chē; run over someone yà-'rén.

ACCOMPANY. dày, gēn, sùng. ‖He was accompanied by two policemen. tā 'dày-le lyǎng-ge-shywún-'jīng-lay. *or* yěw lyǎng-ge-shywún-'jǐng 'gēn-je ta. ‖May I accompany you home? wǒ 'ké-yi 'sùng-ni hwéy-'jyā-ma?

Be accompanied by fù-je. ‖His letter was accompanied by a receipt. tā-de-'shìn-li fù-je yì-jāng-shēw-'tyáw.

ACCOMPLISH. 'dé-dàw, dzwò-dàw. ‖He accomplished his purpose quickly. tā hěn-'kwày-de dé-daw 'mù-dì. *or* tā hěn-'kwày-de jyèw 'dzwò-daw-le tā-'shyǎng-yàw-dzwò-de.

Accomplish something yěw swǒ-chéng-'jyèw. ‖A man should accomplish something during his life. yí-ge-'rén yì-'shēng dzǔng 'yīng-dang yěw swǒ-chéng-'jyèw.

Not accomplish anything yī wú-swǒ-'chéng (*literary*). ‖He hasn't accomplished anything. tā yī wú-swǒ-'chéng.

Be an accomplished .... 'hěn shì ge-.... ‖He's an accomplished musician. tā 'hěn shì ge-yīn-ywè-'jyā.

ACCORDING TO. 'àn-jàw, 'àn-je, 'gēn-jywu, jywù, 'yī-jàw. ‖According to my orders, I must leave tomorrow. 'yī-jàw mìng-'lìng, wǒ 'míng-tyan 'bì-shywū-děy 'dzěw. ‖According to the latest rumor, there will be a change in policy. 'gēn-jywù dzwèy-'jìn-de-'yáw-chwán, jèng-'tsè yàw yěw 'byàn-dùng. ‖According to the weather report it'll rain tomorrow. jywù chì-shyàng-'táy-de-bàw-'gàw 'míng-tyan yàw shyà-'ywǔ.

ACCOUNT. (*Financial*) jàng, 'jàng-mù. ‖Have you figured out the account? 'jàng 'swàn-chu-lay méy-yew? ‖The company's accounts were in good order. gūng-'sž-de-'jàng-mù hěn 'chīng-chu.

(*That which is said*) tā- (wǒ-, rén-, *etc.*) 'shwō-de. ‖His account is different from hers. (*Pointing at those concerned*) 'tā-shwō-de gēn 'tā-shwō-de bù-yí-'yàng.

Account for jyě-shì. ‖How do you account for that situation? 'jèy-jǔng-chíng-shing nǐ 'dzěme-yàng 'jyě-shì?

On account of yīn (*formal*). ‖The game was postponed on account of rain. bǐ-'sày yīn-'ywǔ jǎn-'chī.

On no account 'wú-lwèn-rú-hé bū-. ‖On no account must you mention the subject in his presence. nǐ dzày tā-'myàn-chyán 'wú-lwèn-rú-hé bù-néng 'tí-daw 'jèy-ge-wèn-ti.

ACCOUNTANT. kwày-jì-'shṛ.

ACHE. Have a headache 'téw-téng; have a toothache 'yá-téng or nàw-'yá; have a stomach ache 'dù-dz-téng or nàw 'dù-dz; the expressions with téng are used for an ache in any part of the body, but those with nàw are confined to tooth, stomach, and throat. ‖My tooth aches. wǒ 'yá-téng. or wǒ dzày nàw-'yá. ‖My headache has stopped. wǒ bù-'téw-téng-le. ‖Have you got a headache? nǐ 'téw-téng-ma?

ACID. swān.

ACORN. shyàng-shù-'dzěr.

ACOUSTICS. (Science) 'yīn-shywé.

ACRE. yīng-'mǔ (see Appendix B). ‖How many mǔ are there in this farm? jèy-ge-núng-'chǎng yěw 'dwō-shaw-mǔ? ‖How many acres are there in your farm? nǐ-de-núng-'chǎng yěw 'dwō-shaw-yīng-'mǔ?

ACROSS. Across the street (road, river, etc.) from ... dzày ...-'dwèy-gwò (or -'dwèy-myàn, -'dwèy-mér, last term only for street). ‖The restaurant is across the street from the hotel. fàn-'gwǎn-dz dzày lywǔ-'gwǎn-'dwèy-mér.
Go across gwò; walk (ride, run, etc.) across dzěw-(kāy-, pǎw-) gwò. ‖Walk across the bridge. 'dzěw-gwò 'chyáw chyǜu.

ACT. 'shíng-wey, 'jywǔ-dùng. ‖His act was rather unbecoming. tā-de-'shíng-wey yěw shyē bú-'jèng-dang. ‖He's acting in a suspicious way. tā 'jywǔ-dùng kě-'yí. ‖He's been acting strangely lately. 'jìn-lay tā 'jywǔ-dùng hěn ckí-'gwày. ‖He acts like a child. tā 'jywǔ-dùng 'yèw-jṛ.
To act like. ‖Don't act like a child. byé shyàng ge-'háy-dz shṛ-de.
(On the stage) byǎw-'yǎn. ‖He acted very well (on the stage). tā dzày 'táy-shang byǎw-'yǎn-de hěn 'hǎw.
To act out a play yǎn-'shì. ‖They act well. tām yǎn-'shì yǎn-de hěn 'hǎw.
Act of a play mù. The third act of the play 'shì-de-dì-'sān-mù.
(Do) dzwò, bàn. ‖I'm prepared to act on your suggestion. wǒ 'jwěn-bèy àn-je nǐ-de-'jyàn-yi chywù 'dzwò. ‖Now is the time to act. shyàn-'dzày shṛ kǎy-shṛ 'dzwò de-shṛ-hew-le. ‖When will this matter be acted on? 'jèy-jyàn-shṛ 'shéme-shṛ-hew 'bàn-ne?
Be in the act of 'jèng dzày. ‖I was in the act of packing. 'nà-shṛ-hew wǒ 'jèng dzày dǎ 'shíng-li.

Act as, act in place of dày-'lǐ. ‖Who's acting as principal of the school? 'shwéy shṛ dày-'lǐ shyàw-'jǎng? ‖Who'll act in your place after you're gone? nǐ 'dzěw-le 'shwéy dày-'lǐ?
(Legal). Act or resolution of a governing body yì-jywé-àn; -fǎ in compounds such as Child Labor Act túng-gūng-'fǎ. ‖The Child Labor Act is no longer in force. túng-gūng-'fǎ yǐ-jing wú-'shyàw-le. ‖It'll take an act of Congress to change that. is expressed as It'll take Congress to change that. !jèy-ge fēy-děy yéw gwó-'hwèy láy 'gǎy.

ACTION. 'dzwò-yùng. Chemical action 'hwà-shywé-'dzwò-yùng; involuntary action bù-swéy-'yì-'dzwò-yùng.
(Military) jàn-shṛ. ‖There's no action on the western front. shī-'shyàn wú-jàn-'shṛ.
(Person's behavior) 'shíng-wéy. ‖His actions show his character well. tsúng tā-de-'shíng-wéy-shang hěn 'kàn-de-chū tā-de-'shìng-gé lay.
Put into action shíng. ‖The plan sounds good, but how are you going to put it into action? jèy-ge-'jì-hwà 'tīng-je hǎw shyàng bú-'tswò, kě-shr dzěme néng 'shíng-nga?

ACTIVE. (Of a child) 'hwó-bwo. ‖His son is very active. tā-de-'ér-dz hěn 'hwó-bwo.
(In political life) hwó-dùng. ‖The communist element hasn't been active lately. gùng-chǎn-'fèn-dz 'jìn-lay méy-yew shéme-'hwó-dùng.
(Of exercise) 'měng-lyè. ‖This sort of exercise is too active for a little boy. 'jèy-jǔng-'ywùn-dùng wèy yí-ge-shyǎw-'hár yěw dyǎr-tày-'měng-lyè. ‖I don't feel like doing anything active. is expressed as I'm too lazy to move around. wǒ 'lǎn-de 'dùng-tan.
Active life. ‖He leads an active life. (Political) tā-'jè-ge-rén hěn 'hwó-dùng. (General) tā-dzwò-de-'shṛ hěn 'dwō. (Sarcastically, meaning that he seeks publicity) tā hěn chū 'fēng-tew.

ACTOR. (Drama) chàng-'shì-de, 'shì-dz; (drama or movies) yǎn-'ywán.

ACTUAL. shṛ-'dzày-de, shṛ-'jì(-de); in some compounds shṛ or jēn. Actual cost shṛ-'jyà; the actual situation shṛ-'chíng or jēn-'chíng or jēn-'shyàng. ‖What's the actual cost of this book? jèy-běr-'shū-de-°shṛ-'jya (or °shṛ-'dzày-de-'jyà-chyán) shṛ 'dwō-shaw? ‖The actual damage isn't heavy. shṛ-'jí-'swěn-shr bú-'jùng. ‖The actual situation in this matter isn't clear yet. 'jèy-ge-shṛ-de-°jēn-'chíng (or °jēn-'shyàng or °shṛ-'chíng) háy bù-'míng-bay.
Actually jēn; shṛ-'jì-shang. ‖Actually, he's wrong. shṛ-'jì-shang tā 'tswò-le. ‖He actually came! tā 'jēn láy-le!

ADD. jyā. ‖Add water to the soup. 'tāng-li 'jyā dyǎr-'shwěy.

Add up 'jyā-chǐ-láy. ‖Add up this list of figures. bǎ jèy-háng-'shù-mù 'jyā-chi-lay.

Add together 'jyā-dzày yí-'kwàr, 'jyā-dàw yí-'kwàr. ‖Add those two men together and they still wouldn't be as heavy as you. tā-men-'lyǎng-ge-rén jyā-dàw yí-'kwàr, háy 'méy-yew 'nǐ jùng.

Add to 'jyā-dzày. ‖You've got to add this figure to the others. nǐ 'děy bǎ 'jèy-ge-shù-mu gēn 'nèy-shyē-shù-mu jyā-dzay yí-'kwàr.

Add it to my bill. is expressed as Figure it onto my bill. swàn-dzay wǒ-de-'jàng-shang.

Add up to. ‖How much does the account add up to? is expressed as The account altogether is how much? 'jàng yí-'gùng-dzǔng shr̀ 'dwō-shaw?

ADDING MACHINE. jì-swàn-'jī.

ADDITION. In addition chú-tsż-yǐ-'wày; in addition to chú-le ... (yǐ-'wày). ‖Do you need anything in addition? chú-tsż-yǐ-'wày nǐ 'háy děy-yàw 'shéme? ‖In addition to her original demands, she also wants a car. chú-le tā-'běn-lay-de-'yāw-chyéw yǐ-'wày, tā 'háy yàw yí-lyàng-chì-'chē.

(Result of adding). ‖Is my addition correct? is expressed as Have I added (or calculated) correctly? wǒ-'jyā-de (or 'swàn-de) 'dwèy-bu-dwèy?

(Thing added). ‖The bathroom is an addition to the house. is expressed as The bathroom was added later. shǐ-dzǎw-'fáng shr̀ 'hèw-jyā-de.

(Person added). ‖We need many additions to our staff is expressed as We must add personnel. wǒm 'shywǔ-yàw 'dzēng-jyā rén-'ywán. or as We must add quite a few people. wǒm 'děy 'tyān bù-'shǎw-de-rén.

ADDRESS. (Place) 'dì-fang; (place at which some function is to be held) dì-'dyǎn; (on an envelope) dì-'jř; (place of residence or business) jù-'jř; (place to which mail should be sent) tūng-shìn-'chù. ‖Send the package to this address. bǎ jèy-bāw-'dūng-shi sùng-daw 'jèy-ge-dì-fang-chywu. ‖The wedding will be held at this address. jyē-'hwēn-de-dì-'dyǎn jyèw dzày-'jèr. ‖What address shall I put on this letter? jèy-fēng-'shìn-de-dì-'jř yīng-dāng 'dzěme-yàng 'shyě? ‖My address is .... wǒ-de-jù-'jř shr̀ .... ‖What's your address? nǐ-de-tūng-shìn-'chù shr̀-'nǎr?

To address a communication. ‖To whom should I address this letter? is expressed as To whom should this letter be written? jèy-fēng-'shìn yīng-dāng 'shyě-gey 'shéy?

To address, to give an address (formal talk) yǎn-'jyǎng, yǎn-'shwō; (of a superior speaking to subordinates) shywùn-'hwà. ‖I have to listen to an address tonight. wǒ jīn-tyan-'wǎn-shang děy tīng yí-ge-yǎn-'jyǎng. ‖The President is going to give an address tomorrow. dà-dzǔng-'tǔng 'míng-tyan yǎn-'shwō. ‖The principal addressed the students. shyàw-'jǎng shyàng 'shywé-sheng yǎn-'shwō. ‖The officer addressed his men. jywūn-'gwān dwèy-'bù-shyà shywùn-'hwà.

To address A as B yǐ B cnēng-hu A. ‖I should address you as uncle. wǒ yīng-dāng yǐ lǎw-'bwó 'chēng-hu nín. ‖Mr. Jāng (who is a bank manager) should be addressed as Manager Jāng. is expressed as Mr. Jāng's title is Manager Jāng. 'jāng-shyān-sheng-de-dzwēn-'chēng shr̀ 'jāng-dzǔng-'lǐ.

ADHESIVE TAPE. shyàng-pí-'gāw.

ADJUTANT. fù-'gwān.

ADMIRAL. hǎy-jywūn-'jyàng-gwān; rear admiral shàw-'jyàng; vice-admiral jūng-'jyàng; (full) admiral shàng-'jyàng.

ADMIRE. (Respect) 'pèy-fu. ‖I admire the Chinese people. wǒ hěn 'pèy-fu 'jūng-gwo-rén.

(Enjoy, contemplate) 'shīn-shǎng. ‖I'm admiring the sights. wǒ dzày 'shīn-shǎng 'fēng-jǐng.

ADMISSION. (Price of entrance) 'pyàw-jyà. ‖How much is the admission? 'pyàw-jyà shr̀ 'dwō-shaw?

No admission 'jìn-jř rù-'nèy (literary).

ADMIT. chéng-'rèn, rèn. ‖He himself admitted it quite frankly. tā-'dž-jǐ háw-wú-yǎn-'shr̀-de chéng-'rèn-le, ‖I admit I was wrong. wǒ chéng-'rèn wo 'tswò-le. ‖He admits no mistake. tā bú-rèn-'tswèr.

Admit someone shēw (formal); shywǔ (or jyàw) ... 'jìn-lay. ‖Not a single school would admit him. ywàn-yi-'shēw-tā-de-shywé-'shyàw 'yí-ge yě 'méy-yew. ‖Don't admit them! bù-'shywǔ-tam 'jìn-lay! or byé 'jyàw-tam 'jìn-lay! ‖Ask for me and you'll be admitted. is expressed as Say you're hunting me and you'll be able to go in immediately. nǐ 'shwō jǎw-'wǒ jyèw ké-yi 'jìn-chywu-le. ‖When were you admitted to the university? is expressed as When did you enter the university? nǐ 'jǐ-shŕ jìn-de 'dà-shywé?

ADOPT. (A child) bàw. ‖They're going to adopt a son from the foundlings' home. tām yàw tsúng ywù-yīng-'táng bàw yí-ge-nán-'háy-dz. But ‖His uncle has adopted him (where adoption is within the family). is expressed as He has already gone over into his uncle's family. tā 'yǐ-jing 'gwò-jì-gěy tā-'shū-shu-jyā-le.

(Take over and use) tsǎy-'chywǔ, tsǎy-'nà, tsǎy-'yùng. ‖We've decided to adopt this method. wǒm jywé-'dìng tsǎy-'chywǔ 'jèy-ge-bàn-fa. ‖I can't adopt your plan. wǒ bù-néng tsǎy-'yùng nǐ-de-'bàn-fa.

ADULT. chéng-'nyán-rén (formal); 'dà-rén (informal). ‖An adult may be mentally quite immature. yí-ge-chéng-'nyán-rén-de-'sž-shyǎng hwèy hěn 'yèw-jr. ‖Children must be accompanied by adults. shyǎw-'háy-dz-men bì-děy yěw 'dà-rén 'gēn-je.

‖Adults only is expressed as Sorry, children aren't welcome. yèw-'túng shù bù-jāw-'dày.

Become an adult chéng-'rén, chéng-'dīng, chéng-'nyán. ‖He's not yet an adult. tā háy méy-chéng-'rén. ‖Adults have to pay the tax. chéng-'dīng-de-rén (or chéng-'nyán-de-rén) děy nà-'shwèy.

ADVANCE. (Progress) jìn-'bù. ‖What advances have been made in medicine? 'yī-shywé yěw shéme-jìn-'bù?

 (In battle) jìn-'jǎn. ‖No advance has been made by the enemy troops. 'dí-jywūn wú jìn-'jǎn.

 Advance! (Battle) chyán-'jìn!

Be advanced (promoted) shēng; be advanced in grade shēng-'jí; be advanced in official position shēng-'gwān; be advanced to a certain position 'shēng-dàw. ‖He's about to be advanced. tā jyèw yàw 'shēng-le. ‖You can be advanced for excellent service. nǐ-de-'chéng-jì 'hǎw, jyèw ké-yi 'shēng. ‖He's recently been advanced to foreman. tā 'jìn-lay shēng-daw gūng-'téw-le.

Get an advance in salary jyā-'shīn, jyā-'chyán. ‖As soon as he became foreman, he got an advance in salary. tā yī dzwò gūng-'téw jyèw jyā-'shīn-le.

To advance prices jǎng-'jyàr. ‖There'll be an advance in price after six o'clock. 'lyèw-dyǎn-jūng-yǐ-'hèw yàw jǎng-'jyàr.

In advance shyān, ywù, ywù-'shyān. ‖Let me know in advance if you're coming. nǐ rú-gwo 'láy de-hwà, 'shyān 'gàw-sung wo yí-shyàr.

To advance money, to give (loan, etc.) money in advance. ‖Could you advance me some money? nǐ néng 'shyān 'jyè-gey wo dyǎr-'chyán-ma? ‖He asked the company to advance him $150. tā yàw tsúng gūng-'sž 'ywù jř 'yì-bǎv-'wǔ-shr-kwày-'chyán.

ADVANTAGE. lì. To have advantage, be advantageous yěw-'lì; to be disadvantageous yěw-'bì. ‖This is to your advantage. 'jèy-ge 'dwèy-ni yěw-'lì. ‖This method has advantages and disadvantages. 'jèy-ge-fāng-fa yěw-'lì yě yěw-'bì. ‖Since you have the advantage of position over me, I can't compete with you. is expressed as Since your position is better than mine, I can't compete with you. yīn-wey 'nǐ-de-dì-wèy bǐ 'wǒ-de 'hǎw, wǒ méy-'fár 'gēn-ni jēng.

ADVERTISE. (To have a notice appear in a newspaper) dēng-'bàw; (to put an ad in a paper) dēng gwǎng-'gàw; (to pass out notices or handbills) sàn gwǎng-'gàw or sàn chwán-'dān; (to post bills) tyē gwǎn-'gàw or tyē chwán-'dān. The purpose of the advertising is expressed separately, with a verb, such as shwō (saying that); jǎw (hunting for); jēng-'pìn or jēng-'chyéw (when wanting a person). ‖They're advertising in the paper for a cook. tām dzày dēng-'bà jǎw 'chú-dz. ‖They're advertising in the paper for a teacher. tām dēng-'bàw jēng-'pìn yí-wèy-'jyàw-ywán. ‖He advertised in the paper for a companion. tā dēng-'bàw jēng-'chyéw bàn-'lywǔ. ‖They've already advertised

three times in the paper. tām 'yǐ-jing dzày 'bàw-shang dēng-le 'sān-tsž-gwǎng-'gàw-le. ‖This store is advertising a big three-day sale. jèy-ge-'pù-dz dēng gwǎng-'gàw shwō shǐ dà-jyǎn-'jyà 'sān-tyān.

 (To spread propaganda) shywān-'chwán. ‖This store is advertising a sale. jèy-ge-'pù-dz shywān-'chwán dà-jyǎn-'jyà.

ADVERTISEMENT. gwǎng-'gàw. ‖A full-page advertisement costs a lot of money. chywán-'myàn-de-gwǎng-'gàw děy hěn-dwō-de-'chyán. ‖I saw your advertisement. wǒ 'kàn-jyan nǐ-'dēng-de-gwǎng-'gàw-le.

ADVICE. jūng-'gàw, 'yì-sz. ‖Your advice has worked well. nǐ-de-jūng-'gàw hěn yěw-'shyàw. ‖I can't act on your advice. wǒ bù-'néng àn-je nǐ-de-'yì-sz 'dzwò. ‖My advice is to leave here immediately. is expressed as I advise that you leave here immediately. wǒ jǔ-'jāng 'gǎn-jǐn 'lí-kay jèr.

 Advices 'shyāw-shì. ‖Late advices from Washington do not prove to be informative. hwá-shēng-'dwèn-dzwèy-'jìn-láy-de-'shyāw-shì méy-'shwō shéme.

ADVISE. jǔ-'jāng, shwō, chywàn. ‖I advise against going. wǒ jǔ-'jāng bú-'chywù. ‖What do you advise me to do? 'nǐ shwō wǒ 'yīng-dang 'dzěme-yàng 'bàn? ‖I advise you to take a rest. wǒ 'chywàn-ni 'shyēw-shi yí-shyà.

 Be advised of 'jyē-daw ...-de-'shyāw-shì. ‖His parents have been advised of his disappearance. tā-de-jyā-'jǎng yǐ-jing 'jyē-daw tā-shř-'dzūng-de-'shyāw-shì-le.

AERIAL. (Radio) tyān-'shyàn.

AFRAID. Be afraid pà, hày-'pà. ‖Don't be afraid! byé hày-'pà!

 Be afraid of 'dzày-hu, pà. ‖I'm not afraid of you! wǒ bú-'dzày-hu ni! ‖He's not afraid of anything. tā 'shéme dēw bú-'pà.

 Be afraid that jywé-de, kě-'shī, kǔng-'pà. ‖I'm afraid it's too late. wǒ 'jywé-de tày 'wǎn-le! or wǒ kě-'shī tày 'wǎn-le! ‖I'm afraid I can't go. wǒ kǔng-'pà bù-néng 'chywù.

AFTER. hèw, yǐ-'hèw; the former most usually after one-syllable nouns, the latter generally. ‖Can you see me after dinner? nǐ 'fàn-hèw néng 'jyàn-wo-ma? ‖Come any time you like after nine. 'jyěw-dyǎn-yǐ-'hèw swéy-'byàn 'shéme-shf-hew 'láy. ‖Wait until after I come back. děng wǒ 'hwéy-lay yǐ-'hèw (dzày shwō).

 After that, afterwards 'hèw-lay. ‖What happened after that? 'hèw-lay 'dzěme-yàng?

 After this tsúng-jīn-yǐ-'hèw, tsž-'hèw. ‖After this please let us know in advance. tsúng-jīn-yǐ-'hèw (or tsž-'hèw) chǐng 'shyān 'tūng-jr wǒ-men.

Day after day, year after year, *etc.* yì-tyān-yì-'tyān-de, yì-nyán-yì-'nyán-de, *etc.* ‖He worked on it day after day. tā yì-tyān-yì-'tyān-de 'dzwò-shya-chywu. ‖We tried store after store, but weren't able to find what we wanted. *is expressed as* We went through all the stores, but weren't able to find what we wanted. wǒm 'pù-dz dēw dzěw-'byàn-le, yě méy-'jǎw-jáw wǒm-shyǎng-'yàw-de-dūng-shi.

After all dàw-'dǐ, jyēw-'jìng, bú-lwèn-rú-'hé. ‖You're right, after all. dàw-'dǐ háy-shr 'nǐ 'dwèy. ‖After all, why do you object? nǐ jyēw-'jìng 'wèy-shéme fǎn-'dwèy? ‖After all, don't forget that he saved your life once. bú-lwèn-rú-'hé, byé 'wàng-le tā 'tséng-jīng 'jyēw-gwo nǐ-de-'mìng.

Be after. (*Search for*) jǎw; (*pursue*) jwēy. ‖The police are after him. shywún-'jǐng 'jǎw-ta-ne. ‖There are three girls after him. yěw 'sān-ge-'gū-nyang 'jwēy-ta-ne.

(*Modeled on*) fǎng, fǎng-'shyàw, fáng-'jàw, 'fǎng-je. ‖This dress is designed after a Parisian style. jè-'yī-fu-dzwò-de-'yàng-dz shr fǎng 'bā-lí-'shr.

(*Next in order*). ‖What's the next street after this? *is expressed as* What's the name of the next street? 'shyà-yì-tyáw-jyē jyàw shéme-'míng-dz? *or as* The next one is what street? 'nèy-byar shr shéme-'jyē?

AFTERNOON. 'shyà-wǔ, 'gwò-wǔ, 'hèw-ban-tyan, 'hèw shǎng, 'shyà-ban-tyan, wǔ-'hèw. ‖I'm leaving in the afternoon. wǒ 'shyà-wǔ 'dzěw. ‖It came yesterday afternoon. 'jèy-ge shr dzwó-tyan-'shyà-wǔ 'láy-de. ‖Can you come this afternoon or tomorrow afternoon? nǐ 'néng-bu-néng 'jīn-tyan-shyà-wǔ hwò-je-shr 'míng-tyan shyà-wǔ 'láy? (*Both English and Chinese mean either (1) these times are suggested rather than any other time, or (2) the hearer is asked to choose definitely between one time and the other, with no other possibilities.*)

AFTERWARD(S). yǐ-'hèw, 'hèw-lay; 'dǐ-shya (*only if referring to a half-finished story*). ‖What happened afterwards? yǐ-'hèw 'dzěme-yàng-le-ne? ‖See me afterwards. *is expressed as* Come see me when it's over. wán-le yǐ-'hèw láy 'kàn-wo. ‖He waited until ten and left shortly afterward. *is expressed as* He waited until ten, then a moment more and left. tā yì-'jŕ 'děng dàw-le 'shŕ-dyǎn, 'yèw dāy-le yì-'hwěr jyèw 'dzěw-le.

AGAIN. dzày; (*yet*) again yèw. ‖Try once again. 'dzày 'shr yí-shyà. ‖I hope to see you again later. yǐ-'hèw dzày 'jyàn. ‖Here I am again. wǒ 'yèw láy-le. ‖I hope to see you again. (*Formal*) *is expressed as* Later there may be an occasion. 'hèw hwèy yěw-'chī.

Never again dzày yě bū-, yǔng bú-'dzày, yǔng-ywǎn bú-'dzày. ‖Never again will I make that mistake. wǒ 'dzày yě bú-'fàn 'nèy-jǔng-tswòr-le.

Again and again, time and time again 'yí-tsż-'yèw-yí-'tsż-de, 'dzwǒ-yí-tsż-'yèw-yí-'tsż-de, *and the same expressions with* byàn *instead of* tsż; wú-shù-'tsż. ‖I could do this again and again. 'jèy-ge wǒ 'ké-yi 'dzwǒ-yí-tsż-'yèw-yí-'tsż-de 'dzwò. ‖I've told you again and again. wǒ yí-tsż-'yèw-yí-'tsż-de 'gàw-su-ni. ‖He tried time and time again. tā 'shr-le wú-shù-'tsż.

AGAINST. (*Against wind, storm*) chyāng(-je), dǐng(-je,, yíng(-je). ‖It isn't exactly easy to run against the wind. chyāng-je 'fēng 'pǎw bú-'dà rúng-yì.

Against *wind, rain, storm, snow, gunfire* màw(-je). ‖They went ahead against the storm. tām màw-je fēng-'ywǔ wǎng-'chyán dzěw-le.

Against *the stream, the current, current opinion, wind* nì. ‖A boat goes much slower against the current than with the current. 'chwán 'nì-shwěy 'dzěw, bǐ 'shwèn-shwěy màn-de 'dwō. ‖His thinking is against current opinion. tā-de-'sz-shyǎng shr 'nì-je shŕ-'dày-de cháw-'lyéw-de.

Lean against kàw, yǐ. ‖He's leaning against a tree. tā 'yǐ-je yì-kē-'shù 'jàn-je. ‖Lean it against the wall. kàw-dzay 'chyáng-nèr.

(*Facing, near*) dwèy, jèng dwèy, chùng. ‖Our house is built against the sea. wǒm-de-'fáng-dz shr chùng-je 'hǎy 'gày-de.

Be against (*of subordinate to higher authority*) fǎn-'kàng. ‖Those soldiers are against the government. 'nà shr fǎn-'kàng-'jèng-'fǔ-de-jywūn-'dwèy.

Be against *a person, policy, etc.* fǎn, fǎn-'dwèy. ‖I'm against war! wǒ fǎn-'jàn! ‖Is everyone against him? dà-'jyā dēw fǎn-'dwèy ta-ma?

Be against *a person* gēn . . . dzwò-'dwèr; bú-'shyàng-je. ‖He's against me. tā 'gēn-wo dzwò-'dwèr. *or* tā bú-'shyàng-je wǒ.

Be against (*attack, a person, policy*) 'gūng-jí. ‖He wrote an article against the president. tā 'shyě-le yì-pyān-'wén-jāng 'gūng-jí dà-dzǔng-'tǔng.

Be against *a proposal, idea* bú-'dzàn-chéng. ‖Are you for or against the proposal? nǐ shr 'dzàn-cheng háy-shr 'bú-dzàn-cheng jèy-ge-tí-'yì?

Be against *the law* wéy, wéy-fǎn, wéy-'fàn, bù-'fú-tsúng. ‖That's against the law. 'nà shr wéy-'fǎn fǎ-'lywù.

Be against *one's conscience* bèy-je. ‖I'd never do anything against my own conscience. wǒ 'jywé bù-néng bèy-je 'lyáng-shīn.

To work against time *is expressed as* to exert effort in order to finish sooner nǔ-'lì 'dzǎw wán.

Against one's will myǎn-'chyǎng. ‖He came against his will. tā myǎn-'chyǎng 'láy-le.

Bring action against gàw, kùng-'gàw. ‖He brought action against me. tā bǎ-wo gěy 'gàw-le.

Talk against gěy . . . shwō hwày-'hwà. ‖He was talking against you. tā gěy-ni shwō hwày-'hwà láy-je.

(*Contrasted with*). ‖The bill was passed by 150 votes

against 100. yì-'àn yǐ 'yì-bǎy-'wǔ-shr dwèy 'yì-bǎy-pyàw 'tūng-gwò-le.

(*Detrimental to*). ‖His looks are against him. tā-de-shyàng-'màw bú-'lì-ywú ta. *or* tā-de-shyàng-'màw ywú-ta bú-'lì.

AGE. *In asking one's age, one uses* swèy (*calendar year of one's life*). *Year of age in the Western sense is* 'shŕ-nyán; *if one is born in December, then in January, it being the following calendar year, one's age is* 'lyǎng-swèy. ‖What is your age? (*To a child less than ten*) nǐ 'jīn-nyan jǐ-'swèy-le? (*To someone in the teens*) nǐ 'jīn-nyan shŕ-jǐ-'swèy-le? (*To an adult*) nǐ 'jīn-nyan dwō-shaw-'swèy-le? (*To an older person, very politely*) nín 'jīn-nyan gāw-'shèw-le? (*To anyone; rather brusque except when said by a doctor to a patient or in similar circumstances*) nǐ dwō-'dà-le?

(*Terms not used in asking one's age*) 'nyán-líng, 'swèy-shù(r), 'nyán-jì. Age required for admission to a school rù-'shywé-nyán-líng; age required for admission to the armed forces fú-'yì-nyán-líng. ‖Sex and age make no difference. 'shìng-byé túng 'nyán-líng bú-'lwèn. ‖Excitement isn't good for a man of my age. shyàng-wǒ-jème-'dà-swèy-shù-de-rén bù-'yīng-dang 'tày shīng-'fèn-le. ‖It's really something that she could do such a thing at such an age. 'tā jème-dà-nyán-jì-de-rén, 'háy néng 'gàn-chu-lay 'nèy-jǔng-shř 'jēn-shř 'kě-yì-de.

Aged (*people*) shàng-'swèy-shu-de-rén, yěw-'nyán-jì-de-rén, 'lǎw-nyán-rén, shàng-'nyán-ji-de-rén. ‖We should aid the aged and the poor. wǒm 'yīng-dang 'bāng-jù shàng-'swèy-shù-de-rén gēn 'chyúng-rén.

To age lǎw. ‖He's aged a great deal lately. tā 'jìn-lay 'lǎw-de 'dwō-le.

(*Era*) shŕ-'dày. ‖This is the age of invention. je-shŕ fā-'míng-de-shŕ-'dày.

AGENT. (*Representative*) dày-'byǎw. ‖Your agent has already called on me. nǐ-de-dày-'byǎw yǐ-jing láy 'jyàn-gwo wo.

(*Person*) 'jīng-lǐ-rén; (*store*) jīng-lǐ(-'dyàn). ‖We must find an agent in every large city for our new merchandise. měy-ge-'dà-chéng-li dēw děy 'jǎw yíge-'jīng-lǐ-rén 'dày-shyāw dzám-de-'shīn-'hwò. ‖We're the sole agent for this make of radio. 'jèy-ge-páy-dz-de-wú-shyàn-'dyàn-shēw-yīn-'jī wǒ-men shř 'dú-jyā-jīng-'lǐ.

(*Operator*) bàn-'shř-de. ‖I'm a government agent. wǒ shř tì-'jèng-fǔ-bàn-'shř-de.

AGO. chyán, yǐ-'chyán. ‖Two years ago I was in America. 'lyǎng-nyán-chyán wǒ dzày 'měy-gwo. ‖I was here two months ago. 'lyǎng-ge-ywè-yǐ-'chyán wǒ dzày-'jèr láy-je.

A while ago gāng . . . (*verb*) yì-'hwěr. ‖I got here a while ago. wǒ gāng 'dàw yì-hwěr. ‖He left a while ago. tā gāng 'dzěw(-le) bú-'dà-hwěr.

Long ago 'shywǔ-jyěw-yǐ-'chyán, 'hǎw-jyěw-yǐ-'chyán.

Not very long ago bù-hěn-'jyěw-yǐ-'chyán.

AGREE. (*Be in accord*) shyāng-'fú; (*have the same opinion*) túng-'yì; (*be the same*) yí-'yàng *or* shyāng-'túng. ‖The two statements don't agree. lyǎng-jywù-'hwà °bú-shyāng-'fú. *or* °bù-yí-'yàng. ‖We agree on everything. wǒm wàn-'chywán túng-'yì. ‖Their ideas agree to some extent. tā-men-de-'yì-jyàn yěw-shyē shyāng-'túng-de-dì-fang.

Agree to *something* 'jyē-shèw. ‖I agree to your terms. wǒ 'jyē-shèw nǐ-de-'tyáw-jyàn.

Agree with (*an idea or proposition*) 'dzàn-chéng. ‖Do you agree with me? nǐ 'dzàn-cheng (wǒ-de-'yì-sz)-ma?

Agree with one (*of food*) *expressed as* agree with one's stomach ywǔ 'wèy-kěw 'hé. ‖This food doesn't agree with her. jèy-jǔng-'shŕ-wu ywǔ tā-'wèy-kew bù-'hé.

(*Of weather*). ‖She was afraid that the weather wouldn't agree with her. *is expressed as* She was afraid that she wouldn't endure the climate. tā 'pà bù-'fú shwěy-'tǔ.

AGRICULTURE. (*As field of endeavor*) núng-'yè; (*as field of study*) 'núng-shywé.

AHEAD. chyán, 'chyán-byan, 'chyán-byar, 'chyán-tew, 'chyán-myan, 'chyán-myar. ‖Are there any roads up ahead? 'chyán-byar 'yěw-méy-yew 'lù? ‖Go straight ahead. yì-'jŕ wàng-'chyán dzěw. ‖Look ahead. wàng-chyán kàn. ‖The car ahead of us has stopped. dzày-wǒm-°'chyán-tew- (*or* °'téw-li *or* °'téw-le-) de-chē 'tíng-jù-le.

Be ahead (*in a game*) 'yıng(-je). ‖Who's ahead? shwéy 'yíng-je-ne?

Be ahead *is often expressed as* not to have fallen behind méy-'là-shya. ‖I'm ahead in my work wǒ-de-'gūng-dzwo méy-'là-shya. ‖He's way ahead of his class. *is expressed as* He's left his classmates far behind. tā bǎ tā-de-túng-'bān-de 'là-de hěn 'ywǎn.

To get ahead 'kāy-gwò-chywù. ‖I was working hard to get ahead of Jāng. wǒ hěn-nǔ-'lì-de shyǎng bǎ lǎw-'jāng 'kāy-gwò-chywù.

That which is ahead chyán-'tú. ‖It's pretty hard to say just what's ahead of him. tā-de-chyán-'tú hěn nán-'shwō.

AID. bāng, bāng . . . 'máng. ‖Let me aid you. 'ràng-wo láy 'bāng-ni ('máng). ‖I'd welcome any aid. 'dzěme 'bāng-yi-bāng dēw 'shíng. *or* 'gěy shéme dēw 'yàw.

(*Pension; as a reward for services or help in an undertaking*) jīn-'tyē. ‖He receives aid from the government. tā tsúng 'jèng-fǔ lǐng jīn-'tyē.

(*Money for study*) jù-shywé-'jīn. ‖Why don't you apply for financial aid? nǐ 'wèy-shéme bù-chǐng-'chyéw jù-shywé-'jīn?

Aid (*from a charitable society*) 'jēw-jì; (*to receive such aid*) shèw 'jēw-jì.

Emergency aid (*in time of flood or other calamity, from charitable societies or from the government*) 'jyèw-ji. ‖The Red Cross is soliciting funds to aid the victims of the calamity. 'húng-shŕ-dz-'hwèy yàw jywān-chyán 'jyèw-jì 'nàn-mín.

To distribute ... as aid (*to those in distress*) 'shŕ-shĕ ....

AIM. mù-'byāw. ‖What's your aim in life? nǐ-rén-'shēng-de-mù-'byāw shŕ 'shéme?

(*Ambition in life*) 'jŕ-shyang. ‖He aims high. tā-de-'jŕ-shyang hĕn 'dà.

To aim *a weapon* myáw, myáw-'jwĕn. ‖Aim higher. wàng-'shàng 'myáw-dyar. *or* 'myáw-de 'gāw-dyar. ‖Aim the gun this way. *meaning* in this manner. 'jème-yàng myáw-'jwĕn. ‖Don't fire until you've aimed. ı. yáw-'jwĕn-le dzày 'fàng. ‖Is your aim good? *is expressed as* Is your technique with firearms good? nǐ-de-'chyāng-fǎ 'hǎw-bu-hǎw?

To aim to 'dǎ-swàn, shyàng. ‖What do you aim to do? nǐ 'dǎ-swàn dzwò 'shéme? ‖Enemy troops aim to capture the town. 'dí rén shyǎng bǎ-'chéng 'gūng-shyà-lay. *or* (*literary*) 'dí-rén 'jŕ-dzày dwó-'chéng.

To aim at 'jŕ-je ... shwō. ‖Who is your remark aimed at? nǐ shŕ 'jŕ-je 'shwéy shwō-de?

What are you aiming at? *is expressed as* What's the point you're trying to make? nǐ shŕ shéme-'yì-sz?

AIR. (*Atmosphere*) 'kūng-chì. ‖I'm going out for some fresh air. wǒ yàw 'chū-chywu 'hū-shi dyǎr 'shīn-shyan-'kūng-chì. ‖The air in this room isn't good. jèy-'wū-dz-li-de-'kūng-chi bù-'hǎw.

(*Sky, weather*) 'tyān-chi. ‖The air is clear today. 'jīn-tyan 'tyān-chi bú-'tswò.

(*Sky*) 'tyān. ‖The swallows are soaring in the air. 'yàn-dz dzày 'tyān-shang 'fēy.

(*Manner*) 'tày-dù. ‖But her air reveals that she's lying. kĕ-shr tā-de-'tày-du 'shyǎn-chu-lay tā shŕ dzày sā-'hwǎng.

By air (*for passengers*) dzwò fēy-'jī; (*for freight or mail*) yùng fēy-'jī; (*for mail*) yùng háng-kūng-'shìn. ‖I want to go by air if possible. rú-gwo 'kĕ-néng de-hwà, wǒ shyàng dzwò fēy-'jī chywù.

Be on the air gwǎng-'bwò. ‖This radio station hasn't been on the air for three days. jèy-ge-wú-shyàn-'dyàn-táy yĕw 'sān-tyan méy gwǎng-'bwò-le.

Open-air lù-tyān-. ‖They've built an open-air theater. tām 'gày-le yí-ge-lù-tyān-shì-'ywán-dz.

To be airtight bú-lèw-'chì.

To air (*a room, etc.*) bǎ ... jyàw-'fēng 'chwēy(-yi-chwēy), bǎ ... 'tūng(-yi-tūng) 'fēng. ‖Would you please air the room while I'm out? wǒ 'chū-chywu yǐ-'hèw chǐng-ni bǎ jèy-ge-'wū-dz jyàw-'fēng 'chwēy-yi-chwēy.

To air (*oneself or clothes, thoroughly*) (bǎ ...) tèw-'fēng. ‖You should air your fur coat every now and then. nǐ 'yīng-dang 'shŕ-cháng bǎ nǐ-de-pí-dà-'yī 'tèw-yi-tèw 'fēng.

To air (*bedding, clothes, laundry, etc.*) lyàng. ‖To prevent fermentation, you should air it once a day. rè-shr-shyǎng jyàw 'jèy-ge-dūng-shi bù-jǎng-'máwr. nǐ 'yīng-dang 'mĕy-tyan 'lyàng-ta yí-'tsz̀.

AIRCRAFT CARRIER. fēy-jī-mǔ-'jyàn, háng-kūng-mǔ-'jyàn.

AIRFIELD. fēy-jī-'chǎng.

AIR FORCE. kūng-'jywūn.

AIR MAIL. háng-kūng-'shìn. By air mail yùng háng-kūng-'shìn, yùng fēy-'jī.

AIRPLANE. fēy-'jī. ‖There are three airplanes in the sky. yĕw 'sān-jyà-fēy-'jī dzày 'tyān-shang 'fēy. ‖How long does it take by airplane? dzwò fēy-'jī chywù dĕy 'dwō-shaw-shŕ-hew?

AIRPORT. fēy-jī-'chǎng.

AIRSHIP. chì-'chwán.

AIRWAY. háng-'shyàn.

AISLE. yǔng-'dàwr, yǔng-'lù.

ALARM. jǐng *in compounds like* fire alarm hwǒ-'jǐng. ‖There were two fire alarms yesterday. 'dzwó-tyan yĕw 'lyǎng-tsz̀-hwǒ-'jǐng.

(*Danger signal*) jǐng-'bàw. Air-raid alarm kūng-shí-jǐng-'bàw; (*first signal*) ywù-bèy-jǐng-'bàw; (*second signal*) jǐn-jí-jǐng-'bàw; (*all-clear signal*) jyĕ-chú-jǐng-'bàw. ‖What was that alarm for? 'nèy-ge-jǐng-'bàw shŕ wèy-'shéme?

To alarm jǐng-'dùng. ‖The noise alarmed the whole town. 'shēng-yīn jǐng-'dùng chywán-'chéng.

Be alarmed fā-'chéw, hwāng, jǐng-'hwāng, 'jāw-jí. ‖I'm quite alarmed at the recent military developments. dzwèy-'jìn-de-'jàn-kwàng hĕn jyàw-wo fā-'chéw. ‖Don't be alarmed. byé 'hwāng. *or* byé jǐng-'hwáng. ‖Don't be so alarmed at your son's sickness. byé 'tày wèy nǐ-'ér-dz-de-'bìng 'jāw-jí.

Be alarming kĕ-'lywù. ‖The situation is quite alarming. 'chíng-shr hĕn kĕ-'lywù.

ALARM CLOCK. 'nàw-jūng. ‖Do you sell alarm clocks? nǐ mày 'nàw-jūng-ma? ‖Set the alarm (clock) for six. bǎ 'nàw-jūng shàng-daw 'lyèw-dyǎn-jūng. *or* jyàw 'nàw-jūng dzày 'lyèw-dyǎn-jūng 'shyǎng.

ALBUM. jì-nyàn-'tsè(-dz).

ALCOHOL. hwǒ-'jyěw.

ALF. mày-'jyěw.

ALFALFA. 'mù-shywu.

ALGEBRA. dày-'shù.

ALIEN. 'wày-gwo-rén, wày-'chyáw.

ALIKE. shyāng-'túng, yí-'yàng. ‖If the cases were all alike, we wouldn't need to discuss them. yàw-shr 'chíng-shíng dēw yí-'yàng de-hwà, wǒm jyěw 'yùng-bu-jáw tǎw-'lwèn-le. ‖These places are all alike. jèy-shyē-'dì-fang dēw yí-'yàng.

To be alike (in appearance, superficially) shyāng-'fàng. ‖These two are somewhat alike. jèy-'lyǎng-ge yěw 'shyē shyāng-'fǎng. ‖These twins don't look alike. is expressed as Those twins haven't grown similarly. jèy-dwèr-'shwàng-sheng 'jǎng-de bú-'shyàng.

(Same way). ‖We treat all the visitors alike. is expressed as We treat all visitors as equals. wǒm dwèy 'swǒ-yěw-de-yéw-'kè yí-shr 'túng-rén.

ALIVE. hwó, shēng, dzày. ‖Get him dead or alive! 'dǎy-ta! sž-'hwó bú-'lwèn. ‖(The reports we get aren't very reliable.) It's not clear whether he's dead or alive. tā shēng-'sž bù-'míng. ‖He's better off dead than alive. (If not yet dead) tā ('hwó-je) háy bù-'rú 'sž-le-ne. (If already dead) tā 'sž-le dàw bǐ 'hwó-je 'hǎw. ‖Is he still alive? tā 'shr-bu-shr háy 'dzày? ‖The legend of his gallantry is still alive. tā-de-'yīng-míng réng 'dzày.

(Figuratively). ‖The war kept the hatred alive. 'jàn-jēng shǐ chéw-'hèn 'lyéw-dzay rén-'shīn-li (literary).

Be alive to dzày 'dī-fang-je. ‖I'm very much alive to the danger. wǒ 'lǎw dzày 'dī-fang-je (nèy-jǔng-'shèr).

Be alive with 'jìng-shr, 'mǎn-shr. ‖This place is alive with crackpots and half-wits. jèy-ge-'dì-fang 'jīng-shr bàn-'fēngr gēn bèn-'dàn. ‖The station was alive with soldiers. hwǒ-che-'jàn-li 'mǎn-shr 'bīng.

ALKALI. jyǎn-'shìng-de.

ALL. dēw, chywán, 'chywán-dēw; the following, if they precede the verb, usually require one of the above three, directly before the verb: dà-'jyā, jěng-'gèr, 'wán-chywán, fán, 'rèn-hé, 'swǒ-yěw-de, yī, yì-'jěng, yí-'chyè. ‖Do you need all of it? nǐ 'dēw 'děy-yàw-ma? ‖Is it all over? dēw 'wán-le-ma? ‖It's all used up. dēw yùng-'wán-le. ‖That's all. dēw 'wán-le. ‖We must all work harder. dzám dēw děy jyā-'yéw. ‖We all know him. wǒm chywán 'rèn-shr ta. ‖Please don't take all of it; leave some for the others. chǐng byé 'chywán-dēw 'ná-chywu; gěy 'páng-rén 'lyéw-dyǎr. ‖Let's all

go. 'dà-jyā 'dēw chywù-ba. ‖Did you all go? nǐm (-dà-'jyā) dēw 'chywù-le-ma? ‖Better do it all over again. 'dǐng hǎw 'jěng-gèr 'dzày 'láy yì-hwéy. ‖I want all of it. wǒ 'jěng-gèr dēw 'yàw. ‖I understand all of it. wǒ 'wán-chywán 'dǔng. ‖All men are mortal. fán-'rén bì 'sž. ‖All vehicles are prohibited from crossing this bridge. 'rèn-hé-'chē-lyàng dēw bù-néng gwò jèy-ge-'chyáw. ‖All dogs must have a tag. 'swǒ-yěw-de-'gěw dēw děy dày-'pár. ‖This is all there is. 'swǒ-yěw-de 'dēw dzày-jèr-le. ‖This is all the money I have. wǒ-'swǒ-yěw-de-'chán jr 'yěw 'jèy-dyǎr-le. or wǒ 'swǒ-yěw-de-'chán jr ywú-'tsž-le. ‖I've been waiting all day long. wǒ 'děng-le yì-'tyān-le. ‖She cried all night. tā 'kū-le yì-jěng-'yè. ‖All I said was true. yí-'chyè dēw-shr shr-'hwà.

All about it tūng-'tūng-de. ‖Tell me all about it. tūng-'tūng-de 'gàw-sung wo.

All along tsúng 'chǐ-téwr, tsúng 'chǐ-chū. ‖He's known it all along. tā tsúng 'chǐ-téwr jyěw 'jr-dàw (-le).

All around 'swǒ-yěw-de ... chywán, yí-ge-'yí-ge-de ... dēw. ‖He shook hands all around. tā gēn 'swǒ-yěw-de 'rén chywán lā-le 'shěw-le. But ‖I've looked all around the city. chywán-'chéng wǒ dēw kàn-'byàn-le.

All at once 'hū-rán(-jyān) jyěw, 'tù-rán(-jyān). ‖All at once something happened. 'hū-rán-jyán jyěw chū-le 'shr-le.

All but jī-hu děng-'ywú. ‖He's all but dead. tā jī-hu děng-'ywú 'sž-le.

All kinds of jǔng-'jǔng-de, gè-'jǔng-de. But ‖It takes all sorts (of men). 'shéme-yàngr-de(-rén) dēw 'yěw.

All the better gèng 'hǎw-le. ‖If that's true, all the better. rú-gwo shǐ 'nà-yàng, dāng-rán gèng 'hǎw-le.

All the same méy-yew shéme-'fēn-bye, dēw shr yí-'yàng-de. ‖You can take either car, it's all the same. nǐ swéy-'byàn dzwò 'nǎ-lyǎng-chē, méy-yew shéme-'fēn-bye. ‖It's all the same to him. dzày tā-('shīn-li) dēw shr yí-'yàng-de. But ‖But I hate you all the same. wǒ 'háy-shr 'hèn-ni.

All the time shr-'jūng.

All the way yí-'lù. ‖He ran all the way. tā yí-'lù 'pǎw-je chywù-de.

In all yí-'gùng. ‖How many are there in all? yí-'gùng yěw 'dwō-shaw?

Not at all 'gēn-běn ... bū, yì-'jr ... méy, 'wán-chywán ... bū, shr-'jūng ... méy, 'yì-dyǎr yě bū. ‖I don't know him at all. wǒ 'gēn-běn bú-'rèn-de ta. ‖I didn't speak at all. wǒ yì-'jr méy-shwō-'hwà. ‖Didn't you go away at all? nǐ yì-'jr méy-'dzěw-ma? ‖Don't you know it at all? nǐ 'wán-chywán bù-'jr-dàw-ma? ‖Haven't you been here at all? nǐ shr-'jūng méy-'láy-gwo-ma? ‖I'm not at all tired. wǒ 'yì-dyǎr yě bú-'lèy.

All right. hǎw. or shíng. or 'ké-yi.

Special expressions in English. ‖I can't do this all alone. 'jèy-ge wǒ-'dz-jǐ bàn-bu-'lyǎw. ‖I'll be there before eight, if at all. wǒ rú-gwo 'chywù de-hwà, 'bā-dyǎn-yǐ-'chyán 'dàw. ‖(Thank you.) Not at all! 'méy-yew shéme! ‖It's all over now. 'yǐ-jing 'gwò-chywu-le. or dēw 'wán-le. or dēw 'lyǎw-le. ‖It's all over the town by now. chywán-'chéng dēw chwán-'byàn-le. ‖That's all the same to me. 'dzěme-je dēw 'shíng, wǒ bú-'dzày-hu. ‖That's all I can do for you. wǒ néng gěy-ni 'bàn-de, jǐ ywú-'tsž-le. ‖I'll do all I can. wǒ jìn-'lì 'bàn-yi-bàn. ‖He ate it, bones and all. tā lyán 'gú-tew dēw 'chī-le. ‖That's all there is to it! bú-gwò rú-'tsž. or jyèw-shr 'jème-je jyèw 'wán-le. ‖As a soldier, he isn't all there. dāng-'bīng tā bù-hé-'gé. ‖What you say is all very well, but my mind is made up. 'hwà 'swéy-rán shr̀ 'jème shwō, bú-gwo wǒ-de-'jú-yì yǐ-jing dǎ-'dìng-le. ‖The score is two-all. 'fēn-shù shyàn-'dzày shr̀ èr-'píng.

ALLEY. hú-'tùng(r), shyǎw-'shyàngr.

ALLIANCE. (Countries bound by an agreement) túng-méng-'gwó, lyán-hé-'gwó, lyán-méng-'gwó; **to make an alliance** jyē-'méng.

ALLIGATOR. è-'ywú.

ALLOW. (Informal) jyàw, ràng; (formal) shywǔ, jwěn. ‖She won't allow me to go. tā bú-'ràng-wo 'chywù. ‖They allow you fifty pounds of baggage without extra charge. jwěn myǎn-'fèy dày 'wǔ-shr-bàng-de-'shíng-li.

(Leave large) 'ràng-chu-lay. ‖Allow one inch on the waistcoat. bèy-'shīn 'ràng-chu yí-'tswèn-lay.

(Figure in) 'dǎ-chu-lay. ‖Allowing a tenth for breakage, you can still make some profit. jyèw-shr 'dǎ-chu 'shí-fēn-jr-'yī-de-swěn-'hàw-lay, 'háy kě-yi 'yěw-de 'jwàn-ne.

Allow for (make allowances for) tǐ-'lyàng. ‖You must allow for his youth. nǐ děy tǐ-'lyàng tā 'nyán-chīng.

Allow so much for (pay, or loan on security). ‖How much will you allow me for this? 'jèy-ge nǐ 'dǎ-swàn gěy-wo 'dwō-shaw-chyán?

ALLY. (Country) túng-méng-'gwó, lyán-méng-'gwó.

ALMANAC. nyán-'jyàn, lì-'shū, dà-shr̀-'jì.

ALMOND. shìng-'rér, shìng-'rén.

ALMOST. 'chà-bu-dwō, 'chà-yì-dyǎr, 'jī-hu. ‖He almost died. tā 'chà-bu-dwō 'sž-le. or tā 'chà-yi-dyǎr méy-'sž. or tā 'chà-yì-dyǎr 'sž-le.

(With reference to time) jyèw, kwày. ‖I'm almost done. 'jyèw 'wán-le. or 'kwày 'wàn-le. ‖We're almost there. 'jyèw (or 'kwày) 'dàw-le.

ALONE. 'dž-jǐ, 'yí-ge-rén, jǐ yěw . . . . ‖Can you do it alone? nǐ-'dž-yǐ néng 'dzwò-ma? ‖I came alone. wǒ shr̀ 'yí-ge-rén 'láy-de. ‖You alone can help me. jǐ yěw-'nǐ néng 'bāng-wo.

‖I'm all alone. wǒ 'gū-shēn 'yì-rén.

‖Leave me alone! 'lí-wo 'ywǎn-dyǎr! or byé jāw-wo! or byé 'rě-wo. or byé 'gwǎn-wo. or nǐ gwǎn-de-'jáw-ma! or yùng-de-'jáw nǐ 'gwǎn! or nǐ gwǎn-bu-'jáw!

ALONG. yán. ‖A fence runs along the road. yán-'lù yěw yí-dàw-'lí-ba. ‖The submarine coasted along the shore. chyán-shwěy-'tǐng yán-je hǎy-'àn màn-'mār-de dzěw.

Along with gēn, túng, hé. ‖Come along with me. 'gēn-wo láy. ‖Put it along with the others. bǎ 'jèy-ge túng (or gēn, hé) 'byé-de fàng-dzay yí-'kwàr.

Take along dày. ‖How much baggage should I take along? wǒ yīng-dang dày 'dwō-shaw-shíng-li?

Push along. ‖Will you push this along, please? chǐng-ni gěy 'kwày bàn.

To get along. ‖How are you getting along? nǐ 'jìn-lay 'dzěme-yàng? or nǐ 'jìn-kwàng rú-'hé? ‖Are you getting along all right together? nǐ-men(-'lyǎng-ge-ren) shyāng-'chǔ háy 'hǎw-ma?

ALPHABET. dž-'mǔ.

ALREADY. yǐ-jing. ‖I'm late already. wǒ 'yǐ-jing 'wǎn-le. ‖I'm already done. wǒ 'yǐ-jing (dzwò-)'wán-le. ‖Are you already finished? nǐ 'yǐ-jing dzwò-'wán-le-ma?

(Unexpectedly soon) 'jywū-rán. ‖Are you finished already? nǐ 'jywū-rán dzwò-'wán-le(-ma)?

ALSO. yě. ‖I'd also like to have that one. wǒ ('túng-shí) yě shyǎng-yàw 'nèy-yí-ge.

(In addition, furthermore) 'èw, háy, dzay 'jyā-shang. ‖There was a policeman there also, so what else could I do? 'yèw (or 'háy or dzày 'jyā-shang) yěw ge-jīng-'chá; nǐ shwō, wǒ 'háy néng yěw 'byé-de-bàn-fa-ma?

See also TOO.

ALTAR. táy, shèng-'tán, jì-'tán, -tán.

ALTHOUGH. 'swéy-rán (often followed in next part of sentence by kě-shr or bú-'gwò). ‖Although there were three of them against me, I wasn't at all afraid. 'swéy-rán tā-men (shr̀) 'sān-ge-rén dǎ wǒ-'yí-ge, (kě-shr) wǒ yì-'dyǎr yě bú-'pà. (kě-shr can also follow wǒ.) ‖Although I was somewhat in the wrong too, his fault was greater than mine. wǒ 'swéy-rán 'yě yěw 'bú-shr, kě-shr 'tā-de-tswèr bǐ-'wǒ 'dwō. ‖They still see each other often, although they've been divorced. tām 'swéy-rán lí-le 'hwēn, kě-shr 'háy cháng jyàn-'myàr.

In all the above sentences, if kě-shr or bú-'gwò is kept, 'swéy-rán can be dropped.

(*Except that*) bú-'gwò. ‖I'll be there, although I may be late. wǒ yí-'dìng 'dàw-nàr, bú-'gwò wǒ 'shywǔ-hwèy 'wǎn yì-dyǎr.

ALTITUDE. gāw-'dù.

ALWAYS. (*Past, present and future*) dzǔng(-shr̀), lǎw (-shr̀). ‖Down south the weather is always bad. 'nán-byan 'ty⁻n-chi 'dzǔng-shr̀ bù-'hǎw. ‖Are you always so busy? nǐ 'lǎw-shr̀ jème-'máng-ma? ‖He's always letting his mind wander. tā 'lǎw-shr̀ (*or* 'dzǔng-shr̀) bú-jù-'yì.

(*In the past, since some remote point of time*) 'shyàng-láy, 'tsúng-láy, yì-'jŕ, yí-'shyàng. ‖In Shang-hai the fifth of June has always been a holiday. dzày shàng-'hǎy, 'lyèw-ywè-'wǔ-hàw 'shyàng-láy shr̀ fàng-'jyà. ‖This train always runs on time. jèy-lyè-'chē 'tsúng-láy bú-wù-'dyǎn. ‖He's always been like that. tā yì-'jŕ shr̀ 'nà-yàng. ‖Having always had a very easy life, he doesn't know what hardship means. tā-yí-'shyàng-'gwò-de shr̀ 'shū-fu-r̀-dz, bù-'jŕ-dàw 'shéme jyàw chr̄-'kǔ.

(*From now on*) yǔng-'ywǎn, cháng-'cháng(-de). ‖Always remember to be on time. (*Ordinarily*) cháng-'cháng-de jì-'jù-le byé.'wǎn 'dàw. (*Emphatically*) yǔng-'ywǎn jì-'jù-le shěw shŕ-'kè.

Not always wèy-bì-'jìn-rán. ‖Crows aren't always black. *meaning* not necessarily 'wū-ya wèy-bì-'jìn-rán shr̀ 'hēy-de. ‖He isn't always like that. tā 'bú-shr̀ 'lǎw 'nà-me-yàng-de. *or* tā bù-'lǎw shr̀ 'nà-me-yàng-de.

See also EVER, OFTEN, NEVER.

AMBASSADOR. dà-'shr̀.

AMBULANCE. bìng-'chē, jyèw-hù-'chē.

AMENDMENT. shyēw-jèng-'fǎ.

AMERICA. (*The continent*) 'měy-jēw; North America běy-'měy-jēw; South America nán-'méy-jēw.

United States 'měy-gwó. ‖This is an American movie. jè shr̀ 'měy-gwo-dyàn-'yěngr. ‖I'm an Ameri-can. wǒ shr̀ 'měy-gwo-rén.

(*Flowery flag country*) hwā-chí(-'gwó). *Unofficial designation of the U. S. A. appearing in names like* hwā-chí-yín-'háng *The National City Bank of New York.*

AMONG. dzày . . .-li. ‖Look among the papers. dzày wén-'jyàn-li 'jǎw-yi-jǎw.

Among our (your, them)selves bǐ-'tsž *or* 'dž-jǐ. ‖They quarreled among themselves. tā-men bǐ-'tsž bàn-'dzwéy. ‖Divide this among yourselves. nǐm bǎ 'jèy-ge 'dž-jǐ 'fēn-le-ba. ‖Just among ourselves, I don't think he's going to succeed. 'jè-hwà jyèw-shr̀ dzám-'dž-jǐ shwō; wǒ 'jywé-de tā bú-'hwèy chéng-'gūng.

One among others 'chí-jūng-jr̀-'yī. ‖Among other titles, he has that of a scoutmaster. tā-de-gwān-'sh/án hěn 'dwō; túng-dž-'jywūn dwèy-'jǎng 'yě-shr̀ 'chí-jūng-jr̀-'yī.

Among the rest, among them dzày-'nèy. ‖Among them they've spoiled the whole thing. tā-men dēw dzày-'nèy, bǎ jèy-jyàn-'shèr gěy nùng-'dzāw-le. ‖Fifty passed the exam, and he was among them. yěw 'wǔ-shr-rén jí-'gé, 'tā yě dzày-'nèy.

‖You're among friends. dēw 'bú-shr̀ 'wày-rén. *or* jè 'dēw-shr̀ (dzám-)'dž-jǐ(-de)-rén.

AMOUNT. 'shù-mu. ‖This isn't the right amount. 'jèy-ge-shù-mu bú-'dwèy. ‖What's the total amount? *is expressed as* Altogether it's how much? yí-'gùng shr̀ 'dwō-shaw?

Amount to swàn. ‖My knowledge of Chinese doesn't amount to much. wǒ-'dǔng-de-jūng-gwo-'hwà bú-swàn 'dwō. ‖What does the bill amount to? *is expressed as* How much is this bill in all? jèy-bǐ-'jàng yí-'gùng shr̀ 'dwō-shaw(-chyán)?

AMUSE. (*A child*) hǔng. ‖Try to amuse the children. shyàng-'fár hǔng-hung 'háy-dz.

(*An adult*) gěy . . . dèw-shyàwr, gěy . . . kāy-kay 'shīn, (jyàw) . . . jywé-de kě-'shyàw. ‖Tell them a story to amuse them. shwō ge-'shyàw-hwar, gěy tā-men °dèw-dew 'shyàwr. *or* °kāy-kay 'shīn. ‖What she says amuses me very much. tā-shwō-de-'hwà wǒ jywé-de kě-'shyàw.

Amuse oneself jyě-'mèr. ‖How do you amuse your-self? nǐ 'džéme-yàng jyě-'mèr?

Amusing kě-'shyàw, yěw-'chywù(r)(-de). ‖Do you find this comedy amusing? nǐ 'jywé-de jèy-ge-shǐ-'jywù kě-'shyàw-ma? ‖Tell them an amusing story. 'gěy tā-men shwō ge-yěw-'chywùr-de-'gù-shr.

AMUSEMENT. ywú-'lè. ‖Are there many amusements here? jèr yěw shéme-ywú-'lè-ma?

Place of amusement kě-'wár-de-dì-fang. ‖Are there many places of amusement here? jèr 'yěw-méy-yew kě-'wár-de-dì-fang?

Expressed with to amuse. ‖Where can you go around here for amusement? jèr yěw 'shéme-dì-fang ké-yi chywù kāy-kay 'shīn?

ANATOMY. 'jyě-pěw-shywé (*the branch of study*).

ANCHOR. máw; weigh anchor bá-'máw; cast anchor shyà-'máw.

AND. *In a sentence like* He saw me and I ducked down again *or* He came and then I left, and *is not expressed in Chinese. Instead, one says* When he saw me I ducked down again *or* After he came I left *or* He came, I left, *either showing the relation between the two parts of the sentence more explicitly, or else not showing it at all.*

And *between nouns in English is often not expressed by a separate Chinese word.* Father and mother fù-'mǔ; mother and child mǔ-'dž; man and wife fū-'fù; brothers and sisters dì-shyung-jyě-'mèy.

(*Between nouns*) gēn, hé, túng; 'jí (*literary*). ‖The room had only a bed, a table, and a chair. 'wū-dz-li jǐ yěw yí-ge-'chwáng, yì-jāng-'jwǒ-dz, gēn yì-bǎ-'yǐ-dz. ‖Japan and Germany want to dominate the whole world. r̀-'běn hé 'dé-gwo yàw chēng-'bà chywán-shr̀-'jyè. ‖You and I have a lot in common. nǐ túng-wo shyāng-'jìn-de-dì-fang hěn 'dwō. ‖The guests included bankers and lawyers. láy-'kè-jūng yěw yín-háng-'jyā jí lywù-'shr̄ (*literary*).

Special English expressions. ‖There are doctors and doctors. yěw °gè-jǔng-gè-'yàng-de- (*or* °jǔng-'jǔng-de-) 'yī-sheng. ‖I walked miles and miles. wǒ 'dzěw-le bù-jr̄-dàw-'dwō-shaw-'lǐ-le. ‖She waited for days and days. tā 'děng-le °bù-jr̄-dàw-'dwō-shaw-'tyān-le *or* °'hǎw-shyē-hǎw-shyē-'tyān-le.

(*Between adjectives*). ‖You're getting better and better every day. nǐ ('jēn-shr̀) yì-'tyān bǐ yì-'tyān jyàn 'hǎw.

(*Between verbs*). ‖I called and called, but no answer. wǒ 'jyàw-le 'yèw jyàw kě-shr 'méy-rén dā-'shēngr.

Come and láy; go and chywù. ‖Come and see. nǐ láy 'kàn-yi-kàn. ‖Go and ask when the train leaves. nǐ chywù 'wèn-yi-wèn hwǒ-'chē 'shéme-shŕ-hew 'kāy.

Try and 'shr̀-yi-shr̀, shyǎng-'fár. ‖Try and see him tomorrow. shyǎng-'fár 'míng-tyan chywù °'kàn-ta. *or* °'kàn-yi-kàn ta.

(*Otherwise*). Both . . . and . . . . yèw . . . yèw . . . . ‖He's both dull and boring. tā yèw 'hú-tu yèw tǎw-'yàn.

And so forth 'děng-děng(-de), 'shéme-de. ‖I need towels, soap, and so forth. wǒ 'shywū-yàw 'shéw-jīn, 'yí-dz, °'děng-děng-de-dūng-shi. *or* °'shéme-de(-dūng-shi).

And so 'swǒ-yi, yin-'tsž. ‖And so he quit. 'swó-yi tā jyèw tsž-'jŕ-le.

And yet 'rán-ěr, 'kě-shr, 'bú-gwò. ‖And yet he did that to me! kě-shr tā 'géy-le wo 'nàme-yí-shyà-dz! ‖Such an intelligent man, and yet he does a thing like that! nàme-tsūng-'míng-de-rén kě-shr 'gàn-chu 'nèy-jǔng-shr̀-lay!

And that ér-'chyě. ‖He speaks English, and that almost as a native. tā hwèy shwō 'yīng-gwo-hwà, ér-'chyě shwō-de 'chà-bu-dwō gēn běn-'dì-rén yí-'yàng.

And then. (*Following that*) yǐ-'hèw jyèw; (*right after that*) jǐn 'gēn-je jyèw; (*secondly, after that*) 'rán-hèw dzày, yǐ-'hèw dzày, jǐn 'gēn-je dzày. ‖Cough loudly, and then enter. dà-shēng-de-'ké-su yì-shēng, 'rán-hèw dzày 'jìn-chywu. ‖Look all around and then close the door. 'jēw-wéy 'kàn-yi-kàn, jǐn 'gēn-je bǎ-'mén 'gwān-shang.

(*If . . . then*). ‖Say one word and you're a goner! chū yì-'shēngr nǐ jyèw méy-'mìng-le! *or* nǐ yàw-shr yàw-'mìng nǐ jyèw byé chū-'shēngr.

ANESTHETIC. má-'yàw.

ANGEL. (*Protestant*) tyān-'shŕ; (*Catholic*) tyān-'shén.

ANGLE. jyǎw(r).

ANGRY. shēng-'chì; nù, fā-'nù (*literary*). ‖He became very angry. tā 'bwó-rán 'dà nù. ‖What are you angry about? nǐ 'wèy-shéme shēng-'chì?

Be angry at nǎw, gēn . . . shēng-'chì. ‖Are you angry at him? nǐ 'shr̀-bu-shr̀ 'nǎw-le tā-le? *or* nǐ 'shr̀-bu-shr̀ 'gēn-ta shēng-'chì-le?

Be angry at *or* with dwèy . . . bù-'mǎn-yì. ‖The people are very angry with the government. rén-'mín dwèy 'jèng-fǔ hěn bù-'mǎn-yì.

ANIMAL. *Member of the* animal *kingdom* 'dùng-wu. ‖An amoeba is a kind of animal, not a plant. byàn-shíng-'chúng shr̀ yì-yǔng-'dùng-wu, bú-shr 'jr̄-wu.

(*Livestock*) 'shēng-kew. ‖Do you have any farm animals? nǐ yěw jùng-'dì-de-'shēng-kew-ma?

(*Not including humans or microscopic animals*) 'shèw. ‖Don't feed the animals. jè-shyē-'shèw bù-shywǔ 'wèy.

Wild animals yě-'shèw. ‖The children went to the zoo to see the animals. 'háy-dz-men dàw dùng-wu-'ywán chywu kàn yě-'shèw.

Animal 'chù-lèy, 'chù-sheng *as contrasted with* human 'rén-lèy (*in Buddhist theory*). ‖He called me an animal. tā 'gwǎn-wo jyàw ge-°'chù-lèy. *or* °'chù-sheng.

ANKLE. jyǎw-'wàn-dz, jyǎw-'wàr.

ANNOUNCE. bàw-'gàw, 'hwéy yì-shēng. ‖They just announced that on the radio. wú-shyàn-'dyàn-li tsáy bàw-'gàw-gwo. ‖Shall I announce your name (*to the host*)? wǒ 'ké-yi gěy-nín 'hwéy yì-shēng-ma?

Announce that 'shywān-bù. ‖They just announced that they're engaged. tām gāng 'shywān-bù dìng-'hwēn-le.

ANNOUNCEMENT. tūng-'gàw.

ANNOUNCER. (*Radio*) bàw-gàw-'ywán.

ANOTHER. (*In addition to or replacing*) byé(-de). ‖Tomorrow another man will come. 'míng-tyan yěw 'byé-rén 'láy.

(*Replacing; plus measure*) 'lìng-yī. ‖Tomorrow another man will come. 'míng-tyan 'lìng-yí-ge-rén 'láy. ‖Another method is to put an ad in the paper. 'lìng-yí-ge-fá-dz shr̀ dzày 'bàw-shang dēng gwǎng-'gàw.

(*Again*) lìng, dzày. ‖Who can think of another method? shwéy néng 'lìng (*or* 'dzày) shyǎng-chu ge-'fá-dz-lay? ‖I don't like this room; may I have another? 'jèy-ge-fáng-'jyān wǒ bù-'shǐ-hwān; 'lìng kāy yì-jyān *or* (hwàn-yì-'jyān), 'shíng-bu-shíng? ‖**Please give me another cup of coffee.** chǐng 'dzày gěy-wo yì-bēy-jyā-'fēy.

(*Yet again*) ling, yèw. ‖**That's another matter.** nà 'yèw-shr̀ yì-hwéy-'shèr.

(*There is also*) háy yěw. ‖**There's another person who can do it.** 'háy yěw yí-ge-'rén ké-yi dzwò jèy-jyàn-'shr̀.

One another bǐ-'tsž; **to one another** hù-'shyāng. ‖**They saw one another frequently.** tām bǐ-'tsž cháng jyàn-'myàn. ‖**They're trying to shift the responsibility to one another.** tām hù-'shyāng twéy-'wěy.

Another day. ‖**Let's talk about it another day.** 'gwò (jǐ-)tyān 'dzày shwō-ba. ‖**One day he's all smiles; another day he'll pull a long face on you.** tā 'jyēr-ge 'mǎn-lyǎn 'shyàw-rúngr, 'myéngr-ge jyèw hwèy yì-'lyǎn bù-gāw-'shìng.

‖**He makes a pile one way or another.** tā 'dzǔng néng shyǎng-'fár jwàn-'chyán.

One after another. ‖**They died one after another.** tām 'yí-ge-gēn-je-yí-ge-de dēw 'sž-le.

ANSWER. dá, 'hwéy-dá. ‖**I can't answer that question.** wǒ bù-néng 'dá nèy-ge-'wèn-tí. *or* 'nèy-ge-wèn-ti wǒ °dá-bu-'lyǎw. *or* °dá-bu-'chū. *or* °nèy-ge-wèn-ti wǒ bù-néng 'hwéy-dá.

(*When one's name is called*) 'dā-ying. ‖**When anyone calls your name, don't answer.** yěw-'rén °'jyàw-ni (*or* °jyàw nǐ-de-'míng-dz) byé 'dā-ying.

Answer (to) gēn . . . shyāng-'fú. ‖**That man answers (to) your description perfectly.** 'nèy-ge-rén gēn nǐ-'shwō-de jèng shyāng-'fú.

Be answered yìng-'yàn, líng. ‖**Your prayer has been answered.** nǐ-de-chǐ-'chyéw yìng-'yàn-le. *or* nǐ-de-dǎw-'gàw jēn 'líng.

(*By mail*). ‖**Please answer by return mail.** chǐng 'kwày láy 'hwéy-shìn.

Answer the phone jyē dyàn-'hwà; **answer a letter** shyě 'hwéy-shìn; **answer a telegram** dǎ 'hwéy-dyàn.

An answer (*to a mathematical problem or to a question*) dá-'àn. ‖**The answers are at the back of the book.** dá-'àn dzày shū-'hèw-tew.

An answer (*phone call or telegram*) 'hwéy-dyàn; (*letter*) 'hwéy-shìn. ‖**What's your answer?** nǐ 'dzěme shwō? *or* nǐ yěw shéme-'yì-jyan?

ANTARCTIC. nán-'jí-de(-dì-fang); (*ocean*) nán-bǐng-'yáng.

ANTENNA. tyān-'shyàn.

ANTHOLOGY. (*Of prose*) wén-'shywǎn; (*of verse*) shr̄-'snywǎn.

ANTIDOTE. shyāw-dú-'yàw.

ANUS. gāng-'mén.

ANXIOUS. **Be anxious about** 'dyàn-ji. ‖**I've been anxious about you.** wǒ 'cháng 'dyàn-ji-je ni.

Be anxious (to) hěn shyǎng, 'jí-ywu yàw, jáw-'jí. ‖**I'm anxious to go there.** wǒ 'hěn shyǎng dàw-'nàr-chywu. ‖**He's anxious to know the results of the exam.** tā 'jí-ywu yàw 'jr̄-dàw kǎw-'shr̀-de-jyē-'gwǒ. ‖**But his father is still more anxious.** kě-shr tā-'bà-ba °bǐ-ta 'háy (*or* °'gèng) jáw-'jí.

ANY. 'nǎ-yī *plus measure* . . . dēw; 'rèn-hé . . . dēw; shéme (. . . dēw); *or not expressed by separate word.* ‖**Any policeman can direct you.** 'něy-yí-ge-shywún-'jǐng dēw néng 'gàw-sung ni dzěme 'dzěw. ‖**Any school teaches that subject.** 'rèn-hé-shywé-'shyàw dēw jyāw 'nèy-mén-'gūng-kè. ‖**Any job is better than none.** 'shéme-shr̀ yě bǐ 'méy-shr̀ 'chyáng. ‖**Any time will do.** swéy-'byàn 'shéme-shŕ-hew dēw 'shíng. ‖**Do you have any money?** nǐ yěw-'chyán méy-yew? ‖**Do you have any more?** nǐ 'háy yěw-ma? ‖**I don't have any.** (wǒ) 'méy-yew. ‖**Do you like any of these girls?** jèy-shyē-'gū-nyang-li yěw nǐ-'shǐ-hwān-de-ma? ‖**If you want any more, say so.** yàw-shr 'háy (shyǎng-)'yàw jyèw shwō-'hwà.

Not . . . any 'shéme dēw bū-, 'shéme yě bū-, yi-dyǎr yě bū-, dēw bū-, *etc.* ‖**I don't feel any pain.** 'yì-dyǎr yě bù-'téng. ‖**He didn't give me any money.** tā 'yí-ge chyár yě méy-'gěy-wo. ‖**I don't like any of them.** wǒ 'dēw bù-'shǐ-hwān. ‖**I won't sell it at any price.** 'dwō-shaw-chyán (*or* 'shéme-jyà-chyan) wǒ 'dēw bú-'mày.

Anyone, anybody 'shwéy (dēw *or* yě), 'shéme-rén (dēw *or* yě). ‖**Anyone can say that.** 'shwéy dēw hwèy 'shwō. ‖**I don't want to see anybody.** wǒ °'shwéy (*or* °'shéme-rén) yě bú-'jyàn.

Anyone at all 'bú-lwèn shwéy; **anything at all** 'bú-lwèn shéme. ‖**Anyone at all can tell you.** 'bú-lwèn shwéy dēw néng 'gàw-sung ni

Anything 'shéme dēw, 'shéme yě. ‖**Anything you have will be all right** (*in a store*). nǐ-'mày-de 'shéme dēw 'hǎw. ‖**I'll give you anything but this letter.** wǒ 'shéme dēw néng 'gěy-ni, 'jyèw-shr bù-néng gěy-ni jè-fēng-'shìn.

Special expressions in English. ‖**Is there anything for me?** yěw 'wǒ-de-'dūng-shi-ma? (*In a post office*) yěw 'wǒ-de-shìn-ma? ‖**Can't anything be done?** 'nán-dàw 'yì-dyǎr-bàn-fa yě 'méy-yew-ma? ‖**He's anything but a miser.** tā 'jywé bú-shr̀ ge-kān-tsáy-'nú. ‖**I'll do anything but that.** jywé-'dwèy bú-gàn 'nèy-ge. ‖**He's anything but a hero.** wú-lwèn-rú-'hé dzǔng 'bù-néng shwō tā shr̀ ge-'yīng-shyung. ‖**There's little chance, if any.** jyèw-shr yěw 'shī-wàng yě °bù-'dwō. *or* °'méy-yew dwō-shaw. ‖**If any man can climb that mountain, he can.** 'nèy-dzwò-shān, jř-yàw rén néng 'shàng-de-chywu 'tā jyèw shàng-de-chywù. *or* 'nèy-dzwò-shān, 'tā yàw-shr shàng-bu-'chywù jyèw 'méy-yew rén néng 'shàng-le.

ANYWAY. héng-shù, dzǔng, 'háy-shr. ‖You don't have to phone him; he'll be here anyway. yùng-bu-'jáw dǎ dyàn-'hwà, héng-'shù tā shr̀ dàw-'jèr-lay-de. ‖You'll get paid anyway, so why worry? nǐ 'dzǔng hwèy ná-jáw 'chyán-de, dzěme 'háy bú-fàng-'shīn-ne? ‖It's raining, but we'll go anyway. shyà-jē 'ywǔ-ne, 'bú-gwò wǒm 'háy-shr 'chywù. or expressed with although 'swéy-rán shr̀ shyà-'ywǔ-ne, wǒm yí-'dìng 'chywù.

APART. lìng-'wày. ‖Set this apart for me. bǎ 'jèy-ge lìng-'wày gē-je.

Take apart 'chāy-kāy. ‖Take this alarm clock apart bǎ nàw-'jūng 'chāy-kāy.

Keep apart 'fēn-kāy. ‖Keep the children apart. bǎ 'háy-dz-men 'fēn-kay. But (more specifically; from each other) 'bú-yàw jyàw 'háy-dz-men dzày yí-'kwàr. (From adults) 'bú-yàw jyàw 'háy-dz-men gēn 'dà-rén dzày yí-'kwàr. or bǎ 'háy-dz gēn 'dà-rén 'fēn-kay.

Set apart for 'tè-wèy. ‖This building is set apart for the orphans. 'jèy-ge-léw shr̀ 'tè-wèy gū-'ér-(shè)-de.

Keep oneself apart from 'lí . . . hěn 'ywǎn, 'dwǒ-je . . . . ‖He always kept apart from us. tā 'lǎw-shr̀ 'lí wǒ-men hěn 'ywǎn. or tā lǎw 'dwǒ-je wǒ-men.

Tell apart 'fēn-byàn, 'féń-byé. ‖How do you tell them apart? nǐ 'dzěme-yàng 'fēn-byàn tā-men?

‖All joking apart, do you think you'll take that position? 'shyàw-hwar shr̀ 'shyàw-hwar; nǐ 'jyēw-jìng 'shyǎng-bu-shyǎng 'jyèw nèy-ge-'wèy-jr̀?

APPEAR. (Be published) chū; chū-'bǎn. ‖The paper appears every day. bàw-'jr̀ 'měy-tyān 'chū. ‖When is his latest work going to appear? tā-dzwèy-'jìn-de-'jù-dzwò 'jǐ-shr̀ chū-'bǎn?

(Come into view) chū-'shyàn. ‖A submarine suddenly appeared before our ship. yí-ge-chyán-shwěy-'tǐng 'hū-rán dzày wǒm-'chwán-de-'chyán-hyar chū-'shyàn-le.

(In a play or theater) chū-'yǎn. ‖When did she appear at the Golden Theater? tā 'jǐ-shr̀ dzày 'hwáng-jīn-dà-shì-'ywán chū-'yǎn-de?

(In court, of plaintiff or defendant) dàw-'àn; (of lawyer or judge) chū-'tíng. ‖The defendant didn't appear in court. bèy-'gàw méy dàw-'àn. ‖That judge will not appear in court today. 'nèy-ge-fǎ 'gwān 'jīn-tyan bù-chū-'tíng.

Appear to be 'fǎng-fù (shr̀), hǎw 'shyàng . . . (shr̀-de). ‖This appears to be correct. 'jèy-ge 'fǎng-fù shr̀ 'dwèy-le. ‖He appears to be very sick. tā hǎw 'shyàng 'bìng-de hěn 'lì-hày (shr̀-de).

APPEARANCE. (Looks) wày-'yàngr, wày-'màw, fēng-'tsǎy. ‖Her appearance is pleasing. wày-'yàngr (or wày-'màw) hěn 'pyàw-lyang. (With emphasis on natural features) tā-'jǎng-de jyàw-rén 'shǐ-hwān. (With emphasis on make-up) tā-'dǎ-ban-de jyàw-rén 'shǐ-hwān. ‖Don't judge people by appearances. bù-'kě yǐ 'wày-'màw 'chywǔ-rén.

To keep up appearances. ‖He did that just to keep up appearances. tā-'nà-me-je 'wán-chywán shr̀ 'wéy-chr̀ 'myàn-dz. ‖He keeps up a good appearance. tā 'lǎw-shr̀ hěn tǐ-'myàn-de.

‖Try to improve your appearance. hǎw-'hāwr-de 'dǎ-ban yí-shyà.

Make an appearance. See APPEAR.

Have the appearance of. See appear to be under APPEAR.

APPENDIX. (Anatomy) máng-'cháng; (in a book) fù-'lù.

APPLE. 'píng-gwo. ‖Chinese apples have thinner skins than the American variety. 'jūng-gwo-píng-gwo bǐ 'měy-gwo-jǔngr-de-'pyér 'báw.

‖Quit that apple-polishing! byé nème 'bā-ive-le!

APPLICATION. Written application (for entrance to an organization, for rationed goods, etc.) chǐng-chyéw-'shū; (only for membership in an organization) jr̀-ywàn-'shū. ‖Your application has been received. wǒm yi-jing 'shēw-dàw nǐ-de-chǐng-chyéw-'shū-le. ‖Your application must be accompanied by two letters of introduction. nǐ-de-jr̀-ywàn-'shū děy 'fù-je lyǎng-fēng-jyè-shàw-'shìn.

Entrance application (for a school) rù-'shywé-°chǐng-chyéw-'shū or °jr̀-ywàn-'shū; oral application 'kěw-téw-chǐng-'chyéw. ‖Will an oral application do? 'kěw-téw-chǐng-'chyéw 'shíng-ma?

Application blank jr̀-ywàn-'shū-byǎw-'gé, chǐng-chyéw-'shū-byǎw-'gé; (in a library, for a book) jyè-shū-'dān.

(Of medicine). ‖This medicine is only for external application. 'jèy-ge-yàw jr̀ néng 'wày-yùng. or 'jèy-ge-yàw jr̀-shr̀ 'shàng-de, bú-shr̀ 'chr̀-de.

APPLY. yīng-'yùng, shr̀-'yùng. ‖In this case this rule doesn't apply. dzày 'jèy-jyàn-shr̀-shang, jèy tyáw-'gwéy-jywu °bù-néng yīng-'yùng. or °bú-shr̀-'yùng.

(Medicine). shàng. ‖Apply the ointment carefully. nèy-ge-yàw-'gāw 'shyǎw-shīn-je 'shàng. But ‖Apply a hot compress every two hours. měy-gé-'lyǎng-dyàn-jūng yùng rè-'shěw-jīn 'tēng yí-shyà.

(A match) dyǎn. ‖Apply a match to this end. yùng yáng-'hwěr dzày 'jèy-téwr 'dyǎn.

Apply for chǐng-'chyéw. ‖He's qualified to apply for a new tire. tā yěw 'dz-gé chywù chǐng-'chyéw yí-ge-'shīn-chē-'dày.

To apply for a position (particularly but not always by indirect methods or political pull) méw 'chāy-shr. ‖I want to apply for that position. wǒ shyǎng 'méw nèy-ge-'chāy-shr.

‖To whom do I apply? wǒ 'yīng-dang jyàn-'shwéy?

APPOINT. (*General*) pày. ‖The divisional commander appointed him inspector of air-raid shelters. shŕ-'jǎng 'pày-ta dzwò fáng-kūng-'dùng-de-shŕ-chá-'ywán.

(*More formal; for non-commissioned officers, company officers, or similar grades in government*) wěy (-'rèn).

(*To an office of intermediate or high rank, except the highest*) rèn-'mìng. ‖The National Government appointed him Minister to Finland. gwó-mín-'jèng-fǔ rèn-'mìng ta dzwò jù-fẹn-'lán-gūng-'shŕ.

(*To the highest offices*) tè-'rèn. ‖The National Government appointed him Ambassador to the United States. gwó-mín-'jèng-fǔ tè-'rèn ta dzwò jù-'měy-'dà-shŕ.

APPRECIATE. (*Art, scenery, etc.*) 'shīn-shǎng. ‖You should learn to appreciate music. nǐ 'yīng-dang 'shywé 'shīn-shǎng yīn-'ywè.

(*A favor or kindness*) 'gǎn-jī. ‖Don't think I don't appreciate all you've done for me. nǐ 'gěy-wo 'bàn-le jème-shyē-'shŕ, 'bú-yàw yǐ-'wéy wǒ bù-gǎn-'jī ni.

(*Characteristics of someone of lower rank*) shǎng-'shŕ. ‖He really appreciates your ability. tā jēn shǎng-'shŕ nǐ-de-tsáy-'gàn.

APPROACH. (*Method*) fá-dz. ‖Am I using the right approach? wǒ-yùng-de-'fá-dz 'dwèy-bu-dwèy?

(*Entrance*) jìn-'kěwr; byār *in such compounds as* approach to a bridge chyáw-'byār. ‖The approaches to the bridge are under repair. 'chyáw-'lyǎng-byān-de-jìn-'kěwr jèng dzày 'shyēw-li. ‖The approach to the bridge is a high slope. chyán-'byār shŕ gāw-'pwō(er).

To approach *a person* gēn ... jyē-'jìn. ‖You can approach the governor through that man. ké-yi yéw 'nèy-ge-rén gēn shěng-'jǎng jyē-'jìn.

To approach 'lí-je 'jìn (*or* bù-'ywǎn). ‖The (camel) caravan is approaching. lwò-two-'dwèy 'lí-je hěn 'jìn-le.

To approach (*of an enemy*) bī-'jìn. ‖The enemy is approaching from three directions. 'dí-rén (yéw) 'sān-myàn bī-'jìn-le.

To approach *a person; about something* jǎw. ‖Is it all right to approach him about this matter? gwān-ywu 'jèy-jyàn-shŕ wǒ 'ké-yi-bu-ké-yi 'jǎw-yi-jǎw ta?

Be approaching *is expressed as* quickly arrive kwày dàw. ‖Let's approach his house carefully. 'kwày dàw tā-'jyā-le; 'shyǎn-shīn-je 'dzěw. ‖We're approaching the end. 'kwày dàw-'téwr-le.

APPROVE. (*Higher authority, in writing*) pī-'jwěn; (*higher authority, not necessarily in writing*) tsǎy-'nà. ‖Make a draft of your plans and send them in; I'll approve them. nǐ bǎ nǐ-de-'jì-hwà ní ge-'gǎw-dz 'jyāw-jìn-lay, wǒ jyèw pī-'jwěn.

Be approved (*by a legislative body*) 'tūng-gwò. ‖Has this plan been approved? jèy-ge-'jì-hwà yǐ-jing 'tūng-gwò-le-ma?

Approve of 'dzàn-chéng, rèn-'kě, 'byǎw-shŕ shyⱳu-'kě. ‖I don't approve of his conduct. wǒ bú-'dzàn-chéng tā-de-'shíng-wéy. ‖I can't approve of your use of my name to borrow money. nǐ yùng wǒ-de-'míng-yì chywù jyè-'chyáh wǒ 'bù-néng rèn-'kě. ‖His father hasn't approved of his engagement to that girl. tā gēn nèy-wèy-nywǔ-'shŕ dìng-'hwēn, tā-'fù-chin méy 'byǎw-shŕ-shywǔ-'kě.

APRICOT. shyèngr; (*the tree*) shìng-'shù.

APRIL. 'sż-ywè.

APRON. (*Clothes*) 'wéy-chywún.

ARCH. (*Architectural term*) hú; (*arched doorway*) gūng-'mén, 'gūng-shíng-de-'mén; (*of foot*) jyǎw-'gǔ.

ARCHEOLOGY. 'kǎw-gǔ-shywé.

ARCHITECT. 'jyàn-jù-'shŕ.

ARCHITECTURE. 'jyàn-jù-shywé.

ARCTIC. běy-'jí-de(-dì-fang); (*ocean*) běy-bīng-'yáng.

AREA. (*Measure of extent*) 'myàn-jí; (*region*) 'dì-fang(r).

ARGUE. Argue *about noisily* chǎw.. ‖What are they arguing about? tām dzày 'chǎw shéme?

(*Noisily*) chǎw-'dzwèy. ‖He likes to argue with people. tā 'ày 'gēn-rén chǎw-'dzwěy.

(*Belligerently*) dǎ-'jyà. ‖What are they arguing about? tām 'wèy-shéme dzày dǎ-'jyà?

(*Seriously*) 'byàn-lwèn, jēng-'byàn. ‖They're arguing about the methods of treating war criminals. tām-jēng-'byàn-de shŕ dwèy-dày-'jàn-shŕ-hwò-'shěw-de-'fāng fa.

(*Dogmatically*) táy-'gàng, chyǎng-'byàn; (*dogmatically; with plays on words for the sake of winning*) 'chyáng-tsź dwó-'lǐ. ‖Now he's arguing dogmatically. tā 'nà-shŕ chyǎng-'byàn.

Argue *something* **out** bǎ ... 'byàn-chū ge-jyē-'gwǒ-lay, bǎ ... byàn shwěy-'lè-shŕ-'chū. ‖We must argue this out. dzám bǎ jèy-ge-'wèn-tí děy 'byàn-chū ge-jyē-'gwǒ-lay.

Argue *someone* **out of** bǎ ... shwō-de bū-; argue *someone* **out of** *something or* **into** *something* shwō-'fu. ‖We argued him out of quitting. wǒm 'bǎ-ta 'shwō-de bù-tsź-'jŕ-le. *or* wǒm shwō-'fú-le tā-le; tā bù-tsź-'jŕ-le.

Other English expressions. ‖There's no use arguing any more. 'háy yěw shéme kě-'shwō-de-ne? *or* 'háy yěw shéme kě-'byàn-de-ne? ‖You can't argue with him. gēn-'tā dzěme 'shwō (*or* 'byàn) yě méy-yew 'yùng. *or* gēn-'tā 'dzěme néng jyǎng-'lǐ-ne? *or* gēn-'tā 'méy-fár shwō-'lǐ (*or* jyǎng-'lǐ). *or* gēn-'tā shwō-'lǐ (*or* jyǎng-'lǐ) yěw shéme-'yùng?

ARGUMENT. *Expressed with verb meaning* **to** argue. ‖He got into quite an argument with his wife. tā túng tă-'tày-tay chăw-'dzwěy 'chăw-de hěn 'lì-hày. ‖I don't follow your argument. nǐ-'shwŏ-de-'lǐ (*or* -lǐ-'yéw) wŏ bú-'dà 'míng-bay. ‖Let's not have an argument about this. dzám bú-'bì wèy 'jèy-ge jēng-'byàn. ‖How can you get the best of an argument with a pretty woman like her? nǐ gēn 'tā-nàme-hăw-'kàn-de-'nywǔ-rén jēng-'byàn 'dzěme néng 'yíng-ne? *But* ‖His argument is based on a false premise. *is expressed as* The premise he follows is wrong. tā-'gēn-jywù-de-chyán-'tí 'tswò-le.

ARITHMETIC. . swàn-'shù.

ARM. (*Of body*) 'gē-be (*or* 'gē-bwo), bèy; upper arm 'shàng-bwò; forearm 'chyán-bwò, (*literary*) jěw, húng, gūng. ‖My arm hurts. wŏ 'gē-be-téng.

Arm in arm 'kwà-je 'gē-be. ‖They went away arm in arm. tām kwà-je 'gē-be 'dzěw-le.

At arm's length. ‖You'd better keep him at arm's length. nǐ 'dzwèy hăw °'ywăn-je ta 'dyăr. *or* °'shū-ywăn ta dyăr.

With arms folded chā-je 'gē-be. *But* ‖They looked on with folded arms. *meaning* with arms in the sleeves of the Chinese upper garment tām shyèw-'shěw páng-'gwān.

With open arms ‖They welcomed him with open arms. tām rè-'lyè-de 'hwān-yíng ta

(*Of a chair, etc.*) 'fú-shew.

Firearms. (*In military usage*) jywǔn-'hwŏ, chyāng-'shyè, wǔ-'chì, bīng-'chì; (*informally*) 'jyā-hwo. ‖We should stop sending arms to Japan. wŏm 'yīng-dang tíng-'jǐ wàng r̀-'běn sùng jywūn-'hwŏ. ‖Do you have any arms in the house? nǐ-'jyā-li yěw chyáng-'shyè-ma?

Be armed (*carry or have arms*) dày (*or* yěw) jywūn-'hwŏ *or* wǔ-'chì, *etc.* ‖Were they armed? tām 'shēn-shang dày-je 'jyā-hwo méy-yew? *or* tām dày-'chyāng-le-ma? *But* ‖Are they fully armed? wǔ-'chì (*or* bīng-'chì) chí-'chywán-ma?

Arms and equipment wǔ-'chì-jwāng-'bèy. ‖This division is completely outfitted in arms and equipment. jèy-'shr̀-de-wǔ-'chì-jwāng-'bèy hěn 'chywán.

To arm someone bǎ . . . wǔ-'jwāng-chi-lay. ‖Arm all the farmers. bǎ 'núng-rén dēw wǔ-'jwāng-chi-lay.

(*Branch of the Army*). (*Personnel*) ('bīng)-kē; (*units*) bīng-'jǔng. ‖We must strengthen these two arms. 'jèy-lyăng-'kē děy jyā-'chyáng. ‖To all Arms: jū-bīng-'jǔng:

‖The arms of the law can't reach him. fǎ-'lywù-de-'lì-lyang gwǎn-bu-'dàw ta. *or* tā 'shyāw-yáw fǎ-'wày.

ARMISTICE. (*Document*) tíng-jàn-'shū; to conclude (*or* make) an armistice tíng-'jàn.

ARMOR. (*For body*) kwēy-jyǎ; (*for vehicle or battleship*) tyé-'jyǎ, tyě-'bǎn.

ARMPIT. gē-je-'wō, yè.

ARMY. (*In contrast to Navy*) lù-'jywūn. ‖The American Army is bigger than the American Navy. měy-gwo-'lù-jywūn-'rén-shù bǐ 'hăy-jywūn-de 'dwō.

(*As a force in the field*) jywūn-'dwèy. ‖There are no such men in the Army. jywūn-'dwèy-li 'méy-yew 'nà-me-yàng-de-rén. ‖He led an army into the jungles, tā 'dày-le yì-jr̀-jywūn-'dwèy dàw shēn-'lín-li chywù-le.

(*Armed forces or major subdivision thereof*) jywūn. ‖The commander of the Seventh Army is a man named Jāng. dì-'chī-'jywūn-de-jywūn-'jǎng shìng-'jāng. ‖These telephones are for army use. 'jèy-shyē-dyàn-hwà-'jī shr̀ 'jywūn-'yùng-de.

To serve in the Army *is expressed as* to serve as a soldier dāng-'bīng. ‖Have you ever served in the Army? nǐ dāng-gwo 'bīng méy-yew?

To send an army to . . . pày-'bīng dàw . . . chywu, pày-jywūn-'dwèy dàw . . . chywu, chū-'bīng dàw . . . chywu. ‖First the United States sent an army to Iceland. 'měy-gwo °'shyān pày-'bīng (*or* one of the other expressions*) dàw bīng-'dǎw-chywu.

AROUND. (*Walk, go, run, etc.*) around . . . wéy-je . . . (dzěw, *etc.*), ràw-je . . . (dzěw, *etc.*). ‖We walked around the lake twice. wŏm wéy-je 'hú 'dzěw-le lyăng-'chywār (*or* -dzāw, -dzāwr). ‖We'll have to detour around the town. wŏm děy 'ràw-je 'chéng 'dzěw.

Around *something is expressed as* something's circumference . . . -jēw-'wéy. ‖How many miles is it around this lake? jèy-ge-'hú-de-jēw-'wéy yěw dwō-shaw-'lǐ?

(*Approximately*) dzwŏ-'yěw, shàng-'shyà. ‖I'll be there around nine o'clock. wŏ 'jyěw-dyǎn-'jūng dzwŏ-'yěw 'dàw-nèr. ‖I have around twenty dollars. wŏ yěw 'èr-shr-kwày-'chyán-shàng-'shyà.

Other expressions in English. ‖Are there any soldiers around? 'jèr yěw-'bīng-ma? ‖It's somewhere around the house. dzwŏ-'yěw bù-'chū jèy-swŏ-'fáng-dz. ‖I'll have to look around for it. wŏ děy 'jăw-yi-jăw. ‖Look around you. sz̀-'shyà (*or* jēw-'wéy) 'kàn-yi-kàn! ‖The store is just around the corner. 'pù-dz gwǎy-'wār jyèw 'shr̀.

‖Turn around! (*Facing me*) 'jwàn-gwo-lay! (*Facing away from me*) 'jwàn-gwo-chywu!

ARRANGE. bǎy. ‖How're you going to arrange the (things on the) table? 'jwŏ-dz-shang-de-dūng-shi nǐ dǎ-'swàn 'dzěme-yàng 'bǎy? ‖How would you arrange these flowers? nǐ 'jywé-de jèy-shyē-'hwār 'dzěme-yàng 'bǎy hǎw?

(*Furniture, etc.*) 'ān-pay. ‖How are you planning to arrange the tables? jèy-shyē-'jwŏ-dz nǐ shyǎng 'dzěme-yàng 'ān-pay?

(*Where the things arranged are mentioned first*) gē. ‖Say, how'll I arrange these things? nǐ shwō, 'jèy-shyē-dūng-shi dzěme 'gē?

(*Books or cards only*) mǎ. ‖Who arranged the books? gwǎn-mǎ-'shū-de shr̀-'shwéy?

(*Straighten out*) 'jěng-li. ‖Please arrange the things on your desk. chǐng-ni bǎ nǐ-'jwō-dz-shang-de-dūng-shi 'jěng-li yí-'shyà.

(*Take care of*) nùng, bàn, bàn-'twǒ. ‖Let me arrange this! 'wǒ láy nùng 'jèy-ge-ba! ‖Can you arrange this for me? 'jèy-ge nǐ néng 'gěy-wo 'bàn yí shyàr-ma? ‖It was arranged long ago. 'dzǎw jyèw bàn-'twǒ-le.

(*Affairs, matters*) 'lyàw-lǐ, 'chǔ-jr̀, 'bàn-lǐ. ‖He didn't arrange that matter well. 'nèy-jyàn-shr̀ tā 'chǔ-jr̀-de bù-dé-'dàng.

(*A game, appointment, etc.*) ywē. ‖The athletic committee has arranged a game for us. tǐ-'ywù-wěy-ywán-'hwèy tì wǒ-men 'ywē-le yí-ge-bǐ-'sày.

(*A schedule*) páy. ‖Who's going to arrange the basketball schedule? 'shwéy gwǎn páy lán-'chyéw-bǐ-'sày-de-tsz̀-shywù?

(*People*) 'páy, 'páy-chéng, páy-'lyè. ‖Arrange the children in two rows. bǎ 'háy-dz-men 'páy-chéng lyǎng-'háng.

(*Prepare*) 'ywù-bèy, jwěn-'bèy, 'ān-pay. ‖Everything has been arranged. yí-'chyè dēw yǐ-jing 'ywù-bèy-'hǎw-le.

Arrange for a job 'ān-jr̀. ‖Can you arrange for him to take this position? nǐ néng 'bǎ-ta 'ān-jr̀-le-ma?

(*Passage, tickets*) dìng. ‖Can you arrange passage (on the boat) for me? nǐ 'néng-bu-néng tì-wo dìng yí-ge-chwán-'wèy?

Arrange with *a person* gēn . . . °'shāng-lyang *or* °'dìng-gwey. ‖Have you arranged things with him? nǐ 'gēn-ta °'shāng-lyang-le-ma? *or* °'dìng-gwey-hǎw (*or* -'twǒ)-le-ma? *or* °'shāng-lyang-'hǎw (*or* -'twǒ *or* 'dìng)-le-ma? ‖Wait until you've arranged things with him. 'děng nǐ gēn-ta 'shāng-lyang-'hǎw-le 'dzày shwō-ba. *or* (*With any of the other combinations given*). ‖Have you arranged with him about the date? nǐ 'gēn-ta 'dìng-gwey(-'hǎw-le) 'r̀-dz-le-ma?

ARREST. dǎy, dēy. ‖The police arrested two men. shywún-'jǐng 'dǎy-le 'lyǎng-ge-rén.

Arrest people ná-'rén, jwō-'rén. ‖The police are arresting people all over town. jǐng-'chá dzày chywán-'chéng-dàw-'chù ná-'rén-ne.

Be arrested bèy-'bǔ. ‖He was arrested and put in prison once. tā 'tséng-jīng bèy-'bǔ shyà-gwo 'ywù. Why've you been arrested? nǐ 'wèy-shéme bèy-'bǔ?

‖You're under arrest! dàw gūng-ān-'jywú-chywu! *To a person of high rank, this would be preceded by* chǐng(-ni).

Arrest someone's attention shī-'yǐn jù-'yì. ‖That hat will certainly arrest his attention all right. nèy ge 'màw-dz jwěn 'ké-yi shī-'yǐn ta jù-'yì.

ARRIVE. (*At a place*) dàw. ‖When will I arrive in New York? wǒ 'jǐ-shŕ ké-yi dàw nyēw-'ywē?

(*At a decision*). ‖Did they arrive at a decision? tām tǎw-'lwèn yěw-le jyē-'gwǒ méy-yew?

ARROW. jyàn.

ARSENAL. (*Storage*) bīng-chì-'kù, jywūn-chì-'kù; (*production*) bīng-gūng-'chǎng.

ART. měy-'shù *includes* hwèy-'hwà painting, dyāw-'kè sculpture, 'jyàn-jù architecture. ‖He came here to study art. tā dàw-'jèr-lay shywé měy-'shù.

(*More inclusive term*) yì-'shù. ‖Drama is one of the arts. 'shì-jywù shŕ yì-jǔng-yì-'shù.

‖There's an art to it. yěw chyǎw-'myàw-de-'fāng-fa.

The useful arts shěw-'yì; industrial arts gūng-'yì; liberal arts wén, wén-'yì; art of self-defense chywán-'shù, wǔ-'shù, gwó-'shù.

ARTERY. (*Blood vessel*) (dà-)dùng-'mày.

ART GALLERY. měy-shù-'gwǎn.

ARTHRITIS. gǔ-jyé-'yán.

ARTICLE. 'dūng-shi. ‖Did they distribute any articles of clothing? tām fā 'chwān-de-dūng-shi méy-yew? ‖I have no articles of value to declare. wǒ 'méy-yew shéme-jŕ-de-yí-'bàw-de-dūng-shi.

In compounds wù, pǐn, wù-pǐn. Article of food yì-jǔng-'shŕ-wù; article of merchandise shāng-'pǐn; toilet articles hwà-jwāng-'pǐn.

(*In a document*) tyáw, shyàng, tyáw-'kwǎn. ‖Article Three isn't clear to me. dì-'sān-tyáw wǒ bú-'dà míng-bay. ‖There are forty-one articles in the treaty. tyáw-'ywē lǐ yí-'gùng yěw sz̀-shr̀-'yì-'tyáw.

(*Writings*) wén-'jāng. ‖There was an article about this in the newspaper. bàw-'jr̀-shang 'tséng-jīng yěw-gwo yì-pyān-wén-'jāng lwèn-daw 'jèy-jyàn-shr̀.

ARTILLERY. (*Weapons*) (dà-)'pàw; (*troops*) pàw-'bīng; (*branch of service*) pàw-'kē; (*science*) 'pàw-shywé, pàw-'shù.

ARTIST. (*Painter*) hwà-'jyā; *more general term* yì-shù-'jyā; (*sculptor*) dyāw-kè-'jyā; (*calligrapher; rated highly as an artist in China*) shū-'jyā; (*painter, sculptor, or architect*) měy-shù-'jyā. ‖The artist is painting a picture. yì-shù-'jyā dzày hwà-'hwàr.

AS. 1. *Followed by a verbal expression, showing manner; expressed with* how dzěme, *thus* jème, *accordingly* jàw, *etc.* ‖Do as you're told. dzěme-'gàw-sung-nǐ-de, nǐ 'jyèw dzěme 'bàn. *or* 'jyàw-ni dzěme-bàn, nǐ 'jyèw jàw 'bàn. ‖Do it as he does. jàw-je 'tā-de-'bàn-fa láy 'bàn. *or* jàw 'tā-jèy-yàngr bàn. *or expressed as* Follow his example. gēn-'tā shywé. ‖Do it exactly as he does. 'tā dzěme-je jyèw ('yě) dzěme-je. ‖Leave it as it stands. jàw °'ywán-yàngr (or °'ywán-'láy-de-yàngr), byé °'gǎy. or °'dùng. ‖Things are bad enough (even) as it is. jyèw 'dzěme-je (or °jyèw 'jèy-yàngr or °jyèw jàw 'jèy-yàngr or °jàw shyàn-'dzày 'jèy-yàngr) yǐ-jing 'gèw dzǎw-de-le. ‖Send it as is. jyèw jàw 'jèy-yàngr (or °jàw 'ywán-yàngr) 'sùng-chywu. ‖I wish you had left them as they were. *is expressed as* It's worse than it would be if you had done nothing. háy 'bù-rú nǐ °'bù-gwǎn-ne. or °'bú-dùng-ne. or nǐ 'nèy-ge-shf-hew °'bù-gwǎn (or °'bú-dùng) dàw 'hǎw-dyar. ‖Do as you please. (*Showing approval*) 'swéy-byàn dzěme-je. or 'dzěme-je děw °'hǎw. or °'shíng. or °'chéng. or nǐ 'chyáw-je 'bàn-ba. *but* (*Showing disgust or sarcasm*) 'swéy nǐ-de-'byàn! or nǐ 'ày dzěme-je dzěme-'jè-ba! ‖He doesn't speak as other people do. *is expressed as* He speaks with other people not the same. tā shwō-'hwà gēn 'byé-rén bù-yí-'yàng. or *as* He not with other people speaks the same. tā 'bù-gēn 'byé-rén shwō-de yí-'yàng. or *as* He doesn't follow other people's speaking manner in his speaking. tā 'bú jàw-je 'byé-rén-shwō-'hwà-de-yàngr láy 'shwō. or tā bú-'shyàng 'byé-rén 'nèy-yàngr shwō-'hwà. ‖It's as you told me. jàw-je 'nǐ gàw-sung-wǒ-de 'bàn-de. or *meaning* It happened as you told me. gēn nǐ-'gàw-sung-wǒ-de yí-'yàng. ‖Why didn't you do as I told you? nǐ 'dzěme méy-'jàw-je 'wǒ-shwō-de-'fá-dz 'bàn-ne?

2. *Same as above, but with the verb omitted and understood.* ‖Here "èw" is pronounced as in "sew," not as in "few." *is expressed as* Here the sound represented by "èw" resembles that in the English word "sew," not that of the word "few." dzày-'jèr, "'èw"-dày-'byǎw-de-'mǔ-yīn shyàng 'yīng-wén-li-de-"'sew"-dž, bú-shyàng "few"-dž. ‖It's "hwà" as in "hwà-'hwàr," not as in "shwō-'hwà." shř hwà-'hwàr-de-'hwà, 'bú-shr shwō-'hwà-de-'hwà. ‖He's late as usual. tā 'jèy-tsž °jàw-'cháng (or °'háy-shr nèm- or °gēn 'píng-cháng yí-'yàng nèm-) 'wǎn 'dàw-de. ‖It is to be done as before. shyàng (or jàw) yǐ-'chyán nèm 'bàn. or gēn (or jàw-je) yǐ-'chyán-de-bàn-fa °yí-'yàng. or °láy 'bàn.

3. *Followed by a verbal expression, showing reason* 'yīn-wèy, jì. ‖I must go, as it is late. wǒ 'fēy-dey dzěw-le, yīn-wey 'tyān yǐ-jing bù-'dzǎw-le. ‖As we've already refused the offer, let's stick to that answer. dzám jì 'hwéy-le rén-jya-le, jyèw 'byé gǎy-'dzwěy-le.

4. *Followed by a verbal expression, showing time de-shf-hew.* ‖Count the people as they enter. rén 'jìn-lay de-shf-hew 'shǔ-je yì-dyǎr. ‖Did you see anyone as you came in? nǐ 'jìn-lay de-shf-hew 'kàn-jyan shéme-'rén méy-yew? ‖All the way he prayed as he went. *is expressed as* All the way on one hand he went, on the other hand he prayed. tā yí-'lù-shang yì-byār 'dzěw yì-byār 'dǎw-gàw.

5. *Followed by a verbal expression, giving a general connective or condition or introductory phrase.* ‖I thought I could be saved the trouble; as it is, I'll probably have to make a trip. wǒ 'yǐ-wéy wǒ kě-yi 'bú-yùng fèy-'shèr-le; °jàw 'jèy-yàngr (or °shyàng 'jèy-yàngr or °shyàng 'dzěm-ge-yàngr or °jàw shyàn-'dzày jèy-yàngr or °shyàng shyàn-'dzày jèy-yàngr) wǒ 'dà-gay děy 'chywù yí-tàng. ‖As I was saying just now, he's hopeless. *is expressed as* I was just saying, he's hopeless. wǒ 'gāng-tsáy 'shwō-gwo, 'jèy-ge-rén méy-'jyèwr-le. ‖As the saying goes, time is gold. *is expressed as* There is a saying that an inch of time is equal to an inch of gold, but even an inch of gold can't always buy an inch of time. yěw yí-jywù-'sú-hwàr, 'yí-tswèn-'gwāng-yīn 'yí-tswèn-'jīn, 'tswèn-jīn 'nán mǎy 'tswèn-gwāng-'yīn. ‖As Americans would say, "It ain't hay," which may be translated by the Chinese saying "It's not to be trifled with." 'měy-gwo-rén yěw jywù-'hwàr, "'bú-shr gān-'tsǎw," 'fān-chéng 'jūng-gwo-'sú-hwàr jyèw-shr "'bú-shr 'wár-de."

6. *As if* hǎw 'shyàng (. . . shř-de). ‖He acts as if he thinks he's the officer in charge. 'tā nèy-yàngr hǎw 'shyàng 'jywé-je dž-'gěr shř 'jǔ-gwǎn-jǎng-'gwān shř-de. ‖He talks as if he were afraid of something. tā shwō-hwà nèy-yàngr hǎw-'shyàng 'pà shéme shř-de. ‖It isn't as if he were destitute. *is expressed as* He certainly isn't destitute. tā °'bìng (or °'yèw) bú-shr dzěm 'chyúng-de méy-'fár-le. ‖Act as if nothing had happened. 'jwāng(-je hǎw 'shyàng) 'méy nème-hwéy-'shèr shř-de. or jř 'dāng 'méy 'nème-hwéy-'shèr shř-de.

7. *So as to* 'wèy-de-shř, hǎw. ‖He's placating her like that so as not to make a scene. tā 'nème 'hǔng-je ta °'wèy-de-shř (or °hǎw) 'byé nàw-gey rén 'kàn.

8. *In giving ratios and proportions* 'děng-ywú. ‖Three is to nine as six is to eighteen. 'sān bǐ-'jyěw děng-ywu 'lyèw bǐ shř-'bā.

9. *Before a nominal expression, meaning* in the role of *or* in the function of dāng, shř, yǐ. ‖As your superior, I'd say don't do it, but as a friend, I'd say by golly, go ahead and sock him. (yīn-wey) wǒ shř 'gwǎn-ni-de, wǒ yīng-gay shwō "'byé nèm-je"; bù-gwò yàw-shr tsúng wǒ shř nǐ -de-'péng-yew 'jèy fāng-myan láy 'jyǎng-nga, wǒ 'gǎy shwō "'gwǎn-ta-de, 'dzěw-ta yí-dwèn dzày 'shwō." ‖As a musician he's a flop, but as a politician he'll be tops. tā dāng 'yīn-ywè-jyā shř ge-'èr-wǔ-'yǎn; bú-gwo dāng 'jèng-kèr hwèy shř dì-'yī-lyéw-de. ‖They employed her as a secretary. tām 'gù-ta dāng 'shū-jì. ‖He was famous as a painter. tā yǐ hwà-'hwàr chū-'míng. ‖He started as an apprentice. tā chǐ-'téwr dāng shywé-'tú-de.

10. *As a rule* jàw 'gwēy-jywu, píng-'cháng. ‖As a rule we don't take anyone's check. jàw 'gwēy-jywu wǒm 'shéy-de-jř-'pyàw yě bù-'shēw.

11. *As of, as from a date* tsúng . . . chǐ. ‖The contract starts as of January first. 'hé-túng tsúng 'yī-ywè-'yí-hàw 'chǐ yěw 'shyàw.

12. As against (*compared to*). ‖The expenditure amounts to ten thousand dollars this year as against nine thousand last year. *is expressed without* as against *in Chinese:* chū-'kwǎn 'jīn-nyan shr̀ yí-'wàn-kwày, 'chywù-nyan shr̀ 'jyěw-chyán.

13. Such as (*like, similar to*) shyàng. ‖Books such as dictionaries, encyclopedias, Who's Who's, and so forth, are called reference books. shyàng dz̀-'dyǎn-na, bǎy-kē-chywán-'shū-wa, 'míng-rén-shyǎw-'jwàn-na, 'děng-děng-de-'shū, 'dēw jyàw 'tsān-kǎw-'shū. ‖Such men as you require special treatment. shyàn-'nǐ-jèy-yàngr-de-'rén děy 'lìng-yǎn kàn 'dày.

14. As to, as for 'jr̀-ywu. ‖As for that, I don't know. jr̀-ywu 'nèy-ge wǒ yì-'dyǎr yě bù-jr̀-'dàw. ‖As for that, I have nothing to add. jr̀-ywu 'nèy-ge wǒ 'méy-yew shéme-'yì-jyan kě-'jyā-de. ‖There's no doubt as to who will be elected. jr̀-ywu 'shwéy dāng 'shywǎn 'yǐ-jing méy-yew yí-'wèn-le.

15. *In comparisons.* Be the same as gēn . . . yí-'yàng. ‖This is the same as that. 'jèy-ge gēn 'nèy-ge yí-'yàng. ‖That's the same as before. 'nèy gēn yǐ-'chyán yí-'yàng.

Just as *good, bad, etc.* yě (. . .) nème. ‖This is just as good. 'jèy-ge yě nème 'hǎw. ‖This is just as important. 'jèy-ge 'yě nème 'yàw-jǐn. ‖I can walk just as far without being tired. wǒ 'yě néng dzěw nème-'dwō-de-'lù bù-jywé-je 'lèy. ‖You can do it just as easily this way. nǐ (yàw-shr) 'dzème-je, 'yě-shr nème 'rú yi-de.

As . . . as, so . . . as shyàng . . . nème; shyàng . . . jème; gēn . . . yí-'yàng(-de); gēn . . . 'chà-bu-dwō; *and other expressions involving these elements.* ‖He's grown as tall as his father. tā 'jǎng-de shyàng tā-'fù-chin nème-'gāw-le. ‖If he works as quickly as I do, he's in. tā yàw-shr dzwò-de shyàng 'wǒ jème-'kwày, jyèw jyàw-ta 'gàn-ba. ‖This is as good as that. 'jèy-ge gēn 'nèy-ge °yí-'yàng-de (*or* °'chà-bu-dwō) 'hǎw. *or* 'jèy-ge 'yě shyàng 'nèy-ge shr̀-de nème-'hǎw. ‖Is this as good as that? 'jèy-ge yě shyàng 'nèy-ge shr̀-de nème 'hǎw-ma? ‖He thinks he knows as much as you. tā-'dz̀-ji jywé-je gēn 'nǐ-jr̀-dàw-de-'shèr yí-'yàng nème-'dwō. ‖This one is as long as that. 'jèy-ge gēn 'nèy-ge yí-'yàng-de (nème-)'cháng. ‖It'll take as long as three months. děy yùng 'sān-ge-ywè °nème-'jyēw. *or* °'nème-'cháng-de-gùng-fu. ‖I can't do it as well as before. wǒ-'dzwò-de 'méy yǐ-'chyán-nème-'hǎw-le. ‖He talks as much as his wife. tā gēn tā-'tày-tày °yí-'yàng-de (*or* °'shr̀-de) nème ày shwō-'hwà.

As soon as yī . . . jyèw. ‖We'll start planting as soon as it stops raining. 'ywǔ yí 'jù dzám jyèw shyà-'jǔng-dz. ‖Take this as soon as you feel a pain. nǐ 'gāng-yi jywé-je 'téng jyèw chr̄ 'jèy-ge. ‖His face turned red as soon as he realized what he was saying. tā yì 'míng-bay-gwo-lay tā-'shwō-de shr̀ shéme-'hwà, 'lyǎn jyèw 'húng-le.

Special expressions with as . . . as *or* so . . . as. ‖He can't be so foolish as to believe that. tā 'bú-hwèy 'shǎ-dàw lyán 'nèy-ge dēw 'shìn-de-ba. ‖As strong as he is, he won't be able to stand it. (jyèw-shr *or* lyán) shyàng 'tā-nème-'jwàng-de yě 'bú-hwèy shèw-de-'jù. ‖As far as I can see, he's out. *is expressed* As I see it, he's out. jywù 'wǒ kàn, tā swàn 'chwéy-le. ‖I'll go with you as far as the door. *is expressed as* I'll accompany you to the door over there. wǒ 'péy-ni dzěw-daw 'mén-nàr̲. ‖You may stay there as long as you behave. nǐ yàw hǎw-'hāwr-de, dāy 'dwō-shaw-shí-hew dēw 'shíng. ‖He'll pay as much as a thousand dollars for it. tā hwèy 'chū-dàw yì-'chyán-kwày-chyán láy 'mǎy.

16. As well (as) (*in addition*) lyán . . . yě, yě. ‖Take this as well. lyán 'jèy-ge yě 'ná-je-ba. *or* 'jèy-ge yě 'ná-chywu-ba. ‖They, as well as you, have been cheated. 'tām, lyán 'nǐ yě dzày-'nèy, 'dēw jyàw-rén gěy 'pyàn-le.

17. May as well jr̀ 'hǎw, jì 'nème-je . . . jyèw. ‖If it's really like you just said, we may as well forget all about it. yàw 'jēn-shr shyàng 'nǐ dzème 'shwō-de, dzám 'jr̀ hǎw dàng-dzwò 'méy nème-hwéy-'shèr-ba. ‖You may as well go. jì 'nème-je nǐ jyèw 'chywù-ba.

18. *Special combinations after a verb.* ‖Treat A as B *or* Treat A as if it were B ná A dàng B dày; dày A gēn B shr̀-de. ‖They treat him as (if he were) a member of the family. tām ná-ta dàng 'yì-jyā-rén nème 'dày. *or* tām dày-ta gēn 'yì-jyā-rén shr̀-de.

Take A as B ná A dàng B. ‖Take it as a joke. 'ná-je dàng(-dzwò) 'shyàw-hwar kàn-ba. ‖He took a real diamond as glass. tā ná yí-kwày-'jēn-dzwàn-'shr̀ dàng 'bwō-li.

Use A as B ná A dàng B yùng; *be used as* dàng B yùng. ‖It may be used as a knife. 'kě-yi dàng 'dāw-dz yùng.

Consider A as *closed, finished, etc.* ná A dàng; 'yǐ-wéy A. ‖They considered the case as closed. tām ná jèy-'àn-dz dàng (*or* tām 'yǐ-wéy jèy-ge-'àn-dz) 'nème-jé jyèw 'lyǎw-le.

Regard A as *worthy, good, etc.* jywé-je; ná-je A dàng. ‖He doesn't regard his job as worthy of his attention. tā 'jywé-je tā-de-'shèr bù-'jr̀-de yí-'bàn. *or* tā bù-'ná-je tā-de-'shèr dàng hwéy-'shèr.

ASBESTOS. shr̀-'myán.

ASH. (*Tree*) yáng-'shù; (*wood*) yáng-'mù; (*residue of fire*) (yān-)'hwēy.

ASHAMED. bù-hǎw-'yì-sz; tsán-'kwèy; hày-'shyēw, hày-'sàw. ‖I was ashamed to ask for his help. wǒ bù-hǎw-'yì-sz chǐng-ta bāng-'máng. *or* jyàw-ta bāng-'máng, wǒ hěn tsán-'kwèy. ‖I was quite ashamed when I asked for his help. wǒ chǐng-ta bāng-'máng de-shf-hew 'shīn-li hěn bù-hǎw-'yì-sz-de. ‖As old as you are, don't you feel ashamed? 'jǎng-le nàme-'dà-le, nán-'dàw háy bù-dǔng-de hày-'sàw?

(*Very serious*) jř shyēw-'chř. ‖Aren't you ashamed of yourself? nǐ nán-'dàw bù-jř shyēw-'chř-ma?

Be ashamed, feel ashamed (ywú-'shīn) yěw-'kwèy; be unashamed (ywú-'shīn) wú-'kwèy. ‖Don't you feel ashamed? nǐ ywú-'shīn wú-'kwèy-ma?

ASH TRAY. yān(-hwēy)-'dyéer, yān-(hwēy-)'pár.

ASK. Ask *someone to do something* chǐng; (*more beggingly*) chyéw. ‖Ask him in. chǐng-ta 'jìn-lay. ‖He asked me to let him leave an hour early. tā °'chǐng-wo (*or* °'chyéw-wo) 'jwěn-ta 'dzǎw dzěw 'yì-dyǎn-jūng.

Ask about 'dǎ-tīng. ‖Mr. Jāng is asking about trains. 'jāng-shyan-sheng 'dǎ-tīng hwǒ-'chē-'jūng-dyǎn.

Ask (*a question; something; somebody*) wèn. ‖Ask who it is. 'wèn-wen shř-'shwéy. ‖Did you ask him his name? nǐ 'wèn tā 'shìng shéme-le-ma? ‖Ask him if he can come. 'wèn tā 'néng láy 'bù-néng láy.

Ask for yāw-'chyéw. ‖He asked for a raise. tā yāw-'chyéw jyā-'shīn.

Ask for *someone* jǎw. ‖Who's asking for me? shwéy 'jǎw-wo? *or* Who wants to see me? 'shwéy yàw 'jyàn-wo? ‖He's asking for Jāng. tā shř jǎw lǎw-'jāng-de.

Ask about *someone* wèn ... 'hǎw. ‖He asked about you. tā 'wèn-ni 'hǎw.

Sometimes expressed in Chinese with to want yàw. ‖I went to that store and asked to see their diamonds. wǒ 'dzěw-jìn nèy-ge-'pù-dz yàw jīn-gāng-'shř 'kàn-yi-kàn. ‖Ask Dad for it. gēn 'bà-ba 'yàw-chywu. *or* wèn 'bà-ba 'yàw-chywu. ‖You can have it for the asking. yǐ 'yàw jyèw 'gěy-ni. ‖What are you asking for that (*in a shop*)? 'nèy-ge nǐ yàw 'dwō-shaw-chyán?

ASLEEP. Fall asleep shwèy-'jáw. ‖He's fallen asleep. tā shwèy-'jáw-le. ‖I must have been asleep. wǒ yí-'dìng shř shwèy-'jáw-le.

ASPARAGUS. lúng-shywū-'tsày, lú-'swěn.

ASPHALT. dì-lì-'chīng, shř-nǎw-'yéw.

ASPIRIN. ā-sž-bǐ-'líng, yǎ-sž-bǐ-'líng.

ASSIST. bāng. ‖Who assisted you? 'shwéy 'bāng-ni láy-je?
See also AID, HELP.

ASSISTANT. 'jù-shěw, jù-'lǐ.

ASSURE. bù-'ywān. *Expressed informally with* not cheat. ‖That's not so, I assure you. 'bú-shr 'nème-yì-hwéy-'shř, wǒ bù-'ywān-ni.

Assure you that (*formal*) dān-'bǎw, gǎn 'bǎw, gǎn dān-'bǎw. ‖I can assure you that he's the man for the job. wǒ dān-'bǎw 'tā dzwò 'nèy-jyàn-shř hěn hé-'shř.

(*Say that ... certainly*) shwō ... yí-'dìng. ‖He assured us that he would be there. tā shwō tā yí-'dìng 'dàw.

ASTHMA. chwǎn-'bìng.

ASTRONOMY. 'tyān-wén-shywé.

ASYLUM. (*Mental hospital*) fēng-rén-'ywàn; (*orphans*) gū-ér-'ywàn.

AT. 1. At *a place* (*specifying position*) dzày, *occasionally* dàw; *if the specification of place is first in the sentence there may be no word for* at. ‖He's at his office. tā dzày gūng-shř-'fáng-ne. ‖He wasn't at his office when I phoned there. wǒ gěy tā-gūng-shř-'fáng dǎ dyàn-'hwà láy-je, 'nèy-ge-shř-hèw tā bú-dzày-nàr. ‖I'll be at home. wǒ yí-'dìng dzày-'jyā. ‖He stood at the street corner. tā dzày gwǎy-'jyǎwr-nàr 'jàn-je láy-je. ‖I'll be at that corner at 10 P.M. sharp. wǎn-shang-'shř-dyan 'jěng, wǒ 'jwěn °dzày gwǎy-'jyǎwr-nàr. *or* °dàw gwǎy-'jyǎwr-nar-chywu. ‖(Where did you buy it?) At Joe's (store). dzày lǎw-'jēw-nàr. ‖At the top there's a star. (dzày) 'dyěngr-shàng yěw ge-'shīng-shing. ‖You stand at that end. 'nǐ dzày 'nèy-téwr jàn-je. ‖He peeped in at the door. tā dzày 'mén-nàr wàng-'lǐ bā-'téwr. ‖There's a commotion at the station. (dzày) hwǒ-chē-'jàn-nàr chū-le-ge-'dà-lwàn-dz.

2. At *a time* (*specifying time when*) dzày, *which is often omitted.* At noon (dzày) 'shǎng-wu *or* (dzày) 'jūng-wǔ; at night (dzày) 'yè-li; at the beginning of *something* (dzày) ... chǐ-'téwr de-shř-hew; at the end of *something* (dzày) ... 'wán de-shř-hew. ‖It rings twice a day, at noon and at midnight. yì-'tyān shyǎng 'lyǎng-tsž, 'jūng-wu 'yí-tsž, bàn-'yè yí-'tsž. ‖Be there at 10 A.M. dzǎw-chen-'shř-dyǎn-jūng yí-'dìng yàw 'dàw-nèr. ‖I'll be there (at) about seven. wǒ (dzày) 'chǐ-dyǎn °dzwǒ-'yèw (*or* °chyán-'hèw) 'dàw-nèr. *or* wǒ chà-bu-dwō 'chǐ-dyǎn kě-yi 'dàw-nèr. ‖At that time he was a major. 'nèy(-ge)-shř-hèw tā-shř ge-shàw-'shyàw. ‖At that moment I heard two shots. 'jèng dzày 'nèy-shř-hew, wǒ 'tīng-jyan-le 'lyǎng-shēng chyāng-'shyǎng. ‖At the time of Confucius, the word was pronounced with a nasal ending. (dzày) 'kǔng-dž-'nèy-shř-hew, jèy-ge-'dž shēw-'wěy shř 'bí-yīn. ‖At the moment he was stumped. tā 'yì-shř 'dá-bu-shang-'láy-le.

When an expression with at *means* as soon as, *it is expressed with* yī ... jyèw. ‖Free him at the first opportunity. 'yì yěw 'jī-hwey jyèw bǎ-ta 'fàng-le. ‖Shoot him at sight. (yí) 'kàn-jyan ta jyèw 'kāy-chyāng 'dǎ-ta. ‖That's what I call love at first sight. *is expressed as* That's what's called one look and the whole heart is poured out. 'nèy jyèw-shr swǒ-'wèy 'yí jyàn chīng-'shīn (*literary*).

Occasionally a different translation is called for. ‖He failed at the first attempt. *meaning* but not at the second. 'téw-yì-hwéy tā méy-bàn-'dàw. *or meaning* then and with no more chances. 'téw-yì-hwéy tā jyèw bàn-'dzāw-le. ‖You may do it at any time (you please). swéy-'shř děw 'shíng. *or* 'shéme-shř-hew děw 'shíng.

3. **At** (*implying both place and time*). ‖He's at dinner now. *is expressed as* He's just now eating dinner. tā 'jèng dzày chř-je 'fàn-ne. ‖He was at dinner then. *is expressed as* At that time he was just eating dinner. tā 'nèy-ge-shŕ-hew 'jèng chř-je 'fàn. ‖At that time the two countries were at war. lyǎng-'gwó ('nèy-shŕ-hew) 'jèng dǎ-'jàng.

4. **At** *a place or thing* (*specifying direction in which or place to which*); *usually a single Chinese verb covers the meaning of the verb of the English sentence and the meaning* at. Aim at jàw (*or* chùng) ... myáw-'jwěr, myáw-'jwèn, chyáw-'jwěn, kàn-'jwěn. ‖Aim at that light. jàw-je (*or* chùng-je) nèy-ge-'dēng myáw-'jwěr. ‖Aim at that light and fire. myáw-'jwěn-le (*or* chyáw-'jwěn-le *or* kàn-'jwěn-le) nèy-ge-'dēng jyèw kāy-'chyāng.

Look at kàn, chyáw, chěw; chùng ... kàn, wǎng ... kàn. ‖We looked at him. wǒm 'kàn-je (*or* 'chyáw-je *or* 'chěw-je) ta. *or, If emphasizing that others were not looked at* wǒm °chùng- (*or* °wàng-) 'tā-nèr 'kàn. ‖Have a look at his hands. 'chyáw-chyaw tā-de-'shěw.

Laugh at shyàw, 'shyàw-hwa. ‖They're laughing at us. tām nèy-shr °'shyàw (*or* °'shyàw-hwa) dzám-ne.

Arrive at. (*A place*) dàw; (*a decision*) 'tán-chū-láy, 'shāng-lyang-chu-láy. ‖He arrived at the border without a penny. tā dàw gwó-'jyè de-shŕ-hew yì-'dyǎr-chyán yě 'méy-yew. ‖We haven't arrived at a decision yet. wǒm 'háy méy °'tán-chu (*or* °'shāng-lyang-chu) yí-ge-yí-'dìng-de-'bàn-fa láy-ne.

Guess at. ‖I'm just guessing at it. wǒ 'bú-gwò shř 'tsǎy-ne.

See also specific verbs for such combinations with at.

5. **At** *a place or thing* (*specifying place from which*) tsúng. ‖Start at the beginning. tsúng-'téwr shwō. *or* tsúng 'téwr-shang shwō. *or* tsúng 'téwr-shang 'shwō-chǐ. *or* tsúng chǐ-'téwr shwō.

6. **At** *an age, expressed without a separate word for* at. ‖He became a professor at (the age of) twenty-three. tā èr-shŕ-'sān-swèy dāng-le jyàw-'shèw-le.

7. **At** *a rate or price, expressed in various ways, none of which involve any equivalent of* at. Sold at three dollars 'sān-kwày-chyán mày-de; bought at three dollars 'sān-kwày-chyán mǎy-de. ‖At ten dollars it's a real bargain. 'shŕ-kwày-chyán, °'mǎy-de (*or* °'mày-de) 'jēn pyán-yì. ‖It's sold at cost. *is expressed as* It just barely covers the cost. 'gāng gèw-'běr. ‖He sold them at a loss. 'nèy-shyē tā-shŕ 'péy-běr 'mày-de. ‖Don't buy things when prices are at their highest. 'jyà-chyán gāw-'jí-le de-shŕ-hew, 'byé 'mǎy dūng-shi. ‖At this (slow) speed we'll miss the boat. yàw-shr 'dzěw-de 'lǎw 'dzème-màn dzám yí-'dìng 'gǎn-bu-shàng 'chwán-de. ‖At this speed we'll certainly catch the boat. yàw-shr 'dzěw-de 'lǎw jème-'kwày, dzám yí-'dìng gǎn-de-'shàng 'chwán-de.

8. **Be good** (*or* **fair** *or* **bad,** *etc.*) **at** *doing something, expressed without any equivalent for* at, *usually with the parts of the sentence in the opposite order from that found in English.* ‖He's clever at magic tricks. *is*

---

expressed as He does magic tricks cleverly. tā byàn-shì-'fǎr byàn-de tǐng-'chyǎw-de. ‖He's quick at lettering. *is expressed as* He letters quickly. tā shyě 'měy-shú-'dž shyě-de tǐng-'kwày-de. ‖I'm not good at that. *is expressed as* I do that, I'm not so good. dzwò 'nèy-ge wǒ bú-'dà °'shíng. *or* °'hwèy.

Be frightened (*or* **surprised** *or* **annoyed**) **at** *something, where* at *indicates* when *and also because of, calls for similar change in method of expression.* ‖He's frightened at the sight of the police. *is expressed as* When he sees the police he gets frightened. tā 'chyáw-jyàn-le jǐng-'chá 'shīn-li hěn hày-'pà. ‖I was surprised at the large size of the footprint. *is expressed as* That footprint being so large made me jump a bit. nèy-ge-jyǎw-'yèr 'dà-de jyàw-wo 'shyà-le yí-tyàw. ‖She was annoyed at your ceaseless joking. *is expressed as* Your joking so much made her feel annoyed. nǐ nème 'lǎw jyǎng 'shyàw-hwar jyàw-ta jywé-je 'nán-yi-wéy 'chíng.

9. *So many at a time usually expressed with one time* yí-'tsž, *or a similar phrase, with no word corresponding to* at. ‖One question at a time! 'yí-tsž 'jǐ néng °wèn 'yí-ge-wèn-tí. *or* °'yěw 'yí-ge-rén 'wèn. ‖He ran up the steps two at a time. tā 'yí-bù tyàw 'lyǎng-dèng-de 'pǎw-shàng-chywu-le. ‖Hey! One at a time, please! 'hèy! yí-gè-yí-'gè-de láy! *or expressed negatively as* Don't come all at once that way! 'byé nème yí-'kwàr láy!

10. **Be at a loss to** *do something.* ‖I'm at a loss to understand it. 'nèy-ge-shèr wǒ °'háw-wú téw-'shywù. *or* °'yì-'dyǎr yě bù-'míng-bay.

11. **At the same time.** (*Literally*) 'túng-shŕ, dzày 'jèy-ge-shŕ-hew; (*concessive*) 'kě-shř-ne. ‖You think it over at the same time. 'túng-shŕ nǐ 'pán-swan-pán-swan. *or* dzày-'jèy-ge-shŕ-hew, nǐ 'yě kě-yi 'pán-swan-pán-swan. ‖At the same time, he might've done it. 'kě-shr-ne, yě-shywu 'shř-ta gàn-de.

12. **At any rate** 'dzěme-je, 'wú-lwèn rú-'hé, 'bù-gwǎn dzěme-'yàng. ‖At any rate he consented. 'dzěme-je (*or etc.*) tā yě-shř 'dā-ying-le.

13. **At first** yì-chǐ-'chū de-shŕ-hew, yì-chǐ-'téwr de-shŕ-hew, chǐ-'chū, chǐ-'téwr, chǐ-'shyān. ‖At first we didn't like this place. yì-chǐ-'chū de-shŕ-hew (*or etc.*) wǒm bù-'shǐ-hwan jèy-ge-'dì-fang.

14. **At once** lì-'kè jyèw, lì-'shŕ jyèw, dāng-'shŕ jyèw, děng-'shŕ jyèw, shyàn-'dzày, 'jè-jyèw, shwō-'hwà jyèw. ‖Do you want it at once or can you wait awhile? (nǐ-shř) °lì-'kè jyèw (*or etc.*) 'yàw, háy-shr kě-yi 'děng-hwer? ‖I'll leave at once. wǒ °lì-'kè jyèw (*or* °lì-'shŕ jyèw *or* °shyàn-'dzày jyèw *or* °jè-jyèw *or* °shwō-'hwà jyèw, *but not the others*) 'dzěw. ‖Can you come at once? nǐ néng °lì-'kè jyèw (*or* °lì-'shŕ jyèw *or* °děng-'shŕ jyèw *or* °shyàn-'dzày jyèw, *but not the others*) láy-ma? ‖I'll be there at once. wǒ °lì-'kè jyèw (*or* °lì-'shŕ jyèw *or* °děng-'shŕ jyèw *or* °shyàn-'dzày jyèw *or* °shwō-'hwà jyèw) 'dàw. ‖He handed the

money over at once. tā °lì-'kè jyèw (or °lì-'shŕ jyèw or °dāng-'shŕ jyèw or °děng-'shŕ jyèw) bǎ-'chyán dì-gwo-chywu-le. ‖When he heard that, his face at once broke out in a big smile. tā 'yì tīng-jyan 'nèy-ge, °lì-'kè jyèw (or °lì-'shŕ jyèw or °dāng-'shŕ jyèw or °děng-'shŕ jyèw) 'mǎn-lyǎn-de 'shyàw-rúngr.

15. At times 'yéw-de-shŕ-hew or 'nème yí-'jèn-dz-yí-'jèn-dz-de. ‖At times I'm doubtful. 'yéw-de-shŕ-hew (or 'nème yí-'jèn-dz-yí-'jèn-dz-de) wǒ yěw dyár-hwáy-'yí.

16. At last in a context indicating relief after a long wait kě. ‖So you're here at last! nǐ 'kě láy-le! ‖At last the train's arrived! hwǒ-'chē kě dàw-le! ‖At last I'm allowed to talk! 'kě shywǔ wǒ shwō jywù-'hwà-le! ‖At last we can start working! dzám 'kě néng chǐ-'téwr dzwò-'shèr-le! ‖At last I won a hand! wǒ 'kě yíng-le yì-'páy. ‖At last my luck changed! wǒ-de-'ywùn-chi 'kě hǎw-dyár-le!

At last in a context indicating finality 'jyē-gwǒ, dàw-'lyǎwr, dàw-'téwr. ‖At last HE won. 'jyē-gwǒ (or dàw-'lyǎwr or dàw-'téwr) shŕ-'tā yíng-le. ‖At last he was caught. 'jyē-gwǒ (or etc.) tā gěy-rén 'dǎy-jáw-le. ‖At last we found the key to the problem. 'jyē-gwǒ (or etc.) wǒm 'jŕ-dàw-le jèy-'shèr 'gāy dzěme 'bàn-le.

17. At (some) length bàn-'tyān. ‖He spoke at some length about it. 'nèy-shèr tā shwō bàn-'tyān.

18. At most 'jŕ- (or 'dǐng- or 'dzwèy) dwō (yě 'bú-gwò), dwō-'jí-le yě bú-°'gwò (or °'dàw); if there is a specific adjective in the context, dwō should be replaced by it in the above expressions, or one can say ... (adjective)-dàw-'téwr yě bú-gwò. ‖He's at most six feet tall. tā 'jŕ-dwō yě bú-gwò 'lyèw-chǐ(-gāw). or tā 'jǐ-dwō yě bú-gwò 'lyèw-chǐ(-gāw). or tā 'dǐng-gāw yě gāw-bu-'gwò 'lyèw-chǐ chywu. or tā 'dwō-shwō-je yě bú-gwò 'lyèw-chǐ(-gāw). ‖It'll take three days at most. 'jŕ-dwō °(yě) bú-gwò 'sān-tyān. or °yùng 'sān-tyān. or °yě 'yùng-bu-lyǎw 'sān-tyān. ‖At most he can only give you a recommendation. tā jŕ-'dwō ʸě 'bú-gwò néng 'bǎw-jywǔ ni yí-shyàr.

At least 'jŕ-shǎw (or °'dǐng-shǎw or °'dzwèy-shǎw) yě. ‖He's at least six feet tall. tā 'jŕ-shǎw yě yěw 'lyèw-chǐ(-gāw). or tā 'dǐng-ǎy̌ yě 'ǎ-bu-shyà 'lyèw-chǐ-chywu. or tā 'shǎw-shwō-je yě yěw 'lyèw-chǐ (-gāw). or tā jŕ-bú-'jì yě yěw 'lyèw-chǐ(-gāw). ‖It'll take three days at least. 'jŕ-shǎw °yě děy 'sān-tyān. or °yě děy yùng 'sān-tyān. ‖At least a thousand men arrived. 'jŕ-shǎw yě yěw yì-'chyān-rén dàw-le. or 'dàw-de 'jŕ-shǎw yě yěw yì-'chyān-rén. ‖At least he should've sent us a note. tā °jŕ-'shǎw (or 'jŕ-bú-'jì) yě gāy láy fēng-'shìn-na.

19. At best. ‖This is a poor meal at best. jèy-dwèn-'fàn 'dzěme shwō yě 'bù-néng swàn 'hǎw-de. ‖This is at best a second-rate picture. nèy-ge-dyàn-'yěngr °dzwèy-'hǎw (or °'dǐng-hǎw or °'jŕ-dwō or °hǎw-'jí-le or °'dzěme-shwō) yě 'bú-gwò shŕ ge-'èr-děng-pyān-dz.

20. At all costs wú-lwèn rú-'hé, 'bù-gwǎn 'dzěme-je, 'bù-gwǎn dzěme-'yàng, 'dzěme-je. ‖We must do it this way at all costs. 'wú-lwèn rú-'hé (or etc.) dzám 'yě děy 'dzěme 'gàn-shya-chywu.

21. At will swéy-'byàn, swéy-'yì. ‖They come and go at will. tām swéy-'byàn chū-'rù. or expressed as When they want to come in they come in, when they want to go out they go out. tām 'shyǎng 'jìn-lay jyèw 'jìn-lay, 'shyǎng chū-chywu jyèw 'chū-chywu. ‖He can discharge anyone at will. tā °swéy-'byàn (or °swéy-'yì) ké-yi 'tsáy-rén.

22. ‖At ease! 'shàw-shi!

23. (Not) at all yì-'dyǎr ... yě. ‖I haven't any money at all. wǒ °yì-'dyǎr-chyán (or °yí-ge-'dà or °yí-ge-'dzěr) yě 'méy-yew. ‖There's no pain at all. yì-'dyǎr yě bù-'téng. or 'wán-chywán 'jywé-bu-chu 'téng-lay. ‖He couldn't do it at all. tā yì-'dyǎr yě bú-'hwèy. or tā 'wán-chywán bú-'hwèy.

‖Not at all! bú-'kè-chi! or 'bú-swàn shéme! or 'méy shéme. or 'shyǎw-yì-sz.

ATHLETE. ywùn-dùng-'ywán.

ATHLETICS. tǐ-'ywù.

ATMOSPHERE. 'kūng-chì.

ATOM. ywán-'dž.

ATTACHÉ. (Civilian) swéy-'ywán; (military) wǔ-'gwān.

ATTACK. (Advance and attack; military) jìn-'gūng. ‖We've already attacked the enemy position here. wǒm 'yǐ-jing jín-'gūng 'dí-jywūn-jèn-'dì-le.

(Military and nonmilitary) 'gūng-jí. ‖I think a dawn attack will carry that hill. wǒ shyǎng yí-tsž-fú-'shyǎw-'gūng-ji jyèw néng jàn-'lǐng nèy-ge-'shān. ‖The morning paper has an editorial attacking the governor. dzǎw-'bàw yěw yì-pyān-shè-'píng gūng-ji shěng-'jǎng.

(Viciously or without regard to truth) hwěy-'bàng, mà. ‖Someone's attacked him for taking money illegally. yěw-'rén 'mà-ta tān-'dzāng.

(Begin to work on) jáw-'shěw. ‖Let's attack that problem from this angle. nèy-ge-'wèn-tí dzám tsúng 'jèy-'fāng-myàn jáw-'shěw-ba.

Be attacked shèw 'gūng-jí. ‖He was violently attacked in the paper. tā hěn shèw bàw-'jŕ-de-'gūng-jí.

Attack of indigestion. ‖I've had an attack of indigestion. wǒ yěw yí-jèn-dz 'shyāw-hwa bù-'lyáng.

ATTEMPT. shŕ. ‖That was the first time she had attempted to cook. nà shŕ tā-dì-'yí-tsž-'shŕ-je-dzwò-'fàn.

‖An attempt was made on his life. tā ywù-'tsž láy-je. or yěw-'rén 'hày-ta láy-je.

‖He attempted suicide once. tā 'yěw-yí-tsž dž-'shā, kě-shr méy-'sž.

(Legal) wèy-'swéy. Attempted murder méw-'shā-wèy-'swéy; attempt on someone's life 'shā-rén-wèy-'swéy.

See also **TRY.**

ATTEND. Attend a meeting dàw-'hwèy, láy (or chywù) kāy-'hwèy. ‖Did you attend the meeting? nǐ dàw-'hwèy-le ma? or nǐ chywù kāy-'hwèy-le ma?

Attend a funeral. *See* FUNERAL.

Attend to bàn. ‖I have something to attend to. wǒ yěw jǐ-yàng-'shř děy 'bàn-yi-bàn. ‖I must attend to my business first. wǒ děy 'shyān bàn wǒ-de-'shř.

Attend (*a patient*) gěy . . . kàn-'bìng (*for illness, not for minor ailments or childbirth*). ‖What doctor attended you? 'něy-ge-'dày-fu gěy-ni kàn-de 'bìng? *But also* nǐ-'jyàn-de 'něy-ge-'dày-fu?

ATTENTION. Pay attention jù-'yì. ‖I can't get anyone to pay attention. wǒ shwō-'hwà shéy yě bú-jù-'yì.

Pay attention (*be attentive, be careful*) lyéw-'shīn, yùng-'shīn. ‖Pay attention to what he says. tā-'shwō-de-'hwà yàw lyéw-'shīn 'tīng.

Stand at attention lì-'jèng. ‖The soldiers stood at attention. 'bīng lì-'jèng-le.

AUDIENCE. (*If listening*) 'tīng-de-rén, tīng-'jùng; (*if watching*) 'kàn-de-rén, gwān-'jùng.

AUDITOR. (*Of accounts*) chá-jàng-'ywán; to audit accounts chá-'jàng.

AUDITORIUM. dà-lǐ-'táng.

AUGUST. 'bā-ywè or 'bá-ywè.

AUTHOR. (*Professional*) dzwò-'jyā; (*of a certain work*) jù-'jě.

AUTHORITY. 'chywán-bìng. ‖What authority do you have to do this? nǐ yěw shéme-'chywán-bìng láy 'jème bàn?

(*Permission*) shywǔ-'kě. ‖On whose authority did you do that? nǐ 'nàme bàn dé-le 'shwéy-de-shywǔ-'kě-le? or shéy 'jyàw-ni nème bàn-de.

Authorities. (*Governmental*) dǎng-'jywú; (*local*) dì-fang-'gwān; (*in general*) fù-dzé-'rén. ‖I want to speak to the authorities. wǒ yàw túng dǎng-'jywú (*or etc.*) 'gwān-jàw yí-shyà.

Have authority fù-'dzé, gwǎn-'shř, jǎng-'chywán, jǔ-'chř. ‖Who has authority here? (Who's the authority here?) 'shwéy shř 'jèr-jǔ-'chř-de-rén?

Be an authority on . . . dwèy . . . (yěw) 'yán-jyēw. ‖He's an authority on China. tā dwèy 'jūng-gwo-chíng-shing hěn yěw 'yán-jyēw. ‖I'm not an authority on that. wǒ dwèy 'nèy-ge méy-'yán-jyēw-gwo.

AUTOBIOGRAPHY. dž-'jwàn.

AUTOCRACY. jwān-jř-'jèng-tǐ, dú-tsáy-'jèng-tǐ, dú-tsáy-jèng-'jř.

AUTOMATIC PISTOL. dž-dùng-shěw-'chyāng.

AUTOMOBILE. chì-'chē; *when the context is clear one uses simply* vehicle chē. ‖My automobile broke down. wǒ-de-'chē 'hwày-le. ‖Can you go there by automobile? dzwò chì-'chē ké-yi 'dàw-nèr-ma?

AUTUMN. 'chyēw-tyan. ‖I hope to stay through the autumn. wǒ 'shī-wàng néng dzày-'jèr gwò 'chyēw-tyan.

(*Season; term at school*) chyēw-'jì. ‖The autumn here is quite warm. 'jèy-ge-dì-fang chyēw-'jì hěn 'nwǎn-he. ‖There aren't quite so many students this autumn. jīn-nyan-chyēw-'jì-de-'shywé-sheng 'shǎw-shye.

AVALANCHE. *Expressed as* a mountain of snow slides down shywě-'shān 'beng-le; *or as* a mountain of ice slides down bīng-'shān 'bēng-le; *or as* the mountain slides down 'shān 'bēng-le.

AVENUE. mǎ-'lù, lù, dà-'lù, dà-'jyē. ‖Take me to 246 Third Avenue. 'lā-wo dàw 'sān-mǎ-'lù 'èr-bǎy-'sž-shr-'lyèw-hàw.

Avenue of escape kě-'táw-de-'lù-dz. *Or as in this sentence:* ‖That'll open up an avenue of escape for him. 'nà jyèw 'gěy-ta 'kāy-chu yì-tyáw-'lù-lay 'jyàw-ta ké-yi 'táw-le.

See also ROAD, ROUTE, STREET.

AVERAGE. píng-'jywūn. ‖Average this column of figures for me. tì-wo bǎ jèy-yì-'háng-de-'shù-mù píng-'jywūn yí-shyà. ‖On the average the class's grades are lower than before. chywán-'bān-de-chéng-'jì píng-'jywūn 'jyáw-bǐ yǐ-'chyán 'dī. ‖On the average I go to the movies once a week. wǒ píng-'jywūn yí-ge-lǐ-'bày kàn 'yí-tsž-dyàn-'yǐng. ‖In this town there is, on the average, one car to every three persons. jèy-ge-'chéng-li píng-'jywūn 'sān-ge-rén yěw 'yí-lyàng-chē. ‖A'verage out his grades and they're better than anyone else's. tā-de-'fēn-shù píng-'jywūn-chi-lay bǐ 'byé-rén dēw 'hǎw. ‖What's the average temperature here? 'jèy-ge-dì-fang píng-'jywūn-wēn-'dù shř 'dwō-shaw?

The average yì-'bān(-de). ‖He's below average height. *is expressed as* He's shorter than people in general. tā bǐ yì-'bān-rén 'ǎy.

Average out méy-yew chū-'rù-le, méy-yew 'fēn-bye-le. ‖It averages out in the end. dàw-le mwò-'lyǎwr jyèw méy-yew chū-'rù-le.

AVIATION. háng-'kūng; (*the study*) 'háng-kūng-shywé.

AVOCATION. fù-'yè.

AVOID. (*A thing, doing something*) 'bì-myǎn. ‖Avoid (doing) that at all costs. wú-lwèn-rú-'hé yàw 'bì-myǎn 'nèy-ge.

(*General term*) dwǒ, 'dwǒ-kāy. ‖He avoided her. tā 'dwǒ-ta. ‖You simply can't avoid him. jyǎn-'jŕ dwǒ-bu-'kāy ta. ‖In times of danger he avoids responsibility. dàw-le 'wéy-shyǎn de-shŕ-hew tā jyèw 'dwǒ-kāy-le.

AWAIT. děng. ‖We await your reply. wǒm 'děng nǐ-de-'hwéy-shìn.

See also **WAIT.**

AWAKE. Be awake shǐng, bú-shwèy-'jáw, bú-shwèy-'jyàw. ‖Are you still awake? nǐ 'háy 'shǐng-je-ne. *or* nǐ 'háy méy-shwèy-'jáw-ne. ‖Stay awake tonight. jīn-tyan-'yè-li byé shwèy-'jyàw. ‖I was awake most of last night. *is expressed as* I hardly closed my eyes all night. wǒ 'chà-bu-dwō yī-'yè méy-bì-'yǎn.

Be wide awake jǐng-'jyè jēw-'mì; (*in the literal sense*) jǐng-'shǐng. ‖The enemy didn't know that we were wide awake. 'dí-rén bù-'jŕ-dàw wǒ-men jǐng-'jyè-de hěn jēw-'mì. ‖You'd better stay wide awake throughout the night. nǐ yī-'yè yàw jǐng-'shǐng-je.

See also **WAKE.**

AWAY. Be away (*by such and such a distance*) lí . . . (*place*) yěw . . . (*distance*). ‖It's thirty kilometers away. lí-'jèr yěw 'sān-shr-gūng-'lǐ.

Keep away lí . . . (*place, person*) ywǎn-dyǎr. ‖Keep away from them. lí tā-men 'ywǎn-dyǎr.

Expressions like go away, take away, move away, *and other such expressions are in Chinese compound verbs with* chywù, dzěw, *or* kāy *as second element.* ‖Please take this away. chǐng bǎ 'jèy-ge 'ná-chywu (*or* -kāy). ‖My work's too important, I can't go away. 'shŕ tày yàw-'jǐn, wǒ bù-néng 'lí-kāy. ‖They carried the wounded soldier away. tām bǎ shāng-'bīng táy-'dzěw-le. ‖They carried the wounded soldier away to the hospital. tām bǎ shāng-'bīng táy-daw yī-'ywàn-li chywù-le. ‖I don't like this soup; take it away. jèy-ge-'tāng jēn nán-'hē, gěy-wo 'ná-kāy. ‖He looked away. tā 'nyěw-gwò 'téw chywù-le. ‖He's away at school. tā dàw shywé-'shyàw chywù-le. *or* tā shàng-'shywé chywù-le. ‖He's away in the country. tā shyà-'shyāng chywù-le.

Go away, be away (*from one's usual territory*) chū-'mén. ‖Have you been away? *is expressed as* Did you go away? nǐ chū-'mén-lc-ma?

Put away 'shēw-chǐ-láy, 'shēw-shr-chǐ-láy. ‖Put it away. 'shēw-chi-lay-ba. ‖Put away those books. bǎ nèy-shyē-'shū 'shēw-shr-chi-láy.

Throw away 'rēng(-dyàw). ‖Don't throw anything away. 'shéme yě byé 'rēng(-dyàw) (-le).

‖Go away! 'chywù! (*Go!*) *or* 'dzěw-ba! (*Scram!*) *or* 'kwày gěy-wo 'gwěn! (*Very emphatic and slangy.*)

‖Look away! *is expressed as* Don't look this way. byé 'kàn!

‖He's away (*from home*). tā bú-dzày-'jyā.

‖He's been away for three months now. tā 'dzěw-le yěw 'sān-ge-'ywè-le.

‖He can't keep away from her. tā láw 'gēn-je ta. *or* tā lí-bu-'kāy ta. *or* tā 'gēn-ta 'byàw-shang-le.

‖We're giving this away free. wǒm 'jèy-ge shŕ báy-'sùng-de.

For other combinations see under the verb **DO.**

AWFUL. hěn bú-'shìng(-de), hěn 'hwày. ‖An awful accident happened yesterday. 'dzwó-tyan 'chū-le yí-jyàn-hěn-bú-'shìng-de-'shŕ. ‖We've been having awful weather. 'jìn-lay 'tyān-chi hěn 'hwày.

‖He looked awful. tā-'myàn-sè hěn bù-hǎw-'kàn.

‖That's awful! What an awful shame! (*Really too bad!*) jēn dzāw-'gāw! (*Really face-losing!*) jēn 'dyēw-rén! (*Really out of luck!*) jēn dáw-'méy! (*What is there to say?*) 'jèy, kě-shr dzěmē 'shwǒ-de!

Awful(ly) hěn, jēn, 'fēy-cháng, dǐng. ‖He's awfully boring. tā 'fēy-cháng tǎw-'yàn. *or* tā 'jēn jyàw ge-tǎw-'yàn-le.

AWNING. 'péng-dz.

AX. 'fǔ(-dz).

AXIS. jéw-'shīn; (*mathematics*) jéw-'shyàn; (*of the earth*) dì-'jéw.

AXLE. chē-'jéw.

B

BABY. 'háy-dz, hár, shyǎw-'háy-dz, shyǎw-'hár. ‖The baby's crying. shyǎw-'hár (dzày) 'kū-ne. ‖Whose baby is this? jèy shŕ 'shwéy-de-'háy-dz? ‖She's sewing baby clothes. tā dzày 'dzwò (*or* 'féng) shyǎw-'hár-chwān-de-'yī-fu.

(*Youngest*) lǎw-'gā-da. ‖She's the baby of our family. tā shŕ wǒ-men-'jyā-de-lǎw-'gā-da.

To baby hǔng, shyàng shyǎw-'hár shŕ-de 'dày, dàng shyǎw-'hár 'dày. ‖Don't always baby her, or you'll spoil her. nǐ byé lǎw 'húng-je ta, bù-'rán nǐ hwèy

'bǎ-ta gwàn-'hwày-le. ‖She likes people to baby her. tā 'ày jyàw-'rén °'hǔng-je. *or* °shyàng shyǎw-'hár shŕ-de 'dày-ta. *or* °ná-ta dàng shyǎw-'hár dày.

BACHELOR. dú-shēn-'nán-dz, gwāng-'gwèr.

BACK. (*Upper part, human*) 'jí-nyang; (*upper part, human; or of an animal*) bèy; (*small of the back, human*) yāw. ‖My back itches. wǒ-de-'jí-nyang 'yǎng-yang. ‖Scratch my back. gěy-wo 'jwā-jwa 'bèy. ‖Strap the saddle tightly, or the horse's back will be hurt, by the rubbing. bǎ mǎ-'ān-dz kwěn-'jǐn-le, bù-'rán hwèy bǎ mǎ-'bèy mwó-'pwò-le. ‖The Mongols are brought up on horseback. 'měng-gu-rén dēw shṝ dzày mǎ-'bèy-shang jǎng-'dà-de. ‖He fell from the roof and broke his back. tā tsúng fáng-'dǐng-shang 'dyàw-shya-lay bǎ-'yāw shwāy-'hwày-le.

(Of a chair, etc.) bèr. ‖This chair has a high back. jèy-bǎ-'yǐ-dz-de-'bèr hěn 'gāw.

(Space back of anything) 'hèw-byan, 'hèw-byar, 'hèw-myan, 'hèw-myar, 'hèw-tew, 'hèw-tewr. ‖There's a flower garden at the back of the house. fáng-dz-'hèw-myan yěw yí-ge-hwā-'ywár.

(Reverse side) 'bèy-myar, 'fǎn-myar. ‖The photo is attached to the back of the letter. shyàng-'pyār dzày 'shìn-de-'bèy-myar. ‖Look at the back (the other side). 'kàn-'kàn 'fǎn-myar.

Back door hèw-'mén. ‖Please leave by the back door. chǐng tsúng 'hèw-mén 'chū-chywu.

To back ·(a vehicle) dàw. ‖Please back your car slowly. chǐng-ni 'màn-dyar dàw-'chē.

To back (a request) 'dzàn-jù. ‖We'll back him in his request. tā-chǐng-'chyéw-de-'shṝ wǒm yí-'dìng 'dzàn-jù.

To back out 'shwō-le bú-'swàn; 'twèy-chū. ‖You shouldn't back out. nǐ bù-'néng 'shwō-le bú-'swàn. ‖You can't back out now. shyàn-'dzày nǐ bù-'néng 'twèy-chū.

To come (go) back hwéy. ‖Let's hurry back to our hotel. 'gǎn-jǐn hwéy dzám-de-lywǔ-'gwǎn-ba. ‖They got back from their trip. ·tām lywǔ-'shíng 'hwéy-lay-le.

To give back 'hwán-gey. ‖Give it back to me! 'hwán-gey wo!

To hold something back lyéw. ‖Tell everything; don't hold anything back. ·'chywán 'shwō-chu-lay; 'shéme yě bù-shywǔ 'lyéw. But Holding back on me, eh? yěw-'hwà bú-'gàw-sung wǒ-a! ‖Why did you hold that back? (Not tell it all) nǐ 'dzěme bù-'dēw 'shwō-chu-lay-ne? (Purposely conceal some facts) nǐ 'wèy-shéme bù-kěn' 'shwō? ‖They held back the names of the gamblers. tām bù-'kěn bǎ dǔ-'tú-de-'míng-dz °'shwō-chu-lay. or °'shywān-'bù-chu-lay. ‖The buyers held back. 'mǎy-de-rén bù-kěn jyā-'jyàr. ‖I can't hold back (keep) from interfering. wǒ bù-néng bù-°gǎn-'shè. or °gwǎn.

To hold someone back 'lán-hwéy, 'lán-jù. ‖They held the people back. tām bǎ-'rén 'lán-hwey-chywu-le. ‖I couldn't hold him back, he was so angry. tā chì-'jí-le, wǒ méy néng 'lán-jù tā.

To move back(wards) (wǎng-'hèw) twèy. ‖The crowd all moved back. 'rén-rén dēw wàng-'hèw twèy-le.

To pay back 'hwán-gěy, 'hwán. ‖We must pay back what we owe him. wǒm-'chyàn-tā-de jyèw děy 'hwán tā.

To repeat back. ‖Repeat the numbers back to me. wǒ-'shwō-de-nèy-shyē-'shùr 'nǐ dzày 'shwō yí-byàn, wǒ 'tīng-ting.

To send back 'twèy-hwéy. ‖Send this back; I don't want it. bǎ-'jèy-ge 'twèy-hwey-chywu, wǒ bú-'yàw.

To turn one's back jwǎn-'lyǎr, jwǎn-'shēn, jwǎn-gwò 'shēn chywù. ‖He turned his back on them and left. tā jwǎn-'lyǎr (or either of the other expressions) jyèw 'dzěw-le.

Behind someone's back dzày . . .'bèy-hèw. ‖They talked about her behind her back. tām dzày tā-'bèy-hèw shwō-tā shyán-'hwà.

BACKBONE. jí-'jwēy, 'jí-nyang-gǔ.

BACKGROUND. 'láy-lì, bèy-'jǐng. ‖The background of this war is very complicated. 'jèy-tsṝ-shṝ-'jyè-dà-'jàn-de-bèy-'jǐng hěn 'fù-dzá. ‖He has a dubious background. tā-'láy-lì bù-'míng.

(Visual) dyèr. ‖Doesn't it look nice against a purple background! 'pèy-shang 'ěw-sè-de-'dyèr 'dwō-me-hǎw-'kàn-na! ‖A darker background would be better. 'dyèr 'dzày 'shēn-yì-dyǎr tsáy 'hǎw.

In the background (not prominent) dzày hèw-'táy, 'àn-jūng. ‖He dominates the party but remains in the background himself. tā 'tsāw-dzùng dǎng-'wù, kě-shr 'běn-rén 'dwō-dzày hèw-'táy. ‖He's still active in the background. tā háy 'àn-jūng hwó-'dùng.

BACON. yān-'rèw.

BACTERIA. wēy-shēng-'wù, shì-'jywǔn.

BAD. hwày, bù-'hǎw. ‖He's a bad egg. tā shṝ ge-hwày-'dàn. ‖He does all sorts of bad things. tā shéme-hwày-'shèr dēw 'gàn. ‖He's acquired some bad habits. tā 'shywé-le shyē-hwày-'máw-bìng. ‖His grades are bad. tā-de-chéng-'jì °hěn 'hwày. or °hěn bù-'hǎw. ‖That's bad or That's a bad thing to do. 'nàme-je bù-'hǎw. ‖Here's some bad news. jèy-ge-'shyāw-shi bú-dà 'hǎw. ‖We've had some bad weather lately. 'jìn-lay jèr-de-'tyān-chi °bú-dà 'hǎw. or °hěn bù-'hǎw. ‖The weather's pretty bad. 'tyān-chi hěn 'hwày. ‖(How is the patient?) Pretty bad. ('bìng-rén dzěme-'yàng?) bú-dà 'hǎw.

To go bad hwày-le. ‖The machine's gone bad. 'jī-chi 'hwày-le. (Of fruits, vegetables, etc.) hwày-le or làn-le. ‖The apple's gone bad. 'píng-gwo 'làn-le. (Of oils and foods cooked with shortening) hwày-le or 'hā-la-le. ‖The butter's gone bad. hwáng-'yéw 'hā-la-le. (Of rice, bean curd, bread, etc.) sēw-le. ‖The bean curd has gone bad. 'dèw-fu 'sēw-le. ‖He got sick from eating bad food (food that had gone bad). tā chṝ bù-'shīn-shyàn-de-'dūng-shi chṝ-'bìng-le.

To smell bad (of food) chèw. ‖The fish smells bad. 'ywú 'chèw-le. (Of air) yěw-'wèr. ‖The air in the room smells bad. 'wū-dz-li-de-'kūng-chi yěw-'wèr-le.

‖There's a bad smell somewhere. yěw yì-gǔ-dz-'wèr. ‖He has bad breath. tā 'dzwéy-li yěw-'wèr. or tā shr̀ chèw-'dzwěr.

To have bad weather nàw-'tyār. ‖The weather's been bad for quite a few days. nàw-'tyār nàw-le hǎw-shyé-'r̀-dz-le. ‖You may catch cold in the bad weather. nàw-'tyār de-shŕ-héw nǐ yé-shywu 'hwèy jāw-'lyáng.

(Of work or conditions) dzāw. ‖The management is pretty bad. bàn-'lǐ-de hěn 'dzāw.

(Of parts of the body) yěw-'bìng-de, 'hwày-le-de. ‖That's his bad arm. tā-'nèy-ge-gē-be shr̀ yěw-'bìng-de. But ‖This is my bad ear. meaning a little deaf wǒ-'jèy-ge-'ěr-dwo yěw dyǎr-'lúng. or meaning totally deaf wǒ-'jèy-ge-'ěr-dwo tīng-bu-'jyàn.

(Of money) jyǎ-de (counterfeit); bù-jŕ-'chyán, hwàn-bu-'chū 'chyán-lay. ‖This doesn't look like a bad coin to me. 'jèy-ge-chyán 'wǒ kàn-bù-'chū shr̀ 'jyǎ-de-lay. ‖That's a bad check. 'nèy-jāng-jr̄-'pyàw hwàn-bu-'chū 'chyán-lay-le.

Bad luck. ‖Don't do that; it's bad luck. bvé 'nème-je; °jāw-'dzǎr. or °bù-'jí-lì. or °bù-'hǎw-jyā. ‖It's bad luck to say that. shwō 'nà-yàng-de-hwà bù-jí-lì.

Bad manners. ‖In China that's not considered to be bad manners. dzày 'jūng-gwo 'nà bú-'swàn shr̄-'lì.

Bad temper. ‖He has a bad temper. tā 'pí-chi hěn °hwày. or °dà.

(Unskillful) bù-'hǎw, bù-'shíng, bù-'chéng; (of calligraphy or painting) bù-hǎw-'kàn. or bú-shr̀ 'yàngr. ‖His ideas are good but the presentation is bad. tā-de-'yì-sz bú-'tswò, kě-shr̀ 'shwō-de 'fāng-fa bù-'hǎw. ‖His handwriting is bad. tā-'shyě-de bú-shr̀ 'yàngr.

(Serious, severe) 'lì-hày, 'jùng. ‖He has a bad case of t.b. tā-de-'fèy-bìng hěn 'lì-hày. ‖He has a bad case of jitters. tā (hày-)'pà-de 'lì-hày. ‖I caught a bad cold. wǒ shāng-'fēng shāng-de hěn 'lì-hày.

Be bad for ywú ... yěw 'hày or (limited to stomach or eyes) shāng. ‖This food is bad for you. 'jèy-jǔng-dūng-shi 'chr̄-le °ywú-nǐ yěw-'hày. or °shāng-wèy. ‖It's bad for your eyes to go to too many movies. 'dyàn-yǐng kàn 'dwō-le shāng 'yǎn-jing. ‖Running too hard is bad for your heart. 'pǎw-de tày 'lì-hày-le ywú 'shīn-dzàng yěw 'hày.

Be in pretty bad shape (of clothes, houses, etc.) 'pwò-làn bù-'kān-le; (of machinery, etc.) 'hwày-de bú-shyàng 'yàng-dz or 'hwày-de bù-'chéng 'yàng-dz; in these expressions hwày may be replaced by pwò (clothes), 'dzāw (situations), bìng (patients). ‖My car is in pretty bad shape. wǒ-de-'chē 'yǐ-jing 'hwày-de bù-chéng 'yàng-dz-le.

From bad to worse ywè 'láy ywè 'hwày (or pwò, dzāw, bìng); 'hwày-de (or 'pwò-de, 'dzāw-de, 'bìng-de) ywè-'láy ywè 'lì-hày. ‖His affairs went from bad to worse. tā-de-'shr̀-ching ywè 'láy ywè 'hwày.

Bad idea. ‖It's not a bad idea. bú-'tswò. ‖It was a bad idea to wait so long. děng nème-'jyěw bú-dà 'hǎw.

‖That's too bad! (General) 'jè shr̀ dzěme-'shwō-de! or (unsympathetic) hwó-'gāy!

BAG. 'kěw-dày; (shyǎw-)kěw-'dàr; (small bag with drawstring) 'hé-bāwr. ‖Will that bag hold it all? nèy-ge-'kěw-dày chywán jwāng-de-'shyà-ma? ‖This bag isn't big enough. jèy-ge-'kěw-dày bú-gèw 'dà. ‖He bought a small leather bag to keep his tobacco in. tā 'mǎy-le ge-shyǎw-pí-kěw-'dàr jwāng yān-'yè-dz. ‖I can't move a man-sized bag all alone. yì-rén-'gāw-de-ge-'dà-'kěw-dày wǒ 'yí-ge-rén káng-bu-'dùng.

Bag of 'kěw-dày, 'dày-dz, 'dàr, kěw-'dàr. ‖He can carry three bags of flour on his back. tā néng 'bēy 'sān-kěw-day-'myàn-('fěn). ‖A bag of flour costs fifteen dollars now. shyàn-'dzày °yí-dàr- (or °yì-'kěw-dày-, °yì-kěw-'dàr-, °yí-'dày-dz-) 'myàn yàw shŕ-wǔ-'kwày.

(Hand luggage in bag shape; not leather cases) shěw-tí-'bāw. ‖Where can I check my bags? shěw-tí-'bāw tswén-'nǎr?

Flour bag myàn-kěw-'dàr. ‖That flour bag can be washed and used as a rag. nèy-ge-myàn-kěw-'dàr 'shǐ-shi ké-yi dzwò 'jǎn-bù.

Burlap bag má-'dày.

Sandbag shā-'náng or shā-dz-'kěw-dày or shā-'dày. ‖Pile up those sandbags. bǎ shā-dz-'kěw-day 'lwò-chi-lay.

Barracks bag shíng-jywūn-'náng. ‖Pack your barracks bag. bǎ nǐ-de-shíng-jywūn-'náng 'jwāng-hǎw-le.

To bag (bring down) 'dǎ-shyà(-lay). ‖He bagged ten planes. tā 'dǎ-shyà-lay 'shŕ-jyà-fēy-'jī.

To bag (swell out) 'gǔ-chū-lay. ‖His trousers bag at the knees. ta-de-kù-'twěr dzày gē-le-'bàr-nàr 'gǔ-chū-lay-le.

Bag and baggage. ‖He moved in, bag and baggage. tā bǎ 'swǒ-yěw-de-'jyā-dāngr 'dēw bān-lay-le.

(Of hunting). ‖We made a good bag today. 'jyēr-dǎ-'lyè-de-chéng-'jì bú-'hwày.

Holding the bag. ‖He left us holding the bag. tā bǎ wǒ-men 'shyàn-dzay 'lǐ-tew, 'dǎ-jǐ kě 'pǎw-le. ‖You're going to leave us holding the bag; you can't get away with it. nǐ 'gwāng-jyàw 'dzám 'wéy-'nán-na; 'nà kě bù-'shíng.

‖He let the cat out of the bag. jyàw-ta gěy shwō-'pwò-le.

‖It's in the bag! méy 'wèn-tí!

BAGGAGE. 'shíng-li; (bedding only, frequently an item of baggage in China) pū-gay-'jywǎr. ‖I want to send my baggage on ahead. wǒ yàw bǎ wǒ-de 'shíng-li shyān ywùn-'dzěw. ‖How many pieces of baggage have you? nǐ yěw 'jǐ-jyàn-shíng-li? ‖Take my baggage up to my room. bǎ wǒ-de-pū-gay-'jywǎr ná-daw wǒ-'wūr-chywu.

To check baggage dǎ (or chǐ) shíng-li-'pyàw. ‖These three pieces of baggage are to be checked; I'll take the rest along with me. 'jèy-sān-jyàn shr̀ dǎ shíng-li-'pyàw-de; 'shèng-shya-de swéy-shēn 'dày-je.

Baggage car shíng-li-'chē; baggage room shíng-li-'fáng; baggage check shíng-li-'pyàw.

BAIL. (*Money to release someone from arrest*) băw-shr̀-'jīn.

BAIT. (*For catching fish*) ywú-'shŕ.

BAKE. kăw. ‖Was this bread baked this morning? jèy-ge-myàn-'bāw shŕ jīn-tyan-'dzăw-chen 'kăw-de-ma?

To bake (*on a griddle*) làw; *any food so cooked is a variety of* bĭng (*breadlike, cakelike food*). ‖Can you bake bĭng? nĭ hwèy làw-'bĭng-ma? ‖The bĭng he baked were delicious. tā-làw-de-'bĭng jēn hăw-'chŕ. ‖It takes half an hour to bake ten bĭng. làw 'shŕ-jāng-'bĭng dĕy yùng 'bàn-dyăn-jūng.

(*In a pastry shop.*) ‖Do you bake every day? nĭ 'mĕy-tyān dzwò·'dyăn-shīn-ma?

BAKERY. (*Chinese*) bāw-dz-'pù, *which produces and sells* mán-tew *and similar steamed products;* bĭng-'pù *or* shāw-bĭng-'pù, *which produces and sells* bĭng' *and similar breads;* dyăn-shīn-'pù *for pastries and cakes. Bakeries which cater to the foreigners' trade are called* myàn-bāw-'fáng, myàn-bāw-'dyàn.

See also **BREAD, CAKE, COOK.**

BALANCE. (*Scales; large*) chèng; (*small; f jewels, jewelry, etc.*) tyān-'píng, 'dĕng-dz. ‖Weigh it on the balance. yùng 'chèng (*or* 'dĕng-dz, tyān-'píng) °'chēng-yi-chēng. *or* °'yăw-yi-yăw.

Bank balance. ‖What's my (bank) balance? yín-'háng-de-tswén-'kwăn 'háy yĕw 'dwō-shav?

(*Remainder*) 'shèng-shyà-de. ‖Pay one-third down and the balance in monthly installments. 'shyān gĕy sän-fēn-jr-'yī, 'shèng-shyà-de àn-'ywè 'gĕy.

Balance of power jywūn-'shŕ. ‖Their policy is to keep the balance of power in Europe. tā-men-de-jèng-'tsè shŕ yàw băw-'chŕ 'ēw-jēw-de-jywūn-'shŕ.

In the balance 'chyān-jywūn-yì-'fă. ‖His fate hung in the balance. tā-de-'chyán-tú jyèw dzày jè-'chyān-jywūn-yì-'fă-de-shŕ-hew láy jywé-'dìng-le.

To keep one's balance. (*While standing*) jàn-'wĕn; (*while walking*) dzĕw-'wĕn. ‖Even standing still I can't keep my balance on such a narrow bridge. dzày nàme-'jăy-de-'chyáw-shang wŏ lyán 'jàn yĕ jàn-bu-'wĕn. ‖That drunk can't keep his balance. nèy-ge-hē-'dzwèy-le-de-rén dzĕw-bu-'wĕn.

To lose one's balance wāy, 'lyè-chye. ‖I lost my balance and fell off the step. wŏ yī 'wāy jyèw 'shwāy-daw táy-'jyēer-'shyà-byar chywù-le.

To balance fàng-'píng. ‖Balance the shoulder-pole on your shoulder. bă 'byăn-dàn dzày jyān-'băngr-shang fàng-'píng-le.

(*To balance a pole on the shoulder with loads hanging down from each end*) tyāw-'píng, dān-'píng. ‖Balance the pole (and load) on your shoulder. bă 'tyāw-dz tyāw-'píng-le.

To balance each other, be balanced (*in weighing*) píng-'jywūn, píng-'héng, shyāng-'dĕng, shyāng-'chèn.

‖The two weights balance each other. 'lyăng-byān-de-'jùng-lyàng shyāng-'dĕng.

To balance each other *in strength* shŕ-'jywūn lì-'dí. ‖I'd say that the two teams balance each other. jywù wŏ 'kàn, jèy-'lyăng-dwèy shŕ-'jywūn lì-'dí.

Be balanced (*be compensated for*) 'chèn-gwò-lay. ‖He makes some mistakes but that's balanced by his speed. tā 'yĕw-de-shŕ-hew chū-'tswèr, kĕ-shr tā dzwò-'shŕ 'kwày, swó-yi 'chèn-gwo-lay-le.

To balance, be balanced (*of an account*) chū-'rù shyāng-'fú; *not be balanced* chū-'rù bù-'fú. ‖Does this account balance? jèy-bĭ-'jàng chū-'rù shyāng-'fú-ma? ‖This account isn't balanced. jèy-bĭ-'jàng chū-'rù bù-'fú.

BALCONY. yáng-'táy.

BALE. (*As of cotton*) bāw.

BALL. chyéw(r). ‖He rolled the string into a ball. tā bă 'shéng-dz 'jywăn-chéng-le yí-ge-'chyéw. ‖The ball rolled away. 'chyéwr 'gwĕn-kay-le.

(*In names of ball games*) chyéw. ‖Do you want to play baseball, football (soccer), or basketball? nĭ yàw wár 'bàng-chyéw, 'dzú-chyéw, háy-shr 'lán-chyéw?

To play (*with a*) ball dă-'chyéw(r), wár-'chyéw. ‖They played ball all afternoon. tām 'dă-le yí-'shyà-wŭ-de-'chyéw. *But* ‖What if he won't play ball (*co-operate*)? tā bù-hé-'dzwò dzĕme 'bàn-ne?

(*A dance*) tyàw-wŭ-'hwèy. ‖At the ball they danced until very late. dzày tyàw-wŭ-'hwèy tām yì-'jŕ 'tyàw-daw hĕn 'wăn.

All balled up. ‖He got all balled up. tā ràw 'hú-dū-le.

BAMBOO. 'jú-dz.

BANANA. shyāng-'jyāw.

BAND. tyáw; (*stripe*) dàwr. Rubber band héw-'jyēr, shyàng-pí-'chywār. ‖The room was trimmed with a blue band near the ceiling. jèy-wū-dz-lĭ lí fáng-'dĭng bù-'ywăn yĕw yì-tyáw-lán-'dàwr. ‖Put an iron band around this box. ná tyĕ-'tyáw bă jèy-ge-'shyāng-dz 'gū-shang. ‖Can you get me a box of rubber bands? nĭ néng 'gĕy-wo măy yì-hér-héw-'jyēr-ma?

(*Music*) ywè-'dwèy. Military band jywūn-ywè-'dwèy. ‖The band played marches and led the parade. ywè-'dwèy dzĕw-je jìn-shíng-'chywŭ lĭng-je rén yéw-'shíng.

To band together 'hé-chĭ-láy, tsèw-daw yí-'kwàr. ‖They banded together to hire a guide. tām 'hé-chi-lay (*or* tām tsèw-daw yí-'kwàr) 'jăw-le °ge-shyăng-'dăw. *or* °yí-ge-lĭng-'lù-de.

BANDAGE. bēng-'dày.

BANDIT. tú-'féy.

BANK. (*Shore*) àn, byār. ‖The river overflowed its banks. 'hé 'màn-gwò lyǎng-'àn chywù-le. ‖He swam to the nearest bank. tā fù-daw dzwèy-'jìn-de-'nèy-byǎr.

(*Heap or pile*) dwēy. ‖There's a bank of snow outside the gate. dà-mér-'wày-byan yěw yì-dwēy-'shywě.

(*For money*) yín-'háng. ‖The bank will exchange our money. yín-'háng ké-yi bǎ dzám-de-'chyán 'hwàn-le. ‖We should deposit this money in a bank. wǒm yīng-dang bǎ jèy-'chyán tswén yín-'háng-li.

To open a bank account lì ge-'jé-dz. ‖I'd like to open a bank account. wǒ shyǎng lì ge-'jé-dz.

To bank a fire yùng-'hwēy péy. ‖Please bank the fire so it will burn slowly. chǐng bǎ-'hwǒ yùng-'hwēy 'péy-shang hǎw jáw-de 'màn.

To bank a plane wāy. ‖He banked the airplane when he turned. ta 'jwàn de-shŕ-hew bǎ fēy-'jī 'wāy-le yí-shyàr.

BANKER. yín-háng-'jyā.

BANK NOTE. 'pyàw-dz, chāw-'pyàw.

BANQUET. yàn-'hwèy

BARBED WIRE. yěw-'tsź-de-tyě-'sź.

BARBER. lǐ-fǎ-'jyàng. (*Specializing in shaving the head*) tì-'téw-de; (*specializing in clipping the hair*) twēy-'téw-de.

Barbershop lǐ-fǎ-'gwǎn. ‖Please direct me to a barbershop. chǐng-ni 'gàw-sung wo 'dzěme-yàng chywù yí-ge-lǐ-fǎ-'gwǎn.

BARGAIN. (*Cheap things*) 'pyán-yi-de-dūng-shi; (*specially priced things*) 'jàn-hwò. ‖You'll find many bargains there. nǐ yí-'dìng ké-yi dzày-'nèr chyáw-jyan bù-'shǎw-de-'pyán-yi-de-dūng-shi. ‖Tomorrow is bargain day at this store. *is expressed as* Tomorrow this store will sell specially priced things. 'míng-tyan jèy-gē-'pù-dz mày 'ìvàn-hwò.

Be a bargain 'pyán-yì. ‖This book was a great bargain. jèy-běn-'shū 'mǎy-de jên 'pyán-yì.

To bargain hwán-'jyà(r), jyǎng-'jyà(r). ‖We bargained with the man a long time before buying. wǒm méy-'mǎy yǐ-chyán gēn-ta 'hwán-le bàn-tyan-'jyàr. ‖They bargained for the house. tā-men wèy nèy-ge-'fáng-dz-de-shŕ-ching jyǎng-'jyàr.

(*Agreement*). ‖According to our bargain you were to pay half in advance. *is expressed as* What we agreed on was that you were to pay half in advance. dzám-shwō-'hǎw-le-de nǐ 'shyàn gěy yí-bàr-'chyán.

To make a bargain. ‖I'll make a bargain with you. *is expressed as* If it's to be that way I have a condition to make. yàw-shr 'nème-je, wǒ yěw ge-'tyáw-jyàn.

BARK. (*Of a tree*) shù-'pí.
To bark (*of a dog*) jyàw.

BARLEY. dà-'mày(-dz).

BARN. (*For grain only*) tsāng-'fáng. ‖The barn was filled with hay and grain. tsāng-'fáng-lǐ-tew 'chywán shŕ gān-'tsǎw gēn 'lyáng-shŕ.
See also STABLE.

BAROMETER. chíng-ywǔ-'byǎw.

BARRACKS. bīng-'yíng, 'yíng-pan; (*buildings*) yīng-fáng.

BARREL. tǔng; (*with cylindrical sides, not bulging*) 'tǔng-dz; (*with bulging sides*) pí-pá-'tǔng or dà-'dù-dz-de-'tǔng. ‖A barrel is a tǔng-like container, with a circumference at the middle larger than that at the ends. Barrel shŕ yì-jǔng-chéng-'dūng-shi-de-'tǔng; 'jūng-bù-'jēw-wéy 'cháng-cháng shŕ 'gǔ-chū-lay-de. ‖The truck was loaded with barrels of beer. dzày-jùng-chì-'chē-shang 'jwāng-le bù-shǎw-'tǔng-'pí-jyěw.

(*Of a gun*) chyáng-'gwǎr, chyáng-'shēn, pàw-'gwǎn, pàw-'shēn, hwǒ-'shēn. ‖Clean out the barrel of this rifle. bǎ jèy-'chyáng-de-chyǎng-'gwǎr 'tsǎ-yì-tsǎ.

BARRIER. (*Of any kind, literally or figuratively*) dzǔ-'ày.

BASE. (*Of a statue, tower*) dzwòr; (*foundation*) jī, 'jī-chu, 'gēn-ji; (*of a mountain or hill*) shān-'jyǎw, shān-'gēr. ‖The base of the statue was still there. jèy-ge-'shyàng-de-'dzwèr háy dzày-nèr-ne. ‖His orchard extends to the base of the hill over there. tā-de-gwěr-'ywán-dz yì-'jŕ daw shān-'gēr-nàr.

(*Military*) gēn-jywù-'dì. ‖Telephone to the base for instructions. dǎ dyàn-'hwà daw gēn-jywù-'dì chǐng-'shŕ. ‖The soldiers were sent back to their base. nèy-shyē-'bīng dēw 'dyǎw-hwéy gēn-jywù-'dì chywù-le.

Be based on yǐ ... wéy 'gēn-jywù, yùng ... wéy 'gēn-jywù, gēn-jywù ... dzwò-de. ‖His report is based on the available statistics. tā-de-bàw-'gàw shŕ yǐ shyàn-'yěw-de-tǔng-'jì wéy 'gēn-jywù. or tā-de-bàw-'gàw shŕ 'gēn-jywù shyàn-'yěw-de-tǔng-'jì 'dzwò-de. But ‖His success is based on honesty. *is expressed as* His success is fundamentally because he's honest. tā-de-'chéng-gūng shŕ 'gēn-běn yīn-wey tā 'chéng-shr.

BASEBALL. bàng-'chyéw.

BASEMENT. dì-'yìn-dz.

BASIN. pén, shwěy-'pén, lyǎn-'pén; (*of a river*) lyéw-'ywù.

BASKET. 'kwāng-dz, 'lán-dz, 'lěw-dz, lěwr. ‖He brought a basket of fruit. tā 'dày-lay yì-kwāng-dz shwěy-'gwǒ. ‖Put the groceries in this basket. bǎ 'dzá-hwò fàng-dzày jèy-ge-'lán-dz-li. ‖Buy a basket of olives. mǎy yì-lěwr-gān-'lǎn-lay.

BASKETBALL. lán-'chyéw.

BAT. (*Animal*) 'byān-fu or byǎn-'fú; (*club*) bàng; (*baseball*) chyéw-'bàng.

BATH. Take a bath shǐ-'dzǎw. ‖Where can I take a bath? wǒ dzày-'nǎr ké-yi shǐ-'dzǎw?
(*Bathroom*) (shǐ-)dzǎw-'fáng, ywù-'shr̀. ‖Does this room have a bath? jèy-ge-'fáng-jyān yěw shǐ-dzǎw-'fáng-ma?
(*Bathtub*) dzǎw-'pén. ‖Please fill the bath half full. bǎ dzǎw-'pén-li fàng yí-bàr-'shwěy.
(*Bathhouse*) (shǐ-)dzǎw-'táng-dz. ‖He's gone to the baths. dàw dzǎw-'táng-dz-chywu shǐ-'dzǎw-chywu-le.

BATHING SUIT. (*For going swimming*) fù-shwěy-'yī, véw-yǔng-'yī.

BATHROBE. 'ywù-yī.

BATH TOWEL. shǐ-dzǎw-'jīn, shǐ-dzǎw-'bù.

BATTERY. (*Electric*) dyàn-'chí; (*criminal*) ēw-'dǎ; (*military*) lyán.

BATTLE. jàn. To join battle jyāw-'jàn; to meet in battle (*of several armies*) hwèy-'jàn; a land battle lù-'jàn; a sea battle hǎy-'jàn; battle situation jàn-'jywú. ‖That battle came to a draw. 'nèy-tsz̀-jyàw-'jàn °'dǎ-le ge-píng-'shěw. or °bù-'fēn shèng-'fù. ‖The Battle of Gettysburg stopped the northern advance of the Confederate Army. Gettysburg-yí-'jàn (or Gettysburg-'nèy-tsz̀-hwèy-'jèn) dzǔ-'jr̀-le nán-'jywūn-de-'běy-jìn. ‖That was a great sea battle. 'nèy-shr̀ yí-tsz̀-'dà-hǎy-'jàn.

In certain combinations jàng *is used instead of* jàn: to battle *or* to do battle dǎ-'jàng; this battle jèy-'jàng; that battle nèy-'jàng; which battle něy-'jàng; to see battle *or* experience battle 'jyàn-gwo 'jàng *or* 'jīng-gwo 'jàng. ‖That battle was fought at the river. 'nèy-yí-jàng shr̀ dzày nèy-ge-'hé-nèr 'dǎ-de. ‖These soldiers haven't seen battle yet. jèy-shyē-'bīng háy méy-°'jyàn-gwo (or °'jīng-gwo) 'jàng-ne.
To battle dǎ-'jàng, jyāw-'jàn, hwèy-'jàn.

BATTLESHIP. jàn-dèw-'jyàn.

BAY. wān; (*specifically of the sea*) hǎy-'wān. ‖The bay made a good harbor. jèy-ge-hǎy-'wān chéng-le yí-gé-hěn-'hǎw-de-gǎng-'kěw. ‖The boat sailed into the bay. jèy-ge-'chwán kāy-jìn 'wān chywù-le.

BAYONET. tsz̀-'dāw.

BE. (AM, ARE, IS, WAS, WERE, BEEN, BEING.)
1. *Followed by a noun.* (*Denoting merely classification*) shr̀; (*indicating profession or function*) dzwò, dāng, *only the latter if the function is that of a soldier.* ‖We're American soldiers. wǒm shr̀ 'měy-gwo-bīng. ‖She's an old hag. tā-shr̀ ge-lǎw-'gwày-wu. ‖When I was a soldier things were different. 'wǒ dāng-'bīng de-shf-hew bú-'jème-je. ‖He's a lawyer. tā °shr̀ ge- (or °dāng or °dzwò) 'lywù-shr̀. ‖They asked him to be chairman. tām 'chǐng-ta °dāng (or °dzwò) jǔ-'shí. But ‖Be a good boy and bring it to me. *is expressed without any word for* be: 'hǎw-háy-dz, gěy-wo 'ná-gwo-lay.

2. *Followed by an adjective.* (*Denoting temporary or relative description*) *the Chinese adjective is used without any separate word for* be; (*denoting general classification*) shr̀ . . .-de. ‖The sky is blue. (*At the moment*) 'tyān hěn 'lán. (*Statement of a general truth*) 'tyān shr̀ 'lán-de. ‖He's OK. 'tā 'jēn °bú-'hwày. or °bú-'tswò. ‖HE'S OK. tā chéng. or 'tā méy-'wèn-tí. ‖I'm thirsty. wǒ 'kě-le. or wǒ hěn 'kě. ‖Be careful! 'shyǎw-shīn-dyǎr! ‖Are you ready? ywù-bey-'hǎw-le-ma?

In other cases the specific words other than be *call for an expression in Chinese which contains neither a word for* be *nor an adjective.* ‖Be sure to be there. yí-'dìng yàw 'dàw-nèr. or byé 'bú-chywù! or byé 'bú-dàw! ‖Be calm! 'chén-jù-le 'chì! or byé 'hwāng-jang! or byé jāw-'jí! ‖Be natural! or Be yourself! 'dz̀-dz-rán-'rán-de! or byé 'jwāng-mu dzwò-'yàngr-de! ‖Do be careful! 'kě yàw 'shyǎw-shīn-je. or 'chyān-wàn 'shyǎw-shīn-je!

3. *Followed by an expression of place* dzày; (*if there is an idea of arriving*) dàw. ‖When I was in Peiping I went to see the Imperial Palace. wǒ dzày běy-'píng de-shf-hew chywù 'gwàng-gwo 'gù-'jūng. ‖The books are on the table. 'shū dzày 'jwōr-shang. ‖He wasn't home when we called. wǒm chywù 'jǎw-ta de-shf-hew tā bú-dzày-'jyä. ‖Be here at nine tomorrow. 'míng-tyan 'jyěw-dyǎn 'dàw-jèr.

In other cases the specific words other than be *call for an expression in Chinese using a verb other than one meaning* be. ‖The sun is up. *is expressed as* The sun has come up. 'tày-yang °'chǐ-láy-le. or *as* The sun has risen high. °'gāw-le. or *as* The sun has come out. °'chū-lay-le. ‖I'm up. *is expressed as* ‖I've already gotten up. wǒ 'yǐ-jing 'chǐ-láy-le. ‖Mr. Jones is in conference. *is expressed as* Mr. Jones is there conferring. 'jēw-shyān-sheng ('dzày-nèr) kāy-'hwèy-ne.

4. Be . . .-ing (*referring to action going on at the time of speaking or at some reference point of time*) *often* dzày *before the verb, frequently with an adverb of present time before it; sometimes* (*also, or instead of* dzày) je *added to the verb or* ne *at the end of the sentence or both.* ‖What're you doing? dzwò 'shéme-ne? ‖I'm winding my watch. shàng-'byǎw-ne. or wǒ jèng dzày shàng-'byǎw-ne. ‖What're YOU doing?

nǐ 'dzày-nàr (*or* nǐ 'nà-shr *or* nǐ-shr̀ *or* nǐ dzày) dzwò 'shéme-ne? ‖I'M winding my watch. 'wǒ ᴗdzày-jèr (*or* 'wǒ jè-shr *or* 'wǒ dzày) shàng-'byǎw-ne. ‖They're **eating dinner right now.** tām chř-je 'fàn-ne. *or* tām 'jèng chř-je 'fàn-ne. *or* tām 'dzày-nèr·chr-'fàn-ne. *or* tām dzày chř 'fàn-ne. *or* tām 'jèng dzày-nèr chř(-je) 'fàn-ne. ‖He was **reading when I entered the room.** wǒ 'jìn-chywu de-shf-hew °tā dzày-nèr kàn-'shū-ne. *or* °tā jèng dzày-nèr kàn-'shū(-ne). *or* °tā jèng kàn-'shū-ne. *or* °tā dzày kàn-'shū. *or* (*putting the other part of the sentence first*) tā °'jèng kàn-je 'shū (*or* °'jèng dzày-nèr kàn-'shū *or* °'jèng dzày-nèr kàn-je 'shū) wǒ jyèw 'jìn-chywu-le.

Be . . .-ing (*referring to an event in the future*) yàw *or omitted.* ‖I'm **going to Chungking tomorrow.** (*If one is fairly near Chungking*) 'míng-tyan wǒ yàw dàw chúng-'chìng chywù. *or* (*If one is far away*) wǒ yàw dàw chúng-'chìng-chywù; 'míng-tyan 'dzǒw. ‖The **President is speaking tomorrow evening.** dzǔng-'tǔng (yàw dzày·) 'míng-tyan-'wǎn-shang yǎn-'jyǎng. ‖Be **seeing you!** 'hwéy-téw 'jyàn! *or* hwéy 'jyàn!

5. Be . . .-ed *expressed with* jyàw *followed by mention of the agent, by* bèy *or* ràng *similarly, by* bèy *or* gěy *with no agent specified, by nothing at all except the verbs used, or by turning the sentence around and making the agent come first.* ‖He was **seen entering the house through the rear door.** tā tsúng 'hèw-mén 'jìn-chywù-de, jyàw-rén 'kàn-jyàn-le. *or* yěw-'rén 'kàn-jyan ta tsúng 'hèw-mén 'jìn-chywu-de. ‖The thief **was caught last evening.** 'dzéy dzwór-'wǎn-shang jyàw-rén 'dǎy-jáw-le. *or* 'dzéy shr̀ 'dzwór-'wǎn-shang jyàw-rén 'dǎy-jáw-de. ‖This job **has never before been done right.** 'jèy-ge-shèr yí-'shyàng °'méy- (*or* °'méy-rén) dzwò 'dwey-le-gwo. ‖He **was shot at sunrise.** tā-shr 'tày·yang 'chū-lay de-shf-hew chyāng-'bì-de. ‖The job **was finished two days ago.** 'nèy-ge-shèr shr̀ 'lyǎng-tyān-yǐ-chyán dzwò-'wán-de.

6. To be *to do something, expressed with a word such as* have to děy, *etc.* ‖You are **to report to the Captain at nine this morning.** jyēr-'dzǎw-chen-'jyěw-ᴗyan nǐ děy chywù jyàn lyán-'jǎng. ‖You and **Jones are to work together in this.** 'jèy-ge-shèr °'nǐ děy (*or* °'yàw-'nǐ) gēn lǎw-'jēw yí-'kwàr dzwò.

There is, there are, there were, *etc.* yěw. ‖There's **a pebble in my shoe.** wǒ 'shyé-li yěw ge-shf-tew-'dzěr. ‖There're **several other things I want to say.** wǒ 'háy yěw 'jǐ-jyàn-'shèr děy 'gǎw báy-gǎw-báy. ‖There **were thirteen at the dinner party.** chř-'fàn de-shf-hew yěw shf-'sān-ge-rén dzày 'dzwò. ‖There isn't **any more sugar.** méy-yew 'táng-le. *or expressed as* The sugar's **all used up.** 'táng dēw yùng-'wán-le. ‖Is there **any more sugar?** 'háy yěw-'táng-ma? ‖Aren't there **any other ways to do this?** háy yěw 'byé-de-'fá-dz-ma?

7. *For other specific combinations of* be *and another word, see under the other word.*

BEADS. jū-dz.   **String of beads** yí-chywàr-'jū-dz.

BEAK.   dzwěy, nyǎw-'dzwěy.

BEAM.   (*Building support*) lyáng; (*of light*) yí-dàw-'gwāng, yí-dàw-gwāng-'shyàn; (*radio*) dyàn-'bwō; (*of a pair of scales*) chèng-'gǎr; (*width of a ship*) chwán-'fǔ.

BEANS. dèw-dz. ‖Do **they have beans on the menu?** tsày-'dār-shang yěw 'dèw-dz méy-yew? ‖Do **you like beans?** nǐ 'shǐ-hwān chř 'dèw-dz-ma? ‖The **beans are growing well this year.** 'dèw-dz 'jīn-nyan 'jǎng-de bú-'tswò.

   Bean soup dèwr-'tāng.

   To plant beans jùng 'dèw-dz. ‖Do **you have beans in your garden?** nǐ tsày-'ywán-dz-li jùng 'dèw-dz-le méy-yew?

   String beans byǎn-'dèw *or* dèw-'jyǎwr; **lima beans** tsán-'dèw; **soya beans** dà-'dèw *or* hwáng-'dèw (*the most important kind in China*); **black beans** hēy-'dèw; **bean curd** (*made from soya beans*) 'dèw-fu.

   To spill the beans gěy 'shwō-chū-lay.

BEAR.   (*Animal*) shyúng. ‖That **bear came from Africa.** nèy-jř-'shyúng·shr̀ 'fēy-jēw láy-de. ‖Bears **like honey.** 'shyúng ày chř fēng-'mì.

   To bear. (*Of plants*) chū. ‖This **orchard bears good peaches.** jèy-ge-gwǒ-'ywán-dz chū hǎw-'táwr. (*Of humans.*) shēng *or* yǎng. ‖She's **borne three children.** tā 'shēng-gwo 'sān-ge-'háy-dz. (*Of animals*) shyà.

   To bear arms káng. ‖All **men who can bear arms must become soldiers.** néng-káng-'chyǎng-de-rén dēw děy chywù dāng-'bīng.

   To bear weight 'jīn-jù. ‖This **board won't bear your weight.** jèy-'bǎn-dz jīn-bu-'jù ni.

   (*To endure*) rěn, 'rěn-de, 'shèw-lyǎw, 'rěn-jù. ‖He **bore the pain in silence.** tā nème-'téng de-shf-hew, 'rěn-je méy-chū-'shēngr. ‖I can't **bear to see them leave.** wǒ bù-'rěn-de kàn tā-men 'dzǒw. ‖I can't **bear it any more.** wǒ 'dzày yě shèw-bu-'lyǎw-le. *or* wǒ 'dzày yě rěn-bu-'jù-le. ‖I can't **bear his attitude any more.** tā-de-'tày-du jyàw-wo 'dzày yě rěn-bu-'jù-le.

   To bear responsibility fù-'dzé. ‖I had **to bear the responsibility for his mistake.** shr̀ 'tā-de-'tswèr, kě-shr 'wǒ děy fù-'dzé.

BEARD.   (*Any facial hair*) 'hú-dz. ‖It's **that man with a long beard!** nèy-ge-cháng-'hú-dz-de!

   To grow a beard (*naturally*) jǎng 'hú-dz; (*intentionally*) lyéw 'hú-dz. ‖He **grew a fuzzy beard in twenty days.** 'èr-shr-tyān-li tā ·'lyéw-le yì-'dzwěy-de-'hú-dz.

   Beard *of a goat is also* 'hú-dz.

   In the literary language rán *means hair growing from cheeks and jaw,* shywū *means a short beard from*

the chin, hú *refers to hair on the chin just below the lower lip, and* tsž *means hair on the upper lip. Some colloquial expressions borrowed from the literary language use these words.* **A man with a beautiful beard** měy-rán-'gūng.
See also MUSTACHE.

BEARING. (*Direction*) 'fāng-shyàng; (*to prevent friction*) jéw-'chéng.

BEAST. yě-'shèw.

BEAT. (*Of music*) 'pāy-dz. ‖**The beat of the music wasn't clear.** yīn-'ywè-de-'pāy-dz bù-'chīng-chu.
(*Of a drum*) gǔ-'dyǎr. ‖**Follow the drumbeats.** gēn-je gǔ-'dyǎr.
(*Of a policeman*) dwàn, dwàr. ‖**What policeman is on this beat?** 'něy-ge-shywún-'jǐng °gwǎn jèy-'dwàr? *or* °'lwén-daw jèy-'dwàr-le? ‖**O'Connor makes this beat at night.** 'jèy-yí-dwàr 'yè-li gwēy lǎw-'kɔng 'gwǎn.
To beat dǎ. (*With a stick*) chyāw, 'chyāw-dǎ; (*with a whip*) chēw; (*with a flat surface, such as the palm of the hand*) gwǎy, pǎy, 'gwǎy-dǎ, 'pǎy-dǎ. ‖**Please beat this carpet.** chǐng bǎ jèy-ge-dì-'tǎn °'dǎ-yi-dǎ. *or* °'chyāw-yi-chyāw. *or* °'chyāw-da-chyāw-da. *or* °'gwǎy-da-gwǎy-da. *or* °'pǎy-da-pǎy-da. ‖**Beat the egg before putting it in.** 'shyān bǎ jī-'dzěr 'dǎ-le, 'dzày 'fàng-jìn-chywu.
To beat time dǎ 'pāy-dz. ‖**He beat time with his foot.** tā yùng-'jyǎw dǎ 'pāy-dz.
To beat a drum dǎ-'gǔ, chyāw-'gǔ. ‖**He sure can beat that drum.** tā dǎ-'gǔ dǎ-de jēn 'hǎw.
(*Of the heart*) tyàw. ‖**His heart was beating regularly.** tā 'shīn 'tyàw-de hěn 'ywún.
(*To win*) yíng; **be beaten** *meaning* lose shū; **be beaten by** 'shū-gěy. ‖**Who beat who?** shwéy 'yíng-le? *or* shwéy 'shū-le? ‖**He beat me at a game of chess.** tā 'yíng-le wo yì-pán-'chí. *or* wǒ 'shū-gey ta yì-pán-'chí.
To beat back, beat off bǎ … dǎ-'dzěw *or* dǎ-'pǎw *or* dǎ-'twèy. ‖**He beat off the dogs with a stick.** tā yùng 'gwèn-dz bǎ-'gěw dǎ-'pǎw-le. *or* 'gěw jyàw-ta yùng 'gwèn-dz gěy dǎ-'pǎw-lè. ‖**Has the enemy been beaten back yet?** 'dí-rén bèy dǎ-'twèy-le-ma?
To beat up dǎ yí-'dwèn; **get beaten up, get a beating** 'āy yí-'dwèn-'dǎ. ‖**They beat him up.** tām bǎ-ta 'dǎ-le yí-'dwèn. ‖**He was beaten up by a gang of hoodlums.** tā jyàw yì-chywún-'gwāng-gwen gěy 'dǎ-le yí-'dwèn. ‖**He got beat up.** tā 'āy-le yí-dwèn-'dǎ.

BEAUTIFUL. hǎw; (*a bit literary*) měy. ‖**What a beautiful day!** 'tyār dwō 'hǎw-wa! ‖**The scenery there is quite beautiful.** nèr-de-'jǐng-jř hěn 'hǎw. ‖**The scenery is very beautiful.** 'jǐng-jř hěn 'měy.
(*To the eye*) hǎw-'kàn. ‖**This picture is very beautiful.** jèy-jāng-'hwàr 'hwà-de hěn hǎw-'kàn. ‖**His wife is a beautiful woman.** tā-'tày-tay hěn hǎw-'kàn.

(*To the ear*) hǎw-'tīng. ‖**She has a beautiful voice.** tā chàng-'gēer chàng-de hěn hǎw-'tīng.
(*Of a person*) jǎng-de 'hǎw, 'pyàw-lyàng. ‖**His wife is a beautiful woman.** tā-'tày-tay 'jǎng-de hěn 'hǎw. *or* tā-'tày-tay hěn 'pyàw-lyàng.

BECAUSE. yīn-wèy. ‖**He didn't come because he got sick.** tā yīn-wey 'bìng-le méy-'láy. ‖**I didn't buy it because of the high price.** yīn-wey 'jyà-chyan tày 'dà wǒ méy-'mǎy.
Expressed with **therefore** swó-yi *introducing the result.* ‖**He didn't come because he was sick.** tā 'bìng-le, swó-yi méy-'láy.
Because of this (that, it) yīn-'tsž. ‖**He treats people so thoughtfully; I like him all the more because of that.** tā 'dày-rén hěn jēw-'dàw, wǒ yīn-'tsž 'gèng 'shǐ-hwān ta.

BECOME. chéng; 'byàn-chéng. ‖**He became famous overnight.** tā 'mǎ-shàng jyèw 'chéng-le 'míng-le. *or* (*Literary*) tā 'yì-'jywǔ chéng-'míng'-le. ‖**What is to become of her?** tā 'hèw-lay bù-'jř-dàw hwèy 'byàn-chéng 'shéme-yàng-de-rén. ‖**She's borrowed it so many times that it's become hers.** tā 'jyè-gwò jǐ-'tsž, jyèw 'byàn-chéng 'tā-de-le (*sarcastic*).
(*Changing to a higher status*) 'chéng, 'dāng-shang, 'shēng-dàw, 'dzwò. ‖**He became a major general at only twenty-nine.** tā èr-shr-'jyěw-swèy jyèw 'chéng-le (*or* 'dzwò-le *or any of the other expressions*) shàw-'jyàng-le.
(*To reach an age*) dàw. ‖**When he became twenty-one he left home.** dàw-le èr-shr-'yí-swèy tā jyèw 'lí-kay 'jyā-le.
Becoming to wèy … hǎw-'kàn, wèy … 'pyàw-lyàng. ‖**That color is very becoming to you.** jèy-ge-'yán-sè wèy-ni hěn hǎw-'kàn. ‖**The red dress becomes her.** 'húng-yī-shang wèy-ta tè-'byé 'pyàw-lyàng.
Often not expressed with a separate Chinese word, as in the following: ‖**The secret has gradually become known.** jèy-ge-'bì-mì jyàn-'jyàn-de gěy-'rén 'jř-dàw-le. ‖**This invention will become more and more important as time goes on.** jèy-ge-fā-'míng yǐ-'hèw ywè-'láy ywè 'jùng-yàw. ‖**What became of them?** tām 'hèw-lay dzěme-'yàng-le? ‖**What's become of the original plan?** 'ywán-lày-de-'jì-hwà shyàn-'dzày dzěme-'yàng-le?

BED. chwáng. ‖**I want a room with two beds.** wǒ yàw yì-jyān-yěw-'lyǎng-ge-'chwáng-de-'wū-dz. ‖**When I came in he was lying in bed.** wǒ 'jìn-lay de-shŕ-hew tā 'tǎng-dzay 'chwáng-shang.
To make a bed pū(-shàng) 'chwáng. ‖**My bed hasn't been made.** wǒ-de-'chwáng méy-'pū. ‖**Please make my bed.** chǐng bǎ wǒ-de-'chwáng 'pū-shang.
To go to bed 'tǎng-shyà, shàng-'chwáng, dǎw-shyà, dzwān bèy-'wōer, 'shwèy(-le). ‖**He's already gone to bed.** tā 'yǐ-jing 'tǎng-shyà-le (*or using any of the other expressions*).

Bedclothes (*sheets or bedspread*) 'chwáng-'dān-dz. To change a bed hwàn chwáng-'dān-dz. ‖When was this bed last changed? jèy-ge-chwáng-'dān-dz shǐ 'shéme-shŕ-hew 'hwàn-de?

Bedroom wò-'shŕ. ‖Let's make this the bedroom! 'jèy-jyān dzwò 'wò-shŕ-ba!

Flower bed hwār-'tán, hwār-'táy. ‖The chrysanthemums in the flower bed are blooming. hwār-'táy-shang-de-'jywú-hwār 'kāy-le.

River bed hé-'dàw. ‖Follow the old river bed for two miles. shwèn-je jyèw-hé-'dàw dzěw èr-lǐ-'dì.

(*Base, foundation*) táy, dzwèr. ‖The machine is set in a bed of concrete. 'jī-chi 'ān-dzay 'shwěy-ní-'táy-shang.

BEDBUG. 'chèw-chung.

BEDDING. 'pū-gav, 'bèy-rù.

BEDROOM. wò-'shŕ, chǐn-'shŕ.

BEE. Honeybee mì-'fēng; bumblebee dà-'fēng *or* yě-'fēng.

Beehive mì-fēng-'wō, fēng-'wō.

To make a beeline. ‖He made a beeline for home. tā yì-'jŕ 'gǎn-hwéy 'jyā chywù-le.

BEECH. (*Tree*) 'jywú-shù; (*wood*) jywǔ-'mù.

BEEF. nyéw-'rèw. ‖This piece of beef is tough. jèy-kwày-nyéw-'rèw °yěw dyǎr-'lǎv. *or* °wǒ jyáw-bu-'dùng. ‖I'll take the roast beef. wǒ chŕ kǎw-nyéw-'rèw. ‖The market has fresh beef today. 'jīn-tyan 'shŕ-shàng yěw 'shyān-nyéw-'rèw.

To beef. ‖What're you beefing about? nǐ 'bàw-ywan shéme?

BEEFSTEAK. nyéw-'páy.

BEEHIVE. (mì-)fēng-'wō.

BEER. 'pí-jyěw.

BEET. tyán-'tsày, dž-'lwó-ba.

BEFORE. (*In front of a person*) dzày (*or* dàw) ... 'myàn-chyan. ‖He was taken before the judge. tā bèy 'dày-daw shěn-pàn-'gwān-myàn-chyan.

(*In front of a thing*) (dzày) ... °'chyán-byan *or* °'chyán-byar *or* °'chyán-tew. ‖Who's standing before that tree? 'shéy dzày 'shù-chyán-tew 'jàn-je? *or* 'shù-chyán-tew-'jàn-je-de shŕ-'shéy?

(*Figuratively*) 'mù-chyán, dāng-'chyán. ‖The question before us is a hard one. 'mù-chyán-de-'wèn-tí hěn nán 'bàn.

(*In time*) yǐ-'chyán; bú-dàw ... (jyèw); *or expressed in terms of* early dzěw. ‖Come before two.

'lyǎng-dyǎn-yǐ-'chyán 'láy. ‖I'd never been there before. wǒ yǐ-'chyán méy-'dàw-gwo nèr. ‖I'll telephone you before I start. wǒ méy-'dzěw yǐ-'chyán shyān gěy-ni dǎ dyàn-'hwà. ‖Before that she lived alone. dzày 'nèy-ge-yǐ-'chyán tā-'dž-jǐ gwò-'r̀-dz. ‖We should have done this before. wǒm 'dzǎw jyèw gāy bǎ 'jèy-ge dzwò-'hǎw-le. ‖We should have done it this way before. wǒm 'dzǎw jyèw gāy 'jème bàn. ‖We should have gone long before this. wǒm 'yīng-dang 'dzǎw jyèw 'lí-kay jèr. ‖The telegram should come before evening. dyàn-'bàw yīng-dang bú-dàw 'wǎn-shang jyèw-'láy.

Before long kwày, bù-jyěw jyèw, yì-hwěr jyèw. ‖They'll come before long. tām 'kwày 'láy-le.

When **before** *indicates a time prior to which something does not or cannot happen, the Chinese has* tsáy, *or* háy ... jyèw. ‖It was past midnight before he came in. 'shyà-bàn-yè tā 'tsáy 'jìn-lay-de. ‖They hadn't been married a month before they quarreled. tām jyē-'hwēn háy 'bú-dàw yí-ge-'ywè jyèw fǎn-'mù-le. ‖I can't leave before I finish this. *is expressed as* While I haven't finished this I can't leave. wǒ méy-bàn-'wán de-shŕ-hew bù-néng 'dzěw-kay.

When **before** *indicates a time prior to which something does happen, Chinese often has* (háy) méy-...jyèw, *or* (háy) méy-...-de. He left before he'd even eaten breakfast. tā (háy) méy-chŕ dzǎw-'fàn jyèw 'dzěw-le. *or* tā lyán dzǎw-'fàn dēw méy-'chŕ jyèw 'dzěw-le. ‖He left before breakfast. tā méy-chŕ dzǎw-'fàn 'dzěw-de.

(*First, earlier*), shyān. ‖Business before pleasure. 'shyān gàn-'shŕ, 'hèw 'wár. ‖Do this before anything else. 'shyān bǎ 'jèy-ge 'dzwò-le.

Before Christ ('shī-lì-)jì-ywán-'chyán; (*among Chinese Christians*) 'jǔ-chyán. ‖This temple was built in the first century B.C. jèy-dzwò-'myàw shŕ ('shī-lì-)jì-ywán-'chyán 'yí-shŕ-'jì 'gày-de. ‖Confucius was born in 551 B.C. 'kǔng-dž 'shēng-dzay 'shī-lì-jì-ywán-'chyán 'wǔ-'wǔ-'yī-nyán.

BEG. To beg *someone* to chyěw. ‖They begged us to help them. tām 'chyěw wǒ-men 'bāng tā-men.

To beg for yàw. ‖The children begged for pennies. (*In one's own home*) shyǎw-'hár yàw-'chyán. (*In the streets, of beggar children*) shyǎw-'hár yàw shyǎw-'chyár. ‖The man came to the door to beg for food. tā dàw mén-'kěwr láy yàw-'fàn. *Except in the situations just given,* yàw *means* beg *only if an expression for* beggar *is used in the sentence.*

To beg for alms hwà-'ywán. ‖That monk comes once a month begging from door to door. nèy-ge-'hé-shang měy-ywè láy yí-'tsž āy-'mér hwà-'ywán.

To beg *someone* to stay wǎn-'lyéw (*especially in the sense of not leaving a job*). ‖We begged him to stay on. wǒ-men wǎn-'lyéw ta láy-je.

‖I beg your pardon. (*For a social error*) dwèy-bu-'chǐ. *or* dwèy-bu-'jù. (*For a misunderstood remark, requesting repetition*) chǐng(-ni) 'dzày shwō.

Beggar yàw-'fàn-de, jyàw-'hwā-dz, 'hwā-dz; (*literary*) chǐ-'gày.

BEGIN. Begin (to) 'chǐ-shř, 'kǎy-shř. ‖Haven't you begun yet? nǐ 'háy méy-'chǐ-shř-ma? ‖We must begin work right away. wǒm děy lì-'shř 'kǎy²shř 'gūng-dzwo. ‖This building was begun many years ago. jèy-ge-'jyàn-ju hǎw-dwō-'nyán-yǐ-'chyán jyèw kāy-shř 'dzàw-le.

Begin to . . . -chǐ . . .-láy (*postverb after main verb, and* láy *final*). ‖Right away they began to fight. tǎm jyèw dǎ-chi 'jàng-lay-le.

(*Of a performance*) kāy-'yǎn. ‖The performance begins at 8:30 P.M. 'wǎn-shang-'bā-dyǎn-'sān-shř kāy-'yǎn.

Begin at *or* with tsúng . . . 'chǐ. ‖Begin at the second chapter. tsúng dì-'èr-jāng 'chǐ.

Not begin to yì-'dyǎr dēw (*or* yě) bū-. ‖The supply doesn't begin to meet our requirements. hwò-'láy-de yì-'dyǎr dēw bú-'gèw.

From the beginning kāy-'téw, tsúng 'chǐ-téwr; from beginning to end tsúng-'téwr dàw-'lyǎwr *or* tsúng-'téw dàw-'wěy. ‖He's been wrong right from the beginning. tā tsúng 'chǐ-téwr jyèw 'tswò-le. ‖He was in charge of the job from beginning to end. tā tsúng-'téwr dàw-'lyǎwr 'gwǎn jèy-jyàn-'shř.

To begin with dì-'yī. ‖To begin with, he's too old. dì-'yī, tā tày 'lǎw.

‖Let's begin with the soup. 'shyān shàng-'tāng.

‖It's beginning to rain. dyàw-'dyǎr-le.

BEHIND. (dzày) . . . 'hèw-myan, 'hèw-byan, 'hèw-byar, 'hèw-tew. ‖The car is parked behind the house. 'chē 'tíng-dzay 'fáng-dz-de-'hèw-byar. ‖Their seats are behind ours. 'tǎ-men-de-'dzwò-wèy dzày wǒ-men-de-'hèw-myan.

Be behind time *or* behind schedule wù-'dyǎn. ‖The train is behind time. hwò-'chē wù-'dyǎn-le.

Behind *in many verb groups is expressed with* shyà *as postverb*; leave behind 'rēng-shyà, 'dyēw-shyà, (*intentionally*) 'lyéw-shyà; fall behind *or* leave behind 'là-shyà. ‖We had to leave our trunk behind. wǒm děy bǎ 'shyāng-dz 'rēng-shyà. ‖He left his home behind him. (*Escaped in spirit as well as physically*) tā 'dyēw-shya 'jyā jyèw 'dzěw-le. ‖He's fallen behind in his work. tā-'gūng-dzwo 'là-shya-le bù-'shǎw. ‖Have you left anything behind? nǐ 'là-shya-le shéme-'dūng-shi méy-yew?

Be behind (*in the sense of supporting, backing*) 'jř-shr. ‖There must be some plan behind it. jèy-jyàn-'shř yí-'dìng yěw-'rén 'jř-shr. ‖He has tremendously powerful groups behind him. jèy-ge-'rén 'láy-téw dà-de 'hěn.

Be behind (*in the sense of scheming*). ‖Someone must be behind this. 'hèw-byar yí-'dìng yěw-'rén. ‖Who's

behind this? jèy-jyàn-'shř shř-'shwéy dzày 'hèw-táy 'tsāw-dzùng-de?

BELIEVE. Believe (in) (*with firm conviction*) shìn. ‖Do you believe what he told us? nǐ 'shìn tā-'gàw-sung-wǒ-men-de-ma? *or* tā-'shwō-de nǐ 'shìn-na? ‖I don't believe he did it. wǒ bú-'shìn jèy shř 'tā-dzwò-de. ‖Do you believe in God? (*Catholic*) nǐ shìn tyān-'jǔ-ma? (*Protestant*) nǐ shìn shàng-'dì-ma? What religion do you believe in? nǐ shìn shéme-'jyàw?

(*Sincerely but not religiously*) shìn-li 'shyǎng. ‖I personally believe that what he said is right. wǒ 'shìn-li 'shyǎng tā-'shwō-de 'dwèy.

(*Think, suppose*) 'jywé-de, shyǎng. ‖Do you believe he's sincere? nǐ 'jywé-de tā 'chéng-shr-ma? ‖I believe he's gone. wǒ shyǎng tā 'dzěw-le. ‖I believe you're mistaken. wǒ shyǎng nǐ 'tswò-le.

The indefinite answer I believe not *depends on the question. Thus* ‖(Has he gone?) I believe not. 'méy-yew-ba. *or* 'háy méy-'dzěw-ba. ‖(Did he do it?) I don't believe so. bú-shr 'tā-ba. ‖(Did that really happen?) I believe not. bú-'hwèy-ba. *or* méy-yew 'nème-hwéy-'shř-ba. ‖(Is that yours?) I believe not. 'dà-gày 'bú-shr. *or* wǒ shyǎng 'bú-shr.

Make-believe jyǎ-'jwāng. ‖It's just make-believe. 'bú-gwò shř jyǎ-'jwāng-je.

BELL. (*Large*) jūng; (*small*) líng, lyéngr, 'líng-dang. ‖That bell is cracked. nèy-kěw-'jūng 'lyè-le. ‖This bell won't ring. jèy-ge-'líng-dang bù-'shyǎng le. ‖You can see the bells in the tower. nǐ ké-yi 'kàn-jyan 'tǎ-shang-de-'jūng.

Doorbell mén-'lyéngr; (*electric*) dyàn-'líng. ‖The doorbell is ringing. mén-'lyéngr 'shyǎng le.

To ring a bell (*by striking*) dǎ-'líng, dǎ-'jūng; (*by moving with the hand*) yáw-'líng; (*by pulling a bell-cord*) lā-'líng, lā-'lyéngr, lā-'jūng; (*by pushing a button*) èn-'lyéngr. ‖Has the bell rung yet? 'jūng 'dǎ-gwo-le-ma? *or* dǎ-gwo 'jūng-le-ma? *or* dǎ-gwo 'líng-le-ma? *or* yáw-gwo 'líng-le-ma? ‖On shipboard time is marked by (ringing) a bell every half hour. dzày 'chwán-shang měy-'bàn-dyǎn-jūng 'dǎ yì-hwéy-'jūng. ‖The bell rings half an hour before services. dzày dzwò-lǐ-'bày-yǐ-'chyán-'bàn-dyǎn-jūng dǎ-'jūng.

Bell tower jūng-'léw(r).

BELLIGERENT. (*Country participating in a war*) jyāw-jàn-'gwó.

BELLOWS. (*For producing a stream of air*) 'fēng-shyāng.

BELLY. 'dù-dz.

BELONG. Belong to (*be a member of*) dzày. ‖He belongs to the Nationalist Party. tā dzày gwó-mín-'dǎng.

Belong to (*be the property of or under the control of*) shǔ. ‖That island belongs to China. nèy-ge-'dǎw shǔ 'jūng-gwo.

Belong to *or* **in** *a place* (*be property of or customarily be kept at*) shr̀ . . .-de. ‖Does this book belong to you? jèy-běn-'shū shr̀ 'nǐ-de-ma? ‖Who does this belong to? jèy shr̀ 'shéy-de? ‖This old chair belongs in the kitchen. jèy-bǎ-'pwò-'yǐ-dz shr̀ chú-'fáng-li-de.

Belong (*be properly or comfortably at a place*). ‖I don't belong here. *is expressed as* I don't fit in. wǒ dzày-'jèr bù-hé-'shr̀. *or as* I'm an outsider. dzày-'jèr wǒ shr̀ 'wày-rén. *or as* I'm looked on as an outsider. tā-men-jèr ná-wo dàng 'wày-rén 'kàn. ‖This flower vase doesn't belong here. *is expressed as* This flower vase shouldn't be put here. jèy-ge-hwā-'pyéngr bù-'gāy fàng-'jèr. ‖This book belongs on that shelf. *is expressed as* This book should be put on that shelf jèy-běn-'shū gāy 'gē-dzày 'nèy-tséng-'jyàr-shang.

BELOW. 'shyà-byan, 'shyà-byar, 'shyà-myan, 'shya-myar, 'dǐ-shyà. ‖From the window they could watch the children below. yéw 'chwāng-hu tā̲m kàn-de-'jyàn shyà-byan-de-'háy-dz. ‖Try the floor below. 'shr̀-shr 'shyà-myan-'nèy-tséng-léw. ‖Watch out below! 'shyà-myar ̣yéw-'shén! ‖Who has the room below me? 'shéy ̣ju wǒ-'dǐ-shya? *or* wǒ-'dǐ-shyà-nèy-jyān-'wūr 'shwéy 'jù? *or* dzày wǒ-'dǐ-shyà-nèy-jyān-'wūr-'jù-de shr̀ 'shéy?

(*On a page or graduated scale*) yǐ-'shyà. ‖The temperature here seldom gets below zero. jèr-de-'tyān-chi hěn 'shǎw lěng-daw líng-'dù-yǐ-'shyà. ‖What he said is given below. *meaning* From here on I'm quoting his words. yǐ-'shyà shr̀ 'tā-shwō-de.

Be given below rú-'shyà (*literary*). ‖The chart is given below. byǎw-'gé rú-'shyà. *In a Chinese text, running from top to bottom and from right to left, the equivalent phrase is* The chart is given to the left. byǎw-'gé rú-'dzwǒ.

Be below (*in rank*) ('jyē-jí) 'dī. ‖A colonel is below a brigadier in rank. shàng-'shyàw bǐ shàw-'jyàng ('jyē-jí) 'dī.

Below deck dzày 'tsāng-li. ‖He works below deck. tā dzày 'tsāng-li dzwò-'gūng.

(*In height*). ‖He's below average height. tā bǐ yī-'bān-rén 'ǎy.

BELT. 'dày-dz, 'dàr; (*at the waist*) yāw-'dày; (*for trousers*) kù-'dày *or* kù-yāw-'dày; (*of leather, for any use*) pí-'dày; (*for a machine*) pí-'dày, lwén-'dày; life belt jyèw-shēng-'dày; fan belt shàn-'dày; (*for a skirt*) chywún-'dày. ‖Do you wear a belt or suspenders? nǐ jì yāw-'dày háy-shr jì bēy-'dày? ‖Put your belt on. jì-shang yāw-'dày. ‖We need a new belt for this machine. jèy-jyà-'jī-chi děy-yàw yì-tyáw-'shīn-de-lwén-'dày.

To tighten one's belt. ‖All you can do is tighten your belt a bit. nǐ jǐ 'hǎw 'shěng-yi-dyǎr 'gwò.

Belt of trees yí-dày-shù-'lín-dz. ‖This is the cotton belt. ' jèy-yí-dày(-'dì-fang) chū 'myán-hwa.

BENCH. (cháng-)bǎn-'dèng, (cháng-)'dèng-dz.

BEND. wān. ‖He fastened the papers together with a bent pin. tā yùng wān-le-de-'jēn bǎ-'jǐ dēw 'byé-chi-lay-le. ‖These nails are bent too much. jèy-shyē-'dīng-dz yěw dyǎr-tày-'wān-le. ‖You've bent this too much. nǐ bǎ 'jèy-ge 'wān-de tày 'lì-hày-le.

To bend *something* **into** 'wān-chéng. ‖Bend this wire into a circle. bǎ jèy-tyáw-dyàn-'shyàṇ wān-cheng ge-'chywār. ‖He bent the rod into a hook. tā bǎ tyǒ-'tyáw ̇wān-cheng-le yí-ge-'gēwr.

To bend *something* **to a certain degree** 'wān-dàw. ‖How much will this rod bend without breaking? jèy-ge-'gwèn-dz néng wān-daw shéme-chéng-'dù háy bù-'shé?

To bend down wān-shyà 'yāw. ‖You'll have to bend down to get through here. nǐ děy wān-shīya 'yāw-lay tsáy néng tsúng-'jèr gwò-de-'chywù.

(*Of a person*) wān-'yāw(r), máw-'yāw. ‖He's bent with age. tā 'lǎw-de °dēw máw-le 'yāw-le. (*or* °dēw wān-le 'yāw-le). ‖He walks bent over. tā wān-je 'yāwr 'dzěw.

(*Submit*) 'chywū-fú. ‖He won't bend a bit under any pressure. dzěme-yàng 'bǐ-ta, tā 'yě bù-'chywū-fú.

A bend wār. ‖Follow the bend of the river. shwèn-je hé-de-'wār 'dzěw. ‖That house is beyond the bend in the road. ʻnèy-swǒ-'fáng-dz-a, shwèn-je 'lù, gwǎy-le 'wār jyèw 'dàw-le.

BENEATH. (dzày) . . . 'dǐ-shyà. ‖He was buried beneath the tree. tā shr̀ 'máy-dzày shù-'dǐ-shya-le.

Be beneath (*in the social scale*) bǐ . . . 'dī. ‖She is far beneath him. tā-de-'jyā-shr̀ bǐ-chi 'tā-lay dī-de 'dwǒ. *or* tā bǐ-'tā 'jyā-shr̀ hán-'wēy (*literary*).

To consider *someone* **as beneath one** shyǎw 'kàn. ‖Don't look on these people as beneath you. byé shyǎw 'kàn jèy-shyē-'rén.

Be beneath one's notice. ‖That remark is beneath our notice. 'nèy-jǔng-hwà bù-'jŕ-de °yì-'tīng. *or* °yí-'kàn. *or* °yí-'mà. *or* 'nèy-jǔng-hwà bù-'jŕ yí-'gù (*literary*).

Be beneath one's dignity. ‖It's beneath his dignity to say something like that. tā shwō 'nèy-yàngr-de-'hwà °yěw-shr̀ 'dzwēn-yán. *or* °yěw-shr̀ 'shēn-fèn. *Both of the foregoing are literary phrases often quoted.*

BENEFIT. 'hǎw-chù; lì (*literary*). ‖The new law gives us very little benefit. jèy-ge-'shīn-de-fǎ-'lywù wèy wǒ-men yì-dyǎr-'hǎw-chù yě 'méy-yew. ‖We don't get any benefit out of it. wǒm yi-dyǎr-'lì yě dé-bu-'jáw.

To benefit ywú . . . yěw-'lì. ‖Who benefits by it? ywú-'shwéy yěw-'lì-ne? ‖Whom does that law benefit? nèy-tyáw-fǎ-'lywù ywú-'shwéy yěw-'lì-ne?

369

To benefit *is also expressed as* **To have good result** yĕw-'shyàw. ‖**We benefited from the medicine.** jèy-ge-'yàw wǒm 'chř-le hěn yĕw-'shyàw.

Benefit. (*Performance of a play*) yì-wu-'shì; (*party, variety show given to raise funds*) mù-'jywān-yéw-yì-'hwèy; (*dance to raise funds*) mù-'jywān-tyàw-wǔ-'hwèy.

BENT. 'tyān-tsáy. ‖**He has a bent for art.** tā yĕw 'yì-shu-'tyān-tsáy.

Be bent on yí-'dìng yàw, jř 'shyǎng, yí-ge-'jyèr-de 'shyǎng. ‖**In spite of everything he is bent on going.** wú-lwèn-rú-'hé tā yí-'dìng yàw 'chywù. ‖**He's bent on making money.** tā jř 'shyǎng jwàn-'chyán.

See also **BEND.**

BERTH. (*Sleeping place*) wò-'pù; (*for a ship*) dìng-bwò-'chù *or* dìng-bwó-'chù.

BESIDE. (*By the side of a person*) dzày ... 'shēn-byǎr. ‖**The boy stood beside his mother.** shyǎw-nán-'hár jàn-dzay tā-'mǔ-chin-'shēn-byǎr.

(*By the side of a thing*) dzày ... 'páng-byǎr. ‖**The boy stood beside the table.** shyǎw-nán-'hár jàn-dzay 'jwō-dz-'páng-byǎr.

Beside and leaning on kàw-je. ‖**Please put the trunk beside the bureau.** bǎ jèy-ge-'shyāng-dz kàw-je yī-'gwèy 'fàng.

Be beside the point. ‖**That's beside the point.** 'jèy bú-shř jèng-'tí. *or* 'jèy shr 'lìng-yí-jyan-'shèr. *or* 'jèy wèy-'myǎn lí-le 'tí-le. ‖**His answer was beside the point.** tā-swǒ-'dá fēy swǒ-'wèn (*literary*).

Be beside oneself. ‖**He's beside himself with anger.** tā 'chì-de 'lì-hày. *or* tā 'chì-de 'lyǎn-sè dēw 'byàn-le. *or* tā 'chì-de dēw gǎy-le 'yàngr-le. ‖**He's beside himself with joy.** tā 'lè-de (*or* 'lwò-de) 'wǎng-chí swó-'yǐ-le. *or* tā 'lè-de (*or* 'lwò-de) fā-'kwáng.

BESIDES. (chú-le) ... yǐ-'wày; chú-le ... lìng-'wày. ‖**Others must help besides me.** chú-le 'wǒ yǐ-'wày 'byé-rén yě děy bāng-'máng. ‖**We need these and more besides.** jèy-shyē-yǐ-'wày wǒm 'háy 'yàw-dyǎr. *or* chú-le 'jèy-shyēer lìng-'wày háy děy-'yàw.

Besides (this) tsž-'wày ... háy, lìng-'wày háy. ‖**What do you have besides this?** tsž-'wày nǐ 'háy yěw 'shéme? ‖**What do you want besides this?** nǐ lìng-'wày 'háy yàw 'shéme?

(*Replacing*) lìng. ‖**I hate the work; you'll have to get someone besides me.** wǒ bù-'shǐ-hwān jèy-'shř; nǐ 'lìng 'jǎw-rén-ba.

(*Moreover*) ér-chyè 'yě, 'dzày jyā-shang, yèw. ‖**I'm not feeling well; besides, I haven't time.** wǒ bú-'dà 'shū-fu; ér-chyè 'yě méy-yew 'gūng-fu.

BEST. dzwèy 'hǎw, dǐng 'hǎw (*etc., with other words like* dzwèy). ‖**I work best in the morning.** wǒ 'dzǎw-chen dzwò 'shř-ching (dzwò-de) dzwèy 'hǎw. ‖**The**

best work was done by the young men. dzwèy-'hǎw-de-'gūng-dzwò dēw-shř nyán-'chīng-de-rén-'dzwò-de.

(*Top grade*) (dzwèy-)shàng-'děng(-de). ‖**We want only the best.** wǒm jyèw yàw (dzwèy-)shàng-'děng-de.

At best dzwèy 'hǎw yě bú-'gwò. ‖**At best he's a dirty politician.** tā dzwèy 'hǎw yě bú-'gwò shř ge-fǔ-'bày-de-jèng-'kè.

Be at one's best dzwèy dé-'yì. ‖**He's at his best when he plays baseball.** tā dǎ 'bèng-chyéw dzwèy dé-'yì.

(*As well as possible*) hǎw-'hāw(r)-de. ‖**Do your best.** hǎw-'hāwr-de 'gàn. ‖**We have few supplies, but we must make the best of what we have.** wǒ-men-de 'gùng-jǐ 'shǎw-le, děy jyèw 'shyàn-yěw-de hǎw-'hāwr-de 'yùng. ‖**We must make the best of the situation.** dà-'jyā děy hǎw-'hāwr-de gàn tsáy 'shíng.

To do one's best for. ‖**I'll do my best for you.** wǒ jyé-'lì (*or* jìn-'lì) gěy-ni 'bàn-yi-bàn.

To get the best of pyàn, (dwō) 'jàn-le ... de 'pyán-yi. ‖**We must be careful that he doesn't get the best of us.** wǒm děy 'shyǎw-shīn-dyǎr, °byé 'ràng-ta 'pyàn-le. *or* °byé 'ràng-ta dwō 'jàn dzǎm-de 'pyán-yi.

To make the best of. ‖**Make the best of the time you have.** jyé-'lì 'lì-yùng shŕ-'jyān.

Best man (*at a wedding*) bàn-'láng.

The best part of one's life jèng-dāng-'nyán-de-shŕ-hew.

Other English expressions. ‖**Let's hope for the best.** bú-'bì tày bēy-'gwān. ‖**Is that the best you can do?** nǐ jyèw hwèy 'jè-ge-ma? *or* jř ywú-'tsž-le-ma? ‖**That's the best he can do.** tā-néng-'dzwò-de yě jyèw jř ywú-'tsž-le. ‖**Show me your best.** nǐ 'háy hwèy shéme?

BETTER. bǐ ... 'hǎw; háy 'hǎw; hǎw-de 'dwō; 'hǎw-dyǎr(-de). ‖**I can't do better than this.** wǒ-'dzwò-de dzày bù-néng bǐ 'jèy-ge 'hǎw-le. ‖**Show me a better way.** nǐ yěw bǐ-'jèy-ge-háy-'hǎw-de-'fá-dz-ma? ‖**They did much better after they'd had some experience.** tām yěw-le jīng-'yàn yǐ-'hèw dzwò-de 'hǎw-de 'dwō-le. ‖**We'll be better off if we move.** wǒm 'lí-kay jèr yí-'dìng hǎw-de 'dwō. ‖**I felt much better this morning.** jīn-tyan-'dzǎw-chen wǒ 'jywé-de hǎw-de 'dwō-le. **I want a better room than this.** wǒ yàw yì-jyān-'hǎw-dyǎr-de-'wū-dz. ‖**Is this any better?** (*Thing*) 'jèy-ge 'hǎw-dyǎr-ma? (*Way*) 'jème-je 'hǎw-dyǎr-ma?

The ... the better ywè ... ywè 'hǎw; **better and better** ywè 'lǎy ywè 'hǎw. ‖**The sooner you go there the better it will be.** nǐ ywè 'dzǎw 'chywù ywè 'hǎw.

(*Of a sick person*) jyàn-'hǎw. ‖**The doctor says he's (getting) better.** 'dày-fu shwō tā jyàn-'hǎw.

To get the better of 'chī-fu, jàn ... de 'pyán-yi. ‖**He'll try to get the better of you.** tā shyǎng-'yàw 'chī-fu ni. *or* tā shyǎng-'yàw jàn nǐ-de 'pyán-yi.

Imperial Palace, Beijing

Jade Buddha Temple, Shanghai

The better part of dwō-'bàn. ‖It took him the better part of a month to do it. tā 'dzwò-le dwō-'bàn-ge-'ywè tsáy dzwò-'hǎw-de.

To know better. ‖You should know better than to do anything like that. nǐ bù-'gāy dzwò-chu 'jèy-yèngr-de-'shèr-lay.

(Had) better gāy, 'yīng-gay. ‖I('d) better go. wǒ gāy 'dzěw. ‖I('d) better go now. wǒ gāy 'dzěw-le. But ‖Better not suggest it. 'jèy-ge-shr̀ yǐ bù-'tí wéy-'myàw.

BETWEEN. Between X and Y X (gēn, hé, or túng) Y jr̄-'jyān. ‖There aren't any large cities between Los Angeles and San Francisco. lwò-shān-'jī sān-fán-'shr̀ jr̄-'jyān méy-yew 'dà-chéng.

(The) Z between X and Y X (gēn, hé, or túng) Y jr̄-'jyān-de Z. ‖The struggle between Germany and France has a long history. 'dé-gwo gēn 'fà-gwo jr̄-'jyān-de jìng-'jēng yěw hěn-'cháng-de-lì-'shr̀.

(Of time). Between X and Y X dàw Y jr̄-'jyān. ‖It happened between six and seven o'clock this morning. jin-tyan-'dzǎw-chen 'lyèw-dyan dàw 'chī-dyan jr̄-'jyān chū-de 'shr̀. ‖I'll meet you between six and seven. dzám lyèw-'chī-dyǎn-jūng 'jyàn.

(In) between jūng-'jyàr. ‖He lives five miles down the road and there are no houses (in) between. tā-'jù-de-dì-fangr lí-'jèr yěw 'wǔ-lǐ-'dì, jūng-'jyàr méy-yew 'byé-de-fáng-dz

Between (the two) ... 'lǐ-tew; jr̄-'jyān; dāng-'jūng. ‖You must choose between the two. nǐ 'yīng-dang 'lyǎng-ge-°lǐ-tew (or °jr̄-'jyān) tyāw 'yí-ge. ‖Between the two of them who would you choose? tām-'lyǎ-dāng-'jūng nǐ tyāw 'něy-ge?

Between them (us, you) meaning jointly tām- (or wǒm-, nǐm-) dà-jyā-'hwěr; meaning separate or divide bǐ-'tsz̄. ‖They killed six ducks between them. tām-dà-jyā-'hwěr 'dǎ-le 'lyèw-jr̄-yě-'yā-dz̄. ‖We mustn't let anything come between us. wǒm bǐ-'tsz̄ bù-'yīng-dang yěw rèn-hé-wù-'hwèy.

To choose between tyāw. ‖It was difficult to choose between the colors. nèy-shyē-'yán-sè hěn nán-'tyāw.

To divide between fēn, 'fēn-gey. ‖Shall we divide it between us? dzám-dà-'jyā bǎ 'jèy-ge 'fēn-le, 'hàw-bu-hǎw? ‖He divided his property between his two sons. tā bǎ tsáy-'chǎn 'fēn-gey lyǎng-ge-'ér-dz le.

To come between (cut off) 'jyé-jù. ‖We nearly caught up with him, but the traffic came between. wǒm 'chà-bu-dwō 'jwěy-shang ta-le, kě-shr̀ 'hèw-lay 'chē-shéme-de bǎ wǒ-men 'jyé-jù-le.

Other English expressions. ‖He's always eating between meals. tā 'lǎw chr̄ 'líng-shr̀. ‖This is just between you and me. 'jè-hwà yě 'jyèw-shr dzám-'lyǎrén 'shwō. or jè-ge "bù-'dzú wèy 'wày-rén 'dàw." ‖He found himself between two fires. tā-dz̄-'jǎw-de dzwò-'yèw wéy-'nán. ‖He can't distinguish between right and wrong. tā shr̀-'fēy bù-'míng. or tā-'jèy-ge-rén bù-

néng 'fēn-byàn shr̀-'fēy. ‖Between you two I think this can be done. yěw 'nǐ-men-lyǎ, wǒ shyǎng jèy-ge-'shèr bàn-de-'chéng. ‖There's no comparison between those two men. tā-men-'lyǎng-ge-rén 'dzěme néng "shyāng-'tí 'bìng-'lwèn"-ne?

BEYOND. dzày (or dàw) ... 'nèy-byan, 'nèy-byar. ‖The address you want is beyond the river. nǐ-jǎw-de-dì-fang shr̀ dzày 'hé-nèy-byar. ‖The ship has gone beyond the horizon. 'chwán yǐ-jing dzěw-daw shwěy-píng-'shyàn-'nèy-byan chywù-le.

(Having passed a point) gwò-le. ‖Are there any more streets beyond this one? gwò-le 'jèy-tyáw-jyē háy yěw 'jyē-ma? ‖There aren't any more inns beyond this village. gwò-le jèy-ge-'tswēr jyèw méy-yew kè-'dyàn-le.

Be beyond one's powers chū-le ... fàn-'wéy. ‖That's beyond my power now. 'nèy-ge yǐ-jing chū-le wǒ-de-néng-'lì-fàn-'wéy-le.

Beyond (us, here) 'chyán-myan(-de). ‖We looked to the mountains beyond. wǒm 'kàn 'chyán-myan-de-'shān. ‖There's nothing beyond. 'chyán-byar méy-yew 'dūng-shi-le.

(Forward) wàng-'chyán. ‖We can't go beyond this point. wǒm bù-néng 'dzày wàng-'chyán dzěw-le.

Be beyond help méy-'jyèw. ‖When we arrived he was beyond help. děng-daw wǒm 'dàw-le de-shr̀-hew tā 'yǐ-jing méy-'jyèw-le.

Beyond one's reach. ‖That's beyond my reach. (Literally) 'nèy-ge wǒ gèw-bu-jǎw' (or gèw-bu-'dàw). (Figuratively, in the sense of not being qualified for something) wǒ gèw-bu-'shàng 'nèy-ge.

Beyond hope. ‖He's so ill that he's beyond hope. tā 'bìng-de nème-'lì-hày hǎw-bu-'lyǎw-le.

Beyond one's expectations. ‖It's beyond my expectations. 'chū-hu wǒ-de-yì-'lyàw jr̄-'wày (literary).

Beyond one's comprehension. ‖This is totally beyond his comprehension. 'jèy-ge tā 'dzěme néng °'dǔng? or °'lyáw-'jyě. ‖It's quite beyond me. wǒ 'jēn °bù-'jr̄-dàw (or °bù-'míng-bay or °'shyǎng-bu-chū) shr̀ 'dzěme-hwéy-'shr̀.

Beyond one's means. ‖She's living beyond her means. tā-'hwā-de bǐ 'jèng-de 'dwō.

BIBLE. shèng-'jīng.

BICYCLE. dz̄-shíng-'chē, jyǎw-tà-'chē.

BID. (Want to) bid (kěn) 'chū; gěy-'jyàr. ‖How much would you bid for this? 'jèy-ge nǐ kěn 'chū 'dwō-shaw-chyán? ‖Who bids five dollars? 'shwéy kěn 'chū 'wǔ-kwày? ‖Who was it that bid five dollars? chū-'wǔ-kwày-de shr̀ 'nǎ-yí-wèy? ‖He bid only five dollars for the rug. nèy-tyáw-dì-'tǎn tā gěy-'jyàr jr̄ gěy-le 'wǔ-kwày-chyán. ‖I don't want to bid too high. wǒ gěy-'jyàr bú-'ywàn-yi gěy-de tày 'gāw. or wǒ bù-'kěn chū 'dà-jyàr.

To enter a bid téw-'byāw. ‖The bid he entered was too low to get the contract. tā téw-'byāw tày-'dī-le, méy-'dé-daw.

(*To order*) jyàw, shwō. ‖We must do as he bids us. tā 'jyàw-dzám dzě̀me 'dzwò, dzám jyèw 'dě̌y dzě̀me 'dzwò. ‖He wouldn't do as I bid him. wǒ jyàw-ta 'nè̀me dzwò, tā bú-'gàn. *or* tā bú-'àn-je wǒ-'shwō-de 'dzwò.

To bid fair to be hǎw 'shyàng hwèy ... (shr̀-de). ‖Our journey bids fair to be pleasant. wǒ-men-'jèy-tsz̀-lywǔ-'shŕng hǎw 'shyàng hwèy hěn yěw 'yì-sz (shr̀-de).

BIG. dà. ‖Their big game is on Saturday. tām lǐ-bày-'lyèw yěw yí-tsz̀-'dà-bǐ-'sày. ‖Is this big enough? 'jèy-ge gèw 'dà bú-gèw 'dà? ‖A big man's going to talk at the meeting. yí-wèy-dà-rén-'wù yàw dàw-'hwèy yǎn-'jyǎng. ‖He talks big. tā shwō dà-'hwà. *or* (*literary*) tā 'dà-yán bù-'tsǎn. ‖They live in a big house. tām jù-dzày yí-swǒ-'dà-fáng-dz-li. ‖We need a bigger box. wǒm děy-'yàw yí-ge-'dà-dyǎr-de-'hé-dz. ‖What's the big idea? nǐ 'shéme-yì-sz? *or* (*fighting talk*) nǐ 'dǎ-swàn 'dzě̀me-je?

(*Boastfully*). ‖He talks (*or* acts) big. tā hěn dz̀-'dà. *or* tā hěn 'jyàw-àw. *or* tā hěn 'shén-chì.

BILL. (*To be paid*) jàng-'dār. ‖The bill includes both labor and materials. 'gūng hé-'lyàw dēw dzày jèy-jàng-jàng-'dār-lǐ-tew.

To pay a bill hwán-'jàng. ‖We must pay the bill today. wǒm 'jīn-tyan 'bì-shywū-děy hwán-'jàng.

To send a bill kāy-'jàng(-láy). ‖They haven't sent their bill yet. tām háy méy bǎ-'jàng 'kāy-lay-ne. ‖They'll bill us after sending the goods. tām bǎ 'dūng-shi 'sùng-lay yí-'hèw dzày °kāy-'jàng-lay. *or* °kāy jàng-'dār(-lay). ‖Bill me at this address. bǎ jàng-'dār gěy-wǒ kāy-daw 'jèy-ge dì-fang chyu.

(*Paper money*) 'pyàw-dz, pyàwr, chyán-'pyàwr. ‖Can you change a five-dollar bill? nǐ néng 'pwò (yì-jāng-) 'wǔ-kwày-chyán-de-'pyàw-dz-ma? ‖I only have twenty-dollar bills. wǒ 'jř yěw 'èr-shr-kwày-de-'pyàw-dz.

(*Theater program*) 'jyé-mù, shì-'dār, shì-'bàw-dz. ‖What's on the bill at the theater this evening? jyèr-'wǎn-shang shì-'ywán-dz-li yěw shéme-'jyé-mù. ‖What does it say on the bill? shì-'dār-shang dzě̀me 'shwō-de?

(*Proposed law*) yì-'àn. ‖The bill will be voted on by Congress. gwó-'hwèy yàw bǎ jèy-ge-yì-'àn fù 'byǎw-jywé. ‖We don't have enough votes to pass the bill. wǒ-men-de-'pyàw-shù bú-'gèw tūng-gwò jèy-ge-yì-'àn-de.

‖Post no bills. (*Literary*) jīn-'jř °jāw-'tyē (*or* °jān-tyē).

(*Of a bird*) dzwěy. ‖The bird held a worm in its bill. 'nyǎw 'dzwěy-li dyàw-je vì-tyáw-'chúng-dz. ‖This bird has a long bill. jèy-jǔng-'nyǎw-de-'dzwěy hěn 'cháng.

Bill of fare tsày-'dān; bill of health jyàn-'kāng-'jèng-shū; bill of lading tí-hwò-'dān; bill of exchange hwèy-'pyàw.

BILLBOARD. gwǎng-gàw-'páy.

BILLFOLD. *Usually of leather, and so usually called* pí-'bāw, pí-'jyā-dz; *but also* pyàw-'jyā-dz, chyán-'bāw, chyán-'jyā-dz.

BIN. chú-tswén-'shyāng.

BIND. kwěn, 'kwěn-chǐ-láy. ‖Bind him up. bǎ-ta 'kwěn-chǐ-lay. ‖His hands are still bound. tā-de-'shěw háy 'kwěn-je-ne.

Bind together 'bǎng-shàng, 'kwěn-shàng. ‖Bind his hands together. bǎ tā-de-'shěw 'bǎng-shang.

Bind *someone* to *something* 'bǎng-dzày, 'kwěn-dzày. ‖Bind him to the post. bǎ-ta 'bǎng-dzay 'jù-dz-shang.

Bind (*a wound*) gwǒ. ‖That wound was bound up too tightly. ('shāng-de-dì-fang) 'gwǒ-de tày 'jǐn-le.

Bind (*a book*) jwāng-'dīng, dīng-chǐ-láy. ‖The book was bound in leather. 'shū shr̀ yùng 'pí-dz jwāng-'dīng-de. ‖The magazines aren't bound yet. dzá-'jr̀ háy méy-yew 'dīng-chi-lay.

(*To put under legal obligation*). ‖Both parties are bound by the contract. 'shwāng-fāng bù-néng 'hwèy.
See also BOUND, TIE.

BIOGRAPHY. (*Book*) (shyǎw-)'jwàn.

BIOLOGY. 'shēng-wù-shywé.

BIPLANE. fù-yè-fēy-'jī.

BIRD. nyǎw(r), nyǎw(r)-'lèy, 'fēy-chín. ‖The bird flew into the tree. 'nyǎw fēy-daw 'shù-li chywù-le. ‖What kind of a bird is this? 'jèy shr̀ shéme-'nyǎw?

Queer bird 'gwày-wu. ‖He's a queer bird! tā hěn 'gwày. *or* tā shr̀ ge-'gwày-wu.

Birds of a feather tūng-'lèy; (*good or bad*) yí-'lèy-de-rén; (*bad*) 'hú-péng-gěw-'dǎng. *But* ‖Birds of a feather flock together (*good or bad*) 'wù yǐ-'lèy 'jywù (*literary*).

Early bird chǐ-'dzǎwr-de.

‖A little bird told me. yěw ge-'rér shwō-de.

Kill two birds with one stone yì-'jywù lyǎng-'dé *or* yí-'jyàn shwāng-'dyāw.

‖A bird in the hand is worth two in the bush. shŕ-'shē bù-rú yí-'shyàn (*literary*).

BIRTH. Give birth to yǎng, shēng. ‖She's just given birth to twins. tā gāng 'yǎng-le yí-dwèy-'shwàng-sheng.

By birth. ‖Are you an American by birth? nǐ shr̀ 'měy-gwo-'shēng(-de)-rén-ma?

Date of birth. ‖What's the date of your birth? nǐ shr̀ 'shéme-shŕ-hew 'shēng-de? *or* nǐ 'shéme-shŕ-hew shēng-'rén?

(*As an event*). ‖They announced the birth of their child. *is expressed as* They announced the happy event to everyone. tām shyàng dà-'jyā bàw-'shí.

(*Background*). ‖The governor was a man of humble birth. *is expressed as* The governor's background is quite humble *or* quite poor and low. shĕng-'jăng-de-'chū-shēn hĕn 'pín-hán.

BIRTHDAY. 'shēng-r̀.

To celebrate a birthday (*anyone's*) gwò 'shēng-r̀; (*older person's*) dzwò-'shèw *or* bàn-'shèw; (*40th, 50th, 60th, etc.*) dzwò jĕng-'shèw. To celebrate the fiftieth birthday dzwò 'wŭ-shf-jĕng-'shèw.

BISCUIT. bĭng-'gān, bĭng-'gār.

BIT. (*Tool*) dzwan. ‖I need a bit to drill a hole with. wŏ 'shywū-yàw yí-ge-'dzwàn hăw dă-'yăr. ‖Do you have a larger bit? nĭ yĕw 'dà-yi-dyăr-de-'dzwàn-ma?

(*Of bridle.*) 'jyáw-dz; (*literary*) shyán. ‖This bridle doesn't have a bit. jèy-ge-'lúng-tew méy-yew 'jyáw-dz. *But* ‖He took the bit between his teeth. tā jywé-'dìng kăy-shŕ yăw-'yá 'gàn.

Bit by bit yì-dyăr-yì-'dyăr(-de). ‖We learned about it bit by bit. jèy-jyàn-'shr̀ wŏm shr yì-dyăr-yì-'dyăr 'tīng-lay-de.

Bit (*of*) dyăr; (*small piece of material thing*) shyăw-'kwàr. ‖I only want a little bit. wŏ 'jŕ yàw yì-'dyăr. ‖It doesn't make a bit of difference. (*Literally*) yì-dyăr-'fēn-bye yĕ 'méy-yew. *If said with personal feeling, this is expressed as* méy-yew 'gwān-shi. *or* wŏ bú-'dzày-hu. ‖They only had a bit of cake left. tām jŕ 'shèng-shya-le yì-shyăw-'kwàr-dàn-'gāw.

Bits (*small broken pieces*) swèy-'kwàr; (*very small broken pieces*) 'fĕn-swèy. ‖He broke the candy into bits. tā bă-'táng 'bāy-chéng-le swèy-'kwàr. ‖The whole house was blown to bits. jĕng-gèr-'fáng-dz 'jà-de 'fĕn-swèy.

A bit more . . . *or* a bit . . .-er . . .-(yì-)dyăr. ‖They arrived a bit later than the others. tām-'dàw-de bĭ 'byé-de-rén 'wăn-dyăr.

Bit of advice. ‖May I give you a bit of advice? nĭ 'ywàn-yi-bu-ywàn-yi tīng wŏ-yí-jywù-'hwà?

BITE. yăw. ‖Did you get bitten (*by an insect*)? nĭ āy 'yăw-le-ma? ‖I got a mosquito bite. 'wén-dz 'yăw-le wo yì-'kĕw. ‖Does this dog bite (*people*)? jèy-'gĕw 'yăw-rén bù-yăw? ‖He bit (*into*) the apple. tā yăw 'píng-gwo.

Bite off 'yăw-shyà. ‖The dog bit some flesh off his leg. tā-de-'twĕy jyàw-'gĕw 'yăw-shya yí-kwày-'rèw-lay.

(*With front teeth*) kĕn. ‖Don't bite the orange skin. byé 'kĕn jywú-dz-'pí.

(*Of fish*) shàng-'gĕw(r). ‖The fish are biting well today. 'ywú 'jīn-tyan shàng-'gĕw shàng-de hĕn 'hăw.

‖I haven't had a bite all day. yì-jēng-'tyān-de-gūng-fu lyán 'yí-ge-ywú dēw méy-láy shàng-'gĕwr. *meaning* I haven't had anything at all to eat all day. wŏ yì-'tyān-li yì-dyăr-'dūng-shi dēw méy-'chŕ-ne.

(*Frostbite*) ‖His ears were bitten by the frost. ta bă 'ĕr-dwo 'dung-le.

Biting cold. ‖It's a biting cold day. 'jīn-tyan gān-'lĕng. *or* 'jīn-tyan 'lĕng-de shyàng 'dăw-dz 'lá shr̀-de.

Biting (*caustic*). ‖She often makes biting remarks. tā shwō-'hwà 'cháng-cháng hĕn 'kè-bwo.

A bite, bite of kĕw. ‖I have two bites on my arm from the mosquito. wŏ-de-'gē-be jyàw-'wén-dz dīng-le lyăng-'kĕw. ‖I just took one bite of the orange. wŏ jŕ 'yăw-le 'yì-kĕw-'jywú-dz. ‖There are several bites apiece. 'mĕy-ge-rén dēw yĕw 'jĭ-kĕw 'chŕ.

BITTER. (*Taste*) kŭ. ‖The quinine tastes bitter. jīn-jī-nà-'shwāng hĕn 'kŭ. ‖This coffee is too bitter. jyă-fēy tày 'kŭ.

(*Deep*) shēn. ‖After the war they still continued in their bitter hatred. 'jàng dă-'wán-le kĕ-shr tām bĭ-'tsž-jŕ-'jyàn-de-shēn-'chéw 'bìng méy-yew jyăn-'shyăw. *or* (*Literary*) jàn-'hèw bĭ-'tsž chéw-'hèn-jŕ-'shīn wèy 'jyăn.

(*Implacable*). ‖They are bitter enemies. (*Literary*) tām-'lyă chéw-'shēn shr̀-'hăy.

(*Painful*). ‖He's had some bitter experiences. tā 'shèw-le °shyē-'kŭ. *or* °shyē-'dzwèy.

A bitter pill to swallow jyàw-'rén °nán-'kān-de-'shŕ *or* °nán-'rĕn-de-'shŕ.

To utter bitter words chū ywàn-'yán.

(*Of wind*). ‖A bitter wind was blowing. 'fēng 'gwă-de yèw 'lĕng yew 'lì-hày. *or* (*Literary*) hán-'fēng nù-'hĕw.

Bitter quarrel. ‖He had a bitter quarrel with his brother. tā gēn tā-'gē-ge dà 'chăw-le yí-'jyà.

Bitter end. ‖They fought to the bitter end. tām pīn-'mìng 'pīn-le ge-nĭ-sž-wŏ-'hwó. ‖He held himself back to the bitter end. tā yì-'jŕ rĕn-daw 'dĭ.

BLACK. (*Dark*) hēy, àn. Black ink hēy-mwò-'shwĕr. ‖Many black clouds began to come up. hăw-dwō-'hēy-'ywún-tsay 'shàng-lay-le. ‖The night was very black. 'yè-li 'tyān hĕn 'hēy (*or* 'àn).

(*Color of an object*) hēy, chīng. ‖Do you have a black dress? nĭ 'yĕw-méy-yew 'hēy-'yī-fu-wa? ‖She's dressed in black satin. tā 'chwān-le yì-shēn-'chīng-dwàn-dz-'yī-shang. ‖Where's my black suit? wŏ nèy-shēr-'chīng-'yī-shang dzày-'năr?

(*Color of bruised skin*) chīng. ‖He got a black eye from someone. tā-de-'yăn-jing-nàr jyàw-'rén dă-'chīng-le.

(*Unpromising*) àn-'dàn *or* hēy-'àn. ‖Their future is black. tā-men-de-'chyán-tú hĕn 'àn-dàn.

(*Morally bad*) hwày, bù-'hăw. ‖He's not as black as he's painted. tā 'méy-yew rén-'shwō-de-nà-me-'hwày.

(*Mourning*) shyàw (*Note that the color of mourning*

clothes in China is white). ‖She's worn black (*mourning clothes*) since her husband died. tā dź-tsúng tā-'jàng-fu 'sź-le yǐ-'hèw yì-'jf̄ chwān-'shyàw. *(Since the period of mourning for different relatives is rigorously prescribed in China, this sentence would be said only of a Westerner in China or possibly of a Chinese Christian.)*

Black and blue chīng-'jǔng. ‖He was beaten black and blue all over by someone. tā (ràng-'rén) 'dǎ-de chywán-'shēn chīng-'jǔng.

In black and white (*written down, printed*). ‖I want it put down in black and white. 'jèy-ge děy 'shyě-shyà-lay. ‖Do you have it in black and white? nǐ yí-'dìng yàw °'shyě-chū-lay-de-ma? *or* °'yìn-chū-lay-de-ma?

A black look. ‖He gave me a black look. tā 'dèng-le wo yì-'yǎn.

Black sheep (*of a family*) bày-jyā-'dzěr; (*of any other group*) hày-'chywún-jf̄-'mǎ (*literary*). ‖He's the black sheep of our family. tā shf̄ wǒ-men-'jyā-de-bày-jyā-'dzěr. ‖We have a black sheep in our midst. wǒ-men-yì-ohywún-'rén-li yěw yí-ge-"hày-'chywún-jf̄-'mǎ."

To black. ‖He blacked his face. tā bǎ-'lyǎn tú-'hēy-le.

To black out (*keep dark*) bú-tèw-'gwāng; (*eliminate*) 'tú-cìywù. ‖The house must be blacked out by dark. hēy-'tyān-yǐ-'hèw 'wū-dz-le bù-néng tèw-'gwāng. ‖This line should be blacked out. jèy-tyáw-'shyàn děy 'tú-le-chywu.

BLACKBOARD. hēy-'bǎn.

BLACKSMITH. 'tyě-jyang.

BLADDER. (*In body*) 'páng-hwang, 'swēy-paw.

BLADE. (*Razor*) dāw-'pyàr, dāw-'pyàn; (*of a knife*) dāw-'kěw; a blade of grass yì-gēr-'tsǎw.

BLAME. (*Hold responsible*) gwày, gwéy-'dzwèy ywú. ‖You must blame the taxi driver for our being late. láy-'wǎn-le-'jèy-jyàn-shf̄, nǐ děy 'gwày kāy-chì-'chē-de. ‖This road has worn out; they blame the engineer for it. jèy tyáw-'lù 'hwày-le, tām gwéy-'dzwèy ywú gūng-chéng-'shf̄. ‖If anything goes wrong, you can't blame me. yàw-shr chū-le 'chàr, bù-néng 'gwày-wǒ.

(*Shift the responsibility unjustly to*) lày, (bǎ-'tswèr) 'twēy-gěy. ‖You can't blame others for the mistakes you made yourself. nǐ-'dź-jǐ-chū-de-'tswèr bù-néng twēy-gey 'byé-rén. ‖He blamed us (unjustly) for the accident. tā chū-'shf̄-le lày 'wǒ-men.

To take the blame dāng, 'dān-chéng, dān-dāng. ‖One should have the courage to take the blame for what one does. yí-ge-'rén děy gǎn 'dzwò gǎn 'dāng ‖He took the blame for their mistake. shf̄ 'tā-men-de-'tswèr, kě-shr 'tā gěy 'dān-chéng-le. ‖I take all the blame for this mistake. jèy-ge-'tswèr wǒ-'yí-ge-rén 'dān-chéng.

(*Be responsible*). ‖Who's to blame for this? shf̄ 'shwéy-de-tswèr? *or* 'shéy yīng-gay fù dzé-'rèn?

BLANKET. 'tǎn-dz; (*wool*) máw-'tǎn(-dz).

BLESS. ‖He's blessed with a good temper. 'tyān 'tsź-gěy-ta hǎw 'pí-chi. *or* tā-de-'pí-chi 'hǎw, 'jēn shf̄ yěw-'fú.

(*Strong thanks*). ‖Bless you for doing this! gǎn-'jī hú-'jìn!

BLIND. shyā, shyā-'yǎn; (*partially*) 'yǎn-jīng 'hwày, máng (*literary*). ‖He was too blind to read letters. tā 'shyā-de lyán-'shìn dēw kàn-bu-'chīng-le. *or* tā 'yǎn-jing 'hwày-de, lyán-'shìn *etc.* ‖He's blind in one eye. tā 'shyā-le 'yì-jf̄-yǎn-jing. ‖Are you blind? (*Literally or figuratively*) nǐ shyā-'yǎn-le-ma? *or* nǐ 'yǎn-jing 'shyā-le! ‖Don't be a blind follower. (*Literary*) byé máng 'tsúng! *or* byé 'shyā gēn-je 'rén 'pǎw!

(*To dazzle*) kàn-bu-'jyàn. ‖The lightning blinded me for a while. dǎ-'shǎn de-shf̄-hew wǒ 'yěw-yi-hwěr 'shéme dēw kàn-bu-'jyàn

To blind someone nùng-'shyā; (*by striking*) dǎ-'shyā; (*by puncturing*) chwō-'shyā. ‖He was blinded in the accident. nèy-tsź-chū-'shf̄ tā bǎ 'yǎn-jing nùng-'shyā-le.

Be blind to rèn-bu-'chīng, fēn-bu-'chū, bù-'míng. ‖He was blind to the (true) facts. tā rèn-bu-'chīng shf̄-'shf̄. *or* tā bù-'míng jēn-'jyǎ. *or* tā fēn-bu-'chū shéme shf̄ 'jēn-de, shéme shf̄ 'jyǎ-de. *Or* (*with* bù-'jf̄-daw). ‖I'm not blind to her shortcomings. tā-de-nèy-shyē-'dwǎn-chù, wǒ 'bú-shr bù-'jf̄-daw.

Blind person 'shyā-dz, shyā-le-'yǎn-de-rén. ‖We helped the blind man across the street. wǒ-men bāng-je nèy-ge-'shyā-dz gwò-'jyē láy-je. *or* wǒ-men 'lǐng nèy-ge-'shyā-dz gwò-'jyē láy-je. *In China the blind live by begging or by fortunetelling. A blind fortune-teller is called* swàn-'mìng-de-shyān-sheng.

Blind alley. sź-hú-'tùngr. ‖This is á blind alley. jè shf̄ yì-tyáw-sź-hú-'tùngr. ‖He ran up a blind alley. tā-'dzěw-de shf̄ yì-tyáw-sź-hú-'tùngr. *or* (*Figuratively*) tā-pèng-'bì-le.

Window blinds chwāng-hu-'lyár, chwāng-hu-'lyán-dz. ‖Please pull down the blinds. bǎ chwāng-hu-'lyár 'lā-shya-lay.

BLISTER. shwéy-'pàw(r).

BLIZZARD. kwáng-fēng dà-'shywě.

BLOCK. (*Solid piece of*) kwày; (*in a city, meaning the distance between two streets*) yì-tyáw-'jyē.

BLOOD. shyě *also pronounced* shywè, *literary pronunciation* shywě. ‖After the accident there was blood on the ground. shf̄-'hèw 'dì-shang yěw-'shyě. ‖Blood flowed from the wound. 'shywè tsúng 'shāng-kěw 'lyéw-chu-lay.

(*If visible through the skin*) shyĕ-'sēr. ‖His eyes had blood in them. tā 'yăn-li yĕw shyĕ-'sēr.

To lose blood lyéw-'shyĕ. ‖He lost a good deal of blood. tā 'lyéw-le hĕn-dwō-'shyĕ.

To let blood fàng-'shyĕ, chywŭ-'shyĕ. ‖The doctor let his blood twice. 'yī-sheng gĕy-ta 'fàng-le 'lyăng-tsż-'shyĕ.

To have a blood test yàn-'shyĕ. ‖Have you had your blood test yet? nĭ 'yàn-gwo 'shyĕ-le-ma?

Blood pressure shyĕ-'yā. ‖I have high blood pressure. wŏ-de-shyĕ-'yā hĕn 'gāw.

Blood type shyĕ-'shíng. ‖What's your blood type? nĭ-de-shyĕ-'shíng °shŕ 'shéme? or °'nĕy-jŭng?

(*Of race or family*) blood relatives shywè-dzú-'chīn. ‖He has some (American) Indian blood in him. tā-de-dzŭ-'shyān-li (or tā-de-shywĕ-'tŭng-li) yĕw yìn-di-'ān-rén. ‖Blood is thicker than water. 'chīn-chi 'dzŭng shŕ shyàng-je 'chīn-chi. or (*Literary*) 'shū bú-'jyàn 'chīn.

In cold blood hĕn 'shīn. ‖They murdered him in cold blood. tām 'shā-ta de-shŕ-hew, jēn shŕ hĕn 'shīn shyà-'shĕw.

Other English expressions. ‖He has blood on his hands. (*Literally*) tā 'shĕw-shang yĕw-'shyĕ. (*Figuratively*) tā 'hày-gwo rén. ‖He's a hot-blooded individual. tā-de-'pí-chi hĕn 'dà. or 'jèy-ge-rén ày shēng-'chì. or 'jèy-ge-rén bù-hăw-'rĕ. or jèy-ge-rén ày fā 'pí-chi. ‖His blood was up. tā hĕn shēng-'chì. ‖Freedom is bought with blood. dż-'yéw shŕ lyéw-'shyĕ 'hwàn-lay-de.

BLOTTER. shī-mwò-'jŕ, chŕ-mwò-'jŕ.

BLOW. (*Of wind*) gwā-'fēng. ‖The wind blew hard. 'fēng 'gwā-de hĕn 'lì-hày. ‖The wind has been blowing all night. 'fēng yĭ-jīng 'gwā-le yī-'yè-le. ‖The wind will blow hard tonight. 'fēng jīn-tyan-'wăn-shang yí-'dìng hwèy 'gwā-de hĕn 'lì-hày.

Blow over (*of a storm*) 'gwā-gwò-chywù. ‖This storm will blow over soon. jèy-jèn-'fēng 'kwày 'gwā-gwò-chywu-le.

Blow up (*of a storm*) chĭ-'fēng. ‖It may blow up a storm this afternoon. jīn-tyan-'shyà-wŭ yé-shywu hwèy chĭ-'fēng.

Blow away gwā-'păw, chwēy-'păw. ‖This tent's going to blow away. jèy-ge-'jàng-péng hwèy jyàw-'fēng gwā-'păw-le. ‖My hat blew away. wŏ-de-'màw-dz gĕy chwēy-'păw-le.

Blow down chwēy-'dăw. ‖That tree blew down. nèy-kē-'shù jyàw-'fēng gĕy chwēy-'dăw-le.

Blow *an instrument, bugle-call, horn, whistle, with the mouth* chwēy; *by pressing a button* èn; *by pulling a cord* lā. ‖They blow taps at eleven o'clock. tām shŕ-'yì-dyăn-jūng chwēy shí-dēng-'hàw. ‖Blow the horn three times when you come. nĭ 'láy de-shŕ-hew èn 'sān-shyàr-'lă-ba. ‖Has the whistle blown? lā-'byéer-le méy-yew?

Blow on *something to cool it* chwēy-'lyáng; *to warm it* chwēy-'nwăn-he. ‖You can blow on your soup to cool it. 'tāng nĭ 'chwēy-yi-chwēy jyēw 'lyáng-le. ‖You can blow on your hands to warm them. nĭ ké-yi bă nĭ-de-'shĕw chwēy-'nwăn-he-le.

Blow out *a light* chwēy-'myè. ‖Blow the lamp out before you go. nĭ 'dzĕw yĭ-'chyán bă-'dēng chwēy-'myè-le.

Blow a bubble chwēy-chi yí-ge-'pàwr-lay.

Blow up *a tire* (*inflate*) 'dă-chì-lay, dă-'dzú-le 'chì. ‖Please blow up this tire for me. chīng-ni bă jèy-ge-'dày-dz °'dă-chi-lay. or °gĕy dă-'dzú-le 'chì.

Blow up (*explode*) jà, bēng, jà-'lyè, bēng-'lyè, jà-'hwày. ‖Be careful that it doesn't blow up (*from inner pressure or from the outside*). 'shyăw-shīn byé 'jyàw-ta 'jà-le. ‖The enemy will try to blow up the bridge. 'dí-rén hwèy-yàw bă-'chyáw 'jà-le. ‖The (steam) boiler blew up. chì-'gwō 'jà-le.

Blow out (*of a tire*) jà, fàng-'pàw. ‖The old tire blew out. 'lăw-chē-'dày fàng-'pàw-le.

Blow one's nose shĭng 'bí-dz; (*to get rid of mucus*) shĭng 'bí-tì.

Blow over (*of trouble, situation*) 'fēng-cháw-gwò-chywu, 'gwò-chywù, 'nàw-gwò-chywù. ‖Wait until all this blows over. 'dĕng-je 'jèy-ge 'fēng-cháw gwò-chywu 'dzày shwō. or 'dĕng-je jèy-jyàn-'shŕ 'gwò-chywu 'dzày shwō. or 'dĕng-je jèy-jyàn-'shŕ nàw-gwo-chywu 'dzày shwō.

A blow (*shock*) dă-jí. ‖Can he stand the blow? jèy-yàngr-de-'dă-jí tā shèw-de-'lyăw-ma? ‖He suffered a terrible blow. tā 'shèw-le yí-ge-'dà-dă-jí.

To receive a blow shèw swĕn-'shŕ. ‖If things go that way wholesale trade will receive a terrible blow. 'nàme-je pī-'fā-de-'shāng-jya yàw 'dà shèw swĕn-'shŕ-le.

To strike a blow dă yí-'shyà-dz, dă yí-'shyàr; (*with the fist*) dă yì-'chywán; (*with the palm*) dă yì-'bā-jang; (*with a stick*) dă yí-'gwèn-dz; (*with a sword*) kăn yì-'dāw; (*with the back of a sword*) dă yì-'dāw-byèr.

(*Oratorical*). ‖We must strike the first blow. 'wŏm déy 'shyān °dùng-'shĕw. or °'shyà-'shĕw.

Come to blows. ‖They came to blows. (*With hands*) tām dùng-chi 'shĕw láy-le. (*With fists*) tām dùng-chi 'chywán-tew láy-le. (*General*) tām 'dă-chi 'jyà láy-le.

BLUE. lán, 'lán-sè, 'lán-shăr. ‖Blue was in vogue last year. 'chywù-nyan 'lán-sè shŕ-'shíng. ‖Give me a blue one. wŏ yàw °'lán-shăr-de. or °'lán-de. ‖It's that book with a blue cover. shŕ nèy-bĕn-'lán-pyér-de-'shū. ‖This shade of blue is very pleasant. 'jèy-jŭng-lán(-shăr) °hĕn 'réw. or °bú-tsż-'yăn. ‖Please let me see a blue tie. wŏ shyăng yàw 'kàn yì-tyáw-'lán-lĭng-'dài. ‖She always wears blue. tā 'lăw chwān 'lán-de. ‖Do you have any blue ink? nĭ yĕw 'lán-mwò-'shwĕr-ma?

Dark blue 'shēn-lán; light blue 'chyǎn-lán; very dark blue 'dzàng-chīng; sky blue 'tyān-lán; (*A shade a little darker than sky blue*) ywǔ-gwò-tyān-'chīng. ‖Have this dyed dark blue. bǎ 'jèy-ge rǎn-chéng 'shēn-lán-de. *But* ‖Do you have a darker shade of blue? (*In this garment or material*) 'dzày 'shēn-dyǎr-de 'háy yěw-ma? *or* nǐ yěw bǐ 'jèy-ge dzày 'shēn-dyǎr-de-ma?

(*Of a mood*) nán-'shèw, bù-'gāw-shìng. ‖After his family left he felt blue. tā-'jyā-li-de-rén 'dzǒw-le yǐ-'hèw tā yěw yì-dyǎr-nán-'shèw. ‖Why're you blue this morning? nǐ jīn-tyan-'dzǎw-chen 'wèy-shéme bù-'gāw-shìng?

Have the blues bú-'tùng-kway, 'mèn-de-hwang. ‖I get the blues when it rains. shyà-'ywǔ de-shŕ-hew wǒ 'lǎw °bú-'tùng-kway. *or* °'mèn-de-hwang.

Blues (*music*). (*Lyrics*) yēw-ywàn-'chywǔ; (*tune*) yēw-ywàn-'dyàwr.

Out of the blue hū-rán-jyān jyèw. ‖He arrived out of the blue. tā hū-'rán-jyān jyèw 'láy-le.

Blueprint. (*Method*) lán-'shày; (*actual design on paper*) lán-'tú. Blue bloods (*nobility*) gwèy-'dzú; bluebook (*government document*) lán-pí-'shū; *compare* book with blue cover lán-pyér-de-'shū.

BOARD. 1. (*Wood*) (mù-tew-) 'bǎn-dz, (mù-tew-) 'bǎr. ‖We need some boards to make the top of the box with. wǒm děy-yàw jǐ-kwày-'bǎn-dz hǎw dzwò hé-dz-'gàr.

To board up yùng mù-'bǎn 'jē-shàng. ‖The front is all boarded up. lín-'jyē-de-yī-'myàr dēw yùng mù-'bǎn 'jē-shang-le.

Ironing board tàng-'yī-fu-'bǎn-dz; blackboard hēy-bǎn.

(*For chess or checkers*) chí-'pán. ‖I still had three men left on the board. (dzày) chí-'pán-shang wǒ 'háy 'shèng-shya 'sān-ge-'dzěr.

Bulletin board bù-gàw-'bǎn. ‖Nail this on the bulletin board. bǎ 'jèy-ge 'dīng-dzay bù-gàw-'bǎn-shang.

2. (*Meals*) bāw-'fàn. ‖They advertise board and rooms. tām dēng gwǎng-'gàw shwō yěw 'wū-dz chū-'dzū háy ké-yi bāw-'fàn. ‖Is the board good there? nàr-de-(bāw-) 'fàn kě-'chŕ-ma?

(*To take meals*) chŕ bāw-'fàn. ‖Are you boarding at your hotel? nǐ shŕ dzày nǐ-lywǔ-'gwǎn chŕ bāw-'fàn-ma? ‖How many people does she board? dzày tā-'nèr chŕ-bāw-'fàn-de yěw 'dwō-shaw-rén? ‖Is there a place to board near your work? nǐ-dzwò-'shŕ-de-dì-fang-fù-'jìn yěw chŕ-bāw-'fàn-de-dì-fang-ma?

(*Cost of meals*) shàn-'fèy. ‖His scholarship includes room and board. tā-de-jyǎng-shywé-'jīn-li 'bāw-kwò 'sù-fèy gēn 'shàn-fèy.

3. To board *a vehicle or boat* shàng. ‖Can we board the train early? wǒm ké-yi 'dzǎw-dyǎr shàng hwǒ-'chē-ma? ‖He's already boarded the train. tā 'yǐ-jing shàng-'chē-le. ‖The whistle has already blown to get on board. yǐ-jing lā-'byéer jyàw-rén 'shàng-chywù-le.

On board (dzày) 'chwán-shang *or with name of other vehicle replacing* chwán boat. ‖This boat has a fugitive on board. (dzày) jèy-jŕ-'chwán-shang yěw yí-ge-táw-'fàn.

‖All aboard! 'kè-rén shàng-°'chē! *or* °-'chwán! *or* °fēy-'jī! *or* 'chē (*or* 'chwán, *etc.*) yàw 'kāy-le.

4. (*Official body*) wěy-ywán-'hwèy (*usually an especially appointed commission*); -jywú, -shǔ, -chù, *with preceding elements indicating the function, is used for regularly constituted parts of the government.* ‖The Board of Health has issued new regulations. 'gūng-gùng-'wèy-shēng-wěy-ywán-'hwèy 'fā-chu shīn-'jǎng-cheng láy-le.

Board of trustees (*of a school*) shyàw-dǔng-'hwèy, (*of a business*) 'dǔng-shŕ-'hwèy; board of examiners (*of a school*) 'kǎw-shŕ-wěy-ywán-'hwèy, (*governmental*) 'shěn-chá-wěy-ywán-'ywèy.

BOAT. chwán; (*in some compounds*) tǐng, tíng. ‖He'll take the boat for America soon. tā kwày yàw dzwò-'chwán dàw 'měy-gwo chywù-le. ‖The boat trip will take five days. 'chwán děy 'dzěw 'wǔ-tyān. ‖We can cross the river in this boat. wǒm ké-yi dzwò jèy-tyáw-'chwán gwò-'hé. ‖Will this small boat hold all five of us? jèy-tyáw °shyǎw-'chwán (*or* °shyǎw-'chwár) jīn-de-'jù dzám-'wǔ-ge-rén-ma?

To go boating hwá-'chwán, yáw-'chwán. ‖We went boating. wǒm hwá-'chwán chywù-le.

‖We're all in the same boat. (*Not necessarily unhappy*) °wǒm-de 'chíng-shing shyāng-'túng. *or* wǒm-de-'dzāw-ywù yí-'yàng. (*Of an unfortunate situation*) wǒ-men shŕ túng-'bìng-shyāng-'lyán (*literary*).

BODY. shēn, 'shēn-dz. ‖This soldier has a healthy body. jèy-ge-bīng-de-'shēn-dz hen jyàn-'kāng. ‖He has a red rash on his body. tā 'shēn-shang jǎng húng-'bān. ‖His legs are too short for his body. tā 'shēn 'cháng 'twěy 'dwǎn.

(*Dead*) 'sž-shŕ. ‖They buried the two bodies in one grave. tām bǎ lyǎng-jywù-'sž-shŕ máy-dzay yí-'kwàr-le.

(*Of a car*) chē-'shēn.

(*Main part; of a fleet or army*) běn-'dwèy; (*of a speech*) 'nèy-rúng. ‖The body of his speech was technical. tā-yǎn-'jyǎng-de-'nèy-rúng hěn jwān-'mén.

Body of troops yí-dwèy-'bīng (*in formation*) *or* yì-chywún-'bīng (*not in formation*); body of men yì-chywún-'rén; body of water yí-pyàn-'shwěy, (*large*) wāng-yáng-dà-'hǎy; political body jèng-jŕ-twán-'tǐ; legislative body lì-fǎ-jī-'gwān.

In a body chywán-'tǐ (dēw). ‖They left in a body. tām chywán-'tǐ dēw 'dzěw-le.

‖They couldn't keep body and soul together. tām 'chyúng-de méy-'fàn chŕ.

BODYGUARD. bǎw-'byāw-de.

BOIL. jŭ. ‖Please boil the egg two minutes. bǎ jī-'dzěr jŭ 'lyǎng-fēn-jūng. ‖We want boiled potatoes for dinner. wǒm 'wǎn-fàn yàw chř jŭ-tŭ-'dèwr.

(*Of water or other liquids*) kāy. ‖In a few minutes the water will boil. dzày dāy jǐ-fēn-'jūng 'shwěy jyèw 'kāy-le. ‖The engine (*i.e., the water in the engine*) is boiling. jī-chi 'rè-de dēw 'kāy-le.

To boil away, boil dry jŭ-'gān. ‖Don't let the pot boil dry. byé jyàw ('hú-li-de-)'shwěy jŭ-'gān-le.

To boil over gwěn-'kāy, fèy. ‖The coffee's boiling over. jyā-'fēy gwěn-'kāy-le. ‖The soup's boiling over. 'tāng 'fèy-le.

(*Infection*) bāw; (*festered and open*) chwāng. ‖He's suffering from boils. tā jǎng-'chwāng-le. ‖This boil is painful. jèy-ge-'bāw hěn 'téng.

To boil down. ‖It all boils down to this. 'gwēy-le bāw-'dzwēy shř 'jème-yì-hwéy-'shř. *or* 'gwēy-chí shř 'jème-yì-hwéy-'shř. ‖What does all this boil down to? 'jèy-ge jyěw-'jìng shř 'dzéme-hwéy-'shř?

(*Be angry*). ‖That remark made me boil. 'nèy-jǔng-hwà hěn jyàw-wǒ shēng-'chì.

BOILER. (*On a steam engine*) jēng-chì-'gwō; (*for hot water*) rè-shwěv-'gwō, rè-shwěy-'shyāng.

BOLD. dǎn-dz 'dà. ‖He's always bold in the face of danger. 'yī yěw wéy-'shyǎn, tā-de-'dǎn-dz jyèw 'dà-le. ‖He was bold enough to talk back to the (school) principal. tā-de-'dǎn-dz °hěn 'dà (*or* °jēn 'dà, *or* °jēn gèw 'dà-de), gǎn gēn shyàw-'jǎng jyàng-'dzwěy.

(*Forthright*) màw-'shyǎn-de. ‖They followed a bold policy. tām 'tsǎy-chywǔ-le hěn-màw-'shyǎn-de-'bàn-fa.

Be bold enough to gǎn. ‖He was bold enough to go in alone. tā gǎn 'yí-ge-rén 'jìn-chywu.

(*Forward*) méy-yěw 'lǐ-màw, bú-yàw-'lyǎn, 'lyǎn-pi 'hèw, bú-'kè-chi. ‖I can't stand bold people. wǒ shèw-bu-'lyǎw méy-yěw-'lǐ-màw-de-rén. ‖He's too bold with strangers. tā gēn 'shēng-rén tày bú-'kè-chi.

BOLT. (*For a nut*) lwó-sž(-'dīng); (*door fastener*) mén-'shwān-dz; (*of cloth*) yì-kwěn (*or* -jywǎn, -jywǎr)-'bù.

BOMB. jà-'dàn.

BOMBER. hūng-jà-'jī.

BOND. (*Surety, bail*) dān-'bǎw, shú-(dzwèy-)'jīn; bonds (*securities*) gūng-jày-'pyàw.

BONE. 'gú-tew, 'gǔ-tew; *in compounds* -gǔ, *e.g.,* leg bone twěy-'gǔ, cow bone nyéw-'gǔ *or* nyéw-'gǔ-tew. ‖Are these human bones? nà shř 'rén-'gú-tew-ma? ‖Those are made of bone. nà shř yùng 'gú-tew 'dzwò-de. ‖Cut the bone from this meat. bǎ 'gǔ-tew 'tī-chu-chywù. ‖I feel chilled to the bone. 'lěng-daw 'gú-tew-li chywù-le. (*or simply* wǒ lěng-'jí-le.) ‖In the accident he broke two bones. chū-'shř de-shř-hew tā 'shé-le lyǎng-gēr-'gú-tew.

(*Of snake or fish*) tsž. ‖A fish bone caught in his throat. yì-gēr-ywú-'tsž 'chyǎ-dzay tā-'sǎng-dz-li-le.

To bone (*a fish*) bǎ-'tsž (*or* -'tsèr) 'tyāw-chu-chywu. ‖Has this fish been boned? jèy-tyáw-ywú-de-'tsèr 'tyāw-chu-chywu-le méy-yew?

Special English expressions. ‖He made no bones about what he wanted. tā yī 'shàng-lay jyèw 'shwō tā 'yàw shéme. *or* tā yì-'dyǎr méy-ràw-'wār. ‖I feel it in my bones that he isn't coming. *is expressed as* I feel that he certainly is not going to come. wǒ 'jywé-de tā yí-'dìng bù-'láy-le. ‖I have a bone to pick with you. wǒ yěw yí-jyàn-'shř děy gēn-ni 'tí-yi-tí.

BONFIRE. yān-'hwǒ.

BOOK. shū. ‖I want a book to read on the train. wǒ yàw yì-běn-'shū hǎw dzày hwǒ-'chē-shang 'kàn. ‖My books are in that trunk. wǒ-de-'shū dzày nèy-ge-'shyāng-dz-li.

(*Fascicle*) běn-dz, běr. ‖Keep your accounts in this blank book. bǎ nǐ-de-'jàng jì-dzay jèy-ge-'běn-dz-li.

Bookstore shū-'pù, shū-'dyàn. ‖Do you know of a good bookstore? nǐ 'jř-daw 'nǎr yěw yí-ge-'hǎw-shū-'pù?

Bookselling trade shū-'yè; booklet shyǎw-'tsè-dz; book collector tsáng shū-'jyā; bookcase shū-'jyà-dz (*open shelves*), shū-'gwèy *or* shū-'chú (*closed*); bookmark shū-'chyān-dz.

Book of tickets chéng-'běr-de-'pyàw. ‖A book of tickets will save you money. chéng-'běr-de-'pyàw 'pyán-yì-shyě.

To keep books jì-'jàng; bookkeeper gwǎn-'jàng-de; bookkeeping bwó-'jì. ‖Did he keep books for his business? tā-de-'mǎy-mày jì-'jàng-le méy-yew?

To bring *someone* to book jř-'wèn. ‖He's been brought to book on that. wèy 'nèy-ge tā 'yǐ-jing ràng-'rén jř-'wèn-le.

BOOKCASE. (*Open*) shū-'jyà; (*with doors*) shū-'gwèy.

BOOKENDS. shū-'jyā-dz.

BOOKKEEPER. gwǎn-'jàng-de, kwày-jì-'ywán.

BOOKLET. běr, shyǎw-'tsè-dz.

BOOKSTORE. shū-'pù, shū-'dyàn.

BOOTH. (*In a market*) 'tān-dz, tsày-'tān(-dz); (*telephone*) dyàn-hwà-'gé-dz.

BOOTS. shywē-dz.

BOOTY. (*In war*) shèng-lì-'pǐn.

BORDER. (*Between countries*) gwó-'jyè; (*area near the border-line*) byān-'jǐng; (*of a piece of cloth, etc.*) byār.

BORN. Be born shēng, 'shēng-shyà(-lay); be born in or at *a place, time, or in certain circumstances* 'shēng-dzày. ‖Their child was born last March. (*In this calendar year*) tā-men-de shyǎw-'hár shr̀ °'sān-ywè 'shēng-de. (*In previous calendar year*) °'chywù-nyan-'sān-ywè 'shēng-de. ‖Were you born in America? (*Emphasis on place of birth*) nǐ shr̀ dzày 'měy-gwo 'shēng-de-ma? or (*Emphasis on the past history of a particular person*) nǐ shr̀ 'shēng-dzay 'měy-gwo-de-ma? ‖He was born rich. tā 'shēng-shyà-lay jyèw yěw-'chyán. or tā shēng-dzày fù-'jyā.

BORROW. jyè. ‖He's borrowed money at the bank. tā gēn yín-'háng jyè-'chyán-le. ‖May I borrow this book overnight? 'jèy-běn-shū wǒ 'jyè-chywu 'míng-tyan-'dzǎw-chen 'hwán, 'shíng-bu-shíng?

In telling someone that he may borrow something the polite expression is Take it and use it. *Thus question* ‖May I borrow your umbrella? jyè nǐ-de-'sǎn 'yùng-yi-'yùng, 'shíng-ma? or jyè nǐ-de-'sǎn 'dǎ, 'shíng-bu-shíng? *but statement* ‖You may borrow my umbrella to get home. nǐ ké-yi 'dǎ wǒ-de-ywǔ-'sǎn hwéy-'jyā.

BOTANY. 'jŕ-wù-shywé.

BOTH. lyǎng ... dēw, lyǎng-ge ... dēw, 'lyǎng-ge-rén ... dēw. ‖Both roads will take you into the town. 'lyǎng-tyáw-'dàwr dēw tūng chéng-'lǐ. ‖I'll buy both of those books. 'nèy-lyǎng-běn-'shū wǒ dēw 'mǎy. ‖We've asked both soldiers to come. 'lyǎng-ge-bīng wǒm dēw 'chǐng. ‖I can't take both. 'lyǎng-ge wǒ bù-néng dēw 'yàw. ‖Both of us saw it happen. wǒm-'lyǎng-ge-rén dēw 'dāng-chǎng 'chýáw-jyàn-le.

(*With things that come in pairs*). ‖He lost both his shoes. tā 'lyǎng-jř-'shyé dēw 'dyēw-le. or tā yì-shwāng-'shyé dēw 'dyēw-le. ‖Both sides fought hard, (*Literary*) shwāng-'fāng lì-'jàn. *But* ‖He lost both pairs of shoes. tā 'lyǎng-shwāng-'shyé dēw 'dyēw-le.

Both X and Y (*nouns*) X (gēn) Y ... dēw. ‖Both boys and girls play here. 'nán-hár 'nywǔ-hár dēw dzày-'jèr 'wár.

Both X and Y (*adjectives*) yèw X yèw Y. ‖It's both good and cheap. 'yèw 'hǎw 'yèw 'pyán-yi.

BOTTLE. 'píng-dz, pyéngr. ‖The bottle broke in my suitcase. 'píng-dz dzày wǒ-de-'shyāng-dz-li 'pwò-le (or 'lyè-le or 'swèy-le).

Bottle of píng, 'píng-dz, pyéngr. ‖This bottle of milk was prepared this morning. jèy-píng-nyéw-'nǎy shr̀ 'jīn-tyan-'dzǎw-chen-de. ‖He drank the whole bottle of milk. tā bǎ yì-jěng-'píng-dz-de-nyéw-'nǎy dēw 'hē-le. ‖I'd like a bottle of ink. wǒ yàw yì-pyéngr-mwò-'shwěr.

Water bottle shwěy-'píng; milk bottle nyéw-nǎy-'píng; *and so on, with* píng *for* bottle.

To bottle jwāng-daw 'píng-dz-li. ‖They bottle the water and sell it. tām bǎ-'shwěy jwāng-daw 'píng-dz-li 'mày.

‖He can't stay away from the bottle. *is expressed as* He can't keep from drinking, tā 'bù-néng bù-hē-'jyěw.

BOTTOM. 'dǐ-shyà, dyěr. ‖The potatoes in the bottom of the sack are all rotten. kěw-'dày-'dǐ-shya-de-tǔ-'dèwr dēw 'làn-le. ‖I can't reach the bottom. (*With the hand*) wǒ gèw-bu-'jáw 'dyěr. (*In swimming*) wǒ fù-bu-'dàw 'dyěr. ‖There were tea leaves at the bottom of the cup. chá-bēy-'dyěr-shang yěw chá-'yè. ‖The ship went to the bottom. 'chwˊn chén-'dyěr-le.

(*Seat, as of a chair*) dzwèr. ‖The bottom of this chair is broken. jèy-jāng-'yǐ-dz-de-'dzwèr 'hwày-le.

(*Buttocks*) 'pì-hu, 'pì-gu. ‖The child fell on its bottom. shyǎw-'hár shwāy-le ge-'pì-hu-dwēr.

(*With bottom down*) 'píng-je. ‖Set the box on its bottom. bǎ 'shyāng-dz 'píng-je 'fàng.

At bottom chí-'shr̀. ‖At bottom there's nothing unusual. chí-'shr̀ 'bìng méy-yew shéme-lyàw-bu-'dé-de. ‖At bottom he's honest. chí-'shr̀ tā hěn 'chéng-shr̀.

To get to the bottom of *something* chá ge-shwěy-'ḷwò-shŕ-'chū, chè-'dǐ 'chá-yi-chá. ‖His actions are so strange that we must get to the bottom of them. tā-de-jywǔ-'dùng hěn 'gwày; wǒm děy 'chá ge shwěy-'ḷwò-shŕ-'chū.

‖Bottoms up! *is expressed as* Dry the cup! gān-'bēy!

Be at the bottom of *something*. ‖I'll bet you she's at the bottom of this. dzám 'dǔ-dyǎr shéme; wǒ shwō yí-'dìng shr̀-'tā tsúng-'jūng jǔ-'shr̀.

BOUGH. shù-'gǎr, shù-'jř, shù-'jēr.

BOULDER. dà-'shŕ-tew.

BOULEVARD. dà-mǎ-'lù.

BOUND. Be bound to yí-'dìng (yàw), yí-'dìng děy, fēy-děy ... bù-'kě, bù-néng bū-, bì-'dìng (yàw). ‖He's bound to be late. tā yí-'dìng wǎn-'dàw. ‖I promised his father I would, so I'm bound to let him go. wǒ yǐ-jing 'dā-ying-le tā-de-'fù-chin-le, swˊ-yi °fēy-děy 'jwěn-ta 'dzěw bù-'kě. or °bù-néng bù-'jwěn-ta 'dzěw. or °yí-'dìng děy 'jwěn-ta 'dzěw. ‖He's bound to fail. tā bì-'dìng shr̄-'bày. ‖I'm bound to take care of them. *is expressed as* If I didn't take care of them it couldn't be explained away within the limits set by custom and ethics. wǒ 'bù-gwǎn tā-men, dzày 'lǐ-shang shwō-bu-gwò-'chywù. ‖My luck is bound to change. wǒ-de-'ywùn-chì yí-'dìng hwèy 'jwǎn-de.

Be bound (for) *a place* dàw ... chywù, chywù, shàng. ‖I'm bound for the park. wǒ dàw gūng-'ywán-chywu. ‖Where are you bound? nǐ dàw-'nǎr-chywu? or nǐ shàng-'nǎr? ‖Are you bound for America? nǐ shr̀ chywù 'měy-gwo-ma?

To bound tyàw, bound back 'tyàw-hwéy. ‖The ball bounded back to his hand. 'chyéwr tyàw-hwéy tā-'shĕw-li-chywu. ‖He jumped to the other side in one bound. tā yí-'tyàw jyèw tyàw-daw 'nèy-byar-chywu-le. ‖Try to catch the ball on the first bound. dzày 'chyéwr dì-'yí-tsż-'tyàw-chi-lay de-shŕ-hew jyèw shyăng-'fár 'jyē-jù.

Bounds (limits, borders). ‖His pride had no bounds. tā-jyāw-'àw-de lyăw-bu-'dć. ‖The ball fell out of bounds. 'chyéw 'păw-daw 'wày-byan chywù-le.

Be bounded by. ‖The valley was bounded by high mountains. jèy-ge shān-'gŭ-sż-jēw-'wĕy chywán shŕ gāw-'shān. ‖The United States is bounded on the north by Canada. 'mĕy-gwo-de-'bĕy-byan gēn jyā-ná-'dà jyāw-'jyè.

Be bound up with. ‖His success is bound up with politics. tā-de-swó-yi-chéng-'gūng hĕn yĕw 'jèng-jŕ-bĕy-'jǐng.

BOUNDARY. (Between countries) gwó-'jyè; (any geographical dividing line) byān-'jyè. Boundary line jyè-'shyàn.

BOW. (Weapon) 'gūng; bow and arrow gūng-'jyàn; bow tie lǐng-'jyéer; (front end of a ship) chwán-'téw; (of a plane) fēy-jī-'téw, fēy-jī-chyán-'bù.

BOWELS. (Intestines) 'cháng-dz. To move the bowels lā-'shŕ, dà-'byàn.

BOWL. wăn.

BOWLING. (Game) (dă-)dì-'chyéw.

BOX. (Container) 'hé-dz, 'shyá-dz, 'snyāng-dz; in compounds 'héer, 'shyár, 'shyāngr, 'gwèy, 'hé, !shyá, 'shyāng; (large box) dà-'hé-dz; (large paper box for packing) dà-jŕ-'shyāng-dz; (large wooden box) dà-mù-tew-'shyá-dz; (jewel box) shĕw-shr 'shyá-dz; (small money box) chyán-'shyāngr, chyán-'shyár; (large money box) chyán-'gwèy. ‖We need a larger box for packing. wŏm dĕy-yùng yí-ge-'dá-dyăr-de-'hé-dz láy 'jwāng dūng-shi. ‖We can break up this box to make a fire. wŏm ké-yi bă jèy-ge-'hé-dz 'chāy-le lŭng-'hwŏ. ‖Fill up that box for me. gĕy-wo bă nèy-ge-'hé-dz jwāng-'măn-le. ‖Please put it in a box. fàng-dzay yí-ge-'shyá-dz-li 'hăw-le. ‖This candy is cheaper by the box. jèy-'táng lwèn-'shyár mĕy 'pyán-yi.

Box of (with any of the above expressions). ‖She ate a whole box of chocolates. tā 'chŕ-le yì-jĕng-'héer-de-kēw-kew-'táng.

To box (up) jwāng(-dzay) 'héer-li, jwāng-'shyár. ‖Box up what is left. shèng-'shyà-de dēw jwāng (-dzay) 'héer-li. ‖I had a hundred pounds boxed in one

hour. wŏ 'yì-dyăn-jūng-li jwāng-'shyár jwāng-le yì-băy-'bàng.

To come boxed dày-'shyár. ‖The cheap candy isn't boxed. 'pyán-yi-de-táng bú-dày-'shyár.

(In theater) bāw-'shyāng. ‖We took a box at the theater. wŏm-dzày-shì-'ywán-dz-li-dzwò-de shŕ bāw-'shyāng.

To box (sport) dă-'chywán. ‖Do you like boxing? nĭ 'shi-hwan dă-'chywán-ma? ‖He boxes well. tā 'chywán 'dă-de hĕn 'hăw.

Boxcar yĕw-'dĭng-hwò-'chē.

BOY. nán-'háy-dz, nán-'hár (nán male is omitted when it is not necessary to specify sex). ‖Boys grow fast. nán-'hár 'jăng-de dĭng 'kwày. ‖That boy is growing fast. nèy-ge-'háy-dz 'jăng-de hĕn 'kwày. ‖My boy doesn't do that. 'wŏ-nèy-ge-háy-dz bú-'nème-je. ‖They have two boys and a girl. tām yĕw 'lyăng-ge-'nán-hár, 'yí-ge-'nywŭ-hár. ‖Boys and girls! Come here! 'háy-dz-men, dàw-'jèr-lay! ‖Boys will be boys. shyăw-'hár dēw. 'wán-pi.

Boys' school. ‖That's a boys' school. nà shŕ ge-'nán-shywé-'shyàw.

The boys (meaning grown-ups) tām-yì-'hwŏ-dz. ‖The boys are having a game of poker tonight. tām-yì-'hwŏ-dz jyēr-'wăn-shang dă 'pū-kè-páy.

(Servant or help; in a hotel) 'chá-fang; (in a restaurant or store) 'hwŏ-ji; (in a' home) tīng-'chāy (-de). ‖Please send a boy up for our luggage, 'dă-fā yí-ge-'chá-fang shàng-lay gĕy wŏ-men ná 'shíng-li. ‖Boy, please bring me some icewater. 'hwŏ-ji, ná dyăr-bīng-'shwĕy-lay. ‖He's serving as a boy in that house. tā dzày nèy-'jyār dāng tīng-'chāy. In calling to a servant, Boy!, use the servant's full name, such as 'lĭ-'shēng, or, for a male servant, use lăw and the surname lăw-'lĭ. It is customary to ask a servant what his name is so that you can use it; ask him nĭ 'jyàw shéme? or, more politely, nĭ gwèy-'shìng?

(Exclamation). ‖Boy oh boy! What a night! hăw-'jyā-hwo, jèy-yì-'wăn-shang!

BRACE. (Tool) bă-'lĭng; bit jyā-'mù.

BRACELET. 'jwó-dz, shĕw-'jwó.

BRAID. (Of hair) yì-gŭ-de-'téw-fa, yí-swèr-de-'téw-fa, yì-lyĕwr-de-'téw-fa; (woven band) (yì-lyĕwr)-fàng-'byàn.

BRAIN. 'năw-dz.

BRAKE. já; (technical term) jŕ-dùng-'chì.

BRAKEMAN. (Railroad) gwăn-'já-de.

BRAN. kāng.

BRANCH. (*Of a tree*) shù-'chà-dz, shù-'jř-dz, shù-'jěr, dà-'jř-dz, shyǎw-'jěr, shyǎw-shù-'jěr. ‖The bird is on that highest branch. 'nyǎw dzày dzwèy-'gāw-de-shù-'jěr-shang. ‖Several big branches blew off in the wind. hǎw-'jǐ-ge-shù-'chà-dz děw gwā-'dwàn-le.

Branch *of a family* jř. ‖Our household is of the New York branch of the family. wǒm-'jyā shř nyēw-ywē-'shěng-'nèy-jř. ‖We come from the western branch of the family. (*Specifically Chinese, referring to the typical situation in which one of a man's sons, with his wife and servants and children, live in the western part of the house.*) wǒm-'jèy-yì-jř shř shī-'fáng-de.

Branch *of a river* jř-'lyéw. ‖No, this is only a branch of the river. 'bú-shr, jè jř shř yì-tyáw-'jř-lyéw.

Branch road jř-'lù, chà-'dàw. ‖Wait for us where there's a branch road to the right. dzày dà-'lù-shang-věw-shyàng-'yèw-de-jř-'lù-nàr 'děng wǒ-men.

Branch of service. (*Of military personnel*) kē; (*of military units*) bīng-'jǔng. ‖What branch of service are you in? (*Asked of an officer*) nǐ shř 'nǎ-yì-'kē-de? ‖What branch of service is that company? 'nèy-yì-lyán shř shéme-bīng-'jǔng?

Branch of study (*or learning*) kē, jǔng. ‖Optics is a branch of physics. 'gwāng-shywé shř wù-'lǐ-shywé-de-yì-'kē.

If a business or official organization has branches at various locations, the terms for them follow the pattern post office yéw-jèng-'jywú; branch post office yéw-jèng-'fēn-jywú *or* (*short form*) 'fēn-jywú; east branch (west branch, *etc.*) (yéw-jèng-)'dūng-jywú. *Names of other such organizations end with a different element from* jywú; *this other element is substituted as above.* ‖Get the stamps at the branch post office. dàw (yéw-jèng-)'fēn-jywú chywù mǎy yéw-'pyàw. ‖You can read the newspapers at the branch library across the street. nǐ kě-yi dzày dwèy-'gwèr-de-tú-shū-'fēn-gwǎn kàn-'bàw.

Branch off from lí, 'lí-kāy. ‖We branched off from the main road. wǒm 'lí(-kay)-le 'dà-lù-le. ‖When he gives a speech he always branches off from his subject. tā yǎn-'shwō de-shŕ-hew 'cháng-cháng lí-'tí.

Branch out into dǎ-'rù. ‖That company has branched out into oil now. nèy-ge-gūng-'sž-de-yíng-'yè yǐ-jing dǎ-'rù-le 'yéw-yè-le.

BRAND. (*Of product*) 'páy-dz.

BRANDY. báy-lán-'dì.

BRASS. (hwáng-)'túng.

BRASSIERE. nǎy-'jàwr.

BREAD. (*Western-style bread or rolls*) myàn-'bāw. ‖We need two loaves of bread. wǒm děy yěw 'lyǎng-kwày-myàn-'bāw. ‖I must slice the bread. děy bǎ myàn-'bāw 'chyē-chéng-le 'pyàr.

Bread is not a part of the Chinese diet. The equivalent staple is some variety of rice fàn *or wheat product* myàn, *the former being prevalent in the south, the latter in the north. Baked products which more or less resemble Western bread or other things, called bread* (*corn bread, etc.*) *are* bǐng, dà-'bǐng *shortened dough in flat, thin, round shape, baked on a griddle;* fā-myàn-'bǐng *the same with yeast;* 'gwō-bǐng *a thick variety;* dž-yéw-'bǐng, *the same with small pieces of lard;* tsūng-hwār-'bǐng *the same with slices of scallion* (*kind of onion*) *in it;* báw-'bǐng *unshortened and very thin. Breadlike products made by steaming are* 'mán-tew *raised with yeast;* hwā-'jywǎr *same in roll shape;* 'bāw-dz *with some stuffing, as dumplings.*

Bread and butter (*a living*). ‖How does he earn his bread and butter? tā 'jř-je shéme chř-'fàn?

To be on the breadline *is expressed as* to receive porridge lǐng-'jēw. ‖Many people are on the breadline today. 'jīn-tyan lǐng-'jēw-de-rén hěn 'dwō.

BREAK. *If something breaks of itself, the terms are* pwò (*break to pieces*); hwày (*break to pieces, get out of order, become useless*); lyè (*to crack*); swèy (*break to bits, disintegrate*); shé (*to fracture, as a glass rod*); dwàn (*to break into segments, of any long object*); sǎn (*of a box or hollow object*). *If something or someone breaks something, the terms are compound verbs of which the second elements are those given; the first elements expressing the method or means of breaking;* dǎ (*by striking a blow*); dzá (*by striking a blow with a heavy object*); chyǎw (*by a light sharp blow*); shwǎy (*by dropping*); pèng (*by colliding with an object*); tī (*by kicking*); yā (*by squeezing down from above*); jǐ (*by squeezing, or by pressure from inside*); lā (*by pulling*); chěw (*by jerking sharply*); twēy (*by pushing*); rēng (*by throwing*); shwǎy (*by swinging and shaking*); 'děw-lu (*by shaking rapidly*); 'yáw-hwàng (*by shaking or swinging back and forth*); jywē (*by applying a bending force to the two ends of a long object*); bǎy (*by applying a bending force to other than a long object*); n·ng *more general, not specifying exact method. These first parts may also combine with the second elements* dàw *or* chéng *as the equivalent of English* break *something* into *so many pieces, such a shape, or* break *something* to *such-and-such a degree. Some of these combinations would not call for the English word* break, *but rather for some other word such as* fracture, destroy, crack. *There are also other less common words and combinations. Some of the above are illustrated below*

‖Be careful not to break this. 'shyǎw-shǐn byé bǎ 'jèy-ge 'dzá-le (*or* 'dǎ-le, 'shwǎy-le, 'pèng-le, pèng-'hwày-le, *etc.*) ‖The waiter broke three plates when he fell. paw-'tángr-de 'shwǎy-le yì-jyāw, 'dzá-le sān-ge-'pán-dz. ‖Does it break easily? hěn 'rúng-yì 'hwày-ma? (*or* 'sǎn-ma?, *etc.*) ‖Who broke the window? 'shwéy bǎ 'bwō-li dǎ-'swèy-le? ‖He fell down and broke his leg. tā bǎ-'twěy shwǎy-'shé-le. ‖He fell down and broke his nose. tā bǎ 'bí-dz shwāy-'pwò-le. ‖The cup didn't break when I dropped it. 'bēy-dz 'dyàw 'dì-shya méy-'swèy. ‖I broke the cup when I dropped it. 'bēy-dz jyàw-wo shwāy-'pwò-le. ‖Has the car broken down already? 'chē 'yǐ-jing 'hwày-le-ma? ‖His health has broken down. tā-'shēn-dz 'hwày-le. ‖The car didn't break down until yesterday. 'chē yì-'jř dàw 'dzwó-tyan háy méy-'hwày. ‖Please break off a piece for me. 'bāy yí-kwàr 'gěy-wo. ‖The ice is breaking up. 'bīng 'lyè-le. ‖The box had (been) broken up. 'hé-dz 'san-le.

(Of dikes, dams, or teeth) bēng. ‖I've broken a tooth on this candy. jèy-kwày-'táng jēn 'yìng, bǎ wǒ-de-'yá gěy 'bēng-le. ‖The dike broke. nèy-ge-'tí 'bēng-le.

Break relations 'fēn-kāy. ‖He broke with his family. tā gēn tā-'jyā 'fēn-kay-le.

Break off relations jywé-'jyāw. ‖They've broken off relations. tām jywé-'jyāw-le.

Break camp bá-'yíng. ‖We're going to break camp tonight. jīn-tyan-'wǎn-shang bá-'yíng.

Break down (refute) bwō-'dǎw. ‖They broke down his argument. tām bǎ tā-de-lì-'yéw gěy bwō-'dǎw-le.

Break down (take apart) 'chāy-kāy. ‖Break down this gun. bǎ-'chyāng 'chāy-kay.

Break into a house 'jìn-daw ...-li. ‖A thief may break into the house. yé-shywu yěw-'dzéy hwèy 'jìn-daw 'fáng-dz-li-chywu.

Break someone's heart jyàw ... shāng-'shīn. ‖It really breaks my heart. (Seriously) jēn jyàw-wo shāng-'shīn. (Seriously or lightly) 'nà tsáy 'jyàw-wo shāng-'shīn-ne.

Break out (of fire) chǐ, fā-'shēng. ‖The fire broke out about midnight. 'hwǒ shř 'bàn-yè 'chǐ-de. ‖A fire broke out near here yesterday. 'dzwó-tyan jè-li-'fù-jìn fā-'shēng 'hwǒ-jīng.

Break out (of war) 'dǎ-chǐ-lay. ‖We hope war won't break out. wǒm 'shī-wàng 'dǎ-bu-chǐ-láy.

Break out with a skin disease chū 'jěn-dz. ‖The child is breaking out with measles. shyǎw-'hár chū 'jěn-dz-le.

Break the law fàn-'fǎ. ‖We mustn't break the law. bù-'yīng-gay fàn-'fǎ.

Break up a crowd 'gǎn-kāy, 'sàn-kāy. ‖Break (it) up! 'sàn-kay!

Break up (of ice) jyě-'dùng. ‖The ice is breaking up. 'bīng jèng-dzày jyě-'dùng.

Break out of jail ywè-'ywù. ‖There was a jail-break yesterday. 'dzwó-tyan yěw-'rén ywè-'ywù.

Break one's journey 'tíng-yí-shyàr. ‖He must break his journey in order to see the cathedral. tā dzày bàn-'dàw děy 'tíng-yí-shyàr hǎw chywù kàn nèy-ge-jyàw-'táng.

Break an engagement jyě-'chú. ‖Her parents broke her engagement. tā-de-fù-'mǔ gěy-ta bǎ hwēn-'ywè jyě-'chú-le.

Break a date. ‖He's broken his date. tā bù-'láy-le. or tā 'shwō-le tā bù-'láy-le.

Break a promise. ‖He won't break his promise. tā bú-'hwèy 'shwō-le bú-'swàn.

Break the ice. ‖They were very formal until somebody broke the ice with a joke. tā-men chǐ-'shyān hěn 'jywū-shù, 'hèw-lay yěw-'rén shwō-le yí-ge-'shyàw-hwar jyèw bǎ chén-'mèn-de-'kūng-chi gěy dǎ-'pwò-le.

‖I'll break your neck! wǒ bǎ nǐ-de-'nǎw-day 'bá-shyà-lay!

A break. ‖Let's give him a break. meaning Let him try again. 'gěy-ta ge-'shīn-'jī-hwey-ba. or 'dzày gěy-ta ge-'jī-hwey-ba. or jyàw-ta 'dzày 'shř-yi-shř. or meaning Let him pass unpunished this time. 'ráw-ta 'jèy-tsż-ba. or meaning Give him a chance. 'gěy-ta ge-'jī-hwey-ba. ‖The breaks were against us. wǒm bù-dzěw-'ywùn.

BREAKFAST. dzǎw-'fàn, dzǎw-'tsān, dzǎw-'dyǎn. ‖Have you had breakfast yet? dzǎw-'dyǎn 'chř-gwo-le-ma? ‖What do you have for breakfast? dzǎw-'fàn yěw 'shéme? ‖What time is breakfast? dzǎw-'tsān 'jǐ-dyǎn-jūng?

BREAST. rǔ-'fáng, shyūng(-'púr).

BREATH. (Mouthful of air) yì-kěw-'chì. ‖Hold your breath to stop the hiccups. 'byē yì-kěw-'chì jyèw bù-dǎ-'géer-le. ‖Now take a deep breath. shyàn-'dzày shēn-'shēn-de shī yì-kěw-'chì.

Breath of air yì-dyǎr-'fēng. ‖There isn't a breath of air today. 'jyér yì-dyǎr-'fēng yě 'méy-yew.

Be out of breath 'chwǎn-bu-chū 'chyèr-lay. ‖She ran up the hill and was out of breath. tā 'pǎw-shang 'shān-chywú pǎw-de 'chwǎn-bu-chū 'chyèr-lay-le.

To catch one's breath chwǎn-'chì, chwǎn-'chyèr. ‖Let's stop here and catch our breath. dzám dzày-'jèr 'tǐng-hwěr hǎw chwǎn kěw-'chyèr. ‖We stopped to catch our breath. wǒm 'jàn-ju-le 'chwǎn-chwan 'chyèr.

To have bad breath 'dzwěy-li yěw-'wèr.

To save one's breath. ‖You might as well save your breath. nǐ yùng-bu-'jáw 'shwō shéme-le. or nǐ 'háy bù-'rú bù-'shwō shéme-ne.

BREATHE. chwǎn-chū 'chyèr-lay. ‖He'd be running so hard he could hardly breathe. tā 'pǎw-a tày 'lì-hày-le, jyǎn-jř 'chwǎn-bu-chū 'chyèr láy-le.

(Exhale and inhale) hū-'shī. ‖He's breathing regularly. (Doctor speaking) tā hū-'shī jèng-'cháng.

Be breathing (showing presence of life; as of an injured person) 'bí-dz yěw-'chì. ‖He's still breathing. tā 'bí-dz háy yěw-'chì.

Breathe freely 'chwǎn-chwan 'chyèr. ‖Now that he's gone we can breathe freely again. tā kě 'dzěw-le, jyàw-'rén ké-yi 'chwǎn-chwan 'chyèr-le.

Breathe hard. ‖She was breathing hard from climbing the stairs. tā shàng 'léw-tī shàng-de jř 'chwǎn.

To have a breathing spell 'shyē-yi-shyē. ‖When do we get a breathing spell? wǒm 'shéme-shŕ-hew néng 'shyē-yi-shyē? ‖Let's take a breathing spell and have a smoke. 'shyē-shye 'chwǎn-chwan chēw dày-'yān.

(*Disclose*). ‖Don't breathe a word of this to anyone. 'jèy-ge gēn-'shwéy yě byé 'shwō.

BREEZE. shyǎw-'fēng(r), wéy-'fēng(r).

BRICK. 'jwān; a brick of . . . yí-'kwày, yí-'kwàr.

BRICKLAYER. 'wǎ-jyang.

BRIDE. shīn-'nyáng-dz.

BRIDEGROOM. shīn-'láng.

BRIDGE. chyáw. ‖This boat can go under the bridge. jèy-jř-'chwán ké-yi tsúng chyáw-'dǐ-shya 'gwò-chywu. ‖We must go around; the bridge is out. dzám děy 'ràw-je dzěw, yīn-wey 'chyáw 'hwày-le.

(*Of a ship*) chwán-'chyáw; (*of warship*) jyàn-'chyáw. ‖The bomb fell on the bridge. jà-'dàn lwò-dzay chwán-'chyáw-shang. ‖Can you see the captain on the bridge? nǐ 'kàn-de-jyàn °jyàn-'jǎng-ma, dzày jyàn-'chyáw-shang-nàr? or °chwán-'jǎng-ma, dzày chwán-'chyáw-shang-nàr?

(*For false teeth*) (jyǎ-'yá-de-)'chyǎ-dz. ‖The dentist says I need a new bridge for that false tooth. yá-'yī shwō wǒ 'nèy-ge-jyǎ-'yá děy hwàn yí-ge-'chyǎ-dz. ‖That dentist does excellent bridge work. nèy-ge-vá-'yī shyāng jyǎ-'yá hěn yěw 'gūng-fu.

(*Of nose*) bí-'lyáng-dz, bí-'lyángr. ‖His nose has a low bridge. tā-de-bí-'lyáng-dz 'byě.

(*Game*). *The few Chinese who play it use the English word* bridge. To play bridge dǎ-'bridge.

To bridge (*a gap*) 'bǔ-shang. ‖These books will bridge the gaps in the library. tú-shū-'gwǎn-li-'chywē-de-shū yěw-le 'jèy-shyē-jyèw 'bǔ-shang-le.

To bridge over a difficulty gwò nán-'gwān.

‖He burned his bridges behind him. (*Literary expressions*) tā na shř pwò-'fǔ-chén-'jēw-le. or tā nà shř běy-chéng-jyè-'jī-le.

BRIDLE. mǎ-'lē-dz.

BRIEF. dwǎn. ‖I've written him a brief note. wǒ gěy-ta 'shyē-le yì-fēng-'dwǎn-'shìn. or wǒ gěy-ta 'shyē-le jǐ-ge-'dzèr. ‖Please make your speech brief. nǐ yán-'shwō-a, 'dwǎn-yi-dyǎr 'shíng-bu-shíng?

In brief dzǔng-ér-'yán-jř, jyàn-'dwàn-jyé-'shwō. ‖In brief, our plan is this. dzǔng-ér-'yán-jř, wǒ-men-de-'jì-hwà shř 'jème-yàng.

A brief. (*Summary*) jyé-'lywè, (*outline*) dà-'gāng. Send me a brief of that document. nèy ge-wén-'jyàn (chǐng-ni) gěy-wo sùng ge-jyé-'lywè-lay.

To brief bǎ dzwò-jàn-'jì-hwa 'dzé-yàw 'gàw-sung. ‖The squadron leader has already briefed the flyers. jūng-dwèy-'jǎng yǐ-jing bǎ dzwò-jàn-'jì-hwa 'dzé-yàw 'gàw-sung-le jyà-shr-'ywán-le.

BRIEFCASE. shū-'bāw, 'gūng-shř-bāw.

BRIGHT. (*Of light, or of things that reflect it*) lyàng; (*local Peiping*) chùng. ‖This mirror isn't bright enough. jèy-myàn-'jìng-dz bú-gèw 'lyàng. ‖The sunlight is quite bright. tày-yang-'gwāng hěn 'lyàng (or 'chùng).

(*Of colors*) chyǎn, shyān-'yàn, shyān-'míng. ‖This flower is a bright yellow. jèy-jǔng-'hwǎr shř chyǎn-'hwáng-sè. ‖The colors aren't bright enough. 'yán-sè bú-'gèw shyān-'yàn-de.

(*Of a fire*). ‖I like to see a bright fire! shyúng-'shyúng-de-hwǒ-'gwāng jēn 'hǎw!

(*Of a person*) 'tsūng-ming, 'nǎw-dz 'kwày. ‖He's a bright boy. tā shř ge-'tsūng-ming-'háy-dz. or tā-'jèy-ge-háy-dz hěn 'tsūng-ming. ‖He wasn't bright enough to catch the idea. tā-de-'nǎw-dz bú-gèw 'kwày-de, swó-yi tīng-bu-'dǔng.

Bright and cheerful gāw-'shìng. ‖Everyone was bright and cheerful at the dinner party. fù-'yàn-de-rén dēw hěn gāw-'shìng.

(*Of prospects*) shwèn- lì, ké-yi lè-'gwān. ‖The prospects are bright enough. chyán-'tú gèw shwèn-'lì-de. or chyán-'tú hěn ké-yi lè-'gwān.

Bright ideas. ‖Do you have any bright ideas? nǐ 'yěw-méy-yew hǎw-'fá-dz? or nǐ 'yě láy tsān-'jyā yì-dyǎr-'yì-jyàn-ba.

(*Of weather*). ‖We'd better wait for a bright day. děng hǎw-'tyār 'dzày shwō-ba.

BRING. *The idea of motion towards the speaker (in contrast to "take", motion away from the speaker), is expressed in Chinese by the use of* láy *after any of a number of verbs of bringing and taking. With* dày, *one such verb of bringing and taking, combinations include* 'dày . . . láy bring, 'dày-hwéy-láy bring back, 'dày-jìn-láy bring in, 'dày-chū-láy bring out, 'dàw-dàw . . . láy bring to (*a place*), 'dày-gwò . . . láy bring over. *English sentences with examples of this type of translation are given first.*

Examples of dày (*and combinations*). ‖I've brought more clothes than I need. wǒ 'yī-fu dày-de tày 'dwō le. ‖The father brought the children a present. 'fù-chin gěy 'háy-dz 'dày-le jyàn-'lǐ-wu. ‖May I bring a friend with me? wǒ ké-yi dày yí-wèy-'péng-yew láy-ma? ‖Please bring the book back with you. chǐng-ni bǎ-'shū 'dày-hwéy-lay. ‖Bring him in. (*As of a prisoner*) bǎ-ta 'dày-jìn-lay. ‖He asked someone to bring me word that he's not coming. tā twō-'rén dày-'hwàr-lay, shwō tā bù-'láy.

Examples of ná (*and combinations*). ‖How many matches should I bring? wǒ 'yīng-dang ná dwō-shaw-yáng-'hwǒ-lay? ‖Please bring me that book. chǐng-ni gěy-wo bǎ nèy-běn-'shū 'ná-lay.

(*To a waiter*) láy alone. ‖Waiter! Bring another bowl of rice! 'hwŏ-ji! 'dzày láy wăn-'fàn! ‖Bring me a glass of water. *is expressed as* Pour and bring a glass of water for me. gěy-wo 'dàw běy-'shwěy-lay.

Bring about (*cause*) jáw-'shěw, jìn-'shíng, shŕ-shíng. ‖We hope in this way to bring about a change very soon. 'pàn-wang bù-'jyěw jyèw yàw jáw-'shěw găy-'dzŭ-le.

Bring action against (*legal*) gàw. ‖He brought action against you. tā 'gàw-ni-le.

Bring *someone* around *or* over (*convince*) 'chywàn-gwò-lay, 'shwō-de 'jwǎn-le 'yì-le, shwō-'fú. ‖At first they didn't agree but we brought them around. tām chǐ-'chū bú-'dzàn-chéng, 'hèw-lay wǒm jyèw bǎ tā-men °'chywàn-gwo-lay-le. *or* °'shwō-de 'jwǎn-le 'yì-le. ‖We brought him over to our point of view. wǒm 'bǎ-ta shwō-'fú-le.

Bring *a subject* forward (*or* up) 'tí-chū-lay. ‖If you have any suggestions bring them forward. nǐ rú-gwo yěw shéme-'yì-jyàn chǐng 'tí-chu-lay. ‖I'll bring the·plan up at the next meeting. shyà-'tsẑ-kāy-'hwèy de-shŕ-hew, wǒ bǎ 'jì-hwa 'tí-chu-lay.

Bring (in) *money, profits* dé, néng 'mǎy, yěw . . . (*amount*)-de-shěw-'rù. ‖This transaction will bring in a large profit. jèy-jwāng-'mǎy-mày ké-yi 'dé bù-shǎw-de-'lì. ‖How much does this bring in the market? 'jèy-ge dzày 'shì-shang néng 'mày 'dwō-shaw-chyán? ‖It brings (him) in three hundred dollars a month. tā měy-'ywè yěw 'sān-bǎy-ywán-de-shěw-'rù.

Bring (in) *an audience* shī-'yǐn. ‖This speaker ought to bring (in) a big crowd. jèy-wèy-jyǎng-'ywán 'yīng-dang shī-'yǐn bù-shǎw-tīng-'jùng.

Bring on *a cold* jyàw . . . jāw-'lyáng; bring on a *fever* jyàw . . . fā-'shāw. ‖This bad weather will bring on many colds. 'tyān-chi jème-'lěng yí-'dìng jyàw bù-'shǎw-rén jāw-'lyáng.

Bring on (*or* about) *a calamity* rě-chu 'hwò-lay; bring on (*or* about) *a crisis, an accident* rě-chu 'shèr-lay.

Bring out *a play* chū-'yǎn, yǎn. ‖They're getting ready to bring out a new play. tām 'jwěn-bèy chū-'yǎn yì-chū-'shīn-de-'shì.

Bring out (*qualities, characteristics*). ‖The emergency brought out all his good qualities. *is expressed as* When the emergency came all his good qualities came out. dàw-le wéy-'jí de-shŕ-hew tā-de-'hǎw-chù dēw 'shyǎn-chu-láy-le.

Bring *someone* to (*from a faint*) 'jyèw-gwo-lay. ‖Cold water will bring him to. ké-yǐ yùng lyáng-'shwěy bǎ-ta 'jyèw-gwò-lay.

Bring up (*a child*) dày-'dà, yǎng-da, 'yàng-chǐ-lay. ‖They didn't bring their children up carefully. tām méy-yùng-'shīn bǎ 'háy-dz dày-'dà-de. ‖Their grand-

mother brought them up. tām shŕ dzŭ-'mǔ 'yǎng-chi-lay-de.

Bring . . . to bear on yùng . . . gūng . . .; yùng . . . chywù 'gàn. ‖They brought all the fire to bear on that fort. tām yùng chywán-'bù-de-pàw-'hwǒ gūng nèy-ge-pàw-'táy. ‖You must bring all your attention to bear on this. 'jèy-jyàn-shì nǐ děy yùng chywán-'shén chywù 'gàn

Bring pressure to bear on bī. ‖Can't you bring some pressure to bear on him? nǐ 'néng-bù-néng 'bī-ta yí-shyà? ‖They brought a lot of pressure to bear on him but he wouldn't budge. tām 'bī-ta bī-de hěn 'lì-hay, kě-shr tā yì-'dyǎr yě bù-'kěn twèy-'ràng.

Bring tears to the eyes. ‖That music brought tears to her eyes. nèy-ge-'chywǔr jyàw-ta 'yǎn-li 'lwèy-wāng-wāng-de.

Bring *someone* to *his* senses. ‖You must bring him to his senses. nǐ děy 'jyàw-ta 'míng-bay-gwò-lay.

Bring *someone* to do *something* chywàn. ‖I can't bring him to do it. wǒ bù-néng 'chywàn-ta 'dzwò nèy-ge. (*or* tā bù-'tīng wǒ-de-'chywàn.)

Be unable to bring oneself to do *something* gàn-bu-'chū. ‖I can't bring myself to do that sort of thing. 'nèy-yàng-de-shèr wǒ gàn-bu-'chū.

(*To cause to come*). ‖What brings you to town? nǐ wèy-!shéme jìn-'chéng-lay-de? *or* nǐ gàn 'shéme jìn-'chéng-lay-ya? ‖What brings you here? nǐ gàn 'shéme 'láy-le? *or* (*slangy*) 'nǎ-jèn-'fēng bǎ-ni 'chwěy-lay-le? ‖What (important matter) brings you to town? yěw shéme-'yàw-jǐn-de-'shèr ràng-'nǐ jìn-'chéng-lay?

Bring before a court. ‖I'll certainly bring this before the court. 'jèy-jyàn-shŕ wǒ yí-'dìng děy dzày fǎ-'tíng chǐ-'sù.

BROADCAST. gwǎng-'bwō.

BROKE. ‖He's dead broke. tā 'yí-ge-dzěr yě 'méy-yew-le.

BRONZE. chǐng-'túng.

BROOK. shyǎw-'hé(er).

BROOM. 'tyáw-shu, 'sàw-shu.

BROTH. chīng-'tāng.

BROTHER. (*Kinship term*). *See Appendix A.*

Brother *in the sense of fellow-member of an organization is not part of Chinese culture, except that in certain Chinese secret societies the term* 'dà-gē *is used for a fellow member; where Western lodges are found, English terms are used.*

BROW. (*Of eye*) 'méy-maw, méy.

BROWN. 'dzūng-shăr, 'hé-sè; *but instead of these, the closest equivalents, the Chinese usually classify what English calls* **brown** *as shades of other colors; if yellow is predominant* hwáng, 'hwáng-shăr; *if red is predominant* húng; *if green is predominant* 'chá-sè, 'chá-shăr; *chestnut* **brown** 'lì-sè, 'lì-dz-shăr. ‖I like the **brown** bag better than the black one. wǒ 'kàn, (nèy-ge-)'hwáng-chyán-'bāw bǐ (nèy-ge-)'hēy-de 'hǎw. ‖The **brown** is too dark. jèy-ge-'hwáng-shăr tày 'shēn-le.

Brown shoes hwáng-'shyé; **brown** bread hēy-myàn-'bāw; **brown** sugar húng-'táng.

To **brown** (*in cooking*). ‖The cake was browned just right over the fire. 'dyăn-shīn 'kăw-le yì-tséng-hwáng-'gār.

(*Of skin*). ‖The sun made his skin brown as coffee. tā 'shày-de jēn 'hēy.

BRUISE. (yí-kwày)-'chīng, -'dž.

BRUSH. 'shwā-dz. ‖You may use this brush to brush your hair. nǐ ké-yi yùng jèy-bǎ-'shwā-dz shwā-'téw. ‖I need a new brush to paint the walls with. wǒ děy-yàw yì-bǎ-'shīn-de-'shwā-dz hǎw shwā-'chyáng. ‖Please scrub this sink with a brush. bǎ jèy-ge-'pén yùng 'shwā-dz shwā-'gān-jìng.

(*Underbrush*) shù-'kē-dz. ‖The workmen are cutting the brush. 'gūng-rén dzày jyǎw shù-'kē-dz.

(*Chinese writing implement*) (jūng-gwo-)'bǐ, máw-'bǐ. ‖He doesn't know how to write with a brush. tā bú-'hwèy yùng máw-'bǐ shyě-'dž.

Artist's brush hwà-'bǐ.

To **brush**. (*With a brush*) shwā; (*with a duster*) dăn; (*with a cloth*) tsā; (*by accidental glancing contact*) 'hú-lu, pèng. ‖I must brush my teeth. wǒ děy shwā-'yá. ‖Please brush these clothes for me. bǎ jèy-shyē-'yī-fu 'shwā yí-shyàr. ‖I've brushed off the top of the table. jwō-'myàr wǒ yǐ-jing °'dăn-gwo-le. *or* °'tsā-gwo-le. ‖I brushed the plate off the table and broke it. wǒ bǎ 'pán-dz 'hú-lu-dàw 'dì-shya chywù-le, jyêw (dǎ-)'swèy-le.

To **brush against** tsèng. ‖I brushed against the paint. wǒ tsèng-'yéw-le.

To **brush away** hūng-'pǎw. ‖He brushed away the fly. tā bǎ 'tsāng-ying hūng-'pǎw-le.

To **brush past** 'tsèng-gwò-chywu, 'dzěw-gwò-chywu, 'tsā-gwò-chywu. ‖She brushed past us without seeing us. tā tsúng wǒ-men-'shēn-byar 'tsèng-gwò-chywu, kě-shř méy-'kàn-jyan wǒ-men.

To **brush up** (*clean up, wash up*) tsā bǎ-'lyăn, 'tsā-yi-tsā 'lyăn (*or* 'shěw), 'shǐ-yi-shǐ (lyăn *or* 'shěw). ‖Do you want to brush up before dinner? nǐ méy-chř-'fàn de-shř-hew shyǎng tsā bǎ-'lyăn-ma?

To **brush up on** 'wēn-shi. ‖I'm brushing up on my French. wǒ dzài 'wēn-shi fà-'wén.

To **brush aside.** ‖He brushed my protests aside. wǒ 'shwō-le 'bàn-tyan, °tā jyăn-'jř 'dàng-dzwò ěr-páng-'fēng-le. *or* °tā 'mǎn méy-tīng-'tí. *or* °tā chywán bú-dzày-'yì.

To **brush off** (*figuratively*). ‖She got brushed off. *or* She got the brush-off. tā jyàw 'rén-jya gěy 'shwăy-le. *or* tā āy 'shwā-le.

BUBBLE. pàwr.   Soap bubble yí-dz-'pàwr.

BUCKET. shwěy-'tǔng.

BUCKLE. dày-'kèw.

BUD. hwā-'gū-du, hwā-'léy.

BUDGET. ywù-swàn-'shū.

BUG. chúng, chúngr, 'chúng-dz.

BUGLE. 'lǎ-ba.

BUGLER. lǎ-ba-'shěw, chwēy-'hàw-de

BUILD. To **build** a *bridge* (*if very simple*) dā; dzàw, shyēw, jyà. ‖They built a bridge across the bay. tām dzày hǎy-'wān-shang 'dzàw-le yí-dzwò-'chyáw.

To **build** a *house or building* gày, dzàw, shyēw. ‖The men are building a new house. tā-men dzày 'gày yì-swěr-'shīn-'fáng-dz.

To **build** a *house or ship* dzàw, shyēw. ‖The ship was well built. 'chwán 'dzàw-de hěn 'hǎw.

To **build** a *nest* dā. ‖The birds are building a nest in the tree. 'nyǎw dzày 'shù-shang dā-'wō.

To **build** a *foundation of a building* lì, dzàw, dzí, shyēw. ‖The foundation is well built. dì-'jī 'lì-de 'hǎw.

To **build** a *pillar, column, lighthouse* dzàw, lì, shyēw. ‖They built a memorial column for him. tā-men wèy-ta 'lì-le yí-ge-jì-nyàn-'tǎ.

To **build** a *city wall, fortification* jǔ, dzàw, shyēw. ‖It took 50,000 men to build that city wall. 'jù nèy-ge-chéng-'chyáng yùng-le 'wǔ-wàn-rén.

To **build** a *fire* 'lǔng-chí-láy. ‖Please build a fire in the fireplace. bǎ chyáng-'lú-dz-de-'hwǒ 'lǔng-chi-lay.

To **build** a *barricade.* ‖They've built a barricade across the street. tām yùng 'dūng-shi bǎ-'lù 'lán-chi-lay-le.

To **build** (**up**) an *empire, big business* jyàn-'shè. ‖It took Japan 70 years to build (up) her empire. ř-'běn jyàn-'shè dì-'gwó yùng-le 'chī-shr-nyán.

To **build** (**up**) a *business* 'jīng-yíng-chǐ-lay, 'dzwò-chǐ-lay, 'dzwò-chū-chywu. ‖His business was built up in thirty years. tā-de-'mǎy-may shř yùng-le 'sān-shr-nyán 'dzwò-chi-lay-de.

To **build up** a *business, product* chwàng 'páy-dz. ‖The advertisement will build up the business. gwǎng-'gàw ké-yi gěy 'mǎy-may chwàng 'páy-dz.

To **build up** a *reputation* làw ge-hǎw-'myéngr, 'shù-lì shēng-'wàng. ‖He's trying to build up a reputation.

(*Informal*) tā shyǎng tì 'dž-jǐ làw ge-hǎw-'myéngr. *or* (*Formal*) tā jyé-'lì yàw (gěy 'dž-jǐ) 'shù-lì shēng-'wàng.

Built-in (*in the wall*) dzày-'chyáng-li-dzwò-'hǎw-le-de. ‖The room has a built-in bookcase. jèy-jyān-'wū-dz-li yěw dzày-'chyáng-li-dzwò-'hǎw-le-de-shū-'jyà-dz. *But* ‖He bought a radio with built-in antenna. tā 'mǎy-le yí-ge-'lǐ-tew-dày-tyān-'shyàn-de-wú-shyàn-'dyàn(-shēw-yīn-'jī).

To build up (*fill with houses*) gày-chi ('fáng-dz)-lay. ‖This region wasn't built up yet when I first came. wǒ chū 'dàw de-shf-hew jèy-ge-'dì-fang(-de-'fáng-dz) háy méy-'gày-chi-lay-ne.

To build on *something* (*add to it, using it as foundation*). ‖He took a simple story and built on it until it became a long novel. tā bǎ yí-ge-hěn-jyǎn-'dān-de-'gù-shr fā-'jǎn chéng-le yì-běn-'cháng-pyān-shyǎw-'shwēr.

A build (*physique*). ‖He has a good build. tā 'shēn-dz 'jǎng-de hěn 'hǎw.

BUILDING. (*Two stories or more*) léw; (*residence*) 'fáng-dz; (*tower*) tǎ; 'jyàn-jù (*used where in English one might say* structure). ‖Both offices are in the same building. 'lyǎng-ge-gūng-shr̀-'fáng dēw dzày 'yí-dzwò-'léw-li. ‖What building is that? (*Pointing*) 'nèy-ge-léw shr̀-'shéme? ‖That building with a spire is a church. nèy-ge-yěw-tǎ-'jyār-de-'jyàn-jù shr̀ ge-lǐ-bày-'táng.

BULB. (*Electric*) (dyàn-)dēng-'pàwr; (*plant*) 'gū-dwor.

BULL. gūng-'nyéw.

BULLET. dž-'dàn, chyāng-'dàn, chyāng-'dzěr.

BULLETIN. (*Notice*) tūng-'gàw, 'gàw-shr; (*published statement of an organization*) hwèy-'bàw; (*of a school*) jyàn-'jāng.

BUMP. (*Raised place; as on the head*) bāw.

BUNCH. bǎ(r) *of something bunched in the hand, or for vegetables like celery that are sold in bunches, not by weight;* kwěn *or* kwěr *for a bunch with a band around it, like tobacco leaves;* chwàr *for keys;* 'dū-lu *for a bunch of things joined at one end of each but loose and randomly arranged at the other, like grapes, keys;* chywún *for a group of human beings or animals.* A bunch of dirty crooks yì-chywún-'dǎy-rén. ‖I'll take two bunches of flowers. wǒ yàw 'lyǎng-bǎr-'hwār. ‖She's lost a bunch of keys. tā bǎ yí-chywàr-'yàw-shr 'dyēw-le. ‖How much is this bunch of grapes? jèy-yì-dū-lu-'pú-taw 'dwō-shǎw-chyán?

To bunch together at *a place* 'jywù-daw, 'jywù-dzay, 'jǐ-daw, 'jǐ-dzay. ‖The passengers were all bunched

together at the front end of the car. dzwò-'kè dēw gěy °'jywù-daw 'chē-'chyán-tew-le. *or* °'jǐ-daw 'chē-'chyán-tew-le.

To bunch together 'jywù-dzay yí-'kwàr, 'jǐ-dzay yí-'kwàr. ‖The passengers were all bunched together. dzwò-'kè dēw gěy 'jywù-dzay yí-'kwàr-le. *But* ‖The shots were all bunched together chyāng-'dzěr dēw 'dǎ-daw yí-'kwàr chywù-le.

BUNDLE. (*Of anything*) kwěn, bāw.

BUOY. fú-'byāw, féw-'byāw.

BUREAU. (*Furniture*) yī-'gwèy, 'gwèy-dz. *See* OFFICE.

BURGLAR. (*At night*) yè-'dàw, yè-'dzéy.

BURROW. (*Animal's home*) wō, dùng.

BURST. (*By freezing*) dùng-'lyè. ‖In the winter the pipes freeze and burst. 'dūng-tyan-li 'gwǎn-dz 'cháng-cháng dùng-'lyè-le.

(*With a bang*) fàng-'pàw. ‖The tire was so old that it burst easily. chē-'dày 'lǎw-de yī 'láy jyèw fàng-'pàw.

(*Of a bomb*) jà. ‖A bomb had burst in the next block. 'páng-byār-nèy-tyáw-'jyē-shang yěw yí-ge-jà-'dàn 'jà-le.

(*Of flowing water or a water barrier*) kāy 'kěw-dz; (*of dike or dam*) bēng, bēng-'lyè. ‖The river burst its banks. 'hé kāy 'kěw-le. ‖Last year the dam burst. 'chywù-nyan 'já kāy 'kěw-dz-le. *or* 'chywù-nyan 'já °'bēng-le. *or* °bēng-'lyè-le.

To burst out 'jǐ-chū-lay. ‖The contents burst out of the trunk. 'dūng-shi tsúng 'shyāng-dz-li 'jǐ-chū-lay-le.

To burst into 'chwǎng-jìn, 'měng-rán-jyān 'jìn. ‖He burst into the room. tā 'chwǎng-jìn 'wū-dz. *or* tā 'měng-rán-jyān jìn-le 'wū-dz.

To burst into flame hū-rán 'jáw-chi 'hwǒ-lay. ‖The airplane burst into flame. fēy-'jī hū-rán jáw-chi 'hwǒ-lay-le.

(*With emotion*). ‖He's bursting with anger. tā 'chì-de kwày rěn-bu-'jù-le. ‖She burst out crying. tā rěn-bu-'jù-le, jyèw 'kū-chi-lay-le. *or* tā hū-rán 'dà 'kū.

A burst 'lyè-de-dì-fang. ‖Did you find the burst in the water pipe? 'gwǎn-dz-'lyè-de-dì-fang nǐ 'jǎw-jáw-le méy-yew?

Burst of jèn. ‖There was a burst of applause after his speech. tā yǎn-'shwō 'wán-le yí-jèn-gǔ-'jǎng. ‖There was a burst of gunfire in the street yesterday. 'dzwó-tyan 'jyē-shang yěw yí-jèn-'pàw-shēng.

BURY. máy (*informal*); ān-'dzàng (*quite polite*); be buried rù-'tǔ, shyà-'dzàng. ‖The dog is burying the bone. 'gěw dzày 'máy 'gǔ-tew. ‖They'll bury the body tomorrow. 'míng-tyan jyèw 'máy-le. *or* 'míng-tyan rù-'tǔ. *or* 'míng-tyan ān-'dzàng. ‖They buried him yesterday. tā shr̀ 'dzwó-tyan shyà-de 'dzàng.

(*To perform burial rites for*) gěy ... shíng dzàng-'lǐ. ‖They want a priest to bury the child. tām yàw chǐng yí-ge-'shén-fù láy gěy 'háy-dz shíng dzàng-'lǐ.

Bury alive hwó 'máy. ‖They buried him alive. tām bǎ-ta 'hwó 'máy-le.

Bury at sea hǎy 'dzàng. ‖Did they bury him at sea? tām shr̀ bǎ-ta hǎy 'dzàng-le-ma?

Be buried under *or* among (*be hidden*) 'yā-dzay. ‖My passport was buried under the other papers. wǒ-de-hù-'jàw 'yā-dzay 'byé-de-wén-'jyàn-'dǐ-shya-le.

Be buried in (*absorbed*). ‖He's buried in his work. tā máy-'téw kǔ-'gàn-ne.

BUS. (*City or suburban*) gūng-gùng-chì-'chē; (*long-distance*) cháng-tú-chì-'chē. ‖Where can I catch the bus? wǒ dzày-'nǎr néng shàng gūng-gùng-chì-'chē? ‖We want to go by bus. wǒm dǎ-'swàn dzwò cháng-tú-chì-'chē chywù. ‖Does a bus go to that town? cháng-tú-chì-'chē 'dàw nèy-ge-'chéng-ma?

Bus-driver (*polite term*) sz̀-'jī; (*impolite if used in direct address*) kāy-'chē-de. ‖The bus-driver will tell you where to get off. sz̀-'jī hwèy 'gàw-sung ni yīng-dang dzày-'nǎr shyà-'chē.

BUSH. (shyǎw-)'shù.

BUSINESS. (*Buying and selling, trading, commerce*) 'mǎy-mày; (*commerce, used in compounds*) -shāng; (*affairs, matters, work*) shr̀; (*the business world, business men as a group*) shāng-'jyè; business man 'shāng-rén, jīng-'shāng-de, 'shāng-jyā; business section (*of a city*) 'shāng-yè-chywū, dà-'jyē, 'rè-nàw-dì-fang; big business dà-'shāng-jyā; big business (*particularly finance*) tsáy-'fá. ‖They're selling their business. tām-de-'mǎy-may yàw °chū-'shěw-le. *or* °dǎw-'shěw-le. ‖He's in business. tā dzwò 'mǎy-may. *or* tā shr̀ dzwò-'mǎy-may-de. *or* tā jīng-'shāng. *or* tā shr̀ 'shāng-rén. *or* tā dzày shāng-'jyè. ‖Will your son join the business? lìng-'láng °yàw láy bāng-'máng-ma? *or* °yě yàw láy dzwò-'shr̀-ma? *or* °yě yàw láy 'shywé-shí-shywé-shí-ma? *or* °yě yàw láy 'shyǎw-yi-shyǎw-ma? ‖What's his business? tā shr̀ dzwò-'shéme-de?

Business school 'shāng-yè-(kē-)shywé-'shyàw; business night school 'shāng-yè-'yè shyàw; business college 'shāng-yè-jwān-'mén-shywé-'shyàw; business (*as a branch of study*) shāng-'kē. ‖He's studying business. tā shywé 'shāng-kē.

Business conditions shāng-'chíng, shāng-yè-chíng-'kwàng, shāng-yè-jwàng-'kwàng.

(*Affairs, work*) shr̀, shèr. ‖Another part of a dentist's business is to pull teeth. yá-'yī-shang-dzwò-de-'shr̀-li 'háy yěw bá-'yá-ne. ‖It's your business to keep

the staff satisfied. jyàw rén-'ywán dzwò-'shr̀-gāw-'shìng shǐ 'nǐ-de-shr̀. ‖Can you understand this business? 'jèy-yàng-de-shèr °nǐ 'dǔng-ma? *or* °nǐ 'hwèy-ma? *or* °nǐ hwèy 'dzwò-ma? *or* nǐ 'kàn, 'jè shr̀ 'dzěme-yí-hwèy-'shèr-a? ‖He told us to mind our own business. tā 'jyàw wǒ-men 'shǎw gwǎn shyán-'shèr. (*or* tā shwō wǒ-men gwǎn-bu-'jáw.) ‖That's my business; you can't interfere. nà shr̀ 'wǒ-de-shr̀, nǐ gwǎn-bu-'jáw. ‖Let's settle this business right away. dzám bǎ jèy-jyàn-'shèr shyàn-'dzày jyèw 'lyǎw-le-ba.

To have no business (*have no right*). ‖He had no business to ask such questions. 'jèy-yàng-de-wèn-'tí tā píng-'shéme láy 'wèn? *or* tā gwǎn-bu-'jáw. *or* tā jyàn-'jr̀ shr̀ dwō-'dzwěy. *or* ywǔ-ta-wú-'gwān-de-shr̀ tā wèn-bu-'jáw.

BUSY. (*Of a person*) máng, yěw-'shèr; (*harshly*) méy-'gūng-fu. ‖I was busy all day. 'máng-le yī-'tyān. ‖This morning I was too busy to read the newspaper. wǒ jīn-tyan-'dzǎw-chen tày 'máng-le, méy-néng kàn-'bàw. ‖When he called I was busy eating. tā 'láy de-shŕ-hew wǒ jèng "máng-je chr̄-'fàn. ‖He's busy. (*Occupied*) tā jèng 'máng-ne. *or* tā hěn 'máng. *or* tā yěw-'shèr. *or* (*Speaking harshly*) tā méy-'gūng-fu. ‖He's always busy. tā 'lǎw-shr̀ 'máng. *or* tā 'lǎw-shr̀ yěw-'shèr. *or* tā 'lǎw-shr̀ méy-'gūng-fu. ‖He's too busy to see anybody. tā 'máng-de méy-'gūng-fu 'jyē-dày rén.

(*Of a place*) 'rè-nàw. ‖They live on a busy street. tām 'jù-dzay yì-tyáw-hěn-'rè-nàw-de-'jyē-shang.

(*Of a telephone number*) yěw-rén 'jyàw. ‖The operator says that the line is busy. sz̀-'jī-de shwō yěw-rén 'jyàw.

BUT. 'kě-shr̀, 'dàn-shr̀; *or often expressed by a pause.* ‖It wasn't me but my brother that you met. nǐ-'jyàn-gwo-de bú-shr̀ 'wǒ, shr̀ wǒ-'gē-ge. ‖It's not that I don't like him as a person, but I just can't work with him. 'bú-shr̀ wǒ bù-'shǐ-hwan tā-jèy-ge-'rén, shr̀ wǒ bù-'néng gēn-ta gùng-'shr̀. ‖This is right, but that is wrong. 'jèy-ge 'dwèy-le, kě-shr̀ 'nèy-ge tswò-le. ‖I thought I could go, but I can't. wǒ 'shyǎn yǐ-'wéy wǒ néng 'chywù-ne, dàn-shr̀ shyàn-'dzày bù-néng 'chywù-le.

(*Except that*) 'bú-gwò. ‖We can go with you but we will have to come back early. gēn-ni 'chywù dàw-shr̀ 'ké-yi, 'bú-gwò wǒm děy 'dzǎw-dyar 'hwéy-lay.

All but ... jyèw shèng ... bū-, jř yěw ... bū-, jř shèng ... bū-. ‖All are ready but you. jyèw shèng-'nǐ háy méy-ywù-bèy-'hǎw.

All but *did something* jyèw shèng bū-, jř shèng bū-, 'chà-dyar bū-. ‖He was so nervous that he all but wrecked the machine. tā 'hwāng-de jyèw shèng-le méy-bǎ 'jī-chi 'hwèy-le.

(*Except*) chú-le ... (yǐ-'wày). ‖The library is open every day but Sunday. tú-shū-'gwǎn chú-le shīng-chī-'r̀ (yǐ-'wày) 'měy-tyān dēw 'kāy. ‖We could do nothing but wait. chú-le 'děng-je méy-yew byé-de-'fár. ‖Who can do it but you? or Who but you could have done it? chú-le 'nǐ háy yěw 'shéy-ne?

Nothing but. ‖They have no meat but chicken. tām 'jǐ yěw 'jī-rèw. ‖She does nothing but grumble. tā 'chéng-tyan-jya 'bàw-ywàn-jè-ge-'bàw-ywàn-nà-ge-de.

(Exclamation) kě. ‖Lord, but it's cold! lǎw-'tyān-yé, kě 'jēn gèw 'lěng-de!

But for. ‖I would have drowned but for him. rè-fēy 'tā 'jyèw-wo (or yàw 'bú-shr 'tā 'jyèw-wo) wǒ jyèw 'yān-sž-le.

‖It never rains but it pours. (Literally) bú-shyà-'ywǔ dzé-'yǐ, yī 'shyà jyèw-shr (chīng-pén-)'dà-ywǔ. (Figuratively) bù-chū-'shr dzé-'yǐ, yī 'chū jyèw-shr bù-dé-'lyǎw.

BUTCHER. (Meat seller) mày-'rèw-de.

Butcher shop rèw-'pù; since Mohammedans do not eat or handle pork, one often says jū-rèw-'pù for a butcher shop that sells pork, and yáng-rèw-'pù lamb meat shop for a butcher shop run by Mohammedans.

BUTT. (Of gun) chyāng-'bàr; (of cigarette) yān-'téwr.

BUTTER. nǎy-'yéw, nyéw-'yéw, hwáng-'yéw.

To butter mwǒ hwáng-'yéw (or either of the others). ‖Shall I butter your toast? kǎw-myàn-'bāw-shang, nǐ 'yàw-bu-yàw mwǒ hwáng-'yéw?

(Figuratively). ‖He doesn't know which side his bread is buttered on. tā-jèy-rén 'bù-jř-dàw hǎw-'dǎy.

BUTTERFLY. hú-'dyè, hú-'tyěr, hǔ-'tyèr, fú-'dyè, fú-'tyěr, fú-'tyèr.

BUTTON. 'nyěw-dz, nyěw-'kèwr, 'kèw-dz, kèw-'pàn-dz, kèw-'pàr, nyěw-'pàr. Chinese buttons consist of two parts, made of thread; one contains a loop, one ends in a knot. The terms given apply to the whole set, and similarly for English button and buttonhole. ‖This button has come off. jèy-ge-'nyěw-dz 'dyàw-le. ‖Do you have a button like this one? nǐ 'jèr yěw gēn-jèy-ge-yí-'yàng-de-nyěw-'kèwr-ma? ‖I've lost two buttons. wǒ 'dyēw-le lyǎng-ge-'kèw-dz.

(Emblem) hwēy-'jāng. ‖He's wearing a Red Cross button. tā 'dày-le yí-ge-'húng-shŕ-dz-'hwèy-de-hwēy-'jāng.

To button (up) 'kèw-shàng (used with kèw-'pàr or Western buttons); 'jì-shàng. ‖Button (up) your overcoat. bǎ nǐ-de-dà-'yī 'kèw-shang. ‖Button (up) your collar. bǎ 'líng-dz 'jì-shang.

To push a (bell) button èn-'lyéngr. ‖To call the elevator, push the button. yàw yùng dyàn-'tī de-hwà, èn-'lyéngr jyèw 'shíng-le.

To press a (light) button èn dyàn-'mén. ‖When I pressed the button the light went out. wǒ yī èn dyàn-'mén 'dēng 'myè-le.

BUTTONHOLE. kèw-'mér.

BUY. mǎy. ‖Have you bought your ticket yet? (nǐ) 'pyàw 'mǎy-le-ma? ‖I bought these shoes in London. wǒ jèy-shyē-'shyé shř dzày lwén-'dwēn 'mǎy-de. ‖Did I buy the right thing? wǒ-'mǎy-de 'dwèy-bu-dwèy? ‖I'll buy our tickets tomorrow. wǒ 'míng-tyan yí-'dìng bǎ-'pyàw 'mǎy-le.

Buy up (chywán, dēw) 'mǎy-láy (or -chywù). ‖All the trucks have been bought up by the government. 'swǒ-yěw-de-dzày-jùng-chì-'chē dēw jyàw 'jèng-fǔ 'mǎy-chywu-le.

Buy out (chywan, dēw) 'mǎy-gwò-láy. ‖He bought out his partners. tā bǎ 'byé-rén-de-'gǔ-dz dēw 'mǎy-gwò-lay-le.

(Bribe) mǎy-'tūng. ‖You can't buy the police of this town. 'jèy-chéng-de-shywún-'jǐng nǐ bù-néng yùng-'chyán láy mǎy-'tūng-le.

Be bought (receive a bribe) shèw 'hwèy-lu.

A buy. ‖That's a good buy. 'nèy-ge 'mǎy-de hěn 'jŕ.

BY. (Location) kàw (be next to); dzày ... 'páng-byar, dzày ... yì-'byàr, dzày ... jèr (or nàr). ‖The hotel is by the sea. lywǔ-'gwǎn kàw-'hǎy. ‖Stand by the window. kàw 'chwāng-hu 'jàn-je. ‖Come and sit by me. láy dzwò-dzay 'wǒ-jèr. Go there and sit by him. dzwò-dzay 'tā-nàr-chywu. ‖He's sitting by my side. tā dzwò-dzay wǒ-'páng-byar. or tā dzày wǒ-'páng-byar 'dzwò-je. or tā kàw-je wo 'dzwò-je. ‖He stood by me. (Literally) tā 'jàn-dzay wǒ-°'páng-byar. or °yì-'byàr. or tā dzày wǒ-°'páng-byar 'jàn-je. or tā 'kàw-je wo 'jàn-je. (Figuratively) tā yì-'jŕ °'bāng-wo. or °'shyàng-je wo. or °dzày 'wǒ-jèy-byar.

Near by dzwǒ-'jìn, 'fù-jìn. ‖Is there a restaurant near by? dzwǒ-'jìn yěw fàn-'gwǎr-ma?

(Motion past an object) tsúng ...-gwò(-láy, -chywù) with some verb of motion before gwò. ‖He passed by me. tā tsung wǒ-'shēn-byar 'dzěw-gwò-chywu-le. ‖The bus went by without stopping. gūng-gùng chì-'chē méy-'tíng jyèw 'kāy-gwò-chywu-le.

By a period of time (in renting or paying) àn. ‖It's rented by the hour. àn 'jǔng-dyǎr 'dzū.

By a quantity (in buying) lwèn. ‖Do you sell this by the pound? nǐ 'jèy-ge lwèn-'bàng mày-ma? ‖No, by the piece. lwèn-'gèr.

By a means of transportation (if a passenger) dzwò; (if traveling on a horse, bicycle, or anything else one straddles) chí. ‖He came to this country by boat. tā shř dzwò-'chwán láy-de 'jèr. ‖Can we get there by rail? wǒm dzwò hwǒ-'chē ké-yi 'dàw-nèr-ma?

By a means of communication, or transportation for freight yùng, tsúng, yéw. ‖Send this by mail. bǎ 'jèy-ge (yéw yéw-jèng-'jywú) 'jì-chywu. ‖Send this by air mail. bǎ 'jèy-ge yùng fēy-jī-'shìn 'jì-chywu.

By someone or something who causes an event jyàw, ràng, bèy. ‖He was struck by lightning. tā jyàw- (or ràng- or bèy-)'léy 'jī-jaw-le. ‖The thief was shot in the leg by the police. nèy-ge-shyǎw-'tēwr-de-'twéy-shang jyàw (or ràng) chǐng-'chá (gěy) 'dǎ-le yì-'chyāng. ‖He was beaten up by a gang of hoodlums. tā jyàw (or ràng) yì-chywún-gwāng-'gwèr (gěy) 'dǎ-le (yí-dwèn). Or expressed as follows without any of the above words. ‖This book was written by a Frenchman. jèy-běn-'shū shř yí-ge-'fà-gwo-rén 'shyě-de. ‖His speech was written by someone I know. tā-de-yǎn-'shwō-'gǎw-dz shř wǒ-'rèn-shr-de-yí-ge-rén (gěy-ta or tì-ta) 'shyě-de.

By an instrument yùng. ‖This wood was sawed by a machine. jèy-ge-'mù-tew shř yùng 'jī-chi 'jywù-de.

By (on or before) a time. ‖He should have been here by now. tā shyàn-'dzày yīng-dang 'dàw-le. or 'jèy-ge-shŕ-hew tā gāy 'dàw-le. ‖I must leave by next week. wǒ jŕ-'wǎn 'shyà-lǐ-bày-'lǐ-tew děy 'dzěw. ‖Please return these clothes by Saturday. lǐ-bày-'ř-yì-chyán bǎ 'yī-shang 'sùng-hwéy-lay. or jŕ-'wǎn lǐ-bày-'lyèw bǎ 'yī-shang 'sùng-hwey-lay. ‖I must finish this by tomorrow. 'jèy-ge wǒ 'míng-tyan fēy-děy dzwò-'wán bù-'kě.

By (during) a time. ‖He sleeps by day and works by night. tā 'báy-tyan shwèy-'jyàw, 'yè-li dzwò-'shř.

By so much excess. ‖He's taller by three inches. tā 'gāw sān-'tswèn. ‖This board is thicker than the other by a couple of inches. 'jèy-kwày-'bǎn-dz bǐ 'nèy-kwày 'hèw jǐ-'tswèn. ‖Of those two, he's the taller by half an inch. 'tām-lyǎng-ge-rén-li, 'tā gāw bàn-'tswèn. ‖The winning horse beat the next by a length. nèy-pǐ-'téw-mǎ bǎ dì-'èr-mǎ 'là-le yì-mǎ-('shēn-dz-nàme-) 'cháng.

By far. ‖This is by far the best hotel in town. 'jè shř jèr-dzwèy-'hǎw-de-lywǔ-'gwǎn, bǐ 'byé-de hǎw-de 'dwō. or 'jèr-de-lywǔ-'gwǎn 'jèy-jyā bǐ 'byé-de dēw hǎw-de 'dwō. or 'jèr-de-lywǔ-'gwǎn shǔ 'jèy-jyār dzwèy-'hǎw-le. or 'jèr-de-lywǔ-'gwǎn 'jèy-jyā 'ywán bǐ 'byé-de 'hǎw.

X by Y (dimensions). ‖The room is ten feet by twelve feet. jèy-jyàn-'wū-dz shř 'yí-jàng 'kwān, 'yí-jàng-'èr-chř 'cháng. ‖This picture frame is nine by nine (inches). jèy-ge-jìng-'kwàngr shř 'jyěw-tswèn jyàn-'fāng.

One by one yí-jyàn-yí-'jyàn-de, yí-ge-'yí-ge-de, yí-kwày-yí-'kwày-de, etc.; two by two lyǎng-ge-'lyǎng-ge-de, etc.; (if taking something two by two) 'yí-tsž 'lyǎng-ge-de or 'yí-tsž ... 'lyǎng-ge. ‖We'll take these matters up one by one. jèy-shyē-'shř dzám yí-jyàn-yí-'jyàn-de 'bàn.

Day by day 'měy-tyān yī or 'yì-tyān yī. ‖Turn in your reports day by day. bàw-'gàw yì-tyān yì-'jyāw.

By (means of) ... -ing 'jř-je, 'jyè-je. ‖He makes a living by selling apples. tā 'jř-je mày 'píng-gwo wéy-'shēng. ‖He made his pile by selling that stuff. tā ('jř-je or 'jyè-je) mày 'nèy-jǔng-dūng-shi fā-de 'tsáy.

By (according to) àn-je, 'jàw-je. ‖We need a map to go by. wǒ-men àn-je yì-jāng-dì-'tú dzěw tsáy 'hǎw. ‖He's not playing by the rules. tā bú-'àn-je 'gwēy-jywu láy.

By (with respect to) àn (or jàw) ... láy shwō. ‖She's an engineer by education. àn tā-de-jyàw-'ywù láy shwō, tā shř ge-gūng-cheng-'shř. ‖She's a model now by profession but she used to be a teacher. jàw tā-shyàn-'dzày-de-jř-'yè láy shwō, tā shř ge-mwó-tè-'ér, kě-shr tā yǐ-'chyán dāng-gwo jyàw-'ywán.

By virtue of (because of). ‖What did you understand by his remark? nǐ 'míng-bay tā 'wèy-shéme shwō 'nèy-jǔng-hwà-de-ma? or tā-'nèy-jywù-hwà nǐ 'míng-bay tā-de-'yì-sz-ma? ‖What do you mean by that (remark)? nǐ ('jèy-jywù-hwà) shř shéme-'yì-sz?

By order of fèng ... de-'lìng. ‖By order of the police (department). fèng jǐng-'chá-tīng-de-'lìng. or fèng jǐng-chá-'jywú-de-'lìng.

By oneself (alone) 'dž-jǐ, dž-jǐ-'gěr, 'yí-ge-rén. ‖He did that by himself. 'nèy-ge shř tā-'dž-jǐ (or -dž-jǐ-'gěr or -'yí-ge-rén) 'dzwò-de.

By way of (route) tsúng (or dǎ, or yéw) ... 'nèy-tyáw-lù. ‖They went by way of the Cape of Good Hope. tām yéw hǎw-wàng-'jyǎw-'nèy-tyáw-lù 'dzěw-de.

Do well by dày ... hǎw, 'dwèy-ywu ... hǎw. ‖He did well by those kids. tā dày nèy-shyē-'háy-dz hěn 'hǎw.

By accident, chance. ‖This happened purely by accident. wán-'chywán shř méy-'shyǎng-dàw-de-'shř. or 'jèy-hwéy-shèr °wán-'chywán chū-hu 'yì-wày. or °jēn shř 'yì-dyǎr yě méy-'shyǎng-dàw. or °yì-dyǎr yě 'bú-shr gù-'yì.

Meet by accident, chance 'pèng-shang. ‖We met by chance the other day. 'nèy-tyān wǒ-men-'lyǎ 'pèng-shang-le. ‖Some inventions have come by chance. yěw-de-fā-'míng shř 'éw-ér 'pèng-shang-de.

By surprise. ‖The rain caught me by surprise. wǒ méy-'shyǎng-dàw hwèy shyà-'ywǔ. or hū-rán shyà-chi 'ywǔ-lay-le, bǎ-wo gěy 'lwén-le.

By the way 'hèy! or wǒ 'shyǎng-chi-lay-le!

By and large tsúng dà-'tǐ-shang 'kàn. ‖By and large the results were satisfactory. tsúng dà-'tǐ-shang 'kàn, 'jyē-gwǒ háy 'hǎw.

‖Stand by! byé 'dzěw-kāy!

BY-LAW. shì-'dzé.

BYPASS. shyǎw-'lù, shyǎw-'dàw(r).

C

CAB. (*Taxi*) líng-'gù-de-chì-'chē, *often simply called* chì-'chē *or* chē.

(*On locomotive*) jī-gwān-chē-'shr̀, ywùn-jwàn-'shr̀.

CABBAGE. yáng-báy-'tsày. **Celery cabbage** báy-'tsày, *a Chinese vegetable which is similar but not identical.*

CABIN. (*On ship or plane*) tsāng. **First-class cabin** téw-děng-'tsāng; **second-class cabin** 'èr-děng-tsāng *or* fáng-'tsāng.

(*Pilot's cabin on plane*) sz̄-jī-'shr̀.

(*Small rough-built house*) shyǎw-'wūr, shyǎw-'fáng-dz.

CABINET. (*Cupboard*) 'gwèy-dz, chú. (*For dishes*) wǎn-'gwèy, wǎn-'chú.

(*Of a government*) nèy-'gé.

CABLE. (*Steel*) tyě-'làn; (*fiber*) dà-'shéng-dz; (*undersea*) hǎy-dǐ-dyàn-'shyàn; (*message*) (hǎy-dǐ-)dyàn-'bàw.

To send a cable fā (*or* dǎ) (hǎy-dǐ-)dyàn-'bàw.

CAGE. 'lúng-dz. (*In a prison*) jyān-'ywù.

CAKE. (*Pastry*) *general terms* 'dyǎn-shīn, 'gāw-dyǎn; **Western-style cakes and pastries** yáng-'dyǎn-shīn; *including any sweet eatables* 'tyán-shŕ. *Designations for specific types of cake end in the following elements:* (*Cakes made with yeast-rising dough, but not in flat and round shape*) gāw; (*flat and round cakes*) bǐng *or* byěngr *or* byěr; (*cakes made with especially shortened dough*) sū; (*cakes in a finger shape, but smaller than lady-fingers*) tyáwr. *Some specific types are* **date cake** dzǎwr-'gāw; **egg cake** dàn-'gāw *or* tsáw-dz-'gāw; **nut cakes** (*made with rice flour, in thin oblong slices*) ywún-pyàn-'gāw; **pan-baked cakes** gwō-tswèy-'byěngr *or* gwō-dz-'byěngr *or* má-'bǐng; **almond cake** shìng-rér-'bǐng; **mooncake** (*made especially for the moon festival on the fifteenth day of the eighth month of the lunar calendar*) 'ywè-bǐng; **shortened almond cake** shìng-rér-'sū; (*cake so fragile that it breaks as it enters the mouth*) dàw-kěw-'sū; (*fried finger-cakes made with rice flour*) jyāng-mǐ-'tyáwr. ‖**I want a catty (*Chinese pound*) of egg cake.** gěy-wo 'nǎ 'yì-jīn-tsáw-dz-'gāw. ‖**What kind of cake do you have?** nǐ 'jèr gāw-'dyǎn dēw yěw shéme-'yàngr-de? ‖**I'd like some cake with my coffee.** wǒ shyǎng 'dyǎn-shīn gēn jyā-'fēy yí-'kwàr chr̄. ‖**Do you have fish cakes?** nǐm yěw ywú-'byěngr-ma?

Cake of (*hunk, piece*) kwày. ‖**Could I have a towel and a cake of soap?** wǒ 'ké-yi-bu-ké-yi yàw yì-tyáw-'shěw-jīn gēn yí-kwày-'yí-dz?

To cake nìng, 'nìng-shàng; (*to dry*) gān; (*to dry into lumps*) gān-chéng 'kwàr. ‖**The oil caked in the cold weather.** tyār 'lěng, 'yéw 'nìng-shang-le. ‖**The mud caked.** 'ní 'gān-le.

CALENDAR. *The Chinese have several calendric systems* 'lì-fǎ: **lunar calendar** yīn-'lì, *also called* **old calendar** jyèw-'lì, *or* **discarded calendar** fèy-'lì; **solar calendar** yáng-'lì, *also, since its adoption by the National Government, called* **official calendar** gwó-'lì, *or* **Western calendar** shī-'lì, *or* **official international calendar** gūng-'lì, *or* **new calendar** shīn-'lì; **Mohammedan calendar** hwéy-'lì *or* hwéy-hwey-'lì.

In the Chinese lunar calendar a year is divided into twenty-four solar periods, determined by the days on which the sun enters the first or the fifteenth degree of a zodiacal sign. The periods are called jyé *or* 'jyé-chì.

‖**April 18, 1908 (of the Western calendar), corresponds to the eighteenth day of the third month of the thirty-fourth year of the gwāng-shywù period.** 'yáng-lì 'yī-jyěw-'líng-'bā-'nyán 'sz̀-ywè 'shf-bā(-hàw) shr̀ 'yīn-lì gwāng-'shywù sān-shr-'sz̀-nyán 'sān-ywè 'shr̀-bā(-'r̀). ‖**A Chinese family usually celebrates two New Year's Days per year, one by the solar calendar and one by the lunar calendar.** 'jūng-gwo-rén-'jyār 'cháng-cháng gwò 'lyáng-ge-nyán, gwò 'yí-ge-'yáng-lì-nyán, yèw gwò 'yí-ge-'yīn-lì-nyán. ‖**In the lunar calendar seventeen intercalary months are added every nineteen years.** 'yīn-lì měy-shŕ-'jyěw-nyán-li jyā 'chī-ge-'rwèn-ywè. ‖**A lunar year may have twelve or thirteen months.** 'yīn-lì 'yì-nyán yěw shŕ-'èr-ge-ywè-de, yě yěw shŕ-'sān-ge-ywè-de. ‖**The old Chinese calendar is based on the calculation of one complete revolution of the moon around the earth, in 29.530588 days.** 'yīn-lì swǒ-'gēn-jywù-de-swàn-'fǎ shr̀ 'ywè-lyang wéy-je dì-'chyéw ràw 'yì-dzāwr, yùng 'èr-shr-'jyěw-'dyǎn-'wǔ-'sān-'líng-'wǔ-'bā-'bā-'tyān. ‖**In the lunar calendar a month is either twenty-nine or thirty days.** 'yīn-lì yí-ge-'ywè yěw 'èr-shr-'jyěw-tyān-de, yěw 'sān-shr-tyān-de. ‖**This country has a different calendar.** 'jèy-gwó-de-'lì-fǎ gēn 'byé-de-'gwó-de bù-yí-'yàng. ‖**What year is this by the Western calendar?** 'jīn-nyan shr̀ 'shī-lì 'shéme-nyán?

(*Device to show the date*). (*On wall or desk*) ywè-fēn-'pár; (*in booklet form, with both lunar and solar dates, sometimes more like an almanac*) 'hwáng-lì *or* 'shyàn-shū.

(*Schedule*). ‖**What events are on the calendar this month?** *is expressed as* What business is there this month? 'jèy-ge-ywè 'dēw yěw shéme-'shr̀?

CALF. shyǎw-mǔ-'nyéw(r). (*Leather*) shyǎw-nyéw(r)-'pí; (*of leg*) shyǎw-'twěy, shyǎw-'twěr.

CALL. 1. (*By name*) jyàw. ‖**What do you call this in Chinese?** 'jūng-gwo-hwà 'jèy-ge jyàw 'shéme? ‖**Someone's calling you(r name).** yěw-'rén °'jyàw-ni. *or* °'jyàw nǐ-de-'míng-dz. ‖**Call him by name.** jyàw tā-de-'míng-dz. ‖**I didn't call you.** wǒ méy-'jyàw-ni-ya.

(*Use as a term of address*) jyàw; (*formal*) 'chēng-hu. ‖**What shall I call her?** (*ordinarily*). wǒ 'jyàw-ta 'shéme-ne? ‖**Call her by (given) name.** jyèw 'jyàw tā-'míng-dz 'hăw-le. ‖What shall I call her (*under more formal circumstances*)? wŏ 'dzěme 'chēng-hu ta-ya? ‖You may call her Aunt Jew. nĭ 'chēng-hu ta 'jēw-bwó-'mŭ-ba. ‖In China, husbands and wives never call each other "dear" or "darling" in public. dzày 'jūng-gwo, fū-'chī jř-'jyān méy-yew dzày 'byé-rén-'myàn-chyán bĭ-'tsž yùng "dear, darling," 'jèy-jŭng-'chēng-hu-de. ‖Some couples call each other by their given names. 'yěw-de-fū-'chī bĭ-'tsž 'chēng-hu yùng 'míng-dz.

(*Classify person or object as such-and-such*) chēng (or jyàw)...wéy... (*Classify oneself as*) 'dž-mìng wéy. ‖Some people call him an old China hand. yěw-'rén 'chēng-ta wéy jūng-gwo-'tūng. ‖He calls himself an old China hand (*presumptuous*). tā 'dž-mìng wéy jūng-gwo-'tūng.

(*Awaken*) jyàw, jyàw-'shĭng. ‖Please call me at 7 A.M. míng-tyan-dzăw-chen-'chī-dyăn-jūng 'jyàw-wo.

(*Summon*) jyàw, hăn. ‖Would you call a porter for me? nĭ gěy-wo jyàw ge-jyàw-'háng shíng-ma?

(*Summon by using the name*) jyàw, hăn, 'jāw-hu. ‖Call him back (*said after he's started to leave*) 'hăn-ta 'hwéy-lay. or jyàw-ta 'hwéy-lay. or bă-ta hăn-'hwéy-le. ‖Try calling his name once. nĭ 'jāw-hu ta yì-shēng 'shř-shr.

2. Call a meeting 'jāw-jí...-'hwèy(-yì). ‖How about calling a special meeting tomorrow? 'míng-tyan 'jāw-ji yí-ge-lín-shŕ-'hwèy-yì 'hăw-bu-hăw? *But* ‖A meeting was called for March third. 'dìng-de shř sān-ywè-'sān-hàw kāy-'hwèy.

Call *people* **to a meeting** 'jāw-jí...kāy-'hwèy. ‖You should call the members to a special meeting to discuss this matter. nĭ 'yīng-gay 'jāw-ji hwéy-'ywán kāy yí-ge-lín-shŕ-'hwèy-yì tăw-'lwèn jèy-jyàn-'shř.

Call a meeting to order 'shywān-bù kāy-'hwèy. ‖The chairman is calling the meeting to order. jŭ-'shí jèng-dzày 'shywān-bù kāy-'hwèy.

3. Call *something* **big, small, cheap, etc.** 'jywé-de, shwō. ‖I don't call this cheap. wŏ 'bìng bù-'jywé-de jèy-ge 'pyán-yì. ‖I don't call her cheap. wŏ 'bìng bù-'jywé-de tā 'chīng-tyaw. ‖Someone called her cheap. yěw-'rén shwō tā 'chīng-tyaw.

4. Call on (*visit*) (láy or chywù) 'jyàn (or 'kàn or 'jăw). ‖I'll call on him later. wŏ 'gwò yì-hwěr chywù 'jyàn-ta. ‖The insurance agent called to see you this afternoon. mày-băw-'shyàn-de 'shyà-wŭ láy 'jyàn-ni láy-je. ‖Someone called on you while you were out. nĭ 'chū-chywù de-shŕ-hew yěw-'rén láy 'jāw-gwo ni.

(*Make a*) **formal call** (**on**) bày-'făng. ‖The ambassador called on you. dà-'shř láy bày-'făng ni láy-je. ‖I'm going out to make a call. wŏ yàw 'chū-chywu bày-'făng yí-ge-rén.

Call at *someone's* **house** dàw...-'jyā chywù. ‖I'll call at his house later. wŏ 'dāy-hwěr dàw tā-'jyā-chywù.

5. Telephone call dyàn-'hwà. ‖Were there any calls for me? yěw wŏ-de-dyàn-'hwà-ma?

Make a phone call dă dyàn-'hwà, jyàw dyàn-'hwà. ‖Who made that call (to me)? 'shwéy gěy-wo dă dyàn-'hwà-le?

Make a phone call to, call *someone* **up** gěy...dă dyàn-'hwà, jăw.... ‖I intended to call him up, but I forgot. wŏ 'běn-láy shyăng 'jăw-ta, kě-shr 'wàng-le.

Put through a phone call jyàw-'tūng, tūng dyàn-'hwà. ‖Please put the call through right away. 'găn-jĭn jyàw-'tūng-le.

Call *someone* **back** (gěy...) dă 'hwéy-dyàn, (gěy...) hwéy dyàn-'hwà. ‖Your friend said he would call back later. nĭ-de-'péng-yew shwō tā 'dāy-hwěr hwéy dyàn-'hwà.

6. Be called down (*informal*) āy (yí-dwèn-)'shwō (or 'tsēng or 'mà); áy (yí-dwèn-)'mà; (*formal*) shèw 'shēn-chr. ‖I was late and got called down for it. wŏ yīn-wey wăn 'dàw 'āy-le yí-dwèn-'shwō. ‖When the company commander went to see the divisional commander he got called down. lyán-'jăng jyàn 'shř-jăng de-shŕ-hew 'shèw-le yí-dwèn-'shēn-chr.

7. Be called away (*temporarily*) jyàw-'dzěw. ‖Someone called him away just a moment ago. yěw-'rén gāng bă-ta jyàw-'dzěw-le. (*Transferred*) ‖I expect to be called away soon. wŏ bù-'jyěw yé-shywu hwèy dyàw-daw-'byé-de-dì-fang chywù.

8. Be on call jŕ-'bān. ‖The doctor will be on call all night. 'dày-fu jěng-'yè jŕ-'bān.

Be within call yì 'jāw-hu jyèw 'láy.

Call after *someone* (jwēy-je) hăn. ‖He called after me (*as I was leaving, running after me and calling*) tā 'jwēy-je 'hăn-wo.

9. Call at *a port* (*of a plane or ship*) dàw. ‖Does this ship call at New York? jèy-ge-'chwán 'dàw-bu-dàw nyēw-'ywē?

10. Call back (*remind someone of*). ‖The sight of that picture calls my school days back to me. 'kàn-jyan nèy-jāng-'hwàr jyàw-wo 'shyăng-chi dzày-shywé-'shyàw-de-shŕ-hew-le.

11. Call for (*require*) shywū-'yàw, děy. ‖What does this plan call for? jèy-ge-'jì-hwa shywū-'yàw shéme? ‖This matter calls for prompt attention. jèy-jyàn-'shř děy 'kwày bàn.

Call for *a person* (*come to meet and accompany*) (láy or chywù) 'jyē (or 'jăw). ‖Can you call for me at the hotel? nĭ néng dàw lywŭ-'gwăn-lay 'jyē-wo-ma?

Call for *a thing* (*come and fetch*) (láy or chywù) 'chywŭ. ‖He'll call for it later. tā 'dāy-hwěr láy 'chywŭ.

Call for *a person* (*shout to*) hăn. ‖He's calling for you. tā 'hăn-ni-ne.

Call for help yàw-rén chywù °'jyèw (or °'bāng); hăn-'jyèw, răng jyèw-'mìng. ‖He's calling for help. (*Out of danger*) tā yàw-'rén chywù 'jyèw-ta. or (*In doing something*) tā yàw-'rén chywù 'bāng-ta. ‖They didn't hear him call for help. tām méy-'tīng-jyan ta hăn-'jyèw.

12. Call in *a person* (*summon*) chĭng...láy. ‖If you don't get well, call in a specialist. nĭ-de-'bìng rú-gwo háy bù-'hăw, 'găn-jĭn chíng yí-wèy-jwān-'mén-de-'dày-fu láy.

Call in (remove from circulation) 'shēw-hwéy, wàng-'hwéy shēw. ‖These notes are being called in. jèy-shyē-'pyàw-dz jèng wàng-'hwéy shēw-ne.

13. Call someone's attention to chĭng ... jù-'yì, chĭng ... lyéw-'shīn °'tīng (or °'kàn). (Addressing an audience) ‖I want to call your attention to this. 'jèy-jyàn-shř chĭng 'jū-wèy °lyéw-'shīn 'tīng-je. or °jù-'yì. ‖May I call your attention to this letter, sir? jèy-fēng-'shìn chĭng-'nín lyéw-'shīn 'kàn-kàn?

Call attention tūng-jr. ‖Please call our attention to any errors you find. rú-gwo yěw-'tswèi de-hwà, chĭng-ni 'tūng-jr wǒ-men yì-shēng.

14. Call a roll, call off names from a list dyăn-'míng (-dz). ‖Who's to call the roll today? 'jyēr-ge 'shwéy dyăn-'míng? ‖He wasn't present when the roll was called. dyăn-'míng de-shŕ-hew tā méy-'dàw. ‖Has my name been called (off)? 'dyăn-daw wǒ-de-'míng-dz méy-yew?

15. Call off (cancel) chywŭ-'shyàw-le, 'méy-yew-le. ‖The game has been called off this afternoon. jyēr-'shyà-wŭ-de-bĭ-'sày 'méy-yew-le.

16. Call on someone to do something chĭng, jyàw. ‖My friend was called on to make a speech. yěw-'rén chĭng wǒ-'péng-yew yăn-'jyăng. ‖They called on me to make a speech. tā-men chĭng-wo yăn-'shwō.

17. Call out reserves 'jāw-jí, dùng-'ywán, jēng-'dyàw. ‖Japan has called out all the reserves. r̀-'běn yĭ-jīng bă ywù-bèy-yĭ-'bīng dēw 'jāw-ji-le.

18. Call someone names mà ... yí-dwèn. ‖He was so angry that he began calling them names. tā chì-'jí-le, 'mà-le tām yí-'dwèn. ‖You shouldn't have called him names in the first place. dì-'yī, ni bù-gāy 'mà-ta.

Call someone a certain name shwō ... shŕ ... ‖No? Didn't you just call him a fool? 'méy-yew-ma! ni 'bú-shr gāng shwō tā shŕ ge-hwén-'dàn-ma?

19. Call someone's bluff gěy (or jyàw) ... 'wèn-chu-lay. ‖He said he was out of money, but I called his bluff. tā shwō tā méy-'chyán-le, kě-shr jyàw-wo gěy 'wèn-chu-lay-le.

20. Call (of an animal) jyàw, 'jyàw-hwan. ‖Can you imitate the call of an owl? ni hwèy 'shywé yè-'māw-dz 'jyàw-ma?

Bugle call hàw-'shēng, lă-ba-'shēng. ‖Can you hear the bugle call? ni tīng-de-'jyàn hàw-'shēng-ma?

21. A close call. ‖That was a close call! 'hèy! jēn 'shyăn! or hăw-'jyā-hwo, shyăn-'jí-le!

CALM. Be calm (of people) 'jèn-jìng, 'tsúng-rúng, wěn, 'yĭ-dyăr yě bù-'hwāng-jang. ‖That girl is very calm. nèy-ge-'nywŭ-háy-dz hěn 'jèn-jìng.

To calm (a child) hŭng. ‖The children were frightened, so we sang several songs to calm them. 'háy-dz-men 'shyà-jaw-le, swó-yi wǒ-men chàng-le ji-ge-'gēer 'hŭng tā-men.

Calm down. 'ān-jìng-shyà-chywu. (Of children) hŭng-'hăw; (of adults) chywàn-'năw, 'ān-wèy; (from crying) chywàn-de bù-'kū; (from being angry) chywàn-de bù-shēng-'chì. ‖We did our best to calm her down wǒ-men shyăng-'făr bă-ta chywàn-'hăw-le. or wǒ-men shyăng-'făr 'ān-wey ta. ‖We've just done our best to calm her down and now you make her cry again! wǒ-men 'hăw-'rúng-yi bă-ta chywàn-de bù-'kū-le, 'ni yěw láy 'bă-ta 'rě-de 'kū-chi-lay-le! ‖It took her some time to calm down. tā gwò-le 'bàn-tyan 'tsáy 'ān-jing-shya-chywu-de.

Keep calm byé 'hwāng, wěn-'jù-le. ‖Keep calm, everybody! 'jū-wèy byé 'hwāng! or dà-'jyā wěn-'jù-le!

(Of weather). ‖The sea is calm after the storm. fēng 'píng làng 'jìng-le (literary). or fēng 'tíng-le, làng yě 'shyàw-le. ‖The sea was calm about half the voyage. yī-'lù-shang 'chà-bu-dwō yěw yí-'bàr shŕ méy-yew-fēng-'làng-de. ‖It was a calm voyage. chwán-'dzěw-de hěn 'wěn. ‖There's been a calm all afternoon. yì-jēng-'shyà-wŭ 'yì-dyăr-fēng yě 'méy-yew.

CAMEL. 'lwò-two.

CAMERA. jàw-shyàng-'jī, (jàw-)shyàng-'shyá-dz.

CAMP. bīng-'yíng; (en route) lù-'yíng.

CAMPHOR. jāng-'năw, 'cháw-năw.

CAMPUS. shyàw-'ywán.

CAN (COULD). hwèy; 'ké-yi; néng; resultative compound with de, or with bu for negative; -de-'lyăw (negative -bu-'lyăw). The differences can be shown as follows:

‖I can do it. meaning know how to 'nèy-ge wǒ 'hwèy. or 'nèy-ge wǒ 'ké-yi 'dzwò. or meaning am qualified to take it on and finish it 'nèy-ge wǒ dzwò-de-'lyăw. or 'nèy-ge wǒ bàn-de-'dàw. or meaning am qualified to do it 'nèy-ge wǒ 'shíng. or 'nèy-ge wǒ néng 'bàn. o 'nèy-ge wǒ néng 'gwàn. or meaning am of the mind to do it, though it is cruel or harsh 'nèy-ge wǒ dzwò-de-'chū or 'nèy-ge wǒ gàn-de-'chū. or wǒ néng shyà-'shěw.

‖I can't do it. meaning I don't know how to 'nèy-ge wǒ bú-'hwèy. or meaning am not equipped to 'nèy-ge wǒ dzwò-bu-'lyăw. or meaning can't make a successful try 'nèy-ge wǒ bàn-bu-'dàw. or in refusing a favor or meaning to make out a plan, or conclude a transaction 'nèy-ge wǒ bù-néng 'bàn. or 'nèy-ge wǒ bù-'shíng. or meaning can't take on someone else's responsibility 'nèy-ge wǒ bù-néng 'gwàn. or meaning can't be harsh enough to 'nèy-ge wǒ dzwò-bu-'chū(-lay). or 'nèy-ge wǒ gàn-bu-'chū(-lay). or wǒ bù-néng shyà-'shěw.

(*Examples with* hwèy). ‖Can you speak English? nǐ hwèy shwō 'yīng-wén-ma? ‖You can't mean that, can you? nǐ 'bú-hwèy shr̀ 'nèy-ge-yì-sz-ba! *or* nǐ-'shwō-de bú-'hwèy shr̀ 'jēn-shīn-hwà-ba!

(*Examples with* 'ké-yi). ‖Can I help you in your work? wǒ 'ké-yi-bu-ké-yi bāng-ni 'dzwò yí-shyàr? ‖Can you give me some help here? nǐ 'ké-yi-bu-ké-yi 'bāng-wo yí-shyàr-'máng? ‖You can go now if you wish. nǐ shyàng 'dzěw de-hwà, shyàn-dzày ké-yi 'dzěw-le.

(*Examples with* néng). ‖Can you direct me to a bank? wǒ yàw 'jǎw yí-ge yín-'háng; (nǐ néng 'gàw-sung wo) dzěme 'chywù-ma? ‖You can't go swimming in this lake. nǐ bù-néng dzày jèy-ge-'hú-li fù-'shwěy. ‖Can't we have these windows open? dzám bù-néng bǎ 'jèy-jǐ-ge-'chwāng-hu dǎ-'kāy-ma?

(*Examples with* de *or* bu *in resultative compounds*). ‖He can't see without his glasses. tā méy-yew yǎn-'jyèngr kàn-bu-'jyàn. ‖(Can you see it?) Yes, I can see it. wǒ kàn-de-'jyàn. ‖I can even see that flagpole. lyán nèy-ge-chí-'gān wǒ dēw kàn-de-'jyàn. ‖I can't see his point. tā-'jyēw-jìng snr̀ 'dzěme-ge-'yì-sz, wǒ kàn-bu-'chū-lay.

(*The word for* CAN *is sometimes not included in Chinese*). ‖I don't see how that can be true. wǒ jyēw kàn-bu-chū-'láy °'dzěme néng 'jēn yěw 'nàme-yì-hwéy-'shèr. *or* °'nèy-ge dzěme hwèy shr̀ 'jēn-de. *or* wǒ 'jywé-de bú-'hwèy 'shŕ yěw chí-'shr̀. ‖He can't read or write. tā bù-shŕ-'dz̀. *or* (*emphatic or impolite*) tā shyǎ-'dz̀ bù-'shŕ. ‖I can't understand French. wǒ bù-'dǔng 'fà-wén.

CAN. (*For food*) 'gwàn-tew (*also means* canned food). ‖Is this fruit out of a can? jèy-'gwǒ-dz shr̀ 'gwàn-tew-de-ma? ‖Do you have any canned vegetables? nǐ 'yěw-méy-yew 'gwàn-tew-chīng-'tsày?

Can of (*food*) 'gwàn-tew, gwàr. ‖Give me a can of soup. gěy-wo yí-gwàr-'tāng.

To can (*to manufacture canned goods*) dzwò 'gwàn-tew; to can (*food*) jwāng 'gwàn-tew. ‖That's a canning factory. nèy-ge-gūng-'chǎng shr̀ dzwò-'gwàn-tew-de.

CANAL. ywùn-'hé.

CANARY. (báy-)ywù-'nyǎw(r), jīn-sz̄-'chywè.

CANCER. dú-'lyéw(-bìng). **To contract cancer, grow a cancer** jǎng dú-'lyéw.

CANDIDATE. 'hèw-shywǎn-rén, 'hèw-bǔ-rén.

CANDLE. là, là-'jú. *For Western style more often* yáng-'là, yáng-là-'jú.

CANDLESTICK. là-(jú-)'tár, là-'táy-dz. *If with a prong over which fits a hole bored in the end of the candle,* là-'chyār.

CANDY. táng, táng-'gwěr.

CANE. (*For walking*) 'gwèn-dz, gwǎy-'gwèr, shěw-'gwèn, shěw-'gwèr, shěw-'jàng. **Sugar cane** 'gān-je.

CANNON. (dà-)'pàw.

CANOE. yéw-'chwán, shyǎw-'chwán.

CAN OPENER. kāy-'gwàn-tew-de, 'kāy-dz, gwàn-tew-'kāy-dz.

CANTEEN. (*For water*) shwěy-'hú; shwěy-'tǔng (*both ends open but stopped up with something*). (*For recreation*) jywù-lwò-'bù.

CANVAS. fān-'bù. (*For an artist's use*) hwà-'bù.

CAP. byǎn-'màw; (*with a visor*) shé-tew-'màw(r). ‖He was wearing a cap. tā 'téw-shang dāy-le dǐng-byǎn-'màw. ‖Where'd you put my cap? nǐ bǎ wǒ-de-shé-tew-'màwr fàng-'nǎr-le? (*Cover for a small object*) gàr. ‖Put the bottle cap on. bǎ píng-dz-'gàr 'gày-shang.

CAPE. (*Garment*) 'děw-péng (*full size*); pēy-'jyān (*short*). (*Of land*) dì-'jyǎw(r), tǔ-'jyǎw(r).

CAPITAL. (*Of a province or state*) shěng-'chéng; (*of a country*) jīng-'chéng, shěw-'dū. **Capital letter** dà-dz̀-'mǔ. (*Money invested*) 'běn-chyán, běr. **Capital punishment** sz̀-'shíng.

CAPITALIST. dz̄-běn-'jyā.

CAPITOL. yì-'ywàn.

CAPSULE. (*Medicine*) 'wán(-dz), yàw-'wán(-dz), wán-'yàw, jyāw-'náng, yàw-'pyér.

CAPTAIN. (*Of a ship*) chwán-'jǎng. ‖The captain commands the men on his ship. chwán-'jǎng 'gwǎn tā-'chwán-shang-de-rén. (*Of a team*) dwèy-'jǎng. ‖Let's choose a captain. dzám 'shywǎn ge-dwèy-'jǎng-ba! ‖The captain led his teammates into the game. dwèy-'jǎng dày-je dwèy-'ywán chān-jyā bǐ-'sày. (*Navy rank*) shàng-shyàw. ‖That's Captain Davis of the U. S. Navy. 'nèy-wèy shr̀ 'měy-gwo-'hǎy-jywūn-shàng-'shyàw 'Davis-shyān-sheng. (*Of a naval vessel*) jyàn-'jǎng. ‖He's captain of a destroyer. tā shr̀ yí-gè-chywū-jú-'jyàn-de-jyàn-'jǎng. (*Army rank*) shàng-'wèy, shàng-ywù. ‖The soldier saluted the captain. 'bīng shyàng shàng-'wèy jìng-'lǐ.

(*Of a company, battery, troop*) lyán-'jăng. ‖Who's the captain of that company? 'ney-lyán-lyán-'jăng shr̀-'shwéy?

CAPTIVE. (*Prisoner*) fú-'lwŏ.

CAR. Car *means automobile, streetcar, or railroad car; depending on context;* chē *with M* lyàng *means any wheeled vehicle, depending on context.* ‖Would you like to ride in my car? nǐ 'ywàn-yi dzwò wŏ-de-'chē-ma? ‖Which car goes downtown? 'nă-yí-lyàng-'chē dàw chéng-'lǐ chywù?

Streetcar dyàn-'chē; railroad car hwŏ-'chē (*with M* lyàng); automobile chì-'chē; baggage car shíng-li-'chē; dining car fàn-'chē; freight car hwŏ-'chē; sleeping car wò-'chē. ‖This train has no dining car. 'jèy-lyè-hwŏ-'chē 'méy-yew 'fàn-chē.

CARAVAN. (*Of camels*) yí-lyèw- (*or* yí-dwèy- *or* yí-'chwàn-de-) 'lwò-two; (*of trucks, particularly military*) yí-lyè- (jywūn-yùng-) 'chē.

CARBON. (*Element*) tàn; (*collected in a gasoline engine*) yéw-'yān-dz.

CARBON PAPER. fù-shyĕ-'jr̆.

CARBURETOR. tàn-hwà-'chì, tàn-hwà-'wù.

CARD. kă-'pyàn, kă-'pyàr; (*postal*) míng-shìng-'pyàn; (*playing*) (jr̆-)'páy; (*calling*) míng-'pyàn.

CARDBOARD. jr̆-'băn, jr̆-'băr, mă-fèn-'jr̆, jr̆-'kéer.

CARE. (*More or less impersonally*) gwăn, gwăn-'jáw; (*with more feeling*) gwān-'shīn, gwà-'shīn. ‖What do you care? *meaning* Is it your affair? 'nǐ gwăn-de-'jáw-ma? *or* nǐ 'gwăn-ne? *or* yùng-de-'jáw 'nǐ 'gwăn? *or meaning* Does it affect you? ày 'nǐ shéme-'shr̀-le? *or meaning* What's it to you? ywú-'nǐ yĕw shéme-'gwăn-shi? *or* ywú-'nǐ yĕw shéme-shyāng-'gān? *or meaning* Why should you worry about it? 'nǐ shr̀ bú-'hwèy °gwăn-'shīn-de! *or* °gwà-'shīn-de! *or* 'nǐ shr̀ bú-'hwèy 'gwăn-de! *or meaning* How could YOU care! 'nǐ tsáy gwăn- (*or* gwà-)'shīn-ne! ‖I may never come back. But what do you care? wŏ 'yé-shywu hwéy-bu-'láy-le. 'bú-gwò 'nǐ shr̀ 'bú-hwèy gwăn-'shīn-de! ‖I don't care. 'méy-yew wŏ-de-'shr̀. *or* 'bú-shr wŏ-de-'shr̀. *or* ywú-'wŏ 'méy-yew 'gwăn-shi. *or* 'wŏ gwăn-bu-'jáw. *or* ywú-'wŏ yĕw shéme-shyāng-'gān? *or* wŏ bù-'gwăn. *or* wŏ bú-'dzày-hu. ‖I do care! wŏ 'dzĕme gwăn-bu-'jáw? *or* wŏ fēy-'gwăn bù-'kĕ! *or* wŏ 'dzĕme bù-gwăn-'shīn-ne? *or* wŏ 'dzĕme néng bù-'gwăn-ne? ‖Who cares? 'shéy yĕ gwăn-bu-'jáw. ‖You needn't care a bit. nǐ yì-'dyăr yĕ bú-yùng 'gwăn. ‖He cares a lot. tā hĕn gwăn-'shīn. ‖He doesn't care a bit. tā yì-'dyăr yĕ bù-gwăn-'shīn. ‖He may go anywhere he

likes for all I care. tā 'ày shàng-'năr 'shàng-năr, wŏ tsáy gwăn-bu-'jáw-ne. ‖I don't care what he thinks. wŏ bù-'gwăn tā dzĕme 'shyăng. *or* tā 'ày dzĕme 'shyăng 'jyĕw dzĕme shyăng, wŏ tsáy bù-'gwăn-ne. ‖I don't care (*even*) if it is so. jyèw 'shr̀ nème-je wŏ yĕ bù-'gwăn. ‖I still don't care. wŏ 'háy-shr bù-'gwăn.

Care (*if something happens*) 'dzày-hu, jyè-'yì. ‖Do you think they'll care if we're late? dzăm yàw-shr 'wăn-le de-hwà nǐ 'jywé-de tām hwèy 'dzày-hu-ma?

Care to (*do something*) shyăng, 'ywàn-yi. ‖We could go to the movies, but I don't care to. wŏm kàn dyàn-'yĕngr chywu dàw-shr 'ké-yi; bú-gwò wŏ bù-'shyăng chywù.

Care for (*like*) 'shǐ-hwăn. ‖I don't care for this book. wŏ bù-'shǐ-hwan jèy-bĕn-'shū. ‖Don't you care for him even a little? nǐ yì-'dyăr yĕ bù-'shǐ-hwan ta-ma? *or* nǐ jyēw-jìng 'yĕw yì-dyăr 'shǐ-hwan ta méy-yew?

Take care to (*do something*) 'shyăw-shīn. ‖Take care not to hurt his feelings. 'shyăw-shīn byé jyàw-ta nán-'gwò.

Give care to, take care to, do with care (jyā) 'shyăw-shīn, lyéw-'shén. ‖Please do this with great care. dzwò 'jèy-ge de-shŕ-hew chǐng tè-'byé jyā 'shyăw-shīn. *or* chǐng chyán-'wàn 'shyăw-shīn-dyăr 'dzwò. ‖You should give more care to what you are doing. nǐ dzwò-'shr̀ de-shŕ-hew dĕy 'dwō lyéw dyăr-'shén.

Take care of (*people*) 'jàw-lyàw, 'jàw-gù, 'jàw-ying. ‖There was no one to take care of the children. 'méy-yew rén 'jàw-gù jè-shyē-'háy-dz! ‖You take good care of him, don't you? nǐ 'jàw-ying tā 'jàw-ying-de jēn 'hăw, á?

Take care of (*guests*) 'jāw-hu, 'jāw-dày. ‖You take care of the mayor; I'll attend to the rest (*only in the meaning indicated*). 'nǐ 'jāw-hu shr̀-'jăng, wŏ gwăn 'byé-rén.

‖Take care of yourself! 'dwō-dwō băw-'jùng!

Take care of (*things*) jù-'yì, dzăy-'yì, kān, băw-'gwăn, 'jàw-lyàw. ‖He takes no care of his things. tā-'dz̆-jǐ-de-'dūng-shi yì-'dyăr yĕ bú-jù-'yì. ‖Take care of my money for me. gĕy-wo 'kān-je-dyăr 'chyán.

Leave *something* in the care of jyāw, 'jyāw-gĕy . . . (gwăn), 'jyāw-gĕy . . . 'lyàw-lǐ, jyàw . . . láy 'lyàw-lǐ. ‖I'll leave this in your care. 'jèy-ge wŏ jyāw-'nǐ-le. ‖He left it in my care. tā 'jyàw-wo láy 'lyàw-li. ‖I'll leave my valuables in your care. wŏ jr̆-'chyán-de-dūng-shi 'jyāw-gey nǐ 'gwăn-ba.

Leave *children* in the care of gwèy . . . 'yăng. ‖The children were left in the care of their grandfather. 'háy-dz-men gwèy dzŭ-'fù 'yăng-le.

Care of . . . (*of mail*) chǐng . . . (gĕy) 'gwăn. ‖He addressed the letter care of Mr. Jăng. tā-de-'shìn chǐng 'jăng-shyān-sheng 'jwăn.

Take care to. ‖Take care to have enough money with you. 'chyán kĕ chyán-'wàn dày-'gèw-le.

(*Worry*). ‖He doesn't have a care in the world. tā yì-'dyăr-fán-'shīn-de-shr̀ yĕ 'méy-yew. *or* (*literary*) tā 'jēn yēw-yéw dz̆-'dzày, wàn-'lywù jyē-'kūng. ‖It's family cares (that are worrying him). shr̀ tā-'jyā-shr̀ fán-'shīn. ‖He has too many cares. tā-fán-'shīn-de-shr̀ tày 'dwō-le.

(Aid). ‖Where can I get immediate medical care? wǒ yàw lì-'shŕ 'jǎw-je 'dày-fu, dàw-'nǎr chywù 'jǎw-ne?

CAREFUL. (a) 'shyǎw-shīn; (b) (meticulous, attentive to detail) dž-'shì; (c) (same) shì-'shīn; (d) (mindful, conservative, regardful) jǐn-'shèn; (e) (same) shèn-'jùng; (f) (attentive, heedful, alert, watchful) lyéw-'shén; (g) (same) lyéw-'shīn; (h) (same) yùng-'shīn; (i) (attentive, respectful) 'jēw-dàw; (j) (attentive to one's own needs) jyàng-'jyēw; (k) (careful in dealing with things) dzày-'yì; (l) (attentive about or to) jù-'yì; (m) (on guard against) 'dī-fang; (n) (take care of oneself; jocular) bǎw-'jùng. ‖Be careful in your work. or Work carefully. dzwò-'shr̀ yàw 'shyǎw-shīn (or with b, c, d, e, f, g, h, or l instead of 'shyǎw-shīn). ‖You've got to be careful in dealing with people. dày-'rén děy yàw 'shyǎw-shīn (or with d, e, i, l, or m). ‖You've got to be careful in dealing with your employees. yùng-'rén yàw 'shyǎw-shīn (or with b, c, d, e, h, or l). ‖Handle the furniture carefully. 'shyǎw-shīn yùng jwō-'yǐ. or yùng jwō-'yǐ děy 'shyǎw-shīn (or with b, c, f, g, or k. Similarly for handling other things). ‖Spend your money carefully. yùng-'chyán děy 'shyǎw-shīn (or with b, d, e, or 'k). ‖Be careful of your conduct. dwèy 'dž-jǐ-de-'shíng-wéy děy 'shyǎw-shīn (or with b, d, e, f, l, or n). ‖Be careful with your clothes (don't wear them out too quickly). chwān 'yī-fu děy 'shyǎw-shīn (or with b, c, d, e, g, h, j, k, or l). ‖Be careful with him. or Handle him carefully. nǐ 'shyǎw-shīn ta (or with f, l, or m). ‖He hasn't been careful. tā méy-'shyǎw-shīn (or with f, g, h, l, or m). ‖He's a careful man. tā shr̀ ge-hěn jǐn-'shèn-de-rén (or with a, b, c, e, f, or g). ‖Be careful not to break this. 'shyǎw-shīn byé bǎ 'jèy-ge 'shwāy-le (or with f). ‖Accidents occur when people aren't careful. 'rén yàw-shr̀ bù-lyéw-'shén de-hwà jyèw hwèy chū-'shr̀ (or with a, l, m). ‖Give this matter your careful attention. jèy-jyàn-'shr̀ chǐng-ni 'tè-byé jù-'yì.

CARGO. hwò.

CARPENTER. 'mù-jyang.

CARPET. dì-'tǎn.

CARRIAGE. (Horse-drawn) mǎ-'chē; (if open) chǎng-'chē or chǎng-péng-'chē; (if enclosed) jyàw-'chē. ‖Let's take a ride in a carriage. dzám dzwò mǎ-'chē 'ràw yí-shyàr.

(Bearing). (Appearance) 'shén-chì; (gait) fēng-'tsǎy; (conduct) 'tày-dù or 'jywǔ-jǐ. ‖He has the carriage of a soldier. tā-de-°'shén-chì (or °'fēng-'tsǎy or °'tày-dù or °'jywǔ-jǐ) hěn 'shyàng ge-'jywūn-rén. or tā hěn yěw 'jywūn-rén-de-°'shén-chì. or °'fēng-'tsǎy. or °'tày-dù. (But not °'jywǔ-jǐ).

CARRIER. (Ship that carries planes) fēy-jī-mǔ-'jyàn, háng-kūng-mǔ-'jyàn.

CARROT. hú-'lwó-be.

CARRY. 1. In the meaning convey, transport, bear, support, hold up, Chinese distinguishes a number of different methods of carrying. A sentence with one of these words which implies motion toward the speaker may have in the nearest English equivalent sentence the word **bring**; if motion away from the speaker is implied the English may have **take**; hence all information below is relevant to the treatment of the English words **bring** and **take**.

(Most general word) ná. ‖It was carried away by two waiters. lyǎng-ge-'chá-fang ná-'dzěw-le. ‖He carried it with him. tā ná-'dzěw-le. ‖What are you carrying in your hand? nǐ 'shěw-li 'ná-je-de shr̀ 'shéme?

(General, but limited to carrying by a single person) dày. ‖He carried it with him. 'nèy-ge tā dày-'dzěw-le. ‖Are you carrying arms? nǐ dǎy-je 'chyāng-ne-ma?

(In the hand, with arm held down along the side of the body) 'dī-le, 'dī-lew, 'dī-lyew, tí. ‖The porter will take charge of carrying the bags. jyǎw-'háng gwǎn 'dī-le 'shyāng-dz.

(In the hand(s), with arms stretched out part way) dwān. ‖He carries trays in the dining hall. tā dzày shr̀-'táng-li dwān 'pán-dz.

(In the hand(s), with arms stretched overhead) jywǔ. ‖The soldier is wading across the brook, carrying his rifle over his head. 'bīng jywǔ-je 'chyāng tāng-'shwěy gwò-'hé.

(In palm(s) face up; also when the edges of the palms are pressed together to form a bowl-shape) pěng, twō. ‖That bronze statue depicts a man carrying a child in his hand. nèy-ge-'túng-'shyàng 'shěw-li twō shyǎw-'hár. ‖The two women carried the tray on their palms. lyǎng-ge-'nywǔ-rén yùng shěw-'jǎng twō-je nèy-ge-'pán-dz. ‖He was carrying a handful of rice. tā 'shěw-li pěng-je yì-bǎ-'mǐ.

(With thumb and finger pinched together, or with tweezers) nyē. ‖The four men carried the flag by the corners. nèy-ge-'chí tǎm-'sž-ge-rén 'yí-ge nyē-je 'yí-ge-jyǎwr 'dzěw.

(Between two fingers other than thumb, or between arm and side of body) jyā. ‖He carried the papers between his fingers. nèy-jāng-'jř tā yùng shěw-'jř-tew 'jyā-je 'dzěw. ‖He's carrying a couple of books under his arm. tā 'jyā-je lyǎng-běr-'shū.

(Supporting with the arm(s)). jyà. ‖They carried the drunk out. tām bǎ dzwèy-'gwěy 'jyà-chu-chywu-le.

(By making a hook with a finger, or at the elbow or wrist) gēw. ‖You can carry the bag by using your finger as a hook. nèy-ge-'dày-dz, ké-yi yùng shěw-'jř tew 'gēw-je.

394

(*On shoulder or neck or high on the back*) káng. ‖I can't carry this bag. wǒ káng-bu-'dùng jèy-ge-kěw-'dày.

(*On the back*) bēy. ‖Carrying the child on his ıck, he went upstairs. tā bēy-je shyǎw-'hár shàng-'léw.

(*On the head*) dǐng. ‖He's carrying a basin of water on his head. tā 'téw-shang dǐng-je yì-pén-'shwěy.

(*In the mouth*) hán, hén. ‖He's carrying a piece of ice in his mouth. tā 'dzwéy-lu hén-je yí-kwày-'bīng.

(*Between the teeth*) dyǎw. ‖He's carrying a pipe between his teeth. tā dyǎw-je ge-yān-'déw.

(*Carry something that hangs from some part of the body or the clothing, particularly if it hangs by a strap*) gwà, kwà. ‖He carries a ring of keys on his belt. tā yāw-'dày-shang gwà-je yí-chwàn-'yàw-shr. ‖He carries a Mauser at his side. ta 'yāw-li kwà-je yì-gǎn-dz-láy-'dé. ‖He went away carrying the bag (*hanging by a strap from his arm*). tā bǎ kěw-'dày dzày 'gē-be-shang 'gwà-je 'dzěw-de.

(*In a pocket, or in one's clothes near the chest*) chwǎy. ‖The boy was carrying two cricket containers in his clothes. shyǎw-'hár chwē̄y-je lyǎng-ge-'gwō-gwèr-'hú-lùr.

(*In a pocket made by folding the lower part of a long gown upward*) dēw. ‖He walked off, carrying the rice in the skirt of his gown. tā bǎ-'mǐ yùng dà-'gwàr dēw-'dzěw-le.

(*On a pole held horizontally, resting on a man's shoulder or on the shoulders of two men, fore and aft*) dān, tyǎw. ‖The peddler was carrying two baskets slung from either end of a pole. mày-'dūng-shi-de dān-je ge-'tyǎwr.

(*On one end of a pole, holding the other end*) tyǎw. ‖He entered the room carrying a snake on one end of a bamboo pole. tā yùng jú-'gǎn-dz tyǎw-je gēn-'cháng-chúng jyèw 'jìn-lay-le.

(*On one end of a pole held vertically*) dǎ. ‖Carrying a large flag, he led the student procession. tā 'dǎ-je gǎn-dà-'chí 'lǐng-je 'shywé-sheng yéw-'shíng.

(*Lift up and carry, when done by two or more people*) táy. ‖They carried the sick man to the hospital. tām bǎ 'bìng-rén táy-daw yī-'ywàn chywu-le. ‖They carried the sedan chair with a swinging motion. tām bǎ-'jyàw táy-de nème-'yēw-je dzěw. ‖They carried him here in a sedan chair. tām yùng-'jyàw bǎ-ta 'táy-lay-le.

(*Same as* táy *but with arms stretched down to lift*) dā. ‖A palanquin is a kind of sedan chair which you carry with arms stretched down. palanquin 'jèy-jǔng-jyàw shr̀ 'dā-je dzěw-de.

By vehicle, animal, conduit, etc.:

(*Of a horse, mule, donkey, camel*) twó, 'twó-dzày. ‖A mule can carry more than a donkey. 'lwó-dz bǐ-'lywú 'twó-de-dūng-shi 'dwō. ‖Two army mules can carry one piece of mountain artillery. 'lyǎng-j̄r-jywūn-'lwó ké-yi 'twó-dzày 'yì-mén-shān-'pàw.

(*Of a vehicle, animal, boat, plane, pipe line*) ywùn. ‖Does this railroad carry freight? jèy-tyáw-tyě-'lù ywùn-'hwò bú-ywùn? ‖This pipe line carries enough oil to supply these states. jèy-ge-'gwǎn-dz-ywùn-de-'yéw gèw 'jè-jǐ-shěng 'yùng-de. ‖One plane carries passengers and another carries the luggage. 'yí-jyà-fēy-'jī ywùn chéng-'kè, 'yí-jyà ywùn 'shíng-li.

(*Of vehicle, boat, plane*) jwāng, dzày. ‖That car can carry twenty tons. 'nèy-lyàng-chē ké-yi jwāng èr-shr-'dwèn.

Be able to carry so much (*pulling some vehicle*) lā-de-'dùng, *or* (*pushing it*) twēy-de-'dùng. ‖Can you carry that much on your cart? nème-'jùng nǐ lā-de-'dùng-ma?

Carry *something* along *with oneself* swéy-'shēn dày-je. ‖These two pieces of luggage are to be checked; those two I'm going to carry with me. 'nèy-lyǎng-jyàn dǎ shíng-li-'pyàw, 'jèy-lyǎng-jyàn wǒ swéy-'shēn dày-je.

2. *Other meanings of* carry.

Be able to carry (*support*) so much weight jīn-de-'jù. ‖How much weight will this bridge carry? jèy-ge-'chyáw jīn-de-'jù dwō-me-'jùng? *or expressed as* What's this bridge's load-limit? jèy-chyáw-de-dzày-jùng-'lyàng shr̀ 'dwō-shaw?

(*Have in stock*) mày, 'jīng-shèw. ‖Do you carry men's shirts? nǐm mày 'nán-rén-chwān-de-chèn-'shān-ma? ‖We carry imported goods. (*Literary*) 'běn-dyàn 'jīng-shèw bwó-láy-'pǐn.

(*Take care of*) yěw. ‖That store carries our account. nèy-ge-'pù-dz yěw wǒ-men-de-'jàng.

(*Persuade, move*) gǎn 'dùng. ‖The speech carried the crowd. yǎn-'jyǎng hěn gǎn-'dùng rén.

(*Of posture*). ‖He carried his head high. (*Literally*) tā 'yáng-je-téwr 'dzěw. (*Metaphorically*) tā hǎw 'shyàng méy-'shr̀-rér shr̀-de. ‖The captain carries himself well. chwán-'jǎng-de-'shén-chì hěn 'hǎw.

Be carried (*of a motion*) 'tūng-gwò. ‖His motion was carried. tā-de-'tí-yì 'tūng-gwò-le.

Carry weight (*authority*) yěw 'lì-lyàng. ‖His remarks carried great weight. tā-de-'hwà hěn yěw 'lì-lyang.

(*In arithmetic*) jì. ‖Nine plus five plus eight is twenty-two; write two, carry two. 'jyěw jyā-'wǔ jyā-'bā, èr-shr-'èr; shyě-'èr, jì-'èr.

(*Conduct sound*) chwán. ‖Water carries sound faster than air. 'shwěy bǐ 'kūng-chì chwán 'shēng-yīn chwán-de 'kwày.

Carry on (*an inherited business*) 'jyē-je dzwò. ‖He's been carrying on the business since his father retired. tsúng tā-'fù-chin twèy-'shyéw(-le) yǐ-'hèw, tā jyèw 'jyē-je bǎ 'mǎy-may 'dzwò-shya-chywu-le. ‖Can you carry on from here? nǐ néng tsúng-'jèr 'jyē-je 'dzwò-ma?

Be carried out, be carried into effect shŕ-'shíng. ‖When will this new ruling be carried into effect? jèy-ge-'shīn-'gwēy-dìng jǐ-'shŕ shŕ-'shíng?

Carry *something* **through** (*to completion*) 'bàn-daw 'dĭ. ‖Do you think you can carry it through? nĭ 'shyǎng nĭ néng 'bàn-daw 'dĭ-ma?

Carry off (*win, take*) dé. ‖Who carried off the first prize? 'shwéy 'dé-le °téw-'jyǎng-le? or (*in a lottery*) °téw-'tsǎy-le?

(*Be sufficient to get someone somewhere*) jyàw ... (néng) ‖Five dollars will carry you there. yěw 'wǔ-kwày-chyán jyèw 'jyàw-ni néng 'dàw-nàr. ‖Bluffing has carried him to his present position. jìng kàw-je chwēy-'nyéw jywū-ran jyàw-ta néng dàw 'jīn-tyan-jèy-ge-'dì-wey.

Carry *someone* **back to** (*remind someone of*) jyàw ... 'shyǎng-chǐ-láy. ‖That poem of yours carried him back to the days when he was courting his wife. nǐ-nèy-shěw-'shř jyàw-ta 'shyǎng-chi-lay gēn-ta-'tày-tay-chyéw-'hwēn-de-shŕ-hew-le.

Carry (*an election*) dé-'shèng. ‖He carried thirty-two states this time. 'jèy-ṭsž(-jìng-'chywǎn) tā dzày sān-shr-'èr-'shěng dé-'shèng.

Carry (*an enemy position or fortress*) jàn-'lǐng. ‖We carried those three forts within an hour. dzày 'yì-shyǎw-shŕ-li wǒm bǎ 'sān-ge-pàw-'táy dēw jàn-'lǐng-le.

CART. 'dà-chē. chē *in terms like* **ox cart, mule cart,** *formed in Chinese as in English.* nyéw-'chē, lwó-dz-'chē. *A* 'dà-chē *is drawn by one or more horses or mules;* jyàw-'chē, jyàw-'chēer *has a framework for a covering, and is for passengers;* 'péng-dz-chē *has a shade above it.* ‖He'll bring the groceries in a cart. tā hwèy bǎ dzá-'hwò yùng-'chē 'sùng-lay.

To cart yùng-'chē *followed by a verb of moving.* ‖The sand was carted away. 'shā-dz shŕ yùng 'dà-chē 'ywùn-chywu-de.

CARTOON. màn-'hwà(r); (*borrowed from English*) kǎ-tūng(-'hwàr).

CARTRIDGE. hwǒ-yàw-'tǔng(r), dàn-yàw-'tǔng(r); (*entire projectile*) dž-'dan.

CARVING KNIFE. chyē-rèw-'dāw.

CASE. 1. (*Container*). (*Usually small, of any material. but not flexible*) -hé, 'hé-dz, héer, 'shyá-dz, shyár; (*large box or crate*) shyāngr, 'shyāng-dz, -shyāng; (*of soft material*) bāw(r); (*of soft material and sheath-like*) tàwr. ‖I lost my cigarette case. wǒ bǎ yān-'héer 'dyēw-le. ‖He sent us a set of silver in a beautiful case. tā sùng-le wǒ-men yí-tàw-dāw-'chǎr, dày-je yí-ge-hěn-hǎw-'kàn-de-'shyá-dz. ‖Don't take the bottles out of the case. byé bǎ 'píng-dz tsúng 'shyāng-dz-li 'ná-chu-lay. ‖I received a case of oranges. wǒ 'shēw-dàw-le yì-shyāng-'jywú-dz.

By the case chéng-'shyāng-de, jěng-'shyāng-de, lwèn-'shyāng-de. ‖This fruit is exported by the case. jèy-ge-shwéy-'gwǒ shŕ chéng-'shyāng wàng-'wày 'ywùn-de.

Pencil case chyān-bǐ-'bāwr *or* chyān-bǐ-'héer; **glass case** *or* **spectacle case** *if of soft material* yǎn-jyèngr-'tàwr, *if hard* yǎn-jyèngr-'héer; **book case** *with door* shū-'gwèy, *without door* shū-'jyà-dz; **show case** *or* **display case** 'gwèy-dz, *with glass top* bwō-li-'gwèy-dz. ‖The shopkeeper took the watch from the showcase. jǎng-'gwèy-de bǎ-'byǎw tsúng 'gwèy-dz-li 'ná-chu-lay-le.

2. (*Legal*) 'àn-dz, 'gwān-sz; (*set of facts for one side of a case*) 'àn-yéw. ‖Who's handling this case? 'shéy bàn jèy-ge-'àr-dz. ‖He's lost his case. tā 'gwān-sz dǎ-'shū-le. ‖He presented his case well. tā bǎ 'àn-yéw 'chén-shù-de 'tyáw-tyáw yěw-'lǐ.

Make out a case (*legally or otherwise*) 'byàn-hu. ‖You'll have no trouble making out a case for yourself. nǐ tì-'dž-jǐ 'byàn-hù, jywé-bu-'hwèy yěw shéme-'kwèn-nan.

Case of *some crime* jyàn; (*if detailing successive crimes at a single place*) tsž; (*if detailing simultaneous crimes at different places*) chù. ‖Yesterday there were two cases of robbery. 'dzwó-tyan yěw 'lyǎng-°jyàn-(*or* °chù-)chyǎng-'àn. ‖Are there many cases of robbery in this city? 'chéng-li chyǎng-'àn 'dwō-ma?

3. (*Other uses*). **In any case** bú-'lwèn dzěme-'yàng(r), wú-'lwèn-rú-'hé. ‖In any case I would follow his advice. bú-'lwèn dzěme-'yàng wǒ yàw 'àn-je tā-'shwō-de chywù 'dzwò. ‖In any case I don't want to go. wú-'lwèn-rú-'hé wǒ bù-shyǎng 'chywù.

In case (*that*) *meaning if* yàw-shr, 'rú-gwo, ywù. (**Just**) **in case** (*that*) *meaning on the long chance* 'wàn-yī, yǐ-fáng-'wàn-yī; **just in case** *meaning because there may be need or use for it* yě-shywu 'yùng-de-jáw. ‖Wait for me in case I'm late. wǒ yàw-shr 'wǎn-le de-hwà, 'děng-wo yì-hwěr. ‖In case you don't know, ask Information. nǐ rú-gwo bù-jŕ-'dàw, wèn tàn-shywūn-'chù. ‖In case there's a fire, walk, don't run. ywù yěw hwǒ-'jing, màn-'mār-de dzěw, byé 'pǎw. ‖Take warm clothes in case the weather is cold. dày-je dyǎr 'nwǎn-he-'yī-fu-ba, 'wàn-yī 'tyār 'lyáng-ne. ‖It may not rain but you'd better take an umbrella just in case. 'ywǔ yě shywu shyà-bu-'chǐ-láy, bú-gwò 'dǐng hǎw háy-shr bǎ ywǔ-'sǎn 'ná-je, yǐ-fáng-'wàn-yī. ‖You'd better take it along, just in case. nǐ 'háy-shr dày-je jèy-ge, yě-shywu 'yùng-de-jáw.

In that case *or* **if that's the case** rú-gwo shŕ 'nème-hwéy-shŕ de-hwà.

‖That's not the case! 'bú-shr 'nème-hwéy-'shŕ! ‖She's a sad case! tā 'jēn kě-'lyán.

(*Medical*). ‖The doctor's out on a case. *is expressed as* The doctor has gone out to see a sick person. 'dày-fu 'chū-chywu kàn 'bìng-rén chywù-le.

(*Typographical*). **Upper case** (*capitals*) 'dà-dž-'mǔ; **lower case** (*small letters*) 'shyǎw-dž-'mǔ.

CASH. (*Contrasting with credit*) shyàn-'chyán, shyàn-'kwǎn. ‖I'll sell it for cash. 'jèy-ge-dūng-shi wǒ yàw mǎy. 'shyàn-chyán. ‖I can make a cash payment. wǒ 'ké-yi gěy 'shyàn-chyán. ‖All purchases are on a cash basis. 'shyàn-chyán jyāw-'yì gày bù-shē-'chyàn.

(*Money*) chyán. ‖Is there any cash in the drawer? 'chēw-ti-li yěw-'chyán-ma?

(*Small change*) 'líng-chyán. ‖I haven't enough cash with me; may I pay you tomorrow? wǒ 'shēn-byar-dày-de-'líng-chyán bú-'gèw, 'míng-tyan hwán-ni 'shíng-bu-shíng?

To cash hwàn, dwèy-'shyàn, chywǔ. ‖Will the manager cash a traveler's check? jīng-'lǐ néng 'hwàn jèy-jāng-lywǔ-'shíng-jǐ-'pyàw-ma? ‖I think I can cash it for you. wǒ shyǎng wǒ 'néng gěy-ni 'hwàn. ‖Will you cash a check for me? jèy-jāng-jǐ-'pyàw nǐ néng gěy-wo dwèy-'shyàn-ma? (*Either give me cash for or get me cash for; in the first meaning only, one also says*): wǒ ná yì-jāng-jǐ-'pyàw, gēn-ni 'hwàn yì-dyǎr-'chyán 'shíng-bu-shíng? ‖I must go to the bank to cash a check. wǒ jyèw děy dàw yín-'háng 'chywù yí-tàng, chywù chywù jāng-jǐ-'pyàw.

CASHIER. chū-nà-'ywán gwǎn-'jàng-de.

CASKET. 'gwān-tsay.

CAST. Cast a net sā-'wǎng. ‖The fisherman cast his net. dǎ-'ywú-de sā-'wǎng. ‖He pulled up a cartload at one cast of the net. tǎ 'yì-wǎng 'dǎ-de gèw-jwāng-yì-'chē-de.

Cast the lead (*or line, in fishing*) rēng-'dzwèr, pyě-dzwèr. ‖Cast the lead farther out. bǎ-'dzwèr 'dzày rēng 'ywǎr-dyar.

Cast anchor pāw-'máw, téw-'máw, shyà-'máw. ‖We'll cast anchor at daybreak. wǒm 'tày-yang 'chū-lay de-shǐ-hew pāw-'máw.

Cast off (*of a ship*) kāy-'chwán. ‖The captain says we're ready to cast off. chwán-'jǎng shwō wǒ-men jyèw yàw kāy-'chwán-le.

Be cast ashore 'pyāw-dàw 'àn-shang. ‖He was cast ashore after five days. 'wǔ-tyān yì-hèw tā pyāw-daw 'àn-shang láy-le.

Cast (*a shadow*) 'jàw-chu. ‖The weak light casts a weird shadow on the wall. 'gwāng hěn 'rwò; dzày-'chyáng-shang-'jàw-chu-lay-de-'yǐng-dz gwày kě-'pà-de.

Cast (*a light*) 'shè-chu. ‖The spotlight cast a cone of light on the stage. hú-gwāng-'dēng dzày 'táy-shang 'shè-chu yí-ge-ywán-jwēy-'shíng-de-'gwāng-lay.

Cast *someone* into prison shyà-'ywù. ‖He was cast into prison for beating up a judge. tā yīn-wey 'dǎ-le ge-fǎ-'gwān shyà-'ywù-le.

Cast ballots téw-'pyàw. ‖How many people cast ballots today? 'jīn-tyan téw-'pyàw-de yěw 'dwō-shaw-rén?

Be cast for (*of ballots*) dé (*number*) -'pyàw. ‖How many ballots were cast for their candidate? tā-men-de-hèw-'shywǎn-rén yí-'gùng dé-le 'dwō-shaw-pyàw?

Cast (off) a skin (*of a snake*) twō-'pí. ‖That snake just cast (off) its skin. nèy-tyáw-'shé gāng twō-le 'pí.

Cast dice jǐ 'shǎy-dz. ‖At one cast he got a four-five-six (*winning throw in a Chinese dice game*). tā yì-'jǐ jyèw 'jǐ-le ge-sz̀-wǔ-'lyèwr. ‖Watch his hand when he casts the dice. tā jǐ ('shǎy-dz) de-shǐ-hew 'kàn-je tā-de-'shěw.

Cast a horoscope swàn ge-'mìng. ‖Let's cast a horoscope. 'dzám swàn ge-'mìng-ba.

Cast-off (*discarded*) yàw-'rēng-de, bú-'yàw-le-de. ‖They want to collect our cast-off clothing. tām yàw 'shēw-'lyán wǒm-yàw-'rēng-de-'yī-fu.

Cast (*people for a play*) fēn-'pèy (yǎn-'ywán), shywǎn. ‖He's casting a group of amateurs for that show. tā jèng-dzày 'fēn-pèy nèy-shyē-pyàw-'yěw láy 'yǎn nèy-chū-'shì. *or* tá 'shywǎn-le shyē-pyàw-'yěw yàn nèy-chū-'shì.

Be cast for (*such-and-such a role*) dāng, chy ᵕ n. ‖Who was cast in the leading role? 'shwéy 'dāng jǔ-'jyǎw?

Cast (*metal*) jù. ‖They cast plates from liquid iron. (*if large*) tām yùng 'rúng-'tyě jù °tyě-'bǎn *or* (*if small and thin*) °(tyě-)'páy-dz.

(*For a broken bone*) shǐ-'gāw. ‖His broken arm was placed in a cast. tā-'shé-le-de-'gē-be yùng shǐ-'gāw 'bāw-chi-lay-le.

(*Of a show*) (dēng-chǎng-)yǎn-'ywán. ‖The cast (of players) has not been chosen. dēng-chǎng-yǎn-ywán háy 'méy-yew fēn-péy-'hǎw.

CASTOR OIL. bì-má(-dz)-'yéw.

CASUALTIES. sž-'shāng, shāng-'wáng.

CAT. māw. ‖Our cat keeps the mice away. wǒ-men-de-'māw bǎ 'lǎw-shu 'shyà-de bù-gǎn láy 'nàw. ‖They've got a tomcat, a she cat, and a litter of kittens. tām yěw yì-jǐ-'gūng-māw, yì-jǐ-'mǔ-māw, háy yěw yì-wō-'shyǎw-māwr. ‖When you scratch a cat under its chin it purrs. gěy māw-'bwó-dz-dǐ-shya jwā-'yǎngr, 'māw jyèw dǎ 'hū-lu. ‖Lions and tigers belong to the cat family. shǐ-dz gēn 'lǎw-hǔ shǐ 'shǔ-ywú māw-'kē-de.

Catcalls dàw-'hǎwr. ‖The catcalls angered the actor. yěw-'rén jyàw dàw-'hǎwr, bǎ chàng-'shì-de gěy chì-'hwày-le.

Special expressions in English. ‖You're their cat's-paw. nǐ 'jyàw tā-men lì-'yùng-le. ‖They're leading a cat-and-dog existence (*specific lly of husband and wife*). tā-men-'gǔ-mu-lyǎ lǎw bàn-'dzwěy. ‖A cat has nine lives. *The equivalent Chinese saying is.* ‖A cat has seven lives, a dog has eight. 'māw yěw 'chī-mìng 'gěw yěw 'bā-mìng.

CATALOGUE. 'mù-lù. (*In book form*) mù-lù-'bĕn-dz or mù-lù-'bĕr; (*sent out by a school*) shwō-míng-'shū, jyǎn-'jāng.

CATCH. Catch *a person* (*with one's hand or legally*) ná, dǎy, dĕy, dēy, dzwō, jwā; *or any of these plus* -jù *giving the meaning* catch and hold on to, catch and stop. ‖The police are trying to catch the criminals. shywún-'jǐng dzày shyǎng-'fár 'dĕy nèy-shyē-'fàn-rén (*any of the above can be substituted for* dĕy *in this sentence*). ‖The polic caught two of them. shywún-'jǐng 'dĕy-ju 'lyǎ-le (*or any of the others with* -jù). ‖We caught two thieves last night. wŏm 'yèr-ge ná-ju lyǎ-'dzéy (*same comment*).

Catch *a child doing mischief* 'chyáw-jyàn, 'dēy-jù, 'dǎy-jù. ‖Don't let your mother catch you doing that. nĭ gàn 'nèy-ge byé jyàw nĭ-'mā 'chyáw-jyàn. ‖You'll get caught if you do that again. nĭ yàw 'dzày gàn 'nèy-ge jyèw yàw jyàw-'rén 'dēy-ju-le.

Catch *someone running* (*just in fun*) dēy. ‖See if you can catch me! 'kàn nĭ néng 'dēy-wo-ma! *or* jyàw-ni 'dēy!

Catch *someone by grasping part of his body or clothes* jyēw, 'jyēw-jù. ‖Catch him by his ear! 'jyēw-ju tā-de-'ĕr-dwo!

Catch *hold of something in order to move it.* (*If the thing is at rest*) 'ná-jù, 'dzwàn-jù; (*if the thing is already lifted*) 'táy-jù. ‖Catch hold of the other end and we'll move this. 'dzwàn-ju-le 'nèy-téwr dzám hǎw bǎ 'jèy-ge 'nwó-kay.

Catch *one's breath* chwǎn (yì-)kĕw-'chyèr.

Catch *an insect.* (*With swatter or insecticide*) dǎ, 'dǎ-jáw; (*with fly paper*) jān, 'jān-jù, 'jān-shàng; (*by hand*) 'dzwàn(-jù), 'chwā(-jù), 'jwā(-jù).

Catch *fire* jáw, jáw-'hwŏ, jáw-chi 'hwŏ-lay. ‖The car caught fire when it turned over. 'chē 'fān-le de-shŕ-hew jáw-chi 'hwŏ láy-le. ‖The wood's so dry that it will catch fire easily. 'mù-tew 'gān-de yī 'dyán jyèw 'jáw.

Catch *a disease* dé; catch *a cold* jāw-'lyáng. ‖I think you must have caught the flu. wŏ shyǎng nĭ yí-'dìng shŕ 'dé-le lyéw-shíng(-shìng)-gǎn-'màw-le. ‖There's danger of catching the flu in this weather, 'jèy-jǔng-tyān-chi hěn 'rúng-yì dé jùng-shàng-'fēng. ‖I caught a cold over the weekend. wŏ jēw-'mwò de-shŕ-hew jāw-'lyáng-le.

Catch *a missile flying through the air* 'jyē(-jù). ‖Here, catch this! 'hèy! 'jyē-je! *or* 'hèy! 'jyē-jù! *or* 'jyē jèy-ge! ‖The boy caught the ball. shyǎw-'hár bǎ-'chyéwr 'jyē-jù-le.

Catch *a vehicle scheduled at a certain time* gǎn, 'gǎn-shàng. ‖Hurry up if you want to catch the bus. nĭ yàw shyǎng gǎn gūng-gùng-chì-'chē kĕ dĕy 'kwày-dyǎr-le. ‖I have to catch the 5:15 train. wŏ dĕy 'gǎn wŭ-dyǎn-shŕ-'wŭ-de-'chē.

Catch *fish.* (*With a net*) dǎ; (*with a rod*) 'dyàw-shang-lay. ‖They caught a lot of fish with one cast of

the net. yì-'wǎng dǎ-le hěn-dwō-de-'ywú. ‖They caught twelve fish. tām 'dyàw-shang-lay shŕ-'èr-tyáw-'ywú.

Catch *a word or a name* tīng-'chīng-chu. ‖I didn't catch his name. wŏ méy-tīng-'chīng-chu tā-'míng-dz shŕ shéme.

Catch *the fancy of some group of people* dzày . . .-li shŕ-'shīng-chi-lay. ‖This has caught the fancy of the women. 'jèy-ge dzày 'nywŭ-rén-li shŕ-'shīng-chi-lay-¹ .

⸗atch *one's eye* yĭn-'rén jù-'yì. ‖The neckties in the window caught one's eye. 'chwāng-hu-li-de-líng-'dày hěn yĭn-'rén jù-'yì.

Catch *sight of* 'chyáw-jyàn. ‖If you catch sight of him, let us know. nĭ 'rú-gwò 'chyáw-jyàn ta de-hwà, 'gàw-sung wŏ-men yì-'shēng.

Catch *up* (*having fallen behind*) 'gǎn-shàng-chywu. ‖We're behind and are trying to catch up. wŏm lwò-'hèw-le, dĕy 'gǎn-shang-chywu.

Catch *up with someone* 'jwēy-shàng, 'gǎn-shàng. ‖Since I walked faster than he did, I soon caught up with him. yīn-wey 'wŏ bĭ-ta 'dzŏu-de 'kwày, wŏ yì-'hwĕr-de-gūng-fu jyèw 'jwēy-shàng ta-le. ‖Go on ahead and I'll catch up with you. nĭ 'shyān dzŏu-ba, yì-'hwĕr jyèw 'jwēy-shang ni.

Catch *on* (*to an idea, suggestion*) shywé-'hwèy, 'míng-bay. ‖We told him how and he caught on quickly. 'jīng-wŏm 'yì jŕ-'dyǎn tā hěn-'kwày-de jyèw shywé-'hwèy-le. ‖Do you catch on? nĭ 'míng-bay-le-ma?

Catch *on* (*of a fashion, habit*) (shŕ-)'shīng-chĭ-láy. ‖This fashion caught on very recently. jèy-ge-'yàng dz shŕ dzwèy-'jìn tsáy shŕ-'shīng-chi-lay-de.

Catch *onto a rope or part of a man's body, or clothing* 'jyēw (jù). ‖Catch onto this rope. 'jyēw-jù-le jèy-'shéng-dz. ‖Catch onto his arm. 'jyēw-ju tā-de-'gē-be.

Get *caught by traffic; in a traffic jam.* ‖I got caught in a traffic jam. 'chē dĕw 'jĭ-shàng-le, wŏ bù-néng 'dzŏu-le.

Get *caught in the rain.* ‖He got caught in the rain. tā jyàw-'ywŭ gĕy 'lwén-le.

Get *caught in a trap* (*of a mouse*). ‖The mouse got caught in the trap. (*Snapping-type trap*) 'hàw-dz jyàw 'jyā-dz 'jyā-jù-le. (*Wire trap*) 'hàw-dz jìn-le 'kwāng-dz, chū-bu-'láy-le. (*Box trap*) 'hàw-dz °jìn-le 'hé-dz, chū-bu-'láy-le. *or* °dzày 'hé-dz-li 'dǎy-ju-le. *or* °gwān-dzay 'hé-dz-li-le.

Get *caught in a trap* (*of a human being falling for a scheme*). ‖He got caught in their trap. tā 'shàng-le tā-men-de-chywān-'tàwr-le.

Get *caught in a room, etc.* ‖He got caught in the room. (*Shut up in*) bǎ-ta 'gwān-dzay 'wū-dz-li-le. (*Surprised by someone's arriving*) bǎ-ta 'dŭ-dzay 'wū-dz-li-le.

Get *caught by something closing; as a door* jĭ, 'jĭ-jù, yǎn, 'yǎn-jù. ‖My hand was caught in the door. wŏ-de-'shĕw jyàw-'mén gĕy 'jĭ-le. ‖The door caught his sleeve. 'mén bǎ tā-de-'shyèw-dz 'jĭ-ju-le.

Get **caught** *under something pressing down.* (*Of something that moves only up and down*) 'yà(-jù); (*of something that moves horizontally*) 'nyǎn'(-jù), 'yà (-jù). ‖**My foot was caught** °**under the leg of the table.** wǒ-de-'jyǎw jyàw °jwǒ-dz-'twěr 'yà-le. *or* °**under the wheel of the car.** °chē-'lwén-dz 'nyǎn-le.

Get **caught** *by a ring or loop-shaped object* 'gwà-shàng, 'tàw-shàng. ‖**His neck got caught** (*in the loop*). tā-de-'bwóer gěy 'tàw-shang-le.

Get **caught** *by a hook-shaped object* 'gēw, 'gēw-shàng, 'gēw-jù.

Get **caught** *by any hook-shaped object so that the thing caught hangs down* 'gwà, 'gwà-shàng, 'gwà-jù.

Get **caught** *and torn* gwǎ, gwǎ-'pwò. ‖**My coat got caught on that hook and was torn.** wǒ-de-shàng-'yī jyàw nèy-ge-'gēwr gěy gwǎ-'pwò-le.

Play **catch** rēng-'chyéwr wár. ‖**Let's go play catch.** dzám rēng-'chyéwr wár chywù-ba.

Catch (*on a door, etc.*) 'chā-gwār, chā-'shyàw. ‖**The catch on the door is broken.** mén-'chā-gwār 'shé-le.

Special expressions in English. ‖**That's his catch word.** 'nèy jyèw-shr tā 'lǎw-ày-'shwō-de-'hwà. ‖**But there's a catch to it.** kě-shr 'lǐ-tew 'háy yěw ge-'wèn-tí.

Catch as catch can. ‖**We'll have to catch as catch can for the time being.** wǒm mù-'chyán jř 'hǎw bù-'gwǎn-sān-chī-èr-shr-'yī-de 'néng dzěme-je jyèw 'dzěme-je.

CATERPILLAR. 'máw(-maw)-chúng.

CATHOLIC. Catholicism tyān-jǔ-'jyàw; a Catholic tyān-jǔ-jyàw-'tú, shìn-tyān-jǔ-'jyàw-de(-rén).

CATTLE. nyéw.

CAULIFLOWER. (yáng-)tsày-'hwār.

CAUSE. -yīn *in such forms as the following:* cause of death sž-'yīn; immediate cause jìn-'yīn; ultimate (*remote*) cause ywǎn-'yīn; cause and effect yīn-'gwó; (*reason*) ywán-'yīn, ywán-'yéw, 'ywán-gu. ‖**Can you explain the cause for the delay?** dān-'wù-le-de-ywán-'yīn nǐ néng (gěy-wo) 'jyǎng-yi-jyǎng-ma? ‖**That's not the cause, that's the result.** 'nèy-ge bú-shr 'ywán-yīn, nèy shř jyē-'gwǒ. ‖**The cause of his death was heart failure.** tā-de-sž-'yīn shř 'shīn-dzàng shwǎy-'rwò.

(*A movement, great purpose*). A good cause jèng-'yì. ‖**He died for a good cause.** tā wèy jèng-'yì 'sž-de.

Cause ... *to* (be) ràng, jyàw. ‖**Sorry to cause you any inconvenience.** dwèy-bu-!jù, jyàw-nǐ 'má-fan.

Cause (*trouble, unpleasantness*) rě, 'rě-chū(-lay), 'neng-chū(-lay). ‖**He caused a lot of trouble for us.** tā 'gěy wó-men °'rě-le hěn-dwō-'shř. *or* °'rě-chu hěn-dwō-'shř-lay.

Cause (*an accident*) chū, 'fā-shēng. ‖**What caused the accident?** jèy-ge-'shèr dzěme 'chū-de?

CAVE. (shān-)'dùng.

CEDAR. (*Tree*) 'bǎy-shù; (*wood*) bǎy-'mù.

CEILING. wū-'dǐng-dz; (*if of paper*) 'dǐng-péng. ‖**There's a crack in the ceiling.** wū-'dǐng-dz yěw ge-lyé-'wér. ‖**Can you reach the ceiling?** nǐ gèw-de-'jáw 'dǐng-peng-ma? ‖**All the rooms have high ceilings.** *is expressed as* All the rooms are very high. swǒ-věw-de-'wū-dz dēw hěn 'gāw.

(*Aeronautical*). ‖**The airplanes are flying despite the low ceiling.** 'swéy-rán 'ywún-tsay hěn 'dī, fēy-'jī 'réng-jyèw 'fēy.

Ceiling prices gwān-'jyà, dǐng-'jyà. ‖**The salesman is asking more than ceiling prices.** mày-'dūng-shi-de-rén-yàw-de-'chyán bǐ 'gwān-jyà 'gāw.

CELEBRATE. jì-'nyàn; (*formal*) chìng-'hè, chìng-'jù. ‖**What holidays do you celebrate?** nǐ 'dēw jì-'nyàn 'něy-jǐ-ge-jyà-'chī? ‖**Let's celebrate.** dzám děy chìng-'hè.

Celebrate the memory of chúng-'bày, dzàn-'měy. ‖**People in general celebrate the memory of their heroes.** yì-'bān-rén chúng-'bày yīng-'shyúng.

Celebration (*large formal party*) chìng-jù-'hwèy. ‖**They celebrated by giving a party.** tǎm 'kāy-le yí-ge-chìng-jù-'hwèy.

CELERY. chín-'tsày.

CELL. (*Small room*) jyān-'fáng; (*in a jail*) ywù-'fáng; (*unit of protoplasm*) shì-'bāw.

CELLAR. dì-'jyàw, dì-'yìn-dz; (*for wine*) jyěw-tsáng-'shř, tsáng-jyěw-'shř.

CELLOPHANE. tèw-mɪng-'jř, bwō-lí-'jř.

CELLULOID. (*Literally false ivory*) jyǎ-shyàng-'yá.

CEMENT. (*Not clearly distinguished from concrete*) yáng-'hwēy, shwěy-'ní, shwěy-mén-'tǐng.

CEMETERY. gūng-'mù, fén-'dì.

CENSOR. To censor jyǎn-'chá. (*An official*) jyǎn-chá-'shř; (*old term for one sent by central government to provinces*) ywù-'shř; (*one who censors mail*) jyǎn-chá-'ywan.

CENSUS. (*Data*) rén-kěw-tǔng-'jì, rén-kěw-dyàw-'chá; (*of individuals*) hù-'kěw; (*of families*) hù-'jì.

CENT. chyán *with measure* fēn; ten cents chyán *with measure* máw; twenty-five cents lyǎng-máw-'wǔ(-fēn-chyán); fifty-seven cents wǔ-máw-'chī(-fēn-chyán);

fourteen cents shŕ-'sž-fēn-chyán *or* yì-máw-'sž. ‖Got a three-cent. stamp? yěw 'sān-fēn-chyán-de-yéw-'pyàw-ma? ‖I haven't a cent in change. wǒ °yì-'dyǎr-líng-chyán (*or* °yí-ge-'dà) yě 'méy-yew.

CENTER. jūng-'shīn; (*center point*) jūng-shīn-'dyǎn; 'jèng-dāng-jūng. ‖Aim for the center of the target. wàng 'bǎ-de-jūng-'shīn 'myáw. ‖At the center of the pool is a fountain. dzày 'chŕ-dz-de-'jèng-dāng-jūng yěw yí-ge-pēn-'chywán.

Center of gravity 'jùng-shīn.

Center of a circle (*geometry*) 'ywán-shīn. ‖A radius (of a circle) is the straight line from the center to any point on the circumference. tsúng-'ywán-shīn-dàw-ywán-'jēw-shang-rèn-'hé-yì-'dyǎn-de-'jŕ-shyàn jyàw bàn-'jìng.

To (be at, put at) center jèng, bù-'wāy; (*in photography*) dwèy-'jèng. ‖This way it'll center right. 'jème-je jyèw °'jèng-le. *or* °bù-'wāy-le. ‖You didn't center (the shot) right. nǐ méy-bǎ 'jìng-téw dwèy-'jèng-le. ‖That's not centered right. 'wāy-le yì-dyǎr.

To center (*thoughts, attention*) on jí-'jūng. ‖The attention of that crowd is centered on the policeman. 'nèy-chywún-rén-de-yǎn-'gwāng 'chywán jí-'jūng-dzày jīng-'chá-shēn-shang-le. ‖All his thoughts were centered on her. tā chéng-'tyār jìng 'shyǎng-ta.

Industrial center 'gūng-yè-jūng-'shīn; mining center 'kwàng-yè-jūng-'shīn; *etc.* ‖Isn't this city an industrial center? jèy-'chéng 'bú-shr ge-'gūng-yè-jūng-'shīn-ma?

CENTRAL. (*Governmental; in contrast to local or provincial*) 'jūng-yāng. ‖The central government is in Chungking. 'jūng-yāng-'jèng-fǔ dzày chúng-'chìng.

(*Most important*) dzwèy-'jùng-yàw-de. ‖He's left out the central point. tā méy-'tí dzwèy-'jùng-yàw-de-yì-'dyǎn.

Central office dzǔng-'jywú, dzǔng-'chù, dzǔng-'háng, *depending for the second element on the official designation of the particular office.*

(*Telephone term*) dzǔng-'jywú. ‖Central doesn't answer. dzǔng-'jywú 'méy-rén gěy 'jyē dyàn-'hwà.

Central location. ‖This hotel has a central location (near the stores). jèy-ge-lywǔ-'gwǎn lí shywǔ-'dwō-de-'pù-dz dēw 'jìn.

CENTURY. 'shŕ-jì.

CERTIFICATE. (*Official*) 'jèng shū, jèng-míng-'shū, jèng-míng-wén-'jyàn.

CHAIN. 'lyàn-dz; watch chain byǎw-'lyàr, byǎw-'lyàn-dz; old watch chain jīn-byǎw-'lyàr; iron chain tyě 'lyàn-dz, tyě-'lyàr. ‖Must I put a chain on the dog? wǒ 'féy-děy bǎ-'gěw yùng 'lyàn-dz 'swǒ-chi-lay-ma?

‖A link of this chain is broken. jèy-gēn-'lyàn-dz yěw yí-ge-'hwán-dz 'lyè-le.

To chain (up) swǒ, 'swǒ-chi-lay. ‖The dog was chained up all night. 'gěw 'swǒ-le yí-'yè. ‖Then he was put in chains. rán-'hèw 'bǎ-ta gěy 'swǒ-chi-lay-le.

Chain bridge swǒ-'chyáw.

Mountain chain shān-'mày.

Chain of events shŕ-'shŕ-de-yǎn-'byàn. ‖I haven't kept up with the chain of events. wǒ méy-'dé jī-'hwèy lyéw-'yì shŕ-'shŕ-de-yǎn-'byàn.

Chain of stores *or* restaurants lyán-'hàw. ‖He operates a chain of restaurants. tā 'kāy-le hǎw-'shyē-ge-fàn-'gwǎr, 'dēw-shr lyán-'hàw.

CHAIR. yǐ-dz. ‖This is a more comfortable chair. 'jèy-bǎ-yǐ-dz 'bǐ-jyǎw 'shū-fu-dyǎr. ‖Please sit down on this chair. chǐng dzwò(-dzay) jèy-bǎ-yǐ-dz(-shang).

Sedan chair 'jyàw(-dz).

(*Chairman*) jǔ-'shí. ‖Will the chair permit such a motion? jǔ-'shí hwèy 'jyē-shèw 'jèy-yàng-de-tí-'yì-ma?

Take the chair dāng jǔ-'shí; (*literary*) jyèw (jǔ-shí-) 'wèy. ‖The meeting began with the president taking the chair. hwèy-'jǎng dāng-le jǔ-'shí, shywān-bù kāy-'hwèy.

(*Professorship*) jyǎng-'dzwò. ‖That chair was established especially for him. nèy-ge-jyǎng-'dzwò shŕ 'jwān-wèy tā 'shè-de.

CHALK. (*In natural state; geological term*) báy-'è; (*for writing*) fěn-'bǐ.

CHAMBER. (*Sleeping room*) 'wò-shr̀.

(*In machinery terms*) -shr̀; firing chamber 'dàn-shr̀. ‖The firing chamber of this gun is empty. (*Technical military*) jèy-gǎn-'chyāng-de-'dàn-shr̀ shr̀ 'kūng-de. (*Less technical*) jèy-gǎn-'chyāng méy-'jwāng dž-'dàn.

Chamber of commerce shāng-'hwèy. ‖The chamber of commerce holds regular meetings. shāng-'hwèy àn-'chī kāy-'hwèy.

Chamber pot yè-'hú, nyàw-'pén, nyàw-'pér. ‖The chamber pot is kept in the washstand. yè-'hú dzày shǐ-lyǎn-'gwèy-de-'lǐ-myan.

CHAMBERMAID. nywǔ-'pú.

CHANCE. (*Opportunity*) 'jī-hwèy. ‖He has no chance to get ahead. tā méy-yew °wàng-'chyán-jìn-de-'jī-hwey. *or* °'shēng-de-jī-hwey.

(*Hope, prospect*) 'shī-wàng. ‖I believe you have a good chance to succeed. wǒ shyāng-'shìn nǐ-chéng-gūng-de-'shī-wang hěn 'dà. ‖He stands a good chance to win. tā hěn yěw 'yíng-de-shī-wang. ‖Is there any chance of catching the train? 'háy yěw 'shī-wang gǎn-shang hwǒ-'chē-ma?

Be a chance that yé-shywu hwèy, yé-shywu néng. ‖There's a chance that he may be alive. tā 'yé-shywu hwèy háy 'hwó-je. ‖I came because I thought there might be a chance of buying a pack of cigarettes here. wǒ shyǎng 'yé-shywu dzày-'jèr néng mǎy-daw yì-bāw-'yān, 'swó-yi láy-le.

Give *someone* a chance to rúng . . ., gěy . . .'jī-hwey. ‖Give me a chance to explain. 'rúng-wo jyě-'shř yí-shyàr. ‖Give him a chance. gěy-ta ge-'jī-hwey-ba. or, *meaning* Let him go unpunished once. 'ráw-ta yí-'tsž-ba.

Take chances màw-'shyàn, dà-'yì. ‖Don't take any chances. byé màw-'shyàn. or 'yì-dyǎr byé dà-'yì.

Take a chance 'pèng-yi-pèng 'ywùn-chì. ‖Let's take a chance on staying here. dzám 'pèng-yi-pèng 'ywù-chì, 'jù-shya-ba. ‖He decided to take a chance, and bingo, he won the jackpot! tā shyǎng 'pèng-yi-pèng 'ywùn-chì; shwéy 'jř-daw 'yí-shyà-dz jyèw 'dēw gěy 'yíng-le chywù-le!

Take a chance (*try once*) 'shř yí-shyàr. ‖He may not be in, but we'll take a chance (and go on the possibility that he is). tā 'yé-shywu méy-dzày-'jyā, dzám ké-yi 'shř yí-shyàr.

A chance (*lottery ticket*) tsǎy-'pyàw.

Game of chance (yì-jǔng-)dǔ-'bwò.

Meet by chance 'ywù-shàng, (ěw-'rán) 'pèng-shàng, (lite, *ry*) bù-'chī ěr 'ywù. ‖I met him by chance. wǒ gēn-ta shř 'ywù-shang-de. ‖He chanced upon that invention. tā 'nèy-ge-fǎ míng shř ěw-'rán 'pèng-shang-de.

CHANGE. gǎy to change *partially or gradually, as by repentance, or as a rug fades and changes color when exposed to the sun;* byàn *to change radically, sometimes suddenly and into a state hardly recognizable, as water to ice, or magically, as a witch to a dog;* hwàn *to change one thing for another, to replace, substitute;* hwà *to change from one physical state to another, but only in the direction of solid to liquid, or liquid to gas, not vice versa. These words occur in compounds with combined meanings:* gǎy-'byàn, gǎy-'hwàn, byàn-'hwàn, byàn-'hwà; *with any of the four* chéng *may be used as a postverb to give the meaning* change into, *or* dàw *to give the meaning* change to (*a degree, an extent*). *Also:* to be changed bù-yí-'yàng, bú-'dà yí-'yàng, yěw-'shyē-bù-yí-'yàng, *etc. Examples of most of these will be found below.*

Change appearance gǎy-'yàngr, gǎy-'byàn. ‖This place hasn't changed any since you left. dž-tsúng nǐ 'dzěw-le yǐ-'hèw, 'jèr 'yì-dyǎr yě méy-gǎy-'yàngr. ‖I don't see any change in your appearance, but your voice has changed a lot. nǐ-de-'myàn-màw wǒ kàn-bu-'chū shéme-gǎy-'byàn-lay, kě-shr 'shēng-yin 'gǎy-le hěn 'dwō. ‖You've changed a lot since I last saw you (*general, of appearance, habits, speech, or anything*). nǐ gēn wǒ 'shàng-tsž 'kàn-jyan nǐ de-shf-hew 'tày bù-yí-'yàng-le. ‖You've changed (*specifically of ways of*

thinking). nǐ byàn-le. ‖You seem almost to have changed into another person. nǐ hǎw 'shyàng 'byàn-cheng 'lìng-yí-ge-'rén shř-de.

Change a date. ‖They've changed the date. tām 'gǎy-le (or 'hwàn-le) ge-'ř-dz. ‖Would you like to change the date? nǐ shyǎng 'gǎy (or 'hwàn, or 'lìng tyāw *literally* again choose) ge-'ř-dz-ma?

Change. (*for the better*). ‖I changed two lines in your manuscript. nǐ-de-'gǎw-dz wǒ gěy 'gǎy-le lyǎng-'háng. ‖You must change your bad habits. nǐ-de-'hwày-máw-'bìng °děy gǎy-yi-gǎy. or (*more seriously*) °fēy-'gǎy-le bù-'kě. ‖Habits are hard to change. shí-'gwàn hěn nán-'gǎy.

Change *one's mind* gǎy (or byàn) 'jú-yì; (*of loyalty, or in a love affair*) byàn-'shīn. ‖I thought of staying, but I've changed my mind. wǒ 'běn-lay shyǎng dzày-'jèr dāy-je, kě-shr wǒ gǎy 'jú-yì-le. ‖When a woman changes her mind there is no way to prevent it. 'nywǔ-rén byàn-le 'shīn méy-'fár wǎn-'hwéy. ‖She changes her mind every minute. *is expressed as* Her mind isn't fixed; one minute it's this way, the next minute it's that way. tā-de 'shīn bú-'dìng; yì-hwěr 'jème-je, yì-hwěr !nème-je-de.

Change clothes. (*Of style*) ‖He changed to wearing Western-style clothes. tā 'gǎy chwān 'shī-fú-le. (*To a different outfit*) ‖He changed into a new suit. tā 'hwàn-le yì-shēn-'shīn-yī. ‖Change into a clean suit before you go out. 'hwàn yì-shēr-'gān-jing-'yī-shang dzày 'chū-chywu. ‖I've got to change. wǒ děy hwàn-'yī. ‖She's changing her clothes now. tā shyàn-dzày 'jèng dzày hwàn 'yī-fu.

Change *personnel*. ‖Ten of their servants have been changed already. tām 'yǐ-jing 'hwàn-le 'shf-ge-'dǐ-shya-rén-le.

Change *merchandise*. ‖I think I'll go back to the store and change this. wǒ shyǎng 'dzày dàw 'pù-dz 'chywù-yi-tàng bǎ 'jèy-ge 'hwàn-le. ‖No changes allowed after the merchandise leaves the store. 'hwò-wù chū-'mén, gày bú-twèy-'hwàn.

Change *trains, planes, etc.* ‖We have to change trains at the next station. dzám shyà-'jàn děy hwàn-'chē. *But in changing from one type of vehicle to another* ‖(You can't get there by train, so) you'll have to change to a bus at Cambridge. nǐ děy dzày jyàn-'chyáw 'gǎy dzwò gūng-gùng-chì-'chē ('tsáy néng 'dàw-nàr-ne).

Change hands dǎw-'shěw, hwàn-'jùr. ‖The hotel has changed hands several times. lywǔ-'gwǎn °'dǎw-gwo hǎw-jǐ-'tsž-'shěw-le. or °'hwàn-le hǎw-jǐ-ge-'jùr-le.

Change (*of a person*). ‖You've changed; you're a man now. nǐ 'byàn-cheng ge-'dà-rén-le. ‖He's changed (*i.e., formerly he was good-natured, now he's a mule*). tā 'byàn-le. ‖The ghost mopped his face and changed into a beautiful woman (*magic*). nèy-ge-'gwěy bǎ-'lyǎn yì-'mwǒ jyèw 'byàn-cheng-le ge-pyàw-'lyàng-de-'nywǔ-rén. ‖She suddenly changed into a large white cat (*magic*). tā 'hū-rán 'byàn-le ge-dà-báy-'māw.

(*Weather*). ‖Do you expect a change of weather to-day? nǐ 'jywé-de 'jīn-tyan hwèy byàn-'tyǎr-ma?

(*Color*). ‖In the evening the clouds change color constantly. hwáng-'hwēn-de-ywún 'shŕ-shŕ byàn-'shǎr. ‖Let's change the color of this room. dzám bǎ jèy-ge-'wū-dz-de-'yán-sè 'hwàn-yi-hwàn, 'hǎw-bu-hǎw?

For a change. ‖Let's have shrimp for a change. dzám chŕ tsž-dà-'shyā 'hwàn-hwan kěw-'wèy. ‖Let's go to the north this year for a change. dzám 'hwàn-yi-hwàn 'dì-fang, 'jīn-nyan shàng 'běy-byar chywù-ba.

(*Governmental*). ‖There'll be a change in the political setup. jèng-'jywú yàw chǐ byàn-'hwà. ‖The minister will be changed for another. bù-'jǎng yàw hwàn-'rén-le. ‖I heard that at first it was planned to make so-and-so the minister, but later it was changed to so-and-so (*gossip before the appointment is made known*). wǒ 'tīng-shwō bù-'jǎng 'shyān yàw pày 'měw-měw, kě-shr 'hèw-lay yàw 'gǎy pày 'měw-měw-měw-le. ‖If the government is bad, change it. 'jèng-fǔ bù-'hǎw, 'hwàn ge-'shīn-de. ‖A coup d'état is (a change of government) made by military force. jèng-'byàn shŕ wǔ-'lì 'dzàw-chéng-de.

To change one's tune hwàn (*or* gǎy, byàn) kěw-'wěn. ‖He used to talk against the governor, but now he's changed his tune. tā 'tsúng-chyán 'fǎn-dwèy shěng-'jǎng, kě-shr shyàn-'dzày 'hwàn-le kěw-'wěn-le.

(*Money; small change*) 'líng-chyán; (*to give or get smaller currency for currency of higher denomination*) hwàn; (*to adopt a new monetary system*) 'gǎy(-yùng); (*money returned to purchaser in excess of cost of article purchased*) 'jǎw-de-chyán, 'jǎw-hwéy-láy-de-'chyán. ‖Can you change these bills for me? nǐ 'tì-wo 'hwàn yí-shyàr jèy-shyē-'pyàw-dz, 'ké-yi-ma? ‖China changed to the new monetary system in 1935. 'jūng-gwo dzày 'yī-'jyěw-'sān-'wǔ-'nyán 'gǎy-yùng-de 'shīn-bì-'jŕ. ‖Do you change American money (*into your currency*)? nín dwèy-'hwàn 'měy-gwo-chyán-ma? ‖Here's your change. 'jè shŕ jǎw(-gey-ni)-de-'chyán.

Chemical change hwà-shywé-byàn-'hwà. ‖A chemical change took place. 'chǐ-le hwà-shywé-byàn-'hwà.

CHANNEL. (*Deep part of a stream*) 'hé-chwáng; (*ditch*) gēw; (*strait*) 'shwěy-'dàw, hǎy-'jyá, hǎy-'shyá.

CHAPTER. (*Of a book*) (yì-)jāng(-'shū); (*of an organization*) fēn-'hwèy

CHARACTER. (*Qualities*) pǐn-'shìng. ‖That boy has character. nèy-ge-'háy-dz-de-pǐn-'shìng hěn 'hǎw. ‖I was disappointed in his character. wǒ dwèy tā-de-pǐn-'shìng bù-'mǎn-yì.

(*Good qualities*) hǎw-pǐn-'shìng; *sometimes* rén, *from the expression* dzwò-'rén *play the part of a man, do a man's share;* (*good reputation*) hǎw-shēng-'míng. ‖He's a man of character. tā-jèy-ge-'rén hěn 'hǎw, *or* tā-de-shēng-'míng hěn 'hǎw.

A man of strong character yì-jŕ-jyān-'chyáng-de-rén.

To have a bad character shēng-'míng láng-'jì, *or* shēng-'míng bù-'hǎw, *or* (*figurative and strong*) 'chèw-le.

Without character píng-'fán. ‖His face has no character. tā-de-'lyǎn hěn píng-'fán.

Be in character (gēn ... jèy-ge-rén) shyāng-'chèn. ‖That new hat of hers is really in character. tā-de-'nèy-dǐng-'shīn-'màw-dz gēn 'tā-nèy-ge-rén hěn shyāng-'chèn. *But* ‖His doing that is in character (*said of a foible of a great man; literary*). 'nèy shŕ yīng-'shyúng běn-'sè.

Be out of character shyàng 'byàn-le-ge-rén shŕ-de, 'gǎy-le cháng-'tày-le. ‖His fit of anger was out of character. tā 'nèy-yì-fā-'pí-chi shyàng 'byàn-le-ge-rén shŕ-de.

(*Person who stands out*). ‖He's quite a character! 'jèy-ge-rén hěn tè-'byé. *or* tā 'hěn shŕ ge-rén-'wù. ‖That person is a familiar character here. *meaning* everyone knows him dzày 'jèy-kwàr 'tí-chi ta-lay, 'shwéy dēw 'jŕ-daw. *or* jèr-'yí-dày-de-'dì-fang dēw 'rèn-shr ta. *or meaning* Everyone knows he's odd tā dzày 'jèy-kwàr shŕ ge-'rén-rén-dēw-'jŕ-daw-de-'gwày-wu.

(*Person*). (*In a book*) rén-'wù; (*on the stage*) 'jyǎwr. ‖Who are the principal characters in the book? 'shū-li-'jǔ-yàw-de-rén-'wù dēw yěw-'shéy? ‖He's a character actor. tā 'jwān-chywù yí-'lù-de-'jyǎwr.

(*Unit of the Chinese writing system*) dž. ‖Please read these characters for me. chǐng bǎ jèy-shyē-'dž gěy-wo 'nyàn yí-shyàr.

CHARCOAL. tàn.

CHARGE. (*Legal*) *expressed with* dzwèy (*guilt*); dzwèy-'míng (*category of guilt*); gàw (*to accuse someone*). ‖What's the charge? shéme-dzwèy-'míng? *or* 'wèy-le shéme? ‖On what charges was he held? tā gěy 'yā-chi-lay shŕ 'fàn-le 'shéme-dzwèy? ‖What crime is he charged with? tā shŕ shéme-dzwèy-'míng? *or* tā-de-dzwèy-'míng shŕ 'shéme? ‖You can't make up charges against people. nǐ bù-néng swéy-'byàn jyā-'rén dzwèy-'míng. ‖You can charge him with anything you like, but can you back up the charges with facts? nǐ 'ày 'jyā-ta shéme-dzwèy-'míng dēw 'shíng, 'bú-gwò nǐ yěw jèng-'jywù-ma? ‖He pleaded guilty to the charge. tā chéng-'rèn tā yěw-'dzwèy. (*or* tā-'jāw-le.) ‖I charge this soldier with insubordination. jèy-ge-'bīng, wǒ 'gàw-ta bù-fú-'tsúng. ‖He pleaded guilty to the charge of speeding. tā chéng-'rèn tā 'kāy tày 'kwày-le.

(*Monetary*) yàw-'chyán, swàn-'chyán; charge extra jyā-'chyan. ‖They charge for any added service. lìng-'wày jyǎw-tam dzwò 'shéme tām 'dēw yàw-'chyán. ‖You've charged me too much. nǐ 'dwō swàn-wo 'chyán-le. ‖Is there any extra charge for this service?

'jème-je 'yàw-bu-yàw. 'jyā-chyán? ‖No extra charge. 'bú-yùng 'jyā-chyán. or myăn-'fèy. or 'bú-yàw-chyán.

Open a charge account (and get an account-book held by the purchaser) lì 'jé-dz. ‖How does a charge account work? lì 'jé-dz shř 'dzěme-ge-'bàn-fa?

Charge something to an account (with record kept by the store) jì-'jàng. (By verbal agreement without record) shē. ‖Charge this to Mr. Lyéw's account. 'jèy-ge jì 'lyéw-shyān-sheng-de-'jàng. ‖Charge that off to profit and loss. 'nèy-ge 'jì-dzay lyéw-shwéy-'jàng-shang.

Charge or recharge (a battery) (dzày dyàn-'chŕ-li) jyā-'dyàn. ‖Have you charged the battery for me? nèy-ge-dyàn-'chŕ jyā-'dyàn-le méy-yew? ‖This battery needs recharging. jèy-ge-dyàn-'chŕ děy jyā-'dyàn.

To charge (of a bull, etc.) (to rush) 'chwàng-gwò (-láy, -chywù), 'chūng-gwò(-láy, -chywù); (with the head) 'dǐng-gwò(-láy, -chywù). ‖Watch out or the bull will charge at us. dāng-'shīn, 'nyéw yàw 'chwàng-gwò-lay. ‖He charged at me with his head. tā dī-je ge-'téw jyèw 'chùng-je wo 'dǐng-lay-le.

To charge (attack, military) 'gūng-jí, chūng-'fēng. ‖The soldiers are preparing to charge the enemy. 'bīng jwěn-'bèy °'gūng-jí 'dí-rén. or °shyàng 'dí-fāng chūng-'fēng.

(Expressions meaning control). Take charge (of) gwăn, (formal) fù ... de-dzé-rèn, 'jàw-gù, 'jàw-lyàw. ‖Who took charge after he left? tā 'dzěw-le yǐ-'hèw shř shwéy 'gwăn? ‖You take charge of that section. nǐ 'jàw-gù 'nèy-bù-fen(-de-'shř).

Take charge of (doing) gwăn. ‖You take charge of entertaining that crowd. nǐ gwăn jāw-'dày nèy-yì-'bāng. ‖You take charge of feeding the babies. 'nǐ gwăn wèy shyǎw-'hár.

Be in charge shř gwăn-'shř-de; (formal) shř fù-dzé-'rén; (official) shř (jǔ-gwăn-)jǎng-'gwān. ‖Who's in charge here? (General) 'shwéy shř jèr-gwăn-'shř-de? (Military) 'shwéy shř jèr-de-(jǔ-gwăn-)jǎng-'gwān? (Formally, expecting the person in charge to answer) 'nǎ-yí-wèy shř 'jèr-de-fù-dzé-'rén? or 'nǎ-yí-wèy shř jǔ-gwǎn-jǎng-'gwān? or wǒ gēn 'nǎ-yí-wèy shwō-'hwà?

X is in charge of Y Y gwēy X 'gwăn, Y shǔ X 'gwăn. ‖He's in charge of this office. jèy-ge-'dì-fang gwēy-ta 'gwăn.

Put X in charge (of) jyàw X 'gwăn, jyāw-gěy X 'gwăn. ‖Who put him in charge of that matter? 'nèy-jyàn-shř shř-'shwéy jyàw-ta 'gwăn-de?

Put X (a person) in Y's charge bǎ X jyāw-gěy Y gwăn. ‖I'll put him in your charge. wǒ 'bǎ-ta jyāw-gey 'nǐ gwăn. ‖He's in your charge from now on. tsúng-'jīn yǐ-'hèw tā gwēy-'nǐ 'gwăn-le. ‖He's in your charge, not mine. tā gwěy (or 'shǔ) 'nǐ 'gwăn, 'méy-yew 'wǒ-de-shř.

Be in someone's charge (for safekeeping) 'jyāw-géy (or 'gwēy) ... bǎw-'gwăn. ‖These documents were in your charge, weren't they? jèy-shyē-wén-'jyàn 'bú-shř gwēy-'nǐ bǎw-'gwăn-de-ma?

Be in charge of a class 'dān-rèn. ‖The class Mr. Wáng is in charge of is grumbling against him. 'wáng-shyān-sheng-'dān-rèn-de-nèy-bān-'shywé-sheng 'bàw-ywàn ta-le.

CHARM. (Of scenery) jǐng-'jŕ. ‖The lakes here have great charm. jèy-shyē-'hú-de-jǐng-'jŕ hěn 'měy.

(Fascination, attractiveness) mwó-'lì. ‖Your eyes have great charm. nǐ-de-'yǎn-jing yěw hěn-'dà-de-mwó-'lì.

(Talisman) fǎ-shù, shyé-'shù. ‖That lama from Tibet claims he has a charm. nèy-ge-shī-'dzàng-láy-de-'lǎ-ma dž-'chēng yěw (mí-'rén-de-)fǎ-'shù. ‖They say he can use a charm to kill people. tām shwǒ tā néng yùng shyé-'shù 'shā-rén.

(To fascinate, attract) jyàw ... jáw-'mí, jyàw ... shén-'hwén dyān-'dǎw, jyàw ... 'ày. ‖She can charm any man. tā néng jyàw 'rén-rén jáw-'mí. ‖Any man who looks at her is charmed. 'nán-rén 'kàn-jyan ta dēw hwèy °jáw-'mí-de. or °shén-'hwén dyān-'dǎw-de.

Have charm jyàw-rén 'ày, mí-'rén. ‖Your eyes have great charm. nǐ-de-'yǎn-jīng °'shŕ-dzày mí-'rén. or °jēn jyàw-rén 'ày.

Be charming (of a person) jyàw (or tǎw)-'rén 'shǐ-hwān; (of a child only) shř ge-mí-rén-'jīng. ‖His sister is very charming. tā-de-'mèy-mey hěn 'tǎw-rén 'shǐ-hwan-de. ‖What a charming child! jèy-ge-'háy-dz 'dwō-me jyàw-rén 'shǐ-hwan! or jèy-ge-'háy-dz jyàn-'jŕ shř ge-mí-rén-'jīng. ‖She has a charming personality. tā hěn jyàw-rén 'shǐ-hwan.

Be charmed by (scenery) hěn 'shīn-shǎng. ‖We were charmed by the beautiful sights. wǒm hěn 'shīn-shǎng nèy-ge-dì-fang-de-'jǐng-jŕ.

CHART. byǎw, yì-lǎn-'byǎw; (of land) tú-'byǎw, dì-'tú; (mariner's) hǎy-'tú, háng-hǎy-'tú.

CHASSIS. (Of car, truck) chē-'pán, chē-'pár, dǐ-'pár.

CHAUFFEUR. (Courteous) sz-'jī-de, jī-'shř; (less polite) kāy-'chē-de, (chì-)'chē-fu.

CHEAP. 'pyán-yì, jyàn. ‖Do you have anything cheaper than this? nǐ yěw bǐ-'jèy-ge-'pyán-yì-dyǎr-de-ma? ‖Do you have a cheap room for rent? nǐ yěw 'pyán-yì-de-'wū-dz chū-'dzū-ma? ‖Are the rates cheap at this hotel? jèy-ge-lywǔ-'gwǎn-de-'jyà-chyán 'pyán-yì-ma? ‖He usually goes for cheap things. tā 'píng-cháng 'ày mǎy °'pyán-yi-'hwò. or °'jyàn-hwò. ‖This is for sale cheap. 'jèy-ge 'jyàn-jyà chū-'mày. ‖We buy it cheap, so we sell it cheap. 'jyàn 'mǎy-lay jyàn 'mày.

(Undignified) yěw-'shř shēn-'fèn, 'fěy-li fěy-'chì-de; (low-class) shyà-'jyàn. ‖He looked cheap in those clothes. tā-'chwān-de-'fěy-li fěy-'chì-de. or tā-chwān-de-'nèy-yàngr-de-'yī-shang °('shyǎn-de) 'fěy-li fěy-'chì-de. or °'shyǎn-je shyà-'jyàn. or °yěw-'shř shēn-'fèn.

(*Showy but unsound, of things*) is expressed as second-grade tsz̀-'děng-de, or as not good bú-shr 'hǎw-de. ‖That's a cheap watch. 'nèy shr tsz̀-'děng-de-'byǎw. or nèy-ge-'byǎw bú-shr 'hǎw-de.

To feel cheap (jywé-de) yěw-'kwèy, (jywé-de) bù-hǎw-'yì-sz-de. ‖His kindness made me feel cheap. tā dày-wo jème-'hǎw, jyàw-wo 'jywé-de yěw-'kwèy.

Cheap trick. ‖He played a cheap trick on me. tā 'gěy-wo 'shr̀-le (yì-)hwéy-'hwày.

CHECK. (*Receipt*) shēw-'jywù; (*made of metal*) 'páy-dz, pár; (*of cardboard*) 'pyàn-dz, pyàr; (*of paper*) 'tyáw-dz, tyáwr. ‖Be sure to keep this check. chyān-'wàn 'lyéw-je jèy-ge-'páy-dz. ‖Give your check to the baggage man. bǎ nǐ-de-'pár jyàw-gey nèy-ge-gwǎn-'shíng-li-de-rén.

(*For money*) jr̆-'pyàw; traveler's check lywǔ-shíng-jr̆-'pyàw; blank check kùng-tew-jr̆-'pyàw; checkbook jr̆-pyàw-'běn-dz, jr̆-pyàw-'běr; make out a check kāy jr̆-'pyàw. ‖I'll send you a check in the morning. wǒ míng-tyan-'dzǎw-chen bǎ jr̆-'pyàw gěy-ni 'sùng-chywu. ‖Who shall I make the check out to? wǒ jèy-jāng-jr̆-'pyàw yīng-dang kāy-gey 'shwéy?

(*Small mark to draw attention*) gēwr. ‖Put a check beside each price. měy-yàng-'jyà-chyán-páng-byar dǎ yí-ge-'gēwr.

(*To stop by law*) jìn-'jr̆. ‖Such lawlessness should be checked. jèy-jǔng-bù-'fǎ-de-shíng-'dùng yīng-gay jìn-'jr̆.

To check oneself (*in doing something*) 'tíng-jù; (*in speaking*) 'rěn-jù. ‖He was about to speak, but checked himself. tā 'gāng yàw kāy-'kěw yèw 'rěn-jù-le.

To check speed (*slow down*) 'màn-shyà-lay. ‖The car checked its speed as it went around the corner. chì-'chē gwǎy-'wār de-shŕ-hew 'màn-shya-lay yì-dyǎr.

(*Chess*). ‖Check! jyāng!

(*Examine for accuracy*) dwèy. ‖Have you checked those sheets? nèy-jǐ-jāng-'jr̆ nǐ 'dwèy(-gwo)-le-ma? ‖Check these (*documents*) for me. gěy-wo 'dwèy-yi-dwèy.

Check something against … gēn … 'dwèy-yi-dwèy, yùng … 'dwèy-yi-dwèy. ‖Check these figures against that table. jèy-shyē-'shr̀r yùng nèy-ge-'byǎw 'dwèy-yi-dwèy.

Check with (*be in agreement with*) gēn … yí-'yàng. ‖Does this timetable check with the new schedule? jèy-ge-shíng-chē-'byǎw gēn shīn-'dìng-ge-'shŕ-jyan yí-'yàng-bu-yí-yàng?

Check with (*someone*) wèn, 'wèn-yi-wèn. ‖I must check with the manager first. wǒ děy-'shyān 'wèn-yi-wèn jīng-'lǐ. ‖I've checked with the police bureau; it's no go. wǒ 'yǐ-jing 'wèn-le jǐng-chá-'jywú-le; bù-'shíng.

‖Check! Correct! 'dwèy!

(*Look at officially*) yàn, chá. ‖They're ready to check our passports. tām 'yǐ-jing ywù-bèy-'hǎw-le yàw yàn wǒ-men-de-hù-'jàw-le.

(*Take a look at*) 'kàn-yi-kàn. ‖Please check the oil in my car. chǐng 'kàn-yi-kàn wǒ-'chē-li-de-'yéw háy 'gèw-bu-gèw.

Check up on (*investigate*) dyàw-'chá. ‖They're checking up on your records now. tām 'jèng-dzày dyàw-'chá nǐ-de-lywǔ-'lì-ne.

(*Leave for safekeeping*) tswén. ‖Check your hat and coat here. bǎ nǐ-de-'màw-dz gēn dà-'yī tswén-dzay 'jèr. ‖Where can I check my baggage? wǒ dzày-'nǎr ké-yi bǎ 'shíng-li 'tswén-chi-lay?

Check baggage through to a place. dàw … chywù, gwà-'hàw (yì-'jŕ) sùng-daw … (láy, chywù). ‖I want this baggage checked through to…. wǒ yàw bǎ jèy-shyē-'shíng-li gwà-'hàw yì-'jŕ sùng-daw … -chywu. or jèy-shyē-'shíng-li dàw … -chywu.

(*Put a check mark on*) jì, hwà, gēw. ‖Check the items that are important. bǎ 'yàw-jǐn-de dēw °'jì-shya-lay. or °'hwà-chi-lay. or °'gēw-chu-lay.

Check in at (*a hotel, etc.*) dēng-'jì. ‖Have you checked in at the hotel? nǐ 'yǐ-jing dzày lywǔ-'gwǎn dēng-'jì-le-ma?

Check in at (*an office, headquarters, etc.*) bàw-'dàw. ‖At this office we check in at nine o'clock. dzày jèy-ge-gūng-shr̀-'fáng wǒm shr̀ 'jyéw-dyǎn-jūng bàw-'dàw.

Check out dzěw. ‖I'm checking out; have my bill ready. wǒ yàw 'dzěw-le; bǎ-'jàng 'swàn-chu-lay. ‖Sign here when you check out. 'dzěw-de-shŕ-hew dzày-'jèr chyàn-'míng.

Get a (*physical*) check-up jyǎn-'chá. ‖Report to the doctor for a physical check-up. dàw 'dày-fu-nèr-chywu jyǎn-'chá yí-shyàr.

CHECKERS. (*Game*) chí; (*pieces used*) chí-'dzěr. To play checkers shyà-'chí.

CHEEK. lyǎn with M byǎr, one cheek yì-byar-'lyǎn or 'bàn-byar-'lyǎn; sāy-'bāng-dz, sāy, dzwěy-'bà-dz; left cheek (for right cheek substitute yèw for dzwǒ) 'dzwǒ-lyǎn, 'dzwǒ-sāy, 'dzwǒ-byār-de-°'lyǎn or °sāy-'bāng-dz or °dzwěy-'bà-dz; cheekbone 'chywán-gǔ. ‖He has a birthmark on his cheek. tā (yì-byar-)'lyǎn-shang yěw kwày-'jì. ‖I think it's his left cheek. wǒ shyǎng-shr̀ tā-'dzwǒ-sāy-shang. ‖His cheek is swollen from a toothache. tā yá-'téng-de ('bàn-byar-)'lyǎn dēw 'jǔng-le. ‖She had a lot of rouge on her cheeks. tā 'lyǎn-shang 'tsā-le bù-'shǎw-de-'yān-jr.

Tongue in cheek. ‖He had his tongue in his cheek when he said it. tā shwō 'nèy-shyē-shèr 'ywān-ni-ne. or tā 'shwō-je 'wár-ne. or expressed as While saying it he traced the character "no" with his foot. tā 'shwō de-shŕ-hew jyǎw-'dǐ-shya hwà 'bū-dzèr.

CHEERFUL. (*Of a person*) 'kwày-hwo, 'shwǎng-kway, 'tùng-kway, gāw-'shìng. ‖He has a cheerful personality. or He's always cheerful. tā-'jèy-ge-rén 'lǎw nème-°'kwày-hwo. or °'gāw-'shìng. or °'shwǎng-kway.

or °'tùng-kway. ‖They're cheerful donors. tām jywăn-'chyán hĕn °'tùng-kway. or °'shwăng-kway. ‖You seem very cheerful this morning. nĭ jyēer-'dzăw-chen hăw 'shyàng shŕ gāw-'shìng.

(Of a room) 'lyàng-tang. ‖What a cheerful room! jèy-jyān-'wŭ-dz jēn 'lyàng-tang.

(Of a color) shyān-'míng, shyān-'yàn. ‖Pink is a cheerful color. fĕn-'húng-jèy-jŭng-'yán-sè hĕn shyān-'míng.

Cozy and cheerful. ‖The fire makes the room cozy and cheerful (both warm and comfortable). jèy-ge-'hwŏ bă-'wŭ-dz nùng-de yèw.'nwăn-he yèw 'shū-fu.

(Sarcastic). ‖That's a cheerful thought! (If in agreement with the remark made) 'nèy kĕ jēn 'dzāw! (If displeased by the remark made, literally) You can certainly sing pleasant songs! nĭ 'jēn hwèy chàng shĭ-'gēr!

CHEESE. (nyéw-)năy-'bĭng; (from English word) 'jì-sz.

CHEF. 'dà-shŕ-fu, chú-dz-'téwr.

CHEMICALS. hwà-shywé-'pĭn; chemical products hwà-shywé-jŕ-'pĭn; medicinal chemicals hwà-shywé-yàw-'pĭn.

CHEMIST. hwà-shywé-'jyā, hwà-shywé-'shŕ.

CHEMISTRY. 'hwà-shywé.

CHERRY. (Fruit) 'yīng-taw; (tree) 'yīng-taw-shù; (wood) yīng-taw-'mù.

CHESS. (Game) 'shyàng-chí; to play chess shyà 'shyàng-chí; chess...an (shyàng-)chí-'dzĕr.

CHEST. (Part of body) shyūng, shyūng-'púr; (lower part only) shīn-'kĕw(r).

(Box) 'gwèy(-dz), 'shyāng(-dz). Chest of drawers chēw-tì-'gwèy; chest of seven drawers (yí-ge-)'chī-tì-'gwèy (similarly with any number of drawers).

CHESTNUT. 'lì-dz.

CHICKEN. jī; (male) gūng-'jī; (female) mŭ-'jī; (young) shyăw-'jyēr; (meat) jī-'rèw, or if shredded jī-'sž, boned and diced jī-'dyēngr, cooked whole jĕng-'jī, chywán-'jī. Chicken breast 'jī-shyūng-púr. ‖Does this farmer raise chickens for their eggs? jèy-ge-'núng-fu yăng-'jī 'wèy-de-shŕ shyà-'dàn-ma? ‖Roast chicken isn't on the menu tonight. jyēer-'wăn-shang tsày-'dān-dz-shang 'méy-yew °kăw-'jī. or °shāw-'jī.

CHICKEN POX. 'shwĕy-dèwr.

CHIEF. (Familiar term of address for one's superior) téwr; (formal) jăng-'gwān; dwèy-'jăng for the chief

of an organization whose designation ends in dwèy; (of a clan) dzú-'jăng; (of a tribe, as among the Mongols or the Miaos) chyéw-'jăng, shĕw-'lĭng. ‖Our chief is quite lenient. wŏm-de-'téwr hĕn 'sūng. ‖Who's your chief? nĭm-de-jăng-'gwān shŕ-'shwéy? ‖He's the chief of a mountain tribe. tā shŕ 'shān-li yì-dzú-'rén-de-chyéw-'jăng. ‖The firemen reported to their chief. shyāw-fáng-'dwèy shyàng tā-men-de-dwèy-'jăng bàw-'dàw.

Chief of police jĭng-chá-'jywú-jywú-'jăng; chief of staff tsān-méw-'jăng or, of the U.S.A. tsān-méw-dzŭng-'jăng; chief of (a department under the chief of staff) shŭ-'jăng, as in chief of ordnance 'bīng-gūng-shŭ-shŭ-'jăng; chief engineer 'dzŭng-gūng-cheng-'shŕ.

(Main) jŭ-'yàw(-de); sometimes in Chinese by dzwèy followed by an adjective. ‖What's your chief complaint? (Sickness) nĭ-de-jŭ-'yàw-de-bìng-'jèng shŕ shéme? (Otherwise) nĭ dzwèy-bù-măn-'yì-de shŕ 'shéme? ‖What are the chief points of interest here? jèr-dzwèy-yĕw-'yì-sz-de-dì-fang dēw dzăy-'năr?

CHILD. 'háy-dz; (literary) ér-túng-. ‖They took the child with them on the trip. tām lywŭ-'shíng dày-je 'háy-dz. ‖He's acting like a child. tā 'nème-yàng shyàng yí-ge-'háy-dz shŕ-de-a. ‖I'm interested in child-welfare. wŏ dwèy ér-túng-fú-'lì-de-wèn-tí hĕn 'găn-daw 'shìng-chywu.

Child psychology ér-túng-shīn-'lĭ(-shywé).

CHIMNEY. 'yān-tŭng. ‖Smoke is coming out of the chimney. 'yān tsúng 'yān-tung 'màw-chu-lay. or 'yān-tung màw-chu-'yān. ‖I want this chimney repaired. wŏ yàw 'shyēw-li-shyēw-li jè-ge-'yān-tung. (Of a lamp) ('yéw-dēng-)dēng-'jàwr. ‖Where's the chimney for the lamp? dēng-'jàwr dzăy-'năr?

CHIN. shyà-be-'kéer. (Often one simply says lyăn face.) ‖I cut my chin while shaving. wŏ gwā-'lyăn de-shŕ-hew bă-°'lyăn (or °shyà-ba-'kéer) gwā-'pwò-le.

Chin strap. (Of a helmet) (gāng-'kwēy-de-)'dày-dz; (of a hat) màw-'dàr.

CHOCOLATE. (Non-Chinese) jū-gŭ-'lì from the English word, or else the English word itself. Chocolate candy kēw-kēw-'táng.

CHOICE. Usually expressed in Chinese by a verb. See CHOOSE.

CHOKE. (On gasoline motor) (kūng-)chì-'mén.

CHOLERA. hŭ-lyè-'lā, hwŏ-'lwàn.

CHOOSE (CHOICE). (General) tyāw; (persons or books) shywăn. ‖I chose the books carefully. jèy-shyē-'shū wŏ 'shywăn-de (or 'tyāw-de) hĕn 'shyăw-shīn. or wŏ tyāw (or shywăn) jèy-shyē-'shū hĕn 'fèy-le dyăr-'shīn. ‖They were unable to choose between the candidates. dzày jè-'lyǎng-ge-hèw-bǔ-rén-'shywǎn-lǐ-tew tām bù-néng jywé-'dìng 'shywǎn něy-ge. ‖You can choose a leader from among yourselves. nǐ-men ké-yǐ 'shǐywǎn yí-ge-lǐng-'shyèw. ‖I have to choose the lesser of two evils. wǒ jǐ 'hǎw tyāw nèy-ge-'bǐ-jyàw-'hǎw-yì-dyǎr-le. ‖I've chosen the black hat. wǒ 'tyāw-le nèy-ge-'hēy-màw-dz-le. ‖What is there to choose? or ‖What choice is there? yěw shéme-kě-'tyāw-de? ‖Do we have our choice of rooms? wǒm ké?yǐ swéy-'byàn tyāw fáng-'jyàn-ma? or yěw 'fáng-dz kě-'tyāw-ma? ‖Take your choice. 'tyāw-ba. or nǐ 'tyāw hǎw-le. or 'ày nǎ-ge 'tyāw nǎ-ge. ‖After all, he's the people's choice. gwēy-le bāw-'dzwēy, tā shǐ rén-'mín-'shywǎn-de. ‖My first choice is red; second, black. dì-'yí-ge wǒ tyāw 'húng-de, 'chí-tsz shǐ 'hēy-de. ‖There's no choice between those two. nèy-'lyǎng-ge dēw yí-'yàng, méy-fár 'tyāw. ‖He's the man of her own choice. nèy shǐ tā-'dz-jǐ-'tyāw-de-rén. ‖How many titles have you chosen from the book list? tsúng nèy-ge-shū-'dàn-dz nǐ 'tyāw-chu 'dwō-shaw-'jǔng-lay? ‖If you choose the red, I'll take the black. yàw-shr nǐ tyāw nèy-ge-'húng-de, wǒ jyèw yàw nèy-ge-'hēy-de. ‖Which one do you choose? nǐ tyāw (or yàw) 'něy-ge?

(*Especially a hotel*) tyāw-'hǎw; jǎw-'hǎw. ‖Have you chosen a hotel for the night? jīn-tyan-'wǎn-shang nǐ 'yǐ-jing jǎw-'hǎw-le lywǔ-'gwǎn méy yew?

Choose to shyǎng, dǎ-'dìng-le 'jú-yì. ‖I chose to remain in my room. (*Mild*) wǒ shyǎng háy-shr dzày-'jyā bù-'chū-chywu 'hǎw. (*Strong*) wǒ dǎ-'dìng-le 'jú-yì, 'jyèw-shr bù-'chū-chywu.

Other English expressions. ‖I've just heard a choice bit of news. wǒ gāng 'tīng-jyàn yí-jyàn-hěn-hǎw-'wár-de-shīn-'wén. ‖This is the choice part of the meat. jè shǐ rèw-de-dzwèy-'hǎw-de-yí-'bù-fen. ‖I had no choice in the matter. wǒ 'méy-yew byé-de-'bàn-fa. or wǒ jǐ hǎw 'nème-je. ‖My first choice is red; second, black. (*See also version in first paragraph.*) wǒ dzwey-'shǐ-hwan 'húng-de, chí-'tsz shǐ 'hēy-de.

CHOW MEIN. chǎw-'myàn.

CHRISTIAN. (*Protestant*) jī-dū-'tú, shìn-yě-sū-'jyàw-de, shìn-jī-dū-'jyàw-de; (*Catholic*) shìn-tyān-jǔ-'jyàw-de. ‖Is there a Christian church in town? jèy-'chéng-li yěw-'méy-yew yě-sū-jyàw-'táng?

CHRISTMAS. shèng-dàn-'jyé, yě-sū-shèng-'dàn. ‖Merry Christmas! shèng-dàn-jǐ-'shǐ. or gūng-'hé shèng-'dàn.

CHROMIUM. kè-lwó-'mǐ; (*element*) gè.

CHRYSANTHEMUM. jywú-'hwǎr, ivěw-'hwǎr.

CHUNK (OF). kwày, kwàr.

CHURCH. jyàw-'táng, lǐ-bày-'táng.
     Go to church (*to worship*) dzwò lǐ-'bày (láy, chywù); dàw °lǐ-bày-'táng (*or* °jyàw-'táng) chywù.

CHUTE. (*Steep slide*) 'shyé-gwǎr. (*Parachute*) jyàng-lè-'sǎn.

CIGARETTE. yān, yān-'jywǎr, jǐ-'yān, shyāng-'yān. ‖Have a cigarette! chēw jǐ- (*or* gēr-)'yān-ba! ‖Do you carry American cigarettes? nǐm mày 'měy-gwo-yān-ma?
     Cigarette case yān-'héer. ‖I've lost my cigarette case. wǒ bǎ yān-'héer 'dyēw-le.

CIRCLE. (ywán-)'chywǎr. ‖Draw a circle. hwà yí-ge-ywán-'chywǎr. ‖The sign has a red circle on a white field. 'jì-hàwr shǐ báy-'dyèr-shang (yěw) ví-ge-húng-'chywǎr.
     (*In city streets*) ywán-'chǎng. ‖These streets meet in a circle. jè-jǐ-tyáw-'jyē dzày jè-ywán-'chǎng hwèy-'hé.
     Circle of *friends, etc.* (*Large*) yì-bāng; (*small*) jí-ge. ‖I have a small circle of friends here. wǒ 'jèr yěw jí-ge-'péng-yew.
     Circles (*governmental, official, etc.*) jyè. ‖He's known only in scholastic circles. tā jǐ dzày 'shywé-jyè yěw dyǎr-'míng.
     (*Make a circular mark around*) yùng (ywán-)'chywǎr °'gēw-chū-lay *or* °'chywǎn-chū-lay. ‖Please circle the words that are misspelled. chǐng bǎ pīn-'tswò-de-dž yùng ywán-'chywǎr 'gēw-chu-lay.
     Go around in a circle wáy-je ... ràw ('chywǎr); (*if number of times is specified*) ràw ...-chywǎr, ràw ...-dzāwr; (*if the motion is flying, running, etc.*) fēy ...-chywǎr, pàw ...-chywǎr, *etc.* ‖We drove around in a circle. wǒm kāy-je 'chē wéy-je ràw-'chywǎr. ‖We drove around in a circle three times. wǒm kāy-je 'chē wéy-je ràw-le 'sān-°chywǎr, *or* °dzāwr. ‖The plane circled around the field several times. fēy-'jī dzày fēy-jī-'chǎng-shàng-tew 'fēy-le hǎw-jǐ-'chywǎr.

CITIZEN. gūng-'mín; *sometimes expressed with* **person** rén. ‖I'm a citizen of the United States. wǒ shǐ 'měy-gwo-gūng-'mín. ‖What country are you a citizen of? nǐ shǐ 'nǎ-yì-gwó-de-'rén?

CITY. chéng (*theoretically, a city with a city wall, of any size*). ‖How far is the nearest city? dzwèy-'jìn-de-chéng lí-'jèr yěw 'dwō-ywǎn? ‖I never lived in the city until this year. wǒ 'jīn-nyan-yǐ-'chyán méy-'jù-dzay chéng-'lǐ-gwo. ‖The whole city was aroused by the news. 'shyāw-shì hūng-'dùng chywán-'chéng.
     (*Municipality*) shǐ; *either a city on the governmental level of a* shyàn (*county*), *directly under provincial government, or one on the governmental level of a province, directly under the national government.*

(*In contrast with country, rural area*) chéng-'shr̀. ‖She's not accustomed to city life. tā méy 'gwò-gwàn 'chéng-shr̀-'shēng-hwó. *or* tā dzày 'chéng-lǐ méy-'gwò-gwàn.

CIVIL. (*Of citizens*) gūng-'mín(-de). ‖The governor pays great attention to civil liberties. shěng-'jǎng hěn jù-'yì °gūng-mín-chywán-'lì. *or* °gūng-mín-dz̀-'yéw.

Civil rights gūng-'chywán. ‖He was deprived of his civil rights. tā chr̀-'dwó gūng-'chywán-le.

(*Nonreligious or nonmilitary*) pǔ-'tūng(-de), pǔ-tūng-'rén-de, mín-'shr̀(-de). ‖He was married by a civil ceremony, not by a religious ceremony. tā àn-je pǔ-'tūng-yí-'shr̀ jyē-de 'hwēn, bú-shr àn-je dzūng-'jyàw-yí-'shr̀.

Civil authorities 'mín-shr̀-dāng-'jywú; **civil officials** wén-'gwān. ‖The civil authorities must be consulted in this. 'jèy-ge děy gēn 'mín-shr̀-dāng-'jywú tǎw-'lwèn-le tsáy 'shíng.

Civil engineering 'tǔ-mù-'gūng-cheng; **civil engineer** 'tǔ-mù-gūng-cheng-'shr̀.

(*According to civil law, not criminal law*) mín-'fǎ, mín-'shr̀; **civil code** mín-'fǎ, 'mín-shr̀-fǎ-'gwēy.

Civil service personnel gūng-wù-'ywán. ‖Has he ever been employed in civil service? tā 'dāng-gwo gūng-wù-'ywán-ma?

Civil war nèy-'lwàn, nèy-'jàn. **The Civil War** (*U.S.A.*) 'měy-gwo-nán-'běy-jàn-'jēng.

(*Polite*) 'kè-chi, yěw lǐ-'màw. ‖At least he was civil to us. tā dwèy wǒ-men jr̀-'shǎw háy °swàn 'kè-chi. *or* °yěw lǐ-'màw.

CLAIM. To claim that *is expressed as* shwō (*say*); shywān-'bù (*shwō*) (*proclaim*); dz̀-'chēng (*profess*). ‖The government claims the mineral rights. gwéy 'jèng-fú. ‖He claims to have a copy of that book. néy-ge-'shū tā 'dz̀-jǐ shwō 'tā yěw yì-běr. ‖He claims that the traffic delayed him. tā shwō lù-shang hěn 'jǐ, swó-yi °'wǎn-le. *or* °'wù-le jūng-dyǎr. ‖He claims to be your relative. tā-'dz̀-jǐ shwō tā gēn-ní yěw (*or*, shr̀) 'chīn-chì. ‖He claims to be a specialist. tā dz̀-'chēng shr̀ 'jwān-jyā.

(*To pick up*) lǐng. ‖Where do I claim my baggage? wǒ dzày 'nǎr lǐng wǒ-de-'shíng-li?

(*Demand*) 'yāw-chyéw. ‖They have no claim on us. tā-men méy-yew 'lǐ-yéw-láy gēn wǒ-men 'yāw-chyéw shém-me. ‖You can't justify your claims. nǐ-de-'yāw-chyéw méy-yew 'gēn-jywù.

(*Indemnity*) péy-cháng-'fèy. ‖The insurance company paid all claims against it. bǎw-shyǎn-'gūng-sz̀ bǎ swǒ-yěw-de-péy-cháng-'fèy dēw °'gěy-le. *or* °'fù-le.

To file a (*legal*) **claim for** chéng (yí-ge-)'jwàng-dz yāw-chyéw. ‖I wish to file a claim for damages. wǒ yàw chéng yí-ge-'jwàng-dz, (shr̀) yāw-chyéw péy-cháng-'swěn-shr̀(-de).

CLASS. (*Sort, kind; general term*) jǔng, lèy. ‖Don't associate with that class of people. byé gēn 'nèy-jǔng-rén 'láy-wang.

(*Grade, quality*) děng. **First class** (*on boat*) téw-děng-'tsāng; (*on train*) téw-děng-'chē; (*in theater*) téw-děng-'dzwèr; **second class** *with* èr *instead of* téw. ‖These accommodations are first class. jèy-shyē-shè-'bèy jēn děy swàn-shr gāw-'děng. ‖Give me one second-class ticket to Chungking. (gěy-wo) yì-jāng-chywù-chúng-'chìng-de-'èr-děng-'pyàw.

(*Style*). ‖This bar has class. jèy-jyěw-'gwǎr hěn jyǎng-'jyēw.

(*Social level*) 'jyē-jí, jí, děng. **The higher classes** gāw-'jí, gāw-'děng; **moneyed class** yěw-'chyán 'jyē-jí; **propertied class** yěw-'chǎn-'jyē-jí; **middle class** jūng-'chǎn-'jyē-jí; **moneyless class** wú-'chǎn-'jyē-jí, 'chyúng-rén; **low classes** shyà-'jí, dī-'jí. ‖The educated class is supporting this measure. 'jr̀-shr̀-jyē-ji-de-'rén 'dzàn-chéng jèy-ge-'bàn-fa.

(*Second terms*). *A class or course in a particular subject* yì-mén-(gūng-)'kè, yì-bān-(gūng-)'kè; *a class session, class period* yì-táng-'kè. ‖I have a class at nine. wǒ 'jyěw-dyǎn yěw-'kè. ‖I must go to (my) class. wǒ děy chywù shàng-°'kè. *or* °'bān. ‖Wait until after the class. děng shyà-le °'kè (*or* °'bān) 'dzày shwō. ‖How many classes are you teaching a week? *meaning* how many different courses nǐ 'yí-ge-lǐ-'bày jyāw °'jǐ-mén-gūng-'kè? *or* °'jǐ-bān-gūng-'kè? *meaning* how many class periods nǐ 'yí-ge-lǐ-'bày jyāw 'dwō-shaw-°dyǎn-'jūng? *or* °táng-'kè?

Classroom kè-'shr̀, kè-'shr̀, kè-'táng, jyǎng-'táng.

(*Students of a single year*) bān, jí, 'nyán-jí; (*certain schools*) chī. ‖He's one class higher. tā 'gāw yì-°bān. *or* °'nyán-ji. *or* °'jí. ‖The freshman class is bigger than it was last year. 'jīn-nyan-de-'yī-nyán-ji-de-shywé-sheng bǐ 'chywù-nyan-de 'dwō. ‖The class of 1946 are juniors now. yī-jyěw-sz̀-lyèw-'bān shyàn-dzày shr̀ 'sān-nyán-ji. ‖The class of 1928 held a reunion dinner. yī-jyěw-èr-'bā-bān-bì-yè-'shēng 'kāy-le ge-jywù-tsān-'hwèy. ‖He's a graduate of the fourteenth class of the Central Military Academy. tā shr̀ 'jūng-yāng-jywūn-'shyàw-dì-shr̀-'sz̀-chī bì-'yè-de.

Classmate túng-'bān(-de), túng-'jí(-de), túng-'chī(-de).

Be classed as 'swàn-shr, 'fēn-dzay . . .-'lèy. ‖These can be classed as finished. 'jèy-shyē ké-yi °swàn-shr 'wán-le. *or* °fēn-dzay dzwò-'wán-de-'nèy-lèy-li. *or* *expressed as* These can be put with the finished ones. 'jèy-shyē ké-yi 'gē-dzay dzwò-'wán-de-'nèy-byar.

CLAY. (jyāw-)'ní, (nyán-)'tǔ; ní *is also mud*, tǔ *is also dust*. ‖This kind of clay can be made into porcelain. 'jèy-jǔng-ní ké-yi dzwò-'tsź. ‖Brick is made of clay. 'jwān shr̀ yùng-'ní dzwò-de. ‖The Chinese sometimes used to print cheap books with type made of clay. 'jūng-gwo-rén yǐ-'chyán yìn 'pyán-yi-shū, 'yěw-de-shŕ-hew yùng yì-jǔng-yǔng-'ní-dzwò-de-hwó-'dz̀.

‖The clay roads are impassable because of the rain. tǔ-'dàw (or tǔ-'lù, ní-'dàw, ní-'lù) yīn-wey shyà-'ywǔ bù-'tūng-le.

CLEAN. 'gān-jìng. ‖Can you give me a clean towel? yěw 'gān-jìng-'shěw-jīn-ma? ‖The hotels here are kept unusually clean. jèr-de-lywǔ-'gwǎn 'shēw-shr-de tè-'byé 'gān-jing.

To clean. *A compound is used with* 'gān-jìng *as second element, the first element specifying the manner or method of cleaning.* **To sweep clean** sǎw-'gān-jìng; **to rub clean** tsā-'gān-jìng; *etc.* ‖He didn't sweep the floor clean. dì-'bǎn tā méy-sǎw-'gān-jìng. ‖Clean the car with that piece of cloth. yùng nèy-kwày-'bù bǎ-'chē tsā-'gān-jìng-le. ‖You can wash it clean with water. yùng-'shwěy ké-yi shǐ-'gān-jing-le. ‖The rain washed the street clean. ywǔ-'shwěy bǎ-'jyē chūng-'gān-jìng-le.

To clean with a broom 'dǎ-sǎw. ‖Has the maid cleaned the room? lǎw-'mā-dz bǎ 'wū-dz 'dǎ-sǎw-le méy-yew?

To clean with a feather duster yùng 'dǎn-dz 'dǎn. ‖She only cleaned it with a feather duster. tā jř yùng 'dǎn-dz 'dǎn-le yí-shyàr.

To clean with a strainer yùng 'lèw-'děwr 'lìn-gwò.

To clean house (*literally*) dǎ-sǎw 'wū-dz; (*figuratively*) chīng-'chú (or táw-'tày) fǔ-hwà-fèn-'dž. ‖The new administration will begin by cleaning house. shīn-gwān-dàw-'rèn, shyān yàw °chīng-'chú (or °táw-'tày) fǔ-hwà-fèn-'dž.

To clean up (*to wash up*) 'shǐ-yi-shǐ, shǐ-'shěw. ‖I'd like to clean up before dinner. méy-chř-'fàn yǐ-'chyán wǒ shyǎng 'shyān 'shǐ yí-shyàr 'shěw.

To clean up (*to straighten up*) 'shěw-shr. ‖The room needs cleaning up for a new guest. jèy-jyān-'wū-dz děy 'shěw-shr yí-shyàr, yěw 'shīn-fáng-'kè yàw 'bān-jìn-lay.

To clean up (*to finish*) dzwò-'wán. ‖You may go home when you clean up the work. 'shr-ching dzwò-'wán-le yǐ-'hèw, nǐ ké-yi hwéy-'jyā.

To clean out chīng-'lǐ. ‖I'll look for it when I clean out my trunk. wǒ chīng-'lǐ 'shyāng-dz de-shŕ-hew 'jǎw yí-shyàr.

(*Free from obscenity*) bù-'tsū, bù-'yě. ‖The new play is clean and amusing. shīn-'páy-de-jèy-chū-hwà-'jywù-li-de-'tsér hěn dèw-'shyàwr, ké-shr 'yì-dyǎr yě bù-'tsū.

Clean cut, clean break. ‖That's a clean cut (*wound*). nèy shr yì-'jŕ-jìn-chywu-de-'shāng. ‖It's a clean break (*of bone*). 'gú-tew-'dwàn-de-dì-fang hěn 'jěng-chí. ‖He has a clean-cut face. tā-de-'lyǎn 'jǎng-de hěn °píng-'jèng. or °dwān-'jèng. ‖She has a clean-cut face. tā 'méy-chīng-mù-'shyèw-de. ‖They made a clean break. tām wán-'chywán dwàn-'jywé 'gwān-shi-le.

(*Free of guilt*). ‖My hands are clean in the matter. wǒ gēn 'nèy-jyàn-shř 'yì-dyǎr-'gwān-shi yě 'méy-yew.

‖I wash my hands clean of the whole thing. tsúng-'jīn-yǐ-'hèw wǒ gēn 'jèy-jyàn-shèr wán-'chvwán dwàn-'jywé 'gwān-shi.

Clean sweep. ‖He made a clean sweep of the old plans. tā bǎ 'ywán-láy-de-'jì-hwà wán-'chywán 'gǎyle. ‖He made a clean sweep of the prizes. jyǎng-'pǐn jyàw-'tā ná-de yì-sǎwr-'gwǎng.

Clean record. ‖The prisoner doesn't have a clean (*criminal*) record. 'fàn-rén 'bú-shr 'chū-fàn.

Clean lines. ‖The new cars have clean lines. shīn-'chē-de-'shŕ-yang méy-léng-méy-'jyǎwr-de hěn shwǎng-'mù.

CLEAR. (*Of the sky or weather*) chíng, shyàng-'chíng. ‖The sky is clear tonight. jyěr-'wǎn-shang 'tyān °hěn 'chíng. or °shyǎng-'chíng. ‖The weather has been clear all week. tyān 'chíng-le yí-ge-lǐ-'bày-le.

(*Of water*) chīng. ‖The water is clear and deep. shwěy yèw 'chīng yèw 'shēn. ‖The spring is clear as crystal. chywán-shwěy 'chīng-de °shyàng 'shwěy-jìng shř-de. or °ké-yi 'kàn-daw dyěr.

(*More general term*) 'chīng-chu. ‖His voice was clear over the radio. tā-de-'shǎng-yīn dzày wú-shyàn-'dyàn-lǐ hěm 'chīng-chu. ‖I don't have a clear idea of what you mean. nǐ-de-'yì-sz wǒ bú-dà °'chīng-chu. or °'míng-báy. ‖This seat has a clear view of the stage. 'jèy-ge-dzwòr kàn shì-'táy ké-yi 'kàn-de hěn 'chīng-chu.

(*Of the head*) 'chīng-shǐng. ‖Try to keep a clear head. shyàng-'fár bǎw-'chŕ 'chīng-shǐng-de-'téw-nǎw.

(*Of an idea in writing; literary*) yí-'mù-lyǎw-'rán.

(*Of handwriting or copy*) yì-'bǐ-yí-'hwàr-de hěn 'chīng-chu.

(*Of a road freed from obstructions*) hǎw-'dzěw. ‖Is the road clear up ahead? 'chván-byar-de-'lù hǎw-'dzěw-ma?

(*Understandable*). ‖Is it clear? 'míng-bay-bu-míng-bay? or 'dǔng-bu-dǔng? or 'míng-bay-le-ma? or 'dǔng-le-ma?

To clear (*up or off*) (*of weather*) chíng. ‖The skies are clearing now. yàw 'chíng (tyān)-le. ‖It may clear up this afternoon. jyěr-'shyà-wǔ 'tyān yě-shywǔ hwèy-'chíng. ‖We will leave as soon as the weather clears up. 'tyār yī 'chíng wǒm jyèw dzěw. ‖The fog has cleared off. wù 'sàn-le.

To clear (*to remove obstructions from*). ‖Have they cleared the road? (tām bǎ) lù-'jàng 'chīng-chú-le 'méy-yew? or lù 'tūng-le-ma? or tām bǎ-'lù nùng-'tūng-le-ma?

To clear away. ‖Ask her to clear away the dishes. 'jyàw-tā bǎ 'dyé-dz 'shěw-chi-lay.

To clear off. ‖Ask her to clear off the table. 'jyàw-tā bǎ 'jwō-dz 'shěw-shr-le.

To clear out (*to empty*). ‖Please clear out this bureau. 'chīng-nǐ bǎ jèy-ge-'gwèy-dz 'téng-chu-lay.

To clear out (*to leave*). ‖When the police came he had already cleared out. jǐng-'chá dàw-le, tā 'yǐ-jīng °'pǎw-le. or °'lí-kay-le. or °'dzěw-kay-le.

To clear up (*explain*). ‖Would you mind clearing up a few points for me? yěw jǐ-'chù nǐ 'géy-wǒ °jyě-'shř yí-shyàr 'ké-yi-ma? *or* °'jyǎng-yi-jyǎng, 'ké-yi-ma?

To clear up (*settle*). ‖I want to clear up some affairs before I go. wǒ méy-dzěw yǐ-'chyán yěw jì-jyàn-'shř děy 'chīng-lǐ yí-shyàr.

To be cleared. (*Of physical obstacles*) ‖The road has been cleared. lù 'méy-yew 'jàng-ày-le. *or* lù 'tūng-le. *or* lù 'gwò-de-chywù-le. ‖The track has been cleared (*of other trains*). byé-de-'chē dēw 'ràng-kay-le. (*Of legal obstacles or requirements*) ‖All my debts are cleared. wǒ-de-'jàng dēw hwán-'chīng-lᴏ. ‖The ship has been cleared. chwán 'chū-kěw shěw-'shywù-°bàn-'chīng-le. *or* °('yǐ-jing) 'lyǎw-le. ‖The account has been cleared. swàn 'chīng-le. ‖The passport has been cleared. (*Issued*) hù-'jàw °bàn-'hǎw-le *or* °'fā-shya-lay-le. (*Checked by foreign authorities*) hù-'jàw °jyǎn-'chá-wán-le. *or* °'fā-hwey-lay-le.

To be cleared (*of a title*) méy-yew 'wèn-tí *or* méy-yew "jǐ-jyé *or* chyán dēw fù-'chīng-le; (*of a title or deed cleared by the authorities*) shř húng-'chì; (*of a document passed by higher authorities*) pī-'jywǔn-le.

(*Of profit*). ‖It is clear profit. shř chwén-'lì. *or* shř 'jìng-dé-de.

To be cleared (*of wooded land*) 'kāy-chu-lay-le *or* kāy-'hǎw-le.

Be cleared (*of checks*). ‖We must wait until the checks are cleared. wǒm dzǔng děy 'děng jř-'pyàw chá-'chīng-le yǐ-'hèw dzày 'shwō.

Be cleared (*of mortgages*). ‖Has the mortgage on this house been cleared off? jř-je 'jèy-swǒr-fáng-dz-'jyè-de-chyán dēw hwán-'chīng-le-ma? *or* yùng-'jèy-swǒr-fáng-dz-dzwò-dǐ-'yā-jyè-de-chyán dēw hwán-'chīng-le-ma?

To clear out *stock*. ‖Wait until we have cleared out the stock. děng 'tswén-hwò dēw màv-'wán-le dzày 'shwō. *or* děng 'tswén-hwò 'chīng-yi-ching dzày 'shwō.

Special expressions in English. ‖He cleared his throat and continued to speak. tā 'ké-sù-le yí-shyàr yèw "jyě-je shwō-shya-chywu. ‖His frank statement cleared the air. tā-shwō-de-'hwà hěn tǎn-'báy, bǎ jǐn-jāng-de-kūng-'chì nèng hwàn-'hé-le. ‖He cleared up the misunderstanding. tā bǎ wù-'hwèy °jyě-'chú-le. *or* °jyě-shř 'chīng-chu-le. *or* °jyě-shř 'míng-bay-le. ‖We can clear the enemy from this region in three days. yùng 'sān-tyan jyèw néng bǎ 'dí-rén tsúng jèy-kwàr-'dì-fang chywán °'gǎn-chu-chywu. *or* °'sǎw-chú jìng-'jìn. ‖The boat cleared the rock by inches. nèy-jř-'chwán gwò 'yán-shf de-shf-hew 'lí-je bù-jǐ-'tswèn. ‖The plane barely cleared the treetops. 'fēy-jī 'fēy-gwò-chywu de-shf-hew 'chà-dyǎr jyèw 'tsèng-jaw shù-'jyǎr. ‖Can we clear that bridge? chyáw 'pèng-de-shàng-ma? (*For width*) chyáw 'rúng-de-kāy-ma? (*For vertical clearance*) chyáw-'dǐ-shya gwò-de-chywù-ma? *or* chyáw gèw 'gāw-de-ma? (*For clearance in an arch*) chyáw-'dùng gèw gāw-de-ma? ‖Clear (the

deck) for action. jwēn-'bèy kāy-jàn. ‖He got clear away. tā-'pǎw-de °wú-yǐng-wú-'dzūng-le. *or* °méy-'yěngr-le. ‖It was clear out of reach. jyǎn-'jf 'gèw-bu-jáw. ‖Keep clear of politics. byé gēn 'jèng-jř 'fā-shēng 'gwān-shi. *or* 'dwǒ-kāy 'jèng-jyè. *or* gēn 'jèng-jř lí 'ywǎn-dyar. ‖Keep clear of in-laws. 'chīn-chì ywǎn-lí-shyāng. ‖He's in the clear. tā méy-yew 'shèr. *or* méy-yew 'tā-de-'shèr. *or* gēn-tā 'méy-yew 'gwān, shi. ‖His name has been cleared. méy 'shèr-le. ‖He's been cleared (*of an accusation in court*). shywān-'gàw wú-'dzwèy-le.

CLERK. (*Salesman; in a small shop*) 'hwǒ-ji; (*in any store*) 'dyàn-ywán. ‖The clerk is looking up the price. nèy-ge-'hwǒ-ji dzày-nar chá jyà-'chyán shř 'dwō-shǎw.

(*Accountant or bookkeeper, not necessarily highly trained*) gwǎn-'jàng-de(-shyān-sheng). *or* 'shyān-sheng.

(*Employee, in a somewhat responsible position*) 'jǐ-ywán; (*otherwise*) 'gù-ywán.

(*Secretary*) 'shū-jì; (*typist*) dǎ-'dz-ywán; (*copyist*) 'lù-shř *or* 'shàn-shyě-ywán.

Chief government clerk dzǔng-wù-'sz-sz-'jǎng *or* dzǔng-wù-'kē-kē-'jǎng *or* dzǔng-wù-'chù-chù-'jǎng. *The chief clerk of any government division the word for which ends in X is* X-jǎng.

Noncommissioned military clerk 'wén-shū-jywǔn-'shř.

Desk clerk gwèy-'táy-shang-de-rén. ‖Leave the key with the clerk at the desk. bǎ 'yàw-shr jyāw-gěy gwèy-táy-shang-de-rén.

(*Court recorder*) shū-jì-'gwān. ‖The clerk kept on file all the records of this court. běn-'ywàn-de-'jì-lù dēw gwěy shū-jì-'gwān fēn-'lèy bǎw-'gwǎn.

To clerk. *Use* dzwò *or* dāng *plus the appropriate noun for* clerk. ‖She hasn't had much experience in clerking. tā °dzwò (*or* °dāng)-'shū-jì-de-'jīng-yàn méy-yew 'dwō-shǎw.

CLEVER. 'tsūng-míng, líng, 'líng-lì. ‖The kid is pretty clever. shyǎw-'hár tǐng °'tsūng-míng. *or* °'líng. *or* °'líng-lì. ‖That's a clever horse. nèy-pǐ-'mǎ jēn 'tsūng-míng. ‖It was clever of you to think of that. nǐ néng-'shyǎng-chū 'nèy-ge-lay, jēn shř 'tsūng-míng.

(*Skillful, talented*) chyǎw. ‖That cat is clever (*e.g., at catching mice*). nèy-jř-'māw hěn 'chyǎw.

(*Of a move, play, or maneuver*) hǎw, myàw, chyǎw, chyǎw-myàw, 'jī-ling. (*Literally*) ‖Your friend made a clever chess move. nǐ-nèy-wèy-'péng-yew dzěw-le yí-'bù-hǎw-'chí. ‖He made a clever bridge play. tā jèy-jāng-'páy chū-de 'myàw. (*Literally or figuratively*) ‖He made a clever move. tā jèy-yí-'bù 'dzěw-de jēn °'jī-ling. *or* °'myàw. *or* °chyǎw-'myàw. *or* °'chyǎw. *or* °'hǎw. (*Figuratively*) ‖He made a clever move. tā jèy-'shěwr 'wàr-de 'myàw.

CLIMATE. 'chì-hew. ‖**The climate here is similar to that in Italy.** jèr-de-'chì-hew hěn-shyàng 'yì-dà-'lì.

(*Weather*). ‖**Is the climate here always so hot?** jèr-de-'tyān-chi lǎw shr̀ jèm 'rè-ma?

(*Place*). ‖**I'd like to visit a warmer climate.** wǒ 'shyǎng dàw yí-ge-'nwǎn-he-yì-dyar-de-'dì-fang-chywu

CLIMB. shàng. ‖**I prefer not to climb stairs.** wǒ bú 'ywàn-yì shàng léw-'tī.

(*Using both hands and feet, or involving other difficulties; crawl, creep*) pá. ‖**I have not climbed Mount Lú.** wǒ méy 'pá-gwo 'lú-shān. ‖**The plane began to climb rapidly.** 'fēy-jī pá-'gāwr 'pá-de hěn kwày. ‖**You will find the climb steep and difficult.** nǐ 'dàw-nèr jyèw 'jr̄-dàw yèw 'jr̄ yèw 'nán-pá. ‖**Is it much of a climb to the top?** yàw 'pá-dàw 'dyěngr-shàng-chywu shr̀-bu-shr̀ hěn chr̄-'lì?

To climb down 'pá-shyà-lay, 'shyà-lay. ‖**Tell that lineman to climb down.** 'gàw-su nèy-ge-'shf́-dwo-dyàn-'hwà-de-rén ('pá-) 'shyà-lay.

To climb (*in society or rank*) wàng-'shàng dzwān, wàng-'shàng pá. ‖**He's trying hard to climb to** (*worm his way into*) **a higher position.** tā 'yí-ge-'jyèr-de shyǎng wàng-'shàng dzwān.

To climb (*only of official position*) shēng-'gwār. ‖**He is trying hard to climb to a higher office.** tā yí-ge-'jyèr-de shyǎng shēng-'gwār.

CLOCK. jūng; **tower clock** 'dà-jūng; **table or mantel clock** 'dzwò-jūng; **clock with four faces** sž-myàr-'jūng; **hall clock** 'lì-jūng; **alarm clock** 'nàw-jūng. ‖**What time does your clock say?** nǐ-de-'jūng jǐ-'dyǎn-le? ‖**Before I went to bed, I set the clock for seven.** wǒ méy-shwèy yǐ-'chyán bǎ 'nàw-jūng °shàng (or 'bwō)-dàw 'chī-dyǎn. ‖**We've set the clock by the radio.** wǒm gēn wú-shyàn-'dyàn bàw-'gàw-de jūng-dyǎr 'dwèy-de.

To clock (*record time used*) jì 'shf́-hew. ‖**We'll clock you while you do this.** nǐ dzwò 'jèy-ge, wǒm gěy-ni jì 'shf́-hew.

See also **O'CLOCK.**

CLOSE. 1. **To close** (*most general terms*) gwān, 'gwān-shàng; shàng-'mén, shàng-'bǎr; *sometimes expressed negatively as* **not open** bù-'kāy. *These same terms sometimes cover the meanings* **close out** *and* **close up.** ‖**Close the door.** gwān-'mén. or 'gwān-shàng 'mén. or bǎ-'mén 'gwān-shang. ‖**Why don't you close the drawer?** nǐ 'dzěme bù-bǎ 'chēw-ti 'gwān-shang? ‖**The zoo closes at six P.M.** dùng-wù-'ywán wǎn 'lyèw-dyǎn gwān-'mén. ‖**It closed an hour ago.** 'yì-dyǎn-jūng yǐ-'chyán jyèw 'gwān-le. ‖**That bookshop closed long ago.** nèy-ge-shū-'pù 'dzǎw jyèw gwān-'mén-le. ‖**That store down the street is closing out.** jyē-'nèy-byar-de-nèy-ge-'pù-dz yàw gwān-'mén. ‖**Today is Sunday; the library is closed all day.** jyèr lǐ-bày-'r̀, tú-shū-'gwǎn yì-'tyān bù-'kāy. ‖**The museum is closed every evening**

after six. bwó-wù-'gwǎn 'měy-tyan-'wǎn-shang-'lyèw-dyǎn yǐ-'hèw jyèw bù-kāy-'mén-le. ‖**They close up the store at six.** tām-de-'pù-dz shr̀ 'lyèw-dyǎn-jūng °shàng-'mén. or °shàng-'bǎr. ‖**They close up promptly at sundown.** 'tày-yang yí 'lè jyèw shàng-'mén-le.

To close *a stall or stand* shēw, shew-'tār. ‖**That stall closes at seven.** nèy-ge-'tān-dz 'chī-dyǎn jyèw °'shēw-le. or °shēw-'tār-le.

To close *something* **tight** gwān-'jǐn, gwān-'yán. ‖**He didn't close the door tight.** tā méy-bǎ-'mén °gwān-'yán-le. or °gwān-'jǐn-le.

To close (*without barring or locking*) yǎn, 'yǎn-shàng; (*and bar*) chā, 'chā-shàng; (*and lock*) swǒ, 'swǒ-shàng. ‖**Close the door, but don't bar or lock it.** bǎ-'mén 'yǎn-shang, kě-shr byé 'chā-shang, yě byé 'swǒ-shang.

To close (*by official order*) fēng. ‖**That store was closed.** nèy-ge-'pù-dz fēng-le 'mén-le.

To close (*of a school*). (*If unscheduled and temporary*) tíng-'kè; (*for a regular holiday*) fàng-'jyà; (*permanently*) tíng-'bàn, or gwān-'mén. ‖**The school is closed today.** shywé-'shyàw jyèr tíng-'kè. or (*for a holiday*) shywé-'shyàw jyèr fàng-'jyà. ‖**The school is closed for the summer vacation.** shywé-'shyàw fàng shǔ-'jyà-le. ‖**That school closed up because of a deficit.** nèy-ge-shywé-'shyàw yīn-wey 'kwěy-kùng °tíng-'bàn-le. or °gwān-'mén-le.

To close *a box, trunk, etc.* 'gày-shang, 'gwān-shang; (*if cover is hinged*) 'hé-shang, 'yǎn-shang. ‖**Close the box.** bǎ-'héer °'gày-shang. or °'gwān-shang. or bǎ hé-dz-'gàr °'gày-shang. or °'gwān-shang. ‖**Close the suitcase.** bǎ shēw-tí-'shyǎng °'gày-shang. or °'gwān-shang. or °'hé-shang. or °'yǎn-shang. or bǎ shēw-tí-shyǎng-'gàr °'gày-shang, or etc. ‖**Close the trunk, but don't lock it.** bǎ dà-'shyāng-dz-de-'gàr 'hé-shang, kě-shr byé 'swǒ.

To close *a knife* 'hé-shang, 'gwān-shang; (*a bottle; with a cork*) 'sāy-shang, (*with a cap*) 'gày-shang; (*a safety pin*) 'byé-shang, or byé-'hǎw. ‖**Please close the knife after using it.** shyǎw-'dāwr yùng-'wán-le jyèw °'hé-shang. or °'gwān-shang. ‖**Have the safety pin closed before you give it to the baby to play with.** bǎ 'byé-jēr 'byé-shang dzày gěy háy-dz 'wár.

To close *the eyes* hé, 'hé-shang, bì, 'bì-shang. ‖**He closed his eyes before he said that.** tā bì-shang 'yǎn tsáy 'shwō-de. or tā hé-shang 'yǎn tsáy 'shwō-de. or tā °bì-'yǎn (or °hé-'yǎn) tsáy 'shwō-de.

To close *the eyes to something* (*figuratively*). ‖**Don't close your eyes to such matters.** jèy-yàng-de-'shèr nǐ bù-néng (jyǎ-) 'jwāng °kàn-bu-'jyàn. or °bù-jr̄-'dàw. or °bù-'gwǎn.

To close *a road* 'lán-jù. ‖**Let's close the road here.** dzám dzày-'jèr bǎ-'lù 'lán-jù. ‖**Road closed!** *is expressed as* **Road not open!** tsž-'lù °bù-'tūng! or °bù-tūng-'shíng!

To close *an office, particularly a branch office* shēw, jyē-'shù, chywǔ-'shyāw. ‖Our Hankow branch was closed. wǒm hàn-'kěw-fēn-'hàw yǐ-jing °jyē-'shù-le. *or* °chywǔ-'shyāw-le. *or* °'shēw-le.

To close *an account* jyē *or* swàn (*followed by* account, bill, debt jàng); chywǔ (*followed by* money chyán). ‖I intend to close my account before I leave. wǒ (méy-)'dzěw yǐ-'chyán shyǎng-chywu °bǎ-'jàng 'jyē-le. *or* °bǎ-'jàng 'swàn-le. *or* °bǎ-'chyán 'chywǔ-le.

To close *a deal* 'chéng-jyāw. ‖The deal was closed this morning. jèy-pyàwr-'mǎy-mǎy jyēr-'dzǎw-shang °'chéng-de 'jyāw. *or* °chéng-'jyāw-de.

To close *a letter or speech, expressed with end, conclusion* mwò-'lyǎwr. ‖I'll close this letter with some gossip. mwò-'lyǎwr shyě dyǎr-jèr-de-'shyān-hwà. ‖He closed the speech with a prayer. tā(-de)-yǎn-'shwō mwò-'lyǎwr dzwò-le ge-dǎw-'gàw.

To close up *ranks.* ‖Close up! (*If marching*) gēn 'jǐn-yi-dyǎr! *or* 'gēn-shang chywù! *or* byé dzày 'hèw-tew 'là-la-je! (*If standing still*) āy 'jǐn-yi-dyǎr! *or* wàng-°'chyán (*or* °'hèw *or* °'dzwǒ *or* °'yèw, *depending on the direction of motion which will fill the gaps*) 'nwó-yi-nwó!

To close up on, close on, close in (*get nearer*). ‖They're closing in on him. tām jyàn-'jyán-de lí-ta 'jìn-le. ‖They're closing in. tām 'lí-de ywè 'láy ywè 'jìn-le.

Be closed (*of a legal case*) 'lyǎw-le, lyǎw-'jyē-le. ‖The case is closed. jèy-ge-'àn-dz °'lyǎw-le. *or* °'lyǎw-'jyē-le.

Behind closed doors. ‖The people are frightened and are hiding behind closed doors. rén dēw 'shyà-de gwān-'mén-bì-'hùr-de 'dwǒ-chi-lay-le.

‖Closed. Use side entrance. chǐng dzěw 'páng-mén.

2. The close (*of a letter, speech, article, etc.*) mwò-'lyǎwr.

A close *is in other cases expressed in different terms.* ‖At the close of the meeting, everyone left. *is expressed as* When the meeting was over everyone left. 'hwèy 'wán-le de-shŕ-hew, dà-'jyā dēw 'dzěw-le. ‖By the time the exhibition came to a close, it was already snowing. *is expressed as* When the exhibition concluded, it was already snowing. jǎn-lǎn-'hwèy bì-'mù de-shŕ-hew, yǐ-jing 'shyà-chi 'shywě láy-le. ‖The year is drawing to a close. 'jèy-yì-nyán kwày 'wán-le. ‖The magistrate's term is drawing to a close. shyàn-'jǎng kwày bàn-'jyāw-dày-le.

3. (*Near*) lí ... jìn. ‖The hotel is close to the station. lywǔ-'gwǎn lí hwǒ-chē-'jàn hěn 'jìn.

Close relatives (*including only brothers, sisters, parents, and children*) běn-'jyā-de; (*including other comparatively close relatives*) jìn-'chīn. ‖Do you have any close relatives here? dzày-'jèr yěw jìn-'chīn, běn-'jyā-de-ma?

Close neighbors 'lín-jywu. ‖They're close neighbors of ours. tām-shŕ wǒ-men-de-'lín-jywu.

Close friends hǎw-'péng-yew *or* chīn-'jìn-de-péng-yew. ‖I'm staying with some close friends. wǒ shyàn-dzày 'jù-dzay °jǐ-ge-hǎw-'péng-yew-'jyā. *or* °jǐ-ge-chīn-'jìn-de-'péng-yew-'jyā.

Give *something* close attention 'tè-byé jù-'yì. ‖Please give this your close attention. 'jèy-ge chǐng-ni 'tè-byé jù-'yì.

(*Of air in a room*) mēn. ‖The air is very close in this room. jèy-ge-'wūr-li mēn-de 'hěn.

(*Of a vote*). ‖The vote was very close. tā-men-de 'pyàw-shù chà-bu-'dwō. ‖He won by a close vote. tā 'chà-dyǎr shywǎn-bu-'shàng.

A close call. ‖That was a close call! hǎw 'shywán-le! *or* jēn 'shyǎn! ‖The car didn't hit me, but it was a close call. chì-'chē méy-'jwàng-jáw wo, bú-gwò °jyǎn-jŕ shŕ 'chà-yi-dyǎr. *or* °'jī-ji-hu méy-'jwàng-shang. *or* °'chà-dyǎr méy-'jwàng-shang.

Closely (*carefully*) dž-'shì. ‖Examine it closely. dž-'shì °'kàn-yi-kàn. *or* °'chá-kàn yí-shyà. *or* °'yán-jyēw yí-shyà.

CLOTH. (*Of cotton, rarely of wool*) 'bù; (*of cotton only*) bù-'lyàwr; (*material*) 'lyàw-dz *or* lyàwr; (*clothing material*) 'yī-lyàwr; (*cotton sheer, lace, gauze, yarn*) 'myán-shā, 'shā-lyàwr; (*cotton or silk sheer, lace, gauze, yarn*) shā; (*finest cotton sheer*) chán-yí-'shā; (*cotton crepe*) yáng-'jèw *or* jèw-'shā; (*wool*) 'ní-dz *or* 'ní-lyàwr (*angora*) 'máw-rúng *or* rúng-'bù; (*velvet*) rúng *or* 'sž-rúng; (*felt*) 'jān-dz; (*raw silk*) sž; (*silk*) chéw-'dwàn; (*fine silk*) 'chéw-dz; (*satin*) 'dwàn-dz; (*linen*) 'má-bù. A cloth bù; dust cloth 'jān-bù *or* 'mà-bù; table cloth jwō-'bù. ‖Wipe off the car with a clean cloth. bǎ-'chē yùng 'gān-jing-'bù 'tsā-yi-tsā. ‖Do you have a better quality of (cotton) cloth? nǐm yěw 'hǎw-dyǎr-de-'bù méy-yew? ‖Where do you keep your dust cloths? nǐ bǎ 'jān-bù 'fàng-dzay nǎr? ‖Change the table cloth. hwàn yí-kwày-jwō-'bù. ‖This cloth is half cotton and half silk. jèy-jǔng-'lyàw-dz shŕ bàn-'sž-bàn-'myán-de. ‖Silk cloth is more expensive than wool. 'chéw-dwàn(-lyàw-dz) bǐ °'ní-dz (*or* °'ní-lyàwr) háy 'gwèy.

Out of whole cloth. ‖He made the story up out of whole cloth. jěng-'gèr-de shŕ tā-'dž-jǐ shyā-'byān-de. *or* tā-shwō-de-nèy-jyàn-'shèr wán-'chywán shŕ tā-'dž-jǐ shyā-'byān-de.

CLOTHE. chwān. ‖You have to keep warmly clothed in this climate. jèy-jǔng-'tyān-chi nǐ 'yīng-dāng chwān 'nwǎn-he-le. ‖He needs this money to feed and clothe his family. tā yàw jèy-'chyán hǎw 'gūng tā-yì-jyā chŕ 'chwān.

CLOTHES. 'yī-shang, 'yī-fu, 'chwān-de ('chwān-de *means simply what is worn.*) ‖What (clothes) shall I wear? wǒ yīng-dāng 'chwān shéme ('yī-shang, 'yī-fu)? ‖I want these clothes cleaned and pressed. jèy-jǐ-jyàn-'yī-fu 'gān-shǐ. ‖I found this in the clothes closet. jè shř dzày gwà-yī-fu-de-shyǎw-'wūr-li 'jǎw-jaw-de.

Sport clothes 'ywùn-dung-yī. ‖Do you have any sport clothes? yěw shéme-'ywùn-dung-yī-ma?

Evening clothes yè-lǐ-'fú. ‖Evening clothes must be worn to the party. chywù nèy-ge-'hwèy fēy-děy chwān yè-lǐ-'fú.

‖Clothes make the man. is expressed as Clothes make the man as the saddle makes the horse. 'rén pèy 'yī-shang 'mǎ pèy 'ān.

CLOUD. ywún, 'ywún-tsǎy. ‖It got chilly when the sun went behind the clouds. ywún-tsay bǎ 'tày-yang 'jē-chi-lay yì-'hèw, tyǎn 'lyáng-le dyǎr. ‖The plane is flying above the clouds. 'fēy-jī dzày ywún-tsay 'shàng-myan fēy.

To cloud up (of the sky) 'yīn(-shang-lay); (with word sky expressed) chǐ-'ywún. ‖Just after we started (eating) on the picnic, it began to cloud up. wǒm gāng chř-chi 'yě-tsān-lay de-shŕ-hew, tyān jyèw 'yīn-shang-lay-le. ‖It's starting to get cloudy. tyān yàw 'yīn-le. or chǐ-'ywún-le. or yàw 'yīn-tyān.

Cloudy day or sky 'yīn-tyān.

(Figuratively). ‖The car left in a cloud of dust. chē kāy-'dzěw de-shŕ-hew 'yáng-chi yí-jèn-'chén-tǔ-lay. ‖Clouds of dense smoke are coming out of the chimney. yì-twánʲyì twán-de-'núng-yān jèng tsúng 'yān-tung-li 'màw-chu-lay. ‖The grasshoppers came in clouds. 'hwáng-chung yí-'pyàn-yí-pyàn-de 'fēy-gwo-lay. ‖One of the partners is a practical man, but the other has his head in the clouds. tām-lyǎ dā-'hwǒ; yěw 'yí-ge bàn-'shř hěn 'chyè-shŕ; 'nèy-ge-ya, jyǎn-'jŕ °shř ge-hú-dū-'chúng. or °hú-sz̀ 'lwàn-shyǎng-dẹ. or °bú chyè shŕ-'jì.

To be cloudy. (Of the memory). ‖The facts are clouded in my memory. 'shř-chíng-de-'jīng-gwò wǒ jì-bu-da-chīng-chu-le. (Of thinking) ‖His mind was clouded by age. tā shàng-le 'swèy-shur-le, °shīn-li nèm 'mwó-mwo-hu-hu-de. or °shīn-li bú-dà míng-bay-le.

To cloud (to darken). ‖His face clouded when I mentioned his name. wǒ 'tí-chi tā-de-'míng-dz de-shŕ-hew, tā-lyǎn lì-shŕ 'chén-shya-chywu-le.

CLUB. (Weapon) chwéy, 'chwéy-dz, 'bàng-chwey. Wooden club 'mù-chwéy; iron club 'tyě-chwéy; policeman's club 'gwèn-dz, 'bàng-dz, jǐng-'gwèn, jǐ hwéy-'gwèn. ‖The policeman was forced to use his club. jǐng-'chá bù-'dé-yǐ tsáy yùng-de °gwèn-dz. or °bàng-dz. or °jǐng-'gwèn. or °jǐ-hwéy-'gwèn. ‖The police said the victim had been clubbed. 'shywún-jīng shwō shèw-'hày-de-rén jyàw-rén yùng 'chwéy-dz dzày téw-shang dǎ-de yì-'chwéy. ‖The girls beat the wet clothes with clubs to clean them. nèy-shyē-nywǔ-'háy-dz bǎ shř-'yī-shang yùng 'bàng-chwey 'chyāw (or 'chyāw-dǎ, or dǎ) gān-jìng-le.

To use a rifle as a club yùng chyāng-'bàr dǎ.

(Organization) hwèy, shè; (for dancing, gambling, or political activities) jywù-lè-'bù. ‖Are you a member of the club? nǐ shř °hwèy-ywán-ma? or 'shè-ywán-ma? ‖Our club will meet next Thursday. běn-'shè (or běn-'hwèy) shyà-lǐ-bày-'sz̀ kāy-hwèy. ‖The tennis court is reserved for club members. wǎng-chyéw-'chǎng shř wèy hwèy-'ywán-men yùng-de.

(To band together) 'tsèw (yí-kwàr), dā-'hwǒ(r). ‖Let's club together and rent a car. dzám °tsèw yí-kwàr (or °dā-'hwǒ) dzū yí-lyàng-'chē-ba. ‖Let's club together (pooling our money). dzám tsèw-'chyán-ba. or dzám tsèw-chǐ chyán-lay-ba.

(Suit in cards) 'méy-hwār. ‖I bid one club. wǒ jyàw-yǐ-ge-'méy-hwār. ‖He took the trick with the ace of clubs. tā ná méy-hwar-'èy-sz yíng-de.

Clubfooted dyǎn-'jyǎwr.

COAL. méy. ‖The fire needs more coal. jèy-hwǒ děy tyān-'méy. ‖I want to order a ton of coal. wǒ yàw jyàw yì-dwēn-'méy. ‖This room is heated by a coal stove in winter. jèy-jyān-'wū-dz dūng-tyan shēng-de shř méy-'lú-dz. ‖Some red-hot coals fell from the grate. yěw jǐ-kwàr-húng-je-de-'méy tsúng tyě-'bì-dz-shang °dyàw-shya-lay-le. or °lèw-shya-lay-le. ‖That's a coal-burning furnace. nèy-ge-lú-dz shāw-'méy. ‖The ship will stop at that port to take on coal. chwán yàw tíng-dzày nèy-ge-'hǎy-kěw shàng-'méy.

Hard coal 'yìng-méy; bituminous coal 'yān-méy, 'yǎr-méy.

‖He will rake us over the coals for this. tā wèy 'jèy-ge yí-dìng hwèy gēn wǒ-men 'dà-nàw yí-'dwèn-de.

COARSE. (Not fine) tsū. ‖This cloth is too coarse for me. jèy-bù (wèy-wo) tày 'tsū. ‖The only flour he had was very coarse. tā jŕ yěw yì-jǔng-hěn-'tsū-de-myàn-'fén. ‖His hands are coarse from hard work. tā-de-shěw 'yīn-wey dzwò kǔ-'gūng swǒ-yǐ hěn 'tsū.

(Vulgar). tsū, yě, 'tsū-yě, 'tsū-sú. ‖She was offended by his coarse manners. tā jywǔ-jŕ 'tsū-yě, rě-de rén-jya hěn bù-gāw-'shìng. ‖His language was coarse and abusive. tā-shwō-de-'hwà yèw-'yě yèw-'tswēn.

COAST. àn, hǎy-'àn. ‖So far we have seen only the coast. jŕ dàw 'jèy-ge-shŕ-hew wǒ-men kàn-jyan-de jŕ sl hǎy-'àn. ‖The ship sails down the coast. chwán yan-je-àn 'dzěw. ‖Follow the coast road to Boston. shwèn-je hǎy-àn-dà-'lù dàw bwō-shř-'dwēn.

To coast lyēw. ‖Let's try coasting down this next hill. dzám 'shř-shř lyēw-shyà chyán-byar-de-shān-'pwōr-chywu.

‖Let me know when the coast is clear. (If the point is that no one is in the way) chyǎw-chyǎw 'nèr, méy 'rén de-shŕ-hew, 'gàw-sung wǒ. (If the point is that some particular person is not in the way) 'chyǎw-je dyǎr, tā yì-'dzěw-kāy jyèw 'gàw-sung wǒ. (If the *point is that the danger is over*) děng shèr 'gwò-le (*or*, děng shèr píng-'jìng-shya chywu-le, *or* děng méy-yew 'wéy-shyǎn-le), jyèw 'jř-hwèy wǒ.

COAT. Suit coat 'shàng-yī; overcoat, topcoat 'dà-yī, wày-'tàwr. ‖You can go without a coat in this weather. jèy-jǔng-'tyār 'rùng-bu-jaw chwān 'dà-yī. ‖You will need a heavy coat for winter. 'dūng-tyār nǐ dzǔng-děy yěw yí-jyàn-'hèw-dǎ-yī. ‖The pants and vest fit, but the coat is too small. 'kù-dz gēn 'kǎn-jyār dàw 'hé-shř, bú-gwò 'shàng-yī tày shyǎw.

(*Layer*) tséng; (*of paint only*) dàw. ‖This room needs another coat of paint. jèy-wū-dz 'háy děy shàng yí-dàw-'yéw-chī.

'To coat (*to cover with a layer*) shàng *plus the layer of substance;* (*with paint· mud, molasses, or some other sticky substance, using e hand or a brush*) 'mwǒ-shang yì-tséng . . . , 'tsā-shang yi-tséng . . . , 'tú-shang yì-tséng . . . (*or* yí-dàw *with* 'yéw-chī *only*) ; (*paper with paste*) 'hú-shang yì-tséng . . . ; (*paper with gum, glue, or mucilage*) 'jān-shang yì-tséng . . . ; (*with splashed mud*) 'jyàn(-shang) yì-tséng . . . . ‖The car was completely coated with mud. chì-chē-'wày-byar mǎn-'mǎr-de yì-tséng-'ní.

(*Of the tongue*). ‖My temperature is above normal and my tongue is coated. wǒ yěw 'shāw, 'shé-tew-shang yě yěw 'tāy.

See also OVERCOAT, RAINCOAT.

COFFEE. 'jyā-fēy, 'kā-fēy; (*ready for drinking*) jyā-fēy-'chá, kā-fēy-'chá. Pound of coffee yí-bàng-'jyā-fēy. ‖I'd like a second cup of coffee, please. chǐng-nǐ dzày gěy-wǒ yì-bēy-°'jyā-fēy. *or* °'kā-fēy. ‖Will you have your coffee now or later? nǐ shyàn-'dzày yàw 'jyā-fēy, háy-shř 'děng-yi-hwěr? ‖Would you like to drop in for a cup of coffee? láy 'dzwò-dzwò hē bēy-'jyā-fēy 'hǎw-bu-hǎw? ‖Please give me finer-ground coffee. wǒ yàw mwò-de-'shì-yi-dyar-de-'jyā-fēy. ‖Do you have any coffee(-flavored) ice cream? ni yew dày-jyā-fēy-'wèr-de-bīng-jī-'líng-ma?

COIN. fǔ-'bì, cnyár (*less than a dollar in value*). ‖I just gave a coin to the porter. wǒ gāng gěy-le jyǎw-'háng °yí-ge-chyár. *or* °yí-ge-fǔ-'bì. ‖Could you give me some coins for this bill? jèy-jāng-'pyàw-dz nǐ ké-yi-bu-ké-yi gěy-wǒ °'hwàn-chéng fǔ-'bì? *or* °'hwàn-chéng shyǎw-'chyár? *or* °'hwàn-chéng 'máw-chyár (*or other term indicating the denomination of the coins desired*). ‖Let's toss a coin to decide. dzám rēng ge-'chyár-lay (kàn-kàn shř 'dzěr shř 'mèr, dzày) jywé-'dìng-ba.

To coin *money* jù (chyán); (*figuratively*) jwàn (chyán). ‖The government needs to coin more money. 'jèng-fǔ yīng-gāy dwō 'jù shyē-chyán. ‖Businessmen are coining money right and left. 'mǎy-mày-rén shyàn-'dzày hěn jwàn-'chyán.

(*Invent*). ‖He coined that phrase himself. tā nèy-jywù-'hwà shř °'dù-jwàn. *or* °tā 'dž-jǐ 'byàn-de.

COLD. lěng, 'lyáng. (lyáng *usually means cool, but when referring to air or drinks it means cold.*) ‖The weather has grown cold. 'tyān-chì 'lěng-le. ‖Is it too cold for you in this room? nǐ-'jywé-de dzày jè-jyān-'wū-dz-li tày 'lěng ma? ‖This drink is not cold enough; please put some more ice in it. jèy-'hē-de-dūng-shi (*or name the particular drink*) bú-gèw 'lyáng; dzày fàng dyǎr-'bīng. ‖It feels cold in here. 'jèy-lǐ-byār yěw dyǎr-'lyáng. ‖The nights are getting cold. 'yě-lǐ shř ywè 'láy ywè 'lěng.

The cold. ‖Let's go in and get out of the cold. dzám 'jìn-chywu-ba, byé dzày-jèr 'dùng-je.

(*Illness*). ‖I feel that I'm coming down with a cold. wǒ 'jywé-de wǒ jáw 'lyáng-le. ‖Do you have something for a head cold? nǐm yěw jř-'shāng-fēng-de-'yàw-ma?

(*Not friendly*). ‖After that incident, he grew cold toward us. dž-tsúng 'nèy-jyàn-shř 'fā-shēng yǐ-'hèw, tā dwèy wǒ-men hěn 'lěng-dàn. ‖We received a cold welcome. 'rén-jyā °bù dzěm-me 'dǎy-jìng wǒ-men. *or* °méy dzěm-me 'hwān-yíng.

Other expressions in English. ‖He did it in cold blood. (*Of serious matters, such as murder*) tā hěn-shīn shyà-'shěw. (*Of a less serious matter*) tā-de-shěw-'dwàn jēn-'là. *or* tā jēn shř yì-dyar bù-lyéw-'chíng. ‖When the new jobs were assigned, he was left out in the cold. pày-shīn-'chǎy-shř de-shf-hew, bǎ-ta gěy °'pyē-shya-le. *or* °'shwǎy-le. ‖The blow knocked him cold. yí-'shyà-dz bǎ-ta 'dǎ-de °'hwēn-gwo-chywu-le. *or* °'ywūn . . . . ‖He got cold feet. tā-shyà-de 'swō-hwéy-chywu-le. *or* tā-shyà-de wàng 'hwéy-shya-li swō. *or* tā dǎr-'shyǎw-le. *or* (*literary*) tā dǎn-'chywè-le. ‖He got cold feet about coming. tā bù-gǎn 'láy-le.

Cold cuts lyáng-'rèw, lěng-'hwēn.

COLLAR. 'lǐng-dz. ‖I take a size fifteen collar. wǒ yùng shf-wǔ-'hàwr-de-'lǐng-dz. ‖Do you want your collars starched or soft? lǐng-dz 'jyǎng bu-jyǎng?

To collar. ‖They collared him after a short chase. tām jwēy-le bù-'ywǎr jyèw bǎ-ta °'jwā-ju-le. *or* °'děy-ju-le.

COLLECT. (*Receive*) shěw; (*gather*) lyǎn. ‖Tickets are collected at the gate. rù-'mén shěw-'pyàw. *or* dzày dà-mén-'kěwr shěw-'pyàw. ‖Who'll collect the money? shwéy shěw-'chyán-ne? *or* shwéy gwǎn shěw chyán? ‖He is in charge of collecting the contributions at all church services. měy-tsž dzwò lǐ-'bày de-shf-hew tā gwǎn shěw-'chyán. ‖We need more men to collect taxes. shěw-'shwèy háy děy 'jyā-rén tsáy 'shíng. ‖How much money has been collected so far? chyán-'lyǎn-le yěw 'dwō-shǎw-le? ‖The ent collector is here. shěw-'dzū-de-rén 'láy-le. ‖Someone at the door says he's collecting old clothes for charity. mén-'wày-tew yěw-rén shwō-shř gěy 'chyúng-rén lyǎn jyèw-'yī-shang-de.

To collect a bill shēw-'chyán, shēw-'jàng, yàw-'chyán, yàw-'jàng, chywǔ(-chyán). (chywǔ-'chyán *may also mean to draw money from a bank.*) ‖The laundry man is here to collect the bill. shǐ-'yī-de láy yàw-'chyán-le. ‖In China debts are collected on New Year's Eve. jūng-gwo gwò-'nyán de-shŕ-hew yàw-'jàng. ‖They'll go to your home to collect it. nèy-ge tā-men yǐ-'hèw dàw nǐ-'jyā-chywu 'chywǔ.

(*To accumulate, as a hobby or by research*) 'shew-tsáng, 'sēw-jí, dzǎn. (dzǎn *is used only for hobby collecting, or meaning to save money.*) ‖I am interested in collecting stamps. wǒ 'sh⸳ \wān 'shēw-tsáng (*or* 'sēw-jí, *or* dzǎn) yéw-'pyàw. ‖He has collected a lot of evidence. tā 'sēw-jí-le hěn-dwō-de 'jèng-jywù.

(*Of mail*) chywǔ. ‖When is the mail collected here? 'jèr 'shìn shéme-shŕ-hew (yěw-rén láy) 'chywǔ?

(*To come together*) jywù; (*to gather around*) wéy. ‖A crowd collected around the accident. chū-'shr̀-de-dì-fang wéy-le (*or* jywù-le) yì-chywún-'rén. ‖A large crowd collected there to hear him. yí-dà-chywún-'rén jywù-dzày nàr 'tīng-ta. *But* ‖He collected about ten children and opened a primary school. tā shēw-le shŕ-lay-ge-shyǎw-'hár kāy-le ge-'méng-gwan.

(*Of dust*) jī. ‖Dust has been collecting on that shelf for years. nèy-gè-'jyà-dz 'jī-le hǎw-shyē-'nyán-de °'chén-tǔ. *or* °'tǔ.

To collect oneself, be calm and collected. bù-'hwāng, jèn-'dìng, (*literary*) jèn-jìng-dz̀-'rú, lěng-'jìng, bù-'hwāng-jāng, bù-hwāng-bù-'máng-de, 'dz̀-rán, 'dz̀-dz-rán-ran-de. ‖He was somewhat confused at first, but collected himself quickly. tā 'chǐ-téwr yěw-dyǎr mwò-míng-chí-'myàw shŕ-de, kě-shr yì-hwěr jyèw °bu-'hwāng-le. *or* °jen-'dìng, *etc.*

(*Of thoughts*) 'kǎw-lywù-yi-shyar, 'kǎw-lywù-kǎw-lywu, 'shyǎng-yi-shyǎng. ‖Give me a chance to collect my thoughts. ràng-wǒ 'kǎw-lywù-yi-shyar. *or* ràng-wǒ 'kǎw-lywù-kǎw-lywù. *or* rúng-wǒ 'shyǎng-yi-shyǎng.

(*Regain*). ‖He collected his courage and made the final dash. tā 'gǔ-le-gǔ yùng-'chì jyèw 'pǎw-gwo-chywu-le.

‖Send it collect. 'nèy-byār gěy-'chyán. *or* 'shēw-de-rén gěy-'chyán. ‖Please wire (*me*) collect. dyàn-'bàw-chyán gwēy (*or* yéw) 'wǒ fù (*or* gěy).

COLLECTION. *Expressed with words meaning COL-LECT.*

‖Mail collections at 9 A.M. and 3 P.M. 'shàng-wǔ 'jyěw-dyǎn, shyà-wǔ 'sān-dyǎn chywǔ-'shìn. ‖The library has a famous collection of books on America. tú-shū-'gwǎn shēw-tsáng-de-gwān-ywú-'m^xy-jēw-de-shū hěn yěw-'míng. ‖They took up a collection after the meeting. hwèy-'wán-le-yǐ-hèw tām shēw-le yí-tsz̀-'chyán. ‖May I see your collection of rare books? gwèy-gwǎn (shēw-tsáng-)de-shàn-běn-'shū ké-yi 'kàn-yi-kan-ma? ‖His collection of Ming porcelain has

been auctioned. tā-shēw-tsáng-de- (*or* tā-sēw-jí-de-) míng-chaw-'tsz̀-chì yǐ-jīng pāy-'mày-le. ‖The collection of scrap iron is a success. `jèy-tsz̀-'shēw-jí-r̂ey-tyé-de-chéng-'jì hěn 'hǎw.

COLLEGE. (*An institution higher than high school, lower than university; or a college or school within a university*) shywé-'ywàn; (*university; or education beyond high school*) 'dà-shywé. College of arts wén-shywé-'ywàn; college of sciences lǐ-shywé-'ywàn; college of arts and sciences wén-lǐ-shywé-'ywàn; college of political science and law jèng-fǎ-shywé-'ywàn; college of engineering gūng-shywé-'ywàn. ‖There is a famous college in our town. jèy-'chéng-li yěw yí-ge-hěn-yěw-'míng-de-°'dà-shywé. *or* °'shywé-'ywàn. ‖Where did you go to college? nǐ-'dà-shywé dzày-'nǎr-shàng-de? *or* nǐ dzày-nǎr nyàn-de 'dà-shywé? ‖He has had two years of college. tā dzày 'dà-shywé-li 'nyàn-gwo lyǎng-nyán-'shū. ‖Lots of college students come here. hěn-dwō-de-dà-shywé-'shēng dēw láy-'jèr.

(*Technical school of college standards*) jwān-mén-'shywé-shyàw.

College degree shywé-'wèy. ‖He didn't get his college degree. tā méy 'dé-je shywé-'wèy. ‖He has a college degree. tā 'dà-shywé bì-'yè-le. *or* tā shr̀ ge-'dà-shywé-bì-yè-'shēng.

COLOR. shǎy, shǎr, (*literary*) sè, 'yán-sè, 'yán-shǎy, 'yán-shǎr. ‖We have this pattern in several colors. jèy-yàng-'hwār-de wǒm yěw hǎw-jǐ-jǔng- °'yán-shǎr-de. *or* °'shǎy-de. *or* °'yán-sè-de, *etc.* ‖Write down the color of your hair, eyes, and complexion. bǎ nǐ-'téw-fa, 'yǎn-jing, gēn 'pí-fǔ-de-'yán-sè shyě-dzày 'jèr. ‖What color eyes does she have? tā-yǎn-'jūr shémme °'shǎr-de? (*or* °'shǎy-de? *or* °'yán-sè-de? *etc.*). ‖In China the color of the hair and eyes is rarely used for identification. dzày 'jūng-gwo hěn-shǎw yùng 'téw-fa gēn yǎn-'jūr-de-'yán-shǎr-láy 'byàn-byé rén. ‖Once you get out in the air, your color will improve. nǐ chū-chywu 'tèw-tew 'chyèr yǐ-hèw, 'yán-sè jyèw hwèy hǎw-'dwō-le. ‖That color is too bright. nèy-ge-'yán-se tày 'shyàn-le. ‖Do you have anything that is of a lighter color? yěw yán-sè-'chyǎn-yì-dyǎr-de-ma?

Colors, colored (*as opposed to black, white, or gray*) dà-húng-dà-'lywù-de, yán-shar-shyān-'míng-de. ‖She likes to wear colors. tā ày chwān dà-húng-dà-'lywù-de. *or* tā ày chwān yán-shar-shyān-'míng-de(-'yī-shang).

Colors. (*Flag*) chí; (*of a nation*) gwó-'chí; (*of a regiment*) twán-'chí.

To color (*blush*) húng. ‖Her face colored. tā-lyǎn 'húng-le.

To color (*give color to*). To color X a Y color shàng X Y shǎr; to paint X a Y color shwā(-cheng) X Y shǎr. ‖She wants the walls colored green. tā yàw 'lywù-yán-shay-de-chyáng.

Colored 'people (*other than white*) yěw-'sè-rén-'jǔng.

(*Vividness, brightness*). ‖The flowers added color to the table. yěw nèm yì-pén-'hwār shyǎn-de 'jwōr-shang 'rè-re-naw-nàw-de.

(*To misrepresent*). ‖The news in that paper is generally colored to suit the publisher. nèy-ge-'bàw-li-de-'shīn-wén 'cháng-cháng °dày 'sè-tsǎy. *or* °yěw pyàn-'jyàn. ‖He colored his report a bit to protect you. wèy-le 'hwéy-hù nǐ tā bǎ bàw-'gàw shvě-de gēn shř-'shř yěw dyǎr-chū-'rù.

COLORFUL. (*Including many colors*). ‖Her clothes are colorful. tā-de-'yī-shang 'yán-sè hěn-dwō. *or* tā-de-'yī-shang yěw hěn-dwō-'shǎr.

Too colorful (*gaudy, too loud*). ‖Her clothes are too colorful. tā-de-'yī-shang wǔ-'yán-lyèw-'sè-de. *or* tā-de-'yī-shang tày 'hwā.

(*Adventurous; of life*). ‖He led a colorful life. (*Of an old man*) tā-yí-'bèy-dz hěn bù-píng 'fán. (*Of a young man*) tā-gwò-de-'shēng-hwo bù píng-'fán.

COLUMN. (*Shaft, pillar*) 'jù-dz, X-'jù, X-'jù-dz. X *represents the material; e.g.* stone column shŕ-'jù. ‖You can recognize his house by its white columns. 'chyán-tew yěw dà-báy-'jù-dz-de jyèw shŕ tā-'jyā. ‖Whose statue is on top of that column? 'jù-dz-'dyěngr-shang shŕ shéy-de-'shyàng.

Memorial column, obelisk jì-nyàn-'bēy, jì-nyàn-'tǎ.

(*Of smoke*) 'gǔ-dz. ‖I wonder where that column of smoke comes from? nèy-gǔ-dz-'yān yě bú-shr tsúng-'nǎr láy-de.

(*Formation*) 'dzùng-dwèy. ‖The soldiers marched in a column of twos. bīng 'páy-je èr-lù-'dzùng-dwèy chyán-'jìn.

(*Of print*) háng. ‖There are two columns per page. měy-'yè lyǎng-'háng.

(*Regular feature in a newspaper*). ‖His column on foreign affairs appears in twenty newspapers. tā-de-gwó-jì-'shŕ-píng 'dēng-dzày 'èr-shr-jí-jyā-'bàw-shang.

COMB. 'lǔng-dz, 'lǔng-shū, 'shū-dz, 'mù-shū; (*fine-toothed*) 'bì-dz. ‖I left my comb on the dresser. wǒ bǎ 'lǔng-dz (*or* 'lǔng-shū, 'shū-dz, 'mù-shū, 'bì-dz) gē-dzày shū-jwāng-'táy-dz-shang-le. ‖She always wears several combs in her hair. tā-'téw-shang lǎw dày-je hǎw-jǐ-ge-'lǔng-dz.

To comb lǔng, shū. ‖My hair needs combing. wǒ děy 'lǔng-lung téw. *or* wǒ-de-'téw-fa děy 'shū-yi-shu-le.

(*Search thoroughly*) dzày . . . jī-le-gā-'lár-de 'jǎw. ‖We had to comb the city to find him. dzày chywán-'chéng-li jī-le-gā-'lár-de jǎw tsáy bǎ-ta-'jǎw-jaw-de.

(*Honeycomb*) fēng-'wō. ‖They have honey in jars, but not in combs. tām-jèr-de-fēng-'mì shŕ píng-dz-'jwāng-de, méy-yew dzày-ywán-lay-de-fēng-'wō-li-de.

COME. 1. (*Specifying motion toward or to the speaker's position*) láy; (*specifying motion not toward the speaker's position*) chywù; (*definitely indicating arrival*) dàw, *often with* láy *or* chywù *later in the sentence.* ‖Coming! (wǒ) jyèw 'láy! *or* (wǒ) jyèw 'chywù! (*depending on whether the speaker speaks in terms of his position as he says it or in terms of the position he will have after the motion is done*). ‖He came before nine. tā 'jyěw-dyǎn yǐ-'chyán °'láy-de. *or* °'dàw-de. ‖Did you come at nine? *meaning* Was nine o'clock one of the times that you came? nǐ-shŕ 'jyèw-dyǎn 'láy-gwo yí-'tsz̀-ma? *but meaning* Was it at nine o'clock that you came? nǐ-shŕ 'jyèw-dyǎn 'dàw-de-ma? ‖He's come before. tā yǐ-'chyán láy-gwo. ‖They came after him (*or after he did*). tām-shř dzày tā yǐ-'hèw láy-de. ‖Some letters came in the mail today. 'jīn-tyan yěw-'shìn láy-le. *or* 'jīn-tyan láy-le jǐ-fēng-'shìn. ‖When did he come? tā 'jǐ-shŕ 'láy-de? ‖Come forward! dàw 'chyán-byan láy!

Come *followed by a word like* here *or* home *that specifies the terminus of the motion.* (*see* come to *below*) dàw . . . láy (*or* chywù); *if the motion is a return to a place from which one has come earlier* hwéy . . . láy (*or* chywù). ‖Come here! dàw-'jèr láy! *often shortened to* 'jèr láy! ‖Why not come home with me for dinner tonight? gēn-wo hwéy-'jyā-chywu chŕ-'fàn, 'hǎw-bu-hǎw?

Come *specifying position in some series.* ‖She comes first. *is expressed as* The first one is her. 'téw-yí-ge shŕ-'tā. ‖Your turn comes next. *is expressed as* The next one turns to you. 'shyà-yí-ge lwén-daw 'nǐ. ‖It comes at the end of the book. *is expressed as* That is at the end of the book. nèy-ge dzày shū-de-mwò-'lyǎwr. ‖When does Easter come this year? *is expressed as* When is Easter this year? fù-hwó-'jyé jīn-nyan shŕ 'něy-tyān?

To come natural. ‖Dancing comes natural to her. *is expressed as* She, as an innate trait, likes to dance. tā tyān-'shēng-de shǐ-hwan tyàw-'wǔ.

Come *meaning* be available *or* be produced yěw. ‖Does this cloth come in other colors? jèy-ge-'bù yěw 'byé-de-'yán-shǎr-de-ma?

Come, coming, to come *specifying future time.* This coming Saturday *is expressed as* this week's Saturday 'jèy-ge-lǐ-bày-'lyèw *or* 'běn-lǐ-bày-'lyèw; this coming Tuesday *is expressed as* this week's Tuesday 'jèy-ge-lǐ-bày-'èr *or* 'běn-lǐ-bày-'èr, *or as* next week's Tuesday 'shyà-lǐ-bày-'èr, *depending on what day it is as one speaks;* in time to come yǐ-'hèw *or* 'jyāng-láy; in the years to come yǐ-'hěw jǐ-'nyán-li *or* 'jyāng-láy jǐ-'nyán-li. ‖The time will come when everyone will be literate. *is expressed as* Sooner or later there will be this kind of a day, that everyone will be literate. 'dzǎw-wǎn yěw 'nème-yì-tyān, 'rén-rén dēw shŕ-'dz̀.

2. Come to *or* come and (*specifying motion and purpose*) láy. ‖He came to see you. tā láy 'kàn-ni. ‖Come

and listen to the radio. láy tīng wú-shyàn-'dyàn. ‖I've come to ask about a room. wǒ láy 'dǎ-ting 'fáng-dz.

Come to (*specifying change*). ‖I've come to believe that he didn't do it. *is expressed as* Now I'm somewhat of the belief that it wasn't he who did it. wǒ shyàn-'dzày yěw dyǎr-shyàng-'shìn 'bú-shr tā 'gàn-de-le. ‖How did you come to think of this? *is expressed as* How did you think to this? nǐ dzěme shyǎng-daw 'jèy-ge-de?

3. *Special expressions.* **To come and go** (*socially*) cháng 'hwàn. ‖Secretaries come and go, but his position is always there. 'bù-jǎng cháng 'hwàn, kě-shr 'tā-de-wèy-jr bú-'dùng.

Come to think of it 'dž-shì 'shyǎng-yi-shyǎng. ‖Come to think of it, it does look suspicious. 'dž-shì 'shyǎng-yi-shyǎng, 'shr yěw dyǎr-kě-'yí.

‖How are things coming?. dzěme-'yàng-le?

‖Easy come, easy go. 'láy-de rúng-yi, 'chywù-de rúng-yi.

‖How come? 'dzěme-ne? *or* 'dzěme-hwéy-'shèr? ‖How come YOU weren't there? dzěme jyèw-shr 'nǐ méy-'dzày-nàr-ne?

‖Come, now, don't try to frighten me! 'swàn-le-ba, byé 'jìng shyǎng 'shyà-hu wo-le!

‖Come come! Do you think I'll bite a second time? 'hèy! wǒ 'háy néng shàng 'lyǎng-tsž-'dàng-ma?

4. (**Come** *with an adverb or preposition*) **Come about** (*happen*) chéng, dàw. ‖How did all this come about? dzěme jyèw chéng 'jèy-yangr-le? *or* dzěme chéng-le 'jème-ge-'jywú-shr? *or* dzěme dàw-le 'jème-ge-'dì-bù?

Come across *something* (*cross over something towards the speaker*) gwò (...láy); wàng ...'jèy-byar láy. ‖The car's coming across the bridge now. chì-'chē jèng wàng 'chyáw-'jèy-byar láy-ne.

Come across *something* (*find*) 'kàn-jyan, 'ywù-jyan. ‖Let me know if you come across anything with my name on it. nǐ yàw-shr °'kàn-jyan (*or* °'ywù-jyan) shéme-'dūng-shi yěw wǒ-'míng-dz-de, chǐng-ni 'gàw-sung wo yì-shēngr.

‖Come across! (*Fork over*) 'ná-chu-lay! *or* 'gěy-wo! (*Confess or inform*) 'shwō-chu-lay! *or* 'gàw-sung wo!

Come after (*come to get*). (*If a thing*) chywǔ, ná, lǐng; (*if a person*) jǎw; (*if a person, in the sense of arresting*) ná, děy; *all of these preceded by* láy. ‖I've come after my passport. wǒ láy °'chywǔ (*or* °'ná *or* °'lǐng) wǒ-de-hù-'jàw láy-le. ‖They came after him. tām láy 'jǎw-ta.

Come along *something* (*follow a route*) dzày ... láy. ‖Whose car is that coming along the road? dzày-'dàwr-shang-wàng-'jèr-láy-de-nèy-lyàng-'chē shr-'shéy-de?

‖Come along! (*Hurry up*) 'kwày-dyǎr! *or* 'kwày-je! *or* 'kwày láy! *or* 'kwày dzěw!

Come along (*come also, accompany*) yě láy, yě chywù, gēn-je. ‖Mind if we come along? wǒm 'yě chywù (*or* wǒm 'gēn-je), nǐ 'dzày-hu-ma?

Come along *in a way* (*develop*). ‖Everything is coming along well, thanks. *is expressed as* Everything is quite smooth, thanks. yí-'chyè dēw hěn 'shwèn-lì, twō-'fú. ‖How's your work coming along? *is expressed as* How is your work progressing? nǐ-'gūng-dzwò jìn-'shíng-de dzěme-'yàng-le?

Come around (*to our place; see* come up, come over).

Come around *a corner* dzày ... 'gwǎy-gwo-láy. ‖He just came around the corner. tā 'gāng dzày 'jyē-jyǎwr-nèr 'gwǎy-gwò-láy.

Come around (*recover from illness*) jyàn hǎw. ‖She was very sick, but she's coming around now. tā 'shyān bìng-de hěn 'lì-hay, kě-shr 'yǐ-jing jyàn 'hǎw-le.

Come around to *a point of view* gēn ... yí-'jr-le. ‖He disagreed for a while, but now he's come around to our point of view. yěw yí-'jèn-dz tā hěn 'byè-nyew, kě-shr shyàn-'dzày tā 'yǐ-jing gēn 'wǒm-de-'yì-jyan yí-'jr-le.

Come away from *a place* lí ... dzěw, 'lí-kay. ‖Come away from there! 'lí-kay nàr! *or* 'dzěw-kay!

Come back (*return*) 'hwéy-lay (*sometimes* 'hwéy-chywu). ‖Hey! Come back here! 'hèy! 'hwéy-lay! ‖I'll come back in a minute. wǒ 'jè-jyèw 'hwéy-lay. *or* wǒ yì-'hwěr jyèw 'hwéy-lay.

Come back. ‖He retired ten years ago but he's now trying to come back (*or* make a come-back). 'shr-nyán-chyán tā jyèw bú-'gàn jèy-ge-le, kě-shr shyàn-dzày 'yèw shyǎng °'gàn. *or* °'dzài láy.

Come back to *a place* hwéy ... láy, 'hwéy-dàw ... láy. ‖I hope to come back to China often. wǒ 'shī-wang 'cháng-cháng néng hwéy(-daw) 'jūng-gwo-lay.

Come back to (*be recalled by*) *expressed with* to recall 'shyǎng-chi-lay. ‖Suddenly it all came back to me. 'hū-rán-jyān wǒ dēw 'shyǎng-chi-lay-le.

Come before *a meeting* (*arise, be considered*) 'tí-chu-lay, tǎw-'lwèn. ‖That question will come before the meeting this morning. nèy-ge-'wèn-tí jyēr-'dzǎw-chen kāy-'hwèy hwèy °'tí-chu-lay. *or* °'tǎw-lwèn-de.

Come before (*in arrangement or protocol*) dzày ... 'chyán-byan. ‖The Secretary of State comes before the Secretary of War. 'wày-jyāw-bù-'jǎng dzày 'lù-jywūn-bù-'jǎng-'chyán-byan.

Come beyond *expectations*. ‖The results came far beyond our expectations. *is expressed as* The results were much better than the expectations. 'jyē-gwǒ (*or* 'chéng-jì) bǐ 'ywù-lyàw-de 'hǎw-de 'dwō.

Come by, come past gwò, 'gwò-láy, dǎ-jèr 'gwò. ‖I was just coming by and thought I'd drop in. wǒ jèng dǎ-jèr 'gwò, swǒ-yi 'jìn-lay 'kàn-yi-kàn.

Come by (*or* come past) *a place* 'lù-gwò, 'jīng-gwò, dǎ ... 'gwò, tsúng ... 'gwò. ‖He comes by our house every morning at this hour. tā 'měy-tyān-'dzǎw-chen jèy-ge-'shŕ-hew °'lù-gwò wǒm-'jyā. *or* °'jīng-gwò wǒm-'jyā. *or* °'dǎ wǒm-'jyā 'gwò. *or* °'tsúng wǒm-'jyā 'gwò.

Come by *a route* yéw (tsúng, dǎ) . . . láy. ‖He's coming by the shorter route. tā-shr yéw 'jìn-dàwr wàng-'jèr láy-ne.

Come by (*acquire*) 'dé-dàw, láy. ‖How did you come by this? 'jèy-ge nǐ 'dzěme 'dé-dàw-de? ‖How did he come by all that money? tā 'nǎr láy-de nème-shyē-'chyán?

Come close to *doing something* (*see* **come near to**).

Come down 'shyà-láy; (*if from upstairs*) shyà-'léw láy; (*if from further north; see* **come up**). ‖Come down here and we'll talk it over. 'shyà-lay (*or* shyà-'léw lay), dzám hǎw 'tán-tan.

A come-down. ‖His new job is quite a come-down. *is expressed as* He's really taken a lower position. tā 'jēn-shr̀ dī-'jyèw-le.

Come down from *a place; in Chinese one omits the* down *idea* tsúng . . . láy. ‖I came down from Peiping by plane this morning. wǒ 'jīn-tyan-'dzǎw-chen tsúng běy-'píng dzwò fēy-'jī láy-de.

Come down from *a higher position* tsúng . . . shyà-láy. ‖When he came down from the platform the crowd gathered around to congratulate him. tā tsúng 'táy-shang 'dzěw-shyà-láy de-shŕ hèw, dà-'jyā-hwǒr bǎ-ta 'wéy-shàng-le.

Come down off. ‖Come down off your high horse! (*referring to haughty talk*) byé 'chwēy-le! *or* shǎw 'chwēy-dyǎr-ba! (*but said about facial expressions or about actions*) byé 'nème 'shén-chi-le! *or* shǎw 'shén-chi-yì-dyǎr-ba!

Come down on *someone* (*with a verbal attack*). mà, 'jŕ-wèn; (*with a physical attack*) dǎ. ‖He came down on him sharply. tā 'mà-de ta hěn 'lì-hay. ‖They came down on him as soon as he sat down. tā gāng yí 'dzwò-shya, tām jyèw °'jŕ-wèn ta. *or* °'mà-ta. *or* °'dǎ-ta.

Come down with *a disease* dé. ‖I think I'm coming down with the flu. wǒ 'dà-gày shr̀ 'dé-le jùng-shāng-'fēng-le.

Come forward to *do something* (*see* **come out**).

Come from *a place* tsúng . . . láy; *in the sense of having that place as one's original home* tsúng . . . láy-de. ‖Do you come from America? nǐ 'shr̀-bu-shr̀ tsúng 'měy-gwo láy-de? ‖How long did it take you to come from America this time? 'jèy-tsz̀ tsúng 'měy-gwo láy 'yùng-de 'dwō-shaw-shŕ-hèw?

Come from (*or* **come of**) *a family, stock, etc.* ‖He comes from (*or* of) a very old family. tā shr̀ yí-ge-'shr̀-jyā-de-'hèw-dày.

Come in (*enter a place*) 'jìn-láy. ‖I just saw him come (*or* coming) in. wǒ gāng-tsáy 'kàn-jyan ta 'jìn-lay. ‖Won't you come in and have a drink? 'jìn-lay 'hē dyǎr-'shéme. ‖Come on in! 'jìn-lay! *or* (*more politely*) chǐng 'jìn! ‖This is where I came in. wǒ jyèw-shr dzày-'jèr 'jìn-lay-de. *or expressed as* I ought to leave. gāy 'dzěw-le.

Come in (*be received*). (*Of money*) 'shēw-jìn-láy, jìn. ‖The money due us is coming in slowly. (*Of debts*) wày-byar-de-'jàng jèng dzày màn-'mār-de 'shēw-jìn-lay. (*Of other funds*) nèy-shyē-'kwǎn-dz jèng dzày yì-bǐ-yì-'bǐ-de 'jìn, bú-gwò 'màn-dyǎr.

Come in (*other meanings*). ‖Where do I come in? *meaning* Where do I speak (*or* start to act)? (*as on the stage*) 'wǒ dzày-'nǎr 'chā-jìn-chywu? *meaning* Where in the line do I fit? (*as in a parade*) 'wǒ dzày-'nǎr jyā-'rù? *meaning* What part of it am I supposed to do? (*as when plans are being drawn up*) 'wǒ dzwò 'shéme-ne? *or* wǒ gàn 'shéme-ne? *meaning* Why'd you leave me out of consideration? *or* What do I get out of it? 'wǒ bǎy-'nǎr-ne? *or* 'wǒ dzày-'nǎr 'bǎy-ne? ‖Where does the joke come in? *is expressed as* Where's the funny part? 'nǎ-yì-dyǎr shr̀ kě-'shyàw-de? *or* kě-'shyàw-de-dì-fang dzày-'nǎr? ‖When did this style come in? 'jèy-jǔng-'jwāng-shù (*or* 'jèy-ge-yàngr) 'shéme-shŕ-hew 'shīng-chi-lay-de?

Come in for *something* (*be the butt or object of*) jǎw-je jyàw-rén . . . . ‖He came in for a lot of kidding. tā 'jǎw-je jyàw-rén °'wā-ku. *or* °gēn-ta kāy wán-'shyàw.

Come in handy 'yùng-de-jáw. ‖This tool will come in handy during the trip. jèy-jyàn-'jyā-hwo dzày 'lù-shang jyèw 'yùng-de-jáw-le.

Come into *a place* jìn, 'jìn-láy. ‖He just came into the house. tā gāng jìn 'wū-dz láy-le.

Come into money (*acquire; the verb depends on context*). ‖He came into a lot of money after the lawsuit. nèy-shyē-'chyán shr̀ tā-dǎ-'gwān-sz̀-'dǎ-lay-de.

Come into play (*or effect*) shŕ-'shíng. ‖When your plan comes into play, there will be no more profit for those scoundrels. nǐ-de-'jì-hwa yì shŕ-'shíng, jèy-chywún-hwén-'dàn jyèw 'lǎw-bu-jáw shéme-le.

Come into *power* 'dé-dàw, dǎng. ‖The revolutionists came into power. gé-mìng-'dǎng °'dé-dàw-le 'jèng-chywán. *or* °'dǎng-'chywán.

Come into sight (*or view*) chū, 'shyǎn-chu-lay, kàn-de-'jyàn. ‖The ship came into sight over the horizon just a minute ago. nèy-tyáw-'chwán gāng tsúng tyān-'byǎr-shang 'shyǎn-chu-lay.

Come loose sūng-le. ‖The knot came loose. jì-de-'kèwr 'sūng-le.

Come near (*approach*) dzěw (*or* pǎw *or another verb of motion*) 'jìn-yi-dyǎr. ‖Wait until he comes near. děng tā dzěw 'jìn-yi-dyǎr.

Come near *doing something,* **come near to** (*or close to*) *doing something* 'chà-dyǎr (méy-). ‖I came near throwing the thing at him. wǒ 'chà-dyǎr (méy-) ná nèy-ge 'cháw-ta °'jwāy-gwo-chywu. *or* °'kǎn-gwo-chywu.

Come of (*see* **come from**).

Come off (*be removable*) hwó; (*by being lifted*) 'ná-shyà-lay; (*by falling*) 'dyàw-shyà-lay; (*by other means*) *the appropriate verb plus* shyà-lay. ‖Is this lid fastened or does it come off? jèy-ge-'gàɪ °'hwó-de-ma? or °ná-de-'shyà-lay-ma? ‖We can't use the table because a leg has come off. jèy-jāng-'jwō-dz yěw ge-'twěr 'dyàw-shya-lay-le, swǒ-yi bù-néng 'yùng.

Come off (*happen*) gwò-le, wán-le. ‖Has the high hurdle race come off yet? gāw-lán 'pǎw-°'gwò-le-ma? or °'wán-le-ma?

Come off *in a way, expressed with* the outcome 'jyē-gwǒ. ‖How did it come off? 'jyē-gwǒ dzěme-'yàng? ‖The concert came off as we expected. yīn-ywè-'hwèy-de-'jyē-gwǒ gēn wǒm-'ywù-lyàw yí-'yàng. ‖He came off a loser. tā 'jyē-gwǒ shř-'bày-le.

Come on (*begin*) láy. ‖A storm came on before we got home. wǒm méy-dàw-'jyā yǐ-'chyán, láy-le yí-jèn-'kwáng-fēng-bàw-'ywǔ.

The come-on. ‖Is she giving us the come-on? tā-'nèy shř gēn-dzám yěw 'yì-sz-ma?

Come on stage dēng-'táy, chū-'táy. ‖When she came on stage the lights went out. tā °dēng-'táy (*or* °chū-'táy) de-shf-hew 'dēng 'myè-le.

Come out (*exit, or appear*) 'chū-láy. ‖Come on out! 'chū-láy-ba! ‖The sun didn't come out all day. 'tày-yang yì-'tyān méy-'chū-lay.

Come out (*appear, other than of the sun*) 'shyǎn-chū-láy. ‖If you put lemon juice on the paper, the invisible writing will come out. yàw-shr ná 'níng-méng-'jř-dz shàng-dzay nèy-jāng-'jř-shang, shyàn-dzày-kàn-bu-'jyàn-de-'dz jyèw 'shyǎn-chū-láy.

Come out (*grow*) chū. ‖A rash came out on his face. tā 'lyǎn-shang chū °húng-'dyǎn-dz. or °húng-'bān.

Come out (*be published; of a news account*) dēng; (*of a publication*) 'chū-láy or chū-'bǎn. ‖The story hasn't yet come out in the papers. nèy-dwàr-'shīn-wén 'bàw-jř-shang háy méy-'dēng. ‖When is that book coming out? nèy-běn-'shū 'shéme-shf-hew °'chū-lay? or °chū-'bǎn? ‖When is the next issue of that magazine coming out? 'shyà-yì-chī 'shéme-shf-hew °'chū-lay? or °chū-'bǎn?

Come out (*be extracted, eliminated, or made to disappear*). (*Of a tooth*) 'bá, 'bá-shyà-lay; (*of a sentence or word to be deleted*) lá, 'lá-shyà-chywu, bù-'lyéw; (*by rubbing*) 'tsā-shyà-chywǔ; (*be eliminated*) 'méy-le; *other conditions call for other verbs plus* shyà-lay *or* shyà-chywu. ‖That tooth's got to come out. nèy-ge-'yá děy 'bá(-shyà-lay). ‖That sentence has got to come out. nèy-jywù-'hwà děy 'lá-shya-chywu. ‖If you put lemon juice on the cloth, the grease spot will come out. 'bù-shang-de-nèy-kwày-yéw-'dyǎn-dz yùng 'níng-méng-'jř-dz yì 'tsā jyèw °'tsā-shya-chywu-le. or °'méy-le.

Come out *in a way, expressed with* result 'jyē-gwǒ. ‖Everything came out all right. yí-chyè-'jyē-gwǒ háy dēw bú-'tswò. ‖It (*a calculation*) didn't come out right. *is expressed as* The figure is wrong. 'shùr bú-'dwèy.

Come out against shywàn-'bù-le (*or* shwō-le) 'fǎn-dwèy. ‖The governor came out against the bill. shěng-'jǎng °shywàn-'bù-le (*or* shwō-le) 'fǎn-dwèy jèy-ge-yì-'àn.

Come out of *a place* tsúng... 'chū-láy. ‖He came out of the room. tā tsúng 'wū-dz-li chū-lay.

Come out on top yíng. ‖Who came out on top in the election? 'shywǎn-jywǔ-'jyē-gwǒ 'shéy 'yíng-le?

Come out (*or* forward) to *do something* chū-láy. ‖No one came out to put in a word for him. lyán 'yí-ge-chū-lay-'gěy-ta-shwō-jywù-'hwà-de yě 'méy-yew.

Come out with. (*Information*) 'shwō-chu-lay; (*a statement*) 'shywàn-bù, shwō; (*a suggestion*) 'tí-chu-lay; (*object or money*) 'ná-chu-lay. ‖At long last he came out with it. dàw-'lyǎwr tā °'shwō-chu-lay-le. or °'ná-chu-lay-le. ‖He came out with a denial. tā °'shywàn-bù (*or* °shwō) méy 'nème-hwéy-'shèr. ‖He came out with a good suggestion. tā 'tí-chu(-lay) yí-ge-hěn-'hǎw-de-'yì-jyan.

Come over (*or* around) láy 'kàn. ‖We have friends coming over this evening. jyēr-'wǎn-shang yěw 'péng-yew yàw láy 'kàn wǒ-men.

Come over *something* dzày... gwò-láy. ‖Who's that coming over the hill? nèy-ge-dzày-'shān-shang-'dzěw-gwo-lay-de shř-'shéy?

Come over (*take possession of*). ‖What's come over you? nǐ-shr 'dzěme-le?

Come past (*see* come by).

Come short of. ‖He came short of what we expected. tā jyàw wǒ-men shř-'wàng.

Come through *something* (*motion*) tsúng... 'dzwān-chu-lay. ‖The train's coming through the tunnel. hwǒ-'chē tsúng shān-'dùng-li 'dzwān-chu-lay-le.

Come through (*arrive*) gwò-láy, dàw, láy. ‖The mail can't come through. 'yéw-jyàn °gwò-bu-'láy. or °'dàw-bu-lyǎw. or °'láy-bu-lyǎw.

Come through (*survive*) hǎw-le, méy-'shèr-le, 'gwò-lay. ‖The operation was serious, but he came through. 'shěw-shù hěn 'wéy-shyǎn, bú-gwò °tā 'yǐ-jing 'hǎw-le. or °tā 'yǐ-jing méy-'shèr-le. or °jèy-ge-'gwān tā swàn 'gwò-lay-le.

Come to (*from a faint*) 'hwán-shǐng-gwò-láy, 'shǐng-gwò-láy. ‖The woman who fainted is coming to. 'ywūn-gwo-chywu-de-nèy-ge-'nywǔ-rén 'yǐ-jing màn-'mār-de (hwán-)'shǐng-gwo-lay-le.

Come to. (*A place*) dàw... láy; (*a person*) dàw...-jèr láy *or* dàw...-nèr láy. ‖When did you come to China? nǐ 'shéme-shf-hew dàw 'jūng-gwo láy-de? ‖He came to you, didn't he? tā dàw 'nǐ-jèr láy-le, 'bú-shr-ma? *or* tā láy 'nǐ-jèr, 'bú-shr-ma? ‖Come to me. dàw 'wǒ-jèr láy. *or* (*if the speaker will be elsewhere when the coming takes place*) dàw 'wǒ-nàr chywù.

Come to (*amount to*) yí-'gùng shř. ‖The bill comes to two dollars. 'jàng yí-'gùng shř 'lyǎng-kwǎy-chyán.

Come to (*result in*) dàw, *or expressed with* a result 'jyē-gwǒ. ‖Who knows what all this will come to? shéy 'jř-daw 'jyàng-láy dàw 'dzěme-ge-'dì-bu? *or* shéy 'jř-dàw 'jyàng-lay 'jyē-gwǒ dzěme-'yàng? *or* jey-shyē-'shèr 'jyàng-lay 'chéng ge-shéme-'jyē-jywú hěn nán 'ywù-lyàw. ‖Has it come to this? dàw-le 'dzěme-ge-'dì-bu-le-ma?

Come to blows dùng-chi 'chywán-tew lay. ‖They came to blows. tām dùng-chi 'chywán-tew láy-le.

Come to a conclusion dé-dàw. ‖How did you come to that conclusion? nèy-ge-'jyē-lwèn nǐ 'dzěme 'dé-dàw-de?

Come to an end. ‖It's a pity all this came to an end. kě-'shī báy 'fèy-le yì-hwéy-'shèr.

Come to a head (of a boil or pimple) jàng-'jyār, chū-'téwr; (of a situation) dàw 'jǐn-yàw-gwān-'téw. ‖The boil has come to a head. nèy-ge-'gē-de °'jàng-chu 'jyār láy-le. or °'chū-le 'téwr-le. ‖When things come to a head, he'll dodge the issue. děng dàw-le 'jǐn-yàw-gwān-'téw, tā jyèw yàw 'twēy-twō-le.

Come to pieces (of something composed of parts) sǎn; (of a single but fragile thing) swèy. ‖It'll come to pieces if you touch it. yí 'pèng jyèw °'sǎn. or °'swèy.

Come to an understanding 'dé-dàw; come to an understanding shwō-'hǎw-le. ‖I think we'll be able to come to an understanding soon. wǒ 'shyǎng wǒ-men bù-'jyěw jyèw kě-yi °'dé-dàw yì-jǔng-lyàng-'jyě. or °'shwō-'hǎw-le.

Come true dwèy-le, 'yìng-yàn-le. ‖Everything he predicted came true. tā-'ywù-lyàw-dàw-de 'yí-jyàn-yí-'jyàn-de dēw 'dwèy-le. or tā-'shwō-de-nèy-shyē-'hwà yí-jyàn-yí-'jyàn-de dēw 'yìng-yàn-le.

Come under something tsúng ...-dǐ-shya °gwò or 'chywù or etc. ‖The boat's coming under the bridge. 'chwán jèng tsúng 'chyáw-dǐ-shya °'gwò-ne. or °'chwān-gwo-chywu-ne.

Come under (be subject to) àn ... láy 'bàn. ‖What regulations does this come under? 'jèy-ge àn 'něy-jǔng-'fǎ-gwèy láy 'bàn?

Come up (from a lower position) 'shàng-láy; (if from downstairs) shàng-'léw-lay. ‖Come up here and we'll talk it over. 'shàng-láy (or shàng-'léw-lay); dzám hǎw 'tán-tán. or (if from farther south, in which case the idea of up is omitted in Chinese) expressed as Come to where I am and we'll talk it over. shàng 'wò-jèr-lay, dzám hǎw 'tán-tán.

Come up something (proceed along) dzày ... °'dzèw-gwò-láy or °'gwò-láy, etc. ‖He came up the walk limping a bit. tā dzày shyǎw-'dàwr-shang 'dzěw-gwo-lay de-shŕ-hew yěw dyǎr-'chywé.

Come up (present itself) yěw. ‖This problem comes up every day. jèy-ge-'wèn-tí tyān-'tyār-de yěw.

Come up (of the sun) expressed as come out 'chū-láy. ‖The sun's come up. 'tày-yang 'chū-lay-le.

Come up (of things planted) chū or 'jǎng-chu-lay. ‖Our tomatoes didn't come up this spring. wǒm-de-shī-húng-'shŕ jīn-nyán méy-°'chū. or °'jǎng-chu-lay.

Come up (or around or over; to a person's residence or place of business) expressed as come láy. ‖Come over and see me some night. něy-tyān-'wǎn-shang láy 'kàn-kan wo. ‖Won't you come up and have some tea? láy hē bēy-'chá, 'hǎw-bu-hǎw?

Come up (of something eaten) expressed with to vomit tù. ‖My dinner came up. wǒ 'tù-le.

Come up from a place; Chinese omits the idea of up and says come from tsúng ... láy. ‖I came up from Chungking on the early plane. wǒ tsúng chúng-'chìng dzwò 'dzǎw-bār-de-fēy-'jī láy-de.

Come up on one (of something eaten) wàng-'shàng yàng. ‖My dinner keeps coming up on me. wǒ-'chŕ-de-dūng-shi jŕ wàng-'shàng yàng.

Come upon (find) 'dé-dàw. ‖I came upon the answer by accident. wǒ-shr pèng-'chyǎw 'dé-dàw jèy-ge-dá-'àn-de.

Come within (fall within the range of) dzày ... yǐ-'nèy. ‖Does this come within the terms of our agreement? jèy-ge dzày dzám-shwō-'hǎw-le-de-'tyáw-jyàn-yǐ-'nèy-ma?

COMFORT. To comfort. ‖This news may comfort you. jèy-ge-'shyāw-shī yě-shywǔ jyàw nǐ gāw-'shìng yì-dyar. or nǐ 'tīng-jyan jèy-ge yě-shywú 'shīn-li ké-yi 'dé dyar-'ān-wèy.

(Physical). ‖This bed was not built for comfort. jèy-ge-'chwáng bù-'shū-fu.

(Material). ‖The Red Cross saw to their comfort. 'húng-shŕ-dz-'hwèy 'jàw-gu tām.

(Relief). ‖The medicine gave me little comfort from the pain. jèy-ge-'yàw 'yì-dyar bù-jŕ-'téng.

Comforts. ‖They lacked many comforts. tām hǎw-shyē-'dūng-shi dēw méy-'yěw.

COMFORTABLE. 'shū-fu. ‖This chair is soft and comfortable. jèy-bǎ-'yǐ-dz yèw 'rwǎn yèw 'shū-fu. ‖Were you comfortable sleeping here? dzày-jèr 'shwèy-de háy 'shū-fu-ma? ‖He makes a comfortable living at it. tā-de-'shèr hěn 'gèw gwò 'ŕ-dz-de.

Comfortably. ‖He's living comfortably. tā(-de-'ŕ-dz) 'gwò-de hěn °'shū-fu. or °'hǎw.

COMMAND. (To order) jyàw; (more officially) 'mìng-lìng. ‖He commanded his son to break the engagement. tā °jyàw (or °'mìng-lìng) tā-'ér-dz jyě-chú hwēn-'ywē.

To command, to be in command of tǔng-'shwày, 'shwày-lǐng, 'jŕ-hwèy, gwǎn, dày, lǐng, dày-'lǐng. ‖He commands (or is in command of) fifteen destroyers. tā °tǔng-'shwày (or °shwày-'lǐng or °'jŕ-hwèy or °'gwǎn or °'dày or °'lǐng or °dày-'lǐng) shŕ-'wǔ-jŕ-chywū-jú-'jyàn. ‖This expedition is commanded by an old general. jèy-ge-'ywàn-jēng-'jywūn °shǔ (or °gwēy) yí-ge-lǎw-'jyāng-jywūn °dày-'lǐng. or °tǔng-'shwày. etc. ‖The three divisions under his command (or which he commands) suffered heavily. tā-°'gwǎn-de-(or °'dày-de- etc.)sān-'shŕ-'rén 'swěn-shŕ hěn 'jùng. ‖He was given command of the nineteenth division. dì-shŕ-'jyěw-'shŕ °gwēy (or °jyàw-gey) ta °'dày. or °'gwǎn. etc.

To be commanded (to be ordered) fèng-'mìng. ‖We were commanded to take to the life boats. wǒm fèng-'mìng shàng jyèw-shēng-'chwán.

To command *a view.* ‖That hill commands an excellent view of the city. *is expressed as* On that hill you can see the whole city. dzày nèy-ge-'shān-shang kàn-de-'jyàn chywán-'chéng.

(*A charge: military, with various expressions used in Chinese*). ‖He was relieved of his command. tā gāng chè-le 'jŕ. ‖A new officer has taken command of the troops. 'shīn-láy-de-°sŕ-'lìng (*or* °jăng-'gwān) jyē-'rèn-le. ‖Have you ever served under his command? nĭ 'gēn-gwo ta-ma? *or* nĭ dzày tā-nèr dzwò-gwo 'shŕ-ma?

Military and Naval Terms. Officer in command *or* commanding officer jŭ-gwān-jăng-'gwān, jăng-'gwān, sŕ-'lìng, jŕ-'hwēy, sŕ-lìng-'gwān, jŕ-hwēy-'gwān. Commander (*Navy rank*) ('hăy-jywūn-) jūńg-'shyàw; lieutenant commander ('hăy-jywŭn-)shàw-'shyàw. Company commander lyán-'jăng; battalion commander yíng-'jăng; *and so forth, with* jăng *preceded by the designation of the unit commanded.* Commander-in-chief dzŭng-sŕ-'lìng, jŭ-'shwày, tŭng-'shwày, dà-'jyàng, dà-ywán-'shwày, dà-jyāng-'jywūn. ‖He was transferred to command another division. *is expressed as* He was transferred to another division to be the commander. tā dyàw-dàw lìng-yi-'shŕ dzwò shŕ-'jăng. ‖Who is in command here? *is expressed as* Who is the commanding officer? jèy-ge-'dì-fang °shwéy shŕ (jŭ-gwăn-)'jăng-gwān? *or* °shwéy shŕ 'sŕ-lìng? *or* °shŭ shwéy 'gwăn?

A command (*an order*) 'mìng-ling. ‖Has he issued his command? tā-de-'mìng-ling 'fā-shya-lay 'méy-yew?

A command (*mastery*). ‖Does he have a good command of English? (*Spoken*) tā-'yīng-wén-'shwō-de 'hăw-ma? (*Written*) tā-'yīng-wén-'shyĕ-de 'hăw-ma?

‖He commands respect. tā 'jyàw-rén bù-néng bù-'dzwēn-jing.

COMMERCE. shāng-, 'shāng-yè, 'măy-mày, màw-'yì, 'shāng-wù. ‖This port is a center for foreign commerce. jèy-ge-hăy-'kĕw shŕ °chū-jìn-kĕw-'măy-mày-de-'jūng-shīn. *or* °chū-jìn-kĕw-'shāng-yè-de-'jūng-shīn. *or* °chū-jìn-kĕw-'shāng-wù-de-'jūng-shīn. *or* °'gwó-jì-màw-'yì-de-'jūng-shīn.

Of commerce, commercial. Department of Commerce 'shāng-bù; Chamber of Commerce 'shāng-hwèy; commercial treaty 'shāng-ywē *or* tūng-shāng-'tyáw-ywē; commercial code 'shāng-fă; commercial attaché 'shāng-wù-tsān-'dzàn; the commercial world, commercial circles 'shāng-jyè.

See also BUSINESS, TRADE.

COMMITTEE. wĕy-ywán-'hwèy. ‖Who is on the committee? shwéy dzày wĕy-ywán-'hwèy-li? ‖There is a committee meeting tonight. jyēr wăn-shang wĕy-ywán-'hwèy kāy-'hwèy.

Committee member, on the committee 'wĕy-ywán. ‖She is on the committee. tā shŕ 'wĕy-ywán.

Committee chairman wĕy-ywán-'jăng, 'jŭ-shí (-'wĕy-ywán).

The Subcommittee on Foreign Affairs of the Military Affairs Committee 'jywūn-shŕ-wĕy-ywán-'hwèy (-de) 'wày-shŕ-wĕy-ywán-'hwèy; the Overseas-Chinese Affairs Commission. 'chyáw-wù-wĕy-ywán-'hwèy.

COMMON. (*General*). ‖How common is this practice? jèy-jŭng-'bàn-fă hĕn 'pŭ-tūng-ma? ‖It is common knowledge that you can't believe everything he says. shwéy dēw 'jŕ-daw tā-de-hwà bù 'wán-chywán kĕ-'kàw. ‖A common saying is that .... (yĕw) yí-jywù-°'sú-ywŭ (*or* °'sú-ywĕr *or* °'sú-hwàr), jyèw-shŕ ....

(*Ordinary*). (*Of a style or thing*) píng-'cháng-de; (*of a person*) píng-'fán, píng-. Common alley cat hĕn píng-'cháng-de-'māw; made of common material píng-'cháng-de-'yī-lyàw-dz-'dzwò-de; a man of no common ability fēy-cháng-'néng-gàn-de-rén. ‖He says this is the century of the common man. tā shwō jèy shŕ °píng-'mín-de-'shŕ-dày. *or* °'lăw-băy-'shìng-de-shŕ-dày.

(*Shared*). ‖These laws are for our common good. jèy-jŭng-fă-'lywù shŕ wèy dà-jyā 'hăw. ‖It was done by common consent. shŕ dà-jyā túng-'yì tsáy nèm-'bàn-de.

In common. ‖The two have nothing in common. nèy-'lyă yì-dyăr yĕ bù-yí-'yàng. ‖Have they any trait in common? tā-men-de-'shìng-ching yĕw shyāng-'túng-de-dì-fang-ma?

Common sense cháng-'shŕ, 'jyàn-wén, 'jyàn-shŕ. ‖He lacks common sense. tā cháng-'shŕ bú-'gèw. *or* tā 'jyàn-wén bù-'gwăng. *or* tā 'jyàn-shŕ 'chā-yi-dyar. *But* ‖If other problems arise, use your common sense. yàw-shŕ yĕw 'byé-de-wèn-tí-de-'hwà, nĭ chyáw-je 'bàn hăw-le.

COMMUNICATION. Be in communication tūng-'shyàw-shi, tūng-'shìn. ‖We have not been in communication with them. wŏm méy-yĕw gēn-tām °tūng-'shyàw-shi. *or* °tūng-'shìn. ‖Our communication lines have been broken by storms. wŏm-de jyāw-tūng-'shyàn jyàw 'kwáng-fēng-bàw-'ywŭ gĕy dwàn-le. ‖The only mean of communication is by radio. jŕ yĕw yùng wú-shyàn-'dyàn ké-yi tūng-'shìn.

(*Official*) 'gūng-wén. ‖The messenger brought two communications from headquarters. chwán-lìng-'bīng tsúng· sŕ-lìng-'bù dày-láy lyăng-jyàn-'gūng-wén.

(*Physical*) 'jyāw-tūng. Ministry of Communications jyāw-tūng-'bù; land communication lù-shang-'jyāw-tūng; sea communication hăy-shàng-'jyāw-tūng; communication center 'jyāw-tūng-jūng-'shīn. *But* rail communication tyĕ-dàw-'ywùn-shū.

COMMUNITY. (*Place, area*) 'dì-fang, dày. ‖**How many families are living in this community?** jèy-ge-dì-fang (*or* jèy-yí-'dày) yèw dwō-shǎw 'jyā? ‖**The whole community is behind this plan.** *is expressed as* All the people of this area are behind this plan. jèy-yí-'dì-fang-de-rén (*or* , jèy-yí-'dày-de-rén) chywán 'dzàn-chéng jèy-ge-'bàn-fǎ.

Community center dà-hwèy-'táng, gūng-gùng-hwèy-'táng, 'dì-fang-'gūng-swǒ; **community chest** gūng-yí-'jywān, tsź-shàn-'jywān.

(*Communities with definite limits, often used where we use community*). (*District or county*) shyàn; (*sub-divisions of a shyàn*) shyāng, jèn; (*subdivision of a shyāng or jèn, equal to about 100 families*) bǎw; (*ten families*) jyǎ; (*a city, usually walled*) chéng; (*suburb of a city*) shyāng; (*large town*) jèn; (*small town or large village*) jwāng; (*village*) tṣwēn; (*street*) jyē; (*district of a city*) chywū.

COMPANION. túng-'bàr-de. ‖**That old lady was traveling with a companion.** nèy-ge-lǎw-'tày-tay yěw ge-túng-'bàr-de.

To be companions dzwò-'bàr. ‖**We were companions on the trip.** wǒm yí-'lù dzwò-'bàr.

(*Matching*). ‖**There is a companion picture to this one.** jèy-jāng-'hwàr háy yěw ge-'dwèr-ne. ‖**There are three companion pictures to this one.** háy yěw 'sān-jāng gēn 'jèy-jāng shr̀ °yí-'tàw. *or* °yí-'fù. *or* °yí-fù-sź-shàn-'píng.

COMPANY. (*Visitors, guests*) 'kè-rén. ‖**I'm expecting company tonight.** jyēr 'wǎn-shang yěw °'kè-rén láy. *or* °'rén láy 'jǎw wǒ.

(*Companions*). ‖**You are known by the company you keep.** *Chinese has several corresponding proverbs, all literary quotations; thus:* One who is near red gets red, one who is near black gets black. jìn-'jū-jě-'chr̀, jìn-'mwò-jě-'hè. Things follow their kind; birds of a feather flock together. wù-tsúng-chí-'lèy. Things of a kind gather together. wù-yí-lèy-'jywù. Look at one's friend and you know one's person. gwān chí-'yěw ěr jř chí-'rén.

(*Companionship*). ‖**I find him very good company.** wǒ hěn 'shǐ-hwān gēn tā °'láy-wǎng. *or* °'jyāw-wǎng. *or* °dzwò 'péng-yew. ‖**He is poor company.** gēn-tā 'láy-wǎng méy 'yì-sz. ‖**Would you stay a little longer and keep me company?** nǐ 'ywàn-yi dzày 'dāy-hwer gēn-wo dzwò-'bàr-ma?

(*Business firm*) hàw, jyā, gūng-'sž. (*hàw is confined to certain uses; jyā means* house; *dyàn, háng and other terms that occur as the last syllable of firm names may also mean* company.) ‖**This company** (*of ours*) **was founded 15 years ago.** bèn-'haw (*or* shyǎw-'hàw *or* běn-'dyàn, běn-'háng, *etc.*) shr yì-bǎy-wǔ-shr̀-'chī-nyán-chyán kāy-'bàn-de. ‖**What company do you represent?** bǎw-'hàw? *or* bǎw-'hàw shr̀ 'něy-jyā? ‖**We will have to order this from the Sanger**

Company. jèy-ge wǒm děy tsúng 'shèng-jyā-gūng-'sž shyàn-'dìng.

(*Theatrical*). ‖**The leading actor is good, but the rest of the company is poor.** bān-dz-li-de-'jǔ-jyǎw hěn hǎw, 'byé-de-rén bù-'shíng.

(*Military*) lyán. ‖**A battalion has three companies.** yì-'yíng yěw sān-'lyán. ‖**The captain will review his company tomorrow.** lyán-'jǎng míng-tyān jyǎn-'ywè chywán-'lyán. ‖**We have a company of engineers here.** dzày-jèr yěw °yì-lyán-'gūng-bīng. *or* °yí-ge-gūng-bīng-'lyán.

COMPARATIVELY. ‖**Comparatively speaking, this hotel isn't bad.** *or* This hotel is comparatively good. *is expressed as* Compare this hotel with others and you can't call it bad. jèy-ge-lywǔ-'gwǎn gēn 'byé-de yì-'bǐ, yě 'bìng bú-swàn-'hwày. *or* jèy-ge-lywǔ-'gwǎn gēn 'byé-de 'bǐ-jyàw-chi-'lay, yě háy bú-swàn-'hwày.

COMPARE. bǐ, 'bǐ-jyǎw, 'bǐ-jyàw. ‖**We compared the two methods and chose this one.** wǒm bǎ lyǎng-jǔng-'fāng-fǎ bǐ-jyàw-le yí-shyàr, jywē-'dìng yùng 'jèy-ge. ‖**This hotel doesn't compare with others I have stayed in.** jèy-ge-'lywǔ-gwǎn gēn 'wǒ-jù-gwò-de 'bǐ chà-'ywǎn-le. ‖**Compare these two.** jèy-lyǎ nín 'bǐ-yi-bǐ. ‖**How can this one be compared with yours?** 'jèy-ge dzěm-me néng gēn 'nǐ-nèy-ge 'bǐ-ne? ‖**His book is awfully dull compared to yours.** tā-nèy-běn-'shū (yàw-shr 'ná-lay) gēn 'nǐ-nèy-běn 'bǐ jyěw °swǒ-rán-wú-'wèy-le. *or* °shyǎn-de hěn méy-yew 'yì-sz-de. ‖**He's a dwarf compared to the captain.** tā gēn lyán-'jǎng (jàn yí-kwar) yì-'bǐ shyàng ge-shyǎw-rén-'gwór shr̀-de. ‖**They don't compare.** bù-néng 'bǐ. *or* jèy-ge gēn 'nèy-ge bù-néng 'bǐ. *or* jèy-ge bù-néng (ná-lay) gēn 'nèy-ge 'bǐ.

COMPARISON. The comparison between them *is expressed as* when you compare them; to make a comparison *is expressed as* to compare; by comparison *is expressed as* when you compare them. ‖**They asked us to make a comparison.** tām jyàw-wǒm 'bǐ yí-shyàr. ‖**There is no comparison between the two towns.** lyǎng-ge-'chéng gēn-běn bù-néng 'bǐ. ‖**It doesn't bear comparison.** yì-'bǐ jyěw °bù-'shíng-le. *or* °'chà-le. *or* °'shyǎn-chu-lay-le. ‖**In comparison with that one this isn't a bad bargain.** gēn 'nèy-ge yì-'bǐ, mǎy 'jèy-ge bú-swàn 'shàng-dàng.

COMPASS. (*For determining direction*) jř-nán-'jēn, fāng-shyàng-'pan; (*navigator's*) 'lwó-pán. ‖**A compass will be useful on your trip.** nǐ lywǔ-'shíng-de-'shr̀-hew yěw ge-jř-nán-'jēn hǎw-dyǎr. ‖**The ship's compass was broken.** 'chwán-shang-de-'lwó-pán 'hwày-le. ‖**Can you box the compass?** 'lwó-pán-shang-de-sān-shr-'èr-ge-'fāng-shyàng °nǐ hwèy 'bèy-ma? *or* °nǐ néng àn-je 'tsź-shywù dēw 'shǔ-chu-lay-ma?

(*For drawing a circle*) 'ywán-gwēy, lyǎng-jyǎw-gwēy. ‖This circle was drawn with a compass. jèy-ge-'chywār shr rùng 'ywán-gwēy (*or* lyǎng-ˈyǎw-'gwēy) 'hwà-de.

(*Scope*). ‖The compass of his work was limited. tā-gūng-'dzwò-de-'fàn-wéy hěn shyǎw.

COMPLAIN. (*Mildly*) bù-mǎn-'yì. **To complain that** (*mildly*) shwō; (*violently*) chǎw, nàw, dǎ-'jyà; (*by shouting*) rǎng, 'rāng-rang; (*by mumbling*) 'dū-nang, 'dū-du-nāng-nāng-de. **Complain about** *a person* (*to an authority*) gàw; (*to an equal*) shwō. **Complain about** *something* ywàn, 'bàw-ywàn. ‖What are you complaining about? nǐ yěw shém-me-bù-mǎn-'yì-de-'dì-fang? ‖She left work early, complaining of a headache. tā dzǎw °'dzěw (*or* °shyà-'bān)-de shwō shr téw 'téng. ‖We complained to the manager about the p or accommodations. wǒ-men gēn jīng-'lǐ shwō 'shè-bèy tày °'chā. *or* °'bù-'shíng. *or* °'hwày. *or* 'shè-bèy tày 'hwày-le, wǒm gēn 'jīng-lǐ °'chǎw-le yí-'dwèn. *or* °'dǎ-le yí-dwèn-'jyà. *or* °'nàw-le yí-'dwèn. *or* °'rǎng-le 'bàn-tyān. *or* °'rāng-rang-le 'bàn-tyān. ‖She's always complaining. tā 'dzǔng-shr̀ bù-mǎn-'yì. *or* tā 'lǎw-shr̀ °'bàw-ywàn jè-ge 'bàw-ywàn nà-ge-de. *or* °'dū-du-nāng-'nāng-de, jè-ge yě bù-'hǎw, nà-ge yě bù hǎw. *or* °'dū-nang jè-ge yě bù-'hǎw .... *or* °'shwō jè-ge yě bù-'hǎw .... ‖I'm not complaining about you. wǒ bú-shr̀ shwō-'nǐ. *or* wǒ bú-shr̀ ywàn-'nǐ. ‖He complained about you (*about your work*). tā wèy-le hǐ-dzwò-de-'shèr 'shwō-nǐ-láy-je. ‖He complained to the manager about you. tā gēn jīng-'lǐ 'shwō-nǐ-lay-je. *or* tā dàw jīng-'lǐ-'nàr 'gàw-ni-lay-je.

COMPLETE. (*To finish*) wán, dé, hǎw, chéng, dìng. *These words are placed after the word which specifies the thing or action which is completed.* hǎw *implies the satisfaction given in the completion;* dìng *refers to something being settled.* ‖Be sure to complete the work before you go home. méy hwéy-'jyā yǐ-chyán, yí-'dìng yàw bǎ jèy-ge-'shèr °dzwò-'wán-le. *or* °dzwò-'hǎw-le. *or* °dzwò-'chéng-le. ‖The plans are not yet complete. 'jì-hwà háy méy °'nǐ-hǎw. *or* °'nǐ-dìng. *or* °'nǐ-chéng. ‖Is it completed? (*Of a piece of writing*) shyě-'hǎw-le-ma? ‖Have you completed the organization? 'gǎy-dzǔ 'wán-le-ma? ‖The preparations were completed. dēw 'jwěn-bèy (*or* 'ywù-bèy) 'hǎw-le.

(*Full, finished*) 'wán-chywán, chywán, 'chywán-dēw, dēw, 'swǒ-yěw-de (dēw *or* chywán). (*These words also mean* all.) ‖This machine does the complete operation (*all the work*). swǒ-yěw-de-'shèr jèy-jyǎ-'jī-chì dēw dzwò-'wán-le. ‖Please make a complete list of your books. chǐng bǎ nǐ-swǒ-yěw-de-'shū kǎy yí-ge-'dān-dz. ‖This is the complete list of the names of persons arrested. bèy 'dày-bǔ-de-rén-de' 'míng-dz dēw dzày jèy-jāng-'dān-dz-shang. *or* jèy-jāng-'dān-dz-shang, 'kǎy-de shr̀ 'swǒ-yěw-de-'dǎy-

chywù-de-rén-de-'míng-dz. ‖That's a complete victory for them. tā-men 'dé-dàw-le chywán-'shèng.

(*Thorough*). ‖As a soldier, he's a complete flop. tā dāng 'jywūn-rén, jyǎn-'jf °yì-twán-'dzǎw. *or* °bú-shr nèm-ge 'tsày-lyǎwr. *or* °bù-'chéng. *or* °bù 'shíng. *or expressed as* he would force a duck to climb a ladder. °shr ná 'yā-dz shàng-'jyà.

COMPOSE. **To compose** (*something in writing*) shyě, dzwò. ‖He composes poems. tā shyě-'shr̀. *or* tā dzwò-'shr̀. ‖He composes music. tā dzwò-'pǔ. **To be composed of** yěw ... 'hé-chéng-de. ‖Compose yourself! byé 'hwāng-jang!

COMPOSITION. (*Musical*). 'yīn-ywè (*music*); ywè-'pǔ (*musical score*). ‖What compositions will the orchestra play tonight? yīn-ywè-'dwèy jyēr 'wǎn-shang 'yǎn-dzèw shém-'yīn-ywè? ‖Whose compositions will be played tonight? jyēr wǎn-shang 'dēw shr yǎn-dzèw nǎ-shyē-'rén-de-°'yīn-ywè. *or* °ywè-'pǔ.

(*Graphic*) 'bù-jywú. ‖The composition of the painting seems defective. nèy-jāng-hwàr-de-'bù-jywú hǎw-shyàng yěw dyǎr-'máw-bing.

(*Literary*) wén. A composition yì-pyān-'wén; class in English composition 'yīng-wén-dzwò-wén-'bān; composition book dzwò-wén-'běr.

(*Chemical*) 'chéng-fen. ‖The chemist will analyze the composition of this metal. hwà-yàn-'shr̀ yàw 'hwà-yàn (*or* 'yán-jyēw) yí-shyàr jèy-jǔng-'jīn-shǔ-de-'chéng-fen.

(*In printing*) páy-'bǎn. ‖The printer will need a week for composition. yìn-'dž-de-rén dzǔng-děy rùng yí-ge-lǐ-'bày láy páy-'bǎn.

CONCERN. (*To involve*). ‖This concerns you. jèy gēn-nǐ yěw 'gwān-shi. ‖Which people were concerned in the matter? jèy-jyàn-'shèr dēw-shr gēn-'shéy yěw 'gwān-shi? *or* jèy-jyàn-'shr̀ ˈi dēw yěw-°'shwéy? *or* °'shéme-rén?

(*Involvement or interest*). ‖She said it was no concern of hers. tā shwō °méy tā-de-'shèr. *or* °bú-shr tā-de-'shèr. *or* °tā bú 'gwǎn. *or* °tā 'gwǎn-bu-jáw. ‖This doesn't concern me. jèy ywǔ wǒ wú-'gǎn. *or* jèy ywǔ wǒ wú-'gwān. *or* jèy-ge gēn-'wǒ méy-yěw 'gwān-shi. ‖Is it any concern of yours? nǐ 'gwǎn-de-jáw-ma? *or* (*More mildly*) ywǔ-nǐ yěw shém-me-'gwān-shi?

To be concerned with (*be interested in*) 'dzày-hu, gwǎn. ‖I'm not concerned with the details. wǒ bú 'dzày-hu (*or* 'gwǎn) °shyǎw-de-'dì-fang. *or* °shyǎw-'jyé-mù.

(*Worry*). ‖She is showing a great deal of concern over her husband. tā 'shyǎn-chu-lay (*or* tā 'shyǎn-je) dwèy tā-de-'jàng-fu hěn 'gwān-shin. *or* 'kàn-shang-chywu tā dwèy tā-de-'jàng-fu hěn 'gwān-shīn-de-'yàng-dz.

(*Business*) 'mǎy-mày, gūng-'sž, 'shāng-dyàn, 'pù-dz, chù, 'dǐ-fang. ('shāng-dyàn *and* 'pu-dz *also mean* store, shop; chù *and* 'dì-fang *simply mean* place.) ‖How long have you been with this concern? nǐ dzày jèr (*or* nǐ dzày jèy-ge-'dì-fang) dzwò-'shř yěw dwō-'jyěw-le? *or* nǐ dzày jèy-ge-gūng-'sž (*or* 'shāng-dyàn, *or* 'pù-dz, *or* 'mǎy-màay) dzwò-le (*or* dāy-le) dwō-shǎw 'shř-hew?

CONCERNING. 'gwān-ywú. ‖Nothing was said concerning this matter. 'gwān-ywú jèy-jyàn-'shèr méy 'tí. ‖I have a question concerning these tickets. 'gwān-ywú jèy-jǐ-jāng-'pyàw wǒ yěw °ge-'wèn-tí. *or* °dyǎr-bù-'míng-bay-de-'dì-fang.

CONCERT. yīn-ywè-'hwèy. ‖Is there to be a concert tonight? jyēr 'wǎn-shang yěw yīn-ywè-'hwèy-ma? ‖We must allow time to pick up the concert tickets. dzám dzǔng-děy 'lyéw-shya (*or* 'ywén-shya, *or* 'téng-shya) 'shř-hew hǎw chywù chywǔ yīn-ywè-hwèy-de-'pyàw.

CONDITION. (*State*) 'yàng-dz, 'yàngr. ‖You are in no condition to leave the house. nǐ 'nèm-ge-yàng-dz bù-néng 'chū-chywu. *or* nǐ-bíng-de-'nà-yàngr bù-néng 'chū-chywu. ‖The house was in poor condition. fáng-dz pwò-jyèw-bù-'kān (*literary quotation*).

  Good condition. ‖The porcelain arrived in good condition. 'tsź-chì hǎw-'hāwr-de 'ywùn-dàw-le. *or* 'tsź-chì ywùn-dàw-le, yì-dyǎr méy-'hwày.

  Physical condition 'shēn-dz, 'shēn-tǐ, 'tǐ-gé; mental condition 'shīn-lǐ jwàng-'kwàng, 'shīn-lǐ jwàng-'tày.

  (*Circumstances; social, political, financial, etc.*) 'chíng-shíng, jwàng-'kwàng, 'chíng-kwàng, -shíng; financial conditions 'tsáy-jèng-jwàng-'kwàng; business conditions 'shāng-chíng, 'shāng-yè-chíng-'kwàng. ‖She said she would not attend under any conditions. tā shwō tā dzày rèn-hé-'chíng-shíng jř-shyà yě bú-'chywù. *or* tā shwō tā 'dzěm yě bú-chywù.

  In conaition. (*Of persons*) jwěn-bèy-'hǎw, 'shēn-tǐ jwěn-bèy-'hǎw. ‖The athletes are not in condition. ywùn-dùng-'ywán méy jwěn-bèy-'hǎw. *or* ywùn-dùng-'ywán-de-'shēn-tǐ méy jwěn-bèy-'hǎw. (*Of things*) 'jwěn-bèy-twǒ-'dàng, néng 'yùng, ké-yi 'yùng. ‖The tanks are not in condition (*for combat*). jàn-'chē méy °jwěn-bèy-twǒ-'dàng. *or* °bù-néng 'yùng. *or* °bù-ké-yí 'yùng.

  (*Stipulation*). ‖I will accept the offer on three conditions. wǒ yěw sān-ge-'tyáw-jyàn, dēw 'hé-le wǒ jyèw 'dā-ying. ‖I will go on condition that I pay my own way. yàw-shr jyàw wǒ-'dž-jǐ chū-'chyán wǒ jyèw chywù.

  (*To influence*). ‖His decision was conditioned by his religious beliefs. tā-de-'jywé-dìng shř shèw tā-'dzūng-jyàw-shìn-yǎng-de-yíng-'shyǎng. ‖The quality of the work is conditioned by the time limit. gūng-dzwò 'hǎw-hwày děy kàn 'yěw-méy-yew 'shř-jyān-de-'shyàn-jř.

CONDUCT. (*To lead*) lǐng, dày, dǎw, 'dày-lǐng, 'lǐng-dǎw. ‖A guide will conduct the party through the art museum. yí-ge-shyǎng-'dǎw hwèy 'lǐng-je rén dzày chén-lyè-'swǒ-lǐ 'ràw-yi-shyar. *or* yěw jāw-dày-ywán dày-je dzày měy-shù-'gwǎn-lǐ 'dzěw-yi-chywar. ‖Conducted tours leave from here. dǎw-'yév tsúng-jèr chū-'fā.

  (*Of electricity*). ‖We need a wire to conduct electricity to the barn. wǒm děy yàw yì-gēr-dyàn-'shyàn hǎw bǎ-'dyàn tūng-dǎw tsāng-'fáng-li-chywu.

  (*To manage*) gwǎn. ‖Who conducted the business in his absence? tā méy dzàv de-'shř-hew shwév ꝺwǎn-'shř?

  (*Music*) 'jř-dǎw. ‖Who conducts the symphony tonight: shwéy 'jř-dǎw ~jyēr-'wǎn-shang-de-jyāw-shyǎng-'ywè?

  (*To behave*). ‖He conducted himself well during the meeting. kāy-'hwèy-de-shř-hew tā-de-'tày-du hěn bú-'tswò.

  (*Behavior*) 'shíng-wey; (*general or usual*) 'pǐn-shíng. ‖The children's conduct was satisfactory. 'háy-dz-men-de-'shíng-wey hěn hǎw. *or* 'háy-dz-men tǐng 'gwēy-jywù. ‖His conduct is beyond criticism. tā-de-'pǐn-shíng méy-yew kě 'pī-píng-de.

  (*Management*). ‖The conduct of the business affairs should be honorable. dzwò-'mǎy-màay yīng-dāng °'ɡwēy-jy ᵕǔ. *or* °'gwēy-gwey-jywu-'jywǔ-de. ‖They constantly criticized the conduct of the war. tām 'lǎw-shř 'pī-ping 'jàn-shř-jř-'hwēy-de bù-'dé-dàng.

CONNECT. jyē. ‖Please connect these wires to the battery. bǎ jèy-jǐ-tyáw-'shyàn jyē-dàw dyàn-'píng-shang. ‖Operator, please connect me with .... gěy wǒ jyē .... *or* wǒ yàw .... ‖All trains connect with busses at the station. swǒ-yěw hwǒ-'chē dàw-'jàn de-shř-hew dēw yěw 'gūng-gùng-chì-'chē jyē.

  Be connected. ‖What firm are you connected with? bǎw-'hàw shř 'něy-jyā? ‖He's connected with an oil company. tā gēn (*or* dzày) yí-ge-'yéw-gūng-sž dzwò-'shř. ‖The two families are connected by marriage. tām-lyǎng-'jyār °shř 'chīn-chì. *or* (*if the daughter of one family is married to the son of the other*) °shř 'chìng-jya. *or* °yěw chywún-dày-'gwān-shi.

  (*Associate*). ‖I always connect war with Napoleon. wǒ yì-shyǎng-dàw dǎ-'jàng jyèw shyǎng-dàw ná-pwò-'lwén.

CONNECTION. (*Physical*). ‖There is a loose connection somewhere in the engine. 'jī-chì yěw dì-fang 'sūng-le. ‖The telephone operator gave us a bad connection. sž-'jī lǎw gěy bǎ-shyàn 'jyē-de bú-dwèy-'jyèr.

  (*Traveling*). ‖The connections for that town are very poor. dàw-'nàr-chywù-de-shř-jyān-'byǎw-páy-de hěn bù-'hǎw. ‖You make connections at the next station. dàw-le 'shyà-jàn hwàn-'chè.

(*Business*). ‖These people have extensive business connections. jèy-shyē-'rén gēn hěn-dwō 'măy-may dēw yew 'lyán-lè.

(*Family*). ‖I'm not clear about their family connections. wǒ bù-'míng-bay tām-'jyā-li-de-'gwān-shi. o tām shř dzěm-me-ge-'chīn-chi, wǒ bú-dà 'chīng-chu.

(*Meaning*). ‖I don't understand the connection between their statements. wǒ bù-'míng-bay tām-nèy-lyǎng-jywù-ʼhwà-de-'gwān-shi. ‖I don't get the connection. jèy gēn 'nèy-ge wǒ'kàn (*or* 'tīng)-bu-chu-láy shř dzěm-me-ge-'gwān-shi. *or* jèy-ge-jyé-gu-'yǎr (*or* jèy-ge-jyé-gwān-ʼyǎr) dzày 'nàr wǒ 'kàn (*or* 'tīng)-bu-chu-láy. ‖Is there any connection between the two cases? No. jèy-lyǎng-ge-'àn-dz 'bǐ-tsž 'yěw-méy-yew 'gwān-shi? bù-shyāng-'gān. ‖It seems that his answer does not have any connection with what you asked. tā-de-'hwà gēn nǐ-'wén-de hýw shyàng méy-yew yì-dyǎr-'gwān-shi. *or* tā hwéy-dʼ nǐ-de-'hwà hǎw shyàng °'lywú-chwén bú-dwèy ɤ.á-'dzwěy. *or* °swǒ-'dá fěv, swǒ-'wèn. *or* °'wén bú-dwèy 'tí.

CONSENT. (*To agree*) 'dā-ying, kěn. ‖Has he consented? tā 'dā-ying-le-ma? *or* tā 'kěn-le-ma? ‖When asked to stay, he consented. yì-'lyéw-tā tā jyèw °'dā-ying-le. *or* °'kěn-le. *or* yì-'lyéw-tā jyèw 'lyéw-shya-le.

(*Agreement*). ‖His consent is absolutely necessary. yí-ʼdìng děy tā 'dā-yǐng tsáy 'shíng. ‖He won't give his consent. tā bú-hwèy 'dā-ying-de. ‖I can't do it without his consent. bù-jīng tā shywǔ-'kě wǒ bù-néng 'bàn. ‖If he is under age, the consent of his parents is required. tā 'rú-gwǒ shàng-wèy 'chéng-nyán tā-'jyā-jǎng-de-shywǔ-'kě shř. bì-'shywū-de. *or* tā 'yàw-shr háy méy-'chéng-nyán yèw děy dé tā-'fù-mu-de-shywǔ-'kě.

CONSIDER. (*Think about and discuss*) 'kǎw-lywù; (*investigate, look into*) 'yán-jyēw; (*think, regard*) shyǎng; (*be concerned with*) gù, 'gù-lywù. ‖We are considering all angles of your proposal. wǒm 'jèng-dzày tsúng gè-'fāng myàn 'kǎw-lywù nǐ-tí-de-nèy-jyàn-'shèr (*or use* 'yán-jyēw *instead of* 'kǎw-lywù *if that meaning is intended*). ‖Have you ever considered it from that angle? nǐ tsúng 'nèy-fāng-myàn °'kǎw-lywù-gwo-me? *or* °'yán-jyēw-gwo-ma? *or* °'shyāng-gwo-ma? ‖He considers too many angles and then never acts. tā 'lǎw-shř 'gù-lywù ʼtày-dwō, rán-hèw 'shém-me yě bú-'bàn. ‖I wouldn't consider him for the job. nèy-ge-'wèy-jř wǒ kàn tā bù-'hé-shř. *or* wǒ shyǎng tā bù-néng dzwò nèy-ge-'shř. ‖He never considers the feelings of others. tā 'yǔng-ywǎn bú-'gù byé-rén dzěm 'shyǎng. *or* tā yí-shyàng bù-gwǎn byé-rén 'shèw-de-lyǎw 'shèw-bu-lyǎw. *or* tā yí-shyàng bú-tì byé-rén 'shyǎng yi-shyǎng.

(*Take into account*). ‖Considering his youth, he has achieved a great deal. àn tā-de-'nyán-jì láy shwō, tā-de-'chéng-jyèw hěn kě-'gwān.

CONSIDERATION. (*Examination*). ‖We'll take the matter under consideration. jèy-jyàn-'shř wǒm 'kǎw-lywù-kǎw-lywù.

(*Regard*). ‖The hotel manager showed us every consideration. lywǔ-gwǎn-'jīng-lǐ-'jàw-gù-de hěn 'jēw-dàw. ‖Don't you have any consideration for other people's feelings? nǐ 'nán-dàw(-shwō) °yì-dyǎr yě bù-'gwǎn byé-rén dzěm-me 'shyǎng-ma? *or* °'jyèw bú-'tì byé-rén 'shyǎng-shyǎng?

(*Compensation*). ‖He will probably expect a consideration for his services. tā 'dà-gày shyǎng 'dé dyǎr-'bàw-chéw. ‖We present this to you in consideration of your services. nín gěy 'dzwò-le dzěm-shyē-'shř, 'jè jyèw-shr wǒm-de-yì-dyar-'yì-sz.

CONSIST. Consist of yěw. ‖The meal consists of fish, vegetables, and tea. nèy-dwèn-'fàn yěw 'ywú, chīng-'tsày, gēn 'chá. ‖What does this consist of? jèy-li dēw yěw 'shéme?

CONSTANT. yì-'jŕ, lǎw, 'lǎw-shr. ‖Constant rains made the roads very muddy. yì-jŕ 'shyà-ywǔ bǎ-'lù 'nùng-de mǎn shř 'ní. ‖The constant noise kept me awake all night. yì-'jŕ (*or* lǎw, *or* 'lǎw-shr) yěw 'shēng-yin, chǎw-de wǒ yī-'yè méy-shwèy-'jáw. *or* 'shēng-yin 'lǎw-shr bù-'tíng, chǎw-de ...

CONTAIN. yěw, ...-lǐ shř. (...-lǐ shř *refers to the total contents.*) ‖What does this package contain? jèy-ge-'bāwr-lǐ shř shéme? ‖It contains three items. 'lǐ-tew yěw 'sān-yàng-dūng-shi. ‖The trunk contains (*is packed full of*) clothing. 'shyāng-dz-li-'jwāng-de shř 'yī-fu. ‖The newspaper contains some interesting reports. bàw-shang yèw jǐ-shyàng-yěw-'yì-sz-de-'shīn-wén. *or* bàw-shang 'dēng-le shyē-ge-yěw-'yì-sz-de-'shyāw-shi. ‖How many liters are contained in a gallon? yì-'jyā-lwén yěw 'dwō-shǎw 'gūng-shēng? ‖How many catties of rice are contained in a standard burlap bag? yì-bāw-'mǐ shř (*or* yěw) dwō-shaw 'jīn?

(*Restrain*). ‖You must learn to contain your temper. nǐ děy 'shywé-je 'gwǎn nǐ-de-'pí-chì. *or* nǐ-de-'pí-chì, nǐ děy 'lyàn-shí-je 'yā-jŕ-dyar. ‖He contained himself throughout the quarrel. dǎ-'jyà-de-shŕ-hew tā yì-jŕ °bú-dùng 'shēng-sè. *or* °'píng-shīn-jìng-'chì-de.

CONTENT. (*Contents*) ‖I don't understand the content of this letter. wǒ bù-'míng-bay jèy-fēng-'shìn-de-'nèy-rúng. ‖The contents of your trunk must be examined. 'fēy-dey 'jyǎn-chá yí-shyàr nǐ-'shyāng-dz-li-de-'dūng-shi. ‖List the contents of your trunk. bǎ nǐ-shyāng-dz-li-de-'dūng-shi 'yí-shyàng-yí-'shyàng-de 'kāy-chu-lay. ‖I have seen only the table of contents. wǒ jŕ 'kàn-le-yī-kàn 'mù-lu.

(*Satisfied*) mǎn-'yì, jŕ-'dzú, 'gān-shīn. ('gān-shīn *means* willing, content to ....) ‖He was content with the price we offered him. wǒm gěy tā-de-'jyàr tā hěn °'mǎn-'yì. *or* °jŕ-'dzú. ‖He's content with his lot. tā hěn mǎn-'yì. *or* tā hěn jŕ-'dzú. ‖A contented wife is hard to find. jř-'dzú-de-'tày-tay nán 'dé. ‖Are you still discontented? nǐ háy bù-jř-'dzú-ma? ‖His contented look is unbearable. tā-nèy-ge-shīn-mǎn-yì-'dzú-de-'yàngr jyàw-rén 'shèw-bu-lyǎw. ‖I am not content with those arrangements. nèy-jǔng-'bàn-fa wǒ bù-mǎn-'yì. ‖I am not content to pay that price. wǒ bù-'gān-shīn gěy nèm-shyē-'chyán. or chū nèm-dà-de-'jyà-chyan wǒ yěw-dyǎr bù-'gān-shīn.

CONTEST. ‖This is the point of the contest. shyāng-'jēng-de-yì-'dyǎn jyèw-shr 'jèy-ge. ‖The winners of this contest will get prizes. jèy-tsž-'bǐ-sày-'yíng-de dé-'jyǎng. ‖Prizes will be given to the winner of the contest. yěw 'jyǎng-pǐn gěy 'yíng-de-rén. ‖There was a bitter contest in the elections. 'shywǎn-jywǔ-de-shŕ-hew jìng-'jēng hěn 'jī-lyè.

(To dispute). (A legal decision) 'kàng-gàw; (other things) jēng. ‖The judge's decision is being contested. yěw-rén 'kàng-gàw fǎ-gwān-de-'pàn-jywé. ‖I'll contest your claim to the property. nǐ shwō 'chǎn-yè shr 'nǐ-de; wǒ yí-'dìng gēn-ni 'jēng. ‖He is preparing to contest every inch of the ground. tā 'ywù-bey pīn-'mìng-chywu 'jēng, yí-bù bú-'ràng. ‖They contested a minor point. tām wèy-le shyǎw-'jyé 'jēng-ge bù-lyǎw. ‖His candidacy is not contested. tā dzwò 'hèw-shywǎn-rén méy-rén gēn-ta 'jēng.

CONTINUALLY. 'lyán-shywù-bú-'dwàn-de, 'jyē-lyán-bù-'tíng-de, yì-'jŕ. ‖He talked in his sleep continually for an hour. tā shwō 'mèng-hwà °yì-'jŕ (or °'lyán-shywù-bú-'dwàn-de, or °'jyē-lyán-bù-'tíng-de) shwō-le 'yì-dyǎn-jūng.

CONTINUE. (Go on) 'jyē-je, or expressed as not stop méy-'tíng. ‖You may continue (talking) now. shyàn-'dzày ké-yi jyē-je 'shwō-shya-chywu. ‖We'll continue (working) from here. wǒm dzài-jèr jyē-je 'dzwò-shya-chywu. ‖I want to continue (walking) on to the city. wǒ shyǎng 'jyē-je dzěw-dàw 'chéng-lǐ. ‖They continued his pay until he died. 'jŕ-dàw tā sž tām méy-'tíng tā-de-'shīn.

To be continued 'dày-shywù, 'wèy-wán. ‖The novel has been continued for seven issues and still isn't finished. nèy-pyān-shyǎw-'shwōr dēng-le chī-'chī, háy méy-'dēng-wán. ‖The story will be continued in the next issue. běn-'wén (or jèy-ge-shyǎw-'shwōr) shyà-chī 'shywù-dēng.

(To resume). ‖The entertainment will continue after a ten-minute intermission. yéw-'yì 'shyēw-shi 'shŕ-fēn-jūng yì-'hèw jì-'shywù byǎw-'yǎn.

CONTROL. gwǎn. ‖The assistant manager controls the expenditures. fù-'jīng-li gwǎn yí-chyè-de-'kāy-jŕ. ‖She is good at controlling children. tā hwèy gwǎn 'háy-dz. ‖Can you control your men? nǐ-de-'rén nǐ 'gwǎn-de-jù (or -lyǎw)-ma? But ‖You must learn to control your temper. nǐ děy 'lyàn-je byé fā 'pí-chi.

To have control over, to control. ‖He has control over three sections. tā gwǎn sān-'bù-fen-de-'shŕ.

Compare also: ‖He is in control. tā gwǎn-'shŕ. ‖This office is under the control of the Army Service Forces. běn-'jywù shǔ 'hèw-fāng-chín-wù-'bù gwǎn. ‖This municipality is under the control of the Executive Ywàn. běn-'shŕ jŕ-shyá-'ywú shíng-jèng-'ywàn. ‖This child is beyond all control. jèy-ge-'háy-dz 'gwǎn-bu-lyǎw-le. ‖The fire is beyond control now. hwǒ 'jyèw-bu-lyǎw-lè. ‖The control of the business has passed to the son. 'mǎy-mèy gěy tā ér-dz 'gwǎn-le. ‖The plane seems to be out of control. 'fēy-jī fǎng-fu chū 'máw-bing-le. ‖The mob is out of control now. nèy-chywún-rén 'gwǎn-bu-jù-le. ‖Everything is under control. méy-yew shém-me °'bù-dé-lyǎw-de. or °'lyǎw-bu-dé-de. or °'jū-shŕ rú-'yì. ‖The fire was brought under control. 'hwǒ-shŕ yěw 'jyèw-le. ‖The fire can't be brought under control. 'hwǒ-shŕ méy-'jyèw-le.

Controls. ‖Are all the controls in order? 'jī-chì dēw 'líng-ma? ‖Would you mind taking over the controls for a while? nǐ láy 'kān (or 'gwǎn, or 'kāy if referring to a plane, train, or large machinery) yì-hwěr, dzěm-'yàng?

CONVENIENT. 'fāng-byan. ‖The bus service here is convenient. jèr-de-'gūng-gùng-chì-'chē hěn 'fāng-byan. ‖Come whenever it is convenient for you. 'shémme-shŕ-hew 'fāng-byan jyèw 'láy. or 'shém-me-shŕ-hew néng 'láy, jyèw 'láy. ‖Transportation is convenient here. jèr 'jyāw-tung 'fāng-byan. ‖Only if it is convenient for you. jŕ-yàw 'nǐ °fāng-byan. or °bù-wéy-'nán.

Other expressions in English. ‖What place would be most convenient for us to meet? dzám dzày-'nǎr jyàn hǎw? ‖It was a very convenient accident. jèy-tsž chū-'shèr jēn jyàw ge-'chyàw-le. or jèy-tsž-chū-'shèr chū-de jèng-shr 'shŕ-hew. ‖The accident was a convenient way for him to get out of it. 'jèng-hǎw oi 'chyà-chyǎw chū-le 'shèr, jyàw tā yěw-'hwà shwō.

CONVERSATION. ‖We had a bit of a conversation. wǒ-men 'tán-le yì-hwěr. or wǒ-men 'tán-le-yì-tán 'hwà. ‖On the train I fell into conversation with a stranger. dzày hwǒ-'chē-shang wǒ gēn yí-ge-'shēng-rén °'lyáw-chi-lay-le. or °shwō-chi 'hwàr-lay-le. or °'lyáw-chi 'tyār-lay-le. or °'tán-chi-lay-le. ‖I had a long conversation with the boss. wǒ gēn dzám-de 'téwr 'tán-le °yí-jèn (or °'bàn-tyān, or °hěn jyěw). ‖I overheard a conversation about it wǒ 'tīng-jyàn ron 'shwō-gwo.

COOK. dzwò-'fàn or dzwò plus the particular kind of food cooked. ‖Start cooking the dinner now. dzwò-'fàn-i a. ‖He knows how to cook. tā hwèy dzwò-'fàn. ‖How do you want your meat cooked? nèy-ge-'rèw °dzěm 'dzwò? or °nǐ yàw dzěm-me 'dzwò-de? ‖He can cook several special dishes. tā hwèy dzwò jǐ-yàng-hǎw-'tsày. ‖He cooked all day long in the kitchen.

tā dzày 'chú-fáng-li °dzwò-'fàn dzwò-le 'yì-jěng-tyān. or °dzwò-le yì-tyān-'fàn. ‖The secret of Chinese cooking is in the correct use of soya sauce. dzwò-jūng-gwo-'tsày-de-'mì-jywé shŕ yùng 'jyàng-yéw yùng-de 'dé-fă. ‖Sometimes the mistress cooks. is expressed as goes to the kitchen. 'yěw-de-shŕ-hew tày-tay 'dž-jĭ shyà 'chū-fang.

Cookstove 'lú-dz or hwǒ; cooking time 'hwǒ-kew.

Cooking (as part of domestic science) 'pēng-rèn. ‖Is there a cooking class? yěw pēng-rèn-'bān-ma?

Cookbook pēng-rèn-'fǎ. or jyǎng pēng-rèn-'fǎ-de 'shū. or shŕ-'pǔ.

To cook in particular ways. Boil, in water or soup) jǔ; (bake, roast) kǎw; (roast over an open fire, barbecue) shāw; (boil or simmer after frying or searing) pēng; (deep-fry) já; (pan-fry; vegetables, pieces of meat, etc.) chǎw; (flat slices, eggs, etc.) jyān; (steam) jēng; (apply heat to evaporate water) kàw. ‖This needs to cook a little longer. 'hwǒ-kew děy 'dà-dyar. or jèy-ge 'háy děy (dwǒ) °'jǔ-hwěr. or °'jǔ-yi-jǔ. or substitute any of the other terms for jǔ.

To cook up (a story) dzēw, byān, 'shyā-dzēw, 'shyā-byān; cooked up (of a story). 'hú-dzēw-de, 'hú-dzēw-bay-'lyě-de. ‖They cooked up a story for us. tām shyā-dzēw-le (or tām 'shyā-byān or tām 'dzēw-le or tām 'byān-le) ge-'hwàr yàw 'pyàn-dzám. ‖That's a fantastic story they cooked up. nèy-shr tām-°'hú-dzēw-de (or °'hú-dzēw-bay-'lyě-de, or °'shyā-dzēw-de, etc.), jyàw-rén hěn nán 'shìn.

‖What's cooking? ('chū-le) shém-me-'shèr?

A cook. In many cases, one of the verbal expressions listed above is used. ‖My younger sister is an excellent cook. wǒ 'mèy-mey °'hěn 'hwèy dzwò-'fàn. or °'dzwò-'tsày dzwò-de hěn-'hǎw. ‖We must hire a cook. děy 'gù ge-dzwò-'fàn-de.

A cook. (Other terms) 'chú-dz; (professional; polite terms) 'dà-shŕ-fu, 'chú-shŕ-fu; (chief chef) jǎng-'sháw-de; (assistant chef) bāng-'sháw-de; (apprentice chef) shywé-'tú-de; (cook's helper, mess boy) dǎ-'dzár-de; (in the army) 'hwǒ-fu. ‖This is a specialty of our cook. jèy-shr wǒm-'chú-dz-de-ná-shěw-'tsày.

COOL. lyáng. ‖It gets pretty cool here toward evening. 'wǎn-shang jèr tǐng 'lyáng. ‖The water is pretty cool (for swimming). shwěy yěw yì-dyǎr-°'lyáng. or °'lěng. ‖Stop the engine and let it cool off; then start it again. bǎ 'jī-chì 'tíng-le, děng 'lyáng-yi-dyar dzày 'kāy.

Cool and comfortable 'lyáng-kwày. ‖This is the coolest room in the house. jèy-shr jèy-swǒ-'fáng-dz-li-dzwèy-'lyáng-kwày-de-'wū-dz. ‖Wait until I change into something cooler. děng wǒ 'hwàn jyàr-'lyáng-kwày-dyǎr-de-'yī-shang. ‖Let's go out on the porch and cool off. dzám dàw lyáng-'táy-shang-chywu 'lyáng-kwày yí-shyàr.

To cool something lyàng. ‖Don't let this soup cool too long. byé bǎ jèy-ge-'tāng lyàng tày-'jyěw-le. ‖(To a child) Let it cool off a bit before you eat it.

is expressed as Let it cool a little bit, little doggie, wait and sit. 'lyàng-lyang 'lěng-leng, shyǎw-'gěwr děng-deng.

Keep something cool jyàw . . . 'lyáng-kwày, jyàw . . . bú-'jŕ-ywu rè, jyàw . . . bú-'rè. ‖Let's keep the house cool by shutting all the windows. dzàm bǎ 'chwāng-hu chywán 'gwān-shang hǎw jyàw 'fáng-dz-li, °'lyáng-kwày. or °bú-('jŕ-ywu) tày-'rè.

Keep cool (of temper) rěn. ‖I tried to keep cool when he insulted me. tā 'mà-wo de-shŕ-hew wǒ jyé-'lì-de °'rěn-je. or °bú-dùng shēng-'sè. ‖It was impossible for me to keep cool when he said that. tā shwō-le 'nèy-ge wǒ jyěw °'rěn-bu-jù-le. or °bù-néng dzày 'rěn-le.

COPPER. túng. ‖The chest is lined with copper. shyāng-dz-'lyěr shŕ 'túng-de. or shyāng-dz-'lǐ-tew 'shyāng-je yì-tséng-'túng-pyàr (sheet copper). ‖Bring me three feet of copper wire. gěy-wǒ 'sān-chŕ-cháng-de-°'túng-sž. or °'túng-sēr.

Other compounds can be similarly constructed: copper coin 'túng-chyán; copper plate 'túng-bǎr; etc.

COPY. To copy (by writing) chāw. ‖Copy each character exactly as it is written. bǎ měy-ge-'dž °'jàw-'yàngr 'chāw-shya-lay. or °'jàw-ywán-'yàngr yì-dyǎr-bú-'chà-de 'chāw-shya-lay. ‖Make ten copies of this report (by hand). jèy-ge-'bàw-gàw chāw 'shŕ-fèr.

To copy (by typing) dǎ (. . . fèr). ‖Type ten copies of this report. jèy-ge-'bàw-gàw dzày dǎ 'shŕ-fèr.

To copy (by photography) yìn, shǐ; (or if the plate is ready for prints to be made) 'jyā-yìn, 'jyā-shǐ. ‖Make ten copies of this print. jèy-jāng-shyàng-'pyàr 'jyā-yìn (or 'jyā-shǐ, or yìn, or shǐ) 'shŕ-jāng.

To copy (in facsimile or by tracing) myáw. ‖Copy (or make a copy of) that painting for me. bǎ nèy-jāng-'hwàr gěy-wǒ °'myáw yì-jāng. or °'jàw-yàngr. or °'hwà yì-jāng. ‖Copy it (by tracing) on a thin piece of paper. yùng 'báw-jŕ 'myáw-shya-lay.

(To imitate) 'jàw-jr. ‖She copies the new styles of clothes in the movies. tā-dzày-dyàn-'yǐng-shàng-'kàn-jyàn-le-shīn-'yàngr-de-'yī-shang jyèw 'jàw-jr dzwò. ‖They like to copy new American styles. tām 'shĭ-hwan 'jàw-jr měy-gwo-'shŕ-yàng fáng-'dzàw.

A copy (specimen). (If it consists of several sheets) (yí-)'fèr; (if it consists of one sheet) (yì-)'jāng; (if it is bound) (yì-)'běr; etc. ‖Do you have a copy of this morning's newspaper? nǐ yěw yí-fèr-jyēr-'dzǎw-chen-de-'bàw-ma? ‖This is a brand new copy (book). jèy-běr shŕ jǎn-'shīn-de.

A copy. (Imitation) is expressed as model on fáng. ‖This is a copy of a very expensive style. jèy-shr fáng-je yí-ge-hěn-'gwèy-de-yàng-dz-'dzwò-de. (Not the original) ‖That's a copy, not the original painting. nèy-shr 'jyǎ-de, bú-shr ywán-'hwàr.

Copy (manuscript) 'gǎw-dz. ‖Copy has been sent to the printer. 'gǎw-dz yǐ-jing 'sùng-dàw yìn-'dzèr-de-nèr-chywu-le.

CORDIAL. (*Of social acts*) 'kè-chi(-de). ‖The host gave us a cordial welcome. 'jǔ-ren hěn 'kè-chi-de 'jyē-dày wǒm. *or* 'jǔ-ren 'jyē-dày wǒm 'jyē-dày-de hěn 'kè-chi. ‖He gave us a cordial invitation to his birthday party. tā gwò-'shēngr (chǐng-'kè) gěy-wǒm °shyě-le fēng-hěn-'kè-chi-de-'shìn chǐng-wǒm chywù (*an invitation by letter*). *or* °shyà-le ge-hěn-'kě-chi-de 'chǐng-tyě (*an invitation by card*).

(*Hearty*). ‖This plan met with a cordial reception at the meeting. kǎy-'hwèy-de-shŕ-hew jèy-ge-'jì-hwà dà-jyā yì-'tīng dēw hěn 'dzàn-chéng.

(*Liqueur*). ‖He offered us a glass of cherry cordial. tā gěy-le wǒm-'měy-rén yì-bēy-yīng-taw-'ivěw.

CORN. 'ywù-mǐ, lǎw-'ywù-mi, 'bàng-dz. ‖They planted corn in some fields and wheat in others. tām dzày jǐ-kwày-'dì-li 'jùng-de shŕ lǎw-'ywù-mi, 'byé-de-'dì-li jùng-de shŕ 'mǎy-dz.

Ear of corn yí-ge-lǎw-'ywù-mǐ; one corn plant yì-kē-°'ywù-mǐ. *or* °lǎw-'ywù-mǐ. *or* °'bàng-dz. ‖He picked ten ears of corn and husked them. tā jāy-le shŕ-ge-lǎw-'ywù-mi bǎ-'pyér dēw 'hāw-le.

Grains of corn 'ywù-mǐ, ywù-mǐ-'lyèr. ‖The corn for the chickens is kept in this bin. gěy 'jī-chŕ-de-lǎw-'ywù-mi chéng-dzày jèy-ge-'pén-li.

Corn meal ywù-mǐ-'myàr, *or* bàng-dz-'myàr.

To corn (*with salt or in brine*) yān; corned yān, shyán; corned beef yān-nyéw-'rèw, shyán-nyéw-'rèw.

(*Callus; if it is painful*) 'jī-yǎn; (*if it is not painful*) 'jyǎng-dz. ‖He said that those shoes hurt his corns. tā shwō nèy-shwāng-'shyé 'mwó (*or* 'gè) tā-de-jyǎw-'jī-yǎn.

CORNER. (*Of an object*) jī-'jyǎwr, -jyǎw, -jyǎwr. ‖One corner of the box was broken open. 'hé-dz-yí-ge-jī-'jyǎwr 'lyè-kay-le. ‖He hit his head on the corner of the table. tā bǎ-'téw pèng-dzay jwō-dz-'jyǎwr-shang-le. ‖The sender's address is put at the upper left corner of the envelope. fā-'shìn-rén-'jù-jŕ shyě-dzày dzwǒ-shàng-'jyǎw. ‖You may sit over at that corner. nǐ ké-yi 'dzwò-dzay nèy-ge-jī-'jyǎwr-nèr.

(*Of a room*). *The same terms may be used, or if the idea of hiding or getting away from the crowd is included, use* 'gā-lár. ‖The man you want is sitting in that corner. nǐ-'jàw-de-nèy-ge-rén dzày nèy-ge-'jī-jyǎwr-nèr 'dzwò-je. ‖He hid himself in a corner. tā dwǒ-dzay yí-ge-'gā-lár.

(*Of a street*) 'jyē-jyǎwr, 'jyē-kěwr, gwǎy-'wār-de-'dì-fang. ‖Let's meet at the corner of 96th and Broadway. dzám dzày jyěw-shr-'lyèw-jyē gēn bwó-lǎw-'hwèy-lù 'jyē-kěwr (*or* 'jyē-jyǎwr, *or* gwǎy-'wār-de-dì-fang)-nèr jyàn. ‖Please let me off at the next corner. wǒ dzày 'shyà-yi-ge-'jyē-kěwr-nèr shyà-chywu. ‖Stop at that corner. dzày nèy-ge-gwǎy-'wār-de-dì-fang 'tíng-shya. ‖This is a corner lot. jèy-kwày-'dì dzày 'jyē-jyǎwr-shang.

(*Difficult or embarrassing position*). ‖His line of argument drove me into a corner. tā nèy-júng-'shwō-

fǎr °jyàw-wǒ gwày nán(-yǐ)-wéy-'chíng-de. *or* °jyàw-wǒ méy-fǎr 'hwéy-dá. *or* °bǐ-rén 'bǐ-de tày-'jǐn.

To corner (*drive into a corner*). ‖The thief was cornered at his mother's house. shyǎw-'tēwr dzày tā-'mā-de-'jyā jyàw-rén °gěy 'dēy-je-le. *or* °bǐ-de méy-lù 'dzěw-le. *or* °'dǔ-jù-le. *or* °'bǐ-jù-le. ‖He was cornered (*in an argument*). tā (jyàw-rén) °gěy 'dēy-je-le. *or* °*any of the other variants given in previous sentence*. *or* °bǐ-de méy-hwà 'shwō-le, *or* °dǔ-de méy-hwà 'shwō-le.

To corner (*get a monopoly of*). ‖Some people have cornered the supply of cigarettes. yěw-'rén bǎ jǐ-'yān 'twén-jí-chi-lay-le.

CORRECT. (*Right*) dwèy. ‖Is this the correct address? jèy-ge-'jù-jŕ 'dwèy-ma? ‖Yes. dwèy-le. ‖He got the correct answer to the (*nonmathematical*) problem. nèy-ge-'wèn-tí tā-de-jyě-jywé-de-'fāng-fa hěn 'dwèy. ‖He got the correct answer to the (*mathematical*) problem. nèy-ge-'swàn-tí tā-dá(-de) 'dwèy-le. *or* ney-ge-'wèn-tí tā 'swàn-chu-lay-le. ‖Your answer is not correct. nǐ-de-dá-'àn bú-'dwèy. *or* nǐ-'dá-de bú-'dwèy. ‖How many correct answers did you get? nǐ dá-'dwèy-le jǐ-ge(-'swàn-tí)?

To correct gǎy; (*of manuscripts or copy*) jyàw, 'jyàw-dwey, dwèy. ‖Please correct my mistakes in French. chǐng bǎ wǒ 'fà-wén-de-'tswòr 'gǎy-yi-gǎy. ‖That has been corrected. nèy-ge 'yǐ-jīng 'gǎy-gwo-le.

Corrected copy (*or manuscript*) 'jyàw-gwo-de-'gǎw-dz. ‖Correct the proof against the manuscript. ná 'ywán-gǎw gēn jyàw-dwèy-'gǎw-dz 'dwèy-yi-dwèy. ‖The teacher has corrected the examination papers. 'shyān-sheng 'yǐ-jīng bǎ kǎw-'jywàr °gǎy-'wán-le. *or* °kàn-'wán-le.

To correct (*reprove*). ‖She was constantly correcting the child. tā lǎw 'shwō tā-de-shyǎw-'hár 'dzèm-jr bú-'dwèy, 'nèm-jr bú-'dwèy-de.

Correct (*proper*). ‖What is the correct dress for this ceremony? wèy jèy-jyàn-'shèr yīng-dāng chwān 'shém-me?

CORRECTION. *Generally, verbal expressions are used. See* **CORRECT.**

‖Please make the necessary corrections. chǐng bǎ 'gāy-gǎy-de-'dì-fang dēw 'gǎy-lew. ‖Correction of the proofs will take three hours. 'jyàw-dwèy 'gǎw-dz. děy yùng sān-ge-jūng-'téw. ‖Behavior like this needs correction. 'lèy-sz jèy-yàngr-de-'jywǔ-dung shywū-yàw 'jyàw-jeng. *or* shyàng jèy-yàngr-de-'shíng-wey děy gǎy.

COST. To cost jŕ, děy. ‖What does this article cost? jèy-'dūng-shi jŕ (*or* děy) 'dwō-shaw-chyán? ‖How much will it cost to have this watch repaired? jèy-ge-'byǎw shyēw-li yí-shyàr děy yùng 'dwō-shaw-chyán?

To cost (*nonmonetary*). ‖His recklessness cost him his life. tā lǎw 'bù-gwǎn-bú-'gù-de (*or* tā (yīn-wèy) lǎw bù-'shyǎw-shīn-dyar or tā yīn-wey bù-kěn 'shyǎw-shin or tā 'tày dà-yì-le), °jyèw bǎ-'mìng 'sùng-le. or °yīn-tsž bǎ-'mìng sùng-le. or °(nèm) sùng-de 'mìng.

(*Financial expense*) 'jyà-chyán, jyàr. ‖He buys clothes without regard for the cost.. tā mǎy 'yī-fu bù-gwǎn °'jyà-chyán shř 'dwō-shaw. or °'jyàr shř 'dwō-shaw. ‖The cost is too much. 'jyà-chyán tày 'dwō (or 'gāw). or 'jyàr tày 'gāw. ‖The cost of living is rising. 'shēng-hwó-'fèy-yùng jŕ wàng-shàng-'jǎng.

(*What was paid earlier*). ‖He was forced to sell his stock (*merchandise*) at less than cost. bī-de tā ba 'tswén-hwò péy-je 'běr-de 'mày-le. ‖This hospital sells medicine at cost. jèy-ge-yī-'ywàn-de-'yàw shř àn-je 'ywán-jyàr mày.

(*Nonfinancial price*). ‖The cost is too high. 'dày-jyà tày-'gāw.

(*Sacrifice*). ‖Think of the cost of human lives! chǐng 'shyǎng-shyang děy °sž 'dwō-shaw-rén! or °'shī-sheng 'dwō-shaw-rén-'mìng! or °yùng 'dwō-shaw-tyáw-'mìng láy-'hwàn! ‖He succeeded at the cost of some pain and suffering. tā 'shèw-le shyē-'dzwèy, chř-le shyē-'kǔ, kě-shr 'chéng-le. ‖They won the battle at a tremendous cost. jèy-jàng tām 'shèng-le, kě-shr 'swèn-shř chí-'jùng. ‖He finished his book at the cost of his health. tā-shū swàn shyè-'wán-le, kě-shr bǎ 'shēn-dz 'dzǎw-tā-le.

At any cost, at all costs bù-gwǎn 'dày-jyà dwō-'gāw or bù-gwǎn 'shī-sheng dwō-'dà. ‖He determined to see the reorganization through at all costs. tā 'jywé-dìng yàw bǎ 'gǎy-dzǔ-de-'shěw-shywù bàn-'wán-le, °bù-gwǎn 'dày-jyà dwō-'gāw. or °bù-gwǎn 'shī-sheng dwō-'dà. ‖Carry out these instructions at any cost. jàw-je 'shywùn-lìng chywú bàn, bù-gwǎn 'shī-sheng (yěw) dwō-'dà.

COTTON. (*Raw*) 'myán-hwā. ‖This country imports two million tons of cotton a year. jèy-ge-'gwó měy-nyán-'jìn-kěw-de-'myán-hwā yěw èr-bǎy-'wàn-dwēn.

(*Medical*) 'yàw-myán-hwa. ‖Wipe away the blood with cotton. bǎ-shyě yùng 'yàw-myán-hwa 'tsā-chywu. (*as cloth*) bù, myán-'bù. ‖She bought a couple of yards of cotton. tā mǎy-le lyǎng-mǎ-°myán-'bù. or °'bù. ‖Printed cottons are in style this spring. yìn-hwār-de-myán-'bù (or yìn-hwār-'bù) 'jīn-nyan 'chwēn-tyan hěn 'shŕ-shīng. ‖She had on a cotton dress and a pair of white cotton stockings. tā chwān-le yì-shēn-(myán)-'bù-'yī-fu gēn yì-shwāng-báy-myán-shyàn-'wà-dz.

(*Thread*) shyàn. ‖Please give me a spool of white cotton (*thread*). gěy-wo yì-jéwr-báy-'shyàn.

COUGH. 'ké-sèw. ‖The baby has been coughing all night. shyǎw-'hár ké-sèw-le yì-'wǎn-shang. ‖I heard a light cough. wǒ 'tīng-jyan yěw-rén shyǎw-shēngr 'ké-sèw. ‖A cough from him warned me. tā 'ké-sèw-le yì-shēng, jyàw wǒ 'shyǎw-shin. ‖Do you have something that's good for a cough? nǐ yěw-'shém néng jř 'ké-sèw-ma?

(*Of a motor*) 'pū-chr. ‖We must be out of gas because the motor is coughing. wǒm yí-'dìng shř méy-'yéw-le 'yīn-wey 'jī-chì jŕ 'pū-chr.

COULD. (*Referring to ability*) néng, or a resultative compound with -de- (*negative -bu-*) inserted. ‖He did everything he could think of. tā néng 'shyǎng-dàw-de dēw 'dzwò-le. ‖When could you start working? nǐ °'shém-shf-hew néng °'kāy-shř dzwò-'gūng? or °chǐ-'téwr? ‖He could get here if he wanted to. tā 'shyǎng láy jyèw 'néng láy. ‖Who could have thought of that? 'nèy-ge shéy 'shyǎng-de-dàw-ne?

(*Referring to social propriety*) néng, gǎn. ‖I couldn't think of taking such a gift. dzěm-yàng-de-'lǐ-wù °wǒ dzěm néng 'shēw-ne? or °wǒ bù-gǎn 'shēw. ‖I couldn't do it! *meaning* It's too much of an honor for me. bù-gǎn-'dāng.

(*Referring to possibility*) hwèy. ‖Who could have called while I was out? wǒ 'chū-chywu de-shŕ-hew yěw shwéy hwèy 'láy-gwò-ne? *But* ‖I don't know what the trouble could be. wǒ mwō-bu-chīng shř dzěm-ge-'máw-bìng.

(*Asking permission*) 'ké-yi, néng, shíng. ‖Could I look at this, please? wǒ 'ké-yi 'kàn-yi-kan jèy-ge-ma? or néng jyàw-wo 'kàn yi-shyàr 'jèy-ge-ma? or jèy-ge wǒ 'kàn-yi-kan 'shíng-ma?

COUNT. (*Compute, enumerate*) shǔ. ‖Please count your change. chǐng-nín bǎ jǎw-hwéy-lay-de-'chyán 'shǔ yí-shyàr. ‖Count this for me. gěy-wǒ 'shǔ-yi-shǔ. ‖Have the towels been counted? 'máw-jīn 'shǔ-gwò-le-ma? ‖The boxer got up on the count of nine. dǎ-'chywán-de dzày shǔ-dàw-dì-'jyěw-shyàr de-shŕ-hew 'jàn-chǐ-lay-le. *But* ‖The count has not yet been taken. háy méy-gwò-'shù(r)-ne.

(*Include*). ‖There are fifteen people here, counting the guests. jèr lyán 'kè-ren dēw 'swàn-shang yěw shŕ-'wǔ-ge-rén. ‖The bill is five dollars, not counting the tax. jàng shř 'wǔ-kwày-chyán °'jyā-jywān dzày-'wày. or °'bú-'swàn-shang 'jyā-jywān.

(*Consider*). ‖I count myself lucky to be here. wǒ néng dzày-'jèr jēn 'swàn-shr 'ywùn-chì.

(*Matter*). ‖I'm in a great hurry; every minute counts. wǒ yěw 'jí-shèr; 'yì-fēn-jūng dēw bù-néng 'dān-wu. ‖In this broad outline, the details don't count. jèy-jǔng-'tsù-fēn-de-dà-'gāng, 'shyǎw-jyé-'mù °méy-yew 'gwān-shì. or °'bú-dà-'jùng-yàw. or °'bú-dà-'yàw-jǐn. ‖He doesn't count. tā 'wú-gwān 'jǐn-yàw. or tā 'swàn-bu-lyaw shém-me. or shǔ-bu-jáw 'tā.

To count on. (*A person*) kàw. ‖We are counting on you. wǒm chywán 'kàw-nǐ-le. ‖We can count on him. tā 'kàw-de-jù. (*A thing happening*) 'yǐ-wéy. ‖Don't count on a reply too soon. byé yǐ-wéy hěn 'kwày-de jyèw hwèy yěw 'hwéy-shìn.

(*A charge*). ‖He was convicted by the court on three counts. 'fǎ-ywàn dìng-tā sān-°shyàng-(*or* °tyaw-) 'dzwèy(-míng).

(*Nobleman*). ‖What is the proper address for a count? 'héw-jywé dāng-'myàr dzěme 'chéng-hu?

COUNTRY. (*Nation*) gwó. ‖What country were you born in? nǐ shēng-dzày 'nǎ-yì-gwó. or nǐ dzày 'nǎ-gwó shēng-'rén? ‖What country are you a citizen of? nǐ shr 'nǎy-yì-gwó-de-rén. ‖How long have you been in this country? nǐ dzày-'jèr (or nǐ dzày . . .-gwo) yěw 'dwō-shǎw-nyán-le. ‖The whole country is behind him. 'chywán-gwó-'rén-min yí-jř 'yūng-hù tā.

(*District*). ‖This is good wheat country. *meaning* It produces good wheat jèy-yí-'dày-de-'mày-dz hěn 'hǎw. or *meaning* It is good land for wheat jèy-yí-dày jùng 'mày-dz hěn 'hǎw. ‖We haven't yet visited the mountain country. wǒm háy méy 'dàw-gwo yěw-'shān-de-'dì-fang.

(*Rural region*) 'shyāng-shya. ‖I'm going to the country for the weekend. wǒ yàw dàw 'shyāng-shya-chywu gwò 'jēw-mwò. ‖The country air will do you good. 'shyāng-shya-de-'kūng-chi wèy-nǐ yí-dìng hěn 'hǎw. ‖The country roads are in bad shape. 'shyāng-shya-de-'lù dēw 'hwày-le.

COUPLE. (*Two*) lyǎng, lyǎ. ‖I want a couple of eggs. wǒ yàw lyǎng-ge-'jī-dzěr.

(*Few*) jǐ. ‖There are only a couple of pieces left. 'shèng-shya-de jř yěw 'jǐ-kwàr-le.

(*Pair*). ‖Those young people make a very nice couple. tǎm-lyǎ hěn shř yí-'dwèr. ‖We are inviting several couples for dancing this evening. wǒm jyèr 'wǎn-shang chǐng-le jǐ-dwèr-'rén láy 'tyàw-wǔ.

To couple gwà, lyán. ‖The private car has been coupled to the last car. nèy-lyàng-'jwǎn-chē 'gwà-(or lyán-)dzày 'mwò-yí-lyàng-'chē-'hèw-tew-le.

COURAGE. (*The quality; also, to be courageous*) 'yǔng-gǎn; (*somewhat literary*) 'yǔng-chì; (*daring, or a specific act of courage*) 'dǎn-dz; 'dǎn-lyàng. ‖Courage is a virtue. 'yǔng-gǎn (or yěw 'dǎn-lyàng) shr 'yì-jǔng-'dé-shing. ‖That's courage for you. chyáw 'rén-jya-de-'dǎn-dz. or chyáw 'rén-jya-de-'dǎn-lyàng. or chyáw rén-jya dwō-me 'yǔng-gǎn. or nà 'jēn swàn yěw 'dǎn-lyàng. ‖He showed courage in saying what he did. tsúng tā-nèm-'jf-chéng-bú-'hwèy ké-yi 'kàn-chu-lay °tā yěw 'yǔng-chi. or °tā 'gǎn-dzwǒ gǎn-'dǎng. ‖He has the courage to talk back to that man. tā 'jywū-rán °yěw 'dǎn-dz (or °gǎn) gēn nèy-ge-rén jyàng-'dzwèy. ‖He has the courage of his convictions. tā 'jywé-je nèm-je 'dwèy, jyèw gǎn nèm °'bàn (or °'shwō).

‖Keep up your courage. byé hwēy-'shīn.

COURSE. (*Direction*) 'háng-shyàn, or one of many roundabout ways of saying it. ‖The plane is flying a straight course. 'fēy-jī-de-'háng-shyàn 'bǐ-jř. or 'fēy-jī yì-'jř shyàng-'chyán 'fēy-ne. ‖The captain says we will have to change our course. chwán-'jǎng shwō wǒm děy gǎy-byàn °'lù-shyàn. or °'háng-shyàn. ‖He

must either change his course or go back. tā bú-shr gǎy ge-'fāng-shyàng, jyèw-shr děy wàng-hwéy 'dzěw.

(*Of action*). ‖That's the proper course. nèy-shr jèng-dàng-de-'shěw-shywù. ‖That's the best course. nèy-shr °'shàng-tsè. or °'dzwèy-hǎw-de-'fá-dz. ‖That's the only course open to me. wǒ jř néng 'dzèm-je. or wǒ jř néng dzěw 'jèy-yì-tyáw-'lù. or wǒ méy-yew 'byé-de-'fá-dz.

(*Of a river*). ‖The course of the river has been changed by the dam. já bǎ 'hé-dàw gěy 'gǎy-le.

(*Golf*). ‖When is the course open for golf? 'chyéw-chǎng-shang 'shéme-shf-hew néng dǎ 'gāw-ěr-'fū? ('chyéw-chang *also means ball park*.)

(*Part of a meal*) dàw, dàwr. Main course 'jèng-pár. ‖What do you want for the main course? 'jèng-pár shyǎng chř 'shém-me? ‖There were six courses at the dinner. yěw 'lyèw-dàw-tsày. ‖How much is the five-course dinner? yì-tsān-'wǔ-dàwr-tsày shř 'dwō-shaw-chyán?

(*Of instruction*) -kē, 'kè-chéng. ‖He never finished the medical course. tā 'yī-kē tsúng-láy méy-nyàn-'wán. ‖What courses are being offered in chemistry? hwà-shywé-'shì dēw yěw shéme 'kè-chéng?

In the course of. ‖I heard from him twice in the course of the year. wǒ 'yì-nyán-li 'jyē-dàw-gwo tā lyǎng-fēng-'shìn.

In due course. ‖You will be notified in due course. dàw 'shf-hew jwěn 'gàw-sung-ni.

As a matter of course 'dāng-ran-rú-'tsž. ‖He takes everything as a matter of course. tā yì-wéy shém-me-'shèr dēw-shr 'dāng-ran-rú-'tsž. *Compare* of course 'dāng-rán, 'dž-rán. ‖Of course I know what you mean. wǒ 'dāng-rán 'míng-bay nǐ-de-'yì-sz. ‖There will be a small charge for this service, of course. jè-ge 'dž-rán děy shēw dyǎr-'shěw-shywù-'fèy.

COURT. (*Courtyard*) ywàn-dz. ‖We have several rooms facing the court. wǒm yěw hǎw-jǐ-jyān-'wǔ-dz dēw shr 'chùng-je-'ywàn-dz-de. ‖Dogs are not allowed in the court. bù-shywǔ gěw jìn 'ywàn-dz-li-lay.

(*Game area*) 'chǎng-dz. ‖This court is too wet for a game. 'chǎng-dz tày shř.

(*Judicial body*). (*Referring to the place*) 'fǎ-ywàn; (*referring to the session*) 'fǎ-tíng. ‖When will the court be in session? 'fǎ-ywàn shéme-shf-hew 'kāy-tíng? ‖I have to attend court to pay a fine. wǒ děy dàw 'fǎ-ywàn (or 'fǎ-tíng)-chywù jyāw yì-bǐ-'fá-kwǎn. ‖The court is adjourned. *is expressed as* The judge has adjourned the session. shěn-pàn-'gwān twèy-'tíng-le.

(*Royal residence*). ‖The ambassador has not yet been received at court. dà-'shř háy 'méy-yew dzày 'hwáng-gūng 'jyē-jyàn-gwo-ne.

To court (*a girl*). ‖He used to court her years ago. dwō-nyán-yǐ-'chyán tā gēn-tā 'jy ng-gwo 'lyàn-ày. or hǎw-shyē-nyán-'chyán tā 'jwéy-gwo-tā.

(*To invite*). ‖You're courting trouble by making such a remark. nǐ shwō nèy-jǔng-'hwà shř 'dž-jǎw 'má-fan.

COVER. (*Lid or cover that belongs with the thing that is covered*) gàr, gày. Trunk cover shyāng-dz-'gàr; cover of a teapot chá-hú-'gàr; cover of a bottle (*bottle cap, not cork*) píng-dz-'gàr; etc. ‖There is a cover that goes with it. jèy-ge háy yěw ge-'gàr-ne. ‖Where are the covers for these boxes? jèy-shyē-'hé-dz-de-'gàr-ne?

Cover (*shaped like an inverted bowl, but not necessarily airtight*) jàw, jàwr.

(*Sheath, fitted case*) tàw, tàwr. Pillow cover (*pillowcase*) jěn-tew-'tàw; bed-roll cover rù-'tàw; chair cover yǐ-dz-'tàwr. ‖The room must be cleaned and the covers removed from the furniture. jèy-'wū-dz děy hǎw-hāwr-de 'shēw-shr yi-shyàr, yǐ-dz-'tàwr yě dēw děy 'jāy-le.

(*Binding*) pí, pyér, myàr. Book cover shū-'pí, shū-'pyér, shū-'myàr, fēng-'myàr. ‖The cover of this book has been torn off. jèy-běr-'shū-de-'pyér dyàw-le. ‖The design on the cover of that book is really a masterpiece. nèy-běn-'shū-shū-'pyér (or nèy-běn-'shū-fēng-'myàr)-shang-de-'tú-àn jēn-shr 'jyé-dzwò. ‖Do you want it with a cloth or paper cover? shū-'pyér yàw 'bù-de yàw 'jř-de? or 'yàw 'bù-myàr (or 'bù-pyér) yàw 'jř-myàr (or 'jř-pyér)? ‖The title on the cover is embossed in gold. shū-'pyér-shang (or shū-'myàr-shang)-de-'byāw-tí shř gǔ-chu-lay-de 'jīn-dzěr.

Magazine cover dzá-jř-'pyér, dzá-jř-de-fēng-'myàr; cover girl fēng-'myàr měy-'rér. *But* ‖I read the book from cover to cover. wǒ bǎ jèy-běr-'shū tsúng-'téwr dàw-'lyǎwr kàn-le yí-byàn.

(*Mail*). ‖Send it under separate cover. lìng jwǎng-ge-shìn-'fēngr.

(*For a bed*). (*Quilt*) bèy; (*blanket*) 'tǎn-dz; (*sheet*) běy-'dān-dz. ‖I didn't have enough covers last night. wǒ dzwór-'wǎn-shang °bèy (or 'tǎn-dz) méy-gày 'gèw. or °méy-gày 'gèw.

(*Shelter*) ‖ nat building served as a better cover than we thought it would. méy-shyǎng-'dàw dzày nèy-ge-'léw-li 'dwǒ-je bǐ 'byé-chùr 'chyáng. ‖Take cover! 'dwǒ-chi-lay! ‖Let's take cover under that tree. dzám dzày nèy-kē-shù-'dǐ-shya 'dwǒ-yi-dwǒ. ‖They took cover under that tree. tām dzày nèy-kē-shù-'dǐ-shya 'dwǒ-je. or tām dwǒ dzày nèy-kē-shù-'dǐ-shya.

To cover (*spread on, cover a flat surface*) pū. ‖The floor was completely covered by a large rug. kě-je-wū-dz-de-'dì-shang 'pū-le yí-kwày-dà-dì-'tǎn. ‖The floor is covered with a mat. 'dì-shang pū-je 'shí. ‖They used fine silk to cover the bottom of the trunk. tām dzày-'shyāng-dz-'dyěr-shang pū 'chéw-dz. or tām yùng 'chéw-dz pū shyāng-dz-'dyěr. ‖The mattress won't even cover a small bed. 'rù-dz lyán 'shyǎw-chwáng dēw 'pū-bu-mǎn. ‖Cover the road with gravel first. shyàn-dzày 'lù-shang· pū yì-tséng-'shř-tew-'dzěr.

To cover (*spread over, cover an object or a person*) 'gày(-shang). ‖He covers the bed with a blanket and covers himself with his overcoat. tā ná 'tǎn-dz pū-'chwáng, 'dž-jǐ gày-je dà-'yī. or tā ná 'tǎn-dz pū-dzay 'chwáng-shang, yèw ná dà-'yī gěy dž-jǐ 'gày-shang. ‖That hole should be filled, not covered. nèy-ge-'kū-lung děy 'tyán-shàng, bù-néng shwō-shř 'gày-shang jyèw 'swàn-le. ‖It's best to have the well covered. jǐng 'gày-shang-dyar tsáy 'hǎw. ‖Cover him with the quilt. ná-'bèy gěy-ta 'gày-shang. or gěy-ta 'gày-shang 'bèy. ‖Cover the bowl with this book. ná jèy-běn-'shū bǎ-wǎn 'gày-shang. ‖He's too tall and the quilt is too short; when his head is covered, his feet stick out. tā tàv 'cháng, bèy tày 'dwǎn; 'gày-shang 'téw, lèw-je 'jyǎw. ‖Cover the pot if you want to boil the water. yàw shyǎng bǎ-shwěy jǔ-'kāy-le děy bǎ-hú 'gày-shang. ‖Cover the pot with the lid. ná-'gàr bǎ-hú 'gày-shang. ‖Put the vase here to cover this cigarette burn. bǎ hwā-'píng fàng-'jèr hǎw bǎ yān-shāw-de-'dì-fang 'gày-shang (or 'jē-shang). ‖Cover it with the tablecloth; then it won't show. ná jwō-'bù 'gày-shang (or 'méng-shang) jyèw 'kàn-bu-jyàn-le. ‖Tack a calender there to cover the stain. ná fēn-'ywè-fen-páy yùng èn-'dyēngr dīng-dzay nàr, hǎw bǎ nèy-kwày-'dzāng-de-dì-fang 'gày-shang. ‖You can cover it by sticking a piece of paper on it. ná jāng-'jř 'jān-shang jyèw 'kàn-bu-jyàn-le.

To cover *a part of the body, or an object with something flexible* méng(-shang). ‖Those girls cover their heads with veils. nèy-shyē-'nywǔ-rén ná méng-téw-'shā méng-je 'téw. ‖You can make a tracing by covering it with a piece of thin paper. ná jāng-báw-'jř 'méng-shang (or 'pū-shang, or 'jàw-shang) jyèw ké-yi 'myáw-shya-lay-le. ‖Cover his eyes (*blindfold him*). bǎ tā-de-'yǎn 'méng-shang. ‖Cover the dough with a wet cloth and wait until it rises. ná kwày-shř-'bù bǎ-myàn 'méng-shang, děng-dàw 'fā-chi-lay. ‖They covered the dead man's face with a handkerchief. tām yùng shěw-'jywàr bǎ sž-rén-de-lyǎn 'méng-shang (or 'gày-shang).

To cover *with the hands in order to hide something* wǔ. ‖He covered it with his hands. tā (yùng-'shěw) 'wǔ-je. ‖Don't cover it up (*with your hand*). byé 'wǔ-je. ‖There was a letter on the desk; she covered it with her hands and asked me to guess who it was from. shū-'jwōr-shang yěw yì-feng-'shìn; tā bǎ-shìn 'wǔ-je jyàw-wo tsāy shř shwéy-'shyě-de. ‖The child covers his eyes with his tiny hands and says, "I'm gone!" shyǎw-'hár yùng shyǎw-'shěwr bǎ 'yǎn-jīng 'wǔ-shang, jyèw 'shwō-lā "wǒ méy-le!" ‖When the guns are fired he covers his ears with his hands. fàng-'pàw-de-shř-hew tā wǔ-je 'ěr-dwo. ‖She covers her mouth with her hand, then giggles. tā wǔ-je 'dzwěn 'gēr-a-gēr-de 'shyàw.

To cover *with something that drapes over the edges* jàw. ‖Cover the sofa (*with a sofa cover*) before you dust the room. bǎ 'shā-fā 'jàw-shang dzày dǎn ('wū-dz). or (*with newspapers or similar materials for protection*) bǎ 'shā-fā 'gày-shang dzày . . . . ‖She wears a satin gown but covers it with a cotton one. tā chwān-de shř 'dwàn-páwr, 'wày-tew kě-shr 'iáw-je jyàn-'bù-gwàr.

To cover (*in order to imprison, protect, preserve, etc.*) kèw. ‖They caught a frog and covered it with a large bowl. tā-men 'dày-le ge-'há-ma, ná ge-wăn 'kèw-shang-le. ‖He covered the butterfly with a (*bag-shaped*) net. tā ná-'dēwr bǎ hú-'tyěr 'kèw-ju-le ‖Cover the sugar so the flies won't get at it. bǎ-'táng 'kèw-shang (*or* 'gày-shang, *or* 'jàw-shang, *or* 'méng-shang), byé jyàw 'tsāng-ying dzūng.

To cover (*to avoid light or curious stares*) jē. ‖He covered his face with a newspaper (*as on the beach*) and went to sleep. tā ná 'bàw-jř 'jē-shang (*or* 'méng-shang) 'lyǎn jyèw shwèy-'jáw-le. ‖He covered his face with a newspaper when he left the court. tā tsúng 'fǎ-ywàn chū-lay de-shŕ-hew ná 'bàw-jř °'jē-je lyǎn. *or* °'gày-je lyǎn. *or* °'dǎng-je lyǎn.

To cover (*conceal from sight*) dǎng. ‖He hung the mirror there to cover a black spot on the wall. tā bǎ 'jìng-dz gwà-dzay nàr 'wèy-de-shr bǎ 'chyáng-shang-de hēy-'dyǎn-dz °'dǎng-shang. *or* °'gày-shang. *or* °'jē-shang.

To cover (*shade from the sun with an awning*). ‖The porch is not covered. láng-dz-shang méy-(gày)-'dyēngr.

To cover with clothes. (*The head*) dày; (*the back*) pēy; (*entire body*) gwǒ, wéy. ‖Keep your head covered in this weather. jèy-jǔng 'tyān-chi dzwèy-hǎw 'téw-shang dày dyǎr-'dūng-shi. ‖She covered herself with a blanket. tā 'pēy-je (*or* gwǒ-je, *or* wéy-je) tyáw-'tǎn-dz.

To be covered with (*Chinese uses expressions meaning is all, as we sometimes do*. ‖He was covered with blood (*he was all blood*). tā-mǎn-'shēn dēw-shr 'shyě. ‖He was covered with mud. tā-mǎn (*or* chywán)-shēn dēw-shr 'ní. *or* tā nùng-le yì-shēn ní. ‖His face was covered with mud. tā-mǎn-'lyǎn dēw-shř 'ní. *or* tā-'lyǎn-shang chywán shř 'ní. ‖The car was covered with mud. mǎn-'chē-shang dēw shř 'ní. ‖He was covered with embarrassment by her remark. tā nèm yì-'shwō jyàw-ta (chywán-shēn) 'shyǎn-je 'jywū-tsù bù-'ān.

To cover (*with dirt, sand, or gravel, but not by actual burial*) máy-shang. ‖They covered the gun with sand. tām ná 'shā-dz bǎ-'chyāng 'máy-shang-le. ‖Cover it with earth. ná-'tǔ 'máy-shang.

To cover up (*referring to mistakes, crimes, etc.*). (*By keeping people ignorant of something bad*) mán; (*to conceal from higher authorities*) 'méng-bì; (*to conceal by making alterations in the unpleasant facts*) 'yǎn-shř; (*by confusing others*) 'méng-hwèn, mēng, hwèn; (*something which is not necessarily bad*) 'jē-gày, 'jē-yǎn. ‖Can we ask him to cover it up for us? chǐng-tā gěy 'jē-gày-jē-gay (*or* 'jē-yǎn-jē-yǎn) 'shíng-ma? ‖He tried to cover it up so his superior wouldn't know. tā shyǎng-'fár °jyàw 'shàng-sž bù-jř-'dàw. *or* °'mán-je 'shàng-sž. *or* °bǎ 'shàng-sž 'mán-ju. *or*

°'yǎn-shř-yǎn-shř hǎw jyàw 'shàng-sž bù-jř-'dàw. *or* °'yǎn-shř-yǎn-shř hǎw bǎ 'shàng-sž 'mán-gwo-chywu. *or* tā shyǎng 'méng-bì 'shàng-sž. ‖He tried to cover up his own obvious mistakes by confusing others. míng-'míng-shř tā-dž-jǐ-de-'tswòr, kě-shr tā shyǎng °'hwèn-gwo-chywu. *or* °'mēng-gwo-chywu. *or* °méng-hwèn-de byé-rén 'kàn-bu-chu-láy. ‖He's only trying to cover up his embarrassment when he acts so nonchalant. tā-nà-mǎn-bú-'dzày-hu-de-yàng-dz bú-'gwò-shr yàw rén 'kàn-bu-chū tā-'shīn-li dwō-me bù-'ān. ‖That's something that needs to be covered up. nèy-shr mán-'rén-de-shèr. ‖That's something you can't cover up (*though you are trying*). nǐ-nà-shr yǎn-'ěr-dàw-'líng-nga (*literary quotation*). ‖He did that to cover up. tā-jè-shr yàw yǎn-rén-'ěr-'mù (*literary quotation; referring to covering people's ears and eyes*). ‖He carefully covered up all his mistakes. tā bǎ tā-de-'tswòr mán-de hěn 'dž-shì. ‖He acts as if he has something to cover up. tā nèm 'jē-je-yǎn-'yǎn-de hǎw 'shyàng yěw dyǎr-'shèr děy mán-'rén-shr-de. ‖He used his high social position to cover up (*as a cover for*) his crimes. tā yùng tā-dzày-shè-'hwèy-shang-'gāw-gwèy-de-'dì-wey láy 'jē-yǎn tā fàn-'dzwèy-de-'shíng-wéy. *or* tā jìng-gàn 'hwày-shèr; tā-dzày-shè-'hwèy-shang-de-'dì-wey bú-gwò-shr 'ná-lay yǎn-rén-'ěr-'mù.

To cover (*to include or comprehend*). ‖This book covers the subject pretty well. nèy-jyàn-'shèr jèy-běn-'shū jyǎng-de hěn 'shyáng-shì. ‖He covered all angles of the problem in 45 minutes. nèy-ge-'wèn-tí tā tsúng gè-'fāng-myàn jyǎng (ěr-chyě jyǎng)-de hěn 'shyáng-shì, kě-shr jř yùng-le sž-snr-'wǔ-fēn-jūng. ‖I've covered a lot of ground today. wǒ jīn-tyān 'jyǎng-le bù-shǎw-'shèr (*in speaking or discussing*). *or* wǒ 'jīn-tyān 'dzěw-le bù-shǎw-'lù (*in physical traveling*). ‖The train covers the distance in two hours. 'kwày-chē dzěw lyǎ-'jūng-téw jyèw 'dàw.

Under cover. ‖He carried out his plan under cover. tā jàw-je tā-de-'jì-hwà °'àn-jūng, jyèw dēw 'bàn-le. *or* °àn 'dì-li, ... *or* °'tēw-je, ... *or* °bú-jyàw rén 'jř-dàw, ... ‖He's been under cover for a year. tā °'dwǒ-le (*or* °dwǒ-chi-lay) yěw 'yì-nyán-le. *or* tā °'tsáng-le (*or* °tsáng-chi-lay) yěw 'yì-nyán-le. ‖He did it under cover of darkness. tā dwǒ (*or* tsáng)-dzày hēy-'dyěr-li 'gàn-de. *or* (*At night*) tā dzày 'yè-li 'gàn-de.

(*Handle*). A new salesman has been taken on to cover this territory. gù-le yí-ge-shīn-de-twèy-shyā v-'ywán gwǎn jèy-yí-dày-'dì-fang. *or* shīn-'gù-le-ge-rén dzày jèy-yí-'dày 'twèy-shyāw.

(*Threaten*). ‖He had us covered with a revolver. tā ná shěw-'chyāng bǐ-je wǒ-men.

(*Protect*). ‖Are you covered by insurance? nǐ yěw bǎw-'shyǎn-ma? ‖Artillery covered the enemy's retreat. 'dí-rén-'twèy-chywè-de-shŕ-hew yěw (*or* yùng) 'pàw-hwǒ 'yǎn-hù. ‖The bombers are covered by fighters. hūng-jà-'jī yěw jàn-dēw-'jī 'yan-hù.

(*Include*). ‖I believe that covers everything. wǒ shyǎng 'gāy-shwō-de dēw 'shwō-le.

COW. nyéw. ‖The milk comes from their own cows. nyéw-'nǎy shr̀ tām-dz-jī-de-'nyéw-de. ‖The cows are milked at six. *is expressed as* The milking is done at six. 'lyèw-dyǎn-jūng jǐ-'nǎy.

(*To intimidate*). ‖I felt somewhat cowed in his presence. dzày tā-'gēn-chyar wǒ-'jywé-de yěw-dyar-dǎn-'chywè.

COWARD. dǎr-'shyǎw-de-rén; (*a chicken-hearted person*) 'jī-dǎn-dz. ‖He's a coward. tā shr̀ dǎr-'shyǎw-de-rén. *or* tā shr̀ 'jī-dǎn-dz.

To be a coward *or* to be cowardly dǎr-'shyǎw, dǎn-dz hěn 'shyǎw, méy 'dǎn-dz, shyǎw-'dǎr, dǎn-'chywè. ‖Like a coward, he gave up the fight. tā hǎv shyàng dǎr-'shyǎw-shr-de, jyèw rèn-'shū-le.

CRACK. To get cracked (*without falling apart*) 'lyè. ‖The windows in my room are cracked. wǒ-'wūr-li-de-'chwǎng-hù 'lyè-le.

Crack. (*a split; if the sides are still together*) 'lyè-wén, 'lyè-wér; (*if the sides have separated*) 'lyè-kěwr, 'lyè-fèngr, 'lyè-dz, fèngr; (*crack in a large object, which allows something to come through*) nwō-'kěw-dz, 'kěw-dz. ‖This crack must be repaired. jèy-tyáw-'lyè-wén (*or* 'lyè-wér, 'lyè-kěwr, 'lyè-fèngr, 'lyè-dz, 'fèngr) yí-dìng děy 'shyēw-li. *or* jèy-ge-hwō-'kěw-dz (*or* jèy-ge-'kěw-dz) yí-dìng děy 'dǔ-le. ‖The crack in the dike is getting wider. tí (*or* dī)-shang-de-hwō-'kěw-dz ywè-láy ywè-'dà, *or* tí-shang-kǎy-de-'kěw-dz ywè-láy ywè-'dà.

To get cracked (*and broken to pieces*) swèy ‖Be careful that the records don't crack. 'shyǎw-shin byé bǎ 'pyān-dz nùng 'swèy-le. ‖Could you send some cracked ice to my room? sùng dyar-swèy-'bīng shàng-lay 'shíng-bu-shíng?

To crack *something.* *Any number of resultative compounds may be constructed from the following combinations. For the first element, expressing the way in which the cracking is done, use* yā (*to press down on*); jyā (*press on two sides*); jǐ (*press on two or more sides*); dzá (*crush with a heavy object*); chyǎw (*to give a light, sharp blow*); pèng (*to collide with*); jwàng (*to swing something against horizontally*). *For the second element, expressing the result, use* kǎy (*to open*); pwò (*be broken*) swèy (*be shattered*); lyè (*be cracked*); *or expressions such as* chū 'lyè-wér (*be cracked but still holding together*), chéng lyǎng-'bàr (*be cracked in two*); cheng fēn-swèy (*be cracked to pieces*). *For example* 'dzá-kǎ (*to crack open by hitting something with a heavy object, as a coconut*); 'chyǎw-lyè (*to crack but not break by a light, sharp blow, as an eggshell*). ‖If we can't open the safe (*any other way*) we'll have to crack it (open). baw-shyan-'shyāng 'yàw-shr kǎy-bu-'kǎy-de-hwa wǒm jyéw děy 'dzá-kǎy. ‖This is a tough nut to crack. (*Literally,*

of a walnut) jèy-ge-'hé-tew jēn 'yìng, jǐ-bu-'pwò. (*Figuratively*) hěn nán 'bàn.

Crack up. *Similar resultative compounds are used.* ‖I was afraid that the driver would crack up the car. wǒ 'pà-de jyèw-shr̀ kǎy-'chē-de hwèy bǎ-'chē jwàng-'hwày-le. ‖The plane cracked up near the landing field. 'fēy-jī dzày jyàng-lwò-'chǎng-'fù-jìn shwāy-'hwěy-le.

(*Sharp sound*). ‖I thought I heard the crack of a rifle. wǒ 'fǎng-fu 'tīng-jyàn yì-'shēngr-chyāng-shyǎng shr̀-de.

(*Wisecrack*). ‖I don't mean that as a dirty crack. nèy-jywù-'hwà wǒ bìng méy-yew hwày-'yì-sz. ‖He made a crack about her looks. tā ná tā-de-lyǎn 'kǎy wán-shyàw-lay-je. ‖He cracked several jokes before beginning the speech. tā yǎn-'shwō yǐ-chyán shyān shwō-le hǎw-jǐ-ge-'shyaw-hwàr.

(*Try*). ‖Would you like to take a crack at the job? nǐ shyǎng 'shr̀ yí-shyàr-ma?

(*Expert*). ‖She is a crack typist. tā shr̀ ge-hěn-hǎw-de-dǎ-'dz-de *or* tā dǎ-'dz hǎw-'jí-le.

CREAM. (*Top milk*) nǎy-'yéw, nǎy-'pí. ‖Do you take cream with your coffee? nǐ hē kā-'fēy yàw °nǎy-'yéw-ma? *or* °nǎy-'pí-ma?

(*Choice part*) 'dzwèy-hǎw-de. ‖Only the cream of the candidates will be accepted jǐ chyw̌ 'hèw-shywǎn-rén-li 'dzwèy-hǎw-de. *or* jǐ yěw 'dzwèv-hǎw-de tsáy chyw̌ǔ-de-shàng. ‖We were shown only the cream of the crop. jyàw-wom-'kàn-de jǐ shr̀ 'dzwèy-haw-de(-'jwāng-jya *if referring to a literal crop*).

(*Medicinal*) yàw-'gāw, gāw-dz-'yàw. ‖Apply this cream twice a day. jèy-ge-yàw-'gāw (*or* jèy-ge-gāw-dz-'yàw) méy-'tyān shàng 'lyǎng-tsz̀. ‖Do you have any (*medicinal*) facial cream? nǐ yěw tsē-'lyǎn-de-yàw-'gaw-ma?

Cold cream shywè-hwār-'gāw.

(*Color*) 'yá-shǎr(-de). ‖The walls are cream with a blue border. chyáng shr̀ 'yá-shǎr-de děy 'lán-byār.

CREATURE. 'hwó-wù(r), *or, if a particular type of creature is intended, Chinese names it.* ‖If you keep a living creature you must feed it. 'yàw-shr yǎng 'hwó-wù(r) jyèw děy-'wèy. ‖The poor creatures (*meaning kittens*) haven't been fed. kě-'lyàn-de-shyǎw-'māwr háy méy-'wèy-ne.

(*Detestable person*) 'jyā-hwo, 'dūng-shi. ‖Who is that creature at the information desk? dzày-wèn-shr̀-'chù-de-nèy-ge-°'jyā-hwo (*or* °'dūng-shi) shr̀ 'shwéy?

CREDIT. (*In finance, loans*) 'shìn-yùng. Credit loan 'shìn-yùng-dày-'kwǎn. ‖His credit is very good. tā-de-'shìn-yùng hěn 'hǎw. ‖His credit is bad. tā méy-yew 'shìn-yùng. *or* tā-'shìn-yùng °bú-dà 'hǎw. *or* °hěn 'hwày.

(*In buying*) To buy on credit jì-'jàng; on credit bú-yùng fù shyàn-'kwǎn. ‖Will they give us credit at this store? jèy-'pù-dz néng jyàw-wǒm jì-'jàng-ma? ‖His credit is good anywhere. tā dzày-'nǎr dēw néng jì-'jàng. ‖The manager said that my credit is good.

'jīng-lǐ shwŏ wŏ 'ké-yǐ jì-'jàng. ‖They are willing to sell the furniture on credit. tām 'ywàn-yi bǎ 'jyā-jywù 'mày-gey-wom, bú-yùng fù 'shyàn-kwǎn.

(Balance). ‖The books show a credit of five dollars in your favor. 'jàng-shàng háy 'tswén-je nín 'wǔ-kwày-chyán.

(Honor) 'gūng-law. To give credit to gwēy-'gūng-ywú, *(praise)* chēng-'dzàn, *(to an underling)* 'kwā-jyǎng. ‖The credit is entirely his. 'gūng-law chvwan-shr 'tā-de. ‖He takes the credit, but we get the blame. 'gūng-law shř 'tā-de, 'tswòr-shr 'dzám-de. ‖We have to credit him with finding it. jèy-ge néng 'jǎw-jəw, °wǒm děy gwēy-'gung-ywú 'tā. *or* °wòm 'bù-néng bù-'shwō shř 'tā-de-'gūng-law. ‖They give him credit for his foresight. tām chēng-'dzàn tā yěw shyan-'jyàn-jř-'míng. ‖The commander-in-chief gives him credit for his quick decision. dzǔng-sž-'lìng 'kwā-jyǎng tā pàn-'dwàn-de 'kwày. ‖The President gives him credit for doing that. tā dzwò nèy-jyàn-'shèr 'dzǔng-tǔng hěn. 'kwā-jyǎng-ta. ‖They gave the doctor credit for curing him. tā-de-'bìng wán-chywár jř-'hàw-le tām shwō dēw-shr nèy-ge-'dày-fu-de-'gūng-law. ‖He takes all the credit. tā 'dž-jǐ shwō dēw-shr tā-de-'gūng-law. *or* tā wán-chywán gwēy-gūng-ywu tā-'dž-jǐ. ‖He took credit for the planning, though others did the work. swéy-ran shèr dēw-shr 'byé-rén-'dzwò-de, kě-shr tā shwō chéw-'bèy-de-'gūng-law shř tā-de.

(Source of praise). ‖He is a credit to his profession. tā wèy 'túng-yè °'dzēng-gwāng. *or* °'jēng-gwāng.

(To believe) shìn. ‖Can you credit the reports in that newspaper? nǐ néng 'shìn nèy-ge-bàw-de-'shyāw-shi-ma?

(Academic) shywé-'fēn, shywé-'fēr. ‖He needs three more credits in order to graduate. tā háy děy nyàn sān-ge-shywé-'fēr tsáy néng bì-'yè.

CRIME *(Case)* 'àn-dz. ‖The police are investigating the crime. jīng-'chá jèng-dzav 'dyàw-chá nèy-ge-'àn-dz.

(Offense) 'àn-chíng. ‖This is a serious crime. 'àn-chíng jùng-'dà.

(Violation of law). Chinese uses expressions derived from verbal phrases. To commit a crime fàn-'fǎ, fàn-'dzwèy; crime *(in general)* fàn-'fǎ-de-shèr, bù-fǎ-'shíng-wéy. ‖He committed a crime. tā fàn-'fǎ-le. *or* tā fàn-'dzwèy-le. ‖What is his crime? tā fàn-de shémme °'dzwèy? *or* °'fǎ? *or* tā-de-'dzwèy-míng shř 'shémme? ‖Crime has decreased since the declaration of martial law. 'shywān-bù jyè-yán-'lìng yǐ-hèw 'fàn-'fǎ-de-shèr 'shǎw-le. *or* 'bù-fǎ-'shíng-wéy 'shǎw-le.

(Disgraceful act). (Mild terms) kě-'chǐ, bú-'dwèy, kě-'hèn, tǎw-'yàn; *(strong terms)* gǎy-'sž, gǎy-'shā, dà-nì-bú-'dàw. ‖It's a crime! jēn-shr *(or* 'jyàn-jŕ*)* °kě-'chǐ. *or* °bú-'dwèy, *etc.* ‖The way they run these busses is a crime! 'gung-gung-chì-'chē bàn-lǐ-dàw dzěm-ge-'dì-bu jyàn-jŕ shř °gǎy-'sž, *etc.*

CROP. 'jwāng-jyà; *(yield)* 'shēw-chéng. ‖They get three crops a year. tām yì-'nyán shēw 'sān-tsž-'jwāng-jya. ‖How are the crops around here? *(In regard to growing conditions)* jèr-'fù-jin-de-'jwāng-jya dzěm-'yàng? *(In regard to yield)* jèr-'fù-jin-de-'shēw-cheng dzěme-'yàng? ‖The farmers expect a good crop this year. 'núng-rén pàn-je 'jīn-nyán shēw-cheng 'hǎw.

A crop of . . . *(a yield of . . .)* 'shēw-de-. . .: *(a growing crop of . . .)* . . . 'jǎng-de; *(specifying one of several in a period of time)* tsž . . . . ‖That's a good crop of wheat. *(Growing)* 'jīn-nyán 'mày-dz 'jǎng-de hěn 'hǎw. *(Harvested)* (nèy-tsž-) (shēw-de-) 'mày-dz hěn 'hǎw. ‖The price of land is high here because it yields three crops of wheat a year. jèr dì-'jyà 'gāw, yīn-wey kě-yi yì-'nyán-li shēw 'sān-tsž-'mày-dz. ‖Have you harvested that wheat (crop)? *is expressed always without crop in Chinese.* shyàw-'mày 'gē-le méy-yew?

A crop of *(figurative)* jen. ‖A new crop of rumors grew up after the conference. 'hwèy 'wán-le yǐ-'hèw, yí-jèn-'yáw-yán yew 'chǐ-lay-le.

To crop up fā-'shēng *or expressed with* many 'dwō. ‖Many new questions are sure to crop up. hěn-'dwō-de-'shīn-'wèn-tí yí-'dìng hwèy fā-'shēng. *or* 'chyáw-je-ba, °'shèr háy 'dwō-je-ne. *or* °'wèn-tí háy 'dwō-je-ne.

CROSS. *(Religious symbol)* shŕ-dz-'jyà *(literally, a framework shaped like the character for shŕ, meaning ten).* ‖Do you see that church with the big cross on the steeple? nǐ 'kàn-jyen nèy-ge-lǐ-bày-'táng-le-ma? nèy-ge-tǎ-'jyār-shang yěw ge-dà-shŕ-dz-'jyà-de?

(Crisscross mark). (X-shaped) chǎr; *(+-shaped)* shŕ-'dzèr. ‖Put a cross (X) on the map to show where we are. dzày-dì-'tú-shang dǎ *(or* hwà*)* ge-'chai hǎw 'jř-chū-láy wǒm dzày-'nǎr. ‖If you can't sign your name, make a cross instead. nǐ yàw bú-hwèy chyān-'míng, hwà ge-shŕ-'dzèr yě 'shíng.

To cross gwò. ‖Cross the street on the green signal. dēng-'lywù-de-shŕ-hew gwò-'jyē. ‖Where can we cross the river? wǒm dzày-nǎr ké-yi gwò-'hé?

To cross out 'lá-(shya-)chywu, 'hwà-(shya-)chywu, 'hwà-dyàw. ‖Cross out the items you don't want. bǎ nǐ bú-'yàw-de dēw °'lá-shya-chywu. *or* °'lá-le-chywu. *or* °'hwà-shya-chywu. *or* °'hwà-dyàw-le.

Cross *one's* fingers. ‖Keep your fingers crossed! *is expressed as* Hope for us to succeed. 'shī-wàng wǒm chéng-'gūng-ba. ‖I've got my fingers crossed. *is expressed as* My heart's in my mouth. wǒ shywán-je ge-'shīn. *or as* I'm worried. wǒ hěn dān-'shīn.

Cross *someone's* path. ‖I've never happened to cross his path. wǒ 'tsung-láy méy-'ywù-jyàn-gwo tā.

Cross *one's* mind. ‖It never crossed my mind that he would object. wǒ 'tsúng-láy méy-'shyǎng-dàw 'tā hwèy fǎn-'dwèy.

(Hybrid). ‖The mule is a cross between the horse and the donkey. 'lwó-dz shř 'mǎ gēn-'lywú 'pèy-chu-lay-de.

CROWD. *(Mob or set)* chywún, ('dà-)shyē, bāng, hwǒ-dz *(all these terms are measures:* 'hwǒ-dz *and* bāng *imply a certain amount of organization)*; rén, dà-'dwèy-de-rén. ‖A crowd gathered on the street corner. jyē-'kěwr-shang 'jywù-le °yì-'chywǔn-rén. or °yì-'bāng-rén. or °yì-'hwǒ-dz-rén. or °yí-('dà-)shyè- (ðr̃ °'hǎw-shyǎ-)rén. ‖Let's follow the crowd. dzám 'gēn-je rén 'dzěw-ba. or dzám gēn-je dà-'dwèy-de-rén 'dzěw-ba. ‖He runs around with a different crowd. tā gēn lìng yì-'bāng-rén 'hwèn. or tā gēn lìng yì-'hwǒ-dz-rén 'hwèn. *(etc.)* ‖That's a smart crowd. nèy-'hwǒ-dz (-rén) hěn 'hwā-shaw. or nèy-'bāng-rén . . . *(etc.)* ‖This is a mixed crowd. jèy-'chywún-rén *(etc.)* hěn 'dzá. ‖He is running around with a bad crowd. tā gēn yì-chywún *(etc.)* -°'hwày-rén láy-wang. or °'hú-péng-gěw-'dǎng láy-wang.

To crowd *(push forward)* yūng; *(press from all sides)* jǐ. ‖More and more people crowded into the square. jǐ-jìn-'chǎng-dz-láy-dè-rén ywè-'láy ywè-'dwō. ‖Don't crowd me! byé 'jǐ-wo! ‖The people crowded against the window to look in. rén dēw 'yūng-dzày (or 'jǐ-dzày) 'chwāng-hu-nàr wàng-lǐ 'chyáw. ‖The theater was crowded to capacity. shì-'ywán-dz-li jǐ-'mǎn-le rén.

CRUEL. *(Physically; of a person, when the cruelty is apt to result in death or mutilation)* tsán-rěn; *(of an act or of treatment)* hěn, kǔ; to be cruel to 'nywè-dày. ‖The kidnappers were very cruel to the child. bǎng-'pyàwr-de 'nywè-dày nèy-ge-'bǎng-chywu-de-shyǎw-'hár láy-je. or bǎng-'pyàwr-de dày nèy-ge-'bǎng-chywu-de-shyǎw-'hár dày-de tǐng °'tsán-rěn-de. or °'hěn-de. or °'kǔ-de.

(Severe, of laws or punishments) yán; not severe sūng, kwān. ‖The punishments under the new laws are less cruel than under the old. shīn-fǎ-'gwēy-dìng-de-'chěng-fá °méy-yew yǐ-'chyán-nàme-'yán. or °bǐ yǐ-'chyán-de sūng 'dwō-le. or °bǐ yǐ-'chyán-de kwān 'dwō-le.

(Mentally) 'kè-be, swěn; to be cruel to 'wā-ku. ‖I didn't pay any attention to his cruel remarks. tā-nèy-jǔng-'kè-be-'hwà wǒ jr̃-jr̃-bù-'lǐ. or tā-shwō-de-'hwà hěn °'kè-be (or °'swěn), kě-shr wǒ méy-'lǐ-ta. or tā-de-'hwà 'wā-ku rén 'wā-ku-de hěn 'lì-hay, kě-shr wǒ méy-'lǐ-ta.

CRUSH. *Many resultative compounds can be constructed by combining the following elements. For the first element, describing the way in which the crushing is done, use* yā *(to apply steady pressure from above)*; jǐ *(to press from two or more sides)*; yà *(to crush by moving or rolling pressure)*; dzá *(to give a heavy blow)*; pèng *(to collide)*; *etc. For the second element, describing the result, use* pwò *(be broken)*; hwày *(be broken or*

ruined).; sz *(to die)*; byǎn *(to be flat)*; swèy *(to be shattered)*; lyè *(to crack)*; sǎn *(to be in parts)*; byě *(to be dry, flat, empty)*; *etc. For example to crush flat by pressure* 'yā-byǎn; to crush *to death by a collision* 'pèng-sž; *etc.* ‖The package was crushed in transit. 'bāw-gwǒ ywùn-de-shŕ-hew °jǐ-'hwày-le. or °jǐ-'byǎn-le, *etc.* ‖I want this (crushed) hat repaired. wǒ shyǎng bǎ jèy-ge-'yā-hwày-le-'màw-dz 'páy-yi-shyar. ‖We were nearly crushed (to death) while leaving the theater. wǒm chū shì-'ywán-dz de-shŕ-hew 'chà-dyǎr (méy-) 'jǐ-sž.

See also BREAK, CRACK.

A crush *(crowd).* ‖There was a crush when they opened the gates. dà-mén yì-'kāy dà-'jyā °lwàn-'jǐ. or °'yì-yūng ěr-'rù.

(Broken in spirit). ‖We were crushed by the announcement. wǒm 'tīng-jyàn bàw-'gàw yi-hèw, jēn shŕ 'shāng-shin 'jí-le. ‖The telegram contained crushing news. dyàn-bàw-de-'shyāw-shi hěn 'hwày.

(Infatuation). ‖She has a crush on that actor. tā jyàw (or tā ràng) nèy-ge-'shì-dz gěy 'mí-le. or tā 'mí-shang-le nèy-ge-'shì-dz-le. or nèy-ge-'shì-dz jyàw-tā °jáw-'mí-le or °rù-'mí-le.

CRY. *(To weep)* kū; *(to weep loudly)* háw, háw-táw dà-'kū. ‖The baby cried all night. shyǎw-'hár °kū-le yí-'yè. or °háw-le yí-'yè. ‖She cried when she heard the news. tā tīng-jyàn nèy-ge-'shyāw-shi yǐ-'hèw, 'kū-le yì-chǎng. ‖She cried loudly. tā háw-táw dà-'kū. ‖She cried loudly and shouted. tā yèw 'kū yèw 'hǎn. or tā 'dà-kū dà-'hǎn. or tā yì-byār háw-táw dà-'kū, yì-byār 'hǎn. ‖She had a good cry and felt better. tā 'kū-le yì-'chǎng (or yí-'jèn) hǎw 'dwō-le.

To cry out 'jyàw-hwan, hǎn. ‖The pain was so great that he cried out. tā téng-de jŕ 'jyàw-hwan.

(Of animals) 'jyàw(-hwan), háw. ‖The dog cried for a while. gěw 'háw-le (or 'jyàw-hwar-le) yì-hwer. ‖The cat cried for a while. máw 'jyàw(-hwan)-le yì-hwěr. ‖You can hear the cry of gulls from this window. nǐ tsúng jèy-ge-'chwāng-hu kě-yǐ tīng-jyan hǎy-'ēw 'jyàw-hwàn.

(To shout) hǎn. ‖"Stop him!" she cried. tā dà-shēng 'hǎn, °byé jyàw-ta 'pǎw-le. or °'dǎng-tā. ‖There was a cry of "Man overboard!" yěw-rén 'hǎn, yěw-rén dyàw 'hǎy-li chywù-le!

Far cry. ‖The accommodations are a far cry from what we wanted. jèr-de-'shè-bèy gēn wǒm-yàw-de shyāng-chà tày 'ywǎn-le.

CUP. bēy, 'bēy-dz. *(In some cases* wǎn *meaning* bowl, *and* jūng *or* jūngr, *meaning* a small bowl, *may be used where we say* cup.*)* Teacup chá-'bēy or chá-'wǎn or chá-'jūng; cup for liquor jyěw-'bēy or jyěw-'jūng. ‖This cup is not full. jèy-ge-bēy(-dz) bù-'mǎn. ‖I have to buy more paper cups. wǒ děy 'dwō mǎy dyǎr-jŕ-'bēy-dz. ‖Will you have a cup of coffee? nǐ shyǎng hē bēy-'jyā-fēy-ma? ‖Whoever wins the race this afternoon will get the cup. (*Trophy cup*) jyēr 'shyà-wŭ-de-bǐ-'sày shéy 'yíng shéy dé nèy-ge °jì-nyàn-'bēy or (*Victory cup*) yēw-shèng-jì-nyàn-'bēy. or (*Gold cup*) jīn-'bēy. or (*Silver cup*) yǐn-'bēy. ‖He keeps the silver cups he won enclosed in a glass case. tā bǎ tā-'dé-de-yín-'bēy dēw yùng 'bwō-li-jàwr 'jàw-je.

To cup. ‖You can light the cigarette if you cup your hands around the match. ni yùng-shéw (bǎ yáng-'hwŏr) 'wŭ (or 'jàw)-je-dyar jyèw 'ké-yi (bǎ-'yāṇ) 'dyăn-jáw-le.

CURE. To be cured (*get well*) hǎw. ‖It will be three weeks before he's cured. tā-děy 'sān-ge-lǐ-bày tsáy néng 'hǎw.

To cure (*make well*) jǐ-hǎw, 'kàn-hǎw, 'yī-hǎw (*resultative compounds*); *if the person cured is not mentioned, simply* jǐ *or* kàn *or* yī *may be used.* kàn *is said only of a person, as a doctor;* jǐ *and* yī *are said of a person or a treatment.* ‖We can trust the doctor to cure him. wǒm kě-yi jǐ-je, jèy-ge-'dày-fu bǎ-tā °jǐ-hǎw-le. or °'kàn-hǎw-le. or °'yī-hǎw-le. ‖That can't be cured by medicine. 'nèy-ge bú-shr 'yàw néng jǐ-de-'hǎw-de. ‖That can't be cured by medicine alone. 'nèy-ge bù-néng gwǎng-kàw 'yàw láy 'jǐ (or 'yī). or 'nèy-ge gwǎng-kàw 'yàw shr °'jǐ-bu-hǎw-de. or °'yī-bu-hǎw-de. ‖Who cured him? shéy bǎ-tā jǐ-'hǎw-le-de? or 'shéy gěy 'jǐ-de? or shéy gěy 'kàn-de?

(*To correct*). ‖This will cure him of that (*bad*) habit. jèy-ge 'ké-yi bǎ tā-'máw-bìng °'gǎy-gwo-lay. or °'jǐ-gwo-lay. or °'jǐ-hǎw-le. or °'gwǎn-gwò-lay.

(*Remedy*) jǐ-de-'fǎr, jǐ-de-'fá-dz, jǐ-de-'fāng-fa, 'jǐ-lyáw, -lyáw, jǐ ('jǐ-lyáw *and* -lyáw *are more formal*). ‖Is there a cure for this disease? jèy-bíng yěw-fǎr 'jǐ-ma? ‖There is no cure for that. nèy-ge-'bìng méy-fǎr 'jǐ. ‖I have a cure for that. nèy-ge wǒ yěw ge-fǎr 'jǐ. or nèy-ge wǒ yěw ge-fāng-fa lay 'jǐ. ‖Would the water cure do him any good? 'shwěy-lyáw (or yùng-shwěy jǐ-de-'fāng-fa, or yùng-shwěy 'jǐ or yùng-shwěy láy 'jǐ) wèy-tā néng yěw shéme-hǎw-chù-ma? ‖The title of this book is "Cures for Common Colds." jèy-běn-shū-de-'tí-mù shr: pǔ-tūng-shāng-'fēng-jǐ-lyáw-fǎ.

(*To preserve by drying, etc.*). (*Of herbs, hides, tobacco*) 'páw-jǐ. (*this is not the same* jǐ *as the one meaning heal*); (*over a slow fire*) 'péy-jǐ, 'péy-gān; (*in the sun*) shày, 'shày-gān; (*with smoke*) shywūn; (*with sugar*) jyā-táng 'páw-jǐ; (*with syrup*) 'mì-jyàn. ‖They cure tobacco in these buildings. tām dzày jèy-jǐ-ge-'féw-li 'páw-jǐ 'yān-tsǎw.

Cured ham. hwǒ-'twěy.

CURL. (*Of hair*). (*The Chinese do not have naturally curly hair and do not curl the hair, so roundabout expressions must be used.*) ‖She went to the beauty parlor to have her hair curled. *is expressed as* She went to the beauty parlor to have heat applied to the hair. tā chywù měy-rúng-'ywàn tàng 'téw-fa. ‖To most Chinese it is silly to have the hair curled. 'jūng-

gwo-rén dwō-'bàn dēw jywé-je bǎ 'téw-fa tàng-de 'chywū-le-gwǎy-wār-de shr jyàn-'shǎ-shèr. ‖Some Westerners have naturally curly hair. yěw-de 'shī-yang-rén-de-'téw-fa °dz-'rán dày-'chywār. or °tyān-shēng-de 'chywū-le-gwǎy-wār-de.

To curl up (*the body*) chywán. ‖The dog curled up and went to sleep. gěw 'chywán-chi-lay jyèw 'shwěy-jáw-le.

(*Spiral*). ‖A curl of smoke is coming out of the chimney. yì-lywǔ-'yān tsúng 'yān-tung-li (wǎn-wan-chywu-'chywū-de) 'chū-lay-le.

CURRENT. (*Of water*) lyèw. ‖The current is very strong. lyèw hěn 'dà. or lyèw hěn 'jí. ‖Does this river have a strong current here? 'hé-dzày-jèr-de-'lyèw 'dà-bu-'dà? Or use the verb meaning flow. hé-shwěy-dzày-jèr-lyéw-de-'jí-ma?

(*Of electricity*). dyàn, 'dyàn-lyéw. ‖My electric current has been cut off. wǒ-nèr méy-'dyàn-le. or wǒ-nèr-de-'dyàn °'tíng-le. or °'chyā-le. ‖The current passes through here and is connected into that room. 'dyàn-lyéw dǎ-jèr 'gwò, yèw 'tūng-dàw nèy-jyàn-'wū-li. ‖What kind of current do you have here? nǐ-jèr yùng shéme-'dyàn? ‖Direct current. jǐ-lyéw-'dyàn. ‖Alternating current. jyāw-lyéw-'dyàn.

(*Circulating*). ‖This story is now current in many papers. jèy-jyàn-shr hǎw-shyē-'bàw-shang °dēw 'yěw-le. or °'dà-'dēng.

(*Present*). ‖What is the current value of the franc? 'fá-láng shyàn-dzày shém-me-'háng-shr? ‖I have no time to pay attention to current events. wǒ méy-'gūng-fu jù-yì 'shf-shr-'shīn-wén. ‖I read that in the current issue of the magazine. wǒ shr dzày jèy-yì-'chī-de-dzá-'jǐ kàn-jyàn-de. or wǒ shr dzày dzwèy-jìn-yì-'chī-de-dzá-'jǐ kàn-jyàn-de.

CURSE. (*Of profanity*) mà. ‖The beggars cursed us when we didn't give them anything. yàw-'fàr-de mà-le-wǒm yí-dwèn 'yīn-wèy wǒm méy-'gěy-tam shém-me. ‖All he did was mutter a few curses. tā jǐ 'mà-le jǐ-shēngr. or tā shyàw-shēngr 'mà-le jǐ-jywù(-jyē) jyèw °'wán-le. or °'swàn-le. or °'lyǎw-le.

(*Affliction*). ‖The mosquitoes were a curse. 'wén-dz jēn tǎw-'yàn. or 'wén-dz jēn jyàw-rén shèw-'dzwèy. ‖We were cursed with bad weather the whole trip. jēn dǎw-'méy, (or wǒm 'ywùn-chi jēn-'hwày,) yí-lù 'hwày-tyār.

(*Evil spell*). ‖They say the house has a curse on it. tām shwō nèy-swǒr-'fáng-dz nàw-'gwěy. or tām shwō nèy shr ge-'shyūng-jáy.

CURTAIN. (*In a house*) lyár. ‖I want curtains for all the windows. wǒ-méy-ge-'chwāng-hu dēw yàw chwāng-hu-'lyár. ‖Pull the curtain shut. bǎ-lyǎr 'lā-shang.

(*In a theater*) mù. ‖Drop the curtain. bǎ-mù 'lā-shya-lay. ‖The curtain goes up at eight-thirty. shì 'bā-dyǎn-'bàn °kāy-'mù. or °'kāy-chǎng. or °'chǐ-shr.

(*Figurative*). ‖There was a curtain of smoke over that area. 'nèy-byar 'wū-yān-jàng-'chì-de. *or* 'nèy-byar jyàw-'yān dēw 'jàw-shang-le. *or* 'nèy-byar jyàw 'yān gěy 'jē-ju-le.

(*The end*). ‖It'll be curtains for him. nà tā jyèw swàn-'wán-le.

CUSTOM. (*Habitual practice of a group or locality*) 'fēng-tǔ-'rén-chíng, 'fēng-shú. ‖I'm not yet familiar with the local customs. běn-dì-de-°'fēng-tǔ-'rén-chíng (*or* °'fēng-shú) wǒ háy bú-'dà shéw.

(*Habitual practice of an individual or family*) 'gwēy-jywu (*regulation*); *but more commonly expressed as* often *or* always dzǔng *or* lǎw *or* 'cháng-cháng. ‖Is it your custom to eat breakfast early? nǐ-dzǎw-'fàn dzǔng shř 'chř-de hěn 'dzǎw-ma?

(*Ordered*). Custom-made 'dìng-dzwò-de; a custom tailor 'tsáy-feng. ‖He wears only custom-made clothes. tā 'gwāng chwān dìng-dzwò-de-'yī-fu. ‖There's a good custom tailor down the street. jyē-'nèy-téwr yěw yí-ge-hǎw-'tsáy-feng.

Customs (*inspection at the border*) hǎy-'gwān-jyǎn-'chá *or* hǎy-'gwān-jyǎn-'yàn; (*tax imposed at customs*) 'shwèy-ehyán *or* shwèy; customs inspector hǎy-'gwān-chá-'ywán, hǎy-'gwān-jì-'chá, chá-'shwèy-de, *or* hǎy-'gwān-shang-chá-'shwèy-de; custom house hǎy-'gwān; (*rate of*) customs *or* income from customs 'gwān-shwèy. ‖We were delayed by customs. wǒm 'yīn-wey °hǎy-'gwān-jyǎn-'chá (*or* °hǎy-'gwān-jyǎn-'yàn) swǒ-yǐ 'dān-wù-lè. ‖Is there a customs inspection at the border? 'byān-jyè-ner yěw °hǎy-'gwān-jyǎn-'chá-ma? *or* °hǎy-'gwān-jyǎn-'yàn-ma? *or* (*an inspector*) °chá-'shwèy-de-ma? ‖Do we have to pay customs on this? jèy-ge wǒm yě děy °jyāw 'shwèy-chyán-ma? *or* °shàng-'shwèy-ma? ‖The customs on this sort of thing are awfully high. 'jèy-jǔng-dǔng-shi 'gwān-shwèy hěn 'jùng.

CUT. *In many cases only one Chinese word can be used, depending on how the cutting is done. These are listed first. In other cases, listed later, there is a choice of several Chinese words.*

(*Most general term*) lá. ‖He cut himself with a pocket knife. tā ná shyǎw-'dāwr bǎ-'shěw lá-le. ‖He cut his chin while shaving. tā-gwā-'lyǎn-de-shř-hew bǎ 'shyà-ba 'lá-le. ‖You can use a diamond to cut glass. ké-yi yùng jīn-gāng-'shř lá 'bwō-li. ‖I cut my hand while I was cutting up the vegetables. wǒ-chyē-'tsày-de-shř-hew bǎ-shěw 'lá-le. ‖Cut diamonds are in the show window. lá-hǎw-le-de-'dzwàn-shŕ dēw dzày 'chwāng-hu-li.

(*To chop with a heavy instrument, swinging it with the arm*) kǎn. ‖He cut the tree down with an ax. tā ná 'fǔ-dz bǎ-shù kǎn-'dàw-le. ‖They have cut down most of the trees for firewood. tām bǎ-'shù chà-bù-dwō dēw 'kǎn-le 'wèy-de-shř shāw-'hwǒ yùng.

(*To chop many times, with force*) dwò. ‖Cut the meat into sausage. bǎ-'rèw dwò-chéng rèw-'mwòr.

(*To chop up or cut into slices*) chyē. ‖Cut the meat into slices. bǎ-'rèw chyē-cheng-le sēr. ‖I cut my hand while I was cutting up the vegetables. wǒ-chyē-'tsày-de-shř-hew bǎ-shěw 'lá-le.

(*To cut into and then slide through; split; trim*) pī. ‖Cut the board in two. bǎ 'bǎn-dz pī-chéng 'lyǎng-kwày. ‖Cut this stalk of bamboo into strips. bǎ 'jú-dz pī-cheng 'tyáwr.

(*To punch*) dzáw, dzá. ‖Cut a hole with a chisel. ná 'dzáw-dz °dzáw ge-'yǎr. (*or* °dzá ge-'yǎr, *or* °dǎ ge-'yǎr). ‖Use a chisel and a hammer to cut off a piece. ná 'dzáw-dz gēn 'chwéy-dz 'dzáw (*or* 'dzá)-shya yí-kwày-chywu.

To cut *with a fodder knife* já. ‖They used a fodder knife to cut up the rice stalks to feed the cow. tām ná 'já-daw bǎ 'dàw-tsǎw já (*or* chyē)-le wèy-'nyéw.

To cut off *a thin strip or slice* shyāw. ‖Cut a thin slice off the surface of the stick. tsúng 'gwèn-dz-shang 'shyāw-shya yí-pyàr-lay.

(*To slice thin, as meat*) pyàn. ‖Cut off a thin slice of the beef. bǎ 'nyéw-rèw 'pyàn-shya yí-pyàr-lay.

To cut *a gash or furrow* hē *or* hwō.

To cut *with a sharp point* hwà, hwá. ‖That wound was cut by a pen point. nèy-ge-'kěw-dz shř ná bǐ-'jyār hwà-de (*or* hwá-de).

To cut *with a hooked point* gwà.

(*To carve*) kē, dzāw. ‖He cut a design on the piece of wood. tā dzày 'mù-tew-shang 'kē-le (*or* 'dzāw-le) ge-'hwār.

(*To scratch intentionally*) jwā, náw. ‖She made the cut with her fingernails. jèy-ge-'dàw-dz shř tā-'jwā-de (*or* tā-'náw-de).

To cut *paper or cloth* tsáy. ‖Fold the paper and cut at the folded edge. bǎ-ir̆ 'dyé-chi-lay, dzày dyé-de-'dàwr-nàr 'tsáy.

To cut *cloth* jyé. ‖This piece of cloth can be cut in two. jèy-kwày-'bù ké-yi 'ivé-cheng (*or* 'tsáy-cheng) lyǎng-kwày.

To cut *with scissors* jyǎn. ‖Cut here. dzày-jèr 'jyǎn-kāy.

To cut *with a saw* jywù. ‖They cut the board in two. tām bǎ mù-'bǎr jywù-cheng lyǎng-'bàr.

To cut *with a rotating saw or blade* shywàn. ‖They cut the wooden ball with a lathe. tām dzày shywàn-'chwáng-dz-shang shywàn-le ge-'mù-téw-chyéwr.

(*To amputate, cut off, or to cut grain*) gē. ‖They use a sickle to cut the grass. tām yùng 'lyán-dāw 'gē-tsǎw. ‖During the operation the doctor used seven kinds of scalpels to cut out the tumor. shíng-'shěw-shù-de-shř-hew 'dày-fu yǔng-le 'chī-jǔng-'dàw-dz bǎ nèy-ge-'lyéw-dz °'gē-shya-lay-de. *or* °'lá-shya-lay-de.

To cut *hair* lǐ (*or* jyǎn; *see above*); with clippers yùng 'twéy-dz twéy-'téw. ‖I must get my hair cut. wǒ děy 'lǐ-fǎ-le. *or* wǒ děy 'jyǎn-fǎ-le.

Cases in which there is a choice of several of the above words. ‖He cut his hand when he fell. tā 'shwāy-de-shř-hew bǎ-'shěw °lá-le. *or* °gwà-le. *or* °hwá-le. *or* °hwà-le. *or* tā 'shwāy-de-shř-hew bǎ-'shěw lá-le (*etc.*)

ge-'kěw-dz. ‖Cut off all the loose ends. bǎ 'swèy-téwr dēw °'jyǎn-shya-chywu. *or* °'lá-shya-chywu. *or* °'dwò-shya-chywu. *etc.*

Cut (*a wound*) 'kěw-dz, kěwr, 'shāng-kěwr. ‖The cut in my finger is nearly healed. wǒ-shěw-'jř-tew-shang-'lá-de-nèy-ge-'kěw-dz kwày 'hǎw-le.

Cut (*of meat*). ‖Choice (*cuts of*) meat for sale. yěw 'hǎw-rèw chū-'mày. ‖When you buy pork you have to specify what cut you want; for example, shoulder, ham, and so on. mǎy-'jū-rèw-de-shŕ-hew nǐ děy 'shwō nǐ yàw tsúng-'nǎr-lá-shya-lay-de-rèw, pì-rú 'jěw-dz, hèw-'twěr, shém-me-de. ‖What other cuts do you have? háy yěw 'byé-de-dì-fang-'lá-shya-lay-de(-réw)-ma? ‖We are having cold cuts for supper. jyěr-wǎn-shang chř 'cháng-dz hé rèw-'dùngr.

Cut flowers. ‖Should we send a plant or cut (*fresh*) flowers? wǒm shř sùng yì-'pér-hwār háy-shr sùng dyǎr-'shyān-hwār? ‖These flowers were cut from our garden. jèy-shyē-'hwār shř ywán-dz-li °'chyǎ-shyà-lay-de. *or* °'jāy-shyà-lay-de. *or* °'jyǎn-shyà-lay-de.

To cut (*divide*) fēn. ‖Shall we cut the cake now? shyàn-dzày fēn dàn-'gāw hǎw-ma? ‖Did all of them get their cut? tām 'dēw fēn-'dàw-le-ma? ‖When the deal was finished they asked for their cut. jyāw 'yì-shwǒ hǎw-le, tām jyěw yàw-chi °'yùng-chyán-lay-le. *or* °'tām-nèy-'fèr-lay-le. *But* ‖The cake was dry and did not cut easily. dàn-'gāw gān-le bù-hǎw 'chyē. (*See above.*)

To cut (*cards*) yāw. ‖Have these cards been cut? páy 'yāw-le-ma?

(*To shorten, reduce*). ‖The movie had to be cut in several places. 'pyān-dz yěw 'jǐ-chù bù-néng-bù-'jyǎn-le chywù. ‖The report had to be cut down to half its length. bàw-'gàw °'lá-shya yí-'bàr chywù. *or* °'shyǎw-shya yí-'bàr chywù. *or* °'shyāw-chywu yí-'bàr. *or* °'jyǎn-chywu yí-'bàr. ‖We are trying to cut down expenses. wǒm jèng-dzày shyǎng-'fār 'shěng-chyán. *or* 'shǎw yùng-'chyán. *or* °'jyé-shěng-dyar. *or* °'jyǎn-shěng-dyar. ‖These prices will be cut next month. shyà-ywè jèy-shyē-'jyàr dēw yàw 'làw.

(*To dig*). ‖They are cutting ground for a new building. tām jèng-dzày pwò-'tǔ gày shīn-'fáng-dz.

To cut in. ‖We were talking very quietly until he cut in. tā méy dǎ-'chà yǐ-chyán wǒm shwō-hwà 'shēng-yin hěn shyǎw. ‖He was going slow, and we cut in ahead of him. tā dzěw-de 'màn, wǒm jyěw bǎ-tā 'gǎn-gwo-chywu-le. ‖He's cutting in and out of traffic to get ahead. tā jèng nème 'ràw-láy-ràw-'chywù-de wàng-chyán 'chyǎng.

To cut loose. ‖When the president got there, they cut loose and raised the roof. dzǔng-tǔng 'dàw-le, tām 'dà-hǎn dà-'jyàw-de láy 'hwān-yíng.

To cut short. ‖Our trip was cut short by the bad news. wǒm 'tīng-jyàn-le (nèy-jyàn-shèr) jyěw 'méy-dzày wàng-chyán 'dzěw. ‖His speech was cut short by the news. tā 'tīng-jyàn-le (nèy-ge) jyěw méy-dzày wàng-shyà 'shwō.

To cut off. ‖The flood has cut off all communication with that town. dà-'shwěy jyàw 'nèy-ge-dì-fang-de-swó-'yěw-de-'jyāw-tung dwàn-'jywé-le. ‖Operator, I've been cut off! wèy! dyàn-hwà shyàn 'dwàn-le!

To cut out. ‖He is not cut out for studying languages. tā shywé 'ywǔ-yán bú-dà hé-'shř. ‖He used to have a good business but was cut out by competition. tā-'mǎy-mày yǐ-chyán bú-'tswò-lày-je; 'hèw-láy jyàw-'rén gěy 'chyǎng-gwò-chywù-le. ‖Tell 'em to cut out the noise. jyàw-tām 'shyǎw-dyǎr shēngr. ‖Cut it out! (*Of actions*) byé 'nèm-je! *or* (*of talking*) byé 'shwō-le! *or* (*of talking nonsense*) byé 'hú-shwō! *or* (*of lies, bragging, etc.; very vulgar*) byé fàng-'pì!

To cut up. ‖This house has been cut up into apartments. jèy-ge-'fáng-dz 'gé-kay-le jǐ-'jyār 'jù. ‖He was terribly cut up over the loss of his baggage. tā bǎ 'shíng-li 'dyēw-le, hěn nán 'shěw. ‖Have the children been cutting up? 'háy-dz-men 'fǎn-láy-je méy-yěw? *or* 'háy-dz-men hú-'nàw-láy-je méy-yěw?

Cut (*of clothes*). ‖She always wears clothes of the latest cut. tā yǔng-'ywǎn chwān dzwèy-mwò-'dēng-de-yī-fu. *or* tā 'chwān-de-'yī-fu lǎw shř 'dzwèy-shīn-shř-de. ‖I'd rather have a suit of a loose cut. wǒ ywàn-yì yàw 'féy-yi-dyǎr-de-'yī-fu.

To cut corners. ‖The job will take five days; four days if we cut corners. dzwò-'jèy-ge-hwór děy 'wǔ-tyān, (yàw-shr) jyā-'jǐn-de-hwà 'sz̀-tyān yě kě-yǐ 'wán.

To cut across, cut through. ‖It will save time to cut across the field. tsúng 'chǎng-dz-li 'chwān-gwò-chywù °'shěng 'shŕ-hew. *or* °'chāw-'jyèr. *or* °'jìn-dyar. ‖When we are in a hurry we cut through the park. wǒm-'máng-de-shŕ-hew jyěw tsúng gūng-'ywán-li 'chwān-gwo-chywu.

Cut (*a reduction*). ‖He asked us to take a salary cut of ten per cent. tā jyàw-wǒm shǎw 'ná 'shŕ-fēn-jř-'yī-de-chyán. *or* tā jyàw-wǒm jyǎn 'shŕ-fēn-jř-'yī-de-'shīn.

To cut (*to ignore*). ‖They are old friends, and I didn't mean to cut them. tā-men shř wǒ-de-'lǎw-péng-yew; wǒ 'bìng bú-shř yàw bù-'lǐ tā-men.

To cut (*a class*). ‖He had to cut the class in order to meet us. tā wèy 'jyē-wǒm 'shwā-le yì-táng-'kè. *or* °'nèy-táng-'kè méy-'shàng. ‖During the term he cut two lectures. yí-'jì-de-gūng-fu tā yěw 'lyǎng-táng-kè méy-'tīng.

Cut (*illustration*). ‖We're making a cut of your latest photograph for our next issue. nǐ-de-'jàw-shyàng wǒ-men yàw dzwò ge-'túng-bǎn 'dēng-dzày 'shyà-yì-chī. ‖There are three cuts in the book. jè-běn-'shū-li yěw 'sān-jāng-chā-'tú.

To cut a figure. ‖Their ambassador cut a big figure at the conference. tā-men-de-dà-'shř dzày-kāy-'hwèy-de-shŕ-hew tǐng 'shén-chì.

D

DAILY. (*Day by day, referring to a continuous process*) 'yì-tyān-yì-'tyān-de. ‖He is getting better daily. tā 'yì-tyān-yì-'tyān-de jyàn-'hǎw. *or* tā 'yì-tyān bǐ 'yì-tyān jyàn-'hǎw.

(*Every day, referring to a repeated action*) 'měy-tyān, 'tyān-tyan. ‖He comes daily. tā 'měy-tyān láy. *or* tā 'tyān-tyan láy. ‖An inspection of the passports is made daily. 'měy-tyān (*or* 'tyān-tyan) jyàn-'chá hù-'jàw. ‖He makes a daily news broadcast. tā °'měy-tyān (*or* °'tyān-tyan) dzày wú-shyàn-'dyàn-li bàw-'gàw 'shīn-wén.

Daily newspapers *are usually called either* morning papers dzǎw-'bàw *or* evening papers wǎn-'bàw. ‖There are two (evening) dailies published in this town. jèy-'chéng-li yěw 'lyǎng-jǔng-wǎn-'bàw. ‖Morning dailies in New York are put on sale the night before. nyěw-ywē-měy-tyān-chū-de-dzǎw-'bàw téw-tyan wǎn-shang jyèw 'màr-le. *But in the names of some papers* ř-'bàw; The World Daily (*a Peiping paper*) 'shř-jyè-ř-'bàw.

DAMAGE. To damage (*physically*) 'dzāw-ta, nùng-'hwày, gěy 'hwěy; (*by collision*) jwàng-'hwày; (*by a sharp blow or by something falling*) dzá-'hwày; (*and other resultative compounds, see* BREAK). ‖He damaged my car. tā bǎ wǒ-de-'chē 'dzāw-ta-le. *or* tā bǎ wǒ-de-'chē °nùng-'hwày-le (*or* °gěy 'hwěy-le). *or* tā nùng-'hwày-le wǒ-de-'chē-le. *or* tā bǎ wǒ-de-'chē jwàng-'hwày-le. *or* tā jwàng-'hwày-le wǒ-de-'chē-le. ‖He did a lot of damage to our furniture. tā bǎ wǒm-de-jyā-jywu 'dzāw-ta-de bù-'chǐng. ‖He did a lot of damage in our factory. tā dzày wǒm-de-gūng-'chǎng-li nùng-'hwày-le hěn-dwō-'dūng-shi. ‖What kind of damage? nùng-'hwày-le 'nǎr-le? ‖How was the damage done? dzěm nùng-'hwày-de? ‖How much damage? hwày-dàw dzěm-ge-'dì-bu? ‖The car was damaged. chì-'chē 'hwěy-le. *or* chì-'chē jwàng-'hwày-le. *or* (*by a falling object*) chì-'chē dzá-'hwày-le. ‖The hail damaged the wheat crop. báw-dz bǎ 'jwāng-jya dēw dzà-'hway-le.

Damage (*physical*) 'dzāw-ta-de, nùng-'hwày-de. *See above.*

Damage (*physical or otherwise*) 'dzāw-ta-de, 'swen-shř. ‖How much damage was done? 'swen-shř 'dwō-shaw? *or* 'swen-shř 'dà-bu-dà? *or* 'swen-shř yěw 'dwō-jùng? *or* 'dzāw-ta-de 'lì-hay-bu-lì-hay? ‖He has done enough damage around here. tā bǎ-jèr 'dzāw-ta-de °'gèw chyáw-de-le. *or* °'gèw shèw-de-le. ‖He did a lot of damage to the name of our factory. tā jyāw wǒm-gūng-'chǎng-de-'míng-ywù shèw hěn-dà-de-'swen-shř. *or* tā bǎ wǒm-gūng-'chǎng-de-'míng-ywu °'dzāw-ta-de bù-'chǐng. *or* °'hwěy-de bù-'chǐng. ‖Serious damages were suffered on the east coast (*newspaper style*). 'dūng-àn-'swen-shř °'chí-jùng. *or* °'hěn-jùng.

‖The damage is done. 'yǐ-jing nùng-chéng 'jè-yàngr-le. *or* 'shēng-mǐ yǐ-jing 'jǔ-cheng shéw-'fàn-le.

To pay damages péy, 'péy-cháng 'swen-shř, péy-'chyán. ‖He'll have to pay damages to the owner of the car. tā děy 'péy-cháng chē-'jǔ-de-'swen-shř. ‖You'll have to pay damages for this. jèy-ge nǐ děy °'péy. *or* °: ʿy-'chyán. ‖I'll sue you for damages. wǒ chywù 'gàŵ-ni, jyàw-ni 'péy.

DANCE. To dance tyàw, tyàw-'wǔ; to dance a certain *kind of* dance *or* to dance *so many* dances tyàw....-'wǔ; a dance, dancing tyàw-'wǔ, wǔ; a dance (*a party for dancing*) tyàw-wǔ-'hwèy; dancing girl wǔ-'nywǔ; dancing partners wǔ-'bàr; sword dance wǔ-'dāw; snake dance wǔ-'shé; tea dance chá-'wǔ; *waltz* 'hwá-er-dz-'wǔ; *fox trot* hú-bù-'wǔ; dancing (*instruction*) wǔ-'dǎw. ‖They used to dance on the stage. tām yǐ-'chyán dzày wǔ-'táy-shang tyàw-'wǔ. ‖The next number is a dance. 'shyà-yí-ge-'jyé-mù shř tyàw-'wǔ. ‖Any dance music among these records? jèy-shyē-'pyān-dz-li yěw tyàw-wǔ-yīn-'ywè-ma? ‖We're invited to a dance at their home. wǒm bèy 'chǐng chywù tām-'jyā tyàw-'wǔ. ‖There's a dance at the YWCA tonight. jyēr-'wǎn-shang 'nywǔ-chīng-nyán-'hwèy kāy tyàw-wǔ-'hwèy. ‖I don't dance. wǒ bú-'hwèy tyàw-'wǔ. ‖He only knows how to dance the fox trot. tā 'jř hwèy tyàw hú-bù-'wǔ. ‖The next dance is a long one. 'shyà-yí-ge-'wǔ hěn 'cháng. ‖They're dancing partners. tām-shr wǔ-'bàr. ‖The dancing teacher in this school is a foreigner. jèy-ge-shywé-'shyàw jyāw-wǔ-'dǎw-de-shyān-sheng shr ge-'wày-gwo-rén. ‖Let's dance some more. 'dzày tyàw-'hwěr-ba. *or* 'dzày tyàw hwěr-'wǔ-ba. ‖They had three dances. tām tyàw-'wǔ tyàw-le sān-'tsž. *or* tām tyàw-le 'sān-tsž-'wǔ.

(*To jump about*) tyàw, bèng, 'lwàn-tyàw. ‖The little girl was dancing with joy. nèy-ge-'shyǎw-hár °'lè-de jř 'tyàw. *or* °'lè-de jř 'bèng. *or* °'gāw-shìng-de jř 'tyàw. *or* °'gāw-shìng-de jř 'bèng. *or* °'lè-de yí-tyàw-yí-'bèng-de. *or* °'lè-de 'lwàn-tyàw.

DANGER. 'wéy-shyǎn; the danger 'wéy-shyǎn-de-'dì-fang. *See also* DANGEROUS. ‖The danger is this, that.... 'wéy-shyǎn-de-'dì-fang dzày-'jèr, jyèw-shr.... ‖The only danger is that he might forget himself and talk with a native accent. jř yěw 'yí-yàng-'wéy-shyǎn (*or* wéy-'yī-de-'wéy-shyǎn *or* jř yěw 'yì-dyǎn jyàw-rén bú-fàng-'shīn-de) jyèw-shr tā wú-'yì-jūng yě-shywǔ 'shwǒ-chu běn-'dì-ren-de-'kěw-yīn-lay. ‖There wasn't any danger to speak of. 'méy-yew shémme 'wéy-shyǎn °kě-'shwō-de. *or* °'jř-de yì-'tí-de. ‖There are going to be plenty of dangers, but I won't mind. 'wéy-shyǎn °yí-'dìng bù-'shǎw- (*or* °yí-'dìng yěw hěn-dwō-) 'wéy-shyǎn, 'kě-shr 'wǒ bú-'dzày-hu. ‖Would he

438

be able to face real danger unflinchingly? dàw-le 'jēn-'wéy-shyǎn de-shŕ-hew, tā néng bù-dǎn-'chywè-ma? ‖That's the real danger. (*Emphasis on* that) 'nà tsáy-shŕ 'jēn-jèng-'wéy-shyǎn-de-dì-fang-ne. (*Emphasis on* real) nà tsáy-shŕ 'jēn-jèng-'wéy-shyǎn-de-dì-fang-ne. ‖There lies the real danger. jēn-'jèng-de-'wéy-shyǎn dzày-'nàr. ‖Danger lurks in every corner. 'dàw-chù dēw hwèy yěw 'wéy-shyǎn. or (*Literary*) 'wéy-jī sż-'fú.

Special expressions in English. ‖He sensed the danger in the dark. 'hēy-gu-lung-'dūng-de tā 'jywé-je yěw dyǎr-'bú-'myǎw. ‖Don't shirk dangers. (*Literary quotations*) bú-yàw lín-'nàn gěw-'myǎn, or lín-'nàn wǔ gěw-'myǎn. ‖He's a danger to peace. tā shŕ ge-'hwò-gēn. or tā shŕ ge-dǎw-'lwàn-fèn-'dž. ‖That large chimney is a danger to night flying. 'yè-jyàn fēy-'shíng de-shŕ-hew nèy-ge-dà-'yān-tung hwèy rě-'hwò.

In danger; out of danger. ‖He's in danger. tā yěw 'wéy-shyǎn. ‖The patient is still in danger. 'bìng-rén háy yěw 'wéy-shyǎn. ‖The patient is out of danger now. 'bìng-rén méy-yew 'wéy-shyǎn-le. or 'bìng-rén 'chū-le. 'wéy-shyǎn-le. ‖When we're out of danger I'll let you know. děng 'chū-le wéy-shyǎn (or děng 'méy-yew wéy-shyǎn-le) wǒ jyèw 'gàw-su nǐ. ‖He's in danger of losing his life. tā yěw 'shìng-mìng-de-'wéy-shyan. or (*Literary*) tā jèng-dzày 'shēng-sž-gwān-'téw. ‖That company is in danger of being surrounded. 'nèy-lyán yěw bèy-bāw-'wéy-de-'wéy-shyǎn. or 'nèy-lyán °hěn 'wéy-shyǎn (or °hěn 'jīn-jí), yě-shywu hwèy ràng-rén 'bāw-wéy. ‖The country is in danger. 'gwó-jyā jèng dzày °wéy-'jí-de-shŕ-hew. or °gwó-'nàn dāng-'chyán.

Less serious danger. ‖We're in danger of being late. kwày yàw 'wǎn-le. or yàw 'wǎn-le. or yě-shywu hwèy 'wǎn-le.

DANGEROUS. (*Perilous*) 'wéy-shyǎn, shyǎn, shywán. ‖That's a dangerous game. wár 'nèy-ge hěn °'wéy-shyan. or °'shyǎn. or °'shywán. ‖It is dangerous to swim here. dzày-'jèr 'fù-shwěy yěw dyǎr-°'shywán. or °'shyǎn. or °'wéy-shyan. ‖It's no more dangerous than what I went through last time. bìng bù-bǐ 'shàng-tsż (wǒ jīng-yàn-de) 'wéy-shyǎn. ‖That's a dangerous undertaking. dzwò 'nèy-yàng-de-shŕ °yěw dyǎr-'shyǎn. or °yěw 'wéy-shyǎn. or °yěw-de hěn.

(*Bad, serious*) 'wéy-shyǎn, *and other expressions.* ‖Is her condition still dangerous? tā-de-'chíng-shing (or tā-'bìng-de) 'háy-shr hěn °bù-'hǎw-ma? or °wéy-shyǎn-ma? ‖That's a dangerous remark. nèy-jywù-hwà shwō-le °yěw 'hày-chù. or °bù-'hǎw. or shwō nèy-yàng-de-'hwà hěn 'wéy-shyan. ‖That's a dangerous habit. nèy-jǔng-'shí-gwàn yěw-'hày.

(*Of person or animal*). ‖He's a dangerous character. (*Unreliable*) nèy-ge-rén bù-kě-'kàw. (*Smooth but mean*) nèy-ge-rén hěn 'yīn-shyǎn. (*Can stand watching*) nèy-ge-rén děy 'dī-fang-je-dyǎr. (*Bad*) tā shŕ ge-'shyǎw-rén. (*Extremely dangerous*) tā shŕ ge-'è-rén. (*Desperate*) tā hwèy hày-'rén-de. or tā hwēy shā-'rén-de. or tā hěn-'shyūng. (*Needs special watching*) děy 'tè-byé 'shyǎw-shīn-je ta. or děy 'tè-byé 'dī-fang-je ta. (*Violently desperate*) tā 'chyúng-shyūng jí-'è. (*Violently desperate and ruthless*) tā shŕ 'shā-rén-bù-ján-'yǎn-de-'mwó-wáng. ‖That's an extremely dangerous criminal you're going to deal with. nǐn-yàw-'bàn-de shŕ ge-'shā-rén-bù-jǎn-'yǎn-de-'shyūng-shew. ‖That's a dangerous beast. nèy shŕ ge-'è-shèw. or nèy-ge-'shèw °hěn-'shyūng. or °hwèy hày-'rén-de. or °hwèy chŕ-'rén-de. or °hwèy shāng-'rén-de. ‖He's a dangerous person to associate with. gēn-tā 'láy-wang (or gēn nèy-ge-ren 'láy-wang) °děy 'dī-fang-je-dyar. or °hwèy yěw 'wéy-shyǎn(-de). or °hěn shyǎn. or °hwèy chū-'shèr(-de). or °hwèy rě-'hwò(-de).

DARE. Dare *to do something* gǎn. ‖Do you dare take the responsibility? nǐ gǎn 'dāng (or 'dān) jèy-ge-'dzé-rèn-ma? Do you dare go there alone? 'nǐ 'gǎn 'yí-ge-rén chywù-'nèr-ma? ‖Don't you dare! 'nǐ 'gǎn! ‖Don't you dare move! 'nǐ 'gǎn 'dùng! or 'nǐ 'gǎn 'dùng-yi-'dùngr! ‖Don't you dare move it! 'nǐ 'gǎn 'dùng! or 'jèy-ge nǐ gǎn 'dùng-yi-dùng-kan! ‖Don't you dare take it. 'nǐ 'gǎn 'ná! ‖Let me see if you dare take it! nǐ gǎn 'ná gěy-wo 'chyǎw-chyaw! ‖I didn't dare leave the baby. wǒ méy-gǎn 'lí-kāy shyǎw-'hár. ‖How dare you! nǐ hǎw-'dà-de-'dǎn-dz! ‖How dare you say that to me! nǐ hǎw-'dà-de-'dǎn-dz, ('jywù-rán) 'gǎn gēn-wo tí 'nèy-ge!

(*Challenge*). jyàng. ‖My friends dared me to go. wǒ-de-'péng-yew-men 'jyàng-wo 'chywù. ‖My friends DARED me to go (and that's why I went). wǒ-de-'péng-yew-men 'jyàng-wo chywù-de. ‖My friends dared me to go, so I went. wǒ-de-'péng-yew-men 'jyàng-wo 'chywù; wǒ jyèw 'chywù-le.

To take a dare chŕ-'jyàng. ‖He always takes a dare. tā 'dzǔng-shŕ chŕ-'jyàng.

DARK. (*Without light*) hēy, àn. *Only* hēy *is used with* tyān *to refer to the darkness of the sky at night.* ‖Wait until it gets dark. děng tyān 'hēy-le-je. or děng tyān 'hēy-le dzày shwō. or děng tyān 'hēy-dyǎr dzày shwō. ‖It's too dark outside. wày-tew tày 'hēy. ‖It gets dark earlier and earlier. tyān 'hēy-de 'ywè láy ywè 'dzǎw. ‖Dark clouds are looming ahead. 'chyán-tew chǐ hēy-'ywún-le. ‖This place is very dark. jèy-ge-dì-fang °'hěn hēy. or °hěn-'àn. or °'hēy-gu-lung-'dūng-de. or °'chī hēy, or °'chywù hēy. or °'jēn hēy, or °'hēy-jr-ne, or °'hēy jí-le. or °hēy-de 'hěn. or *expressed as* This place is so dark that you can't see your hand in front of your face. °'hēy-de shēn-'shèw bú-jyàn-'jǎng. or *as* This place is so dark that you can't see someone else even face to face. °'hēy-de dwèy-'myàr 'kàn-bu-jyàn 'rén. ‖When you come to a very dark room suddenly, you can't see anything for a while. 'hū-ran 'jìn-le °hěn-'àn-de-'wū-dz, (or °hěn-'hēy-de-'wū-dz, or °'chī-hēy-de-'wū-dz, or °'chywù-hēy-de-'wū-dz,) 'yǎn-jīng yěw yì-hwěr 'shém-me dēw kàn-bu-'jyàn.

Darkroom àn-'shr̀, hēy-'wū-dz.

In the dark (*literally*). ‖That place is hard to find in the dark. nèy-ge-'dì-fang °méy-'dēng (*or* °'hēy-gu-lung-'dūng-de, *or* °mwō(-je)-'hèr, *or* °chī-'hēy-de, *or* °chywù-'hēy-de) hěn 'nán 'jǎw. *or* nèy-ge-'dì-fang yè-li °mwō-je-'hèr (*or* °'hēy-gu-lung-'dūng-de) hěn 'nán 'jǎw.

In the dark (*figuratively*). ‖My friend has kept me in the dark about his movements. wǒ-de-'péng-yew 'yì-jŕ méy-'gàw-sung wǒ tā-de shíng-'dzūng. ‖I'm completely in the dark about it. jèy-hwéy-shŕ 'shéy yě méy-'gàw-su-gwo wo. *or* wǒ 'wán-chywán bù-jŕ-dàw (*or* bù-'shyǎw-de) jèy-hwéy-'shŕ. ‖He kept his reasons dark. tā méy-'shwō-chū-lay 'tā-de-'lǐ-yéw.

(*Unenlightened*). The Dark Ages 'hēy-àn shŕ-'dày.

(*Adverse*). ‖Those were dark days for me. nèy-shŕ-hew wǒ hěn 'tsǎn. *or* nèy-shŕ-hew wǒ jèng-dzay 'dǎw-'méy. *or* °dzěw bèy-'dzèr.

(*Of a color*) shēn, jùng *unless special terms for dark shades of a color are used*. ‖His house is a dark brown. tā-de-'fáng-dz shŕ °'shēn-hwáng-shǎr-de. *or* °'dzūng-sè-de, *or* °'hé-sè-de. *Other terms for dark brown, more commonly used, are* copper color 'túng-shǎr; bronze color gǔ-'túng-shǎr; tea color 'chá-shǎr; pig-liver color jū-'gān-shǎr. ‖This color is too dark. jèy-ge-'shǎr °tày 'shēn-le. *or* °tày 'jùng-le. ‖I want a darker shade of this color. wǒ yàw jèy-ge 'shǎr, kě-shr dzày °'jùng-(*or* °'shēn-)yi-dyǎr.

Darkness *is expressed with the various terms given above for* dark. ‖At midnight the darkness was complete. 'dàw-le bàn-'yè jyèw 'chywán hēy-le. ‖The wires were cut and we were left in darkness. dyàn-'shyàn 'jyàw-rén gěy 'jyǎn-le, 'jěng-gèr dēw 'hēy-le. ‖The reasons for going were kept in darkness. wèv-'shém-me dàw-nàr 'chywù, shéy yě méy-'gàw-su. *or* chywù-'nèr-de-'ywán-gù 'méy-yew 'fā-byǎw.

DATE. (*On the calendar*) tyān; (*formal*) r̀. (*Month and day*) N-ywè N-hàw (*N stands for a numeral*); (*day of the month*) N-hàw; (*within the first ten days of the month*) chū-N; (*within the second ten days of the month*) shŕ-N; (*within the third ten days of the month*) èr-shr-N; (*of an event*) 'r̀-dz; (*formal*) 'r̀-chī. **What date** (*local Peiping*) 'jyèr *or expressed as* when 'dwō-hwer *or* 'dwō-dzen. (*Referring to a year*) nyán. ‖What's the date today? It's the tenth. jīn-tyan 'jǐ-hàw? 'shŕ-hàw. ‖What's the date today? It's the tenth of March. jīn-tyan 'jǐ-ywè 'jǐ-hàw? jīn-tyan 'sān-vwè 'shŕ-hàw. ‖What's the date today? It's the third. jīn-tyan chū-'jǐ? jīn-tyan chū-'sān. ‖What's the date today? It's the fourteenth. jīn-tyan 'nǎ-yì-tyān? (*or* jīn-tyan 'něy-tyān? *or* jīn-tyan 'jyěr-le? *or* jyèr (shŕ) 'jyěr? *or* jīn-tyan shŕ-'jǐ?) jīn-tyan shŕ-'sz̀(-hàw). ‖What is the date (*of something*)? (shŕ) 'nǎ-yì-tyān? *or* (shŕ) 'něy-tyān? *or* (shŕ) 'jyěr? *or* (shŕ) 'jyěr-a? *or* (shŕ) 'dwō-hwer? *or* (shŕ) 'dwō-dzen? ‖Has the date been set? dìng-le 'r̀-dz-le-ma? (*especially of a wedding*). *or* 'r̀-chī dìng-

le-ma? ‖What is the date on that letter? nèy-fēng-'shìn-shang-'shyě-de-°'r̀-chī (*or* °'r̀-dz) shŕ 'nǎ-yi-tyān? *or* nèy-fēng-'shìn shŕ 'nǎ-tyān shyě-de? ‖The date of coronation has been advanced. shíng-jyā-myǎn-'lǐ-de-'r̀-chī tí-'chyán-le. ‖Under this line write the date of your arrival. dzày jèy-tyáw-shyàn-'dǐ-shya shyě nǐ-'dàw-jèr-de-'r̀-chī. ‖The date on the letter is Jan. 12, 1945. (*very formal*) shìn-shang-'shyě-de-'r̀-chī shŕ yī-jyěw-sz̀-'wǔ-nyán 'yí-ywè shŕ-'èr-°hàw (*or* °r̀). ‖The date of their marriage has not been set. (jyē-'hwén-de-)'r̀-dz háy méy-dìng-hǎw. *or* 'nǎ-tyān jyē-'hwēn háy méy-dìng-'hǎw. ‖There are three dates to be remembered. yěw 'sān-ge-'r̀-dz děy jì-je. ‖What were the dates of your employment at the bank? nǐ yì-'chyán dzày 'yín-háng dzwò-'shr̀ shŕ 'tsúng 'něy-tyān 'chǐ dàw 'něy-tyān jŕ? *or* °tsúng 'shém-me-shŕ-hew 'chǐ dàw 'shém-me-shŕ-hew? ‖What is the date of your birth? (*including year*) nǐ shŕ 'nǎ-yi-nyán 'jǐ-ywè 'jǐ-r̀ shēng-'rén? *or* (*formal; not necessarily including year*) nǐ shŕ 'jǐ-shŕ shēng-'rén? *or* (*informal*) *is expressed as* When is your birthday? nǐ-'shēng-r shŕ °'dwō-hwer? *or* °'něy-tyān? *or* °'jyěr? ‖What is the date (*year*) of Confucius' birth? 'kǔng-dž 'nǎ-nyán 'shēng-de? ‖Do you know the dates of Confucius' birth and death? 'kǔng-dž de-'shēng-'dzú-'nyán nǐ jŕ-daw-ma? ‖What is the date of the founding of the Chinese Republic? 'jūng-hwá-mín-'gwó 'nǎ-nyán chéng-'lì-de? ‖The letter was dated April 10. 'shìn shŕ 'sz̀-ywè 'shŕ-hàw 'shyě-de. *or* shìn-shang-shyě-de-'r̀-dz shŕ 'sz̀-ywè 'shŕ-hàw. *or* shìn-shang shyě-je 'sz̀-ywè-'shŕ-hàw-de-'r̀-dz. ‖You forgot to date your letter. nǐ 'shìn-shang méy-shyě 'r̀-dz.

At an early date. *meaning* very soon in the future. ‖I'll do it for you at an early date. gwò shyē-'shŕ-hew wǒ gěy-ni 'bàn. ‖The game was temporarily postponed, but will be played at an early date. bǐ-'sày jàn-shŕ yán-'chǐ-le, kě-shr bù-'jyěw hwèy 'jywǔ-shǐng-de. *meaning* very long ago. ‖This building has been here from an early date. jèy-dzwò-'léw shŕ hěn-'jyěw-yǐ-'chyán gày-de.

To date from. ‖The Great Wall dates from the Ch'in Dynasty. cháng-'chéng 'chín-cháw jyèw 'yěw-le. ‖This custom dates from the American pre-Revolutionary days. jè-jǔng-'fēng-su °shŕ méy-gwo-gé-'mìng-yǐ-'chyán °chǐ-de (*or* °yěw-de).

To date (*until now*) 'jŕ dàw shyàn-'dzày *or* 'jŕ dàw 'jīn-tyan. ‖We have not heard from him to date. wǒm 'jŕ dàw shyàn-'dzày yě méy-'jyē-je tā-de-'shyāw-shi.

Up to date. ‖Let's make a new edition and bring it up to date. jèy-běn-shū dzám 'dzay chū yì-'bǎn, bǎ dzwèy-'jìn-de-shèr jyā-jin-chywu. ‖I'm not up to date on this subject. jèy-jyàn-'shŕ-de-shìn-'fā-jǎn wǒ háy bù-'jŕ-daw. ‖This will bring you up to date. děng-wo gàw-su-le nǐ 'jèy-ge, nǐ jyèw dēw 'jŕ-daw-le. ‖His ideas are not up-to-date. tā 'sz̄-shyǎng °'chén-fǔ. *or* °hěn 'jyèw. ‖Try to get the up-to-date information. shyǎng-'fár 'dé-dàw dzwèy-'jìn-de-'shyāw-shi.

Out-of-date, dated jyèw, 'lǎw-shŕ-de, 'jyèw-shŕ-de, gwò-'shŕ-de; 'chén-fǔ (*only of ideas, customs, etc.*). ‖He drives an out-of-date car. tā kāy yí-lyàng-°'jyèw-chē. *or* °'jyèw-shŕ-de-'chē. *or* °'lǎw-shŕ-de-chē. *or* °gwò-'shŕ-de-chē. ‖Her clothes seem out-of-date. tā-'chwān-de-'yī-fu hǎw 'shyàng shŕ °gwò-'shŕ-le. *or* °'lǎw-shŕ-de. *or* (*with* 'jyèw, *meaning* old and worn) °'jyèw-shŕ-de. ‖His books are dated now. tā-de-'shū gwò-'shŕ-le. ‖His style of dancing dates him. *meaning it's old-fashioned* tā-de-wǔ-'bù gwò-'shŕ-le. *or* (*meaning that one can tell when he learned to dance*) tsúng wǔ-'bù-shang ké-yi 'kàn-chu-lay nèy-ge-rén shém-me-'shŕ-hew shywé-de tyàw-'wǔ.

(*Fruit*) dzǎwr. ‖How much per pound are these dates? 'dzǎwr shŕ 'dwō-shaw-chyán yí-'bàng?

(*Appointment*) 'ywē-hwèy. ‖I have a date for noon today. wǒ 'jīn-tyan 'shǎng-wu yěw yí-ge-'ywē-hwèy.

To be dated up méy-'gūng-fu. ‖I'm all dated up this week. wǒ jèy-ge-lǐ-'bày méy-'gūng-fu.

(*Appointment with a girl or fellow*). ‖Who do you have a date with this evening? nǐ jīn-tyan-'wǎn-shang gēn-'shwéy 'chū-chywu? ‖He's been dating her regularly. tā 'cháng dày-ta 'chū-chywu. ‖I haven't had a date in a year. wǒ 'yì-nyán méy-'gēn-rén 'chū-chywu.

DAUGHTER. 'nywǔ-ér, 'nywǔ-háy-dz; (*local Peiping*) 'gū-nyang; (*polite*) 'shyǎw-jye; (*old polite term*) 'chyān-jīn. ‖He has one son and two daughters. tā yěw 'yí-ge-'ér-dz 'lyǎng-ge-'nywǔ-ér. ‖This is my youngest daughter. jèy-shr wǒ dìng-shyǎw-de-'nywǔ-háy-dz. ‖That's Mr. Li's eldest daughter. nèy-shr 'lǐ-shyān-sheng-de-'dà-gū-nyang. ‖The lady has a beautiful daughter. nèy-wèy-'tày-tay yěw yí-wèy-'hěn-hǎw-'kàn-de-shyǎw-jye. ‖How old is your daughter? nín jèy-wey-'chyān-jīn jīn-nyan 'jǐ-swèy-le?

DAY. tyān, (*literary except in certain combinations*) r̀; (*a specific day*) 'r̀-dz, r̀-'chī; (*as opposed to night*) 'báy-tyān, báy-'r̀, (*literary*) báy-'jèw; (*a period of twenty-four hours*) yí-jèw-'yè. **Every third day** 'gé-lyǎng-'tyān *or* 'jyē-lyǎng-'tyān; **in a day or two** yì-lyǎng-'tyān °yì-'nèy *or* °-'li; **in a few days** 'jǐ-tyār *or* jǐ-'tyān-li *or* 'bù-jǐ-tyār; **day before yesterday** 'chyán-tyan *or* (*local Peiping*) 'chyár-ge; **day after tomorrow** 'hèw-tyan *or* (*local Peiping*) 'hèwr-ge; **some day** *or* **one of these days** 'dzǔng yěw nème-yì-'tyān *or* 'jyāng-láy dzǔng; **the other day** 'nèy-tyan; **one day** yěw yì-tyan; **for days on end** jyē-lyán hǎw-shyē-'tyān; **some other day** 'gǎy-tyan *or* yì-'hèw; **the next day** dì-'èr-tyan; **on the day of maturity** mǎn-'chī-de-nèy-'tyān *or* mǎn-'chī-de-r̀-dz; **D-day** dzwò-'jàn dì-yí-'r̀; **the Day of Judgment** 'shŕ-jyè mwò-'r̀; **days of grace** kwān-'shyàn-'r̀-chī. ‖The day is breaking. 'tyān °'míng-le. *or* °kwày 'lyàng-le. ‖He works by day. tā 'báy-tyan dzwò-'gūng. ‖He worked a whole day. tā dzwò-le yì-'jěng-tyan-de-'gūng. ‖He worked on it day and

night for two weeks. tā jèw-'yè-bù-'tíng-de gàn-le lyǎ-lǐ-'bày. ‖We spent three days in the country. wǒm dzày 'shyāng-shya jù-le 'sān-tyān. ‖A day has twenty-four hours. yì-'tyān yěw èr-shr-'sz̀-'shyáw-shŕ. ‖One day he said to me, "From this day on I'm going to come every other day." 'yěw-yì-tyān tā gēn-wo 'shwō, "tsúng 'jīn-tyan 'chǐ wǒ 'gé-yì-tyān yì 'láy." ‖What day of the week is today? 'jīn-tyan lǐ-bày-'jǐ? ‖What day of the month is today? jīn-tyan jǐ-'hàw? ‖He's paid by the day. tā-de-'gūng-chyán °àn-'tyān (*or* °'lwèn-'tyān) 'swàn. ‖He's paid every day. tā-de-'gūng-chyán 'měy-tyan yì 'fā. ‖It's only a day('s journey) away now. jǐ yěw 'yì-tyān-de-'lù-le. ‖It's three years to the day today. dàw 'jīn-tyan jěng 'sān-nyán. ‖One day she says yes, the next day she says no. 'yì-tyān tā shwō 'shíng, ('lìng-)yì-tyān yèw shwō 'bù-shíng. ‖Has she named the day yet? tā dìng-le 'r̀-dz-le-ma? ‖That's a day to be remembered. 'nèy-shr bù-néng-'wàng-de-°yì-'tyān. *or* °ge-'r̀-dz. ‖I'll give you a day's grace. gěy-ni kwān-'shyàn-yì-tyān. ‖All employees work an eight-hour day. 'swǒ-yěw-de-'gù-ywán 'měy-tyan 'gūng-dzwò 'bā-'shyǎw-shŕ. ‖My day begins at seven o'clock. *meaning* I start work at seven o'clock. wǒ-de-'gūng-dzwò 'měy-tyan 'chī-dyǎn-jūng 'kāy-shŕ. *or,* *meaning* I get up at seven o'clock. wǒ 'měy-tyan 'chī-dyǎn-jūng 'chǐ. ‖This is the day of the celebration. ɡjīn-tyan shŕ chìng-'jù-de-'r̀-dz.

(*The day of some special occasion* jyé *in a compound, but* r̀ *if the occasion is not a Chinese festival*. ‖Christmas day is a holiday. shèng-dàn-'jyé (nèy-'tyān) fàng-'jyà. ‖Today is Memorial Day. jīn-tyan shŕ 'chīng-míng-'jyé. ‖Today is Lantern Day. 'jyēr dēng-'jyéer. ‖This is Flag Day. (*Non-Chinese*) 'jīn-tyan shŕ ('měy-gwo-)gwó-'chí-r̀-'dìng-jì-nyàn-'r̀.

(*Era, epoch, period, time*). ‖They're still using that to this day. tām shyàn-'dzày háy yùng 'jèy-ge-ne. ‖That custom is practised to this day. 'nèy-ge-'fēng-su dàw shyàn-'dzày háy 'yěw-ne. ‖That's the fashion of the day. nèy-shr 'rú-jīn dzwèy-lyéw-'shíng-de-'shŕ-yang. ‖Present day customs differ greatly from those of the old days. shyàn-'dzày-de-'fēng-su-shŕ-'gwàn gēn yǐ-'chyán 'dà bù-shyāng-'túng. ‖In America people don't realize such poverty exists in this day and age. dzày 'měy-gwo yì-'bān-rén shyǎng-bu-dàw shyàn-'dzày háy hwèy yěw-rén 'jème-chyúng. ‖The writers of those days had to pay for the printing of their own books. nèy-'shŕ-hew-de-dzwò-jyā shyě-le-'shū děy dz̀-'jǐ ná-chyán chywù 'yìn. ‖He was a naughty boy in his school days. tā shàng-'shywé de-shŕ-hew hěn táw-'chì. ‖Oh, the good old days! háy-shr 'nèy-ge-°nyán-'téwr! *or* °'shŕ-hewr! *or* °shŕ-hew 'hǎw! ‖He's seen better days. tā 'dāng-nyán 'gwò-gwo 'hǎw r̀-dz. ‖He's had his day. tā 'yǐ-jing gwò-'shŕ-le. ‖This is the day of air transportation. 'rú-jīn shŕ 'háng-kūng-ywùn-'shū-de-'shŕ-dày. ‖Let's stop work and call it a day. jyèw 'swàn-le-ba, wǒm 'béng dzwò-shya-chywu.

DEAD. (*See also* DEATH, DIE). 'sž-de, sž-; **to be dead** 'sž-le. *Not used in polite reference to a person's death.* ‖**Two dead horses lay there.** nàr 'dǎw-je 'lyǎng-pǐ-sž-'mǎ. ‖**They suffered the loss of 5,000 men, including dead, wounded, and captured.** tām swēn-shr-le 'wǔ-chyān-rén 'bāw-kwò 'sž-de, 'shāng-de, gēn 'fú-lwŏ-de. ‖**He's dead all right, and no mistake.** méy-'tswòr, yí-'dìng shŕ 'sž-le.

Monument to our honored dead. 'jēn-wáng 'jyàng-shŕ bēy.

(*Polite circumlocutions*). ‖**His father is dead.** tā-'fù-chin °'yǐ-jing chywù-'shŕ-le. *or* 'bú-'dzài-le. *or* °'gù-chywù-le. *or* °'gwò-chywù-le.

‖**Over my dead body!** chú-fēy wǒ 'sž-le! *or* nǐ děy 'shyān bǎ-'wǒ dǎ-'sž! *or* 'jywé-'dwèy 'bù-'shíng!

Shoot dead, strike dead, beat dead, etc. *Use resultative compounds, describing the type of action in the first element, and using sž as the second element; e.g.* ‖**They shot him dead with only one bullet.** tām 'yì-chyāng bǎ-ta 'dǎ-sž-le. ‖**Hang him till he's dead.** bǎ-ta dyàw-'sž. *or* bǎ-tā 'jyàw-sž. (*Figuratively*) ‖**She said she was dead with fatigue.** tā 'shwō tā·'lèy-sž-le.

Dead end street 'sž-hú-'tùngr.

(*Dull*). ‖**It's terribly dead around here in the summer.** 'shyà-tyan-de-'shŕ-hew jèr hěn méy-'yì-sz. ‖**The movie was pretty dead.** dyàn-yěngr 'shyāng-dāng gān-'dzàw (wú-'wèy).

(*Complete, completely*). ‖**I'm dead tired.** wó lèy jǐ-le. *or* wǒ 'lèy-sž-le. ‖**The car stopped dead.** chì-'chē jěng-'gèr tíng-'jù-le. ‖**Are you dead certain you can do it?** nǐ 'jwěn 'jŕ-dàw nǐ néng-'dzwò-ma? ‖**She fell in a dead faint.** tā 'hwēn-gwo-chywu-le. ‖**He's dead set against this plan.** 'jèy-ge-'jì-hwà tā °'shŕ-'jūng fǎn-'dwèy. *or* °'yí-ge-'jyèr-de fǎn-'dwèy. ‖**Whatever we say to him, he's dead set against this plan.** jèy-ge-'jì-hwà dzěm-me gēn-ta shwō, tā háy-shr fǎn-'dwèy. ‖**Come to a dead stop!** 'jàn-ju! ‖**He came to a dead stop.** tā jěng-'gèr 'jàn-ju-le. *or* tā yì-dyǎr yě bú-'dùng-le.

(*Obsolete, outdated*). ‖**That insurance law is dead.** nèy-ge-'bǎw-shyǎn-'fǎ 'yǐ-jing °'shŕ-'shyàw-le. *or* wú-'shyàw-le.

(*Inoperative*). ‖**The battery is dead.** dyàn-'chŕ bù-'jáw-le. ‖**The furnace is dead.** 'lú-dz 'myè-le.

(*Heavy and useless*). ‖**This trunk is so much dead weight.** jèy-ge-'shyāng-dz yèw 'chén yèw méy-'yùng.

DEAF. lúng; (*hard of hearing*) 'jùng-tīng. ‖**He's a little deaf.** tā(-'ěr-dwǒ) yěw dyǎr-'lúng. *or* °'jùng-tīng. ‖**He's stone deaf.** tā-'ěr-dwo jěng-gèr 'lúng-le. *or* tā-'lúng-de shém-me dēw tīng-bu-'jyàn. ‖**He's deaf in the left ear.** tā-'dzwŏ-ěr-dwo yěw dyǎr-°'lúng. *or* °'jùng-tīng. ‖**He doesn't go to concerts because he's deaf.** tā-'ěr-dwo lúng, 'swŏ-yǐ bú-'chywù tīng yīn-ywè-'hwèy. ‖**He became deaf lately.** tā 'jìn-lay 'lúng-le. ‖**The poor child was born deaf and dumb.** nèy-ge-'háy-dz 'jēn kě-'lyán, 'shēng-shya-lay yèw 'lúng yèw 'vá.

Deaf man 'lúng-dz.

(*Intentionally unhearing*). ‖**He is deaf to my requests for help.** wǒ chyéw-ta bāng-'máng, tā 'jwāng tīng-bu-'jyàn.

DEAL. (*Treat*) dày. ‖**He dealt fairly with me.** tā dày-wo °'shyāng-dāng 'gūng-ping. *or* °'háy 'gūng-ping. *or* °'háy bú-'hwày.

To deal with (*a person or situation*). ‖**That man is hard to deal with.** nèy-'ge-rén hěn nán °'yìng-fu. *or* °'dwèy-fu. ‖**That boy is hard to deal with** (*manage*). nèy-ge-'háy-dz jēn jyàw-rén hěn nán °'bàn. *or* °'gwǎn. ‖**He dealt with the situation superbly.** 'nèy-jyàn-shèr tā 'yìng-fu-de jēn 'hǎw. ‖**To deal with that kind of person you need a little finesse.** 'dwèy-fu 'nèy-jǔng-rén děy yùng dyǎr-'shěw-dwàn.

(*Treatment*). ‖**You can expect a square deal from him.** tā yí-'dìng bú-'hwèy gēn-ni °'shwǎ hwá-'téw. *or* °'shŕ-'hwày. *or* tā yí-'dìng bú-hwèy-'tswò-dày-ni-de. ‖**The workmen say they got a raw deal.** 'gūng-rén shwō 'tā-men °'āy-'kēng-le. *or* °'shèw-'pyàn-le. *or* °'chŕ-'kwēy-le.

(*Inflict*). ‖**The regulation deals a severe blow to my plans.** jèy-jǔng-'shyàn-jŕ gěy wǒ-de-'jì-hwà yí-ge hěn-'dà-de 'dǎ-jī. ‖**That kind of rule dealt a severe blow to the morale here.** 'nèy-jǔng-'gwēy-jywu jyàw jèr-'gūng-dzwò-de-'jīng-shen hěn 'shèw 'dǎ-jī.

(*Have charge over*) gwǎn. ‖**This office deals with passports.** 'jèy-ge-'jì-gwǎn shŕ gwǎn hù-'jàw-de.

(*Cards*) fā. ‖**Who dealt this hand?** 'jèy-tsž shŕ-'shwéy fā-de 'páy? ‖**Who dealt this mess?** jèy-shyē shŕ-'shwéy 'nùng-chu-lay-de? ‖**Whose deal is it?** gāy-shwéy 'fā-'páy-le? ‖**It's your deal.** gāy-'nǐ fā-'páy-le. *But* ‖**Deal me in** (*in cards or otherwise*). bǎ-wǒ 'swàn-jìn-chywù. *or* swàn-'wǒ yí-ge.

To deal in (*sell*) mày. ‖**That merchant deals in smuggled wine.** 'nèy-ge-rén (*or* nèy-ge-dzwǒ-'mǎy-may-de) mày 'sž-jyéw.

(*Business*) 'mǎy-may, 'jyāw-yì. ‖**They said the deal was off.** tām shwō nèy-pyàwr-'mǎy-may °'bù-néng chéng-'jyāw-le. *or* °'chǎ-le. *or* °'hwáng-le. ‖**He made a lot of money on that deal.** nèy-tsž-'jyāw-yì (*or* nèy-pyàwr-'mǎy-may) tā 'jwàn-le bù-'shǎw. ‖**Did you close that deal?** nèy-pyàwr-'jyāw-yì (*or* nèy-pyàwr-'may-may) 'chéng-le-ma? ‖**We don't deal with him any more.** wǒm bú-dzài gēn-tā °'yěw 'jyāw-yì-le. *or* °'dzwò 'mǎy-may-le. *or* °'yèw 'láy-wang-le.

(*Agreement*). ‖**It's a deal!** 'shíng. 'jyèw nèm-'jè. *or* dzám shwō-'hǎw-le-a (*or* dzám kě shwō-'hǎw-le), jyèw nèm-!jè. *or* (*Literary quotation*) yì-yán-jì-'chū, 'sž-mǎ nán-'jwēy. *or* bù-shywǔ 'fǎn-hwèy-le. ‖**If they make a deal with each other we're lost.** tām 'yàw-shr ('bǐ-tsž) shwō-'hǎw-le-(de-hwà) (*or* tām 'yàw-shr ('bǐ-tsž) lyán-he-chǐ-láy), 'dzám jyèw °'chwéy-le. *or* °'swàn-'wán-le. ‖**I made a deal with him.** wǒ gēn-tā shwō-'hǎw-le. *or* wǒ gēn-tā shwō-'chéng-le. *or* wǒ gēn-tā 'lyán-he-le.

(*Amount*). ‖A good deal remains to be done. gāy-dzwò-de háy °tày 'dwō-ne. *or* °tíng 'dwō-ne. ‖I haven't a great deal of money to spend. wǒ méy-'dwō-shǎw-chyán kě 'hwā. ‖I smoke a good deal. wǒ 'chēw-yān 'chēw-de hěn-'lì-hay.

DEAR.

(*Beloved*). ‖My (oldest) sister is very dear to me. wǒ-de-'dà-jyě gēn-wǒ 'dzwèy-hǎw.

(*Term of endearment*). *No special term is used in Chinese. The idea is expressed in the use of a personal name or a relationship term.*

Dear sir *expressed by one of many terms after the name, e.g.*, 'dà-jyàn, 'rú-wù.

‖Oh dear! kě 'lyǎw-bu-dé! *or* jēn 'dzāw-gāw! *or* jè-shr dzěm-me 'shwō-de! ‖Oh dear, we're late again! kě 'lyǎw-bu-'dé, (wǒ-men) 'yèw 'wǎn-le!

DEATH. *Most expressions include* sž *to die.* ‖His father met a strange death. tā-'fù-chin-'sž-de hěn 'lǐ-chí. ‖The death of the manager threw the whole company out of gear. °jīng-lǐ/yì-'sž, jéng-'gèr-de-'gūng-sž yěw dyǎr-jwā-'shyā. ‖His death was announced in the papers. 'bàw-shang dēng-je tā-sž-de-'shyàw-shi. ‖He was condemned to death by the military court. 'jywūn-shr̄-fǎ-'tíng pàn-tā 'sž-shíng. ‖Even death is better than this. 'sž-le dēw bǐ 'jèm-me 'hǎw. *or* jyèw-shr 'sž yě bǐ 'jèm-me hǎw. ‖It's a matter of life and death. jèy shr̄ 'shēng-sž-'gwān-téw.

In the following, sž *is not used.* ‖It's a matter of life and death. jèy-ge-shèr 'gwān-shi rén-'mìng. *or* jèy shr̄ jyèw-'mìng-de-'shr̄. ‖He isn't going to die a natural death. tā hwèy bù-dé shàn-'jūng-de. ‖I'm sorry to hear of the death of your friend. wǒ 'tīng-shwō nǐ-de-'péng-yew/bú-dzày-le; wǒ hěn nán-'shèw. ‖He'll fight you to the death. tā hwèy gēn-nǐ pīng-'mìng-de.

Death notice (*obituary*) 'fù-wén, bàw-sàng-'tyě-dz.

. . . **to death** (*kill by some means*). *Use a word meaning kill, or resultative compounds, of which the first element expresses the method of killing, and the second element is* sž, *e.g.*, **to do to death with** . . . bǎ . . . 'nùng-sž; *or* bǎ . . . 'shā-le; *or* bǎ . . . 'hày-le. ‖He was burned to death. tā 'shāw-sž-le. ‖They whipped him to death. tām ná 'byàn-dz bǎ-tā 'dǎ-sž-le. (*Figuratively*) ‖I'm bored to death. wǒ nì-'sž-le. *or* wǒ 'nì-de yàw-'mìng.

DEBT. (*Financial obligation*) jàng, jày, gāy-de-°'chyán (°'jàng, °'jày), chyàn-de-°'chyán (°'jàng, °'jày), lā-de-°'jàng (°'jày). **A debt** yì-bǐ-'jàng. *or* yì-bǐ-'jày. *or* yì-bǐ-'chyán. ‖How are you going to pay your debts? nǐ-de-nèy-shyē-'jàng (*or* -'jày, *or* nǐ-gāy-de-'chyán, *or* nǐ-gāy-de-'jàng, *or* nǐ-gāy-de-'jày, *or* nǐ-chyàn-de-'chyán, *or* nǐ-chyàn-de-'jàng, *or* nǐ-chyàn-de-'jày, *or* nǐ-lā-de-'jàng, *or* nǐ-lā-de-'jày) dzěm 'hwán-ne? ‖I'll try to pay these debts by the end of the month. wǒ shyǎng-'fár dzày ywè-dǐ yì-'chyán bǎ-'jàng (*or* bǎ nèy-jī-bǐ-'jàng, *or* bǎ-nèy-shyē-'jàng) 'hwán-le.

To be in debt chyàn-'jàng, chyàn-'jày, chyàn-'chyán, chyàn-'rén 'jàng, *etc., or use* gāy *instead of* chyán, *or* lā-'jàng-le, lā-'jày-le. ‖Are you in debt now? nǐ shyàn-dzày °chyàn-'jàng-ma? *or* gāy-rén 'jày-ma? *or* lā-'jàng-le méy-yew? *etc.*

National debt. (*General*) gwó-'jày; (*internal*) gūng-'jày.

(*Non-financial obligation*) chíng. ‖I'm in debt to him. wǒ 'chyàn tā-de-'chíng. *or* wǒ 'chyàn-tā yì-bǐ-'chíng. ‖I owe him a debt of gratitude. wǒ 'jēn-shr 'chyàn-tā bù-shǎw-chíng.

DECEMBER. shŕ-'èr-ywè; (*Lunar calendar*) 'là-ywè.

DECIDE. (*To make up one's mind*) 'jywé-dìng (*or* 'ná-'dìng) jú-yì, 'dǎ-dìng jú-yì. **To decide to** . . . 'jywé-dìng . . . ‖I've decided to go to the theater. wǒ 'jywé-dìng (yàw) chywù 'tīng-shì. ‖Wait until he's decided. děng-tā 'jywé-dìng-le (*or* děng-tā ná-dìng-le 'jú-yì, *or* děng-tā dǎ-dìng-le 'jú-yì) dzày 'shwō. ‖He can't decide which one to take with him. tā 'jywé-dìng-bu-'lyǎw (*or* tā bù-néng 'jywé-dìng, *or* tā 'ná-bu-dìng 'jú-yì, *or* tā 'dǎ-bu-dìng 'jú-yì, *or* tā yéw-'yí bù-jywé, *or* tā yéw-'yí bú-dìng) dàw-'dǐ shr̄ dày 'něy-ge. ‖We're still undecided as to which road to follow. dàw-'dǐ shr̄ dzěw 'něy-tyáw-'lù, wǒm háy-shr °'jywé-dìng-bù-'lyǎw. *or* °'bù-néng 'jywé-dìng. *etc.*

(*To judge*) pàn, dwàn, dìng, 'pàn-dwàn, 'pàn-dìng, 'dwàn-dìng; (*only legal*) 'pàn-jywé. ‖The referee decided in their favor. tsáy-pàn-'ywán dìng-de (*or* 'pàn-dwàn-de, *etc.*) shr̄ °tām 'yíng-le. *or* °tām 'dwèy-le. *or* tām-de-'fēr. ‖The Supreme Court decided in his favor. dzwèy-gāw-fǎ-'ywàn 'dwàn-de (*or* dwàn-dìng-de. *etc.*, *or* 'pàn-jywé-de) shr̄ tā 'yíng-le. *or* dzwèy-gāw-fǎ-'ywàn 'dwàn-dìng-le (*etc.*), shr̄ 'tā yíng. ‖The judge decided fourteen cases today. fǎ-'gwān pàn-le (*etc.*) shŕ-'sž-ge-'àn-dz.

(*To solve*) 'jyě-jywé. ‖It isn't easy to decide that question. nèy-ge-'wèn-tí bù-'rúng-yì 'jyě-jywé.

Decided, decidedly tày, méy-'wèn-tí, bú-yùng 'wèn. ‖His height gave him a decided advantage in the game. tā-de-'gèr nèm-'gāw dǎ-'chyéwr-de-shŕ-hew 'tày jàn 'pyán-yi-le. ‖He's decidedly the better of the two. tām-'lyǎ-rén-li méy-'wèn-tí (*or* tām-'lyǎ-rén-li bú-yùng 'wèn) shr̄ 'tā hǎw.

Deciding (*most important*) 'dzwèy jǔ-'yàw-de, 'dzwèy 'yàw-jǐn-de. ‖The expense was the deciding factor. 'kāy-shyaw tày-'dà shr̄ °'dzwèy jǔ-'yàw-de 'ywán-gù. *or* °'dzwèy 'yàw-jǐn-de-'ywán-gù.

DECISION. *See also* **DECIDE.** (*Act of making up one's mind*) *expressed by verbal forms.* (*When any number of persons is involved*) 'jywé-dìng; (*when specifically more than one is involved*) shwō-'hǎw, 'shāng-lyang 'hǎw, 'shāng-lyang-chu(-lay). ‖We haven't come to a decision yet. wǒ-men háy 'méy-yew 'jywé-dìng 'dzěm-me-yàng 'dzwò. *or* wǒ-men háy méy-shwō-'hǎw-le. *or* wǒ-men háy méy-'shāng-lyang 'hǎw-le-ne. or wǒ-men háy méy-'shāng-lyang-chū ge-'jyē-gwǒ láy-ne. We'll follow your decision. nǐ 'dzěm-me jywé-'dìng, wǒm jyèw-°jàw-je (or °dzěm-me) 'bàn.

(*Verdict*) 'pàn-jywé-de. The decision of the court will be announced tomorrow. 'fǎ-ywàn dzěm-me 'pàn-jywé-de 'míng-tyan ké-yi 'shywān-bù.

(*Determination, persistence*). He showed great decision in carrying out the plan successfully. tā 'jàw-je nèy-ge-'jì-hwà 'bàn-de hěn 'hǎw, tsúng-jèr kě-yǐ 'kàn-chu tā °yěw 'jywé-shin. or °yěw 'gwǒ-dwàn. or °néng 'jyān-chf dàw-'dǐ. or °néng yǎw-je yá 'gàn. or °bú-shr 'yéw-yí-bù-'jywé-de-rén.

DECK. On deck jyǎ-'bǎn, tsāng-'myàn, tsāng-'myàr; below deck 'tsāng(-li); a particular deck tséng (-tsāng). Let's go up on deck. dzám dàw jyǎ-'bǎn-shang-chywu-ba. or dzám dàw tsāng-'myàn (or -'myàr)-shang-chywu-ba. Let's go below deck. dzám dàw 'tsāng-li-chywu-ba. or dzám shyà-'tsāng-ba. Our stateroom is on C deck. wǒm-de-'fáng-jyān shr̀ dzày dì-'sān-tséng(-'tsāng-li).

On deck (*ready*). We're usually on deck early in camp. wǒ-men-mù-'yíng-de-shf-hew, lǎw-shr yì-chǐng-'dzǎwr jyew dēw jwěn-bèy 'hǎw-le chywù 'gūng-dzwò.

(*Cards*) fù. Do you have a deck of cards? nǐ yěw yí-'fù-páy méy-yew?

(*Decorate*). The building was decked with flags for the occasion. 'léw-shang gwà-'mǎn-le 'chí-dz. She was decked out with cheap jewelry. tā 'dày-le yì-'shēn-de 'jyǎ-'shěw-shr.

DECLARE. (*To say, claim*) 'rèn-wéy, shwō. The newspapers are declaring that he's innocent. 'bǎw-jǐ 'rèn-wéy (or shwō) tā méy-'dzwèy.

(*Legal verdict*) shywān-'gàw. The court declared him guilty. 'fǎ-tíng shywān-'gàw tā yěw-'dzwèy.

To declare *oneself* byǎw-'shr̀, 'shywān-bù. He declared himself against that kind of law. tā 'tséng-jīng byǎw-'shr̀ (or 'shvwān-bù) tā fǎn-'dwèy nèy-jǔng-'fǎ-lywù.

(*To announce*) 'shywān-bù. The two countries have declared an armistice. nèy-lyang-ge-'jyǎw-jàn-'gwó shywān-'bù tíng-'jàn-le.

To declare war shywān-'jàn. Declaration of war shywān-jàn-'shū. Russia (has) declared war on Germany. 'ē-gwo dwèy 'dé-gwo (or 'ē-gwo shyàng 'dé-gwo) shywān-'jàn.

To declare a dividend. The company has declared a dividend. nèy-ge-'gūng-sz̄ ('shywǎn-bù yàw) 'fēn húng-'lì.

(*To register*) bàw. Must I declare these goods at the customs? jèy-shyē-'hwò yí-dìng děy (or jèy-shyē-'hwò 'bì-shywū yàw) °bàw-'gwān-ma? or °dzày hǎy-'gwān-shang 'bàw-le-ma? You must declare everything in your possession at the customs. yěw 'shémme dēw děy 'bàw(-gwān). or dzày 'hǎy-gwān-nàr yěw 'shém-me dēw děy 'bàw.

DEED. (*Action*) shr̀. The soldier was decorated for a brave deed. nèy-ge-'bīng dzwò-le yí-jyàn-yǔng-gǎn-de-'shr̀, swǒ-yǐ lǐng °'jyǎng-jǎng. or °'shywūn-jǎng.

Deeds (*behavior*) 'shíng-wéy. They should be held responsible for all their deeds. tām-yí-'chyè-de-'shíng-wéy 'yīng-dāng gwēy tām-'dž-jǐ fù-'dzé.

(*To property*) chì; official deed 'húng-chì; privately drawn deed 'báy-chì. I received the deed from my lawyer. wǒ tsúng wǒ 'lywù-shr̀-nèr 'shēw-daw-de nèy jāng-'chì. He went to the magistrate's office to register a deed. tā dàw shyàn-gūng-'shù chywù shwèy-'chì-chywu-le.

To deed (*transfer*) 'ràng-gěy. The land was deeded to its new owner. 'nèy-kwày-'dì 'ràng-gěy nèy-ge-shīn-dì 'jǔ-le. *But* The land was deeded to his son (*by inheritance*). nèy-kwày-dì °'chwán-gěy (or °'lyéw-gěy) tā-'ér-dz-le.

DEEP. (*Literally and figuratively; but see exceptions below*) shēn. That's a deep well. nèy-shr ge-'shēn-jǐng. or nèy-ge-'jǐng hěn 'shēn. That well is the deepest. 'nèy-ge-'jǐng 'shēn. This lake is very deep. jèy-ge-'hú shēn-'jí-le. The mine is half a mile deep. jèy-ge-'kwàng yěw bàn-lǐ-'dì-shēn. Is the wound very deep? 'shāng-kěw 'shēn-bu-shēn? They dug deeper and deeper into the mine. tām dzày 'kwàng-li wā-de 'ywè-láy ywè-'shēn. They dug deeper and deeper into that subject. nèy-ge-'wèn-tí tām yán-jyew-de 'ywè-láy ywè-'shēn. That subject is too deep for me. nèy-ge-'wèn-tí 'wèy-wǒ tày 'shēn-le. Take a few deep breaths and you'll feel better. 'shēn-shēn-de chwǎn jǐ-kěw-'chì nǐ yí-dìng 'jywé-de hǎw 'dwō-le. Beyond them are deep forests. tām 'chyán-byar shr̀ hěn-'shēn-de shù-'lín-dz. The hotel is deep in the mountains. 'fàn-dyàn dzày shēn-'shān-li. The sky was a deep blue. tyān shr̀ 'shēn-lán-'shǎr-de. He studied deep into the night. tā nyàn-'shū nyàn-dàw 'shēn-jīng-bàn-'yè. He has given the question deep study. tā bǎ nèy-ge-'wèn-tí 'kǎw-lywù-de hěn °'shēn. or °'dž-shì.

But (*as noted above*) That doctrine is very deep. nèy-ge-'dàw-li hěn 'àw-myàw. That family is always deep in debt. nèy-'jyār-rén lǎw-shr̀ 'chyàn bù-shǎw-'jàng. He is a man of deep feelings. tā shr̀ yí-ge-'gǎn-chíng-hěn-'jùng-de-rén. His voice is a lot deeper than it used to be. tā-de-'sǎng-mér bǐ yǐ-chyán °dī 'dwō-le. or °tsū 'dwō-le.

DEFEAT. (*In battle*). A defeat (yí-)bày, (yí-tsž-)bày-'jàng; to defeat someone bǎ . . . dǎ-'bày; to be defeated bày-le, dǎ-'bày-le, dǎ bày-'jàng-le. This defeat decided the whole war. jèy-tsž-bày-'jàng 'yǐng-shyǎng 'chywán-jywú. or jèy-yí-'bày 'yǐng-. . . . We defeated the enemy. wǒm bǎ 'dí-rén dǎ-'bày-le. They were defeated three times (*in a row*). tām 'jyē-lyán (dǎ-)bày-le 'sān-tsž. or tām dǎ-le 'sān-tsž-bày-'jàng. (*Without emphasis on the defeats being consecutive*) tām 'jyē-lyán dǎ-le 'sān-ge-bày-'jàng. They suffered

Lion, closeup, Beijing

Lotus, West Lake, Hang Chow

repeated defeats. (*Literary quotations; may also mean* They were defeated three times.) tām 'sān-jàn 'sān-běy. *or* tām 'sān-jàn 'sān-bày (*literally*).

To defeat someone (*in sports*) bǎ . . . 'yíng; to be defeated 'shū-le. ‖We defeated our opponents in the last game. wǒm 'shàng-yí-tsž bǎ 'dwèy-fāng 'yíng-le. ‖They were defeated three times. tām 'shū-le 'sān-tsž.

(*Work against*). ‖They're defeating their own purposes. nà shř 'dž-shyāng máw-°'shywǔn. *or* °'dwèn (*literary quotation*).

.(*To dispose of*). ‖We defeated their plans at one stroke. wǒm 'yí-'shyà-dz jyèw bǎ tām-de-'jì-hwà (*or* -'yīn-méw) 'pwò-hwày-le.

DEFEND. (*Against physical attack*) 'fáng-shěw, shěw, 'bǎw-wèy. ‖That position is well defended. nèy-ge-'jèn-dì °'fáng-shěw-de hěn 'hǎw. *or* °'shěw-de hěn 'hǎw. *or* °'bǎw-wèy-de hén 'hǎw. ‖They decided not to defend the city. tā-men 'jywé-dìng °'bù-shěw nèy-ge-'chéng. *or* °'bù-bǎw-wèy nèy-ge-'chéng. *or* °'bù-fáng-shěw nèy-ge-'chéng. *or* °'fàng-chì nèy-ge-'chéng. ‖That boxer has a strong attack but he can't defend himself well. nèy-ge-dǎ-'chywán-de hwèy 'gūng, bú-hwèy 'shěw. *See also* **PROTECT**, take care of *under* **CARE.**

(*In court*) tì (*or* gěy) . . . dǎ 'gwān-sz; tì (*or* gěy) . . . 'byàn-hù. ‖He should get a lawyer to defend him. tā 'yīng-dāng chǐng yí-ge-'lywù-shř-lay 'tì-tā (*or* gěy-tā) °dǎ-'gwān-sz. *or* °'byàn-hù.

Other English expressions. ‖He issued the report to defend his reputation. (*Against attacks already made*) tā fā-chu nèy-ge-'bàw-gàw-lay wèy-de shř gěy tā-dž-jǐ-de-'míng-ywù láy 'byàn-hù. (*Against possible attacks*) tā fā-chu nèy-ge-'bàw-gàw-lay wèy-de shř 'fáng-bèy yěw-rén 'gūng-jí tā-de-'míng-ywù. ‖She always defends him. tā lǎw tì-tā 'byàn-hù. *or* tā lǎw 'hù-je tā shwō-'hwà. ‖He said it in that way to defend himself. (*Against past accusations*) tā-'nèm-shwō ɛhř wèy 'dž-jǐ 'byàn-hù. (*Against possible attacks*) tā-'nèm-shwō shř °'fáng-bèy yěw-rén 'shwō-tā. *or* °'dī-fáng-je yěw-rén 'shwō-tā. *or* °gěy 'dž-jǐ lyéw 'dì-bu. *or* °'yàw 'dǔ-ju 'byé-rén-de-'dzwěy.

DEFENSE. (*National*) 'gwó-fáng. ‖He has a job in a defense plant. tā dzày yí-ge-'gwó-fáng-'gūng-yè-'gūng-chǎng dzwò-'shř. ‖The defenses of the country have stood the test. 'gwó-fáng 'gūng-dzwò bàn-de 'hǎw, yǐ-jīng jèng-'shř-le.

(*Physical*). *See also* **DEFEND, PROTECT,** take care of *under* **CARE.** ‖We lost the game because of our poor defense. wǒm 'shū-le, 'yīn-wèy 'shěw-de 'bù-hǎw.

(*Legal*). ‖The defense rested its case. 'bèy-gàw-'fāng-myàn 'tíng-jř 'byàn-hù, 'jīng-hèw shywān-'pàn. ‖The lawyer summarized the defense for the accused in only three minutes. 'lywù-shř wèy 'bèy-gàw 'byàn-hù jř 'shwō-le 'sān-fēn-jūng, jyèw 'wán-le.

Self-defense. ‖He said it in self-defense. tā shř dž-wèy tsáy 'nèm 'shwō-de. ‖What can you say in your defense? nǐ yěw 'shém-me °kě-'shwō-de? *or* °'hwà shwō?

DEFINITE. yí-'dìng-de, -dìng, jwěn. Definitely yí-'dìng. ‖Can you name a definite date? nǐ néng 'shwō-chu-lay yí-ge-yí-'dìng-de-'ř-dz-ma? ‖Nothing is definite. 'shem-me dēw háy méy-'dìng-ne. ‖He was definite in his refusal. tā shwō tā yí-'dìng bú-'gàn. ‖That's definitely not mine. nèy yí-'dìng bú-shř 'wǒ-de. *or* nèy 'jwěn bú-shř 'wǒ-de. ‖He says definitely that it's yours. tā yí-'dìng (*or* tā yì-'kěw yǎw-'dìng-le) shwō shř 'nǐ-de. ‖He says that it's definitely yours. tā shwō nèy °yí-'dìng shř nǐ-de. *or* °méy-yew 'wén-ti shř nǐ-de. ‖When can you give me a definite answer? nǐ 'shém-me-shř-hew néng gěy-wǒ ge-°'jwěn-hwàr? *or* °yí-'dìng-de-'hwéy-hwà? ‖Is that a definite answer? dzám 'yì-yán wéy-'dìng-le-ma? ‖Now this is a definite agreement, and no backing out! dzám 'yì-yán wéy-'dìng, 'bù-néng fān-'hwěy! ‖I can't say definitely. wǒ háy bù-néng shwō-°'jwěn-lc. *or* °'dìng-le. ‖The plans for the trip aren't definite. lywù-'shíng-'jì-hwà háy méy-°'dìng. *or* °'dìng-'jwěn. *or* °'dìng-'hǎw.

(*Precise*.) ‖This sentence doesn't have a definite meaning. jèy-jywú-hwà-de-'yì-sz °'hán-han-hū-'hū-de. *or* °dzày lyǎng-'kě-jř-'jyān. ‖He never answers definitely. tā 'hwéy-dá-de-'hwà lǎw-shr °dzày lyǎng-'kě-jř-'jyān. *or* °'hán-hán-hū-'hū-de. *or* tā lǎw bù-kěn° 'tùng-tung-kwāy-'kwǎr-de °shwō ge-'jwěn-hwàr. *or* °'dā-ying.

DEGREE. ·(*Unit of measurement*) dù. ‖A centigrade thermometer is a thermometer which divides the range from the freezing point of water to its boiling point into 100 degrees. bǎy-dù-'byǎw shř yì-jǔng hán-shǔ-'byǎw, tsǔng shwěy-de-'jyē-bīng-dyǎn dàw 'fèy-dyǎn 'fēn-chéng yì-bǎy-'dù. ‖At night the temperature sometimes drops forty degrees. yěw-'shř-hew 'yè-li yí-'jyàng·jyàng 'sž-shr-dù. *or* . . . drops to forty degrees below zero. . . . yí-'jyàng jyàng-dàw líng(-dù-yǐ)-shyà 'sž-shr-dù. ‖The pilot recorded the degrees of latitude and longitude. nèy-ge-jyà-shř-'ywán bǎ 'jīng-wěy-dù 'jì-shya-lay-le. ‖The lines form an angle of 45 degrees. lyǎng-tyáw-'shyàn 'chéng yí-ge-sž-shr-wǔ-dù-'jyáw. ‖20° 35′ 59″ N., 118° 10′ 0″ E. běy-'wěy èr-shr-'dù, 'sān-shr-wǔ-'fēn, 'wǔ-shr-jyěw-'myǎw; dūng-'jīng 'yì-bǎy-'shř-bā-'dù, shř-'fēn, líng-'myǎw. ‖What degree of progress have you made in English? nǐ 'yīng-wén 'yǐ-jing jìn-bù dàw shém-'chéng-dù-le?

(*Extent*). ‖That book is useful only to a small degree. nèy-běr-'shū-de-'yùng-chu bú-'dà. *or* nèy-běr-'shū yěw dyǎr-'yùng kě-shr bú-'dà. ‖The workmen have reached a high degree of efficiency. 'gūng-rén-de-'shyàw-lywù yǐ-'jīng hěn-'gāw-le. ‖You'll have to use your own judgment to a certain degree. yí-'bù-fèn (or yěw-de-'shr̀, or yěw-de-'shf-hew) nǐ děy 'dz̀-jǐ 'jywé-dìng.

(Academic) 'shywé-wèy. B.S. (degree) lǐ-'shywé-shr̀(-'shywé-wèy); LL.B. (degree) fǎ-'shywé-shr̀ (-'shywé-wèy). ‖What degrees have you received? nǐ dé-de dēw shr̀ 'shém-me-'shywé-wèy? ‖He holds a B.A. (degree). tā yěw 'yí-ge-wén-'shywé-shr̀ (-'shywé-wèy).

By degrees. (See also GRADUALLY). ‖He's getting well by degrees. tā jyàn 'jyān-de 'hǎw-le.

The third degree 'yùng-shíng; (if condemning it) yung 'fēy-shíng. ‖He wouldn't confess until after they gave him the third degree. méy-yěw 'yùng-shíng yǐ-chyán tā °bù-kěn chéng-'rèn. or °bù-kěn 'jāw. ‖It's illegal to use the third degree to get a confession. yùng 'fēy-shíng jyàw-rén rèn-'dzwèy shr̀ 'fēy-fǎ-de. or (literary) 'chywū-dǎ-chéng-'jāw shr̀ 'fēy-fǎ-de.

First degree murder 'ywù-méw 'shā-rén. ‖He's accused of murder in the first degree. tā-de-'dzwèy-míng shr̀ 'ywù-méw 'shā-rén.

DELAY. 'dān-gé, dān-wù. ('dān-wù usually refers to a more serious or irreparable delay.) Be delayed is expressed as be late wǎn, bù-'dzǎw. ‖The delay caused us to miss the train. nèm-yì-'dān-gé jyàw wǒ-men bǎ-chē 'wù-le. ‖He delayed me. 'tā jyàw-wo 'wǎn-de. or wǒ jyàw-'tā (gěy) 'dān-gé-de. ‖She blames her parents for delaying her marriage. tā 'mán-ywàn tā-dyē-'mā °bǎ tā-de-'jūng-shēn-dà-'shr̀ gěy 'dān-wù-le. or °bú-jyàw-ta 'dzǎw jyē-'hwēn. ‖She blames her parents for delaying her marriage two weeks. tā 'mán-ywàn tā-dyē-'mā bǎ tā-de-'hwēn-chī 'dān-ge-le lyǎng-ge-lǐ-'bày. ‖Don't delay the child's education. byé 'dān-wu-le háy-dz shàng-'shywé. or byé jyàw háy-dz shàng-'shywé shàng-'wǎn-le.

Don't delay is expressed as hurry up. ‖Don't delay sending the letter. 'gǎn-jǐn bǎ-'shìn 'sùng-chywu.

(Postpone) 'jǎn-chī. ‖We'll delay the trip a week. wǒm 'jywé-dìng bǎ 'lywǔ-shíng 'jǎn-chī yí-ge-lǐ-'bày.

DELICIOUS. hěn hǎw 'chr̄. ‖This candy is delicious. jèy-ge-'táng hěn hǎw 'chr̄. ‖They served us a delicious supper. tām 'gěy-le wǒ-men yī-dwèn-hěn-hǎw-'chr̄-de-'wǎn-fàn.

DELIGHT. (Please) gāw-'shìng. ‖The play delighted everyone. nèy-ge-'shì jyàw dà-jya-'hwǒr tǐng gāw-'shìng. ‖Buying clothes is her greatest delight. mǎy-'yī-fu shr̀ tā-°'dzwèy-gāw-'shìng-de-'shr̀. or °'dzwèy-ày-dzwò-de-'shr̀.

Delight in 'shǐ-hwān, ày. ‖He delights in teasing her. tā 'shǐ-hwān 'dèw-tā. or tā (hěn) ày 'dèw-tā.

Be delighted. ‖I'd be delighted! 'hǎw-'jí-le. ‖I'll be delighted to have you come. 'nǐ néng láy hǎw-'jí-le.

‖I'll be delighted to oblige you. ké-yi gěy-nín 'bàn. or (more politely) yěw 'jī-hwèy gěy-'nín shyàw-'láw, jēn-shr 'chyéw-jr-bu-'dé. ‖I'll be delighted to help you out. jèy-ge-shr̀ wǒ 'ké-yi 'dā-ying. ‖I was delighted with the trip. jèy-tsz̀-'chū-chywu 'wár-de 'hěn-hǎw.

DELIVER. (Send, bring) sùng. ‖The mailman delivers the mail at nine o'clock. sùng-'shìn-de 'dzǎw-chen 'jyěw-dyǎn láy sùng-'shìn. ‖Do you deliver? 'nǐm-jèr gwǎn-'sùng-ma? ‖Please deliver these packages to my hotel. bǎ jèy-shyē-'bāw-gwo 'sùng-dàw wǒ-de-'lywǔ-gwǎn. ‖It'll be delivered Monday. shīng-chī-'yī sùng-dàw. ‖No delivery on Saturdays. 'shīng-chī-'lyèw bú-sùng-'hwò.

(Produce orally). ‖The professor delivered a course of ten lectures. jyàw-'shèw 'lyán-je gěy-le shf-ge-'yǎn-jyǎng. ‖The jury delivered its verdict. péy-'shěn-de-'wěy-ywán-men 'yǐ-jīng 'shywān-bù-le tā-men-shěn-chá-de-'jyé-gwǒ.

Deliver the goods. ‖He promised to do it for us, but he couldn't deliver the goods. tā 'dā-yìng tì wǒ-men 'bàn, kě-shr méy-gěy bàn-'dàw.

Deliver a child. ‖The doctor was called on to deliver two babies last night. 'dày-fu dzwór-'wǎn-shang 'chīng chū-chywu 'lyǎng-tsz̀ shēw-'shēng.

DEMAND. (If a person demands) yí-'dìng yàw, 'fēy-yàw ... bù-'shíng, shwō (...) děy ... (or jyàw may be substituted for yàw if the demand is made upon another person). ‖When she was sick she demanded that we visit her every day. tā-'bìng-de-shf-hew, °yí-'dìng yàw (or jyàw) wǒ-men 'tyān-tyar chywù 'kàn-ta. or °'fēy-jyàw wǒ-men 'tyān-tyar chywù 'kàn-ta bù-'shíng. or °shwō wǒ-men děy 'tyān-tyar chywù 'kàn-ta. ‖He demands immediate payment. tā shwō 'chyán 'lì-kè děy 'hwán-tā. or tā shwō děy 'lì-kè hwán-tā 'chyán. or tā yí-'dìng yàw 'lì-kè hwán-'chyán. or tā 'fēy-yàw 'lì-kè hwán-'chyán bù-shíng.

(If a situation demands). ‖This matter demands your immediate attention. 'jèy-jyàn-shr̀ nǐ °(yí-'dìng) děy 'lì-shf 'bàn. or °'fēy-děy 'lì-shf 'bàn (bù-'shíng).

Other English expressions. ‖His constant demands get on our nerves. tā 'chéng-tyar 'má-fan rén 'jēn yěw-dyǎr jyàw-'rén tǎw-'yàn-ta. ‖They make many demands on our time. tām 'jàn-le wǒm 'bù-shǎw-'shf-hew. ‖The library isn't big enough to supply the demand for books. 'tú-shū-gwǎn-de-shū bú-'gèw yùng-de. ‖This is in demand now. 'shyàn-dzày 'yàw-'jèy-ge-de hěn 'dwō. ‖He was in great demand as a speaker. 'chīng-tā 'yǎn-jyǎng-de hěn 'dwō.

DENTIST. 'yá-yī, 'yá-yī-sheng, 'yá-dày-fu. ‖Is there a good dentist around here? jèr yěw ge-hǎw-'yá-yī (etc.) 'méy-yew?

DENY. fěw-'rèn, bù-chéng-'rèn. ‖He denies he was ever a member of that party. tā fěw-'rèn tā 'jyā-rù-gwò nèy-ge-'dǎng. ‖The prisoner denies all the charges. 'fàn-rén bù-chéng-'rèr yěw-'dzwèy. ‖He denies that he is the father of this child. tā bù-'chéng-rèn 'tā shř jèy-ge-háy-dz-de-'fù-chin.

(Technically, in law). ‖The judge asks the prisoner, "Are you going to deny these charges?" 'fǎ-gwān wèn 'fàn-rén shwō, "nǐ háy bù-'jāw-ma?"

Other English expressions. ‖I couldn't deny him such a small favor. 'jèm-dyǎr-'shyǎw-shèr wǒ 'bù-hǎw-'yì-sz bù-'dā-ying tā. ‖She never denied herself anything. tā 'dž-jǐ 'yàw (or 'shyǎng) dzěm-je, jyèw 'fēy dzěm-je bù-'kě. or tā 'dž-jǐ shyǎng 'mǎy shém-me, jyèw 'fēy-mǎy bù-'kě.

DEPARTMENT. -bù, 'bù-fēn, or sometimes chù. Book and magazine department 'shū-bàw-bù; men's clothing department 'nán-yī-bù; stationery department 'wén-jywù-bù. ‖He works in the accounting department. tā dzày 'kwày-ji-bù (or 'kwày-ji-chù) 'dzwò-shř. ‖What department does he work in? tā dzày shém-me-'bù-fēn dzwò-'shř? ‖You'll have to see someone from the State Department. nǐ děy chywù 'jyàn-yi-jyàn 'měy-gwó-wày-jyāw-'bù-de-'rén.

Department store bǎy-'hwò-gūng-'sz; fire department 'shyāw-fáng-'dwèy. ‖Smoking forbidden by order of fire department. 'shyāw-fáng-'dwèy yěw-'lìng, bù-'shywǔ chēw-'yān.

DEPEND. Depend on (to trust to something) kàw. ‖We have to depend on the radio for our news. wǒm 'yàw-shyǎng 'dé-dàw 'shīn-wén jǐ néng 'kàw-je wú-shyàn-'dyàn.

Depend on (to be determined by) děy 'kàn, děy 'chyáw. ‖My plans depend on the weather. wǒ-de-'jì-hwà děy 'kàn (or 'chyáw) 'tyān-chi dzěm-'yàng. ‖Our trip depends on whether we can get a passport. wǒm 'chywù-bu-'chywù děy 'kàn hù-'jàw 'ná-de-dàw-'ná-bu-dàw. ‖That depends on what she says. děy 'kàn (or 'chyáw) tā 'dzěm-me shwō. ‖It depends on him. děy kàn-'tā. or děy chyáw-'tā. ‖That depends. děy 'kàn-yi-kan. or děy 'chyáw-yi-chyáw (dzày 'shwō).

Depend on (to rely on a person to do something) jǐ. ‖Don't depend on me alone. byé jìng 'jǐ-je 'wǒ. ‖You can't depend on just a child to do all the housework for you. 'jyā-li-de-'shèr byé gwāng 'jǐ-je yí-ge-shyǎw-'háy-dz 'dēw gěy-nǐ 'dzwò-le. ‖He thinks he'll depend on that son-in-law of his to help him. tā shyǎng 'jǐ-je (or 'kàw-je) tā-nèy-ge-'nywǔ-shywù-lay 'bāng-tā.

Depend on (to consider someone reliable). Expressed either by saying someone is dependable, using resulta-

tive compounds with kàw, or by saying that someone is certain about a person. ‖You can depend on him. tā 'kàw-de-jù. or tā kě-'kàw. ‖You can't depend on him. is expressed as He can't be depended on. tā 'kàw-bu-jù. or tā bù-kě-'kàw. ‖Can I depend on his keeping his promise? tā-dā-ying-de-'hwà °kàw-de-'jù-ma? or °kě-'kàw-ma? ‖You can depend on him to see the thing through. tā 'jwèn (or tā yí-'dìng) hwèy bǎ jèy-jyàn-'shèr bàn-dàw-'dǐ-de. or tā 'jywé-bu-hwèy méy-bàn-wán jyèw bù-'gwǎn-de. ‖You can depend on him to spill the beans. jwèn méy-'tswòr, yì yěw-'shèr tā jyèw gěy 'dēw 'shwō-chu-chywu-le.

DEPTH. shēn. ‖The well is fifty feet in depth. jǐng yěw 'wǔ-shf-chř-'shēn. ‖Measure the depth with this stick. yùng jèy-gēr-'gwèr 'lyáng-yi-lyáng yěw dwō-'shēn. ‖He has great depth of mind. tā-de-'sz-shyǎng hěn 'shēn. ‖That music shows great depth of feeling. nèy-ge-'yīn-ywè °hán-'chíng hěn 'shēn. or meaning it moves people very much. °hěn 'dùng-rén.

(Interior space, as a hall, stage, etc.) 'jìn-shen. ‖Because of its depth the stage can accommodate a large cast. shì-'táy-de-'jìn-shen hěn 'shēn, ké-yi 'rúng-shya hěn-dwō-de-yǎn-'ywán.

Out of (beyond) one's depth. ‖I feel out of my depth when I talk to him. hé-'tā tán-hwà, wǒ jyǎn-'jf shř 'jywé-de wǒ yí-'chyǎwr bù-'tūng. ‖I don't go beyond my depth. (Literally, in swimming) wǒ yí-'dìng bú-'fù-dàw 'tày-shēn-de-dì-fang-chywu. (Figuratively, of physical, mental or other difficulties) wǒ yěw 'dž-jŕ-jŕ-'míng. or wǒ bú-hwèy bú-'dž-lyàng-'lì-de. (Last two are literary quotations.)

DESCRIBE. (By telling about) 'shwō-yi-shwō, 'shwō-chu-lay, shwō-gěy ... 'tīng-ting; (By writing or telling about) 'myáw-shye ('myáw-shye); (by drawing a picture) 'hwà-chu-lay; (by picturing in words) 'shíng-rúng(-chu-lay). ‖Describe the kind of work you have been doing. nǐ-dēw-shr-dzwò-gwo-'shém-me-shèr °shwō-yi-shwō wǒ 'tīng-ting. or °shwō-gey wǒ 'tīng-ting. ‖Can you describe his appearance? tā-'jǎng-de shém-me-'yàngr nǐ néng 'shwō-chu-lay-ma? ‖Describe his appearance. bǎ tā-'jǎng-de-shém-me-'yàngr gěy-wo °'shwō-yi-shwō. or °'myáw-shye 'myáw-shye. or °'hwà-chu-lay. ‖I can't describe it. nèy-ge wǒ 'shíng-rúng-bu-cháy. ‖I can't describe it; it's too horrible. 'tày kě-'pà-le; wǒ jyǎn-'jf 'shíng-rúng-bu-chū-láy. ‖You can feel it but you can't describe it. shīn-li 'jywé-de-chū, kě-shr 'shíng-rúng-bu-chu-láy. ‖He described her perfectly. tā bǎ-tā 'shíng-rúng-de jēn-'shyàng.

DESERT. (Waste region) 'shā-mwò. ‖The desert begins a few miles beyond the town. chéng-'nèy-byar jǐ-lǐ-'dì jyèw shř 'shā-mwò. ‖We will soon have to cross a desert region. wǒ-men bù- jyěw jyèw děv 'gwò shā-mwo-'dì-le.

DESERT. (*Leave, run away*) păw; (*military*) táw; *and other expressions.* ‖The woman deserted her husband and ran off with another man. nèy-ge-nywŭ-rén 'dwŏ kay-le 'jàng-fu, gēn 'byé-rén păw-le. ‖The town was completely deserted when we got there. wŏm 'dàw-le nàr yí-'kàn, rén-'yīng dēw méy-'yĕw. ‖The town was deserted. nèy-ge-'dì-fang-de-rén 'dēw păw-le. ‖At midnight the streets have a deserted look. dàw-le bàn-'yè, 'jyē-shang-de-'yàng-dz hĕn 'shyāw-tyáw.

    Deserter (*military*) 'táw-bīng. ‖When a soldier deserts, he is shot if caught. 'tíw-bīng dzwŏ-'dàw-le, jyèw chyāng-'bì. ‖That soldier deserted. nèy-ge-'bīng °táw-le. *or* °păw-le.

DESERVE. 'yīng-dāng 'dé, găy 'dé. ‖Such a steady worker deserves better pay. shyàng-'tā-nèm-'chín-jin-de-rén 'yīng-dāng (*or* găy) dé 'gāw-yi-dyar-de-'shīn-shwey.

    ‖You deserve it! (*Something bad*) 'găy! *or* hwó-'găy! (*Something good*) 'lĭ-swŏ 'dāng-rán (*literary*). *or* 'yīng-dāng rú-'tsž (*literary*). *or* jèm-je 'dwèy-le. ‖He deserves it. (*Something bad*) tā 'găy nèm-je. *or* nèm-je 'dwèy-le. *or* 'sž-gwèy yàw-'jàng, hwó-'găy. (*But said of something good*) 'nèm-je tsáy jyàw 'gūng-ping. ‖He doesn't deserve it. nà 'shŕ-dzày bù-°'gūng-ping. *or* °'dwèy. ‖It's my mistake; I deserve it. shŕ wŏ-de-'tswòr; méy-de-'ywàn. ‖I don't deserve it. (*Bad treatment*) wŏ 'ywān-de-hwang. *or* 'ywān-wang wŏ-le. (*Overly good treatment*) wŏ ('shŕ-dzày) bú-'pèy. *or* wŏ ('shŕ-dzày) bù-găn-'dāng.

DESIGN. (*Pattern*) 'hwā-yàng. ‖The tablecloth has a simple design in the center. jwŏ-'bù-de-dāng-'jūng yĕw yì-dyăr-'hwā-yàng.

    (*To make a plan*) (shè-)'jì; (*make a drawing*) (hwà-)'tú(-àn); (*make a blueprint*) (hwà) 'lán-tú; (*draw a design*) (hwà) shè-jì-'tú. ‖Draw a design (*for this*). hwà yì-jāng-'tú(-àn), *or* hwà yì-jāng-shè-jì-'tú. *or* (*if a blueprint*) hwà yì-jāng-'lán-tú. ‖He is good at designing (*making general plans*). tā-shè-'jì-de hĕn-hăw. ‖He is working on the design for a new machine. tā 'jèng-dzày shè-'jì, shyăng 'dzàw yí-ge-shīn-de-'jī-chì. *or* (*if he is drawing the design*) tā shyăng 'dzàw yí-ge-shīn-de-'jī-chì, 'jèng-dzày hwà-'tú(-àn). ‖The architect is designing an addition to the building. gūng-cheng-'shŕ jèng-dzày shè-'jì, shyăng bă-'léw gày-'chū-chywu yí-'kwày.

    To paint designs hwà tú-àn-'hwàr. ‖She's an expert in painting designs. tā shŕ hwà-tú-àn-'hwàr-de-jwān-'jyā.

    (*To pattern*). ‖She designs her own clothes. tā-'yī-fu-de-'yàng-dz shŕ 'dž-jì-'shyăng-chū-lay-de.

    (*Purpose*). ‖What's your design in going that way? nĭ wàng-'nèm dzĕw shŕ (*or* yĕw) shém-me-'yì-sz?

DESIRE. To desire shyăng-'yàw. ‖What do you desire most of all? nĭ 'dzwèy-shyăng-'yàw-de shŕ 'shém-me?

    A desire (*for something in particular*) 'yì-sz. ‖He's expressed a desire to meet you. tā yĕw °'shyăng-'jyàn-nĭ-de-'yì-sz. *or* °'yì-sz láy 'jyàn-nĭ.

    Desires (*for luxuries, etc.*) 'ywù-wàng. ‖My desires are easily satisfied. wŏ-de-'ywù-wàng hĕn 'rúng-yì 'măn-dzú.

    See also **WANT, LIKE.**

DESK. (*For writing or studying*) shū-'jwōr; (*counter; as in a hotel*) gwèy-'táy. ‖Hand your application to the secretary at that desk. bă nĭ-de-'chīng-chyéw-shū 'jyāw-gĕy dzày °gwèy-'táy-nèr-de-gwăn-'shŕ-de. *or*, (*depending on the kind of desk*) °shū-'jwōr-nèr-de-gwăn-'shŕ-de. ‖Leave your key at the desk. bă 'yàw-shr 'jyāw-gĕy gwèy-'táy-nèr.

    (*For a section, or department, even if located at one desk*) -bù, -chù. Information desk 'wèn-shŕ-'chù. ‖Ask at the information desk over there. dàw 'wèn-shŕ-'chù-chywu 'dă-tīng.

    City desk (*newspaper*) 'bĕn-dì-shīn-'wén(-byān-jì)-'bù.

DESTROY. (*General*) hwĕy. ‖This delay will destroy our chances of success. jèy-yī-'dān-wù bă wŏ-men-'chéng-gūng-de-'jī-hwèy dēw 'hwĕy-le. ‖The town was entirely destroyed. chywán-'chéng dēw gĕy-'hwĕy-le.

    Destroy evidence hwĕy, 'shyāw-myè. ‖He destroyed all the evidence. tā bă 'jèng-jywù dēw 'hwĕy-le, (*or* 'shyāw-myè-le.)

    (*Military*) hwĕy-'myè. ‖First destroy their tanks. shyān hwĕy-'myè-le tām-de-'jàn-chē.

    (*By fire*) expressed with to burn shāw *or* with a resultative compound whose first part is shāw, and whose second part is destroy hwĕy, finish wán, stripped gwāng, ruined hwày, caved in tā, *etc.* ‖All my papers were destroyed in that fire. nèy-tsž-jáw-'hwŏ bă wŏ-de-'wén-jyàn chywán-'shāw-le. ‖That house was destroyed by fire. nèy-swŏ-'fáng-dz jyàw (*or* bèy *or* ràng) hwŏ °'shāw-le. *or* °'shāw-'wán-le. *or* °'shāw-'tā-le. *etc.*

    (*By gunfire*) hūng *or* resultative compounds similarly constructed, *or* dă-'hwày.

    (*By other means*). Similar resultative compounds, which can be constructed by looking up the appropriate elements.

DESTRUCTION. (*See also* **DESTROY**). ‖The destruction of the bridge held us up for an hour. chyáw 'hwĕy-le, 'dān-wù-le wŏ-men yí-ge-'jūng-téw. ‖The flood caused a lot of destruction. 'húng-shwĕy 'hwĕy-le hĕn-dwō-de-'dūng-shi. ‖The destruction of the enemy fleet is our chief task. wŏ-men-de-jŭ-yàw-'rèn-wù shŕ 'hwĕy-myè 'dí-rén-de-'jyàn-dwèy.

DETAIL. (*Full information*) details 'shyáng-shì-de-'chíng-shíng. In detail 'shì, 'shyáng-shì-de, shì-'shì-de. ‖Today's paper gives further details. jyĕr-'bàw-shang dwō-'dēng-le-dyăr 'shyáng-shì-de-'chíng-shíng.

No details have been given out as yet. 'shyáng-shì-de-'chíng-shíng háy méy-'fā-chu-lay. ‖I'll go into detail if you want me to. nǐ 'yàw-shyǎng 'jǐ-dàw-de-hwà wǒ kě-yǐ gěy-nǐ 'shyáng-shì-de 'shwō-yi-shwō. ‖The story is too long to be detailed here. 'hwàr tày 'cháng-le, bù-néng °'shì shwō. or °shì-'shī-de shwō. or °'shyáng-shì-de shwō. But ‖He loves to talk about his travels in great detail. tā yì-'shwō-chi tā 'dàw-gwo-de-'dì-fang-lay jyèw °méy-'wán. or méy-'téwr.

(Minor point) 'shyǎw-de-dì-fang, 'shyǎw-jyé-mu. ‖The battalion commander demands great attention to detail. yíng-'jǎng l.ěn jù-'yì °'shyǎw-de-dì-fang, or °'shyǎw-jyé-mu. But ‖That's a mere detail. nèy-ge shì 'shyǎw-shì-yí-'dwàr.

(Miscellany) 'dzá-shr. ‖The details of the trip will be arranged by the guide. lywǔ-'shíng-de-'dzá-shr yéw 'shyǎng-dǎw 'gwǎn.

In detail (technical military term, meaning group by group) 'gè-ge. ‖We defeated the enemy troops in detail. wǒ-'jywūn jyāng dí-jywān 'gè-ge 'jí-pwò.

(To send, dispatch; or the group sent; the noun is expressed in a roundabout way by using the verb) pày. ‖Policemen were detailed by the police chief to hold back the crowd. 'jǐng-chá-jywú-'jǎng pày-le shywún-'jǐng-chywu 'tán-yā kàn-rè-'nàwr-de-rén. ‖I sent out a detail of six soldiers to take charge. wǒ pày-le 'lyèw-ge-'līng-chywu 'tán-yā.

DETERMINE. (Decide, resolve, settle) 'jywé-dìng; (expressing more of the sense of come to a decision) dìng. ‖We must try to determine the best course of action. wǒm děy 'jywé-dìng (or wǒm děy 'dìng) yí-ge-'dzwèy-hǎw-de-'bàn-far. ‖This matter is to be determined by the chief of staff. 'jèy-jyàn-shr děy yéw tsān-mew-'jǎng láy °'jywé-dìng. or °'dìng. ‖We determined to stay on until the end. wǒm 'jywé-dìng (or wǒm dìng-'hǎw-le) 'jyān-chí dàw-'dǐ. ‖The subject of the lecture is already determined. 'yǎn-jyǎng-de-'tí-mù 'yǐ-jīng °'dìng-le. (or °'jywé-dìng-le.)

Be determined by (depend on) děy 'kàn ... dìng, děy 'chyǎw ... dìng. See also DEPEND. ‖My answer will be determined by what happens today. wǒ-de-'hwéy-dá děy 'kàn 'jyēr-de-'chíng-shíng láy 'dìng.

Determining factor 'gwān-jyàn (also means key). ‖What is the determining factor in this case? jèy-ge-'àn-dz-de-'gwān-jyàn dzày-'nǎr?

Be determined (uncovering, obstinate). ‖She is determined to have her way. tā 'sž 'nìng. or tā 'fēy-yàw jàw-je tā-'dž-ji-de-'yì-sz bù-'kě. or tā 'yàw dzěm-je jyèw 'fēy dzěm-je bù-'kě. or tā yì-'sěr yàw 'àn-je tā-'dž-ji-shyǎng-de láy bàn. or tā yì-'dyǎr bù-'kěn ràng-'rén. ‖She is determined to get back her child. tā yì-'sěr yàw bǎ tā-de-'háy-dz 'yàw-hwey-lay. or tā ná-dìng-le jú-yi yàw bǎ .... or tā yí-'dìng yàw bǎ .... or tā 'fēy-yàw bǎ tā-de-'háy-dz 'yàw-hwey-lay bù-'kě. or tā bù-bǎ tā-de-'háy-dz 'yàw-hwey-lay bù-sž-'shīn. ‖They had a determined look about them

when they came. tā-men hǎw-'shyàng hěn yěw 'jywé-shīn-de-'yàng-dz jyèw 'láy-le. (Of soldiers going into battle) tām láy-de-shŕ-hew yěw yì-jǔng-shŕ-'sž-rú-gwēy-de-'yàng-dz (literary quotation). (Of an angry mob) tām láy shŕ shyūng-'shyūng (literary quotation).

(Calculate) 'swàn(-chu-lay). ‖Can you determine the exact height of that hill? nǐ néng 'swàn-chu-lay nèy-ge-'shān jyēw-'jìng yěw dwō 'gāw-ma?

DEVELOP. (Of strength, skill) lyàn. ‖His skill is well developed. tā-de-'gūng-fu lyàn-de hěn-'shēn. ‖These exercises will develop the strength of your fingers. jèy-shyē-'lyàn-shi ké-yi 'lyàn nǐ-shěw-'jŕ-téw-de-'jyèr.

(Of plans) 'jìn-jǎn, jìn-'shíng, bàn. ‖Are your plans developing to suit you? nǐ-de-'jì-hwà 'jìn-jǎn-de (or jìn-'shíng-de, or 'bàn-de) háy rú-'yì-ma?

Develop into ... chéng (that which precedes chéng describes the method). ‖He developed a simple story (by writing) into a two-volume affair. tā bǎ ge-hěn-'jyǎn-dān-de-'gù-shr 'shyě-chéng-le 'lyǎng-dà-běn-de-'shū. ‖He developed his store (by expansion) into the largest in this town. tā bǎ tā-de-'pù-dz fā-'jǎn chéng-le jèr-dzwèy-dà-de-'mǎy-may-le. ‖The girl developed (by a process of growth) into a great beauty. nèy-ge-'shyǎw-'gū-nyang jàng-'chéng-de ge-yěw-'míng-de-měy-'rér-le.

To develop film shǐ. ‖Can you develop these films right away? nǐ néng 'lì-shŕ bǎ 'jyàw-jwǎr 'shǐ-chū-lay-ma?

(Invent) 'fā-míng. ‖Our research men have developed a new process. wǒm-jèr-dzwò-'yán-jyēw-'gūng-dzwò-de-rén 'fā-míng-le yì-jǔng-'shīn-de-'fāng-fǎ.

DIAMOND. (Gem) jīn-gāng-'shŕ, jīn-gāng-'dzwàr, dzwàn-'shŕ. ‖Where are diamonds produced? nǎr chū 'jīn-gāng-'shŕ? or nǎr chū 'jīn-gāng-'dzwàr? or nǎr chū 'dzwàn-shŕ? ‖He gave her a diamond engagement ring. tā 'sùng-gěy tā yí-ge-'dzwàn-shŕ-de-'dìng-hwēn-'jyè-jr. ‖There are one large diamond and several small ones mounted on that ring. nèy-jŕ-'jyè-jr-shang shyāng-je yí-kwày-'dà-'dzwàn-shŕ, háy shyāng-je jǐ-kwày-'shyǎw-dyǎr-de. ‖He's put his diamonds in the safe. tā bǎ tā-de-'jīn-gāng-shŕ 'gē-dzay bǎw-shyǎn-'shyāng-lǐ-le.

(Suit in cards) 'fāng-kwàr. ‖Did you bid two diamonds? nǐ 'shŕ-bu-shŕ jyàw 'lyǎng-ge fāng-'kwàr-ma? ‖I think he has a flush in diamonds. tā 'dà-gày-shr ná-le yì-shěw-'túng-hwār, háy-shr 'fāng-kwàr.

(Baseball). ‖There is enough room here for a diamond. jèy-'dì-fang 'gèw yí-ge-bàng-chyéwr-'chǎng-dz.

DICE. 'shǎy-dz. ‖There are several games you can play with dice. jǐ (or wár) 'shǎy-dz yěw 'jǐ-ge-fár. ‖A dice game can be played several ways. jǐ 'shǎy-dz yěw jǐ-jǔng-'wár-fa. ‖O.K., let's play the dice game your way. hǎw-ba, jǐ-'shǎy-dz jyèw jàw 'nǐ-de-'fár-ba. ‖No dice. bù-'chéng.

DICTIONARY. dž-'dyăn; (*an old term for a dictionary of characters*) dž-'hwèy. ‖Where do you keep your dictionaries? nǐ-dž-'dyăn 'fàng-dzày năr-le? ‖Do you have a small Chinese-English dictionary? nǐ yěw shyăw-běr-de-hàn-'yīng-dž-'dyăn-ma?

(*Dictionaries of special types are compounds with -dyăn.*) Dictionary of chemical terms 'hwà-shywé-'tsž-dyăn; dictionary of personal names 'rén-míng-'tsž-dyăn; dictionary of place names 'dì-míng-'tsž-dyăn; military dictionary 'jywun-ywǔ-'tsž-dyăn; pocket dictionary 'shyèw-jēn-dž-dyăn.

DIE. sž. *Like the English word* die, sž *is often replaced by euphemisms when referring to the death of some person.* ‖I'm not afraid to die. wǒ bú-pà 'sž. ‖He died a pauper. tā-sž-de-shŕ-hew 'chyúng-dᵒ yàw-'fàn. *or* °méy-'fàn-chŕ. ‖He died of starvation, but left ten thousand dollars for a decent funeral. tā-shr 'è-sz-de, kě-shr lyéw-shya yí-'wàn-kway-chyán hǎw 'chū-ge dà-'bìn. ‖I'm not going to die. (*Will not*) wǒ bú-'hwèy sž-de. (*Don't want to*) wǒ bú-ywàn-yi 'sž. ‖How did he die? tā dzěm-me 'sž-de? ‖He died of illness. tā 'bìng-sž-de. ‖He died of an operation. tā gē-'bìng sž-de. *or* tā !á-'bìng sž-de. ‖He died of a tumor. tā jǎng-'lyéw-dz sž-de. ‖He died of rabies. tā jyàw 'fēng-gěw 'yěw-sž-de. ‖He died of a snakebite. tā jyàw 'cháng-chung 'yǎw-sž-de. ‖He died of overeating. tā 'chēng-sz-de *or* tā chŕ-'dwᵒ-le 'chēng-sz-de. ‖He died of excessive drinking. tā hē-'jyéw hē-'dwō-le sž-de. ‖He died of intoxication. tā 'dzwèy-sž-de. ‖He died of starvation. tā 'è-sz-de. ‖He died of overwork (*or* exhaustion). tā 'lèy-sz-de. (*Figuratively*) ‖He died laughing. tā 'shyàw-je sž-de. ‖I just about died laughing when I heard it. wǒ 'tīng-jyan yí-'hèw 'chā-dyǎr méy 'shyàw-sž.

(*Euphemisms, like our* pass away) tsž-'shŕ, shyà-'shŕ, chywù-'shŕ, 'gwò-chywu, 'gù-chywu, bú-'dzay, dzwò-'gǔ; (*Taoist terms*) 'shyān-chywù, 'shyān-shŕ; (*referring to the exact time of death*) yàn-'chì, dwàn-'chì; *referring to relatives who have died,* shyān- *is prefixed to the relationship term.* ‖When did your father die? (*Not asking the precise moment*) lìng-'dzwēn jǐ-'shŕ °tsž-'shŕ-de? *or* °shyà-'shŕ-de? *or* °bú-'dzày-de? *or* °'shyān-shŕ-de? *or* °'gù-chywu-de? *etc.* (*Asking the precise moment*) °yàn-de 'chì? *or* °'dwàn-de 'chì? ‖My father died three years ago. 'shyān-yán 'sān-nyán chyán tsž-'shŕ-de. *or* wǒ-'fù-chin 'sān-nyán chyán 'gwò-chywu-de. *etc.* ‖He died at two o'clock this morning. tā 'jīn-tyān 'dzǎw-chen 'lyǎng-dyǎn 'yàn-de chì.

(*Terms less polite than* sž, *but not actually insults*) to meet the kings of Hades (*a Buddhist reference*) jyàn 'yán-wáng; to go to Hades yí-'mìng gwēy-'yīn; (*quoted at end of obituaries*) 'wū-hu-'āy-jay (shàng-'shyǎng); 'wan(-le), 'méy(-le).

(*Very rude terms*) wán-shŕ dà-'jí, wár-'wán; to stare dèng-'yǎr; to be stiff-legged chēn-'twěr. ‖He

died after a short illness. (*Normal statement*) tā bìng-le 'méy-jǐ-'tyān °jyèw 'sž-le. (*Polite*) °jyèw 'gù-chywu-le. *etc.* (*Less polite*) °jyèw 'wū-hu-'āy-jay-le. (*Very impolite*) °jyèw wár-'wán-le.

Die (*in line of duty and while in action*) 'jèn-wáng, jàn-'sž; (*naturally, but while on official duty*) yīn-'gūng shywùn-'jŕ. ‖He died in action. tā 'jèn-wáng-le. *or* tā jàn-'sž-le. ‖He died in line of duty (*natural death*). tā yīn-'gūng shywùn-'jŕ-le.

Die off màn-'mār-de 'dēw sž-le. ‖The old inhabitants are dying off. jèr-de-'lǎw-rén màn-'mār-de 'dēw sž-le.

Die out. (*Literally, as of animals*) sž-'gwǎng; (*of a family*) sž-'jywé. ‖The deer have almost died out around here. jèr-fù-'jìn-de-'lù dēw 'kwày sž-'gwǎng-le. ‖His family has died out. tā-nèy-'jyār sž-'jywé-le. ‖The old families here are all dying out. jèr-de lǎw-'jyār kwày 'dēw sž-'jywé-le. (*Figuratively*) ‖The custom of wearing vests is dying out. 'chwān kǎn-'jyār yǐ-'jìng kwày °bù-shŕ-'shīng-le. *or* °gwò-shŕ-le.

(*Figurative uses*). ‖After she came in, the conversation died out. tā 'jìn-lay yǐ-'hèw 'méy-rén shwō-'hwà-le. ‖The noise of the train died away in the distance. hwǒ-'chē dzěw-'ywǎn-le, 'chē-shēng tīng-bu-'jyàn-le. ‖The motor died before we got to the top of the hill. méy-dàw 'shān-dyěngr yǐ-chyán, (chē-de-) 'jī-chì °bú-'dùng-le. *or* °'tíng-ıe. ‖The racket died down when the teacher came in. 'shyān-sheng 'jìn-lay yǐ-'hèw, dà-'jyā dēw 'ān-jìng-le. ‖After dinner we'll let the fire die down. chŕ-wán-le 'fàn, wǒm jyàw 'hwǒ 'dž-jì 'myè. ‖We know the truth now, but old stories die hard. shyàn-'dzày wǒ-men jŕ-dàw shŕ 'dzěm-yì-hwéy-'shŕ-le, kě-shr nà-shyē-'yáw-yán yì-'shŕ hěn nán 'shyāw-myè. ‖He's a die-hard. (*A compliment*) tā shŕ ge-'jyān-chŕ-dàw-'dǐ-de-rén. (*An insult; literally* He's like a bull.) tā shŕ ge-'nyéw-shìng-dz-de-rén. *or* (*literary*) tā shŕ ge-'dzwǎn-nyéw-'jī-jyaw-de-rén. *or* *meaning* not adaptable tā-jèy-ge-rén 'sž-shīn-'yěr. ‖I'm dying to meet him. wǒ 'hèn-bu-néng 'lì-shŕ jyèw 'rèn-shŕ tā. ‖She's dying to find out what he said. tā 'hèn-bu-nᴉng 'lì-shŕ jyèw 'jŕ-dàw tā shwō 'shém láy-je.

DIFFERENT. (*Comparing things*) bù-yí-'yàng (*not the same*); bù-shyāng-'túng (*not similar*). ‖He's quite different from what I expected. tā 'gēn wǒ-shīn-li-'shyǎng-de hěn °bù-yí-'yàng. *or* °bù-shyāng-'túng. ‖He's different (*from others*). tā gēn 'byé-rén bù-yí-'yàng. ‖He's different (*from what he used to be*). tā gēn yǐ-'chyán hěn bù-yí-'yàng. ‖These two seem to be the same, but they're really different. jèy-lyǎng-ge kàn-je hǎw-'shyàng shyāng-'túng (*or* yí-'yàng), 'chí-shŕ 'bù-yí-'yàng.

(*Individualistic*) bù-'túng. ‖This wine has a really different flavor. jèy-jyèw-de-'wèr hěn bù-'túng.

(*Varying with each individual*) bù-'yī, bù-'túng. ‖Different people tell different versions of the incident. 'chwán-shwō °bù-'yī. *or* °bù-'túng. *or* nèy-jyàn-'shèr 'gè-rén-'shwō-fǎ °bù-'túng. *or* °bù-'yī. *or* nèy-jyàn-'shèr yì-rén yí-gè-'shwō-fǎ.

(*Another*) 'lìng-yi . . . , 'hwàn-yi . . . . ‖A **different** person might have considered it an insult. 'lìng-yi-ge-rén (*or* 'hwàn-yi-ge-rén) yě-shywǔ hwèy 'jywé-de nèy-shr 'mà-ta-ne. ‖He seems to be a different person now. tā hǎw-'shyàng °'hwàn-le-ge-rén shr̀-de. *or* °byàn-chéng 'lìng-yi-ge-rén shr̀-de. *or* nà 'nǎ-shr̀ 'tā-ya! jyàn-'jr̀ chéng-le 'lìng-yi-ge-'rén-le. ‖That's a different person. nà shr̀ 'lìng-yi-ge-rén. *or* nà shr̀ 'byé-yi-ge-rén. *or* nà 'yèw-shr yí-ge-rén-le. ‖Let's have someone different. dzám 'hwàn yí-ge-rén-ba. *or* dzám 'lìng yàw ge-rén-ba. *or* dzám 'lìng jǎw ge-rén-ba. ‖That's a different story. nà shr̀ 'lìng-yi-hwèy-'shèr.

‖I saw him three different times today. wǒ 'jīn-tyān 'kàn-jyan tā 'sān-tsz̀.

DIFFICULT. (*Hard to do*) nán, bù-'rúng-yì. ‖The lessons are getting more and more difficult. 'gūng-kè 'ywè-láy ywè-'nán. ‖It's difficult for me to say it to his face. gēn-tā dāng-'myàr hěn 'nán shwō-chu 'kěw-lay. ‖I'm in a difficult position now. wǒ 'jèng-dzày wéy-'nán. ‖That job is difficult. nèy-jyàn-shèr hěn nán 'bàn. ‖I've always found him difficult to talk with. wǒ yí-'shvàng jywé-de hěn 'nán gēn-tā shwō-'hwà. ‖He's difficult to work with. hěn 'nán gēn-tā gùng-'shr̀. ‖Don't leave all the difficult problems to me. byé bǎ 'nán-tí (*o* 'nán-de) dēw 'lyéw-gey wǒ. ‖It's difficult to understand what he means. bú-dà-'rúng-yì 'míng-bày tā-de-'yì-sz. ‖I won't make it difficult for you. wǒ bú-hwèy 'jyàw-nǐ wéy-'nán.

(*Requiring effort*) fèy-'shèr. ‖It was an awfully difficult job explaining this to that blockhead. gěy nèy-ge-hwén-'dàn bǎ jèy-ge 'jyě-shr̀-chīng-chu-le jēn 'fèy-'shèr. ‖That design is difficult to draw. hwà nèy-ge-'tú-àn hěn fèy-'shèr. ‖He's a difficult person to reason with. gēn-tā jyǎng-'lǐ hěn fèy-'shèr.

(*Troublesome, of a person*) dǎw-'lwàn, hú-'nàw, hú-'jyǎw, shyā-'nàw. ‖He's being difficult on purpose. tā gù-'yì °dǎw-'lwàn. *or* °hú-'nàw, *etc.* ‖Don't be difficult! 'byé 'shyā-'nàw. *or* 'byé dǎw-'lwàn. *etc.*

DIFFICULTY. nán, *meaning* difficult, *is frequently used.* ‖No difficulty at all! yì-dyar yě bù-'nán! *or* hěn 'rúng-yì! ‖The difficulties of the job are greater than he thinks. nèy-ge-'shr̀ bǐ tā-'shyǎng-de 'nán 'dwō-le.

(*In accomplishment*) 'nán-chù, 'kwèn-nán, kwèn-nán-de-'dì-fang, wéy-'nán-de-'dì-fang. ‖The difficulty of the job is greater than he thinks. (*See also above.*) nèy-jyàn-shr̀-de-'nán-chù bǐ tā-'shyǎng-de dà-'dwō-le. ‖I have my own difficulties. wǒ yěw 'wǒ-de-'nán-chù. ‖What seems to be the difficulty? kwèn-nán-de-'dì-fang dzày nǎr?

Difficult situation 'nán-shèr, nán-'gwān. ‖Any difficulty can be overcome if one keeps on working. yàw-shr 'jyàn-chf dàw-'dǐ °shém-me 'nán-shèr 'dēw néng

bàn-'hǎw-le. *or* °shém-me nán-'gwān dēw néng gwò-.ae-'chywù. *or* (*Literary*) °'shr̀-shang wú-nén-'shf, jǐ-'pà yěw-'shīn-rén.

(*Expenditure of effort*). Have difficulty fèy (. . .) 'shèr. ‖We had difficulty finding that hotel. wǒm 'fèy-le bàn-tyān-'shèr tsáy 'jǎw-jáw nèy-ge-'lywǔ-gwǎn.

(*Financial troubles*) 'kwèn-nan, wéy-'nán. To be in (financial) difficulty jǐn. ‖I have my own difficulties. wǒ 'dz̀-ji yě shr̀ hěn 'jǐn-de. ‖He is in financial difficulties. tā wèy-le 'chyán jèng-dzày wéy-'nán. *or* tā shyàn-'dzày shěw-'dǐ-shya hěn 'jǐn.

(*Problem*) wèn-'tí. ‖If he had saved his money he wouldn't be having these difficulties. tā dāng-chū 'yàw-shr bǎ-chyán 'shěng-shyà-lay de-hwà, tā shyàn-'dzày jywé-bu-'hwèy yěw jèy-shyē-wèn-'tí.

(*Trouble*) shèr. ‖He's always getting into difficulties. tā lǎw chū-'shèr.

(*Disagreements, quarreling*). ‖We're having difficulty with him. wǒm 'jèng gēn-tā °dǎ-'jyà, *or* °chǎw-'dzwéy, *or* °bú-dwèy-'jyèr.

DIG. Dig *into, in, out of, etc.* (*with hands or paws or with a pick or mattock, but not with a shovel or spade, and not when digging a hole*) páw. ‖They're digging with a mattock. tām yùng-'chú páw-'tǔ-ne. ‖The dog dug up the bone. gēw bǎ máy-le-de-'gú-tew 'páw-chu-lay-le. ‖These potatoes are ready to dig now. jèy-shyē-tǔ-'dèwr ké-yi 'páw-chu-lay-le. ‖We'll have to dig up this apple tree and put it over there. wǒm děy bǎ jèy-kē-'píng-gwǒ-shù 'páw-chū-lay 'nwó-dàw 'nèy-byar-chywu.

Dig *a hole, ditch, trench, well, etc.,* (*with a shovel, spade, or other tool; excavate*) wā, kāy. ‖Dig this hole a little deeper. bǎ jèy-ge-'kēng wā 'shēn-dyǎr. ‖They dug a tunnel under the river. tām dzày hé-'dǐ 'dǐ-shya 'wā (*or* 'kāy)-le ge-dì-'dùng. ‖They dug a canal three hundred miles long. tām 'wā (*or* 'kāy, *or* 'jywé; *see below*)-le tyáw-'sān-bay-lǐ-'cháng-de-'ywùn-hé. ‖They dug a ditch there. tām dzày 'nàr 'wā (*or* 'kāy, *or* 'jywé)-le dàw-'gēw. ‖We can't get through because they're digging up the pavement. wǒm 'gwò-bu-chywù 'yīn-wey tām bǎ 'jwān-dàw 'wā-chǐ-lay-le (*or* 'jywé-chǐ-lay-le).

Dig *with a shovel, especially by pushing deep and prying; literary* jywé.

Dig *down into something in order to get something out* wā; (*literary*) wān. ‖They dug up a chest full of gold and silver and jewels. tǎm 'wā-chù-lay yì-'shyāng-dz-de-'jīn-yín-jū-'bǎw-de. ‖Dig up some asparagus. wā (*or* wān) dyǎr-lúng-shywū-'tsày.

Dig *ground for the foundation of a building* pwò (-'tǔ). ‖They're going to start digging today. tām 'jyěr pwò-'tǔ.

Dig (*reach into something to get something or to remove an obstacle*) tāw. ‖Gentlemen, dig in your pockets! dà-'jyā děy tāw yàw-'bāwr!

Dig in (*fortify*). ‖**How long will it take your company to dig in?** nǐ-'nèy-lyán-rén shè-'bèy 'fáng-ywù-'gūng-shř děy yùng 'dwō-shǎw 'shŕ-hew?

Dig in (*work hard*). ‖**It's a hard job, but he's digging right in.** 'shř-chíng hěn 'nán, 'kě-shr tā 'pīn-mìng gàn.

Dig into. (*Investigate*) 'dyàw-chá; (*do research on*) 'yán-jyew. ‖**I've been digging into the history of that town.** wǒ 'jèng-dzày 'dyàw-chá (*or* 'yán-jyew) nèy-ge-'chéng-de-'fāng-jř. ‖**They dug into his private affairs, but found nothing to point to as a fault.** tām dyàw-chá (*or* tām dǎ-'tīng) tā-de-'sž-shř, kě-shr 'méy-jǎw-chu shém-me ké-yi 'jŕ-jáy-de-lay. *But* ‖**He's digging into his books for some material.** tā 'jèng-dzày 'shū-li jǎw 'tsáy-lyàwr-ne. ‖**He's digging into the books.** tā 'bàw-je-shū 'sž-nyàn.

Dig up (*find out*) 'jǎw-chu-lay. ‖**See what you can dig up about him.** 'chyáw-nǐ néng 'jǎw-chu-lay 'shém-me 'gwān-ywu tā-de-'shř.

A dig (*nudge*). **To give a dig** (*to someone*) tǔng chǔ. ‖**If he starts talking too much, give him a dig in the ribs.** tā yàw-shr 'shwō-hwà tày 'dwō-de-hwà, 'tǔng-tā (*or* 'chǔ-tā) yí-'shyà.

A dig (*verbal*). **To take digs** (*at*) mà. ‖**That editor is always taking digs at the mayor.** nèy-ge-'jǔ-bǐ lǎw 'mà shř-'jǎng.

DINE. chŕ-'fàn. ‖**Dining On The Roof Garden.** dzày 'wū-dǐng-hwā-'ywán chŕ-'fàn. ‖**They're dining with the Ambassador tonight.** tām jyēr 'wǎn-shang gēn (*or* péy-je) 'dà-shř (yí-kwàr) chŕ-'fàn. ‖**We always dine out on Sundays.** wǒm 'lǐ-bày-tyān 'lǎw-shř 'chū-chywu chŕ-'fàn. *But* ‖**They wined and dined him but in the end he made complete fools out of them.** tām chǐng-tā 'dà-chŕ 'dà-hē kě-shr dàw-le 'mwò-lyǎwr tā 'bǎ tā-men 'pyàn-le ge-bú-yì-'lè-hu.

Diner, dining car fàn-'chē. ‖**There's no diner on this train.** jèy-lyè-hwǒ-'chē-shang méy-yew fàn-'chē.

Dining room (*at home*) fàn-'tīng. ‖**Bring another chair into the dining room.** dzày bān bǎ-'yǐ-dz dàw fàn-'tīng-chywu. ‖**We use this room as a dining room.** wǒm ná jèy-jyān-'wūr dàng fàn-'tīng. *or* wǒm dzày-'jèr chŕ-'fàn.

Dining room (*in a hotel*) 'shŕ-táng. ‖**The dining room closes at 10.** 'shŕ-táng shŕ-dyǎn gwān-'mén.

DINNER. fàn, wǎn-'fàn. ‖**Dinner's ready!** fàn 'dé-lèw. *or* chŕ-'fàn-lèw. ‖**We are giving a dinner in his honor next Friday.** wǒ-men shyà-'lǐ-bày-'wǔ chǐng-tā °chŕ-'fàn. (*or* °chŕ wǎn-'fàn). ‖**Won't you come over and have dinner wit us tomorrow night?** nǐ-men 'míng-tyan 'wǎn-shang néng láy chŕ (wǎn-) 'fàn-ma? ‖**I have a dinner engagement tonight.** jyēr 'wǎn-shang wǒ yěw °fàn-'jywú. *or* °ge-chŕ-fàn-de-'ywē-hwèy. ‖**Has the dinner bell rung?** (chŕ-)'fàn-lyéngr 'shyǎng-le 'méy-yew?

DIRECT. (*Opposite of indirect*) 'jŕ-jyē (*or* 'jŕ-jyé), 'yì-jŕ. ‖**I shall make a direct appeal to the colonel.** wǒ yàw 'jŕ-jyē (*or* 'yì-jŕ) chywù 'chyéw shàng-'shyàw. ‖**Let's go direct to the hotel.** dzám 'yì-jŕ (*or* 'jŕ-jyē) chywù 'lywǔ-gwǎn-ba. ‖**His answers are always direct and to the point.** tā-de-'hwéy-dá yī-'shyàng shř °'jŕ-jyé (*or* cogent °'jyǎn-jyé, *but not* 'yì-jŕ) lyǎw-'dàng.

(*Short; opposite of roundabout*) jìn. ‖**This is the most direct route to the city.** 'jèy-ge shř dàw-'chéng-li-chywù-dzwèy-'jìn-de-'dàwr.

Direct descendant 'dí-shì. ‖**She is a direct descendant of Confucius.** tā shř 'kǔng-dž-de-'dí-shì.

(*Exact*) jèng. ‖**The result is the direct opposite of what we expected.** 'jyē-gwǒ gēn wǒm-'shyǎng-de 'jèng shyǎng-'fǎn. ‖**The post office is directly opposite the theater.** yéw-jèng-'jywú jèng 'dwèy-je shì-'ywán-dz.

(*Forthright*) jŕ, 'chéng-kěn. ‖**He has always been direct and honest with me.** tā 'dwèy-wǒ yī-'shyàng hěn 'chéng-kěn. ‖**He's a direct person.** tā hěn 'jŕ. *or meaning* just and straightforward tā hěn 'jèng-jŕ. *or* (*literary quotation*) tā 'shīn-jŕ-kěw-'kwày-de. *or* tā-dzwò-shř-shwō-'hwà-de 'bú-hwèy ràw-'wār.

To direct (*tell*). ‖**I was directed to wait until he returned.** yěw-'rén 'jyàw-wǒ 'děng tā 'hwéy-láy.

To direct (*guide*). ‖**Can you direct me to the post office?** chǐng-'wèn, dàw yéw-jèng-'jywú-chywu dzěm-me-'dzěw?

Direct traffic jŕ-hwēy chē mǎ. *But* ‖**Ask the policeman who's directing traffic.** wèn nèy-ge-jàn-'gǎng-de-jǐng-'chá.

Direct a play dǎw-'yǎn. ‖**Who's directing the play?** jèy-ge-'shì 'shwéy dǎw-yǎn-ne?

Direct attention. ‖**May I direct your attention to rule No. 3?** chǐng-nǐ 'kàn-yi-kan dì-'sān-tyáw.

DIRECTION. In *this, that, one, etc., but not our, your, my, etc.,* direction; (*location*) dzày ... byàr (*or* byān); (*motion*) wàng ... byàr ‑ shyàng ... byàr; (*facing*) chùng(-je) ... byàr. ‖**The village is a mile away in that direction.** tswēn-'jwāngr dzày 'nèy-byàr yì-lǐ-'dì. ‖**He went in that direction.** tā wàng 'nèy-byàr-chywu-le. ‖**He went in an easterly direction.** tā wàng 'dūng(-byàr)-chywu-le. ‖**They came from all directions.** tām tsúng 'sž-byàr (*or* 'sž-myàr) láy-le.

In the direction of (*motion*) wàng ..., shyàng ...; (*facing*) chùng(-je) ... ‖**Look out! He's coming in our direction!** hèy! tā 'chùng-je 'dzám láy-le! ‖**He's aiming in our direction! Duck!** tā 'chùng-je 'dzám myáw-ne! kwày 'dwǒ! ‖**He went in the direction of that house.** tā wàng 'nèy-swǒ-fáng-dz-nèr chywù-le. ‖**He went in that direction** (*in the direction of that place*). tā wàng (*or* shyàng) 'nèr-chywu-le.

In different directions. ‖**They went in different directions.** tām 'fēn-dàw yáng-'byāw (*literary quotation*). *or* tām 'gè dzěw yì-tyáw-'lùr-le.

(*Tendency*). ‖**Since he came the work has taken a new direction.** 'dž-tsúng tā láy-le yì-'hèw 'gūng-dzwò-de-'fāng-jēn 'gǎy-le.

(*Instructions for getting somewhere*) dzĕw-de-'lù, lù-'shyàn. ‖Here are the directions for finding my house. 'jèy-shr chywù-wŏ-'jyā dzĕw-de-'lù. ‖Follow the directions printed in the guide book. 'àn-je jĭ-'nán-shang-gĕy-de-lù-'shyàn 'dzĕw.

(*Instructions for doing something*). ‖Are there directions (with it)? (*meaning a pamphlet or booklet giving directions*) yĕw 'méy-yew shwō-míng-'shū? ‖This booklet gives all the directions for using this machine. jèy-ge-jī-'chĭ-de-yùng-fă dēw dzày jèy-bĕr-shwō-míng-'shū-li-le. ‖Can you give me some directions on how to use this? nĭ gĕy-wŏ 'jyáng-jyang jèy-ge dzĕm-me 'yùng, shíng-ma? ‖Better follow the divisional commander's directions. háy-shr jàw-je shī-'jăng-de-'shywùn-lìng bàn-ba. ‖Please give me some directions. chĭng 'jĭ-dyăn-jĭ-dyăn. or 'dwō-dwō chĭng-'jyàw. *See also* COMMAND.

(*Control*) 'lĭng-dăw. ‖They have made great progress under his direction. dzày tā-'lĭng-dăw-jī-'shyà tām hĕn yĕw 'jìn-bù.

DIRTY. (*Soiled*) dzāng, bù-'gān-jing. ‖These dirty clothes must be sent to the laundry. jèy-shyē-'dzāng-'yī-fu dĕy °'sùng-dàw 'shī-yī-fáng chywù-le. or °'sùng-chywu 'shī-le. ‖The floor of my room is dirty. wŏ-'wū-dz-de-'dì hĕn °'dzāng. or °bù-'gān-jing. ‖I've never seen a hotel as dirty as that. wŏ 'shyàng-lay méy-'kàn-jyàn-gwo 'nèm-'dzāng-de-lywŭ-'gwăn. ‖Don't get my clothes dirty. byé bă wŏ-de-'yī-shang nùng-'dzāng-le.

‖We've been having a spell of dirty weather. 'jèy-shyē-'r̆-dz 'jìng-shr 'hwày-tyār. ‖Don't let such dirty stories fall into the hands of children. byé 'ràng jèy-jŭng-'hwày-shyăw-'shwō lè-dzày háy-dz-men-de-'shĕw-li. ‖He's telling dirty stories. tā jyăng 'hwày-shèr-ne. or tā-'jyăng-de bú-shr 'hăw-shèr. ‖Don't listen to that sort of dirty story. yĕw-rén jyăng nèy-jŭng-'hwày-shèr de-shŕ-hew, byé 'tīng. ‖That was a dirty trick he played on us. tā 'nèy-tsz 'jĕn-shr 'gĕy wŏmen shr-'hwày-le. ‖That's a dirty trick. (*Mild*) jēn 'hwày. or 'jĕn táw-'chì. (*Seriously*) 'wèy-myăn tày 'swĕn-le! or 'hày-rén bù-'chyăn! *or* jēn 'chywē-'dé!

‖He gave us a dirty look. tā 'dèng-le wŏ-men yì-'yăn.

DISAPPEAR. (*From sight*) (kàn-)bu-'jyàn-le. ‖The man disappeared over the hill. nèy-ge-rén 'gwò-le shān-'jyār yì-hèw, jyèw (kàn-)bú-'jyàn-le. ‖It's going to disappear soon. dĕng-yi-hwĕr jyèw (kàn-)bu-'jyàn-le.

(*From a place*) 'méy-le. ‖The old houses are disappearing from the city. 'chéng-lǐ-de-lăw-'fáng-dz màn-'már-de 'méy-le.

(*Socially*). ‖He disappeared three years ago. sān-nyán-'chyán °tā shŕ-'dzūng-le. or °'shéy yĕ bù-jŕ-'dàw tā dàw-năr 'chywù-le.

DISAPPOINT. ‖The new play was rather disappointing. nèy-ge-gāng-'shàng-yăn-de-shì 'bìng bù-'hăw. ‖I was disappointed with the results. 'jyē-gwŏ jyàw-wŏ 'hĕn °bù-măn-'yì. or °săw-'shìng. ‖Please don't disappoint me by not coming. 'byé bù-láy, jyàw-wŏ săw-'shìng. ‖He is awfully disappointing to us. tā jyàw-rén 'dà-shŕ swŏ-'wàng. ‖We're disappointed in you. nĭ 'jyàw-wŏm shŕ-'wàng.

DISCOVER. (*Find*) 'jăw-jáw, 'fā-shyàn. ‖We have discovered a new restaurant that's very good. wŏm 'jàw-jaw-le yí-ge-'tĭng-hăw-de-'fàn-gwăr. ‖Was Columbus the first to discover America? gē-lwén-'bù shŕ 'jàw-jáw (or 'fā-shyàn)-'méy-jēw-de-'téw-yi-ge-rén-ma?

(*Invent, develop*) 'fā-míng, 'yán-jyēw-chu-lay. ‖He discovered a new process for making glass. tā 'fā-míng-le (or tā 'yán-jyēw-chu-lay-le) yì-jŭng-'shīn-fá-dz láy dzwò 'bwō-li.

(*Find out*) 'dyàw-chá, 'fáng-wèn (*both also mean investigate*). ‖There is no truth in the story, so far as I can discover. jywù wŏ-'dyàw-chá-de (or jywù wŏ-'fáng-wèn-de) láy 'shwō, nèy-jyàn-shèr 'háw-wú-'gēn-jywù.

DISCUSS. (*Talk about*) 'tán(-yi-tán); (*consult about*) 'shāng-lyáng; (*debate about*) 'tăw-lwèn. ‖There are lots of things left to discuss. 'háy yĕw hăw-'shyē-shŕ dĕy °'tán-yi-tán. or °'shāng-lyáng. or °'tăw-lwèn. ‖Let's discuss this question first. dzám 'shyān °'tăw-lwèn-tăw-lwèn 'jèy-ge-wèn-tí. or °'bă 'jèy-ge-wèn-tí 'tăw-lwèn-le. ‖We were just discussing our plans. wŏm 'jèng-dzày 'tăw-lwèn (or 'shāng-lyáng, or 'tán-yi-tán) wŏm-de-'jì-hwà.

DISCUSSION. ‖We reached our decision after a long discussion. wŏm 'tán-le (or wŏm 'tăw-lwèn-le, or wŏm 'shāng-lyáng-le) bàn-'tyān tsáy yĕw 'jyē-gwŏ. ‖There will be a discussion period after the lecture. jyăng 'wán-le yĭ-'hèw, yĕw yí-'dwàn-shŕ-hew 'tăw-lwèn.

A discussion meeting 'tăw-lwèn-'hwèy.

DISEASE. bìng. ‖That disease is quite easy to catch. nèy-jŭng-'bìng hĕn 'rúng-yì 'jăw-sheng. ‖The disease rate here is very low. jèr mĕy-'nyán 'bìng-de-rén hĕn 'shăw. ‖His behavior stems from a diseased mind. tā lăw 'nèm-je shŕ 'yīn-wey tā yĕw 'shén-jīng-'bìng.

DISH. 'dyé-dz. *If several kinds of dishes are referred to,* 'dyé-dz *means saucer or small plate, and the other kinds have their own terms. See under each.* ‖He dropped the dish and broke it. tā bă 'dyé-dz shwāy-'pwò-le. ‖Let me help wash the dishes. wŏ láy 'bāng-nĭ shĭ 'dyé-dz

Dishes (*all dishes and utensils needed for cooking and serving*) 'gwō-pér-wăn-'dzàwr. ‖We'll have to buy dishes (*all kinds*). 'gwō-pér-wăn-'dzàwr-de 'dēw dĕy 'măy.

(*Type of food*) tsày. ‖What is your favorite dish? nǐ-dzwèy-'shǐ-hwān-'chř-de-tsày shř 'shém-me?

To dish out (*food*) chéng; (*serve in quantities*) kāy(-'fàn). ‖The cook dished out the food on our plates. 'dà-shr-fu bǎ-tsày 'chéng-dzày wǒm-de-'pán-dz-lǐ-le. ‖The cook is dishing out the food now. 'chú-dz 'jèng-dzày chéng 'tsày-ne. ‖The canteen will start dishing out the food at 6 o'clock. 'jywūn-rén-jywù-lè-'bù 'lyèw-dyǎn kāy-'fàn.

Dish it out. ‖He can dish it out but he can't take it. tā gwāng-'hwèy jàn 'pyán-yì (*or* tā gwāng-'hwèy 'chǐ-fu rén), 'dž-jǐ chř dyǎn-'kwēy jyèw shèw-hu-'lyǎw-le.

DISLIKE. 'tǎw-yàn, bù-'shǐ-hwān. ‖I dislike him very much. wǒ hěn 'tǎw-yàn tā. *or* wǒ hěn bù-'shǐ-hwān tā. ‖I dislike traveling by boat. wǒ bù-'shǐ-hwān (*or* wǒ 'tǎw-yàn) dzwò hwǒ-'chē 'chū-mér. ‖I dislike interruptions when I'm concentrating. wǒ 'jèng shyǎng-'shèr de-shŕ-hew bù-'shǐ-hwan rén dǎ-'jyǎw. ‖I dislike interruptions when I'm talking. wǒ shwō-'hwà de-shŕ-hew bù-'shǐ-hwan rén dǎ-'chà. ‖Your strong dislike of him is just prejudice on your part. nǐ nèm bù-'shǐ-hwan tā (*or* nǐ nèm 'tǎw-yàn tā) shř nǐ-'dž-jǐ-pyān-'shīn. ‖I can't explain my dislike for the city. wǒ 'shwō-bu-chu-lay wèy-'shém-me wǒ 'tǎw-yàn nèy-ge-'chéng.

DISPOSE. Dispose of (*arrange, settle*) bàn. ‖We still have some business to dispose of. háy yěw hǎw-shyē-'shř 'děy 'bàn-ne. *or* °méy 'bàn-ne.

(*Get rid of by ignoring*) 'jř-jř-bū-'lǐ *or* 'jř-jr-bù-'lǐ (*variant pronunciations*), bú-dà-'lǐ. ‖He disposed of our objections in short order (*as with a shrug of the shoulders*). wǒm-'fǎn-dwèy-de-'dì-fang tā °'jř-jr-bù-'lǐ. *or* °bú-dà-'lǐ.

(*Answer satisfactorily*) bàn-'hǎw, bàn-de hěn mǎn-'yì. ‖He disposed of our objections one by one. wǒm-'fǎn-dwèy-de-'dì-fang tā 'yí-jyàn-yí-'jyàn-de 'děw °bàn-'hǎw-le. *or* °bàn-de hěn mǎn-'yì.

(*Sell*) mày. ‖They will leave as soon as they dispose of the furniture. tām bǎ 'jyā-jywu 'mày-le yǐ-'hèw, jyèw 'dzěw.

(*Throw away*) rēng. ‖Where can we dispose of the garbage? 'lā-jī 'rēng-dàw 'nàr-chywu?

(*Get rid of: a person*) 'dǎ-fā(-'dzěw). ‖Let's think of a way to dispose of that fellow. dzám shyǎng ge-'fár bǎ nèy-ge-'jyā-hwo 'dǎ-fā(-'dzěw)-le-ba.

(*Hide*) tsáng. ‖Where did he dispose of the corpse? tā bǎ 'sž-shř tsáng-'nǎr-le?

Dispose (*arrange in a certain order*) páy. ‖The soldiers were disposed in a thin line. bǎ-'bīng páy-chéng-le 'sǎn-bīng-'shyàn-le.

Disposed (*mentally inclined*). ‖He was disposed to take things too seriously. tā-jèy-ge-rén 'sž-shīn-'yǎr, *or* tā-jèy-ge-rén ày jáw-'jěr. *or* tā 'wǎng-wǎng bǎ 'shř-ching 'kàn-de tày 'yán-jùng.

Well disposed toward 'dzàn-chéng. ‖I found him well disposed toward our suggestion. tā hěn 'dzàn-chéng wǒm-de-'jyàn-yì.

DISTANCE. (*Sometimes translated by* jywù-'lí, *but more commonly by expressions including* ywǎn *and other terms. See also* DISTANT.) ‖What is the distance to Kunming? tsúng-'jèr-dàw-'kwēn-míng-de-jywù-'lí shř 'dwō-shǎw? *or* 'kwēn-míng lí-'jèr yěw dwō 'ywǎn? *But* ‖We can cover the distance in three hours. yùng 'sān-ge-jūng-téw-de-'gūng-fu jyèw kě-yi 'dàw-de.

At (*or from*) a distance. ‖You can see the tower from a distance. lǎw-'ywǎn jyèw 'ké-yi 'kàn-jyàn nèy-ge-'tǎ. *or* nèy-ge-'tǎ nǐ lǎw-ywǎn-de jyèw 'kàn-de-jyàn. ‖At a distance the building seems attractive. nèy-ge-'léw tsúng-'ywǎn-chù kàn (*or* nèy-ge-'léw lǎw-ywǎn-de 'kàn-je) háy bú-'tswò. ‖The plane disappeared in the distance. *is expressed as* The plane disappeared in the sky. 'fēy-jī 'fēy-dàw 'tyān-byār bú-'jyàn-le. ‖Keep at a distance (*from a place*). lí 'ywǎn-dyǎr.

(*Coolness of manner*). ‖The distance in her manner is caused by shyness. tā 'yīn-wey 'myǎn-tyǎn 'swó-yi tày-dù (shyǎn-je) °hěn 'lěng-dàn. *or* °'lěng-lěng-dàn-dàn-de. *or* °'lěng-bu-jyēr-de. ‖I wanted to be friends with him, but he always kept at a distance. wǒ shyǎng 'gēn-tā dzwò 'péng-yew, kě-shr tā °'háw-wú 'byǎw-shř. *or* °'lěng-bu-jyēr-de. *or* °'lěng-lěng-dàn-'dàn-de. ‖Keep him at a distance. gēn tā 'shū-ywǎn-dyǎr. ‖Since our argument he keeps his distance. 'dž-tsúng wǒ-men 'bàn-dzwěy yǐ-'hèw, °tā bù-'lǐ-wo-le. *or* °tā 'dwǒ-je-wo.

To out-distance (*pass*) 'là-shya, 'kāy-gwò. ‖We can easily out-distance them. yàw-shyǎng bǎ tā-men °'kāy-gwò-chywu hěn 'rúng-yì. *or* °'là-shya hěn 'rung-yì.

DISTANT. (*Far away*) ywǎn. A distant view ywǎn-'jǐng. ‖My brother lives in a distant part of the country. wǒ-'gē-ge 'jù-dzày 'lí-jèr-hěn-'ywǎn-de-yí-ge-'dì-fang. ‖She is a distant relative of mine. tā shř wǒ-de-'ywǎn-'chīn. *But* ‖The river is five miles distant. hé 'lí-jèr yěw wǔ-lǐ-'dì (nà-me-'ywǎn).

In the distant future jyāng-láy yěw yì-'tyān. ‖Some time in the distant future I may learn to read Chinese characters. 'jyāng-láy yěw yì-'tyān wǒ yě-shywǔ shywé rèn-'dž.

In the distant past hěn jyěw yǐ-'chyán. *But* ‖The origin of this custom is shrouded in the forgotten recesses of the distant past. jèy-jǔng-'fēng-sú 'láy-ywán hwāng-'ywǎn, 'dzǎy-jì wú-'jēng. (*About as literary as the English.*)

Distant (*cool in manner*) 'lěng-dàn. ‖She seems very distant today. tā jyér 'fǎng-fu (dày-rén) tǐng 'lěng-dàn shř-de.

See also FAR, AWAY.

DISTRIBUTION. (*Passing out to many people or in many places*) expressed *with* to distribute fēn. ‖When is the first distribution of mail? 'shìn 'tèw-yí-tsż shém-'shf-hew 'fēn?

(*Spreading of many things in their places*) expressed *with* to distribute 'fēn-pěy. ‖The distribution of population in this country is uneven. 'gwó-nèy-'rén-kěw 'fēn-pèy-de bù-'jywūn.

(*Handing out in shares*) expressed *with* to release fàng. ‖He is in charge of the distribution of relief. tā 'gwǎn fàng-'jèn.

DISTRICT. (*General vicinity*) 'dì-dày, 'dì-fang. ‖The town is in a mountainous district. nèy-chéng dzày dwō-'shān-de-°'dì-dày. *or* °'dì-fang.

(*Administrative subdivision*) chywū. ‖The city is divided into ten administrative districts. jèy-ge-'chéng 'fēn-chéng-le shf-ge-('shíng-jèng-) 'chywū.

(*Administrative unit in China, something like a county*) shyàn. ‖The Chinese Republic is divided into 28 provinces and two border regions; the provinces are divided into about 2,000 districts. 'jūng-hwá-mín-'gwó yěw èr-shr-'bā-ge-'shěng hé lyǎng-gé-'byān-chywū; jèy-èr-shr-bā-'shěng yèw 'fēn-chéng lyǎng-chyān-lay-ge-'shyàn.

DISTURB. (*Objects, by moving or deranging*) 'nùng-lwàn, 'dùng. ‖Someone's disturbed my papers! yěw-rén 'dùng (*or* 'nùng-lwàn) wǒ-de-'wén-jyàn 'láy-je!

(*Call; as after a nap*) jyàw. ‖I don't want to be disturbed until ten. shf-dyǎn-yǐ-'chyán byé 'jyàw-wǒ.

(*Bother*) jyǎw, nàw, chǎw. ‖Don't disturb me again until this is done. jèy-ge méy-'wán yǐ-chyán, 'byé dzày láy °'jyǎw-wo. *or* °'nàw-wo. *or* °'chǎw-wo. ‖Don't disturb them (*from sleep*). byé bǎ-tām °'nàw-shǐng-le. *or* °'chǎw-shǐng-le. *or* (*if no noise is made*) °'jyǎw-shǐng-le.

Be disturbed (*emotionally*) jāw-'jí, 'shīn-li 'lwàn, 'shīn-li fán, 'shīn-li nán-'gwò. ‖I'm disturbed to hear that news. wǒ 'tīng-jyan nèy-ge-'shyāw-shi yǐ-'hèw, °yěw-dyǎr jāw-'jí. *or* °'shīn-li yěw-dyǎr 'lwàn. *or* °'shīn-li hěn-nán-'gwò. *or* °'shīn-li 'fán-de-hwang. ‖She's easily disturbed. ta yì-láy jyèw °jāw-'jí. *or* °'shīn-li 'lwàn. *or* °'shīn-li fán. *or* °'shīn-li nán-'gwò. *or* °'fā-hwāng. ‖This is disturbing news. jèy-ge-'shyāw-shi jyàw-rén °jāw-'jí. *or* °'shīn-li 'lwàn. *etc.*

Disturb *someone emotionally* (*alarm, excite*) 'jīng-dùng. ‖Don't disturb the others. byé 'jīng-dùng 'byé-rén.

DITCH. gēw. ‖There is a ditch on each side of the road. dàw lyǎng-'páng yěw 'gēw. ‖The car was ditched (*or* fell in the ditch) three kilometers up the road. chì-'chē dzày 'lù-'chyán-byàr-sān-'gūng-lǐ-de-'dì-fang dyàw-dzày 'gēw-li-le.

Irrigation ditch gwàn-gày-'chywū, chywū, *or* (*if it is small*) gēw.

‖Let's ditch these people and have some fun. dzám 'dwǒ-kay (*or* dzám 'shwǎy-kay) jèy-shyē-rén hǎw wár-de-'tùng-kway-dyar.

DIVIDE. fēn. Divide equally píng-fēn *or* 'jywūn-fēn. ‖Divide the money among you. nǐm bǎ-'chyán 'fēn-le-ba. ‖Here the river divides into two streams. hé dzày-jèr 'fēn-chéng lyǎng-'tyáw(-'jř-lyéw). ‖A road divides the town (*into two parts*). 'yì-tyáw-'lù bǎ-chéng 'fēn-chéng lyǎng-'bù. ‖Let me divide it for you. 'wǒ láy gěy nǐ-men 'fēn. ‖On the question of taxes Congress (*is*) divided into two camps. 'gwān-ywu 'jywān-shwèy-'wèn-tí gwó-hwèy 'fēn-chéng lyǎng-'pày. *But* ‖The committee (*was*) divided on the question of taxes. 'gwān-ywu 'jywān-shwèy-'wèn-tí wěy-'ywán-hwèy yì-jyan 'bù-yí-(jř).

(*Watershed*) shān-'jí. Continental Divide fēn-shwěy-'lǐng. ‖The hotel is on the divide between the two valleys. 'lywǔ-gwǎn shř dzày 'shān-jí-shàng.

Divided by. X divided by Y X bèy Y chú, X yùng Y chú, Y chú X. ‖14 divided by 2 equals 7. shf-'sż bèy-'èr 'chú dé-'chī. *or* shf-'sż yùng-'èr 'chú dé-'chī. *or* èr chú shf-'sż dé-'chī.

DIVISION. (*Section*) 'bù-fēn. ‖What division of the office do you work in? nǐ dzày 'gūng-shr-'fáng-li nǎ-yí-'bù-fēn dzwò-'shř?

(*Disunity*) 'fēn-fēn, 'bù-yí, bù-yí-'jř. ‖There was a division of opinion on that subject. 'gwān-ywu nèy-ge-'wèn-tí °'yì-lwen-'fēn-fēn. *or* °'yì-jyan-bù-'yī. *or* °'yì-jyan-bù-yī-'jř. ‖There's a division of authority in that office. dzày nèy-ge-'gūng-shr-fáng-li °'bú-shr 'yí-ge-rén 'gwǎn-shř. *or* °'shr-chywán bù-tǔng-'yī.

(*Military*) shř. ‖Three infantry divisions were sent. 'pày-chywu-le sān-ge-'bù-bīng-shř.

(*Mathematical*) 'chú-fǎ. ‖The children haven't started division yet. 'háy-dz-men háy 'méy-shywé 'chú-fǎ.

DO. 1. (*Perform, accomplish*) dzwò; bàn (*perform; more formal*); nùng (*less formal, used especially when the result of the action is in mind, often a bad result*); gàn (*implying mental ability, energy, or effort*); gǎw (*informal, used especially in Peiping*); *or occasionally some special expression confined to a few usages.* ‖What sort of work does he do? tā dzwo shém-me 'shèr? ‖What is he doing? tā dzwǒ 'shém-me-ne? *or* tā gàn 'shém-me-ne? *or* tā nùng 'shém-me-ne? *or* tā gǎw 'shém-me-ne? ‖How do you do this? 'jèy-ge dzěm-me °dzwò-ne? *or* °bàn-ne? *or* °nùng-ne? *or* °gǎw-ne? (gàn *is not used here, but might be used in the following sentence.*) ‖How did you ever do it? 'jèy-ge nǐ dzěm-me 'gàn-de? ‖Are you going to do it or not? nǐ 'jyēw-jing-shr 'gàn-bu-gàn? ‖He's doing three men's work here. tā 'yí-ge-rén dzày jèr dzwò 'sān-ge-rén-de-'shèr. ‖He can do as much as three men can where you come from. tā 'yí-ge-rén-'dzwò-de 'dǐ-de-shàng 'nǐm-nar-láy-de-'sān-ge-rén-dzwò-de nàm 'dwō. ‖The secretary does her work well. jèy-ge-'nywǔ-'shū-ji 'gūng-dzwò hěn hǎw. ‖He did his work well. tā-'dzwò-de hěn 'hǎw. ‖He didn't do his work well. tā-'dzwò-de 'bù-hǎw. ‖He didn't do that job well. nèy-ge-shèr tā méy-dzwò 'hǎw. ‖It certainly was his doing. méy-'tswòr, 'jwěn-shr 'tā-gàn-de. ‖He's doing his duty. tā 'dzwò tā-de-'shr̀-ne. or tā-nà-shr̀ jìn 'tā-de-'dzé-rèn. ‖He does odd jobs for people around here. tā gěy 'jèy-kwàr-de-'rén °dzwò 'líng-hwó. or °dzwò líng-swèy-'shèr. or °dzwò líng-chī-bā-swèy-de-'shèr, or °dzwò 'dzá-shèr. or °dǎ-'dzár. ‖Well done! dzwò-de 'hěn hǎw. or hǎw-'jí-le. ‖Is this the right thing to do? jèy-ge-'shèr shr̀ 'gāy-dzwò-de-ma? ‖Is this the right way to do it? jèy-jyàn shr̀ 'gāy jèm dzwò-ma? or jèy-jyàn 'jèm dzwò 'dwèy-ma? ‖If he can do it, so can I. 'tā yàw néng 'gàn nèy-ge, 'wǒ yě néng. ‖You'd better do as you're told. 'dzěm-me-'gàw-sung-nǐ-de jyèw dzěm-me °'bàn. or °'dzwò. or °'nùng. ‖You do it! nǐ dzwò-yi-dzwò 'kàn! or 'nǐ shr̀-yi-shr̀ 'kàn! ‖Let me see you do it. 'nǐ 'dzwò-yi-hwèy gěy-wǒ 'kàn-kan. ‖You can't do it that way. nǐ 'bù-néng 'nèm-je. ‖Now (that) you've done it, how do you feel? shyàn-dzày nǐ 'yǐ-jīng °bàn 'hǎw-le (if it was good; if bad, 'bàn 'dzāw-le) shīn-li jywé-je 'dzěm-me-yàng? ‖Now you've done it! (scolding). nǐ 'kàn! dēw °nùng-'hwày-le. or °nùng-'dzāw-le. ‖How is your brother doing at his new job? nǐ-de-'gē-ge 'jèy-ge-'shīn-shr̀-ching 'dzwò-de dzěm-me-'yàng? ‖He's doing pretty well. tā 'nùng-de hěn 'hǎw. or tā 'nùng-de háy bú-'tswò. ‖Something should be done about the high price of meat. 'dzěm-me-gāw-de-'rèw-jyàr 'yīng-gāy 'shyǎng-dyar 'bàn-fa. ‖My pen won't work; what did you do to it? wǒ-de-'gāng-bǐ bù-néng 'yùng-le; nǐ 'dzěm-me °'nùng-le-lay-je? or °'hwò-hwo-lay-je? ‖See what you've done! 'kàn nǐ-'hwò-hwo-de. or 'kàn nǐ-'nàw-de. or 'kàn nǐ-'nùng-de. ‖He's a hard man to do business with. gēn-'tā °láy-'wǎng hěn 'nán. or °dǎ 'jyāw-dày hěn 'nán. or °'gùng-shr̀ hěn 'nán. or °'dzwò 'mǎy-may hěn 'nán. ‖I've got to go downtown and do a little shopping. wǒ děy 'jìn-chéng chywù 'mǎy dyǎr-'dūng-shi.

2. *When some other word can easily be used in place of* do, *specifying the type of action more accurately, use the word in Chinese that corresponds to the more specific English word; e.g., for* do the dishes *use* wash the dishes. ‖Do (tie) the package up good and tight. bǎ 'bāw-fu °gwǒ-'hǎw-le, gwǒ-'jǐn-le. or °gwǒ-de hǎw-'hǎwr-de, jǐn-'jyēr-de. ‖The maid wants to do (put in order) this room now. shyàn-dzày nywǔ-'dǐ-shyà-rén yàw 'shr̀-dwò (or 'shr̀-daw, or 'shēw-shr) 'jèy-jyàn-'wū-dz. ‖On a bad road like this I can't do (drive) more than twenty miles an hour. 'jèm-hwày-de-'lù wǒ 'yì-shyǎw-shr bù-néng 'kāy-gwo 'èr-shr̀-lǐ. ‖This car only does (goes) twelve miles to the gallon. jèy-ge-'chē yì-'jyā-lwén jr̀ chěw shr̀-'èr-lǐ. ‖I'd better do (read, study) tomorrow's history lesson now. wǒ shyàn-'dzày 'háy-shr °'nyàn-nyàn (or °'ywù-bey-ywù-bey) myér-de-lì-'shr̀(-nèy-táng-'kè)-ba. ‖Could I help you do (wash, wipe) the dishes? wǒ 'bāng-ni °shǐ (or

°tsā) 'dyé-dz 'hǎw-ma? ‖Where can I get this laundry done (washed)? jèy-shyē-'yī-shang dzày-'nǎr shǐ 'hǎw-ne? ‖He is doing (writing) a magazine article on local customs. tā 'jèng-dzày shyě yì-pyān-'gwān-ywú-'dāng-dì-'fēng-su-shí-'gwàn-de-'wén-jang, yàw dzày yí-ge dzá-'jr̀-shang 'dēng. ‖This variety of melon does (grows) better in sandy soil. 'jèy-jǔng-'gwā dzày 'shā-dì-lǐ 'jǎng-de hǎw. ‖If we got caught, we'd have to do (sit) at least five years. 'yàw-shr 'dzám jyàw-rén 'děy-jaw, jyèw děy jr̀-shǎw dzwò 'wǔ-nyán-jyān-'jìn-na. ‖Do you think this color will do (be OK)? nǐ 'jywé-je jèy-ge-'shǎr °'chéng-ma? or °'shíng-ma? or °'háy, 'tsèw-hū-ma? ‖We'll have to make this do (serve). jèy-ge méy-'fár, jǐ-hǎw 'tsèw-hū-je. or 'jǐ-hǎw 'tsèw-hū-je yùng 'jèy-ge-ba. ‖That'll do (serve) all right for us, but she's more particular. 'wǒ-men ké-yi 'tsèw-hū-le, kě-shr tā hěn 'tyāw-tì. ‖She does (fixes) her hair up in a knot. tā bǎ 'téw-fa dzày 'téw-shang 'shū-le yí-ge-'jyēwr. ‖It takes her an hour to do (fix) her hair. tā shū-'téw fèy-le 'yí-ge-'jūng-téwr. ‖She's getting her hair done (professionally) for the party. tā yīn-wèy yàw chǐng-'kè dàw měy-rúng-'ywàn-chywu-le.

3. *When* do *is used as a substitute for another word earlier in the sentence, Chinese repeats either the first word, or uses none at all, or repeats some other word which is to be emphasized.* ‖If you want to ask any questions, do it now. 'yàw-shr nǐ yàw 'wèn shém-me, shyàn-'dzày jyèw wèn 'hǎw-le. ‖He drinks wine the way I do water. tā 'shyàng-wǒ-hē-'shwěy-shr̀-de nàm hē-'jyěw. ‖He gets up early and so do I. tā 'chǐ-de 'dzǎw; wǒ yě 'chǐ-de 'dzǎw. ‖Whatever he does, you do it too. (Here, do is not expressed in either part of the sentence.) 'tā dzěm-je; 'nǐ 'yě dzěm-je. ‖Who was it who saw him? I did. (shr̀-)shéy 'kàn-jyan-de-ta? shr̀-wǒ. ‖Did anyone see him? I did. (yěw-)shéy 'kàn-jyan tā-le? 'wǒ kàn-jyan-le. ‖We have to pay more than you (do) for cigarettes. 'wǒ-men mǎy 'yān-jywǎr děy bǐ-nǐ °'hwà-de 'dwō. or °'dwō chū-'chyán. ‖He works harder now than (he did) last year. tā shyàn-'dzày bǐ 'chywù-nyán mày 'lì-chi mày-de 'dwō-dyar. ‖I always have written home every week, and I still do. wǒ yí-'shyàng gěy 'jyā-li 'yí-ge-lǐ-'bày shyě 'yì-fēng-'shìn; 'shyàn-dzày 'háy-shr °'jèy-yàngr. or °'dzěm-je.

4. *As an auxiliary verb in questions (Does he go?), negatives (He doesn't go), and emphatics (He does go), do is expressed respectively by an interrogative form, a negative word or an emphatic word.* ‖Do you like the food here? nǐ 'shǐ-hwan 'jèr-de-'fàn-ma? ‖Does he live here? tā jù-'jèr-ma? ‖What do you want? nǐ yàw 'shém-me? ‖Why did he say that? tā 'wèy shém-me shwō 'nèy-ge? ‖Did you want to see me now? 'shr̀-bu-shr nǐ yàw shyàn-dzày 'jyàn-wo? ‖I don't want to trouble you. wǒ 'bú-ywàn-yì 'má-fàn nǐ. ‖Why doesn't he like this hotel? tā 'wèy shém-me bù-'shǐ-hwan jèy-ge-lywǔ-'gwǎn? ‖Didn't you have

enough to eat? nǐ méy-chr̄-ʰbǎw-ma? ‖I didn't say I liked him. wǒ 'méy-shwō-gwo wǒ 'shǐ-hwān tā. ‖Don't lean out the window. byé dzày 'chwāng-hu-nar 'tàn-chu-chywu. ‖Don't do it in that case. yàw-shr 'nèm-je, jyèw béng 'gàn-hǎw-le. meaning Let it go. 'nàm jyèw 'swàn-le-ba. or. meaning Oh, nuts! Forget it! 'ày-gàn-bú-'gàn. ‖But we DO want you. 'bú-gwò wǒ-men shr̀ 'jēn yàw-nǐ ('bú-shr 'jyǎ-de). ‖I do wish we could finish today. wǒ 'jēn-shr 'pàn-je 'jīn-tyān néng dzwò-'wán. ‖No matter what you say, I did see the man. bù-'gwǎn nǐ 'shwō shém-me, wǒ 'shr̀ 'jyàn-le tā-le. ‖You did say it! nǐ 'shwō-gwo!

5. *Combinations of do with other words.* **Do good, do well, etc.** ‖He has done a lot of good. tā 'dzwò-le hěn-'dwō-de-hǎw-'shr̀. (*See 1 above.*) ‖It will do you good. ywú-nǐ yěw 'hǎw-chù. ‖But it didn't do me any good. 'wǒ kě 'méy-dé-daw shém-me 'hǎw-chù. or ywú-'wǒ kě-shr méy-shém-me 'hǎw-chù. or (*if referring to medicine*) 'wǒ yùng-le kě méy-shém-me 'shyàw. ‖The drug does some good, but it's not a cure. yàw yěw dyǎr-'shyàw, bú-gwo bù-néng 'wán-chywán jr-'hǎw-le. ‖It won't do any good to complain to the police. gēn 'jǐng-chá 'mán-ywàn 'méy-yew shém-me 'yùng. ‖A vacation will do you lots of good. 'shyē-shye-'jyà hwèy-gěy-nǐ bù-'shǎw 'yí-chù. ‖He did pretty well by me. tā 'dày-wǒ hěn 'hǎw. ‖I see the army's done pretty well by you. hè! jywūn-'dwèy 'dày-nǐ háy bú-'hwày. or hè! nǐ dzày jywūn-'dwèy dāy-de háy bú-'hwày. ‖He did pretty well for himself in politics. tā dzày 'jèng-jyè gàn-de (*or* hwèn-de) 'hěn hǎw. ‖He's out of danger now and is doing as well as can be expected. tā méy-'wéy-shyǎn-le, 'yí-chyè dēw háy 'shwèn-li. ‖I'll do my best to have it ready on time. wǒ yàw 'jìn-lì dàw 'shr̄-hew gěy 'ywù-bey 'chū-lay. ‖Do your best; that's all. jìn-'lì-ěr-'wéy-jr̄, jyèw 'shr̀-le (*literary quotation*). ‖Do your best and leave the rest to Providence. jìn-'rén-shr̀, tīng-tyān-'mìng (*literary quotation*). ‖I have no illusions about it; I just do my best, and that's all. wǒ yě bú 'wàng-shyǎng tyān-'gāw, jìn-'lì-ěr-'wéy-jr̄ jyèw 'shr̀-le (*literary quotation*).

Do harm. ‖Will it do any harm if we talk over the matter? 'tán-tán nèy-jyàn-'shr̀ yěw shém-me 'hwày-chu-ma? ‖His unfriendly report did our work a lot of harm. tā-nèy-ge-bàw-'gàw gěy-wǒm shwō hwày-'hwà-lay-je, jyàw 'wǒm-de-'gūng-dzwò °dà shèw 'yǐng-shyǎng. or °shèw-'hày bù-'chyǎn. ‖The new tax has done much harm to retail trade. shīn-'shwèy 'yǐ-jīng jyàw 'shyǎw-mǎy-may 'shèw-le bù-'shǎw-de-'hày-le. or shīn-'shwèy bǎ 'shyǎw-mǎy-may 'hày-le bù-'chyǎn. ‖He did us a lot of harm by refusing to testify for us. tā bù-kěn tì-wǒm dzwò 'jyàn-jèng °jyàw-wǒm 'shèw-hày bù-'chyǎn. or °jyàw-wǒm dà shèw chí-'hày. or °jēn 'hǎy-le wǒm-le.

Do away with 'chywǔ-shyāw. ‖They plan to do away with most of these regulations. tā-men 'dǎ-swàn 'chywǔ-shyāw yí-dà-bàr-de-'gwéy-jywū.

Do out of. ‖He did me out of ten dollars. tā 'nùng-le wǒ 'shr̄-kwày-chyán-chywu.

Do with (*dispose of, use*) bàn. ‖What can I do with the leftover vegetables? (*Either "How can I use them?" or "Where shall I throw them out?"*) 'shèng-shya-de-'tsày wǒ 'dzěm-me bàn?

Do with (*use, welcome*). ‖We could do with several more people to come and help us. dzày 'láy jǐ-ge-rén bāng-'máng yě hǎw.

Have something to do with (*be related to*). ‖That has nothing to do with the question. 'nèy-ge gēn 'jèy-ge-wèn-'tí méy-'gwān-shi.

Do without. ‖Can you do without this pencil for a while? nǐ néng 'dāy-hwer dzày yùng 'jèy-gwǎn-chyān-'bi-ma? ‖If we can't get fresh fruit, we'll have to do without. · yàw mǎy-bu-'jáw 'shyān-gwǒ-dz, wǒ-men jyèw 'jr̄-hǎw bù-'chr̄. ‖I can't do without you. méy-'nǐ bù-'shíng. ‖We can't do without him. 'wǒm-jèr méy-'tā °bù-'shíng. or °'bàn-bu-lyǎw.

6. *Miscellaneous uses.* ‖Someone do something! 'kwày-je! 'kwày-je! ‖Yes, do! hǎw-'jí-le! ‖I do! (shr̀) 'jēn-de! ‖I do (*take this woman, etc.*). shr̀! ‖Well, I do. (*spoken with emphasis on "I"*) 'wǒ kě 'nèm-je. or 'wǒ ... (*with specific indication of what is done*). ‖Do I? 'wǒ? (*Point at your nose when you say it.*) ‖Did I? meaning Did I say it? shr̀-'wǒ shwō-de-ma? or meaning Did I do it? shr̀ 'wǒ nùng-de-ma? ‖Oh, I did, did I? nǐ shwǒ shr̀ 'wǒ °shwō-de (*or* °dzwò-de, *etc.*), éy? ‖Easy does it. (*Be careful*) 'shyǎw-shīn-je; or (*slower*) 'màn-dyar; or (*more lightly*) 'chīng-dyar; or (*don't get excited*) byé 'hwāng. ‖Do or die! bú-'nèm-je jyèw-'sž! ‖How do you do? 'nǐ hǎw! ‖That'll do! meaning It's OK. 'shíng-le. or 'chéng-le. or 'hǎw-le. or 'yěw-le. or meaning It's enough. 'gèw-le. (or *sarcastically*) 'dé-le-ba. or 'swàn-le-ba! or 'dzěm-me 'méy-'gèw-wa? or 'háy bú-'gèw-ma? or nǐ háy yěw-wán méy-'wán-na? ‖That'll do now; no more of that! háy bú-'gèw-ma? byé dzày °'nèm-je-le! or °'shwō-le!

Done (*cooked, finished*). **done for, done in, done with.** *See* **DONE**.

DOCTOR. (*Medical*) 'yī-sheng, 'dày-fu. ‖He's a doctor. tā 'shr̀ ge-'yī-sheng (*or* -'dày-fu). ‖Will you please send for a doctor? láw-nǐ-'jyà chywù 'jǎw ge-'dày-fu-lay. ‖Is there a doctor in the house? dzày jèy-'wū-dz-rén-li yěw °'dày-fu-ma? or °'yī-sheng-ma? ‖May I introduce Dr. Fáng. 'jèy-wèy shr̀ 'fáng-'dày-fu.

Doctor of philosophy 'bwó-shr. ‖He is a Ph.D. tā shr̀ ge-'jé-shywé-'bwó-shr. ‖May I introduce Dr. Féng. 'jèy-wèy shr̀ 'féng-bwó-shr.

(*Treat medically*) jr̄. ‖I'm doctoring myself for a cold. wǒ-de-shāng-'fēng wǒ 'dž-jǐ 'jr̄-ne.

(*Take care of*) kàn. ‖Who's doctoring you? shwéy 'kàn nǐ-de-'bìng?

Doctor up. ‖The documents appear to have been doctored up. jèy-jyàn-'gūng-wén 'kàn-shang-chywu hǎw 'shyàng yěw-rén gěy °dzwò-le 'jyǎ-le. or °'gǎy-gwo.

or °'tyān-jēr chywù-'yèr-de-le (*literary quotation*). ‖The editor's doctored up the story for publication. !byān-jì bǎ nèy-dwàr-shīn-'wén 'pū-jāng-de hěn 'dà.

DOG. gěw. ‖Have you fed the dog? wèy-'gěw-le-ma? *or* gěw 'wèy-le-ma? ‖Please take the dog out for a walk. dày-gěw 'chū-chywu 'dzěw-dzěw.

Dog-tired lèy 'pā-shya. ‖They came in dog-tired after sightseeing all day. gwàng-le yì-'tyān tā-men dēw lèy 'pā-shya-le.

To go to the dogs. ‖He used to be successful, but now he's going to the dogs. tā yí-'shyàng hěn dé-'yì, kě-shr 'shyàn-dzày °'twēy-táng-le. *or* °'làw-daw-le. *or* °'dǎw-méy-le. *or* °'lè-'pwò-le. ‖He thinks the world is going to the dogs. tā shyǎng 'jèy-ge-'shr̀-jyè jyǎn-'jŕ shr̀ hwèn-'jàng.

Dog-house. ‖He's in the dog-house now. tā shr̀-'chǔng-le.

To dog bī. ‖They say they'll dog him until he gives in. tā-men shwō yàw bǎ-tā 'bī-dàw °'bù-'dā-ying bù-'jŕ. *or* °'tā 'dā-ying-le wéy-jŕ. *or* °'tā 'dā-ying-le t̑áy 'swàn-wán.

DONE. (*For most uses, see* **DO**; *the following are uses of* **DONE** *not common to* **DO**.) (*Cooked*) 'dé-le, dzwò-'hǎw-le. ‖In ten minutes the rice will be done. 'shf-fēn-'jūng-nèy fàn jyèw °'dé-le. *or* °'dzwò-'hǎw-le. *or* °'nùng-'hǎw-le.

Well done shéw, 'hwǒ-kěw 'dà. ‖I want the meat well done. 'rèw dzwò 'shéw-le. *or* 'rèw dzwò-de 'hwǒ-kěw 'dà-dyar. ‖I don't want the meat well done. rèw 'byé dzwò-de 'hwǒ-kěw 'dà-le. *or* rèw dzwò-de 'hwǒ-kěw 'shyǎw-dyar.

Half done (*of food*) 'bàn-shēng bù-'shéw-de. ‖It was only half done when he served it. háy 'bàn-shēng bù-'shéw-de jyèw gěy-wǒm 'dwān-shang-lay-le.

(*Finished*). ‖It's only half done. gāng dzwò-le yí▾ 'bàr. (*But usually use* wán.) ‖It's not done yet. háy méy-'wán. ‖All my lessons are done. wǒ-de-'gūng-kè chywún dzwò-'wán-le. ‖I can't leave before the job is done. shèr méy-'wán wǒ bù-néng 'dzěw-kāy.

Done for swàn-'wán-le, swàn-'lyǎw-le, swàn-wár-'wán-le, swàn-'hwěy-le. ‖These tires are done for. jèy-jī-'tyáw-'chē-dày swàn-'wán-le. *etc.* ‖If the boss finds this out I'm done for. téwr yàw 'chá-chu-lay wǒ jyèw swàn-'wán-le.

Done in 'lèy-sž-le. ‖I'm done in, working in all this heat. dzày ʾ-me-'rè-tyār-li 'gūng-dzwò wǒ 'lèy-sz-le.

Done with. ‖Are you done with these scissors? nǐ shr̀-'wán (*or* nǐ yùng-'wán) jʾy-bǎ-'jyǎn-dz-le-ma? ‖If he gets drunk again, I'm done with him. tā yàw dzày hē-'dzwèy-le, wǒ 'gēn-tā °'swàn-'wán-le. *or* °'rwàn-'wán-le. *or* °'swàn-'lyǎw-le. *or* °'swàn-'chwēy-le.

DOOR. mén, mér. ‖The dining room has two doors. 'jèy-ge-fàn-'tīng yèw lyǎng-ge-'mén. ‖The china closet has two glass doors. chéng-'tsź-chì-de-'gwèy yèw lyǎng-ge-'bwō-li-mér. ‖Please open the door for me. láw-'jyà tì-wǒ 'kāy-kāy 'mén. *or* láw-'jyà gěy-wǒ bǎ-mén 'kāy-kay. ‖His house is three doors down the street from ours. dǎ-'wǒm-jer wàng-'nèy-byar 'shǔ, dì-'sān-ge `dà-mér jyèw-shr tā-'jyā. *or* 'tā-jyā gēn 'wǒm 'jyē-je 'lyǎng-ge dà-mén.

Outdoors (dzày) !wày-byan. ‖Let's have the game outdoors. dzám dzày 'wày-byan 'wár-ba.

Other English expressions. ‖If he gets insulting, show him the door. tā 'yàw-shr wū-'rǔ-rén °chǐng-tā 'chū-chywu. *or* °'yàw-tā 'chū-chywu. *or* °'bǎ-tā 'gǎn-chu-chywu. *or* °'jyàw-ta 'gwěn (*vulgar*). ‖His remarks closed the door to further discussion. tā 'nèm yì-s̄hwō, jyèw °'chǎ-le. *or* °'yùng-bu-jáw dzày 'tán-le.

DOUBLE. bèy. ‖His income was double what he expected. tā-de-'shēw-rù bǐ tā 'ywù-lyàw-de dwō yí-'bèy. ‖I'll double his offer. wǒ jyā-'bèy chū-'chyán, *or* wǒ jyā-bèy gěy-'chyán. ‖He doubled my offer. tā bǐ-'wǒ dwō-'chū yí-'bèy-de-'chyán. *or* tā yàw bǐ-wǒ dwō-'gěy yí-'bèy-de-chyán. ‖If you lose, you lose double. nǐ yàw 'shū-le, nǐ-shū-de jyèw děy jyā-'bèy. ‖Double (*in bridge*)! jyā-'bèy! ‖Redouble! jyā-'bèy-de-jyā-'bèy!

(*Two*) lyǎng. ‖May I have a double portion (*two parts*) of ice cream? 'bīng-jī-líng wǒ 'kě-yǐ láy 'lyǎng-fèr-ma? ‖The double doors (*literally* two-fan-gate) open onto the terrace. nèy-ge-'lyǎng-shàn-'mén 'chùng-je 'shày-táy 'kāy. ‖Only double rooms (*literally* two-person rooms) are left. 'jŕ yèw 'lyǎng-ge-rén-'jù-de-'fáng-jyān-le. *or* jŕ-yèw 'shwāng-rén-'fáng-jyān-le.

(*Pair of*) shwāng. ‖That word has a double meaning. nèy shr̀ yí-ge-'shwāng-gwān-'dzèr. ‖There's a double-track railroad between the two towns. lyǎ-chéng-'jŕ-jyān-de-tyě-'lù shr̀ shwāng-'gwěy-de. ‖Let's play doubles. dzám dǎ 'shwāng-dǎ-ba.

To double (*back*) hwéy. ‖The burglar must have doubled on his tracks. dzéy yí-'dìng shr̀ dzěw 'ywán-lù hwéy-chywu-le. ‖The road doubles back toward town. jè-tyáw-'lù 'jwàn-hwéy-láy háy hwéy-dàw 'chéng-li.

(*Image*). ‖He looks enough like you to be your double. tā-'jǎng-de 'shyàng-nǐ 'shyàng-de hěn 'ké-yi dzwò nǐ-de-'tì-shēn.

Double up. ‖There's only one room, so we must double up. jŕ yèw 'yì-jyān-'kūng-fáng, dzám lyǎ-rén děy jù-yí-'kwàr.

(*Fists*). ‖He doubled his fists in anger. tā 'chì-de (jŕ-) 'dzwàn 'chywán-tew.

(*Life*). ‖He's leading a double life. tā 'yán-shíng bù-'fú. *or* 'tā 'jyǎ-màw wéy-'shàn. *or* tā shr̀ 'láw-hu dày 'sù-ju, 'jyā-chūng 'shàn-rér (*literary*). *or meaning* He's keeping a mistress. tā 'yèw ge-'shyǎw-gūng-'gwǎn.

Other expressions in English. ‖You must be seeing double. nǐ yí-'dìng shr̀ yǎn-'lí-le. ‖He's doubled up with pain. tā-'dù-dz 'téng-de °'wān-yāw. *or* °'máw-yāw. *or* °'jŕ-bu-chi 'yāw-lay. ‖Double time, march!

'păw-bù, 'dzĕw! ‖Double the order! jàw-'yàngr dzày 'yàw yí-'fèr! or jàw-'yàngr dzày 'láy yí-'fèr! ‖Do you boys mind sleeping in a double bed? nĭ-men-'lyă shwèy 'yì-jāng-chwáng, 'shíng-ma? ‖This room has a double bed. jèy-'wū-li yĕw yí-ge-'dà-chwáng. ‖He's doubled his capital in two years. tā lyăng-'nyán-de-'gūng-fu jyèw bă 'bĕn-chyán 'jwàn-hwéy-lay-le.

DOUBT. To doubt (not believe) bú-'shìn; (suspect) 'yí-shīn like the English, this latter can be used of a person, as to doubt someone; but when saying to doubt that . . . you have to say to suspect that . . . not . . ., using a negative; not to doubt that . . . (believe certainly) shyāng-'shìn . . . . ‖I don't doubt that in the least. wŏ shyāng-'shìn yí-'dìng shr̀ 'nèm-hwéy-'shèr. ‖I doubt if he meant it that way. wŏ 'yí-shīn tā-de-'yì-sz 'bú-shr nèm-je. or wŏ bú-'shìn tā yĕw 'nèy-ge-yì-sz. ‖I'm beginning to doubt his intentions. shyàn-'dzày wŏ 'yĕw dyăr-°'yí-shīn tā 'bù-hwáy-hăw-'yì-le. or °'bú-'shìn tā shr̀ 'shàn-yì-de-le. ‖I don't doubt him at all. wŏ yì-dyăr yĕ 'bù-'yí-shìn tā. ‖I don't doubt that he meant it. meaning what he said about the past. wŏ shyàng-'shìn tā-'nà-shr 'jēn shīn-'hwà. meaning what he threatened wŏ shyàng-'shīn tā 'jēn°yàw 'nèm-je. or °'hwèy 'gàn-de-chu-'láy. ‖I still have some doubts about him. wŏ háy yĕw-dyăr 'yí-shīn tā. or wŏ háy yĕw-dyăr bù-néng shyàng-'shìn tā. ‖I doubt if the story is true. wŏ 'yí-shīn 'méy-nèm-me-'hwéy-shr̀.

No doubt yí-'dìng, wú-'yí-de, wú-yí-'wèn. ‖There's no doubt about it. 'háw-wú-yí-'wèn. ‖No doubt the train will be late. hwŏ-chē yí-'dìng 'wù-dyăn.

Without doubt 'dāng-rán. ‖Without doubt he's the best man for the job. wèy dzwò nèy-jyàn-'shr̀ tā 'dāng-rán shr̀ dzwèy-'hé-shr̀-de-rén.

Be in doubt 'bù-yí-dìng. ‖The result is still in doubt. 'jyē-gwŏ háy 'bù-yí-'dìng.

Be in doubt about bù-'jwĕn jr̀-dàw. ‖When in doubt about the enemy's intentions, it's best to strike first. bù-'jwĕn jr̀-daw 'dí-rén-de-láy-'yì de-shf-hew, háy-shr 'shyān shyà-'shĕw wéy-'chyáng. (The last four syllables are a literary quotation.)

DOUBTFUL. See also **DOUBT**. ‖I'm doubtful about when he plans to come. wŏ 'bú-dà 'jr̀-dàw (or wŏ bù-'jwĕn jr̀-daw) tā 'dă-swàn 'shém-me-shf-hew láy. ‖It's doubtful whether he'll get well. tā bù-yí-'dìng hăw-de-'lyăw. or tā 'yĕ-shywŭ hăw-bu-'lyăw-le.

(Not beyond reproach) bù-kĕ-'kàw. ‖The guides here are of doubtful character. 'jèr-de-'shyŏ .g-dăw 'dēw bù-kĕ-'kàw.

DOWN. (To a lower place) shyà. ‖Come down from there! 'shyà-láy! ‖Step down! 'shyà-chywu! ‖Sailing downstream is much faster. 'shyà-shwéy 'dzĕw-de 'kwày-de 'dwō. ‖Down! (lowering something) dzày wàng-°'shyà-dyar! or °'dī-dyar! (See also **LOWER**.) ‖Lie down! (to a dog) 'tăng-shya! ‖Sit down. 'dzwò-shya. or (in a greeting or invitation) chĭng 'dzwò. ‖Is

this elevator going down? jèy-ge-'dyàn-tī shr̀ wàng-'shyà-chywù-ma? ‖The ship went (sank) down with all hands, five miles off shore. lyán-'chwán dày-'rén dzày lí-'àn-'wŭ-li-dì-de-'dì-fang 'chén-shyà-chywu-le. ‖Put on the brakes, or the car will roll down the hill. 'găn-jǐn tsăy-'já, bù-rán chē yàw 'gwĕn-shyà 'shān-chywu-le. ‖This thing moves up and down. jèy-ge-dūng-shi yí-'shàng-yí-'shyà-de dùng. ‖He stepped down from the porch. tā tsúng 'lyáng-táy-shang 'dzĕw-shyà-lay-le. ‖He downed (drank) his drink quickly. tā bă-'jyĕw hĕn 'kwày-de jyĕw 'hē-shya-chywu-le. ‖Swallow it down. 'yàn-shya-chywu. ‖Put that thing down. bă nèy-ge °'gē-shya. or °'fàng-shya. ‖In Chinese, to cut with a downward stroke is lá, kăn, chyē, dwò, or já. jūng-gwo-hwà wàng-'shyà yùng-lì "cut" shr̀ 'lá, 'kăn, 'chyē, 'dwò, 'já, 'jèy-jǐ-ge-'dz. ‖The price is going down. 'jyà-chyan dzày wàng-shyà °'làw. or °'jyàng. or (without -shyà) 'jyà-chyan kàn 'làw. ‖Wait until the price has come down a little. dĕng-dàw 'jyà-chyan 'làw-shya-dyăr-lay dzày-'shwō. ‖The balloon is coming down. chì-chyéw dzày wàng-shyà °'lè. or °'làw. or °'jyàng. ‖The mercury (in the thermometer) is coming down. 'hán-shŭ-byăw dzày wàng-shyà °'lè. or °'làw. or °'jyàng. ‖The sun is just going down. 'tày-yang jèng wàng-shya °'làw-je. or °'lè-je. ‖The sun has gone down. 'tày-yang °'làw-le. or °'lè-le.

When the place or terminus is specific, down is not usually expressed separately. ‖Put the suitcase down there. bă 'shyāng-dz °'gē-dzày nàr. or °'fàng-dzày nàr. ‖The mercury went down to zero. 'hán-shŭ-byăw lè-dàw 'líng-dù-le.

Down is sometimes expressed with shyà when a physically lower place is not referred to. ‖Write down your address. bă nǐ-de-'jù-jǐ 'shyĕ-shyà-láy. ‖The police took down his statement. 'shywún-jǐng bă tā-de-kĕw-'gùng 'jì-shya-lay-le. ‖She calmed down after a while. gwò-le-hwĕr tā jyèw 'ān-jìng-shya-lay-le.

Down is not expressed at all in some cases, usually those in which it may also be omitted in English. ‖He fell down. tā 'dăw-le. ‖He lost his balance and fell down. tā shwāy (or dyē)-'dăw-le. or 'tā 'shwāy (or 'dyē)-le ge-'jyăw. ‖He tripped and fell down. tā 'bàn (or 'hwá)-le ge-'jyăw. ‖He fell down on the floor tā 'dăw-dzày dì-'băn-shang-le.

Of directions or geographical locations, Chinese say go down only when the motion is actually downhill or away from Peiping; otherwise use go up, as we sometimes do in English, or neither. ‖I went down (downhill or from Peiping) to Tientsin last week. 'shàng-lǐ-bày wŏ shyà 'tyān-jīn-le. ‖In the winter I go down (up) to Shanghai. 'dūng-tyar-de-'shŕ-hew wŏ shàng 'shàng-hăy. ‖I saw him walking down the street. wŏ 'kàn-jyàn tā wàng jyē-'nèy-téwr-dzĕw. ‖He lived down south two years. tā dzày 'nán-fāng jù-le lyăng-'nyán. ‖It's way down that way. dzày 'nèy-byar 'ywăn-je-ne.

‖They live down by the river. tām 'jù-dzày 'kàw-hé-byār-nèr. ‖He comes down here once a week. tā měy-lì-'bày dàw-jèr láy yí-'tsź.

Calm down. (*Be patient*) byé 'chǎw-le; (*don't be excited*) byé 'hwāng. ‖Pipe down! byé 'rāng-rang.

Up and down (*back and forth*). ‖He was walking up and down the room. tā dzày 'wū-li 'láy-hwéy-de 'dzěw.

Up and down (*better and worse*). ‖Business goes up and down. 'mǎy-mày yěw-'péy yěw-'jwàn. ‖He has his ups and downs. (*Emotionally, physically, financially, etc.*) tā yěw-shf-hew 'hǎw yěw-shf-hew 'hwày.

Come down with (*catch*) jāw, dé. ‖I'm coming down with a cold. wǒ jāw-'lyáng-le.

Boil down, cut down 'swō-dwǎn. ‖This report needs to be boiled down to half its length. 'jèy-ge-'bàw-gàw děy 'swō-dwǎn yí-'bàr.

It boils down to this. (*Literary quotations*) 'jyǎn-dwàn 'jyé-shwō shf 'jèm-je. *or* 'gwēy-le bāw-'dzwēy shf 'jèm-je.

Burn down shāw-'hwěy, shāw-'tā. ‖The building has burned down. jěng-'gèr-léw dēw °shāw-'hwěy-le. *or* °shāw-'tā-le.

Pay down, down payment. To pay ... down (*to make the first payment*) téw (*or* dì)-yí-tsź °'jyāw ... *or* °'fù ... *or* °'shyà ... *or* °shyān ...; (*pay cash*) fù-'shyàn. Down payment téw (*or* dì)-yí-tsź-'jyāw-de-chyán; (*or any of the other combinations plus* -de-chyán); *or* (*deposit to reserve something*) téw-yí-tsź-'jyāw-de-'dìng-chyán. ‖How much is the down payment? *is expressed as* How much must be paid down? dì-yí-tsź děy jyāw (*or* fù *or* shyà) 'dwō-shǎw ('dìng)-chyán? *or* shyàn jyāw (*etc.*) 'dwō-shaw 'chyán? *or* 'shyàn-chyán shyān jyāw (*etc.*) 'dwō-shaw? *or* 'dìng-chyán shf 'dwō-shaw? ‖They want half (paid) down and the rest in monthly installments. tām yàw yí-'bàr fù-shyàn, 'shèng-shya-de àn-'ywè fēn-'chī gěy. *or* tām 'shyàn yàw yí-'bàr-chyán, shèng-....

Go down (*lose in card games*) shū. ‖We went down two on the last hand. shàng-yī-bǎ-'páy, wǒ-men shū-le 'lyǎng-dwēn (*or* -fù).

(*Unfortunate*). ‖Don't hit a man when he's down. (*Figuratively*) byé 'chī-fu dǎw-'méy-de-rén. *or* (*literary quotation*) bú-yàw lè-jīng shyà-'shf. ‖They used to be well off, but they're down and out now. tām-jyā yǐ-chyán hěn 'kwò, shyàn-dzày °'lwò-twò-le. *or* °'làw-le.

Be down on (*be disgusted with*) tǎw-'yàn; (*attack verbally*) 'gūng-ji, mà. ‖The others are down on him because he can't keep his temper. 'tām hěn tǎw-'yàn tā 'yīn-wèy tā jìng fā 'pí-chì.

‖Let's get down to work. dzám hǎw-'hǎwr-de 'gàn yí-shyàr.

‖She is loaded down with packages. tā 'bàw-le yí-'dà-dzwēy-'dūng-shi.

Down (*of a bird*) rwǎn-'máwr, rúng. ‖This pillow is filled with swan's down. jèy-ge-'jěn-tew-lǐ-téw 'jwāng-de shf 'tyān-é-°de-rwǎn-'máwr. *or* °rúng.

DOZEN. dá. ‖Please give me a dozen eggs. gěy-wǒ yì-dá-'jī-dzěr.

(*Indefinite quantity*). ‖There are dozens of people in line already. yǐ-'jīng yěw hǎw-shvē-rén jàn-'páy-le.

DRAFT. (*Drawing power of a chimney*). To have a draft tèw-'chyèr. ‖This chimney doesn't have enough draft. jèy-ge-'yān-tung bú-'dà tèw-'chyèr.

Draft regulator fēng-'mér. ‖Please open the draft of the furnace. bǎ lú-dz-de-fēng-'mér kāy-kay.

(*Breeze*) fēng(-'kěwr). ‖I'm sitting in a draft. wǒ dzwò-dzày fēng-'kěwr-shàng-le. ‖There's a draft here. jèr yěw-'fēng.

To draft (*draw*) hwà. ‖The plans were drafted in the engineer's office. tú shf dzày 'gūng-chéng-shf-nèr 'hwà-de.

To draft (*draw up a plan*) ní, ní-'dìng, ní-'hǎw. ‖The plan of the offensive was drafted in the Pentagon Building. 'gūng-jí-de-'jì-hwà shf dzày wǔ-byān-'léw-li °ní-de. *or* °ní-'dìng-le. *or* °ní-'hǎw-le.

To draft (*write*) shyě. ‖The committee is drafting a message of welcome. wěy-ywán-'hwèy jèng-dzày shyě 'hwān-yíng-'tsź.

First draft, rough draft tsǎw-'gǎwr. To make a first draft chǐ-'tsǎw, dǎ (*or* chǐ) tsǎw-'gǎwr. ‖He has made a rough draft of his speech. tā bǎ 'yǎn-jyǎng 'dǎ-le (*or* 'chǐ-le) ge-tsǎw-'gǎwr. ‖It has been drafted (*but not in final form*). yǐ-jīng chǐ-'tsǎw-le. ‖Do you have a draft of your plan? nǐ-de-'jì-hwà yěw ge-tsǎw-'gǎwr-ma? (*But formally, a first draft is* tsǎw-'àn.) ‖This is the first draft of the Constitution. jèy-shr 'shyàn-fǎ-dì-'yí-tsź-tsǎw-'àn.

Bank draft 'hwèy-pyàw. ‖The bank will cash this draft for you. nǐ-jèy-jāng-'hwèy-pyàw 'yín-háng ké-yi gěy-nǐ dwèy-'shyàn. ‖This draft is on the Central Bank of China. 'jèy-shr yì-jāng-'jūng-yāng-yín-háng-de-'hwèy-pyàw.

(*For military service*) jēng. Draft board jēng-bīng-'jywú *or* bīng-yì-'jywú; draft laws bīng-yì-'fǎ. ‖He's due to be drafted next month. tā 'shyà-ywè yàw bèy-'jēng chywù 'dāng-bīng. ‖The draft has taken half our men. wǒm-jèr-yí-bàr-'rén yǐ-jīng bèy-'jēng chywù 'dāng-bīng-le.

Draft horse (wǎn-) 'mǎ. ‖The roads are so bad that we'll have to get draft horses to haul our equipment. lù tày 'hwày-le, dzám-de-'dūng-shi 'fēy-děy yùng (wǎn-) 'mǎ 'lā bù-'kě.

(*Displacement, of a boat*) chř-shwěy-'lyàng, (*not commonly used; replaced more frequently by*) to have a draft of ... chř ... shwěy. ‖This boat has a draft of six feet. jèy-ge-'chwán chř-shwěy 'lyèw-chř. *or* jèy-ge-'chwán chř 'lyèw-chř-de-'shwěy. ‖What's the draft? chř 'dwō-shaw shwěy? *or* chř-shwěy-'lyàng shf dwō-shaw?

DRAW (DREW, DRAWN). 1. (*Pull, drag, haul*) lā; (*only stationary things*) jwày. ‖Two horses are used to draw that cart. này-lyǎng-'chē yùng 'lyǎng-pǐ-mǎ 'lā. ‖Have you seen a dog-drawn cart? ní 'jyàn-gwo gěw-lā-de-'chē-ma? ‖It took six horses for them to draw that piece of stone out. tām yùng lyèw-pǐ-'mǎ bǎ nèy-kwày-'shŕ-tew ·jwày-kāy-de. ‖Draw it tight. lā-'jǐn-le. or jwày-'jǐn-le. or dèn-'jǐn-le.

2. (*Pull, something small; pull with a jerk*) chēw; (*pull out*) bá; (*take out*) tāw; (*withdraw*) twèy; (*pull in*) swō; (*a knife*) dùng. ‖He drew out a piece of paper from the pile. tā tsúng yì-dwēy-'jŕ-li 'chēw-chu yì-'jāng-láy. ‖Draw the sword out and look at the blade. bǎ-'dāw chēw (or bá, or lā)-chu-lay 'chyáw-chyaw nèy-ge-'rèr. ‖He drew a piece of paper out of his pocket. tā tsúng kěw-'dàr-li 'tāw- (or 'ná-, *take*) chu yì-'jāng-'jŕ-láy. ‖He drew his hands out of his pockets. tā bǎ-'shěw tsúng kěw-'dàr 'twèy (or 'ná, *take*)-chu-lay-le. ‖Don't draw back your hand. byé bǎ-'shěw 'chēw (or 'swō)-hwey-chywu. ‖The turtle drew in its head. gwēy bǎ-'téw 'swō-jin-chywu-le. ‖When he drew a knife on me I shot him. tā 'gēn-wǒ dùng 'dāw-dz, 'swǒ-yǐ wǒ ná-'chyāng 'dǎ-tā. ‖They came out with drawn (*flashing*) swords. tām lyàng-je-'dāw láy-de.

3. (*Of air or smoke*) shī, chēw; (*but referring to a chimney*) tūng-'chyèr. ‖When it was over he drew a deep breath. 'wán-le yǐ-'hèw, tā shēn-'shēn-de 'shī-le (or 'chēw-le) yì-kěw 'chì. ‖This pipe draws well. jèy-ge-'yān-děw hěn hǎw 'chēw. (shī *would not be used here.*) ‖This pipe doesn't draw. jèy-ge-'yān-děw °'chēw-bu-jìn 'yān-lay. or °'shī-bu-jìn 'yān-lay. or °'shī-bu-'jáw. or °chēw-bu-'jáw. or (*it is clogged*) °'dǔ-shang-le. ‖When the wind is in this direction the chimney draws well. fēng wàng 'jèy-byar gwä de-'shŕ-hew 'yān-túng hěn tūng-'chyèr. ‖The chimney doesn't draw well. ·'yān-túng bú-dà tūng-'chyèr.

4. (*Attract*) jāw ..., yǐn ..., 'jāw-yǐn ..., jyàw ...; *the construction with each is* to cause *someone to do something.* (*Of a magnet*) shī. To draw attention 'jāw-yáw; to draw a crowd *or* to be a drawing card jyàw-'dzwòr. ‖This concert is sure to draw a big crowd. jèy-ge-yīn-ywè-'hwèy yí-dìng néng °jyàw-'dzwòr. or °'jāw (or yǐn, or 'jāw-yǐn, or 'jyàw) hěn-'dwō-rén láy ('tīng). ‖Her little hat drew a lot of attention. tā nèy-dǐng-shyǎw-'màwr hěn °'jāw (or 'yǐn, or 'jāw-yǐn, or 'jyàw)-rén jù-'yì. or °'jyàw-rén 'kàn. or °'jyàw-rěn 'chyáw. or °'jāw-yáw. ‖She wears that on the street just to draw attention to herself. tā chwān-je 'nèy-ge shàng 'jyě jyèw-shŕ yàw °'jāw (or 'yǐn, or 'jāw-yǐn, or 'jyàw)-rén jù-'yì. or °'jāw-yáw-jāw-yáw. or °jyàw-rén dwō 'chyáw-tā lyǎng-yǎn. ‖His remark drew applause from the audience. tā 'nèy-jywù-hwà jyàw 'tīng-de-rén gǔ-'jǎng. ‖The magnet draws these pieces of iron toward it. 'shī-tyě-'shŕ bǎ jèy-shyē-kwàr-'tyě 'shī-gwo-lay. ‖He is a big draw(ing) card) wher-

ever he goes. tā 'dàw-nar děw °jyàw-'dzwòr. or, *expressed as* He is welcomed by all. °shèw-rén 'hwǎn-yíng.

5. (*Money*) chywǔ. ‖I'll have to draw fifty dollars out of the bank. wǒ děy tsúng 'yín-háng chywǔ 'wǔ-shŕ-kwày-chán. ‖I've drawn most of my money out of the bank. wǒ-de-'chán chā-bu-dwō 'děw tsúng 'yín-háng 'chywǔ-chu-lay-le. ‖You're overdrawn. nǐ-'chywǔ-de-chán gwò-le 'shùr-le. or (*Your deposit is insufficient*) nǐ-'tswén-de-chán bú-'gèw-le.

(*Interest*) shēng. ‖I'm letting my money draw interest. wǒ bǎ-'chyán 'tswén-chi-láy shēng-°'lì. or °'shì. or °'lì-shi.

6. Draw water dǎ-('shwěy); (*with a rope*) shì. ‖Go out and draw a bucket of water. 'chū-chywu 'dǎ yì-tǔng-'shwěy-láy. ‖The rope they use for drawing water is too short. tām-'yùng-láy-shì (or -dǎ)-'shwěy-de-'shéng-dz tày 'dwàn. ‖They drew him out of the well with a rope. tām (yùng 'shéng-dz) bǎ-tā tsúng-'jǐng-lǐ 'shì-shang-lay-le.

7. Draw blood (*to bleed*) lyéw-'shyě, chū-'shyě. ‖The scratches were deep enough to draw blood. jwā-de-'shēn-de lyéw (or chū)-'shyě-le.

8. Draw *so much* water (*displace*) chŕ (...)-shwěy. ‖On this river a boat has to draw less than three feet. dzày 'jèy-tyáw-'hé-li chwán chŕ-'shwěy bù-néng 'gwò 'sān-chŕ.

9. Draw (*pictures, maps, etc.*) hwà. ‖Everybody can draw (*pictures*). 'rén-rén néng hwà-'hwàr. ‖I can't draw (*pictures*). wǒ bú-'hwèy hwà-'hwàr. ‖Won't you please draw me a map of the route? nǐ 'néng-bu-néng bǎ lù-'shyàn gěy-wǒ 'hwà-chu-lay? ‖Draw a map. hwà yì-jāng-dì-'tú. ‖Draw (a picture of) me. hwà-'wǒ. ‖Draw a tiger. hwà yí-ge-'hǔ. ‖Draw a circle. hwà yí-ge-'ywán-chywār. ‖Draw a line here. dzày-'jèr hwà yì-tyáw-'shyàn. ‖The officer drew a map of the area. 'jywūn-gwān 'hwà-le yì-jāng-fú-'jìn-de-'shíng-shŕ-tú.

10. Draw conclusions 'dé-dàw °jyē-'lwèn, or °'kàn-fǎ, or °'jyàn-jyě. ‖They drew different conclusions from the same facts. tsúng yí-'yàng-de-'shŕ-ching-shang tām dé-'dàw-le bù-'túng-de-jyē-'lwèn. ‖What conclusion can you draw from that? nǐ-de-'kàn-fǎ (or nǐ-de-'jyàn-jyě) dzěm-me-'yàng. or nǐ yěw shém-me-°'jyàn-jyě? or °'kàn-fǎ? ‖Each one will draw a different conclusion. gè-rén-kàn-fǎ (or gè-rén-jyàn-jyě) bù-'túng. or, *to express the same idea by a literary quotation*, The kind can see only kindness; the wise can see only wisdom. 'rén-jě jyàn-'rén, 'jŕ-jě jyàn-'jŕ.

11. (*In games, etc.*). To end in a draw píng, 'bù-fēn shèng-'fù; a draw (*between sides*) 'píng-shěw (*but not* píng *alone*). ‖The game ended in a draw. 'jyē-gwǒ 'píng-le. or 'jyē-gwò 'bù-fēn shèng-'fù. ‖They fought to a draw. tām 'dǎ-le ge-'píng-shěw. or tām 'dǎ-le ge-'bù-fēn-shèng-'fù. *But* (*in Chinese chess*) ‖It's a draw. shŕ 'hé-chí. or 'hé-le.

12. Draw (*lots*) chēw(-'tyáwr), chēw(-'chyār), jwā(-'jyēwr), nyǎn(-'jyēwr). ‖Let's draw straws to see who goes first. dzám chēw-'tyáwr kàn 'shwéy shyān 'dzěw. ‖The opposing team won the draw. wèy-tyāwr-'byār jwā-'jyēwr 'dwèy-fāng 'yíng-le. ‖He drew a winning number. tā 'chēw-de-'hàw-mǎr jùng-le. *But* (*in cards*) ‖Would you like to draw for partners? dzám-ná-'páy-de-dà-'shyǎw láy dìng 'shéy gēn-shéy yì-'byār, hǎw-bu-hǎw?

13. Draw into (*enter*) jìn. ‖The train is just drawing into the station. hwǒ-'chē gāng jìn-'jàn.'

14. Draw near *or* to kwày(-dàw). ‖The. train is drawing near the station. hwǒ-'chē kwày-dàw 'jàn-le. ‖The time is drawing near. kwày-dàw 'shŕ-hew-le. ‖The campaign is drawing to a close. 'jìng-shywǎn kwày 'jyē-shù-le. *But* ‖Draw near the fire. kàw-hwǒ 'jìn-dyar.

15. Draw out (*encourage*). ‖I did my best to draw him out. wǒ shyǎng-'jìn-le 'fāng-fa °'yǐn-tā shwō-'hwà. *or* °bǎ tā-de-'hwà 'yǐn-chu-lay.

16. Draw up (*An object*) lā . . . gwò-láy (*See* 1.); (*in writing*) shyě; (*drive up and stop*) 'kāy (. . .) láy; (*for inspection*) 'páy-dwèy. ‖As soon as I get the information I'll draw up a report. wǒ 'dé-dàw 'tsáy-lyàw yì-'hèw, 'lì-shŕ shyě yí-ge-'bàw-gàw. ‖Just then a car drew up. 'jèng-dzày-nèy-shŕ-hew yí-lyàng-chì-'chē 'kāy-gwo-láy-le. ‖Draw up here. kāy-dàw 'jèr-lay. ‖The men were drawn up for inspection. bīng 'páy-dwèy shèw jyǎn-'ywè. *or* yàw jyǎn-'ywè-le; bīng dēw 'páy-chi 'dwèy-lay-le.

17. Draw the line. ‖You have to draw the line somewhere. (*Between right and wrong*) 'shŕ-fēy dzǔng-děy 'fēn-yi-shyàr. (*Set a limit*) dzǔng-děy 'dìng ge-'jyè-shyàn. ‖I draw the line right here! wǒ 'jyèw-tsž dǎ-'jù! *or* wǒ dàw-'jèr wéy-'jŕ! *or* 'nèm-je wǒ jyèw bú-'gàn-le!

18. Draw a blank. (*Run into a wall*) pèng-'bì; (*run into a nail*) pèng 'dīng-dz; (*exert effort in vain*) 'báy-fèy hwéy-'shèr. ‖He drew a blank everywhere he looked. ta 'dàw-chù pèng °-'bì. *or* °'dīng-dz. ‖I drew a blank there. wǒ 'pèng-le ge-'dīng-dz. *or* wǒ pèng-'bì-le. *or* wǒ 'báy-fèy-le hwéy-'shèr.

19. Draw back (*See* 2.) ‖Suddenly he drew back into the shade. 'hū-rán tā bǎ-'shēn-dz 'chēw-hwéy hēy-'yěngr-li-chywu-le. ‖The enemy drew back to his second line of defense. dí-rén 'twèy-dàw dì-'èr-tyáw-'fáng-shyàn.

20. Drawback 'dwǎn-chù. ‖That's his drawback. nèy-shr tā-de-'dwǎn-chù.

21. Drawbridge 'dyàw-chyáw.

DRAWER. 'chēw-tì. ‖My passport is in the top drawer. wǒ-de-'hù-jàw shŕ dzày 'tew-yì-tséng-'chēw-tì-li. ‖This drawer is stuck. jèy-ge-'chēw-tì °'kāy-bu-kāy. *or* °'lā-bu-chu-'láy. *or* °'jwày-bu-chu-'láy. *or* °'sž-'jǐn. ‖Pull out that drawer. bǎ nèy-ge-'chēw-tì 'lā (*or* 'chēw) -chu-lay.

Drawers (*clothes*) 'chèn-yī. ‖He advised me to wear heavy drawers. tā 'chywàn-wǒ chwān 'hèw-de-'chèn-yī.

DRAWN. (*See* **DRAW**, *except for the following uses in which* **draw** *is impossible.*)

Long drawn-out. ‖This will be a long drawn-out battle. jèy-yí-'jàng děy 'dǎ shyē-'ř-dz.

Drawn with pain. ‖Her face was drawn with pain. tā 'lyǎn-shàng 'dày-je hěn-'tùng-kǔ-de-'yàng-dz. *or* 'téng-de tā-'lyǎn dēw gǎy-le 'yàngr-le. *or* téng-de tā 'yǎw-yá lyě-'dzwěy-de.

DREAM. mèng. ‖I had a strange dream last night. wǒ dzwór 'wǎn-shàng 'dzwò-le yí-ge-hěn-chí-'gwày-de-'mèng. ‖It could happen only in a dream. jǐ-yew 'mèng-li tsáy hwèy yěw 'nà-yang-de-shŕ. ‖That's only a dream. 'bú-gwo shŕ ge-'mèng. ‖In the dream I seemed to have walked miles and miles. dzày 'mèng-li wǒ hǎw-shyàng (*or* . . . wǒ 'fǎng-fú) dzěw-le 'hěn-dwō-hěn-'dwō-de-'lù. ‖Last night I dreamed I was home. dzwór 'wǎn-shang wǒ 'mèng-jyàn dzày 'jyā-li. ‖I dreamed of you. wǒ 'mèng-jyàn 'nǐ-le. *or* wǒ 'mèng-jyàn-le 'nǐ. ‖I've been dreaming (*thinking*) about buying a car. wǒ 'dzwò-le 'bù-shǎw-'ř-dz-mǎy-'chē-de-'mèng-le.

Day-dream. ‖Don't waste time dreaming. byé 'hú-shyǎng-le.

‖I wouldn't dream of doing that. wǒ 'jywé-bu-hwèy gàn 'nèy-ge.

‖Their new house is a dream. 'tām-de-shīn-'fáng-dz jēn-shr shwō-bu-'chū-de-'hǎw.

DRESS. (*Woman's garment*) 'yī-fu, 'yī-shang; (*These words may also refer to clothing in general, and so may designate other garments as well. The measure* jyàn, *however, specifies a single garment rather than an outfit; and since most other garments have special terms, these will usually be understood to mean a dress, in this usage.*) ‖She wants to buy a new dress before she leaves. tā yàw dzày méy-'dzěw yì-'chyán mǎy yí-jyàn-shīn-'yī-fu. (*or* -'yī-shang). ‖That looks like a cool dress. nèy-jyàn-'yī-fu (*or* nèy-jyàn-'yī-shang) 'kàn-shang-chywu hěn 'lyáng-kwày.

(*To put on clothes*) chwān (*put on, wear, must be followed by a word for clothes*); *meaning* get dressed 'dá-bàn (*includes toilet preparations and all the trimmings*). ‖I'm not dressed yet. wǒ háy méy-chwān-'hǎw-le 'yī-fu-ne. ‖We've got to dress (*put on evening clothes*) for the occasion. 'jèy-tsž dzám děy chwān 'lǐ-fú. ‖I'll have to dress up to go there. wǒ děy 'chwān-shang 'lǐ-fú tsáy néng chywù-'nèr. ‖It took her a whole hour to dress. tā 'yùng-le 'jèng yí-ge-jūng-'tew tsáy 'dá-bàn-'hǎw-le.

(*Clothing, style*). ‖She appeared in students' dress. 'chū-lay-de-shŕ-hew tā °chwān-je 'shywé-sheng-'yī-fu. *or* °chwān-je 'shywé-sheng-'jwāng. *or* °'yì-shēn 'shywé-sheng 'jwāng-shù. *or* °'yì-shēn 'shywé-sheng 'dá-bàn.

(*Formal*) 'lúng-jùng(-de); (*military full dress*) 'chywán-fù 'wǔ-jwēng. ‖The reception is a dress affair.

'hwān-yíng-'hwèy shr̀ hěn 'lúng-jùng-de. ‖It's a dress parade. jèy-tsž yéw-'shíng yàw 'chywán-fù 'wǔ-jwāng. ‖You have to be present in full (*military*) dress. dàw-'chǎng-de-shŕ-hew yàw 'chywán-fù 'wǔ-jwāng

(*Decorate*) 'jwāng-shr. ‖They dress the store windows in the evening. tām 'wǎn-shang bǎ 'chwāng-hu 'jwāng-shr-chi-láy.

(*Treat medically*) shàng yàw. ‖When was this wound dressed? jèy-ge-'shāng 3hŕ 'shém-me-shŕ-hew-'shàng-de-'yàw?

(*Of poultry*). *In China, only live poultry is retailed; dressing must be expressed by more detailed words such as*, slaughter dzǎy; pluck twèy. ‖Does he sell dressed chickens? tā mày dzǎy-'hǎw-le twèy-'gān-jìng-le-de-'jī-ma? ‖You have to dress the chicken yourself. nèy-jr-'jī nǐ děy 'dž-jǐ chywù 'dzǎy, dž-jǐ chywù twèy-'gān-jìng-le.

DRILL. (*Boring tool*) dzwàn. ‖They need another drill. tām děy 'dzày yàw yí-ge-'dzwàn. ‖The bit in this drill has got to be changed. jèy-bǎ-'dzwàn-de-'téwr děy 'hwàn.

(*To bore*). (*Open*) dzwàn, kāy; (*punch open, drill with considerable force*) 'dzáw-kay. ‖The dentist has to drill (*a hole in*) this tooth. yá-'yī děy bǎ jèy-ge-'yá dzwàn yí-ge-'kū-lung. ‖The engineers are drilling a tunnel. gūng-chéng-'shŕ dzày °kāy yí-ge-'swéy-dàw. or (*especially through rock*) °dzáw-kay yí-ge-'swéy-dàw. or (*with a machine drill*) °yùng 'jī-chì dzwàn yí-ge-'swéy-dàw. ‖They are drilling for oil (*opening an oil well*). tām dzày kāy yéw-'jǐng.

(*To train or practice*) lyàn *followed by a term designating the persons trained, as to drill soldiers* lyàn-'bīng; *or designating the thing practiced as to drill in typing* lyàn-dǎ-'dž.

To drill *in a military sense is either* practice drilling lyàn-'tsāw, *or go to drill* shàng-'tsāw. ‖He'll drill us in typing every day. tā měy-'tyān jyàw wǒ-men lyàn dǎ-'dž. ‖The officer is drilling his men. jywūn-'gwǎn dzày lyàn-'bīng. ‖We drill every day on that field. wǒm měy-'tyān dzày 'nèy-ge-tsāw-'chǎng-shang lyàn-'tsāw. ‖They're tired of drilling. tām lyàn-'tsāw lyàn-'nì-le. ‖The soldiers have (*go to*) drill at 8 A.M. and 2 P.M. 'bīng (měy-'tyān) 'dzǎw-chen 'bā-dyǎn gēn 'shyà-wǔ 'lyǎng-dyǎn shàng-'tsāw.

DRINK. To drink hē. ‖Drink plenty of water. 'dwǒ hē-'shwěy. ‖Don't drink too much at the party. fù-'hwèy-de-shŕ-hew shǎw 'hē-dyǎr. ‖May I have a drink of water? wǒ yàw dyar-'shwěy hē. or wǒ shyǎng hē dyǎr-'shwěy. ‖He drinks too much (*liquor*). tā hē-'jyěw hē-de tày 'dwǒ.

A drink (*of liquor*) jyěw. ‖Can I bring you a drink? yàw-'jyěw-ma? or láy bēy-'jyěw hǎw-bu-hǎw?

Drink to (*toast*). ‖Let's drink to your speedy return. 'jù-nǐ 'dzǎw-r̀ 'hwéy-láy.

DRIP. dī, 'dī-da. ‖His clothes are dripping wet. tā-de-'yī-shang shŕ-de jŕ dī(-da) 'shwěy. ‖Let it drip for a while. dzày 'dī-yi-hwer.

DRIVE. Drive away, drive out, etc. gǎn; (*by force; impolitely; impatiently*) hūng, (*local Peiping*) nyǎn. ‖They drove him out. tām bǎ-tā 'gǎn-chū-chywu-le. or tām bǎ-tā 'hūng-chu-chywu-le. or tām bǎ-tā 'nyǎn-chu-chywu-le. ‖Drive the dogs away. bǎ-gěw 'hūng (or gǎn)-dzěw. ‖He's using a fan to drive the flies away. tā yùng 'shàn-dz gǎn (or hūng, or nyǎn) 'tsāng-yíng-ne. ‖They drove the cattle this way. tām bǎ-'nyéw gǎn-dàw 'jèy-byar-lay-le. ‖The crowd was driven back. nèy-chywún-'rén gěy 'gǎn (or hūng)-hwéy-chywu-le. ‖The cows were driven to pasture. bǎ-nyéw gǎn-dàw tsǎw-'dì-li-chywu-le. *But* ‖The soldiers drove (*fought*) the enemy back. jywūn-dwèy bǎ 'dí-rén 'dǎ-hwéy-chywu-le.

Drive *a vehicle*. (*If horse-drawn*) gǎn; (*if mechanical*) kāy. ‖He drives a cart. tā gǎn-'chē. or tā shŕ ge-gǎn-'chē-de. or tā gǎn 'mǎ-chē. ‖The car was driven by a woman. nèy-ge-'chē shr̀ ge-'nywǔ-rén-'kāy-de. ‖Can you drive a truck? nǐ hwèy kāy 'dzày-jùng-chē-ma? ‖I don't know how to drive (*a car*). wǒ bú-hwèy kāy-'chē. ‖Let's drive (*a car*) out into the country. dzám 'kāy-chē dàw 'shyāng-shyà-chywu.

Drive *a person* (*in a vehicle*). (*Coming or going*) dày; (*going only*) sùng; (*coming only*) jyē. ‖I'll drive you over. wǒ 'sùng (or dày)-nǐ-chywu. ‖I can call for you and drive you back. wǒ ké-yi chywù 'jǎw-nǐ, bǎ-nǐ 'jyē (or dày)-hwey-lay. ‖The boss drove me home in his new car. wǒ-de-'shàng-sz yùng tā-de-'shīn-chē bǎ-wǒ 'sùng-hwéy-'jyā-chywu-le.

Go for a drive. ‖Would you like to go for a drive in my car? nǐ 'ywàn-yi dzwò wǒ-de-chē 'chū-chywu 'wár-yi-wár-ma?

A drive (*a road*) mǎ-'lù. ‖The drive goes around the lake. nèy-tyáw-mǎ-'lù shr̀ 'wey-je hú-'byǎr dzěw.

Drive *a nail* dìng. ‖Drive the nail into the wall. bǎ 'dīng-dz dìng-dàw 'chyáng-li-chywu.

Drive *a screw* nǐng. ‖Drive the screw straight. bǎ lwó-sž-'dyěr nǐng-'jèng-le. ‖I can't drive this screw in. jèy-ge-lwó-sž-dyēngr wǒ nǐng-bu-'jìn-chywu.

Drive (*force to do something*) bŕ; (*be driven; literary*) pwò; (*urge, hurry*) tswēy; *and other less direct ways of saying it*. ‖Hunger drove him to stealing. jī-hán 'bī-de tā dzwò-'dzéy. or tā wéy 'jī-nán swǒ-'pwo, swó-yi tēw 'dūng-shi. or tā 'chyúng-de (or tā 'e-de) dzwò-'dzéy. or tā 'chyúng-de (or tā 'è-de) mey-'fǎr-le jyěw 'bī-de dzwo-'dzéy. ‖The foreman drives the workmen continually. gūng-'tewr lǎw 'tswēy-je (or 'bī-je) gūng-rén dzwò-'gūng.

Drive (*vigor, energy*). ‖He has a lot of drive. tā hěn yěw °gǔ-dz-'gàn-jyer. or °'jīng-shen.

Drive (*tennis, golf, etc.*) chēw. ‖He has a powerful drive. tā 'chēw-chyéw chēw-de hěn 'yìng.

Other English expressions. ‖He drives a hard bargain. (*Literally*) tā jyǎng-'jyàr jyǎng-de tày °'kè-le. or °jàn 'pyán-yi-le. (*Literally or figuratively*) tā jìng yàw jàn 'pyán-yi. ‖The town is staging a drive to raise money for the poor. nèy-ge-dì-fang 'jěng-dzày 'jywǔ-shíng mù-'jў̌wǎn-'ywùn-dung tì 'chyúng-rén 'jywān-chyán. ‖We made our way home through a driving rain. wǒm 'màw-je yí-jèn-'bàw-ywǔ hwéy-'jyā-de. ‖What are you driving at? nǐ shr̀ shéme-'yì-sz?

DRIVER. (*Of a coach or cart*) gǎn-'chē-de; (*of a motor-driven vehicle*) kǎy-'chē-de. ‖He's a cart driver. tā shr̀ ge-gǎn-'chē-de. ‖Where's the driver of this car? kǎy-'chē-de nǎr 'chywù-le?

DROP. (*To drip*) or a drop of fluid dī. ‖There isn't a drop of water left. lyán yì-'dī-de-'shwěy yě 'méy-le. ‖Put (*drop*) two drops of medicine in a glass of water. yì-bēy-'shwěy-li dī 'lyǎng-dī-'yàw (jyèw 'gèw-le). ‖Just a few drops (*of rain fell*). 'bú-gwo jǐ-'dī. (*Put in, of medicine, etc.*) jř 'gē jǐ-'dī. *But also* ‖A few drops of rain fell. 'dyàw-le jǐ-ge-'dyǎr.

(*Fall*) dyàw. ‖The pencil dropped out of my hand. 'chyān-bǐ tsúng wǒ-'shěw-li 'dyàw-chu-chywu-le. ‖Something dropped on his hat. 'yěw dyǎr-shém-me 'dyàw-dzay tā-'màw-dz-shang-le. ‖Let it drop. jyàw jèy-ge-'dūng-shi dž-jǐ 'dyàw.

(*Let fall, set aside*). (*Throw*) rēng; (*fling*) pyē; (*set aside, leave*) lyàw; (*let go, lose*) dyēw; (*put*) gē; (*place*) fàng; *or appropriate combinations with* -shyà (*down*), *or* -kāy (*away*). ‖I dropped the letter in the street. wǒ bǎ-'shìn dyēw-dzày dà-'jyē-shang-le. ‖Drop the letter in the box. bǎ-'shìn gē-dzày shìn-'shyāng-li. ‖Drop anchor! shyà-'māw! ‖Drop the anchor overboard. bǎ-'māw rēng-dzày 'shwěy-li. ‖I can't just drop my work and go with you. wǒ bù-néng bǎ wǒ-de-shèr 'dyēw-shya (*or* 'lyàw-shya, *or* 'pyē-shya, *or* rēng-shya, *or* 'gē-shya) jyèw gēn-ni 'dzěw. ‖Why don't you drop her? dzěm nǐ bù-bǎ-tā °'dyēw-kay-ne? *or* °'lyàw-kay-ne? ‖Let's drop the subject for the time being. dzám bǎ jèy-jyàn-shèr 'gē-shya (*or* 'fàng-dzay yì-'byǎr, *or* 'dyēw-kay, *or* 'lyàw-shya) yì-'hèw dzày 'shwō. *or* dzám 'jàn-shŕ 'shyān bù-tǎw-'lwèn °jèy-ge-'wèn-tí. *or* °jèy-jyàn-'shèr.

(*Fall down, fall over*) 'pā-shya. ‖The messenger dropped from exhaustion. sùng-'shìn-de lèy 'pā-shya-le.

(*Go down, of temperature*) jyàng. ‖The temperature dropped very rapidly. 'wēn-dù 'jyàng-de hěn 'kwày.

(*Omit*) jyē. ‖Drop every other letter and you can read the code. fān-dyàn-'mǎr-de-shŕ-hew 'jyē yí-ge-'dzèr yī-'nyàn.

Other English expressions. ‖If I don't pay my dues I'll be dropped from the club. wǒ 'rú-gwǒ bù jyāw hwèy-'fèy, 'hwèy-li jyèw yàw bǎ-wǒ kāy-chú-le. ‖From the second floor there is a drop of twenty feet

to the ground. dì-'èr-tséng-léw lí-'dì yěw 'èr-shr-chř. ‖Please drop me (off) at the corner. wǒ dàw lù-'kěwr-nèr 'shyà-lay. ‖Drop in to see me tomorrow. 'míng-tyan 'láy jyàn-wǒ. ‖I dropped off to sleep immediately. wǒ lì-'kè jyèw shwèy-'jáw-le. ‖She dropped a hint that she wanted to go. tā-'hwàr-li dày-je yàw-'dzěw-de-'yì-sz. ‖Lemon drops are my favorite candy. wǒ dzwèy-'shǐ-hwan chř níng-'méng-táng-'chyéwr. ‖He'll fight at the drop of a hat. tā 'dùng-bu-dùng jyèw dǎ-'jyā.

DROVE. (*See also* **DRIVE.**) (*Herd*) chywún. ‖There was a drove of cattle crossing the road. yěw yì-chywún-'nyéw dǎ-jèr 'gwò.

DROWN. (*Die by drowning*) 'yān-sž. ‖Many people have drowned at this beach. jèy-ge-hǎy-'byǎr-shang 'yān-sz-gwò 'bù-shǎw-'rén.

(*Covered with water*) yān. ‖The field was drowned out by the spring rains. jèy-pyàn-'dì yàw 'chwēn-tyan-de-'ywǔ-shwéy gěy 'yān-le.

Drown out (*of sound*) yān. ‖The noise drowned out his remarks. 'dzá-lwàn-de-'shēng-yīn bǎ tā-de-hwà 'yān-jù-le.

‖He's just trying to drown his sorrows. tā 'bú-gwò shr̀ shyǎng shyāw-'chéw jyèw shr̀-le.

DRUG. yàw. (*Intoxicating drug, sleep-producing drug, or anesthetic*) 'mí-yàw, 'méng-yàw; (*paralyzing drug or local or general anesthetic*) 'má-yàw. Poisonous drug 'dú-yàw, 'dú-wù; to drug *is expressed as* to give a drug; drugstore 'yàw-pù *or* 'yàw-fáng. ‖This drug is sold only on a doctor's prescription. jèy-ge-'yàw děy yěw 'dày-fu kāy 'fāng-dz tsáy néng 'mǎy. ‖Opium is a (*medical*) drug. yǎ-'pyàn shr̀ yì-jǔng-'yàw. ‖Opium is a (*poisonous*) drug that has ruined I don't know how many people. yǎ-'pyàn jèy-jǔng-'dú-wù hwěy-le bù-jř-dàw-'dwō-shǎw-rén-le. ‖He's a drug addict. tā 'shī-shŕ 'dú-wù. *or* (*expressed by a pun meaning both addict and recluse*) He's a gentleman of peculiar habits. tā shr̀ ge-'yǐn-jywūn-'dž. ‖They drugged his coffee. tām bǎ tā-de-jyā-'fēy-li 'shyà-le 'yàw-le. ‖They drugged him. tām gěy-tā °'mí-yàw chř-le. *or* °'méng-yàw chř-le. *or* °'má-yàw chř-le. *or* °'dú-yàw chř-le (*depending on the kind of drug*). ‖He thought he'd been drugged. tā 'jywé-je yěw-rén gěy-tā shàng 'méng-yàw-le (*etc.*).

Other expressions in English. ‖I felt drugged with sleep. wǒ kwèn-'jí-le. ‖This year grapes are a drug on the market. 'jīn-nyan 'pú-taw 'kě jēn 'dwō.

DRUM. (*Percussion instrument*) gǔ. Noise of drums 'gǔ-shēng, 'gǔ-shyǎng; drummer gǔ-'shěw *or* chyāw-'gǔ-de *or* dǎ-'gǔ-de. Drum beats gǔ-'dyǎr. ‖Please don't give our boy any more drums for Christmas.

yǐ-hèw shèng-dàn-'jyé chyān-'wàn byé dzày sùng wǒm-nèy-ge-háy-dz 'gǔ-le. ‖This drum needs fixing. jèy-ge-'gǔ děy 'shyēw-li-shyēw-li-le. ‖We have eight drums, but no drummer. wǒm yěw 'bā-ge-gǔ kě-shr méy-yew °hwèy-'chyāw-de. or °hwèy-'dǎ-de. or °gǔ-'shěw. or °chyāw-'gǔ-de. or °dǎ-'gǔ-de. ‖Can't you hear the drums yet? nǐ háy 'tīng-bu-jyàn 'gǔ-shyǎng-ma? ‖The drums are fading out. 'gǔ-shēng jyàn-'jyān-de shyǎw-dàw tīng-bu-jyàn-le. ‖He can't follow the beat of the drums. tā 'gēn-bu-shang gǔ-'dyǎr.

(*Container*). ‖They unloaded six drums of gasoline. tā-men 'shyè-le 'lyèw-tǔng-chì-'yéw.

(*To tap*) chyāw. ‖Please stop drumming on the table. chǐng-nǐ 'byé chyāw 'jwō-dz.

To drum into. ‖These rules have been drummed into me. nà-shyē-'gwēy-jywū wǒ 'tīng-le bù-jř-dàw yěw 'dwō-shǎw hwéy-le. or tām bǎ nèy-shyē-'gwēy-jywū 'lywǔ-tsž-sān-'fān-de 'shwō-gěy wǒ 'tīng.

To drum up. ‖He's trying to drum up trade. tā dzày-nàr shyǎng-'fár °'jāng-lwo 'mǎy-may-ne. or °'lā 'mǎy-may-ne

DRUNK. (*Intoxicated*) to be drunk, to have gotten drunk hē-'dzwèy-le; to get drunk hē-'dzwèy; a drunk (*person*) dzwèy-'gwěy. ‖He got drunk (*or* He's drunk) tā hē-'dzwèy-le. ‖He gets drunk every night. tā 'měy-tyān 'wǎn-shang hē-'dzwèy. ‖We had trouble with a drunk. yí-ge-dzwèy-'gwěy gēn-wǒm dǎw-'lwàn-lay-le. ‖He looks like he's been on a drunk. tā 'hǎw shyàng shř °hē-dzwèy-le 'jyěw shř-de. or °dà 'hē-le yí-'jèn shř-de.

(*Figuratively*). ‖He's hard to work with because he's drunk with power. gēn-tā hěn 'nán gùng-'shř, yīn-wèy tā °ày 'dé-yì wàng-'shíng. or °tày 'bà-dàw. or °nà-shr 'shyǎw-rén dé-'jř. ‖They were drunk with joy at the outcome of the trial. shěn-'pàn-de-'jyē-gwǒ ràng tā-men °'hwān-shǐ-de 'lyǎw-bù-dé. or °'hwān-shi-sž-le. or °hwān-shǐ-de yàwᵣsž.

DRY. (*Not wet*) gān, bù-'shř; (*not damp*) bù-'cháw. Dry and pleasant 'gān-shwǎng; keep dry bù-'lín-jaw, bù-'lwén-jaw; *to dry by fire or heat* kǎw, hūng, kǎw-'gān, hūng-gān; *to dry in the sun* shày, shày-'gān; dry by airing lyàng, lyàng-'gān; dry in the wind chwēy, chwēy-'gān. ‖Change into some dry clothes. 'hwàn-shang dyǎr-°gān-yī-shang. or °bu-'shř-de-yī-shang. ‖These towels are still damp; get some dry ones. jèy-shyē-'shěw-jīn háy 'cháw-ne; ná dyǎr-°'gān-de-lay. or °'bù-'cháw-de-lay. ‖I wore a raincoat and kept dry. wǒ 'chwān-je ywǔ-'yī-le, °'shēn-shang méy-'shř. or °lǐ-tew méy-'lín-jaw. ʼor °'lǐ-tew méy-'lwén-jaw. ‖The streets are dry now. 'jyē-shang shyàn-dzày 'gān-le. ‖The well's gone dry. jèy-ge-'jǐng 'gān-le. ‖Have your clothes dried out? nǐ-de-'yī-shang °'gān-le-ma? or (*by fire or heat*) °kǎw-'gān-le-ma? or °'hūng-'gān-le-ma? or (*by the sun*) °shày-'gān-le-ma? or (*by airing*) °lyàng-'gān-le-ma? or (*by the wind*) °chwēy-'gān-le-ma? ‖Dry yourself by

the fire. nǐ dàw 'hwǒ-nà⟍ chywù °'hūng-yi-hung. or °'kǎw-yi-kǎw. ‖The paint dried in five hours. 'yéw-chī 'wǔ-ge-jūng-téw jyèw 'gān-le. ‖Every summer this stream dries up. yí-dàw 'shyà-tyān jèy-tyáw-'hé jyèw 'gān-le. ‖After the long rains this dry air feels swell. shyà-le 'jèm-shyē-shř-hew-de-'ywǔ-le. jèy-jǔng-'gān-shwang-de-kūng-'chì jyàw-rén jywé-de 'jēn shū-fu.

(*Arid; of weather*) hàn, dwǎn 'ywǔ(-shwěy), chywē 'ywǔ(-shwěy), 'ywǔ-shwěy bú-'gèw. ‖It's been a dry summer. jīn-nyan 'shyà-tyān hěn °'hàn, or °dwǎn 'ywǔ-(shwěy). or °chywē 'ywǔ(-shwěy). or °'ywǔ-shwěy bú-'gèw.

(*Dehydrated; of foods*) gār. ‖Give me a pound of dried apples. gěy-wǒ yí-bàng-'píng-gwǒ 'gār.

(*Thirsty*) kě. ‖I'm dry; let's have a drink. wǒ yěw dyǎr-'kě; dzám 'hē dyǎr-shém-me-ba.

(*Not giving milk*). ‖The cow has been dry a month. jèy-tyéw-'nyéw yí-ge-'ywè °méy-'nǎy-le. or °bù-chū-'nǎy-le.

To dry (*wipe; dishes*) tsā. ‖Who's going to dry the dishes? shéy láy tsā 'dyé-dz?

(*Not sweet*) bù-'tyán. ‖I'd like a good dry wine. wǒ yàw bù-'tyán-de-hǎw-'jyěw.

(*Boring*) 'gān-dzàw-wú-'wèy. ‖The lecture was so dry that I walked out. yǎn-'jyǎng 'gān-dzàw-wú-'wèy, wǒ jyèw 'dzěw-le.

Dry land àn or lù-'dì. ‖It's good to be on dry land after such a long voyage. dzày 'shwěy-shang dzěw-le jèm-'jyéw yí-shàng-'àn (or -lù-'dì) 'jēn shū-fu.

Dry up (*stop talking*). ‖Tell him to dry up. jyàw-tā byé 'shwō-le. or jyàw-tā byé 'dāw-daw-le. or jyàw-tā jù-'dzwěy-ba.

DUCK. (*Fowl*) 'yā-dz. ‖My father brought home three ducks. 'fù-chin dày-le 'sān-jř-'yā-dz-hwey-lay. ‖We're having roast duck for dinner. 'wǎn-fàn wǒ-men chř °'kǎw yā-dz. or °'shāw-yā-dz. ‖Don't walk like a duck waddling along. dzěw-'lù byé shyàng ge-'yā-dz 'jwǎy-ya-jwǎy-de. ‖A duck quacks. 'yā-dz 'gwā-'gwā-de 'jyàw.

‖Duck! dī-'téw! ‖Duck your head! 'dī-yi-dī 'téw-ba!

‖He took a quick duck in the lake. tā 'yí-shyà-dz jyèw 'dzwǎn-jìn 'hú-li chywù-le.

‖Let's duck him in the lake. dzám bǎ-tā 'twēy-dàw °'hú-li-chywu-ba. or (*in the water*) ‾'shwěy-li-chywu-ba. or (*to hold under water a while*) dzám bǎ-tā 'èn-dzày 'shwěy-li 'gwàn-ta-yi-shyar.

‖Let's duck him (*get away from him*). dzám bǎ-tā 'shwǎy-kay-ba. or dzám 'dwǒ-kay tā-ba. ‖Let's duck out of here. dzám tēw-'tēwr-de 'chū-chywu-ba. or dzám 'lyēw-chū-chywù-ba. or dzam 'dwǒ-chū-chywù-ba.

Duck (*cloth*) 'fān-bù, 'shyè-wén-'bù. ‖Lots of summer clothes are made of white duck. 'shyà-tyān-de-

'yī-shang hěn dwō shr̀ °báy-fān-'bù-dzwò-de. or °báy-shyé-wén-'bù-dzwò-de. ‖He's 'wearing white ducks. tā-chẁan-de shr̀ °'báy-bù-'kù-dz. or °'báy-fān-bù.'kù-dz. or °'báy-shyé-wén-bù-'kù-dz.

DUE. (*Owed*) gāy, chyàn (*overdue, to a person*) méy-'fā-gey. ‖I have three weeks' pay due me. wǒ háy yěw 'sān-ge-lǐ-'bày-de-°'shīn-shwey (*salary*) or °'gūng-chyan (*wages*) or -°'shyǎng (*soldier's pay*) méy-'fā-gey wǒ-ne. or háy 'gāy-wǒ (or háy 'chyàn-wǒ) 'sān-ge-lǐ-'bày-de-°shīn-shwey-ne. or °'gūng-chyán-ne. or °'shyǎng-ne. or wǒ háy yěw 'sān-ge-lǐ-'bày-de-°chyàn-'shīn. or °chyàn-'shyǎng. (*No separate term for* **owed wages** *in this construction.*)

Be due, come due. (*With the thing due as object*) ('yīng-)gāy 'jyàw, yàw 'jyàw; (*arrive at the day, with the thing due as subject*) dàw-'chī, dàw 'r̀-dz. **Be overdue** gwò-'chī, gwò 'r̀-dz. ‖The rent will be due again next Monday. shyà-lǐ-bày-'yī yèw gāy (or yàw) jyàw 'fáng-chyan-le. ‖The rent was due five days ago. 'fáng-chyan 'wǔ-tyān yǐ-'chyán jyèw ('yīng-)gāy 'jyàw-le. ‖Your report is due tomorrow. nǐ-de-bàw-'gàw 'míng-tyān gāy 'jyàw-le. ‖Your note will be due soon. nǐ-de-'jyè-ywē kwày °dàw-'chī le. or °dàw 'r̀-dz le. ‖Your insurance payment is overdue. nǐ-gāy-'jyàw-de-bǎw-shyǎn-'fèy yǐ-jing gwò-'chī-le. or nǐ-de-'bǎw-shyǎn yǐ-jīn 'gwò-le jyàw-'kwǎn-de-'r̀-dz-le.

Dues hwèy-'fèy. ‖The dues are five dollars a year. hwèy-'fèy shr̀ 'wǔ-kwày-chyán yì-'nyán.

Due to arrive yīng-dāng 'dàw. ‖The train is due at noon. hwǒ-chē 'yīng-dāng 'jūng-wǔ 'dàw.

(*Deserved*). ‖Gratitude is due him. 'yīng-gāy 'gǎn-jī tā. or 'yīng-dāng 'gǎn-jī tā. ‖Gratitude is due these retired veterans who defended our country. jèy-shyē-'bǎw-wèy-'gwó-jyā-de-'twèy-wǔ-'jywūn-rén, wǒm 'yīng-gāy (or 'yīng-dāng) 'gǎn-jī. ‖Respect is due these men. jèy-shyē-rén wǒm 'yīng-gāy 'dzwēn-jìng. or jèy-shyē-rén 'jf-de wǒm 'dzwēṇ-jìng. ‖We should pay him due respect for his courage. tā-de-'yǔng-chì °'jf-de wǒm 'pèy-fu. or °'wǒm 'yīng-dāng 'pèy-fu. ‖I pay him due respect. *is expressed as* He deserves my respect. tā jf-de wǒ 'dzwēn-jìng. or *as* I respect him. wǒ hěn 'dzwēn-jìng tā. or *as* I pay him as much respect as he is worth. wǒ shyāng-'dāng-de 'dzwēn-jìng tā. ‖With due respect for your learning, I can't agree with you on this point. nǐ-de-'shywé-wèn wǒ hěn 'pèy-fu, bú-gwo 'jèy-yì-dyǎn wǒ bù-'néng gēn-nǐ túng-'yì. or wǒ bú-shr bú 'pèy-fu nǐ-de-'shywé-wèn, bú-gwo 'jèy-yì-dyǎn wǒ gēn nǐ-de 'yí-jyàn bù-yí-'yàng.

One's due. ‖You must give a person his due (*treat him fairly*). dǎy-'rén děy 'gūng-píng. ‖You have to give each person his due. *is expressed as* Treat a person the way you judge him. dǎy-rén 'hǎw 'hwày, děy fēn-'rén-láy. or *as* Each person has his good points and his bad points. 'shéy-dēw yěw 'cháng-chù, yěw 'dwǎn-chu.

Due (*straight, in one direction*) yì-'jf. ‖Go due west and you'll hit the river. nǐ yì-'jf wàng-'shī dzěw jyèw-dàw 'hé-byār-le.

Due to. (*See* BECAUSE.) ‖His death was due to malaria. tā (yīn-wey) fā 'yàw-dz 'sž-de. ‖His failure is due to overcautiousness. tā (yīn-wey) tày dǎr-'shyǎw-le, swǒ-yǐ shr̄-'bày-de. or tā-shr̄-'bày-de-'ywár -yīn shr̀ 'tày dǎr-'shyǎw-le.

DULL. (*Not sharp*) dwèn; (*of an edge only*) bú-'kwày or méy-'rèr; (*of a point only*) bù-'jyàn; (*edge only, when it is bent*) jywǎn-le-'rèr-le; (*edge only, when it is chipped*) bēn-le-'rèr-le. To dull (*something*) bēn; or nùng-'dwèn-le. ‖This knife is dull. jèy-bǎ-'dāw °dwèn-le. or °bú-'kwày. or °yěw dyǎr-'dwèn (a bit dull). or °bú-dà (or bù-hěn)-'kwày (a bit dull). or °méy-'rèr-le. etc. ‖This needle is awfully dull. jèy-ge-'jēn °hěn 'dwèn. or °hěn bù-'jyàn. ‖He dulled the knife (*blade*). tā bǎ dāw-'rèr °bēn-le. or °nùng-'dwèn-le. ‖Don't cut the nail with the knife; it'll dull the blade. byé ná 'dāw-dz lá 'dīng-dz; yí-dìng bǎ-'rèr °'bēn-le-de. or °nùng-'dwèn-le-de. ‖Don't dull the knife. byé bǎ 'dāw-dz bēn-le. ‖If you use it that way it'll get dull. yàw-shr 'nèm yùng, yí-'dìng hwèy 'bēn-de.

To dull the appetite. (*Seriously*) bǎ 'wèy-kew nùng-'hwày-le. (*Mildly*) jyàw . . . 'bù-shyǎng chī 'dūng-shi. ‖A cigarette might dull my appetite. chēw-'yān yě-shywǔ 'hwèy jyàw-wǒ 'bù-shyǎng chī 'dūng-shi-le. ‖I think that drug dulled my appetite. wǒ shyǎng nèy-ge-'yàw bǎ wǒ-de-'wèy-kew nùng-'hwày-le.

Dull (*of light or colors; general descriptions*) fā-'hwēy, fā-'wū, bú-'lyàng, 'àn-dàn, 'wū-chī-mā-'hèy-de; (*technical definitions*) dull green 'hwēy-lywù (-shǎr); dull red 'hēy-húng(-shǎr); (*pig-liver color*) jū-'gān-shǎr. ‖That's a sort of dull green. nèy-shr yì-jǔng-bú-'lyàng-de-lywù-shǎr. ‖That green is too dull. nèy-jǔng-'lywù-shǎr tày °'àn-dàn-le. or °bú-'lyàng-le. or °fā-'hwēy-le. or °'wū-chī-mā-'hēy-de. or °fā-'wū-le. ‖The floor is painted a sort of dull red. 'dì-bǎn-'yéw-de shr̀ yì-jǔng °'hēy-húng-shǎr. or °jū-'gān-shǎr. ‖They have only a dull light to see by. tām-de-'dēng °bú-'lyàng. or °hěn 'àn(-dàn). or °'wū-chī-mā-'hēy-de.

(*Of day or sky*) 'hwēn-(or 'yīn-)chén-'chén-de. ‖If it's a dull day, let's not go. tyār yàw-shr 'hwēn-(or 'yīn-)chén-'chén-de, dzám jyèw byé 'chywù.

(*Of sound*) 'tày bú-'tswèy-sheng. or bēng-a-'bēng-de. or pu-'tūng-pu-tūng-de. ‖The dull thumping of that drum depresses me. nèy-ge-'gǔ-chyāw-de °'tày bú-'tswèy-sheng-le (or °bēng-a-'bēng-de, or °pu-'tūng-pu-tūng-de), jyàw-rén 'tīng-je 'mèn-de-hwang.

Dull thud. (*Resonant*) 'bēng-de-yi-'shēng, 'pēng-de-yi-'shēng; (*heavy*) pu-'tūng-yi-'shēng; (*of a flat thing*) pā-'jī; (*as a pail of water on the ground*) 'pū-de-yi-'shēng; (*as cards on a table*) kwā-'chā-yi-'shēng; (*as a door closing*) gwā-'dā-yi-'shēng; (*as a door clos-*

ing in an empty place) kwāng-'dāng-yi-'shēng, gwāng-'dāng-yi-shēng, 'gwāng-de-yi-'shēng. ‖The book hit the floor with a dull thud. shū 'bēng-de-yi-'shēng (*or any other appropriate expression*) jyèw dyàw-dzày dì-'bǎn-shang-le.

(*Of pain*). ‖She feels a dull pain in her chest. tā jywé-je shyūng-'kěw mèn-bu-jī-de-'téng. ‖It's a dull sort of pain. 'téng, kě-shr bù-'lì-hay.

(*Of persons; uninteresting, stodgy, foolish*) dāy, mù, shǎ, nyé, 'dāy (*or* 'mù *or* 'shǎ *or* 'nyé)-le-gwāng-'jī-de, 'dāy (*etc.*)-bu-'jī-de, yěw-dyǎr-'dāy (*etc.*), méy-'yì-sz, (hěn) 'bèn; (*in studying*) (hěn) 'bèn, bù-'tsūng-ming; (*of speech*) (hěn) méy-'yì-sz, (hěn) 'bèn, (hěn) 'dāy-bàn. ‖He's dull. 'tā-nèy-ge-rén °méy-'yì-sz. *or* °'mù-bu-jī-de. *or* °'shǎ-le-gwāng-'jī-de. *etc.* ‖Their son is a dull student. 'tām-nèy-ge-háy-dz nyàn-'shū °hěn 'bèn. *or* °bù-'tsūng-ming. ‖His talk is very dull. tā shwō-'hwà shwō-de °hěn méy-'yì-sz. *or* °hěn-'bèn. *or* °hěn 'dāy-bǎn. ‖Our neighbors are nice but dull. wǒm-de-'jyē-fang 'rén háy bú-'hwày, 'jyèw-shr °méy-shém-'yì-sz. *or* °yěw-dyǎr fā-'nyé. *etc.*

(*Of an event*) méy-'yì-sz; méy-'jìn; 'kě-jyàw rén 'mèn-sz-le. ‖What a dull evening! 'jèy-yi-'wǎn-shang °'jēn méy-'yì-sz. *or* °jēn méy-'jìn. *or* °'kě-jyàw rén 'mèn-sz-le.

DURING. (*Of a period that has to be specified at some length; not regular units*) (dzày) ... de-shf-hew. (*The addition of* dzày *puts more emphasis on the particular period.*) ‖I met him during the last war. 'shàng-tsz dà-'jàn de-shf-hew wǒ 'rèn-shr-de-ta. ‖It was during the last war that I met him. wǒ 'rèn-shr tā shr dzày 'shàng-tsz dè-'jàn de-shf-hew. ‖We were close friends during school days. wǒm dzày shywé-'shyàw de-shf-hew °shr hěn-'hǎw-de-péng-yew. *or* °'hěn 'shéw. (*In this sentence the* dzáy *goes with* shywé-'shyàw, *not with the whole construction.*)

During the day 'báy-tyan(-li); during the night (dzày) 'yè-li; during a year yì-'nyán-li. ‖He eats five times during the day. tā 'báy-tyan chr 'wǔ-tsz.

DUST. tǔ, 'chén-tǔ; (*only in the air or settled on furniture*) 'hwēy-chén. ‖She swept the dust under the rug. tā bǎ-'tǔ dēw sǎw-dàw 'dì-tǎn-'dǐ-shya-chywu-le. ‖The car raised a cloud of dust. 'chì-chē 'yáng (*or* 'jywǎn)-chǐ-láy yí-jèn-°'hwēy-chén. *or* °'chén-tǔ. ‖Look at the coat of dust on the window sill! 'chyáw chwāng-hu-'tár-shang nèy-tséng-°'tǔ! *or* °'chén-tǔ! ‖The bureau has collected a layer of dust as thick as a silver dollar. 'gwèy-shang-de-'tǔ (*or* 'gwèy-shang-de-'chén-tǔ, *or* 'gwèy-shang-de-'hwēy-chén) 'jī-de yěw yí-kwày-'chyán nà-me 'hèw. ‖Dust shows clearly in a beam of sunlight. 'hwēy-chén dzày yí-dàw-r-'gwāng-li shyǎn-de hěn 'chīng-chu. ‖The dog must have rolled in the dust. gěw yí-'dìng shr dzày °'tǔ (*or* °'chén-tǔ)-li dǎ-'gwěr lay-je. ‖The horse is

taking a dust bath. mǎ dzày-'tǔ (*or* 'chén-tǔ)-li dǎ-'gwěr-ne.

To dust (*with a duster*) dǎn, 'dǎ-pu; (*with a cloth*) tsā, 'gān-tsā. ‖Please dust my desk. (ná 'dǎn-dz) bǎ (wǒ-de-)'jwō-dz °'dǎn-yi-dǎn. *or* °'dǎ-pu-dǎ-pu. *or* (yùng-'bù) bǎ (wǒ-de-)'jwō-dz °tsā-yi-tsā. *or* °'gān-tsā-ỳi-shyar.

To bite the dust. ‖The enemy sniper in the tree bit the dust. *meaning* tumbled down nèy-kē-'shù-shang-'tsáng-je-de-nèy-ge-'dí-bīng °'dǎ-shya-lay-le. *or meaning* was killed °'dǎ-sz-le. *or meaning* was wounded °'dǎ-shāng-le.

(*Figuratively*). ‖He threw dust in her eyes with his clever excuses. tā 'hwā-yán-chyǎw-'ywǔ-de bǎ-tā °'pyàn-le. *or* °'kwāng-le. *or* °shwō-de 'shìn-yǐ-wéy-'jēn-le.

DUTY. (*Natural, common responsibility*) 'běn-fèn, yīng-'jìn-de-'běn-fèn, 'běn-fèn-li 'yīng-gāy-dzwò-de-'shr̀; 'tyān-jf̀ (*literary; of national defense especially*). ‖It's your duty as a citizen to buy bonds. mǎy gūng-'jày shr̀ nǐ-dzwò-gūng-'mín-yīng-'jìn-de-'běn-fèn. ‖To help one's younger brother is one's duty. bāng dz̀-'jǐ-de-'dì-di shr̀ 'běn-fèn-li 'yīng-gāy-dzwò-de-'shr̀. ‖To defend one's country is the duty of all military men. 'bǎw-wèy 'gwó-jyā shr̀ 'jywūn-rén-de-'tyān-jf̀.

(*Social; under specific circumstances, duty toward others*) 'dzé-rèn. ‖It's your duty to have your children educated. jyàw nǐ-de-'háy-dz-men shèw 'jyàw-ywù shr̀ nǐ-de-'dzé-rèn.

(*Particular duty in a job*) 'gūng-dzwò, shèr. ‖What are your duties as a secretary? nǐ dāng 'shū-jì dēw °yěw shém-me 'gūng-dzwò? *or* °dzwò shém-me 'shèr? ‖Answering the phone is one of my duties. tīng dyàn-'hwà yě shr̀ wǒ-de-'shèr. ‖It's not my duty to clean the wastebaskets. dàw fèy-jǐ 'bú-shr 'wǒ-de-shèr. *or* wǒ-de-'gūng-dzwò-li 'méy-yew gwǎn dàw fèy-jǐ-'tǔng nèm yì-'shwō.

Go off duty 'shyà-gūng, 'shyà-bān, 'wán-shèr. ‖I go off duty at 5:30. wǒ 'wǔ-dyǎn-bàn shyà-gūng.

Go on duty 'shàng-bān. ‖I go on duty at 8:30. wǒ 'bā-dyǎn-bàn shàng-bān.

Be on duty 'jf̀-bān. ‖Who's on duty now? shyàn-dzày 'shéy jf̀-bān?

(*Customs*). ‖How much duty on this tobacco? 'jèy-jǔng-yān shàng 'dwō-shǎw 'shwèy?

DWELL. jù. ‖Once upon a time there dwelt a prince in a beautiful castle. tsúng-'chyán yěw yí-ge-'chīn-wáng jù-dzày yǐ-'swǒr-hěn-hǎw-'kàn-de-wáng-'fǔ-li.

To dwell on. ‖Stop dwelling on your own troubles! *meaning* Stop thinking about them! hày! byé 'jìng-shyǎng nǐ-dz̀-'gěr-de-nán-chu-le. *or meaning* Stop talking about them! 'dé-le-ba! byé 'jìng dāw-daw nǐ-dz̀-'gěr-de-nán-chu-le.

E

EACH. (*Every*) yī, měy; *for emphasis* 'měy-yī *plus measure.* ‖How many beds are there to each room? 'yì-jyān-'wū-dz yěw 'jǐ-jāng-chwáng? ‖Issue three of these to each person. 'jèy-ge, měy-'rén gěy 'sān-ge. ‖Please give me one sheet from each pile (of papers). 'měy-yì-'dwēy-li chǐng-nǐ 'gěy-wǒ yì-'jāng. ‖I want one copy of each of the following books. yi-'shyà gè-'shū wǒ 'měy-jǔng yàw yì-'běn. (*Informal*) ‖Please give me one of each kind. 'yí-yàngr 'láy yí-ge. *or* wǒ 'yí-yàngr 'yàw yí-ge.

(*Every person*) 'měy-rén. ‖Each of them has two rooms. tām 'měy-rén yěw 'lyǎng-jyān-'wū-dz.

When the idea is every . . . its own . . . use měy, yī *or* gè ('gè-dz); měy *and* yī *are more general,* gè *is literary and formal and sometimes more limiting.* ‖Each of us has his own duties. *is expressed as* Every person has his own responsibility. 'měy-rén dēw yěw tā 'dz-jǐ-de-'dzé-rèn. ‖Each of these men has his own peculiar temperament. 'jèy-shyē-rén 'gè yěw 'gè-de-gwǎy-'pí-chi. ‖Each country has its own customs. 'yí-chù yěw 'yí-chù-de-'fēng-su. *or* 'gè-chù-'fēng-su bù-'túng.

(*Apiece*) yí-'gè. ‖These apples are a penny each. 'jèy-shyē-ge-'píng-gwo yī-fēn-'chán yí-'gè.

Each other 'bǐ-tsž; (*literary*) 'hù-shyǎng. ‖They're accusing each other in court. tām dzày 'fǎ-tīng 'hù-shyǎng 'gàw-jà. ‖We don't understand each other. wǒ-men 'bǐ-tsž bù-'míng-lyǎw. (*If the misunderstanding is one of language*) wǒm shwō-de-'hwà 'bǐ-tsž bù-néng dǔng. *In many sentences each other is not expressed directly.* ‖They just look at each other. *is expressed as* They're facing (*one another*) and looking. tām 'gwāng dzày-nar 'dwèy-je 'kàn. ‖Let's never fight each other again. *is expressed as* Let's never fight again. dzám 'tsúng-tsž 'byé dzày dǎ-'jyà-le. ‖They're killing each other! (*of a fist fight*) tām dǎ-'jyà 'dǎ-de 'pīn-mìng-le!

EAGER. (*To want very much*) 'hěn shyǎng. ‖I am eager to meet your friends. wǒ 'hěn shyǎng jyàn-jyan nǐ-de-'péng-yew. ‖He's eager to learn. tā 'hěn shyǎng shywé. ‖I'm eager to get home. *is expressed as* I want to get home as early as possible. wǒ yàw 'dzǎw-dyar dàw-'jyā. (*But note the following, when the action has already taken place*): ‖He has been quite eager to learn so far, but we'll have to wait and see. *is expressed as* Up to now he's exerted a great deal of effort in learning, still we must wait and see what it will be like. tā dàw shyàn-'dzày 'shywé-de háy-shr hěn chǐ-'jyèr, yī-'hèw dzěm-yàng jyèw děy 'dzěw-je 'chyáw-le.

EAR. 'ěr-dwo. ‖My ear hurts. wǒ 'ěr-dwo téng. ‖He pricked up his ears as soon as they lowered their voices.

tām shwō-'hwà-de-'shēng-yin 'gāng yī-'dī-shya-chywu, tā jyèw 'jř-leng-je ěr-dwo yàw 'tīng. ‖She spoke something in his ear and he smiled. tā dzǎy tā ěr-'byān-shang 'shyǎw-shēngr shwō-le dyǎr-mār, tā wēy-'wēy-de yí-shyàw.

All ears. ‖Go on with your story; I'm all ears. *is expressed as* Continue with what you were saying; I'm here listening. 'jyē-je 'shwō-shya-chywu-ba, wǒ jèr 'tīng-je-ne.

Burning ears. ‖Were your ears burning last night? dzwór 'wǎn-shang nǐ 'ěr-dwo °fā-'shāw-le-ma? (°fā-'rè-le-ma?) (*In Chinese this means either that someone was talking about you or that someone was thinking about you.*)

A deaf ear. ‖He turned a deaf ear to all their pleas. *is expressed as* He pretended he didn't hear what they pleaded. tām 'dzěm chyéw tā 'jyèw-shr 'jwāng tīng-bu-'jyàn.

An ear to the ground. ‖He keeps his ear to the ground. *is expressed as* He's very careful to learn other people's opinions. bvé-rén-de-'yì-jyan, tā hěn 'lyéw-shīn yàw 'jř-daw.

An ear for music. ‖I don't have an ear for music. *is expressed as* I don't understand music when I hear it. 'yīn-ywè wǒ 'tīng-bù-'dǔng. *or as* ‖I don't know how to enjoy music. wǒ 'bú-hwèy 'shǐr-shang 'yīn-ywè.

(*Head of grain*) swèr; *but* ear of corn 'ywù-mǐ-'bàngr. ‖The ears of wheat are nearly ripe. mày-'swèr kwày 'shéw-le. *or* 'mày-dz kwày shyèw-'swèr-le.

EARLY. (*Sooner than expected or sooner than normal*) dzǎw. ‖You are early. 'dzǎw-wa. ‖Am I too early? wě-'láy-de (*or* wǒ-'dàw-de) tày 'dzǎw-le-ma? ‖He always arrives early. tā 'lǎw-shr 'dzǎw dàw. ‖It's still early. háy 'dzǎw-ne. ‖He arrived very early today. 'jīn-tyan tā dzǎw-'dzāwr-de jyèw 'dàw-le. ‖Be sure to get here as early as possible. yí-'dìng dzǎw-'dzāwr-de 'chǐ-lay ya. *or* 'chǐ-lay-de 'néng dwō 'dzǎw jyèw dwō-'dzǎw. *or* 'chǐ-lay-de ywè 'dzǎw ywè 'hǎw. ‖I'll be there early. wǒ yí-'dìng 'dzǎw-dyǎr 'dàw. ‖Please call me early. láw-jyà 'dzǎw-dyǎr jyàw-wǒ. ‖You are two minutes early. nǐ 'dzǎw-le 'lyǎng-fēn-jūng. *or* nǐ 'tày dzǎw-le, 'dzǎw-le 'lyǎng-fēn-jūng. ‖Let's not get there too early. wǒ-men byé 'chywù(-de) (*or* 'dàw (-de)) tày 'dzǎw-le. ‖He's been arriving earlier than before. tā-'láy-de bǐ yǐ-'chyán 'dzǎw(-dyǎr)-le. ‖Let us have an early reply from you. chǐng 'dzǎw-dyǎr 'dá-fù. *or* chǐng 'dzǎw-dyǎr 'hwéy-dá. *or* chǐng 'dzǎw gěy 'hwéy-shìn. *or* chǐng 'dzǎw láy 'hwéy-shìn. ‖Spring is early this year. 'jīn-nyán 'chwēn-tyān-láy-de 'dzǎw.

(First of two or more) dzăw, 'téw-yī, dì-'yī. *(In combinations such as these,* dzăw *often refers to* **morning,** *rather than merely to* **first.)** ‖**What time does the early show begin?** *(Morning show)* 'dzăw-chăng-'dyàn-yěngr *(or, meaning* **First show in afternoon or evening** 'téw-yì-chăng-'dyàn-yěngr *or* dì-'yì-chăng-'dyàn-yěngr*)* 'jĭ-dyàn-jūng 'kǎy-shř? ‖**Has the early mail come?** *(morning mail)* 'dzăw-bān-de-shìn 'láy-le méy-yew?

(First part of). *Often* dzăw, *but also expressed by other terms for* **the first part,** *some of them technical.* **Early life** 'shyǎw-shŕ-hew *or* 'dzăw-nyán. ‖**Tell me something of your early life.** 'gàw-su wǒ dyǎr-nĭ-'shyǎw-shŕ-hew-de-'shř-ching. *or* 'gàw-su wǒ dyǎr-nĭ-'dzăw-nyán-de-'shř-ching. ‖**He came early in the morning.** *(Very early, 5 or 6 A.M.)* tā (yì-)'chĭng-dzăwr láy-de. *or* tā (yí-)'dà-dzăwr láy-de. *(About 7 to 9 A.M.)* tā 'dzăw-chen láy-de ('dzăw-chen *also means simply* **morning**).

Early in the day 'dzăw-chen. ‖**The boat docked early in the day.** chwán 'dzăw-chen kàw-de 'mǎ-tew.

Early in the afternoon *(hardly past noon)* 'gāng gwò 'jūng-wǔ. ‖**The boat docked early in the afternoon.** chwán kàw 'mǎ-tew de-shŕ-hew, 'gāng gwò 'jūng-wǔ.

Early in the evening *(not long after dark)* tyān 'gāng hēy-le bù-'jyěw. *(Used in sentences as with* **early in the afternoon.)**

Early in the month ywè-'chū; **in the early months** 'téw-jĭ-ge-'ywè.

Early in the season 'chū-X *or* 'X-chū *(X represents the name of a season; (literary, uncommon); for* **spring** *and* **fall** *only)* 'dzăw-X, *or* gāng dàw 'X-tyān **de-shŕ**-hew, gāng rù 'X-tyān de-shŕ-hew. *Or use the term for the first month of any season, which in the lunar calendar is two months before the corresponding month in the Western calendar.*

Early in the year. *(January and February)* 'jēng-èr-'ywè-li; *(spring)* 'chwēn-tyān; *(not long after the passing of the year)* 'gāng gwò-nyán bù-'jyěw; **early in 1948** 'yī-jyèw-sż-'bā-nyán °'gāng gwò-nyán bù-'jyěw *(or with either of the other phrases after* °*).*

Early in *(a certain period)* gāng . . . bù-'jyěw *(with a verbal expression enclosed),* or *expressed as* **in the early years of . . .** 'chū-nyán. ‖**He went to school early in the Chinese Republican period.** tā mín-gwó-'chū-nyán shàng-de 'shywé. ‖**He was wounded early in the war.** gāng kāy-'jàng bù-'jyěw, tā shèw-de 'shāng.

Early in the book shū kāy-'téwr-nar, shū 'téw-jĭ-dwàr-li. ‖**It's mentioned early in the book.** shū kāy-'téwr-nar *(or* shū 'téw-jĭ-dwàr-li) 'shwō-gwo.

See also **SOON.**

EARN. *(Financially, be paid)* jèng *(of wages, salary, and fees only)* ; jwàn *(also of profit).* ‖**How much do you earn a week?** nĭ yí-ge-lĭ-'bày jèng *(or* jwàn) 'dwō-shaw chyán? ‖**The boy earned fifty cents by**

mowing the lawn. 'nèy-ge-háy-dz twēy-'tsăw jèng-le 'wǔ-máw-chyán. ‖**He didn't earn that wealth; he inherited it.** tā-de-chyán 'bú-shr 'dż-jĭ 'jèng-lay-de; shř 'chéng-shèw-lay-de.

(Figuratively, merit) *sometimes translated by words meaning* **deserve,** *sometimes by literary expressions.* ‖**He earned his reputation.** tā-'míng fù-chí-'shŕ. *or* tā-'míng bù-shywū-'chwán. *or* tā 'shŕ-dzày 'pèy shèw-rén nèm 'chēng-dzàn. ‖**He didn't earn his reward.** tā 'wú-gūng shèw-'shăng. *or* tā shèw 'nèy-yàng-de-'shăng yěw dyǎr-bú-'pèy. ‖**His behavior earned him the respect of everyone.** tā-de 'shíng-wéy 'rén-ren dēw 'pèy-fu.

EARTH. *(As a planet)* dì-'chyéw. ‖**The earth is mostly covered with water.** dì-'chyéw-shang 'dwō-bàn shr 'shwěy.

(Ground) dì. ‖**There are many treasures buried in the earth.** dì-'dĭ-shya *(or* dì-'lĭ-téw) máy-je 'hěn dwō 'băw-bey.

(Dirt) tǔ. ‖**These holes must be filled with earth.** jèy-shyē-'kŭ-lung děy ná-'tǔ °'dǔ-shang. *or* °'tyán-shang. ‖**There is a thin layer of earth on top of the rock.** 'yán-shŕ-shang yěw báw-'báw-de-yì-tséng•'tǔ.

(World). *(The inhabited world)* 'shř-jyè; *(that which is under heaven)* tyān-'dì-shya; *(literary; opposed to* 'tyān(-shàng) **heaven)** 'dì(-shyà); *(among men; literary)* 'rén-jyān. ‖**There is nothing on earth like it.** 'shř-jyè-shang (jyèw) 'méy-yěw 'jèy-yàngr-de-'shŕ. *or* °'dūng-shi. *or* tyān-'dĭ-shya (jyèw) . . . *or* *(literary)* *meaning* **Actually there are few in heaven, no duplicates on earth.** 'jēn-shr 'tyān-shang shăw 'yěw, 'dì-shyà wú-'shwāng *or* 'jēn-shr 'rén-jyān shăw 'yěw.

On earth *(added for emphasis).* ‖**What on earth is that?** *(Showing merely surprise)* 'āy-ya! 'nà jyàw 'shéme-ya? *or* 'āy-ya! 'nà shŕ ge 'shéme-ya? *(Showing disapproval)* 'hāy! 'nà jyàw 'shéme-ya? ‖**What on earth did you do that for?** *(Mild)* nĭ 'dzěm 'nèm-je-ya? *(With strong disapproval)* nĭ 'nèm-je dàw-'dĭ-shr 'dzěm-ge-'yì-sz-a? *or* °'wèy-de 'shém-ma? ‖**Who on earth could have seen that far ahead?** 'shéy yèw *(or* 'shéme-rén) néng 'jyàn-de 'nèm 'ywǎn-ne? ‖**Where on earth did you buy that?** 'āy-ya. 'nǎr mǎy-de?·

Back to earth *or* **down to earth.** ‖**The trip was very pleasant, but now we have to get back to earth.** 'jèy-yí-tsż-lywǔ-'shíng wár-de hěn gāw-'shìng; shyàn-'dzày kě děy °'gāy gàn shém-me 'gàn shém-me-le. *or* °'shèw-'shìn-le. ‖**Oh, come back to earth!** *meaning* **Stop dreaming!** 'hāy! 'byé dzwò-'mèng-le. *or* *meaning* **Let's talk sense.** 'hāy! shwō 'jèng-jĭng-de. *or* 'hāy! shwō jēn-'gé-de. ‖**He has a down-to-earth attitude.** tā hěn 'shŕ-shr chyéw-'shŕ.

EASILY. *(Without difficulty)* 'rúng-yì, bù-'nán, bǔ-fèy-'shŕ, *or* bǔ- *plus other words for* **DIFFICULT. HARD,** *which see.* ‖**It's easily done.** hěn 'rúng-yì. *or* bú-fèy-'shr̀. ‖I learned it quite easily. wǒ 'rúng-rung-yì-'yì-de jyèw shywé-'hwèy-le. or wǒ shywé-de hěn 'rúng-yì. or wǒ shywé-de bú-fèy-'shr̀. ‖I learned how to ride a bicycle quite easily. wǒ shywé chí-'dz̀-shíng-chē shywé-de °'hěn rúng-yì. or °'hěn bú-fèy-'shr̀. or wǒ 'rúng-rúng-yì-'yì-de jyèw °bǎ chí-'dz̀-shíng-chē shywé-'hwèy-le. or °shywé-'hwèy-le chí-'dz̀-shíng-'chē-le. ‖He doesn't make friends easily. tā bù-'rúng-yì (or tā hěn 'nán) jyāw 'péng-yew. or (with the additional idea that he doesn't care to) tā bù-°'chīng-yì jyāw 'péng-yew. or °'swéy-swey-byan-'byàn-de jyāw 'péng-yew. ‖It's easier (more easily) said than done. 'shwō-je (or 'kàn-je) 'rúng-yì, 'dzwò-chǐ-lay jyèw 'nán-le.

Other expressions in English. ‖We are expecting him, but he could easily be late. wǒ-men dzày-jèr jèng 'děng-je tā 'láy, kě-shr °tā hěn 'kě néng láy 'wǎn-le. or °tā 'jyèw-shywǔ hwèy láy 'wǎn-le. ‖That is easily the best I've seen. dzày wǒ-swǒ-'jyàn-gwo-de-'lǐ-tew, 'nèy-ge bǐ 'byé-de dēw 'hǎw-de 'dwō.

See also **EASY.**

EAST. dūng; *in many cases combinations are required, as* to the east of, ...-de-'dūng-byār; the East (*part of a country*) 'dūng-bù, 'dūng-byār; the (Far) East 'dūng-fāng, *or* 'ywǎn-dūng; Near East 'jìn-dūng; the east end 'dūng-téwr. ‖Where do I turn east? wǒ dzày-'nǎr wàng-'dūng gwǎy? ‖An east wind usually comes up in the afternoon. 'píng-cháng 'shyà-wǔ chǐ (or gwā) 'dūng-fēng. ‖I lived in the East (*of a certain country*) for ten years. wǒ dzày 'dūng-bù (or 'dūng-byār) jù-le (or jù-gwo) 'shŕ-nyán. ‖It's just east of the highway. (nèy) jyèw dzày gūng-lù-de-'dūng-byār yì-dyǎr. ‖We get most of our tea from the East (*the Orient*). wǒ-men-hē-de-'chá 'dwō-bàn (or 'dà-bàn) dēw shŕ tsúng 'dūng-fāng láy-de. ‖The plane is north by east of the airport now. jèy-ge-'fēy-jī shyàn-dzày shŕ dzày fēy-jī-'chǎng-de-běy-wěy-'dūng-de-fāng-shyàng.

EASTERN. dūng. Eastern Asia dūng-'yǎ; eastern China 'jūng-gwo-de-'dūng-bù; the Near Eastern question 'jìn-dūng-'wèn-tí.

The Eastern Church (*here, The Greek Church*) shī-lā-'jyàw.

See also **EAST.**

EASY. (*Not difficult*) 'rúng-yì, bù-'nán; (*requiring little effort*) bú-fèy-'shr̀. *In a few combinations,* hǎw (*good*) *is used.* ‖English would be easy for you. nǐ shywé 'yīng-wén yīng-dāng hěn 'rúng-yì. ‖It looks easy, but actually it's quite complicated. 'kàn-je rúng-yì, chí-'shŕ hěn 'má-fan. ‖He is easy to see *or to* approach. tā 'rúng-yì jyàn. ‖It isn't so easy as that. 'méy nèm 'rúng-yì. ‖Bicycling is easy to learn. chí-'dz̀-shíng-chē °'rúng-yì shywé. or 'hǎw shywé. ‖He's easy to deal with. tā 'rúng-yì dá-dyan. or tā 'hǎw bàn. ‖Is it easy? nèy-ge 'rúng-yì-ma? or nèy-ge 'rúng-yì-bù-rúng-yì. ‖It's very easy. 'hěn rúng-yì. or

yì-'dyǎr yě bù-'nán. ‖It's easier said than done. 'shwō-je (or 'kàn-je) rúng-yì, 'dzwò-chǐ-lay jyèw 'nán-le.

(*Comfortable*) 'shū-fu. Easy chair 'shū-fu-de-'yǐ-dz. ‖He leads an easy life. (*In regard to physical comforts*) tā-'gwò-de hěn 'shū-fu. (*In regard to mental attitude*) tā-'shīn-lǐ hěn 'shū-fu.

(*Of writing*). ‖He writes in an easy style. tā-'shyě-de °hěn 'lyèw-lì. or °hěn 'tūng-shwèn.

(*Not harsh, hurried, etc., especially in such expressions as* take it easy). *There is a wide range of meaning for most phrases here.* ‖Take it easy! *or* Easy! *meaning* Don't hurry. byé-'máng! or màn-'mār-de! or *meaning* Don't be excited! byé 'hwāng! or byé 'hwāng-jāng! or byé 'jāng-hwáng! or 'chén-jù-le 'chì! *or meaning* Don't be noisy! byé 'nàw! or byé 'chǎw! ‖Easy does it! màn-'mār-de! *meaning* Be alert! lyéw-'shén-dyar! or *meaning* Be careful! 'shyǎw-shīn-je-dyar! ‖Let's take things easy (*slowly*). dzám màn-'mār-de dzwò. ‖His manners are free and easy. tā ('tày-dù) hěn °'shyāw-sǎ. or °'dà-fāng. or °'swéy-byàn. or °'bù-bǎy 'jyà-dz. or °'dz̀-rán. ‖Go easy on the sugar; it's hard to get. 'shěng-je-dyar yùng-'táng (or chǐ-'táng); hěn nán 'mǎy-dàw-ne. ‖Take it easy on your sprained ankle. nǐ-'nyěw-le-de-'jyǎw yàw °'shǎw yùng. or °'shyǎw-shīn-je. ‖She's easy on the eyes. tā-'jǎng-de hěn shwèn-'yǎn.

Easy-going. ‖Their boss is very easy-going (*good-natured*). tām-de-'téwr °'hěn hǎw shwō-'hwàr. or °'pí-chì 'hěn hǎw. or °hǎw 'pí-chyèr. or °hěn 'hé-chi. or °'shīn hěn 'kwān-dà-de. ‖He's an easy-going sort of person (*lazy*). tā-nèy-ge-rén hěn 'lǎn.

Easy street. ‖He has been living on easy street since his father died. tā-'fù-chin yì-'sž, tā jyèw 'gwò-chi 'shū-fu-'r̀-dz lay-le.

See also **HARD, DIFFICULT.**

EAT. (*As a particular action, or to eat a particular thing*) chŕ. ‖I want something to eat. wǒ yàw 'chŕ dyǎr-'dūng-shi. or wǒ 'yàw dyǎr-'chŕ-de-dūng-shi. ‖Did you EAT that? 'nèy-ge nǐ shŕ 'chŕ-le-ma? ‖Have you really eaten that? nèy-ge nǐ 'jēn 'chŕ-le-ma? ‖Are these good to eat? *meaning* Do they taste good? 'jèy-shyē-dūng-shi °hǎw 'chŕ-ma? or °hǎy 'chŕ-de-ma? *meaning* Are they edible? °'néng chŕ-ma? or °'chŕ-de-ma? ‖He likes to eat it raw. jèy-ge tā ày °chŕ 'shēng-de. or °'shēng(-je) chŕ. ‖They ate up everything. tām 'dēw gěy chŕ-'gwāng-le.

(*To have a meal*) chŕ-'fàn; *occasionally* chŕ *alone.* ‖Where shall we eat after the show? kàn-'wán-le dyàn-'yǐng dàw-'nǎr chŕ-'fàn-ne? ‖Have you eaten? chŕ-'gwò (fàn)-le-ma? ‖We take turns to eat. wǒm 'lwén-bār chŕ-'fàn. ‖Shall we eat out tonight? jyér 'wǎn-shang °'chū-chywu chŕ(-'fàn), 'hǎw-ma? ‖Are we going to eat out tonight? jyér 'wǎn-shang wǒ-men dzày 'wày-tew chŕ-'fàn-ma?

Eat up (*damage, destroy*). ‖The rifle barrel was eaten up with rust. chyāng-'gwǎn-dz dēw 'shyèw-de bù-chéng-'yàngr-le. ‖The clothes were eaten up by moths. 'yī-shang jyàw 'chúng-dz dēw gěy °'chř-le. *or* °'dǎ-le.

(*Figuratively*). ‖What's eating you? nǐ 'dzěm-la? *or* nǐ shēng 'něy-mén-dz 'chì-ya? *or* nǐ wèy-'shéme 'byè-nyew? ‖She is eating her heart out. tā 'shāng-shīn 'jí-le.

EDGE. byār (*or* byān), *most general term, refers particularly to the area near the edge or the side surface* (*see also below*). ‖It is on the edge of town. dzày chéng-'byār-shang. ‖She moved the glass from the edge to the center of the table. tā bǎ bwō-li-'bēy tsúng jwō-dz-'byār-nar nwó-daw dāng-'jūng-chywu-le. ‖Don't fall over the edge of the rock. byé tsúng shŕ-tew-'byār-shang 'dyàw-shyà-chywu. ‖Keep away from the edge of the platform. lí 'táy-byār 'ywǎn-dyar.

(*Boundary*) 'byān-jyè. ‖How far is the edge of town? dàw jèy-ge-chéng-de-'byān-jyè yěw 'dwō ywǎn?

(*Long, narrow side of a flat, thin object; side surface*) byār (*or* byān); *often expressed as* line along the border of a surface léngr (*or* léng, *or, in combinations, sometimes* 'léng-er). ‖The edge of the glass is very sharp. bwō-li-'byār (*or* bwō-li-'léngr) hěn 'kwày. ‖Old style cars have many edges and corners. jyèw-shŕ-de-'chē 'léng-er-'jyǎwr-de hěn 'dwō.

(*Of a cliff, bank, etc.*) yàr. ‖There are rails on the edge of the cliff. 'yán-shŕ-de-'yàr-shang (*or* 'yán-shŕ-de-'byār-shang) yěw 'lán-gan.

(*Of a book*) kěw. ‖The book has gilt edges. shū-'kěw shř 'jīn-de. *or* shū shř 'jīn-byār-de. *But* ‖The book was placed on its edge (*standing upright*); he picked it up and laid it flat. shū shyān-shr 'shù-je-de; tā 'ná-chi-lay gěy fàng-'píng-le.

(*Extended edge of a roof; eave*) fāng-'yár, wū-'yár.

(*Cutting edge of a blade*) rèr, dāw-'kěw. ‖The edge of this razor is too dull. jèy-ge-'gwā-lyǎn-dāw-de-°'rèr tày 'dwèn. *or* °'dāw-'kěw tày 'dwèn.

To put an edge on. (*For the first time*) kāy-'kěw; (*to sharpen*) 'mwó. ‖I want an edge put on this blade. *meaning* I want it sharpened. gěy-wǒ 'mwó-mwo jèy-bǎ-'dāw. ‖This knife has not yet had an edge put on it. jèy-bǎ-'dāw háy méy kāy-gwo 'kěw.

To edge along (*to go slowly and carefully along the side of a building, a wall, etc.*) 'lyēw-je . . .-'byār dzěw; 'shwèn-je . . .-'byār dzěw; 'kàw-je . . .-byār dzěw; pǎw *or other verbs of motion can be used instead of* dzěw. ‖The soldiers edged along the buildings while the bullets were flying in the street. bīng dēw 'shwèn-je (*or* 'lyēw-je, *or* 'kàw-je) léw-'byār dzěw, nèy-shŕ-hew 'dž-dàn dzày 'jyē-shang 'lwàn-fēy. ‖The child edged along the wall and went out of the room. shyǎw-'hár 'lyēw-je (*or* 'shwèn-je, *or* 'kàw-je) chyáng-'byār jyèw 'dzěw (*or* 'lyēw)-chū-chywu-le. ‖The thief edged away along the wall. dzéy 'lyēw-je chyáng-'byār pǎw-le.

To edge (*press; as in a crowd*) jǐ. ‖I edged my way to the front of the room. wǒ (snyé-je 'shēn-dz) jǐ-dàw wū-dz-'chyán-byar chywù-le. ‖I just edged in. wǒ yì-'jǐ jyèw 'jìn-chywu-le. ‖The man edged through the crowd. nèy-ge-rén dzày rén-'dwēy-li ('pyān-je shēn-dz, *or* 'shyé-je shēn-dz) 'jǐ-gwò-chywu-le. ‖He edged into the crowd unnoticed. tā 'shén-bù-jř-'gwěy-bù-jywé-de jyèw 'jǐ-jìn nèy-'chywún-'rén-li chywù-le.

To have the edge on *someone*. A has the edge on B A bǐ B 'chyáng *or* B bù-'rú A. ‖I think you have the edge on me, at least in foreign languages. wǒ jywé-je nǐ 'jř-shǎw 'wày-gwo-ywú bǐ wǒ 'chyáng. *or* wǒ jywé-je wǒ 'jř-shǎw 'wày-gwo-ywú bù-'rú nǐ.

On edge. ‖His nerves have been on edge for days now. (*From excitement*) tā 'shīn-li °fā-'dzàw, (*or* °'jè-teng-le *or* °'fán-de-hwang *or* (*From impatience*) °jáw-'jí *or* °'jí-de-hwang *or* °bú-ày-'fár) 'yěw shyē-'ř-dz-le.

To take the edge off (*weaken*). ‖That certainly took the edge off the enemy's attacking power. nèy kě 'jēn bǎ 'dí-rén-de-'rwèy-chì 'jyǎn-le hěn-'dwō. ‖Your statement took the edge off his enthusiasm. nǐ 'nèm yì-shwō °jyàw tā-de-'shīn 'lěng-le yí-'bàr. *or* (*literary, alluding to throwing cold water on the head*) °gěy-le tā ge-'lěng-shwěy-jyàw-'téw. ‖His mother-in-law's visit took the edge off their enjoyment of the vacation. tā jàng-mu-'nyáng nèm yì-láy 'kàn-tam, jyàw tām-'wár-de 'bú-dà dzěm gāw-'shìng-le.

EDUCATION. 'jyàw-ywù. Department of education (*in a school*) 'jyàw-ywù-shì; mass education 'mín-jùng-jyàw-'ywù *or* 'píng-mín-jyàw-'ywù; adult education 'chéng-nyán jyàw-'ywù *or* 'pǔ-tung-jyàw-'ywù. ‖Where did you receive your education? nǐ dzày-'nǎr °shèw-de jyàw-'ywù? *meaning* Where did you go to school? °shàng-de 'shywé? *or meaning* Where did you study? °nyàn-de 'shū? ‖How much education have you had? nǐ 'shèw-gwo shém-me (*or* dwō-shǎw) jyàw-'ywù? *or expressed as* What schools have you entered? nǐ 'rù-gwo shém-me-'shywé-shyàw? *or as* How much have you studied? nǐ 'nyàn-gwo 'dwō-shǎw 'shū?

Other than formal schooling is expressed as experience. 'jīng-yàn; benefit 'yí-chù; *or* knowledge 'jř-shr. ‖Going out with her is an education in itself. gēn-'tā chū-chywu 'wár °jyàw-rén 'dé hěn-dwō 'jīng-yàn. *or* °jyàw-rén 'dé hěn-dwō 'yí-chù. *or* °ké-yi 'jǎng hěn-dwō 'jř-shr. *or* °jyèw-shr ge-dé-'jyàw-ywù-de-'jī hwey.

EFFECT. (*Final result; result as opposed to cause; or an indirect and incidental result*) 'jyē-gwǒ. Cause and effect 'ywán-yīn hé 'jyē-gwǒ; *or* (*fixed combinations*) 'yīn-gwǒ, 'chyán-yīn-hèw-'gwǒ. ‖Let's examine the cause and effect of this incident. dzám 'yán-jyew-yan-'jyèw jèy-jyàn-shř-de-°'yīn-gwǒ. *or* °'ywán-yīn hé 'jyē-gwǒ. *or* °'chyán-yīn-hèw-'gwǒ. ‖What do you think the effect of his speech will be? nǐ 'jywé-je 'tā-de-jyǎng-yǎn hwèy dzày rén-'shīn-li yěw 'shéme-yàng-de-'jyē-gwǒ-ne?

(*Immediate, direct or intended result, usually desirable*) 'shyàw-lì, *or sometimes expressed as* potency 'lì-lyang; (*particular effect of a specific action*) 'shyàw-gwǒ; (*an experimentally proved result*) 'shyàw-yàn; (shyàw *alone is used only in negative or indefinite expressions*). *For* no effect *and* take effect *see below.* ‖His speech had a great deal of effect. *or* His speech was very effective. tā-de-'yǎn-jyǎng hěn yěw 'shyàw-lì. ‖The full effect of this medicine hasn't been felt yet. jèy-ge-yàw-de-'shyàw-lì (*or* jèy-ge-yàw-de-'lì-lyang) háy méy-'wán-chywán 'jyàn (*or* 'shyǎn)-chu-lay-ne. ‖What is the effect of this medicine? jèy-ge-'yàw yěw shém-me 'shyàw-lì? ‖What will be the effect of this medicine (*when it is applied*)? jèy-ge-'yàw yěw shém-me 'shyàw-yàn? ‖What was the effect of this medicine? jèy-ge-'yàw yěw shém-me 'shyàw-gwǒ? ‖Will this medicine have any effect? jèy-ge-'yàw yěw-'shyàw méy-yew? ‖His speech had exactly the desired effect. tà-yǎn-'jyǎng-de-'shyàw-gwǒ 'jèng gēn 'ywán-láy-'shyǎng-de yì-'dyǎr bú-'chà.

No effect *is expressed by one of the terms already discussed, or by others covering a wider range of meaning.* ‖This medicine had no effect at all. jèy-ge-'yàw °yì-'dyǎr 'shyàw-lì (*or* 'shyàw-yàn, *or* 'shyàw-gwǒ, *or* 'shyàw) yě 'méy-yěw. *or meaning* It was no use. °yì-'dyǎr 'yùng-chu yě 'méy-yěw. *or meaning* It was no help. °'sz-háw-wú-'bǔ. *or* °'wú-jì-ywú-'shr̀. *or* °yì-'dyǎr yě bú-jì-'shr̀. *or meaning* It didn't cure. °yì-'dyǎr yě bú-jr̀-'bìng.

Good or bad effect chù, *e.g.,* good effects 'hǎw-chù. ‖Living in these places has many bad effects on the children. dzày jèy-shyē-'dì-fang jù wèy shyǎw-'hár yěw hěn dwō 'hwày-chù.

Take effect (*begin to show results*) chǐ 'dzwò-yùng, yěw 'dùng-jìng; 'shàng-lay (*said of the potency of the substance*). ‖The medicine is beginning to take effect (*or* is taking effect); I can feel it. 'jèy-ge-yàw yǐ-jīng chǐ 'dzwò-yùng-le (*or* 'jèy-ge-yàw yǐ-jīng yěw 'dùng-jìng-le); wǒ jywé-de-chū-'láy. ‖These drinks are beginning to take effect. jèy-ge-'jyěw-jyèr shàng-lay-le.

(*Of a law, etc.*) 'shyàw, *except in the phrase* 'shŕ-shíng, be put into effect. ‖The law will take effect (*or* go into effect) a week from today. jèy-tyáw-'fǎ-gwēy 'chī-tyān yǐ-'hèw jyèw °yěw-'shyàw-le. *or* °'shēng-'shyàw-le. ‖When does this regulation go into effect? jèy-ge-'gwēy-dzé 'shém-me-shŕ-hew 'chǐ °yěw-'shyàw. *or* °'shēng-'shyàw. ‖The new law is not in effect yet. shīn-'fǎ-lywù háy méy 'shŕ-shíng-ne. ‖The law is still in effect. nèy-ge-'fǎ-gwēy háy 'yěw-shyàw. ‖The law is no longer in effect. nèy-ge-'fǎ-gwēy yǐ-jīng °'wú-shyàw-le. *or* °'shŕ-shyàw-le.

(*Influence*) 'yǐng-shyǎng. ‖The effect of climate on these plants is tremendous. jèy-shyē-'jŕ-wù shèw 'chì-hèw-de-'yǐng-shyǎng hěn 'dà. ‖You can see the

effect of the mountain air on him. shān-shang-de-'kūng-chì gěy-tā-de-'yǐng-shyǎng kě-yǐ 'kàn-de-chu-láy.

(For) effect. (*See also* **SHOW OFF**.) ‖I'm not trying to produce an effect. wǒ bìng 'bú-shr yàw 'shyǎn-bay. ‖She's wearing those clothes for effect. tā chwān 'nèy-jǔng-de-'yī-fu jyèw 'wèy-de shr̀ yàw °'yīn-rén jù-'mù. *or* °'shyǎn-nùng-'shyǎn-nùng. *or* °chū 'fēng-tew.

In effect (*really; for all practical purposes*) 'shŕ-dzày 'shwō-chǐ-lay; 'chí-shŕ. ‖His career began, in effect, when he was twelve. 'shŕ-dzày 'shwō-chi-lay, tā-de-'shr̀-yè shr̀ tsúng shŕ-'èr-swèy kāy-'shǐ-de. *or* 'chí-shŕ, tā-de-....

To effect bàn. *See also* **DO**. ‖He effected the change without difficulty. jèy-tsz̀-'gǎy-byàn tā 'bàn-de hěn 'shwèn-lì.

See also **RESULT**.

EFFECTS. (*Possessions*) 'dūng-shi. ‖His effects are still in his room. tā-de-'dūng-shi háy dzày tā-de-'wū-dz-li-ne.

EGG. Chicken eggs 'jī-dàn, jī-'dzěr; 'báy-gwǒr (*literally white fruit, local Peiping*); *in certain combinations or when chickens are mentioned elsewhere in the sentence* dàn *or* (*local Peiping*) gwǒr, *but not* dzěr. Scrambled eggs 'chǎw-jī-dàn; boiled eggs 'jǔ-jī-dàn; poached eggs 'wò-jī-dàn *or* wò-'gwǒr. ‖How much are eggs by the dozen? 'jī-dàn (*or* jī-'dzěr) 'dwō-shǎw-chyán yì-'dá. ‖That hen laid two hundred eggs last year. 'nèy-jr̀-jī 'chywù-nyán 'shyà-le 'èr-bǎy-ge-'dàn. ‖Those eggs are for hatching (chicks). nèy-shyē-'dàn shr̀ 'fū-shyǎw-'jyěr-de. ‖I like fried eggs. wǒ 'shǐ-hwān °'yān-jī-dàn. *or* °'já-gwǒr. *or* °hé-bāw-'dàn. ‖I'd like two poached eggs in my soup. 'tāng-li wǒ lyǎ-'gwǒr. *or* 'tāng-li wǒ 'lyǎng-ge-jī-dàn.

Eggs (*of any bird*) dàn, dàr. ‖There are four eggs in the swallow's nest. yàn-dz-'wō-li yěw 'sz̀-ge-'dàr.

To egg on 'chywàn, 'gǔ-dùng; (*local Peiping*) 'tswān-deng. ‖He was egged on by his friends. tā-de-'péng-yew-men °'chywàn-de (*or* °'gǔ-dùng-de, *or* °'tswān-deng-de) tā nèm-je.

A good egg, etc. (*of a person*). ‖He's a good egg. *is expressed as* He's not bad. tā-jèy-ge-rén °hěn 'hǎw. *or* °bú-'hwày. *or* °bú-'tswò. ‖He's a bad egg. *is expressed as in English* tā shr̀ ge-hwày-'dàn. *or as* tā shr̀ ge-'hwày-dūng-shi. *or* tā shr̀ ge-'hwày-jǔng. *or* tā 'bú-shr ge-'hǎw-rén. *or expressed as* Don't associate with him. 'byé gēn-tā 'láy-wang.

A bad egg (*literally*). (*Stale*) 'chén-jī-dàn; (*bad to the point where the yolk and the white mix*) shyè-le-'hwángr-de-jī-dàn; (*rotten*) 'chòw-jī-dàn.

All one's eggs in one basket. (*Literary quotations*) ‖He failed because he put all his eggs in one basket. *is expressed as* He didn't understand the teaching that a wise rabbit has three holes, so he couldn't succeed.

tā bù-dǔng 'jyǎw-tù-sān-'kū-de-'dàw-li, swǒ-yǐ bù-néng 'chéng-gūng. *or as* **He depended on just one tree to hang himself, so what could he do?** tā jìng jǐ-je 'yì-kē-shù-shang 'dyàw-sž, nà dzěm-me 'shíng-ne? ‖**He's putting all his eggs in one basket.** *is expressed as* **He's betting all his chips at once.** tā-nà shŕ 'gū-jù-yí-'jŕ (*or* -yì-'jŕ).

To lay an egg (*figuratively*). ‖**The comedian laid an egg.** nèy-ge-'chěwr shwō-le jywù-'hwà, méy-rén °'lǐ-hwèy. *or* °'shyàw.

EIGHT. bā. **One eighth** 'bā-fēn-jr-'yī; **the eighth** dì-'bā.

EIGHTEEN. shŕ-'bā. **One eighteenth** shŕ-'bā-fēn-jr-'yī; **the eighteenth** dì-shŕ-'bā.

EIGHTY. 'bā-shŕ. **One eightieth** 'bā-shr-fēn-jr-'yī; **the eightieth** dì-'bā-shŕ.

EITHER. (*One of*) něy-yī-... dēw. ‖**Does either of these roads lead to town?** jèy-'lyǎng-tyáw-lù 'něy-yì-tyáw dēw 'tūng-dàw 'chéng-lǐ-ma? ‖**Either one will do.** ('lyǎng-ge-li) 'něy-yì-ge dēw °'chéng. *or* °'hǎw. *or* °'shíng. *But* ‖**Either way will do.** dzěm-je dēw 'shíng. *See* ANY.

(*Both*) 'lyǎng ... dēw. ‖**There were trees on either side of the road.** nà-tyáw-'lù-de-'lyǎng-byār 'dēw yěw 'shù láy-je.

(*Negative of also*) yě. ‖**If you won't go, I won't either.** 'nǐ yàw bú-'chywù, 'wǒ yě bú-'chywù-le.

Either ... or .... *Two degrees of emphasis are distinguished.* (*If the choice is a matter of indifference*) **either X or Y** X Y(-de) dēw, X hwò-shr Y (dēw), X hwò-jr Y (dēw), (dēw *being used only in cases where* both *can be used in English*); (*if the choice is urgent*) (yàw-shr) 'bū ..., (háy-shr) 'jyèw ...; (*definitely*) 'bū ..., -... 'jwěn. ‖**Either today or tomorrow will do.** 'jyēr 'myér(-de) 'dēw chéng. *or* 'jyēr hwò-shr (*or* hwò-jr) 'myér 'dēw chéng. ‖**You may fill it out with either pen or pencil.** 'tyán-de-shŕ-hew yùng 'gāng-bǐ 'chyán-bǐ 'dēw shíng. ‖**I shall leave either tonight or tomorrow.** (*It doesn't matter which*) wǒ jyēr 'wǎn-shang hwò-shr 'myéngr-ge dzěw. (*Definitely one of the two*) wǒ 'jyēr wǎn-shang 'bù-dzěw, 'myéngr-ge jyèw jwěn 'dzěw. ‖**Either you go there or he does.** bú-shr 'nǐ chywù, jyèw-shr 'tā chywù. *or* nǐ hé-tā nǐm-'lyǎng-ge-rén-lǐ-tew 'dzǒng-děy yěw 'yí-ge 'chywù-de. ‖**Either you marry her, or you drop her entirely.** nǐ bù-'chywǔ-tā jyèw děy 'dwàn-kāy. *or* nǐ 'bù-gēn-tā jyē-'hwēn, jyèw byé 'gēn-'hǎw. ‖**Either take it or leave it.** 'bú-yàw jyèw 'byé 'shyǎng yàw. ‖**There is no middle ground; you either go the whole way or stop right now.** méy-yěw 'lyǎng-'kě-de-'bàn-fa; nǐ yàw-shr 'bù-shyǎng 𝑔̣n-dàw 'dǐ, háy-shr 'jyèw-tsž dǎ-'jù wéy-'myàw.

ELECT. shywǎn; 'shywǎn-jywú; (*less formal*) jywǔ, twēy. ‖**Have you elected a chairman?** nǐ-men 'shywǎn-le (*or* 'shywǎn-jywǔ-le, *or* 'jywǔ-le, *or* 'twēy-le) jǔ-'shí-le-ma?

Elected; -elect 'dāng-shywǎn. ‖**Who was elected president?** shéy 'dāng-shywǎn dsǔng-'tǔng-le? ‖**The President-elect will speak tomorrow.** 'dāng-shywǎn-'shyà-rèn-de-dà-dzǔng-'tǔng (*or* háy-méy-yěw-jyèw-'jŕ-de-'shīn-dà-dzǔng-'tǔng) 'míng-tyān jyǎng-'hwà.

ELECTRIC. dyàn. **Electric power** *or* **electricity** 'dyàn-chì; **electric power** *or* **electric current** (*used to operate something*) 'dyàn-lì; **electric iron** 'dyàn-làw-tǐ; **electric range** 'dyàn-lù-dz. ‖**Are there electric lights?** yěw 'dyàn-děng-ma? ‖**His girl friend sent him an electric razor.** tā-de-'nywǔ-péng-yew 'sùng-le tā yí-ge-yùng-'dyàn-de-gwā-lyàn-'dāw. ‖**It's electr-** (*electrically operated*). shŕ yùng-'dyàn-de. ‖**He received an electric shock.** tā jyàw 'dyàn 'dǎ-le. ‖**He got the electric chair.** (*Punishment executed*) tā dzwò dyàn-'yǐ-dz-le. (*Sentence passed*) tā-pàn-de shŕ dzwò dyàn-'yǐ-dz. ‖**Is the electric train still operating?** 'dyàn-lì-hwǒ-'chē háy 'tūng-ma? ‖**Is the electric train still running (at this hour)?** 'dyàn-lì-hwǒ-'chē háy °'dzěw-je-ne-ma? *or* °'yěw-ma? *or* °'kāy-je-ne-ma?

ELEVEN. 'shŕ-yī(-). ‖**He is eleven years old.** tā 'shŕ-yí-swèy.

Eleventh hour. kwày-dàw 'shŕ-hew-le. *or* dàw-le mwò-'lyǎwr-le. ‖**At the eleventh hour he starts to worry.** kwày-dàw 'shŕ-hew-le (*or* dàw-le mwò-'lyǎwr-le) tā fā-chí 'chéw-lay-le.

ELSE. (*Other*) *usually* byé(-de), *often with* háy *in the same sentence; if* háy *occurs,* byé(-de) *is sometimes omitted.* ‖**There is no one else here.** jèr 'méy-yěw 'byé-rén. ‖**Everyone else has gone.** 'byé-rén chywán 'dzěw-le. ‖**What else can we do?** 'háy yěw shèr-ma? *or* háy yěw 'byé-de-ma? *or* háy yěw 'byé-de-shèr kě-'dzwò-de-ma? *or* háy-yěw 'byé-de-'fár-ma?

(*Otherwise*) ('yàw) bù-'rán, 'fěw-dzé. ‖**How else can I manage?** *is expressed as* **If not that way, then how?** bú-'nèm-je nǐ jyàw-wǒ 'dzěm-je? *or* yàw bù-'rán wǒ 'dzěm-me 'bàn-ne? ‖**Hurry, or else we'll be late.** 'kwày-dyǎr, 'fěw-dzé (*or* yàw bù-'rán) wǒ-men jyèw 'wǎn-le. ‖**You do as I tell you, or else!** wǒ dzěm shwō nǐ dzěm dzwò (*or* wǒ 'jyàw-nǐ dzěm-je nǐ 'jyèw dzěm-je), °'rú-rè bù-'rán-na, 'hm! *or* °yàw bù-'rán-na, 'hm! *or* °'fěw-dzé-ya, 'hm!

EMPIRE. 'dì-gwó. ‖**They discussed the history of the British Empire.** tā-men 'tǎw-lwèn 'yīng-dì-gwó-de-lì-'shŕ (láy-je).

EMPLOY. (*To use; of persons or tools*) yùng; (*use a tool*) shŕ; (*of servants only*) 'shŕ-hwàn; (*hire*) gù; (*polite; of lawyers, etc.*) chǐng. **Be employed** (*work*) dzwò-'shŕ, (*especially of labor*) dzwò-'gūng. ‖**How**

many workers are employed here? jèr yùng-je 'dwŏ-shăw °rén? or °'gūng-rén (laborers)? ‖We used to employ five hundred workers. wŏm yĭ-chyán yùng-gwo 'wŭ-bay-rén. ‖We plan to employ about 1,000 men. wŏm 'ywù-bey yùng (or gù) yì-'chyān-rén. ‖They have employed all the workers available. 'néng-dzwò-'gūng-de-rén tām 'dēw °'yùng-le. or °'gù-le-chywu-le. ‖He knows how to employ people to the best advantage. tā 'hěn hwèy yùng-'rén. ‖He employs a flock of servants. tā 'yùng-je (or 'shŕ-hwàn-je) yì-chywún-'dĭ-shya-rén. ‖He's trying to employ the services of a good lawyer in an advisory role. tā 'hěn shyǎng chĭng ge-hăw-'lywù-shŕ dzwò 'gù-wèn. ‖We were fortunate in being able to employ his help. wŏm 'shìng-kwēy néng chĭng-dàw 'tā lǻy bāng-'máng. ‖Are you employed here? nĭ dzày-'jèr °dzwò-'shŕ-ma? or (of labor) °dzwò-'gūng-ma? ‖In whose employ are you? is expressed as Where (or for whom) do you work? nĭ dzày-'năr dzwo-'shŕ? or nĭ gěy-'shéy dzwo-'shŕ? ‖He employed himself (he employed his time) in reading. tā yùng tā-dè-'shŕ-jyān dú-le 'shū-le. ‖She employs herself in practising shorthand. tā yùng °shyán-je-de-'gūng-fū (or °shyán-je-de-'shŕ-jyān) 'lyàn-shí sù-'jì. ‖You have to employ caution (literally be careful) in crossing this river. gwò jèy-ge-'hé nĭ děy jyā dyăr-'shyăw-shīn.

EMPTY. 1. **(To be) empty** (of contents other than people) kūng; (emptied to make space) 'kùng-chu-lay; 'téng-chu-lay; 'téng-jìng. **An empty house** (yì-swŏr-) 'kūng-fáng-dz; **empty space** (on the ground) 'kūng-di or kùngr. ‖**Do you have an empty box?** yěw 'kūng (-de)-hé-dz-ma? ‖**The room is empty now** (of furniture, etc.). wū-dz 'kūng-le. or wū-dz 'kūng-chu-lay-le. or wū-dz 'kùng-chu-lay-le. or wū-dz 'téng-chu-lay-le. or wū-dz 'téng-jìng-le. ‖**The room is almost empty.** wū-dz-li 'kūng-kung-dung-'dùng-de. or wū-dz-li 'kūng-kung rú-ye. or wū-dz 'jyǎn-jŕ shŕ 'kūng-de (or -je). or meaning has been almost emptied wū-dz 'jyèw-yaw 'téng-chu-lay-le. or wū-dz 'kwày téng-'jìng-le. or wū-dz 'kwày kūng-chu-lay-le. or wū-dz 'kwày kùng-chu-lay-le. ‖**The trunk is empty.** shyāng-dz shŕ 'kūng-de. ‖**The trunk is (still) almost empty.** shyāng-dz 'jyǎn-jŕ (shŕ) 'kūng-de (or -je). ‖**The trunk is (already) empty.** shyāng-dz °'kūng-chu-lay-le. or °'kùng-chu-lay-le. or °'téng-chu-lay-le. ‖**The trunk has been emptied.** (By someone) shyāng-dz gěy ná-'kūng-le. (By a thief) shyāng-dz gěy tēw-'kūng-le. ‖**He came with an empty stomach.** tā 'kūng-je dù-dz láy-de. or tā 'kūng-dùr láy-de. ‖**He came back empty-handed.** tā 'kūng-shěw (or 'kūng-je shěw) hwéy-lay-de.

(To be) empty (of people; no people in it; everyone gone out; etc.). ‖**Is this an empty** (unoccupied) **room?** jèy-jyān-'wū-dz °'méy-rén 'jù-ma? or °'yěw-rén 'jù-ma? or °'yěw méy-yew rén 'jù? ‖**The theater was emptied in five minutes.** shì-'ywán-dz-li-de-rén 'wŭ-fēn-jūng-de-gūng-fu jyèw 'dēw dzěw-'jìng-le.

Empty talk 'kūng-hwà. ‖**That's just empty talk.** nà shŕ 'kūng-hwà.

Empty-headed. (Silly) shă; 'shăw-le-ge-shīn-'yăr; (stupid) 'hú-du, bèn.

Empty threats. ‖**He always makes empty threats.** tā lăw-shr 'kūng (or jyă-'jwāngr) 'shyà-hu rén, shyà-hu 'wán-le jyèw 'swàn-le. or tā lăw-shr 'shwō-de hěn 'shyūng, kě-shr shwō-'wán-le jyèw 'swàn-le. or expressed as He always thunders, never rains. tā lăw-shr 'gān-dă-'léy 'bú-shyà-'ywǔ. ‖**He made a few empty threats.** tā 'kūng shyà-hu-le jĭ-'jywŭ jyèw 'swàn-le. or tā jyă-'jwāngr-de 'shyà-hu-le jĭ-'jywù jyèw 'swàn-le.

2. **To empty** (or be emptied in proper constructions). There are several types of constructions, depending on the nature of the action or of the contents, as follows. When all the contents of a container are emptied (by taking them out) 'ná-chu-lay, 'ná-chu-chywu, ná-'jìng(-le), ná-de 'gān-gan-jìng-'jìng-de; (by lifting and carrying them out) táy instead of ná in the same constructions; (by moving them out; as furniture) bān instead of ná in the same constructions; (by chasing living beings out) găn instead of ná in the same constructions; or use other verbs with meanings such as throw, carry, etc., in the same constructions. ‖**The room was emptied of everything.** wū-dz-li-de-'dūng-shi dēw bān-'jìng-le. ‖**Empty everything out of the trunk.** bă 'shyāng-dz-li-de-'dūng-shi dēw °'ná-chu-lay. or °'chīng-chu-lay. etc.

When a container is emptied and room is being made for other contents 'téng-chu-lay, 'kùng-chu-lay, 'kūng-chu-lay. See above. ‖**Can you empty these things?** (containers) nĭ néng bă jèy-shyē-'dūng-shi °'kūng-chu-lay-ma? or °'téng-chu-lay-ma? or °'kùng-chu-lay-ma?

When either containers or their contents are emptied, and the emptying is done in a particular way. (By inverting or tipping) dàw, dàw-'wán(-le), dàw-'jìng(-le), dàw-'gān-jìng(-le); (after emptying) dàw-de yì-'dĭ yě méy-'yěw-le, dăw-de 'gān-gan-jìng-'jìng-de; (by suspending in an inverted position and letting it drip, as a sieve) kùng instead of dàw in the same constructions; (by letting it drip, drop by drop) dī instead of dàw in the same constructions; (by flowing or letting it flow) lyéw instead of dàw in the same constructions; (by letting it out) fàng instead of dàw in the same constructions. **Empty into** 'dàw-dzày, 'kùng-dzày, 'dī-dzày, 'fàng-dzày or 'fàng-dàw, 'lyéw-dàw; (lyéw is used only of a container; and only with jyàw as co-verb; the other words are used of container or contents, with bă as co-verb). ‖**Empty the ash tray** (ashes) **here.** bă 'yān-hwēy 'dàw-dzày jèr. ‖**Empty all the ash trays.** bă 'yān-dyér dēw 'dàw-le. ‖**Empty the garbage (can) in that bag.** bă 'tǔng-dz-li-de-'dzāng-dūng-shi 'dàw-dzày 'kěw-day-li. ‖**Can you empty these things?** (Contents or containers) nĭ néng bă jèy-shyē-'dūng-shi °'dàw-le-ma? or (By letting the contents out) °'fàng-le-ma? ‖**The bottle is empty** (of something that dripped

out). píng-dz kùng-'wán-le. *or* píng-dz 'kùng-de yì-'dī
yě méy-'yěw-le. *or* píng-dz 'dī-de 'gān-gan-jìng-'jìng-
de. *etc.* ‖**Empty all the cod-liver oil out of the bottle** (*by
letting it drip*). bǎ nèy-ge-píng-dz-li-de-'ywú-gān-yéw
kùng-de °'gān-gan-jìng-'jìng-de. *or* °-'gān-jing-le. *etc.*
‖**This oil tank empties in about five minutes.** jèy-ge-
yéw-'tǔng dà-gày dzày 'wǔ-fēn-jūng-yǐ-'nèy kě-yǐ
°lyéw-'jìng-le. *or* °fàng-'wán-le. (*etc., with* lyéw *and*
fàng.) ‖**This stream empties into a big lake.** jèy-tyáw-
'hé lyéw-dàw yí-ge-dà-'hú-li-tew chywù.

ENCLOSE. (*To shut up, shut in*) fù, 'fēng-dzày ...,
'jwāng-dzày .... ‖**Enclose this with the message.** bǎ
'jèy-ge gēn-'shìn °'jwāng-dzày 'yí-ge-shìn-'fēngr-li.
(°'fēng-dzày yí-ge-shìn-'fēngr-li.) *or* bǎ 'jèy-ge 'fù-
dzày 'shìn-fēngr-li. ‖**Enclosed is the sum you requested.** (*Literary*) swǒ-'shywū-jř-'kwǎn rú-'shù fù-
'shàng. *or* nǐ-yàw-de-'chyán jàw-'shùr 'fù-dzày jè-
fēng-'shìn-li.

(*To surround*) 'wéy(-chǐ-láy), 'chywān(-chǐ-láy).
‖**The property is enclosed by a fence.** jèy-kwày-'dì sž-
jēw-'wéy chywān-chǐ-láy-le. *or* jèy-kwày-'dì yěw (*or* ná,
or yùng) yí-dàw-'dwǎn-chyáng °'wéy-je. *or* °'chywān-
je. ‖**Our house is enclosed on four sides by tall buildings.** wǒm-de-fáng-dz 'sž-myàr jyàw 'gāw-léw ° wéy-
chǐ-láy-le. (°'chywān-chǐ-láy-le.)

ENCOURAGE. 'gǔ-lì; (*to encourage someone to do
something*) 'myǎn-lì; (*to encourage by praising*) 'kwā-
jyǎng. ‖**He encouraged us to go ahead.** tā 'gǔ-lì wǒ-
men 'gàn-shya-chywu. ‖**She should have discouraged
the child from saying that sort of thing; instead, she
encouraged him.** tā 'gēn-běn jyèw yīng-gāy 'gwǎn-
je-dyar háy-dz 'bú-jyàw. tā shwō 'nèy-yàngr-de-'hwà,
kě-shr (háy-dz 'shwō de-shŕ-hew) tā 'fǎn-dàw 'kwā-
jyǎng tā. ‖**So far he hasn't encouraged us to do it this
way.** jŕ-dàw shyàn-'dzày tā bìng 'méy-yew 'gǔ-lì
wǒm yùng 'jèy-ge-fāng-fa 'dzwò-shya-chywu. ‖**So far
he hasn't ventured to encourage us to do it this way.**
jŕ-dàw shyàn-'dzày tā 'bù-kěn 'gǔ-lì wǒm yùng 'jèy-
ge-fāng-fa 'dzwò-shya-chywu. *But* ‖**Do you feel more
encouraged now?** *meaning* **Do you feel better?** shīn-li
'hǎw-dyǎr-le-ma? *or meaning* **You're not hesitating
any more?** bú-nèm fā-'chù-le-ba? *or meaning* **You're
not depressed any more?** bú-nèm fā-'chéw-le-ba?

Not encourage (*discourage*) *is expressed as* **dislike**
bù-'shǐ-hwan *or* bú-'ywàn-yi; *or as* to discourage someone from doing something gwǎn ... bú-jyàw. ‖**We do
not encourage that conduct here.** *is expressed as* **We
don't like people to do that sort of thing here.** 'wǒm
jèr bù-'shǐ-hwan rén 'nèm-je dzwò 'nèy-yàngr-de-'shř.
‖**Don't encourage the child to say that!** *is expressed as*
**In managing the child, don't let him say that kind of
thing.** 'gwǎn-je-dyar háy-dz 'byé jyàw tā shwō 'nèy-
yàngr-de-'hwà.

END. 1. (*Of something long and narrow*) téwr. ‖**You
hold this end and I'll take the other.** nǐ 'ná-je 'jèy-
téwr; wǒ chywù ná 'nèy-téwr. ‖**Stretch it at both
ends.** 'dzwàn-je 'lyǎng-téwr yì-'chēn (*or* yí-'dèn).
‖**He searched from one end of the street to the other.**
tā tsúng jyē-'jèy-téwr 'jǎw-dàw 'nèy-téwr. ‖**Is this the
end of the street?** jyē dàw-'téwr-le-ma? *or* jèy shř
jyē-de-jìn-'téwr-ma? ‖**It's at the very end of the
street.** dzày jèy-tyáw-'jyē-de-jìn-'téwr-shang.

2. (*Of something pointed*) jyār. *See also* **POINT**
‖**Use the sharp end.** yùng nèy-ge-'jyār. *or* yùng 'jyān-
de-nèy-téwr. ‖**The crab caught the end of the dog's
tail.** 'páng-shye bǎ 'gěw-de-yǐ-ba-'jyār 'jyā-ju-le.

3. (*Of something rectangular or irregularly shaped*)
byān, byār, téwr. ‖**That end of the building is not finished.** fáng-dz-'nèy-byār (*or* -'nèy-téwr) méy wán-
'gūng-ne. ‖**This end of the island is rocky.** 'dǎw-de-
jèy-téwr (*or* -jèy-byār) dēw shř dà-'shŕ-tew. ‖**Put the
blue label on this end.** bǎ 'lán-jř-'tyáwr 'tyē-dzay
'jèy-byār (*or* 'jèy-téwr). ‖**Put blue labels on both ends.**
bǎ 'lán-jř-'tyáwr 'tyē-dzay 'lyǎng-téwr. *or* lán-jř-
'tyáwr 'lyǎng-téwr 'dēw tyē-shang. ‖**Stand it on this
end.** lì-chi-lay-de-shŕ-hew, jyàw 'jèy-téwr 'cháw-
'shyà. *or* °dzày 'dǐ-shya. *But* ‖**Stand it on end.** *is expressed as* **Stand it upright.** (bǎ jèy-ge) 'lì-chi-lay.

4. (*Result*) 'jyē-gwǒ, 'jyē-jywú. ‖**It's going to be
quite unpleasant in the end.** 'jyē-gwǒ (*or* 'jyē-jywú)
'jwěn bú-hwèy jyàw-rén gāw-'shìng-de. ‖**Who knows
what the end will be?** 'shéy jř-dàw °hwèy dàw 'dzěm-
me-ge-'jyē-gwǒ? (*or* -'jyē-jywú?) *or* °'jyē-gwǒ (*or*
'jyē-jywú) hwèy 'dzěm-yàng? ‖**This will end in disaster.** 'jyē-gwǒ (*or* 'jyē-jywú, *or* 'wán-de-shŕ-hew,
see below) 'jwěn yàw dzāw-'gāw. ‖**Their marriage
came to an unhappy end.** tām-de-'hwēn-yin 'jyē-jywú
hěn bù-'hǎw.

5. (*Conclusion, ending*) (mwò-)'lyǎwr; (*last part of
the time*) dzwèy-'hèw(-de-shŕ-hew); (*conclusion of a
story, etc.*) shēw-'wěy; (*ending time*) 'wán-de-shŕ-hew
or 'jyē-shù(-de-shr-hew); *in some combinations* -dì.
To come to an end wán, lyǎw, 'jyē-shù, 'lyǎw-jywú;
(*stop*) tíng; (*of work*) bú-'dzwò-shya-chywu; (*come
to a stop*) wéy-'jř; **bring to an end** dzwò-'wán *or other
words for* dzwò; dzwò-'chéng; (*conclude*) dzwò-'jyē.
‖**I read the book from beginning to end at one sitting.**
wǒ yí-'chyèr bǎ jèy-běn-'shū °tsúng-'téwr kàn-dàw
'lyǎwr. *or* °tsúng chǐ-'téwr kàn-dàw mwò-'lyǎwr. ‖**At
last the end is in sight.** 'kě kwày yàw 'wán-le. *or* 'kě
dàw-le °kwày-'wán-de-shŕ-hew. *or* °kwày-'jyē-shù-de-
shŕ-hew. ‖**Is there an end to it?** hày yěw-'wán-ma?
or háy yěw-'téwr-ma? *or* háy yěw ge-'wán-de-shŕ-
hew-ma? *etc.* ‖**I don't like the ending.** wǒ bù-'shǐ-
hwān °mwò-'lyǎwr-de-nèy-dwàr. *or* °nèy-ge-shēw-
'wěy. ‖**Will you stay with us to the end?** nǐ 'ywàn-yi
gēn wǒm yí-'kwàr gàn-dàw 'dǐ-ma? ‖**She slept to the
end of the show.** tā yì-'jŕ shwèy-dàw °'sàn-'chǎng-de-
shŕ-hew. *or* °dyàn-'yǐng yǎn-'wán-le. ‖**There is an end

to everything. 'shéme dēw yěw ge-'wán(-de-shŕ-hew). ‖I'll pay you at the end of the month. wó ywè-'dǐ hwán-nǐ. ‖I'll pay you at the end of one month. wǒ ywè-'téwr hwán-nǐ. ‖Before the end of this year the war will end. 'jīn-nyán-nyán-'dǐ (or 'jīn-nyán-nyán-'jūng) yǐ-'chyán 'jàn-shŕ jyèw 'wán-le. ‖He ended by saying, "This is the end." tā-dzwèy-'hèw (or tā-mwò-'lyǎwr)-shwō-de shŕ, "'wán-le." ‖His whole project ended in nothing. tā jéng-'gèr-de-'jì-hwà 'gǎw-le bàn-'tyān °'jyē-gwǒ 'yì-chǎng-'kūng? or °dàw-'téw-lay shŕ 'yì-chǎng-'kūng. or °dàw-'lyǎwr yě méy 'gǎw-chu shéme-lay. or °'méy shéme-'jyē-gwǒ jyèw 'wán-le. ‖The work will be ended next month. 'jèy-ge-shèr 'shyà-ywè °dzwò-'wán. or °'jyē-shù. or °dzwò-'chéng. ‖He ended the book with a proverb. tā dzày shū-de-mwò-'lyǎwr 'yùng-le jywù-'chéng-ywǔ dzwò-'jyē. or tā-de-shū 'mwo-yí-jywù-hwà 'yùng-le jywù-'chéng-ywǔ. ‖When does the performance end? 'shì shéme-shŕ-hèw (yǎn-)'wán? ‖There's no telling how this will end. '(shéy yě) bù-jŕ-daw 'jèy-ge (jyāng-lay) °dzěme 'jyē-shù. or °dzěme 'lyǎw-jywú. or °dàw-'lyǎwr dzěm-yàng. or °dàw-'téwr dzěm-yàng. or °'wán-de-shŕ-hew shŕ ge-'shém-yàng-dz. ‖The enterprise ended with his death. nèy-jyàn-shŕ tā yì-'sž jyèw °'wán-le. or °'lyǎw-le. or °'jyē-shù-le. or °méy-'jyē-je 'dzwò-shya-chywu. or °'tíng-le. ‖The history of ancient Europe ends with the fall of the Roman Empire. 'ēw-jēw 'shàng-gǔ-shŕ dàw 'lwó-mǎ-'dì-gwó-'myè-wáng wéy-'jŕ.

Rear end or end of the line jīn-'hèw-téw. ‖You've got to go to the end of the line. nǐ yàw shŕ jàn-'páy děy dàw jīn-'hèw-téw-chywu. ‖Look! He's standing at the end. 'kàn-na! tā dzày °mwò-'lyǎwr-nar-ne. or °'mwo-mwo-lā-'lyǎwr-ner-ne. or °jīn-'hèw-tew-ne.

6. (Objective). ‖To what end (for what) are you working so hard? 'dzěm mày 'lì-chi °wèy-le 'shém-me? or °wèy-de shŕ 'shém-me? ‖This is only a necessary means to the end. jèy 'bú-gwo shŕ wèy-'dá-daw-nèy-ge-'mù-dǐ-'děy-yùng-de-'shěw-dwàn.

7. (Referring to death). ‖His father came to an unhappy end. tā fù-chin chywù-'shŕ de-shŕ-hew hěn 'tsǎn. ‖He finally had to end his own life. mwò-'lyǎwr tā jyèw 'fěy dž-'shā bù-'kě-le. See also DEATH.

8. Combinations. Put an end to, make an end of (abolish) chywǔ-'shyǎw; (forbid) 'bù-shywǔ; (stop) 'jèn-yā-shya-chywu; (finish) 'lyǎw. ‖As soon as the new director came, he put an énd to that nonsense. shīn-jǔ-'rèn yí-dàw jyèw °bǎ 'nèy-ge chywǔ-'shyǎw-le. or °'bù-shywǔ nèm hú-'nàw-le. ‖He put an end to the riot. tā bǎ 'lwàn-dz gěy °jèn-yā-shya-chywu-le. or °'lyǎw-le. ‖He put an end to their fight by pointing out the cause of the misunderstanding. tā bǎ 'lyǎng-byār-'wù-hwey-de- ywán-gu jyě-'shŕ-le yí-shyàr °tām jyèw 'bù-dǎ-'jyà-le. or °jyèw gěy-tām 'hé-le.

Loose ends. ‖Matters are still at loose ends. shèr háy méy dzwò-'wán-ne. or shèr háy bù-néng 'jyē-shù-ne. or shèr háy méy 'wán-chywán 'lyǎw-ne. ‖A

few loose ends remain to be cleared up. háy 'shèng-shya 'dzá-shŕ děy °nùng-'wán-le. or °'chīng-li-chīng-li. ‖He always leaves some loose ends for me to clear up for him. tā dzwò-'shŕ lǎw 'shèng dyar-'dzá-shr (or dyar-'líng-tewr) 'bú-dzwò-'wán-le.

No end. ‖He'll give you no end of trouble. tā hwèy 'má-fan nǐ, 'má-fan °méy-'téwr-de. or °méy-'wán-de. ‖We had no end of trouble on the trip. wǒm yí-'lù °'jìng-chu 'shèr. or °'jìng-chu 'má-fan-'shèr. ‖We had no end of trouble with him on the trip. tā yí-'lù °jìng dǎw 'má-fan. or °jìng jyàw-rén fèy-'shŕ.

Make ends meet chū-rù-shyāng-'dǐ. ‖It'll be hard to make ends meet that way. 'nèm-je 'chū-rù-shyāng-'dǐ jyèw hěn 'nán-le.

Odds and ends (objects) 'líng-chī-bā-'swèy-de-dūng-shi; (matters) 'ling-chī-bā-'swèy-de-shŕ. ‖The room is full of odds and ends. wū-dz-li 'mǎn dēw shŕ 'líng-chī-bā-'swèy-de-dūng-ski. ‖We keep him to take care of the odds and ends. wǒm jyǎw-tā 'dzày-jèr hǎw 'jàw-gwǎn 'líng-chī-bā-'swèy-de-'shŕ.

‖This is the end! (the last straw) 'jè kě bù-'shíng-le!

ENEMY. (Personal). 'chéw-rén. ‖We are enemies. wǒm shŕ 'chéw-rén. or wǒm yèw-'chéw.

(In war; a single individual or the group) 'dí-rén. Enemy nation 'dí-gwó; enemy national or enemy alien 'dí-chyáw. ‖Where is the enemy? 'dí-rén dzày-'nǎr-ne? ‖Are there any enemy nationals here? jèr yěw 'dí-chyáw (or 'dí-gwo-de-rén, or 'dí-gwó-'chyáw-mín)-ma?

ENERGY. (Potential power, especially mental) 'jīng-shen; (a capacity for work) 'gàn-jyèr. ‖He is a man of energy. or He is full of energy. tā-'jèy-ge-rén hěn °yěw 'jīng-shen. or °yěw ge-'gàn-jyèr.

(Expended power) 'jīng-shen; (mind and strength) 'jīng-lì; (strength) jyèr or jìn; (strength) 'lì-chi. ‖A lot of energy will be needed in this work. jèy-ge-'gūng-dzwò hěn fèy °'jīng-shen. or °'jīng-lì. or °'jyèr. or °'jìn. or °'lì-chi. ‖His energy is waning gradually. tā-'jīng-shen (or tā-'jīng-lì, or tā-'lì-chi) jyàn-'jyàn-de 'shwāy-shya-chywu-le. ‖His energy seems to be unlimited. tā-de-'jīng-shen (or tā-de-'jīng-lì, or tā-de-'lì-chi) hǎw shyàng yùng-bu-'wán shŕ-de.

ENGINE. (Motor; general term for any power-driven machine; automobile motor) 'jī-chì; (technical term; especially for an airplane motor) 'fā-dùng-'jī; (rare, from English engine) 'yǐn-jīng. Diesel engine 'cháy-yéw-fā-dùng-'jī. ‖One engine on the airplane stopped. fēy-'jī-de-'yí-ge-fā-dùng-jī 'tíng-le. ‖My engine needs repairing. wǒ-de-'jī-chì děy °'shyēw-li-le. or °'shēw-shr-shēw-shr-le. ‖Can someone fix an automobile engine? shéy hwèy 'shyēw-li chì-chē-'jī-chi?

(Locomotive) chē-'téw, 'jī-chē. ‖The train has two engines. jèy-lyè-'chē yěw 'lyǎng-ge °chē-'téw. or °'jī-chē. ‖Does it have a steam or electric engine? nèy-lyè-'chē-de-chē-'téw (or -de-'jī-chē) 'shŕ yùng 'jēng-chì háy-shr yùng-'dyàn?

ENGINEER. (*One whose profession is engineering*) gūng-chéng-'shř. **Electrical engineer** 'dyàn-chì-gūng-chéng-'shř; **mechanical engineer** 'jī-shyè-gūng-chéng-'shř; **civil engineer** 'tǔ-mù-gūng-chéng-'shř; **hydraulic engineer** 'shwěy-lì-gūng-chéng-'shř; **aeronautical engineer** 'fēy-jī(-jř-'dzàw)-gūng-chéng-'shř. ‖**What kind of an engineer are you?** nǐ shř 'nǎ-yì-kē (*or* -mén)-dè-'gūng-chéng-'shř?

(*In government employ*) 'jì-shř. **Chief engineer** jì-'jèng.

(*In army service; individual or group*) 'gūng-bīng. **A regiment of engineers.** yì-twán-'gūng-bīng. ‖**I am a Pfc., 3rd Co. Engrs.** wǒ shř 'gūng-bīng-dì-'sān-lyán-de-'yī-děng-bīng. *or* wǒ shř 'gūng-sān-lyán-de-'yī-děng-bīng. ‖**I'm Major Swēn, 17th Engrs.** wǒ shř 'gūng-bīng-shŕ-'chī-twán-de-'swēn-shàw-shyàw. ‖**I am a captain in the Engineers, U. S. Army.** wǒ shř 'měy-gwo-'lù-jywūn-'gūng-bīng-shàng-'wèy.

(*Of a train*) kāy-'chē-de, sž-'jī. ‖**The engineer brought the train to a stop.** nèy-ge-kāy-'chē-de (*or* nèy-ge-sž-'jī) bǎ-chē 'tíng-jù-le.

Engineering (*as a subject of study*) 'gūng-kē. ‖**I was in the engineering department in the military academy.** wǒ-dzày-'jywūn-gwān-shywé-'shyàw-nyàn-de shř 'gūng-kē.

To engineer. ‖**He engineered the building from beginning to end.** nèy-ge-'léw (tsúng shè-'jì dàw-'lyǎwr) chywán shř tā-'yì-shǒw-'jyàn-dzàw-de. ‖**He engineered his scheme successfully through a good deal of opposition.** tā-de-'jì-hwà yěw hěn-'dwō-rén 'fǎn-dwèy, kě-shr tā gěy 'shū-tūng-de tūng-'gwò-le. ‖**Who engineered the robbery?** jèy-ge-'chyǎng-àn °shř 'shéy-chū-de-'jú-yì? *or* °shéy shř 'jǔ-méw? *or* °shř shéy-'jǔ-dùng-de? *or* °shř shéy-jǔ-'shř-de? *or* °shř shéy-'jì-hwa-de? ‖**He engineered the scheme very well.** tā 'jì-hwà-de hěn 'hǎw. ‖**He engineered** (*planned*) **the whole thing.** 'dēw shř 'tā-chū-de-'jú-yì. *or* 'dēw shř 'tā-'jì-hwà-de.

ENGLISH. (*Of England*) 'yīng-gwo(-de). **English** (*made*) 'yīng-gwo-dzwò-de *or* 'yīng-gwo-dzàw-de. ‖**Do you like English cigarettes?** nǐ 'shǐ-hwān 'yīng-gwo-'jř-yān-ma? ‖**She likes English china.** tā 'shǐ-hwān 'yīng-gwo(-dzwò, *or* -dzàw)-de-'tsź-chì. ‖**Is this of English make?** jèy shř 'yīng-gwo-dzwò-de-ma? *or* jèy shř 'yīng-gwo-dzàw-de-ma? ‖**This is English merchandise.** jèy shř 'yīng-gwo-hwò. ‖**He's English.** *or* **He's an Englishman.** tā shř 'yīng-gwo-rén. ‖**He married an Englishwoman.** tā-'chywǔ-de shř 'yīng-gwo-tày-tay. (*or* 'yīng-gwo-rén.) ‖**His actions are English, but he talks like a German.** tā 'jywǔ-dùng shyàng 'yīng-gwo-rén, kě-shr shwō-'hwà shyàng 'dé-gwo-rén. ‖**He speaks (English) with an English (British) accent.** tā-shwō-de-'yīng-wén dày 'yīng-gwo-'kěw-yīn (*or* 'yīng-gwo-'dyàwr). ‖**He's English all over.** tā jěng-'gèr-de yīng-gwo-'pày-téwr. ‖**He came of pure**

English stock. tā-de-'shywè-tǔng shř 'chwén-yīng-gwo-'jǔng-de. *or* tā-de-'dzǔ-shyān 'dēw shř 'yīng-gwo-rén.

(*The English language*) 'yīng-wén, 'yīng-gwo-hwà. ‖**Do you speak English?** nǐ hwèy shwō 'yīng-wén-ma? *or* nǐ 'hwèy-bú-hwèy shwō 'yīng-gwo-hwà? ‖**He is in the English Department.** tā dzày 'yīng-wén-shì. ‖**He can read and write English.** tā 'yng-wén hwèy 'shwō hwèy 'shyě. ‖**English is not difficult.** 'yīng-wén bù-nán. ‖**His English is excellent.** tā-'yīng-wén °'chéng-dù hěn 'shēn. *or* °hǎw-'jí-le.

ENJOY. *In general, an action is described and followed by* yěw 'yì-sz, yěw 'chywù-wèy, yěw-'chywùr; *sometimes* hěn 'hǎw. ‖**Are you enjoying yourself?** 'wár-ne háy yěw °'yì-sz-ma? *or* °'chywù-wèy-ma? *or* °-'chywùr-ma? ‖**How do you enjoy staying home alone every evening?** 'tyān-tyar wǎn-shang 'dž-ji dzày-'jyā dāy-je yěw °'yī-sz-ma? *or* °'chywù-wèy-ma? *or* °-'chywùr-ma? ‖**I enjoyed myself very much.** wǒ-wár-de 'hěn hǎw. *or simply* 'hěn hǎw, 'hěn hǎw. ‖**Did you enjoy his speech?** tā-'jyǎng-de nǐ 'tīng-je yěw 'yì-sz (*or* 'chywù-wèy, *or* -'chywùr)-ma? ‖**I didn't enjoy it at all.** yì-'dyǎr-yì-sz (*or* yì-'dyǎr-chywù-wèy *or* yì-'dyǎr-chywùr) yě méy-'yěw. ‖**How do you manage to enjoy yourself** (*literally* **how do you entertain yourself**) **staying home alone every evening?** 'tyān-tyar wǎn-shang 'dž-jī dzày-'jyā dāy-je °dzwò shém-'shyāw-chyǎn? *or* °dēw ná shém-jyě-mèr?

To enjoy life shyǎng-'lè, shyǎng-'fú. ‖**He knows how to enjoy life.** tā hwèy shyǎng-'lè. *or* tā hwèy shyǎng-'fú.

To enjoy *doing something* (*like to*) ày, hǎw, 'shǐ-hwān. ‖**He enjoys eating good food.** tā (hěn) 'ày (*or* 'hàw, *or* 'shǐ-hwān) chř (hǎw-de). ‖**He enjoys kidding people.** tā 'ày (*etc.*) gēn-rén 'dèw-je wár.

Enjoy good health *is expressed as* **health is good.** ‖**He enjoys good health as a rule.** tā-'shēn-ti yí-'shyàng hěn 'hǎw.

In polite formulas such as **I hope you enjoyed yourself** *the Chinese say nothing of the sort, but rather apologize for being bad hosts.* ‖**I hope you enjoyed the party** (*or the dinner, etc.*), *is expressed as* **We treated you half-heartedly.** 'dày-màn-de 'hěn. ‖**I hope you enjoyed the dinner.** *is expressed as* **I'm sorry; there was not enough prepared** (*or nothing fit to eat*). dwèy-bu-'jù, 'jīn-tyān méy °'dzěme-'ywù-bey. *or* °shém-m. kě-'chř-de. *or as* **I'm sorry; you didn't eat well.** dwèy-bu-'jù, nín dēw 'méy-chř 'hǎw-ba. ‖**I hope you enjoyed the party.** *is expressed as* **I'm sorry; you didn't have a good time.** dwèy-bu-'jù, nín dēw 'méy-wár 'hǎw-ba. *The proper answer to these statements,* **I enjoyed myself very much,** *would be* hǎw 'shwō, hǎw 'shwō. *or* 'hěn hǎw, hěn hǎw. *or* (*If a party*) wǒ-wár-de 'hěn hǎw. *or* yěw 'yì-sz. *or* yěw 'chywù-wèy. *or* yěw-'chywùr. *or* (*In any situation*) byé 'kè-chi.

ENOUGH. (*Sufficient*) gèw; (*only of eating; one's fill*) -băw. ‖Do you have enough money? nǐ-'chyán 'gèw-ma? *or* nǐ-'chyán 'gèw-bu-gèw? ‖Is that enough (*of anything*)? 'gèw-le-ma? ‖That's enough! 'gèw-le. *or meaning* Don't say any more. byé 'pín-le. *or* byé 'shwō-le. ‖Have you had enough? 'gèw-le-ma? *or* (*Of a beating*) nǐ 'fú-bù-fú? *or* (*Of exertion, bad luck, etc.*) nǐ shèw-'gèw-le-ma? ‖I've had enough (*food*). wǒ chr̄-'băw-le. *or* wǒ chr̄-le ge-'jyéw-dzú-fàn-'băw.

(*Rather*) hěn. ‖He seemed glad enough to do it. tā (hǎw-shyàng) 'hěn gāw-shing 'dzwò shr̀-de. ‖He's willing enough. tā hěn 'ywàn-yì.

ENTER. (*Come, or go, into a place*) jìn, 'jìn-dàw . . . lǐ; *either expression may be followed by* láy *or* chywù, *depending on whether the motion is toward or away from the speaker; or any of these may be preceded by a verb specifying the type of action, whether walking, running, driving, etc., in which case the combination means* enter by X *or* X in; *e.g.*, 'dzěw-jìn, enter by walking *or* walk in. ‖We might as well enter now. dzám 'bù-fáng 'shyàn-dzày 'jìn-chywù-ba. ‖The boat is entering the harbor. chwán 'jèng-dzày jìn °hǎy-'kěw(-lay *or* -chywu). *or* °-'gǎng (. . .). *or* °-'jyàng (. . .). ‖You enter here. dzày-'jèr jìn(-lay *or* -chywu). ‖My orders from the chief are that no one is allowed to enter this room unescorted. 'shàng-tew yěw-'hwà, 'méy-rén-gēn-je 'shéy yě bù-néng jìn 'jèy-jyàn-'wū-dz. ‖He entered on foot. tā 'dzěw-jìn-láy-de. ‖When you enter a cave, it takes a little while before you can see. jìn-'dùng (*or* jìn-dáw 'dùng-li) yǐ-'hèw děy 'dāy-hwěr tsáy 'kàn-de-jyàn.

(*To enter.* An *organization*) jìn; (*literary, but commonly used in certain combinations*) rù; (*go to, of a school*) shàng. ‖When did you enter the army? nǐ 'shéme-shr̄-hew jìn-de (*or* rù-de) jywūn-'dwèy? ‖Do you plan to enter a university? nǐ 'yàw (*or* 'dǎ-swàn) jìn (*or* rù, *or* shàng) dà-'shywé-ma?

(*To list or write in*) 'shyě-jìn; (*fill in*) 'tyán-jìn; (*report in*) 'bàw-jìn. ‖Your name was entered yesterday. nǐ-de-'míng-dz shr̀ 'dzwór shyě- (*or* tyán-, *or* bàw-)jìn-chywu-de.

(*To register*) bàw-'míng. ‖Who is entered in the race? nèy-ge-sày-'pǎw 'shéy bàw-'míng-le? ‖He entered his name as a candidate. tā bàw-le 'míng-le, yàw dzwò 'hèw-shywǎn-rén.

(*Join*) 'tsān-jyā, 'jyā-rù. ‖He entered the discussion without introduction. yě méy-rén 'jyè-shàw tā 'dz̀-jǐ jyèw 'tsān-jyā (*or* 'jyā-rù) 'tǎw-lwèn-le.

ENTERTAINMENT. (*Amusement in the abstract*) 'ywú-lè, ké-'wár-de-dì-fang, kě-'shyāw-chyǎn-de-dì-fang. *The latter two mean* place for entertainment, *but all correspond to English* entertainment *in contrast to* an entertainment, the entertainment, entertainments, *etc., for which see below.* ‖Is there any enter-

tainment in this town? chéng-'lǐ-tew yěw shéme-°'ywú-lè-ma? *or* °kě-'wár-de-dì-fang-ma? *or* °kě-'shyāw-chyǎn-de-dì-fang-ma?

An entertainment (*show put on for amusement; amateur performances*) 'yéw-yì-hwèy. ‖When does the entertainment begin? 'yéw-yì-hwèy 'shéme-shr̄-hew chǐ-'téwr? ‖Is the entertainment good? nèy-ge-'yéw-yì-hwèy (*or* (*If the person questioned is a performer*) nèy-ge-'yéw-yì-hwèy 'wár-de *or* (*If the person questioned has seen it*) nèy-ge-'yéw-yì-hwèy 'kàn-de) °'hǎw-ma? *or* °yěw 'yì-sz-ma?

ENTIRE (ENTIRELY). (*Whole, as a unit*) jěng-'gèr-de . . . dēw (*or* chywán), *sometimes* yī . . . dēw (*or* chywán). ‖His entire attitude is wrong. *or* His attitude is entirely wrong. tā jěng-'gèr-de-'kàn-fa dēw 'tswò-le. ‖He spent his entire fortune on her. tā bǎ-tā jěng-'gèr-de-'jyā-chǎn 'chywán hwā-dzay 'tā shēn-shang-le. ‖This requires your entire attention. jèy-ge nǐ děy bǎ jěng-'gèr-de-'shīn dēw 'yùng-shang. *or* jèy-ge nǐ děy 'chywán-shén-'gwàn-jù. ‖The entire trip was pleasant. yí-'lù dēw jyàw-rén 'tùng-kway. ‖His entire family came. tā-'chywán-jyā (*or* tā-'yì-jyā) dēw láy-le.

(*Pertaining to everything, distributively*) 'swǒ-yěw-de; *or a sentence with* altogether yǐ-'gùng. ‖Is this the entire cost? (*the cost of everything*). yí-'gùng dzèm-me-shyē-'chyán-ma? *or* 'swǒ-yěw-de-'fèy-yùng dēw dzày-'nèy-ma?

Entirely (*completely*) 'wán-chywán. ‖It's entirely up to you. 'wán-chywán děy nǐ 'dz̀-jǐ dǎ 'jú-yi. ‖He's entirely reliable. tā 'wán-chywán kě-'kàw.

ENTRANCE. (*Place to enter*) 'rù-kěw, mén; *or a sentence including an expression meaning* to enter. *See* **ENTER.** ‖Where is the entrance? 'rù-kěw dzày 'shéme-dì-fang? *or* 'mén dzày-'nǎr? *or* tsúng-'nǎr jìn-chywu? ‖Is the entrance closed? 'rù-kěw (*or* 'mén) 'gwān-le-ma?

(*Act of entering*). *See also* **ENTER.** ‖Is there an entrance fee? 'jìn-chywu yàw-'chyán-ma? *or* jìn-chywu yàw mǎy-'pyàw-ma? *or* yàw rù-'chǎng-fèy-ma? ‖Her sudden entrance took us by surprise. tā 'hū-rán-jyān yí 'jìn-lay, wǒ-men 'chywán shyà-le yí-'tyàw. ‖What an entrance she staged! tā-nèy-yí-'jìn-lay-de-'jyèr jēn jyàw ge-'dzú-le.

Entrance *onto the stage* chū-'chǎng. ‖Everyone applauded the actor's entrance. nèy-ge-'yǎn-ywán chū-'chǎng de-shr̄-hew °rén chywán gǔ-'jǎng. *or* °'dà-jyā-hwǒr 'chywán-dēw pāy-'shěwr.

ENVELOPE. shìn-'fēngr. ‖This envelope has the wrong address. jèy-ge-shìn-'fēngr-shang-shyě-de-dì-'myéngr (*or* -dì-'jř) 'tswò-le. ‖I need a larger envelope for this letter. 'jèy-fēng-shìn wǒ děy yùng yí-ge-'dà-dyǎr-de-shìn-'fēngr.

EQUAL. (*In mathematics and some other circumstances*) děng-. To be equal shyāng-'děng; to equal 'děng-ywú. ‖Two times two equals four. 'èr chéng-'èr děng-ywú 'sz̀. or *expressed as* Two times two amounts to four. 'èr chéng-'èr dé-'sz̀. ‖This is an "equals" sign: =. jèy shr̀ 'děng-hàwr; =. ‖This angle equals that angle. 'jèy-ge-jyǎw 'děng-ywú 'nèy-ge-jyǎw. ‖These two angles are equal. jèy-'lyǎng-ge-jyǎw shyāng-'děng. ‖They are of equal (*official*) rank. tām 'gwān-jyē shyāng-'děng. ‖A lieutenant in the navy is equal in rank to a captain in the army. 'hǎy-jywun-'shàng-wèy gēn 'lù-jywun-'shàng-wèy gwān-jyē shyāng-'děng.

In general, in comparing two or more things, use the same yí-'yàng; *fair and equal* píng-('děng); *other expressions meaning* same; *other roundabout expressions; sometimes one of the expressions listed above.* ‖We traveled at equal speeds. wǒ-men-'dzěw-de °yì-'byār-kwày. or °yì-'bān-kwày. or °yí-'yàng-kwày. ‖Adjust the three wheels to rotate at equal speeds. jyàw jèy-'sān-ge-'lwén-dz jwàn-de °yì-'bān-kway. or °yí-'yàng-kwày. or °yì-'byār-kwày. (byār *is used only with* kwày.) or *in technical language* jèy-'sān-ge-'lwén-dz yàw 'tyáw-jěng-dàw 'shywán-jwàn-de-'sú-dù shyāng-'děng. ‖These two bottles are equal in size or are equally large. jèy-'lyǎng-ge-'píng-dz °yì-'bān-da. or °yì-'bār-da. or °yí-'yàng-da. ‖Divide this into two equal parts. bǎ jèy-ge °'fēn-chéng yí-'yàng-de-'lyǎng-fèr. or °'fēn-chéng shyāng-'děng-de-'lyǎng-fèr. or °'fēn-chéng lyǎng-'děng-fèn. or *expressed as* Divide it into halves. °'fēn-chéng yí-'bàr yí-'bàr. or *expressed as* Divide it equally. °'píng-fēn-le. or *expressed as* Divide it into matching parts. 'dwèy-'bàr fēn-le. ‖Divide this into three equal parts. bǎ jèy-ge 'fēn-chéng °'yí-'yàng-de-'sān-fèr. or °'shyāng-'děng-de-'sān-fèr. ‖All men should have equal rights. 'swǒ-yěw-de-rén dēw 'yīng-gāy yěw °'yí-'yàng-de-'chywán-lì. or °'píng-'děng-de-'chywán-lì.

To equal (*to correspond to in other terms or in another system*) shr̀. ‖How much does that equal in American money? 'nèy-ge hé (or 'hé-chéng, or 'swàn-chéng) 'měy-gwo-chyán shr̀ 'dwō-shǎw?

To equal (*come up to*) *usually* 'gǎn-shang. ‖We'd been behind in the game, but we equalled their score. bǐ-'sày-de-shf-hew 'shyàn-shr tā-men-de-'fēn-shùr 'dwō; 'méy-dwō-dà-'hwěr °wǒ-men jyèw 'gǎn-shang-le. or *meaning* overtook °wǒ-men jyèw 'jwēy-shang-le. or *meaning* the two sides become even °lyǎng-byar jyèw 'píng-le. ‖His record will be hard to equal. tā-de-'jì-lù bù-rúng-yì 'gǎn-shang. ‖It will be hard to find his equal. gēn-'tā-yí-'yàng-de-rén (or shyàng-'tā-nèy-yàngr-de-rén) 'bù-hǎw jǎw. or 'hěn-nán jǎw-jáw 'gǎn-de-shang-'tā-de-rén.

An equal; to be one's equal. *In the negative, Chinese usually uses* superior *instead of* equal; *in most cases verbs are used. e.g.,* compare with bǐ; match dwèy, pèy. ‖He doesn't think of anyone here as his equal. tā jywé-je 'jèr °shéy yě 'bǐ-tā bú-'shàng. or °shéy yě 'bǐ-tā bǐ-bú-'shàng. or °shéy yě 'bù-néng gēn-tā 'bǐ. or °'méy-rén bǐ-de-'shàng tā. or (*Of physical strength*)

°'shéy dēw 'bú-shr tā-de-'gèr. or (*Of social or other rank*) °'shéy dēw bǐ tā-'dī. ‖His mother thinks he ought to marry his equal. tā-'mǔ-chin jywé-je tā gāy 'chywǔ ge-'mén-dāng-hù-'dwèy-de. ‖Do you regard her as his equal? nǐ jywé-je tā 'pèy-de-'shàng tā-ma?

Equal to (*able to bear*) 'shèw-de-'lyǎw. ‖I don't feel equal to the trip. dzěw 'jèy-yí-tàng wǒ pà (wǒ) 'shèw-bu-'lyǎw.

Equal to (*qualified for, able to do*). ‖Do you think he is equal to such a job? nǐ jywé-je tā 'pèy-dzwò (or 'dzwò-de-lyǎw, or 'dāng-de-chǐ, or 'dān-de-chǐ) 'jèn-yàng-de-'shr̀-ma?

ERROR. tswòr; or *expressed in the verb* tswò make a mistake, or bú-'dwèy. ‖Pardon me; my error. dwèy-bu-'jù (or dwèy-bu-'chǐ), °'wǒ tswò-le. or 'shr̀ 'wǒ-de-tswèr. ‖Look for errors and check them with a red pencil. bǎ-'tswèr (or bǎ 'tswò-de-dì-fang, or bǎ bú-'dwèy-de-dì-fang) 'jǎw-chu-laỳ, yùng 'húng-chyān-bǐ yì-'gēw. ‖Please try not to make any errors. láw-'jyà, lyéw dyǎr-'shén, byé chū-'tswèr. ‖Some errors are unpardonable. 'yěw-de-tswèr 'bù-néng 'ráw-shù. ‖There seems to be an error in the bill. jèy-ge-'jàng-'dār-shang hǎw shyàng °yěw ge-'tswèr. or °yěw dyǎr-'tswèr. or °'tswò-le. or °'bú-dà 'dwèy.

ESCAPE. *The noun is usually expressed verbally. But* ‖We had a narrow escape. *is expressed as* We almost had it. wǒ-men chà-'dyǎr. or *as* We were in great danger. wǒm 'shyǎn-de 'hěn.

To escape. (*To get away* (*from*) *physically, escape in flight*) táw, 'táw-pǎw, 'táw-dzěw, 'táw-twō, 'táw-kāy, *also* (*literary*) 'táw-bì; (*to get away from, hide from*) 'dwǒ-kāy, 'dwǒ-bì; (*to run away from*) 'pǎw-kāy, 'pǎw-dzěw; (*to get away*) twō, 'twō-kāy; (*to escape from danger*) twō-'shyǎn; (*to leave*) 'twō-lí; (*in certain rather literary combinations*) bì; (*to escape to asylum*) bì-'shyǎn; (*to escape as a refugee*) bì-'nàn. ‖Where can we escape to? 'táw-dàw 'nǎr chýwù-ne? ‖Is there any way to escape from the prison? tsúng 'jyān-ywù-li yěw fár °'táw-ma? (°'táw-pǎw-ma?, °'táw-chū-chywu-ma?) ‖There is no way to escape bombings. 'hūng-jà 'méy-fǎr °'dwǒ-bì (°'dwǒ-kāy, °'táw-kāy, °'pǎw-kāy). ‖Did anyone escape? yěw °'táw-le-de-ma? (°'pǎw-le-de-ma?, °'táw-'pǎw-le-de-ma?, °'táw-'dzěw-le-de-ma?) ‖Where can we escape the crowds? *is expressed as* Where shall we go to avoid the crowds? dzám dàw-'nǎr °'dwǒ-kāy (or °'dwǒ-dwo) jè-yì-'chywún-yì-chywún-de-rén-ne? or, *if the situation seems hopeless, as* With all these crowds, where can one escape? jè-yì-chywún-yì-chywún-de-rén 'nǎr dwǒ-de-'kāy-ya? ‖He escaped with his life. tā swàn 'táw-le 'mìng-le. ‖You can't escape the consequences. nǐ 'twō-bu-kāy 'gwān-shi. or nǐ 'twō-lí-bù-lyǎw 'gwān-shi. ‖Did the criminal (make good his) escape? nèy-ge-'fàn-rén °'pǎw-le-ma? (°'táw-le-ma?)

(To get away mentally). *See also* **FORGET**. ‖He **took to drinking for escape.** tā wèy-le jyě-'mèr hē-chi 'jy̆ew láy-le. ‖He **went to live in the mountains to escape from worldly worries.** tā dàw 'shān-shang chywù 'jù hăw °'táw-kay (or °'dwŏ-kay, °'twō-lí) 'chén-shr̀-de-'fán-năw. ‖Her **face is familiar but her name escapes me.** *is expressed as* I recognize her face as familiar, but I can't think of her name. wŏ 'kàn tā hĕn myàn-'shú, kĕ-shr̀ 'shyăng-bù-chĭ tā-'míng-dz-lay.

ESPECIALLY. *(Unusually or most of all)* 'yéw-chí (-shr̀); tè-'byé(-shr̀), dzwèy. dzwèy *is limited in use, not occurring before* shr̀. ‖I **want THIS one especially.** wŏ 'yéw-chí-shr̀ (or tè-'byé, or dzwèy) shyăng-yàw 'jèy-ge. ‖Everybody **must give, especially you.** 'shéy dēw dĕy 'gĕy, tè-'byé-shr̀ (or 'yéw-chí-shr̀) 'nĭ. ‖It **is this child especially who needs correction.** 'jèy-ge-háy-dz 'dzwèy (or 'yéw-chí-shr̀, or tè-'byé) dĕy 'gwăn. ‖That **is an especially unpardonable mistake.** tè-'byé-shr (or 'yéw-chí-shr) 'nèy-ge-tswòr shr̀ bù-néng-'ráw-shù-de. or 'nèy-ge-tswòr shr̀ 'dzwèy-bù-néng-'ráw-shù-de. ‖Cantonese **food is especially good.** 'gwăng-dūng-'fàn 'yéw-chí (or tè-'byé, or dzwèy) 'hăw chŕ.

(Particularly) tè-'byé. ‖This **dish is made especially for you.** 'jèy-dyér-tsày shr̀ tè-'byé-wèy-'nĭ-dzwò-de. ‖This **was arranged especially for you.** jèy-ge shr̀ tè-'byé-wèy-'nĭ-ywù-bey-de.

ESTABLISH. Establish *an organization* shè, 'shè-lì, 'chéng-lì; *(especially of a government or church)* 'jyàn-shè; *(especially of a business, school, or other organization)* 'kāy-bàn; *(to found; not used of a branch)* 'chwàng-bàn. ‖A **new government was then established.** yĭ-'hèw jyèw 'shè-le (or 'shè-lì-le, or 'chéng-lì-le, or 'jyàn-shè-le) yí-ge-'shīn-jèng-'fŭ. ‖The **new government was established in 1946.** 'shīn-jèng-'fŭ shr̀ 'yī-jyĕw-sz̀-'lyèw-nyán-°'shè-de. or °'shè-lì-de. or °'chéng-lì-de. or °'jyàn-shè-de. ‖The **new government was established at the old capital.** 'shīn-jèng-'fŭ 'shè-dzày 'jyèw-dū. or dzày 'jyèw-dū 'shè-lì-le (or 'chéng-lì-le, or 'jyàn-shè-le) 'shīn-jèng-'fŭ. ‖Our **business was established forty years ago.** bĕn-'hàw shr̀ 'sz̀-shr-nyán-'chyán-°'shè-lì-de. or °'chéng-lì-de. or °'kāy-bàn-de. or °'chwàng-bàn-de. ‖We **also established three branches in this town.** wŏm yèw dzày bĕn-'shr̀ 'shè-le (or 'shè-lì-le, or 'chéng-lì-le, or 'kāy-bàn-le) 'sān-ge-'fēn-hàw.

Establish *an account* lì 'jé-dz; *(colloquial, only for an account in a bank)* kāy 'hù-téw(r). ‖I **should like to establish an account.** wŏ yàw lì yí-ge-'jé-dz. or *(if a banking account)* wŏ yàw kāy yí-ge-'hù-téwr.

Establish *a reputation (especially in government or military exploits)* 'lì-shya 'gūng-míng, 'lì-shya 'míng-shēng, chéng-'míng, bă 'shēng-míng lì-'dìng; **be established** *(as to reputation)* 'chéng-le. ‖You **might be able to establish a reputation for yourself.** nĭ 'yĕ-shywŭ néng °'lì-shya dyăr-'gūng-míng. or °'chéng ge-'míng.

‖Establish **a reputation** *(or a name)* **first, and then carry out your plans.** 'shyān bă 'shēng-míng lì-'dìng-le (or 'shyān 'lì-shya ge-'míng-shēng), dzày jàw-je nĭ-de-'jì-hwà chywù 'bàn. ‖He's **established, after that write-up.** tā swàn 'chéng-le, 'hăw-jyā-hwo nèm 'pĕng-tā.

Establish *a brand of merchandise* 'chwàng(-chu-chywu). ‖That **brand is established.** nèy-ge-'păy-dz 'chwàng-chu-chywu-le.

Establish *residence* 'jù-shya-lay. ‖Are **you comfortably established here?** nĭ dzày-jèr 'jù-shya-lay jywé-je 'shū-fu-ma?

Establish *a fact or claim (prove)* jèng-'míng, jèng-'shŕ. ‖His **presence was established by several witnesses.** tā 'dāng-shŕ dzày-'chăng, yĭ-jīng yĕw 'hăw-jĭ-ge-'jèng-rén °jèng-'míng-le. or °jèng-'shŕ-le. ‖Can **you establish your claim?** nĭ-de-'hwà néng yĕw fá-dz °jèng-'míng-ma? or °jèng-'shŕ-ma?

EVEN. 1. *(Level)* píng; *(smooth and level)* 'lyēw-píng. Be **even with** píng or lyēw *in some combinations;* gēn ... píng; gēn ... chí. ‖Is **the surface even?** 'myàr-shang 'píng-ma? ‖The **ice froze even(ly).** bīng 'dùng-de hĕn 'píng. or bīng 'dùng-de 'jyēw-píng. ‖The **water in the river is nearly even with the top of the dikes.** hé-li-de-'shwĕy °gēn 'àn-shang-de-dī kwày 'píng-le. or °kwày píng-'tsáw-le. ‖Fill **it with water almost even with the rim.** dàw-de-'shwĕy chà-bu-dwō °'lyēw-byàr-lyēw-yàr-de. or °gēn-'kĕwr 'píng-je. or °gēn-'kĕwr 'chí-je.

(Constant; of motion) ywún. At **an even speed** *or* **steadily** *(of vehicles, etc.)* ('píng-)wĕn. ‖The **train traveled at an even speed.** hwŏ-'chē-dzĕw-de-°'kwày-màn hĕn 'ywún. or °hĕn 'wĕn. or °hĕn 'píng-wĕn. ‖The **wheel turned at an even speed.** lwén-dz-'jwàn-de °-'kwày-màn hĕn 'ywún. or °hĕn 'wĕn. or °hĕn 'píng-wĕn. ‖His **heartbeat is even.** tā-shīn-'tyàw-de hĕn °'ywún. or °'wĕn or °'píng-wĕn.

(Impartial; of distribution) 'píng-jywūn, jywūn-ywún. ‖There **was an even distribution of food.** 'lyáng-shŕ-'fēn-pèy-de ˉn °'píng-jywūn. or °'jywūn-ywún.

(Calm; of disposition) 'hé-píng, 'wĕn-jùng. ‖He **has an even disposition** *(or temper)*. tā hĕn 'hé-píng. or tā hĕn 'wĕn-jùng. or tā-de-'pí-chì (or tā-de-'shìng-dz, or tā-de-'shìng-ching) hĕn 'hé-píng (or 'wĕn-jùng).

(Equal, well-balanced) yí-'yàng, chí, jywūn. ‖The **two teams were almost even in strength.** jèy-'lyăng-dwèy-de-'lì-lyàng °'chà-bu-dwō. or °'chà-bu-dwō yí-'yàng. or *(Not one up, one down)* °'bù-shyàng shàng-'shyà or °hĕn 'chí. or jèy-'lyăng-dwèy 'chà-bu-dwō 'shr̀-jywūr-lì-'dí.

(Neither in debt to the other). ‖This **check makes us even.** 'fù-le jèy-jāng-'jŕ-pyàw °jyèw shéy yĕ bù-'gāy-shéy-le. or °'dzám jyèw chīng-'jàng-le. or °jyèw 'lyăng bù-'gāy-le.

(Exact; of a number) jĕng or 'gāng-hăw *before a verb*. ‖When **the last couple arrived, we had an even**

dozen. 'nèy-lyǎng-ge-rén 'dàw-le yī-'hèw, wǒ-men jyèw 'jěng (or 'gāng-hǎw) yěw shŕ-'èr-ge-rén.

(*Divisible by two*) shwāng; *but in mathematics* 'ěw. ‖Does it make any difference whether this game is played by an odd or even number of people? wár-'jèy-ge-de 'rén-shù 'dān-shùr 'shwāng-shùr 'dēw shíng-ma? ‖Four is an even number. 'sż shŕ 'ěw-shù. *or* 'sż shŕ 'shwāng-shù.

2. To even (*make equal*). (*General*) nèng-'chí, nùng-'chí; (*with scissors*) jyǎn-'chí; (*with knife*) lá-'chí. *Similar resultative compounds can be constructed with other meanings of even, using many of the Chinese equivalents as second members.* ‖Please even the sleeves of this coat. láw-jyà, bǎ wǒ-jèy-jyàn-'yī-fu-de(-lyǎng-jŕ)-'shyèw-dz °nèng-'chí-le. *or* °nùng-'chí-le. *or* °'jyǎn-chí-le.

To even the score (*catch up with*) 'gǎn-shang, 'jwéy-shang. ‖Let's even the score. dzám 'gǎn-shang 'tā-men. *or* dzám 'jwéy-shang tā-men.

3. To break even. (*Just meet expenses*) gāng gèw 'kāy-shyāw; (*just make enough to eat*) gāng gèw 'chŕ-de *or* (*local Peiping*) gāng gèw 'jyáw-gu; (*no profit or loss*) 'bù-péy bú-'jwàn. ‖His business doesn't make much; he just breaks even.° tā-de-'mǎy-mày 'méy-jw... dwǒ-shǎw-'chyán; yě jyèw-shr °gāng gèw 'kāy-shyāw. *or* °gāng gèw 'chŕ-de. *or* °gāng gèw 'jyáw-gu. *or* °'bù-péy bú-'jwàn.

To get even (*get revenge*) bàw-'chéw. ‖I'll get even with you sooner or later. 'dzǎw-wǎn wǒ yàw 'bàw jèy-ge-'chéw. *or expressed with the proverb* For a gentleman to get revenge, even ten years is not too late. 'jywūn-dz bàw-'chéw, 'shŕ-nyán bù-'wǎn.

4. Even (*for emphasis*). *Chinese usually puts an emphatic word both before and after the word to be emphasized, though sometimes only one occurs. Those occurring before are* indeed, even if 'jyèw-shr; including, also lyán; even though 'swéy-rán. *Those occurring after the word emphasized, and just before the verb, are* also yě; all, altogether, also dōw, yě . . . dēw; still, furthermore háy(-shr); still, more gèng; still, also yě(-shr). ‖Even the little children took cold. lyán (or 'jyèw-shr) shyǎw-'háy-dz-men yě dēw jāw-'lyáng-le. ‖Even he didn't go. jyèw-shr (or lyán-)'tā yě (or dēw) 'méy-'chywù-ya. ‖Even he couldn't go. jyèw-shr (or lyán-)'tā yě (or dēw) 'méy-néng chywù. ‖Even he will say no to your request. jyèw-shr (or lyán-)'tā dēw hwèy 'bù-kěn 'dā-ying-de. ‖He'll refuse even his own mother, let alone you. jyèw-shr tā-'dz̀-jǐ-de-'mǔ-chin (chyéw-tā) tā yě bú-hwèy 'kěn-de, 'hé-kwàng 'nǐ-ne? ‖He refused even his own mother; what chance do you have? tā lyán tā-'mǔ-chin dēw 'bù-kěn 'dā-ying, 'hé-kwàng 'nǐ-ne? ‖Yes, even you have to go. 'dwèy-le, jyèw-shr (or lyán-)'nǐ yě děy chywù. ‖He couldn't feed even himself. tā 'lyán 'dz̀-ji dēw 'yǎng-bù-'lyǎw. *or* tā-'jèng-ge 'háy bú-gèw 'dz̀-ji-chŕ-'fàn-de-ne. ‖He can do even better if he tries. tā yàw-shr 'yùng-shīn dzwò, jyèw néng 'dzwò-de háy (or gèng) 'hǎw-dyar-ne. ‖They don't just wear coats;

they even wear neckties (too). tā-men 'bú-dàn chwān 'shàng-yī; ('ěr-chyě or 'jywū-rán) háy 'jì lǐng-'dày-ne. *or* tām 'bù-jŕ chwān 'shàng-yī; lyán lǐng-'dày dēw (or yě) 'jì-je-ne. ‖The clothes were dirty even after (*even though*) they were washed. jèy-shyē-'yī-fu (swéy-rán, or jyèw-shr) 'shǐ-le, 'háy-shr 'dzāng. ‖The stain remains even after washing with soap. jyèw-shr (or lyán, or swéy-rán) yùng 'yī-dz shǐ-le, 'dyǎn-dz 'háy-shr (or 'yě-shr) bú-'dyàw. ‖Even so, I don't agree with you. jyèw-shr 'dzèm-je, wǒ yě bú-'dzàn-chéng nǐ. ‖Even so, I still think I'm right. jyèw-shr 'dzèm-me-je, wǒ 'háy-shr jywé-je 'wǒ dwèy. ‖Even so, I couldn't swing him around. lyán 'dzèm-je, wǒ háy bù-néng bǎ-tā-'shwō-de 'hwéy-shīn jwǎn-'yì-le-ne. ‖Even if we left early, it would take an hour to get there. wǒ-men 'jyèw-shr chywù-de 'dzǎw, yě děy dzěw yì-'dyǎn-jūng tsáy néng 'dàw-nèr-ne. ‖He can't do it even if he tries. tā 'jyèw-shr 'shyǎng gàn, yě 'gàn-bu-'chéng. ‖I must say he's a good man, even though I don't like him. 'swéy-rán wǒ bù-'shǐ-hwān tā, wǒ yě děy shwō tā shŕ yí-ge-'hǎw-rén.

EVENING. 'wǎn-shang; *in compounds* wǎn, yè. This evening jyēr-'wǎn-shang; last evening 'dzwó-tyān-wǎn-shang, 'dzwór-wǎn-shang; tomorrow evening 'míng-tyān (or 'myéngr, 'myér)-wǎn-shang; two evenings ago 'chyán-tyān-wǎn-shang; three evenings ago 'sān-tyan-yǐ-chyán-de-'wǎn-shang. ‖He comes in about this time every evening. tā 'měy-tyān-wǎn-shang bāng-je 'jèy-ge-shŕ-hew dàw. ‖She feels pretty lonesome during the day, but worse in the evening. tā 'báy-tyan yǐ-jīng 'gèw mèn-de-le, 'wǎn-shang 'gèng nán-'gwò. ‖What time does the evening show begin? 'yè-chǎng (or 'wǎn-chǎng) shéme-shŕ-hew kāy-'shǐ? ‖He attends an evening school. tā shàng 'yè-shyàw.

‖Good evening! nǐ 'hǎw? or nín 'hǎw? or 'hǎw-wa?

EVENT. (*Happening*) shŕ. A happy event 'shǐ-shŕ. ‖I always try to keep up with current events. wǒ 'shyàng-láy hěn 'jù-yì 'shŕ-shŕ. ‖It's an important event in her life. dzày tā-yì-'shēng-li jèy shŕ jyàn-°'dà-shŕ. °hěn-'jùng-yàw-de-'shŕ. ‖In this town the arrival of a foreigner is an event. dzày 'jèy-ge-'dì-fang dàw-le yí-ge-'wày-gwo-rén dēw shŕ yí-jyàn-°'dà-shŕ. °'shīn-shyan-'shŕ. *But* ‖A thing like that couldn't happen in the normal course of events. dzày píng-'cháng-de-'chíng-shing-jŕ-'shyà, 'jèy-jǔng-'shŕ shŕ 'chū-bu-láy-de.

(*Item on a program*) shyàng, 'jyé-mù. ‖What's the next event? shyà °'yí-shyàng (°'yí-ge-'jyé-mù) shŕ 'shéme?

In any event 'wú-lwèn-rú-hé, 'dzěm-je, 'bù-gwǎn-'dzěm-je, 'fǎn-jèng. ‖I'll be there waiting for you in any event. 'bù-gwǎn-'dzěm-je wǒ yě 'dzày-nar děng nǐ.

In the event of 'yàw-shr . . . . ‖In the event of an accident, please notify my father. *is expressed as* If anything happens to me, please inform my father. wǒ 'yàw-shr chū-le-'shř chǐng-nǐ 'tūng-jř wǒ-'fù-chin yì-shēngr.

EVER. (*At any time at all; said of past events or customary actions*) -gwo. ‖Have you ever done it this way? nǐ 'dzèm-je nùng-gwo-ma? ‖Have you ever been in America? nǐ (yǐ-chyán) 'dàw-gwo 'měy-gwo-ma? ‖Have I ever met you before? dzám yǐ-'chyán 'jyàn-gwo-ma? ‖Have I ever told a lie? wǒ 'yí-shyàng shwō-gwo 'hwǎng-ma? ‖I hardly ever play cards. *is expressed as* I have hardly ever played cards. wǒ jyàn-'jř-de 'méy-dzěm-me 'wár-gwo 'páy. *or* wǒ 'yí-shyàng 'méy-dà 'wár-gwo 'páy. ‖He seldom if ever is on time. tā 'jyàn-jř 'méy-àn 'shř-hew 'dàw-gwo. *or expressed as* If he is ever on time, it is most unusual. tā jyèw-shr 'yěw-de-shř-hew ǎn-'shř-hew 'dàw, nà yě-shr 'bù-cháng-'yěw-de-'shř.

(*At some time in particular; said of present or future events, wishes, questions, etc.*) yěw ... de-shř-hew; yěw ... (*when the words following yěw refer to an event*). ‖Will that woman ever stop wrangling? 'nèy-ge-'nywǔ-rén yě yěw ge-bù-'chǎw-bú-'nàw-de-'shř-hew-ma? ‖Is she ever home? tā yěw dzày-'jyā-de-'shř-hew-ma? ‖I don't think she's ever home. wǒ jywé-de tā 'méy-yěw dzày-'jyā-de-'shř-hew. ‖Could a thing like that ever happen? 'yěw chū-'nèy-yang-shř-de-shř-hew-ma? *or* yěw 'nèy-yangr-de-shř-hew-ma? ‖Will there ever be a chance like this again? 'háy néng 'dzày yěw shyàng-'jèy-yàngr-de-'jī-hwey-ma? ‖If you ever find it, let me know, will you? nǐ yàw-shr 'jǎw-jáw-le (*or* nǐ yàw-shr yěw ge-'jǎw-jáw-de-shř-hew), jyèw gěy-wǒ ge-'shyèr; 'shíng-ma? ‖Do you think he'll ever change? nǐ shyǎng tā yěw ge-'gǎy (-de-shř-hew)-ma? ‖Will he ever believe in you again? tā 'háy-yěw shyàng-'shìn-nǐ-de-shř-hew-ma?

(*Before; especially in than ever*) yǐ-'chyán. ‖I like this more than ever. wǒ bǐ yǐ-'chyán gèng 'shǐ-hwān jèy-ge-le. ‖He is drinking more than ever. tā bǐ yǐ-'chyán hē-de 'gèng dwō-le.

Ever (*used only for emphasis*) -ne, -a, (-ya, -na, -nga, -wa). ‖Why did I ever get into this? wǒ 'dzěm-me hwèy dàw-le °'jèy-bù-'tyán-dì-ne? *or* °'jèm-ge-'dì-bù-ne? ‖Why did I ever say that? wǒ nà-shr 'dzěm-le, 'dzěm shwō 'nèy-yangr-de-'hwà-ya? ‖How did you ever hit on such a plan? nǐ 'dzěm 'shyǎng-dàw-de 'nèm-ge-'fár-ne? ‖How did you ever find out? nǐ 'dzěm 'jř-dàw-de-ya?

Ever since tsúng, 'dz̀-tsúng. ‖I've been taking it easy ever since she left. 'dz̀-tsúng tā 'dzěw-le (yǐ-'hèw), wǒ jyèw 'yěw-yéw-dz̀-'dzày-de. ‖I've left this alone ever since he said that. 'dz̀-tsúng tā 'nèm yì-'shwō, wǒ jyèw méy-'gwǎn-gwo jèy-ge.

See also NEVER.

EVERY. měy *or* měy-yī *plus a measure;* (*limited in usage except in literary contexts*) gè; *certain nouns are repeated to give the collective idea, as* every person

'rén-rén, *or* every day 'tyān-tyan. *If the emphasis is collective rather than distributive,* altogether dēw *or* chywán (*or, stronger,* chywán-'dēw) *is placed after the noun before the verb. Sometimes when one of these expressions for* altogether *is included there is no other expression of collectivity.* ‖Every person gets three dollars. 'měy-rén °dé (*or* °ná) 'sān-kwày-chyán. ‖Every man gets three dollars; why don't you take it too? 'rén-rén (*or* 'měy-rén *or* 'shéy) dēw dé 'sān-kwày-chyán; 'nǐ dzěme bú-'yàw-ne? ‖He knows every man, woman, and child in the village by name. jèy-ge-'tswēn-dz-li-de-°'měy-yí-ge-'nán-rén, 'nywǔ-rén, shyǎw-'háy-dz (*or* °'nán-nywǔ-lǎw-'shàw *or* °'yí-ge-'yí-ge-de) tā dēw 'jyàw-de-chū 'míng-dz-lay. ‖I see him every day. wǒ 'měy-tyān 'kàn-jyàn ta. ‖It rains every day. 'tyān-tyān shyà-'ywǔ. ‖Every year there's been a flood. 'měy-nyán (*or* 'nyán-nyán) fā-'shwěy. *or expressed as* One year, one flood. 'yì-nyán fā 'yí-tsz̀-'shwěy. ‖Every time I see him he's busy. 'měy-tsz̀ wǒ 'kàn-jyan ta de-shř-hew, tā °'lǎw-shr (*or* °'dēw-shr *or* °'dzǔng-shr) nème-'máng. ‖I've given him every opportunity to make good. wǒ 'gěy-le ta 'gè-shř-gè-'yàngr-de-'jī-hwey ràng-ta 'chéng dyǎr-'shř. ‖Every dynasty has its founders. 'měy-cháw (*or* gè-'cháw) dēw yěw 'kāy-gwó-de-rén-'wù. ‖Every time he makes the same mistake. 'měy-hwéy (*or* 'měy-tsz̀ *or* 'hwéy-hwéy) chū jèy-ge-yàngr-dé-'tswòr. ‖Every village has a school. měy-ge-'tswēn-dz yěw ge-shywé-'shyàw. *or* 'gè-ge-tswēn-dz dēw yěw ge-shywé-'shyàw. *or* 'yí-ge-tswēn-dz yěw 'yí-ge-shywé-'shyàw. ‖Every man has his specialty. 'gè yěw swǒ-'cháng. ‖Every bill is marked. 'měy-jāng(-chyán-'pyàw-dz)-shang dēw °yěw (*or* °jì-le) 'jì-hàwr. ‖Every dog has his day. *is expressed as* Everyone has his lucky time. 'shéy dēw yěw dzěw-'ywùn-de-shř-hew.

Every kind of gè-'jǔng-de *or* 'gè-shř-gè-'yàngr-de *or* 'gè-yàngr-de *or* 'jǔng-jǔng-de.

Every other (*skipping one*) 'jyē-yì *plus a measure;* (*all but this one*) 'byé-de-... dēw. ‖They have movies here every other day. jèr 'jyē-yì-tyān 'yǎn yì-hwéy-'yàn-'yěngr. ‖Take every other book, from left to right. tsúng-'dzwǒ dàw-'yěw 'jyē yì-běr 'ná yì-'běr.

Every now and then *or* every once in a while 'sān-tyān-lyǎng-'téwr-de. ‖He takes a drink every now and then. tā 'sān-tyān-lyǎng-'téwr-de hē dyǎr-'jyěw.

EVERYBODY. 'měy-rén, 'měy-yí-ge-rén, 'rén-rén, 'gè-rén, shéy, 'dà-jyā; (*in statements only*) 'swǒ-yěw-de-(rén); *or any of these followed by* dēw; *or* dēw *alone.* ‖Did everybody have a good time? 'dà-jyā-wár-de yěw 'yì-sz-ma? *or* (*If referring to a meal*) dēw chř-'hǎw-le-ma? ‖I'm willing if everybody else is. dà-jyā dēw 'ywàn-yì-de-hwà wǒ yě 'swéy-je. ‖Nearly everybody likes the climate here. chà-bu-dwō °'měy-yí-ge-rén (*or* °'rén-rén) dēw 'shǐ-hwan jèr-de-'tyān-chi (*or* jèr-de-'chì-hew). ‖Is everybody here? 'dēw dzày-jèr-ne-ma? *or* 'swǒ-yěw-de-rén (*or* 'dà-jyā) 'dēw dzày-jèr-ne-ma? ‖Everybody does it; why shouldn't I?

ʲrén-rén dēw 'nèm-je; dzěm 'wǒ jyèw bù-'shíng-ne? ‖Not everybody enjoys this kind of music. 'jè-yàngr-de-'yīn-ywè bú-shr̀ 'rén-rén (or 'shéy, or 'měy-yí-ge-rén) dēw °ày-'tīng-de. or °néng-'shīn-shang-de.

See also **EVERY.**

EVERYTHING. *If referring to objects of all sorts, use* 'swǒ-yěw-de-'dūng-shi, 'měy-yí-jyàn-dūng-shi, 'shém-me(-dūng-shi), *or any of these followed by* dēw. *When referring to all objects or actions of a particular sort, replace* dūng-shi *by the particular word for the object or action.* ‖I want to see everything you have about engineering. wǒ yàw 'kàn-kan nǐ-jèr-'swǒ-yěw-'gwān-ywú-'gūng-chéng-de-°'dūng-shi. or °'shū. ‖He lost everything when his ship was sunk. tā-de-chwán 'chén-le de-shŕ-hèwr tā °'měy-yí-jyàn-dūng-shi 'dēw dyēw-le. or °'swǒ-yěw-de-dūng-shi 'dēw dyēw-le. or °'shém-me(-dūng-shi) 'dēw dyēw-le. or °'jyèn-jyàr-dūng-shi 'dēw dyēw-le. or °'dūng-shi 'dēw dyēw-le. ‖Everything is expensive these days. 'jìn-láy 'shém-me-dūng-shi dēw 'gwèy. ‖Everything in the house is insured. jèy-ge-'fáng-dz-li 'měy-jyàn-dūng-shi (or 'jyàn-jyàr-dūng-shi, or shém-me-dūng-shi, or swǒ-'yěw-de-dūng-shi, or shém-me) 'dēw bǎw-le 'shyǎn-le. ‖We can't all do everything. wǒ-men 'bù-néng 'měy(-yí-ge)-rén 'shém-me(-'shŕ-chìng) 'dēw hwèy-'dzwò. ‖An officer should be able to do everything his men can do. fán 'shŕ-bīng-hwèy-dzwò-de 'gwān-jǎng jyèw 'yīng-gāy 'dēw hwèy.

It means everything (*it's most important*). ‖In this business a good start means everything. gàn 'jèy-ge 'dzwèy-yàw-'jǐn-de shŕ yàw chǐ-'téwr chǐ-de 'hǎw.

See also **EVERY.**

EVERYWHERE. 'chù-chù (dēw); 'dàw-chù (dēw); 'gè-chù (dēw); 'nǎr dēw; dēw . . . 'byǎn. ‖I've looked everywhere for it. wǒ 'dàw-chù dēw 'jǎw-le. or wǒ 'chù-chù dēw 'jǎw-le. or wǒ 'gè-chù dēw 'jǎw-le. or wǒ 'nǎr dēw 'jǎw-le. or wǒ 'dēw jǎw-'byàn-le. ‖Everywhere he goes he, is welcome. tā 'dàw-chù (or 'gè-chù or dàw-'nǎr dēw) 'shèw-rén 'hwān-yíng.

See also **EVERY.**

EXACT. (*Without deviation*) . . . yě bú-'chà, *where the words which precede specify a division, detail, or characteristic of the thing referred to.* ‖These are his exact words. jēy shr̀ tā-'shwō-de, 'yí-ge-dż yě bú-'chà. ‖Tell me his exact words. *is expressed as* Tell me exactly what he said. tā-'dzěm-shwō-de, nǐ 'yí-ge-dż-yě-bú-'chà-de shwō-gey wǒ 'tīng-ting. ‖This is an exact reproduction of the original edition. jèy-ge-'fān-yìn-běn gēn 'ywán-bǎn 'fēn-háw (or 'yì-dyǎr) bú-'chà.

(*Without error*) . . . yě bú-'tswèr, *used like the above;* 'bù-chū-'tswèr, 'jwěn-chywè. (*See also the two following paragraphs.*) ‖His work is very exact. tā dzwò-'shr̀ °'bù-chū-'tswòr. or °'yì-dyǎr yě bú-'tswèr. or °hěn 'jwěn-chywè. ‖This answer is only approximate,

not exact. 'jèy-ge-'hwéy-dá-de 'bú-gwò-shr̀ dà-gà 'chí, bìng 'bú-shr̀ °'jwěn-chywè-de. or °'yì-dyǎr méy 'tswèr. or °'yì-dyǎr bú-'chà.

(*In precise detail*) 'yī . . . 'yī . . . (*may also mean* every). ‖I'm giving you his exact words (*every word, word for word*). wǒ 'yí-ge-dż-yí-ge-'dż-de gàw-su nǐ tā shwō 'shém-me láy-je.

(*Precise; in mathematics, work, etc.*) 'jwěn-chywè. ‖The exact location of the city is 29° 34′ N., 106° 35′ E. 'jèy-ge-chéng-de-'jwěn-chywè-'dì-wèy shr̀ 'běy-wěy èr-shŕ-'jyěw-dù sān-shŕ-'sż-fēn, 'dūng-jīng 'yì-bǎy-líng-'lyèw-dù sān-shŕ-'wǔ-fēn. ‖Are these figures exact jèy-shyē-'shùr 'jwěn-chywè-ma?

(*Accurate; of news, information, etc.*) 'jèng-chyw 'chywè-shŕ. ‖Is that information exact? nèy-ge-shyāw-shi °'jèng-chywè-ma? or °'chywè-shŕ-ma?

(*In hours and minutes; of time*). ‖Do you have the exact time? shyàn-dzày shr̀ 'jǐ-dyǎn 'jǐ-fēn-le?

The exact . . . (*just the . . . ; see also* **JUST**) *usually* 'jèng. ‖We live in the exact center of town. wǒm jù-dzày chéng-'lǐ-de-'jèng-dāng-jūng. ‖That's the EXACT solution. 'nèy-yàng (or 'nèm-jyě-jywé) 'jèng dwèy.

EXACTLY. (*In questions*) dàw-'dǐ, 'jyēw-jìng. ‖Exactly what do you mean? nǐ 'jyěw-jìng (or dàw-'dǐ) shr̀ shém-'yì-sz?

(*In statements*) jèng, jyèw; *sometimes other expressions;* (*whole, with no fractions*) jěng. ‖It's exactly four-thirty. 'jěng (or 'jèng) 'sż-dyǎn-'bàn. ‖We both arrived at exactly the same time. wǒm 'jèng-hǎw (or 'chyà-hǎw) 'túng-shŕ dàw-de. ‖I can make you do exactly what I want. wǒ 'yàw nǐ dzěm-je, nǐ 'jyèw 'fēy nèm-je bù-'shíng. ‖That's exactly the amount he gave me. nèy 'jèng-shr̀ tā-gěy-wǒ-de-nèy-ge-'shùr. or tā-gěy-wǒ-de 'jyèw-shr̀ 'nèm-shyē.

‖Exactly! *or* That's exactly it! 'jèng dwèy! *or* 'jyèw-shr̀ 'nèm-je! or 'yì-dyǎr bú-'chà! or kě bú-'shr̀-ma! ‖That's exactly what I want. nèy 'jèng-shr̀ wǒ-'yàw-de.

(*In comparisons*) jēn, jyǎn-'jŕ. ‖He walks exactly like his father. tā 'dzěw-lù 'jēn (or jyǎn-'jŕ) shyàng tā-'dyē shr̀-de. or tā 'dzěw-lù jyǎn-'jŕ gēn (or 'jyèw-shr̀) tā-'dyē yí-'yàng.

(*Simply*) 'jyǎn-'jŕ. ‖He said exactly nothing. tā 'jyǎn-jŕ jyèw 'swàn-shr̀ 'shém-me yě 'méy-'shwō.

See also **JUST.**

EXAMINATION. *Most of the terms listed below also mean* examine.

(*Physical: by eyes or instruments*) 'jyǎn-chá, 'jyǎn-yàn. To reveal by examination 'chá-chū-láy. ‖He is still under examination. tā háy dzày 'jyǎn-chá. ‖How did your (physical) examination come out? nǐ ('jyǎn-chá shēn-'tǐ) 'jyǎn-chá-de °'dzěm-'yàng. or °'-jyē-gwǒ dzěm'-yàng? ‖The examination of the (contents of the) trunk revealed nothing. 'shyāng-dz-lǐ-de-'dūng-shi 'jyǎn-chá-le, °'méy-'kàn-chu shém-me-lay. or °'méy-'chá-chu shém-me-lay. or 'shyāng-dz-lǐ-de-'dūng-shi méy-'chá-chu shém-me-lay. ‖You ought to have a

483

thorough physical examination. nǐ děy dzwǒ yì-hwéy-'shyáng-shì-'tǐ-ge-'jyǎn-chá-le. *or* . . . 'jyǎn-yàn-le.

(*Investigation*) 'kǎw-chá, 'shěn-chá, 'yán-jyēw. ‖I have made a careful examination of the situation. wǒ 'yǐ-jīng bǎ jèy-ge-'chíng-shíng 'dž-shì-de 'kǎw-chá-le (*or* 'shěn-chá-le, *or* 'yán-jyēw-le) yí-shyàr.

(*Test*) 'kǎw-de, kǎw-'shr̀ (*the verb is* kǎw). To pass an examination 'kǎw-shang-le; jí-'gé-le; civil service examination 'wén-gwān-kǎw-'shr̀. ‖How did you make out in your examinations? nǐ-'kǎw-de (*or* nǐ-de-'kǎw-shr̀) °dzěm-'yàng? *or* °-'jyē-gwǒ dzěm-'yàng?

EXAMINE. (*Look over carefully*) 'jyǎn-chá, chá, yàn, 'jyǎn-yàn; *sometimes* (*for perfunctory examinations*) kàn; chyáw. ‖The police went to examine their passports. 'jǐng-chá chywù 'jyǎn-chá (*or* 'jyǎn-yàn, *or* chá, *or* yàn) tām-de-hù-'jàw-chywu-le. ‖Let me examine your passport again. wǒ 'dzày kàn-kan (*or* chyáw-chyaw) nǐ-de-hù-'jàw. ‖Has the doctor examined you yet? 'dày-fu 'jyǎn-chá (*or* 'jyǎn-yàn, *or* 'chá-le, *or* yàn-le) nǐ-le-ma? *or simply* 'jyǎn-chá (*or* 'jyǎn-yàn) 'gwò-le-ma?

(*Investigate*) 'yán-jyēw; (*with particular care*) 'kǎw-chá, 'shěn-chá; (*with deep thought*) 'kǎw-lywù; (*by merely looking around*) 'chá-kàn. ‖We should examine the claims made on both sides. wǒ-men 'yīng-gāy bǎ 'lyǎng-byār-de-hwà dēw °'yán-jyēw-yán-jyēw. *or* °'kǎw-lywù-kǎw-lywù. *etc.* ‖The police are examining the circumstances of the accident. 'chū-shr̀-de-'chíng-shìng, 'jǐng-chá jèng-dzày °'yán-jyēw. *or* °'kǎw-chá, *or* °'shěn-chá. *or* °'chá-kàn.

(*To question in court*) shěn, wèn, 'shěn-wèn. ‖When examined in court, he denied everything. dzày 'táng-shang (*or* dzày gwò-'tíng) 'shěn-tā (*or* 'wèn-tā, *or* 'shěn-wèn tā) de-shŕ-hew, tā dēw méy-'chéng-rèn.

EXAMPLE. (*Illustration, case in point; in speech*) 'bǐ-fang; (*in action*) 'lì(-dz); *or sometimes expressed indirectly.* ‖Let me give you an example. (*In speech*) wǒ gěy-nǐ dǎ (*or* shwō) ge-'bǐ-fang-ba. (*In action*) wǒ gěy-nǐ dzwò °ge-'lì-dz-ba. *or* °'yí-tsž nǐ 'kàn-kan. ‖For example, if you come late, you will be punished. 'bǐ-fang shwō, nǐ yàw-shr láy 'wǎn-le, jyèw děy āy-'fá. ‖Take this one, for example. ná 'jèy-ge dzwò ge-°'bǐ-fang-ba. *or* °'lì-ba. *or* 'pì-rú 'jèy-ge-ba. *or* (*jyèw*) ná 'jèy-ge láy 'shwō-ba.

(*Specimen, sample; for purposes of study and imitation*) 'lì-tí; (*for purposes of comparison*) 'yàng-dz; *or sometimes expressed indirectly.* ‖Study the example carefully and answer the questions the same way. bǎ 'lì-tí 'dž-shì kàn-le; swǒ-yěw-de-'wèn-tí dēw jàw-'yàngr 'hwéy-dá. ‖Show me an example of his writing. tā-'shyě-de-dūng-shi gěy-wǒ °ge-'yàng-dz kàn-kan. *or meaning* a bit °'ná-dyar-lay (*or* °'ná-ge-lay) kàn-kan. ‖Is this a typical example of his work? *is expressed as* Is all his work like this? tā-dzwò-de 'dēw 'jèy-yàngr-ma? ‖This painting is a good example of his

art. *is expressed as* This painting will illustrate his art. 'jèy-jāng-hwàr 'hěn kě-yǐ 'dày-byǎw tā-h*w*à-'hwàr-de-'gūng-fu. *or* tsúng-'jèy-jāng-'hwàr jyèw '*k*ě-yǐ 'kàn-chu tā-(hwà-'hwàr-)de-'gūng-fu-lay. ‖This is (an example of) how the machine works. jèy-ge-'jī-chi 'dzèm-je °'dùng. *or* °'yùng*,or* °'kāy. *or* °'shŕ.

(*Precedent*) 'bǎng-yàng; (*only in a voluntary sense*) 'byǎw-shwày; *or sometimes expressed indirectly.* ‖You ought to set an example for the others. nǐ děy gěy 'byé-rén dzwò °ge-'bǎng-yàng. *or* °'ge-'byǎw-shwày. ‖The way he is treated will be an example for the others. (*Good or bad*) 'tā 'jèy-jyàn-shr̀-a, jyèw-shr ge-'bǎng-yàng. *or* (*Bad; a warning*) jè jyèw-shr 'shā-yī-jǐng-'bǎy. ‖He ought to be made an example of. (*Good or bad*) děy ná-'tā-lay dzwò ge-'bǎng-yàng. *or* (*A warning*) děy ná-'tā-lay 'jǐng-jyè-jǐng-jyè 'byé-rén.

EXCELLENT. 'jēn hǎw. ‖That was an excellent dinner. nèy-dwèn-fàn 'jēn hǎw. ‖He is an excellent tennis player. tā-de-'wǎng-chyéw dǎ-de 'jēn hǎw. ‖She gave an excellent performance last night. dzwér 'wǎn-shang tā-yǎn-de 'jēn hǎw.

EXCEPT. (*Excluding; occurs initially only*) 'chú-le; (*if it were not that, if it had not been that; occurs initially only*) yàw 'bú-shr; (*only for, just that; occurs after the general statement*) 'jyèw-shr *or* 'jyèw yěw, *or* 'jř-shr *or* 'jř yěw. (*See* JUST.) ‖Everything was fine, except one thing. chú-le 'yí-yàngr, 'dēw hǎw. *or* 'dēw-hǎw, 'jyèw-shr (*or* 'jyèw yěw, *or* 'jř-shr, *or* 'jř yěw) 'yí-yàngr °'bú-hǎw. *or* °'chà-dyǎr. *or* °bú-jyàw-rén 'mǎn-yì. *or other expressions meaning* bad, *etc.* ‖There are no rooms available except on the top floor. chú-le jīn-'dyěngr-shang-yì-'tséng 'méy-yěw 'kùng-fáng. ‖There is no way out except giving him what he wants. 'chú-le tā 'yàw-shéme 'gěy-tā shéme (yǐ-'wày), jyèw 'méy-yew 'byé-de-fár. *or expressed as* There's no other way; give him what he wants. 'méy-yew 'byé-de-fár; tā 'yàw-shéme 'gěy-tā shéme hǎw-le. ‖I don't have any reason except that I don't like him. 'chú-le wǒ 'bù-'shǐ-hwān tā (yǐ-'wày), 'méy-yew shéme-'lǐ-yéw. *or expressed as* There's no reason; I just don't like him. shéme-'lǐ-yěw yě méy-'yěw; wǒ 'jyèw-shr bù-'shǐ-hwān tā me. ‖I would have been here much sooner except for some trouble on the way. yàw 'bú-shr dzày 'dàwr-shang 'chū-le dyǎr-'má-fan, wǒ 'dzǎw jyèw kě-yǐ 'dàw-le. ‖I like the book pretty well except for the last two chapters. 'jèy-běr-shū, 'chú-le dzwèy-'hèw-lyǎng-'jāng wǒ 'dēw hěn 'shǐ-hwān.

EXCEPTION. lì-'wày; *or expressed indirectly.* ‖There's an exception to everything. 'shém-me-shr̀ 'dēw yěw lì-'wày. ‖That's an exception. nèy shr̀ lì-'wày. *or expressed as* That doesn't count. 'nèy bú-'swàn. ‖We allow no exceptions for anyone. *is expressed as* We treat everyone the same way. wǒm-jèr 'shéy dēw 'yí-lywù 'kàn-dày. ‖Make an exception (for him) this time. 'jèy-tsž swàn lì-'wày hǎw-le. *or expressed as*

Allow him to do it that way this time. 'jèy-tsz̀ 'ràng-ta nèm-je hǎw-le. ‖However, I'll make an exception in your case. 'kě-shr, 'jèy-tsz̀ °'swàn-le. *or* °'swàn-dzwò lì-'wày-le. *or expressed politely as* In your case it calls for different treatment. 'kě-shr ('nín-ne), 'nín jèy-tsz̀ 'yèw-dāng 'byé-lwèn-le.

EXCHANGE. *To exchange one thing for another* hwàn. ‖I'd like to exchange this book for another one. wǒ shyǎng ná 'jèy-běr-shū 'hwàn yì-běr(-'byé-de). ‖Could I exchange this (for something else)? jèy-ge shywǔ 'hwàn-ma? *or* jèy-ge 'hwàn-hwan 'shíng-bu-shíng? *or* jèy-ge 'hwàn 'byé-de, 'shíng-bu-shíng?

To exchange *mutually* 'jyāw-hwàn. ‖Prisoners of war are going to be exchanged within a year. 'fú-lwǒ dzày yì-'nyán-yí-nèy 'jyāw-hwàn. ‖I've been exchanging information with your friend. wǒ gēn nǐ-de-'péng-yew °'jyāw-hwàn-le bù-shǎw-de-'shyāw-shì. *or (Talking with him)* °'tán-le-tán. ‖They exchanged ideas before reaching a decision. dzày 'méy-'jywé-dìng yǐ-'chyán tā-men 'jyāw-hwàn 'yì-jyàn láy-je. ‖Would you exchange with me? dzám 'jyāw-hwàn, nǐ 'ywàn-yi-ma? *or expressed as* Would you exchange yours for mine? (*See above.*) nǐ ywàn-yi °ná 'nǐ-de hwàn 'wǒ-de-ma? *or* °ná 'nǐ-nèy-ge hwàn wǒ-'jèy-ge-ma?

Rate of exchange 'hwéy-lywù, 'hwéy-dwèy-'lywù, 'hwéy-dwèy-de-'háng-shr. ‖What's the rate of exchange today? jyēr-de-'hwèy-lywù (*or,* jyēr-de-'hwèy-dwèy-'lywù, *or,* jyēr-de-'hwèy-dwèy-de-'háng-shr) shr̀ 'dwō-shǎw?

In exchange for hwàn *or an indirect expression.* ‖Would you like to give me your tickets in exchange for this fountain pen? nǐ 'ywàn-yi ná (*or* yùng) nǐ-de-'pyàw láy 'hwàn jèy-gwǎn-'dz̀-lay-shwéy-'bǐ-ma? ‖We'll feed you in exchange for some information. *is expressed as* You give us some news, we'll give you a meal. nǐ 'gàw-su wǒm dyǎr-'shyāw-shi, wǒm gěy-nǐ yí-dwèn-'fàn chr̄.

EXCITE (EXCITED, EXCITING). *Chinese uses no general terms for excitement, but specifies several ways in which a person becomes excited, as by happiness, anger, etc.*

Excite. ‖Don't excite him (*an animal or person*). (*By intentional or unintentional teasing; with pleasant or unpleasant results*) byé 'jāw-ta. *or (by intentional teasing, kidding, or nagging; with pleasant or unpleasant results)* byé 'dèw-ta. *or (by irritating)* byé 'rě-ta. ‖Don't excite the patient. *or* Don't let the patient get excited. (*crossed, angered*) byé jyàw 'bìng-rén °jāw-'jí. *or (angered)* °shēng-'chì. *or (too happily excited, as by good news)* °tày gāw-'shìng-lè. *or (too dangerously excited; a medical term not widely understood)* °tày 'shīng-fèn-le. ‖The book is too specialized to excite (*draw out*) popular interest. 'jèy-běr-shū tày jwān-'mén-le, bù-néng 'yǐn-chǐ 'pǔ-tūng-rén-de-'shìng-chywu.

Excited. ‖The kids were excited (*very happy*) when you said you would take them to the circus. nǐ shwō yàw dày 'háy-dz-men chywù kàn 'mǎ-'shì-lay-je, jyàw-tam 'shì-hwān °'jí-le. *or* °-de 'lyǎw-bu-dé. ‖The excited mob (*like madmen*) threatened to break in. nèy-chywún-rén fā-'fēng-shr-de yàw 'chwǎng-jìn-lay. ‖Don't get excited! *is expressed as* Be calm! 'wěn-je-dyar! *or as* Don't be impatient! nǐ shyān byé jāw-'jí! *or as* Don't be agitated! nǐ shyān byé 'hwāng! *or as* Don't get angry! nǐ shyān byé °'hwǒr. *or* °shēng-'chì. *or as* Go slowly. mày-'már-lay. *or* màn-'mān-lay. *or as* Don't be too happy. byé tày gāw-'shìng-le. *or as* Be quiet and calm (*a literary quotation*). nǐ 'shǎw-ān-wú-'dzàw.

Exciting. ‖That was an exciting story. (*Moving*) nèy-ge-'gù-shr hěn °'dùng-'rén *or (Interesting)* °'yěw 'yì-sz. *or* nèy-ge-'gù-shr jyàw-rén 'tīng-le dùng-'shīn. ‖Isn't it exciting? 'dwō yěw 'yì-sz-a?

EXCUSE. (*Pardon, forgive; or in expressions of politeness*) *the Chinese expressions fit narrower contexts than the English. Thus the equivalents of* Excuse me! *are as follows:* (*most general, also usable in most of the more specific contexts stated below*) dwèy-bu-'chǐ! *or* dwèy-bu-'jù! (*if preceding a request for information made to a stranger*) jyè-'gwāng! *or* chǐng-'wèn! (*if preceding a request for a favor*) láw-'jyà! (*in extremely formal circumstances*) hěn bàw-'chyàn! (*less formal apology for a shortcoming*) 'ywán-lyàng! ‖Excuse me; where's the railroad station? jyè-'gwāng; hwǒ-chē-'jàn dzày-'nǎr? ‖Excuse me; didn't you say ten cents at first? chǐng-'wèn, nín-chǐ-'shyān-shwō-de bú-shr 'shf-fēn-chyán-ma? ‖Excuse me; would you move over a bit? láw-'jyà, 'nwó-nwór 'shíng-ma? ‖Excuse me; please repeat that. láw-'jyà (*or* dwèy-bu-'chǐ), chǐng 'dzày shwō yì-hwéy. ‖Excuse me for appearing in informal clothes this evening. (wǒ) hěn bàw-'chyàn, jyēr-'wǎn-shang chwān 'byàn-yī jyèw 'láy-le. ‖Excuse me for coughing. chǐng 'ywán-lyàng wo; wǒ yěw dyǎr-'ké-su. ‖Please excuse my bad Chinese; I'm just learning the language. chǐng 'ywán-lyàng, wǒ 'gāng shywé 'jūng-gwo-hwà, shwō bù-'hǎw.

Less often, where English may have Excuse me, *the following two expressions are used:* don't hold me up to ridicule byé 'shyàw-hwa; don't feel outraged byé jyàn-'gwày. ‖You'll have to excuse the way the house looks. nín byé 'shyàw-hwa, wǒ-men-de-'wū-dz 'lwàn-chǐ-bā-'dzāw-de. ‖Please excuse me! The child doesn't have any manners. chǐng byé jyàn-'gwày! 'háy-dz bù-dǔng 'lǐ-màw.

EXERCISE. (*Bodily movement*) 'ywùn-dùng. Take exercise yěw 'ywùn-dùng; (*practice*) (yěw) 'lyàn-shí. ‖In a job like this it's hard to get enough exercise. jèy-yàngr-de-'gūng-dzwò 'ywùn-dùng 'tày bú-'gèw. ‖You ought to take exercise at least three times a week. yì-'shīng-chī nǐ jr̄-shǎw děy yěw sān-tsz̀-'ywùn-dùng.

(*Particular set of motions*) 'dùng-dzwò. ‖**Each exercise should be performed fifty times.** 'mĕy-yí-ge-'dùng-dzwò dĕy dzwò 'wŭ-shŕ-hwéy.

To give exercise to (*a horse*) lyèw. ‖**We exercised the horses twice a day.** wŏ-men-de-'mă 'yì-tyān lyèw 'lyăng-hwéy. ‖**He went out·to exercise the horse.** tā lyèw-'mă-chywu-le.

(*To use*) yùng, *or indirect expressions.* ‖**He has exercised a good deal of ingenuity in this matter.** (*Literary*) dzày nèy-jyàn-'shŕ-ching-shang tā °hĕn 'dú-chū 'shīn-tsáy. *or* °yùng-le bù-shăw-de-'shīn-fá-dz. *or* °yùng-le bù-shăw-de-'chyăw-jāwr. ‖**Exercise care in handling that horse.** shŕ 'nèy-pĭ-mă dĕy °jyā 'shyăw-shīn. *or* °'tè-byé yùng-'shīn.

(*Problem*) 'shí-tí. ‖**Do all the exercises at the end of the lesson.** bă 'jèy-kè-shū-'hèw-myàn-de-'shí-tí 'dēw dzwò-le.

(*Formal program*) hwèy, dyăn-'lǐ. ‖**The graduation exercises will be held at 10 o'clock.** bì-yè-'hwèy dzày 'shŕ-dyăn-jūng kāy. *or* 'bì-yè-dyăn-'lǐ 'shŕ-dyăn 'jywŭ-shíng.

EXIST. (*Have being*) yĕw. ‖**I doubt if such a person exists.** wŏ 'bú-shìn yĕw 'dzèm-ge-'rén. *or* 'shŕ-jyè-shang 'năr yĕw 'jè-yàngr-rén? ‖**Such conditions shouldn't be allowed to exist in oùr neighborhood.** 'gēn-bĕn jyèw 'bù-gāy ràng 'dzám-jèr yĕw 'jèy-jŭng °-shŕ. *or* °-'chíng-shíng.

(*Sustain life*) hwó. ‖**He existed on water and fish only.** tā 'jŕ kàw-je 'ywú gēn-'shwĕy hwó-je. *or expressed as* He ate only water and fish. tā 'gwāng chŕ-'shwĕy hé-'ywú. ‖**Who can exist on such a meager ration?** fēn 'jèm-dyăr-'dŭng-shīn °jyàw-rén dzĕm 'hwó-de-'lyàw-ne? *or expressed as* Who gets enough to eat on such a meager ration? °gèw 'shéy-chŕ-de? ‖**How does he manage to exist on what he makes?** tā jèng-de 'nèy-dyăr-chyán dzĕm-me °hwó-de-'lyàw-ne? *or* °gèw 'chŕ-de-ne? *or* °gèw chŕ-'fàn-de-ne?

EXPECT. (*Think, suppose*) shyăng. ‖**When do you expect the train to get in?** nĭ shyăng hwŏ-chē 'shém-me-shŕ-hew jìn-'jàn? ‖**I expect you had a hard time finding this house.** wŏ shyăng nĭ 'jăw-dàw 'jèr láy hĕn 'kwèn-nán-ba.

(*Think of in advance*) shyăng-'dàw *only with negative preceding;* 'yĭ-wéy *only without negative preceding.* ‖**I never expected to see him again.** wŏ 'tsúng-láy méy-shyăng-'dàw néng 'dzày jyàn-de-'jáw tā. ‖**It's more than I expected.** méy-shyăng-'dàw 'jèm-dwō. ‖**He gave me more than I expected.** méy-shyăng-'dàw tā gĕy-wŏ 'jèm-dwō. ‖**It's easier than I expected.** wŏ 'ywán-láy 'yĭ-wéy °'méy-jèm 'rúng-yi. *or* °bĭ·'jè-ge 'nán.

(*Want*) shyăng 'yàw. ‖**Does he expect a tip?** t 'shŕ-bu-shr shyăng 'yàw shyăw-'fèy? ‖**Well, what did you expect?** (*A bit impolite unless said with a smile.*) háy 'shyăng yàw dzĕm-je-ne?

(*Count on something happening*) 'dă-swan; shyăng. ‖**You can't expect good weather here at this time of the year.** dzày 'jèy-ge-'jyé-chi-li, 'béng 'dă-swan (*or* shyăng) 'jèy-ge-dì-fang 'néng yĕw 'hăw-tyār.

' (*Count on someone for something*) 'jŕ-wàng. ‖**Don't expect too much of him.** byé 'tày 'jŕ-wàng tā. ‖**Don't expect too much of others.** byé jìng 'jŕ-wàng 'byé-rén. ‖**I never expected such gratitude froḿ him.** wŏ 'tsúng-láy méy-'jŕ-wàng (*or* méy-'shyăng-dàw; *see above*) tā neng 'dzèm 'bàw-dá wŏ. ‖**You have no right to expect him to have everything done for you.** nĭ 'bù-gāy 'jŕ-wàng 'rén-jyā gĕy-nĭ 'shém-me dēw dzwò-'hăw-le.

(*Hope for*) 'shī-wàng. ‖**Don't expect too much.** 'shī-wàng 'byé tày 'gāw.

(*Wait for*) dĕng; hèw. ‖**I'll expect you at six.** 'lyèw-dyăn-jūng wŏ °'dĕng-je nín. *or* °'hèw-je nín.

As well as can be expected háy 'hăw. ‖**He's doing as well as can be expected.** *is expressed as* If you say he's doing well, he is. shwō 'hăw-ne, yĕ háy 'hăw.

EXPENSE. kāy-'shyāw, 'fèy-yung; *or expressed by money* chyán *preceded by a word meaning* use, spend, much, little, *etc.; or by a compound built on to spend* fèy. ‖**I'd like to do it, but I can't afford the expense.** wŏ 'dzwò dàw-shr 'shyăng dzwò, bú-gwò °'méy nèm-shyē-'chyán. *or* °chū-bu-'chī nèm-shyē-'chyán. *or* °'dān-fu-bù-'lyăw nèm-'dà-de-'kāy-shyāw. *or* °'dān-fu-bù-'lyăw nèm-'dà-de-'fèy-yung. *or* °'fèy-yung (*or* 'kāy-shyāw) tày 'dà, wŏ chū-bu-'chī. ‖**The expense is more than I can afford.** 'fèy-yung (*or* 'kāy-shyāw) tày 'dà, wŏ 'dān-fu-bu-'chī. *or* yùng-'chyán tày 'dwō, wŏ 'dān-fu-bù-'lyăw. ‖**I must cut down expenses** (*economize a little*). wŏ dĕy 'jyàn-shĕng dyăr. *or* wŏ dĕy 'shăw-yùng-dyăr (*or* 'shăw-hwā-dyăr) 'chyán. ‖**He built the whole thing at his own expense.** jĕng-'gèr-de 'dēw-shŕ tā °yùng tā-'dz-jĭ-de-chyán 'gày-de. *or* °'dz-jĭ chū-chyán 'gày-de. *or expressed as* digging into his own pocket °'dz-jĭ tāw-yāw-'bāwr gày-de. ‖**I don't want to go to much expense for this party.** wŏ 'jèy-tsz-chĭng-'kè 'bù-shyăng hwā (*or* yùng, *or* chū) 'tày-dwō-de-chyán. ‖**Please don't go to any expense on my account.** byé wèy-wŏ °dwō hwā (*or* yùng)-'chyán. *or meaning* don't bother °tày fèy-'shīn-le.

Daily expenses *or* **miscellaneous expenses** 'líng-yùng-de-chyán, *or* 'líng-hwàr-de-chyán, *or* 'r̀-yùng-de-chyán, *or* 'dzá-fèy; **incidental expenses** (*paid by others*) bàn-'gūng-fèy; **traveling expenses** (*paid by others*) chū-'chāy-fèy; (*paid privately or by others*) 'lywŭ-fèy. ‖**He gets a straight salary and expenses in this job.** tā-jèy-ge-shŕ-ching 'jèng-shīn yĭ-'wày háy yĕw °bàn-'gūng-fèy. *or* °chū-'chāy-fèy.

At one's expense (*other than ṕnancial*). ‖**We had a good laugh at his expense.** tā gàn-le jyàn-'shă-shèr, jyàw-wŏm 'dà-shyàw. *or* tā gĕy-wŏm dèw-'shyàwr-lay-je.

EXPERIENCE. (*Time spent and knowledge gained; general term*) 'jīng-yàn; (*with resulting good judgment*) 'jyàn-shr̀; (*contacts with people, "getting around"*) ·'shr̀-myan. **Have experience** *or* **be experienced** yěw 'jīng-yàn, yěw 'jyàn-shr̀, jyàn(-gwo) 'shr̀-myan; (*literary, referring metaphorically to having been in battle*) jīng-gwo 'jèn; (*be expert; see also* **EXPERT**) dzày-'háng; *indirect expressions such as* **to see ..., to do ..., to learn about ..., to know ....** ‖**He has had a good deal of experience.** tā hěn yěw °'jīng-yàn. *or* °'jyàn-shr̀. *or* tā 'jyàn-gwo hén-dwō-'shr̀-myan. *or* tā .shr̀ jīng-gwo-'jèn-de. ‖**I am experienced in this.** jèy-ge wǒ °yěw 'jīng-yàn. (*or* °yěw 'jyàn-shr̀, *which implies too much conceit about one's judgment to say it of oneself; or* 'jyàn-gwo 'shr̀-myan, *which implies an admission of utter naïveté.*) ‖**He's as inexperienced as a ten-year-old.** tā gēn ge-'shŕ-swèy-de-'háy-dz shr̀-de nèm °méy-'jīng-yàn. *or* °méy-'jyàn-shr̀. *or* °méy-jyàn-gwo 'shr̀-myan. *or* °méy-jīng-gwo 'jèn. ‖**He's quite experienced in this sort of thing.** jèy-jǔng-'shr̀ tā·°hěn dzày-'háng. *or* °hěn, shr̀ ge-'háng-jya. *or* °hěn yěw 'jīng-yan. *or* (*an old hand*) °shr̀ ge-'lǎw-shěwr. ‖**He's quite inexperienced in this sort of thing.** jèy-jǔng-'shr̀ tā °méy-yěw 'jīng-yàn. *or* °méy-'jīng-yàn-gwo. *or* (*in xpert*) °shr̀ 'wày-háng. *or* °'bú-dzày-'háng. *or* °méy-'jyàn-gwo. ‖**I've learned by experience that this is the best way.** jywù (*or* jàw) wǒ-de-'jīng-yàn wǒ 'jř-daw jèy shr̀ 'dzwèy-hǎw-de-'bàn-fa. ‖**What experience do you have?** nǐ yěw 'dwō-shǎw-'jīng-yàn? *or* nǐ dēw 'dzwò-gwo 'shém-me-'shr̀? ‖**Is experience necessary?** yǐ-dìng yàw yěw 'jīng-yàn-ma? ‖**You might take that as an opportunity to gain some experience.** ná 'nèy-ge dàng °ge-dé-'jīng-yàn-de-'jī-hwey (*or* °ge-jǎng-'jyàn-shr-de-'jī-hwey) bù-yě-'hǎw-ma? *or* 'nèm-je jǎng-jang 'jyàn-shr bù-yě-'hǎw-ma? *or* (*To someone young*) 'nèm-je jyàn-jyan 'shr̀-myan bù-yě-'hǎw-ma? ‖**I haven't had much experience with cars.** *meaning* **haven't learned much about** chì-'chē-de-'shr̀ wǒ °bù-'shéw-shr. *or meaning* **don't know much about** °bù-'jř-daw shéme. *or* °'méy-yěw shéme-'jīng-yan.

(*Particular thing experienced; expressed indirectly*). ‖**That was really an experience!** *is expressed as* **That really wasn't lived through in vain.** nèy jēn méy-'báy gwo! ‖**I'll never forget the experience I had last night.** wǒ 'yǔng-ywǎn ·wàng-bu-lyǎw dzwér 'wǎn-shang nèy-jyàn-'shr̀. ‖**I'll never forget the bitter experience I had last night.** dzwér-'wǎn-shang-'shèw-de-'dzwèr wǒ 'dzày yě bù-néng 'wàng. ‖**I'll never forget the pleasant experiences I had with their family that summer.** wǒ gēn 'tām-jya yí-kwàr 'jù-de (*or* 'wár-de) nèy-yí-'shyà-tyan 'jēn shr̀ 'kwày-hwo; wǒ 'yǔng-ywǎn wàng-bu-'lyǎw.

(*Past time and circumstances*). **In all one's experience** 'tsúng-láy, 'yí-shyàng, 'shyàng-láy. ‖**In all my experience I've never seen such a thing happen.** wǒ 'tsúng-láy (*or* 'yí-shyàng, *or* 'shyàng-lay) méy 'jyàn-

gwo jè-yàngr-de-'shr̀. (*Note this possible translation:* **In all my experience I've never experienced such an experience.**)

(*Undergo, meet up with*) 'ywù-jyàn; (*have*) yěw. ‖**We may experience some difficulties.** wǒ-men hwèy 'ywù-jyàn shyē-ge-'kwèn-nán. ‖**We've never experienced such a debacle.** nèm-wéy-'nán-de-shr̀ wǒm-jèr 'shyàng-láy méy °'ywù-jyan-gwo. *or* °'yěw-gwo.

EXPERT. (*Specialist*) 'jwān-jyā, jwān-'mén-de-rén; (*in the trade, practised*) dzày-'háng; (*practised; one who is expert*) 'nèy-háng; (*experienced*) yěw-'jīng-yàn; (*an old hand*) 'lǎw-lyàn-de; (*expert in ...*) ... 'jīng; (*good at, skillful*) hǎw. ‖**He is considered an expert in his field.** rén 'dēw shwō tā dzày 'tā-nèy-háng-lǐ shr̀ ge-'jwān-jyā. ‖**He's an expert in that kind of work.** nèy-jǔng-'shr̀ tā °shr̀ ge-'nèy-háng. *or* °hěn 'nèy-háng. *or* °hěn yěw 'jīng-yàn. *or* °(hěn) dzày-'háng. ‖**The experts decided the documents were a forgery.** 'jwān-jyā 'dwàn-dìng nèy-shyē-'wén-jyàn shr̀ 'jyǎ-de. ‖**I need some expert advice.** wǒ děy 'chǐng-jyàw °'jwān-jyā. *or* °jwān-'mén-de-rén. *or* °yěw-'jīng-yàn-de. ‖**We need an expert mechanic for this job.** jèy-ge-'shr̀-ching děy jǎw °ge-'hǎw-jī-chi-'jyàng (*or* °ge-yěw-'jīng-yàn-de-jī-chi-'jyàng, *or* °ge-'lǎw-lyàn-de-jī-chi-'jyàng) láy dzwò. ‖**He is an expert at all kinds of games.** wár-'shéme tā dēw °'wár-de 'jīng. *or* °'wár-de 'hǎw.

EXPLAIN. (*Make clear*) jyǎng; (*speak; of mental problems only*) shwō; (*clarify; especially of a misunderstanding*) 'jyě-shr̀; *or any of these three as the first element of a resultative compound of which the second element is* 'míng-bay *or* 'chīng-chu. ‖**Could you explain how this machine works?** jèy-ge-'jī-chi dzěm 'shř gěy-wǒ 'jyǎng-yi-jyǎng shíng-ma? ‖**He can explain anything (clearly) in ordinary language.** shéme tā 'dēw néng yùng píng-'cháng-de-hwà °jyǎng-'míng-bay-le. *or* °'jyǎng-'chīng-chu-le. *or* °'shwō-'míng-bay-le. *or* °'shwō-'chīng-chu-le. *or* °'jyě-shr-'míng-bay-le. *or* °'jyě-shr-'chīng-chu-le. *or* °'jyǎng-de (*or* °'shwō-de, *or* °'jyě-shr-de) 'míng-míng-bay-'báy-de. (*or* 'chīng-chīng-chu-'chǔ-de). ‖**He explained and explained, but still nobody understood.** tā 'shwō-le yèw 'shwō *or* tā 'shwō-láy· shwō-'chywù, kě-shr 'háy méy-rén 'dǔng. (*Or substitute* jyǎng *or·* 'jyě-shr *for* shwō *in every case.*) ‖**It's hard for me to explain what that word means.** nèy-ge-dž-de-'yì-sz hěn nán °shwō-'míng-bay-le. *or* °'jyǎng-'chīng-chu-le. *or* °'jyě-shr-'míng-bay-le. *etc. or* °'jyǎng-de (*etc.*) jyàw-rén 'míng-bay. *or* °'jyě-shr-de (*etc.*) jyàw-rén 'tīng-de 'chīng-chu. ‖**I can explain everything.** wǒ láy °'shwō-shwō (*or* °'jyě-shr̀-jyě-shr) jyèw 'dēw míng-bay-le. ‖**Let me explain** (*a misunderstanding*). wǒ láy (*or* 'tīng-wǒ) 'jyě-shr̀-jyě-shr. ‖**Let me explain it to him.** 'jèy-ge-shr̀ ràng-'wǒ-lay gēn-tā °'shwō-shwō. *or* 'jyě-shr̀-jyě-shr. *or* 'jyǎng-jyang.

(*Justify, make excuses for; expressed indirectly*) ‖**Explain yourself.** 'dzěm-me-le? ‖**Can you explain** your behavior last night? nǐ dzwér 'wǎn-shang shr̀ 'dzěm-me-le? *or expressed as* Do you dare tell about it openly? nǐ gǎn bǎ dzwér-'wǎn-shang-de-'shr̀-ching gūng-kāy-de 'shwō-shwō-ma?

EXPRESS. (*Say in words*) shwō, shwō-chu-lay; (*talk about*) tán. Express oneself shwō(-'hwà); *also some indirect expressions.* ‖I want you to feel free to express your opinions. 'yěw shém-me-'hwà 'swéy-byàn °tán. *or* °shwō. *or* °shwō-chu-lay. ‖He expresses a desire to join the new political party. tā shwō shyǎng 'jyā-rù 'shīn-jèng-dǎng. ‖He expressed his opinion very clearly in a few words. tā yùng 'jǐ-'jywù-hwà bǎstá-de-'yì-jyàn shwō-de hěn 'chīng-chu. ‖I have difficulty expressing myself in Chinese. *meaning* often the words don't convey meaning wǒ shwō 'jūng-gwo-hwà °cháng-chang 'tsź-bù-dá-'yì. *or meaning* I can't express what I mean. °'bù-néng 'shyǎng-shém 'shwō-shém. *or meaning* It's an effort to express the meaning clearly. °yàw bǎ 'yì-sz shwō-'chīng-chu-le hěn fèy-'shr̀. ‖You can express yourself clearly if you use plain words. nǐ yàw-shr̀ yùng píng-'cháng-shwō-de-'hwà, jyèw kě-yǐ shwō-de jyàw-rén °'míng-bay-le. *or* °'dǔng. ‖He doesn't know how to express himself. tā 'bú-hwèy shwō-'hwà. *or* tā 'yěw-hwà bù-'jř-daw dzěm 'shwō. *or* tā 'yěw-hwà bú-hwèy 'shwō.

Express company 'jwǎn-ywùn-gūng-'sž. ‖Is it quicker to send this by mail or express? bǎ 'jèy-ge sùng-chywù shr̀ 'yéw-jèng-'jywú kwày, háy-shr 'jwǎn-ywùn-gūng-'sž kwày?

Express train. (*Fast train*) 'kwày-chē; (*super-express*) 'tè-byé-'kwày-chē. ‖Is the next train an express or a local? 'shyà-yí-tàng-'chē shr̀ 'kwày-chē háy-shr 'màn-chē? ‖Does the express train stop here? jèr 'kwày-chē tíng-ma? ‖Can I get an express train here? jèr yěw 'tè-byé-'kwày-chē-ma?

EXPRESSION. (*Manner of statement*) (shwō-de-)hwà. ‖That sounds like an old-fashioned expression. nèy-ge 'tīng-je hǎw shyàng shr̀ jywù-'lǎw-nyán-jyān-de-rén-shwō-de-'hwà.

(*Facial appearance*) 'lyǎn-sè; lyǎn-shang-de-'shén-chi. ‖I can tell what you're thinking by the expression on your face. wǒ kàn nǐ-de-'lyǎn-sè *or* wǒ kàn nǐ-de-'lyǎn-shang-de-'shén-chi, jyèw 'jř-dàw nǐ-de-'shīn-shr̀.

(*Token*) 'yì-sz; *this may include by implication the thing expressed, as* an expression of love, an expression of gratitude, *etc.* ‖I give you this book as a small expression of my gratitude. sùng-nín jèy-běr-'shū bú-gwo shr̀ ge-'shyǎw-yì-sz. *or* (*highly literary*) dzèng-'shū-yí-tsè, 'lywè-byǎw-'shyè-yì.

(*Feeling*) 'byǎw-chíng; 'yì-sz. Without expression 'sž-bu-la-jī-de. ‖He plays the piano without much expression. tā-de-gāng-'chín-tán-de °'méy shém-me-'byǎw-chíng. *or* °'sž-bu-la-jī-de. *or* °'méy shéme-'yì-sz.

EXTEND. (*Be extensive, reach a distance*) *expressed indirectly by expressions of distance, definitions of limits, etc.* ‖This road extends for miles in that direc-

tion. *is expressed as* That end of the road is far away. 'jèy-tyáw-'lù wàng 'nèy-téwr 'ywǎn-le chywù-le. ‖This farm extends for many miles to the east. *is expressed as* The eastern boundary of this farm is many miles away. jèy-ge-núng-'chǎng-'dūng-byar yěw 'hǎw-shyē-lǐ-'dì ywǎn. ‖The battle line extends (*literally is long*) from the mountains to the coast. jàn-'shyàn hěn 'cháng, tsúng-'shān dàw-'hǎy.

(*Lengthen*) 'yán-cháng; (*add; followed by what is added*) 'jyā. ‖The enemy extended his line along the river to the coast. 'dí-rén bǎ jàn-'shyàn yán-je hé-'àn 'yán-cháng-daw hǎy-'byār-shang-chywu-le. ‖They plan to extend the railroad to the coast next year. tā-men 'dǎ-swàn 'gwò-nyán bǎ 'jèy-tyáw-tyě-'lù 'yán-cháng-dàw hǎy-'àn. ‖They extended the fence to enclose the lake. tām bǎ-'chyáng 'jyā-le yí-dwàn, bǎ-'hú 'chywān (*or* 'tàw)-jìn-lay-le.

(*Postpone the date of expiration*) jǎn-'chī. ‖I'd like to get this visa extended. chǐng bǎ 'jèy-ge-hù-'jàw jǎn-'chī. ‖I'd like to get this visa extended to next June. chǐng bǎ 'jèy-ge-hù-jàw jǎn-'chī-dàw 'lyèw-ywè. ‖I'd like to get this visa extended for three months. chǐng bǎ 'jèy-ge-hù-jàw jǎn-'chī 'sān-ge-'ywè.

(*Offer*) gěy. ‖May we extend to you our heartiest congratulations? 'gěy nín dàw-'shǐ.

EXTRA. (*In addition*) *expressed adverbially by* 'lìng-wày; (*special*) 'gé-wày, wày; (*of an extra amount or number*) dwō; *expressed verbally by* ADD jyā. *Sometimes both adverb and verb occur.* ‖Do I get extra pay for this job? wǒ dzwò jèy-ge-'shr̀-ching °'gé-wày 'jyā-chyán-ma? *or* °'yěw 'lìng-wày-'jyā-de-chyán-ma? *or* °'yěw jyā-'jǐ-ma? *or* °'yěw wày-'jyā-de-chyán-ma? *or* wǒ dzwò 'jèy-jyàn-shr̀ ('jèng-shīn-jř-'wày, *or* 'gūng-chyán-jř-'wày) háy gěy-'chyán-ma? ‖How much extra pay do you get for doing this? nǐ dzwò 'jèy-ge dé 'dwō-shaw-wày-'jyā-de-chyán? ‖We must put in some extra time in order to finish this on time. děy ('gé-wày, *or* 'lìng-wày) jyā-'gūng tsáy néng bú-'wù-chī-ne. ‖You probably need only five tickets, but I'm giving you a few extras. nǐ dà-gày 'wǔ-jāng-pyàw jyèw 'gèw-le, bú-gwò wǒ dzày (*or* lìng-'wày) dwō 'gěy-nǐ 'jǐ-jāng.

(*Special*) 'tè-byé, 'gé-wày. ‖Pay extra attention to this. jèy-ge 'tè-byé (*or* 'gé-wày) lyéw-'shén.

(*Superfluous*) 'fù-ywu-de. Have extra 'fù-ywu. ‖Do you have an extra pencil you could lend me? nǐ yěw 'fù-ywu-de-chyán-'bǐ 'jyè-gěy wǒ yì-'jř-ma? ‖I have two extra blankets. wǒ 'fù-ywu 'lyǎng-jāng-'tǎn-dz.

(*An actor without assigned parts*). To be an extra dāng 'shyán-jyǎwr, pǎw 'lúng-tàw. ‖He worked for years as an extra before he got his first part. tā dāng-le 'jǐ-nyán 'shyán-jyǎwr (*or* tā 'pǎw-le hǎw-jǐ-nyán 'lúng-tàw) yǐ-'hèw, tsáy 'dāng-de 'pèy-jyǎwr.

EXTREME (EXTREMELY). ‖This is an extreme case. *is expressed as* This isn't frequent. 'jèy-ge bú-shr 'cháng-yěw-de. *or as* This isn't often seen. 'jèy-ge bù-'cháng jyàn. *But usually when we say something is* extreme, *Chinese says it is* extremely . . . . *The terms for* extremely *are* . . . 'jí-le, dǐng . . ., 'fēy-cháng . . ., 'shf-fēn . . ., 'jí-chi . . ., (*too, very*) tày . . .; *with some adjectives* jí . . .; *with* poor chyúng *and* bad hwày *only,* . . . tèw. ‖This is an extreme case. *meaning* This is an extremely serious crime. jèy shr 'jí-dà-de-'dzwèy. *or* jèy shr 'jí-jùng-de-'àn-dz. *or* jèy shr 'fēy-cháng-'jùng-dà-de-'àn-dz. *or* 'jèy shr !dǐng-dà-de-'dzwèy; *or other combinations with* 'shf-fēn, 'jí-chi, dǐng, 'fēy-cháng. ‖Such an operation is necessary only in extreme(ly serious) cases (of illness). 'jèy-yàng-de-'shěw-shù jř yěw °'lì-hay-'jí-le-de-'bìng (*or* -'jèng-hèw *for* -bìng, *or* °'jí-lì-hay-de-'bìng *or* °'jí-shyūng-de-'bìng *or* °'dǐng-shyūng-de-'bìng *or* °'dǐng-lì-hay-de-'bìng *or* °'fēy-cháng-'lì-hay-de-'bìng *or* °'jí-chi-'lì-hay-de-'bìng *or other combinations with* shyūng *instead of* 'lì-hay) tsáy 'yùng-de-'jáw. ‖He was reduced to extreme poverty. tā 'hèw-lay °chyúng-'jí-le. *or* °chyúng-'tèw-le, *or* °lè-pwò-'jí-le. ‖He is extremely sensitive about his baldness. tā 'fēy-cháng (*or* 'shf-fēn, *or* 'jí-chi, *or* tày) 'jì-hwèy rén shwō tā 'tū. ‖He is in extreme danger. tā 'jí-chi 'wéy-shyǎn. *or* tā 'wéy-shyǎn 'jí-le. *or expressed as* He is in danger to the 10,000th degree. tā 'wéy-shyǎn-dàw 'wàn-fēn-le. ‖This weapon is extremely useful in jungle warfare. jèy-jǔng-'wǔ-chì dzày 'sēn-lín-jàn-de-shf-hew °'yùng-chu dà 'jí-le. *or* °'fēy-cháng yěw-'yùng. *or* °'dǐng yěw-'yùng. ‖We never have any extremes in temperature here. *is expressed as* It's never too hot nor too cold. jèr-'tyān-chi shyàng-lay méy-yěw 'tày-lěng-'tày-rè-de-shf-hew. *or as* It's always mild. jèr-'tyān-chi shyàng-lay hěn 'wēn-hé.

Go to extremes, be extreme (*be excessive*) gwò-'fèn; *or, in cases in which the meaning is appropriate, the expressions described above may be used.* ‖Let's not go to extremes. dzám byé tày 'nèm-je-lew. *or* dzám byé (tày) gwò-'fèn-lew. ‖She is extreme in her tastes. tā 'shǐ-hwān shém, jyèw 'shǐ-hwān-de gwò-'fèn. ‖You may tease him, but don't go to extremes. 'dèw-dèw-ta bú-'yàw-jǐn, 'kě byé dèw-de °'tày 'lì-hay-lew. *or* °('tày) gwò-'fèn-lew. ‖If he goes to extremes in this matter, you'll have to let him learn his lesson. 'jèy-jyàn-shr tā yàw-shr 'bàn-de gwò-'fèn-le, nǐ jyèw děy gěy-tā ge-'jyàw-shywun.

Go from one extreme to the other *is expressed as* change extremely byàn-de hěn 'lì-hay. ‖He always goes from one extreme to the other. *is expressed as* He always changes extremely, in one change to the opposite end. tā 'lǎw-shr byàn-de hěn 'lì-hay, yí-'byàn jyèw 'byàn-de °'jèng shyàng-'fǎn. *or* °'tsúng 'jèy-téwr dàw 'nèy-téwr. ‖He went from one extreme to the other and married a chorus girl. tā 'byàn-de 'tày 'lì-hay-le; 'chywǔ-le ge-wǔ-'nywǔ.

EYE. (*Organ of vision*) 'yǎn-jing; *in compounds and some phrases* yǎn *or occasionally* yǎr. **Before the eyes** yǎn-'chyán; **cross-eyed** 'dèw-yǎr; **left eye** 'dzwò-yǎn; **right eye** 'yèw-yǎn; **eyelash** yǎn-'máw; **eyebrow** yǎn-'méy; **eyeball** yǎn-'jūr (*used also in referring to the color of eyes*). ‖My eyes are tired. wǒ 'yǎn-jīng lèy-le. ‖Small type hurts the eyes. 'shyǎw-dzèr shāng 'yǎn-jīng. ‖Open your eyes wide. bǎ 'yǎn-jīng jěng-'dà-lew. ‖Close your eyes. 'bì-shang 'yǎn-jīng. ‖This eyewash will relieve the strain on your eyes. yùng 'jèy-ge-shǐ-'yǎn-yàw-'shwěy kě-yǐ jyàw 'yǎn-jīng 'shū-fu. ‖It's right before your eyes. 'jvèw dzày nǐ-yǎn-'chyán-ner. ‖I have something in my eye. wǒ 'yǎn-jīng-lǐ 'jìn-chywu dyǎr-'dūng-shi. ‖He is blind in one eye. tā 'yì-jř-'yǎn-jīng shyā-le. ‖He is nearsighted in his left eye, and astigmatic in the right. tā 'dzwǒ-yǎn 'jìn-shr, 'yèw-yǎn 'sǎn-gwāng. ‖He is cross-eyed. tá shr 'dèw-yǎr. ‖Her eyelashes and eyebrows were burned, but her eyes weren't hurt. tā-yǎn-'máw yǎn-'méy dēw 'shǎw-le, kě-shr 'yǎn-jīng hǎw-'hāwr-de. ‖One of his eyes (*eyeballs*) is false. tā yěw yí-ge-'jyǎ-yǎn-jūr. ‖His eyes are blue. tā-de-yǎn-'jūr shr 'lán-de. *or* tā shr 'lán-yǎn-jūr. ‖Have you got anything good for a black eye? 'yǎn-jīng-nar dǎ-'chīng-le, 'yěw-fár 'jr-ma? ‖She gave me the eye, but I went right by. tā gēn-wo fēy-'yǎr, kě-shr wǒ méy-'lǐ-ta. ‖It's invisible to the naked eye. 'rèw-yǎn bù-néng 'kàn-jyan.

To eye *or* have one's eyes on *something or someone* pyāw, byāw, kàn. ‖He's been eyeing me for the last half hour. tā (ná-'yǎn-jing) 'pyāw-wǒ pyāw-le (*or* 'byāw-wǒ byāw-le, *or* 'kàn-wǒ kàn-le) 'bàn-dyǎn-jūng-le.

Set eyes on 'kàn-jyàn. ‖I never set eyes on her before in my life. wǒ 'jèy-bèy-dz 'téw-yì-hwéy 'kàn-jyàn-ta. *or* wǒ 'shàng-láy méy-'kàn-jyan-gwo tā.

Catch one's eye ràng . . . 'kàn-jyan *followed by a pronoun referring to the subject.* ‖I've been trying to catch your eye for the last half hour. yěw 'bàn-dyǎn-jūng-le wǒ shyǎng-'fár ràng nǐ 'kàn-jyan wǒ.

Keep an eye on 'kān; chyáw. ‖Keep an eye on him. 'kān-je-tā-dyar. *or* 'chyáw-je-tā-dyar. ‖Be sure to keep an eye on the children. 'chyān-wàn 'kān-je-dyar (*or* 'chyáw-je-dyar) háy-dz-men.

Be all eyes *phrases with* look kàn. ‖The boy was all eyes. shyǎw-'hár kàn-de chū-'shér-le. *or* shyǎw-'hár 'mù-bu-jwǎn-'jīng-de kàn.

Have an eye to *or* have one's eye on 'chyáw-shang. ‖He has an eye to her fortune. tā 'chyáw-shang-le tā-de-'tsáy-chǎn-le. ‖He has his eye on that position. tā 'chyáw-shang-le 'nèy-ge-'wèy-jr-le.

Keep an eye out for lyéw-'shén. ‖Keep an eye out for escaped prisoners. yěw 'fú-lwǒ 'táw-le, 'lyéw-dyar-'shén.

Have a good eye (*aim*). ‖He has a good eye. tā hwèy myāw-'jwěn.

Have a good eye for yěw 'yǎn-lì. ‖He has a good eye for horses. tā kàn-'mǎ hěn yěw 'yǎn-lì.

Make eyes at (*fish for*) dyàw. ‖Don't make eyes at married women. byé dyàw jyē-le-'hwēn-de-'nywǔ-rén.

In one's eyes (*opinion*). ‖In the eyes of his parents he's a little angel. tā-de-dyē-'mā kě 'ná-tā 'dàng ge-bǎw-'bèr kàn-nye.

Pull the wool over one's eyes. jyàw ... 'shàng ... 'dàng-de. or jyàw ... 'shèw ... 'pyàn-de. ‖His suave manner is likely to pull the wool over your eyes. tā nèy-jǔng-'tǎw-rén-'shī-hwān-de-yàngr hwèy jyàw-nǐ °'shàng tā-de-'dàng-de. or °'shèw tā-de-'pyàn-de.

Close one's eyes to (*pretend not to be able to see*) 'jwāng kàn-bu-'jyàn. ‖He closes his eyes to his pupils' mischievous pranks. 'shy.wé-sheng-men táw-'chì, tā 'jwāng kàn-bu-'jyàn.

With one's eyes open míng-'míng-de 'jř-daw. ‖He did it with his eyes open. míng-'míng-de 'jř-daw-me. ‖His eyes were open all right, but he married her anyway. tā míng-'míng-de 'jř-daw, kě-shr 'háy gēn-ta jyē-'hwēn-le. *Compare* ‖That'll open his eyes. 'nèy jyèw 'jyàw-ta 'míng-bay-le.

With one's eyes shut 'hú-li-hú-'dū-de. ‖He went into that marriage with his eyes shut. tā 'hú-li-hú-'dū-de jyèw jyē-le 'hwēn-le.

With dry eyes (*not crying*). ‖She went through the funeral with dry eyes. shíng-dzàng-'lǐ-de-shŕ-hew tā yì-'dyǎr méy-'kū.

See eye to eye. *Chinese refers to the point of view* (kàn-fǎ) *being the same.* (*See* SAME). ‖I don't see eye to eye with you on this question. 'jèy-ge-wèn-tí wǒ gēn 'nǐ-de-kàn-fǎ °bù-'túng. or °bù-yí-'yàng. ‖They don't see eye to eye on much of anything. tām 'jī-hu 'shéme-shř dēw °'yì-'jyàn bù-'hé. or °bù-yí-'yì. or 'jī-hu 'shéme-shř tām-de-'kàn-fǎ dēw °bù-'túng. or °bù-yí-'yàng. ‖We do see eye to eye, don't we? 'dzám kàn-fǎ yí-'yàng (or shyāng-'túng). 'dwèy-ma? or 'dzám yì-jyan shyāng-'hé, 'dwèy-ma?

Eye (*small round hole*) yǎr. The eye of a needle jēn-'yǎr. *But for* hook and eye *Chinese merely says* hook gēwr, 'gēw-dz. ‖This coat fastens at the neck with a hook and eye. jèy-jyàn-wày-'yī líng-dz-ner shř yùng-'gēwr-gēw-shang-de. *However, when the two parts have to be distinguished, use* yǎr. ‖The eye is squeezed shut; I can't hook it. yǎr 'jǐ-jǐn-le; wǒ 'gēw-bu-jin-chywu.

‖My eye! *is expressed as* How strange! tsáy-'gwày-ne! ‖Hasn't she been kind to you? Kind, my eye! tā bú-shr 'dày-nǐ hěn 'hǎw-ma? 'tā dày-'wǒ hǎw!? tsáy-'gwày-ne!

F

FACE. (*Physical features*) lyǎn, lyǎr; myàn, myàr (*especially the appearance, or when speaking of looking at someone's face*). ‖When he gets angry his face gets red. tā yì shēng-'chì, 'lyǎn jyèw 'húng. ‖His face is oval. tā shř ge-'é-dàn-lyǎr. ‖His face is pockmarked. tā 'lyǎn-shang yěw 'má-dz. or tā shř ge-'má-dz. ‖What an ugly face! 'nèy-lyǎr hǎw °'hán-chen-le! or °nán-'kàn-le! or (*fierce*) °'shyūng-shyàngr! ‖Lie on the bed face down. lyǎn cháw-'shyà pā-je. ‖He was laid on the bed face up. tām bǎ-tā lyǎn-cháw-'shàng gē-dzày 'chwáng-shang. ‖Ever since she lost her job she's been going around with a long face. 'dž-tsúng tā bǎ-'shèr dyēw-le, °tā-'lyǎn-shang jyèw méy-'dày-gwo 'shyàw-rúngr. or °tā jyèw 'lǎw běng-je ge-'lyǎn. or °tā jyèw 'lǎw kū-sang-je ge-'lyǎn. or (*pouting*) °tā jyèw lǎw jywē-je 'dzwěy. ‖He said it with a straight face. tā 'běng-je lyǎn 'shwǒ-de. ‖I'd call him that right to his face. wǒ jyèw 'dāng-je tā-de-'myàr nèm 'mà-ta-le. ‖He has an intelligent face. tā-'myàn-màw hěn 'tsūng-míng. or (*He looks intelligent*) tā-'jǎng-de-'yàng-dz hěn 'tsūng-míng. ‖His face looks familiar to me. jèy-rén wǒ kàn-je myàn-'shéw. ‖His face is unfamiliar to me. jèy-rén wǒ kàn-je myàn-'shēng. ‖How can you look me in the face (*with a shameless face*) and say that? nǐ dzěm 'tyěn-je lyǎn shwō shyā-'hwàr-a? *But* ‖Can you look me in the face and say that (*is the truth*)? nèy shř shŕ-'hwà-ma?

(*Surface, side*) myàr. (*But, of a cliff,* yáy *is usually used, though* yáy-'myàr *is possible.*) ‖I can't see the face of the clock from here. jūng-de-'jèng-myàr wǒ tsúng-'jèr chyáw-bu-'jyàn. ‖The face of the coin has been rubbed almost smooth. chyán-yěw-'dzèr-de-nèy-myàr kwày mwó-'gwāng-le. ‖A poem was inscribed on the face of the cliff. 'yáy-shang 'kè-je yì-shěw-'shř. ‖The face of the cliff is steep and forbidding. 'shywán-yáy 'dwàn-bì kàn-je 'shèn-rén.

(*Honor, social prestige*) lyǎn, 'myàn-dz; lose face *is expressed with the foregoing, or also as* dzǎy 'gēn-dew (*fall flat*). ‖He felt that he had lost face when you said that to him in front of other people. nǐ dāng-je 'byé-rén gēn-tā shwō nèy-jywù-'hwà de-shŕ-hew, tā jywé-je °dyēw-'lyǎn-le. or °dzǎy 'gēn-dew-le. or °hěn méy 'myàn-dz. ‖When you said "No!" to him like that, it made him lose face. nǐ 'nèm-je gēn-tā shwō: 'bù-'shíng, jyàw-tā 'jywé-je hěn °dyēw-'lyǎn. or °méy 'myàn-dz. ‖They're afraid of losing face in the community. tām 'pà dzǎy 'jyē-fang-'lín-jywu gēn-chyan °dyēw-'lyǎn. or °dzǎy 'gēn-dew. ‖You should have been more considerate of his "face", and not have said that to him in front of others. nǐ yīng-gāy gěy-tā lyéw dyǎr-'myàn-dz, 'bù-gāy nèm 'dāng-je 'rén shwō-tā. ‖He was trying to save his face when he gave those excuses. tā nèm 'jyé-lì-de 'jě-shwō shř °'pà dyēw-'lyǎn. or °yàw 'gù-chywán tā-dž-'gěr-de-'myàn-dz. ‖He's so ashamed that he doesn't dare show his face. tā ('sàw-de) °bù-gǎn lèw-'myàr-le. or *meaning* doesn't dare to see people ˇbu-găn jyàn-'rén-le. *or meaning* doesn't have the face to see people °'méy-lyăr jyàn-'rén-le,

To face (*physically*). (*Of position*) chùng-je *or* cháw-je; (*of position or motion*) shyàng-je; (*especially of facing a counterpart*) dwèy-je. (*When speaking of one person facing another or others*, kàn *is often added.*) ‖**Turn around and face the wall.** 'jwăn-gwo-chywu chùng-je (*or* cháw-je) 'chyáng. ‖**Our windows face the street.** wŏm-de-'chwāng-hu shyàng-je (*or* chùng-je, *or* cháw-je, *or* dwèy-je) dà-'jyē. ‖**He lives in the house facing ours.** tā jù wŏm-dwèy-'mér-de-nèy-swŏr-'fáng-dz-li. ‖**Suddenly he turned his head and faced her.** tā 'hú-rán jwăn-gwo 'téw láy 'cháw-je (*or* 'chùng-je) tā kàn.

(**To**) **face** (*in military commands*) shyàng . . . 'jwăn. ‖**About, face!** shyàng-'hèw 'jwăn! ‖**Left, face!** shyàng-'dzwŏ 'jwăn! ‖**Right, face!** shyàng-'yèw 'jwăn!

To face (*meet with; also in the face of*) lín. ‖**He faced death unflinchingly.** tā lín-'sž 'myàn bù-găy-'sè. *or* tā lín-'sž 'shén-sè bú-byàn. ‖**He can face any crisis and remain steady.** tā lín-je 'shéme-'dà-shŕ 'dēw néng 'jèn-jìng. *or* tā 'lín-shŕ 'jèn-jìng. ‖**He remained cool in the face of great danger.** tā 'dà-nán-lín-'téw 'shīn-li 'háy-shr nèm 'jèn-jìng.

To face (*deal with*) 'yìng-fù. ‖**You should face your troubles like a man.** nĭ 'yìng-fù jèy-shyē-'nán-shŕ yīng-gāy shyàng ge-'nán-dz-hàn-dà-'jàng-fu tsáy chéng.

Be faced (*covered on the outside*). (*All around*) 'wày-myàr shŕ . . .; (*in front*) 'chyán-myàr shŕ . . . (*both followed by the material*). ‖**The building is faced with red brick.** jèy-ge-léw-'wày-myàr (*or* jèy-ge-léw-'chyán-myàr) shŕ yì-tséng-'húng-jwān.

Be faced (*hemmed*) yán-shang . . . byār. ‖**She had the collar and cuffs faced in red.** tā bă 'lĭng-dz gēn shyèw-'kĕwr dēw yán-shang 'húng-byār.

Face to face myàn-dwèy-'myàr-de. ‖**They sat through the meeting face to face, but neither one would say a word to the other.** kāy-'hwèy-de-shŕ-hew tām myàn-dwèy-'myàr-de dzwò-je, kĕ-shr yì-'jŕ shéy yĕ bù-'lĭ-shéy. ‖**Let's get together and talk the whole thing over face to face.** dzám 'jywù-yi-jywù, °myàn-dwèy-'myàr-de (*or* °'jŕ-jyē, *literally* directly) bă 'jèy-jyàn-shèr 'dž-shì 'tán-yi-tán.

Come face to face with (*figuratively*) 'ywù-jaw; 'pèng-jaw. ‖**Suddenly we came face to face with a difficult problem.** 'mĕng-rán-jyàn wŏm 'ywù-jaw-le (*or* 'pèng-jaw-le) yí-jyàn-nán-'bàn-de-'shŕ.

Make faces dzwò 'gwĕy-lyăr. ‖**Stop making faces at me.** 'byé gēn-wŏ dzwò 'gwĕy-lyăr.

Make a face lyĕ-'dzwĕy; dzèw bí-dz. ‖**He made a face when he tasted it.** tā 'cháng-le yì-kĕw, jŕ °lyĕ-'dzwĕy. *or* °dzèw 'bí-dz.

Face down (*not of people*) 'kèw-je; **face up** 'fān-je. ‖**Put your cards on the table face down.** bă-páy 'kèw-je fàng-dzay 'jwŏr-shang.

Face value. ‖**This banknote is still worth its face value.** jèy-jāng-'pyàw-dz °'háy-shr 'bù-jé-bú-'kèw-de (*literally, no discount*). *or* °'háy néng àn-je pyàw-'myàr hwàn-'chyán (*or* dwèy-'shyàn) (*literally, can be exchanged according to its face*). ‖**Don't take his word at its face value.** tā-de-'hwà °dĕy dă 'jé-kèw. *or* °'bù-néng chywán shìn.

On the face of it tsúng byăw-'myàr-shang kàn. ‖**His idea seems to be absurd on the face of it.** 'tā-jèy-ge-'jú-yí tsúng byăw-'myàr-shang kàn 'hăw shyàng' shŕ bù-'tūng shŕ-de.

Face card dày-rén-'téwr-de-páy.

Face the music. ‖**I guess I'd better go home and face the music.** wŏ shyăng wŏ háy-shr hwéy-'jyā °āy-'shwō-chywu-ba. *or* °'gāy shèw shéme-'dzwèy jyèw 'shèw-chywu-ba.

FACT. (*The real situation*) 'jēn-shŕ, 'jēn-yĕw-de-shŕ, 'shŕ-dzày(-yĕw)-dę-shŕ; *or expressed adjectivally by* 'jēn-de (*true*); *or expressed adverbially by* jēn (*really*) *or similar adverbs.* ‖**Is this a fact or is it just your own opinion?** 'jèy shŕ 'jēn-shŕ (*or* 'jèy shŕ 'jēn-yĕw-de-shŕ *or* 'jèy shŕ 'shŕ-dzày(-yĕw)-de-shŕ), háy-shr °nĭ-'dž-jĭ-de-'yì-jyan? *or* °nĭ 'jywé-je shŕ dzèm-je? ‖**Is that a fact?** shŕ 'jēn-de-ma? *or* 'jēn-de-ma? *or* 'jēn yĕw nèm hwéy-'shŕ-ma? *or* nèy-jyàn-'shŕ-ching shŕ 'jēn-de-ma? ‖**Tell him the facts.** *meaning* Whatever there is 'yĕw-shéme jyèw gēn-tā 'shwō-shéme. *or meaning* What you actually saw bă nĭ-'chīn-yăn-'kàn-jyan-de-shŕ gàw-sung tā. *or meaning* What you actually heard bă nĭ-'chīn-ĕr-'tīng-jyan-de-shŕ gàw-sung tā. *or* bă 'jēn-yĕw-de-shŕ gàw-su tā.

(*In a legal case*) 'shŕ-shŕ, 'shŕ-ching, 'jēn-shyàng, 'chíng-yéw. ‖**Do you understand the facts in this case?** jèy-ge-'àn-dz-de-'shŕ-shŕ (*or* jèy-ge-'àn-dz-de-'shŕ-ching, *or* jèy-ge-'àn-dz-de-'jēn-shyàng, *or* jèy-ge-'àn-dz-de-'chíng-yéw) nĭ dēw 'chīng-chu-ma?

(*Situation, referring to something already mentioned*) shŕ, shèr, 'shè-ching; **the fact that . . .** . . . nèy-jyàn-shŕ; . . . jèy-jyàn-shŕ; *or simply omitted.* ‖**That fact makes no difference to me.** 'nèy-jyàn-shŕ wŏ °bù-'gwăn. *or* °bú-'dzày-hu. ‖**What about the fact that you were late for work today?** (*What do you have to say?*) nĭ 'jīn-tyan chŕ-'dàw, (jèy-jyàn-shŕ) nĭ yèw dzĕm °'shwō-ne? *or* (*What are you going to do about it?*) °'bàn-ne?

(*Something assumed to be true*). ‖**His facts** (*what he says*) **are definitely open to question.** tā-'shwō-de (-nèy-shyē-shŕ) 'dēw °bú-jyàn-de shŕ 'jēn-de. *or* °yĕw kĕ-'yí-de-dì-fang.

The facts of life 'rén-shèr. ‖**It's time he learned the facts of life.** tā 'gāy jŕ-dàw dyăr-'rén-shèr-le.

As a matter of fact *or* **in fact** chí-'shŕ. ‖**As a matter of fact, I couldn't go if I wanted to.** chí-'shŕ wŏ jyèw-shr yàw chywù °háy· chywù-bu-'lyăw-ne. *or* °yĕ chywù-bu-'lyăw-wa. ‖**In fact, he's a Ph.D.** chí-'shŕ tā háy shŕ-ge-'bwó-shŕ·ne.

FAIL. (*Not succeed*) bū or méy *with a verb* (*usually* néng *or some other verb expressing ability*), *or a resultative compound with* bū. ‖I failed to convince him. wǒ 'méy-néng °jyǎw-tā 'shìn. *or* °bǎ-tā shwō-de 'hwéy-shǐn-jwàn-'yì-le. *or* °bǎ-tā shwō-'fú-le. ‖I failed to find him. wǒ 'méy-jǎw-'jáw tā. ‖I still fail to see the point of your argument. wǒ háy méy-'tīng-chu-lay nǐ-'shwō-de 'jyēw-jìng shǐ shéme-'yì-sz. ‖I tried to do it alone, but failed. wǒ 'běn-lay shyǎng dž-'gěr dzwò-de, bú-gwò °bù-'shíng. *or* °bù-'chéng. *or* °méy bàn-'dàw. *or* °dzwò-bù-'lyǎw. *or* °bàn-bú-'dàw.

(*Of crops*). (*Not good*) bù-'hǎw; (*none at all*) 'méy-yěw .... ‖The crops failed last year. chywù-nyán 'shēw-chéng bù-'hǎw. *or* chywù-nyán 'méy-yěw 'shēw-chéng.

(*Of business*). (*Fail*) dǎw; (*lose money*) péy; (*close doors*) gwān-'mén; (*go bankrupt*) pwò-'chǎn; (*not succeed*) *negative with* dzwò-'chéng *or* dzwò-'hǎw. ‖His business failed. tā-de-'mǎy-may °dǎw-le. *or* °'péy-le. *or* °gwān-'mén-le. *or* °pwò-'chǎn-le. *or* °'méy-dzwò-'chéng. *or* °'méy-dzwò-'hǎw.

(*In school*) 'bú-jì-'gé. ‖Five students in the class failed. nèy-'bān yěw 'wǔ-ge-shywé-sheng 'bú-jì-'gé.

(*Of a sick person*). (*At a particular moment*) yàw bù-'shíng-le; (*over a long time*) bìng-de 'ywè láy ywè 'lì-hay. ‖The patient is failing rapidly. 'bìng-rén yàw bù-'shíng-le. *or* 'bìng-rén bìng-de 'ywè láy ywè 'lì-hay.

To fail (*a person*), *many varied expressions.* ‖I won't fail you. wǒ 'shwō dzěm-je 'jyèw dzěm-je. *or* wǒ 'shwō-le jyèw 'swàn. ‖I won't fail to help you out of this jam. nǐ-'jèy-jyàn-shǐ wǒ 'jwěn gěy-nǐ 'bàn. *or* °'shwō-le bāng-ní jyèw 'jwěn bāng-nǐ. ‖He failed me when I needed his help most. wǒ 'jí-ywu yùng-de-jáw tā de-shí-hew tā méy-°'bāng-wǒ. *or* °'lǐ-wǒ. ‖This rifle of mine never fails me. (*It is accurate*) wǒ-'jèy-gǎn-chyāng °hěn 'jwěn. *or* °'shwō dǎ-nǎr dǎ-'nǎr. *or* (*It is reliable*) °hěn dé-'jì. ‖Words fail me. wǒ 'yěw-hwà 'shwō-bu-chū 'láy.

‖Be there without fail. *or* ‖Don't fail to be there. 'byé bú-'dàw.

FAINT. (*Lose consciousness*) 'hwēn-gwo-chywu; 'ywǔn-gwo-chywu. ‖Someone fainted. yěw-rén 'hwēn-gwo-chywu-le. *or* yěw-rén 'ywūn-gwo-chywu-le. *or* (*figuratively*) 'shyà yí-'tyàw. ‖You'll faint when you hear this. nǐ 'tīng-jyan jèy-ge děy 'shyà yí-'tyàw.

(*Dizzy and weak*) hwēn (*said of* téw, *the head*); ywùn. ‖I feel faint. wǒ-'téw yěw dyǎr-'hwēn. *or* wǒ (yěw dyǎr-) 'téw-hwēn. *or* wǒ yěw dyǎr-'ywùn.

(*Weak, of color*) dàn. ‖The color is too faint. shǎr tày 'dàn.

(*Not distinct, of ideas, etc.*) *constructions with* shadow·yǐng. ‖I have only a faint idea of what you said. nǐ-'shwō-de wǒ 'yǐng-ying-chaw-'chāwr-de jì-de yì-dyǎr. ‖I don't have the faintest idea of what you're talking about. nǐ-shwō-de-hwà wǒ yì-dyǎr-'yěngr dēw mwō-bu-'jáw.

Faint-hearted 'shyǎw *or* 'chywè (*said of* 'dǎn-dz *or* dǎn *or* dǎr, *courage*). ‖He's a faint-hearted individual. tā dǎr-'shyǎw. *or* tā dǎn-'chywè, *or* tā shǐ ge-shyǎw-'dǎr. *or* tā-'dǎn-dz tày 'shyǎw.

FAIR. (*Just, honest*) 'gūng-píng, 'gūng-daw. (*Only* 'gūng-ping *is used of people's treatment of each other; only* 'gūng-daw *is used of a price; some more general expressions are also used.*) ‖That's a fair way to say it. 'nèm-shwō-de hěn 'gūng-píng (*or* 'gūng-daw). ‖They made a fair distribution. tǎm-fēn-de hěn 'gūng-píng (*or* 'gūng-daw). ‖He always treats me fairly. tā dày-wǒ 'lǎw-shr °hěn 'gūng-píng-de. *or* °hěn 'hǎw-de. *or* °hǎw-'hāwr-de. *or* (*He never cheats me*) tā 'shyàng-lay bù-'chī-fu wǒ. ‖That's a fair price. 'jyàr hěn 'gūng-daw. ‖Give me a fair price and I'll let you have it. gěy ge-'gūng-daw-jyàr wǒ jyèw 'mày. ‖They said he wasn't playing fair (*literally or figuratively*). tǎm shwō tā °bù-'gūng-píng. *or* °bù-'gūng-daw. *or* (*wasn't being reasonable*) °bù-jyǎng-'lǐ. *or* (*wasn't going according to the rules*) °bú-jàw 'gwēy-jywu bàn-'shǐ.

(*Moderately good*). ‖The work is only fair. 'dzwò-de °píng-'cháng. *or* °bú-tày hǎw yě bú-tày 'hwày. *or* °'háy hǎw. *or* °shyàng-'dāng-de 'hǎw.

(*Moderate in size*). ‖He has a fair chance of winning. tā-'yíng-de-jī-hwèy °bù-'shyǎw. *or* °shyàng-dāng 'dà.

(*Moderate in amount*). ‖Give me a fair amount of it. gěy-wǒ-de byé tày 'dwō yě byé tày 'shǎw. *or* 'bù-dwō-bù-'shǎw-de gěy-wǒ-dyar jyèw 'shíng. *or* 'byé gěy-wǒ tày-'shǎw-lew.

(*Light in color*). (*Of complexion*) báy; (*of hair*) chyǎn. A fair-haired baby 'chyǎn-shǎr-téw-fa-de-háy-dz. ‖Her complexion is fair. tā-de-'pí-fu hěn 'báy.

(*Of weather*) hǎw, chíng. ‖Is the weather fair? tyān-chi 'hǎw-ma? *or* tyān-chi 'chíng-ma? ‖The weather is going to be fair tomorrow. myéngr-ge shǐ 'chíng-tyān. *or* myéngr-ge tyān-chi 'hǎw. ‖Fair and warmer (*weather report*). tyān-chíng shǎw-'nwǎn.

Fair and square. ‖The contest will be run off fair and square. 'bǐ-sày 'bàn-lǐ-de yí-'dìng bú-hwèy yěw 'jyǎ-de (*or* 'gwěy-de). *or* 'bǐ-sày yí-'dìng 'gūng-píng bàn-'lǐ.

A fair jí (*a sort of market day, held at regular intervals, usually at a monastery*); 'bwó-lǎn-hwèy (*a modern, large-scale exposition*). The New York World's Fair nyēw-ywē-shǐ-'shǐ-jyè-'bwó-lán-'hwèy. ‖Are you going to the fair? nǐ gǎn-'jí-chywu-ma? ‖There isn't any fair today. 'jyěr 'bú-shǐ 'jí-ya. *or* 'jyěr 'méy-yěw 'jí-ya. ‖He bought it at the fair. tā dzày 'jí-shàng mǎy-de.

FALL. (*Drop*) dyàw; làw (*or* lwò, *or* lè) (*especially of things falling of their own accord*). ‖Did you hear something fall? nǐ 'tīng-jyàn yěw 'dūng-shi 'dyàw-shya-lay-ma? ‖The leaves are beginning to fall. shù-'yèr 'chǐ-téwr °'làw-le. *or* °'dyàw-le. ‖The lid fell off. 'gàr dyàw-le. ‖When the curtain fell, he came to the front of the stage. mù 'làw-shya-lay dé-shŕ-hew tā dzěw-dàw táy-'chyán-tew-lay-le. ‖The curtain has already fallen. 'mù yí-jīng 'làw-shya-lay-le. ‖He tripped over a fallen branch. dyàw (or lǎw, or lwò, or lè)-dzày-'dì-shang-de-shù-'jěr bàn-le tā yì-'jyāw. ‖He fell into the well. tā 'dyàw-dzày 'jǐng-li-le. ‖This letter would cause trouble if it fell into the hands of the wrong people. 'jèy-fēng-'shìn 'rú-gwǒ lwò-dzày 'dǎy-rén-'shěw-li hwèy 'nàw-chu 'lwàn-dz-lay. ‖He fell out of the boat. tā tsúng 'chwán-shang °'dyàw-chu-chywu-le. or °'dyàw-shya- chywu-le. ‖Be careful, it's a bad fall if you slip. 'shyǎw-shīn-dyar; jèr 'hǎw 'gāw-de (or jèr hěn 'shēn-de), yí-'dyàw-shya-chywu jyèw 'bú-shr 'wár-de. ‖It's dangerous to cross the bridge until the river falls. 'chú-fēy děng 'hé-shwěy 'làw-le, gwò-'chyáw hěn 'wéy-shyǎn.

(By stumbling or tripping) shwǎy or dyē; fall over something jyàw ... bàn yì-'jyāw. ‖Where did you fall? nǐ dzày 'shem-me-dì-fang shwǎy-'dǎw-le láy-je? ‖I fell down. wǒ shwǎy-'dǎw-le. or wǒ shwǎy-le yì-'jyāw. or wǒ dyē-le yì-'jyāw. ‖She had a bad fall last winter. tā 'chywù-nyán 'dūng-tyān 'shwǎy-de bù-chīng. ‖I fell over a chair last night in the dark. dzwér 'wǎn-shang wǒ mwō-je 'hēr °jyàw 'yǐ-dz 'bàn-le yì-'jyāw. or °shwǎy-dzày 'yǐ-dz-shàng-le.

(Go lower; of prices and other things) dī; làw. (Only dī is used of a voice falling in pitch or volume.) ‖The stock market fell slightly today. 'jīn-tyān 'gǔ-pyàw-'háng-shŕ 'dī-le (or 'làw-le, or 'lwò-le, or 'lè-le) yì-'dyǎr. ‖Let's wait for a fall in prices before we buy. dzám děng 'jyà-chyán dī (or làw)-shya-chywu dzày 'mǎy. ‖His voice fell when he mentioned her name. tā tí-dàw tā-'míng-dz de-shŕ-hew, 'shēng-yīn 'dī-shya-chywu-le.

(Go lower; of temperature) jyàng. ‖There was a sudden fall in temperature last night. dzwó-tyān 'yè-li 'wēn-dù 'hū-rán 'jyàng-le.

(Be overthrown in war) shyàn; shŕ-'shěw. ‖The day the city fell is still celebrated every year. chéng-'shyàn-de-'r̀-dz (or chéng-shŕ-'shěw-de-'r̀-dz) dàw shyàn-'dzày háy 'nyán-nyar yěw 'jì-nyàn-'lì. ‖The fall of the fort was announced yesterday. 'pàw-táy-shŕ-'shěw-de-'shyāw-shi dzwó-tyan fā-'byǎw-le.

A fall of (precipitation) jèn. ‖We were delayed by a heavy fall of snow. wǒm ràng yí-jèn-dà-'shywě gěy 'dān-wu-le.

Falls (waterfall) 'pù-bù. ‖There are a lot of falls and rapids on this river. jèy-ge-'hé yěw bù-'shǎw-de 'pù-bù gēn 'jí-lyèw.

(Be inherited by) gwēy; 'lyéw-gey. ‖His property falls to his wife. tā-de-'tsáy-chǎn gwēy (or 'lyéw-gey) tā-'tày-tay.

(Shine on; of light) jàw-dzày. ‖The sunlight fell directly on his book. 'tày-yang-'gwāng jèng jàw-dzày tā-de-'shū-shang.

(Autumn) 'chyēw-tyān. ‖I'll be back next fall. wǒ 'chyēw-tyān 'hwéy-láy. ‖Is that your new fall outfit? nèy shr nǐ-'chyēw-tyān-de-'shīn-yì-shang-ma?

(Occur, as of accent on a word) azay. ‖Where does the accent fall in this word? jèy-ge-dz̀-de-'jùng-yīn dzày-'nǎr?

(Occur on a date) shr. ‖The holiday falls on Monday this year. 'fàng-jyà-'r̀ jīn-nyán shr shīng-chī-'yī.

Fall asleep shwèy-'jáw. ‖Did you fall asleep? nǐ shwèy-'jáw-le-ma?

Fall back on kàw-je; (depend on) jr̀-je. ‖We can always fall back on our savings. dzám 'dzǔng néng kàw-je (or jr̀-je) dzám-de-tswén-'kwǎn láy 'gwò.

Fall behind (in). ‖He's fallen behind in his payments. tā 'gwò-le 'r̀-dz méy-jyāw-'chyán.

Fall down on the job. ‖Can you be sure he won't fall down on the job? nǐ 'jwěn néng shwō tā 'bú-hwèy dzwò-bù-'hǎw-ma?

Fall due dàw-'chī. ‖The rent falls due next Monday. fáng-'dzū shyà-shīng-chī-'yī dàw-'chī.

Fall for 'mí-shang. ‖Boy, I really fell for her! 'hǎw-jyā-hwo, wǒ 'jēn jyèw 'mí-shang tā-le. But (of words) ‖His story sounded convincing, so I fell for it. tā-de-hwà 'tīng-je hěn-yěw-'lǐ-de, swǒ-yǐ wǒ °'shīn-yí-wèy-'jēn-le. or °shàng-le 'dàng-le. or °shèw le 'pyàn-le.

Fall in(to). ‖Fall in! jàn-'páy! or (Military command) jí-'hé! ‖They fell into line. tām jàn-de yì-'páy-yì-'páy-de. ‖I've fallen into the habit of reading newspapers on the train. wǒ dzày 'chē-shang kàn-'bàw, yǐ-jing chéng-le 'shí-gwàn-le. ‖All these documents will fall into three classes. swǒ-'yěw-de-jèy-shyē-'wén-jyàn kě-yǐ 'fēn-chéng 'sān-lèy.

Fall in love. ‖They fell in love with each other at first sight. tām yí-jyàn °chīng-'shīn. or °jūng-'chíng. ‖He fell in love with her. tā 'ày-shang ta-le.

Fall off. ‖His income from farming has been falling off lately. tā jùng-dì-de-'shēw-rù 'jìn-lay °jyàn 'shǎw-le. or °ywè láy ywè 'shǎw-le.

Fall on. ‖They fell on the food as though they were starving. tām 'chyǎng-je chr̄ 'hǎw shyàng 'dwō-shǎw-shŕ méy-chr̄-'fàn shr̀-de.

Fall out. ‖Fall out! bàn-'dwèy! ‖They used to be good friends, but now they've fallen out because of some woman. tām ywán-láy shr̀ 'hǎw-péng-yew, kě-shr shyàn-dzày wèy-le ge-'nywǔ-rén °'dǎ-chi-láy-le. or °'nǎw-le.

Fall short of. ‖The dinner fell short of our expectations. nèy-dwèn-fàn 'bù-rú (or nèy-dwèn-fàn 'méy-yěw) ywán-láy-'shyǎng-de nèm 'hǎw.

Fall to. ‖He fell to work with enthusiasm. tā 'gāw-gàw-shìng-'shìng-de dzwò-chī 'shr̀-lay-le.

Fall through. ‖The plans for the park fell through. dzàw-gūng-'ywán-de-'jì-hwà °méy-chéng. or °'chwēy-le.

Fall to pieces. ‖This typewriter is ready to fall to pieces. 'jèy-jyà-dǎ-dz̀-'jī swéy-'shŕ kě-yǐ 'sǎn-de.

Fall under. ‖All those expenses will fall under the same heading. swǒ-yěw-de-'kāy-shyāw 'děw kě-yǐ lyè-dzày (or fēn-dzày) yí-shyàng-li.

Fallen arches. ‖He wears special shoes because he has fallen arches. tā chwān tè-'byé-de-shyé 'yīn-wey tā-de-jyǎw-'jǎng yěw dyǎr-'pīng.

FALSE. (*Not true, not genuine*) jyǎ (*not used for statements or ideas*). ‖Is this true or false? jèy shr̀-'jen shr̀ 'jyǎ? ‖Is this real or false? jèy shr̀ 'jēn-de shr̀ 'jyǎ-de? ‖She's having trouble getting used to her false teeth. tā-'jyǎ-yá lǎw 'yùng-bú-'gwàn. ‖This drawer has a false bottom. jèy-ge-'chēw-ti-de-dyěr shr̀ 'jyǎ-de.

(*Not right*) bú-'dwèy, 'tswǒ(-le), 'bú-shr nèm hwéy-'shèr; (*of a way of saying or thinking*) bú-'jèng-chywè; *also several more specific expressions.* ‖That's a false statement. 'nèm-shwō bú-'dwèy. or 'nèm shwō jyèw 'tswò-le. or nèy-ge-'shwō-fa yěw-'tswèr. ‖That's a false idea. 'nèm shyǎng bú-'dwèy. or 'nèm shyǎng jyèw 'tswò-le. or 'nèy-ge-'shyǎng-fǎr bú-'jèng-chywè. ‖His account of the accident is all false (*not deliberately*). tā-shwō-de-chū-'shèr-de-'chíng-shíng 'chywán °bú-'dwèy. or °'tswò-le. or °'bú-shr nèm hwéy-'shèr. ‖He gave me a false (*wrong*) answer. 'tā-gàw-su-wǒ-de °bú-'dwèy. or °'tswò-le. or (*entirely false*) °'chywán 'tswò-le. or °'yì-'dyǎr bú-'dwèy. or °'chywán bú-shr nèm hwéy-'shèr. or °'wán-chywán méy nèm hwéy-'shèr. or (*local Peiping*) °mǎn-'níng. ‖These are true-and-false questions. 'jèy-shyē-'wèn-tí yěw 'dwèy-de yěw 'bú-dwèy-de. ‖Many people get false ideas from movies. hěn-'dwō-rén yīn-wey kàn dyàn-'yěngr dé-le °bú-'jèng-chywè-de-sž-'shyǎng. or °'hwāng-nyèw-de-sž-'shyǎng. or (*yet fooled by the movies*) hěn-'dwō-rén shèw dyàn-'yěngr-de-'pyàn. or hěn-'dwō-rén shàng-dyàn-'yěngr-de-'dàng. ‖One false step and you're washed up. (*Literally*) 'yì-shr̄-'dzú chéng 'chyān-gǔ-'hèn. or (*Figuratively*) nǐ yí-bù dzěw-'tswò-le jyèw 'yǔng-ywǎn bù-néng fān-'shēn-le. ‖Don't condemn him because of his one false step. bú-yàw yīn-wey tā tswò-le 'yí-tsž (or bú-yàw yīn-wey tā dzěw-'tswò-le 'yí-bù) jyèw bǎ-tā dàng 'hwày-rén 'kàn. ‖Don't get any false ideas. (*suspicions; perhaps including plans*) byé dwō-'shīn. or (*literary; meaning* impressions; *often used as a joke*) byé shyǎng-rù fēy-'fēy.

(*Deliberately deceptive*). *Many varied expressions.* ‖That's a false (*lying*) statement! nà shr̀ 'shyā-shwō! or 'nèm shwō jyèw-shr yàw pyàn-'rén! or 'nèy shr̀ shyā-hwàr! or 'nèy shr̀ 'hú-shwō-bā-'dàw! or 'nèy shr̀ wú-'jì-jr̄-'tán! or 'nèy 'bú-shr 'shr̀-hwà! ‖He gave a false (*falsified*) account of the accident. tā bǎ chū-'shèr-de-'chíng-shíng °'shwō-le yí-'byàn, kě-shr shwō-de 'bú-shr 'shr̀-hwà. or °'shwō-le yí-'byàn, dēw shr̀ 'hú-dzěw-de. or °'shwō-le yí-'byàn, dēw shr̀ 'shyā-shwō-bā-'dàw. or °'shwō-le yí-'byàn, dēw shr̀ 'hú-dzěw-bay-'lyě-de. or °'shyā-'dzěw-le yí-tàw-'hwàr. or °'hú-shwō-bā-'dàw-de shwō-le yí-byàn. ‖She got the job under false pretenses. tā-nèy-'shèr shr̀ 'pyàn-lay-de. or tā jǎw nèy-ge-'shr̀ de-shŕ-hew, °shwō 'shyā-

hwàr-lay-je. or °méy-shwō 'shŕ-h·à. or °shwō-de bú-shr 'shŕ-hwà. or °shwō-'hwǎng .ay-je. or °pyàn-'rén-lay-je.

False alarm. ‖The rumer turned out to be a false alarm. 'jyē-gwǒ shr̀ 'waw-yán. or 'jyē-gwǒ 'méy nèm hwéy-'shèr. ‖The fire engines were called out on a false alarm. jyèw-hwǒ-'dwèy jyàw-chū-chywu-le; yí-'kàn shr̀ °'shywū-jīng. or °'méy-yěw 'hwǒ. or °'yěw-rén 'shywū-bàw. or °'yěw-rén dǎw-'gwěy.

FAMILIAR. (*Acquainted with*) shéw, bù-'shēng; (*recognize*) 'rèn-shr or 'rèn-de. Unfamiliar bù-'shéw, shēng, bú-dà 'rèn-shr or bú-dà 'rèn-de; (*strange*) (kàn-je) hěn 'gwày. ‖I'm not familiar with him. wǒ gēn-tā bù-'shéw. or wǒ gēn-tā 'bú-dà 'rèn-shr. ‖He looks familiar. tā hěn myàn-'shéw. ‖His face doesn't look at all familiar to me. tā yì-'dyǎr yě bú-myàn-'shéw. ‖It's good to see a familiar face. kàn-jyan ge-'shéw-rén jēn jyàw-wǒ gāw-'shìng. ‖I'm not familiar with the place or the people. wǒ 'rén-shēng-'dì-bù-'shéw-de. ‖That word (*or character*) is not quite familiar (*or quite unfamiliar*) to me. 'nèy-ge-dž °hěn yǎn-'shēng. or °wǒ kàn-je hěn 'gwày. or °wǒ 'bú-dà 'rèn-de. ‖After you've become familiar with the people here, they're quite friendly. děng tām gēn-nǐ 'shéw-le, hwèy 'hěn hé-chi-de.

(*Accustomed to*) hú-shi; (*negative*) bù-'shú-shi; bú-dà 'jr̄-daw-de. ‖I'm not yet familiar with your customs. nǐm-jèr-de-'fēng-sú wǒ háy °'bù-'shú-shi-ne. or °'bú-dà 'jr̄-daw-ne. or (*not acquainted with*) °bù-'shéw-ne. ‖I'm not familiar with this system. 'jèy-ge-bàn-fa wǒ °bù-'shú-shi. or °bù-'shéw. or hěn 'shēng. ‖After a while our system will be familiar to you. 'gwò-shyē-shŕ wǒm-de-'bàn-fa nǐ ivèw °'shú-shi-le. or °'shéw-le.

(*Intimate*) lā 'jìn-hu, jyāw-de 'shēn. ‖Don't get too familiar with them. 'byé gēn-tām °tày lā-'jìn-hu. or °jyāw-de tày-'shēn. or °tày 'shéw-lew.

(*Taking undue liberties*) shyā-'nàw(-de). ‖If you aren't careful with him, he's likely to get familiar. nǐ yàw bù-'shyǎw-shīn-je tā-dyar, tā hwèy gēn-nǐ shyā-'nàw-de. or 'byé gēn-tā tày 'shéw-le, tā ày shyā-'nàw.

(*Common*). ‖Tall buildings have become a familiar sight nowadays. 'shyàn-dzày 'gāw-léw-dà-'shà-de °'dàw-chù 'kàn-de-'jyàn. or °'rén dēw jyàn-'gwàn-le. or °'rén 'jyàn-le bù-chí-'gwày-le. or °'rén 'jyàn-le bù-jywé-je yǎn-'shēng-le. or °'rén 'jyàn-le méy shéme-'shī-chi-le.

FAMILY. *Three rather subtle distinctions may be observed:*

1. jyā (*which also means* home) *is the family as a group of people living together, a household, but without any particular emphasis on its social unity.* ‖She has to work to support her family. tā děy dzwò-'shr (tsáy néng) yǎng-'jyā. ‖This farm has been in their

family for seven hundred years. nèy-kwày-'dì dzày 'tām-jyā-li yěw 'chī-bǎy-nyán-le. ‖**Which are the leading families of the town?** jèr 'néy-jǐ-jyār yěw 'shŕ-li? or jèr-de-'dà-jyār dēw shŕ néy-jǐ-'jyā? ‖**That temper of his is a family trait.** tā-yì-'jyā 'dēw shŕ nèy-ge-'pí-chyer. ‖**That's a family heirloom.** nèy shŕ (wǒm-)'jyā-chwán-jŕ-'bǎw. or (*inherited from ancestors*) nèy shŕ (wǒm-)'dzǔ-chwán-de. ‖**He can't cut his family ties.** tā bù-néng gēn tā-'jyā-li 'dwàn-jywé 'gwān-shì.

2. 'jyā-li-de-rén *is the family as several related individuals, the members of the family; hence also* yì-'jyā-de-rén (*the whole family*). ‖**He has a large family.** tā-'jyā-li rén 'dwō. or tā-'jyā-li rén-kew 'dwō. or tā 'jyā-li-de-rén hěn 'dwō. or tā yěw yí-'dà-jyā-de-'rén. ‖**His whole family came.** tā-'chywán-jyā (or tā-'yì-jyā, or tā-yì-'jyā-de-rén) 'dēw láy-le. ‖**Her family always comes first in her mind.** tā-shīn-li lǎw 'shyàng-je tā-'dž-jǐ-'jyā-de-rén.

3. 'jyā-tíng *and* 'jyā-dz *refer to the family as a closely knit social unit.* ‖**The Chinese have very strong feelings for family ties.** 'jūng-gwo-rén 'jyā-tíng-gwān-'nyàn hěn 'jùng. ‖**There are fewer large families as industrialization progresses.** 'gūng-yè ywè 'fā-dá, 'dà-jyā-tíng jyèw 'ywè láy ywè 'shǎw. ‖**He has family troubles.** tā 'jyā-tíng jŕ-jyān °jìng nàw-'shŕ. or °bú-shwèn-'shīn. or °bù-rú-'yì. ‖**He is on good terms with his family.** tā-'jyā-tíng jŕ-jyān 'chǔ-de 'hǎw. ‖**Small families are now in vogue.** shyàn-dzày 'shŕ-shīng 'shyǎw-jyā-tíng. ‖**We're just one big, happy family.** wǒm yí-'dà-jyā-dz-rén °'yì-twán hé-'chì. or °'hé-hé-mù-'mù-de. or °hěn 'hé-mù. or (*sarcastic*) 'wǒm-jyā 'nà tsáy jyàw 'hé-mù-ne! or 'dzám-jyā dzěm-'dzèm 'hé-mù-a?

In some cases, the family is referred to indirectly by speaking of outsiders as 'wày-rén. ‖**He is almost one of the family.** wǒm 'bù-ná-tā dàng 'wày-rén kàn. ‖**When the family is alone, we eat in the kitchen.** méy-'wày-ren-de-shŕ-hew or (*of guests* méy-'kè-ren-de-shŕ-hew) wǒm dzày 'chú-fáng-li chŕ-'fàn. ‖**Keep it in the family.** *is expressed as* **Don't sell it to an outsider.** byé jyàw 'wày-rén 'dé-chywu. or as **Don't tell it to an outsider.** byé jyàw 'wày-rén 'jŕ-dàw. or as **Family skeletons should not be exposed outside.** 'jyā-chěw bù-kě 'wày-yáng.

(*Of animals and birds*) wō (*nest, litter, brood, etc.*). ‖**There's apparently a family of weasels living under the front porch.** 'láng-dz-'dǐ-shya yí-'dìng yěw yì-wō-'hwáng-shu-'láng.

FAMOUS. yěw-'míng, yěw 'míng-chì, chū-'míng. **Become famous** chéng-'míng, chū-'míng. ‖**He is quite famous.** tā 'hěn yěw-'míng. or tā 'hěn yěw 'míng-chì. ‖**This road is famous for its view.** 'jèy-tyáw-lù yǐ 'fēng-jīng-'hǎw °yěw-'míng. or °chū-'míng. or 'jèy-tyáw-lù-chū-'míng-de-'fēng-jīng-hǎw. ‖**His book made him famous.** nèy-běn-'shū jyàw-tā °chū-'míng. or °'chéng-'míng. or tā yīn-wey nèy-běr-'shū yěw-'míng.

FAR. (*Distant*) ywǎn. ‖**Don't go far.** byé dzěw-'ywǎn-le. or byé wàng-'ywǎn-lew 'chywù. ‖**Do you live very far from the station?** ní-jù-de lí chē-'jàn 'hěn ywǎn-ma? ‖**Is it far away?** lí-jèr 'ywǎn-ma? or lí-jèr 'ywǎn-bu-ywǎn? ‖**How far are the mountains?** shān yěw 'dwō-ywǎn? or 'shān lí-jèr (yěw) 'dwō-ywǎn? ‖**Have you ever been in the Far East before?** ní 'yǐ-chyán dàw-gwo ywǎn-'dūng-ma? ‖**We heard, far off in the distance, a ship's whistle.** ywǎn-'ywǎn-de tīng-jyan yěw-'chwán lā-'byér. *But* ‖**This tunnel goes pretty far down** (*deep*). jèy-ge-'swéy-dàw (or jèy-ge-'dì-dàw) hěn 'shēn. ‖**His house is on the far** (*other*) **side of the woods.** tā-de-'fáng-dz dzày shù-'lín-dz-de-'nèy-byār.

Other expressions, without special reference. ‖**That young fellow will go far.** 'nèy-ge-háy-dz (or 'nèy-ge-shyǎw-'hwǒ-dz) 'chyán-chéng ywǎn-'dà. ‖**The meeting lasted far into the night.** 'hwèy yì-jŕ kāy-dàw °bàn-'yè-li. or °'shēn-jīng-bàn-'yè-de. ‖**This joke has gone far enough.** jèy-ge-'wán-shyàw kāy-de 'gèw-lì-hay-de-le. ‖**Are you feeling well now? No, far from it.** ní 'shyàn-dzày 'jywé-je 'hǎw-le-ma? °'hāy! tsáy 'bù-ne. or °'hāy! yì-'dyār dēw bù-'hǎw. ‖**It's far from perfect, but it will do.** jèy-ge 'chà-de hěn 'dwō, bú-gwò kě-yǐ 'tsèw-he-je yùng. ‖**That's not far wrong.** nèy-ge chà-de (or nèy-ge 'tswò-de) bú-'tày °dwō. or °'lì-hay. ‖**This is far more important than that.** 'jèy-ge bǐ 'nèy-ge yàw-'jìn-de 'dwō. or 'jèy-ge 'ywǎn bǐ 'nèy-ge yàw-'jìn. ‖**She is by far** (or **far and away**) **the best cook we ever had.** wǒm 'yí-shyàng-gù-de-'chú-dz-li °tā bǐ 'byé-rén 'dēw hǎw. or °'byé-rén 'ywǎn bǐ-bu-'shàng tā. ‖**He is by far the better of the two.** 'tām-lyǎ-li tā chyáng-de 'dwō.

Few and far between. (*Literally*) ‖**In this country gasoline stations are few and far between.** 'jèy-ge-dì-fang mày-chì-'yéw-de hěn 'shǎw, 'lí-de yě 'ywǎn. (*Figuratively*) ‖**Men like that are few and far between these days.** mù-chyán shyàng-tām-nèy-yàngr-de-rén jēn shŕ °tày 'shǎw-le. or °'fèng-máw-lín-'jyǎw.

As far as. (*Literally*) dàw. ‖**We walked together as far as the gate.** wǒm yí-'kwàr dzěw-dàw dà-'mén-nar. (*Figuratively*) ‖**As far as I'm concerned, you do as you please.** 'gwāng ná-'wǒ láy shwō (or yǐ-wǒ 'gè-ren ěr-'lwèn) ní 'ày dzěm-je 'jyèw dzěm-je. or (*rude*) ní 'ày dzěm-je 'jyèw dzěm-je, 'wǒ gwǎn-bu-'jáw. ‖**This is a good idea as far as it goes.** jyèw-'shŕ-lwèn-'shŕ 'jèy-ge-jú-yi háy bú-'hwày.

Far be it from me. ‖**Far be it from me to criticize, but I think you should use that word more carefully.** *is expressed as* **I don't like to criticize, . . .** wǒ bìng 'bú-shr ày 'pī-píng, bú-gwo wǒ 'jywé-je ní yùng 'nèy-ge-dzèr de-shŕ-hew 'yīng-gāy 'shyǎw-shīn-dyar. or as **I don't like to criticize you, . . .** wǒ bìng 'bú-shr yàw 'pī-píng ní, ... or as **I'm not qualified to criticize, . . .** chí-'shŕ wǒ 'méy dz-ge láy 'pī-píng, ... ‖**Far be it**

from me to criticize, but I don't like your hat. *is expressed as* It's none of my business, ... chí-shŕ méy 'wŏ-shéme-shèr, bú-gwo wŏ 'chyáw-je nĭ-de-'màw-dz bú-shwèn-'yăn.

Far-fetched. (*Far from the subject*). ‖**That argument is pretty far-fetched.** 'nèm-ge-'shwō-far lí-'tí tày 'ywăn-le. (*Without force*) ‖**What she said is too far-fetched.** tā-shwō-de tày méy-'lĭ-le.

Far-sighted. (*Literally*) 'ywăn-shŕ-yăn; (*figuratively*) jyàn-de 'ywăn *or* yĕw 'ywăn-jyàn. ‖**Are you near-sighted or far-sighted?** nĭ shŕ-'jìn-shŕ-yăn háy-shr 'ywăn-shŕ-yăn? ‖**Their plans proved to be far-sighted.** jyē-gwŏ jèng-'míng-le tām-de-'jì-hwà jyàn-de 'ywăn. *or* yĕw 'ywăn-jyàn.

FARM. (*Field*) tyán; (*land*) dì; (*farmed land*) jùng-de-'dì; (*large-scale farm*) núng-'chăng, ‖**A brook runs through their farm.** yĕw yí-dàw-hé-'gēw-dz tsúng tām-de-'tyán-li (*or* tām-de-'dì-li) 'lyéw-gwo-chywu. ‖**He owns the farm now.** shyàn-dzày (tā-jùng-de-) nèy-kwày-'dì (*or* -'tyán) shŕ 'tā-de-le. ‖**Does the farm have a mortgage on it?** *is expressed as* Is the farm's deed clear? jèy-kwày-'dì (*or* jèy-kwày-'tyán, *or* jèy-ge-núng-'chăng)-de-'chì shŕ-bu-shr 'yā-chū-chywu-le? ‖**This farm seems to be well taken care of.** jèy-kwày-'dì (*or* jèy-kwày-'tyán) jùng-de 'hăw. *or* jèy-ge-núng-'chăng 'jīng-yíng-de hěn 'hăw. ‖**They're short of farm hands.** tām 'gù-bu-jáw 'rén jùng-'dì. *But* ‖**They have a chicken farm.** *is expressed as* They raise chickens. tām yăng-'jī. ‖**Have you ever lived on a farm?** *is expressed as* in the country? nĭ dzày 'shyăng-shya jù-gwo-ma? **Have you ever lived in a farm house?** *is expressed as* Have you ever lived in a farmer's house? nĭ dzày jùng-'jwāng-jya-de-rén-jyā-li 'jù-gwo-ma? *or* nĭ dzày 'jwāng-jya-rén-jyā-li 'jù-gwo-ma? ‖**There is a (farm) house over there.** 'nàr yĕw ge-'rén-jyār. *or* 'nàr yĕw-ge-jáy-dz. *or* 'nàr yĕw-rén 'jù.

To farm jùng(-'dì), gēng(-'dì); (*local Peiping*) jīng(-'dì). ‖**Their family has been farming the same piece of land for generations.** tām-jyā 'hăw-shyē-dày jùng (*or* gēng, *or* jīng) nèy-'yí-kwày-'dì. *or* tām-jyā jùng (*or* gēng, *or* jīng) 'nèy-kwày-'dì yĕw 'hăw-shyē-'dày-le. ‖**Their family has been farming for generations.** tām-jyā 'hăw-shyē-dày jùng-'dì (*or* gēng-'dì, *or* jīng-'dì).

Farm out 'jì-yăng. ‖**He farms out his children.** tā bă 'háy-dz dēw °'jì-yăng dzày 'byé-rén-'jyā-li. *or* °'jì-dzày 'byé-rén-jyā-li 'yăng-je.

FARMER. (*As a social class*) 'núng-rén, ‖**The farmers want to be left alone by the government.** 'núng-rén ʼbú-ywàn-yì jyàw 'jèng-fú ʼgwăn. ‖**Farmers and industrial laborers must cooperate.** 'núng-rén gēn 'gūng-rén děy hé-'dzwò tsáy 'shíng.

(*As an occupation*) 'jwāng-jya-rén, jùng-'dì-de; (*rare*) 'núng-fu; (*those who live in the country*) 'shyăng-shya-rén. **To be a farmer** shŕ *plus any of the above.* *or* jùng-'dì *or* wù-'núng *or* wù-'néng. ‖**The**

farmers bring their vegetables to town every morning. 'jwăng-jya-rén (*or* jùng-'dì-de, *or* 'shyăng-shya-rén) 'tyān-tyan 'dzăw-chen bă 'chīng-tsày dày-dàw 'chéng-li-lay. ‖**My (maternal) uncle is a farmer.** wŏ-'jyèw-jyew °wù-'núng. *or* °wù-!néng. *or* °jùng-'dì. *or* °shŕ ge-'núng-rén. *or* °shŕ ge-'jwāng-jya-rén. *or* °shŕ ge-jùng-'dì-de. *or* °shŕ ge-'núng-fu.

FARTHER. (*More distant*) ywăn, *with another word such as* still háy *or* again dzày *elsewhere in the sentence.* ‖**How much farther do we have to go?** 'háy děy dzěw 'dwō-ywăn? *or* (*How much road?*) 'háy yĕw 'dwō-shăw lù? ‖**His house is farther away than mine.** 'tā-jyā bĭ 'wŏ-jyā lí-de háy 'ywăn-dyar. ‖**Move the chair a little farther from the fire.** bă 'yĭ-dz nwó-de lí-'hwŏ 'dzày ywăn-dyar. ‖**The farther he goes the less homesick he becomes.** tā 'ywè dzěw-de 'ywăn ywè 'bù-shyăng-'jyā. *But* ‖**The post office is farther down that way.** (*Still that way*) 'yéw-jèng-'jywú 'háy dzày 'nèy-byar-ne. *or* (*Still ahead*) 'yéw-jèng-'jywú 'háy děy wàng-'chyán dzěw. ‖**They went toward the farther** (*other*) **side of the park.** tām wàng gūng-ywăn-'nèy-byar chywù-le.

(*Not referring to distance*). ‖**He never got farther than grade school.** shàng-le 'shyăw-shywé yĭ-'hèw tā 'dzày yě méy-shàng-'shywé.

See also **FAR.**

FASHION. shŕ-'shīng; (*showing disapproval*) shŕ-'máw. *Both of these terms are verbs, meaning* to be in fashion, to be the fashion, to be fashionable. ‖**Is it the fashion here to wear straw hats?** jèr shŕ-'shīng dày tsăw-'màwr-ma? ‖**During the last few years women have given up the fashion of wearing long dresses.** 'jìn-jĭ-nyán-lay 'nywŭ-rén bù-shŕ-'shīng chwān 'cháng-'yī-fu-le. ‖**We don't try to keep up with all the latest fashions here.** wŏm-jèr 'bù-jyăng shŕ-'máw. ‖**Long hair has gone out of fashion.** shyàn-dzày 'bù-shŕ-shīng 'cháng-téw-fa-le. *or* shyàn-dzày 'cháng-téw-fa °bù-shŕ-'shīng-le. *or* °bù-shŕ-'máw-le.

(*Manner*). ‖**He has a habit of rubbing his hands together in this fashion.** tā yĕw ge-'máw-bing, ày 'dzèm-je tswō-'shĕw.

(*Set the fashion*). ‖**They set the fashion.** *is expressed as* They lead at the head 'tām lĭng-'téwr. *or as* Everyone imitates them 'dà-jyā dēw 'shywé-tām. ‖**The dancing girls here set the fashion in dress.** *is expressed as* The dancing girls here lead in the way of dressing. jèr-de-'wŭ-nywŭ lĭng-'téwr găy 'yī-shang-'shŕ-yang. *or as* Everyone imitates them in manner of dress jèr 'dà-jyā dēw shywé 'wŭ-nywŭ-de-'jwāng-shù.

FAST. (*Speedy, quick*) kwày. ‖**If you get a fast train you can get there in two hours.** dzwò 'kwày-chē yĕw 'lyăng-dyăn-jūng kě-yĭ 'dàw-nàr. ‖**You're setting too fast a pace for the others.** nĭ dzwò-de tày 'kwày-le, 'byé-rén 'gēn-bu-'shàng. ‖**Tell him about the new rules,**

and make it fast. bǎ 'shīn-mìng-lìng gěy-tā 'jyang-yi-jyǎng, kwày-'kwār-de. ‖Not so fast, please! láw-'jyà, byé nèm 'kwày! or (slower) láw-'jyà, 'màn-dyar. ‖Hurry as fast as you can. or The faster the better. ywè 'kwày ywè 'hǎw. ‖It can be done as fast as you want. 'yàw dwō-kwày 'néng dwō-'kwày. ‖My watch is ten minutes fast. 'wǒ-de-byǎw 'kwày 'shŕ-fēn-jūng. ‖Your watch is fast too. 'nǐ-de-byǎw 'yě kwày-le. ‖The horses have a fast track today. is expressed as The horses can run fast on the track. 'jyēr-de-'chǎng-dz mǎ-pǎw-de 'kwày. ‖This is a fast (tennis) court. 'jèy-ge-(wǎng-chyéw-)'chǎng-dz-shang kě-yǐ 'pǎw-de 'kwày.

(Tight) jǐn. ‖Hold it fast. jǐn-'jǐn-de 'dzwàn-je. ‖He held it fast. tā dzwàn-de hěn 'jǐn. ‖Make the boat fast. bǎ-chwán shwān-'jǐn-le. ‖The ship was stuck fast in the mud. chwán dzày 'ní-li 'jyāw-de hěn 'jǐn. or chwán dzày 'ní-li jǐn-'jǐn-de 'gē-jù-le. ‖We don't have any hard and fast rules here. wǒm-jèr méy-yěw shéme-tày-'jǐn-de-'gwēy-jywu. or (severe) wǒm-jèr méy-yew shéme-hěn-'yán-de-'gwēy-jywu.

(Permanent, of color) bù-rúng-yi 'dyàw, bù-rúng-yi 'twèy. ‖Are these colors fast? jèy-shyē-'yán-shǎr rúng-yi °'dyàw-ma? or °'twèy-ma? or jèy-shyē-'yán-shǎr 'rúng-yi-bù-rúng-yi 'dyàw (or 'twèy)? ‖This color is fast. jèy-shǎr bù-rúng-yi 'dyàw (or 'twèy).

(Of friends). ‖They are fast friends. tām 'láy-wang (or tām 'jyāw-chíng) °hěn 'chín. or °hěn 'shēn. or tām shŕ 'hǎw-peng-yew.

(Of sleep) shéw, 'shŕ-dzay, sź. ‖I was fast asleep. wǒ-'shwèy-de hěn °'shéw. or °'shŕ-dzày. or °'sź.

(Of people) expressed as like to play ày-'wár. ‖He travels in fast company. tā gēn yì-chywún-ày-'wár-de-rén 'láy-wang. ‖She's too fast to suit me. tā 'tày ày-'wár-le, jyàw-wǒ 'bú-dà 'shǐ-hwān.

(Abstain from food: entirely) jìn-'shŕ (usually used by Catholics): (stop eating, go on a hunger strike) jywé-'shŕ; (stay away from meat, fowl, and fish) chŕ-'jāy (a Buddhist expression). ‖Are you fasting? or Are you keeping the fast? nǐ jèng-dzày jìn-'shŕ-ne-ma? ‖She is fasting. shyàn-dzày tā chŕ-'jāy.

FAT. (Of animals) féy; (fat part of the flesh) 'féy-rèw. ‖This is a nice fat chicken for roasting. 'jèy-jŕ-dà-féy-jī 'kǎw-je chŕ 'hǎw. ‖This pork is too fat. jèy-kwày-jū-rèw °tày-'féy-le. or °'féy-rèw tày 'dwō. ‖There's too much fat on this meat. jèy-kwày-'rèw-shang 'féy-de tày 'dwō. or jèy-kwày-rèw tày 'féy-le.

(Vegetable or animal fat used for cooking) yéw (also means oil). ‖What is the best fat for frying? 'jyān dūng-shi yùng shéme-'yéw dzwèy-'hǎw?

(Of people) pàng; (politely) fā-'fú. ‖I'm getting too fat, don't you think? wǒ (jǎng-de) tày 'pàng-le, nǐ shwō 'shŕ-bu-shŕ? ‖You're getting a bit fat. nín fā-'fú-le.

FATHER. (Kinship term.) See Appendix A.
(Priest) 'shén-fù.

To father. ‖He fathered the whole idea. jèy-ge-'ju-yi chywán shŕ 'tā-chū-ḍe.

FAULT. (Mistake; does not stress the idea of blame) tswèr; (wrong-doing, something worthy of blame) 'bú-shr. ‖Sorry, it's my fault. dwèy-bú-'jù, shŕ 'wǒ-de-°tswèr. or °'bú-shr. ‖I can't be blamed for other people's faults. 'wǒ bù-néng gěy 'byé-rén dān 'bú-shr. or 'byé-rén-de-'tswèr 'bù-néng gwày-'wǒ. ‖Whose fault is it? jèy shŕ 'shéy-de-tswèr? ‖It's no one's fault. or No one is at fault. 'shéy yě 'méy-yew 'bú-shr. ‖It's nobody's fault but your own. shŕ nǐ-'dz̀-jǐ-de-'tswèr, gēn 'byé-rén méy-'gwan-shi.

(Defect, in a person) 'dwǎn-chù; (bad habit) 'máw-bìng. ‖In spite of her faults, she is easy to get along with. tā 'swéy-rán yěw shyē-ge-'dwǎn-chù, kě-shr °'rén hěn 'swéy-he. or °'rúng-yi shyāng-'chù. ‖His worst fault is that he talks too much. tā 'dǐng-hwày-de-'máw-bìng jyèw-shr °ày shwō-'hwà. or °shwō-'hwà tày 'dwō.

(Find fault) tyāw-'tswèr, 'tyāw-ti, 'chwēy-máw-chyéw-'tsź. ‖You're always finding fault. nǐ 'lǎw-shr °'tyāw-ti. or °tyāw-'tswèr. or °'chwēy-máw-chyéw-'tsź. ‖I don't mean to find fault with you, but that won't do. wǒ 'bú-shr 'chéng-shīn 'tyāw nǐ-de-'tswèr (or wǒ 'bú-shr gù-'yì-de 'tyāw nǐ-de-'tswèr, or wǒ 'bú-shr 'chwēy-máw-chyéw-'tsź), 'bú-gwo 'nèm-je 'jēn-shr bù-'chéng.

(Defect; in something material) 'máw-bìng, 'chywē-dyǎn. ‖The collapse of the bridge was caused by a fault in one of the beams. chyáw 'dǎw-le shŕ yīn-wey yěw yì-gēn-'lyáng yěw °'máw-bìng. or °'chywē-dyǎn.

Faulty. ‖The collapse of the bridge was caused by faulty construction. chyáw 'dǎw-le shŕ 'yīn-wey gày-de °-'fāng-fa bú-'dwèy. or °-shŕ-hew 'méy-gày-'hǎw. or °-shŕ-hew yěw-'tswèr.

FAVOR. (Kindness, privilege) In statements, (mercy) ēn or (honor, "face") 'myàn-dz may be used; in questions, the idea is expressed in words such as (request, please) chǐng, (beg, ask very politely) chyéw, (please) láw-'jyà. ‖As a great favor, he let me use this camera for a day. tā dà-'dā-de kāy-'ēn (or tā gēn-wǒ 'hǎw-dà-de-'myàn-dz), bǎ jèy-ge-jàw-shyàng-'jī jyàw-wǒ ná-lay 'yùng yì-tyān. ‖I want to ask you a favor. wǒ yěw dyar-shŕ 'chyéw-nǐ. ‖Would you do me a favor? chyéw-nǐ gěy 'dzwò dyǎr-'shŕ, 'shíng-bu-shíng? or láw-'jyà gěy 'dzwò dyǎr-'shŕ, 'shíng-bu-shíng? or (wǒ) yěw yí-jyàn-'shŕ chyéw-nǐ. ‖Would you favor us with your attention? chǐng 'jìng tīng.

(Advantage). In one's favor (be of benefit) ywú... yěw-'lì; (enable one to gain an advantage) jyàw... jàn 'pyán-yi. ‖That's a point in your favor. is expressed as What you said was right. nǐ-'jèy-dyǎn-shwō-de 'dwèy. or nèy-dyǎn ywú-'nǐ yěw-'lì. or (grudgingly) nèy jyàw-'nǐ jàn 'pyán-yi. ‖That's in my favor. nèy ywú-'wǒ yěw-'lì. *or* nèy jyàw-'wǒ jàn 'pyán-yi.

(*Gift, especially at a party*) 'lǐ-wù. ‖What shall we give as favors at the children's party? shyǎw-'hár láy 'wár de-shŕ-hew dzám gěy dyǎr-shéme-'lǐ-wù hǎw-ne?

(*Prefer*) 'shyàng-je. ‖Which side do you favor? nǐ 'shyàng-je 'něy-byar?

(*Resemble*) shyàng. ‖The little boy favors his mother's side of the family. jèy-háy-dz shyàng tā-'lǎw-law-jyā-de-rén.

(*Deal gently with*) 'bú-dà 'gǎn-yùng. ‖He seems to be favoring his right leg. tā 'hǎw-shyàng 'bú-dà 'gǎn-yùng yèw-'twěy shŕ-de.

(*In favor of*) 'dzàn-chéng. ‖I'm in favor of immediate action. wǒ 'dzàn-chéng jí-kè 'gàn-chi-lay.

FAVORITE. 'dzwèy-shǐ-hwǎn-de, 'dzwèy-ày-de, *or verbal constructions without -de, meaning* to like best; *also* dzwèy *or* dǐng *with other verbs of similar meaning.* ‖Red is my favorite color. wǒ-'dzwèy-shǐ-hwǎn-de shŕ 'húng-shǎr. ‖Who is your favorite movie actress? 'nywǔ-míng-'shīng-li nǐ 'dzwèy shǐ-hwān 'něy-ge? ‖This book is a great favorite with children. jèy-běn-'shū shyǎw-'háy-dz-men °'dzwèy ày 'kàn. *or* °'dzwèy shǐ-hwān 'kàn. ‖The boy is his father's favorite. jèy-háy-dz shŕ tā-'fù-chin-dzwèy-°'shǐ-hwān-de. *or* °'ày-dé. *or* °'téng-de. *or* °'chǔng-de. ‖He's the favorite of the boss. tā shŕ 'téwr-de-'húng-rén (*literally,* red person, *used for* favorite *in this sense*). *or* dzày 'téwr-nar 'tā dǐng 'húng. *or* téwr dǐng 'shǐ-hwān tā. *or* téwr dǐng chǔng-tā.

‖The favorite (*horse*) dropped out of the race early. 'dà-jyā-jywé-je-yèw-'yíng-de-mǎ 'méy-pǎw 'dwō ywǎn jyèw 'là-dzay 'hèw-tew-le.

FEAR. *The noun is usually expressed verbally: three types of fear may be distinguished.*

Be full of fear, be scared stiff hày-'pà. ‖His actions were strongly influenced by fear. tā-de-nèy-shyē-'jywǔ-dùng 'dwō-bàn 'dēw shŕ yīn-wey ('shīn-li) hày-'pà. ‖He doesn't know the meaning of fear. tā 'bù-dǔng 'shéme jyàw hày-'pà.

Fear *something or someone*, fear that, fear to pà; (*be anxious about*) wèy ... dān-'shīn; *not fear also expressed as* put the mind at rest fang-'shīn. ‖She lives in constant fear of her mother-in-law. tā pà tā-'pwó-pwo pà-de 'lǎw-shr 'shīn-jīng dǎn-'jàn-de. ‖Never fear! He'll take care of you there. (*There's nothing to be afraid of*) 'méy shéme-kě-'pà-de. yěw-'tā dzày jàw-ying nǐ-ne. *or* (*Don't be scared*) 'byé (*or* 'bú-yùng) hày-'pà .... ‖I have no fears for myself, but I'm worried about them. wǒ dàw 'bú-shr wèy wǒ-'dz̀-jǐ dān-'shīn, wǒ shŕ dān-'shīn-je 'tā-men. *or* wǒ-'dz̀-jǐ 'méy shéme-kě-'pà-de, wǒ shŕ pà 'tā-men yěw-shéme 'chà-tswò. ‖I can say this without fear of contradicting myself. jèy-ge wǒ 'kě-yǐ 'fàng-shīn-dà-'dǎn-de shwō, yīn-wey 'bú-hwèy 'dz̀-shyàng-máw-'dwèn-de.

‖There's no fear of anything like that happening. 'nèm-yàng-de-shř (bú-yàw 'pà, *or* fàng-'shīn-ba), 'jwěn bú-hwèy 'yěw-de.

(*Be afraid in a very weak sense, with no actual fear*) kǔng-'pà. ‖He went to the station early for fear of missing the train. tā dzǎw-'dzāwr-de shàng chē-'jàn-chywu-le, yīn-wey (kǔng-)'pà 'wù-le 'chē. ‖I hurried home for fear I'd miss you. wǒ kwày-'kwār-de hwéy-'jyā-lǎy, yīn-wey (kǔng-)pà 'jèy-tsz̀ jyàn-bu-'jáw nǐ.

FEATHER. máw (*especially soft feathers that can be used for stuffing*); 'líng-dz (*especially larger feathers with a good-sized shaft*); *but* chicken feathers *are always called* 'jī-máw *unless referring to a long tail-feather.* ‖They make dusters out of chicken feathers. tām ná 'jī-máw dzwò 'dǎn-dz. ‖Peacock feathers are long and colorful. 'kǔng-chyǎw-'líng-dz yèw 'cháng yèw yěw 'hǎw-jǐ-jǔng-'yán-se. ‖Her new hat has a red feather on it. tā-de-'shīn-màw-dz-shang 'chā-je yì-gēn-°'húng-de-'líng-dz. *or* °'húng-máwr.

Light as a feather 'jēn chīng. ‖This coat is as light as a feather. 'jèy-jyàn-dà-yī 'jēn chīng.

A feather in one's cap. ‖If he could get his book published, it would really be a feather in his cap. tā yàw-shr néng bǎ tā-nèy-běr-'shū chū-le-'bǎn, 'jēn kě-yǐ 'jyāw-àw-yí-shyàr.

‖Birds of a feather flock together. *is expressed with a literary proverb* Everything goes with its own kind. 'wù-tsúng-chí-'lèy.

FEBRUARY. 'èr-ywè.

FEEL. (*Touch, handle, grope*) mwō. ‖Feel it. Isn't it smooth? 'mwō-yi-mwo. bú-shr hěn-'gwāng-hwar-de-ma? ‖He felt her head with his hand. tā ná-shěw 'mwō-le-mwo tā-de-'téw. ‖It looks like leather and feels like leather, but it isn't. kàn-je shyàng 'pí-dz, mwō-je 'yě shyàng 'pí-dz, kě jyèw-shr 'bú-shr pí-dz. ‖He felt for the light switch. tā 'mwō-je jǎw dyàn-'mén. ‖It was so dark I had to feel my way around the room. wū-li 'hěn hēy, wǒ děy °mwō-je 'hēr dzěw. *or* °mwō-je 'shyār dzěw. ‖I felt his pulse. wǒ 'mwō-le-mwo °tā-de-'mày, *or* °tā-de-'mwò. *But* ‖The doctor is feeling his pulse (*technical medical term*). 'dày-fu gěy-tā °'hǎw-'mwò-ne. *or* °'hǎw-'mày-ne.

(*Weigh in the hand*). (*By holding on the palm*) dyān; (*by suspending from the hand*) 'dī-lew; (*by lifting*) táy; (*by moving*) nwó; *these terms are usually double* dyān(-yi)-dyān, *etc.* ‖He put the coin on his palm to feel how heavy it was. tā bǎ-'chyán gē-dzày shěw-'jǎng-shang dyān-dyan yèw 'dwō-jùng. ‖Feel how heavy this chair is. 'jèy-bǎ-yǐ-dz nǐ 'dī-lew-dī-lew (*or* 'táy-yi-táy, *or* 'nwó-yi-nwó) kàn yěw 'dwō-jùng. ‖This box feels heavy. jèy-ge-'shyá-dz 'dyān-je hěn 'chén.

(*Perceive, be aware of, have feelings about, think*) jywé-je (*always refers to a person; ... feels ... to one is paraphrased as* one feels ... is ...). ‖I feel a pain here. wǒ 'jywé-je wǒ 'jèr téng. ‖I feel the need of a little exercise. wǒ-'shēn-shang 'jywé-je wǒ děy 'ywùn-dung-ywùn-dung tsáy 'hǎw. ‖I never feel the cold. wǒ lǎw jywé-bu-chu 'léng-lay. ‖How do you feel about this? jèy 'nǐ jywé-je dzěm-'yàng? ‖I felt that this would be a bad move. wǒ 'jywé-je dzèm bàn bú-dà 'hǎw láy-je. ‖I've never felt such heat. wǒ yí-shyàng 'méy jywé-je dzèm 'rè-gwo. ‖I felt tired last night. dzwó 'wǎn-shang wǒ (jywé-je) hěn 'lèy. ‖I feel sure he'll come. 'wǒ jywé-je (or, I think 'wǒ shyǎng) tā yí-'dìng láy. ‖It feels like (it's going to) rain today. 'jyēr jywé-je yàw shyà-'ywǔ shr̀-de. ‖Does the room feel cold to you? nǐ 'jywé-je wū-dz 'lěng-ma? ‖Does this feel all right to you? nǐ 'jywé-je jèy 'shíng-ma? ‖I don't like the feel of woolen shirts. 'máw-rúng-bù-de-'chèn-shān wǒ 'chwān-shang jywé-je 'bù-hǎw 'shèw. ‖I feel pretty well. wǒ jywé-je (or wǒ 'shēn-shang) hěn 'shū-fu. ‖I feel a little uneasy about my brother. wǒ-lǎw-'dì jyàw-wǒ jywé-je 'bú-fàng-'shīn. ‖I feel a little tired. wǒ jywé-je yěw dyár-'lèy. ‖Do you feel hungry? nǐ jywé-je 'è-le-ma? ‖I feel as if I'm going to get sick. wǒ jywé-je shyàng yàw yěw-'bìng shr̀-de. ‖I feel certain of it. wǒ 'jywé-je (or wǒ shyǎng) yí-'dìng shr̀ 'nèm-je(-le). ‖I feel like I'd been cheated. wǒ jywé-je hǎw shyàng wǒ 'shàng-le 'dàng-le. ‖I feel like a fool. wǒ 'jywé-je shyàng °ge-'shǎ-dz shr̀-de. or °ge-shǎw-ge-'shīn-yǎr shr̀-de. or °ge-'hú-du-'chúng. ‖I feel very strongly about women smoking (that it's bad). 'nywǔ-rén shī-'yān wǒ jywé-je 'hěn bù-hǎw. ‖I don't feel up to (or equal to) playing tennis right now. yàw wǒ lì-'kè jyèw dǎ wǎng-'chyéwr wǒ jywé-je wǒ chr̀-bu-'jù. But ‖I felt sure (I knew) it would happen. wǒ 'dzǎw jyèw jr̄-daw yàw 'dzèm-je.

Feel like (want to) 'ywàn-yì, shyǎng. ‖Do you feel like taking a walk? nǐ 'ywàn-yì (or nǐ shyǎng chywù) 'lyèw-da-lyèw-da-ma? ‖I feel like (having) another beer. wǒ shyǎng dzày 'hē bēy-pí-'jyěw.

Feel out. ‖Let's feel out the situation before we do anything more. dzám 'kàn-kan 'chíng-shing dzày dzěw 'shyà yí-bù.

Get (or have) the feel of . . . . . . 'shéw; . . . 'shú-shi; . . . 'dé-shīn-yìng-'shěw; . . . jywé-je 'dz̀-rán. ‖If you keep on practising you'll get the feel of it. nǐ yàw-shr bú-'dwàn-de 'lyàn-shí jyèw °'shéw-le. or °'shú-shi-le. or °'dé-shīn-yìng-'shěw-le. or °jywé-je 'dz̀-rán-le. ‖I still don't have the feel of it. 'jèy-ge wǒ háy °bù-'shéw-ne. or °méy-'shú-shi-ne. or °bù-néng 'dé-shīn-yìng-'shěw-ne. or °bù-néng jywé-je 'dz̀-rán-ne.

Other expressions in English ‖This city didn't feel the full force of the hurricane. *meaning* it died down first 'dà-fēng dàw 'běn-chéng de-shí-hew 'yǐ-jīng 'bú-lì-hay-le. or *meaning* the center didn't come here 'dà-fēng dzày 'běn-chéng yě jyèw-shr 'shāw-je yì-dyǎr-'byàr. ‖Do you know how it feels to have a hangover? nǐ 'jr̄-daw jyěw-'shìng de-shí-hew dwō nán-'shèw-ma? ‖I know how you feel, because I had the measles too.

'wǒ yě chū-gwo 'jěn-dz, swǒ-yǐ wǒ 'jr̄-daw nǐ 'dwō-me bù-'hǎw 'shèw. ‖I really feel for you. wǒ hěn 'chyān-gwà-je ni. or wǒ hěn 'dyàn-ji-je nǐ.

FELT. (*Compressed wool or fur*) 'jān-dz. ‖Is this felt or cloth? jèy-shr 'jān-dz háy-shr 'bù? ‖He has an old felt hat that he always wears in the rain. tā yěw dìng-'jyèw-jān-'màwr, 'yí shyà-'ywǔ jyèw 'dày.

FEVER. (*High body temperature*) shāw; to have a fever fā-'shāw. ‖Do you have a fever? nǐ fā-'shāw-ma? ‖His fever is going down. tā-shāw jyàn 'dī. ‖His fever went down. tā méy-yew 'shāw-le. or tā twèy-'shāw-le. or tā-shāw 'twèy-le.

(*In names of diseases*) rè, rè-'bìng, rè-'jèng; *e.g.*, scarlet fever shīng-húng-'rè; yellow fever 'hwáng-'rè-'bìng or 'hwáng-rè-'jèng. ‖He nearly died of yellow fever a year or two ago. tā 'yí-èr-nyán-chyán dé 'hwáng-rè-'jèng-le, 'chà-dyar (méy-)'sž-le.

(*Figuratively*). ‖The good news put them all into a fever of excitement. 'nèy-ge-hǎw-'shyāw-shi 'jyàw-tām 'shf-fen gāw-'shìng.

FEW. (*With emphasis on the fact that there are some, even though not many*) jǐ. ‖We asked him to say a few words at the meeting. wǒm chǐng-tā dàw-'hwèy shwō jǐ-jywù-'hwà. ‖A few of these books are torn. jèy-shyē-shū-li 'yěw jǐ-běr 'pwò-le. ‖I want to stay a few days. wǒ yàw 'jù jǐ-tyān. ‖I'd like to borrow a few of your cups. wǒ shyǎng gēn-nǐ jyè jǐ-ge-'wǎn yùng. ‖I know only a few words. wǒ jř jř-daw jǐ-ge-'dzèr. ‖It's only a few miles away. lí-jèr bú-gwò jǐ-lǐ-'dì. ‖Say it over a few more times. 'dzày shwō jǐ-byàn.

(*With emphasis on the fact that there are not many, even though there are some*) 'méy jǐ- (*followed by a measure*); bù-'dwō, (hěn) 'shǎw. ‖Few people realize it, but it's true. 'jèy-shèr shr̀ 'jēn-de, 'bú-gwò °'méy jǐ-ge-rén 'jr̄-dàw. or °'jr̄-dàw-de-rén bù-'dwō. or °'jr̄-dàw-de-rén hěn 'shǎw. ‖Very few children draw as well as he does. 'méy jǐ-ge-háy-dz néng shyàng 'tā hwà-de nèm 'hǎw-de. or shyàng-'tā-hwà-de-nèm-'hǎw-de-háy-dz °bù-'dwō. or °hěn shǎw. ‖Few of them like the idea. 'tām-nèy-shyē-rén-lǐ 'shǐ-hwān-'jèy-gē-bàn-fa-de °hěn 'shǎw. or °bù-'dwō. ‖Fewer people come here every year. láy-'jèr-de-rén 'yì-nyán bǐ yì-nyán 'shǎw. ‖The fish in this river are few and far between. 'jèy-hé-li 'ywú hěn 'shī-shǎw.

Quite a few bù-'shǎw, hěn 'dwō, hěn bù-'shǎw. ‖Quite a few people objected. 'fǎn-dwèy-de-rén °bù-'shǎw. or °hěn 'dwō. or °hěn bù-'shǎw.

FIELD. (*Tract of land*) dì; (*with measure*) kwày. ‖Let's cut across this field. dzám tsúng jèy-kwày-'dì-shang 'chwān-gwo-chywu-ba. ‖That's a fine-looking field of corn. nèy-yí-'dì-lǎw-'ywù-mǐ jǎng-de bú-'hwày.

(*For playing*) 'chǎng-dz. ‖The teams are coming onto the field. bǐ-'sày-de-rén yàw jìn 'chǎng-dz-le.

(For other purposes) -chǎng. **Magnetic field** tsź-lì-'chǎng or tsź-'chǎng; **airfield** fēy-jī-'chǎng; **battlefield** jàn-'chǎng; more properly, the field of battle 'jèn-dì.

The field (in combat) 'jèn-dì. ‖He is a correspondent who spent months in the field with the troops. tā shř ge-'shìn-wén-jì-'jě, dzày 'jèn-dì-li gēn shř-'bīng dzày yí-'kwàr gwò-le 'hǎw-jǐ-ge-'ywè.

(Sphere, range). (Range of study) yán-jyēw-de-'fàn-wéy; (specialty of study, course) mér; (profession) háng. ‖Political questions aren't in my field. 'jèng-jì-wèn-tí bú-dzày 'wǒ-yán-jyēw-de-'fàn-wéy yí-'nèy. ‖He's the best man in his field. 'tā-nèy-'háng-li (or 'tā-nèy-'mér-li) tā 'dzwèy hǎw. But ‖They were out of our field of vision. wǒm kàn-bu-'jyàn tām.

(On a flag) dyèr. ‖Their flag has white stars on a blue field. tām-de-'chí shř lán-'dyèr-shang yěw 'báy-shyēngr.

(Away from base of operations) 'wày-byar. ‖He is doing field work now. or He is working in the field now. tā pày-daw 'wày-byar °chywù-le. or (Collecting materials) °'sēw-jí 'tsáy-lyawr chywù-le. or (Doing investigation) °dyàw-'chá-chywu-le. or (Excavating) °fā-'jywé-chywu-le.

FIERCE. (Of persons or animals) shyūng; (of animals, in some combinations) měng. ‖Is your dog fierce? nǐ-de-gěw 'shyūng-bu-shyūng? ‖This is a fierce dog. jèy shř měng-'gěw. ‖He has a fierce-looking face. tā-lyǎn-shang hěn 'shyùng. or tā-lyǎn 'shyūng shyàng. ‖He fought fiercely. tā 'dǎ-de hěn 'shyūng. But ‖He gave me a fierce look. tā gěy-wǒ 'lyǎr kàn. or tā 'dèng-le wǒ yì-'yǎn. or tā hěn-'hēn-de 'dèng-wǒ. or tā gēn-wǒ 'lyǎn-shang hěn 'shyūng.

(Of actions or characteristics) 'lì-hay. ‖How can you stand that fierce heat all day? rè-de 'nèm 'lì-hay nǐ yì-'jěng-tyān dzěm shèw-de-'jù-wa? ‖You're going to come up against fierce competition. hwèy yěw-rén gēn-nǐ 'jēng-de hěn °'lì-hay-de. or (since this may be considered as personal) °'shyūng-de. ‖They fought fiercely. tām 'dǎ-de hěn °'lì-hay. or °'shyūng.

FIFTEEN. shf-'wǔ. **One fifteenth** shf-'wǔ-fēn-jr-'yī; **the fifteenth** dì-shf-'wǔ.

FIFTH. One fifth 'wǔ-fēn-jr-'yī; **the fifth** dì-'wǔ.

FIFTY. 'wǔ-shf. **One fiftieth** 'wǔ-shr-fēn-jr-'yī; **the fiftieth** dì-'wǔ-shf.

Fifty-fifty. ‖We'll split fifty-fifty. dzám dwèy-'bàr fēn. or dzám-'lyǎ 'píng-fēn. or dzám-'lyǎ 'jywūn-fēn. or 'nǐ yí-'bàr, 'wǒ yì-'bàr. or (literary) dzám 'èr-yi-tyān-dzwò-'wǔ-ba.

FIGHT. (Between individuals, physically). **To fight** dǎ-'jyà; especially, **start to fight** dùng-'shěw (dǎ-'rén); (especially in combinations or when the type of fighting is described) dǎ; (with the fists) dùng 'chywán-tew; **fight back** hwéy-'shěw. ‖They had a fight. tām 'dǎ-le yí-dwèn-'jyà. or tām dǎ-'jyà-lay-je. ‖Let's not start a fight. dzám byé 'dǎ-'jyà. or dzám byé 'dǎ-chī-lay. ‖There's a fight on the street. 'jyē-shang yěw-rén °dǎ-'jyà. or °'dǎ-chī-lay-le. ‖Have you been fighting with the boy next door again? nǐ 'yèw gēn jyè-'byěr-de-háy-dz dǎ-'jyà-la! ‖He started the fight. tā 'shyān dùng-de 'shěw. ‖They had a fist fight. tām dùng-le yì-hwéy-'chywán-tew. ‖They fought with their fists. tām dùng-chi 'chywán-tew-lay-le. ‖They fought and kicked each other for an hour. tām 'chywán-dǎ-jyǎw-'tī-de (or tǎm 'lyán-tī-dày-'dǎ-de) dǎ-le yì-dyǎn-'jūng-de-'jyà. ‖I'm afraid we're going to have a fight about this. 'jèy-shèr 'kǔng-pà dzám děy 'dǎ yí-dwèn-'jyà. ‖How did the fight come out? dǎ-de-'jyē-gwǒ rú-'hé? or (Who won?) 'shéy dǎ-'yíng-le? or (Who lost?) 'shéy dǎ-'shū-le? or (See fight it out below) shèng-'fù rú-'hé? ‖What can I do if he doesn't fight back? tā yàw 'bù-hwéy-'shěw (or tā yàw 'bù-gēn-wǒ 'dǎ) wǒ yěw dzěm-'bàn-ne? ‖What could I do? He wouldn't fight back. tā 'bù-hwéy-'shěw (or tā 'bù-gēn-wǒ 'dǎ), wǒ yěw yěw shéme-'fá-dz-ne?

(Verbally, sometimes) dǎ-'jyà; but (specifically) chǎw-'dzwěy; (curse) 'mà(-chi-lay); yěw 'chwén-shé, chū.'chǎw-dz or dǎ 'chǎw-dz. ‖They had a fight. tām chǎw-'dzwěy láy-je. or tām bǐ-tsž dwèy 'mà-lay-je. ‖I'm afraid we're going to have a fight about this. 'jèy-shèr 'kǔng-pà °dzám děy yěw yì-fán-'chwén-shé. or °'yàw chū 'chǎw-dz.

(In court) dǎ; (argue, contend) jēng; (explain reasons) jyǎng-'lǐ; all are said of a lawsuit 'gwān-sz; the combination dǎ 'gwān-sz is also possible. ‖I intend to fight that suit to the bitter end. nèy-ge-'gwān-sz wǒ yí-'dìng yàw dǎ-dàw 'dǐ. ‖I intend to fight them on that suit. nèy-ge-'gwān-sz wǒ yàw gēn-tām °'dǎ-yi-dǎ. or °'jēng-yi-jēng. or °jyǎng-jyang 'lǐ.

(In war) dǎ-'jàng; (sometimes) 'jàn-dèw; (in combination) dǎ, jàn. ‖He fought through the worst campaign. 'dǐng-lì-hay-de-nèy-yí-'jàng tā yě dzày-nàr 'dǎ láy-je. ‖The enemy has fought on the flat country rather than through the mountains. dí-rén yì-'jř dzày píng-'ywán-shang dǎ-'jàng (or 'jàn-dèw), 'bù-kěn dàw 'shān-lù-shang-chywu. ‖They fought up the beach to the railroad. tām tsúng 'hǎy-àn dǎ (or jàn)-dàw tyě-'lù-nar.

(In most of the above senses, but with emphasis on the vigorous life-or-death nature of the fight) pīn-'mìng. ‖We must all unite in fighting the common enemy. (Of a nation) dzám děy 'lyán-hé-chī-lay gēn dzám-de-°'dì-rén pīn-'mìng. or (Of a person) °'chéw-rén pīn-'mìng.

Fight it out. (In speaking of others) fēn ge-shèng-'fù, dǎ ge-'tùng-kwày; (including oneself) dǎ-dàw 'dǐ, pīn-'mìng; (to the death) dǎ ge-'nǐ-sž-wǒ-'hwó. (nǐ and wǒ do not necessarily mean literally you and I *here, and the whole expression can be used figuratively.*) ‖**Stand back and let them fight it out.** 'dwǒ-kāy-dyar jyàw-tām °'fēn ge-shèng-'fù. *or* °dǎ ge-'tùng-kwày. ‖**We're going to have to fight it out with them.** wǒm děy gēn-tām °dǎ-dàw 'dǐ. *or* °pīn-'mìng. *o*. °dǎ ge-'nǐ-sž-wǒ-'hwó.

Fight off. (*In combat*) dǎ-'twèy. ‖**They fought off the enemy.** tām bǎ 'dí-rén dǎ-'twèy-le. (*In personal inner struggle*) yǎw-je-'yá *plus a negative and a verb.* ‖**I was very sleepy, but I fought it off.** wǒ kwèn-'jí-le, kě-shr yǎw-je-'yá méy-'shwèy.

Fight against (*figuratively*). ‖**You've got to fight against that habit of yours** (*bite your teeth and change it*). nǐ-nèy-ge-'máw-bìng nǐ děy yǎw-je-'yá gwǎn-gwo-lay. ‖**They're fighting against** (*trying hard to get rid of*) **syphilis.** tām 'jyé-lì yàw 'chǎn-chú 'méy-dú.

Fight about, fight over, fight for wèy … *plus most of the words used above for* fight. ‖**I think I'm right, but I'm not going to fight about it.** wǒ shyǎng 'wǒ yěw-'lì, bú-gwo wǒ 'bù-shyǎng chywù wèy nèy-ge °'jēng. *or* °dǎ-'jyà. *or* °dǎ 'gwǎn-sz. *or* °pīn-'mìng. *or* °chǎw-'dzwèy.

Put up a good fight ('dǎ-de) hěn mày 'lì-chi. ‖**He put up a good fight but lost anyway.** tā ('dǎ-de) hěn mày 'lì-chi, bú-gwo 'háy-shr 'shū-le.

FIGURE. (*Numeral*) shùr. ‖**These figures don't add up right.** jèy-shyē-'shùr jyā-yí-kwàr bú-'dwèy. ‖**Those figures show that the population is decreasing.** tsúng nèy-shyē-'shùr-shang kě-yǐ kàn-chu shyàn-dzày 'rén-kew jyàn-'jyǎn-de 'shǎw-le. ‖**Delete that figure.** bǎ nèy-ge-shùr 'shān-chywu.

(*Compute*) swàn. ‖**Figure up how much it amounts to.** swàn-yi-swan yí-'gùng dwō-shǎw (*plus* -chyán *if money is referred to*).

(*Computation*) 'swàn-shywé, 'swàn-fa. ‖**Are you good at figures** (*or* at figuring)? nǐ-'swàn-shywé hǎw-ma? *or* nǐ-'swàn-fa hǎw-ma?

(*To judge*) kàn. ‖**I figure it's about time we were going.** wǒ kàn dzám kwày gāy 'dzěw-je-le. ‖**The way I figure (it), we can get it done in time.** jàw wǒ-'kàn dzám dàw-le 'shŕ-hew 'kě-yǐ dzwò-'wán.

(*To plan, predict*) 'dǎ-swàn, 'swàn-ji, dǎ 'swàn-pan; (*think*) shyǎng; (*guess*) tsǎy; (*form an idea*) dǎ 'jú-yì. ‖**He figured it wrong.** tā 'dǎ-swàn-tswò-le. *or* tā 'tsǎy-tswò-le. *or* tā 'swàn-ji-tswò-le. *or* tā 'shyǎng-tswò-le. *or* tā dǎ-tswò-le 'jú-yi-le. *or* tā dǎ-tswò-le 'swàn-ᵖ ‖**Don't just figure for** (*or* on) **yourself.** 'byé jìng gˌey nǐ-'dž-ji 'dǎ-swàn. ‖**How did you figure on going?** nǐ dǎ-swàn 'dzěm chywù-ya?

Figure out. (*By guessing*) 'tsǎy-chū; (*by thinking*) 'shyǎng-chū; (*by calculation*) 'swàn-ji-chū; (*by looking*) 'kàn-chu. ‖**I couldn't figure out what he was going to do.** wǒ 'tsǎy-bu-chū (*or* wǒ 'shyǎng-bu-chū, *or* wǒ 'swàn-ji-bu-chū) tā yàw dzěm-'bàn-lay. ‖**I can't figure him out.** wǒ 'tsǎy-bu-jáw (*or* wǒ 'kàn-bu-chu) tā shr̀ ge-'dzěm-yàng-de-rén. ‖**Can you figure out this**

problem? (*mathematics*) 'jèy-ge-tí nǐ 'shyang de-chū dzěm 'swàn-ne? *or* (*not mathematics*) ˌjèy-ge 'wèn-tí (*or* jèy-jyàn-'shŕ) nǐ 'shyǎng-de-chū ge-'bàn-fa-lay-ma?

Figure on 'shyǎng-dàw, 'swàn-ji-dàw. ‖**That's something I hadn't figured on.** wǒ méy-'shyǎng-dàw 'jèy-ge. *or* wǒ méy-'swàn-ji-dàw 'jèy-ge.

Figure in (*have a part in*). ‖**This didn't figure in my plans.** 'wǒ-de-'jì-hwà-li méy-bǎ jèy-ge 'dǎ-jìn-chywu.

(*Shape: human*) shēn-'jyà-dz, 'shēn-dz; *or sometimes not expressed.* ‖**She has a nice figure.** tā-shēn-'jyà-dz jǎng-de 'hǎw. *or* tā-'shēn-dz jǎng-de °hǎw-'kàn. *or* °'myáw-tyáw. *or* °'fēng-mǎn. *or* °'líng-lúng. *or* °'shì-lyew. *or* °shwèn-'yǎn. ‖**What a figure!** (*Nice*) ('shēn-dz) jǎng-de 'jēn hǎw-'kàn! *or* (*Ugly*) 'shēn-dz) jǎng-de 'jēn nán-'kàn. ‖**I have to watch my figure.** wǒ děy 'shyǎw-shīn-je, byé tày 'pàng-le.

(*Personage*) 'rén-wu, 'yàw-rén, yàw-'jǐn-de-'rén-wu, 'dà-rén-wu, 'shēn-shr. ‖**He's a mighty important figure in this town.** tā shr̀ jèy-ge-dì-'myàr-shang-de-'yàw-rén. *or* tā shŕ 'jèy-dì-fang-°'hěn-yàw-'jǐn-de-rén wu. *or* °de-'dà-rén-wu. *or* °de-'shēn-shr. ‖**He cut a fine figure in national politics.** tā dzày 'jèng-jr̀-wǔ-'táy-shang dž-jǐ gǎw-de chéng-le ge-'rén-wu-le.

(*Small statue*) shyàng; (*human*) shyǎw-'rér. ‖**How do you like that little bronze figure?** nèy-ge-shyǎw-túng-'shyàng (*òr* nèy-ge-'dž-túng-de-shyǎw-'rér) nǐ 'shǐ-hwān-ma?

(*Illustration*) tú. ‖**Figure 7 shows the parts of a machine gun.** dì-'chī-tú shŕ jī-gwān-'chyāng-'chǎy-kay-de-gè-'bù-fen.

(*Pattern*) hwǎr. ‖**The material is white with a little green figure.** lyàw-dz shŕ 'báy-de, shàng-tew yěw shyǎw-lywù-'hwǎr. ‖**He had on a figured necktie.** tā dày-je ge-yěw-'hwǎr-de-lǐng-'dày.

Figure of speech 'bǐ-fang, 'bǐ-ywù. ‖**I didn't mean it that way; it was only a figure of speech.** wǒ 'bú-shr nèy-ge-'yì-sz; nèy bú-gwo shŕ °ge-'bǐ-fang. *or* °ge-'bǐ-ywù.

FILL. *Chinese uses resultative compounds in almost all cases; the first element indicates the type of action; the second element indicates the result. The second element is usually* mǎn *full, but sometimes, especially when speaking of filling up holes,* shàng *is used, corresponding to English* up *in* fill up; *in a few cases only* shàng *is used.*

(*Of a hole or gap*) 'tyán-shang *and* tyán-'mǎn (*especially of vertical holes*); 'sǎy-shang *and* sǎy-'mǎn (*plug up; of vertical and horizontal holes*); 'dǔ-shang (*stop up; especially* stop up the opening; *of vertical and horizontal holes*); 'bǔ-shang *patch up.* ‖**Fill up the holes in the road with gravel.** bǎ 'lù-shang-de-'kēng yùng swèy-shŕ-tew °'tyán-shang. *or* °'tyán-'mǎn-le. ‖**They filled up the well with earth.** tām bǎ-'jǐng ná-tǔ °'tyán-shang-le. *or* °'tyán-'mǎn-le. *or* °'sǎy-shang-le. *or* °'sǎy-'mǎn-le. *or* °'dǔ-shang-le.

‖This cavity (*in a tooth*) will have to be filled pretty soon. jèy-ge-'yá-kū-lung děy kwày-dyar °'tyán-shang. *or* °'bǔ-shang. *or* °'sāy-shang. *or* °'dǔ-shang. ‖The ditch has been filled in. nèy-ge-'gēw yǐ-jīng 'tyán-shang-le. ‖That cave has been filled in. nèy-ge-'dùng yǐ-jīng °'dǔ-shang-le. *or* °'sāy-shang-le.

(*Of a gap, figuratively, left by the absence of a person*) 'bǔ(-shang). ‖There are several jobs here that need to be filled. jèr yěw 'jǐ-ge-'wèy-jr̀ (*or* jèr yěw 'jǐ-ge-'chywē-é) °děy 'bǔ-shang. *or* °háy 'méy-rén bǔ. ‖All the jobs are filled now. 'swǒ-yěw-de-'wèy-jr̀ (*or* 'swǒ-yěw-de-'chywē-é) dēw 'bǔ-shang-le. ‖I'm just filling in here temporarily. wǒ 'bú-gwo dzày-jèr 'bǔ ge-lín-'shŕ-de-'chywē.

(*Of space on paper*). Fill up (*completely*) bǔ-'mǎn *and* tyán-'mǎn; fill (up) (*with something*) 'bǔ-shang *and* 'tyán-shang; fill in *or* fill out tyán; *or* (*write*) shyě. ‖Fill up that space (*as in a newspaper*). bǎ nèy-kwày-'kùng-báy °'bǔ-'mǎn-le. *or* °'tyán-'mǎn-le. ‖Fill (up) that space with this story. ná 'jèy-dwàr-'shīn-wén bǎ nèy-kwày-'kùng-báy °'tyán-shang. *or* °'bǔ-shang. ‖Fill out the blanks first. shyān bǎ 'dān-dz dēw °'tyán-shang. *or* °'tyán-le. ‖Fill in your name and address here. (bǎ) nǐ-de-'shìng-míng-jù-'jr̀ °'tyán-dzày 'jèr. *or* °shyě-dzày 'jèr.

(*Of a container*) the second element is always mǎn; the first may be pour dàw; pack, contain jwāng; contain (*especially of a mass*) chéng. ‖That bottle is filled (up) with hot water. nèy-ge-'píng-dz (*or* nèy-ge-'dày-dz) °mǎn-'mān-de 'jwāng-je rè-'shwěy. *or* °-lǐ jwāng-'mǎn-le rè-'shwěy. ‖Fill this bottle full of hot water. bǎ jèy-ge-'píng-dz jwāng-'mǎn-le (*or* dàw-'mǎn-le) rè-'shwěy. ‖They filled two trucks with furniture. tām bǎ 'jyā-jywù jwāng-'mǎn-le 'lyǎng-lyàng-dà-kǎ-'chē. ‖Fill up his cup first. shyān gěy-'tā dàw-'mǎn-le bēy. ‖They filled his bowl with rice. tām gěy-tā 'chéng-le yì-'mǎn-wǎn-'fàn. ‖His pocket is all filled up with candy. tā-de-kěw-'dày-li jwāng-'mǎn-le 'táng-le. *or* tā 'jwāng-le yì-kěw-'dàr-de-'táng. ‖Our students filled up a whole bus. wǒm-de-'shywé-sheng jwāng-'mǎn-le yí-'lyàng-gūng-'gùng-chì-'chē. ‖There isn't enough rice to fill three bowls. fàn bú-gèw chéng sān-'wǎn-de. ‖Fill 'er up (*with gas*). jwāng-'mǎn-le. *or* dàw-'mǎn-le.

(*Of an area filled with objects*) the second element is mǎn, *unless such an expression as* the whole *occurs, in which case no second element is needed; some of the verbs used as first elements are* arrange in order bǎy; put gē *or* fàng; cover pū *or* gày; set up ān; park (*a car*) tíng. ‖The sofa just about fills that end of the room. shā-'fā jyāng-'jyāngr-de bǎ wū-dz-nèy-téwr bǎy-'mǎn-le. ‖They filled the shelves with odds and ends. tām dzày 'jyà-dz-shang bǎy-'mǎn-le (*or* gē-'mǎn-le, *or* fàng-'mǎn-le) 'líng-swèr. ‖He filled the room with antiques. tā bǎy-le yì-'wū-dz-de-gǔ-'wán. ‖He filled the room with electric lamps. tā ān-le yì-'wū-dz-de-dyàn-'dēng. ‖This rug will fill up the living room (*floor*). jèy-kwày-'dì-tǎn kě-yǐ bǎ kè-tīng-de-dì-'bǎn pū-'mǎn-le. ‖The parking place is filled with out-of-town cars. tíng-chē-'chǎng tíng-'mǎn-le wày-'láy-de-'chē.

(*Of a space filled with people*) the second element is mǎn; first elements are (*by sitting*) dzwò; (*by standing*) jàn; (*by crowding together*) jǐ; (*by gathering together*) jywù; (*by living*) jù. ‖The theater was slowly filling with people. shì-'ywán-dz màn-'mān-de dzwò-'mǎn-le rén-le. ‖The hall was filled with people standing there listening. 'tīng-li °jàn-'mǎn-le rén dzày-nàr 'tīng. *or* °jǐ (*or* jywù)-'mǎn-le rén, dēw 'jàn-dzày nàr 'tīng. ‖The barracks are filled to the full with recruits. 'yíng-pán-li jù-'mǎn-le 'shīn-bīng. *or* 'shīn-bīng bǎ 'yíng-pán dēw jù-'mǎn-le.

Be filled with *without the means being specified.* mǎn *and other expressions; see* FULL. ‖The room is filled with smoke. yì-'wū-dz-li 'mǎn shr̀ 'yān.

Have one's fill. (*Of food*) bǎw; (*of an experience, etc.*) gèw. ‖Have you had your fill of it? (*Food*) 'bǎw-le-ma? (*Otherwise*) 'gèw-le-ma? ‖Don't be bashful; go ahead and eat your fill. 'byé bù-hǎw-'yì-sz; 'chr̄-ba, chr̄-de bǎw-'bāwr-de.

FINAL. (*Last*) mwò-'lyǎwr(-de) *or* 'dzwèy-hèw(-de) (*followed by a numeral or demonstrative and a measure before the noun*). ‖This is the final lecture of the semester. jèy 'shr̀ 'běn-jì-'dzwèy-hèw-de (*or* jèy shr̀ 'běn-jì-mwò-'lyǎwr-de) °-yì-táng-'kè-le. *or* °-yì-'bān-le. ‖Did you go to the final lecture of the semester? 'běn-jì-'dzwèy-hèw-nèy-táng-'kè nǐ 'dàw-le-ma?

Final examination 'dà-kǎw; (*of a semester*) 'jì-kǎw *or* jì-'jūng-kǎw-shr̀; (*of a school year*) 'shywé-nyán-kǎw-shr̀; (*for graduation*) bì-'yè-kǎw-shr̀. ‖Did he pass his French final? tā 'fà-wén-'dà-kǎw (*etc.*) jí-'gé-le-ma?

(*Definite*). (*Already decided*) yí-'dìng-de; (*determinable*) néng-'dìng-de. ‖There's nothing final about it yet. (*Already decided; as of a plan*) 'jèy-shr̀ háy 'méy-yěw yí-'dìng-de-'bàn-fa-ne. *or* (*Determinable, as of something now happening*) 'jèy-shr̀ 'jyē-gwǒ dzěm-'yàng háy bù-néng 'dìng-ne.

(*Ultimate*) final outcome 'jyē-gwǒ, 'jyē-jywú. ‖You can already tell what the final outcome is going to be. 'jyē-gwǒ (*or* 'jyē-jywú) shéme-'yàngr yǐ-jīng 'kàn-de-chū-'láy-le.

(*Beyond appeal; legal*) 'bù-néng 'kàng-gàw *or* 'bù-néng shàng-'sù-le. ‖The decision of the Supreme Court is final. 'dzwèy-gāw-'fǎ-ywàn °-pàn-jywé-de 'bù-néng 'kàng-gàw. *or* °pàn-jywé yǐ-'hèw. ivc̀ 'bù-néng shàng-'sù-le.

(*Leaving nothing to be said or done*). ‖Is that final? *meaning* absolutely necessary 'fēy-'shr̀ bù-'kě-le-ma? *or meaning* Is there any other way? 'háy néng yěw 'byé-de-'bàn-fǎ-ma? *or meaning* Can it be discussed? háy néng 'shāng-lyang-shāng-lyang-ma? *or meaning* It's settled, then? 'yì-yán-wéy-'dìng-le, ā? ‖His word is final. *meaning* What he says goes. 'tā shwǒ 'dzěm-je 'jyèw děy 'dzěm-je.

Finals (*in competition*) 'jywé-sày. ‖He was eliminated before he got to the finals. tā 'jywé-sày yǐ-chyán jyèw 'shyà-chywu-le. *or* tā 'méy-dàw 'jywé-sày jyèw 'shyà-chywu-le.

FIND. 1. (*Discover*). *Chinese distinguishes several ways in which things are found; most of the expressions are resultative compounds.*

Find accidentally, pick up shŕ *or* jyàn. ‖I found a coin in the street. wǒ dzày 'jyē-shang shŕ-le (*or* jyàn-le) yí-ge-'chyán. ‖I found this five-dollar bill in the street. jèy-jāng-'wǔ-kwày-chyán-de-'pyàw-dz shŕ wǒ-dzày-'jyē-shang-°shŕ-de. *or* °jyàn-de.

Find by looking for (*general term*) 'jǎw-jáw. ‖They looked everywhere for him, but couldn't find him. tām 'dàw-chù 'jǎw-tā kě-shr °méy jǎw-'jáw. *or* °jǎw-bu-'jáw. ‖When you find him tell him there is nothing for him to worry about any more. 'jǎw-jaw tā de-shŕ-hew, 'gàw-su tā 'shéme dēw kě-yǐ fàng-'shīn-le. ‖They found him. tām bǎ-tā 'jǎw-jáw-le. ‖Put everything back where you found it. dzày-nǎr 'jǎw-jáw-de háy dēw 'gē-hwéy 'nǎr-chywu. *or* dzày 'shéme-dì-fang 'jǎw-jáw-de háy dēw 'gē-hwéy nèy-ge-'dì-fang-chywu. ‖I can't find my keys anywhere. wǒ-de-'yàw-shr 'nǎr dēw jǎw-bu-'jáw. ‖Did you find it? 'jǎw-jáw-le-ma? ‖Where did you find it? (dzày-)'nǎr jǎw-jáw-de? ‖Can you find it? jǎw-de-'jáw-ma? ‖Could you find him for me? nǐ néng 'tì-wǒ bǎ-tā 'jǎw-jáw-ma? ‖Find him and bring him here. bǎ-tā 'jǎw-lay.

Find by turning things up *or* **over.** 'fān-jáw *or* 'fān-chū-lay. ‖I found this five-dollar bill in that book. jèy-jāng-'wǔ-kwày-chyán-de-'pyàw-dz shŕ wǒ-dzày-nèy-běr-'shū-li-°'fān-jaw-de. *or* °'fān-chu-lay-de.

Find by searching, research, *or* **inspection** 'chá-chu-lay *or* 'chà-jaw. ‖They found a gun in his trunk. tām dzày tā-'shyāng-dz-li °'chá-chu-lay (*or, with meanings given above,* °'jǎw-jáw-le, *or* °'fān-jaw-le, *or* °'fān-chu-lay) yì-gǎn-'chyāng.

Find by reading *or* **looking around** 'kàn-chu-lay. ‖I found five mistakes on one page. dzày 'yì-pyār-shang wǒ 'kàn-chu-lay (*or* 'chá-chu-lay, *or* 'jǎw-jaw) 'wǔ-ge-'tswèr. ‖I found many mistakes in that book. 'nèy-běr-shū-li wǒ 'kàn-chu-lay (*or* 'jǎw-jáw-le, *or* 'chá-chu-lay, *or* 'fān-chu-lay) 'hǎw-shyē-'tswèr.

Find by looking for and uncovering 'jǎw-chū-lay (*literally and figuratively*). ‖You can find faults with (*or* in) anyone. nǐ yàw 'jǎw de-hwà 'shéy-shēn-shang dēw 'jǎw-de-chū 'tswèr-lay.

Find by thinking 'shyǎng-chū-lay. ‖How did you ever find such an illuminating word to describe him? nǐ 'dzěm shyǎng-chu 'dzèm-chyà-dang-de-'dzèr láy 'shíng-rung tā? ‖I can't find the right word to describe her. wǒ 'shyǎng-bu-chu ge-'chyà-dang-de-dzèr láy 'shíng-rung tā. ‖He couldn't find anything to say. tā 'shyǎng-bu-chu 'hwà láy 'shwō-le. ‖I haven't found a solution yet. wǒ háy méy 'shyǎng-chu ge-'bàn-fa láy-ne. ‖Can you find an answer to this problem? jèy-jyàn-shèr nǐ 'shyǎng-de-chū ge-'bàn-fa-láy-ma?

‖I've found the best answer to it. wǒ 'shyǎng-chu ge-'dzwèy-hǎw-de-'bàn-fa-láy. ‖Let's try to find a way out. (*Of a difficulty*) shyǎng ge-shyà-'táy-de-'bàn-fa-ba. *or* (*Of a place*) jǎw yì-tyáw-'lù hǎw 'chū-chywu-ba.

Find by scientific research 'yán-jyew-chū-lay. ‖They found a new drug. tām 'yán-jyew-chū yì-jǔng-'shīn-yàw-lay.

Find by experimentation 'shŕ-yan-chū-lay. ‖They found a new way to cure diabetes. tām 'shŕ-yan-chū (*or* tām 'yán-jyew-chū) yì-jǔng-shīn-'fá-dz láy j̀r 'táng-nyàw-'jèng.

Find by exploration 'fā-jyàn *or* 'fā-shyàn. ‖They found gold in those streams. tām dzày nèy-shyē-'hé-li 'fā-shyàn (*or* 'fā-jyàn, *or* 'jǎw-jaw, *or* 'kàn-jyàn) 'jīn-dz-le.

Find by digging 'jywé-chu *or* 'wā-chu (*plus* láy). ‖They found gold in those mountains. tām dzày nèy-shyē-'shān-lǐ °'jywé-chu (*or* 'wā-chu) 'jīn-dz-lay-le. *or* °'fā-shyàn (*or* 'fā-jyàn, *or* 'jǎw-jaw, *or* 'kàn-jyàn) 'jīn-dz-le.

Find by diagnosis 'jyǎn-chá-chu-lay. ‖The doctor found him to be a mental case. dày-fu 'jyǎn-chá-chu-lay (*or* dày-fu 'chá-chu-lay, *or* dày-fu 'jèng-míng-le) tā yěw 'shén-jīng-'bìng.

2. (*To see*) 'kàn-jyàn. ‖I found a note on my desk. wǒ dzày wǒ-shū-'jwōr-shang kàn-jyàn yì-jāng-'dž-tyáwr. ‖I found a book missing from the shelf. wǒ kàn-jyàn (*or* wǒ chá-chu-lay) shū-'jyàr-shang 'dwǎn-le (*or* 'shǎw-le, *or* 'dyēw-le) yì-běn-'shū. ‖Who found the body? 'shŕ-shew shŕ 'shéy-shyān-'kàn-jyàn-de? *or* 'shŕ-shew shŕ 'shéy-'jǎw-jáw-de? ‖I found her staring at me. wǒ kàn-jyàn tā (dzày-nàr) 'dèng-je yǎn 'chyáw-wo-ne. ‖I found her writing something. wǒ kàn-jyàn tā dzày-nàr 'shyě shém-me-ne. ‖They found him breaking into a house. tām kàn-jyàn tā yàw 'jìn rén-jyā-'fáng-dz tēw 'dūng-shi.

3. (*Learn by experience, perceive, feel*) 'jywé-je. ‖We've always found this place peaceful. wǒm yí-'shyàng jywé-je jèr hěn 'ān-jing-je. ‖If you ever find yourself in a tight spot, call on me. nǐ 'yì-jywé-je méy-'bàn-fa-le, jyèw jǎw-'wǒ hǎw-le. ‖I found the book interesting. wǒ 'jywé-je jèy-běn-'shū hěn yěw 'yì-sz. ‖They thought they were going to meet a dull girl, but they found her quite interesting. tām 'yǐ-wéy yàw-'jyàn-de shŕ ge-shǎ-'yā-tew-ne; méy-shyǎng-'dàw jyàn-'myàr yǐ-'hěw (tām) jywé-je tā 'hěn yěw-'chywèr. ‖I found him quite a bore. wǒ(-shīn-li) jywé-je tā 'jēn jyàw-rén 'nì-wey-de-hwang.

4. *In some cases the English* **find** *may be interpreted in more than one of the above ways, and is sometimes not translated at all.* ‖They found him already dead. tā 'yǐ-jīng 'sž-le. *or* tām 'kàn-jyàn tā de-shŕ-hew (*or* tām 'jǎw-jaw tā de-shŕ-hew) tā 'yǐ-jīng 'sž-le. *or meaning* **after looking him over** tām 'kàn-chu-lay tā yǐ-jīng 'sž-le. *or meaning* **upon investigation** (*as in files*) tām 'chá-chu-lay tā 'yǐ-jīng 'sž-le. ‖I found her

sick in bed. (wǒ 'kàn-jyàn tā de-shŕ-hew) 'tā jèng bìng-dzày 'chwáng-shang. ‖When I got home I found my brother waiting for me. wǒ dàw-'jyā de-shŕ-hew, °kàn-jyàn (*or* °tsáy jŕ-dàw, *see* find out *below*) wǒ-'gē-ge dzày-nàr 'děng-wǒ-ne. ‖How did you find her? *meaning* By what means? · nǐ 'dzěm jǎw-jaw-tā-de-ya? *or* nǐ 'dzěm bǎ-tā jǎw-jaw-de-ya? *or meaning* In what condition? nǐ 'kàn-jyan tā de-shŕ-hew, tā 'dzěm-yàng? *or meaning* What is your impression of her? nǐ 'jywé-je tā 'dzěm-yàng? ‖I found her just as you told me. (*In that way*) wǒ 'wán-chywán jàw-je 'nǐ-de-hwà bǎ-tā 'jǎw-jáw-de. *or* ⸲*In that condition*) wǒ 'kàn-jyàn tā de-shŕ-hew, tā 'háy-shr shyàng 'nǐ-shwō-de nèy-yàngr. *or meaning* She impressed me as you described. 'wǒ jywé-je nǐ 'shíng-rung-de tā 'jēn shyàng. *or* 'wǒ jywé-je tā gēn 'nǐ-shwō-de 'yì-mú-yí-yàngr.

5. (*Of a court or judge*). (*To prove*) 'jèng-míng; (*to decide*) pàn. ‖The court finds him guilty of murder. 'fǎ-ywàn 'jèng-míng-le tā shŕ 'shyūng-shew. *or* 'fǎ-ywàn 'pàn-tā yěw 'shā-rén-dzwèy. ‖The court found him innocent (*or* not guilty). 'fǎ-ywàn 'pàn-tā 'méy-yěw-'dzwèy.

6. *Combinations.* Find out (*seek out, look up*) 'jǎw-chu-lay; (*same, with successful result*) 'jǎw-jaw *or* 'jǎw-dàw; (*by investigating*) 'chá-chu-lay; (*by asking*) 'dǎ-tīng-chu-lay, 'wèn-chu-lay, 'dǎ-tīng-jaw, 'wèn-jaw; (*obtain, of information or material*) 'dé-jaw; (*know as a result of finding out*) 'jŕ-dàw. ‖Find out all about him. bǎ tā-de-'dǐ-shì dēw °'jǎw-chu-lay. *or* °'dǎ-tīng-chu-lay. *or* °'chá-chu-lay. ‖How much did you find out? nǐ 'dé-jaw 'dwō-shǎw-'tsáy-lyàwr. *or* nǐ 'jŕ-dàw 'dwō-shǎw-le? *or* nǐ 'dǎ-tīng-chu-lay 'dwō-shǎw-le? *or* nǐ 'wèn-chu-lay 'dwō-shǎw-le? *or* nǐ 'chá-chu-lay 'dwō-shǎw-le? *or* nǐ 'jǎw-jáw 'dwō-shǎw-le? ‖Don't let him find out. 'byé jyàw-tā °'jŕ-dàw. *or* °'chá-chu-lay. *or* °'dǎ-tīng-jaw. *or* °'wèn-jaw. ‖How did you find out that we live here? wǒm jù-'jèr nǐ dzěm °'jŕ-dàw-de? *or* °'jǎw-jáw-de? *or* °'dǎ-tīng-chu-lay-de? *or* °'wèn-jaw-de? *or* °'wèn-chu-lay-de? *or* °'jǎw-dàw-de? ‖They found out that he was hiding in town. tām 'jŕ-dàw-le (*etc.*) tā dzày jèy-ge-'dì-fang 'tsáng-je-ne.

Lost and found department 'shŕ-wù-bǎw-gwǎn-'chù.

Find the mark. (*Literally*) dǎ-'jùng, dǎ-'jáw, 'dǎ-shàng; (*figuratively: of something said*) shwō-'jáw. ‖The bullet found its mark. 'nèy-chyāng °'dǎ-'jùng-le. *or* °'dǎ-'jáw-le. *or* °'dǎ-shàng-le. ‖Your accusation really found its mark. 'nǐ-nèy-jywù-hwà 'jēn-shr shwō-'jáw-le.

Find oneself. ‖I think he'll find himself some day. *meaning* know himself wǒ shyǎng 'dzǔng yěw yì-tyān tā néng jŕ-dàw tā 'dz̀-jǐ shŕ 'dzěm hwéy-'shèr. *or meaning* understand himself wǒ shyǎng tā 'dzǔng yěw yì-tyān néng 'dz̀-jǐ 'míng-bay-gwo-lay. *or* wǒ shyǎng tā hwèy dz̀-jǐ-'jywé-wu-de, 'dzǔng yěw 'nèm-yì-tyān.

FINE. (*Very good*) hǎw *and combinations; see* **GOOD.** ‖That's fine! 'hǎw! *or* hǎw-'jí-le! ‖We gave him the finest watch that money could buy. wǒm gěy-tā yì-jŕ-'dzwèy-hǎw-de-'byǎw, 'dzày yě mǎy-bu-chū-láy bǐ 'nèy-ge-'hǎw-de-le. ‖I had a fine time last night. wǒ 'dzwér 'wǎn-shang wár-de °'hěn 'hǎw. *or* °'hěn 'kwày-hwo. *or* °'hěn yěw 'yì-sz. ‖That's a fine job for him. 'nèy shŕ jyàw-tā dzwò hǎw-'jí-le. ‖That was a mighty fine thing for him to do. tā 'nèm-je jēn shŕ 'dzwò-le hǎw-'shŕ-le. ‖He has a fine disposition. tā-'pí-chyer 'jēn hǎw. ‖I'm feeling fine, thanks. 'hěn hǎw, 'hěn hǎw; 'dwō 'shyè, 'dwō 'shyè. ‖It's a fine day today. 'jyēr tyār 'jēn hǎw. *or* 'jyēr tyār shyǎng-'chíng. ‖That's a fine way to put it. nèy-hwà 'nèm shwō °'hěn hǎw. *or* °'hěn 'dwèy. *or* °'wǎn-jwǎn-de hǎw. *or* 'jēn hwèy shwō-'hwàr-a. (*Also ironically*) ‖That's fine! (*or* A fine thing!) I lend you money to eat and then you spend it all on her! 'hǎw(-wa)! wǒ jyè-gěy nǐ 'chyán, nǐ 'dēw hwā-dzày 'tā-shēn-shang-le. ‖That's a fine way to treat a friend! hǎw! dày 'péng-yew 'nèm-ge-dày-far!

(*Thin*) shì. ‖You can draw finer lines with a hard pencil. ná-'yìng-chyān-bǐ-hwà-de-'shyàn kě-yǐ 'dzày shì-dyar. ‖There are some fine hairs on her shin. tā-shyǎw-t-twěy-shang yěw shyē-'shì-máwr. ‖This thread is too fine for sewing on buttons. 'jèy-ge-shyàn féng 'kèw-dz tày 'shì-le.

(*Sharp*) jyān. ‖Don't sharpen it to such a fine point. 'byé shyāw-de 'dzèm jyān-na. ‖I'd like a fine-pointed one, please. wǒ yàw ge-'jyān-de. ·

(*Powdery*) shì. ‖The pharmacist ground the drug into fine powder. yàw-jì-'shŕ (*or* mày-'yàw-de) bǎ-yàw 'yán-chéng °shì-'myàr. *or* °hěn-shì-de-'myàr.

(*Subtle, in detail*) shì. ‖There is no need of making such fine distinctions. 'bú-yùng fēn-de 'dzěm 'shì. *or* 'bú-yùng dzěm 'shì-fēn.

(*Expert; of workmanship*) shì, jīng, chyǎw. ‖What fine workmanship! 'dzwǒ-de (*or* jèy-'gūng) 'jēn °shì. *or* °jīng. *or* °chyǎw.

(*Acute; of musical ear*) 'líng-mǐn. ‖She has a fine ear for music. tā-'ěr-dwo tīng 'yīn-ywè hěn 'líng-mǐn.

Fine arts 'měy-shù. Museum of fine arts 'měy-shù-gwǎn.

Fine gold 'chwén-jīn.

A fine fá-'kwǎn. Pay a fine jyāw (yì-bǐ-)fá-'kwǎn; be fined fá(-le). ‖If he's convicted he'll have to pay a stiff fine. yàw-shr 'pàn-tā yěw 'dzwèy, tā děy dà-'dā-de jyāw yì-bǐ-fá-'kwǎn. ‖I paid a five-dollar fine. wǒ jyāw-le 'wǔ-kwày-chyán-de-'fá-kwǎn. ‖You may pay the fine now or have your case tried in court. nǐ hè-shr shyàn-dzày jyāw 'fá-kwǎn, hè-shr dàw 'fǎ-ywàn-chywu gwò-'táng. ‖He was fined five dollars. tā fá-le (*or* fá-le tā) 'wǔ-kwày-'chyán.

FINGER. shěw-'jŕ-ţew (*or* shěw-'jŕ-tew); *especially in combinations* -jŕ; *sometimes* shěw-'jŕ. Index finger 'èr-jř; **middle finger** 'jūng-jř; **fourth finger** 'wú-míng-jř (*nameless finger*); **little finger** 'shyǎw-jř *or* shyǎw-shěw-'jř-tew. (Thumb *is* 'dà-jř, 'dà-shěw-jř-tew, dà-mǔ-'gē, *or* dàm-'gē.) **Fingernail** shěw-'jř-jyǎ. ‖**He has six fingers on each hand.** tā 'lyǎ-shěw 'dēw shř 'lyèw-ge-shěw-'jř-tew. *or* tā shř 'lyèw-jěr. ‖**I cut my thumb and middle finger opening that can.** wǒ kāy 'gwàn-tew de-shř-hew bǎ 'dà-jř gēn 'jūng-jř 'lá-le. ‖**She fingered** (*felt with her fingers*) **the material appraisingly.** tā yùng shěw-'jř-tew mwō-le-mwo yī-lyàwr kàn ˇshř shéme-'chéng-shar. *or* °shř-'tsū shř-'shì. *or* °hǎw-bu-'hǎw. ‖**Watch out or you'll burn your fingers.** (*Literally*) 'shyǎw-shīn-dyar byé 'shāw-le shěw-'jř-tew. (*Literally or figuratively*) dāng-'shīn-dyar byé 'tàng-le shěw-'jř-tew. (*Figuratively*) dāng-'shīn-dyar, °byé 'dž-tǎw 'kǔ-chř. *or* °byé 'dž-shywún 'fán-nǎw. ‖**You can count them on your fingers.** jēn shř 'chywū-jř-kě-'shǔ. (*Unlike Westerners, who start with a closed fist and count to five by sticking out the fingers, the Chinese start with the hand open and bend the fingers one at a time until the fist is closed. then count from 6 to 10 by sticking out the fingers again, so that they can count to 10 on each hand.*)

To snap the fingers dǎ 'fěy-dz. ‖**Don't snap your finger at me.** byé gēn-wǒ dǎ 'fěy-dz.

Other expressions in English. ‖**I know there is a mistake somewhere, but I can't put my finger on it.** wǒ 'jř-daw 'yěw ge-dì-fang 'tswò-le, bú-gwo 'jř-bu-chū-láy. ‖**I'm sure I know his name, but I just can't put my finger on it.** wǒ 'jř-daw tā jyàw-shéme, 'jyèw-shr °shyǎng-bu-chu-'láy. *or* °shwō-bu-chu-'láy. *or* °jyàw-bu-shang-'láy. ‖**Don't let him slip through your fingers.** byé bǎ-tā 'fàng-gwo-chywu. ‖**He had a fine opportunity, but he let it slip through his fingers.** tā yěw-gwo yí-ge-'hǎw-jī-hwey, kě-shr °'tswò-gwo-chywu-le. *or* °'fàng-gwo-chywu-le. ‖**He had all that information at his fingertips.** 'dzèm-dwō-de-'shèr tā 'dēw jì-de, 'yàw shwō jyèw ⸍yěw. ‖**He always keeps some spicy jokes at his fingertips.** tā yěw jǐ-ge-'nèm-yàngr-de-'shyǎw-hwàr dzày dzwěy-'byār-shang, 'yàw shwō jyèw 'yěw.

FINISH. *Chinese usually uses resultative compounds. The first element indicates the action being finished, such as* dzwò (*do, make*), nùng (*make*), shyě (*write*), shwō (*speak*), *and any number of others. The second element indicates completion* wán, lyǎw, chéng (*usually of a piece of work*), hǎw (*complete and well done*), bǎw (*of eating only*), *and some others. When the type of action is not specified, the second element may be used alone. Occasionally, when the action is the important thing, only the first element occurs.* ‖**Let's finish this job tonight.** dzám jyēr 'wǎn-shang bǎ jèy-shèr °nùng-'wán-le-ba. *or* °dzwò-'wán-le-ba. *or* °gǎn-'wán-le-ba. ‖**Wait until he finishes eating.** děng

tā °chř-'wán-le-je. *or* °chř-'hǎw-le-je. *or* °chř-'bǎw-le-je. ‖**Don't hurry; finish what you're doing.** 'bú-yùng máng; nǐ 'jèng dzwò-shéme °dzwò-'wán-le dzày shwō. *or* °dēw 'lyǎw-le dzày shwō. *or* °dzwò-'hǎw-le dzày shwō. *or* °dēw 'wán-le dzày shwō. ‖**Have you finished the book yet?** nèy-běr-'shū °kàn-'wán-le-ma? *or* °nyàn-'wán-le-ma? *or* yùng-'wán-le-ma? ‖**I'll be with you as soon as I finish this drink.** wǒ hē-'wán-le jèy-ge, jyèw 'láy. ‖**It's finished.** yǐ-jīng 'wán-le. ‖**There's only a little bit left; finish it off.** (*Of food*) shèng 'nèm-dyǎr-le, °dēw 'chř-le-ba. (*Of drink*) °dēw 'hē-le-ba. (*Of work*) °dzwò-'wán-le-ba. *or* °nùng-'wán-le-ba. (*Mowing a lawn*) °twēy-'wán-le-ba. *etc.* ‖**I'd like to borrow your paper if you're finished with it.** 'bàw nǐ kàn-'wán-le de-hwà, 'wǒ shyǎng jyè-lay 'kàn-kan. ‖**The maid has finished (making) the beds.** lǎw-'mā-dz bǎ chwáng dēw °pū-'hǎw-le. *or* °pū-'wán-le. ‖**The carpenter has just finished the cabinet.** 'mù-jyang 'gāng bǎ 'gwèy-dz °dzwò-'chéng-le. *or* °dzwò-'wán-le. *or* °dzwò-'hǎw-le. ‖**When she finishes talking, wake me up.** tā shwō-'wán-le de-shř-hew, bǎ-wǒ jyàw-'shǐng-le. ‖**You can never finish it that way.** 'nèm-je nǐ jyèw 'yǔng-ywǎn °dzwò-bú-'wán-le. *or* °méy ge-'wán-le. *or* °dzwò-bu-'chéng-le.

When speaking of finishing in a certain order (first, last, etc.) Chinese uses wán *or* dàw, *or names the position alone.* ‖**He finished first.** tā 'téw-yí-ge 'wán-de. *or* tā 'téw-yí-ge 'dàw-de. *or* tā shyān 'wán-de. *or* tā dì-'yī. ‖**Who finished second?** shéy dì-'èr-ge °wán-de? *or* °dàw-de? *or* shéy dì-'èr? ‖**He finished last.** tā mwò-'lyǎwr wán-de. *or* tā dzwèy-'hèw wán-de. *or* tā shř 'dàw-shǔ dì-'yī. *or* tā shř mwò-'lyǎwr-de-'yí-ge. *or* tā dzày 'mwò-mwo-lā-'lyǎwr. *or* tā dzày 'jīn-hèw-tew. *or* (*in an examination*) tā shř dzwò-húng-'yī-dz-de.

Be finished (*of a person*) chwēy, lyǎw, wán, wár-'wán, 'wár-shř-dà-'jí, 'méy-shì-'chàng, (*very vulgar*) wár-'dàn. (*These words are usually preceded by* swàn, *meaning* to consider as, be as good as, *and are usually followed by* -le.) ‖**He's finished.** tā swàn 'chwēy-le. *or* tā swàn 'lyǎw-le. *etc.* ‖**He's finished as a politician.** dzày 'jèng-jř-wǔ-'táy-shang tā swàn 'chwēy-le. *etc.*

To finish (*of a person*) bǎ . . . 'jyē-shù, bǎ . . .-de-táy 'chǎy-le, bǎ . . . dǎ-'dǎw; (*especially of possessions*) bǎ . . . nèng-'gwāng, bǎ . . . nèng-'jìng, bǎ . . . nèng-'kūng, bǎ . . . nèng-de-'yì-gān-èr-'jìng, bǎ . . .-'shěw-lǐ-de 'dēw nèng-chu-lay. ‖**That finished him.** 'nèm-yì-láy tā jyèw swàn 'chwēy-le (*etc., see last paragraph above*). *or* 'nèm-yì-láy jyèw bǎ-tā °'jyē-shù-le. *or* °-de-táy 'chǎy-le. *or* °'dǎ-'dǎw-le. *or* °nèng-'gwāng-le. *or* °nèng-de 'yì-gān-èr-'jìng-le. *or* °-'shěw-lǐ-de 'dēw nèng-chu-lay-le.

(*Polish, paint, etc.*). (*Lacquer*) chī; (*oil or lacquer*) yéw; (*to polish with sandpaper*) 'dǎ-me; (*put on color or paint*) shàng-'shǎr. ‖**This table has a nice finish.** jèy-ge-'jwō-dz °'chī-de hǎw. *or* °'yéw-de hǎw. *or* °'dǎ-me-de 'hǎw. *or* °'shàng-'shǎr shàng-de hǎw. ‖**How** would you like it finished? *meaning* **What kind of lacquer?** shàng 'shéme-'chī? *or meaning* **Do you want it lacquered?** shàng-'chī bú-shàng? *or meaning* **Do you want lacquer added?** jyā-'chī bù-'jyā? *or meaning* **How many coats of lacquer?** shàng 'jǐ-dǎw-'chī? *or (of oil)* shàng 'shéme-'yéw? *(etc.) or meaning* **What color?** yàw 'shéme-shǎr-de? *or meaning* **Polished?** yàw-bú-yàw 'dá-me-le? ‖**I'd like a natural finish.** wǒ 'shī-hwān ywán-lay-de-'mù-tew-'shǎr, bù-'jyā-shéme.

FIRE. *(Flames)* hwǒ. **Catch fire** jáw-hwǒ; **build a fire** 'shēng-hwǒ; **start a fire** *(conflagration)* 'chǐ-hwǒ; **set afire** 'fàng-hwǒ; **light a fire** 'dyǎn-hwǒ. ‖**Fire! Fire!** 'jáw-hwǒ-le! 'jáw-hwǒ-le! *or* 'chǐ-hwǒ-le! 'chǐ-hwǒ-le! ‖**Build a good fire.** hǎw-'hāwr-de shēng ge-'hwǒ. ‖**It's very hard to build a fire when there are cross winds.** fēng lwàn-'chwēy (*or* fēng lwàn-'gwā) de-shǐ-hew 'hwǒ hěn nán 'shēng-de-'jáw. ‖**I can't get this fire going.** 'jèy-hwǒ wǒ shēng-bu-jáw. *or* 'jèy-hwǒ wǒ dyǎn-bu-jáw. ‖**They built a fire to warm their hands and feet.** tām shēng-le ge-'hwǒ láy bǎ 'shěw-wa-'jyǎw-de 'kǎw-yi-kǎw. ‖**Will you light the fire?** nǐ bǎ-'hwǒ dyǎn-jáw. ‖**He likes to relax with a fire in the fireplace and all the lights out.** ta 'shī-hwān bǎ-'dēng dēw 'shī-le, dzày chyáng-'lú-dz-li shēng-je (*or* dyǎn-je, *or* jáw-je) 'hwǒ, nèm 'dāy-je yàng-'shén. ‖**The fire is going strong.** 'hwǒ jáw-de hěn 'wàng. ‖**Let the fire go out.** ràng-hwǒ 'shī-le-ba. *or* ràng-hwǒ 'myè-le-ba. ‖**The fire died out.** hwǒ 'myè-le. ‖**That building burned down in a fire.** 'nèy-ge-léw 'yì-bǎ-'hwǒ shāw-'gwāng-le. ‖**The (light from the) fire lighted up the whole town.** 'hwǒ-gwāng bǎ yì-'chéng dēw jàw-de hěn 'lyàng-de. ‖**How much fire insurance do you carry?** nǐ bǎw-le 'dwō-shǎw-chyán-de-'hwǒ-shyǎn? ‖**This material doesn't catch fire easily.** 'jèy-jǔng-'tsáy-lyàwr 'bù-rúng-yì jáw-'hwǒ. ‖**The rug caught (on) fire and burned the house down.** dì-'tǎn 'jáw-le ('hwǒ-le), bǎ-'fáng-dz dēw 'shāw-le. *or* tsúng-dì-'tǎn-jáw-de-hwǒ bǎ 'fáng-dz gěy 'shāw-le. ‖**That was no accident; someone set the house on fire.** 'nèy tsáy bú-shr 'ěw-rán-de-shr-ne; jwěn-shr 'yěw-rén 'fàng-hwǒ bǎ fáng-dz 'shāw-de.

Fire station 'jyèw-hwǒ-'jywú *or* 'jyèw-hwǒ-'dwèy *or* 'shyāw-fáng-'jywú *or* 'shyāw-fáng-'dwèy; fireman jyèw-'hwǒ-de *or* 'shyāw-fáng-'dwèy-de-rén *or (one who tends a fire)* 'hwǒ-fū; firebug *(arsonist)* fàng-'hwǒ-de.

Set fire to ... ; set ... on fire *also* bǎ ... dyǎn-'jáw, bǎ ... shāw-'jáw, bǎ ... 'shāw. ‖**The people set fire to their own homes before leaving.** nèy-shyē-rén bǎ 'dz-jǐ-de-'fáng-dz °dyǎn-'jáw-le tsáy 'dzěw-de. *or* °dyǎn-'jáw-le hwǒ tsáy 'dzěw-de. *or* °shāw-'jáw-le tsáy 'dzěw-de. *or* °shāw-le tsáy 'dzěw-de. *or* °fàng-hwǒ 'shāw-le tsáy 'dzěw-de. ‖**Set fire to that haystack at midnight.** dàw-le 'yè-li shr-èr-'dyǎn bǎ tsǎw-'dwēy dyǎn-'jáw-le.

Be on fire *also* jáw. ‖**The basket's on fire.** 'kwāng-dz 'jáw-le.

To fire *(bake, of pottery, etc.)* shāw. ‖**They're firing bricks.** tām shāw-'jwān-ne. ‖**They fire the pottery in primitive ovens.** tām yùng hěn-'tsū-de-lú-dz shāw 'tsź-chì.

To fire *(keep a fire going)* tyān-'hwǒ; *(with coal)* tyān-'méy. ‖**Fire the boiler.** 'chì-gwō děy tyān-'hwǒ. ‖**They're firing the furnace.** tām jèng tyān-'méy-ne.

To fire *or* **to open fire** *(of guns)* kāy-'hwǒ; *(with small arms)* kāy-'chyāng; *(with artillery)* kāy-'pàw, *also* fàng-'chyāng, fàng-'pàw; *(shoot)* 'shè-jí. **Gunfire** 'pàw-hwǒ, 'chyāng-lín-dàn-'ywǔ. ‖**Wait until they open fire.** děng-tām 'shyān kāy °-'hwǒ. *or* °-'chyāng. *or* °-'pàw. ‖**Don't fire!** *(not in military connection)* byé fàng-'chyāng! ‖**Fire!** *(military)* 'shè-jí! ‖**Cease firing!** 'tíng-jr shè-'jí! ‖**He fired a couple of shots in our direction.** tā 'chùng-je wǒm 'fàng-le (*or* 'kāy-le) lyǎng(-sān) 'chyāng. *or* °kāy-'chyāng. *or* °fàng-'chyāng. ‖**How does it feel to be under fire?** 'chyāng-lín-dàn-'ywǔ-li shīn-li jywé-je 'dzěm-yàng? ‖**They were under fire for three days and nights before they attacked.** dzày 'gūng-jí yǐ-'chyán tām °dzày 'chyāng-lín-dàn-'ywǔ-li áw-le 'sān-tyān sān-'yè. *or* °dzày 'dí-rén-pàw-hwǒ-jr̄-shyà áw-le 'sān-tyān sān-'yè.

(Discharge from employment) tsź, shwā, *and some indirect expressions.* ‖**That man was fired last week.** nèy-ge-rén 'shàng-lǐ-bày (jyàw 'rén-jya) gěy °'tsź-le. *or* °'shwā-le. *or* nèy-ge-rén 'shàng-lǐ-bày jyàw 'rén-jya chǐng-tā 'dzěw-le. ‖**You can fire him, can't you?** nǐ 'tsź-le tā, bù-'shíng-ma? *or* nǐ jyàw-tā jywǎn 'pū-gay bú-jyèw 'wán-le-ma? *or* *(vulgar)* nǐ jyàw-tā gwěn-'dàn bú-jyèw 'wán-le-ma?

Other expressions in English. ‖**Better be careful; you're playing with fire.** shyǎw-'shīn-dyar-ba, °nèy 'bú-shr 'wár-de. *or* °nǐ-nà-shr jáw-'dzwèy-'shěw-wa. *or (Of a person)* °nèy-ge-rén 'rě-bu-de. *or (Of a thing)* °nèy-ge shr̀ 'dzwò-bu-de. *or (Of an action)* °nǐ 'nèm-je jáw-'dzār. *or* °nǐ 'nèm-je hwèy rě-'hwò-de. *or* °nǐ 'nèm-je hwèy chū-'shèr-de. *or* °nǐ 'nèm-je shr̀ 'méy-bìng-jáw-'bìng. *or* °nǐ nèm-je shr̀ 'méy-shèr-jáw-'shèr. ‖**Where's the fire?** *(Literally)* 'nǎr jáw-'hwǒ-le! *or (Figuratively)* **What's the hurry?** 'jí-de shr̀ shém? *or* 'máng-de shr̀ shém? *or* 'hwāng ge-shéme-'jyèr? ‖**That's fighting fire with fire.** nèy shr̀ 'hwǒ-shang jyā-'yéw. *or (proverbs)* nèy shr̀ yǐ-'jèn jr̄-'kě. *or* nèy shr̀ yǐ-'láng jywù-'hǔ. ‖**He's out of the frying pan and into the fire.** *(Literary proverbs)* tā 'chū-le lwó-be-'jyàw dyàw-dzày 'shyán-tsày-'gāng-li-le. *or* tā 'yì-pwō wéy-'píng 'yì-pwō yèw-'chǐ. *or* tā 'fú-wú shwāng-'jr̀ 'hwò-bù dān-'shíng. ‖**The scheme has been hanging fire for weeks now.** 'nèy-shèr nèm 'shywán-je (*or* nèy-shèr nèm 'gē-je) yěw hǎw-jǐ-ge-lǐ-'bày-le.

†*(Of something said)* ‖**I'm ready. Fire away.** wǒ 'tīng-je-ne. nǐ 'shwō-ba! ‖**They fired a lot of caustic questions at him.** tām wèn-le tā °shyē-hěn-'swěn-de-'wèn-tí. *or* °shyē-hěn-'wā-ku-rén-de-'wèn-tí. *or* °shyē-hěn-'kè-bwó-de-'wèn-tí.

To be fired with. ‖They were fired with enthusiasm about the plan by his speech. tā-de-yǎn-'jyǎng jyàw-tăm dwèy-ywu nèy-ge-'jì-hwà hĕn °shàng-'jìn. or °re-'shīn.

FIRM. (*Solid; literally*) 'jyē-shr, 'dzwò-shr, 'láw-kaw; (*tight*) jīn; (*hard*) yìng; (*steady*) wĕn; *also negatives of words meaning* weak, soft, *etc.* ‖The ground is firmer here. 'jèr dì 'jyē-shr-dyar. *or* 'jèr dì 'yìng-dyar. *or* 'jèr dì 'bú-nèm 'rwǎn. *or* 'jèr dì 'bú-nèm wàng-shya 'shyàn. ‖This chair is not firm. 'jèy-bǎ-yǐ-dz 'bù-'jyē-shr. *or* °bú-'dzwò-shr. *or* °bù-'láw-kaw. *or* °bù-'wĕn. *or* °yĕw dyar-'yēw-da. *or* °jf-'hwó-dung. ‖Have the chair nailed firm. bǎ 'yǐ-dz dìng °'jyē-shr-le. *or* °'dzwò-shr-le. *or* °'láw-kaw-le. *or* °'jīn. *or* °-de bù-'yēw-da-le. *or* °-de bú-nèm 'hwó-dung-le. ‖The boat has been firmly secured. chwán 'lǎn-de hĕn °'jīn. *or* °'jyē-shr. *or* °'dzwò-shr. *or* °'láw-kaw. ‖Make sure the plank is firm before you walk on it. 'jwĕn jr̄-daw bǎn-dz gē 'láw-kaw-le, dzày dzày 'shàng-tew 'dzĕw. *or* 'jwĕn jr̄-daw bǎn-dz 'gē-de °bù-'yēw-da-le (*or* °bù-'hwó-dung-le), dzày dzày 'shàng-tew 'dzĕw.

(*Tight; of grip*) jīn, sž-'jīn(-de), yùng (*or* shř) 'dà-jyèr. ‖Don't use too firm a grip on the wheel. 'lwén-dz 'byé dzwàn-de 'nèm °jīn. *or* °sž-'jīn-de. *or* 'lwén-dz 'byé shř 'nèm-dà-de-jyèr láy 'dzwàn-je. ‖Hold it firmly. ná-'jīn-le. *or* dzwàn-'jīn-le. *or* (*steady*) ná-'wĕn-le.

(*Strict*) yán, 'rèn-jēn. ‖I intend to be very firm in enforcing that rule. wǒ yàw jàw-je 'nèy-tyáw-gwēy-jywu 'rèn-jēn 'bàn-lì. *or* (*of a law*) fàn 'nèy-tyáw-'fǎ-lywù-de wǒ 'yí-dìng 'yī-fǎ 'yán-chĕng 'jywé bù-'kwān-dày. ‖He is very firm in enforcing that rule. tā jàw-je 'nèy-ge-gwēy-jywu 'bàn-de 'hĕn rèn-'jēn-de, *or* 'nèy-tyáw-'fǎ-lywù tā 'bàn-de hĕn °'yán. *or* °rèn-'jēn-de. ‖You have to be firm with children. gwǎn 'háy-dz-men dĕy °'yán. *or* °'shwō-shéme jyèw 'shř-shéme.

Believe firmly (*of belief or conviction; in a religious sense*) hĕn 'shìn; (*in other senses*) jywé-je (*feel*) *and similar expressions plus some expressions including the idea of necessity or rightness; see* **NECESSARY, RIGHT.** ‖I'm a firm believer in it. (*Religiously*) wǒ hĕn 'shìn jèy-ge. (*Otherwise*) wǒ jywé-dâe jèy-ge °'jēn dwèy. *or* °shř wéy-'yī-de-bàn-fa. ‖He's a firm believer in heaven and hell. tā hĕn 'shìn yĕw 'tyān-tang yĕw 'dì-ywu nèm yì-'shwō. ‖He's a firm believer in letting people alone. tā jywé-je 'bù-gwǎn 'byé-rén-de-'shř shř 'dwèy-de. *or* tā jywé-je bù-yīng-gāy gwǎn 'byé-rén-de-shř. ‖It is my firm conviction that we should take immediate action. jywù 'wǒ-kàn dzám fēy 'lì-shř-jyèw 'gàn-chř-lay bù-'kĕ. *or* jywù 'wǒ-kàn dzám yí-'dìng dĕy lì-'shř-jyèw 'gàn-chř-lay.

Other expressions in English. ‖He was on firm grounds in his argument. tā shwō-de ᵠhĕn yĕw-'lǐ. *or* °yĕw 'gēn-jywù. *or* °dēw shř 'shf-shr-dzay-'dzày-de-'chíng-shíng. ‖We must take a firm stand in this matter. 'jèy-jyàn-shř dzám °dĕy 'jyān-chf dàw-'dǐ. *or* °yì-'dyǎr yĕ 'bù-néng 'ràng. ‖He stood firm on his own

idea. tā 'jyàn-chf tā-'dž-jǐ-de-'yì-jyan, (yì-'dyǎr yĕ bù-kĕn 'ràng). *or* tā yí-'dìng yàw àn-je tā-'dž-jǐ-de-'yì-jyan láy 'bàn.

(*Company, corporation*) jyār, gūng-'sž, (*store*) 'pù-dz; your firm (*polite*) bǎw-'hàw. ‖Whose firm do you represent? bǎw-'hàw shř 'nĕy-jyā? *or* nǐ shř 'nĕy-jyār-de? *or* nǐ shř 'nĕy-ge-gūng-'sž-de? *or* nǐ shř 'nĕy-ge-'pù-dz-de?

FIRST. (*Of a series*) dì-'yī-, 'téw(-yī)-, 'téw-, 'chū-, *sometimes only* yī-; (*each of these is followed by a measure*). ‖Do you remember the way you stared at me the first time I came here? nǐ 'jì-de wǒ 'téw-yi-hwéy dàw-jèr (*or* nǐ 'jì-de wǒ dì-'yí-tsž dàw-jèr, *or* nǐ 'jì-de wǒ 'téw-tsž dàw-jèr, *or* nǐ 'jì-de wǒ 'chū-tsž dàw-jèr) nǐ-'dèng-je-yǎr-'chĕw-wǒ-de-nèy-'yàngr-ma? ‖This is my first trip to China. wǒ jèy shř 'téw-yi-tsž (*or* 'téw-tsž, *or* dì-'yí-tsž, *or* 'téw-yi-mwór, *or* 'chū-tsž) shàng 'jūng-gwo. ‖Where did you first meet him? nǐ 'téw-yi-hwéy (*or* nǐ dì-'yí-tsž, *or* nǐ 'chū-tsž, *or* nǐ 'téw-yi-tsž, *or* nǐ 'téw-yi-mwór) dzày-'nǎr ywù-jyan-de tā? ‖The first day she came here to work she looked like a child. tā 'téw-yi-tyān (*or* tā dì-'yī-tyān) shàng-gūng (láy de-shf-hew), 'kǎn-shang-chywu 'jyàn-jf shř ge máw-'yā-tew. ‖I get paid on the first. wǒ 'yí-hàw (*or* chū-'yī) líng-'shīn. ‖He'll arrive on the twenty-first. tā èr-shr-'yí-hàw dàw. ‖Is this his first offense? tā jèy shř 'chū-fàn-ma? *or* tā jèy shř 'téw-yi-tsž (*etc.*) fàn-'dzwèy-ma? ‖This is only the first step. jèy 'bú-gwo shř °'chū-bù. *or* °'téw-yí-bù. *or* °dì-'yí-bù. *or* °(gāng-)chǐ-'téwr-de-yí-bù. *or* °(gāng-)chǐ-'shf-de-yí-bù. *or* °'gāng-jáw-shĕw-'bàn-de-yí-bù. ‖The first step is the hardest. yì-chǐ-'téwr 'dzwèy nán. *or* gāng-kāy-'shf 'dzwèy nán. *or* 'téw-yí-bù 'dzwèy nán. *or* 'chū-bàn-de-shf-hew 'dzwèy nán. *or* (*Proverb*) 'fán-shř 'téw-nán. *or* (*Literally, of a baby*) shyǎw-'hár dzĕw 'téw-yí-'bù de-shf-hew 'dzwèy nán. ‖It's the first house after you turn the corner. 'gwǎy-le wār °'téw-yì-jyār jyèw 'shř. *or* °'téw-yì-swór-'fáng-dz jyèw 'shř. ‖That's the first good news we've had for a long time. 'dzèm-shyē-'shf-hew-le jèy shř dì-'yí-tsž tīng-jyàn 'hǎw-shyāw-shi. *or expressed as* We haven't heard any such good news for a long time. 'hǎw-shyē-shf-hew 'méy-tīng-jyàn 'dzèm-hǎw-de-'shyāw-shi-le. ‖The first good rainstorm will wash it off. 'yí-shyà-'dà-ywǔ jyèw hwèy 'chūng-shya-chywu-de. ‖First of all, you misunderstood me. dì-'yī (*or, meaning* most important of all 'dzwèy-yàw-jǐn-de shř) nǐ méy-tīng-míng-bay wǒ-de-'hwà. ‖Give me two tickets on the first (*or* front) row center. gěy-wǒ 'lyǎng-jāng-pyàwr, yàw °'dǐng-chyán-páy dāng-'jūng-de. *or* °'dzwèy-chyán-páy-dāng-'jūng-de. *or* °dì-'yī-páy-dāng-'jūng-de. ‖He's always the first one to complain. tā 'lǎw-shr dì-'yī-ge (*or* 'téw-yí-ge, *or* leading lǐng-'téwr)-'bàw-ywan-de. ‖He was the first to get there. tā shř 'téw-yí-ge (*or* dì-'yí-ge)-dàw-de. *or meaning* He was in front of all tā dàw-de bǐ-'shéy dēw dzày 'chyán-tew.

(*Earlier in time*) shyān. ‖I have to go to the store first. wǒ děy 'shyān dàw 'pù-dz-li-chywù. ‖Put first things first. 'gāy-shyān-dzwò-de jyèw 'shyāŋ dzwò. *or* yěw 'shyān-hèw-'bù-dzèw, 'bù-néng 'lwàn-lay-de. ‖First, let me ask you this. *meaning* Before we do anything else wǒ 'shyān wèn-nǐ 'jèy-ge. *or meaning* Before other questions 'téw-yí-yàngr (*or* 'téw-yí-shyàng, *or,* dì-'yí-jyàn-shr̀) wǒ-yàw-'wèn-nǐ-de shr̀ 'jèy-ge. ‖I'll do this the first thing in the morning. myár 'dzǎw-chen wǒ °'shyān dzwò 'jèy-ge. *or* °'téw-yí-jyàn-shr̀ jyèw dzwò 'jèy-ge.

(*At the beginning of something continuous*) when . . . first . . . . gāng . . . de-shŕ-hew; *or, instead of* gāng, *use* chū, gāng-yī, chǐ-'téwr, yì-chǐ-'téwr, 'chwǎng (*usually with* bàn), *etc.* (chǐ-'téwr *is sometimes used without a verb following*). ‖When we first came here, there was only one store. wǒm 'chū (*or* gāng) dàw de-shŕ-hew, jèr jŕ yěw 'yí-ge-pù-dz. ‖When the firm was first established, there was only one secretary. 'gūng-sz̄ 'chwǎng-bǎn (*or* 'gūng-sz̄ 'gāng kāy-bàn, *or* 'gūng-sz̄ chǐ-'téwr, *or* 'gūng-sz̄ 'yì-chǐ-'téwr, *or* 'gūng-sz̄ 'gāng-yí-bàn, *or* 'gūng-sz̄ 'chū-bàn) de-shŕ-hew, jŕ yěw 'yí-ge-'shū-jì. ‖He was way behind when the race first started. 'gāng-pǎw (*or* 'gāng-yí-pǎw, *or* chǐ-'téwr-pǎw, *or* yì-chǐ-'téwr-pǎw, *or* tsáy-yì-'pǎw, *or* 'chū-pǎw)-de-shŕ-hew, tā là-dzày 'hèw-tew láy-je.

At first chǐ-'shyān, chǐ-'chū, chǐ-'téwr-de-shŕ-hew. ‖I didn't like him at first. wǒ chǐ-'shyān (*or* wǒ chí-'chū, *or* wǒ chǐ-'téwr-de-shŕ-hew) bù-'shǐ-hwān tā.

At first sight. (*Either literally of seeing or figuratively of hearing, etc.*) yī *plus a verb; sometimes* yī *is preceded by* gāng, jà, *or* měng, *and the verb followed by* de-shŕ-hew. (*See also above*). ‖I knew he was a crook at first sight. wǒ yí-'kàn-jyàn tā (*or* wǒ gēn-tā yí-jyàn-'myàn, *or* wǒ 'téw-yí-tsz̀ kàn-jyan tā) jyèw jŕ-dàw tā 'bú-shr̀ hǎw-'rén. ‖The idea is really much better than it looks at first sight. 'jèy-ge-bàn-fa °yì 'tīng-jyàn (*or* °'gāng-yì 'tīng-jyàn, *or* °'jà-yì 'tīng-jyàn, *or* °'měng-yì 'tīng-jyàn, *or* °yí 'kàn-jyàn, *or* °'gāng-yí 'kàn, *or* °jà-yí 'kàn, *or* °měng-yí 'kàn) de-shŕ-hew 'bù-dzěm 'hǎw; chí-'shŕ shr̀ 'hěn-hǎw-de.

First aid 'chū-lyáw, jyèw-'jí-fǎ.

First class (*travel*) 'téw-děng. ‖I always travel first class. wǒ chū-'mér de-shŕ-hew lǎw-shr̀ dzwò 'téw-děng.

First class, first rate, first grade *see* Best. ‖These are first-class rayon stockings. jèy 'děw-shr (dzwèy-)°'shàng-děng-(*or* °'hǎw-)de-'rén-dzàw-sz̄-de-sz̄'wà-dz. ‖He gave a first-class performance. tā yǎn-de 'jēn hǎw. *or* tā yǎn-de 'shŕ-dzày hǎw. ‖He's a first rate comedian. tā shr̀ 'dzwèy-hǎw-de-'chéw-jyǎwr. ‖He doesn't know the first thing about Chinese customs. tā yì-'dyǎr yě bù-jŕ-dàw jūng-gwo-'gwéy-jywu. *or* jūng-gwo-'gwéy-jywu dzěm-yàng tā °yì-'dyǎr yě bù-jŕ-'dàw. *or* °'háy méy-rù-'mér-ne.

FISH. ywú. To fish (*catch fish; by hook*) 'dyàw-ywú; (*by net*) (yùng-'wǎng) 'dǎ-ywú; (*by spear*) 'chā-ywú; *but* to catch (a) fish (*succeed in catching*) 'dyàw-shang 'ywú, 'dǎ-jáw 'ywú, 'chā-jáw 'ywú; fresh-water fish 'hé-ywú *or* 'hé-li-de-'ywú; lake fish 'hú-ywú *or* 'hú-li-de-ywú; salt-water fish 'hǎy-ywú; fresh fish 'shyān-ywú. ‖Do you like fish? (*as food*) nǐ 'shǐ-hwān chŕ 'ywú-ma? ‖I caught a fish. wǒ 'dyàw-shang-lay °yì-tyáw-'ywú. *or* °yì-jŕ-'ywú. *or* wǒ 'chā-jáw (*or* 'dǎ-jáw, *or* (*with the hand*) 'dǎy-jáw) yì-tyáw- (*or* -jŕ-) 'ywú. ‖How many fish did you catch? (*Probably few*) nǐ dyàw-shang °'jǐ-tyáw-ywú-lay? *or* (*Probably many*) °'dwō-shǎw-tyáw-'ywú-lay? ‖What kind of fish do you have? nǐ yěw 'shéme-yàngr-de-'ywú? *or* nǐ 'dēw yěw 'shéme-ywú? ‖How would you like the fish done? ywú 'dzěm-dzwò 'hǎw? *or* ywú 'dzěm-chŕ 'hǎw? ‖They make their living by fishing. *or* They are fishermen. tām shr̀ dǎ-'ywú-de. *or* tām dǎ-'ywú wéy 'shēng. *or* tām dǎ-'ywú gwò-'r̀-dz. ‖Do you want to go fishing? chywù dyàw-'ywú-chywu 'hǎw-bu-hǎw? ‖Are you allowed to fish here? jèr shywǔ dyàw-'ywú-ma? ‖They have a fish pond. tām yěw ge-'yǎng-ywú-'chŕ. ‖That's like a blind man groping for fish. shyàng 'shyā-dz mwō-'ywú shr̀-de.

Fish for (*feel for*) mwō *or* māw. ‖He fished through his pockets for keys, but couldn't find them. tā 'jèy-ge-kěw-dàr-'nèy-ge-kěw-dàr-de mwō 'yàw-shr, 'dzěm mwō yě 'méy-mwō-'jáw. *or* tā yàw jáw 'yàw-shr, kěw-dàr 'dēw mwō-dàw-le yě méy-mwō-'jáw. *or* tā shēn-'shěw dàw tā-'kěw-dàr-li-chywu mwō 'yàw-shr, jǐ-ge-kěw-dàr 'dēw mwō-dàw-le yě méy-mwō-'jáw.

Fish for (*try to get*). *Expressed as* think of shyǎng; want yàw; try tàn *and other similar verbs, plus another verb.* ‖She's fishing for information. tā shyǎng dǎ-tīng 'shèr-ne, *or* tā-nà shr̀ °yàw 'dǎ-tīng shr̀ 'dzěm-hwéy-'shèr. *or* °'tàn-tīng 'shyāw-shi-ne. *or* °yàw 'dé-dàw dyǎr-'shyāw-shi-ne. *or* °'tàn-tīng 'kěw-chì láy-le. ‖He's always fishing for compliments. tā 'lǎw shyǎng 'dé-rén 'chēng-dzàn. *or* tā 'lǎw ày̦ gù-'yì-de dzwò dyǎr-mār hǎw jyàw-rén 'kwā-jyang.

Fish out, fish up 'mwō-chū; *see also* FIND, PULL OUT, TAKE OUT, *etc.* ‖He fished a picture of his son out of his wallet. tā tsúng chyán-'jyā-dz-li 'mwō-chu (*or* 'jǎw-chu) yì-jāng-tā-'èr-dz-de-shyàng-'pyàr-lay. ‖The puppy fell into the brook, but we fished him out. shyǎw-'gěw-dz dyàw 'hé-li-le; 'wǒm bǎ-tā °'jyèw-chu-lay-de. *or* °'jyèw-shang-lay-de. *or* °'lā-chu-lay-de. *or* °'lā-shang-lay-de. ‖I was hunting in the tool box for a hammer, but fished up this screwdriver. wǒ dzày 'hé-dz-li jǎw 'láng-tew, kě-shr mwō-jáw (*or* jǎw-jaw) 'jèy-ge-le, shr̀ ge gǎy-'jwēy.

Fishy (*suspicious*). ‖This sounds fishy to me. wǒ 'jywé-je (*or* wǒ 'tīng-je) °kě-'yí. *or* °yěw dyǎr-'gwěy. *or* °shr̀ pyàn-'rén-de. *But* (*literally*) ‖There's a fishy smell. (wén-je) yěw chèw-'ywú-wèr.

FIT. (*Be the right size, be suitable*) hé-'shr̀; (*be contained in*) 'gē-shya, 'bǎy-shya, 'fàng-jin-chywu, etc. (*See* PUT *and other appropriate words.*) ‖It fits you perfectly. wèy-'nǐ jèng hé-'shr̀. *or* (*Of clothes*) 'nǐ chwān-je jèng hé-'shr̀. *or* (*Of a job*) 'nǐ dzwò jèng hé-'shr̀. *or* (*Of a chair*) 'nǐ dzwò-shang jèng hé-'shr̀. ‖This suit is not a good fit. 'jèy-tàw-yī 'bú-dà hé-'shr̀. ‖Does it fit all right? hé-'shr̀-ma? ‖This pair of shoes fits. 'jèy-shwāng-shyé hé-'shr̀. ‖This pair of shoes just fits. 'jèy-shwāng-shyé 'jèng (*or* 'gāng) hé-'shr̀. ‖We're missing the piece that fits in here. dzày-'jèr-gē (*or* fàng)-de-'shyà-de-nèy-kwàr jǎw-bu-'jáw. ‖This picture just fits this space. 'jèy-jāng-hwàr 'jèng (*or* 'gāng)-hǎw dzày-jèr 'gwà(-de)-'shyà. ‖This typewriter just fits in that cardboard box. 'jèy-jyà-dǎ-dz̀-'jī dzày nèy-ge-'jǐr-shyāng-dz-li °gāng-hǎw 'gē-shya. *or* °gāng-hǎw 'bǎy-shya. *or* °gāng-hǎw 'fàng-jin-chywu. *or* °jèng 'bǎy-de-shyà. *or* °'gē-jìn-chywu (*or* °'fàng-jìn-chywu, *or* °'bǎy-jìn-chywu) jèng hé-'shr̀. *meaning* That box just fits this typewriter nèy-ge-'jǐr-shyāng-dz 'gāng-hǎw 'rúng(-de)-shya (*or* 'gē-shya, *or* 'gē-de-shya, *or* 'bǎy-shya, *or* 'bǎy-de-shya, *or* 'jāw-shya, *or* 'jāw-de-shya) nèy-ge-dǎ-dz̀-'jī. ‖Have you got a key to fit this lock? yěw 'kāy-de-kāy-jèy-bǎ-'swǒ-de-'yàw-shr-ma? *or* 'jèy-bǎ-swǒ nǐ yěw °hé-'shr̀-de-'yàw-shr-ma? *or* °'kāy-de-'kāy-de-'yàw-shr-ma? *But, of a description* ‖The description fits you perfectly. 'shǐng-rúng-de (*or* 'myáw-shyě-de, *or* 'shwō-de-nèy-myàn-kǔng) gēn-'nǐ 'yì-mū-yí-'yàngr-de.

(*Be suitable for a certain purpose*) hé-'shr̀, shyāng-'yí, *and many indirect expressions.* ‖What kind of work is he fit for? tā dzwò 'shéme-yàngr-de-shr̀ °hé-'shr̀. *or* °shyāng-'yí. ‖The food here isn't fit to eat. 'jèr-de-fàn °'bú-shr 'rén-chǐr-de. *or* °jyàw-rén 'chǐr-bu-shyà-'chywù. *or* °'bù-'yí-ywu rén-'chǐr. *or* °'bù-'yí-lyang rén-'chǐr. *or* °'rén-chǐr-le bù-hé-'shr̀. *or* °'chǐr-le bù-'hǎw. *or* °'chǐr-le bù-shyāng-'yí. ‖I'll do whatever you think fit. 'nǐ jywé-je 'dzěm-je hé-'shr̀, wǒ jyèw dzěm 'dzwò. *or* 'nǐ jywé-je gāy 'dzěm dzwò, wǒ jyèw dzěm 'dzwò. ‖He may act as he sees fit. 'tā jywé-je 'gāy dzěm-je jyèw kě-yǐ 'dzěm-je. *or* 'tā jywé-je 'dzěm-je hǎw jyèw kě-yǐ 'dzěm-je. *or* tā yàw 'dzěm-je dēw 'shíng.

(*Physically suited*) 'tǐ-gé gèw ... *or* néng ... (*followed by what the person is fit for*). ‖He was classified as not fit (*or* unfit) for front line duty. tā 'fēn-dzày 'tǐ-gé-'bú-gèw-dàw-'chyán-shyàn-dzwò-'jàn-de-nèy-'lèy-li. ‖He was classified as fit for front line duty. tā 'fēn-dzày 'néng (*or* tā 'fēn-dzày 'tǐ-gé-gèw)-dàw-'chyán-shyàn-dzwò-'jàn-de-nèy-'lèy-li.

(*Healthy*) 'tǐ-gé hǎw, 'shēn-dz hǎw. ‖I feel pretty fit. (wǒ jywé-je) wǒ-'shēn-dz 'hěn hǎw. *or* (wǒ jywé-je) wǒ-'tǐ-gé 'hěn hǎw.

(*Supply, put on*) ān. ‖I want to have a new lock fitted on the door. wǒ shyǎng dzày 'mén-shang 'ān bǎ-'shīn-swǒ. ‖The plane is being fitted with the best

instruments. fēy-jī-shang 'ān-je 'dzwèy-hǎw-de-'yí-chì. ‖The ship is being fitted out with all the latest gadgets. 'chwán-shang 'ān-je dzwèy-'shīn-shr̀-de-'líng-jyàr.

(*Spasm*) jèn; jèn-dz. **Have a fit of ...** chēw yí-jèn-...; *but* **have a fit** (*get dizzy*) téw-'hwēn; (*faint*) 'ywūn-gwo-chywu; *and, figuratively, expressions meaning to become angry.* ‖He had a fit of epilepsy one morning. · yěw-yì-tyān 'dzǎw-shang tā 'chēw-le yí-jèn-('yǎng-jyǎwr-)'fēng. ‖He threw a fit. tā téw-!hwēn-le. *or* tā 'ywūn-gwo-chywu-lę. ‖Every time I mention her name he throws a fit. wǒ 'yì-shwō 'nèy-ge-nywǔ-rén-de-'míng-dz tā jyèw °chǐ-'jí. *or* °shēng-'chì. *or* °'nǎw-le. *or* °'téw-téng. ‖In a fit of anger he swore and swore. tā 'yí-jèn-'dà-nù 'mà-le yèw 'mà. ‖In a fit of energy he cleaned his desk inside and out. tā 'hú-rán yí-'jèn-dz-mày-'jyèr bǎ tā-de-'jwō-dz 'dǎ-lǐ dàw 'wày-de dēw 'shēw-shr-'gān-jing-le. ‖He works by fits and starts. tā dzwò-'shr̀ bù-'lyán-gwàn nèm yí-'jèn-dz yí-'jèn-dz-de. *or* tā dzwò-'shr̀ nèm 'jǐn (*or* 'máng)-yí-jèn 'màn (*or* 'shyán)-yí-jèn-de.

Fit in with gēn ... hé-'shr̀, gēh ... 'chèn, gēn ... 'pèy-shang. ‖That chair won't fit in with the rest of the furniture. jèy-bǎ-'yǐ-dz gēn byé-de-jyā-jywu °bù-hé-'chèn. *or* °'bú-'chèn. *or* °ɪ⌣y-bu-'shàng.

Fit someone in (*to a schedule*). ‖The doctor's very busy today, but he'll try to fit you in somewhere. dàyfu jyēr 'hěn máng, bú-gwo tā dzǔng hwèy 'ywún ge-shf-hew 'kàn-nǐ-de.

FIVE. wǔ.

FIX. (*Repair*) 'shyēw-li; 'shēw-shr (*also means* put in order); (*patch up*) 'shyēw-bǔ *or* bǔ; *also resultative compounds of these plus* hǎw, *etc.* ‖Can you fix this watch? néng bǎ jèy-ge-'byǎw °shyēw-li-'hǎw-le-ma? *or* °shēw-shr-'hǎw-le-ma? ‖Where can I find someone to fix the car? dàw-'nǎr jǎw-de-jáw rén hwèy-'shyēw-li (*or* 'shēw-shr)-'chē-de? ‖We fix flats. wǒm 'shyēw-bu (chì-chē-)lwén-'dày. ‖We're having a little trouble now, but it will be all fixed up soon. (*Of actual repairing*) wǒm 'shyàn-dzày 'chū-le dyàr-'shèr, yì-'hwěr jyèw °'shēw-shr-'hǎw-le. *or* °'shyēw-li-'hǎw-le. *or* (*Of any kind of trouble*) °'hǎw-le.

(*Set in order; usually* fix up) 'shēw-shr. ‖I was just fixing up my room. wǒ 'jèng-dzày 'shēw-shr 'wū-d⌣

(*Establish*) dìng; (*physically, make unmovable*) dìng-'jù, dìng-'sź; (*be unmovable, fixed*) sź(-de); (*definite*) gù-'dìng, yí-'dìng. ‖You fix the date. 'nǐ dìng ge-'r̀-dz. ‖All these prices are fixed by the government. jèy-shyē-'jyà-chyan 'chywán-shr 'jèng-fǔ-'dìng-de. ‖This part of the machine moves, but the rest is fixed. jī-chì-jèy-'bù-fen shr̀ 'hwó-de, byé-de dēw shr̀ °'sź-de. *or* °'dìng-'jù-le-de. *or* °'dìng-'sź-le-de. ‖These aspects show a fixed relationship with the weather. 'jèy-shyē-'chíng-shíng gēn 'tyān-chi 'dēw yěw °'gù-'dìng-de-'yin-gwǒ-'gwān-shi. *or* °'yí-'dìng-de-'yin-gwǒ-'gwān-shi. *But* ‖I'm trying to fix :hat impression in my mind. wǒ 'jèng-dzày yàw bǎ 'nèy-jywù-'hwà 'jì-dzày 'shīn-li. ‖He has fixed (*stubborn*) ideas. tā-shīn-li yěw hěn 'gù-jɼ-de-'jyàn-jye. *or* tā 'yěw-de-dì-fang 'sž-shīn-'yǎr. *or* tā 'gāng-pǐ-dž-'yùng.

Fix on, fix upon (*decide on*) dìng, dìng-gwey. ‖Let's fix on that one. dzám jyèw 'dìng-le (*or* 'dìng-gwey) yàw 'nèy-ge 'hǎw-le. ‖We finally fixed upon the 28th as the best day for the meeting. 'jyē-gwǒ dìng-le (*or* dìng-gwey-le) èr-shɼ-'bā-hàw kāy-'hwèy dzwèy 'hǎw. *But* ‖Her mind is fixed on getting that hat. *is expressed as* She certainly wants to get that hat tā yì-'sěr-de (*or* tā yí-'dìng-de) shyǎng mǎy 'nèy-ge-'màw-dz. *or* tā 'fēy yàw mǎy 'nèy-ge-'màw-dz bù-'kě.

Fix *something for a person* (*take care of*) gěy ... *plus a specific expression for the favor done.* ‖I'll fix you up. 'wǒ gěy-nǐ bàn. ‖I'll fix you up for the night. 'wǒ gěy-nǐ jǎw dì-fang gwò-'yè. ‖Can you fix me up with a place to sleep? (*Arrange a place*) nǐ néng gěy-wǒ nèng ge-dì-fang 'shwēy-ma? *or* (*Find a place*) nǐ néng gěy-wǒ jǎw ge-dì-fang 'shwèy-ma? *or* wǒ shyǎng jǎw ge-dì-fang 'shwèy, nǐ néng (gěy-wǒ) bàn-de-'dàw-ma? ‖I'll fix it up for you with the mayor. *meaning* Talk it over to a satisfactory conclusion 'wǒ gěy-nǐ gēn shɼ-'jǎng chywù °shwō-'hǎw-le-ba. *or meaning merely* Talk it over °'shwō-yi-shwō kàn. *or meaning* Explain it °'jyǎng-yi-jyǎng kàn. *or meaning* Do it °'bàn-yi-bàn kàn. ‖I'll fix a drink for you. wǒ gěy-nǐ dzwò °dyar-'hē-de. *or* °dyàr-'jyěw hē. ‖He fixed my watch for me. tā bǎ wǒ-de-'byǎw gěy-wǒ shyēw-li-'hǎw-le. ‖We were five minutes late to work, but the timekeeper said he'd fix it for us. wǒm 'chɼ-dàw-le 'wǔ-fēn-jūng; gwǎn chyán-'dàw-de-rén shwō 'tā kě-yǐ gěy-wǒm 'bàn-de 'méy-shèr-le.

Fix the eyes *or* **attention.** ‖His eyes were fixed on the door. tā-'lyǎ-yǎr 'dèng-je 'mén-nar. *or* tā-'lyǎ-yǎr yì-'jɼ chěw-je 'mén-nar. *or* tā-'lyǎ-yǎr 'mù-bu-gwǎn-'jīng-de chěw-je 'mén-nar. ‖I want you to fix your attention on this card in my hand. dà-jyā yùng-'shīn kàn-je (*or* chěw-je, *or* chyǎw-je) wǒ-'shěw-li-jèy-jāng-'páy.

Fix blame. ‖They don't know where to fix the blame. tām 'bù-jɼ-dàw shɼ 'shéy-de-'tswèr.

Fix a race. ‖No wonder that horse won; the race was fixed. 'gwày-bu-dé 'nèy-pǐ-mǎ 'yíng-le-ne; °'lǐ-tew yěw-'gwěy. *or* °pǎw-mǎ yì-'chyán yěw-rén 'àn-jūng dìng-le 'nèy-pǐ-mǎ 'yíng-le.

Fix a person. ‖I'll fix him. *meaning* correct him wǒ 'gwǎn-gwan tā. *or meaning* get him into an embarrassing situation 'wǒ kě-yǐ 'shěw-shr tā yí-shyà-dz.

A fix (*predicament*). ‖He got himself into a terrible fix. tā-'dž-jǐ °rě-le 'hwò, 'méy-fár 'lyǎw-le. *or* °'jǎw-de 'shyà-bu-láy-'táy-le. *or* °'nèng-de 'méy bàn-fa twǒ-'shēn-le. *or* °'nèng-de 'chí-hǔ-nán-'shyà-le. *or* (*dilemma*) °gǎw-de 'wǔ-dà-lángr-pán-'gàng-dz, 'shàng-shyà bú-shr 'rér-le. *or* °gǎw-de 'dzwǒ-yèw-wéy-'nán-le.

FLAG. chí *or* (*informally*) chyér. National flag 'gwó-chí; school flag 'shyàw-chí; (*etc. with other compounds*). ‖The Chinese flag is known as "Blue sky, bright sun, all the ground red". jūng-gwo-gwó-'chí jyàw-dzwò 'chīng-tyān 'bwó-ɼ mǎn-dì-'húng. (bwó *here is literary for* báy.) ‖The American flag has three colors. 'měy-gwo-'chí-shang yěw 'sān-ge-shǎr. ‖Did you see that red flag? nǐ chyáw-jyàn °húng-'chí-le-ma? *or* °húng-'chyér-le-ma? ‖That's a white flag. nèy shɼ báy-'chí. ‖They're putting up white flags. tām chě báy-'chí-le. *or* (*surrender flags*) tām gwà-chi téw-'shyáng-de-'chí-le. ‖Raise the flag. gwà-'chí. *or* bǎ-chí 'chě-shang-chywù: *or* bǎ-chí 'lā-shang-chywu. *or* (*formal*) 'shēng-chí. ‖Lower the flag. bǎ-chí 'chě-shya-lay. *or* bǎ-chí 'lā-shya-lay. *or* (*formal*) 'jyàng-chí.

To flag (*stop by a signal*) jyàw ... 'tíng(-shya). ‖The station master flagged the train. (*With a flag*) jàn-'jǎng yùng-'chí jyàw 'hwǒ-chē 'tíng-le. ‖Can you flag a passing truck? nǐ néng jyàw yí-lyàng-gwò-'lù-de-'dà-chì-chē 'tíng-shya-ma?

To flag (*fade, lag*). ‖Public interest flagged after a while. 'gwò-le shyē-shɼ 'dà-jyā-de-shīn dēw 'lěng-le yì-dyǎr. *or* 'gwò-le shyē-shɼ 'dà-jyā-de-gāw-'shìng 'jyǎn-le yì-dyǎr.

FLAME. hwǒ, hwǒ-'myáwr, 'hwǒ-yán. ‖The flames sprang up as high as the ceiling. 'hwǒ (*or* hwǒ-'myáwr, *or* 'hwǒ-yán) 'tswān-dàw fàng-'dǐng-dz něm 'gāw. ‖The flames flared out in all directions. 'hwǒ (*or* hwǒ-'myáwr, *or* 'hwǒ-yán) 'sž-shya-li lwàn-'pū. ‖Heat it in the flame. dzày 'hwǒ-li (*or* dzày hwǒ-'myáwr-shang) 'kǎw. ('hwǒ-yán *is not used here.*)

Be in flames jáw, 'jáw-chí-lay, jáw-chi 'hwǒ-lay. ‖By that time the whole house was in flames. dàw 'nèy-shɼ-hew jěng-'gèr-de-'fáng-dz dēw °'jáw-le. *or* 'jáw-chi-lay-le. ‖The car turned over and burst into flames. chē 'fān-le, 'hū-rán °'jáw-chi-lay-le. *or* 'jáw-chi 'hwǒ-lay-le.

Flame up 'jáw-chi-lay, chǐ hwǒ-'myáwr, 'wàng-chi-lay. ‖He blew on the fire until it flamed up. tā bǎ-hwǒ 'chwēy-de °'wàng-chi-lay-le. *or* °'jáw-chi-lay-le. *or* °chǐ-le hěn-'dà-de-hwǒ-'myáwr.

See also FIRE.

FLASH. (*A burst of light*) shǎn; to flash (*as of lightning*) dǎ-'shǎn. ‖Did you see that flash of lightning just now? nǐ 'kàn-jyan gāng-'dǎ-de-nèy-ge-'shǎn-le-ma? ‖A bright flash of lightning was followed by a loud crack of thunder. dǎ-le yí-ge-'dà-shǎn, 'gēn-je jyèw 'shyǎng-le yì-shēng-dà-'léy. ‖Her diamonds flashed dazzlingly in the light. tā-de-'jīn-gāng-shɼ dzày 'gwāng-li yì-'shǎn-yì-'shǎn-de jēn hǎw 'kàn.

(*To shine a light*) jàw. ‖Flash the light in this corner. 'jàw-yi-jàw jèy-ge-'jyǎwr.

(*An instant*) 'yí-shyà-dz; (*in the twinkling of an eye*) yì-jǎn-'yǎn-de-gūng-fu. ‖It's all over in a flash. 'yí-shyà-dz (*or* yì-jǎn-'yǎn-de-gūng-fu) jyèw 'dēw gwò-chywu-le.

(*To spread, of news*). ‖In a few minutes the news had been flashed over the whole country. (*Spread by telegraph*) 'jǐ-fēn-jūng-li 'nèy-shèr jyèw ?yùng dyàn-'bàw 'chwán-byàn 'chywán-gwó. *or* (*Spread by radio*) °'gwǎng-bwò·de 'chywán-gwó 'dēw jř-daw-le.

(*Item of news*) 'shyǎw-shi. ‖An important flash has just been received. 'gāng jyē-dàw yí-ge-'jùng-yàw-'shyǎw-shì.

Flashlight shěw-dyàn-'dēng. ‖The battery in this flashlight is weak. jèy-ge-shěw-dyàn-'dēng-de-dyàn-'chř méy-'jyèr-le.

‖An idea just flashed through my mind. wǒ-'shīn-li gāng-tsáy 'hū-rán yí-'dùng, shyǎng-chū ge-'jú-yi-lay.

FLAT. (*Level*) píng. ‖His house has a flat roof. tā-de-fáng-'dǐng-dz shř 'píng-de. ‖He has flat feet. tā shř 'píng-jyǎw-'gǔ. ‖Put the flat side against the wall. bǎ 'píng-de-nèy-myàr kàw-'chyáng fàng. ‖Is the country flat? dì 'píng-bu-píng? *or meaning* Are there flat plains? shř píng-'ywán bú-shr?

(*Thin and flat*) byǎn, 'byǎn-píng. ‖What's in that flat package? nèy-ge-'byǎn(-píng)-de-bāw-gwo-li yěw 'shém-me?

(*Deflated*) byě(-le). ‖The car has a flat tire. 'chē yěw ge-lwén-'dày byě-le. *But* ‖We fix flats. wǒm 'shyēw-bǔ lwén-'dày.

(*Tasteless*) 'sù-dàn, 'chīng-dàn, méy-'wèr, méy-yěw 'wèy-daw, bù-jūng 'chř. ‖The food lately has been pretty flat. 'jìn-láy fàn-shř hěn °'sù-dàn. *or* °'chīng-dàn. *or* °méy-'wèr. *or* °méy-yew 'wèy-daw. *or* °bù-jūng 'chř.

(*Uninteresting*) méy-'yì-sz, 'píng-dàn-wú-'wèy. ‖Her conversation is flat. tā-shwō-de-'hwà tīng-je °méy-'yì-sz. *or* °'píng-dàn-wú-'wèy.

(*Decisive*) *expressed with* definitely 'jywé-dwèy. ‖He published a flat denial of the charges. tā děng-de gwǎng-'gàw-li shwō 'gūng-jí-tā-de-jǐ-dyǎn tā 'jywé-dwèy 'bù-chéng-'rèn.

(*Established*) yí-'dìng-de. ‖Can you give me a flat price? dēw swàn yí-'kwàr shwō ge-yí-'dìng-de-jyà-chyán.

(*Low in pitch*) bú-gèw-dyàw-'mér. ‖Her high notes are a little flat. tā-chàng-de-'gāw-yīn 'dēw yěw dyar-bú-gèw-dyàw-'mér.

(*One-floor apartment*) léw-li. ‖There are two flats for rent in that house. 'nèy yěw 'lyǎng-tséng-chū-'dzū-ge-léw-li.

Flatiron 'ywùn-děw *or* 'làw-tyě.

Fall flat. (*Literally*) shwǎy-'pā-shya, shwāy ge-dà-mǎ-'pā; (*figuratively; fail*) shř-'bày *or a more specific expression*. ‖He fell flat on his face. tā shwǎy-le ge-dà-mǎ-'pā. *or* tā shwāy-'pā-shya-le. ‖My prize joke fell flat. wǒ-'dzwèy-dèw-'gén-de-'shyàw-hwàr °shř-'bày-le. *meaning* no one laughed °'méy-rén 'lǐ-hwèy.

FLOOR. (*Of a room or house*) dì; (*wooden only*) dì-'bǎn. ‖Put it on the floor. gē-dzày 'dì-shang. *or* gē-dzày dì-'bǎn-shang. ‖I just swept the floor. 'dì (*or* dì-'bǎn) wǒ gwāng 'sǎw-le yí-shyàr. ‖They're waxing their floor. tām jèng gěy dì-'bǎn dǎ-'là-ne. ‖The floor squeaks. dì-'bǎn 'gē-jr-gē-jr-de 'shyǎng. ‖The floor of the cave is damp. dùng-li-de-'dì-shang fā-'cháw.

(*Story of a building*) léw. ‖What floor are you on? nǐ dzày dì-'jǐ-tséng-léw-shang? *or* nǐ dzày 'jǐ-léw? *or* nǐ dzày 'něy-tséng-'léw-shang? ‖We live on the third floor. wǒm jù-dzày 'sān-tséng-'léw-shang. *or* wǒm jù dì-'sān-tséng-léw-shang. *or* wǒm jù 'sān-léw.

Have the floor (*speak; in a meeting*) jyǎng, shwō-'hwà. ‖Mr. McCarthy still had the floor, and the chairman just yawned. 'mǎ-shyān-sheng 'háy dzày-nar jyǎng-ne. (*or* shwō-'hwà-ne), jǔ-'shí jř dǎ 'hē-shi.

To floor (*stump*) *a person* bǎ . . . 'nán-jù; *or expressed as* to tire someone out bǎ . . . 'lèy-sz. ‖The problem floors us. 'nèy-shèr kě 'jēn bǎ-wǒm °'nán-jù-le *or* °'lèy-sz-le.

To floor (*knock down*) *a person* bǎ . . . dǎ-'pā-shya, bǎ . . . dǎ-'dǎw; (*knock out*) bǎ . . . dǎ-de 'hwēn-gwo-chywu; bǎ . . . dǎ-de 'ywūn-gwo-chywu. ‖Do you think you can floor him at one blow? nǐ jywé-je nǐ néng 'yì-chywán bǎ-tā °dǎ-'pā-shya-ma. *or* °dǎ-'dǎw-le-ma? *or* °dǎ-de 'hwēn-gwo-chywu-ma? *or* °dǎ-de 'ywūn-gwo-chywu-ma?

FLOUR. myàn-'fěn; (*white wheat flour*) 'báy-myàn; (*when specifying the grain of which it is made*) 'myàn-dz, myàr, 'fěn-dz. ‖Flour is three dollars a sack. myàn-'fěn (*or* 'báy-myàn) 'sān-kwày-chyán yí-'dày. ‖Sprinkle the fish with flour, and fry. bǎ-'ywú sǎ-shang 'báy-myàn dzày 'jyān. ‖Millet flour is too sticky. 'shyǎw-mǐ-myàr tày 'nyán. ‖Rice flour is good for steamed dumplings. 'dà-mǐ-myàr jēng-'bāw-dz hǎw. ‖It's first ground into flour. 'shyān mwò-chéng-le °'myàn-dz. *or* °'myàr. *or* °myàn-'fěn. *or* °'fěn-dz.

FLOWER. hwā *or* hwār. ‖The plum blossom is China's national flower. 'méy-hwā (*or* 'méy-hwār) shř 'jūng-gwo-de-'gwó-hwā. ‖He likes to raise flowers. tā ày jùng-'hwār. *or* tā ày yǎng-'hwār.

FLY. (*Of birds, planes, etc.*) fēy. Fly up 'fēy-chǐ-lay; fly to 'fēy-dàw; *etc.* ‖The birds have flown south. nyǎwr dēw fēy-dàw 'nán-byar-chywu-le. ‖The young bird can't fly yet. shyǎw-'nyǎwr háy °bú-hwèy 'fēy-ne. *or* °fēy-bu-'dùng-ne. ‖This plane can fly 300 miles per hour. 'jèy-ge-fēy-'jī yì-dyǎn-jūng néng fēy (*or* go 300) 'sān-bǎy-'lǐ. ‖The higher you fly the harder you fall. 'fēy-de 'gāw, 'dyē-de 'jùng. ‖The bird flew into that tree. nyǎwr fēy-dàw 'nèy-kē-'shù-li chywù-le.

(*Ride in a plane*) dzwò fēy-'jī chywù (*or* láy). ‖He flew down to Brazil. tā dzwò fēy-'jī dàw bā-'shī chywù-le.

(*Pilot a plane*) kāy fēy-'jī. ‖He flew down to Brazil (*as pilot*). tā kāy fēy-'jī dàw bā-'shī chywù-le. ‖She's just learning to fly a plane. tā gāng-dzày shywé-je kāy fēy-'jī.

(*Run fast*) shyàng-'fēy-shr-de 'pǎw; 'fēy-ya-shr-de 'pǎw. ‖She flew down the street that way. tā shyàng-'fēy-shr-de (*or* tā 'fēy-ya-shr-de) wàng jyē-'nèy-téwr 'pǎw.

(*Flutter*) pyāw. ‖Her hair is flying around her face. tā-de-'téw-fa dzày tā-'lyǎn-shang °'pyāw-láy-pyāw-chywù-de. *or* °'wàn 'pyāw. ‖The flag was flying in the breeze. 'chí-dz dzày 'fēng-li °'pyāw-je. *or* °'pyāw-yáng. *or* °'pyāw-dàng. *or* °'jāw-jǎn.

Fly a *flag*. (*On a pole*) gwà; (*holding it*) dǎ. ‖What flag are they flying? tām 'gwà-je 'shéme-chí? *or* tām-'dǎ-je-de shr 'shéme-chí?

Fly a *kite* fàng. ‖Kite flying is good sport for children. shyǎw-hár fàng 'fēng-jeng yěw 'yí-chu.

Fly at (*start a fight with*). ‖They flew at each other. tām 'dǎ-chi-lay-le. *or* tām 'jyēw-chi-lay-le. ‖She flew at me as though I'd said something awful about her. 'tā nèm 'mà-wǒ (*or* tā nèm 'gūng-jí wǒ), 'hwó-shyàng wǒ shwō-le tā shéme-hwày-'hwà shr-de.

Fly into a temper fā-chi 'pí-chi-lay-ya. ‖There's no need to fly into a temper. 'yùng-bu-jáw 'hū-rán fā-chi 'pí-chi-lay-ya.

Fly off the handle. ‖He flies off the handle at every little thing that happens. shéme-'shyǎw-shèr yì-'chū tā jyèw °'jywé-je bù-dé-'lyǎw-le. *or* °'jí-de bù-dé-'lyǎw. *or* °'jí-chi-lay-le. *or* °'jí-de yàw-'mìng. *or* °'nàw ge-'tyān-fān-dì-'fù.

Let fly (*words*). ‖He let fly (with) a few choice remarks. tā 'dà-mà-le jǐ-jywù.

On the fly (*hurrying*). ‖I was late and caught the train on the fly. wǒ 'dàw-de 'wǎn-le-dyar, 'jí-ji-máng-máng-de 'gāng gǎn-shang hwǒ-'chē. ‖I caught the ball on the fly. chyéwr 'fēy-je wǒ gěy 'jyē-jaw-le.

(*Insect*) 'tsāng-yíng, 'yíng-dz. ‖The flies around here are terrible. 'jèy-kwàr-de-'tsāng-yíng (*or* 'jèy-kwàr-de-'yíng-dz) 'nì-sz 'rén.

Flypaper tsāng-yíng-'jǐ.

FOLLOW. (*Be behind, be after*) 'gēn-je (*also means be with*); dzày 'hèw-tew 'gēn-je; 'gēn-shang (*especially with the idea of spying*); *of events in time* X follows Y Y yǐ-'hèw, X. ‖This dog followed me all the way home. 'jèy-ge-gěw gēn-je wǒ yì-'jr dzěw-dàw 'jyā. ‖Don't look now, but I think there's someone following us. 'byé hwéy-tew kàn; wǒ jywé-je yěw-rén °'gēn-je dzám-ne. *or* °'dzày dzám-'hèw-tew 'gēn-je-ne. *or* °'gēn-shang dzám-le. ‖The hot weather was followed by several days of rain. tyān-chi 're-le yí-jèn yǐ-'hèw, 'shyà-le jǐ-tyān-'ywǔ. *or* tyān-chi 're-gwo-le, (jìn) 'gēn-je (*or* ..., 'gēn-shēwr) 'shyà-le jǐ-tyān-'ywǔ. ‖Follow the leader. 'gēn-je 'lǐng-shyèw (dzěw). ‖Follow the guide. 'gēn-je dày-'lù-de dzěw. ‖Follow him. *meaning* walking, *or* spying on him 'gēn-je tā 'dzěw.

or meaning spying 'gēn-shang tā. ‖He's following in his father's footsteps. tā gēn-je tā-'fù-chin-de-'jyǎw-bùr dzěw.

(*Obey*) fú-tsúng; tīng ... de-hwà. ‖Follow your leader. 'fú-tsúng 'lǐng-shyèw. *or* tīng 'lǐng-shyèw-de-'hwà.

(*Imitate*) shywé. ‖Follow him. gēn-ta 'shywé. ‖He's (deliberately) following in his father's footsteps. tā 'shywé tā-'fù-chin-ne.

(*Go along; a road*) 'shwèn-je. ‖Follow this road until you come to the river. 'shwèn-je jèy-tyáw-'lù yì-jr dàw 'hé-nar.

(*Go according to instructions*) 'jàw-je; 'àn-je; (*with military precision*) 'dzwēn-shíng. ‖Just follow these instructions step by step and you can bind the book yourself. 'jyèw jàw-je (*or* 'jyèw àn-je) jèy-ge-shwō-míng-shū 'yí-bù-yí-bù-de 'dzwò, jyèw kě-yǐ 'dz̀-jǐ bǎ-shū jwāng-ding-'hǎw-le. ‖Be sure to follow these instructions exactly. 'chyān-wàn 'wán-chywán jàw-je (*or* àn-je) jèr-'shwō-de bàn, yì-'dyǎr yě 'tswò-bu-de. *or* 'jèy-jǐ-shyàng-'shywùn-lìng yàw 'jywé-dwèy 'dzwēn-shíng.

(*Understand; arguments*) tīng-'míng-bay; tīng-'chǐng-chu. ‖I can't quite follow your arguments. nǐ-'byàn-lwèn-de jǐ-dyǎn wǒ 'tīng-bu-míng-bay. ‖Do you follow me? wǒ shwō-de nǐ tīng-'chǐng-chu-le-ma? *or* wǒ shwō-de nǐ dēw 'chǐng-chu-ma?

(*Be the logical conclusion*). ‖From what you just said this doesn't necessarily follow. jàw nǐ-'gāng-shwō-de, 'bú-jyàn-de jyèw yí-'dìng děy 'dzèm-je.

Follow the news 'jù-yì shīn-'wén; lyéw-'shén 'dà-shr. ‖I haven't been following the news much lately. 'jìn-lay wǒ 'méy-dà 'jù-yì shīn-'wén. *or* 'jìn-lay-de-'dà-shr wǒ 'méy-dà lyéw-'shén.

Follow suit 'gēn-je. ‖You're supposed to follow suit and play a heart too. nǐ yīng-gāy 'gēn-je 'yě chū húng-'shīn tsáy 'dwèy. ‖They left early and we followed suit. tām dzěw-de hěn 'dzǎw, wǒm gēn-je 'yě dzěw-le.

Follow out jàw(-je) ... °bàn (*or* °*another verb meaning* do). ‖We decided to follow out your suggestion. wǒm 'dìng-gwey-'hǎw-le 'wán-chywán jàw 'nǐ-shwō-de chywù 'bàn.

Follow up chè-'dǐ-de bàn; bàn dàw-'dǐ; 'chá-wèn 'chǐng-chu. ‖They try to follow up every case. 'měy-jyàn-shr̀ tām dēw shyǎng yàw °chè-'dǐ-de bàn. *or* °bàn dàw-'dǐ. *or* °'chá-wèn 'chǐng-chu-le.

Following (*after one already mentioned*) dì-'èr .... ‖This took place the following day. dì-'èr-tvǎn chū-de 'jèy-jyàn-shr̀.

Following *or* as follows (*coming next*) yǐ-'shyà; 'dǐ-shyà; 'hèw-myan; (*literary*) rú-'shyà. ‖The following sentence is a quotation from Confucius' Analects. yǐ-'shyà (*or* 'dǐ-shyà, *or* 'hèw-myan) yí-jywù-hwà shr̀ tsúng 'lwén-ywǔ-li yǐn-de. ‖My reasons are as follows. wǒ-de-jǐ-ge-'lǐ-yéw rú-shyà. *or* yǐ-'shyà (*or* 'dǐ-shyà, *or* 'hèw-myan) shr̀ wǒ-de-jǐ-ge-'lǐ-yéw.

FOOD. (*Staple foods, especially rice*) fàn; (*other than staples*) tsày; (*to eat*) chr̄-de-'dūng-shi, 'chr̄-de; (*as prepared*) dzwò-de-'fàn, dzwò-de-'tsày, dzwò-de-'dūng-shi, 'dzwò-de; (*food prepared in quantity*) 'fàn-shr̄; (*foodstuffs*) 'lyáng-shr̄; (*literary*) 'shr̄-wù. ‖Is the food good there? nàr-dzwò-de-'fàn 'hǎw-ma? *or* nàr-dzwò-de-'tsày 'hǎw-ma? *or* nàr-dzwò-de-'dūng-shi 'hǎw-ma? *or* nàr-de-'fàn-shr̄ 'hǎw-ma? *or* nàr-de-'fàn (*or* nàr-de-'tsày) 'hǎw-ma? *or* nàr-'chr̄-de̊ 'hǎw-ma? ‖Is that food? shr̄ 'chr̄-de-dūng-shi-ma? ‖The people need food, not sympathy. rén-men-'yàw-de shr̄ 'chr̄-de (*or* 'lyáng-shr̄), 'bú-shr̄ hǎw-'tīng-de-'hwà. ‖They've had no food for three days. tām 'sān-tyan méy-yěw 'dūng-shi chr̄-le. ‖Food should be kept clean. 'shr̄-wù yàw 'chīng-jyé. ‖I like Chinese food. wǒ hěn ày chr̄ °'jūng-gwo-fàn. *or* °'jūng-gwo-tsày. ‖This news gives us food for thought. jèy-ge-'nyāw-shi dzám děy °'dž-shì shyǎng-shyang. *or* °'dzwó-me-dzwó-me.

FOOLISH. 'shǎ, 'hú-du; (*in action or words*) hú-'nàw, shyā-'nàw; (*in words only*) hú-'shwō, shyā-'shwō, 'hú-shwō-bā-'dàw-de; (*like a fool*) 'shǎ-li-shǎ-'chì-de, shyàng ge-'shǎ-dz shr̄-de; (*be a fool*) shr̄ ge- *plus one of the following* 'shǎ-dz, *or* (*vulgar*) shǎ-'gwā, *or* shǎ-'d , *or* hwén-'dàn; (*foolhardy*) 'shǎ-shyàw-dz; (*muddle-headed*) 'hú-du-chúng. ‖I was foolish (*or* I was a fool) to believe what she said. wǒ jēn 'shǎ-le (*or* wǒ jēn 'hú-du-le), shīn-le 'tā-de-hwà! ‖Don't be foolish! byé hú-'nàw-le! *or* byé shyā-'nàw-le! *or* byé hú-'shwō-le! *or* byé shyā-'shwō-le! *or* byé 'hú-shwō-bā-'dàw-de-le! *or meaning* Don't be a fool! byé shr̄ ge-'shǎ-dz. *etc.* ‖I said a very foolish thing. wǒ shwō-le jywù-'hěn-shǎ-de-hwà. *or* wǒ shwō-le jywù-'hěn-hú-du-de-hwà. ‖I did a foolish thing. wǒ dzwò-le jyàn-'shǎ-shèr. *or* wǒ dzwò-le jyàn-'hú-du-shèr.

FOOT. (*Part of body*) jyǎw. ‖You're stepping on my foot. nǐ tsǎy-le wǒ-de-'jyǎw-le. ‖My feet hurt. wǒ jyǎw 'téng. ‖Are your feet cold? nǐ-de-jyǎw 'lěng-ma? ‖They carried him out feet first. tā-men bǎ-tā 'táy-chū-chywu-le, jyǎw cháw-'chyán. ‖He always keeps his feet on the ground. (*Only figuratively*) 'tā-jèy-rén-'jyǎw tà shr̄-'dì.

(*Bottom*) *in some cases* jyǎw; *otherwise* 'shyà-téwr. The foot of the mountain 'shān-jyǎw. ‖Put your coat at the foot of the bed. bǎ nǐ-de-'yī-shang fàng-dzày chwáng-'jyǎwr-ner. *But* ‖He was sitting at the foot of the stairs. tā dzwò-dzày léw-'tī-de-'shyà-téwr.

(*Twelve inches*) chr̄. ‖The wall is a foot thick. jèy-ge-'chyáng yěw yì-'chr̄-hèw. ‖She's five-foot-two. tā yěw 'wǔ-chr̄-'èr. ‖There's a six-foot drop here. jèr wā-shyà-le lyèw-'chr̄ chywù. ‖He's over six feet tall. tā yěw 'lyèw-chr̄-dwō-gāw. ‖That building is about 200 feet high. nèy-ge-'fáng-dz yěw 'èr-bǎy-dwō-chr̄-gāw.

On foot (*walking*) 'dzěw-je; (*informal*) bù-'nyǎr. ‖We came on foot. wǒm bù-'nyǎr láy-de. *or* wǒm dzěw-je láy-de. *But* ‖There's a plan (on foot) to get rid of him. 'shyàn-dzày jèng yěw yí-ge-'jì-hwà yàw bǎ-tā gǎn-'dzěw-le.

On one's feet. ‖After that illness it took her a long time to get back on her feet again. *is expressed as* ... a long time before she could start walking again. tā yǎng-le hǎw-'jyěw tsáy néng 'chǐ-lay dzěw-'dùng. ‖A good rest will put him back on his feet again. *is expressed as* ... he will return to normal. hǎw-'hǎwr 'shyēw-shi yí-shyàr, tā jyèw hwèy 'hwēy-fù ywán-'jwàng-le. ‖Did he ever get back on his feet (*start up again*) after his store failed? tā 'pù-dz 'dǎw-le yǐ-hèw, yèw 'chǐ-láy-le-ma? ‖He was badly in debt for a while, but he's back on his feet again now. *Meaning* everything has been returned. tā 'gāy-gwo bù-shǎw-'chyán, bú-gwo shyàn-dzày dēw 'hwán-shang-le.

Stand on one's own feet. ‖He's old enough to stand on his own feet now. tā yǐ-jīng 'dà-le, yīng-gāy néng dž-'lì-le.

Put one's foot down 'gwǎn-gwan. ‖This has gone far enough; I'm going to put my foot down. 'yǐ-jīng bú-shyàng 'yàng-dz-le; wǒ fēy 'gwǎn-gwan bù-'kě-le.

Put one's foot in it shr̄ dž-'jǎw-de. ‖I really put my foot in it that time. nèy-tsž wǒ jēn shr̄ dž-'jǎw-de.

Foot the bill fù-'jàng *or* gěy-'chyán. ‖Who's going to foot the bill? shéy fù-'jàng? *or* shéy gěy-'chyán?

FOR. 1. (*On behalf of*) gěy (*also means give*); (*instead of*) tì. ‖Can't you get someone to do this for you? 'jèy-ge nǐ 'jǎw ge-rén gěy-nǐ (*or* tì-nǐ) dzwò, 'shíng-bu-shíng? ‖Who does he work for now? tā gěy-'shéy dzwò-'shr̄-ne? ‖He's a salesman for our company. tā gěy wǒm-gūng-'sž dāng mày-hwò-'shěw. ‖I couldn't be there, so he did my work for me. wǒ méy-néng 'dàw, swǒ-yǐ tā 'tì-wǒ dzwò-de.

(*Because of*) 'yīn-wey (*followed by a verb*); 'wèy-le *or sometimes* yǐ (*followed by a verb or noun*). ‖I kept quiet for fear of trouble. wǒ yīn-wey pà chū 'chǎw-dz swǒ-yǐ méy-'shwō-shéme. ‖She did it for her mother's sake. tā 'wèy-le tā-'mǔ-chin tsáy 'nèm-je-de. *or* tā 'nèm-je shr̄ wèy-le tā-'mǔ-chin-de-ywán-gu. ‖He did a stretch for burglary. tā wèy-le (*or* tā 'yīn-wey) tēw 'dūng-shi shyà-gwo 'ywù. ‖This restaurant is noted for its good food. jèy-ge-'gwǎn-dz yǐ 'tsày hǎw chū-'míng.

(*Adapted to*) wèy *or* gěy. ‖Is this textbook for children or adults? 'jèy-jǔng-'jyàw-kè-shū shr̄ wèy (*or* gěy) shyǎw-'hár-(yùng-)de háy-shr̄ wèy (*or* gěy) 'dà-rén-(yùng-)de? ‖That movie is not for children, 'nèy-ge-dyàn-'yǐng 'bú-shr̄ wèy (*or* gěy) shyǎw-'hár kàn-de.

(*In honor of*) wèy. ‖We're giving a dinner for him. wǒm yàw wèy-'tā chǐng-hwéy-'kè.

(*With reference to*) ywú. ‖This is good for you. jèy 'ywú-nǐ yěw 'yí-chù. ‖As for me, I don't care what you do. jr̆-ywú-'wŏ-ya, nǐ 'dzĕm-je yĕ méy-yĕw 'wŏ-de-shr̆.

(*Throughout; of time or space) expressed only in the designation of time or distance.* ‖He stayed for an hour. tā 'dāy-le yì-dyăn-'jūng. ‖That'll be enough for the time being. nèy-ge 'jàn-shŕ 'gèw-le. or nèy-ge gèw 'jàn-shŕ-yùng-de-le. ‖That'll be enough for three days. nèy-ge gèw 'sān-tyān-de-le. ‖Go straight ahead for ten miles. wàng-chyán yì-'jŕ dzĕw 'shŕ-lĭ. ‖The road goes straight for about a mile, and then curves. lù chà-bu-dwō yĕw 'yì-lĭ-'dì shŕ 'bì-jŕ-de, rán-'hèw jyèw gwăy-'wār-le.

(*In favor of*) 'dzàn-chéng. ‖Are you for or against it? 'jèy-ge nǐ shŕ 'dzàn-chéng háy-shr̆ 'făn-dwèy?

(*According to*) jywù, jàw. ‖For all I know, he may be there yet. jywù (*or* jàw) 'wŏ-jŕ-daw-de tā yĕ-shywŭ háy 'dzày-nàr-ne. ‖He's tall for his age. jàw tā-de-'nyán-líng láy shwō, tā hĕn 'gāw.

(*Because*) 'yīn-wey. ‖I think the book will sell, for it's published at just the right time. wŏ 'jywé-je 'jèy-bĕn-shū 'shyāw-lù yí-'dìng bú-'hwày, yīn-wey 'chū-de 'jèng-shr 'shŕ-hew.

2. *In a large variety of English expressions, for occurs in fixed combinations with other words, or may be omitted by rephrasing the sentence slightly. For any cases which are not included below, see the words with which* **for** *is combined, or related words which can be used without* **for**.

‖For once I don't agree with you. 'jèy-tsz̆ wŏ gēn nǐ-de-'yì-jyan bù-yí-'yàng. ‖For all his friendly remarks, you can't trust him. tā swéy-rán 'shwō-de hăw 'tīng, nǐ yĕ 'bù-néng 'shìn-rèn tā. ‖For one thing, he doesn't know the language of the place. jyèw ná 'jèy-ge láy shwō-ba, tā 'bù-dŭng 'nèy-ge-dì-fang-de-'hwà. ‖For the first time, he was stumped. tā nèy shŕ 'téw-yì-hwéy (*or* 'téw-yi-mwór, *or* 'téw-yi-tsz̆) jyàwrén gĕy 'wèn-ju-le. ‖He's gone for good. (*From a place*) tā 'bù-hwéy-láy-le. (*From a job*) tā 'lí-kāy jèr-le. ‖That's all for now. shyàn-dzày 'méy-yew 'byéde-le.

‖What do you use for firewood? nǐ yùng 'shémeshāw-'hwŏ. or nǐ-shāw-de shr̆ 'nĕy-jŭng-'pĭ-cháy?

‖I took him for a friend. (*Mistaken identity*) wŏ (kàn-'tswò-le,) 'yǐ-wéy tā shŕ wŏ-nèy-ge-'péng-yewne. or (*Mistaken trust*) wŏ 'yǐ-wey 'tā shŕ wŏ-de-'péng-yew-ne. or wŏ 'ná-tā dàng 'péng-yew-lay-je. or wŏ 'dăng-je tā shŕ wŏ-de-'péng-yew-ne. ‖Do you know it for a fact? jèy-ge nǐ 'jŕ-daw shr̆ 'jēn-de-ma? ‖How much do you want for this book? jèy-bĕn-shū nǐ yàw (mày) 'dwō-shăw-chyán? ‖How much can I get for a dime? yì-'máw-chyán măy 'dwō-shăw? ‖I wouldn't do it for any amount of money. gĕy(-wŏ) 'dwō-shăwchyán wŏ yĕ bú-'gàn. ‖What does he do for a living? tā dzwò-'shéme (*or* tā yǐ-'shéme) wéy-'shēng? or tā azwò-'shéme-'shēng-yì?

‖I voted for him last year. chywù-nyán wŏ shywăn-tā láy-je. ‖That book sells for three dollars.

nèy-bĕn-'shū mày 'sān-kwày-chyán. ‖I bought that book for three dollars. nèy-bĕn-'shū wŏ (yùng-le, *or* shŕ-le) 'sān-kwày-chyán 'măy-de. ‖Did you pay for it? (or get it free?) 'nèy-ge nǐ shŕ hwā-chyán-'măy-de-ma? ‖Did you pay for it (or not)? 'nèy-ge nǐ gĕy-'chyán-le méy-yew? ‖Is it hard for you to do this? 'nǐ dzwò jèy-ge jywé-je 'nán-ma? ‖It's time for us to go home. dzám gāy hwéy-'jyā-le. *or* dàw-le dzám-gāy-hwéy-'jyā-de-shŕ-hew-le. ‖It's time for dinner. gāy chŕ-'fàn-le. *or* dàw-le gāy-chŕ-'fàn-de-shŕ-hew-le. ‖What does that symbol stand for? nèy-gé-'jì-hwar yĕw shéme-'yì-sz? ‖Would you like to go for a walk? nǐ ywàn-yì chywù 'dzĕw-dzew-ma? ‖You'd better send for the doctor. nǐ yīng-gāy chĭng 'dày-fu láy tsáy 'hăw. ‖I'm looking for my gloves. wŏ jăw wŏ-jeshĕw-'tàwr-ne. ‖I went out for a cup of coffee. wŏ chywù hē jyā-'fēy-chywu-le. ‖I went out for some flowers. (*To buy*) wŏ chywù măy dyăr-'hwār-chywu láy-je. *or* (*To pick*) chyā *instead of* măy. ‖When does the train leave for the beach? shàg-'hăy-byār-chywu-de-chē jǐ-shŕ 'kāy? ‖The boat made for shore. 'chwán wàng 'àn-nar 'dzĕw. ‖He was elected for four years. tā-'shywăn-shang-de-nèy-'rèn shŕ 'sz̆-nyán. ‖You're in for some trouble. nǐ 'jwèn dĕy yĕw 'máfan. *or* nǐ yí-'dìng yàw yĕw 'má-fan. *or* jèy-'má-fan nǐ swàn °'táw-bu-'kāy-le. *or* °'dwŏ-bu-'kāy-le.

‖The doctor sent me a bill for fifteen dollars. dày-fu gĕy-wŏ kāy-le jang-shŕ-'wŭ-kwày-chyán-de-'jàng-laỳ. ‖He has a great liking for music. tā hĕn shĭ-hwān 'yīn-ywè.

‖There are two pairs of shoes for each person. (*Available*) 'mĕy-rén kĕ-yǐ yĕw 'lyăng-shwāng-shyé. *or* (*Issued*) 'mĕy-rén lĭng 'lyăng-shwāng-shyé. ‖There are three women for each man. mĕy-'sān-ge-'nywŭrén tsáy yĕw 'yí-ge-'nán-rén. ‖There are only four rifles for every five soldiers. mĕy-'wŭ-ge-bīng tsáy yĕw 'sz̆-găn-chyáng. ‖There are fifty prisoners for each M.P. mĕy-'yí-ge-'shyàn-bīng dĕy gwăn 'wŭ-shr-ge-fú-'lwŏ. *or* mĕy-'wŭ-shr-ge-fú-lwŏ tsáy yĕw 'yí-ge-'shyàn-bīng 'gwăn-je.

FORBID. 'bù-jwĕn; 'bù-shywŭ. ‖Smoking is forbidden in the barracks. 'yíng-nèy 'bù-jwĕn (*or* 'bù-shywŭ) shī-yān. ‖They forbade him to leave his house. tām 'bù-jwĕn (*or* 'bù-shywŭ) tā tsúng tā-jyā 'chū-chywu. ‖I forbid you to enter that door again. 'bù-jwĕn (*or* 'bù-shywŭ) nǐ 'dzày jìn nèy-ge-'mér(-le).

‖Heaven forbid! (*Of a possibility*) 'nà kĕ bù-'shíng! *or* 'nà kĕ bù-'hăw! *or* 'nà kĕ bù-dé-'lyăw! *or* (*of something past*) dzĕm 'nèm-je-ya!

FORCE. (*Strength*) 'lì-lyang, lì, jyèr. ‖I had to use a good deal of force to crack that walnut. wŏ yùngle 'hăw-dà-de-'lì-lyang (*or* wŏ shŕ-le 'hăw-dà-de-'jyèr) tsáy bă nèy-ge-'hé-taw 'jǐ-kay. ‖Force is always applied at one end of a lever. gàng-'găr dzŭng-shr dzày 'yì-téwr-shang °yùng-'lì. *or* °shŕ-'jyèr. ‖Don't use so much force when you say "chywù". shwō 'chywù de-shŕ-hew 'byé nèm yùng-'lì. ‖The mill is turned by the force of the wind. 'jèy-ge-mwò shŕ yùng (or jyè-je)°-'fēng-lì-'jwàn-de. or °'fēng-de-lì-lyang-'jwàn-de. or expressed as This is a wind-mill jèy shŕ 'fēng-mwò. ‖Many trees were torn up by the force of the storm. fēng-de-'lì-lyang hĕn 'dà, bă 'hăw-shyē-shù °gwā-'dăw-le. or °'bá-chu-lay-le. or expressed as Many trees were torn up by the storm. 'hăw-shyē-shù jyàw 'dà-fēng °gwā-'dăw-le. or °'bá-chu-lay-le.

(*Physical compulsion, often with violence*). To use force dùng-'yìng-de, dùng-'shĕw; by force yìng; *also many verbs with meanings such as* push, pull, strike, *etc.* ‖The police had to use force to make him come. 'jĭng-chá dĕy gēn-tā dùng-'yìng-de, tā tsáy 'láy-de. or 'jĭng-chá dùng-le-'shĕw tsáy bă-tā °'jyēw-lay-de. or °'dày-lay-de. or °'nèng-lay-de. ‖We took the drunk home by force. nèy-ge-dzwēy-'gwĕy wŏm 'twēy-je (or 'jwày-je, or jyēw-je) tsáy bă-tā nèng hwéy-'jyā-chywu-de. or nèy-ge-dzwèy-'gwĕy shŕ wŏm-'yìng-gĕy-'nèng-hwéy-'jyā-chywu-de. ‖I'm afraid we'll have to use force. 'kŭng-pà dzám bú-dùng-'yìng-de bù-'shíng. or (*against the person addressed*) 'nèm-je wŏm 'jŕ hăw láy-'yìng-de-le.

(*Military action*) 'wŭ-lì; 'bīng-lì. ‖Some say that diplomacy must be backed by force. yĕw-rén shwō 'wày-jyāw dĕy yĕw 'wŭ-lì (or 'bīng-lì) dzwò hèw-'dwèn.

(*Strength of an argument*) 'lì-lyang; jyèr; lĭ. ‖I admit the force of your argument. wŏ 'chéng-rèn 'nĭ-shwō-de-hwà hĕn yĕw °'lì-lyang. or °-'jyèr. or °-'lĭ.

(*Legal validity*) shyàw or 'snyàw-li (*each is used in special combinations*). ‖His decrees have the force of law. tā-de-'mìng-lìng °gēn 'fă-lywù yĕw 'túng-dĕng-'shyàw-li. *meaning* are taken as law °'dĕng-ywú 'fă-lywù. ‖When did that come into force? nèy-ge shŕ tsúng 'shéme-shŕ-hew chĭ yĕw-'shyàw-de?

(*To compel*) bī; be forced *also* bù-'dé bū-; force oneself 'myăn-chyăng. ‖I was forced (by them) to sign the check. (tām) 'bī-de wŏ bù-'dé bú-dzày jŕ-'pyàw-shang chyān-'dż. or (tām) 'bī-de wŏ méy-'fár-le tsáy dzày jŕ-'pyàw-shang chyān-'dż. or nèy shŕ (tām-) 'bī-je-wŏ-dzày-jŕ-'pyàw-shang-chyān-de-'dż. ‖We were forced to change our tactics. wŏm bù-'dé bù-'găy-byàn °jàn-'lywè. or °'fāng-'jēn. ‖We finally forced him to admit that he did it. dàw-'lyăwr wŏm bă-tā 'bī-de 'chéng-rèn-le 'shŕ tā-gàn-de. ‖They forced a confession out of him. tām 'bī-je tā 'jāw-de ('kĕw-gùng). ‖Don't force yourself to eat it if you don't want to. chŕ-bú-'shyà byé °'myăn-chyăng. or (*see above*) °'yìng chŕ. ‖He forced himself to swallow the drug. tā bă-yàw 'myăn-chyăng 'chŕ-shya-chywu-le. ‖His laugh sounded somewhat forced. tā-shyàw-de 'tīng-je yĕw dyăr-'myăn-chyăng.

Force one's way. (*To press*) jĭ; (*to crush*) chwăng; (*to fight*) dă; *plus second elements such as* (*in*) jìn *or* (*through*) gwò. ‖We may have to force our way in.

dzám yĕ-shywŭ.dĕy °(yìng) 'jĭ-jìn-chywu. or °'dă-jìn-chywu. or °'chwăng-jìn-chywu. ‖We forced our way through the crowd. wŏm tsúng nèy-chywún-'rén-ii °(yìng) 'jĭ-gwo-chywu-de. or °'chwăng-gwo-chywu-de.

(*Break open; with a heavy object*) 'dzá-kāy; (*with an ax*) 'pī-kāy; (*by swinging a heavy object*) 'jwàng-kāy; *etc.*; *see* BREAK. ‖The door has been forced. 'mén jyàw-rén gĕy °'dzá-kāy-le. or °'pī-kāy-le. or °'jwàng-kāy-le. ‖The lock has been forced (*broken*). mén-shang-de-'swŏ jyàw-rén gĕy °dzá-'hwày-le. or °nyĕw-'hwày-le.

Force of habit. ‖I go there from force of habit. wŏ dàw-'nàr-chywu shŕ 'yīn-wey chywù-'gwàn-le.

Forced landing. ‖The plane made a forced landing. fēy-jī bèy-'pwò jyàng-'lwò.

Police force 'jĭng-chá. ‖How large is the police force? 'jĭng-chá yĕw 'dwō-shăw-rén?

Armed forces (*especially the army*) 'jywūn-dwèy; (*military personnel*) 'jywūn-rén; (*land, sea, and air forces*) 'lù-'hăy-'kūng-jywūn. ‖Civilians must back up the armed forces in a war. dă-'jàng-de-shŕ-hew 'mín-rén dĕy 'jyé-lì bāng-je °jywūn-'dwèy. or °'jywūn-rén. ‖Which branch of the armed forces were you in? tsúng-'chyán nĭ dzày-'năr fú-'yì, 'lù-jywūn, 'hăy-jywūn, háy-shr 'kūng-jywun?

In force (*in large numbers*). ‖The students turned out in force. 'shywé-sheng °'láy-de hĕn 'dwō. or °'chywù-de hĕn 'dwō. or °'dà-dwèy-chū-'mă.

FOREIGN. (*Of foreign origin*) 'wày-gwo(-de); *in some combinations* yáng-; *in identifying one of several foreign countries*, gwó *alone is used;* foreign countries' 'gwó-jyā. ‖He studied at a foreign university. tā dzày 'wày-gwo shàng-de 'dà-shywé. or tā-'dà-shywé shŕ dzày-'wày-gwo-'nyàn-de. ‖Do you speak any foreign languages? nĭ hwèy shwō 'wày-gwo-hwà-ma? or nĭ 'dēw-shr hwèy shwō 'nĕy-gwó-hwà? or nĭ 'dēw-shr hwèy shwō 'nă-jĭ-gwó-de-hwà? ‖These are all foreign goods. jèy 'dēw shŕ 'wày-gwo-hwò. or jèy 'dēw shŕ 'yáng-hwò. ‖That's a foreign custom. nèy shŕ 'wày-gwo-gwēy-jywu. or nèy shŕ 'wày-gwo-fēng-su. ‖These things were made in a foreign country. jèy-shyē-dūng-shi 'dēw shŕ dzày-'wày-gwo-dzwò-de. ‖Which foreign country do you mean? nĭ shŕ jŕ-je 'nĕy-gwó shwō-de? ‖Not all foreign countries are represented in the conference. 'jèy-tsż-'hwèy-yì bú-shr 'swŏ-yĕw-de-gwó-jyā 'dēw yĕw dày-'byăw-de. ‖He has a thick foreign accent. tā-'wày-gwo-kĕw-yin hĕn 'jùng. ‖He likes to travel in foreign lands. tā shŕ-hwān dàw 'wày-gwo-chywu lywŭ-'shíng. ‖He acquired many foreign manners. tā shywé-le bù-'shăw-de °'wày-gwo-'gwēy-jywu. or °'wày-gwo-rén-de-'jywŭ-dung. ‖He has a prejudice against foreigners. tā 'tīng bù-'shĭ-hwān 'wày-gwo-ren. ‖His manners look quite foreign to me. wŏ kàn tā-de-'jywŭ-jŕ-'dùng-dzwo °hĕn (yĕw) 'wày-gwo-chyèr. or °'wày-gwo-jyèr hěn 'dà (*or* 'dzú). *or* °'wày-gwo-pày-téwr hěn 'dà (*or* 'dzú). *or* °hěn 'yáng-pày. *or* °'yáng-chyèr 'shŕ-dzú. ‖He is foreign born. tā dzày-'wày-gwo-shēng-de-'rén.

(*With foreign reference*) 'gwó-wày; *in some combinations, especially official titles*, wày. Foreign trade (*to other countries, not of foreign origin*) 'gwó-wày-màw-'yì; foreign trade commission 'gwó-wày-màw-yì-'jywú; foreign propaganda (*to, not from foreign countries*) 'gwó-wày-'shywān-chwán; *but* (*from foreign countries*) 'wày-gwo(-de)-'shywān-chwán. Foreign office 'wày-jyāw-'bù; foreign policy 'wày-jyāw-'jèng-tsè; in foreign service dzwò 'wày-jyāw-'gwān; foreign affairs 'wày-jyāw(-shŕ-jyàn).

(*Strange*). ‖His manners are foreign to me. wǒ kàn tā-de-'jywǔ-jŕ-'dùng-dzwo °hěn kàn-bu-'gwàn. *or* °hěn shyàng 'wày-láy-de-rén. *or* °hěn shyàng 'wày-shēng-rén. *or* °hěn chí-'gwày. *or* °hěn tè-'byé.

(*Unknown, unclear*). ‖The whole procedure is foreign to me. jěng-'gèr-de-'bàn-fa wǒ dēw °bù-jŕ-'dàw. *or* °bù-'chīng-chu. *or* °bù-'míng-bay. *or* °'mwō-bu-jaw 'mér.

(*Different from*). ‖His suggestion is completely foreign to what we had in mind. 'tā-shwō-de gēn 'wǒm-shyǎng-de 'wán-chywán °bù-yí-'yàng. *or* °shŕ 'lyǎng-jyàn-'shèr. *or* °bú-shr 'yí-jyàn-'shèr.

FORGET. wàng; 'wàng-ji; (*not be able to remember*) 'shyǎng-bu-chǐ-lay; bú-'jì-de. ‖I forgot (to bring) it. wǒ 'wàng-le. *or* wǒ 'wàng-ji-le. *or* wǒ 'wàng-ji 'dày-lay-le. ‖It's raining, and we forgot to close the windows. shà-'ywǔ-le; wǒm 'wàng(-ji)-le bǎ 'chwāng-hu 'gwān-shang-le. ‖I'll never forget what you just did for me. nǐ-'tsáy-gěy-wǒ-'bàn-de-'jèy-jyàn-'shèr wǒ 'yǔng-ywan °'wàng-bu-'lyǎw. *or* °'bú-hwèy 'wàng-de. *or* °'bù-néng 'wàng-de. ‖We forgot that you were coming. wǒm bǎ nǐ-'láy-de-jèy-jyàn-shèr °gěy 'wàng (-ji)-le. *or* °'wàng-de sž-'sž-de. ‖She's forgotten all her two years of Chinese. tā bǎ 'lyǎng-nyán-de-'jūng-wén 'dēw °'wàng-le. *or* °'wàng-ji-le. *or* °'wàng-'jìng-le. *or* °'wàng-de 'gān-gan-jìng-'jìng-de-le. ‖I've forgotten his name. wǒ 'wàng-le tā 'jyàw-shéme-le. *or* wǒ 'wàng-ji-le tā 'jyàw-shém-le. *or* wǒ bú-'jì-de tā 'jyàw-shéme-le. *or* wǒ 'shyǎng-bu-chǐ-lay tā 'jyàw-shéme-le. *or* wǒ bǎ tā-de-'míng-dz gěy 'wàng-le. ‖Don't forget! byé 'wàng-le!

‖Oh, forget it! 'bú-swàn-shéme. *or* 'swàn-le. *or* 'méy-shéme; 'swàn-le-ba. *or* 'béng-tí-le. *or* 'shyǎw-shŕ-yì-jwāng, 'swàn-le-ba.

FORK. (*Eating utensil*) 'chā-dz; *sometimes* chār; *in compounds* chā; tuning fork 'yīn-chā *or* 'yīn-chār. ‖He's learning to eat with a knife and fork. tā jèng 'shywé-je yùng 'dāw-dz 'chā-dz chŕ-'fàn.

(*Fork-shaped thing*) 'chā-dz, chàr; *in combination* chà; fork of a tree shù-'chà-dz; fork in the road 'chà-dàw. ‖He was sitting in a fork of the tree. tā dzày shù-chàr-nar dzwò-je. ‖Go left when you get to the

fork in the road. dàw-le yěw-'chà-dàw-de-nàr, dzěw 'dzwǒ-byar-nèy-tyáw-'lù. ‖Did you see that forked lightning? nèy-shǎn-fēn-'chàr nǐ 'kàn-jyan-le-ma?

FORM. (*To make, organize*) chéng *as the second element in a resultative compound; the first element indicates the type of action used in forming; also* (*of establishing a group for some purpose*) 'chéng-lì. ‖They formed a long line to get tickets. tām 'jàn-chéng yì-'páy hǎw mǎy-'pyàw. ‖Can you form two triangles with five matches? nǐ néng ná 'wǔ-gēn-yáng-hwǒr 'bǎy-chéng 'lyǎng-ge-sān-'jyǎwr-ma? ‖They formed a new political party. tām 'dzǔ-jr-chéng-le yí-ge-'shīn-jèng-'dǎng. ‖They're going to form a new cabinet. tām yàw 'dzǔ-jr-chéng (*or* tām yàw 'chéng-lì) yí-ge-'shīn-nèy-'gě.

(*To develop, of an idea*) 'shyǎng-chū-lay; (*draft*) 'nǐ-chū *or* nǐ-'dìng *or* nǐ-'hǎw; (*decide on*) dìng. ‖A plan was slowly forming in his mind. tā-shīn-li màn-'mān-de shyǎng-chū yí-ge-'jì-tsè-lay. ‖I havn't formed an opinion on the subject yet. 'nèy-jyàn-shŕ wǒ háy méy-'shyǎng-chū ge-'yì-jyan-lay-ne. ‖They formed a plan but didn't dare to let people know about it. tām 'shyǎng-chū-lay (*or* tām 'nǐ-chū-le, *or* tām nǐ-'dìng-le, *or* tām nǐ-'hǎw-le, *or* tām 'dìng-le) ge-'bàn-fa, kě-shr 'bù-gǎn jyàw-rén 'jŕ-daw.

(*Shape, appearance, model*) 'yàng-dz; 'yàng-shr; 'yàngr; (*an established type*) 'chéng-shŕ. ‖His arguments were the same, only he presented them in a different form. tā-de-'yì-sz shř yí-'yàng-de; bú-gwo tā 'hwàn-le ge-'yàng-dz (*or* ge-'yàng-shr, *or* ge-'yàngr) láy °'shwō jyèw-shr-le. *or* (*if the arguments were written rather than spoken*) °'shyě jyèw-shr-le. ‖Give me a form to follow. gěy-wǒ ge-'yàng-dz hǎw °'jàw-je shyě. *or* °'bǐ-je shyě. ‖That's' only a form letter. *meaning* one form for everyone nèy-fēng-'gūng-hán gěy shéy-de 'dēw yí-'yàng. ‖This document is not written according to the proper form. jèy-jyàn-'gūng-wén bú-shr 'àn-je (*or* 'jàw-je)-'chéng-shŕ-shyě-de. ‖Is this a different character or just another form of the same character? jèy shŕ 'lìng-yí-ge-dzèr, háy-shr °'ywán-'láy-de-nèy-ge-dzèr hwàn-le (*or* gǎy-le) yí-ge-'yàng-dz (*or* yí-ge-'yàng-shr, *or* yí-ge-'yàngr)? *or* (*way of writing, see next paragraph*) °túng-'yí-ge-dž-de lìng-yí-ge-'shyě-far? ‖I play a reasonably good game of tennis, but my form is terrible. wǒ dǎ-de-'wǎng-chyéw háy 'bú-swàn 'hwày; bú-gwo °'yàng-dz hěn nán kàn. *or* (*a special word for physical form in this sense*) °'shěn-dwàn hěn nán kàn.

(*Way of doing something*) verb plus -fa or -far. (*See next to last sentence above.*) ‖This word has two (written) forms; the meaning and pronunciation (*or*, spoken form) are the same, only there are two ways of writing it. jèy-ge-dž yěw 'lyǎng-ge-'shyě-fa; 'yì-sz gēn 'nyàn-fa dēw yí-'yàng; jŕ yěw 'shyě-fa bù-'túng.

(*Style, written*) 'tǐ-tsáy; *the phrase* in the form of *is also often translated by verbal expressions, for which see first paragraph above.* ‖Put your suggestions in the form of a public letter. bǎ nǐ-de-'yì-jyàn °yùng gūng-'hán-de-'tǐ-tsáy shyě-chu-lay. or °'shyě-chéng yì-pyǎn-gūng-'hán. ‖He printed his findings in the form of a dictionary. tā bǎ tā-'yán-jyēw-de-'jyē-gwǒ °yùng tsź-'dyǎn-de-'tǐ-tsáy 'yìn-de. or °'yìn-chéng yì-běn-shyàng-tsź-'dyǎn-shr̀-de-nèm-yì-běn-'shū. *But* ‖Have this bound in book form. bǎ jèy-ge 'jwāng-dìng chéng-'shū.

(*Ceremony*) 'yí-shr̀; (*outward ceremony without appreciation of meaning*) wày-'byǎw, or wày-'yàngr, or 'myàn-dz; (*regulations*) 'shíng-shr̀; (*custom*) 'gwēy-jywu; (*etiquette*) lǐ or lyěr. ‖The prayer meetings here are conducted only as a matter of form. 'jèr-de-'chǐ-dǎw-'hwèy bú-gwo shr̀ yì-jǔng-'yí-shr̀. ‖They attended the prayer meetings only as a matter of form. tām dàw 'chǐ-dǎw-'hwèy-chywu 'bú-gwo shr̀ wèy-le °wày-'byǎw jyèw-shr-le. or °'wày-'yàngr jyèw-shr-le. or °'myàn-dz jyèw-shr-le. ‖Elections in this town are conducted only as a matter of form. 'jèy-ge-dì-fang-de-shywǎn-'jywǔ ,bú-gwo shr̀ °wèy-le 'shíng-shr̀ (or °jàw 'gwēy-jywu) 'bù-néng bú-'bàn jyèw-shr-le. ‖As a matter of form you have to fill out these blanks. jèy bú-gwo shr̀ 'gwēy-jywu (or jèy shr̀ wèy-le 'shíng-shr̀-shang-de-wèn-'tí); nǐ děy bǎ jèy-shyē-'byǎw-gé dēw 'tyán-le. ‖You have to bow to elders as a matter of form. nǐ děy gěy 'jǎng-bèr shíng-'lǐ, nèy 'jyèw-shr nèm-ge-'lyěr. ‖It's considered bad form if you leave her party early. tā chíng-'kè, yàw-shr nǐ- 'dzǎw dzěw, byé-rén jywé-je nǐ bù-dǔng-'lǐ.

(*A blank*) 'byǎw-gé. ‖Did you fill out all the forms? 'byǎw-gé dēw tyán-'hǎw-le-ma?

(*A mold*) 'mú-dz; (*large wooden framework, as for cement*) 'jyà-dz.

Form of government 'jèng-tǐ. ‖Do you think this is the best form of government? 'nǐ jywé-jé ièv shr̀ 'dzwèy-hǎw-de-'jèng-tǐ-ma?

Other expressions in English. ‖This article is not yet in its final form. 'jèy-pyǎn-'wén-jāng °háy méy-dìng-'gǎwr-ne. or °'gǎw-dz háy méy-dǎ-'hǎw-ne. or °háy shr̀ tsǎw-'gǎwr-ne. ‖His request was not presented in written form. tā 'chǐng-chyéw-de-'shr̀ 'bú-shr yùng-'gūng-wén-'tūng-jr̀-de. ‖All questions must be submitted in written form. 'wèn-tí dēw děy 'shyě-chu-lay dzày 'jyāw-jìn-lay. ‖It's in book form. shr̀ ('jwāng-dìng-hǎw-de-)'shū. ‖He was in good form and kept us amused all evening. tā hěn gāw-'shìng, yì-'wǎn-shang jyàw-wǒm jywé-je 'gwày-yěw-'yì-sz-de.

FORMER. (*Earlier*). *Expressed with* **formerly** yǐ-'chyán (*before the verb*); *of a person,* ex-(*president, etc.*) 'chyán-rèn. In former times 'wǎng-r̀, 'wǎng-nyán, 'chyán-shyē-shf-hew, tsúng-'chyán, 'lǎw-nyán-jyān, yǐ-'chyán. ‖He is a former student of mine. tā yǐ-'chyán shr̀ wǒ-de-'shywé-sheng. or wǒ yǐ-'chyán 'jyāw-gwo tā. ‖The former presidents of this uni-

versity had all been lawyers. 'jèy-ge-dà-shywé-yǐ-'chyán-de-shyàw-'jǎng (or 'jèy-ge-dà-shywé-de-'chyán-rèn-shyàw-'jǎng) 'dēw dāng-gwo 'lywù-shr̀. ‖Formerly he was president of our university. yǐ-'chyán tā 'dāng-gwo 'běn-shyàw-de-shyàw-'jǎng. ‖He is a former president of this university. tā shr̀ jèy-ge-'dà-shywé-chyán-rèn-shyàw-'jǎng.

(*First*). ‖Of your two suggestions I think I prefer the former. nǐ-tí-chu-de-'lyǎng-ge-bàn-fa wǒ rèn-wéy °'téw-yí-ge 'hǎw. or °nǐ-'shyān-shwō-de-nèy-ge 'hǎw. *See also* **FIRST**.

FORT. (*Fortification with mounted guns*) pàw-'táy; (*including barracks*) 'bīng-yíng or 'yíng-pán. ‖The old fort is at the top of the hill. jyèw-pàw-'táy (or jyèw-'bīng-yíng, or jyèw-'yíng-pán) dzày shān-'dǐng-shang.

FORTH. (*After verbs*). See **OUT**.

And so forth (*etc.*) děng-'děng-de (*plus* -dūng-shi *of articles,* -shr̀ *of affairs,* -dì-fang *of places, etc., or with nothing added, all of which may be followed by* chywán *and a verb*). ‖I need a whole new outfit: shoes, ties, hat, suit, and so forth. wǒ děy 'dǎ-lǐ-dàw-'wày-de 'chywán hwàn-le, °shéme 'shyé-ya, lǐng-'dày-ya, 'màw-dz-a, 'yī-shang-nga, děng-'děng-de 'chywán děy 'hwàn. or °'shyé, lǐng-'dày, 'màw-dz, 'yī-shang, děng-'děng-de(-dūng-shi). ‖They went sight-seeing and saw the museum, the library, the park, and so forth. tām chywù 'gwàng-chywu-le, °kàn-le 'bwó-wù-'gwǎn, 'tú-shū-'gwǎn, gūng-'ywán, děng-'děng-de-'dì-fang. or °shéme 'bwó-wù-'gwǎn-na, 'tú-shū-'gwǎn-na, gūng-'ywán-na, děng-'děng-de-'dì-fang chywán kàn-le.

Back and forth. (*Coming and going, coming and returning*) láy-'hwéy-de or 'láy-lay-hwéy-'hwéy-de; (*first one way, then the other, with a verb expressing the action*) . . . láy . . . 'chywù(-de); .(*especially of rhythmic actions*) yì-'láy-yì-'wǎng-de. ‖He kept walking back and forth. tā yì-'jŕ nèm °láy-'hwéy-de 'dzěw. or °'láy-lay-hwéy-'hwěy-de 'dzěw. or °'dzěw-láy-dzěw-'chywù-de. ‖He made several trips back and forth between his house and his office before he found his money. tā tsúng tā-'jyā-li dàw tā-dzwò-'shr̀-de-nàr 'láy-'hwéy-de jǎw-le hǎw-jǐ-'tàng tsáy bǎ-chyán 'jǎw-jǎw-de. ‖They sent the letter back and forth, but he never got it. 'nèy-fēng-'shìn 'jwǎn-láy-jwǎn-'chywù yě 'méy-jwǎn-dàw tā-'shěw-li. ‖They hit the ball back and forth for a long while. tām bǎ-'chyéwr ('nǐ-) 'dǎ-gwo-láy(-'wǒ)-dǎ-gwo-'chywù-de dǎ-le bàn-'tyān. or tām bǎ-'chyéwr 'dǎ-gwo-láy-'jyē-hwéy-'chywù-de dǎ-le bàn-'tyān. or tām bǎ-'chyéwr yì-'láy-yì-'wǎng-de dǎ-le bàn-'tyān. ‖They insulted each other back and forth for hours. (*With something of a humorous turn*) tām 'yì-láy-yì-'wǎng-de 'dwèy-mà-le. bàn-'tyān.

FORTY. 'sz̀-shf. One fortieth 'sz̀-shr-fēn-jr-'yī; the fortieth dì-'sz̀-shf.

FOR WARD (FORWARDS). (*To the front*) dàw 'chyán-byan; shyàng-'chyán; wàng-'chyán. ‖**Come forward.** dàw 'chyán-byan láy. *or* shyàng-'chyán láy. *or* wàng-'chyán láy. *or* 'láy. ‖**Forward, march!** shyàng-'chyán kāy-'bù 'dzěw!

Come forward (*figuratively*) 'chū-lay. ‖**No one came forward to confess.** 'shéy yě bù-'chū-lay 'chéng-rèn.

Bring forward (*figuratively, suggest*) 'tí-chū-lay. ‖**Finally he brought forward a new suggestion.** mwò-'lyàwr tā 'tí-chu-le ge-'shīn-bàn-fa-lay.

Look forward to. (*Await*) děng; (*hope that*) 'pàn-je. ‖**I'll look forward to your letters.** wǒ 'děng nǐ láy-'shìn. ‖**I'm looking forward to that day.** wǒ 'pàn-je °'nèy-tyān kwày dàw. *or* °'yěw nèm-yì-tyān.

To forward jwǎn-jyāw. **Forward to** 'jwǎn-dàw. ‖**Please forward.** chǐng 'jwǎn-jyāw. ‖**Please forward my mail to this new address.** bǎ wǒ-de-'shìn-jyàn chǐng 'jwǎn-dàw jèy-ge-'shīn-dì-jr̆-chywu.

Backward(s) and forward(s). *See* back and forth *under* FORTH.

FOUND. (*Establish*) lì; (*especially of a country*) kāy. ‖**He founded a new dynasty.** tā lì-le ge-'shīn-cháw-dày.

Be founded (*be established*) lì-de; 'shè-de; 'chwǎng-bàn-de, 'shè-lì-de; (*opened*) 'kāy-bàn-de, 'kāy-de. ‖**Our company was founded in the first year of the** (Chinese) **republic.** 'běn-hàw shr̆ 'mín-gwó-'ywán-nyán °shè-de. *or* °'chwǎng-bàn-de. *or* °kāy-de. *or* °kāy-bàn-de. ‖**That college was founded in 1908.** nèy-ge-'dà-shywé shr̆ 'yī-jyěw-líng-'bā-nyán °'chwǎng-bàn-de. *or* °'shè-lì-de. *or* °'kāy-bàn-de.

See also FIND.

FOUR. sz̀. **One fourth** 'sz̀-fēn-jr-'yī; **the fourth** dì-'sz̀.

FOURTEEN. shŕ-'sz̀. **One fourteenth** shŕ-'sz̀-fēn-jr-'yī; **the fourteenth** dì-shŕ-'sz̀.

FREE. (*Not enslaved, unrestricted*). (*Self-determined*) dz̀-'yéw; (*self-managed*) dz̀-'jǔ; 'dz̀-jī *plus a verb of action: an actor noun plus* jǔ. ‖**We are free people.** wǒm shr̆ dz̀-'yéw-de-rén. ‖**This is a free country.** *meaning* **not a dependency** jèy shr̆ 'jèng-jr̆-dz̀-'yéw-de-'gwó-jyā. *but meaning* **promoting the people's power** jèy shr̆ jyǎng-'mín-chywán-de-'gwó-jyā. ‖**Free speech does not mean free rein for libel.** 'yán-lwèn-dz̀-'yéw 'bú-shr shwō jyèw nég 'swéy-byàn gěy-rén 'dzàw yáw-'yán-de. ‖**Did you do it of your own free will?** jèy 'wán-chywán shr̆ nǐ-'dz̀-jī-dzwò-'jǔ-gàn-de-ma? *or* jèy shr̆ nǐ-'dz̀-jī-'chíng-gān-ywàn-'yì-de-bàn-de-ma? *or meaning* **were others managing?** nǐ gàn 'jèy-shèr, 'yěw-méy-yew 'byé-rén 'jǔ-shr̆? ‖**Will you give me a free hand in the matter?** 'jèy-shèr 'shr̆-bu-shr °'wán-chywǎn yéw wǒ dzwò-'jǔ? *or meaning* **may I do as I please?** 'swéy wǒ 'dzěm bàn dēw 'shíng?

(*Unrestrained*). (*Freely*) 'swéy-byàn; (*untied*) bù-'kwěn(-je); (*unrestrained by custom, etc.*) bù-'jywū-

shu; *also indirect expressions.* ‖**This robe will keep the baby warm and also leave his arms free.** 'jèy-jyàn-yī-shang shyǎw-hár 'chwān-je nwǎn-he, 'ér-chyě gē-be kě-yí °'swéy-byàn dùng. *or* °bù-'kwěn-je. ‖**Feel free to do whatever you like.** 'swéy-swey-byàn-'byàn-de. *or* bú-yàw 'jywū-shu. *or meaning* **Do whatever you like, without restraint** 'ày (*or* 'shyǎng) dzěm-je, 'jyèw dzěm-je, byé 'jywū-shu. ‖**He's free to leave at any time.** *is expressed as* **Whenever he wants to leave, it's OK.** tā 'shéme-shŕ-hew yàw 'dzěw, °dēw 'shíng. *or as* **Whenever he wants to leave, let him go.** °'jyèw 'ràng-tā 'dzěw. ‖**He seems rather free with his insults.** tā mà-'rén mà-de wèy-myǎn tày swéy-'byàn-le.

(*Release, be released*) fàng; (*forgive*) ráw; (*let go*) jyàw ... dzěw; (*not hold as prisoner*) bù-'yā. ‖**They're freeing the prisoners.** tām bǎ-'chyéw-fàn dēw fàng-'dzěw-le. ‖**They held him for three hours and then let him go free.** tām bǎ-tā yā-le 'sān-dyǎn-jūng, yèw bǎ-tā 'fàng-le. ‖**They let him go free.** tām bǎ-tā 'fàng-le. *or* tām bǎ-tā 'ráw-le. *or* tām jyàw-tā 'dzěw-le. *or* tām 'méy-bǎ-tā 'yā-chi-lay. ‖**When will he be free** (*released*)? tā 'shéme-shŕ-hew 'fàng-chu-lay? *But* **You're freed from all responsibility.** 'méy-yěw nǐ-°shéme-'shèr-le. *or* °-de-'dzé-rèn-le.

(*Having leisure*) yěw 'gūng-fu; (*with nothing to do*) 'shyán-dzay *or* 'shyán-jè; (*finished*) ... 'wán-le; (*having no business*) 'méy-(yew) shèr; (*not busy*) 'bù-máng. ‖**When will he be free?** tā 'shéme-shŕ-hew °yěw 'gūng-fu? *or* °'shyán-dzay-dyar? *or* °'bàn-'wán-le 'shr̆? ‖**Are you free now?** shyàn-dzày °yěw 'gūng-fu-le-ma? *or* °'shr̆ dēw 'wán-le-ma? ‖**I'm free now.** wǒ 'shyàn-dzày °yěw 'gūng-fu-le. *or* °'méy-shèr-le. *or* °'bù-máng-le. *or* °'shyán-je-ne. ‖**Wait until I'm free.** děng wǒ yěw 'gūng-fu dzày 'shwō. *or* děng wǒ 'shyán-je de-shŕ-hew dzày 'shwō. *or* děng wǒ-shèr wán-le dzày 'shwō. *or* děng wǒ méy-'shèr de-shŕ-hew dzày 'shwō. ‖**I don't have any free time today.** wǒ 'jīn-tyan yì-'dyǎr-°gūng-fu yě méy-'yěw. *or* wǒ 'jyēr yì-'tyān bù-dé-'shyár.

(*Without cost*) 'báy-gěy-de, 'báy-sùng-de; **be free** 'bú-yàw-chyán, 'bú-yùng (gěy-)chyán. ‖**This is a free sample.** jèy shr̆ 'báy-gěy-de-dzwò-'yàng-dz-de. *or* jèy shr̆ 'báy-sùng-de-dzwò-'yàng-dz-de. *or either of these plus* 'bú-yàw-chyán. *or* 'bú-yùng gěy-chyán. ‖**This is free of charge.** jèy 'bú-yùng gěy-chyán. *or* jèy 'bú-yàw-chyán. *or* jèy shr̆ 'báy-'sùng-de. *or* jèy shr̆ 'báy-gěy-de. ‖**He never lets a chance go by to get something free.** yěw 'bú-yùng-'chyán jyèw 'dé-de-'dàw-de, tā 'méy-yěw bú-yàw-de-shŕ-hew. *or* yěw 'báy-gěy-de (*or* yěw 'báy-sùng-de), tā 'méy-yěw .... *But* ‖**Do you have any free tickets?** yěw myǎn-'pyàw-ma? *or* yěw 'bú-yùng-hwā-chyán-'mǎy-de-'pyàw-ma?

Free from (*not having*) 'méy-yew *or any other negative plus verb combinations.* ‖**The product is guaranteed (to be) free from defects of any kind.** jèy-jǔng-dūng-shi 'dān-bǎw (*or* 'gwǎn-bǎw) 'rèn-shém-me-'chywē-chyan yě 'mèy-yew.

Pool at Chin Temple, Taiyuan

Reflection in Huaching Hot Springs

Free and easy. ‖He has a free and easy way of doing things. tā dzwò-shr̀ hěn 'dz̀-rán, yì-'dyǎr yě bù-'hwāng-jang.

Free-for-all. ‖It ended in a free-for-all. 'jyē-gwǒ dà-jyā °dǎ-chǐ 'jyà-lay-le. or °'lwàn-dǎ-le yí-jèn-'jyà.

FREEDOM. *Most of the expressions are verbal; see* FREE. ‖Only when there is freedom of speech can there be a true democracy. yěw 'yán-lwèn-dz̀-'yéw tsáy néng yěw 'jēn-jèng-de-'mín-jǔ-jèng-'jr̀. ‖That doesn't leave me much freedom of action. 'nèm-yi-láy jyèw jyàw-wǒ °'hǎw-dwō-shèr bù-néng 'dz̀-jǐ dzwò-'jǔ-le. or °'bàn-shr̀ 'tày bú-dz̀-'yéw-le. *meaning* That limits me too strictly 'nèm-yi-láy jyèw 'shyàn-jr̀ wǒ tày 'yán-le. ‖The neighbors' children were also given the freedom of the house. 'lín-jywū-de-'háy-dz-men 'yě kě-yǐ dzày 'wǒm-jyā-li 'swéy-byàn 'wár. ‖His painting shows a freedom from conventions. tsúng tā-hwà-de-'hwàr kě-yǐ kàn-chu-lay tā °'bù-kěn 'shywún-gwéy dǎw-'jywǔ-de. or °néng 'dú-chū 'shīn-tsáy. ‖When the prison term was up, he was given his freedom. 'tú-shíng-'r̀-chī 'mǎn-le, tā jyèw gěy 'fàng-chu-lay-le. ‖In the United States, church properties enjoy freedom from taxation. dzày 'měy-gwo, jyàw-'hwèy-de-'chǎn-yè 'dēw bú-yùng shàng-'shwèy.

FREQUENT. (*Often*) 'cháng *occurs before the verb; sometimes* 'cháng-cháng. ‖I was a frequent visitor here. 'jèr wǒ yǐ-chyán 'cháng láy. ‖There was a frequent exchange of letters between them, but only for a while. yěw yí-'jèn-dz tām 'cháng tūng-'shìn-lay-je. ‖This restaurant is much frequented by artists. 'jèy-ge-gwǎn-dz 'yì-shù-jyā cháng láy. or (*see next paragraph*) 'jèy-ge-gwǎn-dz-de-'jǔ-gù 'yì-shù-jyā hěn 'dwō.

(*Numerous*) (hěn) 'dwō. ‖The rainstorms have been more frequent than usual this year. 'jīn-nyán bǐ 'wǎng-nyán 'dà-ywǔ-shyà-de 'dwō.

FRESH. (*Not stale, not spoiled*) 'shīn-shyan. ‖Are these eggs fresh? jèy-shyē-'jī-dàn 'shīn-shyan-ma? ‖Let's go out and get some fresh air. dzám 'chū-chywu shī dyar-'shīn-shyan-kūng-'chì-chywu. ‖I like fresh peas better than canned. 'wān-dèw wǒ ày chr̄ 'shīn-shyan-de, 'bú-ày chr̄ 'gwàn-téw-de.

(*New, recent*) shīn (*before noun or verb*); gāng (*before verb only*). ‖Let's open a fresh deck of cards. dzám 'dǎ-kāy yí-fù-'shīn-páy-ba. ‖That was a fresh deck of cards. 'nèy-fù-páy 'gāng (*or* 'shīn)-dǎ-kāy-de. ‖That's fresh paint. 'yéw shr̀ 'gāng (*or* 'shīn)-shàng-shang-de. or (*not dry yet*) 'yéw háy méy-'gān-ne. ‖He's fresh out of school. tā 'gāng (*or* 'shīn) lí-kāy shywé-'shyaw.

(*Not salty*) dàn. Fresh water 'dàn-shwěy; freshwater fish 'dàn-shwěy-'ywú.

(*Full of energy*) yěw 'jīng-shén. ‖After all this work he seems as fresh as when he started. dzwò-le 'nèm-dwō-'shèr tā 'háy shyàng gāng-chǐ-'téwr-nèy-'shŕ-hew nèm yěw 'jīng-shén.

(*Rosy, of complexion*). ‖She has a fresh complexion. tā-'lyǎn-shang °'yěw-húng-shr-báy-de. or °'húng-bu-yangr-de. or °'húng-bu-jyèr-de.

(*Brisk, of wind*) dà. ‖There was a fresh wind blowing. 'nèy-shŕ-hew gwā 'dà-fēng.

(*Impertinent*). ‖Don't be fresh! 'byé táw-'chì. or 'gwéy-jywu-dyar. or 'byé hú-'nàw.

(*Improperly playful*). ‖He got fresh with her. tā gēn-tā nàw-je-'wár-lay-je. or tā gēn-tā hú-'nàw-lay-je.

FRIDAY. 'shīng-chī-'wǔ, or lǐ-bày-'wǔ. Next Friday 'shyà-lǐ-bày-'wǔ or 'shyà-shīng-chī-'wǔ; next week Friday (*with one Friday intervening*) 'shyà-lǐ-bày-de-'lǐ-bày-'wǔ or 'shyà-shīng-chī-de-'shīng-chī-'wǔ.

FRIEND. 'péng-yew. ‖We're old friends. wǒm shr̀ 'lǎw-péng-yew. ‖He's one of my new friends. tā shr̀ wǒ-'shīn-jyāw-de-ge-'péng-yew. ‖He makes friends easily. tā 'rúng-yì gēn-rén 'jyāw 'péng-yew. ‖Only intimate friends were invited. 'chǐng-de jŕ yěw °'lǎw-péng-yew. or °'jyāw-chíng-'shén-dyar-de-'péng-yew. or °hěn-'chīn-jìn-de-péng-yew. ‖You're not my friend. (*Seriously*) nǐ 'bú-gèw 'péng-yew. (*As a joke*) nǐ 'dzěm bú-'shyàng-je wǒ-ya!

Be friends (with) shr̀ 'péng-yew; shyāng-'hǎw; 'láy-wang; yěw 'jyāw-ching (have friendship; 'jyāw-ching *is sometimes used where we say* friend). ‖He's a good friend of mine. tā shr̀ wǒ-de-'hǎw-péng-yew. or tā gēn-wǒ yěw 'jyāw-ching. ‖They're no longer friends. tām bù-shyāng-'hǎw-le. or tām-de-'jyāw-ching 'dwàn-le. or tām-de-'jyāw-ching 'chǎ-le. or tām 'méy-yew 'láy-wang-le. ‖A friend in need is a friend indeed. yùng-de-'jáw-de-shŕ-hew tsáy 'shyǎn-de-chū °'jyāw-ching-lay. or °'jēn-péng-yew-lay. or (*a comparable Chinese proverb*) 'shywě-li sùng-'tàn-de 'tsáy swàn 'péng-yew. ‖He's a real friend!. tā 'jēn gèw 'péng-yew. or tā 'jēn gèw 'jyāw-ching. or tā 'jēn swàn-shr gèw 'péng-yew. ‖Are you still friends with him? nǐ gēn-ta háy °shr̀ 'péng-yew-ma? or °shyāng-'hǎw-ma? or °'láy-wang-ma? ‖I did my best to make friends with him. wǒ 'jyé-lì shyǎng gēn-tā °dǎ 'jyāw-ching-lay-je. or °'láy-wang-lay-je. or °'jyāw-wang-lay-je. or °dzwò 'péng-yew. or *meaning* I did my best to win him over wǒ 'jyé-lì 'lā-lung tā-lay-je. But ‖Let's be friends. *meaning* Let's not disagree. dzám 'byé nàw 'yì-jyan. or *meaning* Let's not fight. dzám 'byé dǎ-'jyà. or *meaning* Let's not be angry at each other. dzám 'byé bǐ-tsz shēng-'chì.

FRIENDLY. 'hé-chi; *often* good hǎw; lā-'jìn-hu *or intimate* 'chīn-jìn. ‖He seemed friendly towards you. tā hǎw shyàng gēn-nǐ hěn 'hé-chi. ‖He's too friendly towards them. tā gēn-tām tày 'hé-chi-le. or tā dày-tām tày 'hǎw-le. ‖He's too friendly with them. tā gēn-tām 'tày lā-'jìn-hu-le. or tā gēn-tām 'tày 'chīn-jìn-le. ‖This dog is friendly. jèy-ge-'gěw gēn-rén 'hǎw. ‖This dog is friendly with anyone. jèy-ge-'gěw gēn-'shéy dēw 'hǎw. ‖Our country has always had friendly relations with yours. 'dzám-lyǎng-gwó yí-shyàng 'bāng-jyāw hěn 'hǎw. ‖He has a very friendly smile. tā-'shyàw-rúngr shyǎn-de hěn 'hé-chi-de. *or* (*meaning* **kindly,** *of an old person*) ¡ā-'shyàw-rúngr hěn 'tsź-shàn-de.

FRIENDSHIP. 'jyāw-ching; 'yěw-ỳì. ‖Our friendship is the only thing that matters. dzám-¿ie-'jyāw-ching (*or* dzám-de-'yěw-yì) shř 'dzwèy-yàw-'jǐn-de. ‖Our long friendship came to an end. wǒm-dwó-nyán-de-'jyāw-ching (*or* wǒm-'dwó-nyán-de-'yěw·yì) °swàn-'lyǎw-le. *or* °tsúng-tsź 'dwàn-le.

See also **FRIEND.**

FROM. (*Of motion in space or time, or of action*) tsúng; *sometimes* dǎ; (*of motion in space only*) chǐ. ‖Where did you come from just now? nǐ 'gāng tsúng-'nǎr láy? *or* nǐ 'gāng dǎ (*or* chǐ)-'nǎr láy? ‖I just came from home. wǒ gāng tsúng (*or* dǎ, *or* chǐ) 'jyā-li láy. ‖Where do you come from? nǐ shř tsúng-'nǎr-lay-de? *or expressed as* **Of what place are you?** nǐ shř 'nǎr-de-rén? ‖I can't reach it from here. wǒ tsúng-'jèr gèw-bu-'jáw. ‖The smell comes from beyond the river. nèy-ge-'wèr shř tsúng-hé-'nèy-byār-gwò-lay-de. ‖The light is reflected from that window across the street. gwāng shř tsúng-gé-'jyē-nèy-ge-'chwāng-hu-'fǎn-gwo-lay-de. ‖I took a pencil from your drawer. wǒ tsúng nǐ-'chēw-ti-li ná-le yì-gwǎn-chyān-'bǐ. ‖Choose any one from those three. tsúng nèy-'sān-ge-li 'swéy-byàn 'tyāw-yí-ge. ‖Look out from here. tsúng-'jèr wàng-'wày kàn. ‖I took it from my hand. tā tsúng wǒ-'shěw-li ná-chywu-de. ‖I got the news from Joe. wǒ tsúng lǎw-'jēw-nar 'tīng-lay-de. ‖I got this from the corner store. jèy shř tsúng-gwǎy-'jyǎwr-de-nèy-ge-'pù-dz-li-'mǎy-de. *or* (*at*) jèy shř dzày-gwǎy-'jyǎwr-de-nèy-ge-'pù-dz-li-'mǎy-de. ‖I brought it from America. wǒ tsúng 'měy-gwo 'dày-lay-de. ‖Take a clean glass from the cupboard. tsúng wǎn-'jyà-dz-shàng ná yí-ge-'gān-jīng-bēy-dz-lay. ‖Take the coat from the hook. bǎ 'yī-shang tsúng 'gēwr-shang 'ná-shya-lay. ‖I took it from the table there. wǒ tsúng 'jwō-dz-shang ná-lay-de. ‖The shot came from the top of that hill. 'nèy-yì-chyāng shř tsúng-nèy-shān-'dǐng-shang-'fàng-de. ‖These country people are from the mountains. jèy-shyē-'shyāng-shya-rén shř tsúng-'shān-li-lay-de. ‖The tax the merchants pay comes from you and me too. shāng-rén-nà-de-'shwèy yě shř tsúng-'nǐ-wǒ-'shēn-shang-chū-de. ‖He pulled the carpet out from under her feet. tā tsúng tā-jyǎw-'dǐ-shya bǎ dì-'tǎn 'chēw-chu-lay-de. ‖The chair slipped out from under him. 'yǐ-dz tsúng tā-'pì-gu-dǐ-shya °'hwá-chū-chywu-le. *or* °'lyēw-chū-chywu-le. *or* °'hwá-kāy-le. *or* °'lyēw-kāy-le. ‖The children slipped away from the house one by one. 'háy-dz-men 'yí-ge-yí-ge-de tsúng 'jyā-li lyēw-je dzěw-le. ‖It takes three days to go from here to Peiping. tsúng-jèr dzěw-dàw 'běy-píng yàw 'sān-tyān. ‖He ran

from his house to the postoffice. tā tsúng tā-'jyā-li pǎw-dàw 'yéw-jèng-'jywú-chywu. ‖It' bad from beginning to end. tsúng-'téwr dàw-'lyǎwr dēw bù-'hǎw. ‖It took him exactly twenty-five years to rise from a street sweeper to the mayor's office. tā tsúng (dāng-)sǎw-'jyē(-de) dàw 'dzwò-shř-'jǎng 'jěng yùng-le èr-shr-'wǔ-nyán. ‖We lived in Peiping from 1901 on. tsúng 'yī-jyěw-líng-'yī-nyán 'chǐ, wǒm jù-dzày 'běy-píng. ‖From now on there isn't anything to worry about. 'tsúng-jīn yǐ-'hèw kě-yǐ fàng-'shīn-le. ‖He stood up from his chair. tā tsúng 'yǐ-dz-shang 'jàn-chi-lay.

(*Of distance*) lí. ‖It's a three-day trip from here. 'lí-jèr dzǔng yěw 'sān tyān-de-'lù. ‖How far is it from here? 'lí-jèr dwō ywǎn? ‖Do you live very far from the station? nǐ-'jù-de lí chē-'jàn hěn 'ywǎn-ma? ‖He lives ten miles from town. 'tā-jù-de-dì-fang 'lí-chéng 'shŕ-lǐ. ‖I'd like to live miles away from town. wǒ ywǎn-yì 'jù-de lí-chéng 'hěn ywǎn tsáy 'hǎw.

(*Of gifts, mail, etc.*). From X X *plus verb often plus* -de). ‖That's from home. (*Sent*) 'jyā-li sùng-láy-de. *or* (*Mailed*) 'jyā-li jì-láy-de. ‖That's from me. nèy-shr 'wǒ-sùng-de. *or* nèy-shr 'wǒ-jì-de. *or* (*given*) nèy-shr 'wǒ-gěy-de. ‖I got a letter from my brother. wǒ 'jyē-dàw wǒ-'gē-ge-shyě-de-yì-fēng-'shìn. *or* wǒ 'jyē-dàw wǒ-'gē-ge-shyě-gěy-wǒ-de-yì·fēng-'shìn. ‖She got her temper from her father. tā-¿ie-'pí-chì °shř tā-'fù-chin-'chwán-gěy-tā-de. *or* °shř tsúng-tā-'fù-chin-nar-'dé-lay-de. ‖She got her money from her aunt. tā-de-'chyán °shř tā-gū-'mā-gěy-tā-de. *or* °shř tsúng-tā-gū-'mā-nar(-dé)-láy-de. ‖He built a house with the profits from that transaction. tā dzwò (*or* tsúng) 'nèy-pyàwr-'mǎy-may-jwàn-de-'chyán ná-lay gày-le yì-swǒr-'fáng-dz. ‖I won't take money from anybody. 'shéy gěy-wǒ chyán wǒ yě bú-'yàw. ‖I won't take such insulting remarks from anybody. 'shéy gěy-wǒ 'jèy-yàngr-de-hwà 'tīng, wǒ yě 'bù-néng 'ràng. *or* 'shéy nèm 'mà-wǒ 'dēw bù-'shíng. ‖Take it from me, you'd better leave him alone. tīng 'wǒ-de-hwà, 'byé gwǎn-ta. ‖I got it from him. (*A thing*) wǒ tsúng 'tā-nar 'ná-de. *or* shř 'tā-gěy-wǒ-de. *or* (*information*) wǒ tsúng 'tā-nar shywé-de. *or* wǒ gēn "tā-nar shywé-de. *or* shř 'tā-gàw-sung-wǒ-de. *or* (*disease or inheritance or secret*) shř 'tā-chwán-gěy-wǒ-de. ‖Who is that letter from? shř 'shéy-láy-de-'shìn? *But* ‖That was sent from my place. nèy shř tsúng-'wǒ-nàr-sùng-lay-de.

Get away from 'lí-kāy. ‖I want to get away from here. wǒ shyǎng 'lí-kāy jèr. *or* wǒ shyǎng tsúng-'jèr dzěw-kāy.

(*As a result of*) yīn-wèy (..., 'swǒ-yǐ). ‖He was tired and nervous from overwork. tā yīn-wèy dzwò-shř tày 'dwō, swǒ-yǐ yèw lèy yèw 'shīn-shén bú-'dìng-de. ‖He got the disease from exposure in the rain. tā yīn-wèy jyàw-'ywǔ lwén-jaw-le dé-de 'bìng. *or* tā jyàw-'ywǔ lwén-jaw-le, °tsúng-'nàr dé-de 'bìng. *or* °'nèm dé-de 'bìng. *But* ‖He suffers from (*has*) high blood pressure. tā (yěw) shyě-yā-'gāw(-de-'bìng).

According to) jàw; àn-je; tsúng ... láy 'kàn. ‖**From** what he says, I don't think we should go. jàw (or àn-je) 'tā-nèm-shwō-de, wǒ shyǎng dzám háy-shr̀ 'byé chywù-ba. ‖**That's** all right from your point of view, but I'll have to take the blame if anything goes wrong. jàw (or àn-je) 'nǐ-de-kàn-fa nèm-je 'bú-yàw-jǐn, bú-gwo yàw-shr̀ yěw-le 'tswèr, '-vǒ děy āy-mà. ‖**What** is your opinion of him, judging from what he said? tsúng tā-shwō-de-'hwà-li láy 'kàn (or tǐng tā-shwō-de-'hwà), nǐ jywé-je 'tā-jèy-ge-rén 'dzěm-yàng?

(*In defining limits of numbers*). **From X to Y** (*definitely between X and Y*) dzày X yǐ-'shàng Y yǐ-'shyà (*and similar expressions*); (*anywhere between X and Y*) (tsúng or dzày) X dàw Y; (*about X or Y, of adjacent numbers*) XY. ‖**There** were from five to six hundred people in the audience. 'tīng-de-rén °dzày 'wǔ-bǎy yǐ-'shàng 'lyèw-bǎy yǐ-'shyà. or °dzày 'wǔ-bǎy dàw 'lyèw-bǎy jr̀-jyān. or °yěw wǔ-lyèw-'bǎy. ‖**This** is for the use of children from eight to twelve years old. jèy shr̀ gěy (tsúng) 'bā-swèy dàw shr̀-'èr-swèy-de-shyǎw-hár yùng-de. ‖**There** are from ten to fifteen thousand men in a division. yì-shr̀ yěw 'yí-wàn dàw yí-wàn-'wǔ-chyān-rén. ‖**It's** anywhere from 30 to 40 miles from here. lí-'jèr 'sān-sz̀-shŕ-lǐ. or lí-'jèr yěw 'sān-shr-dwō-'lǐ 'sz̀-shr-láy-lǐ. or lí-'jèr dzày 'sān-shr-lǐ yǐ-'wày, 'sz̀-shr-lǐ yǐ-'nèy.

Other expressions in English. ‖**Can** you tell him from his brother? tā gēn tā-'dì-di nǐ 'fēn-de-chu-láy-ma? ‖**This** isn't any differei from the other one. jèy-ge gēn 'nèy-ge méy-yèw 'fēn-byé. ‖**How** is this one different from that? jèy-ge gēn 'nèy-ge yěw shéme-'fēn-byé? ‖**He** kept me from making a big mistake. tā gwǎn-je-wǒ 'méy-jyàw-wǒ nàw-chu ge-dà-'tswèr-lay. ‖**He** kept me from knowing. tā yì-jŕ 'méy-jyàw-wǒ 'jr̀-dàw. ‖**Things** went from bad to worse. 'ywè láy ywè 'hwày. or 'ywè láy ywè 'dzāw. ‖**He** sells soap from house to house. tā āy-je-'jyār-de mày 'yí-dz. ‖**He** sells soap from door to door. tā āy-je-'mér-de mày 'yí-dz. ‖**The** situation changes from day to day. 'chíng-shíng tyān-tyān (or 'chíng-shíng 'yì-tyān-yì-'tyān-de) yěw 'gǎy-byàn. ‖**He** comes home drunk from time to time. tā 'gwò shyē-shŕ 'yěw nèm-yí-tsz̀ (or tā 'jyē-cháng-bù-'dyàr-de) 'dzwèy-le-gwāng-jī-de 'hwéy-jyā-lay.

FRONT. chyán. **The front** 'chyán-myàr, 'chyán-byàr, or 'chyán-tew. **Front door** 'dà-mér. ‖**The front of the house is painted white.** fáng-dz-'chyán-myàr shwā-de shr̀ 'báy-shǎr. ‖**The table of contents is in the front of the book.** 'mù-lù dzày °shū-'chyán-byàr. or °shū-'chyán-myàr. or °shū-'chyán-tew. ‖**He served for three months at the front (lines).** tā dzày chyán-'shyàn-shang dǎ-le 'sān-ge-'ywè. ‖**We can both get front seats.** dzám-lyǎ 'dēw néng dzwò 'chyán-páy. ‖**Someone's knocking on the front door.** yěw-rén °chyāw 'dà-mér-ne. or °dzày 'chyán-mér-nar 'chyāw-ne. ‖I

want a front room. wǒ yàw jyān-'chyán-byǎr-de-'fáng-jyān. or *expressed as* facing the street wǒ yàw jyān-lín-'jyē-de-'fáng-jyān. ‖**The house fronts on the river.** mén-chyán jyèw-shr̀ 'hé. or fáng-dz-'chyán-byǎr shr̀ (or lín)-'hé. or *expressed as* The door opens facing the river fáng-dz chùng (or cháw)-'hé kāy-'mér. ‖**That window fronts on (faces) the street.** 'nèy-ge-chwāng-hu °lín-'jyē. or °chùng-je 'jyē. or °shyàng-'jyē kāy-de. or °cháw-'jyē kāy-de.

In front of dzày ... 'chyán-byǎr; dzay ... 'cnyán-tew; (*in the presence of*) 'dāng-je ...; dzày ... myàn-chyan; dzày ... gēn-chyan. ‖**A big crowd gathered in front of the post office.** yí-'dà-chywún-rén dzày 'yéw-jèng-jywú-'chyán-byar láy-je. ‖**Who was that sitting in front of you at the movies?** kàn dyàn-'yǐng de-shŕ-hew, nǐ-'chyán-byan (or nǐ-'chyán-tew)-dzwò-de shr̀-'shéy? ‖**Don't say that in front of others.** 'nèy-ge 'bú-yàw dāng-je 'byé-rén 'shwō-chu-lay. or 'nèy-ge 'bú-yàw dzày 'byé-rén-myàn-chyan (or 'byé-rén-gēn-chyan) 'shwō-chu-lay.

FRUIT. 'shwéy-gwǒ (*juicy fruits*); 'gwǒ-dz or gwǒr (*includes also nuts*). ‖**Oranges are my favorite fruit.** 'shwéy-gwǒ-li wǒ 'dǐng shǐ-hwān 'jywú-dz. ‖**Do you have any fresh fruit?** yěw 'shīn-shyān-shwéy-gwǒ-ma? ‖**That tree bears a non-edible fruit.** 'nèy-kē-shù jyē-de yì-jǔng-'gwǒ-dz bù-néng 'chr̀. ‖**What kind of fruit does that tree bear?** 'nèy-kē-'shù jyē-de shr̀ 'shéme-gwǒr? or *meaning* what kind of a tree is it? nèy shr̀ 'shéme-shù?

(*Results*) 'jyē-gwǒ. ‖**His success is the fruit of long years of hard work.** 'tā 'gūng-chéng-míng-'jyèw, nà shr̀ tā-'dwō-nyán-'shīn-kǔ-de-'jyē-gwǒ. *But* ‖**Kindness always bears fruit.** (*Of business*) *meaning* kindness produces wealth 'hé-chì shēng-'tsáy. or (*in general; a proverb*) 'shàn-yěw-'shàn-bàw.

FULL. (*Filled*) mǎn, *often as second element of a resultative compound; but of a person filled with food,* bǎw. ‖**Give me a full glass of water.** gěy-wǒ yì-'mǎn-bēy-shwéy. ‖**That bottle is full of hot water** 'nèy-ge-'píng-dz (or nèy-ge-'dày-dz) °mǎn-'mān-de 'jwāng-je rè-'shwéy. or °-li jwāng-'mǎn-le rè-'shwéy. ‖**The parking place is full of out-of-town cars.** tíng-chē-'chǎng tíng-'mǎn-le wày-'láy-de-'chē. ‖**I'm full; I can't eat any more.** wǒ chr̀-'bǎw-le, bù-néng dzày 'chr̀-le. ‖**There's a full enrollment (of a school, army, etc.).** 'é-shù yǐ-jīng 'mǎn-le.

(*Containing many*) 'mǎn dēw-shr̀; 'chywán-shr̀; 'dēw-shr̀; 'chywán-dēw-shr̀; yěw (or other appropriate verbs) 'hěn-dwō; yěw 'hǎw-shyē; all of these expressions are followed by what the subject is full of. ‖**That book is full of mistakes.** 'nèy-běr-shū-li °'chywán-shr̀ 'tswèr. or °'chywán-dēw-shr̀ 'tswèr. or °'dēw-shr̀ tswèr. or °'mǎn dēw-shr̀ 'tswèr. or 'nèy-běr-shū yěw °'hěn-dwō-tswèr. or °'hǎw-shyē-tswèr. ‖**The moths got into the wool blanket, and it's full of holes.**

chúng-dz jìn-le 'máw-shyàn-tăn-dz, °gěy-'dă-de 'măn dēw-shr 'kū-lung. or °gěy-'dă-de 'chywán-shr 'kū-lung. or °gěy-'dă-de 'chywán-dēw-shr 'kū-lung. or °gěy-'dă-de 'dēw-shr 'kū-lung. or °gěy-'dă-le 'hĕn-dwō-'kū-lung. or °gěy-'dă-le 'hăw-shyē-'kū-lung. ‖This plan is full of holes. jèy-ge-'bàn-fa-li yĕw 'hĕn-dwō-dì-fang shyăng-de bù-'jēw-daw.

(*Of rooms, vacancies, etc.*) măn *as a second element;* chywán *or* dēw *before a verb.* ‖Do you have any vacant rooms? We're all full up. *or* They're all full. yĕw 'kùng-fáng-ma? wŏm-jèr °jù-'măn-le. *or* °'chywán jù-shang 'rén-le. *or* °-de-'fáng-jyān 'dēw yĕw-rén 'jù-je. ‖Do you have any vacant positions? We're full up. nĭm-nar háy yĕw 'wèy-jr-ma? 'chywán yĕw-'rén-le.

(*Complete*) jĕng-'gèr-de, jĕng, chywán; (*in detail*) 'shyáng-shì; fully 'wán-chywán. ‖The papers carry a full account of the incident. 'bàw-jř-li bă 'nèy-jyàn-shř 'wán-chywán 'dēng-chu-lay-le. *or* °jĕng-'gèr-de 'dēng-chu-lay-le. *or* °'shwō-de hĕn 'shyáng-shì. ‖Are you working full time? nĭ shyàn-dzày shř-bu-shr dzwò 'jĕng-gūng-ne?

(*Entire*) yí-'gùng (altogether, *comes before a verb*). ‖This is far from the full amount you owe me. jèy gēn nĭ-yí-'gùng-gāy-wŏ-de háy 'chà-de 'dwō-ne.

In full 'chywán; dēw. ‖He paid the debt in full. tā-de-'jày (*or* tā-'jyè-de-chyán) 'chywán (*or* 'dēw) °hwán-le. *or* °hwán-shang-le. *or* °hwán-'chīng-le.

To the full (*one hundred percent*) 'shŕ-fēn. ‖I enjoyed the dinner to the full. 'jèy-dwèn-fàn wŏ-chŕ-de 'shŕ-fēn măn-'yì. *or meaning* I ate to my heart's content 'jèy-dwèn-fàn wŏ 'chŕ-le ge-'shīn-măn-yì-'dzú.

See also **FILL.**

FUN. *There is a wide variety of meanings and translations in the following sentences, but the most common expressions contain words such as* to play wár; *meaning or interest* 'yì-sz; *to laugh* shyăw. ‖I think fishing is a lot of fun. wŏ jywé-je dyàw-'ywú hĕn °yĕw 'yì-sz. *or* °yĕw 'chywù-wey. *or* °yĕw-'chywùr. *or* °hăw 'wár. ‖He's a lot of fun. (*Enjoyable*) tā hĕn °yĕw 'yì-sz. *or* °yĕw 'chywù-wey. *or* °yĕw-'chywùr. *or* °hăw 'wár. *or* (*Amusing*) °hwèy 'dèw-rén 'shyăw. *or* °hwèy 'yĭn-rén 'shyăw. *or* °hwèy gĕy-rén dèw-'shyàwr. *or* °hwèy gĕy-rén kāy-'shīn. ‖He's no fun at all. tā-nèy-rén °'yì-dyăr-'yì-sz yĕ méy-yĕw. *or* °'yì-dyăr-'chywù-wey yĕ méy-yĕw. *or* °'yì-dyăr-'chywùr yĕ méy-yĕw. *or* °'yì-dyăr yĕ 'bù-hăw 'wár. ‖We're just having a little fun. *meaning* not being serious about it wŏm jè shř nàw-je 'wár. *or meaning* playing, not working wŏm jèng dzày-jèr 'wár-ne. ‖We were just starting to have a little fun when that killjoy came in and broke it up. wŏm 'gāng wár-de yĕw dyăr-'yì-sz-le (*or* wŏm 'gāng wár-de yĕw dyăr-'chywùr-le *or* wŏm 'gāng wár-de yĕw dyăr-gāw-'shìng-le *or* wŏm 'gāng wár-de chĭ-le dyăr-'jyèr *or* wŏm 'jèng wár-de hăw-'hāwr-de), nèy-ge-'tăw-yàn-'gwèy 'jìn-lay gĕy 'jyăw-le. ‖Let's step out and have some fun.

dzám chū-chywu 'wár-war-ba. *or* dzám chū-chywu hăw-'hāwr-de 'wár-war-ba. ‖Let's try it just for fun. dzám 'shř-yi-shr, 'jř-dàng nàw-je 'wár. *or* dzám 'wár-yi-war kàn. ‖He hid her pocketbook just for the fun of it. 'tā bă tā-de-chyán-'àr tsáng-chi-lay-le, °nèy 'bú-gwo shř gēn-tā nàw-je 'wár. *or* °yàw gēn-tā 'kāy ge-'wán-shyàw. ‖They're making fun of him. (*Ridiculing him*) tām 'shyăw-hwa-ta-ne. *or* (*Amusing themselves with him*) 'tām ná-tā °kāy 'wán-shyàw-ne. *or* °kāy-'shīn-ne. *or* °'dèw-je 'wár. *or* °dèw-'shyàwr. *or* °'shwă-je 'wár. *or* °chywŭ-'lwèr. *or* tām 'dèw-je tā 'wár. ‖Don't make fun of my pronunciation. byé 'shyăw-hwa wŏ-de-'kĕw-yīn-na.

FUNERAL. (*General, covering everything from death to burial*) 'báy-shř *or* 'sāng-shř; (*covering only funeral rites*) 'sāng-yí *or* 'sāng-lĭ. *Other expressions are verbal rather than nominal; the chief ones are* 'bàw-sāng (*to send out obituary notices containing information about the funeral*); rù-'lyàn (*to hold the ceremony of putting the deceased into the coffin*); nyàn-'jīng (*to engage Buddhist priests or others to conduct funeral services*); shàng-'jì (*to offer funeral sacrifices*); chū-'bìn (*to take care of everything connected with the funeral, or just to hold the funeral procession from home to graveyard*); 'fā-sung (*to conduct the body in the funeral procession from home to graveyard*); fā-'sāng (*to hold the funeral procession from home to graveyard*); ān-'dzàng (*to inter*); 'dyàw-sāng *or* dyàw-'shyàw *to come and console and mourn (of people outside the family*); sùng-'bìn (*to follow the bier to the graveyard and be present at the interment*); 'gūng-dzàng (*to hold a funeral ceremony for an eminent person with local authorities and the general public participating*); 'gwó-dzàng (*to hold a state funeral for someone, financed and conducted by the national government*).

‖They're having a funeral but they don't know how to do it properly. tām jèng 'dzày-nàr bàn °'sāng-shř (*or* °'báy-shř), kĕ-shr yì-'dyăr yĕ bù-'dŭng sāng-'lĭ. ‖He said he wanted to have a big funeral when he died. tā 'shwō-gwo ywàn-yi dzày 'sž-de-shŕ-hew 'chū ge-'dà-bìn. ‖We're going to attend a funeral tomorrow. wŏm 'míng-tyan chywù °dyàw-'sāng. *or* °dyàw-'shyàw. *or* °sùng-'bìn. ‖The day of his funeral was rainy. tā °chū-'bìn-de- (*or* °'fā-sung-de- *or* °fā-'sāng-de- *or* °ān-'dzàng-de-) 'nèy-tyān shyà-'ywŭ láy-je.

Funeral home bìn-yí-'gwăn.

FUNNY. (*Laughable, amusing*) dèw-'shyàwr; dèw-'gén; jāw-'shyàwr; kĕ-'shyăw (*sometimes not a compliment*); *and related expressions.* ‖That's the funniest clown I've ever seen. wŏ 'shyàng-láy méy jyàn-gwo shyàng-'tā nèm °dèw-'shyàwr-de-'chĕwr. *or* °dèw-'gén-de-'chĕwr. *or* °néng-jyàw-rén-'shyăw-de-'chĕwr. *or* °néng-jāw-rén-'shyăw-de-'chĕwr. *or* °néng-dèw-rén-'shyăw-de-'chĕwr. ‖He says some awfully funny things. tā-sh̩wō-de-'hwà °jāw-rén 'shyàw. or °dèw-rén' 'shyàw. or °hěn dèw-'gén. or °hěn dèw-'shyàwr. or °hěn jāw-'shyàwr. or °kě-'shyàw. ‖He can tell very funny jokes. tā hwèy shwō hěn dèw-'gén-de-'shyàw-hwar. ‖It was supposed to be serious, but it turned out to be awfully funny. nèy 'běn-láy hěn 'yán-jùng-de, kě-shr nùng-de hěn kě-'shyàw. ‖I saw a very funny show last night. dzwér 'wǎn-shang wǒ kàn-le °ge-hěn-dèw-'gén-de-'shì. or ‑ge-hěn-jāw-'sh̩.yàw-de-'shì. ‖You mean that funny little man? nǐ-shwō-de shr̀ nèy-ge-'jǎng-de-hěn-°kě-'shyàw-de-nèy-ge-'ǎy-dz-ma? or °jāw-'shyàwr-de-nèy-ge-'ǎy-dz-ma? or °hǎw-'shyàw-de-nèy-ge-'ǎy-dz-ma? ‖The one with a funny big nose. shr̀ 'bí-dz-jǎng-de-hěn-°kě-'shyàw-de-nèy-ge. or °jāw-'shyàwr-de-nèy-ge. or °hǎw-'shyàw-de-nèy-ge. ‖The joke isn't funny at all; it's the way he tells it. nèy-ge-'shyàw-hwar yì-'dyǎr yě °bú-dèw-'gén (or °bù-kě-'shyàw, etc.), shr̀ tā-'jyǎng-de hǎw. ‖It's not funny any more. 'bú-nèm kě-'shyàw-le. or 'bú-nèm jāw-'shyàwr-le. or 'nèm-je jyèw méy 'yì-sz-le. or meaning It's been overdone tày gwò-'hwǒr-le. or nèm-je jyèw tǎw-'yàn-le.

(Peculiar) ‖I have a funny feeling in my stomach. wǒ-'dù-dz-li jywé-je yěw dyǎr-'bú-dà-'hǎw. ‖I have a funny feeling that something is going to happen. wǒ-'shīn-li jf-'dùng, 'shyàng yàw yěw shéme-'shèr shr̀-de. ‖Funny, but I can't seem to remember. chí-'gwày (or 'gwày-le, or jēn 'gwày, or jēn chí-'gwày, or 'hǎw chí-'gwày-le, or, implying that it didn't happen, 'jèy-shèr 'shén-le, or 'jèy-shèr yěw-'gwěy), wǒ dzěm bú-'jì-de-ne?

FUR. 'pí-dz; in combinations pí- (these terms also mean skin or leather); furs 'pí-hwò; 'pí-dz; fur as material in a garment 'pí-lyàwr; 'pí-lyàw-dz; pí-'tǔng-dz. ‖She always wears a fur coat; even in warm weather. 'nwǎn-hwo-tyār tā yě chwān 'pí-dà-yī. ‖That fur looks like seal. nèy shyàng shwěy-'tǎ-pí. ‖What kind of fur do you want, lamb, persian lamb, fox, or squirrel? yàw něy-jǔng-'pí-dz; 'yáng-pí, dž-'gāw, 'hú-lǐ-pí, háy-shr 'hwēy-shǔr? ‖What kind of fur do you want to line the satin gown? nèy-ge-'dwàn-páwr gwà 'shéme-pí-dz-de-'lyěr. ‖Would you like the fur faced with satin? nèy-ge-'pí-dz dyàw ge-'dwàn-myàr hǎw-ma?

(The hair of fur) (pí-°dz-de-)'máwr. ‖This fur is very soft. jèy-ge-pí-dz-de-'máwr jēn 'rwǎn-hwor. ‖This fur comes in natural colors or dyed. jèy-jǔng-pí-dz-de-'máwr yěw 'ywán-shǎr-de yěw 'rǎn-de.

FURNISH. (Supply with furniture) one of the following verbs plus **furniture** 'jyā-jywu: (supply oneself with) jr̀ or 'jr̀-bàn; (buy) mǎy; (have, be furnished with) yěw; (be furnished with) dày; (be taken care of in respect to) gwǎn. ‖I haven't furnished my new apartment yet. wǒ-'shīn-dzū-de-dì-fang háy °méy-yěw 'jyā-jywu-ne. or °méy-mǎy-hǎw-le 'jyā-jywu-ne.

or °'méy-jr̀ 'jyā-jywu-ne. or °méy-'jr̀-bàn 'jyā-jywu-ne. ‖I want a furnished room. wǒ yàw yì-jyān-yěw (or -dày, or -gwǎn)-'jyā-jywu-de-wū-dz.

(Supply with furniture and all other necessities and ornaments) 'shè-bèy, 'bǎy-shè, 'chén-shè. ‖This room is very well furnished. 'jèy-jyān-wū-dz °'shè-bèy hěn 'chywán. or °'chén-shè hěn 'jyǎng-jyew. or °'bǎy-shè hěn 'jyǎng-jyew.

(Provide). (Have) yěw; (take charge of) gwǎn; (give) gěy; (supply as one's share) chū; (prepare) 'ywù-bey; (take charge of buying) gwǎn mǎy; (bring) ná-lay; etc. ‖The hotel will furnish you with everything you need. nǐ yàw 'yùng shéme, fàn-'dyàn-li dēw °'yěw. or °'gwǎn. ‖We furnish sheets and towels (free of charge). wǒm gwǎn chwáng-'dān-dz gēn 'shěw-jīn. ‖You furnish your own soap. 'yí-dz 'dž-bèy. ‖If you furnish the paper, I'll print them for you. nǐ yàw-shr chū (or gwǎn, or 'ywù-bèy, or gwǎn mǎy, or gěy-wǒ) 'jr̀ (or, nǐ yàw-shr ná-'jr̀ láy), wǒ jyèw gěy-nǐ 'yìn.

FURNITURE. 'jyā-jywù; (tables and chairs; usually referring to old-fashioned things) 'jwō-yǐ. Living room furniture kè-'tīng-de-'jyā-jywu; a furniture store 'jyā-jywù-'dyàn or 'jwō-yǐ-'pù. See also FURNISH.

FURTHER. (More). dzày before the verb; sometimes dwō or dzày 'dwō, in a few cases háy also before the verb. ‖Let's walk a little further. dzám dzày 'dwō dzěw-dyar. or dzám dzày dzěw 'ywǎn-dyar. ‖If you come any further I'll shoot. nǐ yàw 'dzày dzěw-'jìn-yi-dyar (or nǐ yàw 'dzày dzěw 'yí-bù, or nǐ yàw 'dzày 'jìn yí-bù), wǒ jyèw kāy-'chyāng-le. ‖Do you want to discuss this matter further? 'jèy-shèr nǐ háy shyǎng 'dzày (or 'dwō) tán-yi-tán-ma? ‖Don't you want me to make further investigations? nǐ 'bú-ywàn-yi jyàw-wǒ °dzày 'jìn yí-bù 'chá-yi-chá-ma? or °dzày 'shēn yí-bù 'chá-yi-chá-ma? or °(dzày) 'dwō chá-yi-chá-ma? ‖Let's go ahead without further arguments. wàng-shyà 'dzwò-ba, 'byé dzày 'jěng-le ‖Are there any further instructions? 'háy yěw-'hwà-ma? or 'háy yěw yàw-'fēn-fu-de-ma?

‖Anyone whose work helps to further our cause should be encouraged. bù-jywū shr̀-'shéy, 'jr̀ yàw tā-dzwò-de-'shr̀ ywú 'dzám-de-'jǔ-jāng yěw 'hǎw-chù, jyèw gāy 'gǔ-.'.

FUTURE. (In time still to come). (Afterwards) yǐ-'hèw; (about to come) 'jyāng-láy; (not yet come) wèy-'láy. ‖Try to do better in the future. yǐ-'hèw shyàng-'fár dzwò-de 'hǎw-dyar. ‖If anything like this happens in the future, call me first. yǐ-'hèw (or 'jyāng-láy) dzày yěw jèy-yàngr-de-shèr, 'shyān tūng-jr̀ 'wǒ. ‖That astrologer pretends to know all the future (events). 'nèy-ge-swàn-'gwà-de 'dž-jì shwō néng jr̀-dàw yí-'chyè-°jyāng-'láy-de-'shr̀. or °'wèy-'láy-de-'shr̀. or °yǐ-'hèw-de-'shr̀.

In the near future bù-'jyěw, 'gwò-bu-lyǎw dwō-shǎw-'shŕ-hew. ‖Things are going to blow up in the near future. bù-'jyěw (or 'gwò-bu-l‚ǎw dwō-shǎw-'shŕ-hew) 'nèy-shèr jyèw yàw 'nàw-chǐ-lay-le.

(*Prospects, prospective; road ahead*) 'chyán-tú; (*journey ahead*) 'chyán-chéng; (*hope*) 'shī-wàng; (*something to hope for*) 'shyǎng-tewr‚ ‖The future of that industry is uncertain. 'nèy-jǔng-gūng-yè 'chyán-tú 'bù-gǎn shwō 'dzěm-yàng. ‖This affair ruined his whole future career. 'jèy-jyàn-shèr bǎ tā-°'jyáng-láy-de-'shŕ-yè chywán 'hwěy-le. or °'chyán-tú jěng-'gèr-de 'hwěy-le. or °'chyán-chéng jěng-'gèr-de 'hwěy-le. ‖This job has no future. 'jèy-ge-shèr 'méy shéme-°'shī-wàng. or °'shyǎng-tewr.

G

GAIN. (*Obtain; as an object or objective*) dé (*especially in certain combinations*) ; (*reach*) dàw; (*occupy*) jàn; (*win from an enemy*) 'dé-gwo-lay, 'dwó-gwo-lay; (*add, gain more*) jyā; *and some indirect expressions.* Gain people's confidence dé rén-'shīn; gain votes ('dwō) dé-'pyàw or jyā-'pyàw; gain victory dé-'shèng; gain the upper hand dé-'shř. *For gain ground and gain the ear of, see below.* ‖The victory was gained at a tremendous cost of lives. 'jèy-tsž-dé-'shèng 'swén-shŕ-le hěn-'dwō-rén. ‖Now that he has gained the upper hand, he'll be relentless. tā shyàn-dzày 'dé-le 'shř-le, 'kě jyèw yàw 'bù-rúng-'chíng-le. ‖He gained a lot of votes by his last speech. tā 'shàng-tsž-jyǎng-'yǎn °'jyàw-ta 'dwō dé-le (or °gěy-tā 'jyā-le) bù-'shǎw-de-'shywǎn-jywǔ-'pyàw. ‖His sincerity gained the confidence of everyone. tā hěn 'chéng-shr, swǒ-yǐ 'dé rén-'shīn. or *expressed as* He was so sincere that everyone trusted him. tā 'chéng-shr-de 'jyàw-rén 'dēw shìn-ren ta. or tā hěn 'chéng-shr, swǒ-yǐ 'rén dēw 'shìn-ren ta. ‖He has not gained his objective. tā shyàng-'bàn-de háy 'méy bàn-'dàw-ne. ‖The soldiers have gained the hill beyond the town. *meaning* reached nèy-shyē-'bīng dàw-le chéng-'nèy-byǎr-de-nèy-ge-'shān-shang-le. *or, meaning* won nèy-shyē-'bīng bǎ chéng-'nèy-byǎr-de-nèy-ge-'shān °'jàn-le‚ or °'dé-gwo-lay-le. or °'dwó-gwo-lay-le.

(*Make profit; in business*) dé; jwàn; *each followed by* lì (*profit*), chyán (*money*), or 'lì-chyán. ‖He lost all his gains of the year through speculation. tā yì téw-'jī bǎ yì-'nyán-jwàn-de-'chyán dēw 'péy-chu-chywu-le. ‖How much did he gain last year? chywù-nyán tā 'dé-le dwō-shǎw 'lì? or °'chyán? or °'lì-chyán?

Gains (*winnings in a game*) 'yíng-de; (*money*) yíng-de-'chyán; (*points*) yíng-de-'fēr; (*chips*) yíng-de-chéw-'mǎ. ‖On the last hand I lost all my gains. 'shàng-yì-bǎ-'páy wǒ bǎ °'yíng-de (or °'yíng-de-'chyán, or °'yíng-de-'fēr, or °'yíng-de-chéw-'mǎ) 'dēw shū-chu-chywu-le.

(*Advantage; profit*) lì, 'lì-yì, 'hǎw-chu. ‖Their loss is our gain. 'tā-men shèw 'swén-shř, jyèw-shr 'wǒ-men dé-'lì. or (*literary*) 'dí-jŕ-'bì, 'wǒ-jŕ-'lì. ‖What do you expect to gain by doing that? nǐ nèm-je yěw shéme-°'hǎw-chu-ne? or °'lì-yì-ne? ‖He's interested only in personal gain. tā jŕ gù (tā-)'dž-jǐ-de-°'lì-yì. or °'hǎw-chu.

(*Improve in health*) hǎw. ‖The doctor reports that the patient is gaining rapidly. 'dày-fu shwō nèy-ge-'bìng-rén 'hǎw-de hěn 'kwày.

(*Increase*) 'dzēng-jyā. ‖There has been a recent gain in the population of the city. 'jìn-láy 'jèy-ge-chéng-de-'rén-kěw 'dzēng-jyā-le.

(*Catch up, in a race or game*) yàw 'gǎn-shang-le, yàw 'jwēy-shang-le. Gain on *is expressed with the above two phrases and also* (jyàn-'jyàn-de 'lí . . .) lí-de 'jìn-le (*of literal distance only*). ‖He's gaining (*in distance or points*). tā yàw 'gǎn-shang-le. or tā yàw 'jwēy-shang-le. ‖He's gaining on us. (*Distance only*) tā (jyàn-'jyàn-de 'lí-wom) lí-de 'jìn-le. or (*Distance or points*) tā yàw 'gǎn-shang-lay-le. or tā yàw 'jwēy-shang-lay-le. ‖No. 6 (horse) is gaining on No. 2. dì-'lyèw-hàw(-'mǎ) yàw °'gǎn-shang (or °'jwēy-shang) dì-'èr-hàw-le. or dì-'lyèw-hàw(-'mǎ) jyàn-'jyàn-de 'lí dì-'èr-hàw lí-de 'jìn-le.

Gain back . . . 'hwěy-fù(-le); (*only of health*) . . . fù-'ywán(-le). ‖A week in the country will help you gain back your health. dzày 'shyāng-shya jù 'yí-ge-shīng-'chī jyèw kě-yi jyàw nǐ-de-'shēn-tǐ °'hwěy-fù-le (or °'fù-'ywán-le). ‖All the lost ground has been gained back. 'dyēw-le-de-dì-fang dēw °'hwěy-fù-le. or °'dé-hwéy-lay-le.

Gain the ear of. *Various expressions meaning* make one hear. ‖He hopes to gain the mayor's ear. tā shyāng jyàw shr-'jǎng °'tīng tā-de-'hwà. or °'shìn-ren tā. ‖He gained the mayor's ear through flattery. tā 'bā-jye-de shř-'jǎng hěn 'shìn-ren ta. or tā bǎ shř-'jǎng 'bā-jye-de °'shwō shéme 'tīng shéme. or °tā 'shwō shéme shř-'jǎng 'tīng shéme.

Gain ground (*literally*) chyán-'jìn; (*of one's own side only*) yěw 'jìn-jǎn; (*figuratively*) dé-'shř, or *indirect expressions.* ‖We are gaining ground (*in battle*). wǒ-'jywūn °yěw 'jìn-jǎn. or °'jyàn-'jyàn-de chyán-'jìn. ‖The enemy is gaining ground. 'dí-rén dzày chyán-'jìn. ‖The idea is gaining ground among us. nèy-jǔng-'sž-shyǎng dzày 'wǒm-jèr °'jyàn-'jyàn-de dé-'shř-le. (*meaning* is prospering) °'jyàn-'jyàn-de 'shīng-chi-lay le. *or expressed as* The number of people who believe it is increasing. °'shìn-de-rén jyàn-'jyàn-de 'dwō-chi-lay-le.

Gain time 'hwǎn-yi-hwǎn, 'dwō dé dyǎr-'shŕ-jyan, 'dwō dé dyǎr-'gūng-fu. ‖The attack was postponed to gain time for preparation. 'gūng-ji jǎŋ-'chī wèy-ɑe-shr °'dwō dé dyǎr-'shŕ-jyan (or °'dwō dé dyǎr-'gūng-fu, or °'hwǎn-yi-hwǎn) °hǎw (or °láy) 'jwěn-bèy. ‖The enemy's request for a truce is just to gain time for putting up a stronger defense. 'dí-rén chyéw-'hé bú-gwò shŕ yàw 'hwǎn-yi-hwǎn (or 'dwō dé dyǎr-'shŕ-jyan) lǎy 'jyā-chyáng 'fáng-ywù. ‖His double-talk is just to gain time for a good excuse. tā nèm shyā-'dāw-daw bú-gwo yàw 'hwǎn-yi-hwǎn hǎw 'shyǎng jywù-'hwà shwō.

GAME. (*Contest*) 'yéw-shì; *but usually expressed by a verb, as* play a game (*general*) wár; (*tennis, cards*) dǎ; (*football, soccer*) tī; (*chess, checkers*) shyà; win a game yíng. ‖That's a good game for children. nèy-jǔng-'yéw-shì jyàw shyǎw-'hár °wár (or °dzwò) tǐng-'hǎw-de. or jyàw shyǎw-'hár wár 'nèy-ge tǐng 'hǎw. ‖Let's play a game. dzám 'wár dyǎr-shéme-ba. ‖He plays all sorts of games well. tā wár 'shéme děw wár-de 'hǎw. or shwō-dàw 'wár-de tā °'jyàn-jyàn 'jīng-tūng. or °shéme děw 'hwèy. or °shéme děw (wár-de) 'hǎw. ‖He plays a good game. tā 'wár-de hěn 'hǎw. or (*Of tennis or cards*) tā 'dǎ-de hěn 'hǎw. or (*Of football*) tā 'tī-de hěn 'hǎw. or (*Of chess or checkers*) tā 'shyà-de hěn 'hǎw. or (*Of any game*) *expressed as* He's a good hand at it. tā shŕ ge-hǎw-'shěwr. ‖I'm a little off my game today. wǒ jyěr °'wár-de (or °'dǎ-de, etc.) yéw-dyar °chà-'jìn. or °shyè-'chì. or °bù-chéng 'yàng-dz. or °bú-shr ge-'yàngr. or (*after shyà, of chess only*) °shŕ. ‖You've won the game. nǐ 'yíng-le. ‖Our team has won five games to their three. ˎwǔ bǐ-'sān, 'wǒm yíng.

A game (of). (*One particular instance of its being played*) tsž, hwéy; (*chess only*) pán. ‖We have time for one more game. háy kě-yi °'dzày (or °'dwō) °wár yí-'tsž. or °wár yì-'hwéy. or (*of chess*) 'shyà yì-'pán.

A game of (*style or degree of skill at*). (*If the hands are primarily used in playing*) shěw; play a good game 'hěn yéw lyǎng-'shěwr, or (*of chess only*) 'hěn yéw lyǎng-'jāwr, or (*of games in which something is hit*) 'hěn yéw lyǎng-'shyà-dz. ‖He plays a good game of chess. tā shyà-'chí shyà-de hěn 'hǎw. or tā shyà-de yì-shěw-hǎw-'chí. or tā shyà-'chí 'hěn yéw lyǎng-°'shěwr. or °'jāwr. ‖He plays a good game of tennis. tā dǎ wǎng-'chyéwr dǎ-de hěn 'hǎw. or tā dǎ-de yì-shěw-hǎw-wǎng-'chyéwr. or tā dǎ wǎng-'chyéwr 'hěn yéw lyǎng-°'shěwr. or °'shyà-dz.

Game boards and equipment 'wán-yèr; a store where games are sold 'wán-jywù-dyàn. ‖Do you sell games here? nǐ-men-jèr mày 'wán-yèr-ma?

(*Fun, as opposed to work*) (nàw-je) wár. ‖He thinks of his work as a game. tā ná tā-dzwò-de-'shèr °dàng (nàw-je) 'wár shŕ-de. or 'bú-dàng-'shèr.

(*Athletic meet*) 'ywùn-dùng-'hwèy. Olympic games 'wàn-gwó- (or 'gwó-jì-) 'ywùn-dùng-'hwèy; the autumn games 'chyēw-jì-'ywùn-dùng-'hwèy.

Play the game (*play fairly, literally or figuratively*). ‖He doesn't play the game. tā 'bú-àn 'gwéy-jywu 'láy. or tā 'ày shwǎ-hwā-'jāwr.

(*Trick, intention, shady dealing*). *Chinese uses many indirect expressions and proverbs.* ‖I saw through his game. *is expressed as* I could see through his chess moves. tā 'dzěw-de nèy(-jì)-bù-'chí wǒ 'děw 'kàn-de-chu-lǎy. or (*closely corresponding to the English*) tā 'wár-de °nèy-'jāwr (or °nèy-'shěwr, or °'lyǎng-jāwr, or °'lyǎng-shěwr, or °'jì-jāwr, or °'jì-shěwr, or °nèy-yí-'tàw, or °hwā-'jāwr, or °'bǎ-shì, or °shì-'fǎr) wǒ 'děw kàn-°'chwān-le (or °'tèw-le). or ta-de-gwěy-'jì (or tā-de-shīn-'yǎr, or tā-de-'jú-yì; or tā-de-'shěw-dwàn) wǒ 'děw kàn-°'chwān-le (or °'tèw-le). ‖Does anyone know what his game is? yéw-rén 'jŕ-dàw °tā yàw dzěw 'něy-bù-'chí-ma? or °tā-dǎ-de shŕ dzěm-ge-'jú-yì-ma? or °tā wár-de shŕ 'shéme-'bǎ-shì-ma? or °tā yàw yùng 'shéme-'shěw-dwàn-ma? or °tā yàw 'shŕ 'shéme-shīn-'yǎr-ma? or °tā 'hú-lu-li-'mày-de shŕ 'shéme-'yàw? ‖I can play that game too. (*Literally or figuratively*) nèy-ge 'wǒ yě 'hwèy. or (*Figuratively only*) *meaning* That's a game two can play. 'nèm-je shéy bú-'hwèy-ya! ‖I don't play that sort of game. wǒ 'bú-gàn 'nèy-ge-yàngr-de-shŕ. or wǒ 'bú-gàn 'nèy-jǔng-'shŕ. ‖It takes two to play that game. (*Literally*) 'nèy-ge děy 'lyǎ-rén 'wár. or (*Figuratively*) *expressed as* A single palm can't make any noise clapping. 'dān-'bā-jang 'pāy-bu-'shyǎng. ‖When their secret was discovered, they realized the game was up. tā-men-de-'mì-mì 'shyè-lèw-le yí-'hèw, tā-men 'jŕ-dàw (tā-men) °swàn-'wán-le. or °swàn-'lyǎw-le. or °swàn-'chwéy-le. or (*Literary*) °'dà-shì-'chywù-yi. or (*Vulgar*) °wár-'wán-le. or °wán-'dàn-le.

(*Occupation, thing to do*). *Usually expressed in a verb, as* do gàn, nùng. ‖How long have you been in this game? nǐ °gàn (or °nùng) 'jèy-ge yéw 'dwō-shǎw-'shŕ-hew-le? ‖He plays a dangerous game. tā-'gàn-de shŕ 'shyǎn-shŕ. or tā-'gàn-de hěw-'shyǎn. ‖That's a dangerous game. nèy shŕ 'shyǎn-shŕ. or 'nèy-ge hěn 'shyǎn. or (*Literally or figuratively*) wár 'nèy-ge tày 'shyǎn.

(*Animals; in wild state*) yě-'shěw; (*as food*) 'yě-wèr or 'yě-wèy. ‖Is there any big game near here? jèr-'fù-jìn yéw shéme-yě-'shèw-ma? ‖This restaurant serves game in season. jèy-ge-'gwǎn-dz °'yìng-shŕ-lwèn-'jyér-de mày 'yě-wèy. or °yéw 'yìng-shŕ-lwèn-'jyér-de-'yě-wèr. ‖The game laws are very strict. *is expressed as* The hunting laws are very strict. dǎ-'lyè-de-fǎ-'gwēy hěn 'yán. or dǎ-'lyè 'gwǎn-de hěn 'yán.

(*Plucky*). ‖Their team put up a game fight. 'tā-men-nèy-'dwèy dǎ-de háy °'jēn mày 'lì-chi. or °'jēn pīn-'mìng. or °'yì-'dyǎr bú-shyè-'chì. or °'yì-dyǎr bù-'hán-hu. or °yéw 'yǔng-chì. or °'jēn yéw yì-'gǔ-dz 'gàn-jyèr. ‖They were game to the end. tām yì-'jŕ (dàw-'lyǎwr) méy-shyè-'chì. or tām 'fèn-děw dàw-'dǐ.

(*Ready and willing*). ‖I'm game for anything. wǒ 'dzěme-je děw 'shíng. or 'wǒ 'hǎw shwō-'hwàr.

(*Lame*) 'chywé, yěw 'máw-bing. ‖I have to move slowly because of my game leg. wǒ-jèy-tyáw-'twéy °'chywé (*or* °'yěw 'máw-bing), děy màn-'mār-de.

ARDEN. 'ywán-dz; -ywár; -ywán. ‖These flowers are from our own garden. 'jèy-shyē-hwār shř tsúng wǒ-men-'dž-jǐ-de-hwā-'ywár °'chyā-lay-de. *or* °'jāy-lay-de. *or* 'jèy-shyē-hwár shř wǒm-'dž-jǐ-de-hwā-'ywár-li-'chū-de. ‖The vegetable garden is behind the garage. tsày-'ywán-dz dzày 'chē-fáng-'hèw-tew. ‖His hobby is gardening. tā ày jùng-'ywán-dz. *or* (*If raising flowers*) tā ày °jùng-'hwār. *or* (*If raising vegetables*) °jùng-'tsày. ‖How do I get to the Botanical Gardens? dàw 'jř-wù-'ywán chywù 'dzěm-me 'dzěw? ‖Are the gardens open to the public? (*Of private gardens*) 'hwā-ywár shywǔ rén 'jìn-chywu-ma? *or* (*Of public gardens*) 'gūng-ywán 'kāy-le-ma?

Zoological garden 'dùng-wù-ywán.

GAS. (*Not a liquid or solid; technical term*) 'chì-tǐ; 'chì, 'chyèr. ‖Various gases have been tested for this purpose. 'yǐ-jing 'shř-yèn-le 'gè-jǔng-de-'chì-tǐ, kàn 'nǎ-jǔng hé-'yùng. ‖In its normal state hydrogen is a gas. 'chīng-chì 'cháng-tày shř 'chì-tǐ. ‖The gas escaped from the balloon. chì-'chyéw-de-'chì dēw 'pǎw-le. *or* chì-'chyéw lèw-'chì-le. *or* chì-'chyéw dzěw-'chì-le. ‖Let the gas out before you work on it. shyān bǎ-'chì °'sā-le (*or* °'fáng-le), dzày 'shyēw-li.

Coal gas *or* natural gas méy-'chì. ‖Turn off the gas. bǎ méy-'chì 'gwān-shang. ‖The gas in the kitchen knocked him out. chū-'fáng-li-de-méy-'chì 'bǎ-ta gěy shywūn-'tǎng-shya-le. ‖He was poisoned by gas. tā jyàw méy-'chì shywūn-je-le. *or* tā júng-le méy-'chì-le. ‖They did all their cooking on a gas stove. tā-men yùng 'méy-chì-'lú-dz dzwò-'fàn. ‖The gas exploded. 'méy-chì 'jà-le.

(*Gasoline*) yéw, chì-'yéw. ‖He still had enough gas for a ten-mile ride. tā-de-(chì-)'yéw 'háy gèw dzěw 'shř-yīng-'lǐ-de. ‖Let's stop at the next station and get some gas. dàw 'shyà-yí-ge-mǎy-'yéw-de-nàr 'tíng-shya °'jyā (*or* °'tyān) dyǎr-'yéw.

(*Anesthetic*) má-'yàw. ‖Did the dentist give you gas? 'yá-yī-sheng gěy-ni shàng má-'yàw-le-ma?

Poison gas dú-'chì. ‖The enemy hasn't used gas yet. 'dí-rén háy 'méy-yùng dú-'chì-ne. ‖He was gassed in the last war. tā 'shàng-tsž-dǎ-'jàng-de-shř-hew 'jùng-gwo dú-'chì.

(*On the stomach*) chì *used only with* wèy *for* stomach; *otherwise Chinese merely refers to the* stomach ('dù-dz) *aching*. ‖He was doubled over with gas. tā 'wèy-chì (*or* tā-'dù-dz) 'téng-de, °wān-chì 'yāw láy-le. *or* °'jř-bu-chì 'yāw láy-le.

GATE. (*General, but especially the entrance gate in a high fence surrounding a house*) dà-'mén; (*in an ordinary fence*) 'jà-lar-'mér; (*in a city wall*) chéng-'mén. ‖The crowd poured out through the gate. dà-'hwơr tsúng dà-'mén nèr 'yūng-chū-chywu-le. ‖He closed the

gate behind him on his way out. tā bǎ dà-'mén 'gwān-shang-le 'dzěw-de. *or* tā 'dzěw de-shř-hew bǎ dà-'mén 'gwān-shang-le. ‖There are two stone lions outside the gate. 'dà-mén-'wày-tew yěw lyǎng-ge-'shř-tew-'shř-dz.

Gatekeeper kān-'mér-de; guard at the gate kān-'mér-de. *or* (*if police*) mén-'jīng.

Gate (*of a dam*) já (*which also means the entire dam*). ‖When the water rises too high they open the gates. 'shwěy yàw-shr jǎng-de tày 'gāw-le, tā-men jyèw bǎ-'já 'kāy-kay.

Gate (receipts). ‖The gate totaled $4000. *is expressed as* Altogether they sold $4000 worth of tickets. mén-'pyàw yí-gùng 'mày-le 'sž-chyān-kwày-'chyán. ‖The game drew a gate of 3000. *is expressed as* For this game they sold 3000 seats (*or* tickets). 'jèy-yì-chǎng-chyéwr mày-le 'sān-chyān-°ge-'dzwòr. *or* °jāng-'pyàw.

GATHER. (*Pick up from here and there; put in order*) 'gwéy-jr, 'shēw-shr; (*hurriedly throwing things together*) 'lyǎn-ba. ‖He gathered up his things and left. tā °'gwéy-jr-gwéy-jr (*or* °'shēw-shr-shēw-shr, *or* °'lyǎn-ba-lyǎn-ba) tā-de-'dūng-shi, 'ná-je jyèw 'dzěw-le. ‖Gather up the papers and put them in order before you leave. bǎ-'jř °'gwéy-jr-gwéy-jr (*or* °'shēw-shr-shēw-shr, *or* °'gwéy-jr-'hǎw-le) dzày 'dzěw.

(*Pick up from the ground or floor*) shf, jyàn. ‖Gather up those papers (*from the floor*) and put them in the drawer. bǎ 'nèy-shyē-'jř °'jyǎn-chǐ-lay (*or* °'shf-chǐ-lay), shēw-dzày 'chēw-tì-li. ‖He's out gathering dry branches for a fire. tā chū-chywu °'jyǎn (*or* °'shf) gān-'jř-dz-chywu-le, hǎw 'lǔng ge-'hwǒ.

(*Pick up to put in one place*) lyǎn. ‖Gather the dirty clothes together and pile them on the floor. bǎ 'dzāng-'yī-fu °'lyǎn-chǐ-lay (*or* °'lyǎn-dzày yí-'kwàr, *or* °'lyǎn-dàw yí 'kwàr), dwēy-dzày 'dì-shang.

(*Put into a pile or piles*) dwēy. ‖He gathered the dry leaves into piles. tā bǎ gān-'yè-dz 'dwēy-le jǐ-dwēr.

(*Assemble by any method; of people, things, water, etc.*) jywù; (*of people only*) 'jywù-jí, 'jí-hé, 'hwèy-hé; (*literary*) 'hwèy-tswèy. ‖Gather the people together and make an announcement. bǎ-rén °'jí-hé-chǐ-lay (*or* °'jywù-jí, *or* °'jywù-dzày yí-'kwàr, *or* °'jywù-dàw yí-'kwàr, *or* °'hwèy-hé-dàw yí-'kwàr), 'shywān-bù yí-shyàr. ‖Let's gather the specialists together and hold a meeting. bǎ 'jwān-jyā 'jywù-dzày yí-'kwàr kāy ge-'hwèy-ba. ‖All the talented people have been gathering there for years. nèy-ge-'dì-fang 'rén-tsáy 'hwèy-tswèy-le hǎw-shyē-'nyán-le. ‖He gathered a crowd around him. tā 'jywù-le yì-chywún-'rén 'wéy-je-ta. ‖A crowd gathered around him. 'wéy-je-ta (*or* 'dzày tā-'jēw-wéy) 'jywù-le yì-chywún-'rén. *or* yì-chywún-'rén 'jywù-dzày tā 'sž-jēw-'wéy. *or* yì-chywún-'rén 'jywù-dzày nàr bǎ-ta 'wéy-chǐ-lay-le. *or* yěw yì-chywún-'rén 'wéy-je-ta.

(*Accumulate*) jī. ‖Dust gathers on window sills. *is expressed as* Window sills collect dust. chwāng-hu-'tár-shang jī 'chén-tu jī-de 'dwō.

Gather in (*crops, washing, etc.*) shēw. ‖They're gathering in the crops. tām shēw 'jwāng-jya-ne. ‖Gather in the wash before it rains. 'chèn-je 'méy-shyà-'ywǔ bǎ 'lyàng-de-'yī-fu 'shēw-jìn-lay-ba.

Gather (*flowers, nuts, etc.*) jāy, chyā. ‖She gathered enough flowers from the garden to fill all these vases. tā °'jāy (*or* °'chyā)-le-'hwār gèw bǎ jèy-shyē-'píng-dz dēw chā-'mǎn-le-de.

Gather *in the arms* bàw, lěw. ‖He gathered the two boys in his arms and said, "Don't cry any more." tā bǎ lyǎ-'háy-dz °'bàw- (*or* °'lěw-)chi-lay, shwō: "byé 'kū-le!"

Gather (*of cloth with thread*) chēw-'jǐn, shēw-'jǐn. ‖Her sleeves are gathered at the cuff. tā-de-'shyèw-dz-shyèw-'kěwr shr °'chēw- (*or* °'shēw-)'jǐn-le-de.

Gather *courage* 'gǔ(-chi-lay). ‖She gathered all her courage and walked in. tā 'gǔ-chi 'yǔng-chì-lay, jyèw 'jìn-chywu-le. *or* (*Literary*) tā 'yì-gǔ-dzwò-'chì, jyèw 'jìn-chywu-le.

Gather *one's wits* 'dǎ(-chi-lay). ‖She gathered all aer wits to talk him out of it. tā 'dǎ-chi 'jīng-shen-lay, yàw bǎ tā-'shwō-de 'bú-nèm-je-le.

Gather (*infer*). ‖I gather you don't like him. (*From the way you look*) kàn-'yàngr (*or* 'kàn jèy-ge-'yàngr, *or* kàn 'nǐ-nèy-ge-'yàngr) nǐ bú-'dà 'shǐ-hwān ta. *or* (*From the way you talk*) tīng nǐ-de-'kěw-chì, nǐ bú-'dà 'shǐ-hwān ta. *or* (*From my observation*) jywù wǒ-'chyáw (*or* 'jywù wǒ-'kàn), nǐ bú-'dà 'shǐ-hwān ta. *or* (*From what I hear*) 'jywù wǒ-'tīng-jyàn-de, nǐ bú-'dà 'shǐ-hwān ta.

Gather speed 'kwày-chi-lay; ywè 'dzěw ywè 'kwày. ‖The car slowly gathered speed. chē màn-'mār-de 'kwày-chi-lay-le. *or* chē jyàn-'jyàn-de ywè 'dzěw ywè 'kwày.

GENERAL. 1. (*Pertaining to all or most people; when followed by a noun*) 'dà-jyā-de (*of everyone*); 'dwō-shù-rén-de (*of a majority*); 'dà-dwō-shù-rén-de (*of a large majority*). (*When followed by a verb*) 'dà-jyā (*everyone; may be followed by* chywán *or* dēw); 'dwō-shù(-rén); 'dà-dwō-shù(-rén); dà (*greatly*). ‖By general consent, the doorman was paid a month's extra wages when he left. kān-'mér-de 'dzěw de-shŕ-hew 'dwò gěy-le ta 'yí-ge-ywè-de-'gūng-chyán; 'nèy-shŕ 'dà-jyā-túng-'yì-de. ‖The general opinion is that he is right. dà-'jyā-de-(*or* 'dwō-shù-rén-de-, *or* 'dà-dwō-shù-rén-de-)'yì-jyan shwō tā 'dwèy-le. ‖There is a general feeling of uneasiness about the future. 'shyamg-dàw jyāng-'láy-de-shŕ 'dà-jyā °'chywán (*or* °'dēw) jywé-je 'shīn-li bù-'ān. ‖That is for the general welfare of the people. 'nèy-shŕ 'wèy-le 'dà-jyā-de-'lì-yì. ‖There was general confusion. 'dà-jyā °dēw (*or* °chywán) 'lwàn-chi-lay-le. ‖There was general confusion in the station. chē-'jàn-shang 'dà lwàn-chi-lay-le.

2. (*Pertaining to people of all sorts without distinction*) pǔ-'tūng(-de); yì-'bān(-de); *in some combinations* pǔ-. ‖The general public is often misled by unscrupulous journalists. pǔ-'tūng-rén (*or* yì-'bān-rén) 'cháng jyàw bù-'jyǎng-'lǐ-de-shīn-wén-jì-'jě gěy 'pyàn-le. ‖This is not a book for specialists; it's for the general reader. jèy-běn-'shū bú-shr gěy 'jwān-jyā 'kàn-de; shŕ wèy °pǔ-'tūng-rén-de. *or* °yì-'bān-rén-de. ‖They hold a general election every year. tā-men 'měy-nyán pǔ-'shywǎn yí-'tsz̀.

3. (*Miscellaneous*) dzá. ‖She's been doing general office work. tā-'dzwò-de shŕ °'dzá-shr̀. *or* °gūng-shr̀-'fáng-li-de-'dzá-shr̀. ‖You can get almost anything at the general store. dzày 'dzá-hwò-'pù-li 'chà-bu-dwō-de-'dūng-shi 'dēw mǎy-de-'dàw.

4. (*Comprehensive*) dzǔng. ‖"Far East" is a general term for eastern Asiatic countries. "'ywǎn-dūng" shŕ 'dūng-yǎ-'gè-gwó-de-'dzǔng-míng. ‖"Aircraft" is the general term for airplanes, dirigibles, and balloons. "'háng-kūng-'jī" shr̀ fēy-'jī, fēy-'tǐng, hé chì-'chyéw-de-'dzǔng-míng.

5. (*Not in detail; in broad outline*). *A number of different expressions, depending on the noun.*

(*Brief and clear, of such things as instructions*) 'jyǎn-míng. ‖The general instructions are brief, but not clear. 'jyǎn-míng-'shywùn-lìng °'jyǎn-ěr bù-'míng. *or* °'jyǎn-de 'dēw bù-'míng-bay-le.

(*In summary*) tūng. General history tūng-'shr̀.

General *or* broad outline dà-'gāng, 'gāng-lǐng, 'gāng-yàw. ‖Here's the general outline; we can learn the details later. jè-shr̀ °ge-dà-'gāng (*or* °ge-'gāng-lǐng, *or* °ge-'gāng-yàw); 'shyáng-chíng yǐ-'hèw dzày shwō.

General idea. (*Not too clear*) dà-'gày; (*a shadow, vague idea*) 'yǐng-dz *or* dà-'gày *or* dà-'ji (*probably*) *followed by verb;* (*more or less*) 'dwō-shǎw *or* 'dwō-dwō-shǎw-'shǎw-de *followed by verb.* ‖I have a general idea of the problem. jèy-ge-wèn-'tí wǒ °'jǐr-dàw ge-dà-'gày. *or* °'jǐr-dàw ge-'yǐng-dz. *or* °dà-'gày 'jǐr-dàw-dyǎr. *or* °dà-'jr̀ 'jǐr-dàw-dyǎr. *or* °'dwō-shǎw 'jǐr-dàw-dyǎr. *or* °'dwō-dwo shǎw-'shǎw-de 'jǐr-daw-dyar.

In general, general. (*Looking at it in general*) dà-'tǐ-shang kàn; (*taking it in general*) dà-gày-'chí ěr-'lwèn *or* dà-gày-'chí 'shwō-chi-lay; (*referring to all points mentioned*) 'dzǔng-er-'yán-jr *or* 'dzǔng-chi-lay 'shwō. ‖The general outlook is bright. 'chyán-tú dà-'tǐ-shang kàn háy 'hǎw. *or* 'chyán-tú dà-gày-'chí shwō-chi-lay háy 'hǎw. ‖In general, things are all right. dà-'tǐ-shang shwō (*or* dà-gày-'chí ěr-'lwen) 'chíng-shíng háy 'hǎw. ‖In general, these three points are irrelevant to the question. 'dzǔng-er-'yán-jr (*or* 'dzǔng-chi-lay 'shwō) jèy-'sān-dyan dēw ywú 'běn-tí wú-'gwān.

(*Usual*) 'píng-cháng, cháng-cháng. ‖As a general rule the meetings are held here. 'píng-cháng 'hwèy dzày-'jèr 'kāy. *or* 'hwèy °'píng-cháng (*or* °'cháng-cháng) dzày-'jèr 'kāy.

6. (*Army officer; collective term for officers above colonel*) jyàng-'gwān; (*title for any such officer if* *his exact command is not known*) 'jyāng-jywūn; (*usual title for any such officer, named by his command*) shř-'jǎng (*divisional commander*), jywūn-'jǎng (*army commander*), etc. (*Terms for the three ranks of general in the Chinese Army*) shàng-'jyàng (*highest*); jūng-'jyàng (*middle*); shàw-'jyàng (*lowest*). *For U. S. Army ranks* shàng-'jyàng *is a full general*, jūng-'jyàng *a lieutenant general*, shàw-'jyàng *a major general or brigadier general; the title* General of the Army *may be* ('lù-jywūn-)'ywán-shwày *or* ('lù-jywūn-)'dà-jyāng-jywūn. Inspector General 'dzǔng-jì-'chá. ‖General Li is a general of the middle rank. 'lǐ-'jyāng-jywūn (*or* 'lǐ-shř-'jǎng) shř 'jūng-jyàng.

General (*the highest officer of a given nonmilitary type*) dzǔng-. Consul general dzǔng-'lǐng-shř; general manager dzǔng-jīng-'lǐ.

GENEROUS. (*Opposed to stingy*). ‖He's certainly generous with his money. (*implying either approval or disapproval*) tā hwā-'chyán 'shř-dzày shř °'dà-fang. *or, meaning* big-handed, *and not too approving* °shěw-'dà. *or, meaning* loose-handed °shěw-'sūng. *or, meaning* free from restrictions °méy 'kwěn-jywù. *or, meaning* he follows his will °swéy-'byàn. ‖That's really generous of you. (*Referring to something done to the speaker*) nǐ 'shīn-yǎr jēn 'hǎw. *or* nǐ 'shīn jēn 'hǎw. *or* (*Referring to something done to someone else*) nèy 'jēn-shr shíng-'hǎw-wa. *or* (*Sarcastically*) nín 'jēn-shř 'kwān-húng-dà-'lyàng. *or* nín 'jēn-shř 'dà-fang. ‖It pays to be generous. *is expressed with the literary quotation* Generosity to others is generosity to oneself. ywǔ-'rén fāng-'byàn 'dz-jǐ fāng-'byàn. *or with the literary quotation* Kindness is exchanged for kindness. 'rén-shīn 'hwàn 'rén-shīn.

(*Not strict*). ‖Be generous; don't always pick on his faults. 'dà-fang-dyǎr-ba (*or* 'bāw-han-dyǎr-ba *or* 'dày-rén 'kwān-dyar-ba *or* 'hèw-daw-dyǎr-ba *or* 'dé-rúng-rén-de-'dì-fang jyèw 'swàn-le-ba *or* 'dé-ráw-rén-de-'dì-fang jyèw 'swàn-le-ba *or* 'jēng-je-yí-ge-'yǎn-'bì-je-yí-ge-'yǎn-de-ba *or* 'shíng-shing-'hǎw-ba); byé 'jìng tyāw 'rén-jyā-de-'tswòr. ‖He's very generous toward his subordinates. tā 'dày tā-'shěw-shyà-de-rén °hěn 'kwān-húng-dà-'lyàng-de. *or* °hěn 'hèw-daw. *or* °yì-dyǎr bú-'kè-be. *or* °lǎw 'jēng-je-yí-ge-'yǎn-'bì-je-yí-ge-'yǎn-de. *or* °hěn 'kwān. *or* °hěn kwān-'dà. *or* °hěn néng 'kwān-rúng. *or* °hěn néng 'bāw-han. *or* °hěn 'jūng-hèw.

(*Big*). ‖This restaurant serves generous portions. jèy-ge-fàn-'gwǎn-dz 'gěy-de hěn 'dwō.

(*Loose*). ‖Notice the generous cut of this coat. nín 'kàn jèy-ge-'gwà-dz °'tsáy-de dwō 'sūng-nga. *or* °'tsáy-de dwō-me 'sūng-sung-kwān-'kwān-de-ya.

GENTLE. (*Light, soothing, mild*) chīng; *of hands, also* wěn. Gently chīng-'chīng-de. ‖The nurse has very gentle hands jèy-ge 'kàn-hu-de-'shěw hěn °'chīng. ‖The tap on the door was so gentle that we hardly

heard it. mén 'chyāw-de hěn 'chīng (*or* chyāw-'mén-de-shēngr 'chīng-de) wǒ-men 'jī-hu 'méy-tīng-'jyàn. ‖She gave the child a gentle push. tā bǎ shyǎw-'hár chīng-'chīng-de yì 'twēy.

(*Slow or moderate; of a current*) màn, hwǎn. ‖He was rowing against a gentle current. 'shwěy-lyéw-de hěn °'màn (*or* °'hwǎn), tā 'dzwò-je chwán wàng-'shàng 'hwá.

(*Soft and moderate, of a breeze*) 'wēn-hé, chīng. ‖There is a gentle breeze from the south. chǐ-'nán chwēy-láy-le yí-jèn-'wēn-hé-de-'fēng. *or* chīng-'chīng-de 'chwēy-láy-le yí-jèn-'nán-fēng.

(*Of a person's attitudes and actions*) 'wén-yǎ, 'ān-shyáng, 'lǎw-shŕ; (*of acquired gentleness*) 'gwēy-jywu; (*of innate nature*) 'wēn-réw. ‖He's a gentle old soul. jèy-ge-rén hěn °'lǎw-shŕ. *or* °'ān-shyáng. *or* °'wén-yǎ. ‖Isn't he gentle! (*Complimentary exclamation*) 'nèy-ge-rén 'dwō °'lǎw-shŕ-a! *or* °'ān-shyáng-nga! *or* °'gwēy-jywu-ya! *or* (*Sarcastically*) tā 'bú-shr hěn 'wén-yǎ-de-ma! ‖She's so gentle she'd never hurt a soul. tā 'wēn-réw-de (*or* tā-'nèm-'wēn-réw-de-rén), 'jywé bù-'kěn jyàw-'rén chř-'kwēy-de.

(*Of an animal; tamed, docile*) 'lǎw-shŕ, tīng-'hwà. ‖We'll let you ride this old horse; she's the gentlest one we have. nǐ chí 'jèy-pǐ-lǎw-'mǎ-ba; 'wǒm-jèr 'jyèw-shr 'jèy-pǐ háy °'lǎw-shŕ. *or* °'tīng-'hwà.

GENTLEMAN. (*Well-bred man*) 'jèng-jīng(-rén); be gentlemanly (*of a person*) 'jèng-jīng, (*yěw*) jèng-shíng; (*of actions*) jèng. ‖Can't you act like a gentleman? nǐ 'néng-bu-néng °'jèng jīng-dyǎr-ne? *or* °'jèng-jeng-jīng-'jīng-de-ne? ‖He's no gentleman. tā 'méy-jèng-'shíng. *or* tā bú-'jèng-jīng. *or* tā 'bú-shr ge-'jèng-jīng-rén. ‖He doesn't act like a gentleman. tā 'jywǔ-jř 'bú-shyàng ge-'jèng-jīng-rén. *or* tā 'méy-jèng-'shíng. *or* tā 'shíng-wéy bú-'jèng.

(*Well-born man*) 'jywūn-dz-rén. ‖He's a gentleman of the old school. tā-shř yí-ge-lǎw-'pàr-de-'jywūn-dz-rén.

(*Polite term of address or reference*). *The polite force of our* gentleman *is expressed by the measure* wèy *used with or without* 'shyān-sheng. ‖A gentleman called this morning (*not on the phone*). jyēr-'dzǎw-shang yěw yí-wèy-'shyān-sheng láy-gwo. ‖Who is that gentleman? 'nà-yí-wèy shř-'shéy? ‖Ladies and gentlemen! 'jū-wèy! *or* 'gè-wèy! *But, as a form of address in a business letter,* Gentlemen: *is* jìng-chǐ-'jě.

GEOGRAPHY. dì-'lǐ. ‖The geography of this region has been studied thoroughly. 'jèy-yí-dày-'dì-fang-de-dì-'lǐ yǐ-jing 'yán-jyèw-de hěn chè-'dǐ-le. ‖He studied geography for three years. tā nyàn-le 'sān-nyán-dì-'lǐ. ‖Any specialist in geography ought to know geology as well. dì-lǐ-'shywé-jwān-'jyā 'yě děy dǔng dì-'jř-shywé. ‖How many maps are there in your geography (book)? nǐ nèy-běr-dì-'lǐ(-shū-li) yěw 'dwō-shǎw-jāng-dì-'tú?

GET (GOT, GOTTEN). 1. Get *plus a noun.*

(*Receive*) 'shēw-dàw, 'jyē-jáw; **get word** *or* **news,** *also* dé-'shìn. ‖**When did you get my letter?** nǐ 'shéme-shŕ-hew °'jyē-jáw-de (*or* °'shēw-dàw-de) wǒ-de-'shìn? ‖**I got this book last week.** 'jèy-běn-shū wǒ 'shàng-lǐ-bày 'shēw-dàw-de. ‖**He got word that his father had died.** tā 'dé-le 'shìn shwō tā-'fù-chin 'gwò-chywu-le. ‖**Did you get any news from home?** *is also expressed as* **Did any news come from home?** 'jyā-li láy-'shìn-le-ma? *or* 'jyā-li yěw-'shìn láy-ma? ‖**I got this from my father.** *is expressed as* **This was given me by my father.** (*As a gift*) jèy-shŕ wǒ-'fù-chin-°gěy-wo-de. *or* (*As a legacy or inherited characteristic*) °'chwán-gěy-wǒ-de. *or* (*Of something told*) °'gàw-su-wo-de.

(*Receive money*) ná(-dàw), dé(-dàw); (*of regular pay*) jwàn. ‖**He gets fifty dollars a week.** tā 'yí-ge-shīng-'chī °ná (*or* °dé, *or* °ná-dàw, *or* °dé-dàw, *or* °jwàn) 'wǔ-shr-kwày-chyán.

(*Fetch a thing*) 'ná-láy; (*by finding*) 'jǎw-láy; (*by asking for*) 'yàw-láy; (*by buying*) 'mǎy-láy; (*by borrowing*) 'jyè-láy; (*by hook or crook*) 'nùng-láy; **get back** 'chywú-láy. ‖**Wait till I get my hat.** 'děng(yì-hwěr,) wǒ bǎ 'màw-dz ná-lay. ‖**I'll go and get the book tomorrow.** nèy-běr-'shū wǒ 'myéngr chywù °'ná-lay. *or* °'yàw-lay. *or* °'mǎy-lay. *or* °'jyè-lay. *or* °'chywú-lay. ‖**Can you get me another pencil?** (**Get another** *is also expressed by* 'dzày láy ....) nǐ néng dzày gěy-wo jǎw yì-jŕ-chyān-'bǐ láy-ma? *or* 'dzày láy yì-jŕ-chyān-'bǐ, shíng-ma? *or* 'dzày °jǎw, (*or* °yàw, *or* °ná, *or* 'nùng) yì-jŕ-chyān-'bǐ-lay, shíng-ma?

(*Fetch; a person*) bǎ *plus the person, followed by one of the following.* (*By asking him*) 'chǐng-láy; (*by calling him; not very polite*) 'jyàw-láy; (*by finding him*) 'jǎw-láy; (*by dragging him*) 'lā-láy; *etc., with other verbs of action.* ‖**Go and get him.** chywù bǎ-ta 'chǐng-láy. *etc.*

(*Find, as a job; or reach, as a person by phone*) 'jǎw-jáw *or* 'jǎw-dàw. ‖**She got herself a good job.** tā 'dž-jǐ 'jǎw-jáw-le ge-hǎw-'shèr. ‖**Did she get a job?** tā °'jǎw-jáw (*or* °'jǎw-dàw) 'shèr-le-ma? ‖**I couldn't get him by phone.** wǒ dzài dyàn-'hwà-li jǎw-bu-'jáw (*or* jǎw-bu-'dàw) ta.

Get (*prepare*) **a meal** dzwò-'fàn. ‖**When are you going to get dinner?** nǐ 'shéme-shŕ-hewr dzwò-'fàn?

Get the right answer dá-'dwèy; 'dá-chū-lay; shwō-'dwèy; nùng-'dwèy; (*of numbers*) 'dé-de-'shùr 'dwèy. ‖**You still haven't got the right answer.** nǐ 'háy méy-°dá-'dwèy-le-ne. *or* °'shwō-'dwèy-le-ne. *or* °'nùng-'dwèy-le-ne. *or* °'dá-chū-lay-ne. *or* (*Mathematical calculation*) nǐ-'dé-de-'shùr háy bú-'dwèy-ne.

Get *a* **disease** 'jāw(-shang); 'chwán(-shang). ‖**Aren't you afraid of getting a cold?** nǐ bú-'pà jāw-'lyáng-ma? ‖**Aren't you afraid of getting that disease?** nǐ bú-'pà 'jāw-shang (*or* 'chwán-shang) nèy-jǔng-'bìng-ma?

Get a (**mental**) **shock** chŕ-'jīng. ‖**He's going to get the shock of his life when he sees her.** tā yí 'kàn-jyan ta hwèy 'dà chŕ yì-'jīng-de.

Get the idea *or* **geι** (*understand*) **it** dǔng; (*be clear about*) 'míng-bay; (*see clearly*) 'kàn-chū-lay; (*think clearly*) 'shyǎng-chū-lay; (*feel the implications of*) mwō-'chīng-chu; (*know*) 'jŕ-dàw; (*hear clearly*) 'tīng-chū-lay. ‖**Do you get the idea?** jèy-ge-'yì-sz nǐ °'dǔng-le-ma? *or* °'míng-bay-le-ma? *or* °'kàn-chū-lay (*or* 'shyǎng-chū-lay, *or* mwō-'chīng-chu-le) shŕ 'dzěm-hwéy-'shèr-le-ma? ‖**I don't get it.** (wǒ) bù-'dǔng (*or* bù-'míng-bay, *or* méy-'tīng-chu-lay) shŕ 'dzěm-hwéy-'shèr. ‖**Do you get me?** (*The idea of what I'm saying*) nǐ 'míng-bay-le-ma? *or* nǐ 'jŕ-daw shì 'dzěm-hwéy-'shŕ-le-ma?

Get *so many* **years** (*imprisonment*) pàn (*or* nùng, *or* làw, *or* nàw) ge-...-nyán-jyān-'jìn. ‖**He got ten years.** tā °'nùng-le (*or* °'làw-le, *or* °'nàw-le, *or* °'pàn-le) ge-'shŕ-nyán-jyān-'jìn. ‖**He may get ten years.** tā yě-shywǔ °'pàn (*or* °'yàw 'nùng, *or* °yàw 'làw, *or* °yàw 'nàw) ge-'shŕ-nyán-jyān-'jìn.

Get (*a station or a place*) **on a radio** wú-shyàn-'dyàn 'tīng-dàw. ‖**Can you get Tokyo on your radio?** nǐ-de-wú-shyàn-'dyàn 'tīng-de-dàw dūng-'jīng-ma?

Get a divorce lí-'hwēn. ‖**They got a divorce.** tām 'jèng-shŕ lí-'hwēn-le.

Get *so many* **miles per gallon** (chē) yì-'jyā-lwén (-chì-'yéw) dzěw ...-lǐ. ‖**I can get twenty-two miles a gallon with this car on the open highway.** wǒ-'jèy-lyàng-chē dzày dà-'lù-shang yì-'jyā-lwén(-chì-'yéw) kě-yi dzěw èr-shŕ-'èr-lǐ.

Get *a* **person.** (*Catch*) bǎ ... 'dēy-jù; (*wound*) bǎ ... dǎ-'shāng; (*kill*) bǎ ... dǎ-'sž; (*hit*) bǎ ... 'dǎ-jáw. ‖**They got him.** tām bǎ-ta °'dēy-jù-le. *or* °'dǎ-'shāng-le. *or* °'dǎ-'sž-le. *or* °'dǎ-jáw-le. ‖**The blow got him on the chin.** 'yí-shyà-dz dǎ-jaw tā-de-'shyà-ba-'ké-dz-le.

Get *a* **person.** (*Leave him without a comeback*) bǎ ... wèn-'jù(-le). *or* jyàw ... 'dá-bu-shàng-'láy(-le). *or* jyàw ... méy-'hwà shwō(-le). *or* bǎ ... 'wèn-de °méy-hwà shwō(-le). *or* °'jāng-kěw-jyē-'shé(-le). *or* °'dá-bu-shàng-'láy(-le). ‖**You've got me there.** 'jèy-shyà-dz kě °bǎ-wo wèn-'jù-le. *or* °jyàw-wǒ 'dá-bu-shàng-'láy-le. *or* °jyàw-wǒ méy-'hwà shwō-le. ‖**They got him that time.** tām 'nèy-shyà-dz °kě bǎ-ta wèn-'jù-le. *or* °bǎ-ta 'wèn-de 'jāng-kěw-jyē-'shé-le. *or* °bǎ-ta 'wèn-de 'dá-bu-shàng-'láy-le. *or* °bǎ-ta 'wèn-de méy-'hwà shwō-le.

Get *a* **person.** (*Annoy*) jyàw-... *followed by* 'nì-wey, 'nì-fan, tǎw-'yàn, tǎw-'shyán; *or expressed as* **to annoy to death** kě bǎ ... nì-'sž-le, kě-jēn tǎw-yàn-'sž-le. ‖**What gets me is the way he cracks his knuckles.** tā něm 'èn 'shēw-shang-de-gǔ-téw-'jyér 'zā-běr-'gā-běr-de 'shyǎng, °jyàw-rén nì-wéy. *or* °'jyàw-rén 'nì-fan. *or* °jyàw-rén tǎw-'yàn. *or* °'jyàw-rén tǎw-'shyán. *or* °kě bǎ-wo nì-'sž-le. *or* °kě jēn tǎw-yàn-'sž-le.

Get *a person (ruin)* bǎ ... hwěy. ‖The opium habit finally got him. 'dà-yān-'yǐn dàw-'lyǎwr bǎ-ta 'hwěy-le.

2. Get *plus an adjective or expression of action; usually expressed by an adjective plus -le or by a verb.*

‖**Get ready.** (*For something to happen*) 'ywù-bèy-'hǎw-le. or (*For a visitor, or to go*) 'jwěn-bèy-'hǎw-le. or (*To go*) 'shěw-shr-'hǎw-le. ‖His feet got wet. tā-'jyǎw 'shŕ-le. ‖He got tired of waiting. tā 'děng-de bú-'này-fán dzày 'děng-le. ‖She got sick. tā 'bìng-le. ‖He got thin. tā 'shěw-le. ‖He got hurt. tā shèw-'shāng-le. ‖The train got under way at last. (*Began moving*) 'hèw-lay hwǒ-'chē yě jyèw °'kāy-le. or (*Began to gather speed*) °'kāy-chǐ-lay-le. or °'dzěw-chǐ-lay-le. ‖Ge usy! 'gǎy dzwò shéme kwày 'dzwò-ba! or *meaning* Hurry up 'kwày-je-dyǎ!

Get murdered. ‖Someone's going to get murdered if we don't get paid today. 'jyěr yàw 'bù-fā-'chyán-na, děy 'chū ge-'rén-mìng-'àn-dz.

Get caught jyàw-rén 'dǎy-ju; jyàw-rén 'ná-ju. ‖Aren't you afraid of getting caught? nǐ bú-'pà jyàw-rén °'dǎy-ju-ma? or °'ná-ju-ma?

Get fired jyàw-rén gěy 'tsź. ‖He got fired for coming in drunk. tā dzwò-'shŕ láy de-shŕ-hew hē-de 'dzwèy-le-gwāng-'jī-de, jyèw 'jyàw-rén gěy 'tsź-le.

Get hit by ràng ... 'dǎ-jáw. ‖Did you get hit by the ball? nǐ ràng-'chyéwr 'dǎ-jáw-le-ma?

Get rid of (*a person*) 'dwǒ-kāy; bǎ ... 'shwǎy-kāy; bǎ ... 'dyěw-shya; bǎ ... 'dǎ-fā-dzěw; (*kill*) bǎ ... 'nèng-sź. ‖How can we get rid of him? (*In what way?*) dzám yěw-'fár 'dwǒ-kāy ta tsáy 'hǎw. or °bǎ ta 'shwǎy-kāy (or 'dyěw-shya, or 'dǎ-fā-'dzěw-le, or 'nèng-sź) tsáy 'hǎw. or (*Is there no way?*) dzám 'dzěm °dwǒ-de-'kāy ta-ne? or °'shwǎy-de-'kāy tà-ne? or °néng bǎ-ta 'dyěw-shya-ne? or °néng bǎ-ta 'dǎ-fā-de-'dzěw-ne?

Get rid of (*a thing*). (*Sell*) mày, chū-'shěw; (*throw away*) rēng; (*give away*) sùng-'rén. ‖I got rid of my car while prices were high. chèn 'jyà-chyán 'dà de-shŕ-hew wǒ bǎ-'chē °'mày-le. or °chū-'shěw-le. ‖He got rid of all his old books. tā bǎ tā-de-jyèw-'shū dēw °'mày-le. or °'rēng-le. or sùng-'rén-le.

Get rid of (*a disease*). ‖I can't get rid of this cold. *is expressed as* This cold doesn't get better. jèy-tsź-shāng-'fēng 'lǎw bù-'hǎw. or °'lǎw 'hǎw-bu-lyǎw. or °'lǎw 'jŕ-bu-'hǎw. or °'shāng-chǐ-lay méy-'téwr-le.

‖**Get going!** 'dzěw! or 'dzěw-kay! or 'dzěw-ba!

For other combinations, see the word combined with **get.**

3. Get *plus a noun followed by a preposition or adjective or adverb; often constructions with* bǎ *or* jyàw *or* ràng.

Get ... done (bǎ ...) dzwò-'wàn-le. ‖I'm afraid we won't get this job done in time. wǒ 'kǔng-pà wǒm 'bù-néng (bǎ 'jèy-jyàn-shr) àn 'shŕ-hew dzwò-'wán-le.

Get ... down. ‖She gets me down. (*Intentionally or unintentionally, pleasantly or unpleasantly*) tā 'jyàw-wo 'shěw-bu-lyǎw. or (*Intentionally*) kě 'jyàw-ta bǎ-wo mwó-'hwày-le.

Get ... elected bǎ ... 'shywǎn-shàng(-le). ‖They got him elected mayor. tā-men bǎ-ta 'shywǎn-shàng shŕ-'jǎng-le. ‖That group got him elected mayor. 'nèy-chywún-rén °'bàn-de (or °'gǎw-de) bǎ-ta 'shywǎn-shàng shŕ-'jǎng-le.

Get ... going. ‖He'll be able to get the work going. 'tā néng °'jyàw (or °'ràng) jèy-ge-'gūng-dzwò 'jìn-shíng-de hěn 'shwèn-li. or 'tā néng bǎ jèy-ge-'shèr 'bàn-de shwèn-'shěw-le.

Get ... in. ‖Get the report in tomorrow. 'míng-tyan bǎ bàw-'gàw 'jyàw-jìn-chywu. ‖Please get the clothes in before it rains. 'chèn-je 'ywǔ háy méy-'shyà bǎ (lyàng-de-) 'yī-fu °'ná-jìn-lay-ba. or °'shēw-jìn-lay-ba. or °'lyǎn-jìn-lay-ba.

Get ... in(to). ‖Get this into your head! (*Listen well*) hǎw-'hāwr-de 'tīng-je! or yùng-'shīn 'tīng-je! or (*Somewhat angrily*) nǐ 'dǔng-bu-'dǔng-nga? or nǐ 'byé dzày 'hú-dū-je-le! ‖Do you expect to get all these things in(to) your suitcase? nǐ shyǎng bǎ 'nèm-shyē-dūng-shi dēw °'fàng-jìn (or 'gē-jìn, or 'sāy-jìn) nǐ-de-shěw-tí-'shyǎng-li chywù-ma?

Get ... off. ‖I can't get my shoe off. wǒ-'shyé 'twō-bu-shyà-'láy-le.

Get ... open. ‖I can't get this drawer open. jèy-ge-'chēw-tì wǒ °kāy-bu-'kāy. or °'dǎ-bu-'kāy. or °nèng-bu-'kāy. or °'nùng-bu-'kāy. or °'lā-bu-chū-'láy. or °'lā-bu-'dùng. or wǒ 'kāy-bu-kāy (*etc.*) jèy-ge-'chēw-tì.

Get ... out (of) bǎ ... *plus one of the following.* (*By any means*) 'nùng-chū-chywu or 'nèng-chū-chywu; (*by throwing*) 'rēng-chū-chywu; (*by chasing*) 'gǎn-chū-chywu or 'hūng-chū-chywu. *etc.* ‖Get that thing out of the house! bǎ 'nèy-ge-dūng-shi °'rēng-chū-chywu! or °'nùng-chū-chywu! or °'nèng-chū-chywu! ‖Get that dog out of the house! bǎ nèy-ge-'gěw °'hūng-chū-chywu! or °'gǎn-chū-chywu! or °'dǎ-chū-chywu! or °'jyàw-chū-chywu!

Get ... over. ‖I finally got the point over. wǒ dàw-'lyǎwr ràng-°ta (or °tām) 'míng-bày-le.

Get ... started. ‖I can't get the engine started. fā-dùng-'jī (kāy-)bú-'dùng.

Get ... there. ‖You can get a letter there by Monday. *is expressed as* A letter you mail today will get there Monday. shìn nǐ 'jyěr fā, shīng-chǐ-'yī 'néng-gèw 'dàw-nèr. or °'jyèw 'dàw-nèr-le.

Get someone to .... *Use one of the following followed by the person and the action.* jyàw; ràng; (*invite*) chǐng; (*persuade*) chywàn; (*compel by pulling*) lā or jwày; (*by a trick*) dyàw; *etc.* ‖Can you get him to come to the theater? nǐ néng shyǎng-'fár °ràng-ta (or °chywàn-ta, *etc.*) shàng shì-'ywán-dz láy-ma?

Get ... together. (*things*) bǎ ... 'shěw-dàw yi-'kwàr; (*persons*) bǎ ... 'jywù-dzày yí-'kwàr. ‖We'll get all the papers together before the meeting. kāy-'hwèy yǐ-'chyán wǒm děy bǎ 'wén-jyàn 'shēw-dàw yí-'kwàr.

Get . . . wet bǎ . . . nùng-'shř-le. ‖I don't want to get my feet wet. wǒ pà bǎ-'jyǎw nùng-'shř-le.

For other combinations, see the words combined with get.

4. Get *plus a preposition or an adverb.*

Get across. ‖I was finally able to get the meaning across. dàw-'dǐ wǒ bǎ nèy-ge-'hwàr °ràng-tam tīng 'míng-bày-le. *or* °'tèw-gwo-chywu-le.

Get along. ‖How are you getting along? 'jìn-lay 'dzěm-yàng? ‖Oh, he gets along. tā-ya, 'háy 'gwò-de-chywù. ‖I'll get along somehow. (*Manage to survive*) wǒ 'dzǔng néng (yěw-'fár) °'gwò-de-chywù. *or* °'gwò-ba. *or* (*In work*) wǒ 'dzǔng hwèy yěw-'fár 'bàn-de. *or* (*With any context; literary*) 'tyān wú-'jywé-rén jř-'lù. ‖He's getting along in years. tā 'lǎw-le. *or* tā shàng 'nyán-jì-le. ‖It's late; I'd better be getting along. bù-'dzáw-le, wǒ děy 'dzěw-le.

Get along (*with someone*). ‖Those two don't get along. tām-'lyǎ (*or* tā-men-'lyǎng-ge-rén) °'yì-jyàn bù-'hé. *or* °'bù-'hé. *or* °'hé-bu-láy. *or* °'shwō-bu-dàw yí-'kwàr. ‖I get along with him very well. wǒ gēn-ta °'hěn hé-de-'láy. *or* °'hwèn-de tǐng bú-'tswò-de.

Get anywhere; get somewhere. ‖We're not getting anywhere doing the work this way. 'dzěm-ge-bàn-fa °'bàn-bu-'tūng. *or* °'báy fèy-'jìn.

Get around (*of a person*). ‖He gets around a lot. (*Is very active*) tā hěn 'hwó-dùng. *or* tā 'gè-chùr 'pǎw. *or* (*In order to get ahead*) tā 'bēn-dzěw-de 'lì-hay. *or* tā 'dzwān-yíng-de 'lì-hay. ‖Get around a bit; don't just sit at home and complain about everything. 'gè-chùr 'dzěw-dzew; 'byé jìng 'dzwò-dzày 'jyā-li °'hǎy-shēng-tàn-'chì-de. *or* °'bàw-ywàn-'jèy-ge-'bàw-ywàn-'nèy-ge-de. ‖For an old man, he gets around very well. tā 'nèm-dà-'swèy-shùr-le, 'twèy-jyǎwr °'jēn 'líng. *or* °'háy swàn hěn 'líng. *or* °'jēn 'yìng-lang. ‖He'll be able to get around in no time at all. jǐ-'tyār tā jyèw néng gēn-'hǎw-rén-yí-yàng-de °'dzěw-a-'pǎw-de-le. *or* (*Especially of a child*) °'tyàw-a-'bèng-de-le. ‖Oh, I get around! *is expressed as* I hear things. hà! wǒ 'shyāw-shi 'líng-tūng. *or as* I've had experience. hà! 'wǒ °'shř 'gwò-lay-rén. *or* °-dzěw-de-'dì-fangr kě 'dwō-le. *or* °'chř-le 'dwō-shaw-wǎn-'fàn-le-ne. ‖He gets around. tā-shř yěw-'jīng-yàn-de. *or* tā 'fù-yěw-'jīng-yèn-dé. *or* tā jyàn-gwo 'shř-myàn. *or* tā jyàn-gwo 'chǎng-myàn. *or* tā 'shéme méy-'jyàn-gwo? *or* tā-shř 'dzěw-byàn-'jyāng-hú-de-rén. *or* tā 'shyāw-shi 'líng.

Get around (*of a story*). ‖The story will get around in a little while. 'nèy-ge-shř-ching yì-'hwěr jyèw hwèy °'chwán-'byàn-le. *or* °'chwán-de 'shéy dēw 'jř-dàw-le. *or* °'chwán-chū-chywu-le. *or expressed proverbially as* Paper won't contain fire. 'jř-li 'dēw-bu-jù 'hwǒ. *or as* A good deed doesn't get out; a bad deed spreads a thousand miles. 'hǎw-shř 'bù-chū-'mén; 'hwày-shř 'chwán chyān-'lǐ. ‖The story got around

(*someone said*) that he was an enemy agent. 'yěw-rén shwō tā shř ge-'dí-rén-de-'jyàn-dyé.

Get around (*plus a noun*). ‖That girl certainly gets around him. nèy-ge-'nywǔ-háy-dz jēn ná-de-'jù ta. ‖Can you get around that regulation (in this case)? 'jēy-jyàn-shèr (jàw 'gwěy-jywu shř bù-'shíng-de, bú-gwò) néng °'tūng-rúng-ma? *or* °'tūng-rúng bàn-'lǐ-ma? *or* °'tūng-rúng-de gwò-'chywù-ma? ‖Can you get around it for me? láw-jyà gěy °'tūng-rúng-tūng-rúng, shíng-ma? *or* °'tūng-rúng yí-shyàr, 'shíng-ma? *or* °'tūng-rúng bàn-'lǐ, shíng-ma?

Get at. ‖I can't get at my luggage. (*Can't reach it*) wǒ 'gèw-bu-jáw wǒ-de-'shíng-li *or* (*Temporarily can't get it*) wǒ-'shíng-li ná-bu-dàw. ‖Our fortifications were so strong that the enemy couldn't get at us. wǒ-men-'fáng-ywù-de hěn 'jyān-gù, 'dí-rén dǎ-bu-dàw wǒm-'jèr-lay. ‖Someday I'll get at the real reason. wǒ 'dzǔng yěw 'nèm-yì-tyān bǎ jèy-ge °'nèng(-de) 'míng-bay-le (*or* 'míng-míng-bay-'báy-de). *or* °'nèng(-de) 'chīng-chu-le (*or* 'chīng-chīng-chu-'chǔ-de). *or* °'chá(-de) . . . . *or* °'nèng (*or* chá, *or* wèn, *or* jwēy-wèn) ge-'shwěy-lè-'shř-chū.

Get away. ‖I'd like to go, but I'm afraid I can't get away. wǒ 'ywàn-yì (*or*, wǒ-'shīn-li shyǎng) 'dzěw, 'bú-gwò kǔng-'pà °'dzěw-bù-lyǎw. *or* °dzěw-bù-'kāy. ‖We chased him for two blocks, but he got away. wǒm 'jwēy-le ta 'lyǎng-tyáw-'jyē (nèm-'ywǎn), kě-shr tā °'háy-shr 'pǎw-le. *or* °'pǎw-de méy-'yěngr-le. ‖I want to get away from this place. wǒ yàw 'dwǒ-kāy (*or* 'lí-kāy) jèy-ge-'dì-fang.

Get away with. ‖He gets away with murder. tā (jyèw-shr) 'shā-le 'rén yě méy-'shèr. ‖I'm sure I can get away with it. wǒ 'jwěn jř-dàw wǒ °'bú-hwèy chū shéme-'wèn-tí-de. *or* °méy-'shèr. *or* °'bú-jř-ywu chū-'shř. *or* (*literary*) wǒ 'jí-rén-tyān-'shyàng, méy-'shèr.

Get back (*return*) 'hwéy(-lay); (*retrieve*) 'ná-hwéy-lay. ‖When did you get back? nǐ 'shéme-shř-hew 'hwéy-lay-de? ‖Did you get your umbrella back? nǐ-de-ywǔ-'sǎn 'ná-hwéy-lay-le-ma? ‖Let's get back to the dormitory. dzám 'hwéy sù-'shè-ba. ‖Let's get back home. dzám hwéy-'jyā-ba. ‖Let's get back to town. dzám hwéy-dàw chéng-'lǐ chywù-ba. ‖Let's get back to the original question. dzám háy-shr 'hwéy-dàw běn-'tí-shang láy-ba.

Get back at. ‖How can I get back at him? wǒ yěw 'shéme-fár yě gěy-'tā láy yí-'shyà-dz-ne? *or* wǒ yěw 'shéme-fár hwéy-'jìng ta yí-'shyàr-ne? *or* (*more seriously*) wǒ yěw 'shéme-fár 'bàw-fù yí-'shyàr-ne?

Get by (*pass*) gwò-chywu. (*May be preceded by a verb such as sneak.*) ‖Can I get by the guard? kān-'mér-de néng ràng-wo 'gwò-chywu-ma? *or* (*Slip by*) kān-'mér-de-nàr wǒ néng 'tēw-je 'lyěw-gwò-chywu-ma? ‖Let me get by. ràng-wo 'gwò-chywu.

Get by (*get along*). ‖I'll get by if I have a place to sleep. wǒ 'yěw ge-dì-fang 'shwèy, jyèw °'chéng (*or* °'shíng). ‖I'll get by somehow if I have a place to sleep. wǒ 'yěw ge-dì-fang 'shwèy, yě jyèw °'tsèw-he-je-le. or °'tsèw-he-gwo-chywù-le. or °'jyāng-jyew-gwo-chywù-le. ‖Do you think I can get by with it? nǐ shwō wǒ °'lèng (or °'yìng, or °'jyèw) nèm 'gàn, shíng-bu-shíng?

Get in (to a place) jìn. ‖What time did you get in last night? dzwór-'wǎn-shang 'jǐ-shŕ °'jìn-lay-de (or °'jìn-chywu-de)? ‖How did HE get in? 'tā dzème °'jìn-lay-de (or °'jìn-chywu-de)? ‖What time does the train get in? hwǒ-chē 'shém-me-shŕ-hew jìn-'jàn?

Get in (be elected) 'shywǎn-shàng-le. ‖Did your candidate get in? 'nǐ-yàw-jywǔ-de-'hèw-shywǎn-rén 'shywǎn-shàng-le-ma?

Get in with. ‖Did you get in with his crowd? nǐ gēn 'tā-de-nèy-'hwǒ-dz °'láy-wǎng-shàng-le-ma? or °'jyàw-shang-le-ma? or °'nèng-dàw yí-'kwài le-ma?

Get into. ‖Get into the house! 'jìn-chywu. or dàw 'wū-li chywù. But ‖He got into the car. tā shàng-'chē-le. (See also Get on, below.)

Get into (of clothes) chwān. ‖It will take me only a minute to get into my bathing suit. 'yéw-yǔng-'yī wǒ yì-'hwěr-de-gūng-fu jyèw kě-yi 'chwān-shang-le.

Get off. ‖Get off the grass. is expressed as Don't step on the grass. 'byé tsǎy tsǎw-'dì. ‖I want to get off at the next stop. wǒ 'shyà-yí-jàn °'shyà-chywu. or 'shyà-'chē. ‖Get off your high horse! 'byé nèm 'shén-chi-le. or byé 'chwēy-le. or byé chèw-'měy-le. or byé 'jwǎy-le. or byé jwāng-'swàn-le. ‖He got off to a flying start. tā chǐ-'téwr 'chǐ-de hěn °'kwày (or °'má-lì). or (In working) tā dùng-'shěw jyèw 'gàn-chi-lay-le. or (In running) tā sā-'twěy jyèw 'pǎw. ‖He got off with very light punishment. tā-'fá-de hěn 'chīng, 'jēn-shŕ 'pyán-yi ta-le.

Get on (mount) shàng. ‖Don't get on the train yet. shyān byé shàng-'chē-ba.

Get on (in other senses). ‖It's getting on toward twelve o'clock. 'kwày shŕ-'èr-dyǎn-le. ‖That whistling gets on my nerves. nèm chwēy-'shàwr jyàw wǒ (-'shīn-li) 'fán-de-hwang.

Get out (of) (usually an expression with chū). ‖Get out of this house! (Impolite) (gěy-wǒ) 'gwěn-chū-chywu. or (gěy-wǒ) 'chū-chywu. or (Urgent, as in case of fire) kwày 'chū-chywu. ‖We mustn't let this news get out. dzám kě-'bù-néng bǎ jèy-ge °'chwán-chū-chywu. or °'jyàw-rén 'jŕ-dàw-le. or °'shyè-lèw-le. ‖They are getting out a new book on the subject. tām yàw 'chū yì-běr-jyǎng-'jèy-ge-de-'shīn-shū. ‖He tried to say the man's name, but couldn't get the words out before he died. tā 'jyé-lì yàw 'shwō-chu 'nèy-ge-rén-de-'míng-dz-lay, kě-shr 'méy-néng 'shwō-chu-lay jyèw dwàn-le 'chì-le. ‖How did you ever get out of it? (Escape) nǐ 'dzěm-me 'táw- (or 'pǎw-)chū-lay-de? or (Avoid doing something) nǐ 'dzěm-me 'dwó-kāy-de?

Get out of the car shyà-chē. See also Get off, above.

Get (meaning) out of. ‖What did you get out of his lecture? nǐ 'tīng tā-yǎn-'jyǎng yì-'hèw °'yěw shéme-snīn-'dé. or °'dé-jaw shéme-le-ma?

Get (profit) out of. ‖What do I get out of it? ywú-'wǒ yěw shéme-°'hǎw-chù-ne? or °'yí-chù-ne? ‖How much did you get out of the deal? (Money) 'nèy-yí-shyàr nǐ °'jwàn-le 'dwō-shǎw? or °'làw-le 'dwō-shǎw? or (Advantage) 'dé-jaw shéme-'hǎw-chù-le?

Get over. ‖I got over my cold quickly. wǒ 'jèy-tsž-shāng-'fēng hǎw-de hěn 'kwày. ‖You feel badly now, but you'll get over it. mù-'chyán yěw dyǎr-nán-'shèw, 'gwò shyē-'shŕ jyèw 'hǎw-le. ‖I can never get over it (forget it). wǒ 'yǔng-ywǎn bù-néng 'wàng-de. ‖She got over it in a short while. tā 'gwò-le-hwěr jyèw °'hǎw-le. or °'bú-nèm-je-le. or °'wàng-le. or °yě jyèw 'swàn-le. ‖How did you get over that difficulty? ('nèm-nán-de-shŕ) nǐ shŕ dzěme °'bàn-de-ne? or °'lyǎw-de-ne? or 'nèm-yàng-de-'nán-gwān nǐ dzěme 'gwò-lay-de-ne?

Get to (a place) or get there, get somewhere, etc. dàw; (finish) wán. ‖I'll get there in an hour. wǒ dzày yì-'shyǎw-shŕ yǐ 'nèy 'dàw-nèr. ‖We have a lot of work left, but we'll get there eventually. háy 'shèng-shya bù-'shǎw-de-shŕ, bú-gwò 'dzǎw-wǎn °yěw 'wán-de-shŕ-hew. or °yěw ge-'wán.

Get together. ‖Let's get together at my house to-night. jyēr-'wǎn-shang dzày wǒ-'jyā-li 'jywù-hwey-jywù-hwey. ‖They never seem to get together on anything. tā-men hǎw 'shyàng °shém-me-'shŕ yě nùng-(or shwō-, or gǎw-)bu-'dàw yí-'kwàr. or (literary) °'shwěy-hwǒ bù-shyāng-'rúng.

Get up. ‖I get up at seven every morning. wǒ 'měy-tyān-'dzǎw-chen 'chī-dyǎn-jūng 'chǐ-lay. ‖Get up from that chair! 'jàn-chi-lay! ‖They're getting up a party. tām 'jèng-dzày °'ywù-bey-je (or °'shāng-lyang-je, or °'dǎ-swàn-je) chǐng (yì-)'hwéy-'kè.

GIFT. (Somewhat formal) 'lǐ-wù; or expressed with verbs such as sùng (send); gěy (give). ‖This is a gift (from someone to me). jèy-shr 'rén-jyā-°'sùng-gey-wo-de-'lǐ-wù. or °'sùng-gey-wo-de. or °'sùng-wo-de. or °'gěy-wo-de. ‖This is a gift from him (to me). jèy-shr tā-°'sùng-gey-wo-de-'lǐ-wù. (or alternates as above). ‖This is a (little) gift for you (from me). jèy-shr °'sùng-gey-ni-de (or °'gěy-ni-de, or 'sùng-ni-de) (-yì-dyǎr-'dūng-shi). or 'jèy-dyǎr-dūng-shi shr °'sùng-gey-ni-de. (°etc.) or 'jèy-shr yì-dyǎr-'shyǎw-'yì-sz (a small token). ‖Here is a gift for you (from someone else). jèr yěw gěy-'nǐ-de (etc.) -'lǐ-wù. or jèr yěw dyǎr-'dūng-shi, shr gěy-'nǐ-de (etc.). ‖We must send them some sort of gift. yí-'dìng děy 'sùng-tam °dyǎr-'lǐ-wù (or °'dyǎr-shéme, or °'dyǎr-'dūng-shi) tsáy 'hǎw. ‖Whose gift is that? (To whom) 'nèy-shr gěy-'shéy-de? or (From whom) 'nèy shr-'shéy 'gěy-de? (or sùng for gěy.) ‖Thank you for your Christmas gift. 'shyè-shye nín 'shèng-dàn-'jyé-de-'lǐ-wù. or 'shyè-shye nín-na! 'shèng-dàn-'jyé °'jyàw-nín fèy-'shīn-le. or °nín náy 'sùng dūng-shi. ‖That's a free gift. 'nèy-shr báy-'gěy-de. ‖I wouldn't have it even as a gift. báy-'gěy (or báy-'sùng) wǒ yě bú-'yàw.

(*Talent*) !tyān-tsáy; **to be gifted** tyān-'shēng-de; tyān-'fù-de (*followed by* hwèy *to express the activity*). ‖**He has a gift for drawing.** tā yěw hwà-'hwàr-de-'tyān-tsáy. *or* tā tyān-'shēng-de hwèy hwà-'hwàr. ‖**She's very gifted musically.** tā yěw 'yīn-ywè-de-'tyān-tsáy. ‖**To be able to sing like that is a gift.** 'chàng-de 'nèm hǎw 'jēn-shr °'tyān-tsáy. *or* °'tyān-'shēng-de. *or* °'tyān-'fù-de.

GIRL. nywǔ-'háy-dz *and* nywǔ- *in other combinations;* 'shyáw-jye, 'gū-nyang (*both mean especially* **young lady**). ‖**The new baby is a girl.** 'shīn-shēng-de-shyǎw-'hár shr °'nywǔ-de. *or* °'ge-'shyáw-jye. *or* °'ge-'gū-nyang. ‖**It's a girl again.** 'yèw shr ge-°'nywǔ-de. *or* 'gū-nyang. *or* °'shyáw-jye. *or* (*Literary allusion*) 'yèw nèng-'wǎ-le. ‖**Are there any pretty girls in town?** chéng-'lǐ-tew 'yěw-méy-yew 'pyàw-lyǎng-de-°'nywǔ-'háy-dz? *or* °'shyáw-jye? *or* °'gū-nyang? ‖**She's quite a girl.** (*Complimentary or insulting*) hǎw-('lǐ-hay-)de-yí-wèy-°'shyáw-jye-le. *or* °'gū-nyang-le. *or* 'nèy-wèy-shyáw-jye-ya (*or* 'nèy-wèy-'gū-nyang-nga) °'jēn-shr ('lǐ-hay). *or* °'jēn 'lyǎw-bu-dé. ‖**I just got a letter from my girl (friend).** wǒ 'gāng jyē-dàw wǒ-nywǔ-'péng-yew yì-fēng-'shìn. ‖**We pay our (hired) girl fifty dollars a month.** wǒ-mel-de-nywǔ-'yùng-rén (*or* wǒ-men-de nywǔ-'dǐ-shya-rén, *or, if older*, wǒ-men-de-lǎw-'mǎr) 'měy-ywè 'wǔ-shŕ-kwày-chyán. ‖**Jimmy certainly made a hit with the girls here.** lǎw-'jāng jyàw jèr-de-nywǔ-'háy-dz (*or* jèr-de-'nywǔ-rén) dēw 'shǐ-hwan-ta. ‖**Well, girls, it's time to go.** (*Including both married and unmarried women*) 'hèy! 'tày-tay-'shyáw-jye-men, dàw 'shŕ-hewr-le, gāy 'dzéw-le. *or* (*Unmarried women only*) 'shyáw-jye-men, gāy 'dzěw-le. *or simply* dàw-le 'shŕ-hew-le, gāy 'dzěw-le. *or* (*If not on intimate terms*) dà-'jyā gāy 'dzěw-le.

[VE (GAVE, GIVEN). 1. (*Transfer, present; general term*) gěy. ‖**This watch was given to me by my mother.** jèy-ge-'byǎw shr wǒ-'mǔ-chin-gěy-wǒ-de. ‖**Who gave you this?** jèy shr 'shéy-gěy-nǐ-de? ‖**Was this given to you by someone I know?** gěy-nǐ-'jèy-ge-de-rén wǒ 'rèn-de-ma? ‖**Give him a dollar.** 'gěy-tā yí-kwày-'chyán. ‖**I'll give you five dollars for it.** 'nèy-ge-dūng-shi wǒ gěy-nǐ 'wǔ-kwày-chyán. ‖**They gave him a very large room.** tām gěy-tā yì-jyān-'hǎw-dà-de-'wū-dz. ‖**They gave him a job.** tām 'gěy-le tā ge-'shèr dzwò. ‖**Give him a letter of recommendation.** gěy-tā yì-fēng-jyàn-'shìn.

With the thing given expressed by a verb in Chinese, gěy *is followed by the person to whom it is given or for whom it is done.* ‖**They gave him a raise.** tām gěy-tā jyā-'chyán-le. ‖**They gave him a raise of $50.** tām gěy-tā jyā-le 'wǔ-shŕ-kwày-chyán. ‖**We're planning to give him a farewell party.** wǒm shyǎng chǐng-'kè, gěy-tā jyàn-'shíng. ‖**They gave him a birthday party.** tām gěy-tā gwò-'shēngr. ‖**Give him an injection.** gěy-tā 'dǎ yì-jēn. ‖**Give him a promotion.**

gěy-tā 'shēng yì-'jí. ‖**Give him a recommendation** (*verbal*). gěy-tā shwō jywù-hǎw-'hwà. ‖**Give him some help.** (gěy-tā) bāng-bang 'máng.

(*Hand over; to someone present*) 'dì-gěy; (*to someone absent*) 'jyāw-gěy. ‖**Please give me the letter.** lǎw-'jyà bǎ-'shìn 'dì-gěy wǒ. (*But, when referring to something that was to be brought, Chinese usually asks, more politely,* **Did you bring it with you?** nèy-fēng-'shìn nǐ 'dày-láy-le-ma?) ‖**Give this letter to him and be sure to get a receipt.** bǎ jèy-fēng-'shìn jyàw-gěy tā; yí-'dìng yàw ge-shēw-'tyáwr.

Give as a present sùng, gěy, 'sùng-gěy. (*See also* **GIFT.**) ‖**This watch was given me by my friends.** jèy-ge-'byǎw shr wǒ-'péng-yew-°'sùng-wǒ-de. *or* °'gěy-wǒ-de. *or* °'sùng-gěy-wǒ-de. ‖**What did he give you for your birthday?** nǐ-'shēng-r tā 'sùng-nǐ (*or* 'gěy-nǐ, *or* 'sùng-gěy nǐ) shém-me-le?

Give a name chǐ. ‖**The baby hasn't been given a name yet.** shyǎw-'hár háy 'méy(-gěy)-chǐ 'míng-dz-ne. ‖**They gave him a nickname.** tām gěy-tā 'chǐ-le ge wày-'hàwr. (*Constructed as in second paragraph, above.*)

Give (a disease) to 'chwán-gěy. ‖**I don't want t give you my cold.** wǒ shāng-'fēng-le, kě-byé 'chwán-gěy nǐ.

2. (*Cause, allow*). *Usually* jyàw; (*of trouble*) jāw, tyān; *occasionally expressed indirectly.* ‖**Too much noise gives me a headache** *is expressed as* **Too much noise causes my head to ache.** 'chǎw-de tày 'lì-hay-le jyàw wǒ 'téw-téng. ‖**The heat gave me a headache.** 'rè-de (jyàw) wǒ 'téw-téng. ‖**Tell him the story; it ought to give him a laugh.** bǎ nèy-ge-'shyǎw-hwàr 'gàw-su-ta; yí-'dìng hwèy jyàw-tā 'dà-shyàw-de. ‖**It's guaranteed to give you satisfaction.** 'jwěn-bǎw jyàw-nǐ mǎn-'yì. ‖**They give you your money's worth at this restaurant.** *is expressed as* **What they give you makes you feel it's worth it.** 'jèy-ge-gwǎn-dz-gěy-de-'dūng-shi jyàw-nǐ 'jywé-je °'gèw-'běr. *or* °'méy-'báy-hwā 'chyán. *or as* **The service they give you ...** 'jèy-ge-gwǎn-dz-'tsž-hew-de jyàw-nǐ ... ‖**Don't give the child too much freedom, or you'll spoil her.** 'byé jyàw shyǎw-'hár tày swéy-'byàn-le, hwèy gwàn-'hwày-le. *or* shyǎw-'hár yàw 'gwàn-je-dyar, 'bù-rán hwèy gwàn-'hwày-le-de. ‖**Give him a taste of it and he'll demand it all the time.** jyàw-tā yì-'cháng-jaw tyán-'téwr, tā jyèw 'yàw-chi-lay méy-'wán-le. ‖**Give him an inch and he'll take a mile.** *or* **Give him a finger and he'll take the whole hand.** (*The common Chinese expression is* **If he gets an inch he'll advance a foot.**) tā dé-'tswèn jìn-'chř. ‖**He gave us no end of trouble.** tā gěy-wǒm °'jǎw-le (*or* °'tyān-le) bù-'shǎw-de-'má-fan.

3. *Give when followed by a noun in English is in many cases expressed in Chinese by a verb which has the meaning* **give** *only in certain contexts, or which is equivalent to the entire English phrase. When* gěy *is included in these cases, it can usually be translated by* **to** *or* **for.** *Some indirect expressions are a*

(*Contribute to charity*) shě, 'shŕ-shě. ‖They gave many things to the poor. tām ('shŕ-)shě-le hěn-dwō-'dūng-shi gěy 'chyúng-rén. ‖They gave a good deal of money to the (*Buddhist*) monastery. tām gěy-'myàw-li (shŕ-)shě-le bù-'shǎw-de-'chyán.

(*Be generous, charitable*) 'jywān-jù. ‖Give until it hurts. chǐng 'jyē-li 'jywān-jù. ‖Please give to a good cause. jèy-shr shíng-'hǎw-de-shŕ, chǐng 'dà-jyā 'jywān-jù.

Give permission jwěn. ‖He gave me permission to go. tā jwěn-wǒ 'dzěw-de. ‖I was given permission to stay until midnight. wǒ chǐng-'jwěn-le, kě-yǐ 'dāy-dàw bàn-'yè.

Give one's time 'ywún-chu 'gūng-fu. ‖We've come to ask you to give a part of your time to a good cause. yěw yí-jyàn-shíng-'hǎw-de-shŕ; wǒm láy chyéw-nín 'ywún-chu dyǎr-'gūng-fu-lay 'bāng-bang 'máng.

Give help, give a hand (gěy . . .) 'bāng-bang 'máng, bāng. ‖Give me a hand, will you? (gěy-wǒ) 'bāng-bang 'máng, shíng-ma? *or* bāng-wǒ yí-shyàr, 'shíng-ma? *or* 'bāng-wǒ yì-bǎ-'shěwr, shíng-ma?

Give a light. ‖Will you give me a light? (*Do you have a match?*) yěw yáng-'hwǒ-ma? *or* (*May I borrow a match?*) jyè gēn-yáng-'hwǒr shíng-ma? *or* (*May I use a bit of fire?*) jyè dyǎr-'hwǒr shŕ-shr shíng-ma?

Give information, *etc.*, (*tell, say*). ‖They gave me the wrong information. tā-men-'gàw-sung-wǒ-de bú-'dwèy. *or* tā-men 'gàw-sung wǒ, gàw-su-'tswò-le. ‖He gave me the wrong time. tā-'gàw-su-wǒ-de-nèy-ge-'shŕ-hew bú-'dwèy. *or* tā-'shwō-de-nèy-ge-'shŕ-hew bú-'dwèy. ‖Sorry, I gave you the wrong directions. 'dwèy-bu-chǐ, wǒ °-'shwō-de bú-'dwèy. *or* °shwō-'tswò-le. *or* (*The wrong direction of the compass*) °-shwō-de-'fāng-shyang bú-'dwèy. *or* °-shwō-de-'fāng-shyang 'tswò-le. ‖Did he give a reason? tā shwō-le ge-'lǐ-yěw méy-yew? *or* *is expressed as* Did he explain? tā 'jyě-shr-le-ma? *But* ‖Can you give me the time, please? *is expressed as* What time is it, please? lǎw-'jyà (*or* jyè-'gwāng). °'shéme-shf-hew-le? *or* °jǐ-'dyǎn-le?

Give a speech jyǎng, yǎn-'jyǎng. ‖Who's giving the main speech? shŕ-'shéy jǔ-'jyǎng-ne?

Give a scream hǎn (*or* jyàw) yì-'shēng. ‖She gave a loud scream. tā 'dà-hǎn-le (*or* 'dà-jyàw-le) yì-'shēng.

Give heat 'nwǎn-hwo (*be warm*). ‖The fireplace gives a lot of heat. 'jèy-ge-lú-dz hěn 'nwǎn-he.

Give one an idea. ‖What gave you that idea? *is expressed as* How did you think of that? nǐ dzěm 'shyǎng-dàw-de 'nèm-ge-'fár? *or as* Where does that kind of talk come from? 'nǎr-láy-de-'nèm-yàng-de-hwà? *or as* It wasn't so! 'méy nèm-hwéy-'shèr! ‖What you just said gives me an idea. nǐ 'nèm-yì-'shwō jyàw-wǒ 'shyǎng-chū ge-'fár-lay.

Give *mileage*. ‖This gas will give you 15 miles to the gallon. *is expressed as* If you use this gas, you can go 15 miles on a gallon. yùng 'jèy-jǔng-chì-'yéw yì-'jyā-lwēn kě-yǐ dzěw shŕ-'wǔ-lǐ.

Give service. ‖This clock has given good service. (*Has stood use*) 'jèy-ge-jūng hěn jīn-'yùng. *or* (*Has been used many years*) 'jèy-ge-jūng yùng-le 'hǎw-shyē-nyán-le. ‖He has given the best years of his life to that job. tā-'bàn-bèy-dz-de-'jīng-lì 'dēw yùng-dzày 'nèy-jyàn-'shŕ-shang-le. ‖My old coat still gives me good service. wǒ-nèy-jyàn-'jyèw-dà-yī háy néng 'chwān-ne.

Give a performance (shàng-)'yǎn; (*go on stage*) dēng-'táy. ‖The first performance will be given Tuesday. tā-men shǐng-chī-'èr dì-'yí-tsž °shàng-'yǎn. *or* °dēng-'táy.

Give orders gwǎn-'rén, 'jŕ-shŕ 'rén (*both mean* order people around); shyà 'mìng-ling. ‖He likes to give orders, but doesn't enjoy following them. (*Following orders that others give*) tā ày gwǎn-rén (*or* 'jŕ-shŕ 'rén), bú-ày 'shèw-rén °'gwǎn (*or* °'jŕ-shŕ). *or* (*Following orders that he himself gives*) tā ày shyà 'mìng-ling, kě-shr 'dž-jǐ bù-kěn jàw-'bàn.

Other expressions in English. ‖Give me the good old days! 'háy-shr 'nèy-shŕ-hew, 'jēn yěw 'yì-sz. ‖I don't like cigarettes; give me a pipe any time! wǒ 'bù-shǐ-hwān yān-'jyǎwr; 'háy-shr yān-'děw yěw 'wèy-daw. ‖I'd give a dollar to see her face when she sees him. tā-yì-'chěw-jyan-tā-de-nèy-ge-'shén-chì néng jyàw-wǒ kàn-jyan tsáy 'hǎw-ne. ‖I don't give a damn. wǒ tsáy bú-'dzày-hu-ne.

4. (*Yield*). ‖Be careful; the step might give under your weight. 'lyéw dyǎr-'shén; nèy-ge-'tī-dz yě-shywǔ jīn-bú-'jù nǐ. ‖The elastic has a lot of give. jèy-ge-'sūng-jǐn-'dàr 'jīn-de-jù 'chēn.

5. *Combinations of* give *and a preposition, and a few other fixed phrases.*

Give away. ‖That old coat was given away long ago. (*See* 1 *above.*) nèy-ge-'jyèw-dà-yī 'dzǎw gěy-le (*or* sùng-gěy-le) 'rén-le. ‖Who gave away the bride? *is expressed as* Who acted as head of the bride's family? jyē-'hwēn-de-shŕ-hew dzwò-shīn-'nyáng-dz-de-jyā-'jǎng-de shŕ-'shéy? ‖Don't give me away. *or* Don't give away my secret. *is expressed as* Don't let water out of the bottom. 'byé gěy-wǒ 'shyè-le 'dǐ. *or as* Don't let out this secret for me. (*Speak it out*) 'jèy-dyǎr(-'mì-mi) byé gěy-wǒ °'shwō-chu-chywu. *or* (*Shout it out*) °'rāng-rang-chu-chywu. *or* (*Shake it out*) °'dēw-lew-chu-chywu. *or* (*Pierce a hole*) °'tǔng-le. *or* °'tǔng-'chwān-le.

Give back 'hwán(-gěy). ‖Please give me back my pen. láw-'jyà bǎ-'bǐ hwán-wǒ. (*But this is not too polite; a preferable usage is* Are you through using that pen? nèy-'bǐ yùng-'wán-le-ma?) ‖I'll give it back to you in an hour. wǒ 'yì-dyǎn-jūng yǐ-'nèy jyèw 'hwán-nǐ. ‖When he gave it back to me, it was in even better shape than when I lent it to him. 'jèy-ge tā 'hwán-lay de-shŕ-hew, bǐ 'jyè-chywu de-shŕ-hew háy 'jěng-chǐ.

Give birth to shēng, dé. ‖She gave birth to a baby boy. tā shēng-le ge-'nán-háy-dz. *or* tā dé-le ge-'nán-háy-dz. (*Also figuratively*) ‖The results of the experiment gave birth to a new idea. tsúng 'shȑ-yàn-de-'jyē-gwǒ °shēng-chu yì-jǔng-'shīn-jyàn-jyě-lay. or °'dé-dàw yì-jǔng-'shīn-fāng-fa. ('jyàn-jyě understanding, and 'fāng-fa method, may be interchanged here.)

Give in (admit failure) rèn-'shū. ‖After a long argument I finally gave in. 'byàn-lwèn-le bàn-'tyān wǒ 'jyē-gwǒ rèn-'shū-le.

Give off. Expressed indirectly or by chū, 'fā-chu-lay, or yěw. ‖This flower gives off a strange odor. is expressed as The odor of this flower is strange. jèy-jǔng-'hwār-de-'wèr hěn 'tè-byé. or 'jéy-jǔng-'hwār °yěw yì-jǔng-gwày-'wèr. or °'chū yì-jǔng-gwày-'wèr. or °'fā-chu yì-jǔng gwày-'wèr-lay.

Give out (issue) fā; (distribute) sàn. ‖Who gave out the tickets? 'shéy gwǎn fā mén-'pyàw láy-je? or 'shéy fā-de mén-'pyàw? or 'shéy sàn-de mén-'pyàw? ‖News of the battle casualties won't be given out for several days. 'gwǎn-bīng-'sž-shāng-'míng-tsè děy 'gwò jǐ-tyān tsáy 'fā-byǎw-ne.

Give out (be all gone) méy-'yěw-le. ‖My supply of ink is giving out. wǒ-de-mwò-'shwér kwày méy-'yěw-le.

Give out (fail in operation) bù-'chéng-le, bù-'shíng-le, bù-jūng-'yùng-le. ‖His heart gave out. tā-de-'shīn-dzàng °bù-'chéng-le. or °'bù-jūng-'yùng-le. or °'bù-'shíng-le.

Give-and-take. ‖It was a matter of give-and-take. (A fair exchange). nèy shȑ 'gūng-píng-jyāw-'yì. or (No one got the worst of it) 'shéy yě méy-chȓ-'kwēy. ‖Marriage is a matter of give-and-take. 'fū-fù-jȑ-'jyān děy néng 'rúng-rěn.

Give to understand. ‖I was given to understand that I'd get a raise in a month. is expressed as From what I heard there was the understanding that I'd get a raise in a month. wǒ-'tīng-lay-de-'hwàr-li yěw 'yí-ge-ywè yǐ-'nèy yàw gěy-wǒ jyā-'chyán nèm-yì-'shwō.

Give up (stop trying). ‖I tried hard, but I had to give up. wǒ 'dzěme nùng yě bù-'chéng, 'jȑ-hǎw fàng-'shěw-le. ‖Finally we gave up trying. (Admitted failure) 'jyē-gwǒ wǒm °'rèn-le. or °rèn-'shū-le. or (Admitted that the loss is irreparable) °'rèn dǎw-'méy-le. or (Knew there was no way) °'jȑ-daw méy-'fár-le. or (Let go) °jyèw ràng-'shěw-le. or (Stopped trying) °jyèw bú-dzày 'nùng-le.

Give up something 'jyāw-chū-lay. ‖They had to give up the stolen goods. tām méy-'fár, jȑ-hǎw bǎ-dzāng 'jyāw-chu-lay. But ‖Our maid gave up her job. wǒ-men-de-nywǔ-'gūng-rén °'dzěw-le. or °'bú-'gàn-le. or °'tsź-'shȑ-le. or °chīng cháng-'jyà-le.

Give up a person. ‖After their quarrel she gave him up. (Brushed him off) tā-men 'chǎw-le yí-jèn-'dzwěy, yǐ-hèw, nèy-ge-'nywǔ-rén jyèw °'shwā-le ta-le. or (Flung him away) °'shwāi-le ta-le. or °bǎ-ta 'shwā-le. or °bǎ-ta 'shwǎy-le. ‖He was so ill that the

doctor gave him up (or gave up hope for him). tā-bìng-de 'jen lì-hay, 'dày-ɪu dēw shwō °'méy-făr 'jȑ-le. or °'méy-yěw 'jyèw-le. (Both mean, He said there was no cure.) ‖When he was half starved, he gave himself up. (To the police) tā-'è-de méy-'făr-le jyèw °dž-'shěw-le. or (To the enemy) °'téw-'shyáng-le. or (To fate) °'jȑ-hǎw děng-'sž-le.

Give way (get out of the way; retreat) wàng-hèw 'twèy; (step back) 'ràng-kay. ‖The crowd gave way. nèy-chywún-'rén °wàng-hèw 'twèy-le. or °'ràng-kay-le.

Give way (break down, fail). ‖The bridge gave way. (Couldn't stand the strain) chyáw jīn-bu-'jù-le. or (Broke down) chyáw 'hwày-le. or (Collapsed) chyáw 'tā-le. or (Broke into two or more parts) chyáw 'shé-le. or chyáw 'dwàn-le. or (Fell on one side) chyáw 'dǎw-le. or (Leaned to one side without falling) chyáw 'wāy-le.

GIVEN. See GIVE except for the following cases, in which give is not used.

(Certain) yí-'dìng-de, dìng-'hǎw-le-de, shwō-'hǎw-le-de. ‖I have to finish this in a given time. wǒ děy dzày yí-'dìng-de (or dìng-'hǎw-le-de, or shwō-'hǎw-le-de)-'shŕ-jyān-lǐ bǎ 'jèy-ge dzwò-'wán-le.

(Supposing; under) dzày . . . jȑ-'shyà. ‖Given such a situation, what else could I do? dzày 'jèy-yàngr-'chíng-shìng-jȑ-'shyà, wǒ háy néng yěw 'byé-de-'bàn-fǎ-ma?

(In the habit of) 'cháng-cháng . . . . ‖He's given to making rash statements. tā shwō-'hwà 'cháng-cháng shwō-de tày °'lǔ-mǎng. or °'mǎng-jwàng. or tā shwō-'hwà cháng-cháng °bù-lyéw-'shén. or °bù-'shyǎw-shīn. or tā cháng-cháng 'bù-gwǎn-'sān-chī-èr-shr-'yī-de jyèw 'shwō-chu-lay-le.

Given name 'míng-dz. ‖What is his given name? tā-'míng-dz jyàw 'shém-me?

GLAD. gāw-'shìng; but when glad in English is primarily for politeness Chinese usually has some other polite expression. ‖I'm glad to hear you're better. wǒ 'tīng-shwo nǐ jyàn 'hǎw-le hěn gāw-'shìng. ‖I sensed that they were not glad to see you. wǒ jywé-je tām jyàn-nǐ de-'shŕ-hew 'bú-dà gāw-'shìng. ‖I'm glad to see you again. 'shìng-'hwèy, shìng-'hwèy! ‖Gee, am I glad to see you! 'āy-'ya! nǐ-'láy-de 'jēn 'hǎw. or expressed as You're my rescuing star. 'āy-'ya! nǐ shȑ wǒ-de-'jyèw-shīng. ‖I'm very glad to meet you. 'jyěw-yǎng, jyěw-'yǎng. ‖I'm glad you warned me. 'dwō-shyè nǐ 'jȑ-jyàw. or 'dwō-shyè nǐ 'gàw-su wǒ.

GLASS. (A substance) 'bwō-li. ‖I cut my hand on a piece of glass. wǒ jyàw 'bwō-li bǎ-'shěw 'lá-le. or wǒ jyàw 'bwō-li lá-le 'shěw-le. ‖I cut myself on a piece of glass. (In answer to How did you cut yourself? wǒ dž-'gěr ná 'bwō-li 'lá-de. or (In answer to What happened?) wǒ dž-'gěr bù-'shyǎw-shīn, jyàw 'bwō-li 'lá-le. ‖I cut my hand on a piece of broken glass. wǒ jyàw bwō-li-'chá-dz lá-le 'shěw-ie. ‖Be careful of the pieces of broken glass on the floor. lyéw-'shén, 'dì-shang yěw °bwō-li-'chá-dz. or °'swèy-bwō-li (-'chá-dz). ‖The library keeps his manuscripts under glass. (In a glass case). tú-shū-'gwǎn bǎ tā-de-shew-'gǎwr 'bǎw-tswén dzày bwō-li-'gwèy-li. or (Covered with glass) °yùng 'bwō-li(-jàwr) jàw-je. ‖These roses were grown under glass. jèy-shyē-'méy-gwèy-hwār dēw-shr yùng-bwō-li-'jàw-je-jǎng-de. ‖That's made of glass. nèy-shr 'bwō-li-dzwò-de. ‖I bought a glass vase. wǒ mǎy-le yí-ge-bwō-li-'hwā-pyéngr. or °yí-ge-'bwō-li (-dzwò)-de-'hwā-pyéngr.

Drinking glass (the object) 'bwō-li-'bēy; (a measure) bēy. ‖I knocked a glass off the table. wǒ bǎ yí-ge-'bwō-li-'bēy tsúng 'jwōr-shang 'pèng-shyà-chywu-le. ‖May I have a glass of water? láw-'jyà gěy-wǒ yì-bēy-'shwěy.

Looking glass 'jìng-dz.

Eyeglasses yǎn-'jyèngr or yǎn-'jìng-dz. ‖I wear glasses only for reading. wǒ-kàn-'dzèr-de-shf-hew (or wǒ-kàn-'shū-de-shf-hew) tsáy dày yǎn-'jyèngr (or yǎn-'jìng-dz).

Field glasses 'wàng-ywǎn-'jìng. ‖I want to buy a pair of field glasses. wǒ yàw mǎy yí-jyà-'wàng-ywǎn-'jìng.

GLORIOUS. (Illustrious) 'gwāng-rúng(-de). ‖Our country has a glorious history. wǒ-men-de-'gwó-jyā yěw yí-ge-hěn-'gwāng-rúng-de-'lì-shǐ.

(Beautiful) 'měy-lì; (colorful) 'tsǎn-làn; (of weather) hǎw. ‖The leaves have glorious colors at this time of year. 'nyán-nyan jèy-shf-hew shù-'yè-dz-de-'yán-shar jēn °'měy-lì. or °'tsǎn-làn. ‖This is certainly a glorious day. 'jīn-tyan 'tyān-chi jēn 'hǎw.

GO (WENT, GONE). 1. Denoting simple motion, without indication of direction, destination, or purpose, dzěw (means walk when used with other verbs); dùng-je, dùng-'shēn (to get a move on); lí-kay (leave a place). ‖Let's go. dzám 'dzěw-ba. or dēw 'dzěw-wa. ‖It's time to go. gāy 'dzěw-le. or gāy 'dzěw-je-le. or gāy 'dùng-je-le. or dàw-le gāy-'dzěw-de-shf-hew-le. or dzám gāy dùng-'shēn-le. or dzám gāy 'lí-kay jèr-le. ‖When did he go? tā 'shém-shf-hew °'dzěw-de? or °'dùng-de shēn? or °'lí-kay-de? ‖He's gone. tā 'yǐ-jīng 'dzěw-le. ‖There goes the man we've been talking about. nàr-'dzěw-je-de-'nèy-ge-'rén 'jyèw-shr dzám gāng-tsáy-'shwō-de-nèy-ge. or (There he is) 'jyèw-shr 'nèy-ge-rén! ‖You go first. or Go ahead. nǐ 'shyān dzěw yí-bù. (See also Go ahead, below.) ‖He went on ahead. tā 'shyān dzěw-de.

2. Indicating direction, destination, or purpose of going chywù. (Compare **COME**. When direction or destination is expressed, chywù is usually at the end of the sentence; when purpose is expressed, the thing to be done usually follows chywù.) ‖Is he going (to some place)? 'tā chywù-ma? or 'tā chywù-bu-chywù? ‖Where are you going? shàng (or dàw)-'nǎr

chywù? ‖We're going the same way. dzám dàw 'yí-ge-dì-fang-chywu. or (With no destination in mind) dzám dzěw 'yì-tyáw-lù. ‖He went that way. tā wàng 'nèy-byar-chywu-le. ‖The road goes due south. jèy-tyáw-'lù wàng 'jèng-nán chywù. ‖He won't go. (Somewhere) tā 'bù-kěn 'chywù. or (He won't leave) tā 'bù-kěn 'dzěw. ‖Let's go for a walk. dzám chywù °'lyèw-da-lyèw-da. or °'dzěw-yi-dzěw. ‖He went swimming. tā fù-'shwěy-chywu-le. or (if already back) tā fù-'shwěy-chywu-lay-je. or tā chywù fù-'shwěy láy-je. ‖Go and see it. chywù 'kàn-kan chywù. ‖Go (ahead) and ask her. chywù 'wèn-wen tā-chywu. or (Defiantly) nǐ 'wèn-tā-chywu-ba. ‖Now see what you've gone and done! 'kàn nǐ-chywù-'gàn-de jè-jyàw 'shéme-shèr! ‖Since her husband died, she hasn't gone out much. tā-'jàng-fu sž-le, tā jyèw 'méy-dà 'chū-chywu 'wár-gwo. ‖I'm going out to dinner. wǒ 'chū-chywu chǐ-'fàn. ‖He went from Peiping to Nanking. tā tsúng 'běy-píng dàw 'nán-jīng chywù-de. (chywù is used also after verbs indicating a type of motion, to show that the motion is in a direction away from the speaker.)

3. When a word indicating a more specific variety of motion can be substituted for go, Chinese uses the more specific word. With màn slow and kwày fast Chinese often uses no word for the motion itself. ‖Go slow! (Walking or in general) 'màn dzěw! or (Running) 'màn-dyar pǎw! or (Driving) 'màn-dyar kāy! or (General) 'màn-dyar! or byé nèm-'kwày! ‖Ready! Get set! Go! jàn-'hǎw! ywù-'bèy! 'pǎw! ‖The time goes very fast. 'shf-jyan 'gwò-de jēn 'kwày. or 'ř-dz (or other terms for periods of time) 'gwò-de jēn 'kwày. ‖My watch goes slow. wǒ-de-'byǎw (dzěw-de) 'màn. ‖The train is certainly going fast. jèy-ge-'hwǒ-chē 'kāy-de (or 'dzěw-de) jēn kwày.

4. (Be done away with, finished, spent, sold). Chinese uses the more specific terms. ‖This rule must go (be abolished). 'jèy-ge-gwēy-jywù děy chywǔ-'shyāw. ‖Everything they had went (was burned up) in the fire. nèy-tsž jáw-'hwǒ °tām-swǒ-'yěw-de 'shéme dēw shāw-'wán-le (or shāw-'gwāng-le). or °bǎ-tām shāw-le ge-'jīng-gwāng (or ge-shéme dēw méy-'shèng). ‖All his money would be gone (spent) by this time. dàw 'jèy-shf-hew 'dà-gài tā-de-'chyán °gāy hwā-'gwāng-le. or °gāy hwā-'wán-le. or °gāy hwā-'jìng-le. or °hwā-de 'shèng-bu-shya shéme-le. ‖All her money goes for clothes. tā-chyán 'dēw hwā-dzày 'yī-fu-shang-le. ‖The brandy is all gone (used up). báy-lán-'dì °dēw yùng-'wán-le. or °'méy-le. or °yì-'dyǎr méy-'shèng. or yì-'dī yě méy-'yěw-le. ‖The pain is gone. shyàn-dzày bù-'téng-le. or 'téng yí-jīng 'jř-le. ‖They're all gone. (Sold) 'chywán mày-'wán-le. or (Bought) 'chywán gěy-rén (or jyàw-rén) °'mǎy-chywu-le. or °mǎy-'gwāng-le. ‖They're going at a dollar apiece. (Here sold is not expressed.) yí-kwày-'chyán °yì-tyáwr. or °yí-ge. or °yī plus another appropriate measure.

5. (*Be, become*). *Followed by an adjective, Chinese expresses only the adjective, or uses* 'byàn-chéng *become with a noun followed by* -de, *or uses an indirect expression.* ‖**Let him go hungry.** jyàw-tā 'è-je-ba. ‖**He went crazy.** tā 'fēng-le. ‖**I'll go crazy if this keeps up.** yàw 'lǎw jè-yàngr wǒ 'jēn yàw 'fēng-le. ‖**He went blind.** tā 'shyā-le. ‖**Everything has gone wrong.** 'shém-me-shr̀ dēw °'tswò-le *or* °mǎn-'nǐng. ‖**Everything goes wrong when I leave.** wǒ 'yì-dzěw jyèw 'shéme-shr̀ 'dēw chū °-'tswòr. *or* °'léw-dz. ‖**Things were going pretty well until he came along.** 'ywán-lay shèr hěn 'shwèn-lì; tā yì-láy jyèw chū 'léw-dz-le. ‖**This meat has gone bad.** rèw 'hwày-le. ‖**The well has gone dry.** jǐng 'gān-le. ‖**I hope the incident will go unnoticed.** 'shī-wàng 'méy-rén 'lǐ-hwèy tsáy ' 'hǎw. ‖**They're still going strong.** tām háy-shr 'jyèr-hěn-'dzú-de.

6. (*Be, but not become, referring to the character or details of something*) shr̀ *or indirect expressions.* ‖**So the story goes.** (*As told*) jyèw-shr 'jèm-yì-hwéy-shèr. *or* (*So people say*) 'rén-jyā nèm 'shwō.' ‖**The story goes like this.** shr̀ 'jèm-yì-hwéy-shèr. *or* (*if fiction*) nèy-ge-'shyàw-hwàr shr̀ 'dzèm-shwō-de. ‖**The building goes like this.** (*Demonstrating shape with hands*) 'léw shr̀ 'jèy-yàngr-de. ‖**How does that tune go?** nèy-ge-'dyàwr dzěme 'chàng? *or* nèy-ge shr̀ ' dzěme-ge-'dyàwr? ‖**As writers go these days, he's not exceptional.** 'jèy-nyán-téwr mày-'wén-jang-de 'dēw (shr̀) nèy-yàngr; (tā yě bú-shr lì-'wày).

7. (*Be placed, fit in*). *Chinese uses the specific terms.* ‖**That chair goes in the corner.** 'nèy-bǎ-'yǐ-dz fàng-dzay (gē-dzay, bǎy-dzay) nèy-ge-jī-'jyǎwr-nar. ‖**Will that umbrella go in your suitcase?** 'nèy-bǎ-sǎn nǐ-de-'shyāng-dz-lǐ °jāw-de-'shyà-ma? *or* °'fàng-de-'kāy-ma? ‖**Is that umbrella to go in your suitcase?** 'nèy-bǎ-sǎn shr̀-bu-shr fàng-nǐ-'shyāng-dz-lǐ-de?

8. *Going to* ... *usually* yàw .... ‖**The roof is going to fall in one of these days.** fáng-'dǐng-dz 'dzǎw-wǎn (yěw yì-tyān) yàw 'tā-shya-lay. ‖**I'm going to go right away.** wǒ 'jyèw yàw 'dzěw. *or* wǒ 'jè-jyèw 'dzěw.

9. *Combinations in which the idea of motion is not included; for the same combinations including motion, see above or under the second word of the combinations.*

Go ahead. (*Polite*) *meaning* **You first, please** (nín) 'chǐng; *meaning* **you may** do it shíng *or* hǎw *or* 'kě-yǐ *or* 'jyèw nèm-je-ba. ‖**Go ahead** (*and eat*). 'chr̄-ba. ‖**Go ahead** (*and write*). 'shyě-ba. ‖**Go ahead** (*and talk*). 'shwō-ba. ‖**I'll go ahead then.** (*And do as we agreed*) 'nèm-je wǒ 'jyèw nèm 'bàn-le. *or* (*And eat*) 'nèm-je wǒ 'jyèw 'chr̄-le.

Go around (*be enough for all*). ‖**There's barely enough to go around once.** 'gāng gèw jwàn 'yì-dzāwr-de. ‖**There isn't enough to go around.** 'bú-gèw 'fēn-de.

Go at (*do*) dzwò. ‖**He went at the job with a lot of enthusiasm.** tā dzwò 'nèy-jyàn-shr̀ dzwò-de 'hěn chī-'jyèr.

Go back on shr̄-'shìn, fān-'hwěy, 'shwō(-le) bú-'swàn. (*All these mean* **to fail to keep faith** *and may be preceded by a verb or by* gēn *plus a personal noun.*) ‖**Don't go back on your word.** byé shr̄-'shìn. *or* byé fān-'hwěy. *or* byé 'shwō-le bú-'swàn. ‖**He went back on me.** tā gēn-wǒ °shr̄-'shìn-le. *or* °'fān-'hwěy-le. *or* °'shwō-le bú-'swàn-le. ‖**I don't go back on my friends.** wǒ gēn 'péng-yew °bù-shr̄-'shìn. *or* °'shwō-shéme 'swàn-shéme. *or* °'méy-yěw fān-'hwěy-de-shŕ-hew. ‖**He won't go back on his promise.** tā 'dā-ying-le jyèw 'bú-hwèy °shr̄-'shìn-de. *or* °fān-'hwěy-de. *or* °'shwō-le-bú-'swàn-de.

Go bail for ... bǎ ... 'bǎw-chū-lay. ‖**I offered to go bail for him.** wǒ 'dz̀-jǐ shwō-de, wǒ yàw bǎ-tā 'bǎw-chū-lay. ‖**Will you go my bail if I get caught?** yàw shr wǒ jyàw-rén 'dǎy-jaw, nǐ kěn bǎ-wǒ 'bǎw-chū-lay-ma?

Go begging (*not be wanted*). ‖**The hats went begging.** 'nèy-shyē-'màw-dz °'méy-rén 'yàw. *or* °'shéy dēw bú-'yàw.

Go by (*act according to*) àn-je ... 'bàn, jàw-je ... 'bàn; (*use*) yǔng. ‖**Those are the rules we go by.** wǒm 'jyèw àn-je (*or* jàw-je) 'nèy-shyē-'gwēy-dzé láy 'bàn. ‖**He goes by a false name.** tā yùng yí-ge-'jyǎ-míng-dz.

Go down. (*Be defeated*) dǎ-'bày(-le); (*be passed on*) 'lyéw-chwán(-de). ‖**Their best troops went down before ours.** 'jyèw-shr tām-'dzwèy-hǎw-de-jyw̄ïn-'dwèy 'yě jyàw-wǒm dǎ-'bày-le. ‖**That speech will go down in history.** nèy-ge-'yǎn-jyǎng yí-'dìng hwèy dzày lì-'shr̄-shang 'lyéw-chwán-de.

Go far. ‖**A dollar doesn't go very far nowadays.** 'jèy-nyán-téwr 'yí-kwày-chyán 'mǎy-bu-chu shéme-lay. ‖**A man like that should go far in politics.** shyàng-nèm-ge-rén dzwò-chǐ 'gwār-lay yīng-gāy 'chyán-chéng-wú-'lyàng.

Go for. ‖**The dog went for me.** nèy-jr̄-'gěw °chùng-je-wǒ jyèw 'pū-lay-le. *or* °yàw 'yǎw-wǒ. ‖**This goes for only that much.** 'jèy-ge 'jř néng mày 'nèm-dwō-'chyán. ‖**I go for Chinese food.** wǒ hěn 'ày chr̄ 'jūng-gwo-fàn. ‖**All his efforts went for nothing.** tā 'báy gàn-le.

Go fifty-fifty. ‖**I'll go fifty-fifty with you on the candy** (*dividing it, not paying for it*). jèy-ge-'táng dzám °'dwèy-fēn. *or* °'píng-fēn. *or* °'dwèy-'bàr fēn. *or* °'nǐ yí-bàr, 'wǒ yí-bàr.

Go in with (*do together*). ‖**Would you like to go in with me on this proposition?** jèy-jyàn-shr̀ nǐ 'ywàn-yi °gēn wǒ 'hé-bàn-ma? *or* °'jyā-rù-ma?

Go in for (*like*). ‖**I don't go in for that sort of thing.** 'nèy-jǔng-shr̀ wǒ bù-('shǐ-hwān) 'gàn. ‖**Do you go in for sports?** nǐ 'shǐ-hwān (*or* nǐ ày) 'ywùn-dung-ma? ‖**He goes in for loud ties.** tā ày 'hwā-hwa-líng-'dày.

Go into. (*Enter an occupation or profession*). ‖**He's planning to go into medicine after the war.** tā 'dǎ-wàn jàn-'hèw shíng-'yī. ‖**He's planning to go into the**

ministry after the war. tā 'dǎ-swàn jàn-'hèw chwán-'dàw. ‖He's planning to go into business after the war. tā 'dǎ-swàn jàn-'hèw dzwò 'mǎy-may. ‖Let's not go into (talk about) that subject now. shyàn-dzày dzám 'shyàn byé shwō (or tán, or tǎw-lwˀ a) 'nèy-ge.

Go off. ‖The rifle went off by accident. chyāng dzěw-'hwǒ-le. ‖Her tea parties go off very smoothly. tā-chǐng-de-'chá-hwèy 'dēw hěn 'shwèn-li. ‖He went off his head. tā fā-'fēng-le. or tā fā-'kwáng-le. ‖He went off on a tangent. tā hú-'nàw-chi-lay-le.

Go on. (Continue) ... shyà-chywu; (start) ... chǐ-lay; (exclamation) 'dé-le-ba! ‖He went right on talking. tā 'jyē-je 'shwō-shya-chywu-le. ‖I can't go on like this. wǒ 'dzèm shyà-chywu (or 'hwó-shyà-chywu, or 'twō-shyà-chywu), kě-bù-'shíng. ‖He went on a rampage. tā shyā-'nàw-chi-lay-le. ‖He went on all fours. tā 'gwèy-je 'pá-chi-lay-le. ‖Go on! You can't fool anyone. 'dé-le-ba! nǐ 'shéy yě ywān-bu-'lyǎw. But ‖What's going on here? shéme-'shr̀? or 'dzěme-la?

Going on (approaching an age) kwày. ‖He's going on fifty. tā kwày wǔ-'shf-le.

Go someone one better. ‖That's a good story, but I can go you one better. 'nǐ-shwō-de bú-'hwày, 'bú-gwò 'wǒ yěw ge-'háy-hǎw-de. ‖I'll go you one better. wǒ dzày 'dwō-lay-yi-dyar.

Go out. (Be extinguished) myè(-le); (of fashion) gwò-'shf, bù-shf-'shīng. ‖Suddenly the lights went out. děng 'hū-rán 'dēw myè-le. ‖That song will go out with the war. dǎ 'wán-le 'jàng, nèy-ge-'gēr jyèw yàw °gwò-'shf-de. or °'bù-shf-'shīng-de.

Go over (succeed) chéng-'gūng. ‖Do you think this song will go over? nǐ shyǎng jèy-ge-'gē néng °chéng-'gūng-ma?

Go over (change one's position, literally or figuratively). ‖He went over to their side. tā 'pǎw-dàw 'tām-nèy-byar-chywu-le.

Go over or **go through.** ‖Let's go over this carefully once. (Discussing) dzám 'dž-shì °'tǎw-lwèn yí-'byàn. or (Searching or checking) °'chá yí-byàn. or (Proofreading) °'jyàw-dwèy yí-byàn. ‖Let's go over (or through) this scene once more. jèy-yì-'chǎng dzám 'dzày yǎn yí-'byàn.

Go through (be successful) chéng-'gūng; (receive, undergo) shèw. ‖Do you think your application will go through? nǐ shyǎng nǐ-'jǎw-de-nèy-ge-shf néng chéng-'gūng-ma? ‖The soldiers went through severe training. 'bīng-'shèw-de-'shywùn-lyàn hěn 'yán.

Go through with (do to the end) dzwò-dàw 'téwr-de. ‖She'll never go through with it. tā 'bú-hwèy dzwò-dàw 'téwr-de.

Go to (attend) shàng; (be given to) gěy. ‖What school do you go to? nǐ 'shàng-de shr̀ 'nèy-ge-shywé-'shyàw? ‖A fifty-dollar prize will go to the best student. yěw 'wǔ-shf-ywán-de-'jyǎng-jīn gěy dzwèy-hǎw-de-'shywé-sheng.

Go to ... trouble. ‖Don't go to any trouble. byé 'tày fèy-'shf-le.

Go to bed. ‖It's time to go to bed. gāy 'shwèy-le. or gāy shàng-'chwáng-le.

Go to press. ‖It has already gone to press. 'yǐ-jīng fù-'yìn-le.

Go to pieces swèy. ‖The eggshell went to pieces when he touched it. 'jī-dàn-'kér tā yì-'mwō jyèw 'swèy-le. ‖She (literally, her heart) went to pieces when he died. tā yì-'sž tā-'shīn dēw 'swèy-le.

‖**Go to the devil!** 'gāy-'sž! But ‖We told him to go to the devil. wǒm bǎ-tā 'mà-le yí-dwèn.

Go under (fail, of business) gwān-'mér. ‖His business went under last year. tā-de-'mǎy-mày chywù-nyán gwān-de-'mér.

Go under a name yùng. ‖He goes under an assumed name. (False name) tā yùng 'jyǎ-míng-dz. (Pen name) tā yùng 'bǐ-míng.

Go up (in price) jǎng-'jyàr. ‖Apples have gone up. 'píng-gwo jǎng-'jyàr-le.

Go together or **go with** (match) pèy; (keep company) shyàng-'hǎw. ‖These curtains don't go with the other furnishings. 'jèy-shyē-chwāng-'lyár gēn 'byé-de-'jyā-jywù 'dēw °bú-pèy. or °'pèy-bu-'shàng. ‖They have been going with each other (or, going together) for years. tā-men shyàng-'hǎw 'yěw shyē-nyán-le.

Go well with (of foods). ‖Dried shrimp goes well with wine (or Dried shrimp and wine go well together). 'gān-shyā-mi jyèw-jyèwr hǎw 'chf.

Go without (get along without). ‖If there isn't enough meat, someone will have to go without. yàw-shr 'rèw bú-'gèw, 'yěw-rén jyèw 'méy-de 'chf. ‖You'll have to go without it. nǐ 'méy-yěw jyèw 'jr̀-hǎw °'méy-yěw-ba. or °'swàn-le.

Let go (release). ‖Let go of the rope. bǎ 'shéng-dz °'fàng-kay. or °'sūng-'shěw. or °'sā-kay 'shěw. or byé 'dzwàn-je 'shéng-dz. ‖Let go of my hand. byé 'dzwàn-je wǒ-de-'shěw. ‖Let him go (release him or pardon him). 'ráw-le-ta-ba. or jyàw-tā 'dzěw-ba.

‖**Let it go at that.** 'jèm-je jyèw 'swàn-le-ba. or 'béng dzày 'tí-le.

Let oneself go. ‖He'd have a better time if he'd let himself go. 'tā shyǎng-de-'kāy-dyar, jyèw 'tùng-kway 'dwō-le.

10. *Nominal expressions.* ‖For an old man, he has a lot of go. tā 'jèm-dà-nyán-ji-de-'rén-le, 'dwō-men yěw 'jīng-shen-na. ‖It's just no go. (It won't do) 'bù-shíng. or (It hasn't worked) méy-'chéng. ‖He's on the go day and night. tā 'hēy-shya-'báy-r̀-de 'gàn. ‖Did he make a go of his marriage? tā-de-'hwēn-yīn mǎn-'yì-ma? ‖He can't make a go of his business. tā-de-'mǎy-may tā lǎw 'bàn-bu-'hǎw. ‖Let's make a go of it. dzám bǎ-'jèy-ge 'bàn-de hǎw-'hāwr-de.

11. *Other expressions in English.* ‖Tell him to go mind his own business. gàw-su tā byé-'gwǎn shyán-shr̀. ‖Whatever he says goes. 'tā dzěm shwō jyèw 'dzěm-je. or 'tā shwō dzěm-je 'jyèw dzěm-je. ‖Here goes! kāy-'téwr-la! ‖Let's go! or Let's get going! (Especially of working) dùng-'shěw-wa!

GOD. (*Common Protestant term*) shàng- dì, *but some Protestants use* shén; (*Roman Catholic*) tyān-'jǔ; (*the name* **Jehovah**) yě-hé-'hwá; (*Buddhist, Taoist, Confucian*) tyān (*heaven*). ‖**The minister gave thanks to God.** 'mù-shr 'gǎn-shyè shàng-'dì. ‖**God knows what we'll be doing next.** 'tyān jr̄-daw 'shyà-tsz̄ gàn 'shéme-ne. (*Some Christians may avoid using* tyān *here, but it is not universally considered irreverent, even in orthodox circles. However, when a Christian says this with a theological meaning, he would say* shàng-'dì jr̄-daw ...) ‖**Oh, my God!** (*Reverent, not profane, Protestant*) shàng-'dì-ya! (*Profane for most Christians, but not necessarily so for Buddhists, etc.*) 'tyān-na!

(*An idolized person*) shén, 'shén-shyan. ‖**His admirers have made a god of him.** 'chúng-bày-'tā-de-'rén bǎ-tā dàng 'shén(-shyan) kàn.

By God. *Chinese has no exactly equivalent oath.* ‖**By God, I'm not going to let him get away with that.** hn! wǒ 'kě bù-néng 'ráw-le-ta. *or* hn! wǒ 'jywé-bù-néng jyàw-tā 'nèm-je jyèw 'swàn-le.

GOLD. 'jīn-dz, jīn. **Solid gold** *or* **pure gold** 'chwén-jīn(-de), 'dzú-jīn(-de), 'chr̄-jīn(-de); **made of gold** 'jīn-dz-dzwò-de *or* 'jīn-de; **gold watch** jīn-'byǎw; **gold watch chain** 'jīn-byǎw-'lyàr *or* 'jīn(-byǎw)-'lyàn-dz; **gold coins** 'jīn-bì, 'jīn-hwò; **gold coin** *or* **gold** (*money*) 'jīn-chyán; **gold thread** jīn-'shyàn, jīn-'sz̄, *or* jīn-'sēr; **gold leaf** jīn-'yè-dz; **gold standard** 'jīn-běn-'wèy; **overlaid with gold** 'bāw-jīn; **gold-plated** (*metal*) 'dù-jīn; **gold-painted** *or* **gilded** (*woodwork*) 'jwāng-jīn 'tú-jīn; **gold** (*color*) 'jīn-sè, 'jīn-shǎr; (*and many other such compounds*). ‖**These dishes are solid gold.** jèy-shyē-'pán-dz shr̀ °'chwén-jīn-de. *or* °'dzú-jīn-de. *or* °'chr̄-jīn-de. ‖**How much is that gold ring?** nèy-ge-jīn-'yè-jr 'dwō-shaw-chyán? ‖**He can't be bought with gold.** 'jīn-dz (*or* 'chyán) 'mǎy-bu-'dùng tā-de-'shīn. ‖**The dome was painted in gold.** ywán-'dyěngr tú-de 'jīn-shǎr. ‖**The frame was done in gold.** kwàng-dz shr̀ °'tú-jīn-de. *or* °'jwāng-jīn-de. ‖**The box was inlaid with gold lines.** 'hé-dz-shang 'shyāng(-chyàn)-je jīn-'sz̄. ‖**Their flag is blue and gold.** tā-men-de-'chí-dz-shang 'lán-de gēn 'jīn-de 'lyǎng-shǎr. *or* tām-de-'chí-shang shr̀ 'lán hé-'jīn 'lyǎng-shǎr. ‖**It has silver stripes on a gold background.** shàng-tew shr̀ 'yín-dàwr 'jīn-dyèr. ‖**Do you have this in gold** (*color*)? 'jèy-ge yěw 'jīn-shǎr-de-ma?

Gold mine (*figuratively*). ‖**You've got a gold mine in that idea.** nǐ-nèy-ge-'fá-dz hwèy jyàw-nǐ fā-'tsáy-de.

Goldbricking. ‖**Soldier, cut out the goldbricking!** lǎw-'shyūng, byé 'mwó-tseng-le.

GOOD. (*See also* **BETTER, BEST.**) 1. (*Of outstanding quality*) hǎw; (*not bad*) bú-'hwày, bú-'tswò. *In some cases more specific adjectives are used.*

Expressions of direct judgment. **Good!** (*Approving something already said or done*) 'hǎw! *or* 'hěn-hǎw! *or* bú-'hwày! *or* 'jēn-hǎw! *or* 'jēn-bú-tswò! (*and similar combinations*). (*Approving a request, meaning,* **You may,** *or* **I will**) 'hǎw! *or* 'hǎw-ba! *or* 'chéng! *or* 'shíng! *or* 'kě-yǐ. *or* 'jyèw nèm-je-ba. ‖**That one is good.** *or* **There's a good one.** 'nèy-ge hǎw. *or* 'nèy-ge bú-'hwày. *or* 'nèy-ge bú-'tswò. ‖**That's very good.** 'hěn-hǎw. *or* 'jēn-hǎw. *or* hǎw-de 'hěn. *or* 'dǐng-hǎw. *or* 'tǐng-hǎw. ‖**That one is very good.** 'nèy-ge 'jēn bú-hwày. *or* 'nèy-ge 'hěn bú-hwày. *or* 'nèy-ge hǎw-de 'hěn. ‖**That one is not so good.** 'nèy-ge 'bú-dà hǎw. *or* 'nèy-ge 'bú-tày hǎw. *or* 'nèy-ge 'chà-dyar(-'jìn). *or* 'nèy-ge hěn 'tsz̄. ‖**Well, that one is neither good nor bad; it's what you'd call so-so or medium.** m̄, nèy-ge yě bù-'hǎw yě bú-'hwày; kě-yǐ shwō shr̀ 'bú-gwò rú-'tsz̄, 'bú-shàng-bú-'shyà-de. ‖**This one is no good at all.** jèy-ge yì-'dyǎr dēw bù-'hǎw. *or* jèy-ge tày 'chà-le. *or* jèy-ge hěn chà-'jìn. ‖**That's a good one!** *or* **That's good!** (*Of a true or fictitious story*) 'shwō-de 'hǎw. (*Of a fictitious story only*) 'byān-de 'hǎw. *or* 'dzēw-de 'hǎw. (*Ironically*) *meaning* **What a tall one!** hǎw 'hú-shwō bā-'dàw-le! *or* shyā-'bāy! ‖**That will be good for him** (*will teach him a lesson*). 'nèy shr̀ 'wěy-tā 'hǎw. ‖**Good for you!** *meaning* **You did the right thing.** 'jēn-hǎw! *or* jēn-'chéng. *or* jēn-'shíng. *or* 'jēn-dwèy. *or* 'yěw-nǐ-de. *or meaning,* **I didn't think you could do it.** ('jywū-rán) nèng-'hǎw-le. *or* ('jywū-rán) 'chéng-le. *or* ('jywū-rán) 'shíng-le. *or* ('jywū-rán) 'dwèy-le.

(*Referring to a specific object*) ‖**Is the milk still good?** nyéw-'nǎy méy-'hwày-ma? *or* (*Not sour*) nyéw-'nǎy méy-'sēw-ma? *or* nyéw-'nǎy háy 'hǎw-je-ne-ma? ‖**He gave me some good advice.** tā gàw-su wǒ yí-ge-hěn-hǎw-de-'fá-dz. *or* tā 'jyāw-gěy-wǒ-de-'bàn-fa 'hěn hǎw. ‖**This is a good meal.** 'jèy-dwèn-fàn °'hěn hǎw *or* °'jēn hǎw. *or* °'hǎw-de 'hěn. ‖**Are those mushrooms good to eat?** nèy-shyē-'mwó-gu hǎw 'chr̄-ma? ‖**The medicine is good for you.** jèy-ge-'yàw ywú-nǐ yěw °'hǎw-chù. *or* °'yí-chù. ‖**He's got a good body.** tā-'shēn-dz bú-'hwày. *or* (*Strong, healthy*) tā-'shēn-dz hěn 'jwàng. *or* (*Local Peiping*) tā yěw ge-'hǎw-shēn-dz-'gǔr. ‖**Does he have a good brain?** *is expressed as* **Is he bright?** tā rén 'tsūng-míng-bù-tsūng-míng?

(*Referring to persons in general*). ‖**He's a good man.** tā 'hěn hǎw. *or* (*Especially of innate character*) tā shr̀ ge-'hǎw-rén. *or* tā 'wéy-rén 'hěn hǎw. *or* (*Of ability*) tā hěn jūng-'yùng. *or* (*Of reliability*) tā hěn kě-'kàw. ‖**He's not a good man.** tā 'bù-hǎw. *etc.* ‖**He's no good.** (*Innately*) tā bú-shr̀ 'hǎw-rén. (*For a job*) tā 'méy-yěw 'yùng. *or* tā bù-'chéng. *or* tā bù-'hǎw. *or* tā bù-'shíng. ‖**Be good.** *or* **Be a good boy.** *etc.* hǎw-'hāwr-de! ‖**He's a very good child.** jèy-háy-dz 'hěn hǎw. *or* (*Likable*) jèy-háy-dz jyàw-rén °'shǐ-hwān. *or* °'ày. *or* °'téng. *or* (*Obedient*) jèy-háy-dz hěn tīng-'hwà (*or* -'shwō).

(*Referring to persons in their treatment of others*). ‖**She's very good with children.** 'tā dày 'háy-dz hěn 'hǎw. or (*Kind*) tā dày 'háy-dz hěn 'tsź-shàn (or hěn 'rén-tsź). or (*She likes children*) tā hěn ày (or téng) shyǎw-'háy-dz. or (*Children like her*) shyǎw-'háy-dz dēw 'ày (or 'shǐ-hwān)-ta. ‖**He has always been good to his family.** tā yí-'shyàng dày tā-'jyā-li-de-rén hěn 'hǎw. or (*To his children*) tā dày 'dž-nywǔ (or tā bǎ 'dž-nywǔ 'jyàw-ywu-de) 'hěn hǎw. ‖**He's very good to people who come for help.** 'shéy láy 'chyéw-tā tā 'dēw hǎw-'hāwr-de 'jyē-dày. ‖**It's good of you to think of us.** *is expressed as* **Many thanks for thinking of us** dwō 'shyè nǐ 'dyàn-ji-je wǒ-men. or nǐ 'jēn hǎw, háy nèm 'dyàn-ji-je wǒ-men.

(*Referring to persons as good in a certain profession or field*). ‖**He's a very good mechanic.** tā-jèy-ge-'jī-chì-jyàng °hěn 'hǎw. or (*capable*) °hěn yěw 'běn-lǐng. or °hěn 'chéng. or °hěn 'shíng. or tā shì ge-hǎw-'jī-chì-jyàng. ‖**He's a good writer.** tā shyě 'wén-jang shyě-de 'hǎw. or *expressed as* **His writings are good.** tā 'wén-bǐ hěn 'hǎw. ‖**He's not a very good mechanic.** tā-jèy-ge-'jī-chì-jyàng bú-'tày hǎw. or tā 'bú-shì ge-'dǐng-hǎw-de-'jī-chì-jyàng. ‖**He's a good doctor.** tā shì ge-'hǎw-yī-sheng. or tā-jèy-ge-'yī-sheng 'jēn hǎw. or tā jì-'bìng 'hěn yěw 'běn-lǐng. ‖**He could have been a good politician.** tā yàw-shr dzwò ge-'jèng-kèr, yí-'dìng bú-'hwày. ‖**He's a good Christian.** tā shì ge-'hǎw-(de-)jī-dū-'tú. or (*Earnest*) tā shìn-'jyàw hěn 'jēn. or (*Pious*) tā shìn-'jyàw shīn hěn 'chéng. ‖**Do you call that being a (good) Christian?** nèy yě jyàw jī-dū-'tú-ma? ‖**He's a good soldier.** tā shì ge-'hǎw-jywūn-rén. or 'tā-jèy-ge-'jywūn-rén hěn 'hǎw. ‖**He's a good man for the job.** tā dzwò 'jèy-shr hěn °hé-'shì. or °shyàng-'yí.

(*Special combinations*). ‖**Wait until he's in a good humor before asking him.** děng tā-gāw-'shìng-de-shǐ-hew (or děng tā-shīn-li-'tùng-kway-de-shì-hew) dzày wèn-tā. ‖**He's not in a good humor today.** tā jyēr °bù-gāw-'shìng. or ᵇ('shīn-li)-bú-'tùng-kway. or °('shīn-li) bú-'dž-dzay. ‖**Who do you get your good looks from?** nǐ-jǎng-de 'nèm hǎw, swéy-'shéy-ya? ‖**She's good-looking.** tā-jǎng-de hǎw 'kàn. ‖**Don't waste your good money on it.** hǎw-'hāwr-de-'chyán 'byé vùng-dzày 'nèy-shàng-téw. or °byé 'nèm hwā. ‖**They're making good money.** tām 'hěn jwàn-'chyán. or tām 'jwàn-chyán hěn 'dwō. ‖**The teacher is a good-natured old man.** lǎw-'shyān-sheng 'wéy-rén hěn °hé-ǎy. or °'hèw-dàw. or °'wēn-hèw. or °'hé-chì. or 'shyān-sheng shì ge-hěn-'hé-ǎy (*etc.*) -de-lǎw-'téwr. ‖**He's good-tempered.** tā-'pí-chi hěn 'hǎw. ‖**They keep things in good order.** tām bǎ 'dūng-shi 'shēw-de °hěn yěw 'tsź-shywu. or °hěn yěw tyáw-li. or °yěw-tyáw-yěw-'lǐ-de. ‖**It's a good thing you came early.** nǐ láy-'dzǎw-le 'hǎw-wa. or (*Lucky for you*) 'kwēy-le (or 'shìng-kwēy) nǐ láy-'dzǎw-le. ‖**It would be a good thing for him to go away to school.** tā yàw-shr shàng-'shy̌wé-chywu tsáy 'hǎw. ‖**Of course he's interested in your idea; he knows a good thing when he sees it.**

tā 'dāng-rán jywé-je nǐ nèy-ge-'fá-dz bú-'hwày-le; °tā shì shí-'hwò-de. or °tā dǔng-de hǎw-'hwày. ‖**Of course he likes your idea; he wouldn't let a good thing like that slip through his hand.** tā 'dāng-rán shǐ-hwān nǐ-de-'fá-dz-le; nèm-hǎw-de-'fá-dz tā 'jywé-bú-hwèy 'fàng-gwo-chywu-de. ‖**One good turn deserves another.** (*Proverbial*) 'shàn yěw 'shàn-bàw. ‖**Let's ask him; he's got a lot of good sense.** wèn-wèn 'tā-ba; tā°-'shīn-li hěn 'míng-bay. or °shì ge-'míng-bay-rén. ‖**Did you have a good time?** wár-de 'hǎw-ma? or wár-de 'tùng-kway-ma? or wár-de yěw 'yì-sz-ma? ‖**Do you have good soil for farming?** nǐm-nàr-'dì-tǔ °'féy-ma? or °jùng 'jwāng-jya 'shíng-ma? ‖**Put in a good word for me.** gěy-wǒ 'shwō jywù-hǎw-'hwà.

2. (*Outstanding in quantity or thoroughness*). *Often* hǎw, *but also many other expressions, depending on the circumstance.* ‖**Give him a good talking-to.** bǎ-tā hǎw-'hāwr-de shwō yí-'dwèn. or bǎ-tā hěn-'hěn-de shwō yí-'dwèn. ‖**Let's give this matter a good going-over.** dzám bǎ 'jèy-jyàn-shì chè-'dǐ-de (or hǎw-'hāwr-de) 'yán-jyew yí-shyàr.

Good deal, good many. ‖**The operation gave me a good deal of pain.** shēw-'shù (or 'lá-de or kāy-'dāw) 'téng-'jí-le. or °hěn 'téng. or °hǎw 'téng. or °'téng-jr-ne. ‖**A good many people don't like him.** 'hǎw-dwō-rén (or 'hěn-dwō-rén) 'bù-shǐ-hwān tā. ‖**I haven't seen him for a good while.** wǒ 'hǎw-jyěw (or 'hěn-jyěw) méy 'kàn-jyàn tā-le.

(*Fully, at least*). ‖**It's a good eight miles.** yěw 'bā-lǐ-dwō-dì. ‖**We waited a good hour.** wǒm 'děng-le yì-'dyǎn-dwō-jūng.

3. *Nominal uses.* **For one's (own) good** *or* **to do one good** 'wèy . . . 'hǎw, 'wèy . . . yěw 'yí-chù, 'wèy . . . yěw 'hǎw-chù. ‖**This is for your own good.** jèy shì 'wèy nǐ-'dž-jǐ °'hǎw. or °yěw 'yí-chù. or °yěw 'hǎw-chù. ‖**This medicine will do you good.** jèy-ge-'yàw ywú-nǐ yěw 'yí-chù.

Do (*any or some*) **good** yěw-'yùng, yěw 'hǎw-chù, yěw 'yùng-chù. ‖**I'd like to go and see him, but what good would it do?** wǒ 'hěn shyǎng chywù 'jyàn-tā, bú-gwò yěw shém-me °'yùng-ne? or °'hǎw-chù-ne? or °'yùng-chù-ne? *But* ‖**He's always going around doing good for people.** tā 'lǎw-shr 'gè-chù 'pǎw-láy-pǎw-'chywù-de °'bāng-jù rén. or °gěy-rén bàn-'shì. or °shíng-'hǎw.

Be to the good (*of winnings*) *expressed in the verb* yíng; (*of benefits*) yěw 'yí-chù, yěw 'hǎw-chù, yěw 'lì. ‖**At the end of the poker game I was eight dollars to the good.** 'pū-kè-páy dǎ-'wán-le, wǒ 'yíng-le 'bā-ywán. ‖**Whatever he brings us is all to the good.** 'wú-lwèn tā gěy-wǒm dày-shéme-lay 'dēw yěw °'yí-chù. or °'hǎw-chù. or °-'lì.

Up to no good. ‖**They're up to no good.** tām dzày-nàr °'méy 'hǎw-shèr. or °'gàn-bu-chu 'hǎw-shèr-lay. or °dǎw shéme-'gwěy-ne. or °'gwěy-gu shéme-ne.

4. Good *in combinations with other words.* **Good and . . . .** *Expressed by doubling an adjective.* ‖**Make**

the tea good and strong. 'chá chī-de °núng-'núng-de. or °yàn-'yān-de.

As good as jyǎn-'jŕ jyèw swàn . . . . ‖The job is as good as done. jèy-jyàn-'shŕ jyǎn-'jŕ jyèw swàn-'chéng-le. ‖He's as good as elected right now. shyàn-dzày tā 'yǐ-jīng jyǎn-'jŕ jyèw swàn 'shỳwǎn-shàng-le. But ‖He's as good as his word. tā 'bù-shŕ-'shìn. or tā-shwō-de-hwà 'méy-yěw bú-'swàn-de. ‖We can't find anyone as good as he (see 1 above). wǒm 'jǎw-bu-jáw shyàng-'tā nèm-'hǎw-de.

For good. ‖Let's fix it for good this time. is expressed as Let's fix it well in order to save labor. jèy-tsž dzám nùng-de hǎw-'hāwr-de, hǎw °yǐ-'hèw shěng-'shŕ. or (literary) °'yì-láw-yǔng-'yì. ‖She's gone for good is expressed as She's gone and won't return. tā 'dzěw-le, 'bù-hwéy-lay-le.

Is she gone for good? is expressed as Will she return? tā háy 'hwéy-lay-ma? or as Won't she return? tā 'bù-hwéy-lay-le-ma?

Be good at. (Know how to) hwèy . . .; (be an expert) . . . shŕ 'nèy-háng or . . . shŕ 'háng-jyā. ‖He's very good at that sort of thing. 'tā 'hěn hwèy nèy-yàngr-de-'shŕ. or 'nèy-yàngr-de-shŕ tā shŕ °'nèy-háng. or °'háng-jyā. ‖He's good only at talking. tā 'jŕ hwèy shwō-'hwà. or 'jŕ yěw shwō-'hwà tā shŕ 'nèy-háng (or 'háng-jyā). ‖Are you good at this sort of thing? Usually, for courtesy's sake, Chinese says, Do you have any experience in this? dwèy-ywú 'jèy-yàngr-de-'shŕ yěw 'jīng-yàn-ma? or, if said by a superior, expressed as Do you have confidence in yourself to do this? nǐ dzwò 'jèy-jǔng-shŕ yěw 'bǎ-wò-ma? or, said by a superior, as Can you do this well? nǐ dzwò 'jèy-jǔng-shŕ 'dzwò-de 'hǎw-ma? or (Referring to something of no great importance) 'jèy-jǔng-shèr nǐ 'hwèy-ma?

Good for. ‖That watch is good for a lifetime. 'jèy-jŕ-byǎw kě-yǐ yùng yí-'bèy-dz. ‖This fur coat is still good for several seasons. 'jèy-jyàn-'pí-dà-yī háy kě-yǐ chwān 'hǎw-jǐ-'jyèr-ne. ‖He's good for the damages to your car. nǐ-de-'chē yěw 'shém-me-swěn-shr tā 'dēw péy-de-'chǐ. ‖He's sort of a good-for-nothing. tā shŕ nèy-jǔng-méy-'yùng-de-rén. or tā shŕ ge-'fèy-wù. or tā shŕ ge-'fèy-wù-'dyǎn-shīn.

Have a good mind to 'shīn-li 'hěn yěw-dyǎr-shyǎng; had a good mind to 'chà-dyǎr. ‖I have a good mind to go with you. wǒ-'shīn-li 'hěn yěw-dyǎr shyǎng 'gēn-nǐ 'dzěw. ‖I had a good mind to leave her there. wǒ 'chà-dyǎr méy 'bù-gwǎn-tā jyèw 'dzěw-le.

Hold good. ‖Does the rule hold good here? 'jèy-tyáw(-'gwēy-jywu) dzày-'jèr yùng-de-'shàng-ma? ‖Does this rule still hold good? jèy-tyáw-'gwēy-jywu háy yěw-'shyàw-ma?

Make good. ‖I'm sure he'll make good. (Accomplish something) wǒ jŕ-dàw tā (néng) °'chéng dyǎr-shém-me. or °'yěw (dyǎr-)'chéng-jyèw. or °'dzwò-chu-dyar-mar-lay. or (Become famous) °chéng-'míng. ‖I'm sure he'll make good in business. wǒ jŕ-dàw tā dzwò 'mǎy-màym yí-'dìng dzwò-de 'hǎw. ‖If I break it, I'll make

good the damage. yàw-shr wǒ gěy nùng-'hwày-le, wǒ yí-'dìng 'péy(-cháng). ‖He always makes good his promises. tā-'dā-ying-de jyèw 'jwén bàn. or tā-'dā-ying-de 'méy-yěw bú-'swàn-de-shŕ-hew.

5. (In greetings and exclamations).

‖Good morning. or Good afternoon. or Good evening. (Greeting) 'hǎw-wa? or nín 'hǎw? or nǐ 'hǎw? ‖Good morning (only). 'dzǎw-wa?

‖Good day. or Good-by. dzày-'jyàn. or dzày-'hwèy. ‖I'll say good-by now. dzám dzày-'jyàn-le. or (If parting for a long time) 'jyèw-tsž gàw-'tsž-le. ‖If you do that again, it'll be good-by for you. nǐ yàw 'dzày nèm-je-a, nà nǐ jyèw swàn chǐng-cháng 'jyà-le.

‖Good night. 'míng-tyan 'jyàn. or 'myéngr-jyàn. or 'myár-jyàn.

‖Good heavens! or Good Lord! or Good night! or My goodness! hǎw 'jyā-hwo! or 'jè shŕ dzěm-'shwō-de!

‖Good old Jones! (Referring to him when he's absent) 'háy-shr rén-jyā lǎw-'jēw. or (Greeting him) jè 'bú-shr lǎw-'jēw-ma!

GOODS. 'hwò-wu (-hwò in compounds); (things) 'dūng-shi; (merchandise) shāng-'pǐn. Foreign goods yáng-'hwò, wày-gwo-'hwò. ‖This store has a large stock of goods. jèy-ge-'pù-dz-lǐ-téw yěw 'hěn-dwō-'tswén-hwò. ‖This store sells all sorts of goods. jèy-ge-'pù-dz mày 'gè-shŕ-gè-'yàngr-de-°'hwò-wu. or °'shāng-pǐn. or °'dūng-shi.

GOT. See GET, except for the following cases, in which GET is not used.

Have got (have) yěw. ‖I've got lots of work to do. wǒ yěw 'hǎw-shyē-shèr děy 'dzwò-de. ‖What have you got to say now? nǐ 'jè háy yěw shéme-°kě-'shwō-de-ne? or °'hwà shwō?

Have got to (have to) děy. ‖I've got to leave early. wǒ yí-'dìng děy 'dzǎw-dyǎr dzěw. or wǒ 'fēy-děy 'dzǎw-dyǎr dzěw bù-'kě.

GOVERNMENT. 'jèng-fǔ. ‖All governments will have to cooperate in this matter. 'swǒ-yěw-de-'jèng-fǔ dwèy-ywú 'jèy-jyàn-shŕ 'yīng-dāng hé 'dzwò. ‖He works for the government. tā gěy 'jèng-fǔ dzwò-'shŕ. ‖He is a government employee. tā shŕ 'jèng-fǔ-de-'gù-ywán. ‖He is a government official. tā shŕ ge-'gwān. ‖He is an important official in the government. tā shŕ 'jèng-fǔ-de-'yàw-rén. ‖Put your money into government bonds. chǐng mǎy 'jèng-fǔ-'gūng-jày-°'pyàw. or -°'chywàn. ‖That's an example of good government. 'hǎw-de-'jèng-fǔ-'yīng-gāy-dzwò-de-'shŕ, 'jèy jyèw-shr ge-'lì-dz. or 'hǎw-'jèng-fǔ 'yīng-gāy dzwò 'nèy-yàngr-de-shŕ.

Note the following combinations. Central government 'jūng-yāng-'jèng-fǔ; federal government 'lyán-bāng-'jèng-fǔ; local government 'dì-fāng-'jèng-fǔ; provincial (or state) government 'shěng-'jèng-fǔ; district government 'shyàn-'jèng-fǔ; coalition government 'gè-'dǎng-'pày-'lyán-hé(-'dzǔ-jr̄-de)-'jeng-fǔ; one-party government 'yì-dǎng-jwán-'jèng-de-'jèng-'fǔ; the United States Government 'měy-gwo(-'lyán bāng)-'jèng-fǔ.

Form of government 'jèng-tǐ; constitutional (form of) government lì-'shyàn-jèng-'tǐ; democratic (form of) government 'mín-jǔ-'jèng-tǐ; republican (form of) government 'gùng-hé-'jèng-tǐ; monarchist (form of) government 'jywūn-jǔ-'jèng-tǐ; dictatorial or fascist (form of) government 'dū-tsáy-'jèng-tǐ. ‖This country has a republican form of government. 'jèy-gwó(-de-'jèng-fú) shr̀ 'gùng-he-'jèng-tǐ.

Power or control over the government 'jèng-chywán. ‖The people control the government. 'rén-mín yěw 'jèng-chywán.

GRAB. (See also HOLD.) Grab at jwā; (in order to pull) jyēw. ‖She reached out her hand and grabbed at the end of the rope. tā shēn-'shěw-chywu °'jwā (or °jyēw) shéng-dz-'téwr.

Grab (grab at and succeed in catching) jwā-'jáw-le; jyēw-'jáw-le. ‖She reached out her hand and grabbed the end of the rope. tā 'shēn-shěw bǎ shéng-dz-'téwr °'jwā-jaw-le. or °'jyēw-jaw-le.

(Take hold of and hold tightly) 'jwā-jù; 'jyēw-jù; (if the thing has already been held loosely) 'dzwàn-jù. ‖She grabbed the broom handle and pulled. tā yì-'bǎ °'jwā-jù (or °'jyēw-jù or °'dzwàn-jù) tyáw-shu-'bàr jyèw 'dèn. ‖He said he could grab the end of the rope in one try. tā shwō tā yì-'bǎ jyèw 'kě-yi °'jwā-jù (or °'jyēw-jù) nèy-ge-shéng-dz-'téwr. ‖She reached out to grab the end of the rope, but couldn't make it. tā shēn-'shěw-chywu °'jwā (or °'jyēw) shéng-dz-'téwr, kě-shr °méy-jwā-'jù. or °méy-jyēw-'jù.

(Pick up in the hand) 'chāw-chǐ-láy, 'ná-chǐ-láy, 'shr̄-chǐ-láy, 'láw-chǐ-láy, 'jwā-chǐ-láy. ‖She grabbed a broomstick and let him have it. tā °'chāw-chi (or °'shr̄-chi, etc.) 'tyáw-shu-lay 'dǎ-le ta yí-'dwèn.

(Move quickly to accept, an offer or opportunity). ‖He grabbed at the offer. is expressed as He accepted immediately. tā lì-'kè jyèw 'dā-ying-le. or as The minute it was offered he grabbed it. tā yì 'shwō jyèw 'kěn-le.

GRADE. (Class of things of one quality) děng. Best grade 'shàng-děng or 'dzwèy-gāw-'děng; high grade 'gāw-děng; medium grade 'jūng-děng; low grade 'shyà-děng; cheaper grade 'tsz̀-děng. ‖We buy the best grade of silk. wǒ-men mǎy 'shàng-děng-'chéw-dz. ‖This is a cheaper grade of yarn. jèy-shr 'tsz̀-děng-de-rúng-'shyàn.

(To classify) fēn-. To grade (without specifying how) fēn-'děng, fēn-'děng-jí; grade according to ... 'àn(-je) ... 'fēn-chū-láy (or 'fēn-kāy, or láy fēn, or 'fēn), or fēn ...; grade according to size 'fēn dà-'shyǎw or 'àn(-je) dà-'shyǎw 'fēn-chū-láy, etc.; grade by quality 'fēn hǎw-'hwày, etc.; grade by length 'fēn cháng-'dwǎn, etc.; grade by thickness 'fēn hèw-'báw,

etc.; grade by depth or closeness in relationship 'fēn shēn-'chyǎn, etc.; grade into N classes 'fēn-chéng N-'děng or -'jǔng (kinds) or -'lèy (kinds) or -'dwēy (piles). ‖Oranges are graded by size and quality. 'jywú-dz dēw shr̄ 'àn-je 'dà-shyǎw gēn hǎw-'hwày °'fēn-chū-láy-de. or °'fēn-kāy-de. or °láy 'fēn-de. or °'fēn-de. ‖Grade these eggs by size. bǎ jèy-shyē-jī-'dàn àn dà-'shyǎw °'fēn-kāy. or °'fēn-chū-lay. ‖Grade these eggs into three sizes. bǎ jèy-shyē-jī-'dàn àn dà-'shyǎw 'fēn-chéng sān-°'děng. or °'jǔng. or °'lèy. or °'dwēy. ‖These eggs must be graded by size. jèy-shyē-jī-'dàn děy °'fēn dà-'shyǎw. or °àn dà-'shyǎw 'fēn-kāy.

(Class in school) 'nyán-jí; in some cases bān, which is not used in numbering grades, except when counting from the highest. ‖What grade do you teach? nǐ jyāw 'něy-bān? or nǐ jyāw 'jǐ-nyán-jí? ‖He's in the second grade now. tā dzày 'èr-nyán-jí.

(Marks in school) 'fēn-shur. ‖He received the highest grades in the class. tā dzày 'tā-nèy-'bān-lǐ 'fēn-shur °'dzwèy-hǎw or °'dzwèy-gāw.

(Slope) pwōr; (degree of slope) 'pwō-dù, 'chīng-shyé-'dù; grade of a road (up) 'shàng-pwōr-lù; (down) 'shyà-pwōr-lù. ‖The railroad has a 3 per cent grade. 'tyě-lù-de-'pwō-dù shr̄ 'bǎy-fēn-jr̄-'sān. ‖There is quite a steep downgrade on the other side of the hill. shān-'nèy-byār-de-' ɔwō-dù hěn 'děw. or (Dangerous) °'pwōr 'shyǎn-de hěn. ‖I like to bicycle only on the downgrade. wǒ 'jyèw shǐ-hwān dzày 'shyà-pwōr-lù-shang 'chí dz̀-shíng-'chē. But ‖The car had trouble making the grade. 'ièy-ge-chē shàng-'shān-de-shŕ-hewr hěn chr̄-'lì.

On the downgrade (figuratively). ‖Business has been on the downgrade for the last month. 'shēng-yì tsúng 'shàng-ywè chǐ °'yì-tyān bù-rú yì-'tyān. or °'ywè láy ywè 'dzāw. or °'měy-kwàng-ywù-shyà.

On the upgrade (figuratively). ‖Business is on the upgrade. 'mǎy-mày °'hěn yěw 'chǐ-sè. or °'yì-tyān bǐ yì-tyān 'hǎw. or °hěn 'fā-dá. or °'jēng-jēng-r̀ shàng.

To make the grade (figuratively; come up to standard) 'gǎn-de-'shàng; (succeed) 'chéng-de-'lyǎw. ‖If you work hard, you can make the grade. nǐ yàw-shr 'dwō mày dyar-'lì-chi, jyèw °'néng 'gǎn-de-'shàng. or °'chéng-de-'lyǎw.

To grade (level) nùng-'píng, 'píng. ‖The laborers graded the land. 'gūng-rén-men bǎ nèy-kwày-'dì °'nùng-'píng-le. or °'píng-le-yì-píng. ‖The land has been graded. nèy-kwày-'dì °'píng-le. or °'nùng-'píng-le.

GRAIN. (Wheat, corn, etc.). (Grain of all kinds) wǔ-'gǔ-dzá-'lyáng; (harvested) 'lyáng-shr; (an amount of any kind of grain not to be used for food; also, especially millet) 'gǔ-dz or 'gǔ-dz; lyáng- in combinations. ‖This year the grain crop is much better than the tobacco crop. 'jīn-nyán-shēw-de 'lyáng-shr (or 'jīn-nyán-shēw-de wǔ-'gǔ-dzá-'lyáng) bǐ yān-'yè-dz 'chyáng-de 'dwō. ‖These trucks are designated for transporting grain. 'jèy-shyē-kà-'chē shr̀ ywùn 'lyáng-shr-de. ‖Grain merchants had a good year last year. 'lyáng-shāng (or mày-wǔ-'gǔ-dzá-'lyáng-de) 'chywù-nyán 'mǎy-mày bú-'hwày. ‖This is pure grain alcohol. jèy-jǔng-jyěw-'jīng shr̀ 'chwén-yùng-'lyáng-shr-'dzwò-de. ‖This grain is being saved for seed. jèy-shyē-'gū-dz (or -'gǔ-dz) lyéw-je dzwò 'jǔng-dz (or 'jǔngr).

(*Small particle*) lì, lyèr; a grain of rice yí-lì-'mǐ. ‖I got most of the sand out of the spinach, but there are a few grains left. wǒ bǎ 'bwō-tsay-li-de-'shā-dz chà-bu-dwō 'dēw 'děw-lěw-chū-chywu-le, kě-shr háy 'shèng-le jǐ-'lì (or jǐ-'lyèr).

Unit of weight, 1/7000 of a pound av., 1/5760 of a pound troy. Chinese does not have a commonly known measure for this unit; do not use lì *or* lyèr, *because in case of pills or capsules containing N grains of something, these measures mean* pill, capsule, *not* grain; yí-lì-yǎ-sz-bǐ-'líng *is an aspirin tablet, not a grain of aspirin.*

(*Small amount*) yì-'dyǎr. ‖There isn't a grain of truth in what he said. 'tā-shwō-de °yì-'dyǎr-'jēn-hwà (or, *more emphatic* °yì-'dī-di-dyǎr-'jēn-hwà *or* °yì-'dīng-dyǎr-'jēn-hwà) dēw méy-'yěw.

(*Of wood*) wén, wér. ‖This wood has a beautiful grain. 'jèy-ge-'mù-tew-de-'wér hěn hǎw 'kàn. ‖What a fine-grained pipe! jèy-ge-yān-'děw 'wén dwō 'shi-ya!

Go against the grain. ‖Does loud conversation go against the grain with you? *is expressed as* Do you dislike loud conversation? nǐ shr̀ bù-'shǐ-hwān (or nǐ shr̀ 'nì-wey, or nǐ shr̀ 'tǎw-yàn) 'dà-shēngr shwō-'hwà-ma? *or as* Does loud conversation make you displeased? 'dà-shēng shwō-'hwà shr̀ jyàw-nǐ °bù-'shǐ-hwān-ma? *or* °'nì-wey-ma? *or* °'tǎw-yàn-ma? *or as* Does loud conversation make you irritated? °'byèn-nyew-ma?

GRAMMAR. wén-'fǎ. ‖I've never studied English grammar. wǒ 'tsúng-láy méy-'shywé-gwo 'yīng-wén-wén-'fǎ. ‖Have you got a good grammar (book) for a beginner? nǐ yěw wèy-'chū-shywé-de-rén-'yùng-de-'hǎw-yì-dyǎr-de-wén-'fǎ-(shū-)ma?

(*Isolated cases of linguistic usages*) shwō-de (*of spoken language*) or 'wén-lǐ (*of literary language*) *qualified as* clear tūng; *as* using proper word order shwèn; *as both of these* 'tūg-shwèn; *as* unclear bù-'tūng; *or as* using poor word order bu-'shwèn. ‖His grammar in Chinese is bad. tā-shwō-de-'jūng-gwo-hwà (shwō-de) 'bù-'tūng. or °bú-'shwèn. ‖His bad grammar (*according to the established rules of literary Chinese*) shows he's uneducated. tā-'wén-lǐ bù-'tūng, kě-'jyàn tā 'méy-nyàn-gwo 'shū.

GRAND. (*Splendid*). ‖It's grand weather for tennis. jèy-ge-'tyān-chi dǎ wǎng-'chyéw 'jēn hǎw. ‖He's a grand old man. 'nèy-wèy-'lǎw-shyān-sheng ('rén) jēn 'hǎw. or (*Literary; implying great virtue, good*

reputation, and advanced years) tā 'jēn shr̀ 'dé-gāw-wàng-'jùng. or tā jēn shr̀ ge-'dé-gāw-wàng-'jùng-de-lǎw-'yé-dz.

(*Luxurious*). ‖They live in very grand style. tām hěn 'shē-chr̀. or tām-'páy-chǎng hěn 'dà. or tām-'jyā-li hěn 'jyǎng-jyēw.

(*Big*). ‖They are dancing in the grand ballroom. tā-men jèng dzày 'dà-tyàw-wǔ-'tīng-li tyàw-'wǔ-ne.

(*Complete*). ‖What is the grand total? 'dzǔng-shùr shr̀ 'dwō-shǎw? or 'dzǔng-jyē shr̀ shém-'shùr?

For Grandfather, Grandmother, *etc., see Appendix A.*

GRANT. To grant permission or a request *is expressed as* to permit jwěn (*rather formal*); ràng (*informal*); 'dā-ying jyàw; be granted gàw-shya-lay (*only of a request for leave*). ‖Did they grant him permission to leave? (*No matter who asked permission for him*) tā-men 'jwěn (or 'ràng, or 'dā-ying jyàw)-tā 'dzěw (-le)-ma? or (*Specifically at his own request*) tā-men 'dā-ying tā jyàw-tā 'dzěw(-le)-ma? ‖Did they grant him his request for a leave? tām 'jwěn (or 'ràng, or 'dā-ying) tā-de-'jyà-le-ma? or tā gàw-'jyà-°tām 'jwěn-le-ma? or °tām rèn-'ke-le-ma? or °tām 'dā-ying tā-le-ma? or °'gàw-shya-lay-le-ma? ‖They granted him a three-day leave. tām 'jwěn-le (*etc.*) tā 'sān-tyan-jyà.

(*Give*) gěy; (*especially of government appropriations*) 'bwō-gěy. ‖The government granted the school $10,000 for research. 'jèng-fǔ (bwō-)gěy shywé-shyàw yí-'wàn-kwày-chyán, dzwò 'yán-jyēw-'gūng-dzwò.

(*Gift*). gěy-de(-'kwǎn-dz); (*especially governmental*) bwō-de(-'kwǎn-dz), 'jīn-tyē. ‖The school is supported by a government grant. jèy-ge-shywé-'shyàw-de-jīng-'fèy shr̀ 'kàw-je °'jèng-fǔ-'gěy-de-'kwǎn-dz. or °'jèng-fǔ-'bwō-de-'kwǎn-dz. or °'jèng-fǔ-de-'jīn-tyē.

To grant that (*concede, admit*) 'chéng-rèn, jyèw 'swàn; *in the construction* granted that ..., still ..., 'chéng-rèn *is followed by* 'bú-gwò, *but* jyèw-'swàn *is followed by* yě. ‖For the time being let's grant that (*for the sake of argument*). dzám jàn-shŕ 'chéng-rèn nèy-ge ('dwèy-le or yěw-'lǐ). or dzám jàn-shŕ jyèw 'swàn nèy-ge °'dwèy-le. or °yěw-'lǐ. ‖Granted that we were late, still you had no reason to be so mad about it. jyèw 'swàn wǒm 'wǎn-le, nǐ yě 'fàn-bu-shang 'nèm jāw-'jí-ya. or wǒm 'chéng-rèn wǒm 'wǎn-le, bú-gwò nǐ 'fàn-bu-shang .... ‖Granted that you're right, still that's not the way to say it. jyèw 'swàn nǐ 'dwèy-le, yě 'bù-gāy nèm 'shwō-ya. or wǒ 'chéng-rèn nǐ 'dwèy-le, 'bú-gwò nǐ 'bù-gāy 'nèm shwō-'hwà.

Take it for granted (*no need to ask*) 'yùng-bu-jáw 'wèn; (*know, of something that turned out as expected*) 'jř-dàw; (*think, of something that didn't turn out as expected*) 'yǐ-wey or 'dǎ-je; (*suppose, with the tentativeness sometimes implied by the English phrase*) jywé-je. *None of these is normally expressed when referring to future actions of the person addressed; the idea is then expressed by* 'yí-dìng (*certainly*), *which is also used with the above constructions.* ‖I take it for granted that you'll be there. nǐ shr̀ 'yí-dìng 'dàw-de. ‖I take it for granted that he'll be there. 'yùng-bu-jáw 'wèn-le, tā shr̀ 'yí-dìng 'dàw-de. *or* (*tentatively*) wǒ 'jywé-je tā shr̀ 'yí-dìng 'dàw-de. ‖I never thought to ask whether you were coming; I just took it for granted. *meaning* Supposed I could take it for granted wǒ méy-'wèn nǐ 'láy-bu-lay, yīn-wey wǒ °'dǎ-je 'yùng-bu-jáw 'wèn-(nǐ-)le-ne. *or meaning* You came as expected °'jr̄-dàw nǐ 'yí-dìng hwèy 'láy-de. *or meaning* You didn't come as expected °'yǐ-wey (*or* 'dǎ-je) nǐ 'yí-dìng hwèy 'láy-ne.

‖You take too much for granted. (*Friendly advice*) nǐ-'jèy-ge rén °'tày 'bù-kěn shěn-'jyěw. *or* °'rén-jyā shwō-'shéme dēw 'rèn-yǐ-wéy 'jēn. *or* °'tày 'dà-yì. *or* °'tày 'mā-hu. *or* °'tày 'mā-ma-hu-'hū-de. *or* °'shéme dēw bù-'dž-shì 'shyǎng-shyang. *or* (*Rebuke*) nǐ 'jìng-yàw jàn 'pyán-yi. *or* nǐ 'wèy-myǎn tày 'chī-fù 'rén. *or* nǐ 'yǐ-wéy 'shéy dēw hǎw 'chī-fu shr̀-de.

GRASP. Grasp *or* grasp at *an object, see* **GRAB, HOLD.**

To grasp *an idea, expressed as* to understand 'míng-bay, dǔng, 'jr̄-daw. ‖He grasped the idea at once. (*From something said*) tā °'yì 'shwō (*or, from something written,* °'yí 'kàn) jyèw °'míng-bay-le. *or* °'dǔng-le. *or* °'dēw 'jr̄-daw-le. *or* (*Literary*) tā 'yí-mù 'lyǎw-rán. ‖He has a good grasp of the subject under discussion. tǎw-'lwèn-de-'tí-mù tā °'dǔng-de (*or* °'jr̄-dàw-de *or* °'lyǎw-jyě-de) hěn 'tèw-chè.

GRASS. tsǎw; (*ground with grass growing on it*) 'tsǎw-dì; grassland 'tsǎw-dì. *or* (*grazing ground*) 'dà-tsǎw-'ywán. ‖Who's going to cut the grass? shéy chywù kǎn (*or* gē)-'tsǎw? ‖Keep off the grass. 'bú-yàw dzěw 'tsǎw-dì. *or* byé dzày 'tsǎw-dì-shang 'dzěw. *or* (*Formal, literary, does not express a word for* grass, *like our* Please keep off) 'chǐng wù 'jyàn-tà. *or* 'jìn-jr̄ 'jyàn-tà. ‖They often play on grass courts. tā-men 'cháng-chang dzày 'tsǎw-dì-shang dǎ-'chyéw. ‖These grasses grow best in a dry climate. jèy-shyē-'tsǎw dzày 'chì-hèw-gān-'dzàw-de-dì-fang 'jǎng-de 'dzwèy 'hǎw.

‖Don't let grass grow under your feet. cháng 'hwó-dùng-je-dyar. *or* 'byé dāy-'lǎn-lew.

GRATEFUL, GRATITUDE. Be grateful to 'gǎn-shyè; be extremely grateful 'gǎn-jī-bú-'jìn; express gratitude for bàw; express gratitude to 'bàw-da. ‖I am grateful to you for your help. nǐ bāng wǒ-de-'máng, wǒ hěn 'gǎn-shyè nǐ. *or* 'méng nǐ bāng-'jù, 'gǎn-jī-bú-'jìn. *or* 'dwō méng dá-'jyèw, yí-'dìng yàw 'bàw nín-de-'ēn-de. ‖That's his way of showing you his gratitude. tā-'nèy shr̀ yàw 'bàw-da-'bàw-da nǐ-ya. *or* (*Sarcastically*) tā-'nèm-je jyèw swàn 'bàw-dá nǐ-le. *or* 'nèy shr̀ yí-'bàw-hwán-yí-'bàw. ‖That's gratitude

for you! *is sarcastically expressed as* That's certainly conscienceless jyǎn-'jr̄-shr méy-'lyáng-shīn.

GRAY. hwēy(-shǎr)(-de). ‖Gray goes well with red. hwēy gēn-'húng °'pèy-de-láy, *or* °'pèy-chi-lay hěn 'hǎw. *or* 'hwēy-shǎr gēn 'húng-shǎr hěn 'chèn. ‖It is a gray stone building. nèy shr̀ yí-dzwò-'hwēy(-shǎr)-de-shŕ-tew-'gày-de-'léw. ‖She has gray eyes. tā yǎn-'jūr shr̀ 'hwēy-de. *or* tā shr̀ 'hwēy-yǎn-'jūr. ‖Her eyes are bluish gray. tā-de-yǎn-'jūr 'hwēy-li dày 'lán.

To gray (*of hair*) báy. ‖He's graying fast. tā-'téw-fa 'báy-de jēn 'kwày. *But* ‖He's graying at the temples. *is expressed as* His temples are getting streaked. tā-'lyǎng-bìn 'bān-le.

(*Cloudy*) yīn. ‖The sky was gray all morning. (tyān) 'yīn-le yì-'dzǎw-shang. *or* 'tyān yì-dzǎw-shang dēw 'yīn-je. *or* yì-'dzǎw-shang 'tyān nèm 'yīn-chen-chen-de.

GREAT. Great big. (*Of things*) 'dà, hǎw-'dà-de, hěn-'dà-de, tǐng-'dǎ-de, yèw-'kwān-yèw-'dà-de (*wide and big*); (*of persons or things*) gāw-'dà-de, 'gāw-gaw-dà-'dà-de, 'yèw-gāw-yèw-'dà-de (*tall and big, of persons only*); 'kwéy-wěy. ‖He owned a great big house. tā yěw yì-swǒr °'dà-fáng-dz. *or* °'hǎw-dà-de-fáng-dz. (*etc.*) *or* °'yèw-'gāw-yèw-'dà-de-fáng-dz. ‖He's a great big fellow. tā (shr̀ g) yèw-'gāw-yèw-'dà(-de-rén). *or* tā (shr̀ ge-)gāw-'dà(-de-rén). (*etc.*) *or* tā (shr̀ ge-) hěn-'kwéy-wěy(-de-rén). ‖They brought in a great (big) coffin. tām 'táy-lay-le yí-ge-yèw-'kwān-yèw-'dà-de-'gwān-tsay.

Great deal, great many hěn 'dwō (*much or many*); 'hǎw-shyē (*many only*); *in exclamations* 'dwō-shaw. ‖He caused a great deal of trouble for us. tā gěy-wǒm 'rě-le hěn-'dwō-de-'má-fan. *or* tā gěy-wǒm 'rě-le 'dwō-shǎw-'má-fan-na! ‖A great many people don't know the difference. 'hěn-dwō-rén (*or* 'hǎw-shyē-rén) bù-jr̄-dàw jèy-ge-'fēn-byé. *or* 'bù-jr̄-daw-'jèy-ge-'fēn-byé-de-rén °'dwō-je-ne. *or* °'dwō-le-chywu-le. *or* °'dwō-'jí-le.

Great (*outstanding*). *Chinese has no single word with this wide range of meaning, but emphasizes the particular quality referred to by some emphatic word. Before words indicating an occupation or calling, Chinese uses simply* dà *or* 'wěy-dà-de. *Elsewhere, an adjective meaning* good, bad, important, *etc., is emphasized by saying* dà . . ., 'tǐng . . ., hěn . . ., . . .-jí-le; *or emphasis is expressed elsewhere in the sentence.* ‖He's a great statesman. tā shr̀ ge-'dà-'jèng-jr̄-'jyā. *or* tā shr̀ ge-'wěy-dà-de-'jèng-jr̄-jyā. ‖He's a great inventor. tā shr̀ ge-'dà-'fā-míng-'jyā. *or* tā shr̀ ge-'wěy-dà-de-'fā-míng-'jyā. ‖He's a great man. (*Very good*) tā shr̀ ge-'dà-hǎw-'én. *or* tā-jèy-ge-rén °'hǎw-'jí-le. *or* °'shŕ-fen 'hǎw. (dà-rén *means* adult.) (*Very famous*) tā-jèy-ge-rén nén yěw-'míng. *or* tā shr̀ ge-'wěy-rén. *or* tā shr̀ ge-'dà-rén-wu. ‖He's a great speaker. tā 'hěn hwèy (or néng) 'yǎn-shwō. or tā shṛ̌ ge-'dà-'yǎn-shwō-'jyā. ‖He's a great scoundrel. tā shṛ̌ ge-'dà-hwày-rén. or tā shṛ̌ ge-'dà-hwày-dàn. or tā 'tǐng bú-shr ge-'dūng-shi-le. ‖He's a great talker. (Endless, but not necessarily boring) tā 'shwō-chi-lay 'tāw-taw-bù-'jywé-de. or tā 'shwō-chi-lay jyèw 'méy-'téwr. or (Long and tiresome) tā 'lǎw-shwō-lǎw-'shwō-de. or meaning He loves to talk tā 'lǎw-ày shwō-'hwà. ‖He was a great favorite with everybody. 'rén-rén dēw 'shǐ-hwan tā. ‖That was a great day in my life, (Happy, successful) nèy shṛ̌ wǒ yí-'bèy-dz-li-°'tǐng-de-'yì-de-yì-'tyān. or (important) °'tǐng-yàw-'jǐn-de-yì-'tyān. or (memorable) °'tǐng-jyàw-wǒ-'lyéw-lyàn-de-yì-'tyān. ‖The conference accomplished great things. jèy-tsz̀-hwèy-'yì 'jyē-gwǒ 'fēy-cháng 'hǎw. ‖They're great friends. tām shṛ̌ 'tǐng-hǎw-de-'péng-yew. or tām shṛ̌ hěn-'chīn-jìn-de-'péng-yew. or tām-lyǎ hǎw-'jí-le. or tām-lyǎ 'hǎw-je-ne. ‖I was in great pain. wǒ 'nèy-shŕ-hew °téng-'jí-le. or °'téng-sž-le. ‖It was a great injustice. nèy 'jēn-shr °(tày) bù-'gūng-píng(-le). or °(tày) 'ywān-wang(-le). ‖That was a great help! (Sincerely) nèy kě 'jēn yěw-'yùng. or (Sarcastically) 'nèy kě yěw shéme-'yùng-nga? or 'nèy jyàw yěw-'yùng, tsáy-'gwày-de-ne! ‖There's a great difference between these two men. 'tām-lyǎ 'chà-byé hěn 'dà. or 'tām-lyǎ yěw 'hěn-bù-'túng-de-dì-fang. or 'tām-lyǎ 'fēn-byé hěn 'dà. ‖That'll make a great difference. hà kě jyèw °'dà bù-'túng-le. or °'dà bù-yí-'yàng-le. or °'chà-de-'ywǎn-le. ‖That's great news. 'nèy kě hǎw-'jí-le. or 'nèy kě 'jēn hǎw ‖That's great! hǎw-'jí-le! or ('nèy kě) 'jēn hǎw!

GREEN. (The color alone) lywù(-shǎr)(-de). Green hat (yì-dǐng-)'lywù-màw-dz. (Note that it is a vicious insult to say that a man wears a green hat.) Greenish dày-'lywù-shǎr-de, or yěw dyǎr-'lywù, or dày dyǎr-'lywù; emerald green 'lywù-bǎw-'shŕ-shǎr(-de); pea green dèw-'lywù(-de); grass green tsǎw-'lywù(-shǎr-de); apple green 'píng-gwǒ-'lywù; sea green shwěy-'lywù; blue green 'lywù-shǎr-'dày-dyǎr-'lán. ‖Bring me my green sweater. bǎ wǒ-'lywù-rúng-shéngr-'gwà-dz 'ná-lay. ‖The book (cover) is green. shū-'pyér shṛ̌ 'lywù-de. ‖Green is not becoming to her. 'lywù-shar 'pèy-tā °'bù-hé-'shṛ̌. or °'bù-hǎw-'kàn. or tā chwān 'lywù-de 'bù-hǎw-'kàn.

Green and fresh (of vegetables) chīng. Green grass 'chīng-tsǎw or 'lywù-tsǎw; green vegetables (including some not actually green, as celery-cabbage, but fresh) chīng-'tsày; (or, specifically green in color) dày-'lywù-shǎr-de-chīng-'tsày; fresh green (color) 'chīng-tswèy or 'shīn-lywù; evergreen 'cháng-chīng-'shù; green tea (leaves) 'chīng-chá-yè or 'lywù-chá-yè. But turnip greens lwó-be-'yèr, or lwó-be-'yēngr, or lwó-be-'yīng-dz. ‖They passed miles of fresh green countryside. tām gwò-le 'hǎw-shyē-lǐ-'dì, 'dēw-shr 'shīn-lywù-de (or 'chīng-tswèy-de)-'tyán-yě. ‖Let's buy some greens for dinner. mǎy dyǎr-'chīng-tsày hǎw dzwò wǎn-'fàn.

(Unripe) fā-'chīng-de (literally, still green); 'shēng (literally, not ripened); (half ripe) 'bàn-shēngr-de. ‖Don't eat green apples or you'll get sick. 'byé chṛ̌ 'shēng-píng-gwo (or fā-'chīng-de-píng-gwo, or 'bàn-shēngr-de-píng-gwo), hwèy 'bìng-de. But ‖That wood won't burn well; it's still green. 'nèy-kwày-'mù-tew bù-hǎw 'jáw; háy 'lywù-je-ne.

A green. (Grass-covered land) 'tsǎw-dì; (park) gūng-'ywán; (in golf) 'chǎng-dz, chyéw-chǎng. ‖The drought has ,ruined the greens. jèy-tsz̀-'hàn-de bǎ chyéw-'chǎng (or 'chǎng-dz) gěy 'hwěy-le.

Green (inexperienced) shēng (also means unripe); (not having experience) 'méy-yew 'jīng-yàn; a green hand 'shēng-shéwr. ‖When I first came, I was green at selling. wǒ tsáy 'láy de-shŕ-hew, mày 'dūng-shi °'méy-yew 'jīng-yàn. or °-shang 'hěn shṛ̌ ge-'shēng-hěwr. or °-shang hěn 'shēng. ‖He's still green at it. tā 'háy shṛ̌ ge-'shēng-shěwr-ne. or tā 'háy 'shēng-ne. or tā 'háy yěw dyar-wày-'háng. or tā 'háy yěw dyar-'lì-ba.

Green with envy. ‖He's green with envy. is expressed as He was so angry that his face turned green. tā-'chì-de 'lyǎn dēw 'chīng-le. or as He is extremely jealous. tā 'tsù-jyèr-'dà-le. or as He was so jealous that his face turned half green and half white. tā 'jì-dù-de 'lyǎn-shang 'chīng-yí-kwày-'báy-yí-kwày-de.

GRIEF. Be in grief nán-'gwò, shāng-'shīn. ‖Her grief over the death of her husband is pitiful indeed. tā 'jàng-fu 'sž-le, tā-nán-'gwò-de (or tā-shāng-'shīn-de) 'jēn kě-'lyán. ‖We have deep sympathy for her in her grief. tā 'nèm nán-'gwò (or tā 'nèm shāng-'shīn) jyàw 'wǒm yě hěn nán-'shèw. or expressed as Her suffering such an unfortunate thing makes us sympathetic. tā dzǎw-le (or tā-jyā 'chū-le) 'nèm-bú-'shìng-de-shṛ̌ (or 'nèm-yàngr-de-'shṛ̌) °'jyàw-wǒm 'hěn nán-'shèw. or °'jēn jyàw-wǒm 'jywé-je tā kě-'lyán.

GRIND (GROUND). (By rubbing two things together, as millstones or mortar and pestle; of something hard) mwó (or mwò). ‖They are using the small millstones to grind beans. tām yùng 'shyǎw-mwòr mwó (or mwò) 'dèw-dz-ne. ‖He ground the ax to a sharp edge. tā bǎ 'fǔ-dz mwó-de hěn 'kwày. ‖It's quite a trick to grind lenses. mwó jìng-'téw (a lens to be mounted; or yǎn-'jìng-dz, eyeglass lens· or 'tèw-gwāng-'jìng, an unmounted lens) hěn děy ge-'běn-lìng. or expressed as grind glass into lenses bǎ 'bwō-li 'mwó-chéng-le 'jìng-'téw (or yǎn-'jìng-dz, or 'tèw-gwāng-'jìng) hěn děy ge-'běn-lìng, ‖This is almost ground flat (or smooth). jèy-ge dēw kwày °mwó-'píng-le. or °mwó-'gwāng-le. or °mwó-'gwāng-hwa-le. ‖He kept turning around on one heel until the heel ground a hole in the surface. tā jàn-dzay 'yí-ge-jyǎw-'hèw-gēn-shang dǎ-'jwàr, yì-'jŕ dàw bǎ 'myàr-shang 'mwó-le ge-'kǔ-lung. ‖We grind our coffee by hand. (Here, although a screw mechanism is sometimes used, mwó is used because coffee beans are hard.) wǒm mwó 'jyā-fēy (yùng-de-'jī-chì) yùng-shéw 'yáw (or 'jwàn). ‖Please have the coffee ground. chǐng bǎ 'jyā-fēy (-dēwr) °mwó-'swèy-le. or °mwó-chéng 'mwèr.

(By a screw-action machine; of something soft, as meat) jyǎw. ‖Grind the meat into hamburger. bǎ-'rèw jyǎw-chéng rèw-'mwèr. ‖The meat grinder doesn't work; I'll have to chop it by hand. 'jyǎw-dāw hwày-le; děy wǒ 'dž-jǐ 'dwò (or 'mwò, but this 'mwò is never 'mwó, and means cut up, chop up, not grind). ‖Please have the meat ground for me. chǐng gěy bǎ-'rèw °'jyǎw-le. or (cut up into bits) °'dwò-le, or °'mwò-le.

Grind (pulverize) yán. ‖The pharmacist ground the medicine into powder. 'yàw-jì-shř bǎ-'yàw °yán-chéng-le 'mwèr. or °'mwó-chéng-le 'mwèr.

Grind the teeth yǎw-'yá (yǎw also means bite). ‖He grinds his teeth in his sleep. tā-shwèy-'jyàw-de-shř-hew yǎw-'yá.

Ground glass (rough-surfaced glass) 'máw-bwō-li. ‖The windows are of ground glass. 'chwāng-hu-shang shř'máw-bwō-li.

(Figuratively). ‖He has an ax to grind, you may be sure. méy-'tswòr, tā yěw 'tā-de-'ywán-gu. ‖Learning any language is a long grind. shywé 'shém-me-'ywǔ-yán dēw děy 'shyà hěn-'dà-de-'gūng-fu. ‖During examinations he turns into a grind. 'kǎw-shř-de-shř-hew tā 'byàn-chéng yí-ge-hěn-yùng-'gūng-de-rén. ‖He grinds out three songs a day. 'yì-tyān-li tā 'tsèw-chū 'sān-ge-'gēer-lay.

GRIP. (A strong hold) 'shěw-jyèr. Loosen one's grip fàng-'shěw or sūng-'shěw; break one's grip bāy-kay 'shěw; vise-like grip (literally tiger-head pincers) 'hǔ-téw-'chyán-dz. ‖He has a powerful grip. tā-'shěw-jyèr hěn 'dà. ‖He was holding the rifle with a vise-like grip. tā dzwàn-'chyāng dzwàn-de °shyàng 'hǔ-téw-'chyán-dz shř-de. or meaning holding tight °hěn 'jǐn. ‖He didn't loosen his grip on the man's throat until the man was dead. tā chyā-je nèy-ge-rén-de-'sǎng-dz, yì-jř chyā-'sž-le tsáy °fàng-'shěw or °sūng-'shěw.

(A strong hold; figuratively) ‖He has the whole nation in his grip. tā bǎ 'chywán-gwó 'tǔng-jř-de hěn 'yán. or 'chywán-gwó 'dēw dzày tā-'jǎng-wò-jř-jūng.

(Handle) bàr. ‖The grip of the revolver is broken. 'shěw-chyāng-bàr 'hwày-le.

(Suitcase) shěw-tí-'bāw. ‖I have a clean shirt in my grip. wǒ-shěw-tí-'bāw-li yěw jyàn-'gān-jīng-'chèn-yī.

(Hold on to tightly). See HOLD, GRASP.

Come to grips with a person jwā, jyèw; come to grips with a subject 'jwā-ju. ‖They argued for hours, but never really came to grips with the central issue; but they did come to grips with each other. tǎm 'chǎw-le bàn-'tyān, 'shéy yě méy-'jwā-ju jèng-'tí; kě-shr tǎm bǐ-tsz 'jwā (or 'jyèw)-chi-lay-le.

Gripping. ‖It was a gripping speech. yǎn-'jyǎng jyǎng-de jyàw-rén °ày 'tīng. or °bù-'néng bú-yùng-'shīn 'tīng.

GROUND. (Surface of the earth) 'dì-shang; (land) dì; (particular place) 'dì-fang; (soil) tǔ. This ground (piece of land) jèy-kwày-'dì or (area) jèy-pyàn-'dì or (section) jèy-dwàn-'dì or (region) jèy-dày-'dì-fang. ‖The ground was very rocky. 'dì-shang yěw 'hěn-dwō-'shř-tew. or 'nèy-dày-'dì-fang 'dēw-shr dà-'shř-tew. ‖This ground is not rich enough for a good crop. jèy-ge-'tǔ bù-'féy (or 'jèy-kwày-dì 'bú-gèw-'féy-de), 'jùng-bu-chu hǎw 'jwāng-jya-lay.

To ground (electricity) is expressed as to connect the ground wire ān(-shang) dì-'shyàn. ‖Is the radio grounded? wú-shyàn-'dyàn ān-le dì-'shyàn méy-yěw?

To be grounded, run aground (of a boat) gē-'chyǎn (-le). ‖The boat is aground. chwán gē-'chyǎn-le.

To be grounded (of a plane) is expressed as can't begin to fly 'bù-néng 'chī-fēy. ‖The plane was grounded by bad weather. yīn-wey 'tyān-chi bù-'hǎw, fēy-jī 'bù-néng 'chī-fēy.

Ground or grounds (logical basis) 'gēn-jywù. ‖What grounds do you have for saying that? nǐ 'nèm shwō yěw shéme-'gēn-jywù? ‖Your opinions are well grounded. nǐ-de-'yì-jyàn 'dēw yěw 'gēn-jywù.

Ground (background, as on a flag) 'dyèr, 'dì-dz. ‖The flag has white stars on a blue ground. chí shř 'lán-dyèr-shang (or chí shř 'lán-dì-dz, 'shàng-tew) yěw shyē-'báy-shyēngr.

Be grounded in (have a good background in) dǎ 'gēn-dǐ; dǎ 'gēn-jī. ‖They are well grounded in history. tā-men (dwèy-ywu) lì-'shř, (dǎ de) 'gēn-dǐ (or 'gēn-jī) hěn °'hǎw (or °'jyē-shr).

On dangerous ground, on solid ground (in an argument). ‖You're on dangerous ground when you say that. nǐ 'nèm-ge-'shwō-fǎr °'jàn-bu-'jù. or °bù-'láw-kàw. or °yì-'bwō jyèw 'dǎw. ‖He was (standing) on solid ground when he made that argument. tā-'shwō-de-nèy-'dyǎn hěn °'yìng. or °'jàn-de-'jù. or °nán bwō-'dǎw ta.

Cover ground. ‖My men covered the ground thoroughly (literally searched everywhere). 'wǒ-de-rén 'yǐ-jīng dzày jèy-yì-dày (or dwàn or pyàn)-'dì-fang 'dēw jǎw-'byàn-le. ‖If I drive, I can cover a lot of ground (literally a great distance) in one day. yàw-shr wǒ kāy-'chē, yì-tyān néng 'kāy-de hěn 'ywǎn. ‖He covered the ground thoroughly. (In a speech) tā (bǎ jèy-jyàn-'shř) shwō-de °hěn 'shyáng-shì. or °hěn 'tèw-chè. or °'dēw shwō-'dàw-le. or 'dēw shwō-'byàn-le. (In research) tā bǎ gwān-ywu jèy-jyàn-'shř-de-'tsáy-lyàw dēw °jǎw-'dàw-le. or °jǎw-'byàn-le.

Ground floor (of several) dì-'yì-tséng-léw; (of two) léw-'shyà. ‖I don't want a room on the ground floor. wǒ bú-yàw dì-'yì-tséng-léw-de-'fáng-jyān. or wǒ bú-yàw léw-'shyà-de-'fáng-jyān

From the ground up. ‖He changed the entire personnel from the ground up (*from bottom to top in rank*). tā tsúng-'shyà dàw-'shàng bá-rén 'dēw hwàn-le. ‖He changed everything from the ground up (*not in special rank*). tā shéme dēw géy 'gǎy-le.

Hold one's ground. ‖He held his ground against all opposition. (*Didn't give in*) nèm 'fǎn-dwèy tā, tā yě méy-ràng-'bù. ‖Hold your ground! (*Don't retreat; fight it out, etc.*) byé 'twèy! or yì-dyǎr byé 'twèy. or ná-'dìng-le 'jú-yì, yì-'dyǎr byé 'ràng. or bú-yàw ràng-'bù. or 'jàn-jù-le 'jyǎw, yì-'dyǎr byé-'ràng.

Grounds (*gardens*) 'ywán-dz. ‖A gardener takes care of the grounds. 'ywán-dz yěw ge-hwǎr-'jyàng (or ge-kān-'ywán-dz-de) 'jàw-gu-je.

Grounds (*area used for a particular purpose*) chǎng(-dz). ‖The circus grounds are on the east side. mǎ-'shì-chǎng(-dz) dzày 'dūng-byar.

Coffee grounds jār. ‖Rinse out the coffee grounds. bǎ 'jyā-fēy-'jār ná-'shwěy 'chūng-shya-chywu.

GROUP. (*Of people*) chywún; (*more informally, especially of a group or crowd of people who happen to be together*) chywúr; dwēy, (*more informally*) dzwēy; (*a group with a common characteristic or interest*) hwǒr, 'hwǒ-dz, bāng; (*a closely-knit organized group*) 'twǎn-tǐ; (*a well-organized group, a party*) dǎng; (*an organization or society*) hwèy; (*a group or division within an organization*) pày; (*a group or section for discussion or work*) dzǔ. *All these except* 'twǎn-tǐ *and* hwèy *are measures.* ‖A group of men stood in the street and watched. yì-'chywún-rén (or yì-'dwēy-rén) dzày 'jyē-shang 'jàn-je 'chyáw. ‖Don't associate with that group. 'byé gēn 'nèy-chywún-rén (or 'nèy-hwǒ-dz-rén, or 'nèy-bāng-rén) 'láy-wang. ‖They will be hard to deal with if they form a group. tām 'jyē-chéng yì-'dǎng (or 'yí-ge-twǎn-'tǐ) jyèw 'bù-hǎw 'yìng-fu-le. ‖They organized themselves into a group. tām 'jyē-chéng °yì-'dǎng. or °yí-ge-twǎn-tǐ. or °yí-ge-'hwèy. ‖They belong to another group. tām shř 'lìng-yì-°dǎng-de. or °ge-'hwèy-de. or (*within a larger organization*) °'pày-de. ‖There are different groups in the party. 'dǎng-lǐ-tew yěw-'pày. ‖The party was divided into several groups over the controversy. 'jèy-jyàn-shř yì-'dǎng-de-rén 'yì-jyàn-bù-'hé, 'fēn-chéng-le jǐ-'pày. ‖Let's divide the members into three groups to discuss these three items. dzám bǎ hwèy-'ywán fēn-chéng sān-'dzǔ láy 'tǎw-lwèn jèy-'sān-jyàn-'shř. ‖The group met every Wednesday. 'nèy-ge-hwèy r.ěy-shīng-chī-sān 'jywù-hwèy yí-'tsž. ‖They went out in groups of two or three. tām 'sā-yì-'chywún 'lyǎ-yì-'hwěr-de jyèw 'dzěw-le.

(*Group; or pile of things*) dwēy or dzwēy; (*pile*) lwò; (*set*) tàw; (*of moving objects that can be scattered*) chywún; (*technical, of an air force*) dwèy; (*several; may be used when grouping is expressed in the verb*) shyē. ‖That's a beautiful group of trees. nèy-yì-dwēy-'shù hěn-hǎw-'kàn. ‖The textile design

has groups of red squares on a white background. nèy-jǔng-bù-de-'hwā-yangr shř 'báy-dyèr-shang yěw yì-'dzwēy-yì-dzwēy-de-húng-fāng-'kwàr. ‖He arranged the cards into groups of four. tā bǎ-'páy 'fēn-chéng-le 'sž-ge-yí-'lwò (or 'sž-ge-yì-'dzwēy). ‖How many buildings are there in that group? nèy-yí-'tàw (or nèy-yì-'dwēy; or nèy-yí-'kwàr, or nèy-yí-kwày-'dì *in that place*, or nèy-yí-ge-'shř-yang-de *in that style*) yěw 'dwō-shǎw-swǒr-'fáng-dz. ‖How many planes are there in that group? (*Non-technical*) nèy-yì-chywún-fēy-'jī-li yěw 'dwō-shǎw-'jyà? ‖How many planes are there in a group? (*Technical*) yí-'dà-dwèy yěw dwō-shǎw-jyà-fēy-'jī? ‖You'll have to memorize this group of letters in the given order. 'jèy-shyē-dž-'mǔr nǐ děy 'jàw-je ywán-'láy-de-'tsž-shywu 'lyán-chi-lay 'jì-dzay 'shīn-li.

To group (*divide into groups*) 'fēn-chéng yì-'dzǔ-yì-dzǔ-de. or *instead of* dzǔ *use* lèy (*class*) or dwēy, or lwò, or tàw, or dwèy, or pày. ‖Group the words according to meaning. bǎ jèy-shyē-dž àn-je 'yì-sž 'fēn-chéng °yì-'dzǔ-yì-'dzǔ-de. or °yí-'lèy-yí-lèy-de.

To group together (*by organization*) 'lyán-chi-lay; 'lyán-hé-chi-lay; 'jyē-chéng yí-chì (or yì-twán); (*informally, of people*) 'jywù-dzay yí-kwàr; hé-'lǔng-lay; (*put together, of things*) 'hé-dzay yí-kwàr. ‖They grouped together to resist him. tām 'lyán-chi-lay (or tām 'lyán-hé-chi-lay, or tām 'jyē-chéng yí-chì, or tām 'jyē-chéng yì-twán) láy 'gēn-tā 'dǐ-kàng. ‖Those cards can be grouped together. nèy-shyē-'chyǎ-pyàn kě-yǐ 'hé-dzay yí-kwàr.

GROW (GREW, GROWN). (*Become larger physically*) jǎng. ‖She grew two inches in six months. tā 'lyèw-ge-ywè-li 'jǎng-le 'lyǎng-tswèn. ‖He's six feet tall and still growing. tā yěw 'lyèw-chř-'gāw-le, 'háy(-dzay) 'jǎng-ne. ‖Weeds grow fast. 'yě-tsǎw jǎng-de 'kwày. ‖He grew to his full height before he was eighteen. tā 'méy-dàw shŕ-'bā-swèy jyèw 'jǎng-de nèm-'gāw-le. ‖Tall trees grow (or trees grow tall) near the river. hé-'byar-de-'shù jǎng-de 'gāw. ‖His daughter is growing up rapidly (*growing into an adult*). tā-de-'nywǔ-ér hěn-'kwày-de jyèw yàw 'jǎng-chéng 'rén-le. ‖My son is quite grown up now. wǒ-de-'ér-dz shyàn-'dzày jyàn-'jŕ-de °'jǎng-chéng 'dà-rén-le. or *meaning* become an adult, *with* grown *not expressed* °chéng-'rén-le. ‖Wait until he's grown up. děng tā (jǎng-)'dà-le dzài 'shwō-ba. *But* ‖He's a grown man (*an adult*) now. tā shyàn-'dzày shř ge-'dà-rén-le.

(*Raise crops*) jùng. ‖These farmers grow fruit. jèy-shyē-'núng-rén 'dēw jùng 'gwǒ-mù-shù.

(*Raise a moustache or beard*) lyéw. ‖How long did it take you to grow the moustache? nǐ lyéw nèy-ge-shyáw-'hú-dz yùng-le 'dwō-shaw-shŕ-hew?

Be grown over with 'dēw-shř, jǎng-'byàn-le. ‖The field is all grown over with weeds. yí-'dì dēw-shr 'yě-tsǎw. or 'tyán-li (or 'dì-li) jǎng-byàn-le 'yě-tsǎw. or 'tyán-li (or 'dì-li) 'yě-tsǎw jǎng-'byàn-le.

(*Increase in respect to some characteristic*). *Occasionally expressed by* -le *or* -de *after the verb describing the characteristic; but more commonly by constructions meaning* **by degrees** jyàn-'jyān-de . . .; *or meaning* **the more . . . the more** . . . ywè . . . ywè . . .; *or meaning* **start up** . . . chǐ-lay(-le). ‖**Hasn't she grown fat!** tā-'jǎng-de 'hǎw-bu-'pàng-nga! *or* tā (jǎng-de) 'pàng-chi-lay-le! *or* tā 'ywè-láy (*or* 'ywè-jǎng) ywè-'pàng! *or* tā jǎng-'pàng-le. ‖**The crowd grew rapidly:** nèy-chywún-rén yì-hwěr-de-'gūng-fu ywè-'jywù (*or* 'ywè-láy) ywè-'dwō. ‖**He grew careless,** tā (jyàn-'jyān-de) °'dà-yì-chi-lay-le. *or* °'bú-nèm-'shyǎw-shīn-le. ‖**He's growing old.** tā (jyàn-'jyān-de) 'lǎw-le. ‖**After a while he grew used to the change in climate,** shīn-de-'chì-hew tā °'jyàn-'jyān-de (*or* °'ywè láy ywè) 'jywé-je 'gwàn-le. ‖**He grew away from his family.** tā jyàn-'jyān-de (*or* tā 'ywè-láy ywè) gēn tā-'jyā-li-de-rén 'shēng-fen-le. *or* tā gēn tā-'jyā-li-de-rén jyàn-'jyān-de (*or* 'ywè-láy ywè) 'shēng-fen-le. ‖**That song grows on me.** wǒ 'ywè-láy ywè 'shǐ-hwan nèy-ge-'gēr-le. ‖**The taste for liquor has been growing on him.** tā jyàn-'jyān-de 'ày hē-'jyéw-le. *or* tā 'ywè-láy ywè ày hē-'jyěw-le. ‖**A new political group is growing up here.** 'jèr yěw yí-ge-'shīn-de-jèng-'dǎng (*or* yí-ge-'shīn-de-'jèng-jř-twán-'tǐ) °'hwó-dùng-chǐ-lay-le. *or* °'fā-jǎn-chǐ-lay-le. ‖**His business has grown rapidly.** tā-de-'mǎy-mày 'chǐ-láy-de (*or* 'fā-jǎn-de) hěn 'kwày.

GROWTH. ‖**The dog reached full growth** (*grew up*) **in a year.** jèy-ge-'gěw yì-'nyán jyèw jǎng-'chéng-le. ‖**He has an ugly growth** (*has grown a tumor*) **on his neck.** tā-'bwó-dz-shang jǎng-le ge-'è-chwāng. ‖**We forced our way through the thick growth** (*dense forest*) **of pines.** wǒm dzày 'mì-mi-chén-'chén-de-sūng-shù-'lín-dz-li yìng 'chwǎng-gwo-chywu-le. ‖**He has a two-day growth of beard.** *is expressed as* **He hasn't shaved for two days.** tā 'lyǎng-tyān méy-gwā-'lyǎn-le. *or as* **He has let his beard grow, purposely, for two days.** tā-'hú-dz lyéw-le 'lyǎng-tyān-le.

GUARD. (*Defend or watch a person or place*) kān(-je); (*referring to a place only*) 'bǎ-shěw(-je). ‖**Soldiers guard the place day and night.** dà-bīng 'hēy-shya-'báy-r̀-de 'kān-je (*or* 'bǎ-shěw-je) nèy-ge-'dì-fang. ‖**Guard the prisoner carefully.** hǎw-'hāwr-de kān-je nèy-ge-'chyéw-fàn. ‖**They stood guard over the fallen bridge until the police came.** chyǎw 'tā-le; tām 'jàn-nar 'kān-je děng 'shywún-jīng 'láy-le tsáy 'dzěw-de. ‖**They kept close guard of the bridge.** nèy-ge-'chyáw tām 'bǎ-shěw-de (*or* 'kān-de) hěn 'jǐn (*or* 'yán, *or* 'yán-mì).

(*Take precautions against a person or attack*) 'dì-fang(-je); (*prepare for*) 'fáng-bèy(-je); (*try to prevent*) 'ywù-fáng. ‖**This is just to guard against burglary.** jèy 'bú-gwo shř 'fáng-bèy-je (*or* 'ywù-fáng *or* 'dì-fang-je) 'bú-jyàw-rén 'tēw. ‖**They tried to guard**

against a spread of the disease. wèy-le 'ywù-fáng (*or* 'fǎng-bèy) jèy-ge-'chwán-rǎn-'bìng, 'bú-jyè 'nàw-chi-lay, tām 'hěn mày 'lì-chi-lay-je. ‖**She's always on guard against me.** tā 'lǎw nèm 'dī-fang-je wǒ. ‖**We had to be on guard constantly.** wǒm 'yì-shŕ-yí-'kè děy 'dī-fang-je (*or* 'fáng-bèy-je).

(*Be careful*) 'shyǎw-shīn(-je), lyéw-'shén; **be off guard** (*not on the alert*) 'shū-hu *or* 'sūng-shyè; (*be lazy*) 'shyè-dày; (*be insufficiently alert*) 'jīng-shen bú-'gwàn-jù. ‖**We had to be on guard constantly.** wǒm 'yì-shŕ yí-'kè °děy 'shyǎw-shīn-je. *or* °děy lyéw-'shén. *or* °'bù-néng yěw 'yì-dyǎr-'sūng-shyè. *or* °'bù-néng yěw 'yì-dyǎr-'shū-hu. ‖**You'd better guard your words.** shwō-'hwà děy °'shyǎw-shīn-dyar. *or* °lyéw dyǎr-'shén. *or* (*Lest someone hear or take you up on them*) °'dī-fang-je-dyar. ‖**For a moment his guard was down.** 'yěw nèm-yì-hwěr tā °'méy-lyéw-'shén. *or* °'bú-tày 'shyǎw-shīn. *or* °'sūng-shyè-le yí-shyàr: *or* (*Against a person or attack*) °'dī-fang-de 'chà-dyar. ‖**You can never catch him off guard.** (*Common literary quotation*) tā 'lǎw-shr jyàw-nǐ wú-'shyè-kě-'jí. *or* tā 'chù-chù lyéw-'shén (*or* 'shyǎw-shīn), 'méy ge-jyàw-ni-'dēy-jaw-de-shŕ-hew. *or* nǐ 'yàw-shyǎng 'jǎw tā bù-lyéw-'shén (*or* bù-'shyǎw-shīn, *or* 'shū-hu, *or* 'shyè-dày, *or* 'jīng-shen-bu-'gwàn-jù) de-shŕ-hew, 'nà kě méy-'yěw.

(*Person who guards; military, especially bodyguard*) 'wèy-bīng; (*military, police, or civilian guard on duty*) jàn-'gǎng-de; (*guard at a door or gate*) bǎ-'mér-de *or* kān-'mér-de; (*police guard at a door or gate*) mén-'jīng; (*bodyguard*) bǎw-'byāw-de *or* 'hù-wèy; (*a guard over . . .*) kān . . . de. ‖**There are always two guards at the entrance.** dà-'mén-nar lǎw yěw 'lyǎng-ge-°'wèy-bīng. *or* °jàn-'gǎng-de. *or* °'bǎ-'mér-de. *or* °kān-'mér-de. *or* °'mén-'jīng. ‖**He has two guards who accompany him everywhere.** tā dàw-'nǎr-chywu dēw yěw 'lyǎng-ge-°'bǎw-'byāw-de 'gēn-je. *or* °'hù-wèy 'gēn-jè. ‖**They hired a guard for the house.** tām 'gù-le °'ge-kān-'fáng-dz-de. *or* °'ge-rén kān 'fáng-dz.

Lifeguard *is expressed as* **a good swimmer** hwèy-'shwěy-de.

(*Protective device*) bǎw-shyǎn . . . (. . . *indicates the type of object used for protection*); **mudguard** 'dǎng-ní-'bǎn. ‖**He has a guard on his pin so that he won't lose it.** tā-de-byé-'jēn-shang yěw bǎw-shyǎn-'hwár, hǎw 'bú-jř-ywu 'dyēw. ‖**There's a guard on the machine to keep the blade from cutting anyone.** 'jī-chì-shang yěw bǎw-shyǎn-'bǎr, hǎw jyàw dāw-'rèr 'lá-bu-jáw 'rén.

GUESS. (*Conjecture*) tsāy; shyǎng (*think, suppose*); kàn (*see, decide from appearances*). ‖**Just guess!** *or* ‖**I'll let you guess.** nǐ 'tsāv(-yi)-tsay (kàn). ‖**Guess who it is.** nǐ 'tsāy shř-'shéy. ‖**Let me guess.** ràng-wǒ 'tsāy(-yi)-tsay (kàn). *or* ràng-wǒ 'shyǎng-shyang (kàn). ‖**I'll give you three guesses.** rúng-nǐ tsāy 'sān-hwéy (*or* 'sān-tsž, *or* 'sān-shyàr). ‖**That was a good guess.** tsāy-de 'hǎw. ‖**I'd say there were twenty-five**

divisions, but that's just a wild guess. wǒ shwō yěw 'èr-shr-wǔ-shɾ̄-rén, bú-gwo jèy shɾ̀ °shyā-'tsāy jyèw 'shɾ̀-le. *or* (*a wild dream*) °shyā-'mēng jyèw 'shɾ̀-le. ‖One guess is as good as another. 'fǎn-jèng shɾ̀ 'tsāy. ‖I guess he's sick. wǒ shyǎng (*or* kàn, *or* tsāy) tā 'bìng-le. *But* ‖Your guess is as good as mine. *is expressed as* I don't know either. 'wǒ yě bù-'jɾ̄-'dàw *or as* Whatever you guess is OK. by me. nǐ 'dzěm tsāy dēw 'shíng. ‖It's anybody's guess. *is expressed as* No one knows. 'shéy yě bù-'jwěn jɾ̀-dàw.

(*Find the answer by conjecture*) 'tsāy-jaw, 'tsāy-jr; be able to guess tsāy-de-'jáw *or* (*afterthought*) shyǎng-de-'dàw; not be able to guess tsāy-bu-'jáw, shyǎng-bu-'dàw. ‖Let's see if you can guess. 'kàn nǐ tsāy-de-'jáw-ma? ‖You won't guess (*right*) anyway. nǐ 'dzěm yě tsāy-bu-'jáw-de. ‖Did you guess the end of the story? jèy-ge-gù-shr-'jyē-gwǒ dzěm-yàng, nǐ 'tsāy-jaw-le-ma? ‖Can you guess my age? nǐ 'tsāy-de-jáw wǒ dwō-'dà-ma? ‖How did you ever guess it? nǐ dzěm 'tsāy-jr-de-ne? ‖You'd never guess it! *or* Who could ever guess it? 'shéy shyǎng-de-'dàw-°wa! *or* °ne! ‖You guessed wrong. nǐ tsāy 'tswò-le. *or* bú-'dwèy, bú-'dwèy! *But* ‖You guessed it! 'dwèy-le! *or* (*Of a thing*) 'jyèw-shr 'nèy-ge! *or* (*Of something abstract*) 'jyèw-shr 'nèm-je.

GUEST. 'kè-rén; (*an invited guest*) 'chǐng-láy(-'jù)-de(-'kè)-rén, *if* jù *is used, it means a guest who stays overnight or longer*. Be a guest at … dzāy … 'jù; invite someone as guest chǐng ('kè-)rén, *or* (*to stay*) chǐng … jù. ‖The hotel does not permit guests to keep dogs. jèy-ge-lywǔ-'gwǎn-li 'bù-shywǔ 'kè-rén °yǎng-'gěw. *or* °dày-'gěw. ‖When the guests arrive, you answer the door. 'kè-rén-'dàw-de-shɾ́-hew 'nǐ chywù kāy-'mén. ‖Don't ever do that again when there are guests. yěw-'kè-rén-de-shɾ́-hew 'bù-shywǔ 'dzày nèm-je-le. ‖How many guests did you invite? nǐ chǐng-le 'jǐ-ge(-kè)-rén? ‖How many guests did you invite to stay? nǐ chǐng-le 'jǐ-ge(-kè)-rén láy 'jù? ‖I was (only) a guest at his house. wǒ dzāy 'tā-jyā °shɾ̀ 'kè-rén. *or* °'jù-gwo. *or* °tām 'chǐng-wǒ chywù 'jù-gwo. ‖I was a guest at his house for three days. wǒ dzāy tā-'jyā jù-gwo 'sān-tyan. *or* tā chǐng-wǒ dzāy tā-'jyā jù-le 'sān-tyan. ‖I was a guest at his house last week. 'shàng-lǐ-bay wǒ dzāy 'tā-jyā 'jù-lay-je.

GUIDE. (*Physically*) lǐng, dày. ‖He guided the group through the woods. tā °'lǐng-je (*or* °'dày-je) nèy-shyē-rén gwò-de shù-'lín-dz. ‖A trained dog guided the blind man through the traffic. 'shyā-dz dzày dà-'jyē-shang 'dzěw de-shɾ́-hew, yěw ge-'shywùn-lyàn-chū-lay-de-'gěw °'lǐng-je. *or* °'dày-je.

(*Mentally or otherwise*). X guides Y *is always translated as* Y is guided by X. Be guided by (*go according to*) àn-je *or* jàw-je; (*referring to*) 'tsān-kǎw-je; (*rely on*) píng; (*listen to*) tīng. *These words are usually followed by a verb of motion or action*. ‖Don't be

guided by his advice. 'byé tīng °'tā-de-'hwà. *or* °tā-de-'sēw-jú-yi. *or* byé àn-je (*or* jàw-je) tā-de-'hwà (*or* tā-de-'sēw-jú-yi) 'dzěw. ‖This schedule will guide you in planning your work. nǐ kě-yǐ àn-je (*or* jàw-je, *or* 'tsān-kǎw-je) jèy-ge-shɾ́-jyàn-'byǎw-lay 'dìng-gwey dzwò-shɾ̀-de-shyàn-'hèw. ‖Let your conscience be your guide. píng 'lyáng-shīn 'dzwò, jyèw 'shíng. *But* ‖Try not to be guided by your own personal feelings in this matter. (*Literary quotation*) jèy-jyàn-'shèr yàw 'shyǎw-shīn-je; byé 'gǎn-chíng-yùng-'shɾ̀.

(*Person who guides; general*) 'shyǎng-dǎw; (*one who leads the way through difficulties*) lǐng-'lù-de, dày-'lù-de. ‖The guide took me around. 'shyǎng-dǎw 'lǐng-je wǒ dàw 'gè-chù chywù 'kàn. ‖You must have a guide to go through the enemy country. gwò 'dí-jìng děy jàw °ge-'shyǎng-dǎw. *or* °ge-lǐng-'lù-de. *or* °ge-dày-'lù-de. *or* (*literally*, someone to guide) °rén 'lǐng-je. *or* °rén 'dày-je.

Guidebook (*for a city, etc.*) 'yéw-lǎn-jɾ̀-'náh; (*of instructions*) shwō-míng-'shū. ‖Where can I buy a guide(book) to the city? 'jèy-dì-fangr yěw 'yéw-lǎn-jɾ̀-'nán-ma? dzày-'nǎr mǎy?

Guide card byāw-tí-'pyàr.

(*Device for steadying or directing a moving part*) 'gwǎn-téwr.

GUILTY. Be guilty. (*Legal term*) yěw-'dzwèy; (*colloquial*) shɾ̀ … 'gàn-de. **Be guilty of** *or* **be to blame for** yěw … 'dzwèy; **plead guilty** 'chéng-rèn. ‖Is he guilty? tā yěw-'dzwèy-ma? *or* 'shɾ̀ tā-'gàn-de-ma? ‖What am I guilty of? *meaning* I admit doing it, but how does that make me guilty? (*Compare next paragraph.*) 'wǒ yěw 'shéme-'dzwèy? ‖I'm not guilty of anything. (*In any respect*) wǒ yì-'dyǎr-dzwèy yě méy-'yěw. *or meaning* I didn't have anything to do with it ywú-'wǒ 'háw-wú-gwān-'shì. ‖He's guilty, all right. 'jwěn-shr tā-'gàn-de. ‖He's guilty of burglary. tā yěw 'tēw-chyè-dzwèy. ‖Guilty or not guilty? nǐ 'chéng-rèn bù-'chéng-rèn? *or* 'shɾ̀-bu-shr nǐ-'gàn-de? ‖Guilty. (*To the first version of the previous sentence*) 'chéng-rèn. *or* (*To the second*) shɾ̀. ‖Not guilty. (*To either version*) wǒ 'méy-gàn nèy-ge. *or* 'bù-shr wǒ. ‖The prisoner was found guilty. 'shěn-chá-'jyē-gwǒ 'fàn-rén 'yěw-dzwèy. *or expressed as* The crime of which he was accused was a fact. 'fàn-rén(-de)-'dzwèy-jwàng jèng 'shɾ́-le.

Be guilty of … fàn …'dzwèy. ‖What am I guilty of? 'wǒ fàn-le shéme-'dzwèy-le? ‖He's guilty of burglary. tā fàn-le 'tēw-chyè-dzwèy. ‖I'm not guilty of anything. wǒ yì-'dyǎr-dzwèy yě méy-'fàn.

(*Suffering from guilt*) yěw-'kwèy. ‖I have a guilty conscience. wǒ 'shīn-li yěw-'kwèy.

‖The boy has a guilty look. *is expressed as* His expression isn't right. jèy-'háy-dz °'shén-chi bú-'dwèy. *or as* He's skulking around. °nèm 'gwěy-gwey-swèy-'swèy-de. *or as* He looks as if he had done something bad. °'hǎw shyàng 'dzwò-le shéme-hwày-'shèr shɾ̀-de. *or as* He looks as if he had a guilty conscience. °'hǎw shyàng 'shīn-li yěw-'kwèy.

GUN. (*Small arms*) chyāng. **One gun** yì-gǎn-'chyāng, yì-jř-'chyāng, yì-gēn-'chyāng; **machine gun** 'jī-gwān-chyāng. ‖**He spends a lot of time cleaning his gun.** tā-dzày-tsā-'chyāng-shang-yùng-de-'shŕ-hew 'hěn bù-'shǎw.

(*Cannon*) pàw; **One gun** yì-mén-'pàw, yì-dzwēn-'pàw. ‖**Every gun on the ship had been put out of action by enemy bombs.** 'chwán-shang-'swǒ-yěw-de-'pàw dēw jyàw 'dí-rén-de-jà-'dàn 'jà-de bù-néng 'yùng-le. ‖**The ship fired a salute of 21 guns.** *is ex-pressed as* **The ship fired 21 sounds of a gun.** 'chwán-shang fàng-le °èr-shr-'yì-shēng-'pàw⸗ *or* °èr-shr-'yì-shēng-lǐ-'pàw.

To stick to one's guns. ‖**He couldn't prove his point, but he stuck to his guns.** tā bù-néng 'dž-ywán-chí-'shwō, kě-shr lǎw 'jyān-chŕ dž-jǐ-de-'yì-jyàn.

To gun for (*figuratively*). ‖**He's gunning for you.** tā jèng-dzày 'jǎw-je-nǐ yàw gēn-nǐ °swàn-'jàng-ne. *or* °dǎ-'ᵤyà-ne.

H

HABIT. 'shí-gwàn. **Good habit** hǎw 'shí-gwàn; **bad habit** hwày 'shí-gwàn *or* 'máw-bìng. ‖**I'm trying to break myself of the habit.** wǒ 'jèng-dzày shyǎng bǎ wǒ-de-'máw-bìng 'gǎy-le-ne. ‖**It's a good habit to get up early.** dzǎw-'chǐ shř ge-'hǎw-shí-gwàn. ‖**That's a bad habit.** nèy shř ge-'máw-bìng. *or* nèy shř ge-'hwày-máw-bìng. *or* nèy shř ge-'hwày-shí-gwàn. ‖**While I was abroad I got into the habit.** wǒ dzày ᵥwày-'yáng de-shŕ-hew 'yǎng-chéng-le nèm-ge-'shí-gwàn. ‖**Don't get into such a habit.** byé 'yǎng-chéng 'nèm-ge-'shí-gwàn. ‖**I've never gotten into the habit of smoking.** wǒ méy-'yǎng-chéng-gwo 'chēw-yān-de-'shí-gwàn.

To be in the habit of (*to do something habitually*) *is expressed as* **always** 'lǎw-shr *or as* **love to** ày *or as* **always love to** 'lǎw-ày. ‖**I'm in the habit of sleeping late on Sundays.** wǒ yí-'dàw lǐ-bày-'tyān lǎw-shr (*or* ày *or* 'lǎw-ày) chì-de hěn 'wǎn-de.

HAD. ‖**If I had known that, I wouldn't have come at all.** wǒ dāng-'chū yàw-shr 'jř-dàw de-hwa, yí-'dìng bù-láy. ‖**If I'd known it was such a mess, I'd have refused to come.** 'dzǎw (*or* wǒ yàw-shr, *or* wǒ yàw-shr dāng-'chū, *or* wǒ yàw-shr 'nèy-shŕ-hew) jř-daw shř 'jèm-yì-twán-'dzǎw(-de-'hwà-ya), jyèw 'bú-hwèy dā-ying láy-le. *Or the same alternatives with the elements in differen' order, within the limits of grammatical possibilities.*

Had better. *See* **BETTER.**
Had rather (*would rather*). *See* **RATHER.**
For other uses see **HAVE.**

HAIR. (*On human head*) 'téw-fa, -fǎ. ‖**What color is her hair?** tā-'téw-fa shř shéme 'yán-shǎr-de? ‖**All his hair turned white.** tā-de-'téw-fa ᶫdēw báy-le. *or* tā 'báy-fǎ-tsāng-'tsāng-le. ‖**Look at that fuzzy-haired boy!** kàn nèy-ge-háy-dz, yì-téw 'rúng-hū-hur-de-'téw-fa. ‖**There is a hair** (*from human head only*) **on your coat.** nǐ-'yī-fu-shang yěw yì-gēn-'téw-fa. ‖**You should have had your hair cut shorter.** nǐ-de-'téw-fa yīng-gāy jyǎn 'dwǎn-dyar láy-je. ‖**I like her hair-do.** tā-téw-fa-'shū-de-nèy-ge-'yàngr bú-'hwày. *But* ‖**Want your hair** (*head*) **washed?** 'shǐ-téw-ma?

(*On the temples*) bìn, bìn-'jyǎw, bìn-'jyǎwr.

(*On other parts of the body; fine hair*) 'hàn-máw, 'hán-mawr; (*coarse or thick*) máw, máwr.

(*On animals*) máw, máwr; (*very soft hair*) rúng, 'rwǎn-mawr; (*near the mouth*) 'hú-dz, 'shywū-dz. ‖**Feel the fuzzy hair on this dog!** nǐ 'mwō-me jèy-ᵤge-gěw-de-'máwr, 'rúng-hū-hur-de.

To miss by a hair. ‖**His shot just missed me by a hair.** tā-nèy-yi-'chyāng chà yì-'dī-dī-dyǎr méy-'dǎ-jáw wǒ.

To hang by a hair. ‖**His life hangs by a hair.** tā-de-'shìng-mìng hěn (*or* jēn) 'wéy-shyan. ‖**The situation is hanging by a hair.** 'chíng-shíng hěn (*or* jēn) 'wey-shyan. *or* (*Literary*) *expressed as* **A thousand 40-pound weights, one hair.** 'chíng-shíng jēn-shr 'chyān-jywūn yì-'fǎ.

HALF. bàn (bàr *when not followed by another word; or, in some cases, expressed as* **not all, not finished,** *etc.*). **Half a mile** 'bàn-lǐ-dì; **a half dollar** 'bàn-kwày-chyán *or* 'wǔ-máw-chyán. ‖**Give me a half pound of pork.** gěy-wǒ bàn-'bàng-'jū-rèw. ‖**Bring home half a pound of butter.** 'dày-hwéy bàn-'bàng-hwáng-'yéw-lay. *or* hwéy-'jyā-lay-de-shŕ-hew dày bàn-'bàng-hwáng-'yéw. ‖**This shirt will take a yard and a half of material.** jèy-jyàn-chèn-'shǎn děy yùng yì-mǎ-'bàn-de-'lyàw-dz. ‖**I'll be back in half an hour.** wǒ bàn-dyǎn-'jūng yǐ-'nèy jyèw 'hwéy-lay. ‖**I've been waiting the last half hour.** wǒ děng-le yěw bàn-dyǎn-'jūng-le. ‖**I got this at half price at a sale.** 'jèy-ge, wǒ shř dzày jyǎn-'jyàr-de-shŕ-hew 'bàn-jyà mǎy-de. ‖**I bought a half interest in that store.** nèy-ge-'pù-dz-de-'běn-chyán yěw wǒ yí-'bàr. ‖**I'll give him half of my share.** wǒ bǎ wǒ-de-nèy-'fèr fēn-gěy tā yí-'bàr. ‖**The enemy's fighting efficiency was reduced by half.** 'dí-rén-de-'jàn-dèw-'lì jyǎn-le yí-'bàn. ‖**Your half is larger than mine.** (*Of an object*) nǐ-nèy-bàn-'lǎ bǐ wǒ-de (*or* ... bǐ wǒ-jèy-bàn-'lǎ) dà. (*Of something abstract*) 'nǐ-nèy-bàr bǐ 'wǒ-de (*or* ... bǐ 'wǒ-jèy-bàr) dwō. ‖**It's only half done** (*finished*). gāng-wán-le yí-'bàr. *or* háy chà yí-'bàr méy-'wán-ne. ‖**That's only half true** (*or* **only a half truth**). nèy-ge bù-'wán-chywán shř 'jēn-de. ‖**The meat is only half done.** rèw háy 'bàn-shēng-bàn-'shéw-de-ne. *or* rèw náy 'bàn-shēngr-ne. *or* rèw háy méy-shéw-'tèw. ‖**I was half afraid** (*a little* *afraid*) **you weren't coming.** wǒ yěw-dyar 'yí-shīn nǐ 'bù-láy-le. ‖**I said it half jokingly.** wǒ shr̀ 'bàn-shwō-bàn-'shyàw-de 'shwō-de. *or* wǒ-'shwō-de-shŕ-hew yí-'bàn shr̀ kāy 'wán-shyàw. ‖**This way it'll cost only half as much.** 'jèm-je jyèw 'shǎw chū yí-'bàr-de-chyán. ‖**He's not half as clever as his wife.** tā-de-'tsūng-míng lyán tā-'tày-tay yí-'bàr dēw 'gǎn-bu-shàng. ‖**I was lying on the couch half asleep** (*nodding*). wǒ jèng dzày tǎng-'yǐ-shàng °chùng-'dwěr. *or* °'mí-mi-hu-'hū-de. *or* °'méy-shwèy-'jyáw. *or* °'bàn-shǐng-bàn-'shwèy-de. ‖**He's been only half awake all day.** tā yì-'jěng-tyān nèm 'bàn-shǐng-bàn-'shwèy-de. ‖**I have half a mind to chuck the whole thing and scram.** wǒ hěn shyǎng yì-shwǎy-'shěw jyèw 'dzěw-kay. ‖**He's doing it half-heartedly.** tā-dzwò-de 'hěn bú-rè-'shīn. ‖**He's half cracked.** tā shr̀ ge-bàn-'fēngr. ‖**I'll be there at half past eight.** wǒ bā-dyǎn-'bàn dàw-'nèr. ‖**Shall I cut this in half?** wǒ bǎ jèy-ge 'chyē-chéng lyǎng-'bàr hǎw-ma? ‖**Will you go halves with me?** dzám-lyǎ dwèy-'bàr dzěm-yàng? *or* dzám-lyǎ dwèy-bàr-'fēn dzěm-yàng? *or* dzám-lyǎ píng-'fēn dzěm-yàng? *or* dzám-lyǎ jywūn-'fēn dzěm-yàng? ‖**He always does things by halves.** (*Literary*) tā lǎw-shr yěw-'shŕ-wú-'jūng. ‖**He never does things by halves.** tā lǎw-shr yěw-'shŕ-yěw-'jūng. *or* tā 'shyàng-lay bú-shr yěw-'shŕ-wú-'jūng-de.

HALL. (*Passage or entrance*) gwò-'dàwr. ‖**Please wait in the hall.** chǐng dzày gwò-'dàwr 'děng. ‖**It's the second door down the hall.** shwèn-je gwò-'dàwr dzěw, dì-'èr-ge-mér.

(*Assembly room*) lǐ-'táng. ‖**There were no seats, so we stood at the back of the hall.** 'yīn-wey méy-'dzwòr-le, 'swǒ-yǐ wǒm 'jàn-dzày lǐ-'táng 'hèw-byār.

(*Public building*) -tīng, -fǔ. ‖**His office is in City Hall.** tā-de-gūng-shr̀-'fáng shr̀ dzày °shr̀-jèng-'tīng-li. *or* °shr̀-jèng-'fǔ-li.

Reception hall kè-'tīng.

Hall *in such places as the old Imperial Palace, large monasteries, etc., is expressed with* -dyàn (*also means* **court, courtyard**). **Main hall** 'dà-dyàn; **front hall** 'chyán-dyàn. ‖**The emperor used to receive foreign diplomats in this hall:** tsúng-chyán 'hwáng-dì dzày 'jèy-ge-dyàn-li jyē-jyàn 'wày-gwó-'shr̀-chén. ‖**The Buddhist monks are chanting the liturgy in the main hall.** 'hé-shang dzày 'dà-dyàn-li nyàn-'jīng-ne.

HAMMER. 'chwéy-dz. ‖**Could I borrow a hammer?** jyè 'chwéy-dz shř-yi-shř 'shíng-ma? *or* jyè 'chwéy-dz yùng-yi-yùng 'shíng-ma?

To hammer chwéy, dǎ; (*with repeated sharp blows*) chyāw. ‖**Someone is hammering at the door.** yěw-rén 'dà-shēng °chyāw-'mén. *or* 'dǎ-'mén. ‖**He hammered him with his fists.** tā ná 'chywán-tew °'chwéy-ta. *or* °'dǎ-ta. ‖**The blacksmith hammered horseshoes out of that piece of iron.** 'tyě-jyàng ná nèy-kway-'tyě dǎ-chéng-le (*or* chwéy-chéng-le) mǎ-'jǎng-le.

To hammer (*figuratively*). ‖**I tried in vain to hammer it into his head that that's no way to treat people.** wǒ shyǎng-'jìn-le fár jyàw-tā míng-bay 'nèm dày-'rén bù-'shíng, kě-shr dzěm shwō tā yě bù-'tīng.

HAND. (*Part of the body*) shěw. ‖**Where can I wash my hands?** wǒ dzày-'nǎr shǐ-shi 'shěw? ‖**What's that in your hand?** nǐ-'shěw-li-'ná-je-de shr̀ 'shém-me? *or* nǐ-'shěw-lǐ-de nèy shr̀ 'shém-me? *or* (*Grasped*) nǐ-'shěw-lǐ-'dzwàn-je-de shr̀ 'shém-me? *Or, for other kinds of holding and carrying, use other verbs in place of* ná *and* dzwàn *in the above examples* (*see* **CARRY**). ‖**Take him by the hand.** 'lā-je tā-de-'shěw. ‖**I shook hands with him and left.** wǒ gēn-tā 'lā-shěw yǐ-'hèw jyèw 'dzěw-le. ‖**His hand shakes.** tā-de-'shěw fā-'chàn. ‖**Hands up!** jywǔ-chǐ 'shěw-lay! ‖**Hands off!** *expressed as* **Don't touch!** bù-shywǔ 'mwō! *or* byé dùng-'shěw! *or as* **Take your hands away!** bǎ-'shěw ná-kāy! *but in a figurative sense, meaning* **Don't get messed up in that.** 'yùng-bu-jáw 'nǐ-gwǎn. *or* 'shéy yě bù-shywǔ 'gwǎn. ‖**My advice is, hands off** (*figuratively*). yǐ-'wǒ kàn-na, 'byé 'gwǎn.

Hand drill shěw-'dzwàn; **hand grenade** 'shěw-lyéw-'dàn; **hand brake** 'shěw-já; **hand car** (*railroad*) shěw-yáw-'chē; **hand cart** shěw-twéy-'chē; **to clap the hands** pāy-'shěw. ‖**He made this with his own hands.** tā 'dz`-jǐ 'dùng-shěw dzwò-de. *or* tā 'chīn-shěw dzwò-de. ‖**They came in, hand in hand.** tām 'shěw-lā-je-'shěwr jyèw 'jìn-lay-de. ‖**He pulled himself up by the rope, hand over hand.** tā 'dǎw-je-shěw (*or* tā 'dzwǒ-yi-shěw-'yèw-yi-shěw-de) pá 'shéng-dz, jyèw 'pá-shang chywu-le. ‖**He is waiting for him, hat in hand.** tā 'shěw-lǐ ná-je 'màw-dz 'děng-tā.

(*Applause*) *is expressed as* **to clap hands** pāy-'shěw. ‖**The audience gave her a big hand.** 'tīng-jùng 'dà gěy-tā pāy-'shěw. ‖**Give him a hand, please!** 'dà-jyā-pāy-'shěw!

(*In cards*) shěw *or* bǎ, *as a measure with* páy, *or in some cases simply* páy. ‖**This is the worst hand I've had all evening.** jèy-shr wǒ-'yì-wǎn-shang-'dzwèy-hwày-de-°yì-shěw-'páy. *or* °yì-bǎ-'páy. ‖**Let's play out this hand.** 'jèy-bǎ-páy dzám dǎ-'wán-le-ba. ‖**Don't look at my hand.** byé 'kàn wǒ-de-'páy. ‖**I've been having bad hands all evening.** wǒ 'yì-wǎn-shang ná 'hwày-páy. *or* wǒ-'yì-wǎn-shang-ná-de-'páy °dēw 'bù-hǎw. *or* °'yì-bǎ-yì-'bǎ-de dēw hèm 'hwày. ‖**What a hand!** (*Good or bad*) 'hǎw-yì-bǎ-'páy-le! *or* 'nèm-yì-bǎ-'páy!

By hand 'shěw-, yùng-'shěw; **handmade, handcraft** 'shěw-gūng-dzwò-de *or* 'rén-gūng-dzwò-de; **handicrafts** (*handwork industry*) 'shěw-gūng-'yè. ‖**All this sewing had to be done by hand.** jèy-shyē-'hwó dēw shr̀ 'shěw-gūng-dzwò-de. ‖**You've got to do it by hand.** 'fēy-dey yùng-'shěw láy dzwò bù-'kě.

Hand (*pointer*) jēn, jēr. **Hour hand** 'shŕ-jēn *or* 'shyǎw-jēr; **minute hand** 'dà-jēn *or* 'dà-jēr; **second hand** 'myǎw-jēn *or* 'myàw-jēr. ‖**The hour hand is**

broken. 'shŕ-jēn (or 'shyǎw-jēr) 'shé-le. ‖Both hands are broken. 'lyǎng-ge-jēn 'dēw shé-le. ‖The minute hand is bent. 'dà-jēr wān-le. ‖Watch the second hand moving. kàn nèy-ge-'myǎw¹-jēr 'dùng. ‖The hand (*picture of a human hand drawn*) on the signpost points that way. fāng-shyàng-'bǎr-shang-'hwà-je-de-'shěw jŕ-je 'nèy-byar.

(*Worker*). ‖I worked a couple of years as a farm hand. wǒ dzày dì-li gěy 'rén-jya dzwò-le lyǎng-nyán-'hwór. ‖He is a farm hand. tā shŕ ge-'cháng-gūng. *or* tā shŕ ge-'dwǎn-gūng. ‖He's one of the hands (*not on a farm*). tā shŕ ge-dzwò-'hwór-de. *or* tā shŕ ge-dǎ-'dzár-de. *or* tā shŕ ge-²gūng-rén. ‖The ship sank with all hands. lyán-'chwán-dày-'rén 'dēw chén-le. ‖We are short of hands. *or* We are short-handed. wǒm 'chywē-rén.

(*Help*). ‖Would you lend me a hand in moving that furniture? nǐ néng 'bāng-wǒ bān yí-shyàr 'jyā-jywù-ma? ‖Give him a hand. 'bāng-ta yí-shyar (-'máng)-ba. ‖Lend me a hand. láy 'bāng-bang 'máng.

(*Share*). ‖Did you have a hand in this? 'jèy-jyan-shèr yěw °'nǐ-de-'fèr méy-yew? *or* °'nǐ dzày 'lǐ-tew ma? ‖You could see his hand in this (*with a bad meaning*). nǐ 'ké-yi 'kàn-chu-lay yěw 'tā dzày 'lǐ-byar (dǎw-'lwàn). ‖It's obvious that he had a hand in this. (*In any sense*) míng-'shyǎn-je jèy-'lǐ-tew yěw 'tā °yí-'fèr. *or* °yì-'shěwr. *or* (*In a bad sense*) °shŕ-'hwày.

(*Style of writing*). ‖He writes in a round hand. tā shyě-'dz (shyě-de) hěn 'ywán-rwèn. *or* tā-de-'bǐ-fǎ 'ywán-rwèn. ‖Is this signature in his hand? jèy-ge-'dz shŕ tā-'chyàn-de-ma? *or* jèy-ge-'dz shŕ tā-chyàn-de-°'míng-ma? *or* °'dz-ma? *or* 'jèy-ge shŕ tā-'chīn-bǐ-'shyě-de-ma?

To hand (*to give, of small objects conveyed by hay* 'dì-gěy, gěy, 'ná-chu-lay. ‖Will you hand me that pencil? bǎ nèy-jŕ-'chyān-bǐ 'dì-gěy wǒ. ‖Hand it over! 'gěy-wǒ! *or* 'ná-chu-lay! *or* 'gěy-wǒ 'ná-chu-lay!

To hand (*transfer*) jyāw -chu-lay), 'jyāw-dày, 'yí-jyāw, jyāw-gěy. ‖Hand him over to the police. bǎ-tā 'jyāw-gěy 'jǐng-chá. ‖He handed over all his documents. tā bǎ 'wén-jyàn 'dēw jyāw-chu-lay-le. ‖He handed over the documents to the new man. tā bǎ 'wén-jyàn 'yí-jyāw-le. *or* 'jyāw-dày-le. ‖He is just now handing over his office to the new mayor. tā jèng-dzày gēn 'shīn-shŕ-'jǎng bàn 'jyāw-dày.

To hand (*to tell*). ‖Don't hand me that sort of stuff. 'nèy-jǔng-hwà 'byé gēn-'wǒ shwō. *or* 'nèy-jǔng-hwà gēn-'wǒ 'shŕ-bu-'shàng. *or* nǐ 'dǎng wǒ shŕ 'shéy-ya, gēn-wǒ shwō 'nèy-jǔng-hwà.

To hand it to (*to give credit to*) 'pèy-fu. ‖You've got to hand it to him for this. 'jēn děy 'pèy-fu tā, *or* 'tā jèy-yi-'shěwr 'shŕ-dzày ké-yi 'pèy-fu.

To lay (one's) hands on. ‖Wait until I lay my hands on him! děng wǒ 'děy-jaw tā dzày 'shwō. *or* (*Figuratively only*) děng tā 'lè-dzày 'wǒ-shěw-li dzày 'shwō.

In one's hands (*in one's charge*). ‖The affair is in my hands. 'jèy-ge-shèr gwēy 'wǒ gwǎn-le. ‖I'll leave the whole matter in your hands. *is expressed politely as* I'll hand it over to you. nàm, wǒ jyèw bǎ 'jèy-jyàn-shèr 'chywán jyāw-gěy 'nǐ-le. *or* (*Even more polite*) nàm, 'yí-chyè bày-'twō-le. *or* (*To a subordinate*) nàm, 'jèy-jyàn-shèr yéw-'nǐ-fù-'dzé chywù 'bàn. ‖Don't let this (*either an object or an affair*) fall into their hands. byé jyàw 'jèy-ge 'lè-dzày 'tām-shěw-li.

Change hands hwàn-'jǔr, hwàn 'dūng-jya, 'dǎw-shěw. ‖The business has changed hands. 'mǎy-mày °hwàn-le 'dūng-jya-le. *or* °'dǎw-le 'shěw-le. *or* °hwàn-'jǔr-le. ‖The store has changed hands. 'pù-dz hwàn-le 'dūng-jya-le. *etc.*

Wash one's hands of. ‖I wash my hands of the whole thing here and now! 'jèy-jyàn-shèr tsúng-'tsž wǒ 'dzày bù-'gwǎn-le. *or* wǒ gēn 'jèy-jyàn-shèr jyèw-'tsž 'dwàn-jywé 'gwān-shì. *or* (*Of something evil*) súng-'tsž yǐ-'hèw wǒ shǐ-'shěw bú-'gàn-le.

Hand in hand (*closely related*). ‖(The advance of) science and the standard of living go hand in hand. 'kē-shywé gēn 'shēng-hwo-'chéng-dù yěw 'lyán-dày-de-'gwān-shi.

Hand in glove. ‖Oh, he's hand in glove with that man! hǎy! tā gēn 'nèy-ge-rén 'láy-wǎng-de hěn 'mì.

A free hand. ‖Give him a free hand. ràng-tā 'dz-jǐ dzwò. *or* 'yéw-tā dzwò-'jǔ. *or* byé 'chè tā-de-'jěw. ‖I don't have a free hand in this. jèy-ge-shèr bù-'chywán yéw-wǒ dzwò-'jǔ. *or* jèy-ge-shèr 'yěw-rén chè-'jěw.

Hands tied. ‖My hands were tied. (*Literally*) wǒ-de-'shěw 'kwèn-je-ne. (*Figuratively*) wǒ 'bù-néng 'dz-yéw. *or* wǒ 'jēn-shr méy-'fár.

First hand, second hand, *etc.* Second-hand store 'jyèw-hwò-'dyàn. ‖I got this information at first hand. jèy-ge-'shyāw-shi wǒ shŕ 'jŕ-jyē 'dé-lay-de. ‖I got this information at second hand. jèy-ge-'shyāw-shi wǒ shŕ 'jyàn-jyē 'dé-lay-de. ‖It is second-hand. (*Old*) shŕ 'jyèw-de. *or* (*Used*) shŕ 'yùng-gwo-de. *or* (*Worn before, of clothes*) shŕ 'chwān-gwo-de.

In hand, out of hand. ‖The situation is well in hand. 'yí-chyè shwèn-'l. . , 'bàn-de hěn dé-'shěw. *or* 'bàn-de hěn 'dé-shīn yìng-'shěw. ‖The crowd got out of hand. 'nèy-chywún-·rén 'gwǎn-bú-'jù-le. ‖Don't let the students get out of hand. byé jyàw 'shywé-sheng dzàw-'fǎn.

Eat out of someone's hand (*figuratively*). ‖I can nake him eat out of my hand. wǒ ké-yi bǎ-ta 'gwǎn-de 'jyàw-tā dzěm-je tā 'jyèw dzěm-je.

On hand. ‖He's never on hand when I want him. wǒ yàw 'yùng-tā de-shŕ-hew, tā dzǔng bú-'dzày. ‖There is only one battalion on hand. 'gēn-chyán (or 'yǎn-chyán) 'jŕ yěw yì-'yíng-rén. ‖I have only a small amount on hand. wǒ 'shěw-°téwr(°-byār) jŕ yěw bù-'dwō-de-chyán (*or use other words for* chyán *if one refers to something other than money*).

On the other hand. ‖As you say, he's a good man; but on the other hand he hasn't had much experience.

nǐ-'shwō-de 'hěn-dwèy; kě-shr, tsúng lìng-yì-fāng-myàn 'kàn, tā 'chywē-fá 'jīng-yàn. ‖Yes, he did cuss you out; on the other hand, you weren't entirely in the right yourself. bú-'tswò, tā 'shr̀ 'mà-nǐ láy-je; bú-gwò 'fǎn-gwo-lay-shwō-ne, 'nǐ yě yěw 'bú-shr̀-a.

On one's hands, off one's hands. ‖I've got a lot of work on my hands today. 'jīn-tyān wǒ(-'shěw-lí)-'gāy-dzwò-de shr̀ hěn 'dwō. ‖ I still have her on my hands. *is expressed as* I can't get rid of her. háy yěw 'tā wǒ 'méy-fár 'dǎ-fa. *or as* She is still my responsibility. háy yěw 'tā wǒ děy 'gwǎn-ne. ‖I'm glad I got that off my hands. bù-gwǎn nèy-ge-le 'jēn 'shū-fu. *or expressed as* I'm glad it's finished. bǎ 'nèy-ge nùng-'wán-le 'jēn shū-fu. *or as* I'm glad it's been turned over to someone else. bǎ 'nèy-ge 'twēy-chu-chywu bù-'gwǎn-le 'jēn shū-fu.

On the right hand dzày (nǐ-)'yěw-byar; on the left hand dzày (nǐ-)'dzwǒ-byar. ‖The house is on your left hand as you go up the street. nǐ wàng jyē-'nèy-byar dzěw, nèy-swǒr-'fáng-dz (shr̀) dzày nǐ-'dzwǒ-byar.

Hand down (*by inheritance, or referring to a secret or a recipe, etc.*) chwán; (*referring to an object, as clothing, given by one person to another*) gěy. ‖The recipe has been handed down in our family for generations. jèy-ge-'dzwò-fǎr dzày 'wǒm-jyā 'chwán-le hǎw-jī-'dày-le. *or* jèy-shr 'wǒm-jyā-'chwán-de-'dzwò-far. ‖It was handed down from our ancestors (*may refer to an object*). shr̀ wǒm-'dzǔ-shyān chwán-shya-lay-de. ‖This is a hand-me-down from my brother. jèy shr̀ 'gē-ge-gěy 'wǒ-de.

Hand in. ‖I'm going to hand in my resignation tomorrow. (*To a higher authority*) wǒ 'míng-tyān bǎ tsź-'chéngr °dì-shang-chywu. *or* (*Not specifying to whom*) °'jyāw-jìn-chywu. ‖My report has been handed in. (*To a higher authority*) wǒ-de-bàw-'gàw °chéng-shang-chywu-le. *or* (*Not specifying to whom*) °jyāw-jìn-chywu-le.

Hand out (*distribute*) 'sā-chu-chywù, 'sàn-chu-chywù. ‖Take these tickets and hand them out. bǎ jèy-shyē-'pyàw °'sā-chu-chywu. *or* °'sàn-chu-chywu.

Handout. ‖He wants a handout. tā yàw shyǎw-'chyár.

Hands full (*figuratively*). ‖He certainly has his hands full with that new job. tā dž-'tsúng yěw-le nèy-jyàn-'shīn-shèr yǐ-'hèw 'jēn shr̀ 'máng-de 'lì-hay.

Hands full (*literally*). ‖He had his hands full of papers. tā-'lyǎ-shěw-lǐ-ná-de 'chywan shr̀-'jř. *or* tā 'jwā-le lyǎng-'dà-bǎ-'jř.

Handful. (*Literally*) ‖He picked up a handful of snow and threw it at me. tā jwā-le yí-'dà-bǎ-'shywě (*or* . . . yì-'mǎn-bǎ-'shywě) jàw-je-'wǒ jyěw 'kǎn-lay-le. (*Figuratively, very few*) ‖There was only a handful of people there. nàr 'jř yěw bù-jī-'gèr-rén.

HANDLE. (*Holder*) bàr. ‖This hoe needs a new handle. jèy-bǎ-'chú děy hwàn ge-('shīn-de-)'bàr.

To handle (*touch*) 'mwō-swō, 'mā-sā; (*move*) nwó, dùng, bān; (*pick up*) ná; (*handle carelessly*) 'shyā-nùng, 'lwàn-dùng, 'hwò-hwo, ná-je 'wár; (*use*) yùng.

See also CARRY, HOLD, USE, MOVE. ‖Look at it all you want, but don't handle it. 'dzěm-me kàn dēw 'shíng, kě byé °'mwō-swō. *or* °'mā-sā. *or* °'dùng. *or* °'ná-chi-lay. *etc.* ‖Handle with care. 'bān (*or* 'ná, *or* 'nwó, *or* 'yùng, *etc.*) -de-shŕ-hew °'lyěw-'shén. *or* °'yàw 'shyǎw-shīn. ‖That child must have handled it. yí-dìng shr̀ nèy-ge-'háy-dz °'mā-sā-láy-je. *or* °'mwō-swō-láy-je. *or* °'ná-láy-je. *or* °'dùng-láy-je. *or* °'ná-je wár láy-je. *or* °'nùng-láy-je. *or* °'shyā-nùng-láy-je. *or* °'lwàn-dùng-láy-je. *or* °'hwò-hwo-láy-je. (*Each is more serious than the preceding.*) ‖Don't handle the watch like that; you might break it. byǎw byé 'nèm 'mwō-swō (*or* 'mā-sā, *or* 'shyā-nùng, *etc.*); 'nèm-je hwèy nùng-'hwày-le. ‖When you handle a priceless thing like that, you've got to be careful. dzày 'shěw-lǐ ná-je 'nèm-yàng-de-'wú-jyà-jī-'bǎw, bù-'néng bù-'shyǎw-shīn.

To handle (*manage, control*) gwǎn. ‖Can you handle the students? nǐ 'gwǎn-de-jù 'shywé-sheng-ma? ‖Students nowadays are hard to handle. 'jèy-ge-nyán-téwr 'shywé-sheng nán °'gwǎn. *or* °'yìng-fu. *See also* CONTROL.

To handle. (*Operate; of tools, weapons, etc.*) yùng, shŕ; (*of a car*) kāy; (*of sharp weapons*) shwǎ. ‖He can handle any kind of firearm. tā shém-me-yàngr-de-'chyāng-pàw dēw hwèy °'yùng. *or* °'shŕ. ‖He handles the car very well. tā-chē-'kāy-de hěn 'hǎw. *or* tā kāy-'chē kāy-de hěn 'hǎw. ‖He shouldn't be allowed to handle the sword the way he does, or he'll get hurt. 'bù-yīng-gāy jyàw-tā 'nèm shwǎ-'dāw; tā hwèy bǎ tā-'dž-jī 'lá-jaw-de. ‖This car handles well. jèy-ge-'chē hěn hǎw 'kāy. ‖This machine handles easily. jèy-ge-'jī-chi hěn hǎw °'yùng. *or* °'shŕ.

(*Deal with*). ‖He handled the situation well. tā-'chǔ-jř-de (*or* tā-'yìng-fu-de, *or* tā-'bàn-lǐ-de) hěn dé-'dàng.

(*Deal in*). ‖We don't handle that brand. wǒm bú-'mày nèy-ge-'páy-dz-de.

HANDSOME. (*Good-looking*) hǎw, bú-'hwày, bú-'tswò, 'pyàw-lyàng, hǎw-'kàn, měy. *Any of these may be preceded by* 'jǎng-de, *referring to appearance.* ‖I don't think he's very handsome. wǒ jywé-de tā 'bù-dzěm-me 'pyàw-lyàng (*etc.*).

(*Generous*) hěn 'hǎw, bú-'tswò; (*of money*) hěn-'dwō, bù-'shǎw; (*of price*) hěn 'dà. ‖He made me a handsome offer for my farm. wǒ-nèy-kwày-'dì tā °'gěy-le ge-hěn-hǎw-de-'jyàr. *or* °chū-de-'jyàr hěn-'dà.

HANG (HUNG). (*Fasten, suspend*) gwà. *This is the most general term; for details and special cases, see below.* ‖He hung the picture over the desk. tā bǎ-'hwàr gwà-dzày shū-'jwōr-shàng-byar-le. ‖Hang this on the wall. bǎ 'jèy-ge gwà-dzày 'chyáng-shang. ‖They hung a "Do not disturb" sign on the doorknob. tām dzày mén-'bàer-shang gwà-le ge-'pár, pár-shang shwō: bú-yàw dǎ-'mén. ‖Is that your hat hanging on the hook? gwà-dzǎy-'gēw-dz-shàng-tew-de shř 'nǐ-de-'màw-dz-ma? ‖Hang up your hat and coat. bǎ nǐ-de-'màw-dz gēn dà-'yī gwà-chǐ-láy-ba. ‖He hung up (*the telephone receiver*) on me. tā méy-děng wǒ shwō-'wán-le jyèw bǎ dyàn-'hwà 'gwà-shang-le. ‖They hung out a lantern in front of the house. tām dzày 'mén-chyán gwà-le ge-'dēng.

To hang (*with a tack*) èn; (*with a nail*) dìng; (*with paste*) jān, hú, tyē. ‖Hang it on the wall with a thumbtack. ná èn-'dǐng èn-dzày 'chyáng-shang. ‖Hang it on the wall with a nail. ná 'dǐng-dz 'dìng-dzày 'chyáng-shang. ‖Call in a paperhanger. jyàw yí-ge-byǎw-hú-'jyàng-lay.

To hang (*of a person's death, but not legal punishment*) dyèw. ‖They hanged him by the wrists. tām 'kwěn-je tā-de-shěw-'wàn-dz bǎ-tā 'dyàw-chi-lay-le. ‖He hanged himself. tā shàng-'dyàw-le. *or* (*Literary*) tā shywán-'lyáng dz-'jìn-le. ‖He died by hanging. tā shř 'dyàw-sž-le.

To hang (*as legal punishment*) jyǎw. ‖He died by hanging (*as punishment*). tā shř 'jyǎw-sž-de. ‖The man will be hanged for his crime. nèy-ge-rén-'fàn-de °dzwèy děy 'jyǎw-sž. *or* °dzwèy gāy 'jyǎw. *or* °shř 'jyǎw-dzwèy.

To hang (*tie up; literary, confined to a few uses*) shywán. ‖They hung up lanterns and festoons to celebrate the Double-Tenth Festival. tām 'shywán-dēng jyē-'tsǎy chìng-jù °shwāng-shŕ-'jyé. *or* °gwó-chìng-'r̀.

To hang (*naturally, as fruit*) chwéy. ‖There are several bunches of bananas hanging on the tree. yěw jǐ-'dū-lu-shyāng-'jyāw dzày 'shù-shang 'chwéy-je. *or* 'shù-shang 'chwéy-je jǐ-'dū-lu-shyāng-'jyāw. ‖The fruits are hanging down. jyē-de-'gwǒr wàng-shyà 'chwéy-je. ‖The nobles stood in front of the throne with hands hanging down (*a mark of respect*). wáng-'gūng dzày bǎw-'dzwò-chyán-byan 'chwéy-shěwr 'jàn-je.

To hang *something over something* dā. ‖They propped up a bamboo pole and hung the dyed threads over it to dry. tām 'jř-chi yì-gēn-'jú-gān-dz-lay, bǎ rǎn-le-de-'shyàn 'dā-dzay shàng-tew 'lyàng.

To hang one's head, *or* (*of a dog*) to hang the tail 'dā-la; (*only of head*) dī, chwéy; (*not lift*) bù-'táy. ‖He hung his head and sneaked away. tā 'dā-la-je téw jyèw 'lyěw-le. ‖The dog shrank back with its tail hanging (*between its legs*). nèy-ge-'gěw 'dā-la-je 'yǐ-ba, wàng-hèw 'twèy. ‖He's been hanging his head since the divorce. tā 'lí-hwēn yǐ-'hèw yì-'jŕ °bù-'gǎn táy-'téw, *or* 'lǎw-shr 'dī-je téw 'bù-gǎn jyàn-'rén. *or* °méy-lyǎn jyàn-'rén. ‖Why are you hanging your head? nǐ wèy-'shéme °'chwéy-téw sàng-'chì-de? *or* °'chwéy-je téw? *or* °'dī-je téw? *or* °'dā-la-je téw? *or* °bù-'táy 'téw-wa?

Hang *from a finger or hook* gēw. ‖He has a string of fish hanging down from his left index finger. tā yùng 'dzwǒ-shěw-de-'shŕ-jř 'gēw-je yí-chwàr-'ywú.

Hang *from the elbow* kwà. ‖She came back with a basket hanging from her left elbow, and carrying a

huge watermelon with both hands. tā 'hwéy-lay de-shŕ-hew, dzwǒ-gē-bwo-'jěwr-shang kwà-je ge-'lán-dz, lyǎng-jř-'shěw-li 'bàw-je ge-dà-'shī-gwā.

Hang (*of clothes*). To hang well *on someone* 'chēn-two. ‖The dress hangs well on you. jèy-jyàn-'yī-fu chwān-dzày nǐ-'shēn-shang hěn 'chēn-two. ‖She improved the hang of the skirt by shortening the waist a little. tā bǎ 'chywún-dz-'yāw-nar 'shěw-jìn-chywu-le-dyar. jyèw bǎ 'chywún-dz-nùng-de-'chēn-two-le shyē.

Hang out (*from a window*) 'tàn-chu, 'shēn-daw. ‖Don't hang out the window. byé bǎ 'shēn-dz 'tàn-chu (*or* 'shēn-daw) chwāng-hu-'wày-byar chywù.

The hang (*knack*). ‖Now you're getting the hang of it. *is expressea as* You've found the door by groping. nǐ 'kě mwō-jaw 'mér-le. ‖You have to use your head to get the hang of it. nǐ děy 'fèy dyar-'shǐn-sž tsáy 'mwō-de-jáw 'mér-ne. ‖Did you get the hang of it? nǐ 'mwō-jaw 'mér-le-ma? *or, meaning* the trick, nǐ dé-jaw jèy-ge-'jywé-chyàw-le-ma? *or, meaning* the idea, nǐ dǔng-de jèy-ge-'yì-sz-le-ma? *or, meaning* the method, nǐ 'míng-bay jèy-ge-'fá-dz-le-ma? ‖I can't get the hang of it. wǒ 'mwō-bu-jáw 'mér. *or* wǒ 'dé-bu-dàw 'jywé-chyàwr. *or* wǒ bù-'dǔng-de shř shém-me 'yì-sz. *or* wǒ bù-'míng-bay shř dzěm-me-ge-'fá-dz.

Hang around (*wait*) děng, bù-'dzěw; (*walk back and forth*) 'dzěw-láy-dzěw-'chywù; (*stay*) 'lyéw-lyán, 'dāy-je; (*walk around*) 'jwàn-yew; (*mix in the crowd; make a sort of living*) hwèn. ‖He's always hanging around the racetrack. tā yǔng-'ywǎn shř dzày pǎw-mǎ-'chǎng-nàr 'hwèn. ‖Hang around awhile. dzày-jèr 'děng-hwer, byé-'dzěw. ‖Some suspicious people are hanging around their neighborhood. tām-nàr fù-'jìn yěw jǐ-ge-kě-'yí-de-rén dzày nàr °jwàn-yew. *or* °'dāy-je. *or* °'dzěw-láy-dzěw-'chywù. ‖He hangs around that joint every night. tyān-tyan 'wǎn-shang tā dzày 'nèy-ge-dì-fang 'dāy-je. ‖They already hinted to him that he's not wanted, but he still hangs around. tām 'yǐ-jing 'tèw-gwo bú-'yàw tā-de-'yì-sz-le, kě-shr tā háy 'lyéw-lyán-je bù-kěn-'dzěw. ‖Why you're still hanging around her is beyond me. nǐ 'háy dzày 'tā-gēn-chyan nèm 'jwàn-yew, wǒ 'jēn shyǎng-bu-chū shř 'dzěm-ge-'dàw-li.

Hang out. *See* Hang around. *But* ‖That's a place where thieves hang out. *or* That's a hang-out for thieves. nèy shř 'dzéy-wō.

Hang on (*hold tightly; by pulling*) lā, chēn, dèn, jwày; (*by holding fast to*) jwày, jyéw; (*in a clasp*) bàw; (*in the hand*) jwā, dzwàn; *all are used with postverbs* jǐn *or* jù. ‖Hang on (*as to a rope*). lā-'jǐn-le. *or* lā-'jù-le. ‖I hung on as tight as I could. wǒ 'jyèw néng 'lā-de (*or* 'chēn-de, *or* 'dèn-de, *or* 'jwày-de, *or* 'jyéw-de, *or* 'bàw-de, *or* 'jwā-de, *or* 'dzwàn-de) 'nèm jǐn. ‖She hung on to his arm and screamed. tā 'jyēw-je tā-de-'gē-be jyèw 'dà-jyàw-chǐ-láy-le.

Hang on to (*of possessions*) *meaning* don't spend byé 'hwā-lew; *meaning* don't lose byé 'dyēw-lew; *meaning* watch hǎw-'hāwr-de 'kān-je; *meaning* keep hăw-'hāwr-de 'shĕw-je. ‖Hang on to this money. jèy-ge-'chyán °byé 'hwā-lew. or °byé 'dyēw-lew. or °hăw-'hāwr-de 'ḵăn-je. or °hăw-hāwr-de 'shĕw-je.

Hang together. ‖They swore to hang together, whatever happens. tām chĭ-le 'shr̀ shwō 'bú-lwèn dzĕm-'yàng tām yĕ °bú-'sàn-kay. or °'jywù-dzay yì-'chĭ.

Other expressions in English. ‖His fate hangs in the balance. tā-de-'jyē-jywú háy dzày lyăng-'kĕ-jr̄-'jyàn. ‖Everything hangs on his decision. (*See* DE-PEND.) 'yí-chyè 'dēw dĕy 'kàn tā 'dzĕm-me 'jywé-dìng-le. ‖Hang the door (*on the hinges*). bă-'mén dzăy mén-'jéwr-nar 'ān-shang. or bă-mén (yùng hé-'yè) 'ān-shang. ‖They hung up a swing for the children. tām gĕy 'háy-dz-men 'ān-le ge-'chyēw-chyan. ‖The fear of losing his job hangs over him like a sword. tā 'pà jyaw rén-jya gĕy-'tsź-le; 'jèy-jyàn-'shèr dzày tā-'shin-shang 'shywán-je shyàng yì-bă-'dāw shr̀-de. ‖How was the hangover? jyĕw-'shǐng-le yĭ-'hèw, 'jywé-je 'dzĕm-yàng? ‖Hang it all! tăw-'yàn.

HAPPEN. *Most commonly expressed by a verb (usually there is yĕw or come out, occur chū) plus affair, event, a happening shr̀ or shèr; in short phrases the verb is often omitted.* ‖What happened? 'dzĕm-le? or 'dzĕm-hwéy-'shèr? or (yĕw) 'shéme-shèr. or (chū-le) 'shéme-shèr. ‖What happened while I was gone? wŏ dzĕw-le yĭ-'hèw °yĕw (or °chū-le) shéme-'shr̀ láy-je? ‖Nothing happened at all. 'méy-shèr. or 'méy-shém-me. or 'shém-me-shr̀ yĕ 'méy-yew. ‖Plenty happened! 'shèr kĕ 'dwō-je-ne. ‖Nothing happens here. 'jèr 'méy-yew shém-me-'shèr. ‖Nothing ever happens around here! 'jèr jyăn-'jŕ 'shéme-shèr yĕ 'méy-yĕw! ‖Think of it! All these things happened just in that five minutes. nĭ 'shyăng-shyang! 'jèm-dwō-de-'shèr dēw 'chū-dzày nèy-'wŭ-fēn-'jūng-li. ‖Were you there when the accident happened? chū-'shèr-de-'shŕ-hew nĭ 'dzày-nèr-ma? ‖How did it happen? shr̀ 'dzĕm hwéy-shèr? or 'dzĕm găw-de? ‖It happened this way. shr̀ 'jèm hwéy-shr̀. ‖So it happened THAT way! 'ywán-láy shr̀ 'nèm hwéy-shr̀-a. ‖Did it really happen that way? 'jēn shr̀ 'nèm-yàng-de yì-hwéy-'shr̀-ma? ‖So it really happened! ywán-láy 'jēn yĕw nèm hwéy-shr̀-a! ‖How could such a thing happen? 'dzĕm hwèy yĕw 'jèm-yàng-de-'shr̀? ‖Did it really happen? 'jēn yĕw nèm hwéy-'shr̀-ma? ‖What happened to you? nĭ 'dzĕm-me-le? ‖I just knew it would happen to me this way. wŏ 'dzăw jyèw jywé-de yàw 'jèm-je. ‖Everything happens to me. 'shéme-'shèr dēw jyàw-'wŏ pèng-shang-le. ‖What happened to this typewriter? 'jèy-jyà-dă-dz̀- jī jè shr̀ 'dzĕm-le? ‖What happened to the man who found the body? 'téw-yi-ge-kàn-jyan-'shŕ-shew-de-nèy-ge-ren dzĕm-me-'yàng-le-ne? ‖A wonderful thing happened to me last night. 'dzwór wăn-shang wŏ yĕw yí-jyàn-dà-'shǐ-de-'shèr. ‖A thing like that WOULD happen to me now! 'jèy-ge-shŕ-hew 'pyān-pyān °yĕw (or °jyàw-wŏ 'pèng-shang, or

°jyàw-wŏ 'ywù-jyan) 'nèy-yàng-de-'shèr. ‖I couldn't help it; it just happened. 'jyèw nèm-je-le 'mwō, 'wŏ yĕw shém-'fár-ne? or *expressed as* It wasn't intentional. wŏ 'bú-shr gù-'yì-de. or jè 'wán-chywán shr̀ găn-'chyăw-le, 'wŏ méy-fár. ‖Could anything ever have happened so opportunely? néng yĕw 'nèm-'chyăw-de(-'shr̀)-ma? ‖How did you happen to find me? nĭ 'dzĕm jáw-je 'wŏ-de? or dzĕm nèm 'chyăw nĭ jyèw bă-wŏ 'jăw-jáw-le.

Happen to, happen that (*just at that time*) jèng 'găn-shang; (*fortunately or by chance*) jèng 'hăw, jèng 'chyăw; (*unluckily*) (jèng) bù-'chyăw; (*not as usual*) kĕ. *Sometimes the idea of chance is implied rather than expressed.* ‖It happened that they were having a marriage ceremony. jèng 'găn-shang tām bàn 'shĭ-shr̀. ‖It happens that we can't do anything about it. jèng 'găn-shang wŏm yì-dyăr-'bàn-fa yĕ 'méy-yew. ‖It happened that I was called away at the time. jèng 'găn-shang (or jèng 'chyăw, or bù-'chyăw) nèy-ge-'shŕ-hew wŏ yĕw 'byé-de-shr̀, bú-'dzày-nàr. ‖It happened that we were all there. jèng 'hăw (or jèng 'chyăw, or jèng 'găn-shang) nèy-ge-'shŕ-hew wŏm 'dēw dzày-nàr. ‖I happen to be the man you've been looking for. jèng 'năw (or jèng 'chyăw) 'wŏ jyèw-shr nĭ-yàw-'jăw-de-nèy-ge-rén. or nĭ-yàw-jăw-de-'nèy-ge-rén (jèng-hăw) jyèw shr̀ 'wŏ. ‖Did you say that you happened to be there when the shot was fired? nĭ 'shr̀ shwō-gwo fàng-'chyāng-de-shŕ-hew nĭ jèng 'găn-shang 'dzày-nàr-ma? ‖I happened to meet him on the street once. yĕw yí-'tsz̀ wŏ dzày 'jyē-shang °'ywù-jyan-le tā. or °'pèng-jyan-le tā. ‖I happened to bump into him in a crowd. wŏ dzày yí-'dà-chywún-rén-li ('jèng chyăw) 'pèng-jyàn tā-le. ‖I happen to agree with you this time. 'jèy-tsz̀ wŏ kĕ gēn 'nĭ-de-yì-jyan shyāng-'túng. ‖That happens to be THE Mrs. McGuire. 'nèy-ge-rén-na! kĕ-'chyăw 'jèng-shr 'mă-dà-'mā. ‖Guess who it is! It happens to be your honorable wife! nĭ 'tsāy-tsay 'nèy-ge-rén shr̀ 'shéy? 'ywán-láy shr̀ lìng-'jèng!

HAPPINESS. (*The emotion*) 'kwày-lwo; (*technical, literary*) lè. ‖Happiness lessens with age. rén ywè-'dà ywè-nán 'jywé-de-chu 'kwày-lwo-lay. ‖Contentment breeds happiness. 'kwày-lwo tsúng jr̄-'dzú shēng-chu-lay. or néng jr̄-'dzú, jyèw 'kwày-lwo. or (*Literary quotation*) jr̄-'dzú-de cháng-'lwò. ‖The Chinese regard happiness as one of the seven emotions; these emotions are pleasure, anger, sorrow, happiness, love, hate, and fear. 'jūng-gwo-rén yĭ 'lè wéy 'chī-'chíng-jr̄-'yī; chī-'chíng jyèw shr̀ 'shǐ, 'nù, 'āy, 'lè, 'ày, 'wù, 'jywù.

(*Good luck, good fortune*). ‖He knows how to enjoy happiness. tā shr̀ hwèy-shnyăng-'fú- ə-rén. ‖Let's drink to your happiness. hē (bēy-) 'shi-jyĕw. ‖Here's to your happiness. (*A toast*) dà-'shǐ, dà-'shǐ. ‖Here's happiness to you! 'jū-shř rú-'yì. ‖Happiness can't last. 'hǎw-shř wú-'cháng. ‖I've never had much happiness. wǒ méy-'shyǎng-jaw shém-'rén-shēng lwò-'chywèr. ‖Next year you'll have great happiness coming to you. (*Especially of marriage*) 'míng-nyán dà-'shǐ. or (*General*) 'míng-nyán °nín 'ywùn-chi 'háw. or °nín jyāw 'hǎw-ywùn. or °nín 'shǐ-shř chúng-'chúng. or °nín 'fú-shīng-gāw-'jàw.

HAPPY. 'kwày-le, 'kwày-lwo, 'kwày-hwo, gāw-'shìng. Feel *or* act happy lè (*literary*) ; (*of dogs or children*) sā-'hwār; (*be contented*) jř-'dzú; (*be satisfied*) 'mǎn-yì; (*be successful*) 'dé-yì; (*be lucky*) dzěw-'ywùn, ywùn-chì 'hǎw, yěw-'fú, shyǎng-'fú; (*be pleased with*) -shǐ, 'shǐ-hwan, 'hwān-shi. ‖I don't feel happy about ฅ. wǒ bìng bù-jywé-de gāw-'shìng. ‖Oh, those happy days! hāy! 'nèy-shř-hew 'dwŏ-me-'kwày-hwo! ‖You don't look happy these days. jèy-shyē-'ř-dz nǐ 'hǎw-shyàng bú-dà 'kwày-hwo. ‖If you don't feel too happy when you're successful, then you won't be too depressed when you aren't. 'dé-yì-de-shř-hew bú-yàw 'tày gāw-'shìng, 'shř-yì-de-shř-hew jyèw 'bú-hwèy 'tày nán-'shèw-le. ‖He's always happy. tā lǎw-shr 'kwày-hwo-de. ‖If you feel too happy when something turns out your way, then you're likely to feel very unhappy if it doesn't. 'dé-yì-de-shř-hew 'tày 'gāw-'shìng-le, 'shř-yì-de-shř-hew yě jyèw hwèy tày nán-'gwò-le. ‖This is the happiest day of my life. jè shř wǒ-yī-'shēng-'dzwèy-kwày-le-de-yì-'tyān. or wǒ yì-shēng-li 'méy-yew yì-'tyān shyàng 'jèm-'kwày-le-de.

(*Of the face*). ‖Look at his happy (*smiling*) face! kàn tā nèm-'méy-kāy-yǎn-'shyàw-de! or kàn tā nèm 'yì-lyǎn 'shyàw-rúngr! or kàn tā 'lè-de 'bì-bu-shang 'dzwěr!

Happy-go-lucky. ‖He's a sort or happy-go-lucky person. tā shř yì-jǔng-'jīn-jāw-yěw-'jyěw-jīn-jāw-'dzwèy-de-rén (*literary quotation*).

Happy ending. ‖The movie had a happy ending. 'pyān-dz-mwò-'lyǎwr shř ge-'dà-twán-ywán (*literary*). ‖Many happy returns. 'jū-shř rú-'yì.

HARBOR. (*Port*) 'gǎng-kěw, -gǎng (or 'jyǎng-kěw, or -jyǎng, *different pronunciations of the same words*). ‖New York is a natural harbor. 'nyéw-ywē shř ge-'tyān-rán-de-'gǎng-kěw. ‖What's the difference between a commercial harbor and a naval base? 'shāng-jyǎng gēn 'jywūn-jyǎng yěw 'shéme-'fēn-byé? ‖All the harbor facilities were destroyed. 'gǎng-kěw-de-'gūng-shř dēw 'hwěy-le.

(*To give shelter to*) tsáng. ‖Do you know it's against the law to harbor an enemy in your house? nǐ 'jř-dàw bǎ 'dí-rén tsáng-dzay nǐ-'jyā-li shř fàn-'fǎ-ma?

Harbor a grudge. ‖I don't harbor a grudge against him any more. wǒ bú 'jì-hèn tā-le.

HARD. (*Not soft*) yìng, bù-'rwǎn. ‖I don't like to sleep on a hard bed. wǒ bù-'shǐ-hwan shwèy 'yìng-chwáng. ‖Sitting on that hard chair all day certainly tires

one out. dzày nèy-ge-'yìng-yı-dz-shang dzwò yì-'jěng-tyān, 'shéy yě hwèy jywé-je 'lèy-de. ‖You'd better change to a hard pencil; soft lead smears easily. háy-shr hwàn ge-'yìng-chyān-bǐ 'hǎw; rwǎn-chyān rúng-yì 'dzāng. ‖We burn hard coal. wǒm shāw 'yìng-méy. ‖This is made of hard wood. jèy shř 'yìng-mù-dzwò-de. ‖The ground becomes hard in winter. dàw-le 'dūng-tyan 'dì jyèw 'yìng-le. ‖This wood is hard enough for wood carving. jèy-jǔng-'mù-tèw yìng-de ké-yi dzwò mù-'kē yùng. ‖That's a hard nut to crack (*literally ; for figurative expression see next paragraph*). jèy-ge-'gwǒr jēn-'yìng, jǐ-bu-'kāy. ‖You can drive over fifty miles an hour if the road is hard. lù-'myàn yàw-shr 'yìng-de, jyèw ké-yi kāy 'gwò yì-dyǎn-jūng 'wǔ-shř-lǐ. ‖After the first few miles they came to a hard road. dzěw-le jǐ-lǐ-'dì yì-'hèw tām 'shàng-le yì-tyáw-°'mǎ-lù. or °'lù, lù-'myàn shř 'yìng-de. ‖Don't wash clothes in hard water. byé dzày 'yìng-shwěy-lǐ shı 'yī-fu. ‖The water here is hard; it has too high a mineral content. 'jèr-de-shwěy 'yìng; hán-de-'kwàng-jř tày 'dwō. ‖The ice cream didn't freeze hard (*become solid*). bīng-jì-'líng méy-dùng-°'tsź-shr-le. or °'jyē-shr-le. or °'yìng-le. ‖Wait until the river is frozen hard. děng hé dùng-°'yìng-le. or °'jyē-shr-le. or °'tsź-shr-le.

(*Not easy*) nán, bù-'rúng-yì, bú-'yì; (*requiring energy or effort*) fèy-'shř, fèy-'lì, fèy-'jìn, chř-'lì; (*requiring mental effort*) fèy-'shīn-sz, or in a few cases bù-'hǎw. ‖That's a hard nut to crack (*figuratively*). 'nèy-jyàn-shř 'hěn nán 'bàn. or 'jēn shř ge-'nán-tí. ‖I had a hard time getting here. wǒ 'fèy-le 'bàn-tyān-'shř tsáy 'dàw-jèr. ‖It's hard to say. hěn 'nán shwō. or bù-'hǎw shwō. or *expressed as* It's hard to predict. hěn 'nán 'ywù-lyàw. or bù-hǎw 'ywù-lyàw. ‖Don't make it so hard for me. byé jyàw-wǒ wéy-'nán. ‖It's hard to make a living. chř-'fàn °bù-'rúng-yì. or °bú-'yì. or °hěn 'nán. ‖No job is too hard for him. tā dzwò 'shéme dēw °bù-wéy-'nán. or, *meaning* can do, °shíng. ‖Isn't this job too hard for him? 'jèy-jyàn-shř jyàw-'tā dzwò bú-'tày-nán-dyǎr-ma? ‖This mathematics problem is hard to solve. 'jèy-ge-tí 'jyě-chi-lay hěn fèy-'shīn-sz. ‖Farming is hard. jùng-'dì °bú-shr 'rúng-yì-de-shř. or °bú-'yì. or °hěn 'nán. or °hěn chř-'lì. or °hěn 'shīn-kǔ. ‖This kind of box is hard to make without the right tools. méy-yew hé-'shř-de-'jyā-hwo, jèy-jǔng-'hé-dz °bù-hǎw 'dzwò. or °hěn nán 'dzwò. or °'dzwò-chī-lay hěn fèy-'shř. or °'dzwò-chī-lay hěn fèy-'lì. or °'dzwò-chī-lay bù-'rúng-yì. ‖If you like hard work, there is plenty here. nǐ yàw-shr 'shǐ-hwan dzwò fèy-jìn-de-'hwór, jèr 'yěw-de 'shř. ‖This job is hard to tackle. jèy-jyàn-'shř dzwò-chi-lay hěn °fèy-'shř. or °fèy-'shīn-sz. or °fèy-'jìn. or °fèy-'jyèr. or °fèy-'lì. or °'nán. ‖It looks easy, but it's really quite hard. 'kàn-shang-chywu 'rúng-yì, dzwò-chi-lay jyèw 'nán-le. ‖The work gets harder and harder. gūng-dzwò 'ywè-láy ywè-°'nán. or °bù-'rúng-yì. or °'má-fan. or °chř-'lì. *etc.*

(*Strenuous; of work*) shř-'jìn, shř-'jyèr, mày 'lì-chi, chū-'lì; (*of trying to do something*) fèy . . . jìn, fèy . . . 'lì-chi, fèy . . . jyèr. *Compare some of the expressions in previous section.* ‖He is a hard worker and does a good job. tā dzwò-'shř hěn mày 'lì-chì, ěr-chyě 'dzwò-de yě hěn 'hǎw. ‖He gets ahead because he works hard. tā dzwò-'shř kěn chū-'lì, swǒ-yǐ néng dzěw-dàw 'byé-rén-'chyán-tew-chywu. ‖He tried hard to do it right, but failed. tā 'fèy-le hěn-'dà-de-jìn shyǎng bǎ 'nèy-ge dzwò-'dwèy-le, 'kě-shr méy-'chéng-gūng. *or* tā 'hěn shyǎng dzwò-de-'hǎw, kě-shr fèy-le hǎw-'dà-de-'lì-chi (*or* kě-shr 'báy-fèy-le hěn-'dà-de-'jyèr) yě bù-'shíng.

(*Tight*) jǐn. ‖He tied the rope into a hard knot. tā bǎ 'shéng-dz dǎ-le yí-ge-hěn-'jǐn-de-'kèwr.

Hard (and fast). (*Strict*) yán, jǐn; *or expressed as* fierce hěn; *or as* ungracious 'kè-bwo. ‖We have no hard and fast rules here. 'wǒm-jèr 'méy-shéme-hěn-'yán (*or* -'jǐn)-de-'gwēy-jywù. ‖Hard rules are hard to apply. tày-yán (*or* tày-jǐn)-de-'gwēy-dzé nán 'shíng. ‖He's hard on people. tā dày-rén tày °'yán. *or* °'jǐn. *or* °'hěn. *or* °'kè-bwo.

(*Harsh; of words*). ‖Those are hard words. nèy-shyē-'hwà °hěn 'shyūng. *or* °hěn 'swèn. *or* °hěn 'kè-bwo. *or* °yěw dyǎr-gwò-'fèn.

(*Hurt; of feelings*). ‖No hard feelings? shèr 'gwò-le jyèw 'swàn-le, hǎw-ma? *or* byé 'jì-dzày 'shīn-shang, hǎw-ma? ‖I know he left with some hard feelings. wǒ 'jř-dàw tā-'dzěw-de-shř-hew 'shīn-li °hěn bú-'tùng-kay. *or* °hwáy-'hèn.

To be hard on. ‖He's hard on shoes. tā chwān-'shyé hěn 'fèy.

(*Of rain*). ‖It was raining hard when he left the house. tā 'lí-kay jyā de-shř-hew, ywǔ-'shyà-de ,hěn °'dà. *or* 'jǐn. *or* °'lì-hay.

(*Of persuasion*). ‖Don't press him too hard. byé 'bǎ-tā 'bī-de tày °'jǐn-le. *or* °'jí-le.

(*Of physical condition*). ‖He's been training for two months and is hard as nails. *is expressed as* . . . like a small iron ball. tā 'lyàn-le yěw· 'lyǎng-ge-ywè-le, °gēn ge-shyǎw-tyě-'dàr shř-de. *or as* . . . trained to where he's like iron. °'lyàn-de shyàng 'tyě-dǎ-de shř-de. *or as* . . . trained so that his body is solid. °lyàn-de 'shēn-dz hěn 'jyē-shr.

Hard of hearing. ‖You'll have to speak louder, because he's hard of hearing. nǐ děy 'dà-dyǎr-shēngr 'shwō, tā 'ěr-dwo yěw dyǎr °'bèy. *or* °'lúng.

Hard up (*short of cash*). ‖He's always hard up before pay day. yí-'kwày-dàw fā-'chyán-de-nèy-'jǐ-tyān tā jyèw °hěn 'jyǔng. *or* °hěn 'jǐn. *or* °shěw-'dǐ-shya hěn 'jǐn-de.

HARDLY. (*Not quite, just*) gāng X, jyèw Y; *or* tsáy X, jyèw Y (*X and Y must include a verb*). ‖He had hardly begun to speak when he was interrupted. tā 'gāng yī-'shwō de-shř-hew, jyèw 'jyàw-rén gěy 'chà-kāy-le. *or* tā 'gāng (*or* tsáy) kāy-'kěw, jyèw gěy 'chà-gwo-chywu·le.

(*Scarcely*) 'chà-dyǎr, 'jī-hū, 'jyǎn-jř *plus a negative or a word meaning the opposite of the English; these terms mean* almost, *so that one must say* almost not. ‖There were hardly any people there when the picture started. 'dyàn-yěngr-'kāy-de-shř-hew, °'jyǎn-jř 'méy-jī-ge-rén. *or* °'jī-hu méy-yew rén. ‖I could hardly believe my eyes when I saw him. wǒ 'gāng yí-'kàn-jyan_tā 'chà-dyǎr yǐ-wéy wǒ kàn-'tswò-le rén-le. ‖I could hardly believe my eyes when I saw the food on the table. wǒ yí-'kàn-jyan jwōr-shang-'bǎy-de-chř-shr, 'jī-hu 'yǐ-wéy wǒ °kàn-'tswò-le. *or* °yǎn-'lí-le. *or* °shř dzwò-'mèng-ne. ‖Hardly any people came. 'jī-hu 'méy-yew rén 'láy. ‖He hardly ever shows up any more. tsúng 'nèy-tsž yǐ-'hèw, tā 'jyǎn-jř bú-lèw-'myàr-le.

(*Not quite to the point of*) bú-'dàw. ‖He's hardly twenty. tā háy 'bú-dàw 'èr-shr-swèy.

(*Polite expression for* definitely not). ‖You can hardly expect me to believe what he just said. tā-'gāng-tsay-shwō-de-'hwà °nǐ shyǎng 'wǒ néng 'shìn-ma? *or* °nǐ 'bú-yàw yǐ-wéy wǒ hwèy 'shìn-de. *or* °nǐ 'fàng-shīn, wǒ 'bú-hwèy 'shìn-de. ‖You can hardly expect me to be taken in like that. nǐ shyǎng 'wǒ 'nèm-'rúng-yi 'pyàn-ma? ‖It's hardly right to say that about him. 'nèm 'jyǎng-lwèn tā bú-dà 'dwèy. ‖You can hardly blame him for losing his temper. bù-hǎw 'gwày tā fā 'pí-chi-de. *or* dzěm néng 'gwày-tā fā 'pí-chi-ne? ‖You can hardly call him a scholar. tā 'chēng-wéy 'shywé-jě bú-dà 'pèy.

HAT. 'màw-dz. ‖Where can I buy a hat? wǒ yàw may 'màw-dz dzày-'nǎr mǎy hǎw? *or* wǒ yàw mǎy 'màw-dz, dàw-'nǎr mǎy-ne? *or* 'nǎr yěw mày-'màw-dz-de?

HATE. hèn. ‖She hated her husband because he had left her. tā 'hèn tā-'jàng-fu, yīn-wey tā bǎ-tā 'rēng-shya-le. ‖They hate him because he worked them to death. tā 'bī-tām dzwò-gūng tày 'jǐn-le, swǒ-yǐ tām 'hèn-tā. ‖They hate her because she is more intelligent than they. tā bǐ-tām 'jīng-ming, swǒ-yǐ tām 'hèn-tā. ‖He hates that family because they forced his father to commit suicide. tā 'hèn nèy-'jyā-de-rén, yīn-wèy tām bǎ tā-'fù-chin 'bī-de dz̀-'shā-le. *or* tā gēn nèy-'jyā-de-rén yěw-'chéw, yīn-wèy . . . (chéw *means* a serious grievance). ‖She hates you for saying that. nǐ shwō 'nèy-ge láy-je, tā jyèw °'hèn-nǐ-le. *or* °('shīn-li) hwáy-'hèn-le. *or* °nǎw-le nǐ-le. ‖Hate is anger perpetuated. shēng-'chì shēng-de méy-'wán-le, nà jyèw-shr 'hèn. ‖You could see hate in her eyes. tā 'yǎn-li dày-je 'hèn-de-yì-sz.

(*Milder dislike*). ‖I hate to get up in the morning. 'dzǎw-shang wǒ bù-'shǐ-hwan 'chǐ-láy.

HAVE (HAS, HAD). (*To possess*). *Often directly translated by* yěw; *sometimes indirectly translated by other expressions:* yěw *in some cases also demands the translation* there is *or* there are. ‖I have two tickets to the theater. wǒ yěw 'lyǎng-jāng-shì-'pyàw. ‖Do you have any brothers and sisters? nǐ yěw 'dì-shyūng jyě-'mèy-ma? ‖He has a dog. tā yěw yì-jř-'gěw. ‖He has a fine library. tā yěw 'hěn dwō 'hǎw-shū. or expressed as His book collection is large. tā-'tsáng-shū bù-'shǎw. ‖I have a sore foot. is expressed as My foot hurts. wǒ-'jyǎw téng. or wǒ yěw yì-jř-'jyǎw téng. or wǒ-yì-jř-'jyǎw yěw dyǎr-'téng. ‖He has a funny nose. is expressed as His nose grows funny. tā-de-'bí-dz-jǎng-de kě-'shyàw. ‖What do you have in your hands? is expressed as What is in your hands? nǐ-'shěw-li-ná-de shř 'shéme? ‖He has a bit of a southern accent. tā dày (or tā yěw) lyǎr-'nán-fang-'kěw-yīn.

(To take along) dày. ‖I had some money with me. wǒ-(-'shēn-shang) 'dày-je dyǎr-'chyán láy-je. ‖I had my dog with me when I went there. wǒ dày-je 'gěw chywù-de. ‖I had my gun with me when I came downstairs. wǒ dày-je 'chyāng shyà-de 'léw. or wǒ-shyà-'léw-de-shf-hew dày-je 'chyāng-lay-je. ‖I had a gun with me all the time. wǒ yì-jř dày-je 'chyāng-láy-je. But ‖I didn't have any money (at all). as distinguished from I didn't have any money with me. wǒ méy-yew 'chyán.

(To keep). Various expressions, usually not direct translations. ‖I had the gun under the pillow the whole night. jěng-'yè chyāng dēw dzày 'jěn-léw 'dǐ-shya. ‖I had him with me the whole evening. yì-'wǎn-shang tā dēw gēn-'wǒ dzày yí-'kwàr. ‖They're going to have a guest staying with them for some time. 'tām-nàr kwày yàw °yěw ge-'kè-rén láy 'jù shyē-shf-hew. or °láy ge-'kè-ren 'jù shyē-r̀-dz.

(To give birth to) shēng, or, more commonly, expressed by euphemisms. ‖Is she going to have a baby? is expressed as Does she have happiness? tā yěw-'shǐ-le-ma? or as Has she conceived a child? tā yěw shyǎw-'hár-le-ma? or, medical, as Is she pregnant? tā yěw-'ywùn-le-ma? ‖When is she going to have the baby? tā 'jǐ-shf shēng shyǎw-'hár? or expressed as When will she reach the month? tā 'jǐ-shf dzwò. 'ywè-dz? ‖My wife is going to have a baby. is expressed in modern speech as She's going to the hospital. wǒ-'tày-tay yàw shàng yī-'ywàn-le. or (Old-fashioned speech) nèy-rén kwày dàw-'ywèr-le. or nèy-rén yàw dzwò 'ywè-dz-le. or (Plain talk) wǒ-'tày-tay yàw shēng 'háy-dz-le.

(To take, of food, lessons, etc.). Expressed by more specific verb in Chinese, as to eat chř; to drink hē; to study shywé, etc. ‖Let's have dinner at six o'clock. dzám 'lyèw-dyǎn-jūng chř-'fàn-ba. ‖I've had one drink too many. wǒ 'dwō hē-le nèm-yi-dyar. ‖Have you had dinner yet? chř-'fàn-le-ma? ‖Do have another cup of coffee. dzày 'hē (or dzày 'láy) bēy-'jyā-fēy-ba. ‖I have piano lessons twice a week. wǒ 'měy-lǐ-bày shywé 'lyǎng-tsž-chín. ‖When do you have a holiday? nǐ 'jǐ-shf yěw (or fàng)-'jyà?

(To speak) as in have a word with. ‖May I have a word with you? wǒ yěw 'hwà yàw gēn-ni 'tán-tan.

(To experience). ‖I had a hard time getting up this morning, because of my sore legs. wǒ-'twéy téng-de jyěr 'dzǎw-chen 'chǐ-de hěn fèy-'shř. ‖I had a hard time buying it. 'jèy-ge wǒ mǎy-de hěn fèy-'shř. or 'jèy-ge wǒ 'fèy-le hǎw-'shyē-shf-hew tsáy 'mǎy-jáw-de.

(To know) 'jř-dàw. ‖I have the idea clearly in mind. nèy-ge wǒ-'jř-dàw-de hěn 'chīng-chu. or nèy-ge wǒ-'jř-dàw-de 'chīng-ching-chu-'chū-de.

(To cause, let). Have something done bǎ . . .; have someone do something jyàw . . . . ‖Have this cleaned thoroughly. bǎ 'jèy-ge 'dž-dz-shì-'shì-de tsā-'gān-jing-le. ‖I'll have the room ready for you in fifteen minutes. yěw shf-'wǔ-fēn-jūng wǒ jyèw bǎ 'wū-dz gěy-nǐ 'shēw-shr-chū-lay-le. ‖He had the janitor discharged. tā bǎ tìng-'chāy-de gěy tsáy-le. ‖He had all the cards marked as you told him. tā bǎ 'pyàn-dz dēw jàw nǐ-'shwō-de nèy-yàngr hwà-'hǎw-le. ‖I'll have two men here tomorrow to cut down the trees. myér wǒ jyàw 'lyǎng-ge-rén láy kǎn-'shù. ‖I had him do it. wǒ jyàw-'tā dzwò-de. ‖I had him do it over and over again. wǒ jyàw-tā 'yí-byàn yèw yí-'byàn-de dzwò. ‖He has the laundry do his shirts. tā jyàw shǐ-'yī-f-de shǐ tā-de-chèn-'shār. But ‖I have my teeth cleaned twice a year. wǒ 'měy-nyán shǐ 'lyǎng-tsž yá and ‖I had it made to order. nèy shř wǒ dìng-'dzwò-de.

Have to (must) děy; or, more emphatic, 'bū . . . bù-'shíng, 'bū . . . nǐ 'jyàw-wǒ 'dzěm-je, 'fēy-děy, 'fēy . . . bù-'shíng, 'bù-néng bū; not have to bù-yí-'dìng děy; 'bū . . . yě 'shíng, 'bū . . .hǎw, bú-'bì. ‖I had to leave early. wǒ děy 'dzǎw dzěw. ‖She has to go home now. tā děy hwéy-'jyā-le. ‖I simply had to hit him. wǒ bù-'dǎ-tā bù-'shíng. or wǒ fēy 'dǎ-tā bù-'shíng. or wǒ bù-'dǎ-tā nǐ 'jyàw-wǒ 'dzěm-je-ne? or wǒ 'bù-néng bù-'dǎ-tā. ‖Do I HAVE to have tickets? 'fēy-děy yěw-'pyàw-ma? ‖Do you HAVE to say that? nǐ 'fēy nèm shwō bù-'shíng-ma? or nǐ yí-'dìng děy nèm shwō-ma? or (Sarcastically) nǐ 'dzěm jyèw 'fēy dwō 'dzwěy bù-'shíng-ne? or nǐ 'dzěm jyèw 'fēy-děy 'shwō-chu-lay-ne? ‖Does he have to wear patent leather shoes? tā 'fēy-děy (or tā . .-'dìng děy) chwān 'chī-pí-shyé-ma? or tā 'bù-chwān 'chī-pí-shyé bù-'shíng-ma? ‖She had to say yes. tā bù-'néng bù-'dā-ying. ‖You don't have to do anything you don't want to. nǐ-'bú-ywàn-yì-dzwò-de jyèw 'béng-dzwò, hǎw-le. ‖You don't have to come. (nǐ) 'bù-láy yě 'shíng. or (Impatiently) 'bù-láy jyèw 'bù-láy-ba. ‖You don't have to pay me now. nǐ 'shyàn-dzày 'bù-hwán yě 'shíng. or nǐ 'bú-bì 'shyàn-dzày jyèw 'hwán-wǒ. ‖I don't have to go, do I? wǒ 'bú-shř yí-'dìng děy 'chywù-ba, á? or wǒ 'bú-chywù yě 'shíng-ba, nǐ 'shwō-ne? ‖You don't have to be THAT polite. nǐ 'bú-bì 'nèm 'kè-chi. or nǐ 'yùng-bu-jáw 'nèm 'kè-chi.

(To permit) usually shywǔ. ‖I won't have noise in this room any longer. 'dzày bù-shywǔ dzày 'jèy-jyān-wū-dz-li 'chǎw-le. ‖I won't have it! 'bù-shywǔ 'nèm-je. or 'bù-néng 'nèm-je.

(Before a verb, indicating past time or completed action) -le or -gwo (negative forms are méy- or méy . . .-gwo, but never méy . . .-le; 'méy-yew is sometimes

*used by southerners, and always as the negative alter-
native of a question)* ; *sometimes expressed by a phrase
ending in* -de; *when a specific time is indicated, there
is often no additional expression.* ‖Have you read this?
jèy-ge nǐ kàn-'wán-le-ma? *or* jèy-ge nǐ kàn-'wán-le
méy-yew? ‖I've read it. 'kàn-le. *or* kàn-'wán-le. ‖I've
read it three times. wǒ 'kàn-gwo 'sān-byàn-le.
‖I haven't read it. méy-'kàn-gwo. *or* méy-'kàn. *or
sometimes, by southerners,* méy-yew 'kàn. ‖Has he
gone home? tā ('yǐ-jīng) hwéy-'jyā-le-ma? *or* tā
hwéy-'jyā-le méy-yew? *or expressed as* Has he returned home yet? tā 'hwéy méy-hwéy 'jyā? ‖Has he
taken the medicine? tā chī-'yàw-le méy-yew? ‖I have
lived here twelve years. wǒ dzày-'jèr (jù-le) shí-'èr-
nyán-le. ‖What I have done, I have done. 'yǐ-jīng
nèm-je-le, jyèw 'swàn-le. *or* (*Literary*) 'mù-yǐ-chéng-
'jēw-le, jyèw 'swàn-le. ‖Has he done his job well? tā-
de-shī-'dzwò-de hǎw-bu-hǎw? ‖He has had his day.
tā gwò-'shí-le. ‖I have known her since kindergarten
days. tsúng yèw-jī-'ywán-de-shí-hew wǒ jyèw 'rèn-
de tā. ‖I've been watching him since he came in.
tsúng tā yí-'jìn-lay wǒ jyèw 'dīng-je tā.

Have it in for. ‖They'll have it in for us if we do
that. yàw-shr 'jèm-yàng tā-men 'bú-hwèy 'ráw wǒ-
men-de.

Have it out (*figuratively*). ‖It's better to have it out
now than later. háy-shr shyàn-dzày shwō-'míng-bay-
le hǎw. *or* (*Proverbial*) 'shyǎn shyǎw-rén 'hèw jywūn-
dz-ba.

Other expressions in English. ‖Let him have it! *is
expressed as* Give it (*something*) to him. 'gěy-tā.
or as Shoot him! 'gěy-tā yí-'shyà-dz. ‖Have it your
way, then. *is expressed as* I won't restrain you. swéy
'nǐ-ba. *or as* We'll do it your way. yī (*or* swéy) 'nǐ-
shwō-de 'bàn, hǎw-le. ‖He can be had (*bribed*). tā kě-
yǐ mǎy-gwo-lay. *or* tā kě-yǐ 'mǎy-de-'tūng. *or* 'tā-ya,
gěy-tā 'chyán jyèw shíng.

HAY. 'tsǎw (*also means* grass *and* straw). ‖They saw
field after field of hay. tām yí-'kàn, 'nǎr dēw shr
'tsǎw. *or* tām 'kàn-jyan yí-'kwày-yí-kwày-de-'dì-li
'dēw shr 'tsǎw.

Other expressions in English. ‖Let's make hay while
the sun shines. *is expressed as* While there's a chance,
let's hurry and do it. 'chèn-je yěw 'jī-hwèy, dzám
'gǎn-jǐn kwày-'gàn. *or as* Don't let this chance slip
away. byé 'tswò-gwò-le jèy-ge-'jī-hwey. *or as* If we
don't leave now, what other time are we waiting for?
(*Literary quotation*) 'tsž-shí bù-'dzěw 'gèng-dàw-
'hé-shí? ‖I'm tired; let's hit the hay. wǒ 'lèy-le;
shwèy-'jyàw-ba.

HE (SHE). tā; him, her tā; his, her, hers tā *or* 'tā-de.
‖Who is he? 'tā shr-'shéy? ‖If anyone can do it, he
can. (yàw-shr) 'rén-néng-'dzwò-de-shr, shr-'tā jwěn
néng 'dzwò. ‖I've seen him once. wǒ 'kàn-jyan-gwo
tā yí-'tsž. ‖Oh, HIM! 'èw, 'tā-ya! ‖Give this to him.

bǎ jèy-ge gěy-'tā. ‖I saw her last week. wǒ 'shàng-lǐ-
bày 'kàn-jyan ta-le. ‖This is her hat. jèy-shr 'tā-de-
màw-dz. ‖Where's her hat? tā-de-'màw-dz dzày-
'nǎr-ne? ‖Do you have his address? nǐ yěw tā-de
'jù-jr-ma? ‖His father was a minister. tā-'fù-chir
shr ge-'mù-shr. ‖Hers is blue. 'tā-de shr 'lán-de.

He *and* she *used to specify sex are expressed as*
male *and* female (*for human beings*) nán *and* nywǔ;
(*for animals*) gūng *and* mǔ. ‖It's a HE. shr ge-'nán-
rén. *or* shr ge-'nán-de *or* (*of animal*) shr ge-'gūng-de.
‖It's a he-goat. shr ge-'gūng-yáng.

The simple form tā *is often lengthened to* tā-'nèy-
ge-rén *or* (*specifying sex*) tā-nèy-ge-'nán-ren, tā-nèy-
ge-'nywǔ-rén; *sometimes one says just that fellow*
nèy-ge-'rén, *etc.*

Himself, herself. *See* SELF.

HEAD. (*Part of the body*) téw, or, *in certain localities,*
'nǎw-day. ‖My head hurts. wǒ 'téw-téng. ‖He shakes
his head. tā yáw-'téw. ‖He's raising his head. tā
'táy-chi 'téw-lay-le. ‖He nods his head in recognition.
tā dyàn-'téw. ‖He turned his head that way. tā
chùng-je 'nèy-byar 'nyěw-téw. ‖I fell head first. wǒ
'téw-cháw-'shyà 'shwāy-shya-chywu-le. ‖The child's
head is covered with dust. nèy-ge-háy-dz-'téw (*or*
-'nǎw-day)-shang 'chywán shr 'tǔ. ‖The head of that
monkey is almost human. nèy-ge-'héw-dz-de-'téw
jyǎn-jí shyàng 'rén-de.

(*Of a nail*) téw, téwr. ‖We want some nails with
larger heads. wǒm yàw téwr-'dà-dyǎr-de-'dīng-dz.

(*Of workmen or an informal group*) 'téwr, líng-
'téwr. ‖Mr. Wáng is the head man. 'wáng-shyān-
sheng shr °'téwr. *or* °líng-'téwr-de.

(*Of a family*) jyā-'jǎng. ‖Who is the head of the
family? jyā-'jǎng shr shéy?

(*Of an organization*) jǔ-'shr-de. ‖I want to speak to
the head of the organization. wǒ yàw jyàn jǔ-'shr-de.

(*Climax*). ‖Matters are coming to a head. dàw-le
'jǐn-yàw-gwān-'téw-le. *or* 'shr-chíng 'dzày bù-néng
'twō-le. *or* 'shr-chíng dàw-le 'fēy-bàn-bù-'kě-de-shí-
hew-le. ‖When did this trouble come to a head? jèy-
ge-'lwàn-dz 'shéme-shí-hew 'nàw-'lì-hay-le-de?

(*Unit; in counting cattle*) téw; (*in counting vegetables*) kē; (*in counting people*) rén. ‖How many head
of cattle are there on the farm? 'chǎng-shang yěw
'dwō-shǎw-téw-'nyéw? ‖The cabbage is ten cents a
head. 'yáng-báy-tsày yì-'máw-chyán yì-'kē. ‖At ten
dollars per head (*person*) that would amount to
seventy-five million dollars. 'měy-rén 'shr-kwày-
chyán jyèw-shr 'chī-chyān-'wǔ-bǎy-'wàn. ‖We need
two heads of cabbage. wǒm děy-yàw 'lyǎng-kē-báy-
'tsày

(*Intelligence*) 'běn-lǐng, 'tsáy-gàn. ‖He has a good
head for business. tā yěw dzwò-'mǎy-may-de-°'běn-
lǐng. *or* °'tsáy-gàn.

(*Top*) 'gàr. ‖We'll have to knock in the head of the
barrel. tǔng-dz-'gàr yí-'dìng děy 'dzá-shyà-chywù.

(*Beginning; of a page*) chǐ-'téwr. ‖Begin at the head of this page. dzày jèy-'pyār-shang tsúng chǐ-'téwr nyàn.

(*Top or front*) 'chyán-byar, dì-'yī. ‖You are at the head of the list. nǐ dzày 'míng-dār jǐn 'chyán-byar. ‖The mayor was at the head of the procession. shr-'jǎng dzày dwèy-'chyán-byar lǐng-je. ‖The boy heads his class (*is at the head of his class*) in school. jèy-ge-'háy-dz dzày tā-'bān-li dì-'yī.

(*Source*) 'fā-ywán-'dì. ‖How far is it to the head of the river? (jèy-tváw-'hé) lí 'fā-ywán-'dì yèw 'dwō-ywǎn?

(*To move or face in a direction; go*) shàng; (*return*) hwéy; (*go toward*) wàng, shyàng; (*face toward*) 'chùng-je, 'dǐng-je. ‖Where are you headed? 'nǐ shàng-'nǎr? ‖It's about time for me to head home. 'dàw-le wǒ-gǎy-hwéy-'jyā-de-shŕ-hew-le. *or* 'dàw-le wǒ gǎy-wàng-'jyā-dzěw-de-shŕ-hew-le. ‖I saw the plane heading east. wǒ 'kàn-jyan nèy-jyà-fēy-'jī shyàng (*or* wàng)-'dūng fēy. ‖He is heading that way. tā 'jèng wàng (*or* shyàng, *or* chùng-je) 'nèy-byar 'dzěw (*or* 'pǎw *if he is in a rush*). ‖The pilot headed the plane into the wind. jyà-shǐ-'ywán bǎ 'fēy-jī 'chùng-je (*or* 'dǐng-je) fēng 'kāy-chywu-le.

Head wind. ‖A head wind all along the way delayed our arrival. *is expressed as* We were heading into the wind the whole way, so we were late. yí-'lù 'dǐng-je 'fēng, swǒ-yǐ 'wǎn-dàw-de. (*See also preceding paragraph.*)

Head-on. ‖It was a head-on collision. jèng-'chwàng-shang. *or* (*Of vehicles only*) chē-'téw pèng (*or* 'jwàng, *or* chwàng) chē-'téw.

To head off. ‖Head him off! *is expressed as* Stop him. bǎ-tā 'jyé-jù. *or* bǎ-tā 'lán-ju. *or as* Force him to go in another direction. jyàw-tā byé wàng 'nèy-byar chywù. *or as* Get him to change his ideas. jyàw-tā byé wàng 'nèy-byar 'shyàng.

Head over heels (*literally*). ‖He fell out of the car head over heels. tā tsúng 'chē-shang 'dyàw-chu-chywu de-shŕ-hew, 'fān-le jǐ-ge-'gēn-dew.

Head over heels (*figuratively*). ‖My friend is head over heels in love. wǒ-de-'péng-yew jèng-dzay °lyàn-'ày lyàn-de 'hwǒ-rè-de. *or* °'rè-lyàn-de-shŕ-hew. *or* (*of a man only*) °'bày-dǎw 'shŕ-lyew-'chywún-shyà.

Heads (*in tossing a coin*) dzèr. ‖Heads I win, tails I lose. yàw-shr 'dzèr, wǒ jyèw 'yíng; 'mèr, wǒ jyèw 'shū.

Out of one's head 'fēng(-le). ‖That man is positively out of his head. 'nèy-ge-rén jyàn-'jŕ shr 'fēng-le.

Over one's head (*beyond one's understanding*). ‖That problem is over my head. nèy-ge-wèn-'tí wǒ 'mwò-míng-chí-'myàw.

Over one's head (*to a higher authority*). ‖It may be necessary to go over his head on this. 'jèy-jyàn-shŕ, yě-shywǔ děy 'ywè-gwo tā-chywu.

Go to one's head. ‖The success has gone to his head. tā yěw dyǎr-'dé-yì-wàng-'shing.

Hit the nail on the head. ‖You hit the nail on the head that time. 'nèy-tsž nǐ kě shwō-'jáw-le. *or* 'nèy-tsž nǐ shwō-de jèng 'dwèy.

Keep one's head bù-'hwāng, 'lěng-jìng, 'jèn-jìng; lose one's head hwāng, 'hú-dū. ‖Everyone kept his head in the excitement. dzày 'jin-jāng-de-shŕ-hew, dà-jyā dēw °hěn 'lěng-jìng. *or* °hěn 'jèn-jìng. *or* °méy-'hwāng. ‖Everyone lost his head. dà-jyā dēw °hwāng-le. *or* °'hú-dū-le. *or* °'bù-jŕ-dàw dzěm-me 'bàn-le. ‖She got angry and lost her head. tā jí-de 'hú-du-le. *or* tā chì-de 'hú-du-le.

Keep one's head above water. ‖He can hardly keep his head above water. (*Literally*) tā dzày 'shwěy-li dž-jǐ jyǎn-jŕ 'táy-bu-chǐ 'téw-lay. (*Figuratively*) tā 'jyǎn-jŕ dž-gù-bù-'shyá.

Make head or tail of. ‖I can't make head or tail of the story. wǒ 'māw (*or* 'mwō)-bu-chīng shr 'dzěm hwéy-shr.

Put heads together. ‖Let's put our heads together and figure it out. dzám 'jywù-jīng-hwèy-'shén-de 'yán-jyēw yí-shyàr.

Take it into one's head. ‖The maid suddenly took it into her head to leave. nywǔ-'shyà-rén 'hú-rán °shyǎng (*or* yàw) 'dzěw (*or* bú-'gàn). *or* °'fēy-yàw 'dzěw (bù-'kě).

Turn *someone's* head (*make one conceited*). ‖His flattery turned her head. tā bǎ-tā 'kwā-de 'wàng-chí swǒ-'yǐ-le. *or* tā yí-'jèn 'hwā-yán-chyǎw-'ywǔ bǎy-tā 'shwō-de 'gǎy-le 'jú-yì-le.

HEALTH. 'shēn-dz, 'shēn-tǐ (*both also mean body, bodily condition*); (**in**) **good health** 'jyàn-kāng; (*health measures, health protection*) wèy-'shēng. ‖How is your health? nǐ 'shēn-dz dzěm-yàng? *or* nǐ 'shēn-tǐ dzěm-yàng? *or* (*Medical*) nǐ 'jyàn-kāng dzěm-yàng? ‖If you keep on that way you'll ruin your health. nǐ yàw 'lǎw nèm-je, jyèw bǎ 'shēn-dz nùng 'hwày-le. ‖You should guard your health. 'shēn-dz (*or* 'shēn-tǐ) yàw bǎw-'jùng. *or* yàw 'bǎw-chŕ 'jyàn-kāng. *or* yàw jyǎng wèy-'shēng. ‖He's in good health. tā-shēn-dz (*or* tā-'shēn-tǐ) hěn 'hǎw. *or, meaning* in sound health, tā-'shēn-dz (*or* tā-'shēn-tǐ) hěn 'jyē-shr. *or* tā hěn 'jyàn-kāng. ‖This is the Public Health Bureau. jèy shr 'gūng-gùng-wèy-'shēng-'jywú. ‖It's good for your health. jyàw nǐ-de-'shēn-dz 'hǎw. *or* jyàw-nǐ 'jwàng. *or* jyàw-nǐ 'chyáng-jwàng. ‖She has been in poor health lately. tā jìn-lay 'shēn-dz bú-dà 'hǎw. ‖Health is appreciated only after it is lost. dàw-le 'bú-jyàn-kāng-de-shŕ-hew rén tsáy 'jŕ-dàw 'jyàn-kāng (*or* 'shēn-dz) 'dwō-me yīng-gay 'ày-shī. *But* ‖Here's to your health! 'jìng-nǐ yì-'bēy. *or* 'fú-shèw-kāng-'níng. *or* 'jìng-nǐ yì-bēy-'fú-shèw-kāng-'níng.

HEALTHY. ‖I feel healthy enough. (*Strong*) wǒ 'jywé-de wǒ-shēn-dz gèw °'jwàng-de. *or* (*Well*) °'hǎw-de. *or* (*Sound*) °'jyē-shr-de. *or* °'tsž-shr. ‖He's healthy. tā(-shēn-dz) hěn °'jwàng. *or* °'chyáng-jwàng. *or*

°'hǎw. or °'jyē-shr. or °tsźź-shr. or tā hěn 'jyàn-kāng. or tā 'méy-yew 'bìng. ‖**You look healthier, now.** nǐ-'shēn-dz (or, referring to facial color nǐ-'chì-shǎr, or nǐ-'lyǎn-shǎr) kàn-shang-chywu hǎw 'dwō-le. or nǐ 'jīng-shén hǎw 'dwō-le.

(Conducive to health). ‖**This isn't a healthy climate to live in.** jèr-de-'chì-hew 'rén jù-je bù-shyāng-'yí. ‖**This isn't a healthy job.** 'jèy-ge-shèr ywú 'jyàn-kāng yěw-'hày. or dzwò 'jèy-ge-shèr dzwò-'cháng-le jyàw 'shēn-dz bù-'hǎw. ‖**This is a healthy sport.** 'jèy-jǔng-'ywùn-dung jyàw-rén 'shēn-dz 'chyáng-jwàng. ‖**This is a healthy place to be in.** jèy-ge-'dì-fang dāy-je °'ywú-rén yěw-'yí. or °'ywú-rén shyāng-'yí. or °jyàw-rén yěw 'jīng-shen. or °jyàw-rén 'kāng-jyàn. or °jyàw-rén 'shēn-dz hǎw. or °jyàw-rén 'dwō-hwó-jǐ-nyán.

(Figuratively). ‖**The pupils showed a healthy respect for their teacher.** shywé-sheng hěn 'dzwēn-jing tām-de-'shyān-sheng.

HEAP. dwēy (Peiping pronunciation dzwēy). Small heap dwēr. ‖**Don't leave those things in a heap.** byé bǎ 'dūng-shi 'dwēy-je (or 'dwēy-ner) jyèw bù-'gwǎn-le. ‖**Heaps of sand dotted the yard.** 'ywàn-dz-li yěw yì-'dwēy-yì-'dwēv-de-'shā-dz. ‖**Throw all this stuff in the rubbish heap.** bǎ 'jèy-shyē dēw 'rēng-dàw 'lā-shi-'dwēy-shang-chywu. ‖**What is that canvas-covered heap?** yùng-'fān-bù-gày-je-de-nèy-'dwēy shr̀ shémme? ‖**The children piled sand into small heaps.** shyǎw-'hár bǎ 'shā-dz dwēy-de yì-'dwēr-yì-'dwēr-de. ‖**The table was heaped with all kinds of food.** 'jwō-dz-shang dwēy-'mǎn-le 'gè-shr-ge-'yàngr-de-'chr̄-de. ‖**Heap everything onto the bed.** dēw dwēy-dzày 'chwáng-shang hǎw-le. ‖**I just can't heap any more on the table.** 'jwōr-shang 'dzày yě dwēy-bu 'shyà shéme-le. or jwōr-shang-nèy-'dwēy dzày yě bù-néng 'jyā shéme-le. But ‖**He put two heaping teaspoons of sugar in his coffee.** jyā-'féy-lì-téw tā 'fàng-le mǎn-'mān-de-lyǎng-sháwr-'táng.

(Figuratively). ‖**That's heaping insult upon insult.** nèy shr̀ jyā-'bèy-de 'chī-fù rén. or (Literary) nà shr̀ 'chī-rén tày 'shèn-le.

HEAR (HEARD). (Simple perception) 'tīng-jyàn. ‖**I hear someone coming from there.** wǒ 'tīng-jyàn yěw-'rén tsúng-'nàr láy. ‖**Did you hear anything?** nǐ 'tīng-jyàn-le dyǎr-'shēng-yīn-ma? ‖**Can you hear it?** nǐ 'tīng-de-jyàn-ma? ‖**Do (or did) you hear it?** nǐ 'tīng-jyàn-le-ma? ‖**I just heard the telephone ring.** wǒ gāng 'tīng-jyàn dyàn-'hwà shyǎng-le. ‖**I hear a scratching sound.** wǒ tīng-jyàn-le 'kwā-cha-kwa-chā-de-'shēng-yīn. ‖**I can't hear a thing.** wǒ shém dēw 'tīng-bu-jyàn. ‖**I didn't hear a thing.** wǒ 'shém dēw méy-'tīng-jyan. ‖**All you can hear is his endless prattle.** nǐ 'jř-néng tīng-jyàn tā 'yí-ge-rén-de-'shēng-yīn, dzày-nàr shyā-'shwō. ‖**He pretends that he didn't hear me.** tā 'jwāng tīng-bu-jyàn.

(Clear perception) tīng-'chīng-chu. ‖**I can't hear you very well.** wǒ tīng-bu-'chīng-chu nǐ-'shwō-de shr̀ shéme.

(Listen to, listen for) tīng. ‖**I hear good music every night.** wǒ 'méy-tyān 'wán-shang tīng hǎw-'yīn-ywè. ‖**Hear me to the end.** nǐ 'tīng-wǒ shwō-'wán-le(w). ‖**I heard an interesting story yesterday.** wǒ dzwór 'tīng-le yí-dwàr-hěn-yěw-'yì-sź-de-shèr. ‖**Let me hear the arguments from both sides.** 'lyǎng-byàr-de-'lǐ dēw 'jyǎng-gěy wǒ 'tīng-ting. ‖**Hear ye, hear ye!** 'tīng-nga! 'tīng-nga!

To hear that, hear of is expressed as to hear it said that tīng-'shwō. ‖**I hear that the play was a success.** wǒ tīng-shwō 'shì hěn chéng-'gūng. ‖**I never heard of such a thing.** 'jèy-ge wǒ 'tsúng-láy méy-tīng-'shwō-gwo. or (without tīng-shwō) nǎr yěw 'nà-yàng-de shr̀. or (Literary and emphatic) nà jēn 'chí-yěw-tsź̌-'lǐ. ‖**I never heard of him.** jèy-ge-rén 'méy-tīng-jyàn 'shwō-gwo.

Hear in court shěn. ‖**The judge hears different kinds of cases every day.** fǎ-'gwǎn 'méy-tyān shěn gè-jǔng-'àn-dz. ‖**The case was heard in open court.** nèy-jyàn-'àn-dz dēw shr̀ 'gūng-kāy-'shěn-de.

Not hear of (not stand for). ‖**They offered to put me up for the night, but I wouldn't hear of it.** tām 'lyéw-wǒ 'jù-shya, °wǒ bú-'gàn. or °wǒ méy-'tīng.

(Of news). ‖**What do you hear from home?** jyā-li yěw-'shyèr-ma?

HEART. (Physical) 'shīn-dzàng. ‖**He has a weak heart.** tā-'shīn-dzàng yěw dyǎr-'shwāy-rwò. ‖**His heartbeat is weak today.** jyēr-ge tā-'shīn-dzàng (or tā-de-'mwò, his pulse) yěw dyǎr-'rwò. ‖**He has heart disease.** tā yěw 'shīn-dzàng-bìng.

(Emotional) shīn. ‖**She has a soft heart.** tā-shīn 'rwǎn. ‖**I'm glad to do it for you with all my heart.** jèy-jyàn-'shr̀ wǒ shr̀ 'jēn-shīn-chíng-'ywàn-de yàw shyàw-'láw. ‖**His heart is in the right place.** tā-'shīn hǎw. or tā-de-'shīn jǎng-de-'jèng. ‖**He wears his heart on his sleeve.** (Complimentary) tā 'shīn-jŕ-kěw-'kwày-de. or tā shr̀ ge-'jŕ-shīn-yǎr-de-rén. or tā shr̀ ge-'jŕ-shīn-cháng-de-rén. or tā 'yì-jywǔ-yí-'dùng dēw néng jyàw-rén 'kàn-de-chū tā-de-'shīn-shr-lay. (Not complimentary) tā-jèy-ge-rén bù-'shēn-chén. or tā 'shǐ-'nù shíng-ywú-'sè. ‖**He'll do it heart and soul.** tā hwèy 're-shīn-chywù-'bàn-de. ‖**He expressed his heartfelt gratitude toward you.** tā shwō tā 'jēn-shīn 'gǎn-jí nǐ. ‖**In his heart of hearts he probably doesn't mean it.** chí-'shŕ tā 'shīn-li dà-gày 'bú-shr nèm hwéy-shr̀. ‖**Don't lose heart.** byé 'hwēy-shīn. ‖**My heart was in my mouth when I said that.** wǒ shwō nèy-jywù-'hwà de-shŕ-hew, °'tí-shīn-dyàw-'dǎn-de. or °jěng-'gèr-de shǐn-'shywán-je. ‖**He's a man after my own heart.** tā gēn-wǒ 'shīn-téw-'yì-hé. or 'jèy-ge-rén 'jēn jyàw-wǒ 'shǐ-hwān. ‖**At heart he is really a nice fellow.** chí-'shŕ tā-nèy-ge-rén 'shīn-dì hěn 'hǎw. ‖**He broke her heart when he left.** tā-'dzěw-de-shŕ-hew 'jēn jyàw-tā shāng-'shīn. ‖**His mother died of a broken heart** while he was serving the sentence. tā-dzày-'jyān-de-shŕ-hew tā-'mǔ-chin shāng-'shīn sž-de. ‖It does my heart good to see them happy. tām gāw-'shìng 'wǒ-shīn-li yě hěn 'tùng-kwày. ‖Don't take it to heart. byé 'tày gē-dzay 'shīn-shang. or byé 'tày rèn-'jēn. ‖His dog and his gun are the things nearest his heart. tā shīn-li-'dzwèy-ày-de shŕ tā-de-'gěw gēn tā-de-'chyāng.

Other expressions relating to emotions. ‖Have a heart. 'shíng-shing-'hǎw-ba. ‖He has no heart. tā 'hěn-je-ne. or tā-shīn 'hěn. or tā-jèy-ge-rén 'méy-yew 'chíng-yì. or (*Literary*) tā-jèy-ge-rén wú-'chíng. or (*Literary*) tā-jèy-ge-rén 'kè-ḅwó-gwǎ-'ēn. ‖I haven't the heart to do it. wǒ bù-'rěn-de. ‖I haven't the heart to leave him here unattended. wǒ bù-'rěn-de bǎ-tā 'lyàw-shya jyèw 'dzěw. ‖Do you have the heart to treat him that way? ni 'nèm dày-tā shīn-li 'rěn-de-ma? or nǐ néng 'rěn-shīn 'nèm dày-tā-ma?

(*Heart-shaped figure*) shīn, táw. ‖Give me the box of candy with the heart on it. gěy-wǒ nèy-'hé-dz-shang-dày-'shīn (or -'táw)-de-'táng.

(*Suit in cards*) húng-'táwr. ‖I bid two hearts. wǒ jyàw-le 'lyǎng-ge húng-'táwr.

(*Central part*) jūng-'bù; (*precise center*) jèng-dāng-'jūng, 'jūng-shīn, 'jūng-shīn-dyǎn. ‖The store was located in the heart of town. 'pù-dz shŕ dzày chéng-de-°jèng-dāng-'jūng. or °'jūng-shīn(-'dyǎn). or °jūng-'bù.

Get at the heart of. ‖I intend to get at the heart of this matter. wǒ yàw 'jŕ-dàw jèy-jyàn-shŕ dàw-dǐ (or 'jyēw-jing) shŕ 'dzěm-me hwéy-shŕ. or jèy-jyàn-shŕ wǒ yí-'dìng yàw 'chè-dǐ chá-'chīng-le. or jèy-jyàn-shŕ-de-'dǐ-shì wǒ yàw 'dēw jŕ-daw-le.

By heart. ‖He learned the poem by heart. tā bǎ-'shŕ 'bèy-shya-lay-le.

HEAT. (*Hotness; usually natural*) rè; (*especially artificial; hot air*) rè-'chì, rè-'chyèr; (*strength of heat*) 'rè-jyèr. (rè *also means* be hot, hot, to heat.) *Compare also* nwǎn, **warm.** **White heat** 'báy-rè. ‖I can't bear the heat in this place during the summer. wǒ 'shèw-bu-lyǎw jèr-'shyà-tyan-de-'rè. or jèr-'shyà-tyan-rè-de wǒ 'shèw-bu-lyǎw. ‖Heat can be produced by rubbing. mwó-'tsā néng shēng-'rè. ‖Iron is a better conductor of heat than stone. tyě bǐ 'shŕ-tew rúng-yì chwán-'rè. ‖You can feel the heat from here. tsúng jèr jyèw 'jywé-de-chū °'rè-lay. or °'rè-'chì-lay. or °'rè-'chyèr-lay. ‖There is no heat in this radiator. 'nwǎn-chì-'lú-dz-li °'méy-rè-'chyèr. or °'(yì-dyǎr yě) bú-'rè. or °'méy-yew nwǎn-'chì. ‖The heat of the furnace warmed the whole house. lú-dz-de-rè-'chyèr bǎ jěng-ge-'fáng-dz dēw 'nwǎn-gwò-láy-le. ‖I can't stand the heat in this room. 'jèy-wūr tày 'rè (or 'nwǎn), wǒ shèw-bu-lyǎw. or 'jèy-jyān-wū-dz-de-'rè-jyèr wǒ shèw-bu-lyǎw. ‖In July the heat is intense. 'chī-ywè-rè-de 'lì-hay. ‖The (*degree of*) heat must be as high as 1,000° centigrade. 'rè-dù děy 'gāw-dàw 'tǎy-dù-byǎw yì-'chyān-dù. ‖There is more heat in this place

than necessary. jèr yùng-bu-'jáw nùng-de 'nèm-rè. ‖I'll heat up the soup for you. wǒ bǎ-'tāng gěy-ni 'rè-yi-rè.

(*Method of heating, furnace heat*) hwǒ. To heat with (*to burn*) shāw; steam heat 'nwǎn-chì. ‖They've had no heat there for three days now, and in such weather, too! 'tām-nàr 'sān-tyān méy-yew 'hwǒ-le, 'tyān-chi yèw jèm-'lěng. ‖You provide your own heat. 'méy-hwǒ-chyán nǐ dž-jǐ 'chū. ‖This apartment house has no heat as yet. jèy-ge-gūng-'ywù háy méy shēng-'hwǒ. ‖That building has oil heat. nèy-ge-'léw shāw-'yéw. ‖What kind of heat do you have? ('dūng-tyan) shāw-'shéme? ‖The (*steam*) heat should be turned on. (*At the radiator*) 'nwǎn-chì yīng-dāng 'kāy-kay-le. (*From the furnace*) 'nwǎn-chì yīng-dāng 'láy-le. ‖This house is hard to heat. *is expressed as* This house uses much fire. jèy-ge-'fáng-dz yàw shyǎng 'nwǎn-he hěn fèy 'hwǒ. ‖She is heating the iron. tā bǎ 'làw-tye 'shāw-shang-le. ‖She heated the iron. tā bǎ 'làw-tye shāw-'rè-le.

(*Figuratively*). ‖They hit each other in the heat of the argument. tā-men 'byàn-dàw hěn-'jí-de-shŕ-hew, 'dǎ-chi-lay-le. or tām ywè-'jēng ywè-'chì jyèw 'dǎ-chi-lay-le. ‖They had a heated argument. tām-'jēng-byàn-de hěn 'lì-hay.

(*Of a race*). ‖He qualified in the first heat, but lost out in the final race. tā 'ywù-sày 'chywú-shang-le, kě-shr 'jyé-sày 'shū-le.

HEAVY. (*Of weight*) jùng, chén, jùng-. Heavy oil 'jùng-yéw; heavy water 'jùng-shwěy. ‖Is that too heavy for you? tày 'chén-le-ma? or tày 'jùng-le-ma? ‖How heavy you are! nǐ jēn 'chén. or nǐ jēn 'jùng. ‖How heavy is this? jèy-ge yěw dwō(-me) °'chén? or °'jùng? ‖That's a heavy trunk. nèy-ge-'shyāng-dz hěn °'chén. or °'jùng. ‖Heavy industry depends on coal and iron. 'jùng-gūng-yè yàw 'kàw-je 'méy gēn 'tyě. ‖We need the support of your heavy artillery unit. wǒm děy yěw nim-de-'jùng-pàw-dwèy 'yǎn-hù. ‖Guns of 155 mm. caliber are in the heavy artillery class. yí-wǔ-'wǔ-gūng-'lí-'kěw-jìng-de-'pàw shŕ 'jùng-pàw. ‖The enemy has two heavy machine guns. dí-rén yěw 'lyǎng-jyà (or 'lyǎng-tǐng)-'jùng-jī-gwān-'chyāng.

Other uses are sometimes expressed by large dà; much dwō; (*of sleep only*) chén. ‖He was tired and fell into a heavy sleep. tā 'lèy-le; °'hū-hu dà-shwèy chǐ-lay-le. or °'shwèy-de hěn 'chén. or °'shwèy-de hěn 'sž. ‖He is a heavy sleeper, so he couldn't have heard it. tā shwèy-'jyàw hěn 'chén, swǒ-yǐ 'bú-hwèy tīng-de-'jyàn-de. ‖His eyes are heavy with sleep. (*For want of sleep*) tā 'kwèn-de yǎn-jing 'jēng-bu-kāy-le. or tā 'kwèn-de yǎn-'pí fā-'chén. (*Because he just woke up*) tā 'shwèy-de 'yǎn-jing 'mwō-me-hu-'hū-de. ‖In the morning there was a heavy rain. 'dzǎw-chen shyà-le yí-jèn-'dà-ywǔ. ‖There will be a heavy vote if the weather is good. tyān-chi 'hǎw, téw-'pyàw-de-rén jyèw 'dwō. ‖The heavy strain these last few days is beginning to tell on him. 'jèy-jǐ-tyān 'tày 'jǐn-jāngle, bǎ-tā 'lèy-de dēw dày-'shyàngr-le. ‖We had three days of heavy sea. yěw 'sān-tyān ('hǎy-shang) 'fēnglàng hěn 'dà. ‖That was a heavy meal. (*Too much of everything*) nèy-dwèn-'fàn-chr̄-de 'jēn dwō. (*Too much fat*) nèy-dwèn-'fàn tày 'yéw-nì-le. ‖He is a heavy buyer. tā-'mǎy-de 'dwō. ‖He is a heavy gambler. tā 'dǔ-chi-lay jyèw shyà 'dà-jù-dz. *or* tā hàw-'dǔ. ‖Use a soft pencil to draw these heavy lines. jèy-jǐ-tyáw-'tsū-shyàn yùng 'rwǎn-dyǎr-de-chyān-'bǐ hwà. ‖This dough is still heavy. 'myàn háy méy fā-'hǎw. ‖His heavy features attract attention. tā-de-'tsū-bèn-de-'yàng-dz 'jāw-rén jù-'yì. ‖Are you a heavy drinker? nǐ hē-'jyěw hē-de 'lì-hay-ma? ‖He is well known for his heavy drinking. tā yǐ 'jyěw-lyàng-'dà chū-'míng. ‖He's a heavy drinker. tā 'jyěw-lyàng hěn 'dà. *or* tā shǐ ge-'dzwèy-gwěy. ‖My duties are heavy this week. wǒ-'jèy-ge-lǐ-'bày 'shèr tǐng °'dwō. *or* °'lèy. *or* °'fèy-shin. *or* °chř-'lì. ‖It is a heavy problem. wèn-'tí hěn °'má-fan. *or* °'fǔ-dza. ‖This book is heavy reading. jèy-běr-'shū 'kàn-chǐ-lay °'tǐng fèy-'jìn. *or* °hěn 'gān-dzàw. ‖Traffic is heavy today. 'jīn-tyan 'lù-shang hěn 'jǐ. *or* 'jīn-tyan chē hěn 'dwō.

HEEL. (*Back of the foot*) jyǎw-'hèw-gen. ‖I cut my heel on stone. 'shŕ-tew bǎ wǒ-jyǎw-'hèw-gen 'lá-le. ‖Something is hurting my heel. yě bú-shr 'shéme 'dūng-shi jř 'gè wǒ jyǎw-'hèw-gen.

(*Back of a shoe, etc.*) 'hèw-gen, hèw-'gēr. ‖My shoes are worn down at the heels. wǒ-shyé-de-'hèw-gen 'mwó-shya-chywù-le. ‖There are holes in the heels of these socks. 'wà-dz-de-'hèw-gen (*or* 'wà-dz-de-hèw-'gēr) pwò-le. ‖Put heels on (*the shoes*). ān (shyé-) 'hèw-ger. *or* hwàn (shyé-) 'hèw-ger. ‖Darn the heels. bǔ (wà-dz-) 'hèw-ger.

(*Of bread*). ‖Only the heel of this loaf is left. 'jyèw shèng-le myàn-bāw-'tèwr-le.

Down-at-the-heel. ‖He's been out of work for a long time and looks down-at-the-heel. tā fù-'shyán-le hǎw 'jyěw, 'yàng-dz hěn 'lán-léw. *or* tā hǎw-shyē-'shŕ-hew méy-dzwò-'shř-le, yěw-dyar 'pwò-yī-lan-'shān-de.

(*Cad*). ‖He's a heel. tā shř ge-'shyǎw-rén.

To heel (*of a ship*) wāy. ‖The ship heeled as it made the turn. chwán 'wāy-je jwǎn-de 'wār. ‖The ship heeled and turned over. chwán 'wāy-de 'fān-le.

To take to one's heels. ‖He took to his heels when I said, "Hey!" wǒ yì-shwō, "dèy!" tā jyèw 'pǎw-le.

To cool one's heels. ‖He's been cooling his heels outside the office since noon. tā tsúng 'jūng-wǔ jyèw dzày mén-'wày-tew děng-je. ‖Let him cool his heels for a while. jyàw-tā 'děng-deng.

HEIGHT. (*By measurement*) gāw. ‖What is the height of those hills? (nèy-shyē-)'shān yěw 'dwō gāw? ‖This plane can fly at a great height (*or* at great heights). jèy-jyà-fēy-'jī kě-yǐ 'fēy-de 'hěn 'gāw.

Heights (*hills, high places*) shān, 'gāw-dì. ‖His house is on the heights west of the town. tā-jyā dzày chéng-'shī-byar shān-shang. ‖He suffered no loss during the flood because his house is on the heights. tā-jyā dzày 'shān-shang (*or* tā-jyā dzày 'gāw-dì-shang), swǒ-yǐ fā-'shwěy-de-shŕ-hew méy-'yān-jaw.

(*Limit*). ‖He has reached the height of success. tā yǐ-jīng 'dèw-le dzwèy-dé-'yì-de-shŕ-hew-le. *or* (*Literary*) tā yǐ-jīng 'dàw-ie 'jí-shèng shŕ-'dày-le. ‖There is a Chinese proverb, "The height of success must be followed by a decline." 'jūng-gwo yěw jywù-'súhwàr: "shèng-'jí bì-'shwāy."

HELLO. ‖Hello! How are you? 'hèy! nǐ 'hǎw-ma? *or* 'ā! 'hǎw-ma? *or* 'dzěm-yàng?

‖Hello! (*On the telephone*). 'wèy! *or* 'èy! *or* 'ày!

HELP. (*Assist, assistance; give assistance to*) bāng-'máng; (*help do something, or help financially*) bāng; (*help financially*) bāng-'jù; (*help a number of people financially*) 'jēw-jì; (*help financially in an emergency*) jyèw; (*help a number of people financially in an emergency*) 'jyèw-jì; (*help physically in an emergency*) jyèw, jyèw-'mìng; (*of medicine*) jř, gwǎn, 'gwǎn-jř. ‖Can someone help? 'shéy 'gwò-lay 'bāng-bang 'máng? *or* 'shéy 'gwò-lay 'bāng yì-bǎ-'shěwr? *or* yěw-'rén-ma? ‖Help! jyèw-'mìng-ew! *or* jyèw-'mìng-nga! *or* jyèw-'mìng! ‖Please help me. láw-'jyà, °'bāng shyar-'máng. *or* °'bāng-bang 'máng. *or* °'bāng yì-bǎ-'shěwr. ‖Please help him hold this up. láw-'jyà, 'bāng-tā 'táy-je-dyar. ‖Do you need any help? yàw-rén bāng-'máng-ma? ‖I need your help. fèy yěw 'nǐ láy bāng-'máng tsáy 'shíng. *or* wǒ gēn-nǐ chyěw-'bāng-lay-le. *or expressed as* I can't get along without you. 'wǒ-jèr méy-yew 'nǐ bù-shíng. *or as* I can use you. wǒ 'yùng-de-'jáw nǐ. ‖When I need your help I'll let you know. wǒ 'yùng-de-jáw nǐ de-'shŕ-hew jyèw 'gàw-su nǐ. ‖Whenever you need any help from me (*can use me*), let me know. nǐ 'shém-me-shŕ-hew 'yùng-de-'jáw wǒ, jyèw shwō-'hwà. ‖Can you help me (get) out? bāng-wǒ (*or, meaning* pull me, lā-wo) yì-'bǎ wǒ hǎw 'chū-chywu. ‖Help him up. bāng-je (*or* fú-je) tā 'shàng-chywu. ‖I helped him a good deal. wǒ hěn 'bāng-gwo ta. ‖Won't you give something to help the poor? nín 'shě dyǎr-shém-me 'jēw-jì 'chywún-rén shíng-bu-shíng? ‖Would you like to give something to help the poor children? chǐng-nín ('shř-)shě dyǎr-'mār (*or* dyǎr-'shéme) 'bāng-bang (*or* 'jēw-ji-jēw-ji) 'chyúng-háy-dz-men. ‖The stricken area needs immediate help. 'lì-kē yàw 'jyèw-jì 'jāy-chywū-de-'nàn-mín. ‖He needs some (financial) help. děy 'bāng-tā dyǎr-'chyán. *or* děy 'bāng-bang tā. ‖Can you help him (*financially*)? nǐ 'bāng-tā yí-shyàr 'shíng-bu-shíng? *or* nǐ néng 'bāng-tā dyǎr-shém-me-ma? *or* nǐ 'fú-tā yì-bǎ 'shíng-bu-shíng? ‖Can you help him (*physically*)? nǐ néng 'bāng-bang tā-de-'mángma? ‖Can you help him finish it? nǐ néng 'bāng-je tā nùng-'wán-le-ma? ‖Help will come in two days

(*military*).   'lyǎng-tyān-li 'jyèw-bīng néng 'dàw.
‖**Help came too late** (*military*).   jyèw-bīng 'dàw-le, yǐ-jīng 'wǎn-le. ‖**It's a help.** *is expressed as* It's useful. 'yěw dyǎr-'yùng. ‖**He's a big help.** tā 'hěn yěw 'yùng. ‖**He'll be a big help.** tā 'hěn néng 'bāng-máng. ‖**He's been a big help.** tā hěn 'bāng-le shyē-'máng. ‖**He's no help at all.** tā jyǎn-'jf °'méy-yew 'yùng. *or* °shr̀ ge-'fèy-wu. ‖**Help me put away the books.** bāng-wǒ 'shěw-shr̀'shěw-shr shū. *or* bāng-wǒ 'jyǎn-jyan shū. ‖**I was just helping her wash dishes.** wǒ 'gāng-tsáy bāng-tā shǐ-'wǎn láy-je. ‖**Come and help!** 'láy bāng-bang 'máng! *or* láy 'bāng yì-bǎ-'shěw. ‖**Come help lift it.** gwò-lay 'bāng-je 'táy-tay. ‖**I helped that old man cross the street.** wǒ 'bāng-je (*or, by leading him*, wǒ 'lǐng-jē *or, by holding his arm*, wǒ 'jyà-je *or* wǒ 'fú-je *or* wǒ 'chān-je) nèy-ge-lǎw-'téwr gwò-'jyē láy-je. ‖**Help the old lady across the street.** bǎ lǎw-'tày-tay fú (*or* chān, *or* lǐng, *or* jyà, *but not* 'bāng *here*) gwò-'jyē-chywu. ‖**I. would have drowned if he hadn't come to help me.** yàw bú-shr̀ tā láy 'jyèw-wo wǒ jyèw 'yān-sz-le.

    (*Persons who help*). ‖**It's difficult to get help these days.** 'rú-jīn hěn nán jǎw °'yùng-rén. *or* °'dǐ-shya-rén. ‖**Our help didn't show up this morning.** wǒm 'yùng-de-rén jyěr 'dzǎw-chen méy-'láy ‖**I want to hire some help.** wǒ shyǎng 'gù ge-°bāng-'mángr-de. *or*, *meaning* **an odd-job man,** °dǎ-'dzár-de. *or, meaning* a **short-term laborer,** °'dwǎn-gūng. *or, meaning* a **seasonal laborer,** °'cháng-gūng. *or, meaning* a **boy,** °shyǎw-'hwór.

    (*Prevent*). ‖**Sorry, it can't be helped.** 'dwèy-bu-chǐ, 'méy-yew 'fǎ-dz. *or* °'méy-fǎr 'bàn. ‖**Well, it just can't be helped.** 'hāy! 'méy-fǎr 'bàn-na! ‖**I can't help it.** 'wǒ méy-'fǎr. *or* 'wǒ yěw shém-me-'fǎr-ne? ‖**I can't HELP it** (*weeping or anger*). *is expressed as* I can't hold it back any longer. wǒ 'rěn-bu-'jù-le. ‖**I couldn't help but tell him.** wǒ 'jǐ-hǎw 'gàw-sung tā. *or* wǒ bù-'néng bǔ-'gàw-sung tā. *or expressed as* I couldn't hold it back any longer. wǒ rěn-bu-'jù-le jyèw 'gàw-sung tā-le.

    (*Serve*). ‖**Can I help you to something?** yàw dyǎr-'shéme? (wǒ gěy-nín ná.) ‖**Help yourself.** dz̀-'jǐ láy byé 'kè-chi.

HEN.   (*Fowl*) mǔ-'jī. ‖**He has a rooster and several hens.** tā yěw yì-jř-'gūng-jī, jǐ-jř-'mǔ-jī.

    (*Woman; colloquial*). ‖**It's strictly a hen party.** nèy-ge-'hwèy dēw-shr 'nywǔ-rén. *or* nèy-ge-'hwèy jř yěw 'nywǔ-rén. *or* nèy-ge-'hwèy 'jywé-dwèy 'bú-yàw 'nán-rén.

HENCE.   (*Therefore*) yīn-'tsž, 'swǒ-yǐ. ‖**He ran away, hence it appears that he's guilty.** tā táw-'pǎw-le, yīn-'tsž (*or* 'swǒ-yǐ) 'hǎw shyàng tā yěw 'dzwèy shř-de. ‖**He realized that he couldn't get along without you; hence the change of attitude.** tā 'míng-bay-le méy-yew 'nǐ tā 'dzwò-bu-shya-chywù, yīn-'tsž (*or* 'swǒ-yǐ) °'gǎy-de 'tày-du. *or* °'gǎy-lé 'tày-du-le. ‖**From this**

evidence we can conclude that he is a spy; hence we **must act at once.** tsúng jèy-shyē-'jèng-jywu-shang kàn, tā yí-'dìng shr̀ ge-'jyàn-dyé; 'swǒ-yǐ (*or* yīn-'tsž) dzám děy lí-'kè jyèw shyà-'shěw.

    (*From this time*) gwò ..., ... yǐ-'hèw, tsúng-tsž yǐ-'hèw gwò .... ‖**Forty years hence nobody will care about this.** 'sž-shr-nyán yǐ-'hèw 'shéy háy gwǎn 'jè-ge? *or* gwò 'sž-shr-nyán jyèw 'méy-rén gwò-'wèn-le. ‖**He said he would come a week hence.** tā shwō tā 'gwò yí-ge-lǐ-'bày láy. ‖**Women will still be women a thousand years hence.** jyèw-shr dzày gwò yì-'chyān-nyán 'nywǔ-rén 'háy-shr 'nywǔ-rén.

HER (HERS). *See* HE.

HERE.   (*This place*) jèr (*especially used in Peiping*) 'jè-li, 'jè-her, 'jè-ge-dì-fang, 'jèy-ge-dì-fang; (*this locality*) 'jèy-kwàr; *all preceded by* dzày *when* at this place *is meant*. ‖**Meet me here at six o'clock.** 'lyèw-dyǎn dzày-'jèr gēn-wǒ jyàn-'myàr. *or* dzám 'lyèw-dyǎn-jūng dzày-'jèr jyàn. ‖**Stand here and don't move.** nǐ jàn-dzày 'jèr, byé 'dùng. ‖**We've never had any snow here.** 'wǒm-jèr (*or* 'wǒm-jè-li, *or* 'wǒm-jèy-ge-'dì-fang *or* 'wǒm-jèy-kwàr) 'tsúng-láy méy 'shyà-gwo 'shywě. ‖**We don't have anyone here by that name.** 'wǒm-jèr 'méy-yew rén jyàw 'nèy-ge-'míng-dz-de. ‖**We have a man here who answers your description.** wǒm-jèr 'yěw ge-rén shyàng nǐ-'shwō-de nèy-ge-'yàngr. ‖**We've had no electricity here for three days.** 'wǒm-jèr (*or, if a town, etc.,* 'wǒm-jèy-kwàr) 'sān-tyan méy-yew 'dyàn-le. ‖**Here's the book** (*in this place*). shū dzày-'jèr. ‖**Your hat is here.** (nǐ-de-) 'màw-dz dzày-'jèr. (*But for* Here's your hat, *when handing it to a person, see below*.) ‖**Come here.** dàw-'jèr láy. *or* láy-'jèr. *or* 'gwò-lay. ‖**Here I am!** (*over here, not there*) (wǒ dzày-)'jèr-ne! ‖**There's something for you here.** 'jèr yěw dyǎr-'dūng-shi shř 'nǐ-de. ‖**Here it is.** dzày-'jèr-ne.

    (*At this point, at this time*) 'tsž. ‖**Here's where I draw the line.** wǒ jyèw 'tsž wéy-'jř.

    (*Exclamatory*). ‖**Here, take this!** èy, 'ná-je 'jèy-ge. *or* 'èy, gěy-nǐ 'jèy-ge. ‖**Here, let me help you.** 'wǒ láy (gěy-nǐ nùng). ‖**Here, watch ME do it.** 'láy-ya, kǎn 'wǒ-de. ‖**Here! (Look here!) This isn't right!** 'hèy! (*or* 'èy!) 'jè-kě bú-'dwèy. ‖**Look here! See what I got!** 'kàn-na! kàn 'jè-shr shém-me. ‖**Now, look here! You can't do that to me!** 'hèy! (*or* 'èy!) 'nǐ bù-néng 'nèm dày-wǒ. ‖**Here I am!** *meaning* I've come. wǒ 'láy-le. ‖**Well, here we are** (*in a mess*). wǒm jyèw 'dàw-le 'jèy-ge-dì-bu-le. ‖**Here I am, without a cent, while they dine and make merry.** chyáw-chyaw 'wǒ, yí-ge-'dzěr yě 'méy-yew; chyáw-chyaw 'tām-ne, yèw 'chī yěw 'wár-de. ‖**Here you are.** *meaning* You've come. nǐ 'láy-le. ‖**Here you are.** *meaning* This is what you wanted. 'jèy jyèw-shr nǐ-'yàw-de. ‖**Here you are, holding the bag.** chyáw-chyaw 'nǐ, dzày-jèr shěw-'dzwèy. ‖**Here it is.** *meaning* Look at it. nǐ 'chyáw-chyaw. ‖**Here goes!** chyáw 'jèy-shěwr-de.

(*This*). ‖Here's something for you. ʼjè-shr gěy-ʼnǐ-de. ‖Here's your hat. nǐ-ʼmàw-dz. ‖Here is a man who has never complained about anything. ʼjèy-wèy ʼshyàng-láy méy-ʼbàw-ywàn-gwo shém-me. ‖My friend here will take you to the station. wǒ (jèy-wèy-) ʼpéng-yew kě-yǐ ʼsùng-nǐ dàw chē-ʼjàn. ‖This man here wants to see you. ʼjèy-ge-rén yàw ʼjàn-nǐ. ‖Do you know this man here? ʼjèy-ge-rén nǐ ʼrèn-de-ma? ‖Now, take Mr. Wáng here. I'm sure he wouldn't do it. jyèw ná-(-jèr jèy-wèy-) ʼwáng-shyàn-sheng shwō-ba. wǒ ʼjwěn jř-dàw ʼtā bú-hwèy-de.

(*Present*). ‖Here! ʼdàw! *or* ʼyěw! *or* ʼdzày! ‖Only six of the men answered, "Here!" chí-ʼjūng jř yěw ʼlyèw-ge-rén dá ʼ"ʼdàw!" láy-je.

Here and there. ‖The stores are scattered here and there throughout the city. ʼpù-dz dzày chéng-ʼlǐ ʼdàw-chu dēw ʼyěw. ‖He looked here and there and left without a word. tā ʼjèr kàn-kan, ʼnàr kàn-kan, ʼyí-jywù-hwà yě méy-ʼyán-ywu jyèw ʼdzěw-le. ‖Here and there a star twinkles. tyān-shang-de-ʼshīng ʼjèy-ge yí-ʼlyàng, ʼnèy-ge yí-ʼlyàng-de. ‖A little here, a little there, and it's all gone. ʼjèr yì-dyǎr, ʼnàr yì-dyǎr, jyèw dēw ʼméy-le. ‖He talks to someone here and talks to someone there, and the whole day is wasted. tā gēn ʼjèy-ge tán-tan, gēn ʼnèy-ge tán-tan, yì-ʼtyān jyèw ʼbáy-gwò-le. ‖That's neither here nor there. *is expressed as* I still don't get the main point. ʼháy-shr ʼbù-dé yàw-ʼlǐng. *or as* What's been said has no relation to the main point. jè ywú ʼběn-tí méy-yěw ʼgwān-shi. *or as* The problem still isn't solved. ʼwèn-tí háy-shr ʼjyě-jywé-bù-ʼlyǎw.

HIDDEN. (*See* **HIDE**, *except for the one usage below, which is peculiar to* **HIDDEN**.) ‖Is there any hidden meaning in what he said? tā-de-ʼhwà-li yěw méy-yew àn-ʼhán-je-de-ʼyì-sz?

HIDE (HID, HIDDEN). (*Conceal*) tsáng. Hide oneself tsáng, dwǒ. ‖He hid his money in a bureau drawer. tā bǎ-ʼchyán ʼtsáng-dzày yí-ge-gwèy-dz-ʼchēw-tì-lǐ-le. ‖He hid it somewhere. nèy-ge tā ʼtsáng-chǐ-lay-le. ‖Have you hidden anything? nǐ ʼtsáng-le shéme láy-je-ma? *or* nǐ yěw-shém ʼtsáng-chi-lay-de-ma? ‖Look! He seems to be hiding something. kwày ʼkàn! tā °yěw-dyǎr ʼtsáng-tsang-yan-ʼyǎn-de. *or* °dzày-nar ʼtsáng-shéme-ne. ‖The men are hiding in those woods. rén dēw ʼtsáng-dzày (*or* ʼdwǒ-dzày) nèy-pyàn-shù-ʼlín-dz-lǐ-le. ‖He hid himself under the bed. tā tsáng-dzày (*or* ʼdwǒ-dzày) chwáng-ʼdǐ-shya-le. ‖Go and hide! kwày ʼtsáng-chi-lay. *or* kwày ʼdwǒ-chi-lay. ‖Hide it under the blanket. ʼtsáng-dzày tăn-dz-ʼdǐ-shya. *or expressed as* Cover it with a blanket. ná tăn-dz °ʼgày-shang. *or* °ʼméng-shang. (*See* **COVER**.)

(*Keep from sight by an obstruction*) dǎng, jé (*only* jé *is used to express concealment of emotion*). ‖The sign hides the view. ʼpáy-dz ʼdǎng-jù-le. *or* ʼpáy-dz ʼjé-jù-le. ‖This tall building hides everything from

view. jyàw jèy-ge-léw ʼdǎng-ae (*or* ʼjé-de) ʼshém dēw kàn-bu-ʼjyàn. ‖He became cross just to hide his embarrassment. tā nèm shēng-ʼchì bú-gwò-shr yàw jé-ʼshyēw.

(*Animal skin*) ʼshēng-pí-dz *or* ʼshēng-X-ʼpí (*where* X *is the name of an animal*). Cowhide ʼshēng-nyéw-ʼpí. ‖They are selling hides in the market. tām dzày ʼjí-shang mày ʼshēng-pí-dz.

To save one's hide (*figuratively*). ‖He did that to save his own hide. tā nèm-ʼgàn shř yàw lín-ʼnàn gěw-ʼmyàn (*literary*).

HIGH. (*By measurement*) gāw; (*not low*) bù-ʼdī. High jump tyàw-ʼgāwr; (*aeronautics*) high dive tsúng ʼgāw-chù fǔ-ʼchūng; high climb pá-ʼgāwr; high-flying ʼgāw-fēy *or* ʼgāw-kūng fēy-ʼshíng; high-ranking officers ʼgāw-jí-jywūn-gwān; the higher courts ʼgāw-jí-ʼfǎ-ywàn. ‖That's high enough. nèy jyèw ʼgèw-gāw-de-le. *or* nèy jyèw ʼbú-swàn ʼdī-le. ‖The building is eight stories high. ʼléw yěw ʼbā-tséng gāw. ‖Hang it high. ʼgwà-de gāw-ʼgāwr-de. ‖Hang it higher. dzày gwà ʼgāw-dyar. ‖This is as high as I can reach. wǒ ʼgèw-de bù-néng bǐ ʼjè-ge dzày ʼgāw-le. *or* wǒ ʼjř néng gèw-dàw ʼjèr. ‖The mountains are so high that their tops are always snow-capped. shān ʼgāw-de ʼdyěngr-shang lǎw jàw-je ʼshīywě. ‖It's always the other mountain that looks higher. (*Proverb*) ʼjè-shān ʼwàng-je ʼnà-shān ʼgāw. ‖The highest mountain peak has never been reached by man. ʼdzwèy-gāw-de-(shān-)ʼfēng háy méy-yew rén ʼdàw-gwo. ‖He climbed up so high that we couldn't see him. tā wàng-shang ʼpá, ʼgāw-de wǒm dēw kàn-bu-ʼjyàn tā-le. ‖The temperature will be pretty high today. jīn-tyān ʼwēn-dù yí-dìng hwèy hěn ʼgāw. ‖She sang a high note. tā chàng-le yí-ge-hěn-ʼgāw-de-ʼyīn. ‖Your voice is too high. nǐ ʼshēng-yin tàw ʼgāw. ‖He is in a higher class. (*In school*) tā-de-bān ʼgāw. (*In native ability*) tā ʼběn-lìng ʼgāw-dyar. (*In acquired skills*) tā ʼshěw-yì ʼgāw-dyar. (*Socially*) tā ʼdì-wèy ʼgāw-dyar.

(*Of price*) gāw, dà, gwèy. ‖This price is too high. jèy-ge-jyàr tàw °ʼgāw. *or* °ʼdà. *or* °ʼgwèy.

(*Of hopes*) gāw, dà. ‖Don't let your hopes fly too high. byé bàw-je (*or* byé tswén-je) °ʼtàw-dà-de-ʼshī-wàng. *or* °ʼtàw-gāw-de-ʼshī-wàng. *or* (*More emphatic*) byé ʼwàng-shyǎng (tyān-ʼkāy).

High and dry (*figuratively*). ‖She was left high and dry. bǎ-tā gěy jěng-ʼger-de °ʼpyé-kay-le. *or* °ʼpyé-shya-le.

High and low. ‖I looked high and low, but couldn't find it. wǒ ʼnǎr dēw ʼjǎw-le, ʼjyèw-shr jǎw-bu-ʼjáw. *or* wǒ ʼshém-me-dì-fang dēw jǎw-ʼbyàn-le, yě ʼméy-jǎw-ʼjáw.

A new high. ‖Prices have reached a new high. ʼwù-jyà ʼyèw wǎng-ʼshàng jǎng-le yi-shyàr. *or* ʼdūng-shi yèw jǎng-ʼjyàr-le.

High-class ʼgāw-děng-de; (*expensive*) gwèy; (*wealthy, of people*) kwò, bù-ʼchyúng. ‖A high-class restaurant serves the same food, but charges extra for the atmosphere. 'gāw-děng-de-'gwǎn-dz-li 'fàn bìng 'bú-jyàn-de 'tè-byé 'hǎw, bú-gwo jyè-je 'shè-bey é-'chyán. ‖This is a high-class restaurant. jèy-ge-'gwǎn-dz 'gwèy. ‖This is a high-class neighborhood. 'jèy-kwar-'jù-de dēw shr̀ • 'kwò-rén. *or* 'jèy-kwar 'chyúng-rén 'jù-bu-'chǐ.

High (*gear*) *is expressed as* third dì-'sān *or as* fast kwày. ‖He shifted into high. tā dǎw-dàw dì-'sān-dàw-já﹕or tā gǎy-dàw 'kwày-já-le.

High grade hǎw; *or expressed as* of high quality 'chéng-shǎy °'hǎw *or* °'gāw. ‖This is high-grade silver. jèy-ge-'yín-dz 'chéng-shǎy °'hǎw. *or* °'gāw.

High-handed. jwān-'jr̀, 'bà-daw, 'bà-chi. ‖He is too ·gh-handed to suit me. tā tày °jwān-'jr̀ (*or* °'bà-daw, *or* °'bà-chi), jyàw-wǒ bù-'shǐ-hwān.

To high-hat *someone* gēn ... chūng dà-'yé; 'shyǎw kàn. ‖Don't you high-hat her! nǐ gēn 'rén-jyā byé 'chūng shéme-dà-'yé. *or* 'bù-shywǔ nǐ 'shyǎw kàn rén-jyā.

High-minded (*having high principles*) 'fēng-du bù-'sú *or* (hěn) 'jwāng-jùng; (*proud*) 'àw-chi *or* 'jyàw-aw. ‖He's a high-minded person. tā 'fēng-dù bù-'sú. *or* tā hěn 'jwāng-jùng. ‖He's too high-minded. tā tày 'àw-chi. *or* tā tày 'jyàw-aw.

Have a high opinion of 'pèy-fu. ‖I have a high opinion of him. wǒ hěn 'pèy-fu tā.

High-powered (*of force*) dà; (*of horsepower*) dà *or* gāw. ‖This air-rifle is high-powered. jèy-ge-'chì-chyāng lì-lyang hěn 'dà. ‖This is a high-powered engine. jèy-ge-'jī-chì 'lì-lyang hěn 'dà. ‖This car is high-powered. jèy-lyàng-'chē 'mǎ-lì hěn °'gāw. *or* °'dà.

High pressure dà. ‖This boiler can't stand such high pressure. jèy-ge-chì-'gwō 'jīn-bu-jù 'jèm-dà-de-'yā-lì.

High-pressure (*figuratively, of a sales talk*) *is expressed by a proverb meaning* to make flowers fall from heaven by talking shwō-de 'tyān-hwār-lwàn-'jwèy, *or as* to talk *someone* into bǎ ... 'shwō-de, *or as* nothing would do but that 'fēy chywàn ... bù-'kě. ‖The salesman high-pressured him into buying a high-priced car. 'mày-chē-de shwō-de 'tyān-hwār-lwàn-'jwèy, jyē-gwo bǎ-tā shwō-de mǎy-le lyàng-'tǐng-gwèy-de-'chē. *or* 'mày-chē-de bǎ-tā 'shwō-de mǎy-le lyàng-'tǐng-gwèy-de-'chē. *or* 'mày-chē-de 'fēy chywàn tā mǎy lyàng-'tǐng-gwèy-de-'chē bù-'kě, 'jyē-gwǒ tā 'mǎy-le.

Highest respect. ‖He commands the highest respect in his circle. 'tā-nèy-chywār-li-de﹐rén dzwèy 'dzwēn﹐jìng tā.

High speed *is expressed as* fast kwày. ‖How high a speed will this car reach? 'jèy-ge-chē kě-yǐ kāy 'dwō kwày? ‖At high speeds it's likely to develop engine trouble. kāy-de 'kwày de-shŕ-hew, 'jī-chi hwèy chū 'máw-bìng.

In high spirits. gāw-'shìng. ‖Why is he ɪn such high spirits today? tā 'jīn-tyān wèy 'shéme jèm gāw-'shìng.

High-strung. 'shén-jīng 'jǐn-jāng. ‖He's too high-strung to be a good driver. tā 'shén-jīng tày 'jǐn-jāng, kāy-'chē 'bú-hwèy kāy-de-'hǎw-de.

High tide. shàng-'cháw. ‖Let's wait until high tide. děng shàng-'cháw dzày shwō.

High time. ‖It's high time you came. nǐ-'láy-de kě 'jēn bú-swàn 'dzǎw. ‖It's high time you should do something about it. kě 'jēn gāy 'bàn-le. *or* nǐ-'bàn-de kě 'jēn bú-swàn 'dzǎw-le.

High﹒wind ('fēy-cháng) 'chyáng-de-fēng. ‖The airplanes met high winds. fēy-'jī 'ywù-jyan-le 'fēy-cháng-'chyáng-de-fēng.

High above (dzày) ... 'shàng-byar. ‖We were high above the clouds. wǒm dzày 'ywún-tsay-'shàng-byar.

HILL. shān, 'shyǎw-shān, 'ǎy-shān (shāń *also means* mountain; *the other terms are used only to contrast the meaning*). ‖We must cross a range of hills before we reach the mountains. wǒm dàw 'gāw-shān yǐ-'chyán děy gwò yí-dàw-°'shyǎw-shān. *or* °'ǎy-shān. ‖What is beyond the hills? shān-'hèw-byar yěw 'shém-me?

(*Slope, road on a hill*) shān, pwō, pwǒr, shān-lù. ‖That's a bad hill. nèy-ge-pwō (*or* nèy-ge-pwǒr, *or* nèy-ge-shān, *or* nèy-ge-'shān-lù) hěn 'děw. ‖That hill is icy. nèy-ge-'shān-shang hěn 'hwá. *or* nèy-ge-'shān-lù hěn 'hwá. *or* nèy-ge-pwǒr hěn 'hwá.

HIM. *See* HE.

HIS. *See* HE.

HISTORY. lì-'shr̀, -shr̀. ‖The history of this country is very interesting. 'jèy-gwó-de-lì-'shr̀ yěw °'yì-sz. *or* °-'chywèr. ‖This picture has quite a history. jèy-jāng-'hwàr yěw shyāng-'dāng-de-lì-'shr̀. ‖He is writing a history of historiography. tā jèng-dzày shyě yì-běn-'shr̀-shywé-'shr̀. ‖He wrote several works on the history of printing. tā 'shyě-le jǐ-běn-gwān-ywu-'yìn-shwā-'shr̀-de-'shū. ‖His field is history. *meaning* He's studying history. tā shr̀ nyàn-lì-'shr̀-de. *or meaning* He's majoring in history. tā-de-'jǔ-shyēw-kē shr̀ lì-'shr̀. *or meaning* He teaches history. tā jyāw lì-'shr̀. *or meaning* He works on history professionally. tā jr̀ 'shr̀-shywé. *or meaning* He's a historian. tā shr̀ 'shr̀-shywé-jyā. *or meaning* He writes history books. tā 'shyě lì-'shr̀-shū.

HIT. (*General term; can be used in almost any connection*) dǎ; (*hit with a sharp blow*) chyāw; (*hit a heavy blow, especially with something in the hand*) dzá; (*especially with hammer, fist, or club*) chwéy; (*especially with hammer and chisel, and with downward motion*) dzáw; (*hit by throwing, or hit and cut with a sword*) kǎn; (*by throwing*) rēng, pyě, jwāy; (*by accident*) pèng, jwàng; (*with an arrow*) shè; (*by bombing*) jà. *Or use resultative compounds, with one of the above words as the first element, and one of the following for the second; (hit the mark)* jùng *or* jáw; *(open, broken)* kāy; *(broken)* hwày; *(to pieces)* swèy; *(reach)* dàw; *(wound)* shāng; *(dead)* sž, *etc. Or use as a second object (a number of blows)* yí-'dwèn; *(a blow)* yí-shyà *or* yí-shyàr; *or a numeral, plus the object used in hitting.* Be hit *by also* jùng. ‖The *(deaf)* mute hit the lama with his trumpet, and the lama hit back with his sole *(fish). (A popular tongue-twister.)* 'yǎ-ba dǎ-le 'lǎ-mā yì-'lǎ-ba, 'lǎ-ma dǎ-le 'yǎ-ba yì-'tǎ-ma. ‖He hit me, and I hit back. tā 'yì-chywán 'dǎ-láy, wǒ yě 'yì-chywán 'dǎ-chywù. *or expressed as* He hit me, and I returned the compliment. tā dǎ-le wǒ yì-'chywán, wǒ yě 'hwéy-jìng-le yì-chywán. ‖The ball hit the wall and bounced back to my hand. chyéwr dǎ (*or* pèng)-dàw 'chyáng-shàng, yèw 'pèng-hwéy (*or* 'hwéy-dàw) wǒ-'shěw-li. ‖He was trying to hit the nail, but hit his own finger instead. tā yàw dzá 'dīng-dz, 'kě-shr bǎ dž-'jǐ-de-shěw-'jř-tew dzá-le. ‖The blacksmith hits the iron with a hammer. 'tyé-jyang ná 'chwéy-dz dǎ-'tyě. ‖He hit the clock with a hammer and broke it to pieces at one blow. tā ná 'chwéy-dz bǎ-'jūng 'yí-shyà-dz jyèw dǎ-'swèy-le. ‖I hit my knee against the door. wǒ-gé-le-'bàr jwàng (*or* pèng)(-dzày) 'mén-shàng-le. ‖The door suddenly opened and hit him in the face. 'mén yì-'kāy 'pèng (*or* 'jwàng)-le tā-de-'lyǎn-le. ‖He was hit by a streetcar, but fortunately didn't get under the wheels. tā jyàw 'dyàn-chē 'pèng-le (*or* 'jwàng-le), kě-shr 'jyǎw-shìng méy 'yà-jaw. ‖Did the ball hit him? chyéwr 'dǎ-jáw tā-le-ma? ‖He was hit by a ball. tā jyàw ge-'chyéwr 'dǎ-jáw-le. ‖He was hit by a bullet. tā 'jùng-le yì-kē-'dž-dàn. *or* tā jùng-'dàn-le. ‖I hit him with a bullet. wǒ fàng-'chyāng bǎ-tā 'dǎ-jaw-le. ‖I hit him with a piece of stone. wǒ ná (*or* rēng, *or* jwāy, *or* pyě) 'shŕ-tew bǎ-tā 'kǎn-jaw-le. ‖Let's see if you can hit that tree. kàn nǐ dǎ-de-'jáw (*or* kǎn-de-'jáw) nèy-kē-'shù-ma. ‖If you can hit that coin with this one, you get both. nǐ yàw-shr néng ná 'jèy-ge-chyár bǎ 'nèy-ge-chyár 'dzá-shang, 'lyǎ-chyár nǐ 'dēw 'yíng-le chywu. ‖He hit the bull's-eye. tā dǎ-'jùng-le húng-'shīn-le. ‖He hit the bull's-eye nine shots out of ten. tā 'shŕ-chyāng-li kě-yi °jùng 'jyěw-tsž. *or* °bǎ húng-'shīn dǎ-jùng 'jyěw-tsž. ‖You might get hit (*by bullets*) if you stand in the open. nǐ dzày

'kùng-dì-shang jàn-je yě-shywù hwèy jyàw °'dž-dàn 'dǎ-jaw. *or (By a bomb)* °'jà-dàn 'jà-jaw. *or (By splinters)* °'jà-dàn-pyàr 'dǎ-jáw. ‖The bombardier got three hits. 'hūng-jà-shěw jǎ-'jùng-le 'sān-tsž. ‖It's a hit! *(Not a miss)* 'jùng-le. ‖Did you hit it? *(With a bomb)* jà-'jùng-le-ma? ‖He hit the deer with an arrow. tā (yùng-'jyàn) 'shè-jaw nèy-ge-'lù-le. ‖He made just four hits. tā jyèw (*or* jř) 'dǎ-jáw-le 'sž-shyàr. *(If referring to archery, use* shè *instead of* dǎ, *or if referring to bombing, . . .* 'jà-jùng-le 'sž-tsž.) ‖He hit the jackpot *(won first prize, as in a lottery)*. tā jùng-le 'téw-tsǎy. *or* tā 'dà-yíng. ‖It's a hit! *(Baseball)* dǎ-'jùng-le! *or* 'dǎ-jáw-le! ‖He hit the ball so hard that it sailed out of the park. tā-nà-yí-'bàng jyèr 'jēn dzú, bǎ-chyéwr dǎ-de fēy-dàw 'chǎng-dź-'wày-tew-chywu-le.

To hit *(shine brightly upon)*. ‖The light hit his eyes and made him blink. gwāng 'jàw-je (*or* gwāng 'hwǎng, *or* gwāng 'shè-dàw) tā-de-yǎn, jyàw-tā jř-'jǎ-me.

(Success). ‖The movie was a hit. *meaning* It made a lot of money. nèy-ge-'pyān-dz hěn °'jwàn-chyán. *or meaning* It was well received. °shèw 'hwān-yíng. ‖He made a hit with her family. tā hěn shèw tā-'jyā-li-rén 'hwān-yíng. *or* tā-'jyā-li-rén yí-jyàn-myàn jyèw dēw 'shǐ-hwan tā.

To hit hard *(affect severely)*. ‖The news hit me very hard. tīng-jyàn nèy-ge-'shyāw-shi jyàw wǒ 'hěn nán-shèw. ‖The death of her son hit her so hard that she never left her sick bed. tā-ér-dz-nèy-yi-'sž jyàw-tā 'shīn-li 'hěn nán-'gwò, tsúng-nèr chǐ tā yì-'jř méy chǐ-'chwáng.

Hit or miss. ‖He works in a hit-or-miss fashion. tā dzwò-'shr °tày 'mǎng-jwàng. *or* °tày 'měng. *or* °'yěw dyǎr-shyā-'mēng. *or* °'yěw dyǎr-shyā-'pèng. ‖It was sort of hit-or-miss, but he was lucky. bú-gwò-shr 'mēng (*or* 'pēng)-yi-shyar, kě-shr tā jyèw 'mēng (*or* 'pēng)-shang-le.

Hit it off *(agree)*. ‖They hit it off well from the beginning. *(Of friendship only)* tām yí-'jyàn rú-'gù. *or (Of friendship or love at first sight)* tām yí-'jyàn chīng-'shīn.

Hit on *(find)*. ‖How did you hit on that? *(mentally)* nǐ dzěm 'shyǎng-chū-láy-de? ‖I just hit on that pun. nèy-ge-shwāng-'gwān-de-hwàr shr̀ wǒ-'ěw-rán shyǎng-'dàw-de.

HOLD (HELD). 1. *Within the meaning* **hold up, support, carry, grasp,** *Chinese distinguishes a number of different methods of holding. The most general verb corresponding to* **hold** *is* ná, *which also means* **carry.** *Almost all of the other numerous words meaning* **carry** *may also be used to mean* **hold.** (*See* **CARRY.**) *Just a few of these are listed here, along with some words which are not used when one speaks of carrying something from one place to another.*

(*General term*) ná. ‖**Will you hold this package a minute for me?** jèy-ge-'bāwr nǐ gěy-wǒ 'ná-hwer, shíng-ma?

To hold *between thumb and finger, or with tweezers* nyē. ‖**He held the snake in his fingers by its tail and shook it.** tā nyē-je 'cháng-chūng 'yǐ-ba-'jyǎr, jǐ 'déw-lew.

To hold *in the fist* (*grip*) dzwàn. ‖**He is holding a fistful of sand.** tā 'dzwàn-je yì-bǎ-'shā-dz. ‖**He held both ends of the iron rod and bent it at one twist.** tā 'dzwàn-je tyě-'gwèn-dz-de-lyǎng-'téwr yì-'jywē jyèw jywē-'wān-le.

To hold *in the fist or hand, take hold of* (*grasp*) jwā. ‖**He reached out and took hold of his collar.** tā 'yì-bǎ bǎ tā-de-'lǐng-dz 'jwā-jù-le.

To hold *in the fist or hand* (*grip; but only in certain combinations*) bǎ. ‖**The captain held the tiller in one hand, and a long pipe in the other.** chwán-jǔ 'yì-shěw bǎ-'dwò, 'yì-shěw ná-je ge-'hàn-yān-'dày.

To hold *with the palms face up, especially when pressed together to form a bowl shape* pěng. ‖**He did not have any container for the rice, so he could only hold it in his hands.** tā 'méy-yew dūng-shī 'chéng-mǐ, jǐ hǎw ná-shěw 'pěng-je.

To hold *in the hand or hands, with arm partially outstretched* dwān. ‖**He held the tray with both hands while the other man piled dishes on it.** tā lyǎ-shěw 'dwān-je yí-ge-twò-'pár, 'lìng-yi-ge-rén wàng-shang lwò 'pán-dz 'dyé-dz-de. ‖**He held the gun level and faced me.** tā 'chùng-je wǒ píng-'dwān-je chyāng.

To hold *in the palm or palms, with arms stretched out, hands not joined* twō. ‖**He held the tray balanced on one palm.** tā 'yì-jǐ-shěw 'twō-je twō-'pár.

To hold *in the hand*(*s*), *with arm*(*s*) *stretched overhead* jywǔ. ‖**He held up his hat as if he were going to put it on.** tā jywǔ-je 'màw-dz hǎw 'shyàng yàw-dày-shang-shr-de. ‖**He held the flag and walked ahead of the parade.** tā jywǔ (*or* dǎ)-je dà-'chí dzày 'dà-dwèy-'chyán-byan 'dzěw. ‖**Hold up your right hand.** jywǔ 'yèw-shěw.

To hold *in the arms, in an embrace* lěw, bàw (bàw *may also include lifting up, as of a baby*). ‖**They stood there and looked at each other for a while, and then he suddenly held her in his arms.** tām jàn-nàr 'bǐ-tsž awèy-'kàn-le yì-hwěr; tā 'hū-rán yí-shyà-dz bǎ-tā 'lěw (*or* 'bàw)-dzày 'hwáy-li-le. ‖**They held each other in a clinch while the referee tried to break them up.**

tām jǐn-'jīn-de 'lěw-je (*or* 'bàw-je), 'nèy-shŕ-hew tsáy-pàn-'ywán shŕ-jyèr yàw bǎ-tām 'fēn-kāy. ‖**The drunk held on to the lamp post.** dzwèy-'gwěy jǐn-'jīn-de lěw-je (*or*, bàw-je) dyàn-dēng-'jù-dz. ‖**As soon as he held her** (*a baby*) **in his arms, she stopped whimpering.** tā bǎ-tā 'bàw-chi-lay-le, tā jyèw bù-'kū-le. ‖**Hold the baby and let her burp.** 'bàw-je háy-dz 'jyàw-tā dǎ ge-'gér. ‖**Hold the baby on your lap.** bǎ shyǎw-'hár gē-dzày dà-'twěy-shang 'bàw-je. ‖**Hold me tight!** bǎw-'jǐn-le!

(*Support in the arms*) jyà, chān, fú. ‖**Hold him or he'll fall.** 'chān-je tā dyǎr, yàw bù-rán tā hwèy 'tǎng-shya (*or use* 'jyà-je *or* 'fú-je).

2. To hold *meaning* to contain *is variously expressed according to the nature of the things contained.*

(*General terms*) rúng, jāw, *resultative compounds with* -kāy, -shyà, -lyǎw. ‖**That box can hold all this rice and then some.** jèy-shyē-'mǐ, nèy-ge-'shyāng-dz 'dēw 'rúng-de-'shyà, háy yěw-'ywú-ne. ‖**Can your pocket hold all these things?** nǐ-de-kěw-'dàr néng ng (*or* jāw) jèm-dwō-'dūng-shi-ma?

(*Of things in liquid or granular form*) jwāng, chéng, *resultative compounds with* -shyà, -lyǎw. ‖**This bottle holds a thousand cubic centimeters.** jèy-ge-'píng-dz néng chéng (*or* jwāng, *or* rúng) yì-'chyān-lì-fāng-gūng-'fēn. ‖**That box can't hold all this rice.** nèy-ge-'shyāng-dz 'chéng-bu-shyà (*or* 'chéng-bu-lyǎw) nèm-dwō-'mǐ.

(*Of things that are put in the container one by one, packed or arranged*) jwāng, gē, fàng, *resultative compounds with* -kāy, -shyà, -lyǎw. ‖**Will this box hold all these books?** jèy-ge-'shyāng-dz, nèy-shyē-'shū dēw °'jāw-de-kāy-ma? *or* °'jwāng-de-shyà-ma? *or* °'gē-de-shyà-ma? *or* °'fàng-de-lyǎw-ma? *etc.* ‖**One box won't hold all those books.** 'nèm-shyē-shū yí-ge-shyāng-dz 'gē-bu-shyà. *etc.* ‖**You'd be surprised how much a woman's pocketbook can hold.** nǐ yàw 'jŕ-dàw-le 'nywǔ-rén-de-kěw-'dàr-li néng gē 'dwō-shǎw dūng-shi nǐ jyèw děy 'shyà yí-'tyàw. ‖**Our garage can hold three cars.** wǒm-de-'chē-fáng rúng-de-shyà (*or* gē-de-shyà, *or* fàng-de-shyà, *etc.*) 'sān-lyàng-'chē.

To hold *in a limited space, or arranged for artistic purposes* bǎy, páy. ‖**That shelf holds fifty books in two rows.** 'nèy-tséng-shū-'jyàr, yàw-shr fēn 'lyǎng-páy, kě-yǐ bǎy 'wǔ-shr-běn-'shū.

(*Of persons in an auditorium, hotel, etc.*) dzwò. ‖**The car holds five people.** 'jèy-lyàng-chē néng dzwò 'wǔ-ge-rén. ‖**Will the car hold one more?** chē néng dzày dzwò (*or* jāw, *or* rúng) 'yí-ge-rén-ma? ‖**It can't hold one more as fat as you.** shyàng-'nǐ nèm-'pàng-de jyèw rúng (*or* dzwò)-bu-shyà-le.

(*Of passengers*) dzày, dā, ('dā-dzày). ‖**This plane can hold thirty-five passengers.** jèy-ge-'fēy-jī °kě-yǐ dā (*or* °kě-yi dzày *or* °'rúng-de-shyà *or* °'dzwò-de-lyǎw, *etc.*) 'sān-shr-'wǔ-ge-'kè-rén.

(*Of liquor in a person*). ‖**How much can he hold?** tā néng hē 'dwō-shǎw? *or* tā-de-'lyàng °dzěme-yàng? *or* °'dà-shyǎw?

3. (*To stand the strain, support*). **Be able to hold** (*of weight*) 'jīn-de-jù. ‖**Will this bridge hold?** jèy-ge-'chyáw 'jīn-de-jù-ma? ‖**How much weight will the bridge hold?** 'chyáw néng 'jīn-de-jù 'dwō-jùng. ‖**Will this chair hold me?** jèy-bǎ-'yǐ-dz 'wǒ dzwò-shang 'jīn-de-jù-ma? *or* jèy-bǎ-'yǐ-dz 'wǒ dzwò-de-'shyà-ma? (*See 2 above.*) ‖**Will this nail hold the picture in place?** jèy-ge-'dīng-dz 'jīn-de-jù jèy-jāng-'hwàr-ma?

(*Military*). ‖**Our lines held.** 'wǒ-jywūn 'jēn-dì 'jyān-gù-rú-'cháng.

(*Remain fast*). ‖**That knot will hold.** nèy-ge-'kèwr 'kāy-bu-lyǎw. *or* nèy-ge-'kèwr hěn 'jǐn.

4. **Hold back, hold down.** (*Of a person: to restrain, suppress with the hands*) 'jyēw-jù, 'lā-jù; (*with a rope in the hands*) 'lā-jù, 'chyān-jù; (*with a rope tied to something*) 'shwān-jù; (*detain, restrain, not let go*) 'kèw-jù, 'lyéw-jù, 'kèw-shyà, 'lyéw-shyà, 'yā-chi-lay, 'kān-chí-lay, 'gwān-chi-lay, 'bù-shywǔ (tā) 'dzěw, 'bú-jyàw (tā) 'dzěw ('kèw ... *and* 'lyéw ... *indicate especially official detention*); (*stop by obstructing the way*) 'lán-jù, 'jyé-jù, 'dǎng-jù. ‖**You hold him while I get my gun.** nǐ bǎ-tā 'jyēw-jù (*or* 'lā-jù, *or* 'lán-jù, *or* 'jyé-jù, *or* 'dǎng-jù), děng-wǒ bǎ-'chyāng ná-lay. ‖**Hold that horse!** bǎ-mǎ 'lā-jù (*or* 'chyān-jù, *or* 'jyēw-jù, *or* 'shwān-jù). *or* bǎ-mǎ 'lán-jù (*or* 'jyé-jù *or* 'dǎng-jù). *or expressed as* **Don't untie that horse!** byé bǎ-mǎ 'jyě-kay. ‖**When the little boy wants to go somewhere there's no holding him,** shyǎw-'hár yàw shyǎng 'shàng-nǎr 'pǎw, jyèw 'méy-fár bǎ-tā 'lā-jù. ‖**He's being held by the police.** tā jyàw jǐng-chá °'kèw-jù-le. *or* °'lyéw-jù-le. *or* °'yā-chì-lay-le. *or* °'kān-chǐ-lay-le. *or* °'gwān-chǐ-lay-le. ‖**Hold your horses!** byé jáw-'jí. 'máng shém-me?

5. (*To keep*) 'tswén-je, 'lyéw-je; (*keep safely*) 'shēw-je; (*keep from going out, as a document*) kèw, yā, gē. ‖**She held the check for a long time.** tā bǎ jī-'pyàw 'kèw-le (*or* 'yā-le, *or* 'gē-le) hǎw-shyē-'r̄-dz. ‖**We'll hold the letter for you.** wǒm bǎ-'shìn gěy-nǐ °'tswén-je. *or* °'lyéw-je. *or* °'shēw-je.

6. *Miscellaneous other meanings.* (*Maintain oneself*). ‖**He held himself ready for all emergencies.** tā 'yí-chyè 'dēw yěw 'jwěn-bèy.

Hold the lead. ‖**Our team held the lead to the end.** wǒm-'dwèy dé-de 'fēr yì-'jf dzày 'chyán-tew. ‖**Can we hold the lead from now on?** dzám 'néng-bu-néng yì-'jf bú-jyàw tām 'gǎn-gwo-chywu?

A hold (*grip*). ‖**He lost his hold and fell.** tā 'tū-lu shēw-le (*or* tā 'jwā-bu-jù-le *or* tā 'jyēw-bu-jù-le *or* tā 'dzwàn-bu-jù-le), jyèw 'dyàw-shyà-chywù-le. (*See 1 above.*)

(*Influence*). ‖**Say, what hold does he have on you?** *meaning* **Why do you believe in him so implicitly?** hèy! nǐ dzěm 'nèm 'mí-shìn tā? *or* (*Implying that there is cause for blackmail*) nǐ yěw shém 'dwǎn-chu jyàw-tā 'ná-jù-le-ma?

Hold attention (*by a speech*). ‖**He holds (your) attention.** tā jyàw-rén ày 'tīng. *or* tā jyàw-rén 'tīng-je 'chǐ-jyèr.

Hold attention (*by general personality*). ‖**The teacher couldn't hold our attention.** 'shyān-sheng 'jyǎng-de °méy-'jìn. *or* °'wú-jīng-dǎ-'tsǎy-de. *or* °'jyàw-wǒm 'tīng-je bù-chí-'jyèr.

To hold one's eyes. ‖**He held my eyes.** wǒ 'dīng-le tā yì-'yǎn. *or* wǒ yì-jf 'kàn-je-ta.

To hold one's tongue. ‖**Hold your tongue!** (*Don't start to speak*) byé 'shwō. *or* (*Stop speaking*) byé 'shwō-le.

To hold one's head high. ‖**He holds his head high in spite of all.** kě-shr tā háy néng 'mǎn-bu-'dzǎy-hu. ‖**He can hold his head high in any group.** tā dàw-'nǎr dēw néng 'páng-rè wú-'rén.

To hold one's breath. ‖**Hold your breath.** byé 'chwǎn-chì. *or* 'bì-jù (yì-)kěw-'chì. ‖**Hold your breath until I say OK.** bì-je 'chì, děng wǒ shwō 'hǎw-le, dzày 'chwǎn. ‖**Everybody held their breath when she missed a rung of the ladder.** tā dzày 'tī-dz-shang 'yì-jyǎw tsǎy-'tsz̄-le, shyà-de-'rén-ren 'bì-je (yì-)kěw-'chì.

Be held in respect. ‖**He is held in great respect by his fellows.** tā-nèy-'dǎng-de-rén dēw tǐng 'dzwēn-jìng-ta.

To hold (*believe and maintain*) 'yǐ-wéy, yi-'dìng shwō. ‖**They held that the earth was flat.** tām yí-'dìng shwō (*or* tām 'yǐ-wéy) dì-'chyéw shr̄ 'píng-de.

To hold (*judge*). (*In court*) pàn; (*otherwise*) shwō. ‖**The court held him guilty.** fǎ-'ywàn pàn-tā yěw-'dzwèy. ‖**The police held him responsible for the accident.** jǐng-'chá shwō (jèy-tsz̄-chū-de-'shr̄) shr̄ 'tā-de-tswòr. *But* ‖**We'll hold you responsible if it turns out otherwise.** yàw-shr 'bú-nèm-je, jyèw 'dēw shr̄ 'nǐ-de-tswèr.

To hold a meeting. *Usually* 'kāy; (*hold ceremonies*) shíng; (*hold church services*) dzwò. **Hold a discussion** kāy 'tǎw-lwèn-hwèy; **hold a dance** kāy 'tyàw-wǔ-hwèy; **hold a tea party** kāy 'chá-hwà-hwèy; **hold a church service** dzwò lǐ-'bày. ‖**The meetings of the club are held once a week.** 'měy lǐ-bày kāy yí-tsz̄-'hwěy. ‖**When will the wedding be held?** 'jǐ-shf shíng 'jyē-hwēn-'lǐ?

(*Of a rule*). ‖**The rule won't hold in this case.** 'jèy-jyàn-shr̄, nèy-tyáw-'gwēy-jywu 'yùng-bu-'shàng.

(*Retain a position or office*). ‖**He held office for a long time.** tā dzày-'rèn bù-shǎw 'nyán.

(*Keep a job*). ‖**There must be some reason why he can't hold a job.** tā nèm 'nǎr dēw dǎy-bu-'jù (*or* tā nèm 'nǎr dēw dzwò-bu-'cháng) yí-'dìng yěw ge-'ywán-gù.

(*Have possession of*). ‖**They held the land under a ten-year lease.** dzày 'dzū-chī-de 'shf-nyán-lǐ jèy-'dì shǔ 'tā-men.

(*In music*). ‖**She held the high note for a long time.** nà-ge-'gāw-yīn tā 'lā-le hěn 'cháng.

(*Exclamation*). ‖Hold it! *meaning* Carry it. 'ná-je! (*etc. see* 1, *above*) *meaning* Don't move! byé 'dùng! *meaning* Don't leave! byé 'dzěw! *meaning* Stop! 'dǎ-jù! *meaning* Hold that pose. 'hǎw! 'jyèw nèm-je byé-'dùng.

(*Exhortation*). ‖Hold the line! (*Military*) *is expressed as* Defend to the death. 'sž-shěw 'jèn-dì! *or as* Don't retreat. 'dzěm-je yě bú-yàw 'twèy! *or* (*Against inflation*) 'bú-yàw jyàw 'wù-jyà dzày 'jǎng. *or* (*Telephoning*) *as* Don't hang up. byé 'gwà-shang.

Hold back. ‖I wanted to go but held myself back. wǒ běn-lay yàw 'chywù, kě-shr 'hèw-lay wǒ 'gwǎn-je wǒ-'dž-jǐ méy-'chywù. *or* wǒ-shīn-lǐ 'shyǎng chywù láy-je, bú-gwò yǎw-je 'yá méy-'chywù. ‖Hold that crowd back. bǎ nèy-chywún-rén 'lán-hwéy-chywu. *or* 'byé jyàw nèy-chywún-'rén shàng-'chyán-lay. ‖He held me back. (*Literally*) tā bú-jyàw-wǒ 'gwò-chywu. *or* (*Literally or figuratively*) tā bǎ-wǒ 'lán-jù-le. (*See* 4 *above.*)

Hold forth. ‖The professor has been holding forth for an hour about some scientific theory. jyàw-'shèw-men tǎw-lwèn yì-jǔng-kē-shywé-'ywán-lǐ, tǎw-'lwèn-le 'yì-dyǎn-jūng.

Hold good. ‖Does that rule still hold good? nèy-tyáw-'gwēy-jywū háy yěw-'shyàw-ma?

Hold in (*of feelings*). ‖I was simply furious, but I held it in until he had left. wǒ-shīn-lǐ chì-'jí-le, kě-shr 'rěn-je 'jŕ dàw tā 'dzěw-le.

Hold off (*literally*) ná 'ywǎn-dyǎr. ‖Hold off the picture to get a better view of it. nèy-ge-'hwàr ná 'ywǎn-dyǎr 'gèng hǎw 'kàn.

Hold off (*figuratively; delay*) táng. ‖The butcher wants us to pay our bill, but maybe we can hold him off for a few days. mày-'rèw-de shyǎng yàw-'chyán, bú-gwò dzám yě-shywǔ néng dzày 'táng lyǎng-tyān.

Hold on. (*See* 1, *above.*) ‖Hold on! *meaning* Don't let go. 'dzwàn-je. *or* 'ná-je. *etc. or* byé fàng-'shěw. *or meaning* Wait a moment! 'děng-yi-hwěr! ‖Hold on to me when we cross the street. gwò-'jyē-de-shŕ-hew, 'lā-je-wo-dyar. ‖Why don't you hold on to (*keep*) that house until prices rise? nǐ wèy-'shéme bù-děng 'jyà-chyan 'jǎng-le dzày mày-'fáng-ne? ‖Try to hold on (*keep going*) a little longer. dzày 'rěn yì-hwěr. ‖Hold on (*stop*) and let me explain that. nǐ shyān tīng 'wǒ shwō.

Hold out. ‖They held out against all odds. *meaning* . . .wouldn't let go tām 'sž-bù fàng-'shěw. *or meaning* . . . wouldn't give in tām 'sž-bú-kěn-'ràng. *or* (*Military; of the enemy only*) tām 'wán-chyáng 'dí-kàng ('shŕ-dzay gāy-'dž). *or* (*Military; of one's own men*) tām 'jyān-shěw bú-'dùng ('shŕ-dzay kě-'jyā). ‖They held out longer than I thought. méy-shyǎng-'dàw tām néng 'nèm 'chén-de-jù 'chì.

Hold over. ‖Let's hold this over until the next meeting. jèy-ge dzám děng 'shyà-tsž kāy-'hwèy dzày 'shwō-ba. ‖The movie will be held over ᴧn extra week. nèy-ge-'pyān-dz háy dzày 'dwō yǎn yì-shīng-'chī.

Hold together. ‖This coat has been mended so much it will hardly hold together. jèy-ge-wǎy-'tàwr 'bǔ-le-yèw-'bǔ-de dēw yàw 'sǎn-le. ‖The box was barely holding together after the trip. dzěw-le yì-'dzāwr, nèy-ge-'hé-dz jyǎn-'jŕ jyèw yàw 'sǎn-le. ‖Let's hold together to the end. dzám 'twán-jyē dàw-'dǐ.

Hold up (*support; see* 1, *above*). ‖She's such a poor skater that we had to hold her up to keep her from falling. tā lyēw-'bīng 'jyǎn-jŕ bù-'shíng, háy děy rén °'jyà-je-ne. *or* °'fú-je-ne. *or* °'chān-je-ne.

Hold up (*stop*). ‖The work was held up for three weeks. gūng-dzwò 'dāng-gē-le 'sā-lǐ-bày. ‖What's holding up traffic? 'dzěm dēw bù-'dzěw-le? *or* 'dzěm dēw bú-'dùng-le? *or* 'chyán-tew 'chū-le shém-'shŕ-le?

Hold up (*endure*). ‖He held up well under the strain. nèm-yàng-'nán-de-shŕ tā 'jywū-rán néng 'dīng-de-jù.

Hold up. (*Rob; at home*) chyǎng; (*on the road*) jyé; a holdup on the road lù-'jyé. ‖I was held up last night. wǒ dzwór 'wǎn-shang jyàw-'rén gěy °'chyǎng-le. *or* °'jyé-le. ‖People avoid this road because there have been several holdups here. 'jèy-tyáw-'lù-shang 'yěw-le 'jǐ-ge- (*or* 'jǐ-tsž-)lù-'jyé, swǒ-yǐ 'rén dēw 'bù-kěn 'dǎ jèr 'dzěw.

Hold water. (*Literally*) chéng-'shwěy; . (*figuratively, of reasoning*) 'chūng-dzú; (*of a plan*) 'twǒ-dàng. ‖This canvas can't hold water long. jèy-ge-'fān-bù chéng-'shwěy yì-'hwěr jyèw 'lèw. ‖Your arguments won't hold water. nǐ-shwō-de-'lǐ-yéw bù-'chūng-dzú. ‖Your plan won't hold water. nǐ-de-'bàn-fa bú-dà 'twǒ-dàng.

(*Below decks in a ship*) tsāng(-li). ‖The boat carried planes on the deck, and all sorts of merchandise in the hold. chwán-'myàn-shang dzày fēy-'jī, 'tsāng-li-jwāng-de shŕ 'gè-jǔng-de-'hwò-wù.

HOLE. 'kū-lung; dùng; *or, if the hole is quite round and regular*, yǎr. Pinhole (*yùng*) 'jēn-jā-de-ge-'kū-lung, *or* jēn-'jyār-dà-de-ge-'kū-lung (*or* 'dùng *instead of* 'kū-lung); hole of a doughnut (*empty place in center*) dāng-jūng-'kūng-de-fang. ‖In Chinese a doughnut may be defined as a fried-in-deep-fat, made-of-risen-dough, round, sweet pastry, empty at the center (*or*, with a hole in the center). 'jūng-gwo-hwà doughnut shŕ yùng-yéw-'já-de, 'fā-myàn-dzwò-de, ywán-de-tyán-'byěngr, °dāng-jūng shŕ 'kūng-de. *or* °dāng-jūng yěw ge-'kū-lung. ‖There is a hole in that glove. shěw-'tàwr-shang yěw (*or* pwò-le) yí-ge-'kū-lung (*or* yí-ge-'dùng). ‖His hat was shot full of holes. tā-de-'dà-lǐ-màw-shang 'dǎ-le hǎw-shyē-'kū-lung. ‖The mouse ran into his hole. 'hàw-dz dzwān °'dùngr-li-chywù-le. *or* °'kū-lung-li-chywu-le. ‖Did you find any holes in the screen? *meaning* Is the screen broken? shā-'chwāngr pwò-le-ma? *or meaning* Are there any holes in the screen? shā-'chwāngr-shang yěw °'kū-lung-ma? *or* °'dùng-ma? ‖Drill a hole two inches deep on the table here. dzày jwō-dz-'jèr dzwàn ge-'lyǎng-tswèn-de-°'kū-lung. *or* °'dùng. *or* °'yǎr.

Hole in the ground (or a dent) kēng, kēngr. ‖They dug a hole and planted the tree. tām 'wā (or 'páw)-le ge-'kēng bǎ-shù 'jùng-shang-le. ‖They dug a deep hole and buried the gold. tām 'wā (or 'páw)-le ge-'shēn-kēng bǎ jīn-dz máy-le.

‖That restaurant is just an old hole. nèy-ge-fàn-'gwǎr 'pwò-làn-bu-'kān.

Other expressions in English. ‖She suddenly found herself in a hole financially. (*In debt*) tā 'hū-rán jř-dàw-le tā ('dž-jǐ) °'kwēy-kùng-le bù-'shǎw. or (*Unable to raise money*) °'jēw-jwàn-bù-'lǐng-le. ‖The trip made a big hole in her funds. 'jè-yi-tàng 'hwā-le (or 'pwò-fèy-le) tā bù-'shǎw-chyán. ‖He picks holes in everything I say. bú-lwèn wǒ shwō 'shéme, tā dzǔng tyāw-'tswòr. or tyāw-'yǎr. ‖He's a square peg in a round hole. tā yùng-dzày 'nàr bù-hé-'shř. or tā bù-'yí-wú dzwò 'nèy-ge.

HOLIDAY. (*Time off from work*) fàng-'jyà (*also means* have a holiday, be a holiday; *literally* give time off) ; (*the specific day*) fàng-jyà-'ř; a holiday of N days N-tyān-'jyà; holiday period 'jyà-chī. ‖Is today a holiday? jyēr fàng-'jyà-ma? ‖When does the holiday season begin? fàng-'jyà tsúng 'něy-tyān 'chǐ? ‖October tenth is a holiday in China. 'shŕ-ywè 'shŕ-hàw dzày 'jūng-gwo shř fàng-jyà-'ř. ‖Sunday is a holiday. lǐ-bày-'ř fàng-'jyà. ‖I want to take a holiday for a few days. wǒ shyǎng gàw 'jǐ-tyān-'jyà. ‖I'll see you during the holiday(s). dzám 'jyà-chī-li 'hwèy. or dzám fàng-'jyà-de-shŕ-hew 'jyàn.

However, the modern Western concept of a holiday as a vacation is recent in China, and is common only in government circles, schools, and Western-style business concerns. In other circles, a holiday is really a festival, and is called jyé. *The three main festivals (all by the old calendar) are the fifth day of the fifth month* (wǔ-ywè-'jyé *or* dwān-'wǔ), *the fifteenth day of the eighth month* (bā-ywè-'jyé *or* 'jūng-chyēw), *and the turn of the year* (gwò-'nyán). ‖We passed the New Year's holiday season (*old festival*) by feasting several days. wǒm gwò-'nyán 'dà-chŕ-le jǐ-'tyān.

HOME. (*Referring only to the building; house*) 'fáng-dz; 'jáy-dz. ‖They have a beautiful home in the country. tām dzày 'shyāng-shyà yěw yì-swǒr-hěn-'hǎw-de-°'fáng-dz. or °'jáy-dz. ‖Whose home is this? jèy shř 'shwéy-de-°'fáng-dz? or °'jáy-dz?

Including other associations, like English home, jyā (*also means family in some cases*). (*Polite forms*) your (honorable) home 'fǔ-shàng; my (humble) home 'shè-shyà, 'bǐ-ywù. ‖Where is your home? My home is at No. 15 Sun Yat-sen Road. nǐ 'jù-dzày nǎr? °wǒ 'jù-dzày or °wǒ-jyā dzày 'jūng-shān-'lù shŕ-'wǔ-hàw. or (*Polite*) 'fǔ-shàng dzày 'nǎr? 'bǐ-ywù 'jūng-shān-'lù shŕ-'wǔ-hàw. ‖How many persons are there in your home? (*Polite*) 'fǔ-shàng yěw 'dwō-shǎw rén? ‖There are five persons including me in my home. (*Polite answer*) 'shè-shyà lyán-wǒ 'wǔ-kěw-rén. ‖This

is my home. jè shř wǒ-de-'jyā. ‖Here is my home. wǒ-'jyā dzày 'jèr. or jèr shř wǒ-de-'jyā. ‖Come to my home tomorrow evening at six. myér 'wǎn-shang 'lyèw-dyǎn dàw wǒ-'jyā-lay. ‖What is the street number of your home? (*Polite*) 'fǔ-shàng-mén-'páy 'dwō-shǎw hàw? or (*Common*) nǐ-'jyā-mén-'páy 'dwō-shǎw hàw? ‖I have to go home. wǒ děy hwéy-'jyā-le. ‖He'll drive me home. tā kě-yǐ kāy-'chē sùng-wǒ hwéy-'jyā. ‖See her home, will you? 'sùng-tā dàw-'jyā, á? ‖I was at home all day yesterday. wǒ 'dzwó-tyān yì-'jěng-tyān dzày-'jyā. ‖They are at home every Wednesday evening (*to receive guests*) tām 'dìng-gwēy-de shř měy-'shīng-chī-'sān 'wǎn-shang dzày 'jyā-li jyē-dàiy 'péng-yew. ‖This is just like home cooking. jèy-ge hěn shyàng 'jyā-li-dzwò-de-'fàn. ‖This is home cooking (*plain style*). jèy shř 'jyā-cháng-'fàn. or jèy shř 'byàn-fàn. ‖Make it a sort of home atmosphere. 'nùng-de jyàw-rén 'jywé-je shyàng dzày 'jyā-li shř-de. ‖He makes all his guests feel at home in his place. dzày 'tā-nar 'shéy dēw gēn dzày-dž-jǐ-'jyā-li shř-de nèm swéy-'byàn. or (*Literary*) 'tā-nar 'jēn-shr 'bīn-jř-rú-'gwēy.

Make yourself at home. byé 'kè-chi. or bú 'kè-chi. or dzày-'jèr gēn dzày 'dž-jǐ-'jyā-lǐ shř-de.

(*Place to stay*). ‖You can always find a home with us (*live with us*). 'wǒm-jèr nǐ 'jǐ-shŕ yàw 'jù, jyèw láy 'jù.

(*Native*). ‖He went back to his home state. tā hwéy tā-de-běn-'shěng-chywu-le. ‖My home state is California, but now I'm living in New York. wǒ shř 'jyā-shěng-rén, bú-gwò shyàn-'dzày jù-dzày 'nyéw-ywē. ‖Where is your home town? (*Polite*) gwèy-'chù shř shéme-'dì-fang? or gwèy-'chù shř 'nǎ-yì-chéng? or (*Common*) nǐ shř 'nǎ-chéng-de-rén? or nǐ shř 'nǎr-de-rén? ‖My home town is Tày-ywán. (*Polite*) bì-'chéng (or bì-'chù) tày-ywán. or (*Common*) wǒ shř 'tày-ywàn-de-rén.

(*Institution for the poor, old, sick, etc.*) -ywàn. Old people's home lǎw-rén-'ywàn; orphans' home gū-ér-'ywàn. ‖There is a home for old ladies up on the hill. 'shān-shang yěw ge-jwǎn-shēw-'nywł-rón-de-'lǎw-rén-'ywàn.

(*Of birds, animals, etc.*) *use* nest wō, *and other expressions.* ‖This tree is the home of a family of squirrels. jèy-kē-'shù-shang yěw yì-'wō-sūng-'shǔr. ‖Several squirrels make this tree their home. yěw jǐ-ge-sūng-'shùr dzày jèy-kē-'shù-shang dǎ-'wō. ‖This is the home of a delicious kind of carp. 'jèy-ge-dì-fang chū (*produces*) yì-'jǔng hǎw-'chŕ-de-'lǐ-ywú.

Home-grown. ‖Are these vegetables home-grown? (*grown by yourselves*). jèy-shyē-'chīng-tsày shř dž-'jǐ-jùng-de-ma?

(*To the place aimed at*). ‖He drove his point home. tā 'shwō-de (or tā 'jyǎng-de) jùng-'kěn. or tā 'yì-ywǔ pwò-'dì. or (*Literary*) tā 'shwō-de (or tā 'jyǎng-de) hěn 'jùng kěn-'chì. ‖He brought home the point that the enemy is tough. tā bǎ 'dí-rén-hěn-'shyūng jèy-yì-'dyǎn shwō-de (or jyǎng-de) hěn °'tèw-chè. or

°'chīng-cnu. or ''míng-bay. ‖He brought home to all of the children why they should be polite. tā jyàw swŏ-y w-de-'háy-dz dēw 'míng-bay (or ... dēw 'lyǎw-jyě, or ... dēw 'jĭ-dàw) wèy-'shéme tām děy yěw 'lǐ-màw.

HONEST. (*Upright*) 'chéng-shf́, 'lǎw-shf́; or *expressed as* not being capable of lying 'bú-hwèy-shwō-'shyā-hwàr-de, 'bú-hwèy-shwō-'hwǎng-de, 'bú-hwěy-sā-'hwǎng-de. ‖Is he honest? tǎ-rén 'chéng-shf́-ma? or ta shr̀ ge-'chéng-shf́-rén-ma? or tā shr̀ ge-'bú-hwèy-shwō-'shyā-hwàr-de-rén-ma? etc. ‖Here is an honest man. Let's have his opinion. tā shr̀ ge-'lǎw-shf́-rén etc.), dzám wèn-wen 'tā-ba.

(*Just*). ‖That wouldn't be honest. 'nèy jyèw tày chywǔ-'chyǎw-le. or nà bú-shr̀ sā-'hwǎng-ma? or nà bu-shr shwō 'shyā-hwàr-ma? or nèy jyèw 'bú-shr 'kāy-chéng-bù-'gūng-de-le.

(*Frank*) 'chéng-shf́, 'lǎw-shf́. Be honest, speak honestly shwō 'shf́-hwà. ‖He has an honest face. tā-lyǎn-'jǎng-de hěn shyàng °ge-'lǎw-shf́-rén. or °ge-'chéng-shf́-rén. ‖Tell me honestly what you think of that plan. shwō 'shf́-hwà, nǐ 'jywé-je nèy-ge-'bàn-fa 'dzěm-yàng? ‖Be honest with me and I'll see that your name is kept out of it. nǐ gēn-wǒ shwō 'shf́-hwà, wǒ jyèw 'bú-jyàw nǐ-de-'míng-dz 'lyè-dzay 'lǐ-taw. ‖Women are usually not honest about their age. 'nywǔ-rén jān-le 'dž-jǐ-de-'nyán-líng cháng-chang °bù-kěn shwō 'shf́-hwà. or °'mán-je-dyar.

(*Fair to all concerned*) 'gūng-dàw, 'gūng-píng. ‖That's an honest bargain. nèy-ge-jyàr hěn °'gūng-dàw. or °'gūng-píng.

(*Exact; of weight*) jwěn. ‖That scale gives honest weight. nèy-ge-'chèng 'fèn-lyàng hěn 'jwěn. ‖I don't believe your scale gives honest weight. wǒ jywé-je nǐ-nèy-ge-'chèng °'fèn-lyàng bù-'jwěn. or (*if a buyer thinks the scale reads high*) °'shyǎw. or (*if a seller thinks the scale reads low*) °'dà.

(*Really*). ‖Honest? (shr̀) 'jēn-de-ma? ‖Honest, I didn't say anything. (shr̀) 'jēn-de; wǒ yí-jywù-'hwà yě méy-'shwō.

HONEY. mì; fēng-'mì (*literally* bee honey, *used especially of prepared honey as eaten*). Honeybee 'mì-fēngr. ‖I'd like some bread and honey. wǒ shyàng chr̄ dyàr-myàn-'bāw gēn fēng-'mì. ‖The clover is full of bees gathering honey. 'dīng-shyang-'shù-shang jìng shr̀ 'mì-fēngr dzày-nar tsǎy-'mì.

(*Figuratively*). ‖That's a honey of a dress. nèy-'yī-fu kě jēn 'pyàw-lyàng. ‖She's a honey. (*Looks only*) tā jēn hǎw-'kàn.

HONOR. (*Personal glory, personal privilege*) lèw-'lyǎn (*also means* honored), 'mǎn-myàn-dz, or *expressed as* give face 'tǐ-myàn, or *frequently expressed in roundabout ways*. ‖What an honor to be invited to dinner by the governor! shěng-'jǎng (or shěng-jǔ-'shf́) chǐng chr̄-'fàn jēn shr̀ °'mǎn-myàn-dz. or °'tǐ-myàn. ‖It is a

real honor to be asked to speak to such a learned audience. (*As a comment about the fact*) rén-jyā 'chǐng chywù gēn 'nèm-yěw-'shywé-wèn-de-rén yǎn-'jyǎng 'jēn-shr °lèw-'lyǎn. or °'tǐ-myàn. (*but not* °'mǎn-myàn-dz *here*). (*As an introduction to the speech*) *meaning* gives me great pleasure gēn 'jū-wèy-'jèm-yěw-'shywé-wèn-de-rén láy yǎn-'jyǎng, 'shf́-dzày shr̀ jyàw-wǒ jywé-je 'rúng-shìng. ‖I consider it a great honor to be elected president of this association. *meaning* it makes me feel uneasy chéng jū-wèy-'jywù (or chéng jū-wèy-'shywǎn-jywù) wǒ dzwò běn-'hwèy-de-hwèy-'jǎng, jyàw-wǒ jywé-de shf́-dzày shr̀ °'tsán-kwèy. or *meaning* it makes me surprised at such an honor °shèw-'chǔng-rè-'jīng. (*Or, each time* wǒ *occurs in the above sentence, substitute* 'shyūng-dì or 'bì-rén, *more modest forms*.) *But* ‖I feel honored to meet you. *is expressed as* I've heard of you for a long time. jyěw-yǎng, 'jyěw-yǎng. ‖He has won great honors. tā 'hěn lèw-'lyǎn. or *more commonly expressed as* People praise him. tā 'hěn shèw-rén 'chēng-dzàn. or tā 'hěn shèw-rén 'kwā-jyǎng. or 'rén-ren dēw shwō tā 'hǎw.

Honors (*at school, etc.*) ‖He won highest honors at school. *is expressed as* His school record is very good. tā-dzày-shywé-'shyàw-de-'chéng-jì hěn °'hǎw. or °'gāw. ‖He expects to graduate with honors. *meaning* among the highest few tā shyǎng-yàw bì-'yè-de-shf́-hew dzày 'téw-jǐ-'míng-li. or *meaning* with prizes tā shyǎng-yàw bì-'yè-de-shf́-hew dé-'jyǎng.

Be an honor to wèy ... °dzēng-'gwāng or °jēng-'gwāng. ‖He was an honor to his country. tā wèy-'gwó °jēng-'gwāng. or °dzēng-'gwāng. ‖He is an honor to his family. tā wèy 'mén-hù dzēng-'gwāng. or (*Colloquial*) tā gěy 'jyā-li lèw-'lyǎn.

To honor, in honor of, *often included in meaning of* invite chǐng or give gěy. ‖They gave a dinner to honor us (or in our honor). tām 'chǐng-wǒm chr̄-'fàn. or (*Literary*) tām shè-'yàn 'kwǎn-dày wǒ-men. ‖We gave a birthday party in his honor. wǒm 'chǐng-le shyè-rén-lay 'gěy-tā gwò 'shēng-r̀.

(*Good faith*). ‖You are a man of honor. nǐ shr̀ ge 'jywūn-dz. or nǐ shr̀ ge-'hǎw-rén.

(*Oath*). ‖I swear on my honor. wǒ píng 'lyáng-shīn chǐ-'shr̀.

Your honor. *Use the person's official title; thus* ‖Would your honor please repeat that? chǐng 'shěn-pàn-gwān 'dzày shwō yí-tsž. ('shěn-pàn-gwān *is the commonest term for* judge.) *But in* Yes, your honor *the title is not used. See* YES.

Do the honors. ‖You do the honors tonight at the banquet. (*Be in charge, be toastmaster, be speaker, etc.*) jyēr-wǎn-shang-de-yàn-'hwèy nǐ dzwò 'jǔ-shí. ‖Let me do the honors (*pay the bill*). ràng-'wǒ chǐng. or 'wǒ chǐng-ba. or ràng-'wǒ dzwò 'dūng-daw. or 'wǒ dzwò 'dūng-daw-ba. or (*Peiping*) 'wǒ hwèy-le-ba.

(*Accept for payment*). ‖We can't honor this check. jèy-jāng-jr̄-'pyàw wǒm bù-néng 'shēw.

HOOK. 'gēw-dz, gēwr. Fishhook ywú-'gēw, ywú-'gēwr, ywú-'gēw-dz. ‖Is there a hook to hang my coat on? yěw gwà-'yī-fu-de-'gēw-dz-ma? ‖That stick has a hook at one end. nèy-gēn-'gwèr yěw yì-'téwr yěw ge-'gēwr. ‖We went fishing with a hook and line. wǒm dày-je ywú-'gēwr gēn ywú-'gār jyèw dyàw-'ywú-chywu-le. ‖This dress is fastened with hooks and eyes. jèy-jyàn-'yī-fu yùng 'gēw-dz jì-shang.

To hook (fasten with a hook) 'gēw(-shang), kèw-(shang). ‖Help me hook this. bāng-je wǒ bǎ jèy-ge °'gēw-shang. or °'kèw-shang. ‖This dress buttons; it doesn't hook. jèy-shēr-'yī-fu shř yùng 'kèwr (or 'kèw-dz) 'kèw-de; 'bú-shř yùng 'gēw-dz-de. ‖He hooked his arm around the post. tā yùng 'yèw-gē-bey bǎ 'jù-dz °'gēw-ju-le. or °'bàw-ju-le.

(In fishing). ‖I hooked a big fish. wǒ 'dyàw-shang yì-tyáw-'dà-ywú-lay.

(In boxing). ‖He gave him a left hook to the jaw. tā yùng 'dzwǒ-shěw yì-'chywán 'dǎ-dzày 'nèy-ge-rén-de ('yèw-)yá-'chwáng-shang.

By hook or crook. ‖He'll get the job by hook or crook. tā 'bú-lwèn 'dzěm-je yě yàw bǎ nèy-ge-'shèr 'chyǎng-dàw 'shěw-li. or tā 'wèy-le chyǎng 'nèy-jyan-shèr 'shéme dēw 'gàn-de chū-'láy.

Hookup. ‖He spoke on a coast-to-coast hookup. tā-(dzày-wú-shyàn-'dyàn-shang-shwō-)de-'hwà chywán-gwó 'gè-dyàn-táy dēw 'gwǎng-bwò.

HOPE. (Expect, desire) 'shī-wàng; (especially desire) 'pàn-wàng; (especially expect, depend on) 'jř-wàng; (of things already past; to expect, think, plan on) 'dǎ-je, 'dǎ-swàn, 'yǐ-wéy; (wait and see) děng-je 'chyáw. ‖I hope you can come. wǒ 'shī-wàng. (or wǒ 'pàn-wàng) nǐ 'néng láy. ‖I hope it will turn out all right. wǒ 'shī-wàng (or wǒ 'pàn-wàng) jèy-ge-shèr 'bù-chū 'lwàn-dz. ‖There is nothing to hope for. yì-dyǎr-'jř-wàng (or yì-dyǎr-'shī-wàng) yě méy-'yěw. ‖There is still hope. háy yěw dyǎr-'shī-wàng. or háy yěw dyǎr-'jř-wàng. ‖There is still hope that he'll change his mind. děng-je 'chyáw-ba, tā 'yě-shywǔ hwéy 'hwéy-shīn-jwǎn-'yì. ‖It is my hope to go back to school. wǒ 'shī-wàng hwéy shywé-'shyàw-chywu. ‖I don't see any hope in this job. jèy-ge-shèr wǒ jywé-je 'méy-shéme-'shī-wàng. or °méy-shéme-'jř-wàng. or °méy-shéme-kě-'shī-wàng-de. or °méy-shéme-kě-'jř-wàng-de. ‖Let's hope for the best. děng-je 'chyáw-ba. ‖We had hoped that after he came the situation would improve. wǒm 'ywán-láy 'shī-wàng (or 'pàn-wàng, or 'jř-wàng, or 'dǎ-swàn, or 'dǎ-je, or 'yǐ-wéy) tā yì-'láy jèy-shèr jyèw hwèy 'hǎw-de. ‖We hoped you would come. wǒm 'dǎ-je (or 'dǎ-swàn-je) nǐ hwèy 'láy-de.

Other expressions in English. ‖Don't give up hope. byé 'hwéy shīn. ‖He gave up hope. tā 'hwéy-shīn-le. ‖I have hopes of seeing you again (literary). dzám 'hèw-hwèy yěw-'chī. ‖The new player is the only hope of the team. jèy-yí-dwèy jyèw 'chyáw (or . . . jyèw 'jř-je) nèy-ge-'shīn-láy-de °shywǎn-'shěw-le. or

°shywǎn-'shěw dzěm-'yàng-le. ‖We hoped against hope (or, We hoped against expectation) to get a ticket. wǒm 'míng jř-dàw bù-'shíng, kě-shr háy 'pàn-je 'néng dé-dàw jāng-'pyàw.

HORN. (Of an animal) 'jī-jyaw; -jyǎw preceded by the name of the particular animal, as goat's horn yáng-'jyǎw. Horns of insects (feelers) 'chù-'jyǎw. ‖Be careful, the bull has sharp horns. lyéw-'shén, nyéw-'jī-jyaw 'jyān-je-ne. ‖This is made of horn. jèy shř nyéw-'jyǎwr-dzwò-de. ‖The two bucks locked horns (fought with heads bull-fashion). lyǎ-'lù dǐng-'nyéwr-ne.

(Wind instrument) hàw-'jyǎw; (trumpet) 'lǎ-ba. ‖Horns were once used by the Mongolian Army. yǐ-chyán 'méng-gu-jywūn-'dwèy-li yùng hàw-'jyǎw. ‖Don't blow the horn so much. byé lǎw chwěy 'lǎ-ba.

Horn in (interfere). ‖I don't like to horn in. wǒ bú-'ywàn-yi gwǎn 'shyán-shř.

To pull in one's horns. ‖All you have to do is say that, and he'll pull in his horns. nǐ 'nèm yì-'shwō tā jyèw °hwèy 'nyān-le. or °hwèy 'lǎw-shr-le. or °bú-nèm shén-'chì-le.

HORSE. mǎ. One horse yì-pǐ-'mǎ; wild horse 'yě-mǎ; white horse 'báy-mǎ; horse-drawn carriage 'mǎ-chē; horse-drawn cart, wagon 'dà-chē, 'mǎ-lē-de-'chē. ‖Where can I get a horse? wǒ dzày-'nǎr néng jǎw-je yì-pǐ-'mǎ? ‖Take care of my horse. 'chyáw-je-dyǎr (or 'kān-je-dyǎr, or 'jàw-yīng-je-dyǎr) (wǒ-de-)'mǎ. ‖Let's go to the horse races. dzám kàn sày-'mǎ chywù-ba. or dzám kàn pǎw-'mǎ chywù-ba. ‖Saddle the horse. 'bèy-mǎ.

Special expressions in English. ‖He works like a horse. tā dzwò-'shř chín-'kěn. ‖He was up on his high horse. tā 'ywè-wǔ-yáng-'wéy-de. or tā 'jř-gāw-chì-'yáng-de. ‖You're putting the cart before the horse. nǐ-nà-shr 'chīng-jùng dàw-'jř. or nǐ-nà shř 'chyán-hèw dyān-'dǎw. or shř-ching 'bú-shr nèm 'bàn-de.

HOSPITAL. 'yī-ywàn. ‖Where is the hospital? 'yī-ywàn dzày 'nǎr? ‖You will have to go to the hospital. nǐ děy jìn 'yī-ywàn. ‖We took the puppy to the dog hospital. wǒm bǎ shyǎw-'gēwr sùng-dàw 'shèw-yī-ywàn-chywu-le.

HOST. 'jǔ-rén; act as host dzwò 'jǔ-rén, dzwò-'dǔng, chǐng(-'kè); perform the duties of a host (welcome and take care of guests) 'jāw-dày. ‖The host sits here, and the honored guest sits there. 'jǔ-rén dzwò-'jèr, 'gwèy-kè dzwò-'nèr. ‖I am the host. wǒ shř 'jǔ-rén. ‖I'll be the host today. jyēr 'wǒ dzwò 'jǔ-rén. or jyēr 'wǒ dzwò-'dūng. or jyēr 'wǒ chǐng(-'kè). ‖Who is the host? nǎ-wèy shř 'jǔ-rén? or shéy 'chǐng(-kè)? ‖You are a wonderful host. nǐ-'jāw-dày-de jēn jēw-daw.

HOT. (*High in temperature*) rè. ‖Do you have hot water? nǐm-jèr yěw 'rè-shwěy-ma? ‖This is too hot. (jè) 'tày rè-le. ‖I want a hot dinner. wǒ shyǎng chr̄ 'rè-de. ‖The motor is running hot. 'jī-chi 'rè-le. ‖His forehead is hot. tā-nǎw-'mén-dz °fā-'rè. or, meaning is burning up, °fā-'shāw. ‖The sun is shining awfully hot today. jyēr 'tày-yang °shày-de jēn 'rè. or (harsh) °hěn 'dú. or (shines like fire) °shày-de shyàng-'hwǒ-shr̄-de. ‖The water must be boiling (hot). (Chinese omits hot.) děy 'kāy-je-de-'shwéy. or shwéy děy 'gwěn-kāy.

(*Pungent*) 'là. ‖I don't like hot foods. wǒ 'bú-ày chr̄ 'là-de. ‖Is this pepper hot? jèy-ge-'chín-jyāw 'là bú-là?

(*Violent, of temper*) bàw. ‖He has a hot temper. tā-'pí-chi hěn bàw.

(*Wanted by the police*). ‖He's hot. 'jīng-chá jèng 'jǎw-tā-ne.

(*Stolen*) ‖This string of pearls is hot. jèy-chwàn-'jēn-jū shr̀ 'dzéy-dzāng.

(*Fresh, of a scent*). ‖The dog followed the hot scent. gěw wén-jaw 'wèr-le, jyèw gēn-je wèr 'pǎw.

(*Close*). ‖We thought we were hot on the trail. wǒm háy 'yǐ-wéy jǎw-de bú-'tswò-ne.

HOTEL. (*Western style, with dining room*) fàn-'dyàn. ‖Where is the (Western) hotel? fàn-'dyàn dzày-'nǎr?

(*Other hotels, high grade*) lywǔ-'gwǎn. ‖Are there any other hotels? yěw 'byé-de-lywǔ-'gwǎn-ma? ‖I'm looking for a cheap hotel. wǒ jèng-dzày jǎw yí-ge-'pyán-yi-de-lywǔ-'gwǎn.

(*Inn, guest house*) kè-'jàn, jàn-'fáng, kè-'dyàn.

(*Country inn*) shyǎw-'dyàr.

HOUR. (*Sixty minutes*) dyǎn(-'jūng) (dyǎn, *a measure, refers particularly to the point of time, not the space of time; it may be used without -'jūng only when it is clear that time is being talked about*); jūng-'téw, shyǎw-'shŕ. ‖I'll be back within an hour. wǒ 'yí-ge-jūng-'téw yí-'nèy hwéy-láy. or wǒ 'yì-dyǎn-jūng yǐ-nèy 'hwéy-láy. or wǒ 'yí-ge-shyǎw-'shŕ yí-nèy 'hwéy-láy. ‖I'll be back in about an hour. wǒ 'gwò yí-ge-jūng-'téw 'hwéy-láy. or wǒ 'gwò yí-ge-shyǎw-'shŕ 'hwéy-láy. or wǒ 'gwò yì-dyǎn-'jūng 'hwéy-láy. ‖A day has twenty-four hours. yì-tyān yěw èr-shr-'sz̀-°dyǎn-jūng. or °ge-jūng-'téw. or °ge-shyǎw-'shŕ. ‖That city is about four hours from here by plane. 'nèy-ge-dì-fang lí-'jèr (or dàw 'nèy-ge-dì-fang chywù) dzwò fēy-'jī yàw °'sz̀-ge-jūng-'téw. or °'sz̀-ge-shyǎw-'shŕ. or °'sz̀-dyǎn-jūng. ‖The big clock struck the hour. dà-'jūng dǎ-'dyǎn-le. ‖Wait a quarter of an hour. děng yí-'kè-jūng. ‖Wait a half-hour. děng 'bàn-dyǎn-jung. or děng 'bàn-ge-jūng-'téw. ‖Wait an hour and a half. děng yí-ge-'bàn-jūng-'téw. ‖The train leaves every hour on the hour. hwǒ-'chē 'měy-dyǎn-'jūng yí-'tsz̀, dzày 'jèng-dyǎn 'kāy. ‖The train

leaves every hour on the half hour. hwǒ-'chē 'měy-dyǎn-jūng yí-'tsz̀, dzày 'bàn-dyǎn-shang 'kāy. ‖We waited for hours. wǒm děng-le °hǎw 'bàn-tyān. or 'hǎw dà 'bàn-tyān. or °'hǎw-jǐ-dyǎn-jūng. But ‖We are open twenty-four hours (all day, all night). wǒm 'jěng-tyān jěng-'yè kāy-je.

(*Time, more generally*) shŕ-hew. ‖Are you available at all hours? nǐ 'shéme-shŕ-hew dōu 'fāng-byàn-ma? ‖When do you take your lunch hour? 'shéme-shŕ-hew (shr̀ nǐ-)chr̄-wǔ-'fàn-de-shr-hew? or 'shéme-shŕ-hew chr̄ wǔ-'fàn?

(*Academic unit*) shywé-'fēn; (*hours per week*) dyǎn-'jūng. ‖How many hours of French are you taking? nǐ nyàn 'jǐ-ge-shywé-'fēn-de-'fà-wén? or nǐ-'fà-wén yí-ge-lǐ-'bày 'jǐ-dyǎn-jūng?

Working hours. ‖This is after (working) hours. 'shyàn-dzày yǐ-jīng 'bú-bàn-'gūng-le. or 'shyàn-dzày yǐ-jīng 'gwò-le shyà-'bān-de-shŕ-hew-le. ‖You'll have to see me during working hours. nǐ děy dzày wǒ bàn-'gūng-de-shŕ-hew láy 'jyàn-wǒ.

Late hours. ‖He keeps late hours. tā bàn-'gūng bàn-de hěn 'wǎn. or tā shyà-'bān shyà-de hěn 'wǎn.

‖He's the man of the hour. (*Favorite*) tā shr̀ yì-'shŕ-de-'húng-rén. (*Important*) tā shr̀ yì-'shŕ-de-'yàw-rén.

Hour-glass lèw.

HOUSE. (*Dwelling place*) 'fáng-dz, *occasionally* fáng. ‖I want to rent a house. wǒ děy 'dzū yì-swǒr-'fáng-dz. ‖They sold their house. tām bǎ-'fáng-dz 'mày-le. ‖This house has three courtyards. jèy-swǒr-'fáng-dz yěw 'sān-ge-'ywàn-dz. ‖This house has three courtyards arranged one behind another. jèy-swǒr-'fáng-dz yěw sān-'jìn. ‖All the houses are packed together in the city. chéng-'lǐ-de-'fáng dōu 'jǐ-dzày yí-'kwàr.

(*Household*) jyā. The imperial house 'hwáng-jyā or 'hwáng-shr̀; royal house 'wáng-fǔ; a noble house 'gwèy-dzú. ‖The whole house turned out to greet him. chywán-'jyā dōu chū-lay 'hwān-yíng tā. ‖Eighty generations of the house of Kǔng have lived in this city. 'kǔng-jyā dzày 'jèy-ge-chéng-li jù-le 'bā-shr-'dày-le. ‖This is from the collection of a noble (royal) house. jèy shr̀ tsúng yì-jyā-'wáng-fǔ-li 'chū-lay-de. ‖He is a descendant of a noble house. tā shr̀ 'gwèy-dzú-de-'hèw-yi. ‖I'm not used to keeping house for others. gěy 'byé-rén gwǎn jyā-'shr̀ wǒ yǐ-chyán méy 'dzwò-gwo. ‖We made a house-to-house search. wǒm āy-'jyā(r)-de 'sēw-le.

(*Business firm; store*) 'pù-dz. ‖His house sells clothing. tā-de-'pù-dz mày 'yī-fu.

(*Theater*) -'ywàn. ‖Let's go to the movie house around the corner. dzám chywù jí-'jyǎwr-nèr-de dyàn-yǐng-'ywàn-ba.

(*Audience*). ‖The whole house enjoyed the play. láy-'kàn-de-rén 'dōu jywé-je shì 'hǎw. or (*Formal, literary*) 'chywán-tǐ-'gwān-jùng dōu hěn 'shīn-shǎng nèy-chū-'shì. ‖We had a full house. mǎn-'dzwòr-le. or mày-le ge-'mǎn-dzwòr.

(*Legislative*) 'yì-ywàn. House of Representatives 'jùng-yì-ywàn; member of the House of Representatives 'jùng-yì-ywàn-yì-'ywán. ‖The law was just passed by the Upper House. 'jèy-tyáw-'fǎ-àn 'shàng-yì-ywàn 'gāng tūng-'gwò.

To house. ‖Where are the visitors to be housed? 'kè-rén jù-dzày 'nǎr? ‖We can house your car in the barn. wǒm 'kě-yǐ bǎ nǐ-de-chē gē-dzày 'tsāng-fáng-li.

Housing. ‖Can you provide housing for all of us? nǐ néng gěy-wǒm .chywán-dēw jǎw-jaw 'dì-fang 'jù-ma?

HOW. (*In what way*) dzěm, dzěme, 'dzěme-yàng. ‖How shall I do this? 'jèy-ge 'dzěm dzwò? ‖How did you do it? (*Of an affair*) nǐ 'dzěm bàn-'chéng-de? or (*Of an object*) 'jèy-ge 'dzěm dzwò-de? ‖How did he get here? tā dzěm 'láy-de? ‖**How does this sound to you?** 'jèm shwō nǐ 'tīng-tíng ('dzěm-yàng)? ‖How do you feel? nǐ jywé-de 'dzěm-yǎng? ‖How do you like your new house? *is expressed as* Are you satisfied with your new house? 'shīn-fáng-dz (nǐ) mǎn-'yì-ma? ‖How do you like her for a mother-in-law? yàw 'nèy-ge-rén dāng nǐ-de-'jàng-mǔ-'nyáng 'dzěm-yàng?

To know how hwèy. ‖Do you know how to swim? nǐ hwèy fù-'shwěy-ma?

To show *someone* how to jyāw. ‖Show me how to tie that knot. 'jyaw wǒ 'jì nèy-ge-'kèwr.

(*The way, like this*) jèm(e), nèm(e). ‖This is how he walks. tā 'jèm-je dzěw. ‖That's how the accident happened. jyèw-shr 'nèm chū-de-'shr. ‖That's how I would interpret your remark. nǐ 'nèy-jywù-'hwà 'wǒ jywé-de jyèw-shr 'nèm-ge-'yì-sz.

(*At what price*). ‖How do you sell this? jèy-ge (mày) 'dwō-shaw-chyán? ‖How do you sell this, by the pound or by the piece? jèy-ge 'dzěm mày, lwèn 'bàng háy-shr lwèn 'gèr?

(*At what extent*) dwō *for example* how wide? dwō-'kwān? ‖How much? 'dwō-shaw? ‖How many? 'dwō-shaw? (*If the expected answer is less than ten,* 'jǐ-ge?) ‖How long? (*Spatial length*) 'dwō-cháng? (*Length of time*) 'dwō-jyěw or 'dwō-shaw 'shŕ-hew? ‖How much did he pay? tā gěy-le 'dwō-shaw-chyán? ‖How long have you waited? nǐ 'děng-le 'dwō-shaw 'shŕ-hew-le? *But* ‖How often does he go to church? *is expressed as* Does he go to church often? tā 'cháng chywù dzwò-lǐ-'bày-ma? ‖How soon can you finish the book? jèy-běn-shū nǐ gǎn-'kwày kàn, děy 'shém-shŕ-hew kàn-'wán?

How is it that . . . (*why*) wèy-'shém. ‖How is it you didn't come? nǐ °wèy-'shém (or °'dzěme) méy-'láy?

How . . .! dzěm 'nèm . . .! ‖How kind of you! dzěm 'nèm 'kè-chi-ya! or nǐ-de-'shīn dzěm 'nèm 'hǎw-wa! ‖How smart he is! tā dzěm 'nèm 'jī-ling-nga!

Special expressions in English. ‖How do you do? nǐ 'hǎw? ‖How are you getting along? 'jìn-lay 'dzěm-yàng? or jìn-lay 'hǎw-wa? or yí-shyàng 'hǎw-wa? or dzěm-ge 'hǎw-far? ‖How about you? 'nǐ dzěm-yàng?

‖That's a fine how-do-you-do! dzěm-'hǎw-wa! or dzěm 'bàn-ne! or 'jěn-shr dzwò-'là! or 'jěn-shr 'méy-far 'bàn! or 'jěn jyàw-rén wéy-'nán! ‖How is that? *meaning* How can that be? 'dzěm-hwéy-shèr? or *meaning* I didn't catch it. nǐ shwō 'shém láy-je? ‖How come? 'dzěm-ne? ‖Was his face red! And how! *is expressed as* Right away his whole face got red. You can really call it red! tā 'lì-kē mǎn-lyǎn tùng-'húng. 'jěn jyàw ge-'húng-le! ‖He made a mess of the whole thing. And how! *is expressed as* He made a mess of it. You can really call it messy. tā gěy nùng-ge 'lwàn-chī-bā-'dzāw-de. kě 'jěn jyàw ge-'dzāw-le. ‖Wait till he gets this. He'll be mad all right; and how! *is expressed as* Wait till he sees this. He'll be mad; you wait and see! děng tā 'chyáw-jyàn 'jèy-ge-je. tā jyèw hwèy 'jí-le. 'chyáw-je-de-ba.

HOWEVER. (*In whatever way*) dzěm (or bù-gwǎn 'dzěm) . . . °yě-shr (°dzǔng-shr). ‖However you do it, do it well. bù-gwǎn nǐ 'dzěm dzwò, 'dzǔng-shr dzwò 'hǎw-le. ‖However you tell him, he won't listen. bù-gwǎn nǐ 'dzěm gàw-su tā, tā 'dzǔng-shr bù-'tīng-de.

(*To whatever degree*) bù-gwǎn °dwō-me (or °dzěm) . . . yě (or 'dzǔng-shr or 'háy-shr or, *more emphatic,* 'jyèw-shr). ‖However ungrateful he is, I still treat him the same way. bù-gwǎn tā 'dwō-me méy 'lyáng-shīn, wǒ háy-shr jàw 'yàngr 'hǎw dày tā. ‖However cold it gets, I still won't wear my fur coat. tyān 'dwō-me-lěng wǒ yě 'bù-chwān pí-dà-'yī. ‖However persuasive you are, I just won't go. 'bù-gwǎn nǐ shwō-de 'dwō-me hǎw-'tīng, wǒ °'jyèw-shr (or °yě or °'yě-shr or °'háy-shr, *but not* 'dzǔng-shr) bú-'chywù.

(*In spite of everything*). *In exclamations where* however *means* Oh! *or still, Chinese uses* hǎy! *or nothing.* ‖However, let's forget it. (hǎy!) 'swàn-le-ba.

Where a judicious statement is being made, there are a number of Chinese expressions. Thus, although this is said 'jǐn-gwǎn nèm 'shwō; but, still 'kě-shr-ne; although this is so 'swéy-rán rú-tsž; no matter what you say bù-gwǎn 'dzěm shwō, *meaning* after all 'shwō-láy shwō-'chywù, *etc.* ‖However, he's still better than anyone else. 'jǐn-gwǎn nèm 'shwō, tā háy-shr bǐ 'shéy dēw 'chyáng-nga.

HUMAN. (*Pertaining to man*) rén-de, rén. ‖The human skull is much larger than the monkey's. rén-de-'nǎw-gǔ bǐ héw-dz-de dà-de 'dwō. ‖The human mind is quite unfathomable. rén-'shīn nán-'tsè. ‖Will the human race become extinct? 'rén-lèy yě hwèy 'shyāw-myè-ma?

In many sentences there is no direct equivalent. ‖It's only human to make mistakes. *is expressed as* We're all people, no one can help making mistakes. 'dēw shr 'rén,' 'shwéy néng méy 'tswòr? ‖I'm only human. *is expressed with the literary quotation* A human being is not a plant that can go without feeling. 'rén-fēy-'tsǎw-'mù, 'shú-néng-wú-'chíng? or *the literary quotation* A human being who is not a sage, how can he avoid mistakes? 'rén-fēy-'shèng-shyán 'shú-néng-wú-'gwò? ‖It's not human to make people do such things. *is expressed as* Can one who does that sort of thing be called a human being? jyàw rén dzwò-'nèy-jǔng-shr̀-de háy-shr 'rén-ma?

Human (being) rén. ‖This food isn't fit for human beings. jèy 'bú-shr̀ 'rén-chr̄-de. ‖There were more animals than humans on the island. nèy-ge-'dǎw-shang 'yě-shèw bǐ 'rén dwō.

HUMOR. (*Amusing quality*). ‖I don't see any humor in the situation. *is expressed as* I don't think the situation is amusing at all. wǒ 'bìng bù jywé-de 'jèy-jǔng-'chíng-shing kě-'shyàw. ‖He's full of humor. *is expressed as* What he says makes people amused. tā shwō-'hwà hěn °dèw-'gén. *or* °dèw-'shyàwr. *or in literary language as* He's amusing, both in speech and action. tā hěn 'hwá-jì.

(*Ability to be amused*). ‖Keep your sense of humor. *is expressed as* It's just kidding, don't take it seriously. kāy 'wán-shyàw, byé rèn-'jēn. *or* (*Of a situation*) *as* One laugh and it's over. yí-'shyàw jyèw 'gwò-chywu-le. *or* (*Of a serious situation*) *as* Be sure you don't flare up. chyān-wàn byé fā-'pí-chi.

Some Chinese use 'yēw-mwò, *a term based on the English word.* ‖Humor carried too far becomes sarcasm. 'yēw-mwò gwò-'fèn-le jyèw byàn-'chéng-le fěng-'tsz̀-le.

To humor hǔng. ‖You'll have to humor him. nǐ děy 'hǔng-je tā.

HUNDRED. bǎy. One one-hundredth 'bǎy-fēn-jr-'yī; the hundredth dì-yì-'bǎy.

(*A great many*). ‖Hundreds of refugees left the stricken area. hěn-'dwō-nàn-'mín lí-kay-le 'jāy-chywu-le. ‖I've come across that word a hundred times. 'nèy-ge-dž wǒ 'jyàn-le °bù-'jř-daw 'dwō-shaw-tsz̀-le. *or* °'hǎw-shyē-'hwéy-le.

HUNGRY. è. ‖I'm hungry. wǒ 'è-le. ‖I'm a little hungry. wǒ yěw dyàr-'è. ‖Are you hungry AGAIN? nǐ dzěm 'yèw è-le? ‖The child seems hungry. shyǎw-'hár hǎw-shyàng 'è-le.

(*Craving*). ‖He's hungry for knowledge. *is expressed as* His anxiety to learn is very strong. tā chyéw-'shywé-de-shīn hěn 'chyáng. ‖She's hungry for love. *is expressed as* With her whole heart she wants someone to love her. tā 'mǎn-shīn shyǎng yàw rén ày. *or as* She's thinking of men. tā shyǎng 'nán-rén-le.

HUNT. (*To chase game*) dǎ; to hunt for dǎ-'lyè; to hunt lyè *in combinations.* A hunter (*sportsman*) dǎ-'lyè-de; (*professional*) 'lyè-hu. ‖Do you like to hunt? nǐ shǐ-hwān dǎ-'lyè-ma? ‖They are out hunting deer. tā 'chū-chywù dǎ 'lù chywù-le. ‖Good hunting! *is expressed as* Get more than usual. dwō 'dǎ jǐ-ge.

(*To harry*) jwēy; (*to chase*) gǎn; (*to look for*) sēw, jǎw. ‖They hunted the fugitive from city to city.

is expressed as They chased the fugitive from this city to that. tā bǎ 'dzéy 'jwēy-de pǎw-dàw 'jèy-ge-chéng pǎw-dàw 'nèy-ge-chéng. ‖How long has the hunt for the criminal been going ? *is expressed as* How long have they been hunting for the criminal? nèy-ge-'fàn-rén 'jǎw-le 'dwō-shaw shŕ-hew-le?

(*To search*) sēw, jǎw; (*to search for something by turning over things*) fān; (*if successful*) 'chá-chu, 'jǎw-chu. ‖What are you hunting for? nǐ jǎw 'shémne? ‖I hunted high and low and couldn't find it. wó 'nǎr dēw 'fān-le, jyèw-shr jǎw-bù-'jǎw. ‖Try to hunt up that telephone number. shyàng-'fár bǎ nèy-ge-'dyàn-hwà-hàw-'mǎr 'chá-chu-lay.

A hunt. *No Chinese equivalent.* ‖Are you going on the hunt? *is expressed as* Are you going to hunt? nǐ chywù .dǎ-'lyè-ma? ‖I made a thorough hunt for the missing bracelet; guess where I found it? nèy-ge-'dyēw-le-de-'jwó-dz wǒ 'nǎr dēw jǎw-'byàn-le; nǐ 'tsāy-tsay dzày-'nǎr jǎw-jaw-de?

To hunt down 'jǎw-jaw, 'jwā-ju, 'dēy-ju. ‖They hunted him down. tām bǎ tā 'jǎw-jaw-le.

To hunt up. (*To invent*) 'byàn-chu; (*to make up*) 'dzēw-chu; (*to manufacture*) 'dzàw-chu. ‖He could always hunt up an excuse. tā dzǔng néng 'byàn-chu yī-ge-'lǐ-yéw láy.

HURRY. To hurry 'kwày-je, 'gǎn-je, 'máng-je, gǎn-'máng, gǎn-'jǐn, gǎn-'kwày. ‖Hurry up! (*In general*) 'kwày-je! *or* 'kwày-dyar. *or* (*If the person is running or walking; already moving*) dzěw (*or* pǎw, yáw, kāy) 'kwày-dyar. *or* (*If the person is doing something without moving, like thinking, talking, packing, etc.*) 'kwày (-je)-dyar 'shwō (*or* 'shyǎng, 'shēw-shr, *etc.*) *or* 'gǎn-jǐn-bàn, 'gǎn-máng-bàn, gǎn-'kwày-bàn, *etc.* ‖Let's hurry or we'll be late. 'kwày(-je)-dyar-ba, bù-rán jyèw 'wǎn-le. ‖Hurry! Hurry! 'kwày-je! 'kwày-je! ‖Don't hurry. byé 'máng. *or expressed as* Slow down. 'màn-dyar. ‖They hurried all the way home. tām yí-lù 'gǎn-je hwéy-'jyā-le. *or* tām hwéy-'jyā-de-shŕ-hew yì-lù 'gǎn-gan-máng-'máng-de.

(*To make haste in doing something*) gǎn. ‖We're hurrying to have this done before five o'clock. wǒm 'gǎn-je yàw dzày 'wǔ-dyǎn yǐ-chyán dzwò 'hǎw-le. ‖Hurry and have this typed in half an hour. *is expressed as* Hurry and get this out in half an hour. dzày 'bàn-dyǎn-jūng-li bǎ jèy-ge 'gǎn-chu-lay. *or as* Hurry to type this out in half an hour. 'kwày-je bǎ jèy-ge dzày 'bàn-dyǎn-jūng-li 'dǎ-chu-lay.

(*To cause to move quickly*) tswēy, jyàw . . . 'kwày-dyǎr; (*to hurry someone too much*) gǎn-lu. ‖Hurry them out. *is expressed as* Tell them to hurry out. jyàw tām 'kwày-dyǎr 'chū-chywu. *or as* Urge them to hurry and go. 'tswēy-je tām jyàw tām 'kwày wán-le hǎw 'dzěw. *or* (*If the process is quite involved*) *as* Hurry up the process of getting them out. 'kwày-dyar bǎ tām 'dǎ-fā 'dzěw-le-ba. *or* (*If you're chasing them out*) kwày bǎ tām 'gǎn-chu-chywu. ‖Hurry him up a bit. 'tswēy-tswey tā. *or* jyàw tā 'kwày-dyar. ‖If you hurry him too much, he can't turn out a good job. nǐ yàw-shr 'gǎn-lu-de tày 'jīn-le, tā jyèw bù-néng dzwò-de 'hǎw. ‖Don't hurry the decision. *is expressed as* Don't hurry; discuss it slowly. byé 'máng, màn-'mān-de 'shāng-lyang. ‖Time is short. Can you hurry up the packing? *is expressed as* There isn't much time. Can you hurry to pack? méy-yew dwō-shaw 'shŕ-hew-le. néng-bu-néng 'kwày-dyar 'shēw-shr?

A hurry. *Expressed with a verb.* ‖What's the hurry? 'máng shéme? ‖I'm in a hurry. wǒ tǐng 'máng. ‖We were surprised that he was in such a hurry. *is expressed as* We were surprised that he was hurrying so. wǒm méy shyǎng-'dàw tā hwèy 'nèm 'máng-mang-daw-'dāw-de.

Hurried. ‖That's a hurried job. nèy-ge-'dzwò-de tày 'kwày-le (*or* 'gǎn-lū-le).

Hurry-up. ‖This is a hurry-up job. *is expressed as* This must be done quickly. jèy-ge děy 'kwày dzwò.

HURT. 1. *With the meaning* injure, wound, *Chinese either uses the word* shāng, *which has a general meaning but is of limited use, or distinguishes any number of means by which the hurt is inflicted and any number of degrees of injury.* shāng, *which also commonly means wound, is used independently to mean* hurt *in only a few constructions, but there are the combinations* shēw-'shāng get hurt *and* dǎ-'shāng hurt, inflict injury, wound, *which are used more commonly.* ‖How many were hurt? shāng-le 'jǐ-ge-ren? ‖I hurt a muscle. wǒ shāng-le 'jīn-le. *or* wǒ-de-'jīn 'shāng-le. *or* wǒ de-'jīn shēw-'shāng-le. ‖I hurt the bone. wǒ shāng-le 'gú-tew-le. (*etc.*) ‖Was anyone hurt? yěw-rén shēw-'shāng-le-ma? ‖I hurt him. wǒ bǎ-ta dǎ-'shāng-le. *or* wǒ jyàw-tā shēw-'shāng-le.

Any number of resultative compounds can be constructed which specify the means of inflicting injury and the extent of the injury. Any action which might result in injury can be used as the first element; any descriptive word appropriate to the extent of the injury can be used as the second element. The following is only a partial list, with cross-references. As first element use cut lá (*see* CUT *for other words*); hit dzá *or* pèng (*see* HIT); knock kē (*see* KNOCK); burn shāw; press, squeeze yà *or* jí; fall, drop shwāy; stretch, strain chēn; *etc. As second element use* be pained téng; be broken pwò *or* shé *or* lyè (*see* BREAK); lose skin dyàw-le 'pí; bleed lyéw-'shyě; be wounded, bruised shāng; be swollen jǔng; be black and blue, *or* black (*of eye*) chīng; be black and blue dž; be paralyzed má; fallen tǎng-shya-le; *etc.*

The first elements may also be used alone, without specifying the extent of injury. ‖I hurt my hand. (*By hitting it*) wǒ bǎ-'shēw 'dzá-le. *or* (*Bruised it or made it black and blue, by hitting it*) wǒ bǎ-'shēw °dzá-'chīng-le. *or* °dzá-'dž-le. *or* (*Hit it and broke the surface*) °dzá-'pwò-le. *or* (*Hit it and scraped off some*

skin). °'dzá dyàw-le 'pí-le. *or* (*Hit it and injured it in some or any way*) °dzá-'shāng-le. *or* (*Hit it so that it swelled*) °dzá-'jǔng-le. *or* (*Hit it so that it pains so much I can't move it*) °dzá-de 'téng-de bù-'néng dùng-le. *or* (*By cutting it*) wǒ lá-le 'shēw-le. *or* wǒ bǎ-'shēw °'lá-le. *or* (*Cut it so that it bled*) °'lá-de lyéw-'shyě-le. *or* (*Cut it into the flesh*) °lá-'pwò-le. *or* wǒ lá-'pwò-le 'shēw-le. *or* (*By burning it*) wǒ shāw-le 'shēw-le.

‖I hurt my head by bumping into the door, and raised a bump on it. wǒ-'téw pèng-dzày 'mén-shang, 'pèng-le ge-'gā-da. ‖The stone hurt my arm so that it is paralyzed. shŕ-tew bǎ wǒ-'gē-be yà-'má-ıe. ‖He hurt his back in a fall. tā shwāy-'hwày-le 'yāw-le. *or, meaning* sprained, tā shwāy-de 'nyěw-le 'yāw-le. ‖Where are you hurt? nǐ-'nǎr shēw-'shāng-le. *or* lá-le 'nǎr-le? *etc. But* ‖Where were you hurt? *meaning* Where were you when you got hurt? nǐ dzày-'nǎr shēw-de-'shāng? *or* nǐ-shēw-'shāng-de-shŕ-hew jàn-dzày-'nǎr?

2. (*Pain*) téng. ‖My arm hurts. wǒ-'gē-bey 'téng. ‖It hurt badly. téng-de 'lì-hay. *or* 'hěn téng. *or* 'jēn téng. *or* téng-de bù-néng shwō-'hwà-le. *or* téng-de jŕ 'hǎy-yěw. *or* téng-de yǎw-'yá. ‖Where does it hurt? 'nǎr téng?

3. (*Offend, distress*). ‖His feelings are hurt. jyaw-tā °shāng-'shīn-le. *or* °('shīn-li) nán-shèw-le. *or* °'shīn-li bù-hǎw 'gwò. *or* °'shīn-li 'byè-nyēw. *or* °shēng-'chì-le. ‖I hope your feelings aren't hurt. nǐ 'bú-hwèy jywé-je °shāng-'shīn-ba. *or* °nán-'shèw-ba. *or* °shēng-'chì-ba. *or* nǐ-shīn-li 'bú-hwèy °bù-hǎw 'gwò-ba. *or* °'byè-nyēw-ba. ‖This hurts me more than it does you. jè jyàw-'wǒ bǐ-'nǐ háy °nán-'shèw. *or* °bù-hǎw 'gwò. ‖Whenever I think of his ingratitude, it hurts. yì-'shyǎng-chǐ tā 'dwō-me méy-'lyáng-shīn-lay, jyèw jyàw-wǒ °nán-'shèw. *or* °shāng-'shīn. *or* °shīn-li bù-hǎw 'gwò. *etc.* ‖She has a hurt look. tā hǎw shyàng hěn °shāng-'shīn shŕ-de. *or* °nán-'shèw shŕ-de. *or* °'byè-nyěw' shŕ-de.

4. (*Have a bad effect on*). ‖This will hurt business. 'nèm-je hwèy jyàw 'mǎy-may shèw 'swěn-shŕ-de.

5. (*Matter*). ‖Will it hurt if I'm late? wǒ 'wǎn-dyǎr 'yàw-jīn-bú-yàw-jīn?

HUSBAND. (*As opposed to a bachelor, brother, etc.*) 'jàng-fu; (*informal, colloquial*) 'nán-rén. ‖A husband has his responsibilities. 'jàng-fu yěw 'jàng-fu-de-'dzé-rèn. *or* dzwò-'jàng-fu-de yěw 'jàng-fu-de-'dzé-ren. ‖Some husbands pamper their wives. 'yěw-de-'jàng-fu °'gwàn-je chī-dz. *or* °bǎ 'tày-tày gwàn-'hwày-le. ‖Don't pamper your husband. 'bú-yàw bǎ °'jàng-fu (*or* °'nán-rén) gwàn-'hwày-le.

(*Of a particular person; polite term*) 'shyān-sheng; (*common terms, rarely used to refer to the husband of the woman spoken to*) 'nán-rén, 'yé-men, jàng-'gwèy-de, dāng-'jyā-de; (*vulgar and insulting*) 'hàn-dz. *Or, when talking to or about a wife, refer to the husband by his title, such as* the shopkeeper jǎng-'gwèv-de.

When acquainted with the family, always refer to the husband by his given name or by his relation to the person addressed (your brother, your cousin, etc.). Do not ask a woman if her husband is living; get such information, when it is necessary, by some indirect method, such as asking her one of the two following questions. Thus ‖**What does your husband do?** 'shyān-sheng (*or* nǐ-de-'jàng-fu) dzwò shéme-'shr̀? *or* ‖**Where is your husband?** nín-'shyān-sheng dzày-'nǎr? *or* (*If you know the family*) lù-'dūng (*or whatever his name is*) dzày-'nǎr? ‖**Her husband is a good-for-nothing.** tā(-de)-'shyān-sheng bù-chéng-'tsáy. *or* (*Very insulting*) tā(-de)-'hàn-dz bù-chéng-'tsáy. ‖**Who's her husband?** tā-de-'shyān-sheng shr̀-'shéy? ‖**Does your husband like this color?** jèy-jǔng-'yán-

shǎr nín-'shyān-sheng 'shǐ-hwan-ma? ‖**He thinks that no man on earth is worthy to be her husband.** tā 'jywé-je 'shr̀-shang 'méy-rén 'pèy °dāng tā-de-'jàng-fu. *or* °'chywǔ-ta. ‖**What kind of a husband would you like to have?** nǐ 'shyǎng 'jyà ge-'shéme-yàng-de-rén? ‖**My husband is not home.** 'shyān-sheng bú-dzày-'jyā. *or* wǒm-dāng-'jyā-de 'chū-chywù-le.

Husband and wife fū-'fù, 'fū-chī; a husband and wife yí-dwèr-fū-'fù, lyǎng-fú-'fù, lyǎng-'kěw-dz, gū-mu-'lyǎ; husbands and wives 'lǎw-yé (gēn) 'tày-tay, 'shyān-sheng (gēn) 'tày-tay. ‖**Husband and wife should live harmoniously.** fū-'fù gwò 'r̀-dz yàw °'hé-mù. *or* °'hé-he-mù-'mù-de. ‖**Husbands and wives shouldn't sit together.** 'lǎw-yé (*or* 'shyān-sheng) gēn 'tày-tay yàw 'fēn-kay 'dzwò.

I.

(ME). wǒ. ‖**She phoned me but I wasn't home.** tā gěy-wǒ dǎ-dyàn-'hwà-lay-je, kě-shr wǒ méy dzày 'jyā. *But* ‖**Did you go? No, I didn't.** nǐ 'chywù-le-ma? 'méy-chywù. *or* 'méy,yew.

Mine wǒ-de. ‖**I gave him mine.** wǒ bǎ-wǒ-de gěy-le tā-le. ‖**Mine stinks.** wǒ-de dzāw-'tèw-le.

My (*belonging to me*) wǒ-de; *elsewhere*, wǒ, *or* wǒ A-de, *where A describes the relationship; in polite speech referring to one's own relatives, see Appendix I.* ‖**My pen leaks.** wǒ-de bǐ lèw mè-'shwěr. ‖**My bank pays a higher interest.** wǒ-tswén-chyán-de yín-'háng gěy-de-lì-chyán 'dwō-dyar. ‖**My feet hurt.** wǒ 'jyǎw-téng. ‖**So, imagine my annoyance!** nǐ 'shyǎng-shyang wǒ yěw 'dwō-me 'byè-nyew-ba!

MYSELF. *See* **SELF.**

ICE. bīng. ‖**Put some ice in the glasses.** dzày 'bēi-dz-li 'gē dyǎr-'bīng. ‖**Is the ice thick enough for skating?** bīng 'dùng-de néng 'lyēw-le-ma?

(*To cool with ice*) bīng; to put on ice 'bīng-shang, *or* gē-dzày 'bīng-shang, *or* (*to put in the icebox*) gē-dzày bīng-'shyāng-li. ‖**This orange juice ought to be iced.** jèy-ge-'jywú-dz-'shwěy 'yīng-gay 'bīng-yi-bīng. ‖**Put the meat on the ice right away.** 'gǎn-jǐn bǎ-'rèw 'bīng-shang.

(*To put frosting on*) bǎ yì-'tséng-táng-'pyér 'nùng-shang. ‖**Ice the cake as soon as it's cool.** dàn-'gāw yì 'lyáng děy bǎ nèy-tséng-táng-'pyér 'nùng-shang.

Icebox bīng-'shyāng; (*electric*) dyàn-bīng-'shyāng. **Ice cream** bīng-jì-'líng. **Ice water** bīng-'shwěy *or* bīng-'jèn-lyáng-kāy-'shwěy. **Iced** bīng, *or* (*cool*) lyáng. ‖**Let's order iced drinks.** dzám yàw dyǎr-'lyáng-dūng-shi 'hē-ba. **To break the ice** (*break up the stiff atmosphere*) bǎ jyāng-'jywú dǎ-'pwò-le. ‖**She broke the ice by telling a joke.** tā 'shwō-le ge-'shyàw-hwà jyěw bǎ nèy-ge-jyāng-'jywú gěy dǎ-'pwò-le. *or expressed as* She told

a joke and immediately everyone was less stiff and formal. tā 'shwō-le ge-'shyàw-hwà dà-'jyā jyèw 'bú-nàme-'jyāng-le.

IDEA. (*Thought, suggestion*) 'jú-yì; (*understanding*) 'jyàn-jyě; (*meaning, opinion*) 'yì-sz; (*viewpoint, opinion*) 'yì-jyàn; (*point of view*) 'kàn-fǎ. ‖**Do you have any ideas on the subject?** dwèy-ywú 'jèy-jyàn-shr̀ nǐ yěw shéme-'yì-jyàn-ma? *or* gwān-ywu jèy-jǔng-'wèn-tí nǐ yěw shéme-'jyàn-jyě? ‖**That's a good idea.** nèy-ge-'jú-yì bú-'tswò. ‖**My idea is to go by car.** wǒ-de-'yì-sz shr̀ dzwò-'chē chywù. ‖**What's the big idea?** nǐ-shr̀ shéme-'yì-sz? ‖**Was this party your idea?** jèy-dwèn-'fàn shr̀ nǐ-de-'jú-yì-ma? ‖**His idea is that the war will be over quickly.** jywù tā-de-'kàn-fǎ 'jàng hwèy hěn 'kwày-de jyèw dǎ-'wán-le. ‖**Don't you give him any ideas now!** *is expressed as* Don't you teach him wrong! nǐ jyèw byé 'jyāw-ta 'hwày-le! ‖**He hasn't an idea in his head.** *is expressed as* He doesn't understand anything. tā 'shéme yě bù-'dǔng. ‖**I had an idea this would happen.** *is expressed as* I knew before that it would be this way. wǒ 'dzǎw jyèw 'jr̄-dàw yàw 'jèy-yàngr. ‖**I haven't any idea where he is.** *is expressed as* I don't know at all where he is. tā dzày-'nǎr wǒ lyán-'yěngr yě bù-jr̄-'dàw. ‖**The idea is to get there early.** *is expressed as* The best thing is to get there early. 'dzwèy hǎw shr̀ 'dzǎw-'dàw-nèr dyǎr.

(*Plan*) 'bàn-fǎ, 'fá-dz, 'fāng-far; *or, colloquial,* jāwr. ‖**He has an idea for making money.** tā yěw yí-ge-'fāng-far jwàn-'chyán. ‖**Say, I have an idea!** hēy, wǒ 'shyǎng-chū yí-ge-'jāwr-lay!

‖**That's the idea!** 'jyèw shr̀ 'nèy-yàngr! *or* jyèw děy 'jème-je! *or* 'dwèy-le!

IDEAL. (*Aim*) 'jr̄-shyàng; shyǎng yàw 'dzwò(-dàw)-de. ‖**He has very high ideals.** tā 'jr̄-shyàng hěn 'gāw. ‖**His father has always been his ideal.** tā yì-'jr̄ °shyǎng yàw dzwò-dàw tā 'fù-chin nàm-yàngr-de ge-'rén. *or* °jywé-je tā 'fù-chin shr̀ shr̀-jyè-shang 'dzwèy-hǎw-de rén.

(Perfect). (Existing only in the imagination) 'lǐ-shyǎng-de; (model) mwó-'fàn; (best) dzwèy 'hǎw; (nothing better) 'dzày-hǎw 'méy-yew. ‖His ideal woman is too hard to find. tā-'lǐ-shyǎng-de-'nywǔ-rén 'tày nán 'jǎw-le. ‖He's an ideal student. tā shŕ ge-'mwó-fàn-'shēng. ‖He is the ideal man for the job. 'tā dzwò nèy-jyàn-'shèr °'dzày-hǎw 'méy-yew-le. or °dzwèy 'hǎw. ‖A situation like that would be ideal. 'nèm-je kě jyèw hǎw-'jí-le.

IDLE. Idle time (free time) kùngr; (leisure time) shyán-'kùngr.

To be idle (have free time; of a person) yěw-'kùngr; (not be busy) bù-'máng; (not be working) bú-gàn- (or bú-dzwò-)'shŕ. ‖Are you idle at the moment? nǐ shyàn-'dzày yěw-'kùngr-ma? or nǐ shyàn-'dzày bù-'máng-ba? ‖He never has an idle moment. tā 'yì-dyǎr-shyán-'kùngr yě 'méy-yew. ‖Come over sometime when you have an idle afternoon. něy-tyān-'shyà-wǔ yěw-'kùngr ꞊e-shŕ-hew 'gwò-lay 'wár-a. ‖I spent an idle morning. wǒ yì-'dzǎw-chen shém yě méy-'gàn. But ‖I hate idle (lazy) people. wǒ dzwèy 'hèn bú-gàn-°'lǎn-rén. or °'yěw-shěw-hàw-'shyán-de-rén.

To be idle (a factory). (Stop work) tíng-'gūng; (close up) gwān-le. ‖The factory stood idle for years. jèy-ge-gūꞏꞏr-'chǎng °tíng-'gūng 'tíng-le (or °'gwān-le) hǎw-jǐ-'nyán-le.

IF. 'yàw(-shr) (or 'rè-shr, or 'rwò-shr, or 'rú-gwo) . . . (de-hwà); often omitted; the if-clause coming first in a sentence; even if see EVEN. ‖If I had any suggestions, I'd give them to you. 'yàw-shr yěw shéme-'yì-jyàn de-hwà, wǒ yí-'dìng hwèy 'gàw-su ni. ‖Stop me if you've heard this before. nǐ yàw-shr 'tīng-gwo jèy-ge jyèw byé 'ràng-wo dzày wǎng-shyà 'shwō-le. ‖If anyone asks for me, say I'll be right back. yěw-'rén 'jǎw-wo, nǐ shwō wǒ jyèw 'hwéy-lay. ‖What if it rains? 'yàw-shr (or rè-shr) shyà-'ywǔ-ne?

(Whether). Expressed by alternatives. ‖See if there's any mail for me. 'kàn-kan yěw wǒ-de-'shìn méy-yew. or 'kàn-kan 'yěw-méy-yew wǒ-de-'shìn. ‖I don't know if he's left yet. wǒ bù-'jŕ-dàw tā 'dzěw-le 'méy-yew. ‖Ask her if she's coming with us. nǐ 'wèn-wen tā 'shŕ-bu-shŕ yàw 'gēn-wom chywù.

As if gēn . . . shŕ-de; (the appearance of it seems) . . . de-'yàng-dz 'sż-hu . . . shŕ-de, or . . . de-'yàng-dz hǎw-'shyàng . . . shŕ-de. ‖He walks as if he were crippled. tā dzěw-'dàwr gēn ge-'chywé-dz shŕ-de. ‖She talks as if she were a movie star. tā shwō-'hwà gēn ge-dyàn-'yǐng-míng-'shīng shŕ-de. ‖He talked as if he had been there. tā-'shwō-de-yàng-dz °'sż-hu (or °hǎw 'shyàng) tā 'dàw-gwo nàr shŕ-de. ‖As if you didn't know! (Sarcastically) hǎw 'shyàng nǐ bù-jŕ-'dàw shŕ-de!

If only. ‖If today were only pay day! is expressed as If today they gave out pay, it would be swell. 'yàw-shr jyēꞏ fā-'shīn °dwō 'hǎw-wa. or °'jyèw 'hǎw-le. ‖If

she'd only stop talking! is expressed as Would that she didn't talk so incessantly! tā byé nèm 'shywù-shywu-dāw-dāw-de-le! ‖If he had only come home earlier, nothing would have happened. tā yàw-shr dzǎw-dyǎr 'hwéy-lay de-hwà, yě jyèw méy-'shèr-le.

ILL. bìng; (uncomfortable, not well) bù-'shū-fu. ‖He has been seriously ill. tā 'bìng-de hěn 'lì-hay láy-je. ‖Are you feeling ill? nǐ 'jywé-de bù-'shū-fu-ma?

Ill at ease. (Shy, nervous) fā-'máw; (timid) 'jywū-nì; (unnatural) bú-'dż-rán; (restrained, held back) 'jywū-shù; (uncomfortable) bù-'shū-fu.

IMAGINE. (Think) shyǎng; (feel) 'jywé-de; (think something is true which isn't) 'yǐ-wéy. ‖I imagine the shops will be open. wǒ 'shyǎng 'pù-dz hwèy kāy-'mér. ‖I imagine so. wǒ 'shyǎng °'shŕ-ba. or °'shŕ-de. or °'dwèy-ba. ‖You're just imagining things. nà 'jŕ-shr nǐ nèm 'shyǎng ér-'yǐ. or nà 'jŕ-shr 'yǐ-wéy shŕ 'nèy-yàngr. ‖She imagined there was someone in the room. tā °'yǐ-wéy (or °'jywé-de) 'wūr-li yěw yí-ge-'rén. ‖He imagined himself the ruler of the world. tā 'dż-yǐ-wéy shŕ shŕ-'jyè-'bà-wáng.

Other expressions in English. ‖I can't imagine what you mean. is expressed as I can't think out what you mean. wǒ 'shyǎng-bu-chū nǐ-shŕ 'shéme-'yì-sz. ‖I can't imagine him doing that. is expressed as I certainly wouldn't expect him to do that. wǒ 'jēn-shŕ 'shyǎng-bu-dàw tā hwèy gàn 'nèy-ge. ‖Just imagine you're on a boat. is expressed as Close your eyes and think you're on a boat. nǐ bì-'yǎn yì 'shyǎng nǐ dzày 'chwán-shang shŕ-de. ‖Imagine living in a place like that! (of a desirable or undesirable place) is expressed as Think of living in a place like that! jù-dzày 'nèm-ge-dì-fangr, nǐ 'shyǎng-shyǎng kàn. or (of an undesirable place only) is expressed as How could anyone live in a place like that! dzěm 'néng 'jù-dzày 'nèm-ge-'dì-fang!

IMMEDIATE. (First) mù-'chyán-de. ‖This is our immediate problem. wǒm mù-'chyán-de-'wèn-tí shŕ 'jèy-ge. ‖Our immediate job is to fill up the swamp. wǒm mù-'chyán shꞏꞏān děy bǎ shwéy-'kēng 'tyán-shang.

(Earliest) dzwèy-'chū-de. The immediate future dzwèy-'jìn. ‖The immediate result was not what they expected. dzwèy-'chū-de-'jyē-gwǒ 'chū-hu tā-men-wù-'lyàw-jr-'wày. ‖We don't know what's going to happen in the immediate future. wǒm bù-jŕ-'dàw dzwèy-'jìn hwèy dzěm-'yàng.

(Urgent) jǐn-'jí-de. ‖The need is immediate. jèy-shŕ jǐn-'jí-de-shŕ.

(Closest). ‖There is a river ꞏꞏ the immediate neighborhoood. is expressed as There is a river right in the neighborhood. yěw yí-dàw-'hé 'jyèw dzày 'fù-jìn. ‖There's no school in the immediate vicinity. is expressed as There's no school in the neighborhood here. jèr-'fù-jìn méy shywé-'shyàw. ‖Our immediate neighbo-s live in a big house. *is expressed as* **Our next door neighbors have a big house.** wǒ-men-jyè-'byǎr-de-rén yěw yì-swǒr-'dà-fáng-dz.

(*Occurring at once*). ‖**We must take immediate action.** *is expressed as* **We must do it immediately.** wǒmen bì-'děy mǎ-'shàng jyèw 'dzwò. ‖**There was an immediate rise in prices.** *is expressed as* **Things immediately rose in price.** 'dūng-shi lì-'shŕ jyèw jǎng-'jyàr-le.

IMMEDIATELY. jyèw; lì-'kè, lì-'shŕ, mǎ-'shàng, 'gǎn-jǐn, kwày-'kwǎr-de, *all followed optionally by* jyèw. ‖**You'd better go home immediately.** nǐ 'háy-shr lì-'kè' jyèw hwéy-'jyā-ba. *or* nǐ 'háy-shr kwày-'kwǎr-de hwéy-'jyā-ba. ‖**We heard the news immediately after it happened.** jèy-jyàn-'shèr yì fā-'shēng, wǒ-men jyèw 'dé-jaw 'shyāw-shi-le.

IMPORTANT. 'yàw-jǐn, 'jùng-yàw; (*grave, serious*) 'yán-jùng; (*extremely significant*) 'lyǎw-bù-dé; (*of people; famous, esteemed*) yěw-'míng-de, *or* (*powerful, influential*) yěw-'shŕ-li-de. ‖**I want to see' you about an important matter.** wǒ yěw yí-jyàn-'yì-jyàn-jǐn-de-'shŕ-ching děy 'jyàn-ni. ‖**There were no important letters in the mail.** 'láy-de-'yěw-jyàn-lǐ-tew 'méy shéme-'yàw-jǐn-de-'shìn. ‖**He's never accomplished anything very important.** tā méy-'dzwò shéme-'lyǎw-bu-dé-de-'shŕ. ‖**Why is she going around looking important?** *meaning* Why does she think she's important? tā gàn-'má 'yǐ-wéy 'dz̀-jǐ tǐng 'lyǎw-bù-dé shŕ-de? ‖**He's the most important man in the municipal government.** tā-shŕ shŕ-'jèng-fǔ-li dzwèy-'yàw-jǐn-de-'rén. ‖**He was the most important man in town.** tā-shŕ jèy-'chéng-li °dzwèy-yěw-'míng-de-rén. *or* °dzwèy-yěw-'shŕ-li-de-rén.

IMPOSSIBLE. *Expressions using* It's impossible to . . . *in English are often expressed by* méy-'fǎr *meaning* There's no way to . . . *in Chinese.* ‖**It's impossible to describe the scene.** jyǎn-'jŕ méy-'fǎr 'myáw-shyě nèy-ge-'jǐng-jr̀. ‖**It's impossible to get there except by plane.** 'chú-le dzwò fēy-'jī yǐ-'wày méy-'fǎr néng 'dàw-nèr.

Be impossible for one to . . . *is expressed also by* bù-'néng *or* -bu-lyǎw, *or* jyǎn-'jŕ . . . bū. ‖**It's impossible for her to come.** tā 'láy-bu-lyǎw. *or* tā bù-'néng láy 'jyàn-ni. *or* tā méy-'fǎr láy 'jyàn-ni. ‖**I found the book impossible to understand.** nèy-běr-'shū wǒ jyǎn-'jŕ shŕ kàn-bu-'dǔng.

‖**Impossible!** 'bù-shíng *or* 'bù-chéng *or* bàn-bù-'dàw *or* dzwò-bù-'dàw. ‖**According to my point of view, it's impossible.** 'jywù wǒ 'kàn °'bù-shíng. *or* °'bù-chéng. *etc.* ‖**That's an impossible task.** 'jèy-shr̀ dzwò-bù-'dàw-de-'shŕ. ‖**Don't try to do the impossible.** bàn-bù-'dàw-de-'shŕ jyèw 'byé bàn.

(*Unendurable, obnoxious; of a person*) yàw-'mìng. ‖**She's impossible!** tā 'jēn shr̀ yàw-'mìng. ‖**She's an impossible snob.** tā jyāw-'àw-de yàw-'mìng.

IMPROVE. (*To get better*) 'hǎw-le. *Also many other expressions applying to particular cases, such as,* (*of a situation; take a turn for the better*) jyàn-'hǎw *or* (*progress*) yěw jìn-'bù; (*of a neighborhood; become more desirable*) shyàng-'yàngr; (*of someone's work; show progress*) jǎng-'jìn; (*of social behavior; change*) 'gǎy-le *or* (*be softened*) hé-'hwǎn-le. ‖**Do you think his health has improved?** nǐ 'jywé-de tā 'hǎw-yì-dyǎr-le-ma? ‖**The war situation has improved a lot.** jàn-'jywù °hǎw-de 'dwō-le. *or* °hěn jyàn-'hǎw. *or* °hěn yěw jìn-'bù. ‖**This neighborhood hasn't improved any.** jèy-yí-'dày-jù-de-rén 'háy-shr nèm 'bú-shyàng-'yàngr. ‖**This neighborhood has improved a lot.** jèy-yí-'dày-de-rén °shyàng-'yàngr 'dwō-le. *or* °hǎw 'dwō-le. ‖**Has his work improved?** tā dzwò-'shèr °jǎng-'jìn-le-ma? *or* °'hǎw-dyar-le-ma? ‖**His manners have improved a lot.** tā-de-'tày-du °'gǎy-le bù-'shǎw. *or* °hé-'hwǎn-de 'dwō-le. *or* °hǎw-de 'dwō-le.

(*To make better*) gǎy-'lyáng; (*of a house*) jyàn-'shīn. ‖**To what extent have they improved the soil?** tā-men bǎ jèy-kwày-'dì-de-tǔ-'rǎng gǎy-'lyáng-le 'méy-yew? ‖**They've really managed to improve their product.** tām jywū-'rán bǎ chū-'pǐn gǎy-'lyáng-le. ‖**They haven't made any attempt to improve the house.** tām méy-bǎ 'fáng-dz jyàn-'shīn.

(*To increase*) dzēng-'jìn *or* dzēng-'jyā. ‖**They're trying to improve the efficiency of the work.** tām 'jèng dzày shyǎng-'fár dzēng-'jìn 'gūng-dzwò-'shyàw-lywù.

To improve on *something* (*change*) gǎy; (*add the finishing touches*) shyēw-'gǎy. ‖**Can you improve on my dissertation?** nǐ 'néng bǎ wǒ-de-lwèn-'wén °'gǎy-yi-gǎy-ma? *or* °'shyēw-'gǎy yí-'shyà-dz-ma? ‖**The picture is so beautiful it can't possibly be improved upon.** *is expressed as* The picture is painted so well there are no points that can be improved on. nèy-jǎng-'hwàr 'hwà-de hǎw-de méy-shéme-kě-shyēw-'gǎy-de-'dì-fang-le.

IN. (*Physical location, participation in a group*) (dzày) . . . °-li *or* °-'lǐ-tew; . . . -li yěw. ‖**There's no heat in my room.** wǒ-'wū-dz-li méy-'hwǒ. ‖**The dress is in that pile of clothes.** nèy-jyàn-'yī-fu dzày nèy-dwèy-'yī-fu-li. ‖**Is he in the Army?** tā-shr dzày jywūn-'dwèy-li-ma? ‖**There are fifty members in the club.** jèy-ge-jywù-lwò-'bù-lǐ-tew yěw 'wǔ-shŕ-ge-hwèy-'ywán.

(*Using as a medium*) yùng. ‖**Write it in ink.** yùng mwò-'shwěr 'shyě. ‖**Say it in English.** yùng 'yīng-wén 'shwō.

(*At, concerning*). ‖**Are you good in arithmetic?** *is expressed as* Is your arithmetic good? nǐ-de-'swàn-shywé 'hǎw-bu-hǎw?

(*During a period of*) . . . de-shŕ-hew. ‖**He broke it in anger.** tā shēng-'chì de-shŕ-hew bǎ nèy-ge dǎ-'pwò-de.

(*Engaged in*) dzwò. ‖**He's in business for himself.** tā gěy 'dz̀-jǐ dzwò 'mǎy-may.

Be in *is often expressed as* to have entered jìn (*or* rù *or sometimes* shàng) . . .-le. ‖His boys are all in college. tā-de-'háy-dz-men dēw °jìn (*or* °rù *or* °shàng) 'dà-shywé-le.

(*Location in time*) . . .-li, . . . de-shŕ-hew, *sometimes omitted.* ‖It gets hot here in the daytime. jèr 'ŕ-li 'rè. *or* jèr 'báy-tyan-de-shŕ-hew 'rè.

(*Marking period of time before the end of which something is done*) dzày (*or* yùng) . . . -de-shŕ-hew, dzày . . . yǐ-'nèy, *or sometimes just the term for the period of time.* ‖I can finish this in a week. yí-ge-lǐ-'bày wǒ néng dzwò-'wán jèy-ge. *or* wǒ yùng yí-ge-lǐ-'bày-de-shŕ-hew néng dzwò-'wán jèy-ge.

(*Marking period of time before the end of which something is not done*) gwò . . .; *or often just the term for the period of time.* ‖You can begin this in one hour. gwò yí-ge-'jūng-téw, nǐ jyèw kě-yi 'dzwò jèy-ge-le. ‖I'll be back in a week. wǒ yí-ge-lǐ-'bày jyèw 'hwéy-lay.

(*Marking resultant state*) chéng *as postverb.* ‖Cut it in half. bǎ nèy-ge 'chyē-chéng lyǎng-'bàr.

Be in (*at home*) dzày-'jyā.

For other combinations, such as **come in, go in, put in,** *and so forth, see under the verb.*

INCH. tswèn (*see Appendix B*).

Every inch (*every bit*) ¹swǒ-yěw-de . . . dēw. ‖I used up every inch of cloth. 'swǒ-yěw-de-'bù dēw jyàw-wo yùng-'wán-le. ‖We covered every inch of ground looking for it. wǒm 'swǒ-yěw-de-'dì-fang dēw jǎw-'dàw-le.

‖The bullet missed him by inches. *is expressed as* The bullet almost hit him. nèy-ge-chyáng-'dzěr chà-'dyǎr jyèw 'dǎ-je ta. ‖He was beaten within an inch of his life. *is expressed as* He was almost beaten to death. tā chà-'dyǎr jyàw-rén 'dǎ-sž.

‖To inch along gǔng, nwó, tsèng. ‖The traffic is just inching along. *or* The traffic is just moving ahead by inches. chē-'mǎ yí-'bù-yí-'bù-de wàng-'chyán 'gǔng.

INCLINE. (*To lean*) shyé, pyān, wāy. ‖Doesn't that tower incline to the right? nèy-ge-'tǎ 'shŕ-bu-shŕ shyàng-'yèw 'shyé?

(*To tend to, be a little* . . .) yěw-'dyǎr; (*often* . . .) cháng; *or* (*like to* . . .) 'shǐ-hwān. ‖He's inclined to be late. tā cháng 'wǎn. ‖He's inclined to boast. tā 'shǐ-hwan shwō dà-'hwà. ‖She's inclined to stoutness. *meaning either* She's on the stout side. *or* She's apt to get fat if she's not careful. tā yěw-dyǎr 'pàng. ‖He's inclined to act queer. tā yěw-'dyǎr 'fēng-fēng-dyān-'dyǎn-de. ‖I'm inclined to believe you. wǒ 'yěw-dyǎr 'shìn-ni-le. *or expressed as* I think I can believe you. wǒ 'shyǎng wǒ 'hwèy shyǎng-'shìn ni.

(*A slope*) pwǒr. ‖How steep is the incline? nèy-ge-'pwǒr yěw dwō-'děw?

INCLUDE. (*Within a whole*) bāw-'kwò; (*have*) yěw; (*have in a container*) chéng *or* jwāng; (*count* . . *in*) 'swàn . . . °dzày 'lǐ-tew (*or* °dzày-'nèy *or* °dzày . . .-jr-'nèy); (*give* . . . *a share*) 'swàn . . . yí-'fèr. ‖All his friends were included in the party. tā 'swǒ-yěw-de-'péng-yew dēw dzày bèy-'chǐng-jr-'nèy. ‖We're going to include the most common words in this dictionary. wǒm jèy-běr-dz-'dyǎn-li bāw-'kwò 'swǒ-yěw-de-dzwèy-cháng-'jyàn-de-'dzèr. ‖His criticism included some very unkind remarks. tā-de-'pī-ping-lǐ-tew yěw hǎw-shyē-'hwà tǐng 'swěn nán-'tīng. ‖This chest includes all the tools you need. jèy-'shyá-dz-li °'chéng-je (*or* °'jwāng-je) 'swǒ-yěw-de-nǐ-yàw-'yùng-de-'jyā-hwo. ‖Be sure to include him at your dinner party. chǐng-'kè de-'shŕ-hew byé 'wàng-le bǎ-'tā 'swàn-dzày °'lǐ-tew. *or* °-'nèy. ‖He felt hurt because he wasn't included. tā tǐng nán-'gwò-de 'yīn-wèy méy tā-de-'fèr. ‖My name wasn't included on the list. wǒ-de-'míng-dz bú-dzày míng-'dār-jr-'nèy.

Including . . . lyán . . . dzày-'nèy. ‖This is the price, including tax. 'jyà-chyan lyán-'shwèy dzày-'nèy. ‖He sold everything he owned, including his car. tā bǎ 'swǒ-yěw-de-'dūng-shi dēw 'mày-le, lyán-'chē dzày-'nèy.

INCREASE. (*Become greater*) 'dà-le; (*become more*) 'dwō-le. ‖His power is increasing all the time. tā-de-'shŕ-lì ywè 'láy ywè 'dà. ‖His power has increased a lot. tā-de-'shŕ-li dà 'dwō-le. ‖The demand for refrigerators has increased a great deal. yàw dyàn-bīng-'shyāng-de dwō 'dwō-le. ‖The population has increased by fifty percent. 'rén-kěw 'dwō-le 'bǎy-fēn-jr-'wǔ-shŕ.

(*Of taxes*). (*Get heavier*) 'jyà-le *or* jyā-'jùng-le *or* (*get higher*) tí-'gāw-le.

(*Of prices*). (*Rise*) ¹jǎng-le *or* (*get higher*) tí-'gāw-le.

(*Make greater*). (*Add to*) dzēng-'jyā *or* (*improve, make even better*) dzēng-'jìn. ‖You must increase production. nǐ děy dzēng-'jyā chǎn-'lyàng. ‖The population has been increased by fifty percent. 'rén-kěw dzēng-'jyā-le bǎy-fēn-jr-'wǔ-shŕ.

(*Growth*) *expressed in terms of the forms given above.* ‖There was a sudden increase in prices. *is expressed as* Suddenly prices went up. 'hū-rán jyèw jǎng-'jyàr-le. ‖They're expecting an increase in the family. *is expressed as* Their family will soon add a baby. tām-'jyā kwày °'tyān (*or* °'dwō) yí-ge-shyǎw-'hár-le. ‖Do you expect an increase in salary? *is expressed as* Do you hope they will add to your salary? nǐ shyǎng tām yàw gěy-ni jyā-'shīn-ma?

INDEED. (*Really*) 'jēn. ‖Indeed! (*either for surprise or disbelief*) 'jēn-de! ‖She's very sick indeed. tā 'bìng-de 'jēn-shŕ hěn 'lì-hay. ‖There are, indeed, some people who disagree. 'jēn yěw shyē-'rén bú-'dzàn-chéng.

‖Indeed not! *meaning* Certainly not! 'dāng-rán 'bù!

INDEPENDENT. Become independent (*of nations or people*) dú-'lì. ‖I used to have an allowance, but now I'm financially independent. wǒ tsúng-'chyán 'lǐng-gwo jàn-yǎng-'fèy, shyàn-'dzày wǒ dž-'jǐ 'jīng-ji dú-'lì-le.

(*Of people only*). (*Not need to ask other people for things*) 'bú-yùng chyéw-'rén; (*not need to depend on people*) 'yùng-bu-jáw kàw-'rén; (*be able to stand on one's own feet*) néng dž-'lì-le; (*of personalities: have a strong personality*) 'gè-shing hěn 'chyáng. ‖Those farmers are completely independent. néy-shyē-jùng-'dì-de 'yì-dyǎr dēw 'bú-yùng chyéw-'rén. ‖You're getting pretty independent. nǐ shyàn-'dzày 'yùng-bu-jáw kàw-'rén-le. *or* shyàn-'dzày nǐ hěn néng dž-'lì-le. ‖He's an independent fellow; he never takes anyone's word for anything. tā jèy-ge-'rén 'gè-shing hěn 'chyáng, gàn 'shéme yě bù-tīng 'byé-rén-de-'hwà.

(*Separate*). ‖Her interests are independent of her husband's. *is expressed as* Her interests and her husband's aren't the same. tā-de-'shìng-chywu gēn tā-de-'jàng-fu-de bù-yí-'yàng. ‖This company is completely independent of that one. *is expressed as* This company has no connection at all with that one. jèy-ge-gūng-'sz gēn 'nèy-ge 'yì-dyǎr-'gwān-shi dēw 'méy-yew. ‖She has an independent income. *is expressed as* She has her own income. tā yěw tā-'dž-jǐ-de-shēw-'rù.

INDICATE. (*Point out*) 'jǐr-chū-láy. ‖The policeman indicated the way traffic was to go. shywūn-'jǐng 'jǐr-chū-lay chē-'mǎ 'yīng-dang wàng 'něy-byār 'dzěw.

(*Show*). (*Tend to show*) 'shyǎn-je; (*show definitely*) 'shyǎn-chū-lay; (*explain*) shwō-'míng; (*express*) 'byǎw-sh̀r; (*prove*) jèng-'míng. ‖This indicates that he has nothing to do with it. 'jèm kàn-lay méy tā-de-'shèr. ‖The results of the examination indicated that the class had really studied. jèy-ge-kǎw-'shr̀-de-'jyē-gwǒ 'shyǎn-chū-lay chywán-'bān-de-'rén dēw jēn-'jèng nyàn-'shū láy-je. ‖This pointer indicates the room temperature. jèy-ge-jyàn-'téwr 'wèy-de-shr̀ °shwō-'míng (*or* °'byǎw-shr̀ *or* °'jǐr-chū-lay) 'wū-dz-li-de-wēn-'dù yew 'dwō-'gāw. ‖A footnote is indicated by an asterisk. *is expressed as* An asterisk shows there is a note at the bottom. shǐng-'hàwr shr̀ 'byǎw-shr̀ 'hèw-tew yěw ge-'jùr.

(*State*) 'shwō. ‖Indicate briefly your experience in this kind of work. 'jyǎn-dān-de 'shwō-shwo nǐ-dwèy-'nèy-jǔng-'gūng-dzwò-de-'jīng-yàn.

Indicate (*with a mark*) jù-'míng; *or*-(*make a cross*) 'hwà ge-'chār. ‖Indicate which of these jobs you'd prefer. jù-'míng nǐ 'shǐ-hwān 'něy-jǔng-'shr̀-ching. ‖Indicate with a cross which school you went to. nǐ 'shàng-gwo-de shr̀ 'něy-ge-shywé-'shyàw dzày 'shàng-tew °'hwà ge-'chār. *or* °'dǎ ge-'chār.

(*Mean*). ‖What is that symbol supposed to indicate? *is expressed as* That symbol has what meaning? nèy-ge-'jì-hawr shr̀ shéme-'yì-sz? ‖His rash might indicate

measles. *is expressed as* His body has red spots on it, perhaps it's measles. tā-'shēn-shang-de-húng-'dyǎr. 'yě-shywǔ 'jyèw-shr̀ 'jěn-dz.

INDUSTRY. gūng-'yè. ‖Steel is one of the main industries here. gāng-'tyě shr̀ jèr-'jǔ-yàw-de-gūng-'yè-de-yì-'jǔng. ‖How fast has heavy industry developed here? jèr-de 'jùng-gūng-'yè fá-'jǎn-de yěw dwō-'kwày?

INFLUENCE. (*Effect*) 'yǐng-shyǎng. ‖His travels had a tremendous influence on him. tā 'yéw-li-de-'jīng-yàn dwèy-ywu ta yěw hěn-'dà-de-'yǐng-shyǎng. ‖You can see the influence of the French painters in his work. nǐ 'kě-yi 'kàn-chū-lay 'tā-hwà-de-'hwàr shr̀ 'shèw-le 'fà-gwo-hwà-'jyā-de-'yǐng-shyǎng. ‖Your friendship has always been a good influence on him. tā gēn-nǐ dzwò-'péng-yew °ywú tā hěn yěw 'hǎw-chù. *or* °dé-le bù-'shǎw-de 'yí-chù. ‖I don't think he's a very good influence on you. *meaning* I think you can't learn anything good with him. wǒ 'jywé-de gēn-'tā yí-kwàr 'shywé-bù-lyǎw 'hǎw-de.

(*Power*) 'shr̀-lì. ‖The church has a big influence in politics here. 'jèr-de-jyàw-'hwèy dzày jèng-'jyè-li hěn yěw 'shr̀-lì.

(*To persuade*) chywàn; (*draw into something*) lā; (*talk into*) 'shwèy-shwō. To be influenced (*listen to*) tīng *or* (*believe*) 'shìn. ‖I'm not trying to influence you. wǒ bìng 'bú-shr yàw láy 'shwèy-shwō ni. ‖She influenced him to stay. tā bǎ-ta 'chywàn-de 'dāy-shya-le. ‖Try not to be influenced by his flattery. byé °'tīng (*or* °'shìn) tā nèy-'tàw-hwā-yán-chyǎw-'ywǔ.

INFORM. (*Notify, orally or by a written message*) 'tūng-jr; (*tell*) 'gàw-su. ‖They informed him that his brother had died. tām °'gàw-su (*or* °'gàw-sung *or* 'tūng-jr) ta tā-'gē-ge 'gwò-chywù-le. ‖I was not informed in time. tā-men-'gàw-su-wo-de tày 'wǎn-le.

Be well informed (*know a lot*). 'dǔng-de (*or* 'jǐr-daw) hěn 'dwō. ‖He is quite well informed on the subject. 'gwān-ywu jèy-ge-'wèn-tí tā 'dǔng-de hěn 'dwō.

INFORMATION. (*News*) 'shyāw-shi; *also various other expressions, as illustrated in the following sentences.* ‖Can you give me some information? nǐ néng 'gàw-su wo dyǎr-'shyāw-shi-ma? *or expressed as* Can you advise me? nǐ néng 'jǐr-dyǎn-jǐr-dyan wǒ-ma? ‖I want some information about train schedules. wǒ shyǎng °'jǐr-daw (°'dǎ-tīng-dǎ-ting) hwǒ-'chē-de-jūng-'dyǎr. ‖We haven't had any information about him in a long time. wǒm hěn 'jyěw méy-'jyē-je tā-de-'shyāw-shi-le. *or expressed as* We haven't had any word from him in a long time. wǒm hěn 'jyěw méy-'jyē-je tā-de-'yīn-shìn-le. ‖The information he gave me was wrong. *is expressed as* He told me wrong. tā-'gàw-sung-wo-de 'tswò-le.

Information desk wèn-shywùn-'chù.

INK. mwò-'shwĕy *or* mwò-'shwĕr. ‖She uses green ink. tā yùng 'lywù-mwò-'shwĕr. ‖Please use ink. chǐng-ni yùng mwò-'shwĕr 'shyĕ. *or expressed more naturally as* Please write with a fountain pen. chǐng-ni yùng 'gāng-bǐ 'shyĕ. *or as* Please write with a Chinese brush. chǐng-ni yùng 'mwò-bǐ 'shyĕ.

To ink. ‖Don't ink the pad too heavily. *is expressed as* Don't pour too much ink on the stamp pad. 'byé dzày yìn-shǎy-'hé-dz-li dàw tày-'dwō-mwò-'shwĕr.

To ink in yùng mwò-'shwĕr 'tú-shang. ‖Ink in the letters on the sign. bǎ páy-dz-shang-de-'dzèr yùng mwò-'shwĕr 'tú-shang.

ꓥQUIRE. *(Ask about)* 'wèn *or* 'dǎ-tīng. ‖I want to inquire about rooms. wǒ yàw °'dǎ-ting-dǎ-ting (*or* °'wèn-wen) 'fáng-dz. ‖Several people stopped to inquire what was going on. yĕw 'hǎw-jǐ-ge-'rén 'jàn-jù-le 'wèn shr̀ 'dzĕm-hwéy-'shèr. ‖He inquired about you, and I said you were fine. tā 'dǎ-tīng ni láy-je, wǒ 'gàw-sung ta nǐ tǐng bú-'tswò.

Inquire into *(investigate)* 'dyàw-chá; *or (study)* 'yán-jyew. ‖A committee was appointed to inquire into the matter. 'yǐ-jing 'dzǔ-jr-le 'yí-ge-wĕy-ywán-'hwèy 'wèy-de-shr̀ 'dyàw-cha jèy-jyàn-'shr̀. ‖Let's inquire into the truth of the matter. dzám láy 'yán-jyew-yán-jyew dàw-'dǐ shr̀ 'dzĕme-yì-hwéy-'shr̀. *or* dzám dĕy bǎ jèy-jyàn-'shr̀ 'dyàw-cha-'chīng-chu-le.

INSECT. 'kwēn-chúng *(scientific name for insect class)*; 'chúng-dz *or* chúngr *(colloquial for insect, bug, or worm).* ‖Are there any poisonous insects here? jèr yĕw 'yĕw-dú-de-'kwēn-chúng-ma?

INSIDE. 'lǐ-tew, 'lǐ-myan, *or* 'lǐ-byan. ‖May I see the inside of the house? wǒ 'kĕ-yi 'kàn-kan fáng-dz-'lǐ-byar shr̀ shém-'yàngr-ma? ‖The inside of the overcoat is red. dà-'yī-lǐ-byar shr̀ 'húng-shǎr-de. ‖The fruit looked good, but the inside was rotten. jèy-ge-'gwǒ-dz 'kàn-je hĕn 'hǎw, kĕ-shr 'lǐ-tew 'làn-le. ‖She kept on the inside of the sidewalk. tā dzày byàn-'dàw-shang kàw 'lǐ-byar 'dzĕw. ‖Let's go inside. dzám dàw 'lǐ-tew chywù-ba. ‖Leave it inside. 'gē-dzày 'lǐ-tew 'hǎw-le. ‖Inside the house, everything was in confusion. dzày wū-dz-'lǐ-byǎr, shém dēw tǐng 'lwàn-de. ‖Give me an inside room. *is expressed as* Give me a room facing in. gĕy-wo yì-jyān-chùng-'lǐ-de-'wū-dz-ba.

An inside job. ‖The theft must have been an inside job. *is expressed as* This must have been done by (their) own people. jèy yí-'dìng shr̀ 'dz̀-jǐ-de-'rén 'gàn-de. *or as* This must have been done by the people inside. jèy yí-'dìng shr̀ 'lǐ-byàr-de-'rén 'gàn-de.

Inside of . . . dzày . . . yǐ-'nèy. ‖I think I can have it done inside of five minutes. wǒ 'shyǎng wǒ 'wǔ-fēn-jūng-yǐ-'nèy kĕ-yi bǎ 'nèy-ge dzwò-'wán-le.

Inside out fǎn; to turn inside out 'fān-gwo-lay. ‖Your sweater's on inside out. nǐ bǎ rúng-'yī-shang chwān-'fǎn-le. ‖Turn the coat inside out. bǎ 'yī-shang 'fān-gwo-lay.

INSIST. fēy 'shwō; *or' (say again)* 'háy-shr shwō. ‖I insist that I know nothing about it. wǒ 'háy-shr shwō wǒ wán-'chywán bù-jr̄-'dàw. ‖He insists that you're wrong. tā fēy 'shwō nǐ 'tswò-le.

Insist on. *Various expressions using* definitely yí-'dìng *or* persistently sž-chi-báy-'lyē-de, jyàn-'chr̄-je, *or* yì-'sĕr-de. ‖Why do you insist on going? nǐ 'wèy-shéme yí-'dìng yàw 'dzĕw? ‖He insists on knowing more about it. tā yì-'sĕr-de yàw 'dwō 'jr̄-daw dyǎr.

INSTANT. yì-'hwĕr. ‖Don't wait an instant. 'yì-hwĕr yĕ béng 'dĕng.

In an instant, this instant *(or other expressions meaning* immediately*)* lì-'kè, 'gǎn-jǐn, dāng-'shŕ, lì-'shŕ, mǎ-'shàng. ‖He was ready in an instant. tā lì-'kè jyĕw 'ywù-bey-'hǎw-le. ‖Come this instant. *is expressed as* Come right now. 'gǎn-jǐn 'láy. *or* shyàn-'dzày jyĕw 'láy. ‖Let me know the instant he arrives. *is expressed as* When he arrives, please tell me immediately. tā yí 'dàw de-'shŕ-hew, chǐng-ni lì-'kè 'gàw-su wo. ‖The play had instant success. *is expressed as* The play was immediately successful. jèy-chū-'shì lì-'shŕ jyĕw chū-'míng-le. ‖When the product was advertised, there was an instant demand for it. *is expressed as* Once the thing was advertised, people immediately wanted to buy it. jèy-ge-'dūng-shi-de-gwǎng-'gàw yì 'dēng-chū-láy rén lì-'kè jyĕw yàw 'mǎy.

INSTEAD. Instead of *someone* tì. ‖He went instead of his brother. tā tì tā-'gē-ge 'chywù-de. ‖I got bawled out instead of him. wǒ 'tì-ta āy-le dwèn-'mà.

Other English sentences with instead *are expressed as follows.* ‖I don't want that; give me this instead. *is expressed as* I want this, not that. wǒ yàw 'jèy-ge, 'bú-yàw 'nèy-ge. *or as* I don't want that; change it for this. wǒ 'bú-yàw 'nèy-ge-le, hwàn 'jèy-ge-ba. ‖They decided to walk instead of ride. *is expressed as* They decided to walk, not ride. tām jywé-'dìng 'dzĕw-je chywù, 'bú-dzwò-'chē. ‖Can I pay you later instead of now? *is expressed as* Is it all right to pay you later? wǒ yǐ-'hèw gĕy-ni 'kĕ-yi-ma? *or as* Is it all right not to pay you right now? wǒ jàn-'shŕ shyān 'bù-gĕy-ni 'kĕ-yi bù-'kĕ-yi? ‖Would you like this instead? *is expressed as* Will this do then? nème 'ièv-ge 'shíng-bu-shíng?

INSTRUMENT. *(Thing)* 'dūng-shi; *(tool)* 'jyā-hwo; *or (literary)* 'yùng-jywù, 'chì-jywù. ‖That doctor uses the latest surgical instruments. nà-wèy-'dày-fu yùng dzwèy-'shīn-shr̀-de-°'wày-kē-'yùng-jywù. *or* °'wày-kē-'chì-jywù. *or* °'wày-kē-shr̀-de-'jyā-hwo. *or* °'wày-kē-shr̀-de-'dūng-shi.

(Musical instrument) 'ywè-chi. To (know how to) play an instrument hwèy 'ywè-chi, *or* hwèy yīn-'ywè. ‖This store sells musical instruments. jèy-ge-'pù-dz mày 'ywè-chi. ‖Does anyone here play an instrument? jèr yĕw-'rén hwèy °'ywè-chi- (*or* °yīn-'ywè-) ma?

(*Means*). ‖Money was the instrument by which he achieved his purpose. tā bàn-chéng-le nèy-'shèr °shř yīn-wey tā kĕṇ hwā-'chyan. *or* °dēw-shr 'chyán-de-'gūng-law.

INTEND. ˬṇyăng; *also* (*plan, but never viciously*) 'dă-swàn. ‖What do you intend to do? nĭ 'dă-swàn dzĕme-'yàng? *or expressed as* What plans do you have? nĭ yĕw shéme-'jì-hwa? ‖I didn't intend to hit him. *is expressed as* I didn't deliberately intend to hit him. wŏ méy-chéng-'shīn shyăng 'dă-ta. ‖He had intended to do harm to her. tā 'shyăng 'bă-ta gĕy 'hàyle láy·je. ‖I intended you to have it. *is expressed as* I wanted to give you that froṃ the very first. wŏ 'bĕn-láy jyèw shyăng bă 'nèy-ge 'gĕy-ni.

‖Is this intended for me? *is expressed as* Is this mine? 'jèy-shř 'wŏ-de-ma?

ṆTEREST. (*Share*) fèr. ‖Do you have an interest in the business? jèy-ge-'măy-may-lĭ-tew nĭ yĕw-'fèr-ma?

(*Legal claim*) chywán-'yí. ‖He hired a lawyer to protect his interest in the property. tā 'chĭng-le lywù-'shř láy băw-'jàng tā-dzày-nèy-fèr-'chăn-yè-lĭ-de-chywán-'yí.

(*Money return*) 'lì(-chyán). ‖How much interest does it pay? gĕy 'dwō-shaw-'lì-chyán? ‖They pay 3% interest. tām gĕy 'sān-fēn-'lì.

(*Advantage*). ˬ(*Benefit*) 'hăw-chù; *or* (*advantage or disadvantage*) lì-'hày. ‖He's only thinking of his own interests. tā 'jř shř wèy tā-'dz̆-jĭ-de-'hăw-chù 'shyăng. ‖For your own interest, you ought to look into the matter. wèy nĭ-'gè-rén-lì-'hày-shè-'shyăng, nĭ 'yīng-dang 'chá-cḥa shř 'dzĕme-hwéy-'shèr.

Be of interest (*concern*) shyàng-'gān, yĕw 'gwān-shi. ‖It's of no interest to me whether we win or lose. shū-'yíng gēn-'wŏ °bù-shyàng-'gān. *or* °méy-'gwān-shi. *or expressed as* Win or lose, I don't care. shū-'yíng wŏ bú-'dzày-hu.

Interests (*group*) -jyè. ‖The business interests in the city want a new bridge. jèy-'chéng-li-de-shāng-'jyè 'chĭng-chyèw 'dzàw yí-dzwò-'shīn-'chyáw.

To interest, be of interest yĕw 'yì-sz. ‖That book didn't interest me at all. wŏ 'jywé-de nèy-bĕr-'shū 'yì-dyăr-'yì-sz yĕ 'méy-yew.

To be interested in, show interest in. (*Like*) 'shí-hwān; (*Be enthusiastic about*) dwèy . . . yĕw 'shìng-chywu. ‖Do you take an interest in sports? nĭ 'shí-hwan 'ywùn-dung-ma? *or* nĭ 'dwèy-ywu 'ywùn-dung yĕw 'shìng-chywu-ma? ‖I'm not interested in the problem. wŏ dwèy nèy-ge-'wèn-tí 'háw wú-'shìng-chywu. ‖Would you be interested in going to a movie? *is expressed as* Do you want to go to a movie? nĭ °yàw (*or* °shyăng) kàn dyàn-'yĭng chywù-ma? *or* °as What do you say to going to a movie? kàn dyàn-'yĕngr chywù nĭ shwō 'dzĕm-yàng? ‖Sorry, I'm not interested. wŏ 'bú-yàw 'chywù. *or* wŏ 'bù-shyăng 'chywù. ‖Would you be interested in buying a second-hand car? *is expressed as* What about buying a sec-

and-hand car? măy lyàng ˬjyèw-'chē dzĕm-'yàng? ‖Sorry, I'm not interested. *is expressed as* I have no such idea. 'méy-yew nèy-jŭng-'yì-sz.

‖He tried to inṭerest me in the property. *is expressed as* He wanted me to buy the property. tā shyăng yàw wŏ 'măy °jèy-swŏr-'fáng. *or* °jèy-kway-'dì.

INTO. jìn, *preceded by a verb of motion; thus* **walk into** 'dzĕw-jìn (láy *or* chywù); **run into** 'păw-jìn (láy *or* chywù); *etc.* ‖He went into the house. tā dzĕw-jìn 'wū-dz-li chywù-le.

For s̤ecial combinations like **get into trouble, break into pieces,** *etc., see under the other words involved.*

INTRODUCE. (*Introduce two people of about equal rank*) 'jyè-shaw; (*pr̤ṿent someone to a superior*) 'yĭn-jyàn. **To be introduced** *also expressed as* **to meet** jyàn. ‖Have you two been introduced (to each other)? yĕw-'rén 'gĕy nĭ-men 'jyè-shaw-le-ma? ‖Allow me to introduce you two. wŏ láy gĕy nĭ-men 'jyè-shaw yí-shyàr. ‖Can you introduce me? nĭ gĕy-wo 'yĭn-jyan-yĭn-jyan, shíng-ma? ‖I'd like to introduce you to my father. wŏ shyăng 'dày-ni chywù 'jyàn-jyan wŏ-'fù-chin.

(*Propose*) 'tí-chū-láy. ‖Who introduced that law? jèy-tyáw-fă-'lywù shř 'shéy 'tí-chu-lay-de? ‖The bill has been introduced in Congress. jèy-ge-fă-'àn yĭ-jìng dzày gwó-'hwèy-li 'tí-chu-lay-lè.

(*Start*) *expressed as* do something first (chǐ-'téwr) ‖She introduced the fashion of short hair for women. dzày 'nywŭ-rén-li tā chǐ-'téwr jyàn dwăn-'tĕw-fa.

(*Present*) ˬhū, gĕy; (*present orally*) 'shwō-chū-láy. ‖He introduced a new problem for our consideration. tā °'chū-le (*or* °'gĕy-le *or* °'shwō-chū-láy-le) yí-ge-'shīn-de-'wèn-tí jyàw wŏ-men 'shyăng.

INVENT. fā-'míng. ‖Who invented this contraption? jèy-ge-gwày-wán-'yèr shř-'shéy 'fā-míng-de?

(*Make up a story*) dzĕw, byàn. ‖Did you invent that story? nèy-ge-'gù-shr shř-'nĭ 'dzĕw-de-ma?

INVITATION. An invitation (*oral*) *is expressed indirectly, sometimes using the verb* to request chǐng; an invitation (*written*) chǐng-'tyē. ‖Thanks for your invitation *is expressed as* You're too kind, °I'll certainly go. nín tày 'kè-chi-le, °wŏ yí-'dìng dàw. *or* °I'm sorry I can't go. °dwèy-bu-'jù wŏ 'bù-néng 'dàw. ‖I didn't receive your invitation. wŏ méy-'jyē-je nĭ-de-chǐng-'tyē.

Be an invitation *is expressed with* to request chǐng. ‖The applause was an invitation for him to sing another song. dà-jyā dēw pāy-'shĕw 'chǐng-ta 'chàng yí-ge-'gēr.

Be an invitation to trouble. jàw 'má-fan.

INVITE. chǐng. ‖Who is invited for dinner tonight? jyèr-'wăn-shang chř-'fàn dēw yĕw-'shéy bèy 'chǐng-le? ‖The speaker invited questions. yăn-'jyăng-de-rén chǐng dà-'jyā fā 'wèn-tí.

(*Arouse*) 'yĭn-chǐ. ‖His painting invited a lot of criticism. tā-de-'hwàr 'yĭn-chi-le hěn-'dwō-de-'pī-ping.

Look inviting (*literally*, move people's hearts) ràng-'rén shyǎng .... ‖The water looks very inviting. jèy-ge-'shwěy 'chyáw-je hěn ràng-'rén shyǎng 'jìn-chywu 'fù.

IRON. (*The metal*) tyě. ‖This stove is made of iron. jèy-ge-'lú-dz shr̀ 'tyě-dzwò-de. ‖Go as far as the iron gate. yì-jŕ 'dzěw-dàw tye-'mér-nàr.

(*The instrument*) 'làw-tye. Electric iron dyàn-'làw-tye; charcoal iron 'ywùn-dew. ‖Have you got an iron I can borrow? nǐ yěw 'làw-tye méy-yew, 'jyè-wo 'yùng-yung?

To iron tàng, làw, ywùn. ‖Iron my dress carefully, please. chǐng-ni 'shyǎw-shīn yì-dyǎr 'tàng wǒ-de-'yī-fu.

(*Figuratively*). ‖There are still a few problems to be ironed out. is expressed as There are still a few problems to be solved. háy yěw 'jǐ-ge-'wèn-tí děy 'jyě-jywé yí-shyàr. or as There are still a few problems to be got rid of. há yěw 'jǐ-ge-'wèn-tí děy 'lyǎw-le.

ISLAND. dǎw. ‖They swam out to the island. tā-men 'fù-dàw 'dǎw-nèr chywù-le.

ISSUE. (*To publish*) chū. ‖When was the paper issued? jèy-ge-'bàw shr̀ 'shéme-shŕ-hew 'chū-de?

(*Send out, distribute*) fā. ‖A bulletin will be issued to each department in the University. dà-'shywé-li měy-yí-'shì dēw 'fā yí-ge-tūng-'jř. ‖A new series of government bonds is being issued. yì-chī-'shīn-de-'jèng-fǔ-gūng-'jày gāng 'fā-chū-lay. ‖Our raincoats haven't been issued to us yet. wǒm-de-ywǔ-'yī háy méy-'fā-gěy wǒ-men-ne. ‖These are G. I. shoes. jèy-shyē-'shyé shr̀ 'jèng-fǔ-'fā-de.

(*Publication; number, of a periodical*) chī; (*edition or printing, of a newspaper, book, etc.*) bǎn. ‖The story was in the November issue. nèy-ge-'gù-shr shr̀ dzày shŕ-'yī-ywè-nèy-'chī-li. ‖When does the next issue of the paper come out? jèy-ge-'bàw-de-'shyà-yì-'bǎn 'shéme-shŕ-hew 'chū?

(*Problem, dispute*) 'wèn-tí. ‖The issue is whether or not they'll be allowed to participate. 'wèn-tí shr̀ 'shywǔ-bu-shywǔ tam chū-'shí.

At issue. ‖What's the point at issue, then? is expressed as What are you quarreling about then? 'nàme, nǐm shr̀ 'wèy-shéme 'chǎw-ne? or as Then what are you arguing about? 'nàme, nǐm 'jēng-de shr̀ 'něy-yì-'dyǎn-ne?

Make an issue of ... (*raise a question about*) 'gwān-ywu ... 'jēng-jŕ. ‖He insists on making an issue of the problem. 'gwān-ywu nèy-ge-'wèn-tí tā 'fēy yàw 'jēng-jŕ yí-shyàr bù-'kě. ‖I don't want to make an issue of it. wǒ bú-'ywàn-yi 'jēng-jŕ 'nèy-yì-dyǎn.

Take issue with ... (*oppose*) fǎn-'dwèy. ‖Why do you always take issue with what I say? 'wèy-shéme wǒ 'shwō shéme nǐ fǎn-'dwèy shéme?

IT. (*As substitute for noun*). When the noun is in the sentence, it is not expressed. When the noun is not in the sentence, it is usually not expressed, but may be expressed by jèy-ge or nèy-ge plus the noun. ‖This suit is nice, but it costs too much. jèy-tàw-'yī-fu dàw bú-'tswò, kě-shr tày 'gwèy. ‖I don't like this book; it's too dull. wǒ bù-'shǐ-hwan jèy-běr-'shū, tày 'gān-dzàw. ‖I like it. wǒ 'shǐ-hwan. ‖Sell it. 'mày-le-ba. ‖How long was the movie? It lasted two hours. dyàn-'yěngr yěw dwō-'cháng? 'yǎn-le (or, less natural, dyàn-'yěngr 'yǎn-le or nèy-ge-dyàn-'yěngr 'yǎn-le) yěw 'lyǎ-jūng-'téw. ‖Did the car work all right? No, it broke down. chē 'dzěw-de 'hǎw-ma? bù-'shíng, °bàn-'dàwr (or °chē bàn-'dàwr or °nèy-ge-'chē bàn-'dàwr) 'hwày-le. ‖It went that way. wàng 'nèy-byar chywù-le. ‖It's an hour late. (*Of a train, etc.*) 'wǎn-le 'yí-ge-jūng-'téw. ‖How's it going? dzěme-'yàng?

Its (*of children*) tā-de. ‖The baby's lost its rattle. shyǎw-'hár bǎ ('tā-de-)hwā-'gǔr 'dyēw-le. In all other instances its is expressed as follows: if the noun for which its is a substitute is in the sentence, its is not expressed (unless the sentence is very long and there might be some ambiguity). If the noun is not in the sentence, its is either not expressed or is expressed by the noun plus -de or (rarely) by tā-de or 'dz̀-jǐ-de (its own.) ‖This city is famous for its parks. jèy-ge-'chéng yǐ gūng-'ywán chū-'míng. ‖The dog is chasing its tail. 'gěw dǎ-'jwàr 'wár 'yǐ-ba-ne. ‖The dog led us to its master. nèy-tyáw-'gěw bǎ wǒ-men lǐng-dàw tā-'jǔ-rén-nàr chywù-le. ‖I don't like its smell. (*Of a flower*) wǒ bù-'shǐ-hwan nèy-ge-'hwār-de-'wèr. or wǒ bù-'shǐ-hwan nèy-ge-'wèr.

(*As demonstrative*) it is expressed by jèy(-ge) or nèy(-ge) or is not expressed at all. ‖What is it? 'nèy (-ge) shr̀ 'shéme? or shr̀ 'shéme? or shéme? ‖Who is it? nèy(-ge) shr̀-'shéy? or shr̀-'shéy? or shéy? ‖I can't do it. nèy-ge wǒ 'bàn-bu-lyǎw. or wǒ 'bàn-bu-lyǎw.

(*With impersonal verb*) it is omitted. ‖It's five o'clock. shr̀ 'wǔ-dyǎn. or 'wǔ-dyǎn-le. ‖Is it raining? (shr̀) shyà-'ywǔ-ne-ma? ‖It's a beautiful day. shr̀ ge-'hǎw-tyār. or 'tyār jēn bú-'tswò. ‖It snowed last night. wór-'yè-li shyà-'shywě-le.

It is (or was) .... which (or that) 'nèy jyèw-shr, shr̀. ‖It was that house that I saw yesterday. 'nèy jyèw-shr wǒ-'dzwó-tyān-'chyáw-jyàn-de-nèy-swǒ-'fáng-dz. ‖It was a friend of mine who phoned. 'shr̀ wǒ-yí-ge-'péng-yew 'dǎ-láy-de dyàn-'hwà.

(*Anticipating the subject*). ‖It's hard to get a ticket. is expressed as Getting a ticket isn't easy. 'mǎy-jaw 'pyàw bù-'rúng-yi. ‖It's impossible to get there by tomorrow morning. is expressed as To get there by tomorrow morning is definitely impossible. yàw 'shyǎng myéngr-'dzǎw-chen jyèw 'dàw-nèr 'gēn-běn bù-kě-'néng. ‖Is it necessary for us to go? is expressed as Must we go? dzám 'fēy-děy 'chywù-ma?

J

JACK. (*Tool*) jywǔ-jùng-'jī, 'chyān-jin. ‖I need a jack to change my tire. wǒ hwàn chē-'dày děy 'yùng ge-jywǔ-jùng-'jī. *or* gěy wǒ yí-ge-jywǔ-jùng-'jī hǎw 'hwàn chē-'dày.

To jack up (*to raise with a jack*) bǎ . . . 'jř-chǐ-láy. ‖You'll have to jack up the car. nǐ děy bǎ-'chē 'jř-chǐ-láy.

To jack up prices wù-'jyà tí-'gāw; (*without any reason*) jyā-'jyà méy 'dàw-li. ‖At that time prices were jacked up. nèy-tsž 'yěw-de-wù-'jyà (jyàw-tām) wú-'gù tí-'gāw-le. *or* nèy-tsž 'yěw-de-'dūng-shi jyā-'jyà hěn méy 'dàw-li.

JANUARY. (*Modern calendar*) 'yī-ywè; (*old lunar calendar*) 'jēng-ywè.

JAR. (*Container*) gwàn, gwàr, 'gwàn-dz (*usually a small jar*); earthen jar wǎ-'gwàr (wǎ-'gwàn-dz); china *or* porcelain jar tsž-'gwàr (tsž-'gwàn-dz); glass jar bwō-li-'gwàr, bwō-li-'gwàn-dz, (bwō-li-)'pyéngr, (bwō-li-)'píng-dz; candy jar táng-'gwàr; sealed jar mēn-'gwàr; sealed jar shaped like a gourd mēn-'hú-lu-'gwàr. ‖I bought a jar of cherry preserves. wǒ mǎy-le °yí-'gwàr- (*or* °yì-'píng-)mì-'jyàn-de-'yīng-taw.

(*Large jar with small opening, for granular things like rice*) wèng; jar of rice yí-wèng-'mǐ. ‖There is rice in the jar. wèng-li yěw 'mǐ.

(*Large jar with small opening, for liquids, like vinegar, soybean sauce, wine, liquor, etc.*) tán-dz. ‖Those jars are for wine. nèy-shyē-'tán-dz shř chéng-'jyěw-de.

(*Large jar with large opening*) gāng. ‖Pour the water in that jar. bǎ-'shwěy dàw-dzày (shwěy-)'gāng-li.

(*Jolt*) jèn; (*earthquake*) dì-'jèn; *less violent in action* jēn (*to jar the nerves, etc.*). ‖One jar and it will explode. yí-'jèn jyèw 'jà. ‖That drill jars my hand. nèy-ge-'dzwàn 'jèn-dǎ wǒ-de-'shěw. ‖That drill jarred out of my hand. nèy-ge-'dzwàn 'jèn-de wǒ ná-bu-'jù-le. ‖That drill jars on my nerves. *is expressed as* That drill jars so that my nerves can't stand it. nèy-ge-'dzwàn 'jèn-de wǒ 'shīn-li shěw-bu-'lyǎw.

(*To jolt up and down*) dyàn (*at the end of a sentence* 'dyàn-da); (*to jolt sideways*) 'yáw-hwang. ‖When you hold the bottle, be sure you don't jar it. ná-je jèy-ge-'píng-dz de-shŕ-hew, 'chyān-wàn byé °'dyàn-da. *or* °yáw-hwang.

JEALOUS. Be jealous (*apprehensive of rivalry*) 'jì-dù. ‖He (*or* she) is jealous. tā ày 'jì-dù. ‖She is jealous of her husband's secretary. tā 'jì-dù tā-'jàng-fu-de-nywǔ-'shū-jì.

Be jealous (*envious*) 'jì-dù *or* extremely jealous hèn. ‖They are jealous of him. tām 'jì-dù (*or* 'hèn) ta. ‖His successes made them jealous. tā tày dé-'yì-le jyàw-'tām yěw dyǎr-°'jì-dù. *or* °'hèn.

Be jealous of (*be watchful of*) bú-fàng-'sūng (*literally* not loosen). ‖Journalists must be jealous of their right of free speech. *is expressed as* Journalists can't loosen a bit in regard to the right of free speech. 'shīn-wén-jyè-de-rén dwèy-ywu 'yán-lwèn-dž-'yéw yì-'dyǎr yě bù-néng fàng-'sūng.

JELLY. (*Congealed substance*) dùngr. ‖It becomes a sort of jelly if you leave it in the icebox overnight. dzày bīng-'shyāng-li gē yí-'yè jyěw chéng-le 'dùngr-le.

Jelly (*or* jam) táng-'jyàng *or* gwǒ-dz-'jyàng. ‖I want bread and jelly. wǒ yàw myàn-'bāw 'gēn táng-'jyàng.

Petroleum jelly fán-shr-lín-'yéw.

To jelly nìng, *or* chéng 'dùngr. ‖Wait until it has jellied, then put it away. děng 'nìng-le dzày 'shěw-chi-lay.

JEWEL. (*Precious stone*) bǎw-'shŕ. ‖My watch has seventeen jewels. wǒ-de-'byǎw yěw shŕ-'chī-kwày-bǎw-'shŕ.

(*Jewelry, ornaments in general*) 'shěw-shŕ (*woman's jewels*); 'gwèy-jùng-de-'shěw-shŕ (*expensive jewels*); (*in general*) 'jēn-jū-bǎw-'shŕ (*pearls and other stones*) *or* 'jū-bǎw-'ywù-chì (*pearls, other stones, and jade*): (*jewelry and other precious things*) jū-'ywù, 'jēn-bǎw, 'jū-bǎw. ‖She has many jewels in that box. tā nèy-ge-'shyá-dz-li yěw hěn-'dwō-'shěw-shr. ‖I have no jewels worth declaring. wǒ 'méy-yew shém-jŕ-de-'bàw-de-°'shěw-shr. *or* °'jēn-jū-bǎw-'shŕ yí-lèy-de-'dūng-shi. *or* °'jū-bǎw-'ywù-chì.

Jeweled shyāng-bǎw-'shŕ-de. ‖She has a beautiful pair of jeweled earrings. tā yěw yí-fù-shyāng-bǎw-'shŕ-de-ěr-'jwèy-dz, jēn hǎw-'kàn.

Jewelry store shěw-shr-'léw (*small one*); jīn-'dyàn (*large one*); gǔ-wán-'pù (*one selling antique jewelry*).

JOB. (*Piece of work*). (*Small; as repairing one car*) hwó; (*any size*) gūng; hwó *and* gūng *both involve manual labor*. ‖That job took longer than I thought. nèy-ge-°'hwó (*or* °'gūng) shyàng-bu-'dàw yùng 'nèm-dwō-shŕ-hew. ‖How many hands would this (*large-scale*) job require? jèy-ge-'gūng děy 'dwō-shaw-rén 'dzwò?

(*Permanent employment, or work that requires mental effort*) shŕ. ‖He's looking for a job. tā shyǎng jǎw-'shŕ. ‖How many men does this job require? jèy-jyàn-'shŕ yàw yùng 'dwō-shaw-rén?

586

To have as a job gwăn (*to be in charge of*) ‖My job is to wash the dishes. *is expressed as* **I'm in charge of washing the dishes.** wŏ 'gwăn shì-'wăn.

‖**Do a good job.** hăw-'hāwr-de 'dzwò. *or* dzwò-de hăw-'hāwr-de. *But usually a specific word is used:* (*if repairing*) hăw-'hāwr-de 'shyēw-li; (*if washing*) hăw-'hāwr-de 'shĭ; *etc.* ‖**They did a good job on my car.** wŏ-de-'chē ţăm °'shyēw-li-de hěn 'hăw. *or* °'shĭ-de hěn 'hăw. *etc.*

JOIN. (*To connect something*) jyē. To join hands lā-'shěw. ‖**Join these pipes together.** bă jèy-shyē-'gwăn dz °'jyē-shang *or* °jyē-chi-lay. ‖**Let's join hands.** 'láy, wŏ-men lā-je 'shěw.

(*To connect, come together*) hé. ‖**Where do the two roads join?** *is expressed as* **Where do the two roads meet and become one road?** 'lyăng-tyáw-lù dzày-'năr 'hé-chéng 'yì-tyáw?

To join a group 'jyā-rù. ‖**Do you want to join us?** nĭ yàw 'jyā-rù-ma? ‖**Everybody join in the chorus!** dàw 'hé-chàng-'nèy-yí-dwàr dà-'jyā 'dēw 'jyā-rù! ‖**After his vacation the actor joined his company.** *is expressed as* **After his vacation the actor returned to his former company.** yăn-'shì-de 'jyà-chī 'măn-le yèw 'hwéy-dàw tā ywán-láy-de-'bān-dz chywù-le. *or* (*If a new company*) yăn-'shì-de 'jyà-chī 'măn-le yĭ-'hèw, 'jyā-rù-le yí-ge-'shīn-bān-dz.

To join the army 'jyā-rù jywūn-'dwèy, dāng-'bīng, rù-'wŭ.

To join battle jyē-'jàn, kāy-'hwŏ. ‖**The battle was joined at 1325.** shŕ-'sān-dyăn èr-shŕ-'wŭ-fēn °jyē-'jàn-de. *or* °kāy-de wŏ.

JOKE. 'shyàw-hwar; to joke shwō 'shvàw-hwar. ‖**He's always telling jokes.** tā lăw shwō 'shyàw-hwar. *or* tā lăw shwō dèw 'shyàwr-de-hwà. ‖**This is no time for joking.** jè 'bú-shŕ shwō 'shyàw-hwar de-shŕ-hew-wa!

To play a joke nàw-je 'wár, kāy ge-'wán-shyàw. ‖**I was only playing a joke on you.** wŏ 'bú-gwo shŕ gēn-ni °nàw-je 'wár láy-je. *or* °kāy ge-'wán-shyàw. ‖**This is no joking matter.** jèy 'bú-shŕ °nàw-je 'wár-de. *or* °shwō-je 'wár-de. *or* °kāy 'wán-shyàw-de-shŕ.

To make a joke of *something* 'nùng-chéng ge-'shyàw-hwar. ‖**They made a joke of the whole thing.** tā-men jyăn-'jŕ bă jĕng-'gèr-de-'shŕ 'nùng-cheng-le ge-'shyàw-hwar-le.

JOURNEY. (*To travel*) lywŭ-'shíng. ‖**They journeyed all the way to the east coast.** tā-men yì-'jŕ lywŭ-'shíng-dàw 'dūng-àn.

(*Trip*) lù. ‖**It's a three-day journey.** shŕ 'sān-tyān-de-'lù. *or expressed as* **You must travel three days to get there.** děy dzěw 'sān-tyān tsáy 'dàw. ‖**Is it more than a day's journey?** 'yì-tyān 'dàw-de-'lyăw-ma? *or* 'yì-tyān néng 'dàw-ma? ‖**It is more than a day's journey.** 'yì-tyān 'dàw-bu-'lyăw. *or* děy dzěw 'yì-tyān-'dwō.

JOY. (*Pleasure*). ‖**I wish you joy in your marriage.** *is expressed as* **May your marriage be satisfactory.** jù ni-'hwēn-yīn °'měy-măn. *or as* **May your marriage be as you like it.** °rú-'yì.

(*Source of pleasure*). ‖**The baby is a joy to watch.** (*Gets more and more interesting*) jèy-ge-shyăw-'hár 'ywè kàn ywè °yěw 'yì-sz. *or* (*Gets more and more likeable*) °jyàw-rén 'shĭ-hwān. *or* °jyàw-rén 'ày.

JUDGE. (*In a law court: general, comprehensive term, indicating any law official, including prosecuting attorneys*) 'fă-gwān; (*any official who conducts trials and passes judgment*) 'twēy-shŕ; (*one of three or more judges, each of whom is a* 'twēy-shŕ, *presiding over a serious case*) 'shĕn-pàn-gwān; (*the chief judge of such a trial*) 'shĕn-pàn-jăng; (*chief justice of an established court-district, high or circuit, or supreme*) ywàn-'jăng; (*head of one of the divisions, civil or criminal, of one of the established courts*) tíng-'jăng. ‖**He is a judge.** tā shŕ ge-'fă-gwān. ‖**Where is the judge?** 'twēy-shŕ dzày-năr? *or* ywàn-'jăng dzày-năr? *or* tíng-'jăng dzày-năr? *etc.* ‖**He is a judge in the circuit court.** tā shŕ 'gāw-děng-fă-'ywàn-de-'twēy-shŕ. ‖**He is the (chief) district court judge.** tā shŕ 'dì-fang-fă-'ywàn-ywàn-'jăng. ‖**Is the head of the civil court going to serve as the chief judge in this case?** 'jèy-ge-àn-dz shŕ-bu-shr yéw ('mín-shr-fă-'tíng-)tíng-'jăng dzwò shĕn-pàn-'jăng? ‖**The three judges agreed to postpone the trial of this case.** 'sān-wèy-'twēy-shŕ (*or* 'sān-wèy-'shĕn-pàn-'gwān) yì-'jywé bĕn-'àn 'yán⌐chī dzày 'shĕn. ‖**The judge asked the prosecutor to repeat.** 'twēy-shŕ (*or* 'shĕn-pàn-gwān) chĭng 'jyăn-chá-gwān 'dzày shwō yí-byàn.

(*In a contest*) 'tsáy-pàn-ywán, 'píng-pàn-ywán, 'gūng-jèng-rén. ‖**The judges picked that bulldog as the winner in the show.** 'tsáy-pàn-ywán (*or* 'píng-pàn-ywán, *or* 'gūng-jèng-rén) 'pàn-dìng nèy-ge-'lăw-hŭ-gěw °dì-'yī. *or* °dé 'téw-jyăng.

To judge *or* to be a judge of (*be expert in*) kàn; judge by appearance shyàng; (*make a final judgment about*) 'pàn-dwàn; judge critically 'pī-píng; (*understand*) dŭng; (*be expert*) 'nèy-háng; (*be inexpert, be no judge*) 'wày-háng; *and a few special expressions in certain cases.* ‖**He is a good judge of men.** tā kàn-'rén kàn-de hěn 'jwěn. *or* tā néng 'kàn-chū rén-de-'pĭn-gé-lay. *or* tā yěw 'jŕ-rén-jr-'míng. *or* tā 'shàn-ywú 'fēng-jyàn. *or* tā hwèy shyàng-'myàn. ‖**Don't judge him by that alone.** byé 'gwāng àn-je nèy-'yí-jyàn-shŕ láy °'pàn-dwàn tā. *or* °'kàn-tā. ‖**Don't judge people too harshly.** 'pī-píng rén 'bù-yīng-gāy tày 'kè-le. ‖**Don't judge people only by appearance.** 'kàn-rén 'bù-néng 'gwāng kàn 'wày-byăw. *or* bú-yàw ɣĭ-'màw chywŭ-'rén. ‖**He is a good judge of horses.** *or* **He can judge horses.** tā kàn-'mă kàn-de hěn 'jwěn. *or* tā 'cháng-ywú shyàng-'mă. ‖**I'm no judge of art.** wŏ 'bú-pèy 'pī-píng 'měy-shù. *or* dwèy-ywú 'měy-shù wŏ shŕ 'wày-háng. ‖**He is a good judge of art.** tā hěn 'dŭng-de 'měy-shù. *or* tā 'dwèy-ywú 'měy-shù hěn 'nèv-háng. *or expressed as* **He specializes in art.** tā 'jwan-mén 'měy-shù.

To judge *or* **to be the judge of** (*to decide about*) 'jywé-dìng; 'kàn(-chu-lay); dìng; shwō; 'píng; dwàn; 'pàn-dwàn. ‖**You be the judge of that.** nèy-ge nǐ 'dž-jī láy (*or* chywù) 'jywé-dìng-ba. ‖**You'll have to judge it for yourself.** nǐ děy 'dž-jī chywù °'kàn. *or* °'jywé-dìng. ‖**Can you judge who is right** (*and who is wrong*)? nǐ néng 'shwō (*or* 'dìng, *or* 'jywé-dìng, *or* 'píng-yi-píng, *or* 'dwàn-yi-dwàn, *or* 'kàn-chu-lay, *or* 'pàn-dwàn) shéy 'dwèy shéy 'tswò-ma?

JUDGMENT. (*Not in court; in general*) 'kàn-de; (*particular case*) 'kàn-fǎ; *or expressed verbally by* kàn *or* chyáw. ‖**He always shows good judgment.** tā-kàn-de hěn 'jwěn. *or* (*Of events*) tā kàn-'shř kàn-de hěn 'jwěn. *or* (*Of persons*) tā kàn-'rén kàn-de hěn 'jwěn. ‖**The judgment he made was not very sound.** tā-de-'kàn-fa bú-dà 'gāw-míng. ‖**In my judgment, you're doing the wrong thing.** jywù 'wǒ kàn (*or* jywù 'wǒ chyáw, *or* yī 'wǒ kàn, *or* yī 'wǒ chyáw, *or* jàw wǒ-de-'kàn-fǎ), nǐ jè-ge-shř °'dzwò-de bú-'dwèy. *or* °dzwò-'tswò-le.

(*In court*). ‖**How large was the judgment against you?** 'fǎ-tíng jyàw-nǐ péy 'dwō-shǎw-chyán?

To pass judgment. shyà 'dwàn-ywǔ. ‖**Don't pass judgment too quickly.** shyà 'dwàn-ywǔ °'bú-yàw tày kwày-le. *or* °'yàw 'jēn-jwò-jēn-jwò.

JUICE. 'jř-dz, -jř; -jyāng; (*liquid, secretion*) -yè. ‖**He is preparing some orange juice for us.** tā 'jèng dzày-nàr gěy-dzám 'dzwò (*make*; *or* 'jǐ *squeeze*; *or* 'yà *press*) jywú-dz-'jř-ne. ‖**Just squeeze it with your fingers and the juice will come out.** yì-'nyē, 'jř-dz jyèw chū-lay-le. ‖**They take the juice from sugar cane and sell it to sugar manufacturers.** tām tsúng 'gān-jē 'dǎw-chū táng-'jyāng-lay mày-gěy dzwò-'táng-de. ‖**Gastric juice contains acid.** wèy-'yè-li yěw 'swān.

JULY. 'chī-ywè. ‖**July Fourth is the national birthday of the United States.** 'chī-ywè 'sž-hàw shř 'měy-gwo-de-gwó-chìng-'r̀. ‖**"chī-chī" is the shortened form of July Seventh in Chinese, on which day in 1937 the Sino-Japanese War began.** 'chī-chī jyèw-shr 'chī-ywè-'chī-hàw-de-'jyǎn-chēng; dzày 'yī-jyěw-sān-'chī-nyán-de-'nèy-tyān 'jūng-r̀-'jàn-shř kāy-'shř-de.

JUMP.

Chinese distinguishes three types of jumping.

tyàw *and* (*Peiping*) bèng *refer to jumping or leaping in general, including jumping up and down and jumping involuntarily as when frightened.*

tswàn *and* tswān (*two pronunciations of the same word;* tswān *is more common colloquially*) *refer to jumping for a particular purpose, or jumping to reach an object or get to a place.*

pū *refers to jumping more or less horizontally in order to grasp something, often* **to jump at.**

‖**He jumped onto the table.** tā 'tyàw-dàw 'jwōr-shang-chywu-le. ‖**He reached the door in one jump.** tā yì-'tswān (*or* tā yí-'tyàw, *or* tā yì-'pū) jyèw °'tswān-dàw (*or* °'tyàw-dàw, *or* °'pū-dàw) 'mén-nar-le. ‖**The tiger jumped at the deer.** 'láw-hu chùng-je 'lù 'pū-gwo-chywu. ‖**The tiger reached the deer with one jump.** 'láw-hu yì-'pū 'pū-dàw 'lù-nar. ‖**Jump down.** 'tyàw-shya-lay. *or* 'tyàw-shya-chywu (*depending on where the speaker is*). ‖**The child jumped up and down with joy.** shyǎw-hár 'lè-de jř °'tyàw. *or* °'bèng. ‖**The man jumped up and down with rage.** nèy-ge-rén 'chì-de lwàn. °'tyàw. *or* °'bèng. ‖**Jump!** (*for safety*) 'tyàw! (*Not* bèng, tswān, *or* pū.) ‖**See how high you can jump.** 'kàn (*or* 'chyáw) nǐ néng °'tyàw (*or* °'bèng, *or* °'tswān) 'dwō gāw. ‖**Jump over it.** 'tyàw-gwo-chywu. *or* 'bèng-gwo-chywu. *or* 'tswān-gwo-chywu. (*or* -lay *instead of* -chywu). ‖**Jump your horse over the fence.** jyǎw nǐ-de-'mǎ tyàw-gwo nèy-ge-'lán-gān-chywu. ‖**He can jump up, and reach the ceiling.** tā yí-'tyàw (*or* tā yì-'tswān) kě-yǐ gèw-jaw fáng-'dǐng-dz. ‖**He jumped out the window.** tā tsúng 'chwāng-hu 'tyàw-chu-chywu-le. ‖**The girl is so short that she has to jump up to hang up her coat.** shyǎw-'gū-nyang tswó-de děy 'tswān-chi-lay tsáy néng bǎ 'yī-fu 'gwà-shang. ‖**You made me jump.** nǐ bǎ-wǒ 'shyà-le yí-'tyàw. *or* nǐ 'shyà-le wǒ yí-'tyàw. *But* ‖**Suddenly he jumped up from his chair.** tā 'hú-rán tsúng 'yǐ-dz-shang 'jàn-chi-lay-le.

High jump tyàw-'gāw(r); **broad jump** tyàw-'ywǎn, *or* tyàw-'ywǎr; **hop, skip, and jump** 'sān-jí-'tyàw (-ywǎn).

(*Distance*). ‖**It's quite a jump from one side of the brook to the other.** tsúng hé-'jè-byar dàw hé-'nà-byar bú-'jìn. ‖**It's quite a jump from the main topic.** shwō-de lí 'běn-tí tày 'ywǎn-le.

(*Sudden rise*). ‖**There's been quite a jump in the temperature.** 'tyān-chì 'hú-rán 'rè-le. *or* 'wēn-dù 'hú-rán 'gāw-le. *or* 'wēn-dù 'hú-rán 'jǎng-le.

‖**He jumped at the offer.** tā lì-'kè jyèw 'dá-yīng-le. *or* tā 'chyǎng-je jyèw 'dá-yīng-le.

JUNE. 'lyèw-ywè.

JUST. 1. (*Fair, honest, reasonable, etc.*)

(*Of a person*) 'gūng-píng, 'gūng-jèng, 'jèng-jř. ‖**Even his enemies admit he's a just man.** lyán tā-de-'chéw-rén dēw chéng-rèn tā-jèy-ge-rén hěn °'gūng-píng. *or* °'gūng-jèng. *or* °'jèng-jř.

(*Of decisions, judgments, or opinions*) 'gūng-píng, 'gūng-dàw, dwèy. ‖**His decisions are always just.** tā-'pàn-de (*or* tā-'dwàn-de, *or* tā-'dìng-de)-shř-chíng dēw hěn °'gūng-píng. *or* °'gūng-dàw. *or* °'dwèy.

(*Of punishments*) gāy (nèm 'fá), (nèm 'fá hěn) 'dwèy, (nèm 'dà hěn) 'dwèy, *and other expressions meaning* **that punishment is right, that punishment** is deserved, *etc.* ‖His punishment was just. nèm 'fá-tā hěn 'dwèy. *or* tā 'gāy nèm 'fá. *or* tā ('yīng-)gāy shèw 'jèm-yàng-de-°'chěng-fá. *or* °'shíng-fá. ('chěng-fá *is any sort of punishment;* 'shíng-fá *is legal punishment.*)

To be just (*of claims, rights, reasons, etc.*) (hěn) yěw-'lǐ, 'bú-shr méy-'lǐ. ‖We felt that he had a just claim to this piece of land. wǒm 'jywé-je tā yàw jèy-kwày-'dì (yàw-de) °hěn yěw-'lǐ. *or* °'bú-shr méy-'lǐ.

(*Of a report; fair*) 'jwěn-chywè. ‖He gave a just account of what happened at the meeting. tā bǎ nèy-tsz̀-kāy-'hwèy-de-'chíng-shíng 'bàw-gàw-de hěn 'jwěn-chywè.

2. (*Exactly, except in expressions of time*)

(*In questions*) dàw-'dǐ, 'jyēw-jìng. ‖Just what do you mean? nǐ dàw-'dǐ (*or* nǐ 'jyēw-jìng) shr̀ 'shéme-yì-sz? ‖Just how much do you want? nǐ dàw-'dǐ (*or* nǐ 'jyēw-jìng) (shr̀) yàw 'dwō-shǎw? ‖Just who do you think you are? nǐ 'jywé-je nǐ 'jyēw-jìng shr̀ lǎw-'jǐ-ya?

(*In simple statements*) *usually* jèng, *occasionally* jyēw *or other expressions.* ‖That's just what I want. nèy-ge 'jèng shr̀ wǒ-'yàw-de. ‖That's just the one I had in mind. nèy 'jèng-shr wǒ-'shīn-li-'shyǎng-de-nèy-ge. ‖Just so! 'jèng dwèy! ‖Just right! 'jèng dwèy! *or* 'jèng shr̀! ‖He must have everything just right. tā yí-'dìng yàw 'shéme-shr dēw shr̀ °'jèng 'hǎw. *or* °'jèng dwèy tā-de-'shēn-sz. ‖You must do it just right or you'll spoil everything. nǐ děy 'dzwò-de °'jèng 'dwèy (*or* °'yì-dyǎr yě 'bú-'chà) bù-rán jyēw 'chywán 'hwěy-le. ‖That's just the trouble. 'nán-chù 'jèng dzày jèy-ge-'dì-fang. *or* jèy 'jèng shr̀ jyàw-rén-wéy-'nán-de-dì-fang. ‖That's just the way it should have been done (*but wasn't*). yàw-shr 'nèm-je, jyēw 'dwèy-le. ‖Everything he does is just right. tā-'shéme-dēw-dzwò-de °'jèng 'dwèy. *or* °'chyà-dàw 'hǎw-chù. ‖Just that much will be enough. 'jyēw nèm-'shyē jyēw 'gèw-le. ‖It fits just beautifully. 'jèng hé-'shr̀. *or* 'chyà-chya hé-'shr̀. *or* 'gāng-hǎw hé-'shr̀.

Just as, just like (*in expressed or implied comparisons*) jēn, jyǎn-'jí. (*Either may be followed by* shyàng *resembling, like;* jyǎn-'jí *is often followed by* gēn . . . yí-'yàng *or* 'jyēw-shr . . . yí-'yàng *the same as.* . . .) ‖It turned out just as I told you. 'jēn jyēw shyàng wǒ-'gàw-su-nǐ-de-nèy-'yàngr. ‖It was just like a dream. 'jēn (*or* jyǎn-'jí) shyàng dzwò(-le yí-ge) 'mèng shr̀-de. ‖It's just like spring. 'jēn (*or* jyǎn-'jí) shyàng 'chwēn-tyān (shr̀-de). *or* jyǎn-'jí jyēw-shr 'chwēn-tyān yí-'yàng. *or* jyǎn-'jí gēn 'chwēn-tyān yí-'yàng. ‖He walks just like his father. tā 'dzěw-lù 'jēn (*or* jyǎn-'jí) shyàng tā-'dyē shr̀-de. *or* tā 'dzěw-lù jyǎn-'jí °gēn (*or* °'jyēw-shr) tā-'dyē yí-'yàng. *But* ‖I'm just as tall as you are. wǒ gēn-'nǐ yì-'bān-'gāw. *or* wǒ 'bìng bù-'bǔ nǐ-'ǎy. ‖Do just as much as you can. 'néng dzwò 'dwō-shǎw, jyēw dzwò 'dwō-shǎw.

3. (*By a small margin; except in expressions of time where* just as, just when, *etc., are used*) gāng, tsáy.

Just a while ago 'gāng-tsáy. ‖He won't know; he just came in. 'tā bú-hwèy 'jr̄-dàw; tā 'gāng (*or* 'tsáy). 'jìn-lay. ‖They had just arrived here. tām 'gāng (*or* 'tsáy) dàw-de. ‖Did you just come? (*Friendly question*) 'gāng láy-ya? *or* 'tsáy láy-ya? *or* (*Simple question, emphasizing* just) nǐ 'shr̀-bu-shr 'gāng láy? *or* nǐ 'shr̀-bu-shr 'tsáy láy? *or* (*With surprise, sarcasm, or impatience*) nǐ 'tsáy 'láy-ya? ‖He was here just a while ago. tā 'gāng(-tsáy) háy 'dzày-jèr-ne. *or* tā 'gāng(-tsáy) 'dzày-jèr-lay-je. ‖You just said so yourself. nǐ 'dz̀-jǐ 'gāng nèm 'shwō-lay-je. ‖He just made the train. hwǒ-'chē tā 'gāng-gang 'gǎn-shang. ‖He just missed the train. hwǒ-'chē, tā 'gāng-gang 'méy-néng 'gǎn-shang. *or* hwǒ-'chē, tā 'jī-ji-hu 'gǎn shang. *or* hwǒ-'chē, tā chà-'dyǎr jyēw 'gǎn-shang-le (*almost made it*). ‖The bullet just missed him. chyāng-'dzěr 'gāng-gang méy 'dǎ-jaw tā. *or* chyāng-'dzěr chà-'dyǎr jyēw 'dǎ-jaw tā. *or* chyāng-'dzěr 'jī-ji-hu 'dǎ-jaw tā. ‖That's just enough for the three of us. (*Barely enough*) nèy-ge dzám-'sā 'gāng gèw. *or* (*Exactly enough; see* 2 *above*) nèy-ge dzám-'sā °'gāng-hǎw 'gèw. *or* °'chyà-hǎw 'gèw.

4. Just as, just when, *or* just (*at that moment*) 'jèng-dzày . . . de-shŕ-hew; 'gāng (yī), gāng, 'gāng-hǎw, 'gāng-chyǎw. ‖Just as I was opening the door I heard a shot. 'jèng-dzày wǒ kāy-'mén de-shŕ-hew, wǒ (*or* wǒ 'gāng yì-kāy-'mén, jyēw) tīng-jyàn 'pāng-de yì-'chyāng. ‖Just as she was stepping into the bathtub the doorbell rang. tā gāng 'mày-jìn 'dzǎw-pén-chywu, mén-'lyéngr jyēw shyǎng-le. ‖He just left when you came. nǐ 'jìn-lay de-shŕ-hew, tā 'gāng dzěw. ‖You were just coming in when he left. tā-'dzěw-de-shŕ-hew, nǐ 'gāng jìn-lay.

5. (*Only, simply, nothing more than*). *Several shades of meaning are distinguished, some of them difficult to express in English.*

Just (and nothing but) 'bú-gwò. ‖He's just a little boy. tā 'bú-gwò shr̀ ge-'háy-dz. ‖He's just acting (*or* pretending). tā nà shr̀ jwāng-'swàn. ‖He's just trying to be smart. tā nà bú-gwò shr̀ yàw 'shyǎn-nung-shyǎn-nung. ‖He's just a crackpot. tā 'bú-gwò shr̀ ge-bàn-'fēngr. *or* (*More emphatic, with the implication that he should therefore be avoided; see below*) tā 'jyǎn-jí shr̀ ge-bàn-'fēngr.

Just (and nothing further) 'jŕ(-shŕ), gwāng, 'jŕ-ywú. ‖He just shook his head and said nothing. tā 'gwāng (*or* tā 'jŕ-ywú, *or* tā 'jŕ-shr) yáw-le yàw-'téw, méy. 'shwō shém-me. ‖He just said that word and everyone understood what he meant. tā 'gwāng (*or* tā 'jŕ-shr, *or* tā 'jŕ) shwō-le nèy-yí-ge-'dzèr, kě-shr 'rén-ren dēw jŕ-daw tā shr̀ shéme-'yì-sz.

Just (and that's final *or* enough) jyēw, jyèw-shr. ‖I just won't let you do it. wǒ 'jyēw-shr bu-'jyàw-nǐ 'nèm-je. ‖Just let me go this once (*and never again*). jyèw 'jyàw-wǒ chywù jèy-yì-'hwéy. ‖I just don't understand! wǒ 'jyēw-shr bù-'dǔng-me! *or* (*see below*) wǒ jyǎn-'jí bù-'dǔng(-me)! ‖Just a little bit! That's enough! 'jyēw nèm yì-'dyǎr. 'gèw-la! *But* ‖Just a little lower! Hold it! (*Still a little lower.*) dzày 'dī nèm yì-'dyăn-dyăr! 'shíng-la! ‖In that case, let's just pretend that we don't know who he is (*and let it go at that*). 'nèm-je-ne dzám jyèw 'jwāng bù-'jř-dàw tā shř 'shéy, hăw-le.

Just (*used primarily for emphasis*) 'jyăn-jř or jyăn-'jř; kě (*used especially in wishes*). ‖I'm just tired to death! wǒ kě 'lèy-sz-le! or wǒ 'jyăn-jř 'lèy-sz-le! ‖Just let me go there once! kě 'jyàw-wǒ 'chywù-yi-hwéy-ba. ‖I just don't understand. wǒ jyăn-'jř bù-'dǔng. or (*see above*) wǒ 'jyèw-shr bù-'dǔng(-me). ‖He's just a crackpot. tā 'jyăn-jř shř ge-bàn-'fēngr. or (*As a simple statement*) tā 'bú-gwò shř ge-bàn-'fēngr. But ‖Just you wait (*and see*)! nǐ 'děng-je 'chyăw-ba.

If . . . just 'jř-yàw (*if only*) ; or 'yàw-shr *followed by some other expression for only.* ‖If he would just say it! 'jř-yàw tā yì-kāy 'kéw-wa! ‖If he'd said just another word, I'd have let him have it. tā 'yàw-shr jīn-'jīn-de dzày shwō 'yí-ge-dzèr, wǒ jyèw bù-néng 'ráw-ta-le.

6. Just about (*almost*) 'chà-bu-dwō. *See* ALMOST.

JUSTICE. (*Fairness*) *Expressed in verb phrases; see* JUST *for various meanings and terms.* ‖Don't expect justice from him. *is expressed as* Don't expect him to be just. nǐ byé 'wàng-shyang tā hwèy 'gūng-píng. ‖We must admit the justice of his demands. *is expressed as* We must admit that his demands are just. wǒ-men 'bù-néng bù-'chéng-rèn tā-'yāw-chéw-de yěw-'lǐ.

(*Trial*). ‖He will be brought to justice for his crimes. (*General*) tā 'wéy-fēy-dzwò-dǎy-de yí-'dìng bù-dé hǎw-bàw. or tā yí-'dìng yěw 'è-gwàn-mǎn-'yíng-de-yì-'tyān. or (*Legal only*) tā fàn-le jèy-shyē-'dzwèy yí-dìng 'nán-táw fǎ-'wǎng.

Do justice to. ‖This work certainly doesn't do justice to your abilities. jàw 'nǐ-de-'néng-gàn láy shwō. dzwò 'jèy-yàng-de-shř 'shŕ-dzày shŕ °'wěy-chywū-le. or °'dà-tsáy shyǎw-'yùng-le. or °chywū-'tsáy-le. or °'dī-jyèw-le. or nín dzwò 'jèy-yàng-de-shř 'shŕ-dzày shř °etc. ‖Are you doing justice to his talents? nǐ 'yùng-tā yùng-de dé-'dàng-ma? or jàw tā-de-'tsáy-gàn láy shwō, nǐ 'shŕ-bu-shr yěw dyǎr-'wěy-chywū tā? ‖You're not doing justice to his talents. nǐ 'dày-tā 'wèy-myǎn 'dà-tsáy shyǎw-'yùng-le.

K

KEEP. 1. *Cases in which no other word need follow.* (*Remain in good condition*). *This meaning is expressed as* still be good háy hǎw-'hāwr-de; still be edible háy néng 'chř; still be drinkable háy néng 'hē; *or by a negative word with* be spoiled hwày *or* be sour swān; *or by resultative compounds with* lyéw (*keep in the sense of* retain; *see* 2 *below*) *such as* not (be able to) keep for long lyéw-bù-'jyéw; (be able to) keep until 'lyéw-de-dàw. ‖Did the milk keep all right? 'nǎy-dz háy hǎw-'hāwr-de-ma? or 'nǎy-dz háy néng 'hē-ma? or 'nǎy-dz méy-'hwày-ma? or 'nǎy-dz méy-'swān-ma? ‖This milk won't keep until tomorrow. jèy-ge-'nǎy-dz 'lyéw-bu-dàw 'míng-tyan-le. But ‖The story will keep. nèy-shèr yǐ-'hèw dzày 'shwō.

(*Means of living*). *This meaning is expressed as* enough for *doing something* (*such as eating, using, etc.*) gèw-. . .-de. ‖Does he earn his keep? tā-jwàn-de gèw-°'gwòr-de-ma? or °'chř-de-ma? or °'yùng-de-ma? or °'jyǎw-gwer-de-ma?

For keeps. ‖We're playing this game for keeps *is expressed as* This is real gambling. jèy shř dǔ-'jēn-de.

For keeps (*permanently*) *is expressed with* yì-'jř. ‖We expect to stay here for keeps. wǒm shyǎng yàw dzày-'jèr yì-'jř dāy-shya-chywu.

2. *When followed by a noun after which no other word need follow.* (*Retain in one's possession, save*). (*Preserve*) lyéw; (*put away*) shěw; (*keep on hand for future use, keep in stock, etc.*) tswén; *and several indirect expressions.* ‖I kept this book for you. 'jèy-běn-shū wǒ gěy-nǐ 'lyéw-je-ne. or 'jèy-běn-shū shř wǒ-gěy-nǐ-'lyéw-je-de. ‖Let's keep this candy and eat it later.

'jèy-táng °'shěw-chi-lay (or °'shěw-je, or °'lyéw-chi-lay, or °'lyéw-je, or °'tswén-chi-lay, or °'tswén-je) yì-'hèw dzày chř-ba. ‖We kept the champagne for her wedding. wǒm bǎ 'shyāng-bīn-jyěw °'shěw-je (or °'lyéw-je, or °'tswén-je) děng tā-jyē-'hwēn-de-shŕ-hèw dzày 'hē. ‖What do you keep in stock? nǐ dēw tswén-le shéme-'hwò-le? or *expressed as* What is all your stock? nǐ dēw-shr yěw 'shéme-'tswén-hwò. ‖Do you want to keep this? 'jèy-ge nǐ shyǎng °'shěw-je-ma? or °'lyéw-je-ma? or °'tswén-je-ma? or keep *expressed as* later still want °yǐ-'hèw háy 'yàw-ma? ‖May I keep this picture? 'jèy-jāng-shyàng-'pyār wǒ 'lyéw-shya, shíng-ma? or *expressed as* I want this picture; OK.? °'wǒ yàw-le, shíng-ma? or as Let this picture be mine; OK.? °swàn 'wǒ-de-le, shíng-ma? ‖Keep the change. *When making payment this is expressed as* Don't bother bringing change. béng (or 'bú-yùng) jǎw-'chyán-le. or *When the change is being offered this is expressed as* That's for you. nèy-ge gěy-'nǐ-le. or as That's yours. nèy-ge shř 'nǐ-de-le. or as Keep that. nèy-ge nǐ 'lyéw-shya-ba. ‖I can't keep a fountain pen two weeks *is expressed as* If I have a fountain pen, in two weeks it's lost. wǒ 'yěw-le dž-láy-shwěy-'bǐ, 'lyǎng-ge-lǐ-'bày jyèw 'dyēw-le. ‖Do you keep soap? (keep *is expressed as* have) yěw 'yí-dz-ma? ‖Where do you keep (*put*) your stamps? nǐ-de-yěw-'pyàw °gē- (or °'fàng-, or °'shěw-)'nǎr-le?

(*Observe or guard*) shěw. ‖They keep all the Christian holidays. 'swǒ-yěw-de-jī-dū-jyàw-'jyé-chi tām 'dòw shëw. ‖If you keep the law and keep your temper, you ought to keep out of trouble. nǐ yàw-shr °shëw-'fǎ (or expressed as not violate the law °byé fàn-'fǎ), byé fǎ 'pí-chi, dà-gày jyèw 'bú-jr̀-ywu 'jāw-dzār-rě-'hwò-de-le. ‖Can you keep a secret? nǐ néng 'shëw mì-'mì-ma?

Keep a promise or keep one's word. ‖You kept your promise. (Congratulation) nǐ jēn shr̀ yán-ěr-yěw-'shìn-na. or (Warning or encouragement) nǐ-'dā-yìng-de 'yǐ-jīng 'dēw bàn-'dàw-le. ‖He always keeps his promise. tā 'yán-ěr-yěw-'shìn. or tā-'dā-yìng-de jyèw 'yí-dìng °gěy bàn-'dàw-le. or °bàn-de-'dàw. or tā lǎw shr̀ shëw-'shìn-de. or 'tā-de-hwà 'kàw-de-'jù. ‖I always keep my word. wǒ 'shwō-le jyèw 'swàn.

(Support or raise) yǎng; but of a garden jùng. ‖Do you earn enough to keep your family? nǐ jwàn-de gèw-yǎng-'jyā-de-ma? ‖Do you keep chickens? nǐ yǎng-'jī-ma? ‖They keep chickens, draft animals, and bees. tām yǎng-'jī, yǎng shēng-kew, háy yǎng 'mì-fēngr. ‖Why don't you keep a garden? nǐ wèy-shéme bú-jùng 'ywán-dz-ne?

(Detain a person) bǎ . . . 'dān-wù, bǎ . . . 'lyéw, jyàw . . . dzày . . . (a place) 'dāy; jyàw . . . bù-néng 'láy. ‖I'm sorry to be late; the dentist kept me longer than I expected. 'dwèy-bu-jù, 'láy-de 'wǎn-le; wǒ méy shyǎng-'dàw yá-'yī-shēng °bǎ-wǒ 'dān-wu-le 'nèm dà-'bàn-tyān. or °bǎ-wǒ 'lyéw-le 'nèm dà-'bàn-tyān. or °jyàw-wǒ dzày-nàr 'dāy-le 'nèm dà-'bàn-tyān. ‖What's keeping him? tā yěw shéme-'shèr jyàw-tā 'bù-néng 'láy-ne? ‖What kept you? is expressed as What were you doing? nǐ dzwò-'shéme láy-je?

Keep one's looks. ‖She's certainly kept her good looks all these years. tā 'jēn hwèy 'bǎw-yǎng, 'dzēm-shyē-nyán-le 'háy nèm °'měy. or °hǎw-'kàn. or (a literary quotation) 'shywú-nyáng 'bàn-lǎw, 'fēng-ywùn 'yéw-tswén.

Keep house. (Manage a house) gwǎn-'jyā; (take care of the housework) 'jàw-ying 'jyā-li-de 'shèr; keep house by oneself (live by oneself) 'dz̀-jǐ gwò. ‖Who's keeping house for them? 'shéy gěy-tām gwǎn-'jyā-ne? or 'shéy gěy-tām 'jàw-ying 'jyā-li-de-'shèr-ne? ‖They're going to keep house by themselves. tām yàw 'dz̀-jǐ gwò-le.

Keep a job. ‖He kept the same job for the last ten years. is expressed as He has done his job straight through for ten years. tā-de-'shèr yì-'jŕ dzwò-le 'shŕ-nyán-le. or as He has done that one job for ten years. tā dzwò nèy-'yí-ge-shèr dzwò-le 'shŕ-nyán-le. ‖He can't keep a job is expressed as He does work can't work long. tā dzwò-'shèr dzwò-bu-°'cháng. or °'jyéw. or as He does work can't stay long. tā dzwò-'shèr dāy-bu-°'jù. or °'jyéw.

Keep accounts jì-'jàng. ‖Can you keep accounts? nǐ hwèy jì-'jàng-ma?

Keep a diary jì r̀-'jì. ‖Do you keep a diary? nǐ jì r̀-'jì-ma?

Keep one's balance or keep one's footing (be able to stand firmly) jàn-de-'wěn or (be able to place the foot

firmly) wěn-dę-jù 'jyǎw. ‖It's very hard to keep your balance on that tiny spot. 'nèm-shyǎw-de-yí-kwày-'dì-fang-shang 'jàn-je hěn nán °jàn-dę-'wěn. or °wěn-de-jù 'jyǎw(-bùr). ‖The road was so slippery that I couldn't keep my footing, and I kept falling down. lù tày 'hwá-le, wǒ lǎw 'wěn-bu-jù jyǎw-'bùr, yì-'jŕ shwāy 'gēn-dew.

Keep one's head or keep one's wits about one; see Keep cool under 3 below.

Keep one's temper bù-shēng-'chì, bù-fā 'pí-chi, 'rěn-shya-chywu; 'rěn-je, 'rěn yí-shyàr, 'rěn-jù-le 'chì. ‖Keep your temper. 'byé shēng-'chì. or 'byé fā 'pí-chi. or 'rěn-shyà-chywu. etc. as above.

Keep good time (of a timepiece) dzěw-de 'jwěn. ‖Does your watch keep good time? nǐ-de-'byǎw dzěw-de 'jwěn-ma?

Keep time (mark time with a beat) dǎ 'pāy-dz; keep time to music gēn-je 'yīn-ywè °dǎ 'pāy-dz or (by jumping) °'tyàw (etc., with other verbs of motion); keep time to a drumbeat gēn-je gǔ-'dyǎr °dǎ 'pāy-dz or (perfectly marking accented and unaccented beats) °pāy-da-de 'yěw-bǎn-yěw-'yǎn-de (etc., with other verbs). ‖He kept time to the music with his fingers. tā gēn-je 'yīn-ywè yùng shěw-'jŕ-tew dǎ 'pāy-dz.

Keep watch shěw, kān. ‖I kept watch through the night. wǒ 'shěw-le yí-'yè. or (in my turn) shěw-'yè shr̀ 'wǒ-jŕ-de-bān. ‖I'll keep watch. 'wǒ shěw-je. or 'wǒ kān-je. ‖You keep watch over the patient tonight. jyēr 'yè-li 'nǐ °shěw-je (or °kān-je) 'bìng-rén-ba.

3. When followed by an adjective or an action word ending in -ing. The commonest expressions are constructions with lǎw (always), yì-'jŕ or bú-'dwàn-de or yì-'jŕ-bú-'dwàn-de (continually), or 'jyē-je (continue) before a verb of action, -je following a verb of action, or a negative word with a verb of opposite meaning.

Keep cool (physically) lǎw dzày 'lyáng-kwày-dì-fang dāy-je; Keep cool (mentally) or Keep your head byé 'hwāng, or 'jèn-jìng-je, or 'wěn-jù-le 'shīn. (See also Keep your temper under 2 above.) ‖Keep cool; don't let them make you nervous. 'wěn-jù-le ''shīn; byé jyàw-tām bǎ-nǐ °rě-'jí-le. or °rě-'hú-du-le. ‖They built a fire to keep warm. tām shēng-le ge-'hwǒ hǎw °nwǎn-he-dyǎr. or expressed as in order not to feel cold. °'bú-jr̀-ywu 'dùng-de-hung. ‖Keep quiet. is expressed as Don't speak. 'byé shwō-'hwà. or as Don't make any racket. byé 'chǎw. or byé 'nàw. or byé 'rāng-rang. or as Don't make a sound. 'byé chū-'shēngr. or as Stop talking. byé 'shwō-le. or as Stop the racket. byé 'nàw-le. or byé 'chǎw-le. or byé 'rāng-rang-le. ‖He keeps bothering me. tā lǎw 'má-fan wǒ. or tā bú-'dwàn-de 'má-fan wǒ. ‖We kept telling her you'd come. wǒm yì-'jŕ-bú-'dwàn-de 'gàw-su tā shwō nǐ hwèy 'láy-de. ‖The policeman told us to keep moving. 'jīng-chá jyàw-wǒm °byé 'jàn-ju. or °'wàng-chyán 'dzěw-je-dyǎr. ‖Keep (on) trying. is expressed as

Don't stop. byé dǎ-'jù. *or* 'bú-yàw 'tíng. *or* byé 'tíng-ju. *or as* **Don't lose heart.** byé hwēy-'shīn. *or as* **Continue working.** 'jyē-je 'gàn-shya-chywu. *or as* **Continue calling.** jyē-je 'jyǎw-shya-chywu. *or as* **Continue searching.** jyē-je 'jǎw-shya-chywu. *etc.*

4. *When followed by a preposition, a prepositional phrase, or one of a few other phrases. Most of the expressions are similar to those described in 3 above.*

Keep at. ‖**Keep at it.** 'byé dǎ-'jù. *or* jyē-je 'gàn-shya-chywu. *or* dzày 'jyē dzày 'lì. ‖**We kept at her until she told us.** wǒm °bù-'tíng-de (*or* 'bú-'jù-de, *or* °bú-'dwàn-de) wèn-tā yì-'jŕ-dàw tā 'shwō-chu-lay-le. *or* wǒm 'jyē-gwò 'bī-de tā 'shwō-chu-lay-le.

Keep away from. ‖**Keep away from here.** 'byé dzày dàw-'jèr láy. *or* 'lí-jèr 'ywǎn-dyar. ‖**Keep away from her; she's a vicious gossip.** 'byé gēn-ta láy-wang (*or* 'dwǒ-je tā-dyar, *or* lí-tā 'ywǎn-dyar), tā 'nà-tsáy ày 'chwán shyán-'hwà-ne.

Keep from. ‖**We couldn't keep from laughing, he looked so funny.** wǒm méy-fár bú-'shyàw-le (*or* wǒm rěn-bu-jù jyèw 'shyàw-le), tā-de-'yàngr 'jēn kě-'shyàw.

Keep in. ‖**I like to play the piano, but I'm so busy I can't keep in practice.** wǒ 'ày tán 'gāng-chín, bú-gwò tày 'máng-le, °méy gūng-fu 'lyàn-shi. *or* °bù-néng 'jyē-je lyàn-shi. ‖**Keep in touch with me.** cháng gěy-wǒ láy ge-'hwàr. *or* 'jyē-cháng-bú-'dwàn-de gēn-wǒ 'jyē-jye 'téw. *or* cháng 'gwān-jaw wǒ-dyar. ‖**Keep in step.** *See* **Keep step** *under 2 above.*

Keep off. ‖**Keep off the grass.** byé dzày tsǎw-'dì-shang 'dzěw.

Keep on. *When followed by an action word ending in -ing, see 3 above.* ‖**Keep on the job.** byé bǎ nǐ-de-'shèr dyěw-le. *or* nǐ-de-'shèr yì-'jŕ 'dzwò-shya-chywu-ba. ‖**Keep on the watch for him.** *or* **Keep on the lookout for him.** nǐ hǎw-'hāwr-de (*or* nǐ lyéw-je 'shén) děng-je tā 'láy.

Keep out byé 'jìn-láy. ‖**I'll try to keep out of trouble.** wǒ yí-'dìng shyǎng-fár 'bù-rě-°'shŕ. *or* °'hwò.

Keep to. ‖**Do I keep to the right or the left?** kàw-'dzwǒ dzěw háy-shr kàw-'yèw dzěw? ‖**Keep to the subject, please.** byé lí-'tí.

Keep track of. ‖**He changes jobs so often we have a hard time keeping track of him.** tā 'sān-tyan-lyǎng-'téwr-de hwàn-'shèr, wǒm 'jyǎn-jŕ °gēn-bu-'shàng tā-le. *or* °bù-jŕ-dàw tā 'shéme-shŕ-hew 'dzày-nǎr-le.

Keep up. ‖**Keep up the good work.** jàw 'jèy-yàngr 'dzwò-shya-chywu-ba. *or* (dzwò-de 'hǎw) 'lǎw. nèm-je tsáy 'hǎw. *or* jèy shr 'hǎw-shèr, byé 'jyàn-dwàn tsáy 'hǎw. ‖**Keep it up.** jyē-je 'gàn-shya-chywu. *or* byé dǎ-'jù. *or* 'lǎw nèm-je tsáy 'hǎw. ‖**We have to keep up appearances.** *or* **We have to keep face.** wǒm 'bù-néng °'bú-gù (*or* °'bù-gwǎn) 'chǎng-myàn. *or* wǒm fēy-děy 'gù-chywan-je dyǎr-'myàn-dz. ‖**Isn't it expensive to keep up your car?** 'yǎw (*or* 'yàw) nèm-ge-'chē bú-fèy-'chyán-ma? *or* 'cháng nèm 'shyēw-li chē bú-fèy-'chyán-ma? ‖**I'll keep up my end of the bar-**

gain. 'wǒ-jèy-téwr dzěm 'shwō-de jwěn °bàn-de-'dàw. *or* °jàw 'bàn. ‖**They're trying to keep up the prices.** tām yàw bǎ 'jyà-chyán 'wéy-chŕ-jù-le. *or* tām yàw bú²-jyàw 'jyà-chyán 'làw-shya-chywu.

Keep up with. ‖**Do you have any trouble keeping up with the others?** nǐ 'gēn-de-shàng (*or* nǐ 'gǎn-de-shàng) 'rén-jyā-ma? ‖**Did you have any trouble keeping up with the others?** nǐ 'nèm gēn-tām 'bǐ-je, 'fèy-jyèr-ma?

5. *When followed by a noun and then an adjective. Many of the constructions are similar to those described in 3 above: the noun is usually preceded by jyàw if one refers to a person, otherwise by bǎ.*

‖**Sorry to keep you waiting.** 'dwèy-bu-jù, jyàw-nǐ 'děng-le 'bàn-tyān. ‖**This will keep him amused for a while.** jèy jyèw kě-yǐ °jyàw-tā 'wár-hwěr-le. *or* °jyàw-tā 'lǎw-shr hwěr-le. *or* °gèw tā-'wár-hwěr-de-le. ‖**Keep him busy.** byé jyàw-tā 'shyán-je. *or* 'jyàw-tā 'lǎw yěw 'shèr dzwò. *or* (*To distract his attention*) 'jyàw-tā 'máng-bu-gwo-láy. *or* 'jyàw-tā 'máng-de 'gù bu-gwo-láy. ‖**Keep dinner warm for me.** bǎ-fàn gěy-wǒ 'wēn-je.

6. *When followed by a noun and then a prepositional or other phrase or an adverb. Sometimes in these constructions the adverb may precede the noun in English, as* **Keep on your shoes** *as well as* **Keep your shoes on; these are listed here nevertheless. Most of the constructions are similar to those described in 3 and 5 above.*

Keep . . . away. ‖**If the food is good you can't keep him away.** 'tsày yàw-shr hǎw 'chŕ, nǐ 'hūng-tā tā yě bù-'dzěw-de. ‖**She keeps insulting him, but even that doesn't keep him away.** tā lǎw 'mà-tā, kě-shr jyèw 'nèm-je tā 'háy-shr °bù-kěn fàng-'shěw. *or* °bù-kěn dǎ-'jù. *or* °bù-kěn 'dzěw. *or* °bù-kěn 'lí-kay. *or meaning* **but even at that he keeps annoying her** °'chán-me-je tā.

Keep . . . down. ‖**He pretends to be helping the workers, but actually he wants to keep them down.** tā 'jwāng-je gěy 'láw-gūng bāng-'máng, shŕ-'jì-shang tā shŕ yàw °bǎ-tām 'yā-jù-le-de. *or* °'yā-jŕ tām-ne. ‖**He's so sick that he can't keep anything down (***or* **keep down anything) but water.** tā bìng-de 'jŕ néng hē-'shwěy, chŕ-le (byé-de) 'shéme dēw 'tù-chi-lay.

Keep . . . from. ‖**You'd better put a bandage on to keep the dirt from getting into that cut.** nǐ-lá-'pwō-le-de-nar 'háy-shr °chán-shang (*or* °gwǒ-shang) dyǎr-bēng-'dày-ba, hǎw byé °jyàw 'dzāng-dūng-shi jìn-chywu. *or* °jān-je 'dzāng-dūng-shi. ‖**The doctor quarantined the house to keep other people from getting the disease.** dày-fu 'bù-shywǔ rén dzày 'nèy-jyāer chū-'rù, wèy-de shr 'bú-ràng 'byé-rén °'chwán-rǎn-shang (*or* °'jáw-shang) nèy-jǔng-'bìng. ‖**We wrote often to keep him from feeling blue.** wǒm cháng gěy-tā shyě-'shìn, hǎw 'bú-jyàw tā-'shīn-li nán 'gwò.

Shore of Li River, Gweilin

Soldier of Xian

Keep . . . in. ‖We were furious at her, but we managed to keep in our feelings (*or,* keep our feelings in) until she left. tā jyàw-wǒm hěn shēng-'chì, kě-shr 'dž-jǐ 'yā-je yì-'jŕ děng tā 'dzěw-le. ‖This work keeps him in a great deal. jèy-shèr jyàw-tā °lǎw děy dzày 'wū-dz-li dzwò. *or* °'hěn shǎw 'chū-chywù. *or* tā dzwò 'jèy-shèr lǎw děy 'gwān-dzay 'wūr-li. ‖I'm working on another job now, but I'm trying to keep my hand in the old importing business at the same time. wǒ 'lìng yěw ge-'shèr, bú-gwò wǒ 'hěn shyǎng 'túng-shr °háy gàn-je 'jìn-kěw-de-'shēng-yi. *or* °háy bù-'dyēw-kay 'jìn-kěw-de-'shēng-yi.

Keep . . . off. ‖They're doing that to keep people off the new cement path. tām nèy shř yàw 'jyàw-rén 'byé dzày 'shīn-'yáng-hwēy-'lù-shang 'dzěw.

Keep . . . on. ‖Keep your coat on.' byé 'twō-yī. *or* 'yī-shang 'chwān-je-ba. ‖Keep a watch on that man. *or* Keep your eyes on that man. nǐ 'dīng-je-dyar nèy-ge-rén. *or* nǐ 'kān je-dyar, nèy-ge-rén. *or* nǐ 'lyéw dyǎr 'shén kàn-je nèy-ge-rén. ‖Keep your shirt on. *See* Keep one's temper *under 2 above.* ‖Keep your feet on the ground. jàn 'wěn-lew. *or* 'lì-jù-le 'jyǎw. *See also* Keep one's footing *under 2 above.*

Keep . . . out. ‖We'll keep him out of mischief. wǒm ví-'dìng bú-hwèy jyàw-ta °rě-'shèr-de. *or* °hú-'nàw-ca. *or (Of children only)* °táw-'chì-de.

KEY. (*Lock opener*) 'yàw-shr. ‖I have a pair of keys to that door. 'nèy-ge-mén wǒ yěw 'lyǎng-bǎ-'yàw-shr. ‖This key doesn't fit (*can't open*) that lock. 'jèy-ge-yàw-shr kāy-bu-kāy nèy-bǎ-'swǒ.

(*Solution; way of doing*) 'bàn-fa; (*way of translating, as a code*) 'fān-fǎ; (*printed directions giving the key to something*) 'shwō-míng-shū; *or expressed verbally by* bàn, fān, *and similar words.* ‖I don't know the key to this code. wǒ bù-jŕ-dàw jèy-jǔng-'mì-mǎr-de-'fān-fa. *or* jèy-jǔng-'mì-mǎr wǒ bù-jŕ-dàw dzěme 'fān. ‖I don't know the key to this problem. wǒ bù-jŕ-dàw jèy-ge-'wèn-tí-de-'bàn-fa. *or* jèy-ge-'wèn-tí wǒ bù-jŕ-dàw dzěme 'bàn. ‖Here is the key to this code. jèy-jǔng-'mì-mǎr °shř 'jèm-ge-'fān-fa. *or* °'jèm-yàng 'fān. *or* jè shř jèy-jǔng-'mì-mǎr-de-'shwō-míng-shū.

(*Lever of typewriter, piano, etc.*) 'jyàn-dz. ‖The typewriter keys are terribly stiff. dǎ-dž-jī-de-'jyàn-dz sž-'jǐn-de.

(*In music*) dyàwr. ‖The symphony is written in the key of G. nèy-jyāw-shyǎng-'chywǔ shř °'jī-dyàwr. *or* °'yùng-'jī-dyàwr-shyě-de.

(*Most important*) dzwèy-'yàw-jǐn-de. ‖He's the key man in the plant. gūng-'chǎng-li tā shř dzwèy-yàw-'jǐn-de-rén.

‖Keyed up for . . . děng-je . . . , shīn-li hěn 'jǐn-jāng; *or* 'yì-shīn děng-je . . . . ‖He's all keyed up for his (stage) appearance. tā děng-je chū-'táy, shīn-li hěn 'jǐn-jāng. *or* tā 'yì-shīn děng-je yèw chū-'táy-le.

KICK. (*With the foot*) tī; give a kick 'tī yì-jyǎw *or* 'tī yí-shyàr; (*of a hoofed animal kicking with hind feet*) !yàw 'jywě-dz. ‖He kicked her. ´tā 'tī-tā láy-je. ‖He gave her a kick. tā 'tī-le tā °yì-'jyǎw. *or* °yí-shyàr. ‖Kick the ball! tī-'chyéwr! ‖Give it a kick and let it roll over this way. nèy-ge nǐ °yì-'tī (*or* °'tī yì-'jyǎw) jyèw 'gú-lu-gwo-lay-le. ‖That horse gave you some kick! nèy-pī-mǎ °'tī-le nǐ yí-shyàr 'hǎw-de! *or* °'tī-de nǐ hěn bù-'chīng-nga! ‖I hope this horse doesn't kick. shī-wang 'jèy-pī-mǎ °'bú-lyàw 'jywě-dz. *or* °'bù-tī-'rén.

(*A recoil*) hèw-dzwò-'lì; (*to recoil*) wàng-'hèw dzwò. ‖The kick of the rifle can hurt your shoulder. 'bù-chyāng-de-hèw-dzwò-'lì (*or* 'bù-chyāng wàng-'hèw yí-'dzwò) kě-yi bǎ jyān-'bǎng jwàng-'shàng-le.

(*Gripe, complain*) 'bàw-ywan; (*find fault*) 'tyāw-tì (*grumble*) 'dū-nang. ‖What are you kicking about? nǐ nèm 'bàw-ywan, shř wèy-le 'shéme. ‖What are you kicking about then? nèm-je nǐ yěw 'bàw-ywan shéme-ne? ‖He's always kicking about something. tā 'lǎw dzày-nàr °'bàw-ywan. *or* °'tyāw-tì. *or* °'dū-nang. *or* °'bàw-ywan-jèy-ge-bàw-ywan-nèy-ge-de. *or* °'tyāw-ti-jèy-ge-tyāw-ti-nèy-ge-de. *or* °'dū-du-nang-nang-de.

Get a kick out of *doing something.* yī . . . jyèw 'jywé-je °'tǐng-yěw-'chywèr-de, *or* °'tǐng-gāw-'shìng-de, *or* 'hěn shí-hwān . . . , 'tǐng shí-hwān . . . , 'tǐng ày . . . , 'hěn ày . . . ; **get a kick out of** *someone or something* is expressed in the same way by stating the action enjoyed in connection with the person or thing. ‖He gets a big kick out of telling that story about the mayor. tā yì-'jyǎng-chi shř-'jǎng-de-nèy-dwàn-'gù-shr-lay jyèw 'jywé-je °'tǐng-yěw-'chywèr-de. *or* °'tǐng-gāw-'shìng-de. *or* tā 'hěn shí-hwān (*or* tā 'tǐng ày) gàw-sung rén shř-'jǎng-de-nèy-dwàn-'gù-shr.

KID. (*Young goat*) 'shyǎw-shān-'yáng, 'shyǎw-yáng, 'shyǎw-yángr, 'yáng-gāw-dz, 'gāw-yáng. ‖That kid is always following the she-g at around. nèy-jř-'shyǎw-yángr lǎw 'gēn-je nèy-jř-'mǔ-yáng.

(*Leather*) 'jī-pí. ‖She is very proud of her kid gloves. nèy-fù-'jī-pí-shěw-'tàwr tā tǐng dé-'yì-de. *or* tā 'tǐng dé-'yì tā-nèy-fù-'jī-pí-shěw-'tàwr.

(*Child*) shyǎw-'hár *or* 'háy-dz; (*children*) shyǎw-'hár-men, 'háy-dz-men. ‖Send the kids to bed. jyàw 'háy-dz-men chywù shwèy-'jyàw-ba.

(*To joke*) shwō-je 'wár; kid *someone* (along) gēn . . . nàw-je 'wár. ‖Are you kidding? nǐ shwō-je 'wár-ba. ‖I was just kidding with him. wǒ-nà 'bú-gwò shř gēn-tā nàw-je 'wár.

(*To fool*) ywān, dzwàn, pyàn. ‖Who're you kidding? nǐ-nà shř ywān-'shéy-ya? *or* nǐ yàw dzwàn-'shéy-ya? *or* nǐ yàw pyàn-'shéy-ya?

KILL. (*Put to death; by a blow, shot, or beating*) 'dǎ-sž *and any number of other resultative compounds with* sž die *as the second element, such as* (*do to death* *by any means*) 'nĕng-sž, (*do to death after scheming*) 'hày-sž, (*by stabbing*) 'jā-sž, (*by kicking*) 'tī-sž, (*by burning*) 'shāw-sž (*vy electric shock*) 'dyàn-sž, (*by poisoning*) 'dú-sž, (*by running over*) 'yà-sž, (*by a collision*) 'jwàng-sž, (*by lightning*) jyàw-léy 'jì-sž, *etc.*; (*murder*) shā; (*murder with premeditation*) 'méw-shā; (*unintentional manslaughter*) 'wù-shā; (*hit, but the meaning sometimes includes killing*) 'dǎ-jaw; *sometimes expressed with* die *sž alone; a killer* shā-'rén-de-rén *or* shā-'rén-de-'shyūng-shĕw *or* 'shyūng-shĕw. ‖**Who killed him?** 'shéy shā-de tā? *or* 'shéy bǎ-tā 'dǎ-sž-d r 'shěy bǎ-tā 'nèng-sž-de? *or* 'shéy bǎ-tā 'hày-sž-de? ‖**How was he killed?** tā 'dzěm sž-de? *or* tā jyàw-rén dzěm 'nèng-sž-de? *or* tā jyàw-rén dzěm 'hày-sž-de? ‖**They killed him.** tām bǎ-tā (gěy) °'dǎ-sž-le. *or* (*By starving him*) °'è-sž-le. *or* (*By hanging*) °'dyàw-sž-le. *or* (*By poisoning*) °'dú-sž-le. ‖**This man was killed °by a blow on the head.** jèy-ge-rén shř °jyàw-rén-dzày-'téw-shang-'dǎ-le-yí-shyàr-'dǎ-sž-de. *or* °**by a gun.** °jyàw-rén-yùng-'chyāng-dǎ-sž-de. *or* °**by being stabbed with a bayonet.** °jyàw-rén-yùng-'tsž-dāw-'tsž-sž-de. *or* °**by being strangled.** °'lēy-sž-de. *or* °**by lightning.** °jyàw-'léy gěy-'jì-sž-de. *or* °**by being hit by a car.** °jyàw-chē 'jwàng-sž-de. *or* °**by being smothered.** °'byē-sž-de. *or* °'mēn-sž-de. *or* °**by a falling rock.** °jyàw-yí-kwày-shŕ-tew-'dzá-sž-de. *or* °**by coal gas.** °jyàw-méy-chì-'shywūn-sž-de. ‖**He kills a man as if he were killing a fly.** tā shā ge-'rén gēn 'nèng-sz-ge-'tsāng-ying shř-de. *or* tā dǎ-sž ge-'rén gēn 'dǎ-sž ge-'tsāng-ying shř-de. ‖**You didn't raise a finger, yes, but you killed him just the same.** nǐ 'lyán ge-shĕw-'jŕ-tew dēw méy-'dùng, bú-'tswò, kě-shr °tā 'háy-shr jyàw-nǐ-'hày-sž-de. *or* °tā 'háy-shr jyàw-nǐ-'bǐ-sz-de. *or* °tā 'háy-shr yīn-wey 'nǐ tsáy 'sž-de. *or* °nǐ gēn 'chīn-shĕw bǎ-tā 'shā-le yí-'yàng. *or* °tā-'sž-de gēn nǐ-'chīn-shew bǎ-tā 'shā-le yí-'yàng. *or* °tā-'sž-de-'ywán-yīn jyèw-shr 'nǐ.

Figuratively, other resultative compounds with sž *as the second element, as* (*by laughter*) 'shyàw-sž; (*by overwork*) 'lèy-sž; (*by pain*) 'téng-sž; (*by boredom*) 'mèn-sž; (*by noise*) 'chǎw-sž; *etc.* ‖**You're killing me!** nǐ kě jyàw-wǒ 'shyàw-sž-le! *or* nǐ kě bǎ-wǒ 'lèy-sž-le! ‖**This is killing me!** (*Overwork*) kě bǎ-wǒ 'lèy-sž-le. *or* (*Pain*) kě bǎ-wǒ 'téng-sž-le. *or* (*Boredom*) kě bǎ-wǒ 'mèn-sž-le. *etc.*

The kill (*act of killing*), *expressed verbally as* **drop the raised hand** shyà-'shĕw. ‖**They closed in for the kill.** tām 'wéy-lŭng-láy (*or* tām 'bī-jìn-láy) yàw shyà-'shĕw.

The kill (*animals killed in hunting*) 'dǎ-sž-de, 'dǎ-jaw-de, 'shā-le-de. ‖**The hunters brought home the kill.** dǎ-'lyè-de bǎ 'dǎ-sž-de-'shĕw dày-hwéy-'jyā-chywu-le.

(*Of time; pass, spend*) gwò; (*enjoy in a leisurely way*) 'shyāw-mwó *or* 'shyāw-chyǎn. **Have time to kill** yĕw 'gūng-fu méy-'shèr *or* yĕw 'gūng-fu 'shyán-je *or* yĕw 'gūng-fu 'shván-je méy-'shèr. ‖**Let's go to the**

park and **kill a few hours.** dzám dàw gūng-'ywán chywù °'gwò (*or* °'shyāw-mwó, *or* °'shyāw-chyǎn) jǐ-dyǎn-'jūng-ba. ‖**We have four hours to kill.** dzám yĕw 'sž-dyǎn-jūng-de-'gūng-fu °méy-'shèr. *or* °'shyán-je. *or* °'shyàn-je méy-'shèr.

Figurative meanings ranging from **suppress** *to* **eliminate.** (*Suppress*) bǎ . . . 'yā-shya-chywu; (*rob, as of flavor*) bǎ . . . 'dwó-chywu; (*destroy*) bǎ . . . 'hwěy; (*eliminate*) bǎ . . . chywǔ-'shyāw; (*not publish, as an article*) bù-'dēng *or* bù-fā-'byǎw; (*not bring up for discussion*) bù-bǎ . . . 'tí-chu-lay 'tǎw-lwèn. ‖**Too much salt will kill the flavor.** gē-'yán tày 'dwō hwèy bǎ-'wèr °'dwó-le-chywu-de. *or* °'yā-shya-chywu-de. *or* °'hwěy-le-de. ‖**The mayor killed their plan.** shř-'jǎng bǎ tām-de-'jì-hwà gěy °'yā-shya-chywu-le. *or* °chywǔ-'shyāw-le. *or* shř-'jǎng méy-bǎ tām-de-'jì-hwà 'tí-chu-lay 'tǎw-lwèn. ‖**Let's kill that article.** nèy-pyān-'wén-jang °'byé dēng-ba. *or* °'byé fā-'byǎw-ba.

KIND. (*Benevolent; of persons*). (*Good*) hǎw; (*philanthropic, a somewhat literary term*) shàn; (*philanthropic*) 'shàn-lyáng; (*mild, polite*) 'hé-chi; (*mild and liberal*) 'wēn-hèw; (*generous*) 'hèw-daw; (*faithful and liberal*) 'jūng-hèw; (*compassionate*) tsž-bēy; (*of actions, most of the above and also* hǎw-'hǎwr-de; (*helpful*) kěn-'bāng-ju-rén-de *or* kěn-gěy-rén-bāng-'máng-de; **do a kind deed** *is also expressed as* shíng ge-'hǎw. ‖**He's a very kind man.** tā-rén hěn °'hǎw. *or* °'shàn. *or* °'shàn-lyáng. *or* °'hé-chi. *or* °'wēn-hèw. *or* °'hèw-dàw. *or* °'jūng-hèw. *or* °'tsž-bēy. ‖**He's the kindest person I've ever met.** 'méy-jyàn-gwo nèm-°hǎw-'shīn-de-rén. *or* °'shàn-lyáng-de-rén. *or* °'hé-chi-de-rén. *or* °'hèw-daw-de-rén. *or* °'jūng-hew-de-rén. *or* °'tsž-bēy-de-rén. ‖**He's very kind-hearted.** tā-'shīn hěn °'hǎw. *or* °'shàn. *or* °'shàn-lyáng. *or* °'hèw-dàw. *or* °'jūng-hèw. *or* °'tsž-bēy. ‖**He treats people kindly.** tā 'dày-rén hěn °'hǎw. *or* °'shàn-lyáng. *or* °'hé-chi. *or* °'wēn-hèw. *or* °'hèw-dàw. *or* °'jūng-hèw. *or* °'tsž-bēy. ‖**Be kind to others.** dày-'rén yàw °hǎw-'hǎwr-de. *or* °'hé-chi. *or* °'hèw-dàw. *or* °'jūng-hèw. *or* °yĕw 'tsž-bēy-shīn. *or* °'tsž-bēy-je-dyar. ‖**Be kind to animals.** dày 'shēng-kew (*work animals; or* dày 'shyàw-shèwr, *pets*) yàw °hǎw-'hǎwr-de. *or* °'tsž-bēy-je-dyar. ‖**You'll gradually find the people here very kind.** nǐ màn-'mār-de jyèw jŕ-dàw-le, 'jèr-de-rén °-'shīn hěn °'hǎw. *or* °hěn 'hé-chi. *or* °hěn 'hèw-dàw. *or* °'dày-rén 'hěn hǎw. *or* °hěn kěn-'bāng-ju-rén-de. *or* °hěn kěn-gěy-rén-bāng-'máng-de. ‖**Do a kind deed every day.** 'měy-tyān 'dzwò jyàn-'hǎw-shèr. *or* 'měy tyān 'dzwò jyàn-'shàn-shèr. *or* 'měy-tyān 'shíng ge-'hǎw.

Give kindest regards 'wèn-hèw (*literary, but used for elders*) ; wèn-'hǎwr; dày-'hǎwr; shāw-'hǎwr. ‖**Give my kindest regards to your family.** 'fŭ-shang 'dēw tì-wǒ °'wèn-hèw. *or* °wèn ge-'hǎwr. *or* °wèn yì-shēng-'hǎwr. *or* °dày ge-'hǎwr-chywu. *or* °shāw ge-'hǎwr-chywu.

‖**You've been very kind.** 'jēn-shr fèy-'shīn-le. *or* fèy-'shīn, fèy-'shīn. *or* dwō-'shyè, dwō-'shyè. *or* láw-'jyà, láw-'jyà.

Be kind enough to chǐng (*see also* **PLEASE**); (*sarcastic*) 'fā-fa 'tsź-běy *or* 'shíng-shing 'hǎw(-ba). ‖**Would you be kind enough to help me?** chǐng-nǐ 'bāng-bang-'máng. *or* chǐng-nǐ 'bāng-ju-bāng-ju-ba. *or* (*sarcastically*) nín 'fā-fa 'tsź-běy, 'bāng-bang wǒ-ba. *or* nín 'shíng-shing 'hǎw-ba, 'bāng-bang wǒ-ba.

(*Sort; especially of inherent type, as species*) jǔng; (*especially of types distinguished by external characteristics as shape, form, mannerisms*) yàng *or* yàngr *or* jǔng-'yàngr; (*type*) pày; (*grade*) děng; (*of people distinguished by their way of life; also means* **road, way**) lù; (*class characterized by some point of similarity in all members*) lèy; *when referring to actions,* **that kind** *may be expressed by* (*thus*) nèm(-je), **this kind** *by* jèm *or* dzèm, **what kind** *or* **any kind** *by* dzěm. ‖**What kind of a person is he?** tā shr̀ 'shéme-yàngr-de-ge-'rén? *or* tā shr̀ 'dzěm-yàngr-de-ge-'rén? *or* tā shr̀ 'dzěm-ge-'rén? ‖**That kind of person is hard to deal with.** 'nèy-jǔng- (*or* 'nèy-yàngr-, *or* 'nèy-jǔng-'yàngr-, *or* 'nèy-lèy, *or, of social class,* 'nèy-děng-) (de-) rén hěn nán °'yìng-fu. *or* °'dwèy-fu. *or* °'chán. *or* °'dèw. ‖**Do you have any more of this kind of paper?** 'háy yěw 'jèy-jǔng-jř-ma? *or* 'háy yěw 'jèy-yàngr-de-jř-ma? ‖**There are several kinds of people here.** jèr yěw ji-'jǔng-de-rén. *or* jèr yěw ji-'lèy-de-rén. *or* jèr yěw ji-'jǔng-'yàngr-de-rén. *ŏr* jèr yěw jĭ-'pày-de-rén. ‖**He's a different kind of person.** tā shr̀ 'lìng-yí-pày-de-rén. *or* tā shr̀ 'lìng-yì-jǔng-de-rén. *or* tā shr̀ 'lìng-yí-lèy-de-rén. *or* tā shr̀ 'lìng-yí-lù-de-rén. ‖**He's the same kind of a man as Lincoln.** tā gēn lín-'kěn shr̀ yí-'lèy-de-rén. ‖**This is the same kind of work I've done before.** 'jèy-shèr gēn wǒ-yì-'chyán-dzwò-gwo-de yí-'yàng. ‖**He's not my kind.** tā gēn-wǒ bú-shr yí-'pày-de-rén. *or* tā gēn-wǒ bú-shr yí-'lù-de-rén. ‖**This kind of book doesn't sell.** 'jèy-jǔng-shū (*or* 'jèy-yàngr-de-shū, *or* 'jèy-jǔng-'yàngr-de-shū, *or* 'jèy-lèy-de-shū) 'mày bu-'dwō. ‖**This is a new kind of glass.** jèy shr̀ yì-jǔng-'shīn-bwō-li. ‖**What kind** (*species*) **of dog is he?** jèy-gěw shr̀ shéme-'jǔngr-de? *or* jèy shr̀ 'něy-jǔng-'gěw? *or meaning* **What is this kind of dog called?** 'jèy-jǔng-gěw jyàw 'shéme-míng-dz? ‖**I like all kinds of food.** 'gè-jǔng-'chř-shŕ wǒ 'dēw ày chř. *or expressed as* ‖**I like all foods that people eat.** 'fán-shr-'rén-chř-de wǒ 'dēw ày chř. ‖**He's an engineer or something of the kind.** tā shr̀ ge-gūng-chéng-'shŕ, yàw-'bú-shr-de-hwà yě shr̀ (dzwò-de) nèy-yí-'lèy-de-shr̀. ‖**So that's the kind of friend you are!** nǐ 'ywán-láy shr̀ °'nèm-yì-jǔng-de-'péng-yew-wa! *or* °'nèy-yàngr-de-'péng-yew-wa! *or* °'nèm-yàngr-de-yí-ge-'péng-yew-wa! ‖**I'll do nothing of the kind!** 'nèy-yàng-shèr 'wǒ tsáy bú-'gàn-ne! *or* wǒ 'jywé bú-'nèm-je! *or* 'wǒ tsáy bú-'nèm-je-ne! *or* wǒ 'pyān bú-'nèm-je! *or* wǒ 'jyew-shr bú-'nèm-je! ‖**She's a journal-**

ist of a kind. (*Sarcastic*) tā shr̀   m yì-'jǔng-de 'shīn-wén-j^u-'jě.

In kind (*in a similar way*) jàw-'yàngr. ‖**He answered the challenge in kind.** tā jàw-'yàngr 'hwéy-le yí-jywù. *But* ‖**Workers on farms here are not paid in money but in kind** (*in produce*). jèr-'dì-li-gù-de-rén bù-gěy 'gūng-chyán °gěy 'lyáng-shŕ. *or* °dì-li 'chū-shéme 'gěy-shéme.

Kind of yì-dyǎr *or* dyǎr. ‖**It's kind of lonesome here.** jèr yěw-(yì-)dyǎr 'mèn-de-hung. ‖**We're kind of busy right now.** wǒm 'jèy-hwer 'yěw dyǎr-'máng. ‖**Yes, kind of!** ěy, 'yěw nèm-yì-dyǎr!

KINDLY. *See* **KIND** *except for the following uses.* (*Please*) chǐng, láw-'jyà; (*see* **PLEASE** ‖**Kindly stop when your time is up.** 'dàw-le 'shŕ-hew jyèw chǐng °'tíng-ju. *or* °'bú-yàw wàng-shyà 'dzwò-le. ‖**Kindly mind your own business.** láw-'jyà, 'byé dwō gwǎn shyán-'shèr. *or expressed as* **I'll thank you to mind your own business** 'shyè-shye 'nín-na, 'byé dwō gwǎn shyán-'shèr. *or as* **Don't tire yourself out sticking your nose into other people's business.** nín 'shǎw gwǎn dyǎr-shyán-'shèr-ba, kàn 'lèy-'jaw.

Take kindly to 'shǐ-hwān; *or expressed as* **like to hear** ày 'tīng. ‖**He didn't take kindly to my advice.** wǒ-'chywàn-tā-de-hwà tā 'bú-dà °'shǐ-hwān. *or* °ày 'tīng.

KINDNESS. 'ēn-dyǎn *or* 'ēn (*grace, a literary term, but used of superiors or sarcastically*); *more commonly expressed indirectly with words meaning* **kind.** ‖**I can never forget your kindness,** nǐ dày-wǒ 'nèm hǎw (*or* nín-de-'ēn-dyǎn) wǒ 'yǔng-ywǎn wàng-bu-'lyǎy "**How can I ever repay you for such kindness?** nín dày-wǒ 'dzěm hǎw, wǒ dzěm 'bàw-dá nín-ne? ‖**Her kindness knows no bounds.** tā dày-'rén hǎw-dàw-'jyā-le. *or* tā 'hèw-dàw jí-le. *or* (*Sarcastic, a literary quotation*) tā 'jēn shr̀ 'tsź-háng pǔ-'dù-wa. ‖**Even this is an exceptional kindness from him.** jyèw 'jèy-yàngr dzày-ta 'yǐ-jīng shr̀ °'dày-rén tè-'byé 'hǎw-le. *or* °'dà-'dá-de kāy-'ēn-le. *or* °'tè-ēn-le. *or* (*Literary quotation*) °'ēn-chū-gé-'wày-le. ‖**I appreciate your kindness very much.** wǒ hěn 'gǎn-ji nǐ. *or* 'gǎn-shyè bú-'jìn. *or* 'jēn-shr fèy-'shīn-le. *or* dwō-'shyè, dwō-'shyè.

KISS. 'chīn-chin (*used especially of kissing children; public or indiscriminate kissing among adults, even as a merely friendly gesture or between relatives, is not generally approved in China*); chīn-'dzwěr *or* dzwō 'gwǎy-gway *or* jyē-'wèn (*said of both participants or of A and B, expressed as A gēn B*). ‖**When they kissed on the screen, someone whistled.** tām dzày dyàn-'yǐng-li °'chīn-dzwěr (*or* °'dzwō 'gwǎy-gway, *or* °jyē-'wèn) de-shŕ-hew, 'yěw-rén 'chwēy-le yì-shēng-'shàwr. ‖**Let me kiss you, you precious little thing.** (*Strictly confined to infants*) wǒ 'chīn-chin-nǐ, nǐ jèy-ge-shyǎw-bǎw-'bèr.

KITCHEN. 'chú-fáng. ‖The kitchen is large and clean. 'chú-fáng yèw 'dà ·yèw 'gān-jing. ‖From the kitchen window you can see the river. dǎ chū-'fáng-de-'chwāng-hu-nar kě-yi kàn-jyan 'hé. ‖Who is in charge of the school kitchen? shywé-'shyàw-li 'shéy gwǎn chú-'fáng?

KITTEN. shyǎw-'māw *or* shyǎw-'māwr.

KNEE. bwō-le-'gàr; 'shī-gày *or sometimes* 'chī-gày (*literary, but used technically as in medicine*). ‖My knee hurts. wǒ-bwō-le-'gàr 'téng. ‖I tore a hole in the knee of my pants. wǒ bǎ 'kù-dz dzày bwō-le-'gàr-nar gwà-le ge-'kěw-dz.

On one's knees *is expressed verbally as* kneel 'gwèy. ‖On your knees! 'gwèy-shya! ‖He was down on his knees begging. tā 'gwèy-je 'chyéw.

KNIFE. dāw *or* 'daw-dz. ‖Give me the big knife to cut the bread. gěy-wǒ 'dà-dāw láy chyē myàn-'bāw.

To knife ná 'dāw-dz lá. ‖He was knifed in a street fight. tā dzày 'jyē-shang-dǎ-'jyà jyàw-rén ná 'dāw-dz °'lá-le. *or meaning* and killed °'lá-sž-le.

KNOCK. (*Bump*) pèng; (*more violently; usually accidental*) jwàng. ‖Don't knock against the table. 'byé pèng 'jwō-dz. *or* 'byé pèng-jaw 'jwō-dz. *or* byé 'pèng-dzày 'jwō-dz-shang. *or sometimes* byé 'jwàng-dzày jwō-dz-shang. ‖He was knocked down by a car. tā jyàw chì-'chē °pèng-'dǎw-le. *or* °jwàng-'dǎw-le. ‖Be careful not to knock anything down. shyǎw-'shīn-je byé bǎ shéme-dūng-shi 'pèng-shya-chywu. ‖He knocked his head against the wall. tā-'téw °jwàng- (*or* °pèng-)dzày 'chyáng-shang-le.

(*Rap or tap*) chyāw; knock on a door chyāw-'mén *or* dǎ-'mén *or* jyàw-'mén (*especially of shouting to have a door opened, but may be confined to persistent knocking*). ‖Knock before you open the door. 'chyāw-chyaw (*or* 'chyāw-yi-shyar) °'mén dzày 'kāy. *or* °dzày kāy-'mén. ‖Someone is knocking on the door. 'yěw-rén chyāw-'mén-ne. *or* 'yěw-rén dǎ-'mén-ne. *or* 'yěw-rén jyàw-'mén-ne. ‖He broke the glass rod by knocking it on the rim of the cup. tā dzày wǎn-'byār-shang bǎ 'bwō-li-gwèr °chyāw-'dwàn-le-de. *or* °'chyāw-da-dwàn-le-de.

(*Strike or pound*) dzá; (*with sharp blows*) chyāw; (*with a hammer*) chwéy; (*punch or strike in order to break something from what it is fastened to*) dzáw; (*ram*) dǎw; (*hit, especially with a missile*) dǎ; (*with a hard sharp blow*) 'chyāw-da; *see also* HIT. ‖Knock the bottom out of the barrel. bǎ 'tǔng-de-'dyěr °'dzá-shya-chywu. *or* °'chyāw-shya-chywu; *or* °'chwéy-shya-chywu. *or* °'dǎw-shya-chywu. ‖Knock the box apart and burn it. bǎ shyá-dz °'dzá-kāy (*or* °dzá-'sǎn-le) shāw-'hwǒ. ‖They knocked all the legs off the table. tām bǎ jwō-dz-'twěr dēw °'dzáw-shya-chywu-le. *or* °'dzá-shya-chywu-le. *or* °'chyāw-da-shya-chywu-le. ‖The book fell from the shelf and knocked him on the

head. 'shū tsúng 'jyà-dz-shang 'dyàw-shya-lay, 'dzá-dzày tā-'téw-shang-le. ‖The bullet missed him and knocked a picture off the wall. chyāng-'dzěr méy-'dǎ-jaw tā, bǎ chyáng-shang-gwà-de-'hwàr dǎ-'dyàw-le.

To knock (*in a motor*) 'gāng-dēng, 'gwāng-dēng, 'gāng-dāng, 'gē-dēng; (*make a noise*) shyǎng. ‖Do you hear the knock in the motor? 'jī-chì jř °'gāng-dēng (*or* °'gwāng-dēng, *or* °'gāng-dāng, *or* °'gē-dēng-gē-dēng-de), 'tīng-jyàn-le-ma? ‖See what you can do to stop this motor from knocking. nǐ gěy 'shēw-shr-shēw-shr, byé jyàw 'jī-chì nèm °'shyǎng. *or* °'gāng-dēng-gāng-dēng-de. *or* °'gwāng-dēng-gwāng-dēng-de. *or* °'gāng-dāng-gāng-dāng-le. *or* °'gē-dēng-gē-dēng-de.

(*Criticize*) 'pī-píng. ‖They're always knocking the administration. tām lǎw 'pī-píng 'shyàn-jèng-'fǔ.

Knock around (*wander aimlessly*) gwàng. ‖I've been knocking around town for a couple of days. wǒ dzày-jèr 'gwàng-le lyǎng-sān-'tyān-le.

Knock *someone* cold bǎ . . . dǎ-'hwēn-gwo-chywu, bǎ . . . dǎ-'ywūn-gwo-chywu, bǎ . . . dǎ-'mēng-gwo-chywu. ‖The punch caught him on the jaw and knocked him cold. nèy-yì-'chywán dǎ-dzày tā-'shya-ba-'kér-shang, bǎ-tā °dǎ-'hwēn-gwo-chywu-le. *or* °dǎ-'ywūn-gwo-chywu-le. *or* °dǎ-'mēng-gwo-chywu-le. ‖He was knocked cold. tā gěy °dǎ-'hwēn-gwo-chywu-le. *or* °dǎ-'ywūn-gwo-chywu-le. *or* °dǎ-'mēng-gwo-chywu-le.

Knock down (*dismantle*) chāy. ‖Knock down the scaffolding. bǎ jyà-dz 'chāy-le.

Knock down (*sell at auction*) pāy-'mày. ‖He knocked down the painting for only a hundred dollars. nèy-'hwàr tā yì-'bǎy-kwày-chyán jyèw pāy-'mày-le.

Knock down (*reduce: of a price*) *is expressed as* reduce by *a certain amount* jyǎn *or* 'jyǎn-shyà-chywu; *or as* deduct *a certain amount* 'shǎw-yàw (*see* knock off *below*). ‖Can't you knock down the price a couple of dollars? 'jyà-chyán háy néng °'jyǎn jǐ-kwày-ma? *or* °'jyǎn-shyà jǐ-kwày-chywu-ma? *or* °'shǎw-yàw jǐ-kwǎy-ma?

Knock off (*deduct*) 'shǎw-yàw, jyǎn, 'jyǎn-shyà-chywu. ‖Knock a couple of dollars off the price and I'll take it. 'shǎw-yàw jǐ-kwày-chyán (*or* 'jyǎn jǐ-kwày-chyán, *or* 'jyǎn-shyà jǐ-kwày-chyán-chywu), wǒ jyèw 'mǎy.

Knock off (*stop work*). (*Not work any more*) bú-'dzwò-le; (*stop*) dǎ-'jù; (*leave*) dzěw; (*cease work, especially at the regular quitting time*) shyà-'gūng. ‖Let's knock off at five o'clock. dzám 'wǔ-dyǎn °jyèw 'dzěw-ba. *or* °jyèw byé-'dzwò-le. *or* °dǎ-'jù-ba. *or* °shyà-'gūng-ba.

Knock *someone* out (*hit into unconsciousness*). *See* Knock cold *above*.

Knock *someone* out (*exhaust*). Be knocked out lèy-'hwày-le *or* lèy-'pā-shya-le *or* méy-'jyèr-le. ‖He was knocked out after playing tennis for only a little while. tā dǎ 'wǎng-chyéwr dǎ-le yì-'hwěr jyèw °lèy-'hwày-le. *or* °lèy-'pā-shya-le. *or* °méy-'jyèr-le.

Knock together (*construct hastily*). ‖**Be knocked together** gày-de tǐng 'mǎ-hu-de *or* gày-de tǐng 'hánghu-de; (*boards taken and nailed up*) ná-'mù-tew-bǎr-°'dīng-da-shang-de. *or* °'dìng-da-shang-de. *or* °'dzáda-shang-de. ‖**That garage is just knocked together.** nèy-ge-'chē-fáng °gày-de tǐng 'mǎ-hu-de. *or* °bú-gwò-shr ná-'mù-tew-bǎr-'dīng-da-shang-de.

Knock the bottom out of. ‖**That knocked the bottom out of my plans.** wǒ-de-'jì-hwà dzèm-yì-láy °'chywán wán-le. *or* °mǎn-'nǐng-le. *or* °'chywán gěy twéy-'fān-le. *or* °'wán-chywán méy-'yùng-le. *or* °jěng-'gèr-de dzá-'gwò-le. *or* °'chywán-chéng-le pàw-'yǐng-le.

Knock someone for a loop. (*With charm: intentionally*) bǎ . . . 'mí-ju; (*unintentionally*) jyàw . . . jáw-'mí; **be knocked for a loop** gěy 'mí-jù-le *or* jáw-le 'mí-le (*mí in all of these expressions means* **to bewitch**). ‖**That gorgeous actress has knocked him for a loop.** nèy-ge-'pyàw-lyang-nywǔ-'shì-dz 'kě jyàw-tā jáw-le 'mí-le. ‖**He was knocked for a loop.** tā gěy 'mí-jù-le. *or* tā jáw-le 'mí-le.

Other expressions in English. ‖**I'll knock your block off.** wǒ bǎ nǐ-'nǎw-dày 'jyēw-shya⋁ay. ‖**They finally knocked some sense into his head.** 'jyē-gwò tām jyàw-tā 'míng-bay-gwo-lay-le.

KNOT. (*The place tied; especially a fastening*) kèwr; (*especially an obstruction, which may be a knot unintentionally tied, a knot tied to keep a rope from passing through a hole, or simply a bump in the rope caused by a fault in weaving*) 'gā-da *or* ¹gē-da *or* 'gē-de; **tie a knot** jì-'kèwr *or* jì 'gā-da *or* dǎ-'jyēr. ‖**Can you untie this knot?** jèy-ge-'kèwr nǐ jyě-de-'kāy-ma? ‖**Could you untie this knot for me?** láw-'jyà gěy bǎ jèy-'kèwr 'jyě-kāy. ‖**He knotted the rope securely.** tā bǎ 'shéng-dz jǐn-'jīn-de °jì-le ge-'kèwr. *or* °jì-le ge-'gā-da. *or* °dǎ-le ge-'jyēr. ‖**There are a lot of knots in this rope.** jèy-ge-'shéng-dz yěw 'hǎw-jǐ-ge-°'kèwr. *or* °¹'gā-da.

(*Hard mass, as in wood*) 'jyē-dz, 'gā-da (*see above*). ‖**I can't saw through this knot.** jèy-ge-'jyē-dz (*or* jèy-ge-'gā-da) wǒ 'jywù-bu-kāy.

(*Group*) dzwēy *or* chywún. ‖**A knot of people gathered around the accident.** chū-'shèr-de-nàr jywù-le °yì-'dzwēy-rén. *or* °yì-'chywún-rén.

(*Nautical miles per hour*) yì-'dyǎn-jūng . . . N (hǎy-)'lǐ (*with a verb of motion in the blank space*). ‖**This ship can make fifteen knots.** jèy-ge-'chwán yì-'dyǎn-jūng kě-yi ¹dzěw shŕ-'wǔ-(hǎy-)'lǐ.

KNOW. (*Be sure of or have knowledge about*) 'jŕ-dàw. ‖**I'm not guessing; I really know.** wǒ 'bú-shŕ 'tsāy; wǒ 'jēn 'jŕ-dàw. ‖**I know he's ill.** wǒ 'jŕ-dàw tā 'bìng-le. ‖**I knew something was wrong.** wǒ jyēw 'jŕ-dàw °chū-le dyǎr-'shèr. *or* °'yěw dyǎr-bú-'dwèy. ‖**Who knows?** shéy jŕ-'dàw-ne? ‖**Who else knows?** 'háy yěw-shéy jŕ-'dàw? ‖**That's a known fact.** nèy shŕ 'yǐ-jīng-'jŕ-dàw-de-shèr-le. *or* 'nèy-shèr 'yǐ-jīng 'jŕ-dàw shŕ 'jēn-de-le. ‖**Wait until all the facts of the case**

are known. děng 'àn-chíng dēw °'jŕ-dàw-le (*or expressed as* clear °'chīng-chu-le *or* °nèng 'míng-bay-le) dzày 'shwō. ‖**Not that I know of.** 'wǒ bù-jŕ-'dàw. *or expressed as* I haven't heard. 'méy-tīng-shwō.

(*Be skilled in: know how to, know*) hwèy; (*to have studied*) 'shywé-gwo; (*understand*) dǔng. ‖**He knows Arabic.** tā 'shywé-gwo (*or* tā dǔng, *or* tā hwèy, *or* tā hwèy shwō, *or* tā hwèy shyě) yǎ-lā-'bé-⋁ ɛ́n. ‖**I don't know how to drive a car.** wǒ ƀú-hwèy kāy-'chē. *or* wǒ méy-'shywé-gwo kāy-'chē.

(*Be acquainted with: be familiar with, well acquainted with*) 'rèn-shr, 'rèn-de, gēn . . . shéw, (*be friendly with*) gēn . . . yěw 'jyāw-chíng; (*be able to pick out*) kàn-de-chū-lay. ‖**Do you know him?** nǐ 'rèn-shr tā-ma? *or* nǐ 'rèn-de tā-ma? *or meaning* **Do you have any knowledge about him?** nǐ 'jŕ-dàw jèy-ge-rén-ma? *or* nǐ gēn-tā yěw 'jyāw-chíng-ma? *or* nǐ gēn-tā 'shéw-ma? ‖**I know him only by sight.** *is expressed as* I've only seen him to know (*be sure of*) who he is. wǒ bú-gwò 'kàn-jyàn tā jŕ-dàw tā shŕ-'shéy jyèw-shŕ-le. ‖**I know him only by name.** *is expressed as* I have only heard his name. wǒ bú-gwò 'tīng-ìyàn-gwo tā-de-'míng-dz. ‖**Do you know him well enough to speak to?** nǐ gēn-tā yěw tán-'hwà-de-'jyāw-chíng-ma? ‖**Do you know what that boat is over there?** nàr-nèy-ge-'chwán nǐ °'rèn-de-ma? *or* °'jŕ-dàw shŕ 'shéme-chwán-ma? ‖**Do you know a real ruby when you see one?** 'jēn-de-húng-bǎw-'shŕ nǐ °'kàn-de-chū-láy-ma? *or* °'rèn-de-chū-láy-ma? ‖**I don't know this character.** jèy-ge-'dž wǒ °bú-'rèn-shr. *or* °bú-'rèn-de. ‖**I wish I'd known you before.** wǒ 'jēn ywàn-yì dzǎw-jyěw 'rèn-shr-ni.

Know better than 'jŕ-dàw 'bù-néng (*followed by a verb*). ‖**He knew better than to tell his wife.** tā 'jŕ-dàw 'bù-néng gàw-su tā-'tày-tay. ‖**You ought to know better than that.** nǐ yīng-gāy 'jŕ-dàw 'bù-néng nèm-jꜟ.

In the know. ‖**He's in the know around there.** *is expressed as* They haven't concealed (anything) from him. tām 'méy-mán-je tā. *or as* They let him know everything. tām 'shéme dēw jyàw-tā 'jŕ-dàw.

You know (*comment added to a statement*) 'bú-shr-ma. ‖**She's going to have a baby, you know.** tā yěw-'ywùn-le, 'bú-shr-ma.

‖**What do you know?** *is expressed as* **Tell me all about everything.** yěw shéme-'shèr-ra, shwō-shwo wǒ 'tīng-ting.

‖**Whaddaya know!** (*Surprise*) ǎ? 'jywū-rán rú-'tsž! *or* (*Astonishment*) 'shéy shyǎng-de-'dàw?! *or* (*Confirmation*) ǎ? jēn jyèw 'nèm-je! *or* (*Pleasure*) 'jēn chǐ-'gwày.

Knowing (*giving the appearance of knowing all*). ‖**He gave her a knowing smile, as if to say, "I know all about it."** tā gēn-tā nèm yí-'shyàw, 'hǎw shyàng shŕ shwō, 'hm̀, wǒ 'dēw jŕ-dàw. ‖**His knowing smiles make his sister mad.** tā lǎw nèm 'shyàw, hǎw shyàng 'shéme dēw jŕ-dàw shŕ-de, jyàw tā-'mèy-mey hěn shēng-'chì.

KNOWLEDGE. *Expressed indirectly by verbs meaning to know; see* KNOW. ‖To the best of my knowledge, he didn't go. jywù 'wǒ-jr̄-dàw-de, tā 'méy-chywù. ‖Do you have any knowledge of this matter? 'jèy-shèr nǐ yì-'dyǎr yě bù-jr̄-'dàw-ma? ‖He has a tremendous amount of knowledge. tā-'jr̄-dàw-de hěn 'dwō. *or* tā-'jr̄-dàw-de hěn 'shēn. *or* tā 'shywé-wèn hěn 'shēn.

L

LABOR. (*Work or effort*) gūng; (*stressing the activity*) 'gūng-dzwò; (*a job*) hwór; (*handwork*) 'shěw-gūng. ‖Mining is very hard labor. kāy-'kwàng shr̀ hěn-°'kǔ- (*or* °'jùng-)de-'gūng-dzwò. *or* 'kwàng-gūng gūng-dzwò hěn °'kǔ-de. *or* chr̄-'lì. *or expressed as* Being a miner is very hard. dzwò 'kwàng-kūng hěn °'láw-kǔ. *or* °chr̄-'lì. ‖He was sentenced to three years' hard labor. fá-ta dzwò 'sān-nyán-'kǔ-gūng. ‖How much did you pay for the labor on this, and how much for the materials? jèy-yàngr-'dǔng-shi-de-'shěw-gūng-chyán nǐ gěy-le 'dwō-shaw, 'lyàw-dz-chyán 'dwō-shaw? *or* jèy-jyàn-hwór 'gūng ˉ shr̀ 'dwō-shǎw (-chyán), 'lyàw-dz shr̀ 'dwō-shǎw(-chyán)? ‖This kind of labor is inhuman. 'jèy-jǔng-'hwór 'bú-shr 'rén-gàn-de.

(*Organized workers or pertaining to workers*) 'láw-gūng. ‖Labor favors an eight-hour day. 'láw-gūng (-fāng-myan) 'dzàn-chéng 'měy-tyān °'gūng-dzwò 'bā-shyǎw-shŕ. *or* °dzwò bā-dyǎn-'jūng-de-'gūng. ‖He became a very powerful labor leader. tā chéng-le yíge-'hěn-yěw-'shr̀-lì-de-'láw-gūng-'lǐng-shyèw. ‖Do you know the labor laws? nǐ 'dǔng-de láw-gūng-'fǎ-ma?

(*Exert effort*) kǔ-'gàn; mày 'lì-chì; (*struggle*) fèn-'dèw. ‖He labored under difficulties. tā dzày hěn-'kwèn-nán-de-'hwán-jìng-lǐ °kǔ-'gàn. *or* °mày 'lì-chì. *or* °fèn-'dèw. ‖He labored hard on it. 'jèy-shèr tā-dzwò-de hěn mày 'lì-chì. *or* wèy 'jèy-shèr tā 'jēn-shr kǔ-'gàn láy-je.

(*To elaborate*). ‖Don't labor the point. byé 'láw chyúng 'dāw-daw jèy-'yì-dyǎn. *or* 'byé jìng-dzày jèy-'yì-dyǎn-shang chyúng 'dāw-daw.

(*In childbirth*). To labor *or* be in labor shēng 'háy-dz, 'shēng-chǎn, 'fēn-myǎn (*literary*); labor 'shēng-chǎn-de-shŕ-hew, 'fēn-myǎn-de-shŕ-hew. ‖She was in labor for nine hours. tā shēng 'háy-dz (*or* tā-'shēng-chǎn, *or* tā-'fēn-myǎn) tsúng 'fā-dùng dàw 'shēng-shya-lay 'jīng gwò-le 'jyěw-ge-jūng-'téw.

Be labored (*of breathing*) fèy-'jìn (*require strength*). ‖His breathing is labored. tā chwàn-'chyèr tǐng fèy-'jìn.

LACK, LACKING. (*Be somewhat deficient, be somewhat deficient in*) 'chà-dyar, 'chyàn-dyar, *or* 'chywē-dyar; (*not have, be entirely lacking in*) 'méy-yěw; (*be short of*) dwǎn; (*be not enough; said of the thing lacked*) bú-'gèw; (*be little; said of the thing lacked*) (hěn) 'shǎw; (*be deficient in strength; said of the thing lacked*) chà-'jìn; *also some indirect expressions.* ‖He lacks the courage of his convictions. tā chyàn-dyar (*or* tā chywē-dyar, *or* tā chà-dyar) 'jr̄-yán-bú-'hwèy-de-'jīng-shen. *or expressed as* When he has opinions he doesn't much dare to speak them out. tā 'yěw-le °'jú-yì (*or* °'jyàn-jyě)bú-dà gǎn 'shwō-chū-lay. ‖He lacks common sense. tā-'rén-chíng-'shr̀-gù 'dǔng-de hěn 'shǎw. *or* tā-'rén-chíng-'shr̀-gù-'jr̄-daw-de bú-'gèw *or* tā 'rén-chíng-'shr̀-gù-shang °chyàn-dyar ('gūng-fu). *or* °chywē-dyar 'gūng-fu. *or* °'chà-dyar ('gūng-fu). ('gūng-fu *in these cases refers to the time spent in acquiring common sense*.) ‖He lacks tact. tā 'yìng-fu-rén-shang °chà-dyar ('gūng-fu). *or* °chywē-dyar 'gūng-fu. *or* °chyàn-dyar ('gūng-fu). *or* tā-'yìng-fu-rén-de-'gūng-fu °chà-dyar. *or* °chyàn-dyar. *or* °bú-'gèw. ‖His lack of knowledge was obvious. 'nèy-ge-rén yí-'kàn jyèw kě-yǐ 'jr̄-dàw tā °méy shéme-'shywé-wén. *or* °méy shéme-'jr̄-shŕ. *or* °dwǎn 'jyàn-shŕ. ‖Nothing was lacking to make the party a success. jèy-ge-'yàn-hwèy 'chéw-bèy-de hěn 'jēw-dàw, bù-'chywē-shéme. ‖The area was lacking in defenses. 'jèy-yí-dày-de-fáng-'ywù-gūng-'shr̀ °bú-'gèw. *or* °chà-'jìn. ‖He lacks emotion. *is expressed as* He has no human feelings (*a literary quotation*). 'tā-jèy-rén 'má-mù-bù-'rén. *or as* He is emotionally very cool. tā 'gǎn-chíng-shang hěn 'lěng. *or as* His heart is harsh. tā-rén-'shīn-cháng hěn 'yìng. *or as* He has no emotions. tā méy-yěw 'gǎn-chíng. *or as* He is entirely lacking in emotion. tā yì-'dyǎr-gǎn-chíng yě méy-'yěw. ‖For lack of anywhere else to stay, I have to live in a hotel. 'yīn-wèy 'méy-yěw byé-de-'dì-fang kě 'jù, wǒ 'jr̄ hǎw jù lywǔ-'gwǎn.

LADY. (*Woman*) 'tày-tay (*married*); 'fū-ren (*married; a somewhat politer term*); young lady 'shyáw-jye *or* (*in Peiping*) 'gū-nyang (*apparently unmarried*); nyán-'chīng-de-'tày-tay (*married*); (*as a term of address*) 'nywǔ-shr̀; ladies (*married and unmarried*) 'shyáw-jye 'tày-tay-men. ‖Is that lady at the door your mother? dzày mén-'kěwr-de-nèy-wèy-lǎw-'tày-tay shr̀ nǐ-'mǔ-chin-ma? ‖Do you wish to speak to the lady of the house? nǐ yàw gēn (jèy-jyār-de-) 'tày-tay shwō-'hwà-ma? *or* nǐ yàw jyàn wǒm-'tày-tay-ma? ‖Let the ladies go first. chǐng 'shyáw-jye 'tày-tay-men 'shyān dzěw. *But* ‖Ladies and gentlemen! jū-'wèy-láy-'bīn.

Ladies' room 'nywǔ-tsè-'swǒ.

Well-bred woman *is expressed indirectly or by* 'dà-jyā-gwēy-shyèw (*literary*). ‖She acts like a lady. *is expressed as* She very much understands etiquette. tā 'hěn dǔng 'lǐ-jyé. *or* tā yěw 'dà-jyā-gwēy-shyèw-de-'fēng-dù.

LAKE. hú. ‖I want to row around the lake. wǒ yàw wéy-je 'hú °'hwá (or °'yéw) yì-dzāwr.

    The Great Lakes 'běy-měy-jēw-wǔ-dà-'hú.

LAME. (Crippled) 'twěy (or 'jyǎw) yěw dyǎr-°'chywé or °'gwǎy-le-gwǎy-le-de; or (expressed as a noun; a cripple) 'chywé-dz or (clubfoot) dyān-'jyǎwr. ‖The little boy is lame. shyǎw-'hár shr̀ ge-'chywé-dz. or shyǎw-'hár shr̀ ge-dyān-'jyǎwr. or shyǎw-hár-'twěy (or shyǎw-hár-'jyǎw) yěw dyǎr-°'chywé. or °'gwǎy-le-gwǎy-le-de.

    To (make) lame for life jyàw . . . 'tsán-fèy yí-'bèy-dz; (jyàw . . .) làw ge-yí-'bèy-dz-de-°'tsán-jí or °chywé-'twěy; jyàw . . . °twěy (or °jyǎw) chywé yí-'bèy-dz. ‖The fall lamed him for life. tā-nèy-yì-'shwāy jyèw-ta 'tsán-fèy-le yí-'bèy-dz.

    (Sore and temporarily unable to move comfortably) twěy-'swān-de (or twěy-'téng-de) dēw dzěw-bú-'dùng-le; (dzěw-'lù) yì-'chywé-yì-'gwǎy-de; dzěw-'lù t̆ĭng fèy-'jyèr; yí-mày-'bùr jyèw 'téng. ‖I was lame after the horseback ride. chí-mǎ yǐ-'hèw wǒ-twěy-°'swān-de (or °'téng-de) dēw dzěw-bú-'dùng-le. or wǒ chí-wán-le 'mǎ, °(dzěw-'lù) yì-'chywé-yì-'gwǎy-de. or °dzěw-'lù t̆ĭng fèy-'jyèr. or °yí-mày-'bùr jyèw 'téng.

    (Poor). ‖That's a lame excuse. nèy-'lǐ-yéw tày 'chyān-chyǎng. or nèm shwō shéy 'shìn-na? ‖That's a lame excuse for giving up. 'yīn-wey °'nèy-ge (or °'nèm-je) jyèw bú-'gàn-le, shéy 'shìn-ne?

LAMP. dēng; kerosene lamp 'méy-yéw-dēng; oil lamp 'yéw-dēng; gas lamp 'méy-chì-dēng; safety lamp bǎw-'shyǎn-dēng; electric lamp 'dyàn-dēng. ‖Let's light the lamp. 'dyǎn-dēng-ba. ‖Light the lamp. bǎ-dēng 'dyǎn-jáw. ‖Blow out the lamp. bǎ-dēng 'chwēy-le. ‖Turn up the lamp. bǎ-dēng nyǎn-'dà-le. or (the lampwick) bǎ dēng-'nyǎn-dz nyǎn-'dà-le. ‖Turn down the lamp. bǎ-dēng nyǎn-'shyǎw-le. or bǎ dēng-'nyǎn-dz nyǎn-'shyǎw-le. ‖Turn on the lamp (of an electric lamp). bǎ-dēng 'kāy-kay. ‖Turn off the lamp. bǎ-dēng 'gwān-shang.

LAND. dì; (real estate) 'dì-chǎn. ‖He inherited a great deal of land. tā 'chéng-shew-le shywǔ-dwō-°'dì-chǎn. or °'dì.

    (Soil) tǔ or dì. ‖The land here is too poor for farming. jèr-de-'tǔ jùng-'dì bú-gèw 'féy-de. or jèr-de-'dì bù-néng jùng 'dūng-shi.

    (Nation) gwó. Native land or fatherland 'dzǔ-gwó; (from the viewpoint of one living in it) běn-'shyāng; (from the viewpoint of one living away from it) gù-'shyāng. ‖He had a great love for his native land. tā hěn 'ày tā-'dzǔ-gwó. or tā dwèy 'dzǔ-gwó yí-'shyàng hěn rè-'shìn. or (If away from it) tā hěn 'lyéw-lyàn 'gù-shyāng. or (If living in it) tā dwèy běn-'shyāng-de-'shr̀ hěn rè-'shìn.

    (Shore) àn; (land in contrast to water) lù-'dì. ‖When do you expect to reach land? nǐ shwō shéme-'shr̀-hew kě-yǐ °'kàw-'àn? or °jyàn-je lù-'dì?

    (Rural territory) núng-'tswēn. ‖He always wanted

to get back to the land. tā dzǔng shyǎng hwéy-dàw núng-'tswēn-chywu. or expressed as He's always wanted to return to the happiness of country life. tā dzǔng 'pàn-je néng 'chúng shyǎng 'tyán-ywán-jr̄-'lè.

    (Come to earth) làw, jyàng-'lè, lè-'dì. ‖About a hundred planes take off and land here every day. měy-tyān yěw yì-'bǎy-láy-jyà-fēy-'jī dzày-jèr °'chǐ-ya-'làw-de. or °yěw-de chǐ-'fēy yěw-de jyàng-'lè. or °yěw-de chǐ-'fēy yěw-de lè-'dì. ‖The pilot landed the plane at night. jyà-shr̀-'ywán (or kāy-fēy-'jī-de) dzày 'yè-li bǎ fēy-'jī °'làw-dzày 'dì-shang-de. or °jyàng-'lè-de. or °'lè-dì-de.

    (Fall) dyàw (drop); shwāy (slip or stumble); dzwò (sit down). ‖The car landed in the ditch. chì-'chē dyàw 'gēw-li-le. ‖Too many of my golf balls have landed in that pond. wǒ-de-gǎw-ěr-fū-'chyéwr bù-jr̄-dàw yěw 'dwō-shǎw dēw dyàw-dzày nèy-shwěy-'kēng-li-le. ‖He slipped on the ice and landed with a thud. tā dzày 'bīng-shàng yì-'hwá jyèw pā-'jī-de yí-shyàr °'shwāy-nàr-le. or °'dzwò-nàr-le.

    (Catch; of fish) dēy, dáy, 'dyàw-shang-lay. ‖You should have seen the fish I almost landed. wǒ-chà-'dyǎr-méy-'dēy-je- (or wǒ chà-'dyǎr-méy-'dyàw-shang-lay-)de-nèy-tyáw-'ywú, °kě-'shr̀ nǐ méy-'kàn-jyàn. or °nǐ 'jen yīng-dāng 'chyáw-jyàn-lay-je.

    (Of a contract) bàn-'chéng, shwō-'chéng. ‖I landed a big contract today. wǒ jyèr °bàn-'chéng-le (or °shwō-'chéng-le) yì-jwāng-dà-'mǎy-may.

    (Of a job) 'jǎw-jáw. ‖He finally landed a job. 'jyě-gwǒ tā 'jǎw-jáw-le ge-'shèr dzwò.

LANGUAGE. 'ywǔ-yán (somewhat literary); hwà or shwō-de-'hwà (spoken language); 'wén-dz or (in combinations) wén (written language). ‖He studied the science of language. tā 'nyàn-gwo (or tā 'shywé-gwo, or tā 'yán-jyew-gwo) 'ywǔ-yán-'shywé. ‖Some nations have several spoken languages, and some have no written language. yěw 'jǐ-gwó-li yěw hǎw-jǐ-jǔng-'ywǔ-yán; yěw 'jǐ-gwó méy-yěw 'wén-dz. ‖Language is one of the things that distinguish human beings from animals. 'rén-lèy-gēn-'chín-shèw-bù-túng-de-'dì-fang yěw 'yì-dyǎr jyèw-shr̀ rén °néng shwō-'hwà. or °yěw 'ywǔ-yán. ‖This is a textbook on the Japanese language, spoken and written. jèy-běn-jyàw-ke-'shū jyǎng-de shr̀ °r̀-běn-'hwà gēn r̀-běn-'wén. or °dzěme shwō r̀-běn-'hwà gēn dzěme shyě r̀-běn-'wén. ‖What languages do you know? nǐ dēw tūng (or hwèy) 'něy-jǐ-'gwó-de-°'wén-dz? or °'hwà? ‖The baby speaks a language all her own. jèy-háy-dz-shwō-de-'hwà 'méy-rén 'dǔng.

    (Way of speaking, words used) hwà; use bad language may be expressed by constructions with hwà, or also as sā-'tswēn (of vulgar language) or mà-'jyē or mà-'rén (of profane or abusive language). ‖Try not to use bad language here. dzày-jèr néng bù-shwō °'bù-hǎw-'tīng-de-hwà (or °'dzāng-hwà, or °'tǔ-hwà. or °nán-'tīng-de-hwà), jyèw 'byé shwō. or dzày-jèr lyéw-'shén byé °sā-'tswēn. or °mà-'jyē. or °mà-'rén.

LARGE. dà (*of size*) ; dwō *or* bù-'shǎw *or* shyē (*a large amount or number of*). ‖This room is not large enough. jèy-'wū-dz bú-gèw-'dà-de. ‖I want a larger desk. wǒ yàw ge-'dà-dyǎr-de-shū-'jwōr. ‖This is the largest building in town. jèy shř jèr-'dzwèy-dà-de-'lèw(-le). ‖He wants a larger share. tā shyǎng 'dwō yàw-dyar. ‖He wants a larger share of responsibility. tā shyǎng 'dwō gwǎn-dyǎr 'shèr. ‖A large crowd gathered to watch the fire. chǐ-'hwǒ-de-nàr jywù-le °'hǎw-shyē-rén (or °hěn-'dwō-rén, or °yí-dà-'chywún-rén) dzày-nàr 'kàn. ‖Large quantities of food and ammunition can be shipped by plane. hěn-'dwō-de (or bù-'shǎw-de)-'lyáng-shr hé jywūn-'hwǒ dēw kě-yǐ yùng fēy-'jī láy 'ywùn. ‖He spent a large part of the time talking about politics. tā yùng-le 'hǎw-shyē-gūng-fu tán (or tā yùng-le 'hǎw-shyē shŕ-hew tán, or tā tán-le 'hǎw-bàn-tyān-de, or tā tán-le yí-dà-bàn-tyān-de) 'jèng-jř-shang-de-'shèr. ‖To a large extent we'll have to raise our own food. yí-'dà-bàn-de- (or 'hǎw-shyē-, or hěn-'dwō-de-)'chř-shŕ děy wǒm-'dž-jǐ láy °'bàn. or °'jùng.

At large *is expressed as* taking it easy outside the law (*literary*) 'shyāw-yáw-fǎ-'wày; *or as* to have escaped pǎw-le. ‖The thief has been at large for two days. shyǎw-tēwr 'shyāw-yáw-fǎ-'wày yěw 'lyǎng-tyān-le. or dzéy 'pǎw-le lyǎng-'tyān-le.

At large (*as a whole*) chywán. ‖The country at large is interested in the problem. 'chywán-gwó 'dēw hěn 'jù-yı jèy-ge-'wèn-tí. ‖He's a congressman-at-large. tā-jèy-ge 'shyà-yì-ywàn-yì-'ywán shř 'dày-byǎw-chywán-'shěng-de.

LAST. (*Final*) dzwèy-'hèw(-de); mwò *or* mwò-'lyǎwr (-de); 'dàw-shǔ dì-'yī (*first counting backwards*) ; *or expressed indirectly as* there is only 'jř yěw, *or as* and then no more dzày 'méy-yěw-le, *etc.* ‖I spent my last dollar for lunch. wǒ bǎ °dzwèy-'hěw- (or °mwò-'lyǎwr-de-, or °'mwò-)yí-kwày-'chyán 'hwā-dzày wǔ-'fàn-shang-le. ‖The last battle of the war was fought here. dzwèy-'hèw- (or 'mwò-, or mwò-'lyǎwr-de-) yí-'jàng shř dzày-'jèr-dǎ-de. ‖He was the last to leave. tā shř °dzwèy-mwò-mwò-'lyǎwr- (or °dzwèy-mwò-'lyǎwr-, or °dzwèy-mwò-mwo-lā-'lyǎwr-, or °'mwò-yí-ge-, or °mwò-'lyǎwr-de-yí-ge-)dzěw-de. ‖He's the last one left now. *is expressed as* There only remains he alone. 'jyèw shèng-shya tā-'yí-ge-rén-le. ‖She said she wouldn't marry him if he were the last man on earth. tā shwō, jyèw-shr 'shř-jyè-shang jř (or jyèw) 'shèng tā-'yí-ge-nán-rén tā yě-shr bú-'jyà-ta. ‖He was last. tā shř 'mwò-yí-ge. or tā shř dzwèy-'hèw-de-yí-ge. ‖He came last. tā dzwèy-'hèw dàw-de. or tā shř dzwèy-'hèw-de-yí-ge-dàw-de. or tā shř 'mwò-yí-ge-dàw-de. or (On a list or in turn) tā dzày dzwèy-mwò-'lyǎwr-nar. or tā dzày 'dàw-shǔ-dì-'yī-nar. ‖These were his last words before he died. jè shř tā-°'méy-'sž-yǐ-'chyán-dzwèy-'hèw-de-jǐ jywù-'hwà. or (*literary*) °'lín-jūng-'yí-yán. ‖This is my last word. *is expressed as* After speaking this time I'll say no more. 'jèy-tsž shwō-le yí-'hèw wǒ jyèw 'dzày bù-shwō-le.

‖This is your last chance. jèy shř nǐ-'dzwèy-hèw-de-'jī-hwey-le. *or expressed as* After this time there is no more such chance. 'jèy-tsž yǐ-'hèw 'dzày méy-yěw jèm-ge-'jī-hwey-le. *or expressed as* There is only this chance. 'jř yěw 'jèy-tsž-'jī-hwey-le. ‖She believed to the last that her husband would be saved. tā yì-'jř dàw-'lyǎwr (or, to death tā yì-'jř dàw-'sž) háy 'yǐ-wéy tā-'jàng-fù yěw-'jyèwr-ne. ‖That was the last straw. *is expressed as* That is simply impossible to bear any more. nà 'jyán-jř shř °'bù-néng (or °'wú-kě) dzày 'rěn-le.

(*Most recent(ly)*) dzwèy-'jìn; 'shàng(-yī-) (*of events, times*) ; 'chyán(-yī) (*the former*) ; jèy (*this or these last*). Last night dzwér (or 'dzwó-tyān) 'wǎn-shang; last week 'shàng-shīng-'chī; last month 'shàng-ywè; last year 'chywù-nyán; night before last 'chyán-tyān 'wǎn-shang; week before last dà-'shàng-shīng-'chī or 'shàng-shang-shīng-'chī; month before last 'chyán lyǎng-ge-'ywè or dà-'shàng-ywè; year before last 'chyán-nyán. ‖When were you in Chungking last? nǐ-dzwèy-'jìn shř shéme-shŕ-hew dzày chúng-'chìng-lay-je? or nǐ 'shàng-yí-tsž dzày chúng-'chìng shř 'shéme-shŕ-hew? ‖I went shopping last night. wǒ dzwér 'wǎn-shang mǎy 'dūng-shi chywù-le. ‖Did you see the name of the last station? nǐ 'kàn-jyàn 'shàng-yí-jàn jyàw shéme-'míng-dz-le-ma? ‖The weather has been beautiful for the last few weeks. dzwèy-'jìn- (or jèy-)jǐ-ge-lǐ-'bày tyār 'tày hǎw-le. ‖This is the last word. (*Most recent style*) jèy-shr 'dzwèy-jìn-de-'shř-yang. or jèy-shr 'dzwèy-shīn-de-'shř-yang. or (*Best style*) jèy-shr 'dzwèy-hǎw-de-'shř-yang.

At last kě; dàw-'lyǎwr; 'jyē-gwò (*the final result*) ; dzwèy-'hèw. ‖At last we found the place. wǒm 'kě (or wǒm dàw-'lyǎwr, or wǒm 'jyē-gwò, or wǒm dzwèy-'hèw) bǎ nèy-ge-'dì-fang 'jǎw-jáw-le.

The last of. ‖You haven't heard the last of it yet. *is expressed as* This isn't finished yet. jèy-shèr háy méy-'wán-ne. ‖You'll never hear the last of it. *is expressed as* You wait and see, it will never end. nǐ 'chyáw-je-ba, 'chyě méy-'wán-ne. ‖I hope we've seen the last of her. *is expressed as* I hope this is the last time we see her. 'shī-wàng jèy-shr 'mwò-(yí-)tsž chyáw-jyàn tā. *or as* I hope that hereafter she won't trouble us any more. 'shī-wàng yǐ-'hèw tā 'dzày bù-láy 'má-fan dzám-le. *or as* I hope from now on we won't have any more dealings with her. 'shī-wang tsúng-'tsž dzám 'dzày bù-gēn-ta dǎ 'jyāw-day-le.

(*Most unlikely*). ‖That was the last thing I expected him to do. *is expressed as* I thought he'd never be able to do that. wǒ 'yǐ-wey tā 'jywé-bu-hwèy 'gàn-chū 'nèy-jǔng-shř-lay-ne. *or as* I never thought he'd be able to do that. wǒ 'méy-shyǎng-'dàw tā hwèy gàn-chū 'nèy-jǔng-shř-lay.

To last *is expressed by any verb followed by an expression of time, especially* yùng (*be used or usable, use*) ; jīn-'yùng (*stand use*) ; dǐng or 'jř-chr (*hold out*) ; last long *may also be expressed simply by* jyèw or cháng; not last long *may also be expressed as* one moment, then it's past yì-'hwěr jyèw 'gwò-le *or as one* moment, then it's finished yì-'hwěr jyèw 'wán-le. ‖**How long does this ride last?** 'jèy-tàng-'chē děy 'dzwò 'dwō-shǎw-shŕ-hew? ‖**It lasted an hour.** yěw yì̀-dyǎn-'jūng (nèm-'jyěw). ‖**The battle lasted five days.** nèy-jàng dǎ-le 'wǔ-tyǎn. ‖**Do you think you can last another mile?** nǐ jywé-je ᵇháy néng 'dīng (*or* °néng dzày 'jŕ-chr, *or* ᵇháy néng 'pǎw, *of running*) yì-lǐ-'dìma? ‖**It doesn't last very long.** nèy bú-hwèy 'jyěw-de. *or* nèy bú-hwèy 'cháng-de. *or* nèy yì-'hwěr jyèw 'gwò-le. *or* (*Of the effect of medicine*) yàw-de 'lìlyang °bú-hwèy 'jyěw-de. *or* °bú-hwèy 'cháng-de. *or* °yì-'hwěr jyèw 'gwò-le. *or* (*Of pain*) 'téng yì-ḣwěr jyèw 'bù-téng-le. *or* (*Of someone's anger*) tā shēng-'chì yì-'hwěr jyèw 'wán. *etc.* ‖**This chair won't last very long.** jèy-bǎ-'yǐ-dz 'bú-hwèy °jīn-'yung-de. *or* °yùng-de 'cháng-de. *or* °yùng-de 'jyěw-de. *or* °'yùng-bu-lyǎw jǐ-tyǎr jyèw hwèy 'hwày-de. ‖**I didn't think my money would last me until today.** wǒ méy-shyř ng-'dàw wǒ-de-'chyán néng °'yùng (*or* °'hwā)-dàw 'jyēr-ge. ‖**This butter will have to last us a week.** jèy-dyǎr-hwáng-'yéw dzám děy chŕ 'yí-ge-lǐ-'bày.

LATE. (*Far advanced in time*) wǎn; **late in the day** 'hèw-bàn-shǎngr *or* 'hèw-bàn-ṯyān; hwáng-'hwēn-de-shŕ-hew *or* bāng-'hēy-chyar *or* bāng-'hēy-de-shŕ-hew (*dusk, late afternoon*); 'wǎn-shang (*evening*); **late at night** *or* **at a late hour** 'shēn-jing-bàn-'yè-de; **late in life** 'hǎw-dà-'swèy-shur-lᵉ **late summer** (*etc.*) 'shyà-tyān (*etc.*) -kwày-'wán-ᵉ-ue-shŕ-hew; **late show** dzwèy-'hèw-yì-'chǎng *or* (*night show*) 'yè-chǎng; **stay up late** dāy-de 'wǎn *or* áw-'yè (*watch out the night*). ‖**Its getting awfully late.** (tyān) tày 'wǎn-le. ‖**He keeps late hours.** *or* **He goes to bed late.** *is expressed as* **He goes to sleep late.** tā-'shwèy-de hěn 'wǎn. ‖**He sleeps late.** *is expressed as* **He gets up late.** tā-'chǐ-de hěn 'wǎn. ‖**Should we come at eight P.M. or later?** wǒm shř 'yīng-dāng 'wǎn-shang 'bā-dyǎn-jūng dàw, háy-shr dzày 'wǎn-dyar? ‖**It was late in the day when she came.** tā shř °'hèw-bàn-shǎngr (*or* °'hèw-bàn-tyān, *or* °hwáng-'hwēn-de-shŕ-hew, *or* °bāng-'hēy-chyar, *or* °bāng-'hēy-de-shŕ-hew, *or* °'wǎn-shang) dàw-de. ‖**The mountains are beautiful in the late afternoon.** shān dzày °hwáng-'hwēn-de-shŕ-hew (*or* °bāng-'hēy-de-shŕ-hew, *or* °bāng-'hēy-chyar) hěn hǎw 'kàn. ‖**You shouldn't have waked them up at such a late hour.** dzèm 'wǎn-le (*or* dzèm 'shēn-jing-bàn-'yè-de) nǐ 'bù-gāy bǎ rén-jya jyàw-'shǐng-le-de. ‖**He learned to read and write late in life.** tā 'hǎw-dà-'swèy-shur-le tsáy shywé-de 'nyàn-shū-shyě-'dz-de. ‖**I always take my vacation in late summer.** wǒ 'lǎw-shř dzày 'shyà-tyān-kwày-'wán-le-de-shŕ-hew shyē-'jyà. ‖**It was the late show he went to.** tā kàn-de shř °dzwèy-'hèw-yì-'chǎng. *or* °'yè-chǎng. ‖**Don't stay up too late.** byé áw-'yè. *or* byé áw-'yèr. *or* byé dāy-de tày 'wǎn-le.

(*Tardy*) wǎn; chŕ (*used of arriving, with* dàw, *especially in school*); wù-le jūng-'dyǎr-le (*miss the*

hour); bù-néng àn 'shŕ-hew (dàw). ‖**I'll be late if I don't take a taxi.** yàw 'bú-dzwò chì-'chē chywù, wǒ jyèw °'hwèy 'wù-le-jūng-'dyǎr-de. *or* °'wù-le jūng-'dyǎr-le. *or* °'bù-néng àn 'shŕ-hew 'dàw-le. *or* °'wǎn-le. *or* (*For. work*) °'bù-néng àn 'shŕ-hew dàw 'bān-le. *or* (*For work or school*) °chŕ 'dàw-le. ‖**Don't be late at the theater.** tīng-'shì (*or* kàn-'shì) byé °chywù 'wǎn-le. *or* °'wǎn dàw.

Of late *or* **lately** 'jìn-láy. ‖**The news has been better of late.** 'jìn-lay 'shyāw-shi 'hǎw-dyǎr-le.

Latest dzwèy-'hèw-de (*final*); dzwèy-'jìn-de (*most recent*); dzwèy-'shīn-de (*newest*). ‖**You can read the latest news in the evening paper.** nǐ kě-yǐ dzày 'wǎn-bàw-shang 'kàn-dàw dzwèy-°'hèw- (*or* °'jìn-, *or* °'shīn-)de-'shyāw-shi.

At the latest 'dzwèy-wǎn *or* 'jŕ-wǎn bú-gwò. ‖**You said you'd be here by five at the latest.** nǐ 'dz̀-jǐ shwō-de °'dzwèy-wǎn (*or* °'jŕ-dwō bú-gwò) 'wǔ-dyǎn jwēn 'dàw-jèr.

(*Recently deceased*) 'gāng-chywù-'shř-de. ‖**Your late Secretary of War was a fine man.** 'gwèy-gwó-'gāng-chywù-'shř-de-'lù-jywūn-bù-bù-'jǎng 'jēn shř ge-'hǎw-rén.

LATTER. dì-'èr(-ge), 'hèw-yī(-ge), 'hèw-tew-de; hèw *in some other combinations.* ‖**Of the two reports, I prefer the latter.** jèy-lyǎ-bàw-'gàw-li, wǒ 'jywé-de dì-'èr-ge 'hǎw-dyǎr. ‖**I said the latter, not the former.** wǒ-'shwō-de shř °dì-'èr-ge, bú-shr dì-'yí-ge. *or* °'hèw-yí-ge, bú-shr 'chyán-yí-ge. *or* °'hèw-tew-de-nèy-ge, bú-shr 'chyán-tew-de-nèy-ge. ‖**He was very successful in the latter part of his life.** tā 'hèw-bàn-bèy-dz tǐng dé-'yì.

LAUGH. shyàw (*show mirth*); **have a laugh** shyàw yí-'jèn. ‖**We laughed at each other.** wǒm 'bǐ-tsz dwèy shyàw-le yí-'jèn. ‖**We had a good laugh over the matter.** wǒm jywé-de nèy-jyàn-shř hěn kě-'shyàw. *or* 'nèy-shèr jyàw-wǒm °'dà-shyàw-le yí-'jèn. *or* °'hūng-táng-'dà-shyàw.

(*Sound of laughter*) 'shyàw-de-shēng-yin. ‖**He has a hearty laugh.** tā-'shyàw-de-shēng-yin hěn-'dà.

Laugh at (*make fun of*) 'shyàw-hwà. ‖**He was always afraid that people were laughing at him.** tā 'dzǔng yì-wéy 'byé-rén dzày-nàr 'shyàw-hwà-ta.

Laugh off yí-'shyàw jyèw 'swàn-le *or* yí-'shyàw jyèw 'gwò-chywu-le. ‖**When we found a mistake, he tried to laugh it off.** wǒm jǎw-jaw-le ge-'tswòr, tā shyǎng nèm yí-'shyàw jyèw °'swàn-le. *or* °'gwò-chywu-le.

Laugh out of. ‖**We laughed him out of his bad temper.** tā shēng-'chì jyàw-wǒm 'lyán-shwō-dày-'shyàw-de 'hūng-gwò-chywu-le.

No laughing matter. ‖**It's not a laughing matter.** yì-'dyǎr yě 'bù kě-'shyàw. *or* 'bú-shr nàw-je-'wár-de.

LAUGHTER. shyàw-de-'shēngr. (*sound of laughing*) *or* 'shyàw-de (*action of laughing*). ‖**We heard loud laughter behind us. wǒm 'tīng-jyàn 'hèw-byār yěw 'hā-hā-dà-'shyàw-de-'shēngr. ‖She shook with silent laughter. tā-'shyàw-de bù-chū-'shēngr, kě-shr jf !yáw-hwang 'shēn-dz.

LAUNDRY. (*Place where clothes are washed*) shǐ-yī-'dyàn or shǐ-yī(-shang)-'fáng or shǐ-'yī(-shang)-de-nàr or shǐ-'yī(-shang)-de-dì-fang or (*Peiping*) shǐ-yī-'dzwō. ‖These clothes are ready to go to the laundry. jèy-shyē-'yī-fu gāy sùng-dàw shǐ-yī-'dyàn chywù-le. ‖There's a lack of help in the laundry. shǐ-yī-'fáng-lí chywē-'rén.

(*Clothes washed*) 'shǐ-de-yī-fu or 'shǐ-de-dūng-shi. ‖My laundry just came back. wǒ ná-chywu-'shǐ-de-'yī-fu 'gāng hwéy-lay.

(*Clothes to be washed*) gāy-'shǐ-de-yī-fu or gāy-'shǐ-de-dūng-shi. ‖I've got to take my laundry out. wǒ kě děy bǎ wǒ-gāy-'shǐ-de-'dūng-shi 'sùng-chū-chywù-le.

LAW. (*Legal institutions*) 'fǎ-lywù; 'fǎ-gwēy (*laws and regulations*); 'fǎ-dyǎn (*legal code*); fǎ after one-syllable verbs and in many combinations. Civil law 'mín-fǎ; criminal law 'shíng-fǎ; national law or law of the land 'gwó-fǎ or gwó-jyā-'fǎ-lywù; international law 'gwó-jì-fǎ or 'gwó-jì-gūng-fǎ; maritime law 'hǎy-shang-fǎ; military law 'jywūn-fǎ. ‖You'll have to obey the law. nǐ děy shěw-'fǎ. ‖You can't expect to break a law and escape the consequences. nǐ béng hyǎng °'fàn-le-fǎ (or °'wéy-le-fǎ) háy néng 'shyàw-°áw fǎ-'wày. ‖He'll be punished according to the law. i-'dìng yàw yī-'fǎ °bàn-ta. or °chǔ-fen-ta. ‖It's against the law to park here. dzày-jèr tíng-'chē °fàn-'fǎ. or °wéy-'fǎ. ‖Is there a law against speeding? *is expressed as* Is speeding against the law? pǎw-'chē fàn-'fǎ-ma? or as Is it forbidden to speed? shr̀ 'bù-shywǔ pǎw-'chē-ma? or as Is there a law prohibiting driving a car too fast? shr̀ yěw 'fǎ-lywù 'jǐn-jr̀ bǎ-chē kāy-de tày 'kwày-ma? ‖He is studying law now. tā shyàn-dzày nyàn (or shywé) °'fǎ-lywù-ne. or °'fǎ-kē-ne. ‖Who makes the laws in this country? jèy-gwó-de-°'fǎ-lywù (or °'fǎ-gwēy, or °'fǎ-dyǎn) yéw-'shéy láy 'dìng? or expressed as The legislative power of this country is in whose hands? jèy-gwó-de-'lì-fǎ-chywán dzày 'shéy-shěw-li? ‖He took the law into his own hands. *is expressed as* He didn't follow the law (or He didn't go through official procedure), (but) himself punished people. tā bù-yī-'fǎ (or tā bù-jīng-'gwān), 'dž-ji jyèw °fá-'rén. or (*Took revenge*) °bàw-'chéw. ‖My brother is practicing law. is expressed as My brother is a lawyer. wǒ-'gē-ge dāng lywù-'shr̄-ne.

(*Statement of invariable relationships*) lǐ. Natural law or laws of nature lǐ or tyān-'lǐ (*especially in relation to man or life*), 'dž-rán-lywù (*in physics and other sciences*); law of averages lǐ; law of gravity *is expressed as* earth core has attractive force, that theory 'dì-shīn yěw 'shí-lì nèm-yì-'shwō or as the attractive force of the earth's core 'dì-shīn-de-'shí-lì. ‖That's

against the laws of nature. nèy jyǎn-'jf shr̀ bù-hé °'lǐ. or °tyān-'lǐ. or °'dž-rán-lywù. ‖According to the laws of nature (or of averages), this is bound to happen. jàw-'lǐ shwō, yí-'dìng hwèy 'dzèm-je-de. ‖Haven't you ever heard of the law of gravity? nǐ 'nán-dàw 'méy-tīng-jyàn-gwo 'dì-shīn yěw 'shī-lì nèm yì-'shwō-ma?

Lay down the law (gěy . . .) 'dìng ge-'gwēy-jywu, jyàw . . . shěw (*establish a rule and make sor one obey*); (gēn . . .) 'ywē-fǎ-sān-'jāng (*literary quotation, meaning literally to make three stipulations*). ‖He laid down the law to them. tā gěy-tam 'dìng-le ge-'gwēy-jywu, jyàw-tam 'shěw. ‖My father laid down the law to me last night. wǒm-lǎw-'yé-dz dzwér 'wǎn-shang gēn-wo 'ywē-fǎ-sān-'jāng.

(*Authority*). ‖His word is law around here. or He lays down the law around here. *is expressed as* Everybody has to listen to his word here. dzày-'jèr tā-de-hwà 'shéy dēw děy 'tīng. or as He dictates the affairs of this place. tā 'dú-dwàn (or tā 'wǔ-dwàn) jèy-ge-dì-fang-de-'shr̀-ching.

LAWYER. lywù-'shr̄. ‖Try to find a good lawyer to handle the case. shyǎng-'fár jǎw yí-ge-yěw-'míng-de-lywù-'shr̄ láy 'dǎ jèy-ge-'gwān-sz. ‖My brother is a lawyer. wǒ-'gē-ge dāng lywù-'shr̄-ne.

LAY (LAID). (*Put*) gē; fàng; bǎy (*arrange, put in proper place*). ‖Lay the book here. bǎ-shū gē-'jèr. or bǎ-shū fàng-'jèr. or bǎ-shū bǎy-'jèr. ‖Lay the baby on the bed gently. bǎ shyàw-'hár chīng-'chyēngr-de °fàng-dzày (or °gē-dzày) 'chwáng-shang. ‖All your clothes are laid out on the bed. nǐ-de-'yī-fu dēw °gē (-dzày) (or °fàng, or °fàng-dzày) 'chwáng-shang-le. ‖Lay the board down flat. bǎ 'bǎn-dz °fàng-'píng-le. or °gē-'píng-le. or °'píng-je fàng-shya. or °'píng-je gē-shya. ‖Lay those books down. (*Flat, not standing on end*) bǎ 'nèy-shyē-shū °fàng-'píng-le. or, etc. after °, as in preceding sentence. or (*Set them down, any way*) °'fàng-shya. or °'gē-shya.

(*Spread out*) pū. (*Unfold or unroll and spread out*) 'pū-kāy, or 'tān-kāy, or 'dǎ-kāy, or (*to full length*) 'pū-jǎn-kāy; (*spread out to cover*) méng or jàw. ‖There was a Persian rug laid on the floor. dì-shang pū-je 'bwō-sz-dì-'tǎn. ‖The floor was laid with linoleum. dì-shang pū-je chī-'bù-dì-'tǎn. ‖The painted scroll was laid out on the floor for him to examine. nèy-jywǎn-dz-'hwàr °pū-dzày 'dì-shang (or °dzày 'dì-shang 'pū-kāy, or °dzày 'dì-shang 'dǎ-kāy, or °dzày 'dì-shang 'tān-kāy) gěy-ta 'kàn. ‖She laid a damp cloth over the bowl. tā 'ná yí-kwày-'shr̄-bù °'méng-dzày (or °'jàw-dzày) 'wǎn-shang. ‖A satin cover was laid on the table. jwēr-shang °pū-je (or °méng-je, or °jàw-je) yí-kwày-'dwàn-dz. ‖He laid a cement path across his garden. tā dzày 'ywàn-dz-li tsúng 'jèy-téwr dàw 'nèy-téwr pū-le yì-tyáw-'yáng-hwēy-'lù. ‖Laying concrete is backbreaking work. pū 'yáng-hwēy (or pū 'sān-hé-tǔ) 'lèy-sz 'rén.

Lay down (*of weapons*) 'rēng-shya, 'dyēw-shya, 'lyàw-shya (*throw down*). ‖He laid down his weapons and ran. tā bǎ 'jyā-hwo 'rēng-shya jyèw 'pǎw-le.

(*Of bricks*) chì; *but to lay bricks in a pile with a design* mǎ. ‖He didn't lay the bricks carefully. tā 'méy-bǎ-jwān chì-'hǎw-lew. ‖He laid the bricks in a neat pile. tā bǎ-jwān mǎ-'hǎw-le.

(*Of tiles*) ān, shàng, chì. ‖He didn't lay the tiles evenly. tā 'méy-bǎ-wǎ ān-°'jěng-chi-lew. *or* °'chí-lew.

(*Of a cornerstone*) ān *or* lì. ‖The cornerstone was laid in 1900. chyáng-'jyàwr-de-nèy-kwày-'shŕ-tew shŕ 'yī-jyěw-líng-'líng-nyán-°ān-de. *or* °'lì-de.

(*Of a keel*) ān. ‖It took only two months to build this ship, from the time the keel was laid until it was launched. nèy-chwán tsǔng ān lúng-'gǔ dàw shyà-'shwěy yí-gùng 'lyǎng-ge-ywè jyèw dzàw-'chéng-le.

(*Of a foundation*) dǎ, dzá, gày, *or* shyēw; (*figuratively*) dǎ *or* lì. ‖The foundation was laid forty years ago. 'dì-jī shŕ 'sz-shŕ-nyán-'chyán-°dǎ-de. *or* °'dzá-de. *or* °'gày-de. *or* °shyēw-de. ‖He laid a solid foundation for the business. tā bǎ 'mǎy-may-de-gēn-jī °'dǎ-de (*or* °'lì-de) hěn 'láw-kaw. *or* °dǎ-de (*or* °'lì-de) hén 'jyē-shŕ.

(*Of dust*) 'yā-shya-chywu. ‖The rain laid the dust. 'ywǔ bǎ 'chén-tǔ 'yā-shya-chywu-le.

(*Of eggs*) shyà. ‖This hen lays a lot of eggs. jèy-ge-mǔ-'jī shyà-'dàn tǐng 'dwō.

(*Of a wager or money in a wager*). *See* **BET**.

(*Of a tax*) dìng (*fix*); jyā (*add*); shēw (*put*); jyàw-rén shàng *or* yàw-rén shàng (*make people pay*). ‖They laid a heavy tax on wool. tām gěy máw-'rúng °dìng-le (*or* °jyā-le) hěn-jùng-de-'shwèy. ‖They laid a tax on everything. tām 'shéme dēw °jyàw-rén shàng-'shwèy. *or* °yàw-rén shàng-'shwèy. *or* °shēw-'shwèy.

(*Of a trap*) ān; shè (*of a large or complicated device*); shyà (*of a small device*); 'shyà-shang *or* 'ān-shang (*only of a net* wǎng); (*figuratively, of a scheme*) dìng *or* 'ān-pay *or in some cases* 'shè. ‖They laid a trap for that tiger. tām ān-le (*or* tām shè-le) °ge-shyàn-'jǐng (*a pit; or* °ge-'lúng-dz, *a cage*) yàw dǎy nèy-jŕ-'lǎw-hǔ. ‖We've laid a trap for that woodpecker. wǒm yǐ-jīng °'shyà-shang wǎng-le (*a net; or* °'ān-shang wǎng-le, *or* °'shyà-le ge-'wǎng, *or* °ān-le ge-'wǎng, *or* °shyà-le ge-'tàwr *a loop, or* °ān-le ge-'tàwr, *or* °shyà-le ge-'jyā-dz *a snapping trap, or* °ān-le ge-'jyā-dz) yàw 'dǎy nèy-ge-'bēn-der-'mù. ‖They laid a trap for you. tām 'shè-le ge-'chywān-tàwr (*or* tām 'shè-le ge-'jì-tse, *or* tām 'dìng-le ge-'chywān-tàwr, *or* tām 'dìng-le ge-'jì-tse, *or* tām 'dìng-le ge-'jāwr, *or* tām 'dìng-le ge-'gwěy-jāwr, *or use* 'ān-pay *instead of* 'dìng *anywhere*) yàw °'hày-ni (*to hurt you, physically or otherwise*). *or* °jyàw-ni shàng-'dàng (*to take you in*). *or* °jyàw-ni chŕ-'kwēy (*to make you lose*). *or more commonly expressed as* They intend to hurt you. tām yàw (shyàn-) 'hày-ni.

To lay *a corpse in a* **coffin** lyàn *or* rù-'lyàn. ‖The body was already laid in a coffin. 'shŕ-shew yǐ-jīng rù-'lyàn-le.

To lay the blame on gwày, 'mán-ywàn, bǎ-tswèr twey-dàw … shēn-shang. ‖Don't lay the blame on me. byé gwày-'wǒ-ya. *or* byé 'mán-ywàn 'wǒ-ya. *or expressed as* I can't be blamed. 'gwày-bu-jaw 'wǒ-ya. *or* 'mán-ywàn-bu-jáw 'wǒ-ya. *or as* It wasn't my doing. méy 'wǒ-de-shèr-ra. *or* byé bǎ-tswèr twey-dàw 'wǒ-shēn-shang-nga.

To lay claim to. ‖You'd better lay claim to the estate while you can. háy bú-chèn-je 'jèy-shŕ-hew 'gǎn-kwày 'shēng-míng nèy-fèr-'chǎn-yè °nǐ yěw 'chywán-láy-'chéng-jì? (*of inheritance rights*). *or* °shŕ 'nǐ-de? (*of ownership*).

To lay emphasis on 'jù-jùng, 'jyǎng-jyew, dzày … tǐng °jù-'yì *or* °'jyǎng-jyew *or* °jáw-'yì. ‖They lay great emphasis on sports at this school. tām jèy-ge-shywé-shyàw °hěn 'jù-jūng 'ywùn-dùng. *or* °hěn 'jyǎng-jyew 'ywùn-dùng. *or* °dzày ywùn-dùng-shang tǐng jù-'yì (*etc.*).

To lay plans 'dǎ-swàn, 'jì-hwà, 'swàn-ji, dìng 'jì-hwà, shyǎng 'fá-dz. ‖They laid their plans carefully, but still failed. tām-'dǎ-swàn-de (*or* tām-'jì-hwà-de, *or* tām-'swàn-ji-de, *or* tām-dìng-de-'jì-hwa, *or* tām-shyǎng-de-'fá-dz) hěn 'jēw-daw, bú-gwo 'jyē-gwǒ 'háy-shr bù-'shíng.

To lay a scene *somewhere*. ‖The scene of his last play is laid abroad. *is expressed as* The background (*or* The scenery) of his last play is abroad. tā-dzwèy-'jìn-nèy-chù-'shì °'yùng-de-'bèy-jǐng (*or* °chywǔ-'jǐng, *or* °chywǔ-'tsáy) shŕ dzày wàȳ-'yáng. *or as* His last play enacts a foreign incident. tā dzwèy-jìn-nèy-chù-'shì yǎn-de shŕ 'wày-gwo-shèr.

Lay aside *or* lay away. (*Of an object*) 'gē-shya *or* 'fàng-shya; (*of a piece of work*) 'gē-shya, 'gē-je, 'fàng-shya, 'fàng-je, 'lyéw-shya, 'lyéw-je, 'lyàw-shya, *or* 'lyàw-je; (*of something for future use*) tswén(-je), 'tswén-chi-lay, 'shēw-chi-lay, 'lyéw-je, *or* (*of money only*) 'jī-shywu. (*See also* Lay up, *below, and* Put aside *under* PUT.) ‖Lay aside your book and listen to me. 'gē-shya (*or* 'fàng-shya) shū tǐng-wo shwō-'hwà. ‖If you can't do it now, lay it aside and do it later. yàw-shr 'yì-shŕ 'bù-néng 'dzwò jyèw 'lyéw-je děng yǐ-'hèw dzày shwō-ba. ‖He laid aside a good sum of money. tā 'tswén-le (*or* tā 'tswén-je, *or* tā 'jī-shywu)-bù-shǎw-de-'chyán. ‖Lay that aside against an emergency. bǎ nèy-ge °'tswén-chǐ-lay lyéw-je (*or* °'tswén-chi-lay děng, *or* °'shēw-chǐ-lay lyéw-je, *or* °'shēw-chǐ-lay děng, *or* °'lyéw-je děng) yěw-'shŕ-de-shŕ-hew yùng-ba.

Lay *something* before *someone* bǎ … 'tí-chu-lay (jyàw … *or* dà-jyā) 'tǎw-lwèn. ‖The chairman laid the plan before us. jǔ-'shí bǎ nèy-ge-'bàn-fǎ 'tí-chu-lay (jyàw-wǒm, *or* dà-jyā) 'tǎw-lwèn.

Lay for *someone* dīng. ‖They're laying for him. tām dzày-nàr 'dīng-je tā-ne.

603

Lay a hand on 'jān-yi-jān, 'pèng-yi-pèng, 'āy-yi-āy, 'dùng-yi-dùng, 'mwō-yi-mwō. ‖**Don't you dare lay a hand on that child!** nǐ gǎn 'jān-yi-jān nèy-ge-'háy-dz-de!

Lay one's hand on (*be able to find*) néng 'jǎw, néng 'ná-lay, 'jǎw-de-jǎw, 'jwā-de-jù, 'ná-de-jù; yěw-'fár. ‖**I think I can lay my hands on those papers right away.** wǒ shyǎng wǒ lì-'shŕ néng bǎ nèy-shyē-'wén-jyàn °'jǎw-je. *or* °'ná-lay. ‖**The trouble is that you can't lay your hand on a thing to prove that he did it.** 'wèn-tí jyèw-shr °'méy-fár láy jèng-míng shř tā-'gàn-de. *or* °'jǎw-bu-jǎw (*or* °'jwā-bu-jù, *or* °'há-bu-jù) yì-dyǎr-'jèng-jywu láy jèng-míng shř tā-'gàn-de.

Lay hold of *or* **lay hands on** 'jyēw-ju, 'jwā-ju, 'dzwàn-ju, 'lā-ju. ‖**He laid hold of him.** tā bǎ-ta 'jyēw-ju-le. *See also* **Take hold of.**

Lay into *someone* bǎ . . . gěy 'dzèw. ‖**They laid into him as though they'd kill him.** tām bǎ-ta gěy 'dzèw-de gēn yàw bǎ-ta gěy 'dzèw-sž shř-de.

Lay off *an employee* kāy, tsáy, sàn, 'dǎ-fa-'dzěw. ‖**They laid off ten men today.** tām jīn-tyan °'kāy-le (*or* °'tsáy-le, *or* °'sàn-le, *or* °'dǎ-fa-'dzěw-le) 'shŕ-ge-rén. ‖**He got laid off.** tā (jyàw rén-jyā) gěy °'kāy-le. *or* °'tsáy-le. *or* °'sàn-le. *or expressed as* **He lost his job.** tā-shèr °'dyēw-le. *or* °'dyàw-le. *or* °'shyà-lay-le.

Lay open. ‖**The blow laid open his skull.** nèy-yì-shyàr °'bǎ tā-'téw gěy 'dǎ-pwò-le. *or* (*Peiping*) °'bǎ-tā gěy kāy-'pyáwr-le. ‖**Eventually the whole scandal was laid wide open.** dàw-'lyǎwr nèy-jyàn-°'chěw-shèr (*or* °'dyēw-'rén-de-shèr) dà-jyā-'hwěr 'dēw jř-dàw-le. *or* °'chěw-shèr (*or* °'dyēw-'rén-de-shèr) 'wán-chywán gūng-'kāy-le.

Lay *someone* **out cold.** bǎ . . . gěy dǎ-°'mēn- (*or* °'ywūn, *or* °'mēng-, *or* °'hwēn-)gwò-chywu. ‖**That sock on the jaw laid him out cold.** sāy-'bāng-dz-shang nèy-yì-'chywán bǎ-ta gěy dǎ-'mēn-gwò-chywu-le.

Lay *something* **to** *someone('s account)* shwō shř . . .-de (*with the person and the action in the blank*). ‖**The theft was laid to him.** shwō shř 'tā-tēw-de.

Lay *something* **to** *a cause* shwō . . . shř 'yīn-wey . . . . ‖**If he loses all his money I'll lay it to his drinking.** rè-shr tā bǎ tā-de-'chyán dēw 'hwā-le de-hwà, wǒ jyèw shwō 'wán-chywán shř 'yīn-wey tā hē-'jyěw.

Lay up (*store away*) 'shēw-chi-lay, 'lyéw-chi-lay, 'tswén-chi-lay; *see also* **Lay aside** *above*. ‖**We have a lot of vegetables laid up for the winter.** wǒm 'shēw-chi bù-'shǎw-de-chīng-'tsày-lay °'wèy-de (*or* °'wèy-le) 'dūng-tyan chŕ. *or* °'hǎw gwò-'dūng.

Be laid up (*sick*) bìng; (*sick in bed*) bìng- (*or* tǎng-)dzày 'chwáng-shang. ‖**He's been laid up with a cold all week.** tā shāng-'fēng °'bìng-le yí-ge-lǐ-'bày. *or* °'bìng- (*or* °'tǎng-)dzày 'chwáng-shang yí-ge-lǐ-'bày-le.

Lay waste *is expressed by resultative compounds whose second element is* hwěy *or* hwày, *or by* bǎ . . . hwěy-le. ‖**The whole region was laid waste by the**

storm. 'jèy-yí-dày 'wán-chywán jyàw-fēng gěy gwā-°'hwěy-le. *or* °'hwày-le. ‖**The war laid waste many large cities.** 'jèy-tsž-'jàn-shř bǎ 'hǎw-shyē-'dà-chéng dēw 'hwěy-le.

Lay down the law. *See* **LAW.**

Lay down one's life jywān-'chywū, shī-'shēng, jìn-'jūng. ‖**He laid down his life for his country.** tā wèy-'gwó jywān-'chywū.

Lay in a supply of . . . mǎy dyǎr . . . tswén-je (*for other forms instead of* tswén-je, *see* **Lay aside,** *above*). ‖**We'd better lay in a supply of rice.** dzám mǎy dyǎr-'mǐ tswén-je tsáy 'dwèy.

Lay it on thick. ‖**Don't you think he was laying it on a bit thick when he was describing that wonderful job of his?** shř-bu-shř (*or* nǐ 'jywé-de-bu-jywé-de) tā shwō tā-'dž-jǐ-dzwò-de-'shř °de-shŕ-hew 'chwēy-de tày 'lì-hay-le? *or* °'dzèm hǎw 'nèm hǎw-de, 'shwō-de yěw dyǎr-gwò-'hwǒr? *or* °'dzèm hǎw 'nèm hǎw-de, 'shwō-de yěw dyǎr-gwò-'fèn? ‖**Aren't you laying it on a little too thick?** nǐ 'wèy-myǎn chwēy-de yěw dyǎr-°'gwò-'fèn-le-ba. *or* °'gwò-'hwǒr-le-ba. *or* °'tày-'lì-hay-le-ba. *or* nǐ 'wèy-myǎn shwō-de yěw dyǎr-gwò-'fèn-le-ba (*etc., as above*). *or* nǐ 'wèy-myǎn 'gwò-shèn chí-'tsž-le (*literary allusion*). *or* (*Meaning* **Aren't you praising me too much?**) 'gwò-jyǎng, 'gwò-jyǎng. *or* 'bù-gǎn-dāng, 'bù-gǎn-dāng. *or* 'nèm shwō jyàw-wo 'tày nán-yǐ-wéy-'chíng-le.

Lay on the table (*in parliamentary procedure*). ‖**His motion was laid on the table.** (*Temporarily filed for future action*) tā-tí-de-!yì-àn 'jàn-shŕ °'tswén-àn. *or* (*Temporarily not put to a vote*) °'bú-fù 'byǎw-jywé.

The lay of the land (*literally*) 'dì-shang-de-'yàng-dz, 'shíng-shr̀, dì-'shíng. ‖**From this hill you can see the lay of the land.** tsúng jèy-'shān-shang 'kě-yǐ 'kàn-jyàn sž-jēw-wéy-°'dì-shang-de-'yàng-dz. *or* °de-'shíng-shr̀. *or* °'de-dì-'shíng. (*Figuratively*) ‖**I'd like to get the lay of the land around here before I start work.** wǒ shyǎng 'shyān jŕ-dàw °'jèr shř dzěm hwéy-'shèr (*or* °'jèy-kwàr-dà-'gày-de-'chíng-shing) dzày chǐ-'téwr.

LAZY. lǎn. ‖**I'm too lazy to get up.** (*Out of bed*) wǒ 'lǎn-de 'chǐ-láy. (*From elsewhere*) wǒ 'lǎn-de 'dùng-tán. ‖**Aren't you being a bit too lazy?** nǐ 'wèy-myǎn tày 'lǎn-dyǎr-le-ba. ‖**You can't help being lazy in this hot weather.** 'jèm-rè-de-tyār, rén dž-'rán fā-'lǎn. ‖**It's a very lazy way of doing things.** 'nèm-je jyàn-'jŕ shř tēw-°'lǎn. *or* °'lǎr. ‖**This** (*the way I'm doing it*) **is the lazy man's way.** wǒ-jèy shř 'lǎn-rén-de-'lǎn-fá-dz.

LEAD (LED). (*Guide*) lǐng (*conduct, or lead by the hand*); dày (*conduct*); chyān (*with a rope*); lā *or* jwày *or* dèn (*pull with force; see* **PULL**). ‖**Please lead us to the U. S. Consulate.** chǐng bǎ-wǒm °'dày- (*or* °'lǐng-)dàw 'měy-gwo-'lǐng-shř-'gwǎn-chywu. ‖**He led the people onward.** tā (dzày 'chyán-tew) 'lǐng-je 'rén-mín chyán-'jìn. ‖**He led us on a little further.** tā lǐng-je (*or* tā dày-je) wǒm 'yèw wàng-chyán 'dzěw-le-dyar. ‖He led the child across the street by the hand. tā ná-'shěw lǐng-je shyǎw-hár gwò-'jyē. ‖He led the horse to the stable. tā bǎ-'mǎ chyán-dàw mǎ-'hàw-chywu-le. ‖The dog led us to his master. nèy-tyáw-'gěw bǎ-wom lǐng-dàw tā-'jǔ-rén-nàr-chywu-le. *or expressed as* We followed the dog and found his master. wǒm gēn-je nèy-tyáw-'gěw dzěw, jyèw bǎ tā-'jǔ-rén 'jàw-jaw-le.

(*Be at the front of*) dzày (. . .) 'chyán-tew lǐng-je. ‖The general was leading the parade. 'jyāng-jywun dzày 'dwèy-wu-'chyán-tew lǐng-je.

Lead the way *or* **take the lead** 'shyān dzěw (*go first*) ; dzày 'chyán-tew lǐng-je; lǐng-'téwr (*be the leader*) ; 'téw-chyán dày-'lù (*literary quotation*). ‖You lead the way. chǐng nǐ 'shyān dzěw. *or* chǐng dzày 'chyán-tew 'lǐng-je. *or* nǐ 'téw-chyán dày-'lù. ‖The guide should take the lead and direct us. dày-'lù-de (*or* lǐng-'lù-de) 'yīng-dāng dzày 'chyán-tew °'jāng-lwo-je-dyǎr. *or* °'jāng-le-je-dyǎr. *or* °'jàw-ying-je-dyǎr. *or use* 'téw-le (*or* 'téw-li) *in place of* chyán-tew. ‖When we are together he always takes the lead. wǒm dzày yí-'kwàr de-shǐ-hew, 'lǎw shǐ tā lǐng-'téwr.

Follow one's lead 'gēn-je (*followed by a person and a verb of action*) ; (*of an example*) jàw-je . . . -de-'bàn-fa (*followed by a verb of action*), *or expressed as* see someone do something, *also do it* thus kàn . . . yě nème . . . ; (*of directions*) tīng . . . de-°'hwà. *or* °'jǐr-hwēy. *or* °'dyàw-dùng. ‖We followed his lead and entered by the window. wǒm 'gēn-je tā (shywé), 'yě dǎ 'chwāng-hu jìn-chywu-de. *or* wǒm jàw-je 'tā-de-bàn-fa, 'yě dǎ 'chwāng-hu jìn-chywu-de. *or* wǒm kàn 'tā dǎ chwāng-hu jìn-chywu-de, 'yě nèm jìn-chywu-le. ‖They followed his lead in voicing opposition to my plan. tām 'gēn-je tā, (*or* tām tǐng 'tā-de-°'hwà, *or* °'jǐr-hwēy, *or* °'dyàw-dùng,) 'yě fǎn-dwèy-chǐ 'wǒ-de-'bàn-fa-lay-le. ‖They always follow his lead. tām 'lǎw 'gēn-je tā 'dzěw. *or* (*Imitate him*) tām 'lǎw gēn-ta 'shywé. *or* (*Of directions*) tām 'lǎw tīng tā-de-°'hwà. *or* °'jǐr-hwēy. *or* °'dyàw-dùng. *or* (*Of example*) tām 'lǎw °jàw-je 'tā-de-bàn-fa láy 'bàn. *or* °kàn-je 'tā dzěm-je tām 'yě dzěm-je.

(*Conduct; in music*) lǐng. ‖He led them in singing. tā 'lǐng-je tām 'chàng.

(*Be ahead in a contest*) dzày 'téw-li *or* dzày 'chyán-tew (*in a race*) ; yíng (*by points in a game*) ; dwō (*by votes in an election*). ‖Our horse is leading, but only by a neck. wǒm-de-'mǎ dzày 'téw-li, bú-gwò shyǎng-'chà jǐr yěw yì-'dyǎr. ‖Our team is leading by seven points. wǒm-jèy-dwèy 'yíng-je 'chī-fēr-ne. ‖He's leading (*or* He's in the lead) by 2,000 votes. tā bǐ 'nèy-ge-rén dwō 'lyǎng-chyān-'pyàw. ‖How much of a lead (*in the election*) does he have now? tā 'shyàn-dzày dé-de-'pyàw-shu dwō 'dwō-shaw?

(*Of a road, etc.*) tūng (*go through*). ‖This road leads to the bridge. 'jèy-tyáw-lù tūng-dàw 'chyáw-nar. ‖Where does that road lead? 'nèy-tyáw-lù tūng-'nǎr? ‖It leads to Rome. tūng 'lwó-mǎ. *But* ‖This road leads to a dead end (*literally and figuratively*) *is expressed as* If you follow this road, somewhere along the way it doesn't go through. dzěw 'jèy-tyáw-lù 'dzěw-láy dzěw-'chywù jyèw bù-'tūng-le. *or as* The other end of this road is a blind alley. 'jèy-tyáw-lù-'nèy-téwr shǐ ge-'sž-hú-'tùngr.

(*In cards*) (shyān) chū-'páy (*put out a card*), *or* (shyān) chū *followed by the name of a card or suit.* ‖Who leads? gǎy-'shéy (shyān) chū-'páy-ya? ‖Why did you lead spades? nǐ wèy-'shéme chū hēy-'téwr-ne?

(*Clue*) 'shyàn-swǒ; (*suggested route*) 'mén-lù. ‖The thief hasn't been caught yet, but the police have some leads. dzéy háy méy-dǎy-'jáw-ne, bú-gwò jǐng-chá yěw dyǎr-'shyàn-swǒ. ‖When I was looking for a job, he gave me a lead. wǒ jǎw-'shèr de-shǐ-w, tā °'jǐr-dyan gěy-wo (*or* °gěy-le-wo) yí-ge-'mén-lù.

(*In drama*) 'jǔ-jyǎwr. ‖She had the lead in the play. tā chywù (*or* dzwò, *or* dāng, *or* shǐ) nèy-'shì-li-de-'jǔ-jyǎwr.

Lead *a certain kind of* **life** 'gwò-de(-ř-dz) . . .; (*as a way of making a living*) dzwò-de-'shǐ. . . . ‖He's leading a quiet life. tā-shyàn-dzày-'gwò-de(-ř-dz) hěn 'ān-shyán. ‖He leads an exciting life. tā-dzwò-de-'shǐ hěn 'jǐn-jāng. *or* tā-'gwò-de(-ř-dz) °hěn 'rè-naw. *or* °yěw-'shēng-yěw-'sè-de.

Lead astray (*by setting example, perhaps unintentionally*) yǐn-'hwày; (*by teaching*) dày-'hwày *or* jyāw-'hwày *or* lǐng-'hwày. ‖He led the child astray. tā bǎ háy-dz dày-'hwày-le.

Lead *someone* **on** (*get someone to do or say something*) 'yǐn-dèw. ‖He's leading her on. tā-nàr 'yǐn-dèw tā-ne. *or* (*To say something*) tā-nàr 'yǐn-dèw-je tā shwō-ne. *or* (*To do something*) tā-nàr 'yǐn-dèw-je tā jyàw-ta 'nèm-je-ne.

Lead to (*result in, or guide to, indirectly*). ‖That plan is going to lead to disaster. jàw-je 'nèy-ge-fá-dz 'bàn, jwěn 'dzz ‖The information supplied by that woman led to his hiding place. ná nèy-ge-'nywǔ-rén-gěy-de-'shyèr dàng 'shyàn-swǒ jyèw bǎ tā-'dwǒ-je-de-dì-fang 'jàw-jáw-le.

Lead *someone* **to** *do something* jyàw; shwō (*tell*) ; chywàn (*advise*) ; 'jǐr-dǎw (*direct*) ; bǎ . . . pyàn (*fool*). ‖I led him to change his plans. shǐ 'wǒ 'jyàw (*or* °shwō-de, *or* °chywàn-de)-ta gǎy-de 'jú-yì. *or* tā gǎy 'jú-yì shǐ °'wǒ-shwō-de. *or* °'wǒ-chywàn-de. °'wǒ-jǐr-dǎw-de. *or* °yīn-wey 'wǒ-de-ywán-gu. ‖He led the police to believe that he planned to run away. (*Intentionally or unintentionally*) tā jyàw 'jǐng-chá 'jywé-je tā yàw 'pǎw shǐ-de. *or* (*Intentionally*) tā gù-'yì-de jyàw 'jǐng-chá jywé-je tā yàw 'pǎw shǐ-de. *or* (*By deception*) tā bǎ 'jǐng-chá 'pyàn-de yǐ-wey tā yàw 'pǎw-ne.

Lead up to (*a conclusion or request*) shyǎng shwō, *or* yàw shwō, *or* shyǎng yàw shwō (*want to say*) ; *when the object is a word like* **this, that,** *or* **what?,**

lead up to ... *may be expressed as* shr̀ ... 'yì-sz. ‖What did his talk lead up to? tā-de-hwà 'jyēw-jing shr̀ 'shéme-yì-sz-ne? *or* tā 'jyēw-jing shr̀ shyǎng yàw shwō 'shéme-ne? ‖He's trying to lead up to something. tīng tā-de-'kěw-chì hǎw shyàng yěw shéme-'hwà yàw 'shwō shr̀-de. ‖What are you leading up to? nǐ 'jyēw-jing shr̀ °'shéme-yì-sz? *or* °shyǎng shwō 'shéme-ne?

Leading (*outstanding*) dzwèy-'hǎw-de (*best*); dzwèy-yěw-'míng-de (*most famous*). ‖He's the leading chemist of our time. tā shr̀ rú-'jīn-dzwèy-'hǎw-de hwà-shywé-'jyā.

LEAD. (*Metal*) chyān. ‖Is this made of lead? jèy shr̀ 'chyān-dzwò-de-ma? ‖The house is fitted with lead pipes. fáng-dz-lǐ-'ān-de shr̀ 'chyān-gwǎn-dz. ‖I prefer a lead pencil to a pen. wǒ shǐ-hwān yùng 'chyān-bǐ, 'bù-shǐ-hwān yùng 'gāng-bǐ. ‖The lead in the pencil is broken. 'chyān-bǐ-'lǐ-tew-de-'chyān shé-le.

(*Figurative*). ‖My feet feel like lead. wǒ-jyǎw 'lèy-de jyǎn-'jŕ 'táy-bu-chǐ-'láy-le. ‖They filled him full of lead. *is expressed as* They shot him °until he was like a broken-down beehive. tām ná-'chyǎng bǎ-ta gěy 'dǎ-de °chéng-le làn-fēng-'wō shr̀-de. *or* °a body full of holes. °yì-'shēn-de-kū-lung.

LEADER. (*A person fitted to lead*) 'lǐng-shyèw. ‖He's a born leader. tā tyān-'shēng-de jyèw shr̀ ge-'lǐng-shyèw.

(*Chief*). (*In a good sense, a leader of men*) 'lǐng-shyèw; (*good or bad*) téwr (*especially in certain combinations, as* dǎ-'téwr-de vanguard *or* guide, dzéy-'téwr leader of a gang, leader of bandits, ringleader); (*leader of a party, usually bad*) dǎng-'kwéy; (*in a bad sense only; of bandits*) fěy-'shěw; platoon leader páy-'jǎng. ‖He was the leader of the movement. (*Good*) tā shr̀ nèy-pày-de-'lǐng-shyèw. *or* (*Bad*) tā shr̀ nèy-'dǎng-de-dǎng-'kwéy. ‖We haven't caught the leader of the gang yet. dzéy-'téwr háy méy dǎy-'jáw-ne.

(*Conductor; in music*) jř-'dǎw. ‖The leader of the band was a very tall man. ywě-'dwèy-de-jř-'dǎw °'gèr (*or* °'shēn-lyang, *or* °'jǎng-de) tǐng 'gāw.

LEAF. (*Part of plant*) 'yè-dz *or* 'yèr, *or* yè *in combinations;* tea leaves 'chá-yè *or sometimes* chá. ‖I like to see the leaves on the trees turn color. wǒ 'shǐ-hwān kàn ('shù-shang-de)'shù-'yè-dz byàn 'yán-shar. *or expressed as* I like to see red leaves. wǒ ày kàn húng-'yè. ‖They're picking tea leaves. tām dzày-nàr tsǎy 'chá-ne. ‖There are some tea leaves left in the cup. wǎn-'dyěr-shang yěw jǐ-pyàr-'chá-yè.

(*Page*) pyār. ‖Many leaves of this book are torn. jèy-běr-'shū-li yěw bù-shǎw-'pyar dēw 'chě-le.

Gold leaf jīn-'jř *or* jīn-'yè-dz.

(*Section of a table*) bǎr. ‖Add another leaf to the table. 'jwō-dz-shang dzày jyā yí-kwày-'bǎr.

Turn over a new leaf gǎy-gwò dž-'shīn *or* 'shǐ-shīn gé-'myàn. ‖If you don't turn over a new leaf soon, you'll be sorry. nǐ 'yàw-shr bù-gǎn-'kwày °gǎy-gwò dž-'shīn (*or* °'shǐ-shīn gé-'myàn) de-hwà, (jyǎng-láy) 'dzǔng yěw hèw-'hwěy-de-nèm-yì-'tyān.

LEAN. To lean against *or* to lean on (*support oneself; °of a person*). (*With the whole body*) 'yǐ-je, 'yǐ-dzày ...-shang; 'kàw-je (*less common; also means* be close to *and* depend on), 'kàw-dzày ...-shang, bǎ 'shēn-dz 'kàw-dzày ...-shang; (*with the hands or sometimes the arms*) 'fú-je, bǎ-'shěw fú-dzày ...-shang; (*forward, with the arms or elbows or sometimes the hands*) 'pā-dzày ...-shang; (*on a stick or cane*) 'jǔ-je. ‖He leaned against the wall and tied his shoes. tā °'yǐ-je chyáng (*or* °'yǐ-dzày 'chyáng-shang, *or* °bǎ 'shēn-dz kàw-dzày 'chyáng-shang) bǎ shyé-'dàr jì-shang-le. ‖He's leaning back in the chair. tā dzwò-dzày 'yǐ-dz-shang wàng-'hèw °'yǐ-je. *or* °'kàw-je. ‖Here, lean on this cushion. yǐ-je (*or* kàw-je) jèy-ge-'dyàr. *or* yǐ- (*or* kàw-)dzày jèy-ge-'dyàr-shang. ‖As he leaned against the door to listen, it suddenly gave. tā yǐ- (*or* tā bǎ 'shēn-dz kàw-)dzày 'mén-shang 'tīng; 'hū-rán mén °'yěw-kāy-le. *or* °'dž-jǐ kāy-le. ‖He leaned on my arm for support. tā 'fú-je wǒ-de-'gē-bwo. *or* tā 'yǐ- (*or* tā 'kàw-)dzày wǒ-de-'gē-bwo-shang. ‖He leaned on the table. (*With hand or hands*) tā 'fú-dzày 'jwō-dz-shang. *or* (*With elbows or forearms*) tā 'pā-dzày 'jwō-dz-shang. ‖He leaned against the table (*with back, side, or leg*). tā 'yǐ-je (*or* tā 'kàw-je) 'jwō-dz. ‖He has to lean on his cane to rest awhile before walking on. tā děy jǔ-je 'gwèr 'shyē-hwer tsáy néng dzày 'jyē-je dzěw.

Lean against (*rest against, of an object*). (*On side or end*) 'yǐ-dzày (*or* 'kàw-dzày) ...-shang; (*on end only*) 'lì-dzày *or* 'yǐ-je (*or* 'kàw-je) ... 'lì; (*on end, with top touching*) 'dǐng-dzày ...°.-shang *or* 'dǐng-je; (*of something normally vertical*) 'dǎw-dzày ...-shang; lean *something* against bǎ ... 'yǐ-dzày ...-shang, bǎ ... 'kàw-dzày ...-shàng, bǎ ... 'lì-dzày, bǎ ... 'dǐng-dzày ...-shang; (*on end, with part of the top extending above the point of support*) bǎ ... 'dā-dzày ...-shang (*without* bǎ ..., this would refer to being supported horizontally at two points, as boards on a scaffold*); lean one's head against bǎ-'téw kàw-dzay ...-shang. ‖Bring me the ladder that's leaning against the tree, not the one lying on the ground. bǎ °'yǐ-dzày-'shù-shang- (*or* °'kàw-dzày-'shù-shang-, *or, meaning* on end °'dǐng-dzày-'shù-shang-, *or* °'lì-dzày-'shù-nàr-)de-nèy-ge-'tī-dz ná-láy; bú-yàw ná nèy-ge-'dǎw-dzày-'dì-shang-de. ‖The flagpole is leaning against the wall. 'chí-gān ('yì-téwr) dǎw-dzày 'chyáng-shang-le. ‖Lean the ladder against the wall. bǎ tī-dz °'yǐ- (*or* °'kàw, *or, with top touching*, °-'shàng-téwr dǐng, *or* °-'shàng-téwr yǐ-, *or* °-'shàng-téwr kàw-, *or with top sticking over*, °-'shàng-téwr dā-)dzày 'chyáng-shang. ‖Lean the ladder against the eaves. bǎ 'tī-dz-'shàng-byar dā-dzày fáng-'yán-shang.

To lean on. (*Depend on; of a person*) 'kàw-je; (*if depending on another person only, also*) 'jř-je, or 'yǐ-kàw-je, or 'jàng-je, or 'yǐ-lày. ‖She leans on her mother in everything. tā 'shéme dēw °'kàw-je (*or* °'jř-je, *or* °'yǐ-kàw-je, *or* °'jàng-je, *or* °'yǐ-lày) tā-'mǔ-chin. ‖In that case I'll have to lean heavily on my memory. nà-me-je, wǒ jyèw děy 'jwǎn (*or* 'jìng) kàw-je wǒ-de-'jì-shing. ‖He was leaning heavily on his imagination for what he said. *is expressed as* He mostly was talking through his hat. tā jìng 'shyā-shwō.

To lean *in a certain direction.* (*Of an object*) wāy, shyé; (*lean vertically while the base remains horizontal and stationary, as a table whose legs all slant in one direction but touch the floor, and the top remains horizontal*) yēw. (*Of a person leaning to see, hear, speak, etc.; to the side only*) wāy(-je) 'shēn-dz; (*forward or to the side*) tàn or tàn(-je) 'shēn-dz; (*to the side or back, turning at the same time*) nyěw(-je) 'shēn-dz; (*lean over or down, bending at the waist*) wān(-shya) 'yāw or máw-'yāw; (*stretching the neck as if to see*) tàn(-je) 'téwr; (*stretching the neck to see over something*) bā(-ba) 'téwr; (*stretch the body in any direction*) shēn(-shen) 'yāw; (*stretch forward*) hā-'yāw; (*backwards, with face up*) yǎng; 'pā-dzày (*followed only by* 'ěr-dwo-shang, *to lean over to talk into someone's ear.* The leaning tower shyé-'tǎ *or* wāy-'tǎ. ‖The bookcase seems to be leaning over a little to this side. shū-'jyà-dz hǎw shyàng yěw-dyǎr wàng 'jèy-byar °'wāy. *or* °'shyé. *or* °yēw. ‖He leaned over and whispered something to his wife. tā 'wāy-je shēn-dz (*or* tā 'tàn-je shēn-dz, *or* tā 'nyěw-gwo 'shēn-dz-lay) gēn tā-'tày-tay °'shyǎw-shēngr-de 'shwō-le dyǎr-shéme. *or* °dǎ 'chā-cha. *or* tā 'pā-dzày tā-tày-tay-'ěr-dwo-shang °'shyǎw-shēngr-de 'shwō-le dyǎr-shéme. *or* °dǎ 'chā-cha. ‖If you lean forward, you can see. nǐ wàng-'chyán °tàn-tan 'shēn-dz (*or* °tàn-tan 'téwr, *or* °yǐ-'tàn, *or* °bā-ba 'téwr, *or* °shēn-shen 'yāw, *or* °hā-dyar 'yāw), jyèw néng 'kàn-jyàn-le. ‖He leaned over backward in his chair. tā dzwò-dzày 'yǐ-dz-shang wàng-hèw 'yǎng. ‖I love to see the way he leans back and laughs when he hears a good joke. wǒ 'tǐng ày kàn tā 'tīng-jyàn-le 'shyǎw-hwàr jyèw nèm wàng-hèw 'yǎng-jc dà-'shyǎw de-'shén-chi. ‖He leaned over (*or down*) to pick up the baby. tā wān-shya 'yāw-lay (*or* tā yì-máw-'yāwr) bǎ shyǎw-'hár °bàw-chǐ-lay-le. *or* °jywǔ-chǐ-lay-le. *or* °shf-chǐ-lay-le.

To lean toward *or* **to lean** *in some direction* (*incline in opinion*) '-sž-shyàng 'pyàn-shyàng; lean **towards the left** (*or* **right**) *in politics may also be expressed as* 'sž-shyǎng °yěw dyǎr-'dzwǒ-chīng (*or* °yěw dyǎr-'yèw-chīng); jywé-je . . . 'dwèy (*feel that . . . is right*); lean this way and that yěw dyǎr-'swéy-fēng-'dǎw (*lie down as the wind blows*). ‖He leans toward the left (*in politics*). tā-(-'jèng-jř)-'sž-shyàng °yěw dyǎr-'dzwǒ-chīng. *or* °yěw-dyǎr shyàng-'dzwǒ pyān. *or* °'pyàn-shyàng 'dzwǒ-byǎr yì-dyǎr. ‖He leans toward the right (*in politics*). tā-(-'jèng-jř-)'sž-shyàng °yěw dyǎr-'yèw-chīng. *or expressed as* His (political)

thought °keeps to the old. °yěw-dyǎr shěw-'jyèw. *or as* °is a bit conservative. °yěw dyǎr-'wán-gù. *or as* °is partial to the side of keeping the old. °'pyàn-shyàng 'shěw-'jyèw-nèy-byǎr. ‖I've been leaning toward your viewpoint lately. jìn-láy wǒ ywè láy ywè 'jywé-je 'nǐ-de-'yì-jyàn 'dwèy. ‖He's been leaning this way and that lately, without any opinion of his own. tā jìn-láy yěw dyǎr-'swéy-fēng-'dǎw, 'dž-jǐ yì-dyǎr-'jú-yì yě méy-'yěw.

To lean over backward (*figuratively*). (*Overdo it*) tày gwò-'fèn; (*do all in one's power*) shyǎng-'jìn fár-lay *or* jyé-'lì(-de). ‖I only asked you not to yell; you don't have to lean over backward and whisper. wǒ 'hú-gwò shř shwō byé 'dà-shēng °'rǎng (*or* °'hǎn); 'yùng-bu-jáw jyèw nèm dǎ 'chā-char-ra; nà 'chǐ bú-shř tày gwò-'fèn-le-ma? ‖He leaned over backward to please her. tā shyǎng-'jìn-le fár-lay (*or* tā jyé-'lì-de) °'bā-jye tā. *or* °'fēng-chéng tā. ‖He leaned over backward to make her like him. *is expressed as* To make her like him he °was willing to suffer. tā wèy-le 'tǎw tā-de-'shǐ-hwān °'nìng-kě 'dž-jǐ shěw-'wěy-chywu. *or* °yielded to her. °hěn 'ràng-je tā.

(*Not fat*) shěw; a tall lean person *is also expressed as* shì-gāw-'tyǎwr. ‖I like lean meat. wǒ 'shǐ-hwān 'shěw-rèw. ‖I'd like some lean meat. gěy-wǒ 'shěw-de. ‖Who's that tall lean individual over there? 'nèy-byǎr nèy-ge-°'shì-gāw-'tyǎwr (*or* °'yěw-'gāw-yèw-'shěw-de-rén) shř shéy?

(*Unproductive*) 'bù-hǎw (*bad*) *preceded by a verbal expression describing the activity in question.* ‖It's been a lean year for farmers. 'jèy-yì-nyán 'shěw-chēng 'bù-hǎw. ‖It's been a lean year for black market racketeers. 'jèy-yì-nyán 'hēy-shř-de-mǎy-may 'bù-hǎw.

LEAP. (*General term*) tyàw; (*over a distance, to a higher level, or straight up*) tswān; (*more vertically than horizontally*) bèng. ‖He leaped from the boat to the shore. tā tsúng 'chwán-shang °tyàw- (*or* °tswān-)dàw 'àn-shang-chywu-le. ‖The horse leaped over the fence. mǎ tsúng 'jà-lar-lǐ °'bèng- (*or* °'tyàw-, *or* °'tswān-)chū-chywu-le. ‖The frog made a big leap. 'há-ma 'tswān-le yí-shyàr. ‖He leaped out of the window. tā tsúng 'chwāng-hu 'tyàw-chu-chywu-le. ‖He leaped to his death (*from a high building*). tā tyàw-'léw dž-'shā-de. *or* tā tsúng 'léw-shang 'tyàw-shya-lay dž-°'jìn-de. *or* °'shā-de. ‖The thief leaped over the wall. dzéy °tswān- (*or* °tyàw-)gwo 'chyáng-chywu-le. *or* dzéy dǎ chyáng-shang °'tswān- (*or* °'tyàw-)gwo-chywu-le. ‖He made a ten-foot leap. tā tyàw-le (*or* tā tswān-le) yěw yí-'jàng-ywǎn. *But* ‖It's a ten-foot leap across the brook. *is expressed as* The brook is ten feet wide. hé-'gēwr yěw yí-'jàng-kwān.

Leaps and bounds. ‖His fame increased by leaps and bounds. tā-de-'míng-shēng chǐ-lay-de 'jēn kwày.

LEARN. (*Receive knowledge*) 'jr̄-dàw-jr̄-dàw; (*by experience*) 'cháng-chang (*taste*) ; (*by suffering*) shèw-'dzwèy. ‖I want to learn all about this country. 'jèy-gwǒ-de-yí-'chyè wǒ 'dēw shyǎng 'jr̄-dàw-jr̄-dàw. ‖Let him learn a lesson. jyàw-ta °shèw dyǎr-'dzwèy yě 'hǎw. *or* °'jr̄-dàw-jr̄-dàw (*or* °'cháng-chang) nèy-ge-'dź-wèr yě 'hǎw.

(*Acquire knowledge by studying*) shywé; (*of a skill only*) lyàn. ‖He learns quickly. tā 'shywé-shéme dēw 'shywé-de hěn 'kwày. *or* tā 'shywé dūng-shi hěn 'kwày. ‖That language is very difficult to learn. 'nèy-gwó-de-hwà (*or* 'nèy-jǔng-hwà) hěn 'nán shywé. ‖Are you learning how to type? nǐ 'lyàn (*or* 'shywé) dǎ-'dź-ne-ma?

Learn by heart 'bèy-shya-lay. ‖She learned the part by heart. tā bǎ-'tsér dēw 'bèy-shya-lay-le.

Learn that *or* learn of *or* learn about *is expressed as* hear 'tīng-jyàn, hear tell 'tīng-shwō, *or, in some cases,* know 'jr̄-dàw. ‖I didn't learn of his death until today. wǒ jŕ-dàw 'jīn-tyān tsáy °'tīng-shwō (*or* °'tīng-jyàn, *or* °'jr̄-dàw) tā 'sź-le.

LEARNED. (*Erudite*) yěw-'shywé-shŕ(-de); yěw-'shywé-wèn(-de); bwó-'shywé(-de). ‖He gives the impression of being a learned man. 'kàn tā (nèy-'yàngr) (*or* tā nèy-yàngr jyàw-rén 'jywé-je tā) °hěn yěw 'shywé-wén shŕ-de. *or* °hěn bwó-'shywé shŕ-de. *or* (*Somewhat sarcastically*) kàn tā-'nèy-jǔng-'shén-chì 'fǎng-fu shŕ ge-'shyāng-dāng °yěw-'shywé-shŕ-de-rén. *or* °yěw-'shywé-wèn-de-rén. *or* °bwó-'shywé-de-rén.

LEARNING. (*Erudition*) 'shywé-wèn. Have learning yěw 'shywé-wèn *or* 'bú-shŕ 'bù-shywé-wú-'shù (*literary quotation*) ; *or* shèw-gwo 'jyàw-ywù (*having received education*). ‖The book shows a great deal of learning. jèy-běr-'shū-li 'shywé-wèn 'dà-le. ‖He has no learning to speak of. 'tā-nèy-ge-rén °jēn shŕ 'bù-shywé-wú-'shù. *or* °'méy shèw-gwo shéme-'jyàw-ywù. *or* °'méy shéme-'shywé-wèn.

LEAST. (*Smallest amount*) 'dzwèy shǎw, dǐng shǎw; (*less than all other people*) bǐ-'shéy dēw 'shǎw. ‖He worked the least but was paid the most. tā-dzwò-de-shèr 'dzwèy shǎw, kě-shr ná-de-'chyán dzwèy 'dwō. ‖A got less than B, but C got the least. lǎw-'dà-dé-de bǐ lǎw-'èr shǎw; lǎw-'sān-dé-de °bǐ-'shéy dēw 'shǎw. *or* °'dzwèy shǎw. ‖He was the one who did the least work but got the most money. 'tā jyèw-shr nèy-ge-bǐ-'shéy-dzwò-de-shèr-dēw-'shǎw-kě-shr-bǐ-'shéy-ná-de-chyán-dēw-'dwō-de-nèy-ge-rén.

(*Smallest; in the smallest degree*) dzwèy *or* dǐng (*most*) *followed by an adjective or descriptive phrase of opposite meaning from the one in English.* ‖The least capable ones should be discharged at once. 'dǐng- (*or* 'dzwèy-)'bù-'shíng-de (*or* °bù-'chéng-de, *or* °méy-'běn-shr̀-de) yīng-gāy lì-'kè jyèw 'tsź-le. ‖I like this

one least of all. wǒ-°'dǐng- (*or* °'dzwèy-)bù-shr̄-hwān-de shr̀ 'jèy-ge. ‖Of the four boys, he seemed to have the least chance of success at that time. (*Of future possibilities*) nèy-shŕ-hew nèy-'sz̀-ge-háy-dz-li 'tā hǎw shyàng shŕ °'dzwèy-méy-yěw-'chū-shi-de. *or* (*Of a particular situation; here* have the least chance *is expressed as* be entirely unable to do anything; *see next paragraph*) °'jywé-chéng-bu-lyǎw-shéme-'shŕ-de. ‖That's the least of my worries. *is expressed as* That is my most-useless-to-worry-about. 'nèy shr̀ wǒ-'dzwèy-yùng-bu-jáw-'chéw-de. *or* as I worry but little about that. 'nèy-ge wǒ dàw 'bù-dzěme chéw.

(*Even a little*) yì-'dyǎr(-. . .) (*in negative sentences,* yě *usually follows, before the negative; a noun after* least *in this construction is usually an action noun and often is expressed by a verb in Chinese*) : not have the least chance (to do . . . or for . . .) *is often expressed as* if you want to . . ., that is certainly an impossibility, yàw shyǎng . . ., nà shŕ °'jywé (*or* °'jywé-dwèy, *or* °'wàn-wán)-bàn-bu-'dàw-de-'shŕ, *or* as be entirely unable to . . . shŕ jywé-. . .-de (*with a negative resultative compound in the blank*). ‖He doesn't have the least concern for his appearance. tā yì-'dyǎr yě bù-'jyǎng-jyew wày-°'yàngr. *or* °'byǎw. ‖He hasn't the least consideration for other people's feelings. tā yì-'dyǎr vě méy-yěw 'tǐ-tyē-'byé-rén-de-°'shīn. *or* °'yì-sz. *or* ā yì-'dyǎr yě 'bù-gwǎn 'byé-rén shèw-de-'lyǎw shè v-bu-lyǎw. ‖If you had the least consideration for other people's feelings, you wouldn't say that. nǐ yàw-shr yěw yì-'dyǎr-'tǐ-tyē-byé-rén-de-'shīn-ha, nǐ °yě bú-hwèy shwō-chū 'nèy-jǔng-hwà-lay. *or* °jyèw bú-hwèy shwō-chū 'nèy-jǔng-hwà-lav-le. ‖You haven't the least chance of winning him over. nǐ yàw shyǎng bǎ-'tā lā-gwo-lay, nà shr̀ °'jywé-(dwèy-) (*or* °'wàn-wán-)bàn-bu-'dàw-de-'shr̀. ‖You haven't the least chance of doing that. nǐ yàw shyǎng 'nèm-je, nà shr̀ °'jywé-(dwèy-) (*or* °'wàn-wán-)bàn-bu-'dàw-de-'shr̀. *or* °yì-'dyǎr-shī-wang yě méy-yěw.

Not in the least yì-'dyǎr yě bū-. ‖I don't mind the noise in the least. wǒ yì-'dyǎr yě bú-'dzày-hu nèy-ge-'shēng-yin.

At least 'jr̄ shǎw *or* 'dǐng shǎw; (*as the least desirable thing*) 'jr̄ bú-jì *or* dǐng bú-'jì; (*in any case*) 'wú-lwèn-rú-'hé; (*no matter what*) bù-gwǎn 'dzěm-yàng. ‖The trip will take at least three days. jèy-yí-'tàng 'jr̄ shǎw děy yùng sān-'tyān. ‖You might at least have written to me. nǐ 'wú-lwèn-rú-'hé yě °'gāy (*or* °'kě-yǐ) gěy-wǒ láy fēng-'shìn-ne.

The least (*one can do, etc.*) *is expressed as* at least. ‖That is the least you can do. bù-gwǎn 'dzěm-yàng (*or* 'jr̄ shǎw, *or* 'jr̄ bú-jì, *or* 'dǐng shǎw, *or* dǐng bú-'jì, *or* 'wú-lwèn-rú-'hé) 'nèy-ge nǐ dzǔng kě-yǐ dzwò-'dàw-le(-ba).

To say the least *is expressed as* at least, *or as* 'byé-de 'bú-yùng shwō-le, 'jr̄ shǎw. ‖He made a brave attempt, to say the least. 'jr̀ shǎw tā 'gǎn-nèm 'gàn-le yí-shyàr. ‖We were surprised, to say the least. 'byé-de 'bú-yùng shwō-lɔ, 'jr̀ shǎw wǒm shyà-le yí-'tyàw.

The least possible *is expressed by an adjective or descriptive phrase in the construction* 'ywè . . . ywè 'hǎw. ‖This work has to be done in the least possible time. 'jèy-jyàn-shèr děy kwày-'kwàr-de gǎn-'wán-le, °wán-de 'ywè kwày ywè 'hǎw. *or* °fèy-de-'shf́-hewr ywè 'shǎw ywè 'hǎw. *or* jèy-ge 'fēy-děy gǎn-'kwày dzwò-chū-lay tsáy 'shíng, wán-de 'ywè kwày ywè 'hǎw.

LEATHER. 'pí-dz *or* (*especially in combinations*) pí. ‖Is this saddle made of the best leather? jèy-(mǎ-) 'ān-dz shr̀ yùng-'dzwèy-hǎw-de-'pí-dz-dzwò-de-ma? ‖This isn't made of real leather. jèy 'bú-shr 'jēn-pí-dz-dzwò-de. ‖This book is bound in leather. jèy-shū shr̀ 'pí-pyér-de. *or* 'shū-pyér shr̀ 'pí-de. *or* 'shū-pyér shr̀ 'pí-dz-dzwò-de.

LEAVE (LEFT). (*Not take, including especially* **leave behind;** *of something that was already there*) lyéw (-shya) (*intentionally*) ; shèng(-shya) (*so that some remains*) ; 'là-shya (*go away without*) ; 'dyēw-shya (*drop or throw down*) ; 'lyàw-shya (*throw down*) ; *or expressed as* **not take, make stay, not let go,** *etc.* ‖He took all the money but left these jewels. tā bǎ-'chyán dēw ná-dzěw-le, kě-shr bǎ jèy-shyē-'shěw-shr̀ °'lyéw-shya-le. *or* °'là-shya-le. *or* °'lyàw-shya-le. *or* °'dyēw-shya-le. *or expressed as* He took all the money but didn't take these jewels. tā bǎ-'chyán dēw ná-dzěw-le, kě-shr 'méy-bǎ jèy-shyē-'shěw-shr̀ ná-chywu. ‖We were left behind. bǎ wǒ-men gěy °'lyéw-shya-le. *or* °'shèng-shya-le. *or* °'là-shya-le. (*See also* **Leave behind,** *meaning outdistance, below.*) ‖Leave him behind to watch things. 'lyéw-shya tā kān-je 'dūng-shi. ‖I don't like him around; let's leave him behind. wǒ bú-'ywàn-yi gēn-tā dzày yí-'kwàr; °bǎ-ta 'lyéw-shyà-ba. *or expressed as* °let's make him stay here. °jyàw-ta dzày-jèr 'dāy-je-ba. *or as* °let's not let him go along. °'byé jyàw-ta 'gēn-je. *or* °'byé jyàw-ta 'chywù. ‖I left my hat in the restaurant. wǒ bǎ 'màw-dz °là- (*or* °dyēw-)dzày fàn-'gwǎr-lĭ-le. *or expressed as* When I left the restaurant I forgot to take my hat. wǒ tsúng fàn-gwǎr 'dzěw de-shf́-hew, wàng-le ná 'màw-dz. ‖He left half a bowl of rice. tā 'shèng-(shya-)le 'bàn-wǎn-'fàn. ‖Don't leave any rice in your bowl. wǎn-lĭ yì-'dyar-fàn yě 'bú-yàw 'shèng(-shya).

(*Put or cause to remain when leaving; of something that was not there before*) lyéw(-shya). ‖Leave a note saying we called. lyéw(-shya) ge-°'tyáwr (*or* °'dzèr) shwō dzám 'láy-lay-je. ‖He left a message for you. tā gěy-ni lyéw-le ge-°'dzèr (*written*). *or* °'hwàr (*verbal*). ‖We must leave a sentry here. jèr děy 'lyéw ge-rén 'kān-je. ‖I left three dollars for him. wǒ gěy-ta 'lyéw (-shya)-le 'sān-kwày-ch.yán.

Lo something to something °*when leaving, or* °*before leaving, or* °*and then leave is expressed by saying what is done and adding the verb* dzěw. ‖He dragged the suitcase out of the car and left it on the road. tā bǎ shěw-tí-'shyang tsúng 'chē-li 'jwày-chū-lay, °fàng- (*or* °gē-, *or* °rēng-, *or* °dyēw-)dzày 'lù-shang jyèw 'dzěw-le. ‖He left his desk clean. tā bǎ jwō-dz shěw-shr-'gān-jing-le 'dzěw-de. ‖He always leaves his desk clean. tā 'lǎw bǎ jwō-dz shěw-shr-'gān-jing-le tsáy 'dzěw.

(*For future reference or safekeeping, including especially* **leave with**) gē, fàng, tswén. ‖May I leave my books here for a while? wǒ bǎ-'shū dzày-jèr 'gē (*or* 'fàng, *or* 'tswén) yì-hwěr, 'shíng-ma? ‖May I leave my trunks °with you? *or* °at your place? wǒ bǎ 'shyāng-dz 'gē (*or* °fàng, *or* °tswén) 'nĭ-nàr, 'shíng-ma? ‖May I leave it with you for a few days? wǒ bǎ 'jèy-ge dzày 'nĭ-jèr °tswén (*or* °'gē, *or* °'fàng) jĭ-tyān, 'shíng-ma? ‖I'll leave it with you, then. 'nèm-je jyèw °tswén (*or* °'gē, *or* °'fàng) 'nĭ-jèr-ba. *or* (*Permanently*) 'nèm-je jyèw 'lyéw nĭ-jèr-le. ‖I left three dollars with him. wǒ °gē (*or* °tswén) tā-nàr 'sān kwày-chyán.

(*Hand over for care or use, including especially* **leave with**) 'jyāw-gěy, lyéw, gē, fàng, tswén. ‖I left three dollars with him (*to use in a certain way*). wǒ 'jyàw-gěy tā 'sān-kwày-chyán. ‖I left two dollars with the next-door neighbors to pay the newsboy for me. wǒ 'jyāw-gěy jyè-'byěr (*or* wǒ gěy jyè-'byěr lyéw-le, *or* wǒ °tswén- *or* °gē-, *or* °fàng-dzày jyè-'byěr-nàr) 'lyǎng-kwày-chyán hǎw 'tì-wǒ gěy sùng-'bàw-de. ‖Leave the baby with us if you want to go. nĭm yàw shyǎng 'chywù de-hwà, bǎ 'háy-dz °jyāw-gěy 'wǒm-ba. *or* °lyéw(-dzày) 'wǒm-jèr-ba. *or* °gē(-dzày) 'wǒm-jèr-ba. *or* °fàng(-dzày) 'wǒm-jèr-ba.

(*Bequeath, including especially* **leave to**) 'lyéw (-gěy); (*by a will*) jyàw . . . 'chéng-shèw. ‖She will leave the house to her son. tā yàw bǎ nèy-swěr-'fáng-dz lyéw-gěy tā-'ér-dz. *or* tā yàw bǎ nèy-swěr-'fáng-dz jyàw tā-'ér-dz 'chéng-shèw.

(*Be survived by*) 'shēn-hèw 'lyéw-shya, 'shēn-hèw 'pyē-shya. ‖He leaves a wife and three children. tā 'shēn-hèw 'lyéw-shya 'shí-fer gēn sā-'háy-dz. *or* tā 'shēn-hèw 'pyē-shya-le-ge-'gwǎ-fu hé sā-'háy-dz.

(*Let remain unchanged*) *is expressed by a negative word with a verb expressing a change, or by a verb indicating the status quo usually followed by* -je; *if it is an object that is left unchanged,* lyéw *is sometimes added; see also* **Leave someone alone,** *below.* ‖Leave it at that nèm-je 'swàn-le. ‖They left all the lights on. *is expressed as* They didn't turn off a single light. tām 'yí-ge-dēng yě méy-'gwān. ‖They left all the lights on and went to sleep. tām 'yí-ge-dēng yě méy-'gwān, jyèw 'shwèy-le. *or* 'swǒ-yěw-de-dēng 'chywán °kāy-je (*or* °dyǎn-je), tàm jyèw 'shwèy-le. ‖I left the door open. wǒ méy-gwān-'mén. ‖He left everything as it was. *is expressed as* He didn't touch anything. tā 'shéme dēw méy-'dùng. *or as* **When he left he put everything in its original place.** tā 'dzěw de-shŕ-hew 'shéme dēw jàw 'ywán-yàngr 'gē-je. ‖**He left his food untouched.** tā 'fàn yì-'dyăr dēw méy-°'dùng. *or* °'chŕ. ‖**Leave everything as it is.** 'shéme dēw byé-°'dung. *or* °'mwō. *or* dzěw-de-shŕ-hew 'shéme dēw jàw 'ywán-yàngr gē-'hǎw-le. ‖**Leave your coat off.** byé (*or* béng) chwān 'shàng-yī-le. ‖**Leave your hat on.** 'dày-je 'màw-dz-ba. *or* byé (*or* béng) jāy 'màw-dz-le. ‖**Many items were left for the next meeting.** 'hǎw-shyē-shèr dēw méy-'fù byǎw-jywé, lyéw-je děng 'shyà-tsż kāy-'hwèy dzày shwō. ‖**A great many things were left unsaid.** (*Undiscussed*) 'hǎw-shyē-hwà (*or* 'hǎw-shyē-shèr) dēw méy-°'tí. *or* (*Not said for lack of time or opportunity*) °dé 'jī-hwèy shwō, *or* °yěw 'jī-hwèy shwō. *or* °láy-de-'jí shwō. *or* °'dyé-de shwō. ‖**Let's leave it at that.** 'jyew nèm-je 'swàn-le. ‖**Let's leave the matter open.** jèy-shèr°'yĭ-'hèw dzày jywé-'dìng-ba. *or* °'shyàn-dzày 'bù-jywé-'dìng hǎw-le. ‖**I left the door unlocked.** wǒ méy-swǒ-'mén. *But* ‖**I left the door unlocked for you.** (*A special expression for this case*) wǒ gěy-nĭ 'lyéw-je mén-ne.

Be left (*remaining*) háy *with a verb, as* háy yěw (*still are some*) *or* háy dzày ... (*still at ...*); shèng (-shya) (*remaining*); 'fù-ywu (*be surplus*); *or by a negative with a verb such as* mày (*sell*) *or* gěy (*give*). ‖**Are there any tickets left for tonight?** jyēr-'wǎn-shang-de-'pyàw °háy 'yěw-ma? *or* °yěw 'shèng-shya-de-ma? *or* (*Surplus*) °yěw 'fù-ywu-de-ma? *or* (*Unsold*) °yěw méy-'mày-chū-chywu-de-ma? *or* (*Not given out*) °yěw méy-'gěy-chū-chywu-de-ma? ‖**All sold out; nothing left.** chywán 'mày-le; yì-'dyǎr méy-'shèng. ‖**They've all gone; I'm the only one left.** tām dēw 'dzěw-le; °'jyew shèng-shyà 'wǒ-le. *or* °jř-yěw-'wǒ háy dzày-jèr.

(*Depart*) dzěw; (*for some place*) chywù. ‖**I must leave now to catch that train.** wǒ kě 'jěn děy 'dzěw-le, hǎw 'gǎn-shang nèy-tàng-hwǒ-'chē. ‖**I'm leaving.** wǒ yàw 'dzěw-le. ‖**He has left already.** tā 'yǐ-jīng 'dzěw-le. *or* (*Gone to a place*) tā 'yǐ-jīng 'chywù-le. ‖**He has left for home.** tā hwéy-'jyā chywù-le.

(*Depart from a place or person*) tsúng (*or* dǎ) ... dzěw; (*especially permanently*) lí *or* 'lí-kāy; (*leave the country*) chū-'gwó *or* chū-yáng (*go abroad*); (*leave home*) chū-'mér (*go out the door*). ‖**He left the station at seven and must be home by now.** tā 'chī-dyǎn-jūng tsúng (*or* dǎ) hwǒ-chē-'jàn dzěw-de, 'jèy-shŕ-hew yí-'dìng dàw-'jyā-le. ‖**I'm leaving this place.** wǒ yàw 'lí-kāy jèr-le. ‖**I'm going to leave you now.** wǒ yàw 'lí-kāy nĭ-le. ‖**He left home when he was sixteen.** tā shŕ-'lyèw-swèy °lí-de 'jyā, *or* °tsúng (*or* dǎ) 'jyā-li dzěw-de. *or* °'jyew lí-'jyā-le. *or* °'jyèw tsúng (*or* dǎ) 'jyā-li dzěw-le. ‖**I'm going to leave this country within a month.** wǒ yí-ge-'ywè yĭ-'nèy yàw °'lí-kāy jèr. *or* °chū-'gwó. *or* °chū-'yáng. ‖**This time he left home for good.** tā 'jèy-tsż °'lí-jyā (*or* °chū-'mér) jyèw 'bù-hwéy-lay-le.

(*Start; of a train, bus, etc.*) kāy; (*start from*) tsúng (*or* dǎ) ... kāy. ‖**The train leaves at six.** hwǒ-chē 'lyèw-dyǎn 'kāy.

(*Quit a job*) bú-'dzwò-le (*stop doing*); bú-'gàn-le (*stop working; need not take an object*). ‖**I'm leaving my job.** wǒ yàw bú-'gàn-le. *or* jèy-'shèr wǒ yàw bú-'dzwò-le.

(*Desert a husband or wife*) 'bù-gēn ... yí-kwàr 'gwò-le (*stop living with*); gēn ... lí (*separate or divorce*); *or expressed as* **run off with someone (else)** gēn-rén 'pǎw(-le). ‖**She left her husband.** tā 'bù-gēn tā-'jàng-fu yí-kwàr 'gwò-le. *or* tā gēn tā-'jàng-fu 'lí-le. *or* tā gēn-rén 'pǎw-le.

Leave *someone* **alone** (*figuratively*) bù-'gwǎn (*not interfere with*); bù-'lĭ (*not do anything for; e.g., not comfort a crying baby*); bù-'jyǎw *or* bù-'dǎ-jyǎw (*not disturb*); ràng ... °'yí-ge-rén (*or* °'dž-gěr) nèng (*let someone do something by himself*); 'swéy ... chywù (*let someone do as he likes*); (... 'ày dzěm-je, jyèw) 'jyàw ... 'dzěm-je (*let someone do anything he pleases*). ‖**Leave me alone.** byé 'gwǎn-wo. *or* (*Rude, something like our* **What's it to you?**) nĭ gwǎn-de-'jáw-ma? *or* (*Rude, something like our* **One side, please!** *or* **Go chase yourself!**) 'chywù nĭ yì-'byār chywù. ‖**Leave him alone.** byé 'gwǎn-ta. *or* byé 'lĭ-ta. *or* byé 'jyǎw-ta. *or* byé 'dǎ-jyǎw ta. *or* 'swéy-ta chywù-ba. *or* tā 'ày dzěm-je jyèw °'jyàw-ta dzěm-je-ba. *or* °'swéy-tā chywù-ba. *or* ràng-ta 'yí-ge-rén nèng-ba. *or* ràng-ta 'dž-gěr nèng-ba.

Leave *someone* **behind** (*outdistance*) 'là(-shya); *for other meanings see first paragraph, above.* ‖**We were left behind.** wǒm jyàw-rén gěy 'là-shya-le. ‖**We walked so fast that we left them far behind.** wǒm dzěw-de tĭng 'kwày-de, bǎ-tām °'là-le hǎw 'ywǎn-de. *or* °'là-de tĭng 'ywǎn.

Leave *someone* **cold** (*unaffected*) bú-'jyàw ... dùng-'shīn; ... bù-'jywé-de dzěm-'yàng. ‖**That speech left me cold.** wǒ 'tīng-le nèy-ge-'yǎn-jyǎng yĭ-'hèw, yì-'dyǎr yě °bù-'jywé-de dzěm-'yàng. *or* °bú-'jyàw-wǒ dùng-'shīn.

Leave *something* **out** 'là-shya; bù-'gē-jìn-chywu *or* bú-'fàng-jìn-chywu (*not put in*). ‖**When you copy it, don't leave anything out.** 'chāw-de-shŕ-hew 'shéme yě 'byé 'là-shya. ‖**Leave it out.** bú-yùng (*or* byé) °'gē- (*or* °'fàng-)jìn-chywu.

Leave *something* **to** *someone* (*of an action*) jyàw *followed by the person and a verb expressing the action;* ràng (*allow*) *in the same construction;* 'gē-je (*or* 'lyéw-je) děng (*put or leave in someone's hands*) *in the same construction;* (*of a thing, by inheritance, see* (*Bequeath, above*). ‖**Leave it to him!** (*sarcastically, meaning* **That's the way he does it every time,** *or* **It never fails**). tā lǎw 'nèm-je. ‖**Leave it to him.** (*To manage*) jyàw-ta °'gwǎn-ba. *or* (*to do*) °'nèng-ba. *or* °'bàn-ba. *or* (*to wash, as dishes or laundry*) °'shĭ-ba. *or* (*to say*) 'shwō-ba. *etc.* ‖**Leave everything to me.**

'dēw jyàw-'wǒ gwǎn-'hǎw-le. or 'shéme dēw ràng-'wǒ láy hǎw-le. or 'gē-je (or 'lyéw-je) děng-'wǒ láy 'néng-ba. etc.

Leave a way open or out; leave is expressed by lyéw. ‖Leave a way open for him. gěy-ta 'lyéw °ge-'dì-bù hǎw shyà-'táy. or °ge-'twèy-shēn-de-'dì-bù. or (to escape confinement) °ge-'lùr. ‖He always leaves himself a way out. tā lǎw gěy 'dz-jǐ lyéw °ge-'twèy-shēn-de-'dì-bù. or °ge-'twèy-shēn-de-'lùr. or °ge-shyà-'táy-de-'dì-bu.

Leave (of absence) jyà. ‖He took a three months' leave from his job. tā 'gàw-le sān-ge-ywè-de-'jyà. ‖When he was on leave he came home. tā dzǎy-'jyà (or, tā fàng-'jyà) de-shŕ-hew, hwéy-'jyā-lay-le.

LEFT. dzwǒ. ‖My home is over there on the left. wǒ-'jyā dzày 'dzwǒ-byǎr-nèy-byar. ‖Take the other bag in your left hand. 'nèy-ge-'kěw-dày yùng 'dzwǒ-shěw 'ná-ba. ‖Make a turn to the left at the next corner. dzěw dàw 'shyà-yí-ge-jyē-'kěwr wàng-'dzwǒ gwǎy. ‖I sat on the principal's left. wǒ 'dzwǒ-dzày shyàw-'jǎng-de-'dzwǒ-byǎr. ‖This newspaper follows a leftist policy. 'jèy-ge-'bàw-jŕ °'dzwǒ-chīng. or expressed as This newspaper's policy is radical. °-de-'lwèn-dyàw 'jǐ-lyè. ‖He's always been on the left politically. tā yí-'shyàng shŕ 'sz-shyǎng 'dzwǒ-chīng.

LEG. twěy. or, sometimes, especially informally, derogatorily, or of animals, twěr. ‖My right leg hurts. wǒ 'yèw-twěy 'téng. ‖One of the dog's legs is lame. nèy-'gěw chywé-le yì-tyáw-°'twěy. or °'twěr. ‖Try to buy a leg of lamb for dinner. mǎy dyǎr-yáng-'twěy dzwò wǎn-'fàn chŕ.

(Of inanimate objects) twěr or sometimes twěy. I've torn the leg of my trousers. wǒ bǎ kù-'twěr chě-le. ‖The leg of the chair is broken. yǐ-dz-'twěr shé-le. ‖Steady the table by putting some paper under that leg. dzày 'nèy-tyáw-'jwō-(dz-)twěr 'dǐ-shyà dyàn dyǎr-'jǐ jyew bù-'yěw-hwang-le.

(Stage in trip, etc.) dwàr. ‖We're on the last leg of our journey. jèy shŕ dzám-'mwò-yí-dwàr-'lù-le.

(Side of a triangle) yāw. ‖Measure the legs of the triangle. 'lyáng-lyang sān-jyǎw-shíng-de-lyǎng-'yāw.

Leg it dzěw-je °chywù (or °láy), bù-'nyǎr °chywù (or °láy). ‖Let's leg it. dzám 'dzěw-je chywù-ba. or dzám bù-'nyǎr chywù-ba.

On one's last legs kwày wár-'wán-le or kwày bù-'shíng-le. ‖He's on his last legs. tā kwày wár-'wán-le. or tā kwày bù-'shíng-le.

Not have a leg to stand on is expressed as simply be without basis for argument jyǎn-'jŕ shŕ 'hǎw-wú-'dàw-lǐ, or as have not a bit of reasonableness yì-'dyǎr-'lǐ-yéw yě méy-'yěw. ‖He didn't have a leg to stand on. tā jyǎn-'jŕ shŕ 'hǎw-wú-'dàw-lǐ. or tā yì-'dyǎr-'lǐ-yéw yě méy-'yěw.

Pull one's leg pyàn, jyàw . . . shàng-'dàng. ‖He's trying to pull your leg. tā shyǎng °'pyàn-'nǐ-ne. or °'jyàw-nǐ shàng-'dàng-ne.

LENGTH. (Long dimension) 'cháng-li or 'cháng-shya-li, but more often expressed indirectly by cháng (long). ‖What length boards do you need? mù-tew-'bǎr (or 'bǎn-dz) yàw 'dwō-cháng-de? ‖The length of the room is twice its width. jèy-'wū-dz-'cháng-(shya-)li bǐ 'kwān-(shya-)li dwō yí-'bèy. or (Width is half the length) jèy-'wū-dz-'kwān-shya-li jǐ yěw 'cháng-shya-li-de-yí-'bàr. ‖What is the length of the table? jwō-dz yěw 'dwō cháng?

(Distance) ywǎn (far).; lù (road). ‖What is the length of the trip? (dzěw) jèy-yí-tàng yěw 'dwō ywǎn? or (dzěw) 'jèy-yí-lù yěw 'dwō ywǎn? or jèy-yí-'tàng (or yí-'gùng) yěw 'dwō-shǎw 'lù?

(Piece measured in long dimension) jyéer. ‖We need more than one length of pipe. 'yì-jyéer-'gwǎn-dz bú-gèw 'yùng-de.

The length of (as long as) . . . jèm 'cháng. ‖He had a cut on his face the length of this pencil. tā-'lyǎn-shang lá-le °yí-dàw-'kěw-dz, yěw 'jèy-gwǎn-chyān-'bǐ jèm 'cháng. or °jèy-gwǎn-chyān-'bǐ-jèm-'cháng-de-yí-dàw-'kěw-dz.

The length of (from one end to the other) tsúng (or dǎ) . . . 'jèy-téwr dàw 'nèy-téwr. ‖He swam the length of the pool. tā tsúng (or dǎ) 'yéw-yǔng-chŕ-'jèy-téwr fù-dàw 'nèy-téwr. or tā dzày yéw-yǔng-'chŕ-li dǎ (or tsúng) 'jèy-téwr fù-dàw 'nèy-téwr.

Length of time shyē-'shŕ-hew: shyē plus a word for a unit of time, as day or year; referring to several hours as a long time 'dà-bàn-tyān; as a long time in general jyéw. ‖We were surprised at the length of time you were away. nǐ dzěw-le °'nèm-shyē-'shŕ-hew (or °'nèm-shyē-tyān, etc., or °'nèm-dà-bàn-tyān, or °'nèm jyéw) wǒm 'dēw jywé-de tíng chí-'gwày-de.

At length (in great detail) 'shyáng-shyáng-shì-'shì-de, 'dž-dž-shì-'shì-de, 'tsúng-téwr dàw-'lyǎwr. ‖He described his trip at length. tā bǎ yì-'lù-de-'shŕ °'shyáng-shyáng-shì-'shì-de (or °'dž-dž-shì-'shì-de, or °'tsúng-téwr dàw-'lyǎwr) shwō-le yí-byàn.

Go to any length. 'shéme dēw gàn-de-chū-'láy. ‖They would go to any length to get what they wanted. tām 'jǐ yàw néng bǎ 'nèy-ge dé-dàw 'shěw-li, 'shéme dēw gàn-de-chū-'láy.

At arm's length. (Literally) ‖Hold the picture at arm's length to look at it. 'ná-je jèy-'hwàr bǎ 'gē-bèy shēn-'jŕ-le 'kàn. (Figuratively) ‖If you take my advice, you'll keep him at arm's length. nǐ yàw-shr tīng 'wǒ-de-hwà, °'lí-ta ywǎn-'ywǎr-de. or °'dwō-je tā-dyar.

LESS. (Smaller amount, or to a smaller degree) 'shǎw-dyǎr; (few, or little) shǎw in constructions with ywè . . . ywè . . . (the more . . . the more . . .), with bǐ (than), with háy (still); similar constructions with negated words of opposite meaning, such as much dwō, many shyē, etc.; reverse constructions with words of opposite meaning; less plus an adjective is often expressed by the corresponding Chinese adjective in reverse constructions, as less noisy expressed as more quiet 'ān-jìng-dyǎr; **A is less than B** *may be ex-pressed as* A bǐ B shǎw *or as* A méy(-yěw) B dwō *or as* A háy 'bù-rú B̄ dwō. ‖**Eat less but exercise more.** shǎw 'chŕ-dyar, dwō 'yùwn-dùng. ‖**Less noise, please!** láw-'jyà, 'ān-jìng-dyar. *or* (*Of verbal noises*) láw-'jyà, 'shǎw rāng-rang-dyar. *or* láw-'jyà, 'byé nèm 'chǎw-le. *or* láw-'jyà, 'byé nèm 'rāng-rang-le. ‖**I've always paid less for such things.** *is expressed as* **I've never paid so much for such things.** wǒ mǎy 'jèy-jǔng-dūng-shi yí-'shyàng méy-°'hwā- (*or* °'chū-)gwo 'jèm-shyē-'chyán. ‖**You should talk less and think more.** nǐ yīng-dāng 'shǎw shwō-dyar hwà, 'dwō yùng-dyar 'shīn. ‖**Give me less sugar this time.** 'jèy-hwéy 'shǎw °láy (*or* °gěy-wǒ)-dyǎr 'táng. ‖**I seem to be getting paid more now, but in reality I'm getting less.** wǒ-'shyàn-dzày-hǎw-shyàng-ná-de-chyán 'dwō-le, chí-'shŕ wǒ-'jēn-ná-dàw-de-chyán °gèng 'shǎw-le. *or* °háy 'shǎw-le-ne. *or* °háy 'méy-yěw yǐ-chyán-'dwō-ne. *or* °háy 'bù-rú yǐ-chyán-'dwō-ne. ‖**The less said about it the better.** 'jèy-ge ywè 'shǎw tí (*or* shwō) ywè 'hǎw. ‖**We saw him less and less after that.** dǎ nèy-hwéy yǐ-'hèw wǒm ywè láy jyàn-de tā ywè 'shǎw-le. ‖**He's less enthusiastic now** (*than before*). tā méy-yěw yǐ-'chyán nèm chǐ-'jyèr-le. *or* tā 'bù-rú yǐ-'chyán nèm chǐ-'jyèr-le. *or* tā 'bú-nèm chǐ-'jyèr-le. ‖**He's less intelligent than I thought.** wǒ 'méy-shyǎng-dàw tā nèm 'bèn. *or* wǒ jywé-je (*or* wǒ yǐ-wéy, *or* wǒ dǎ-je) tā (bǐ 'jèy-ge) háy °'tsūng-míng-dyar-ne. *or* °'jīng-ming-dyar-ne. ‖**A square bottle takes less space than a round one in packing.** jwāng-'shyàng-de-shŕ-hèw (sž-)'fāng-píng-dz bǐ 'ywán-píng-dz °jàn-de (*or* °'yùng-de, *or* °fèy-de) 'dì-jyar shǎw. ‖**I have less money than he.** 'wǒ-de-chyán °bǐ 'tā-de shǎw. *or* °'méy(-yěw) 'tā-de-dwō. *or* °'méy(-yěw) 'tā-nèm-'dwō. ‖**There's even less money in this racket than in your old one.** gàn-'jèy-ge bǐ gàn-nǐ-ywán-'láy-de-nèy-ge-nèng-de-'chyán háy 'shǎw-ne. *or* gàn-'jèy-ge háy 'bù-rú gàn-nǐ-ywán-'láy-de-nèy-ge-nèng-de-'chyán 'dwō-ne. ‖**I have less money with me than I thought.** wǒ ywán-'láy 'yǐ-wéy wǒ-de-'chyán bǐ jèy-ge 'dwō-ne. *or* wǒ 'dǎ-je wǒ-dày-de-'chyán bǐ jèy-ge 'dwō-ne.

Less than (*not in comparisons of parallel things*). (*Not up to*) bú-'dàw; (*not enough for*) 'bú-gèw; (*not fully*) 'bù-dzú; (*are or have not*) méy-'yěw. ‖**We have less than two divisions.** wǒm-jèr °'bú-dàw (*or* °'bú-gèw, *or* °'bù-dzú) 'lyǎng-shŕ-rén. *or* wǒm-jèr 'lyǎng-shŕ-rén háy °'bú-'dàw-ne. *or* °'méy-'yěw-ne. ‖**Less than a hundred people were at the play.** kàn-'shì-de °'bú-dàw yì-'bǎy-rén. *or* °'háy méy-yěw yì-'bǎy-rén-ne. *or* °'lyán yì-'bǎy-rén háy bú-'dàw-ne.

No less than jř 'shǎw (*at least*); (*of status*) dzày 'dī-le *or* dzày 'dī-de-wèy-jr *plus a negative* (*nothing lower*). ‖**There were no less than a hundred people at the play.** kàn-'shì-de 'jř-shǎw yěw yì-'bǎy-dwō-rén. ‖**He wants no less a position than that of associate professor.** tā jř 'shǎw shyǎng dāng ge-'fù-jyàw-'shèw. *or* bǐ 'fù-jyàw-shèw dzày °'dī-le (*or* °'dī-de-wèy-jr) tā 'bù-kěn 'jyèw. ‖**He's no less than the**

president of our company, *is expressed as* **He's no other; he's the president of our company.** tā bú-shr 'byé-rén, shř 'běn-gūng-'sž-de-jīng-'lǐ.

(*Minus*) jyǎn, 'jyǎn-chywù, chywù; (*in payment*) mwǒ (*deduct*) *or* bù-'gěy (*not pay*); *in computing discounts*, **less 10%** *may be expressed by using* jyǎn, 'jyǎn-chywù, *or* chywù, *or by* **(take) nine parts** (dǎ) 'jyěw-jé *or* (dǎ) 'jyěw-kèw (*and so on with other multiples of ten*). ‖**Five less three is two.** 'wǔ °jyǎn- (*or* °chywù-, *or* °jyǎn-chywù) 'sān dé (*or* shèng, *or* děng-ywú)-'èr. ‖**$75 less 20% discount would be $60.** chī-shr-'wǔ-kwày chywù 'bǎy-fēn-jř-èr-'shř-de-'jé-kèw (*or* chī-shr-'wǔ-kwày dǎ 'bā-jé, *or* chī-shr-'wǔ-kwày dǎ 'bā-kèw, *or* chī-shr-'wǔ-kwày 'bā-jé, *or* chī-shr-'wǔ-kwày 'bā-kèw) 'jyěw-shr (*or* °'shř, *or* 'jyěw děng-ywú; *or* °'děng-ywú, *or* °'háy shèng, *or* °'háy yěw) 'lyèw-shr-kwày. ‖**$75 less 2% would be $73.50.** chī-shr-'wǔ-kwày °chywù (*or* °jyǎn, *or* °'jyǎn-chywù) bǎy-fēn-jř-'èr. °'jyěw-shr (*or* °'shř, *or* 'jyěw děng-ywú, *or* °'děng-ywú, *or* °'háy shèng, *or* °'háy yěw) chī-shr-'sān-kwày-'wǔ. ‖**She'll pay the amount of the note for you, less interest.** tā shyàng tì-ni 'hwán nèy-bǐ-'jàng, bú-gwo °'bù-shyǎng gěy 'lì-chyán. *or* °'shyǎng bǎ 'lì-chyán 'mwǒ-le.

(*Lacking*) 'chywē(-je), 'chyàn(-je), 'chà(-je), shǎw, dwǎn. ‖**We have two divisions, less three battalions.** wǒm(-jèr) chà (*or* chyàn, *or* chywē) 'sān-yíng bú-dàw 'lyǎng-shŕ-rén. *or* wǒm(-jèr) yěw 'lyǎng-ge-shŕ, kě-shr °háy 'chywē-je (*or* °háy 'chyàn-je, *or* °háy 'chà-je, *or* háy 'shǎw, *or* °háy 'dwǎn) 'sān-yíng. *or expressed as* **but there are three battalions not here.** °yěw 'sān-yíng 'bú-dzày-jèr.

‖**In less than no time it was all finished.** yì-'jwǎn-yǎn (*or* yì-'jwǎn-yǎn-de-gūng-fu, *or* yì-jǎn-'yǎn-de-gūng-fu, *or* yì-jǎm-'yǎr-de-gung-fu, *or* 'yí-shyà-dz, *or* yì-'hwěr-de-gūng-fu, *or* 'lì-shř, *or* 'děng-shř, *or* mǎ-'shàng, *or* 'dāng-shř) jyèw dēw 'wán-le.

LESSON. (*Material to be learned, or assignment*) 'gūng-kè. ‖**The boy is good at his lessons.** shyǎw-hár 'gūng-kè (dzwò-de) tǐng 'hǎw. ‖**He has to finish his lessons before he can go out and play.** tā děy 'shyān bǎ 'gūng-kè dzwò-'wán-le tsáy néng 'chū-chywù 'wár-ne.

(*Learning unit*) kè. ‖**The book is divided into thirty lessons.** jèy-běn-'shū fēn 'sān-shr-kè. ‖**This is Lesson Twelve.** jèy shr dì-shŕ-'èr-kè.

Take lessons in *something*, **take . . . lessons** shywé (*study*). ‖**He was taking dancing lessons.** tā shywé tyàw-'wǔ láy-je.

(*Instructive experience*) 'jyàw-shywùn. ‖**This failure should be taken as a lesson.** 'jèy-tsž-shř-'bày 'yīng-gāy dàng-dzwò yí-ge-'jyàw-shywùn kàn. ‖**Let this be a lesson to you.** jèy shr gěy-ni yí-ge-'jyàw-shywùn. ‖**The experience taught him a great lesson.** tā °'jīng-le nèm-jyàn-'shèr (*or* °'shèw-le nèm-hwéy-'dzwèy, *or* °'shàng-le nèm-hwéy-'dàng, *or* °'chŕ-le nèm-hwéy-'kwēy) dé-le yí-ge-hěn-'dà-de-'jyàw-shywùn.

‖I'll teach you a lesson. wǒ 'fēy-děy 'jyàw-shywùn-'jyàw-shywùn nǐ bù-'kě. *or* (*Somewhat stronger*) wǒ 'fēy-děy 'gwǎn-jyàw-gwǎn-jyàw nǐ bù-'kě. *But* ‖You learned a lesson from that, didn't you? *is expressed proverbially, as* No experience, no increase in wisdom, right? bù-'jīng yí-'shř, bù-'jǎng yí-'jř, dwèy-ma? *or as* Having had the experience, you learned a little about cleverness, eh? 'shàng-le hwéy-'dàng (*or* 'chř-le hwéy-'kwēy, *or* 'shèw-le hwéy-'dzwèy), °swàn 'shywé-le-dyar 'gwāy-ba, á? *or as* Having had the experience, you quieted down a bit! °'lǎw-shr-le-ba.

LET. (*Permit: in a strong sense, used in negative statements or in questions or exclamations*) jwěn *or* shywǔ (*give permission*); jyàw *or* ràng (*allow*); swéy *or* yéw *or* 'bù-gwǎn (*allow without interference*); fàng (*permit passage, let go, let loose*); *or expressed by saying that something* is permitted néng *or* shywǔ, *or that it* is OK. shíng *or* chéng; *or other indirect expressions.* ‖He won't let me see his sister any more. tā 'bú-jyàw (*or* tā 'bú-ràng, *or* tā 'bù-jwěn, *or* tā 'bù-shywǔ) wǒ 'dzày chywù jǎw tā-'mèy-mey-le. ‖He wanted to stay, but they won't let him. tā shyǎng 'bù-dzěw (*or* tā shyǎng hǎy 'dāy-je), bú-gwo tām yí-'dìng °bú-jyàw tā 'dzày-nàr 'dāy-je. *or expressed as* . . . but they're going to make him go. °jyàw-ta 'dzěw-de. *or as* . . . but they won't retain him. °bù-'lyéw-ta. ‖Will the customs officials let us go through? nǐ kàn hǎy-'gwān-shang-de-rén 'hwèy °jyàw- (*or* °ràng-, *or* °fàng-)dzám 'gwò-chywu-ma? *or* bǎ-dzám 'fàng-gwo-chywu-ma? ‖Aw, let him do it hāy! °'swéy-ta-de-ba. *or* °'swéy-ta chywù-ba. *or* °'yew-ta-de-ba. *or* °'yéw-ta chywù-ba. *or* °'byé gwǎn-ta-le. ‖I won't let you! wǒ bù-'jwěn-ni! *or* wǒ bù-'shywǔ-ni! *or* (*Very strong prohibition*) dǎ 'wǒ-jer shwō jyèw bù-°'shíng! *or* °'chéng! *or* (*Courteous protests*) 'byé nèm-je! *or* 'kě byé nèm-je! *or* 'bù-néng nèm-je! *or* 'bù-shywǔ nèm-je! *or* 'háy-yěw 'nèm-je-de-ma? *or* nà jyèw 'bú-shyàng 'hwà-le. *or* nà jyèw 'bù-chéng 'hwà-le. *or* 'nǎr-de-'hwà? *or* 'byé dǎw-'lwàn. *or* 'byé hú-'nàw. *or* 'nèm-je wǒ kě bù-'dá-ying-ni.

(*Allow; in a weak sense, as used in affirmative statements or mild commands*) jyàw *or* ràng; fàng (*let go, let loose*); let someone have *is often expressed as* give gěy; let me see *is often expressed by* wǒ 'kàn-kan *or* wǒ 'chyáw-chyaw; let someone know *is often expressed as* tell 'gàw-su; *a negative with a word opposite in meaning to what follows* let *is sometimes used; when an action follows,* let *is sometimes expressed as* watch kàn. ‖Let him try once. jyàw- (*or* ràng-)'tā °láy-yi-shyar kàn-kan. *or* °shř-yi-shr(-ba). *or* kàn-'tā láy-yi-shyar-de. ‖Don't let the fire go out. 'byé jyàw-hwǒ 'myè-le. ‖He let the cup fall from his hands and broke it. (*Unintentionally*) tā bù-hǎw-'hāwr-de ná-je 'wǎn (*or* tā méy-bǎ-'wǎn ná-'jù-le) gěy 'shwāy-le. *or* (*Intentionally*) tā gù-'yì-de °bù-hǎw-'hāwr-de ná-je 'wǎn (*or* °bù-bǎ-'wǎn ná-'jù-le) gěy 'shwāy-le. ‖Don't let him get the better of you.

byé °jyàw- (*or* °ràng-)ta 'jàn-le rǐ-de-'pyán-yi. ‖He always lets his dog run loose on the street. tā 'lǎw jyàw-gěw 'swéy-byàn dzày 'jyē-shang pǎw. ‖Please let me have the menu. bǎ tsày-'dār dì-gěy wǒ. ‖Please let me see the menu. jyàw-wo 'kàn-kan tsày-'dār. *or* wǒ 'chyáw-chyaw nèy-ge-tsày-'dār. ‖I'll let you know. wǒ yí-'dìng (hwèy) °jyàw- (*or* °ràng-)ni 'jř-dàw-de. *or* wǒ yǐ-'hèw 'gàw-su nǐ. ‖The police let the burglar go in order to follow him to his fence. 'jǐng-chá bǎ-dzéy 'fàng-le, hǎw 'àn-jūng 'gēn-je tā bǎ 'wō-°jyā (*or* °jǔ) 'dǎy-jáw. ‖Let me see it. 'wǒ kàn-kan. *or* ràng- (*or* jyàw-, *or* gěy) 'wǒ kàn-kan. ‖Let it stand. *is expressed as* Don't change it. 'bú-yàw gǎy. *or* 'byé gǎy. *or* byé 'dùng. *or as* It's all right not to change it. bù-'gǎy 'hǎw-le. *or* 'bá-yùng gǎy-le. *or* jyèw nèm-'jè-ba. *or* 'jyèw nèm-je 'swàn-le.

Let's *is expressed by* -ba *at the end of a sentence, with* dzám *or* wǒm *as the subject only if the reference is clearly to* us; *when the expression is virtually a command rather than a suggestion,* -ba *is not used.* ‖Let's go to a show. dzám chywù kàn dyàn-'yěngr-ba. ‖Let's give him a little more time. dzày 'rúng-ta dyǎr-'shř-hew-ba. ‖Let's leave it until tomorrow. myéngr dzày 'shwō-ba. ‖Let's face the facts. *is expressed as* The facts are displayed in front of us, let's (see) how we should go about it. 'shř-ching dēw 'bǎy-dzày yǎn-'chyán-le, (kàn-kan) dzám gāy dzěme 'bàn-ba. *or as* Let's look at it according to the facts. dzám àn-je 'shř-dzày-de-'chíng-shíng láy °'kàn-kan-ba. *or* °'shyǎng-shyǎng-ba. ‖Let's see you do it. (*Without sarcasm*) 'chyáw-chyaw 'nǐ-de. *or* 'kàn-kan 'nǐ-de. *or* (*With or without sarcasm*) 'nǐ láy-lay kàn. *or* 'nǐ shř-shr kàn.

Let me see (*said very slowly*) *and other verbal delaying actions are expressed as* let me think and see wǒ 'shyǎng-shyǎng kàn, *or as* wait a bit and see 'děng-yi-děng kàn, *and similar constructions using verbs for* think, calculate, *etc.* ‖Let me see; two by two, times fifty, that's two hundred square feet. wǒ 'shyǎng-shyǎng kàn (*or* wǒ 'swàn-yi-swàn, *or* 'děng-yi-děng kàn), 'èr chéng-'èr, dzày chéng wǔ-'shŕ; yí-gùng 'èr-bǎy-chř-jyàn-'fāng. ‖Let's see; today is Tuesday; it must have been last Friday then. wǒ 'shyǎng-shyǎng kàn (*or* wǒ 'swàn-yi-swàn, *or* 'děng-yi-děng kàn, *or,* don't rush me 'byé máng byé máng), 'jyēr shř shīng-chī-'èr; nà-me nèy yí-'dìng shř 'shàng-shīng-chī-'wǔ-le. ‖Let me think for a while. wǒ láy (*or* wǒ, *or* ràng-wo, *or* rúng-wo) °'shyǎng-yi-shyǎng. *or* °'dzwó-me-dzwó-me. *or* °'jwó-me-jwó-me. *or* °'swàn-ji-swàn-ji.

To let (*may be rented*) jāw-'dzū, chū-'dzū, chū-'lìn. ‖The sign says "House to Let." nèy-shang 'shyě-je: 'jí-fáng °jāw-'dzū. *or* °chū-'dzū. *or* °chū-'lìn. *See also* RENT.

Let something *or* someone alone; Let something *or* someone be; *see* Leave someone alone, *under* LEAVE.

Let *someone* **by** ràng (*etc.*) . . . 'gwò-ckywu. ‖**Let me by.** *is usually expressed by a polite request similar to our* **Please** jyè-'gwāng. *or* ràng-wo 'gwò-chywu.

Let *something* **down** (*by releasing*) 'fàng-shya. ‖**Let down the curtain.** bǎ 'lyán-dz 'fàng-shya-lay. ‖**She let down her hair.** (*Literally*) tā bǎ 'téw-fa °'fàng-shya-lay-le. *or* °'sā-kāy-le. *or Figuratively, meaning* **She told all about it.** tā 'chywán-dēw °'shwŏ- (*or* °'jyǎng-)chū-lay-le.

Let down (*relax efforts*) 'sūng-shyè-shya-chywu; 'shyè-dày-shya-chywu, 'màn-shya-chywu (*slow down*), shyè-'jìn. ‖**They let down in their work.** tām gàn-'hwór °shyè-le 'jìn-le. *or* °'sūng-shyè-shya-chywu-le. *or* °'shyè-dày-shya-chywu-le. *or* °'màn-shya-chywu-le. *or expressed by a proverb,* **The way they work is like an old ox pulling a cart; the start is all right, but it doesn't keep up.** tām jyàn-'jŕ shŕ lǎw-'nyéw lā-'chē, yěw-chyán-'jìn méy-hèw-'jìn.

Let *someone* **down** (*disappoint*) dwèy-bu-'chĭ, *or* dwèy-bu-'jù; (*seriously*) jyàw . . . shāng-'shīn; (*purposely*) bǎ . . . gěy 'shwǎ(-le) *or* bǎ . . . gěy 'pyàn-le; *or expressed indirectly.* ‖**They let him down badly.** tām kě 'jēn °dwèy-bu-'chĭ tā. *or* °dwèy-bu-'jù tā. *or* °'jyàw-ta shāng-'shīn. *or* °'bǎ-ta gěy 'shwǎ-le. *or* °'bǎ-ta gěy 'pyàn-le. ‖**I won't let you down.** wŏ 'jwěn dwèy-de-'chĭ nĭ-de. *or* wŏ 'jwěn dwèy-de-'jù nĭ-de. *or* wŏ 'jwěn bú-hwèy jyàw-nĭ shāng-'shīn. *or* wŏ 'jwěn bú-'pyàn-ni. *or* wŏ 'jwěn bú-hwèy 'pyàn-ni-de. *or expressed as* **I won't do anything inappropriate to friendship.** wŏ 'bú-hwèy dzwò-chu 'bú-gèw-'péng-yew-de-shèr-lay-de.

Let go (**of**) (*release hold*) bǎ . . . 'sā-kāy; bù-'chě-je, bù-'lā-je, bù-'jyēw-je; **let go of** *anything is often expressed as* **release** (*your*) **hand** fàng-'shĕw *or* sā-'shĕw, *without the thing being held expressed.* ‖**Don't let go of the rope until I tell you.** wŏ bù-shwō-'hwà nĭ bye °bǎ 'shéng-dz 'sā-kāy. *or* °fàng-'shĕw. *or* °sā-'shĕw. ‖**Let go of my coat!** sā-'shĕw! *or* fàng-'shĕw. *or* 'byé °chě-je (*or* °'lā-je, *or* °'jyēw-je) wŏ-de-'yī-shang.

Let go (**of**) (*sell*) mày; chū-'shĕw (*let get out of one's hand*). ‖**Don't let go of your car yet.** nĭ-de-'chē shyān byé °'mày. *or* °chū-'shĕw.

Let *oneself* **go.** ‖**Let yourself go!** *is expressed as* **Don't be so self-conscious; relax.** 'byé nèm 'sž-bu-la-'jĭ-de. *or* 'byé 'pà-jèy-ge-pà-'nèy-ge-de. *or* 'byé nèm 'jywū-jywu-shù-'shù-de. *or* 'byé nèm 'chēw-chew-chè-'chè-de. *or as* **Be a little more active.** 'hwó-dùng-dyǎr-ba. *or* 'hwó-pwo-je-dyǎr-ba. *or as* **Be less inhibited.** 'sūng-sung 'shīn-ba. *or* 'fàng-shīn dà-'dǎn-de 'láy yí-shyàr-ba. *or* (*In crying*) (yàw 'kū, jyèw) °kū ge-'tùng-kway-ba. *or* °'tùng-tung-kwāy-'kwār-de 'kū-ba. *or* °'fàng-shēng 'dà kū-ba. *or as* **Enjoy yourself to the full.** 'tùng-tung-kwār-'kwār-de °'láy yí-shyàr-ba. *or* °'láy-lay. *or* (*Of playing*) °'wár-war. *or* shŕ-'jyèr-de 'láy-lay. *or* pīn-'mìng-de 'láy-lay. *or* bú-yàw 'mìng-de 'láy-lay. (*or* 'wár-war *or* 'láy yí-shyàr-ba *or* 'láy yí-shyà-dz *in place of* 'láy-lay *in any of these.*)

or (*In dancing*) shŕ-'jyèr-de (*etc.*) 'tyàw yì-'hwéy. *or* (*In speaking*) byé nèm 'twēn-twen-tu-'tŭ-de. *or* 'tùng-tung-kwār-'kwār-de 'shwō-bá. *or* yàw 'shwō jyèw shwō ge-'tùng-kway. *or* 'fàng-shīn-dà-'dǎn-đe shwō-ba. ‖**She took the news of his death calmly, but when she was alone she let herself go.** tā 'tīng-jyàn tā 'sž-shyèr de-shŕ-hew dàw hěn 'jèn-jìng-de, kě-shr dàw-le méy-'rén-de-shŕ-hew °'tùng (*or* °'dà-'dār-de) kū-le yì-cháng.

Let it go (**at that**) 'swàn-le. ‖**We'd better just let it go at that.** 'jyèw nèm-je 'swàn-le-ba. ‖**He didn't mean it; just let it go** (**or pass**). tā 'bú-shr yěw-'yì-de (*or* tā 'bú-shr gù-'yì-de, *or* tā 'bú-shr chéng-'shīn-de), °'jyèw 'swàn-le-ba. *or* °'gwò-chywu-le jyèw 'swàn-le-ba.

Let *someone* *or* *something* **in** ràng (*etc.*) . . . 'jìn-°lay (*or* °chywu); *but, of air, also* tūng *or* jìn; *of light* tèw *or* jìn. ‖**Let us in.** ràng-wŏm 'jìn-chywu. ‖**He won't let us in.** tā 'bú-ràng (*or* tā 'bú-jyàw) wŏm 'jìn-°chywu (*or* °lay). ‖**Let the dog in.** jyàw-gĕw 'jìn-lay. ‖**Windows let in light.** 'chwāng-hu 'tèw-'gwāng. *or* °'tèw-'lyàngr. *or* °'jìn-'gwāng. *or* yĕw 'chwāng-hu shŕ wèy-le-yàw-°tèw-'lyàngr-de. *or* °'tèw-'gwāng-de. *or* °'jìn-'gwāng-de. *or* tsúng (*or* dǎ) 'chwāng-hu-nar kě-yǐ °'tèw-jìn 'gwāng-lay. *or* °'yĕw-'gwāng jìn-lay. ‖**Windows let in air and light.** chwāng-hu shŕ tūng-°'fēng (*or* °'chyèr) tèw-'lyàngr-de. ‖**That opening is to let in air.** nèy-ge-'kĕwr shŕ °jìn-'chyèr-de. *or* °'tūng-'chyèr-de. *or* °'tūng-'fēng-de. *or* °'jyàw-kūng-'chì-jìn-lay-de-dì-fang. *or* °'fàng-jìn 'chyèr-lay-de. *or* tsúng (*or* dǎ) nèy-ge-'kĕwr-nar kě-yǐ °'fàng-jìn 'chyèr-lay. *or* °'jìn-'chyèr. *or* °'tūng-'chyèr. *or* °'jyàw kūng-'chì jìn-lay.

Let *someone* **in on** *something* (*tell*) 'gàw-sung *or* 'gàw-su; (*include*) 'swàn-jìn-chywu *or* 'swàn-shang. ‖**I'll let you in on a little secret.** wŏ 'gàw-sung nĭ dyǎr-mì-'mì. ‖**Let me in on the deal.** bǎ-'wŏ swàn-shang. *or* bǎ-'wŏ yě 'swàn-jin-chywu. *or expressed as* **There's surely a part for me!** yĕw 'wŏ-yí-'fèr, á!

Let *oneself* **in for** *something.* ‖**Well, you let yourself in for it.** 'nĭ shŕ dž-'jǎw. *or* 'nĭ shŕ gān-'shīn-lè 'yì. *or* nĭ jè shŕ dž-'jǎw-de, háy yĕw shéme-kě-'shwō-de.

Let loose (*express anger fully*) 'fā-dzwò, shŕ 'shìng-dz, fā 'pí-chì, nàw 'pí-chì. ‖**When he really lets loose, he can fight like mad.** tā 'jēn °'fā-dzwò-chĭ-lay (*or* °'shŕ-chĭ 'shìng-dz-lay, *or* °'fā-chĭ 'pí-chì-lay), kě-yǐ nàw-de 'tyān-fān-dì-'fù-de. *But* ‖**It seemed as though all hell had let loose.** hǎw shyàng °'tyān-fān-dì-'fù shŕ-de. *or* °'tyān-tā-dì-'shywàn shŕ-de. *or* °'hǎy-dǎw-shān-'bēng shŕ-de. ‖**He let loose** (**with**) **a torrent of invective.** tā 'pwò-kĕw dà 'mà. *or* tā 'yí-jèn 'chèw mà. *or* tā 'yí-jèn 'dà mà.

Let *someone* **off** (*a train, bus, etc.*) ràng (*etc.*) . . . 'shyà-chywu. ‖**Please let us off at the next corner.** dàw 'shyà-yí-ge-jyē-'kĕwr-nèr ('tíng-shyà-lay) ràng-wŏm 'shyà-chywu.

Let *someone* **off** (*set free*) fàng. ‖Will they let him off? tām hwèy bǎ-tā 'fàng-le-ma? *or* tām hwèy 'fàng-tā-ma?

Let *someone* **off** (*easy, etc.*). ‖He was let off with a light sentence. pàn-de tā bú-jùng, 'pyán-yi tā-le.

Let off steam (*literally*) sā-'chì *or* fàng-'chì; (*figuratively*) sā-sā 'chyèr, sǎn-sǎn 'shīn; (*of anger*) jyě-jyě 'hèn; (*of boredom*) jyě-jyě 'mèr. ‖The locomotive is letting off steam. hwǒ-chē-'téw °sā- (*or* °fàng-)'chì-ne. ‖He played a fast game of tennis to let off steam. tā wèy-le yàw °sā-sā 'chyèr (*or* °sǎn-sǎn 'shīn) shǐ-'jyèr-de dǎ-le yì-chǎng-wǎng-'chyéw. ‖Their argument doesn't mean anything; they're just letting off steam. tām dǎ 'chǎw-dz (*or* tām chǎw-'dzwěy) bìng 'méy shéme-me; 'bú-gwo shǐ °sā-sā 'chyèr (*or* °jyě-jyě 'hèn, *or* °jyě-jyě 'mèr, *or* °sǎn-sǎn 'shīn) jyèw 'shǐ-le.

Let on (*tell*) shwō(-chū-lay); (*to someone*) 'gàw-su . . .; jyàw . . . 'jǐ-dàw; not let on *is also expressed as feign ignorance* jwāng bù-jǐ-'dàw. ‖He knew it all the time and never let on. tā yì-'jǐ jyèw 'jǐ-dàw, kě 'jyěw-shr °'méy-shwō-chū-lay. *or* °'bú-gàw-su 'rén. *or* °'méy-gàw-su 'rén. *or* °'méy-jyàw rén (*or* wǒ, *or any other person*) jǐ-dàw. *or* °jwāng bù-jǐ-'dàw.

Let *something or someone* **out** fàng(-chū-chywu); (*of water, let flow out*) jyàw . . . 'lyéw-shyà-chywu *or* jyàw . . . 'lyéw-chū-chywu. ‖Will you let the dog out? nǐ bǎ-'gěw 'fàng-chū-chywu dzěm yàng? ‖Let the water out of the sink slowly. bǎ-shwěy màn-'mār-de 'fàng-lew. *or* jyàw-shwěy màn-'mār-de 'lyéw-°shyà- (*or* °chū-)chywu.

Let up (*stop*) tíng *or* jù; (*reduce*) 'shyǎw-dyǎr(-le). ‖Do you think the rain will let up soon? nǐ jywé-je 'yǔ kwày °'tíng-le-ma? *or* °'jù-le-ma? *or* °'shyǎw-dyǎr-le-ma? ‖The rain hasn't let up (*or* It has rained without letup) for two days. ywǔ bù-'tíng-de shyà-le yěw 'lyǎng-tyān-le.

Let alone (*to say nothing of*). (*Expressions occurring after the rest of the sentence*) jyèw béng 'tí-le, gèng bú-yùng 'tí-le, gèng tán-bu-'dàw-le; (*expressions occurring before the rest of the sentence*) háy 'shwō-shéme *with -ne at the end;* 'nǎr néng *with -a* (*or -wa, or -nga, etc.*) *at the end.* ‖I can't even speak Chinese well, let alone read it. jūng-gwo-'hwà wǒ háy shwō-bu-'hǎw-ne, °kàn (jūng-gwo)-'shū jyèw béng 'tí-le. *or* °kàn (jūng-gwo)-'shū gèng bú-yùng 'tí-le. *or* °kàn (jūng-gwo)-'shū gèng tán-bu-'dàw-le. *or* °háy 'shwō-shéme kàn (jūng-gwo)-'shū-ne? *or* °'nǎr néng kàn (jūng-gwo)-'shū-wa!

Letdown méy-'yì-sz-de, méy-'chywùr-de, méy-'jìn-de; (*also, of feelings, unhappy*) bù-gāw-'shìng-de. ‖The point of the joke was an awful letdown. nèy-ge-'shyàw-hwar yì-'míng-bày-gwo-lay tǐng méy-°'yì-sz-de. *or* °'chywùr-de. *or* °'jìn-de. ‖I had an awfully letdown feeling when he said he wasn't coming. tā 'yì-shwō bù-'láy jyàw-wǒ jywé-je tǐng °bù-gāw-'shìng-de. *or* °méy-'yì-sz-de. *or* °méy-'chywùr-de.

LETTER. (*Message*) shìn; (*form letter*) 'gūng-hán; (*important message with instructions or orders*) 'gūng-shǐ *or* 'gūng-wén. ‖Are there any letters for me today? 'jyēr yěw wǒ-de-'shìn-ma? ‖He wrote me a letter. tā gěy-wo shyě-le yì-fēng-'shìn-lay. ‖These are all business letters. jèy dēw shr °'gūng-hán. *or* °jyàng-'mǎy-may-shr-ching-de-'shìn. ‖We got a letter from the War Department. wǒm 'jyē-jaw-le lù-jywūn-'bù-láy-de-°'yí-jyàn-'gūng-shǐ. *or* °'yí-jyàn-'gūng-wén. *or* °'yì-fēng-'gūng-hán. *or* °'yì-fēng-'shìn. ‖That's a personal letter for him. nèy shr (gěy-)tā-de-'sz-shìn. *or* nèy shr gěy-ta-'běn-rén-de-'shìn. ‖He was nice enough to give me a letter of introduction. 'tā gěy-wǒ 'shyě-le fēng-'jyè-shàw-'shìn, 'jēn shr gèw 'myàn-dz.

(*Of an alphabet*) dzèr (*also means a Chinese character*); dž-'mǔr (*used for a letter of an alphabet in contrast to a character*). ‖These letters are not very clear. jèy-jǐ-ge-'dzèr bú-dà 'chīng-chu. ‖Have you learned all the letters of the alphabet? nǐ ('swǒ-yěw-de-)dž-'mǔr dēw 'rèn-de-le-ma?

To letter shyě-'dzèr; (*in artistic style*) shyě 'měy-shù-dž; (*on large signs*) shyě 'jāw-pay. ‖He does lettering. tā gěy-rén shyě°-'dzèr. *or* °'měy-shù-dž. *or* °'jāw-pay. ‖Letter the sign carefully. 'páv-dz-shang-de-'dzèr yàw hǎw-'hāwr-de sḣ ȯ.

To the letter. (*In every minute and necessary detail*). ‖I want these instructions followed to the letter (*completely*). 'jèy-shyē-'shywùn-lìng-shang-de-'hwà yàw 'wán-chywán °'jàw-bàn. *or* °'dzwēn-shěw. *or add to these, for emphasis* even a little bit may not be °neglected. 'yì-sz-yì-'háw yě 'bù-néng °'hū-lywè. *or* °disobeyed. °'wéy-bèy. *or* °changed. °'gǎy-dùng. *or* (*add*) not the slightest deviation is permitted. 'bù-shywǔ yěw yì-'dyǎr-'chā-wù. (*In every minute and perhaps unnecessary detail*). ‖He obeyed the law to the letter. *is expressed as* He looks upon every word in the law as sacred, and doesn't dare disobey. tā bǎ 'fǎ-lywù-shang-měy-yí-ge-'dzèr dēw kàn-dzwò 'jīn-kē-ywù-'lywù shr-de, 'bù-gǎn 'wéy-bey. (*The literal meaning*) dž-'myàr-shang-de-'yì-sz. ‖According to the letter of the law, it is possible to do that. àn-je 'tyáw-wén-dž-'myàr-shang-de-'yì-sz láy 'jyě-shǐ, yàw 'nèm bàn yě 'kě-yǐ.

LEVEL. (*Horizontal*) píng. ‖Is Peiping on level terrain or on a mountain? běy-'píng shr dzày píng-'dì-shang háy-shr dzày °'shān-shang? *or* °'dwō-'shān-de-dì-fang? ‖Is Szechwan level or mountainous? sz̀-'chwān 'dì-shr 'píng-bu-píng? ‖The table is not level. jwō-dz °bù-'píng. *or* °méy-gē-'píng-le. *or* °méy-fàng-'píng-le. *or* °-'twěr bù-'píng. *or* (*Its legs aren't the same length*) °-'twěr bù-'chí. ‖Hold the basin level. bǎ-'pén dwān-'píng-le.

(*To make horizontal*) nèng-'píng; (*by filling in earth*) dyàn-'píng *or* tyán-'píng; (*by removing earth*) chǎn-'píng; (*of wood, with an adze*) bàw-'píng. ‖This slope has to be leveled. jèy-ge-'pwēr děy ˇdyàn-'píng-le. or °tyán-'píng-le. or °chǎn-'píng-le. ‖This road has to be leveled. jèy-lù děy nèng-'píng-le.

(*To flatten by destruction*). Be leveled 'gwāng-le (*destroyed*); 'hwěy-le (*be in ruins*); leveled place 'hwāng-dì (*a wilderness*); 'jyāw-tǔ (*scorched earth*). ‖The shelling leveled the town. 'pàw bǎ-'chéng 'hūng-chéng yí-pyàn-°'jyāw-tǔ-le. or °'hwāng-dì-le. or pàw bǎ chywán-'chéng dēw °hūng-'hwěy-le. or °dǎ-'gwāng-le. or °hūng-'píng-le.

(*Equal in height*) chí (*of the same kind of things*); yì-bār- (or yì-bān-, or yì-mǎr-)°'píng (*same level*) or °'chí (*same length or height or level of termination*) or °'gāw (*same height*). ‖The book shelf is level with the top of the table. shū-'jyà-dz gēn jwō-'myàr °'chí-je. or °yì-bār-'píng. or °yì-bār-'chí. or °yì-bār-'gāw. ‖The shrubs are clipped all to the same level. shyǎw-'shùr dēw jyǎn-de °yì-bār-'píng (etc.). or °'chí-chi-jyē-'jyēr-de. ‖The river is level with the top of the dike. 'hé-shwěy jǎng-de °gēn-dī (or °gēn-tí) yì-bār-'píng-le. or °'píng-le 'tsáwr-le.

(*Tool to test level*) shwěy-píng-'chř. ‖A level would be handy. yěw ge-shwěy-píng-'chř jyèw 'hǎw-le.

Level-headed. ‖He's level-headed (or, He has a level head) in emergencies. tā ywù-'shř 'jèn-jìng. or tā yěw-'shèr de-shŕ-hew tsúng-láy °bù-jwā-'shyā. or °(shīn-li) bù-'hwāng. or °(shīn-li) bú-'lwàn. or °hěn 'jèn-jìng-de. or °'bù-hwāng-bù-'máng-de.

On a level or **on the same level** (*figuratively*) chí or yí-'yàng or yì-'bān or yì-'byàr plus a word to indicate what is on the particular level, or in what respect the things are level. ‖Try to keep the work of the two classes on a level. (*By teaching at the same speed*) 'lyǎng-bān-de-'gūng-kè yàw jyāw-de °yí-'yàng (or °yì-'bān)-kwày tsáy 'hǎw. or (*Degree of attainment the same*) néng jyàw 'lyǎng-bān-de-'chéng-dù lǎw shř °chí-de (or °yí-'yàng-de) tsáy 'hǎw. ‖The two classes are not on the same level of intelligence. 'lvǎng-bān-de-'chéng-dù bù-°'chí. or °yí-'yàng.

On the level. (*Of something said*) jēn-de (*true*); bù-'ywān (*not cheat, not make a fool of, when followed by a person*); (*of something said or done*) bú-'pyàn (*followed by a person, not to fool*); (*of a person*) numerous expressions are used which are clear in the sentences below. ‖Is that tip on the level? nèy-ge-'shyèr shř 'jēn-de-ma? ‖What I said is on the level. wǒ-shwō-de °shř 'jēn-de. or °bù-'ywān-nǐ. or °bú-'pyàn-ni. ‖I don't think he's on the level. wǒ jywé-je tā °yěw-dyǎr bù-'chéng-shr. or °yěw-dyǎr bú-'jèng-jŕ. or °yěw dyǎr-'jyǎ. or °yěw-dyǎr bù-kě-'kàw. or °bú-shr 'jèng-jīng-rén. or °shř ge-'shyǎw-rén. ‖He's entirely on the level. tā hěn 'chéng-shr. or tā hěn kě-'kàw. or tā hěn 'jèng-jŕ. or tā shř ge-'jèng-jīng-rén. or °tā shř ge-'jywūn-dz. or tā bú-hwèy jwāng-jyǎ.

One's level best. ‖He tried his level best. tā 'jēn mày 'lì-chi-lay-je. or tā 'jēn shŕ-'jyèr-lay-je. or tā yì-'dyǎr yě méy°-shwǎ hwá-'téw. or °-shř shīn-'yǎr. or °'tēw-gūng-jyǎn-'lyàw.

LIBERTY. (*See also* **FREEDOM, FREE.**) (*Political*) dž-'yéw; liberty and equality dž-'yéw píng-'děng; civil liberties (*rights*) 'mín-chywán; (*independence of a country*) dž-'jǔ. ‖This new law puts our civil liberties in danger. 'shīn-fǎ-lywù 'wēy-shyé 'mín-chywán. ‖There is no absolute liberty. 'méy-yěw 'jywé-dwèy-de-dž-'yéw.

(*Legal*). Get one's liberty chū-'ywù (*get out of prison*); 'fàng-chū-lay (*be set free*). ‖The prisoner got his liberty. 'chyéw-fàn 'yǐ-jīng °chū-'ywù-le. or °'fàng-chū-lay-le.

Be at liberty (*to do something*) kě-yǐ (or néng) 'swéy-byàn or kě-yǐ (or néng) 'swéy-yì (*be able freely*); néng (*be able*). ‖Are you at liberty to talk? nǐ 'shyàn-dzày kě-yǐ °'swéy-byàn (or °'swéy-yì) shwō-'hwà-ma? ‖I'm not yet at liberty to talk. wǒ háy bù-néng °'swéy-byàn (or °'swéy-yì) shwō-'hwà. or 'yěw-de-hwà wǒ háy bù-néng °'shwō-chū-lay. or °'jyǎng-chū-lay. or °'gàw-su rén.

Take liberties 'swéy-byàn (*act freely*); 'fàng-sż (*be unrestrained, disorderly*). ‖He took too many liberties when he was here. tā dzày-'jèr de-'shŕ-hew tày °swéy-'byàn-le. or °'fàng-sż-le.

Take the liberty (*to do something*) 'dà-dǎn-de (*literally, with great courage*). ‖May I take the liberty of making a suggestion? wǒ 'dà-dǎn-de °shwō jywù-'hwà, shíng-ma? or °chū ge-'jú-yì, shíng-ma?

LIE (**LAY, LAIN**). (*Assume a horizontal position; of human beings*) tǎng or (*Peiping*) dǎw (*on back or side*); pā (*face down*); (*of animals*) wò (*curled up*); pā (*head up or on the paws*). ‖Don't lie on the damp grass. 'byé tǎng-dzày 'shř-de-tsǎw-'dì-shang. ‖He lay on the sofa and took a rest. tā tǎng-dzày shā-'fā-shang 'shyē-le-hwěr. ‖The soldiers just lay down on the ground and went to sleep. bīng °tǎng- (or °dǎw-)dzày 'dì-shang jyèw dēw shwèy-'jáw-le. ‖Lie down (*on back or side*). 'tǎng-shya. ‖Lie down, face down. 'pā-shya. ‖You'd better lie down for a while. nǐ 'tǎng-hwěr-ba. ‖I want to lie down for a few minutes. wǒ shyǎng 'tǎng-shya 'shyē-yi-hwěr. ‖Let him lie on his side only; don't let him lie face up or down. jyàw-tā 'jáy-leng-je (shēn-dz) 'tǎng-je, byé 'yǎng-je yě byé 'pā-je. ‖He was lying facing this way. tā chỉ-'shyān lyǎn-cháw 'jèy-byar tǎng-je. ‖Lie down! (*to a dog*) 'wò-shya! or 'pā-shya! ‖The cat just lay there motionless and with her eyes closed, but she jumped at the mouse as soon as it showed itself. māw 'pā-nàr (or māw 'wò-nàr), 'bì-je-yǎr yì-'dyǎr yě bú-'dùng; kě-shr 'hàw-dz 'gāng-yi lèw-'téwr māw jyèw 'pū-shang-chywu-le.

(*Be located at*) dzày; (*after being put at*) dzày . . . 'fàng-je. ‖Most of the town lies on the east bank of the river. 'dà-bàn-ge-'chéng dzày hé-de-'dūng-°'àn-shang. or °byar. ‖The book is lying on the table. shū dzày 'jwōr-shang (fàng-je)-ne.

(*Be buried at*) 'máy-dzày; *or expressed as* . . .'s
tomb is at . . .-de-'fén dzày. ‖**His body lies in the International Cemetery.** tā 'máy-dzày 'gwó-jì-gūng-'mù-le. *or* tā-de-'fén dzày 'gwó-jì-gūng-'mù-li.

(*Consist in*) shŕ 'yīn-wey (*be because of*); dzày
(*be located at*); **A lies in B** *may also be expressed as*
B shŕ A. ‖**The appeal of this book lies in its humor.**
jèy-bĕr-'shū swó-yĭ-ràng-rén-'shĭ-hwān-de shŕ 'yīn-wey 'shyĕ-de °hĕn dèw-'gén. *or* °hĕn 'yēw-mwò. *or* °'néng yĭn-rén fā-'shyàw. ‖**Therein lies his weakness.** tā-de-'chywē-dyăn jyèw dzày-'nàr. *or* nèy jyèw-shr tā-de-'chywē-dyăn.

Lie around shyán, 'shyán-gwo-chywu, shyán-'dāy, 'shéme yĕ bú-'gàn (*do nothing at all*). ‖**I've just been lying around all day.** wŏ yì-'tyăn-de-gūng-fu. °jyèw nèm 'shyán-gwo-chywu-le. *or* °jyèw nèm shyán-'dāy-je láy-je. *or* °'shéme yĕ méy-'gàn. ‖**He's been lying around all this time.** tā yì-'jŕ jyèw nèm °'shyán-je. *or* °shyán-'dāy-je. *or* (*As a habit*) °'yéw-shĕw hàw-'shyán-de.

Lie down. *See first paragraph above.*

Lie down on the job bú-'gàn-le (*stop working*); bă-shŕ 'lyàw-shya *or* bă-shŕ 'rēng. ‖**He lay down on the job.** tā bú-'gàn-le. *or* tā bă-shŕ 'lyàw-shya-le. *or* tā bă-shŕ 'rēng-le.

Lie idle (*of a factory*) 'tíng-dwèn; **lie fallow** (*of ground*) hwāng *or* méy-'jùng *or* méy-'jùng-shéme, *or* méy-rén 'jùng; (*of other things, unused*) méy-'yùng *or* (*unmoved*) méy-rén 'dùng. ‖**The factory has been lying idle for a year.** 'gūng-chăng 'tíng-dwèn-le yĕw yì-'nyán-le. ‖**This ground has been lying fallow for two years.** jèy-dì yĕw 'lyăng-nyán méy-°'jùng-le. *or* °'jùng-shéme-le. *or* jèy-dì 'hwāng-le lyăng-'nyán-le. ‖**This machine has been lying idle for two years.** jèy-ge-'jī-chi yĕw 'lyăng-nyán méy-°'yùng-le. *or* (*unmoved*) °'rŕ dùng-le.

Lie low 'dwŏ-yi-dwŏ *or* 'dwŏ-dwĕr (*avoid trouble, hide*); bù-'yán-ywu (*keep still*). ‖**You'd better lie low for a while.** nĭ 'jàn-shŕ °'dwŏ-yi-dwŏ-ba. *or* °'dwŏ-dwĕr-ba. *or* °byé 'yán-ywu.

Lie in wait for 'byē, dĕng, tsáng-je 'dĕng. ‖**It's there that the enemy's ships are lying in wait for us.** 'dí-rén-de-chwán shŕ dzày-'nàr °'byē-je wŏm-ne. *or* °'tsáng-je 'dĕng-wŏm-ne. *or* °'dĕng-je wŏm-ne.

LIE (LIED). (*With meanings ranging from false information to cheating, so that the listener will err only in knowledge*) **a lie** *or* **lies** 'jyă-hwà, 'hwăng-hwà, 'shyā-hwàr, hwăng; *or expressed by a negative plus a word for truth*, 'shŕ-hwà *or* 'jēn-hwà; **to lie** *is expressed by* shwō *with any of the above, by* chĕ *with any of the first four, or by* sā *with* hwăng *alone;* **to tell a lie** *is expressed in the same ways, but with* yī (*one*) *and a measure before the noun;* **lying,** (*false*) 'jyă-de; **to lie by trickery** nèng ge-'shywán-shywū (*play a trick*). ‖**He never told a lie in his life.** tā

'píng-shēng méy-°shwō-gwo (*or* °chĕ-gwo) 'yí-jywù-'jyă-hwà. *or* °shwō-gwo (*or* °chĕ-gwo) 'yí-jywù-'hwăng-hwà. *or* °shwō-gwo (*or* °chĕ-gwo) 'yí-jywù-'shyā-hwàr. *or* °shwō-gwo (*or* °chĕ-gwo, *or* °sā-gwo) 'yí-ge-'hwăng. ‖**He told a lie.** tā 'shwō-le yí-jywù-'hwăng-hwà. (*etc.*) ‖**Don't lie to me.** byé gēn-wo °shwō 'jyă-hwà. *or* °sā-'hwăng. (*etc.*). *or* shwō °'shŕ-hwà. *or* °'jēn-hwà. ‖**There's no doubt that he's lying about it.** tā-'nèy 'jwèn °shŕ sā-'hwăng-ne. (*etc.*) *or* °'bú-shr 'shŕ-hwà. *or* °'bú-shr 'jēn-hwà. ‖**He's trying to lie his way out.** tā shyăng shwō ge-'shyā-hwàr (*etc.;* *or* tā shyăng nèng ge-'shywán-shywū) jyèw °'táng-gwo-chywu. *or* °'dăng-gwo-chywu. *or* °'méy tā-de-'shèr-le. *or* °'dwŏ-gwo-chywu. *or* °'pyàn-gwo-chywu. *or* °'hwèn-gwo-chywu. *or* °'mēng-gwo-chywu. ‖**He told a (little white) lie to ease his mother's mind.** tā yàw jyàw tā-'mŭ-chin bù-fán-'shīn, swŏ-yĭ shwō-le ge-'shyā-hwàr (*etc.*). ‖**He's lying.** tā-shwō-de shŕ °'hwăng-hwà. *or* °'shyā-hwàr. *or* °'jyă-hwàr. *or* °'jyă-de. *or* tā-nèy shŕ °sā-'hwăng-ne. *or* °shwō 'shyā-hwàr-ne (*etc.*). *or* tā-shwō-de bú-shr °'shŕ-hwà. *or* °'jēn-hwà.

(*With meanings ranging from false impressions to slander, so that the listener will err also in attitudes and feelings*) **a lie** *or* **lying** *as an act* 'hú-shwō-bá-dàw, 'hú-dzēw-báy-'lyĕ, 'shyā-chĕ, 'shyā-shwō; **lying** (*false*) hú-'dzēw-de, 'byān-de ge-'shyā-hwàr, 'jyă-de; **to be** (*entirely*) **a lie** méy(-yĕw) (*or* năr yĕw) nèm hwéy-'shèr; **tell lies** *may also be expressed as* méy-yĕw 'yí-jywù-°'shŕ- (*or* °'jēn-)hwà. ‖**He's lying!** (*Compare last sentence in preceding paragraph*) tā-nèy shŕ °hú-shwō-bá-'dàw. *or* °'hú-dzēw-báy-'lyĕ. *or* °shyā-'chĕ. *or* °'shyā-shwō. *or* °hú-'dzēw-de. *or* °'byān-de ge-'shyā-hwàr. ‖**That's a lie!** nèy shŕ 'hú-shwō-bá-'dàw (*etc.*). *or* 'năr yĕw (*or* méy, *or* méy-yĕw) nèm hwéy-'shèr. ‖**Everything he says is a lie.** tā méy-yĕw 'yí-jywù-°'shŕ-hwà. *or* °'jēn-hwà. *or* tā-shwō-de 'wán-chywán shŕ °'hú-shwō-bá-'dàw. *or* °'hú-dzēw-báy-'lyĕ. *or* °shyā-'chĕ. *or* °'shyā-'shwō. *or* °hú-'dzēw-de. *or* °'jyă-de. *or* 'hwăng-'hwà (*etc.*) *or* tā-shwō-de 'wán-chywán 'méy-nèm hwéy-'shèr.

LIFE. 1. (*Being or remaining alive, or behavior of organic matter*) 'shēng-mìng, mìng; *in some combinations* shēng; *or expressed indirectly by* live hwó *or* die sž. ‖**Biology is the science of life.** 'shēng-wù-shywé shŕ 'yán-jyēw-'shēng-mìng-de-'kē-shywé. ‖**The Buddhists teach that killing even an ant is °destroying life.** 'fwó-jyā shwō nèng-sž ge-'má-yi yĕ shŕ °shā-'shēng. *or* °hày yì-tyáw-'mìng. *or* °'hày yì-tyáw-'shēng-mìng. *or expressed as* °**destroying a living thing.** °'hày-sz ge-'hwó-wùr. *or* °'hày-sž ge-'hwó-je-de-dūng-shi. ‖**He barely escaped with his life.** tā-nèy shŕ 'sž-lĭ-táw-'shēng. *or* tā-nèy shŕ 'hŭ-kĕw-ywú-'shēng. *or* tā 'gāng-gang táw-chū yì-tyáw-'mìng-lay. *or* tā-nèy-tyáw-'mìng jyăn-'jŕ shŕ °'shŕ-lay-de. *or* °'jyăn-lay-de. ‖**His life is hanging in the balance.**

tā-'mìng bù-jŕ-dàw bǎw-de-'jù-bǎw-bu-'jù. *or* tā yě-shywǔ hwèy 'sž-de. *or* tā shŕ-'sž shŕ-'hwó háy bù-jŕ-'dàw. ‖It's his life against (*or* or) mine. bú-shr 'tā sž jyèw-shr 'wǒ sž. *or* bú-shr 'tā hwó-je jyèw-shr 'wǒ hwó-je. *or* wǒ gēn-'tā nèy shŕ pīn ge-'nǐ-sž-wǒ-'hwó-de-'shŕ. ‖His life depends on you now. tā-de-'mìng shyàn-dzày dzày 'nǐ-'shěw-li-le. *or* tā 'hwó-de-lyǎw-'hwó-bu-'lyǎw 'chywán kàw-'nǐ-le. ‖He worked as though his life depended on it. tā 'bú-yàw-'mìng-de gàn. *or* tā 'pīn-(je-)'mìng-de gàn. *or* tā méy-'mìng-de gàn.

Life preserver, (*the ring-shaped type*) jyèw-shēng-'chywān; (*the jacket, belt, or Mae West type*) jyèw-shēng-°'dày *or* °'yī; **lifeboat** jyèw-shēng-'chwán; **lifeguard** jyèw-hù-'ywán.

Life line (*figuratively, supply line, etc.*) 'shēng-mìng-'shyàn.

Life insurance rén-'shèw-bǎw-'shyǎn.

Life after death (*as a concept*) *is expressed as* **after death there is a soul** sž-'hèw yěw-'hwén *or* sž-'hèw yěw 'líng-hwén, *or as* **there is a heaven and hell** yěw 'tyān-táng 'dì-ywù, *or as* **when the body dies the soul still lives** 'shēn-dz 'sž-le 'líng-hwén háy 'dzày. ‖Almost every religion teaches (that there is) a life after death. chà-bu-dwō 'shéme- (*or* chà-bu-dwō 'něy-jǔng-)'dzūng-jyàw dēw jyàw-rén 'shìn °sž-'hèw yěw-'líng-hwén. *or* °*etc.*

Signs of life chyèr (*breath*) *or* 'jŕ-jywé (*sensory reaction*). ‖Are there still signs of life in the child? shyǎw-'hár háy yěw °'chyèr (*or* °'jŕ-jywé) méy-yěw?

A matter of life and death *is expressed as* **may result in death or life** 'shìng-mìng-jyāw-'gwān-de, 'gwān-shì rén-'mìng, 'shēng-sž-jyāw-'gwān-de; *or as* **done to save life** jyèw-'mìng-de-shèr; (*figuratively; of utmost importance*) 'gwān-shì dà-le, yàw-'jǐn-de 'lì-hay. ‖This is a matter of life and death. jèy-jyàn-shèr °'shìng-mìng-jyāw-'gwān-de. *or* °*etc.*

For the life of (*one*) yàw-le (. . .-de-)'mìng. ‖I can't for the life of me understand this. yàw-le (wǒ-de-)'mìng, wǒ yě 'bù-dǔng jèy shŕ 'dzěm hwéy-'shèr.

Lose (*one's*) **life** sž. ‖He lost his life in the flood. tā fā-'shwěy-de-shŕ-hèw 'sž-de.

Give (*one's*) **life** jywān-'chywū, jìn-'jūng; 'shā-shēn-chéng-'rén, sàng-'mìng. ‖He gave his life for his country. tā 'wèy-gwó °jywān-'chywū-le. *or* °jìn-'jūng-le. *or* °'shā-shēn-chéng-'rén-le. *or* °sàng-'mìng-le.

2. (*Way of living*) 'shēng-hwó; 'gwò-de (*passing time*); 'hwó-de (*living*); 'wár-de (*playing, of an enjoyable life*); *or expressed verbally as* **to pass** (*one's*) **days** gwò 'r̀-dz, *or as* **to be dwelling** jù-je; *also some indirect expressions.* ‖Life in the country is dull. dzày chéng-'wày-tew (*or* dzày 'shyāng-shya) °jù-je méy 'yì-sz. *or* °jù-je tǐng wú-'lyáw. *or* °'gwò 'r̀-dz méy 'yì-sz. *or* °gwò 'r̀-dz tǐng wú-'lyáw. *or* 'shyāng- (*or* 'núng-)tswēn-'shēng-hwó yì-'dyǎr yě bú-'rè-naw. ‖I hope your married life will be very happy. 'jù-ni (yěw) 'měy-mǎn-de-'jyā-tíng-shēng-'hwó. ‖Their mar-

ried life is very happy. tām lyǎng-'kěw-dz gwò-de tǐng °'hǎw. *or* °'hé-mù. *or* tām fú-'fù-jŕ-jyān tǐng °'hé-mù. *or* °'kwày-lè. ‖He leads a high life. tā-gwò-de hěn 'shē-chŕ. ‖He leads a simple life. tā-gwò-de hěn 'pǔ-sù. ‖He leads a busy life. *is expressed as* **He's very busy every day.** tā 'tyān-tyār hěn 'máng. *or as* **He's busy all day.** tā jěng-'tyān-jya (*or* tā 'yì-tyān dàw-'wǎn-de) °'máng. *or* °hěn 'máng-de. *or* °yěw hěn-'dwō-shèr. *or* °'máng-je-ne. *or* °'lǎw yěw-'shèr. *or* °'máng-mang-daw-'dāw-de.

Night life. ‖There is very little night life in this town. jèy-ge-'chéng-li °'yè-li 'méy shéme-'rè-naw. *or* °'yè-li 'méy-yěw shéme-kě-'wár-de-dì-fang.

‖This is the life! 'jè tsáy jyàw °'hwó-de (*or* °'wár-de) 'tùng-kway-ne!

3. (*Spirit*). **Full of life** (*of a person*) (yěw) 'jīng-shen; 'hwó-pwō-de, 'hwó-bwō-de, *or* 'hwān-shr (*active*); (*of other things; as eyes*) (yěw) 'jīng-shen; yěw-'shén. ‖The children seem full of life. háy-dzmen tǐng °(yěw) 'jīng-shen. *or* °'hwó-bwō-de. *or* °'hwó-pwō-de. *or* °'hwān-shr. ‖His eyes are full of life. tā-'yǎn-lǐ yěw-'shén. *or* tā-'yǎn-jīng hěn (yěw) 'jīng-shen.

‖He was the life of the party. 'nèy-tsž-'jywù-hwèy jyàw-'tā nèng-de tǐng °'rè-naw-de. *or* °yěw-'yì-sz-de. *or* °yěw-'chywùr-de.

4. **Life span** 'shèw(-mìng), *or expressed as* **may live** kě-yǐ hwó. ‖The average life of a dog is ten years. gěw 'píng-jywūn kě-yǐ hwó 'shŕ-nyán.

5. **Lifetime** yí-'bèy-dz (*a complete life*); 'shēng-píng *or* 'píng-shēng *or* yì-'shēng (*the whole life up to the present*); *or expressed as* **until old** dàw-'lǎw; *or as* **from youth** (*until adulthood*) tsúng-'shyǎwr (dàw-'dà); *or as* **straight through** yì-'jŕ (*of the past*); *or in other indirect ways.* ‖He was crippled all his life. tā 'tsán-fèy-le yí-'bèy-dz. ‖He was (*became*) crippled for life. tā làw-le ge-yí-'bèy-dz-de-'tsán-jí. ‖I've lived here all my life. wǒ yì-'jŕ jù-'jèr. *or* wǒ tsúng-'shyǎwr jyèw jù-'jèr. *or* wǒ tsúng-'shyǎwr dàw-'dà méy-dzày 'byé-chùr jù-gwo. *or* (*Of an old man whose life is complete*) wǒ dzày-'jèr jù-le yí-'bèy-dz-le. *or expressed as* **I grew up nowhere but here.** wǒ jǎng dzèm-'dà méy-dzày 'byé-chùr jù-gwo. *or as* **I was born here and brought up here.** wǒ shŕ jèr-'shēng-de jèr-'jǎng-de. ‖You can't expect to have such a chance twice in a lifetime. 'jèm-ge-'jī-hwèy jèy-yí-'bèy-dz 'béng-shyǎng 'dzày yěw-le. ‖That's a lifetime job. 'nèy-shèr kě-yǐ dzwò yí-'bèy-dz. *or* 'nèy-ge děy dzwò °yí-'bèy-dz. *or* °dàw-'lǎw. ‖He can have that job for life if he wants it. nèy-shèr tā shyǎng dzwò yí-'bèy-dz yě 'shíng. ‖He never told a lie in his whole life. tā yí-'bèy-dz (*or* tā 'shēng-píng, *or* tā 'píng-shēng, *or* tā yì-'shēng) méy-'shwō-gwo yì-jywū-'hwǎng-hwà. ‖He had a long and happy life. tā yí-'bèy-dz yèw shyǎng-'shèw, yèw shyǎng-'fú. *or* tā 'fú 'shèw shwāng-chywán.

Life membership 'yǔng-jyěw-hwèy-'ywán **Life imprisonment** 'wú-chī-'tú-shíng.

‖I had the time of my life. wǒ-ˈwár-de hěn ˈtùng-kway.

6. (*Living things*) *is expressed as* human beings rén, *or as* animals ˈhwó-wùr, *or as* signs of human life ˈrén-yān; *or indirectly with a verb meaning* live shēng *or* hwó, *or* grow jž̩ng; no life *may also be expressed as* not even a blade of grass lyán gēn-ˈtsǎw dēw méy-ˈyěw; wild life ˈyě-shèw. ‖There was no life on the island. ˈdǎw-shang °méy-yěw ˈrén. *or* °méy-yěw ˈhwó-wùr. *or* °méy-yěw ˈrén-yān. *or* °lyán gēn-ˈtsǎw dēw méy-ˈyěw. ‖No life can exist in such a place. ˈjèm-ge-dì-fang ˈshéme dēw °ˈhwó-bu-ˈlyǎw. *or* °ˈbù-néng ˈshēng. *or* °ˈbù-néng ˈjǎng. ‖There's a lot of wild life in these forests. ˈjèy-yí-dày-shù-ˈlín-dz-li yěw bù-ˈshǎw-de-ˈyě-shèw.

7. (*Person, or person's life*) rén, ˈrén-mìng, mìng, ˈshìng-mìng. ‖Many lives were lost in the flood. nàw-shwěy-ˈdzǎy de-shŕ-hew sž̩-le bù-ˈshǎw-de-ˈrén. ‖Peace was gained only through the loss of tens of millions of lives. ˈhé-píng shŕ jǐ-ˈchyān-wàn-°ˈrén-mìng- (*or* °tyáw-ˈmìng-, *or* °tyáw-ˈshìng-mìng-)ˈhwàn-láy-de. ‖They saved two lives. tām jyèw-le ˈlyǎng-tyáw-ˈmìng. *or* tām jyèw-ˈhwó-le ˈlyǎng-ge-rén.

8. (*Biography*) ˈjwàn-jì (*book-length*); shyǎw-ˈjwàn (*shorter*). Write a book on someone's life bǎ . . .-de-ˈshēng-píng-ˈshŕ-jì shyě yì-běn-ˈshū *or* shyě yì-běr-. . .-de-ˈjwàn-ji. ‖I'm reading the life of a great novelist. wǒ jèng kàn yí-ge-dà-shyǎw-ˈshwōr-jyā-de-°ˈjwàn-jì. *or* °shyǎw-ˈjwàn. ‖He wrote a book on the life of the President. tā bǎ dzǔng-tǔng-de-ˈshēng-píng-ˈshŕ-jì shyě-gwo yì-běn-ˈshū. *or* tā shyě-gwo yì-ˈběr-jèy-wèy-dzǔng-ˈtǔng-de-ˈjwàn-jì.

LIFT. (*See also* **HOLD, CARRY.**) *In the meaning to* raise, *Chinese distinguishes numerous ways of lifting by using different main verbs; these often occur in combinations such as* to lift (up) (*in order to test weight, carry, or move*) . . .-chǐ-lay; to lift up (*and leave at a place or level*) . . .-shàng-chywu; to lift to a place . . .-dàw . . . chywu; to lift out . . .-chū-chywu; to lift over . . .-gwò-chywu; to lift high . . . gāw; be able to lift . . .-de-dùng *or* . . . de-chǐ-lay; *main verbs which mean* pull, push, *or* move *have the meaning* lift *only in combination with* -shàng-chywu *or* gāw; *the important main verbs follow.*

(*The most general term; of lifting with hands or arms*) jywǔ. ‖Lift these boxes over the fence. bǎ jèy-shyē-ˈhé-dz tsúng ˈlán-gār-shang-nar ˈjywǔ-gwò-chywu. ‖Lift it up a little higher so I can reach it. dzày jywǔ ˈgāw-dyar, wǒ tsáy ˈgèw-de-ˈjáw. (*Or any of the following may be used for* jywǔ *here.*)

(*By two or more persons using their hands*) táy *or* dā. ‖The trunk is full of books; I don't think one person can lift it. yì-shyāng-dz-li ˈchywán shŕ ˈshū, wǒ kàn ˈyí-ge-rén táy- (*or* °dā-, *or* °jywǔ-)bú-ˈdùng. *or* °táy- (*or* °dā-, *or* °jywǔ-)bu-chǐ-láy. ‖Be careful

when you lift him out; don't hurt him. bǎ-tā °ˈtáy- (*or* °dā-)chū-chywu de-shŕ-hew yàw ˈdwō-jyā ˈshyǎw-shīn; byé bǎ-tā pèng-ˈténg-le. ‖They lifted the patient from the bed to the operating table. tām bǎ ˈbìng-rén tsúng ˈchwáng-shang °táy- (*or* °dā-)dàw ˈkǎy-dāw-ˈjwō-shang-chywu-le. ‖Give me a lift with this trunk, will you? láw-ˈjyà, gēŋ-wǒ °ˈdā- (*or* °ˈtáy-)yi-shyar ˈshyāng-dz.

(*Of raising one's own head, hand, or arm*) yáng; (*including feet also*) táy. ‖He was too weak to lift his hand. tā rwǎn-de lyán-ˈshěw dēw ˈbù-néng °yáng-le. *or* °táy-le. *or* °jywǔ-le. *or* °tǎv-chǐ-lay-le. *or* °jywǔ-chǐ-lay-le.

(*In the arms*) bàw. ‖Lift the baby up so he can see. bǎ shyǎw-hár °ˈbàw- (*or* °ˈjywǔ-)chǐ-lay hǎw jyàw-tā kàn-de-ˈjyàn.

(*In the hand, especially with arm down and hand holding a handle*) dī-lew, tí. ‖Lift the suitcase and see how heavy it is. bǎ ˈshyāng-dz ˈtí-chi-lay, kàn-kan yěw dwō ˈjùng.

(*With both hands stretched forward, palms up, especially balancing something*) dwān. ‖There are so many things on the tray that I can hardly lift it. ˈtwō-pár-shang-de-ˈdūng-shi tày ˈdwō-le, wǒ ˈchà-bu-dwō °dwān- (*or* °twō-)bu-chǐ-ˈlay-le.

(*With both hands, palms up, especially of something that must be handled with care*) twō. ‖Lift his head up and give him a drink of hot tea. bǎ tā-de-ˈtéw twō-chi-lay gěy-ta bēy-rè-ˈchá hē.

(*On the shoulders*) káng. ‖The crowd lifted him to their shoulders. dà-jyā-ˈhwǒr bǎ-ta °ˈkáng- (*or* °ˈjywǔ-)chǐ-lay-le.

(*With a crowbar or other lever*) chyàw. ‖Lift the stone with a crowbar. ná gēn-tyě-ˈgwèn bǎ ˈshŕ-tew ˈchyàw-chi-lay.

Similarly with other verbs listed under **HOLD** *or* **CARRY,** *as* pěng (*with both hands, palms together*), dǐng (*with the head or a pole*), *etc.*

(*By picking up*) ná. ‖That suitcase is too heavy for you to lift. nèy-ge-shyāng-dz tày ˈjùng, nǐ °ná- (*or* °jywǔ-)bu-ˈdùng.

(*Of raising the corner or side of something, as a cover, curtain, or rug; only the following combinations with* -kāy *occur*) ˈshyān-kāy; ˈjyē-kāy (*used of flexible things only if strength is required*); ˈdǎ-kāy (*not used of flexible things*). ‖Lift up the cover and see what's inside. ˈshyān-kāy (*or* ˈjyē-kāy, *or* ˈdǎ-kāy) ˈgàr kàn-kan ˈlǐ-tew dēw yěw-ˈshéme. ‖He lifted up a corner of the rug and swept the dirt underneath it. tā bǎ dì-ˈtǎn shyān-kāy-le-ge-ˈjyǎwr, jyèw bǎ ˈdzāng-tǔ ˈsǎw-jìn-chywu-le.

(*By pulling, pushing, and other motions*). (*Pull*) lā *or* chě; (*push*) twēy; (*transport*) ywùn; (*get to move*) nèng *or* ˈgǔ-du. ‖They had to lift the heaviest boxes with a pulley. tām yùng hwá-ˈchēr tsáy bǎ dǐng-ˈjùng-de-jǐ-ge-ˈshyāng-dz °lā- (*or* °chě-, *or* °ywùn-, *or* nèng-, *or* °gǔ-du-)shàng-chywu.

(*To rise; as a fog*) sàn (*disperse*). ‖The fog lifted quickly. 'wù hěn 'kwày-de jyèw 'sàn-le.

(*Upward' force*) (shàng-)'shēng-lì. ‖The plane didn't have enough lift to get off the ground. fēy-'jī-shàng-shēng-lì bú-'gèw(-'dà-de), swǒ-yǐ 'méy-néng °lí-'dì. *or* °'fēy-chǐ-lay.

Give *someone a lift* (*in a car*) shwèn-'byàn °dày *or* °sùng. ‖May I give you a lift? wǒ shwèn-'byàn 'dày-ni-chywu, hǎw-bu-hǎw? ‖Someone gave him a lift (*or He got a lift*) to the station. 'yéw-rén kāy-'chē bǎ-ta shwèn-'byàn 'dày-dàw chē-'jàn-chywu-de.

Give *someone a lift* (*emotionally*). (*Make happy*) jyàw . . . gāw-'shìng; (*encourage*) jyàw . . . 'jīng-shén °yí-'jèn. *or* °'hwàn-fā. *or* °'jèn-dzwò-chǐ-lay. *or* bǎ . . . 'jīng-shén °'tí-chǐ-lay. *or* °'jèn-dzwò-chǐ-lay. ‖His letter really gave me a lift. tā-nèy-fēng-'shìn jyàw-wo hěn gāw-'shìng. ‖That speech of the general's gave the soldiers quite a lift. 'jyāng-jywun-de-tán-'hwà (*or* 'jyāng-jywun-de-shywùn-'hwà) jyàw 'shr̀-bīng-'jīng-shén °yí-'jèn. *or* °'hwàn-fā. *or* °'jèn-dzwò-chǐ-lay-le. *or* 'jyāng-jywun-de-tán-'hwà (*or* 'jyāng-jywun-de-shywùn-'hwà) bǎ 'shr̀-bīng-de-'jīng-shén °'tí-chǐ-lay bù-'shǎw. *or* °'jèn-dzwò-le bù-'shǎw.

Not lift a hand (*or finger*) to help yì-'dyǎr yě bù-bāng-'máng. ‖She wouldn't lift a hand to help. tā yì-'dyǎr yě °méy- (*or* °bù-'kěn) bāng-'máng. ‖He won't lift his little finger to help unless there's something in it for himself. yàw-shr tā-'dž-jǐ dé-bu-dàw 'hǎw-chù de-hwà, tā yì-'dyǎr yě 'bù-kěn 'bāng byé-rén-de-'máng.

LIGHT (LIT). 1. *In relation to vision.*

(*Luminous energy*) gwāng; *sometimes expressed indirectly by saying something is* bright lyàng, *or* (*for lack of light*) dark àn *or* 'hēy-gu-lūng-dūng-de; *a* light-year yí-ge-'gwāng-nyán; light waves 'gwāng-bwō. ‖The velocity of light is 186,000 miles per second. 'gwāng-sù 'méy-myǎw shr̀-'bā-wàn-'lyèw-chyān-yīng-'lǐ. ‖The light is reflected from that window. 'gwāng shr̀ tsúng nèy-ge-(bwō-li-)'chwāng-hu-shang 'fǎn-°shè- (*or* °'jàw-)gwo-lay-de. ‖There was a flash of light over there. nèy-her yěw-'gwāng nèm yì-'shǎn láy-je. ‖A ray of light is let into the grotto through a cleft in the stone. yěw yí-dàw-'gwāng tsúng shf-tew-'fèngr 'tèw-jìn 'dùng-li-lay. *or* tsúng 'dùng-li-de-yí-ge-shf-tew-'fèngr-nàr tèw-jìn yí-dàw-'gwāng-lay. ‖A point of light shows up clearly in the deep darkness. 'dǐng-hēy-de-dì-fang (*or* 'dǐng-àn-de-shf-hew, *and other similar combinations*) °yì-shyēngr-de- (*or* °yì-'dyǎn-dyar-, *or* °yì-'dyǎr-)gwāng dēw shyǎn-de tǐng-'lyàng-de. ‖The soft light in the room made it cozy and restful. 'wū-li-de-'gwāng tǐng 'réw, jyàw-rén jywé-je hěn 'shū-fu, hěn yǎng-'shén-de. ‖The light was so strong that he had to close his eyes. nèy-ge-'gwāng °hěn 'chyáng, jàw-de (*or* °'lyàng-jí-le, jàw-de, *or* °'lyàng-de jyàw-)tā bù-'dé bù-bǎ 'yǎn-jīng 'bì-shang. ‖The light on the snow was blinding. shywě fǎn-

'gwāng, jàw-de (jyàw-ren) 'jēng-bu-kāy 'yǎn. *or* shywě 'lyàng-de jyàw-rén 'jēng-bu-kāy 'yǎn. ‖The (lamp-)light is bad in here. jèr-de-'dēng-gwāng °'bú-gèw-'lyàng-de. *or* °tày 'àn. *or* *expressed as* It's not bright enough here. jèr bú-gèw-'lyàng-de. *or* *as* It's too dark here. jèr tày 'àn. *or* jèr 'hēy-gu-lūng-dūng-de.

(*Brightness or bright; of day or sun*) lyàng; (*of morning only*) míng. ‖There is a strong contrast between light and shade in that painting. nèy-jāng-'hwàr-shang bǎ 'lyàng-de-dì-fang gēn °'àn-de- (*or* °yěw-'yēr-de-)dì-fang 'hwà-de tǐng 'fēn-míng-de. ‖There's some light here. jèr yěw dyǎr-'lyàngr. ‖That bulb doesn't give enough light. 'nèy-ge-dyàn-dēng-'pàwr °bú-gèw-'lyàng-de. *or* °'gwāng bú-gèw-'lyàng-de. *or* °'gwāng bú-gèw-'dà-de. ‖That room is light and airy. 'nèy-wūr yě 'lyàng, 'kūng-chì yě hǎw. *or* 'nèy-wūr yèw 'lyàng-tang yèw 'fēng-lyáng. ‖We can work outdoors as long as it's light. jř yàw tyān háy 'lyàng-je (*or* jř yàw háy yěw-'lyàngr) wǒm jyèw néng dzày 'wày-tew dzwò-'hwór. ‖Wait until it's light. děng tyān °'lyàng-le (*or* °'míng-le) dzày 'shwō. ‖Wake me up as soon as it's light. tyān yí 'lyàng jyèw 'jyàw-wo.

(*To make bright, especially* light up) bǎ . . . jàw-de 'lyàng; *be lit up* lyàng. ‖The candle lit up the table. 'là bǎ 'jwō-dz (*or* 'là-jù jàw-dzày 'jwō-dz-shang) jàw-de tǐng 'lyàng-de. ‖The fire lit up the whole street like day. hwǒ-bǎ yi-tyáw-'jyē jàw-de gēn 'báy-tyān shr̀-de nèm 'lyàng. ‖The house is all lighted up. nèy-swōr-'fáng-dz-li dēng tǐng 'lyàng.

(*Source of artificial illumination*) dēng. Electric light 'dyàn-dēng; light bulb dyàn-dēng-'pàwr; flashlight shěw-dyàn-'dēng; lighthouse 'dēng-tǎ. ‖Please turn on the light. bǎ-'dēng (*or* bǎ 'dyàn-dēng) kāy-kay. ‖Give me a light bulb. gěy-wǒ yí-ge-dyàn-dēng-'pàwr. ‖Did you turn off the lights? nǐ bǎ-dēng 'gwān-shàng-le-ma? ‖We'll leave a light on in the hall. gwò-'dàwr-li lyéw-ge 'dēng-ba. ‖I bought a flashlight and some batteries. wǒ-mǎy-le ge-shěw-dyàn-'dēng, háy mǎy-le jǐ-ge-dyàn-'chf.

(*To cause to burn*). (*Without flame, as an electric light*) bǎ . . . 'dyǎn-shang; (*with flame or smoke, as a candle or pipe*) bǎ . . . dyǎn-'jáw-le. ‖Light the lamp as soon as it gets dark. tyān yí 'hēy jyèw bǎ-'dēng dyǎn-shang. ‖Light the candles. bǎ 'là-jù dyǎn-'jáw-le. ‖Light up your pipe and stay awhile. bǎ yān-'děwr dyǎn-'jáw-le °'dāy-hwěr. *or* °'dzwò-hwěr. *or* *expressed as* Smoke a pipeful of tobacco and stay awhile. chēw dàr-'yān (*or* chēw kěw-'yān) dzwò-'hwěr.

(*Something that causes to burn, especially for smoking*) hwǒr (*fire*); yáng-'hwěr (*match*). ‖May I have a light? jyè (*or* láy) gēn-yáng-'hwěr (shf-shr) 'shíng-ma? *or* jyè-'hwěr shf-shr.

(*Pale*) báy(-jìng). ‖Her complexion is very light. tā-'pí-fu hěn báy(-jìng).

(*Of colors*) chyǎn. ‖The book has a light blue cover. shū-'pyér shr̀ 'chyǎn-lán-(shǎr-)de. ‖He came in a light gray suit. tā chwān-je yí-tàw-'chyăn-hwēy-(shăr-de-)'yī-shang láy-de. ‖I want this color, but in a lighter shade. wǒ yàw jèy-ge-'shăr-de, bú-gwò děy dzày 'chyăn-dyar. ‖A lighter color like silver would be better. dzày 'chyăn-dyar-de-shăr (or shăr dzày 'chyăn-dyar) tsáy 'hăw, yín-'hwēy jyèw 'shíng.

To light up (figuratively, of eyes or face). ‖A smile lit up her face. tā măn 'lyăn 'shyàw-rúngr. or tā 'méy-kāy-yăn-'shyàw-de. ‖As soon as the children heard it, their eyes lit up in anticipation. shyăw-'hár-men yì tīng, dēw °'dèng-je lyă-yăr 'děng-je. or °'bă 'yàn-jīng jēng-de dà-'dá-de 'děng-je.

Throw (a little) light on is expressed by saying that after doing something one will understand 'míng-bay-dyăr or 'dwō-shăw 'jř-daw-dyăr (followed by an expression containing a verb); or as explain somewhat 'dwō-shăw 'jyăng-dyăr (with a noun). ‖This article ought to throw a little light on the subject. kàn-le jèy-pyān-'wér dà-gày kě-yǐ °'míng-bay-dyar (or °'dwō-shăw 'jř-daw-dyar) 'nèy shř dzěm hwéy-'shèr-le. or 'nèy-jyàn-shèr 'jèy-pyān-wér-li yīng-gāy 'dwō-shăw 'jyăng-le-dyăr.

Bring to light (by investigation) 'chá-chu-lay. ‖The investigation brought many new facts to light. nèm-yì-'chá chá-chu-le bù-'shăw-yǐ-'chyán-bù-jř-'dàw-de-shèr-lay.

In the light of 'àn-je or 'běn-je. ‖I made my decision in the light of what you said. wǒ shř 'àn-je 'nǐ-de-'hwà dă-de 'jú-yì.

See the light (figuratively) 'míng-bay-gwo-lay (become clear); 'ràw-gwo nèy-ge-'wār-lay (turn the corner, get the point). ‖At last I've made you see the light. wǒ dàw-'lyăwr ràng-nǐ 'míng-bay-gwo-lay-le.

(Point of view). ‖I don't think you're looking at this thing in the right light. wǒ jywé-de nǐ-dwèy-'jèy-jyàn-shř-de-'kàn-fa bú-tày 'jèng-chywè. or 'gwān-ywu 'jèy-jyàn-shèr wǒ jywé-je nǐ °'kàn-'tswò-le. or °-'kàn-de bú-dà 'dwèy. or °-de-'kàn-fa bú-dà 'dwèy. or °-de-'kàn-fa 'tswò-le.

2. In relation to weight or feeling.

(Of weight only) chīng. ‖Please take light packages with you; don't ask us to deliver. 'chīng-dyăr-de-'bāwr (or 'fèn-lyàng-'chīng-de-'bāwr) chǐng 'dż-jǐ dày-je; 'bú-yàw jyàw-wom 'sùng-le. ‖Light tanks can move much faster. 'chīng-jàn-'chē dzěw-de kwày 'dwō-le. ‖Light artillery won't be enough. jùng kàw-je °'chīng-pàw or (small caliber °'kěw-jìng-'shyăw-de-pàw) bú-'gèw.

(Of blows, knocks, footsteps, etc.; said of their sound) (tīng) 'chīng(-de); or expressed by chīng-'chīng-de followed by a verb. ‖She's very light on her feet for such a heavy woman. tā swéy-rán nèm 'pàng, kě-shr jyăw-'bùr tīng 'chīng(-de). ‖He heard light footsteps in the yard. tā tīng-jyàn 'ywàn-dz-li °yěw tīng-'chīng-de-jyăw-'bùr-shēng-yīn. or °yěw-rén chīng-'chīng-de dzěw-'lù. ‖There was a light knock on the

door. yěw-rén chīng-'chīng-de chyāw-le yí-shyàr 'mén. or yěw-rén chyāw-le yí-shyàr 'mén, chyāw-de-'shēng-yīn tīng 'chīng-de. ‖I heard a light scratch on the other side of the wall. wǒ tīng-jyàn chyáng-'nèy-byar yěw-rén chīng-'chīng-de dzày 'chyáng-shang 'jwā-le yí-shyàr.

(Of losses) bú-'jùng, bù-'dwō. ‖Our losses in the battle were light. wǒm-dzày-'nèy-yí-jàng-lǐ-de-°'swèn-shř (or °'sž-shāng) bú-'jùng. or °'swèn-shř (or °'sž-shāng) bù-'dwō.

(Of snow, rain, etc.) dyăr, bú-'dà(-de). ‖A light snow fell last night. dzwér 'wăn-shang °shyà-le dyăr-'shywě. or °shyà-de-'shywě bú-'dà.

(Of wind) chīng or shyăw. A light breeze 'chīng-fēng or 'shyăw-fēng.

(Of work) 'chīng-sheng-dyăr-de, 'chīng-sung-dyăr-de. ‖Our maid has not fully recovered yet; she can only do light housework. wǒm-de-lăw-'mā-dz (bìng-le) háy méy-'hăw 'lì-saw; 'jř néng dzwò °'chīng-sheng- (or °'chīng-sung-)dyăr-de-'hwǒr.

(Of taxes) 'chīng; (in comparison, lower) jyăn-'chīng(-le) or dī(-le). ‖Our taxes are lighter this year. 'jīn-nyán-de-'shwèy °jyăn-'chīng-le (or °'dī-le) bù-'shăw.

(Of food; in quantity) hèn 'snaw or bù-'dwō. ‖I had only a light lunch today. wǒ 'shăng-wu chř-de °hěn 'shăw. or °bù-'dwō.

(Of food; easy to digest) is expressed by saying the opposite about heavy food 'yěw-nì-de-'dūng-shi. ‖Take light food for a few days. is expressed as Don't eat (or Eat little) heavy stuff for a few days. 'jèy-jǐ-tyān °'b-é (or °'shăw) chř 'yěw-nì-de-dūng-shi.

(Of pastry) 'chī-de hăw or 'fā-de hăw (well risen). ‖My cakes are lighter today than usual. wǒ-'jyěr-dzwò-de-'dyăn-shin bǐ píng-'cháng-de °'chī-de hăw. or °'fā-de hăw.

(Of sleep). ‖He fell into a light sleep. tā dzày-nèr dă-'dwěr-ne.

(Of punishment) chīng. ‖He got off with a very light sentence. 'fá-de tā tīng-'chīng-de (pván-yi tā-le).

(Of moods). In a light mood gāw-'shìng. ‖I'm in a light mood today. wǒ 'jyěr-ge tīng gāw-'shìng.

(Of entertainment). ‖I prefer light reading after work. shyà-'gūng yǐ-'hèw wó-ywàn-yì-'kàn °'bú-yùng-fèy-'shīn-sž-de-shū. or °kě-yǐ-'shyāw-shyán-jyě-'mèr-de-shū. or °'chīng-sūng-dyar-de-shū. or °shyăw-'shwōr-yí-lèy-de shū.

Lighthearted. ‖He's always lighthearted. tā 'lăw shř °'kwày-kway-hwo-hwó-de. or °shyàng 'shīn-li méy shéme-'shèr shř-de. or °'shī-shī-hā-'hā-de.

Lightheaded (dizzy). ‖I feel a little lightheaded. wǒ jywé-je °'ywūn-hu-hu-de. or °yěw dyăr-'ywùn.

To make light of. ‖He made light of the matter. tā bă 'nèy-shèr kàn-de °tīng 'chīng. or °bú-'jùng-yàw. or 'nèy-shèr tā jywé-de °'bú-yàw-'jǐn. or °'méy shéme-'gwān-shì. or °shř 'shyāw-shèr-yì-'jwāng. or tā 'méy-bă nèy-shèr °'gē-dzày 'shīn-shang. or °dàng hwéy-

'shèr. or °dàng hwéy-'shèr kàn. ‖He made light of the danger. 'tā jywé-de 'bú-dà 'wéy-shyǎn.

3. (To come down and land) làw. ‖The birds often light on this tree. nyǎwr 'cháng làw-dzày jèy-kē-'shù-shang.

LIKE. 1. To like.

To like a person 'shǐ-hwān; ày (also means to love, but may be used for to like when speaking of an older person liking a younger person, etc.); in some cases kàn-de-'shàng or jūng-'yì or 'shǎng-shr̀; jywé-de . . . 'hǎw (or other words for good or, in the negative, for bad, etc., instead of hǎw); (if the opinion is derived from appearances) kàn . . . 'hǎw (etc.); A likes B may also be expressed as B dwèy A-de-'shīn-sz; other indirect expressions are also used, especially in the negative. ‖She likes children. tā hěn °'shǐ-hwān (or °'ày) shyǎw-'hár. ‖There are three young faculty members that the president likes very much. jyàw-'ywán-li yěw 'sān-ge-nyán-'chīng-de, shyàw-'jǎng tǐng °'shǐ-hwān(-de). or °kàn-de-'shàng(-de). or °jūng-'yì(-de). or °'shǎng-shr̀(-de). ‖I like you as you are. is expressed as I like the way you are. (See next paragraph.) nǐ shyàn-'dzày jèy-yàngr wǒ tǐng 'shǐ-hwān. or wǒ jywé-je nǐ shyàn-'dzày jèy-yàngr jyèw tǐng 'hǎw-de. ‖He doesn't like her. tā 'bù-shǐ-hwān tā. or tā jywé-je tā °'bù-hǎw. or °tǎw-'yàn. or °tǎw-'shyán. or (Stronger) tā tǎw-'yàn-ta. or tā 'nì-wey tā. or tā 'kàn-bu-'shàng tā. or tā 'kàn-ta °kàn-bu-'shàng 'yǎn. or 'bú-shwèn-'yǎn. or 'bù-jūng-'yì. or °'bú-dwèy 'shīn-sz. ‖I don't like her. wǒ 'bù-shǐ-hwān 'tā(-nèy-ge-rén). or wǒ 'jywé-je tā °'bù-hǎw. or °tǎw-'yàn. or °tǎw-'shyán. or (Stronger) tā-nèy-ge-rén 'tǎw-'yàn. or °jyàw-rén 'nì-wey. or °tǐng tǎw-'shyán-de. or °jyàw-rén kàn-bu-'shàng. ‖I don't like her looks. (As she always is) wǒ kàn-ta bú-shwèn-'yǎn. or wǒ jywé-je tā-'jǎng-de °'chěw. or 'bù-hǎw 'kàn. or 'bú-shwèn-'yǎn. or °nán 'kàn. or (As she looks just now) tā-nèy-ge-'yàng-dz °hǎw nán-'kàn-le. or 'hěn tǎw-'yàn-de. or °jyàw-rén kàn-bu-'shàng. or (She looks sick to me) wǒ kàn-ta yěw-'bìng-le. or (She is sick, and looks seriously ill to me) wǒ kàn-ta bìng-de hěn 'jùng.

To like each other ('bǐ-tsz) shyāng-'dé, ('bǐ-tsž) 'jìng-jùng, 'chǔ-de tǐng 'hǎw-de, tǐng shyāng-'hǎw-de; (of two people in a stated mutual relationship) shyāng-'dé, (chǔ-de) tǐng 'hǎw-de. ‖They like each other very much. tām 'bǐ-tsz shyāng-'dé (etc.). or (If they are brothers) tām-'gēr-men (or tām-'dì-shyùng) tǐng 'hǎw-de.

To like a thing 'shǐ-hwān (may be followed by a verb such as to see kàn); ày (must be followed by a verb such as to see kàn); jywé-de (or kàn-de if judged by appearance) . . . 'hǎw (or other similar words for hǎw); also many indirect expressions. ‖This is the kind of book I like. wǒ-'shǐ-hwān-de jyèw shr̀ 'jèy-jǔng-'shū. or wǒ 'shǐ-hwān kàn 'jèy-jǔng-'shū. or 'jèy-jǔng-shū wǒ 'shǐ-hwān

'kàn. or 'jèy-jǔng-shū wǒ ày 'kàn. or wǒ 'ày kàn 'jèy-jǔng-shū. ‖Do you like this pen? nǐ 'shǐ-hwān jèy-gwǎn-'bǐ-ma? ‖I like your hat. wǒ hěn 'shǐ-hwān (kàn) nǐ-de-'màw-dz. or wǒ 'jywé-je nǐ-de-'màw-dz tǐng hǎw 'kàn. or expressed as Your hat is very good-looking. nǐ-de-'màw-dz hěn hǎw 'kàn. ‖I don't like her hat. wǒ jywé-je tā-de-'màw-dz 'bù-hǎw 'kàn. or wǒ bù-'shǐ-hwān tā-de-nèy-ge-'màw-dz. ‖How do you like my new dress? wǒ-de-'shīn-yī-shang nǐ 'jywé-de °dzěm-'yàng? or °'hǎw-bù-hǎw? or wǒ-de-'shīn-yī-shang nǐ kàn °dzěm-'yàng? or °'hǎw-bù-hǎw? or nǐ 'jywé-de (or nǐ 'kàn) wǒ-de-'shīn-yī-shang °dzěm-'yàng? or °'hǎw-bù-hǎw? ‖I like the way she carries herself. wǒ hěn shǐ-hwān tā-de-'jywǔ-jř-'dùng-dzwò. or wǒ jywé-je tā-'yì-jywǔ-yí-'dùng dēw tǐng 'hǎw-de. ‖I don't like your work. wǒ jywé-je nǐ-dzwò-de °bù-'chéng. or °bù-'shíng. or °chà-'jìn. ‖Do you like it? 'shǐ-hwān-ma? or 'hǎw-bù-hǎw-wa? or jūng-'yì-ma? or 'dwèy nǐ-de-'shīn-sz-ma? or nǐ 'jywé-de (or nǐ kàn) °'dzěm-yàng? or °'hǎw-bù-hǎw? or (Of a taste) nǐ chř-je dzěm-'yàng? or hǎw 'chř-ma? or (Of a smell) nǐ wén-je dzěm-'yàng? or hǎw 'wén-ma? or (Of looks) nǐ kàn-je dzěm-'yàng? or hǎw 'kàn-ma? ‖I like it. hǎw. or shíng. or chéng. or bú-'hwày. or wǒ jywé-je nèy bú-'hwày. or (Of a taste) hǎw 'chř. (etc.) ‖I don't like it. 'wǒ jywé-je 'bù-hǎw. or wǒ 'bú-dà 'shǐ-hwān. or (Stronger) 'bù-hǎw. or 'bú-dwèy. or bú-'shìng. ‖How do you like the food there? nàr-de-fàn nǐ 'jywé-de °dzěm-'yàng? or °'hǎw-bu-hǎw? or °'hǎw chř bù-hǎw 'chř? ‖Do you like fish? is expressed as Do you like to eat fish? nǐ 'shǐ-hwān (or nǐ 'ày) chř-'ywú-ma?

To like °to do something or °a situation expressed verbally ày; 'shǐ-hwān; 'ywàn-yì (enjoy); jywé-je . . . 'hǎw (etc.). ‖I like to be with you. wǒ 'ày (or wǒ shǐ-hwān) gēn-ni dzày yí-'kwàr. or wǒ jywé-je néng gēn-ni dzày yí-'kwàr tsáy 'hǎw. ‖I like my hair cut short. wǒ shǐ-hwān bǎ 'téw-fa jyǎn-de °'dwǎn-le. or °dwǎn-'dwār-de. ‖He likes to show off. tā ày 'shyǎn-nèng. or tā ày shyǎn 'běn-shr̀. or tā ày 'shyǎn-nèng tā dž-'gěr-de-'běn-shr̀.

‖He likes to take charge of things. tā ày gwǎn-'shèr. ‖He doesn't like to read small type. tā 'bú-ày (or tā bù-'shǐ-hwān) kàn 'shyǎw-dzèr-de-shū ‖He likes to be babied. tā 'ywàn-yì (or tā 'ày, or tā 'shǐ-hwān) jyàw-rén 'hǔng-je tā. ‖He doesn't like to be ordered around. tā 'bú-ywàn-yì 'shèw-rén °'gwǎn. or °'jř-shr. ‖He doesn't like to be called by that name. tā bú-ywàn-yì rén 'nèm °jyàw-ta. or °chēng-hu tā. or 'nèm jyàw-ta (or 'nèm chēng-hu tā) tā 'bú-ày 'tīng.

Other expressions in English. ‖Well, how do you like that! jè 'wèy-myǎn 'tày nán-le. or jè 'bú-shr̀ ('chéng-shīn) dǎw-'lwàn-ma? or 'jēn méy-shyǎng-'dàw. or 'jēn méy shyǎng-'dàw hwèy 'dzěm-je. or 'jè kě 'jyàw-rén dzěm 'bàn-ne. ‖She doesn't hesitate to express her likes and dislikes. tā 'shīn-li dzěm 'shyǎng 'dzwěy-li jyèw dzěm 'shwō. or tā 'shīn-jř-kěw-'kwày-de. or tā dzwěy hěn 'jŕ. *or* tā (shīn-li) 'shŕ-hwān 'bù-shŕ-hwān yì-'jŕ jyèw 'shwō-chū-lay. ‖As you like. swéy-'byàn. *or* 'dzěm-je dēw 'shíng. *or* 'hǎw-ba.

2. Would like. (*Followed by a verb*) 'ywàn-yì (*enjoy or be willing*) *or* (hěn) 'shyǎng *or* (shyǎng) yàw (*want*); (*followed by a noun*) (shyǎng) yàw; *also some indirect expressions.* ‖I'd like to be with you. wǒ 'ywàn-yì (*or* wǒ 'hěn shyǎng) gēn-ni dzày yí-'kwàr. ‖Would you like to go there for me? nǐ 'ywàn-yì gěy-wo 'chywù yí-'tàng-ma? ‖I'd like to see his face when he hears this. tā 'tīng-jyàn 'jèy-ge de-shŕ-hew de-'shén-chì 'wǒ 'jēn shyǎng kàn-kan. *or* °wǒ 'jēn ywàn-yì kàn-kan. *or expressed as* It would be worth while to see.... °yí-'dìng jŕ-de yí-'kàn-de. ‖I'd like to, but I can't. wǒ ywàn-yì dàw-shr 'ywàn-yì (*or* wǒ 'shīn-li 'ywàn-yì), 'bú-gwo bàn-bu-'dàw. ‖Would you like (to have) another cup of tea? nǐ shyǎng dzày láy wǎn-'chá-ma? ‖I'd like to have some pork and sausages. wǒ yàw (*or* wǒ shyǎng yàw-dyar) 'jū-rèw gēn 'cháng-dz. ‖Would you like this pen? (*To have it*) nǐ shyǎng yàw jèy-gwǎn-'bǐ-ma? *or* (*To buy it*) nǐ shyǎng mǎy jèy-gwǎn-'bǐ-ma? ‖Would you like it? nǐ 'ywàn-yì-ma? *or* nǐ dzěme 'shwō-ne? *or* nǐ shwō dzěm-'yàng? ‖I'd like it. 'ywàn-yì. *or* 'kě-yǐ. *or* shíng. *or* chéng. ‖I wouldn't like it a bit. wǒ 'bú-ywàn-yì nèm-je. *or* wǒ 'bú-gàn.

Other expressions in English. ‖How would you like THAT? 'nèm-je nǐ yèw dzěm-'yàng-ne? ‖I'd like nothing better. 'nèy-ge (*of a thing, or* 'nèm-je *of an action*) 'dzày hǎw méy-'yěw-le. ‖I'd like to have my hair cut short, please. jyǎn 'dwǎn-le. *or* jyǎn 'dwǎn-dyar. *or* (*Shorter*) 'dwō jyǎn-shyà-dyar chywù.

3. (*Similar to*) gēn...shŕ-de; shyàng...(shŕ-de); shyàng...yí-'yàng; like that nèm(-je), 'nèy-yàngr; like this 'dzèm(-je), 'jèy-yàngr; like what? 'dzěm (-je), shéme-'yàngr. ‖He talks like a minister. tā shwō-'hwà °gēn (*or* shyàng) jyǎng-'dàw shŕ-de. *or* °shyàng ge-'mù-shr. ‖People here are very much like Americans. 'jèr-de-rén °gēn (*or* shyàng) 'měy-gwo-rén shŕ-de. *or* °hěn shyàng 'měy-gwo-rén. ‖You look like your father. nǐ-'jǎng-de °shyàng nǐ-'fù-chin (shŕ-de). *or* °gēn nǐ-'fù-chin shŕ-de. ‖You look exactly like your father. nǐ-'jǎng-de °gēn nǐ-'fù-chin-de-'mú-yàngr yì-'dyǎr bú-'chà. *or* °gēn nǐ-fù-chin yí-ge-'yàngr. *or* °shyàng nǐ-'fù-chin shyàng-'jí-le. *or* °shyàng-'jí-le nǐ-'fù-chin-le. ‖I've never met anyone like him. wǒ tsúng-'láy méy-'pèng-jyàn-gwo shyàng-'tā-nèy-yàngr-de(-rén). ‖He ran like mad (*or, like the wind*). tā 'pǎw-de gēn 'fēng-le shŕ-de. *or* tā gēn 'fēng-le shŕ-de nèm 'pǎw. ‖She's like a mother to him. tā dày-tā jyèw gēn 'mù-chin dày 'ér-dz shŕ-de. ‖Don't talk like that. hwà bú-shŕ 'nèm-shwō-de. *or* byé 'nèm shwō-'hwà-ya. *or* byé shwō 'nèy-yàngr-de-hwà-ya. *or* (*Polite*) jè shŕ 'nǎr-láy-de-'hwà-ya! ‖What is she like? tā 'shéme-yàngr? ‖Is it like this? (*A thing*) shŕ shyàng 'jèy-ge shŕ-de-ma? *or* shŕ shyàng jèy-yàngr-de-ma? *or* shŕ 'jèy-yàngr-de-ma? *or* (*An ac-*

tion) shŕ 'dzèm-yàngr-ma? ‖Oh, so it's like that! 'nèm-je-a, á?

Feel like (*doing something*) shyǎng. ‖Do you feel like dancing? nǐ shyǎng τyàw-'wǔ-ma? *See also* FEEL.

Look like 'chyáw-je hǎw shyàng, 'kàn-je hǎw 'shyàng, kàn-'yàngr, kàn jèy-'yàngr. ‖It looks like (it will) snow. 'chyáw-je hǎw shyàng yàw 'shyà-shywě. (*etc.*)

There's nothing like 'shéme yě °'bù-rú *or* °gǎn-bu-'shàng *or* °bǐ-bu-'shàng. ‖There's nothing like a good cup of hot tea. 'shéme yě 'bù-rú yì-wǎn-'rè-chá.

Something like 'chà-bu-dwō (*almost, about*); ...-de-yàng-dz (*of that sort*); dzwǒ-'yèw *or* chyám-'hèw (*more or less*). ‖He paid something like $1,500 for that car. tā mǎy nèy-lyàng-'chē hwā-le 'chà-bu-dwō yěw yì-chyān-'wǔ-bǎy-dwō-kwày-chyán. ‖It may be something like three o'clock when I get there. wǒ 'dà-gày (dīng) 'sān-dyǎn-jūng-de-yàng-dz 'dàw-nàr. *or* wǒ yě-shywǔ (*or* wǒ 'dà-gày) děy 'sān-dyǎn °dzwǒ-'yèw (*or* °chyán-'hèw) tsáy néng 'dàw-nàr.

And the like (*and so forth*). nèy-yí-lèy-de-°'dūngshi. *or* °'shèr.

Other expressions in English. ‖It's not like you to be irritable. nǐ 'bú-shr (*or* nǐ bú-shyàng) ày-shēng-'chì-de-rén-na. ‖He took to it like a duck to water. (*He learned it quickly*) tā-'nà tsáy jyàw °dé-chí-'swǒ-dzāy-ne. *or* (*He came to it very much*) °shàng-'yǐn-ne. ‖That's more like it! 'nèm-je háy 'hǎw-dyar. *or* 'nèm-je 'shyàng hwéy-'shèr. *or* 'nèm-je 'shyàng jywù-'hwà. ‖Like heck you will! (*Expressing disbelief*) hm! tsáy 'gwày-de-ne! *or* (*A threat, like our* **Over my dead body**) hèy! wǒ-de-'chywán-tew bù-'dá-ying. *or* dǎ 'wǒ-jèr shwō jyèw bù-'shíng.

LIKELY. To be likely to hwèy (*may be*); néng (*can be*). ‖Are we likely to arrive on time? ('chyáw jèy-yàngr) dzám 'néng (*or* hwèy) àn 'shŕ-hewr 'dàw-ma? ‖Is it likely to rain tonight? ('chyáw jèy-yàngr) jyēr 'wǎn-shang 'hwèy (*or* 'néng) shyà-'ywǔ-ma?

Most likely *or* very likely 'dà-gày; 'dwō-bàn (*in all probability*); 'bā-chéngr (*literally*, 80%). ‖The trip will most likely take three days. 'chywù yí-tàng °'dà-gày (*or* °'dwō-bàn, *or* °'bā-chéngr) děy dzěw 'sān-tyān-de-de-'yàng-dz. ‖We'll very likely be seen. ('chyáw jèy-yàngr) dzám °'dà-gày (*or* °'dwō-bàr, *or* °'bā-chéngr) yàw jyàw-rén 'kàn-jyàn.

(*Sarcastic*). ‖That's a likely story! 'nèy-shwō-de háy shyàng-'hwà ma? *or* 'nèy-shwō-de bú-shyàng-'hwà! *or* hwèy (*or* néng) yěw 'nà-yàng-de-'shŕ!

Most likely to succeed dzwèy-yěw-'shī-wang-de-'rén. ‖He was voted most likely to succeed by his classmates. tā-túng-'bān-de shywǎn-de tā shŕ dzwèy-yěw-'shī-wang-de-'rén.

LIMIT. To limit (*control*) 'ywē-shù *or* 'gwǎn-shù; to be limited (*restricted*) yěw-'shyàn *or* yěw 'shyàn-jŕ; (*controlled*) shèw 'ywē-shù *or* shèw 'gwǎn-shù *or* shèw 'shyàn-jr̀; (*insignificant*) 'méy shéme-kě-'chywǔ-de; (*low*) hěn 'dī. ‖The President's powers are limited by law. dzǔng-'tǔng-de-'chywán-lì shèw 'fǎ-lywù-de-°'ywē-shù. *or* °'shyàn-jr̀. ‖His ability is definitely limited. tā-jèy-rén 'tsáy-néng °yěw-'shyàn. *or* °'méy shém-kě-'chywǔ-de. *or* °hěn 'dī.

To limit to *or* to be limited to (*consist of nothing but*) jr̀ yěw; (*not exceed*) bú-'gwò; (*not go beyond the range*) bù-chū 'fàn-wéy. ‖My interest is limited to history. wǒ-'hàw-shi-de (*or* wǒ-'shǐ-hàw-de. *or* wǒ-'shǐ-hwān-de) jr̀ yěw lì-'shř. ‖Limit your speech to twenty minutes. nǐ yǎn-'jyǎng byé gwò 'èr-shr-fēn-'jūng. ‖Limit your remarks to the subject under discussion. shwō-de-'hwà bú-yàw 'chū-le běn-'tí-de-'fàn-wéy.

A limit (*restriction*) (yí-'dìng-de-)'shyàn-jr̀; (*set amount*) yí-'dìng-de-'shùr; *or expressed indirectly as* at the most 'jr̀ dwō *or* only 'jr̀. ‖There's a limit to the amount of work I can do in one day. wǒ yì-'tyān-li °'néng-dzwò-de-'shř yěw yí-'dìng-de-'shyàn-jr̀. *or* °'néng-dzwò-de-'shř yěw yí-'dìng-de-'shùr. *or* °'jr̀ dwō néng dzwò 'nèm-shyē-'shèr. *or* °'jr̀ néng dzwò 'nèm-shyē-'shèr.

To have no limits *or* to know no limit *or* there is no limit to méy-yěw ge-'byār, méy-yěw ge-'téwr; (*referring to a time when one is satisfied*) méy-yěw ge-jr̀-°'dzú-de-shŕ-hew. ‖There is no limit to his ambition. tā 'shyúng-shīn bwò-'bwò-de, méy-yěw ge-°'byār. *or* °'téwr. *or* °'jr̀-'dzú-de-shŕ-hew.

Up to (a limit of) dàw. ‖You may spend up to (a limit of) ten dollars. nǐ 'kě-yǐ 'hwā-dàw 'shŕ-kwày-chyán °(wéy-'jr̀). *or* °(wéy-'shyàn).

Limited yěw-'shyàn; *or expressed as* small. (*see* SMALL); *or expressed indirectly in other ways.* ‖They have a limited income. tām-'jìn-kwǎn °yěw 'shyàn. *or* °bù-'dwō. *or* °hěn 'shǎw. *or* °hěn 'shyǎw. *or* °'méy dwō-shǎw. ‖We have only a limited amount of time to finish this in. dzám 'méy-yěw dwō-shǎw-shŕ-hew jyèw děy bǎ jèy-ge nèng-'wán-le. ‖She lived on a limited diet. (*For reasons of health*) *is expressed as* She could eat only a few things. tā 'jr̀ néng chř 'jǐ-yàngr-dūng-shi. *or as* She was unable to eat many things. tā 'hǎw-shyē-dūng-shi dēw 'bù-néng 'chř. *or* (*For reasons of poverty*) *is expressed as* She ate very thriftily. tā 'chř-de hěn 'shěng.

Time limit *is expressed by constructions including* dìng (*set*) *followed by* 'chī-shyàn *or* 'shŕ-hew *or* 'r̀-dz. ‖We'll have to set a time limit for this job. dzwò jèy-jyàn-'shèr dzám (dzǔng) děy °'gwēy-dìng- (*or* °'dìng-gwēy-, *or* °'dìng-)chū ge-'chī-shyàn-lay. *or* 'jèy-jyàn-shèr dzám (dzǔng) děy °'dìng-gwēy (*or* °'gwēy-dìng, *or* °'dìng) ge-dzwò-'wán-de-°'r̀-dz. *or* °'shŕ-hew. *or* °'chī-shyàn. *or* (*More emphatic*) jèy-jyàn-shèr dzám (dzǔng) děy 'dìng-chū ge-'chī-shyàn-lay, dàw-le 'shŕ-hew yí-'dìng yàw dzwò-'wán-le. ‖You must finish everything within the time limit. shéme dēw děy dzày °yí-'dìng-de- (*or* °'dìng-'hǎw-le-de-, *or* °shwō-'dìng-le-de-)'chī-shyàn-li dzwò-'wán-lew.

City limits chéng-'jyè, chéng-de-'byān-jyè; (*the four boundaries*) chéng-de-sž-°'jr̀ *or* °'wéy; *or expressed as* the place where the city's controlled area stops chéng-(*or* shř-)gwǎn-de-'dì-fang dēw dàw . . . wéy-'jr̀; *outside the city limits is also expressed as* outside the city chéng-'wày. ‖Where are the city limits? chéng-'jyè (*or* chéng-de-'byān-jyè, *or* chéng-de-sž-'jr̀, *or* chéng-de-sž-'wéy) (dēw) °dzày- (*or* °dàw-)'nǎr? *or* běn-shř- (*or* běn-chéng-)gwǎn-de-'dì-fang dēw dàw-'nǎr wéy-'jr̀? ‖We're out of the city limits now. wǒm 'shyàn-dzày °'chū-le chéng-'jyè-le. *or* °'chū-le chéng-de-'byān-jyè-le. *or* °'yǐ-jīng dàw-le chéng-'wày-le.

Speed limit *is expressed indirectly.* ‖Speed limit 25 m.p.h. *is expressed as* Driving at most should not exceed 25 m.p.h. kāy-de 'jr̀ dwō (*or* kāy-de 'dzwèy kwày) bù-néng ('chāw-)gwò èr-shr-'wǔ-lí yì-dyǎn-'jūng. *or as* A speed of 25 m.p.h. is the limit. 'sù-du yǐ 'měy-shyǎw-shŕ èr-shr-'wǔ-lí wéy-'shyàn.

Other expressions in English. ‖Don't overstep the limits of good taste. 'bù-kě ywè-'lǐ. *or* 'fán-shř dēw yěw 'jèng-dàng-de-'lǐ-jyé, bù-néng dzwò-de °gwò-'hwǒr-lew. *or* °gwò-'fèn-lew. *or* bú-yàw 'shř-le 'shēn-fèn. ‖This is the limit! dàw-'tsž wéy-'jr̀. *or* dàw-'jèr jyèw swàn 'jr̀-yǐ-'jìn-yǐ-le. *or* 'dzày bù-néng °'rěn-le. *or* °'shèw-le. ‖He's the limit! 'jèy-jyā-hwo 'jēn shř shǎw 'yěw. *or* 'méy nèy-yàngr-de-'rén! *or* tā 'jēn shř gèw-'chyáw-de-le!

LIMITATION. (*Restriction*) 'shyàn-jr̀. ‖There are limitations on the amount of baggage a passenger may carry. 'chéng-kě-'shíng-li-de-'fèn-lyàng yěw 'shyàn-jr̀.

(*Deficiency or shortcoming*) shyàn; (*lack*) 'chywē-dyǎn; (*shortcomings*) 'dwǎn-chù; (*insecure points*) bù-'twǒ-de-'dì-fang *or* bù-'twǒ-dàng-de-'dì-fang. ‖He has great limitations. tā-de-'néng-li yěw-'shyàn. *or* tā-de-'dwǎn-chù hěn 'dwō. ‖Everyone should recognize his own limitations. *is expressed as* Everyone should know himself. 'shéy dēw yīng-gāy yěw 'dž-jř-jř-'míng. ‖This plan has its limitations. jèy-ge-'bàn-fa yěw °shyē-'dwǎn-chù. *or* °shyē-'chywē-dyǎn. *or* °bù-'twǒ(-dàng)-de-'dì-fang.

LINE. (*Mark*). (*Especially fine, threadlike*) shyàn; (*usually wider*) dàwr. ‖Draw a line between these two points (*connecting them*). dzày jèy-'lyǎng-dyǎn-jř-'jyān hwà tyáw-'shyàn 'lyán-chǐ-lay. ‖Divide the court into two parts with a chalk line. bǎ 'chǎng-dz °yùng 'báy-dàwr (*or* °'hwà yì-tyáw-báy-'shyàn, *or* °'dǎ yì-tyáw-báy-'shyàn, *or* °'hwà yì-tyáw-báy-'dàwr, *or* °'dǎ yì-tyáw-báy-'dàwr) dzày dāng-'jūng 'fēn-kay. *or* bǎ 'chǎng-dz dāng-'jūng °yùng 'báy-dàwr (°etc.) 'fēn-kay. ‖I want a tablet with lines. wǒ yàw °yì-běr-dày-'dàwr-de-'jr̀. *or* °yí-ge-dày-'dàwr-de-jr̀-'běr. ‖Sign on the dotted line. (bǎ 'míng-dz) c'yàn-dzày 'shywū-shyàn-shàng. *But* (*figuratively*) ‖You have no choice but to sign on the dotted line (*as directed*). nǐ 'méy-yěw shéme-'fár, jr̀ hǎw 'chyān-míng rèn-'kě-ba. *or* nǐ 'chyān-míng rèn-'kě-ba, 'háy yěw shéme-'fár-ne?

(*Electric or telephone wire*) shyàn; *or expressed in terms of* a telephone dyàn-'hwà. ‖**The rebels cut the telephone lines.** 'fǎn-pàn bǎ dyàn-hwà-'shyàn gěy °'chyā-le. *or* ¹ °nèng-'dwàn-le. *or* 'fǎn-pàn 'bù-jwěn tūng dyàn-'hwà-le. ‖**I'm sorry, the lines are all busy.** dwèy-bu-'jù, 'jǐ-tyáw-'shyàn dēw °'jàn-je-ne. *or* °yěw-rén 'jyàw. *or* °'yùng-je-ne. *or* °yěw-rén shwō-'hwà-ne. ‖**The line's busy; she must be talking to someone else.** tā-de-dyàn-'hwà yěw-rén 'jyàw (*or* tā-de-dyàn-'hwà jàn-je 'shyàn-ne); tā yí-dìng shr̀ gēn 'byé-rén shwō-'hwà-ne.

(*Cord or rope*) (*For rescue work*) 'shéng-dz; clothesline lyàng-'yī-fu-'shéng-dz; **fish line** ywú-'shyán, dyàw-'ywú-de-°shyán, °shyàn, *or* °'shéng-dz. ‖**Throw out a line!** bǎ 'shéng-dz (yì-téwr) 'rēng-chū-chywu! ‖**Hang the clothes on the line.** bǎ 'yī-fu 'gwà-dzày lyàng-'yī-fu-'shéng-dz-shang. ‖**Is your line strong enough to land a ten-pound fish?** nǐ-de-°ywú-'shyán (*or* °dyàw-'ywú-de-shyán, *etc.*) jīn-de jù yì-tyáw-'shŕ-bàng-jùng-de-'ywú-ma?

(*Series of objects, as cars or trees*) lyèw *or* páy (*measures*). ‖**There's a long line of cars ahead of us.** wǒm-'chyán-tew (*or* wǒm 'téw-le) yěw tǐng-'cháng-de-yí-°lyèw-'chē. *or* °páy-'chē. ‖**How many people are ahead of you in the line?** nǐ-jàn-de-jèy-yì-°'páy (*or* °'lyèw) 'chyán-tew yěw 'dwō-shǎw-rén? ‖**I had to stand in line to get this pack of cigarettes.** wǒ děy jàn-'páy tsáy mǎy-jáw-de jèy-bāw-yān-'jywǎr. ‖**They formed a line** (*or* **They lined up**) **in front of the post office.** tām dzày yéw-jèng-'jywú-'chyán-tew jàn-chéng-le yì-'páy.

(*Of type or writing*) háng (*a measure; refers to a vertical column in Chinese writing*). ‖**Don't skip a line when you write.** 'shyě-de-'shŕ-hew yì-'háng yě byé 'là. ‖**Set these lines in smaller type.** páy jèy-jǐ-'háng de-shŕ-hew yùng 'shyǎw-hàwr-de-chyān-'dz̀. ‖**Leave out these five lines when you copy this.** nǐ 'chāw jèy-ge de-'shŕ-hew °bǎ 'jèy-wǔ-'háng 'chywù-lew. *or* °bǎ 'jèy-wǔ-'háng chywú-'shyǎw-lew. *or* °byé chāw 'jèy-wǔ-háng. ‖**You left out five lines when you copied this.** nǐ chāw-de °'lèw-le (*or* °'là-le, *or* °'dyàw-le) 'wǔ-háng.

(*Of poetry, or sometimes prose*) jywù (*a measure; means also* **sentence**). ‖**Do you know what poem these lines are from?** nǐ 'jŕ-dàw jèy-jǐ-'jywù shr̀ tsúng něy-shěw-'shŕ-shang láy-de-ma?

(*In battle*) shyàn (*alone and in combinations*). ‖**The enemy has shortened his lines.** 'dí-rén 'swō-dwǎn °'fáng- (*or* °'jèn-, *or* °'jàn-)shyàn-le. ‖**He saw action in the front lines.** tā 'shàng-gwo chyán-'shyàn.

(*Of argument*) *is expressed by terms referring to* method, *as* **way of talking** 'shwō-fa, **how?** dzěme?, *etc.* ‖**What line of argument are you going to use to prove that?** 'nèy-ge nǐ shyǎng yùng °'shéme-'fāng-fa láy 'shwō-de (*or* °'dzěm-ge-'shwō-fa tsáy néng) jyàw-ren 'shìn-ne? ‖**What line is the defense following?** 'bèy-gàw fāng-myàn °dzěm 'shwō? *or* °yùng-de shr̀ 'něy-jùng-'shwō-far.

(*In transportation*). (*Route*) lù; (*number, as of a bus*) hàw; (*sign, of busses, etc., that are distinguished by colored signs*) 'páy-dz; (*company*) jyār *or* gūng-'sz̀; *when referring to using or riding on a line, the expression is* dzwò . . .-de- *followed by the name of the type of vehicle in question.* ‖**Which bus line do you use to go home?** nǐ hwéy-'jyā shř dzwò °'něy-'lù- (*or* °'jǐ-hàw-, *or* °'něy-ge-'páy-dz-, *or* °'něy-jyār-, *or* °'něy-ge-gūng-'sz̀-)de-'gūng-gùng-chì-'chē? ‖**I'm planning to go on the Tientsin-Pukow Line.** wǒ 'dǎ-swàn dzwò jīn-'pǔ-'lù-de-'chē. ‖**Have you ever traveled on this air line before?** nǐ 'dzwò-gwo jèy-ge-gūng-'sz̀-de-fēy-'jī-ma? ‖**This is one of the largest railroad lines in the world.** jèy shř 'shŕ-jyè-shang-shù-de-'jáw-de-yí-ge-'dà-tyě-lù-gūng-'sz̀. ‖**That steamship line owns over a hundred liners.** nèy-ge(-'chwán)-gūng-'sz̀ yěw yì-'bǎy-dwō-jř-'dà-chwán.

(*Business or profession*) háng; in . . . line . . . hang-de; (*selling*) mǎy . . .-de. ‖**He's in the dry-goods line.** tā shř mǎy-'bù-de. *or* tā shř 'bù-háng-de. *or* tā shř 'bù-pǐ-háng-de. *or* tā shř 'bù-pǐ-hwā-'byār-háng-de. ‖**We're in the same line.** wǒm shř 'túng-háng.

(*Specialty or sphere of interest*) háng; (*of study*) 'shywé-de *or* 'nyàn-de; in one's line *is expressed by saying that the person is* in the line nèy-'háng-de, *or* specializes in the thing gàn *or* 'jwān-mén, *or is a* specialist 'jwān-jyā *or* jyàng, *or by saying that the* thing is his specialty jwān-'mén-de *or* bĕn-'háng *or* ná-'shĕw-de-hǎw-'shì *or* yĕw-'ná-shĕw-de; out of one's line *is also expressed by saying that the person is* out of that line wày-'háng, *or is an outsider* 'lì-ba *or* 'lì-ba-'téw *or* mén-wày-'hàn. ‖**That's out of my line** (*or* **That's not my line**). nèy 'bú-shr wǒ °'bĕn-háng. *or* °'shywé-de. *or* °'nyàn-de. *or* nèy-ge wǒ shř °mén-wày-'hàn. *or* °'lì-ba. *or* °'lì-ba-'téw. *or* °'wày-'háng. ‖**That's right in his line.** tā 'jèng-shr °'něy-háng-de. *or* °'gàn nèy-ge-de. *or* °'jwān-mén nèy-ge-de. *or* °'ge-'nèy-mér-de-'jwān-jyā. *or* 'nèy-ge tā hěn dzày-'háng. *or* nèy jèng-shr tā-'jwān-'mén-de. *or* °'bĕn-háng. *or* °'ná-'shĕw-de-hǎw-'shì. *or* °yĕw-'ná-shĕw-de.

(*Of goods*). (*Brand*) 'páy-dz. ‖**They sell a good line of radios.** tām-mǎy-de-'wú-shyàn-dyàn °shř ge-'hǎw-páy-dz. *or* °'tǐng-'hǎw-de.

(*Short letter*) shìn; (*a few words*) jǐ-ge-'dzèr. ‖**Drop me a line if you have time.** yěw 'gūng-fu de-shŕ-hew gěy-wo °láy fēng-'shìn. *or* °shyě jǐ-ge-'dzèr.

(*Of talk or action, meant to interest someone*) yí-tàw(-'hwàr); *or expressed by saying someone* knows how to talk hwèy shwō-'hwàr-de. ‖**He has a good line.** tā 'tǐng hwèy shwō-'hwàr-de. *or* tā 'jyàn-le shéme-'rén jyèw yěw yí-tàw-'hwàr. ‖**Don't try that line with me.** 'yùng-bu-'jáw gen-'wǒ láy (*or* shwō, *or* shř) 'nèy-yí-tàw.

Pipe line 'gwǎn-dz; (*for oil*) yéw-'gwǎn-dz. ‖**They built a huge pipe line to transport oil to the north.** tām ān-le yí-dàw-'dà-yéw-'gwǎn-dz, bǎ-yéw wàng-'bĕy ywùn.

Production line 'jř-dzàw-'bù-dzèw. ‖Our production line is working smoothly now. shyàn-dzày 'jř-dzàw-'bù-dzèw 'lyán-jyē-de tǐng 'hǎw-de.

Supply line 'jyāw-tūng-'shyàn, 'jyāw-tūng-lù-'shyàn, 'jǐ-yǎng-lù-'shyàn. ‖Our supply lines are longer now. 'jyāw-tūng-lù-'shyàn bǐ yǐ-'chyán 'cháng-le.

Line of march dzěw-de-lù-'shyàn. ‖The arrows on the map show our line of march. dì-'tú-shang-de-jyàn-'téwr 'jř-chū-lay wǒm-dzěw-de-lù-'shyàn.

Line of fire hwǒ-'shyàn; *or expressed as* the place where the fire power can reach 'hwǒ-lì-gèw-de-'dàw-de-dì-fang. ‖Our troops were out of the enemy's line of fire. wǒm-de-jywūn-'dwèy °chū-le 'dí-rén-de-hwǒ-'shyàn-le. *or* °dzày 'dí-rén-'hwǒ-lì-gèw-bú-'dàw-de-dì-fang-le.

To line up (*form a line*) *see fourth paragraph above;* (*arrange in formation*) bǎy-hǎw-le 'dwèy, chí-'dwèy, páy-chéng-de 'dwèy, jàn-hǎw-le 'dwèy, páy-hǎw-le 'dwèy; (*organize*) 'jwěn-bèy-'hǎw; have lined up (*for a job*) yěw *or* 'jǎw-jáw.(-le) *or* 'dìng-gwey(-le) jyàw . . . 'dzwò(-le) *or* (*in mind*) 'shīn-li yěw. ‖Line up the boys before we start. bǎ 'háy-dz-men 'shyān °bǎy-hǎw-le 'dwèy (*or* °chí-'dwèy, *or* °páy-chéng-le 'dwèy) dzày 'dzěw. *or* shyān jyàw 'háy-dz-men °jàn-hǎw-le 'dwèy (*or* °páy-hǎw-le 'dwèy) dzày 'dzěw. ‖I have everything lined up to start work next week. wǒ 'shéme dēw 'jwěn-bèy 'hǎw-le, shyà-lǐ-bày kǎy-'gūng. ‖Do you have anyone lined up for that job yet? 'nèy-shr̀ nǐ °yěw-'rén-le-ma? *or* 'jǎw-jaw-'rén-le-ma? *or* °'dìng-gwey-le jyàw-'shéy dzwò-le-ma? *or* °'shīn-li yěw-'rén-le-ma?

Be lined with (*have a line on each side*) is expressed indirectly. ‖The street was lined with people watching the parade. 'yán-jyē- (*or* 'jyē-de-lyáng-'páng) °jàn-'mǎn-le (*or* °yì-'páy-yí-'lyèw-de 'dēw-shr) kàn-yéw-'shíng-de-rén. ‖The walls are lined with books. yán-chyáng dēw shr̀ shū-'jyà-dz, shàng-tew °bǎy 'mǎn-le 'shū. · °'jìng shr̀ 'shū.

Be lined with (*have a lining of*) shr̀ . . .-lyěr-de, gwà-de . . .-lyěr. ‖Her coat is lined with red. tā-de-'yī-shang °shr̀ 'húng-lyěr-de. *or* °gwà-de 'húng-lyěr.

Be lined with worry. ‖Her face was lined with worry. tā 'chéw-de 'yì-lyǎn °jèw-'wén. *or* °jèw-'wér.

All along the line. ‖There will have to be improvements all along the line. jěng-'gèr-de-'bàn-fa dēw děy 'gǎy. *or* tsúng-'shàng dàw-'shyà 'swǒ-yěw-de-'bàn-fa dēw děy 'gǎy. *or* tsúng-'téwr dàw-'lyǎw měy-yí-'bù-de-'bàn-fa dēw děy 'gǎy.

Along the lines of (*according to*) 'běn-je, 'jàw-je, 'àn-je; (*similar to*) gēn . . . °shyāng-'sz̀, °hěn 'jìn, °'chà-bu-'dwō. ‖They're working along the lines of my idea. tām jèng-dzày °'běn-je (*or* °'jàw-je, *or* °'àn-je) 'wǒ-de-'yì-sz láy 'dzwò. ‖That's along the lines of what I meant. nèy gēn 'wǒ-shwō-de-'yì-sz °shyāng-'sz̀. *or* °hěn 'jìn. *or* °'chà-bu-'dwō.

Down the line (*including everyone*) is expressed indirectly in terms of each *or* all. ‖He shook hands all down the line. tā āy-je-'gèr-de (*or* tā 'yí-gè-yí-gè-de) lā-'shěw, 'dēw lā-'dàw-le. ‖Everyone got a raise, from the president on down the line. tsúng jīng-'lǐ chǐ yí-'gè-yí-gè-de chywán jyā-'shīn-le. *or* tsúng-'shàng dàw-'shyà °yí-'lywù (*or* °'chywán) jyā-'shīn-le. *or* chywán-'tǐ yí-'lywù jyā-'shīn-le.

In line (*aligned*) dwèy-'jwěn-le. ‖See whether the wheels are in line. 'kàn-kan 'lwén-dz shr̀-bu-shr dwèy-'jwěn-le.

In line (*working together properly*) yí-'jř shíng-'dùng; (*not disagreeing with each other*) bǐ-'tsz bú-nàw 'yì-jyàn; (*under control*) 'jř-fú-'jù-le *or* gwǎn-'jù-le. ‖Try to bring the committee into line. 'shyǎng-fár jyàw 'hwèy-lǐ-de-rén 'tsǎy-chywǔ yí-'jř shíng-'dùng. ‖He managed to keep the whole party in line. tā 'dzǔng swàn-shr̀ 'méy-jyàw 'dǎng-li-de-'rén bǐ-'tsz nàw 'yì-jyàn. *or* tā 'dzǔng swàn-shr̀ bǎ dǎng-li-de-rén °'jř-fú-'jù-le. *or* °'gwǎn-'jù-le.

In line for. ‖He was in line for a promotion. gāy 'lwén-dàw (*or* 'shyà-yí-ge gāy shr̀) 'tā shēng(-'jí)-le.

Wounded in line of duty yīn-'gūng shèw-'shāng *or* gwà-'tsǎy-le; killed in line of duty shywùn-'gwó-le *or* jèn-'wáng-le. ‖His injury was sustained in line of duty. 'tā °shr̀ yīn-'gūng shèw-'shāng. *or* °'gwà-'tsǎy-le.

In the line of . . . yí-lèy-de. ‖Do you have anything in the line of old paintings? gǔ-'hwàr-yí-lèy-de 'yěw-ma?

Come from a long line of is expressed indirectly. ‖He comes from a long line of doctors. tā-'jyā-li °shr̀-'dày shíng-'yī. *or* °bèy-'bēr-de shíng-'yī. *or* 'tā-jyā shíng-'yī °yěw 'hǎw-shyē-'dày-le. *or* °yěw 'hǎw-shyē-'bèy-dz-le. *or* °shr̀ dzǔ-'chwán-de.

Get a line on (*investigate*) 'dyàw-chá; (*find out about by questioning*) 'dǎ-tīng; like to get a line on (*want to know about*) shyǎng 'jř-dàw. ‖Get a line on his background. 'dyàw-chá-dyàw-chá (*or* 'dǎ-tīng-dǎ-tīng) °tā-de-'bèy-jǐng. *or* °tā yǐ-chyán shr̀ dzěm-'yàngr-de-ge-rén. ‖I'd like to get a line on his ability. wǒ hěn shyǎng 'jř-dàw tā-de-'běn-lǐng rú-'hé.

LINEN. (*Type of cloth*). (*General term for Chinese types of linen*) 'shyà-bù. (*Any cloth made of hemp or sometimes flax; likely to be a coarser, rougher cloth than Western linen*) 'má-bù; (*coarsely woven linen, or muslin*) má-'shā(-lyàw-dz); (*finely woven linen, or cambric*) yáng-'shā(-lyàw-dz). ‖Linen is fine, but expensive. 'shyà-bù (*or* 'má-bù, *or* má-'shā-lyàw-dz, *or* yáng-'shā-lyàw-dz) hǎw dàw shr̀ hǎw, kě-shr tǐng 'gwèy. ‖You can buy nice linen handkerchiefs down the street. nǐ 'kě-yǐ dzày jyē-'nèy-téwr mǎy dǐng-hǎw-de-yáng-'shā-shěw-'jywàr.

(*Things made of linen*) expressed as **bedclothes** etc. chwáng-'dān-dz-shéme-de *or* as **tablecloths** etc. jwē-'bù-shéme-de. ‖What laundry do you send your linen(s) to? nǐ-chwáng-'dān-dz-shéme-de (*or* nǐ-jwō-'bù-shéme-de) sùng-'nǎr chywù 'shǐ?

LIP. (*Part of the mouth*). (*When referring to the individual lips*) dzwěy-'chwén; (*when referring to the lips as the whole mouth*) dzwěy; **upper lip** .hàng-dzwěy-'chwén; **lower lip** shyà-dzwěy-'chwén; **a lipstick** tú-'chwén-gāw *or* 'yān-jr; **to put on lipstick** tú-'chwén *or* bǎ dzwěy-'chwén tú-'húng; **to purse the lips** jywē-je 'dzwěy. ‖His lips and cheeks are swollen from frostbite. tā-dzwěy-'chwén gēn lyǎn-'dàr dùng-'jǔng-le. ‖She has lipstick on. tā-dzwěy-'chwén tú-de hěn 'húng. ‖I've been practicing lip-reading. wǒ jèng lyàn-je 'kàn rén-'dzwěy dzěme 'dùng jyèw 'jr-dàw tā-shwō-de shř shéme-'hwà.

(*Of a pitcher*) dzwěr. ‖The lip of the pitcher is broken. shwěy-'gwàn-dz-de-'dzwěr pwò-le.

Lip service. ‖He gives only lip service to that principle. gwà 'yáng-téw mày 'gěw-rèw. *or* mǎn-kěw 'rén-yì dàw-'dé. *or* tā gwāng dzwěy-'téwr-shang shwō (nèy-jǔng-'jǔ-jāng) 'hǎw. *or* tā-'shīn-kěw bù-yí-'jr. *or* tā-'kěw 'shř shīn 'fēy.

‖Keep a stiff upper lip. 'chyèr yàw 'jwàng. *or* 'chyèr yàw 'dzú. *or* 'dǎr dà-dyar.

LIQUID. (*Matter in liquid form, as opposed to gas or solid*) 'yè-tǐ. ‖Some gases change into liquids only at very low temperature and under tremendous pressure. yěw-de-'chì-tǐ 'fēy-děy nèng-de 'hěn lěng, dzày jyā 'hěn-dà-de-'yā-lì, tsáy nìng-chéng 'yè-tǐ.

(*Watery substance*) shwěr. ‖What's this blue liquid? jèy-ge-'lán-shǎr-de-'shwěr shř-shéme? ‖Take a teaspoonful of this liquid (medicine) every two hours. jèy-ge-yàw-'shwěr gé-'lyǎng-dyǎn-jūng 'chř yì-tyáw-'gēng. ‖Do you have liquid shampoo? yěw shǐ-'téw-de-(yí-dz-)'shwěr-ma?

(*Nonsolid foods*). Eat liquid foods chř 'shī-de, bù-chř 'gān-de. ‖Keep him on a liquid diet. *or* Let him eat only liquids. jyàw-ta gwāng chř 'shī-de. *or* byé jyàw-ta chř 'gān-de.

LIST. 'dān-dz *or* (*in combinations*) dār; **make a list** kāy ge-'dān-dz; **make a list of** bǎ ... kāy ge-'dān-dz; **to list** bǎ ... 'kāy-chū-lay; **to list** *something* **on** bǎ ... 'kāy-dzày. ‖This is a list of the materials I need. jèy-'dān-dz-shang 'kāy-de shř wǒ-děy-'yàw-de-°'tsáy-lyàw. *or* °'dūng-shi. ‖List their names in the letter. bǎ tām-de-'míng-dz kāy dzày 'shìn-li. ‖List their names on a separate sheet. bǎ tām-de-'míng-dz °'kāy-dzày 'lìng-yì-jāng-'jř-shang. *or* °'lìng kāy ge-'dān-dz. ‖List the things you lost and give it to the police. bǎ 'dyēw-de-'dūng-shi kāy ge-'dān-dz bàw 'shywún-jīng-'jywú. *or* dàw shywún-jīng-'jywú bàw ge-shř-'dān. ‖Is my name on the list? míng-'dār-shang yěw-'wǒ-ma?

LISTEN. tīng. ‖I like to listen to folk songs. wǒ 'shǐ-hwān (*or* wǒ 'ày) tīng 'yáng-gē. ‖Listen! (nǐ) 'tīng-(yi-)tīng. *or* (*Urgent*) 'tīng-nga! *or* (*Keep listening*) 'tīng-je! ‖I'm listening. wǒ 'tīng-je-ne. ‖Listen for

the sound of a bell. 'tīng-je-dyar 'lyéngr-shyǎng. ‖I told him so, but he wouldn't listen. wǒ nèm 'gàw-sung tā-de, 'kě-shr tā bù-'tīng-me. ‖Listen to what I have to say. (*Of a statement or opinion*) tīng 'wǒ láy shwō. *or* (*Obey me*) 'tīng wǒ-de-'hwà. *or* (*Of long instructions*) 'lyéw-shīn 'tīng-je, jèy shr̀ hěn-yàw-'jǐn-de-hwà. ‖Now you listen to me. (*In turn*) 'shyàn-dzày tīng 'wǒ-de. *or* (*Of a command*) nǐ 'tīng-je!

LITERATURE. (*Literary productions*) 'wén-shywé. ‖The library has an excellent collection of English literature. tú-shū-'gwǎn dzày 'yíng-wén-'wén-shywé-fāng-myàn 'sēw-jí-de°-'jù-dzwò hěn dwō. *or* °hěn 'chywán. ‖He's going into literature. tā yàw °'shywé (*or* °'yán-jyēw) 'wén-shywé. ‖He's taking a course in the history of English literature. tā 'shywǎn-le yì-mér-'yīng-gwo-'wén-shywé-'shř.

(*Writing on a certain subject*) *is expressed as* **books** shū; **the literature of** (*or* **on**) ... *is expressed as* ... yí-lèy-de-'shū. ‖The literature of travel is extensive. yéw-'jì-yí-lèy-de-'shū tǐng 'dwō.

LITTLE. (*Small in size*). (*Of objects*) shyǎw; (*of persons*) shēn-tsáy-'shyǎw-de, gèr-'áy-de, 'shyǎw-shēn-lyang-de, 'shyǎw-gèr-de, shēn-lyang-'shèw-dyar-de; (*of children*) *also* shyǎw (*but* shyǎw-'rén *means a* small (mean) person); (*unimportant*) 'méy-shéme-yàw-'jǐn-de; yì-'dyǎr-dà-de-ge (*literally;* of even the smallest size); **little finger** 'shyǎw-mǔ-'gēr. ‖Give me a little piece of cake. gěy-wo yì-'shyǎw-kwàr-dàn-'gāw. ‖This dress is for a little girl. jèy-jyàn-'yī-fu shř wey-°'shyǎw- (*or* °shēn-tsáy-'shyǎw-de, *etc.*) 'nywǔ-hár-chwān-de. ‖He noticed every little mistake. tā 'shéme-'shyǎw-tswòr (*or* yì-'dyǎr-dà-de-ge-tswòr tā yě, *or* 'méy-shéme-yàw-'jǐn-de-tswòr tā yě, *or* 'tīng-shyǎw-de-'tswòr tā yě) dēw 'kàn-chu-lay-le.

A little (*in amount*). (*In most cases*) yì-dyǎr; *sometimes expressed by* **a few** jǐ *plus a unit measure, as* **a little** *of a language, expressed as* **a few sentences of** jǐ-jywù; **a little** *while* yì-'hwěr, bú-'dà-de-gūng-fu; (*in the past*) 'méy-dwō jyěw, 'méy-dwō-dà-de-°'shř-hew *or* °'gūng-fu; (*later*) (wǎn) 'yí-bù; (*in the future*) 'hwéy-téw, děng yí-shyàr, jyèw; **a little way** jǐ-'bùr. ‖Take a little interest in your work. dzwò-'shř-de-shř-hew yùng dyǎr-'shīn. ‖There's just a little of the cake left. dàn-'gāw jyèw shèng-le °yì-'dyǎr-le. *or* °yì-'dǐ-dyǎr-le. *or* °yì-'dīng-dīng-'dyǎr-le. ‖I think she's a little drunk. wǒ kàn tā yěw dyǎr-'dzwèy-le. ‖I'll tell you what little I know about it. wǒ-swǒ-'jř-daw-de-jèy-dyǎr dēw 'gàw-sung nǐ. ‖It won't do any harm to pamper her just a little. 'chǔng-ta-dyǎr (*or* 'chǔng-ta yì-dyǎr) pà-'mǎr-de? ‖He's a little worried. tā yěw-dyǎr °jāw-'jí. *or* °bú-fàng-'shīn. *or* °dān(-je)-'shīn. ‖He pampers her a little too much. tā 'chǔng-ta 'chǔng-de yěw-dyǎr tày °'lì-hay-le. *or* °gwò-'fèn-le. *or* °gwò-'hwǒr-le. ‖He doesn't love her even a little. tā yì-'dyǎr yě bú-'ày-ta. ‖I can speak a little French.

wǒ néng 'jyǎng jǐ-jywù-'fà-wén. *or* wǒ néng 'shwō yì-dyǎr-'fà-gwo-'hwà. ‖I'll come in a little while. wǒ °yì-'hwěr (*or* °'hwéy-téw, *or* °děng yí-shyàr) jyèw 'láy. *or* wǒ 'jyèw láy. ‖He came a little (while) after you did. 'nǐ dàw-le yì-hèw °bú-dà-de-gūng-fu (*or* °'méy-dwō jyěw, *or* °'yì-'hwěr, *or* °gwò-le yì-'shyǎw-hwěr, *or* °gwò-le 'méy-dwō-dà-de-shŕ-hew, *or* °gwò-le 'méy-dwō-dà-de-'gūng-fu) tā 'yě dàw-le. *or* 'tā-dàw-de bǐ-nǐ °wǎn 'yí-bù. *or* °wǎn nèm yì-'shyǎw-hwěr. ‖I rode a little (while) yesterday. 'dzwér-ge wǒ 'chí-le hwěr-'mǎ. ‖I can walk a little way with you. wǒ 'kě-yǐ gēn-nǐ 'dzěw jǐ-'bùr.

A little (*of activity, ability: not much or not well*) *is expressed as* **sometimes** 'yěw-de-shŕ-hew, **not much** bù-'cháng *or* 'bú-dà; (*said of someone else*) **not too well** bú-'tày hǎw; (*said of oneself*) **not well** bù-'hǎw, **just so-so** 'mā-ma-hū-'hū-de *or* hěn 'èr-wǔ-'yǎn, *or* **very badly** shŕ (*of chess*). ‖**Does he play chess? Oh, a little.** tā hwèy shyà-'chí-ma? hwèy, 'bú-gwo bú-'tày hǎw. *or* tā shyà-'chí-ma? °bù-'cháng shyà. *or* °'bú-dà shyà. *or* °'yěw-de-shŕ-hew shyà. ‖**Do you play chess? Oh, a little.** nǐ shyà-'chí-ma? °'yěw-de-shŕ-hew shyà. *or* °'bù-'cháng shyà. *or* °'bú-dà shyà. *or* °shyà-de bù-'hǎw. *or* shyà-de hěn 'shŕ. ‖**I can shoot a little** (**but not well**). wǒ hwèy 'mā-ma-hū-'hū-de 'fàng lyǎng-shyàr-'chyǎng. *or* wǒ hwèy fàng-'chyǎng, 'bú-gwo hěn 'èr-wǔ-'yǎn.

Little (*not much*) 'méy shéme, bú-'dà, hěn 'shyǎw. ‖**He has little influence there.** tā dzày-nàr °'méy shéme-'shŕ-lì. *or* °'shŕ-lì bú-'dà. *or* °'shŕ-lì hěn 'shyǎw.

Little better than bǐ . . . 'chyáng-bu-lyǎw dwō-'shǎw. ‖**He's little better than a thief.** tā bǐ shyàw-'téwr 'chyáng-bu-lyǎw dwō-'shǎw.

Little by little (*in separate bits*) 'yì-dyǎr-yì-dyǎr-de; (*gradually*) jyàn-'jyàn-de; (*slowly*) màn-'mǎr-de. ‖**Little by little the job's getting done.** shèr °jyàn-'jyǎn-de (*or* °màn-'mǎr-de, *or* °'yì-dyǎr-yì-dyǎr-de) jyèw yàw dzwò-'wán-le.

LIVE. (*To be or remain alive*) hwó; *a negative plus* **die** sž. ‖**I don't know whether he's living or dead.** wǒ 'bù-jŕ-dàw tā shŕ 'sž-le háy-shr 'hwó-je-ne. ‖**He lived to a ripe old age.** tā hwó-dàw 'hǎw-dà-de-'nyán-jì. ‖**Live and let live.** 'dž-jǐ hwó-je yě děy jyàw 'byé-rén hwó-je. ‖**The doctor said the patient would live.** 'dày-fu shwō 'bìng-rén 'néng 'hwó. *or* °'sž-bu-lyǎw. *or* (*has hope*) °'yěw-'jyěwr. ‖**I hope we live to see this finished.** wǒ 'shī-wang jèy-ge 'néng dzày dzám méy-'sž yǐ-chyán dzwò-'wán-le. *or* wǒ shī-wang jèy-ge 'wán de-shŕ-hew dzám háy °'hwó-je. *or* °méy-'sž. *or* (*Be on earth*) °dzày-'shŕ. ‖**He's living on borrowed time.** *is expressed as* He's living each day for itself. 'hwó yì-tyǎr swàn yì-'tyǎr-le. *or as* He has today but not tomorrow. tā yěw 'jīn-tyān méy 'míng-tyān-de-le.

(*To spend one's life*) gwò *plus a noun referring to time, as* **days** 'ŕ-dz *or* **lifetime** yí-'bèy-dz; *occasionally* hwó *in the same construction; see also* **LIFE.** ‖**He lived**

a happy life. *or* He lived happily. tā 'kwày-kway-hwó-'hwér-de gwò-le °yì-'shēng. *or* 'yí-'bèy-dz. ‖**He never really lived** (*well*). tā yí-'bèy-dz méy-'gwò-gwo °'shū-fu-'ŕ-dz. *or* °'hǎw-ŕ-dz. ‖**You've never really lived** (*expressed as* **This life can be said to have been lived in vain**) **unless you've seen Peiping.** nǐ 'yàw-shr méy-'kàn-jyàn-gwo běy-'píng, jèy-'bèy-dz kě 'swàn shŕ 'báy-°'hwó-le. *or* °'gwò-le.

(*To dwell*) jù. ‖**Does anyone live in this house?** jèy-swèr-'fáng yěw-rén 'jù-ma? ‖**Where does he live?** tā 'jù-nǎr? *or expressed as* Where is his home? tā-'jyā dzày-nǎr? ‖**I expect to live here for two months.** wǒ 'dǎ-swàn dzày-'jèr jù 'lyǎng-ge-'ywè.

(*Various combinations referring to income and livelihood*). In **to live on**, live *is expressed in terms of* **passing** (**days**) gwò ('ŕ-dz) *or, in terms of* **eating, by** chŕ *and other terms; in the meaning* **to spend** hwā *is used;* **a living** (*income*) 'jìn-kwǎn; **make one's living doing something** jŕ-je . . . °gwò 'ŕ-dz *or* °'hù-'kěw. ‖**He earns hardly enough to live on.** tā jèng-de jyǎn-'jŕ bú-gèw °gwò-'ŕ-dz-de. *or* °'gwōr. *or* °'chŕ-de. *or* °'jyáw-gwer. ‖**How can you live on that little salary?** 'shīn-shwěy 'nèm dyǎr, dzěme gèw 'gwò-de-ne? ‖**They live on $100 a month.** tām měy-ywè yùng yì-'bǎy-kwày-chyán gwò 'ŕ-dz. ‖**They must be living beyond their income.** tām yí-'dìng shŕ 'hwā-de bǐ 'jwàn-de 'dwō. ‖**Live within your income.** 'jwàn dwō-shǎw-'chyán byé hwā-'gwò-le. ‖**He lives up to his income.** tā 'jìn byé dwō-chyán 'hwā dwō-shǎw. ‖**He make a good living.** tā-'jìn-kwǎn hěn 'fēng-fù. ‖**He ma es his living selling books.** tā jŕ-je mày-'shū 'gwò 'ŕ-dz. *or* °'hù-'kěw.

To live on (*of food*). (*To subsist on*) 'jŕ-je . . . 'hwó-je *or* ('gwāng) chŕ . . . hwó-je; (*to eat nothing but*) 'gwāng chŕ . . .; (*have nothing to eat but*) 'jŕ yěw . . . chŕ. ‖**How can people live on this food?** 'rén dzěm néng °'jŕ-je 'jèy-jǔng-'chŕ-de 'hwó-je? *or* °'gwāng chŕ 'jèy-ge hwó-je? ‖**They lived on nothing but rice for three months.** yěw 'sān-ge-'ywè-de-gūng-fu tām °'gwāng chŕ-'mǐ. *or* °'jŕ yěw-'mǐ chŕ.

To live on *or* **to live off** (*a person*) 'jŕ-je (*or* 'kàw-je) . . . °'hwó-je *or* °'chŕ-'fàn. ‖**They've been living on his parents for years.** tām 'dwō-shǎw-'nyán-le dēw shŕ °'jŕ-je (*or* °'kàw-je) 'lǎw-rén-jyǎr hwó-je. *or* °'jŕ-je (*or* °'kàw-je) 'lǎw-rén-jyǎr chŕ-'fàn.

To live down. ‖**It will take years to live down the gossip.** *is expressed as* **Wait and see; this rumor will be passed on endlessly.** nǐ 'chyáw-je-ba, 'jèy-dwàr-yáw-'yán 'chyè yěw-rén 'chwán-ne.

To live up to. ‖**He didn't live up to my hopes.** *is expressed as* **He disappoints me.** 'tā jyàw-wǒ shŕ-'wàng. *or as* **I formerly had great hopes for him.** wǒ 'ywán-láy dwèy-ta 'chī-wàng hěn 'shēn láy-je.

LIVE. (*Of biological life*) expressed by constructions with **to live** hwó. ‖**That's a live snake, and he's dangerous.** nèy-tyáw-'cháng-chung °'hwó-je-ne (*or* °'shŕ 'hwó-de), ér-chyě háy yěw-'dú. ‖**Buy some live fish.** mǎy dyar-'hwó-ywú.

(*Of an electric wire*) dày-'dyàn-de, tūng-je-'dyàn-de, yěw-'dyàn-de. ‖Never touch á live wire. yǔng-ywǎn byé mwō dày-'dyàn-de-dyàn-'shyàn.

(*Of coals*) shāw-'húng-le-de, háy-'húng-je-de, háy-jáw-je-de, háy-méy-'myè-de. ‖Roast it over live coals. dzày shāw-'húng-le-de-'méy-shang 'kǎw.

(*Of ammunition*) shŕ *in the combination* a live cartridge *or* a live shell 'shŕ-dàn, 'jēn-de; *or expressed by saying that* it might explode hwèy-'jà-de *or* has not yet exploded méy-'jà-kāy-ne. ‖They use live cartridges for practice. tām yùng 'shŕ-dàn dǎ-'bǎ. ‖That's a live shell. nèy shř 'shŕ-dàn. *or* nèy shř 'jēn-de-pàw-'dàn. *or* nèy-ge-pàw-'dàn °hwèy-'jà-de. *or* °méy-'jà-kāy-ne.

(*Of an issue*) *is expressed by saying that* people really have *the issue* 'jēn shř yěw, *or that the issue is* not yet solved háy méy-'jyě-jywé. ‖It's a live issue in some places. hǎw-'shyē-'dì-fang 'jēn shř yěw jèy-jǔng-°'wèn-tí. *or* °'má-fan-'shèr. ‖It's still a live issue. jèy-ge-'wèn-tí háy méy 'jyě-jywé.

LIVELY. (*Of a person, in actions or disposition*) 'hwó-pwo, 'hwó-bwo, 'hwó-be. ‖She has a lively disposition. tā hěn 'hwó-pwo.

(*Vigorous; in emotions or actions connected with emotions, as hatred, fighting*) 'jī-lyè, 'lì-hay.

(*Inspiring; as of music or actions*) 'shyúng-jwàng-de. ‖The band played a lively march. yīn-ywè-'dwèy dzèw-le yí-ge-hěn-'shyúng-jwàng-de-jìn-shíng-'chywǔ.

(*Vivid; of a description*) 'yěw-shēng-yěw-'sè-de. ‖He gave a lively description of the scene. tā bǎ nèy-ge-'chíng-shing 'shíng-rung-de 'yěw-shēng-yěw-'sè-de. ‖Step lively! 'kwày-dyar 'dzěw.

Make things lively for *someone* gēn . . . 'dǎw-dǎw 'lwǎn, gēn . . . 'nàw-yi-nàw, jyàw . . . 'bù-dé ān-'shēng. ‖We'll make things lively for him when he comes back. tā 'hwéy-lay de-shŕ-hew 'dzám děy °gēn-ta 'dǎw-dǎw 'lwǎn. *or* °gēn-ta 'nàw-yi-nǎw. *or* °jyàw-ta 'bù-dé ān-'shēng.

LOAD. *All the Chinese expressions are verbal.* To load *things* (*on a vehicle*) jwāng . . . or shàng . . .; (*on an animal*) bǎ . . . twó (*in each case a noun for the things loaded on must be expressed*); to load *a vehicle* jwāng . . .; to load *a gun* . . . jwāng-shang 'dzěr or . . . jwāng-shang dž-'dàn; to be loaded (*of a gun*) *also* jwāng-'hǎw-le, yěw chyáng-'dzěr, yěw dž-'dàn; to be loaded (with) *or* to carry a load (of) (*of a vehicle*) jwāng *or* dzày, (*of an animal*) twó, (*of a person with arms loaded*) bàw, (*when the things are hanging down*) *is expressed as* hang full (of) gwà-'mǎn(-le); to be fully loaded *or* to carry a full load *may also be expressed as* mǎn-'dzàr(-le); to load *someone* with work gěy . . . bù-'shǎw-de-shèr dzwò.

‖Are the men loading or unloading the vessel? nèy-shyē-rén 'jwāng-chwán-ne háy-shr 'shyè-chwán-ne? *or* (*Referring to the things handled rather than the ship*) nèy-shyē-rén 'jwāng-hwò-ne háy-shr 'shyè-hwò-ne? *or* nèy-shyē-rén 'shàng-hwò-ne háy-shr 'shyà-hwò-ne? ‖It's time to load the truck. gāy jwāng-'chē-le. ‖The men were loading hay onto the wagon. nèy-bāng-rén 'jèng-dzày wàng 'chē-shang °shàng- (*or* °jwāng-)'tsǎw-ne. ‖We've been loading all morning. wǒm yì-'dzǎw-chen jìng °jwāng 'dūng-shi láy-je. *or* °shàng-'hwò láy-je. *or* °jwāng-'hwò láy-je. ‖How heavy is the normal load? píng-'cháng néng 'jwāng (*or* 'dzày, *or, of an animal,* 'twó) 'dwō-shaw-'dūng-shi? ‖How much of a load can that boat carry? nèy-jř-'chwán néng jwāng (*or* dzày) 'dwō-shǎw-°'dūng-shi? *or* °'hwò? *or* (*pounds*) °'bàng? *or* (*tons*) °'dwèn? *or* (*catties*) °'jīn? *or* nèy-jř-'chwán dzày-'jùng 'dwō-shǎw? ‖The load weighs a hundred pounds. *is expressed as* It weighs a hundred pounds. yěw yì-'bǎy-bàng-'jùng. ‖The load on the mule weighs a hundred pounds. lwó-dz-'shēn-shang °'twó-je yěw yì-'bǎy-bàng-jùng-de-dūng-shi. *or* °'twó-je-de-dūng-shi yěw yì-'bǎy-bàng(-jùng). *or* °'twó-de yěw yì-'bǎy-bàng (-jùng). ‖The mule is too heavily loaded. 'lwó-dz twó-de tày °'jùng-le. *or* °'chén-le. ‖Load the packs on the mules; the horses are for riding. bǎ-'bāw °'twó-dzày 'lwó-dz-shang (*or* °jyàw 'lwó-dz twó); mǎ shř (rén-)'chí-de. ‖His arms were loaded with books. tā 'bàw-le yí-'dà-°dwēy- (*or* °bàw-)shū. ‖The plane is carrying a full load now. fēy-jī-shang °jwāng-de (*or* °dzày-de) yǐ-jīng gèw-'jùng-de-le. *or* °jwāng-de (*or* °dzày-de) yǐ-jīng 'bù-néng dzày 'jùng-le. *or* °jwāng-de (*or* °dzày-de) yǐ-jīng 'mǎn-le. *or* °yǐ-jīng mǎn-'dzàr-le. ‖These guys have been running fully loaded planes over the hump for three years. 'jèy-shyē-'háy-dz-men kāy mǎn-'dzàr-de-fēy-'jī gwò 'shī-mǎ-lā-'yǎ-shang yǐ-jīng yěw 'sān-nyán-le. ‖The boat is fully loaded with merchandise. nèy-jř-'chwán-li jwāng-°'mǎn-le 'hwò-le. *or* °de mǎn-'chwán-de-hwò. *or* °de yì-'chwán-de-hwò. *or* °de yì-'mǎn-chwán-de-hwò. *or* °'hwò jwāng-de mǎn-'dzàr-le. ‖The gun was loaded and ready for firing. 'chyáng-lǐ-tew °jwāng-'hǎw-le (*or* °jwāng-shang 'dzěr-le, *or* °'jwāng-shang dž-'dàn-le, *or* °yěw 'chyáng-'dzěr, *or* °yěw dž-'dàn), swéy-'shŕ kě-yǐ 'fàng. ‖Load this gun for me. jèy-chyáng-li gěy-wǒ jwāng-shang °'dzěr. *or* °dž-'dàn. ‖The tree was loaded with Christmas presents. 'shù-shang gwà-'mǎn-le shèng-dan-'lǐ. ‖They loaded us with work. tām 'gěy-le wǒm bù-'shǎw-de-'shèr dzwò. *or* tām-jyàw-wǒm-dzwò-de-'shèr 'tày dwō-le.

LOCK. A lock (*operated by key or combination*) swǒ. (*the metal plates with rings through which a padlock is inserted*) mén-'dyàwr, lyàw-'dyàwr, *or* mén-'byér. ‖Do you have a lock for a trunk? nǐ yěw 'shyāng-dz-shang-yùng-de-'swǒ-ma? ‖The lock on the stable door is broken. mǎ-'hàw-mén-shang-de-°'swǒ hwày-le. *or* °mén-'dyàwr (*or* °lyàw-'dyàwr, *or* °mén-'byér) 'shé-le.

To lock (*with such a lock*) swǒ; bǎ . . . 'swǒ-shang; bǎ . . . swǒ-'hǎw-le. ‖Be sure to lock the door when you leave. 'dzěw-de-shf-hew byé 'wàng-le °swǒ-'mén. *or* °bǎ-mén 'swǒ-shang. *or* °bǎ-mén swǒ-'hǎw-le.

To lock in *a place* 'jywǎn-dzày *or* 'gwān-dzày *or* 'swǒ-dzày; (*without the place being expressed*) 'jywān-chi-lay *or* 'gwān-chi-lay (*see also* lock up *below*). ‖We locked the dog in the cellar. wǒm bǎ-gěw °'jywān- (*or* °'gwān-)dzày dì-'yìn-dz-li-le. ‖Lock the prisoners in their cells. bǎ 'fàn-rén děw °'gwān-chi-lay. *or* °'jywān-chi-lay. *or* °swǒ-dzày 'ywù-li. *or* °'swǒ-dzày 'wūr-li. ‖Lock these prisoners in their cells *is expressed as* Put these prisoners in their cells and lock the doors. jyàw 'jey-shyē(-'fàn)-rén děw jìn 'wūr-li, bǎ-mén děw 'swǒ-shang.

To lock up (*a person*) 'jywān-chǐ-lay, 'gwān-chǐ-lay, 'kān-chǐ-lay, 'yā-chǐ-lay; (*may also mean in chains*) 'swǒ-chǐ-lay. ‖The prisoners were locked up. 'fàn-rén děw 'jywān-chǐ-lay-le.

To lock out (*a person*) bǎ-'mén 'swǒ-shang-le, 'bú-jyàw . . . 'jìn-lay; be locked out (*accidentally*) *is expressed as* not be able to *get the door* open kāy-bu-'kāy. ‖We locked him out. wǒm bǎ-'mén 'swǒ-shang-le, °'méy (*or* °bú)-jyàw-ta 'jìn-lay. ‖We were locked out when we forgot the key last night. wǒm dzwér 'wǎn-shang 'wàng-le dày 'yàw-shr, 'mér kāy-bu-'kāy-le.

(*A stopping device*) 'shyāw-shyer, 'jī-gwān, 'gwǎn-téwr. ‖There's a lock on the gears to keep them from turning backwards. 'lwén-dz-shang (*or* chř-'lwén-shang) yěw 'shyāw-shyer gwǎn-je (*etc.*) °'bú-jyàw lwén-dz wàng-'hèw 'jwàn (*or* 'dzěw). *or* °jyàw 'lwén-dz jǐr néng wàng 'yì-téwr jwàn (*or* 'dzěw).

To lock (*be immovable*) *is expressed as* be stuck 'chyá-shang-le *or* 'chyǎ-shang-le. ‖The brakes locked. já 'chyá-shang-le.

To be locked together (*interlocked*) 'gwà-shang-le, 'chyá-shang-le, 'chyǎ-shang-le. ‖The bumpers of the two cars are locked together. 'lyàng-lyàng-chē-de-chyán-hèw-'dǎng °'gwà-shang-le. *etc.*

(*Of hair*) lyéwr; *sometimes expressed as* one hair yì-sž. ‖She won't go out unless every lock of her hair is in place. tā fēy-děy bǎ 'téw-fa 'nùng-de 'yì-sž bú-'lwàn, 'yàw-bù-rán jyèw bù-'chū-chywu.

(*Of a canal*) já. ‖The second lock of the canal is under repair now. ywùn-'hé-shang dì-'èr-dàw-'já °jèng-dzày 'shyēw-li. *or* °'háy méy-'shyēw-li-'hǎw-ne.

LOG. (*Cut tree*) 'kǎn-shyà-lay-de-'shù; to log (*trees*) kǎn-'shù *or* fá-'shù. ‖The logs are tied into rafts and floated down the river. jěng-'kē-de-kǎn-shyà-lay-de-'shù děw kwěn-chéng-le °mù-'páy (*or* °mù-'fá) shwèn-je 'hé pyāw-shyà-lay. ‖When will they start logging? tām 'shéme-shf-hew chǐ-'téwr °kǎn-'shù? *or* °fá-'shù?

(*A record*) r̂-'jì. To log *or* record in a log 'jì-shyà-lay. ‖There is a complete record of the storm in the

ship's log. nèy-tsž-dà-'fēng chwán-shang-de-r̂-'jì-li jì-de tǐng 'chywán. ‖Don't forget to log the speed. byé wàng-le bǎ 'sú-dù 'jì-shyà-lay.

LONELY (LONESOME). (*Of a person*) 'mèn, 'mèn-de-hung, 'gū-dān. ‖Aren't you lonesome without your friends? nǐ-de-'péng-yew 'děw bú-'dzày-jèr nǐ °bú-'mèn-de-hung-ma? *or* °'bù-jywé-je 'mèn-ma? *or* °'bù-jywé-je 'mèn-de-hung-ma? *or* °'bù-jywé-je 'gū-dān-ma?

(*Of a place*). ‖This must be a lonely place in the winter. 'jèy-ge-dì-fang 'dūng-tyar yí-'dìng hěn °'lěng-jìng (*cold and quiet*). *or* °'chī-lyáng (*sad and cold*).

LONG. (*In space*) cháng; a long way (*far*) ywǎn; *in a few cases* dà (*big*) *is used*. ‖The room is twenty feet long. jèy-jyān-wū-dz °(yěw) 'èr-shr-chř-'cháng. *or* 'cháng-li yěw 'èr-shr-'chř. *or* °'cháng-shya-li yěw 'èr-shr-'chř. ‖Longer ones are better. 'cháng-dyar-de 'hǎw. ‖These are the longest ones we have. 'jèy shř wǒm-jèr-'dzwèy-cháng-de-le. ‖The longest river in China is called the Big River or the Long River, given on foreign maps as the Yangtze. jūng-gwo-'dzwèy-cháng-de-hé jyàw 'dà-jyāng, yě jyàw 'cháng-jyāng, dzày 'yáng-wén-dì-'tú-shang jyàw 'yáng-dž-jyāng. ‖I need a long rope. wǒ děy yàw yì-°tyáw-'cháng-shéng-dz. *or* °gēn-'cháng-shéng-dz. *or* °tyáw-hěn-'cháng-de-'shéng-dz. *or* °gēn-hěn-'cháng-de-'shéng-dz. ‖It's a long story. 'nèy-hwàr tí-chu-lay kě °'cháng-je-ne. *or* °jyěw 'cháng-le. ‖The snake was as long as from here to the table. 'shé yěw tsúng-'jèr dàw nèy-ge-'jwǒ-dz-nar nèm 'cháng. ‖He gave me a long list of names to investigate one by one. tā jyāw-gěy wǒ °yí-'dà-lyèw-rén-'míng-dz (*or* °yí-'dà-dwēy-rén-'míng-dz, *or* °yí-ge-hěn-'cháng-de-rén-'míng-dān-dz), jyàw-wǒ yí-'gè-yí-gèr chywù 'dyàw-chá. ‖It's a long way to the top of the mountain. dàw shān-'dyěngr-shang °tǐng 'ywǎn-de. *or* °'ywǎn-je-ne. *or* °'lù hěn 'ywǎn.

(*In time*) *expressed as* for a long time chyě (*before the verb*), *or* jyěw, shyē-'shf-hew, dwǒ-'shf-hew, dà-de-'gūng-fu (*all after the verb*); *or by specific expressions as* for many years 'dwō-nyán; *or* (*especially for a long wait*) by 'bàn-tyān (*literally*, half a day); *or by* jyěw *or* cháng *with* 'shf-hew; *in expressions indicating a given period of time, as* all night long, long *is not expressed, but the expression for time is put after the verb*. ‖It's quite a long trip by water. tsúng 'shwěy-lù(r) dzěw °'chyě děy 'dzěw-ne. *or* °děy dzěw 'hǎw-shyē-shf-hew. *or* °děy dzěw 'hěn jyěw. ‖It'll still take a long time to finish this job. jèy-jyàn-shèr háy °'chyě děy dzwò-ne. *or* °'chyě děy (*or* °děy 'hǎw-) shyē-'shf-hew tsáy néng dzwò-'wán-ne. ‖The dinner party was a long-drawn-out affair. yí-dwèn-'fàn chř-le 'hǎw-shyē-shf-hew. ‖It may take as long as six months. yě-shywǔ děy yùng 'lyèw-ge-'ywè nèm °'jyěw. *or* °shyē-'shf-hew. ‖We've waited just as long.

wǒm yě děng-le nèm °'jyĕw-le. or °-shyē-'shŕ-hew-le. or °dà-de-'gūng-fu-le. ‖Don't stay away too long. byé 'lí-kay °tày 'jyĕw-le. or °shŕ-hew tày 'cháng-le. or °shŕ-hew tày 'jyĕw-le. ‖The event happened a long time ago. 'nèy shŕ 'hěn-jyĕw-yǐ-'chyán(-de-shèr). or 'nèy shŕ 'shywǔ-jyĕw-yǐ-'chyán(-de-shèr). or 'nèy shŕ 'shywǔ-dwō-shŕ-hew-yǐ-'chyán(-de-shèr). or 'nèy shŕ 'shywǔ-dwō-nyán-yǐ-'chyán(-de-shèr). or 'nèy shŕ 'hǎw-shyē-shŕ-hew-yǐ-'chyán(-de-shèr). ‖He got there long after we did. wǒm dàw-nèr °bàn-'tyān-le (or °'hǎw-shyē-shŕ-hew-le, or °'hǎw-jyĕw) 'tā tsáy láy-de. ‖The play is three hours long. jèy-chū-'shì děy yǎn 'sān-ge-jūng-'téw. ‖The child cried all night long. shyǎw-'hár' 'kū-le yì-'jěng-yè. ‖We can wait as long as you can. 'nǐ-men néng děng 'dwō-jyĕw, wǒm yě néng (děng nèm 'jyew). or 'nǐ-men néng děng 'dwō-shǎw-'shŕ-hew, 'wǒm yě néng (děng 'nèm-shyē-shŕ-hew). or 'nǐ-men néng děng 'dwō-dà-de-'gūng-fu, wǒm yě néng (děng 'nèm-dà-de-'gūng-fu). or expressed as We can outlast you. wǒm 'jwěn néng 'hàw-de-gwò 'nǐ-men.

(To yearn). (Want badly) hěn shyǎng; (hope) 'pàn-wàng. ‖I long to finish that job. wǒ 'hěn shyǎng (or wǒ 'jēn shŕ 'pàn-wàng-je) bǎ 'nèy-jyàn-shèr bàn-'wán-le.

As long as (provided that, if; referring to something still uncertain or unfinished) is usually expressed by a conditional sentence; see IF; also, especially when there is a time element present, the construction . . . yì-'tyān, . . . yì-'tyān is sometimes used in a conditional sentence. ‖As long as you're here I'll have nothing to worry about. 'jŕ yàw 'nǐ dzày-jèr, wǒ jyĕw 'méy-yĕw kě-'bú-fàng-'shīn-de. or 'nǐ dzày-jèr yì-'tyān wǒ jyĕw kě-yǐ °'fàng yì-tyān-de-'shīn. or °'yĕw yì-'tyān-de-gūng-fu bú-yùng tsāw-'shīn. ‖You may play in the yard as long as it doesn't rain. jŕ yàw 'bú-shyà-'ywǔ, nǐm °dzày 'ywàr-li wár 'dwō-shaw-shŕ-hew dēw 'shíng. or °'jyĕw dzày ywàr-li 'wár hǎw-le. or °'jyĕw dzày ywàr-li 'wár-ba. ‖As long as you can wait, so can we. 'jŕ yàw 'nǐm néng děng-de-'lyǎw, 'wǒm yě 'néng (děng-de-lyǎw).

As long as (since, referring to an accomplished fact) 'jì-rán, 'jì-shŕ, jì. ‖As long as you really want it, you can have it. nǐ °'jì-rán (or °'jì-shŕ, or °jì) 'jēn shyǎng 'yàw, jyĕw 'swàn 'nǐ-de-le. ‖As long as no one is asking you about it, you may as well keep quiet. jì 'méy-rén 'wèn-nǐ, nǐ yě jyĕw 'béng tí-le.

Have a long face 'dā-le-'lyǎn, yì-lyǎn bù-gāw-'shìng-de-yàng-dz, 'mǎn-lyǎn dày-je bù-gāw-'shìng-de-yàng-dz, 'mǎn-lyǎn dày-je bú-'tùng-kway-de-yang-dz. ‖Why has he got such a long face today? tā 'jyēr-ge dzěm °'dā-le-je ge-'lyǎn? or °'yì-lyǎn bù-gāw-'shìng-de-yàng-dz? or °'mǎn-lyǎn dày-je bù-gāw-'shìng-de-yàng-dz. or °'mǎn-lyǎr dày-je bú-'tùng-kway-de-yàng-dz.

In the long run 'jyē-gwò (finally); kàw-'cháng-lew. ‖In the long run the more expensive watch would be better. 'jyē-gwǒ (or kàw-'cháng-lew) hay-shr 'gwèy-dyar-de-'byǎw shàng-'swàn.

‖So long! 'hwéy jyàn!

LOOK. (Direct the eyes to see) kàn or chyǎw or chěw; (especially of looking once, or a little) 'kàn-kan or 'chyǎw-chyaw or 'chěw-chew (or 'kàn-yi-kan, etc.); (with more specific meanings) lyěw-'shén (pay attention); nyěw-'téwr (turn the head); jǎw (search). ‖Look this way. wàng (or chùng-je) 'jèy-byar kàn (or chyǎw, or chěw). ‖Let me look. 'wǒ kàn-kan. or 'wǒ kàn-yi-kan or 'wǒ chyǎw-yi-chyaw. etc. ‖Just looking (around). 'jyĕw-shr 'kàn-kan. ‖No harm in looking. 'kàn-kan 'bú-ày-shr. ‖I wasn't looking just at that moment. jèng-hǎw 'nèy-jèr wǒ °méy-'kàn-je. or °méy-'chyǎw-je. or °méy-lyěw-'shén. or °'yì-yǎn méy-chyǎw-'jyàn. ‖Don't look now, but there's someone over there staring at you. 'byé nyěw-'téwr, ā (or ˌbyé kàn, ā, or 'byé chyǎw, ā, or expressed as pretend you don't know 'jwāng bù-jŕ-'dàw), nèy-byar yěw ge-ren 'dèng-je-yǎr 'chěw-nǐ-ne. ‖Did you look everywhere? nǐ 'nǎr dēw °'kàn-le-ma? or °'jǎw-le-ma? ‖Hey! Look! 'hèy! nǐ 'kàn! or 'hèy! nǐ 'chyǎw! or 'hèy! kan-na! or 'hèy! 'chyǎw-wa! or 'hèy! 'kàn-ney! or 'hèy! 'chyǎw-ey! or 'hèy! 'chěw-ey! or (Peiping) 'hèy! 'lēw-yi-lew! or (especially when whispering) simply 'hèy! ‖Hey, look to your right! 'hèy, 'yèw-byar! or 'hèy, wàng nǐ-'yèw-byar °kàn. or °kàn-kan. or °chyǎw. etc. ‖Look where you're going! 'chyǎw-je-dyar! or rudely expressed as Where are your eyes? 'yǎn-jīng jǎng 'nǎr-chywu-le. or as Do you have eyes? yěw 'yǎn-jīng méy-yěw? or as Blind!? 'shyā-le!?

Look at, take (or have, or give) **a look** (at) is expressed as above, and also by dīng (fix the eyes on) 'chá-kàn (examine) 'shyāng or 'dwǎn-shyang (look at carefully and steadily, take a good look); take a (good) look at may also be expressed by kàn (or chyǎw, or chěw, or dīng, or dèng) yì-'yǎn or 'chyǎw yí-shyàr; take one look and . . . yí 'kàn (or 'chyǎw, or 'chěw), jyěw . . . or 'kàn (etc.) yì-'yǎn, jyěw . . .; (especially of looking sideways, out of the corner of the eyes, stealthily, etc.) ná-yǎn 'lyěw yí-shyàr or 'lyǎ-yě 'lyěw yí-shyàr or 'shyé-je-yǎn 'kàn-kan. ‖Look at the beautiful sunset! èy! nǐ kàn nà-°'wǎn-shyá (or °'lwò-'r) 'dwō hǎw 'kàn. ‖May I look at it? ràng-wǒ °'kàn-kan (or °'chyǎw-chyaw) 'shíng-ma? ‖I enjoy looking at pictures. wǒ 'hàw kàn-'hwàr. ‖He looked at her for a long time without moving his eyes, as if he were in a trance. tā 'dèng-je-yǎn (or tā 'mù-bù-jwǎn-'jīng-de) °'kàn-je-ta kàn-le (or °'chyǎw-je-ta chyǎw-le, or °'chěw-je-ta chěw-le, or °'dīng-je-ta kàn-le) bàn-'tyān, 'hǎw shyǎng jǎw-le-'mí shr̀-de. or tā 'sž-dīng-je tā kàn-le bàn-'tyān, ... ‖He took one look and beat it. tā yí 'kàn (or tā yì 'chyǎw, or tā yì 'chěw, or tā 'kàn-le yì-'yǎn) jyěw shyà-'pǎw-le. ‖Take a look from here. tsúng-'jèr °'kàn-yi-kan. or °'chyǎw-yi-chyaw. or °'chěw-yi-chew. ‖Take a good look. 'dž-shì (or hǎw-'hāwr-de) °'kàn-kan. or °'chyǎw-chyaw. or °'shyāng-shyang. or °'dwǎn-shyang-dwǎn-shyang. ‖She took one good look and fainted. tā 'dž-shì °kàn-le yì-'yǎn (or °chyáw-le yì-'yǎn, or °chyáw-le yí-shyàr) jyèw 'hwēn-gwo-chywu-le. ‖She gave him a nasty look. tā hěn-'hěn-de °'dīng-le (or °'chěw-le, or °'kàn-le, or °'chyáw-le, or °'dèng-le) tā yì-'yǎn. ‖I've got a good mind to go there and have a look (around) for myself. wǒ 'hěn shyǎng 'chīn-dz (dàw-nàr) chywù °'chá-kàn-chá-kàn. or °'kàn-kan. etc. ‖She pretended to be reading, but once in a while she looked at him out of the corner of her eyes. tā jwāng-je kàn-'shū, kě-shr 'gwò-yi-hwěr jyèw °ná-'yǎn 'lyēw-ta yǐ-shyàr, or °'lyǎ-yǎr 'lyēw-ta yí-shyàr. or °'pyǎw-ta yì-'yǎn. or °'shyé-je-yǎn kàn-kan-ta.

(To appear, to seem) is often unexpressed, but the rest of the sentence in such cases usually includes some expression referring to the external appearance, as 'lyǎn-shang (face) or hǎw 'kàn (good-looking); or expressed by 'kàn-shang-chywu; look like see LIKE. ‖She looks very pretty today. tā jyēr 'dǎ-bàn-de hěn hǎw 'kàn. or tā jyēr 'kàn-shang-chywu jēn 'pyàwlyang. or tā 'jīn-tyàn hěn 'měy. ‖She looked angry when she said that. tā 'shwō nèy-ge de-shí-hewr °'lyǎn-shang hěn bù-hǎw 'kàn. or °hǎw 'shyàng tǐng yěw-'chì shr-de. or °'lyǎn-shang dày-je shēng-'chìde-yàng-dz. or °'lyǎn-shang dày-je 'nù-róng. ‖How does this hat look to you? 'jèy-dǐng-'màw-dz °'dzěme-yàng? or °'shíng-bu-shíng? or °'shyàng-yàngr-ma? ‖It looks nice on you. 'nǐ chwān-je (or 'nǐ dày-je) 'tǐng °shr ge-'yàngr-de. or °hǎw-'kàn-de. ‖It looks OK. 'kàn-shang-chywu °bú-'hwày. or °'tǐng-hǎw-de. or °hěn shr'-yàngr. ‖It looks like snow. 'chyáw-je (or 'chyáw jèy-yàngr, or 'kàn jèy-yàngr) yàw shyà-'shywe. ‖He looks like a ghost. tā kàn-je (or tā nèyyàngr) shyàng ge-'gwěy shr'-de. ‖You look very much like your father. nǐ-'jǎng-de (or nǐ 'kàn-shangchywu) hěn shyàng nǐ-'fù-chin.

(Appearance) 'yàng-dz, shyàngr (showing strong disapproval) 'dé-shing, 'shén-chì; (see also preceding paragraph). ‖The house has a neat look. 'jèy-swěrfáng-dz °'yàng-dz (or °'kàn-shang-chywu) tǐng 'jěng-chí. or °'yàng-dz (or °'kàn-shang-chywu) hěn 'gān-jing. ‖I don't like his looks. wǒ bù-'shǐ-hwān tā-de-'yàng-dz. or wǒ bú-'dày-jìng 'tā-nèy-ge-°'shyàngr. or °'dé-shing. or tā-nèy-jǔng-'shén-chì ràng-wǒ chǐ 'yǐshin. or 'jèy-rén wǒ kàn-je 'bú-shwèn-'yǎn.' or expressed as Look at the way he looks. 'chyáw tā-nèyge-°'yàng-dz. or °'shén-chì. or °'dé-shing. or °'shyàngr. or (If he looks sick) tā-de-'yàng-dz bù-hǎw kàn, shyàng °yěw-'bìng shr-de. or (If he looks sicker than expected) °'bìng-de hěn 'jùng. ‖I don't like the looks of this situation. wǒ kàn (or wǒ jywé-je) °'jèy-ge-'chíng-shr bú-dà 'dwèy. or °'dà-'shr bù-'hǎw. or °'jèyge-'chíng-shíng yàw 'dzāw.

(In exclamations where actual vision is not referred to) hèy! or 'āy-yā! or not expressed. ‖Look, where are you going? hèy! nǐ yàw shàng-'nǎr? ‖Look who's here! 'āy-yā! (or 'hēy!) 'jèy shr 'shéy láy-le! ‖Look who's talking (now)! (If the person talking, referred to as you or he, has no right to talk) 'nǐ (or 'tā) dung-

shéme (yě 'shyā-shwō). or 'nǐ (or 'tā) yě pèy shwō-'hwà! or dzěme 'shéy dēw néng shwō-'hwà-ya! or (A proverb) jè jyàw 'yì-píng-dz bù-'shyǎng, 'bàn-píng-dz 'gwàng-dang. or (If the person talking has changed sides in an argument) 'éy, dzěm 'nǐ (or 'tā) yě gǎy-le 'dzwěy-le? or (If insincerity is suspected) 'kěw-shr shīn-'fēy.

To look after kān (of children; also means **to guard**); (of an adult, affairs, etc.) 'jàw-lyàw or 'jàwgwǎn or 'jàw-ying. ‖Did you get someone to look after the child? nǐ 'jǎw-jáw rén kān 'háy-dz-le-ma? or nǐ 'jǎw-jáw kān-'háy-dz-de-le-ma? ‖He's getting old and needs someone to look after him. tā 'lǎw-le, děy 'yěw ge-rén °'jàw-ying-je-dyar. or °'jàw-gwǎn-jedyar. or °'jàw-lyàw-je-dyar.

To look ahead to; see **Look forward to,** below.

To look around; see first paragraph above.

To look at; see second paragraph above.

To look back (recollect) 'hwéy shyǎng, shyǎng yǐchyán-de-shèr, shyǎng 'jyèw-shr. ‖Looking back now, those years we spent together were the most memorable in my life. 'hwéy shyǎng-chǐ-lay (or 'shyǎng-shyang yǐ-'chyán-de-shèr, or 'shyǎng-shyang 'jyèw-shr), wǒm-dzǎy-yí-'kwàr-gwo-de-nèy-shyē-'nyán shr wǒ-'jèy-bèy-dz-li-'dzwèy-kě-'lyéw-lyàn-de. ‖Don't look back (on the past). 'byé shyǎng yǐ-'chyánde-shèr.

Look down on kàn-bu-'chǐ, chyáw-bu-'chǐ, 'shyǎwkàn; bǎ . . . kàn-'dī; 'chīng-shr or 'myǎw-shr somewhat literary). ‖He felt that the people there looked down on him. tā jywé-je nàr-de-rén °'kàn-bu-'chǐ tā láy-je. or °chyáw-bu-'chǐ tā láy-je. or °'shyǎw-kàn tā láy-je. or °bǎ-ta kàn-'dī-le. or °'chīng-shr tā láy-je. or °'myǎw-shr tā láy-je.

Look for jǎw; **look for** trouble jǎw and indirect expressions. ‖We're looking for rooms. wǒm jǎw-'fángne. ‖What are you looking for? nǐ jǎw 'shéme-ne? ‖I'm looking for my keys. (wǒ) jǎw 'yàw-shr-ne. ‖I've looked everywhere for him, but no luck yet. wǒ jǎw-ta 'nǎr dēw jǎw-'byàn-le, háy méy-jǎw-'jáw-ne. ‖He's always looking for trouble. tā 'lǎw shr °'méyshr-jǎw-'shr. or °'dž-tǎw-'kǔ-chī. or °'dž-jǐ jǎw 'máfan. or °'dž-jǐ jǎw-'shèr. or tā 'lǎw rě-'shr. or tā 'lǎw (jǎw-)rě 'shr-fēy. ‖Are you looking for trouble? (A threat) nǐ shyǎng jǎw 'má-fan-na! or nǐ shyǎng dǎ-'jyà-a! ‖Aren't you looking for trouble? (Friendly warning) nǐ-nà bú-shr °(dž-jǐ) 'méy-shèr-jǎw-'shèrma? or °'dž-tǎw-'kǔ-chī-ma? or °jǎw-je yàw chī-'kwēy-ma? or °jǎw-je yàw dǎ-'jyà-ma? or °jǎw-je yàw rě-'shèr-ma? or °jǎw-je yàw chū-'shèr-ma?

Look forward to. (Wait impatiently for) 'pàn-je 'kwày-dàw; (Make plans for) wèy . . . dzwò 'dǎ-swàn or 'gù-lywù-dàw. . . . ‖He's looking forward to the time when he'll finish college. tā 'pàn-je 'kwày-dàw 'dàshywé-bì-'yè-de-shí-hew. or tā-nèy shr wèy 'dž-jǐ-'dàshywé-bì-'yè-de-shí-hew dzwò 'dǎ-swàn-ne. or tā-nèy shr 'gù-lù-dàw dž-jǐ-'dà-shywé-bì-'yè-yǐ-'hèw-de-'shèrne. ‖We're looking forward to our vacation. wǒm 'pàn-je 'kwày-dàw fàng-'jyà-de-shí-hew.

Look here! (*Forbidding*) 'hèy! or (*Surprise*) 'ĕy! or '.ă! or (*Mild warning*) nĭ 'shyăng-shyang, nĭ 'dzwó-me-dzwó-me, nĭ tīng 'wŏ shwō, or nĭ tīng 'wŏ-de. ‖**Look here! You can't do that!** 'hèy! 'nà kĕ bù-'shíng. or 'hèy! 'bù-néng 'nèm-je-a! (or 'ĕy! or '.ă! for 'hèy!) or nĭ 'shyăng-shyang (or nĭ 'dzwó-me-dzwó-me), 'nà dzĕme 'shíng-ne? or nĭ tīng 'wŏ shwō (or nĭ tīng 'wŏ-de), 'nèm-je bù-'shíng.

Look into (*investigate*) 'dyàw-chá. ‖**The police will certainly look into the robbery.** jīng-chá-'jywú yí-'dìng hwèy 'dyàw-chá nèy-jyàn-'chyàng-àn-de.

Look on (*as a spectator*) kàn, dzày yì-'byār kàn; (*literary quotation*) dzwò 'bì-shang-'gwān. ‖**The others played, but he just looked on.** 'byé-rén 'dă (or 'wár) de-shŕ-hew tā °gwāng 'kàn láy-je. or °dzày yì-'byār kàn-je. or °dzwò 'bì-shang-'gwān.

Look on *something* **as** (*consider*) 'rèn-wéy, 'jywé-je. ‖**Her father looked on her marriage as unfortunate.** tā-'fù-chin °'rèn-wéy (or °'jywé-je) tā-'jyà-de-rén bù-hé-'shŕ.

‖**Look out!** lyéw-'shén! or shyăw-'shīn! or dāng-'shĭn! or 'kàn-na! or 'chyáw-wa!

Look out, on (*face*) chùng-je or dwèy-je; *see also* FACE. ‖**The big window looks out on a flower garden.** 'dà-chwāng-hu chùng-je hwā-'ywár.

Look over; *see second paragraph above*.

Look to *someone* **for help** 'jŕ-je or 'kàw-je. ‖**He always looked to his father for help.** tā lăw shŕ 'jŕ-je tā-'fù-chin.

Look up *someone* 'jăw(-jaw). ‖**Look me up sometime.** méy-shèr 'jăw-wŏ-lay. or 'méy-shèr láy 'jăw-jaw wŏ.

Look up (*lift the head*) 'táy-téw. ‖**He looked up quickly.** tā lì-'kè bă-téw 'táy-chĭ-lay-le. or tā lì-'kè 'táy-téw yí-'kàn.

Look up (*find out*) 'jăw-jaw; *or expressed as* **examine,** *of the place where the information is found,* 'chá-cha. ‖**If you lose this card you can always look up my address in the phone book.** yăw bă jèy-jàng-'pyàn-dz 'dyēw-le, °dzŭng kĕ-yĭ dzày 'dyàn-hwà-'bĕn-dz-shang 'jăw-jaw wŏ-de-'jù-jŕ-de. or °'chá-cha (or °'chá-yi-cha, or °kàn-kan) 'dyàn-hwà-'bĕn-dz jyèw 'jăw-jáw wŏ-de-'jù-jŕ-le. ‖**Look up the train schedule.** *is expressed as* **Examine the timetable.** 'chá-cha 'hwŏ-'chē-shŕ-jyān-'byăw.

Look up to 'pèy-fu (*admire*); 'jìng-jùng (*respect*). ‖**I can't help looking up to him.** wŏ bù-'néng bú-°'pèy-fu tā. or °'jìng-jùng tā. or tā jēn jyàw-rén °'pèy-fu. or °'jìng-jùng.

Looking up (*improving*). ‖**Things are looking up.** jyàn 'hăw. or yĕw 'chĭ-sè.

LOOSE. (*Not tight: of a fastening or grip*) sūng, bù-'jĭn. **Come loose** 'sūng-le or 'sūng-kāy-le; **be loose** (*because never tightened*) *is expressed by a verb meaning* **to tie, to nail, to screw, to pull,** *etc., in constructions such as* . . .-de sūng, . . .-de bù-'jĭn, méy-. . .-'jĭn; *of a knot, also* 'jì-de 'bú-shŕ 'sź-kèwr (*not tied in a tight knot*); *of a screw, also* méy-'nīng-dàw téwr (*not*

screwed to the head). ‖**If that knot comes loose, the whole bundle will fall apart.** nèy-ge-'kèwr yàw-shŕ 'sūng(-kāy)-le, kwér (or bāwr) jyèw 'săn-le. ‖**The knot is (tied) loose, so it shouldn't be hard to undo it.** nèy-kèwr °'jì-de hĕn 'sūng (or °'jì-de bù-'jĭn, or °'méy-jì-'jĭn, or °shŕ sūng-'sūngr-de 'jì-de, or °'jì-de 'bú-shŕ 'sź-kèwr), bù-gĕy 'nèm nán 'jyĕ-ya. ‖**If the rope around the box is too loose, it will slip off.** 'hé-dz-shang-de-'shéng-dz yàw-shŕ °kwén-de tày 'sūng-le (or °băng-de tày 'sūng-le, or °bù-chēw-'jĭn-le, or °bù-shēw-'jĭn-le), hwèy 'dyàw-shya-lay-de. ‖**Put a loose bandage on his arm.** dzày tā-'gē-be-shang °kwén-shang bēng-'dày kwén-de 'sūng-je-dyar. or °kwén-shang bēng-'dày 'byé kwén-'jĭn-le. or °sūng-'sūng-de kwén tyáw-bēng-'dày. ‖**Doesn't that bolt seem loose?** nèy-ge-'lwó-sz shŕ-bu-shŕ °yĕw-dyăr 'sūng-le? or °'méy-'nĭng-dàw 'téwr. ‖**Hold it loosely.** ná-de 'sūng-je-dyar. or 'sūng-je-dyar °ná-je. or °'dzwàn-je. or 'byé °ná-de (or °'dzwàn-de) tày 'jĭn-le.

(*Not connected tightly: as a wire*) *is expressed in the same way, but also* **come loose** bù-'jyē-je-le. ‖**There must be a loose wire in the plug.** chā-'shyăw-li yĕw yì-tyáw-shyàn °'sūng-kay-le. or °bù-'jyē-je-le. or (*not fastened tightly in the first place*) °méy-nĭng-'jĭn.

(*Not fitting in tightly, as a loose cork*) sūng; tày 'shyăw (*too small*); săy-bu-'jù (*can't plug up*); săy-bu-'jĭn (*can't plug tightly*). ‖**This cork fits too loosely.** jèy-ge-sār °tày 'shyăw. or °săy-bu-'jù. or °săy-bu-'jĭn. or săy-shang tày 'sūng.

(*Not fitting on tightly, as clothes*) tày 'dà (*too large*); 'dà-le (*become large*); 'féy-fey-dà-'dà-de (*too large a size*); 'bù-fū-'shēr or 'bù-hé-'shŕ (*not fitting*); 'gwàng-le-gwàng-dāng-de(-le) (*like a half-full bottle*); *all of these are preceded by* 'chwān-je (*in wearing*). ‖**I've lost so much weight that my clothes are all loose.** wŏ 'shèw-de 'yī-shang dēw chwān-je °'dà-le. or °'féy-fey-dà-'dà-de-le. or °'gwàng-le gwàng-dāng-de-le. or °'bù-fū-'shēr-le. or °'bù-hé-'shŕ-le.

(*Not sewn on tightly, as a button*) yàw 'dyàw (*about to fall off*); 'dā-la-je-le (*hanging by a thread*); 'shyàn-dwàn-le (*a thread broken*). ‖**There's a loose button on your coat.** nĭ-'yī-shang yĕw yí-ge-'nyĕw-dz °yàw 'dyàw. or °'dā-la-je-le. or °'shyàn-dwàn-le.

(*Insecure, not solid*) hwó, 'hwó-dùng, or 'hwó-yĕw (*moving, wiggling*); bù-'láw-kàw (*insecure*); 'hwàng-yĕw, 'gàng-yĕw, or 'gà-yĕw (*shaky*); *of a board, also* 'chĭ-láy-le (*risen, buckled*), or 'chyàw-chĭ-lay-le or yĕw-dyăr 'chyàw-je (*tipped up at one end*). ‖**He has a loose tooth.** tā yĕw yí-ge-'yá 'hwó(-dùng)-le. ‖**This plank is loose.** (*Of a board laid to walk on, as a gangplank*) tyàw-'băn °'dā-de bù-'láw-kàw. or °'méy-dā 'láw-kàw. or °yĕw-dyăr 'hwàng-yĕw. or °yĕw-dyăr 'gàng-yĕw. or °yĕw-dyăr 'gà-yĕw. or °yĕw-dyăr 'hwó-yĕw. or °yĕw-dyăr 'hwó-dùng. or (*Of a board fastened down*) jèy-kwày-'băn-dz (or jèy-kwày-'băr) °yĕw 'hwó-yĕw. or °yĕw-dyăr 'hwó-dùng. or °'chyàw-chĭ-lay-le. or °yĕw-dyăr 'chyàw-jè. or °'dīng-dz sūng-le. or °'méy-dīng-'láw-kàw. or °'dīng-de bù-'láw-kàw.

(*Not tied up or shut in*) 'fàng-kāy(-le), 'fàng-chū-chywu(-le). ‖Isn't that dog allowed to go loose? nèy-'gĕw °bù-néng 'fàng-kāy-ma? or °bú-'fàng-kāy-ma?

(*Individual, not packaged*) lwèn plus a unit measure (*by the piece*) ; or expressed by the appropriate unit measure; or expressed as **buy loose** líng 'mǎy or as **sell loose** líng 'mày. ‖During the cigarette shortage some shopkeepers broke open the packages and sold the cigarettes loose. 'jǐ-yān shǎw de-nèy-shf-hew, yěw-de mày-'yān-de bǎ 'jēng-bāwr 'dǎ-kāy. °'líng mày. or °'lwèn-'gēr mày. ‖I bought some loose cookies. wǒ mǎy-le dyǎr-pǐng-'gān, °shř 'líng-mǎy-de. or °shř lwèn-'gèr-mǎy-de. ‖He has some loose cigarettes in his pocket. tā kěw-'dàr-li yěw jǐ-gēn-'yān.

(*Out of order, disorganized; as papers*) lwàn. ‖Look for it among the loose papers on my desk. dzày wǒ-'jwōr-shang lwàn-'jř-li 'jǎw-jaw kàn.

Loose ends 'swèr, 'swèy-téwr, 'lwàn-chi-bā-'dzāw-de. ‖Cut off the loose ends. bǎ-'swèr (or bǎ 'swèy-téwr, or bǎ 'lwàn-chī-bā-'dzāw-de) °'jyàn-shyà-chywu. or (*cut off even*) °'jyàn-'chí-le.

Loose (*of life*) 'làng-màn, 'fàng-dàng. ‖She leads a loose life. tā-de-'shēng-hwo hĕn °'làng-màn. or °'fàng-dàng.

Loose tongue. ‖She's known for a loose tongue. tā shř chū-le-'míng-de hàw chwán-'shé(-de). or 'shwéy dēw jř-dàw tā shwō-'hwà tày swéy-'byàn.

Loose translation. ‖He made a loose translation from the original. tā 'jř-shř bǎ ywán-'wén-de-dà-'yì 'fān-chū-láy-le.

Loose weave, loose-woven jř-de 'shī-de, jř-de bú-'mì-de. ‖Get material with a loose weave. 'lyàw-dz yàw jř-de 'shī-dyar-de. or 'lyàw-dz yàw jř-de 'shī-shi-lā-lār-de. or 'lyàw-dz bú-yàw jř-de 'mì-de.

Cut loose (*figuratively*) fǎn-de (or 'nàw-de) gèw 'chyáw-de, fǎn-de (or 'nàw-de) 'lì-hay. ‖He certainly cut loose at that dance. nèy-tsž kāy tyàw-wǔ-'hwèy tā 'fǎn-de kě lèn gèw 'chyáw-de.

LOSE. To lose an object bǎ . . . dyēw; (*drop*) bǎ . . . dyàw; or expressed by saying that the object is lost 'dyēw-le or is not seen bú-'jyàn-le. ‖I've lost my fountain pen again. wǒ 'yèw bǎ 'dz-láy-shwěy-'bǐ 'dyēw-le. or wǒ-dz-láy-shwěy-'bǐ 'yèw °dyēw-le. or bú-'jyàn-le. ‖Don't lose it. byé 'dyēw-le. ‖Don't lose this negative. byé bǎ jèy-dǐ-'pyàn dyēw-lew. ‖I've lost a gold ring somewhere. wǒ yě-bú-shř bǎ yí-ge-jīn-'jyè-jř °'dyēw- (or °'dyàw-)dzày 'nǎr-le.

To be lost (*of an object*) 'dyēw-le or bú-'jyàn-le (*see above*) ; (*of a person*) bú-rèn-de 'jyā-le (*see also* **To lose one's way**, *below*) ; **be lost in thought** 'shyǎng-de chū-'shér-le or 'shyǎng-de lèng-le 'shér-le; (*of lives*) see **LIFE**. ‖Are you lost, little boy? hèy, nǐ 'shř-bu-shř 'bú-rèn-de 'jyā-le? ‖He was lost in thought. tā 'shyǎng-de °chū-'shér-le. or °'lèng-le 'shér-le.

To lose in a game or race shū; (*not necessarily last, but not first*) bù-'yíng, méy-'chywú-shàng, (*of horses only*) méy-'pǎw-shàng. ‖I lost. wǒ shū-le. ‖Our team lost. wǒm-dwèy 'shū-le. ‖My horse lost the race. wǒ-de-nèy-pǐ-'mǎ méy-°'yíng. or °'chywǔ-shàng. or °'pǎw-shàng.

To lose something in gambling shū. ‖I lost five dollars. wǒ 'shū-le 'wǔ-kwày-chyán. ‖I lost the most. or I was the biggest loser. 'wǒ-shū-de 'dzwèy dwō. ‖He lost his shirt playing dice. tā jř 'shǎy-dz 'shéme dēw 'shū-le. or °'dēw shū-'gwāng-le. or °'dēw shū-chū-chywu-le. or °'shū-le ge-'jīng-gwāng. or °'shū-le ge-'yì-gān-èr-jìng.

To lose a battle or war 'dǎ-bày. ‖Their army can't afford to lose any more battles. tām-de-'jywūn-dwèy 'bù-néng 'dzày dǎ-bày-'jàng-le. *See also* **DEFEAT**.

To lose (*in*) an election méy-shywǎn-'shàng. ‖He lost the election by 600 votes. tā 'shǎw dé-le 'lyèw-bǎy-jāng-'pyàw, jyèw 'méy-shywǎn-'shàng. ‖That speech lost him the election. tā yīn-wey nèy-tsž-yǎn-'jyǎng jyèw méy-shywǎn-'shàng.

To lose as battle casualties (*in dead and wounded*) 'swĕn-shř or 'shāng-wáng. ‖We lost 2,000 men in that battle. wǒm nèy-yí-jàng °'swĕn-shř-le lyang-chyān-rén. or °'shāng-wáng lyǎng-'chyān.

To lose (*by death; as a loved one*) is expressed by saying that the person lost died 'gwò-chywu-le etc. (*see* **DIE**). ‖He lost his wife five years ago. tā-'tày-tay wǔ-'nyán yǐ-chyán 'gwò-chywu-le.

To lose one's accent (*change from former*) bǎ ywán-'láy-de-'kěw-yīn °'chywù-shyang or °'gǎy or °'byàn; (*change to local*) bǎ 'kěw-yīn °'gǎy-gwò-lay or °'byàn-gwò-lay. ‖He lost his accent within six months. tā 'lyèw-ge-'ywè-li jyèw bǎ °'kěw-yīn chywán 'gǎy-gwò-lay-le. or °'kěw-yīn 'byàn-gwò-lay-le. or °ywán-'láy-de-kěw-yīn chywán 'chywù-dyàw-le.

To lose one's balance yí-'lyè-chye, méy-jàn-'wĕn, méy-tsǎy-'jù. ‖He lost his balance and fell. tā yí-'lyè-chye (or tā 'yí-bù méy-jàn-'wĕn, or tā 'yí-bù méy-tsǎy-'jù) jyèw 'shwǎy-le yì-'jyāw.

To lose control of is expressed indirectly, and in different ways when referring to different objects. ‖He almost lost control of the car. tā chà-'dyǎr méy-néng bǎ-chē 'jwàn-gwo-lay. ‖He lost control of the plane and crashed. tā 'méy-fár bǎ fēy-jī 'jèng-gwo-lay-le, jyèw dyē-dzày 'dì-shang-le. ‖The police lost control of the mob. nèy-yí-'dà-chywún-'rén jīng-'chá °'gwǎn-bu-'jù-le. or °'méy-fár 'gwǎn-le. ‖Don't lose control of yourself. byé 'hú-dū-lew. or byé 'mí-hwen-lew, or yàw dz-jǐ 'ná-dìng-le 'jú-yì. or yàw 'wĕn-jù-le 'shīn.

To lose one's credit shř 'shìn-yung. ‖If I don't pay them now I'll lose my credit. yàw-shr 'shyàn-dzày bù-bǎ-chyán 'hwán-gey tā-men, wǒ jyèw shř-le 'shìn-yung-le.

To lose face dyēw-'rén, dyēw-'lyǎn. ‖He lost face by admitting that. tā nèm yì chéng-'rèn, 'jēn dyēw-°'rén. or °'lyǎn.

To lose one's head (be seriously confused) hwāng or 'hwāng-jāng; (be temporarily mixed up) ywūn-'děwr; lose one's head over someone (emotionally) jyàw ... gěy nèng °'mí-hu-le or °'hú-du-le or °-de 'shén-hwén-dyān-'dǎw-le or °-de ywūn-'děwr-le. ‖Even during the worst of the battle he never lost his head. jyèw-shr 'jàn-shr dzwèy bú-'lì de-shf-hewr tā yě méy-°'hwāng. or °'hwāng-jāng. or °'ywūn-'děwr. ‖Don't lose your head. byé 'hwāng(-jāng). or byé ywūn-le-'děwr. or (Emotionally) byé nèng 'hú-du-le. or byé nèng 'mí-hu-le. ‖He lost his head over that woman. tā jyàw nèy-ge-'nywǔ-rén gěy nèng °'mí-hu-le. or °'hú-du-le. or °-de 'shén-hwén-dyān-'dǎw-de. or °-de ywūn-'děwr-le.

To lose one's hold shr̀-'shěw, 'shěw-li 'hwá, méy-ná-'jù, ná-bu-'jù. ‖He lost his hold and broke the bowl. tā yì shr̄-'shěw (or tā-'shěw-li yì 'hwá, or tā 'yí-shyà-dz méy-ná-'jù) jyèw bǎ-'wǎn (gěy) 'dǎ-le.

To lose hope or to lose heart hwēy-'shīn. ‖Don't lose hope. byé hwēy-'shīn.

To lose one's job is expressed as one's job is lost 'dyēw-le or 'dyàw-le or 'shyà-lay-le or 'méy-le. ‖He lost his job. tā-shèr °'dyēw-le. or °'dyàw-le. or °'shyà-lay-le. or °'méy-le.

To lose one's mind fēng. ‖She lost her mind after her husband died. tā-'jàng-fu sž-le yǐ-'hèw, tā 'fēng-le.

To lose oneself (intentionally). ‖He lost himself in the crowd. tā wàng rén-'dwēy-li yì 'dzwǎn (or 'dwǒ) jyèw bú-'jyàn-le.

To lose an opportunity bǎ 'jī-hwèy °'tswò-gwò-chywu or (by delay) °'dān-wu-gwò-chywu. ‖You've lost a good opportunity by delaying. nǐ yì 'dǎn-wu bǎ yí-ge-'tǐng-hǎw-de-'jī-hwèy (gěy) 'tswò-gwò-chywu-le. or nǐ 'yàw bú-kwày-'kwǎr-de-me bǎ ge-'tǐng-hǎw-de-'jī-hwèy °'tswò-gwò-chywu-le. or °'dān-wu-gwò-chywu-le.

To lose (one's) patience shēng-'chì, fā 'pí-chì, tswǎr, jà. ‖My teacher lost patience with me. wǒ-de-'shyān-sheng gēn-wǒ °'shēng-'chì-le. or °'fā 'pí-chì-le. or °'tswǎr-le. or °'jà-le.

To lose one's reputation 'míng-ywù 'sǎw-dì. ‖He lost his reputation. tā-'míng-ywù 'sǎw-dì.

To lose sight of is expressed in terms of watching or following and letting get away. ‖Don't lose sight of him. 'dīng-je tā-dyar (or 'chyáw-je tā-dyar, or 'kàn-je tā-dyar, or yì-'jŕ gēn-je tā), byé jyàw-ta °'pǎw-le. or °'dzěw-kāy. or °'lyēw-le.

To lose sleep (not be able to sleep) shwèy-bu-'jáw or (technical) shr̄-'myán; (not get enough sleep) shwèy-'jyàw °bú-'gèw or °tày 'shǎw. ‖I've been losing too much sleep lately. wǒ 'jìn-láy °'lǎw shwèy-bu-'jáw. or °'lǎw shr̄-'myán. or °'shwèy-'jyàw bú-'gèw. or °'shwèy-'jyàw tày 'shǎw.

To lose someone (when trying to catch or follow him) is expressed as not see him any more bú-'jyàn ...-le or as not see his shadow any more bú-jyàn ...-de-'yěngr-le, or by saying that the person disappeared bú-'jyàn-le; (when trying to get rid of him) bǎ ... °'shwǎy-kāy or °'dyēw-shya or °'jŕ-shr-kāy. ‖The police chased him all over until they got downtown and lost him in a crowd. 'jǐng-chá 'dàw-chùr ⁻'jwēy-ta, jwēy-dàw 'rè-nàw-dì-fang °'hǎw-shyē-rén yì 'jǐ jyèw bú-'jyàn tā(-de-'yěngr)-le. or °tā wàng rén-'dwēy-li yì 'dzwān (or 'dwǒ) jyèw bú-'jyàn-le. ‖Can't we lose him somehow? dzám 'nán-dàw-shwō jyèw 'méy-fár bǎ-ta °'shwǎy-kāy-ma? or °'dyēw-shya-ma? or °'jŕ-shr-kāy-ma?

To lose one's temper. (Be unable to forbear) rěn-bu-'jù; (get angry) jí or chì-'jí; (burn up) hwǒr; all of these are usually preceded by jēn. ‖Finally I lost my temper and beat him up. mwò-mwò-'lyǎwr wǒ 'jēn °hwǒr-le (or °rěn-bu-'jù-le, or °'jí-le, or °chì-'jí-le), jyèw bǎ-ta 'dzěw-le yí-'dwèn.

To lose the thread of an argument. ‖I lost the thread of his argument when you spoke to me. wǒ jèng tīng-je tā jyǎng tā-de-'lǐ-yéw, 'nǐ nèm yì shwō 'hwà gěy dǎ-'dwàn-le.

To lose time fèy 'gūng-fu, dān-wu 'gūng-fu. ‖I don't want to lose any more time here. wǒ bú-'ywàn-yì 'dzày dzày-jèr °fèy 'gūng-fu-le. or °'dān-wu 'gūng-fu-le.

To lose track of (a person) bù jŕ-daw ... dzày-'nǎr. ‖I've lost track of all my old friends. wǒ-de 'lǎw-péng-yew-men dzày-'nǎr wǒ 'dēw bù-jŕ-'dàw-le.

To lose one's way (or, to be lost) (dzěw-)'mí-le 'lùr, (dzěw-)'tswò 'lùr, bú-rèn-de 'lùr-le, dzěw 'mí-hu-le; lose one's way home bù-rèn-de 'jyā(-le) or 'jǎw-bu-jáw 'jyā(-le). ‖Don't lose your way home. hwéy-'jyā-de-shí-hewr byé dzěw-°'mí-le (or °'tswò) 'lùr. ‖The little boy lost his way home. shyǎw-'hár °bú-rèn-de 'jyā-le. or °'jǎw-bu-jáw 'jyā-le. or °'mí-le 'lù-le. or °dzěw 'mí-hu-le. or °bú-rèn-de 'lùr-le.

To lose weight 'shèw. ‖You've been losing weight, haven't you? nǐ jìn-láy 'shèw-le-ba?

Lost and found department 'shr̄-wù-bǎw-gwǎn-'chù, 'shr̄-wù-jāw-ling-'chù.

LOSS. *All of the expressions except a few noted are verbal; see under the appropriate paragraph of* LOSE.

(By losing an object). ‖I want to report the loss of some jewelry. wǒ yàw 'bàw 'dyēw-le dyǎr-'shěw-shr̄.

(In a game or race). ‖The team took all their losses lightly. dwèy-'ywán měy-tsž 'shū de-shf-hew dēw 'bù-dzěme 'dzày-hu.

(In gambling). ‖My losses amounted to five dollars. wǒ shū-le 'wǔ-kwày-chyán.

(By death). ‖The loss of his wife was a great blow to him. tā-tày-tay yì 'sž, tā shāng-'shīn-de 'lyǎw-bu-dé.

(By burglary or robbery) expressed with the verb shŕ. ‖We are not responsible for the loss of personal property. (As worded on a sign) yī-wù 'gè-dz lyéw-'shén, rú yěw yí 'shŕ, gày-bu-fù 'dzé.

(*By destruction*). 'swĕn-shŕ; *or expressed with the verb* shāng *or* hwĕy. ‖**The drought caused a great loss of crops.** tyān-'hàn °'swĕn-shŕ (*or* °'shāng-le, *or* °'hwĕy-le) bù-'shăw-de-'jwāng-jya.

(*In business*) 'péy-chyán *or* 'kwēy-kùng; *or expressed with the verb* péy. ‖**The company's books showed a loss over a period of several years.** gūng-'sž-de-'jàng-shang 'jì-je 'hăw-shyē-nyán-le lăw shŕ °'péy-chyán. *or* °'kwēy-kùng.

(*Of time*). ‖**There was no reason for the loss of time.** 'dān-wu-le nèm-shyē-'shŕ-hew 'méy 'lĭ-yéw. *or* °'méy 'dàw-lĭ. *or* 'hĕn kĕ-yĭ 'bú-bì (*or* 'yùng-bu-jáw, *or* 'fàn-bu-shàng) 'dān-wu nèm-shyē-'shŕ-hew.

To be at a loss to know. yì-'dyăr yĕ bù-jŕ-'dàw; **be at a loss to explain** (*or say, etc.*) yì-'dyăr yĕ bù-jŕ-'dàw, 'jyăn-jŕ 'shwō-bu-chū-láy, 'jyăn-jŕ shwō-bu-'shàng-láy. ‖**I'm at a loss to know what to do.** wŏ yì-'dyăr yĕ bù-jŕ-'dàw 'dzĕm-je 'hăw. ‖**I'm at a loss to explain his absence.** wŏ yì-'dyăr yĕ bù-jŕ-'dàw (*or* wŏ 'jyăn-jŕ 'shwō-bu-chū-lay, *or* wŏ 'jyăn-jŕ shwō-bu-'shàng-lay) wèy-'shéme tā méy-'láy.

LOT. A lot of *or* **lots of** (*many*) ūwo, shyē, dwō-'dwō-de. ‖**There are lots of ways to get into town.** jìn-'chéng °'dàwr (*or* 'lùr) kĕ 'dwō-le (chywù-le). *or* °'yĕw 'hăw-shyē-lù kĕ 'dzĕw-de. ‖**There are lots of ways to make her conscious of you.** yàw jyàw-ta 'shīn-lĭ 'yĕw nĭ-jèy-ge-'rén, 'făr kĕ 'dwō-le (chywù-le). ‖**There were a lot of people there.** nàr yĕw °'hĕn-dwō-rén. *or* °'hăw-shyē-rén. *or* °'bù-shăw-rén.

A lot of *or* **lots of** (*much*) *is expressed similarly; or before verbs as* **very** hĕn, tĭng, jēn, jìng, *etc.; or after verbs as* **terribly** 'lì-hay *or other appropriate words.* ‖**Put a lot of sugar in my coffee.** gĕy wŏ-de-jyā-'fēy-li °'dwō- (*or* °'dwō-'dwō-de-)gē-'táng. ‖**There was lots of fun at the dance last night.** dzwér 'wăn-shang tyàw-'wŭ 'tĭng (*or* 'hĕn, *or* jēn, *or* jēn-shr) °'yĕw 'yĭ-sz. *or* °'yĕw-chywùr. *or* °'hăw 'wár. ‖**The cats make an awful lot of noise at night.** 'māw dzày 'yè-li jìng 'jyàw-hwàn. *or* 'yè-li nàw 'māw °'chăw-de (*or* °'nàw-de) 'lì-hay. ‖**He caused me a lot of trouble.** tā 'jìng gĕy-wŏ ré-°'shèr. *or* °'hwò. *or* tā jyàw-wŏ 'hĕn fèy-'shèr láy-je.

A lot more, a lot . . . .-er (*with or without a noun following*) . . . -de 'dwō. ‖**She's a lot sicker than when I last saw her.** tā 'bìng-de bĭ wŏ 'shàng-tsž chyáw-jyàn tā 'jùng-de 'dwō-le. ‖**We'll need a lot more food.** dzám dĕy 'yàw-de 'chŕ-de-dūng-shi háy 'dwō-je-ne.

(*Plot of ground*) yí-kwày-'dì. ‖**He bought a lot near my house.** tā dzày wŏ-'fáng-dz-páng-'byār 'măy-le yí-kwày-'dì.

(*Group of people*) chywún, 'hwŏ-dz, bāng, shyē; *see* **GROUP.** ‖**They're a fine lot of soldiers.** nèy(-yì)-°'chywún- (*or* °'hwŏ-dz-, *or* °'bāng-, *or* °shyē-)bīng bú-'tswò.

(*Group or package of things*). (*Group of several*) chyĕr; (*division*) fèr; (*pile*) dzwēy; (*bundle*) kwĕr;

(*package*) bāwr. ‖**I'll send the books in three different lots.** wŏ bă-shū fēn 'sān-°'chyĕr (*or* °'fèr) sùng-hăw-le. ‖**The books were auctioned off by lots.** shū shŕ °'yì-'dzwēy-yì-dzwēy-de (*or* °'lwèn-'dzwēy, *or* °'yì-'kwĕr-yì-kwĕr-de, *or* °'lwèn-'kwĕr) pāy-'mày-de. ‖**The powder is sold in hundred-pound lots.** nèy-jŭng-'fĕn °'yì-'băy-bàng-yì-'bāwr-de 'mày. *or* °'shŕ chéng-'băwr yì-'băy-bàng-yì-'băy-bàng-de 'mày. *or* °'shŕ lwèn-'bāwr mà
y, 'méy-bāwr yì-'băy-bàng.

To draw lots (*if they are slips of paper*) chēw-'tyáwr *or* chēw-'chyăr; (*if they are rolled into balls*) jwā-'jyēwr; (*informal expressions*) jwā dà-'téw *or* pĭ-'lán *or* pyĕ-'lán. ‖**They drew lots to see who would go first.** tām °'jwā-'jyēwr (*or* 'chēw-'tyáwr, *or* °'chēw-'chyăr, *or* °'jwā dà-'téw, *or* °'pĭ-'lán, *or* °'pyĕ-'lán) kàn 'shwéy shyān 'chywù.

LOUD. (*In sound*) dà; *of speaking* 'dà-shēng; *of an explosion* 'hūng-de *or* 'pāng-de *or* 'gwāng-de. ‖**She has a loud, unpleasant voice.** tā-'săng-mér (*or, her speaking voice* tā-shwō-'hwà-de-'shēng-yīn, *or, her singing voice* tā-'chàng-de-'shēng-yīn) yèw 'dà yèw nán 'tīng. ‖**Please speak loud enough to be heard.** 'dà-dyăr-shēngr 'shwō, 'hăw 'ràng-rén 'tīng-jyàn. ‖**Louder, please!** 'shēng-yīn (dzày) 'dà-dyar. ‖**Don't talk so loud.** byé nèm 'dà-shēng shwō-'hwà. ‖**There was a loud report after the flash.** 'gwāng yì 'shăn 'gēn-je jyèw shŕ °'hūng-de- (*or* °'pāng-de-, *or* °'gwāng-de-) yì-'shēng.

(*Vigorous, as of criticism*) dà, tùng, 'lì-hay. ‖**There were loud criticisms in the press.** bàw-'jŕ-shang °'gūng-ji-de hĕn 'lì-hay. *or* °'pī-ping-de hĕn 'lì-hay. *or* °'dà 'mà. *or* °'tùng 'mà.

(*Flashy, of clothes*). (*Flowery*) 'hwā-hwā(r)-de, 'hwā; (*in poor taste*) bú-shyàng ge-'yàngr. ‖**His ties are always too loud.** tā-swŏ-yĕw-de-lĭng-'dày dēw tày 'hwā-le. *or* tā(-dày)-de-lĭng-'dày 'dēw (*or* 'lăw) (shŕ) nèm °'hwā-hwā-de. *or* °'hwā-hwār-de bú-shyàng ge-'yàngr.

Out loud 'dà-shēng; **not out loud** bú-'dà-shēng, yùng shyăw-'shyăwr-de-shēng-yīn, yùng dī-'dī-de-shēng-yīn. ‖**He said it out loud.** tā 'dà-shēng °'shwō-chu-lay-de. *or* °'rāng-rang-chū-lay-de. ‖**Don't talk out loud.** 'byé 'dà-shēng shwō-'hwà. *or* yùng, shyăw-'shyăwr-de-shēng-yīn shwō-'hwà. *or* yùng dī-'dī-de-'shēng-yīn shwō-'hwà.

LOVE. *Most of the cases in which* **love** *is used as a noun in English, as well as the verbal uses, are translated by verbal expressions; the verbs are* (*for love toward persons*) ày *or sometimes* 'shĭ-hwān; (*for love toward things or actions*) 'shĭ-hwān *or sometimes* ày; (*of elders toward children*) 'téng *or* ày; (*of children toward parents*) 'shyàw-shwèn *or* 'shyàw-jìng; (*of brothers, sisters, etc.*) dày (*or* gēn) . . .'găn-chíng 'hăw (*or similar words in place of* hăw); (*toward one's country*) ày; *see also* **LIKE;** *two nouns are also used in some* *cases: (love toward a person of the opposite sex)* 'rè-hu 'jyèr; *(strong liking or habit, of an action)* yĭn. ‖He loves her, but she doesn't like him at all. 'nan-de àv 'nywŭ-de, kĕ-shr 'nywŭ-de yì-'dyăr yĕ 'bù-shĭ-hwān nèy-gɛ-'nán-de. *or expressed as a proverb,* He's an itinerant barber with only one side hot. tā-nèy shr̀ 'tì-téw-'tyāw-dz 'yì-téwr-'rè. ‖I think John really loves her. wǒ shyǎng ywē-'hàn shr̀ 'jēn 'shĭ-hwān tā. ‖He has a deep love for his children. tā 'tĭng ày (*or* téng) tā-de-'háy-dz-men. ‖He has a deep love for his parents. tā 'tĭng °'shyàw-shwèn (*or* °'shyàw-jìng) 'fù-mŭ. ‖He has a real love for his brothers. tā dày (*or* gēn) 'dì-shyŭng-men 'gǎn-chíng tĭng 'jēn (*or* 'shēn). ‖He has a sincere love for his country. tā 'yì-shīn ày-'gwó. *or* tā hĕn ày-'gwó. ‖He made this trip because of his love for his brother. tā 'shŕ-dzày shr̀ 'yīn-wey gēn tā-'gē-ge 'gǎn-chíng tày 'hǎw-le, swǒ-yĭ tsáy 'dzěw jèm yí-'tàng. ‖I love to walk along the river in the morning. wǒ 'tĭng shĭ-hwān 'dzǎw-chen dzày hé-'byār 'lyēw-da-lyēw-da. ‖I love apples. wǒ 'shĭ-hwān chr̄ 'píng-gwǒ. ‖His love probably won't last. -tā-jèy-'rè-hu 'jyèr dà-gày 'cháng-bu-'lyăw. ‖He really loves to fish. tā 'jí shĭ-hwān dyàw-'ywú. *or* tā-dyàw-'ywú-de-'yīn dà-'jí-le.

To fall in love (with) 'ày-shang, *(Of one person, secretly)* 'shīn-li 'ày-shang; *(specifically of two people)* lyàn-'ày-chĭ-lay. ‖He fell in love with the captain's daughter. tā ('shīn-li) 'ày-shang chwán-'jăng-de-'nywŭ-ér-le. ‖They fell in love with each other. tām-lyǎ 'ày-shang-le. *or* tām lyàn-'ày-chĭ-lay-le. ‖They fell in love at first sight. *or* It was a case of love at first sight for them. tām yí jyàn-'myàn jyèw 'bĭ-tsž ày-shang-le.

(In greetings). ‖Give my love to all my old friends. chĭng tì-wǒ wèn 'swǒ-yěw-de-lǎw-'péng-yew 'hǎw. ər jyàn-le lǎw-'péng-yew-men děw tì-wǒ °'wèn-'hǎwr. *or* °'wèn-hew-wèn-hew. *or* gěy lǎw-'péng-yew-men děw shāw (*or* dày) ge-'hǎwr-chywu.

LOVELY. *(To see). (Beautiful)* mĕy; *(good-looking)* hǎw 'kàn; *(good, of a view)* hǎw. ‖There's a lovely view from the bridge. tsúng 'chyáw-ner 'kàn-gwo-chywu 'jĭng-jr̀ °'hǎw-jí-le. *or* °'mĕy-jí-le. *or* °hĕn 'hǎw. *or* °hĕn 'mĕy. ‖I've never seen such a lovely girl. wǒ 'tsúng-láy méy 'kàn-jyàn-gwo 'jèm °hǎw-'kàn- (*or* °'mĕy-) de-nywŭ-'háy-dz.

(To hear) hǎw 'tīng. ‖Isn't that a lovely song? 'nèy-ge-'gēr 'dwō hǎw 'tīng-nga?

LOW. *(Physically). (Especially of level)* dī; *(especially of vertical distance)* ǎy; *sometimes expressed as* not high *or* not tall bù-'gāw; *or as* short dwǎn *or* tswó; *or as* small shyǎw; *or as* down shyà; *or indirectly in other ways; (of the tide)* to be low twēy-'jìng, twēy-'wán, *or* làw-dàw dzwèy-'dī-de-dì-fang; *(of water level) is expressed as* shallow chyǎn; low land 'dī-dì;

low coast line hĕn-'dī-de-hǎy-àn-shyàn. ‖The ceiling is very low. fáng-'dǐng-dz hĕn 'dī. ‖The hill looks very low from here. tsúng-'jèr kàn nèy-'shān hǎw shyàng °'tǐng 'dī (*or* °'tǐng 'ǎy, *or* °'bù-'gāw, *or* °'bù-hĕn 'gāw) (shr̀-de). ‖She prefers low-heeled shoes. tā ày chwān 'hèw-gēr-'dī-de-shyé. ‖That plane is flying too low. nèy-ge-fēy-'jī fēy-de tày 'dī-le. ‖This bed is too low. 'chwáng tày °'ǎy. *or* °'dī. ‖This chair is too low. 'yǐ-dz tày °'ǎy. *or* °'tswó. *or* °'dī. ‖There is a low fence around the house. fáng-dz-jēw-wéy yěw yí-dàw-°'dwǎn- (*or* °'ǎy-, *or* °'shyǎw-)chyáng. ‖Have you a room on a lower floor? 'shyà-yì-tséng yěw fáng-jyān-ma? ‖Please give me a lower berth. gěy-wo yí-ge-'shyà-pù. ‖She has a very low forehead. tā-de-nǎw-'mén-dz hĕn °'dī. *or* (*narrow*) °'jǎy. ‖Hang the picture a little lower. 'hwàr dzày °gwà-de 'dī-dyar. *or* °gwà-de wàng-'shyà-dyar. *or* °wàng-'shyà gwà-dyar. ‖Low tide is at twelve today. jyēr 'jūng-wǔ shŕ-èr-'dyǎn 'cháw(-shwěy) °twèy-'jìng. *or* °twèy-'wár. *or* °làw-dàw dzwèy-'dī-de-dì-fang. ‖The river was so low during the drought that several rocks never seen before stuck out. nàw hàn-'dzāy de-shŕ-hew 'hé-shwěy 'chyǎn-de yěw jĭ-kwày-yĭ-'shyàng-kàn-bu-'jyàn-de-'shŕ-tew dēw 'lèw-chu-lay-le.

(Of rank, position, grade, etc.) dī. ‖He's of lower rank. 'tā-de-'gwān-jyē 'dī. ‖He was then in the lower grades. 'nèy-shŕ-hew tā dzày 'dī-bān-li.

(Of temperature) dī; *or expressed nontechnically in terms of being cold* lĕng. ‖The temperature is very low today. jyēr 'wēn-dù hĕn 'dī. *or* jyēr tĭng 'lĕng-de. ‖The temperature hit an all-time low. 'tyān-chì yí-'shyàng méy-dzème 'lĕng-gwo.

(In pitch). (Of specific notes) dī *or* 'dī-yīn; *of someone's voice)* dī *or* tsū. ‖Sing low. yùng 'dī-yīn 'chàng. ‖The opera singer has a very low voice. nèy-ge-'shì-dz-de-sǎng-'yīn hĕn °'dī. *or* °'tsū.

(In volume) 'shyǎw-shēng(r) *or* 'dī-shēng(r). ‖Sing low. 'shyǎw-shēngr 'chàng.

(Of marks) 'dī, 'hwày, 'bù-hǎw. ‖He got low marks. tā-dé-de-'fēr tĭng °'dī-de. *or* °'hwày. *or* °'bù-hǎw.

(Of prices) 'dī; *or expressed as* low-priced 'pyán-yi; be(come) low(er) làw. ‖Would you consider the price low enough? nǐ 'jywé-de jèy-ge-'jyàr gèw 'pyán-yi-de-lə-ma? ‖This car is in the lower-priced group. 'jèy-jǔng-chē shr̀ dzày °'pyán-yi-chē- (*or* °'jyà-chyán-'dī-de-)nèy-'lèy-li. ‖Prices will be lower again after the war. dǎ-'wán-le 'jàng °shéme jyèw děw 'pyán-yi-le. *or* °'jyà-chyán jyèw hwèy 'làw-de.

(Of supplies) is expressed as almost used up kwày yùng-'wán-le; *or as* not much 'méy-dwō-'shǎw-le *(etc.)*. ‖Our gas is getting low. dzám-de-chì-'yéw kwày yùng-'wán-le. ‖We're low on sugar. wǒm-de-'táng °'méy-dwō-'shǎw-le. *or* °'kwày yùng-'wán-le.

(Humble, of birth or background) dī *or* 'dī-jyàn-de; *(literary)* 'pín-hán. ‖He's not ashamed of his low birth.

tā-'chū shēn (or tā-'jyā-shr̀) hěn 'dī(-jyàn-de), 'kě-shr̀ tā bú-'dzày-hu. or tā 'bù-yǐ tā-°'chū-shēn (or °'jyā-shr̀) 'pín-hán wéy-'chř̌.

(Depressed) nán 'shèw, bù-gāw-'shìng, bú-'tùng-kwày. ‖I'm low today. or I feel very low today. wǒ 'jyēr-ge hěn °nán 'shèw. or °'bù-gāw-'shìng. or °bú-'tùng-kwày.

(Vulgar) tswēn or yě. ‖He has a low type of humor. tā-shwō-de-'shyàw-nwàr tǐng °'tswēn-de. or °'yě-de.

Low gear 'tēw-dàw-já. ‖Put the car in low to climb the hill. shàng-'shān-de-'shŕ-hew ,'ǹg 'tēw-dàw-já.

To have a low opinion of jywé-je . . . °bù-'hǎw, or (as to character) °tǐng 'shyà-jyàn, or (as to possibilities) °tǐng méy-'chū-shi-de, or (as to ability) °tǐng méy-'néng-gàn-de or °tǐng méy-'běn-shr-de; or (despise) chyáw-bu-'chǐ. ‖I have a low opinion of him. wǒ jywé-je tā °bù-'hǎw. or °tǐng 'shyà-jyàn. or °tǐng méy-'chū-shi-de. or °tǐng méy-'néng-gàn-de. or °tǐng méy-'běn-shr-de. ‖He has a low opinion of his staff. tā tǐng chyáw-bu-'chǐ tā-'shǔ-shyà-de-rén.

Low or low-down (mean; of an action) is expressed as cruel 'kè-bwo; or as not right méy-'dàw-lǐ or bù-jyǎng-'lǐ or bú-'dwèy; (of a person) 'shyàw-rén; (of a person or action) 'chǐ-yěw-tsž-'lǐ; (vulgar) chywē-'dé; play a low(-down) trick on someone is also expressed as chī-fu . . . chī-fu-de (or pyàn . . . pyàn-de) hěn °'lì-hay. or °'swēn. or °méy-'dàw-li. or °bú-'dwèy-de. ‖That was a low trick. 'nèy-'shěwr (or 'nèm yì-'shěwr) bàn-de 'tày °'kè-bwo-le. or °méy-'dàw-li-le. or °bù-jyǎng-'lǐ-le. or °bú-'dwèy-le. or °'shyàw-rén-le. or °'chǐ-yěw-tsž-'lǐ-le. ‖It was a low-down trick to kick him out at this stage of the game. dēw 'dzwò-dàw 'jèy-ge-'dì-bù-le, háy bǎ rén-jyā kěy-dzěw-le, 'wèy-myǎn tày °'kè-bwo-le. or °etc. ‖He played a low trick on her. tā 'chī-fu tā chī-fu-de (or tā pyàn-tā pyàn-de) hěn °'lì-hay. or °'swēn. or °méy-'dàw-li. or °bú-'dwèy-de.

Low-down (mean; of a person). ‖He's a low-down skunk. tā 'bú-shr 'dūng-shi. or tā 'shéme-'dūng-shi. or tā shr̀ ge-'hwèn-jàng wáng-bā-'dàn.

The low-down. ‖Give me the low-down. gěy-wǒ 'jyǎng-yi-jyǎng. or 'gàw-su wǒ 'tīng-ting.

LOWER. To lower (physically) is usually expressed by bǎ . . . followed by a combination of an action verb with shyà-lay or shyà-chywu; some of the verbs so used are fall or drop làw, pull lā or chě, put fàng or gē; to lower by ropes 'shì; to lower the head bǎ-tēw 'dī-shya-chywu; with lowered head 'dī-je tēw or 'chwéy-je tēw or 'dā-la-je tēw. ‖Please lower the window. láw-'jyà bǎ 'chwāng-hu °'làw- (or °'lā-, or °'fàng-)shya \dyǎr-lay. ‖Lower the flag at sunset. r̀ 'lè de-shŕ-hew °shyà-'chí. or °bǎ chí-dz 'lā-shyà-lay. or °bǎ chí-dz 'chě-shyà-lay. ‖The crew slowly lowered the body into the sea. 'shwěy-shěw bǎ 'shř̌-shew màn-'már-de 'shì-dàw- 'hǎy-lǐ-chywu-le. ‖He lowered his head and didn't say a thing. tā bǎ-tēw 'dī-shya-chywu, 'yì-shēngr bù-°'shyǎng. or °'yán-ywu. ‖He remained

seated with his head lowered. tā yì-'jŕ dzwò-nàr, °'dī-je téw. or °'chwéy-je téw. or °'dā-la-je téw.

To lower the voice (in speaking) 'dī-dyǎr- (or 'shyǎw-dyǎr-)'shēngr shwō-'hwà. ‖Can't you lower your voice? nǐ 'dī-dyǎr- (or nǐ 'shyǎw-dyǎr-)'shēngr shwō-'hwà 'shíng-ma?

(As opposed to upper) shyà. Lower berth 'shyà-pù.

LUCK. (LUCKY). 'ywùn-chi; (in gambling) 'shěw-chì; (continuing) 'fú-chi. Be in luck, have good luck, or be lucky (at a particular time) dzěw-'ywùn, dzěw hǎw-'ywùn; (always) (shr̀) yěw-'fú-de-rén, 'fú-chi dà, 'fú-chi 'hǎw; (in gambling) shěw-'chì (hěn) hǎw; be out of luck, not have good luck, or be unlucky bù-dzěw-'ywùn, dǎw-'méy; a sign or omen of good luck 'jí-jàw (r). ‖He said his failure was entirely due to bad luck. tā shwō tā ′méy-nèng-'hǎw wán-chywán shr̀ yīn-wey 'ywùn-chi bù-'hǎw. ‖I can't help it if you couldn't go; that's your hard luck. 'nǐ nèy-shŕ-hew bù-néng 'chywù, wǒ yěw shéme-'fár-ne? nèy shr̀ nǐ-'ywùn-chi bù-'hǎw. ‖My luck won't last. 'ywùn-chi 'dēw shr̀ yí-'jèr. or wǒ yě 'jyèw-shr jèy-yì-'shŕ°-de-'ywùn-chi hǎw. or °dzěw-'ywùn. or (In gambling) °-de-'shěw-chì 'hǎw. ‖I was lucky last night; I won twenty dollars. dzwér 'wǎn-shang wǒ-'shěw-chì hěn 'hǎw, yíng-le 'èr-shr-'kwày. ‖You're in luck. (Right now) nǐ-'ywùn-chi 'hǎw. or nǐ jēn dzěw-'ywùn. or (Always) nǐ shr̀ yěw-'fú-de-rén. or nǐ-'fú-chi °'dà. or °'hǎw. ‖I'm out of luck to-day. wǒ 'jyēr °dǎw-'méy. or °bù-dzěw-'ywùn. or °'ywùn-chi bù-'hǎw. or °'ywùn-chi bù-'jyā. ‖That's supposed to be lucky. (To do something) 'nèm-je hwèy dzěw-hǎw-'ywùn-de. or (A sign of good luck) nèy shr̀ 'jí-jàwr. ‖Why, you lucky dog! nǐ jēn dzěw-'ywùn.

Just luck (good or bad) jèng 'chyǎw; (good only) jèng 'hǎw. ‖It was just luck that he happened along at that moment. jèng 'chyǎw (or jèng 'hǎw) dzày 'nèy-shŕ-hew 'tā dàw-nàr-le.

Not just luck 'bìng-fēy 'ěw-rán. ‖This victory is not just a matter of luck. jèy-tsž °dǎ- (or °jàn-)'shèng-le 'bìng-fēy 'ěw-rán.

‖Good luck! 'jū-shr̀ rú-'yì! or fā-'tsáy, fā-'tsáy! or shēng-·gwān fā-'tsáy!

LUMBER. 'mù-tew-bǎr, 'mù-tew-'bǎn-dz, mù-'bǎn-dz, 'mù-lyàw. ‖Where can I buy lumber and nails? wǒ dzày-'nǎr néng mǎy dyǎr-'mù-tew-bǎr gēn 'dīng-dz? ‖We need lumber to build a garage. wǒm gày chē-'fáng děy yàw °'mù(-tew)-'bǎn-dz. or °'mù-lyàw. ‖He's in the lumber business. tā dzwò 'mù-lyàw-'shēng-yì.

(To cut trees) tsǎy-'mù, fá-'mù, nùng 'mù-tew, kǎn-'shù. ‖This company does its lumbering up the river. jèy-ge-gūng-'sž dzày hé-'shàng-yéw tsǎy-'mù.

(To shamble) 'yí-bù-yí-bù-de °'jwǎy. or °'nyěw. ‖The elephant lumbered along. Jà-'shyàng 'yí-bù-yí-bù-de °'jwǎy. or °'nyěw.

LUNCH. (*Noon meal*) 'wŭ-fàn, 'jūng-fàn, 'shăng-wŭ-fàn, wŭ-'tsān. Have lunch *or* to lunch *is expressed as* eat lunch chr̄ *plus one of the above, or more commonly simply as* eat chr̄-'fàn. ‖It's almost time for lunch. kwày dàw chr̄-'wŭ-fàn-de-shŕ-hew-le. ‖What do you want for lunch? nǐ 'shăng-wŭ-fàn shyăng chr̄-'shéme? ‖Will you lunch with me? nǐ 'néng gēn-wŏ yí-'kwàr chr̄ 'wŭ-fàn-ma? *or* 'jūng-wŭ dzám yí-'kwàr chr̄-'fàn hăw-ma?

(*Snack*) *is expressed as* to eat a little bit chr̄ dyăr-'shéme *or* chr̄ dyăr-'fàn *etc.* ‖How about a little lunch before going to bed? 'chr̄ dyăr-shéme dzày 'shwèy-ba.

LUNG. fèy. ‖I'll have to see a doctor about my lungs. wŏ dĕy 'jyàn yí-ge-'dày-fu 'yàn-yan wŏ-de-'fèy. ‖When I breathe deeply, my lungs hurt. wŏ shŕ-'jìn-chwăn-'chì-de-shŕ-hew 'fèy jyèw 'téng.

M

MACHINE. 'jī-chi. ‖She uses a machine in washing and ironing. tā yùng 'jī-chi 'shǐ-yī 'tàng-yī. ‖Will the machine work? 'jī-chi néng 'yùng-ma? ‖It's an electric machine. shŕ yùng-'dyàn-de-'jī-chi. ‖That machine is operated by hand. 'nèy-shr yùng-'shĕw-dùng-de-'jī-chi.

(*Political*) 'dzŭ-jr̄. ‖The machine is backing him in the election. jèy-ge-'dzŭ-jr̄ 'bāng-ta jìng-'shywăn. ‖He's the machine candidate. tā-shr jèy-ge-'dzŭ-jr̄-de-'hèw-shywăn-rén.

MAD. (*Angry*) shēng-'chì, năw, fā 'pí-chi; (*crazy, rabid*) fēng, fā-'kwáng; (*foolish*) shă. ‖That's no reason to get mad. byé wèy 'nèy-ge shēng-'chì. *or* byé wèy 'nèy-ge 'năw-le. *or* 'yùng-bu-jáw wèy 'nèy-ge fā 'pí-chi-ya. ‖He must be mad to take such a chance. tā 'jè-yàng màw-'shyăn, jēn-shr 'fēng-le. ‖Watch out for the mad dog. 'shyăw-shīn fēng-'gĕw. ‖That was a mad thing to do. 'nà-yàng 'gàn jēn 'shă.

Be mad at *someone* gēn . . . 'năw, năw . . . . ‖He's been mad at me for a long time. tā °gēn-wo 'năw-le (*or* °'năw-wo yĕw) 'hăw-shyē-shŕ-hew-le.

Be mad about *someone* 'mí-shàng. ‖She was mad about him from the very first. tā tsúng yí jyàn-'myàn jyèw 'mí-shang ta-le.

Like mad shyàng 'fēng-le shŕ-de. ‖He drove like mad. tā kāy-'chē shyàng 'fēng-le shŕ-de.

MAGAZINE. dzá-'jr̄; (*illustrated news magazine*) hwà-'bàw. ‖Where can I buy a magazine? shéme-'dì-fang kĕ-yi măy dzá-'jr̄? ‖That magazine comes out on Thursdays. nèy-ge-hwà-'bàw lĭ-bày-'sż chū-'băn.

(*For munitions*) dàn-yàw-'shr̀; (*of rifle*) dàn-'shyá.

MAID. (*Servant*) nywù-'yùng-rén; (*if married*) lăw-'mā-dz. ‖Where can I hire a maid? shéme-'dì-fang kĕ-yi 'gù yí-ge-nywù-'yùng-rén?

Old maid lăw-'chŭ-nywŭ. ‖Two old maids live there. lyăng-ge-lăw-'chŭ-nywŭ jù-dzay nàr.

MAIL. (*Materials transmitted*) shìn; (*postal system*) yéw-'jèng, yéw(-jèng)-'jywú, *sometimes* yéw-. ‖Did I get any mail this morning? jīn-tyan-'shàng-wŭ wŏ yĕw-'shìn méy-yew? ‖Mail delivery here is twice a day. jèr 'mĕy-tyān sùng 'lyăng-hwéy-'shìn. ‖The

mails were held up by the storm. tyān-chi bù-'hăw, 'shìn wù-le 'dyăn-le. ‖The mail truck is late. yéw-jèng-'chē láy 'wăn-le. ‖Will this catch the last mail? jèy-ge néng 'găn-shang dzwèy-'hèw-yì-bān-'shìn-ma? ‖He promised to send the check by mail. tā 'dá-ying tsúng yéw-'jywú bă 'jr̄-pyàw 'jì-lay.

To mail jì. ‖Where can I mail this? shéme-'dì-fang kĕ-yi 'jì jèy-ge-dūng-shi?

MAIN. (*Most important*) dzwèy-'yàw-jĭn-de; (*biggest or most prominent*) dzwèy-'dà-de, *sometimes* dà, jŭ-'yàw-de. ‖What's his main reason for wanting to leave? tā yàw 'lí-kay jèr dzwèy-'yàw-jĭn-dé-'ywán-yín shr̀ shéme? ‖Where is the main street? 'dà-jyē dzày-'năr? ‖The main line runs through Sian. jŭ-'yàw-de-'lù-shyàn shr̀ tsúng shī-'ān dzĕw.

(*Conduit*) 'gwăn-dz, dzŭng-'gwăn-dz. ‖The water main has burst. dż-láy-shwĕy-dzŭng-'gwăn-dz 'hwày-le. ‖The gas mains end at the city line. 'méy-chì-'gwăn-dz tūng-daw 'chéng(-shr̀-de)-'byàr-shang.

In the main dà-'jr̀. ‖I agree with him in the main. wŏ 'dà-jr̀ hé-ta túng-'yì.

MAINTAIN. băw-'chŕ, wéy-'chŕ. ‖You'll need more coal to maintain that degree of heat. nǐ yàw băw-'chŕ 'nà-yàng-de-wēn-'dù dĕy 'dwō yùng yì-dyăr-'méy. ‖Those countries have maintained peace for twenty years. nèy-shyē-gwó-'jyā 'wéy-chŕ-le 'èr-shr-lay-nyán-de-hé-'píng.

Maintain *a reputation* 'băw-hù. ‖He's always careful to maintain his good name. tā 'lăw-shr hĕn-'shyăw-shīn-de 'băw-hù tā-de-'míng-ywù.

Maintain a family yăng-'jyā. ‖He needs more money to maintain his family. tā yàw yăng-'jyā háy dĕy 'dwō-dyăr-chyán.

(*To assert*) găn shwō, 'jyān-chŕ. ‖I maintain that I'm not at fault. wŏ 'găn shwō wŏ méy-'tswò. ‖How can you still maintain that? nǐ 'dzĕme háy yàw 'jyān-chŕ 'nèy-ge?

MAKE (MADE). (*To build, create*) dzwò, dă, dzàw; *often a more specific word, thus* to make a hole *is expressed as* to drill a hole dzwăn 'kū-lung *or* chwān-'dùng. ‖He made a bookcase for his room. tā dzwò-le yí-ge-shū-'jyà-dz hăw 'băy-dzày tā-'wū-li. ‖Make a hole in this. dzày-'jèr chwān yí-ge-'dùng. or dzày 'jèy-ge-shang 'dzwǎn yí-ge-'kū-lung.

(*Add up to*) yěw, shř. ‖Twenty dollars per week makes about eighty dollars per month. 'èr-shŕ-kwày-chyán yí-ge-lǐ-'bày °jyèw yěw 'bā-shr-dwō-kwày-chyán yí-ge-'ywè. or °yí-ge-'ywè jyèw-shr 'bā-shr dwō-kwày. ‖That makes the tenth truckload today. 'jīn-tyan 'jèy-shr dì-'shŕ-chē-le.

(*Attain a speed*) dzěw. ‖That car can make eighty miles an hour. 'nèy-lyàng-chē 'yì-dyǎn-jūng néng dzěw 'bā-shr-lǐ.

(*Be, function as*) shř, dāng, dzwò. ‖He makes a good carpenter. tā shř ge-'hǎw-'mù-jyang. ‖He'd make a good carpenter. tā yàw-shr dāng 'mù-jyang yí-'dìng hěn 'hǎw.

(*Succeed in something, the something not always specified*) *expressed with* néng *followed by a specific verb, or by that verb in the potential form of a resultative compound.* ‖Do you think a table this wide can make the doorway? nǐ shyǎng 'jème-kwān-de-'jwō-dz °néng 'táy-gwò 'mén chywù-ma? or °nèy-ge-'mén gwò-de-'chywù-ma?

(*Render someone successful*). ‖The writer was made by his first book. *is expressed as* This writer with his first book immediately became famous. jèy-ge-'dzwò-jyā dì-'yī-běn-shū jyèw chéng-le 'míng-le.

(*Choose someone to perform a function*) jywǔ (or twěy or shywǎn) ... dāng (or dzwò).... ‖They made that man chairman. tām 'jywǔ-ta dzwò jǔ-'shí.

(*Estimate that a thing is such-and-such*) shyǎng, 'gū-me-je. ‖I make the height of the hill five hundred feet. 'wǒ °shyǎng (or °gū-me-je) jèy-ge-'shān yěw 'wǔ-bǎy-chř 'gāw. ‖I make it (the time) eight o'clock. wǒ °shyǎng (or °gū-me-je) shyàn-dzày °shř (or °yěw) 'bā-dyǎn-jūng-le.

(*Cause one thing to be another, or to be a certain way*). ‖Hard work made him a success. *is expressed as* He became successful through hard work. tā-shř kǔ-'gàn °'gàn-chu-lay-de. or °chéng-'gūng-de. ‖He's making a success of his business. *is expressed as* His business he's carrying on very well. tā-de-'mǎy-may dzwò-de hěn 'hǎw. ‖He made himself sick by drinking too much. tā 'jyěw-hē-de tày 'dwō, 'dž-jǐ nèng-'bìng-le. ‖What made you sick? *is expressed as* How did you get sick? nǐ 'dzěme hwèy bìng-le?

Make *something big* (*or good or red, etc.*) nùng *or* nèng *followed by the proper adjective; if a specific action is involved, the verb for that action replaces* nùng *or* nèng. ‖Make the background blue. bǎ-'dyèr °nùng-'lán-le. or °tú-'lán-le.

Make *someone do something* jyàw. ‖Don't make me do that. byé 'jyàw-wo dzwò 'nèy-ge.

Make *a destination* dàw. ‖The train will make New York within two hours. jèy-tàng-'chē 'lyǎng-dyǎn yàw 'dàw nyēw-'ywē. ‖We can make our destination by evening. wǒm jyēr-'wǎn-shang °néng 'dàw. or °'dàw-de-lyǎw.

Make a fire shēng-'hwǒ, bǎ-'hwǒ dyǎn-'jáw-le. ‖Can you make a fire in this wind? nǐ néng dzày jèy-ge-'fēng-lǐ-tew shēng-'hwǒ-ma?

Make both ends meet 'chū-rù-shyāng-'dǐ or chū-rù-shyāng-'fú. ‖It's hard to make both ends meet. 'chū-rù-shyāng-'dǐ shř hěn bù-'rǔng-yi. ‖We can't make both ends meet. rù-bù-fú-'chū.

Make one's living méw-'shēng; make one's living on ... jř-je ... °wéy-'shēng. or °chř. ‖How does he make his living? tā 'dzěme-yàng méw-'shēng? or tā 'jř-je shéme wéy-'shēng-a?

Make a mistake nùng-'tswò-le, nèng-'tswò-le, chū-'tswòr, dzwò-'tswò-le, dzwò tswò-'shř. ‖Someone made a mistake. yí-dìng shr yěw-'rén nùng-'tswò-le. ‖He hardly ever makes a mistake. tā 'chà-bu-dwō 'tsúng-lay °'bú-dzwò tswò-'shř. or °yě 'méy-chū-gwo 'tswòr.

Make money jwàn-'chyán, jèng-'chyán, ná-'chyán, shēw-'rù chyán, nùng-'chyán, nèng-'chyán. ‖How much do you make a week? nǐ yí-ge-lǐ-'bày °jwàn (or °jèng etc.) 'dwō-shaw-chyán?

Make peace jyǎng-'hé. ‖Are they willing to make peace? tām 'ywàn-yi jyǎng-'hé-ma?

Make a point shwō-'chīng-chu. ‖Has he made his point? tā shwō-'chīng-chu-le-ma?

Make a reputation yěw-'míng-le, chū-'míng. ‖He made his reputation early in life. tā dzày nyán-'chīng de-shŕ-hew jyèw °yěw-'míng-le. or °chū-'míng-le.

Make a score dé (or nùng or nèng) 'fēn-shù. ‖Who made the highest score? 'shéy-dé-de-'fēn-shù dzwèy 'dwō?

Make sense yěw 'dàw-lǐ. ‖Does this make sense? 'jèy-ge 'yěw-méy-yew 'dàw-li?

Make time shěng 'shŕ-hewr, 'kwày-dyǎr. ‖We can make (better) time if we take the dirt road. wǒm yàw-shr dzěw 'nèy-tyáw-'tǔ-lù, jyèw °shěng dyǎr-'shŕ-hewr. or °néng 'kwày-dyǎr.

Make a train (or bus, etc.) gǎn-'chē. ‖Do you think we'll make the train? nǐ 'shyǎng wǒm néng 'gǎn-de-shàng hwǒ-'chē-ma?

Make believe (that) (jyǎ) 'jwāng. ‖She's only making believe she doesn't know. tā jyǎ 'jwāng tā bù-jř-'dàw. or tā 'jwāng bù-jř-'dàw.

Make for *a place, expressed with a verb such as* run pǎw, *often with an adverb such as* quickly 'gǎn-jǐn *or* kwày. ‖Let's make for that tall tree. dzám 'pǎw-dàw nèy-kē-'dà-'shù-nèr-ba. ‖The boys made for home at dinnertime. 'háy-dz-men chř-'fàn-de-shŕ-hew 'gǎn-jǐn wàng 'jyā-li 'pǎw.

Make for (*contribute to the possibility of*). ‖Her company made for a pleasant afternoon. *is expressed as* That afternoon as soon as she came it rendered things very interesting. nèy-ge-'shyà-wǔ tā yì 'láy 'nùng-de tǐng yěw 'yì-sz.

Make off with chāw-'dzěw-le, tēw-'dzěw-le. ‖Don't make off with my book. byé bǎ wǒ-de-'shū chāw-'dzěw-le. ‖They've made off with our books. tām bǎ wǒm-de-'shū tēw-'dzěw-le.

Make out *a report* dzwò. ‖It's time to make out our annual report. wǒm dzwò nyán-'bàw de-shŕ-hew̆ 'dàw-le.

Make out *a check or bill* kāy. ‖Have you made the check out yet? jř-'pyàw yǐ-jing kāy-'hǎw-le-ma? ‖Please make out our bill. chǐng-ni bǎ wǒ-men-de-jàng-'dār 'kāy-chu-lay.

Make out *a form* tyán. ‖Come back when you've made out this form. bǎ jèy-ge-'byǎw tyán-'hǎw-le dzày 'hwéy-lay.

Make out (*manage despite possible difficulties*) 'bàn-de-lyǎw, 'bàn-de-chū-láy. ‖Don't worry; I'll make out. byé 'jāw-jí; wǒ 'bàn-de-lyǎw.

Make *something* **out** (*understand when listening*) tīng-'dǔng; (*understand when looking*) kàn-'dǔng; (*general*) dǔng, 'míng-bay. ‖Can you make out what he means? nǐ 'dǔng tā-de-'yì-sz-ma? *or* nǐ 'néng-bu-néng ʿtīng-'dǔng (*or* ʿkàn-'dǔng) nà-shř shéme-'yì-sz? ‖He couldn't make out the sign. tā kàn-bu-'dǔng nèy-ge-'páy-dz.

Make out with (*manage with*). ‖How did you make out with ʿhim? *or* ʿher? *or* ʿthe problem? *etc.*, *is expressed as* What was the result? 'jyē-gwǒ dzěme-'yàng? ‖We'll have to make out with what we've got. *is expressed as* All we can do is do the best we can. wǒm jř 'hǎw jìn wǒ-men-de-'lì-lyang 'dzwò-shya-chywu.

Make it out that shyǎng-'fár shwō. ‖They tried to make it out that we were to blame. tām shyǎng-'fár shwō shř 'wǒ-men bú-'dwèy.

Make *clothing* **over** 'gǎy. ‖She's having her old coat made over. tā bǎ tā-de-'jyèw-dà-'yī ná-chywu 'gǎy-chywù-le.

Make room for ràng-chu (*or* téng-chu) . . .-de-'dì-fangr-láy. ‖Can you make room for one more? nǐ néng 'dzày ʿràng-chu (*or* ʿténg-chu) 'yí-ge-rén-de-'dì-fangr-lay-ma?

Make up (*after a quarrel*) hǎw-le, nèng-'hǎw-le, nùng-'hǎw-le. ‖Do you know whether they've made up yet? nǐ 'jř-dàw tām yǐ-jing (nèng- *or* nùng-) 'hǎw-le méy-yew?

Make up (*use cosmetics*) 'dǎ-ban, dá-ban. ‖She takes a lot of time to make up. tā yùng 'hǎw-shyē-ʿshŕ-hewr láy 'dǎ-ban.

Make up, make good, *a deficit or share* 'tsèw-shàng, 'bǔ-shàng; fù *or* gěy. ‖Collect all you can, and he'll make up the rest. nǐ-men 'jìn-lyàng-de shēw-'chyán-ba, bú-'gèw-de 'tā láy ʿ'tsèw-shang. *or* ʿ'bǔ-shang. ‖I want to make good my share of the bill. nèy-ge-'chyán 'wǒ gěy wǒ-'dž-jǐ-de-nèy-'fèr-bə

Make up (*invent*) *is expressed as* **prepare** 'ywù-bèy *or* 'jwèn-bèy, **make** dzwò, **write** shyě, *etc.* ‖Did he make up the speech himself? tā-de-yǎn-'shwō shř tā-'dž-jǐ-ʿ'ywù-bèy-de-ma? *or* ʿ'jwěn-bèy-de-ma? *or* ʿ'dzwò-de-ma?

Make up (*falsify*) shyā-'byān. ‖Is it true, or did he make that story up? shř 'jēn-de-ma, 'háy-shr tā shyā-'byān-de?

Make up (*arrange print, etc.*) byān-'hǎw-le. ‖The newspaper's already made up. 'bàw yǐ-jing byān-'hǎw-le.

Make up (*prepare*) 'ywù-běy-'hǎw-le. ‖We make up the payroll on the fifteenth of the month. wǒm dzày shŕ-'wǔ-hàw bǎ 'shīn-shwéy dēw ywù-bey-'hǎw-le.

Make up one's mind 'dǎ-dìng jú-'yì, jywé-'dìng. ‖My mind is made up. wǒ yǐ-jing ʿ'dǎ-dìng 'jú-yì-le. *or* ʿ'jywé-ʿ'dìng-le.

Make up for péy; (*of time*) 'bǔ-shang. ‖He's willing to make up for his mistake. tā 'ywàn-yi péy-'tswèr.

(*Brand*) 'páy-dz. ‖He has a car of an old make. tā yěw yí-lyàng-'lǎw-páy-dz-de-chì-'chē.

MAN. (*Human being*) rén; (*adult, not specifying sex*) 'dà-rén; (*male, not specifying age*) 'nán-rén; (*male*) nán-. ‖Men have used that road for hundreds of years. 'nèy-tyáw-'lù 'rén yǐ-jing 'dzěw-le 'jǐ-bǎy-'nyán-le. ‖I need a man to mow the lawn. wǒ yàw 'jǎw yí-ge-rén· gěy-wo twēy-'tsǎw. ‖Is that man this boy's father? nèy-ge-'rén shř jèy-ge-'háy-dz-de-'fù-chin-ma? ‖There are two men and three boys in the party. 'nèy-chywún-rén-li yěw 'lyǎng-ge-'nán-rén, 'sān-ge-nán-'háy-dz. ‖Where's the men's room? nán-tsè-'swǒ dzày-'nǎr? ‖They've asked for a man cook. tām yàw 'gù yí-ge-'nán-chú-dz.

Not a man shwéy ʿyě (*or* ʿdēw) bū-. ‖Not a man believed his story. 'shwéy yě bù-'shyāng-shìn tā-de-'hwà.

(*Manly person*). hǎw-'hàn. ‖He spoke like a man. tā-de-'kěw-chì jēn shyàng ge-hǎw-'hàn. ‖What a man he was! tā 'jēn-shr ge-hǎw-'hàn!

To a man 'chywán-tǐ-yì-'chí. ‖The committee voted for the bill to a man. jèy-ge-'àn-dz shř 'wěy-ywán-'hwèy 'chywán-tǐ-yì-'chí 'tūng-gwò-de.

Man and wife fū-'fù. ‖Are they man and wife? tām-shř fū-'fù-ma?

Man to man píng-'lyáng-shīn. ‖We'll have to have a man-to-man talk about this. dzám-'lyǎ píng-'lyáng-shīn bǎ jèy-jyàn-'shř láy 'tán-tán.

To man a gun. (*Be in charge of it*) gwǎn fàng-'pàw; (*go to operate it*) chywù fàng-'pàw. ‖Man the guns! 'ywù-bèy fàng-'pàw!

To man a boat (*work on it*) dzày 'chwán-shang dzwò-'gūng. ‖Man the lifeboats! shàng jyèw-shēn-'chwán!

MANAGE. (*Succeed in doing something, handle successfully*) *is expressed by a verb meaning* **to do** (*see* **DO**), *or by verbs with more specific meanings appropriate to the circumstances, as* (*of a car*) **to drive** kāy, (*of packages, etc.*) **to carry** ná (*etc., see* **CARRY**), (*of persons*) **to keep under control** 'dwèy-fù; *the common combination* **can manage** *is expressed by resultative compounds made up of such verbs with* -de-'lyǎw *or by the verb* **can do** 'shíng; *in the meaning* **be able to get along,** **can manage** *is expressed as* **have a way of doing**

yěw 'bàn-fa. ‖Can you manage the horse by yourself? nǐ-'dž-jǐ chǐ-'mǎ °bàn-de-'lyǎw-ma? or °nèng-de-'lyǎw-ma? ‖Can you manage those packages by yourself? 'nèy-shyē-bāw-de-'dūng-shi nǐ 'ná-de-lyǎw-ma? ‖How did you manage to get these tickets? jèy-shyē-'pyàw nǐ yùng 'shéme-fá-dz nùng-láy-de? ‖I managed to see him twice last week. wǒ 'bàn-dàw-le shàng-lǐ-bày jyàn-ta 'lyǎng-hwèy. ‖They say he is difficult, but I think I can manage him. dà-jyā 'dēw shwō tā nán 'dwèy-fù, 'wǒ kě yěw 'fá-dz 'dwèy-fù tā. ‖Oh, I'll manage. ē, wǒ 'dzǔng yěw 'bàn-fa. ‖I can manage, thanks. wǒ yěw 'bàn-fa, 'shīn-lǐng yèw shř-le.

(Control, have charge of) gwǎn, 'gwǎn-lǐ; (especially of a store, shop, or business; also means manager) 'jīng-lǐ. ‖Who manages this place? jèy-ge-dì-fang gwēy-'shéy gwǎn? ‖This place is well managed. jèy-ge-dì-fang °'gwǎn-de (or °'gwǎn-lǐ-de, or °'jīng-lǐ-de) hěn 'hǎw.

MANAGER. gwǎn-'shř-de, 'jīng-lǐ. ‖Who's the manager here? gwǎn-'shř-de shř-'shéy? ‖I want to see the manager. wǒ yàw 'jyàn yi-jyàn 'jīng-lǐ.

Be a good manager (in the home) hwèy gwǎn-'jyā. ‖He doesn't make much money, but his wife is a good manager. tā-jwàn-de-'chyán bù-'dwō, dàn-shr tā-de-'tày-tay hwèy gwǎn-'jyā.

MANNER. (Way) yàng-dz. ‖He seems to be doing his work in an efficient manner. tā bàn-'shř hǎw shyàng hěn-'néng-gàn-de-yàng-dz. ‖He answered in a sharp manner. tā-de-'hwéy-dā hǎw 'shyàng hěn-'lì-hày-de-yàng-dz.

Manners (politeness of behavior) lǐ-'màw; (customs) lǐ-'jyé. ‖We must be careful of our manners when we go there. wǒm dàw-'nàr chywù děy jù-'yì yì-dyǎr lǐ-màw. ‖The manners in this country are different from ours. 'jèy-ge-dì-fang-de-lǐ-'jyé gēn 'wǒm-nàr-de bù-yí-'yàng.

In a manner of speaking kě-yǐ shwō. ‖In a manner of speaking she's a nurse, though she never got her certificate. tā 'kě-yǐ shwō shř ge-'kān-hu, 'swéy-rán tā méy-bì-'yè.

MANUFACTURE. dzwò, dzàw, jř-'dzàw. ‖What do you manufacture here? nǐm-'jèr jř-'dzàw shéme? ‖How long does it take to manufacture this? 'jèy-ge-dūng-shi yàw 'dwō-shaw-shř-hewr dzwò-'dé-le? ‖He's developed a new method of manufacture. tā 'fā-míng-le yí-ge-'shīn-de-jř-dzàw-'fǎ.

(Production) chǎn. ‖We're increasing the rate of manufacture here. wǒm 'jèng dzày dzēng-'jyā jèr-de-chǎn-'lyàng.

(Create speciously) 'nyē-dzàw. ‖He'll be able to manufacture a story for the occasion. tā kě-yi wèy jèy-jyàn-'shèr 'nyē-dzàw yí-dwàn-'hwà.

MANY. dwō, hěn 'dwō, shywǔ-'dwō; a great many shywǔ-shywu-dwō-'dwō-de. ‖I have many reasons.

wǒ yěw 'shywǔ-dwō-de-'lǐ-yéw. ‖I have many things to do. wǒ yěw 'shywǔ-dwō-'shř yàw 'dzwò. ‖Are there many coming to dinner? láy-chř-'fàn-de-rén 'dwō-ma? ‖There weren't very many (people) at his house. dzày-tā-'jyā-lǐ-de-rén bù-hěn 'dwō. ‖He knows a good many people in this city. dzày jèy-ge-'chéng-li tā rèn-shr hěn-'dwō-rén. ‖I called you a good many times yesterday. dzwó-tyan wǒ 'jǎw-le nǐ 'hěn-dwō-tsž. ‖I've passed you on the street many a time. wǒ dzày 'jyē-shang 'pèng-gwo nín 'shywǔ-dwō-'hwéy. ‖A great many people use that bank. 'shywǔ-shywu-dwō-'dwō-de-rén gēn nèy-ge-yín-'háng 'wǎng-láy. ‖We have a great many things to do before we leave. wǒm 'dzěw yǐ-'chyán háy yěw 'shywǔ-shywu-dwō-'dwō-de-shř yàw 'dzwò.

How many 'dwō-shaw. ‖How many tickets do you want? nín yàw 'dwō-shaw pyàw? ‖I don't know how many of my friends will turn up this evening. wǒ bù-jř-'dàw jyēr-'wǎn-shang wǒ yěw 'dwō-shaw-péng-yew hwèy 'láy.

MAP. dì-'tú. ‖I want a map of China. wǒ yàw yì-jāng-'jūng-gwo-dì-'tú. ‖Can you show me the town on this map? nǐ 'kě-yi dzày dì-'tú-shang bǎ jèy-ge-'tswēn-dz 'jř gěy-wo 'kàn-ma?

To map an area, etc. hwà, 'hwà-chu-lay. ‖Our next job is to map the coast. 'dzày-láy jyèw-shr yàw bǎ hǎy-àn-'shyàn 'hwà-chu-lay.

To map (plan a route) 'jì-hwà. ‖The guide is mapping our route now. lǐng-'lù-de dzày 'gēn wǒm 'jì-hwà 'lù-chéng-ne.

To map out (plan) dìng. ‖Have you mapped out your schedule yet? nǐ-de-'shř-jyān-'byǎw yǐ-jing dìng-'hǎw-le-ma?

MARCH. (Month) 'sān-ywè. ‖I plan to stay through March. wǒ 'dǎ-swàn dzày-jèr jù-je, gwò-le 'sān-ywè dzày 'dzěw.

(To walk in formation). (Referring primarily to the walking motion) dzěw; (with emphasis on formation) bǎy-je-'dwèy (or páy-je-'dwèy, or páy-'dwèy) dzěw; (when leaving under orders) kāy instead of dzěw in the same constructions; march by gwò in place of or after dzěw or kāy in the same constructions; a march is expressed verbally by the same expressions. ‖They march the prisoners in the yard every morning. tām 'měy-tyān 'dzǎw-chen jyàw 'fàn-rén-men dzày 'ywàn-dz-li °bǎy-je-'dwèy (or °páy-je-'dwèy) dzěw-'chywār. ‖Did you see the soldiers march by? nǐ kàn-jyàn 'jywūn-dwèy tsúng-jèr °bǎy-je-'dwèy gwò-ma? or °'gwò-ma? or °'kāy-gwo-chywu-ma? ‖We had a tough march this morning. wǒm jīn-tyan 'dzǎw-shang 'dzěw-de 'jēn gèw-'shèw-de. ‖They just came in from a twenty-mile march. tām dzěw-le 'èr-shr-lǐ-'lù 'gāng dàw-jèr.

(Military music) 'jìn-shíng-'chywǔ. ‖The band started the concert with a march. ywè-dwèy 'kāy-chǎng dzěw-le ge-'jìn-shíng-'chywǔ.

MARK. (*Written symbol, as a check*) 'jì-hàwr; (*a check*) gēwr; (*a circle*) chywār; **make a mark** dǎ (*or* dzwò, *or* hwà, *or* shyě) ge-'jì-hàwr, dǎ ge-'gēwr, dǎ ge-'chywār; *or expressed verbally as* **to mark** (*with a check*) 'gēw-chū-lay, 'gēw-shyà-lay; (*with a circle*) 'chywān-chū-lay; (*with lines*) 'hwà-chū-lay; (*as a note or record*) 'jì-shyà-lay. ‖**Make a mark after the names of those present.** dzày 'dàw-de-rén-de-'míng-dz-shang °dǎ (*or* °dzwò) ge-'jì-hàwr. *or* °dǎ ge-'gēwr. *or* °dǎ ge-'chywār. *or* bǎ 'dàw-le-de-rén-de-'mìng-dz °'gēw-chū-lay. *or* °'chywān-chū lay. *or* °'gēw-shyà-lay. *or* °'jì-shyà-lay. ‖**This bill has a mark on it.** jèy-jāng-'chyán-pyàw-de-shàng-myàn yěw ge-'jì-hàwr. ‖**Be sure your mark is on your laundry.** nín-yàw-'shǐ-de-'yī-shang-shang yí-'dìng děy dǎ (*or* hwà, *or* shyě) ge-'jì-hàwr. ‖**I've marked the items I want.** wǒ-'yàw-de dēw °'gēw-chū-lay-le. *or* °'gēw-shyà-lay-le. *or* °'chywān-chū-lay-le. *or* °dǎ-le 'jì-hàwr-le. ‖**I've marked the important parts of the notice.** wǒ bǎ jèy-ge-'tūng-gàw-de-'jùng-yàw-'bù-fēn yǐ-jīng °'hwà-chū-lay-le. *or* °'gēw-chū-lay-le. *or* °'chywān-chū-lay-le. *or* °dǎ-le 'jì-hàwr. ‖**I've marked your route on the map.** nǐ-dzěw-de-lù-'shyàn wǒ 'yǐ-jīng dzày dì-'tú-shang gěy-nǐ 'hwà-chū-lay-le. ‖**The river has never gone higher than this mark.** hé-shwěy 'tsúng-láy méy-yěw jǎnẹ-'gwò-le jèy-ge-°'jì-hàwr. *or* (*line*) °'dàwr.

(*Target*) *is usually expressed indirectly, but sometimes by* 'mù-dī *or* bǎ. ‖**The shells fell wide of the mark.** *is expressed as* The shells didn't hit. pàw-'dàn méy-'jùng. *or as* The deviation in firing was too great. 'nèy-jǐ-pàw-'fàng-de-'pyān-chā tày 'dà. *or, more literally* pǎw-'dàn-'le-de-dì-fang lí °'mù-dī (*or* °-'bǎ) tày 'ywǎn.

(*Grade*) fēr *or* 'fēn-shu, *or expressed as* **look over** kàn. ‖**When will you have our examination papers marked?** nín 'shéme-shǐ-hew kàn-wán wǒm-de-'jywàn-dz? ‖**Have you marked those examination papers yet?** nèy-shyē-'jywàn-dz dēw °dǎ-le 'fēr-le-ma? *or* °dǎ-le 'fēn-shu-le-ma? *or* °kàn-'gwò-le-ma?

To mark (*prices on*) *goods* bǎ . . . °shyě- (*or* °jì-, *or* °byāw-) shang 'jyà-chyan. ‖**We must mark these goods today.** dzám 'jyér děy bǎ nèy-shyē-'hwò °shyě- (*or* °jì-, *or* °byāw-) shang 'jyà-chyan. ‖**What price is marked on the tag?** 'pyàr-shang- (*or* 'pár-shang-) °shyě-de- (*or* °byāw-de-) 'jyàr shǐ 'dwō-shǎw?

To mark up prices *or* **to mark up goods** (*in price*) jǎng 'jyà-chyán, jǎng-'jyàr; *or expressed by saying that* the prices have increased jyà-chyan 'jǎng-le *or that* the prices asked are higher than before jyà-chyan yàw-de bǐ yǐ-chyán °'dwō-le *or* °'dà-le. ‖**He seems to have marked up his prices.** tā-de-dūng-shi 'hǎw shyàng jǎng-le 'jyàr-le. *or* tā-de-dūng-shi dìng-de-'jyà-chyan hǎw shyàng °'jǎng-le. *or* °'yàw-de bǐ yǐ-chyán 'dwō-le. *or* °'yàw-de bǐ yǐ-chyán 'dà-le.

To mark down prices *or* **to mark down goods** (*in price*) jyǎn 'jyà-chyan, jyǎn-'jyàr. ‖**These coats have been marked down for our sale.** jèy-shyē-'dà-yī yīn-wey yàw fàng-'pán yǐ-jīng bǎ 'jyà-chyan 'jyǎn-le.

‖**These are marked-down prices.** jèy shǐ 'yǐ-jīng-'jyǎn-le-de-'jyàr.

To reach a mark (*goal*). ‖**Do you think he'll reach the mark he has set for himself?** tā shyǎng (jyǎng-láy) dzwò-dàw 'nèm-ge-'dì-bu, 'nǐ jywé-je tā 'dzwò-de-'dàw-ma?

To be wide of the mark (*of a guess, etc.*). ‖**His guess was wide of the mark.** tā-tsāy-de °'tày chā-le. *or* °kě 'jēn chā-de 'tày ywǎn-le. *or* °kě 'jēn chā-de 'tày dwō-le. *or* °kě 'jēn chā-de 'ywǎn-le chywù-le. (*or chà instead of chā throughout.*)

To miss the mark (*figuratively*). ‖**His answers missed the mark every time.** *is expressed as* Every time he °answered wrong. tā 'měy-tsż 'lǎw-shr °dá-'tswò-le. *or* °didn't answer the question. °'dá-de bú-dwèy-'tí. *or* °didn't answer what was asked. °'dá-fēy swǒ 'wèn. *or* °answered as "when others say east he says west." °dá-de 'rén-jyā shwō-'dūng tā shwō-'shī.

To mark time until 'gān-děng-je, 'jìng-děng-je; (*waste time until*) děng-je . . . hàw 'shf́-hew. ‖**They're just marking time until their boat leaves.** tām 'děng-je kāy-'chwán, dzày-nàr hàw 'shf́-hew-ne. *or* tām dzày-nàr °'gān- (*or* °'jìng-)děng-je kāy-'chwán-ne. ‖**They're marking time until he leaves.** tām dzày-nàr °'gān- (*or* °'jìng-)děng-je tā 'dzěw-kāy-ne.

‖**On your mark!** jàn-'hǎw! ‖**On your mark; get set; go!** jàn-'hǎw; ywù-'bèy; 'pǎw! *or expressed, as in English, as* One, two, three, go! 'yī, 'èr, 'sān, 'pǎw!

Marked. ‖**Business has shown a marked improvement this year.** 'jīn-nyán 'měy-may hěn jyàn 'hǎw.

MARKET. (*Place to buy and sell*) shḟ *or* shèr; (*a country market held on certain days*) jí; (*the same, held in monastery grounds*) myàw-'hwèy; (*a market open at night in large cities, selling produce and used extensively for disposing of stolen goods*) 'yè-shèr; **market place** shř-'chǎng; **fish market** 'ywú-shř *or* 'ywú-shèr; **black market** 'hēy-shèr; **stock market** jyāw-yì-'swǒ; **to market** *goods is expressed as* to send to market sùng-shang 'shř-chywu *or* sùng-dàw 'jí-shang chywù 'mǎy *or as* to send to sell sùng-chywu 'mǎy. ‖**The market is very lively today.** jyēr °'shř-shang (*or* °'jí-shang, *or* °myàw-'hwèy, *or* °'yè-sher, *or* °shř-'chǎng-li, *or* °jyāw-yì-'swǒ) ͭing 'máng. *or* jyēr 'shř-shang (*etc.*) 'měy-may tǐng ͭè-naw. ‖**These eggs were brought to the market this morning.** jèy-shyē-'jī-dzěr shř jyēr-'dzǎw-shang-tsáy-shàng-'shř-de. ‖**When does the market open?** shř-'chǎng shéme-shf́-hew kāy-'mén? ‖**Is there anything new on the market today?** jyēr 'shř-shang °'shīn-dàw-le shém-me-'hwò-ma? *or* °yěw shém-me-'shīn-hwò? ‖**He will market his fruit this month.** 'jèy-ge-ywè tā yàw bǎ 'gwǒ-dz °sùng-shang 'shř-chywu. *or* °sùng-chywu 'màỵ. *or* °sùng-dàw 'jí-shang chywù 'màỵ.

To do marketing, to go marketing, or to go to market (*to buy*) *is expressed as* to buy things mǎy 'dūng-shi. ‖**She does her marketing in the morning.** tā 'dzǎw-shang chywù mǎy 'dūng-shi.

(*Sales field*) 'shyāw-lù; (*customer*) 'măy-jŭr. ‖This country is a good market for cotton cloth. dzày jèy-ge-'gwó-li 'myán-bù°-'shyāw-lù hĕn 'hăw. *or* °kĕ-yĭ 'chàng shyāw. ‖He's trying to find a market for his product. tā shyăng gĕy tā-'dzàw-de-dūng-shi jăw °'shyāw-lù. *or* °ge-'măy-jŭr. ‖There's a heavy market in machinery here. jèy-ge-dì-fang-'jī-chi-de-°'shyāw-lù (*or*, *of high price*, °'háng-shr; *see next paragraph*) hĕn 'hăw.

(*Prices*) 'háng-shr. ‖The tea market is off today. 'jīn-tyān 'chá-yè méy-yĕw 'háng-shr.

Be in the market for (*want to buy*) yàw 'măy. ‖Are you in the market for a good car? nĭ yàw măy lyàng-hăw-chì-'chē-ma?

MARRIAGE. (*Wedding*) 'jyē-hwēn-'lĭ; (*of old traditional style*) 'húng-shr̀ *or* 'shĭ-shr̀; (*of several of them, also*) 'jyà-chywŭ-de-shr̀; to have a marriage shíng 'jyē-hwēn-'lĭ, bàn 'húng-shr̀, bàn 'shĭ-shr̀; *verbal expressions meaning* to get married *or* to marry *are also used; see* MARRY. ‖The marriage will take place on March 1. 'sān-ywè 'yí-hàw °shíng 'jyē-hwēn-'lĭ. *or* °'bàn 'shĭ-shr̀. ‖They have had several marriages in their family within the last year. tām-jyā yì-'nyán-li bàn-le hăw-jĭ-jyàn-°'húng-shr̀. *or* °'shĭ-shr̀. *or* °'jyà-chywŭ-de-shr̀. *or* tām-jyā jèy- -'nyán-li 'gū-nyang °chū 'mén-dz (*or* °chū-'jyà), 'ér-ʊz chywŭ 'shí-fer-de, bàn-le 'hăw-jĭ-'hwéy.

(*Married life*) 'hwēn-yīn. ‖Their marriage has been very successful. tām-de-'hwēn-yīn hĕn 'méy-măn.

MARRY. To get married (*of a couple or an individual*) jyē-'hwēn; (*expressions used in connection with old traditional ceremonies: of a couple*) bày 'tyān-dì, hé-'jĭn, (*of a man*) chywŭ 'shí-fer, (*of a woman*) chū 'mén-dz *or* chū-jyà *or* (*in old ceremonies*) gwò-'mén; to marry *a woman* chywŭ; to marry *a man* jyà *or* 'jyà-gĕy; to give *a woman in marriage* bă . . . 'jyà-gĕy; to marry *a couple* (*of the one performing the ceremony*) gĕy . . . jèng-'hwēn. ‖Do you know when she's to be married? nĭ 'jr̄-daw-bu-jr̄-daw tā 'shéme-shŕ-hew jyē-'hwēn? ‖Is she going to marry him? tā 'hwèy-bu-hwèy 'jyà(-gĕy)-ta? ‖They say he married her for her money. dà-'jyā shwō tā 'chywŭ-tā shr̀ wèy-le tā-de ʊhyán. ‖He married his daughter to an old friend. tā bă tā-de-'nywŭ-er 'jyà-gey-le tā-de-yí-ge-lăw-'péng-yew. ‖When will he be able to marry us? tā 'shéme-shŕ-hewr néng gĕy wŏ-men jèng-'hwēn?

MASTER. (*Of a household or servants*) 'jŭ-rén; master of the house 'jŭ-rén *or* (*man of the house*) 'shyān-sheng *or* (*Peiping*) 'lăw-yé. ‖Who is the master of the house? 'něy-yí-wèy shr̀ 'jŭ-rén? ‖Is the master of the house in? 'shyān-sheng dzày-'jyā-ma?

Master of the ship chwán-'jŭ *or* chwán-'jăng. ‖The master of the ship has sailed the sea for many years. chwán-'jŭ (*or* chwán-'jăng) păw-'hăy păw-le 'hăw-shyē-'nyán-le.

To be master of the situation néng 'yìng-fù-dž-'rú, néng 'tsāw-dzùng-dé-'yí, bàn-de 'chyà-dàw 'hăw-chù. ‖No matter what happens, he's always (the) master of the situation. 'bù-gwăn ywù-jyàn 'shéme-shr̀, tā 'dēw °néng 'yìng-fù-dž-'rú. *or* °néng 'tsāw-dzùng-dé-'yí. *or* °'bàn-de 'chyà-dàw 'hăw-chù.

To master *a subject of study* (*completely*) nyàn-'tūng; (*at all*) shywé-'hăw. ‖He mastered the language in a year. tā bă nèy-gwó-de-'hwà yì-nyán-de-'gūng-fu °nyàn-'tūng-le. *or* °shywé-'hăw-le. ‖I find this language difficult to master. wŏ jywé-je nèy-gwó-de-'hwà hĕn nán shywé-de 'hăw.

To master *one's feelings* (*be unperturbed*) néng 'bú-dùng-'shīn; (*keep feelings hidden or under control*) néng 'rĕn; (*not be swayed by sentiment or tenderness*) néng shyà 'hĕn-shīn. ‖You must master your feelings. nĭ dĕy néng 'bú-dùng-'shīn tsáy 'shíng.

In combinations such as **master key**, dzŭng *is used, or the idea is expressed by a word for* all, *as* 'chywán. ‖Where is the master switch? 'dzŭng-dyàn-mén (*or* 'dzŭng-kāy-gwān) dzày-'năr? ‖This is the master schedule. jèy shr̀ 'dzŭng-shŕ-jyān-byăw.

Master of Arts 'shwò-shr̀ *or* 'wén-kē-'shwò-shr̀; Master of Science 'lĭ-kē-'shwò-shr̀.

MATCH. (*Fire lighter*) yáng-'hwŏ *or* yáng-'hwŏr; (*in Peiping, also*) 'yáng-chywŭ-'dēngr *or* yáng-'chywŭ-dēngr; (*in some other areas*) hwŏ-'cháy. ‖Have you got a match? yĕw yáng-'hwŏ-ma? ‖A box of matches, please. 'gĕy-wo yì-hé-yáng-'hwŏ.

(*Equal of a person*) 'dwèy-shĕw. ‖I'm no match for him. wŏ 'bú-shr̀ tā-de-'dwèy-shĕw. ‖He met his match. tā 'kĕ pèng-jaw 'dwèy-shĕw-le.

(*To equal*) 'găn-shang . . . nèm °dwō *or* °dà, etc. *with other adjectives, depending on whether the reference is to equaling in amount, size, speed, quality, etc.;* yĕ yĕw *instead of* 'găn-shang *in the same constructions;* gēn . . . yí-'yàng °dwō *or* °etc. ‖Can we match their speed? dzám 'găn-de-shang (*or* dzám yĕ néng yĕw) 'tām nèm 'kwày-ma? ‖He matched Jones's record for sales. 'tā-mày-de °găn-shang-le lăw-'jēw-mày-de nèm 'dwō-le. *or* °gēn lăw-'jēw-mày-de yí-'yàng dwō-le.

(*To be of the same set or pair*) *is expressed as* to be one set *or* to be one pair (*see* SET, PAIR). ‖These shoes don't match. jèy-lyăng-jr̄-shyé 'bú-shr̀ yì-'shwāng. ‖These gloves don't match. jèy-lyăng-jr̄-shĕw-'tàwr 'bú-shr̀ yí-'fù. ‖These chairs don't match (with) the table. jey-shyē-'yĭ-dz gēn 'jwō-dz bú-shr̀ yí-'tàw.

(*To fit together physically*) 'dwèy-shang, dwèy-de-'shàng. ‖The broken edges don't match. 'chár dwèy-bu-'shàng.

(*To be of the same kind*) (shr̀) yí-'yàng(-de). ‖Can you match this plate? yĕw gēn-jèy-ge-yí-'yàng-de 'pár-ma?

(*To be of the same color*) (shr̀) yí-ge-'shăr(-de). ‖These two match. jèy-'lyăng-ge dēw shr̀ yí-gé-'shăr. ‖Do you have thread to match this? yĕw 'jèy-shăr-de 'shyàn-ma?

(*To harmonize, go together well*) pèy; (*in color*) 'yán-shăr 'pèy or dwèy-'shăr. ‖These colors aren't a good match. 'jèy-shyē-'yán-se °bú-'pèy. or °'pèy-daw yí-'kwàr 'bú-dà 'hăw. ‖His tie doesn't match his suit. tā-de-lǐng-'dày hé tā-de-'yī-shang °bú-'pèy. or °'yán-shăr bú-'pèy. or °bú-dwèy-'shăr.

(*A contest*) bǐ-'sày. ‖Would you like to see a tennis match? nǐ yàw kàn 'wăng-chyéw-bǐ-'sày-ma?

(*Marriage*). ‖She's making a good match. *is expressed as* The man she's marrying is suitable. tā-'jyà-de-rén tǐng hé-'shr̀. ‖He's making a good match. *is expressed as* He's marrying her; it's very suitable. tā 'chywŭ-tā tǐng hé-'shr̀-de.

‖I'll match you for it. *is expressed as* Let's flip a coin to see who pays (*or other expressions instead of* pays). dzám dŭ ge-'dzèr-m̥èr kàn 'shéy gĕy-'chyán.

MATERIAL. 'tsáy-lyàw; raw material 'ywán-lyàw. ‖What materials do you need to make a bookcase? nǐ dzwò shū-'jyà-dz yàw yùng shéme-'tsáy-lyàw? ‖Do you have enough of this material to make me a suit? nǐ 'yĕw-méy-yew jèy-jŭng-'tsáy-lyàw 'gĕw gĕy-wo dzwò yì-shēn-'yī-shang? ‖He's collecting material for a new book. tā dzày jăw 'tsáy-lyàw shyĕ-'shū. ‖The factory is short of raw materials. jèy-ge-gūng-'chăng 'ywán-lyàw bú-'gĕw.

Writing materials wén-'jywù.

Material comforts wù-'jr̀-de-shyăng-'shèw. ‖They've never had much material comfort. tām shyàng-lay 'méy-yew-gwo dwō-shaw-wù-'jr̀-de-shyăng-'shèw.

Material witness jŭ-'yàw-de-'jèng-rén.

MATTER. (*Material substance*). (*Literary and technical terms*) 'wù-jr̀ or·jr̀; *or expressed as* things in the world 'shr̀-jye-shang-de-'dūng-shi; *specific kinds of matter are expressed by an adjective with* 'dūng-shi *or by specific terms:* (*pus or similar bodily secretion*) néng *or* núng. ‖All matter has one of three forms: gas, liquid, or solid. 'wù-jr̀ 'shíng-tǐ yĕw 'sān-jŭng: 'chì-tǐ, 'lyéw-jr̀, 'shr̀-jr̀. or 'shr̀-jye-shang-de-'dūng-shi yĕw 'sān-jŭng: 'yàw-bu-jyèwr-shr 'chyèr, 'yàw-bu-jyew-shr 'shwĕr, 'yàw-bu-jyèw-shr shr̀-'dzáwr-de. ‖All religions teach the existence of spirit as well as matter. 'swŏ-yĕw-de-'dzūng-jyàw 'dēw shwō °yĕw-'jr̀ yĕ yĕw-'líng. or °'wù-jr̀ yì-'wày háy yĕw 'líng-hwén. ‖Many kinds of coloring matter are obtained from bark. hĕn-dwō-dzwò-'yán-lyàw-de-'dūng-shi dēw shr̀ tsúng shù-'pí-shang 'chywŭ-chū-lay-de. ‖Pine trees secrete a sticky matter. 'sūng-shù chū yì-jŭng-°shyàng-'jyāw-de-'dūng-shi. or (*sap*) °'nyán-jr̀.

Reading matter kĕ-'kàn-de-dūng-shi; 'dūng-shi *if* kàn *is used elsewhere in the sentence; or expressed as* books and magazines shū, dzá-'jr̀. ‖This reading matter will last me a week. jèy-shyē-'dūng-shi °'gĕw wŏ kàn yí-ge-shīng-'chī-de. or °wŏ dĕy kàn yí-ge-shīng-'chī. ‖Got some reading matter? yĕw 'shū-a, dzá-'jr̀-de-ma? or yĕw kĕ-'kàn-de-dūng-shi-ma?

Printed matter 'yìn-shwā-'pǐn. ‖Do I have to declare printed matter? 'yìn-shwā-'pǐn yĕ dĕy °'bàw-ma? or °'shēng-míng-ma?

(*Postal*) matter 'yéw-jyàn. ‖This package will have to go as first-class matter. jèy-ge-'bāw-gwŏ yí-'dìng dĕy àn-je 'yī-dĕng-'yéw-jyàn °dzĕw. or °jì.

Subject matter jyăng-de-'shèr. ‖The subject matter of the book is interesting, but the presentation is dull. nèy-bĕn-shū-jyăng-de-'shèr tǐng yĕw 'yì-sz-de, bú-gwo 'shyĕ-de °nèm 'sz̀-chen-chén-de. or °nèm 'mèn-chen-chén-de. or °bù-'shēng-dùng.

(*Affair*) shr̀ or shèr; *sometimes expressed indirectly:* matters (*indefinite*) 'shéme-shr̀ or 'shr̀-ching. ‖Will you look into the matter? jèy-jyàn-'shr̀ nǐ gĕy 'chá-(yi-)cha ('shíng-ma)? ‖I must settle some business matters. wŏ yĕw jǐ-jyàn-'gūng-shr̀ dĕy bàn-'wán-lew. ‖You take matters too seriously. nǐ 'shéme-shr̀ dēw tày rèn-'jēn-le. or nǐ 'shéme-shr̀ or nǐ bă 'shr̀-ching) dēw kàn-de tày °rèn-'jēn-le. or °'sz̀-le. or °'yán-jùng-le. or °'dà-le. ‖You're only making matters worse. nǐ făn bă-'shr̀ nèng-de gèng °'dzāw-le. or °méy-fár 'bàn-le. *or expressed as* You're simply giving people more trouble. nǐ 'jyăn-jŕ shr̀ gĕy-rén 'tyān má-fan. ‖It's a matter of no importance. 'shyăw-shèr yì-'jwāng. or 'bú-shr shéme-°yàw-'jǐn-de. or °'dà-shr̀. or °'yán-jùng-de-shr̀. or °dà-bu-'lyăw-de-shr̀. or °'jŕ-de-gwān-'shín-de-shr̀. or °'jùng-yaw-de-shr̀. ‖The matter is of absolutely no concern to me. nèy-shèr °gēn-wŏ yì-'dyăr-gwān-shi yĕ méy-'yĕw. or °wŏ yì-'dyăr yĕ gwān-bu-'jáw. ‖Bring the matter up tomorrow. jèy-jyàn-shèr (or jèy-ge) 'myér dzày shwō. ‖Bring the matter to his attention. jèy-jyàn-shèr (or jèy-ge) yàw (or dĕy) jyàw-'tā jŕ-dàw. or bă jèy-jyàn-shèr (or bă jèy-ge) 'gàw-su tā.

To matter *and* to be a matter of concern *are expressed in various indirect ways referring to importance or personal interest and concern.* ‖It doesn't matter. 'bú-yàw-jǐn. or 'méy shéme-'gwān-shi. or 'shyăw-shèr yì-'jwāng. or 'swàn-le. or 'bú-shr shéme-'dà-bu-'lyăw-de-shr̀. or 'yùng-bu-jáw gwăn. or 'yùng-bu-jáw tsāw-'shīn. ‖What does it matter how it's done, so long as it gets done in time? 'gwăn dzĕm 'bàn-ne? (or 'gwăn-ta dzĕm 'bàn-ne? or 'dzĕm-ge-'bàn-fa yĕw shéme-'gwān-shi?) 'jŕ yàw dàw shŕ-hew dzwò-'chéng-le jyèw 'shr̀-le. ‖It matters a great deal to me what he says about you. tā dzĕm shwō-'nǐ °wŏ tǐng gwăn-'shīn-de. or 'jyèw gēn shwō-wŏ yí-'yàng. ‖It matters a great deal to me whether he'll be there or not. tā 'dàw ywù bú-'dàw °tsúng 'wŏ-jèr shyăng 'tǐng yàw-'jǐn-de. or °tsúng 'wŏ-jèr shyăng 'tǐng yĕw-'gwān-shi-de. or (*I'll have to do something about it*) °wŏ 'fēy gwăn bù-'kĕ. ‖His health is a matter of great concern to the people of the whole world. tā-'bìng-de dzĕm-'yàng chywán-shr̀-'jyè-de-rén dēw °'rèn-wéy shŕ yí-jyàn-'dà-shr̀. or °hĕn gwān-'shīn. or °jywé-je hĕn 'jùng-yàw. or °jywé-je yĕw 'gwān-shi. ‖His escape from the insane asylum is a matter of great concern to us. tā tsúng 'fēng-rén-'ywàn 'pǎw-le; jèy-jyàn-shèr °wǒm hěn gwān-'shīn. or (Of worry) °jyàw-wǒm hěn dān-'shīn. or °jyàw-wǒm 'tí-shīn dyàw-'dǎn-de.

The matter (the trouble, wrong, when not followed by with) shř or not expressed. ‖What's the matter? 'shéme-shř? or yěw 'shéme-shř? or 'dzěm-yì-hwéy-shř? or 'dzěm-le? ‖Nothing's the matter. 'méy shéme-shř. or 'méy-shèr. or méy 'dzěm-je.

The matter with is expressed as illness bìng; or as defect 'máw-bing; or as broken 'hwày-le; or in other ways similar to those in the preceding paragraph. ‖Something's the matter with my stomach; I can't eat without getting a stomach-ache. wǒ 'wèy-kew 'jwěn shř yěw dyǎr-'bìng; 'yì chř dūng-shi jyèw 'téng. ‖There's something the matter with my car; it won't start. chē kāy-bu-'dùng-ie; jwěn-shr nǎr °yěw dyǎr-'máw-bing. or °'hwày-le. ‖What's the matter with you? Are you crazy? ní-je shř 'dzěm-le? nǐ °'fēng-la! or °'shǎ-la! or °'hú-du-la! ‖There's nothing the matter with him that a good rest won't cure. tā 'shéme-bìng yě méy-'yěw (or tā hǎw-'hǎwr-de), 'shyē-hwer jyèw 'hǎw-le. ‖There's nothing the matter with him that a good talking-to won't cure. 'tā-ya, 'shwō yí-dwèn jyèw 'hǎw-le.

To be a matter of (depend on) děy kàn. ‖It's a matter of how you look at it. děy kàn nǐ dzěm-ge-'kàn-fa. ‖That's a matter of how you say it. 'nèy děy kàn dzěm 'shwō-le. ‖It's a matter of timing. 'shŕ-hewr děy kàn-de °'jwěn. or °jèng 'dwèy. ‖It's all a matter of time. (Of how much time there is) děy kàn yěw 'dwō-shǎw-'shŕ-hew. or (Of how much time it will take) kàn děy yùng 'dwō-shǎw-'shŕ-hew-le. or (For time to decide) děy kàn 'shŕ-jyān láy 'dìng. or expressed as This is a question of time. jey shř 'shŕ-jyān-wèn-'tí.

(Just) a matter of time (depends only on time) is expressed as above. But ‖It's just a matter of time. may also be expressed as There isn't much time. 'méy dwō-shǎw-shŕ-hew-le. or expressed as In a little while it will be known. 'děng-yi-děng jyèw 'jŕ-dàw-le. ‖His death is just a matter of days. tā 'hwó-bu-lyǎw jǐ-'tyār-le. or tā 'méy jǐ-tyār-de-'hwó-tcwr-le. or tā yǎn-'kàn-je jyèw kwày 'sž-le. or tā méy 'jǐ-tyār jyèw hwèy 'sž-de.

A matter of life and death. ‖This is a matter of life and death. (Literally) jèy-shř 'rén-mìng jyāw-'gwān (-de-shř). or 'yěw-mìng 'méy mìng (or shř-'sž shř-'hwó, or 'shēng 'sž) °jyèw kàn 'jèy-shèr chéng-bu-chéng-le. or °dzáy tsž-yì-'jywǔ-le. or (Literally or figuratively) jèy-shr °'shìng-mìng (or °'shēng-sž) jyāw-'gwān(-de-shř).

A matter of opinion. ‖That's a matter of opinion. is expressed as People's opinions differ. 'gè-rén-'kàn-fa bù-'túng.

A matter of course 'dāng-rán-rú-'tsž-de; or expressed as of course dāng-'rán or dž-'rán. ‖That's a matter of course. nèy shr 'dāng-rán-rú-'tsž-de. or dāng-'rán (or dž-'rán) shř nèm-je.

(To take) as a matter of course gwàn-le, 'bù-yǐ-wéy-'chǐ-le, 'rèn-wéy 'dāng-rán-le. ‖She accepts praise

as a matter of course. tā shèw rén 'gūng-wey °'gwàn-le. or °'bù-yǐ-wéy-'chǐ-le. or °'rèn-wéy 'dāng-rán-le.

As a matter of fact chí-'shŕ(-a); or expressed as simply 'jyàn-jŕ; or as let me tell you the truth gēn-nǐ shwō 'shŕ-hwà-ba. ‖As a matter of fact, this should have been placed under your control in the beginning. chí-'shŕ(-a), 'jèy-shèr yì chǐ-'chū jyèw gāy ràng-'nǐ gwǎn. ‖As a matter of fact, she did go to college. chí-'shŕ-a, tā 'jēn shàng-gwo dà-'shywé. ‖His handwriting is pretty bad; as a matter of fact, I can't read it at all. tā-shyě-de-dž jēn 'bù-chéng-shíng (or tā-shyě-de-dž jēn 'bù-hǎw rèn), wǒ 'jyàn-jŕ °rèn-bu-chū-'láy. or °kàn-bu-'dúng. ‖As a matter of fact, I didn't even know his name. gēn-ni shwō 'shŕ-hwà-ba (or chí-'shŕ-a), wǒ lyán tā 'jyàw-shéme yě bù-jŕ-'dàw.

Matter-of-fact or in a matter-of-fact sort of way is expressed as as if nothing were the matter shyàng 'méy nèm-hwéy-'shèr shŕ-de; or as not changing the attitude 'bú-dùng-'shīn-de; or as not changing the voice or expression 'bú-dùng-'shēng-sè-de; or as unperturbed 'bù-hwāng-bù-máng-de; or as not taking (it) as anything at all ná-je 'bú-dàng (or 'bù-ná-je dàng) hwéy-'shèr. ‖Don't be so matter-of-fact about it! 'byé nèm °ná-je 'bú-dàng (or °'bù-ná-je dàng) hwéy-'shèr láy kàn! or °shyàng 'méy nèm-hwéy-'shèr shŕ-de! or °'bú-dùng 'shīn! ‖He told me in a matter-of-fact sort of way that he had just won ten thousand dollars at the races. tā 'bù-hwāng-bù-máng-de (or tā shyàng 'méy nèm-hwéy-'shèr shŕ-de, or tā 'bú-dùng-'shēng-sè-de) gēn-wǒ shwō tā 'gāng-tsáy dzày mǎ-'chǎng dé-le yí-'wàn-kwày-chyán.

For that matter (so far as this point is concerned) dzày 'jèy-yì-dyǎn-shang; (even) 'jyèw-shr; (also) yě or lyán. ‖He said our work was no good, and we agreed with him, for that matter. tā shwō wǒm-dzwò-de-'shèr chà-'jìn; dzày 'jèy-yì-dyǎn-shang 'wǒm gēn-ta túng-'yì. or . . . ; jyèw-shī wǒm yě 'gēn-ta túng-'yì.

No matter (followed by what, whether, if, how, etc.) bù-'gwǎn, 'píng, 'swéy. ‖We've made up our minds no matter what you say. 'píng (or bù-'gwǎn, or 'swéy) nǐ 'dzěm shwō, wǒm fǎn-'jèng shř ná-'dìng-le 'jú-yì-le. ‖No matter whether he comes or not, we've got to leave. bù-'gwǎn tā láy-bu-lay, wǒm děy 'dzěw. ‖She wants that coat no matter what the cost. tā 'fēy yàw mǎy nèy-jyàn-dà-'yī bù-kě, bù-gwǎn 'dwō-dà-de-'jyàr. or 'bù-gwǎn 'dwō gwèy, tā yě yàw 'mǎy nèy-jyàn-dà-'yī.

No laughing matter. ‖That's no laughing matter. nèy 'bú-shr °kě-'shyàw-de-shèr. or °'yí-'shyàw-jyèw-'iyǎw-de-shèr. or 'nèy-shèr °hěn yàw-'jǐn-de. or °'bù-néng 'chīng-shř. or °'bù-néng 'bú-dàng hwéy-'shèr. or °'bù-néng kàn-'chīng-le.

MAY. (Possibility) expressed with perhaps 'yě-shywu. ‖That may be true. 'nà yě-shywu shř 'dwèy-de. ‖I may go with you tomorrow night. myéngr-'wǎn-shang wǒ 'yě-shywu 'gēn-ni yí-'kwàr chywù.

(*In polite requests; formally, in their answers*) 'kĕ-yi, ké-yi. ‖**May I leave this with you?** wŏ 'kĕ-yi bă 'jèy-ge 'jyāw-gey ni-ma? ‖**May I have this dance?** 'jèy-yí-tsz̀ nín 'kĕ-yi gēn-wo 'tyàw-ma? ‖**Certainly you may.** 'kĕ-yi.

(*Month*) 'wŭ-ywè.

MAYOR. (*Of a city classed as a municipality*) shr̀-'jăng; (*of a city classed as a district*) shyàn-'jăng (*more often translated into English as* **District Magistrate**); (*of a village*) tswēn-'jăng (*often translated as* **village head man**).

ME. *See* **I.**

MEAL. fàn *with measure* dwèn. ‖**Where can I get a good meal?** shéme-'dì-fang wŏ kĕ-yi 'chr̄ yí-dwèn-'hăw-'fàn? ‖**I take some of my meals at home.** yĕw 'jĭ-dwèn-'fàn wŏ dzày 'jyā-li chr̄.

(*Ground grain*) myàn, *usually with type of grain specified;* **corn meal** bàng-dz-'myàr.

MEAN. (*To be defined or explained as; used with* this, that, what, anything, *etc.*). ‖**What does it mean?** (*What is its definition?*) shr 'shéme-yì-sz? (*How is it to be explained?*) 'dzĕm jyăng? (*How is it to be stated? What is it in other words?*) shr̀ 'dzĕm-ge-'shwō-far? (*What is it all about?*) shr̀ 'dzĕm-hwéy-shèr? *Other usages are similarly constructed.* ‖**What does this word mean?** jèy-ge-'dzèr shr̀ 'shéme-yì-sz? ‖**What does this small circle mean?** jèy-ge-shyăw-'chywār °shr̀ 'shéme-yì-sz? *or* °'dzĕm jyăng? *or* °shr̀ 'dzĕm-ge-'shwō-far? *or* °shr̀ 'dzĕm-hwéy-shèr? ‖**Oh! So that's what it means!** 'èw! shr̀ 'nèm-°ge-yì-sz-a! *or* °'hwéy-shèr-a! ‖**That's what this word means, but it can't be used that way.** jèy-ge-dzèr 'shr̀ nèy-ge-'yì-sz, bú-gwo 'yùng-de-shŕ-hew 'bù-néng nèm 'yùng. ‖**I heard what you said, but °I don't understand what it means.** (ni-de-'hwà wŏ) 'tīng-jyan-le, kĕ-shr °'bù-dŭng shr̀ shéme-'yì-sz. *or expressed as* °**I couldn't understand it** (when I heard it). °'tīng-bu-'dŭng. *or* °'tīng-bu-'míng-bay. ‖**What does this word mean literally?** jèy-ge-dzèr bĕn-'shēn shr̀ 'shéme-yì-sz? *or* jèy-ge-dzèr-de-'bĕn-yì shr̀ 'shéme? ‖**What did this word mean originally?** jèy-ge-dzèr-'ywán-láy-de-yì-sz shr̀ 'shéme?

(*To get across a meaning, or to intend, of a person*). (*To get across a meaning*) *is expressed by saying that what the person says* means *so-and-so, the expressions for which are the same as above;* (*to intend*) shyăng, yàw, 'shyăng-yàw, 'dă-swàn, *or expressed in terms of a person's* intention 'yì-sz, *or indirectly, especially with a negative, as* intentionally *or with* malicious purpose gù-'yì-de, yĕw-'yì-de, chéng-'shīn, *or* (*dropping the negative*) *as* unintentionally 'wŭ-shīn-jūng, *or as* carelessly 'méy-lyĕw-'shén *or* bù-'shyăw-shīn, *or as an* unintentional mistake 'wú-shīn-jŕ-'gwò; (*to intend definitely*) yí-'dìng yàw. ‖**That's not what he meant.**

(*Of meaning*) tā-de-'hwà-li-tew méy-yĕw 'nèy-ge-'yì-sz. *or* (*Of intention*) tā bìng 'bú-shr nèy-ge-'yì-sz. *or* tā-de-'yì-sz 'bú-shr 'nèm-hwéy-shèr. ‖**What do you mean by that?** nèy shr̀ 'shéme-yì-sz? *or* nèy dzĕm 'jyăng? *or* nĭ shyăng yàw 'dzĕm-je? ‖**What do you mean by saying that?** (*Of meaning or intention*) nĭ shwō 'nèy-ge °yĕw shéme-'yì-sz? *or* (*Of intention only*) °shr̀ 'dzĕm-ge-'yì-sz? *or* °nà shr̀ shyăng yàw 'dzĕm-je? *or* °nà shr̀ 'dă-swàn 'dzĕm-je? ‖**Perhaps that's what he meant.** tā 'yĕ-shywŭ yàw shwō 'nèy-ge láy-je. *or* tā-shwō-de-'hwà 'yĕ-shywŭ shr̀ °'nèm-ge-yì-sz. *or* °'jèy-ge-yì-sz. *or* °'nèy-ge-yì-sz. ‖**Do you mean this for me?** nĭ shyăng (*or* nĭ-de-'yì-sz shr̀ yàw) bà 'jèy-ge gĕy-'wŏ-ma? ‖**Do you mean to see him before you go?** nĭ 'shr̀ shyăng dzày °'dzĕw (*or* °'méy-dzĕw) yĭ-'chyán 'jyàn-jyan tā-ma? ‖**I meant to do it yesterday, but I forgot.** wŏ ywán-láy °'shyăng (*or* °'dă-swàn) dzwér jyèw bă jèy-ge 'dzwò-le, yí-'shyà-dz gĕy 'wàng-le. ‖**I didn't mean to come today, but I had nowhere to go.** wŏ méy-'dă-swàn 'jīn-tyan láy-de (*or* wŏ méy-shyăng 'jīn-tyan láy-de, *or* wŏ bĕn-láy 'dă-swàn 'jīn-tyan bù-láy-de, *or* wŏ bĕn-láy shyăng jīn-tyan bù-láy-de), kĕ-shr wŏ 'méy-chùr 'chywù. ‖**Please forgive me; I didn't mean to do that.** dwèy-bu-'jù; °wŏ 'bú-shr gù-'yì-de. *or* °'jèy shr̀ wŏ-'wú-shīn-jŕ-'gwò. *or* °shr̀ wŏ 'méy-lyĕw-'shén láy-je. *or* shr̀ wŏ bù-'shyăw-shīn láy-je. ‖**Don't get sore; he didn't mean anything by that remark.** 'byé shēng-'chì-ba; tā nèy-jywù-'hwà yì-'dyăr yĕ bú-shr °'chéng-'shīn- (*or* °'gù-'yì-de, *or* °'yĕw-'yì-de) shwō-de. ‖**She means to have her way about the party.** chĭng-'kè-de-shr̀ tā yí-'dìng yàw àn tā-'dz̀-jĭ-de-'yì-sz láy 'bàn.

To mean (that) ... (*of a condition or situation, to have the effect or meaning that*) *is expressed as* to say shwō, to be shr̀, *or not expressed.* ‖**If he scowls at you, it means you're in; if he's very friendly, you might as well go elsewhere to look for a job.** tā yàw-shr 'dzĕw-je 'méy-téw 'dèng-nĭ, nèy jyèw-shr shwō tā yàw 'yùng-nĭ; tā yàw-shr 'fēy-cháng 'hé-chi-ya, 'nà nĭ jyèw dàw 'byé-chùr jăw-'shèr chywù-ba. ‖**If I don't come before noon, it means I can't come at all.** wŏ yàw-shr 'jūng-wŭ háy méy-'dàw, wŏ jyèw (shr̀) °'bù-láy-le. *or* °'bù-néng láy-le. ‖**If he comes, it'll mean trouble for us.** yàw-shr 'tā láy-ya, 'dzăm kĕ jyèw yàw °yĕw 'má-fan-le. *or* °'méy-yĕw 'ān-jing 'r̄-dz-le. ‖**He means that he wants you to give him a drink.** (*By his gestures or actions*) tā-nà shr̀ °yàw hē-'shwĕy. *or* °shyăng 'gēn-nĭ yàw bēy-'shwĕy hē. *or* (*By his speech, as in another language*) tā-shwō-de shr̀ shyăng gēn-nĭ yàw bēy-'shwĕy hē.

(*To refer to*) shwō; 'jŕ-je ... shwō. ‖**I didn't mean you.** wŏ bú-shr °shwō-'nĭ. *or* °'jŕ-je 'nĭ shwō-de. ‖**I do mean you!** wŏ 'jèng-shr shwō-'nĭ. *or* wŏ-shwō-de jèng-shr 'nĭ. *or* wŏ-shwō-de jyèw-shr 'nĭ. ‖**Which one do you mean?** nĭ-shwō-de shr̀ 'nèy-ge? ‖**That's not the one I meant.** wŏ 'bú-shr shwō-de 'nèy-ge.

(*To stand for; of a symbol*) 'dày-byăw. ‖**The big circles mean field officers, the small circles mean com-**

pany officers. 'dà-chywār 'dày-byǎw 'shyàw-gwān, 'shyǎw-chywār dày-byǎw 'wèy-gwān. ‖Every symbol of this kind means a thousand men. měy-yí-ge-jèy-jǔng-'jì-hawr 'dày-byǎw yì-'chyān-rén.

To mean it, to mean business, to mean *followed by a quotation of what one said is expressed by saying that the thing said is true* 'jēn(-de), the truth 'shŕ-hwà, *not said in fun* 'bú-shŕ shwō-je 'wár, *or that when one says something it goes* jyèw swàn-'shùr, *or, more indirectly, by saying that someone must do something about it.* ‖I mean it. 'jēn-de. *or* shŕ 'jēn-de. *or* wǒ shŕ 'jēn-shīn-'hwà. *or* wǒ 'shwō-le jyèw swàn-'shùr. *or expressed as* If I say one, it's one; if I say two, it's two. wǒ 'shwō-yī shŕ-'yī, shwō-'èr shŕ-'èr. ‖When a woman tells you that she's twenty-one, she doesn't always mean it literally. yàw-shr yě v 'nywǔ-rén gàw-su nǐ tā shŕ 'èr-shŕ-'yī-swèy, nèy 'cháng-chang 'bú-shr °'jēn-de. *or* °'shŕ-hwà. ‖When he tells you to do something, he means business. tā jyàw-nǐ 'dzwò-shéme de-shŕ-hew, 'bú-shr shwō-je 'wár. ‖When I say stop, I mean stop! wǒ shwō byé 'dùng, nǐ jyèw 'bù-néng dzày 'dùng! *or* wǒ shwō 'jàn-ju, nǐ jyèw °děy 'jàn-ju! *or* °'bù-néng dzày 'dzěw!

To mean well, to mean no harm shŕ hǎw-'shīn, shì hǎw-'yì, (bìng) méy-yěw 'è-yì(-de), 'shīn hǎw, shīn hěn-'hǎw-de. ‖He means well, anyway. tā 'wú-lwèn-rú-hé shŕ °hǎw-'shīn. *or* °hǎw-'yì. ‖He makes mistakes, but I'm sure he means well. tā 'cháng nèng-'tswò-le, bú-gwo tā°-'shīn hǎw. *or* °bìng méy-yěw 'è-yi. ‖Don't worry about what he says; he really means well by us. tā ày 'shwō jyàw-tā 'shwō-chywu-ba; tā dwèy-'dzám °shŕ 'hǎw-shīn. *or* °shŕ hǎw-'yì-de. *or* °shīn hěn-'hǎw-de. *or* °shŕ 'méy-yěw 'è-yì-de.

Mean a lot to. ‖This means a lot to me. jèy gēn-'wǒ yěw 'hěn-dà-de-'gwān-shi. *or* tsúng 'wǒ-jèr 'shyǎng 'jèy shŕ °'tǐng-yàw-'jǐn-de-shŕ. *or* °'dà-shŕ.

What do you mean by ... wèy-'shéme, dzěm. ‖What do you mean by calling people names? nǐ 'dzěm (*or* nǐ wèy-'shéme) mà-'rén-na?

To be meant for. ‖That remark was meant for you. (*It meant you; see fourth paragraph above*) nèy-jywù-hwà shŕ °'jǐr-je-'nǐ-shwō-de. *or* (*It was said for you to hear*) 'shwō-gěy-'nǐ-tīng-de. *or* (*It was said because of you*) °yīn-wey-'nǐ-shwō-de. ‖He was meant for that job. *is expressed as* He's really suited to do that job. tā dzwò 'nèy-shèr 'jèng hé-'shŕ. *or as* That job seems to have been made for him. 'nèy-shèr hǎw shyàng wèy-'tā 'shè-de shŕ-de. *or meaning* He was supposed to do that job, not this one. 'běn-láy 'pày-ta dzwò 'nèy-jyàn-shŕ. ‖They were meant for each other. (*They're really °a pair*) tām 'jèng shŕ (*or* tām 'jēn shŕ) °'yí-dwèr. *or* (°*destined*) °'ywán-fer. *or* °'tyan-shēng-dì-'shē-de-yí-'dwèr. *or* °'tyān-shēng-de-yí-'dwèr. *or* °'chyán-shŕ-de-'yīn-ywán. *or* (*Sarcastically, of a couple that doesn't get along*) °'ywān-jyā-lù-'jǎy. *or* °'bú-shr 'ywān-jya 'bú-jywù-'téw.

(*Average*) 'píng-jywūn. ‖The mean temperature here is 65° F. 'tsž-dì 'píng-jywūn-'wēn-dù 'hwá-shŕ 'lyèw-shŕ-'wǔ-dù.

The golden mean (*as a teaching*) 'jung-yung-jŕ-'dàw. ‖Confucius is best known for his teaching of the golden mean. hěn-'dwō-rén dēw jŕ-dàw 'kǔng-dz-de-'jūng-yúng-jŕ-'dàw.

(To be) mean (*fierce*) shyūng; (*hot-tempered*) 'shìng-dz tǐng 'bàw(-dzaw) *or* 'pí-chyer jēn °'lì-hay *or* °'shyūng *or* °'hwày; (*hard to manage*) nán 'gwǎn; (*difficult*) nán-'bàn-de (*etc.*): (*stingy*) 'shyǎw-chi *or* 'lìn-sè; (*cruel, harsh*) 'hěn, hěn-'shīn; *and similar expressions.* To feel mean (*about having done something*) jywé-de méy-'yì-sz, jywé-de bú-'dwèy, (*followed by a person*) jywé-de dwèy-bu-°'chǐ *or* °'jù; to feel mean (*not well*) 'byè-nywew-de-heng. ‖Be careful; that's a mean animal. 'shyǎw-shīn-dyar; nèy-ge-'shēng-kew °nán 'gwǎn. *or* °hěn 'shyūng. *or* °'shìng-dz tǐng 'bàw. ‖She's a pretty girl, but she has a mean temper. tā-jèy-wèy-'shyǎw-jye 'jǎng-de mǎn 'pyàw-lyang; kě-shr °'pí-chyer jēn 'lì-hay. *or* °'pí-chyer jēn 'shyūng. *or* °'pí-chyer jēn 'hwày. *or* °tǐng nán-'chán-de. *or* °tǐng bù-hǎw-'rě-de. *or* °'shìng-dz tǐng 'bàw (-dzaw). ‖I'd borrow some of his books if he weren't so mean about them. tā yàw-shr bú-nèm °'shyǎw-chi (*or* °'lìn-sè), wǒ jyèw gēn-tā 'jyè jǐ-běr-'shū-le. ‖It was mean of him to put his child to bed without any supper, even if she had been misbehaving. jyèw-shr háy-dz 'táw dyǎr-'chì, 'tā nèm 'bù-gěy 'fàn chŕ jyèw jyàw 'háy-dz shwèy-'jyàw yě 'wèy-myǎn tày °'hěn-le. *or* °'hěn-shīn-le. ‖This is the meanest job I've ever done. wǒ yí-'shyàng méy dzwò-gwo dzèm-°'má-fan-de-'shèr. *or* °'bù-hǎw-'bàn-de-'shèr. *or* °'nán-'bàn-de-'shèr. *or* °'jyàw-rén-wéy-'nán-de-'shèr. ‖I felt mean about hurting her feelings that way. wǒ jyàw-tā 'nèm nán-'shèw, 'jēn shŕ jywé-de °méy-'yì-sz. *or* °bú-'dwèy. *or* °'dwèy-bu-'chǐ tā. *or* °'dwèy-bu-jù tā. ‖I feel better now, but I sure felt mean this morning. wǒ shyàn-dzày 'hǎw-dyǎr-le; jyěr 'dzǎw-chen wǒ kě 'jēn 'bye-nyew-de-hung.

No mean *is expressed in ways similar to some of the above, as* not small bù-'shǎw, not easy bù-'rúng-yi, *etc.* ‖That mountain range is no mean obstacle. yàw shyàng 'gwò nèy-dzwò-shān-'lǐng °'bú-shr 'rúng-yi-de-'shèr. *or* °'nán-je-ne. *or* °'nán-le chywù-le.

Means (*a method*) fár, *or* -fa *in combination with many verbs.* ‖We've got to find some means of getting him out of here. dzám yí-'dìng děy shyǎng-'fár bǎ-ta sùng 'byé-chùr-chywu.

By all means yí-'dìng. ‖By all means look up my brother when you get to Peiping. dàw-le běy-'píng yí-'dìng yàw jǎw wǒ-lǎw-'dì-chywu 'tán-tan, á!

By no means tsáy *or* jywé *or* bìng *followed by a negative.* ‖That's by no means the end of the matter. 'nèy-shèr tsáy méy-'wán-ne. *or* 'nèy-shèr 'tsáy bù-néng swàn 'wán-le-ne. *or* 'nèy-shèr 'jywé (*or* 'bìng) bù-néng swàn 'wán-le.

MEASURE. To measure *linear dimensions* 'lyáng-yi-lyang; (*specifically of length*) 'lyáng-yi-lyang (kàn) yěw 'dwō cháng; (*of width*) 'lyáng-yi-lyang (kàn) yěw 'dwō kwān; (*of height*) 'lyáng-yi-lyang (kàn) yěw 'dwō gāw; (*in inches*) 'lyáng-yi-lyang (kàn) yěw 'dwō-shǎw-'tswèn (*etc. for other units*); (*estimate by the eye*) 'gǔ-lyang (or 'gǔ-jì, or, *in Peiping*, 'gū-me) yí-shyàr yěw 'dwō cháng (*etc. for other dimensions or by various units*), or 'kàn-yi-kàn (or 'chyáw-yi-chyáw) yěw 'dwō cháng (*etc.*). ‖Use this ruler to do the measuring. ná jèy-ge-'chř láy 'lyáng-yi-lyang. ‖We'll have to measure the room before we buy the rug. děy bǎ 'wū-dz 'lyáng-yi-lyang dzày mǎy dì-'tǎn. ‖Measure it from here to there. tsúng-jèr dàw-'nàr lyáng-yi-lyang yěw 'dwō cháng. ‖Have you measured (yourself to see) how much cloth you'll need for the suit? nǐ 'lyáng-yi-lyang 'shēn-dz, kàn dzwò 'yī-shang děy yùng 'dwō-shǎw-'bù-le-ma? ‖He measured the distance with his eye. tā (shīn-li) °'gǔ-lyang (or °'gǔ-jì, or °'gū-me) -le yí-shyàr yěw dwō 'ywǎn. or °'gǔ-lyang (*etc.*) -le yí-shyàr yěw dwō-shǎw-'chř ywǎn. or tā 'kàn-le-kàn (or tā 'chyáw-le-chyáw) yěw dwō 'ywǎn.

To measure (*have linear dimensions of*) *is expressed only by stating the dimensions.* ‖This kitchen measures sixteen by ten feet. 'jèy-ge-chú-fáng °shř-'lyèw-chř-cháng 'shŕ-chř-'kwān. or °'cháng(-shya)-li yěw shŕ-'lyèw-chř, 'kwān(-shya)-li yěw 'shŕ-chř.

(*Measurement of the circumference of part of the body*) 'jēw-wéy. ‖What's your waist measure? nǐ 'yāw-nar 'jēw-wéy dwō-shǎw-'tswèn?

To measure (out) (*a specific quantity*). (*To measure out and pour out of the measuring container*) 'dàw-chú; (*to measure out and leave in the container*) 'chéng-chu. ‖First measure (out) a cup of sugar. shyān 'dàw-chu (or shyān 'chéng-chu) yì-bēy-'táng-lay.

A measure *of capacity is expressed by specific words for such measures,* as a peck measure (*or* a peck, *or* a peck of) děw. ‖Take the rice in this peck measure. bǎ-'mǐ ná jèy-ge-'děw chéng-je 'ná-chywu-ba.

Weights and measures dù, lyàng, héng; a system of weights and measures 'dù-lyàng-héng-'jř-du; the Chinese system of weights and measures 'jūng-gwo-'dù-lyàng-héng-'jř-du.

Full measure (*in weight*) gèw-'fèn-lyàng-de, shŕ-'dzú-de-'fèn-lyàng, shŕ-'dzú-de-'chèng, shŕ-'lyèw-lyàng-de-'chèng. ‖I always get full measure at that store. 'nèy-ge-pù-dz 'mày-gěy wǒ 'dūng-shi 'lǎw shř °gèw-'fèn-lyàng-de. or °shŕ-'dzú-de-'fèn-lyàng. or °shŕ-'dzú-de-'chèng. or hŕ-'lyèw-lyǎng-de-'chèng.

A measure (*in music*) pāy. ‖Begin singing after the four-measure introduction. 'sž-pāy yì-'wán jyèw 'chàng-chi-lay.

A measure (*law*) 'fǎ-lìng. ‖Taxes under the new measures will be very high. 'shīn-fǎ-lìng bǎ-shwèy hwèy 'tí-de hěn 'gāw-de.

'Measures (*methods of operation*) 'fāng-fa, 'shěw-dwàn; take strong measures láy 'yìng-de, yùng 'yìng(-dyar)-de-'shěw-dwàn. ‖The doctor took measures to stop the bleeding. dày-fu yùng-le shyē 'fāng-fa bǎ-shyē 'jř-jù. ‖We'll have to take strong measures. dzám děy láy 'yìng-de. or dzám děy yùng 'yìng-dyar-de-'shěw-dwàn.

In some measure 'dwō-shǎw. ‖The mistake was in some measure my fault. jèy-ge-tswèr 'dwō-shǎw °gēn-'wǒ yěw 'gwān-shi. or °shř yīn-wey 'wǒ nàw-chū-lay-de.

To a great measure yì-'dwō-bàr, yí-'dà-bù-fen. ‖To a great measure the plan was his idea. nèy-ge-'bàn-fa °yì-'dwō-bàr (or °yí-'dà-bù-fen) shř 'tā-shyǎng-chū-lay-de.

MEAT. rèw. ‖I want the meat well done. 'rèw wǒ 'shǐ-hwan já-de 'tèw-yì-dyar.

(*Of a nut*) rér.

(*Substance*) 'nèy-rúng. ‖There's very little meat in that book. nèy-běn-'shū 'méy-yew shéme-'nèy-rúng.

MEDICINE. yàw. ‖Did the doctor give you any medicine for your cold? nǐ shāng-'fēng, 'dày-fu gěy-ni 'yàw méy-yew? ‖Are you taking medicine? nǐ dzày chř-'yàw-ma?

To study medicine shywé-'yī; to practice medicine shíng-'yī. ‖He's practiced medicine here for twenty years. tā dzày-'jèr shíng-'yī shíng-le 'èr-shŕ-'nyán-le.

To take one's medicine (*figuratively*) chř 'kǔ-tew. ‖You started the quarrel; now take your medicine. shř-'nǐ shyàn yàw 'chǎw-de; shyàn-dzày nǐ-'dž-jǐ chř 'kǔ-tew-ba.

MEET (MET). 1. (*For the first time, especially by introduction*) jyàn(-'myàn), jyàn-jyan ('myàn), hwèy (-'myàn), hwèy-hwey ('myàn); *often expressed with* to introduce 'jyè-shàw, 'yǐn-jyàn. ‖I want you to meet her one of these days. 'gwò-lyǎng-tyān °wǒ jyàw nǐ-men jyàn-jyàn 'myàn. or °wǒ jyàw nǐ-men hwèy ge-'myàn. or °wǒ gěy nǐ-men 'jyè-shaw-jyè-shaw. or °wǒ gěy nǐ-men 'jyàn-jyan. or °wǒ gěy nǐ-men 'yǐn-jyàn-yǐn-jyan. ‖I'd like you to meet my friend Mr. Lù. (*Expressed desire, with Mr. Lù not present*) wǒ shyǎng gěy 'nǐ gēn wǒ-de-yí-wèy-shìng-'lù-de-péng-yew °'jyè-shaw jyè-shaw. or °'yǐn-jyàn-yǐn-jyan. or wǒ ywàn-yi nǐ gēn wǒ-de-shìng-'lù-de-péng-yew °'jyàn-yi-jyàn. or °'hwèy-yi-hwèy. or °'jyàn-jyàn ('myàr). or °'hwèy-hwey ('myàr). (*Actual introduction*) wǒ 'gěy nǐ-men °'jyè-shaw-jyè-shaw (or °'jyàn-yi-jyàn, or °'yǐn-jyàn-yǐn-jyan); jèy-shr wǒ-de-péng-yew-'lù-shyān-sheng. ‖When you've met and talked to him, you'll know what I mean. děng nǐ gēn-ta jyàn-le 'myàr, yì 'tán jyèw 'jř-daw wǒ-'shwō-de shř shéme-'yì-sz-le. ‖We've never met before, have we? dzám yǐ-'chyán 'méy-jyàn-gwo-ba? or °hwèy-gwo-ba? ‖Have we ever met! Why, we were brought up together! wǒm 'hwèy-gwo méy-yew! 'hǎw! wǒm yí-'kwàr jǎng-'dà-le-de! ‖Come over here; I want to have you meet a friend of mine. 'gwò-láy; wǒ gěy-ni 'jyè-shaw yí-wèy-'péng-yew. ‖I'd like to meet your friend. wǒ hěn 'shyǎng °'jyàn-jyan (or °'hwèy-hwey) nǐ-'nèy-wèy-'péng-yew. ‖We met once long ago. wǒm 'hǎw jyěw yǐ-'chyán °'jyàn-gwo (or °'hwèy-gwo) yí-tsż (-'myàr). ‖Haven't we met before? dzám dzày-'nǎr °'jyàn-gwò-ba? or °'hwèy-gwò-ba? ‖Have you two met before? nǐm-'lyǎng-ge-rén yǐ-'chyán °'hwèy-gwo-ma? or expressed as Were you two acquainted before? °'rèn-shr-ma? ‖I'm glad to meet you. is expressed as Long respected, long respected (your name). 'jyěw-yǎng jyěw-yǎng.

2. (*Get together as prearranged; informal, mainly of just two people*) jyàn, hwèy, (*Peiping*) pèng-'téw; (*informal, of more than two persons, when after meeting they go on elsewhere or do something*) hwèy-'chí, chywǔ-'chí; (*formal, large-scale*) 'jywù-jí, jywù-'hwèy, kāy-'hwèy. ‖I'll meet you (*one person*) there at eight. dzám 'bā-dyǎn dzày-nàr °'jyàn. or °'hwèy. or °'hwèy-'myàn. or °'jyàn-'myàn. or °'pèng-'téw. ‖I'll meet you all there at eight. wǒ 'bā-dyǎn 'dàw-nèr gēn nǐ-men °'jyàn-'myàn. or °'hwèy-'myàn. or °'hwèy-'chí. or °'jywù-'chí. ‖We'll meet at his place at eight and then go to the meeting together. dzám 'bā-dyǎn dzày 'tā-jyā °chywǔ-'chí (or, °'jywù-'chí, or °'jywù-'jí, or °'hwèy-'myàn), rán-hèw yí-'kwàr chywù kāy-'hwèy. ‖We're going to meet next Tuesday (*referring to a formal group*). dzám 'shyà-shīng-chī-'èr °kāy-'hwèy. or °'jywù-'hwèy.

3. (*Come across by chance*) 'ywù-jyàn, 'pèng-jyàn, *so etimes* 'kàn-jyàn. ‖Did you meet anyone on the road? dzày 'lù-shang °'kàn-jyan (or °'ywù-jyan or °'pèng-jyan) shéme-'rén-le méy-yew?

4. (*Receive, opposite of* see off; *at a station, etc.*) jyē; (*to go out of one's house to receive a visitor; a Chinese custom*) 'yíng-jyē; (*to welcome, formal*) 'hwān-yíng; *if A meets B in this sense, then B* yíng A. ‖Is anybody going to meet them at the train? yěw-rén dàw °'chē-shang (or °'chē-'jàn) chywù °'jyē (or °'yíng-jyē or °'hwān-yíng or °yíng) tā-men ma? ‖He came out to the gate to meet us. (*Informal*) tā dàw-le dà-'mén-nàr chywù 'jyē °wǒ-men. (*Formal*) °'yíng wǒ-men. or °'yíng-jyē wǒ-men. ‖A bus meets the train outside the station. hwǒ-'chē 'dàw de-shŕ-hew, yěw 'gūng-gùng-chì-'chē dzày chē-jàn-'wày-tew °'jyē. or expressed as There's a bus waiting. °'děng. ‖I've sent a car to meet him at the station. wǒ 'dǎ-fā-le yí-lyàng-'chē chywù dzày chē-'jàn-nàr °jyē-ta. or °'děng-ta.

5. *Miscellaneous uses.*

(*Of a court*) kāy-'tíng. ‖The **court** doesn't meet again until next week. fǎ-'ywàn shyà-shīng-'chī tsáy dzày kāy-'tíng.

(*Of a class*) shàng-'kè. ‖This class meets every Monday and Thursday. jèy-'bān měy-shīng-chī-'yī hé shīng-chī-'sż shàng-'kè.

(*Of rivers*) hé-'lyéw, hwèy-dzay yí-'kwàr, hé-dzay yí-'kwàr. ‖The two rivers meet below the city. lyǎng-dàw-'hé dzày chéng-'nèy-byar °hé-'lyéw. or °'hwèy-dzay yí-'kwàr. *etc.*

(*Of roads; if two roads combine*) 'hé-chéng 'yì-tyáw-'lù, 'bìng-chéng 'yì-tyáw-'lù, 'hé-dzày yí-'kwàr, 'bìng-dzày yí-'kwàr; (*if two or more roads intersect*) 'jyāw-chā, 'jyāw-chà; (*if three roads meet at approximately 60-degree angles without intersecting*) expressed as three-fork corner 'sān-chā-lù-'kěwr. ‖The two roads meet three miles from here. (*If they combine*) lí-'jèr 'sān-lǐ-dì 'lyǎng-tyáw-'lù °'hé- (or °'bìng-)chéng 'yì-tyáw-'lù. *etc.* (*If they cross*) lí-'jèr 'sān-lǐ-dì 'lyǎng-tyáw-'lù °'jyāw-chā. or °'jyāw-chà. ‖I'll meet you where the three roads meet. (*If they all intersect at a point*) dzám dzày 'sān-tyáw-'lù 'jyāw-chā-de-nàr 'jyàn. (*If they come together without crossing*) dzám dzày 'sān-chā-lù-'kěwr-nàr 'jyàn.

(*Of areas*) 'jyē-shang, fēn-'jyè. ‖My field meets his at that fence. wǒ-de-'dì gēn 'tā-de dzày nèy-dàw-'lí-ba-nàr °'jyē-shang. or °fēn-'jyè. ‖Our two fields meet at that fence. wǒm-'lyǎng-jyār-de-'dì dzày nèy-dàw-!lí-ba-nàr °'jyē-shang. or °fēn-'jyè.

To meet *bills* fù. ‖We have only enough to meet this month's bills. wǒm 'gāng gèw fù 'jèy-ywè-de-'kāy-shyāw(-de-chyán).

To meet *demands* gěy; (*only a demand for money*) gěy-de-'chǐ, gěy-de-'lyǎw. ‖Can you meet their demands? tām-'yaw-de nǐ 'dēw °néng 'gěy-ma? or °gěy-de-'chǐ-ma? or °gěy-de-'lyǎw-ma? ‖Did you agree to meet all their demands? tām-'yàw-de nǐ 'dēw 'dá-ying 'gěy-le-ma?

To meet one's death *is expressed as* to die sž. ‖She met her death in a street accident. tā dzày 'jyē-shang jyàw-'chē 'jwàng-sž-de. or °'yà-sž-de.

To meet with objections. ‖The measure met with objections from all sides. nèy-ge-'bàn-fa °gè- (or °'něy-)'fāng-myan-de-rén 'dēw bú-'dzàn-chéng.

To meet someone halfway (*compromise*). ‖I'll meet you halfway; you pay for the dinner but I'll buy the tickets for the show. OK? dzám 'dzèm-je-ba (or °dzám 'shéy yě byé 'jēng-le or °dzám 'shwāng-fang ràng-'bù-ba), 'nǐ gěy 'fàn-chyán, 'wǒ mǎy shì-'pyàw, 'hǎw-bu-hǎw?

Make ends meet. ‖He can barely make ends meet. *is expressed as* He barely manages to eat. tā 'yě jyěw-shr gāng gèw 'chŕ-de. *See also* MAKE.

A meet hwèy. ‖Are you going to the swimming meet? 'yéw-yǔng-bǐ-sày-'hwèy nǐ 'chywù-bu-chywù?

MELT. hwà; (*technical chemical term, and literary*) rúng; to melt *something* nùng-'hwà-le. ‖The ice in my glass has all melted. wó-'bēy-dz-li-de-'bīng dēw 'hwà-le. ‖The candy is melting from the heat. 'táng 'rè-de 'hwà-le.

To melt away (*of a crowd*) sàn. ‖The crowd melted away when the police came. jǐng-'chá láy-le dà-'jyā jyěw 'sàn-le.

MEMBER. hwèy-'ywán; *when referring to a member of an organization the specific name of which does not end in* hwèy, hwèy *is replaced by the element which is found at the end of the name of the organization.* ‖**What organizations are you a member of?** nǐ-shr shéme-'hwèy-de-hwèy-'ywán? ‖**Only members allowed.** 'jwān wéy hwèy-'ywán jr̄ 'yùng (*literary*). ‖**I'd like to be a member.** wǒ 'shyǎng dzwò hwèy-'ywán.

MEMORY. 'jì-shing; *or expressed verbally as* **to remember** jì, *or as* **to forget** wàng *or* 'wàng-ji, *or as* **to recall** 'shyǎng-chǐ-lay. ‖**My memory isn't very good.** wǒ-'jì-shing °bú-dà 'hǎw. *or* °tǐng 'hwày. ‖**My memory for names isn't very good.** wǒ jì réñ-'míng-dz lǎw jì-bu-'jù. ‖**His memory is bad** (*due to old age or some such condition*) tā ày 'wàng. *or* tā 'lǎw ày 'wàng. *or* tā ày wàng-'shr̀. *or* tā 'lǎw jì-bu-'jù. ‖**He has a clear memory of the accident.** nèy-shèr tā 'jì-de hén 'chīng-chu. ‖**Do you have any memory of that?** nèy-ge nǐ 'jì-de-ma? ‖**The old man lost his memory** (*entirely*). lǎw-'téwr 'shéme dēw °'wàng-le. *or* °bú-'jì-de-le. *or* °'jì-bu-'jù-le. ‖**That's never happened before in my memory.** jywù wǒ-°'jì-de-de, yǐ-chyán 'méy-yěw-gwo 'dzèm-yàng-de-'shèr. *or* wǒ 'bú-jì-de 'yěw-gwo 'dzèm-yàng-de-'shèr. ‖**I'll certainly have pleasant memories of this town** (*of having lived here*). wǒ 'jywé wàng-bu-'lyǎw (*or* wǒ yí-'dìng 'cháng jì-de, *or* wǒ yí-'dìng cháng shyǎng-chǐ-lay, *or* wǒ yí-'dìng wàng-bu-'lyǎw, *or* wǒ yí-'dìng bù-néng 'wàng-ji) dzày jèy-ge-dì-fang jù-de 'dwō-me yěw 'yì-sz. ‖**He can never put her out of his memory.** tā lǎw 'jì-je tā. *or* tā lǎw wàng-bu-'lyǎw tā. *or* tā lǎw 'bù-néng bǎ-tā 'wàng-le.

In memory of 'jì-nyàn. ‖**This tablet was put up in his memory.** jèy-ge-'páy-dz shr̀ wèy 'jì-nyan tā-de. ‖**This monument is erected in memory of the men who were killed in action for their country.** (*A statement*) nèy shr̀ 'jì-nyan-°'jèn-wáng-(*or* °'wèy-gwó-jywān-'chywū-de-)'gwān-bīng-lì-de-'béy. *or* (*The inscription*) 'jèn-wáng-'jyàng-shr̀-'jì-nyàn-'béy. *or* (*Literary*) 'wèy-gwó-'jywān-chywū-'jūng-hwén-jr̄-'béy.

MENTION. (*To speak*) shwō; (*to bring up*) tí, 'shwō-chǐ-láy. ‖**He didn't mention the price.** tā méy-shwō-'jyà. ‖**Did the teacher mention my name?** shyān-sheng tí wǒ-de-'míng-dz méy-yew? ‖**Now that you mention it,** (I remember) **I did hear him say that.** nǐ nèm yì-'shwō, jyàw wǒ 'shyǎng-chi-lay-le; tā 'jēn nèm shwō láy-je. ‖**Don't mention it in his presence.** jèy-ge dzày 'tā myàn-chyán kě byé 'shwō. ‖**Don't mention it!** 'shyǎw-shèr, jr̄-bu-de yì-'tí. *or* 'shyǎw yì-sz. *or* 'méy shéme.

MERCHANT. shāng, shāng-rén. ‖**Who are the leading merchants of this town?** jèy-ge dì-fang °'dà-shāng-rén dēw shr̀ 'shéy? *or* °'dà-shāng-jyā dēw yěw 'něy-jǐ-jyār?

    Merchant ship (shāng-)chwán.

MERE (MERELY). *Expressed adverbially as* **only** 'bú-gwo *or* **entirely** 'wán-chywán, 'chwén-tswèy, *or* (*with a negative*) yì-'dyǎr yě. ‖**This is a mere formality.** jèy 'bú-gwo shr̀ °děy 'jīng dzèm-ge-'shěw-shywù jyèw shr̀-le. *or* °jàw 'gwéy-jywu děy dzèm 'bàn. ‖**This is merely red tape.** jèy 'bú-gwo shr̀ 'lì-shíng-gūng-'shr̀ jyèw 'shr̀-le. ‖**I ran into him by the merest chance.** wǒ 'pèng-jyan tā 'wán-chywán shr̀ 'ywùn-chi. *or* wǒ yì-'dyǎr yě (*or* wǒ 'wán-chywán) méy-shyǎng-'dàw hwèy 'pèng-jyan tā.

    See also **ONLY, JUST.**

MESSAGE. (*Oral*) hwà; (*written*) shìn, shyèr; (*note*) tyáwr. ‖**Is there a message for me?** yěw-rén gěy-wo lyéw-'hwà méy-yew? ‖**I want to leave a message.** wǒ yàw lyéw ge-'tyáwr. ‖**Could you take a message?** láw-'jyà, gěy tā lyéw-ge-'hwàr, shíng-ma?

    (*Significant idea*) 'dàw-li. ‖**His book has a strong message.** tā-de-'shū-li yěw hěn-'shēn-de 'dàw-li.

METAL. tyě (*which usually means iron*); **the metals** wǔ-'jīn. ‖**I'd rather have the metal desk.** wǒ 'ywàn-yi yàw nèy-ge-'tyě-iwō-dz.

METHOD. fá-dz, 'bàn-fa; fāng-fa; **method of X-ing** X-fǎ *or* (*if X is a longer expression in Chinese*) X-de-'bàn-fa. ‖**Your method here is new to me.** nǐ 'jèy-ge-bàn-fa wǒ yǐ-'chyán 'dàw bù-jr̄-'dàw. ‖**I don't understand your method of bookkeeping.** wǒ bù-'dǔng nǐ-jì-'jàng-de-'fá-dz. ‖**He's learning the language much quicker by this new method.** tā yùng jèy-ge-'shīn-'fá-dz shywé jèy-jǔng-'hwà bǐ yǐ-'chyán shywé-de 'kwày-dwō-le.

MIDDLE. (*Of a space*) dāng-'jyàr, dāng-'jūng, jūng-'jyàr. ‖**You'll find them in the middle room.** tām dēw dzày °dāng-'jyàr-de- (*or* °dāng-'jūng-de-, *or* °jūng-'jyàr-de-)nèy-jyān-'wūr-li-ne. *or* nǐ dàw dāng-'jyàr-de- (*etc.*) 'wūr-li 'jyèw 'jǎw-jaw tām-le. ‖**It's in the middle of the street.** dzày 'jyē-de-°dāng-'jūng (*or* °dāng-'jyàr, *or* °jūng-'jyàr) nèy-'kwàr. ‖**Put the vase in the middle of the table.** bǎ hwā-'píng bǎy-dzày 'jwō-dz-de-dāng-'jūng. ‖**He drove in the middle of the road.** tā dzày 'lù-de-dāng-'jūng-nàr kāy-°hē. ‖**Take the middle road.** dzěw dāng-'jūng-de (*or* dzěw jūng-'jyàr-de)-nèy-tyáw-'lù. ‖**He parts his hair in the middle.** tā-'téw-fa dzày dāng-'jūng °fēn-de. *or* °fēn-kāy. ‖**The middle part of the Yangtze Valley is very densely populated.** 'cháng-jyāng-lyéw-'ywù-dāng-'jūng-yí-dày rén-kěw hěn 'mì.

    (*Of an action*) *is expressed as* **just then** (*doing something*) 'jèng *or* 'jèng-dzày; *or as* **not finished** méy . . . 'wán; *or as* **half done** . . . (dàw) yí-'bàr *or* . . . dàw bàn-'jyér-shang. ‖**I'm in the middle of packing.** wǒ 'jèng dǎ 'shíng-li. *or* wǒ 'jèng-dzày dǎ 'shíng-li. *or* wó dǎ 'shíng-li gāng dǎ-°le yí-'bàr. *or* °dàw bàn-'jyér-shang. ‖**In the middle of the battle our planes arrived.** 'nèy-jàng jèng °'dǎ-je (*or* °'dǎ-dàw yí-'bàr de-shf-hew) wǒm-de-fēy-'jī dàw-le. ‖**Don't in-**

terrupt me in the middle of my work.　wǒ 'jèng dzwò-
'shèr (or wǒ 'jèng-dzày dzwò-'shèr, or wǒ-shèr jèng
dzwò-dàw yí-'bàr, or wǒ-shèr jèng dzwò-dàw bàn-
'jyér-shang), byé 'jyǎw-wǒ. ‖He broke off in the middle of a sentence.　tā yí-jywù-'hwà °méy-shwō-'wán
(or °shwō-le yí-'bàr, or °shwō-dàw bàn-'jyér-shang)
jyèw bù-'shwō-le. ‖They called him away while he was
in the middle of dinner.　tā 'jèng chī-je 'fàn (or tā
'jèng-dzày chī-je 'fàn, or tā chī-'fàn gāng chī-dàw
yí-'bàr) tām jyèw bǎ-tā jyàw 'dzěw-de.

　In the middle (*involuntarily involved*) *is expressed
as* (*physically*) in the middle (*see first paragraph
above*). ‖A fight started and I was right in the middle.
tām dǎ-chī 'jyà-lay de-shí-hew °wǒ jèng dzày dāng-
'jūng. or °bǎ-wǒ 'jyā-dzày dāng-'jūng-le. (*etc.*)

　In the middle (*behind the eight-ball*) *is expressed in
the same way or as* getting the blame from both sides
shèw 'jyā-gan-'chyèr. ‖That leaves me in the middle.
nèm-je jyèw bǎ-wo °gē- (or °jyā-, or °lyàw-)dzày
dāng-'jūng-le. or nèm-je 'wǒ děy dzày-nàr shèw 'jyā-
gan-chyèr.

　In the middle of (*in the thick of, involved in*) jyā-
'rù, dzày 'lǐ-tew gwǒ-je, 'gwǒ-dàw 'lǐ-tew-chywu.
‖He always manages to get in the middle of a fight.
yì yěw dǎ-'jyà-de-'shèr tā jwěn °jyā-'rù. or °dzày
'lǐ-tew gwǒ-je. or °'gwǒ-dàw li-tew-chywu.

　Around the middle (*of the body*) *is expressed by
reference to* the waist yāw or the belt 'dù-dz. ‖He's
put on weight around the middle.　tā-'yāw-nar 'tsū-le.
or tā-'dù-dz 'dà-chǐ-lay-le. or (*More polite, He's put on
weight*) tā fā-'fú-le.

　Of middle height. ‖He's of middle height.　tā 'jūng-
děng-'shēn-lyang. or ā 'bù-gāw-bù-'ǎy-de.

　Middle school (*high school*) 'jūng-shywé. ‖He's still
in middle school.　tā háy dzày 'jūng-shywé-ne.

　Middle-aged 'jūng-nyán. ‖He's middle-aged.　tā shì
ge-'jūng-nyán-rén.

　The Middle Ages 'jūng-shǐ-'jì.

　The middle road *or* the middle course (*not extreme*).
‖Take the middle course.　yàw 'bù-pyān bù-'yǐ tsáy
hǎw. or yàw shíng 'jūng-yúng-jī-'dàw tsáy 'dwèy.

MIGHT. (*Possibility*) kě-yi, hwèy, néng, *with* perhaps
'yě-shywu. ‖You might try to reach him at home.　nǐ
'yě-shywu kě-yi wàng tā-'jyā-lǐ chywù 'jǎw-ta. ‖I
might be there.　wǒ 'yě-shywu hwèy 'láy. ‖You might
have changed your mind if you'd heard all the facts.
nǐ yàw-shr 'jī-daw-le 'swǒ-yěw-de-shī-'shí, 'yě-shywu
hwèy gǎy-'byàn nǐ-de-'yǐ-sz.

　(*Strength*) 'chì-li. ‖He tried with all his might to
push the car onto the road.　tā yùng-'jìn-le tā-de-
'chì-li yàw bǎ chì-'chē twēy-daw 'lù-shang chywù.

MIGHTY. (*Strong*) hěn-'dà-de. ‖He made a mighty
effort to swim over to the boat.　tā yùng-le hěn-'dà-
de-'jyěr fú-daw 'chwán-nar chywù.

　(*Very*) hěn; (*extremely*) shí-'dzày tày. ‖I'm mighty
glad to see you.　wǒ hěn 'gāw-shìng 'jyàn-je-le nín.

‖He's done mighty little work today.　tā-'jīn-tyan
dzwò-de-'shǐ shí-'dzày tày 'shǎw.

MILE.　yīng-'lǐ; Chinese mile lǐ (*see Appendix B*). ‖It's
three miles away.　yěw 'sān-yīng-lǐ-'lù ywǎn. ‖The
speed limit here is thirty miles an hour.　sù-'dù 'měy-
dyǎn-jūng bù-néng gwo 'sān-shr-yīng-lǐ.

MILK.　nǎy; *cow's milk* nyéw-'nǎy. ‖Is the milk fresh?
nyéw-'nǎy 'shīn-shyān-bu-shīn-shyān?

　(*Of a coconut*) jī. ‖Will you help me get the milk out
of this coconut?　'bāng 'máng bǎ jèy-ge-'yē-dz-de-'jī
'nùng-chu-lay, hǎw-ma?

　To milk a cow jǐ nyéw-'nǎy. ‖Do you know how to
milk a cow?　nǐ 'hwèy-bu-hwèy jǐ nyéw-'nǎy? ‖Is it
time to do the milking?　shr 'jǐ-nyéw-'nǎy-de-shí-
hewr-ma?

　To milk (*figuratively*) lēw, 'chīn-twēn. ‖The officials
milked the treasury year after year.　yì-nyán-yì-
'nyán-de jī-'ywán-men lēw-le bù-'shǎw-gūng-'kwǎn.

MILL.　(*Machine*) coffee mill mwò-jyā-'fēy-de-jī-chi;
X mill mwò-'X-de-jī-chi.

　(*Establishment for grinding, particularly grain*)
mwò-'fáng. ‖There's a flour mill the other side of the
bridge.　chyáw-de-'nèy-byan yěw ge-myàn-'fěn-mwò-
'fáng.

　To mill (*grind*) mwò. ‖The baker here mills his own
flour.　jèr-de dzwò-myàn-'bāw-de 'dz̀-jǐ mwò myàn-
'fěn.

　(*Manufacturing plant*) gūng-'chǎng; *or* -chǎng *if
type of plant is specified*. ‖How many people work in
the mill?　jèy-ge-gūng-'chǎng-li yěw 'dwō-shaw-rén
dzwò-'gūng? ‖They're building a new cotton mill on
the edge of town.　dzày jèy-ge-'dì-fang-de-'byān-jìng
tām shyǎng-yàw 'bàn yí-ge-'myán-hwā-'chǎng.

　(*To manufacture or produce*) chū. ‖How much steel
does that plant mill per month?　nèy-ge-gūng-'chǎng
yí-ge-ywè chū 'dwō-shaw-gāng?

　To mill around *or* about 'jǐ-láy-'jǐ-chywù, 'jwàn-láy-
'jwàn-chywù. ‖The crowd milled around waiting for
the parade to begin.　nèy-chywún-'rén 'jǐ-láy-'jǐ-
chywù, 'děng-je yéw-'shíng 'kāy-shǐ.

　To have been through the mill (*figuratively*) 'gwò-
láy-le. ‖He's been through the mill already and he
knows what he's talking about.　tā-shr 'gwò-láy-rén,
tā-shwō-de dēw-shr yěw-'jīng-yàn-de-hwà.

MIND.　(*Mental faculty*). (*Brain*) 'nǎw-dz; (*thinking
power*) 'shīn-sz; (*thinking activity*) 'shīn-shywě;
(*thoughts, concentration; also means* heart) shīn;
(*memory*) 'jì-shing; *often expressed indirectly as* to
think shyǎng; a quick mind *also* 'jí-jr *or expressed as*
quick and clever 'jī-líng-de; a good mind *also expressed
as* intelligent líng; *also other indirect expressions*. ‖He
has a good mind.　tā-'nǎw-dz tǐng 'hǎw. or tā-'jì-shing
tǐng 'hǎw. or tā-'shyǎng-de (or tā-'shīn-sz) tǐng °'shì-
mì. or °'jēw-daw. or tā hěn 'líng. ‖He has a very quick

mind. tā hĕn 'jī-ling-de. or tā-'shīn-sź tĭng 'kwày-de. or tā hĕn yĕw 'jí-jr̀. or tā shéme-'shèr yí 'kàn jyèw jr̀-dàw shíng-bu-'shíng. or tā-'shyǎng-de tĭng 'kwày-de. or tā shéme-'shèr yì 'shyǎng jyèw yĕw 'bàn-fǎ. ‖He has a one-track mind. tā-shīn-li lǎw 'ràw-bu-gwo 'wār-lay. or tā 'sź shīn-'yǎr. or tā 'jìng dzwān nyéw-'jī-jyaw. ‖My mind isn't clear on what happened. chū-'shèr-de-'chíng-shíng wǒ(-'shīn-li) bú-dà 'chīng-chu. ‖His mind isn't on his work. tā-'shīn-li yĕw byé-de-'shèr. or tā 'jèy-jèr dzwò-'shèr 'shīn-shén bú-'dìng. or (Literary quotation) tā-'shīn bú-'dzày-yan. ‖He doesn't keep his mind on his work. tā dzwò-'shèr de-shŕ-hew, 'shīn-li yĕw byé-de-'sher. or tā dzwò-'shèr °'shīn-shén bú-'dìng. or °bù-jwān-'shīn. or °bù-hǎw-'hāwr-de. or tā-'shīn bú-'dzày-yan. ‖Keep your mind on your work. 'byé gwǎn shyán-'shr̀. or hǎw-'hāwr-de dzwò nǐ-'dž-jǐ-de-shèr. or yùng-'shīn dzwò-'shr̀. or dzwò-'shr̀ shīn yàw 'jwān.

To have in mind. (Of a person) 'shīn-li yĕw; (of a person; to mean in saying something) 'jr̀-je; (of an action; think about or plan) shyǎng or 'dǎ-swàn. ‖Do you have anyone in mind for the job? nèy-ge-'wèy-jr nǐ°-'shīn-li yĕw 'rén-le-ma? or 'shyǎng gěy-'shéy-ne? or nèy-ge-'shèr nǐ shyǎng °jyàw-'shéy dzwò-ya? or °chū hé-'shr̀-de-'rén láy-le-ma? ‖Did you have her in mind when you said that? nǐ shwō 'nèy-ge de-shŕ-hew shr̀-bu-shr jr̀-je 'tā shwō-de? ‖What do you have in mind to do with him? 'néy-ge-rén nǐ °shỳang (or °'dǎ-swàn) yàw jyaw-tā 'dzěm-je? or 'ney-ge-rén-de-shèr nǐ °shyǎng (or °'dǎ-swàn) 'dzěm bàn? ‖What did you have in mind? (to get or buy). nǐ 'dǎ-swàn yàw (or mǎy) 'shéme-yàngr-de?

To keep in mind (of a thing) gē- (or fàng-) dzày 'shīn-shang (hǎw-le); (take care of) lyéw-'shén (hǎw-le); (to remember) 'jì(-de) or (not forget) 'bú-hwèy 'wàng-le(-de); (of a person, do something for) gěy . . . 'bàn-yi-ban. ‖I'll keep it in mind. wǒ 'jì-de. or wǒ 'jì-je. or wǒ 'bú-hwèy 'wàng-le-de. or wǒ lyéw-'shén hǎw-le. or wǒ gē- (or wǒ fàng-) dzày 'shīn-shang hǎw-le. ‖I'll keep you in mind. 'nǐ-de-shèr wǒ °gěy-nǐ 'lyéw dyǎr-'shén. or °fàng- (or gē-) dzày 'shīn-shang hǎw-le. or wǒ gěy-nǐ 'bàn.

To have on one's mind (with something or what) yĕw 'shīn-shr, 'shīn-li yĕw-'shèr; (to say) yĕw-'hwà. ‖What's on (or What do you have on) your mind? nǐ yĕw shéme-'shīn-shr̀? or nǐ-'shīn-li yĕw 'shéme-shèr? or nǐ shyǎng-'shéme-ne? ‖I think he's got something on his mind. wǒ kàn-tā °'shīn-li yĕw (dyǎr-shéme)-'shèr. or °yĕw 'shīn-shr̀. ‖He's got something on his mind, but he hasn't spoken up. tā yĕw-'hwà 'méy-shwō-chū-'láy. ‖She must have had something on her mind today. tā 'jīn-tyān yí-'dìng shr̀ 'shīn-li yĕw shéme-'shr̀-lay-je. ‖I've got too much on my mind. wǒ-'shīn-li-'shèr tày 'dwō. or jyàw-wǒ dān-'shīn-de-'shèr tày 'dwō.

To make up one's mind is expressed by various constructions which include the element meaning **to determine** dìng. ‖Have you made up your mind what to do about him yet? 'nèy-ge-rén-de-'shèr nǐ °'shyǎng-chū-le (or °yĕw-le, or °'jywé-dìng-le) yí-'dìng-de-'bàn-fa-le-ma? or °dìng-'hǎw-le (or °shyǎng-'dìng-le, or °jywé-'dìng-le, or °ná-'dìng-le 'jú-yi, or °dǎ-'dìng-le 'jú-yi) yàw dzěm 'bàn-le-ma? ‖I've made up my mind to go, and nobody's going to stop me now. wǒ 'yǐ-jīng °ná-'dìng-le 'jú-yi-le (or °dǎ-'dìng-le 'jú-yi-le, or °'jywé-dìng-le) 'fēy chywù bù-'kě, 'shéy yě bù-néng 'bú-jyàw-wo 'chywù. or expressed as I've said I was going to go, and . . . . wǒ 'shwō yàw 'chywù jyèw 'shéy yě bù-néng °'bú-jyàw-wǒ 'chywù. or °'lán-wo. or °bǎ-wo 'lán-jù.

Have one's mind set on yí-'dìng yàw, 'jywé-dìng yàw, dǎ-'dìng-le-'jú-yi yàw, ná-'dìng-le 'jú-yi yàw, 'yì-shīn yàw, fēy yàw . . . bù-'kě. ‖She's got her mind set on going shopping today. tā yí-'dìng yàw 'jyĕr chywù mǎy 'dūng-shi.

Not be able to get °one's mind off or **°off one's mind** or **°out of one's mind** ('shīn-li) lǎw °'nyàn-ji-je, or °'dyàn-ji-je, or °'dyàn-nyan-je, or °'shyǎng-je. or °'gwà-nyan-je, or °'wàng-bu-'lyǎw, or (of a thing, thinking over) °'pán-swàn, or (of a person) °'chyān-gwà-je. ‖I can't get my mind off my office work at night. dàw-le 'yè-li, wǒ-'shīn-li háy-shr lǎw 'nyàn-ji-je 'gūng-shr̀-'fáng-li-de-'shèr. ‖I can't get her out of my mind. wǒ(-'shīn-li) lǎw 'dyàn-ji-je tā.

To change one's mind gǎy 'jú-yi; (not want it so) 'bú-ywàn-yi 'nèm-je. ‖I thought I'd go along with them, but I changed my mind. wǒ 'ywán-láy shyǎng gēn-tām yí-kwàr 'gàn-lay-je, kě-shr 'hèw-láy °gǎy-le 'jú-yi-le. or °'bú-ywàn-yì nèm-je-le.

To slip one's mind is expressed by saying that the person **forgets** (gěy)'wàng. ‖I planned to do it, but it slipped my mind. wǒ 'dǎ-swàn (or wǒ 'shyǎng) dzwò-lay-je, kě-shr yí-shyà-dz (gěy) 'wàng-le.

To one's mind (from one's point of view) jywù '. . . kàn; '. . . jywé-je; '. . . kàn. ‖To my mind, the job will take at least a week. jywù 'wǒ kàn (or 'wǒ jywé-je, or 'wǒ kàn) jèy-shèr 'jr̀-shǎw děy yì-shīng-'chī tsáy dzwò-de-'wán. ‖To my mind he seems sort of simple. 'wǒ jywé-je (or jywù 'wǒ kàn, or 'wǒ kàn) tā yĕw-dyar 'shǎ-bu-jyēr-de.

Be out of one's mind or **lose one's mind** fēng. ‖She's practically out of her mind with worry. tā 'chéw-de (or tā 'jí-de) jyǎn-'jŕ yàw 'fēng-le. ‖I thought I'd lose my mind with all that noise. chǎw-de 'nèm lì-hay, dēw kwày bǎ-wǒ chǎw-'fēng-le.

Be simple-minded shǎ. ‖He's a bit simple-minded. tā yĕw-dyar 'shǎ.

To know one's own mind. ‖He doesn't know his own mind. tā ná-bú-'dìng jú-yi. or tā dǎ-bú-'dìng jú-yi. or tā 'yéw-yí-bù-'jywé. or tā lǎw 'chéw-chú-bú-'dìng-de. or tā `lǎw 'sān-shīn-èr-'yì-de. or tā lǎw 'bù-jr̀-dàw dzěm-je 'hǎw.

To call to mind or **to bring to mind** is expressed by saying that the person **thinks of** 'shyǎng-chǐ-lay. ‖That calls to mind a story I know. 'nèm yì shwō, wǒ 'shyǎng-chǐ-lay °ge-'shyàw-hwàr. or (a true story) °yí-jyàn-'shèr.

A meeting of minds *is expressed as* a decision (on method) 'bàn-fa, *or as* a conclusion 'jyē-gwǒ, *or as* to agree túng-'yì. ‖Let's see if we can't reach a meeting of minds on this thing. 'kàn-kan dzám 'néng-bunéng bǎ jèy-jyàn-shèr 'shāng-lyang chū ge-°'bàn-falay. *or* °'jyē-gwǒ-lay. *or* 'kàn-kan dzám dzày 'jèy-jyàn-shèr-shang 'néng-bu-néng túng-'yì.

To have a mind of one's own. ‖He has a mind of his own. (*Of a child; a compliment*) *is expressed as* He makes his own decisions. tā 'nà-tsáy-jyàw yěw 'jú-yine. *or as* He can think of ways to do things. tā tǐng néng 'dž-jǐ shyǎng 'bàn-fa-de. *or* (*Of a child: not a compliment*) *expressed as* He's disobedient. tā bù-tīng-'hwà. *or* (*Of an adult*) *expressed as* He doesn't listen to what anyone says. tā 'shéy-de-hwà yě bù-'tīng. *or as* He doesn't listen to other people's advice. tā bù-tīng rén-'chywàn. *or as* He's very stubborn. tā-rén tǐng 'nìng-de. *or as* No matter what you say to him, he always follows his own advice. píng nǐ 'dzěm gēn-tā shwō, tā lǎw yěw yí-'dìng jř-'gwēy.

To have half a mind to *or* to have a good mind to 'hěn shyǎng. ‖I've got half a mind to leave tomorrow. wǒ 'hěn shyǎng 'myér jyèw 'dzěw. ‖I've got half a mind to give him a good scolding. wǒ 'hěn shyǎng 'shwō (*or* 'mà) tā yí-'dwèn. ‖I've got a good mind to quit. wǒ 'hěn shyǎng bú-'gàn-le.

Give *someone* a piece of one's mind 'shwō (*or* 'mà) ... yí-'dwèn.

To mind (*take charge of; of persons or things*) kān, 'jàw-ying; (*of persons*) gwǎn; (*of things*) 'jàw-lyàw. ‖Mind the store for me while I go to lunch, will you? láw-'jyà, wǒ chywù chř-'fàn de-shf-hew, gěy-wǒ °'jàw-ying-je-dyar (*or* °'kān-je-dyar, *or* °'jàw-lyàw-je-dyar) pù-dz. ‖Will you mind the baby for a while? nǐ gěy-wǒ °'kān- (*or* °'gwǎn-, *or* °'jàw-ying-)yi-hwěr shyǎw-'nár, shíng-ma? ‖Mind your own business. *is expressed* (*mildly*) *as* Mind other people's business less. 'shǎw gwǎn °'byé-rén-de-'shèr. *or* °'shyán-shèr. *or* (*More strongly*) *as* Why should you mind (this)? nǐ 'gwǎn-de-'jáw-ma? *or as* What's it to you? ày- (*or* yěw-) 'nǐ shéme-'shèr?

To mind (*obey; of obeying a person*) tīng-'hwà, tīng ... -de-'hwà; (*be good*) hǎw; (*of obeying laws*) shěw. ‖Mind your mother. tīng nǐ-'mǔ-chin-de-'hwà. *or* 'mǔ-chin-shwō-de-'hwà yàw 'tīng-je. ‖The child won't mind anybody. shyǎw-'hár gēn-'shéy dēw 'hǎw. ‖He doesn't mind. tā bù-tīng-'hwà. ‖You have to mind the rules when you drive here. dzày 'jèy-kwàr kāy-'chē °děy shěw 'gwēy-jywu. *or* °děy shěw-'fǎ. *or* °bù-neng bù-shěw 'gwēy-jywu.

To mind (*be careful*) 'shyǎw-shīn; (*watch out for*) 'chyáw-je *or* 'kàn-je *or* 'dī-fang-je. ‖Mind how you cross the street. gwò-'jyē-de-shf-hew 'shyǎw-shīn-je-dyar. ‖Mind the traffic when you cross the street. gwò-'jyē-de-shf-hew °'chyáw- (*or* °'kàn-, *or* °'dī-fang-)je-dyar 'chē-a-'mǎ-de.

To mind (*care about or dislike; of active dislike*) (shīn-li) 'dzày-hu, (shīn-li) bú-'ywàn-yi; not mind (*be agreeable*) *is expressed as* not matter (*see* MATTER),

or as be OK shíng. ‖Are you sure you don't mind? nǐ 'jēn bú-'dzày-hu-ma? ‖Do you mind working with him? nǐ gēn-'tā yí-kwàr dzwò-'shř °shīn-li 'ywàn-yi-ma? *or* °shīn-li 'dzày-hu-bu-dzày-hu? ‖I wouldn't mind taking the trip alone, except that I don't have enough money with me. wǒ 'dž-gěr chywù yí-tàng dàw bú-yàw-'jǐn (*or* wǒ 'dž-gěr chywù yí-tàng dàw yě 'méy-shéme, *or* wǒ dàw 'bú-dzày-hu dž-'gěr chywù), 'bú-gwo wǒ-'shēn-shang dày-de-'chán bú-gèw 'hwāde. ‖I don't mind going alone. wǒ dž-'gěr chywù, jyèw dž-'gěr chywù-ba. *or* wǒ dž-'gěr chywù yě 'méyshéme. *or* 'méy gwǎn-shi (*or* méy-shéme), wǒ dž-'gěr chywù 'hǎw-le. ‖Would you mind working over there for a few minutes? láw-'jyà dàw 'nèy-byàr-chywu dzwò-hwer, 'shíng-bu-shíng?

Never mind. *meaning* It isn't important 'bú-yàw-jǐn. *or* 'swàn-le. *or* 'méy-shéme. *or* 'méy-shèr. *or meaning* You don't have to do it 'bú-yùng gwǎn-le. *or* (*Said in a sour way*) 'hǎw-ba! *or* 'bù-gwǎn jyèw bù-'gwǎn-ba! *or* 'ày gwǎn bù-'gwǎn-ba. ‖Never mind that! (*That's enough, let's have order, etc.*) 'nèy yùng-bu-jáw nǐ tsāw-'shīn. ‖Never mind what THEY say. 'byé-gwǎn 'tām dzěm shwō. *or* 'béng 'lǐ 'tām. *or* tām dzěm 'shwō jyèw jyàw-tām 'shwō-chywu-ba. *or* tām 'ày dzěm shwō, dzěm 'shwō-ba. *or* 'swéy tām dzěm 'shwō-chywu-ba.

MINE. (*Belonging to me*) *see* I.

(*Of minerals*) kwàng; iron mine tyě-'kwàng; X mine X-'kwàng. ‖Who owns this mine? jèy-ge-'kwàng shř 'shéy-de? ‖We get our coal from the mines around here. wǒm-de-'méy shř 'fù-jìn-de-méy-'kwàng-li láyde.

To mine *a mineral, expressed as* to produce *such-and-such* a mineral product chū ... -'kwàng-wù *or as* to open (*or* operate) *such-and-such* a mine kāy ... -'kwàng. ‖What do they mine around here? 'jèr 'chū shéme-'kwàng-wù? ‖This company has mined iron here for years. 'jèy-ge-gūng-'sž dzày-'jèr kāy-le-'kwàng kāy-le hǎw-shyē-'nyán-le.

(*Rich source; figurative*). ‖He's a mine of information. *is expressed as* He knows everything. tā 'shéme dēw 'jř-daw. ‖This book is a mine of information. *is expressed as* This book contains a very great many facts. jèy-běn-'shū-li yěw hěn-dwō-hěn-'dwō-de-shř-'shř. ‖He's a mine of information about this localitv. *is expressed as* He's a map. tā-shř ge-dì-lǐ-'tú.

MINUTE. (*One-sixtieth of an hour*) jūng *with measure* fēn; (*one-sixtieth of a degree*) fēn. ‖I'll be back in five minutes. wǒ 'wǔ-fēn-jūng jyèw 'hwéy-lay. ‖They can't wait more than twenty minutes. tām 'jř néng 'děng 'èr-shr-fēn-jūng. ‖The ship is five degrees and forty minutes off its course. 'chwán 'dzěw-chū-le 'lù-shyàn 'wǔ-dù-'sž-shr-fēn.

(*Short period of time*) hwěr. ‖He'll only be a minute. tā 'jř yàw yì-'hwěr. ‖We can only see you for a minute. wǒm 'jř néng gēn-nín tán yì-'hwěr. ‖Can you give me a minute of your time? *is expressed as* **Do you have some leisure so I can have a word with you?** nín yěw 'gūng-fu-ma? wǒ 'gēn-nín shwō yí-jywù-'hwà.

The minute (that) yī . . ., jyèw . . . . ‖**Call the hotel the minute you get home.** ni yí hwéy-'jyā, jyèw gěy lywǔ-'gwǎn-li dǎ dyàn-'hwà. ‖**You'll know the house the minute you see it.** nǐ yí 'kàn-jyan nèy-ge-'fáng-dz jyèw 'rèn-de-le.

The last minute 'lír-lyǎw. ‖**Don't leave everything to the last minute.** byé bǎ 'shéme dēw 'děng-dàw 'lín-lyǎw tsáy dzwò.

Minutes (*of a meeting*) 'jì-lù. ‖**Who's taking the minutes of the meeting?** kāy-'hwèy 'shéy ji 'jì-lù? ‖**Have the minutes of the last meeting been read yet?** 'shàng-tsž-kāy-'hwèy-de-'jì-lù yǐ-jing 'nyàn-le méy-yew?

Up to the minute dzwèy-'jìn-de. ‖**The news in this paper is up to the minute.** jèy-ge-bàw-'jř-li-de-'shīn-wén shř dzwèy-'jìn-de.

(*Small*) shyǎw. ‖**It's hard to read the minute print in this book.** 'shū-shàng-de-shyǎw-'dž hěn nán 'nyàn. ‖**The engineer knows every minute detail of the new machine.** jèy-ge-shīn-'jī-chi-de-rèn-shéme-'shyǎw-dì-fangr gūng-chéng-'shř dēw dǔng-de.

MIRROR. 'jìng-dz. ‖**Is there a mirror in the bathroom?** shǐ-lyǎn-'shř yěw yí-myàn-'jìng-dz-ma?

To be mirrored 'fǎn-jàw. ‖**The trees on the bank are mirrored in the lake.** 'hú-byān-de-'shù-de-'dàw-yǐng 'fǎn jàw-dzay 'shwěy-li.

To mirror (*figuratively*) 'fǎn-yìng.

MISS. (*Unmarried woman*) **Miss** . . . . 'shyáw-jye; (*very formal*) . . . 'nywǔ-shř; (*of a teacher, also means* **Mr.**) . . . 'shyān-sheng; *when calling a waitress, etc.,* **Miss** *is not expressed, or* 'èy, *an exclamation used in getting someone's attention, is used; among the younger people of China, the English word* **Miss** *is sometimes used.* ‖**This is Miss Jones.** (*In making an introduction*) jèy shř 'jēw-°shyáw-jye. *or* °nywǔ-shř. *or* °shyān-sheng. *or* (*In answer to* **Who is this?**) wǒ shìng 'jēw. *or* (*In answer to* **Is this Miss Jones?**) 'wǒ jyèw shř. ‖**We have three Miss Joneses here.** wǒm-jèr yěw sān-wèy-°'jēw-shyáw-jye. *or* °'shyáw-jye dēw shìng 'jēw. ‖**Miss Jones, come here.** 'jēw-shyáw-jye (*or,* Miss 'jēw), dàw-'jèr láy. ‖**Will you please sit over there, Miss?** (èy,) 'chǐng-nín °dzwò-dzày 'nàr-chywu. *or* °'dzày 'nèy-byar dzwò.

(*Not hit*). (*With a missile or bullet*) *is expressed by negative forms of* dǎ-'jùng, dǎ-'jáw, 'jùng; (*by collision*) 'jwàng, 'jwàng-jáw, 'jwàng-shang; **just miss** chà-'dyǎr (*or* chà-yi-'dyǎr, *or* shyàn-yì-'dyǎr) (méy-) °dǎ-shang; **miss by** *a certain distance* dǎ-de. (*or* jwàng-de) °chà-le . . . *or* °lí (*plus the place or thing*) yěw. . . . ‖**He missed twice, but** (*or* **After two misses**) **he finally made a hit.** 'lyǎng-shyàr dēw méy-dǎ-'jáw, dì-'sān-shyàr kě °dǎ-shàng-le. *or* °'dǎ-jáw-le. *or* °'jùng-le. ‖**That was pretty close, but a miss is as good**

as a mile. 'shyǎn kě 'jēn shyǎn; bú-gwo 'jī-shr méy-°dǎ-'jùng (*or* °dǎ-'jáw, *or* °'jwàng-jaw, *or* °'jwàng-shang) yě jyèw 'bú-swàn shéme-le. ‖**The truck just missed (hitting) the boy.** 'dà-chì-'chē ɤchà-'dyǎr (*or* °chà-yi-'dyǎr, *or* °shyàn-yi-'dyǎr) (méy-)bǎ shyǎw-hár 'jwàng-le. ‖**His shot missed the bird by at least five feet.** tā nèy-chyāng 'dǎ-de (nàr) lí-'nyǎwr 'jř-shǎw yěw 'wǔ-chř. ‖**His shot missed by at least five feet.** tā nèy-chyāng dǎ-de 'jř-shǎw chà-le 'wǔ-chř.

To miss *a chance* 'fàng-gwo-chywu; **never miss a chance to . . .** 'méy ge-shwō-'bū- . . .-de.` ‖**He never misses a chance to do a little business.** 'tā-ya, 'yì yěw ge-'jī-hwey dzwò dyǎr-'mǎy-mar, °'méy-yew 'fàng-gwo-chywu-de-'shř-hew. *or* °'méy-yěw 'fàng-gwo-chywu-de nèm yì 'shwō. *or* °'méy ge-shwō-°'bú-dzwò-de.`

To miss *a train* (*not make it*) méy-'gǎn-shang; (*be delayed so that it can't be made*) wù. ‖**Do you think I'll miss my train?** nǐ shyǎng wǒ 'hwèy °gǎn-bu-shang 'chē-ma? *or* °wù-le 'chē-ma?

To miss the mark *when speaking* 'jyàng-de ('wán-chywán) °'bù-jàw 'byān-jì. *or* °'bù-tyē-'tí. *or* °'bú-dwèy. *or* °'bú-shr nèm-hwéy-'shèr. ‖**The speaker missed the mark completely.** yǎn-'jyǎng-de-nèy-ge-rén 'jyǎng-de 'wán-chywán °'bù-jàw 'byān-jì. *or* °'bù-tyē-'tí. *or* °'bú-dwèy. *or* °'bú-shr nèm-hwéy-'shèr. (*See also next paragraph.*)

(*Not hear, or not understand*). (*Not hear at all*) *is expressed by negative forms of* tīng-'jyàn; (*not hear with understanding*) tīng-'dǔng *or* tīng-'míng-bay *or* tīng-'chīng-chu; (*not hear clearly*) tīng-'chīng-chu; (*not have an understanding of*) 'dǔng *or* 'míng-bay *or* 'chīng-chu. ‖**I missed that last remark.** 'gāng-shwō-de-nèy-jywù-'hwà wǒ méy-tīng-'jyàn.

(*Not see, or not find*). (*Not see*) *a negative with* 'chyáw-jyàn *or* 'kàn-jyàn; (*not find*) *a negative with* 'jǎw-jáw; *or expressed indirectly;* **don't miss (seeing)** byé 'wàng-le (*or* yàw 'jì-je, *or* yàw) 'kàn-kan. ‖**I missed you at the meeting last night.** dzwér 'wǎn-shang kāy-'hwèy wǒ méy-°'chyáw-jyàn nǐ. *or* °'jǎw-jaw nǐ. *or expressed as* **Hey! How come you weren't at the meeting last night?** hèy! dzwér 'wǎn-shang nèy-ge-'hwèy nǐ dzěm méy-'dàw-wa? ‖**I missed him at the hotel, so I went on to the station.** wǒ dàw lywǔ-'gwǎn-li méy °chyáw-jyàn (*or* °'jǎw-jaw) tā; (wǒ) jyèw yì-'jř dàw chē-'jàn chywù-le. *or expressed as* **When I got to the hotel he had already left, so . . .** wǒ dàw lywǔ-'gwǎn de-shŕ-hew tā yǐ-jing 'dzěw-le; . . . ‖**Don't miss seeing the Temple of Confucius when you get to that town.** dàw-le 'nèy-ge-'dì-fang, yí-'dìng °byé 'wàng-le (*or* °yàw 'jì-je, *or* °'yàw) kàn-kan kǔng-dz-'myàw. ‖**It's just around the next corner; you can't miss it.** 'yì gwǎy-'wārˋ jyèw 'shř; 'méy ge-jǎw-bu-'jáw-de.

‖**Be missing.** (*Lost*) 'dyēw-le, bú-'jyàn-le; (*not able to be found*) jǎw-bu-'jáw-le; (*gone*) 'méy-le; (*not here*) bú-'dzày-jèr; (*not yet arrived*) háy méy-'dàw;

for someone **to be missing** *something is expressed by saying that the thing is missing;* **missing in action** *is expressed as* **after the battle it was not clear whether he was dead or alive** dzwò-'jàn yǐ-'hèw 'shēng-sž bù-'míng. ‖**Is anything missing from your wallet?** nǐ-chyán-'bāwr-li-de-dūng-shi °yěw 'dyēw-de-ma? *or* °yěw bú-'jyàn-le-de-ma? *or expressed as* °**is everything there?** °dēw 'chywán-ma? *or* °dēw 'dzày-nàr-ma? ‖**Yes, I'm missing my passport.** 'dwèy-le, wǒ-de-hù-'jàw °bú-'jyàn-le. *or* °jàw-bu-'jáw-le. *or* °'méy-le. *or* °'dyēw-le. *or* °'bú-'dzày-ièr. ‖**He was reported missing in action.** yěw bàw-'gàw shwō tā dzwò-'jàn yǐ-'hèw 'shēng-sž bù-'míng.

(*To fail*) *see* **FAIL, SUCCEED.** ‖**You can't miss** (*of physical aim*) (nǐ) yí-'dìng °dǎ-de-'shàng. *or* °dǎ-de-'jáw. *or* °dǎ-de-'jùng. *or* (*in bombing*) °jà-de-'jáw. *or* (*of finding something*) °jàw-de-'jáw. *or* (*Because of a suggested procedure*) (nǐ) yí-'dìng °bàn-de-'hǎw. *or* °bàn-de-'dàw. *or* °nèng-de-'chéng. *or* (*Because of personal ability*) 'nǐ yí-'dìng °bàn-de-'hǎw. *or* °néng-'chéng. *or* °chéng-'gūng. *Or all of these alternants may be used in a construction such as* (nǐ) yí-'dìng bú-hwèy dǎ-bu-'shàng-de. *or* (*You must not miss this time*) 'jèy-tsž nǐ kě 'bù-néng bàn-'dzāw-le. ‖**After two misses, he finally made a hit** (*figuratively*). 'lyǎng-tsž dēw méy-'chéng; kě-shr dàw-'lyǎwr háy-shr °'chéng-le. *or* °'nèng-shang-le.

To miss one's guess tsāy-'tswò-le, tsāy-de bú-'dwèy; **unless I miss my guess** *is expressed as* **as I see it** jywù 'wǒ chyáw *or* jywù 'wǒ kàn. ‖**I missed my guess that time.** nèy-tsž wǒ tsāy-'tswò-le. *or* nèy-tsž wǒ tsāy-de-bú-'dwèy. ‖**Unless I miss my guess, we're going to run into some trouble.** jywù 'wǒ chyáw (*or* kàn), dzám yàw yěw 'má-fan-shèr.

To miss something (*worth while*) *is expressed as* **to lose a chance** shr̄ ge-'jī-hwey, *or as* **what a pity** (*that someone wasn't there*) kě 'shī; **not miss anything** *is expressed as* **it isn't interesting** méy 'yì-sz-de *or as* (*someone's not being there*) **doesn't matter** 'méy-shéme *or* **is all right** dàw-'hǎw. ‖**You sure missed something by not going with us.** nǐ jèy-tsž 'méy-gēn-wǒm dàw-nàr 'chywù 'jēn shr̄ °'shr̄-le ge-'jī-hwey. *or* °kě.'shī. ‖**Oh, you didn't miss anything by not going.** hāy! 'bú-chywù °yě 'méy-shéme. *or* °dàw-'hǎw. *or* hāy! 'tǐng méy 'yì-sz-de.

(*To be lonesome without*) *is expressed as* **think of** shyǎng. ‖**I'll miss you.** nǐ 'dzěw-le wǒ yí-'dìng yàw 'shyǎng nǐ-de. ‖**She missed him very much.** tā 'shyǎng-tā shyǎng-de 'lì-hay.

(*To be at a loss without*) ‖**I miss my car.** *is expressed as* **My car's not being here is a great inconvenience.** wǒ-'chē bú-'dzày-jèr hěn bù-'fāng-byan. ‖**We certainly missed you while you were sick.** (*We were helpless*) 'nǐ nèm yí 'bìng wǒm °tǐng jwā-'shyā-de. *or* (*We didn't know how to do anything right*) °dēw bù-jř-dàw dzěm-je 'hǎw-le. *or* (*We were lonesome*) nǐ 'bìng de-shr̄-hew wǒm 'jēn-shr 'shyǎng-nǐ láy-je.

‖**I miss my library.** *is expressed as* **If my books were all here everything would be fine.** yàw-shr wǒ-de-'shū dēw dzày-'jèr °'tsáy 'hǎw-ne. *or* °dwō 'hǎw-wa.

MISTAKE, tswòr; *sometimes* 'tswò-wù, 'chà-tswò, bú-'dwèy-de-di-fang; **to make a mistake** tswò, chū ge-'tswèr; (*in doing something*) nèng-'tswò, nàw-'tswò, nèng-chū ge-'tswèr (*etc., with other verbs meaning to do*); (*in looking at something*) kàn-'tswò; (*in recognizing someone*) 'rèn-tswò-le 'rén; **to take something by mistake** ná-'tswò; **to mistake** *a person's meaning* (*misunderstand*) 'wù-hwey; **to mistake** *someone* **for** *someone else* 'ná ... dàng ... , 'dǎng(-je) ... shr̄ ....

‖**Sorry, my mistake.** (*In action*) 'dwèy-bu-chǐ, shr̄ 'wǒ°-de-tswèr. *or* °'tswò-le. (*In mistaking identity*) 'dwèy-bu-chǐ, wǒ rèn-'tswò-le 'rén-le. ‖**There must be a mistake somewhere.** yí-'dìng shr̄ 'nǎr °yěw ge-'tswèr. *or* °yěw dyǎr-'tswèr. *or* °'tswò-le. *or* °'tswò-le-dyar. *or* °yěw (dyǎr-)bú-'dwèy-de-dì-fang. *or* °yěw 'tswò-wù. *or* yěw dyǎr-'chà-tswò. ‖**There must be some mistake.** yí-'dìng °yěw dyǎr-'tswèr-ba. *or* °'nèng-'tswò-le-ba. *or* 'nàw-'tswò-le-ba. *or* (*In identity*) °shr̄ rèn-'tswò-le 'rén-le-ba. ‖**Anyone could make such a mistake.** 'jèy-yàngr-de-tswèr 'shéy dēw hwèy °'yěw-de. *or* °'nèng-de-chū-'láy-de. ‖**You must have made a mistake.** nǐ-yí-'dìng shr̄ °nèng-'tswò-le. *or* (*In identity*) °'rèn-tswò-le 'rén-le-ba. ‖**He made a mistake.** tā chū-le ge-'tswèr. *or* tā nèng-chu-le ge-'tswèr-lay. *or* (*He was completely wrong*) tā 'tswò-le. *or* (*In identity*) tā 'rèn-tswò-le 'rén-le. ‖**What a terrible mistake to make!** 'dzěm néng °dzwò- (*or* °'nèng-, *or* °'nàw-, *or* °'bàn-) chū 'nèm-lì-hay-de-ge-'tswèr láy-ya! *or* 'dzěm néng 'tswò-dàw 'nèm-ge-yàngr-ne! ‖**I made a terrible mistake.** wǒ 'nèng-chu ge-'dà-tswèr-lay. ‖**Did you take that by mistake?** nǐ 'shr̄-bu-shr kàn-'tswò-le, jyèw bǎ jèy-ge 'ná-chywu-le? *or* 'nèy-ge nǐ shr̄-bu-shr ná-'tswò-le? ‖**You can't mistake it.** 'jywé bú-hwèy yěw-'tswèr-de. *or* 'méy-tswèr. *or* 'méy ge-bu-'dwèy-de. ‖**Please don't mistake me.** byé 'wù-hwey wǒ-de-'yì-sz. *or* byé 'tswò-gwày-le wǒ. ‖**I mistook her for a friend of mine.** wǒ (kàn-'tswò-le 'rén-le) 'dǎng(-je) tā shr̄ wǒ-de-ge-'péng-yew-ne. ‖**They mistook me** (*or* **I was mistaken**) **for someone else.** tām ('rèn-tswò-le 'rén-le) dàng-wǒ shr̄ 'lìng-yí-ge-'rén-ne. ‖**It's a case of mistaken identity.** shr̄ rèn-'tswò-le 'rén-le. ‖**That's a mistaken belief.** nèm shyǎng °bú-'dwèy. *or* °'jyèw 'tswò-le. *or* yàw shìn 'nèy-ge jyèw 'tswò-le. *or* nèy-ge shìn-'tswò-le.

By mistake *is sometimes expressed also as* **carelessly** 'méy-lyéw-'shén, *or as* **thoughtlessly** 'méy-dž-shi 'shyǎng-shyǎng, *or as* **not on purpose** 'bú-shr gù-'yì-de. ‖**Did you do it by mistake?** 'nǐ jè shr̄ 'méy-°lyéw-'shén (*or* °dž-shi 'shyǎng-shyang) nèng-de-ba. *or* nǐ 'bú-shr gù-'yì-de nèm-je-ba.

‖**Make no mistake about it.** (*You can rest assured*) nǐ jyèw fàng-'shīn-ba. *or* (*I'm telling you!*) nǐ jyèw tīng 'wǒ-de hǎw-le.

MISTER (MR.). 'shyān-sheng. ‖Hello, Mr. Jones. 'jēw-shyān-sheng, nǐ 'hǎw? ‖Are you Mr. Jones? nín shr̀ 'jēw-shyān-sheng-ma?

MIX. (*Combine ingredients*) **to mix** *something* **with** (*or* **into**) *something,* *or* **to mix** *dough* hwò; (*to stir*) 'hwò-lung *or* jyǎw. ‖Mix this flour with two cups of water. jèy-ge-'myàn jyā-jìn lyǎng-bēy-'shwěy chywù 'hwò. *or* yùng lyǎng-bēy-'shwěy láy hwò jèy-ge-'myàn. ‖Don't mix too much sand with the concrete. yáng-'hwēy-li-hwò-de-'shā-dz byé tày 'dwō-le. *or* yáng-'hwēy-li 'shǎw hwò (*or* put gē) dyar-'shā-dz. ‖The cook is mixing the cake now. 'dà-shr̄-fu dzày-nàr hwò dzwò-'dyǎn-shīn-de-'fěn-dz-ne. ‖You'll have to mix it with a large spoon. nǐ děy ná-'sháwr °'jyǎw-yi-jyǎw. *or* °'hwò-lung-hwò-lung.

(*To associate; with people*) 'láy-wǎng, 'lā-lǔng; **to mix well** láy-de-'shàng, 'tán-de-shàng-'láy, 'shwō-de-shàng-'láy; **not mix well** 'tán-bu-shàng-'láy, 'shwō-bu-shàng-'láy, 'gé-gé-bú-'rù. ‖He's a good mixer. tā gēn-'shéy dēw °'láy-de-'shàng. *or* °'tán- (*or* °'shwō-) de-shàng-'láy. ‖He doesn't mix well. tā gēn-rén °'gé-gé-bú-'rù. *or* °'tán- (*or* °'shwō-) bu-shàng-'láy.

To mix well (*of foods*) néng yí-'kwàr chr̄, néng 'chān-he-chǐ-lay chr̄, néng 'hé-chǐ-lay yí-'kwàr chr̄. ‖These two foods don't mix well. jèy-lyǎng-yàngr-dūng-shi 'bù-néng °'yí-'kwàr chr̄. *or* °'chān-he-chǐ-lay chr̄. *or* °'hé-chǐ-lay yí-kwàr chr̄.

To mix up (*disarrange, get out of order*) nèng-lwàn; **be all mixed up** 'lwàn-le; (*of things*) 'lwàn-le 'tàw-le, nèng-'lwàn-le; (*of a situation*) 'lwàn-chī-bā-'dzǎw-de. ‖Who mixed up all these cards like this? shéy bǎ jèy-shyē-'pyàn-dz nèng-de jèm 'lwàn? ‖These cards are all mixed up. jèy-shyē-'pyàn-dz dēw °'lwàn-le. *or* °'lwàn-le 'tàw-le. *or* °nèng-'lwàn-le. ‖What a °mixed-up mess! *or* °mix-up! 'hǎw-jyā-hwo (*or* 'dzāw-gāw)! dzěm °'dzěm 'lwàn-na! *or* °nàw-de dzèm 'lwàn-chī-bā-'dzǎw-de-ya!

To mix up (*confuse in identity*) *or* **to get mixed up** nàw-'hwěn; *or expressed as* not be able to tell which is which 'fēn-bu-kāy (*or* 'fēn-bu-chīng, *or* 'nàw-bu-chīng, *or* 'rèn-bu-chīng) . . . °shéy shr̀-'shéy (*or; of things,* °'něy-ge shr̀ 'něy-ge *or* °shéme shr̀-'shéme). ‖I always get those two brothers mixed up. wǒ 'lǎw bǎ tām-lyǎng-'dì-shyūng nàw-'hwěn-le. *or* wǒ 'lǎw °fēn-bu-kāy (°*etc.*) tām-'lyǎng-'dì-shyūng shéy shr̀-'shéy.

To mix up (*confuse, a person*) bǎ . . . °nùng- (*or* °nàw-, *or* °jyǎw-) 'hú-du-le; *or* (*district*) jyǎw. ‖Don't mix me up. byé bǎ-wo °nùng- (*or* °nàw-, *or* °jyǎw-) 'hú-de-le. *or* byé 'jyǎw-wo. ‖Now you've got me all mixed up. nǐ bǎ-wo 'wán-chywán nùng-'hú-du-le.

To get *someone* **mixed up in** bǎ . . . °'lā- (*or* °'nàw-, *or* °'gwǒ-) jìn-chywu. ‖Don't get me mixed up in your argument. 'nǐ-men 'chǎw, byé bǎ-'wǒ 'lā- (*or* °'nàw-, *or* °'gwǒ-) jìn-chywu.

Mixed (*composed of different kinds of people*). ‖That's quite a mixed crowd. (*As to types*) dàw-de- (*or* nàr-de-) rén hěn 'dzá. *or* nàr 'gè-shr̀-gè-'yàngr-

de-rén dēw 'yěw. *or* nàr 'shéme-yàngr-de-rén dēw 'yěw. *or* (*As to sexes*) dàw-de- (*or* nàr-de-) rén 'nán-nan-nywǔ-'nywǔ-de hěn 'dwō. *or* nàr-de-rén 'nán-ny.wǔ 'hwèn-dzá.

Mixed marriage (*miscegenation*). ‖Mixed marriages are common in Hawaii. bù-túng-'jùng-de-rén jyē-'hwēn dzày tán-shyāng-'shān shr̀ 'cháng-shèr.

Mixed feelings. ‖She took the news with mixed feelings. (*Confused*) tā yì 'tīng-jyàn nèy-ge, 'shīn-li °'lwàn-le. *or* (*With happiness and sadness*) °'bēy-shǐ jyāw-'jí. *or* (*With joy and fear*) °yěw 'shǐ-hwān yèw 'pà. *or* (*With anger and regret*) °yěw 'chì yèw 'hèn. *or* (*With love and hate*) °yěw 'ày yèw 'hèn.

MODEL. (*See also* FORM, EXAMPLE.) (*Small copy*) mwó-'shíng. ‖He's making a model of the bridge. tā dzày dzwò 'chyáw-de-mwó-'shíng. ‖Please show me a model of the boat. láw-'jyà bǎ nèy-ge-'chwán-de-mwó-'shíng gěy-wǒ 'kàn-kan.

(*Form for imitation or copying*) 'yàng-dz *or* 'yàngr; *or more often expressed as* **to model after** (*to follow*) 'jàw-je, 'bǐ-je, 'àn-je, *or* (*sometimes, literary*) 'fǎng-shyàw. ‖Give me a model to follow (*for writing*). gěy-wǒ ge-'yàng-dz °'jàw-je (*or* °'bǐ-je) shyě. ‖Use this model for your writing. nǐ kě-yǐ °'jàw-je (*or* °'bǐ-je, *or* °'fǎng-shyàw) 'jèy-ge láy 'shyě. *or* ná jèy-ge dzwò 'yàng-dz láy °'jàw-je (*or* °'bǐ-je) shyě. ‖American law is modeled after British law, while Continental law follows the model of old Roman law. 'mēy-gwo-'fǎ-lywù shr̀ °'jàw-je (*or* °'bǐ-je) 'yīng-gwo-'fǎ-lywù 'dìng-de; dà-'lù-fǎ-'shì shr̀ °'jàw-je (*or* °'bǐ-je) 'lwó-mǎ-'fǎ-lywù 'dìng-de. ‖We're modeling our plans for the house after that picture. wǒm jèng-dzày àn-je nèy-jāng-'hwàr láy dìng-gwey nèy-'fáng-dz dzěm 'gày.

(*Style, type*) 'yàng-dz, yàngr, 'shr̀-yàng; *the model of a certain year may be expressed as* manufactured in a certain year . . . dzǎw-de. ‖Is that your latest model? nà shr̀ nǐm-dzwèy-'shīn-de-°'yàng-dz-ma? *or* °'yàngr-ma? *or* °'shr̀-yàng-ma? ‖This year's model has a lower body. 'jīn-nyán °chē-'yǎngr (*or* °chē-'yàng-dz, *or* °chē-'shr̀-yang) chē-shēn 'dī-le-dyar. ‖That car is last year's model. nèy-lyàng-'chē shr̀ 'chywù-nyán-dzǎw-de.

A **model** *town* 'mwó-fàn. ‖Ours is a model town. běn-'shr̀ shr̀ 'mwó-fàn-'shr̀.

A **model of good behavior** *is expressed as* really well behaved 'jēn gwěy-jywu, *or* (*of a child*) *as* better behaved than anyone else's children bǐ 'shéy-jyā-de-háy-dz dēw 'gwěy-jywu. ‖Their boy is a model of good behavior. tām-de-'háy-dz °'jēn (*or* bǐ 'shéy-jyā-de-háy-dz dēw) 'gwēy-jywu.

A **model** (*person who poses, or mannequin*) 'mwó-de-ér. ‖She's an artist's model. tā gěy 'hwà-jyā dzwò 'mwó-de-ér.

To model (*clothes*). ‖She modeled the dress for us *is expressed as* She put the dress on for us to see. tā bǎ 'yī-shang 'chwān-shang gěy-wǒm 'kàn-lay-je.

MODERN. (*Recent, of recent years*) 'jìn-dày; (*referring to style*) 'jìn-dày-shr̀-de; **modern times** 'jìn-dày; **modern history** 'jìn-dày-'shr̃. ‖We're thinking of buying some modern furniture. wǒm 'dǎ-swàn mǎy dyǎr-'jìn-dày-shr̀-de-'jyā-jywu.

(*Up-to-date*). (*New*) shīn; (*present, current*) 'shyàn-dày (*referring to style*) 'shīn-shr̀-de, 'shyàn-dày-shr̀-de. ‖Do you have anything more modern? 'háy yěw bǐ jèy-ge 'shīn-shr̀-de-ma? *or* 'shr̀-yàng háy yěw gèng-'shīn-de-ma? ‖Are there any modern conveniences? 'nèy-ge-dì-fang yěw 'shīn-shr̀-de-'shè-bèy méy-yěw? *Or, of a house, usually expressed as* Are there electric lights and running water? 'nèy-ge-dì-fang 'dyàn-dēng dz̀-láy-'shwěy dēw 'yěw-ma?

MOMENT. (*Short period of time*) hwěr. ‖I'll be back in a moment. wǒ yì-'hwěr jyèw 'hwéy-lay. ‖We'll have your change in a moment. wǒm yì-'hwěr jyèw jǎw-gěy-nín 'chyán. ‖Wait a moment. 'děng-yì-hwěr.

(*Instant*) shŕ-'jyān, shŕ-hew. ‖I didn't have a single moment to myself. wǒ-'dz̀-jǐ 'yì-dyǎr-shŕ-'jyān yě 'méy-yew.

The moment (that) yī . . . , jyèw . . . . ‖Let me know the moment he arrives. tā yí 'dàw jyèw 'gàw-sung wo.

At a moment's notice yí-dé-daw 'tūng-jr̃, jyèw . . . . ‖Be ready to leave at a moment's notice. 'ywù-bèy-'hǎw-le, yí dé-daw 'tūng-jr̃, jyèw dùng-'shēn.

At the moment yì-'shŕ. ‖I can't answer your question at the moment. wǒ yì-'shŕ 'dá-bu-shàng nǐ-de-'wèn-tí.

MONDAY. lǐ-bày-'yī, shīng-chī-'yī.

MONEY. chyán. ‖Where can I change my American money? 'měy-gwo-chyán 'shéme-dì-fang kě-yi 'hwàn? ‖Do you accept American money? nǐm yùng 'měy-gwo-chyán-ma? ‖How much is that in American money? yùng 'měy-gwo-chyán swàn-shr 'dwō-shaw? ‖How much money do I owe you? wǒ 'chyàn-ni 'dwō-shaw-chyán? ‖Do you have any money on you? nǐ 'shēn-shang yěw-'chyán-ma? ‖He has lots of money. 'nèy-ge-rén 'hěn yěw-'chyán. ‖He's taking another job to make more money. tā lìng-'wày jǎw-le ge-'shr̃, hǎw 'dwō jwàn dyǎr-'chyán.

MONTH. ywè; one month yí-ge-'ywè. ‖How about joining us on a trip next month? 'shyà-ywè gēn-wǒm 'chū-chywu lywǔ-'shíng, 'hǎw-bu-hǎw? ‖Can we rent this house by the month? jèy-ge-'fáng-dz kě-yi àn-'ywè 'dzū-ma? ‖This job should be finished in a month's time. jèy-ge-'gūng-dzwò kě-yi yí-ge-'ywè dzwò-'wán. ‖They never know where they'll be from month to month. 'měy-ge-ywè tām dēw bù-jr̃-'dàw hwèy wàng-'nǎr chywù.

MOON. 'ywè-lyàng. ‖Is there a full moon tonight? jyěr-ge-'wǎn-shang 'ywè 'yang hwèy 'ywán-ma? ‖The moon is hidden behind the clouds. 'ywè-lyang gěy 'ywún-tsay 'jē-jù-le.

MORAL. (*Ethical*) 'dàw-dé; **not moral** bú-'dàw-dé *or* (*more colloquially*) chywē-'dé; **moral standards** (*of a community*) 'fēng-hwà *or* rén-'shīn. ‖That was hardly a moral thing to do. nèm-je 'wèy-myǎn °chywē-'dé. *or* ˇbú-'dàw-dé. ‖This will have a profound effect on moral standards. 'jèy-ge yěw gwān 'fēng-hwà. ‖This is fundamentally a moral issue. jèy 'gēn-běn shr̃ °'dàw-dé-shang-de-wèn-'tí. *or* °'fēng-hwà-shang-de-wèn-'tí. ‖Let's forget the legal technicalities and get down to the moral issue. (*The question of whether this is morally right or wrong*) dzám byé gwǎn 'fǎ-lywù-shang dzěm 'shwō, shyān kàn-kan jèy-shèr °'dàw-dé-shang shr̃ ʼhǎw shr̃ 'hwày. *or* °'dàw-dé-shang shr̃ 'dwèy háy shr̃ 'tswò. *or* °'dàw-dé-shang shr̃ 'dwèy háy shr̃ bú-'dwèy. *or* (*The question of how this is related to the morals of society*) °dwèy-ywu 'shè-hwèy-'dàw-dé-de-'gwān-shi-ba. *or* °dwèy-ywu 'shè-hwèy-rén-'shīn-de-'gwān-shi-ba. *or* °dwèy-ywu 'shè-hwèy-'fēng-hwà-de-'gwān-shi-ba.

Moral standards (*of an individual*) *or* moral character *is expressed in terms of character* 'pǐn-shíng *being good* 'hǎw, *high* gāw, *upright* 'dwān-jèng, *not upright* bú-'jèng, bù-'dwān, *etc.* ‖Everybody knows him as a man of high moral character (*or* standards). 'rén-ren děw 'jywé-de tā shr̃ ge-'pǐn-shíng-°'hǎw- (*or* °hěn-'gāw-, *or* °'dwān-jèng-) de-rén.

A moral issue (*involving a person*) *is indirectly expressed as above.* ‖The mayor was attacked on a moral issue when other methods failed. 'gūng-jí-shr̃-'jǎng-de-fāng-fa 'dēw bù-'chéng-le, tām jyèw shwō tā-'pǐn-shíng °bú-'jèng. *or* °bù-'dwān.

To be without morals *is expressed as* to be able to do anything (*without restraint*) 'shéme dēw dzwò-de-chū-'láy. ‖She's a woman without morals. tā-jèy-ge-'nywǔ-rén 'shéme dēw dzwò-de-chū-'láy.

A moral (*lesson*) 'jyàw-shywun. ‖I don't get the moral of this story. jèy-gé-'gù-shr̃-de-'jyàw-shywun dzày-'nǎr wǒ 'méy-tīng-chu-'láy.

MORE. (*In amount, as used alone or followed by a noun*) dwō *before a verb, often with* dyǎr *following;* háy *or* dzày *before a verb, with or without* dwō(-dyar) *following;* much more *or* a lot more dwō-'dwō-de *before a verb;* háy *or* dzày *before a verb, with* hěn dwō *following;* need more, want more, *and similar expressions may also be expressed in terms of* enough gèw *or* not enough bú-'gèw; *comparisons with* than *which may be omitted in English are not expressed in Chinese; for necessary comparisons, see below;* to cost more *is expressed as* more expensive, *see next paragraph.* ‖You should eat more (than you do). nǐ yīng-gāy 'dwō chr̃-dyar. ‖I'll allow them more time, then. nèm-je wǒ jyèw 'dwō rúng-tām dyǎr-'shŕ-hew 'hǎw-le. ‖Can you get this man at the regular salary, or do you think he wants more? nèy-ge-rén nǐ gěy-tā jàw-'lì-de-'shīn-shwey tā 'gàn-bu-gàn? nǐ jywé-je tā ʼháy shyǎng 'dwō yàw-ma? ‖How much more time do you need? 'háy děy yàw 'dwō-shǎw-shŕ-hew? ‖Do you need more time? 'shŕ-jyan 'gèw-le-ma? *or* 'shŕ-jyan bú-'gèw-ba? ‖Won't you have some more? háy 'yàw-dyar-ma? *or* dzày 'láy-dyar-ba? *or* dzáy dwō 'láy-dyar-ba? ‖I need more money (than I have on me). wŏ-'shēn-shang-dày-de-'chán bú-'gèw(; háy dĕy 'dwō yĕw-dyar tsáy 'shíng).

(In degree, as used before an adjective) is expressed by the adjective alone; by háy *or* dzày *before an adjective or verb; or, especially with the meaning* even more, *by* gèng *before an adjective.* ‖This one is more expensive. jèy-ge 'gwèy(-dyar). ‖Which do you think is the more careful worker? nĭ kàn nĕy-ge dzwò-de yùng-'shīn-dyar? ‖I don't think I can afford a more expensive one. wŏ shyăng wŏ 'măy-bu-chĭ 'dzày gwèy-de-le. ‖Which one is more important? nèy-ge ('gèng) yàw-'jĭn-ne? ‖I have a more important problem on my hands. wŏ 'shyàn-dzày 'jèng nèng yí-jyàn-'gèng-yàw-'jĭn-de-'shèr.

(In number, preceded by a numeral or other word indicating number) háy *or* dzày *before a verb with a numeral following.* ‖There are two more guests coming. 'háy yĕw 'lyăng-ge-kè-rén méy-'dàw-ne. ‖I'm going to stay three weeks more. wŏ 'háy yàw 'dwō jù 'sān-ge-shīng-'chī. ‖There are a few more left. háy 'shèng-shya jĭ-ge. ‖There are only a few more. *may also be expressed as* Those left are not many. 'shèng-shya-de bù-'dwō-le. ‖Give me a few more, please. 'dzáy gĕy-wŏ 'jĭ-ge ba. *or* dzày 'láy jĭ-ge. ‖Give me two more bottles, please. láw-'jyà, 'dzày gĕy-wŏ 'lyăng-píng. ‖I want two more. 'dzày gĕy-wŏ 'lyăng-ge. *or* wŏ 'háy yàw 'lyăng-ge. *or* 'dzày láy 'lyăng-ge. ‖Try once more. 'dzày láy yí-tsż. *or* 'dzày shŕ yí-shyàr. ‖I'd like to buy some more of these if you still carry them. jèy-ge yàw-shr háy 'yĕw de-hwà, wŏ shyăng °'dwō (*or* °dzày 'dwō) măy-dyar. *or* °'dzày măy 'jĭ-ge.

More than . . . bĭ . . . dwō; **more . . . than . . .** bĭ . . . *plus an adjective;* **more than** *(followed by a numeral) is expressed by* dwō (*or, if the amount more is less than ten, sometimes* jĭ) *after a numeral, or as* dzày . . . yĭ 'shàng; **more than enough** 'dzú-gèw-le, *or expressed as* **too much** tày 'dwō; **more than** *one thought may also be expressed as* didn't think it would be so much (*or other adjective instead of* much) 'méy-shyăng-'dàw hwèy nèm . . . ‖There were a hundred more there today than yesterday. 'jyēr bĭ-'dzwér dwō yì-'băy. ‖Doing a good job is much more important than finishing quickly. dzwò-de 'hăw 'ywăn bĭ dzwò-de 'kwày yàw-'jĭn. ‖I dislike her too, perhaps even more than you do. 'wŏ yĕ tăw-'yàn tā; yĕ-shywŭ bĭ-nĭ 'háy tăw-'yàn tā-ne. ‖They need more time than we did. 'tām dĕy bĭ-'wŏm yùng-de-'shŕ-jyan 'dwō-dyar tsáy 'shíng. ‖There were more than a thousand people there. dàw-le yì-chyán-'dwō-rén. *or* dàw-de-rén dzày yì-'chyán yĭ 'shàng. ‖He's more than forty years old. tā yĕw 'sż-shr-dwō-swèr. *or* tā yĕw 'sż-shr-jĭ-swèr. *or* tā dzày 'sż-shr-swèy yĭ 'shàng. ‖That's more than enough. 'nèy yĭ-jīng tày 'dwō-le. *or* 'dzú-gèw-le. ‖This

costs more than I expected. wŏ 'méy-shyăng-'dàw hwèy nèm 'gwèy. *or* nèy-ge-'jyàr bĭ wŏ-shīn-li-'shyăng-de 'gwèy.

No more than, not any more than *is sometimes expressed similarly; when followed by numerals, often as* **not over** bú-'gwò; *many indirect expressions are also used.* ‖I don't care any more than you do. wŏ 'bìng bù-bĭ-'nĭ háy 'dzày-hu-wa. ‖There were no more than fifty people in the whole town. chywán-'chéng-li yĕ bú-gwò 'wŭ-shr-rén-de-yàng-dz. ‖The price surely can't be more than ten dollars. 'jyà-chán 'jywé bú-hwèy °gwò-le 'shŕ-kwày-chán. *or* °'chāw-gwò 'shŕ-ᴋwày-chán. *or* °bĭ 'shŕ-kwày-chán háy 'dwō. ‖Don't do any more than you have time for. nĭ dzwò-'snŕ yàw 'kĕ-je 'shŕ-hew dzwò, byé tān-'dwō. ‖We're no more ready to start the work now than we were a year ago. wŏm 'háy-shr 'bù-néng chĭ-téwr 'dzwò-chĭ-lay, jyăn-'jŕ gēn 'chywù-nyán °'yí-'yàng. *or* °'méy shéme-'fēn-bye. ‖He's paid $3,000 a year, but it's no more than he's worth. tā 'yì-nyán-de 'shīn-shwey 'sān-chyān-ywán; yàw àn tā-de-'bĕn-lĭng láy shwō, bìng 'bú-swàn 'dwō.

The more the . . .-er ywè 'dwō ywè . . . ; **the more . . . the more . . .** ywè . . . ywè . . . . ‖The more I read it the madder I get. jèy-ge wŏ 'ywè kàn ywè 'chì. ‖The more I read it the less I understand. jèy-ge wŏ 'ywè nyàn ywè bù-'dŭng. ‖The more the merrier. ywè 'dwō ywè 'hăw. ‖The more you eat the more you want. *is popularly expressed as* The more you chew it the tastier it gets. 'ywè jyáw ywè 'shyàng. *or* (*More literally*) 'ywè chŕ ywè 'tsán. *cr* 'ywè chŕ ywè 'shyàng chŕ.

More and more (*as time goes by*) ywè láy ywè . . . . ‖They got more and more out of control as time went by. tām 'ywè láy ywè méy-făr 'gwăn-le. ‖They've been seeing more and more of each other lately. tām 'jìn-láy láy-wăng-de ywè láy ywè °'mì-chye. *or* °'chīn-mì. *or* °'mì. *or* °'dwō. ‖This place seems more (and more) beautiful every time I come here. *is expressed as* Each time I come, this place seems more beautiful than each (other) time. 'jèy-ge-dì-fang wŏ 'láy yí-tsż bĭ yí-tsż kàn-je 'hăw.

More or less (*of amount*) shàng-!shyà, dzwŏ-'yĕw, yĕ-shywŭ 'dwō-dyar yĕ-shywŭ 'shăw-dyar; (*almost*) chā-bu-'dwō; (*in the main*) dà-'jŕ; (*probably*) 'dà-gày, *or expressed by* méy shéme *or* 'bú-hwèy shéme *followed by a word with opposite meaning from that which follows* **more or less.** ‖There were a hundred people there, more or less. dàw-le yĕw yì-'băy-rén °shàng-'shyà. *or* °dzwŏ-'yĕw. ‖It will take two months, more or less. dĕy 'lyăng-ge-ywè °shàng-'shyà. *or* °dzwŏ-'yĕw. *or* °yĕ-shywŭ 'dwō-dyar yĕ-shywŭ 'shăw-dyar. *or* chā-bu-dwō dĕy 'lyăng-ge-ywè-de-gwāng-jĭng. ‖I believe that report is more or less true. jywù 'wŏ kàn, nèy-ge-bàw-'gàw-lĭ-de-shèr °'dà-gày (*or* °'dà-'jŕ) shŕ 'jēn-de. *or* °'dà-gày (*or* °dà-'jŕ) shŕ kĕ-'shìn-de. *or* °'méy shéme-'jyă-de. *or* °'bú-hwèy yĕw shéme-'jyă-de.

Any more (*with a negative*) dzày, 'dzày yě; (*from now on*) 'tsúng-tsž. ‖Don't do that any more. byé 'dzày nèm-je-le! ‖I don't care any more. wǒ 'tsúng-tsž (*or* wǒ 'dzày yě) bú-gwǎn-le.

More to *something* **than you'd think** *and similar expressions are expressed indirectly.* ‖There's more to his plan than you'd imagine at first sight. *is expressed as* There are many things about his plan that you can't see at first glance. tā-de-'bàn-fa 'yěw shyē-dì-fang 'jà yí 'jyàn kàn-bu-chū-'láy-de.

What's more. ‖What's more, I don't believe you. 'dzày shwō-ne (*or* 'háy yěw yì-'tséng, *or* gèng 'jìn yí-bù láy shwō-ne, *or* dzày 'jìn yí-bù láy shwō-ne), wǒ 'gēn-běn bú-'shìn nǐ-de-'hwà.

More than ever, all the more, even more (than that) gèng. ‖After hearing you say that the show was so good, I wanted to go °more than ever. *or* °all the more. *or* °even more. tīng nǐ-shwō-de nèy-chū-shì 'nèm hǎw, wǒ 'gèng shyǎng chywù 'kàn-kan-le. ‖I'd like to go see him, but even more (than that) I'd like to see his daughter again. wǒ 'shyǎng chywù 'jyàn-jyan tā; wǒ yě 'gèng shyǎng chywù 'dzày hwèy-daw 'tā-de-nèy-wèy-'shyáw-jye. ‖I'd like to go to the show, but even more I want to go to this lecture. wǒ dàw 'shyǎng chywù kàn nèy-chū-'shì; bú-gwo wǒ 'gèng shyǎng tīng jèy-ge-yǎn-'jyǎng.

‖**More power to you.** *is expressed as* I certainly hope you succeed. wǒ 'jēn pàn-wang nǐ bàn-de-'dàw. ‖If you want to try to convince him, go ahead, and more power to you. nǐ yàw-shr shyǎng bǎ-ta 'chywàn-gwo-làry, jyèw chywù 'chywàn-ba; wǒ 'jēn pàn-wang nǐ bàn-de-'dàw.

‖**We had more fun than a picnic.** *is expressed as* We never had so much fun. wár-de 'dzày méy-nèm yěw 'yì-sz-de-le.

More fun than a barrel of monkeys *may be expressed literally, except that* crowd chywún *is used instead of* barrel. ‖He's more fun than a barrel of monkeys. tā bǐ yì-chywún-'héw-dz háy néng dèw-rén 'shyàw.

More luck than brains *is expressed as* depending entirely on luck, not at all on ability. ‖Don't brag about winning the game; it was more luck than brains. yíng jyèw 'yíng-le jyèw 'shr̀-le, 'chwēy ge-shéme-'jyèr! nèy shr̀ kàw 'ywùn-chi 'yíng-de, bú-shr̀ 'jìng-píng 'běn-shr̀.

More bother (*or* trouble) **than it's worth** *is expressed as* to expend that energy isn't worth it. fèy 'nèy-ge-shèr bù-'jŕ-de. ‖Don't bother fixing it; it's more bother than it's worth. béng shyǎng-fár 'shēw-shr-le; fèy 'nèy-ge-shèr bù-'jŕ-de.

More than willing. ‖I'd be more than willing to lend you ten, but I simply don't have it. wǒ 'shyàn-dzày 'méy-yěw 'shŕ-kwày-chyán. yàw-shr 'yěw de-hwà °yí-'dìng jyè-gěy nǐ. *or* °byé shwō 'jyè-le, gěy-nǐ dēw 'shíng.

‖**They bit off more than they could chew.** tām-nèy shr̀ 'tān-dwō 'jyáw-bú-'làn. *or* tām 'jēn shr̀ 'bú-dž-lyàng-'lì.

MORNING. 'dzǎw-chen, 'dzǎw-shang; **morning meal** dzǎw-'fàn; **morning X** dzǎw-'X. ‖I'll see you in the morning. myéngr-'dzǎw-chen 'jyàn. ‖He slept all morning. tā 'shwèy-le yì-'dzǎw-shang. ‖Is there a morning train? yěw dzǎw-'chē-ma? ‖Shall I pick up a morning paper? wǒ mǎy fèn-dzǎw-'bàw-ba?

‖**Good morning!** *is usually expressed simply as* Hello! nǐ 'hǎw? *but sometimes one says* It's early! 'dzǎw-a! (*The latter is chiefly used by Chinese from the South.*)

MOST. (*Greatest in quantity or degree, etc.*) dzwèy *or* dǐng *followed by an adjective;* (*when not followed by an adjective in English, and referring to amount*) 'dzwèy dwō, 'dǐng dwō; **at (the) most** 'jǐ dwō, 'dzwèy dwō, 'dǐng dwō; **the most I've ever seen** *is expressed as* I've never seen so much, *etc., with similar expressions.* ‖This is the most fun we've had in a long time. wǒ-men 'hǎw-shyē-ř-dz-li yàw swàn 'jèy-tsž-wár-de 'dzwèy °chǐ-'jyèr-le. *or* 'yěw 'yì-sz-le. ‖Which room has the most space? 'něy-jyān-wū-dz dǐng (*or* dzwèy) 'kwān-chang? ‖Who has done the most work in this job? 'jèy-jyèn-shèr 'shéy-chū-de-'lì dzwèy 'dwō? ‖He's the most reliable person I've ever had. wǒ-'yùng-gwo-de-rén-li tā dzwèy kě-'kàw. ‖That is the most I can pay. wǒ 'jǐ (*or* 'dzwèy) dwō néng chū jèm-ge-'jyàr. ‖That's the most I want to pay. wǒ 'jǐ (*or* 'dzwèy, *or* dǐng) dwō chū-dàw 'jèm-shyē-chyán. *or often expressed as* That's the price, it can't be higher. 'jyèw-shr 'nèm-ge-jyàr, 'dzày bù-néng 'gāw-le. ‖What's the most you can lend me? 'dzwèy dwō nǐ néng jyè-wǒ 'dwō-shǎw? ‖I can pay fifteen dollars at the most. wǒ 'jǐ (*or* 'dzwèy, *or* 'dǐng) dwō néng chū-dàw shŕ-'wǔ-kwày-chyán. ‖Where's the most convenient place to meet you? dzày-'nǎr (*or* 'shéme-dì-fang) jyàn-nǐ dzwèy 'fāng-byan? ‖The train goes there, but you can go most easily by bus. nèy-ge-dì-fang tūng hwǒ-'chē, bú-gwo dzwò 'gūng-gùng-chì-chē 'dzwèy shěng-'shr̀. ‖The hotel can hold three hundred guests at most. lywú-'gwǎn jǐ (*or* dzwèy) dwō (yě 'bú-gwo) néng rúng 'sān-bǎy-rén. ‖This is the most beautiful photograph of a cat I've ever seen. wǒ 'tsúng-láy méy jyàn-gwo gěy-'māw jàw-'shyàng jàw-de 'jèm hǎw-'kàn-de.

(*Almost all, a majority*) *is expressed as* almost all chā-bu-dwō 'dēw (*or* 'chywán); **the greatest number of . . .** all dà-'dwō-shù-de-. . . 'dēw; **very nearly all** 'jī-hu 'dēw. ‖Most people think he did the right thing. dà-'dwō-shù-de-rén (*or* chā-bu-dwō 'shéy, *or* chā-bu-dwō 'rén-rén) 'dēw jywé-je tā-bàn-de 'dwèy. ‖She's already been to most of the stores in town. jèy-ge-dì-fang-de-'pù-dz tā °chā-bu-dwō 'yǐ-jīng 'dēw (*or* 'chywán) dzěw-'byàn-le. *or* °jī-hu (*or* °chā-bu-dwō) 'jyā-jyar dēw 'dàw-gwo-le. ‖He's away from home most of the time every day. tā jěng-'tyān-jya chā-bu-dwō dēw °bú-dzày 'jyā-li. *or* °dzày 'wày-tew.

(*Very*) jēn, hěn, tǐng, 'fēy-cháng, 'shŕ-fēn; (*after an adjectival expression*) 'jí-le, 'lì-hay, hěn. ‖His talk was most interesting. tā-shwō-de °'jēn (or °'hěn, or °tǐng, or °'fēy-cháng, or °'shŕ-fēn) yěw 'yì-sz. or °yěw 'yì-sz 'jí-le. or °yěw-'chywùr-de 'lì-hay. or °yěw-'chywùr-de 'hěn. ‖I found his manner most annoying. wǒ kě jywé-je tā-de-'jywǔ-jǐ-'dùng-dzwo °'tǐng (or °'hěn, or °'shŕ-fēn, or °'fēy-cháng) jyàw-rén 'nì-wey-de.

For the most part dà-'jǐ, 'dwō-bàn; or expressed indirectly. ‖I agree with your plan for the most part. nǐ-de-'jì-hwà wǒ °'dà-'jǐ dzàn-'chéng. or expressed as There aren't many places in which I disagree with your plan. °'méy-yěw dwō-shǎw-'bú-dzàn-chéng-de-'dì-fang.

To make the most of is expressed indirectly. ‖We're not staying here long, so let's make the most of our time. is expressed as We're not staying here long, so let's not waste this chance. dzám dzày-jèr 'dāy-bu-lyǎw dwō 'jywé, háy bú-'chèn jèy-ge-'jī-hwey 'dà gàn (or wár) yí-shyàr. ‖Let's make the most of the money we've got left. is expressed as We'll have to use the rest of the money °in the right place. 'shèng-shya-de-chyán dzám děy °'hwā-de shŕ-'dì-fangr tsáy 'hǎw. or °'well. °hǎw-'hāwr-de hwā-le.

MOTHER. (In a human family) 'mǔ-chin; (somewhat more intimate terms) nyáng, mā; (used by children, mamma) 'mā-ma; **your mother** (terms used for special politeness) lìng-'táng, lìng-'tsź; **my mother** (terms used for special politeness) jyā-'tsź, jyā-'mǔ; **my mother** (if she is deceased) 'shyān-tsź, 'shyān-mǔ; **stepmother** (polite term) 'jì-mǔ or (more colloquial) 'hèw-nyáng; **mother-in-law** (wife's mother, polite term) 'ywè-mǔ or (more colloquial) 'jàng-mǔ-nyáng, (husband's mother) 'pwó-pwo. ‖Mother wants you to go home. 'mǔ-chin (or 'mā-ma, or 'nyáng) jyàw-nǐ hwéy-'jyā. ‖I'd like to have you meet my mother. (Sometime) wǒ shyǎng yàw-nǐ jyàn-jyan wǒ-'mǔ-chin. or (In an introduction, indicating her with a gesture) wǒ-'mǔ-chin. ‖Do you live with your mother? nǐ gēn nǐ-'mǔ-chin yí-'kwàr jù-ma? ‖Did your mother tell you to come here? shŕ nǐ-'nyáng (or shŕ nǐ-'mā-ma, or shŕ nǐ-'mǔ-chin, or shŕ lìng-'táng) jyàw-nǐ dàw-jèr 'láy-de-ma?

(Among animals) is expressed indirectly by the verb to give birth shyà. ‖This one is the mother of the litter (of puppies). nèy-yì-wō-shyǎw-'gěwr shŕ 'jèy-ge-gěw 'shyà-de.

To mother someone is expressed as To care for as a mother (treats a child) shyàng 'mǔ-chin (dày 'ér-dz) shŕ-de nèm °'jàw-ying or °'jāw-hù or °'kān-hù. ‖She mothered him all through his illness. tā bìng de-shŕ-hew, tā shyàng 'mǔ-chin (dày ér-dz) shŕ-de nèm °'jàw-ying (or °'jāw-hù, or °'kān-hù) tā láy-je.

One's **mother country** 'běn-gwó, gwó; (the country of one's ancestors) 'dzǔ-gwó.

One's **mother tongue** is expressed indirectly as to speak natively 'běn-láy shwō. ‖What is your mother tongue? nǐ 'běn-láy shwō °'něy-gwó-'hwà? or °'něy-ge-dì-fang-de-'hwà?

MOTION. (A gesture) 'jāw-hū; **to motion to** someone gēn . . . dǎ-'jāw-hū. ‖Will you motion to that bus to stop? láw-'jyà °'jāw-hū nèy-chì-chē 'tíng-shya. or °gēn nèy-ge-kāy-chì-'che-de dǎ 'jāw-hu, jyàw-ta 'tíng-shya.

(Movement) expressed with to move dùng. ‖The motion of the boat has made me ill. chwán 'dùng-de ràng-wo nán-'shèw.

(Formal suggestion in a meeting) 'tí-yì, ti-'àn. ‖I want to make a motion. wǒ yěw ge-'tí-yì. ‖The motion was carried. tí-'àn yǐ-jing 'tūng-gwò-le.

MOUNTAIN. shān; when contrasting with a hill gāw-'shān. ‖How high is the mountain? nèy-ge-'shān dwō 'gāw? ‖It takes several days to cross through the mountains. gwò jèy-dwàn-'shān děy 'hǎw-jǐ-tyān. ‖We're spending a month in the mountains this summer. 'jīn-nyán-'shyà-tyan wǒm dzày 'shān-li jù-le yí-ge-'ywè. ‖How do you like this mountain view? nǐ 'ày-bu-ày jèy-ge-shān-'jǐng? ‖He's living here for the mountain air. tā jù-dzay 'jèr 'wèy-de-shŕ 'shān-shang-de-kūng-'chì.

(Figurative) yí-'dà-dwēy(-de). ‖I've got a mountain of work to do next week. 'shyà-lǐ-bày wǒ yěw yí-'dà-dwēy-de-'shŕ yàw dzwò.

MOUTH. (Part of the body) dzwěy; in some combinations kěw. ‖His mouth is a little crooked. tā-dzwěy jǎng-de °yěw dyǎr-'wāy. or °bù-hěn-'jèng. ‖He's got a large mouth. tā-dzwěy běn 'dà. ‖Don't put it in your mouth; it's dirty. byé gē-dzay 'dzwěy-li; tày 'dzāng. ‖He opened his mouth as if to say something. tā 'jāng-kay dzwěy (or kěw) hǎw shyàng yàw 'shwō-shéme shŕ-de. ‖He looks frightened, with his mouth open and his eyes staring like that. tā 'jāng(-je)-°kěw (or 'dzwěy) 'dèng(-je)-yǎn-de nèy-'yàngr 'hǎw shyàng tǐng hày-'pà shŕ-de.

. (In constructions referring to speaking) sometimes kěw; more commonly expressed in terms of to speak shwō, or words hwà. ‖I didn't have a chance to open my mouth. wǒ 'jyǎn-jŕ 'méy jī-hwey kāy-'kěw. ‖He kept his mouth shut like a clam. (Over a period of time) tā yì-'jŕ bù-kěn shwō. or (Didn't say a word) tā 'yí-jywù-hwà yě bù-kěn 'shwō-chū-lay. or (Literary) expressed as He kept his mouth like a bottle tā shěw-'kěw rú-'píng. ‖Why did you have to open your big mouth? dzěm nǐ jyèw 'fēy děy °shwō-'hwà (or °'shwō-chū-lay) bù-'shíng-ne? ‖He can't keep his mouth shut (as a habit). tā 'tswén-bu-ju 'hwà. or tā 'yěw-hwà jyèw 'shwǒ-chu-chywu. or tā 'yěw shéme-hwà 'dēw gěy-nǐ 'děw-lew-chū-chywu. or tā shwō-'hwà tǐng bù-'shyǎw-shīn. ‖He couldn't keep his mouth shut (on a particular occasion). tā 'fēy shwō bù-'kě-me. or tā 'yí-ge-bù-'shyǎw-shīn jyèw 'shwō-chū-chywu-le. or tā 'bù-jŕ-bù-'jywé-de (or tā 'shǎ-bu-jī-de, or tā 'hú-li-hú-dū-de) gěy 'shwō-chū-chywu-le.

‖You took the words right out of my mouth. wǒ 'gāng yàw nèm 'shwō. or nǐ-shwō-de 'jēn dwèy. or kě-bú-'shr̀-ma! ‖Don't put words into my mouth. hèy! hèy bú-shr wǒ-°'shwō-de. or °de-'yì-sz. ‖The story was passed from mouth to mouth. nèy-jyàn-shèr °'chwán-yáng-chu-chywu-le. or °chwán-'byàn-le. or °jèy-ge (-rén)-chwán-'nèy-ge-de chwán-de hěn 'ywǎn. ‖The word was passed from mouth to mouth that a date had been set for the general strike. 'dà-jyā 'àn-jūng °'chwán-shwō (or °bǐ-tsź 'gàw-su shwō) dà-bà-'gūng-de-'r̀-dz yǐ-jīng 'dìng-le.

(*Opening, place of emptying*) kěw, kěwr. ‖How far is it to the mouth of the river? dàw hé-'kěw-nar yěw 'dwō-shǎw-'lù? ‖The dog stopped at the mouth of the cave. gěw dàw-le 'dùng-'kěwr-nar jyèw 'jàn-ju-le. ‖Wipe off the mouth of the bottle. bǎ píng-dz-'kěwr tsā-'r̀ǎn-jing-le.

‖It makes his mouth water. (*Literally or figuratively*) jyàw-tā 'chán-de-hung. or jyàw-tā kàn-je yǎn-'chán. (*Figuratively only*) jyàw-tā kàn-je yǎr-'rè.

‖Why are you so down in the mouth? nǐ 'dzěm nèm °bù-gāw-'shìng-de-'yàng-dz? or °'chwéy-tew-sàng-'chì-de?

MOVE. (*To change the location of something*). (*General term*) nwó; (*with the hand*) dùng; (*of heavy things*) bān; *also expressed by a wide variety of specific terms such as* to pull lā, to push twēy, to drive kāy, to carry (*in the hands*) ná, etc.; *see these words and others with similar meanings; these words are also used in combination with* -dùng; to move *something to a place* . . . -dàw; to move *something away* . . . -kāy *or sometimes* . . . -dzěw; be able to move *something* dùng-de-'lyǎw, nwó-de-°'lyǎw or °'dùng, bān-de-°'lyǎw or °'dùng, *other specific terms plus* -de-dùng. ‖Move the table away, please. láw-'jyà bǎ 'jwō-dz °'nwó- (or °'bān-, or °'twēy-, or °'lā, or °táy-, or °'dā-, etc.) kāy. ‖Move the table over there, please. láw-'jyà bǎ 'jwō-dz °'nwó- (°etc.) dàw 'nèy-byar-chywu. ‖He's going to move the car around to the front of the house after dinner. chr̄-wán-le 'fàn tā jyèw chywù bǎ-chē °'nwó- (or °'kāy-)dàw fáng-dz-'chyán-byar-chywu. ‖Don't move these books. 'jèy-shyē-shū byé °'dùng. or °'nwó-kay. or °ná-'dzěw. ‖These things are not to be moved. jèy-shyē-'dūng-shi °yì-'dyǎr yě bú-yàw 'dùng. or (*moved away*) °bye bān-'dzěw. ‖I can't move the table. (*By pushing*) 'jwō-dz wǒ twēy-bu-'dùng. or (*By pulling*) 'jwō-dz wǒ lā-bu-'dùng. or (*By any method*) 'jwō-dz wǒ nwó-bu-'dùng.

(*To change one's position or posture, while remaining in the same general location*) dùng; make a move 'dùng-yi-dùngr; move around (*shift one's position restlessly*) lwàn 'dùng, 'nwó-gwo-láy-nwó-gwo-'chywù-de, 'dāy-bu-jù-shyán-bu-'jù-de; (*when sitting*) dzwò-bu-'jù; (*when standing*) jàn-bu-'jù. ‖Don't move! by 'dùng! ‖I can't move (a muscle). wǒ 'bù-néng 'dùng. or wǒ 'dùng-bu-'lyǎw ('jyèr). ‖If you dare to make a

move I'll shoot. nǐ yàw gǎn dùng-yi-'dùngr wǒ jyèw kāy-'chyāng. ‖Don't move around so much. byé nèm °lwàn 'dùng. or °'nwó-gwo-láy-nwó-gwo-'chywù-de. or dāy-bu-jù-shyán-bu-'jù-de. or °dzwò-bu-'jù. or °jàn-bu-'jù.

(*To change one's location, or to be in motion, of a person*) 'nwó-dùng, dzěw; (*not stand*) bú-'jàn; (*not stay*) bù-'dāy; move over 'nwó-yi-nwó, 'nwó-kāy (-dyar); move up (*forward*) wàng-chyán °'nwó or °'dzěw; move closer (*together*) āy-'jǐn(-dyar), wàng yí-'kwàr 'nwó(-yi-nwó). ‖I can't move (*from here*). wǒ 'nwó-bu-kāy. or wǒ bù-néng 'nwó-dùng. ‖Move on (*or along*)! 'dzěw(-je-dyar)! or 'nwó-dùng-je-dyar! or wàng-chyán 'dzěw! ‖The police kept the crowds moving. shywún-jǐng °jyàw-rén 'nwó-dùng-je. or °jyàw-rén wàng-chyán 'dzěw. or °'bú-jyàw-rén 'jàn-dzay-nar. or °'bú-jyàw-rén dzày-nàr 'dāy-je. ‖Don't move around so much. (*From one place to another*) byé nèm 'nwó(-dàw)-jèr-nwó(-dàw)-'nàr-de. or byé nèm dzày-'jèr-dāy-hwer-dzày-'nàr-dāy-hwer-de. or byé nèm 'dzěw-gwo-láy-dzěw-gwo-'chywù-de. or byé nèm 'dzěw-láy-dzěw-'chywù-de. or (*Of walking back and forth*) byé nèm 'mwò-mwo. or byé nèm 'mwò-me.

(*To be in motion, of a thing*). (*Changing location*) dùng, dzěw; (*of a vehicle*) kāy; really moving along jēn 'kāy-chǐ-lay-le or jēn 'kwày-chǐ-lay-le; (*without changing location*) dùng; (*of wheels, turn*) jwàn. ‖Don't get off the train while it's moving. chē °'dùng- (or °'dzěw-)je-de-shf-hew byé 'shyà-chywu. ‖The train is really moving along! 'hwǒ-chē jēn °'kāy- (or °'kwày-)chǐ-lay-le.

(*To change residence*) bān, bān-'jyā. ‖Do you know where they're moving to? nǐ jr̄-dàw tām yàw wàng-'nǎr bān-ma? ‖Are they going to move? tām yàw bān-'jyā-ma? ‖They've moved out of town. (*To the suburbs*) tām bān-dàw chéng-'wày-chywu-le. or (*elsewhere*) tām bān-dàw 'byé-chùr-chywu-le. ‖Where can I find someone to help me move? yàw 'jǎw-rén láy bāng-wǒ bān-'jyā, dàw-'nǎr-chywu 'jǎw-ne? ‖I've been moving around all my life. wǒ yí-'bèy-dz °méy-dzày 'yí-chùr-dì-fang 'dāy-jù-gwo. or °'lǎw-shr 'bān-dàw-'jèr-bān-dàw-'nàr-de. or °'lǎw-shr 'bān-láy-bān-'chywù-de. ‖When will the house be ready for us to move in? fáng-dz 'shéme-shf-hew nèng-'hǎw-le wǒm hǎw 'bān-jìn-chywu? ‖We have to move out next week. wǒm 'shyà-lǐ-bày děy °bān-chū-chywu. or *expressed as* We have to vacate the nest for others. °gěy-rén nwó-'wōer.

(*In games*) to move dzěw, shyà; (*figuratively*) dzěw, dùng, bàn, dzwò; a move (*literally or figuratively*) bù; the next move (*figuratively*) 'shyà-yí-bù, 'shyà-yí-jyàn-shr̀, or *expressed as* next dz̀ay. ‖Whose move is it now? gǎy-'shéy dzěw-le? or 'jèy-bù 'shr̀- (or °'gǎy-)'shéy dzěw? ‖It's your move. gǎy-'nǐ dzěw. ‖That was a wasted move. 'nèy-yí-bù 'dzěw-de méy-'yùng. ‖He can't make a move without his secre-

tary. méy-yěw tā-de-nèy-wèy-'shū-ji tā °'yí-bù yě bù-néng 'dùng. *or* °'shéme yě bàn-bu-'lyăw. *or* °'shéme yě bù-néng 'bàn. ‖He doesn't dare make a move· at present. tā shyàn-dzày 'yí-bù yě bù-gǎn 'dùng. I'm not going to ask him again; it's his move now. wǒ 'bú-dzày wèn-tā-le; 'shyà-yí-bù gāy 'tā-de-le. ‖Let me know before you make a move. yàw 'dzwò-shéme shyān 'gàw-su wǒ yì-'shēng. ‖My next move is to go for the tickets. wǒ 'shyà-yí-bù (*or* wǒ 'shyà-yí-jyàn-shř. *or* wǒ 'dzày jyèw) gāy chywù mǎy-'pyàw-le.

(*To make a motion, in parliamentary procedure*) 'dùng-yì, 'tí-yì. ‖I move we adjourn. wǒ 'dùng-yì (*or* wǒ 'tí-yì) 'shyàn-dzày sàn-'hwèy. ‖I move that we accept him as a member. wǒ 'dùng-yì (*or* wǒ 'tí-yì) 'jyē-shèw tā dzwò hwèy-'ywán.

(*To affect emotionally*) gǎn, 'gǎn-dùng, 'gǎn-kày. ‖I was very much moved by what he said. 'tā-de-hwà jyàw-wǒ 'hěn shèw 'gǎn-dùng. *or* tīng-le 'tā-de-hwà jyàw-wǒ 'hěn shēng 'gǎn-kày. ‖He gave a moving speech. tā-de-yǎn-'jyǎng hěn °'gǎn-rén. *or* °'gǎn-dùng rén. *or* °'jyàw-rén shèw 'gǎn-dùng. ‖His speech moved the crowd to tears. tīng-le 'tā-de-'hwà, nèv-shyē-rén 'gǎn-dùng-de lyéw-'lèy.

To be moving (*busy, in action, etc.*) *is expressed as* to be busy máng, to be doing gan *or* bàn; (*of matters or business*) to be much dwō, to be fast kwày. ‖Things are really moving now. jēn 'máng-chí-lay-le. *or* jēn 'gàn-chí-lay-le. *or* shèr (jēn) 'dwō-chí-lay-le. *or* shèr (jēn) 'máng-chí-lay-le. ‖Things are moving much faster now. shèr bàn-de kwày-'dwō-le. ‖The new director has really got things moving. 'shīn-jǔ-'rèn kě 'jēn bǎ-shèr nèng-de °'kwày-chí-lay-le. *or* °'máng-chí-lay-le.

To move in (*associate with*) gēn . . . 'láy-wǎng. ‖They enjoy the fact that they move in the best circles. tām 'hàw gēn 'shàng-děng-rén láy-wǎng. ‖She's been moving in fast company lately. tā 'jìn-láy 'láy-wǎng-de 'dēw shř shyē-ày-'wár-de-rén. *or* tā 'jìn-láy 'jìng gēn ày-'wár-de-rén 'láy-wǎng.

Move in 'on (*get closer*) lí . . . 'jìn(-dyar). ‖Move in on them so you can fire at close range. lí-tām 'jìn-dyar, myāw-'jwěr jyèw 'rúng-yi-dyar.

Be on the move (*on the road*) dzày 'lù-shang; (*moving around*) dzěw-dàw-'jèr-dzěw-dàw-'nàr-de, 'bān-láy-bān-'chywù-de. ‖We've been on the move for the last month. dǎ 'shàng-ywè wǒm jyèw °'lǎw dzày 'lù-shang. *or* °'dzěw-dàw-'jèr-dzěw-dàw-'nàr-de. *or* °'bān-láy-bān-'chywù-de.

To have the bowels move dà-'byàn, lā-'shř.

MRS. 'tày-tay; *for the wife of a prominent man, particularly an official, one says rather* Madame 'fū-rén. ‖How do you do, Mrs. Jones! (*greeting, not when first meeting*). 'jēw-tày-tay, nǐ 'hǎw? ‖This is for Mrs. Jones. 'jè-shř gěy 'jēw-tày-tay-de.

MUCH. (*In amount*) dwō, bù-shǎw; (*a measure*) shyē; not much bù-'dwō, méy-'dwō-shǎw; how much 'dwō-shǎw; much of . . . . . . 'dwō-bàn, . . . 'dà-bàn, *or* *expressed as* to a great extent shyāng-'dāng-de. ‖Did you spend much last night? dzwér 'wǎn-shang °'hwā-de-chyán 'dwō-ma? *or* °'hwā-de-chyán 'dwō-bu-dwō? *or* °'hwā-de-chyán shř-bu-shr tǐng-'dwō-de? *or* °'shř-bu-shr hwā-le 'hěn-dwō-chyán? *or* °'shř-bu-shr hwā-le bù-'shǎw-de-chyán? *or* °'shř-bu-shr hwā-le 'hǎw-shyē-chyán? ‖Take as much as you like. nǐ 'yàw dwō-shǎw 'ná dwō-shǎw. *or* nǐ ywàn-yi 'yàw dwō-shǎw jyèw 'ná dwō-shǎw hǎw-le. ‖We don't have much time to spend here. wǒm dzày-jèr 'dày-bu-lyǎw 'dwō-shǎw-'shŕ-hew. ‖How much will it cost me? wǒ děy chū 'dwō-shǎw-chyán-ne? ‖I've done only that much up to now. wǒ 'jŕ dàw shyàn-'dzày 'jyèw dzwò-chū-lay 'nèm-°'shyē. *or* (*that little*) °'dyǎr ‖Much of what you say is true. nǐ-'shwō-de-hwà °'yì-dwō-'bàr (*or* °'dà-bàn) dēw 'dwèy. *or* nǐ-shwō-de shyāng-'dāng-de yěw-'lǐ. ‖Much of what's written here is rubbish. jèr-shyě-de-'dwō-bàn shř 'fèy-hwà.

(*In degree*). (*With verbs*) dà; (*awfully*) 'lì-hay; (*fiercely*) shyūng, *and other more specific expressions;* not much (*with verbs*) bú-'dà, *and indirect expressions;* much *with* more . . . *or with adjectives in the* . . .-er *form* dwō; too much tày; very much (*with verbs*) hěn; much rather shyāng háy-shr . . . hǎw, *or* nìng kě. ‖Was there much fuss about it? nèy-shèr nàw-de °'lì-hay-ma? *or* °'shyūng-ma? *or* nèy-shèr shř-bu-shr nàw-de tǐng-°'dà-de? *or* °'lì-hay-de? *or* °'shyūng-de? ‖Do you feel much pain? nǐ téng-de 'lì-hay-ma? ‖He's not much good at this sort of work. 'jèy-jǔng-shèr tā °'bú-dà 'hwèy. *or* °'bú-dà 'chéng. *or* °'bú-dà 'shíng. *or* °'bú-dà dzwò-de-'láy. *or* °'méy-dà 'yùng. ‖I don't care very much for that. wǒ 'bú-dà 'shǐ-hwān °'nèy-ge. *or* (*Of an action*) °'nèm-je. ‖I don't care much about that (*one way or the other*). 'nèy-ge wǒ 'bú-dà 'dzày-hu. ‖I don't have much faith in what they say. tām-de-'hwà wǒ °'bú-dǎ 'shìn. *or* °'bú-dà shyāng-'shìn. *or* °'bú-dà néng 'shìn. *or* °'bú-dà néng shìn-de-'jí. *or* °'jywé-je 'bú-dà kě 'shìn. *or* °'jywé-je 'bú-dà kě 'kàw. *or* °'jywé-je 'bú-dà kàw-de-'jù. ‖I don't think that car is much of a buy. wǒ jywé-je 'nèy-lyàng-chē °'mǎy-je 'bú-dà shàng-'swàn. *or* (*Not worth buying*) °'bù-'jŕ-de yì 'mǎy. *or* °'bù-jŕ-'dàng-de 'mǎy. ‖I feel much better, thanks. hǎw-'dwō-le, dwō 'shyē. ‖This piece is much bigger. 'jèy-yí-kwàr 'dà-de 'dwō. ‖This one is much more expensive. 'jèy-ge 'gwèy-de 'dwō. ‖That's too much! (*Too much to bear*) nèy wèy-'myǎn tày 'nán-dyǎr-le. *or* (*Excessive*) nèy wèy-'myǎn tày gwò-'fèn-le. *or* (*Too improper*) nèy tày bú-shyàng-'hwà-le. ‖I'd very much like to go, but I can't. wǒ 'hěn shyǎng 'chywù, 'bú-gwo wǒ 'bú-néng chywù. ‖I'd much rather stay home. wǒ shyǎng wǒ 'háy-shr dzày 'jyā-li 'dāy-je hǎw.

Much *of the time.* (*Often*) cháng, 'cháng-chang; (*always*) lǎw, jìng; (*all day, all the time*) 'jěng-tyār, 'chéng-tyār. ‖Do they travel much? tām cháng (*or* tām 'cháng-chang) °chū-'mér-ma? or °chū-chywu lywǔ-'shíng-ma? ‖Did they travel much when they were in Russia? tām dzày 'ē-gwo de-shŕ-hew °'cháng (-chang) chū-chywṵ lywǔ-'shíng-ma? or (To many places) °dàw-de-'dì-fang 'dwō-ma? ‖Don't go out too much; you should do your homework once in a while. 'byé °jìng (or °'lǎw, or °jěng-tyǎr, or °chéng-tyǎr) chū-chywu 'wár, yě gāy dzày 'jyā-li.'ywù-bey-ywù-bey 'gūng-kè-le.

‖Thank you very much. dwō-'shyè. or dwō-'shyè, dwō-'shyè. or (for trouble taken) fèy-'shīn, fèy-'shīn.

‖I don't think he's so much. wǒ jywé-je tā °'méy-shéme. or °'méy shéme-lyàw-bu-'chǐ-de. or wǒ bú-jywé-je tā °dzěm-'yàng. or °dzěm lyàw-bu-'chǐ.

‖Not much! (sarcastically) tsáy 'gwày-de-ne!

(As) much as (although . . . very much) 'swéy-rán (. . .) hěn. ‖(As) much as I'd like to go with you, I'm afraid it's impossible. wǒ 'swéy-rán 'hěn shyǎng gēn nǐ-men 'chywù, shŕ-'shŕ-shang kǔng-pà bù-'shíng.

Inasmuch as (since) 'jì-shr. ‖Inasmuch as I've decided to go myself, I don't think you'll have to write that letter now. wǒ 'jì-shr 'jywé-dìng 'chìn-dz dàw-nàr 'chywù-le, wǒ kàn nǐ jyèw 'béng shyě nèy-fēng-'shìn-le.

So much the better gèng 'hǎw. ‖Well, if she's not coming, so much the better. tā 'bù-láy, gèng 'hǎw.

MUD. ní. ‖Don't step in the mud. byé wàng 'ní-li 'tsǎy. ‖My car is stuck in the mud. chì-'chē 'shyàn-dzay 'ní-li-le ‖My shoes are covered with mud. wǒ-de-'shyé-shang 'mǎn-shŕ 'ní.

MUSIC. yīn-'ywè. ‖Where's the music coming from? yīn-'ywè-de-'shēng-yīn tsúng-'nǎr láy-de? ‖What kind of music do you like? nǐ 'shǐ-hwan 'shéme-yàng-de yīn-'ywè? ‖She's studied music for ten years. tā 'shywé-le 'shŕ-nyán-yīn-'ywè. ‖Who's giving the music course this year? 'jīn-nyán 'shéy jyāw yīn-'ywè?

(Score) ywè-'pǔ(r). ‖Has the band received the music yet? ywè-'dwèy yǐ-jing 'ná-dàw-le ywè-'pǔma? ‖I'd like to practice this music. wǒ shyǎng 'lyàn-lyan jèy-ge-°'pǔ-dz. or °'ywè-'pǔr.

To face the music shèw-'dzwèy. ‖It's your mistake; now you must face the music. nǐ-'dż-jǐ nùng-'dzāw₁le, shyàn-dzày nǐ-'dż-jǐ shèw-'dzwèy-ba.

MUST. děy; or expressed with the adverbs yí-'dìng, 'jwěn-shŕ. ‖We must do what we can to help him. wǒm děy jí-'lì bāng tā-de-'máng. ‖It's my party; you must let me pay. 'wǒ chǐng-'kè, nǐ děy ràng-'wǒ fù-'jàng. ‖They were so nice to us; we must have them over. tām dày wǒ-men hěn 'hǎw; wǒm děy 'chǐng-chǐng 'tā-men. ‖The contract must be signed by the end of the month. jèy-ge-'ywè-'nèy yí-'dìng děy bǎ jèy-ge-hé-túng 'chyān-hǎw. ‖If you MUST catch an earlier train, I'll see you to the station. nǐ yàw-shr yí-'dìng yàw dzwò 'dzǎw-chē dzěw, wǒ jyèw dàw chē-'jàn chywù 'sùng-shíng. ‖He must be there by now. tā 'jèy-ge-shŕ-hewr yí-'dìng 'dàw-nèr-le. ‖I must have left my wallet home. wǒ-de-pí-'bāw 'jwěn-shŕ 'là-dzay 'jyā-li-le. ‖It must be almost four o'clock. 'jwěn-shŕ 'chà-bu-dwō 'sż-dyǎn-jūng-le. ‖This must be my room. 'jèy-ge-wū-dz °'dà-gàv (or °'yīng-gay) shŕ 'wǒ-de.

MY. See I.

N

NAME. (Of a person; full name, or given name as opposed to family name, or formal name as opposed to other names as given below) 'míng-dz; (a person's name) 'rén-míng; (family name) shìng; (full name) 'shìng-míng; (pet name of a child) 'rǔ-míng or 'shyǎw-míng; (school name) 'shywé-míng or dà-'hàw; (some-one's courtesy name, used by others but not by himself) dż or hàw; (courtesy name of the person addressed) 'táy-fǔ; (pen name) 'bǐ-míng; (nickname) wày-'hàwr; (name of a Buddhist priest, who must renounce his family name) shàng-'shyà; or expressed as call, be called, be named (of a person) jyàw; or call (of a person) or be called, of a person's name) 'chēng-hū. ‖In a Chinese name, the surname comes first; e.g., in the name 'hwáng ān-'lǐ, hwáng is the surname and ān-'lǐ the given name. 'jūng-gwo-'rén-míng 'shìng dzày 'chyán-tew; 'bǐ-fāng shwō, 'hwáng ān-'lǐ jèy-ge-'míng-dz-ba, 'hwáng shŕ shìng, ān-'lǐ shŕ 'míng-dz. ‖A Chinese should never be addressed directly by his given name, except by superiors, elders, or close

friends. dāng-'myàr jyàw-rén, chú-le 'shàng-sz, 'jǎng-bèr, hé 'jŕ-jìn-de-'péng-yew, bù-néng jyàw 'míng-dz. ‖So there are also courtesy names. swǒ-yǐ yěw 'dż-a-'hàw-de. ‖A Chinese usually has a formal name and several courtesy names. yí-ge-'jūng-gwo-rén cháng-chang yěw yí-ge-'míng-dz hé jǐ-ge-'dż-a-'hàw-de. ‖Some Chinese have only one name which they use throughout their lives. 'yěw-de-jūng-gwo-rén yí-bèy-dz jř yùng 'yí-ge-míng-dz. ‖When a man grows up, he should never be referred to by his child-hood name, except sometimes by his elders. jǎng-'dà-le-de-rén, chú-le 'jǎng-bèr, 'shéy dēw bù-néng jyàw tā-de-'shyǎw-myéngr (or tā-de-'rǔ-míng). ‖He may be called by his surname, as Mr. So-and-so. kě-yǐ jyàw-tā měw-'shyàn-sheng. ‖Please write your full name here. chǐng bǎ 'míng-dz (or 'shìng-míng) shyě-dzày 'jèr. ‖What is your name? (Polite) gwèy-'shìng? or (Surname and given name) gwèy-'shìng, dà-'míng? or (Only among highly educated people in very formal circumstances) méy-'lìng-jyàw? or (Cour-

tesy name) táy-'fǔ dzěm 'chēng-hū? *or* (*To inferiors*) nǐ jyàw 'shéme-míng-dz? *or* nǐ 'shìng-shéme, 'jyàw-shéme? ‖My name is 'wèy mù-'shř. bì-'shìng (*or* wǒ shìng) 'wèy, jyàw mù-'shř. *or* wǒ jyàw 'wèy mù-'shř. ‖His name is 'chywán lù-'chí. tā jyàw (*or* tā-de-'míng-dz shř) 'chywán lù-'chí. ‖His nickname is Long John. tā-de-wày-'hǎwr shř 'cháng-dz. *or expressed as* Everybody calls him Long John. rén dēw 'jyàw-tā 'cháng-dz. ‖They gave him a nickname. tām gěy-tā 'chǐ-le ge-wày-'hǎwr. ‖I forgot his name. tā-'míng-dz (*or* tā 'jyàw-shéme) wǒ 'shyǎng-bù-chǐ-láy-le. ‖Let's give the baby a (*formal*) name. dzám gěy 'háy-dz chǐ ge-'míng-dz-ba. ‖I know him only by name. wǒ jř 'tīng-jyàn-gwo jèy-ge-'rén-de-'míng-dz. ‖I know him by name. wǒ 'jř-dàw tā-de-'míng-dz. *or* wǒ 'jř-dàw tā 'jyàw-shéme. ‖I'm sorry I can't call you by name. dwèy-bu-'chǐ, 'táy-fǔ wǒ yì-'shŕ jyàw-bu-shang-'láy-le. ‖Great teacher (*to a Buddhist priest*), what is your name? dà-'shŕ-fù, shàng-'shyà dzěm 'chēng-hū?

(*Of something other than a person*) 'míng-dz; -míng; (*trade name*) 'páy-dz; *or expressed by* jyàw; *or in some cases not expressed at all.* ‖What's the name of your store? (*Polite*) bǎw-'hàw shř 'něy-jyā? *or* (*Ordinary conversation*) nǐm-de-'pù-dz °jyàw-'shéme? *or* °shř 'něy-jyār? ‖What's the name of that store? 'něy-ge-'pù-dz °jyàw-'shéme. *or* °shř 'shéme-míng-dz? ‖What's the name of the street she lives on? tā-'jù-de nèy-tyáw-'jyē °jyàw-'shéme-lay-je? *or* °shř shéme-'míng-dz-lay-je? ‖The name of the book is .... 'shū-míng shř .... *or* jèy-běn-'shū-de-'míng-dz shř .... ‖The name of the boat is .... 'chwán-míng shř .... *or* 'chwán-de-'míng-dz shř .... ‖What's the (*trade*) name of that product? 'nèy-jǔng-'dūng-shi shř shéme-'páy-dz-de?

(*Reputation, fame; with a necessarily good connotation*) míng, 'míng-ywù, 'míng-chi. ‖That product has a good name. 'nèy-dūng-shi hěn yěw-'míng. ‖He's just trying to whitewash his father's name. 'tā-nà bú-gwò shř yàw gěy tā-'fù-chin-de-'míng-ywù 'shǐ-shwā-shǐ-shwā. ‖He's a lawyer who has made quite a name for himself. tā shř ge-'lywù-shř, (dz-gěr) gǎw-de 'hěn yěw 'míng-chi-le.

To name. (*Give a name to*) gěy ... chǐ 'míng-dz (*or* 'myéngr); (*very formal*) gěy ... mìng-'míng. *Each may be followed by* jyàw *plus the name given.* Formal naming ceremony mìng-'míng-dyǎn-'lǐ. ‖In China a baby is never named after its parents (*elders*). dzày 'jūng-gwo 'shyǎw-hár 'méy-yěw gēn-'jǎng-bèr-chǐ-yí-'yàng-de-'míng-dz-de. ‖We named the dog Fido. wǒm gěy-'gěw chǐ-le ge-myéngr, jyàw féy-'dèwr. ‖I name you ... (*in a formal naming ceremony*). wǒ gěy-nǐ mìng-'míng, jyàw .... ‖Have you named the baby yet? shyǎw-'hár chǐ-'myéngr-le-ma? *or* nǐm gěy shyǎw-'hár chǐ-'myéngr-le-ma?

To name (*call by name*) 'jyàw-chu 'myéngr-lay, 'shǔ-chu ..., 'shwō-chu .... ‖Can you name all the players? shywǎn-'shěw dēw shř 'shéy, nǐ jyàw-de-chu 'myéngr-lay-ma? *or* shywǎn-'shěw-de-'míng-dz nǐ dēw

°'shǔ-de-chu-láy-ma? *or* °'jyàw-de-chu-láy-ma? *or* °'shwō-de-chu-láy-ma? ‖The burglar refused to name the men who had helped him. shyǎw-tēwr 'bù-kěn bǎ bāng-gwo-tā-de-rén-de-'míng-dz °'shwō-chu-lay. *or meaning* admit °'jāw-chu-lay. ‖Just name one! nǐ 'shwō-chū 'yí-ge-lay wǒ 'tīng-ting.

To name. (*Designate, select*) shwō; (*to set*) dìng; (*to choose*) tyāw. ‖You name the day, and we'll have dinner together. nǐ 'shwō (*or* 'dìng, *or* 'dìng-gwey, *or* 'tyāw) ge-'ř-dz, dzám hǎw yí-'kwàr chŕ-dwèn-'fàn. *or* dzám 'něy-tyān yí-'kwàr chŕ-dwèn-'fàn, °nǐ 'shwō (*or* 'dìng, *etc.*) 'ř-dz-ba. *or* °'ř-dz yéw-'nǐ shwō (*or* dìng, *etc.*). ‖Name a price. shwō yí-ge-'jyàr. ‖We asked him about a good place to eat, and he named several downtown restaurants. wǒm wèn-tā 'nǎr-de-'tsày hǎw, tā shwō-le 'hǎw-jǐ-jyār-dà-'jyē-shang-de-'gwǎn-dz. (*See also* **APPOINT.**)

To call *someone* **names** (*curse*) mà. ‖He likes to call people names. 'tā ày mà-'rén.

In name only yěw-'míng-wú-'shŕ (*literary*); be only a name shř ge-'kūng-míng-dz. ‖He is head of the company in name only. 'tā dāng jīng-'lǐ (*or* tā-nèy-ge-jīng-'lǐ dāng-de) yěw-'míng-wú-'shŕ. *or* tā-nèy-ge-jīng-'lǐ shř ge-'kūng-míng-dz. ‖He's a scholar in name only. 'tā-nèy-ge 'shywe-je yěw-'míng-wú-'shŕ.

In the name of, in *someone's* **name** yùng ...-de-míng-dz, yùng ...-de-míng-yì. ‖I bought the property in her name. jèy-kwày-'chǎn-yè wǒ yùng 'tā-de-'míng-dz (*or* tā-de-'míng-yì) mǎy-de. ‖He's been borrowing money in my name. tā yùng 'wǒ-de-'míng-yì (*or* 'wǒ-de-'míng-dz) °chywù jyè-'chyán. *or* (*without my consent*) °'jāw-yáw-jwàng-'pyàn. *But* ‖Open the door in the name of the law! wǒ fèng 'mìng-lìng láy-de, (jyàw-ni) kāy-'mén! ‖In the name of all that's holy! dàw-'dǐ! *or* 'jyēw-jìng! ‖What in heaven's name did you do that for? nǐ 'nèm-je dàw-'dǐ (*or* 'jyēw-jìng) shř 'dzěm-hwéy-'shř-a?

Other expressions in English. ‖I haven't a cent to my name. wǒ yí-ge-'dà dēw 'méy-yěw. *or* (*Literary*) wǒ 'yì-wén bù-'míng. ‖He was named in the will. 'yí-jū-shang-'tí-dàw-de-yí-chǎn-jì-chéng-rén-li yěw-tā.

NARROW. (*Of spatial dimension*) jǎy, bù-'kwān; *sometimes* (*thin*) shèw *or* shì; *or* (*small*) shyǎw; *or* (*tight*) jǐn; *or* (*not widespread*) bù-'gwǎng. ‖This is a very narrow road. jèy-tyáw-'lù tǐng-'jǎy. ‖Be careful when you are on narrow roads. dzày 'jǎy-lù-shang dzěw de-'shŕ-hew, yàw 'shyǎw-shīn-je. ‖The road narrows down (*or* gets narrow) just beyond the bridge. 'gāng-yī gwò-'chyáw lù-'myàr jyèw 'jǎy-le. ‖This piece of cloth is too narrow. 'jèy-kwày-bù tày 'jǎy. ‖I don't want it that narrow. wǒ 'bú-shr yàw 'nèm-jǎy-de. ‖The pants are very baggy, and narrow at the cuffs. kù-'twěr dū-lu-je, kù-'jyàwr hěn °'jǎy *or* °'shèw. ‖Her eyebrows are narrow and long. tā-de-'méy-maw yèw 'shì yèw 'cháng. *or expressed as* She has willow-leaf eyebrows. tā shř lyěw-'yèr-méy. ‖She has very narrow shoulders. tā-jyān-'bǎngr hěn 'jǎy (*or* 'shyǎw). ‖The waist of her skirt is very narrow. tā-'chywún-dz-'yāw-nar hěn 'jǎy (or 'shì, or 'shyǎw, or 'shèw, or 'jǐn). ‖These shoes are too narrow. 'jèy-shwāng-shyé tày 'jǎy (or 'jǐn). ‖He only had a narrow circle of friends. tā-'péng-yew hěn 'shǎw. or (Literary) tā-'jyāw-yéw bù-'gwǎng.

(Literal) kēw-je dž-'myàr, àn-je dž-'myàr. ‖His decision in this case showed a narrow interpretation of the law. jèy-ge-'àn-dz tā shř 'kēw-je 'jèy-tyáw-'fǎ-lywù-de-dž-'myàr 'dwàn-de. or tā dwàn 'jèy-ge-àn-dz de-shŕ-hew, ywán-yǐn-de-'fǎ-lywù shř àn-je-dž-'myàr-jyě-shř-de.

(Detailed and careful) 'dž-shì. ‖A narrow scrutiny of the case is called for. jèy-ge-'àn-dz háy děy 'dž-shì 'chá-yi-chá.

(Of the mind, views, etc.). ‖She's a narrow-minded person. 'tā-nèy-ge-rén °shīn-'jǎy. or °'shīn-yǎr hěn 'jǎy. or °'shīn-yǎr hěn 'shyǎw. or °'bú-'dà-fang. or °'shyǎw-chì. or °'dù-lyàng hěn shyǎw. or (Especially in thinking) °méy-'jyàn-shř. or °'jyàn-jyě hěn 'dī. or °'jyàn-jyě 'chyǎn-bwó. or (Prejudiced) °yěw 'pyān-jyàn. or °'pyān-shīn-'yǎr. ‖His views on the subject are very narrow. dzày 'jèy-jyàn-'shř-shang tā-de-'yǎn-gwāng (or tā-de-'kàn-fǎ, or tā-de-'jyàn-jyě) hěn 'pyān.

Narrow down. ‖The question narrows down to this: do you want to go, or don't you? 'gān-tswèy (yí-jywù-'hwà), nǐ 'ywàn-yì-bú-ywàn-yì 'chywù-ba? ‖His suspicions have narrowed down to one person. tā-'yí-shīn-de-rén °jř 'shèng-shya 'yí-ge-le. or °'jyǎn-dàw 'yí-ge-le.

Narrow escape. ‖We had a narrow escape yesterday. is expressed as We were in great danger. 'dzwér-ge wǒm 'shyǎn-de (or 'shywán-de) 'hěn. or meaning from death dzwór wǒm chà-'dyǎr méy °bǎ-'mìng dyēw-le. or meaning from being seen and caught °jyàw-rén dǎy-jáw.

NATION. gwó, 'gwó-jyā. The whole nation chywán-'gwó, 'gwó-mín, chywán-gwó-'gwó-mín; (with special reference to the people) 'mín-dzú. ‖Five nations were represented at the conference. nèy-ge-'hwèy yěw °'wǔ-gwó-de-dày-'byǎw chū-'shí. or °'wǔ-ge-'gwó-jyā-de-dày-'byǎw chū-'shí. ‖The whole nation will be affected by the new law. nèy-ge-'shīn-fǎ-gwēy hwèy jyàw chywán-'gwó(-de-rén, or -gwó-mín) shèw 'yǐng-shyǎng.

NATIONAL. (Pertaining to the political entity) gwó-. ‖Stand up when they play the national anthem. 'yǎn-dzèw 'gwó-gē de-shŕ-hew, 'jàn-chǐ-lay.

(Pertaining to the political entity and its people) 'gwó-jyā-de. ‖A national law gives all citizens the right to vote. àn-je-'gwó-jyā-de-'fǎ-lywù 'swǒ-yěw-de-'gwó-mín 'dēw yěw 'shywǎn-jywǔ-'chywán.

(Pertaining to the whole country distributively). Expressed by the noun 'chywán-gwó. ‖This is a matter of national importance. jèy-jyàn-shř gēn 'chywán-gwó yěw 'gwān-shì. ‖He owns a national chain of restaurants. tā-de-'gwǎn-dz 'chywán-gwó dēw yěw 'fēn-hàw.

(A citizen) 'rén-mín, 'gwó-mín. ‖The country requires its nationals to register in time of war. 'gwó-jyā dzày 'jàn-shŕ jyàw 'rén-mín (or 'gwó-mín) 'dēng-jì.

Nationalism 'mín-dzú-jǔ-'yì, 'gwó-jyā-jǔ-'yì.

Nationality (recorded in census, etc.) gwó-jí.

NATURAL. (Pertaining to the physical universe) 'dž-rán. ‖He's studying natural science. tā nyàn 'dž-rán-'kē-shywé.

(In accordance with nature, in a native state) 'tyān-rán. Natural gas 'tyān-rán-'méy-chì. ‖The landscape has been left in its natural state, with none of the works of man added. jèy shř 'tyān-rán-de-'fēng-jǐng, 'yì-dyǎr-'rén-gūng yě méy-'jyā-gwo. ‖There is a natural waterfall there. nèr yěw yí-ge-'tyān-rán-de-pù-'bù.

(Innate, in accordance with inborn nature) tyān-'shēng-de, tyān- only in the phrase 'tyān-tsáy natural talent. ‖He has a natural talent for painting. tā tyān-'shēng-de hwèy hwà-'hwàr. or tā yěw hwà-'hwàr-de-'tyān-tsáy. ‖He's a natural at (playing) tennis. tā dǎ 'wǎng-chyéw yěw 'tyān-tsáy. or tā tyān-'shēng-de dǎ 'wǎng-chyéw dǎ-de 'hǎw. or expressed as One try and he excels. tā dǎ 'wǎng-chyéw 'yì-dǎ jyèw 'jīng.

(Normal) 'dž-rán (or, emphatically, dž-'rán), 'dāng-rán; both mean normally, of course. ‖It was a natural thing to say. 'dž-rán (or 'dāng-rán) děy nèm-'shwō-de. ‖It was only natural for him to feel that way. tā dž-'rán (or dāng-'rán) hwèy 'jywé-je nèm-yàngr-de. ‖It's only natural that he didn't like it. tā dž-'rán (or 'dāng-rán) bú-hwèy 'shǐ-hwān-de.

(Real) jēn-de. ‖The picture looks natural. jèy-jāng-'hwàr kàn-je gēn 'jēn-de shř-de.

(Habitual) 'tsúng-láy; (habitually) yí-'shyàng. ‖Is that your natural posture? nǐ-de-'dž-shř 'tsúng-láy (or yí-'shyàng) jyèw 'nèy-yàngr-ma?

(Unaffected) 'tyān-jēn, 'dž-rán, 'dà-fāng, bú-hwèy jwāng-'jyǎ, bú-hwèy 'jwāng-mú-dzwò-'yàngr-de; (not bound by convention) bù-'sú-chì, bù-'jywū-shù, 'shyāw-sǎ, sǎ-twō. ‖He's a very natural person. 'tā-jèy-ge-rén °hěn 'tyān-jēn. or °hěn 'dž-rán. or °hěn 'dà-fāng. or °hěn 'shyǎw-sǎ. or °bù-'sú-chì. etc. ‖Act natural. 'dž-dz-rán-'rán-de. or 'dà-da-fāng-'fāng-de.

(Not violent). ‖He died a natural death. (Of an old man, literary) tā shř 'shèw-jūng-jèng-'chǐn. or expressed as He died of illness. tā shř 'bìng-sž-de.

NATURE. (System of the physical universe). Chinese uses only the combining form meaning natural(ly) 'dž-rán. ‖Gravity is one of the laws of nature. 'dì-shīn-'shī-lì shř 'dž-rán-'lywù jř-'yī. ‖He won't take medicine; he says, let nature take its course. tā 'bù-chř-'yàw; tā shwō 'yǎng-yi-yang dž-'rán jyèw 'hǎw-le. ‖He won't take medicine; he just lets nature take its course (waits for himself to get well). ta bù-chř-'yàw; děng 'dž-jǐ 'hǎw.

Stairway, Chin Temple, Taiyuan

Temple of Heaven, Beijing

(*Inborn nature*) 'tyān-shìng; *or expressions with the combining form meaning* natural(ly) tyān-'shēng-de. ‖It's not his nature to forget. tā-'tyān-shìng °'bú-hàw 'wàng. *or* (*Of hatred*) -°ay jì-'chéw? *or* (*Of loyalty*) °'jūng-hèw. ‖It's not in his nature to be rude to his parents. *is expressed as* He's naturally respectful to his parents. tā-'tyān-shìng hěn 'shyàw-shwèn. *or* tā tyān-'shēng-de 'shyàw-jìng 'fù-mǔ. *or expressed as* He's not naturally disrespectful to his parents (*despite evidence to the contrary*). tā 'bú-shr tyān-'shēng-de 'bù-kěn 'shyàw-jìng 'fù-mǔ-de-'rén. ‖He's a lazy person by nature. 'tā-jèy-ge-rén °tyān-'shēng-de 'lǎn. *or* °'tyān-shìng 'lǎn-dwò.

(*Characteristic, of other than a person*) 'tè-shìng. ‖It's the nature of this metal to melt at a very low temperature. jèy-jǔng-'dǔng-shi-de, 'tè-shìng shr dzày wēn-dù-hěn-'dī-de-shŕ-hew jyèw kě-yǐ 'hwà-de.

(*Kind*) jǔng *or* yàng(r) (*measures meaning* kind of); (hwéy-) 'shŕ, 'chíng-yéw. ‖Has he explained to you the nature of your work (*what kind of work you're going to do*)? nǐ-'yàw-dzwò-de shr 'něy-jǔng-shr (*or* shr 'shéme-yàngr-de-shr) tā dwèy-nǐ 'jyǎng-gwo-le-ma? ‖What was the nature of the crime? jèy(-jyàn)-'àn-dz(-...-'shì-chíng) shr dzěme-hwéy-'shŕ? *or* jèy (-jyàn)-'àn-dz shr dzěme-ge-'chíng-yéw?

Good-natured. ‖She's a good-natured person. tā pí-chì 'hǎw. *or* tā-jèy-rén °hǎw-'pí-chyer. *or* °tyān-'shēng-de (*or* 'tyān-shìng) 'hèw-daw. *or* °tyān-'shēng-de (*or* 'tyān-shìng) 'jūng-hèw.

NEAR. (*Close in space or relationship*) jìn, bù-'ywǎn; near . . . lí . . . 'jìn, lí . . . bù-'ywǎn. ‖The store is near the station. pù-dz lí hwǒ-chē-'jàn hěn 'jìn. ‖Where is the nearest post office? lí-jèr 'dzwèy-jìn-de-'yéw-jèng-'jywú dzày-'nǎr? ‖He grabbed the arm of the man nearest him. tā bǎ 'lí-tā-'dzwèy-jìn-de-nèy-ge-rén-de-'gē-bwo 'yì-bǎ 'dzwàn-ju-le. ‖We walked near the river. wǒm dzày lí-'hé-byār-bù-'ywǎn-de-nàr 'dzěw-lay-je. ‖He is a near relative of ours. (*Of the same surname*) tā shr wǒm-de-'jìn-běn-jyā. *or* (*By marriage*) tā shr ge-'jìn-chīn. *or* tā shr ge-hěn-'jìn-de-'chīn-chì.

Near here, nearby (*in the neighborhood*) (jèr-) 'fù-jìn, (jèr-) 'dzwó-jìn, 'gēn-chyar, bù-'ywǎn. ‖Is there a hotel near here? jèr-'fù-jìn (*or* jèr-'dzwǒ-jìn) yěw lywú-'gwǎn-ma? ‖We can get milk from one of the nearby farms. fù-'jìn-de-núng-'chǎng-nàr kě-yǐ mǎy nyéw-'nǎy. ‖There are several grocery stores nearby. 'gēn-chyar (*or* fù-'jìn, *or* bù-'ywǎn) yěw 'jǐ-jyā-'dzá-hwò-pùr.

To near. (*Come near, get near, be nearly at*) (lí . . .) 'jìn-le, (lí . . .) bù-'ywǎn-le; (*almost at*) 'kwày-dàw. ‖The boat is nearing land now. chwán 'kwày-dàw 'àn-le. *or* chwán lí-'àn °bù-'ywǎn-le. *or* °hěn 'jìn-le. ‖We're getting near Chicago. dzám 'kwày-dàw jŕ-jyā-'gē-le. *or* dzám lí jŕ-jyā-'gē °'jìn-le. *or* °bù-'ywǎn-le.

Be near, nearly . . ., near at hand. (*Close in time*) 'kwày-dàw; (*almost, just before*) 'chà-bu-dwō, jyèw yàw 'dàw-le; (*be near at hand*) . . . jyèw 'dàw. ‖It will be sometime near Christmas (*or*, It will be nearly Christmas) before he gets back. tā děy 'kwày-dàw (*or* 'chà-bu-dwō) shēng-dàn-'jyé-de-shŕ-hew tsáy néng 'hwéy-lay-ne. ‖The time for the attack is near (at hand), *or*, . . . is nearly here. jìn-'gūng-de-shŕ-jyān °jyèw yàw 'dàw-le. *or* °'shwō-hwà jyèw 'dàw. *or* °'jǎn-yǎn jyèw 'dàw. *or* °kwày 'dàw-le.

(*Soon, early*) dzǎw. ‖We tried to get theater tickets but the nearest date was two months off, so we didn't buy any. wǒm wèy mǎy 'shì-pyàw hěn 'fèy-le dyǎr-shŕ, 'bú-gwò dzwèy-'dzǎw-de yě dzày 'lyǎ-ywè yǐ-hèw, 'swǒ-yǐ méy-'mǎy.

(*Closely resembling*). *See also* LIKE, DIFFERENT. ‖I think this ring is nearer to what I had in mind than that one. wǒ shyǎng 'jèy-ge-jyè-jŕ bǐ 'nèy-ge gēn wǒ-'shīn-li-shyǎng-'yàw-de háy 'shyàng-dyar. ‖We don't have that kind of tobacco, but this is the nearest thing to it. wǒm 'méy-yěw nèy-jǔng-yān-'yè-dz, bú-gwò jèy-ge °'chà yě chà-de bù-'dwō, *or* °'chà-de bù-'dwō *or* °'chà-bu-'dwō. *or* °hěn 'bǐ-de-'shàng. *or* °yě jyèw-shr shywē-wēy yěw yì-dyǎr-bù-'túng (*or* yì-'dyǎr-bù-yí-yàng).

Near miss. ‖It's a near miss. (méy-'jùng, bù-gwo) °'pyān-de bù-'dwō. *or* °'chà-de bù-'dwō. *or* °'chà-de hěn 'shǎw. *or* °chà-bu-'dwō (jyèw 'jùng-le). *or* °'shāw-wēy chà nèm-yì-'dyǎr jyèw 'shŕ-le.

Near at hand *or* near to hand (*easily accessible*) dzày shěw-'byār-shang. ‖The documents are all near at hand. nèy-shyē-'wén-jyàn 'dēw dzày shěw-'byār-shang.

Come near . . .ing *or* nearly . . . kwày . . .; 'chà-dyǎr jyèw . . . . *See also* ALMOST. ‖I came near forgetting how to get here. (*or* I nearly forgot . . . .) wǒ bǎ shàng-jèr-'láy-de-lù °dēw kwày 'wàng-le. *or* °'chà-dyǎr jyèw 'wàng-le.

Near-sighted 'jìn-shŕ(-de), (shr) 'jìn-shŕ-'yǎn. ‖He's near-sighted. tā 'jìn-shŕ. *or* tā shr 'jìn-shŕ-'yǎn. ‖He's so near-sighted that he can't see without glasses. tā 'jìn-shŕ-de 'bú-dày yǎn-'jyèngr 'shéme dēw 'kàn-bu-'jyàn.

NECESSARY. It is necessary to . . . yí-'dìng yàw . . ., yí-'dìng děy . . .; absolutely necessary 'bì-shywū yàw . . ., 'bì-shywū děy . . ., fēy(-dèy) . . . bù-'shíng, fēy (-děy) . . . bù-'chéng, fēy(-děy) . . . bù-'kě, bū . . . bù-'shíng, bū . . . bù-'chéng. . . . is necessary *use* yěw *plus the noun after* děy, yàw, *or* fēy *in the above expressions, or* 'méy-yěw *plus the noun instead of* bū . . . . It is necessary for . . . to *do so-and-so, put the word after* for *before any of the above expressions.* ‖It will be necessary to have a passport (*or* A passport will be necessary) to travel abroad. dàw gwó-'wày chywù lywú-'shíng °yí-'dìng děy yěw hù-'jàw. *or* °'bì-shywū děy yěw hù-'jàw. (*or* yàw *instead of* děy *in either of these.) or* °'fēy(-děy) yěw hù-'jàw bù-'shíng (or bù-'chéng, or bù-'kě). or °'méy-yěw hù-'jàw bù-'shíng (or bù-'chéng). ‖It will be necessary to have everything checked before release. dzày 'fā-chū-chywu yǐ-'chyán °yí-'dìng (or 'bì-shywū) yàw (or děy) dž-shì 'chá yí-byàn. or °'fēy(-děy) 'dž-shì chá yí-byàn bù-'shíng (or bù-'chéng, or 'bù-kě). or °'bú-'dž-shì chá yí-byàn bù-'shíng (or bù-'chéng). ‖It is necessary for you to be here at eight o'clock. nǐ yí-'dìng (or 'bì-shywū) děy (or yàw) 'bā-dyǎn-jūng 'dàw-jèr. or nǐ 'fēy-děy 'bā-dyǎn-jūng 'dàw-jèr bù-'kě (or bù-'shíng, or bù-'chéng). or nǐ 'bā-dyǎn-jūng bú-'dàw bù-'shíng (or bù-'chéng). ‖Is that necessary? 'fēy nèm-je bù-'shíng-ma? or yí-'dìng děy 'nèm-je-ma? or 'bì-shywū yàw 'nèm-je-ma? or 'bú-nèm-je bù-'shíng-ma? etc. or (Emphatically sarcastic) hé-'bì-ne! ‖Is this trip necessary? 'jèy-tsž 'fēy-děy 'chywù-ma? or expressed as Is it worth while? (May be sarcastic) 'yùng-de-jáw dzěw nèm-yí-'tàng-ma?

(Attributive uses) Add -de to any of the above constructions, with a verb in the blank; also 'yīng-dāng . . .-de, referring to things that ought to be: in some cases the sentences are paraphrased with the verbal sentences above. ‖He brought only the most necessary articles of clothing with him. tā swéy-shēn-'dày-de jř yěw jǐ-jyàn-°fēy-chwān-bù-'kě-de-'yī-shang. or °yí-'dìng-děy-chwān-de-'yī-shang. or °'bú-'dày-bù-'shíng-de-'yī-shang. etc. ‖I'll make the necessary arrangements. 'yīng-dang-bàn-de-'shěw-shywu (or yí-'dìng-děy-bàn-de-'shěw-shywu) dēw jyāw-gěy wǒ-ba. ‖Do you have all the evidence necessary to prove the case? 'jèy-ge-àn-dz yí-'dìng-děy-'yěw-de-'jèng-jywu (or 'bì-shywū-děy-'yěw-de-'jèng-jywu) dēw 'chywán-ma? ‖The necessary result will be a great deal of confusion. (Verbal construction, and limited to certainty, not absolute requirement or desirability). 'jyē-gwǒ 'fēy-chéng yì-twán-'dzāw bù-'kě. or 'jyē-gwǒ yí-'dìng yàw nèng ge-'lwàn-chī-bā-'dzāw-de.

NECK. (Part of the body) bwó-dz. ‖He broke his neck. tā bǎ 'bwó-dz nèng-'shé-le. ‖He has a scar on the back of his neck. tā-'bwó-dz-'hèw-tew yěw ge-'bā-la. ‖He has a thick neck. tā-'bwó-dz hěn 'tsū. ‖I've got a stiff (sore) neck. wǒ-'bwó-dz téng. or wǒ-'bwó-dz fā-'swān. or (Stiff from sleeping awkwardly) wǒ lè-'jěn-le.

(Collar) lǐng-dz, lyěngr. ‖She wore a dress with a high neck. tā-chwān-de-nèy-jyàn-'yī-shang 'lǐng-dz hěn 'gāw. or tā chwān-de yì-jyàn-'gāw-lyěngr-de-'yī-shang.

(Narrow par. of a bottle) kěwr. ‖Pick up the bottle by the neck. bǎ 'píng-dz 'ná-chǐ-lay de-shŕ-hew, ná-je 'píng-dz-'kěwr-nar.

(Narrow stretch of land) tǔ-'yāw. ‖There are three necks of land jutting out into the bay. hǎy-'wān-li 'shēn-je 'sān-ge-tǔ-'yāw.

Neck and neck. ‖The two horses finished neck and neck. (Even) lyǎng-pǐ-'mǎ °pǎw-le ge-'píng. or (In a draw, literary) °pǎw-le ge-'bù-fēn-shèng-'fù. or (Arrived together) °yí-'kwàr dàw-'jyā.

Get it in the neck āy(-le) dwèn 'hǎw-de. ‖He got it in the neck when they were caught loafing. tām 'wár-chǐ-lay-le (jyàw-rén) gěy 'dǎy-ju-le; 'nèy-shŕ-hew tā āy-le dwèn 'hǎw-de.

Save one's neck. ‖Never mind about me. You'd better save your own neck. (Think of a way out) byé gwǎn-'wǒ-le. °nǐ gěy nǐ-dž-'jǐ shyǎng 'fá-dz-ba. or (Save your life) °nǐ-'dž-jǐ táw-'mìng yàw-'jǐn.

To neck 'bàw-je 'chīn. ‖Does she neck? tā hwèy 'bàw-je 'chīn-ma?

NEED. *All the Chinese expressions are verbal, even where English uses* need *as a noun.*

(With other verbs) děy (must), gāy, 'yīng-gāy, or 'yīng-dāng, also other words of similar meaning, for which see **NECESSARY.** ‖These clothes need to be washed. 'jèy-shyē-'yī-shang gāy (or děy) 'shǐ-le. ‖He needs to get a haircut. tā gāy (or děy) lǐ-'fà-le. ‖He needs to be taught a lesson. tā gāy (or děy) 'jyàw-shywun-jyàw-shywun. ‖Need you leave now? nǐ 'jēn děy 'dzěw-ma? ‖She needn't have made such a fuss. tā 'bù(-yīng)-gāy 'nèm fā 'pí-chi. ‖Well, he needn't have slapped her. yàw 'nèm shwō-ne, tā 'běn-láy jyèw bù-gāy 'dǎ-tā. ‖The car is in need of repairs (of being repaired). jèy-ge-chē 'yīng-dāng (or 'yīng-gāy, or gāy, or děy) 'shēw-shr-le. ‖I'll go there myself if need be. yàw-shr 'fēy-nèm-je-bù-'kě de-hwà (or yàw-shr yí-'dìng-děy-nèm-je de-hwà or yàw-shr 'bú-nèm-je-bù-'shíng de-hwà) wǒ jyèw dž-'gěr chywù yí-tàng.

(With verbs or nouns in the meaning **have use for**) 'yùng-de-jáw. ‖I don't see any need for me to go personally. wǒ jywé-je yì-'dyǎr yě 'yùng-bu-jáw wǒ běn-'rén chywù. ‖You needn't have bothered. nǐ 'běn-láy 'yùng-bu-jáw 'gwǎn-de. ‖You don't need to thank me. nǐ 'yùng-bu-jáw 'shyè-wǒ. ‖When he needs you he's very nice, but when he doesn't need you any more he gives you the cold shoulder. tā 'yùng-de-jáw rén de-shŕ-hew, 'mǎn-lyǎn péy-'shyàwr; 'yùng-bu-jáw rén de-shŕ-hew, tā-de-'jyà-dz kě jyèw jyàw-rén shèw-bu-'lyǎw-le. or (Proverb) tā 'yùng-jáw rén cháw-'chyán, 'yùng-bu-jáw rén cháw-'hèw.

(With nouns, in the meaning **need to have, need to use**). Also děy yěw (etc.); 'yīng-gāy yěw (etc.); (or yùng in place of yěw); (want, ask for) yàw; (use) yùng, yàw-yùng. ‖I think we (have) need (of) a man of your abilities. shyàng 'nǐ-nèm-néng-gàn-de-'rén wǒm-jèr °'děy yěw yí-wèy. or °'yīng-gāy yěw yí-wèy. or °'yùng-de-jáw. ‖He is in need of a vacation. tā 'yīng-gāy (or 'yīng-dāng, or gāy, or děy) yěw jǐ-tyān 'shyēw-shi-shyēw-shi. ‖We need him here too. 'wǒm-jèr yě yùng-de-jáw tā. ‖We need him badly. 'wǒm-jèr 'fēy yěw (or yàw)-tā bù-'shíng. ‖His needs are very simple. 'tā-yàw-de (or 'tā-yùng-de) 'dēw shř hěn-'rúng-yì-bàn-'dàw-de. ‖I need money. wǒ děy 'yùng dyǎr-'chyán. ‖I need money urgently. wǒ 'jí-ywú yàw yùng dyǎr-'chyán.

(*With nouns, in the meaning* lack) chywē, chà, *also in some cases* yùng *or* yàw *as above.* ‖Take care of his needs. tā 'chywē-shéme (*or* tā 'yùng-shéme, *or* tā 'yàw-shéme) 'jàw-yīng-je-dyar. ‖They are in great need of clothing and medicine. tām yèw chywē 'yī-fu, yèw chywē 'yàw-pǐn. ‖There is a great need for co-operation. dà-jyā 'lyán-lè tày 'chà. *But* ‖I need your help a minute. *is expressed as* I have something right now; please help a bit. wǒ shyàn-'dzày yěw-'shr̀, chǐng-nǐ bāng-bang 'máng.

A friend in need. ‖You certainly are a friend in need. nǐ 'jēn gèw 'péng-yew. *or* nǐ 'jēn gèw 'jyāw-chíng. ‖A friend in need is a friend indeed. *is expressed as* Only one who can be relied on can be called a friend. kàw-de-'jú-de tsáy swàn 'péng-yew. *or* Only one who can be trusted with widow and son can . . . . 'néng-twō-chī-jì-'dž-de tsáy . . . . *or* Only one who sends charcoal when it snows can . . . 'shywě-li-sùng-'tàn-de tsáy . . . .

NEEDLE. (*Sewing, hypodermic, phonograph*) jēn. Magnetic needle. tsź-jēn. ‖Do you have a needle and thread? nǐ yěw-'jēn yěw-'shyàn-ma? ‖She's lost a knitting needle. tā dyěw-le yì-gēn-dǎ-'rúng-shyàn-de-'jēn. ‖Change the needle before playing that record. shyān 'hwàn yí-ge-'jēn dzày chàng 'nèy-ge-pyān-dz. ‖Does the needle point due south? 'tsź-jēn jr̀-je 'jèng nán-ma?

Pine needles 'sūng-máw. ‖We made a bed of pine needles. wǒm dzày 'dì-shang pū-le 'sūng-máw dàng 'rù-dz. *or* (. . . *and slept on it*) wǒm 'dyàn-je 'sung-máw 'shwèy-de.

To needle bī (*force*). ‖Who needled him into this? 'shéy bǎ-tā 'bī-de 'nèm-je-le?

NEGLECT. *Many indirect expressions are used with such meanings as* not be serious, be careless, not put to heart, not do well, forget, not take care of, *etc.*

(*Not be serious about, be careless about*) ‖He's been neglecting his work lately. 'jìn-láy tā °dzwò-'shr̀ bú-shàng-'jìn. *or* °dzwò-'shr̀ yěw dyǎr-'shyè-day. *or* °dzwò-'shr̀ bú-rèn-'jēn. *or* °méy bǎ tā-dzwò-de-'shr̀ gē-dzày 'shīn-shang. *or* °yěw-dyar ná-shr̀-bú-dàng-'shr̀ dzwò. *or* °dzwò-'shr̀ bù-'shyǎw-shīn. *or* °dzwò-'shr̀ bù-lyéw-'shén. *or* °dzwò-'shr̀ tày 'dà-yi. *or* °dzwò-'shr̀ tày 'shū-hu. *or* °dzwò-'shr̀ tày 'tsǎw-shwày. *or* °dzwò-'shr̀ 'shīn-bú-'dzày-yan. ‖He's been neglecting her. tā 'jìn-láy °bú-dà bǎ-tā 'gē-dzày shīn-shang. *or* °dwèy-tā 'bú-dà shàng-'jìn. *or* °dwèy-tā yěw dyǎr-'shyè-day (*or* dyǎr-'shū-hu, *or* dyǎr-'shū-ywǎn). *or* °yěw-dyǎr 'bù-ná-tā-dàng-hwéy-'shèr. *or* (*literary*) °yěw-dyǎr shīn-bú-'dzày-yan. ‖You'd better not neglect that infection. nèy-ge-hwèy-'néng-de-'dì-fang °byé 'dà-yi-le tsáy 'hǎw. *or* °byé 'dān-wù-le tsáy 'hǎw. *or* (*A doctor will have to take care of it.*) °děy 'jř. *or* °děy hǎw-'hāwr-de 'jř-yi-jř. ‖He's been neglecting his disease. tā dwèy-ywu dž-'gěr-de-'bìng tày 'dà-yi-le. *or* tā dž-'gěr-de-'bìng 'lǎw. 'dān-wu-je. *or* °bù-hǎw-'hāwr-de-'jř.

(*Not do well*) bù-hǎw-'hāwr-de. . . . ‖He's been neglecting his duties lately. 'jìn-láy tā 'gāy-dzwò-de-shř 'bù-hǎw-'hāwr-de 'dzwò. ‖Her parents neglected her education. tā-de-'fù-mǔ °'dān-wu-le ta, 'méy jyàw-tā hǎw-'hāwr-de shàng-'shywé. *or* °bǎ tā-nyàn-'shū-de-shèr gěy 'dān-wu-le. ‖You've been neglecting your school work. 'jìn-lay nǐ 'gūng-ke 'méy-hǎw-'hāwr-de nyàn (*or* 'ywù-bey).

(*Not do at all, forget*). ‖I neglected to lock the door. wǒ 'wàng-le swǒ-'mén-le. *or* wǒ tày 'dà-yi-le (*or* wǒ tày 'shū-hu-le), 'méy-swǒ-'mén. ‖He neglected to tell his boss that he'd borrowed some money. tā yì-'shū-hu (*or* tā yí-'dà-yi) méy-bǎ tā-jyè-'chyán-de-shèr gàw-su tā-de-'téwr.

‖The house shows signs of neglect. jèy-ge-'fáng-dz méy-rén 'gwǎn shr̀-de.

NEIGHBOR. 'lín-jywū, 'jyē-fáng; next-door neighbor jyè-'byěr(-jù-de); neighbors (*as a group*) 'lín-jywū-'jyē-fáng-de. ‖He is our next-door neighbor. tā shr̀ wǒm-de-°'jìn-'lín-jywū. *or* °'jyē-fang. *or* °jyè-'byěr. *or* tā jù wǒm-jyè-'byěr. ‖The neighbors formed a committee. 'lín-jywū-'jyē-fang-de 'chéng-lì-le yí-ge-'wěy-ywán-'hwèy.

NEITHER. (*Negative of both*) . . . 'dēw bū-. . .; 'něy-ge . . . yě bū-. . . (*preceded by a noun, followed by a verb*). ‖Neither statement is true. 'lyǎng-jǔng-'shwō-fǎ 'dēw bú-'dwèy. *or* 'něy-ge-'shwō-de yě bú-'dwèy. ‖Neither one of us can be there. wǒm-lyǎ 'shéy-dew bù-néng 'dàw. *or* wǒm-lyǎ 'dēw bù-néng 'dàw.

(*Negative of also*) 'yě bū-. . . (*or* 'yě méy-. . .); *must be followed by a verb; if two parallel negations are expressed,* yě *is used with each; see* neither . . . nor *below.* ‖If she isn't going to write, neither will I. 'tā yàw-shr 'bù-shyě-'shìn-na, wǒ (jyěw) 'yě bù-'shyě. ‖He doesn't have any, and neither do I. tā yě 'méy-yěw, 'wǒ yě méy-yěw.

Neither . . . nor (*negative of both . . . and*) yèw bū . . . yèw bū . . ., yě bū . . . yě bū, jì bū . . . yèw bū . . . . ‖She can neither sew nor cook. tā yèw (*or* yě, *or* jì) 'bú-hwèy dzwò-'yī-shang, yèw (*if* yèw *before, or* yě *after* yě, *or* yèw *after* jì) 'bú-hwèy dzwò-'fàn. ‖I could neither see nor hear the speaker, so I left. nèy-yǎn-'jyǎng-de-rén wǒ °yèw (*or* jì) 'kàn-bu-jyàn yèw 'tīng-bu-jyàn, swǒ-yǐ jyèw 'dzěw-le. *or* °'kàn yě 'kàn-bu-jyàn, 'tīng yě 'tīng-bu-jyàn, swǒ-yǐ jyèw 'dzěw-le.

Neither here nor there (*irrelevant; inconclusive*). ‖That talk is neither here nor there. nèy-shyē-'hwà (dēw) °'wú-gwān 'jǐn-yàw. *or* °'bù-gwān 'tùng-yǎng. *or* °méy-'yùng. *or* °'bú-jùng-'kěn(-chì). *or* nèy dēw-shr 'fèy-hwà.

See also **EITHER.**

NET. (*Mesh*) 'wǎng(-dz). Fish net 'ywú-wǎng (*and most similar combinations*). *But:* mosquito net 'wén-jàng. ‖The nets were loaded with fish. (ywú-) 'wǎng-li 'jìng-shr (*or* 'chywán-shr, *or* 'dēw-shr, *or* 'mǎn-le) 'ywú. ‖The ball went through the net. chyéwr dzày wăng-dz-li 'chwān-gwo-chywu-le. ‖It's safer to sleep under a mosquito net in this climate. dzày 'jèy-jŭng-dì-fang 'háy-shr dzày 'wén-jàng-lì shwèy °'hăw-dyar. or °'jyàw-rén fàng-'shīn.

(*Actual; without apparent or external additions*) jìng, (*actual*) 'shŕ-jì-shang (*both go with verbs*); also net profit 'chwén-lì; net income 'shēw-rù 'dzŭng-'é; net weight chywù-'pí. ‖What was your net profit last year? chywù-nyán °'jìng jwàn (*or* shèng) 'dwō-shăw-chyán? or °'chwén-lì dwō-shăw? ‖We made $3,000 net. wŏm jìng jwàn (*or* shèng) (*or*, wŏm-de-'chwén-lì shr̀) 'sān-chyān(-ywán). ‖The net weight is two catties. 'jìng jùng 'lyăng-jīn. or chywù-'pí 'lyăng-jīn. ‖We made a net gain of ten yards. wŏmen 'shŕ-jì-shang wàng-'chyán jìn-le shŕ-'mă.

To net (*of money*) jwàn; (*of other things*) (jyàw ...) dé. ‖The firm netted a good profit. gūng-'sz̄ jwàn-le hěn-'dwō-de-chyán. or gūng-'sz̄ 'dà jwàn-'chyán. ‖The clever suggestion netted him a reward. tā chū-de-'fá-dz hěn 'chyăw, jyàw-tā dé-le 'jyăng-le.

NEVER. (*Habitually not, including at present*) bū-, méy(-yĕw) .... ‖I never say such things. wŏ 'bù-shwō 'nèy-yàngr-de-hwà. ‖When he starts talking he never stops. tā 'yì-shwō-chī-lay jyèw °méy(-yĕw) 'wán. or °méy(-yĕw) 'téwr. or °bú-jù-'dzwěy. or °bú-jù-'dzwěr. or °bù-'tíng.

(*Habitually not, in past time only*) 'shyàng-láy bū-, 'tsúng-láy bū-, 'yí-shyàng bū-. ‖I've never said such things. wŏ 'shyàng-láy (*or* 'tsúng-láy, or 'yí-shyàng) bù-shwō 'nèy-yàngr-de-hwà.

(*Not once, in past time only*) ('gēn-běn) méy-; or 'shyàng-láy bū- etc., *especially in resultative compounds;* or 'shyàng-láy (etc.) méy-. ‖I never said any such thing. wŏ 'gēn-běn 'méy-shwō-gwo 'nèm-yàngr-de 'hwà. ‖He never even opened the book. 'nèy-běn-shū tā (gēn-'běn jyèw) lyán-'běr děw méy 'dă-gwo. ‖I don't know why she's crying; I never even touched her. 'wŏ bù-jŕ-dàw tā wèy-shéme 'kū; wŏ °(lyán) 'ay děw méy-'ày-jaw tā. or °yě méy-'āy-tā-méy-'pèng-tā-de. ‖I've never felt better in my life. wŏ yí-'bèy-dz méy-jèm-gāw-'shìng-gwo. or *expressed as* I feel swell. wŏ 'shū-fu-'jí-le. or *expressed as* I'm not sick at all! wŏ 'shéme-bìng děw 'méy-yěw.

(*Not again, in future time*) jywé bū-, dzày bū-, dzày yě bù-, jywé bú-dzày, yí-'dìng bù-, yí-'dìng bú-dzày; *in imperatives,* don't ever, *use* 'bú-yàw *or* byé *instead of* bū-. ‖I'll never go there again. wŏ dzày (yě) bú-'dàw-nàr 'chywù-le. or wŏ jywé (*or* yí-'dìng) bú-(dzày) dàw-nàr 'chywù-le. ‖Never do it again. 'dzày byé 'nèm-je-le! or 'yí-dìng 'bú-yàw (*or* byé) 'dzày nèm-je-le.

NEW. (*Not old*) shīn; or shīn *plus a verb, with the meaning* newly ...; or *sometimes* gāng or (*just* ...) tsáy *plus a verb.* ‖This building is new. 'jèy-ge-léw °shr̀ 'shīn-de. or °hěn 'shīn. or °shr̀ shīn-'gày-de or jèy shr̀ ge-'shīn-léw. ‖A new president has just been elected. 'shīn-dzŭng-'tŭng gāng 'shywăn-shang-le. or gāng 'shywăn-le ge-'shīn-dzŭng-'tŭng. or shīn-'shywăn-le ge-dzŭng-'tŭng. ‖They have a (very) new suite of furniture. tām yĕw yí-tàw-'jăn-shīn-de-'jyā-jywu. ‖That's a new style. nèy shr̀ ge-'shīn-shr̀-yang. ‖The ground was covered with new-fallen snow. 'dì-shang 'pū-je yī-tséng-°'shīn-shyà-de-shywĕ. or °'gāng-shyà-de-shywĕ. or °'tsáy-shyà-de-shywĕ. ‖The new man was cross-eyed. shīn-'láy-de (or shīn-'dàw-de, or shīn-'hwàn-de)-nèy-ge-rén (shr̀ ge-) 'dèw-yăr. ‖Do you have any new potatoes? tŭ-'dèw yĕw °'shīn-shyà-lay-de-ma? or °'gāng-dàw-de-ma? ‖I'd like a new one. wŏ shyăng yàw ge-'shīn-de. (*See also next paragraph*) ‖I like the new one better. wŏ 'sh́ĭ-hwān nèy-ge-'shīn-de. ‖There will be a new moon next week. 'shyà-lǐ-bày °yěw 'shīn-ywè. or (*Confined to new moon only*) °'ywè-lyang shr̀ 'shàng-shywán. ‖They're a newly wed couple. tām 'shīn jyē-'hwēn. or tām shr̀ 'shīn-hwēn-de-'fū-fù.

‖Happy New Year! shīn-'shǐ, shīn-'shǐ!

(*Different*). (*Changed, exchanged*) hwàn(-le); (*another*) lìng; *also a few indirect expressions.* ‖I'd like a new one (*a different one*). wŏ shyăng yàw 'hwàn yí-ge. ‖He bought a new car. (*New to him, not necessarily newly made*) tā 'hwàn-le yí-lyàng-'chē. or (*He bought a car again.*) tā 'yèw măy-le yí-lyàng-'chē. ‖After the operation he looks like a new man. kāy-'dāw yí-'hèw tā 'kàn-shang-chywu °shyàng 'hwàn-le ge-'rén shr̀-de. or °shyàng 'lìng-yí-ge-'rén shr̀-de. or (*Doesn't look like himself*) bú-'shyàng tā-le. ‖She got a new man. (*Servant*) tā hwàn-le ge-tīng-'chāy-de. or (*Lover or husband*) tā hwàn-le ge-'nán-rén. ‖I feel like a new man. wŏ 'jywé-de gēn (or shyàng, or hăw shyàng) 'hwàn-lé yí-ge-'rén shr̀-de.

(*Unfamiliar*). ‖This place is new to me. *is expressed as* I just came. 'jèy-dì-fang wŏ °chū 'láy. or °'shīn dàw. or *as* I've never come before. °méy-'láy-gwo. or *as* I'm not familiar with it. wŏ 'jèy-her háy bù-'shéw-ne. or *as* I'm green here. wŏ 'jèy-her hěn 'shēng-ne. or jèy-ge-dì-fang wŏ háy 'rén-shēng-dì-bù-'shéw-de-ne. ‖This is a new experience for him. 'tā jèy shr̀ °'chū-tsż. or °'téw-yì-'hwéy. or °kāy-'hwēn. or °'shīn kāy-'chyàwr. or °dà-'gū-nyáng shàng shì-'jyàw. ‖I'm new at this kind of work. *is expressed as* I've never done it before. 'jèy-jŭng-shŕ wŏ °méy-'dzwò-gwo. or °méy-'gàn-gwo (etc.) or °háy-shr wày-'háng-ne. or °yĕw dyăr-'lì-ba. or °shr̀ ge-'mén-wày-'hàn. or *as* I'm not used to it. °háy bú-'gwàn-ne. or °háy bù-'shéw-ne. or °háy méy-'mwō-jaw 'mér-ne.

NEWS. (*News report*) 'shīn-wén; (*information*) 'shyāw-shi. ‖What's the latest news? yĕw shéme 'shīn-wén? or yĕw shéme-'shīn-dàw-de-'shyāw-shi? ‖Here is the very latest news. jèy shr̀ 'gāng(-dé)-dàw-de-'shīn-wén. ‖What's the latest news about the election? shywăn-'jywŭ-de-'shr̀ °'gāng dé-le shéme-'shīn-shyaw-shi méy-yĕw? or °'shyàn-dzày dzĕm-'yàng-le? ‖Who's going to break the news to him? 'shéy chywù bă jèy-ge-'shyāw-shi 'gàw-su 'tā-ne?

670

To get news. (*Personally*) dé-'shìn; (*by mail or message*) 'jyē-jaw 'shìn *or* 'shēw-dàw 'shìn. *See* **GET**.

News to . . . . ‖That's news to me. wǒ háy méy-'tīng-jyàn-gwo. *or* wǒ 'ywán-lay 'bù-jŕ-daw yěw 'nèm hwéy-shr̀. ‖That's no news to me. nèy wǒ dzǎw °'tīng-jyàn-gwo-le. *or* °'jŕ-dàw-le. *or* °'shyǎng-dàw-gwo-le.

Daily News 'r̀-bàw; **Alumni News** 'túng-shywé-'shyāw-shi.

NEWSPAPER. bàw, bàw-'jŕ, shīn-wén-'jŕ. (*Referring to the publisher or company*) bàw-'gwǎn. ‖Do you have an evening newspaper? nǐ yěw 'wǎn-bàw-ma? ‖What does the newspaper say? 'bàw-shang (*or* bàw-'jŕ-shang) dzěm 'shwō-de? ‖We have eleven newspapers in our library. wǒm-tú-shū-'gwǎn-li yěw shŕ-'yí-fèn-°'bàw. *or* °bàw-'jŕ. *or* °shīn-wén-'jŕ. ‖They're collecting old newspapers. tām jèng-dzày lyǎn jyèw-bàw-'jŕ. ‖He wrapped the bottle with newspapers. tā bǎ 'píng-dz ná 'bàw-jŕ 'bāw-shang-le. ‖He kept all the issues of that newspaper. 'nèy-fèn-bàw °tā àn-je 'tyār-tswén (*or* °tā yì-'tyān-yì-tyān-de 'tswén-je, *or* °tā yì-'chī-yì-chī-de 'tswén-je) tswén-le yěw 'sān-nyán-le. ‖That newspaper is subsidized. 'nèy-jyā-bàw-'gwǎn (*or* 'nèy-ge-bàw-'jŕ, *or* nèy-ge-'bàw) chŕ (*or* yěw-'rén) 'jīn-tyē. ‖This town has no newspaper. jèy-ge-dì-fang méy-yěw °bàw-'gwǎn. *or* °běn-'dì-de-bàw-'jŕ. *or* °běn-'dì-de-shīn-wén-'jŕ.

NEXT. (*In a series of several things or times*) 'shyà (-yī)-, 'dzày(-yī)-; (*below*) 'dǐ-shyà. The·next time 'shyà(-yí)-tsž, *also* dzày; next month 'shyà-ywè; next week 'shyà-lǐ-'bày; next year 'míng-nyán. ‖Who's next in line here? 'shyà-yí-ge shŕ-'shéy? *or* 'shyà-yí-ge gāy-'shéy-le? *or* 'dǐ-shyà gāy-'shéy-le? *or* 'dzày-yí-ge gāy-'shéy-le? ‖You're next. 'shyà-yí-ge gāy-'nǐ-le. ‖I'll tell him that, the next time I see him. wǒ 'shyà (-yí)-tsž (*or* wǒ 'dzày) 'kàn-jyàn tā de-shŕ-hew bǎ nèy-ge 'gàw-su tā. ‖I've finished this questionnaire, and I'm ready for the next one. 'jèy-ge-tí-'jŕ wǒ dēw dá-'wán-le; děng-je dzwò 'shyà-yí-ge-ne. ‖The next train leaves in half an hour. 'shyà-yí-tàng-'chē gwò 'bàn-ge-jūng-'téw kāy. ‖The next one is mine. 'shyà-yí-ge jyèw-shr̀ 'wǒ-de. *or* 'dzày yěw yí-ge, jyèw-shr̀ 'wǒ-de.

(*After one thing or time*). (*The second*) dì-'èr; next in rank, next best chí-'tsž. ‖I went hom·e the next day. dì-'èr-tyān wǒ hwéy-'jyā chywù-le. ‖He's next to. the last. tā·'dàw-shǔ dì-'èr. ‖He's next in authority (*or* prestige, power, *etc*.). (*Merely second*) 'tā dzwò dì-'èr-bǎ-jyāw-'yǐ. *or* (*After naming one*) chí-'tsž shr̀ 'tā. ‖That is the next best thing.·chí-'tsž jyèw shr̀ (*or* shǔ) 'jèy-ge °'hǎw-le. *or* °-'bàn-fa hǎw-le.

(*Afterwards, later*) rán-'hew, yǐ-'hew. ‖Next he put the letter in his pocket. rán-'hew (*or* yǐ-'hew) tā bǎ 'shìn jwāng (*or* chwāy, *or* gē, *or* shēw) -dzày tā kěw-'dàr-li-le. ‖What shall I do next? yǐ-'hew (*or* rán-'hew) dzwò 'shéme-ne? *or* 'shyà-yí-ge dzwò 'shéme-ne? *or* dzwò-wán 'jèy-ge dzwò 'shéme-ne?

(*In location*) 'páng-byār; (*on that side*) 'nèy-byār; the next . . . 'páng-byār-nèy(-ge-· . .), 'nèy-byār-nèy (-ge-. . .), next to . . . . . .(-de-)'páng-byār (*or* 'nèy-byār); next-door jyè-'byér, *in the same constructions*. ‖The next house is mine. 'páng-byār (*or* 'nèy-byār, *or* 'jyè-byér)-nèy-ge-'fáng-dz shr̀ 'wǒ-de. *or expressed as* Next time you pass a gate, that's our home. 'dzày gwò yí-ge-'mér jyèw-shr wǒm-'jyā-le. ‖Who lives next-door? jyè-'byér (*or* 'nèy-byār)-nèy-swǒr-'fáng-dz 'shéy jù? ‖She sat next to me at the theater. kàn-'shì-de-shŕ-hew 'tā dzwò-dzày wǒ-'páng-byār. ‖We live next-door to the school. wǒ-men jù-dzày shywé-'shyàw-de-jyè-'byér.

Next to nothing.·‖She knows next to (*almost*) nothing about world affairs. 'shŕ-jyè-'dà-shŕ tā 'jyàn-jŕ (*or* tā 'chà-bu-dwō) 'shéme dēw bù-jŕ-'dàw.

NICE. *Often* hǎw (*see* **GOOD**), *but sometimes more specific terms*. ‖Did you have a nice time? nǐ wár-de 'hǎw-ma? ‖I had a very nice time, thank you. dwō 'shyè, wǒ wár-de hěn 'hǎw. ‖I thought your friend was very nice. wǒ 'jywé-je nǐ-nèy-ge-'péng-yew hěn °bú-'hwày. *or* (*Friendly*) °'hé-chi. *or* (*Well-mannered*) °yěw 'lǐ-màw. ‖Everyone was very nice to us. 'shéy dēw dày-wǒm (dày-de) hěn 'hǎw. ‖She wears nice clothes. tā chwān °hǎw-yī-fu. *or* (*Well-chosen*) °'jyǎng-jyew-yī-fu. *or* (*Expensive*) °'gwèy-yī-fu. ‖It's nice and warm here. (*Really warm*) jèr jēn 'nwǎn-he. *or* (*Comfortable and warm*) jèr yèw 'shū-fu yèw 'nwǎn-he.

(*Sarcastic*). ‖This is a nice mess! 'hěw-yì-twán-'dzāw-le! ‖You certainly did a nice job of confusing things! nǐ-de-'shéw-dwàn 'jēn gāw-wa, 'dēw gěy nèng-'lwàn-le. *or* nǐ 'jēn yěw 'běn-shr, nèng-de 'nèm-lwàn-chī-bā-'dzāw-de.

NIGHT. 'yè-li (-yè *in combination*). ‖He studies better at night. tā 'yè-li nyàn-'shū nyàn-de 'hǎw. ‖These flowers bloom at night. jèy-shyē-'hwàr dēw dzày 'yè-li kāy. ‖He spent the night on the train. tā dzày 'chē-shang gwò-de-'yè. ‖I spent two nights there. wǒ dzày-'nàr jù-le (*or* gwò-le) 'lyǎng-yè. ‖He snored all night. tā 'jěng-yè (*or* 'yí-yè) dǎ-'hū-lu. ‖He works nights. tā 'yè-li dzwò-'gūng (*or* dzwò-'shr̀). ‖He does night work. *or* He works on a night shift. tā dzwò 'yè-gūng (*or* 'yè-bān).

Midnight bàn-'yè; **in the middle of the night** 'sān-jīng-bàn-'yè-de *or* 'shē·-jīng-bàn-'yè-de; **night and day** 'hēy-yè-'báy-r̀-de; **last night** 'dzwó-tyān 'yè-li *or simply* 'yè-li; **tomorrow night** míng-tyan 'yè-li. ‖Did you sleep well last night? ('dzwó-tyān) 'yè-li shwèy-de 'hǎw-ma?

(*Evening*) 'wǎn-shang. ‖They're going to the movies tomorrow night. 'míng-tyan 'wǎn-shang tā-men chywù kàn dyàn-'yěngr chywù.

‖**Good night.** (*When parting to meet the next day*) 'myéngr-jyàn. *or* 'míng-tyan jyàn. (*When parting for a longer time*) dzày-'jyàn. (*To someone sleeping in the same house*) hǎw-'hāwr-de 'shwèy.

Make a night of it. ‖Let's go to the play and then go dancing, and really make a night of it. wǒ-men 'shyān chywù kàn-'shì, dzày chywù tyàw-'wǔ, 'tùng-tùng-kwàr-'kwār-de 'wár yì-'wǎn-shang.

NINE. jyěw.

NINETEEN. shŕ-'jyěw. **One-nineteenth** shŕ-'jyěw-fēn-jr-'yī; **the nineteenth** dì-shŕ-'jyěw.

NINETY. 'jyěw-shŕ. **One-ninetieth** 'jyěw-shr-fēn-jr-'yī; **the ninetieth** dì-'jyěw-shŕ.

NINTH. One-ninth 'jyěw-fēn-jr-'yī; **the ninth** dì-'jyěw.

NO. *In answer to a question, Chinese has no exact equivalent (see Part E, Section 5, of Introduction).*

Followed by another word, expressed by a negative sentence. See **NOT.** ‖**We have no guns, no rifles, and not even enough swords.** wǒm 'méy-yěw 'pàw, 'méy-yěw 'chyāng, lyán 'dāw dēw bú-gèw 'yùng-de. ‖**There are no women in the club.** 'hwèy-li 'méy-yěw 'nywǔ-rén. ‖**The situation is no better than before.** 'chíng-shing yì-'dyǎr bu-jyàn 'hǎw. ‖**He's no better than she is.** tā bìng 'bù-bǐ-tā 'hǎw. *or* tā yì-'dyǎr dēw bù-bǐ-tā 'hǎw. ‖**There's no hope of our winning.** dzám 'bú-hwèy 'yíng-de. *or* dzám 'méy-yěw 'yíng-de-'shī-wàng. ‖**It's no joke!** 'bú-shr̀ 'wár-de. *or* 'bú-shr̀ shwō-je 'wár-de. ‖**It's no small matter.** 'bú-shr 'shyǎw-shr̀. *or expressed as* It's important. 'gwān-shi hěn 'dà-de. ‖**That sign says: No Smoking, Please.** (*Somewhat literary*) 'páy-dz-shang 'shyě-je: 'shr̀-nèy 'chǐng wù-shī-'yān. ‖**No Smoking** (*smoking not allowed*). 'bù-jwěn shī-'yān. ‖**No meat today.** (*There is none*) 'jīn-tyan 'méy-yew-'rèw. *or* (*None for sale*) 'jīn-tyan 'bú-mày-'rèw. *or* (*Eating it not allowed*) 'jīn-tyan 'bù-shywǔ chr̄-'rèw. *or* (*I don't want to buy any*) 'jīn-tyan 'bú-°yàw (*or* °mǎy) 'rèw. ‖**He's no longer here.** tā 'bú-dzày-jèr-le. ‖**He's been gone no longer than twenty minutes.** tā ('gāng) dzěw-le bú-dàw 'èr-shr-fēn-'jūng-ne. *or* tā 'dzěw-le (háy) bú-gwò 'èr-shr-fēn-'jūng-ne. *or* (*Just twenty minutes*) tā 'dzěw-le tsáy yěw 'èr-shr-fēn-'jūng. ‖**I have no more to say.** (*That's about all*) 'yě jyěw-shr 'nèm-je-le. *or* (*Nothing more that can be said*) 'méy-yěw byé-de(-kě-'shwō-de)-le. *or* (*helplessly*) wǒ méy-'hwà shwō-le. *or* (*angrily*) 'wǒ 'dzày 'méy-de kě-'shwō-le. ‖**No more!** *meaning* There is no more. méy-'yěw-le! *or meaning* I won't give you any more. bù-'gěy-le. *or meaning* Don't ask for any more. 'byé dzày yàw-le. *or* 'bù-shywǔ 'dzày yàw-le.

In some other cases, the sentence is rephrased into an affirmative. ‖**He promised to be gone no longer than necessary** *is expressed as* He promised to return as soon as he was finished. tā shwō-de shr̀ wán-le-'shr̀ lì-'kè jyěw 'hwéy-lay. ‖**No sooner said than done.** *is expressed as* As soon as it's said it's done. 'shwō-wán-le yě 'dzwò-wán-le. *or* shwō-'hwà jr̄-'jyan jyěw dzwò-'wán-le. *or* 'gāng shwō-wán-le jyěw 'dé-le (*or* 'chéng-le). *or as* That's easy. 'nà hǎw-bàn. *or as* That

can be done immediately. 'mǎ-shàng jyèw kě-yǐ 'chéng. ‖**There were no less than** (*there were at least*) **200 men who volunteered to go.** 'jywū-rán yěw 'èr-bǎy-dwō-rén 'dž-gàw-fēn-'yǔng-yàw-'chywù-de.

NOBODY (NO ONE). (*Before a verb*) 'shéy yě bū-, 'dēw bū-, 'chywán bū-, 'chywán-dēw bū-, 'shéy-dēw bū-; *or, in past time,* méy *instead of* bù; *also, in past time only,* 'méy-rén. ‖**Nobody knows where he is now.** 'shéy 'yě (*or* 'dēw, *or* 'chywán, *or* 'chywán-dēw, *or* 'shéy-dēw) bù-jr̄-dàw tā 'shyàn-dzày dzày-'nǎr. ‖**The policeman said that nobody was to leave the room.** (*Note: this is not past time from the policeman's point of view.*) shywún-'jǐng shwō 'jèy-wū-dz-li-de-'rén 'dēw (*or* 'shéy yě, *etc.*) bù-shywǔ 'chū-chywu. ‖**Nobody told me.** 'shéy yě (*or* 'dēw, *etc.*) méy-'gàw-sung wǒ. *or* 'méy-rén 'gàw-sung wǒ.

‖**There is nobody.** 'méy-yěw rén. ‖**There's nobody here.** jèr 'méy-yěw rén. ‖**There's nobody else here.** jèr 'méy-yěw 'byé-rén.

‖**He's a nobody.** tā méy-yěw 'míng-chi. *or* tā shr̀ ge-'wú-míng-shyǎw-'dzúr.

NONE. (*Not one*). (*Of things or persons, expressed after the noun in Chinese.*) dēw *or* chywán *or* 'chywán-dēw *plus a negativ*; *or, emphasizing,* not a single one yí-ge- *before the noun and a negative, with* yě *preceding the negative if the verb comes after the noun;* (*of people only*) shéy *or* 'shéy-dēw *plus a negative word.* ‖**They have none of the things you have.** shyàng 'nǐ-de-jèy-shyē-'dūng-shi 'tā-men dēw (*or* 'chywán, *or* 'chywán-dēw) méy-'yěw. ‖**None of the men spoke to me.** méy-yěw 'yí-ge-rén °'gēn-wǒ shwō-'hwà. *or* °'lǐ-wǒ. *or* (lyán) 'yí-ge-'lǐ-wǒ de-rén yě méy-'yěw.

(*Not any*) *expressed only in the negative word.* ‖**He asked for some money, but we had none (either).** tā yàw 'jyè dyǎr-chyán, °kě-shr 'wǒm yě méy-'yěw. *or* °kě-shr wǒm 'méy-de kě-'jyè-de.

None too . . . 'bú-dà . . . . ‖**He was none too happy about it.** tā 'bú-dà gāw-shìng nèm-je. *or* nèy-shèr 'jyàw-tā 'bú-dà 'tùng-kwày.

None the less 'swéy-rán-ru-tsž . . . háy-shr . . . ; 'bú-gwò . . . háy-shr . . . . ‖**The situation looks hopeless, but none the less we're determined to try.** 'jèy-shèr 'kàn-je 'méy yì-dyǎr-'shī-wang, °'bú-gwo wǒm 'háy-shr yàw 'shr̀-yi-shr. *or* °'swéy-rán-rú-'tsž, wǒm háy-shr yàw 'shr̀-yị-shr̀.

‖**None of that!** (*Talk*) 'bù-shywǔ nǐ 'hú-shwō! *or* byé 'shyā-shwō! *or* (*Action*) 'bù-shywǔ 'nèm-je. *or* 'byé nèm-je.

Have none of it. ‖**They told him of the plan, but he would have none of it.** tām bǎ nèy-ge-'yì-sz gēn-tā 'tí-le yì-tí; tā °'bú-'gàn. *or* °'wán-chywán 'bú-azan-'chéng. *on* °'wán-chywán fǎn-'dwèy. *or* °'jywù-'jywé-le.

None the worse. ‖**He was none the worse for the accident.** chū-le hwéy-'shèr tā 'jywū-rán °méy dzěm-'yàng. *or* °'hǎw-'hāwr-de 'háy nèy-yàngr.

NOON. 'jūng-wǔ; (*Peiping*) 'shǎng-wǔ; (*in combination*) -wǔ. ‖I'll meet you in front of the hotel at noon. dzá-men 'jūng-wǔ (*or* 'shǎng-wu) dzày lywǔ-gwǎn-'chyán-byar jyàn. ‖It's exactly twelve noon. jèng-shr 'jūng-wǔ (*or* 'shǎng-wu) shŕ-èr-'dyǎn. ‖He's arriving on the noon train. tā 'wǔ-chē dàw.

NOR. *See* **NEITHER.**

NORTH. běy. *In many cases combinations are required.* Toward the north wàng-'běy; the north (*part of a country or place*) 'běy-byǎr, 'běy-fāng, 'běy-bù; north pole běy-'jí; north star běy-'jí-shīng; north station 'běy-jàn *or* 'běy-chē-jàn; northeast 'dūng-běy; northwest 'shī-běy. ‖Which way is north? něy byǎr shr̀ 'běy-ya? *or* (*Straight north*) něy-byǎr shr̀ 'jèng-běy-ya? ‖Go north to the bridge; then turn right. wàng-'běy dzěw-dàw(-le) 'chyáw-nèr (dzày) wàng-'yèw gwǎy. ‖Don't go straight east; go a little to the north. byé yì-'jŕ wàng-'dūng; pyān 'běy-yi-dyǎr. ‖The cemetery is just north of the monastery. 'fén-dì jyèw dzày myàw-'běy-byar yì-'dyǎr. ‖I'm from the North, but my friend is from the South. wǒ shr̀ tsúng 'běy-byǎr (*or* 'běy-fāng, *or* 'běy-bù) láy-de, wǒ-de 'péng-yew shr̀ tsúng 'nán-byǎr (*or* 'nán-fāng, *or* nán-bù) láy-de. ‖My room is on the north side of the courtyard. 'wǒ-de-wū-dz dzày 'ywàn-dz-'běy-byar. ‖There's a strong north wind today jyēr 'běy-fēng gwā-de hěn 'dà.

NOSE. (*Physical organ*) 'bí-dz; *in combination* bí-. ‖I have a cold in my nose. wǒ-'bí-dz snāng-'fēng-le. ‖He has a large red nose. tā-de-'bí-dz yèw 'dà yèw 'húng. ‖The bridge of his nose is prominent. tā-'bí-lyáng-dz hěn 'gāw. *or* tā 'gāw-bí-lyángr. ‖The bridge of his nose is deep-set. tā-'bí-lyáng-dz shr̀ 'byě-de. *or* tā 'byě bú-lyángr. ‖Go blow your nose. chywù shīng 'bí-dz-chywu. *or* chywu bǎ 'bí-dz 'shīng-yi-shīng. ‖He talks through his nose. tā 'bí-yīn hěn-'jùng. ‖He is talking through his nose. tā shwō-'hwà yùng 'bí-dz chū-'shēngr. ‖Most dogs have sharp noses. gěw-'bí-dz 'jyān (*or* 'líng). *or* (*Dogs can really smell*) gěw néng 'wén. *or* (*literary*) gěw-de-'shyèw-jywé hěn 'líng.

Other expressions in English. ‖The dog is nosing around (*smelling everywhere*) for the bone he buried. gěw 'gè-chù 'wén-je jǎw tā-máy-de-'gǔ-tew. ‖The nose (*engine head*) of that plane is pointed. nèy-ge-fēy-'jī-de-jī-'téw shr̀ 'jyān-de. ‖The plane nosed (*faced*) into the wind. fēy-jī 'chùng-je-fēng jyèw 'fēy-chywu-le. ‖He led them by the nose. *is expressed as* Whatever he says, they listen. tā 'shwō-shéme tām 'tīng-shéme. ‖You're just being led by the nose (*blindly following*). nǐm jè-shr 'máng-tsúng. ‖He pokes his nose into everything. *meaning* He wants to manage everything. tā 'shéme dēw yàw 'gwǎn. ‖Let's count noses (*count how many people there are*). dzám 'shǔ-yi-shǔ yěw 'dwō-shǎw-rén. ‖She turned up her nose at him (*wouldn't look at him*). tā kàn-bu-'chǐ tā. *or* tā chyáw-bu-'chǐ tā. ‖That reporter has a good nose for

news (*knows how to get news*). nèy-ge-'jì-jě hěn hwèy 'tsǎy-fǎng 'shīn-wén.

As plain as the nose on your face 'shyǎn-er-yì-'jyàn-de; 'shyǎn-rán-yì-'jyàn-de; 'míng-ming-bay-báy-de: míng-'shyǎn-de.

NOT. bū (bú *before fourth tone,* bù *before other tones*) *before a verb other than* yěw *if* -le *is not used in the affirmative;* méy *before* věw *or if* -le *is used in the affirmative, and before nouns with the meaning* there is not a . . .; byé *or* 'bú-yàw *for imperatives.* ‖He's not going to be home today. tā jyēr bù-hwèy-'jyā-lay. ‖I'm not busy right now. wǒ 'shyàn-dzày °bù-'máng. *or* °méy shéme-'shèr. ‖Not everyone can go to college. 'dà-shywé bú-shr 'shéy-dēw-chywù-de-'lyǎw-de. *or* bù-néng 'měy-rén 'dēw shàng dà-'shywé. *or* 'bú-shr 'měy-rén-dēw-néng-shàng-dà-'shywé-de. ‖Not me. *meaning* It isn't me. 'tsáy bú-shr 'wǒ-ne. *meaning* I'm not going to . . . . wǒ tsáy bū-. . . . *meaning* I didn't . . . . wǒ tsáy méy-. . . . ‖Tell him not to leave before seeing me. 'gàw-su tā 'méy-jyàn-jaw wǒ yǐ-'chyán byé 'dzěw-kay. *or* 'gàw-su tā 'jyàn-le wǒ dzày 'dzěw. ‖Not one person offered to help. lyán 'yí-ge shwō yàw-'bāng-bang-'máng-de yě méy-'yěw. ‖That's not so! 'bú-shr nèm hwéy-'shr̀. *or* bú-'dwèy. ‖Not that he isn't right; it's the way he expresses it that irritates me. bìng 'bú-shr tā méy-'lǐ; shr̀ tā-shwō-de-'hwà bú-jùng-'tīng. ‖No, not that! āy-ya! 'kě byé 'nèm-je-a! ‖Not now (*it can't be done now*). shyàn-'dzày bù-'shíng. ‖Not so fast! byé nèm 'jí! *or* byé nèm jǎw-'jí! *or* byé nèm 'kwày! *or* (*slower*) 'màn-dyar! *or* 'màn-je-dyar! ‖Whether he comes or not is nobody's concern. tā 'láy-ywǔ-'bù-láy shéy yě gwǎn-bu-jáw. ‖He doesn't like it; that is, not much. jèy-ge tā bù-'shǐ-hwān, ē, bú-'dà shǐ-hwān. ‖Not in (*at home*). bú-dzày-'jyā. ‖Not bad. bú-'hwày. ‖Not a bit. *or* Not at all. yì-dyǎr yě bù-. . . (*followed by adjective*). *or* 'méy-shéme, 'méy-shéme. ‖Not a bad idea. jèy-'fá-dz (*or* jèy-'jú-yì) bú-'hwày. ‖Not so good, 'bú-dà 'hǎw. ‖Not a soul. 'yí-gè-rén yě méy-'yěw.

NOTE. Notes, a note (*written record or observations*) 'bǐ-jì. Take notes jì bǐ-'jì; make a note of 'jì-shya-lay; take notes on . . . . . . yěw jì-chù-'dì-fang 'jì-shya-lay. ‖His notes on the lecture are very good. 'yǎn-jyǎng-'bǐ-jì tā-jì-de 'hěn hǎw. ‖Do you always take notes during the meetings? kāy-'hwèy-de-shŕ-hewr nǐ 'lǎw jì bǐ-'jì-ma? ‖Make a note of the time he left. tā-'shém-me-shŕ-hewr-'dzěw-de 'jì-shya-lay. ‖I took notes on that lecture. nèy-ge-'yǎn-jyǎng yěw jì-chù-'dì-fang wǒ 'jì-shya-lay-le. ‖That notebook is for chemistry. nèy-ge-'bǐ-jì-běn-dz shr̀ jì 'hwà-shywé-de. *But:* ‖We compared notes (*not necessarily written*) on this case. †jèy-jyàn-shèr (*or, legal case* 'jèy-ge-àn-dz) wǒm °bǎ 'gè-rén-swǒ-jŕ-dàw-de 'dwèy-jàw-le yí-'shyàr. *or* °'jyāw-hwàn-le-shyar 'yì-'jyàn. *or* °'tán-le yi-tán. *or* °'bǐ-tsz 'tsān-kǎw-le yí-shyàr.

Notes (*for a speech, etc.*). (*Original draft, manuscript*) dǐ-'gǎwr; (*outline*) 'dà-gāng. ‖He can't give a speech without using notes. tā jyǎng-'yǎn méy-yěw dǐ-'gǎwr (or 'dà-gāng) bù-'shíng.

Notes (*explanatory annotations*) jù, jùr, 'shyǎw-jùr, 'jù-jyě. ‖I have a copy of Marco Polo with notes. wǒ yěw yì-běr-dày-'jùr-de-'mǎ-kě-bwō-lwó-yéw-'jì. ‖Read the notes. kàn-kan 'jùr (or 'shyǎw-jùr, or 'jù-jyě). ‖Who wrote the notes for that book? nèy-běn-shù-de-'jùr shr̀ 'shéy-shyě-de?

(*Short letter*) 'dwǎn-shìn; shyèr; (*a word*) dzèr. ‖We just had time to write a short note. wǒm 'jǐ yěw shyě-fēng-'dwǎn-shìn-de-'gūng-fu. ‖Drop me a note when you get there. 'dàw-le láy ge-'shyèr (or ge-'dzèr, or fēng-'dwǎn-shìn). ‖Leave a note. 'lyéw ge-'dzèr.

(*Formal communication*) shìn, 'gūng-hán. ‖He sent in a note of resignation. tā shyě-le fēng-tsź-'jŕ-de-°shìn. or °'gūng-hán.

(*Newspaper item*) dwàr (*a measure*). ‖Today's paper has a note about the ship's arrival. jyēr-de-'bàw-shang 'yěw yí-dwàr shwō 'nèy-jŕ-chwán 'dàw-le.

Promissory note 'jyè-dzèr, 'dž-jywù, 'jyè-ywē. ‖I took a note for the amount of money he owed me. tā-'gāy-wǒ-de-chyán wǒ gēn-tā yàw-le yì-jāng-'jyè-dzèr (or yì-jāng-'dž-jywù, or yì-jyāng-'jyè-ywē).

Bank note chyán-'pyàw-dz, chyán-'pyàwr, 'pyàw-dz, pyàwr.

(*Sound with steady pitch*) yīn. ‖She sang the high notes very easily. tā chàng 'gāw-yīn 'bú-yùng fèy-'jyèr. ‖That's a very high note. 'nèy-ge-yīn 'hěn gāw.

(*Written musical symbol*) yīn-'hàw, yīn-'fú.

(*Suggestion, implication*) 'yì-sz. ‖There was a note of anxiety in her voice. tīng tā-shwō-'hwà-de-'shēng-yīn 'hǎw-shyàng dày dyǎr-jāw-'jí-de-yì-sz.

(*Notice*) 'kàn-chu-lay (*see also* NOTICE). ‖He noted that there was a mistake. tā 'kàn-chu-lay yěw ge-'tswèr.

Noted yěw-'míng(-de). ‖This restaurant is noted for its food. 'jèy-jyā-'gwǎn-dz 'tsày hěn yěw-'míng. ‖A very noted man sat opposite us. dwèy-'myàr dzwò-je ge-'míng-rén.

NOTHING. shém-me (*or* shéme) yě *or* shéme-me dēw *or* yì-'dyǎr yě *plus a negative; or, if the affirmative uses* yěw *as the verb,* méy(-yěw) shém-me; shém-me *and* yì-'dyǎr *are often followed by nouns specifying what there is* **nothing** *of; simply* méy(-yěw) *plus the noun is also possible; and in some cases a simple negative sentence is used.* ‖There is nothing for me to do. wǒ 'méy-yěw shém-me-'shŕ-ching. or wǒ 'méy-yěw shém-me-kě-'dzwò-de. or 'méy-yěw 'wǒ-kě-'dzwò-de-'shŕ. or 'méy-yěw 'shŕ gěy-wǒ 'dzwò. ‖Nothing can be done about it. 'méy-fár 'bàn-le. or 'méy fá-dz 'shyǎng-le. or· 'méy-yěw shéme-'fá-dz-le. ‖There's nothing I can do about it. 'wǒ méy-fár 'bàn. ‖Oh, nothing! (*In answer to* **Why?**) 'bú-wèy shéme. (*In answer to* **What?**) 'méy-shéme. or 'bú-yàw-jǐn. ‖Oh, nothing;

forget it! 'méy-shéme. or 'bú-swàn shéme. or 'shyǎw-shr̀-yì-jwāng. or 'bú-yàw-jǐn. or 'gwò-le jyēw 'swàn-le. ‖He said nothing about it to me. 'jèy-shèr tā yì-'dyǎr yě méy-°'gàw-su 'wǒ. or °gēn-'wǒ shwō. ‖Nothing ever happens around here! jèr 'shéme-shèr dēw (or yě) méy-'yěw, jēn 'mèn-de-hwāng. ‖She means nothing to me. tā yì-'dyǎr yě bú-dzày wǒ-'shīn-shang. or tā gēn-wǒ yì-'dyǎr-gwān-shi yě méy-yěw. ‖That's nothing to me. nèy 'wǒ yì-'dyǎr yě bú-'dzày-hu. or 'nèy gēn-'wǒ yì-'dyǎr-gwān-shi yě méy-yěw. ‖That means nothing to me (*has no meaning*). 'nèy wǒ yì-'dyǎr yě bù-'dǔng. ‖I've heard that story before, but there's nothing to it. 'nèy-shèr wǒ 'tīng-jyàn-gwo; yì-'dyǎr yě bù-'jēn. ‖She's so thin that there's nothing to her (*no strength*). tā 'shèw-de yì-dyǎr-'jyèr dēw méy-'yěw-le.

For nothing (*in vain or free*) báy. ‖We did the work for nothing. dzám 'báy fèy-'shèr-le. or dzám báy fèy-'jyèr-le. or dzám swàn-shr 'báy máng-he-le yí-jèn-le. or dzám swàn-shr 'báy fèy-'shèr-le (or fèy-'jyèr-le). ‖He works there every day for nothing. tā 'tyān-tyan dzày-nàr gěy-rén 'báy dzwò-shr̀. or tā tyān-tyan dzày-nàr dzwò-'shr̀, shéme-'bàw-chéw yě bú-'yàw.

Nothing compared to; nothing like gēn . . . yì-'bǐ kě chà-'ywǎn-le. ‖That's nothing compared to some things I've seen. 'nèy-ge gēn 'wǒ-kàn-jyàn-gwo-de-nèy-shyē yì-'bǐ kě chà-'ywǎn-le. ‖He's nothing like his father. tā gēn tā-'fù-chin yì-'bǐ kě chà-'ywǎn-le. ‖Nothing doing! bù-'chéng. or bù-'shíng.

Nothing to . . . . ‖There's nothing to this work. 'jèy 'bú-swàn hwéy-'shèr. or 'jèy-shèr 'méy-shéme. or 'jèy-shèr hěn 'rúng-yì. or 'jèy-shèr yì-'dyǎr yě bù-'nán. ‖See? Nothing to it! 'chyáw, 'méy-shéme! or 'chyáw, 'dwō-rúng-yì-ya? or 'chyáw, 'jyǎn-jŕ bú-swàn hwéy-'shèr. ‖She's pleasant, but there's nothing to her. tā hěn 'hé-chì, bú-gwò °méy-'chywèr, or °'méy-dà 'yì-sz.

Think nothing of bú-'swàn (or bú-'dàng) hwéy-'shèr. ‖He thinks nothing of driving seventy miles an hour. tā ná yì-'dyǎn-jūng kāy 'chī-shr-lǐ bú-'swàn (or bú-'dàng) hwéy-'shèr.

Nothing less than 'jyǎn-jŕ jyèw-shr. ‖That's nothing less than a lie. nà 'jyǎn-jŕ jyèw-shr shwō-'hwǎng-le.

NOTICE. *Posted notice* 'gàw-shr. ‖The police posted a notice about the missing men. 'jīng-chá-jywú chū-le yí-ge-'gàw-shr, jǎw nèy-jǐ-ge-shŕ-'dzūng-de-rén.

Public notice tūng-'gàw. ‖The factory will be closed until further notice. 'gūng-chǎng tíng-'gūng-le, yì-hèw 'dzày-kāy-de-shŕ-hew yěw tūng-'gàw. or (*As printed*) běn-'gūng-chǎng 'jàn-shíng 'tíng gūng, 'jyāng-lay 'kāy-gūng-'r̀-chī 'lìng °yěw (or °shíng) tūng-'gàw.

Advance notice. Expressed verbally by dzǎw . . 'gàw-su. ‖You will have to give your employer two weeks' notice before you leave your job. nǐ yàw-shr tsź-jŕ, děy 'dzǎw lyǎng-ge-'shīng-chi 'gàw-su nǐ-'jǔ-gwǎn-de-rén.

(*Announcement*). (*Handbill*) 'chwán-dān; (*handbill or sign about a play*) shì-'bàw-dz; (*advertisement*) gwǎng-'gàw. ‖Did you see the notices about the new play? nèy-chū-'shīn-shì-de-shì-'bàw-dz (*or* -de-gwǎng-'gàw, *or* -de-'chwán-dān) nǐ 'kàn-jyan-le-ma?

(*Record*). *Expressed with the verb* 'jì-shya-lay. ‖Was any notice taken of his failure to attend the meeting? tā méy-dàw-'hwèy yěw-rén 'jì-shya-lay-le-ma?

To notice. (*Used as paraphrase also in* escape notice, take notice). (*See*) 'kàn-jyàn *or* 'chyáw-jyàn; (*see and notice particularly*) lǐ-'hwèy; (*pay attention to*) 'jù-yì. ‖That paragraph escaped my notice the first time I read the preface. wǒ 'téw-yì-hwéy kàn nèy-pyān-'shywù de-shŕ-hew, 'nèy-yí-dwàr wǒ °méy-lǐ-'hwèy. *or* °méy-kàn-'jyàn. *or* °méy-chyáw-'jyàn. ‖I didn't notice the sign until you spoke of it. nèy-ge-'páy-dz 'nǐ bù-shwō (*or* nèy-ge-'páy-dz bú-shr 'nǐ-shwō) wǒ °méy-jù-'yì. *or* °méy-chyáw-'jyàn. *or* °'jēn-jyèw méy-'kàn-jyàn. ‖Did you notice that his hand was trembling? nǐ 'kàn-jyàn (*or* 'chyáw-jyàn) tā-shěw 'chàn-le-ma? ‖We didn't take any notice of him. wǒm méy 'lǐ-hwèy-ta.

At a moment's notice. ‖I can be ready at a moment's notice. wǒ swéy-shŕ dēw kě-yǐ 'jwěn-bèy 'hǎw-le.

To serve notice shwō. ‖The store has served notice that all bills must be paid tomorrow. 'pù-dz 'shwō-le 'swǒ-yěw-de-'jàng 'míng-tyan °děy yí-'lywù hwán-'chīng. *or* °'dēw děy hwán-'chīng-le.

NOVEMBER. shŕ-'yí-ywè.

NOW. (*Right at this moment*) 'shyàn-dzày. ‖The doctor can see you now. 'dày-fu 'shyàn-dzày kě-yǐ 'jyàn-nǐ. ‖You'd better leave now, or you'll miss the train. nǐ 'dǐng-hǎw 'shyàn-dzày (*or* mǎ-'shàng, *immediately*) jyèw 'dzěw, 'yàw bù-rán hwéy-téw 'wù-le 'chē-le. ‖Now let's see what he's going to do. 'shyàn-dzày kàn 'tā-de-le.

(*At this time*) 'jèy-shŕ-hewr. ‖He ought to be here by now. tā 'jèy-shŕ-hèwr yīng-gāy dàw-jèr-le. ‖From now on the work will be difficult. tsúng 'jèy-shŕ-hew (*or* tsúng 'shyàn-dzày, *or* 'tsúng jīn yǐ-'hèw, **from today**) chǐ, 'shŕ-ching jyèw yàw 'nán-chǐ-lay-le.

Just now (*just a moment ago*) 'gāng-tsáy . . . (háy). (*See* JUST). ‖I saw him on the street just now. wǒ 'gāng-tsáy dzày dà-'jyē-shang háy 'kàn-jyàn tā-le-ne. (*or* tā láy-jè-ne).

(*In this case*) 'jè kě. ‖Now what am I going to do? 'jè kě dzěm-je 'hǎw-ne? ‖Now what? 'jè kě dzěm-je 'hǎw-ne. *or meaning* What next? 'yèw yàw 'dzěm-je? ‖Now we're sure to be late. jè kě 'jēn yàw 'wǎn-le.

(*Sometimes unexpressed except by stronger stress*). ‖Now do you understand? 'dǔng-le-ma? *or* 'míng-bay-le-ma? ‖Now you listen to me! tīng 'wǒ shwō. *or* tīng 'wǒ gàw-su-ni. *or* (*somewhat angrily*) 'tīng-je. *or* 'shyàn-dzày 'nǐ gǎy tīng-'wǒ-de-le. ‖You be careful, now! 'shyǎw-shīn-dyar, ā!

Now and then 'jyē-cháng-bù-'dwǎr-de. ‖I see him now and then. wǒ 'jyē-chng-bù-'dwǎr-de kàn-jyàn tā.

Now that. (*In light of the present situation*) 'shyàn-dzày; (*once something else has happened*) yī-before a verb. ‖Now that the rain has stopped, we can leave. 'shyàn-dzày ywǔ 'jù-le, wǒ-men kě-yǐ 'dzěw-le. ‖Now that you mention it, I do remember seeing her. 'nǐ dzèm-me yì-'shwō, wǒ 'shyǎng-chǐ-lay-le, wǒ 'kàn-jyàn-gwo tā.

NUMBER. (*In a series*) hàw *or* dì . . . hàw; (*after numerals, or words such as* 'dwō-shǎw, 'jǐ) 'hàw-shùr; (*Peiping*) hàw-'mǎr, hàw-'téwr; (*particular figure*) shùr. House number 'mén-páy-'hàw-shù(r), 'mén-páy-hàw-'mǎr, 'mén-páy-hàw-'téwr; page number 'yè-shù. ‖What is the number of your house? nǐ-jyā-'mén-páy °'shéme 'hàw-shù (*or* hàw-'téwr, *or* hàw-'mǎr)? *or* °'dwō-shǎw 'hàw'? ‖They changed all the numbers on this street. tām bǎ jèy-tyáw-jyē-de-mén-pár-'hàw-shur (*or* -mǎr, *or* -téwr) 'dēw hwàn-le. ‖His street (*or* house) number is 409. tā-'mén-páy-'hàw-shu shŕ 'sż-líng-'jyěw. ‖I can never remember telephone numbers. 'dyàn-hwà-'hàw-shù (*or* -hàw-'mǎr, *or* -hàw-'téwr) wǒ lǎw jì-bú-jù. ‖What is your telephone number? nǐ-'dyàn-hwà dwō-shǎw 'hàw? ‖My telephone number is 3–6001. wǒ-de-dyàn-'hwà-hàw-shu shŕ 'sān-lyèw-líng-líng-'yī. ‖No, it's a large number, at least six digits. jèy bú-'dwèy. 'nèy-ge-shùr hěn 'dà, 'jŕ-shǎw yěw 'lyèw-wèy. ‖His room is on the fifth floor, but I've forgotten the number. tā-de-'fáng-jyān dzày 'wǔ-léw; wǒ 'wàng-le shŕ °dwō-shǎw 'hàw-le. *or* °'shéme 'hàw-shu-le. ‖Room number, please? dì-'jǐ-hàw-fáng-jyān? ‖There is a number on the badge. 'pár-shang yěw ge-'hàw-shu. ‖It's a Western superstition to think of 13 as an unlucky number. ná shŕ-'sān dàng 'shyūng-shùr shŕ shī-yang-rén-de-'mí-shìn. ‖He says 5 is his lucky number. tā shwō 'wǔ jèy-ge-shùr dwèy-'tā hěn 'jí-lì. ‖Number 10 is the best player on the team. 'nèy-dwèy-li (dì-)'shŕ-hàwr dǎ-de 'dzwèy-hǎw.

To number (*assign serial numbers to*) jyā 'hàw-shùr (*etc.*); be numbered yěw 'hàw-shùr (*etc.*). ‖He numbered the pages carefully. tā bǎ 'yè-shù yí-'yè-yí-yè-de 'jyā-de hěn 'dž-shì. ‖These are all numbered. 'jèy-shang 'dēw yěw 'hàw-shur (*or* hàw-'mǎr, *or* hàw-'téwr). ‖These have all been numbered. jèy dēw 'jyā-le hàw-'mǎr-le. ‖Have these sheets numbered. bǎ jèy-shyē-jāng-'jŕ 'jyā-shang hàw-'mǎr.

A number of (*see* MANY). ‖He owns a number of houses. tā yěw bù-'shǎw-de-'fáng-chǎn. *or* 'tā chèn 'hǎw-jǐ-swǒr-'fáng-dz. *or* . . . 'hǎw-shyē-. . . . ‖There's a large number of stores on this street. jèy-tyáw-'jyē-shang yěw 'hěn-dwō-de (*or* 'hǎw-shyē-jyāer)-'pù-dz. ‖Only a small number of men volunteered. jŕ yěw 'bù-jǐ-'gèr-rén gàw-fèn-'yǔng.

(*Issue*) chī. ‖The latest number of the magazine arrived today. dzwèy-'jìn-de-yì-'chī-hwà-'bàw 'jyèr-ge dàw-le. ‖We missed three numbers of that weekly magazine. nèy-ge-'jēw-kān wǒm chywē-le 'sān-chī.

(*Performance on a program*) shyàng. ‖There were five numbers on·the program. 'jyé-mù yí-gùng yěw 'wǔ-shyàng.

Numbers (*of· people*) rén-'dwō. ‖They won the battle by sheer force of numbers. nèy-yí-jàng tăm jǐ 'jàng-je rén-'dwō dǎ-'shèng-de. *But* ‖Refugees came to America in large numbers (*by large groups*). 'nàn-mín yí-'dà-pī-yí-'dà-pī-de (*or* 'chéng-chywún-dǎ-'hwǒ-de) dàw 'měy-gwo láy.

To number (*to total*) yí-'gùng shǐ, yí-'gùng yěw. ‖The population of this place numbered 2,000 in 1940. jèy-ge-dì-fang-'rén-kěw dzày 'yī-jyěw-sż-'líng-nyán yí-'gùng shǐ (*or* yěw) 'lyǎng-chyān.

‖His days here are numbered. (*On earth*) tā méy-'jyěwr-le. *or* tā 'hwó-bù-lyǎw jǐ-'tyān-le. *or* (*In this place*) tā dzày-jèr 'dāy-bù-lyǎw jǐ-'tyān-le. *or* (*Impolite*) tā kwày gwěn-'dàn-le. *or* tā kwày jywǎn 'pū-gay-le.

‖His number will be up pretty soon. *meaning* It will be his turn soon. kwày·'lwén-dàw 'tā-le. *or meaning* His serial number (*as in the draft*) is not far off. lí 'tā-de-hàw-'téwr bù-'ywǎn-le. *or meaning* His day is coming. 'tā-de-'ř-dz kwày 'dàw-le.

‖I've got your number. wǒ 'jř-dàw 'nǐ shǐ dzěm-me-hwéy-'shǐ. *or* 'nǐ wǒ swàn chyáw (*or* kàn)-'tèw-le.

NURSE. 1. (*Trained*) 'kàn-hu, 'kān-hu, 'hù-shr. ‖You need (to call in) a nurse. nǐ děy chǐng ge-'kàn-hu (*or* ge-'kān-hu, *or* ge-'hù-shr). ‖When does the night nurse come on? 'yè-bān-de-'kàn-hu (*etc.*) shéme-shǐ-hew jyē-'bān-ne (*or* shàng-'bān-ne, *or* dàw-'bān-ne)? ‖She's a graduate nurse. tā shř 'jèng-shř-bì-'yè-de-'kàn-hu (*etc.*). *or* tā shř 'hù-shr-'hwèy-de.

2. (*Someone to take care of one.*) *Expressed verbally by the following:*

To nurse (*take care of*) 'jàw-ying(-je), 'jàw-gu(-je), 'fú-shr(-je). ‖They nursed him through his illness. tā-'bìng-je-de-shǐ-hew tā-men yì-'jř-de °'jàw-ying-je tā. *or* °'jàw-gu-je tā. *or* °'fú-shr-je tā. ‖You need a nurse (*not trained, but just someone to take care of you*). nǐ děy 'yěw ge-rén 'jàw-ying-je (*or* 'jàw-gu-je, *or* 'fú-shr-je).

Child's nurse băw-'mǔ, kān-'háy-dz-de. ‖The children's nurse has taken them for a walk. kān-'háy-dz-de (*or* băw-'mǔ) dày-je 'háy-dz-men lyèw-'wǎr-chywu-lay-je.

To nurse (*breastfeed*) wèy; gěy . . . 'năy chř. ‖She was nursing the baby when I came in. wǒ-'jìn-lay-de-shǐ-hew tā 'jèng °wèy 'háy-dz-ne. *or* °gěy háy-dz 'năy chř-ne.

To nurse (*a disease, wound, etc.*) yăng. ‖I'm nursing a cold. wǒ shāng-'fēng-le, yăng-je-ne. ‖I'm nursing a wound. wǒ yăng-'shāng-ne.

To nurse (*a fire along*) 'jyèw-hu. ‖We had to nurse the fire (along) carefully to make it burn. jèy-ge-hwǒ děy 'jyèw-hu-je-dyǎr tsáy 'jáw-de-chǐ-láy-ne.

To nurse (*a grudge*). ‖He's nursing a grudge against me. 'tā gēn-wǒ 'byē-je yì-'kěw-'chì-ne. *or* tā 'shīn-li "jèng-dzày 'hèn-wǒ. *or* tā dzày-'nàr 'ywè shyǎng ywè 'hèn-wǒ-ne.

NUT. (*Hard-shelled seed or fruit*). *Chinese has no general term for nut in this sense.* 'gān-gwǒr *may be used for* (dry) nuts, *but it may also mean* dried fruit, *as opposed to* 'shyān-gwǒr fresh fruit. *Here are the names of some varieties of nuts that are common in China:* peanut dà-hwā-'shēng, 'lè-hwā-shēng, 'làw-hwā-shēng, hwā-'shēng; Spanish peanuts (*the small variety*) 'shyǎw-hwā-shēng; hazelnut 'jēn-dz; chestnut 'lì-dz; walnut 'hé-taw *or* 'hé-tew; lichee nut 'lì-jř. ‖Crack the walnut and eat the meat. bǎ 'hé-tew dzá-kāy chř hé-tew-'rér. ‖He's eating peanuts. tā bwō hwā-'shēng chř-ne. *or* tā chř hwā-'shēng-ne. ‖He's eating shelled peanuts (*peanut meats*). tā chř hwā-shēng-'rér-ne. ‖That store sells candy and nuts. nèy-ge-'pù-dz mày 'táng mày 'gān-gwǒr.

(*Figuratively*). ‖I thought the problem would be easy, but it turned out to be a hard nut to crack. (*In mathematics*) wǒ 'ywán-láy dǎng-je jèy-ge-'wèn-tí 'rúng-yì swàn-ne; 'shéy jř-dàw 'dzěm nán 'swàn-na? *or* (*A situation*) wǒ 'ywán-láy dǎng-je 'jèy-shèr hǎw 'bàn-ne; 'shéy jř-dàw jyàw-rén 'dzěm wéy-'nán-na?

(*Counterpart of a bolt*) lwó-sz-'mǔr. ‖The board is held in place by a nut and bolt. (*Chinese says* bolt and nut.) 'jèy-kwày-'bǎn-dz shř yùng lwò-sz-'dyēngr gēn lwò-sz-'mǔr dīng-jù-de.

(*Eccentric person*). ‖He's a nut. *is expressed as* He's a strange thing. tā shř ge-'gwày-wu. *or as* That guy is priceless. 'nèy-jyā-hwo jēn shř kwày-'bǎw-bèy. *or as* He's somewhat abnormal. tā 'fēng-li-fēng-'chì-de. *or* tā shř ge-'mwó-gu. *or* tā shř ge-'mwó-jeng. *or as* He's somewhat subnormal. tā 'shǎ-li-shǎ-'chì-de.

Nuts *or* nutty (*insane*). ‖If this keeps up, I'll go nuts. yàw-shr 'lǎw dzěm-me-yàngr wǒ jyèw 'kwày °dé 'jīng-shen-'bìng-le. *or* °'fēng-le. *or* °dé·'shén-jīng-'bìng-le. ‖It was driving him nuts. nèy-shèr jyàw-tā 'jí-de fā-'fēng.

‖Oh, nuts! (*Said to a person*) shyā-'bāy! (*Said about something that has happened*) 'jè shr dzěm-'shwō-de. *or expressed as* smelly cake 'dzāw-'gāw.

In a nutshell. ‖That's the story in a nutshell. 'jyèw-shr 'dzěm-yì-hwéy-'shèr. *or* 'gwēy-le bāw-'dzwēy (*or* 'jyǎn-dwàn-'jyé-shwō) jyèw-shř 'dzěm-yì-hwéy-dz-'shèr.

O

OBEY. shěw; fú-'tsúng, tīng (. . .-de-)'hwà. ‖Obey the law. fú-'tsúng 'fǎ-lywù. ‖I can't obey that order. nèy-ge-'mìng-ling wǒ bù-'néng fú-'tsúng. ‖The dog obeyed him immediately. 'gěw lì-'kè jyew 'tīng tā-de-'hwǎ-le.

OBJECT. (*Be opposed*) fǎn-'dwèy; (*not approve*) bú-dzàn-'chéng. ‖Will you object to his marriage? tā jyē-'hwēn; nǐ fǎn-'dwey bù-fǎn 'dwèy? ‖I hope you don't object to drinking. wǒ 'shī-wàng nǐ 'bù-fǎn-'dwèy hē-'jyéw. ‖I won't object. wǒ 'bú-hwèy bú-dzàn-'chéng.

    (*Thing*) 'dūng-shi. ‖What's that object on the road? dzày-nèy-ge-'dàwr-shang-de shr̀ shéme-'dūng-shi?

    (*Purpose*) 'mù-dì. ‖The object of the game is to hit the ball over the net. jèy-jǔng-'ywùn-dung-de-'mù-dì shr̀ dzày bǎ-'chyéwr dǎ-gwò 'wǎng-dz-chywu.

    (*Something arousing feeling*). ‖I hate to be an object of sympathy. *is expressed as* I hate to have everybody pity me. wǒ dzwèy 'hèn jyàw 'rén-jyā 'kě-lyán wǒ.

    Object of one's affections . . .-'ày-de-rén. ‖The object of his affections is someone you know. tā-'ày-de-nèy-ge-rén nǐ 'rèn-shr.

OBLIGE. To be obliged to děy, 'fēy-děy (. . . bù-'kě); (*can't not*) bù-'dé bū-, bù-'néng bū-; *see also* have to *under* HAVE. ‖Will I be obliged to attend the meeting? wǒ 'fēy-děy chywù kāy-'hwèy-ma? ‖He's obliged to work nights. tā 'děy dǎ yè-'gūng. ‖After his death she was obliged to go to work. tā-de-'jàng-fu 'sž-le yǐ-'hèw tā bù-'dé bú-chywù dzwò-'gūng.

    To feel obliged to jywé-je . . . °'yīng-dāng *or* °'yīng-gāy. ‖He feels obliged to see her home. tā 'jywé-je tā 'yīng-dāng sùng-ta 'hwéy-chywù.

    (*Require*). ‖His social position obliges him to entertain frequently. *is expressed as* A man in his social position has to entertain often. dzày-'tā-nèy-jǔng-'dì-wèy-de-rén bù-'dé-bù-cháng-chǐng-'kè.

    To oblige (*to do a favor*). ‖I am always glad to oblige you. *is expressed as* I'm glad to do anything for you at any time. 'shéme-shŕ-hew wǒ dēw 'ywàn-yì gěy-nín 'dzwò. ‖Glad to oblige. nǎr-de-'hwà? ‖We asked him to sing for us, and he was glad to oblige. *is expressed as* We asked him to sing for us, and he very pleasantly agreed. wǒ-men 'chǐng-ta gěy wǒ-men 'chàng yí-ge-'gēer, tā hěn-gāw-'shìng-de jyew 'dā-ying-le. ‖Please oblige us by coming early. *is expressed as* Please come early. chǐng 'dzǎw-dyǎr 'láy.

    To be obliged (*to be grateful*) kē-'téw. ‖Much obliged. *is expressed as* Many thanks. dwō-'shyè dwō-'shyè. ‖I'd be much obliged if you'd come early. nǐ 'yàw-shr néng 'dzǎw láy de-'hwà wǒ yí-'dìng kē-'téw.

OBSERVE. 'kàn, chyáw; (*pay attention to*) jù-'yì; (*study closely*) 'yán-jyew. ‖Did you observe her reaction? nǐ 'jù-yì 'tā-de-'fǎn-yìng-le-ma? ‖He was careful not to be observed. tā 'méy-ràng-rén 'chyáw-jyàn ta. ‖We can observe better from above. wǒ-men 'kě-yi dǎ 'shàng-myar 'kàn-de 'gèng 'chīng-chu-dyǎr. ‖The students were observing bacteria under the microscope. 'shywé-sheng-men 'yán-jyew jèy-ge-shyǎn-wéy-'jìng-ǐ-de-wéy-shēng-'chúng-ne.

    (*To obey*) (dzwēn-)'shěw. ‖Be careful to observe all the rules. 'swǒ-yěw-de-gwēy-'dzé 'dēw děy hǎw-'hāwr-de dzwēn-'shěw.

    (*To say*) shwō. ‖"You're late," he observed. "nǐ 'wǎn-le" tā 'shwō.

    To observe a holiday. gwo-'jyé *or* fàng-'jyà. ‖What holidays do you observe? nǐ-men dēw shr̀ shéme-'shŕ-hewr fàng-'jyà? *or* nǐ-men dēw 'gwò shéme-'jyé?

OBTAIN. (*Acquire*) dé, 'dé-dàw; (*fetch*) 'ná; (*buy*) mǎy; *etc.*, *depending on the means of acquisition.* ‖All this information was obtained from his daughter. jèy-shyē-'hwà dēw shr̀ tsúng tā-'nywǔ-ér-nèr 'dé-lay-de. ‖We managed to obtain a favorable settlement. 'jyē-gwǒ bàn-de háy bú-'hwày.

OCCASION. (*Time*) 'shŕ-hew, chǎng-'hé. Happy occasion (*as a wedding, birthday, etc.*) 'shǐ-shr̀; sad occasion (*a funeral*) 'báy-shr̀. ‖Can this be used for all occasions? jèy-ge 'shéme-'chǎng-hé dēw néng 'yùng-ma? ‖This is a happy occasion. 'jèy-shr̀ yí-jyàn-'shǐ-shr̀. ‖It's always a big occasion when the whole family gets together. *is expressed as* When the whole family gets together, it's always bustling. chywán-'jyā-de-rén 'tsèw-daw yí-'kwàr de-'shŕ-hew yǔng-'ywǎn shr̀ hěn 'rè-nàw.

    (*Opportunity*) 'jī-hwèy. ‖I haven't had occasion to attend to it. wǒ 'háy méy-yew 'jī-hwey chywù 'dzwò nèy-ge-ne.

    (*Cause, reason*) 'lǐ-yéw. ‖There's no occasion for you to be angry. nǐ méy 'lǐ-yéw shēng-'chì.

    (*To cause*) jāw, 'yǐn-chi. ‖Her appearance in public with that man occasioned a great deal of gossip. tā 'gēn 'nèy-ge-rén láy, 'jāw-de dà-'jyā-hwǒr jǐ 'shwō shyán-'hwà.

OCCUPY. (*To take up space or time*) jàn. ‖The playground occupies three acres of land. jèy-ge-yéw-shì-'chǎng 'jàn-le sān-mǔ-'dì.

    (*To seize in a military action*). Occupy a position or a place jàn *or* jàn-'lǐng; occupy a place jàn-'jywù. ‖The enemy occupied the town. 'dí-rén bǎ jèy-'chéng gěy jàn-'lǐng-le.

(*To live in*) jù. ‖**What room do you occupy?** ní 'jù-dzày 'něy-jyān-'wū-dz-li? ‖**All our rooms are occupied.** 'fáng-dz chywán yěw-'rén 'jù-le.

Occupied (*taken or reserved*). ‖**Every seat was occupied.** *is expressed as* **The seats were all full.** 'dzwòr dēw 'mǎn-le. ‖**Is this seat occupied?** *is expressed as* **Has anyone reserved this seat?** jèy-ge-'dzwòr yěw-'rén 'dìng-le-ma? *or as* **Has this seat got anyone** (*in it*)? jèy-ge-'dzwòr yěw-'rén méy-yew?

To occupy a position. ‖**What position do you occupy?** *is expressed as* **You are in what occupation?** nǐ shr̀ shéme-'chǎy-shr̀? *or as* **What are you in charge of?** nǐ 'dān-rèn °shéme-'shr̀? *or* °něy-'bù-fen-de-'shr̀? ‖**For the last ten years the position has been occupied by a woman.** *is expressed as* **For the last ten years a woman has done that job.** gwò-'chywù 'shŕ-nyán nèy-ge-'shèr shr̀ yí-ge-'nywǔ-rén dzwò.

To be occupied. (*Be doing something*) yěw-'shr̀; (*be busy*) máng; (*have no time*) méy 'gūng-fu. ‖**I'm occupied at present.** wǒ shyàn-'dzày méy 'gūng-fu.

OCEAN. yáng, dà-'yáng; *sometimes* **big sea** dà-'hǎy. ‖**How near is this to the ocean?** jèr lí dà-'hǎy yěw 'dwō-ywǎn-na?

In the names of the oceans yáng. **Pacific Ocean** tày-píng-'yáng.

O'CLOCK. jūng *with measure* dyǎn, *or* dyǎn *alone.* ‖**The train leaves at seven o'clock.** hwǒ-'chē 'chī-dyǎn-jūng 'kāy. ‖**It's five o'clock.** 'wǔ-dyǎn. *or* 'wǔ-dyǎn-jūng.

OCTOBER. 'shŕ-ywè.

OF. 1. A of B, *equivalent in meaning to* B's A, *is expressed as* **B-A** *or as* **B-de-A.** ‖**There's a hole in the roof of this house.** 'fáng-'dyěngr-shang yěw ge-'dùngr. ‖**I met a friend of yours yesterday.** 'dzwó-tyan wǒ 'pèng-jyan nǐ-de-yí-wèy-'péng-yew. ‖**He's a man of means.** tā-shr̀ ge-°yěw-'chyán-de-rén. *or* °kwò-rén. ‖**Do you have a certificate of good health?** nǐ yěw 'jyàn-kāng-jèng-míng-'shū méy-yew? ‖**I hate the taste of pickles.** wǒ bù-'shŕ-hwan pàw-tsày-'wèr. ‖**The estimate of the cost will have to be revised.** jèy-ge-chéng-'běn-de-'gū-jì děy 'gǎy-yi-gǎy. ‖**Do you have any books of short stories?** nín yěw shéme-dày-dwǎn-'pyān-shyǎw-'shwǒ-de-'shū-ma? ‖**Who's the driver of this car?** *is expressed as* **Who's the drive-this-car-er?** 'shéy-shr̀ kāy̆-jèy-ge-'chē-de? *or as* **Who drives this car?** 'shéy kāy jèy-ge-'chē? *or as* **Who's this car's driver?** 'shéy shr̀ jèy-lyàng-'chē-dè-kāy-'chē-de? ‖**This movie is a story of adventure.** *is expressed as* **This is an adventure movie.** jèy-shr̀ yí-ge-tàn-'shyǎn-de-dyàn-yǐng-'pyān-dz.

2. A of B, *where A indicates a quantity or kind of B, is usually expressed as* A-B, *where A is a measure and* B *a noun.* ‖**I want to buy a carton of cigarettes.** wǒ yàw 'mǎy yì-tyáwr-yān-'jywǎr. ‖**Just a group of friends will be there.** jyèw-shr yì-chywún-'péng-yew-men yàw 'dàw-nèr chywù. ‖**Could I have a glass of water, please?** láw-'jyà gěy-wo yì-bēy-'shwěy, 'shíng-bu-shíng? ‖**A bottle of wine is served with the meal.** shàng-'fàn de-shŕ-hew shàng yì-pyéngr-'jyěw. ‖**I want a pound of rice.** wǒ yàw yí-bàng-'mǐ. ‖**First put a coat of blue on the walls.** 'chyáng-shang 'shyān shwā yí-dàw-'lán-shǎr.

In some cases the noun (B) *is placed first, and the specification of quantity or kind comes later, expressed with numeral plus measure.* ‖**Please give me a piece of that cake.** láw-'jyà bǎ nèy-ge-'gāw gěy-wo yí-'kwàr. ‖**A few of my belongings are missing.** wǒ yěw 'jǐ-jyàn-dūng-shi 'dyēw-le. ‖**Three of the prisoners escaped.** 'fàn-rén 'pǎw-le 'sān-ge. ‖**I'll pay my half of the bill.** nèy-ge-jàng-'dār-shang-de-'chyán wǒ gěy yí-'bàr.

In some cases the specification of quantity does not take the form of a measure. ‖**He wastes a good deal of time.** tā 'dān-wù shywǔ-'dwō-'gūng-fu. ‖**We'll need much more of this silk than we've got.** sz̀ bú-'gèw. ‖**None of us have ever been there.** *is expressed as* **We none has been there.** wǒm 'shéy yě méy-'dàw-gwo nèr.

3. (*Expressing time before an hour.*) **A quarter of eight** chà yí-'kè (bú-dàw) 'bā-dyǎn, *or, more often, expressed as* **seven forty-five** 'chī-dyǎn-sān-'kè.

4. (*Specifying the number included*). ‖**We made up a party of four.** *is expressed as* **The four of us made up a party.** wǒm-'sz̀-ge-rén 'jywù-hwèy-le 'jywù-hwèy.

5. (*Between* **city, state,** *etc., and the name of a particular city or state*). **The city of Peiping** *is expressed as* **Peiping city** 'běy-píng-'chéng; **the province of Anhwei** *is expressed as* **Anhwei province** 'ān-hwēy-'shěng.

6. *In many combinations with other words, of has a special meaning, and such groups should usually be looked for under one of the other words. The following are only a few examples of what may be involved.*

Be afraid of pà. ‖**There's nothing to be afraid of.** 'méy shéme kě-'pà-de.

Build *something* **of** *a material* yùng . . . gày . . . . ‖**The house is built of rough stone.** jèy-ge-'fáng-dz shr̀ yùng 'dà-tsū-'shŕ-tew 'gày-de.

Die of A, A sz̀-de. ‖**His father died of apoplexy.** tā-'fù-chin shr̀ jùng-'fēng 'sz̀-de.

Fall short of méy-. . .-dàw. ‖**He fell short of his goal.** tā méy-'dá-dàw tā-de-'mù-dì.

Hear of 'tīng-shwō. ‖**I've never heard of him.** wǒ 'shyàng-láy méy-'tīng-shwō-gwo ta.

Know of 'jř-daw . . . shr̀ °'shéme *or* °'shéy. ‖**I don't know him personally, but I know of him.** wǒ bú-'rèn-shr ta 'běn-rén, kě-shr wǒ 'jř-daw tā shr̀-'shéy.

On the other side of A, A-de-'nèy-byar. ‖My house is on the other side of the church. wǒ-'jyā dzày jèy-ge-jyàw-'táng-de-'nèy-byar.

Be *so far* north (*or south, etc.*) of lí ... wàng-°'běy (*or* °'nán, *etc.*) yěw .... ‖The hotel is six miles south of here. lywǔ-'gwǎn lí-'jèr wàng-'nán dzěw yěw 'lyèw-lǐ.

On top of A, A-shàng. ‖Put the package on top of the table. bǎ jèy-ge-'bāwr fàng-dzay 'jwō-dz-shang.

Be within *such-and-such a distance* of lí ... bú-dàw .... ‖We're within ten miles of our destination. wǒm lí nèy-ge-dì-fang bú-dàw shŕ-'yīng-lǐ-le.

OFF. (*Away*). *Expressions with* lí (*from, away from*) *or* dàw (*until*); *verb compounds with* -kāy, *e.g.,* **move off** 'nwó-kāy *or* 'dzěw-kāy; **stand off** 'jàn-kāy; **take off** (*away*) 'ná-kāy; *for* **fall off, get off, take off, send off,** *etc., see the verb.* ‖How far off is it? lí-'jèr yěw dwō-'ywǎn? ‖The ship anchored three miles off shore. jèy-ge-'chwán pāw-'máw-de-'dì-fàng lí-'àn 'sān-yīng-'lǐ. ‖June is still three months off. dàw 'lyèw-ywè 'háy yěw 'sān-ge-'ywè-ne.

(*Missing*). *Expressions with* 'dyàw (*to lose*). ‖There's a button off your dress. nín-'yī-fu-shang yěw yí-ge-'kèw-dz 'dyàw-le: *or* nín-'yī-fu-shang 'dyàw-le yí-ge-'kèw-dz.

(*Not working*). **To have time off** shyē-'jyà, fàng-'jyà, shyēw-'jyà. ‖I'm going to have a week off. wǒ yàw shyē yí-ge-lǐ-'bày-de-'jyà.

(*Disconnected*). *See* **turn off, shut off,** *etc.* ‖The power is off. *is expressed as* There's no power. méy-'dyàn-le. *or* The power has stopped. dyàn 'tíng-le.

(*Wrong*). *Expressed with* **to differ** chà. ‖His figures were way off. 'tā-de nèy-ge-shù-mu-'dzèr chà °'dwō-le. *or* °'ywǎn-le.

(*Below standard*) bù-'hǎw; **off grade** (*secondary*) tǐng 'ts̀z; (*bad*) bù-'hǎw, 'hwày-le, *or* bú-'jì. ‖He sold us an off grade of eggs. tā-'mày-gěy-'wǒm-de-jī-'dzěr °tǐng 'ts̀z. *or* °bù-'hǎw. *etc.* ‖It's an off year for crops. jīn-nyán 'shēw-chéng bù-'hǎw.

Off and on (*sometimes*) yěw-'shŕ-hew. ‖I've been studying off and on all year. jèy-yì-'nyán-láy wǒ yěw-'shŕ-hew nyàn-'shū, yěw-'shŕ-hew °'shyē-je. *or* °bú-'nyàn.

Off one's course (*go on the wrong road*) dzěw-'tswò-le 'lù-le.

Well off kwò (*rich*), jīng-kwàng 'hǎw; *badly off* kǔ (*hardship*.) ‖How well off is he? tā yěw dwō-'kwò? *or* *expressed as* How much money has he? tā 'chèn dwō-shaw-'chyán? ‖They're not so badly off. tā-men 'méy-yew nàme-'kǔ. *or* tā-men bú-'tày kǔ.

OFFER. ‖I am willing to offer one hundred dollars for it. *is expressed as* I'm willing to pay out a hundred dollars to buy it. wǒ 'ywàn-yì 'chū yì-'bǎy-kwày-chyán 'mǎy. ‖She offered to preside at the meeting. *is expressed as* She volunteered to be chairman at the meeting. kāy-'hwèy de-'dé-shŕ-hew tā gàw-fèn-'yǔng dzwò jǔ-'shí. ‖He offered to help us. *is expressed as* He wanted to help us. tā 'yàw bāng wǒm-de-'máng. ‖He offered us the use of his car. *is expressed as* He was going to lend us his car. tā yàw bà-'chē 'jyè-gey wǒ-men. ‖Did they offer any resistance? *is expressed as* Did they try to resist? tā-men shyǎng dǐ-'kàng méy-yew?

To offer one's congratulations dàw-'shǐ. ‖May I offer my congratulations? wǒ gěy-'nín dàw-'shǐ.

An offer. ‖They made him an offer of a good job. *is expressed as* They gave him a good job (*which he may or may not have taken*). tā-men yàw 'gěy-ta yí-ge-hǎw-'shèr. ‖Will you keep the offer open? *is expressed as* Can you keep it for a while? nín 'néng-bù-néng gěy-wo 'lyéw shyē-'shŕ-hew? ‖I'd sell the car if I had a good offer for it. *is expressed as* When someone gives me a good price, then I'll sell the car. yěw-'rén gěy hǎw-'jyàr, wǒ jyèw bǎ-'chē 'mày-le.

OFFICE. (*Place or room for business*) gūng-shŕ-'fáng, bàn-gūng-'shŕ. ‖I'll see you at the office tomorrow. wǒ 'myéngr-ge dzày gūng-shŕ-'fáng 'jyàn-ni. ‖His office is to the left. tā-de-gūng-shŕ-'fáng dzày 'dzwǒ-byār.

(*Office staff*) jŕ-'ywán. ‖He arranged a picnic for the whole office. tā gěy chywán-'tǐ-de-jŕ-'ywán 'bàn-gwo yí-'ts`z-yě-'tsān.

(*Department, bureau*) jī-'gwān; *in compounds* -jywú, -chǎng, -swǒ, -hwèy, *and others*. **Patent office** jwān-lì-'jywú; **post office** yéw-jèng-'jywú. ‖All the government offices are having a holiday. 'swǒ-yěw-de-'jèng-fǔ-jī-'gwān dēw fàng-'jyà-ne.

(*Position, rank, title*) 'míng-yì; (*responsibility*) 'jŕ-wù; (*term of office:* or *to hold an office*) rèn. ‖What office does he hold? tā shéme-'míng-yì? *or* tā 'dān-rèn shéme-'jŕ-wù? ‖He's been in office five years. tā dzày-'rèn 'wǔ-nyán-le.

OFFICER. (*Government or military*) gwān, gwār. **Police officer** (*an officer of the police force*) shywún-'gwān *or* (*policeman*) shywún-'jǐng; *in addressing a policeman, call him* shywún-'jǐng *or* 'shyàn-sheng, *or, if very humble about it,* shywún-'jǐng 'lǎw-yè. ‖Were you an officer in the army? nín 'shŕ-bu-shŕ 'dāng-gwo jywūn-'gwān? ‖Are you a police officer? nín shŕ shywún-'gwān-ma? ‖Officer, can you tell me which street goes there? 'shyàn-sheng, dzěw 'něy-tyáw-jyè tsáy néng 'dàw-nar?

(*Of company or club*) jŕ-'ywán. ‖Yesterday the company elected its new officers. 'dzwó-tyān gūng-'sz̀ bǎ shīn-jŕ-'ywán 'shywǎn-chū-láy-le.

OFFICIAL. An official (*government or military*) gwān, gwār; (*company or club*) jŕ-'ywán. ‖He's a government official. tā shŕ dzwò-'gwār-de. ‖Who are those officials? nèy-shyē-'gwār dēw shŕ-'shéy?

(*Public, not personal*) gūng; (*belonging to an official*) gwān; (*verified, authoritative*) jèng-'shr̀-de. **Official car** gwān-'chē; **official news** (*from an official source*) 'gwān-fāng-'shyāw-shì or (*verified news*) 'jèng-'shr̀-de-'shyāw-shi. ‖**Is this official business?** 'jèy 'shr̀-bu-shr̀ gūng-'shr̀? ‖**Is that an official order?** nèy 'shr̀-bu-shr̀ jèng-'shr̀-de-'mìng-lìng?

OFTEN. cháng. ‖**Does this happen often?** 'cháng yěw jèy-yàng-de-'shèr-ma? ‖**I've seen them together often.** wǒ 'cháng 'kàn-jyàn tam dzày yí-"kwàr. ‖**Does he come here often?** tā 'cháng láy-ma? ‖**Did he come to see you often?** tā 'cháng láy 'kàn nǐ-ma? ‖**How often did he come to see you?** *is expressed as* **How many times did he come to see you?** tā láy 'kàn nǐ láy-gwo 'dwō-shaw-tsź?

In referring to trains or buses that run on schedule, **often** *is expressed as* **how many times** (*in same period*) dwō-shaw-°'tsź (*or* °'tàng). ‖**How often do the buses run?** gūng-gùng-chì-'chē °yì-'tyān (*or* °yì-dyǎn-jūng) °kāy 'dwō-shaw-'tsź? *or* °dzěw 'dwō-shaw-'tàng?

OIL. yéw. ‖**What kind of oil is in that can?** dzày-nèy-'gwàr-li-de shr̀ shéme-'yéw? ‖**Please check the oil.** *is expressed as* **Please check whether my car has oil enough or not.** láw-jyà 'kàn-kan wǒ-chē-li-de-'yéw 'gèw-bu-gèw.

Oil painting yéw-'hwà(r). ‖**He does his best work in oils.** *is expressed as* **He paints oil paintings best.** tā hwà 'yéw-hwàr 'hwà-de 'dzwèy hǎw.

To oil *something.* (*Put on oil, apply oil*) shàng-'yéw; (*squirt oil on or into something*) gàw-'yéw; (*rub oil on something*) tsā-'yéw. ‖**The machine needs oiling.** jèy-ge-'jī-chi gāy gàw-'yéw-le.

OLD. (*Of people*) lǎw; (*of children*) *expressed as* **big** dà; (*really aged*) shàng-'swèy-shùr-de, shàng 'nyán-ji. ‖**His grandmother is a very old woman.** tā-de-'nǎy-nay shr̀ ge-hěn-°'lǎw-de-lǎw-'tày-tay. *or* °shàng-'swèy-shùr-de-'tày-tay. ‖**I'm getting old.** (*If you're an adult*) wǒ 'lǎw-le. ‖**He's too old to be treated like a child.** tā 'yǐ-jing 'něm-dà-le bù-néng dzày 'ná-ta dàng shyǎw-'hár dày-le.

(*In asking age*). ‖**How old are you?** (*If said to a young person*) *is expressed as* **How big is your age?** nín dwō-dà-'nyán-jì? *or as* **How big a number of years have you?** nín dwō-dà-'swèy-shù-le? *or as* **How big are you?** nǐ dwō-'dà-le? *or as* **How many years have you?** nǐ 'jǐ-swèy-le? *or* (*If said to an adult*) *as* **How high is your age?** nín gāw-'shèw? ‖**I'm thirty years old.** wǒ 'sān-shr-swèy-le. *or* wǒ 'sān-shŕ-le.

(*Of things; used, dilapidated*) jyèw; (*old but not less good*) lǎw; (*ancient*) gǔ. ‖**Wear old clothes.** chwān 'jyèw-'yī-fu. ‖**This is a very old house.** jèy-swǒr-'fáng-dz hěn 'lǎw-le. ‖**This is a very old city.** jèy-shr̀ dzwò-'gǔ-chéng.

(*Former*) lǎw. ‖**He's an old student of mine.** 'ta shr̀ wǒ-de-'lǎw-'shywé-shēng. ‖**Is this the old type?** jèy 'shr̀-bu-shr̀ lǎw-'yàngr-de?

(*Mature*) 'lǎw-lyàn. **An old hand** lǎw-'shěw. ‖**He's old for his years.** tā-'swèy-shu 'bú-dà 'kě-shr tǐng 'lǎw-lyàn. ‖**He's an old hand at that.** tā 'bàn nèy-ge-'shèr shr̀ ge-lǎw-'shěw-le.

ON. 1. (*On the surface of*) . . .-shang. ‖**What's on the list?** jèy-ge-'byǎw-shang shr̀ 'shéme? ‖**Is chicken on the menu tonight?** jyèr-'wǎn-shang-de-tsày-'dār-shang yěw-'jī méy-yew? ‖**There were two pictures on the wall.** 'chyáng-shang yěw lyǎng-jāng-'hwàr.

(*Next to or facing*) āy, kàw, chùng, shyàng, dwèy, cháw, *all plus* -je. ‖**Do you have a room on the street?** nǐ 'yěw-méy-yew °āy-je- (*or* °'kàw-je. *etc.*) dà-'jyè-de-'wū-dz?

(*In a direction*) dzày. ‖**It's on the left.** dzày 'dzwǒ-byar.

(*Included in*) . . .-li. ‖**There's only one woman on the committee.** jèy-ge-wěy-ywán-'hwèy-li jř yěw 'yí-wèy shr̀ 'nywǔ-de. ‖**Who's on the team?** jèy-ge-'dwèy-li dēw yěw-'shwéy?

(*At a time*). ‖**Are you open on Saturday?** *is expressed as* **Are you open Saturday?** nín lǐ-bày-'lyèw kāy-'mér-ma? ‖**The bell rings on the hour.** jèy-ge-'jūng měy-dàw-'jěng-yí-ge-'jūng-téwr-de-shŕ-hew 'dǎ yí-'tsź.

(*From or on the basis of*) tsúng. ‖**I got this on good authority.** jèy-ge-'shyāw-shi wǒ tsúng kě-'kàw-de-'dì-fang 'dé-lay-de.

(*Concerning*) 'gwān-ywu, 'dwèy-ywu, jyàng. ‖**It's a book on animals.** jèy-shr yì-běr-°'gwān-ywu- (*or* 'jyàng-) 'dùng-wù-de-shū. ‖**What're your ideas on the subject?** nǐ dwèy-ywu jèy-ge-'wèn-tí yěw shéme-'yì-jyàn?

(*Resting on*). ‖**The car went around the corner on two wheels.** *is expressed as* **When the car turned the corner there were only two wheels touching the ground.** jèy-ge-chì-'chē gwǎy jèy-ge-'wār de-shŕ-hew jř yěw 'lyǎng-ge-'lwén-dz jāw-'dì.

(*Using as means of locomotion*). **On foot** 'dzěw-je, 'twěy-je. ‖**Can we go on foot?** wǒm 'néng-bu-néng °'dzěw-je chywù? *or* °'twěy-je chywù?

2. *In a combination with a verb, where* **on** *means* **come to be in a position above and resting on some-thing not specified,** *Chinese has an appropriate verb of motion plus* -shàng *as postverb.* ‖**Climb on!** 'pá-shang-chywù! *or* 'pá-shang-láy! ‖**Jump on!** 'tyàw-shang-chywù! *or* (*if* **jump** *is said just for liveliness*) 'shàng-láy! ‖**Is the coffee on?** jyā-'fēy 'jǔ-shàng-le-ma? *or* bǎ jyā-fēy-'hú 'dzwò-shang-le-ma? ‖**Is the pot cover on?** hú-'gàr 'gày-shang-le-ma?

In similar combinations, where the meaning is **to cause something to be on something not specified,** *Chinese has the appropriate verb of handling plus* -shàng *as postverb; or, occasionally, a different post-verb, such as* hǎw, *indicating satisfactory completion* *of the action.* ‖**Have you got your shoes on yet?** nǐ-de-'shyé yì 'ĭng °chwān-'hǎw-le (*or* °'chwān-shang-le) méy-yew? ‖**Put your coat on.** bǎ dà-'yī 'chwān-shang-ba.

In combinations similar to the last, except that the object on which the thing handled comes to rest is also specified, dzày *is generally used as the postverb, and* -shang *is added to the specification of the object-on-which.* ‖**Put it on the table.** 'fàng-dzay 'jwō-dz-shang. ‖**Put it on ice.** fàng-dzay 'bīng-shang. *or expressed as* **Ice it.** 'bīng-shang.

3. *Combinations in which* on *has the force of* **resume** *or* **continue.** **Be on** (*in process*). ‖**Is the race on yet?** *is expressed as* **Has the race already been started?** nèy-ge-bǐ-'sày yǐ-jìng kāy-'shř-le-ma? *or* tām yǐ-jìng 'sày-chi-lay-le-ma?

Go on (*continue or resume moving forward*) 'háy-shr jyē-je . . . dzěw. ‖**Let's go on towards the mountains.** dzám 'háy-shr 'jyē-je wàng nèy-ge-'shān-nèr 'dzěw-ba.

Go on . . . -ing 'jyē-je, bù-'tíng-de, bú-'dwàn-de. ‖**Let's go on working hard.** wǒm °'jyē-je (*or* °'bù-'tíng-de *or* °'bú-'dwàn-de) kǔ 'gàn-ba.

Keep on with 'jì-shywù, 'jyē-je, 'háy-shr. ‖**Keep on with what you're doing.** nǐ °'jì-shywù (*or* °'jyē-je *or* °'háy-shr) gàn nǐ-de-'hwór.

‖**Move on!** (*Don't loiter*) 'dzěw-wa!

4. *Miscellaneous other combinations* (*for such combinations see also the word or words with which* on *is combined*).

Be on (*at the expense of*). ‖**This one's on me.** 'jèy ràng-'wǒ-ba. *or* 'wǒ hèw-ba. *or* 'wǒ gěy-ba. ‖**The drinks are on the house.** 'jyew dēw-shr lǎw-'bǎn jìng-de. *or* 'jyēw-chyán 'gwèy-shang 'hèw-le.

Bring *something* **on** (*cause*). ‖**What brought on this condition?** 'dzěme 'nùng-chéng 'jèy-yàngr-le-ne? *or* 'jèy-shř dzěme 'nàw-de?

On the contrary 'jèng shyang-'fǎn.

On credit. ‖**Do you sell on credit?** 'gāy-je (*or* 'chyàn-je) 'shíng-bu-shíng? *or* kě-yi shyě-'jàng-ma?

Be on duty jŕ-'bān, jàn-'gǎng, shàng-'bān. ‖**When are you on duty?** nǐ 'shéme-shř-hew °jŕ-'bān? *or* °jàn-'gǎng? *etc.*

Be on fire jáw-le 'hwǒ-le, chǐ-'hwǒ-le, 'jáw-le, shāw-'jáw-le.

To go on *or* **start on** (*in order to do or have*). ‖**He went on an errand.** *is expressed as* **He went out because of some business.** tā yěw-'shř 'chū-chywu-le. *or as* **He went to take care of some business.** tā bàn-'shř chywù-le. ‖**I'm going on my vacation next Monday.** *is expressed as* **Next Monday I start having my vacation.** shyà-lǐ-bày-'yī wǒ jyèw yàw shyēw-'jyà-le. ‖**When do you start on your trip?** *is expressed as* **When do you go to travel?** nǐ 'shéme-shř-hew chywù lywǔ-'shíng? *or as* **When do you start out?** nǐ 'shéme-shř-hew °chǐ-'chéng? *or* °chū-'fā?

Later on yǐ-'hèw, gwò shyē-'shŕ-hewr. ‖**Wait till later on.** děng °'yǐ-'hèw (*or* °'gwò shyē-shŕ-hewr) dzày shwō.

Stand . . . on end bǎ . . . 'shù-chǐ-láy. ‖**Stand the book on end.** bǎ jèy-běn-'shū 'shù-chǐ-láy.

Turn . . . on kāy, 'kāy-kay. ‖**Is the gas turned on?** méy-'chì shř 'kāy-je-ne-ma?

ONCE. yì-'hwéy, yí-'tsž, yí-'byàn. ‖**He feeds the dog once a day.** jèy-ge-'gěw tā yì-'tyān wèy yí-'tsž. ‖**Try it just this once.** jyèw 'shř jèy-yì-'hwéy. ‖**I've seen him once or twice.** wǒ jyàn-gwo tā yì-lyǎng-'hwéy. ‖**If you once read it, you'll never forget it.** nǐ 'jŕ-yàw 'bǎ jèy-ge 'nyàn-gwo 'yí-byàn, jyèw 'yǔng-ywǎn 'wàng-bù-lyǎw-le.

(*Formerly*) tsúng-'chyán, tséng-'jīng. ‖**I was in the army once.** wǒ 'tsúng-chyán dāng-gwo 'bīng. ‖**We lived near here once.** wǒm 'tséng-jīng dzày-jèr-'fù-jìn 'jù-gwo.

Once . . . , (then) yɪ . . . . ‖**Once we get there you'll see how beautiful it is.** yí 'dàw-nèr, nǐ jyèw 'jŕ-dàw nèy-ge-'dì-fang dwō-me hǎw-'kàn.

At once (*immediately*) 'lì-kè, mǎ-'shàng, 'gǎn-jǐn, gǎn-'kwày. ‖**Come at once.** nǐ 'lì-kè 'láy.

At once (*at the same time*) túng-'shŕ; (*together*) yí-'kwàr. ‖**Everyone was shouting at once.** dà-'jyā-hwǒr túng-'shŕ 'rāng-rang. ‖**Everything always happens at once.** shéme-'shèr dēw 'tsèw-dàw yí-'kwàr-le.

Once in a while yěw(-de)-'shŕ(-hewr). ‖**You might be nice to me once in a while.** nǐ yěw-'shŕ-hewr yě 'dày-wo 'haw-dyǎr 'shíng-bu-shíng?

ONE. yī *plus a measure.* ‖**Count from one to a hundred.** nǐ tsúng-'yī 'shǔ-dàw yì-'bǎy. ‖**One or two will be enough.** yì-'lyǎng-ge jyèw 'gèw-le. ‖**One of us can buy the tickets while the others wait here.** wǒ-men kě-yi 'yí-ge-rén chywù mǎy-'pyàw, 'byé-rén dzày-'jèr 'děng-je dé-le. ‖**I have only one thought.** wǒ 'jŕ yěw 'yí-ge-'nyàn-tew *or* wǒ 'shīn-li 'jŕ yěw 'yí-jyàn-shř. ‖**I have only one thought, and that's to go home.** *is expressed as* **With my whole mind I'm thinking of going home.** wǒ yì-'shīn shyǎng hwéy-'jyā.

One at a time, *or* **one by one** yí-ge-'yí-ge- le, *or with another measure replacing* ge *in the same pattern.* ‖**One at a time, please!** chǐng 'yí-ge-yí-'gèr-de láy. ‖**They came in one by one.** tām 'yí-ge-'y -ge-de 'jìn-lay-le.

(*Some person not specified*) rén, *or omitted.* ‖**One has to be careful with fire.** (rén) děy 'shyǎw-shīn 'hwǒ-jù.

One another bǐ-'tsž. ‖**It's up to us to protect one another.** wǒm děy bǐ-'tsž 'jàw-lyàw-je dyǎr.

(*Referring to a single thing, but without specifying what*) yī *plus a measure, without any following noun, or an expression ending in* de *without any following noun.* ‖**You have two horses; will you give me one?** nǐ yěw 'lyǎng-pǐ-mǎ; 'gěy-wo 'yì-pǐ, 'hǎw-bu-hǎw? ‖**I prefer the more expensive one.** wǒ 'shř-hwan nèy-ge-'gwèy-dyǎr-de. ‖**I prefer the more expensive ones.** wǒ 'shř-hwan 'gwèy-dyǎr-de.

ONLY. (*Single, only existing one*) wéy-'yī-de. Only person yí-ge-'rén. ‖It's our only hope. nà shř wǒm-wéy-'yī-de-'shī-wàng-le. ‖It's your only chance. nà shř nǐ-wéy-'yī-de-'jī-hwèy-le. ‖Am I the only one here? *is expressed as* Here is there just me alone? jèr 'jř yěw wǒ-'yí-ge-rén-ma? ‖She's an only child. *is expressed as* Her family has just her alone. tā-'jyā jyèw shř 'tā-nème-'yí-gè.

(*Merely, just, exclusively*) jř, *or* jyèw (*see also* JUST). ‖This is only for you. jèy °'jř (*or* °'jyèw shř) wèy-'nín-de. ‖This seat is only big enough for one person. nèy-ge-'dzwòr 'jř néng 'dzwò 'yí-ge-rén. ‖I only want a little. wǒ °'jř (*or* °'jyèw) yàw yì-'dyǎr. ‖He was here only two weeks. tā °jř (*or* °jyèw) 'dzày-jèr 'dāy-le 'lyǎ-lǐ-'bày.

Only . . . ago tsáy. ‖He died only a month ago. tā tsáy 'sž-le yí-ge-'ywè. ‖I got here only a moment ago. wǒ °'tsáy (*or* °gāng *just now*) 'dàw-jèr yì-'hwěr.

(*But*) kě-shr, *or* bú-'gwò. ‖I was going to buy it, only you told me not to. wǒ 'běn-láy yàw 'mǎy láy-je, 'kě-shr yīn-wey nǐ yì 'shwō, wǒ jyèw méy-'mǎy. ‖He wanted to help, only he didn't have time. tā 'dàw-shř shyǎng bāng-'máng láy-je, 'bú-gwò jēn shř méy 'gūng-fu.

If only (*see* IF). ‖If you could only help me! nín yàw néng 'bāng-wo yí-'shyàr, dwō-'hǎw!

Not only . . . but also . . . (*literary*) bú-'dàn-shr . . . ér-chyě 'yěw . . . ; *or* (*both . . . and . .*) yěw . . . yěw . . . . ‖It's not only snowing, but there's a wind, too. bú-'dàn-shr shyà-'shywě ér-chyě 'yěw gwā-'fēng. *or* yěw shyà-'shywě yěw gwā-'fēng.

Only too dāng-'rán *or* dž-'rán (*naturally, of course*). ‖I'm only too glad to help you. wǒ °dāng-'rán (*or* °dž-'rán) 'ywàn-yi bāng nín-de-'máng. ‖He was only too willing to agree. *is expressed as* That was unexpectedly good, and of course, he agreed. nà jyǎn-'jř shř 'chyéw-jř-bù-dé, tā °dž-'rán (*or* °dāng-'rán) 'dā-ying-le.

OPEN. To open *something. Various compounds containing* kāy, *the first element expressing the means of opening.* Open a door bǎ-'mén 'kāy-kay; open a window 'dǎ-kāy 'chwāng-hu; open a box 'dǎ-kāy 'hé-dz; open a drawer 'lā-kāy 'chēw-tì; open a book 'dǎ-kāy 'shū *or* 'fān-kāy 'shū; open a letter 'dǎ-kāy (*or* 'chāy-kāy) nèy-fēng-'shìn; open one's mouth 'jāng-kāy 'dzwěy (*figuratively*, to speak, kāy-'kěw *or* jāng-'dzwěy); open one's eyes jēng-'yǎn *or* 'jēng-kāy 'yǎn (*also figuratively, wide-eyed*); open a meeting kāy-'hwèy. ‖Open the door, please. chǐng bǎ-'mér 'kāy-kay. *or* chǐng kāy-'mér. *or* 'kāy-kay 'mér. ‖What time do you open shop? nǐ-'pù-dz 'shéme-shŕ-hew kāy-'mér? ‖The doctor told the child to open her mouth. 'dày-fu jyàw jèy-ge-'háy-dz 'jāng-kay 'dzwěy. ‖He never opened his mouth. tā yì-'jř méy-°'kāy-'kěw. *or* °'jāng-'dzwěy. ‖When will they open the meeting? 'tā-men 'shéme-shŕ-hew kāy-'hwèy? ‖Open your eyes. bǎ-'yǎn 'jēng-kāy. ‖That certainly opened my eyes to a few things. nèy kě 'jēn ràng-wo kāy-'yǎn-le.

To open (*of a stove, building, dining room, etc.*) kāy-'mér; (*of a school*) kāy-'shywé; (*of flowers*) 'kāy-le; (*begin: of a meeting*) kāy-'shř. ‖The store opens at ten o'clock. 'pù-dz shř 'shŕ-dyǎn-jūng kāy-'mér. ‖When does school open this year? 'jīn-nyán shywé-'shyàw shéme-'shŕ-hew kāy-'shywé? ‖I'd like some roses that haven't opened too far. wǒ yàw jĭ-'dwǒr-méy-'dà-kāy-de-méy-gwèy-'hwār.

To open into (onto) cháw; (*to face*) 'chùng-je. ‖There's a door opening into the garden. yěw yí-ge-'mén 'chùng-je hwā-'ywár. ‖What do the windows open onto? nèy-shyē-'chwāng-hu 'chùng-je 'něy-byār?

To open up. *See* to open *something and* to open, *in the first two paragraphs.* ‖Open up! (*Open the door!*) 'kāy-kay! ‖He finally opened up and told us everything. *is expressed as* He finally couldn't hold it any longer, and told us everything. tā dàw-'lyǎwr byē-bu-'jù-le, bǎ 'shéme dēw 'gàw-su wǒ-men-le.

Open (*opposite of closed*). ‖Is the door open? mén °méy-'gwān-ba.. 'shř-bu-shř °'kāy-je-ne-ma? *or* °'chǎng-je-ne-ma? ‖He came in through the open window. tā 'tsúng nèy-ge-'kāy-je-de-'chwāng-hu 'jìn-lay-de. ‖Are you open on Sundays? lǐ-bày-'tyān nǐm 'kāy-mér-ma? ‖The book was open at page fifty. nèy-běr-'shū dzày dì-'wǔ-shr-yè-nèr °'dǎ-je (*or* °'kāy-je) láy-je. ‖The roses are fully open. 'méy-gwèy-'hwār dēw 'kāy-kay-le. ‖The pipe is open at both ends. *is expressed as* The pipe has an opening at both ends. 'gwǎn-dz-lyǎng-'téwr dēw yěw-'kěwr.

(*Passable; of a road, pipe, river, communication line, or any passage that has been obstructed*) 'tūng-le. ‖This road is open to traffic. jèy-tyáw-'lù yǐ-jing °'tūng-'shíng-le. *or* °'tūng-'chē-le. *or* nèy-tyáw-'lù °néng (*or* °shywǔ *or* °'kě-yi *or* °ràng) 'dzěw-le. ‖Is the harbor open? gǎng-'wān 'kě-yǐ °'jìn-chywu-ma? *or* °'kāy-le-ma? *or, meaning* Is the harbor cleared of ice? gǎng-'wān kāy-'dùng-le-ma?

(*Frank, on the level*) jēn-'gé-de; (*frankly*) 'tǎn-báy-de. ‖I don't think he was really open with me. wǒ 'shyǎng tā 'méy-gēn-wo °'shwō jēn-'gé-de. *or* °'tǎn-báy-de 'shwō.

(*Generally known*) gūng-'kāy-de; *also several expressions meaning* everybody knows it. ‖That's an open secret. 'nèy shř ge-gūng-'kāy-de-bì-'mì. *or* nèy-jyàn-'shř shř °'rén-swǒ-gùng-'jř-de. *or* °'rén-rér dēw 'jř-daw. *or* °'dà-jyā dēw 'jř-daw. *or* °'shéy dēw 'jř-daw.

(*Undecided*) méy-'jyē-gwǒ. ‖That's still an open question. nèy-ge-'wèn-tí háy méy-'jyē-gwǒ. *or expressed as* No one's decided what to do about that yet. 'nèy-ge dà-'jyā-hwǒr 'háy bù-'jř-daw dzěme 'bàn.

(*Available, accessible*). ‖Is the park open to the public? *is expressed as* Are people allowed to go in the park? jèy-ge-gūng-'ywán 'shywǔ-rén 'jìn-chywu-ma? ‖All our harbors are open to ships of neutral countries. *is expressed as* Neutral ships are allowed to come in all our harbors. wŏm-'swŏ-yĕw-de-găng-'wān dēw 'shywŭ jūng-'lì-gwó-de-chwán-'jř 'jìn-lay. ‖The contest is open to anyone. *is expressed as* Anyone can join this contest. jèy-ge-bĭ-'sày 'shéy dēw néng tsān-'jyā. *or as* This is a public contest. jèy-ge shř gūng-'kāy-bĭ-'sày. ‖The job is still open. *is expressed as* There's still no one working on that job. nèy-jyàn-'shèr háy méy-rén 'dzwò-ne. ‖Is your offer still open? *is expressed as* That thing you mentioned, is it still all right? nĭ-'shàng-hwéy-'tí-de-nèy-ge-'shèr °háy 'shíng-ma? *or as* . . . can we still do it? °háy néng 'bàn-ma? *or as* . . . what about it? °dzěm-'yàng-le? ‖The 23rd is still open, if you want to use the auditorium then. *is expressed as* If you want to borrow the auditorium, it's unoccupied the 23rd. nĭ yàw shyáng 'jyè dà-lĭ-'táng, °èr-shr-'sān-hàw 'shyán-je-ne. *or as* . . . it's all right the 23rd. °èr-shr-'sān-hàw 'shíng. *or as* . . . it's still not taken for the 23rd. °èr-shr-'sān-hàw háy 'kūng-je-ne. ‖There are several possibilities open. *is expressed us* There are several ways, any of them is all right. yĕw 'hăw-jĭ-jŭng-'bàn-fa, 'dzěme-je dēw 'shíng. ‖I'm open to conviction. *is expressed as* I'm not clinging to my idea. wŏ bú-'gù-jř jĭ-'jyàn. *or as* If you have any ideas, speak up. yĕw shéme-'yì-jyàn jìn-'gwăn 'shwō. ‖He's always open to reason. *is expressed as* He's always reasonable. tā-'nèy-ge-rén hěn jyàng-'lì. ‖I have an open mind about it. *is expressed as* I have no prejudice at all about it. wŏ dwèy 'nèy-ge bìng 'méy-yew shéme-'chéng-jyàn.

Open air lù-'tyān. ‖The concert was given in the open air. yīn-ywè-'hwèy shř dzày lù-'tyān 'yăn-de.

Open city (*unfortified*) bú-shè-fáng-chéng-'shř.

Open country 'kūng-kwàng-'dì-fang.

Open fields kwàng-'yě.

Opening remarks *is expressed as* the remarks at the beginning. chĭ-'téwr-jĭ-jywù-'hwà.

Open wound (*unhealed*) méy-shēw-'kěwr-de-'shāng-kěw.

With open arms (*affectionately*) 'chīn-rè.

OPERATE. (*Manage, run; of machines that move*) kāy; (*use; of other machines*) yùng, shř. ‖Can you operate a sewing machine? nĭ hwèy °'yùng (*or* °'shř) féng-yī-'jī-chì-ma? ‖I don't know how to operate this car. wŏ bù-'jř-daw dzěm 'kāy jèy-ge-'chē.

(*Be running; be in use*) yěw-'rén °'yùng-je (*or* °'shř-je); (*of all electric machines*) 'kāy-je; (*be in condition to run*) néng 'yùng, néng 'shř, *or* (*of electrical machines*) néng 'kāy; (*of a factory*) kāy-'gūng. ‖The factory operates twenty-four hours a day. gūng-'chăng 'hēy-yè 'báy-r kāy-'gūng. ‖Is this elevator operating? (*In use*) dyàn-'tī 'kāy-je-ne-ma? (*Usable*) dyàn-'tī néng 'kāy-ma? ‖Is this (*non-electric*) machine operating? (*In use*) jèy-ge-'jī-chi yěw-'rén 'yùng-je-ne-ma? (*Usable*) jèy-ge-'jī-chi néng 'yùng-ma?

(*Act, work*). ‖Just how would your plan operate? *is expressed as* Just how do you do it according to your method? nĭ-de-'bàn-fa shř 'dzěm-je 'dzwò? *or as* What's the method of approach of your plan? nĭ-de-'bàn-fa shř 'dzěme-ge-'dzwò-far? ‖The plan operates to his advantage, of course. *is expressed as* The plan being used is advantageous to him, of course. jèy-ge-'bàn-far 'dzwò-chĭ-láy dāng-'rán wèy-'tā yěw-'lì.

(*Use surgery*) kāy-'dāw; *or* shř (*or* dùng) 'shēw-shù. ‖The doctor said he'd have to operate. 'dày-fu shwō tā děy kāy-'dāw.

Operating room gé-jèng-'shř. ‖He was in the operating room two hours. tā dzày gé-jèng-'shř-li yěw 'lyă-jūng-'téw.

OPERATION. (*Action*) be in operation, *see* OPERATE. Go into (be put into) operation shř-'shíng. ‖Are the street cars in operation? *is expressed as* Are there any street cars (running)? dyàn-'chē 'kāy-je-ne-ma? *or* yěw dyàn-'chē 'méy-'yew? ‖The plan will be put into operation immediately. nèy-ge-'jì-hwa lì-'shř jyèw yàw shř-'shíng. ‖This plan may not be as good in actual operation as in theory. jèy-ge-'jì-hwa shř-'shíng-chi-lay yě-shywu méy-yew 'shyăng-de-nèm-'hăw.

(*Movement, process; movements made by a person*) 'dùng-dzwò; (*processes*) 'bù-dzèw; (*steps*) 'jyē-dwàn; (*procedure*) 'shēw-shywù. In one operation (*at one time*). yí-'shyàr. ‖Everything could be done in a single operation. 'swŏ-yěw-de yí-'shyàr jyèw 'kě-yi 'dzwò-chu-lay. ‖It takes three operations to do this. dzwò 'jèy-ge yěw sān-ge-°'bù-dzèw. *or* °'jyē-dwàn. *or* dzwò 'jèy-ge yěw 'sān-jŭng-'shēw-shywù. ‖It involves too many operations. nèm-je bàn 'shēw-shywù tày 'má-fan.

Military operations (*military movements*) 'jywūn-shr-shíng-'dùng. ‖They kept the military operations a secret. 'jywūn-shr-shíng-'dùng tām 'shěw-je mì-'mì lay-je. ‖He has been in many military operations. *is expressed as* He has many times fought in campaigns. tā 'yĭ-jing dă-gwo 'hăw-jĭ-tsż-'jàng-le.

Surgical operation shēw-'shù. ‖Do I have to have an operation? wŏ 'yí-dìng 'děy 'dùng yí-tsż shēw-'shù-ma?

OPINION. 'yì-jyàn, 'yì-sz. ‖What is your opinion? nín-de-'yì-jyàn dzěme-'yàng?

To have an opinion (*think*) jywé-de. ‖I have a very good opinion of him. *is expressed as* I think he's quite good. wŏ 'jywé-de tā hěn bú-'tswò. ‖I haven't a very good opinion of his ability. *is expressed as* I think he has no ability. wŏ 'jywé-de tā 'méy-shéme-'běn-shr. ‖She has a pretty high opinion of herself. *is expressed as* She thinks that she's pretty good. tā-'dż-jĭ 'jywé-de 'dż-jĭ tĭng bú-'tswò shř-de.

OPPORTUNITY. 'jī-hwey. **Have an opportunity** yěw 'jī-hwey; **get an opportunity** 'dé-dàw 'jī-hwey; **miss an opportunity** 'tswò-gwò 'jī-hwey. ‖**This is a big opportunity for you.** 'jèy-shr̀ nǐ-de-hǎw-'jī-hwey. ‖**Opportunity knocks but once.** *is expressed as* You can't pass up a good opportunity. lyáng-'jī bù-kě 'tswò-gwò. ‖**When will you have an opportunity to see me?** nǐ 'shéme-shŕ-hew néng yěw 'jī-hwey láy 'kàn-wo? *or expressed as* When will you have time to come see me? nǐ 'shéme-shŕ-hew néng yěw 'gūng-fu láy 'kàn-wo?

OPPOSITE. (*Converse*) shyāng-'fǎn. ‖**That is just the opposite of what I meant.** 'nèy-ge gēn wǒ-'shwō-de-'yì-sz 'gāng hǎw shyāng-'fǎn. ‖**This is the opposite of what I expected.** gēn wǒ-'shī-wàng-de gāng-'gǎng shyāng-'fǎng. ‖**He and his wife are exact opposites in looks and personality.** *is expressed as* He and his wife are definitely not alike. tām-'gūng-mǔ-'lyǎ jyǎn-'jŕ bù-yí-'yàng.
  Be opposite. (*To face*) dwèy-je; **opposite side** dwèy-'myàn, dwèy-'gwòr. ‖**What's that opposite us?** dwèy-je-'jèr-de-'nèy-ge shr̀ 'shéme? *or* °'dwèy-'myàr (*or* °'dwèy-'gwòr) shr̀ 'shéme? ‖**The cemetery is just opposite the church.** fén-'dì jyèw dzày lǐ-bày-'táng-de-dwèy-'gwòr. *or* fén-'dì jèng 'dwèy-je lǐ-bày-'táng. ‖**She sat opposite me at the table.** chŕ-'fàn de-'shŕ-hew 'tā 'dzwō-dzày wǒ-dwèy-'myàr. *or* °'tā 'dwèy-je wo 'dzwò-je. *But* ‖**They live on opposite sides of town.** tām-lyǎng-'jyǎ 'yí-ge dzày chéng-'jèy-téwr 'yí-ge dzày 'nèy-téwr. ‖**You should go in the opposite direction.** nǐ děy wàng dwèy-'myàr 'dzěw. *expressed as* You should go that way. nǐ děy wàng 'nèy-byar.

OR. 'háy-shr; *between words meaning the same thing* hwò (*literary*). **One or two** yì-lyǎng, **two or three** lyǎng-sān. ‖**Shall I wait here or come back later?** wǒ dzày-'jèr !děng-je 'háy-shr hwèy-'téw dzày 'láy? ‖**What is the aim, or purpose, of this collection?** jèy-jǔng-'sēw-ji-de-'dzūng-jŕ hwò 'mù-dì shr̀ 'shéme? ‖**Could I have two or three more cookies?** 'néng-bu-néng 'dzày gěy-wo lyǎng-'sān-kwàr-bǐng-'gār?
  (*Otherwise*) 'yàw-bu-rán. ‖**Hurry, or we'll be late.** 'kwày-dyǎr, 'yàw-bù-rán wǒ-men 'hwéy-téw 'wán-le.
  Either . . . or (*if . . . otherwise*) yàw . . . bù-rán. ‖**Either be there on time, or don't come at all.** *is expressed as* If you come, be on time, otherwise don't come at all. yàw 'láy jyèw àn 'shŕ-hew dàw, bù-rán 'gān-tswèy béng 'láy. ‖**He must be either drunk or crazy.** *is expressed as* If he isn't drunk, he's crazy. tā 'bú-shr̀ hē-'dzwèy-le, jyèw-shr 'fēng-le.

ORANGE. (*Fruit*) 'chen-dz; (*loose-peeled, tangerine*) 'jywú-dz; (*large, sweet*) mì-'gān, mì-gān-'jywú; (*red-skinned*) 'húng-jywú. ‖**How much are oranges?** 'chén-dz 'dwōr-chyán? ‖**Do you have orange juice?** nǐm yěw °'chén-dz-'jēr (*or* °'chén-dz-'shwěy) méy-yew?

(*Color*) 'shìng-hwáng *or* 'jywù-hwáng-'sè. ‖**Her dress was orange.** tā-de-'yī-fu shr̀ °'shìng-hwáng-de *or* °'jywù-hwáng-'sè.

ORDER. (*Arrangement*) 'tsż-shywu; **in order** āy-je (*or* àn-je) 'tsż-shywu, (*not messy*) bú-'lwàn; **out of order** lwàn; **put in order** (*arrange*) 'jěng-lǐ, (*file*) páy. ‖**What order should these papers be filed in?** jèy-shyē-wén-'jyàn 'yīng-dāng àn-je 'shéme-tsż-shywu 'páy? ‖**Line up in order of height.** àn-je gāw-'ǎy-de-'tsż-shywu jàn-'páy. ‖**The names were listed in alphabetical order.** 'míng-dz shr̀ àn-je yīng-'wén-dż-'mǔr-'tsż-shywu páy-de. ‖**These are not in the right order.** jèy-shyē 'páy-de bú-'dwèy. ‖**Everything on my desk was in order when I left.** wǒ 'dzěw de-shŕ-hew 'jwōr-shang-de-dūng-shi 'yì-dyǎr yě bú-'lwàn. ‖**Try to bring some order into these papers.** bǎ jèy-shyē-wén-'jyàn jìn-'lì 'jěng-lǐ yí-shyàr. ‖**Are these papers out of order?** jèy-shyē-wén-'jyàn 'lwàn-bu-lwàn?
  (*Discipline, orderliness*) 'jŕ-shywu. **Law and order** (*literary*) fǎ-'jì. ‖**You'll have to keep order in this hall.** dzày jèy-dà-'tīng-li nǐ děy 'wéy-chŕ 'jŕ-shywu. ‖**He has to see that law and order is observed.** tā 'gwǎn 'wéy-chŕ fǎ-'jì.
  (*Command*) 'mìng-lìng; **to order** shyà 'mìng-lìng *or* shyà-'lìng. ‖**Have you got your orders?** nǐ 'jyē-dàw 'mìng-lìng-le-ma? ‖**This is an order from the Captain.** jèy-ge-'mìng-lìng shr̀ 'dwèy-jǎng 'shyà-de. ‖**He ordered them put under arrest.** tā 'shyà-le 'mìng-lìng bǎ tā-men 'jwā-chi-lay-le. ‖**Who ordered you to do this?** *is expressed as* Who told you to do this? shwéy 'gàw-su ni dzwò 'jèy-ge? *or as* Who made you do this? shwéy °'ràng-ni (*or* °'jyàw-ni) 'dzwò 'jèy-ge-de? ‖**He was ordered to appear in court.** *is expressed as* He was summoned by the court to go there. fǎ-'ywàn chwán-ta chywù dàw-'tíng.
  (*List of things wanted*) dìng-'dār. **To order things** jyàw 'dūng-shi *or* dìng-'hwò; **to order a meal** dyǎn-(*or* jyàw- *or* yàw-)'tsày; **to order a meal delivered to your home** jyàw-'fàn; **to order** (*ask for*) yàw; (*reserve*) dìng. ‖**The order was given to the purchasing agent.** nèy-ge-dìng-'dār 'jyāw-gěy bàn-'hwò-de-rén-le. ‖**You can order these things by telephone.** nǐ 'kě-yi yùng dyàn-'hwà jyàw 'jèy-shyē-'dūng-shi. ‖**You can order these things by mail.** nǐ 'kě-yi shyě-'shìn yàw jèy-shyē-'dūng-shi. ‖**Have you ordered** (*dinner*) **yet?** nǐ dyǎn-'tsày-le-ma? ‖**This is not what I ordered.** jèy 'bú-shr̀ wǒ-°'dìng-de. *or* °'yàw-de. ‖**I ordered you a glass of wine.** wǒ gěy-ni 'yàw-le yì-bēy-'jyěw. ‖**I want to give an order for some things.** wǒ yàw dìng dyǎr-'hwò.
  By order of. ‖**The new regulation was put into effect by order of the Mayor.** *is expressed as* The new regulation was ordered made by the Mayor. jèy-ge-'shīn-'jāng-chéng shr̀ shŕ-'jǎng shyà-'lìng 'dìng-de.
  In order *or* **out of order.** ‖**Is the machinery in order?** *is expressed as* Is the machine usable? jèy-ge-'jī-chi néng 'yùng-ma? ‖**The elevator is temporarily out**

of order. *is expressed as* The elevator is temporarily unusable. dyàn-'tī jàn-'shŕ bù-néng 'yùng. ‖Is the machinery out of order? *is expressed as* Is the machine broken? jèy-ge-'jī-chi 'hwày-le méy-yew?

In order to 'wèy-de-shŕ. ‖I came all the way just in order to see you. wǒ lǎw-'ywǎn-de 'pǎw-láy jyèw 'wèy-de-shŕ láy 'kàn-kàn ni.

Made to order. ‖The suit was made to order. *is expressed as* The suit was custom made. jèy-tàw-'yī-fu shŕ .dìng-'dzwò-de. ‖That dish (*food*) will have to be made to order. *is expressed as* That dish will have to be made now. 'nèy-yàngr-tsày děy shyàn 'dzwò. ‖A day like this is made to order. jyēr-de-'tyār tày 'hǎw-le.

To call to order. ‖He called the meeting to order. *is expressed as* He announced the beginning of the meeting. tā shywān-'bù kāy-'hwèy.

To order around 'jŕ-shŕ, *or* hú 'jŕ-shŕ. ‖Stop ordering me around! być nème 'jŕ-shr rén!

ORDINARILY. píng-'cháng. ‖Where do you ordinarily eat? nǐ píng-'cháng dzày-'nǎr 'chŕ? ‖I wouldn't ordinarily do this. *is expressed as* I wouldn't ordinarily act this way. wǒ 'píng-cháng bú-'dzèm-je. *or as* I wouldn't ordinarily do this for anyone. wǒ 'píng-cháng bù-'gwǎn 'jèy-yàngr-de-'shŕ. ‖Ordinarily, we can get cigarettes here. 'píng-cháng 'jèr mǎy-de-'jáw 'yān.

ORDINARY. píng-'cháng-de, pǔ-'tūng-de. ‖Just give me an ordinary room. wǒ jyèw 'yàw yì-'jyān-píng-'cháng-de-'wū-dz. ‖They're very ordinary people. tām shŕ hěn píng-'cháng-de-rén. ‖Is this the ordinary route? *is expressed as* Is this the route people often go on? jèy 'shŕ-bu-shŕ 'cháng-dzěw-de-lù-'shyàn?

Out of the ordinary. (*Queer*) gwày; (*unusual, special*) 'tè-byé-de; (*outstanding*) chū-'sè-de. ‖Is this anything out of the ordinary? jèy yěw-dyǎr 'tè-byé-ma? ‖I didn't notice anything out of the ordinary about him. wǒ 'chyáw-bu-chu-láy tā yěw shéme-chū-'sè-de-dì-fang.

ORIGINAL. (*First*) ywán-'láy-de, dzwèy-'chū-de. Original manuscript ywán-gǎw-'běn; original painting ywán-'hwà; in the original (*language*) ywán-'wén-de. ‖The original site of the house was over there. dzwèy-'chū-de-fáng-'jī shŕ dzày 'nèy-byar. ‖Our original plan had to be changed. ywán-'láy-de-'jì-hwà bù-'dé bù-'gǎy-le. ‖Where is the original of this painting? nèy-jāng-°ywán-'hwà (*or* °ywán-láy-de-'hwàr) dzày-'nǎr-ne? *or is expressed as* Where is the real painted picture? jèy-jāng-jēn-'bǐ-de-'hwàr dzày-'nǎr-ne? ‖The original statue is in London. *is expressed as* The real statue is in London. nèy-ge-'jēn-de-shŕ-'shyàng shŕ dzày lwén-'dwēn. ‖Is this the original manuscript? jèy 'shŕ-bu-shŕ ywán-gǎw-'běn? ‖Have you read this book in the original? jèy-běr-'shū nǐ 'nyàn-gwo ywán-'wén-de-ma? ‖I read the translation, not the original. wǒ 'nyàn-gwo 'fān-yì-de, méy-'nyàn-gwo 'ywán-wén.

(*New, novel*) shīn; (*unusual*) 'tè-byé; (*not like the others*) ywú-jùng-bù-'túng; (*having originality*) 'shīn-chí. ‖That's an original idea. nèy shŕ ge-'shīn-'yì-jyàn. ‖His plan was quite original. tā-de-'jì-hwa °hěn 'tè-byé. *or* °ywú-'jùng-bù-'túng. ‖The style of that dress is very original. nèy-jyàn-'yī-fu-de-'yàng-dz 'jēn-shŕ 'tè-byé. ‖His stories aren't original enough to be published. tā-de-shyǎw-'shwōr 'tsáy-lyawr méy shéme-'shīn-chí, 'jŕ-de chū-'bǎn-de. ‖Is that joke original, or did you read it somewhere? *is expressed as* Did you make up that joke, or did you get it somewhere? nèy-ge-'shyàw-hwar shŕ nǐ-'byān-de, 'háy-shr 'dwēn-láy-de?

OTHER. (*The rest, of things*) chí-'tā-de, chí-'ywú-de; the others (*people*) 'byé-rén, 'páng-rén, *or* tām (*them*). ‖Do you want to know the other reasons? nǐ shyǎng 'jŕ-daw chí-'tā-de-'ywán-gu-ma? ‖The others you sold me were better. nǐ-'mǎy-gey-wo-de-chí-'ywú-de-dūng-shi bǐ 'jèy-ge 'hǎw. ‖Where are the others? 'byé-rén-ne? ‖If the others come, say I'm busy. 'tām yàw 'láy de-hwà jyèw 'shwō wǒ hěn 'máng. ‖I told the others to meet us here. wǒ gēn-tā-men 'shwō-de dzày-'jèr 'jyàn.

(*More, additional*) byé-de; (*besides*) háy. Other people 'byé-rén, 'páng-rén. ‖Sorry, I have other things to do. dwèy-bu-'jù, wǒ 'yěw dyǎr-'byé-de-'shŕ. ‖If any other people come, say I'm busy. 'yàw-shr yěw 'páng-rén 'láy de-hwà, jyèw 'shwō wǒ hěn 'máng. ‖Have you any other books? nǐ 'háy yěw 'byé-de-shū méy-yew? ‖What other things did he say? tā 'háy shwō 'shéme láy-je?

The other *of two* 'nèy(-geỳ. ‖Give me the other one. 'gěy-wo 'nèy-yí-ge. ‖Use your other hand too. 'nèy-jŕ-shěw yě 'shàng-láy. ‖What's on the other side of the mountain? shān-'nèy-byar yěw 'shéme? ‖He waved to her from the other side of the street. tā dzày jyē-'nèy-byar chùng-ta jāw-'shěwr. ‖I don't want this one, but the other. wǒ 'bú-yàw 'jèy-ge, yàw 'nèy-ge. ‖I can't tell one from the other. *is expressed as* I can't tell which is which. wǒ 'fēn-bu-chu-láy 'něy-ge shŕ 'něy-ge.

Every other (*alternating*) 'jyē-yí-ge, 'gé-yí-ge. ‖Trains leave every other hour. hwǒ-'chē měy-'jyē-yí-ge-jūng-'téwr kāy yí-'tàng. *But* ‖Every other time (*but this*) he's come with us. *is expressed as* It's just this time he hasn't come with us. tā jyèw-shr 'jèy-hwéy méy-'gēn wǒ-men 'láy.

On the other hand 'kě-shr, 'bú-gwò. ‖On the other hand, he may be too busy to see you. 'bú-gwò, tā 'yě-shywu méy-'gūng-fu 'jyàn nǐ.

Someone or other *is expressed as* I don't know who bù-('jŕ-daw) shŕ-'shéy. ‖Someone or other phoned you just now. yě 'bú-shŕ 'shwéy gāng gěy-ni dǎ-dyàn-'hwà láy-je.

Something or other *is expressed as* I don't know what bù-('jŕ-dàw) shŕ 'shéme. ‖He wrote something or other in his notebook. tā 'dzày tā-bǐ-jì-'běr-li yě 'bú-shř 'shyě-le shyē-'shéme. ‖He said something or other about meeting you. *is expressed as* He seems to have said he wanted to meet you. tā 'fǎng-fu 'shwō-gwo yàw 'jyàn-ni shř-de.

OUGHT. 'yīng-dang, yīng-gǎy, gǎy; (*certainly must*) yí-dìng 'děy. ‖You ought to help your parents. nǐ 'yīng-gǎy 'bāng-jù nǐ-fù-'mǔ. ‖The cake ought to be done soon. jèy-ge-dàn-'gāw jyèw gǎy 'dé-le. ‖He ought to leave before it rain. tā yí-'dìng děy dzày 'ywǔ méy-'shyà-chi-lay de-'shř-hew 'dzěw.

OUR, OURS. *See* WE.

OURSELVES. *See* SELF.

OUT. 1. (*Not in something*) chū *as postverb with the proper main verb, occasionally itself as verb.* ‖Take your tickets out! bǎ-'pyàw 'ná-chū-láy! ‖Let's go out for a while. dzám 'chū-chywu yì-'hwěr-ba. ‖Let the cat out. bǎ-'māw 'fàng-chu-chywù. ‖The secret is out. jèy-ge-bì-'mì 'lèw-chu-lay-le. *or expressed as* Everyone knows the secret. jèy-ge-bì-'mì 'rén dēw 'jř-daw-le.

  Come out *or* **be out** (*be published*) chū *or* chū-'bǎn. ‖When does the magazine come out? dzá-'jř 'shéme-shř-hew °'chū-lay? *or* °'chū-'bǎn? ‖The new number of that magazine is out today. nèy-ge-dzá-'jř-dzwèy-'jìn-de-yì-'chī jyēr °'chū-láy-le. *or* °'chū-'bǎn-le.

  To give *something* **out** (*distribute*) fā, 'fā-chū-láy. ‖When did they give out the books? jèy-shyē-'shū 'shéme-shř-hew 'fā(-chu-lay)-de?

  2. **Come out** *or* **be out** (*in bloom*) kāy. ‖What flowers are out now? shyàn-'dzày shéme-'hwār 'kāy-je-ne?

  3. **Leave** *something* **out** 'shān-chywù, chywù. ‖Leave the first paragraph out. bǎ 'téw-yí-'dwàr °'shān-chywu-le. *or* °'chywǔ-le.

  4. **Break out** (*of an epidemic, fire or other catastrophe*) 'nàw-chǐ-lay. ‖What'll we do if an epidemic breaks out? yàw-shr nàw-chi-'wēn-yì-lay, dzám dzěme 'bàn-ne?

  5. **Put** *a light* **out** . . . .-myè, *with a main verb specifying the method used* ⸝ 'gwān, 'gwān-shàng *for an electric light.* ‖Put the light out. bǎ-'dēng °nùng-'myè-le! *or* °'gwān-le! *or* ⸝gwān-'dēng!

  6. *Other groups containing* **out**; *for most of these see the word or words with which* **out** *is combined.*

  Out-and-out jyàn-'jř, wán-'chywán, jēn. ‖It's an out-and-out case of murder. 'nèy jyàn-'jř shř yí-jyàn-shyūng-shā-'àn. ‖You're an out-and-out liar! nǐ wán-'chywán shř sā-'hwǎng!

  Be out *so much money* 'dwǎn-le, 'chà-le, 'chyàn-le, shǎw-le. ‖I'm out three dollars. wǒ °'dwǎn-le (*or* 'chà-le, *etc.*) 'sān-kwày-chyán.

  Be out for *something* shyǎng, 'dǎ-swàn.

  Out of (*because of*). ‖Are you acting out of spite? *is expressed as* Are you wanting to take revenge? nǐ-shr yàw bàw-'chéw-ma? *or as* Is hate your reason? nǐ-shř 'wèy-de-shř jyě-'hèn-ma? ‖I did it for him out of gratitude. *is expressed as* I did it for him because I owed him a favor. wǒ 'yīn-wey 'chyàn tā-de-'chínr tsáy nàme 'bàn-de.

  Be out of (*minus*) méy, 'méy-yew, *or expressed by saying that the thing is finished* wán-le, *all sold* mày-'wán-le, *etc. with other appropriate main verbs before* wán. ‖We're all out of cigarettes. wǒm méy-yew yān-'jywǎr-le. *or* wǒm-de-yān-'jywǎr dēw °'wán-le. *or* °'chēw-'wán-le. *or* °'màs-'wán-le. ‖He's been out of work a long time. tā hěn 'jyew méy-'shèr-le. *or expressed as* He's been idle a long time. tā 'shyán-le bù-shǎw-'ř-dz-le.

  Be out of (*beyond*). ‖It's out of my control. *is expressed as* I can't control that. 'nèy-ge wǒ °'kùng-jř-bu-'jù-le. *or* °'kùng-jř-bù-'lyǎw-le. *or* °'gwǎn-bu-'jù-le. *or* °'gwǎn-bu-'lyǎw-le. *or* °'méy-fár 'gwǎn-le.

  Be out of the question shř bàn-bu-'dàw-de. ‖My staying here is out of the question. wǒ 'jù-dzay jèr shř bàn-bu-'dàw-de. *or* wǒ 'jywé-bu jù-dzay 'jèr.

  Be out of step. ‖You're out of step. nǐ-de-'bù-fa 'lwàn-le *or* nǐ-de-jyǎw-'bù °'lwàn-le. *or* °'tswò-le.

  Be out to *do something* 'dǎ-swàn. ‖He's out to break the record. tā 'dǎ-swàh dǎ-'pwò jì-'lù.

  Speak out. ‖He wasn't afraid to speak out in the meeting. *is expressed as* At the meeting he really dared to speak. tā dzày jèy-ge-'hwèy-li hěn 'gǎn shwō-'hwà.

  Stand out. ‖His height makes him stand out in a crowd. *is expressed as* His height is conspicuous in a crowd. tā-gèr-'gāw, dzày rén-'chywúr-li hěn jāw-'yǎn.

  Vote *someone* **out.** ‖They voted him out. *is expressed as* They voted that they didn't want him. tām byǎw-'jywé bú-'yàw ta-le.

OUTSIDE. 'wày-myan, 'wày-byar, 'wày-tew. ‖Is it cold outside? 'wày-byar 'lěng-bu-lěng? ‖Wait outside. dzày 'wày-myan 'děng-je. ‖Step outside, and say that again! dzám shàng 'wày-tew chywù, 'nǐ háy gǎn 'shwō-ma! ‖Three of them sat in the front seat, with the boy on the outside. tām 'lǐ-tew yěw 'sān-ge-rén dzwò dzày 'chyán-tew, nán-'háy-dz 'dzwò-de kàw 'wày-byar. ‖I like the outside of the house very much. jèy-fáng-dz dǎ-'wày-byar-kàn, wǒ tǐng 'shǐ-hwan-de. ‖The bowl is purple outside and blue inside. nèy-ge-'wǎn-de-'wày-byar shř 'dž-shǎr, 'lǐ-byar 'gwà-de 'lán-shǎr. ‖We need the opinion of someone from the outside. wǒm děy 'jǎw yí-ge-'wày-byar-de-rén 'kàn-kan. *or* °'pī-ping-pí-ping. ‖Do you have an outside room? *is expressed as* Do you have a room facing the outside? nǐ 'yěw-méy-yew yì-jyān-cháw-'wày-de-wū-dz?

  (*Figuratively*). ‖Isn't this outside your jurisdiction? *is expressed as* Doesn't this not belong to you to manage? jèy 'bú-shr bù-'gwēy-nín 'gwǎn-ma?

At the outside (*at the most*) dzwèy-'dwō. ‖It won't cost more than ten dollars at the outside. dzwèy-'dwō yě jyèw-shr 'shŕ-kwày-chyán.

Outside of (*besides, or except for*) chú-le . . . yǐ-'wày *or* chú-le . . . jr-'wày. ‖I wouldn't trust anyone outside of you. chú-le 'nǐ yǐ-'wày wǒ 'shéy dēw bú-'shìn. ‖Outside of a few funny remarks his speech was very dull. chú-le jǐ-jywù-dèw-'gén-de-hwà yǐ-'wày, tā-de-yǎn-'jyǎng hěn méy 'yì-sz. ‖Outside of the rent there's still the electric light bill to be paid. 'chú-le 'fáng-chyán yǐ-'wày háy děy 'gěy 'dyàn-chyán.

OVER. (*In a higher position than; spatially*) dzày . . .°-'shàng-myan *or* °-'shàng-myar *or* °-'shàng-tew *or* °-'shàng-byar. ‖His room is directly over mine. tā-de-'wū-dz jyèw-dzày 'wǒ-wū-dz-de-'shàng-tew.

Over someone's head (*figuratively*). ‖His speech was way over my head. *is expressed as* **What he said was too deep; I couldn't understand it.** tā-de-'hwà tày 'shēn; wǒ tīng-bu-'dǔng.

(*In a higher position than; in authority*) dzày . . . 'shàng-tew, bǐ . . . 'gāw, *or expressed by using a term for the higher person which implies his higher position.* ‖Is he over you or do you work together? nǐm dzwò-'shr̀ shr̀ 'píng-děng-'dì-wèy, 'háy-shr tā °dzày nǐ-'shàng-tew? *or* °bǐ-ni 'gāw? ‖How many bosses are over you? nǐ yěw 'dwō-shaw-'shàng-sž? *or* nǐ-de-'shàng-byar yěw 'jǐ-ge-'téwr-a?

(*Relative to someone in a lower position or with less power*). ‖He has the power of life and death over them. tā 'dwèy-ywu tā-men yěw 'shēng-shā-jr-'chywán. ‖We won a complete victory over them. *is expressed as* **We beat them completely.** wǒm bǎ tā-men jěng-'gèr-de dǎ-'bày-le.

(*Moving through a higher position than, spatially*) gwò *alone; or as postverb with a main verb which implies motion over rather than motion through; e.g.,* **climb over** *something* 'pá-gwò-chywù. ‖I threw a stone over the wall. wǒ bǎ yí-kwàr-'shŕ-tew 'rēng-gwò 'chyáng-chywù-le. ‖How can I get over the river? wǒ 'dzěme-yàng gwò-'hé-ne? ‖The horse jumped over the gate. 'mǎ 'tyàw-gwò 'mér-chywù-le.

(*Moving from one position to another, not necessarily through higher points*) gwò *as verb or postverb.* ‖We asked them over for some cards. wǒm 'chǐng tā-men ('gwò-)láy 'dǎ-da 'páy. ‖Bring the chair over here. bǎ-'yǐ-dz 'bān-gwò-lay.

(*Along the surface of*) dzày. ‖We travelled over a very good road. wǒm dzày yì-tyáw-hěn-'hǎw-de-'dàwr-shang 'dzěw láy-je.

(*By tripping or stumbling on*). ‖Don't fall over the rock! *is expressed as* **Don't let the rock trip you.** byé ràng 'shŕ-tew gěy 'bàn-le!

(*From vertical to horizontal*) dǎw *or* 'tǎng-shyà *as postverbs.* ‖Don't knock the lamp over. byé bǎ-'dēng °dǎ-'fān-le. *or* °pèng-'tǎng-shya-le.

(*Upside down*) fān *as postverb or verb;* **to roll over** (*of a dog*) dǎ ge-'gwěr. ‖Turn the eggs over. bǎ jī-'dzěr fān ge-'gèr.

(*Covering completely*) dzày . . .°-'wày-tew *or* °-'shàng-tew. ‖Are you going to wear a coat over your sweater? nǐ dzày máw-'yī-°wày-tew (*or* °shǎng-tew) háy yàw 'jàw-shang yí-jyàn-shàng-'shēr-ma?

(*In a direction*). (*For motion*) wàng, shyàng; (*for location*) dzày. ‖It's ten miles over that way. wàng 'nèy-byar dzěw yěw 'shŕ-lǐ-'dì. ‖What's over there? 'nèr shr̀ 'shéme? ‖It's over there. dzày 'nèy-byar.

(*From one person to another*). **To hand** *something* **over** 'dì-gwò-láy, 'jyāw-chu-láy. ‖Hand over (*or* fork over) the money! jyāw-chu 'chyán-lay! *or* bǎ-'chyán 'dì-gwo-láy!

(*Through, in various parts of, in more or less detail*). **To go over** *a problem* 'yán-jyew, tán; **to count over** shǔ yí-°'dàwr *or* °'gwòr *or* °'hwéy; **to read over** nyàn yí-'byàn; **to look over** 'kàn-yi-kàn. ‖Let's go over the problem together. dzám yí-'kwàr bǎ jèy-ge-'wèn-tí 'yán-jyew-yán-jyew. ‖We've been over this before. jèy dzám 'yǐ-jing 'tán-gwo-le. ‖He counted over the money. tā bǎ-'chyán 'shǔ-le °yí-'dàwr. *or* °yí-'gwòr. *or* °yì-'hwéy. ‖They read over the terms of surrender. tām bǎ téw-'shyáng-'tyáw-jyàn 'nyàn-le yí-'byàn. ‖May I look the house over? ràng-wo 'kàn-yi-kàn jèy-swǒr-'fáng-dz, 'kě-yi-ma?

(*Through a period of time*). ‖How long will it be held over? *is expressed as* **How long will it continue to play?** yàw jyē 'yàn dwō-'jyěw? ‖Can you stay over till Monday? *is expressed as* **Can you stay till Monday?** nǐ néng 'jù-dàw lǐ-bày-'yī-ma?

(*Done*). ‖It's all over now. shyàn-'dzày (*or* 'yǐ-jing) dēw °'wán-le. *or* °'gwò-chywù-le. *or* °jyě-jywé-le. *or* °jyé-'shù-le. *or* °'hǎw-le. *or* °méy-'shèr-le. ‖Let's get this over with. dzám bǎ 'jèy-ge nèng-'wán-le jyèw 'wán-le. ‖The war is over. jàn-'shr̀ °'wán-le. *or* jyē 'shù-le. ‖When is the play over? 'shì 'shéme-shŕ-hęw 'wán?

(*More than*) dwō *or* yì-'shàng *after a numerical expression;* gwò *as verb or postverb; or expressed as* **and a little more** háy líng-'dyǎr *or* háy 'dwō-dyǎr. ‖It'll cost over twenty dollars to have it fixed. 'shēw-shr yí-shyàr děy °gwò 'èr-shr-kwày-chyán. *or* °'èr-shr-'dwō kwày-chyán. ‖Don't drive over forty miles an hour. byé 'kāy-gwò 'sż-shŕ-'lǐ. ‖She's over thirty, if she's a day. tā 'dzěme-je yě 'gwò-le sān-'shŕ-le. ‖Is it over three miles from here to there? tsúng-'jèr dàw-'nèr 'shr̀-bu-shr̀ 'chāw-gwò sān-lǐ-'dì? ‖The meat weighs five pounds and a little over. 'rèw shr̀ 'wǔ-bàng háy °'líng-dyǎr. *or* °'dwō-dyǎr.

(*Again*) dzày; **over and over** láy-'hwéy-de, yí-byàn-yí-'byàn-de, V-le 'yèw V (*where V is a verb*), 'dzwò V 'yèw V (*where V is a verb*). ‖Do it over. 'dzày dzwò yí-byàn. *or* 'dzày tsúng-'téwr 'láy yì-hwéy. ‖He read it over and over. tā láy-'hwéy-de 'nyàn-le hǎw-jǐ-'byàn. *or* tā yí-byàn-yí-'byàn-de 'kàn-le hǎw-jǐ-'byàn. *or* tā 'nyàn-le 'yèw nyàn. *or* tā 'dzwǒ nyàn 'yèw nyàn.

(*About, concerning*) wèy. ‖All that trouble over such a tiny thing! 'swǒ-yěw-de-'mǎ-fan jyèw wèy 'nème-yì-ḋyǎr-'dèwr-dà-de-'shr̀! ‖They're fighting over some woman. tām wèy 'nywǔ-de 'dǎ-chi-láy-le. ‖They quarreled over who should get the money. tām wèy 'shéy yīng-gay 'dé nèy-ge-'chyán táy-'gàng láy-je. ‖It's silly to fight over it. wèy 'jèy-ge 'jēn tày bù-'jŕ-le. ‖We'll laugh over this some day. *is expressed as* In the future some day we'll be able to feel that this is funny. 'jyāng-láy 'yěw-yì-tyān wǒm hwèy 'jywé-de jèy-ge kě-'shyàw.

All over (*in all parts of*). 'He travelled all over the country. jèy- (*or* nèy-)'gwó-li gè-'chùr tā dēw dzěw-'ḣyàn-le. ‖I've been all over this part of the country. jǫy-yí-'dày-de-dì-fang wǒ 'chywán-dēw 'dàw-gwo.

OVERCOAT. dà-'yī, dà-'chǎng, wày-'yī.

OVERLOOK. (*To have a view from a high position*). ‖This window overlooks the garden. *is expressed as* The window faces the garden. 'chwāng-hu 'chùng-je hwā-'ywár. *or as* The garden is beneath the window. 'chwāng-hu-'dǐ-shya shr̀ hwā-'ywár.

(*Neglect; not notice*) méy-lǐ-'hwèy *or* méy-'kàn-jyàn; *or* (*not pay attention to*) méy-lyéw-'shén. ‖Here are some papers you overlooked. jèy-shyē-wén-'jyàn nǐ 'dà-gày méy-lǐ-'hwèy.

(*Excuse*). ‖I'll overlook your mistake this time. *is expressed as* I won't go any further with your mistake this time. nǐ 'jèy-tsz̀-chū-'tswòr wǒ °bù-'jwèy-jyew-le. *or as* I'll excuse your mistake this time. °'ywán-lyàng nǐ-ba. *or as* This time that you've made a mistake, I'll let you go. °fàng-nǐ 'gwò-chywu. *or, if said by some high authority who is really relieving you of some punishment, expressed as* I forgive you your mistake this time. °wǒ 'ráw-le nǐ.

OVERSHOE. tàw-'shyé.

OVERWEIGHT. To become overweight gwò-'jùng. ‖He's twenty pounds overweight. tā gwò-'jùng yěw 'èr-shr̀-'bàng.

OWE. chyàn *or* gāy. ‖How much do I owe you? wǒ 'chyàn-ni 'dwō-shǎw-chyán? ‖You owe me ten dollars. nǐ gāy-wo 'shŕ-kwày-chyán.

(*To be obligated, not as regards money*). ‖To what do you owe your success? *is expressed as* What's your secret of success? nǐ-chéng-'gūng-de-mì-'jywé shr̀ 'shéme? ‖He owes a great deal to his friends' help. *is expressed as* The reason why he is where he is today is not a little credit to his friends. tā 'swǒ yǐ néng 'yěw 'jīn-tyān tā-'péng-yew-men-de-'gūng-law hěn bù-'shǎw. *or as* His friends have helped him a lot. tā-'péng-yew-men 'jēn-shr 'bāng-ta bù-shǎw-'máng. ‖You owe it to yourself to take a vacation. dz̀-ji 'bǎw-jùng-dyar, nǐ 'yīng-dāng gàw-'jyà 'shyē-shye tsáy-'dwèy.

OWN. (*To possess*) yěw. ‖Do you own a typewriter? nǐ yěw dǎ-dz̀-'jī méy-yew? ‖He owns seven houses. tā yěw 'chī-swǒr-'fáng-dz. *But in sentences where* have *would be unnatural in English:* ‖Who owns this property? *is expressed as* Whose property is this? jèy-ge-'chǎn-yè shr̀ 'shéy-de? ‖He owns this house. *is expressed as* This house is his. jèy-swǒr-'fáng-dz shr̀ 'tā-de.

(*Belonging to oneself*) 'dz̀-jǐ-de *or* dz̀-jǐ-'gěr-de; of one's own (*by oneself, alone*) dú *or* 'yí-ge-rén. ‖Are these your own things? jèy-shyē-'dūng-shi shr̀ nǐ-'dz̀-jǐ-de-ma? ‖This is his own car. jèy-shr̀ tā-dz̀-jǐ-'gěr-de-'chē. ‖He has his own horses. tā-'dz̀-jǐ yěw-'mǎ. ‖Can I have a room of my own? wǒ kě-yi 'yí-ge-rén jàn yì-jyān-'wū-dz-ma?

On one's own. (*Live on one's own efforts*). dz̀-'shŕ-chí-'lì; (*having one's own business*) 'dz̀-jǐ dzwò 'mǎy-may. ‖He's been on his own for a year now. tā dz̀-'shŕ-chí-'lì yěw yì-'nyán-le. *or* tā-'dz̀-jǐ dzwò 'mǎy-may yěw yì-'nyán-le.

OWNER. 'jǔ-rén; (*possessor: legal term*) swǒ-yěw-'rén; *in compounds* 'jǔ *or* -'jǔr; *thus* (*owner of the house*) fáng-'jǔr; (*car owner*) chē-'jǔr; (*owner of an inn*) dyàn-'jǔr; (*owner of land, or landlord*) dì-'jǔr. ‖Who is the owner of the house? fáng-'jǔr shr̀-'shéy? ‖The owner of the dog will be fined ten dollars. jèy-jŕ-gěw-de-'jǔ-rén děy gěy 'shŕ-kwày-chyán fá-'kwǎn. *But* ‖Who's the owner of this car? *is expressed as* Whose car is this? jèy-ge-'chē shr̀ 'shéy-de? ‖I am the owner. *is expressed as* It's mine. shr̀ 'wǒ-de.

P

'ACK. (*Put things in a container; said of the container*) jwāng; (*pack in a container; said of the things packed*) jwāng-'shyàng; (*pack in, followed by the name of the container*) jwāng-dzày; (*pack in order*) 'shŕ-dwo *or,* 'shēw-shr; (*pack into the form of*) 'dǎ-chéng; (*used only of baggage*) dǎ; (*bundle up*) kwen, (*make a bundle of*) dǎ-'kwěr; (*make a package of*). dǎ-'bāw. ‖Have you packed your trunk yet? nǐ-'shyāng-dz jwāng-le-ma? ‖Have you finished packing yet? 'shíng-li dēw °dǎ-'hǎw-le-ma? *or* °'shŕ-dwo-'hǎw-le-ma? *or* °'shēw-shr-'hǎw-le-ma? *or* 'shyāng-dz dēw jwāng-'hǎw-le-ma? ‖Start packing at once. lì-'kè jyèw chywù °shēw-shr 'shíng-li-ba. *or* °'shŕ-dwo 'shíng-li-ba. *or* °dǎ 'shíng-li-ba. ‖He packed up his things and left. tā bǎ 'dūng-shi °'shēw-shr-chǐ-lay jyèw (dày-) 'dzěw-le. or °'shŕ-dwo-chǐ-lay jyèw (dày-) 'dzěw-le. or °jwāng-dzày 'shyāng-dz-li jyèw (dày-) 'dzěw-le. or °dǎ-chéng-le shíng-li-'jywǎr jyèw (dày-) 'dzěw-le. ‖Have you packed up your books yet? nǐ-shū °'shēw-chǐ-láy-le-ma? or °jwāng-'shyāng-le méy-yěw-wa? or °dǎ-'bāw-le méy-yěw-wa? or °dǎ-'kwěr-le méy-yěw-wa? or °kwě· ·'hǎw-le méy-yěw wa? ‖I have a good deal of packing to do yet. wǒ 'shēw-shr dūng-shi dǎ 'shíng-li háy yěw 'hǎw-shyē-'shèr-ne. ‖The fruit will soon be packed in boxes for shipping. 'shwěy-gwǒ 'jyèw yàw °jwāng-'shyāng ywùn-'dzěw. or °jwāng-dzày 'shyāng-dz-li hǎw 'ywùn-chu-chywu.

(To crowd, of people in a space) jǐ. ‖The train was really packed this morning. jyēr 'dzǎw-chen 'chē-li jēn 'jǐ. ‖The people packed into the train. rén dēw 'jǐ-jìn 'chē-li-chywu-le. ‖The room was packed with people. wū-dz-li jǐ-'mǎn-le rén. ‖Several hundred men were packed into the boat. hǎw-jǐ-'bǎy-rén dēw 'jǐ-dàw nèy-'yì-jř-chwán-li chywù-le.

(To press together; as earth) yà. ‖They're packing the earth down firmly to make a strong foundation. tām bǎ-tǔ 'yà-de hěn 'jǐn wèy-de shř dzá yí-ge-hǎw-'gēn-jī.

A pack (bundle) bāw; (load carried on the back) bēy-'bāw. ‖T : donkeys were carrying heavy packs. lywú-'twó-de-bēy-'bāw hěn 'jùng.

Ice pack bīng-kěw-'dày. ‖That ice pack made him feel much better. nèy-ge-bīng-kěw-'dày jyàw-tā jywé-de 'shū-fu 'dwō-le.

(Set, of cards) fù. ‖Where is that new pack of cards? nèy-fù-'shīn-jř-páy dzày 'nǎr-ne?

(Group) chywún. ‖A pack of wolves attacked our sheep. yì-chywún-'láng láy chř wǒm-de-'yáng-lay-je.

A pack of lies. ‖His story is a pack of lies. 'tā-shwō-de 'chywán-shr 'shyā-hwàr. or nèy-shr tā-'dzēw-de-yí-tàw-'shyā-hwàr.

To pack off sùng. ‖He packed his wife off to the country. tā bǎ 'tày-tay 'sùng-dàw 'shyāng-shya-chywù-le.

To pack a wallop. ‖That letter really packs a wallop. nèy-fēng-'shìn shwō-de °jēn yěw-'jyèr. or °jēn yěw 'lì-lyang. ‖He really packs a wallop (physically). tā 'dǎ-rén dǎ-de hěn 'jùng. or tā-'chywán-tew hěn °'yìng. or °yěw-'jyèr. or °yěw 'lì-lyang.

PACKAGE. bāwr; (if wrapped) 'bāw-gwǒ; (if wrapped with cloth) 'bāw-fu; (if a box) 'shyāng-dz, 'hé-dz. ‖Has a package arrived for me? wǒ yěw ge-'bāwr (or wǒ yěw ge-'bāw-gwǒ) 'dàw-le méy-yew? ‖Here is a package for you. jèr yěw nǐ-yí-ge-'bāwr, or jèr yěw nǐ-yí-ge-'bāw-gwǒ. or jèr yěw nǐ-yí-ge-'bāw-fu. or (Paper box) jèr yěw nǐ-yí-ge-jř-'shyāng-dz. or jèr yěw nǐ-yí-ge-jř-'hé-dz.

A package of bāw. ‖How much is a package of cigarettes? yì-bāw-'yān 'dwō-shǎw-chyán?

PAGE. (One side of a sheet) myàn, myàr; (one side or the entire sheet) yè; (term used most often in giving

page numbers) yèr; (the entire sheet) pyār. ‖This book is 200 pages long. jèy-běr-'shū yew 'er-bay-·ye. or °'yèr. or °myàn. or °myàr. ‖The illustration is opposite page 1/1. chā-'tú dzày (dì-)yī-líng-'yī-yè-de-dwèy-'myàr. ‖There is a footnote on page 10. dì-'shŕ-yè-'dǐ-shya yěw shyǎw-'jùr. ‖Isn't there a page missing in this book? 'jèy-běr-shū 'shŕ-bú-shř 'dwǎn-le yì-pyār?

To page through fān (yí-byàr). ‖He paged through the book, but didn't read a word. tā bǎ nèy-běr-'shū 'fān-le yí-byàr kě-shr 'yí-ge-dzèr yě méy-'kàn.

To page someone jyàw or 'jāw-hu. ‖If you want me, page me in the dining room. nǐ 'yàw-shr 'jǎw-wǒ de-hwà, jyàw-rén dàw fàn-'tīng-chywu °'jyàw-wǒ. or °'jāw-hu wǒ.

PAID. See PAY except for the following: Paid (on a bill) yǐ-'fù. or 'fù-le. or 'fù-chǐ.·

PAIL. tǔng; (for liquids only) shāw. Water pail shwěy-'tǔng or shwěy-'shāw. ‖Put the rubbish in this pail. bǎ 'lā-jī (or bǎ dzāng-'dūng-shi) dàw-dzày jèy-ge-'tǔng-li. ‖Bring me a pail of water. gěy-wǒ ná (or dǎ) °yì-tǔng-'shwěy-lay. or °yì-shāw-'shwěy-lay.

PAIN. téng (a verb meaning have pain, hurt); but labor pains 'jèn-tùng. ‖I have a pain in my stomach. wǒ 'wèy-téng. ‖I have a pain in the back. wǒ 'bèy-téng. ‖Where is the pain? 'nǎr téng? ‖The pain is gone. téng-'jř-le; or 'bù-téng-le. ‖Do you feel any pain? 'téng-ma? or jywé-de-chu 'téng-lay-ma? ‖The tooth pained me so that I couldn't sleep. 'yá téng-de wǒ 'shwèy-bu-jáw 'jyàw. ‖This shouldn't cause you any pain at all. jèy-ge 'bù-dzěm-me téng. or jèy-ge yì-'dyǎr yě bù-'téng. ‖The pain is unbearable. 'téng-de shèw-bu-'lyǎw. ‖Labor pains come before childbirth. 'shēng-chǎn yǐ-'chyán yěw 'jèn-tùng.

(Mental anguish). ‖His drinking caused his mother a great deal of pain. tā nèm hē-'jyěw jyàw tā-'mǔ-chin(-shīn-li) hěn nán-°'gwò. or °'shèw.

To take pains. ‖Take pains to do your work well. mày 'lì-chi (or shř-'jyèr, or jyé-'lì, or jìn dyar-'shīn) bǎ-shèr dzwò-'hǎw-le.

PAINT. (Pigment) yéw (also means oil). ‖There is wet paint on the door. 'mén-shang-de-yéw méy-'gān. ‖The house needs a new coat of paint. 'fáng-dz děy 'chúng-shīn 'shàng yí-dàw-'yéw-le.

(To cover with paint) shàng-'yéw; (brush on paint) shwā-'yéw; sometimes yéw. ‖They are painting. tām 'jèng-dzày °'shàng-'yéw. or °shwā-'yéw. ‖Paint the house white. bǎ 'fáng-dz °shàng yí-dàw-'báy-yéw. or °yéw-'báy-lew. ‖The house has been painted. fáng-dz 'yéw-le. ‖The house was painted white. fáng-dz yéw-'báy-le.

To paint pictures hwà. ‖He paints very well. tā hwà-'hwàr hwà-de hěn 'hǎw. ‖He painted a very good picture of his mother. tā gěy tā-'mǔ-chin 'hwà-le yì-jāng-hěn-hǎw-de-'shyàng.

PAIR. *Three measures are commonly used,* shwāng *for pairs of things that are identical, as chopsticks, socks, and shoes (not made differently in China for right and left) ;* dwèy *or* dwèr *for pairs of things that match or are set opposite each other but are not normally identical, as a man and a woman, matching vases, eyes ;* fù *(also a set of more than two) for things that are similar and used together, but not necessarily identical, as glasses, gloves, bracelets ; in the case of some things as bracelets either* fù *or* dwèy *may be used ; sometimes* two *is said instead of* a pair*; trousers and scissors and other inseparable objects that we sometimes call* **pairs** *are units in Chinese, and take unit measures.* **A pair of bracelets** yí-fù-'jwó-dz *or* yí-dwèy-'jwó-dz. ‖**Where can I get a pair of skating shoes?** wǒ yàw mǎy (yì-) shwāng-lyēw-'bīng-chwān-de-'shyé, dàw-'nǎr-chywu mǎy. ‖**He owns a fine pair of horses.** tā yěw yí-dwèr hǎw-'mǎ. ‖**He kept a pair of rabbits for breeding.** tā 'yǎng-le yí-dwèr-'tù-dz wèy-de shr °lyéw-'jǔngr. *or* °shyà 'shyǎw-dyer. ‖**You get two pair of trousers with this suit.** jèy-tàw-'yī-fu dày 'lyǎng-tyáw-'kù-dz. ‖**Have you a pair of scissors?** nǐ yěw yi-bǎ-'jyǎn-dz-ma? ‖**The boys and girls paired off for the dance.** nán-nywǔ-'háy-dz tsèw-hǎw-le 'dwèr tyàw-'wǔ. ‖**They all paired off and left her sitting there alone.** tām dēw 'chéng-shwāng-dzwò-'dwèr-de (*or* tām dēw yí-'dwèr-yí-dwèr-de, *or* tām dēw tsèw-chéng-le 'dwèr) dzěw-le, bǎ-tā 'lyàw-nar 'yí-ge-rén dzwò-je.

PAN. *(Any cooking pan)* gwō; *(an earthenware or metal pan, usually without a handle, seldom used for cooking)* pén *or* pér. **Frying pan** chǎw-'sháw; **dust-pan** (tǔ-)'bwò-chi. ‖**Put a cup of water in the pan.** dzày (*or* wàng) 'gwō-li dàw yì-bēy-'shwěy. ‖**Put a pan of water on the stove.** nùng yì-gwō-'shwěy (*or* nùng yì-pén-'shwěy) gē-dzày 'lú-dz-shang.

   To pan *(as gold)* shāy *(sift).* ‖**Those men are panning for gold.** 'nèy-shyē-rén dzày-nàr shāy 'jīn-dz.

   To pan out chéng-'gūng. ‖**My scheme panned out well.** wǒ-de-'jì-hwa hěn chéng-'gūng.

   Pancake bǐng.

   To pancake *(of a plane).* ‖**The airplane pancaked, but did not turn over.** fēy-jī 'pā-je-làw-shya-lay-de, kě-shr méy fān 'gēn-dew.

PAPER. *(As material)* jř. **Writing paper** *(for pen and ink)* 'yáng-jř, 'yáng-shìn-jř; **writing paper** *(for writing Chinese with brush and india ink : a thick, durable variety used for decorative purposes)* 'shywān-jř; *(thin bamboo paper)* 'jú-jř; *(other varieties)* 'fǎng-jř, 'lyán-sž-jř, 'máw-byān-jř; **wallpaper** hú-'chyáng-de-jř; **toilet paper** 'shěw-jř; **fire paper** *(lit with a piece of flint, smolders until blown into flame)* 'hwǒ-jř; **pad of paper** jř-'běn-dz; **ruled paper** dày-'dàwr-de-jř; **paper carton** jř-'shyāng-dz. ‖**Do you have some good writing paper?** nǐ yěw hǎw-'yáng-jř-ma? *or* nǐ yěw hǎw-'jú-jř-ma? *or* nǐ yěw hǎw-shyē-'dž-de-'jř-ma? *(etc.)* ‖**She wrapped up the package with heavy paper.** tā yùng 'hèw-jř bǎ 'bāw-gwǒ 'bāw-chi-lay-le.

   (Document) 'wén-jyàn. ‖**Some important papers are missing.** yěw shyē-'jùng-yàw-de-'wén-jyàn bú-'jyàn-le.

   (Essay) 'wén-jang. ‖**He has written a paper on the production of rubber.** tā 'shyě-le yì-pyār-'gwān-ywu-'jř-dzàw-shyàng-'pí-de-'wén-jang.

   (Newspaper) bàw. ‖**Where's the morning paper?** 'chén-bàw (*or* 'dzǎw-chen-de-bàw) dzày-'nǎr?

   Papers 'shěw-shywù; *(official orders)* 'gūng-shř. ‖**You must see that your papers are in order before you can leave the country.** nǐ děy bǎ 'shěw-shywù dēw shyān-bàn-'hǎw-lew tsáy néng chū-'gwó-ne.

   Paper money (chyán-)'pyàw-dz; *(if of foreign origin)* yáng-chyán-'pyàw-dz; *(technically, as a medium of exchange)* 'jř-bì. ‖**Could you give me coins for this paper money?** wǒ yùng jèy-jāng-(yáng-chyán-)'pyàw-dz gēn-nǐ hwàn dyǎr-líng-'chyán shíng-ma? ‖**Paper money was first used in the Tǎng dynasty.** 'táng-cháw dzwèy-'dzǎw yùng 'jř-bì.

   To paper *a room* hú. ‖**This room hasn't been papered in five years.** jèy-'wū-dz yěw 'wǔ-nyán méy-'hú-je. ‖**Paper this room light blue.** 'jèy-jyàn-wū-dz hú 'chyǎn-lán(-shǎr)-de(-'jř). ‖**Paper the walls blue and the ceiling white.** 'chyáng-shang hú 'lán-de(-jř), fáng-'dǐng-dz hú 'báy-de.

   On paper *(not existing otherwise)* byǎw-'myǎr-shang. ‖**My profits were only on paper.** wǒ yě jyèw-shr byǎw-'myǎr-shang 'jwàn-chyán.

PARALLEL. píng-'shíng. **Parallel lines** 'píng-shíng-shyàn; *except in mathematical discussion, these terms are not usually used.* ‖**These two lines are parallel.** 'jèy-lyǎng-tyáw-shyàn °píng-'shíng. *or* °shř píng-'shíng-de. ‖**Put the figures between the parallel lines.** *is expressed as* **Put the figures between the two straight lines.** bǎ 'shù-mu fàng-dzày °'lyǎng-háng-de-jūng-'jyàr-nàr. *or* °'lyǎng-tyáw-'jř-shyàn-de-jūng-'jyàr-nàr. *or* °'lyǎng-dàw-'jř-shyàn-de-jūng-'jyàr-nàr.

   Parallel with *(along)* 'shwèn-je *or* 'yán-je. ‖**The road runs parallel with the river.** lù shř 'shwèn-je (*or* 'yán-je) hé dzěw.

   (Of latitude) 'wěy-shyàn . . . dù. ‖**The island is located on the 34th parallel.** dǎw dzày 'wěy-shyàn-'sān-shr-'sž-dù-ner.

   (Comparison). ‖**You can draw a parallel between these two events.** ná jèy-'lyǎng-jyàn-shèr yì-'bǐ, kě-yǐ 'bǐ-chū bù-shǎw-°yí-'yàng-de-dì-fang-lay. *or* °shyāng-'túng-de-dì-fang-lay. *or* °shyāng-'shyàng-de-dì-fang-lay.

PARCEL. *(Package : wrapped)* bāwr, 'bāw-gwǒ, 'bāw-fu; *(box)* 'hé-dz, 'shyá-dz. *See also* **PACKAGE, BOX.** ‖**I'm expecting a parcel from the store.** 'pù-dz yàw gěy-wǒ sùng yí-ge-'bāwr-lay. *(etc. instead of* bāwr.*)*

   Parcel post dàng 'bāw-gwǒ *or* *(at parcel rates)* àn 'bāw-gwǒ. ‖**Send it parcel post.** dàng (*or* àn) 'bāw-gwǒ jì.

   To parcel out *(distribute)* 'fēn-fā, 'fā-chu-chywu; *(divide into portions)* 'fēn-pèy. ‖**All the supplies have**

been parceled out. dūng-shi dēw 'yǐ-jīng °'fēn-fa-le. or °'fā-chu-chywu-le. ‖Let's parcel these out before distributing them. dzám bǎ jèy-shyē-'dūng-shi 'fēn-pèy-'hǎw-le dzày 'fā.

(Amount: of land) kwày. ‖He bought a parcel of land. tā 'mǎy-le yí-kwày-'dì.

PARDON. (In polite apologies). ‖Pardon me. or I beg your pardon. (For something to be said or done) láw-'jyà. or jyè-'gwāng. (For something already said or done) dwèy-bu-'jù. or dwèy-bu-'chǐ. or chǐng-ní 'ywán-lyang. ‖Pardon me; let me pass. láw-'jyà (or jyè-'gwāng); 'ràng-yí-bù.

(Forgive, remit penalty; said of a person) shè; (said of a crime or penalty) myǎn or 'shè-myǎn. ‖His pardon was granted by the President. shr̀ dzǔng-'tǔng 'shè-de-tā. or shr̀ dzǔng-'tǔng 'myǎn-de tā-de-'dzwèy. ‖The governor pardoned the thief. shěng-'jǎng bǎ nèy-ge-'dzéy-de-dzwèy °'myǎn-le. or °'shè-myǎn-le.

‖That's unpardonable! nèy-ge bù-néng °'rúng! or °'ráw! or °'ráw-shù!

PARENTS. (Father, mother) 'fù-mǔ; (somewhat more formal) 'shwāng-chīn. ‖Both my parents are still living. wǒ-'fù-mǔ dēw 'dzày. or wǒ-'shwāng-chīn dēw 'dzày. ‖They're good parents. tām shr̀ 'shyán-míng-de-'fù-mǔ. or expressed as They bring up children very well. tām-'jyàw-ywù-de-'dž-nywǔ 'hěn hǎw.

PARK. (Public land) gūng-'ywán. ‖The city has many beautiful parks. 'chéng-li yěw hǎw-'shyē-ge-hǎw-'kàn-de-gūng-'ywán. ‖We camped for two weeks in the National Park. wǒm dzày 'g⸺ lì-gūng-'ywán-lǐ dā 'jàng-píng jù-le 'lyǎng-ge-lǐ-'bà⸺.

To park a car tíng. ‖Where can we park (the car)? meaning Where may we...? 'nǎr shywǔ tíng-'chē? or meaning Where shall we...? 'chē tíng-dzày 'nǎr-ne? ‖There's a parking lot over there. 'nèy-her yěw ge-tíng-chē-'chǎng. ‖Leave a parking space for others. gěy 'byé-rén lyéw-chu 'tíng-chē-de-'dì-fang-lay. or lyéw-chu 'kùngr-lay hǎw jyàw 'byé-rén (yě néng) 'tíng-chē. ‖No parking! 'bù-shywǔ 'tíng-chē!

(Leave something someplace) fàng. ‖You can park your things here. 'dūng-shi fàng-'jèr hǎw-le.

PART. (Division) 'bù-fen; (length, or one of several continuous parts) dwàr or dwàn; (length, only physical) jyér; (a natural division or section, as of an orange) bàr; (half; a different word) bàr; (section, side; of a place) byār. ‖We can divide the work into four parts. wǒm kě-yǐ bǎ 'gūng-dzwò 'fēn-chéng 'sz̀-bù-fen. ‖His part of the work isn't finished. jèy-jyàn-shèr 'tā-de (or 'tā-gwǎn-de, or 'tā-dzwò-de)-nèy-°'bù-fen háy méy-'wán. or (If the work was done in consecutive parts) °yí-'dwàr háy méy-'wán. ‖He cut off part of the rope. tā bǎ 'shéng-dz 'lā-shya °yí-'dwàr-lay. or °yì-'jyér-lay. ‖This part of the road is

muddy. jèy-yí-dwàr-'lù-shang °yěw-'ní. or °hěn 'nèng. ‖The fence is part wood and part stone. is expressed as The fence is wood for a distance, stone for a distance. 'wéy-chyang yí-dwàr shr̀ 'mù-tew-de, yí-dwàr shr̀ 'shŕ-tew-de. or, meaning one layer of each, jyér instead of dwàr. ‖What part of town do you live in? nǐ jù-dzày chéng-'něy-byār?

(Unit measurement) fèr. ‖Mix two parts of samshu with one part of lemon juice. dwèy 'lyǎng-fèr-'shǎw-jyēw 'yí-fèr-níng-méng-'jěr.

(Some) yěw-de. ‖Part of this shipment of apples isn't good. 'jèy-tsz̀-láy-de-'píng-gwo 'yěw-de 'bù-hǎw.

(Role in a play) 'jyàw-sè or jyǎwr. ‖She played her part very well. tā yǎn 'nèy-ge-jyǎw-sè (or tā yǎn 'nèy-ge-jyǎwr) yǎn-de 'hěn hǎw.

(Dividing line in hair) 'fèngr. ‖The part in your hair isn't straight. nǐ-téw-fa-'fèngr 'fēn-de bù-'jŕ.

(Piece of a machine) 'líng-jyàr. ‖Where can I get some new parts for my car? nǎr yěw màyʼ-chì-chē-'líng-jyàr-de?

Parts (places). (Region) dày; (place) 'dì-fang. ‖I haven't traveled much in these parts for a long time. wǒ 'hěn jyéw méy-dà dzày °'jèy-yí-dày 'yéw-lì-le. or °'jèy-shyē-dì-fang 'yéw-lì-le.

(To separate) 'fēn-kāy; fēn-'shěw; 'fēn-dàw-'yáng-byāw (deliberately; somewhat poetic); (divide) 'fēn-dzày 'lyǎng-byār. ‖We parted at the corner. wǒm dzày gwǎy-'jyǎwr-nar °'fēn-kāy-le. or, °fēn-'shěw-le. ‖Our ways parted three years ago. wǒm 'fēn-kāy (or wǒm fēn-'shěw, or wǒm 'fēn-dàw-'yáng-byāw) yěw 'sān-nyán-dwō-le. ‖The best of friends must part. 'dzwèy-hǎw-de-péng-yew yě yěw fēn-'shěw-de-shŕ-hew. ‖The policemen parted the crowd. jǐng-'chá bǎ-rén 'fēn-dzày 'lyǎng-byār.

Part time. Work part time (not do full-time work). 'bú-dzwò 'jěng-gūng or (work half-day) dzwò 'bàn-tyǎr; part-time work 'líng-gūngr or 'líng-hwór. ‖May I work part time? wǒ 'bú-dzwò 'jěng-gūng shíng-bu-shíng? or wǒ dzwò 'bàn-tyǎr shíng-bu-shíng? ‖Is there any part-time work available? yěw shéme-'líng-gūngr (or yěw shéme-'líng-hwór) kě 'dzwò-ma?

Take one's part shyàng-je (favor). ‖He always takes his brother's part in an argument. tā 'yí gēn-rén-'byàn-de-shŕ-hew lǎw-shr shyàng-je tā-'gē-ge.

For the most part. ‖For the most part, this work is very pleasant. 'jèy-shèr dà-'tǐ-shang (or 'jèy-shèr dà-'jŕ, or 'jèy-shèr yěw 'hǎw-shyē-dì-fang) 'hěn jyàw-rén 'shǐ-hwān dzwò. ‖For the most part, the weather has been nice this season. 'dzǔng-chǐ-lay shwō 'jèy-yí-jì-de-'tyān-chì háy bú-tswò. ‖For the most part, I enjoyed this book. jèy-běn-'shū-li yì-'dwō-bàr wǒ háy °'shǐ-hwān. or °'ày kàn.

Part with chū-'shěw. ‖I wouldn't part with that book for any price. 'nèy-běr-shū-wa, shwō-'shéme wǒ yě bù-kěn chū-'shěw.

Take part in 'tsān-jyā. ‖He refused to take part in the game. tā 'bù-kěn 'tsān-jyā bǐ-'sày.

PARTICULAR. *Used to emphasize* this, that, *or* the; *Chinese stresses* jèy *or* nèy, *and often adds the numeral* yī ‖I can't get a ticket for that particular train. wǒ 'may-bu-jáw 'nèy(-yí)-tàng-chē-de-'pyàw. ‖I can't get a ticket for the particular train I want to take. wǒ- 'mǎy-bu-jáw wǒ-yàw-dzwò-de-'nèy(-yí)-tàng-chē-de-'pyàw. ‖I have to take this particular train. wǒ fēy děy dzwò 'jèy(-yí)-tàng-chē bù-'kě. ‖That particular dress costs more. 'nèy-jyàn-'yī-fu bǐ 'byé-de 'gwèy.

(*Special*). (*Especially, occurs before the verb, refers to facts*) 'tè-byé, 'yěw-chi-shr; (*but referring to intentions or possibilities*) 'tè-wèy; *sometimes expressed merely by stress.* ‖He has a particular dislike of sloppy persons. tā tè-'byé bù-shǐ-hwān 'lē-li-le-dē-de-rén. ‖I remember one fellow in particular. yěw 'yí-ge-jyā-hwo wǒ °tè-'byé jì-de. *or* °tè-'byé wàng-bu-'lyǎw. *or* °'yěw-chí-shr jì-de. *or* °'yěw-chí-shr wàng-bu-'lyǎw. ‖Are you going anywhere in particular? nǐ shǐ 'tè-wèy yàw shàng-nǎr 'chywù-ma? ‖Is he a particular friend of yours? tā shǐ nǐ-'hǎw-péng-yew-ma?

(*Fussy*) 'jù-yi; 'jyǎng-jyew (*especially about decorations and luxuries*); (*finicky*) 'shyán-jè-ge-'shyán-nà-ge-de (*disliking this and that*). ‖He's very particular about his appearance. tā 'hěn jù-yi 'dǎ-ban. *or* tā 'hěn jyǎng-jyew 'dǎ-ban. ‖He's very particular about manners. tā 'hěn jù-yi 'lǐ-màw. *or* tā 'hěn jyǎng-jyew 'lǐ-màw. ‖You can't be too particular around here. dzày 'jèy-kwàr nǐ 'bù-néng tày °'jyǎng-jyew-le. *or* °'nèm-'shyán-jè-ge-'shyán-nà-ge-de.

(*Detail; of a situation*) 'shì-chíng, 'shyáng-chíng, 'shyáng-shì-chíng-shíng. ‖We haven't learned the particulars of the accident yet. nèy-ge-shèr-de-°'shì-chíng wǒm háy bù-jr̄-'dàw-ne. *or* °'shyáng-chíng wǒm . . . . *or* °'shyáng-shì-chíng-shíng wǒm . . . .

In every particular 'chù-chùr, 'gè-fāng-myàn, 'yàng-yàngr. ‖The work is complete in every particular. 'jèy-ge-gūng (*or* 'jèy-jyàn-hwór) °'chù-chùr dēw dzwò-'wán-le. *or* °'gè-fāng-myàn dēw . . . . *or* °'yàng-yangr dēw . . . .

PARTY. (*Social gathering*) *Chinese has no single term that covers the range of meaning of the English term* party, *but the following expressions are useful:* chǐng-'kè (*invite guests*); yěw 'kè-rén (*have guests*); chǐng . . . chr̄-'fàn (*invite . . . to eat; have a dinner party for . . .*); chǐng . . . dǎ-'páy (*have a card party for . . .*); *similarly with other kinds of parties;* 'jywù-yi-jywu *or* 'jywù-hwèy-jywù-hwey (*get together*); (*more or less informal dinner party*) fàn-'jywú; (*literary; a very formal dinner party*) 'dà-yàn-hwèy. ‖We're having a party. wǒm-jèr yěw 'kè-rén. ‖I gave a (dinner) party for him. wǒ chǐng-tā chr̄-'fàn. ‖We had a big party last night. dzwér 'wǎn-shang wǒm °yěw hěn-'dwō-de-kè-rén. *or* °'chǐng-lè hěn-'dwō-de-kè-rén. ‖Let's have a party for him before he goes. tā 'méy-dzěw

yǐ-'chyán dzám °'jywù-yi-jywu. *or* °'jywù-hwey-jywu-hwey. ‖I went to a big dinner party last night. wǒ 'dzwér wǎn-shang °chywù (*or* °tsān-jyā)-le yí-ge-'dà-yàn-hwèy. *or* °'dàw-le ge-fàn-'jywú, rén hěn-'dwō-de.

(*Group of people*) chywún. ‖A party of soldiers arrived by car. yěw yì-chywún-'bīng dzwò-je chì-'chē láy-le.

(*Political group*) 'jèng-dǎng; dǎng *in combination.* ‖Which party won the last election? 'shàng-tsž shywǎn-'jywǔ 'něy-ge-'jèng-dǎng 'yíng-le?

(*Participant*) X is a party to . . . . . .-li yěw X *or* X dzày . . .-li yěw 'gwān-shi; party to a crime 'túng-méw-'fàn, (*legal*) gùng-'fàn; both parties 'shwāng-fāng. ‖They couldn't prove that he was a party to the crime. tām 'méy-néng 'jèng-míng °nèy-ge-'àn-dz-li 'yěw-tā méy-yew. *or* °tā dzày nèy-ge-'àn-dz-li 'yěw-méy-yěw 'gwān-shi. *or* tām méy-yěw 'jèng-jywù shwō tā 'jwěn shr̄ túng-méw-fàn. *or* (*Legal*) tām 'wú-tsung 'jèng-míng tā shr̄ gùng-'fàn. ‖Both parties in the lawsuit failed to appear. 'shwāng-fāng dēw méy-'chū-tíng. ‖Both parties agreed. 'shwāng-fāng túng-'yì.

PASS. (*To go by*) gwò. ‖He passed our car at a tremendous speed. tā gwò wǒm-de-'chē de-shf-hew dzěw-de kwày-'jí-le. ‖I pass the bank every day on the way to work. wǒ 'méy-tyān chywù dzwò-'shr̄ de-shf-hew, 'lù gwò yín-'háng. ‖We passed by the park. wǒm dǎ (*or* tsúng) 'gūng-ywán-'páng-byǎr gwò. ‖We passed the building. wǒm dǎ (*or* tsúng) 'léw-nar gwò láy-je. ‖We passed by the building. wǒm dǎ (*or* tsúng) léw-'páng-byār gwò-de. ‖We passed in front of the building. wǒm dǎ (*or* tsúng) léw-'chyán-tew gwò-de. ‖We passed over the bridge. wǒm dǎ (*or* tsúng) 'chyáw-shang gwò-de. ‖he days pass quickly when you are busy. 'máng-de-shf-hew yì-'tyān-yì-tyān-de gwò-de 'jēn kwày. ‖We passed several towns without stopping. wǒm gwò-le 'hǎw-jí-ge-chéng yě méy-'tíng-shya-lay.

Pass through gwò *or* 'chwān-gwo; (*press through*) 'jǐ-gwo. ‖We passed through the park. wǒm dǎ (*or* tsúng) 'gūng-ywán-'lǐ-tew °'chwān-gwo-chywu. *or* °gwò. ‖How long will it take us to pass through the town? dzám dǎ (*or* tsúng) 'chéng-li ('chwān-)gwò-chywu děy yùng 'dwō-shǎw-shf-hew? ‖We passed through the center of the town. wǒm dǎ (*or* tsúng) chéng-dāng-'jūng (chwān-)gwò-chywu-de. ‖When we passed through the town we found it deserted. wǒm 'gwò nèy-ge-'chéng (*or* wǒm dǎ nèy-ge-'chéng gwò) de-shf-hew kàn-jyan 'rén dēw 'pǎw-le. ‖We passed through the crowd with much effort. wǒm dǎ (*or* tsúng) nèy-chywún-rén-li 'jǐ-gwo-chywu de-shf-hew, 'hěn fèy-le dyǎr-'shèr. ‖Pass the rope through here and tie it. bǎ 'shéng-dz dǎ (*or* tsúng) -jèr 'chwān-gwo-chywu jì-shang. ‖Pass the thread through the eye of the needle and double it up. bǎ shyàn dǎ (*or* tsúng) jēn-'yàr 'chwān-gwo-chywu dzày 'shwāng-chi-lay. *But* ‖That manuscript has passed through several hands. nèy-ge-'gǎw-dz 'hǎw-jí-ge-rén dēw 'kàn-gwo-le.

(*Encounter a person*) 'pèng-jyàn. ‖Did you pass him on the road? nǐ dzày 'dàwr-shang 'pèng-jyàn tā méy-yěw?

Hand around (*of food*) 'dì-gwo. ‖Please pass (me) the bread. láw-'jyà, bǎ myàn-'bāw dì-gwo-lay.

(*Send*) sùng, ywùn. ‖The supplies were passed up to the front. 'jywūn-shywū-'pǐn sùng-dàw (*or* ywùn-dàw) chyán-'shyàn-chywu-le.

(*Of an examination*). (*In school*) jí-'gé; (*to undergo*) jīng. ‖Did you pass your examination? nǐ-'kǎw-de jí-'gé-le-ma? ‖Did you pass? nǐ jí-'gé-le-ma? ‖He had to pass a stiff test before he could go. tā děy jīng hěn-'yán-de-'kǎw-shr̀ tsáy néng 'chywù.

(*To approve, of legislation*) 'tūng-gwo. ‖The Senate passed the bill yesterday. shàng-yì-ywàn 'dzwó-tyan 'tūng-gwo nèy-ge-'yì-àn. ‖It passed. 'tūng-gwo-le.

(*Not bid, in cards*) bú-'jyàw-shéme. ‖I had a lousy hand and decided to pass. wǒ-de-'páy hěn 'hwày, swǒ-yǐ 'jywé-dìng bú-'jyàw-shéme.

(*A narrow passage*) 'kěw-dz. ‖You can't get through the mountain pass at this time of the year. 'jèy-shŕ-hew nèy-ge-shān-'kěw-dz gwò-bú-'chywù.

(*Permit*) -jèng; (*door pass*) chū-mén-'jèng; (*pass to go through a place*) 'tūng-shíng-'jèng; *etc. with passes for other purposes.* ‖You'll need a pass to get by the gate. nǐ chū dà-'mér děy yěw chū-mén-'jèng.

To pass (*by inheritance*). ‖The title passes from father to son. (*Literary*) 'jywé-wèy °shr̀ shr̀-'shí-de. *or* °fù-'dz shyāng-'chwān.

Let it pass swàn. ‖He shouldn't have said that, but let it pass. tā jyèw 'bù-yīng-dāng 'shwō nèy-jǔng-hwà, bú-gwò ('gwò-chywu-le jyèw) 'swàn-le-ba.

Pass sentence pàn-'dzwèy, dìng-'dzwèy. ‖The court passed sentence on him today. 'fǎ-ywàn 'jīn-tyan 'pàn-le (*or* 'dìng-le) tā-de-'dzwèy-le.

Pass judgment on shwō . . . dzěm-'yàng, shwō . . . hǎw-'hwày, *and similar expressions depending on the nature of the judgment.* ‖Don't pass judgment on his character until you know him better. nǐ háy 'bú-dà 'rèn-shr̀ rén-jyā de-shŕ-hew byé (*or* nǐ 'děng gēn rén-jyā 'shéw-dyar̀ dzày) shwō rén-jyā-de-'pǐn-shíng dzěm-yàng.

Pass time 'shyāw-mwó. ‖He passed most of his time fishing. tā bǎ 'gūng-fu 'dwō-bàn dēw 'shyāw-mwó-dzày dyàw-'ywú-shang-le.

Pass around (*of a story*) 'chwán-chu-chywù; *with the speaker as subject* 'chwán-shwō. ‖The story passed around that we were about to leave. dà-jyā 'chwán-shwō wǒm 'jyèw °děy 'lí-kāy jèr (*or* nàr). *or* (*of military embarkation*) °yàw kāy-'bá.

Pass away. (*See also* DIE.) ‖She said her mother passed away last week. tā shwō tā-'mǔ-chin shàng-lǐ-bày 'gù-chywu-le.

Pass off as chūng, 'hwèn-chūng, 'màw-chūng. ‖He tried to pass off an imitation as the real thing. tā shyǎng ná 'jyǎ-de °chūng 'jēn-de. *or* °'hwèn-chūng 'jēn-de. *or* °'màw-chūng 'jēn-de.

Pass out. (*Distribute*) sàn; (*give free*) sùng. ‖He's passing out handbills. tā dzày-nar 'sàn chwán-'dān-ne. ‖He passed out a free ticket to each soldier. 'swǒ-yěw-de-bīng tā 'měy-rén sùng-le yì-jāng-'pyàw.

Pass out. (*Faint*) 'ywūn-gwo-chywu; (*lose consciousness from excessive drinking*) dzwèy-'dǎw-le-de; dzwèy-de 'bù-shǐng-rén-'shèr-le. ‖When the gas escaped several people passed out. 'méy-chì lèw hu-lay-le de-shŕ-hew, 'hǎw-jǐ-ge-rén shywūn-de 'yūn-gwo-chywu-le. ‖If you give her another drink, she'll pass out. nǐ dzày jyàw-tā 'hē-dyǎr, tā 'yí-dìng hwèy °dzwèy-'dǎw-le-de. *or* °dzwèy-de 'bù-shǐng-rén-'shèr-le-de.

Pass up 'tswò-gwo, bǎ . . . 'tswò-gwo-chywu, bǎ . . . 'fàng-gwo-chywu. ‖You shouldn't pass up an opportunity like that. nǐ 'bù-yīng-dang °tswò-gwo 'nèm-hǎw-de-jī-hwèy. *or* °bǎ 'nèm-hǎw-de-jī-hwèy tswò-gwo-chywu. *or* °bǎ 'nèm-hǎw-de-'jī-hwèy fàng-gwo-chywu.

PASSENGER. *There is no exact equivalent in Chinese; under varying circumstances it is possible to use* rén (*person*); kè (*guest*); 'chéng-kè (*riding guest*). ‖Our car holds only five passengers. wǒm-de-chē 'jǐ néng dzwò 'wǔ-ge-rén. ‖That (railroad) car is not used for passengers. 'nèy-lyàng-chē bú-shr̀ °'kè-chē. *or* °dzày-'kè-de. ‖Passengers not allowed beyond this line. 'chéng-kè dàw-'tsz̀ jř-'bù.

PAST. (*Gone by, in space or time*) gwò(-le) (*a verb; also used in combination after other verbs of motion such as* pǎw (*run*), kāy (*drive*)). ‖The worst part of the trip is past. 'dzwèy-hwày-de-nèy-yí-dwàr-'lù yǐ-jīng 'gwò-lay-le. ‖Don't worry about a thing that's past. yǐ-jīng-'gwò-chywu-de-shr̀-le, byé 'shyǎng-le. ‖Walk past the church and turn right. 'gwò-le lǐ-bày-'táng wàng-'yèw gwǎy. ‖It's past noon; let's eat. 'gwò-le 'shǎng-wu-le; dzám chř-'fàn-ba. ‖We drove past his house on the way here. wǒm-'láy-de-shr-hew dǎ (*or* tsúng) tā-'jyā-nar 'gwò-lay-je. ‖I thought he was going to stop, but he ran right past. wǒ 'yǐ-wey tā yàw 'jàn-ju-ne, 'shéy jř-daw tā yì-'jŕ jyèw 'pǎw-gwo-chywu-le.

(*Of time only*). In the past tsúng-'chyán, yǐ-'chyán, chyán *plus a period of time, as* past few years 'chyán-jǐ-nyán; 'wǎng *plus* nyán *or* r̀-li; *but the* past month 'shàng-ywè; the past year 'chywù-nyán (*see* LAST); for the past month . . . le yí-ge-'ywè-le (*etc.*); 'shàng-tsz̀ *plus a verb* (*the last time . . .*); jèy (*this just past*). ‖We've been expecting rain for the past week. 'shàng-yí-ge-shīng-chī wǒm yì-'jŕ pàn-je shyà-'ywǔ. *or* wǒm 'pàn-je shyà-'ywǔ pàn-le 'yí-ge-shīng-'chī-le. ‖In the past it's been very difficult to get tickets. tsúng-'chyán (*or* yǐ-'chyán, *or* 'chyán-jǐ-ge-ywè, *etc.*) 'hěn nán mǎy-jaw 'pyàw. ‖The past election made him realize his mistakes. 'shàng-tsz̀ shywǎn-'jywǔ jyàw-tā 'míng-bay-le tā-bàn-de-bú-'dwèy-de-'dì-fang.

(*History*) tsúng-'chyán-de-shèr; 'dāng-nyán-de-shèr; (*recorded history*) lì-'shř, 'gù-shř, 'dyǎn-gù; (*remembered events*) 'wǎng-r̀-de-shr, yǐ-'wǎng-de-shr̀, 'wǎng-shr̀; (*past actions*) 'lǎw-hwàr, yǐ-'chyán-dzwò-gwo-de-shèr; (*past glories*) 'dāng-nyán-'yǔng. ‖That city has a very interesting past. nèy-ge-chéng-de-°'gù-shr (*or* °'dyǎn-gù, *or* °lì-'shř, *or* °tsúng-'chyán-de-shèr, *or* °'dāng-nyán-de-shèr) hěn yěw 'yì-sz. ‖He's always haunted by his past. tā-'dāng-nyán-de-shr̀ (*or* tā tsúng-'chyán-de-shr̀, *or* tā-'wǎng-r̀-de-shr̀, tā-yǐ-'wǎng-de-shr̀) 'lǎw jyàw tā-'shīn-li bù-'ān. ‖He can talk about his past for days on end. tā 'jyǎng-chǐ tā °tsúng-'chyán-de-shèr-lay, 'dwō-shǎw-'tyān yě shwō-bu-'wán. *or* °tā-de-'wǎng-shr̀-lay .... *or* °tā-de-'lǎw-hwàr-lay .... *or* °tā-yǐ-'chyán-dzwò-gwo-de-shèr-lay .... *or* °tā-'dāng-nyán-de-shèr-lay .... ‖Whenever she thinks of the past she starts to weep. tā yì-'shyǎng-chǐ 'dāng-nyán-de-shr̀-lay jyèw 'kū. ‖A great man doesn't talk about past glories. 'hǎw-hàn 'bù-tán 'dāng-nyái-'yǔng.

PATH. 'shyǎw-dàwr *or* 'shyǎw-lù. ‖Take the path that runs along the river. dzěw kàw-hé-'byār-de(-nèy-tyáw)-°'shyǎw-dàwr. *or* °'shyǎw-lù. *But* ‖Our paths had never crossed before that. dzày nèy-jyàn-shr̀ yǐ-'chyán wǒ gēn-tā yí-'shyàng méy-dǎ-gwo 'jyāw-daw.

PATIENT. rěn (*used after* néng, děy, *etc.; said especially of circumstances*); yěw 'này-shīn-'fár (*said especially of patience with people*); 'rěn-này, này 'shìng-dz, bù-jāw-'jí. ‖He's a very patient man. tā hěn néng 'rěn. *or* tā hěn yěw 'này-shīn-'fár. ‖He'd be a better teacher if he were more patient. tā yàw-shr yěw 'này-shīn-'fár de-hwà, yí-dìng jyāw-de 'hǎw-dyar. ‖He's a patient man to wait that long for her to say yes. tā 'jēn néng 'rěn, děng-le 'nèm-jyěw tā tsáy 'dā-ying-de. ‖He's very patient with the children. tā dày háy-dz-men °'hěn yěw này-shīn-'fár. *or* °yì-'dyǎr yě bù-jāw-'jí. ‖You have to be very patient with talkative people like that. gēn 'nèy-jǔng-ày-shwō-'hwà-de-rén 'hěn děy °'rěn-je-dyar. *or* °'rěn-này-je-dyar. *or* °'này-je dyar-'shìng-dz. *or* °yěw 'này-shīn-'fár. ‖Be patient! 'byé jāw-'jí.

(*Sick person*) 'bìng-rén. ‖How's the patient this morning? 'bìng-rén jyēr 'dzǎw-chen 'dzěm-yàng?

PATTERN. (*Design*) 'hwā-yàng. ‖This rug has a nice pattern. 'jèy-kwày-dì-'tǎn-de-'hwā-yàng hěn hǎw.

(*Model*) 'yàng-dz (*see* FORM). ‖Where did you get the pattern for your new dress? nǐ-nèy-jyàn-'shīn-yī-fu-de-'yàng-dz shr̀ 'nǎr-lay-de?

Pattern oneself after 'shyàw-fǎ. ‖I've tried to pattern myself after my father. wǒ 'hěn shyǎng 'shyàwfǎ jyā-'yán.

PAY. (*Make payment for something*) gěy-'chyán; fù-'chyán (*especially an established amount*). ‖I paid him

three dollars. wǒ gěy-le tā (wǒ fù-le tā) 'sān-kwày-chyán. ‖I haven't paid for it yet. wǒ háy méy-gěy-'chyán. *or* wǒ háy méy-fù-'chyán. ‖If you pay a black-mailer once, you have to pay and pay and pay. yàw-shr yěw-rén 'é-nǐ (*or* 'jà-nǐ, *or* 'é-jà-nǐ), °nǐ 'yì-gěy-chǐ chyán-lay jyèw méy-'téwr-le. *or* °nǐ gěy-le 'yí-tsž-chyán jyèw děy 'lǎw gěy.

(*Spend*) hwā *or* yùng *or* ná, *plus* 'chyán *or a certain amount of money followed by* mǎy (*buy*) *or similar words; or simply the amount plus* mǎy, *etc.* ‖How much did you pay for your car? nǐ-de-'chē shr̀ hwā (*or* yùng)-'dwō-shǎw-chyán-mǎy-de? *or* nǐ-de-'chē shr̀ 'dwō-shǎw-chyán-mǎy-de? ‖How much did you get paid for your car? nǐ-nèy-'chē °mày-le 'dwō-shaw chyán? *or* °'dwō-shaw chyán mày-de? ‖I paid five dollars for this watch. jèy-ge-'byǎw wǒ hwā (*or* yùng, *or* ná, *or nothing*) 'wǔ-kwày-chyán mǎy-de.

(*Give as price*) chū. ‖How much do you want to pay for this? jèy-ge nǐ shyǎng chū 'dwō-shǎw-chyán (láy mǎy)?

(*Buy*) *any of the above; also* mǎy; tāw yàw-'bāwr (*dig in the pocket*). ‖You'll have to pay for your own ticket. nǐ děy 'dž-jǐ mǎy-'pyàw. ‖You'll have to pay for it yourself. nǐ děy 'dž-jǐ °mǎy. *or* °chū-'chyán. *or* °ná-'chyán. *or* °gěy-'chyán. *or* °páw yàw-'bāwr. ‖You can't get it for nothing; you have to pay for it. jèy-ge 'bù-néng 'báy-gěy nǐ; nǐ děy °gěy-'chyán tsáy 'shíng. *or* °chū-'chyán tsáy 'shíng. *or* °hwā-'chyán mǎy. *or* °yùng-'chyán mǎy. *or* °ná-'chyán mǎy. *or* °ná-'chyán chū-lay tsáy 'shíng.

(*Of payments coming due regularly*) jyāw (*hand over*). ‖I have to pay the rent every Monday. 'měy-shīng-chī-'yī wǒ děy jyāw fáng-'dzū.

(*Of bills, debts, loans*) hwán (*return*). ‖The bills were paid up yesterday. jàng 'dzwó-tyan dēw 'hwán-le. ‖He pays his debts promptly. 'tā-gāy-de-'jàng dēw °shr̀ 'shwō shéme-shŕ-hew 'hwán 'jwěn hwán. *or* °àn-'shŕ-hew 'hwán. *or* tā hwán-'jàng hwán-de hěn 'má-li. ‖I'll be all paid up after (paying) one more installment. dzày gěy (*or* fù, *or* jyāw) 'yí-tsž wǒ jyèw hwán-'chīng-le. ‖The paid bills are listed in this column. 'yǐ-jīng-'hwán-le-de-jàng lyè-dzày 'jèy-háng. ‖Loan me a dollar now, and I'll pay you back Monday. jyè-wǒ yí-kwày-'chyán, lǐ-bày-'yī hwán-nǐ.

(*Of damages*) péy. ‖You'll have to pay for it. nǐ yí-'dìng děy 'péy. *or* nǐ féy 'péy bù-'shíng.

(*Of gambling debts*) shū-gěy.

(*Of taxes, duty, etc.*) nà *or* shàng *or* jyāw (*of* shwèy, *taxes*); gěy *or* fù *also of tax money*. ‖Pay your taxes or go to jail. bú-nà-'shwèy (*or* bú-shàng-'shwèy, *or, of regular payments*, bú-jyāw-'shwèy) jyèw shyà-'ywù. ‖How much import duty do you have to pay? děy nà (*or* shàng, *or* ná, *or* gěy, *or* fù) 'dwō-shǎw-chyán-de-'jìn-kěw-shwèy?

(*Of wages or salary*). (*Salary*) 'shīn-shwey; (*wages*) 'gūng-chyán; gěy-de-'chyán, jèng-de-'chyán; **to pay** gěy-'chyán *or* jèng-'chyán; **be paid** ná-'chyán *or* kāy-'jř *or* fā-'shīn *or* gwān-'shyǎng. ‖Is the pay good on your new job? nǐ-de-'shīn-shèr °gěy(-de)-chyán 'dwō-ma? or °jèng(-de)-chyán 'dwō-ma? or °'shīn-shwey 'dà-ma (or 'dwō-ma)? or °'gūng-chyán 'dà-ma (or 'dwō-ma)? ‖When áre we going to be paid? 'shéme-shŕ-hew °fā-'shīn? or °gwān-'shyǎng? or °ná-'chyán? or °kāy-'jŕ?

(Be worthwhile) shàng-'swàn, or hé-'swàn, or 'jŕ-de. ‖It doesn't pay to spend too much time on this work. dzày jèy-jyàn-'gūng-dzwò-shang fèy tǐng-dwō-'shŕ-hew °bú-shàng-'swàn. or °bù-hé-'swàn. or °bù-'jŕ-de. ‖It won't pay to settle now for cash. 'jèy-shŕ-hew mày shyàn-chyán °bú-shàng-'swàn. or °bù-hé-'swàn. or °bù-'jŕ-de.

Pay for (figuratively) bàw. ‖I'll make you pay for that! jèy-ge chéw=wǒ yí-'dìng yàw-'bàw-de!

Pay for itself bǎ 'běr 'jwàn-hwéy-lay or bǎ 'běn-chyán 'jwàn-hwéy-lay. ‖This machine will pay for itself in no time. jèy-jyà-'jī-chi 'bú-yùng dwō-shǎw-shŕ-hew jyew kě-yǐ bǎ 'běr (or 'běn-chyán) 'jwàn-hwéy-lay.

Pay a visit kàn . . . yí-shyàr. ‖We ought to pay him a visit before he leaves. wǒm 'yīng-dāng dzày tā 'méy-dzěw yǐ-'chyán chywù 'kàn-tā yí-shyàr.

PAYMENT. *The expressions are all verbal; see* **PAY.** ‖I have' to make three monthly payments of ten dollars each. wǒ jŕ néng 'yí-ge-ywè gěy (or fù, or hwán, or jyāw) 'shŕ-kwày-chyán, y´ 'gùng gěy (etc.) 'sān-ge-ywè. or wǒ děy fù 'sān-ge-ywè-de-chyán, 'měy-tsz gěy 'shŕ-kwày. ‖Prompt payment will be appreciated. nèy-bǐ-'kwǎn-dz chǐng-nín 'kwày-dyar hwán. or (Literary) 'dzwēn-kwǎn chǐng 'dzǎw-r̀ hwán-'chīng. or (Of cash only) 'shyàn-chyán jyāw-'yì.

PEACE. National peacę 'hé-píng or 'tày-píng; however, when speaking of peace as the ending of a present war, verbal expressions are used such as 'bù-dǎ-'jàng-le, 'jàn-shŕ 'wán-le, 'méy-yew 'jàn-shŕ; peace treaty 'hé-ywē; peace conference 'hé-píng-hwèy-'yì. ‖Do you favor a strong peacetime army? nǐ 'dzàn-chéng dzày 'hé-píng (or 'tày-píng)-de-shŕ-hew yǎng hěn-dwō-de jywūn-'dwèy-ma? ‖It cost blood and sweat to win this peace. jèr-shr wǒm-ná-'shywě-'hàn-dé-lay-de-°'hé-píng. or °'tày-píng. or jèy-tsž-'hé-píng shŕ wǒm-ná-'shywě-'hàn-hwàn-lay-de. ‖I hope peace will come soon. wǒ 'pàn-wang 'kwày-dyar 'bù-dǎ-'jàng-le. or wǒ 'pàn-wang 'jàn-shŕ kwày-dyar 'wán-le. ‖I'm going to buy a car as soon as peace comes. 'yì-dǎ-wán-le-'jàng (or 'jàn-shŕ 'yì-wán) wǒ jyew mǎy lyàng-chì-'chē. ‖He wants peace in our time. tā shyǎng jyàw 'dzám-jèy-bèy-dz-li 'méy-yew 'jàn-shŕ.

Domestic peace 'hé-mù (a verb, meaning be harmonious); 'hé-he-mù-'mù-de (harmonious, peaceful). ‖She always manages to have peace in her house. tā 'lǎw bǎ 'jyā-li nèng-de 'hé-he-mù-'mù-de. ‖Their family is always at peace. tām-'jyā-li hěn 'hé-mù. ‖There's no more peace in his home since his mother-in-law came. tsúng tā-jàng-mu-'nyáng láy-le yǐ-hèw tā-'jyā-li jyèw 'bú-nèm 'hé-mù-le.

Peace (and quiet) expressed verbally 'ān-jing, bù-chǎw-'dzwéy, bù-dǎ-'jyà, shǎw dǎ-'jyà; shǎw chǎw-'dzwèy. ‖Can't we have a little peace (and quiet) around here? dzám-jèr °shǎw dǎ dyar-'jyà shíng-bu-shíng? or °shǎw chǎw dyar-'dzwéy shíng-bu-shíng? or °'ān-jing-dyar shíng-bu-shíng?

PEN. (Writing implement). (Western type) 'gāng-bǐ; (Chinese type) bǐ; 'máw-bǐ (actually a brush, but used for writing); mwò or mwò-'jŕ (ink stick); pen point (Western) gāng-bǐ-'téwr or gāng-bǐ-'jyǎr; fountain pen 'dž-láy-shwěy-'bǐ. ‖My pen is dry; can you spare some ink? wǒ-'gāng-bǐ méy-'shwěr-le; nǐ néng 'jyè-wǒ dyǎr-mwò-'shwěr-ma?

Pen name 'bǐ-míng. But ‖It's from his pen. shŕ 'tā-shyě-de.

(Enclosure) jywàn (for pigs, sheep); lán (for cattle). ‖We'll have to build a larger pen for the pigs. dzám děy nùng yí-ge-'dà-dyar-de-jū-'jywàn.

To pen up (animals) jywàn. ‖We keep the sheep penned up at night. wǒm 'yè-li bǎ-yáng 'jywàn-chi-lay.

PENCIL. chyān-'bǐ. ‖Will you sharpen this pencil for me? láw-'jyà gěy jèy-gēr-chyān-'bǐ shyēw-shyew shíng-ma? ‖I lost my pencil. wǒ bǎ chyān-'bǐ dyēw-le. ‖He penciled a short note. tā ná 'chyān-bǐ shyě-le jⁱ⁴ge-'dzèr.

PEOPLE. (Persons) rén. ‖Were there many·péople at the meeting? dàw-'hwèy-de-rén 'dwō-ma? ‖You must consider other people's feelings (desires). nǐ děy shyǎng-shyǎng 'byé-rén ywàn-yì-bú-'ywàn-yì. ‖Several people have asked that question. 'yěw jǐ-ge-rén 'yě nèm 'wèn-gwo-wo.

(Electorate) 'rén-mín, 'mín-jùng, lǎw-'bǎy-shìng. ‖This government is not well supported by the people. jèy-ge-'jèng-fu bú-'dà shèw °'rén-mín-de-'yūng-hù. or °'mín-jùng-de-'yūng-hù. or °'lǎw-'bǎy-shìng-de-'yūng-hù.

(Race) 'jǔng-dzú; (kind of people) rén with measure jǔng. ‖The natives of this region are a distinct people. jèy-yí-dày-de-'jywū-mín °'dān shŕ yì-'jǔng-rén. or °'lìng shŕ yì-'jǔng-rén. or °shŕ 'lìng-yí-ge-jǔng-dzú-de-rén.

(Nation) gwó. ‖Many peoples will be represented at the conference. 'jèy-tsž-'hwèy-yì yěw 'hěn-dwō-'gwó-de-dày-'byǎw chū-'shí.

PER CENT. N per cent bǎy-fēn-jŕ-'N. ‖The cost of living has gone up 10 per cent since last year. r̀-cháng-shēng-hwó-'fèy-yùng bǐ 'chywù-nyán yǐ-jīng 'gāw-le bǎy-fēn-jŕ-'shŕ. ‖What per cent? bǎy-fēn-jŕ-'jǐ?

PERFECT. *There is no single word that expresses the idea of* **perfect,** *but there are four types of expressions used:*

(Good) hǎw *or some other adjective plus* 'jí-le *or* dàw-'jyā-le *or* dàw·'jí-dyǎn-le *(to the last detail).*

(Just) jèng; *(really)* jēn *plus* hǎw *or another adjective or a verb, or expressed with* hǎw *or* dà *and similar adjectives plus a noun.*

(No defects at all) yì-'dyǎr-jǎr yě méy-yěw; *(no mistakes at all)* yì-'dyǎr-tswòr yě méy-yěw; *(beyond criticism)* yì-dyǎr-kě-'pī-píng-de(-dì-fang) yě méy-yěw *or* yì-dyǎr-kě-'tyāw-ti-de(-dì-fang) yě méy-yěw *or* yì-dyǎr-'bāw-han yě méy-yěw; yì-'dyǎr yě *plus a negative verb.*

There are also a few indirect expressions.

‖It's perfect! hǎw 'jí-le! *or* hǎw dàw-'jyā-le! *or* yì-'dyǎr-jǎr *or* yì-'dyǎr-tswòr yǒ méy-yěw. *etc.* yě méy-yěw. ‖They're a perfect match. 'pèy-de 'jèng hé-'shř. *or* 'pèy-de hǎw 'jí-le. *or* 'jèng shř yí-'dwèr. *or* 'jēn shř yí-'dwèr. *or* pèy-dzày yí-'kwàr yì-dyǎr-kě-'pī-píng-de *(etc.)* yě méy-yěw. ‖He's a perfect scoundrel. tā shř ge-'dà-hwày-'dàn. *or* 'tā-jèy-rén hwày 'jí-le. *or* 'tā-jèy-rén jēn shř 'hwèn-jàng dàw-'jyā-le. *or* tā-hwày-de yì-'dyǎr-kě-'chywǔ-de-dì-fang yò méy-yěw. ‖She gave a perfect performance. tā-yǎn-de °jēn shř hǎw dàw 'jí-dyǎn-le. *or* °hǎw 'jí-le. *or* °hǎw-de dàw-'jyā-le. *or* °yì-dyǎr-kě-'pī-ping-de-dì-fang yě méy-yěw. *or* °yì-dyǎr-kě-'tyāw-ti-de-dì-fang yě méy-yěw. *or* °yì-dyǎr-'bāw-han yě méy-yěw. *or* *(without error)* °yì-'dyǎr-tswèr yě méy-yěw. ‖He speaks perfect Chinese. tā shwō 'jūng-gwo-hwà shwō-de hǎw 'jí-le. *or* *(Like a native)* 'tā-shwō-de-jūng-gwo-hwà gēn 'jūng-gwo-rén-shwō-de yí-'yàng. ‖He's a perfect stranger to me. *is expressed as* I don't know him at all. wǒ yì-'dyǎr yě bú-'rèn-shr tā. *or* wǒ gēn-tā 'sù bù-shyāng-'shř. ‖The method hasn't been perfected yet. fāng-fa háy méy-'yán-jyew dàw-'jyā-ne. ‖It's the perfect crime. *is expressed as* Even spirits can't solve it. 'jèy-shèr gàn-de 'shén-shyān yě 'bù-néng jř-chu shř 'shéy-gàn-de-lay. ‖He did a perfect job of ridiculing him. tā bǎ-tā 'swěn-de dàw-'jyā-le. ‖It's a perfect caricature of him. bǎ-tā 'pī-píng-de 'tǐ-wú-wán-'fǔ.

PERFORM. *(On a stage)* yǎn; *(come on stage)* shàng-'táy. ‖She performed very well. *or* She gave a fine performance. tā-yǎn-de hǎw 'jí-le. ‖Who performs next? 'shyà-yí-mù shř 'shéy °yǎn? *or* °shàng-'táy?

Perform an operation 'gěy-rén lá-'bìng, kāy-'dāw. ‖The doctor is performing an operation. 'dày-fu 'jèng-dzày 'gěy-rén lá-'bìng.

See also DO.

PERHAPS. 'yě-shywǔ, shywǔ; *(literary)* 'hè-jě; *(I'm afraid that)* (wǒ) 'kǔng-pà. ‖Perhaps it'll rain today. jyěr yě-shywǔ shyà-'ywǔ. *or* jyēr yě-shywǔ yàw *(or* hwèy) shyà-'ywǔ. *or* jyēr shywǔ yàw shyà-'ywǔ. *or* jyēr hè-jě hwèy shyà-'ywǔ, yě wèy kě-'jř. *or* jyēr kǔng-pà yàw shyà-'ywǔ. ‖Perhaps he forgot. 'yě-shywǔ tā 'wàng-le. *or* tā yě-shywǔ 'wàng-le. *or* tā shywǔ-shr 'wàng-le. *or* tā 'hè-jě 'wàng-le. *or* kǔng-pà tā 'wàng-le. ‖Perhaps it was I who was wrong. yě-

shywǔ *(or* shywǔ) shř 'wǒ tswò-lè-ba. *or* 'hè-jě shř 'wǒ tswò-le. *But* ‖I think perhaps you'd better take an umbrella. wǒ kàn nǐ 'háy-shr dày bǎ(-ywǔ)-'sǎn hǎw. *or* wǒ kàn nǐ (yě-shywǔ) dày bǎ(-ywǔ)-'sǎn **tsáy** 'hǎw.

PERIOD. *(Stretch of time)* 'shř-hew. ‖He worked here for a short period. tā dzày-jèr dzwò-le 'méy **dwō**-shǎw-'shř-hew.

(Limited section of time) chī *or* dwàr *(measures)*; 'shř-dày *(noun; literary).* The glacial period 'bīng-hé 'chī, *or* 'bīng-hé-shř-'dày. ‖The history of this town may be divided into three periods. jèy-dì-fang-de-lì-'shř kě-yǐ fēn-chéng sān-°'chī. *or* °'dwàr. *or* °ge-'shř-dày. ‖The first period is the most interesting. dì-'yī-chī *(or* dì-'yī-dwàr) 'dzwéy yěw 'yì-sz. ‖The Civil War period of American history serves as a good example. 'měy-gwo-shř-li 'nán-běy-jàn-'jēng °jèy-yì-'chī *(or* °jèy-yí-'dwàr, *or* °jèy-ge-'shř-dày) kě-yǐ 'ná-lay dzwò ge-'lì-dz.

(Class hour) táng. ‖I have no classes the third period. dì-'sān-táng wǒ 'méy-kè.

(Punctuation mark) dyǎr *(dot).* ‖You forgot to put a period here. nǐ jèr 'wàng-le dyǎn-'dyǎr-le.

(That's all there is to be said) 'méy-yěw 'byé-de-kě-'shwō-de. ‖He's no good, period. tā 'bú-shr hǎw-rén, 'méy-yěw 'byé-de-kě-'shwō-de.

PERMIT. *(Written permission)* shywǔ-kě-'jèng; special permit 'tè-shywǔ-'jěng. ‖You'll have to get a permit to visit this factory. nǐ děy 'lǐng yí-ge-shywǔ-kě-'jèng tsáy néng 'tsān-gwān jèy-ge-gūng-'chǎng. ‖They're issuing special permits to discharged soldiers. tām jèng-dzày fā-gěy twèy-wǔ 'jywūn-rén 'tè-shywǔ-'jèng-ne.

(To allow) jyàw *or* ràng *(allow without interference)*; shywǔ *or* jwěn *(give authoritative permission)*; rúng *(give a chance)*; be permitted shywǔ *or* jwěn; néng *(be possible)*; shíng *(be OK).* ‖I won't permit you to go. wǒ bú-'jyàw *(or* wǒ bú-'ràng, *or, stronger,* wǒ bù-'shywǔ, *or* wǒ bù-'jwěn) nǐ 'chywù. ‖He never permits me to speak. tā bù-'rúng wǒ shwō-'hwà. ‖No one is permitted to enter this building. 'jèy-dzwò-léw 'shéy yě 'bù-shywǔ *(or* 'bù-jwěn) jìn-chywu. ‖Such behavior as theirs shouldn't be permitted. 'bù-gāy jwěn *(or* shywǔ) tām 'dzèm-je. ‖I won't permit anybody to bully people around here. dzày 'wǒ-jèr 'shéy °yě bù-shywǔ *(or* °yě bù-jwěn, *or* °yě bù-néng) 'chǐ-fu rén. *or* °chī-fu rén dēw bù-'shíng. *or* °'chī-fu rén wǒ yě bù-néng 'rúng.

PERSON. rén. ‖What sort of a person is she? tā shř 'dzěm-yàngr-de-yí-ge-rén? ‖She seems like a different person. 'tā hǎw shyàng °'byàn-le yí-ge-'rén shř-de. *or* °'hwàn-le yí-ge-'rén shř-de. *or* °shř 'lìng-yi-ge-'rén shř-de. ‖(He isn't much of a leader, but) just as a person he isn't bad. ... tā-ya, 'rén-ne, bìng 'bú-hwày. *or* gwāng ná jèy-ge-'rén láy shwō-ne, tā bìng 'bú-hwày.

In person. (*Oneself*) 'běn-rén; (*personally*) 'chin-dž; (*face to face*) dāng-'myàr; *or combinations of these.* ‖She's going to be here in person! 'tā yàw dàw-jèr láy, (shř) ('běn-rén) 'chin-dž láy! ‖Please deliver this to him in person. (*Yourself*) chǐng nǐ 'chin-dž bǎ jèy-ge sùng-dàw 'tā-nar-chywu. *or* (*To himself*) chǐng nǐ bǎ jèy-ge sùng-dàw 'tā-nar, dāng-'myàr jyāw-gěy tā. ‖He came in person and handed me this. tā-'běn-rén 'chin-dž láy-de, dāng-'myàr bǎ jèy-ge 'jyāw-gěy wǒ-de.

PERSONAL. 'dž-jǐ-de *or* 'gè-rén-de; *in a few combinations* sž. Personal affairs 'sž-shř; personal property (*legal term*) 'sz-chǎn. ‖Don't mix personal affairs with business. bú-yàw bǎ 'sž-shř gēn 'gūng-shř 'hwèn-dzày yì-'chǐ. ‖He asked too many personal questions. tā 'jìng wèn rén-jyā-de-'sž-shř. *or* tā 'wèn rén-jyā-de-'sž-shř wèn-de tày 'dwō-le. ‖This is my personal opinion. jèy shř wǒ-'dž-jǐ-de-'yì-jyan. *or* °'gè-rén-de-'yì-jyan. ‖Are these your personal belongings? jèy shř nǐ-'dž-jǐ-de-dūng-shi-ma?

PHOTOGRAPH. shyàng-'pyǎr; take a photograph *or* have a photograph taken jàw-'shyàng. ‖You'll need eight copies of a photograph of yourself. nǐ-'běn-rén-de-shyàng-'pyār děy yěw 'bā-jāng. ‖I haven't had a photograph taken for months. wǒ 'jǐ-ge-ywè-li 'yì-jāng-shyàng yě méy-'jàw. *or* wǒ yěw 'hǎw-jǐ-ge-ywè méy-jàw-'shyàng-le.

To photograph *or* take a photograph of 'jàw-shya-lay. ‖He photographed those fishing boats for the exhibit. tā bǎ nèy-shyē-'ywú-chwán jàw-shya-láy-le, wèy jǎn-'lǎn yùng.

PIANO. gāng-'chín. ‖He really knows how to play the piano. tā jēn hwèy tán gāng-'chín. *or* tā tán gāng-'chín tán-de hěn 'hǎw.

PICK. (*Pluck*) jāy (*fruit*); chyā (*flowers*). ‖Are the tomatoes ripe enough to pick? shī-húng-'shř kě-yǐ 'jāy-le-ma?

(*Choose*) tyāw; shywǎn *or* 'tyāw-shywǎn (*with particular care*). ‖You certainly picked a nice time to start an argument! nǐ kě 'jēn hwèy tyāw 'shř-hewr bàn-'dzwěy-ya! ‖These are all picked men. jèy-shyē dēw shř °'tyāw-chu-lay-de-'jwàng-dīng. *or* °'shywǎn-chu-lay-de-'jwàng-dīng. *or* °'tyāw-shywǎn-chu-lay-de-'jwàng-dīng. ‖We have a hand-picked group. wǒm-de-jèy-shyē-rén 'dēw shř hěn-'dž-shì-de-°tyāw-chu-lay-de. *or* °shywǎn-chu-lay-de. *or* °tyāw-shywǎn-chu-lay-de. ‖I picked (*successfully*) a winner that time. 'nèy-tsž wǒ kě 'tyāw-jàw-le ge-'yíng-de. ‖He picked (out) a very nice bracelet as a gift to his wife. tā 'tyāw-le yí-jyàn-'hěr-hǎw-de-'jwó-dz 'sùng-gěy tā-'tày-tay. ‖He picked out two watches and had a hard time deciding which to buy. tā tyāw-chu 'lyǎng-jř-byǎw-lay; 'dzěm yě ná-bu-dìng 'jú-yi mǎy 'něy-ge.

‖The captain picked me to do the job. lyán-'jǎng tyāw 'wǒ chywù dān-ren 'jèy-ge-'chāy-shr. *or* (*Sarcastically*) lyán-'jǎng 'chyáw-shang wǒ-le (*or* lyán-'jǎng 'kàn-shang wǒ-le, *or* lyán-'jǎng jēn 'shǎng-shř wǒ) gěy-wǒ 'dzèm-ge-'chāy-shr.

(*A digging tool*) gǎw. ‖The men were working with picks and shovels. nèy-shyē-rén yùng-'gǎw gēn 'chǎn-dz dzwò-'hwór.

Pick on (*annoy*) 'chī-fu(-chī-fu); gēn . . . jāw-'chár. ‖Pick on someone your own size. yěw 'néng-ney, 'chī-fu-chī-fu gēn-nǐ-gèr-yì-'byār-dà-de. ‖Stop picking on him. byé dzày 'chī-fu rén-jyā-le. *or* byé dzày gēn 'rén-jyā jāw-'chár.

Pick to pieces. ‖They picked his arguments to pieces. tām bǎ 'tā-shwō-de jǐ-dyǎn °'pī-ping-de 'yì-wén bù-'jř. *or* °'wán-chywán bwó-'dǎw-le.

Pick up (*an object*) 'jyǎn-chi-lay, 'shŕ-chi-lay. ‖Please pick up the papers. láw-'jyà bǎ-'jř °jyǎn-chi-lay. *or* °shŕ-chi-lay.

Pick up (*passengers*) děng rén 'shàng (*wait for people to get on*). ‖The bus is stopping to pick up passengers. 'gūng-gùng-chì-'chē yàw dzày-jèr 'tíng-shya-lay děng rén 'shàng.

Pick up (*information*). (*Unintentionally*) 'tīng-jyàn; (*intentionally*) 'dǎ-tīng-dàw. ‖He picked up some information while in town. tā dzày chéng-'lǐ de-shŕ-hew °'tīng-jyàn-le jǐ-jyàn-'shèr. *or* °'dǎ-tīng-dàw jǐ-jyàn-'shèr.

Pick up (*a bargain*) 'mǎy-jáw. ‖She picked up a good bargain yesterday. tā 'dzwér-ge 'mǎy-jáw-le jvàn-'pyán-yi-'hwò.

Pick up speed 'kwày-chi-lay. ‖The train will pick up speed in a minute. yì-'hwěr hwǒ-chē jyèw 'kwày-chi-lay-le.

Pick up in other uses. *See* GET.

Pick (*one's teeth*) tī. ‖He knows he shouldn't pick his teeth in public. tā 'jř-daw tā 'bù-yīng-dāng dzày 'hěn-dwō-rén-'myàn-chyán tī-'yá.

Pick (*a lock*) (bǎ-swǒ) 'bwō-kāy *or* (*with a lever*) 'chyàw-kāy *or* (*in any way*) 'néng-kāy *cr* 'gǔ-du-kāy. ‖We'll have to pick the lock to get into the house. wǒm děy bǎ-swǒ °'bwō-kāy tsáy néng 'jìn-chywu. *or* °'chyàw-kāy tsáy néng 'jìn-chywu. *or* °shyǎng-fár 'nèng-kāy tsáy néng 'jìn-chywu. *or* °shyǎng-fár 'gǔ-du-kāy tsáy néng 'jìn-chywu.

Pick (*a fight*) dǎ-'jyà. ‖Are you trying to pick a fight with me? nǐ shyǎng 'gēn-wǒ dǎ-'jyà-ma?

PICTURE. (*Painting or drawing*) hwàr (*not of a person*); shyàng (*portrait*). ‖They have some beautiful pictures for sale. tām yěw shyē-hǎw-'kàn-de-hwàr chū 'mày. ‖He drew a picture on the blackboard. tā dzày hēy-'bǎn-shang hwà-le yí-ge-'hwàr. ‖He drew a picture of the mountain on the blackboard. tā dzày hēy-'bǎn-shang bǎ nèy-ge-'shān-de-yàng-dz hwà-le yì-jāng-'hwàr. ‖He drew a picture of her on the blackboard. tā dzày hēy-'bǎn-shang 'hwà-le yì-jāng-tā-de-'shyàng.

(*Photograph*) shyàng-'pyār. **Take a picture, take pictures, have one's picture taken** jàw-'shyàng. ‖**I saw your picture in a show window.** wǒ kàn-jyan ni-de-shyàng-'pyār-le, 'bǎy-dzày yí-ge-'pù-dz-de-'chwāng-hu-li. ‖**I haven't had my picture taken for years.** wǒ 'yěw shyē-nyán méy-jàw-'shyàng-le.

(*Movie*) dyàn-'yěngr. ‖**I like to see a good picture once in a while.** wǒ 'jyē-cháng bú-dwàr-de shyǎng kàn ge-'hǎw-dyàn-yěngr. ‖**She's been in pictures since she was a baby.** tā tsúng hèn-'shyǎw-de-shŕ-hew 'chỉ jyèw yǎn dyàn-'yěngr.

To picture (*in writing*) 'myáw-shyě. ‖**The story pictures life in London a thousand years ago.** nèy-ge-'gù-shr shŕ 'myáw-shyě-yì-'chyan-nyán-yǐ-'chyán-'lwén-dwēn-rén-de-'shēng-hwó.

To picture (*in the imagination*). ‖**In his mind he pictured her as a teen-age kid with pig-tails and a freckled face.** tā-'shīn-li jywé-je tā-de-yàngr yí-'dìng shŕ 'shŕ-jǐ-swèr-de-ge-shyǎw-'gū-nyangr, shū-je shyǎw-'byàr, yì-'lyǎn-de chyǎwr-'bān.

PIECE. *The following measures are used:* (*chunk*) kwày *or* kwàr; (*sheet; also used of flat things where we would not say piece*) jāng; (*of work, or an article of something made*) vàn *or* jyàr; (*natural section, as of an orange*) bàr; (*section or paragraph or piece of music*) dwàr *or* dwàn; (*written article*) pyān; (*a length*) tyáw *or* gēn; (*a section of length*) jyér. *The following nouns are also used:* (*small broken pieces*) 'chá-dz *or* chár; (*crumbs, ground pieces*) 'jā-dz *or* jār. ‖**She cut each cake into six pieces.** tā bǎ yí-kwày-yí-kwày-de-'gēw 'měy-yí-kwày chyē-chéng-le °'lyèw-kwàr. *or* °'lyèw-'shyǎw-kwàr. ‖**He owns a piece of land in the country.** tā dzày 'shyāng-shya yěw yí-kwày-dì. ‖**Write your name on this piece of paper.** bǎ nǐ-'míng-dz shyě-dzày jèy-jāng-'jǐr-shang. ‖**Tear off a piece of that paper for me.** nèy-ge-'jǐr gěy-wǒ 'sž yí-kwàr. ‖**That's a fine piece of furniture.** nèy-jyàr-'jyā-jywu jēn bú-'hwày. ‖**That** (*porcelain*) **is a Ming piece.** nèy-jyàn-'tsž-chì shŕ 'míng-chaw-de. ‖**What is the name of that piece the orchestra is playing?** ywè-'dwèy jèng dzèw-de jèy-dwàn-'yīn-ywe jyàw 'shéme-míng-dz? ‖**Maybe I can fix it with this piece of copper wire.** 'jèy-ge wǒ yùng jèy-tyáw-'túng-sēr (*or* jèy-gēn-'túng-sēr) 'yě-shywǔ néng nèng-'hǎw-lew. ‖**The stick was broken into two pieces.** gwèn-dz dwàn-chéng-le 'lyǎng-jyér. ‖**He picked up all the pieces except this one.** tā bǎ 'swèy-kwàr (*or* tā bǎ 'swèy-chá-dz, *or, of glass,* tā bǎ bwō-li-'chá-dz) 'dēw jyǎn-chi-lay-le, jǐr yěw 'jèy-kwàr 'là-shya-le. ‖**That's a fine piece of work.** (*Of a job*) jèy-jyàn-'hwó dzwò-de 'hěn haw. *or* (*Of a situation*) jèy-jyàn-'shŕ bàn-de 'hěn hǎw. *or* (*Of working or a product*) nèy-ge 'dzwò-de 'hěn hǎw. *or* (*Of writing*) jéy-ge 'shyě-de 'hěn hǎw. *or* jèy-pyàn-'wén shyě-de 'hěn hǎw. *or* (*Of a book*) jèy-běn-'shū shyě-de 'hěn hǎw.

or (*Of a plan*) jèy-ge 'dǎ-swàn-de 'hěn hǎw. ‖**There's a piece missing from the tool shelf.** gē-'jyā-hwor-de-jyà-dz-shang 'dwǎn-le yí-jyàr-shéme. ‖**There's a piece** (*part or thing*) **missing from this machine.** jèy-ge-'jī-chi 'dwǎn-le °yí-ge-'líng-jyàr. *or* °dyàr-'dūng-shi.

Timepiece. (*Clock*) jūng; (*watch*) byǎw; (*stop watch*) 'mǎ-byǎw.

A piece of one's mind yí-dwèn. ‖**She gave him a piece of her mind.** (*To equals or superiors*) tā gēn-tā 'chǎw-le yí-'dwèn. *or* (*to inferiors or equals*) tā bǎ-tā 'shwō-le yí-'dwèn. *or* tā bǎ-tā 'mà-le yí-'dwèn. *or* tā bǎ-tā 'gwǎn-jyàw-le yí-'dwèn.

To pieces; go to pieces. (*Shatter*) swèy; (*come apart*) sǎn; (*collapse*) tā; (*collapse mentally*) lwàn; **break to pieces** *resultative compounds with* swèy *as second element; see* **BREAK.** ‖**The bookcase just fell to pieces all at once.** shū-'jyà-dz 'hū-rán-jyān jyèw °'sǎn-le. *or* 'tā-le. ‖**This shoe is going to come to pieces.** jèy-jř-'shyé kwày yàw 'sǎn-le. ‖**The ball hit the fish bowl and broke it to pieces.** chyéwr bǎ ywú-'gāng dzá (*or* dǎ) -'swèy-le. ‖**She just went to pieces after his death.** tā nèm yì-'sž jyàw tā-de-shīn dēw 'lwàn-le.

Piece together 'dwèy-shang, 'tsèw-dzay yí-'kwàr, 'pīn-dzày yí-'kwàr. ‖**See if you can piece them together again.** kàn nǐ 'néng-bu-néng bǎ jèy-ge dzày °'dwèy-shang. *or* °'tsèw-dzay yí-'kwàr. *or* °'pīn-dzày yí-'kwàr.

PIG. jū. ‖**He raises pigs.** tā yǎng 'jū. ‖**He eats like a pig.** tā 'chŕ-chi-lay gēn-'jū shŕ-de. *or* tā-chŕ-de gēn-'jū shŕ-de nèm 'dwō.

PILE. *See* HEAP, *except for one meaning below.*

To arrange in a neat pile lwò, mǎ; **a neat pile** *is* lwò. ‖**He piled the books on top of each other.** tā bǎ-shū yì-'běr-yì-'běr-de °'lwò-chi-lay-le. *or* °'mǎ-chi-lay-le. *or* °'lwò-chéng yí-'lwò. *or* °'mǎ-chéng yí-'lwò. *or* °'lwò-le yí-dà-'lwò. *or* °'mǎ-le yí-dà-'lwò.

PIN. (*Fastener*) jēn *or* jēr; (*safety pin or any pin that has a fastening device*) 'byé-jēr; **bobby pin** 'chyǎ-dz; **hairpin** 'téw-jēr. ‖**If you haven't got a safety pin, a straight pin will do.** nǐ rú-gwǒ 'méy-yěw byé-'jēr, yùng dzwò-'hwó-de-'jēn yě 'shing. ‖**I need some hairpins and bobby pins.** wǒ děy yàw 'shyē-ge-'téw-jēr gēn 'chyǎ-dz. ‖**She wore a silver pin on her coat.** tā-de-'yī-fu-shang 'byé-le yí-ge-'yín-de-byé-jēr.

(*Fasten with pins*) byé. ‖**Pin some flowers on your hat.** bǎ-'hwār yùng 'byé-jēr byé-dzày nǐ-'màw-dz-shang. *But* ‖**Pin** (*nail*) **this notice on the bulletin board, will you please?** bǎ jèy-ge-'tūng-gàw dìng-dzày gàw-báy-'bǎn-shang, láw-'jyà, láw-'jyà.

Pin down (*a person*). (*Physically*) yā. ‖**The two men were pinned under the car.** lyǎng-ge-rén 'yā-dzày chē-'dǐ-shya-le. (*Mentally*) ‖**You can't pin him**

down to the facts. 'méy-fár gēn-tā jyǎng-chu ge-'lyěr-lay. ‖We couldn't pin him down to a definite agreement. tā 'dzěm-je yě 'bù-kěn gēn-wǒm shwō-'dìng-le.

PINE. (*Tree*) 'sūng-shù. ‖That tree looks like a pine to me. wǒ kàn nèy-kē-'shù shyàng 'sūng-shù. ‖Pines and cedars make good lumber. 'sūng-shù gēn 'bǎy-shù dēw shr̀ 'hǎw-mù-lyaw.

(*Wood*) 'sūng-mù. ‖That pine table is not very strong. nèy-ge-'sūng-mù-jwō-dz 'bú-dà 'jyē-shr.

Pine needles sūng-'jēn or sūng-'jēr.

PINK. 'fěn-húng(-shǎr).

PIPE. (*Tube*) 'gwǎn-dz. ‖There's a leak in that pipe. 'gwǎn-dz 'lèw-le. or (*Water pipe*) 'shwěy-gwǎn-dz 'lèw-le. or (*Steam pipe*) 'chì-gwǎn-dz 'lèw-le. or (*Gas pipe*) 'méy-chì-gwǎn-dz 'lèw-le.

To pipe yùng 'gwǎn-dz 'yǐn. ‖I piped this water here from a spring a mile away. jèr-de-'shwěy shr̀ wǒ-tsúng-'lí-jèr-yì-lǐ-'dì-de-yí-ge-'chywán-ywan-nèr-yùng-'gwǎn-dz-'yǐn-gwo-lay-de.

(*For smoking*). (*The kind familiar to us*) yān-'děwr; (*a long-stemmed Chinese pipe*) yān-'dày; **water pipe** 'shwěy-yān-'dày. ‖If you smoke a pipe, you'll have a hard time getting tobacco here. nǐ yàw-shr chēw yān-'děwr (or yān-'dày), 'jèr hěn nán mǎy-dàw yān-'yè-dz.

‖Pipe down! byé 'rāng-rang-le!

PLACE. (*Location*) 'dì-fang. *Measures with and without* 'dì-fang: (*general*) ge-'dì-fang; (*spot*) 'chù(-dì-fang); (*region*) 'dày(-dì-fang); (*area*) 'pyàn(-dì-fang); (*section*) dwàr. (**In**) **this place** jèy-ge-'dì-fang (*etc.*); (*here*) jèr; (*hereabouts*) 'jèy-her or 'jèy-har; (*in this region*) 'jèy-kwàr; (**in**) **that place** *similar forms with* nèy *and* nàr; (**in**) **which place** or (**in**) **any place** *similar forms with* něy *and* nǎr, *also* 'shéme-dì-fang; **my place** (*where I live, where I work, etc.*) 'wǒ-jèr (*nearby*) or 'wǒ-nàr (*somewhere else*), *and similarly with other pronouns.* ‖Be sure to put it back in the same place. byé 'wàng-lew 'gē-hwéy 'ywán-láy-de-'dì-fang. ‖Is there any place to put the car? yěw gē-'chē-de-dì-fang-ma? ‖There's no parking place around here. 'jèy-her méy-yěw tíng-'chē-de-dì-fang. ‖This place is ten miles from the railroad. 'jèy-ge-dì-fang lí chē-'jàn yěw 'shŕ-lǐ-dì. ‖There's not a single tree in that place. nèy-ge-'dì-fang (or nèy-'dày-dì-fang, or nèy-'dày, or nèy-'kwàr, or 'nèy-her, or nàr) lyán 'yì-kē-shù yě méy-'yěw. ‖We put a cordon around that place. wǒm jyàw-rén bǎ nèy-ge-'dì-fang wéy-chi-lay-le. ‖His place of business is near mine. tā-dzwò-'shèr-de-dì-fang lí 'wǒ-nèr tǐng 'jìn. ‖My place is very noisy. 'wǒ-nèr (or 'wǒ-nàr) hěn 'chǎw. ‖We'll come to your place; OK? wǒm dàw 'nǐ-nèr (or 'nǐ-nàr) chywù, 'hǎw-ma? ‖We have a lot of trees on our place. 'wǒm-nèy-ge-dì-fang yěw 'hǎw-shyē-kē-'shù.

‖They're looking for a good place to open a shop. tām jèng-dzay jǎw ge-'hǎw-dì-fang kāy 'pù-dz̀. ‖There isn't a single place open now. dàw 'jèy-shŕ-hew 'nǎr (or dàw 'jèy-shŕ-hew 'shéme-dì-fang) dēw gwān-le 'mén-le, or dàw 'jèy-shŕ-hew méy-yěw 'yì-jyār kāy-je-de-le. ‖This is hardly the place for dancing. jèr 'jyàn-jŕ bú-shr tyàw-'wǔ-de-dì-fang. ‖The play is weak in several places. nèy-chū-'shì yěw 'hǎw-jǐ-°chùr(-dì-fang) chà-'jìn. or °'dwàr chà-'jìn. ‖I've lost my place in the book I was reading. wǒ 'wàng-le shū kàn-dàw °'nǎr-le. or °shéme-'dì-fang-le.

(*Proper location*). **In place** (*where something belongs*) ywán-'láy-de-dì-fang; (*fitted together*) 'dwèy-shang(-le); (*set*) **out of place** gē-de (or bǎy-de, or fàng-de) 'bú-shr̀ 'dì-fang. ‖Please put the books back in place. chǐng bǎ-'shū fàng-hwéy ywán-'láy-de-dì-fang-chywu. ‖The chairs are all back in place. 'yǐ-dz dēw bǎy-hwéy ywán-'láy-de-dì-fang-chywu-le. ‖The pieces are all in place and yét there still seems to be something wrong. yí-'kwàr-yí-kwàr-de dēw 'dwèy-shang-le, kě-shr 'háy shyàng nǎr yěw dyǎr-'tswòr shr̀-de. ‖This chair is out of place. jèy-bǎ-'yǐ-dz gē-de (or bǎy-de, or fàng-de) 'bú-shr̀ 'dì-fang.

(*Job*) 'wèy-jr̀; (*vacancy*) chywē. ‖There are two places vacant in the office. 'gūng-shr-fáng-li yěw lyǎng-ge-'chywē. ‖I have no place for you here. 'wǒ-jèr °méy-yěw nǐ-de-'wèy-jr. or °méy-fár 'wèy-jr nǐ. ‖I got a place for you to work. wǒ gěy-nǐ jǎw-le °ge-'wèy-jr. or °ge-'dì-fang dzwò-'shr̀.

(*Put*) 'fàng(-dzày), 'gē(-dzày), 'bǎy(-dzày). ‖The table can be placed over there for now. 'jwō-dz kě-yǐ 'jàn-shr fàng-dzày (or gē-dzày, or bǎy-dzày) 'nàr.

(*Find employment for*) gěy ... jǎw(-jáw) 'wèy-jr; gěy ... jǎw(-jáw) 'shèr; 'wèy-jr ...; bǎ ... 'ān-chā; bǎ ... 'ān-jr; yěw 'wèy-jr láy 'ān-chā ...; yěw-'shèr láy 'ān-chā; yěw 'dì-fang láy 'ān-chā. ‖They placed her in a large company as secretary. 'tām gěy-tā dzày yì-jyā-'dà-gūng-sz̄-li jǎw-le ge-'shū-ji-de-wèy-jr. ‖Could you place these three people in your office? 'nǐ-nàr 'néng-bu-néng °bǎ jèy-'sān-ge-rén 'ān-chā (or 'ān-jr) jìn-chywu? or °'wèy-jr jèy-'sān-ge-rén? ‖So many people are looking for jobs; how can I place them all? 'dzèm-dwō-de-rén yàw jǎw-'shèr, wǒ °nǎr yěw 'jèm-dwō-de-'wèy-jr (or 'jèm-dwō-de-'shèr, or 'jèm-dwō-de-'dì-fang) láy 'ān-chā tām-ne? or °'dzěm néng °dēw gěy-tām jǎw-jáw 'shèr-ne (or 'wèy-jr-ne)?

(*Identify*). ‖I'm sure I've met him before, but I can't quite place him. wǒ 'jwěn jŕ-dàw wǒ yǐ-chyán 'jyàn-gwo tā, 'kě-shr wǒ bú-'dà jì-de tā shr̀-'shéy-le.

Out of place (*inappropriate*) bù-'shíng, bú-dwèy-'jyèr, bù-chéng 'tǐ-tǔng, bù-chéng 'yàng-dz, bú-shr̀ 'yàng-dz. ‖Your actions are out of place here. nǐ-'nèm-yàngr-de-'jywǔ-dùng dzày 'jèy-her °bù-'shíng. *etc.*

In the Nth place dì-'N, dì-'N-dyǎn. ‖In the first place, we can't leave until the supplies arrive. dì-'yī (-dyǎn) 'jyē-jì méy-láy yǐ-'chyán wǒm 'bù-néng 'dzěw.

Take the place of (*a person*) tì (*substitute for*) or *indirect expressions such as* **do one's work**; (*other than* *a person*) *indirect expressions such as* be just as good, use as, *etc.: see also* USE. ‖Go and find someone to take his place. chywù 'jăw ge-rén láy °'tì-tā. *or* °dzwò tā-nèy-ge-'shèr. ‖No one can take his place. shéy yĕ 'tì-bu-lyăw tā. *or* tā-de-'shèr shéy yĕ °'dzwò-bu-'lyăw. *or* °dān-fu-bu-'lyăw. *or* °dān-ren-bu-'lyăw. ‖Nothing can take the place of a good spanking to make a child behave. jyàw shyăw-'hár tīng-'hwà, °'shéme-fár yĕ méy-yĕw 'dzwò-dzwo-shr-shŕ-de 'dă-yí-dwèn. *or* °shéme yĕ 'bú-rù 'dzwò-dzwo-shr-shŕ-de 'dă-yí-dwèn.

Take place (*happen*) 'fā-shēng, chū; *see* HAPPEN. ‖This must have taken place while I was away. 'jèy-shèr yí-'dì..g shŕ dzày-wŏ-bú-'dzày-jèr-de-shŕ-hew-°'fā-shēng-de. *or* °'chū-de.

Put someone in his place. ‖Somebody should put you in your place. jyèw-'chyàn yĕw-rén °'jyàw-shywun nĭ yí-'dwèn. *or* °jyàw-nĭ 'jŕ-daw nĭ shŕ ge-lăw-'jĭ.

PLAIN. (*Clear; of statements or arguments*) 'chīng-chu (*especially of pronunciation*); 'míng-bay (*understandable*); *or expressed by saying that a person understands, for which the verbs are the two above and also* dŭng, 'lyăw-jyĕ, *or* 'lyăw-rán. ‖His argument was plain to me. tā-shwō-de 'lĭ-yéw 'wŏ tīng-je hĕn °'chīng-chu. *or* °'míng-bay. ‖I'll put it in the plainest language I can. wŏ yùng 'tīng-'rúng-yì-'míng-bay-de-hwà (*or* 'tīng-'rúng-yì-'dŭng-de-hwà) láy 'jyăng-ba. ‖He made it perfectly plain that he didn't want to leave. tā shwō-de 'chīng-ching-chù-'chŭ-de. (*or* tā shwō-de 'míng-ming-bay-'báy-de) tā 'bú-ywàn-yì 'dzĕw. ‖He writes in a very plain style. 'tā-shyĕ-de-dŭng-shi °hĕn 'chīng-chu. *or* °hĕn 'míng-bay. *or* °jyăw-rén yí-'kàn jyèw 'míng-bay. *or* °jyăw-rén yí-'kàn jyèw 'chīng-chu. *or* °jyăw-rén yí-'kàn jyèw 'dŭng. *or* °jyăw-rén yí-'kàn jyèw néng 'lyăw-jyĕ. *or* °'yí-mù 'lyăw-rán.

(*Clear; in other connections*) 'míng-bay, 'chīng-chu, 'shyăn-rán, 'shyăn-ĕr-yì-'jyàn-de, 'míng-'shyăn-je, yí-'kàn-jyèw(-néng)-'jŕ-daw-de, yì-'tīng-jyèw(-néng)-'jŕ-daw-de, yì-'tīng-jyèw(-néng)-'míng-bay-de, háy 'kàn-bu-chū-'láy-ma (*literally* can't you see thru it); in plain sigh`: dzày 'yăn-chyán (băy-je), 'shéy dēw 'kàn-de-jyàn. ‖It's perfectly plain that that's the case. jèy shŕ 'shyăn-ĕr-yì-'jyàn-de-shŕ. *or* jèy shŕ yí-'kàn-jyèw-néng-'jŕ-daw-de-shŕ. *or* jèy shŕ yì-'tīng-jyèw-'míng-bay-de-shŕ. *or* 'shyăn-rán (*or* míng-'shyăn-je, *or* míng-ming-báy-'báy-de, *or* chīng-ching-chu-'chŭ-de) shŕ nèm-hwéy-'shèr. *or* yăn-'chyán-de-shèr háy kàn-bu-chū-'láy-ma? ‖It's quite plain (*or* It's plain as day) that he isn't going to be a sucker. 'shyăn-rán (*or* 'shyăn-ĕr-yì-'jyàn-de, *or* míng-'shyăn-je, *or* háy 'kàn-bu-chū-'láy-ma, *or* yí-'kàn jyèw 'jŕ-dàw, *or* yì-'tīng jyèw 'jŕ-dàw) tā shŕ 'bú-hwèy °shàng-'dàng-de. *or* °'dzwò-'ywàn-dà-'téw-de. *or* °'shèw-'pyàn-de. ‖It's in plain sight. jyèw dzày 'yăn-chyán (băy-je). *or* 'shéy dēw 'kàn-de-jyàn.

(*Ordinary*) píng-'cháng. ‖It's too bad she's such a plain-looking girl. kĕ-'shī tā °'jăng-de píng-'cháng. *or* °'myàn-màw píng-'cháng. *or* °'shyàng-màw píng-'cháng. ‖They are plain people. tām shŕ píng-'cháng-rén. ‖We have a plain house. wŏm-de-'fáng-dz °hĕn píng-'cháng-de. *or* (*Not fancy*) °méy shéme-'jyăng-jyew. *But* ‖He came from plain stock. tā shŕ píng-'mín-chū-'shēn.

(*Of design*) 'sù-jìn, bù-'hwā-shāw. ‖She wore a plain dress. chwān-de-'yī-fu °hĕn 'sù-jìng. *or* °'yì-dyăr bù-'hwā-shāw.

(*Of color*) sù (*means* plain white *by itself,* plain *when used with words for other colors*) ‖She wore a plain white dress. tā 'chwān-je °'sù-yī-shang. *or* hĕn-'sù-de-yī-shang. ‖She wore a plain blue dress. tā 'chwān-je hĕn 'sù-de-'lán-yī-shang.

(*Of food*) 'jyā-cháng-(byàn-)'fàn; (*not fancy*) 'méy shéme-'hwā-yàngr. ‖That restaurant serves good plain food. nèy-ge-'gwăn-dz-de-fàn 'méy shéme-'hwā-yàngr, kĕ-shr hăw 'chŕ. *or* nèy-ge-'gwăn-dz(-dzwò-de) dēw shr 'jyā-cháng-byàn-'fàn.

(*Level land*) 'píng-ywán, 'dì-dì. ‖I've lived most of my life on the plains where trees and hills are scarce. wŏ yí-'bèy-dz-li 'dwō-bàr dēw shŕ jù-dzày °'dì-dì-shang (*or* 'píng-'ywán-shang), yĕ méy dwō-shăw-'shù, yĕ méy dwō-shăw-'shān. ‖There is a wide plain between the mountains and the coast. tsúng 'shān-nar daw hăy-'byār shr yí-'dày-'píng-ywán.

PLAN. (*Intend*) 'dă-swàn, shyăng. ‖Where do you plan to spend the summer? nĭ 'dă-swàn (*or* nĭ 'shyăng) dzày-năr gwò-'shyà?

(*Intention*) *expressed verbally as above.* ‖What are your plans for tomorrow? nĭ 'míng-tyān °'dă-swàn dzwò-'shéme? *or* °dēw shŕ 'shyăng dzwò-'shéme? ‖I've made all my plans. wŏ 'dēw dă-swàn-'hăw-le.

(*Arrange*) 'ān-pay. ‖I planned the whole thing this way. 'jèy-shèr wŏ 'tsúng-téwr daw-'lyăwr 'dēw shŕ dzĕm-'ān-pay-de. *or* 'jèy-shèr 'yí-bù-yí-'bù-de dēw shŕ wŏ-'ān-pay-de.

(*Arrangements*) *expressed verbally as above.* ‖All my plans are in good order. wŏ-'ān-pay-de dēw 'hăw.

(*Method*) 'fá-dz, 'fāng-fa, 'bàn-fa. ‖I've adopted a simple plan for disposing of such people. yàw 'dă-fa 'jèy-jŭng-rén wŏ yĕw ge-hĕn-'rúng-yì-de-°'fá-dz. *or* °'fāng-fa. *or* °'bàn-fa.

(*Diagram*) tú, 'tú-àn; (*technical*) shè-jì-'tú. ‖Do you have a plan of the house? nĭ yĕw jèy-'fáng-dz-de-°'tú-ma. *or* °'tú-àn-ma? *or* °shè-jì-'tú-ma?

To plan on 'kàw-je, 'jŕ-wàng-je. ‖You'd better not plan on it. nĭ 'dzwèy-hăw byé °'kàw-je nèy-ge. *or* °'tày jŕ-wàng-je nèy-ge.

PLANT. (*Vegetation*). *Chinese has no general term, but several specific or descriptive terms.* (*Grass or a grasslike leafy plant*) tsăw; (*plant with thick woodlike stem, or tree*) mù *the common opposite of* tsăw, *not used independently;* (*a tree*) shù; (*a vegetable*) tsày; (*a flower*) hwār; (*something growing*) jǎng-de; (*something blossoming*) kāy-'hwār-de; *specific vegetable and flower plants are named only by the names of the vegetables or flowers, but may be distinguished as whole plants by the measure* kē (*a single plant*), páy (*a row*), dì (*a patch*), dwēy (*a clump*) ; plants (*plant life*) 'tsǎw-mù *or* 'hwā-tsǎw-'shù-mù *or* 'hwā-tsǎw. ‖No plants will grow in this cold climate. jèm-lěng-de-'chì-hew 'tsǎw-mù (*or* 'hwā-tsǎw, *or* 'hwā-tsǎw-'shù-mù) 'dēw hwó-bù-'lyǎw. ‖What kind of plants are these? 'jèy-shyē shř 'shéme-°hwār. *or* °tsǎw. ‖What is the name of that plant? 'dì-shang-jǎng-de nèy jyàw-'shéme? *or* nèy-kāy-'hwār-de jyàw-'shéme? ‖Do you want cut flowers or a plant? nǐ yàw yì-'dwǒr-yì-'dwǒr-de-hwār háy-shr yàw jěng-'kē-de?

To plant. (*Of seeds or plants*) jùng; (*sow seeds*) shyà-'jǔngr; dzāy (*of plants or trees*). ‖The seeds I planted last week are just beginning to come up. wǒ-'shàng-shīng-chī-jùng-de-'dzěr gāng 'chū-lay. ‖Early spring is the time for planting. 'chū-chwēn shř °shyà-'jǔngr-de-shŕ-hew. *or* °jùng-'dzěr-de-shŕ-hew. ‖I planted a cypress tree in our yard. wǒ dzày ywàn-dz-li jùng-le (*or* 'dzāy-le) kē-'bǎy-shù.

(*Factory*) 'chǎng-dz, gūng-'chǎng. ‖The manager offered to show me around the plant. 'jīng-lǐ yàw dày-wǒ dzày 'chǎng-dz (*or* gūng-'chǎng) -lǐ 'ràw-yi-ràw.

PLATE. (*Dish*). 'pan-dz; (*as measure*) pár. ‖Pass your plate and I'll give you some more food. bǎ nǐ-'pán-dz dì-gwo-lay wǒ gěy-nǐ 'jyā dyǎr-'tsày. ‖This plate of meat will be enough. 'jèy-pár-rèw 'gèw-le.

(*Sheet of metal*) . . .-'bǎn. ‖The sides of the car have steel plates on them. chē-de-lyǎr̄g-'byār yěw gāng-'bǎn.

-plated 'dù-. . .-de. ‖His watch is gold-plated. tā-de-'byǎw shř 'dù-jīn-de.

PLAY. (*Amuse oneself*) wár; (*be at leisure*) shyán; shyán-'wár; (*do something in fun*) nàw-je wár; (*engage in organized recreation*) dzwò 'yéw-shì. ‖The children are playing in the yard. 'háy-dz-men dzày 'ywàn-dz-li 'wár-ne. ‖The children are at play. 'háy-dz-men dzày °''wár-ne. *or* °dzwò 'yéw-shì. ‖Don't play with fire. byé wár-'hwǒ. *or* 'hwǒ bú-shř 'wár-de. *or* (*Figuratively*) 'nèy kě bú-shř 'wár-de. ‖You've been playing around long enough. nǐ wár-le (*or* nǐ shyán-'wár-le, *or* nǐ shyán-le) bù-'shǎw shŕ-hewr-le. ‖You mustn't take it to heart; he was just playing. nǐ byé 'dzày-hu (*or* nǐ byé wǎng 'shīn-li chywù); tā nà shř nàw-je 'wár.

(*Compete*) sày, 'bǐ-sày. ‖When are we going to play their team? wǒm 'shéme-shŕ-hew gēn 'tām-nèy-dwèy 'sày (*or* 'bǐ-sày) ? ‖The teams had just started to play when it began to rain. 'gāng sày(-chi-lay) jyèw shyà-'ywǔ-le.

(*Of games*). (*Tennis and other games in which a ball is hit; also cards*) dǎ; (*games in which a ball is*

kicked) tī; (*chess and checkers*) shyà; *when no specific game is mentioned,* wár *may be used; see also* GAME *for a fuller discussion.* ‖He plays a good game of tennis. tā dǎ 'wǎng-chyéwr 'dǎ-de 'hěn hǎw. ‖He plays a good game of chess. tā shyà-'chí shyà-de 'hěn hǎw. ‖He plays a good game. tā 'wár-de 'hěn hǎw. *or* tā hěn 'yěw lyǎng-'shěwr. ‖We played a good game of tennis. wǒm nèy-chǎng-'wǎng-chyéw dǎ-de 'tǐng hǎw.

(*Of music*) dzèw-'ywè. ‖Listen; the orchestra is playing now. 'tīng-nga, ywè-'dwèy dzèw-'ywè-le.

(*Of musical instruments*). (*Played with a bow*) lā; (*played with the fingers*) tán; (*wind instruments*) chwēy; (*percussion instruments*) dǎ *or* chyǎw. ‖He plays the violin very well. tā lā tí-'chín lā-de 'hěn hǎw. ‖He plays the piano very well. tā tán gāng-'chín tán-de 'hěn hǎw. ‖He plays the trumpet very well. tā chwēy 'lǎ-ba chwēy-de 'hěn hǎw.

(*Of a card in a card game*) chū. ‖He played his high card. tā-'chū-de shř tā-de-'dà-páy. *or* tā. chū-'dà-páy-le.

Play a joke kāy 'wán-shyàw, kāy-'shīn, dǎ 'hā-har, dèw-'shyàwr; play a joke on . . . ná . . . *plus one of the above.* ‖He played a joke on us. tā ná-'wǒm °kāy 'wán-shyàw-lay-je. *or* °kāy-'shīn-lay-je. *or* °dǎ 'hā-har-lay-je. *or* °dèw-'shyàwr-lay-je.

(*Drama*) shì. ‖Are there any good plays in town? chéng-li shyàn-dzày yěw shéme-hǎw-'shì-ma?

(*Act*) yǎn; play the part of yǎn, dāng, chywù. ‖He plays the part of a villain (*or* traitor). tā-chywù-de (*or* tā-dāng-de, *or* tā-yǎn-de) shř ge-°'hwày-rén. *or* °'jyǎn-chén.

(*Looseness*) *expressed verbally* (*be loose*) sūng; (*not tight*) bù-'jǐn. ‖There's a lot of play in this rope. (*Tied around something*) 'jèy-gēn-shéng-dz 'kwěn-de °bù-'jǐn. *or* °tày 'sūng. *or* (*Stretched in a straight line*) 'jèy-gēn-'shéng-dz °'bēng-de bù-'jǐn. *or* °'lā-de bú-gèw-'jǐn-de. *or* °'hěn 'sūng. *or* °tày 'sūng.

Play fair with dày . . . gūng-ping; dày . . . 'gūng; dày . . . jyǎng-'lǐ. ‖He really doesn't play fair with me. tā kě 'jēn dày-wǒ bù-'gūng(-ping). *or* tā dày-wǒ 'jēn bù-jyǎng-'lǐ.

Play on (*influence*) 'lì-yùng. ‖The movies play on your emotions. dyàn-'yěngr 'lì-yùng rén-de-'gǎn-chíng.

Played out gěy lèy-'hwày-le, lèy-de méy-'jyèr-le, lèy-de 'jīn-pí-lì-'jyé-le. ‖After a hard day's work he's all played out. 'dzwò-le yì-tyān-'lèy-hwór (bǎ) tā °gěy lèy-'hwày-le. *or* °lèy-de méy-'jyèr-le. *or* °lèy-de 'jīn-pí-lì-'jyé-le.

Play up. ‖He plays up only the good points of the job. tā 'gwāng shwō (*or* tā 'gwāng jyǎng) nèy-shèr-de-'hǎw-chù. *or* tā 'gwāng bǎ nèy-shèr-de-'hǎw-chù shwō-de 'tyān-hwār-lwàn-'jwèy.

PLEASANT. (*Of a person*). (*Friendly*) 'hé-chì. ‖Your friend is a very pleasant person. nǐ-nèy-ge-'péng-yew hěn 'hé-chì.

(*Of a person's manner*) 'kè-chi. ‖He asked me in a very pleasant way. tā hĕn-'kè-chi-de wèn-wŏ.

(*Of appearance*) 'shĭ-chìng. ‖She has a pleasant face. tā-jăng-de hĕn 'shĭ-chìng.

(*Enjoyable*) jyàw-rén hĕn gāw-'shìng. ‖Our work is very pleasant. 'wŏm-de-shèr dzwò-ie jyàw-rén hĕn gāw-'shìng.

(*Enjoyable and interesting*) yĕw 'yì-sz, yĕw-'chywèr, gāw-'shìng-de. ‖We had a very pleasant talk. wŏm-'tán-de 'hĕn °yĕw 'yì-sz. *or* °yĕw-'chywùr. *or* °gāw-'shìng-de.

In many cases hăw (*good*) *is used.* ‖It was a very pleasant day today. 'jīn-tyan tyān-chi hĕn 'hăw. ‖We had a pleasant time. wŏm-'wár-de hĕn hăw.

PLEASE. (*Be agreeable to*) jyàw . . . 'shĭ-hwān; jyàw . . . 'hwān-shi; (*make happy*) jyàw . . . gāw-'shìng; (*of something said*) jyàw . . . ày 'tīng. *or, instead of saying that something pleases someone, Chinese often says that a person likes something, using* 'shĭ-hwān *or* 'hwān-shi. ‖Does this please you, or do you want something else? nĭ 'shĭ-hwān (*or* nĭ 'hwān-shi) jèy-ge-ma, háy-shr shyăng yàw ge-'byé-de? ‖He's pleased with it. jèy-ge tā 'shĭ-hwān. ‖What you said pleased him very much. 'nĭ-de-hwà jyàw-tā hĕn °'shĭ-hwān. *or* °'hwān-shi. *or* °gāw-'shìng. *or* °ày 'tīng.

(*Satisfy*). (*Serve*) 'tsz-hew; (*deal with*) dwèy-fu. ‖She's a hard person to please. tā-nèy-ge-rén hĕn nán °'tsz-hew. *or* °'dwèy-fu.

(*Wish*). ‖Do as you please. 'swéy-byàn, swéy-byàn. *or* byé 'jywū-shù. *or* 'dzĕm-je dēw 'hăw. *or* 'dzĕm-je dēw 'shíng. *or* (*Impatiently*) 'swéy nĭ-de-byàn.

(*In requests*) chĭng, láw-'jyà. ‖Please shut the door. chĭng (*or* láw-'jyà) bă-'mén gwān-shang.

PLENTY. (*Many or much*) hĕn-'dwō *or* hăw-'shyē; (*enough*) gèw; (*more than enough*) (yĕw) 'fù-ywu. ‖I have plenty of matches. 'wŏ-jèr yáng-hwŏr hĕn 'dwō. *or* 'wŏ-jèr yĕw hăw-'shyē-yáng-'hwŏr. *or* 'wŏ-jèr yĕw hĕn-'dwō-yáng-'hwŏr. *or* 'wŏ-jèr yáng-'hwŏr háy yĕw 'fù-ywu. *or* wŏ-de-'yáng-hwŏr gèw-'yùng-de. ‖There's plenty more in the kitchen. chú-'fáng-li háy yĕw hăw-'shyē-ne.

PLOW. lí *or* 'lí-ba. ‖You need a heavier plow than this. yùng-de-'lí(-ba) dĕy bĭ jèy-ge 'jùng-dyar.

To plow (soil) gēng-'dì *or* jīng-'dì. ‖We started our spring plowing early this year. wŏm 'jīn-nyán chwēn-tyān °gēng-'dì gēng-de 'dzăw-dyar. *or* °jīng-'dì jīng-de 'dzăw-dyar.

To plow (*figuratively*). (*Press*) jĭ; (*to nose along with up-and-down motion, as a porpoise*) gŭng; (*to push along with head down, as a bull*) dĭng. ‖He plowed his way through the crowd. tā tsúng rén-'dzwēy-li 'jĭ-gwo-chywu-le. ‖The ship plowed slowly through the waves. chwán dzày 'làng-tew-li màn-'măr-de gŭng.

POCKET. (*In clothes*) kĕw-'dàr, dēwr; (*only in a secretive sense*) yāw-'bāwr. ‖He put it in his pocket. nèy-ge tā gē-dzày °kĕw-'dàr-li-le. *or* °dēwr-li-le. ‖He paid the bill and pocketed the change. tā bă-'jàng gĕy-le yĭ-'hèw, bă 'jăw-hwéy-láy-de-chyán °gē-dzày kĕw-'dàr-li-le. *or* °gē-dzày 'dēwr-li-le. *or* (*Cheating by so doing*) °rù-le 'dž-jĭ-de-yāw-'bāwr-le.

Pocketknife shyăw-'dāwr. ‖Do you have a pocketknife I can borrow? nĭ yĕw yì-bă-shyăw-'dāwr jyè-wŏ 'yùng-yung-ma?

Air pocket chì-'shywè. ‖The plane hit several air pockets. fēy-jī 'pèng-shang-le hăw-jĭ-'chù-chì-'shywè. (*Of metal in the earth*) kwàng. ‖They discovered a valuable pocket of silver. tām jăw-jăw-le ge-'kĕ-yĭ-chū-hĕn-'dwō-yín-dz-de-'kwàng.

POEM. shr (*also means poetry*); (*poems of irregular meter*) tsź; (*verses for singing in a play*) 'chywŭ-dz. ‖This book contains all his poems. ('swŏ-yĕw-)tā-shyĕ-de-'shr 'dēw dzày jèy-bĕr-°'shū-li. *or* °'jí-dz-li.

POET. 'shr-rén; (*a great poet*) dà-'shr-jyā, dà-'tsź-jyā, dà-'chywŭ-jya (*see* POEM). ‖A new collection of the poet's works will come out this summer. nèy-ge-'shr-rén-de-'shīn-shr-'jí 'shyà-tyān chū-'băn.

POINT. (*Sharp end*) jyār; having a sharp point jyān-de (*sharp*). ‖He broke the point of his knife. tā bă 'dāw-dz-'jyār gĕy °nùng-'shé-le. *or* °'bēn-le. ‖The point on this pencil is not sharp enough. 'jèy-gwăn-'chyán-bĭ °bú-gèw-'jyān-de. *or* °'shyēw-de bú-gèw 'jyān-de. *or* °'jyār háy tày tsū.

(*Place*) 'dì-fang, *etc., see* PLACE; halfway point jūng-'jyàr(-de-dì-fang) *or* dāng-'jūng(-nar) *or* dāng-'jūng-de-dì-fang. ‖The train stopped at a point halfway between the two stations. hwŏ-'chē dzày 'lyăng-jàn-°'jūng-'jyàr(-de-dí-fang) 'tíng-shya-le. *or* °dāng-'jūng-nar (*or* dāng-'jūng-de-dì-fang) 'tíng-shya-le. ‖The enemy has fought to a point four miles from here. 'dí-rén yĭ-jīng 'dă-dàw 'lí-jèr-'sz-lĭ-dì-de-'dì-fang. ‖At one point they're only ten miles from here. dzày 'yí-ge-dì-fang tām lí-jèr 'jr yĕw 'shŕ-lĭ-dì.

(*Land jutting into water*) jyăwr. ‖The boat we saw has sailed around the point. wŏm-'chyáw-jyàn-de-nèy-jr-chwán 'yĭ-jīng 'ràw-gwo nèy-ge-'jyăwr-chywu-le.

(*Dot*) dyăn *or* dyăr. ‖The decimal point in this number is in the wrong place. jèy-ge-shùr-li-de-shyăw-shùr-'dyăr °dyăn-de 'bú-shr 'dì-fangr. *or* °dyăn-'tswò-le (dì-fang-le)

(*Time*) 'shŕ-hew; (*stage, condition*) dì-bu. ‖At that point in the proceedings he suddenly got angry. dàw 'nèy-shŕ-hew tā 'hū-rán fā-chì 'pí-chi-lay-le.

(*Unit of scoring*) fēn *or* fēr. ‖Our team made 23 points in the first half of the game. 'wŏm-jèy-byăr dzày 'chyán-bàn-chăng dé-le èr-shr-'sān-fēr.

(*Degree*) dù. **boiling point** 'fú-dyǎn *or* 'fèy-dyǎn. ‖**The thermometer went down ten points.** hán-shǔ-'byǎw jyàng-le 'shf-dù. ‖**The water was heated to the boiling point.** shwěy jǔ-dàw °'fú-dyǎn-le. *or* °'fèy-dyǎn-le.

(*Of a compass*). (*Mark*) dzèr; (*direction*) 'fāng-shyàng. ‖**He steered several points off the course.** tā bǎ-'dwò jwàn-de chà-le 'hǎw-jǐ-ge-'dzèr.

(*Detail*) dyǎn. ‖**We've gone over that point already.** 'nèy-dyǎn dzám 'yǐ-jīng 'tán-gwo-le. ‖**I disagree with your argument at** (*or* on) **every point.** nǐ-swǒ-'shwō-de wǒ méy-yěw 'yì-dyǎn-°túng-'yì-de. *or* °dzán-'chéng-de. ‖**Every point in your argument needs expanding a little.** nǐ-swǒ-shwō-de-'nèy-yì-dyǎn dēw děy °dwō 'fā-hwēy yí-shyàr. *or* °'dzày shwō-de 'shyáng-shì-dyar.

(*Characteristic, part*) dì-fang. **Good points** 'hǎw-de-dì-fang; **beneficial points** 'hǎw-chù; **bad points** 'hwày-de-dì-fang. ‖**The book has its good and bad points.** jěy-běn-'shū yěw 'hǎw-de-dì-fang yě yěw 'hwày-de-dì-fang. ‖**Can you name just one good point about that book?** 'nèy-běn-shū nǐ néng jř-chu 'yì-dyǎn-'hǎw-de-dì-fang láy-ma? ‖**He has many good points.** tā yěw 'hǎw-shyē-'hǎw-chù. ‖**Don't you think the job has any good points at all?** 'nán-daw-shwō nǐ jywé-je 'jèy-shèr yì-'dyǎr-'hǎw-chù yě méy-'yěw-ma?

(*Of a story*). (*The critical spot*) jyé-gu-'yǎr *or* jyé-gwān-'yǎr; **get the point** 'tīng-chū (*or* 'kàn-chū) jyé-gu-'yǎr-lay, dǔng shř 'dzěm hwéy-'shèr, (*aim, application*) dǔng shř jř-je-'shéme shwō-de. ‖**His answer shows that he missed the whole point of the joke.** tsúng tā-de-'hwéy-dá-li kě-yǐ kàn-chu-lay nèy-ge-'shyàw-hwar°-de-jyé-gu-'yǎr tā 'méy-tīng-chū-láy. *or* °-de-jyé-gu-'yǎr tā 'méy-kàn-chu-lay. *or* °tā 'gēn-běn bù-dǔng shř 'dzěm hwéy-'shèr. *or* °tā 'gēn-běn bù-dǔng shř jř-je-'shéme shwō-de. ‖**What's the point?** jyé-gu-'yǎr dzày 'shéme-dì-fang? *or* shř 'dzěm hwéy-shèr? *or* (*Application*) shř 'jř-je-'shéme shwō-de? ‖**That's just the point.** jyé-gu-'yǎr jyèw-shr dzày 'nèy-ge-dì-fang. *or* 'jyèw-shr 'nèm hwéy-'shèr. ‖**The point is this.** 'jyèw-shr jř-je 'jèy-ge shwō-de.

(*Purpose*) 'wěy-de; (*desire*) 'yàw-de. ‖**Our point is to get the result quickly.** wǒm-'wěy-de (*or* wǒm-'yàw-de) jyèw-shr 'gǎn-kwày dzwò-'wán-lew. ‖**What was the point of his doing that?** tā nà shr 'wèy-de shéme?

To point (*indicate direction*) jř; **to point out** jř-chū-lay. ‖**He pointed to where the house is located.** tā (yùng-shěw) 'jř-je nèy-swǒr-'fáng-dz-nar. ‖**The compass needle points (to the) north.** lwó-pán-'jēn jř-je 'jèng-běy. ‖**Point to** (*or* out) **the one you mean.** nǐ-shwō-de shř 'nèy-ge °gěy-wǒ 'jř-chū-lay. *or* °gěy-wǒ 'jř-yi-jř. *or* °'jř-gěy wǒ kàn. °'jř-gěy wǒ kàn-kan. *or* °'jř-gěy wǒ chyáw-chyaw. ‖**Point out the place you told me about.** nǐ-'gàw-sung-wǒ-de-nèy-ge-'dì-fang gěy-wǒ 'jř-chū-lay.

To be pointed (*aim*) chùng(-je), wàng(-je), shyàng (-je), dwèy(-je). ‖**The gun is pointed north.** pàw chùng-je 'běy-byār. *or* pàw shř wàng-'běy (*or* chùng-'běy, *or* shyàng-'běy, *or* dwèy-'běy)-myáw-de. ‖**Don't point the gun at me.** byé ná 'chyāng-kěw 'dwèy-je 'wǒ.

Make a point of yí-'dìng yàw. ‖**He makes a point of dressing properly.** tā yí-'dìng yàw chwān-de jěng-'chí.

Be on the point of 'jèng-dzay yàw, 'jeng yàw, 'gāng yàw. ‖**We were on the point of leaving when some visitors arrived.** wǒm 'jèng-dzày yàw. (*or* wǒm jèng yàw, *or* wǒm 'gāng yàw) dzěw de-shf-hew, 'kè láy-le.

Beside the point ('háw) bú-'chyè-tí, ('háw) bù-tyē-'tí, gēn běn-'tí méy 'gwān-shi. ‖**That's an interesting statement, but it's quite beside the point.** nèy-jywù-'hwà hěn yěw 'yì-sz, kě-shr °('háw) bú-'chyè-tí. *or* °('háw) bù-tyē-'tí. *or* °gēn běn-'tí méy 'gwān-shi.

To the point 'jèng-shr 'dì-fangr, dwèy-'jyèr, chyè-'tí, tyē-'tí. ‖**His comments are always right to the point.** tā-de-píng-lwèn (*or* 'tā-pī-píng-de) 'lǎw-shr °hěn chyè-'tí. *or* °hěn tyē-'tí. *or* °'jèng chyè-'tí. *or* °'jèng-shr 'dì-fangr. *or* °jèng dwèy-'jyèr.

Point of view 'yì-jyàn; **from . . . point of view** (*on . . . basis*) tsúng . . . fāng-myan kàn; tsúng . . . fāng-myan jáy-'shyǎng; *or* (*on . . . opinion*) àn(-je) (*or* jàw) . . . yì-jyàn; àn(-je) (*or* jàw) . . . yì-sz. ‖**His point of view is nearly the same as mine.** 'tā-de-'yì-jyàn gēn 'wǒ-de chà bù-'dwō. ‖**From his point of view the plan is of course impossible.** tsúng 'tā-nèy-fāng-myan kàn (*or* tsúng 'tā-nèy-fāng-myan jáw-'shyǎng), 'jèy-ge-bàn-fa dž-'rán shř 'dzwò-bu-dé-de. ‖**From our point of view, it is the right thing to do.** àn(-je) (*or* jàw) 'wǒm-de-yì-jyan (*or* 'wǒm-de-yì-sz), 'yīng-gāy dzěm bàn.

Point toward (*indicate*). ‖**All the signs pointed toward a hard winter.** 'chyáw jèy-ge-'yì-sz (*or* 'chyáw jèy-ge-'yàngr) jīn-nyán 'dūng-tyān hwèy tǐng 'lěng-de.

POISON. 'dú-yàw; dú *in combinations.* ‖**This medicine is poison if taken internally.** jèy-yàw bú-shr 'chř-de, chř-le yěw-'dú. *or* (*Literary*) 'dú-yàw, bù-kě nèy 'fú. ‖**This is poison.** jèy-shr 'dú-yàw. ‖**Our dog has been poisoned.** wǒm-de-gěw jùng-'dú-le. ‖**The thief poisoned our dog.** dzéy ná 'dú-yàw gěy wǒm-dc-gěw chř-le. *or* (*So that it died*) dzéy bǎ wǒm-de-'gěw dú-sz-le. ‖**The enemy may attack with poison gas.** dí-rén hwò-je yàw yùng 'dú-chì.

‖**He's poison.** tā shř ge-'dǎy-rén. *or* tā shř ge-'shyǎw-rén. *or* tā shř ge-'háy-chywún-jr-'mǎ.

POLICE. 'jǐng-chá, 'jǐng-gwān. **Military police** 'shyàn-bīng. **To police** 'shywún-chá, 'jì-chá. ‖**Call the police!** jyàw (*or* chǐng) °'jǐng-chá (*or* °shywún-'jǐng) láy.

POLICY. (*Custom*). (*Of a government*) 'jèng-tsè; (*otherwise*) 'gwēy-jywu. ‖**Our foreign policy has**

always been consistent. wŏm-de-'wày-jyāw-'jèng-tsè tsúng-láy shr̀ yí-'gwàn-de. ‖It is the policy of our company never to cash checks. wŏm-gūng-sz̄-de-'gwēy-jywu shr̀ bù-shēw 'jr̄-pyàw.

(Contract) 'dān-c ‖I've just taken out another $5,000 (insurance) policy. wŏ 'gāng yèw líng-le yí-ge-'wŭ-chyān-ywán-de-bǎw-'shyǎn-dān-dz̄.

POLITE. Be polite (proper in action) yĕw 'lǐ-màw, jyǎng 'lǐ-màw, jyǎng 'lǐ-jyé, dǔng 'gwēy-jywu; (according to etiquette) jàw 'gwēy-jyw·i, jàw 'lǐ-jyé, jàw-'lǐ; be polite to . . . 'gūng-jing . . . ; dwèy . . . yĕw 'lǐ-màw; gĕy . . . 'myàn-dz̄; be (considered) impolite 'bú-dà-hǎw-'yì-sz̄. ‖They consider that polite. tām jywé-je 'nèm-je shr̀ 'yĕw 'lǐ-màw. or °jyǎng 'lǐ-màw. or °jyǎng 'lǐ-jyé. or °dǔng 'gwēy-jywu. ‖He's very polite. tā 'hĕn °yĕw 'lǐ-màw. or °jyǎng 'lǐ-jyé. or °jyǎng 'lǐ-màw. or °dǔng 'gwēy-jywu. ‖The polite thing to do is to open the packages at once. jàw 'gwēy-jywu shr̀ lì-'kè bǎ-bāwr 'dǎ-kāy. ‖That is a polite expression. jàw 'gwēy-jywu (or jàw 'lǐ-jyé, or jàw-'lǐ) gāy nèm 'shwō. ‖He isn't very polite to her. tā bú-dà 'gūng-jing tā. or tā dwèy-tā méy-yĕw 'lǐ-màw. or tā hĕn bù-gĕy-tā 'myàn-dz̄. ‖I don't think it'd be polite for us to leave so soon. wŏ jywé-de 'jèm kwày jyèw dzĕw °'bú-dà-hǎw-'yì-sz̄. or °tày méy-yĕw 'lǐ-màw. or °tày bù-dǔng 'lǐ-jyé.

POLITICAL. 'jèng-jr̀; in combinations jèng; political circles 'jèng-jyè; political party jèng-'dǎng; political rights 'jèng-chywán or 'jèng-jr̀-'chywán-lì. ‖Every citizen has certain political rights. mĕy-ge-'gūng-mín dēw 'kĕ-yǐ 'shyǎng-shèw rwò-gān-'jǔng-de-°'jèng-jr̀-'chywán-lì. or °'jèng-chywán. ‖He's an authority in political science. tā shr̀ jèng-jr̀-'shywé-'jwān-jyā. or yán-jyèw jèng-jr̀-'shywé-de tā shr̀ ge-'chywán-wèy. or (A student of) tā shr̀ nyàn-'jèng-jr̀-shywé-de. ‖He is an important political figure. tā dzày 'jèng-jyè-li (or 'jèng-jr̀-wŭ-táy-shang) shr̀ yí-ge-hĕn-'jùng-yàw-de-°'rén-wù. or °'jyǎw-sè. or tā shr̀ ge-'jèng-jyè-de-'yàw-rén. or tā shr̀ ge-'jèng-jr̀-wŭ-táy-shang-de-'yàw-rén. ‖What political party do you belong to? nǐ 'shǔ-ywú nĕy-yí-ge-jèng-'dǎng-ne?

POOR. (Not rich) chyúng; poor people (literary) pín-'mín. ‖Many poor people live in this neighborhood. 'hǎw-shyē-'chyúng-rén jù-dzày jèy-'fù-jìn. ‖She doesn't like being poor. tā 'bù-kĕn shèw-'chyúng. ‖We are taking up a collection for the poor. wŏm dzày tì pín-'mín mù-'jywān.

(Not good). (Poor quality) tsz̀; (something lacking) chà-'jìn or 'chà-dyar; bù-'hǎw; and often more specific terms. ‖This soil is poor for roses. jèy-jǔng-'tǔ jùng 'méy-gwèy-hwār 'tày 'tsz̀. or 'tày chà-'jìn. or °'tày 'chà-dyar. or (Not rich enough) °bú-gèw-'féy de. ‖She gave a poor performance. tā-yǎn-de °'chà-'jìn. or °'chà-dyar. or °bú-'dà hǎw. ‖That's a mighty

poor excuse. nèm-je-'jyĕ-shr̀-de 'tày chà-'jìn-le. or nèm-je-'shwō-de °tày méy-'lǐ-le. or °jyàw-'shéy yĕ bù-néng 'shìn. ‖That's a poor example. nèy-ge-'bǐ-de bú-dà 'dwèy. ‖The workmanship is rather poor. 'gūng hĕn 'tsz̀. or (Rough) 'gūng hĕn 'tsāw. or gūng hĕn 'tsū. or (Careless) 'gūng hĕn 'mǎ-hu. ‖That's a pretty poor job. nèy-ge-dzwò-de °chà-'jìn. or °bù-'hǎw. or °méy 'yì-sz̄. ‖His health is poor. tā-'shēn-dz̄ bù-'hǎw. ‖His poor eyesight explains why he retired so young. tā nèm-'nyán-chīng-'chyēngr-de jyèw-twèy-'shyēw-le shr̀ 'yīn-wey tā-'yǎn-jing °bù-'chéng-le. or °yàw 'shyā-le.

‖The poor fellow! 'jēn kĕ 'lyán! ‖The poor fellow is blind. 'jēn kĕ 'lyán; tā 'shyā-le.

POPULAR. (Much liked). For the most part, Chinese uses indirect expressions to say that many people like something or do something, or that something is often done. ‖He is the most popular mayor the city ever had. jèy-dì-fang-de-shr̀-'jǎng-li °tā 'dzwèy jyàw-rén 'shǐ-hwān. or °tā 'dzwèy shèw-rén 'ày dày. or °dà-jyā 'dzwèy shǐ-hwān tā. ‖This book is quite popular. 'jèy-bĕn-'shū hĕn-'dwō-rén °ày 'kàn. or °'shǐ-hwān 'kàn. ‖That song was very popular last year. nèy-ge-gēr 'chywù-nyán °hĕn-'dwō-rén ày 'chàng. or °'cháng tīng-de-'jyàn. or (In vogue) °hĕn shŕ-'shīng. ‖It's a popular custom in China to have flowerpots in the courtyard. dzày 'jūng-gwo rén-jyāer-li cháng dzày ywàn-dz̄-li bǎy hwā-'pér.

(Of style of writing or speaking) sú, 'tūng-sú. ‖This is not a bad book, in spite of its popular style. jèy-bĕr-'shū swéy-rán 'shyĕ-de hĕn 'sú (or 'tūng-sǔ), bú-gwò háy bú-'tswò.

Popular prices 'bù-yā-'jyàr-le (literally, not at increased prices). ‖The movie will be shown at popular prices pretty soon. nèy-ge-dyàn-'yĕngr gwò-bù-jǐ-'tyār jyèw 'bù-yā-'jyàr-le.

(Of the people) 'rén-mín-de. ‖No government can stand long without popular support. 'rén-mín-bù-'yūng-hu-de-jèng-'fǔ 'dāy-bu-'cháng.

PORCH. (On ground level) 'láng-dz̄; (on roof level) lyáng-'táy (a porch for airing) or shày-'táy (a sun porch).

PORT. (Harbor) hǎy-'kĕw or kĕw. ‖When do you expect the ship to get into port? nǐm kàn jèy-ge-'chwán 'shéme-shŕ-hew néng jìn (hǎy)-'kĕw?

(Harbor city) shāng-'gǎng, shāng-'fǔ; (city along the coast) yán-'àn-de-chéng. ‖This town is one of the principal Pacific ports. jèy shr̀ 'tày-píng-yáng-yán-'àn-de-yí-ge-°'dà-chéng. or °dà-shāng-'gǎng. or °dà-shāng-'fǔ.

(Left side of a ship) chwán-'dzwŏ-byar. ‖There's a man overboard on the port side of the ship. chwán-'dzwŏ-byar yĕw-rén dyàw 'shwĕy-li-le.

(Kind of wine) 'húng-pú-táw-jyĕw (red grape wine). ‖Port is my favorite wine. wŏ dzwèy 'shǐ-hwān hē 'húng-pú-táw-jyĕw.

PORTION. *See* PART. ‖You must take some portion of the responsibility. nǐ 'dzǔng děy fù yí-'bù-fen-de-'dzé-rèn.

POSITION. (*Location*) 'dì-fang (*see* PLACE). ‖From this position you can see the whole city. tsúng 'jèy-ge-dì-fang kě-yǐ kàn-jyàn 'chywán-chéng.

(*Posture*) *Chinese speaks of the way* (yàngr) *in which one stands* (jàn), *sits* (dzwò), *or lies* (tǎng), *combining them in various constructions: or uses expressions such as* standing jàn-je, *etc.* ‖If you're not comfortable, change your position. nǐ 'rú-gwo bù-'shū-fu, hwàn ge-'yàngr °jàn-je. *or* °dzwò-je. *or* °tǎng-je. *or* (*Move a bit*) nǐ 'rú-gwo bù-'shū-fu, 'nwó-nwo jyèw 'hǎw-le.

(*Situation*). (*Circumstances*) 'chíng-shíng; (*high social position*) 'dì-wèy. ‖A man in my position has to be careful what he says. dzày-'wǒ-jèy-jǔng-dì-wèy-de-rén shwō-'hwà děy lyéw-'shén. *or* wǒ dzày 'jèy-jǔng-chíng-shíng jř-'shyà shwō-'hwà děy lyéw-'shén. ‖He's in a similar position; he doesn't know what to do either. 'tā-de-chíng-shíng (*or* 'tā-de-dì-wèy) yě shř yí-'yàng-de, méy 'bàn-fa. *But* ‖This places me in a very difficult position. *is expressed as* This makes things hard for me. 'dzèm-je jyàw-wǒ hěn wéy-'nán.

(*Job*) shèr, 'wèy-jr. ‖He has a good position with a wholesale house. tā dzày yì-jyāer-'pī-fā-'dyàn-li dzwò-'shèr, °ney-shèr hěn 'hǎw. *or* °nèy-'wèy-jr hěn 'hǎw. *or* °'dì-wey hěn 'gāw.

(*Attitude*). (*Opinion*) 'yì-jyàn; (*point of view*) 'kàn-fa. ‖What is your position in regard to this new law? nǐ dwèy-ywù jèy-ge-'shīn-fǎ-'gwēy °yěw shéme-'yì-jyàn? *or* °shř 'dzěm-ge 'kàn-fa?

POSSESSION. (*Property*) 'jyā-dàng. ‖He gave away all his possessions before he went in the army. tā méy-rù-'wǔ yǐ-'chyán bǎ 'jyā-dàng dēw sùng-'rén-le.

(*Of a country*) shǔ-'dì. ‖This island is a possession of the United States. jèy-ge-'dǎw shř 'měy-gwo-de-shǔ-'dì.

Have in one's possession yěw. ‖I have in my possession a book with your name on it. 'wǒ-nar yěw běr-'shū, shàng-tew yěw 'nǐ-de-míng-dz.

Take possession of bǎ . . . 'jyē-gwo-lay. ‖The new owner hasn't taken possession of the house. 'shīn-fáng-'jǔ háy méy-bǎ fáng-dz 'jyē-gwo-lay.

POSSIBLE. (*Within power of performance*). *Chinese uses the verbs* néng (*be able to*) ; shíng (*be workable*) ; *and resultative compounds with* -de-. ‖Be here by nine, if possible. rú-gwó 'shíng (*or* yàw-shr bàn-de-'dàw) de-hwà, jyèw dzày 'jyěw-dyǎn-jūng 'dàw-jèr. ‖I'll come early if it's at all possible. 'dàn-fán 'néng dzǎw 'dàw, wǒ yí-'dìng dzǎw 'dàw. ‖Is it possible? *meaning* for something to be done (néng) bàn-de-'dàw-ma? *or*, *meaning* for something to happen, néng yěw 'nèm-yàngr-de-shèr-ma? *But* ‖It's possible but not proba-

ble. 'nèm-yàngr-de-shèr 'yěw dàw-shr 'yěw, bú-gwo 'jèy bú-hwèy 'shř-de.

(*Of something that may happen*). (*Perhaps*) 'yě-shywǔ; (*it may be*) kě-yǐ. ‖We'd better go prepared for a possible shower. dzám 'chywù de-shŕ-hew 'fáng-bèy-je dyǎr-ba, yě-shywǔ hwèy shyà-'ywǔ-ne. ‖It's possible that the letter will come today. nèy-fēng-'shìn yě-shywǔ (*or* kě-yǐ) 'jīn-tyān dàw.

The best (*or* worst, *etc.*) possible dzwèy . . .-de. néng-de. ‖You'll get the best possible treatment. yí-'dìng yùng 'dzwèy-hǎw-de-'fāng-fa gěy-nǐ 'jř.

POST. *Of a fence* 'jù-dz. ‖The fence needs some new posts. jèy-dàw-'wéy-dz děy hwàn jǐ-ge-shīn-'jù-dz-le.

(*To put up*). (*Put on by sticking*) 'tyē-dàw, 'tyē-dzày; (*hang on*) 'gwà-dzày; (*nail on*) 'dìng-dzay. ‖Post it on the bulletin board. bǎ 'jèy-ge tyē-dàw (*or* tyē-dzày, *or* gwà-dzày, *or* dìng-dzày) bù-gàw-'bán-shang-chywu.

(*Assigned place*) gǎng, 'gǎng-wèy, shìn-'dì. ‖Those soldiers were arrested for being away from their posts. nèy-shyē-'bīng yīn-wey 'sž-lí gǎng-'wèy (*or* shìn-'dì) bèy-'bǔ-de. ‖That soldier has to go to his post at the gate. nèy-ge-'bīng děy chywù dàw dà-'mén-nar jàn-'gǎng.

(*Assign to a place*) pày. ‖We posted a squad to guard that bridge. wǒm pày-le yì-'páy-rén chywù 'shěw nèy-ge-'chyáw. ‖Troops were posted to guard the bridge. 'chyáw-shang pày-le 'bīng chywù.

(*Army camp*). (*The place*) 'yíng-pán; (*the forces at the place*) 'yíng-pán-li-de-rén. ‖The whole post has been notified of the change in rules. 'shīn-gǎy-de-'fǎ-gwēy 'yǐ-jīng 'tūng-jř-le 'yíng-pán-li-'swǒ-yěw-de-rén-le.

(*Job*). (*Appointment*) 'chāy-shr; (*position*) 'wèy-jr. ‖He has just been appointed to a new post in the government. tā 'gāng dzày jèng-'fǔ-li dé-le yí-ge-'shīn-°chāy-shr. *or* °wèy-jr.

Post office 'yéw-jèng-'jywú.

POT. hú. ‖She has a pot of tea ready for us. tā gěy-wǒm 'chī-hǎw-le yì-hú-'chá. (*Pan*) gwō. ‖There's a pot of soup on the stove. 'lú-dz-shang yěw yì-gwō-'tāng.

Flowerpot hwā-'pér. ‖There's a row of flowerpots on the porch. lyáng-'táy-shang yěw yí-lyèw-hwā-'pér.

POTATO. tǔ-'dèwr, 'shān-yaw-'dèwr; (*terms not commonly used*) 'shān-yaw-'dàn, fán-'shǔ.

POUND. (*Unit of weight*) bàng. ‖Give me a pound of tobacco, please. gěy-wǒ yí-bàng-yān-'yè-dz.

(*Unit of money*). English pound 'yīng-bàng. ‖He owes me six pounds. tā gāy-wǒ lyèw-'yīng-bàng.

(*To hit*) dǎ, chyāw; (*with considerable force*) dzá. ‖We pounded on the door for five minutes before they heard us. wǒm chyāw-'mén chyāw-le (or, wǒm dǎ-'mén dǎ-le) yěw 'wǔ-fēn-'jūng tsáy yěw-rén 'tīng-jyàn. ‖They pounded the rock into small pieces. tām bǎ 'shŕ-tew dzá-chéng-le swèy-'kwàr.

POUR. (*Cause to flow*) dàw. ‖Please pour me a cup of tea. láw-'jyà gěy-wǒ dàw yì-bēy-'chá (hē). ‖He poured all the water out of the pail. tā bǎ tǔng-li-de-'shwěy dēw 'dàw-chū-chywu-le.

(*Flow*) chūng; (*of people*) jǐ, yùng, chūng. ‖The water was pouring through a little hole in the dike. 'dī-shang yěw ge-shyǎw-'kū-lung, 'shwěy tsúng-nàr 'chūng-chu-lay-le. ‖The crowd poured out of the theater. rén tsúng shì-'ywán-dz-li °jǐ-chū-lay-le. or °yūng-chū-lay-le. or °chūng-chū-lay-le.

(*Rain hard*) 'ywù-shyà-de tǐng 'dà. ‖Don't go out; it's pouring. 'byé chū-chywu-le; 'ywù-shyà-de tǐng 'dà.

(*Figuratively*). ‖It never rains but it pours. 'hwò-bu 'dān shíng.

POWER. (*See also* **FORCE, STRENGTH.**) (*Mechanical energy*) 'lì-lyàng; electric power 'dyàn-lì or dyàn; hydraulic power 'shwěy-lì or shwěy; horsepower 'mǎ-lì. ‖This machine has more power than that one. 'jèy-ge-'jī-chì bǐ nèy-ge 'lì-lyàng dà. ‖This is run by electric power. jèy shŕ yùng-°'dyàn-de. or °'dyàn-lì-de. ‖Water is the cheapest source of power. 'shwěy-lì dzwèy 'pyán-yi. ‖This factory uses a lot of electric power. 'jèy-ge-gūng-'chǎng yùng-'dyàn hěn 'dwō. ‖The power has been turned off. dyàn 'tíng-le. ‖How much power does this machine have? jèy-ge-'jī-chì yěw °'dwō-dà-de-'mǎ-lì? or °'dwō-shǎw-'mǎ-lì?

Powerhouse or power station 'fā-dyàn-'chǎng.

(*Authority*) 'chywán or 'chywán-bìng; (*influence*) shŕ or 'shŕ-li; come into power *may also be expressed as* take office shàng-'táy, *and* be in power *as* be in office dzày 'táy-shang. ‖When he came into power he forgot all his promises. tā 'yí-shàng-'táy (or tā 'yì-dé-le-'shŕ, or tā 'yì-yěw-le-'chywán, or tā 'yì-yěw-le-'chywán-bìng) jyèw bǎ tā-'dā-ying-de 'dēw wàng-le. ‖This party won't be in power much longer. jèy-yì-'dǎng dzày 'táy-shang 'méy jǐ-tyār-le. ‖The one who has the real power here is not an official. jèy-dǐ-fang-'dzwèy-yěw-°'chywán-de (or °'shŕ-li-de) 'bú-shr ge-'gwār. ‖He has the real power. tā yěw 'shŕ-chywán. ‖What power does he have over you? (*Literally*) tā yěw shéme-'chywán-bìng láy 'gwǎn-nǐ? or (*Figuratively, as of blackmail*) nǐ yěw shéme-'bǎ-bìng dzày tā-'shěw-li? ‖The mayor's power should be limited. shŕ-'jǎng-de-'chywán(-bìng) yīng-gāy °yěw 'shyàn-jř. or (*By legislation*) °yěw 'fǎ-lywù láy shyàn-jř. or (*Reduced*) °dzày 'shyǎw-dyar.

Ability *is expressed by the verb* to be able néng, *or by resultative compounds with* -de- *or, in the negative, with* -bu-. ‖I'll certainly do everything in my power. wǒ-'néng-bàn-de-'dàw-de jyèw yí-'dìng bàn. ‖His powers of concentration are amazing. tā 'jēn-shr jyàw-rén chí-'gwày, dzěme néng 'nème jwān-'shīn-ne.

(*Great nation*) 'lyè-chyáng. ‖Our nation is one of the world powers. wǒ-gwó shř shŕ-jyè-'lyè-chyáng-jŕ-'yī.

PRACTICAL. (*Usable*) *Chinese says a thing is fit for use or that it can be done, using expressions such as* kě-yǐ 'yùng, kě-'yùng, shŕ-'yùng, jūng-'yùng, néng 'yùng, néng 'shíng, bàn-de-'dàw, yùng-de-'shàng, *etc.* ‖That was a very practical suggestion you made. 'nǐ-shwō-de-nèy-ge-'fá-dz hěn °kě-yǐ 'yùng. or °jūng-'yùng. or °kě-'yùng. or °shŕ-'yùng. or °'kě-yǐ bàn-de-'dàw. or °'kě-yǐ yùng-de-'shàng. ‖Is his idea practical? 'tā-de-yì-jyan °kě-'yùng-ma? or °néng 'yùng-ma? or °néng 'shíng-ma? ‖Your suggestion is good, but it isn't practical. nǐ-shwō-de-'yì-sz hěn 'hǎw, 'bú-gwò °bù-shŕ-'yùng. or °bù-néng 'yùng. or °bù-néng 'shíng. or °bàn-bú-'dàw. ‖Your suggestion is good, but it isn't practical so far as this matter is concerned. (nǐ-shwō-de-'yì-sz hěn 'hǎw, 'bú-gwò °dzày 'jèy-jyàn-shř-shang bù-néng 'yùng. or °dzày 'jèy-jyàn-shř-shang yùng-bu-'shàng. or °'jèy-jyàn-shř bù-'néng nèm bàn. or °yùng-dzày 'jèy-jyàn-shř-shang bù-'shíng. ‖His ideas are all impractical. 'tā-de-jú-yì 'dēw °bù-néng 'yùng. or °yùng-bú-'shàng. or °bù-shŕ-'yùng. or °bàn-bu-'dàw. or °bù-néng 'shíng. or (*Rude*) tā jìng chū 'sēw-jú-yì. or tā-chū-de-'jú-yì chywán shř shyā-'nàw. or tā jìng 'hú-chu-jú-yì.

(*Sensible, of a person*) dǔng-'shŕ, jŕ-'chywèr. ‖Your friend is a very practical man. nǐ-jèy-ge-'péng-yew hěn °dǔng-'shŕ. or °jŕ-'chywèr.

PRACTICE (PRACTISE). (*Train oneself*) 'lyàn-shi or lyàn; *Chinese uses these verbs to express* practice *as a noun*. ‖I need a little more practice before I can take you on. wǒ děy shyān 'lyàn-lyan (or wǒ děy shyān 'lyàn-shi-lyàn-shi) tsáy néng gēn-nǐ 'sày. ‖He's practising the piano. tā lyàn-'chín-ne. or tā jèng 'lyàn-shi tán gāng-'chín-ne. ‖Chinese calligraphy requires constant practice before you can master the art. shyě 'jūng-gwo-dž děy shyà (or yùng, or fèy) 'gūng-fu yì-'jŕ-bú-'dwàn-de 'lyàn-shi tsáy néng shyě-de 'hǎw-ne. *But* ‖Practice makes perfect. 'shéw-jūng shēng-'chyǎw. or 'shéw néng shēng-'chyǎw.

Be out of practice 'yěw shyē-shŕ méy . . . le, *with a verb in the blank defining the type of action used in doing what one is out of practice in.* ‖I know how to play chess, but I'm a little out of practice. shyà-'chí wǒ 'hwèy dàw-shr 'hwèy, bú-gwò 'yěw shyē-shŕ méy-'shyà-le.

(*Action*) be in practice *or* put into practice (*use*) yùng; (*make real*) shŕ-'shíng; (*apply*) shŕ-'shíng; (*act according to*) jàw-'bàn; (*try out*) shř(-yi-shř); in practice (*in reality*) shŕ-'jì-shang. ‖His suggestion was put into practice immediately. 'tā-shyǎng-de-'bàn-fa lì-'kè jyèw °'yùng-shang-le. or °shŕ-'shíng-le. or °'yùng-le. or °jàw-'bàn-le. ‖A law becomes a useless document unless it is put into practice. 'fǎ-lywù 'gē-nar bú-'yùng (or 'fǎ-lywù yěw-le kě-shr bù-shŕ-'shíng) jyèw chéng-le 'jywù-wén-le. ‖The law sounds harsh,

---

but in practice it is very fair. jèy-ge-'fǎ-lywù 'tǐng-je hěn 'yán, °shŕ-'jì-shang hěn 'gūng-píng. or °'yùng-chi-lay jyèw jŕ-dàw shŕ hěn-'gūng-píng-de-le. or °shŕ-'shíng-chi-lay jyèw jŕ-dàw shŕ hěn-'gūng-píng-de-le. ‖Let's put your plan into practice and see whether it works. 'nǐ-de-fá-dz dzám 'shŕ-yi-shŕ kàn 'shíng-bu-shíng.

(Custom) make a practice of; make it a practice to (always): 'shyàng-láy, lǎw. ‖We make it a practice to get to work on time. .wǒm 'shyàng-láy (or wǒm lǎw) shŕ àn 'shŕ-hew shàng-'bān.

Practise law is expressed as be a lawyer formally 'jèng-shŕ dāng 'lywù-shŕ. ‖How much longer do you have to study before you can practise law? nǐ 'háy děy nyàn 'dwō-shǎw-shŕ-hew tsáy néng 'jèng-shŕ dāng 'lywù-shŕ.

Practise medicine is expressed as be a physician formally 'jèng-shŕ dāng 'yī-sheng, 'jèng-shŕ shíng-'yī. ‖Are you an intern or in practice now? nǐ shŕ shŕ-'shí-ne háy-shr yǐ-jīng 'jèng-shŕ °dāng 'yī-sheng-le? or °'shíng-'yī-le?

(Clientele) ‖The new doctor has only a small practice. nèy-wèy-'shīn-láy-de-'dày-fu, chǐng-tā-jŕ-'bìng-de-rén bù-'dwō.

PRAY (PRAYER). To pray 'chí-dǎw, 'dǎw-gàw; (to ask for) chyéw; prayer 'dǎw-gàw-de; the Lord's Prayer jǔ-dǎw-'wén. ‖They prayed for rain. tām chyéw-'ywǔ. ‖They prayed to heaven for forgiveness. tām dǎw-'gàw chyéw-'ráw. ‖The prayer was rather long. dǎw-'gàw-de yěw yì-dyǎr-'cháng.

PRECIOUS. 'bǎw-bey (also a precious thing). ‖He regards it as being very precious. nèy-ge tā ná-je dàng 'bǎw-bey shŕ-de. or nèy-ge tā 'bǎw-bey-de 'lyǎw-bu-dé.

PREFER. (Followed by a noun) 'shǐ-hwān, jywé-je ... 'hǎw; (followed by a verb) 'shǐ-hwān, 'ywàn-yì, jywé-je háy-shr, shyǎng háy-shr, ày; prefer X to Y 'shǐ-hwān X, 'bù-shǐ-hwān Y. ‖Whom do you prefer (to use)? nǐ shǐ-hwān 'něy-ge? or nǐ ywàn-yì yùng 'něy-ge? ‖Who do you prefer for president? nǐ ywàn-yì 'něy-ge shywǎn-shang dzwò dzǔng-'tǔng? ‖I still prefer (to smoke) this brand of cigarettes. wǒ 'háy-shr ày chēw 'jèy-ge-páy-dz-de-'yān. or wǒ 'háy-shr jywé-je 'jèy-ge-páy-dz-yān 'hǎw. ‖I prefer to wait until the weather is cooler. wǒ shyǎng wǒ háy-shr (or wǒ jywé-je háy-shr, or wǒ ywàn-yì) děng tyān 'lěng-dyǎr dzày 'shwō. ‖I prefer pork to beef. wǒ 'shǐ-hwān chŕ 'jū-rèw, 'bù-'shǐ-hwān chŕ 'nyéw-rèw.

PREPARE. (Get ready) 'ywù-bèy-'hǎw; (make careful preparations) 'jwěn-bèy-'hǎw; (make, as a report) dzwò-'hǎw. ‖They prepared to leave immediately. tām 'ywù-bèy-hǎw-le, 'shwō dzěw jyèw 'dzěw. ‖He prepared a long and detailed report, and then didn't have a chance to present it at the meeting. tā dzwò-'hǎw-le (or tā 'ywù-bèy-'hǎw-le) yí-ge-hěn-'cháng-hěn-'shyàng-shǐ-de-bàw-'gàw, kě-shr 'méy-yěw 'jī-hwey dzày hwèy-'chǎng-shang 'jyǎng-gěy dà-jyā 'tīng.

Be prepared for, be prepared to. (Expect) shyàng-'dàw; (be qualified for) yěw 'dz-gé; (be able) néng. ‖I'm not prepared for this. 'jèy-ge wǒ méy-shyàng-'dàw. or dzwò 'jèy-ge wǒ 'bú-gèw 'dz-gé. ‖I'm not prepared to say how many divisions of troops we have in China. wǒm dzày 'jūng-gwo yěw 'jǐ-shŕ wǒ °'bù-néng 'shwō. or (shouldn't say) °'bù-néng 'shwō-chu-lay. or (don't know) °'bù-jŕ-'dàw. or °'méy-dé-'chá.

(Cook) dzwò. ‖That was a delicious meal you prepared. nǐ-'dzwò-de-nèy-dwèn-fàn 'jēn shyǎng. ‖That's not the way to prepare fish. ywú bú-shr 'nèm-dzwò-de. or ywú bù-néng 'nèm dzwò. or nèy 'bú-shr dzwò-'ywú-de-'fá-dz.

Prepare (someone) for (something). ‖You'd better prepare him for the news. nǐ shyān ná-hwà 'kāy-dǎw tā yí-shyàr, dzày jyàw-tā 'jŕ-dàw.

PRESENCE. (Being present). ‖His presence is not going to make any difference. is expressed as Whether he comes or not won't make any difference. tā 'dàw-bú-'dàw 'méy-yěw 'gwān-shi.

In the presence of dzày ... 'myàn-chyán. ‖This must be signed in the presence of three witnesses. jèy-ge 'fēy-děy dzày 'sān-ge-'jèng-rén-'myàn-chyán chyān-'dž tsáy-'shíng.

Presence of mind. ‖He showed considerable presence of mind. (Was not ruffled) tā 'jēn néng 'jèn-jìng. or tā 'jēn 'chǔ-jŕ-'tày-rán. or tā 'jēn néng nèm 'bù-hwāng bù-'máng-de. or tā 'jēn néng yì-'dyǎr bù-'hwāng-jāng. (Knew what to do) tā jēn 'jī-líng. or tā 'jēn néng 'swéy-jī-yìng-'byàn.

PRESENT. (Gift). See GIFT. ‖This watch was a present from my wife. jèy-'byǎw shŕ wǒ-'tày-tay-°'sùng-wǒ-de. or °gěy-wǒ-de. or °'sùng-gěy-wǒ-de.

(Not absent) expressed by the verbs dàw (arrive) or dzày (be at). ‖There are five hundred people present. 'dàw-le yěw 'wǔ-bǎy-rén. or yěw 'wǔ-bǎy-rén dàw-'chǎng. or yěw 'wǔ-bǎy-rén dzày-jèr. ‖Everybody is present. 'dēw dàw-le. or 'dēw dzày-jèr. ‖How many people are expected to be present? 'dà-gày yěw 'dwō-shǎw-rén 'dàw?

Referring to this time (right now) 'shyàn-dzày or 'jèng-dzày; (this short period of time, temporarily) 'jàn-shŕ, mù-'chyán, 'tsž-kè, 'tsž-shŕ, 'shyàn-shŕ, 'jèy-shŕ-hew, or 'jèy-jèr; (the present as opposed to the past) 'rú-jīn. ‖The present policy is to hire younger men. 'shyàn-dzày-de (or mù-'chyán-de, 'tsž-kè-de, etc.) bàn-fa shŕ gù nyán-'chīng-dyar-de-rén. ‖The future cannot be any worse than the present. 'jyāng-láy bù-'gwǎn dzěm-yàng yě 'bù-néng bǐ °'shyàn-dzày (or °'tsž-kè or °mù-'chyán or others, except 'rú-jīn) háy 'hwày-dàw 'nǎr chywù. ‖That will be enough for the present. 'jàn-shŕ (or mù-'chyán, and others-meaning temporarily) swàn 'gèw-le. ‖He's too busy to see you at present. tā 'jèy-jèr (or tā 'tsž-kè, or tā 'tsž-shŕ, or tā 'shyàn-dzày, etc.) tày 'máng, 'bù-néng 'jyàn-nǐ.

(Give) gěy, 'sùng-gěy, sùng. See GIVE. ‖They presented him with a gold watch. tā-men 'sùng-le (or tā-men 'gěy-le, *or* tā-men 'sùng-gěy-le) tā yí-ge-'jīn-byăw.

(*Offer to view*) 'kàn-shang-chywu yěw. ‖This assignment presents many difficulties. 'jèy-jyàn-shř 'kàn-shang-chywu hwèy yěw bù-'shăw-de-'nán-chù. ‖The soldiers presented a good appearance. bīng-de-'yàng-dz 'kàn-shang-chywu 'hěn yěw 'jīng-shén.

(*Submit*). (*Say*) shwō. ‖This report presents all the facts. jèy-ge-bàw-'gàw-li °yí-'jyàn-yí-jyàn-de-'shř 'děw shwō-'dàw-le. *or* °'jyàn-jyan-shř 'děw shwō-'dàw-le.

(*Exhibit; of a play*) yăn. ‖That play was presented by a group of young actors. nèy-chū-'shì shř yì-chywún-'chīng-nyán-'shì-jywù-jyā-'yăn-de.

(*Introduce*). ‖Allow me to present Mr. McPherson. *is expressed as* I'll introduce you; this is Mr. Mă. wŏ gěy nǐ-men 'jyè-shaw; 'jèy-wèy shř 'mă-shyān-sheng.

PRESIDENT. (*Of a republic*) dzŭng-'tŭng *or* 'dì-dzŭng-tŭng; (*of a republic governed by a committee of which the president is chairman*) jŭ-'shí; (*of a ywàn in the Chinese government*) ywàn-'jăng; (*of a school*) shyàw-'jăng; (*of a business concern*) 'jīng-lǐ *or* 'dzŭng-jīng-lǐ *or* (*especially of a bank*) háng-'jăng; (*of a society or association*) 'hwèy-jăng.

Vice-president 'fù- *plus any of the above terms.*

PRESS. (*Exert physical pressure*). (*Squeeze, crowd*) jǐ; (*apply weight to*) yā; (*with finger or hand*) èn; (*press down, or with a roller*) yà; (*with foot*) tsăy. ‖The crowd pressed through the gates. dà-jyā-'hwŏr 'jǐ-jìn (*or* 'jǐ-chū) dà-'mén °láy-le. *or* °chywù-le. ‖The crowd pressed against the gates. dà-jyā-'hwŏr jř jǐ dà-'mén. ‖The baby pressed his nose against the window to watch his daddy watering the flowers. shyăw-'hár bă 'bí-dz jǐ-dzày 'chwāng-hu-shang kàn tā-'dyē jyāw-'hwār. ‖Keep the two pieces of wood pressed together until the glue dries. bă lyăng-kwày-'mù-tew °jǐ-dzày (*or* °yā-dzày, *or* °yà-dzày) yí-kwàr jř-dàw 'jyāw 'gān-le. ‖Don't press too hard; that's where it hurts. 'byé shř-'jìn èn; 'jyèw-shr nàr 'téng. ‖When you press the piano key, a little hammer inside strikes the string. nǐ yí-èn gāng-chín-de-'jyàn-dz, lǐ-tew yěw ge-shyăw-'chwéy-dzer jyèw chyāw nèy-ge-'shyán. ‖Press the button and see what happens. èn yí-shyà 'lyéngr kàn-kan °dzěm-yàng. *or* °yěw shéme-'dùng-jyengr. ‖Press the lever at this end. èn gàng-'găr-de-'jèy-téwr. ‖Press the handle down. bă-bàr 'èn-shya-chywu. *or* bă-bàr 'yà-shya-chywu. ‖Press the pedal down. bă 'tà-băn 'tsăy-shya-chywu. ‖After the prints are washed, press them flat with this roller. 'shyàng-pyār shǐ-chu-lay yǐ-'hèw, ná jèy-ge-'gwěn-dz yà-'píng-lew.

(*To iron*) tàng *or* tàng-'píng; (*by hand*) ywùn *or* ywùn-'píng; (*with an old-fashioned flatiron*) làw *or* làw-'píng. ‖Have this suit pressed for me. jèy-tàw-'yī-shang gěy-wŏ °'tàng-yi-tang. *or* °tàng-'píng-le. *or*

°'ywùn-yi-ywun. *or* °ywùn-'píng-le. *or* °'làw-yi-law. *or* °làw-'píng-le. ‖Where can I get my suit pressed? yàw tàng 'yī-shang, dàw 'shéme-dì-fang-chywu? *or* dzày-'năr kě-yi tàng 'yī-fu? *or* năr yěw tàng-'yī-fu-de?

(*To force*) bī. ‖If you press him a little further he'll talk. nǐ yàw-shr 'bī-de tā 'dzày °lì-hay-dyar (*or* °jǐn-dyar), tā jyèw 'shwō-le. ‖They're pressing him for a definite answer. tām 'bī-je-tā gěy ge-'jwěn-hwàr. ‖Don't press people too hard. bú-yàw bī-rén bī-de tày °'lì-hay-le. *or* °'jǐn-le. *or* bù-néng 'bī-rén tày 'shèn. *or* 'bú-yàw 'tày găn-lu rén.

(*Push or urge; an investigation*) 'jwēy-jyēw *or* 'jwēy-wèn. ‖I wouldn't press the matter any further if I were you. 'wŏ yàw shř nǐ de-hwà, jèy-jyàn-shèr wŏ 'bú-dzày °'jwēy-jyēw-le. *or* °'jwēy-wèn-le. ‖The governor is pressing this matter too far. 'jèy-shèr shěng-jăng 'jwēy-jyēw-de tày °'yán-le. *or* °'jǐn-le.

(*Insist on*) 'yì-jř-bú-'dwàn-de shwō. ‖He pressed the point until everyone got the idea. tā bă 'nèy-jyàn-shř 'yì-jř-bú-'dwàn-de shwō, 'jř dàw 'dà-jyā 'děw míng-bay-le.

(*Machine for pressing*) 'yà-já-jī' (*for punching, stamping, or applying steady pressure*); oil press já-'yéw-jī; drill press 'dă-yăn-jī; hydraulic press 'shwěy-yā-jī (*for applying steady pressure only*).

(*Machine for printing*) 'yìn-dz-jī, 'yìn-shwā-'jī-chì. ‖Only trained men can operate this printing press. jèy-jyà-'yìn-dz-jī (*or* jèy-jyà-'yìn-shwā-'jī-chì) fēy-děy 'shèw-gwo 'shywùn-lyàn-de-rén tsáy néng 'yùng.

Go to press. ‖This edition is ready to go to press. jèy-yì-'băn kě-yi °'fù-'yìn-le. *or* °ná-chywu 'yìn-le.

(*Journalists*) 'shīn-wén-jì-'jě. ‖Will the press be admitted to the conference? hwèy-'yì shywŭ 'shīn-wén-jì-'jě jìn-chywu-ma?

(*Newspaper criticisms*) bàw-shang-de-'pī-píng. ‖This play was well received by the press. nèy-chū-'shì bàw-shang-de-'pī-píng 'děw shwō 'hăw.

Hard pressed. ‖He was hard pressed for an answer. tā-jí-de méy-yěw hwà kě-yi 'hwéy-dá. *or* tā jyàw rén-'bī-de 'shyăng-bu-chū făr-lay 'hwéy-dá-le.

Pressing. (*Important*) yàw-'jǐn; (*urgent*) jí. ‖I have a pressing engagement elsewhere. wŏ dzài 'byé-chùr yěw °ge-yàw-'jǐn-de-'ywē-hwèr. *or* °jyàn-'jí-shèr.

PRETTY. (*Pleasing to the eye*) hăw 'kàn. ‖She is a very pretty girl. tā-jăng-de hěn hăw 'kàn.

(*Pleasing to the ear*) hăw 'tīng. ‖That's a pretty tune. nèy-ge-'dyàwr tīng hăw 'tīng.

(*Rather*) hěn, tīng. ‖I've been pretty busy since I saw you last. wŏ 'dz-tsúng 'shàng-tsz jyàn-nǐ yǐ-'hèw, yì-'jř hěn (*or* tīng) 'máng láy-je.

PREVENT. Prevent *someone from doing something* jyàw...bū- (*or* ràng...bū-, *or* bú-jyàw..., *or* bú-ràng...*) plus a verb indicating what is to be prevented; or bă... plus a verb indicating the opposite of what is to be prevented; or expressed as .. ., therefore not ..., using *'swŏ-yǐ *or* 'yīn-tsz *for* therefore. ‖Can you

find a way to prevent him from leaving? nǐ néng shyǎng ge-'fár °jyàw-tā 'bù-dzěw-ma? or °ràng-tā 'byé dzěw-ma? or °bú-jyàw-tā 'dzěw-ma? or °bú-ràng-tā 'dzěw-ma? or °bǎ-tā 'lán-ju-ma? or °bǎ-tā 'lyéw-shya-ma? ‖The bad weather prevented the ship from arriving on time. 'tyān-chì 'bù-hǎw, °bǎ-chwán-dàw-'àn-de-jūng-'dyǎr gěy 'dān-wù-le. or °'swǒ-yǐ chwán dàw-de 'wǎn-le. or °'swǒ-yǐ chwán wù-le 'dyǎn-le. or °'swǒ-yǐ chwán 'méy-néng àn 'shŕ-hew 'dàw. ‖We should try to prevent forest fires. wǒm 'yīng-dāng 'shyǎng-fár 'bú-jyàw (or 'bú-ràng) shù-'lín-dz jáw-'hwǒ. ‖Your timely wink prevented him from spilling the beans. nǐ jǐ-'yǎr jǐ-de 'jèng-shr 'shŕ-hew, °'méy-jyàw-tā (or 'méy-ràng-tā) (bǎ nèy-ge) gěy 'shwō-chu-chywu. or 'bǎ-tā-'gāng-yàw-shwō-de-nèy-ge gěy 'dǎng-hwéy-chywu-le. or °jyàw-tā (or ràng-tā) méy-bǎ nèy-ge gěy 'shwō-chu-chywu. or °'swǒ-yǐ (or yīn-tsž) tā méy-bǎ nèy-ge gěy 'shwō-chu-chywu. or °'bù-ran tā jyèw (bǎ nèy-ge) 'shwō-chu-lay-le. or *expressed as* **Good night! He was just about to spill the beans.** °'hǎw, tā 'gāng yàw (bǎ nèy-ge) 'shwō-chu-chywu.

PRICE. jyàr or 'jyà-chyán; (*price asked*) yàw-de-'chyán; **wholesale price** pī-'fā-de-jyàr or pī-'fā-de-'jyà-chyán; **retail price** 'líng-mày-de-jyàr or 'líng-mày-de-jyà-chyán; **sale price** 'mày-jyàr or 'mày-de-jyà-chyán; **fixed prices** (*no bargaining*) 'dìng-jyàr or yí-'dìng-de-jyà-chyán; **prices** (*of all things*) 'wù-jyà. ‖I like the rooms, but the price is too high. 'wū-dz dēw tǐng-'hǎw-de jyèw-shr °'jyàr tày 'gāw-dyar. or °'jyà-chyán tày 'gāw-dyar. or °yàw-de-'chyán tày 'dwō-le. ‖This price is less than the cost. 'mày-jyàr bǐ 'běn-chyán háy 'shǎw-ne. or jàw 'jèy-ge-jyàr (or jàw 'jèy-ge-jyà-chyán) láy mày háy 'bú-gèw 'běn-chyán-ne. ‖Prices are higher this year. 'jīn-nyan-de-'wù-jyà 'gāw-le-dyar.

PRIDE. (*See* **PROUD.**) (*Gratification*) *expressed by the verb* dé-'yì *and other expressions.* ‖He takes great pride in his work. tā-dzwò-de-dūng-shi tā-'dž-jǐ hěn dé-'yì. ‖The new park is the pride of the city. yì-'chéng-de-rén 'dēw °jywé-je nèy-shīn-'kǎy-de-gūng-'ywán hěn 'hǎw. or °kàn-je nèy-shīn-'kǎy-de-gūng-'ywán hěn dé-'yì-de.

(*Self-righteousness*) *expressed with* **to be proud** àw. ‖His pride won't let him admit he's wrong. tā-'rén (or tā-'shìng-dz) hěn 'àw, 'bù-kěn rèn-'tswòr. or tā 'bù-kěn rèn-'tswèr, yīn-wèy tā-'shìng-dz hěn 'àw.

(*Haughtiness*). ‖Pride goeth before a fall, but a contrite heart the Lord will not despise. (*A corresponding literary proverb*) 'mǎn jāw 'swèn; 'chyān shèw-'yì.

To pride oneself. ‖He prides himself on his good judgment. tā jywé-je tā-'dž-jǐ hěn yěw 'yǎn-gwāng. or tā hěn dž-'fù néng 'pàn-dwàn 'shŕ-fēy.

PRINCIPAL. (*Most important*) 'dzwèy-yàw-'jǐn-de, jǔ-'yàw-de. ‖Cotton is the principal crop in this province. 'myán-hwa shŕ 'běn-shěng °'dzwèy-yàw-'jǐn-de-'núng-chǎn. or °jǔ-'yàw-de-'núng-chǎn. ‖This is his principal argument against your plan. tā 'fǎn-dwèy 'nǐ-de-nèy-ge-'bàn-fa, shwō-le jǐ-tyáw-'lǐ-yéw; 'jèy-shŕ 'dzwèy-yàw-'jǐn-de-yì-tyáw.

(*Head of a school*) 'shyàw-jǎng. ‖The principal called a teachers' meeting. 'shyàw-jǎng 'jāw-jí 'jyàw-ywán kāy-'hwèy.

(*Participant in legal case*) 'dāng-shŕ-rén. ‖The principals in the case were represented by their lawyer. jèy-ge-'àn-dz-li-de-'dāng-shŕ-rén yéw tā-men-de-'lywù-shŕ 'dày-byǎw chū-'tíng.

(*Sum of money*) 'běn-chyán, běr. ‖Principal: $1,000,000. 'běn-chyán: yì-'bǎy-wàn. ‖We'll need a principal of over $100,000. 'běn-chyán děy yàw 'shŕ-wán-ywán yì-'shàng. ‖Don't draw on your principal. byé dùng 'běn-chyán. or byé dùng-'běr.

PRINT. (*By a printing press*) yìn. **Be printed** or **come out in print.** (*Published*) 'yìn-chu-lay, yìn-'hǎw, yìn-'dé, chū-'bǎn; (*recorded*) dēng. ‖How much will it cost to print this? jèy-ge děy 'dwō-shǎw-chyán láy 'yìn? or 'yìn jèy-ge děy 'dwō-shǎw-chyán? ‖Who printed this newspaper? jèy-'bàw shŕ 'shwéy-yìn-de? ‖A printed notice will be sent out tomorrow. yěw ge-'yìn-chu-láy-de-'tūng-gàw (or yěw ge-'yìn-hǎw-le-de-'tūng-gàw) 'míng-tyan fā-chu-chywu. ‖The cloth is printed with a flower pattern. 'bù-shang yìn-je 'hwār. ‖The president's speech has just come out in print. dà-dzǔng-'tǔng-de-yǎn-'jyǎng 'gāng °'yìn-chu-lay. or °chū-'bǎn. or °'yìn-'hǎw-le. or °'yìn-'dé-le. ‖This letter was printed in yesterday's paper. jèy-fēng-'shìn dēng-dzày 'dzwó-tyān-de-bàw-'jŕ-shang.

Printing shop. 'yìn-shwā-'swǒ.

(*Type*) dzèr (*characters*). ‖The print in this book is too small. jèy-běr-'shū-li-de-'dzèr tày 'shyǎw.

Printed cloth 'yìn-hwār-'bù; *but* **a print dress** 'hwār-yī-fu or 'yìn-hwār-bù-de-'yī-shang. ‖We're selling lots of prints this year. 'jīn-nyán wǒm mày-le hěn-'dwō-de-'yìn-hwār-bù. ‖She wore a pretty print dress. tā chwān-le yí-jyàn-'hěn-hǎw-kàn-de-°'hwār-yī-fu. or °'yìn-hwār-bù-de-'yī-shang.

Printed picture yìn-de-'hwàr. ‖The museum of fine arts has a collection of famous prints and paintings. 'měy-shù-'gwǎn-li yěw hěn-yěw-'míng-de-'hwàr, yěw 'yìn-de, yěw 'jēn-de. ‖He collects old prints of sailing ships. tā 'sēw-jí 'jyèw-bǎn-yìn-de-fān-chwán-'hwàr.

(*Photographic positive*) 'shyàng-pyàn; **to print** shǐ (*wash*); yìn. ‖How many prints do you want from this negative? 'jèy-jāng-'dǐ-pyàn nǐ yàw shǐ (or yìn) 'dwō-shǎw-jāng? ‖I'm going to have a few prints made. wǒ yàw chywù yìn (or shǐ) jǐ-jāng-'shyàng-pyàr-chywu.

(*Write like type*) yùng 'jèng-kǎy shyě (*write in formal script*). ‖Please print your name instead of writing it. chǐng bǎ 'míng-dz yùng 'jèng-kǎy shyě-chū-lay

Be out of print; be in print. ‖Is the book still in print? *is expressed as* Do the plates still exist? 'jèy-shū 'bǎn háy 'yěw-ma? ‖This book is still in print. 'jèy-shū 'méy-jywé-'bǎn. ‖That book is hard to get because it's out of print. 'nèy-běr-shū yǐ-jīng ʃywé-'bǎn-le swǒ-yǐ 'hěn nán-ʾmǎy-jaw.

PRISON. (*Penitentiary*) 'jyān-ywù; jyān; láw; ywù; jyān-láw-'ywù. ‖He was sent from the local jail to the state prison. tām bǎ-tā tsúng 'dì-fang-'kān-shěw-swǒ jyě-dàw 'shěng-'jyān-ywù chywù-le. ‖Put him in prison. bǎ-tā gwān-dzày (*or* bǎ-tā sùng-dàw) °'jyān-li-chywu-ba. *or* °'láw-li-chywu-ba. *or* °'jyān-láw-'ywù-li-chywu-ba. *or* °'ywù-li-chywu-ba.

PRISONER. (*Prison inmate*) 'fàn-rén *or* 'chyéw-fàn. ‖A prisoner has just escaped and is headed this way. yí-ge-'fàn-rén (*or* yí-ge-'chyèw-fán) 'gāng °ywè-le-'ywù (*or* °tsúng jyān-'ywù-li 'pàw-chu-lay-le), jèng wàng 'jèy-byàr dzěw-je.

(*Captive*) 'fú-lwǒ. ‖How many prisoners were taken during the last battle? 'shàng-tsż dzwò-'jàn de-shŕ-hew, 'fú-lwǒ yěw 'dwō-shaw?

Take prisoner fú-'lwǒ, 'dǎy-ju. ‖They took him prisoner. tām bǎ-tā fú-'lwǒ-le. *or* tām bǎ-tā 'dǎy-ju-le.

PRIVATE. (*Not public; personal*) 'dž-jǐ-de, 'gè-rén-de, 'dž _-de *with a verb:* sž *in some combinations;* (*not in front of people*) bù-'dāng-je-rén. ‖This is a private car. jèy shŕ 'dž-yùng-de-'chē. *or* jèy shŕ 'dž-jǐ-yùng-de-'chē. ‖This is their private house. jèy shŕ tām-'dž-jǐ-de-fáng-dz. *or* jèy shŕ tām-de-'sž-rén-jù-'jáy. ‖My private opinion is that the man is a thief. wǒ-'gè-rén-de-'yì-jyàn (*or* wǒ-'dž-jǐ-de-'yì-jyàn) 'yí-wey 'nèy-ge-rén shŕ ge-'dzéy. *or expressed as* I believe in my mind that the man is a thief. wǒ 'shīn-li jywé-je tā shŕ ge-'dzéy. ‖I'd like to discuss this matter with you in private. wǒ shyǎng 'sž-shyà-li gēn-nǐ 'tán-yi-tán jèy-jyàn-shŕ. *or* wǒ shyǎng dzám 'dž-jǐ 'tán-yi-tán jèy-jyàn-shŕ.

(*Army rank*) *no exact equivalent, but* shyǎw-'bīng *or simply* bīng *may be used.* ‖He was a private in the last war. 'shàng-tsż-'shŕ-jyè-dà-'jàn de-shŕ-hew tā °shŕ ge-shyǎw-'bīng. *or* °-dāng-de shŕ 'bīng.

PRIZE. (*Award*) jyǎng; (*money*) 'jyǎng-jīn. ‖There will be a fifty-dollar prize for the writer of the best short story. 'shéy shyě-de 'dwǎn-pyān-'shyǎw-shwōr 'dzwèy hǎw jyèw dé 'wǔ-shr-'ywán-°'jyǎng-jīn. *or* °de-'jyǎng. ‖The prize(-winning) story was written by a friend of mine. dé-'jyǎng-de-nèy-ge-shyǎw-'shwōr shŕ wǒ-de-yí-ge-'péng-yew-shyě-de.

(*Best*) 'dzwèy-hǎw-de. ‖That's the prize movie of the year, don't you think? nǐ jywé-de-bù-jywé-de 'nèy-ge-dyàn-'yěngr shŕ 'jīn-nyán-li-'dzwèy-hǎw-de?

Prized possession 'bǎw-bey. ‖This is one of my most prized possessions. *or* I prize this very highly. jèy shŕ wǒ-de-yí-ge-'bǎw-bey.

PROBABLE (PROBABLY). (*Probably, in all probability*) 'dà-gày *or* 'dwō-bàr; (*not for certain*) shwō-bu-'dìng *or* jŕ-bu-'dìng. ‖It's probable that there will be a bad storm tonight. jyěr 'wǎn-shang 'dwō-bar-shr (*or* jyēr 'wǎn-shang 'dà-gày-shr, *or* jyěr 'wǎn-shang shwō-bu-'dìng, *or* jyēr 'wǎn-shang jŕ-bu-'dìng) yàw 'gwā-dà-'fēng-'shyà-dà-'ywù-de. ‖It's possible but not probable that you'll see him on the train. nǐ 'yě-shywǔ néng dzày 'chē-shang 'pèng-jyan tā, bú-gwò 'dwō-bar (*or* 'dà-gày) shŕ 'pèng-bu-jyàn-de.

PROBLEM. (*In mathematics*) 'swàn-tí; (*question; may refer to a problem in mathematics*) 'wèn-tí; (*difficulty*) 'nán-chù, nán-'bàn-de-dì-fang, nán-'bàn-de-shŕ, wéy-'nán-de-shŕ; (*situation; which may be hard to solve,* nán 'bàn, *or easy to solve,* 'rúng-yì 'bàn, *etc.*) shèr. ‖It's a difficult problem to solve. jèy-ge-'swàn-tí (*or* jèy-ge-'wèn-tí) 'hěn nán 'jyě-jywé. ‖There's no problem at all. yì-'dyǎr-'nán-chù (*or* yì-'dyǎr-nán-'bàn-de-dì-fang) yě méy-'yěw. ‖I have a problem here. 'wǒ-jèr yěw °ge-'wèn-tí. *or* °ge-'nán-chù. *or* °jyàn-nán-'bàn-de-shŕ. *or* °jyàn-shèr jyàw-wǒ wéy-'nán. ‖I have a way to solve your problem. 'nǐ-de-'wèn-tí (*or* 'nǐ-de-'swàn-tí) 'wǒ yěw ge-'fāng-fa 'jyě-jywé. *or* 'nǐ-nèy-ge-'nán-chù (*or* 'nǐ-nèy-jyàn-wéy-'nán-de-'shŕ, *or* 'nǐ-nèy-jyàn-nán-'bàn-de-'shŕ) 'wǒ yěw ge-°'bàn-fa. *or* °'fá-dz bàn. ‖That problem is easy to solve; why don't you do it like this? 'nèy-shèr 'hǎw bàn (*or* 'nèy-shèr 'rúng-yì bàn, *or* 'nèy-shèr 'bù-nán, *or* 'nèy-shèr 'bù-nán bàn); nǐ 'dzěm bú-'dzěm-je-ne? ‖He's a problem child. jèy-háy-dz °hěn nán 'bàn (*or* 'gwǎn). *or* °'méy-fár 'bàn (*or* 'gwǎn). *or* °jyàw-rén méy 'bàn-fa.

PROCEED. (*Continue*) 'jyē-je (*general term*); 'jì-shywù (*general and also military*); 'jàw-cháng (*as usual*); *each of these must be followed by a verb describing the action continued.* ‖After the interruption they proceeded with their work. 'dān-wu-le yì-'hèw tām 'jyē-je (*or* 'jì-shywù) dzwò-shya-chywu-le. ‖Despite the bombing, he proceeded with his bath. jà-'dàn yì-byǎr 'làw-je, tā háy-shr 'jyē-je (*or* 'jì-shywù, *or* 'jàw-cháng) shǐ tā-de-'dzǎw. ‖Our orders are to proceed to the bridge (*when already advancing*). 'mìng-lìng-shang shwō jyàw-dzám 'jì-shywù 'chyán-jìn dàw 'chyáw-nar.

(*Start out*).. (*Of motion*) chywù (*go*); (*of other action*) ... chǐ-láy. ‖Despite the bombing, he proceeded to take a bath as usual. jà-'dàn yì-byǎr 'làw-je, tā 'jàw-cháng shǐ-chǐ 'dzǎw-lay-le. ‖Our orders are to proceed to the bridge (*from a stationary position*). 'mìng-lìng-shang shwō jyàw-dzám dàw 'chyáw-nar chywù.

PROCEEDS. 'jìn-kwǎn. ‖He sold his house and put the proceeds in government bonds. tā bǎ fáng-dz 'mày-le, bǎ 'swǒ-yěw-de-'jìn-kwǎn 'dēw mǎy-le gūng-jày-'pyàw-le.

PRODUCE. (*Manufacture*) 'dzwò-chu, 'dzàw-chu, chū. ‖**How many planes does that factory produce per month?** 'nèy-ge-gūng-'chǎng 'yí-ge-ywè °néng 'dzàw-chu(-lay) 'dwō-shǎw-jyà-fēy-'jī? *or* °néng 'dzwò-chu (-lay) 'dwō-shǎw-jyà-fēy-'jī? *or* °chū 'dwō-shǎw-jyà-fēy-'ji?

(*Grow*). (*Of crops*) jǎng; ⸀(*of crops and other commodities*) chū; *or expressed by the noun* 'shēw-cheng (*crop produced*). ‖**This soil ought to have produced better grapes than these.** 'jèy-jǔng-tǔ-li 'yīng-gāy jǎng-de (*or* chū-de) 'pú-taw bǐ jèy-ge 'hǎw-wa. ‖**The farm ought to produce a good crop this year.** 'jīn-nyán 'dì-li °jwāng-jya 'yīng-gāy jǎng-de 'hǎw. *or* °'shēw-cheng 'yīng-gāy bú-'hwày. ‖**This place produces raw silk.** 'jèy-ge-dì-fang chū 'shēng-sz̄.

(*Result in*). (*Give birth to, literally or figuratively*) shēng; dé (*said of* 'jyē-gwǒ, *results*); jyàw *plus a noun and verb; or expressed by the noun* 'jyē-gwǒ (*result produced*). ‖**All these are the effects produced by one cause.** jèy-shyē 'dēw shr̄ 'yí-ge-ywán-yīn 'shēng-chu-lay-de-'jyē-gwǒ. ‖**Well, it produced the right effect.** 'bù-gwǎn dzěm-je, (dé-de-) 'jyē-gwǒ bú-'tswò. ‖**The purpose of the medicine is to produce a high fever.** 'jèy-ge-yàw shr̄ jyàw-rén-fā-'dà-shāw-de.

(*Present; as facts, evidence*) 'ná-chu, 'shwō-chu. ‖**You have to produce the facts to prove your argument.** nǐ-'nèm-ge-shwō-far děy °ná-chu 'jèng-jywu-lay tsáy 'shíng. *or* °yěw 'jèng-jywu ná-de-chū-'láy tsáy 'shíng.

(*Of a play*) 'páy-yǎn. ‖**How much will it cost to produce the play?** 'páy-yǎn jèy-ge-'shì děy 'dwō-shǎw-'běn-chyán?

(*Farm products*) 'cʻ ū-chǎn, 'núng-pǐn, 'núng-chǎn, núng-chǎn-'pǐn. ‖**Th e is no market for our produce.** wǒm-de-'chū-chǎn *or* wǒm-de-'núng-pǐn, *or* wǒm-de-'núng-chǎn) méy shyāw-lù.

ROFIT. (*Financial*) lì, 'lì-chyán; (*net profit*) 'chwén-lì; **to profit** jwàn. ‖**The profits from the business will be divided equally.** dé-le 'lì (*or* dé-le 'lì-chyán, *or* 'lì-chyán, *or* yěw-'lì, *or* 'jwàn-lay-de-chyán) 'dà-jyā-hwǒr píng fēn. ‖**How much profit did you make on that sale?** nèy-pyàwr-'mǎy-may °jwàn-le 'dwō-shǎw (-chyán)? *or* °'chwén-lì 'dwō-shǎw(-chyán)? ‖**I sold my car at a profit.** wǒ mày-'chē jwàn-le dyǎr-'chyán. ‖**I sold my car at a $50 profit.** wǒ mày-'chē jwàn-le 'wǔ-shr-kwày-chyán.

To profit (*gain advantage*) shàng-'swàn. ‖**The store has profited** (*financially or otherwise*) **from its use of advertising.** nèy-ge-'pù-dz dēng gwǎng-'gàw hěn shàng-'swàn.

(*Personal benefit*) 'hǎw-chù, 'jyàw-shywun; **to profit** ywú ... yěw 'hǎw-chù, dé ge-'jyàw-shywun. ‖**I hope he profits by this experience.** pàn-wang tā °'jèy-tsz̀ dé ge-'jyàw-shywun. *or* °jīng-gwo 'dzěm-yí-tsz̀ ywú-tā yěw 'hǎw-chù.

PROGRAM. (*Schedule*) jr̄-shywù-'dār, jř-shywù-'dār, jr̄-shywù-'dān-dz, jř-shywù-'dān-dz. ‖**The programs sell for a dime.** jř-shywù-'dār (*etc.*) yì-'máw-chyán yí-'fèr. ‖**There are eight numbers on the program.** jr̄-shywù-'dān-dz-shang (*etc.*) °shwō yí-'gùng yěw 'bā-shyàng. *or* °-de-'jyé-mù yěw bā-'shyàng. *or* °shwō yěw bā-ge-'jyé-mù.

Number on a program shyàng (*a measure meaning* item); 'jyé-mù (*a noun meaning* item in the order of events; *may have* shyàng *as its measure*); *see last sentence above.* ‖**What's the next number on the program?** 'shyà-yí-shyàng °-'jyé-mù shr̄ 'shéme? *or* °yǎn-'shéme?

(*Period of entertainment or performances*) *expressed indirectly by verbs such as* tīng (*hear*), kàn (*see*), *or any one of several specific verbs describing the type of performance, or not expressed at all; however, a radio program, as one item in a continuous series of entertainments, may be called* 'jyé-mù. ‖**Are there any good programs on now?** 'shyàn-dzày yěw shéme-°'hǎw-jyé-mù? *or* °kě-'tīng-de? *or* (*for television*) °kě-'kàn-de? ‖**I enjoyed the program very much.** wǒ-tīng-de (*or* wǒ-kàn-de) hěn gāw-'shìng. ‖**It will probably be a very good program.** nèy-ge 'dà-gày bú-'hwày. ‖**I thought he was going to be** (*perform*) **on the program.** wǒ 'yǐ-wey yěw 'tā °yǎn-ne. *or* (*sing*) °chàng-ne. *or* (*play the piano*) °tán 'gāng-chín-ne. *or* (*dance*) °tyàw-'wǔ-ne. *or* (*speak*) °shwō-'hwà-ne. *or* (*juggle*) °shwǎ-'chyéwr-ne. (*etc., etc.*). *or* (*Without specifying*) wǒ 'yǐ-wey 'nèy-lì-tew 'yěw 'tā-ne. ‖**What's** (**on**) **the program for tonight?** jyēr 'wǎn-shang dēw °yěw-'shéme? *or* *expressed as* What's going to be done? °gàn-'shéme?

(*A plan*) 'bù-dzèw-byǎw (*chart of steps*), jì-hwà-'byǎw. ‖**He made out a program for his work.** tā dìng-chu-lay yí-ge-'gūng-dzwò-'bù-dzèw-byǎw.

PROGRESS. (*To advance*) jìn-'bù; (*an advance*) *expressed in terms of the verb.* ‖**We've progressed since those days.** wǒm bǐ 'nèy-shyē-r̀-dz jìn-'bù 'dwō-le. ‖**Our country has made a lot of progress lately.** wǒ-'gwó 'jìn-láy hěn yěw jìn-'bù.

(*To continue some action, or continuation of some action*) *expressed by any verb of action, commonly* dzwò, *or with* -je *added to the verb, or with more* dwō. ‖**How are things progressing?** 'shèr 'dzwò-de dzěme-'yàng-le? ‖**Are you making any progress with your report?** nǐ-bàw-'gàw °dzwò-de dzěme-'yàng-le? *or* °'yěw dwō 'shyě-le yì-dyǎr-ma? ‖**Our work is still in progress, but it will soon be done.** wǒm-de-'shèr 'háy dzày-nàr 'dzwò-ne, bú-gwo 'kwày wán-le. *or* wǒm-de-'shèr háy 'jèng-dzày 'dzwò-je-ne, bú-gwo 'kwày wán-le.

PROMISE. (*A pledge, or to pledge*) *expressed with the verbs* 'dā-ying, shwō. **Break a promise** *expressions using these terms, and also* shr̄-'ywē (*of a two-*

sided agreement) ; shř-'shìn (break faith). ‖We promised the child a ride in the car. wǒm 'dā-ying-le (or wǒm-'shwō-de shř) 'dày háy-dz chywù dzwò-'chē. ‖He promised to meet me here. tā 'dā-ying-le (or tā-'shwō-de shř) dzày-'jèr jyàn-wǒ. ‖I promised him. wǒ 'dā-ying-ta-le. ‖You've broken your promise. nǐ-'shwō-de (shř-shéme láy-je), nǐ méy bàn-'dàw. or nǐ-'dā-ying-de (shř-shéme láy-je) nǐ méy bàn-'dàw. or nǐ shř-'ywē-le. or nǐ shř-'shìn-le. or (Only a mild rebuke) nǐ-shwō-de (or nǐ-dā-ying-de) shř-'shéme láy-je, á? ‖A promise is a promise. shwō-le (or 'dā-ying-le) °jyèw děy 'swàn. or °bú-'swàn bù-'shíng. or jì 'dā-ying-le jyèw 'bù-néng shř-'shìn. or 'shwō-le-hwà bú-dàng-'hwà bù-'shíng.

(Indication of later performance). ‖The new planes show great promise. shīn-'chū-de-fēy-jī 'chyˊn-tú bù-kě 'shyàn-lyàng.

PROMPT. (Quick) kẁày; (quickly, immediately) lì-'shř or lì-'kè or 'dāng-shř or 'děng-shř; (on time) 'àn-je shř-hew; (at the appointed time) 'shwō shéme-shř-hew . . . 'jyèw . . . or 'shwō shéme-shř-hew . . . 'jwěn . . . (with the same verb in each blank). ‖She sent a prompt reply to my letter. wǒ-de-'shìn tā lì-'shř (or lì-'kè, or 'dāng-shř, or 'děng-shř) jyèw 'hwéy-le. or wǒ-de-'shìn tā hwéy-de hěn 'kwày. ‖He's prompt in paying his debts. 'tā-jyè-de-chyán 'shwō shéme-shř-hew hwán 'jyèw (or 'jwěn) hwán. or tā hwán-'jàng hwán-de hěn 'kwày.

(Remind) 'tí-shǐng; (tell) 'gàw-su. ‖Don't prompt him. byé 'tí-shǐng tā. or byé 'gàw-su tā.

(Cause). ‖What prompted you to say that? nǐ wèy-'shéme (or nǐ 'dzěm jyèw) tí-chǐ 'nèy-ge láy-le?

PRONOUNCE. (Enunciate). (Say) shwō; (read) nyàn. ‖How do you pronounce that word? nèy-ge-dzèr nǐ 'dzěm °shwō? or °nyàn?

(Declare). (Of a judge) pàn; (say) shwō. ‖The judge pronounced him guilty of murder. 'fǎ-gwān 'pàn-tā shā-'rén-'dzwèy. ‖When he was brought to the hospital, the doctor pronounced him dead. bǎ-tā táy-dàw yī-'ywàn-li yǐ-'hèw, 'dày-fu shwō tā yǐ-jīng 'sž-le.

PROOF. (Evidence) 'jèng-jywu. ‖What proof do you have that he is the man we want? nǐ yěw shéme-'jèng-jywu shwō tā °'jyèw-shr nèy-ge-rén? or (to arrest) °'jyèw-shr dzám-yàw-'dǎy-de-nèy-ge-rén?

In proof of (kě-yǐ) 'jèng-míng. ‖I have here some evidence in proof of his assertion. 'wǒ-jèr yěw shyē-'jèng-jywu, kě-yǐ 'jèng-míng tā-de-hwà shř 'dwèy-de.

(In printing) 'jyàw-dwèy-'gǎw-dz; read proof jyàw. ‖I've just finished reading proof on my book. wǒ 'gāng kàn-wán-le wǒ-nèy-běr-'shū-de-'jyàw-dwèy-'gǎw-dz. ‖Are you through reading proof? 'jyàw-'wán-le-ma? or 'jyàw-dwèy-'gǎw-dz kàn-'wán-le-ma?

PROPER. (Correct according to custom; following custom) jàw 'gwēy-jywu; (agreeing with custom) hé 'gwēy-jywu; (be right) dwèy; (ought) 'yīng-gay or

gǎy; (be permitted) néng or shywǔ; with constructions varying with the types of expressions. The proper time 'shř-hew; do the proper thing 'shywún-gwēy-dǎw-'jywǔ-de. ‖What is the proper way to address a business letter? 'mǎy-may-shìn-shang°-de-'chēng-hū yīng-gǎy dzěm shyè? or °'yīng-gǎy dzěm-yàng 'chēng-hū? ‖The proper thing to do is to send some flowers. jàw 'gwēy-jywu shř sùng-dyǎr-'hwǎr-chywu. or jàw 'gwēy-jywu yīng-gǎy sùng dyǎr-'hwǎr-chywu. or 'yīng-gǎy sùng-'hwǎr. or sùng-'hwǎr tsáy 'dwèy. ‖It's not proper. nèm-je bù-hé 'gwēy-jywu. or nèm-je bú-'dwèy. or bù-'gǎy nèm-je. or bù-'néng nèm-je. or 'bù-shywǔ nèm-je. ‖This will certainly be taken care of at the proper time. jèy-ge dàw 'shř-hew °jyèw 'bàn. or °'jwěn bàn. ‖He always does the proper thing. tā 'lǎw-shr 'shywún-gwēy-dǎw-'jywǔ-de.

(In the strict sense). ‖His office is in a smaller building in the back, not in the building proper. tā-de-bàn-'gūng-de-dì-fang dzày hèw-tew-de-'shyǎw-léwr-li, 'bú-dzày °'jèng-léw-li. or °'dà-léw-li. ‖The city proper ends here; from here on it's suburbs. chéng-běn-'shēn dàw-'jèr wéy-'jř; 'gwò-chywu jyèw-shr sž-'shyāng-le.

PROPERTY. (Possessions; things) 'dūng-shi; someone's property (things) . . . de(-dūng-shi); (family possessions) 'jyā-dàng(r). (Real estate; general) 'chǎn-yè; (land only) dì or 'dì-chǎn; (house) 'fáng-dz; etc., with other buildings. ‖This is my property. jèy shř 'wǒ-de. or jèy shř wǒ-'dž-jǐ-de. ‖The things on my desk are my own property. dzày-wǒ-'jwěr-shang-de-dūng-shi dēw shř wǒ-'dž-jǐ-de. ‖You should be more careful in using other people's property. yùng 'byé-rén-de-dūng-shi (or yùng 'rén-jyā-de-dūng-shi) yīng-gǎy 'dwō-jyā 'shyǎw-shīn. ‖I own some property near the river. wǒ dzày 'hé-nar-yěw dyǎr-°'chǎn-yè. or °'dì. or °'dì-chǎn. ‖His property is not enough to cover his debts. tā-de-'jyā-dàngr (or tā-de-'chǎn-yě) bú-gèw hwán-'jàng-le.

(Attribute) 'shìng-jř. ‖This salt has the property of absorbing moisture from the air. jèy-jǔng-'yán yěw 'shī-shēw-'shwěy-fèn-de-'shìng-jř.

PROSPECT. ‖What are your prospects for the future? is expressed as How do you think the future will be? nǐ shyǎng jyàng-láy dzěm-'yàng-ne? or as What are you thinking of doing in the future? nǐ 'jyāng-lay shyǎng (or hope 'shī-wang, or plan 'dǎ-swàn) dzwò-'shéme? or as Do you have any plans in the future? nǐ yěw shéme-'jyāng-lay-de-'dǎ-swàn-ma? ‖There are no prospects in this job. is expressed as There is nothing to hope for in this job. jèy-shèr jyàw-rén méy shéme-'shyǎng-téwr. ‖The prospect (chance) of a swim appeals to me. 'néng yěw nèm-ge-'jī-hwey chywù 'fù-hwéy-'shwěy, jyàw-wǒ jywé-je gāw-'shìng. ‖I've been looking for someone to fill this job, but I haven't found any prospects yet. *is expressed as* . . . **person who wants the job.** wǒ yì-'jŕ shyǎng jǎw-rén 'bǔ jèy-ge-'chywē, °kě-shr 'yí-ge-shyǎng-'gàn-de háy méy-'yěw-ne. *or as* . . . **qualified person.** kě-shr 'yí-ge-hé-'gé-de háy méy-'yěw-ne. ‖**He's a good prospect** (*for buying*). tā· 'dwō-bàn hwèy 'mǎy-de.

PROTECT. (*Defend*) 'bǎw-hù; (*take protective care of*) 'bǎw-yǎng; **protect X from Y** (*some English sentences which do not have this form are also expressed this way in Chinese*) jyàw X 'bú-jř-ywu Y *or* X 'bú-jř-ywu jyàw . . . Y, *and similar constructions with* jyàw *or* 'bú-jř-ywu, *in which Y is a verb.* ‖**This law is designed to protect the poorer farmers.** jèy-ge-'fǎ-lywù shř wèy-'bǎw-hù-'chyúng-dyar-de-'núng-rén-de. ‖**I wear these glasses to protect my eyes.** wǒ dày jèy-fù-yǎn-'jyèngr wèy-de shř 'bǎw-yǎng wǒ-de-'yǎn-jing. ‖**The dike protects the land from minor floods.** fā-dé-'shwěy bú-'dà de-shŕ-hew, jèy-tyáw-dī kě-yǐ jyàw-dì 'bú-jř-ywu 'yān-le. ‖**This shield protects the worker from the flying sparks.** yěw jèy-ge-'dǎng-tewr dzwò-'hwór-de jyèw 'bú-jř-ywu jyàw hwǒ-'shīng-dz 'shāw-jaw-le. ‖**He hired a lawyer to protect his interests.** (*From loss*) tā chǐng-le ge-'lywù-shŕ hǎw jyàw-tā 'bú-jř-ywu °chŕ-'kwēy. *or* (*From being cheated*) °shàng-'dàng. ‖**Put this oil on; it protects your hands from chapping.** 'tsā-shang jèy-ge-'yéw, shěw jyèw 'bú-jř-ywu 'lyè-le. ‖**He sleeps in a mosquito net to protect himself from snakes.** tā dzày 'wén-jàng-li shwèy-'jyàw, hǎw jyàw 'cháng-chúng yǎw-bu-'jáw.

PROUD. (*Gratified*) dé-'yì *and various indirect expressions;* dé-'yì *is not used politely of oneself, one's own accomplishments, or, in speaking to others, of members of one's own family; in these cases expressions of opposite meaning are more common.* ‖**He's proud of his promotion to the new position.** tā shēng-dàw shīn-'wèy-jř hěn dé-'yì. ‖**You must be very proud to have such a student.** yěw 'nèm-ge-'mén-sheng (*or* yěw 'nèm-ge-'shywé-sheng) děy 'dwō-men dé-'yì-ya. ‖**I'm proud of this student of mine.** jèy shř wǒ-de-dé-'yì-de-'mén-sheng. ‖**I'm proud that my country did the right thing.** wǒ jywé-de 'bì-gwó-jèng-fǔ 'jèy-jyàn-shř bàn-de hěn 'dwèy. ‖**I'm proud of you.** (*For yourself*) nǐ 'jēn hǎw. *or* (*To a child*) nǐ 'jēn shř ge-'hǎw-háy-dz. *or* (*For what you did*) dzwò-de 'jēn hǎw. *or* dzwò-de 'jēn dwèy. *or* (*For your abilities*) nǐ 'jēn chéng. *or* nǐ 'jēn shíng. ‖**I'm proud of my son.** *is expressed as* **He has some few possibilities.** wǒ 'jèy-ge-ér-dz háy 'yěw dyǎr-'chū-shi. ‖**I feel very proud of myself for completing this task alone.** *is expressed as* **It's just luck that I did, I'm not sure whether that's good.** 'hěn jyàw-wú-'shìng-de, 'yí-ge-rén bǎ jèy-ge dzwò-wán-le, kě-shr bù-jř-dàw 'hǎw-bu-hǎw. *or* wǒ 'yí-ge-rén bǎ jèy-ge dzwò-'wán-de, 'jyǎw-shìng-de 'hěn.

(*Independent*) àw. ‖**He is a very proud person and would not ask for any help.** tā-°rén (*or* °'shìng-dz) hěn 'àw, 'bú-ywàn-yi chyéw-'rén.

(*Haughty*). ‖**She's become very proud since she inherited all that money.** tā dž-tsúng 'chéng-jì-le nèy-bǐ-'chyán yǐ-'hèw, °'jyà-dz byàn-de hěn 'dà. *or* °bǎy-chǐ 'jyà-dz-lay-le. *or* °'jyāw-àw-chi-lay-le. *or* °nèm 'chì-shŕ-líng-'rén-le. *or* °jywé-je 'měy-de 'shèw-bu-dé. *or* (*vulgar expressions*) °chèw-'měy-de bù-dé-'lyǎw. *or* °'nà-ge 'měy-ya. ‖**Don't be too proud; you can always find someone better than yourself.** byé tày dž-'mǎn (*or* byé tày jywé-je 'dž-jǐ 'hǎw, *or* byé tày 'jyāw-àw); yàw jř-dàw 'néng-rén bèy-'hèw yěw 'néng-rén.

PROVE. (*Demonstrate*) 'jèng-míng; *or expressed by nouns:* 'jèng-jywù *or* 'gēn-jywù (*evidence*); *or* (*show people*) jyàw-rén 'jř-daw. ‖**I can prove that he didn't do it.** wǒ 'kě-yǐ 'jèng-míng °tā 'méy-dzwò nèy-ge. *or* °nèy 'bú-shr 'tā-gàn-de. ‖**Can you prove your statement?** nǐ-de-'hwà yěw °'jèng-jywù-ma? *or* °'gēn-jywù-ma? *or* °shéme-'jèng-jywù-ne? *or* °shéme-'gēn-jywù-ne? *or* nǐ 'néng-bu-néng ná-chu 'jèng-jywù-lay 'jèng-míng nǐ-de-hwà shř 'dwèy-de? ‖**I know he's guilty, but I have no way to prove it.** wǒ 'jř-dàw shř 'tā-gàn-de; bú-gwo wǒ 'méy-fár °jǎw-chu 'jèng-jywù-lay. *or* °'jèng-míng. ‖**That proves nothing.** 'nèy 'bìng bù-néng 'jèng-míng shéme. ‖**It only proves that his mind is muddled.** jèy 'jř néng 'jèng-míng (*or* jèy 'jř néng jyàw-rén 'jř-daw) tā-shīn-li hěn 'hú-du.

(*Turn out*). ‖**This disease might prove fatal.** jèy-jǔng-'bìng yě-shywǔ hwèy jř-'mìng-de. ‖**The letter proved to be a forgery.** nèy-fēng-shìn 'jyē-gwo jř-daw shř 'jyǎ-de. ‖**The movie proved to be very bad.** nèy-ge-pyàn-dz yí-'kàn, tǐng-'dzāw-de. *or* (*Contrary to expectations*) nèy-ge-pyàn-dz 'jēn jyèw tǐng-'dzāw-de. *or* (*For the producers*) 'nèy-ge-pyàn-dz yí-shàng-'yǎn, 'jyē-gwo tǐng-'dzāw.

PROVIDE. ·(*Supply*) chū. *See also* **SUPPLY.** ‖**If you provide the material, I'll build a garage for you.** nǐ rú-gwo chū 'tsáy-lyaw, wǒ gwǎn gěy-nǐ gày yí-ge-chē-'fáng.

(*Stipulate*) dìng. ‖**The rule provides that you cannot leave the camp without permission.** 'gwēy-jywu-'dìng-de shř 'méy-jīng-shywǔ-'kě 'bù-néng lí-'yíng.

Provide with. (*Give*) gěy. ‖**We were provided with food enough to last two weeks.** gěy-wǒ-men-de-'lyáng-shr gèw yùng lyǎng-shīng-'chī-de.

Be provided for. (*Of a person; have a share*) yěw-'fèr; *or* yěw *with other nouns, as money.* ‖**The family was provided for in the will.** 'jyā-li-de-rén dzày yí-'jǔ-lǐ dēw yěw-'fèr.

Provide against, provide for. (*Plan for*) 'dǎ-swàn *or* 'swàn-ji; (*think of*) shyǎng-'dàw; (*pay attention to*) gù-lywu-'dàw. ‖**My plan provides for that possibility too.** 'wǒ-de-bàn-fa-li lyán 'nèy-ge yě °'dǎ-swàn dzày lǐ-tew-le. *or* °'swàn-ji dzày lǐ-tew-le. *or* °shyǎng-'dàw-le. *or* °'gù-lywu-'dàw-le. *But* ‖**Our (automobile) insurance provides also against the theft of our car.** wǒm-bǎw-de-'chē-shyǎn-li, chē yàw-shr jyàw-rén 'tēw-chywu-le yě 'gwǎn-de.

Provided that 'jř-yěw, 'yàw-shr. ‖I'll come, provided (that) you come with me. 'jř-yěw nǐ gēn-wǒ yí-'kwàr láy, wǒ tsáy 'láy. *or* yàw-shr 'nǐ gēn-wǒ yí-'kwàr láy, (jř-yěw 'nèm-je) wǒ tsáy láy.

PUBLIC. (*All people*). (*Everybody*) 'dà-jyā; (*all the people of the nation*) chywán-'gwó-de-rén *and similar expressions with other place terms instead of gwó.* gūng- *in combinations:* public park 'gūng-ywán'; public interests 'gūng-gùng-'lì-yì *or* 'gūng-yì *or* 'dà-jyā-dę-'lì-yì; public opinion 'dà-jyā-de-'yì-jyàn *or* 'gūng-lwèn *or* 'ywǔ-lwèn. ‖There isn't enough public interest in the election. 'jèy-tsz̀-shywǎn-'jywǔ °'dà-jyā (*or, if a national election,* °chywán-'gwó-de-rén, *or, if a provincial election,* °chywán-'shěng-de-rén, *etc.*) 'bú-gèw °gwān-'shīn-de. *or* °'yǔng-ywè-de. ‖Public opinion is against him. 'dà-jyā-de-'yì-jyàn °bú-'dzàn-chéng tā. *or* °dēw 'fǎn-dwèy tā. *or* 'ywǔ-lwèn 'fǎn-dwèy tā. *or* 'gūng-lwèn 'dwèy-tā bù-'mǎn.

Open to the public gūng-'kǎy-de *or* 'shéy-dēw-néng-'(jìn-)chywù-de. ‖This library is only for members of the society, not open to the public. 'jèy-ge-tú-shū-'gwǎn jř wèy 'hwèy-ywán yùng, 'bú-shr °gūng-'kǎy-de. *or* °'shéy-dēw-néng-'jìn-chywu-de. ‖This is a public meeting, and the admission is free. 'jèy-ge-hwèy shř °gūng-'kǎy-de (*or* °'shéy-dēw-néng-'chywù-de), 'bú-yùng 'mǎy-pyàw.

Audience is expressed as the people who hear *a* speaker 'tīng-. . .-de-rén, the people who read *a* writer's writings 'kàn-. . .-shyě-de-dūng-shi-de-rén, *etc.* ‖His program reaches a large public. 'tīng-tā-de-rén hěn 'dwō. ‖He writes for a small but select public. kàn-'tā-shyě-de-dūng-shi-de-rén bù-'dwō, 'bú-gwò 'dēw shř yí-'pày-de.

Public office 'jèng-jyè; public officer 'gwān. ‖He's held a public office for the last twenty years. tā dzwò-'gwān (*or* tā dzày 'jèng-jyè) yěw 'èr-shr-nyán-le.

In public. (*In front of people*) dzày rén-'myàn-chyán; (*in front of others*) dzày 'byé-rén-'myàn-chyán; dzày hěn-'dwō-rén-'myàn-chyán. ‖That's the way to behave in public. dzày 'rén-myàn-chyán 'yīng-gāy nèm-je.

PULL. (*Cause to move toward the force exerted; draw*) lā; (*especially to start in motion by pulling*) jwày; (*tug*) dèn; (*especially to pull sideways or with a ripping motion*) chě; (*pull out by the roots or from something sticky*) bá; (*contract, pull in*) swō; (*grasp and pull, as hair*) jyēw. *See also* TAKE. ‖We'll have to get a truck to pull this car out of the mud. dzám děy jǎw lyàng-'dzày-jùng-chì-'chē-lay bǎ jèy-'chē tsúng 'ní-li °'lā-chu-lay. *or* °'jwày-chu-lay. ‖I'll pull while you push. wǒ 'lā-je nǐ 'twēy. ‖Pull the shades down. bǎ chwāng-'lyán-dz 'lā-shya-lay. ‖He pulled the blankets over his head. tā bǎ 'tǎn-dz °'lā-shang-lay (*or* °'lā-gwo-lay), bǎ-'téw gày-shang-le. ‖If you pull this cord, the driver will stop the bus. nǐ yì-'lā (*or* nǐ yì-'chě, *or* nǐ yí-'jwày, *or* nǐ yí-'dèn) jèy-'shéngr, kāy-'chē-de jyèw bǎ-chē °'tíng-shya-lay. *or* °'tíng-ju.

However they pull at it, it won't move a bit. tām 'dzěme lā yě lā-bu-'dùng. *or* tām 'dzěme jwày yě jwày-bu-'dùng. ‖This trunk is not well made; I just gave the handle a pull and it came off. shyāng-dz tày bù-'jyē-shr; nèy-ge-'bàr wǒ °yí-'jwày (*or* °yí-'dèn, *or* °yì-'chě, *or* °yì-'lā) jyèw 'dyàw-le. ‖Pull the door shut. bǎ-'mén 'lā-shang. ‖Pull the door shut when you go out. 'chū-chywu-de-shř-hew 'shwèn-shěw bǎ-mén 'lā-shang. ‖He pulled furtively at my coat with the idea of getting to speak to me in private. tā 'tēw-je dèn (*or* chě) wǒ-de-'yī-shang, 'yì-sz shř yàw gēn-wǒ dàw 'bèy-jìng-dì-fang-chywu shwō-'hwà. ‖If you give it too hard a pull, the rope will break. nǐ yàw-shr 'tày shř-'jìn dèn (*or* chě, *or* jwày, *or* lā), shéng-dz jyèw yàw °'shé-le. *or* °'dwàn-le. ‖This tooth has to be pulled. jèy-yá děy 'bá. ‖He's pulling weeds. tā bá yě-'tsǎw-ne. ‖They pulled up the flowers by the roots. tām bǎ-'hwār lyán-'gēr 'bá-chu-lay-le. ‖The turtle pulled in its head and legs. 'wū-gwey bǎ-'téw gēn-'twěy dēw 'swō-jin-chywu-le. ‖They're pulling each other's hair. tām 'jyēw-je téw-fa dǎ-'jyā.

(*Tear, rip*). (*If it can be done with the hands*) chě; (*break*) chǎy. ‖We can pull the box apart for firewood. dzám kě-yi bǎ 'shyá-dz °'chǎy-le (*or* °chǎy-'sǎn-le, *or* °'chě-kāy) dàng 'pǐ-chay shāw. ‖They're going to pull it down and build a new one. tā-men dǎ-swàn 'chǎy-lew gày 'shīn-de.

(*Climb*) pá. ‖This hill is a hard pull for an old car. 'jèy-ge-shān 'gèw jèy-ge-'lǎw-chē 'pá-de.

(*Perform, as a trick*) shř (*use*), *but often expressed indirectly.* ‖He pulled a mean trick on me. tā gěy-wǒ °'shř-'hwày láy-je. *or* °'shř-le ge-'dà-hwày. ‖Don't pull any funny stuff. (*Serious warning*) byé shř 'gwěy-jāwr. *or* (*Friendly*) byé táw-'chì. ‖He pulled a fast one that time. (*Of an action*) tā 'nèy-jāwr shř-de-'chyǎw. *or* tā 'nèy-hwéy nèng-de jēn 'myàw. *or* tā 'nèy-shěwr °shwǎ-de (*or* °wár-de) 'pyàw-lyàng. *or* tā 'nèy-tsz̀ °shwǎ-de (*or* °wár-de) 'hwā-téwr 'tày chyǎw-le. *or* (*Of something said*) tā 'nèy-ge-hwà shwō-de 'tày °chyǎw-le. *or* °'jī-ling-le. *or* tā 'nèy-shyàr bǎ-rén °'dzwàn-de (*or* °'pyàn-de) hǎw 'kǔ-wa.

(*Influence*). (*Favors*) 'rén-chíng; (*means of access*) 'mén-lù; (*influence, power*) 'shř-lì. Have pull yěw (*or* twō, *ask for*) 'rén-chíng, yěw (*or* dzěw) 'mén-lù, yěw 'shř-lì; *or expressed as* ask favors of people twō-'rén. ‖You have to have a lot of pull to get a job here. nǐ děy °yěw tǐng-'dà-de-'rén-chíng (*or* °twō bù-'shǎw-de-'rén-chíng, *or* °dzěw hěn-'dwō-de-'mén-lù, *or* °twō bù-'shǎw-rén) tsáy néng dzày-'jèr dé ge-'chāy-shr. ‖He has a good deal of pull at the municipal government. (*As a member of it*) tā dzày 'shř-jèng-'fǔ-li hěn yěw 'shř-lì. *or* (*As an outsider*) °yěw 'hǎw-shyē-'mén-lù.

Pull in. (*Arrive*) dàw; (*enter the station*) jìn-'jàn. ‖What time do you expect to pull into town? nǐ 'dà-gày 'shéme-shř-hew dàw chéng-'li? ‖The train's just pulling in. hwǒ-chē gāng °'dàw! *or* °jìn-'jàn.

Pull off (*accomplish*) 'dzwò-chū-lay, bàn-de-'dàw, bàn-de-'chéng, 'gàn-de-chū-'láy. ‖It's a good idea if you can pull it off. nǐ yàw-shr néng 'dzwò-chū-lay, yí-'dìng bú-'tswò.

Pull out (*leave*) kāy. ‖The train pulled out on time for once. hwǒ-chē 'kě àn 'shŕ-hew 'kāy-le yì-hwéy.

Pull out (*level off; of a plane that has been diving*) 'gǎy-dàw 'píng-fēy. ‖The plane pulled out of the dive at 2,000 feet. fēy-jī wàng-shyà 'jŕ-chūng dàw 'lyǎng-chyān-chř-'gāw-nar jyèw 'gǎy-daw 'píng-fēy-le.

Pull over (*drive to the side of the road*). (*Including stopping*) kāy-dàw 'byār-shang-chywu; (*remaining in motion*) wàng 'byār-shang kāy. ‖Pull over to the curb and show me your driver's license. kāy-dàw 'byār-shang-chywu, wǒ 'kàn-kan nǐ-de-'kāy-chē-'jŕ-jàw. ‖Pull over a bit. wàng 'byār-shang kāy-yi-dyar.

Pull through (*recover from illness or injury*) hǎw-le, hǎw-de-'lyǎw. ‖She was pretty sick, and we were afraid she might not pull through. tā bìng-de tǐng 'lì-hay, wǒm 'yǐ-wey tā 'hǎw-bu-'lyǎw-le.

Pull oneself together. (*Settle the mind*) dìng-'shén, dìng-'shér, dìng-ding 'shén, bǎ 'shīn-shén 'dìng-ding; (*quiet down*) jēn-jing-shya-chywu; (*one's mind no longer confused*) shīn bú-'lwàn-le; (*recover*) 'hǎw-le. ‖Pull yourself together and let's be on our way. dìng-dìng 'shér (*or* bǎ 'shīn-shén 'dìng-yi-ding, *or expressed as* don't be that way 'byé nèm-je-le), dzám gāy 'dzěw-je-le. ‖Wait until he's pulled himself together. děng tā °'jēn-jing-shya-chywu (*or* 'hǎw-le, *or* °shīn 'bú-nèm 'lwàn-le) dzày 'shwō. ‖After being stunned for a while he pulled himself together and walked on. tā 'lèng-le yì-hwěr, rán-hèw 'dìng-le-dìng 'shén, jyèw 'jyē-je wàng-chyán 'dzěw-le.

Pull up (*stop*) 'jàn-jù. ‖The car pulled up in front of the house. chē kāy-dàw 'fáng-dz-'chyán-tew 'jàn-jù-le.

Pull *a knife* dùng. ‖He pulled a knife on us, so we had to kill him. tā gēn-wǒm dùng 'dāw, wǒm bù-'dé bù-bǎ-tā 'shā-le.

Pull one's punches. (*In boxing*) dǎ-de °bù-shř-'jìn *or* °bú-dày-'jìn (*or* jyèr *instead of* jìn), *but* not pull one's punches *may also be* °shàng-'jìn *or* °yěw-'jìn; (*in speaking*) shwō-de-'hwà °méy 'lì-lyang, *or* °méy-'jìn, *or* °méy-'jyèr, *or* °bú-dày-'jìn, *or* °bú-jùng-'kěn, *or* °chà-'jìn; *or* °'gūng-jí-de °'bú-shr 'dì-fang. *or* °bú-dàw-'jyā. *or* °'lǐ-yew chà-'jìn. ‖He pulls his punches. tā 'dǎ-de °bù-shř-'jìn. *or* °bú-dày-'jyèr. *or* tā shwō-de-'hwà °méy-'lì-lyang. *or* °méy-'jyèr. *or* tā 'gūng-ji-de °'bú-shr 'dì-fang. *or* °'lǐ-yéw chà-'jìn. *etc.*

Pull the wool over one's eyes. (*Cheat*) pyàn . . .; (*fool completely*) bǎ . . . 'pyàn-de °yí-'lèng-yí-lèng-de *or* °'mwò-míng-chí-'myàw-le. ‖He tried to pull the wool over my eyes. tā shyǎng 'pyàn-wo láy-je. ‖He pulled the wool over her eyes. tā bǎ-tā 'pyàn-de °yí-'lèng-yí-lèng-de. *or* °'mwò-míng-chí-'myàw-le.

PUNISH. fá, 'chǔ-fèn; (*deal with*) bàn; (*somewhat literary*) 'chěng-fá. **Be punished** (*especially legal and*

physical) shèw 'shíng-fa; (*by natural suffering rather than inflicted punishment*) shèw-'dzwèy; shèw-'shíng, shèw-'fá, shèw 'chǔ-fèn. ‖How are you going to punish him? nǐ shyǎng dzěme °'fá-tā? *or* °'chǔ-fèn tā? *or* °'bàn-tā? ‖I think he's been punished enough. wǒ jywé-je °'fá-de tā 'bù-chīng-le. *or* °tā-shèw-de-'shíng-fa 'bù-chīng-le *or* °tā-shèw-de-'chǔ-fèn 'gèw-jùng-de-le. *or* °dzème 'fá-tā (*or* °dzème 'chǔ-fèn tā, *or* °dzème 'bàn-tā) yǐ-jing 'gèw-jùng-de-le. *or* (*by the natural consequences of his actions*) °tā-jèy-ge-'dzwèy shèw-de 'gèw-chyáw-de-le. *or* °tā-shèw-de-'dzwèy 'bú-swàn 'shǎw-le. ‖This crime ought to be punished more severely. (*Of a minor crime*) 'jèy-yàngr-de-'gwò-fàn (*or* 'jèy-yàngr-de-'gwò-tswò, *or* 'dzèm-yàng-fàn-'fá-de-shř) yīng-gāy °'fá-de 'dzày lì-hay-dyar. *or* °'chǔ-fèn-de 'dzày lì-hay-dyar. *or* °'bàn-de 'dzày lì-hay-dyar. *or* (*Of a major crime*) 'jèy-yàngr-de-'dzwèy-chíng yīng-gāy jyā-°'jùng- (*or* °'děng-)de °'chěng-fa. *or* °'chǔ-fèn. *or* °'fá. *or* °'bàn.

PUNISHMENT. 'shíng-fa (*legal and physical*); *or expressed verbally; see* PUNISH; *or expressed indirectly.* ‖This punishment is too severe. jèy-ge-'shíng-fa (*or* jèy-ge-'fá-de, *or* jèy-ge-'chǔ-fèn-de, *or* jèy-ge-'bàn-de) tày 'jùng. ‖The punishment for this crime is death. jèy-jǔng-dzwèy-de-'chǔ-fèn shř 'sž-shíng. *or expressed as* This is a capital crime. jèy-shr 'sž-dzwèy. *or as* The violator of this law °is guilty of death. fàn-'jèy-tyáw-'fǎ-lywù-de °shř 'sž-dzwèy. *or as* °is given the death penalty. °chǔ 'sž-shíng. *or as* °receives the death penalty. °shèw 'sž-shíng. ‖The car took a lot of punishment on its last trip. 'jèy-yi-tàng °'jēn gèw nèy-chē 'shèw-de. *or* °'jyàw-chē shèw-le bù-'shǎw-de-'dzwèy.

PUPIL. (*Student*) 'shywé-sheng; (*disciple*) 'mén-sheng.

(*Of the eye*) 'yǎn-rér, 'túng-rér.

PURCHASE. (*Buy*) mǎy. ‖I'm trying to purchase some land on this street. wǒ jèng-dzày shyǎng-fár dzày 'jèy-tyáw-jyē-shang mǎy dyǎr-'dì.

(*Things bought*) ('mǎy-de-)'dūng-shi. ‖I have a few purchases to make in this store. wǒ děy dzài 'jèy-pù-dz-li mǎy jǐ-yàngr-'dūng-shi. ‖Please deliver these purchases for me. láw-'jyà bǎ °'jèy-shyē-'dūng-shi (*or* °wǒ-'mǎy-de-'dūng-shi) gěy-wǒ 'sùng-chywu.

PURE. (*Unadulterated*) chwén; *sometimes* (*real*) jēn. ‖Pure gold should be heavier than this. 'chwén-jīn bǐ jèy-ge 'jùng. ‖The dress is pure silk. 'yī-fu shŕ °'jēn-sž-de. *or* °'chwén-sž-de.

(*Unpolluted*). (*Clean*) 'gān-jing(-de); (*filtered; of liquids*) 'lìn-gwo-de; *or, expressed indirectly.* ‖Is the water pure enough to drink? jèy-'shwěy shŕ °'gān-jing-de-ma (*or* °'lìn-gwo-de-ma)? néng 'hē-ma? *or expressed as* drinkable 'shwěy °kě-yi 'hē-me? *or* °'hē-de-ma?

(*Sheer*). ‖His statement is pure nonsense. tā 'gēn-běn shř °'hú-shwō-bá-'dàw. *or* °'shyā-shwō-bá-'dàw. *or* (*Rather polite*) tā-shwō-de °'wán-chywán méy-'lǐ. *or* °yì-dyǎr-'lǐ yě méy-'yěw. *or* (*Very vulgar*) tǎ jyǎn-'jŕ shř fàng-'pì.

Pure and simple. ‖He's a push-over, pure and simple. tā jyǎn-'jŕ shř 'rúng-yi-'dwèy-fu. *or* tā míng-'bǎy-je shř ge-'rúng-yi-'dwèy-fu-de-rén.

PURPLE. 'dž(-de) *or* 'dž-shǎr(-de) *or* 'dž-sè(-de).

PURPOSE. (*Intention*) 'yì-sz; *or expressed indirectly with* wèy (*because of*), yàw (*want, intend*), 'wèy-de shř (*in order to*; *or, without defining the purpose* shīn (*heart*), 'tswén-shīn *or* 'jywū-shīn (*heart, inner man*). ‖What's the purpose of all this commotion? jèr 'wàn-lwan tēng-tēng-de shř °'wèy-'shéme? *or* °'wèy-le-'shéme? *or* °'yàw 'dzěm-je? *or* °'shéme-'yì-sz-ne? ‖What's the purpose of his visit (here)? tā wèy-'shéme dàw‧jèr láy-de? *or* tā dàw-'jèr-lay shř °'wèy-'shéme? *or* °'wèy-le-'shéme? *or* °'yàw 'dzěm-je? *or* °'shéme-'yì-sz-ne? ‖He comes here for the purpose of starting a branch office. tā 'láy-jèr °'wèy-de shř (*or* °'shř yàw, *or* °'yàw) 'lì yí-ge-'fēn-hàw. ‖I know that his purpose is honorable. wǒ jŕ-dàw tā °'shř 'hǎw-shīn. *or* °-de-'yì-sz hěn 'hǎw. *or* °'méy-yěw 'hwày-yì-sz. *or* °-'tswén-shīn 'jèng-dà-gwāng-'míng-de. ‖His purpose is dishonorable. tā-'tswén-shīn (*or* tā 'jywū-shīn) 'bù-'lyáng. *or* °'bú-'shàn. *or* °'bú-'jèng. *or* tā-'yì-sz bú-'jèng. *or* tā-nèy 'bú-shr 'hǎw-yì-sz. *or* tā 'bù-hwáy 'hǎw-yì. ‖His sole purpose is personal gain. tā 'wán-chywán °'shř 'sž-shīn. *or* °'wèy-le tā-'dž-jǐ-'gěr.

Serve a purpose. (*Have use*) yěw 'yùng; (*have benefit*) yěw 'hǎw-chù; yěw 'yì-sz. ‖It serves no purpose to do it that way. 'nèm-je méy°-'yùng. *or* °'hǎw-chù. *or* °'shéme-'yì-sz. ‖What purpose does it serve to do it that way? 'nèm-je °'yěw shéme-'yùng-ne? *or* °'yěw shéme-'hǎw-chù-ne? *or* °'yěw shéme-'yì-sz-ne? *or expressed as* If that way, then what? °'yěw 'dzěm-je-ne? *or* °'yěw dzěm-'yàng-ne?

Serve the purpose. (*Be satisfactory*) chéng, shíng, néng-'yùng; (*be a necessary substitute*) 'myǎn-chyǎng 'yùng; (*be a poor substitute*) 'jyáng-jyew; (*be a temporary substitute*) 'jàn-shŕ yùng ... 'hǎw-le. ‖I guess this desk will serve the purpose until we get a new one. wǒ kàn dzày wǒm 'méy-nèng-daw 'shīn-jwō-dz yǐ-'chyán, °'jàn-shŕ yùng 'jèy-ge(-jwō-dz) 'hǎw-le. *or* °'jèy-ge yě jyèw 'jyāng-jyew-le. *or* °'jèy-ge yě jyèw 'jyāng-jyew-je-ba. *or* °'jèy-ge yě jyèw 'myǎn-chyǎng 'yùng-je-ba. *or* °'jèy-ge yě 'chéng. *or* °'jèy-ge yě néng-'yùng. *or* °'jèy-ge yě 'shíng.

On purpose chéng-'shīn(-de), gù-'yì(-de); *in some cases* jìng-'yèr(-de); (*for a reason*) 'yěw-swǒ-'wèy. ‖He did this on purpose. tā shř gù-'yì-de dzèm-je. *or* tā shř chéng-'shīn dzèm-je. *or* tā shř jìng-'yèr-de dzèm-je. *or* tā 'nèm-je shř 'yěw-swǒ-'wèy. ‖He threw a monkey wrench into the works on purpose. tā-jè-shr °'chéng-shīn (*or* °'gù-'yì) dǎw-'lwàn. ‖I left my

coat home on purpose. wǒ gù-'yì-de (*or* wǒ chéng-'shīn-de) bǎ wày-'tàwr gē-dzày 'jyā-li-le. ‖I asked on purpose, to see what you'd say. wǒ chéng-'shīn (*or* wǒ gù-'yì) wèn-de °'wèy-de shř (*or* °'yàw) kàn nǐ dzěm 'shwō.

PURSE. (*Moneybag; billfold*) chyán-'jyā-dz; (*bag*) chyán-'bāwr. ‖How much mônev do you have in your purse? nǐ-chyán-'jyā-dz-li (*or* nǐ-chyán-'bāwr-li) yěw 'dwō-shǎw-'chyán?

(*Prize money*) 'yíng-láy-de-chyán. ‖The purse was divided evenly among the winners. 'yíng-láy-de-chyán 'dà-jyā-hwǒr 'fēn-le.

(*To pucker*) 'jywē. ‖He pursed his lips. tā 'jywē-je 'dzwěr.

PURSUE. *Chase* jwēy; (*chase and drive*) gǎn. ‖He pursued the enemy as far as the river. tā-men yì-'jŕ bǎ 'dí-rén °'jwēy- (*or* °'gǎn)-dàw 'hé-ner.

Pursue a course. (*Take a step*) dzěw ... 'bù; (*adopt a procedure*) 'tsǎy-chywǔ 'bù-dzèw; *and indirect expressions.* ‖This is a dangerous course to pursue. dzěw 'jèy-yí-bù 'bú-dà kě-'kàw. *or* 'tsǎy-chywǔ 'jèy-jǔng-'bù-dzèw (*or expressed as* This method ... 'jèy-ge-'bàn-fa, *or as* To follow this method ... jàw 'jèy-ge-fá-dz láy bàn) yěw dyǎr-'shyǎn.

(*Try to get*) chyéw (*ask for, seek*). ‖Do you intend to pursue your education after the war? jàn-'hèw nǐ háy dǎ-swàn chyéw-'shywé-ma?

PUSH. (*Shove*) twēy; (*with the head or with the end of something*) dǐng; (*give an impatient push*) 'sǎng-da; (*from the side or to the side*) 'bā-la; (*force aside, also means chase back*) hūng. ‖Push the table over by the window. bǎ jwō-dz 'twēy-dàw kàw-'chwāng-hu-ner chywù. ‖Give the car a push for me, will you? bǎ 'chē gěy-wǒ 'twēy (*or, if with another car,* 'dǐng) yí-shyàr dzěm-yàng? ‖He pushed me out of the way and went right by. tā bǎ-wǒ °'twēy-kāy (*or* °'sǎng-da kāy, *or* °'bā-la-kāy), jyèw dzèw-gwò-chywu-le. ‖He pushed the dishes aside and laid a map on the table. tā bǎ 'dyé-dz-wǎn-de °'bā-la-kāy (*or* °'twēy-kāy), jyèw bǎ dì-'tú pū-dzay 'jwōr-shang-e.

(*Press: of people*) jǐ; (*of a single person fighting his way through a crowd*) chyǎng; (*with force, especially of an army*) chūng; (*push ahead, as of an army*) twēy-jìn; (*by fighting*) dǎ. ‖The crowd pushed into the elevator. rén 'jǐ-jìn dyàn-'tī-li chywù-le. ‖There's room for everybody. Don't push. 'yěw-de shř 'dì-fangr. byé 'jǐ-le. ‖He was pushed to the front of the crowd. tā‧m bǎ-tā 'jǐ-dàw 'chyán-byar-chywu-le. ‖The policeman pushed his way through the crowd to where the r en were fighting. 'jǐng-chá dǎ 'rén-dwēy-li °jǐ- (*or* °chyǎng‧) dàw 'nèy-shyē-rén-dǎ-'jyà-de-dì-fang. ‖Our armies have pushed to within ten miles of the enemy's divisional headquarters. 'wǒ-jywūn 'twēy-jìn-dàw (*or* 'wǒ-jywūn 'chūng-dàw, *or* wǒm-de-'jywūn-dwèy wàng-'chyán dǎ-dàw) lí-'dí-rén-de-'shŕ-bù-bú-dàw-'shŕ-lǐ-de-dì-fang. ‖The enemy attacked and advanced five miles, but were soon pushed back. 'dí-rén jìn-gūng dǎ-gwò-lay 'wǔ-lǐ, kě-shr 'yí-shyà-dz yèw gěy 'dǎ-hwéy-chywu-le.

(*Back a person*) 'ywùn-dùng, 'twēy-jywù. ‖He's being pushed for the mayor's office. 'yěw-rén jèng-dzày °'ywùn-dùng, shyǎng jyàw-tā (*or* 'twēy-jywǔ tā) dzwò shr̀-'jǎng.

Push off (*of a boat*) lí-'àn (*leave the shore*). ‖The boat pushed off from the shore. chwán lí-'àn-le.

Push *someone* **around** (*treat roughly*) 'chī-fu, 'bā-la-lay 'sǎng-da-chywu. ‖I've been pushed around a good deal for the last three years. wǒ jyàw-rén °'chī-fu-le (*or* °'bā-la-gwo-lay 'sǎng-da-gwo-chywu-de) yěw 'sān-nyán-le.

Push *a claim* **to.** (*Contend for*) jēng; (*contend to the end for*) 'jēng-dàw 'dǐ. ‖I intend to push my claim to the land. jèy-kwày-dì wǒ yí-'dìng yàw °'jēng-de. *or* °'jēng-dàw-'dǐ-de.

Other expressions in English. ‖Don't push your luck. byé tày 'tān-le. *or* byé nèm 'tān-shīn bù-'dzú. *or* 'tān-shīn bù-kě gwò-'fèn. *or* bú-yàw 'tān-dé wú-'yàn. ‖It's a push-over. 'nèy rúng-yì. *or* 'nèy hǎw-'bàn. *or* 'nèy 'méy-shéme.

PUT. (*Place, set*) gē *or* fàng; (*set in proper place, arrange*) bǎy; (*set in order, in proper places*) shēw; (*in one's pocket*) chwāy; (*insert*) chā; (*put on by rubbing*) tsá; (*tear something rather than taking it away*) lyàw; (*drive in, of a car into a garage, etc.*) 'kāy-jìn; (*put more, add*) jyā. *See also* PACK, LAY, SET, PLACE, POUR. ‖Put your suitcase over here. bǎ nǐ-de-shēw-tí-'shyāng °gē-'jèr. *or* °fàng-'jèr. ‖Put the book back where you got it. bǎ-shū °'fàng- (*or* °'gē-, *or* °'bǎy-) hwéy ywán-'láy-de-'dì-fang-chywu. ‖Put the tools away when you're through with them. 'jyā-hwo yùng-'wán-le jyèw °'shēw-chi-lay. *or* (*put back*) °'shēw-hwéy-chywu. *or* °'gē-hwéy-chywu. ‖He put the knife in his pocket. tā bǎ 'dāw-dz °'gē- (*or* °'fàng-, *or* °'chwāy-) dzày °kěw-'dàr-li-le. *or* °'dēwr-li-le. ‖Put the flowers in this vase and put the vase on the table. bǎ-hwār 'chā-dzày jèy-ge-hwār-'píng-li, dzày bǎ hwār-'píng °bǎy- (*or* °'fàng-, *or* °gē-) dzày 'jwōr-shang. ‖Put some of the salve on, and it won't hurt so much. 'gē-shang (*or* 'tsá-shang) dyǎr-jèy-ge-'yéw, jyèw 'bú-nèm téng-le. ‖Put that chair down. bǎ yǐ-dz °'gē-shya. *or* °'fàng-shya. *or* °'lyàw-shya. ‖Put the car in the garage. bǎ-'chē kāy-jìn chē-'fáng-li-chywu.

(*Print, as in a newspaper*) dēng. ‖The notice was put on the front page. nèy-ge-'chǐ-shr̀ dēng-dzày 'téw-yì-pyār-shang-le.

(*Express or record: in writing*) shyě; (*in words*) shwō. ‖The report puts the fact very clearly. jèy-ge-bàw-'gàw, 'nèy-jyàn-shr̀ °'shwō-de (*or* °'shyě-de) hěn 'chīng-chu. ‖Put it in another way. 'lìng yùng ge-'fāng-fa láy shyě. *or* 'hwàn jywù-hwà láy shwō. ‖Put it in writing. 'shyě-shyà-lay.

Put across. (*Make clear*) jyàw-rén 'míng-bay; (*put into action*) 'shíng-chū-chywu; (*make people think something can be used*) jyàw-rén jywé-je kě-yǐ 'yùng. ‖Can this idea be put across successfully? jèy-ge-'yì-sz (*or* jèy-ge-'fá-dz, *or* jèy-ge-'bàn-fa) néng jyàw byé-rén 'míng-bay-ma? *or* jèy-ge-'bàn-fa °'shíng-de-chū-'chywù-ma? *or* °néng 'shíng-ma? *or* °néng jyàw-rén jywé-je kě-yǐ 'yùng-ma?

Put aside *money.* (*Save*) 'lyéw-shyà-lay; (*deposit*) 'tswén-chǐ-lay; (*put away*) 'shēw-chǐ-lay. ‖She's been putting aside a little money each month. tā 'ywè-ywè °'lyéw-shyà (*or* °'tswén-chǐ, *or* °'shēw-chǐ) dyǎr-'chyán-lay.

Put *a price or value* **at** *an amount* gū, dìng. ‖They put the value of the estate at fifty thousand dollars. lyán 'fáng-dz dày-'dì tām °gū-le 'wǔ-wàn-kwày-chyán-de-'jyàr. *or* °'dìng-le 'wǔ-wàn-kwày-chyán-de-'jyàr. *or expressed as* Their estimated price is fifty thousand dollars. °-de-'gū-jyà shr̀ 'wǔ-wàn-kwày-chyán.

Put down (*quell*) dǎ-'píng, jyǎw-'píng, píng. ‖The revolt was put down with little trouble. nèy-'lwàn-dz méy-fèy-'shèr jyèw °dǎ-'píng-le. *or* °jyǎw-'píng-le. *or* 'píng-le.

Put down (*write*) 'shyě-shyà-lay. ‖Put down your name and address. bǎ nǐ-de-'míng-dz gēn 'jù-jr̀ shyě-shyà-lay.

Put an end to *the thing stopped is expressed by a verb in the following constructions* méy . . .-le, . . . 'méy-le, 'bù-néng dzày . . .-le, dzày bū-. . .-le. ‖This news put an end to our hopes. 'jèy-shyà-dz (*or* 'dzèm yì-láy) °méy-'shī-wàng-le. *or* °méy-'jr̀-wàng-le. *or* yì-'tīng-jyàn 'jèy-ge-shyāw-shi wǒm jyèw 'jr̀-dàw °méy-'shī-wàng-le. *or* °méy-'jr̀-wàng-le.

Put in (*of time*) dzwò (*work*). ‖How many hours did you put in at the office last week? nǐ 'shàng-yí-ge-lǐ-bày yí-'gùng dzày gūng-shr̀-'fáng-li dzwò-le 'dwō-shǎw-shŕ-hew-de-shr̀?

Put (*affairs*) **in order** 'lyàw-lǐ, 'lyàw-lǐ-chīng-chu, 'jěng-li; (*wind up*) 'lyǎw-yi-lyǎw *or* 'lyǎw-le; (*set straight*) 'jěng-dwèn. ‖He's putting his affairs in order. tā jèng-dzày bǎ tā-de-'shr̀-ching dēw °'lyàw-li-'chīng-chu-le. *or* °'jěng-li-jěng-li.

Put off (*delay*) 'chyān-yán(-je bú-'bàn), wàng-shyà 'twēy, 'gē-je bú-'bàn; (*neglect*) 'lǎ-hu. **Put off until** 'děng(-dàw), 'chyān-yán-dàw, 'twēy-dàw, 'gē-dàw (*followed by an expression of time and a verb of action*). ‖He likes to put things off and then rush them through hurriedly at the last minute. tā 'cháng-bǎ-shr̀ °'gē-je bú-'bàn (*or* °'chyān-yán-je bú-'bàn, *or* °wàng-shyà 'twēy), dàw-le mwò-'lyǎwr 'jí-ji-mang-máng-de °'fǔ-yǎn-'lyǎw-shr̀. *or* °'tsǎw-shwày-'lyǎw-shr̀. *or* °'yì-hú-'gǔ-dew jyèw 'swàn-le. ‖Let's put off the decision until tomorrow. dzám děng 'míng-tyan dzày dǎ 'jú-yì-ba. ‖Don't put off until tomorrow what you can do today. 'jīn-tyan-néng-'bàn-de 'bù-kě °'twēy- (*or* °'chyān-yán-, *or* °'gē-, *or* °'děng-) dàw 'míng-tyan bàn. *or* 'fán-shr̀ bù-kě °'lǎ-hu. *or* °'chyān-yán.

Put off *a person.* (*Ward off*) táng; (*placate temporarily*) 'fǔ-yǎn; (*stop*) dǎng. ‖Can't you put him off until we have time to think it over? nǐ néng-bu-néng 'táng-tā yǐ-táng (*or* nǐ néng-bu-néng 'fǔ-yǎn-je tā), hǎw jyàw-wǒm yěw 'gūng-fu °'pán-swàn-pán-swàn? *or* °'dzwó-mwo-dzwó-mwo? *or* °'shyǎng-yi-shyǎng? *or* nǐ néng-bu-néng 'fǔ-yǎn tā shyē-'shŕ-hew (*or* nǐ néng-bu-néng 'táng-tā shyē-'shŕ-hew, *or* nǐ néng-bu-néng 'fǔ-yǎn-fǔ-yǎn tā, *or* nǐ néng-bu-néng 'táng-yi-táng tā), hǎw 'rúng-wǒm °'pán-swàn-pán-swàn? *or* °'dzwó-mwo-dzwó-mwo? *or* °'shyǎng-yi-shyǎng? ‖Put him off for three days. 'táng-tā (*or* 'fǔ-yǎn tā) 'sān-tyān dzày shwō. ‖I can't put him off any longer. wǒ 'dzày yě °táng- (*or* °dǎng-, *or* °fǔ-yǎn-) bú-'jù tā-le.

Put on *clothes.* (*Of articles of clothing which a part of the body passes through*) 'chwān(-shàng); (*of hats, gloves, ornaments*) 'dày(-shàng); (*of something tied, as a tie or belt*) 'jì(-shàng); (*of an outer covering, as a cape*) 'pēy(-shàng); (*of suspenders*) 'bēy (-shàng); (*of ornamental pins*) 'chā(-shàng). ‖Wait until I put on my coat and hat. děng wǒ chwān-shang dà-'yī dày-shang 'màw-dz.

Put on (*assume*) jyǎ-'jwāng, jyǎ-'jwāngr; (*only of an accent in speech*) jwāng-'chyāng; (*act*) jwāng. ‖That accent isn't real; it's just put on. nèy-ge-'kěw-yīn 'bú-shr̀ 'jēn-de, yí-'dìng shr̀ °jyǎ-'jwāngr-de. *or* °jyǎ-'jwāng-de. *or* °jwāng-'chyāng-ne. *or* °'jwāng-de.

Put out *a light* myè, shí; (*of electric light only*) gwān. ‖Put out the lights before you leave. 'méy-chū-chywu yǐ-'chyán bǎ-'dēng °myè-lew. *or* °shí-lew. *or* °gwān-lew.

Put out (*publish*) chū. ‖This publisher puts out some very good books. jèy-ge-yìn-shū-'jywú hěn 'chū-le jǐ-běr-'hǎw-shū.

Put *someone* **out.** (*Trouble*) gěy . . . jǎw 'má-fan; (*distract*) bǎ . . .-de-shèr dēw 'dān-wù-le. ‖Don't put yourself out on my account. byé yīn-wèy 'wǒ °bǎ nǐ-'dž-jǐ-de-shèr dēw 'dān-wù-le. *or* °gěy nǐ-'dž-jǐ jǎw 'má-fan.

Be *or* **feel put out.** ‖I feel quite put out about it. nèy-jyàn-shèr °ràng- (*or* °jyàw-)wǒ jywé-je °hěn bú-'tùng-kwày. *or* °'tǐng-'bvè-nyew.

Put something over on. (*Intimidate*) hǔ(-'jù); (*cheat*) mēng(-lyǎw) *or* pyàn(-lyǎw) *or* dzwàn (-lyǎw); (*take in*) jyàw . . . shàng-'dàng. ‖You can't put anything over on him. nǐ hǔ-bù-'jù tā. *or* nǐ béng shyǎng °'mēng(-de-lyǎw) tā. *or* °'pyàn-de-lyǎw ta. *or* °'dzwàn-de-lyǎw tā. *or* nǐ mēng-bu-'lyǎw tā. *or* nǐ pyàn-bu-'lyǎw tā. *or* nǐ dzwàn-bu-'lyǎw tā. *or* nǐ 'méy-fár jyàw-'tā shàng- 'dàng.

Put *a question* wèn. ‖The question was put to the chairman. 'nèy-shèr yěw-rén wèn jǔ-'shí láy-je.

Put through (*vote on and pass*) tūng-'gwǒ. ‖The bill was put through (by) Congress last week. 'nèy-ge-yì-àn gwó-'hwèy 'shàng-lǐ-bày yǐ-jīng tūng-'gwò-le.

Put through *a telephone call* tūng, dǎ, dǎ-'tūng. ‖He put through a call to his home. tā gēn tā-'jyā-li °tūng-le (*or* °dǎ-le, *or* °dǎ-'tūng-le) yí-tsž-dyàn-'hwà.

Put . . . to bed jyàw . . . chywù shwèy-'jyàw. ‖I have to put the kids to bed. wǒ děy jyàw shyǎr-'hár chywù shwèy-'jyàw.

Put . . . to death bǎ . . . 'nèng-sž-le; (*by shooting*) bǎ . . . chyàng-'bì-le; **be put to death** (*by shooting*) chyàng-'bì-le, jyàw-rén 'nèng-sž-le; (*by legal execution*) shèw 'sž-shíng-le. ‖He's already been put to death. tā yǐ-jīng °shèw 'sž-shíng-le. *or* °chyàng-'bì-le. *or* °jyàw-rén 'nèng-sž-le.

Put . . . to expense jyàw . . . hwā bù-'shǎw-de-chyán, ràng . . . hwā bù-'shǎw-de-chyán. ‖This will put me to considerable expense. jèy-ge yí-'dìng yàw °jyàw-wǒ (*or* °ràng-wǒ) hwā bù-'shǎw-de-chyán.

Put . . . to good use. (*Of money*) 'bú-shr̀ 'swéy-swéy-byàn-'byàn-de hwā; (*use rightly*) yùng-de 'jèng-dàng; (*use in the right place*) yùng-dzày 'jèng-chù. ‖You can be sure this money will be put to good use. nǐ 'fàng-shīn, 'jèy-bǐ-chyán °'jywé bù-néng 'swéy-swéy-byàn-'byàn-de jyèw 'hwā-le. *or* °'yí-'dìng yùng-de 'jèng-dàng. *or* °'yí-'dìng yùng-dzày 'jèng-chù.

Put . . . to work jyàw . . . dzwò-chǐ 'gūng-lay. ‖They put him to work as soon as he got there. tā yí-'dàw tām jyèw jyàw-tā dzwò-chǐ 'gūng-lay-le.

Put . . . to trouble; *see* **Put** *someone* **out,** *above.*

Put up (*build*) gày; shyēw (*of an engineering project*). ‖This building was put up in six months. jèy-ge-'léw yùng-le 'lyèw-ge-ywè-de-'gūng-fu jyèw °gày-'dé-le. *or* °'gày-'hǎw-le. *or* °'gày-'chéng-le.

Put up (*accommodate*). ‖Can you put up some extra guests for the night? 'nǐm-jèr yěw 'dì-fangr 'dwō jāw-dày 'jǐ-ge-rén 'gwò yí-yè-ma?

Put up for sale chū-'mày. ‖The farm will be put up for sale this week. núng-'chǎng jèy-lǐ-bày chū-'mày.

Put up (*supply, provide*). See SUPPLY, PROVIDE.

Put . . . up to jyàw . . ., 'tyáw-su . . .; jyàw . . . (*rather polite*). ‖Who put him up to that trick? shr̀ 'shéy °jyàw (*or* °tyáw-su-de, *or* °jyàw) tā nèm shr̀-'hwày-de? *or* °nèy-ge-hwàv-'jāwr shéy 'jyàw-gěy tā-de?

Put up with 'rěn-shèw. ‖I can't put up with this noise any longer. wǒ 'bù-néng dzày 'rěn-shèw 'jèy-jǔng-'chǎw-jyèr-le.

Stay put. (*Not move*) bù-nwó-'wōr; (*remain right at . . .*) hǎw-'hāwr-de dzày . . . 'dāy-je; (*behave*) bù-'hú-nàw *or* 'lǎw-lǎw-shř-'shř-de. ‖I'll stay put right here until you get back. nǐ 'méy-hwéy-lay yǐ-'chyán wǒ yí-'dìng °bù-nwó-'wōr. *or* °hǎw-'hāwr-de dzày-jèr 'dāy-je. *or* *meaning* stay out of trouble, but not necessarily in one spot °bù-'hú-nàw. *or* °'lǎw-lǎw-shř-'shř-de.

Q

QUALITY. (*Property*) -'shìng *or* 'shìng-jř *or* 'shìng-jf (*literary and technical*) ; *more commonly* **to have the property of** *is expressed as* **can** *or* **can be** néng, 'kĕ-yĭ; *or a resultative compound with* -de-; *or as is* shř. ‖**Bamboo has three special qualities; lightness, strength, and elasticity.** (*Technical*) 'jú-dz yĕw 'sān-jŭng-°'tè-shìng (*or* °'tè-'byé-de-'shìng-jř) ; 'chīng, 'jyān, 'rèn. ‖**This medicine has the quality of dissolving in water.** 'jèy-jŭng-yàw °yĕw rúng-jyĕ-'shìng. *or* °néng dzày 'shwĕy-li 'hwà-kāy. *or* °kĕ-yĭ dzày 'shwĕy-li 'hwà-kāy. *or* °'dzày 'shwĕy-li 'hwà-de-kāy.

(*Characteristic*) 'dì-fang (*also means place*) ; chù (*measure used elsewhere with* 'dì-fang), *commonly in combinations as* **good quality** 'hăw-chù *or* 'cháng-chù, **bad quality** 'hwày-chù *or* 'dwăn-chù. ‖**She has many good qualities.** tā yĕw hĕn-'dwō-dè-°'cháng-chù. *or* °'hăw-chù. ‖**He has many qualities that I like.** tā yĕw hĕn-'dwō-de-dì-fang wŏ hĕn 'shĭ-hwān. *or* wŏ-'shĭ-hwān-tā-de-'dì-fang hĕn 'dwō.

(*Grade*) 'chéng-shay (*of things only, not workmanship*) ; *usually expressed simply by saying a thing is* **good** hăw, **bad** hwày, **fine** jīng *or* shì *or* (*especially of workmanship*) 'jīng-shì, **coarse** tsū *or* (*especially of workmanship*) 'tsū-tsaw, **secondary** tsž; 'chéng-shay *may be described by any of these adjectives or as* **high** gāw *or* **low** dī; **quality** *as opposed to* **quantity** *is sometimes expressed by a literary word* jř *or* jf. ‖**There are different qualities of cloth.** bù-de-'chéng-shay bù-'túng. *or* bù yĕw 'hăw yĕw 'hwày. *or* bù yĕw 'jīng yĕw 'tsū. ‖**The better quality is, of course, more expensive.** (chéng-shay) 'hăw-de dz-'rán jyèw 'gwèy. ‖**If it's of good quality, quantity doesn't matter.** jř yàw-'hăw, 'dwō-shăw méy-'gwān-shi. ‖**We want (good) quality, not (large) quantity.** wŏm-yàw-de shř 'jīng (*or* 'hăw), bú-shr 'dwō. ‖**If the quality is good, I won't dicker about the price.** jř yàw °'hăw (*or* °'chéng-shay hăw, *or* °dzwò-de 'hăw, *or* °dzwò-de-'jīng-shì, *or* °'hwò hăw), 'jyà-chyán-shang hăw 'shāng-lyang. ‖**It's quality that's important, not quantity.** (*Literary*) jáw-jùng dzày 'jf, bú-dzày 'lyàng. ‖**The quality of his work has improved a great deal lately.** tā-'jìn-lay-dzwò-de hăw-'dwō-le.

Tone quality 'shēng-yīn.

QUANTITY. lyàng (*literary*), *but more commonly expressed by words such as* **many** *or* **much** dwō *or* shyē (*a measure*) ; **few** shăw; **small** shyăw; **large** dà, *etc.* ‖**He's neglecting quantity for quality.** (*Literary*) tā bú-gù-'lyàng, 'jř chyéw-'jř. *or* tā yàw 'chéng-shăy hăw, dzwò-'dwō-dzwò-'shăw-de bú-'dzày-hu. ‖**He hoarded a large quantity of good liquor.** tā 'twén-jī-le °'hăw-shyē- (*or* °'bù-'shăw-de-, *or* °'bù-'shăw-)'shàng-dĕng-de-'jyĕw. ‖**They say there are (large) quantities of coal underground in this region.** yĕw-rén shwō 'jèy-yí-dày-dì-'dǐ-shya yĕw °'hăw-shyē- (*or* °'bù-'shăw-de-) 'méy.

QUARREL. (*See also* **FIGHT.**) *The Chinese expressions are all verb-noun phrases or verbs but some distinctions of meaning are observable.* dă-'jyà *refers to an angry quarrel, which may include blows.* nàw 'chăw-dz *and* nàw 'yì-jyàn *refer to a violent disagreement.* fān-'lyăn *refers to a serious dispute after which the participants are still angry with each other.* chăw-'jyà, chăw-'dzwéy, dă 'chăw-dz, *and* bàn-'dzwéy *refer to any kind of argument.* nàw, chăw, *and* 'rāng-rang *refer to a noisy wrangling, as among children.* jēng *is about the same, but may include a more serious dispute; it also means* **to compete.** ‖**They haven't been friends since that quarrel.** tām 'dž-tsúng 'nèy-tsž-°chăw-'jyà (*or* °dă-'jyà, *or* °chăw-'dzwéy, *or* °nàw-'chăw-dz, *or* °dă-'chăw-dz, *or* °'bàn-'dzwéy} *or* °nàw-'yì-jyàn, *or* °fān-'lyăn) yĭ-'hèw jyéw méy 'hăw-gwò. ‖**They had a quarrel about some woman.** tām wèy-le ge-'nywŭ-rén °chăw-'jyà. *etc. or* °chăw-le yí-tsž-'jyà. *etc.* ‖**He always quarrels with people.** tā 'lăw gēn-rén °chăw-'jyà. *etc.* (*except* °fān-'lyăn; *which is not appropriate here.*) ‖**What are they quarreling about?** tām wèy-'shéme dzày-nàr °'chăw? *or* °chăw-'jyà? *or* °chăw-'dzwéy? *or* °dă 'chăw-dz? *or* °bàn-'dzwéy? *or* °'rāng-rang. ‖**The children are quarreling about what game they want to play.** shyăw-'hár-mén bù-néng 'dìng-gwèy wár-shéme 'hăw, dzày-nàr °'chăw-chǐ-lay-le. *or* °'chăw-ne. *or* °'nàw-chǐ-lay-le. *or* °'nàw-ne. *or* °'jēng-chǐ-lay-le. *or* °'jēng-ne. *or* °'rāng-rang-chǐ-lay-le. *or* °'rāng-rang-ne.

QUARTER. (*Fourth*) 'sž-fēn-jř- (*followed by a numeral indicating how many*). ‖**Each son received a quarter of the estate.** mĕy-ge-'ér-dz dé-le 'sž-fēn-jř-'yī-de-jyā-chăn.

(*Divide into four parts*). (*By cutting*) 'chye-cneng sž-'bàr; (*by other action*) *substitute other verbs for* chyē. ‖**She quartered the apples.** tā bă 'píng-gwŏ dēw 'chyē-chéng sž-'bàr.

(*Twenty-five cents*) 'lyăng-máw-'wŭ(-fēn-chyán). ‖**It costs a quarter to get to the theater.** dàw shì-'ywán-dz-chywu dĕy hwā 'lyăng-máw-'wŭ.

(*Fifteen minutes*) kè (*measure with* jūng). ‖**The train leaves at quarter of three.** hwŏ-'chē chà yí-'kè sān-dyăn kāy. *or* hwŏ-'chē 'lyăng-dyăn-sān-'kè kāy. ‖**The train leaves at quarter after three.** hwŏ-'chē 'sān-dyăn-yí-'kè kăy. ‖**We waited there for three-quarters of an hour.** wŏm dzày-nàr 'dĕng-le 'sān-kè-jūng.

(*Place*) 'dì-fang, *with* chù *as measure.* ‖**He has a very bad reputation in certain quarters.** *expressed as* **The people of certain quarters** °**speak very ill of him.** *or* °**feel he is worthless.** 'yĕw-jĭ-chù-'dì-fang-de-rén °'mà-tā mà-de 'lì-hay. *or* °jywé-je tā 'bú-shr 'dūng-shi.

Be quartered (*stationed*) 'jù-jā. ‖The soldiers were quartered in an old house near the fort. bīng děw jù-jā-dzày lí-'yíng-pán'-bù-'ywǎn-de-yì-swěr-'lǎw-fáng-dz-li.

Quarters. (*Place to live*) 'jù-de(-dì-fang); (*field headquarters*) shíng-'yíng. ‖His quarters are near the camp. tā-'jù-de(-dì-fang) (*or* tā-dé-'shíng-'yíng) lí 'yíng-pán bù-'ywǎn.

QUEEN. *Wife of the ruler* hwáng-'hèw; *female ruler* nywǔ-'wáng *or* nywǔ-'jǔ. ‖This magazine has a picture of the queen. jèy-běr-'dzá-jř děng-le yì-jāng-°hwáng-'hèw- (*or* °nywǔ-'wáng-, *or* °nywǔ-'jǔ-) de-shyàng-'pyār.

QUESTION. *Inquiry or point of uncertainty* 'wèn-tí; (*something asked*) 'wèn-de; (*the words of something asked*) 'wèn-de-'hwà; (*something someone wants to ask*) yàw-'wèn-de; (*polite terms*): (yàw-)'chǐng-jyàw-de; (*an unclear point*) bù-'míng-bay-de(-dì-fang). *Often expressed verbally as to ask* wèn; (*want to find out about something from someone*) yàw gēn . . . 'dǎ-tīng; (*polite terms*): (*want to get instructions from someone*) yàw gēn . . . 'lǐng-jyàw; (*request someone to give instruction*) (yàw) chǐng . . . 'jř-jyàw. **Questions and answers** 'wèn-tí dá-'àn. ‖What you said is a statement, not a question. nǐ-'shwō-de shř nǐ-de-'yì-jyàn, 'bú-shr ge-'wèn-tí. ‖Why don't you put it in the form of a question? nǐ 'bù-rú bǎ jèy-ge yùng 'wèn-tí láy 'wèn-wen. ‖Have you answered all the questions? 'wèn-de (*or* 'wèn-tí) 'dēw dá-le-ma? ‖What you said didn't answer my question. nǐ-'dá-de bú-shr wǒ-'wèn-de. ‖Do you understand my question? wǒ-'wèn-de-'hwà nǐ 'dǔng-ma? ‖What was your question? nǐ wèn-'shéme láy-je? ‖Any questions? yěw shéme-yàw-'wèn-de-ma? ‖If there are any questions, raise your hand. yěw yàw-'wén-de, jyèw jywǔ-'shěw. ‖Would you like to ask any questions? nǐ yěw yàw-wèn-de-'shř-ma? *or* nǐ shyǎng 'wèn-shéme-ma? *or* nǐ yàw 'wèn-shéme-ma? ‖I have a question here. (*Polite expressions*) 'chǐng-jyàw, 'chǐng-jyàw. *or* wǒ yěw yì-'dyǎn°-yàw-'chǐng-jyàw-de. *or* °-bù-'míng-bay-de. *or* °yàw (gēn-nín) 'lǐng-jyàw. *or* °yàw chǐng-nín 'jř-jyàw. (*Expressions not necessarily polite, but not impolite either*) wǒ-jèr yěw ge-'wèn-tí. *or* wǒ yéw yì-'dyǎn-yàw-'wèn-de. (*Expressions that may be impolite*) wǒ 'wèn-nǐ. *or* wǒ yàw 'wèn-nǐ yí-jyàn-'shř. ‖I want to ask you a question. (*Polite*) 'chǐng-jyàw, chǐng-jyàw. *or* wǒ yěw yì-'dyǎn-bù-'míng-bay-de-dì-fang, °kě-yǐ 'wèn-ma? *or* °gēn-nín 'lǐng-jyàw-lǐng-jyàw. *or* °chǐng-nín gěy 'jř-jyàw-jř-jyàw. (*Neutral*) wǒ yàw gēn-nǐ 'dǎ-tīng-dǎ-tīng. *or* wǒ yàw 'wèn-nǐ yí-jyàn-'shř. ‖They asked me a lot of questions about my past experience. (*See also* to question, *below*.) tām 'pán-wèn wǒ (*or* tām 'wèn-láy-wèn-'chywù-de wèn-wǒ, *or* tām 'dzwǒ-wèn yèw-wèn 'wèn-wǒ) °dēw 'dzwò-gwo shéme-'shèr. *or* °-de-'lywǔ-lì láy-je.

(*Matter of doubt*) 'wèn-tí. ‖Then the question of his qualification came up for discussion. 'hèw-láy

'tǎw-lwèn-dàw tā-de-'dz-gé-'wèn-tí. ‖There is no question about his ability. tā-de-'tsáy-gàn °'méy-yěw wèn-'tí. *or* °'bù-chéng wèn-'tí.

(*Problem*) 'wèn-tí; *often indirectly expressed by saying that something is* hard to do nán 'bàn; *or* easy to do rúng-yì 'bàn, *etc. See* PROBLEM. ‖It's a question to know what to do in this situation. 'jèy-jǔng-'chíng-shíng hěn nán 'bàn. *or* dàw 'jèy-ge-'dì-bu hěn nán 'bàn.

To question *someone*. (*Ask many questions of*) 'pán-wèn; (*by authorities of a person under arrest*) 'shěn-wèn. ‖The prisoners will be held for questioning. 'fú-lwǒ děy 'yā-chi-lay °'shěn-wèn. *or* °'pán-wèn.

To question *something* (*doubt*). (*Suspect that*) 'yí-shīn *or* (*feel that*) 'jywé-je *with a following verb negated*. ‖I question the sincerity of his speech. wǒ 'yí-shīn (*or* wǒ 'jywé-je) tā-'shwō-de °'bú-shr 'jēn-shīn-'hwà. *or* °'yán-bù-yéw 'jūng (*literary*).

Beside the question. *See* beside the point *under* POINT. ‖His remarks are beside the question. tā-shwō-de °gēn 'běn-tí wú-'gwān. *or* °'bù-tyē-'tí.

Beyond question. (*Unquestionably*) 'háw-wú-'yí-wèn-de; (*cannot be questioned*) 'yùng-bu-jáw 'wèn-le. ‖His honesty is beyond question. tā 'háw-wú-'yí-wèn-de shř yí-ge-'hěn-chéng-shř-de-rén. *or* tā hěn 'chéng-shř (*or* tā hěn kě-'kàw), nèy 'yùng-bu-jáw 'wèn-le.

Out of the question yí-'dìng bù-'shíng, 'jywé-dwèy bù-'shíng. ‖It's out of the question for me to leave the job. 'yàw shyǎng 'jyàw-wǒ bǎ-shèr 'rēng-shya °yí-'dìng bù-'shíng. *or* °'jywé-dwèy bù-'shíng.

Without question yí-'dìng, 'jwěn. *See also* CERTAINLY. ‖He'll be there without question. tā yí-'dìng dàw. *or* tā 'jwěn dàw.

QUICK, QUICKLY. *Fast* (*general term*) kwày; (*in a hurry*) gǎn-'kwày; (*immediately*) 'gǎn-jǐn, 'děng-shŕ, lì-'kè, 'dāng-shŕ, mǎ-'shàng; (*quick and efficient*) 'má-lì; (*nimble, active*) hwó *or* 'líng-byan. ‖Shut that door, and be quick about it. bǎ-mén 'gwān-shang, 'kwày-je-dyar. *or* bǎ-mén 'gwān-shang, 'kwày-je, 'kwày-je. *or* bǎ-mén 'gwān-shang, kwày 'chywù. *or* 'kwày bǎ-mén 'gwān-shang. *or* kwày-'kwār-de bǎ-mén 'gwān-shang. *or* gǎn-'kwày bǎ-mén 'gwān-shang. ‖Be quick about it! 'kwày-je! *or* 'kwày-dyar! *or* kwày-'kwār-de! *or* gěy-wǒ °'gǎn-jǐn (*or* °lì-'kè, *or* °'dāng shŕ, *or* °'děng-shŕ, *or* °mǎ-'shàng) jyèw 'bàn. ‖I'll be there as quick(ly) as I can. wǒ dàw-nèr 'néng dwō kwày jyèw dwō 'kwày. ‖Get there as quickly as possible. dàw-de ywè 'kwày ywè 'hǎw. ‖His answer was quick and to the point. tā-'hwéy-da-de yèw 'kwày yèw 'chyà-dang. ‖His hands aren't quick enough for this sort of work. dzwò 'jèy-jǔng-shř tā-de-'shěw bú-gèw °'kwày-de. *or* °'má-lì-de. ‖He's certainly quick on his feet! tā-'pǎw-de (*or* tā-'tyàw-da-de, *or* tā-'twéy-jyǎwr) jēn °'kwày. *or* °'hwó. *or* °'líng-byan. ‖He's a man of quick decisions. tā-jèy-rén 'shéme-shř °'děng-shŕ (*or* °'dāng-shŕ, *or* °lì-'kè, *or* °mǎ-'shàng) jyèw néng 'dwàn.

(*Of temper*) jí, dzàw, 'jí-dzàw. ‖She has a very quick temper. tā-'pí-chì hěn °'jí. *or* °'dzàw. *or* °'jí-dzàw.

Quick-witted (*or* **quick on the trigger**) 'shīn-sz (tǐng-) 'kwày-de, shyǎng-de (tǐng-) 'kwày-de, (tǐng-) 'jī-líng-de, (tǐng-) 'líng-li-de, (*literary*) yěw 'jí-jr̀. ‖He's pretty quick-witted; he'll always have an immediate answer for your questions. tā-'shīn-sz tǐng-'kwày-de (*or* tā-shyǎng-de tǐng-'kwày-de, *or* tā tǐng-'jī-líng-de, *or* tā tǐng-'líng-li-de, *or* tā hěn yěw 'jí-jr̀); yì-'tí-chi 'shéme-lay, tā 'dēw néng lì-'kè jyèw 'hwéy-nǐ yí-tàw-'hwà.

In an instant; also **be quick to . . .** *is expressed as* **one instant** (*or* **one look, one listen,** *etc.*), **immediately** . . . 'yí-shyà-dz (*or* yí-'kàn, yì-'tīng, *etc.*), jyèw . . .-le. ‖It was all over so quickly that I didn't even see it. 'yí-shyà-dz jyèw 'wán-le, wǒ háy 'méy-kàn-jyan. ‖Don't be so quick to take offense. byé nèm 'yí-shyà-dz jyèw 'nǎw-le. ‖He was quick to catch on. tā yì-'shywé jyèw 'hwèy-le. *or* tā yì-'tīng jyèw 'dǔng-le. *or* tā yí-'kàn jyèw 'míng-bay-le. *or* tā 'yí-shyà-dz jyèw 'tūng-le.

Cut *someone* **to the quick** jyàw . . . 'hěn bú-'tùng-kway. ‖His statements cut me to the quick. tā-'shwō-de jyàw-wǒ 'hěn bú-'tùng-kway.

QUIET. *Without noise or confusion* 'ān-jìng, jìng; (*only of a place*) 'chīng-jìng; (*of profound stillness*) 'chén-jìng; (*peaceful and quiet*) 'píng-jìng; (*of a person, quiet in manner*) 'sz̀-sz-wén-'wén(-de); *or negatives of words meaning* **noisy** dzwò-'shēngr, chū-'shēngr, chàw, 'rāng-rang; *or* **rowdy** 'nàw-hung; *or* **mischievous** hú-'nàw *or* táw-'chì. ‖I live in a quiet neighborhood. wǒ-'jù-de-nèy-yí-dày hěn °'ān-jìng. *or* °'jìng. *or* °'chīng-jìng. ‖It's as quiet as night around here. jèr-'ān-jìng-de (*or* jèr-'jìng-de, *or* jèr-'chīng-jìng-de, *or* jèr-'chén-jìng-de) shyàng dzày 'yè-lì shr̀-de. ‖We've learned to enjoy the quiet of the country. wǒm jyàn-'jyān-de néng 'lǐng-hwèy shyāng-shya-°'ān-jìng-de (*or* °'chén-jìng-de-) 'hǎw-chù-le. ‖He's so quiet you'd never know he's around. tā-'ān-jìng-de nǐ tsúng-láy bù-'jywé-de tā 'dzày-jèr. ‖He's very quiet. tā-rén hěn 'ān-jìng. *or* tā 'lǎw bú-dzwò-'shēngr. *or* tā 'lǎw bù-chū-'shēngr. *or* tā nèm 'ān-ān-jìng-'jyèngr-de. *or* tā nèm 'sz̀-sz-wén-'wén-de. ‖Quiet down, please! 'ān-jìng-dyar! *or* byé 'chǎw-le! *or* byé 'rāng-rang-le! ‖He'll quiet down a bit when he grows up. děng tā 'dà-dyǎr jyèw 'bú-nèm °'nàw-hung-le. *or* °'hú-'nàw-le. *or* °'táw-'chì-le.

With little current lyéw-de 'hwǎn, lyéw-de 'màn, lyéw-de bù-'jí. ‖The stream isn't quiet enough. jèy-ge-'hé-gēwr-de-'shwěy lyéw-de tày 'jí. ‖It's very quiet two miles upstream, though. wàng-shàng dzěw 'èr-li shwěy lyéw-de °'hwǎn 'dwō-le. *or* °'màn 'dwō-le.

(*Not bright, of colors*) 'sù(-shǎr-de). ‖She always dresses in quiet colors. tā lǎw shr̀ chwān 'sù-shǎr-de-'yī-fu.

(*To calm someone*) bǎ . . . 'yā-shyà-chywù, bǎ . . . 'jèn-jìng-shyà-chywù. ‖His speech quieted the crowd. tā-nèy-yì-fān-'hwà bǎ-rén dēw °'yā-shyà-chywù-le. *or* °'jèn-jìng-shyà-chywù-le.

QUIT. (*Stop doing something*). ‖Quit it! (*Making trouble*) byé dǎw-'lwàn. (*Being rowdy*) byé h·-'nàw. *or* byé hú-'láy. (*Telling lies*) 'byé shyā-'shwō-le. *or* 'byé shyā-'jyǎng-le. (*Talking nonsense*) 'byé hú-'shwō-le. (*Talking*) 'béng shwō-le. *etc.*

(*Stop work according to schedule*) shyà-'gūng. ‖I quit at five. wǒ 'wǔ-dyǎn-jūng shyà-'gūng.

(*Leave something for a time*) 'gē-shya. ‖Why don't you quit what you're doing and come out for a walk? nǐ 'wèy-shéme bù-bǎ nǐ-dzwò-de-shèr 'gē-shya, gēn-wǒm chū-chywù °'dzěw-dzěw? *or* °'lyēw-da-lyēw-da?

(*Leave a job permanently*) dzěw, bú-'gàn-le. bǎ shr̀-ching 'tsź-le, bǎ shr̀-ching 'lyàw-shya jyèw ḥú-'gàn-le. ‖He quit (his job) yesterday. tā 'dzwér °'dzěw-le. *or* °'bú-'gàn-le. *or* °'bǎ shr̀-ching 'tsź-le. *or* °'bǎ shr̀-ching 'lyàw-shya jyèw bú-'gàn-le.

(*Surrender*) téw-'shyáng; (*ask for peace*) jyǎng-'hé *or* chyéw-'hé. ‖The enemy refuses to quit. 'dí-rén bù-kěn °'téw-'shyáng. *or* °'jyǎng-'hé. *or* °'chyéw-'hé

QUITE. *With meaning ranging from* **somewhat** *to* **very** tǐng, hěn, hǎw. ‖The movie was quite good. dyàn-'yěngr tǐng 'hǎw. *or* dyàn-'yěngr hěn bú-'hwày. *or* dyàn-'yěngr tǐng-yěw-'yì-sz-de. ‖It turned out to be quite cold during the night. 'jyē-gwǒ 'wǎn-shang °'tǐng 'lyáng. *or* °'hěn 'lyáng. *or* °'hǎw 'lyáng-le. ‖I live quite near here. wǒ-'jù-de 'lí-jèr °'tǐng 'jìn. *or* °'hěn jìn. *or* °'jìn-je-ne. ‖He has quite a lot of money in the bank. tā dzày yín-'háng-li 'bě̌n yěw jǐ-ge-'chyár. ‖There were quite °a few (*or* °a number of, *or* °a lot of) people there. 'dàw-de-rén hěn 'dwō. *or* 'dàw-de-rén bù-'shǎw. *or* 'dàw-le 'hǎw-shyē-rén.

Quite a *plus a noun* jēn *plus a description indicating goodness, badness, interest, etc.* ‖That was quite an experience we had yesterday. 'dzwér-ge-dzám-nèy-'dwàr (*or* 'dzwér-ge-dzám-nèy-jyàn-'shèr) jēn °'kě-'yǐ-de-ya! *or* (*All that could be asked for*) °'gèw-'chyáw-de. *or* (*All that could be borne*) °'gèw-'shèw-de.

Not quite (. . .) 'chà-dyǎr *or* 'chà-yi-dyǎr *or* 'chà-bu-dwō (*may be followed by* jyèw *plus a verb*); bú-'dà *plus an adjective*. ‖That's not quite what I wanted. jèy-ge 'chà-dyǎr. *or* (*not quite right*) jèy-ge bú-'dà 'dwèy. ‖It's not quite finished. (*or* I'm not quite finished.) 'chà-yi-dyǎr jyèw 'wán-le. *or* 'chà-bu-dwō jyèw 'wán-le. *or* 'mey-wán-ne, háy 'chà-dyǎr.

Be quite sure that (*in statements, meaning* **in all probability**) 'dwō-bàn; (*in questions, meaning* **know for certain**) 'jwěn jr̀-dàw *or* 'jēn jr̀-dàw *or* *expressed as* **dare to say for certain** gǎn 'jwěn shwō, *or as* **certainly** 'jēn-shr. ‖I'm quite sure I can go. wǒ 'dwō-bàn néng 'chywù. ‖Are you quite sure that you can't go? nǐ 'jēn-shr bù-néng 'chywù-ma? ‖Are you quite sure that he's the guy? nǐ 'jwěn jr̀-dàw (*or* nǐ 'jēn jr̀-daw, *or* nǐ gǎn 'jwěn shwō) shr̀ 'tā-ma?

Quite so. *or* **Oh, quite!** méy-'tswòr. *or* 'hěn dwèy. *or* 'jèng-shr̀. *or* yì-'dyǎr bú-'tswò. *or* 'jyèw-shr 'nèm-je. *or* kě bú-'shr̀-ma?!

R

RACE. (*A contest of speed; competition*) bǐ-'sày, *in compounds* sày-; *also in compounds* pǎw-; horse race sày-'mǎ *or* pǎw-'mǎ; automobile race sày-'chē *or* pǎw-'chē; race between persons sày-'pǎw. ‖The races will be held next week. 'shyà lǐ-'bày °bǐ-'sày. *or* °sày-'mǎ, *etc.* ‖Are you going to the (*horse*) races this afternoon? nǐ jyēr-'shyà-wǔ chywù 'kàn sày-'mǎ-ma? ‖His horse won every race. *is expressed as* His hórse won every time. 'tā-de-mǎ hwéy-'hwér 'yíng. *or as* His horse won every time they raced. 'tā-de-mǎ měy-tsž-'sày dēw 'yíng-le. ‖He made a lot of money on the (*horse*) races. *is expressed as* He bought tickets on the horses and won a lot of money. tā měy mǎ-'pyàw yíng-le bù-shǎw-de-'chyán. ‖It was a race for us to get to the station on time. *is expressed as* We had to rush not to miss the train. wǒm děy 'jǐn-je 'gǎn tsáy méy-'wù-le 'chē. *or as* We ran to the station to get the train. wǒm 'jǐn-je 'pǎw dàw chē-'jàn tsáy 'gǎn shàng-'chē.

(*To have a contest for speed*) sày, bǐ, bǐ-'sày, chyǎng-je (kàn shéy shyān 'dàw). ‖I'll race you. wǒ gēn-nǐ 'sày-say. ‖The two boats raced into the harbor. jèy-lyǎng-jr̄-'chwán 'chyǎng-je 'kāy-jìn hǎy-'gǎng chywù-le. ‖I'll race you to that schoolhouse. *is expressed as* Let's see which of us runs to that schoolhouse first. kàn dzám-'lyǎ 'shwéy shyān 'pǎw-dàw nèy-ge-shywé shyàw-nar chywù.

(*To go fast; of persons or animals*) *is expressed as* run pǎw; (*of vehicles*) 'fēy kwày-de 'kāy. ‖The dog raced down the road. gěw dzày 'jyē-shang jř 'pǎw. ‖The car raced past the bridge. nèy-lyàng-'chē 'fēy kwày-de 'kāy-gwo 'chyáw chywù-le.

To race a motor *is expressed as* to make a motor go fast jyàw 'jī-chi jwàn-de hěn 'kwày. ‖Why are you racing the engine? nǐ 'wèy-shéme jyàw·'jī-chi jwàn-de nèm-'kwày?

(*People of same ancestry*) -'jǔng-de-rén. ‖What is your race? nǐ 'shǔ-ywú 'něy-yì-'jǔng-de-'rén? ‖The French and English belong to the same race. 'yīng-gwo-rén gēn 'fa-gwo-rén túng-'jǔng. Human race rén-'lèy; lèy *means* class *or* group, *and is found in compounds like* 'chù-lèy (*animal class*) *or* 'nyǎw-lèy (*bird class*). ‖He's an enemy of the whole human race. 'tā shř chywán-rén-'lèy-de-gūng-'dí. *or*, *more common.* He hates the whole human race. *is expressed as* He hates absolutely everybody. 'swǒ-yěw-de-'rén tā 'dēw hèn.

RADIO. wú-shyàn-'dyàn; (*receiving set*) shēw-yīn-'jī. ‖Do you have a radio here? nǐ 'jèr yěw wú-shyàn-'dyàn-ma? ‖The news was radioed to us. jèy-ge-'shyāw-shi shř yùng wú-shyàn-'dyàn 'dǎ-láy-de.

RAILROAD. tyě-'lù. (*Railroad company*) tyě-lù-'jywú; (*train*) hwǒ-'chē; (*railroad track*) hwǒ-chē-'dàw; (*railroad station*) hwǒ-chē-'jàn. ‖A new railroad will be built soon. yàw 'shyēw yì-'tyáw-shīn-tyě-'lù-le. ‖The railroad offers a cheap rate on Saturday. tyě-lù-'jywú gwēy-'dìng lǐ-bày-'lyèw chē-pyàw jyàn-'jyà. ‖He works for the railroad. tā dzày tyě-'lù-shang dzwò-'shř. ‖The railroad is torn up beyond the city, chéng-'nèy-byar-de-hwǒ-chē-'dàw 'chāy-le.

To railroad *someone or something*. ‖They railroaded the bill through the House. *is expressed as* They rushed and got the bill passed in the House. shyà-yì-ywàn 'chyǎng-je jyèw bǎ jèy-ge-yì-'àn 'tūng-gwo-le.

RAIN. ywǔ; to rain shyà-'ywǔ. Drop of rain dyǎr; rainstorm 'bàw-ywǔ, dà-'fēng-ywǔ, bàw-'fēng-ywǔ, kwáng-'fēng-bàw-'ywǔ. ‖A light rain made the street wet. yí-jèn-shyǎw-'ywǔ bǎ 'jyē-shang dēw jyàw-'shř-le. ‖It rained hard during the morning. 'dzǎw-shang ywǔ-'shyà-de hěn 'dà. ‖Only a few drops of rain have fallen. gwāng 'dyàw-le jǐ-ge-'dyǎr. ‖It's beginning to rain. dyàw 'dyǎr-le. ‖The rains started late this year. 'jīn-nyán shyà-'ywǔ shyà-de 'wǎn. *or* 'jīn-nyán ywǔ-'shwěy 'wǎn.

RAISE. To raise *an army* jāw, lyàn. ‖The country raised a large army. jèy-yì-'gwó °'jāw-le (*or* °'lyàn-le) hěn-'dwō-de-'bīng.

Raise *crops* jùng; raise *farm animals* yǎng. ‖This farmer raises wheat, but that one raises hogs. jèy-ge-'núng-rén jùng 'mày-dz, 'nèy-ge yǎng-'jū.

Raise *a curtain* kāy. ‖We'd better get in, they've raised the curtain. dzám 'jìn-chywu-ba, 'shì yǐ-jīng kāy-'mù-le.

Raise *a family* yǎng. ‖They raised a big family. tām 'yǎng-le yí-'dà-jyā-dz. *or expressed as* There are a lot of children in their family. tām-'jyā-lǐ 'háy-dz hěn 'dwō. *But* ‖He was raised in China. tā-shr dzày 'jūng-gwō jǎng-'dà-le-de.

Raise *a flag* shēng, 'gwà-chi-láy. ‖The soldiers raised the flag. jèy-shyē-'bīng bǎ 'chí-dz °'shēng-chi-láy-le. *or* °'gwà-chi-láy-le.

Raise *one's hand* jywǔ-'shěw. ‖If you want a ticket please raise your hand. shéy yàw-shr yàw-'pyàw de-hwà, jywǔ-'shěw.

Raise *one's hat* jāy 'màw-dz. ‖When she came by, he raised his hat. nèy-ge-'nywǔ-de gwò-lay de-shf-hew, tā bǎ 'màw-dz 'jāy-le.

Raise *money* jywān. ‖How large a sum did they raise? tām yí-'gùng jywān-le 'dwō-shaw-chyán?

Raise *prices* jàng-'jyàr, jyā-'jyàr, bǎ 'jyà-chyán tí-'gāw-le. ‖He's raised the price of this book. tā bǎ jèy-běr-'shū-de-'jyà-chyán tí-'gāw-le. *or* jèy-běr-'shū tā °'jàng-'jyàr-le. *or* °'jyā-'jyàr-le.

Raise wages jǎng 'gūng-chyán; raise salary jyā-'shīn. ‖Should we raise their wages? wǒm 'yīng-gāy gěy tā-men jǎng 'gūng-chyán-ma?

Raise *a question* 'tí-chu-lay. ‖He raised a very interesting question. tā 'tí-chu-lay yí-ge-hěn-yěw-'yìsz-de-'wèn-tí.

A raise (*in pay*) *is expressed as* to raise wages *or* salary (*see above*). ‖He asked for a raise. tā 'yǎwchyéw °jyā-'shīn. *or* °jǎng-'chyán.

RANGE. (*Variety*). *No one expression.* ‖What is his range of prices? *is expressed as* His prices go from how much to how much? tā-nèr-de-'jyà-chyán shr̀ tsúng 'dwō-shaw dàw 'dwō-shaw? ‖The store had only a small range of colors to choose from. *is expressed as* The store didn't have many kinds of colors to choose from. jèy-'pù-dz 'méy-yěw °'dwō-shaw-jǔng-'yán-shar (*or* °'dwō-shaw-yàngr-'yán-shar) kě 'tyāw-de. ‖He has a wide range of interests. *is expressed as* The things he likes are many. tā-'shǐ-hwān-de-'dūng-shi hěn 'dwō. ‖His voice has a very wide range. *is expressed as* His voice can go high and low. tā-de-'sǎng-dz néng 'gāw néng 'dī. ‖His voice has a very narrow range. *is expressed as* His voice when high can't go very high, and when low can't go very low. 'tā-de-sǎng-dz gāw yé 'gāw-bù-shàng-chywù 'dwō-shǎw, 'dī yě 'dī bú-shyà-'chywù dwō-'shǎw. ‖Prices range from one to five dollars. *is expressed as* Prices go from one to five dollars. 'jyà-chyán shr̀ tsúng 'yí-kwày dàw 'wù-kwày.

(*Distance*). ‖Are we out of (range of) hearing? *is expressed as* Can people hear us? rén 'háy néng 'tīng-de-jyàn wǒm shwō-'hwà-ma? ‖Wait till the wolf is within (firing) range and then shoot. 'děng dàw láng dàw-le shè-'chéng yi-'nèy dzày 'fàng. *or* (*If you're the one who's moving*) *expressed as* Wait till the gun can get the wolf, then shoot. děng dàw 'chyǎng 'gèw-de-'jáw nèy-tyáw-'láng de-'shf-hew dzày 'fàng.

(*Grazing land*) tsǎw-'dì. ‖The cattle were turned out on the range. nyéw dēy 'fàng-chū-chywù dzày tsǎw-'dì-lǐ-ne.

(*Area for practising shooting*) chǎng. Rifle range bǎ-'chǎng. ‖You can find him at the rifle range. nǐ 'kě-yi dàw bǎ-'chǎng chywù 'jǎw-tā.

(*Of mountains*) dàw. ‖We will cross the range of mountains tomorrow. wǒ-men 'myéngr yàw 'gwò jèy-dàw-'shān.

(*Stove*) 'lú-dz. ‖Light the range. bǎ 'lú-dz 'lúng-shang.

(*To wander*). ‖Wolves range over this valley. cháng yěw 'láng dzày jèy-shān-'gǔ-li °ràw. *or* °pǎw-láy pǎw-chywù.

RANK. (*Row*) páy; to form ranks jàn-'dwèy *or* páy-'dwèy. ‖Only the front rank had guns. 'jř yěw 'chyán-páy-de-bīng yěw 'chyāng. ‖The soldiers formed ranks jèy-shyē-'bīng páy-'dwèy-le.

To come up from the ranks dāng-'bīng chū-'shēn *or* dǎ dāng-'bīng-'shēng-shang lay. ‖That major has come up from the ranks. nèy-ge-shàw-'shyàw shr̀ °'dāng 'bīng chū-'shēn. *or* °dǎ dāng-'bīng 'shēng-shang-lay-de.

(*Position, title*) 'jyē-ji. ‖He had the rank of captain. tā-de-'jyē-ji shr̀ shàng-'wèy.

(*Class, grade*) děng, *or* lyéw. ‖That university is of the first rank. 'nèy-ge-dà-'shywé shr̀ °dì-'yī-děng-de-shywé-'fǔ. *or* °dì-'yī-lyéw-de-shywé-'fǔ. *or* °jyà-'děng-de-shywé-'fǔ. *or* (*very good*) °dǐng-'hǎw-de.

(*To be graded as*) *is expressed as* to be shr̀ *or* to count as swàn. ‖He ranks second in popularity among all the movie stars. swǒ-'yěw-de-'dyàn-yěngr míng-'shīng-li tā shr̀ dì-'èr-ge-dzwèy-jyàw-rén-shǐ-hwān-de. ‖This city ranks high in importance. jèy-ge-'chéng 'swàn shr̀ hěn jùng-yàw-de-'yí-ge.

(*To grade*). ‖How would you rank him in efficiency? *is expressed as* How well do you think he works? nǐ 'jywé-de tā bàn-'shr̀ 'dzěme-yàng? ‖He doesn't rank very high with me. *is expressed as* I don't regard him as worth much. wǒ kàn tā °'méy-shéme lyǎw-bù-'dé. *or* °'bù-dzěme-'yàng.

RAPID. *See also* FAST. Rapidly kwày, kwày-'kwār-de, 'gǎn-je, 'máng-je, 'jǐn-je, *or* lyán-'máng. ‖He made a rapid journey. tā °kwày-'kwār-de (°'gǎn-je, *etc.*) 'dzěw-le yí-'tàng. ‖There has been a rapid increase in the population. rén-'kěw dzēng-'jyā-de hěn 'kwày. *or* *expressed as* The population increased suddenly. 'rén-kěw dà-'dzēng.

Rapids chwǎn-'lyéw; (*rapid current*) jí-'lyéw; (*strong current*) shwěy-'lyèw. ‖The rapids are stronger this year than last. jīn-nyán-de-°chwǎn-'lyéw (*or* °jí-'lyéw *or* °shwěy-'lyèw) bǐ 'chywù-nyán °gèng-'jí. *or* °gèng-'dà.

RATE. (*Charge or fee*) fèy, dž; (*price*) jyàr, 'jyà-chyán; special rate yěw-'dày. ‖The postage rate is six cents a pound. 'yéw-fèy (*or* 'yéw-dž *or* 'yéw-jyàr) shr̀ 'měy-yí-'bàng 'lyèw-fēn-chyán. ‖He charges more than the regular rate. tā-'yàw-de bǐ píng-'cháng-de-°'jyà-chyán (*or* °'jyàr) °dwō. *or* °'dà. ‖Is there a special rate for this tour? jèy-yí-tàng-de-lywǔ-'shíng yěw méy-yěw yěw-'dày-'bàn-fǎ?

At the rate of. ‖You can pay for it at the rate of five dollars a week. *is expressed as* You can pay five dollars a week for this. jèy-ge nǐ 'kě-yi 'měy-lǐ-bày 'fù 'wǔ-kwày-chyán. ‖This car can go (at the rate of) sixty miles per hour. jèy-lyàng-'chē 'měy-dyǎn-jūng 'néng dzěw 'lyèw-shf-lǐ.

(*Class, grade*) děng. ‖This book is definitely third rate. jèy-běn-'shū jywé-'dwèy-de shr̀ dì-'sān-děng-de.

To rate (*deserve*) yīng-'dāng 'dé. ‖He rates a reward for that. tā nèy-ge yīng-'dāng dé 'jyǎng-de.

‖That exam paper rates an A. nèy-běr-kǎw-'jywàr yīng-'dāng dé 'ēy.

To rate, *and* to be rated (*be ranked*). *See* RANK. ‖He was rated most popular man in his class. 'tā dzày tā-'bān-lǐ-tew 'swàn shř yí-ge-'dzwèy-shèw-rén-hwān-'yíng-de-rén-le.

At any rate 'bù-gwǎn dzěm-'yàng. ‖He arrived here today; at any rate his baggage is here. tā jīn-tyān 'dàw-le, 'bù-gwǎn dzěm-'yàng, tā-de-'shíng-li 'dàw-le. ‖We think this is the best plan; at any rate we will try it. wǒ-men 'jywé-de jèy-ge-'jì-hwa 'dzwèy hǎw, 'bù-gwǎn dzěm-'yàng, wǒ-men yàw 'shř-shr kàn.

At this rate (at that rate) jàw 'jèy-yàng. ‖The work is too much for one man; at that rate we will need other helpers. jèy-jyàn-'shř 'yí-ge-rén 'dzwò-bù-lyǎw, jàw 'jèy-yàng, wǒ-men 'háy děy 'jàw jǐ-ge-bāng-'mángr-de.

RATHER. (*A little*) dyǎr, shyāng-'dāng-de. ‖It is rather cold on deck. jyǎ-'bǎn-shang 'yěw-dyǎr 'lěng. ‖The play was rather long. 'shì shyāng-'dāng-de 'chang. ‖It seems rather early to decide. shyàn-'dzày 'jywé dìng 'sž-hū háy 'dzǎw-dyǎr.

Or rather (*actually*) chí-'shř-ne. ‖I was running, or rather walking quickly. wǒ 'pǎw-láy-je, chí-'shř-ne, wǒ jř néng 'shwō kwày-'kwār-de 'dzěw-láy-je. ‖His mother, or rather his father, is foreign born. *is expressed as* His mother—no, it's his father—is foreign born. tā-'mǔ-chin shř, 'bú-shř, shř tā-'fù-chin shř dzày-'wày-gwo-shēng-de.

. . . rather than . . . (*actually . . ., not . . .*) chí-'shř . . . bù-néng 'swàn . . . ‖This is a small trunk rather than a suitcase. chí-'shř jèy-ge shř yí-ge-shyǎw-'shyāng-dz bù-néng 'swàn tí-'bāw.

Would rather chíng-'ywàn, 'háy-shr, shyàng, *all expressing a rather mild preference;* 'níng-kě, *expressing a strong preference, making a decision that may entail sacrifice, etc.* ‖Would you rather come with us? nǐ °chíng-'ywàn (*or* °'háy-shr 'ywàn-yi *or* °'shyàng) gēn-wǒm yí-dàwr 'dzěw-ma? ‖I don't feel well and I'd rather stay at home. wǒ 'jywé-de bù-'shū-fu, °'háy-shr dzày-jyā 'dāy-je-ba. *or* °'bù-shyàng 'chū-chywù-le. ‖We would rather stay at home than hurt her feelings. wǒm chíng-'ywàn dzày-'jyā-li 'dāy-je, yě bú-'ywàn-yi 'jyàw-tā nán-'shèw. ‖I'd rather have ice cream. wǒ 'háy-shr yàw bīng-jì-'líng-ba. ‖I'd rather die than do it. wǒ 'níng-kě 'sž yě bú-'gàn.

RAW. (*Uncooked or unprocessed*) 'shēng-de. Raw silk 'shēng-sž; raw cotton 'myán-hwa; raw material ywán-'lyàw. ‖She eats only raw vegetables. tā jř 'chř 'shēng-de-chīng-'tsày. ‖This meat is nearly raw. jèy-kwày-'rèw chà-bu-'dwō háy 'shēng-je-ne. ‖The raw material must be shipped in. ywán-'lyàw yí-dìng yàw 'ywùn-jìn-chywù.

(*Inexperienced*) 'méy-yěw-jīng-'yàn-de; (*new*) shīn; (*untrained*) méy-'shèw-gwo-'shywùn-lyàn-de. ‖He had

only raw soldiers to use for the work. tā 'jř yěw shīn-'bīng (*or* °'méy-yěw-jīng-'yàn-de-bīng *or* °'méy-'shèw-gwo-'shywùn-lyàn-de-bīng) kě 'yùng.

(*Sore; chapped*) 'shān-le; (*scraped*) mwó-'pwò-le. ‖Her face is raw from the wind. 'tā-de-'lyǎn jyàw-'fēng-gwā 'shān-le. ‖The horse has a raw place on its back. mǎ-'bèy-shang mwó-'pwò-le.

(*Damp and cold*) yěw 'cháw yěw 'lyáng. ‖There's a raw wind today. 'jyēr-de-'fēng yěw 'cháw yěw 'lyáng.

RAY. A ray of light yí-'dàw-'gwāng, yí-'dàw, yì-tyáw-gwāng-'shyàn; (*a tiny sliver of light*) yì-'dyǎr-lyàngr *or* yí-'shyàn-de-gwāng. ‖If you turn the lights off, you can see a ray of light through that crack. yàw bǎ-'dēng 'gwān-shang jyèw ké-yi kàn-jyan tsúng nèy-ge-'fèngr-li 'tèw-jin-lay °yí-'dàw-'gwāng. *or* °'yì-tyáw-gwāng-'shyàn. *or* °'yí-'shyàn-de-gwāng. *or* °'yì-'dyǎr-lyàngr. ‖We couldn't see even a ray of light. lyán °'yí-'shyàn-de-gwāng (*or* °'yì-'dyǎr-lyàngr) yě kàn-bu-'jyàn.

A ray of hope yí-'shyàn-de-'shī-wàng. ‖There is not a ray of hope that he will live. tā-jèy-'tyáw-'mìng shř yí-'shyàn-de-'shī-wàng dēw 'méy-yěw-le.

REACH. (*Make a motion toward, without much effort; reach for*) 'shēn-shěw yàw 'ná; (*reach for something in one's pocket*) 'tāw; (*reach for something, when it involves stretching and effort*) 'gèw; (*reach for and touch*) gèw-de-'jáw. ‖He reached for his gun. tā tāw 'chyáng. *or* tā 'shēn-shěw yàw ná-'chyáng. *or* tā 'gèw tā-de-'chyáng. ‖Can you reach the sugar? nǐ 'gèw-de-jáw nèy-táng-'gwàr-ma? ‖Put the candy out of his reach. *is expressed as* Put the candy (*where*) he can't reach it. bǎ-'táng 'gē-de 'jyàw-tā gèw-bù-'jáw.

(*Extend to*) dàw, *or in compounds* -dàw; (*touch*) jān. ‖The garden reaches to the river. jèy-ge-'hwà-ywár yì-'jŕ dàw hē-'byār-nèr. ‖His power reaches everywhere. dàw-'chù dēw 'yěw tā-de-'shŕ-lì, *or* tā-de-'shŕ-lì shēn-'jāng-dàw 'gè-chu. ‖This curtain reaches the floor. 'jèy-ge-lyán-dz 'cháng-de jān-'dì-le. *or expressed as* This curtain drags on the floor. 'jèy-ge-lyán-dz twō-dàw 'dì-shang-le. *or as* This curtain hangs to the floor. 'jèy-ge-lyán-dz 'cháng-de °dā-le-dàw 'dì-shang-le. *or* °'dzày 'dì-shang 'dā-le-je.

(*To arrive at*) dàw. ‖Your letter didn't reach me until today. 'nǐ-dé-'shìn 'jīn-tyān tsáy 'dàw. ‖Tell me when we reach the city. 'dàw nèy-chéng de-'shŕ-hew, 'chǐng nǐ 'gàw-su wǒ yì-'shēngr. ‖He has reached the retirement age. tā 'dàw-le gàw-'lǎw-de-'swèy-shu-le.

(*To find, get at*) 'jáw-jaw. ‖There was no way of reaching him. 'méy-yěw 'fá-dz 'jáw-jaw tā.

Out of reach *or* beyond one's reach. ‖Such patience is out of my reach. *is expressed as* I don't have that great patience. 'wǒ méy-nèm-'dà-de-này-shīn-'fár. *or as* I can't be so patient. 'wǒ kě 'méy-nème-này-'fár.

‖Such food is beyond the reach of poor people. *is expressed as* **Poor people can't buy such food.** 'jèy-jŭng-'dūng-shï 'chyúng-rén 'chř-bù-'chľ

READ. kàn; (*read aloud or study*) nyàn. ‖**Please read the instructions.** chǐng 'kàn jèy-ge-'shwō-míng-shū. ‖**Have you read your mail yet?** nǐ 'kàn-le nǐ-de-'shìn-le-ma? ‖**I have read somewhere that this is false.** wǒ yě bú-'jř-daw shř dzày-'nǎr °'nyàn-gwo (*or* °'kàn-gwo) shwō jèy shř 'jyǎ-de. ‖**Please read it to me.** chǐng nǐ gěy-wǒ 'nyàn-nyan. *or* chǐng nǐ 'nyàn gěy-wǒ 'tīng-ting. ‖**He read the timetable out loud to us.** tā bǎ shř-jyān-'byǎw 'nyàn gěy wǒ-men 'tīng.

(*To predict*) 'twēy-tsè *or* 'ywù-tsè. ‖**He tries to read the future.** tā shyǎng-'fá-dz °'twēy-tsè (*or* °'ywù-tsè) 'jyāng-láy-de-'shř.

READY. To get ready (*in general*) 'ywù-bèy; (*take exactly the right precautions in advance*) 'jwěn-bèy; get ready to go out 'dǎ-bàn. *See also* **PREPARE.** ‖**I can get ready to go in five minutes.** wǔ-fēn-jūng-de-'gūng-fu wǒ jyèw kě-yǐ 'ywù-bèy hǎw-le 'dzěw-le. ‖**After we decided to go, it took her an hour to get ready.** wǒm shwō 'hǎw-le yǎw 'dzěw-le, tā jyèw chywù 'dǎ-bàn, °'yì-dǎ-bàn (*or* °'yí-yùng *or* °'yí-chywù) yùng-le yí-ge-jūng-'téw. ‖**For some time the men have been getting ready to go overseas.** bīng wèy 'hǎy-wày-ywǎn-'jēng 'jwěn-bèy-le 'yěw-shyē-shř-hew-le. ‖**Ready, get set, go!** jàn-'hǎw, ywù-'bèy, 'pǎw!

To be ready (*prepared*) 'hǎw-le, 'ywù-bèy-'hǎw-le, 'jwěn-bèy-'hǎw-le; (*of food*) dé. ‖**When will dinner be ready?** 'fàn shéme-'shř-hew °'dé? *or* °'ywù-bèy-'hǎw-le. *or* °'hǎw? ‖**The coffee is ready.** 'jyā-fēy jǔ-'dé-le. ‖**Is everything ready?** yí-chyè dēw 'jwěn-bèy-'hǎw-le-ma? *or* 'ywù-bèy-'hǎw-le-ma?

To be ready to *or* for. (*Can*) 'kě-yǐ, néng. ‖**Is the manuscript ready to be printed?** 'gǎw-dz 'kě-yǐ fù-'yìn-le-ma? ‖**Everything is ready for shipment.** 'shéme dēw 'kě-yǐ 'lì-shř ná-'dzěw. ‖**I am ready to go anywhere I am sent.** bù-'gwǎn 'pày-wǒ dàw-'nǎr, 'wǒ dēw néng 'chywù. *Also* ‖**Are you ready to forgive him?** nǐ shyàn-'dzày 'néng 'ráw-shù tā-ma? *or expressed as* **Are you planning to forgive him?** nǐ 'dǎ-swàn 'ráw-shù 'tā-ma?

Ready (*at hand*) shěw-byār. ‖**I don't have much ready cash.** wǒ shěw-'byār 'méy-yěw 'dày-je shéme-chyán.

REAL. jēn, jēn-'jèng-de. Really jēn; (*actually*) shř-'jì-shang. ‖**Is this real silk or imitation?** jèy shř 'jēn-sz̄ 'háy-shr řen-'dzàw-sz̄? ‖**This looks like the real thing.** 'jèy-ge gēn 'jēn-de yí-'yàng. ‖**What was his real reason?** tā-de-'jēn-de-'lǐ-yéw shř 'shéme? *or expressed as* **What was his motive at the bottom?** dàw-'dǐ tā-de-'dùng-jí shř 'shéme? ‖**That never hap-**

pens in real life. jēn-'jèng-de-'rén-shēng 'jywè bú-hwèy yěw 'nèy-shř. *or* shř-'jì-shang 'bú-hwèy yěw 'nèy-shř. ‖**It was a real pleasure to meet him.** wǒ 'jēn gāw-'shìng °'pèng-jyàn-le (*or* °'kàn-jyàn-le) tā. ‖**Do you know the real facts?** *is expressed as* **Do you know the truth of the matter?** nǐ 'jř-daw jèy-ge-'shř-de-jēn-'shyàng-ma?

REALIZE. (*Understand*) 'míng-bay; (*catch on*) mwō 'chīng-chu-le; (*see into*) 'chyáw-chū-láy, 'kàn-chū-láy; (*know*) 'jř-dàw, (*literary*) 'shyǎw-dé; (*expect*) shyǎng-'dàw. ‖**I didn't realize that you were interested in it.** wǒ méy-shyǎng-'dàw nǐ dwèy-ywú jèy-ge hěn yěw 'shìng-chywù. *or* wǒ bù-jř-'dàw nǐ 'shǐ-hwan jèy-ge. ‖**Do you realize what this means?** nǐ °'míng-bay (*or* °mwō 'chīng-chu *or* °'chyáw-chū-láy *or* °'kàn-chū-láy) jèy shř 'dzěm-hwéy-'shèr-ma? ‖**It took me a long time to realize what he was trying to say.** wǒ 'fèy-le hǎw-'dà-de-'shř-hew tsáy °'míng-bày (*or* °mwō 'chīng-chu-le) tā-shyǎng-'shwō-de shř 'shéme. ‖**I realize that this is an important job.** wǒ °'jř-daw (*or* °'shyǎw-dé) jèy shř yí-jyàn-hěn-'jùng-yàw-de-'shèr.

(*To achieve*) bàn-'dàw; (*to come true: of a dream*) ywán. ‖**He has never realized his desire to own a house.** tā yàw 'jř yì-swǒ-'fáng-dz shyǎng kě-shr yì-jř 'méy-bàn-dàw. ‖**I'm afraid that's a dream that will never be realized.** wǒ pà nèy-ge-'mèng yǔng-'ywǎn yě 'ywán-bù-lyǎw. *or* wǒ pà nèy-shèr yǔng-ywan yě bàn-bu-'dàw.

To realize a profit (*make money*) jwàn-'chyán. ‖**He realized a big profit on the transaction.** tā dzwò nèy-bǐ-'mǎy-may jwàn-le bù-'shǎw-de-'chyán.

REALLY. chí-'shř, jēn, 'jēn-shr. ‖**I really wanted to stay home.** wǒ 'jēn-shř yàw dzày-'jyā 'dāy-je-de-láy-je. ‖**Will the train really start on time?** hwǒ-'chē 'jēn jwěn-shř 'kāy-ma? ‖**She is really younger than she looks.** chí-'shř tā-de-'swèy-shu 'méy-yěw tā-de-'yàng-dz nèm-'lǎw. *or expressed as* **She looks older than she is.** tā-de-'yàng-dz 'kàn-je bǐ-tā-rén 'lǎw. ‖**Do you really mean that?** nǐ 'jēn shř nèy-ge-'yì-sz-ma? *or expressed as* **Are you speaking on the level?** nǐ shř shwō jēn-'gé-de-ne-ma?

‖Really? 'jēn-de-ma? ‖Well, really! jēn-'gé-de-le!

REASON. (*A cause*) 'ywán-gù, 'ywán-yīn, 'dàw-li, *or* 'lǐ-yéw. The reason why wèy-'shéme. *See also* **WHY.** ‖**What were your reasons for leaving there?** nǐ 'lí-kāy nèr shř 'shéme-°'ywán-gù. *or* °'ywán-yīn, *etc.* ‖**He had a good reason for wanting to leave.** tā yàw-'dzěw 'yěw tā-de-°'dàw-li. *or* °'lǐ-yéw. *etc.* ‖**I can't figure out the reason why he did it.** wǒ jēn 'dzwó-me-bù-chū-láy tā wèy-'shéme 'něm-je. *or expressed as* **I can't figure out what his reasons were for doing it.** wǒ jēn shyǎng-bù-chū-láy, tā dzwò nèy-jyàn-'shř shř shéme-°'dàw-li. *or* °'lǐ-yéw. *etc.* ‖**We have reason to believe that it was murder.** *is expressed as* **We think it was murder and have some evidence.** wǒm 'rèn-wéy jèy shř méw-'shā shr yěw-shyāng-dāng-de-'gēn-jywù-de. ‖**I have reason to believe that we will never**

see him again. *is expressed as* **There are some things that make me think we won't see him again.** yěw hǎw-shyē-°'shř-ching (*or* °'dì-fangr) jyàw-wǒ 'jywé-de wǒ-men dzày jyàn-bù-'jáw tā-le.

(*Intelligence*) 'lǐ-shìng. ‖**Some insects almost seem to have reason.** yěw-de-kwēn-'chúng 'hǎw-shyàng yě 'yěw-dyǎr 'lǐ-shìng 'shř-de. *or* yěw-de-'chúng-dz hǎw-shyàng yě 'dǔng-dyǎr shéme shř-de.

It stands to reason dāng-'rán. ‖**It stands to reason that he wouldn't have done that.** nèy-ge 'dāng-rán 'bú-shř tā-'gàn-de.

To bring . . . to reason bǎ . . . gěy shwō 'míng-bày gwò-láy *or* bǎ . . . gěy °chywàn 'míng-bày, *or* °'chywàn-gwo-láy, *or* °chywàn 'míng-bày gwò-láy. ‖**He was stubborn, but we brought him to reason.** tā chǐ-'chū hěn 'gù-jř-láy-je, 'kě-shr wǒ-men bǎ-tā °gěy shwō 'míng-bày gwò-láy-le. *or* °gěy chywàn 'míng-bày-le. *etc.*

To listen to reason (*be reasonable*) jyǎng-'lǐ. ‖**Please listen to reason.** jyǎng-dyǎr 'lǐ, hǎw-bù-'hǎw? *or* byé bù-jyǎng-'lǐ. ‖**He wouldn't listen to reason.** tā mán bù-jyǎng-'lǐ. *or expressed as* **He didn't listen to good advice.** tā bù-tīng hǎw-'hwà.

To lose one's reason (*go crazy*) yàw-'fēng-le.

Within reason. ‖**He'll pay anything within reason to get it.** *is expressed as* **However much it's worth he can pay it.** jř 'dwō-shaw-'chyán tā 'dēw néng 'gěy. *or as* **If it's worth it, he'll pay any amount of money.** jř yàw-shr 'jř, tā 'dwō-shaw-'chyán dēw 'ywàn-yi 'hwā.

To reason (*think logically; use one's head*) yùng 'nǎw-dz; (*think*) shyǎng; (*think it over*) 'shyǎng-shyǎng, 'sž-swǒ 'sž-swǒ; (*figure out*) 'dzwó-me. ‖**The child can't reason.** jèy-'háy-dz 'bú-hwèy yùng 'nǎw-dz. ‖**He reasoned that she would have gone home first.** tā 'shyǎng tā shř shyān hwéy-'jyā. ‖**Let's try to reason it out.** dzám 'dž-shì °'dzwó-me 'dzwó-me (*or* °'shyǎng-shyǎng *or* °'sž-swǒ 'sž-swǒ) shr dzěm-hwéy-'shèr.

(*Argue, persuade, advise*) chywàn; (*talk to . . .*) gēn . . . 'shwō; (*explain to . . .*) gēn . . . 'jyǎng. ‖**We reasoned with her until she changed her mind.** wǒ-men °'chywàn-tā (*or* °gēn-tā 'shwō *or* °gēn-tā 'jyǎng) yí-'jř dàw bǎ-tā-de-'shīn gěy shwō-'hwó-le.

RECEIPT. (*Act of receiving*) *is expressed as* **to receive** jyē. ‖**Immediately upon receipt of the telegram, he took the train.** tā yì-'jyē-je jèy-dyàn-'bàw, lì-'kè jyèw shàng-le hwǒ-'chē-le.

(*Paper acknowledging receipt*) 'shēw-jywù, shēw-'tyáwr. ‖**Please sign this receipt.** 'chǐng nǐ dzày °'shēw-jywù-shang (*or* °shēw-'tyáwr-shang) chyān ge-'míng. ‖**Be sure to get a receipt when you deliver the package.** bǎ jèy-ge-'bāwr sùng-'dàw-le de-'shř-hew, byé 'wàng-le yàw °shēw-'tyáwr. *or* °'shēw-jywù.

(*Money received*) 'shēw-rù, jìn-'kwǎn, 'jìn-shyàng. ‖**Our receipts will just pay our expenses.** 'wǒ-men-de-°'shēw-rù (*or* °jìn-'kwǎn *or* °'jìn-shyàng) jyang 'gèw 'kāy-shyāw.

To receipt. ‖**Please receipt this bill.** *is expressed as* **Please mark the bill paid.** 'chǐng nǐ bǎ jèy-jāng-jàng-'tyáwr °jù yí-jù 'fù-le. *or* °'shyě-shàng 'fù-le. *or as* **Please strike off this bill.** 'chǐng nǐ bǎ jèy-jāng-jàng-'tyáwr jù 'shyāw-le.

RECEIVE. (*To accept*) jyē; (*accept; also, collect*) shēw; (*get or gain*) dé. ‖**Please wait until you receive the letter.** 'chǐng nǐ 'děng-je 'jyē-je nèy-fēng-'shìn dzài 'shwō. ‖**We just received the news.** wǒ-men gāng 'jyē-je jèy-ge 'shyāw-shi. ‖**The soldier has not received his orders.** jèy-ge-'bīng háy méy-jyē-dàw tā-de-'mìng-ling-ne. ‖**Received payment.** 'shēw-dàw. ‖**He didn't receive any compensation for the work.** tā 'dzwò-chū nèy-jyàn-'hwòr láy, yì-'dyǎr-'bàw-chew yě méy-'dé-je.

(*To experience; especially, to suffer*) shēw. ‖**He received a wound in the war.** tā dǎ-'jàng de-'shř-hew shēw-'shāng-le. ‖**He's received a lot of criticism.** tā 'shēw-le bù-shǎw-de-'pī-píng.

(*To welcome*) hwān-'yíng, 'jāw-dày. ‖**He was on hand to receive the guests.** tā dzày-'chǎng °hwān-'yíng (*or* °'jāw-dày) 'kè-rén.

To be received. ‖**How was your suggestion received?** *is expressed as* **How did everybody consider your idea?** dà-jyā-'hwǒr 'rèn-wéy nǐ-de-jyàn-'yì dzěm-'yàng? ‖**His speech was well received by the audience.** *is expressed as* **Everybody liked to listen to his speech.** tā-de-yǎn-'jyǎng dà-'jyā dēw hěn 'ày tīng. ‖**He was well received in the community.** *is expressed as* **Everyone welcomed him very well.** dà-'jyā jāw-'dày-de tā °bú-tswò. *or* °hěn 'hǎw.

RECENT. shīn-'jìn. ‖**The airplane is a comparatively recent invention.** fēy-jī 'bǐ-jyàw shř yí-ge-shīn-'jìn-fā-'míng-de-'dūng-shi. ‖**Is this a recent issue?** jèy shř shīn-'jìn-'chū-de-ma?

RECENTLY. 'jìn-lay; (*very recently*) dzwèy-'jìn; (*a few days ago*) 'téw-jǐ-tyān. **How recently** (*when*) 'dwō-hwěr. ‖**Have you seen him recently?** nǐ 'jìn-lay 'kàn-jyàn tā 'méy-yěw? ‖**He has recently been promoted.** tā dzwèy-'jìn 'shēng-le. ‖**Only recently I met him on the street.** wǒ 'téw-jǐ-tyān háy dzày 'jyē-shang 'kàn-jyàn tā láy-je. ‖**How recently were you there?** 'nǐ shř 'dwō-hwěr 'dzày-nèr láy-je?

RECOGNIZE. rèn; (*to know*) 'jř-dàw. ‖**I recognize him by his hat.** wǒ 'rèn-de 'tā-de-'màw-dz. ‖**I didn't recognize her in that hat.** tā 'dày-shang nèy-'màw-dz wǒ 'jēn bú-'rèn-de tā-le. ‖**We recognized the place from your description.** wǒm 'àn-je nǐ-swǒ-'shwō-de 'rèn-chu nèy-ge-'dì-fang láy-le. ‖**No one recognized his genius while he was alive.** tā 'hwó-je de-'shř-hew méy-'rén 'jř-dàw tā-de-'tyān-tsáy.

To recognize a claim rèn-'jàng *or* 'chéng-rèn 'yāw-chyéw. ‖**We recognize all claims.** wǒ-men 'chywán rèn-'jàng. *or* wǒ-men 'chéng-rèn swǒ-'yěw-de-'yāw-chyéw.

To recognize a government 'chéng-rèn 'jèng-fŭ. ‖Do they recognize the new government? 'tā-men 'chéng-rèn jèy-ge-shīn-'jèng-fŭ-ma?

To recognize *a speaker* 'ràng ... °fā-'yán *or* °shwō-'hwà. ‖Wait until the chairman recognizes you. 'dĕng-dàw jŭ-'shí 'ràng-nǐ °fā-'yán, nǐ dzày fā-'yán. *or* °shwō-'hwà, nǐ dzày 'shwō.

RECORD. (*Written statement*) jì-'lù; (*financial*) jàng. To keep records jì-'lù; to keep financial records of bă ... jì-dzay 'jàng-shang. ‖Keep a careful record of all expenses. bă 'swŏ-yĕw-de-'fèy-yùng dēw shyáng-'shì-de jì-dzay 'jàng-shang. ‖All the records are kept in a file cabinet. 'swŏ-yĕw-de-'jì-lù dēw dzày jywàn-dzūng-'gwèy-dz-li băw-'lyéw-je-ne.

(*Recorded maximum, optimum, etc.*) jì-'lù. ‖He broke all records for speed. tā-de-'sù-dù dă-'pwò yí-'chyè-de-jì-'lù. ‖This heat spell sets a new record. jèy-tsž-chí-'rè dzàw-le 'shīn-jì-'lù. ‖We had a record crop this year. *expressed as* Our crop this year betters all previous ones. wŏm-'jīn-nyán-de-'shēw-chéng bĭ 'nĕy-nyán-de dēw 'hăw. ‖That's a record for stupidity. *expressed as* There isn't anything more stupid than that. 'dzày yĕ 'méy-yĕw bĭ-'nèy-ge-háy-'bèn-de-le.

(*Phonograph disk*) lyéw-shēng-jī-'pyàn-dz. ‖Do you have many dance records? nĭ-de-tyàw-'wŭ-de-lyéw-shēng-'jī 'pyàn-dz 'dwō-bu-dwō?

(*Known past; of a particular person*) yĭ-'chyán-dzwò-gwo-de-'shř. ‖He has a clean record. tā yĭ-'chyán dzwò-gwo-de-'shř méy shéme-kĕ-'pī-píng-de. ‖He has a criminal record. *is expressed as* He's committed crimes in the past. tā tséng-'jīng fàn-gwo 'dzwèy. ‖He had a fine record in college. *is expressed as* In college his attainments were quite good. tā dzày-'dà-shywé-de-shř-hew-de-'chéng-jì hĕn 'hăw.

Go on record as. ‖Let me go on record as against this idea. *is expressed as* Put it down that I'm opposed to this. 'jì-je, wŏ jèng-'shř-de 'făn-dwèy 'jèy-ge.

The worst (*or* best, *etc.*) ... on record. ‖This is the worst earthquake on record here. *is expressed as* This earthquake is worse than any we've had here before. 'jèy-tsž-de-dì-'jèn yán-'jùng-de-'chíng-shíng shř 'jèr 'tsúng-láy méy-'yĕw-gwo-de.

To record (*in writing*) jì, jì-'lù. ‖Who recorded the proceedings? hwèy-'yì-de-'jīng-gwò shř-'shéy 'jì-de?

To record (*on disks*) gwàn 'pyàn-dz. ‖What company records for you? nĭ dzày 'nĕy-yí-ge-gūng-'sž 'gwàn 'pyàn-dz?

RECOVER. (*Get back*) 'jăw-jáw-le, 'jwéy-hwéy-láy-le, 'ná-hwéy-láy-le, *sometimes other verbs meaning* take *or* get *plus* -hwéy-láy-le. ‖I recovered my watch within a week. wŏ dzày yí-ge-shīng-'chī-yĭ-'nèy, bă wŏ-de-'byăw 'jwéy-hwéy-lay-le.

Recover one's self-control jèn-'dìng. ‖He quickly recovered his self-control. tā lì-'kè jyèw jèn-'dìng-le.

Recover oneself hăw-le. ‖He lost his temper for a moment, but soon recovered himself. tā 'fā-le yì-'hwĕr-de-'pí-chi, kĕ-shr yì-'hwĕr jyèw 'hăw-le.

Recover *from illness* (bìng) 'hăw-le; *from an operation* 'hăw-le, fú-'ywán-le. ‖How long did it take you to recover from your operation? nĭ kāy-'dāw yĭ-'hèw °'yăng-le dwō-jyĕw tsáy 'hăw-de? *or* °dwō-'jyĕw tsáy fú-'ywán-de?

RED. húng. Red color 'húng-sè, 'húng-shăr, 'húng-de-'yán-sè. ‖Red isn't becoming to her. 'húng-de-'yán-sè gēn-ta bù-hé-'shř. *or* tā chwān-je 'húng-de bù-°'hăw-'kàn. *or* °chèn-'pày. ‖I want to buy a red hat. wŏ yàw 'măy yì-dĭng-húng-'màw-dz. ‖Her face was red with embarrassment. tā bù-hăw-'yì-sz, 'lyăn dēw 'húng-le.

(*Politically*). *Expressed as* Communist gùng-chăn-'dăng. To be a Red *may also be expressed as* to carry (political) coloring dày sè-'tsăy. ‖They said that he'd always been a Red. jywù tām 'shwō tā yí-'shyàng jyèw-shr °yí-ge-gùng-chăn-'dăng. *or* °dày sè-'tsăy.

REFUSE. To refuse *a proposal* jywù-'jywé. ‖Has she refused him again? tā 'yèw jywù-'jywé-tā-le-ma?

To refuse *in other contexts is expressed with various other wordings.* ‖I offered him a drink, but he refused it. *is expressed as* I asked him to drink, but he won't. wŏ 'chĭng-ta hē-'jyĕw, kĕ-shr tā bù-kĕn-'hē. ‖The manager refused to accept his resignation. *is expressed as* The manager didn't let him resign. jīng-'lĭ bù-'jwĕn-ta tsź-'jŕ. *or as* The manager didn't accept his resignation. jīng-'lĭ bù-'jyē-shèw tā de-tsź-'chéng.

(*Discarded stuff*). *Expressed as* stuff 'dūng-shi, *with some other element in the sentence expressing the idea of discard.* ‖Throw it out with the rest of the refuse. bă-ta gēn chí-'ywú-de nèy-shyē-'dūng-shi yì-'chĭ 'rēng-le-ba.

REGARD. Regard *someone* (*or something*) *as* 'rèn-wéy ... shř. ‖He's regarded as a great pianist. yì-bān-rén 'rèn-wéy tā tĭng-'haw-de-gāng-chín-'jyā.

Be well regarded. ‖He's well regarded here. *is expressed as* People here all think he's not bad. 'jèr-de-rén dēw 'jywé-de tā bú-'tswò. *or as* He has a very good reputation here. tā dzày-'jèr hĕn yĕw dyăr-míng-'wàng.

(*To look at*) kàn. ‖He regarded her face carefully. tā hĕn dž-'shì-de bă tā-de-'lyăn 'kàn-yi-kàn.

(*Consideration*). ‖Show some regard for your parents. *is expressed as* You ought to think of your parents some. shāw-'wéy yĕ tì nĭ-'fù-mŭ 'shyăng-yi-shyăng.

To send *or* give one's regards chĭng-'ān, wèn-'hăw, wèn-'ān. ‖Send my regards to your mother. tì-wo gĕy nín-de-'lăw-'tày °chĭng-'ān. *or* °wèn-'hăw. *etc.*

Regarding *or* with regard to *or* in regard to 'dwèy-ywu, 'gwān-ywu, 'jŕ-ywu. ‖We'll have to have a little discussion regarding that last point. 'dwèy-ywu dzwèy-'hèw-nèy-yi-'dyǎn, wǒm 'háy děy tǎw-'lwèn-tǎw-lwèn. ‖With regard to your letter of January 1st . . . 'gwān-ywu °nǐ 'yí-ywè-yí-'hàw-de-'shìn . . . or °'yí-ywè-yí-'r̀-láy-'hán . . . .

In that regard 'jr̀-ywu 'nèy-yi-dyǎn. ‖In that regard, I agree with you. jr̀-ywu 'nèy-yì-dyǎn, wǒ 'gēn-ni túng-'yì.

REGRET. To regret *or* to have regrets hèw-'hwěy. ‖I have no regrets for what I've done. wǒ swǒ-'dzwò-de-shr̀ wǒ 'bìng bú-hèw-'hwěy. ‖I've always regretted not having traveled. wǒ 'cháng-cháng hèw-'hwěy méy-'chū-chywu yéw-'lì-gwo.

To send one's regrets dàw-'shyè, (shwō bù-néng chywù). ‖Everyone sent his regrets. rén-jyā 'chywán-dēw dàw-'shyè, shwō bù-néng °chywù. (*or* °láy). *or* rén-jyā 'dēw dàw-'shyè-le.

REGULAR. (*Normal, customary*) 'jàw-lì-de, *or expressed by using* ought 'yīng-gay. ‖This is the regular procedure. 'jèy-ge shr̀ 'jàw-lì-de-°'shěw-shywù. *or* °'chéng-shywù. ‖What's the regular way of writing a business letter? 'shāng-jyè-de-gūng-'hán yīng-gāy 'dzěme-shyě?

(*Orderly*) yěw-'jr̀-shywu-de. ‖He lives a very regular life. tā gwò-je yì-jǔng-hěn-yěw-'jr̀-shywù-de-'shēng-hwó.

(*Of the same pattern*) chí; yí-'yàng. ‖The hills have a regular outline. nèy-shyē-'shān-de 'lwén-kwò °dēw yí-'yàng. *or* °hěn 'chí. .

(*Repeated at regular intervals*). *Expressed with* customarily 'píng-cháng, jàw-'lì; *or as* definite, fixed yí-'dìng-de. ‖This happens at regular intervals. shyàng-'gé yěw yí-'dìng-de-shŕ-jyān. *or* gwò yí-'dìng-de-shŕ-jyān 'jwên yěw yí-tsż. ‖The trains operate on a regular schedule. hwǒ-chē àn-je yí-'dìng-de shŕ-jyān 'kāy. ‖Is there regular bus service to town? jèr 'píng-cháng yěw gūng-gùng-chì-'chē dàw chéng-'lǐ chywù-ma? ‖He makes a regular thing of it. tā 'měy-tyān jàw-'lì dzwò 'jèy-ge.

(*Real, genuine*). *Expressed with* really jēn. ‖That storm was a regular flood. nèy-jèn-bàw-fēng-'ywǔ 'jēn chéng-le shwěy-'dzāy-le.

RELATION. 'gwān-shi, 'jyāw-chíng. ‖That scene has no relation to the rest of the play. 'nèy-yí-mù gēn jèy-chywán-chū-'shì °'háw wú 'gwān-shi. *or* °méy 'gwān-shi. ‖Our relations with the mayor are excellent. wǒm-gēn-shr̀-'jǎng-de-'jyāw-chíng hěn bú-'tswò. ‖You must judge his work in relation to the circumstances. *is expressed as* In judging his work, at the same time you must think of the circumstances. nǐ 'pī-ping tā-de-'gūng-dzwò de-shŕ-hew túng-'shŕ yě 'yīng-dang 'shyǎng-dàw tā-de-hwán-'jìng. *or as* You must think of the circumstances and then say how his work is. nǐ děy 'shyǎng tā-de-hwán-'jìng 'dzày shwō tā-'dzwò-de dzěme-'yàng.

To break off relations (*of countries*) jywé-'jyāw. ‖The two countries have broken off relations. 'jèy-lyǎng-gwó jywé-'jyāw-le.

(*Relatives; in the same household*) 'běn-jyā; (*a larger group*) 'chīn-chì.

RELATIVE. (*Not absolute*) shyāng-'dwèy-de. ‖Everything in life is relative. rén-'shēng-de-'shr̀-ching dēw-shr shyāng-'dwèy-de. *or* 'hwà děy-kàn dzày shém-'dì-fang (shém 'shŕ-hew) láy 'shwō.

Be relative to (*depend on*) děy 'kàn. ‖The merits of this proposal are relative to the particular circumstances. jèy-ge-yì-'jyàn 'hǎw-bu-hǎw yùng-děy 'kàn dzày shéme-'chíng-shíng-jr̀-'shyà.

(*Kin; in the same household*) běn-'jyā; (*a larger group*) chīn-'chì; close relatives jìn-'chīn. ‖They're close relatives. tām shr̀ jìn-'chīn. ‖They invited all their friends and relatives to the wedding. tām jyē-'hwēn de-shŕ-hew lyán běn-'jyā dày 'chīn-chì, 'péng-yew, dēw 'chǐng-le.

RELIGION (RELIGIOUS). dzūng-'jyàw. ‖She's very tolerant in her attitude towards other religions. tā-de-'tày-du dwèy-ywu byé-de-dzūng-'jyàw yě dēw bù-fǎn-'dwèy. ‖Some people say Confucianism isn't a religion. 'yěw-rén shwō 'kǔng-dž-'jyàw 'bú-shr dzūng-'jyàw. ‖He belongs to a religious order. tā 'shìn nèm-yí-ge-jyàw-'mér.

Religious (*pious*) 'rè-shīn. ‖Quakers are religious people. 'gwēy-gé-hwèy-de-rén shìn-'jyàw hěn 'rè-shīn.

REMAIN. To remain *in a certain state* 'háy-shr̀, 'lǎw-shr̀. ‖These things always remain the same. 'jèy-shyē-dūng-shi 'lǎw-shr̀ 'jè-yàng.

To remain at *a place* yì-'jŕ-dzày. ‖He remained at home. tā yì-'jŕ-dzay 'jyā-li.

To remain to be *seen or done, etc.* háy děy. ‖That remains to be seen. 'háy bù-néng 'dìng-ne. ‖Most of the work still remains to be done. nèy-jyàn-'shŕ-li yì-'dwò-bàr háy děy 'dzwò-ne. ‖Nothing else remains to be done. *is expressed as* Everything else is done. 'byé-de dēw dzwò-'wán-le.

Remains (*of a meal*) shèng-de-'tsày. ‖She cleared away the remains of dinner. tā bǎ shèng-de-'tsày dēw 'ná-kay-le.

Remains (*corpse*) 'shŕ-shew. ‖Where did they bury his remains? tām bǎ tā-de-'shŕ-shew máy-'něr-le?

REMARK. To remark on 'lwèn-dàw, 'shwō-dàw. ‖He remarked on her appearance. tā °'lwèn-dàw (*or* °'shwō-dàw) tā-de-°'shén-chì. *or* °'yàng-dz.

To remark that shwō. ‖We've already remarked before that opinions differ on this point. wǒm 'dzǎw jyèw shwō-gwo dà-'jyā dwèy-ywu 'jèy-yì-dyǎn 'yì-jyàn bù-'túng.

(*Casual comment*) hwà *with measure* jywù. ‖That was an unkind remark. 'nèy-jywù-hwà hěn 'swěn. ‖Limit your remarks to five minutes. *is expressed as* Just speak five minutes. 'shyàn-ni shwō 'wǔ-fēn-jūng.

or as **Don't speak for more than five minutes.** byé 'shwō-gwò 'wǔ-fēn-jūng.

REMEMBER. 'jì-de, 'jì-je; (*recall*) 'shyǎng-chǐ-láy. ‖**It was in May, as I remember.** 'wǒ jì-de shr̀ dzày 'wǔ-ywè-li. ‖**Do you remember when he said that?** nǐ 'jì-de tā 'shéme-shŕ-hew 'sh'wō-de nèy-ge-ma? ‖**Remember to turn out the lights.** 'jì-je bǎ-'dēng gěy 'gwān-le. ‖**I can't remember the occasion.** wǒ 'shyǎng-bu-chǐ-'láy 'něy-yì-hwéy-'shr̀.

(*Give a gift to*) 'shyǎng-je . . . yì-dyǎr, 'là-bu-lyǎw. ‖**He always remembers us at Christmas.** tā dzày shèng-dàn-'jyé sùng-'lǐ de-shŕ-hew 'dzǔng °'shyǎng-je wǒ-men yì-dyǎr. *or* °'là-bu-lyǎw wǒ-men. ‖**I'll remember you in my will.** *is expressed as* **When I write my will I won't forget you.** wǒ shyě yí-'jū de-shŕ-hew bú-'hwèy bǎ-'nǐ gěy 'wàng-le.

Remember *someone* to tì . . . gěy . . . chǐng-'ān. ‖**Remember me to your mother.** 'tì-wo gěy nín-de-lǎw-'tày-tay chǐng-'ān.

REMIND. *Expressed as* **to cause to remember** jyàw . . . 'shyǎng-chǐ-lay; *sometimes rearranged and expressed as* **to remember** 'shyǎng-chǐ-lay. ‖**She reminds me of my mother.** kàn-je 'tā wǒ 'shyǎng-chi wǒ-de-'mǔ-chin-lay. ‖**I'm reminded of an amusing story.** shwō 'jèy-ge jyàw-wo 'shyǎng-chi yí-ge-'shyàw-hwar-lay.

Remind *someone (to do something)* 'tí-je . . . yì-dyǎr, 'tí-shǐng . . . yì-shēngr. ‖**Remind me to write him.** nǐ 'tí-je wo dyǎr, 'gěy-ta shyě yì-fēng-'shìn. ‖**If you don't remind me, I'll forget.** nǐ yàw bù-'tí-shǐng wo yì-shēngr, wǒ jyèw-shywù 'wàng-le.

REMOVE. **Remove** *stains, ink spots, etc.* bǎ . . . chywù. ‖**This is guaranteed to remove ink spots.** jèy-ge bǎw-'gwǎn néng bǎ mwò-shwěy-'dyǎr 'chywù-le.

Remove *traces, clues, etc.* ‖**They removed every trace of their presence before they left.** *is expressed as* **When they went they left no traces.** tām 'dzěw de-shŕ-hew, 'yì-dyǎr-'hén-jì dēw méy-'lyéw-shyà. *or as* **First they took everything and fixed it so that it couldn't be discovered that they had been there, and only then did they leave.** tām 'shyān bǎ 'shéme dēw 'nèng-de 'yì-dyǎr yě 'chyáw-bu-chu-láy tām 'dzày-nèr 'dāy láy-je, tsáy 'dzěw-de.

Remove *one's hat* jǎy; (*other garments*) twō. ‖**Please remove your hats.** chǐng nǐ-men bǎ 'màw-dz 'jǎy-le.

Remove *a growth,' an appendix, etc.* 'chywù-chū-láy, 'lá-shyà-láy. ‖**They operated to remove a growth.** tām yùng 'shěw-shù bǎ 'lyéw-dz °'chywù-chu-lay-le. *or* °'lá-shyà-lay-le.

To remove *an official (by higher authority)* gé-'jŕ, myǎn-'jŕ; (*by vote*) méy-yew 'dzày shywǎn-'shàng. ‖**He was removed from office.** tā 'méy-yew 'dzày shywǎn-'shàng. *or* tā bèy gé-'jŕ-le. *or* tā bèy myǎn-'jŕ-le. ‖**It's about time this official was removed.** jēn-shr̀ gāy bǎ-ta 'gé-le.

To remove *someone, as from a room,* **by force** 'tī-chu-chywù, 'rēng-chu-chywù, 'hūng-chu-chywù. ‖**He**

got boisterous and they had to remove him by force. tā 'nàw-de tày 'lì-hay-le, 'rén-jyā jr̀ 'hǎw bǎ-ta gěy °'tī- (*or* °'rēng- *or* °'hūng-)chu-chywù-le.

To remove *a population* jyàw (*or* ràng) . . . bān-'dzěw. ‖**They'll have to remove the people who live in the valley before they can build the dam.** tām 'shyān děy jyàw dzày-shān-'gǔ-li-jù-de-'rén bān-'dzěw-le tsáy néng shyēw-'já.

RENDER. (*Cause to be*) jyàw, ràng; **render** *someone or something* . . . bǎ A nùng-de . . . , *where A denotes a person or thing; or expressed with resultative compounds.* ‖**The (wounds he received in the) accident rendered him completely helpless.** chū-'shèr de-shŕ-hew tā-shèw-de-'shāng °'jyàw-tā (*or* °'ràng-tā, *or* °'bǎ-tā nùng-de) yì-'dyǎr-jyèr yě 'dùng-bu-'lyǎw. ‖**This news renders it probable that nothing will happen.** *is expressed as* **Having this news probably nothing will happen.** yěw 'jèy-ge-'shyāw-shi 'nà jyèw 'dà-gày bú-hwèy chū 'shr̀-le. ‖**The shock rendered him speechless.** *is expressed as* **He was shocked to the point of not being able to speak.** tā 'shyà-de shwō-bu-chū-'hwà-láy-le.

(*Give*). ‖**You have rendered invaluable assistance.** *is expressed as* **You've really helped a lot.** nǐ 'jēn-shr 'bāng-le hěn-'dà-de-'máng. ‖**An account must be rendered monthly.** *is expressed as* **Each month an account must be sent in.** 'měy-yí-ge-'ywè, bì-děy bǎ-'jàng 'jyāw-jin-chywu. ‖**For services rendered, $10.** 'shěw-shywù-fèy shr̀ 'shŕ-kwày-chyán.

RENT. **To rent** (*of the person who acquires*) dzū; (*of the person who receives payment*) chū-'dzū-gěy. ‖**He had to rent a costume for the party.** tā wèy tsān-'jyā nèy-ge-'hwèy dzū-le jyàn-'yī-fu. ‖**He rents boats to tourists.** tā yěw-'chwán 'chū-dzū-gěy 'yéw-kè.

To rent (*of the thing transferred*) dzū. ‖**This car rents for a dollar an hour.** jèy-lyàng-'chē 'dzū 'yí-ge-jūng-tew 'yí-kwày-chyán.

(*Payment*). *Usually expressed with* chyán, dzū *being used elsewhere in the sentence; sometimes* 'dzū-chyán. **House rent** 'fáng-chyán; **X-rent** 'X-chyán. ‖**How much rent do you pay for the house?** nǐ-de-'fáng-dz shr̀ 'dwō-shaw-chyán 'dzū-de? *or* nǐ 'jù-dzay nèy-ge-'fáng-dz děy gěy 'dwō-shaw-°'fáng-chyán? *or* °'dzū-chyán?

REPAIR. **To repair** 'shyēw-li; **repairs, repair job,** *and the like, are expressed in terms of this verb.* ‖**Can you repair my shoes in a hurry?** néng-bu-neng lì-'kè bǎ-jèy-'shyé shyēw-'hǎw le? ‖**The car only needs minor repairs.** jèy-lyàng-'chē 'jř yàw shāw-'wēy 'shyēw-li-shyēw-li. ‖**A complete repair job will take ten days.** yàw-shr 'wán-chywán 'shyēw-li yí-shyàr, děy 'shŕ-tyān. ‖**The house on the corner is in bad repair.** jī-'jyǎw-shang-nèy-jyān-'fáng-dz děy 'dà shyēw-li yí-shyà.

REPEAT. *Expressed with* **again** dzày (*referring to a future action*) *or* yèw (*referring to a past action*), *with the specific verb for the thing done a second time.* **The**

play will be repeated next week. jèy-chū-'shì 'shyà-lǐ-bày 'dzày yǎn. ‖He repeated what he had just 'said. tā 'yew shwō yí-byàr.

Repeat *something* after *someone* 'gēn-je . . . shwō. ‖Repeat this after me. nǐ 'gēn-je wǒ shwō.

(*To pass on by word of mouth*) gàw-su 'byé-rén. ‖Don't repeat what I've told you. wǒ 'gàw-su-nǐ-de-'hwà 'bú-yàw gàw-su 'byé-rén.

REPLY. 'hwéy-dá, hwéy-'hwà, 'dá-fu; *sometimes expressed as* say shwō. ‖What can you say in reply to this? 'jèy-ge nǐ 'dzěme 'dá-fu-fǎr? *or* 'jèy-ge nǐ yěw 'shéme kě-'shwō-de? ‖He replied that they would be glad to go. tā hwéy-'hwà shwō tām dēw néng 'láy. ‖His reply was quick and direct. tā-de-'hwéy-dá (*or* tā-'hwéy-dá-de) yèw 'pyàw-lyàng yèw gān-'tswèy.

REPORT. bàw-'gàw. ‖He reported that everything was in order. tā bàw-'gàw shwō 'shéme dēw nùng-'hǎw-le. ‖It is reported that you are wasting money. yěw-rén gēn-wo shwō nǐ làng-fèy 'chyán. ‖I'll report on this matter tomorrow. wǒ 'míng-tyan bǎ jèy-jyàn-'shr̀-ching 'bàw-gàw-bàw-gàw. ‖They reported him to the police. tām bǎ-ta gěy bàw-'gàw jǐng-'chá-le. ‖It was an illuminating report. nèy-ge-bàw-'gàw-de-'nèy-rúng hěn 'tèw-chè. ‖He gave the report in person. tā 'chīn-dz̀ bàw-'gàw-de.

Report for duty bàw-'dàw. ‖Report for duty Monday morning. lǐ-bày-'yī 'dzǎw-shang bàw-'dàw.

Reporter shīn-wén-jì-'jě; to report, *said of a reporter or correspondent, is often expressed as* to write an account shyě yí-dwàn-'shīn-wén. ‖He reported the fire for his paper. tā bǎ hwǒ-'jǐng-de-'chíng-shíng gěy tā-de-bàw-'gwǎn shyě-le yí-dwàn-'shīn-wén.

To hear a report (*rumor*) that 'tīng-shwō. ‖I heard a report that you're leaving town. wǒ 'tīng-shwō nǐ yàw dàw 'byé-dì-fang chywǔ.

(*Sound of a shot*) chyāng-'shēng, 'bēng-de-yì-shēng. ‖The gun went off with a loud report. jèy-ge-'chyāng 'bēng-de-yì-shēng 'fàng-chu-chywu-le.

REPRESENT. (*Symbolize*). ‖What does this symbol represent? *is expressed as* This symbol is of what meaning? jèy-ge-'jì-hwar shr̀ shéme-'yì-sz? *or as* How do you explain this symbol? jèy-ge-'jì-hawr dzěme 'jyǎng?

(*Portray*) shr̀. ‖This statue represents Bismarck. jèy-ge-shŕ-'shyàng shr̀ bì-sz-'mày.

(*Report, make out*). ‖He was represented to me as a first-rate surgeon, but I have reason to doubt it. *is expressed as* People told me . . . rén-'jyā 'gàw-sung wo (*or as* When people introduced us they told me . . . rén-'jyā 'jyè-shaw de-shf-hew shwō) tā shr̀ ge-'hěn-'hǎw-de-'wày-kē-'dày-fu; wǒ 'jŕ-daw nèy-hwà bú-'dwèy.

(*Exemplify*). ‖He doesn't represent the typical shopkeeper. *is expressed as* You can't take him as the typical shopkeeper. tā 'bù-néng 'swàn-shr̀ jēn-jèng kāy-'pù-dz-de. *or* 'bù-néng ná-'tā 'dàng-dzwo jēn-

jèng kāy-'pù-dz-de. *or as* The typical shopkeeper isn't the kind he is. 'jēn-jèng kāy-'pù-dz-de 'bú-shr 'tā-nèy-yàngr-de.

(*Include representatives of*) yěw. ‖All classes are represented in our membership. wǒm-'hwèy-ywán-li 'něy-yì-'jyē-jí-de-rén dēw 'yěw.

(*Act for; politically*) dày-'byǎw; (*in court*) tì . . . chū-'tíng. ‖He's represented us in Congress for years. tā dzày gwó-'hwèy dāng wǒ-men-de-dày-'byǎw dāng-le 'hǎw-shyē-nyán-le. ‖He represented China at the Paris Peace Conference in 1919. 'yī-'jyěw-'yī-'jyěw-nyán tā dày-'byǎw 'jūng-gwo dzày 'bā-lí-hé-píng-'hwèy chū-'shí. ‖Who represented the defendant? 'shéy tì bèy-'gàw chū-'tíng-le? ‖He engaged a young lawyer to represent him in court. tā 'chǐng-le ge-nyán-'chǐng-de-lywù-'shŕ láy tì-ta chū-'tíng.

REQUEST. To request chǐng; (*demand*) 'yāw-chyéw (*pleading*) chǐng-'chyéw; a request chǐng-'chyéw, (*written*) chǐng-chyéw-'shū, *but sometimes rephrased with one of the verbs.* ‖I'd like to request further (*financial*) assistance. wǒ shyǎng 'dzày chǐng shyē-'jīn-tyè. ‖He requested us to take care of his child. tā 'chǐng wǒ-men 'jàw-gù tā-de-'háy-dz. ‖I am writing you at the request of a friend. yěw yí-wèy 'péng-yew chyéw wǒ gěy-ni shyē-'shìn. ‖We're turning down your request. nǐ-chyéw-de-'shŕ wǒm bù-néng 'dā-ying. ‖ Please file a written request. chǐng 'jyāw yì-jāng-chǐng-chyéw-'shū.

REQUIRE. To require *someone to do something* jyàw; (*less emphatic*) yàw; *often expressed with* have to 'yīng-gay, *or a similar expression.* ‖They required us to pass an examination first. tām jyàw wǒ-men děy 'shyān jīng-gwò kǎw-'shŕ. ‖You are required by law to appear in person. àn fǎ-'lywù shwō nǐ yīng-gay 'dz̀-jǐ °chū-'myàn. *or* (*if in court*) °chū-'tíng.

(*To demand a thing*) yàw. ‖Do you require a deposit? nǐ yàw 'dìng-chyán-ma? *or expressed as* Is it necessary to pay a deposit first? 'shr̀-bu-shr̀ děy 'shyān gěy 'dìng chyán?

(*To need*) yàw, 'shywū-yàw. ‖How much do you require? nǐ yàw 'dwō-shaw? ‖This matter requires consideration. jèy-jyàn-'shr̀-ching °yàw (*or* °'shywū-yàw) 'dwō 'kǎw-lywù-kǎ w-lywù.

RESPECT. (*Esteem*) kàn-de-'chǐ, dzwēn-'jìng. ‖I respect your opinion, but I can't always agree with it. wǒ hěn kàn-de-'chǐ nǐ-de-'yì-jyàn, kě-shr jè 'bìng bú-shr shwō wǒ 'lǎw 'yì-wéy nǐ 'dwèy. ‖He respects his elders. tā hěn dzwēn-'jìng tā-de-'jǎng-bèy.

To respect *or* have respect for 'gù-je, 'pèy-fù. ‖Have some respect for other people's opinions. dzǔng 'yīng-dāng 'gù-je-dyǎr 'byé-rén-de-'yì-jyàn. ‖He has the respect of everyone he works with. gēn-ta-dzwò-'shr̀-de-rén dēw 'pèy-fu ta.

(*Refrain from infringing on*) dzwēn-'jùng, bù-'chī-fù. ‖They should respect our rights. tām 'yīng-gay dzwēn-'jùng wǒ-men-de-'chwán-lì. *or* tām bù-'yīng-gay 'chī-fu wǒ-men.

In what respect 'dzěme-yàng, dzěme 'kàn, tsúng 'něy-yì-'fāng-myàn; in many respects yěw 'hǎw-shyē-'dì-fang. ‖In what respect is this true? 'dzěme-yàng (shwō) jèy-ge 'tsáy shr̀ 'jēn-de-ne? *or* 'jèy-ge děy dzěme 'kàn tsáy shr̀ 'jēn-de'ne? *or* tsúng 'něy-yì-'fāng-myàn kě-yi shwō 'jèy-ge shr̀ 'jēn-de? ‖In many respects I agree with you. yěw 'hǎw-shyē-'dì-fang wǒ 'jywé-de nǐ hěn 'dwèy.

Respecting 'gwān-ywu. ‖There was a question respecting his position. gwān-ywu tā-de-'dì-wèy tséng-'jīng 'fā-sheng gwò 'wèn-tí.

RESPONSIBLE. 'jùng-yaw, fù 'dzé-rèn. ‖It is a most responsible position. nèy-ge-'shr̀-ching děy 'fù hěn-'dà-de-'dzé-rèn. *or* 'nèy-ge shr̀ yí-ge-hěn-'jùng-yaw-de-'chāy-shr̀.

(*Trustworthy*) kě-'kàw-de. ‖I consider him a thoroughly responsible individual. wǒ 'rèn-wéy tā-shr yí-ge-'jywé-dwèy-chéng-'shf-kě-'kàw-de-rén.

Be responsible for (*give rise to*). ‖His strategy was responsible for the victory. *is expressed as* The victory was due to his strategy. 'jèy-tsz̀-dǎ-shèng-'jàng shr̀ 'yéw-ywu tā-de-'jàn-lywè. *or as* Only because of his strategy was the victory possible. 'yīn-wey tā-de-'jàn-lywè tsáy néng dǎ shèng-'jàng.

Be responsible for (*accountable for*). ‖You are responsible for the books you take out of the library. *is expressed as* The books you take out of the library are your responsibility. nǐ-tsúng-tú-shū-'gwǎn-jyè-de-'shū yéw-'nǐ fù-'dzé.

Be responsible to. ‖He is responsible only to the President. *is expressed as* He takes orders only from the President. tā jř̀ tīng dzǔng-'tǔng-de-'mìng-lìng.

REST. shyē, 'shyēw-shi. ‖Rest awhile. 'shyē yì-hwěr. *or* 'shyēw-shi yì-'hwěr. ‖I hope you rest well. wǒ 'shī-wang nǐ hǎw-'hāwr-de 'shyē-je. ‖Try to rest your eyes. 'shyē-shye nǐ-de-'yǎn-jing. ‖A little rest would do you a lot of good. nǐ yàw 'shyē yì-hwěr, jyèw 'hǎw-de 'dwō-le.

To rest with. ‖The power rests with him. chywán-'bìng dzày 'tā shěw-li.

To rest one's head on 'jēn-dzày. ‖She rested her head on the pillow. tā 'jēn-dzày 'jēn-tew-shang.

To rest against (*lean against*) kàw-je. ‖The ladder is resting against the wall. 'tī-dz kàw-je 'chyáng 'bǎy-je-ne.

To rest in. ‖Our hope rests in him. wǒm jyèw °kàn-'tā-le. *or* °kàw-'tā-le. *or* °shī-wang 'tā-le.

To rest on (*depend on*). ‖This argument rests on rather weak evidence. *is expressed as* This evidence isn't very strong. jèy-ge-'lǐ-yéw bú-'dà hěn 'chūng-dzu.

Rest assured that fàng-'shīn. ‖Rest assured that I'll take care of it. fàng-'shīn-ba, 'wǒ yí-'dìng bàn.

Put one's mind at rest (jyàw . . .) 'shīn-li jyèw 'ān-le. ‖This will put your mind at rest. 'jèy-yàng nǐ 'shīn-li jyèw 'ān-le.

Be at rest *or* come to rest 'tíng-jù-le, 'jàn-jù-le. ‖Wait 'till the pointer is at rest. 'děng-je jèy-ge-'jēn 'tíng-jù-le.

(*Remainder*) chí-'ywú, byé, 'shèng-shyà-de. ‖Where is the rest of the gang? chí-'ywú-nèy-shyē-rén (*or* 'byé-de-rén) dēw dzày-'nǎr? ‖I'll do the rest of the job. chí-'ywú-de (*or* 'shèng-shyà-de-'shr̀) 'wǒ dzwò. ‖I understood a little and guessed the rest. wǒ 'jr̀-daw yì-'dyǎr, chí-'ywú-de dēw-shr̀ 'tsāy-de.

RESTAURANT. fàn-'gwǎn-dz, fàn-'gwǎr, gwǎn-dz, fàn-'pùr; (*Western food*) 'shr̀-tsān-gwǎr; (*Moslem restaurant*) 'hwéy-hwey-gwǎr.

RESULT. 'jyē-gwǒ. ‖The results were very satisfactory. 'jyē-gwǒ hěn 'mǎn-yì. ‖One result is that we'll have enough to eat. *is expressed as* Thus we'll have enough to eat. 'jè-yàng yì 'láy wǒm-'chř̀-de-dūng-shi shr̀ 'gèw-le. ‖That fire was the result of your carelessness. *is expressed as* That fire was because you weren't careful. nèy-hwéy-shr̀-'hwǒ shr̀ yǐn-wey nǐ bù-'shyǎw-shīn.

To result from. ‖A lot of trouble results from gossip. *is expressed as* Gossiping causes a lot of trouble. shwō shyán-'hwà °dǐng shēng shr̀-'fēy-le. *or* °dzwèy chū 'lwàn-dz.

To result in. ‖That disagreement resulted in a complete break between them. *is expressed as* Because of that disagreement they broke completely. yīn-wey nèy-tsz̀-de-'yì-jyàn bù-'hé, tām jyèw wán-'chywán jywé-'lyè-le.

RETURN. 'hwéy-láy, 'hwéy-chywù. ‖When did he return? tā 'shéme-shf-hewr 'hwéy-lay-de? ‖He just returned from work. tā 'gāng dzwò-wán 'gūng 'hwéy-lay.

To return *something* hwán. ‖Will you return it when you're through? chǐng-ni yùng-'wán-le de-shr̀-hew jyèw 'hwán-le.

Be returned (by the election) bèy 'shywǎn hwéy . . . . ‖He's been returned to Congress several times. tā bèy 'shywǎn-le 'hǎw-jǐ-tsz̀ hwéy-daw gwó-'hwèy chywù.

To return to (*resume use of*) yèw yùng. ‖He returned to his original plan. tā 'yèw yùng tā-'běn-láy-de-'jì-hwà-le.

(*Time of getting back*) 'hwéy-láy-de-shf-hew; (*act of getting back*) *expressed with* to return 'hwéy-láy. ‖I'll take the matter up on my return. wǒ 'hwéy-láy de-shf-hew 'dzày bàn jèy-jyàn-'shr̀. ‖His return was eagerly awaited by everyone. 'měy-yí-ge-rén dēw 'pàn-je tā 'hwéy-lay.

(*Interest*) 'lì-chyán. ‖How much of a return did you get on your investment? nǐ 'téw-dz °dé-le (*or* °jwàn-le) dwō-shaw-'lì-chyan?

(*Results*) 'jyē-gwǒ. ‖Did the election returns come in yet? shywǎn-'jywǔ-de-'jyē-gwǒ yěw-'shyèr-le-ma?

Return ticket (*for return journey*) hwéy-'pyàw; return half of a ticket 'hwéy-chywù-nèy-yí-'bàr-de-pyàw. ‖I didn't use the return half of the ticket. 'hwéy-chywù-nèy-yí-'bàr-de-pyàw wǒ méy-'yùng.

By return mail. ‖Try to answer these letters by return mail. *is expressed as* Try to answer these letters quickly. shyǎng-'fár bǎ nèy-shyē-'shìn jyèw 'hwéy-le. *or* shyǎng-'fár 'kwày 'shyě-hwéy nèy-shyē-'shìn.

REWARD. To get a reward shèw-'shǎng, dé-'jyǎng; to reward *someone* jyǎng-'lì; to give a reward (*for something lost and recovered*) shywán-'shǎng. ‖You deserve a reward for your hard work. nǐ 'jēn-shr̀ láw-kǔ-'gūng-gāw, yīng-gay °shèw-'shǎng. *or* °dé-'jyǎng. ‖He was rewarded with a promotion. yīn-wey jyǎng-'lì ta, gěy-ta 'shēng-le. ‖She offered five dollars reward for the return of her dog. wèy-le-yàw bǎ-'gěw 'jǎw-hwéy-láy tā shywán-'shǎng 'wǔ-kwày-chyán. ‖His efforts were not rewarded during his lifetime. *is expressed as* He worked a whole lifetime without getting any benefit. tā 'máng-le yí-'bèy-dz méy 'dé-je shéme-'hǎw-chù. *or as* He worked a whole lifetime without anyone knowing it. tā 'máng-le yì-'shēng 'méy-rén 'jr̄-daw. *or as* He worked hard for a lifetime but got no compensation at all. tā kù-'gàn-le yí-'bèy-dz, 'bìng méy-'dé-je shéme-'bàw-chéw. *or as* He worked a whole lifetime but the result was no achievement. tā 'gàn-le yí-'bèy-dz, 'jyē-gwǒ yě 'méy shéme 'chéng-jyèw.

RIBBON. dwàn-'tyáw, sz̄-'dày; (*as of a typewriter*) 'dày-dz. ‖Give me a yard of white ribbon. gěy-wo yì-mǎ-'báy-de-dwàn-'tyáw. ‖The medal had a three-color ribbon. jèy-ge-jyǎng-'jāng yěw yí-ge-sān-'shǎr-de-°sz̄-'dày. *or* °dwàn-'tyáw. ‖I need a new ribbon for my typewriter. wǒ-de-dǎ-dz̀-'jī yīng-gay 'hwàn yí-ge-'shīn-de-'dày-dz.

RICE. (*Growing in the field*) 'dàw(-dz); rice grain (dàw-)'mǐ; (*ready to eat*) mǐ-'fàn *or* (*including also all staple food made from rice or wheat, or even food in general*) fàn. ‖I'd like a catty of rice. wǒ yàw yì-jīn-'mǐ.

RICH. yěw-'chyán. Rich people 'kwò-rén; rich family kwò-rén-'jyā. ‖This law will benefit the rich. jèy-tyáw-fǎ-'lywù dwèy-ywu 'kwò-rén yěw-'lì. ‖He was adopted by a very rich family. tā-shr̀ bèy yí-ge-kwò-rén-'jyā shěw-chywù 'yǎng-de.

(*Abounding*) 'fēng-fù; (*productive*) féy, fù, chǎn-'lyàng dzwèy 'dwō, hěn 'dwō. ‖Spinach is rich in iron. bwó-'tsày-lǐ-tew 'tyě-jr̀ hěn 'dwō. ‖This country is rich in natural resources. jèy ge-gwó-'jyā-de-'tyān-rán-wù-'chǎn hěn 'fēng-fù. ‖This is very rich wheat land. jèy-kwày-'dì jùng 'mày-dz hěn 'féy. ‖This is one of the richest oil-fields in the world. jèy-shr̀ shr̀-'jyè-shang-yí-ge-°dzwèy-'fù-de- (*or* °chǎn-'lyàng-dzwèy-'dwō-de-) 'yéw-tyán.

To strike it rich dzěw-'ywùn. ‖My brother's struck it rich. wǒ-de-'gē-ge jēn dzěw-'ywùn.

RIDE. dzwò; (*if one sits astride the vehicle or animal*) chí. ‖We rode in a beautiful car. wǒm 'dzwò yí-lyàng-hěn-'pyàw-lyàng-de-'chē. ‖I rode past the railroad station. wǒ 'dzwò-gwò-le hwǒ-chē-'jàn-le. ‖We went for a ride in an airplane. wǒm dzwò-je fēy-'jī 'gwàng-le yí-tàng. ‖We rode to the end of the line. wǒm 'dzwò-daw dzwèy-'hèw-de-yí-'jàn. ‖Do you know how to ride a bike? nǐ hwèy chí dz̀-shíng-'chē-ma? ‖He's ridden horses all his life. tā chí-le yí-'bèy-dz-de-'mǎ. ‖We rode (horseback) a lot last year. wǒm 'chywù-nyan cháng-cháng chí-'mǎ.

(*Of the vehicle*) dzěw. ‖This car rides smoothly. jèy-lyàng-'chē dzěw-de hěn 'wěn.

A ride. ‖He gave me a ride the whole way. *is expressed as* The whole way, he driving a car brought me. yí-'lù, tā kāy-je 'chē 'sùng-wo láy-de. ‖It's a short bus ride. *is expressed as* Ride a short spell on the bus and you get there. dzwò yì-shyǎw-'dwàr-de-gūng-gùng-chì-'chē jyèw 'dàw-le.

To ride *someone* gēn . . . dǎw-'lwàn, gēn . . . kāy wán-'shyàw. Oh, stop riding me! 'ày, byé gēn-wo °dǎw-'lwàn-le! *or* °kāy wán-'shyàw!

RIGHT. (*Correct, proper*) dwèy. ‖That's right! 'dwey-le. ‖This is the right answer. 'jèy-ge-hwéy-da shr̀ 'dwèy-de. ‖You're absolutely right. nǐ 'wán-chywán 'dwèy. ‖He's right about everything. tā shwō-de dēw 'dwèy-le. ‖Is this the right way? 'dzème dzěw 'dwèy-ma? *or* 'dzème dzwò 'dwèy-ma?

(*Of a size*) dwèy, hé-'shr̀. ‖This one is the right size. jèy-ge-dà-'shyǎw jèng hé-'shr̀. *or* 'jèy-ge-hàw-'mǎr jèng 'dwèy.

(*Of the weather*) hǎw, *if the weather desired is good weather; if some other type is desired, the appropriate adjective.* ‖We'll leave tomorrow if the weather is right. myéngr tyār 'hǎw wǒm jyèw 'dzěw.

(*Of one's mind*). ‖You're not in your right mind. nǐ 'hú-dù-le. *or* nǐ-'nǎw jīn-bu hīng-chu.

(*Of something that has two sides, one of which is designed to be seen*) jèng. ‖Make sure that only the right side of the material shows. 'chyáw-je-dyǎr jr̀ jyàw nèy-ge-dūng-shi-de 'jèng-myàr chùng 'wày-tew.

(*Privilege; legal*) chywán; (*social*) 'lì-yew; *sometimes expressed with the verb* can *or* may kě-yi. ‖They denied his right to the property. tām bù-chéng-'rèn tā-de-tsáy-chǎn-'chywán. ‖You have no right to behave like this. nǐ méy 'lì-yew 'jè-yang. ‖I have a right to go if I wish. rú-gwo wǒ 'yàw chywù de-hwà, wǒ 'kě-yi chywù. ‖I have my rights! (*In protest against someone's claim or action*)₁ wǒ yěw-'lǐ! *or* wǒ lǐ-'jŕ chì-'jwàng! (*To an officer of the law who is trying to arrest you*) *meaning* I haven't done anything illegal. wǒ 'bìng °méy- (*or* °bú-)fàn-'fǎ! (*To someone who is protesting against your participation in something*) wǒ yěw-'chywán gwò-'wèn! *or* wǒ 'gwǎn-de-jáw!

(*Moral good*) hǎw. Right and wrong hǎw-'dǎy, shṛ-'fēy. ‖You seem to have no idea of right and wrong. nǐ hǎw 'shyàng °bù-'jŕ hǎw-'dǎy. *or* °shṛ-'fēy bù-'míng.

(*Correctly*) dwèy. ‖Do it right or not at all. yàw 'dzwò jyèw dzwò 'dwèy-le, 'yàw-bu-rán 'yì-dyǎr yě byé 'dzwò.

(*Fairly*) 'gūng-píng. ‖You haven't been treated right. tām 'dày-ni bù-'gūng-píng. *or expressed as* You've really gotten a raw deal. nǐ 'jēn-shṛ °shèw-'chywū-le. *or* °áy 'chī-fu-le.

Do the right thing by dwèy . . . jù. ‖You didn't do the right thing by him. nǐ 'dwèy-ta bú-'jù. *or expressed as* You owe him an apology. nǐ 'dwèy-bu-chi 'tā. ‖Do you think we did right by him? *is expressed as* Do you think we can face him? nǐ 'jywé-de wǒm 'dwèy-de-chǐ ta-ma?

Serve *someone* right. ‖It serves him right! tā jyèw 'chyàn nème-yàngr! *or* hwó-'gāy! *or* 'běn-láy jyèw 'gāy nème 'jŕ-ta.

(*Precisely*) jyèw. ‖Ask him; he's right in the room. tā jyèw dzày jèy-ge-'wū-dz-li-ne; nǐ 'wèn-ta. ‖The book's right there on the shelf. 'shū jyèw dzày nèy-ge-'jyà-dz-shang-ne.

(*Immediately, or often added simply to give a polite tone to the sentence*) jyèw; (*if the idea is that of continuing straight ahead*) yì-'jŕ; *sometimes not expressed.* ‖I'll be right there. wǒ jyèw 'láy. ‖Go right in the house. yì-'jŕ dzěw-jìn 'fáng-dz chywù, 'hǎw-le. ‖He drove right on. tā yì-'jŕ 'kāy-gwò-chywu-le. ‖Go right ahead. (*When answering a request for permission to do something*) 'shíng. *or* 'kě-yi. ‖Sit right down. 'dzwò-shya-chywu, 'hǎw-le. *or* 'dzwò-ba.

(*Completely*) yì-'jŕ, dēw, jèng. ‖They fought right to the end. tām yì-'jŕ 'dǎ-dàw 'dǐ. ‖The porch runs right around the house. jèy-dzwò-'fáng-dz-'sṛ-myàn dēw-shṛ 'láng-dz. ‖The bullet went right through him. chyàng-'dzěr jèng tsúng tā-'shēn-shang 'chwān-gwò-chywu.

Right now shyàn-dzày (jèng). ‖I'm busy right now. wǒ shyàn-'dzày jèng 'máng-je-ne. *or* wǒ shyàn-'dzày méy 'gūng-fu.

Right away 'gǎn-jǐn, lì-'kè, 'mǎ-shang, *all followed by* jyèw. ‖Let's go right away, or we'll be late. wǒm °'gǎn-jǐn (*or* °lì-'kè, *etc.*) jyèw 'dzěw-ba, 'yàw-bu-rán jyèw 'wǎn-le.

To right *something* (*turn the proper side up*) 'jèng-gwò-láy. ‖Can you right the boat without any help? nǐ-'yí-ge-rén néng bǎ-'chwán gěy 'jèng-gwo-láy-ma?

All right hǎw. ‖The doctor said you'd be all right in a few days. 'dày-fu shwō nǐ 'jǐ-tyān jyèw kě-yi 'hǎw-le. ‖Everything will turn out all right. *is expressed as* The result will certainly be satisfactory. 'jyē-gwǒ yí-'dìng °ywán-'mǎn. *or* °méy 'wèn-tí. ‖All right, I'll do it if you want me to. 'hǎw, yàw-shr nǐ 'jyàw-wo dzwò wǒ jyèw 'dzwò.

(*Ninety degrees*) jèng. ‖That's bigger than a right angle. 'nèy-ge bǐ 'jèng-jyǎw 'dà-yì-dyǎr.

(*Opposite of left*) yèw. ‖Take the road on the right. dzěw 'yèw-byàr-nèy-tyáw-'lù. ‖I've lost my right shoe. wǒ bǎ 'yèw-jyǎw-de-'shyé 'dyěw-le.

RING. (*On finger*) 'jyè-jr, (shěw-)'lyěw-dz; (*other circular objects*) 'chywār. ‖Keep your napkin in this ring. bǎ nǐ-de-tsān-'jīn fàng-dzay nèy-ge-'chywār-li. ‖They stood in a ring. tām 'jàn-le yì-'chywār. ‖There's a ring of trees around the house. ràw-je jèy-ge-'fáng-dz jùng-le yì-chywār-'shù. ‖They've built a ring of cement around the spring. wéy-je 'chywán-ywan tām pū-le yì-chywār-yáng-'hwēy.

(*Boxing arena*) lèy-'táy, 'táy-dz. ‖We had seats near the ring. wǒ-men-de-'dzwò-wèy lí nèy-ge-°lèy-'táy (*or* °'táy-dz) hěn-'jìn.

To be ringed by 'sž-wéy dēw-shṛ, 'wéy-je dēw-shṛ. ‖The valley is ringed by mountains. jèy-ge-shān-'gǔ °'sž-wéy (*or* °'wéy-je) dēw-shṛ 'shān.

(*Gang*) hwǒr, hwǒ-dz. ‖They broke up the spy ring. tām bǎ jèy-hwǒr-jyàn-'dyé dǎ-'sàn-le.

To ring shyǎng; (*if by striking*) dǎ, chyāw. ‖The bell rings every hour. jèy-ge-'líng 'měy-yì-dyǎn-jūng °'shyǎng-yì-tsž. *or* °'dǎ-yì-tsž. ‖The phone rang. dyàn-'hwà 'shyǎng-le. ‖Two shots rang out. yěw lyǎng-shēngr-'chyāng 'shyǎng.

To ring *something* (*cause to sound*): (*If by pressing a button*) èn; (*if by swinging*) yáw; (*if by striking*) dǎ; *etc.* ‖Ring the bell again. 'dzày èn yí-shyà 'líng. ‖Ring the buzzer. èn nèy-ge-'líng. ‖Have you rung the bell? nǐ jâw-'líng-le-ma?

To ring with (*resound with*). ‖The valley rang with gun fire. *is expressed as* The whole valley was the sound of guns. mǎn-shān-'gǔ-lǐ-tew dēw-shr chyáng-'shēng.

(*Of the ears*) shyǎng, jyàw-'hwàn. ‖His ears were ringing. tā-de-'ěr-dwo jŕ °'shyǎng. *or* °'jyàw-hwàn. ‖The sound is still ringing in my ears. nèy-ge-shēng-'yīn háy dzày wǒ-'ěr-dwo-lǐ-tew 'shyǎng-ne.

Ring *someone* up, *or* give *someone* a ring gěy . . . dǎ dyàn-'hwà. ‖Ring him up some night next week. shyà-lǐ-'bày-'něy-tyān-'wǎn-shang gěy-ta dǎ ge-dyàn-'hwà. ‖Give me a ring tomorrow. 'myéngr gěy-wo dǎ dyàn-'hwà.

(*Sound of ringing*) 'shēng-yīn. ‖That bell has a peculiar ring. nèy-ge-'líng-de-'shēng-yīn hěn chí-'gwày.

To have a false ring. ‖Her laughter had a false ring. tā 'shyàw-de 'jyǎ-le jyǎ-'chì-de.

To ring true. ‖His offer rings true. tā shwō-de hǎw-shyàng shṛ 'jēn-shīn-hwà.

RISE. (*Move upwards; steadily, like a balloon*) 'shēng-chǐ-láy, 'pyāw-chǐ-láy; (*flying, like a bird or plane*) 'fēy-chǐ-láy, 'fēy-shàng-chywù. ‖The balloon rose slowly. nèy-ge-chì-'chyéw màn-'mār-de °'shēng-chi-lay-le. *or* °'pyāw-chi-lay-le. ‖The plane rose and circled the field. fēy-jī 'fēy-chi-láy-le, dzày fēy-jī-'chǎng-shang 'ràw.

(*Of a curtain*) kāy. ‖When will the curtain rise? 'shéme-shŕ-hew kāy-'mù?

(*To extend upwards*) 'gāw-chǐ-láy, lí-'dì yěw. ‖The mountain rises a thousand feet. 'shān °'gāw-chi yì-chyān-'chǐ. *or* °'-dyěngr lí-'dì yěw yì-chyān-'chǐ. ‖The ground rises a little behind the house. fáng-'hèw-tew-de 'dì 'gāw-chi yì-'dyǎr-lay.

(*To stretch upwards*) 'fā-chǐ-láy. ‖The bread has risen. jèy-ge-myàn-'bāw 'fā-chi-lay-le.

(*Of prices*) jǎng. ‖Prices are still rising. 'wù-jyà háy 'jǎng-ne. ‖Sugar has risen to twice its old price. *is expressed as* The price of sugar has risen to double what it was. táng-de-'jyà-chyán 'jǎng-le yí-'bèy.

(*Of a person; get up in the morning*) 'chǐ-láy, chǐ-'chwǎng; (*get up from sitting*) 'jàn-chǐ-láy. ‖The men all rose as we came in. wǒm 'jìn-chywu de-shŕ-hew rén dēw 'jàn-chi-láy-le.

Rise to *a state.* Rise to importance dé-'yì, 'chéng-wey hěn 'jùng-yàw-de-rén; rise to fame chéng-'míng, chū-'míng. ‖He rose to importance when he was still young. tā háy dzày nyán-'chīng de-shŕ-hew jyèw yǐ-jing 'chéng-wey hěn-'jùng-yaw-de-'rén-le. *or* tā dzày shàw-'nyán de-shŕ-hew jyèw hěn dé-'yì-le. ‖He rose to international fame almost overnight. tā yī-'jywǔ chéng-'míng. *or* tā lì-'kè chū-le 'míng-le. *or* tā lì-'kè 'míng mǎn 'tyān-shyà.

Rise to the occasion. ‖You can depend on her to rise to the occasion. nǐ fàng-'shīn-ba, tā 'jŕ-daw dzěme 'bàn. *or* (*always*) 'shém-shèr tā dēw néng yìng-fu-de-'hǎw.

(*Of the sun*) 'chū-lay. ‖The sun rises earlier at this time of the year. 'měy-nyán 'jèy-ge-shŕ-hew 'tày-yang 'chū-lay-de 'dzǎw. ‖The sun hasn't risen yet. 'tày-yang háy méy-'chū-lay-le-ne.

(*Of a voice*). ‖Her voice rose to a scream. *is expressed as* Her voice got bigger and bigger, (until she) called out. tā-de-'shēng-yīn ywè láy ywè 'dà, 'jyàw-chi-lay-le.

(*Of water*) jǎng. ‖The river is rising fast. hé (-'shwěy) 'jǎng-de kwày-'jí-le.

A rise (*of ground*) pwō. ‖The house is on a little rise. nèy-ge-'fáng-dz shŕ dzày yí-ge-shyǎw-'pwōr-shang.

A rise (*of prices*) *expressed with* to rise jǎng. ‖There's been a rise in price since last week. tsúng 'shàng-lǐ-bày chǐ 'jǎng-le 'jyà-le.

A rise (*of temperature*) *expressed with* to rise jǎng. ‖There was a sudden rise in temperature today. jyēr-de wēn-'dù 'hū-rán-de 'jǎng-le.

Give rise to *expressed as* cause people to do so-and-so jyàw (*or* ràng) . . . . ‖The rumor gave rise to a lot of unnecessary worry. jèy-ge-yáw-'yán °'jyàw- (*or* °'ràng-)rén báy dān-'shīn-le yì-'chǎng.

RIVER. hé. ‖That's a good river for fishing. nèy-tyáw-'hé dǎ-'ywú hěn 'hǎw.

Yellow River hwáng-'hé; Yangtze River cháng-'jyāng, dà-jyāng; (*just the lower part*) yáng-dž-jyāng.

ROAD. lù, dàw; main road dà-'lù; side road shyǎw-'lù; branch road chà-'lù; (*thoroughfare*) mǎ-'lù; (*highway*) gūng-'lù. ‖The road is getting steadily worse. *meaning* as one goes along it nèy-tyáw-'lù °ywè 'dzěw ywè 'hwày. *or meaning* from day to day °'yì-tyān-yì-'tyān-de ywè láy ywè 'hwày.

Take the wrong road (*figuratively*) dzěw shyé-'lù. ‖The boy took the wrong road and has been stealing things. jèy-ge-'háy-dz dzěw shyé-'lù, lǎw 'tēw rén-de-'dūng-shi.

Go on the road dzěw mǎ-'téw. ‖When does the show go on the road? jèy-'bān-dz 'shéme-shŕ-hew 'chū-chywu dzěw mǎ-'téw?

ROAST. kǎw, shāw (*see Chinese-English side*).

(*Figuratively*) 'rè-sž-le. ‖I'm roasting in here; how about you? wǒ jèr 'rè-sž-le; 'nǐ dzěme-'yàng?

ROB. chyǎng. ‖I've been robbed. wǒ bèy 'chyǎng-le. *or* (*figuratively*) wǒ °'shàng-'dàng-le. *or* °'jyàw rén 'ywān-le. ‖They'll rob you of everything you've got. tām yàw bǎ nǐ-'swǒ-yěw-de-'dūng-shi dēw 'chyǎng-le. *or* (*Figuratively*) tām hěn 'chyāw jú-'gàng.

ROCK. 'shŕ-tew; a rock (*contrasted with a pebble*) yí-kwày-'dà-shŕ-tew. ‖What kind of rock is this? jè-shr shéme-'shŕ-tew? ‖Don't throw that rock! 'byé rēng nèy-kwày-'shŕ-tew! ‖The ship was wrecked on a rock. 'chwán 'jwàng-dzày yí-kwày-'dà-shŕ-tew-shang-le. ‖That's no pebble, that's a rock. 'nèy-ge 'bú-shr shŕ-tew-'dzěr shŕ yí-kwày-'dà-shŕ-tew.

To rock *a baby* yáw; to rock *a baby to sleep* yáw-'jáw-le; to rock *a house* (*or something big*) yáw-'dùng-le. ‖Rock the baby to sleep. bǎ 'háy-dz 'yáw-je-yáw-je jyèw yáw-'jáw-le. ‖The earthquake rocked the whole house. dì-'jèn bǎ jèy-jěng-'gèr-de-'fáng-dz dēw jèn-de jŕ-'dùng.

ROD. gwèr, tyáw. ‖We need new curtain rods. wǒm děy hwàn 'shīn-de-lyán-dz-'gwèr-le. ‖The parts are connected by an iron rod. jèy-shyē-'dwàr dēw-shŕ yùng yì-gēr-tyě-°'tyáw (*or* °'gwèr) 'lyán-chi-lay-de. Fishing rod ywú-'gār.

ROLL. (*To change location by rotary motion along a surface, or to cause to move thus; of a ball, wheel, ring, person, etc.*) 'gú-lu; (*particularly of a roller or ball*) gwèn; (*to turn around on an axis, either at one location or changing location*) jwàn, *with which a verb indicating the method of causing such motion can be used, e.g.,* by pushing 'twěy-je, by pulling 'lā-je, by kicking 'tī-je. ‖Roll the barrel over here. bǎ nèy-ge-'tǔng gěy °'gú-lu-gwò-lay. *or* °'gú-lu-dàw 'jèr-lay.

‖Turn the barrel sidewise and roll it up the slope. bǎ-'tǔng fàng-'dǎw-le 'twēy-je °'jwàn-daw (or °'gú-lu-daw) 'pwōr-shang-chywu. ‖Put the barrel on top of the plank and it'll roll down by itself. bǎ-'tǔng gē-dzay tyàw-'bǎn-'gāw-de-nèy-'téwr-shang, 'dž-jǐ jyèw kě-yi °'gwěn-shya-chywu-le. or °'gú-lu-shya-chywu-le. ‖Give the barrel a push and it'll roll over here. bǎ-'tǔng °'twēy yí-shyàr jyèw 'gú-lu-gwo-láy-le. or yì 'twēy jyèw 'gú-lu-gwo-láy-le. ‖The ball rolled down the hill. 'chyéwr °'gwěn-shyà (or °'gú-lu-shyà) 'shān chywù-le. ‖The ring rolled ten feet before it toppled over. 'hwán-dz °'jwàn-le (or °'gwěn-le or 'gú-lu-le) 'shŕ-chř nème 'ywǎn tsáy 'dǎw-shyà. ‖I rolled out of bed last night. dzwór-'wǎn-shang wǒ tsúng 'chwáng-shang °'gwěn- (or °'gú-lu or °'yì 'gú-lu gú-lu- or °'yì 'gwěn gwěn- or °'yì fān-'shēn fān-)dàw 'dì-shya chywu-le. ‖The waves keep rolling in. 'làng-téw yí-jèn-yí-'jèn-de °'gwěn-jìn-láy. or °'jywán-gwò-láy.

Roll over (of something lying down, so that the parts facing upwards and downwards are reversed) fān-'shēn, 'fān-gwò-láy; roll over and over (either in one place or moving along a surface) dǎ-'gwěr. ‖Roll over! (Facing the speaker) 'fān-gwò 'shēn-lay! (Facing away from the speaker) 'fān-gwò 'shēn-chywu! ‖He rolled (himself) on the ground when his coat caught fire. tā-'yī-shang 'jáw-le, tā jyèw dzày 'dì-shang dǎ-le ge-'gwěr. ‖The dog rolled over and over on the ground. 'gěw dzày 'dì-shang jŕ dǎ-'gwěr. ‖He rolled back and forth on the bed. tā dzày 'chwáng-shang °jŕ dǎ-'gwěr. or °'fān-gwò-lay dyàw-gwò-'chywù-de. or °jŕ fān-'shēn.

(To shape a flat thing into a spiral) jywǎn; (sleeves only) wǎn. ‖We rolled up the rug. wǒm bǎ dì-'tǎn °'jywǎn-chi-láy-le. or °'jywǎn-chéng-le yí-ge-'jywǎr. ‖He rolls his own (cigarettes). tā-'dž-jǐ 'jywǎn yān-'jywǎr. ‖Roll up your sleeves. bǎ 'shyèw-dz °'jywǎn-chi-lay. or °'wǎn-chi-lay.

Roll something into a ball (with palms or fingers) 'tswō-chéng ge-'chyéwr; (with fingers only) 'nyǎn-chéng ge-'chyéwr; (enlarging it by rolling it along, as a snowball) 'gwěn-chéng ge-'chyéwr. Roll something into a pellet (with palm or fingers) 'tswō-chéng 'jyéwr; (with fingers only) 'nyǎn-chéng 'jyéwr.

(To press something down by rolling something over it) yà; (if with a large roller, making it flat) nyǎn-'píng-le; (to make thin by rolling something over it; only for dough) gǎn. ‖They rolled the field flat with a roller. tām ná nyéw-'jéw bǎ 'chǎng-dz yà-'píng-le. or tām ná 'nyǎn-dz bǎ 'chǎng-dz nyǎn-'píng-le. ‖Roll the dough out thin. 'myàn gǎn 'báw-yi-dyǎr.

(Move along on wheels) dzěw. ‖This car rolls along smoothly. jèy-ge-'chē 'dzěw-de hěn 'wěn.

(Of a ship) yáw, bǎy. ‖The ship rolled heavily. 'chwán °'yáw-de (or °'bǎy-de) hěn 'lì-hay.

To roll by (of time). ‖I get more homesick as the months roll by. wǒ shyǎng-'jyā 'shyǎng-de 'yí-ge-ywè bǐ 'yí-ge-ywè 'lì-hay.

A roll of jywǎr, 'jywǎn-dz. ‖He used a whole roll of wallpaper. tā 'yùng-le jěng-'jywǎr-de-hú-chyáng-'jŕ. ‖He took out a big roll of bills. tā 'ná-chu yí-'dà-jywǎn-dz-chyán-'pyàw-dz-lay. ‖Do you have toilet paper in rolls? nǐ yěw °chéng-'jywǎr-de- (or 'jěng-'jywǎr-de-) shěw-'jŕ-ma?

(List of names) míng-'dān; to call the roll dyǎn-'míng. ‖Have they called the roll yet? tām dyǎn-'míng-le-ma?

ROOF. (Of a house) fáng-'dyěngr; (of a building) léw-'dyěngr. ‖The burglar escaped via the roof of the adjacent house. 'dzéy tsúng 'jyè-byer-de-fáng-'dyěngr-shang 'pǎw-le. ‖The tin roof is only temporary. jèy-ge-'fáng-dz-de-yáng-tyě-'dyěngr 'bú-gwò shř 'jàn-shŕ-de.

To roof pū, or expressed with the nouns given above. ‖The cottage is roofed with tiles. jèy-ge-shyǎw-'fáng-dz°-shàng-tew-'pū-de shř-'wǎ. or 'shř 'wǎ-'dyěngr.

Roof of the mouth shàng-'táng. ‖I burned the roof of my mouth. wǒ 'tàng-le wǒ-de-°shàng-'táng-le.

ROOM. 'wū-dz, wūr; (in a hotel) fáng-'jyān. ‖Where can I rent a furnished room? 'shéme-dì-fang néng 'dzū yì-jyān-dày-'jyā-jywu-de-'wū-dz? ‖It was a big room with plenty of light. nèy-jyān-'wū-dz yèw 'dà yèw 'lyàng.

Room (rent) fáng-'dzū. ‖What do you charge for room and board? 'fáng-dzū gēn 'fàn-chyán yì-'chǐ nǐ yàw 'dwō-shaw?

(Space or place) 'dì-fang. ‖There's no room to sit down. 'jèr méy dì-fang 'dzwò. ‖Is there room for one more? is expressed rather as Can you still seat (or ride) one? 'háy néng dzwò 'yí-ge-ma? ‖I see little room for improvement. wǒ 'jywé-de néng-'ŕ v-de-dì-fang 'méy dwō-shǎw-le. or expressed as As I see it, there isn't much you can improve. wǒ 'kàn, 'méy shém kě-'gǎy-de.

To room jù. ‖Shall we room together? dzám 'jù yí-'kwàr, 'hǎw-ma?

ROOT. gēn. ‖The roots have to be protected. 'gēn děy bǎ-'hǎw-le. ‖He had to have the root of his tooth extracted. tā-de-yá-'gēr děy 'bá-chu-lay. ‖You don't have to pull my hair out by the roots. nǐ 'yùng-bu-jáw bǎ wǒ-de-'téw-fa lyán 'gēr 'bá-chu-lay.

Get to the root of kàn . . . dàw-'dǐ shř . . . . ‖Let's get at the root of the matter. 'kàn-kàn jèy-jyàn-'shř dàw-'dǐ shř 'dzěme-hwéy-'shř.

To root something out 'gēn-běn gěy °'chú-le or °'chǎn-chú or 'chywù-le. ‖They're trying to root out malaria from this region. tām shyǎng bǎ jèy-ge-'dì-fang-de-'yàw-dz 'gēn-běn gěy °'chú-le. or °'chǎn-chú.

To take root jùng-'hwó. ‖Has the rosebush taken root yet? nèy-kē-'méy-gwèy jùng-'hwó-le-ma?

To take root (figuratively) ‖The custom never really took root. nèy-ge-'fēng-sú 'gēn-běn méy 'jēn shēng-chi-lay.

735

ROPE. 'shéng-dz. ‖He slid down the rope. tā shwèn-je 'shéng-dz 'lyēw-shya-chywu-le. ‖Fix it with this piece of rope. ná jèy-tyáw-'shéng-dz 'jì-shàng-'hǎw-le.

To rope off yùng 'shéng-dz 'lán. ‖A large space was roped off in one corner. jī-'jyǎw-nèr yùng 'shéng-dz 'lán-chū yí-'dà-kwày-'dì-fang-chywu.

To know the ropes. ‖Wait till you know the ropes better. shyān bǎ 'chíng-shíng nèng-'shéw-shí-le 'dzày shwō.

To give rope. ‖His father gave him too much rope. tā-de-'fù-chin tày 'dzùng-ta-le. ‖Don't worry; give him enough rope and he'll hang himself. nǐ béng 'gwǎn-ta-le; tā dzǎw-'wǎn dzǔng-'hwèy 'dz-jǐ rě-chū 'shr̀-lay-de.

ROSE. méy-gwèy-'hwār; rosebush 'méy-gwèy(-shù) *with measure* kē. ‖They presented the actress with a bouquet of roses. tām 'shyàn-gey nèy-ge-nywǔ-jǔ-'jyǎw yì-bǎr-méy-gwèy-'hwār. ‖How do you like my rosebushes? wǒ jèy-shyē-kē-'méy-gwèy 'hǎw-bu-hǎw?

(*Color*) méy-gwèy-'dž, méy-gwèy-'shǎr. ‖She's wearing a rose dress. tā chwān yí-jyàn-'méy-gwèy-shǎr-de-'yī-fu.

Bed of roses (*figuratively*). ‖This trip has been no bed of roses. jèy-yí-'tàng kě bù-'shū-fu.

ROUGH. (*Not smooth-surfaced*) tsū; (*of water*) *expressed as* waves big 'làng-'dà; (*of a road*) bù-'píng, hwày. ‖The bark of this tree is very rough. jèy-kē-'shù-'pí hěn 'tsū. ‖This table is made of rough planks. jèy-jāng-'jwō-dz shr̀ tsū-'bǎn-dz dzwò-de. ‖The water's pretty rough today. jyēr-ge 'làng hěn 'dà. ‖How well can this truck take rough ground? jèy-lyàng-dzày-jùng-'chē néng dzěw bù-'píng-de 'lù-ma?

(*Sketchy*) dà-'jř-de; a rough draft tsǎw-'gǎw. ‖This'll give you a rough idea. 'jèy-ge kě-yi jyàw-ni míng-bay-ge-dà-'gày. ‖Here's a rough draft of my speech. jèy-shr̀ wǒ-yǎn-'jyǎng-de-tsǎw-'gǎw.

(*Not gentle*) tsū-'yě. ‖His rough manner frightened the children. tā-nàme-tsū-'yě-de-'yàng-dz bǎ shyǎw-'háy-dz-men dēw 'shyà-jàw-le.

(*Severe, difficult*). ‖They had a rough time of it. *is expressed as* They experienced a lot of difficulties. tām 'jīng-gwò hěn-dwō-'má-fan.

To rough it. ‖He didn't enjoy roughing it last summer. *is expressed as* Last summer he certainly didn't like that kind of rough existence. 'chywù-nyán-'shyà-tyăn tā kě bù-'shǐ-hwan nèy-jǔng bù-'shū-fu-de-'shēng-hwó.

ROUND. 1. ywán. ‖They have a round table in the living room. tām kè-'tīng-li yěw yì-jāng-ywán-'jwō-dz. ‖The medicine is in the little round bottle. 'yàw dzày shyǎw-ywán-'píng-dz-le-ne. ‖What a nice round mirror! 'ày! jèy-myàn-ywán-'jìng-dz jēn 'hǎw! ‖That ball doesn't look round to me. wǒ 'jywé-de nèy-ge-'chyéwr 'bú-shr̀ ywán-de.

(*Both ways*) láy-'hwéy. Round-trip ticket láy-hwéy-'pyàw. ‖How much for the round trip? láy-'hwéy 'dwō-shaw-chyán?

(*Approximate*). In round numbers dà-'gày-de-'shù-mu, *or expressed with* probably dà-'gày. ‖I'm speaking in round numbers. wǒ 'shwō-de shr̀ dà-'gày-de-'shù-mu. ‖It costs a hundred dollars in round numbers. dà-'gày děy yùng yì-'bǎy-kwày-chyán.

(*In a contest*) chǎng. ‖He was eliminated in the second round. dì-'èr-chǎng tā jyēw bèy 'dǎ-shyà-chywu-le. ‖In what round was the boxer knocked out? 'něy-yì-chǎng nèy-ge-dǎ-'chywán-de dzěw 'pā-shyà-le?

A round of dàw. ‖He ordered another round of drinks. tā 'yèw gěy 'dà-jya jyàw-le yí-dàw-'jyěw.

Rounds (*route*). Be on one's rounds sùng-X, *where X is the thing being delivered;* finish one's rounds sùng-'wán. ‖The newsboy is on his rounds. jèy-ge-sùng-'bàw-de-háy-dz sùng-'bàw-ne. ‖When will the milkman finish his rounds? jèy-ge-sùng-nyéw-'nǎy-de 'shéme-shf-hew sùng-'wán?

To make the rounds (*to get around*) chwán-de 'kwày; *or expressed as* everybody knows it 'shwéy dēw 'jř-daw-le. ‖That story sure made the rounds. jèy-ge-'shr̀ jen chwán-de 'kwày. *or* nèy-jyàn-'shèr 'shwéy dēw 'jř-daw-le.

To round a corner gwǎy-'wār; to round *a point or obstruction* 'ràw-gwò. ‖As soon as you round the corner you'll see the store. nǐ yì gwǎy-'wār jyèw 'kàn-jyan nèy-ge-'pù-dz-le. ‖The ship rounded the Cape of Good Hope this morning. jīn-tyan-'dzǎw-shang 'chwán 'ràw-gwo hǎw-wàng-'jyǎw-le.

To round off *an edge* (*smooth down*) nèng-'ywán, mwó-'ywán. ‖Round off the edges a little. bǎ-'byār °nèng-'ywán yì-dyǎr. *or* °mwó-'ywán yì-dyǎr.

To round out *something* (*complete*) bǎ ... tsèw-'chí-le. ‖I need this to round out my collection. wǒ yàw 'jèy-ge hǎw bǎ wǒ-'dzǎn-de tsèw-'chí-le.

2. *Cases in which* round (*or* 'round) *or* around *can be used, perhaps more often the latter.*

To come round a corner 'gwǎy-gwò 'wār-lay; to go round a corner 'gwǎy-gwò 'wār-chywu. ‖He's just coming round the corner. tā gāng 'gwǎy-gwò 'wār-lay.

Round the edge of 'sž-wéy. ‖There's a border round the edge of it. 'sž-wéy 'yán-le yì-tyáw-'byān.

Enough to go round gèw 'fēn-de; gèw dà-'jyā-hwǒr X-de, *where X is an appropriate verb.* ‖Is there enough candy to go round? 'táng 'gèw-bu-gèw 'fēn-de? *or* 'táng 'gèw dà-'jyā-hwǒr 'chř-de-ma?

All the year round 'jěng-nyán, 'wú-'dūng-'lì-'shyà. ‖I live here all the year round now. wǒ shyàn-dzày 'jěng-nyán 'jù-jèr. *or* wǒ-shr̀ 'wú-'dūng-'lì-'shyà-de 'jù-dzày jèr-le.

Round and round. jwàn-je 'wār-de X-láy X-chywù, *where X is an appropriate verb.* ‖The children were dancing round and round. jèy-shyē-'háy-dz-men jwàn-je 'wār-de tyàw-'láy tyàw-'chywù.

ROW. (*Line*) lyèw. ‖He pulled up a whole row of carrots. tā 'bá-le yì-jeng-'lyèw-de-hú-'lwó-be. ‖They stood in a row awaiting their turn. tām 'páy-le yí-'lyèw děng 'lwén-dàw tā-men.

To row yáw, hwá. ‖You'll have to row too. 'nǐ yě děy °'yáw. *or* °'hwá. ‖Who will row this boat? 'shéy °'yáw (*or* °'hwá) jèy-ge-'chwán-ne? ‖Row me across the river. bǎ-wo 'yáw-gwò 'hé-'nèy-byar chywu.

(*A fight*) to have a row chǎw, dǎ-'jyà. ‖We had quite a row on our block last night. dzwó-'wǎn-shang, wǒm-jèy-tyáw-'jyē hěn °'chǎw. *or* °'yěw-rén dǎ-jyà.

RUB. (*With repeated grinding motion*) mwó; (*scraping, polishing, or rubbing something in, or dirt off*) tsā; (*in rubbing the hands together, occasionally in other situations*) tswō; (*with a sideswiping motion*) tsèng. ‖My shoe's rubbing. wǒ-de-'shyé °'jř 'tsèng. *or* °'mwó-'jyǎw. ‖The boat rubbed against the pier. 'chwán 'tsèng-je nèy-ge-'mǎ-téw. ‖He rubbed his hands together. tā 'tswō-'shěw. ‖Better rub the clothes hard or they won't get clean. háy-shř bǎ 'yī-shang shř-'jìn °'tsā-yi-tsā (*or* °'tswō-yi-tswō) yàw-bu-rán shǐ-bu-'gān-jing. ‖Rub her back with alcohol. yùng hwó-'jyěw tsā tā-de-'bèy. ‖You forgot to rub out your name. nǐ 'wàng-le bǎ nǐ-de-'míng-dz gěy 'tsā-le.

Rub it in. ‖I know I'm wrong, so don't rub it in. wǒ 'jř-daw wǒ 'tswò-le, °'jyèw byé 'shwō-le. *or* °byé méy-'wán-le.

RUBBER. shyàng-'pí; *in some compounds* pí. ‖They used a lot of rubber in these tires. jèy-shyē-wén-'dày yùng-le hěn-dwō-shyàng-'pí. ‖Take this piece of rubber hose. 'ná jèy-ge-pí-'gwǎr hǎw-le.

Rubbers (*overshoes*) jyāw-pí-'shyé, shyàng-pí-'shyé. ‖I lost one of my rubbers yesterday. wǒ 'dzwór-ge dyěw-le yì-jř-jyāw-pí-'shyé.

RUG. dì-'tǎn. ‖I like oriental rugs. wǒ 'shǐ-hwan 'dūng-fāng-dì-'tǎn. ‖That's a nine-by-twelve rug. 'nèy-shř yí-ge-'jyěw-chř-'kwān, shř-'èr-chř-'cháng-de-dì-'tǎn.

RUIN. To ruin *or* cause the ruin of *or* be the ruin of hwěy, 'dzāw-ta; go to rack and ruin *or* be in ruins hwěy-le. ‖He caused the ruin of his family. tā-'jyā shř jyàw-'tā gěy 'hwěy-de. ‖The frost will ruin the crop. jèy-tsź-de-'shwāng yàw bǎ 'jwāng-jya gěy 'hwěy-le. ‖He's ruining his health. tā 'dzāw-ta dž-jǐ-de shēn-dz. ‖This material is ruined. jèy-ge-tsáy-'lyàw °'hwěy-le. *or* °'dzāw-ta-le. ‖The place is going to rack and ruin. jèy-ge-'dì-fang 'hwěy-le. ‖Their house is in ruins. tā-men-de-'fáng-dz 'hwěy-le.

Be ruined (*financially*) pwò-'chǎn. ‖He was ruined in the depression. tā dzày 'nyán-téw-bù-'hǎw-de-shf-hew pwò-le 'chǎn-le.

Ruins (*destroyed buildings*) lwàn-'dwēy; (*remnants of ancient buildings*) gǔ-'jì. ‖They were hunting for bodies among the ruins. tām dzày nèy-lwàn-'dwēy-lǐ-tew jǎw sž-'shř-ne. ‖Those are very impressive ruins. nèy-shř hěn-kě-'gwān-de-gǔ-'jì.

RULE. (*Regulation*) 'gwēy-jywu. ‖Smoking is against the rules here. dzày-'jèr chēw-'yān shř fān-'gwēy-jywu-de. *or expressed as* Smoking is prohibited here. 'jèr bù-'shywǔ chēw-'yān.

(*To govern*) 'tǔng-jř. ‖The same family has been ruling for generations. jèy-yí-'shìng yǐ-jing 'tǔng-jř-le 'dwō-shaw-dày-le. ‖This island has been under foreign rule for years. jèy-ge-'dǎw bèy 'way-gwo-rén gwǎn-le hěn 'jyěw-le. ‖He's ruled by his emotions. tā lǎw-shr 'gǎn-chíng yùng-'shř.

To rule *something* out. ‖This doesn't entirely rule out all possibilities. *is expressed as* This isn't to say that there are no other ways. 'jè-yàng 'bú-shr shwō 'méy-yew 'byé-de-fá-dz-le.

Ruled paper dày-'dàwr-de-jř.

As a rule 'shyàng-láy; to be the rule (*be customary*) *is also expressed with this phrase.* ‖As a rule I don't drink. wǒ 'shyàng-láy bù-hē-'jyěw-de. ‖That sort of thing is the rule around here. 'jyèr 'shyàng-láy 'jème-yàng.

RUN. 1. (*Go fast on foot*) pǎw. ‖You'll have to run if you want to catch the train. nǐ yàw shyǎng 'gǎn-shàng nèy-tàng-'chē, nǐ kě děy 'pǎw-le. ‖I can walk faster than you can run. 'wǒ-'dzěw-de bǐ nǐ-'pǎw-de háy 'kwày. ‖He ran two miles in fourteen minutes and thirty-two seconds. tā 'pǎw 'èr-yīng-lǐ yùng shf-'sž-fēn-'sān-shr-èr-'myǎw.

2. (*Sail or move*) dzěw. ‖The ship was running before the wind. 'chwán 'dzěw-de hěn shwèn-'fēng.

(*Be in operation*) kāy. ‖The engine's running. 'jī-chi 'kāy-je-ne.

(*Function*) *expressed with* to use yùng. ‖That car hasn't run well since we bought it. nèy-ge-'chē dž-tsúng wǒ-men 'mǎy-láy yǐ-'hèw jyèw bù-hǎw-'yùng.

(*Be in process*) kāy, yǎn. ‖The movie had been running for half an hour when we went in. wǒm 'jìn-chywu de-shf-hew dyàn-'yǐng yǐ-jing °'yǎn-le (*or* °'kāy-le) 'bàn-ge-'jūng-téw-le.

(*Flow; of colors*) twèy-'sè, twèy-'shǎy, dyàw 'yán-shǎr, dyàw-'shǎr, làw-'shǎr. ‖These colors are guaranteed not to run. jèy-shyē-'yán-sè 'gwǎn-bāw bú-°'twèy-'sè. *or* °'twèy-'shǎy. *etc.*

(*Unravel*) chēw-'sž, tyàw-'sž. ‖Do rayon stockings run worse than silk? rén-dzàw-'sž-de-'wà-dz bǐ jēn-'sž-de 'rúng-yì °chēw-'sž-ma? *or* °'tyàw-'sž-ma?

(*Go; of something quoted or sung*). ‖The tune runs like this. *is expressed as* The tune is like this. jèy-ge-'dyàwr shyàng 'jè-yàng. ‖How does the first line run?

is expressed as How is the first line sung (*or read*)? dì-'yī-háng dzěme °'chàng? or °'nyàn? *or as* How is the first line? dì-'yī-háng shr̀ 'dzěme láy-je?

(*Be mostly*). ‖These apples run small. *is expressed as* These apples are mostly small. jèy-shyē-'píng-gwo chà-bu-dwō 'dēw 'shyǎw. ‖What sizes do these dresses run in? *is expressed as* What sizes are there of these dresses? jèy-shyē-'yī-fu dēw-shr̀ 'dwō-dà-'hàwr-de?

3. Run *an apparatus or machine* yùng. ‖Can you run a washing machine? nǐ 'jr̄-daw dzěme yùng shǐ-'yī-shang-de-'jī-chi-ma?

Run *a business* dzwò, gwǎn. ‖I don't think he knows how to run the business. wǒ 'jywé-de tā bú-'hwèy dzwò 'mǎy-may.

4. Run (on) *an errand* chū-'chāy. ‖How many errands have you run today? 'jīn-tyan nǐ 'chū-le 'jǐ-tsż-'chāy-le?

Run *a race* pǎw (*or* sày) . . . chǎng. ‖The first race has already been run. dì-'yī-chǎng yǐ-jìng °'pǎw-gwo-le. *or* °'sày-gwo-le.

Run *a risk* màw-'shyǎn. ‖He's running a big risk. tā 'màw hěn-'dà-de-'shyǎn.

Run *the risk of* . . .*-ing.* ‖If you wear that pin with the broken catch, you'll run the risk of losing it. *is expressed as* If you wear that pin with the broken catch, it'll be easily lost. nǐ byé-'jēn-de-gēwr dwàn-le, dày-je hěn 'rúng-yi 'dyēw.

5. *Combinations of* run *with adverbs, adjectives, and prepositions.*

Run across *an area* (*on foot*) 'pǎw-dàw . . .°-'nèy-byar-chywù *or* °-'jèy-byar-láy. ‖The chicken ran across the road. shyǎw-'jyēr 'pǎw-dàw dàwr-'nèy-byar chywù-le.

Run across *an area* (*by flowing*) lyéw-dàw . . .°-'nèy-byar-chywu *or* °-'jèy-byar-lay. ‖There was a trickle of water running across the floor. yí-lyèwr-'shwěy tsúng dì-'bǎn-'jèy-byar 'lyéw-dàw 'nèy-byar chywù-le.

Run across *someone or something* (*see by accident*) 'pèng-jyan, 'ěw-rán 'kàn-jyàn. ‖When did you last run across him? nǐ dzwèy-'hèw dzày 'shéme-shr̄-hew 'pèng-jyan ta-de? ‖I ran across an article about him the other day. nèy-tyan wǒ 'ěw-rán 'kàn-jyan yí-'dwàr-'gwān-ywu-ta-de-'wén-jāng.

Run aground gē-'chyǎn. ‖My boat ran aground. wǒ-de-'chwán gē-'chyǎn-le.

Run *something* aground bǎ . . . nùng-de gē-'chyǎn-le. ‖He ran the boat aground. tā bǎ-'chwán 'nùng-de gē-'chyǎn-le.

Run along (*leave*) chywù. ‖Run along now! 'chywù-ba! *or* shàng 'byé-chùr 'chywù-ba! *or* 'dzěw-ba!

Run along *a route* (*on foot*) shwèn-je . . . pǎw. ‖He ran along the path until he reached the lake. tā shwèn-je 'dàwr pǎw, yì-'jŕ-de pǎw-de nèy-ge-'hú-nèr.

Run along *a route* (*extend along*) yán-je. ‖The path runs along the edge of the lake for about a quarter of a mile. nèy-ge-'lù yán-je 'hú yěw 'sż-fēn-jr-'yī-'lǐ.

Run along *a line of thought.* ‖Along what lines does his mind run? tā-shr̀ dzěme-ge-'shyǎng-far?

Run around *a corner or obstruction* (*on foot*) shwèn-je . . . 'pǎw. ‖He ran around the north side of the house and then just seemed to disappear. tā shwèn-je nèy-ge-'fáng-dz-'běy-byàr 'pǎw chywù-le, 'yì hwéy-'téw jyèw kàn-bu-'jyàn-le.

Run around *something* (*extend so as to encircle*) yán-je . . .-de-jēw-'wéy, wéy-je; run halfway around wéy-je . . . ví-'bàr. ‖The path runs around the lake. yán-je 'hú-de-jēw-'wéy dēw yěw 'dàwr. *or* nèy-'dàwr 'wéy-je hú-byar 'ràw. ‖The road runs only halfway around the lake. wéy-je hú-'byār-shang jyèw yěw yí-'bàr yěw-'lù.

Run around (*go out for good times*) wár. ‖He's running around too much; he'll never be able to pass his exams. tā 'wár-de tày 'lì-hay-le, 'kǎw-shr̀ yǔng-'ywǎn yě 'jí-bu-lyǎw 'gé.

The run-around. ‖He's giving her the run-around. tā-shr̀ 'yěw-dyǎr 'shwǎ-je nèy-ge-'nywǔ-de 'wár-ne.

Run around to *a place* (*on foot*) 'pǎw-dàw, 'jwàn-dàw. ‖The thief ran around to the rear of the house and escaped through the back gate. 'dzéy °'pǎw-dàw (*or* °'jwàn-dàw) 'fáng-dz-'hèw-tew chywù, tsúng 'hèw-mér 'pǎw-le.

Run around with (*keep company with*) gēn . . . 'hwèn. ‖He's running around with a fast crowd. tā 'jìng gēn yì-bāng-hú-'nàw-de-rén 'hwèn.

Run away (*leave quickly, with or without the intention of returning*) pǎw. ‖He ran away when he saw me. tā yí 'kàn-jyan wo, jyèw 'pǎw-le. ‖Don't let him run away. byé jyàw-ta 'pǎw-le. ‖My dog ran away. wǒ-de-'gěw 'pǎw-le.

Runaway 'pǎw-le-de; runaway horse 'jīng-le-de-'mǎ. ‖They finally caught the runaways. tām dàw 'lyǎwr bǎ 'pǎw-le-de 'dǎy-hwéy-láy-le. ‖He was killed by a runaway horse. yì-pǐ-'jīng-le-de-'mǎ bǎ-ta gěy chwàng-'sž-le.

Run away from *a place* (*intending to stay away*) tsúng . . . pǎw. ‖He ran away from home when he was eight. tā 'bā-swèy de-shŕ-hewr jyèw tsúng 'jyā-li 'pǎw-le.

Run away from (*figuratively*) 'dwǒ-kāy. ‖He always runs away from danger. tā yǔng-'ywǎn shr̀ 'kàn-jyan bù-'hǎw jyèw 'dwǒ-kāy.

Run away with *someone* (*elope*) gēn . . . pǎw. ‖She ran away with the chauffeur. nèy-ge-'nywǔ-de gēn kāy-'chē-de 'pǎw-le.

Run away with *something* (*abscond*) bǎ . . . chwān-'pǎw-le. ‖He ran away with my best suit. tā bǎ wǒ-dzwèy-'hǎw-de-yí-tàw-'yī-fu gěy chwān-'pǎw-le.

Run away with one (*of the imagination*). ‖Don't let your imagination run away with you. byé hú-'sż-lwàn-'shyǎng-le. *or* byé shyǎng-rù-'fēy-fēy.

Run by *or* past *someone or something* (*on foot*) tsúng . . .-páng-'byār 'pǎw-gwò-chywu. ‖He ran right by us without seeing us. tā tsúng wǒ-men-páng-'byār 'pǎw-gwo-chywu kě-shr̀ méy-'kàn-jyan wǒ-men. ‖He ran right by the house without realizing he had

738

reached it. tā tsúng nèy-ge-'fáng-dz-páng-'byār 'păw-gwo-chywu kě-shr méy-'jywé-chu-láy tā 'dàw-le nèr-le.

Run by or **past** *something* (*extend*) dzày . . .-páng-'byār. ‖The road runs right by my house. jèy-tyáw-'lù jyèw dzày wǒ-de-'fáng-dz-páng-'byār 'gwò.

Run circles around (*figuratively*) bì-je 'yǎn yě bǐ . . . 'chyáng. ‖He can run circles around anyone at that business. 'nèy-jyàn-shr̀ tā bì-je 'yǎn yě bǐ 'byé-rén dzwò-de 'chyáng.

Run down (*stop going*) tíng. ‖Wind up the clock before it runs down. bǎ-'jūng gěy 'shàng-shang byé děng 'tíng-le tsáy-'shàng.

Run down *a route* (*to a lower position; on foot*) păw-shyà . . . chywù. ‖They ran down the hill. tām 'păw-shyà 'shān chywù-le.

Run down *a route* (*to a lower position; by flowing*) iyéw-shyà-lay. ‖The tears ran down her cheeks. tā-de-yǎn-'lèy jǐ 'lyéw.

Run down *a route* (*on foot, but not to a lower position*) dzày . . .-shang păw. ‖He ran down the road as fast as he could go. tā dzày nèy-ge-'dàwr-shang pīn-'mìng-de wàng-chyán-'păw.

Run *someone* **down** (*strike down*) bǎ . . . chwàng-'dǎw-le. ‖He was run down by a truck. yí-lyàng-dà-'chē bǎ-ta gěy chwàng-'dǎw-le.

Run *someone* **down** (*speak ill of*) mà, 'pī-ping. ‖Don't run him down that way; he's doing his best. 'byé nème °'mà-ta (*or* °'pī-ping ta); tā-nèr 'bú-shr 'hǎw-hāwr-de 'dzwò-ne-ma?

Be run down (*of a thing*) hwày-le, 'pwò-le, bù-'shíng-le; **look run down** (*of a person*) 'shēn-tǐ shyàng 'hwày-le-de-yàng-dz. ‖The house is run down. jèy-jyān-'fáng-dz °'hwày-le. *or* °'pwò-le. *or* °'bù-'shíng-le. ‖She looks terribly run down. tā-de-'shēn-tǐ hǎw 'shyàng hěn-'hwày-de-yàng-dz.

Run dry gān-le. ‖The well has never run dry. jèy-kěw-'jǐng méy-'gān-gwo.

Run for *a destination* păw-dàw. ‖It's started to rain; let's run for that tree. shyà-'ywǔ-le, dzám 'păw-dàw nèy-kē-'shù-nèr chywù-ba. *But* ‖Run for it! kwày 'dzěw-ba! *or* kwày 'păw-ba!

Run for *an office* jìng-'shywǎn (dzwo). ‖Do you think he'll run for mayor? nǐ shyǎng tā yàw jìng-'shywǎn dzwo shr̀-'jǎng-ma? ‖Who ran for president that year? 'nèy-nyán shr̀-'shéy jìng-'shywǎn dzǔng-'tǔng?

Run from *someone*. ‖Her dog always runs from strangers. *is expressed as* The minute her dog sees strangers he runs. tā-de-'gěw yí 'kàn-jyan 'shēng-ren jyèw 'păw.

Run from A to B (*of a vehicle on a route*) shr̀ tsúng A kāy-daw B. ‖This bus runs from Peiping to Tientsin. jèy-ge-cháng-tú-chì-'chē shr̀ tsúng běy-'píng kāy 'tyān-jīn de.

Run from A to B (*of a route*) shr̀ tsúng A tūng-dàw B. ‖This railroad runs from the ocean to the center of Shensi province. jèy-tyáw-tyě-'lù tsúng hǎy-'byār-shang tūng-daw 'shǎn-shī-'shěng-de-dāng-'jyàr.

Run in a family (*of a trait*). ‖That trait runs in their family. *is expressed as* Everyone in their family has a bit of that. tām-'jyā-de-rén 'dēw yěw-dyǎr 'nà-yàngr.

Run *someone* **in** (*take to jail*). ‖I'll have to run you in. wǒ děy bǎ-ni °'dày-'chywū. *or* °'dày-de chywū-shang 'kān-chi-láy. *or* °'yā-chi-láy. *or* °'jywān-chi-láy.

Run into *an interior* (*on foot*) păw-dàw . . .-li. ‖He ran into the house. tā 'păw-dàw nèy ge-'fáng-dz-li chywù-le.

Run into *an interior* (*extend*) 'tūng-dàw . . .-li. ‖Does this road run into the city? jèy-tyáw-'lù tūng-daw chéng-'lǐ-tew-ma?

Run into *an obstruction* (*of a vehicle*) kāy-dàw, jwàng. ‖The car ran into a tree. jèy-lyàng-'chē °kāy-daw 'shù-shang chywù-le. *or* °'jwàng 'shù-shang-le.

Run into debt chyàn-'jày, lā-'jàng, gāy-'jàng, chyàn-'jàng. ‖He's running into debt. tā shyàn-dzày °'chyàn-'jày-le. *or* °'lā-'jàng-le. *etc*.

Run *a vehicle* **into** *an interior* bǎ . . . °kāy-dàw . . .-li *or* °kāy-jìn . . . . ‖She ran the car into the garage. tā bǎ-'chē °kāy-daw chē-'fáng-li chywù-le. *or* °kāy-jìn chē-'fáng chywù-le. ‖He ran the boat into the harbor. tā bǎ-'chwán kāy-jìn hǎy-'kěw chywù-le.

Run *a vehicle* **into** *an obstruction* bǎ . . . kāy-dàw. ‖He ran his car into a tree. tā bǎ-'chē kāy-daw 'shù-shang-le.

Run *something* **into** *another* (*thrust into*). ‖I ran a splinter into my finger. wǒ-shěw-'jr̀-tew-shang 'jā-le yí-ge-'tsèr.

Run last. ‖My horse ran last. wǒ-de-'mǎ là 'hèw-tew-le.

Run low ywè láy ywè 'shǎw-le. ‖My money is running low. wǒ-de-'chyán ywè láy ywè 'shǎw-le.

Run off (*hurry away*) dzěw. ‖Don't run off now! I have some other things to say. shyàn-'dzày byé 'dzěw-wa! wǒ 'háy yěw 'byé-de-shr̀-ching gēn-ni 'shwō-ne.

Run off *a route* (*of a vehicle*) kāy-daw . . .-'wày-tew. ‖The car ran off the road. jèy-lyàng-'chē kāy-daw dàwr-'wày-tew chywù-le.

Run off with (*elope or abscond*) *see* **run away with**, *above*.

Run out yùng-'wán-le, yùng-'gwāng-le. ‖Our supply of sugar has run out. wǒ-men-de-'táng yùng-°'wán-le. *or* °'gwāng-le.

Run out of *an interior* tsúng . . . 'păw-chu-láy. ‖He ran out of the house. tā tsúng 'wū-dz-li 'păw-chu-láy-le.

Run out of *something* (*use up*) yùng-'wán-le, yùng-'gwāng-le. ‖We ran out of ammunition. wǒ-men-de-jywūn-'hwǒ yùng-'wán-le.

Run *someone* **out of** *town, a country, etc*. bǎ . . . 'chywū-ju chū-'jìng-le. ‖They ran him out of town. tām bǎ-ta 'chywū-ju chū-'jìng-le.

Run over (*overflow*) 'lyéw-chu-lay, 'màn-chu-lay; (*even if said of the container, expressed in Chinese in terms of the contents*) ‖The water's running over.

'shwěy dēw °'mǎn-de 'lyéw-chu-lay-le. *or* °'màn-chu-lay-le. ‖**The tub is running over.** 'pén-dz-li-de-'shwěy dēw °'mǎn-de 'lyéw-chu-lay-le. *or* °'màn-chu-lay-le.

Run over *an edge* (*overflow*) *expressed in the same terms,* edge *being omitted.* ‖**The milk is running over the edge of the cup.** 'bēy-dz-li-de-nyéw-'nǎy 'mǎn-de dēw 'lyéw-chu-lay-le.

Run (*all*) **over** *something* (*cover*). ‖**There was ivy running all over the wall.** *is expressed as* **The surface of the wall was completely covered with ivy.** 'chyáng-shang pá-'mǎn-le pá-chyáng-'hǔ.

Run over *someone* (*with a vehicle*) yà-'shāng-le, 'yà-le; (*if it results in death*) yà-'sž-le. ‖**Someone got run over.** yěw-'rén rà... ṛ-'chē gěy 'yà-le.

Run over *something* (*review*) 'wēn-shi yí-byàn; (*in one's mind*) 'shyǎng-shyang. ‖**Run over your part before the rehearsal.** 'ywù-yǎn-yǐ-'chyán, bǎ nǐ-nèy-yí-'bù-fen 'wēn-shi yí-byàn. ‖**I ran over in my mind all the persons involved.** wǒ bǎ swǒ-yěw-de (gēn-'jèy-shèr) yěw-'gwān-shi-de-rén dēw 'shyǎng-le yì-shyǎng.

Run over to *a place* (*if on foot*) pǎw; (*if not specifying means*) chywù. ‖**Run over to the store and see if you can get some sugar.** wàng nèy-ge-'pù-dz-li °chywù (*or* °pǎw) yí-tàng, kàn-kan 'néng-bu-néng 'mǎy-jáw dyàr-'táng.

Run short kwày yùng-'wán-le. ‖**Our supplies are running short.** wǒm-de-'dūng-shi dēw kwày yùng-'wán-le.

Run short of *something* kwày yùng-'wán-le. ‖**I'm running short of cash.** wǒ-de-'shyàn-chyán kwày yùng-'wán-le.

Run through *a passage* (*on foot*) dzày . . . pǎw. ‖**He ran through the streets as fast as he could go.** tā pīn-'mìng-de dzày 'jyē-shang kwày 'pǎw.

Run through *one's head* dzày . . .-'nǎw-dz-li 'jwàn-yew. ‖**That tune keeps running through my head.** nèy-ge-'dyàw-dz 'lǎw dzày wǒ-'nǎw-dz-li 'jwàn-yew.

Run through (*be found in all of*). ‖**There's a strange idea running through the whole book.** jèy-běn-'shū-de 'jwàn-jyě °tsúng-'téw dàw-'wěy (*or* °tsúng-'téw dàw-'lyǎwr *or* °dž-'shř jǐ-'jūng) dēw hěn 'gwày.

Run *something* **through** *a machine.* ‖**He ran the meat through the meat-grinder.** tā bǎ-'rèw 'gē-dàw jyǎw-'dāw-lǐ-tew 'jyǎw-chu-láy-le.

Run *something long* **through** *a narrow passage* bǎ . . . 'chwān-gwò . . . ‖**Run the rope through this loop.** bǎ jèy-ge-'shéng-dz 'chwān-gwò nèy-ge-'chywār-chywu.

Run *something pointed* **through** *something* (*thrust*). ‖**He ran a splinter through his finger.** tā shěw-'jǐ-tew-shang 'jā-le ge-'tsèr, jā-'tūng-le.

Run to *a place* (*on foot*) 'pǎw-dàw; **run to** *a person* 'pǎw-dàw . . .-nèr. ‖**The child ran to its mother.** jèy-ge-'háy-dz pǎw-daw tā-'mǔ-chin-nèr chywù-le.

Run to *a place* (*extend*) tūng(-dàw). ‖**All roads run to Rome.** 'tyáw-tyáw-dà-'dàw tūng lwó-'mǎ.

Run until *a time* (*extend*) yì-'jǐ dàw. ‖**His term runs until next year.** tā-de-rèn-'chī yì-'jǐ dàw 'míng-nyan.

Run up *a route* (*to a higher position, by foot*) 'pǎw-shàng . . . chywù. ‖**They ran up the hill.** tām 'pǎw-shàng 'shān chywù-le.

Run up *a route* (*by foot, but without getting to a higher position*) dzày . . . 'pǎw. ‖**He ran up the road as fast as he could go.** tā dzày 'dàwr-shang 'pǎw-de 'néng pǎw dwō-'kwày 'pǎw dwō-'kwày.

Run up *a flag* 'shēng-chǐ-láy, 'gwà-chǐ-láy. ‖**They ran up the flag as soon as they reached the top of the hill.** tām yí dàw shān-'dyěngr-shang 'mǎ-shang jyèw bǎ 'chí-dz °'shēng- (*or* °'gwà-) chi-lay-le.

Run up *a bill.* ‖**She ran up a terrific clothing bill.** tā mǎy 'yī-fu 'hwā-le hěn-'dwō-de-chyán.

Run wild (*of children*). ‖**We're just letting them run wild.** wǒm 'tày yéw-je tām-de 'shyèngr-le.

6. *Special expressions, particularly those with* **run** *functioning nominally.*

On the run. ‖**He's coming on the run.** tā 'pǎw-je láy-de.

A run (*in a stocking*). ‖**Don't look now, but there's a run in your stocking.** byé 'dùng; nǐ-de-'wà-dz chēw-le yì-tyáw-'sž.

A run (*of a play*). ‖**That play had an amazingly long run.** nèy-chū-'shì jēn 'cháng-de 'lì-hay.

A run of luck. ‖**That run of luck pulled him out of debt.** tā 'fā-le jèy-bǐ-'tsáy, bǎ tā-de-'jày dēw 'hwán-le.

The usual run (*of things or events*) píng-'cháng-de. ‖**That's out of the usual run of things.** 'nèy-ge gēn píng-'cháng-de bù-yí-'yàng.

‖**Make a run for it!** kwày 'dzěw-ba!

(*A trip*) tàng. ‖**The truck goes a hundred miles on each run.** jèy-ge-dzǎy-jùng-'chē 'měy-yí-'tàng dzěw 'yì-bǎy-'lǐ. ‖**It's a long run from coast to coast.** *is expressed as* **From this coast to that coast is really not short.** tsúng 'jèy-àn dàw 'nèy-àn kě 'jēn bú-'jǐn.

In the long run dzwèy-'hèw, 'jyāng-láy. ‖**You're bound to succeed in the long run.** dzwèy-'hèw (*or* 'jyāng-láy) yí-'dìng shř 'nǐ chéng-'gūng.

Be out of the running. ‖**After that speech he was out of the running.** tā jyǎng-'wán 'nèy-ge-jyǎng-'yǎn yǐ-'hèw jyèw bù-'tsān-jyā jìng-'shywǎn-le.

An also-ran. ‖**My horse was just an also-ran.** wǒ-mǎy-'pyàw-de-nèy-pǐ-'mǎ 'shū-le.

Running sore núng, núng-'bāw. ‖**He has a running sore on his foot.** tā-de-'jyǎw jǎng-'núng-le. *or* tā-de-'jyǎw-shang yěw yí-ge-núng-'bāw.

RUNG. (*On ladder*) héng-'gwèr. ‖**Is the top rung strong enough?** 'tī-dz-'téw-shang-nèy-ge-héng-'gwèr gěw 'jyē-shr-ma?

RUSH. (*To do something in a hurry*). *Expressed with the appropriate verb for the thing done, and some expression for hurrying such as* 'chyǎng-je, kwày-'kwāy-de. (*To go in a hurry*) pǎw. ‖**They rushed to the bank.**

740

Top of Great Wall, Badalin

Tower with moon, Renmin Peoples

tām 'păw-dàw yín-'háng chywù-le. ‖They rushed through their work. tām 'chyǎng-je bǎ tā-men-de-'shŕ dzwò-'wán-le. ‖They rushed the bill through. tām 'chyǎng-je 'tūng-gwò-le nèy-ge-yì-'àn. ‖Rush him to the hospital. kwày-'kwāy-de bǎ-ta sùng-daw yī-'ywàn chywù. ‖The blood rushed to his face. is expressed as His face became all red. tā-'lyǎn chywán 'húng-le.

(Hurry, tumult). Expressed in terms of to be pressed or crowded jǐ or to be busy máng. ‖At five o'clock there's always a rush. 'wǔ-dyǎn-jūng-de-shŕ-hew, 'cháng-cháng hěn 'jǐ. ‖What's your rush? nǐ °'máng (or °'jí) shéme? ‖This is the rush season in our busi-ness. shyàn-dzày shŕ wǒ-men-jè-jǔng-'shēng-yi-dzwèy-'máng-de-shŕ-hew. ‖It was a rush job. nèy-shŕ 'jí-shŕ. or nèy-ge dzwò-de tày 'jí-le.

(Of water) expressed as to flow lyéw. ‖You could hear the rush of water. 'tīng-de-jyàn 'shwéy-'lyèw-de hěn-'jí-de-'shēng-yīn.

(The plant; growing) lú-'tsǎw; (as material) ú-'gǎr. ‖That swamp is full of rushes. nèy-ge-'shwéy-'kēng-lǐ-tew jǎng-'mǎn-le °lú-'tsǎw. or 'lú-'wěy.

RUST. shyèw; to rust jǎng-'shyèw. ‖The knives are covered with rust. jèy-shyē-'dāw-dz dēw (jǎng-)'shyèw-le. ‖Oil the parts or they will rust. bǎ jèy-shyē-'jī-chi 'shàng-shang 'yéw, shěng-de jǎng-'shyèw.

S

SACK. má-'dày, 'kěw-dày, 'dày-dz. ‖I want a sack of potatoes. wǒ yàw yì-'kěw-dày-tǔ-'dèwr.

To get the sack bèy 'tsáy. ‖How many in the office got the sack? jèy-ge-gūng-shŕ-'fáng-li yew 'dwō-shaw-rén bèy 'tsáy-le?

SAD. (Of a person) fā-'chéw, bù-'gāw-shìng, bú-'tùng-kwày, bù-hǎw-'shèw, nán-'shèw, bù-hǎw-'gwò, nán-'gwò, (literary) 'chéw-méy-bù-'jǎn; (of a thing or situation) 'ràng-rén °fā-'chéw, °bù-'gāw-shìng, etc.; (unfortunate or bad) dzāw, hwày. ‖I don't like to see you looking sad. nǐ 'chéw-méy-bù-'jǎn-de-'yàng-dz jyàw-wǒ shīn-li nán-'gwò. ‖What happened to him was very sad. tā 'dzāw-le 'nèy-yàngr-de-'shŕ-ching jēn ràng-rén nán-'gwò. ‖That's a sad state of affairs. nèy-ge-'chíng-shing hěn 'dzāw. ‖The children's toys are in a pretty sad condition. 'háy-dz-men-de-'wán-'yèr dēw 'hwày-le.

SAFE. (Reliable, dependable) bǎw-'shyǎn, 'láw-kàw, kě-'kàw, méy 'wéy-shyàn; (not likely to suffer harm or danger, out of danger) bú-'jŕ-ywú yew 'wéy-shyàn, bú-hwèy yew 'wéy-shyàn; (not harmed) 'méy shèr, 'ān-rán-wú-'shŕ. ‖Is the bridge safe? jèy-ge-'chyáw bǎw-'shyǎn-ma? ‖You're safe now. nǐ shyàn-dzày 'bú-hwèy yew 'wéy-shyǎn-le.

(Probable, reasonable) yew 'bǎ-wù. ‖That's a safe guess. nèy-ge 'tsāy-de yew 'bǎ-wù.

(Beyond power of causing harm) bú-hwèy 'dzày chū 'má-fan. ‖He's safe in jail; he can't hurt anybody else. tā dzày 'jyān-ywù-li, °'bú-hwèy 'dzày chū 'má-fan-le. or °'shàng-bu-lyǎw 'rén-le.

A safe (box for valuables) bǎw-shyàn-'shyāng, bǎw-shyǎn-'gwèy. ‖Please put these in the safe. láw-'jyà, bǎ jèy-shyē 'gē-dzày bǎw-shyǎn-'shyāng-li.

SAFETY. 'ān-chywán. ‖Safety first. 'ān-chywán dì-'yī. ‖This is for your safety. jèy shŕ wèy nǐ-'ān-chywán. Safety lamp ān-chywán-'dēng.

SAIL. A sail fān, péng. ‖That boat has pretty sails. nèy-ge-chwán-de-'fān hěn hǎw-'kàn.

To sail (of a ship) kāy-'chwán, dzěw. ‖When do we sail? wǒ-men 'shéme-shŕ-hew kāy-'chwán? ‖This boat is sailing slowly. jèy-ge-chwán 'dzěw-de hěn 'màn.

(To handle a sailboat) shŕ, kāy, jyà. ‖Can you sail a boat? nǐ hwèy shŕ 'fān-chwán-ma?

To sail (of a person; move smoothly) dwān-je 'jyà-dz dzěw. ‖She sailed out of the room. nèy-wèy-'tày-tay dwān-je 'jyà-dz tsúng wū-li 'chū-lay-le.

To go for a sail dzwò-'chwán wár-war. ‖Let's go for a sail. dzám dzwò-'chwán 'wár-war chywù-ba.

To sail the seas háng-'hǎy. ‖He's been sailing the seas for years. tā háng-'hǎy yew 'hǎw-shye-'nyán-le.

SAILOR. (Member of a ship's crew) 'shwěy-shěw. ‖How many sailors are on the boat? 'chwán-shang yew 'dwō-shaw-'shwěy-shěw?

(Naval personnel) shwěy-'bīng. ‖She goes out with a sailor in the U. S. Navy. tā gēn yí-ge-měy-gwo-shwěy-'bīng chū-chywu 'wár chywù-le.

SAKE. For the sake of wèy, gěy. ‖This is for the sake of security. 'jèy-ge shŕ wèy bǎw-dyǎr 'shyǎn. ‖Do it for my sake. gěy-'wǒ 'dzwò-dzwo jèy-ge.

For heaven's sake 'jè shŕ dzěme 'shwō-de; (Peiping) lǎw-tyān-'yé. ‖For heaven's sake, cut it out! hày! 'jè-shŕ dzěme 'shwō-de! (or hēy! lǎw-tyān-'yé!) 'swàn-le-ba!

SALE. (Selling). ‖They made a lot of money through the sale of the family heirlooms. is expressed as They sold the family antiques and made a lot of money. 'tā-men bǎ jyā-'chwán-de-'gǔ-dǔng 'mày-le, dé-le yí-'dà-bǐ-chyán.

(Selling at a lowered price) jyǎn-'jyà. ‖Is this on sale? jèy-ge jyǎn-'jyà-ma? ‖When are you holding a sale? nǐ-men 'shéme-shŕ-hew jyǎn-'jyà?

(Amount sold) 'shēng-yì, 'mǎy-mày. ‖Our sales doubled this year. jīn-nyán wǒ-men-de-'mǎy-mày 'jyā-le yí-'bèy.

(*Demand*) 'shyăw-lù, 'mày-chu-chywu. ‖There is no sale for automobiles now. shyàn-'dzày chì-'chē °méy 'shyăw-lù. *or expressed as* Now automobiles don't sell. °'mày-bu-chū-'chywù.

SALT. (*The substance*) yán. Salt mine yán-'kwàng; mined salt 'jǐng-yán; salt well yán-'jǐng; salt tax yán-'shwèy. ‖I want some salt for my meat. wǒ-chř-de-'rèw-li yàw dyăr-'yán.

To salt (*season*) gē-'yán, jyā-'yán, fàng-'yán. ‖Did you salt that soup? nèy-ge-'tāng nǐ gē-'yán-le-ma?

(*Containing salt*) yán, shyán. Salt water yán-'shwěy *or* (*sea-water*) hǎy-'shwěy; salt lake shyán-shwěy-'hú, yán-'hú. ‖Do you have salt pork? nǐ yěw yán-'rèw-ma?

To salt away *or* down (*preserve with salt*) yán, bǎ . . . 'yán-shang. ‖We ought to salt the meat away. wǒ-men děy bǎ jèy-ge-'rèw 'yán-shang.

To salt away (*save*) tswén, dzǎn. ‖I understand he salted away a good deal for his old age. wǒ jř-daw tā 'tswén-le bù-shǎw-de-'chyán wèy yǎng-'lǎw-de.

To take with a grain of salt. (*Be rather doubtful*) yěw-dyăr °'hwáy-yí; (*suspicious*) °yí-'shìn; (*skeptical*) °bú-'shìn; (*mistrusting*) °bù-shyāng-'shìn. ‖I always take what she says with a grain of salt. wǒ dwèy-ywu tā-de-'hwà lǎw yěw-dyăr 'hwáy-yí.

SAME. To be the same yí-'yàng, shyāng-'túng, túng-'yàng(r). ‖Is this the same as the other chair? jèy-bǎ-'yǐ-dz gēn 'byé-de yí-'yàng-ma? ‖He's not the same as he was ten years ago. *is expressed as* He doesn't resemble the way he was ten years ago. tā bú-'shyàng 'shŕ-nyán-yǐ-'chyán-'nà-yàngr-le.

The same *something* (*as that used before*) 'ywán, 'ywán-láy-de; (*one and the same*) yī; (*identical with what it always has been*) *expressed with* still háy; the same day dàng-'tyār, dāng-'tyār, *etc. with other expressions of time;* at the same time túng-'shŕ. ‖Take the same road home that you came on. nǐ tsúng 'ywán-dàwr hwéy-'jyā-ba. ‖We came here on the same train. wǒm shř dzwò 'yí-tàng-chē láy-de. ‖Even though it's the same problem he still can't solve it. jèy swéy-rán shř yí-'yàng-de shèr, tā 'háy-shr jyě-jywé-bù-'lyǎw. ‖Can I leave and be back the same day? wǒ kě-yi dàng-'tyār dǎ láy-'hwér-ma? ‖She didn't come in at the same time he did. tā 'bú-shř gēn-ta túng-'shŕ 'jìn-lay-de.

The same *as someone else has done, expressed with* also yě. ‖I got up, and he did the same. wǒ 'chǐ-láy-le, tā 'yě 'chǐ-láy-le.

Just the same, all the same (*regardless of argument or opposition*) fǎn-'jèng, 'wú-lwèn-rú-'hé, bù-gwǎn 'dzěme-je, 'bú-lwèn-rú-'hé. ‖We're going just the same. bù-gwǎn 'dzěme-je, wǒm yàw 'dzěw.

At the same time (*but*) kě-shř. ‖I think she'll go with us; at the same time, I'm not sure of it. wǒ 'shyǎng tā gēn wǒ-men yí-kwàr 'chywù, kě-shr wǒ yěw bù-gǎn jwěn 'shwō.

All the same (*all one kind*) chywán yí-'yàng, (*no difference*) méy (shéme-) 'gwān-shi. ‖That's all the same to me. *is expressed as* I see no difference, *or* It makes no difference to me. nèy-ge wǒ kàn 'méy shéme-'gwān-shi.

In the same boat *is expressed as* have the same sickness and therefore mutual sympathy 'túng-bìng-shyāng-'lyán. ‖We're in the same boat. wǒ-men shř 'túng-bìng-shyāng-'lyán.

‖Same here! *is expressed as* I agree. wǒ túng-'yì. *or as* I approve. wǒ dzàn-'chéng. *or as* I also . . . wǒ yě . . . . ‖I'm hungry. Same here! wǒ 'è-le. wǒ yě 'è-le.

‖The same to you! *is expressed as* The feeling is mutual. bǐ-'tsž bǐ-'tsž. ‖Happy new year! The same to you! shīn-'shǐ shīn-'shǐ! bǐ-'tsž bǐ-'tsž!

SAND. shā-dz, shā-'tǔ. ‖Let's lie in the sand. dzám dzày 'shā-dz-shang 'tǎng-tang-ba. ‖Our cottage is beyond the sand dunes. wǒ-men-de-'fáng-dz dzày shā-tǔ-'dwēy-de-'nèy-byar.

To sand dǎ-'mwó; (*if sand is actually used*) ná 'shā-dz °'dǎ (*or* °mwó, *or* °dǎ-'mwó) *or* yùng 'shā-dz °'dǎ (*or* °mwó, *or* °dǎ-'mwó). ‖The men are sanding the floors. tām 'dǎ-'mwó dì-'bǎn-ne.

SANDPAPER. shā-'jř.

To sandpaper ná shā-'jř °'dǎ (*or* °mwó, *or* °dǎ-'mwó).

SATISFY. jyě, 'jyě-shř-'chīng-chu. ‖You drink water to satisfy your thirst. nǐ děy hē-'shwěy tsáy néng 'jyě nǐ-de-'kě. ‖Does that satisfy you on this question? nèy-ge bǎ nǐ-de-'wèn-tí 'jyě-shř-'chīng-chu-le-ma?

(*Fulfill conditions*) 'hé-hu, 'mǎn-dzú; (*discharge an obligation*) táng. ‖Does that satisfy your requirements? nèy-ge 'hé-hu nǐ-de-shywǔ-'yàw-ma? ‖Will this payment satisfy his creditors? jèy-bǐ-'chyán néng bǎ 'jày-jǔ 'táng-gwò-chywu-ma?

Be satisfied (*of a person; in general*) mǎn-'yì; (*with a quantity or degree of expenditure*) jř-'dzú; (*convinced*) shìn, shyāng-'shìn; (*sated*) gwò-'yǐn, 'shū-fu, 'tùng-kwày. ‖I'm not satisfied with my new room. wǒ-nèy-jyān-'shīn-'wū-dz wǒ bù-mǎn-'yì. ‖Even though the diamond IS that expensive, she still isn't satisfied. nèy-kwày-dzwàn-'shŕ 'nème gwèy, tā 'háy bù-jř-'dzú. ‖I'm not satisfied that she's guilty. wǒ bú-'shìn tā yěw-'dzwèy. ‖Were you satisfied with your lunch? nǐ wǔ-'fàn chř-de mǎn-'yì-ma? ‖Now are you satisfied! (*Literal or sarcastic*) shyàn-'dzày nǐ gwò-'yǐn-le-ba! *or* (*Sarcastic only*) *expressed as* Look what a good job you've done! 'chyáw nǐ-'gàn-de 'hǎw-'shèr! *or as* It's all to your credit! 'dēw-shr 'nǐ-de-'gūng-láw!

SATURDAY. shīng-chī-'lyèw, lǐ-bày-'lyèw.

SAVE. (*Not spend*) shěng. ‖Save your money. nǐ 'shěng dyăr-'chyán-ba.

(*To spare, avoid the expense of*) shěng, 'yùng-bu-jáw, béng, 'bú-yùng. ‖You can save yourself the trouble. nǐ kě-yi 'shěng yì-hwéy-'má-fan.

(*To keep, hold on to*) lyéw, gē, tswén. ‖Could you save this for me? nǐ 'kě-yi bǎ jèy-ge gěy-wo °'lyéw-lyewr-ma? *or* °'lyéw-chi-lay-ma? ‖I'll save this candy for later. wǒ bǎ jèy-ge-'táng 'gē-chi-lay lyéw-je 'dāy-hwěr dzày 'chř.

(*To reserve*) lyéw, jàn. ‖Is this seat being s;ved for anybody? jèy-ge-dzwòr shř gěy 'byé-rén 'jàn-de-ma?

(*To rescue*) jyèw. ‖He saved her life. tā 'jyèw-le tā-de-'mìng-le.

(*To collect*) tswén, dzǎn, sēw-'jí. ‖He saves stamps. tā 'dzǎn yéw-'pyàw.

(*To be careful of*) lyéw, 'bǎw-yǎng, 'yǎng-yang. ‖Save your voice. 'lyéw-je nǐ-de-'sǎng-dz-ba. *or* 'yǎng-yang nǐ-de-'sǎng-dz-ba. *But* ‖You might as well save your breath. *is expressed as* Just speak fewer idle words. jyǎn-'jř 'shǎw shwō fèy-'hwà-ba. *or as* Don't waste your lips and tongue. bú-yàw 'báy·fèy chwén-'shé-le.

To save the day kàw . . . (gěy) °'dǎng-gwo-chywu *or* °'táng-gwo-chywu. ‖He certainly saved the day. wán-'chywán kàw-'tā gěy 'dǎng-gwo-chywu-de.

SAW. A saw jywù. ‖Could I borrow a saw? jyè wǒ bǎ-'jywù shř-shr.

To saw jywù. ‖He sawed the dogs in half. tā bǎ mù-tew dēw 'jywù-cheng lyǎng-'jyéer.

SAY. shwō, jyǎng. ‖What did you say? nǐ shwō 'shéme láy-je? ‖The paper says it's going to rain tonight. bàw-shang 'shwō jyěr-'wǎn-shang yàw shyà-'ywǔ. ‖What have you got to say for yourself? nǐ háy yěw 'shéme kě-'shwō-de-ma? *or expressed as* Give your reason. nǐ bǎ nǐ-de-'lǐ 'shwō-shwo.

Say, let's say, shall we say jyèw 'swàn (*or* dà-'gày, *or* swàn) . . . °'shéme-'yàng(°-ba). ‖I'll give you enough to cover the expenses, shall we say fifty dollars? wǒ gěy-ni gèw nǐ-'kāy-shyǎw-de, jyèw 'swàn 'wǔ-shŕ-kwày-chyán, 'dzěme-yàng? ‖I'll meet you, say in an hour. wǒ-men 'dāy-hwěr jyàn, dà-gày yí-ge-'jūng-tew yǐ-'nèy-ba.

Let's say (*for example*) *is expressed as* like . . . how about it? shyàng . . . dzěme-'yàng? ‖We'll have·to buy some fruit, let's say oranges and peaches. wǒ-men děy mǎy dyǎr-'gwǒ-dz, shyàng 'jywú-dz-le 'táwr-le, dzěme-'yàng?

To have one's say 'shwō-shwo. ‖I insist on having my say. wǒ yí-dìng děy 'shwō-shwo.

To have the whole say yěw-'chywán, ná-'shř, ná-'chywán, 'shwō shéme 'shř shéme. ‖He has the whole say around here. tā dzày-'jèr yěw-'chywán.

‖I can't say. wǒ bù-jř-'dàw.

‖Say! (*Oh! By the way!*) hèy! ‖Say! Did you see the way she acted on the stage? hèy! nǐ kàn-gwo tā-dzày-'táy-shang-de-nèy-gǔ-dz-'jyèr-le-ma?

‖Say! (*Gosh!*) hē!, āy-'yà! ‖Say! It IS a big one. āy-'yà! jēn 'dà!

‖Say! (*Showing disagreement, or detection of something disagreeable*) éy!, á! ‖Say! What do you mean? 'éy! nǐ 'shéme-'yì-sz? ‖Say! Who do you think you are? 'á! nǐ-shř lǎw-'jǐ-ya?

‖Say! (*Calling someone*) ēy!, hēy!, wēy! ‖Say! Come over here! 'éy! dàw-'jèr láy!

‖Say! (*Oh!*) hèy!, hē!, āy-'yà! ‖Say! I almost forgot. 'hèy! chà-dyǎr 'wàng-le.

SCALE. (*Layer of covering*) lín. ‖The fish had shiny scales. nèy-tyáw-ywú-de-'lín jēn 'lyàng.

(*Weighing machine; a balance*) 'tyān-píng; (*a Chinese scale*) chèng; (*a small Chinese scale*) 'děng-dz; (*a scale that weighs in pounds*) bàng, 'bàng-chèng. ‖Put that on the scale. bǎ nèy-ge 'gē-dzay 'chèng-shang 'yāw-yaw.

(*Series of tones*) yīn-'jyē. ‖She practices scales all day. tā jěng-'tyān jìng lyàn yīn-'jyē.

(*Graded system*) děng, 'děng-jí. ‖What is the scale of wages in this factory? jè-ge-gūng-'chǎng-li °gūng-'dz-de-'děng-jí dzěme-yàng? *or* °gūng-'dz fēn jǐ-'děng?

(*Series of marks at regular intervals for measurement; on a barometer, thermometer, protractor*) 'dù-shur; (*on a ruler*) 'chř-tswèn; (*on a measuring cup, chemical flask, chart, weighing machine*) gé, géer; (*on a Chinese weighing machine*) 'chèng-shyēngr. ‖The scale on this barometer is hard to read. jèy-ge-chì-yā-'byǎw-shang-de-'dù-shur kàn-bu-'chīng-chu.

(*Proportion*) bǐ-'lì, bǐ-'lì-chř. ‖This map has a scale of one inch to one hundred miles. jèy-ge-dì-'tú-de-bǐ-'lì-chř yì-yīng-'tswèn shř yì-bǎy-yīng-'lì. ‖This ship model is made exactly to scale. jèy 'mwó-shíng shř jàw-je ywán-láy-de-chwán àn yí-'dìng-de-'bǐ-lì dzwò-de.

(*Relative size*) gwēy-'mwó. ‖They've planned the improvements on a large scale. *is expressed as* They've planned to improve on a large scale. tā-men 'jì-hwà le yàw 'dà-gwēy-'mwó-de gǎy-'lyáng.

To scale. (*Remove scales*) gwā-'lín, gwā-cha 'lín, 'kwā-cha 'lín. ‖Please scale the fish. láw-'jyà, bǎ ywú-'lín gěy 'gwā-gwā.

(*To come off in scales*) dyàw-'pyér. ‖The paint is scaling off. nèy-tséng-yéw-'chī dyàw-'pyér-le.

(*To climb*) pá. ‖They scaled the cliff with difficulty. tā-men 'pá nèy-ge-'shān pá-de hěn chř-'lì.

To scale down jyǎn. ‖All their prices have been scaled down. tā-men bǎ 'swǒ-yěw-de-'jyà-cnyan dēw 'jyǎn-le.

To turn the scales byàn, jwǎn-'byàn, jwǎn-'byàn 'jywú-shř. ‖That victory turned the scales in our favor. nèy-ge-shèng-'jàng dǎ-le yǐ-'hèw, wǒ-men-de-'jywú-shř byàn 'hǎw-le.

SCARCE. shǎw, 'shī-shǎw, chywē, 'chywē-shǎw, nán, nán-'jǎw, 'kwèn-nàn. ‖Is food scarce? 'chř-de-dūng-shi 'chywe-ma? ‖Jobs are scarce right now. shyán-'dzày 'shř-ching hěn nán 'jǎw.

SCATTER. (*To sprinkle around*) sǎ, rēng. ‖Scatter some food for the pigeons. gěy 'gē-dz 'sǎ dyǎr-'shŕ.

(*To disband*) sàn. ‖Wait until the crowd scatters. děng jèy-chywǔn-'rén 'sàn-le-je.

(*To cause to disband*) (*by force*) bǎ ... 'hūng (*or* 'gǎn)-sàn; (*by scaring*) bǎ ... dēw shyà-'pǎw-le; (*by order*) jyàw ... dēw 'sàn (*or* 'fēn)-kay; *or other resultative compounds with* sàn *or* kāy *as second element.* ‖They scattered the herd of cattle. tām bǎ nèy-chywún-'nyéw gǎn-'sàn-le.

‖I found everything scattered. (*Thrown about*) 'shém dēw rēng-de 'nǎr dēw 'shŕ. *or* (*Not packed*) 'shém dēw 'sǎn-je. *or* (*In disorder*) shém dēw 'lwàn-chi-bā-'dzāw-de (rēng-je).

SCENE. (*Setting*) bù-'jǐng. ‖What is the scene of the play? jèy-chū-'shì-de-bù-'jǐng shŕ shéme?

(*View*) 'jǐng-jer, fēng-'jǐng. ‖That's a beautiful scene. nèy-ge-'jǐng-jer jēn hǎw-'kàn.

(*Situation*) 'chíng-shing. ‖Let's reconstruct the scene of the crime. dzám bǎ 'nèy-ge-'àn-dz-de-'chíng-shing dzày 'yán-jyew-yán-jyew.

(*Environment*) 'hwán-jìng. ‖A change of scene will do him good. 'hwàn-hwan 'hwán-jìng dwèy-ywu 'tā 'hěn yěw 'hǎw-chù.

(*Part of a play*) chǎng. ‖This is the third scene of the second act. jèy shŕ dì-'èr-mù-de-dì-'sān-chǎng.

To make a scene nàw(-hung), nàw 'shyàw-hwar, shyā-nàw. ‖Don't make a scene. byé dāng-je 'rén nàw 'shyàw-hwar. ‖I hate scenes. wǒ bú-'ywàn-yi nàw-gěy-rén-'kàn.

Behind the scenes (*in the theater*) hèw-'táy; (*out of the public view*) hèw-'táy, 'bèy-dì-li, 'àn-dì-li. ‖I met him in the dressing room behind the scenes. wǒ dzày hèw-'táy-hwà-jwāng-'shŕ-li 'pèng-jyan ta-le. ‖The details were worked out behind the scenes. 'shyáng-shì-de-'jyé-mu shŕ dzày 'bèy-dì-li 'dzwò-de.

SCHOOL. (*Place of learning*) shywé-'shyàw. To go to school (*as a student*) shàng-'shywé. ‖That school has a dormitory. nèy-ge shywé-'shyàw yěw sù-'shè. ‖Do you go to school? nǐ shàng-'shywé-le-ma?

(*Membership of a school*) shyàw, shywé-'shyàw. ‖The whole school turned out to welcome him back. chywán-'shyàw dēw 'hwān-yíng tā 'hwéy-lay.

(*Lessons*) shywé. ‖What time does school get out? 'shéme-shŕ-hew fàng-'shywé?

(*Academic division*) ywàn, shywé-'ywàn. ‖He went to the school of law at the university. tā shàng 'nèy-ge-dà-'shywé-'fǎ-shywé-'ywàn-le.

(*Group devoted to a common aim*) pày, pàr. ‖He belongs to a new school of thought. tā-de-'sz̄-shyǎng shŕ 'shǔ-ywú-shīn-'pày-de.

(*Group of water animals*) chywún. ‖A school of fish is coming down the river. yì-chywún-'ywú shwèn-je 'hé 'shyà-lay-le.

(*Used in school*) 'shywé-shyàw-'yùng-de; school building shyàw-'shè; school expenses shywé-'shyàw-jīng-'fèy, *etc.* ‖His school books cost a lot. tā shywé-'shyàw-'yùng-de-'shū hěn 'gwèy.

To school 'shywùn-lyàn; (*if the person instructing is a superior*) 'jyàw-shywùn. ‖They schooled us in military drill. tā-men 'shywùn-lyàn wǒ-men dzwò 'jywūn-shŕ-'dùng-dzwò. ‖My father schooled me in self-discipline. ' wǒ-'fù-chin 'jyàw-gey wǒ 'dzěm 'dž-ji-de-'shīn.

To be schooled shèw 'shywùn-lyàn. ‖He was schooled in patience. tā shèw-gwo 'shywùn-lyàn, ji gwǎn-jù dž-ji-de-'shīn.

SCIENCE. 'kē-shywé. ‖Have you studied any science? nǐ 'yán-jyew-gwo 'kē-shywé-ma?

(*Skill*) 'shywé-wèn. ‖There's a science to cooking. dzwò-'fàn 'jēn-shŕ dyǎr-'shywé-wèn.

SCISSORS. 'jyǎn-dz, jyǎn-'dāw.

SCOOP. A scoop sháwr, 'sháw-dz. ‖Where's the sugar scoop? táng-'sháwr dzày-'nǎr-ne?

To scoop. (*To dig, on a large scale*) wā; (*to dig, on a small scale*) wǎ, wǎy, kwǎy. ‖Scoop out some grain for the pigs. gěy-'jū 'wǎy dyǎr-'lyáng-shr. ‖This machine is for scooping up sand and gravel. jèy-ge-'jī-chi shŕ wèy wā 'shā-dz gēn shŕ-tew-'dzěr-de. ‖She scooped out the inside of the melon. tā ná-'sháwr bǎ gwā-'rángr dēw 'wǎy-chu-lay-le.

SCORE. (*The points in a game*) fēn, fēr, jì-'lù. ‖What was the score? 'dwō-shaw-'fēr-le? *or* jì-'lù shŕ 'dwō-shaw?

(*Twenty*) èr-shŕ. Scores (*a considerable number*) hǎw-jǐ-'shŕ.

Musical score pǔ, ywè-'pǔ, gēer-'pǔ, 'pǔ-dz, 'yīn-ywè-de-'pǔ-dz, chàng-'gēer-de-'pǔ-dz. ‖Can you read a score at sight? ywè-'pǔ nǐ néng yí-'shyàr 'nyàn-shyà-lay-ma? *or expressed as* Can you recognize a score? nǐ néng rèn-'pǔ-ma?

To score (*make points*) dé-°'fēr (°'fēn). ‖He scored five points for our team. tā gěy wǒ-men-'dwèy-shang 'dé-le 'wǔ-fēr.

(*To keep a record*) jì-°'fēr (°'fēn). ‖How does one score this? jèy-ge-'fēr dzěme 'jì?

(*To arrange musically*). ‖This selection is scored for piano. jèy-'pǔ-dz shŕ wèy tán gāng-'chín yùng-de. 'tyāw-chu-lay-de-'yīn-ywè shŕ gěy gāng-'chín gēn ywè-'dwèy 'ywǔ-bèy-de.

On that score dzày 'nèy-ge-shang, wèy 'nèy-ge. ‖You may rest easy on that score. dzày 'nèy-ge-shang nǐ 'kě-yi fàng-'shīn-le.

To pay off (settle) a score (*to pay a debt or to get even*) swàn-'jàng; (*to pay a debt*) hwán-'jàng, 'ìng-'jàng, hwán-'jày, hwán-'chíng; (*to get even*) bàw-'chéw, 'bàw-fu. ‖He's sure to pay off that score sometime. 'dzǎw-wǎn tā děy 'swàn nèy-bǐ-'jàng.

SCRAPE. (*By rubbing*) mwó, tsèng; (*to remove, using something sharp or rough*) gwā, 'gwā-cha, 'kwā-cha, 'kū-cha, 'kā-cha; (*rubbing with something sharp or rough in order to make smooth or clean*) 'dǎ-mwó; (*to scour, wipe*) tsā; (*to file*) tswò; (*by rubbing and* *scratching*) hwá, gwă; *all of the above are used as main verbs with appropriate postverbs such as* off shyà-chywu, *clean* 'gān-jing, *etc.* ‖We can scrape off the paint with a knife. wǒm kě-yi ná-'dāw bǎ nèy-tséng-yéw-'chǐ 'kā-cha-shyà-lay. ‖Scrape your shoes on the mat before you come in. bǎ-'jyǎw dzày shyé-'dyàr-shang 'tsèng-yi-tsèng dzày 'jìn-lay. ‖The bushes scraped against the side of the car. nèy-shyē-shyǎw-'shùr bǎ jèy-ge-'chē-de-'páng-byār gěy 'gwǎ-le.

(*If the result is a hole in the ground*) páw, wā. ‖The puppy scraped a hole just big enough to lie down in. nèy-ge-shyǎw-'gěwr 'páw-le yí-ge-'kēngr tā 'jèng hǎw néng 'tǎng-dzày lǐ-tew.

To scrape *something* together (*collect with difficulty*) *expressed simply as* collect tsèw (*for money*), *the idea of* difficulty *being omitted or expressed by other means.* ‖My son is trying to scrape together enough money to buy a car. wǒ-de-'ér-dz jèng shyǎng-'fár tsèw-'chyán yàw mǎy yí-lyàng-'chē.

To scrape along (*manage with difficulty*) 'tsèw-he, 'jyāng-jyèw, 'fū-yǎn, 'dwèy-fu, 'myǎn-chyǎng. ‖Ever since he died, the family has just earned enough to scrape along. tsúng tā 'sž-le yǐ-'hèw, tām-'jyā yě jyèw-shr 'jèng dyǎr-'chyán 'tsèw-he-je gwò 'r-dz.

A scrape (*difficulty*) 'kwèn-nan; (*trouble*) 'lwàn-dz. ‖His father got into a rather bad scrape financially. tā-de-'fù-chin dzày 'jīng-jì-shang 'ywù-jyàn-le hěn-'dà-de-'kwèn-nàn. ‖He was always getting into scrapes at school. tā dzày shywé-'shyàw-li 'jìng chū 'lwàn-dz.

SCRATCH. (*To rub or mark with something sharp*) hwá; (*to mark slightly with something sharp*) gwǎ; (*to rub with something rough*) tsēng. ‖Try not to scratch the floor when you move the piano. nwó gāng-'chín de-shŕ-hew byé bǎ 'dì-bǎn 'hwá-le.

To scratch *with the nails or claws* (*in order to relieve itching*) kwǎy; (*with the claws*) dāw; (*with nails or claws, whether to relieve itching or not*) jwā, náw. ‖The kitten scratched my hand. nèy-ge-shyǎw-'māw bǎ wǒ'shěw °'jwā-le *or* °'dāw-le *or* °'náw-le. ‖Will you scratch my back? láw-'jyà, gěy-wo °'jwā-jwa (*or* °'kwǎy-kway *or* °'náw-naw) hèw-'jí-nyang.

(*To cut slightly*) lá. ‖Will that stone scratch glass? nèy-ge-'shŕ-tew néng lá 'bwō-li-ma?

To scratch out hwá-le chywù. ‖Scratch out the last line. bǎ dzwèy-'hèw-yì-'háng 'hwá-le chywù.

(*To dig*) páw, wā; (*to dig with the nails*) kēw. ‖We watched the chickens scratching for food. wǒ-men kàn-je nèy-shyē-shyǎw-'jyēr páw 'chŕ-de láy-je.

(*To collect with effort*) tsèw; (*find*) jǎw. ‖They scratched up a little work to keep him out of mischief. tā-men gěy-ta 'jǎw-le dyǎr-'hwór, 'shéng-de tā dǎw-'lwàn.

A scratch (*line made by scratching*) hwá-de- (*or* gwǎ-de-, tsēng-de-, jwā-de-, náw-de-, kway-de-, dāw-de-)'dàw-dz; (*scratch or a scraped place*) yèr; (*wound made by scratching or otherwise*) shāng. ‖The desk is covered with scratches. jèy-ge-shū-'jwō-'myàr-shàng yěw hǎw-shyē-'hwá-de-'dàw-dz. ‖How did you get that scratch on your chin? nǐ shyà-ba-'kéer-shang-de-'dàw-dz shŕ 'dzěme-láy-de?

From scratch (*from the beginning*) tsúng-'téwr láy. ‖The whole job had to be done over again from scratch. jèy-jyàn-'shŕ-ching háy 'děy jěng-'gèr-de tsúng-'téwr dzày 'láy yì-hwéy.

Up to scratch píng-'cháng 'nà-yàngr; píng-'cháng nàme-'hǎw. ‖Don't you think his work hasn't been up to scratch lately? nǐ bù-'jywé-de 'jìn-lay tā dzwò-'shŕ 'bú-shyàng píng-'cháng-nàme-'hǎw-le-ma?

To scratch (*withdraw from a contest; to cancel*) chywǔ-'shyāw; to be scratched gěy chywǔ-'shyāw; (*not come out to the contest*) bù-chū-'chǎng. ‖Our horse scratched. wǒ-men-mǎy-le-mǎ-'pyàw-de-nèy-pǐ-'mǎ méy-chū-'chǎng.

SCREAM. rǎng, hǎn, jyàw, 'ráng-rang. ‖She screamed in terror. tā 'shyà-de jŕ 'rǎng. ‖I thought I heard a scream. wǒ 'jywé-de wǒ 'tīng-jyan 'rǎng-le yì-'shēng. (*To laugh shrilly*) 'hā-hā 'dà 'shyàw. ‖Everybody screamed at his jokes. tā-nèy-ge-'shyàw-hwàr 'dèw-de 'měy-yí-ge-rén dēw 'hā-hā 'dà 'shyàw.

A scream. ‖That movie is a scream. *is expressed as* That movie is funny. nèy-ge-dyàn-'yěngr jēn dèw-'shyàwr. *or as* That movie is laughable. (*Either it's humorous, or it's so bad it's funny.*) nèy-ge-dyàn-'yěngr jēn kě-'shyàw.

SCREW. A screw 'lwó-sz, lwó-sz-'dyēngr. ‖These screws need tightening. jèy-shyē-lwó-sz-'dyēngr děy jǐn-jin-le.

(*To turn, as a screw*) nǐng. ‖Screw it in tightly. nǐng-'jǐn-le.

(*To fasten with screws*) nǐng; (*to fasten with screws or in various other ways*) ān. ‖These pipes screw together very easily. jèy-shyē-'gwǎn-dz hěn 'rúng-yi ān-de ví-'kwàr.

SEA. hǎy. ‖How far are we from the sea? wǒ-men jèr lí-'hǎy yěw dwō-'ywǎn? ‖There was a heavy sea the day we went fishing. *is expressed as* The day we went fishing, the sea, wind and waves were very strong. wǒ-men-chywù-dǎ-'ywú-de-'nèy-tyān hǎy-shang-de-fēng-'làng hěn 'dà.

At sea. (*On the ocean*) dzày 'hǎy-shang; (*in a boat on the ocean*) dzày hǎy-'chwán-shang. ‖They've been at sea for three weeks. tā-men dzày 'hǎy-shang dāy-le sā-shīng-'chī.

At sea. (*Puzzled*) mí-hu, hú-tu; (*can't understand it*) mwò-'míng-chí-'myàw; (*can't understand what it is*) bù-'dǔng shŕ 'dzěme-hwéy-'shŕ. ‖Her answers left me completely at sea. tā 'hwéy-da-de-'hwà jyàn-'jŕ-de shŕ ràng-wo mwò-'míng-chí-'myàw.

To go to sea háng-'hǎy chywù; (*to be a sailor; if member of a ship's crew*) dāng 'shwěy-shěw chywù; (*if member of the navy*) dāng shwěy-'bīng chywù, dāng hǎy-'jywūn chywù.

To put to sea kǎy, dzěw. ‖When does the ship put to sea? nèy-jř-'chwán 'shéme-shŕ-hew 'kāy?

Sea level hǎy-'myàn; above sea level hày-'bá. ‖This land is only 200 feet above sea level. jèy-kwày-'dì 'gāw chū hǎy-'myàn tsáy 'èr-bǎy-chř. or jèy-kwày-'dì hǎy-'bá tsáy 'èr-bǎy-chř.

Seasick. (On a boat) ywùn-'chwán. ‖The rolling of the boat made me seasick. nèy-ge-'chwán 'yáw-de wǒ ywùn-'chwán-le.

SEARCH. jǎw, shywé-me, shywé-le. ‖I've searched everywhere. wǒ shéme-'dì-fangr dēw 'jǎw-le. ‖Is a search necessary? yí-'dìng děy 'jǎw-ma?

(To hunt for something by turning things over in a box, drawer, etc.) fān, 'shŕ-fan. ‖I've searched for that pen in the drawer for a long time, but I haven't found it. nèy-gwǎn-'bǐ wǒ dzày 'chēw-tì-li 'fān-le bàn-'tyān, yě méy-fǎn-'jǎw.

(To look for something concealed) sēw, fān; (to examine) jyǎn-'chá. ‖We'll have to search you. wǒ-men děy 'sēw-sew ni.

SEASON. (One of the four seasons) jì. ‖Fall is my favorite season. 'chyēw-tyan shŕ wǒ-'dzwèy-'shǐ-hwan-dě-yí-'jì.

(Period of the year) 'shŕ-hew; (in special circumstances and rather literary usage) chī; holiday season 'jyà-chī; fishing season 'ywú-chī; etc. ‖This is the best season for tennis. jè-shŕ dǎ-wǎng-'chyéw-dzwèy-'hǎw-de-shŕ-hew. ‖The hotel keeper said this was their best season in many years. lywǔ-'gwǎn-jǎng-'gwèy-de shwō jè-shŕ 'dzème-shyē-'nyán-láy-'dzwèy-hǎw-de-yí-'jyèr. ‖I'll try to get home during the holiday season. 'jyà-chī-li wǒ shyǎng-'fár hwéy-'jyā.

To season (cure, mature; dry in the air) lyàng; (to put aside) gē. ‖Has this wood been seasoned long enough? jèy-ge-'mù-tew 'lyàng-de gēw-'shŕ-hewr-le-ma?

(To flavor; add salt) gē (or jyā) 'shyán-dàr; (to add salt, sauce, or spices) gē (or jyā) 'dzwó-lyàwr. Heavily seasoned kěw-'jùng. ‖Have you seasoned the beef stew? dwèn-nyéw-'rèw-li gē 'dzwó-lyàwr-le-ma? ‖The food is too heavily seasoned. dzwò-de 'tsày tày kěw-'jùng-le.

In season (be ripe) shéw, 'shyà-lay-le; (come to market) shàng-'shŕ. ‖Are strawberries in season yet? yáng-'méy shàng-'shŕ-le-ma?

Off season bù-'hǎw-de-shŕ-hew. ‖The hotel is having an off season. shyàn-'dzày 'jèng shŕ jèy-ge-lywǔ-'gwǎn-'mǎy-may-bù-'hǎw-de-shŕ-hewr.

Seasoned. (Old) lǎw; (experienced) yěw-gwo 'jīng-yàn-de. ‖Those men are seasoned soldiers. jè-shyē-'rén dēw shŕ 'lǎw-bīng.

SEAT. dzwòr, 'dzwò-wèy, 'wèy-dz. ‖You're in my seat. nǐ 'dzwò-dzày 'wǒ-de-'dzwòr-shang-le. ‖I want two seats for the play. jèy-chū-'shì wǒ yàw 'lyǎ-dzwòr.

(Of a chair) dzwòr. ‖The seat of the chair needs repairing. nèy-bǎ-'yǐ-dz-de-'dzwòr-nèr děy 'shēw-shr-shēw-shr-le.

(Of a garment) 'dzwò-de-dì-fangr, 'hèw-tew; (somewhat vulgar, of clothes or the body) 'pì-hu, 'pì-gu. ‖The seat of my pants is torn. wǒ-'kù-dz-de-'hèw-tew 'pwò-le.

(Central location of, source of) ywán-'yīn, 'ywán-gu. ‖Where does the seat of the trouble seem to be? jèy-ge-'lwàn-dz-de-ywán-'yīn shŕ 'shéme?

Seat of government (national) gwó-'dū, shěw-'dū, jīng-'chéng; (provincial) shěng-'chéng, shěng-'hwèy; (district) shyàn-'chéng.

To be seated 'dzwò-shyà, dzwò; to seat someone ràng . . . dzwò; to take a seat 'dzwò-shyà; to seat in the sense of have seats for néng dzwò. ‖May I be seated? wǒ 'kě-yi 'dzwò-shya-ma? ‖Seat them in order. ràng tā-men àn-je 'tsz̀-shywu 'dzwò. ‖Tell him to take a seat. ràng-ta 'dzwò-shya. ‖This theater seats several hundred people. jèy-ge-shì-'ywán-dz néng dzwò 'hǎw-jǐ-bǎy-'rén.

To have a seat in Congress shŕ ge-gwó-'hwèy-de-yì-'ywán.

SECOND. (Following the first) dì-'èr. ‖Who's the second man in line? nèy-yí-'lyèw-li dì-'èr-ge-'rén shŕ-'shéy? ‖My room is on the second floor. wǒ-de-'wū-dz dzày (dì-)'èr-tséng-léw. ‖The second was better dressed than the first. dì-'èr-ge 'dǎ-bàn-de bǐ 'téw-yí-ge 'hǎw.

(Another). expressed as again . . . once dzày . . . yí-'tsz̀. ‖May I have a second helping? wǒ 'kě-yi dzày 'tyān yí-'tsz̀-ma? ‖Give him a second chance. 'dzày 'ywán-lyàng ta yí-'tsz̀.

(A moment) yì-'hwěr, yí-'shyàr. ‖Wait a second. 'děng yì-'hwěr.

(One sixtieth of a minute; of time or angular measure) myǎw.

Seconds (goods of an inferior grade) 'èr-děng-'hwò, 'tsz̀-děng-'hwò. ‖These stockings are seconds. jèy-shyē-'wà-dz dēw-shŕ 'èr-děng-'hwò.

To second (parliamentary procedure) fù-'yì; (to approve) dzàn-'chéng. ‖I second the motion. wǒ fù-'yì. or wǒ dzàn-'chéng 'jèy-ge-tí-'yì.

Second, in the second place dì-'èr, 'dzày-je, 'dzày shwō, chí-'tsz̀. ‖Second, I don't want to. dì-'èr-ne, wǒ bú-'yàw nà-yàngr.

Second-hand (old) jyèw; second-hand goods (handed on goods) 'gwò-shěw-'hwò; jyèw-'hwò. ‖We bought most of the furniture second-hand. dà-dwō-'shùr-de-'jyā-jywù wǒ-men dēw-shŕ 'mǎy-de 'gwò-shěw-'hwò.

SECRET. A secret 'mì-mì, 'bì-mì. ‖Can he keep a secret? tā néng shěw 'mì-mì-ma? or expressed as Is he close-mouthed? tā dzwěy-'yán-ma? ‖Let me in on the secret. 'gàw-su wo 'nèy-ge-'mì-mì.

(Not generally known) 'bì-mì(-de), mì-'mì(-de). ‖It was a secret agreement. nèy-ge shŕ yí-ge-'bì-mì-'shyé-dìng.

(*Hidden, not obvious to the eye*) àn. ‖There's a secret lock on the desk. nèy-ge-shū-'jwōr-shang yěw yí-ge-àn-'swǒ.

To have a secret meaning (*of words, gestures, etc.*) àn-'hán-je yěw 'yì-sz *or* yěw àn-'hán-je-de-'yì-sz.

In secret 'àn-jūng, 'bì-mì, 'mì-mì, tēw-'tēwr-de, bèy-'dì-li. ‖They met in secret to discuss their plans. tā-men 'àn-jūng kāy-'hwèy 'shāng-lyang tā-men-de-'jì-hwa.

SECRETARY. (*Stenographer*) bì-'shū, mì-'shū; *or* (*clerk*) 'shū-ji. ‖He needs two secretaries to answer all his letters. tā děy yùng 'lyǎng-ge-mì-'shū gwǎn tā-de-'shìn-jyàn.

(*Officer of a club or company*) bì-'shū, mì-'shū, wén-'dú, 'wén-shū, 'shū-ji.

(*Government official; minister*) bù-'jǎng. ‖He's the Secretary of War. tā-shř jywūn-jèng-'bù-bù-'jǎng.

SECTION. (*Piece*) kwàr, fèr, bàr, dwàr. ‖Cut this stick of bamboo into sections. bǎ nèy-ge-jú-'gār 'kǎn-chéng jǐ-'dwàr.

(*Of a citrus fruit*) bàr. ‖Cut this orange into sections. bǎ nèy-ge-'jywú-dz 'chyē-chéng 'bàr.

(*Of a class*) dzǔ. ‖What section of the class is he in? tā dzày jèy-'bān-li-'nǎ-yì-'dzǔ?

(*Of a department*) dzǔ, gǔ, kē, bān, bù, chù, tīng. ‖This is the legal section of the department. 'jèy-shr jèy-'sž-li-de-'fǎ-lywù-'kē.

(*Of a written composition*) jyé, dwàn. ‖The part I'm referring to is in chapter one, section three. wǒ jèng 'tí-de nèy-'bù-fen shř dzày dì-'yī-jāng dì-'sān-jyé.

(*Region*) dày, kwàr, 'dì-fangr. ‖I was brought up in this section. wǒ-shr dzày jèy-'dày jǎng-'dà-de.

SECURE. (*Safe*) bǎw-'shyǎn, kàw-de-'jù, kě-'kàw, wěn, 'wěn-dang, 'twǒ-dang, wěn-'gù, twǒ-'kàw. ‖I feel secure in my new job. wǒ 'jywé-de wǒ-de-'shīn-'jŕ-yè hěn 'wěn-dang. ‖I don't think the foundation of the bridge is very secure. wǒ shyǎng nèy-ge-'chyáw-de-'dzwòr bù hěn bǎw-'shyǎn.

(*Firmly fastened*) 'jyē-shr. ‖Is this bolt secure? (*On a door*) jèy-ge-mén-'shwān 'jyē-shr-ma?

To secure (*acquire*) nèng, nùng, 'táw-hwan, dìng. ‖Can you secure a seat on the plane for me? nǐ néng dzày fēy-'jī-shang gěy-wo 'nèng ge-'dzwò-ma?

To secure a loan. (*To guarantee someone else's loan*) dān-'bǎw yì-bǐ-'jàng; (*to offer a house, etc. as security for a loan*) ná . . . ('dǐ-)yā yì-bǐ-'jàng. ‖The bank asked my father to secure the loan before they would lend me the money. yín-'háng jyè-gey wo 'chyán yǐ-'chyán, ràng wǒ-'fù-chin dān-'bǎw jèy-bǐ-'jàng. ‖How much do you require to secure this loan? nǐ yàw ràng-wo ná jŕ-'dwō-shǎw-chyán-de-'dūng-shi °láy 'dǐ-yā jèy-bǐ-'jàng? *or* °dzwò 'dǐ-yā?

Secure from bǎw-'shyǎn (*or* kàw-de-'jù, *or* jywé) bú-'jŕ-ywu. ‖Here we're secure from attack. dzày-'jèr wǒ-men jywé bú-'jŕ-ywu shèw 'gūng-jī-le.

SEE (SAW, SEEN). (*To look at*) kàn, chyáw, chěw. ‖May I see your pass? gěy-wo 'kàn-kan nǐ-de-tūng-shíng-'jèng. ‖We've just seen a good movie. wǒ-men gāng 'kàn-le yí-ge-'hǎw-dyàn-'yěngr.

(*To find out*) kàn. ‖See what can be done to change it. 'kàn-kan nèy-ge néng 'dzěme 'gǎy-gay. ‖I've got to see about getting a new clerk. wǒ děy 'kàn-kan dzěme 'jǎw yí-ge-shīn-'shū-ji láy.

(*To call on*) kàn, jàw. ‖Come to see me tomorrow. myéngr láy 'kàn wo. ‖You'd better see a doctor about that infection. nèy-ge-chwán-rǎn-'bìng nǐ děy °'kàn-kan 'dày-fu. *or* °jyàw 'dày-fu 'kàn-kan.

(*To meet*) jyàn. ‖See you again. dzày 'jyàn! ‖I'd like to see more of you. *is expressed as* I wish we would meet more times. wǒ 'ywàn-yi dzám dwō 'jyàn jǐ-hwéy.

(*To make sure; pay attention*) jù-'yì; (*don't forget*) byé 'wàng-le. ‖Please see that this letter is mailed today. láw-'jyà, jù-'yì jèy-fēng-'shìn 'jyēr děy 'fā-chū-chywu.

(*To understand*) dǔng, 'míng-bay; *also* (*to know*) 'shyǎw-de, 'jŕ-daw. ‖I see what you mean. wǒ 'dǔng nǐ-de-'yì-sz-le. ‖You see, we're planning to leave soon. nǐ 'jŕ-daw, wǒ-men jyèw 'dǎ-swàn 'dzěw-le. ‖See? 'míng-bay-bu-míng-bay? ‖I don't intend to do it, see? wǒ méy-'yàw nàme 'bàn, 'shyǎw-de-ba? (*Both of the last two either friendly or unfriendly.*) *But* ‖I don't see it that way. *is expressed as* My way of looking at it isn't the same. wǒ-de-'kàn-fa 'bú-nà-yàngr.

(*To realize, grasp*) 'kàn-chū-láy. ‖Do you see the point? nǐ 'kàn-chū jèy-'dyǎn láy-le-ma?

(*To experience*) gwò, 'jīng-gwo. ‖He's seen better times. tā 'gwò-gwo (bǐ-jèy-ge-)hǎw(-de)-'ŕ-dz. ‖He's seen some action. *is expressed as* He has experienced battle. tā 'dǎ-gwo 'jàng.

To have seen plenty of service 'chū-le bù-shǎw-de-'lì. ‖These boots have seen plenty of service. jèy-shwāng-'shywē-dz kě jēn 'chū-le bù-shǎw-de-'lì.

(*To escort someone who is leaving*) sùng. ‖Will anyone see me off? yěw-rén 'sùng-wo chywù-ma? ‖Let me see you to the door. wǒ 'sùng-ni dàw mén-'kéwr.

To see *light or objects* through *a window, etc.* 'jyē-je . . . kàn(-de-'jyàn). Can't see through kàn-bu-'gwò-chywu *or* kàn-bu-'jyàn 'nèy-byar. ‖Can you see anything through this glass? 'jyē-je jèy-kwāy-'bwō-li kàn-de-'jyàn 'nèy-byar-ma? ‖This kind of glass lets light through, but you can't see through it. jèy-jǔng-'bwō-li tēw-'lyàngr (*or* tēw-gwang), kě-shr 'kàn-bu-gwò-chywu. ‖This window is so dirty we can't see through it. 'chwāng-hu 'dzāng-de dēw kàn-bu-'jyàn °'nèy-byar-le. (*If looking in, like a Peeping Tom*) °'lǐ-byar-le. (*If looking out*) °'wày-byar-le.

To see through *something* (*be aware of something false*) 'kàn-chū-láy, kàn-'chwān-le. *See also* (*to realize*) *above.* ‖I can see through his politeness. tā nèy-ge-jyǎ-'kè-chi-jyèr, wǒ yí 'kàn jyèw 'kàn-chū-láy-le. ‖I can see through her. *is expressed as* I know what kind of thing she is. wǒ 'jŕ-daw tā shř 'dzěme-hwéy-'shř.

To see *something* through (*to go through with*) dzwò-'wán, wán-'chéng, nùng-'wán, nèng-'wán, gàn-'wán. ‖I intend to see the project through. wǒ 'dǎ-swàn bǎ jèy-jyàn-'jì-hwa dzwò-'wán.

To see *someone* through (*to help through*) bāng-'máng bāng-dàw 'dǐ. ‖Did they see him through the trouble? tā-men 'bāng tā-de-'máng bāng-dàw 'dǐ-le-ma?

To see to (*to take care of*) 'jàw-gù. ‖I'll see to the arrangements. wǒ láy 'jàw-gù yí-chyè-de-'bù-jr̀.

I see … (*So! when you've just learned something*) 'ywán-láy; (*Peiping*) 'gǎn-ching. ‖I see there was a big fire last night. 'ywán-láy dzwór-'wǎn-shang jáw-le yì-cháng-dà-'hwǒ. ‖Oh! I see! *is expressed as* Oh! So it's like that. èw! 'ywán-láy rú-'tsz̀. *or as* A thing like that, eh? 'nèm hwéy-'shèr-a!

Let me see (*let me look*) gěy-wo °'kàn-kan (*or* °'chyáw-chyaw *or* °'chěw-chew; (*let me think*) ràng-wo 'shyǎng-shyang *or expressed as* wait a minute 'děng-yi-děng.

Let's see (*let us look*) 'ràng wǒ-men °'kàn-kan (*or* °'chyáw-chyaw, *or* °'chěw-chew).

SEED. A seed 'jǔng-dz, dzěr; hur, héer, *which in general correspond to our* pit *but may also be used for the seeds of oranges, dates, grapes, or raisins.* ‖These flowers were grown from seed. jèy-shyē-'hwār shr̀ ná-'dzěr 'jǔng-chū-láy-de. ‖Spit out the seeds. bǎ-'húr tǔ-le.

To seed (*to plant*) jùng, shyà-'jǔngr, shyà-'dzěr. ‖When did you seed the lawn? jèy-kwày-tsǎw-'dì nǐ shéme-'shŕ-hew shyà-de-'jǔngr-a?

(*To remove seeds*) chywù-'dzěr, chywù-'húr, chywù-'héer. ‖These raisins have been seeded. jèy-shyē-'pú-taw-'gār shr̀ °chywù-le-'dzěr-de. *or* °chywù-le-'húr-de.

To go to seed dǎ-'dzěr, jyē-'dzěr; (*of a person; be unlucky*) dǎw-'méy. ‖The hedge has gone to seed. jèy-háng-shyǎw-'shùr dǎ-le 'dzěr-le. ‖He looks as if he's going to seed. *is expressed as* He looks unlucky. tā nèy-ge-'yàng-dz shyàng 'dǎw-le 'méy-le shr̀-de.

For seed wèy dǎ-'dzěr-de. ‖The onions were grown for seed. jùng jèy-ge-'tsūng shr̀ wèy dǎ-'dzěr-de. ‖The corn in that field is seed corn. nèy-kwày-'dì-li-de-lǎw-'ywù-mǐ shr̀ wèy dǎ-'dzěr-de.

SEEK (SOUGHT). (*To look for*) jǎw; (*look for and find*) 'shywé-le, 'shywé-me. ‖They sought high and low, but couldn't find him. tā-men 'gè-chùr dēw jǎw-'dàw-le yě jǎw-bù-'jáw ta.

(*To try*) shyǎng-'fár, jìn-'lyèr. ‖He sought to persuade her to go. tā shyǎng-'fár chywàn-ta 'chywù láy-je.

(*To ask for*) chyéw, chǐng. ‖We came here to seek your help. wǒ-men shàng-'jèr láy 'chyéw-ni bāng-bang 'máng.

Be sought after yěw rén-'ywár (*popular*). ‖He's much sought after in local society. 'tā dzày tā-men-nèy-ge-'dì-fangr hěn yěw rén-'ywár.

SEEM. hǎw 'shyàng, shyàng; it seems to me wǒ 'jywé-de. ‖The door seems to be locked. 'mén hǎw 'shyàng shr̀ 'swǒ-shang-le. ‖It seems like a good idea to me. wǒ 'jywé-de 'nèm-je tǐng 'hǎw. ‖How does that seem to you? nǐ 'jywé- -ge dzěme-'yàng?

SEIZE. (*To grasp; literally or figuratively*) jwā, 'jwā-jù; (*literally only*) dzwàn, 'dzwàn-jù. To seize an opportunity 'jwā-jù (*or* 'bǎ-wu *or* bǎ-'wò) 'jī-hwèy. ‖He seized my hand. tā 'dzwàn-je wǒ-de-'shěw. ‖You ought to seize this opportunity. nǐ děy 'jwā-ju jèy-ge-'jī-hwey.

(*To take possession of; with or without force*) jàn, jàn-'jywù; (*with force, someone's personal property*) 'chyǎng-jàn, 'bà-jàn. ‖You have no legal right to seize my property! nǐ 'méy-yew 'chywán-lì 'jàn wǒ-de-'chǎn-yè. ‖We seized the town after a short battle. 'dǎ-le méy 'dwō-jyěw, wǒm jyèw bǎ-'chéng 'jàn-le.

SELDOM. shǎw, bù-'cháng.

SELECT. To select tyāw, shyťwǎn, jyǎn, tyāw-'shywǎn. ‖She selected several dresses to try on. tā 'tyāw-le 'jǐ-jyàn-'yī-fu-lay 'shr̀-le-yi-shr̀.

(*Picked out for superior quality*) 'shywǎn-chū-láy-de, tyāw-'shywǎn-chū-láy-de; (*picked out, either because the articles or people are good or because they're bad*) 'tyāw-chū-láy-de, 'jyǎn-chū-láy-de. ‖These are select peaches. 'jèy-shyē-'táwr shr̀ 'shywǎn-chū-láy-de.

(*Exclusive; of a school, etc.*) *is expressed as* expensive 'gwèy-dzú. ‖She went to a select school. tā 'rù-le yí-ge-'gwèy-dzú-shywé-'shyàw.

SELF. Myself, ourselves, yourself, yourselves, himself, herself, themselves, *are expressed by the proper pronoun plus the following; for intensive effect* 'dz̀-jǐ *or* 'dz̀-gěr; *for reflexive effect* bǎ 'dz̀-jǐ *or* gěy 'dz̀-jǐ *or* gēn 'dz̀-jǐ *or* tì 'dz̀-jǐ, *or by* 'dz̀-jǐ *after the verb of the sentence; for reciprocal effect* bǐ-'tsz̀; *in some cases Chinese leaves the intensive, reflexive, or reciprocal idea unexpressed.* ‖She did it herself. 'nèy-shr̀ tā-'dz̀-jǐ-dzwò-de. ‖She herself said so. tā-'dz̀-jǐ nème 'shwō-de. ‖He hurt himself in the leg. tā bǎ ('dz̀-jǐ-de-) 'twěy 'pèng-le. ‖He must consider himself pretty good to say that. tā 'nème shwō yí-'dìng 'jywé-hu-je 'dz̀-jǐ háy bú-'hwày-ne.

By oneself *the proper pronoun (or noun) plus* one person 'yí-ge-rén. ‖She came by herself. tā-'yí-ge-rén láy-de.

Not be oneself. ‖She isn't herself today. *is expressed as* She isn't usually this way. tā 'píng-cháng bú-'jèy-yàngr.

One's better self *is expressed as* conscience 'lyáng-shīn.

Self *before an adjective* az. Self-confident dz̀-'shìn; self satisfied dz̀-'mǎn; self-sufficient dz̀-'dzú. *In other cases a different expression is used;* to be self-centered *is expressed as* to think first of oneself 'shyān shyăng-daw 'dz̀-jǐ, *or as* to put oneself first bǎ 'dz̀-jǐ gē-dzày 'tēw-le; to be self-supporting *is expressed as* by oneself to support oneself 'dz̀-jǐ 'gūng-jí 'dz̀-jǐ; to be self-conscious *is expressed as* to be unnatural bú-'dz̀-rán; to be self-possessed *is expressed as* to be calm 'lĕng-jìng.

Self *before a noun calls for various modes of expression.* ‖He has no self-control. *is expressed as* He can't control himself. tā bù-néng dz̀-'jr̀. ‖I hit him in self-defense. *is expressed as* I hit him to defend myself. wǒ wèy dz̀-'wèy tsáy 'dǎ-ta. ‖Haven't you any self-respect? *is expressed as* Can't you respect yourself a bit? nǐ 'bù-néng dz̀-'dzwēn yì-dyǎr-ma?

SELL (SOLD). mày. ‖Did you sell your old piano? nǐ bǎ nǐ-de-jyèw-gāng-'chín 'mày-le-ma? ‖They sell furniture. tā-men mày 'jyā-jywu. ‖Sugar sells for six cents a pound. 'táng mày 'lyèw-fēn-chyán yí-'bàng.

(*To betray*) mày, chū-'mày. ‖He sold us to the enemy. tā bǎ 'wǒ-men dzày 'dí-rén-nèr gěy 'mày-le. *or* tā bǎ 'wǒ-men chū-'mày-gey 'dí-rén-le.

(*To persuade to accept*) ràng . . . 'jyē-shèw; (*to make someone believe*) ràng . . . shyǎng-'shìn. ‖If you had been more tactful, you might have sold him the idea. nǐ yàw-shr dzày 'dwō hwèy 'dwèy-fu-dyǎr 'rén, yě-shywu jyèw néng 'ràng-ta 'jyē-shèw nèy-ge-'yì-jyàn-le.

To sell out (*get rid of by selling*) 'mày-chū-chywù-le, mày-'wán-le, mày-'gwǎng-le, mày-'jìng-le. ‖They sold out their whole stock of bicycles. tā-men bǎ dz̀-shíng-'chē-de-tswén-'hwò dēw 'mày-chū-chywù-le.

SEND (SENT). sùng; (*to mail*) jì; (*to send out*) fā. To send a *message* 'dǎ. ‖We've sent the manuscript off to the printers. wǒ-men yǐ-'rán bǎ 'gǎw-dz gěy yìn-shwā-'jywú 'sùng-chywu-le. ‖Have the invitations been sent out yet? chǐng '^vě yǐ-'rán 'sùng-chū-chywu-le-ma?

(*To cause to go*) ràng, jyàw. ‖Send him in. ràng-ta 'jìn-lay.

To send someone for (*to have someone go to . . .*) 'pày-rén chywù . . . , 'ràng-rén chywù . . . , 'jyàw-rén chywù . . . , 'dǎ-fā rén chywù . . . . ‖Can we send him for ice-cream? wǒ-men 'ràng-ta chywù 'mǎy dyǎr-bīng-ji-'líng, 'hǎw-bu-hǎw? *or* wǒ-men 'ràng-ta chywù 'yàw dyǎr-bīng-ji-'líng. ‖They sent to him for help. tā-men pày-'rén chywù 'jǎw-ta bāng-'máng. ‖I'll send for my trunk later. *is expressed as* Later I'll tell you to send me my trunk. yǐ-hèw wǒ dzày 'tūng-jr ni bǎ 'shyāng-dz gěy-wo 'sùng-chywu.

SENSE. (*Faculty of sensation*) 'gǎn-jywé, 'jr̄-jywé. Sense of hearing 'tīng-jywé; sense of seeing 'shr̀-jywé; sense of smelling 'shyèw-jywé; sense of tasting 'wèy-jywé; sense of feeling 'gǎn-jywé.

(*Meaning*) 'yì-sz, 'yì-yì, 'dàw-lǐ. ‖That doesn't make sense. nèy-ge 'méy 'shéme-'yì-sz. ‖There's no sense

in doing that. gàn nèy-ge 'méy 'shéme-'yì-sz. ‖In what sense do you mean what you just said? nǐ gáng-'tsáy-shwō-de-'hwà dàw-'dǐ shr̀ 'dzěme-ge-'yì-sz?

(*Good judgment*). ‖He has sense enough to stay out of trouble. *is expressed as* He is rather sensible, he won't get into trouble. tā háy 'míng-bay (*or* 'chīng-chu), bú-hwèy 'chū 'má-fan.

(*Feeling*). To have a sense of (*to feel*) 'jywé-de, gǎn-jywé-je, 'jywé-hu-je. ‖I have a sense of danger. wǒ 'jywé-de hěn 'wéy-shyǎn. ‖He has a strong sense of responsibility. tā jywé-de tā-'dzé-rèn hěn 'jùng.

To sense 'jywé-de, 'gǎn-jywé-je, 'jywé-hu-je. ‖I sense vaguely what he means. wǒ hwǎng-hu 'jywé-de-chū-dyar tā shr̀ 'shéme-'yì-sz. ‖Do you sense something wrong? nǐ 'jywé-de yěw 'shéme bú-'dwèy-ma?

Common sense 'cháng-shr̀, pǔ-'tūng-cháng-'shr̀. To have common sense dǔng-'shr̀, dǔng-'shèr. ‖That's just common sense. nèy 'bú-gwò-shr cháng-'shr̀. ‖He lacks common sense. tā 'bú-dà dǔng-'shr̀.

To lose one's sense of direction (*to be all turned around*) jwàn-le 'shyàngr-le. ‖He has a wonderful sense of direction. *is expressed as* He never gets turned around. tā yǔng-'ywǎn yě bú jwàn 'shyàngr.

To have a sense of humor jī-'chywùr. 'wár. ‖Do you think he has much sense of humor? nǐ jywé-de tā shr̀-bu-shr jī-'chywùr-de-rén?

In a sense (*from one point of view*) 'yì-fāng-'myàn, dzày 'yì-fāng-'myàn °kàn (°shwō). ‖In a sense, that is true. dzày 'yì-fāng-'myàn shwō, nà shr̀ 'jēn-de.

To come to one's senses (*to come out of a faint*) 'shǐng-gwò-láy-le; (*to be sensible at last*) 'míng-bay-le.

SENTENCE. hwà *with measure* jywù. ‖I didn't understand that last sentence. wǒ bù-'míng-bay dzwèy-'hèw-nèy-jywù-'hwà.

(*Decision of court*) pàn-'jywé. ‖The judge's sentence was unduly severe. fǎ-'gwān-pàn-'jywé-de tày 'jùng-le, *or expressed as* The judge passed judgment on that case too severely. fǎ-'gwān bǎ nèy-ge-'àn-dz pàn-de tày 'jùng-le.

To sentence pàn, dìng. ‖For how long were you sentenced? *is expressed as* They sentenced you to be in prison for how long? 'pàn-le ni 'dwō-shaw-r̀-dz-tú-'shíng?

To serve a sentence (*to be in prison*) jyān-'jìn, tú-'shíng. ‖He's already served his sentence. tā jyān-'jìn-de-r̀-dz yǐ-'rán 'mǎn-le.

SEPARATE. (*To divide*) fēn, 'fēn-kay. ‖Separate the class into five sections. bǎ jèy-'bān 'fēn-chéng wǔ-'dzǔ. ‖We don't want to be separated. wǒ-men bú-'ywàn-yi 'fēn-kay. ‖Separate the yolks from the whites. bǎ jī-'dàn-de-'hwángr gēn-'chyēngr 'fēn-kay.

(*To divide by putting something in between*) gé, 'gé-kay. ‖This partition separates the two rooms. jèy-shàn-'chyáng bǎ jèy-'lyǎng-jyān-'wū-dz 'gé-kay-le.

749

(*To pull apart*) 'lā-kay. ‖Separate the two boys who are fighting. bǎ jèy-'lyǎng-ge-dǎ-'jyà-de-'háy-dz lā-kay.

(*To stop living with someone*) fēn-'jywū. ‖When did she separate from him? tā tsúng 'shéme-shŕ-hew 'gēn-ta fēn-'jywū-le?

(*Apart from others*) 'fēn-je-de, 'fēn-kay-de; *also* (*single*) 'dān-je-de *or* (*another*) lìng-'wày. ‖We want separate rooms. wǒ-men yàw °'fēn-kay-de-'wū-dz. *or* °'dān-jyār-de-'wū-dz. ‖Put that under a separate heading. bǎ nèy-ge 'gē-dzay lìng-'wày-yí-'shyàng-lǐ-tew. ‖I'd like to make a separate settlement. *is expressed as* I'd like to make an agreement alone. wǒ shyǎng 'dān-dú 'dìng ge-'hé-tung. *or as* I'd like to make an agreement separately. wǒ shyǎng 'jèy-ge-'hé-tung 'fēn-je 'dìng-ba.

SEPTEMBER. jyěw-'ywè.

SERIOUS. (*In one's moral attitude*) 'yán-sù; (*in one's moral attitude and also in the way one works*) 'jèng-jǐng, 'jèng-jǐng-ba-běy, *or*, *formal*, jèng-jùng-chí-'shŕ; (*in the way one works*) rèn-'jēn, yùng-'shīn, gē-'shīn; (*on the level*) jēn-'gé-de. ‖He's a very serious young man. tā shŕ 'yí-ge-hěn-'jèng-jǐng-de-'chīng-nyán-rén. ‖He's very serious about his work. tā dzwò-'shŕ hěn °rèn-'jēn. *or* °yùng-'shīn. *or* °gē-'shīn. ‖He's not serious enough about his work. *is expressed as* He doesn't pay much attention to his work. tā 'dwèy-ywú tā-de-'shŕ bú-dà rèn-'jēn. *or* tā 'dwèy-ywú tā-de-'shŕ bú-dà jù-'yì. ‖Are you serious? nǐ shŕ 'shwō jēn-'gé-de-ne-ma? ‖Do you suppose this story is serious? *is expressed as* Do you think this story is real? nǐ 'jywé-je jèy-'shèr shŕ 'jēn-de-ma? ‖Did you make a serious attempt to find him? *is expressed as* Did you really try to find him? nǐ jēn hǎw-'hāwr-de jǎw-ta láy-je-ma? ‖I wasn't serious at all. wǒ nà shŕ 'nàw-je 'wár-ne. *or expressed as* I was just fooling. wǒ nà shŕ 'mǎ-ma hū-'hū. *or as* I didn't take it as anything that counts. wǒ 'gēn-běn jyěw 'méy ná nèy-ge dàng hwéy-'shèr. ‖He's not at all serious about this work. *is expressed as* He doesn't take the work as anything that counts. tā ná-shŕ bú-dàng-'shŕ. ‖They're not taking this matter seriously. *is expressed as* They aren't taking this matter to heart at all. jèy-jyàn-'shèr tām °ná-je 'bú-dàng-hwéy-'shèr. *or* °bàn-de 'mǎ-ma-hū-'hū. *or* jèy-jyàn-'shèr tām 'gēn-běn °méy-wàng-'shīn-li 'chywù. *or* °méy-gē-'shīn. *or* °méy-yùng-'shīn. *or* °méy-jù-'yì. *or as* They aren't putting in any effort on this thing. tām dwèy jèy-jyàn-'shèr bú-shàng-'jìn. ‖Don't take him seriously. 'byé ná-ta 'dàng nèm-yì-hwéy-'shèr. *or expressed as* Don't listen to him. béng tīng tā-de. *or as* Don't believe him. 'byé jēn 'shìn tā-de. *or as* Don't have anything to do with him. béng 'lǐ-ta. *or as* Don't take what he says to heart. béng bǎ-ta 'gē-de 'shīn-shang.

(*Important*) 'jùng-yàw, yàw-'jǐn; (*extremely important*) 'yán-jùng. ‖This is a serious matter. jèy-ge-'shŕ-ching hěn 'yán-jùng.

(*Grave*) 'yán-jùng, 'lì-hay; (*of sickness*) jùng, 'yàw-jǐn. ‖He had a serious accident with his car. tā jwàng 'chē jwàng-de hěn 'lì-hay. ‖Is his illness serious, Doctor? 'shyān-sheng, tā-de-'bìng 'yàw-jǐn-ma?

(*Stern*) 'jwāng-yán. **To look serious** *is expressed as* to tighten one's face 'běng-je 'lyǎn. ‖She looks very serious. tā-de-'yàng-dz hěn 'jwāng-yán. ‖He told the joke with a perfectly serious face. tā 'běng-je 'lyǎn 'shwō-de nèy-ge-'shyàw-hwàr.

SERVANT. tīng-'chāy(-de), dǐ-shya-'rén, bāng-'mángr-de, dǎ-'dzár-de, 'yùng-rén; (*female servant*) lǎw-'mā-dz *or* lǎw-'mār. ‖I want to hire a servant. wǒ shyǎng 'gù yí-ge-tīng-'chāy-de.

(*Employee*) 'jŕ-ywán (*but* 'chín-wù *or* gūng-'yěw *for an office boy*). ‖He has been a faithful servant of this company for a good many years. tā shŕ yí-ge-hěn-'jūng-shŕ-de-'jŕ-ywán dzày 'jèy-ge-gūng-'sž-li dāy-le hǎw-shyē-'nyán-le.

Public servant gūng-wù-'ywán.

SERVE. (*To bring; food or drinks*) shàng, ná, dwāng; (*to bring food*) kāy-'fàn. ‖Serve the drinks now, please. shàng-'jyěw-ba.

(*To wait on*) 'tsž-hew, 'fú-shr. ‖Who serves this table? shéy 'tsž-hew 'jèy-jā r̄-'jwō-dz?

(*To work*) dzwò, gàn; (*to work for an officer*) fú-'wù; (*to work for a person*) 'tsž-hew, 'fú-shr. ‖How long did you serve in that capacity? 'nèy-ge-shŕ-ching nǐ 'dzwò-le dwō-'jyěw-le? ‖He served fifteen years in the army. tā dzày jywūn-'dwèy-shang 'gàn-le shŕ-'wǔ-nyán.

(*To help*) ‖Is there any way in which I can serve you? *is expressed as* Is there anything I can do? yěw shéme-'shèr jyàw-wo 'dzwò-de-ma?

To serve a need. ‖I think this will serve your needs. wǒ shyǎng nǐ yěw 'jèy-ge jyèw 'shíng-le.

To serve the purpose. ‖This will serve the purpose. yùng-'jèy jyèw 'shíng. ‖What purpose does it serve? nà yěw shéme-'yùng-ne? ‖That serves no purpose at all. 'nèm-je yì-dyǎr-'yùng yě měy-'yěw.

To serve a prison term dzwò-'jyān. ‖He is serving a life-term in prison. tā 'dzày-nèr dzwò-'jyān shŕ wú-chī-tú-'shíng.

To serve a summons sùng-chwán-'pyàw. ‖He served a summons on us. tā gěy wo-men 'sùng-lay chwán-'pyàw, chwán wǒ-men dàw-'tíng.

To serve (*in tennis*) fā-'chyéw. ‖He served a mean one. tā jèy-ge-'chyéw 'fā-de jēn 'lì-hay. ‖Whose serve is it? *is expressed as* Whose turn is it to serve? gāy-'shéy fā-'chyéw-le?

To serve as. ‖What will serve as a substitute? *is expressed as* What can you use as a substitute? ná (*or* yùng *or* shŕ) 'shéme láy 'dày-ti-ya?

‖It serves you right! (nǐ) hwó-'gāy!

SERVICE. *There is no direct Chinese equivalent for the noun. The following sentences show how the idea may be expressed.*

(*Performance of labor*). ‖He gave us good service for more than ten years. (*Of an employee*) *expressed as* He worked well for us for more than ten years. tā gěy wǒ-men dzwò-'shŕ 'dzwò-le shŕ-jǐ-'nyán-le děw hěn 'hǎw. (*Of a hotel clerk*) *expressed as* He served us for more than ten years, the serving very good. tā 'tsż-hew wǒ-men 'shŕ-jǐ-'nyán-le 'tsż-hew-de hěn 'hǎw. (*Of a garageman*) *expressed as* He did repair work for us for more than ten years, the repairing very good. tā gěy wǒ-men 'shēw-shr hǎw-jǐ-'nyán-le 'shēw-shr-de hěn 'hǎw. *Etc. There is no general word for* service; *the kind of work must be specified.*

(*Supplying of some need*). ‖Does the rent include maid service? *is expressed as* Does the rent money take care of tidying up the room? dzème-shyē-'chyán-de-fáng-'dzū, gwǎn 'shēw-shr 'wū-dz-ma? ‖Do you have bus service here? *is expressed as* Do you have public buses here? nǐ-men jèr yěw gūng-'gùng-chì-'chē-ma? ‖I want to complain about the service. *is expressed as* The serving here is bad, I must complain. jèr 'tsż-hew-de bù-'shíng wǒ děy 'shwō-shwo.

(*Employment*). ‖In whose service are you? *is expressed as* For whom do you work? nǐ gēn-'shwéy dzwò-'shŕ? ‖Has she a civil service job? *is expressed as* Does she work for the government? tā gěy jèng-'fǔ dzwò-'shŕ-ma?

(*Armed forces*) jywūn-'dwèy. ‖He enlisted in the service. tā dàw jywūn-'dwèy-shang 'chywù-le. ‖Service men are admitted free. *is expressed as* For service people there is no expense. 'jywun-rén myǎn-'fèy.

To service (*as an automobile; to look over*) 'yàn yí-yàn; (*to wash*) tsā-'shǐ; (*to repair*) 'shēw-shr, 'shyēw-lǐ. Service station chì-yéw-'jàn. ‖I'm leaving my car here to be serviced. wǒ bǎ wǒ-de-'chē 'gē-de jèr 'shēw-shr-'shēw-shr.

To be at one's service. ‖I'm at your service. *is expressed as* When you want something, call me. nín yěw 'shéme-shŕ-de-'shŕ-hew 'jyàw wǒ. *or as* If you want something, don't be bashful. nǐ yěw 'shéme-'shŕ, byé 'kè-chi.

To be of service yěw 'yùng. ‖Will this book be of service? jèy-běr-'shū dwèy-ni yěw 'yùng-ma?

To do a service (*to help*) bāng-'máng. ‖Could you do me a small service? nǐ 'ké-yi 'bāng-bang wǒ-de-'máng-ma?

To hold a (*religious*) service dzwò lǐ-'bày. *But* funeral service kāy-'dyàw; marriage service jyē-'hwēn.

To use (*the services of*) yùng. ‖Can you use (the services of) a typist? nǐ néng 'yùng yí-ge-dǎ-dż-'ywán-ma?

SET. (*To put, place*) fàng, gē. ‖Set it over there. bǎ 'nèy-ge fàng-dzày 'nèr. ‖Set this aside for me. bǎ 'jèy-ge gěy-wǒ 'gē-dzày yì-'byār.

(*To put right*) dwèy, bwō. To set an alarm bwo shàng; to set in order páy(-'hǎw). ‖I want to set my watch. wǒ yàw 'dwèy-dwey wǒ-de-'byǎu. ‖Set the alarm for 7 o'clock, will you? bǎ nàw-'jūng 'shàng-daw 'chī-dyǎn-jūng, 'hǎw-ma? ‖Has the type been set yet? 'bǎn páy-'hǎw-le-ma? ‖He set the cards in order. tā bǎ kǎ-'pyàr 'àn-je 'tsż-shywù páy-'hǎw-le.

(*To fix*) dìng. ‖He set the price at fifty dollars. tā bǎ-'jyàr dìng-chéng 'wǔ-shŕ-kwày-'chyán-le. ‖I must set a limit to expenses. wǒ hwā-'chyán yí-'dìng děy 'dìng-chū ge-'shùr-lay.

To set a jewel shyāng. ‖The pin has diamonds set in gold. jèy-ge-byé-'jer shŕ 'jīn-dz-shyāng-dzwàn-'shŕ-de.

To set a trap ān, fàng, shyà. ‖We set traps for the animal. wǒ-men 'shyà-le yí-ge-dǎ-yě-'shèw-de-'jyǎ-dz.

To set a bone jyē. ‖Can you set a broken bone? nǐ hwèy jyē-'gǔ-ma?

(*To become firm*) dìng, nìng.

(*To assign*) jyàw, ràng, pày; (*to invite*) chǐng. ‖They set him to counting the money. tā-men 'ràng-ta láy shǔ-'chyán.

(*To sit on eggs*) fū-'wō, baw-'wō, fū-'dàn; (*of hens*) fū shyǎw-'jyēr; (*to place on eggs*) ràng . . . fū-'wō. ‖The hens are setting. 'jī fū shyǎw-'jyēr-ne. ‖We set a dozen hens each spring. 'měy-nyán-'chwēn-tyān wǒ-men ràng shŕ-'èr-ge-'jī fū-'wō.

(*To go down*) làw. ‖The sun sets at 6 o'clock tonight. jyēr-'wǎn-shang 'lyèw-dyǎn-jūng làw ˙tày-yang.

A set (*collection of things that go together but are not identical*) tàw; (*collection of things that go together and are almost identical*) fù; (*of books*) bù. ‖Do you have a complete set of these dishes? jèy-ge-'dyé-dz nǐ yěw jěng-'tàw-de-ma? ‖These buttons are a set. jèy-shyē-'nyěw-dz shŕ yí-'fù.

(*Form, appearance*) 'yàng-dz, yàngr. ‖Something about the set of his mouth frightened us. tā 'dzwěy-de-nèy-ge-'yàng-dz 'shyà-le wǒ-men yí-'tyàw.

(*Group of people*) yì-'hwǒr (*or* yì-'chywún *or* yí-'mwò-dz)(-rén); *or* shyē-'rén. ‖He doesn't fit in our set. tā gēn 'wǒ-men-jèy-yì-'hwǒr shwō-bù-'láy.

(*Scenery*) bù-'jǐng; (*set and all the stage equipment*) 'chyè-me. ‖Who designed the sets for the play? jèy-chū-'shì-de-bù-'jǐng shŕ-'shéy 'jì-hwa-de?

Radio set wú-shyàn-'dyàn.

(*Ready, prepared*) 'ywù-bey-'hǎw-le, 'jwěn-bey-'hǎw-le, nùng-'hǎw-le, nèng-'hǎw-le. ‖Are you all set to go? nǐ děw ywù-bey-'hǎw-le yàw 'dzěw-le-ma?

(*Decided*) 'gù-jǐ, sž. ‖He has very set opinions. tā-de-'yì-jyàn hěn 'gù-jǐ. *or* tā sž-shīn-'yǎr.

Set expression. ‖He has a very set expression on his face. tā-de-'lyǎn làw 'běng-de hěn 'jǐn.

To set about (*to begin*) chǐ-'téwr, kāy-'shǐ; (*to be going to*) jèng 'yàw. ‖He set about finishing his report. tā 'jèng yàw bǎ tā-de-bàw-'gàw nùng-'wan-le.

To set aside 'gē-dzày yì-'byār, 'gē-chǐ-láy-le. ‖This fund has been set aside for an emergency. jèy-bǐ-'chyán gē-dzày yì-'byār, děng yěw-shŕ-de-shŕ-hew yùng.

To set at ease ràng . . . swéy-'byàn, ràng . . . °byé 'jywū-ni *or* °byé 'jywū-shu. ‖We tried to set them at ease. wǒ-men shyǎng-'fár ràng tā-men byé 'jywū-shu.

To set at liberty jyàw . . . dzěw, bǎ . . . 'fàng-le. ‖You will be set at liberty. hwèy bǎ-ni fàng-le-de. *or* hwèy jyàw-ni dzěw-de.

To set an example 'dzwò ge-'bǎng-yàng, 'dzwò ge-'mwó-fàn. ‖He's set a good example for us to follow. tā gěy wǒ-men 'dzwò-le yí-ge-'hěn-hǎw-de-'bǎng-yàng ràng wǒ-men 'mwó-fǎng.

To set down. (*To land, as a plane*) bǎ . . . làw; (*to write down*) shyě, 'jì(-lu); (*to ascribe*) swàn. ‖He set the plane down on the new airfield. tā bǎ fēy-'jī làw-dzay 'shīn-fēy-jī-'chǎng-li-le. ‖Set down the main arguments. bǎ nèy-ge-byàn-'lwèn-de-yàw-'dyǎn 'shyě-shya-lay. ‖He made a mess of his job, but set it down to bad luck. tā bǎ nèy-ge-'shr̀-ching nùng-'dzāw-le, jyèw swàn 'ywèn-chi bù-'hǎw jyèw 'wán-le.

To set forth shwō, jyǎng, 'jyě-shr. ‖He set forth his position quite clearly. tā bǎ tā-de-'yì-jyan 'shwō-de hěn 'chīng-chu.

To set one's heart on jēn 'shyǎng. ‖I set my heart on going today. wǒ 'jēn shyǎng 'jīn-tyān 'chywù.

To set in (*come*) láy. ‖The rainy season set in early this year. jīn-nyán ywǔ-'jì láy-de 'dzǎw.

To set in motion kāy. ‖By pushing a button he set the machine in motion. tā yí 'èn 'jī-gwan jyèw bǎ nèy-ge-'jī-chi 'kāy-kay-le. *But* ‖Have you set the clock going? nǐ bǎ-'jūng shàng-le-ma?

To set off. (*To start to go*) chū-'fā, dzěw, dùng-'shēn, chǐ-'shēn; (*to increase the effect of*) chèn; (*to cause to explode*) fàng; (*to light*) dyǎn. ‖We're setting off on our hike tomorrow morning. wǒ-men-de-tú-bù-lywǔ-'shíng 'míng-tyān-'dzǎw-shàng chū-'fā. ‖That belt sets off her dress nicely. nèy-tyáw-pí-'dày bǎ tā-de-'yī-shang chèn-de gèng hǎw-'kàn-le. ‖He set off the firecracker. tā bǎ 'pàw-jang dyǎn-'jáw-le.

To set someone on (*or* **against**) **someone else.** ‖They wouldn't have fought, if he hadn't set them on one another. *is expressed as* If he hadn't gone between them finding fault, they wouldn't have started to fight. yàw 'bú-shr tā 'tsúng-jūng 'tyǎw-bwō, tā-men háy 'dǎ-bu-chǐ-'láy-ne. ‖By clever propaganda they set the two countries against each other. *is expressed as* They used clever propaganda and incited the two countries to mutual distrust. tā-men yùng yì-'jǔng-'chyǎw-myàw-de-'shywàn-chwán bǎ 'nèy-lyǎng-'gwó 'tyǎw-bwō-de bǐ-'tsž bù-'hé-le.

To set on fire dyǎn-'jáw; **to be set on fire** jáw, jáw-'hwǒ, chǐ-'hwǒ, shāw. ‖My cigarette set the newspaper on fire. wǒ-de-yān-'jywǎr bǎ bàw-'jř dyǎn-'jáw-le.

To set out. *See* **to set off.**

To set sail kāy-'chwán.

To set right *or* **to set straight** shwō-(*or* jyǎng- *or* 'jyě-shr̀-) °'chīng-chu *or* °'míng-bay. ‖Set me straight on this. bǎ jèy-ge gěy-wo 'jyě-shr̀-'chīng-chu-le.

To set to music. (*To compose*) gěy . . . byān (*or to make* dzwò, *or to write* shyě) ge-'pǔ-dz. ‖Can you set this poem to music? nǐ néng gěy jèy-shěw-'shr̀ byān yí-ge-'pǔ-dz-ma?

To set up (*to start*) kāy-'shř, tsáy, chǐ-'téwr, dùng-'shěw. ‖When did they set up housekeeping? tā-men 'shéme-shŕ-hew kāy-'shř gwǎn 'jyā-li-de-'shř-ching? *But* ‖His father set him up in business. *is expressed as* His father helped him to open a business. tā-'fù-chin bāng-ta ʔkāy ge-'mǎy-mày.

SETTLE. (*To take up residence; to live*) jù; (*to stay*) dāy. ‖In what part of the country did you settle? nǐ-men dzày jèy-'gwó-li-'nǎ-yí-'bù-fen 'jù-shyà-láy-le? ‖It was the English who first settled in that region. 'yīng-gwo-rén shyān 'láy-dàw 'jèy-yí-'dày 'jù-shyà-láy-de.

(*To arrange comfortably; to sit*) dzwò, (*to recline, lean back*) kàw. ‖He settled himself in the chair. tā-'dž-jī 'kàw-dzày 'yǐ-dz-shang-le.

(*To go to the bottom*) chén-'dyěr, 'chén-shyà-chywu, 'làw-shyà-chywu. ‖Wait until the tea leaves settle. děng chá-'yè 'làw-shyà-chywu.

(*To sink, as into the ground*) 'shyàn-shyà-chywu. ‖The wall has settled a little bit. jèy-dwǒ-'chyáng 'shyàn-shyà-chywu-le yì-'dyǎr.

(*To decide*) jywé- lìng, jyě-'jywé, 'pàn-dwàn. ‖Can you settle a question for us? nǐ néng 'gěy wǒ-men jyě-'jywé yí-ge-'wèn-tí-ma?

(*To satisfy; accomplish*) bàn. ‖All legitimate claims will be settled. 'swǒ-yěw-hé-'fǎ-de-'yàw-chyéw dēw bàn-de-'dàw.

(*To quiet*) ràng . . . °bú-'nàw-le *or* °bù-nán-'shèw-le *or* °'shū-fu-le *or* °bù-'téng-le *or* °bú-'nàw-de-heng-le *or* °bù-'jē-teng-le). ‖This medicine will settle your stomach. jèy-ge-'yàw néng ràng nǐ-de-'wèy-li bù-nán-'shèw-le. *or expressed as* Take this medicine and your stomach will feel better. nǐ chř-le 'jèy-ge-'yàw 'wèy-li jyèw bú-'nàw-le.

Settled gù-'dìng; **to be settled** yěw yí-'dìng-jř-'gwēy. ‖He seems very settled in his ways. tā-de-'shēng-hwó-shí-'gwàn hǎw !shyàng dēw °hěn gù-'dìng (°yěw yí-'dìng-jř-'gwēy).

To settle down. (*Live regularly*) ān-jr-'hǎw; (*direct one's attention*) ān-'shīn, tā-shyà 'shīn-chywu. ‖Hasn't he settled down yet? tā-de-'shēng-hwó háy méy ān-jr-'hǎw-ne-ma? ‖The boy couldn't settle down to his homework. nèy-ge-'háy-dz 'tā-bu-shyà 'shīn-chywu dzày 'jyā-li dzwò 'gūng-ke.

To settle (*decide*) jywé-'dìng, 'dìng-gwey-'hǎw-le. ‖They settled the terms of the treaty. tā-men bǎ 'tyáw-jyan dēw 'dìng-gwey-'hǎw-le.

To settle . . . on (*give legally*) gěy, 'lyéw-shyà, gěy . . . 'lyéw-shyà, 'lyéw-gěy. ‖Her husband settled quite a sum on her. tā-de-'jàng-fu 'gěy-ta 'lyéw-shya bù-'shǎw-de-'chyán.

SEVEN. chī. **One seventh** 'chī-fēn-jr-'yī; **the seventh** dì-'chī.

SEVENTEEN. shŕ-'chī. One seventeenth shŕ-'chī-fēn-jr-'yī; the seventeenth dì-shŕ-'chī.

SEVENTY. 'chī-shŕ. One seventieth 'chī-shr-fēn-jr-'yī; the seventieth dì-'chī-shŕ.

SEVERAL. jĭ *plus measure; for emphasis* hăw-jĭ *plus measure.* Several days 'jĭ-tyān; several years 'jĭ-nyán. ‖I want to stay for several days. wŏ yàw dzày-'jèr 'dăy 'jĭ-tyān. ‖There are several ways of doing this. dzwò 'jèy-ge yĕw 'hăw-jĭ-ge-'fá-dz.

SEVERE. 'lì-hay; (*for an illness*) jùng, 'chén-jùng, dà; (*for an accident*) 'yán-jùng-de. Severe illness 'lì-hay-de-'bìng; have a severe pain 'téng-de 'lì-hay; severe criticism 'pī-ping-de hĕn 'lì-hay; severe accident 'lì-hay-de-'shŕ-ching. ‖The judge was very severe. jèy-ge-fă-'gwān hĕn 'lì-hay.

(*Stern*) 'jwāng-yán. ‖I've never seen him look so severe. wŏ 'tsúng-láy yĕ méy 'kàn-jyàn-gwo tā 'dzème-yàngr 'jwāng-yán-gwo.

(*Hard to endure; severely cold, or especially cold*) 'lĕng-de 'lì-hay *or* tè-byé 'lĕng. ‖Is the winter severe? 'dūng-tyān lĕng-de 'lì-hay-ma?

(*Difficult*). ‖This motor will have to undergo a severe test before it is put into service. *is expressed as* This motor must be tested carefully before it is used. jèy-ge-fă-dùng-'jī méy-'yùng yĭ-'chyán dĕy °hăw-hāwr-de 'shŕ-yàn yí-shyàr. *or* °'yán-gé-de 'shŕ-yàn yí-shyàr. *or* °'dž-shi-de 'shŕ-yàn yí-shyàr. *or* °'shyăw-shyăw-shin-'shīn-de 'shŕ-yàn yí-shyàr.

(*Strict*). ‖Don't be so severe with the child. *is expressed as* Don't treat the child too severely. byé bă 'háy-dz gwăn-de tày °'yán. *or* °'lì-hay.

(*Plain*) 'jyăn-dan. ‖That dress has very severe lines. nèy-ge-'yī-fu-de-'yàng-dz hĕn 'jyăn-dan. *or* nèy-ge-'yī-fu-de-yàng-dz jŕ-gu-lūng-'tūng.

SEW. féng. To sew a seam lyáw; (*to hem*) swŏ; to sew on (*a button, etc.*) dĭng; to sew two pieces together (*to piece*) lyán; (*to stitch something, as the sole of a Chinese shoe, to make it strong*) nà; (*to sew the upper part of a shoe to the sole*) shàng; *etc.*; to do sewing (*use a needle and thread*) dzwò-'hwó *or* dzwò 'jēn-shyàn(-'hwó); (*to make clothes*) dzwò 'yī-shang. ‖She makes her living sewing. tā 'jŕ-je dzwò 'jēn-shyàn-'hwó wéy-'shēng. ‖Please sew the buttons on. láw-'jyà bă 'jèy-jĭ-ge-'nyĕw-dz gĕy 'dĭng-shang. ‖Sew up the seam. bă 'jèy-dàw-'fèng gĕy °'féng-shang. *or,* (*if sewing very quickly*) °'lyáw-shang.

To sew on a machine yùng 'jī-chi dzwò-'hwó.
Sewing machine féng-rèn-'jī.

SEX. shìng-'byé (*literary; used only on written documents or when citing them*); *otherwise, when asking about sex, one says* male *or* female (*for humans*) 'nán-de-'nywŭ-de, (*for animals*) 'gūng-de-'mŭ-de.

‖Give your name, age, and sex. bă nǐ-de-shìng-'míng 'nyán-líng, shìng-'byé, dēw 'shyĕ-shang. ‖What sex is the puppy? shyăw-'gĕwr shŕ 'gūng-de háy-shr 'mŭ-de?

Sex appeal *is expressed as* to be physically attractive 'rèw-găn. ‖The new secretary has a lot of sex appeal. jèy-ge-shīn-'shū-ji hĕn 'rèw-găn.

SHADE. (*Place in shadow*) yīn-'lyángr. ‖Let's stay in the shade. dzá-men dàw yīn-'lyángr-li láy-ba. ‖This is a fine shade tree. jèy-kē-'shù-de-shù-yīn-'lyángr hĕn hăw.

(*Dark part*) yīn-'yĕngr, 'àn-de-dì-fang; light and shade 'yīn-yáng. ‖There is too much shade in this photograph. jèy-jāng-shyàng-'pyār yīn-'yĕngr tày dwō-le. ‖Light and shade are well balanced in that painting. nèy-jāng-'hwàr 'yīn-yáng gwāng-'shyàn 'pèy-de hĕn 'ywún.

(*Of color*) 'shēn-chyăn. But ‖Have you any thread to match this shade of blue? *is expressed as* Have you any kind of thread to match this blue color? nĭ yĕw shéme-yàngr-de-shyàn pèy 'jèy-jŭng-'lán-shăr-ma?

(*Minor distinction*). ‖Your translation doesn't get quite the right shade of meaning. *is expressed as* Your translation hasn't grasped the exact meaning. nĭ-de-'fān-yì 'méy-yew 'jwā-ju nèy-ge-jēn-'jèng-de-'yì-sz. *or as* You translated the meaning not quite right. nĭ 'fān-de nèy-ge-'yì-sz bú 'shŕ-fēn 'chyà-dang.

(*Blinds*) 'chwāng-(hu-)lyár. ‖Pull down the shades. bă 'chwāng-hu-lyár 'lā-shyà-lay.

(*To screen*) 'jē-ju. ‖Shade your eyes from the glare. jē-ju-dyăr 'yăn-jīng shĕng-de hwăng-'yăn. *or expressed as* Cut off the light to keep it from shining in your eyes. 'dăng-je-dyăr nèy-ge-'lyàng-'gwāng shĕng-de hwăng-'yăn.

(*To darken*) tú-'shēn, hwà-'shēn, mwŏ-'shēn, myáw 'shēn. ‖Shade this part a little more. bă 'jèy-bù-fen dzày tú-'shēn-dyăr.

(*To change color gradually*) jyàn-'jyàn-de byàn 'yán-shar *or* yì-'dyăr yì-'dyăr-de byàn 'yán-shar. ‖This wool shades from pink to red. jèy-ge-máw-'shyàn-de-'yán-shar yì-'téwr shŕ 'fĕn-de yì-'dyăr yì-'dyăr-de byàn, dàw 'nèy-téwr jyèw chéng 'húng-de-le. ‖The stage lights shaded from green to blue. wŭ-'táy-de-dēng-'gwāng tsúng 'lywù-'yán-shar jyàn-'jyăn-de 'byàn-chéng 'lán-yán-shar-le.

(*Slightly*) (yì-)dyăr. ‖This hat is a shade more expensive than I thought. jèy-ge-'màw-dz-de-'jyà-chyán bĭ wŏ-'shyăng-de shāw-'wēy 'gwèy yì-dyăr. ‖It's a shade too big. nèy-ge tày 'dà-dyăr-le.

To put *someone* in the shade *is expressed as* to cover *someone* up bă . . . gĕy 'gày-gwò-chywu, *or as* to make *someone* seem inferior by comparison. bă . . . gĕy 'bĭ shyà-chywu. ‖She puts her sister completely in the shade. tā bă tā-de-'mèy-méy 'wán-chywán gĕy °'gày-gwò-chywu-le. *or* °'bĭ-shyà-chywu-le.

SHADOW. (*Of a person or thing*) 'yǐng-dz, yěngr. ‖The trees cast a long shadow in the afternoon. 'shyà-bǎn-tyār shù-'yéngr hěn 'cháng. ‖He clings to him like his shadow. *is expressed as* He follows him, form and shadow not apart. tā 'shíng-yǐng-bù-'lí-de 'jwēy-je ta. *But* ‖He's just a shadow of his former self. *is expressed as* He's thin, not the way he used to be. tā 'shèw-de °'bú-shř nà-'yàngr-le. *or* °'gǎy-le 'yàngr-le.

(*A little bit*) yì-'dyǎr, háw . . ., 'sž-háw . . . . ‖There is not a shadow of doubt about the truth of the story. jèy-sher yí-'dìng shr 'jēn-de, °yì-dyǎr (*or* °'sž-háw) méy-yěw kě-'yí-de.

To shadow. (*Watch secretly*) àn-'dì 'jyān-shr; (*follow secretly*) àn-'dì 'gēn-je. ‖I hired someone to shadow him. wǒ 'gù-le yí-ge-'rén àn-'dì 'gēn-je ta.

SHAKE (SHOOK, SHAKEN). yáw, *a general term, meaning to shake in almost any way, but particularly sideways; thus* to ring a bell by shaking it yáw-'líng, to shake one's head sideways to say no yáw-'téw; (*to swing sideways or back and forth*) 'yáw-hwàng, hwàng, 'hwàng-yew. ‖He took the boy by the shoulders and shook him. tā 'jwā-ju nèy-'háy-dz-de-jyān-'bǎngr 'yáw-hwang tā. ‖Shake the bottle well before using the medicine. jèy-'yàw méy-'yùng yǐ-'chyán 'shyān děy bǎ píng-dž 'yáw-yaw.

(*To hold from the tip and shake up and down, to get out dust, etc.*) děw, 'děw-lew. ‖Shake the dust out of these clothes. bǎ 'jèy-shyē-'yī-shang-shàng-de-'tǔ 'děw-lew *or* -'děw-lew.

(*To bump up and down, on horseback or in a car*) dyàn, 'dyàn-de. ‖The road is so bumpy, it feels as if the car would shake apart. 'jèy-ge-dàwr tày bù-'píng, chē hǎw-'shyàng děw kwày 'dyàn sǎn-le.

(*To move*) 'dùng-han. ‖Our whole house shook during the earthquake. dì-'jèn-de-'shŕ-hewr wǒ-men jěng-'gèr-de-'fáng-dz děw jŕ 'dùng-han.

(*To quiver*) fā-'děw, chàn, 'dwō-swo, 'chàn-wey, dǎ-'chàn, děw; (*to shiver and have one's teeth chatter*) dǎ-'jàn, jàn. ‖He was shaking with cold. tā 'lěng-de jŕ fā-'děw. ‖His voice shook. tā-de-'shēng-yīn jŕ 'chàn-wey. ‖He can't stop his hand from shaking. tā-de-'shěw jŕ-bú-'jù-de jŕ 'dwō-swo.

To shake hands 'lā-shěw, 'wò-shěw. ‖We didn't get a chance to shake hands with the hostess. wǒ-men méy 'dé-jaw 'jī-hwèy gēn 'nywǔ-jǔ-rén 'lā-la shěw.

To shake one's head (*meaning no*) yáw-'téw. ‖He shook his head. tā 'yáw-le yáw-téwr.

To shake off (*to fall off*) dyàw, dyàw-le, 'dyàw-shyà-chywu. ‖The mud will shake off your shoes easily when it dries. shyé-shang-de-'ní yì-'gān hěn 'rúng-yi-de jyèw 'dyàw-le.

To shake off (*to get rid of*). To shake off bad temper *is expressed as* to press down bad temper bǎ-'chì 'yā-shyà-chywu; to shake off responsibilities *is ex-*

pressed *as* to unload responsibilities 'shyè-le 'dzé-rèn-le; *etc.* ‖He shook off his depression and went visiting. *is expressed as* He took up good spirits, and went out to see people. tā 'dǎ-chǐ 'jīng-shen láy, 'chū-chywù kàn-'rén-chywu-le.

To shake (up). (*Startle; give a shock to* . . .) bǎ . . . shyà yí-'tyàw *or* (*to make* . . . *receive a shock*) jyàw (*or* shř) . . . shèw yì-'jīng. ‖He was really shaken up by the accident. jèy-tsž-chū-shř 'jēn bǎ-ta shyà yí-dà-'tyàw. *But* ‖The news shook him out of his indifference. *is expressed as* The news made him unable again to be indifferent. jèy-ge-'shyāw-shì shř tā bù-'néng 'dzày 'mwó-bù-gwān-'shīn-le.

A shake. ‖He answered with a shake of his head. *is expressed as* He didn't answer with words; he just shook his head no. tā méy-'hwéy-da 'shéme-'hwà, jyèw 'yáw-le yáw-'téwr.

SHALL. (*In asking someone to express his opinion as to what you should do; not expressed.*) ‖Shall I wait? wǒ 'děng-je-ma? ‖Let's have dinner now, shall we? dzám jyèw chř-'fàn, 'hǎw-bu-hǎw? ‖Shall I close the window? wǒ gwān-shang 'chwāng-hu-ba?

SHAPE. (*Form*) yàngr, 'yàng-dz. ‖Isn't the shape of that mountain odd! jèy-ge-'shān-de-'yàng-dz dwō-'gwày-ya!

To get . . . **into shape** bǎ . . . 'nùng-chū ge-'yàngr-lay. ‖Get your plans into shape before we discuss them. dzày wǒ-men 'shāng-lyang yǐ-'chyán shyān bǎ nǐ-de-'jì-hwà 'nùng-chū ge-'yàngr-lay.

To take shape 'yěw dyǎr-°'gwēy-mwó-le *or* °'yàngr-le. ‖His plan for the dam is taking shape. tā dzwò-'já-de-'jì-hwà 'yěw dyǎr-'gwēy-mwó-le.

To shape up (*take a certain form*) 'nùng-chéng . . . yàngr. ‖How are things shaping up? 'shŕ-ching 'nùng-chéng 'shéme-yàngr-le? *or* 'shŕ-ching dzěme-'yàng?

To shape *something* (*mould with the hands*) sù. ‖He shaped the clay into the image of a human head. tā yùng-'ní 'sù-chéng yí-ge-rén-'téw.

(*Condition*) 'chíng-shíng, 'jwàng-kwàng. ‖The business is in bad shape. jèy-ge-'mǎy-mày-de-'chíng-shíng 'bú-dà 'hǎw. *But* ‖I'm in bad shape. *is expressed as* Lately I haven't felt too good. wǒ 'jìn-láy 'bú-dà 'hǎw. ‖What shape is it in? nèy-ge dzěme-'yàng?

To get into shape (*to arrange in good order*) 'shŕ-dew- (*or* 'gwēy-jr- *or* 'jěng-li-) °'hǎw-le *or* °'lì-lwo. ‖Is the house in shape for visitors? fáng-dz 'gwēy-jew-de 'kě-yi ràng-'rén 'jìn-lay-le-ma?

SHARE. (*Part*) fèr, 'bù-fen. ‖You'll have to do your share. nǐ děy dzwò 'nǐ-nèy-'fèr. ‖Pay your share of the bill. nǐ gěy 'nǐ-nèy-'fèr. ‖We divided the money share and share alike. wǒ-men bǎ-'chyán 'píng-fēn-le.

(*Part ownership of a company*) 'gǔ-dz, gǔr, 'gǔ-fen, gǔ-'běn. ‖How many shares do you hold in that company? nèy-ge-gūng-'sž-li nǐ yěw 'dwō-shaw-'gǔ-dz?

To share (*to divide and use*) fēn. ‖**Let's share the cakes.** dzám bǎ jèy-ge-'gāw fēn-le-ba.

(*To use in common*) dēw yùng, hé yùng. ‖**We three share a bicycle.** wǒm-'sān-ge-rén 'dēw yùng 'yí-lyàng-dž-shíng-'chē. ‖**They share a room.** *is expressed as* They live together in one room. tām-'lyǎ hé 'jù 'yì-jyān-'wū-dz. ‖**May I share your table?** *is expressed as* May I sit here? wǒ 'dzwò-jèr, 'shíng-ma?

(*To have in common*) dēw yěw. ‖**We share the same bad habit of always being late.** wǒm-'lyǎ 'dēw yěw wǎn-'dàw-de-'máw-bìng. ‖**They shared the secret.** *is expressed as* They both knew the secret. tā-men dēw 'jř-daw jèy-ge-'mì-mi-le.

SHAVE. (*To remove facial hair*) gwā-'lyǎn, gwā 'hú-dz, tì 'hú-dz. ‖**I have to shave before dressing for the evening.** jyēr-'wǎn-shang hwàn 'yī-shang yǐ-'chyán wǒ děy 'gwā-gwa 'lyǎn. ‖**I went to the barber for a haircut and a shave.** wǒ shàng lǐ-fǎ-'gwǎn chywù lǐ-le-li 'fǎ, gwǎ-le-gwa 'lyǎn.

(*To remove hair*) gwā, tì. ‖**He shaved my neck for me.** tā gěy-wo 'gwā-le 'bwó-dz-hèw-tew.

(*To remove thin slices; with any instrument, by scraping*) gwā; (*with a plane*) bàw; (*with a knife or axe, etc.*) shyāw. ‖**Use a plane to shave the edge of the door.** ná 'bàw-dz bǎ jèy-ge-mén-de-'byǎr-shang 'gwā-gwa. ‖**If you shave the soap, it will melt faster.** nǐ 'yàw-shr bǎ yí-dz 'shyāw-chéng 'pyàr jyèw hwà-de 'kwày-le.

SHE. *See* HE.

SHEEP. yáng, myán-'yáng. ‖**How many head of sheep have you?** nǐ yěw 'dwō-shaw-téw-'yáng-a?

Black sheep méy-'chū-shi-de-°'háy-dz *or* °rén. ‖**He is the black sheep of the family.** tā shř tā-men-'jyā-li-méy-'chū-shi-de-'háy-dz.

SHEET. (*Of paper*) pyār, jāng. ‖**I want a hundred sheets of paper.** wǒ yàw yì-'bǎy-jāng-'jř.

(*Of cardboard, metal, and other stiff things*) pyàr. ‖**This machine cuts the aluminum into thin sheets.** jèy-ge-'jī-chi bǎ-lywǔ 'chyē-chéng báw-'pyàr.

(*On a bed*) (chwáng-)'dān-dz. ‖**Put clean sheets on the bed.** bǎ-'chwáng 'pū-shang 'gān-jìng-'dān-dz. ‖**The sheets are changed every Saturday.** 'měy-ge-lǐ-bày-'lyàw hwàn chwáng-'dān-dz.

(*Upper sheet; or a sheet sewed to the under side of a quilt, to keep it clean*) bèy-'dān-dz; *also called* bèy-'lǐ-dz, *or* bèy-'lyěr.

(*Under sheet; or a sheet sewed to the mattress to keep it clean*) rù-'dān-dz.

SHELL. (*Hard outer covering*) kér, chyàwr (*both a little literary*); pyér. ‖**The shells on these walnuts are very thick.** jèy-shyē-'hé-tew-de-'kér hěn 'hèw.

(*Of a turtle*) (wáng-ba-)'kér, (wáng-ba-)'gàr.

(*Of an egg*) dàn-'kér, dàn-'pyér, dàn-'chyàwr; (*of a chicken egg*) 'jī-dàn-'kér; (*of a duck egg*) 'yā-dàn-'kér; *etc.*

Sea shell bèng-'kér, gé-li-'bèng-dz.

(*Framework, of a building*) 'chywū-chyàwr (*literary*), 'jyà-dz. ‖**After the fire, just the shell of the house was left.** jèy-ge-fáng-dz shāw-le yǐ-'hèw jyèw 'shèng yí-ge-'chywū-chyàwr-le.

(*Projectile*) dž-'dàn, jà-'dàn, paw-'dàn ‖**A shell nearly hit him.** yí-ge-dž-'dàn 'chà-dyǎr méy 'dǎ-jáw ta.

To shell. (*To remove shells; in general*) bāw-'pyér, chywù-'pyér; (*for nuts only*) chywù-'kér. ‖**Are the peas all shelled?** wān-'dèw dēw bāw-'pyér-le-ma?

(*To bombard*) ná (*or* yùng)-'pàw °'hūng *or* °gūng *or* °dǎ. ‖**We shelled the enemy positions for hours.** wǒ-men yùng-'pàw 'gūng-le 'dí-rén 'hǎw-jǐ-ge-jūng-'téw.

SHELTER. (*Place to stay*) ān-'shěn-de-dì-fangr, ān-'shěn-jr'chù, 'jù-de-dì-fangr. ‖**We had to find shelter for the night.** 'wǎn-shang wǒ-men děy 'jǎw ge-'jù-de-dì-fangr.

(*A shack*) 'wō-peng. ‖**We built a crude shelter out of branches.** wǒ-men yùng shù-'jèr dā-le ge-'wō-peng.

Air raid shelter fáng-kūng-'dùng.

To shelter 'jàw-gu, 'jāw-hu. ‖**Who'll shelter the refugees?** 'shwéy 'jàw-gu 'jèy-shyē-táw-'nàn-de-ya?

SHINE (SHONE). (*To be visible*). ‖**Is the sun shining?** *is expressed as* Is the sun hot or not? 'tày-yang 'dú-bu-dú? *or more commonly, as in English, as* Is the sun out or not? yěw 'tày-yang méy-yew? ‖**The moon is shining very brightly.** *is expressed as* The moon is very bright. 'ywè-lyàng hěn 'lyàng.

(*To give light, of the heavenly bodies or any light*) jàw; (*to dazzle*) hwǎng. ‖**The moonlight is shining on the lake.** 'ywè-gwāng 'jàw-dzày 'hú-shang. ‖**That car's headlights are shining in my eyes.** nèy-lyàng-'chē-de-chē-'dēng 'jàw (*or* 'hwǎng) wǒ-de-'yǎn.

(*To cause to give light*) bǎ . . . jàw. ‖**Shine the light over here.** bǎ 'lyàngr wàng-'jèr 'jàw-jaw.

(*To polish*) tsā. ‖**I want my shoes shined.** wǒ yàw 'tsā-tsa 'shyé. ‖**Can you put a shine on these shoes?** jèy-'shyé néng 'tsā-de 'lyàng-ma?

(*To be outstanding*) chū-'sè, lèw-'lyǎn, chū 'fēng-tew. ‖**He really shone in his math class.** tā dzày 'shù-shywé-'bān-shang jēn lèw-'lyǎn.

To have a shine (*be shiny*) lyàng, fā-'lyàng, shǎn-'gwāng. ‖**That brass platter has quite a shine on it.** nèy-ge-túng-'pár-shang °hěn 'lyàng. *or* °jř fā-'lyàng. *or* °jř shǎn-gwang. ‖**Look at the shine on that car!** nǐ chyáw nèy-'chē dwō 'lyàng!

Rain or shine (*wind and rain no obstacle*) 'fēng-ywù-wú-'dzǔ. ‖**We'll come, rain or shine.** wǒ-men yí-'dìng 'láy, 'fēng-ywǔ-wú-'dzǔ. *or expressed as* Whether it's cloudy or fair, we'll certainly come. bù-gwǎn 'yīn-tyān 'chíng-tyān, wǒ-men yí-'dìng láy.

SHIP. chwán. ‖Who is in charge of this ship? shéy 'gwǎn jèy-jr̄-'chwán?

(*Plane*) fēy-'jī. ‖He was piloting a big four-motored ship. tā 'kāy-de shr̀ 'sz̀-ge-fā-dùng-'jī-de-fēy-'jī.

To ship. (*To send*) sùng; (*to mail*) jì; (*to send by freight*) wùn; (*to dispatch, as troops*) pày-'chyǎn. ‖I want to ship this. wǒ yàw bǎ 'jèy-ge jì-'dzĕw. ‖Has the case been shipped yet? nèy-jr̄-'shyàng-dz ywùn-'dzĕw-l -ma? ‖The government shipped troops to the city to maintain order. 'jèng-fǔ pày-'chyǎn rwò-gān-bù-'dwèy dàw 'chéng-li-chywu 'wéy-chŕ 'jr̀-shywù.

(*Of soldiers*). ‖They expect to be shipped any day now. *is expressed as* At any time they will break camp. tām jyèw yàw kāy-'bá-le.

To leave by ship dzwò-'chwán dzĕw. ‖Has the sailor we met last night shipped out yet? dzám-dzwór-wǎn shang-'kàn-jyàn-de-nèy-ge-shwéy-'shĕw 'yĭ-jing °dzwò-'chwán 'dzĕw-le-ma? *or* °chū-chywù-le-ma?

To ship water. ‖This rowboat is shipping water. *is expressed as* On this rowboat the water floods in over the side. jèy-ge-'hwá-dz 'shwěy 'màn-jìn-láy-le.

SHIRT. chèn-'shān, hàn-'shān; undershirt chèn-'yī.

Special expressions in English. ‖Keep your shirt on! *is expressed as* Don't get excited; take it easy. byé jāw-'jí; màn-'mār-de. ‖He lost his shirt gambling. *is expressed as* He gambled and lost everything, even his pants. tā dǔ-'chyán 'dŭ-de bǎ 'kù-dz dēw-'shū-le. ‖He'd give you the shirt off his back. *is expressed as* He's capable of giving you anything. tā 'néng-gèw bǎ 'shéme dēw 'gěy-ni. *or as* He's extremely generous. tā 'dà-fang 'jí-le.

SHOE. shyé. Cloth shoes 'bŭ-shyé; leather shoes 'pí-shyé; sports shoes 'ywùn-dung-shyé; *etc.*

Horseshoe mǎ-'jǎng.

To shoe *a horse* dīng-'jǎng, dīng mǎ-'jǎng. ‖Who's going to shoe the horses? 'shéy dīng-mǎ-'jǎng-a?

(*Figuratively*). ‖Put yourself in his shoes. *is expressed as* If you were he, what would you think? 'nǐ yàw-shr 'tā nǐ 'yèw dzěme 'shyǎng? *or as* If you were he, what would you do? 'nǐ yàw-shr 'tā nǐ 'yèw dzěme 'bàn? *or as* If you were in his position, what would you do? 'nǐ yàw-shr 'chǔ-dzay 'tā-de-'dì-wèy nǐ 'dzěme 'bàn? ‖I'd hate to be in his shoes. wǒ kě bú-'ywàn-yì 'chǔ-dzày 'tā-de-'dì-wèy.

SHOOT (SHOT). To shoot dǎ-'chyāng; to shoot at *something* kāy-'chyāng 'dǎ, fàng-'chyāng 'dǎ, ná-'chyāng 'dǎ, yùng-'chyāng 'dǎ. ‖How well can you shoot? *is politely expressed as* You shoot well, don't you? nǐ dǎ-'chyāng yí-'dìng 'dǎ-de 'hǎw-ba. *or as* Do you shoot well? nǐ dǎ-'chyāng dǎ-de 'hǎw-ma? ‖What are they shooting at? tā-men (yùng-'chyāng) dǎ 'shéme-ne? ‖He shot me in the arm. tā ná-'chyāng 'dǎ-de wǒ-'gē-be-shang-le.

(*To use; of a gun*) yùng. ‖What kind of bullet does this gun shoot? jèy-gǎn-'chyāng yùng 'shéme-dž-'dàn?

(*To move very quickly; to run*) pǎw, chūng; (*to run, with a puff of dust*) yí-lyèw-'yār-de 'pǎw; (*to run, with a swish*) 'sēw-de yí-'shyà-dz 'pǎw. ‖A squirrel shot across the road. yí-ge-'sūng-shǔr dzày 'lù-shang 'héng-je 'pǎw-gwò-chywu-le. ‖A car shot past us. yí-lyàng-'chē tsúng wǒ-men-'páng-byar 'sēw-de yí-'shyà-dz jyèw 'pǎw-gwò-chywu-le. ‖On the very last lap of the race our horse shot ahead. nèy-'chǎng-sày-'mǎ dàw-le mwò-mwo-'lyǎwr 'wǒ-men-nèy-pǐ-'mǎ 'sēw-de yí-'shyà-dz jyèw 'pǎw-de 'téw-li chywù-le. *But* ‖Sharp pains are shooting up and down my leg. *is expressed as* In my leg, coming up and going down, time after time it pains very severely. wǒ-'twěy-shang 'shàng-láy-shyà-'chywù-yí-'jèn-yí-'jèn-de 'téng-de hěn 'lì-hay.

(*To grow very fast*) jǎng; *or* (*Peiping slang for a child growing fast*) tswān. ‖How fast that child has shot up in the last year! 'nèy-háy-dz 'chywù-nyán yì-'nyán jǎng-le 'dwō gāw-a! ‖Prices have shot up since the war started. kāy-'jàng yǐ-'hèw wù-'jyà dēw 'jǎng-le.

To shoot out (*as flames*) 'pū-chū-láy-le. ‖I opened the furnace door and the flames shot out. wǒ 'yì kāy lú-'mér, hwǒ-'myáw 'pū-de yí-'shyà-dz jyèw 'chū-láy-le.

To shoot an arrow shè-'jyàn.

To shoot a goal gūng-jìn yí-ge 'chyèwr-cnywú. ‖Just at the last moment he managed to shoot a goal. dzwèy-'hèw-yì-'fēn-'jūng tā háy gūng-jìn-le yí-ge-'chyéwr-chywu.

To shoot pictures jàw-'shyàng. ‖We're planning to shoot a few pictures this morning. wǒ-men 'dǎ-swàn jyēr-'dzǎw-chen chywù 'jàw jǐ-jāng-'shyàng.

To shoot questions 'wèn-le yí-jèn-'wèr-tí. ‖He shot questions at us. tā 'wèn-le wǒ-men yí-jèn-'wèn-tí.

(*New growth*) nèn-'yár; shīn-'yár; shīn-'jēr; shīn-'tyáw; 'jyàn-dz. ‖The new shoots are coming up. shīn-'yár 'chū-láy-le.

Bamboo shoots (jú-') swěn.

SHOP. 'pù-dz; *in compounds, with preceding elements specifying the kind of thing sold or done*, pù, dyàn, jwāng, háng, gwǎn, gàng, 'chwáng-dz, táng, léw, jāy, swǒ, fywú, jywū, jyā, shè; *e.g.*, bookshop shū-'pù; barber shop lǐ-fǎ-'dyàn; bicycle shop dž-shíng-chē-'háng; butcher shop (*non-Mohammedan, therefore selling pork*) jū-rèw-'gàng, (*Mohammedan, selling no pork and concentrating on lamb*) yáng-rèw-'chwáng-dz. ‖I'm looking for a tobacco shop. wǒ jèng 'jǎw yān-jywǎr-'pù-ne. ‖You'll have to take these to a shoe repair shop. nǐ děy bǎ 'jèy-shyē-shyé ná-dàw 'shyēw-li-'shyé-de-'pù-dz-li chywù. ‖Let's walk down the street and look in the shop windows. dzám wàng 'nèy-byar 'dzěw-dzěw 'kàn-kan 'pù-dz-de-'chwāng-hu.

(*Factory*) gūng-'chǎng. ‖He's on the night shift at the shop. tā dzày nèy-ge-gūng-'chǎng-li dīng 'yè-bān.

To shop mǎy 'dūng-shi; to shop around 'kàn-yí-kàn. ‖Where are the best places to shop? 'shéme-dì-fang mǎy 'dūng-shi dzwèy 'hǎw-wa? ‖I want to shop around a little before I decide. wǒ děy 'shyān 'kàn lyǎng-jyǎer dzày 'mǎy.

To shut up shop shew-'tǎr. ‖It's late; let's shut up shop and go home. tyān bù-'dzǎw-le, dzám shew-'tǎr hwéy-'jyā-ba.

To talk shop. ‖He's always talking shop. *is expressed as* He never says even three sentences without mentioning his own profession. tā 'sān-jywù-hwà bù-'lí běn-'háng.

SHORE. àn. ‖How far is it from here to the other shore? jèr lí dwèy-'àn yěw dwō-'ywǎn? ‖Let's pull the boat farther up on shore. 'dzám dzày bǎ-'chwán dwǒ wàng 'àn-shang 'lā-la.

(*Seashore*) hǎy-'byǎr-shang, hǎy-'bīn, hǎy-'àn. ‖I want to go to the shore for a vacation. wǒ yàw dàw hǎy-'byǎr-shang chywù 'shyēw-shi-shyēw-shi.

To be on shore leave shyēw-'jyà. ‖I'm on shore leave. wǒ 'jèng-dzày shyēw-'jyà.

SHORT. (*Not long*) dwǎn. Short story dwǎn-'pyān-'shyǎw-shwōr; short wave dwǎn-'bwō. ‖I want my hair cut short. wǒ yàw bǎ 'téw-fa jyǎw 'dwǎn-dyǎr. ‖The days are short now. tyān 'dwǎn-le. ‖This coat is too short. jèy-jyàn-shàng-'shēr tày 'dwǎn-le. *But* ‖It's a short distance from here to the lake. *is expressed as* From here to the lake it's very near. tsúng-'jèr dàw-'hú-nèr 'hěn 'jìn *or* (*meaning* not far) °bù-'ywǎn. ‖We took a short walk in the afternoon. *is expressed as* In the afternoon we walked a little. 'shyà-wǔ wǒ-men 'dzěw-le °yì-dyǎr-'lù. *or* °'jǐ-bù-'lù. *or as* In the afternoon we walked around a little. 'shyà-wǔ 'wǒ-men 'sàn-le-sàn 'bù.

(*Not tall; low*) ǎy. ‖She is a very short girl. tā jèy-ge-nywǔ-'háy-dz 'gèr tày 'ǎy.

(*Not enough*) bú-'gèw; (*less*) shǎw. ‖Don't let them give you short weight in the store. byé ràng nèy-ge-'pù-dz gěy-ni bú-'gèw-'fèn-lyang. *or* byé ràng nèy-ge-'pù-dz 'shǎw gě-ni. ‖That clerk short-changed me. nèy-ge-'hwǒ-ji 'jǎw-gěy wǒ-de-'chyán bú-'gèw. *or* nèy-ge-'hwǒ-ji shǎw 'jǎw-gěy wǒ 'chyán-le.

(*Rude; expressed mildly*) tsū; (*more emphatic*) yě; (*bad mannered*) méy 'gwēy-jywu. ‖He was very short with us. tā gēn wǒ-men tày méy 'gwēy-jywu-le.

(*Abruptly; immediately*) mǎ-'shàng, lì-'kè, lì-shŕ-'kè, dēng-'shŕ, dāng-'shŕ, lì-'shŕ. ‖He stopped short when he saw us. tā 'kàn-jyan wǒ-men mǎ-'shàng jyèw 'jàn-ju-le. ‖She pulled the horse up short. *is expressed as* She reined the horse in firmly. tā bǎ-'mǎ lēy-jù-le.

To be short of *or* to run short of (*to lack*) dwǎn 'dwǎn-dyǎr, chywē, 'chywē-dyǎr, 'chywe-fá, chyàn, 'chyàn-dyǎr; to run short (*to be insufficient*) bú-'gèw, chà. ‖I'm a little short of money. wǒ 'dwǎn-dyǎr 'chyán. ‖Our supplies were running short. *is expressed as* Our supplies were becoming not enough. wǒ-men-de-'dūng-shi yàw bú-'gèw-le. ‖We ran short of paper. *is expressed as* Our paper was not enough. wǒ-men-de-'jŕ háy 'chà-dyǎr.

To cut short swō-'dwǎn-le, tí-'chyán 'jyé-su, ràng . . . 'shǎw. ‖Her mother's illness cut their vacation short. *is expressed as* Her mother being sick made them take fewer days' vacation. tā-'mǔ-chin yí-'bìng °ràng tā-men 'shǎw 'wár-de jǐ-tyān.

To fall short (*not to reach*) méy-. . .-dàw. ‖The factory fell short of its goal. jèy-ge-gūng-'chǎng méy-'dzwò-dàw 'ywán-lay-de-'jì-hwa. ‖The picture fell short of our expectations. jèy-ge-dyàn-'yěngr méy-'shyǎng-dàw nèm chà-'jìn.

In short *or* to make a long story short (*as a whole*) dzǔng-'jŕ, dzǔng-ér-yán-'jŕ; (*simply, in a word*) gān-'tswèy (*to speak simply*) 'gān-tswèy 'shwō-ba; (*to cut it and speak briefly*) 'jyǎn-dwǎn-jyé 'shwō. ‖I have neither the time nor the inclination; in short, I refuse wǒ shŕ 'jì méy 'gūng-fu yèw méy 'shìng-chywù, gān 'tswèy, wǒ bú-'gàn.

Just short of 'chà-dyǎr, 'chà-bu-dwō, 'chà-yì-chǎr, 'jī-hu, jī-jī 'hū, kwày. ‖He came just short of missing the train. tā 'chà-dyar jyèw méy-'gǎn-shàng 'chē. ‖They stopped just short of the railroad tracks. *is expressed as* They almost went on the railroad tracks. tā-men 'chà-dyǎr 'dzěw-daw hwǒ-chē-'dàw-shang. ‖It's just short of ten o'clock. 'kwày dàw 'shŕ-dyǎn-jūng-le. *or* 'chà-yi-dyǎr jyèw yàw dàw 'shŕ-dyǎn-jūng-le.

Nothing short of (*absolutely; certainly*) jyàn-'jŕ-de; (*just*) 'jyèw-shr; (*only*) 'jŕ yěw, chú-'fēy . . . bū-, fēy(-děy) . . . °tsáy *or* °bu-. ‖His action is nothing short of criminal. tā-dzwò-de-'shèr jyàn-'jŕ-de shŕ fàn-'fǎ. ‖Nothing short of a miracle will do any good. 'fēy-děy 'shén-shyān tsáy 'shíng-nga.

Shorthand sù-'shyě, sù-'jì.

Short memory 'jì-shing bù-'hǎw, 'jì-shing tày 'hwày, *or* (*when you can't remember someone you've met before,*) *expressed as* stupid eyes yǎn-'jwō.

Short temper 'pí-chi °bù-'hǎw, °tày 'hwày, 'tù-'dzǎw.

To make short work of. ‖We made short work of that argument. *is expressed as* We in an instant stopped up their mouths. wǒ-men yí-'shyàr jyèw gěy tā-men 'dǐng-hwéy-chywu-le. ‖He made short work of the job. *is expressed as* He had the job done in an instant. tā yí-'shyàr jyèw bǎ nèy-ge-'shŕ-ching 'dzwò-le.

A short (*short circuit*). *Expressed with the verb* to short circuit dyàn-lù bù-'tūng, 'byē-le, 'hwày-le (*to burn out*) shāw-'hwày-le. ‖Check the radio and see where the short is. 'kàn-kan jèy-ge-wú-shyàn-'dyàn nǎr 'byē-le.

Shorts dwǎn-'kù-dz; (*undershorts*) shyǎw-'kù-dz. ‖Don't you think she looks nice in shorts? nǐ shwō tā chwān dwǎn-'kù-dz dwō-hǎw-'kàn-ne?

SHOT. (*Discharge of a gun*) 'chyāng-shyǎng. ‖Did you hear a shot? nǐ 'tīng-jyan yì-shēng-'chyāng-shyǎng-ma? or expressed as Did you hear someone shoot? nǐ 'tīng-jyan fàng-'chyāng-le-ma?

(*Act of shooting*). Take a shot at (*with a gun*) dǎ . . . yì-'chyāng, (*with any weapon*) dǎ yí-'shyà-dz. ‖He took a shot at the sniper. tā chùng-je nèy-ge-'fú-bīng 'dǎ-le yí-'shyà-dz. ‖Let me take a shot at it. wǒ láy 'dǎ-tā yì-'chyāng. or expressed as Let me try. ràng-wo 'shr̀ yí-shyà.

(*Aim*). ‖Good shot! hǎ'-'chyāng! or expressed as Shot very accurately! dǎ le jēn 'jwěn! ‖That was a bad shot. is expressed as The gun was shot poorly. nèy-'chyāng dǎ-de bù-'hǎw.

(*Marksman*) chyāng-'shěw. ‖He's a good shot. is expressed as He's an expert rifleman. tā shr̀ 'yí-ge-shén-chyāng-'shěw. or as He shoots a gun very well. tā dǎ-'chyāng dǎ-de hěn 'hǎw.

(*Lead pellets*) chyāng-'dzěr, 'shā-dz. ‖He loaded the gun with bird shot. tā 'chyāng-li jwāng-de shr̀ dǎ-'nyǎwr-de-'shā-dz.

(*Photograph*) shyàng-'pyār. ‖I took a beautiful shot of the mountains. nèy-jāng-dày-'shān-de-shyàng-'pyār 'jàw-de hěn 'hǎw. But also ‖I took a few good shots of the mountains. is expressed as I took several beautiful mountain views. wǒ 'jàw-le jǐ-jāng-tǐng-hǎw-'kàn-de-'shān-jǐng.

(*Injection*) jù-'shè (*literary*). To get a shot shŕ-'shíng jù-'shè; (*colloquial*) dǎ-'jēn. ‖Have you had your typhoid shots? nǐ dǎ-le shāng-'hán-'jēn-le-ma?

A shot in the arm (*figuratively*) ‖His visit was like a shot in the arm to the office. tā jèy-yí-'láy gěy wǒ-men 'gūng-shr̀-'fángr-li 'dǎ-le yì-mǎ-'fēy-'jēn.

(*Drink*) expressed as a mouthful kěw. ‖I need a shot of whisky. wǒ děy °'hē (or °'láy) yì-kěw-wēy-shr̀-'jì.

A long shot (*term from horse racing*) lěng-'mén; or (*gambling terms referring to a bet on just one number*) 'gū-dìng, dú-'mér. ‖He likes to play long shots, and once in a while he makes a lot of money. tā 'shǐ-hwān yā lěng-'mén, 'kě-shr̀ 'yěw shŕ-hew tā yě néng yíng bù-shǎw-'chyán. But ‖I'm going to try to get a plane reservation for this afternoon; it's a long shot, but maybe I can get one. is expressed as I'm going to go to get a plane reservation for this afternoon; I'm only making a try, but maybe I can get it. jyèr-'shyà-wǔ wǒ yàw chyùw 'dìng yí-ge-fēy-jī-'pyàw, bú-gwò shr̀ °'pèng-peng 'shr̀-shr (or °'mēng-meng 'shr̀-shr, or °'jwàng-jwang 'shr̀-shr) méy-'jwěr wǒ jyèw shywǔ 'dìng-jáw.

A shot in the dark is expressed with to try it once 'mēng (or 'jwàng, 'pèng) yí-shyàr. ‖It's just a shot in the dark. nà 'bú-gwò 'jyèw-shr̀ 'mēng yí-shyàr.

SHOULD. (*Ought to*) 'yīng-gāy, 'yīng-dāng. ‖I should go. wǒ 'yīng-dāng 'dzěw-le. ‖I thought I should go. is expressed as I did think I ought to go. wǒ 'dàw-shr̀ 'shyǎng-gwò wǒ 'yīng-dāng 'chyùw láy-je. ‖They should be here, by this time. tā-men 'jèy-ge-gūng-fu 'yīng-gāy 'dàw-jèr-le.

(*Were to; in a conditional clause*). ‖If it should rain, do you still want to go? is expressed as If it rains, will you still want to go? 'rè-shr̀ shyà-'ywǔ, nǐ 'háy yàw 'chyùw-ma?

SHOULDER. (*Part of the human body*) jyān-'bǎngr, 'bǎng-dz. ‖My shoulder hurts. wǒ jyān-'bǎngr 'téng. ‖Put your head on my shoulder. bǎ nǐ-de-'nǎw-day 'jěn-de wǒ-jyān-'bǎngr-shang.

(*Part of a garment*) 'yī-shang-de-jyān-'bǎngr. ‖I don't want the shoulders padded. wǒ 'yī-shang-jyān-'bǎngr-nèr 'bú-yùng 'dyàn.

(*Animal's upper foreleg*) 'jěw-dz. ‖The butcher has several (*whole*) shoulders hanging in his shop. nèy-ge-jū-rèw-'gàng-li 'gwà-je hǎw-jǐ-'gè-'jěw-dz.

(*Side of a road*) lù-'byār, dàw-'byār. ‖Keep on the pavement, the shoulder's soft. byé chū-le lù-'myàr, lù-'byār-shang tày 'rwǎn.

Give someone the cold shoulder (*be cold to someone*) gēn . . . lěng ('lěng-dàn). ‖What did you give him the cold shoulder for? nǐ 'wèy-shéme gēn-ta 'nà-me-'lěng-dàn-na?

To shoulder (*to take or carry on one's shoulders or upper back; as a pack or person*) káng; (*to carry a pole, weighed at each end, on one shoulder*) dān, tyāw. He was shouldering the pack. tā 'káng-je nèy-bāw-'dūng-shi láy-je. ‖We shouldered our guns and set out. wǒ-men 'káng-je 'chyāng jyèw chū-'fā-le.

(*To push, as with the shoulder*) jǐ. ‖We shouldered our way through the mob. 'wǒ-men tsúng rén-'chywún-li 'jǐ-chū-láy-le.

To shoulder the responsibility fù-'dzé, or fù (or 'dān-fù) 'dzé-rèn. ‖We had to shoulder all the responsibility. wǒ-men děy fù 'wán-chywán 'dzé-rèn. Also Who'll shoulder the blame for this? is expressed as If there's a mistake, who will take the responsibility? yàw-shr 'chū-le-'tswòr shéy fù-'dzé-ya?

SHOW (SHOWN). (*To point out*) jr̆. ‖He showed me where he lived. tā 'jr̆-gey wo tā dzày-'nǎr 'jù. ‖Can you show me the place on a map? nǐ 'kě-yi dzày dì-'tú-shang 'jr̆-gey wo nèy-ge-'dì-fangr-ma?

(*To go with and point out*) dày . . . ('kàn), lǐng . . . 'kàn. ‖Could you show me the way? láw-'jyà 'dày-wo 'chyùw. ‖Will you show me the room? láw-'jyà 'dày-wo kàn-kan 'wū-dz. ‖I'd like to show you around. is expressed as I'd like to take you everywhere to look. wǒ shyǎng 'lǐng-ni 'gè-chùr 'kàn-kan. But ‖Show the man in. is expressed as Tell the man to come in. bǎ 'nèy-ge-rén chǐng 'jìn-lay. ‖Show him out, please. láw-'jyà sùng-ta 'chū-chywu.

(*To let someone see*) ná (*or* dzwò, *etc.*) gěy . . . °'kàn *or* °'chyáw. ‖Please show me some red ties. láw-'jyà ná dyǎr-'húng-yán-shǎr-de-lǐng-'dày gěy-wo 'kàn-kan. ‖Show me how to do it. 'dzwò-gěy wo 'kàn-kan.

(*To instruct*) 'gàw-su. ‖Show me how to do it. *meaning* Tell me how to do it. 'gàw-su wo 'dzěme 'dzwò. (*See above, if the meaning is* Demonstrate how to do it). ‖Could you show me the way? *is expressed as* Please tell me how to go. láw-'jyà 'gàw-su wo dzěme 'dzěw.

(*To be seen*) lèw. ‖Does my slip show? wǒ-de-chèn-'chywún 'lèw-bu-lèw? ‖Put those letters under the book where they won't show. *is expressed as* Put those letters under the book; then they can't be seen. bǎ nèy-shyē-'shìn gē-dzay nèy-ge-'shū-di-shya bú-yàw jyàw-rén 'kàn-jyan. ‖I think my arm is hurt, but it doesn't show. *is expressed as* I think my arm is wounded, but you can't see it. wǒ 'jywé-de wǒ-de-'gē-be shèw-'shāng-le, 'kě-shr kàn-bu-chū-'láy.

(*To let be seen*) bǎ . . . 'lèw-chū-láy. To show one's face lèw-'myǎr; to show one's teeth tsz-'yá. ‖That remark of his shows his mean disposition. tā nèy-jǐ-jywù-'hwà bǎ tā-de-hwày-'pí-chi dēw 'lèw-chū-láy-le. ‖The dog showed his teeth. nèy-ge-'gěw tsz-je 'yá. ‖He won't dare show his face here again. tā bù-'gǎn lèw-'myàr-le.

(*To display*). ‖She doesn't show any consideration for others. *is expressed as* She doesn't think of other people. tā bù-gěy 'byé-rén 'shyǎng-shyang. ‖Try not to show any partiality. *is expressed as* Don't put your heart on one side. byé pyān-shīn-'yǎr. ‖His work showed great concentration. *is expressed as* From his work you can see he expended concentration. tsúng tā-de-'gūng-dzwò-lǐ kàn-de-chū-'láy shr hěn fèy-le yì-fān-'sz-swǒ. ‖Do you think he shows any improvement, Doctor? *is expressed as* Do you think he's getting better, Doctor? nín 'jywé-je (*or* kàn) tā jyàn 'hǎw-ma? ‖His work shows signs of improvement. *is expressed as* His work looks as though it's improving. ta-de-'gūng-dzwò kàn-'yàngr hěn 'yěw 'jìn-bù.

(*To indicate*). ‖The thermometer shows a temperature of 85° in this room. *is expressed as* In this room the thermometer reads 85°. jèy-'wū-li hán-shŭ-'byǎw shr bā-shŕ-'wǔ-dù. ‖This gauge shows that the car needs oil. *is expressed as* From the gauge you can see you must add oil to the car. tsúng jèy-ge-yéw-'byǎw-shang 'ké-yi kàn-chū-lay jèy-ge-'chē děy jyā 'yěw.

(*To prove*) 'jèng-míng. ‖They weren't able to show why they couldn't go. tā-men bù-'néng 'jyě-shŕ 'wèy-shéme tā-men méy-'néng 'chywù. ‖I won't believe it unless it's shown to me. chú-'fēy gěy-wo 'jèng-míng yí-'shyàr, yàw-bù-rán wǒ bú-'shìn.

(*To present, in a theater*) yǎn, 'byǎw-yǎn. ‖What are they showing at the theater? shì-'ywán-dz-li yǎn 'shéme-ne? ‖They're showing one of the new foreign films. tā-men nèr 'yǎn yí-ge-shīn-de 'wày-gwo-dyàn-'yíngr.

(*To present, in a store*) bǎy. ‖The shops are showing some crazy hats this season. jèy-shyē-'pù-dz jèy 'jyèr-li 'bǎy-le shyē-shī-'chí-gǔ-'gwày-de-'màw-dz.

To show off (*to be vain*) 'shyǎn-bey, lèw yì-'shěw; chū 'fēng-téw; to show *something* off ná . . . °'lèw (°'shyǎn-bey) ‖Don't you think he shows off a good deal? nǐ bù-jywé-de tā °tǐng ày 'shyǎn-bey-ma? *or* °hěn chū 'fēng-téw-ma? ‖She was showing off her jewels. tā bǎ tā-de-húng-'hwò hěn 'lèw-le yí-shyà-dz.

To show up (*to appear, of a person; to show one's face*) lèw-'myàr; (*to contrast*) chèn, shyǎn. ‖We waited and waited, but he never showed up. wǒ-men 'děng-le yèw děng tā shr-'jūng méy-lèw-'myàr. ‖The design shows up well against the dark background. dyèr-de-'yán-shar-'àn 'chèn-de jèy-ge-'hwā-yàngr hěn hǎw-'kàn.

(*To expose*). ‖I intend to show up your dishonesty. *is expressed as* I intend to take off your mask. wǒ 'dǎ-swàn bǎ nǐ-de-jyǎ-myàn-'jywù gěy 'jāy-shyà-lay. *or as* I want to uncover the truth about you. wǒ-de-'yì-sz shr yàw 'jyē nǐ-de-'dǐ. *or as* I want to disclose the truth. wǒ-de-'yì-sz shr yàw 'gěy-nǐ 'shyè-shye 'dǐ. *or as* I want to shake out the truth. wǒ-de-'yì-sz shr yàw bǎ nǐ-de-'dǐ gěy 'děw-lew-'děw-lew.

A show (*play*) shì; hwà-'jywù; (*movie*) dyàn-'yěngr; (*stage show, dancing*) tyàw-wǔ; (*musical comedy or opera*) gē-'jywù; (*vaudeville*) dzā-'shwǎr; (*leg show, burlesque*) dà-twěy-'shì. ‖Did you go to the show last night? nǐ dzwó-'wǎn-shang chywù kàn 'shì-chywù-le-ma?

Dog show sày-gěw-'hwèy, gěw-'jǔng-bǐ-'sày. To show a dog ná-gěw chywù 'bǐ-bǐ.

To make a show of (*to pretend*) jyǎ, jwāng, jyǎ-'jwāng. ‖She makes a show of courtesy. tā shr jyǎ 'kè-chi. ‖He makes a show of working hard. tā jwāng-de hǎw-'shyàng tǐng yùng-'gūng-'shŕ-de.

To make a show of oneself (*to act up*) shyàn-'yǎn; (*to lose face*) dyēw-'lyǎn, dyēw-'rén, chū-'chěw; (*to make people laugh*) nàw 'shyàw-hwàr. ‖He made an awful show of himself at that party. dzày nèy-ge-yàn-'hwèy-li tā 'nàw-le ge-'shyàw-hwàr.

To take a show of hands (*to raise hands*) jywǔ-'shěw. ‖We voted by a show of hands. wǒ-men jywǔ-'shěw byǎw-'jywé.

SHOWER. (*Short rain*) yí-jèn-bàw-'ywǔ, yí-jèn-dà-'ywǔ. A shower of hail yí-jèn-'báw-dz. ‖Wait until the shower is over. 'děng jèy-jèn-bàw-'ywǔ 'gwò-chywù.

Shower bath. Take a shower chūng-'dzǎw, shǐ 'pēn-dz, shǐ 'pēn-téwr; *or* (*literary*) lín-'ywù; to take a cold shower 'chūng ge-'lěng-shwěy-'dzǎw *or* ná 'lyáng-shwěy 'chūng-chung. ‖You can take a shower here after the game. wár-'wán-le nǐ 'ké-yi dzày-'jèr chūng ge-'dzǎw.

Shower (*spraying apparatus*) 'pēn-dz, pēn-'téwr. ‖The shower isn't working. jèy-ge-'pēn-dz 'hwày-le.

(*Spray*) dwēy, dzwēy. ‖The wind blew a shower of leaves against the house. 'fēng bǎ nèy-yì-'dzwēy-shù-'yè-dz chùng-je nèy-ge-'fáng-dz 'gwā-gwo-chywu·le. ‖We were caught in a shower of sparks from the burning building. tsúng nèy-ge-jáw-'hwǒ-de-'fáng-dz-nèr láy-le yì-'dwēy-hwǒ-'shyēngr fēy-dàw wǒ-men 'shēn-shang-le.

To shower. ‖Their friends showered them with presents. tā-men-de-'péng-yew sùng-gey tā-men 'hǎw-shye-'lǐ-wù. ‖We were showered with good wishes when we left for our trip. wǒ-men chǐ-'shēn de-shŕ-hew, tā-men gēn wǒ-men shwō-le 'hǎw-shyē-yí-lù-píng-'ān-yí-lèy-de-'hwà.

SHUT. gwān(-shang). ‖Shut the door and sit down. bǎ-mén 'gwān-shang 'dzwǒ yǐ-hwěr. ‖They shut the dog in the house. tā-men bǎ-'gěw 'gwān-dzày 'wū-li-le. ‖Is it shut tight? gwān-'jǐn-le-ma? ‖Something is going on behind those shut doors. nàr gwān-je-'mén jwěn yěw shéme-'shèr-ne.

To shut down (*stop*) gwān, tíng; (*rest*) shyē; (*stop work*) tíng-'gūng, shyē-'yè; (*close the doors*) gwān-'mér; (*fail*) dǎw. ‖How long will this factory be shut down? jèy-ge-gūng-'chǎng tíng 'dwō-shǎw-'shŕ-hew?

To shut off gwān, nìng; (*to break a connection*) 'myè-le. ‖Shut off the motor. bǎ fā-dùng-'jī 'gwān-shang. ‖Shut off the ignition. bǎ-chē 'gwān-le-ba. ‖Shut off the water; it makes too much noise. *is expressed as* Shut off the water valve; the noise is too great. bǎ shwěy-'mén 'gwān-shang, shēngr tày 'dà. *But* ‖The water is shut off in the winter to keep the pipes from freezing. *is expressed as* In the winter the water is stopped to save the pipes from bursting. 'dūng-tyān jyèw bǎ-'shwěy 'tíng-le, 'shěng-de bǎ 'gwǎn-dz dùng-'hwày-le.

To be shut out jìn-bú-'chywù, gwān-de-'wày-tew. ‖Don't forget your key, or you'll be shut out of the house. byé wàng-le 'yàw-shr, bù-'rán jìn-bú-'chywù 'wū-dz-le. ‖He went home, but his wife shut him out. tā hwéy-'jyā-le, 'kě-shr tā-'tày-tay bú-ràng-ta 'jìn-chywu. *or* tā hwéy-'jyā-le, 'kě-shr tā-'tày-tay bǎ-ta 'gwān-dzày 'wày-tew-le.

To shut up (*to close, lock*) swǒ, gwān. ‖When they went·to the country, they shut up their house. tā-men shyà-'shyāng de-shŕ-hew bǎ 'fáng-dz 'swǒ-chǐ-láy-le.

(*To put in jail*) bǎ . . . °'gwān (°'jywān). ‖Shut him up for the night. bǎ-ta 'gwān yí-'yè.

(*To keep indoors*) gwān-dzày 'wū-dz-li. ‖Her work kept her shut up for hours. tā-de-'gūng-dzwò bǎ-ta gwān-dzày wū-dz-li bàn-'tyān. ‖He shut himself up to study for exams. tā bǎ dž-'gěr 'gwān-dzày 'wūr-li 'ywù-bèy kǎw-'shŕ.

‖Shut up! *is expressed as* Don't talk. byé 'shwō-le. *or, more emphatic, as* Don't talk nonsense. byé °hú-'shwō-le. *or* °shyā-'shwō-le. *or, most emphatic* byé °hú-'shwō (*or* °shyā-'shwō) bá-'dàw-le.

SICK. bìng; *or, meaning* indisposed, out of sorts nán-'shèw, bù-'shū-fu, bù·'shū-tan, bù-hé-'shŕ. ‖I'm feeling a little sick. wǒ 'jywé-de yěw-dyǎr bù-'shū-fu. ‖The child has a sick look about him. 'nèy-háy-dz 'kàn-je shyàng yěw-'bìng-de-'yàng-dz. ‖He's sick in bed with pneumónia. *is expressed as* He got pneumonia and is lying in bed. tā dé-le fèy-'yán 'tǎng-dzày 'chwáng-shang-le.

(*Nauseated*) 'ě-shin; (*about to vomit*) yàw 'tù. ‖I'm going to be sick. wǒ 'ě-shin. *or* wǒ yàw 'tù.

(*Sick people*) bìng-'rén. ‖This hospital takes very good care of the sick. jèy-ge-yī-'ywàn dwèy-bìng-'rén-'jàw-gù-de hěn 'hǎw.

To be sick of. (*Not feel like*) 'ıan-de; (*be bored, disgusted*) nì *or* 'nì-fán; (*be disgusted*) tǎw-'yàn; (*not want to*) bú-'ywàn-yi; (*not be pleased at*) bù-gāw-'shing. ‖I'm sick of working. wǒ lǎn-de dzwò-'shŕ. *or* wǒ dzwò-'shŕ dzwò-'nì-le. ‖We're sick and tired of these complaints. jèy-yàngr-'bèw-ywàn-de-'hwà wǒ-men tīng-'nì-le.

To make one sick ràng . . . °'nì-de-heng (°'nì-fán, °tǎw-'yàn); (*be stupid*) méy-'yì-sz; (*be dull, no fun*) wú-'lyáw. ‖That sort of thing makes me sick. nèy-jǔng-'shŕ-ching ràng-wo jywé-je tǎw-'yàn.

SIDE. (*One of the surfaces of an object*) byàr, myàr; (*end*) téw. Front side 'jèng-myàr, 'chyán-byàr, 'chyán-myàr; back side, rear side 'hèw-byàr, 'hèw-myàr, 'hèw-téw, (*if the object has only two sides, like a mirror, also* 'fǎn-myàr, 'bèy-myàr); left side 'dzwǒ-myàr, 'dzwǒ-byàr; right side 'yèw-myàr, 'yèw-byàr; top side 'shàng-myàr, 'shàng-byàr, *or* 'shàng-tew °'nèy-myàr (°'nèy-byàr); bottom side 'dǐ-myàr, 'shyà-myàr, 'shyà-téw, 'shyà-byàr, 'dǐ-shyà °'nèy-myàr (°'nèy-byàr). ‖A dice has six sides. yí-ge-'shǎy-dz yěw lyèw-'myàr. ‖The top side of the silver box is scratched. yín-'héer-'shàng-myàr 'hwá-le shyē-'dàw-dz. ‖The south side of the house needs painting. fáng-dz-'nán-byàr-de-'chyáng děy 'shwā-shwā-le. (*But in the following sentence, only* myàr *can be used.*) ‖The right side of the material is much brighter than the wrong side. jèy-ge-lyàw-dz-de-'jèng-myàr bǐ 'fǎn-myàr lyàng-de 'dwō.

(*Surface not top or bottom*) byàr, 'páng-byàr, 'páng-myàr, 'tsè-myàr. ‖The label is on the side of the box. 'fēng-tyáw dzày 'shyá-dz-de-'tsè-myàr-ne. ‖The picture is taken from the side. jèy-jāng-shyàng-'pyàr shŕ tsúng 'tsè-myàr 'jàw-de. ‖There's a big garden at the side of the house. fáng-dz-páng-'byàr yěw yí-ge-'dà-hwā-'ywár. *But* ‖The lamp has been knocked over on its side. *is expressed as* The lamp has been hit and is lying down. bǎ-'dēng pèng 'tǎng-shya-le. ‖The wrecked car is lying on its side. *is expressed as* The wrecked car is lying down. nèy-ge-pwò-'chē 'tǎng-shya-le.

(*Edge, line bounding a figure*) byān, byàr. ‖The land is in the shape of a triangle, with each side 300 feet long. nèy-kwày-'dì shŕ ge-sān-'jyǎwr-shíng, měy-'byàr shŕ 'sān-bǎy-chŕ-'cháng.

(*Part*) byār, myàr; **east side** (*of a city*) 'dūng chéng, *etc. for other directions.* ‖**When she talks, you can't even hear her on the other side of the room.** tā shwō-'hwà de-shŕ-hew dzày wū-dz 'nèy-byār dēw tīng-bú-'jyàn. ‖**His store is on the east side.** tā-de-'pù-dz dzày 'dūng-chéng.

(*Bank*) byār, àn; (*riverbank*) hé-'yàr. ‖**They crossed to the other side of the river.** tā-men 'gwò-hé dàw 'nèy-byār chywù-le. *or* tā-men gwò-'hé dàw 'dwèy-àn chywù-le. ‖**There are some trees along the side of the river.** hé-'yàr-shang 'yěw shyē-ge-'shù.

(*Slope*) pwōr. ‖**They ran down the side of the hill.** tā-men 'pǎw-shya shān-'pwōr láy-le.

(*Part of the body*) byār. ‖**His left side is paralyzed.** tā 'dzwǒ-byār 'bàn-shēn bù-'swéy. ‖**He's wounded more seriously on the left side.** tā-'shēn-shang 'dzwǒ-byār shèw-de shàng 'jùng. ‖**She told the child to stay close at her side while they crossed the street.** gwò-'jyē de-'shŕ-hewr tā 'gàw-su nèy-háy-dz jīn 'gēn dzày tā-páng-'byār. *But* ‖**He's paralyzed on one side.** *is expressed as* Half of his body is paralyzed. tā 'bàn-shēn bù-'swéy. ‖**He stood with his hands at his side.** *is expressed as* He stood with his hands dangling. tā 'dā-le-je shěw 'jàn-je.

(*Part of an animal's carcass*). shàn. ‖**We bought a whole side of bacon.** wǒ-men 'mǎy-le yí-ge-'jěng-shàn-de-'là-rèw.

(*Partisan group*) byār, téwr; (*point of view*) fāng-'myàn. ‖**Whose side are you on?** nǐ shŕ nǎy-'téwr-de? ‖**He fought for the other side in the last war.** 'shàng-hwéy-dǎ-'jàng tā dzày 'nèy-byār.

(*Aspect*) fāng-'myàn. ‖**Look at every side of the matter.** bǎ jèy-jyàn-'shŕ-ching-de-'gè-fāng-'myàn 'dēw 'kàn-kan. ‖**We discussed the problem from all sides.** wǒ-men bǎ nèy-ge-'wèn-tí tsúng 'gè-fāng-'myàn 'tǎw-lwèn-le-'tǎw-lwèn.

On the side. ‖**He makes some money working on the side.** *is expressed as* He has a job and earns a little money working at odd jobs besides. tā dzwò 'jèng-shŕ yǐ-'wày háy dzwò 'líng-hwó jèng-le-dyǎr 'chyán. ‖**Besides the salary, you can pick up quite a little on the side.** *is expressed as* Besides the salary, you can get quite a lot of extra money. dzày jèng-'shīn yǐ-'wày, nǐ háy néng 'ná bù-'shǎw-de-'líng-chyán. ‖**The store sells mostly clothes, but they carry some household goods on the side.** *is expressed as* This store sells clothes for the most part; besides, they sell some household goods. jèy-ge-'pù-dz 'dà-bù-fèn shŕ mày-'bù, °'lìng-'wày (°dày-'shěwr, °dày-je, °dày-je 'shěwr, °fù-'dày) háy 'mày-dyǎr r-yùng-'pǐn.

Side by side 'bìng-je; (*shoulder to shoulder*) bìng-je 'jyār, bìng-'jyàn; (*together*) dzày yí-'kwàr. ‖**We skated side by side.** wǒ-men bìng-je 'jyār-de lyēw-'bīng.

To choose sides tyāw-'byār. ‖**Let's choose sides and start playing.** dzá-men tyāw-'byār kǎy-shŕ 'láy-ba.

To take sides. ‖**It's difficult to take sides on this question.** *is expressed as* On this question, it's hard

to say who's right and who's wrong. jèy-ge-'wèn-tí hěn nán shwō shèy ·'dwèy shéy bú-'dwèy. ‖**Everybody took sides for or against him.** *is expressed as* If they didn't oppose him they approved of him. tām bú-shr fǎn-'dwèy ta-de, jyèw-shr 'dzàn-chéng ta-de.

(*Not front or center*) páng, páng-'byār-de. ‖**Please use the side door.** chǐng dzěw 'páng-mér. ‖**She's on the side porch.** tā dzày páng-'byār-de-'láng-dz-shang-ne.

(*Not the main: not important*) bú-'jùng-yàw, bú-'yàw-jǐn; (*little*) shyǎw; (*rather irrelevant*) wú-'gwān-jǐn-'yàw, bù-'gwān 'tùng-yǎng, méy 'dà-gwān-shi. ‖**I think you're bringing up only side issues.** wǒ 'jywé-de nǐ jř 'tí-chǐ-le 'shyē-ge-bú-'jùng-yaw-de-'wèn-tí.

To side. ‖**She always sides with us in any argument.** *is expressed as* When there is an argument, she always stands on our side. yěw jēng-lwèn-de-'shŕ-hewr tā 'cháng shř gēn 'wǒ-men 'jàn-dzày yì-'byār. ‖**His wife always sides with him.** *is expressed as* His wife always helps him speak. tā-de-'tày-tay lǎw bāng-je 'tā shwō.

Sideline 'dày-je, fù-'dày, dày-'shěwr; (*extra*) lìng-'wày, gé-'wày, yǐ-'wày. ‖**We carry sports equipment as a sideline.** wǒ-men fù-'dày háy 'mày-dyǎr 'tǐ-ywù-yùng-'pǐn.

Sidelines. ‖**He watched the fistfight from the sidelines.** tā °dzày 'páng-byār (*or* °'dzày yì-'byār) 'kàn-je rén-jya dǎ-'jyà.

Sidetrack (*to change the subject*) dǎ-'chà, bǎ 'hwà-téwr 'chà-kāy, 'chà-gwò-chywu. ‖**He tried to sidetrack me, but I refused to change the subject.** tā 'shyǎng-yàw gēn-wo dǎ-'chà 'kě-shr wǒ háy-shr bǎ nèy-ge shwō-'wán-le. ‖**I'm sorry I'm late; I got sidetracked.** *is expressed as* Excuse me; I had some business and am late. dwèy-bù-'chǐ, wǒ yěw dyǎr-'shř láy 'wǎn-le.

Sideways (*toward one side*) wàng 'páng-byār; (*toward either side*) dzwǒ-'yèw. ‖**The car skidded sideways on the ice.** chē dzày 'bīng-shang dzěw-je jǐ wàng 'páng-byār hwá. ‖**The elevator was so crowded that I couldn't move backward or forward or sideways.** jèy-ge-dyàn-'tī tày 'jǐ-le, wǒ chyán-'hèw dzwǒ-'yèw dēw 'dùng-bu-lyǎw.

SIDEWALK. byàn-'dàw, rén-shíng-'dàw, 'dzěw-dàw.

SIGHT. (*Vision*). ‖**I have poor sight.** *is expressed as* My eyes aren't very good. wǒ 'yǎn-jīng bú-dà 'hǎw. *or as* I can't see things very well. wǒ kàn 'dūng-shi bú-dà 'shíng.

(*Glance, act of seeing*) yǎn. ‖**At first sight I didn't recognize you.** wǒ 'téw-yì-'yǎn méy-'rèn-chū nǐ-láy. *also expressed as* When I first looked at you, I didn't realize it was you. gāng yí 'kàn-jyàn nǐ de-shŕ-hew wǒ méy kàn-chū-'láy shř nǐ. ‖**They fell in love at first**

sight. *is expressed as* They fell in love at the first meeting. tā-men sh̀r yí-jyàn-jūng-'chíng.

To catch sight of 'kàn-jyàn, 'kàn-jyàn yì-'yǎn. ‖I caught sight of you on the railroad platform. wǒ dzày hwǒ-chē-'jàn-shang 'kàn-jyàn 'nǐ-le.

To lose sight of. (*Not be able to see*) kàn-bú-'jyàn; (*be unable to locate*) jǎw-bú-'jáw; (*lose*) 'dyēw-le. ‖I lost sight of him in the crowd. tā dzày 'nèy-chywún-'rén-li wǒ kàn-bú-'jyàn tā-le.

To know by sight. ‖I know him only by sight. *is expressed as* I only know who he is when I see him. wǒ 'kàn-jyan ta, jŕ-daw tā shŕ-'shéy, jyèw-shŕ-le.

In sight. ‖The end is now in sight. (*literally, as a road*) *is expressed as* Now the end can be seen. shyàn-'dzày 'kàn-jyàn 'téwr-le. (*figuratively, as of work*) *is expressed as* We know it's almost done now. wǒm 'jŕ-dàw 'shyàn-dzày kwày 'wán-le.

Out of sight. ‖The ship moved slowly out of sight. nèy-ge-chwán màn-'már-de dzěw-de kàn-bú-'jyàn-le.

On sight yí 'kàn-jyàn, yí 'jyàn-jáw. ‖They had orders to shoot him on sight. tā-men jyē-dàw 'mìng-lìng-le yí 'kàn-jyàn tā jyèw bǎ-ta 'dǎ-sž.

A sight. ‖The children were a sight when they came in out of the snow. *is expressed as* When the children came in out of the snow, you should have seen the way they looked. nèy-shyē-'háy-dz tsúng shywě-'dì-li 'hwéy-láy de-'shŕ-hew nǐ 'chyāw tā-men nà-'yàngr. ‖It was a terrible sight. *is expressed as* It was really hard to look at. nèy-ge 'jēn nán-'kàn. *or as* It wasn't pretty. nèy-ge bù-hǎw-'kàn.

Camera sight *is expressed as* adjusting-focus thing dwèy-'gwāng-de *or as* lens for focusing dwèy-gwāng-'jìng, fǎn-gwāng-'jìng.

Gun sight byǎw-'chŕ.

Sights (*places to be seen*) kě-'kàn-de-dì-fang. ‖Did you see the sights at the fair? 'jí-shang-kě-'kàn-de-dì-fang nǐ dēw 'kàn-le-ma?

To go sightseeing. (*Look everywhere*) gwàng, gè-chù 'kàn-kan; (*make a tour*) 'yéw-lǎn, 'yéw-lì; (*look around*) gwān-'gwǎng. ‖We spent the whole day sightseeing. wǒ-men 'gwàng-le yì-jěng-'tyān.

To sight (*to begin to see*) 'kàn-jyàn. ‖When will we sight land? shéme-'shŕ-hew ké-yi 'kàn-jyàn lù-dì-ya?

(*To look through a gun or camera sight*) myáw, jàw, 'bǐ-hwā. ‖Sight carefully before you shoot the deer. dǎ nèy-ge-'lù yǐ-'chyán děy hǎw-'hǎwr-de 'myáw-myáw jwěn.

SIGN. (*Of wood or metal, or the bulletin board on which signs are posted*) 'páy-dz; (*of paper*) 'tyáw-dz; (*public notice, bulletin*) 'gàw-shr̀; (*marker*) 'fú-hàwr, 'jì-hàwr; (*political sign, or a slogan*) byāw-'ywǔ; (*a wooden tablet with characters carved on it, over a store; or presented to a benefactor, with words of thanks carved on it, to be hung outside his' house*) byǎn; (*a wooden or paper figure hung outside a store, something like a barber's pole or pawnshop's three balls*) 'hwǎng-dz; (*similar, but also containing char-*

acters.) 'jāw-páy. ‖Can't you see the "No Smoking" sign? mwò-fēy nǐ kàn-bu-'jyàn nèy-ge-"jìn-'jŕ-shī-'yān"-de-'páy-dz-ma?

(*Gesture*) 'jāw-hu; (*with the hands only*) jāw-'shěw. ‖The waiter gave us a sign to follow him. nèy-ge-'hwǒ-jì dǎ ge-'jāw-hu ràng wǒ-men 'gēn-je ta.

(*Indication*) 'byǎw-shr̀; (*appearance*) yàngr; (*symptom*) 'shyàn-shyàng, (*literary*) jēng-'jàw; (*omen*) ywù-'jàwr, 'shyān-jàwr; (*good omen*) jí-'jàw; (*bad omen*) 'shyūng-jàw. ‖That's a good sign. 'nèy-ge shr̀ °yí-ge-'jí-jàwr. *or* hǎw-'shyàn-shyàng. ‖All signs point towards a cold winter. kàn jèy-'yàngr, (jīn-nyan-de-) 'dūng-tyan yí-'dìng hwèy hěn- 'lěng. ‖Have you seen any sign of affection between them? nǐ 'kàn-chu-lay tām bǐ-'tsź yěw shéme-'byǎw-shr̀-le-ma?

(*Trace*) yěngr, 'dzūng-jì; *for example*, signs of a wolf láng-de-'dzūng-jì. *But* ‖Have you seen any sign of my friend? nǐ 'kàn-jyàn wǒ-'péng-yew-de-lèw-'myàr-le-ma? *or expressed as* Have you seen my friend? nǐ 'kàn-jyan wǒ-'péng-yew-le-ma?

(*Symbol*) 'fú-hàwr; (*mark on paper, etc.*) hàwr. ‖He got the plus and minus signs mixed up. tā bǎ 'jèng-'fù-hàwr dēw nùng-'lwàn-le.

To sign *one's name* (*formal*) chyān-'dž; (*informal, or in signing in or out*) chyān-'míng; (*of illiterates, with a cross*) hwà-'yā. ‖I forgot to sign the letter. wǒ 'wàng-le dzày jèy-fēng-'shìn-shang chyān-'dž-le. ‖Sign your name here, please. chǐng-ni dzày-'jèr chyān-'míng.

To sign *something* away *or* over lì 'dž-jywù bǎ . . . 'jyāw-gey. ‖He signed away all his property to the bank. tā gěy yín-'háng lì-le ge-'dž-jywù bǎ 'swǒ-yěw-de-'tsáy-chǎn dēw 'jyāw-gěy tā-men-le. ‖He signed over control of the business to his son. tā 'lì-le ge-'dzèr bǎ 'mǎy-may 'jyāw-gey tā-'ér-dz-le.

To sign off. ‖Radio stations here sign off early in the evening. dzày-'jèr-de-wú-shyàn-'dyàn-táy 'wǎn-shang hěn-'dzǎw-de jyèw °tíng-'bwō-le. *or* °tíng-'jǐ 'bwō-sùng-le.

To sign on (*hire*) gù; (*take on*) shěw; *sometimes expressed with* to look for jǎw; (*polite, meaning request the services of*) chǐng. ‖The ship in the harbor is still signing on men. 'mǎ-téw-li-de-nèy-ge-'chwán háy 'dzày-nèr gù-'rén dāng shwěy-'shěw-ne.

To sign on with (*agree to work for*) 'dìng hé-'túng, lì hé-'túng. ‖Will he sign on with us? tā hwèy 'gēn wǒ-men dìng hé-'túng-ma?

To sign up *meaning* A signs B up B gēn A °dìng-'hǎw-le (°shwō-'hǎw-le); *meaning* B signs up dìng hé-'túng. ‖We signed him up for piece work. tā gēn wǒ-men °dìng-'hǎw-le (*or* °shwō-'hǎw-le) dzwò lwèn-'jyàn-gěy-chyán-de-gūng-'dzwò. ‖He signed up for three years. tā 'dìng-le 'sān-nyán-de-'hé-túng.

SIGNAL. (*Sign or mark*) hàw, 'jì-hawr; (*given by an instrument*) 'shìn-hàw. Air raid signal jǐng-'bàw. ‖A pistol shot will be the signal to start. kāy-'shŕ shr̀ yì-fàng-'chyāng wéy 'hàw. ‖A green light is the signal to go ahead. lywù-'dēng shr ràng-nǐ 'dzěw-de yì-jǔng-'jì-hàwr. ‖We sent out an S O S signal. wǒ-men 'fā-chū-chywù yí-ge-gàw-'jí-'shìn-hàw.

To signal. (*To use instruments, or an established code*) fā-'shìn-hàw; (*to make gestures to attract someone's attention*) dǎ 'jāw-hu; (*sound an air raid signal*) fàng (*or* fā) jǐng-'bàw.

SILENCE. (*Quiet*) jìng, 'ān-jìng; (*no sound*) méy-'shēngr, (*no sound or movement*) méy-'dùng-jyèngr: *or* (*literary*) *meaning* from the crow and sparrow no sound yā-chywè-wú-'shēng. ‖I like the silence of the woods. jèy-ge-shù-'lín-dz-li "yā-chywè-wú-'shēng-de" wǒ hěn 'shǐ-hwān. ‖The silence in the room was embarrassing. *is expressed as* No one in the room was talking and it made things a little stiff. jèy-wū-dz-li méy-rén shwō-'hwà, yěw-dyǎr 'jyāng. ‖His silence about the price surprised us. *is expressed as* He didn't mention the price, and we thought it was very queer. tā méy-'tí 'jyà-chyán, wǒ-men 'jywé-de hěn chí-'gwày. ‖There will probably be nothing but silence from the war front during the first days of the invasion. *is expressed as* In the first part of the invasion we won't hear about the situation. dzày jìn-gūng kāy shǐ de-'shǐ-hew chyán-'shyàn-de-'shyāw-shi dà-gày dàw-bu-'lyǎw.

‖Silence! *is expressed as* A little quiet, please! 'ān-jìng-dyǎr! *or as* Don't talk! byé shwō-'hwà-le. *or as* Don't make any noise! byé °'nàw-le! *or* °'chǎw-le! *or as* Don't let out a sound. byé chū-'shēngr!

In silence yì-'shēngr-bù-'yán-ywu-de, bù-'yán-bù-'ywǔ-de, 'ān-ān-'jìng-jìng-de. ‖He went about his work in silence. tā yì-'shēngr-bù-'yán-ywǔ-de dzày-nèr dzwò-'shǐ.

To silence ràng . . . (*or* bǎ . . . nùng) 'ān-jìng-shyà-lay. ‖He silenced the audience and went on speaking. tā bǎ tīng-jùng nùng 'ān-jìng-shyà-lay 'jì-shywù 'shwō-shyà-chywu.

To silence objections 'dǔ-hwéy-chywù, 'dǐng-hwéy-chywù (*to stop . . . from answering*) bǎ . . . 'wèn-jù-le; (*to make . . . stop talking*) ràng . . . méy-'hwà-shwō-le. ‖We finally silenced their objections. dàw-'lyǎwr wǒ-men bǎ 'tā-men 'dǔ-hwéy-chywù-le.

SILENT. jìng, 'ān-jìng, 'jìng-chyaw-'chyāw-de, méy-'shēngr, 'yā-chywè-wú-'shēng; (*of a person, not speak*) bù-shwō-'hwà; be silent about (*not mention*) bù-'tí, ‖The room was silent when we came in. wǒ-men 'jìn-láy de-shǐ-hewr jèy-ge-'wū-dz-li ān-jìng 'jí-le. ‖Why are you so silent? nǐ 'wèy-shéme bù-shwō-'hwà-ya? ‖She's too silent to be good company. tā 'tǎy bú-ày shwō-'hwà, gēn-ta dzày yì-'chǐ méy shéme-dà-'yì-sz. ‖They were silent about their plans. tā-men méy-'tí tā-men-de-'jì-hwa.

Silent partner (*non-participating stockholder*) bù-gwǎn-'shǐ-de-gǔ-'dūng.

SILK. sz; (*raw silk*) shēng-'sz; (*general but rather literary term for silk material*) sz-jr-'pǐn; (*silk material that is shiny on one side and dull on the other, satin*) 'dwàn-dz; (*thin silk material*) 'chéw-dz; (*silk crepe*) yáng-'jèw; (*silk velvet*) (sz-)rúng. ‖How much is silk by the yard? chéw-dz 'dwō-shaw-chyán yì-'mǎ? ‖I'd like to buy some silk dresses. wǒ shyǎng mǎy jǐ-jyàn-'dwàn-dz-de-'yī-shang. ‖I need some silk stockings. wǒ shyǎng 'yàw jǐ-shwāng-sz-'wà-dz. `

(*Silk thread*) sz-'shyàn; (*floss*) rúng-'shyàn. ‖Buy me a spool of silk. gěy-wǒ 'mǎy yì-jéwr-sz-'shyàn. ‖My aunt wants some embroidery silk. wǒ-'gū-gu yàw-dyǎr shyèw-'hwār-de-sz-'shyàn.

SILVER. yín; sterling *or* pure silver 'chwén-yín. ‖Is this sterling silver? 'jèy-ge shr chwén-'yín-de-ma? ‖She's wearing a silver ring. tā 'dày-je yí-ge-'yín-jyè-jer.

(*Utensils of silver*) 'yín-chì, 'yín-dūng-shi. ‖She got a beautiful set of silver for a wedding present. tā shēw-le yí-fèr-jyé-hwēn-'lǐ-wù, shr yí-tàw-hěn-'pyàw-lyàng-de-'yín-chì. ‖A burglar stole all the silver. dzéy bǎ swǒ-yěw-de-'yín-chì dēw 'tēw-le chywù-le.

(*Coins*) máw-'chyár. ‖Give me some silver for these bills. 'jèy-jǐ-jāng-'pyàw-dz 'hwàn-gěy wǒ dyǎr-máw-'chyár.

To silver, plate with silver 'dù-yín; *or* to cover with silver leaf bāw-'yín. ‖The pin is just silver-plated lead. jèy-ge-byé-'jer shr 'chyān-de 'dù-le yì-tséng-'yìn. *or* jèy-ge-byé-'jer shr 'dù-yín-de. ‖Is the teapot sterling silver or just silver plated? jèy-ge-chá-'hú shr 'chwén-yín-de háy-shr 'dù-yín-de? *But* ‖This mirror needs to be silvered. *is expressed as* This mirror needs to be coated with mercury. jèy-ge-'jìng-dz děy 'shàng 'shwěy-yín-le.

SIMPLE. (*Plain*) 'jyǎn-dān. ‖She wears simple clothes. tā-chwān-de-'yī-shang hěn 'jyǎn-dān. ‖He likes the simple life. tā 'shǐ-hwān 'jyǎn-dān-de-'shēng-hwó. ‖They're so poor they can only buy the simplest food. tā-men jēn 'chyúng jyèw néng chr 'dzwèy 'jyǎn-dān-de-chr-de.

(*Easy*) 'jyǎn-dān, 'rúng-yì. ‖That's simple. nèy-ge hěn 'jyǎn-dān. ‖That's a simple matter. nèy-ge-'shǐ-ching hěn 'jyǎn-dān. ‖The work here is fairly simple. jèr-de-'gūng-dzwò 'jyǎn-dān jí-le.

(*Stupid*) bèn, shǎ, chǐ-'dwèn. ‖I may seem simple, but I don't understand it. yě-shywù shr wǒ 'bèn, 'kě-shr jèy-ge wǒ bù-'míng-báy. ‖She's attractive, but rather simple. tā hěn 'tǎw rén 'shǐ-hwān 'kě-shr yěw-dyǎr 'bèn.

(*Single*) yí . . . . ‖He had a simple fracture of the arm *is expressed as* His arm had the bone broken in one place. tā-de-'gē-be-shang yěw-'yí-ge-'dì-fangr 'gú-téw 'shé-le. ‖This test tube contains the simple element. *is expressed as* This test tube contains just one kind of element. jèy-ge-shǐ-'gwǎr-li 'chéng-je 'jyèw-shǐ 'yí-yàngr-ywán-'sù. ‖Even a child could start this machine by a simple twist of the wrist. *is expressed as* Even a child by making one movement could start this machine. 'jyèw-shŕ yí-ge-shyǎw-'háy-dz yě néng °yí-'shyàr (°yí-'nùng, °yì-'bān, °yí-'shyà-dz) jyèw bǎ jèy-ge-'jī-chi 'kāy-kay. *or as* Even a child can operate this machine; it's just as easy as turning over the palm of one's hand. 'jyèw-shŕ shyǎw-'háy-dz kāy jèy-ge-'jī-chi, yě shŕ 'yì-rú-fǎn-'jǎng.

(*Bare*). ‖These are the simple facts. jèy 'dēw-shr míng-'bǎy-je-de-'shŕ. ‖It's the simple truth. *is expressed as* It's certainly that way. nèy-ge-'jyǎn-'jŕ-de 'jyèw-shŕ 'nà-me-je.

SINCE. (*Of something still going on*) tsúng (dž-'tsúng, dǎ) . . . chǐ (*literary*) tsúng ('dž-'tsúng, dǎ) . . . yǐ-'láy, . . . yǐ-'láy; (*of something finished*) tsúng (dž-'tsúng, dǎ) . . . yǐ-'hèw, . . . yǐ-'hèw. ‖I haven't had any fun since I got here. tsúng wǒ 'láy-le yǐ-'hèw méy-'jywé-de yěw shéme-'yì-sz. ‖Has anything exciting happened since I saw you last? tsúng wǒ 'shàng-hwéy 'kàn-jyàn nǐ yǐ-'hèw 'chū-le shéme-tè-'byé-de-'shŕ-ching-ma? ‖He hasn't been here since Monday. tā tsúng shīng-chī-'yī 'láy-le yǐ-'hèw jyèw méy-shàng-jèr 'láy. ‖Since when have you worn glasses? nǐ tsúng shéme-'shŕ-hewr 'chǐ 'dày-de yǎn-'jyèngr? *Also* ‖He broke his leg and has had it in a cast ever since. *is expressed as* Since he broke his leg, it's been wrapped up in a cast. tā-de-'twěy shwāy-'shé-le yǐ-'hèw, jyèw yì-'jŕ yùng shŕ-gāw-'mú-dz 'bāw-je. ‖We quarreled, and I haven't seen her since. *is expressed as* Since we quarreled, I haven't seen her. wǒ-men dǎ-'jyà yi-'hèw, wǒ háy méy-'kàn-jyàn tā-ne.

(*Because*) jì-'rán, 'jì-shŕ, jì; 'yīn-wèy. ‖Since they couldn't be with us, we had to change our plans. tā-men jì-'rán bù-'néng 'tsān-jyā, wǒ-men děy gǎy-'byàn 'jì-hwa. ‖Since you don't believe me, look for yourself. nǐ jì-'rán bú-'shìn, nǐ dž-'jǐ kàn-chywù-ba. ‖Since you're so smart, you do it. nǐ 'jì nème 'néng gàn, 'nǐ dzwò.

SINCERE. 'chéng-shŕ, chéng-'kěn; (*to have a sincere heart*) yěw 'chéng-yì; (*to have a sincere mind and heart*) chéng-'shīn-chéng-yì; (*to be real*) 'jēn-de; (*to come from a sincere heart*) 'chū-ywú °'chéng-yì (°'jŕ-chéng). ‖He's sincere. tā hěn °'chéng-shŕ. *or* °'chéng-kěn. ‖That letter sounds quite sincere. nèy-fēng-'shìn 'kàn-je hěn yěw 'chéng-yì. ‖I don't believe he's sincere in his promises. wǒ bú-'shìn tā shŕ 'jēn-shīn-de 'dā-ying-le. *or* tā swǒ 'dā-ying-de-hwà wǒ bú-'shìn shŕ 'chū-ywú-'chéng-yì-de.

SING (SANG, SUNG). (*Of people*) chàng. ‖I can't sing very well. wǒ 'shàng-de bù-hěn 'hǎw. ‖Try singing the baby to sleep. *is expressed as* Sing a song to the baby and lull it to sleep. gěy háy-dz chàng ge-'chàngr 'hǔng-ta shwèy-'jyàw-ba.

(*Of birds*) jyàw, shàw. ‖The birds have been singing all morning. nyǎwr 'jyàw-le yì-'dzǎw-chen.

(*Figuratively*). ‖Bullets were singing all around us. *is expressed as* Bullets around us sounded with a swish. dž-'dàn 'jyèw dzày wǒ-men sž-jēw-'wéy °'sēw-sēwr-de 'shyǎng. *or* °'rēw-rēwr-de shyǎng.

SINGLE. (*One*) yī. ‖I haven't a single thing to eat. wǒ yì-'kěw-'dūng-shi dēw méy-de 'chŕ. ‖He knocked him down with a single blow. tā 'yí-shyà-dz jyèw bǎ-ta dǎ-'dǎw-le. ‖There isn't a single example of that on record. gwò-'chywù tsúng-'láy yě méy-yěw yí-ge-'jè-yàngr-de-'lì-dz.

(*For one person*) dān, 'dān-rér-de. ‖I want a single room, if possible. yǎw-shŕ bàn-de-'dàw-wa, wǒ 'yàw yì-jyān-'dān-rér-de-'wū-dz. ‖These sheets are for a single bed. jè-shyē-'dān-dz shŕ wèy-'dān-rén-chwáng-'yùng-de.

(*Unmarried*) 'méy-jyé-'hwēn; *if a man, i.e.,* bachelor dǎ-gwāng-'gwèr, gwāng-'gǎr. ‖Are you married or single? nǐ jyé-'hwēn-le 'méy-yěw? *or* nǐ jyé-'hwēn-le háy-shŕ dǎ-gwāng-'gwèr-ne?

To single out. ‖They singled him out for special mention. *is expressed as* They mentioned him alone specially. tā-men bǎ-ta dān-'dú-de tè-byé 'tí-le-'tí.

Single file 'dān-háng *or* 'dān-rén-háng. ‖Form in single file for tickets. mǎy-'pyàw-de 'jàn-chéng 'dān-háng.

Single-handed yí-ge-'rén ǒr dž-'gěr. ‖He shot ten of the enemy single-handed. tā 'yí-ge-rén 'dǎ-sž-le 'shŕ-ge-'dí-rén. *Also* ‖She organized the tea-party single-handed. *is expressed as* She accomplished the organization of the tea-party with one hand. kāy nèy-ge-chá-'hwèy shŕ tā-'yì-shěw-chéng-'bàn.

Singles (*tennis*) dān. ‖Let's play singles. wǒ-men láy dān-'dǎ-de-ba.

SIR. 'shyān-shēng; (*an old-fashioned way of addressing an official*) 'lǎw-yé; (*old-fashioned way of addressing the son of a* 'lǎw-yé) dà-'yé. ‖Yes, sir. 'shŕ, 'nín-ne.

Dear Sir *or* Dear Sirs (*beginning of a letter*) jŕ-'shŕ 'shyān-sheng dà-'jyàn. *or* jìng-chǐ-'jě.

SISTER. *See Appendix A.* (*Catholic nun*) gū-'nǎy-nay; (*Buddhist nun*) 'gū-dz; (*woman who leads a monastic life*) shyēw-'nywǔ, shyēw-'dàw-de. ‖There are two sisters having lunch in the restaurant. yěw lyǎ-gū-'nǎy-nay dzày jèy-ge-fàn-'gwǎr-li chŕ wǔ-'fàn-ne.

Sister ship jyě-mèy-°'hàw (°'jyàn), dž-mèy-°'hàw (°'jyàn). ‖This is the sister ship of the one launched last year. jèy-ge shŕ 'chywù-nyán-shyà-'shwěy-de nèy-ge-'chwán-de-dž-mèy-'jyàn.

SIT (SAT). dzwò. ‖They were sitting when we came in. wǒ-men 'jìn-láy de-'shŕ-hewr 'tā-men nèr 'dzwò-je-ne. ‖Where are we sitting tonight? wǒ-men jyēr-'wǎn-shang 'dzwò-dzày 'nǎr? ‖She made arrangements to sit for her portrait. tā 'ywù-bey 'hǎw-le 'dzwò-dzày nèr ràng-rén gěy tā hwà-shyàng. ‖You won't finish today if you just sit there. *is expressed as* If you just sit without moving, you won't finish today. nǐ 'yàw-shr̀ jyèw 'dzwò-ner bú-'dūng 'ivēr nǐ dzwò-bù-'wán-le:

(*To have been placed*) fàng, gē, bǎy. ‖That vase has been sitting on the shelf for years. nèy-ge-'píng-dz dzày nèy-ge-'jyà-dz-shang 'fàng-le hǎw-jǐ-'nyán-le.

(*To perch*) làw. ‖The pigeons were sitting on the window sill. gē-dz làw-de 'chwàng-hu-'tár-shang-le.

(*Be in session*). ‖The court is sitting. fǎ-'ywàn kāy-'tíng-le.

To sit down 'dzwò-shyà, *sometimes merely* dzwò. ‖He sat down suddenly. tā 'hū-rán jyèw 'dzwò-shyà-le. *Also* ‖Sit down over here, won't you? dzwò-dzày 'jèr, 'hǎw-ma?

To sit in on *something is expressed as* to listen on the side páng 'tīng. ‖He sat in on all the conferences that day. nèy-tyān swǒ-'yěw-de-'hwèy tā dēw °páng 'tīng-le. *or.* (*attended*) °'dàw-le.

To sit on *someone* (*figuratively*) gěy . . . 'dīng-dz pèng. ‖He's very boastful; he just needs to be sat on a little. tā tày dé-'yì-le, děy 'gěy-ta dyǎr-'dīng-dz 'pèng.

To sit out. ‖Let's sit this dance out. *is expressed as* This time let's not dance, let's sit. jèy-'chǎng dzá-men 'béng tyàw-le, 'dzwò-dzwòr-ba. ‖I couldn't sit out that play. *is expressed as* I couldn't finish looking at the play. nèy-chū-'shì wǒ 'kàn-bú-shyà-'chywù-le.

To sit up (*move to an upright position*) 'dzwò-chǐ-láy; (*stay sitting*) dzwò. ‖He sat up suddenly. tā 'hū-rán 'dzwò-chǐ-láy-le. ‖The baby has been able to sit up since he was five months old. *is expressed as* At five months the baby sat up. jèy-háy-dz 'wǔ-ge-'ywè jyèw °'dzwò-chǐ-láy-le. *or as* At five months the baby knew how to sit. °'hwèy 'dzwò-je-le. ‖We sat up all night talking. wǒ-men 'dzwò-de nèr 'tán-le yí-'yè-de-'tyàr. *But* ‖That will make him sit up and take notice. něm-je jyèw jyàw-ta 'bù-néng bù-'gwǎ-le.

SIX. lyèw. One sixth 'lyèw-fēn-jř-'yī; the sixth dì-'lyèw.

SIXTEEN. shŕ-'lyèw. One sixteenth shŕ-'lyèw-fēn-jř-'yī; the sixteenth dì-shŕ-'lyèw.

SIXTY. 'lyèw-shŕ. One sixtieth 'lyèw-shr-fēn-jř-'yī; the sixtieth dì-'lyèw-shŕ.

SIZE. (*Number*) hàw, hàwr. ‖I wear size ten stockings. wǒ chwān 'shŕ-hàwr-de-'wà-dz. ‖What size is this shoe? jèy-ge-'shyé shr̀ 'dwō-dà-'hàwr? ‖These gloves are a size too small. jèy-shyē-shěw-'tàwr 'shyǎw yí-'hàwr.

(*Relative bigness*) dà-'shyǎw; (*bigness of body*) gèr; (*length*) cháng-'dwǎn; (*thickness*) 'hèw-báw (*width*) kwān-'jǎy; (*height*) gāw-'ǎy. ‖Try this for size. shr̀-shr jèy-ge-dà-'shyǎw dzěme-'yàng. ‖You're pretty strong for your size. ná nǐ jèy-ge-'gèr láy 'shwō, nǐ shr̀ gèw 'jwàng-de.

What is the size of . . .? (. . . *is how big?*) . . . yěw dwō-°'dà? or (*Long*) °'cháng? or (*High*) °'gāw? or (*Wide*) °'kwān? or (*Thick*) °'hèw? ‖What size is the house? jèy-swǒ-'fáng-dz yěw dwō-'dà?

To size up. ‖He sized up the situation at a glance. *is expressed as* At one glance he saw the situation clearly. tā 'yì-yǎn jyèw bǎ nèy-ge-'chíng-shing kàn-'chīng-chu-le.

Under-sized (*not up to standard*) shyaw; (*of number*) bú-gèw-'hàwr. ‖Their horse is rather under-sized. tā-men-de-'mǎ 'yěw-dyǎr shyaw.

Out-sized. chū-'hàw-de. ‖He wears out-sized shoes. tā-'chwān-de-'shyé 'dēw shr̀ 'chū-le-'hàw-de.

Good-sized dà. ‖He's a good-sized man. tā jèy-ge rén-'gèr hěn 'dà.

SKIN. (*Of a person*) rèw-'pyér, 'pí-fū. ‖She has very white skin. tā-de-rèw-'pyér hěn 'báy.

(*Of fruits or vegetables; also the bark of a tree*) pí, pyér. ‖The best part of a potato is near the skin. shān-yaw-'dàn dzwèy-'hǎw-de-'dì-fangr shr̀ 'kàw-je 'pyér-de nèy-'dǎr.

(*Of animals; hide*) pí, 'pí-dz. ‖These shoes are made of alligator skin. jèy-'shyé shr̀ è-'ywú-pí-de.

To skin bā-'pí, bāw-'pí. ‖The hunter was skinning the deer. dǎ-'lyè-de jèng 'bā lù-'pí-ne.

By the skin of one's teeth chà-'dyǎr méy. ‖I made the train by the skin of my teeth. wǒ chà-'dyǎr jyèw 'méy-gǎn-shàng 'chē.

Skin deep. ‖The cut is only skin deep. *is expressed as* The skin is cut a little. jyèw lá-'pwò-le-dyǎr 'pyér. ‖Her beauty is only skin deep. *is expressed as* Just her expression is beautiful. tā 'jyèw-shr̀ wày-'byǎw hǎw-'kàn.

To skin out of. ‖She skinned out of her clothes. tā bǎ 'yī-shang °'twō-shyà-láy-le. *or* °'bā-shyà-láy-le. ‖He barely skinned out of that mess. tā jǐ-hu méy-néng twō-'shēn. *or expressed as* He just escaped that situation. tā swàn shr̀ bǎ nèy-ge-'shr̀-ching bǎy-'twō-le.

Thick-skinned. ‖The elephant is a thick-skinned animal. shyàng-de-'pí hěn 'hèw. ‖He's so thick-skinned you can't offend him. *is expressed as* The skin of his face is really thick, you have no way to hurt his feelings. tā-de-lyǎn-'pí jēn 'hèw, nǐ méy-'fár bǎ-ta dzěme-'yàng.

Thin-skinned. ‖I'm very thin-skinned. (*when the meaning is literal*) wǒ-de-rèw-'pyér hěn 'báw. ‖She's too thin-skinned; she can't even take a joke. *is expressed as* The skin on her face is too thin; if you make a joke with her, she can't take it. tā lyǎn-'pyér tày 'bàw, 'gēn-ta 'kāy ge-wán-'shyàw tā jyèw gwà-bú-'jù-le.

Skin and bones. ‖That child is just skin and bones. *is expressed as* That child just has skin covering his bones. nèy-háy-dz jyǎn-'jŕ-de shŕ pí-bāw-'gǔ.

SKIRT. (*Part of a dress from the waist down*) 'yī-shang 'shyà-byǎr; (*woman's garment hanging from the waist*) 'chywún-dz. ‖I don't look good in skirts and blouses. wǒ chwān 'chywún-dz gēn chèn-'shān bù-hǎw-'kàn. ‖The skirt of that dress is too tight. jèy-jyàn-'yī-shang-de-'shyà-byar tày 'shèw.

To skirt 'jwàn-gwò-chywù, 'ràw-gwò-chywù. ‖Can I skirt the business district? wǒ 'ké-yi 'ràw-gwo-chywu bù-dzéw 'rè-naw-dì-fang-ma?

SKY. tyān; *or* tyǎr (*also means* **weather**). ‖How does the sky look today? jyēr 'tyǎr kàn-je 'dzěme-yàng? ‖The sky is cloudy. yīn-'tyān-le.

Out of a clear sky *is expressed as* suddenly hū-'rán (-'jyān), chēw-gu-'lěng-dz, 'lěng-gu-'dīng-de ('měng-gū-'dīng-de). ‖Out of a clear sky he quit his job. tā 'hū-rán jyèw tsź-'jŕ-le.

To the skies. ‖He praised her to the skies. tā bǎ nèy-ge-'nywǔ-de 'pěng-dàw 'tyān-shang chywù-le.

SLEEP (SLEPT). shwèy, shwèy-'jyàw. ‖Did you sleep well? nǐ (shwèy-'jyàw) shwèy-'hǎw-le-ma? ‖I've never slept in this room before. wǒ yǐ-'chyán méy-dzày 'jèy-wū 'shwèy-gwò-'jyàw. ‖I want some place to sleep. wǒ yàw 'jǎw ge-'dì-fangr 'shwèy-shwèy-'jyàw. ‖I must get some sleep. wǒ děy shwèy-hwěr-'jyàw. ‖Did you have a good sleep? nǐ shwèy-'hǎw-le-ma?

(*To find a place for people to sleep*) shwèy-de-'shyà, jù-de-'shyà, ké-yi 'shwèy, ké-yi 'jù. ‖This hotel can sleep 500 people in an emergency. jèy-ge-lywǔ-'gwǎn yěw-'shŕ de-shŕ-hew jù-de-'shyà 'wǔ-bǎy-rén.

To fall asleep, get to sleep, go to sleep shwèy-'jáw. ‖I couldn't get to sleep for hours. wǒ shwèy-le 'hǎw-jǐ-dyǎn-'jūng yě méy-shwèy-'jáw.

To sleep . . . away 'shwèy-gwo-chywù. ‖He slept the afternoon away. tā bǎ yí-'shyà-wǔ dēw 'shwèy-gwò-chywù-le.

To sleep . . . off. ‖He slept off his tiredness. tā 'shwèy-le yí-'jyàw, jyě-le 'fá-le.

SLIGHT. dyǎr, yì-'dyǎr. ‖I have a slight cold. wǒ 'yěw dyǎr-shāng-'fēng. ‖There is a slight difference. yěw dyǎr-'bù-yí-'yàng. ‖There's not the slightest excuse for being late. láy 'wǎn-le, yì-dyǎr-'lǐ yě méy-'yěw *or expressed as* Having come late, what can you say for yourself? láy 'wǎn-le n y yěw shéme kě 'shwō-de?

(*Slender, fragile; either short or thin*) shyaw; (*slender*) 'myáw-tyaw; (*thin*) shèw. ‖She has a rather slight figure. tā-de-'gèr shyāng-'dāng-de-'shyǎw.

To slight (*to belittle, or snub*) kàn-bù-'chǐ. ‖I didn't mean to slight you. wǒ méy-yew kàn-bù-'chǐ-nǐ-de-'yì-sz. *Also* ‖She resented the slight. *is expressed as* Someone slighted her, and she didn't like it. 'rén-jyā kàn-bù-'chǐ tā, tā hěn bú-'tùng-kwày.

SLIP. (*To slide*) hwá, lyēw, 'chū-lyēw; (*to come loose, of something that should be held tight*) 'tū-lu. ‖She slipped and fell. tā yì-'hwá 'tǎng-shyà-le. ‖Don't slip on the ice. byé dzày 'bīng-shang 'chū-lyew 'tǎng-shyà. ‖See that the knife doesn't slip. lyēw-'shén byé ràng 'dāw-dz 'hwá-de 'shěw-shang. ‖The letter slipped off the table into the wastebasket. nèy-fēng-'shìn tsúng 'jwōr-shang 'lyēw-de dż-jŕ-'lěwr-li-le. ‖The canoe slipped down the bank into the water. nèy-ge-shyǎw-'chwár tsúng 'àn-shang 'chū-lyew-de 'hé-li chywù-le. *But* ‖The vase slipped out of my hands. nèy-ge-'píng-dz tsúng wǒ-'shěw-shang °'tū-lu (*or* °hwá, °'lyēw, °'chū-lyēw) 'shyà-chywù-le. ‖Tie the knot tight, so it won't slip. bǎ-kèwr jì-'jǐn-le, byé 'tū-lu-lew.

(*To push with a sliding motion, or stealthily; to put something in a small opening*) sāy, sēy; (*to hand something quickly and unobtrusively*) tēw-'tēwr-de °'rǔ (°'chǔ); (*to pull something out with a sliding motion or stealthily*) 'chēn-chū-láy, 'chēw-chū-láy. ‖He slipped the notebook i to his pocket. tā bǎ nèy-ge-ŕ-jì-'běr 'sāy-de tā-'dēwr li-le. ‖He slipped me a five dollar bill. tā tēw-'tēwr-de °'rǔ (*or* °'sāy)-gěy-wo 'wǔ-kwày-'chyán-de-'pyàw-dz. ‖He slipped the letter out of its envelope. tā bǎ nèy-fēng-'shìn tsúng shìn-'fēngr-li 'chēn-chū-láy-le.

(*To move stealthily, or unobserved*) (tēw-'tēwr-de) 'dzwān *or* 'lyēw. ‖He slipped into the house. tā tēw-'tēwr-de 'dzwān-de nèy-ge-'fáng-dz-li chywù-le. ‖One by one the soldiers slipped past the guard. nèy-shyē-'bīng yí-'gèr yí-'gèr-de tēw-'tēwr-de tsúng wèy-'bīng nèr 'lyēw-gwò-chywù-le. ‖I'm going to slip out of the room for a minute. wǒ yàw 'lyēw-chū yì-hwěr chywù. ‖This party is dull; let's slip away. jèy-ge-'hwèy méy-'yì-sz, 'dzá-men 'lyēw-le-ba.

(*To make a casual mistake*) tswò, chū-'tswòr; (*forget something*) 'wàng dyǎr-shéme. ‖I guess I slipped up somewhere. wǒ 'jywé-de wǒ nǎr 'tswò-le. *or* wǒ 'jywé-de wǒ 'wàng-le-dyǎr 'shéme. ‖It was just a slip that she wasn't invited. bú-shr gù-'yì-de méy-'chǐng tā. ‖Did I make a slip? wǒ chū-'tswòr-le-ma?

(*To escape*) 'tswò-gwò-chywù. ‖Don't let the chance slip, if you can help it. nǐ 'yàw shŕ yèw 'bàn-fǎ, byé ràng 'jī-hwey 'tswò-gwò-chywù. *or expressed as* If you have the means, don't lose this opportunity. nǐ 'yàw-shŕ yěw 'bàn-fǎ, byé bǎ 'jī-hwèy 'dyēw-lew.

(*To say thoughtlessly*) (wù-shīn-'jūng) 'shwō-chū-lay. ‖He let the name slip before he thought. tā wù-shīn-'jūng bǎ nèy-ge-'míng-dz 'shwō-chū-láy-le.

To slip into (*clothes*) bǎ . . . 'chwān-shang; to slip into *a seat* dzày . . . shang 'dzwò.

To slip *something* into sāy, sēy, jǐ. ‖We can slip that announcement into the paper somewhere. wǒ-men 'ké-yi bǎ nèy-dwàn-'shēng-míng 'jǐ-de 'bàw-shang swéy-'byàn 'shéme-'dì-fangr.

To slip out of *clothes* bǎ . . . twō-shyà-láy; to slip out of *a seat* tsúng . . . 'chǐ-láy.

To slip one's mind. ‖The matter slipped my mind completely. *is expressed as* I forgot the whole thing. nèy-jyàn-'shr̀ wǒ jěng-'gèr 'wàng-le.

To slip something over on mēng, dzwàn, ywàn, pyàn. ‖Are you trying to slip something over on me? nǐ shr̀ yàw 'pyàn-wǒ-ma ?

Slip of the pen bǐ-!wù (*rather literary*). ‖That mistake was just a slip of the pen. nèy-ge-'tswòr shr̀ ge-bǐ-!wù. *or expressed as* That mistake was written wrong carelessly. nèy-ge-'tswòr shr̀ méy-lyéw-'shén shyě-de.

Slip of the tongue. ‖I didn't mean to say that; it was a slip of the tongue. wǒ méy-'dǎ-swàn nà-me shwō, wǒ shr̀ 'shwō °'tū-lū 'dzwěy-le. (*or* °'dzěw-le 'dzwěy-le.)

A slip (*woman's undergarment*) chèn-'chywún. ‖Your slip is showing. nǐ-de-chèn-'chywún 'lèw-chū-láy-le.

(*Case, cover*) tàw, tàwr. ‖Please wash the pillow slips. láw-'jyà, bǎ 'jěn-tew-tàwr 'shǐ-shi.

(*Small piece*) tyáwr. ‖Put a slip of paper in the book to keep your place. bǎ 'shū-li 'jyā yí-ge-jǐ-'tyáwr 'dzwò ge-'jì-hawr.

(*Cutting from a plant, for planting or grafting*) jēr, 'jr̄-dz, tyáw. ‖The rose bush grew from a slip. nèy-kē-'méy-gwèy shr̀ ná 'yí-ge-'jēr 'chā-chū-láy-de.

SLOPE. (*An incline*) 'pwō-dù. ‖The hill has a 30 degree slope. jèy-ge-shān-'pwō yěw 'sān-shŕ-'dù.

(*Inclined surface*) pwō, pwōr; (*slope of a hill*) shān-'pwō, shān-'pwōr. ‖My house is on a slope. wǒ-de-'fáng-dz shr̀ dzày 'yí-ge-'pwōr-shang. ‖They raced down the slope. tā-men tsúng shān-'pwōr-shang 'pǎw-shyà-láy-le.

To slope. ‖The land slopes gradually down to the river. *is expressed as* The land is sloping, the nearer to the river the lower. nèy-ge-'dì shr̀ 'pwō-de 'ywè wàng-'hé nèy-byār 'ywè-'dī.

(*Of shoulders only*) lyēw. ‖He has sloping shoulders. *is expressed as* He has shoulders that slide down. tā-'lyēw-jyān-'bǎngr.

SLOW. màn. ‖Is it a slow train? nèy shr̀ ge-'màn-chē-ma ? ‖Don't drive so slow. byé kāy-de dzème-'màn. ‖Go slow, curve ahead. 'wān-lù, màn 'dzěw. ‖My watch is an hour slow. wǒ-de-'byǎw 'màn yí-ge-jūng-'téw.

(*Of a person's thinking or general movements*) 'chŕ-dwèn; (*of specific movements*) màn. ‖He's very slow moving. tā 'dùng-dzwò hěn 'chŕ-dwèn. ‖He was slow in getting the joke. *is expressed as* His thinking is slow: he took half a day over the joke, then under-

stood. tā 'sz-shyǎng 'chŕ-dwèn; nèy-ge-'shyàw-hwàr tā bàn-'tyān tsáy 'míng-báy. ‖Don't walk so slow. byé 'dzěw 'dzème-'màn-ne.

‖She's slow to anger. tā 'bú-dà 'rúng-yì shéng-'chì.

A slow class (*stupid*) yì-'bān-'bèn-'shywé-sheng.

A slow fire 'wén-hwǒ, 'shyǎw-hwǒr, 'màn-hwǒ. ‖Cook the soup over a slow fire. yùng 'wén-hwǒ 'dzwò jèy-ge-'tāng.

To slow down *or* slow up. ‖Slow down! 'màn-dyǎr! ‖He slows down the work a lot. *is expressed as* He delays the work. tā bǎ jèy-ge-'shr̀-ching gěy nàw-de màn-shya-lay-le.

SMALL. shyǎw; (*very small*) yì-'dyǎr (-dà), yì-'dyēw-dyǎr, yì-dyēw-'dyèwr, bú-dà-'dyǎr, (*especially of a person, a tiny tot*) shyǎw-bù-'dyǎr. ‖The room is rather small. 'wū-dz yěw-dyǎr 'shyǎw. ‖It is a very small room. jèy-ge-'wū-dz shr̀ ge-shyǎw-bù-'dyǎr. ‖They began in a small way, and soon had a large business. tā-men chǐ-'téwr 'mǎy-mày 'dzwò-de hěn 'shyǎw, méy-'dwō-shǎw-'r̀-dz jyèw dzwò 'dà-le. ‖She was wearing a small pin. tā-'dày-de nèy-ge-byé-'jēr °yì-'dyǎr-dà. (°'bú-dà-'dyǎr, °yì-dyēw-dyǎr, °'yì-dyēw-'dyèwr.)

(*Small pieces*) swèy, swèy-'kwàr. ‖Chop it up small. chyē-'swèy-le. *or* 'chyē-chéng swèy-'kwàr. ‖Please gather some small pieces of wood. láw-'jyà, 'jyǎn dyǎr-'swèy 'pǐ-cháy-lay.

(*Mean*) shyà-'lyéw. ‖That was an awfully small thing to do. 'nèy-ge shr̀ yí-'jyàn-hěn-'shyà-lyéw-de-'shr̀-ching. *But* ‖He made me feel pretty small. *is expressed as* He made me feel ashamed. tā 'ràng-wo 'jywé-de hěn °'tsán-kwèy. (°bù-hǎw-'yì-sz.)

Small change 'líng-chyán. ‖I haven't any small change. wǒ méy-'yěw 'líng-chyán.

Small farmer jùng-'jwāng-jyā-de, jùng-'dì-de. ‖Her folks are small farmers. tā-'jyā-li shr̀ jùng-'jwāng-jyā-de.

Small letters (*lower case letters*) shyǎw-dž-'mǔ, shyǎw-'shyě-dž-'mǔ. ‖Print it all in small letters. chywán 'yùng 'shyǎw-shyě-dž-'mǔ 'yìn.

A small matter (*unimportant*) 'shyǎw-shr̀; *or* bú-!yàw-jǐn, méy-'gwān-shi, wú-swǒ-'wèy. ‖Where we stay is a small matter. wǒ-men jù-dzày 'nǎr °shr̀ jyàn-'shyǎw-shr̀. *or* °dēw bú-'yàw-jǐn. *But* ‖That's no small matter. 'nèy-ge hěn 'yàw-jǐn. *or* 'nèy-ge hěn yěw 'gwān-shi.

Small talk 'yìng-chew-'hwà. ‖He's good at small talk, but ne's lost in a serious conversation. tā 'hěn hwèy 'shwō 'yìng-chew-'hwà, 'kě-shr yì-'tán jèng-'jīng-de jyèw bù-'shíng-le.

SMELL. wén. ‖Do you smell smoke? nǐ 'wén-jyàn 'yān-wèr-le-me ? *Also* ‖Take a good smell and tell me what you think is in the bottle. hǎw-'hāwr-de wén °-yì-wén (°-yí-'shyàr, °-yì-'bí-dz) rán-'hèw 'gàw-su wǒ 'pyéngr-li shr̀ 'shéme.

A smell wèr, 'wèy-dàw. ‖What is that smell? 'nèy-ge shr̀ 'shéme-'wèr-ra? ‖Do you like the smell of garlic? nǐ 'shǐ-hwān 'swàn-wèr-ma? ‖I don't like the smell. wǒ bù-'shǐ-hwān wén nèy-'wèr.

To smell good hǎw-'wén, bù-nán-'wén; (be fragrant) shyāng. ‖That perfume smells good. nèy-ge-'shyāng-shwěr-de-'wèr hěn hǎw-'wén.

To smell bad bù-hǎw-'wén, nán-'wén; (stink) chèw. ‖It smells bad. 'nèy-ge bù-hǎw-'wén. ‖The garbage smells to high heaven. is expressed as The bad smell of the garbage is great. ⌐nèy-shyē-'lā-jī-de-'chèw-wèr 'dà-le.

To smell a rat. ‖As soon as she mentioned it, I smelled a rat. is expressed as Once I heard her speak, I was a little suspicious. wǒ yì 'tīng-jyàn tā 'shwō, wǒ 'jyèw °'yěw dyǎr-yí-'shīn. or, meaning I felt doubtful. °'jywé-de kě-'yí.

Sense of smell (technical term) 'shyèw-jywé; usually expressed as nose 'bí-dz. ‖A dog has a very keen sense of smell. gěw-de-'bí-dz hěn 'líng.

SMILE. lè, shyàw. ‖I like the way she smiles. wǒ 'shǐ-hwān tā 'shyàw-de nèy-ge-'yàngr.

A smile. (Smiling appearance) 'shyàw-de-'yàng-dz; (cheerful appearance) shyàw-'rúngr. ‖He always has a smile on his face. tā-'lyǎn-shang lǎw 'dày-je shyàw-'rúngr. ‖You have a pretty smile. nǐ-'shyàw-de-'yàng-dz hěn hǎw-'kàn. or expressed as You smile very prettily. nǐ 'shyàw-de hěn hǎw-'kàn.

SMOKE. (Fumes) yān. ‖Open the windows; there's too much smoke in here. bǎ chwāng-hu 'kāy-kay, jè-li-byār yān tày 'chùng.

(To give off smoke) màw-'yān. ‖That stove smokes too much. nèy-ge-'lú-dz màw-'yān màw-de tày 'lì-hay. ‖Do you see any smoke? nǐ 'kàn-jyàn nǎr màw-'yān-le-ma?

(To preserve by smoke) shywūn. ‖The fishermen here smoke most of their fish. jèr-de-dǎ-'ywú-de bǎ yì-'dwō-bàn-'ywū dēw 'shywūn-le.

(To stain by smoke) shywūn-'hēy-le; (to spoil by smoke) shywūn-'hwày-le. ‖The chimney of this lamp is all smoked up. dēng-'jàwr dēw ràng-'yān gěy shywūn-'hēy-le. ‖We can't eat that; it's all smoked up. nèy-ge wǒ-men 'bù-néng 'chr̄-le, dēw ràng-'yān gěy shywūn-'hwày-le.

To smoke (tobacco) chēw-'yān, shī-'yān, chr̄-'yān. ‖Do you smoke? nǐ chēw-'yān-ma? or nǐ chēw-'yān bù-'chēw? ‖No smoking. jìn-'jr̄-shī-'yān. ‖I smoke cigars. wǒ 'chēw shywě-jyā-'yān. ‖I'm dying for a smoke. wǒ 'jēn shyǎng láy gēr-'yān chēw.

To smoke out 'shywūn-chū-láy. ‖We'll have to smoke out the animals. wǒ-men 'děy bǎ 'nèy-shyē-yě-'shèw 'shywūn-chū-láy.

To go up in smoke. (Burn up) shāw-'gwāng-le, shāw-'wán-le; (figuratively, be destroyed) wán-le; or (literary) expressed as dissolve into the shadow of a bubble hwà-chéng-'pàw-yǐng. ‖The house went up in smoke. nèy-ge-'fáng-dz dēw shāw-'gwāng-le. ‖All our plans went up in smoke. 'swǒ-yěw-de-wǒ-men-de-'jì-hwa dēw 'hwà-chéng-'pàw-yǐng.

Smoke screen yān-'mù. ‖The planes laid down a heavy smoke screen. nèy-shyē-fēy-jī 'fàng-le yì-'tséng-hěn-'núng-de-yān-'mù.

SMOOTH. (Level and not rough) píng; (not rough; but not necessarily level; of land, roads, etc.) bù-'kēng-keng-wā-'wā-de; (extremely smooth, often also shiny) 'gwāng-hwa, 'gwāng-lyew; (smooth and also slippery) hwá, 'hwá-lyew. ‖Is the road smooth? dàwr 'píng-ma? ‖The sea was very smooth. hǎy-'shwěy hěn °'píng. or meaning smooth and calm °'píng-wěn. ‖The tires are worn smooth. pí-'dày dēw mwó °'píng-le. or °'gwāng-le. ‖The cloth has a smooth surface. jèy-ge-'bù-'myàr-shang hěn °'gwāng-hwa. or °'gwāng-lyew. or, (of a slippery material like satin) °hwá (or °'hwá-lyew). ‖He got a smooth shave. tā bǎ-'lyǎn 'gwā-de tǐng °'gwāng or °'gwāng-lyew.

(Not lumpy) ywén, bù-'gē-le-gē-'dā-de, méy-'gē-da. ‖I hope the paste is smooth. wǒ 'shī-wàng jèy-ge-'jyàng-dz dǎ-de háy 'ywén. or wǒ 'shī-wàng jèy-ge-'jyàng-dz bú-'nà-me-'gē-le-gē-'dā-de.

(Calm, steady) wěn. ‖We had a very smooth ride. wǒ-men jèy-'tàng-chē-'dzěw-de hěn 'wěn.

(Suave) 'ywán-hwá. ‖He's a smooth salesman. 'tā jèy-ge-mày-hwò-'ywán hěn 'ywán-hwá.

SNAKE. shé, 'cháng-chung. ‖Are there any poisonous snakes around? jèy yí-'dày yěw dú-'shé-ma?

SNOW. shywě. ‖The snow was so thick we couldn't see in front of us. 'shywě-shyà-de 'tày dà-le, dwèy-'myàr dēw 'kàn-bú-jyàn 'dūng-shi. ‖How deep is the snow? 'shywě yěw 'dwō-shēn? ‖This is the first snow this winter. jèy shr̀ lì-'dūng yǐ-láy 'téw-yì-chǎng-'shywě.

To snow shyà-'shywě. ‖It snowed a lot last winter. 'chywù-nyán 'dūng-tyān 'shyà-le bù-'shǎw-de-'shywě. ‖It's snowing! shyà-'shywě-le.

Snowdrift shywě-'dwēy.

Snowfall. ‖We'll have a heavy snowfall tonight. is expressed as A lot of snow will fall tonight. jyēr-'wǎn-shang yàw 'shyà yì-'chǎng-dà-'shywě.

Snowstorm fēng-'shywě, gwā-fēng shyà-'shywě. ‖Snowstorms make traveling difficult. dzày gwā-'fēng-shyà-'shywě-de-'tyār-li lywǔ-'shíng jēn bù-'rúng-yì.

To be snowed in. ‖They were snowed in for a whole week. is expressed as A great deal of snow fell, and for a week they couldn't get out of the house. shywě-'shyà-de 'dà-de tām yěw 'yí-ge-lǐ-'bày méy-'néng tsúng-jyā-li 'chū-láy.

To be snowed under. ‖We are snowed under with bills. is expressed as Our bills are heaped up as high as a mountain. wǒm-de-jàng-'dār 'dwēy-de yěw 'shān-nème-'gāw.

SO. (*In this way*) rú-'tsž (*literary*) ; 'jème, 'nàme, 'dzème, 'nème, 'jème-je, 'nème-je, 'jèy-yàngr, 'nèy-yàngr, jème-'yàngr, nàme-'yàngr, dzème-'yàngr, nème-'yàngr. ‖Do it just so. jyèw 'jème 'dzwò. ‖He's all right now, and I hope he'll remain so. tā shyàn-'dzày hǎw-le, jyèw 'shī-wàng tā néng lǎw jèy-'yàngr. ‖So they say. 'tā-men dzème shwō. ‖Why are you so gloomy? nǐ gàn-'má 'dzème-bù-gāw-'shìng-a? ‖If so, I'll have to go. 'yàw-shř 'nà-yàngr, wǒ děy 'dzěw-le. ‖I told you so. wǒ 'gàw-su-gwo nǐ shř 'dzème-hwéy-'shř. or wǒ 'dzème 'gàw-su-gwo nǐ. ‖That's not so! 'bú-shř 'nème-hwéy-'shèr! ‖It certainly is so. 'dāng-rán shř 'nème-hwéy-'shèr. *But* ‖So? *or* Is that so? *meaning either* I don't believe you. *or* Oh! I didn't know that. á? *or* 'jēn-de-ma? *or* 'shř-ma? *or* shř 'nèm-je? *or* shř 'nème-yàngr-ma?

(*Also*) yě. ‖*Mr. A:* I want to go. *Mr. B:* So do I. *Mr. A:* wǒ yàw 'dzěw-le. *Mr. B:* 'wǒ yě yàw dzěw. ‖If I can do it, so can you. 'wǒ yàw-shř néng 'dzwò, 'nǐ yě néng 'dzwó. ‖They're very nice, and so are their children. 'tā-men rén hěn 'hǎw, tā-men-de-'háy-dz 'yě hěn 'hǎw.

(*Indicating agreement*) 'dwèy-le. ‖*Mr. A:* He left you a letter. *Mr. B:* So he did. *Mr. A:* tā gěy-ni 'lyéw-shyà yì-fēng-'shìn. *Mr. B:* 'dwèy-le. ‖*Mr. A:* The door's open. *Mr. B:* So I see. *Mr. A:* 'mén kāy-le. *Mr. B:* 'dwèy-le. wǒ 'chyáw-jyàn-le.

(*Very; very much*) hěn, jēn, tày, 'shř-fēn, ... 'jí-le, ... 'lì-hay, ...-de hěn. ‖You're so clever. nǐ 'jēn 'tsūng-míng. ‖I'm so glad. nà(-me-je) hǎw 'jí-le. ‖I'd better not go out, my head aches so. wǒ 'téw-téng-de 'lì-hay, 'dǐng hǎw 'byé 'chū-chywù-le.

(*Therefore*) 'swǒ-yí, yīn-'tsž, 'swǒ-yǐ-yīn-'tsž. ‖I'm not feeling well, so I think I'd better not go. wǒ jywé-de yěw 'dyǎr bù-'shū-fu, 'swǒ-yǐ wǒ 'shyǎng 'háy-shř bù-'chū-chywù 'hǎw. ‖They left early and so I missed them. tā-men 'dzěw-de 'dzǎw-dyǎr, 'swǒ-yǐ wǒ méy-'jyàn-jaw tā-men.

(*Well; then*) nème, nèm; *or* shř. So ... finally 'hǎw-ma ...'kě ...; *or* 'hē, ...'kě .... ‖So you think that's a good idea, huh? nèm nǐ 'jywé-de 'nèy-ge háy bú-'tswò, á? ‖So you don't believe me? 'nǐ shř bú-'shyàng-shìn 'wǒ-ya. ‖So you don't like it here! nǐ shř bù-'shǐ-hwān 'jèr-ra. ‖So they lived happily ever after. 'nà-men 'tā-men jyèw 'kwày-kway-hwō-'hwó-de gwò-'r-dz-le. ‖So the work's too hard for you! á? nǐ jywé-je 'shèr tày 'má-fan-le! *or* èw! nǐ shyán shèr tày 'nán-le! ‖So you've finally made up your mind! 'hē! nǐ 'kě jywé-'dìng-le! ‖So you've finally come home! 'hǎw-ma, dàw-'lyǎwr nǐ 'kě 'hwéy-láy-le!

And so forth *or* and so on 'děng-děng, 'shéme-de. ‖He had all the symptoms; fever, headache, nervousness, and so on. tā gè-'jǔng-de-bìng-'shyàng shéme-fā-'shāw, 'téw-téng, 'shén-jīng-gwò-'mǐn 'děng-děng 'dēw yěw.

Or so dà-'gày ... shéme-de. ‖Can you spare me a pound or so of sugar? nǐ 'ké-yi 'fēn-gěy wǒ dyǎr-'táng-ma? dà-'gày yí-bàng shéme-de.

So as to 'wèy-de-shř . . (hǎw); . . . 'hǎw; 'nà-men . . . °'ké-yi (°'hǎw, °'néng.) ‖I did some of the work so as to make things easier for her. wǒ bǎ 'nèy-ge-'shř-ching 'dzwò-le-'dyǎr 'wèy-de-shř ràng-ta 'dzwò-je hǎw 'rúng-yì-dyǎr.

So far (*up to now*) yì-'jř-de, 'jř-dàw shyàn-'dzày wéy-'jř, yí-'shyàng. ‖So far I'm bored. yì-'jř-de wǒ 'jywé-de hěn wú-'lyáw. ‖So far, so good. 'jř-dàw shyàn-dzày háy hǎw.

So far as I know (*according to what I know*) jywù 'wǒ-swǒ-'jř-dàw-de; (*I think*) wǒ 'jywé-de. ‖So far as I know, he still lives there. jywù 'wǒ 'jř-dàw tā 'háy dzày-nèr 'jù.

‖So long! *is expressed as* See you again. dzày-'jyàn. *or as* See you later. hwéy-téw-'jyàn. *or* 'dāy-hwěr-'jyàn. *or* yì-hwěr-'jyàn.

So much. *Usually* 'nème-dwō *etc.* (*See first paragraph*) *But* ‖I wish she wouldn't cry so much. *is expressed as* I wish she wouldn't always cry so. wǒ 'shī-wang tā 'byé 'dzèm lǎw 'kū. ‖Thanks ever so much. 'dwō shyè, 'dwō-shyè. *or* tày 'shyè-shyè-le. ‖So much for that (*that's done*) ; what'll we do next? nèy-ge °'wán-le (°'hǎw-le, °'dé-le), wǒ-men gāy 'dzwò shéme-le?

So-so 'méy-shéme, wú-swǒ-'wèy. ‖*Mr. A:* How are you feeling? *Mr. B:* Oh, so-so. *Mr. A:* nǐ 'jywé-de 'dzème-yàng? *Mr. B:* wú-swǒ-'wèy.

So that (*in order that*) *see* so as to *above*; (*with the result that*) 'swǒ-yǐ, 'nùng-de. ‖He made it sound good, so that I'd help him. tā gù-yì-de 'shwō-de hǎw-'tīng, hǎw 'ràng-wo 'bāng-je-ta. ‖It rained very hard, so that the streets were flooded. ywǔ-'shyà-de hěn 'dà, 'swǒ-yǐ 'jyē-shang 'shwěy dēw 'mǎn-le.

So ... that °tày (°'jème, °'nàme, °'dzème, °'nème, °'jèy-yàngr-de, °'nèy-yàngr-de, °jème-yàngr-de, °'nàme-'yàngr-de, °dzème-'yàngr-de, °nème-'yàngr-de) ... 'swǒ-yǐ (jyàn-'jř-de); *or* ...-de. ‖He ran so fast he got all out of breath. tā 'pǎw-de nème-'kwày, swǒ-yǐ jyàn-'jř-de 'chwǎn-bú-gwò 'chyèr-láy-le. ‖I'm so tired I can hardly keep my eyes open. wǒ tày 'lèy-le, 'swǒ-yǐ jyàn-'jř-de jēng-bù-'kāy 'yǎn-le.

So what? *The Chinese expressions, like the English, are not very polite. The usual equivalents are* 'nèm yèw 'dzème-je-ne? *or* 'nèm yèw 'dzème-'yàng-ne? *or* 'nème 'dzème-le? *or expressed as* What's there to be afraid of? nà 'pà shéme-de?

SOAP. 'yí-dz, 'féy-dzàw. *To describe the form in which the soap is made, use the measure for* cake kwày; long bar tyáwr; box bāw *or* shyāng. ‖I want a bar of soap. wǒ yàw yì-'tyáwr-'yí-dz. ‖Do you want a cake of soap, or soap flakes, or powder? nǐ shř 'yàw yí-'kwày-yí-dz, shř 'yàw yí-dz-'pyàr, 'háy shř·yàw 'yí-dz-'fěn?

To soap (*use soap*) shř 'yí-dz, yùng 'yí-dz; (*apply soap*) dǎ 'yí-dz, shàng 'yí-dz. ‖Soap it thoroughly and then rinse it in hot water. shyān bǎ 'yí-dz dǎ 'mǎn lew, rán-'hèw dzày dzày 're-shwěy-lǐ-tew 'téw-tew.

SOCIETY. (*Social community*) 'shè-hwèy. ‖Civic laws are for the good of society. 'mín-fǎ wèy 'shè-hwèy 'gūng-yì ér-'shè. ‖If boys form into dangerous gangs like tha., our whole society is threatened. 'yàw-shr 'háy-dz-men 'dzème-'yàngr-de yì-'chywún-yì-'chywún-de shyā-'nǎw, wǒ-men-jěn-'gèr-de-'shè-hwèy dēw shèw 'wēy-shyé.

(*Fashionable group of people*) 'gāw-děng-shè-'hwèy, 'shàng-lyéw-shè-'hwèy, 'shàng-děng-shè-'hwèy. ‖She's very prominent in local society. tā dzày 'nèy-ge-'dì-fangr-de-'shàng-děng-shè-'hwèy-li hěn chū-'fēng-téw.

(*Organization*) hwèy, 'dzǔ-jr̀. ‖He didn't want to join our society. tā bú-'ywàn-yì 'jyā-rù wǒ-men-de-'hwèy.

(*Companionship*). ‖I enjoy his society very much. *is expressed as* I like to be with him very much. wǒ hěn 'ywàn-yì gēn-ta °dzày yí-'kwàr. *or* °láy wǎng.

SOCK. (*Short stocking*) 'dwǎn-wà-dz, wà-'tàwr. ‖I want three pairs of socks. wǒ yàw sān-'shwāng-'dwǎn-wà-dz.

(*To hit with the fist*) °'dǎ (°'chwéy, °'dzèw, °'gěy) yí-'shyà-dz. ‖If you do that again, I'll sock you. nǐ 'yàw-shr̀ 'dzày nà-yàngr wǒ fēy 'dzèw-nǐ bù-'shíng. *But* ‖Give him a sock on the jaw. 'gěy-tā yí-ge-'dzwěy-ba.

SOFT. (*Not hard*) rwǎn. ‖This pillow is too soft for my taste. 'jèy-ge-'jěn-tew wǒ 'jěn-je tày 'rwǎn. ‖Is the ground soft? dì 'rwǎn-bù-'rwǎn? ‖The heat makes the pavement soft and sticky. tyār 'rè, mǎ-'ι nèng-de yew 'rwǎn yèw 'nyán. ‖Glass is softer than diamonds. 'bwō-li bǐ jīn-gāng-'dzwàr 'rwǎn. ‖That material isn't soft enough for a dress. nèy-ge-'lyàw-dz yàw 'dzwò 'yí-shang bú-gèw 'rwǎn. ‖Soft wood will burn quicker. 'mù-tew 'rwǎn-de 'jáw-de 'kwày. *or expressed as* Wood with a loose fibre burns quickly. 'mù-tew 'sūng 'jáw-de 'kwày.

(*Not bright; gentle, not harsh*) réw, 'réw-he, rwò; (*dim*) àn. ‖A soft light would be better. 'réw-dyǎr-de-dēng-'gwāng yě-'shywǔ 'hǎw-dyǎr.

(*Not loud*) shyǎw. ‖Make the radio softer. *is expressed as* Make the sound of the radio smaller. bǎ wú-shyàn-'dyàn-de-'shēngr nùng 'shyǎw-dyǎr. ‖She sang in a soft voice. *is expressed as* She sang in a small voice. tā 'shyǎw-shēngr 'chàng-láy-je.

(*Gentle, tender-hearted*) shīn-'rwǎn. ‖You are too soft to be an executive. nǐ-shīn tày 'rwǎn, bù-néng 'dzwò gwǎn-rén-de-'sher.

(*Flabby physically*) rwǎn, 'rwǎn-rwò. ‖I'll get soft if I don't get any exercise. wǒ yàw-shr̀ bú-'ywùn-dùng-nga, shēn-ti jyèw °'rwǎn-le. (°bù-'shíng-le.) *or expressed as* If I don't exercise, my physique will be ruined. wǒ yàw-shr̀ bú-'ywùn-dùng-a, shēn-dz-'gǔr jyèw 'hwày-le. ‖I hate soft men. wǒ bù-'shǐ-hwān yí-ge-'rén tày 'rwǎn-rwò. *or expressed as* I don't like a

man whose body isn't strong. shēn-ti bù-'jyē-shr̀-de-'rén wǒ bù-'shǐ-hwān. *or, meaning a namby-pamby sort of individual, as* I hate indecisive people. wǒ tǎw-'yàn nà méy-jwěn 'jú-yì-de-'rén.

Soft-hearted shīn-'rwǎn. *See above.*

SOIL. dì, 'tyán-dì, 'hàn-dì; (*wet soil for growing rice*) ⁴shwěy-dì. ‖What will grow in this soil? jèy-'dǐ-li néng 'jùng 'shéme? ‖This is good rich soil. jèy-ge-'dì hěn 'féy.

Soiled dzāng, 'āng-dzāng. ‖Don't let it get soiled. 'byé bǎ nèy-ge 'nùng 'dzāng-lew. ‖We'll send the soiled clothes to the laundry tomorrow. wǒ-men myéngr-ge bǎ 'dzāng-'yī-shang 'sùng-dàw shǐ-yī-shang-'fángr-chywu.

SOLDIER. (*Man in uniform, enlisted man or officer, usually soldier, but may also be said of a sailor*) 'jywūn-rén; (*informal term for enlisted man*) bīng; (*enlisted man, rather uncomplimentary term*) dà-'bīng; (*colloquial term for enlisted man*) lǎw-'dzǔng; (*uncomplimentary term for any soldier, enlisted man or officer*) chyēw-'bā. ‖This captain is a fine soldier. 'jèy-ge-lyán-'jǎng 'shr̀ yí-ge-hǎw-'jywūn-rén. ‖Are there any soldiers quartered here? yěw 'bīng dzày-'jèr jù-'já-ma? ‖Is this club for soldiers or officers? 'jèy-ge-jywū-le-'bù shr̀ wèy-'bīng-ywù-bèy-de 'háy shr̀ 'wèy-gwān-'jǎng-ywù-bèy-de?

SOLE. (*Only*) jr̀, 'jǐn-jǐn, 'jǐn-yěw-de; (*just*) jyèw. ‖Are we the sole customers? 'jr̀ yěw wǒ-men shr̀ 'jèr-de 'jǔ-gu-ma? ‖He reads books for the sole purpose of getting knowledge. tā 'nyàn shū 'jyèw 'wèy-de-shr̀ dé 'jr̀-shr.

(*Bottom of the foot*) jyǎw-'jǎngr. ‖I have a pain in the sole of my foot. wǒ-jyǎw-'jǎngr yěw dyǎr-'téng.

(*Bottom of a shoe*). Full sole shyé-'dyěr, chywán-'jǎngr; half sole shyé-'jǎngr, chyán-'jǎngr, 'jǎngr. ‖The soles of these shoes are worn out. jèy-(jǐ-)shwāng-'shyé-de-shyé-'dyěr dēw 'pwò-le. ‖I need new soles on these shoes. wǒ jèy-'shyé děy hwàn-'jǎngr-le.

To resole hwàn-'jǎngr. ‖My shoes need to be resoled. wǒ-de-'shvé děy hwàn-'jǎngr-le.

SOLID. (*Firm, strong; of structures*) 'jyē-shr, 'tsź-shr, 'jyān-gù; (*of persons; local Peiping*) bàng. ‖The construction of the building seems solid enough. jèy-dzwò-'léw gày-de chyáw-'yàngr gèw 'jyē-shr-de. ‖This chair doesn't feel very solid to me. wǒ 'jywé-de 'jèy-bǎ-'yǐ-dz bú-dà 'jyē-shr. ‖His body is very solid. tā-'shēn-dz hěn 'bàng. ‖The lake is frozen solid. 'hú dùng 'jyē-shr-le. ‖Is the ice solid? bīng 'tsź-shr-ma?

(*Not hollow*) sž-ga-°'dár (°'tángr); (*real throughout*) 'shŕ-de, shŕ-'jáwr. ‖Is the beam solid or hollow? fáng-'lyáng shr̀ sž-ga-'dár-de 'háy-shr̀ 'kūng-de?

(*Whole; of units of time*) jěng, jěng-'jēngr; (*full*) dzú, dzú-'dzūr-de. ‖He talked to me for a solid hour. tā gēn-wo 'tán-le jěng-'jēng-de yí-ge-jūng-'téw.

(*Real*). ‖This is solid comfort. *is expressed as* This is really comfort. jèy 'jēn shř 'shū-fu. ‖You'll get solid pleasure out of this pipe. *is expressed as* You'll certainly be completely satisfied with this pipe. jèy-ge-yān-'děwr nǐ yí-'dìng néng 'shŕ-fēn 'mǎn-yì.

(*The same throughout; pure*) chwén; (*also of colors; local Peiping*) yì-'mǎr. Solid gold chwén-'jīn; solid mahogany chwén-'húng-mù *or expressed as* entirely (made of) mahogany chywán shř 'húng-mù-(dzwò-)de. ‖I want a solid blue material. wǒ 'yàw yí-'kwày-yì-mǎr-'lán-de (*or* chwén-'lán-de)-'lyàw-dz.

(*Dependable*) kě-'kàw, kàw-de-'jù; (*creditable*) yěw-'shìn-yùng. ‖You seem to be a solid sort of person. wǒ kàn nǐ shř ge-hěn-'kàw-de-jù-de-'rén. ‖This is a solid concern. 'jèy shř 'yí-ge-hěn-yěw-'shìn-yùng-de-'pù-dz.

A solid 'yìng-dūng-shi; (*of food*) yìng-'shŕ. ‖The doctor told him not to eat solids for a few days. 'dày-fu jyàw-tā 'jèy-jǐ-tyān shyān 'byé chř yìng-'shŕ.

SOME. (*A little*) ɑyar, yì-'dyǎr, shyē, yì-'shyē. ‖Take some meat. 'láy-dyǎr 'rèw. ‖Give me some more water. gěy-wǒ 'dzày láy dyǎr-'shwěy. ‖I want some of that material. wǒ 'yàw yì-'dyǎr-nèy-ge-'lyàw-dz. ‖He objected some, but we persuaded him. tā 'yěw dyǎr-fǎn-'dwèy, 'kě-shř wǒ-men 'bǎ-ta shwō-'fú-le.

(*A few*) jǐ *or* 'hǎw-jǐ *plus measure;* dyǎr, yì-'dyǎr, shyē, yì-'shyē. ‖Could I have some towels? néng 'gěy-wo jǐ-tyáw-'shěw-jīn-ma? ‖Take some of these books. 'jèy-shyē-'shū ná 'jǐ-běr chywù-ba.

(*A fair quantity of*) dyǎr, yì-'dyǎr, shyē, yì-'shyē, shyāng-'dāng-de. ‖He's a man of some reputation. tā-'jèy-ge-rén 'yěw dyǎr-'míng-wàng. ‖I've been working for some time (*days*). wǒ dzwò-'shř 'dzwò-le yěw shyē-'ř-dz-le. ‖The garden is some distance from the house. nèy-ge-hwā-'ywár lí 'jèy-ge-fáng-dz 'yěw-dyǎr dàwr.

(*Unspecified*) 'yí-ge (shéme), ge (shéme), shéme. ‖We've been trying to find some way out of our difficulties. wǒ-men yàw 'shyǎng ge-shéme-'fá-dz dǎ-'pwò nèy-ge-'kwèn-nàn láy-je. ‖Some friend of hers gave it to her. 'tā-de-yí-ge-'péng-yew 'sùng-gěy tā-de.

Some day. *See* SOMETIME. Some place. *See* SOMEWHERE.

(*Certain*) yěw, 'yěw-de. ‖Some fellows didn't like this movie. yěw-de-'rén bù-'shǐ-hwān 'jèy-ge-dyàn-'yěngr. ‖Some types are better suited for printing this (*than this is*). wèy yìn 'jèy-ge 'yěw-de-dż-'tǐ bǐ 'jèy-ge 'hǎw.

(*At least one, with emphasis*) yí(-ge), *another measure, or nothing.* ‖There must be SOME way of finding out! yí-'dìng 'yěw ge-'fá-dz 'chá-chū-láy. ‖No doubt SOME people think so! yí-'dìng 'yěw-rén 'dzème 'shyǎng.

(*Unusually good or bad*) 'hǎw-yí . . . , 'hǎw-ma, 'hǎw-jyā-hwō, jēn kě-'yǐ; (*of a person*) jēn 'shíng; *all of these mean, as in English*, It's terrific!, *either good or bad.* ‖That's some house they live in! tā-men 'jù-de 'hǎw yì-swǒr-'fáng-dz. *or* 'tā-men 'jù-de nèy-swǒr-'fáng-dz 'jēn kě-'yǐ. ‖She's some gal! 'hǎw yí-ge-nywǔ-'háy-dz. *or* 'tā jèy-ge-nywǔ-'háy-dz °'hǎw-ma. (°'hǎw-jyā-hwō, ˇjēn kě-'yǐ, °jēn 'shíng.) ‖This has been some job! jèy-ge-'shř-ching kě jēn kě-'yǐ.

(*About*) yěw, dà-'gài yěw. ‖I played with the baby some twenty or thirty minutes. wǒ gēn 'nèy-háy-dz 'wár-le yěw 'èr-sān-shr-fēn-'jūng.

(*Unspecified ones*) yěw, 'yěw-de. ‖Some of these cups are broken. jèy-shyē-chá-'bēy yěw-de 'shwāy-le. ‖Some of you may disagree with me. nǐ-men jř-'jūng yě-'shywǔ yěw-'rén gēn wǒ-de-'yì-jyàn bù-'túng.

Some . . . or other. (*It doesn't make any difference which*) bú-'lwèn něy(-ge); (*I don't know which*) 'jř-bú-dìng něy. ‖Try to get some typist or other to do the job. shyǎng-'fár bú-'lwèn 'jǎw něy-ge-dǎ-dż-'ywán láy 'dzwò jèy-ge-'shř. ‖It's in some book or other on that shelf. nèy-ge shř 'dzày shū-'jyà-dz-shang 'jř-bú-dìng 'něy-běr-'shú-li.

SOMEBODY. (*An unspecified person*) yěw-'rén; somebody (or other) 'yě bù(-shř)-shéy, 'yě bú(-shř) 'shéme-'rén. ‖Somebody phoned you while you were out. nǐ 'chū-chywū de-'shŕ-hèwr 'yěw-rén 'gěy-ni 'dǎ-dyàn-'hwà láy-je.

(*A person of some importance*) 'rén-wù, 'dà-rén-wù. ‖He's really somebody in that town. dzày 'nèy-ge-'chéng-li tā 'jēn shř ge-'rén-wù.

SOMEHOW. bù-'gwǎn dzěme-je, bú-'lwèn dzěme-je; somehow (*or other*) 'yě bù-dzěme, 'yě bú-shř 'dzěme-hwéy-'shèr. ‖Somehow, I never did meet him. 'yě bú-shř 'dzěme-hwéy-'shèr, wǒ méy-'pèng-jyàn-gwo tā. ‖Somehow or other, that idea seems foolish to me. yě bù-'dzěme wǒ 'jywé-de nèy-ge-jú-'yì hěn 'bèn.

SOMETHING. (*A little*) dyǎr, . . . -dyǎr, 'dwō-shǎw . . . dyǎr. ‖There is something left of the old temper. 'lǎw-'pí-chi háy 'yěw-dyǎr. ‖He knows something about medicine. tā 'dwō-shǎw 'jř-dàw-'dyǎr 'yī-shywé. *But* ‖I saw something of him yesterday. *is expressed as* I saw him for a while yesterday. wǒ 'dzwóer-ge 'kàn-jyàn tā yì-'hwěr. ‖That's something like it. èy! jè háy °'shyàng-dyǎr 'hwà. *or* °'shyàng-dyǎr 'yàngr.

(*An unspecified thing*) shéme. ‖If you want something, ring the bell. nǐ 'yàw-shr ˈyàw shéme de-'hwà, èn-'lyéngr jyèw shíng-le. ‖Wouldn't you like a little something to eat? nǐ bú-'yàw-dyǎr shéme-'chř-ma? *But* ‖Is something the matter? 'dzěme-le? *or* shéme-'shř?

(*A certain thing*) dyǎr, shyē. ‖There is something peculiar here. jèr 'yěw-dyǎr 'gwày. ‖There is something else I want. wǒ háy 'yàw-dyǎr 'byé-de.

(*Some significance*). ‖There's something in what you say. *is expressed as* What you say is rather reasonable. nǐ-'shwō-de 'shyāng-dāng yěw-'lǐ.

To be something of 'swàn yí-ge, 'swàn shr̀ ge. ‖He's something of a pianist. tā 'ké-yǐ swàn yí-ge-gāng-chín-'jyā.

Something or other dyǎr 'shéme-'dūng-shi, dyǎr 'shéme-'shr̀-ching; *or* yě-bú-shr̀ °'shéme (°'dzěme). ‖Something or other reminded me of home. 'yě-bú-shr̀ 'shéme jyàw-wǒ 'shyǎng-chǐ 'jyā láy-le. ‖I'm sure I've forgotten something or other. *is expressed as* I've certainly forgotten °some business. *or* °some thing. wǒ yí-'dìng 'wàng-le-dyǎr °'shéme-'shr̀-ching. *or* °'shéme-'dūng-shi.

SOMETIME. (*In the future*) jyāng-'láy; (*some day in the future*) (jyāng-'láy) něy-'tyān; (*some time in the future*) (jyāng-'láy) 'shéme-'shr̀-hew; (*one of these days*) yěw 'nèm-yì-'tyān. ‖I want to go to Europe sometime. wǒ 'dǎ-swàn jyāng-'láy 'shàng-tàng 'ēw-jew. ‖Can I have a date with you sometime this week? jèy-ge-'shīng-chi něy-'tyān wǒ-men 'chū-chywù 'wár-war, 'hǎw-ma? ‖I'd like to read it sometime or other. wǒ 'shyǎng něy-'tyān 'kàn-kan 'nèy-ge.

(*In the past*) 'yě bú-shr̀ 'shéme-shr̀-hew. ‖The accident happened sometime last night. dzwór-'wǎn-shang 'yě bú-shr̀ 'shéme-shr̀-hew 'chū-de shèr.

SOMETIMES. 'yěw(-de)-shr̀-hew; (*often*) 'cháng-hewr, 'shr̀-cháng, 'cháng yěw-'shr̀-hewr. ‖I get mixed up sometimes. wǒ 'yěw-shr̀-hewr jyèw 'nùng 'hú-du-le. *Mr. A:* Do you ever see her? *Mr. B:* Sometimes. *Mr. A:* nǐ yěw shr̀-hew 'kàn-jyàn tā-ma? *Mr. B:* yěw-'shr̀-hew 'kàn-jyàn.

SOMEWHAT. 'yěw-dyǎr, yì-'dyǎr, shyē, yì-'shyē. ‖This differs somewhat from the usual type. *is expressed as* This and the usual thing are somewhat not the same. 'jèy-ge gēn pǔ-'tūng-de 'yěw-dyǎr 'bú-dà yí-'yàng. ‖That is somewhat more expensive. nèy-ge 'yěw-dyǎr gèng 'gwèy.

SOMEWHERE. nǎr, 'shéme-'dì-fangr, 'yí-ge-'dì-fangr; somewhere (or other) yě bú-shr̀ °'nǎr (°'shéme-'dì-fangr), 'jǐr-bú-dìng °'nǎr (°'shéme-'dì-fangr). ‖I'm sure I've seen her somewhere before. wǒ yí-'dìng yǐ-'chyán dzày-'nǎr 'kàn-jyàn-gwo tā. ‖She comes from somewhere down south. tā yě bú-shr̀ tsúng nán-'fāng shéme-'dì-fang 'láy-de. ‖I want to go somewhere in the country for my vacation. *is expressed as* I want to go to a place out of town for my vacation. wǒ yàw dàw chéng-'wày-yí-ge-'dì-fang chywù shyē-'jyà. ‖That book must be somewhere or other on this shelf. nèy-běr-'shū yí-'dìng dzày jèy-ge-shū-'jyà-dz-shang 'jǐr-bú-dìng 'nǎr. *But* ‖That letter must be somewhere in this desk. *is expressed as* That letter is certainly in this desk. nèy-fēng-'shìn yí-'dìng shr̀ dzày jèy-'jwō-dz-li-ne.

SON. 'ér-dz; (*baby*) shyǎw-'hár; (*child*) 'háy-dz; (*modest way of referring to one's own son*) shyǎw-'chywǎn; (*polite way of referring to someone else's son*) lìng-'láng; (*master, young man*) 'gūng-dž, 'shàw-yé. (*Never address a younger person as* "son" 'ér-dz; *it is very insulting.*) ‖This is my son. 'jèy shr̀ 'wǒ-de-shyǎw-'hár. ‖How many sons do you have? nín yěw 'jǐ-wèy-lìng-'láng? ‖All of you bring your sons and daughters. nǐ-men dà-'jyā 'dēw bǎ 'shàw-ye 'shyáw-jye 'dày-láy.

SONG. (*In general*) gēer; (*melody*) gē-'chywǔ, chywùr; (*folksong*) gē-'yáw; (*children's song*) túng-'yáw; (*hillbilly song*) shān-'gēer; (*anything sung*) chàngr; (*short musical composition*) shyǎw-'chywǔr, shyǎw-'dyàwr.

(*Of birds*) *expressed as* sound 'shēng-yīn. ‖Can you recognize the songs of different birds? nǐ 'tīng-de-chū-láy gè-'jǔng-'nyǎwr-jyàw-de-'shēng-yīn-ma?

For a song (*cheap*) 'pyán-yi, jyàn. ‖Here you can pick up things like that for a song. dzày-'jèr měy 'dūng-shi 'pyán-yi 'íí-le.

SOON. (*In a short while*) jyèw, bù-'jyèw, 'méy-dwō-jyěw, yì-'hwěr, bú-dà-hwěr, méy-dwó-dà-'hwěr, yì-'hwěr-de-'gūng-fu, bú-'dà-de-'gūng-fu. ‖I'll be back soon. wǒ yì-'hwěr jyèw 'hwéy láy. ‖He came soon after I left. wǒ 'dzěw-le yǐ-'hèw 'méy-dwō-dà-'hwěr tā jyèw 'láy-le. ‖The war was soon over. 'jàn-shr̀ bù-'jyěw jyèw 'gwò-chywu-le.

(*Quickly*) kwày. ‖The sooner the better. ywè-'kwày ywè-'hǎw. ‖I won't be back till five at the soonest. wǒ dzwèy-'kwày yě 'děy 'wǔ-dyǎn 'tsáy néng 'hwéy-láy-ne. ‖Why do you have to leave so soon? nǐ 'wèy-shéme yí-'dìng yàw 'dzème-kwày 'dzěw-wa?

(*Willingly*) *expressed as* to be willing 'ywàn-yi, chíng-'ywàn, nìng-'ywàn. ‖I'd just as soon not go. wǒ chíng-'ywàn bú-'chywù. ‖He said he'd stay home as soon as not. tā shwō tā 'ywàn-yi dzày 'jyā-li 'dāy-je. ‖He'd sooner die than give in. tā nìng-'ywàn 'sž yě 'bù-fú-'shū.

As soon as (*of time*) shéme-'snf-hew yī . . . jyèw; (*gāng*) yī . . . jyèw. ‖Let me know as soon as you get here. nǐ yí 'dàw-jèr, jyèw 'tūng-jr wo yì-shēngr. ‖I told you as soon as I knew myself. wǒ yì-'jr̄ daw jyèw 'gàw-su nǐ-le. ‖As soon as you feel any pain; take a dose of this. 'shéme shr̀-hew yì jywé-je 'téng, jyèw hē yí-jì jèy-ge-'yàw.

No sooner . . . than *is expressed as* not yet is . . . finished, then . . . háy méy . . . 'wán-ne, jyèw; *or as* just . . . then . . . gāng . . . jyèw. ‖No sooner said than done. yí-jywù-'hwà háy méy-shwō-'wán-ne jyèw 'dé-le. ‖He had no sooner mentioned her name than she came in. tā gāng yì-'shwō tā-'míng-dz, tā jyèw 'jìn-láy-le.

Sooner or later 'dzǎw-wǎn; *or expressed as* There'll come a day. jwěn yěw yì-'tyān. ‖I'll have to see him sooner or later. wǒ 'dzǎw-wǎn děy 'jyàn-ta. ‖Sooner or later you'll have to make up your mind. 'dzǎw-wǎn nǐ 'děy jywé-'dìng-a.

SORE. téng, tùng. ‖My throat is sore. wǒ-'sǎng-dz 'téng. ‖This bruise is sore to the touch. jèy-kwày-'shāng yí-'pèng jyèw 'téng. ‖Look out for my sore toe. *is expressed as* My toe hurts. Be careful. wǒ 'nèy-ge-jyǎw-'jř-tew 'téng. lyéw-dyǎr-'shén. *or as* Be careful of my hurt toe. lyéw-'shén wǒ-de-'hwày-jyǎw-'jř-tew.

    (*Cut, wound, bruise; some injury received from external causes*) shāng; (*boil, pimple*) pàw; (*swelling*) jǔng. ‖There is a sore on my foot. wǒ-'jyǎw-shang yěw yí-kwày-'shāng. ‖This sore is pretty well healed up now. jèy-kwày-'shāng shyàn-'dzày 'yǐ-jing jǎng-'hǎw-le.

    (*Angry*) shēng-'chì. ‖Don't get sore; I didn't mean anything. byé shēng-'chì, wǒ bú-shr gù-'yì-de.

SORROW. *Expressed as* be sorrowful nán-'gwò, shāng-'shīn; *or as* great unhappiness 'fán-nǎw. ‖He's caused his family a good deal of sorrow. tā 'jēn jyàw tā-'jyā-li-de-'rén nán-'gwò. ‖She's sick with sorrow. tā shāng-'shīn 'jí-le. ‖That is the only real sorrow he's ever had. nà shr tā-shēng-'píng-wéy-'yí-de-jēn-'fán-nǎw.

SORRY. (*Feeling pity*) A is (*or feels*) sorry for B A jywé-je B kě-'lyán; I feel sorry for . . . . . . 'jēn kě-'lyán. ‖He feels sorry for you. tā jywé-je nǐ kě-'lyán. ‖I felt sorry for him and didn't press for payment. wǒ jywé-je tā hěn kě-'lyán-de, jyèw 'méy-wèn-ta yàw nèy-bǐ-'chyán. ‖I feel sorry for you. nǐ 'jēn kě-'lyán. ‖I felt sorry for you; what a fool I was! wǒ 'ywán-láy háy jywé-je nǐ kě-'lyán-ne; wǒ dzěme nèm 'shǎ-ya!

    (*Repentant*) hèw-'hwěy. ‖I'm not sorry I did it. *is expressed as* I did it and am not a bit repentant. wǒ 'gàn-le nèy-'dàng-dz-shr yì-dyǎr yě bú-hèw-'hwěy.

    (*Apologetic*) bàw-'chyàn (*literary*), dwèy-bu-'chǐ, dwèy-bú-'jù; (*be embarrassed*) yěw-'dyǎr bù-hǎw-'yì-sz, yěw-'dyǎr nán-wéy-'chíng. ‖Did I bump you? I'm sorry. wǒ 'pèng-le 'nín-le-ma? dwèy-bù-'chǐ-ya. ‖I'm sorry to be late. wǒ láy 'wǎn-le °hěn dwèy-bu-'chǐ. *or* °jēn yěw-'dyǎr bù-hǎw-'yì-sz.

    (*Poor, bad*) dzāw. ‖She did a sorry job of cleaning this room. jèy-ge-'fáng-dz tā 'dǎ-sǎw-de 'tày dzāw-le.

    (*Pathetic*) láng-bèy-bu-'kān-de. ‖He's a sorry looking person. nèy-ge-'rén 'kàn-je 'jēn shr yěw-dyǎr láng-bèy-bù-'kān-de-'shén-chì.

SORT. jǔng, lèy, yàngr. *See also* KIND. ‖What sort of a man is he? tā shr 'dzěme yì-'jǔng-'rén? *or* tā shr 'shéme-'yàngr-de-'rén? ‖We don't allow that sort

of thing. wǒm-jèr bù-'shywǔ yěw 'nèy-yàngr-de-'shr-ching. ‖They have all sorts of books. tā-men yěw 'gè-jǔng-de-'shū. *or* °'gè-lèy-de-'shū. *or* °'gè-shř-'gè-yàngr-de-'shū. ‖He's not a bad sort. *is expressed as* He's OK. tā 'rén 'bú-'hwày. *or* °háy-'hǎw.

    To sort fēn, fēn-'lèy, 'fēn-kay; (*of people only*) fēn-'dzǔ, fēn-'bār. ‖I must sort these. wǒ děy bǎ 'jè-'shyē 'fēn-fen. ‖Have these been sorted? jèy-shyē-ge 'fēn-gwò-'lèy-ma? ‖We sorted the students according to their ability. wǒ-men bǎ 'shywé-shēng àn-je tā-men-de-'néng-lì °'fēn-kay-le. *or* °fēn-'dzǔ.

    A sort of nèm-yì-'jǔng. ‖It's a sort of gift some people have. yěw-shyē-'rén yew nèm-yì-'jǔng-'tyān-fen. ‖You can't help feeling a sort of admiration for a man like that. nǐ dwèy-ywú 'nà-yàngr-de-'rén děy yěw nèm-yì-'jǔng-'pèy-fu-de-shīn-'lǐ.

    Sort of dyǎr. ‖I'm sort of glad things happened the way they did. 'shr-ching 'chéng-le 'jè-yàngr wǒ yěw-dyǎr gāw-'shìng. ‖I'd sort of like to go. wǒ yěw-'dyǎr shyǎng 'chywù. ‖She's interesting, sort of. tā 'yěw-dyǎr 'yì-sz.

    Out of sorts (*either sick or just nervous and irritable*) bù-'shū-fu. ‖I'm feeling a little out of sorts today. 'jyèr wǒ 'jywé-de 'yěw-dyǎr bù-'shū-fu.

SOUND. (*Noise*) 'shēng-yīn, shēngr, shyǎng. ‖I thought I heard a funny sound. wǒ 'jywé-hu-je wǒ 'tīng-jyàn-le yì-'shēng-hěn-'chí-gwày-de-'shēng-yīn. ‖I don't like the sound of the motor. *is expressed as* The sound of the motor has something wrong. jèy-ge-'jī-chi-de-'shēng-yīn 'yěw-dyǎr bú-'dwèy. ‖What was that sound? 'nèy shr 'shéme-'shyǎng?

    (*Body of water*) hǎy-'jyǎ *or* hǎy-'shyá. ‖Let's go for a sail on the sound. 'dzán-men dàw 'nèy-ge-hǎy-'jyǎ-li 'dzwò-dzwò 'chwán chywù.

    To be soundproof (*be able to cut off sound*) néng gé-'yīn, jyàw 'shēng-yīn gwò-bu-'lay. ‖The telephone booth has soundproof walls. jèy-ge-dyàn-'hwà-'gé-dz-de 'chyáng néng gé-'yīn.

    To be within sound of (*be able to hear*) tīng-de-'jyàn. ‖She didn't know we were within sound of her voice. tā bù-jř-'dàw wǒ-men tīng-de-'jyàn tā shwō-'hwà.

    To sound 'tīng-je. ‖That shout sounded very close. nèy-ge-'rǎng-de-'shēng-yīn 'tīng-je 'lí-jèr hěn 'jìn. ‖Your voice sounds funny over the telephone. nǐ-de-'shēng-yīn 'jyē-je dyàn-'hwà 'tīng-je tǐng tè-'byé. ‖That sounds like thunder. nèy-ge 'tīng-je shyàng dǎ-'léy shr̀-de. ‖It sounds impossible. *is expressed as* It sounds as though it can't be done. nèy-ge 'tīng-je shyàng bù-kě 'néng. ‖How does that sound to you? nèy-ge nǐ 'tīng-je 'dzěme-'yàng? *or expressed as* What do you think about it? nèy-ge nǐ 'jywé-hu-je 'dzěme-'yàng? ‖What you say about him makes him sound very nice. nǐ dzěme yì shwō 'bǎ-ta 'shwō-de tīng hǎw shr̀-de. ‖He sounds very sincere, but he isn't. *is expressed as* His words sound sincere; but he's not at all that way. tā-de-'hwà 'tīng-je hěn 'chéng-kěn, 'kě-shr̀ 'shí-dzày bìng 'bú-shr̀ nà-men-hwéy-'shr̀.

(*To signal by sound*). ‖The bugle sounded retreat. *is expressed as* The bugle blew retreat. 'něy-ge-'chwēy-de shř shyà-chí-'hàw. ‖The police sounded an alarm. *is expressed as* The police department sent out a signal. jǐng-chá-'jywú 'fàng-le ge-'shìn-'hàw. *or as* The policemen blew their whistles. jǐng-'chá chwēy 'shàwr-le.

(*To measure depth*) 'tsè-lyáng 'shēn-dù; 'lyáng-lyang dwó-'shēn *or* 'tsè-lyang-'tsè-lyang dwó-'shēn. ‖They sounded the lake, before they allowed people to swim there. tā-men shyān 'lyáng-lyang něy-ge-'hú yěw dwó-'shēn rán-hèw tsáy shywǔ-'rén chywù yéw-'yǔng-ne. ‖They took soundings of the harbor. tā-men bǎ 'jèy-ge-gǎřg-'wǎn-de-'shēn-dù 'tsè-lyáng-le 'tsè-lyang.

To sound out (*to question*) 'tàn-tīng. ‖He sounded me out on the subject. něy-jyàn-'shř tā 'tàn-tīng wǒ-de-'kěw-chì láy-je.

(*Strong, in good condition*) 'jyē-shr; *or often simply* hǎw. ‖The floor is old but sound. jèy-ge-dì-'bǎn jyěw-le 'kě-shr 'jyē-shr. ‖He's still in sound health. tā-'shēn-tǐ háy hěn °'hǎw (°'jyē-shr.) ‖His mind is still sound. tā-de-'jīng-shen háy hěn 'hǎw.

(*Reliable*) kàw-de-'jù; (*steady*) wěn, 'wěn-dāng. ‖Are you sure the business is sound? nǐ 'shwō něy-ge-'mǎy-may 'wěn-ma?

(*Reasonable*) yěw-'lǐ. ‖She gave him sound advice. tā 'chywàn-ta 'chywàn-de hěn yěw-'lǐ. ‖That's a sound argument. něy-ge-'bwó-de tǐng yěw-'lǐ.

(*Valid; having a basis*) yěw-'gēn-jywù-de, (*legal*) hé-'fǎ-de, (*real*) jēn-'jèng-de, (*reliable*) kàw-de-'jù-de, (*really true*) 'chyān-jēn-wàn-'chywè-de. ‖Can you prove that you have a sound claim to the property? *is expressed as* You say the property is yours; have you any real proof? nǐ shwō 'chǎn-yè shř 'nǐ-de, nǐ yěw shém 'chyān-jēn-wàn-'chywè-de-'jèng-jywu-ma?

Sound sleep. ‖I had a sound sleep last night. dzwóer-'wǎn-shang wǒ 'shwèy-de tǐng °'shyāng (°'jáw, °'hǎw, °'wěn, °'sž).

Safe and sound méy-'shř. ‖Did you get home safe and sound? hwéy-'jyā yí-'lù méy-'shř-ma?

SOUP. tāng. ‖Give me a bowl of chicken soup, please. gěy-wo láy 'wǎn-jī-'tāng.

SOUR. (*Acid to taste, or fermented, spoiled*) swān. Sour pickles swān-'tsày; sweet and sour spareribs táng-'tsù páy-gu *or* 'tyán-swān 'páy-gu. ‖This fruit is sour. jèy-ge-'gwǒ-dz hěn 'swān. ‖The milk is sour. 'nyéw-nǎy 'swān-le.

(*Disagreeable*). ‖She's a sour old maid. *is expressed as* That old maid's disposition is very bad. 'tā jèy-ge-lǎw-'gū-nyang 'pí-chi jēn 'hwày. ‖Look at the old sour-puss. *is expressed as* Look at him with his face so stern and crabby. 'chyáw-ta 'nème °běng-je 'lyǎn *or* °'bǎn-je 'lyǎn.

To sour (*become sour*) byàn 'swān. ‖I'm letting the milk sour. wǒ 'ràng něy-ge-nyéw-'nǎy byàn 'swān-lew.

Sour grapes. ‖That's nothing but a case of sour grapes with him. *is expressed as* It must be because he's jealous. (*Envious*) tā 'něm-je 'bú-gwò shř yīn-wey °yǎr-'rè 'jyèw shř-le. *or* (*Eating vinegar; more commonly said of women*) °chř-'tsù 'jyèw shř-le. *or* (*Covetous*) °kàn-je 'byé-rén yǎn-'húng jyèw shř-le.

(*Damp*). ‖The cellar smells sour. *is expressed as* The cellar has a damp smell. jèy-ge-dì-'yìn-dz-li yěw yì-gǔ-'cháw-chi-wèr.

SOURCE. (*Point of origin*) ywán, 'láy-ywán. ‖Where is the source of this river? *is expressed as* The water source of this river is where? jèy-tyáw-'hé-de-shwěy-'ywán dzày-'nǎr? *or as* Where does this river start? jèy-tyáw-'hé tsúng-'nǎr 'fā-ywán? ‖What is your source of supplies? nǐ-'dūng-shi dēw-shr dǎ-'nǎr nùng-láy? ‖What is your source of information. nǐ jèy-ge-'shyāw-shi tsúng-'nǎr dé-láy-de? *But, of a person* ‖He's a good source of information. *is expressed as* He is always ready with information. tā-de-'shyāw-shi hěn 'líng-tung.

(*Cause*) 'ywán-yīn, (*literary*) 'yīn-sù. ‖Have you found the source of the trouble? chǐ-'hwò-de-'ywán-yīn dzày-'nǎr nǐ 'jǎw-chū-láy-le-ma? *or more naturally expressed as* Did you find out where the trouble is? hwò-'yīn dzày-'nǎr nǐ 'jǎw-chū-láy-ma? ‖His success has been a source of great pride to all of us. *is expressed as* His success gave us no little pride. tā-jèy-yì-chéng-'gūng gěy wǒ-men dzēng-'gwāng bù-'shǎw.

(*Literary material*) 'tsáy-lyàw. ‖This book is based on several published sources. *is expressed as* This book is based on several kinds of published material. jèy-běr-'shū shř 'gēn-jywù hǎw-jǐ-jǔng-chū-bǎn-gwò-de-'tsáy-lyàw shyě-de.

SOUTH, SOUTHERN. nán; 'nán-byar, 'nán-fang. Southern region nán-'bù. ‖This farm extends about a mile from north to south. jèy-kwày-'dì tsúng-'nán dàw-'běy 'chà-bu-dwō yěw 'yì-lǐ-'dì. ‖It's on the south side of town. (*within the town*) 'něy-ge dzày °'nán-chéng. *or* (*outside the town*) °'chéng-'nán. ‖There's a south wind tonight. jyēr-'wǎn-shang gwā 'nán-fēng. ‖We travelled through the south of France. wǒm lywǔ-'shíng 'jīng-gwò 'fà-gwo-de-nán-'bù. ‖Down south they take things easier. 'nán-byar dzwò-'shř 'bú-nème-'máng-mang-dāw-'dāw-de. ‖I want to go south for the winter. 'dūng-tyan wǒ yàw dàw 'nán-byar 'chywù yí-tàng. ‖The southern half is farming country. 'nán-byar-yí-'bàr-dì-fang dēw jùng 'jwāng-jyà. ‖I love southern cooking. wǒ 'shǐ-hwan chř 'nán-fang-'tsày. ‖I'd prefer a room with southern exposure. *is expressed as* I'd prefer a room facing south. wǒ 'ywàn-yì yàw yì-jyān-cháw-'nán-de-'wū-dz.

Southern Hemisphere 'nán-bàn-chyéw.

SPACE. (*Extension*) 'kūng-jyàn. ‖We cannot conceive of things outside space and time. wǒ-men shyǎng 'shéme-shř-ching yě 'chū-bù-lyǎw 'shř-jyān-'kūng-jyàn-de-'chywār. ‖How fast is that star moving through space?

nèy-ge-'shīng-shing dzày 'kūng-jyān 'dzěw-de yěw dwō 'kwày?

To stare into space fā-'lèng. ‖He just sat there staring out into space. tā 'jyèw-shř 'dzwò dzày-nèr fā-'lèng.

(*Part marked off in some way*). ‖Is this space big enough to build a house on? *is expressed as* Is this land enough to build a house on? jèy-kwày-'dì gèw 'gày swǒr-'fáng-de-ma? ‖There's a wide space between the two buildings. *is expressed as* Between the two buildings is a wide piece of vacant land. lyǎ-léw-'jūng-jyàr yěw yí-'dà-pyàn-'kùng-dyèr. ‖There's a narrow space between our building and the next. *is expressed as* Between our building and the next there's a small passage. wǒ-men-'léw gēn tā-men-'léw-de-dāng-'jyàr yěw ̣yí-'lyèw-shyǎw-gwò-'dàwr. ‖How much space do you want between the two desks? *is expressed as* How much emptiness do you want between the two desks? nǐ shwō lyǎ-'jwō-dz-jūng-'jyàr ̣lyéw dwó-dà-'kùngr?

(*Extent of time*). ‖He did the work in the space of a day. *is expressed as* He did the work in a day's time. tā 'nèy-jyàn-'shř 'dzwò-le yěw yì-'tyān-de-'gūng-fu. ‖You ought to have that finished in a short space of time. *is expressed as* You can certainly finish that in a short period of time. nǐ yí-'dìng yì-'hwěr-de 'gūng-fu jyèw 'kě-yi dzwò-'wán.

(*Room*) 'dì-fangr. ‖That piano takes up too much space in his room. tā-'fáng-dz-li nèy-ge-gāng-'chín 'tày jàn 'dì-fangr. ‖Is there any space for my luggage? yěw 'dì-fangr 'gē wǒ-de-'shíng-li-ma? ‖Write small to save space. shyě 'shyǎw-dyǎr 'shěng-dyǎr 'dì-fangr.

To space. ‖The posts are spaced a foot apart. *is expressed as* The posts are set a foot apart. nèy-shyē-'jù-dz dēw 'páy-de 'lí yì-'chř 'ywǎn.

SPARE. ‖Spare me the details. *is expressed as* You don't need to tell me the whole thing in detail. 'yùng-bu-jáw 'shyáng-shyang-shì-'shì-de gēn-wo 'shwō. ‖He was spared that ordeal. *is expressed as* He didn't have to go through that ordeal. tā méy-'shèw-jáw nèy-ge-'dzwèy. *or as* He escaped that ordeal. nèy-ge-'dzwèy tā swàn 'táw-kay-le. ‖I've spared no expense in building the house. gày nèy-ge-'fáng-dz de-shř-hew, dzày yùng-'chyán-shang wǒ yì-'dyǎr yě méy-'shyǎw-chi. ‖His life was spared. *is expressed as* Life was granted him. 'ráw-le tā yí-'mìng.

(*To lend*) jyè; (*to give*) 'ywún-gey, gěy. ‖I can spare you some money. wǒ 'kě-yi 'jyè-ni dyǎr-'chyán. ‖Can you spare a cigarette? nǐ yěw 'fù-ywu-de-yān-'jywǎr 'ywún-gey-wo yì-'gēr-ma? ‖Mister, can you spare a dime? 'shyān-sheng, gěy-wo yì-máw-'chyán-ba. ‖Can you spare a minute? *is expressed as* May I trouble you a minute? wǒ 'dǎ-jyǎw nín yí-'shyàr, shíng-ma?

(*Extra*) 'fù-ywu; a spare room kùng-'fáng-dz; spare time 'fù-ywu-shř-'jyān, (shyán-) 'gūng-fu. ‖I

haven't got much spare cash. wǒ 'méy-yew shéme-'fù-ywu-shyàn-'chyán. ‖Do you have any spare parts for your radio? nǐ jèy-ge-wú-shyàn-'dyàn yěw líng-'jyàr-ma? ‖I'll do it in my spare time. wǒ yěw 'gūng-fu de-shí-hew 'dzwò nèy-ge. ‖I haven't a spare minute. wǒ 'yì-dyǎr-shyán-'gūng-fu dēw 'méy-yew. ‖I got to the station with five minutes to spare. wǒ dàw-le chē-'jàn háy yěw 'wǔ-fēn-jūng-de-'fù-ywu-shř-'jyān.

Spare tire bèy-'dày.

(*Frugal*) 'jyǎn-dan, shěng. ‖They've been living on a very spare diet consisting mostly of rice and cabbage. tām chř-'fàn 'chř-de jēn 'jyǎn-dan, jyèw-shı 'fàn gēn báy-'tsày.

SPEAK (SPOKE, SPOKEN). (*To talk*) shwō, shwō-'hwà, jyǎng *or* jyǎng-'hwà; (*to converse*) tá (-'hwà); (*to discuss*) 'tán-lwèn, 'yì-lwèn. ‖Do I speak clearly enough? wǒ 'shwō-de gèw 'chīng-chu-de-ma? ‖Did you speak to me? nǐ shř gēn-wǒ 'shwō-ne-ma? ‖He speaks with a slight stammer. tā shwō-'hwà 'yěw-dyǎr 'jyē-ba. ‖We were just speaking of you. wǒ-men-jèr 'jèng shwō-'nǐ-ne. ‖Do you speak English? nǐ shwō 'yīng-wén-ma? ‖Since that argument they haven't spoken. tā-men tsúng 'nèy-hwéy bàn-dzwěy yì-'hèw jyèw bǐ-'tsz méy-shwō-'hwà.

(*To make a speech*). jyǎng, jyǎng-'hwà, yǎn-'jyǎng, jyǎng-'yǎn, yǎn-'shwō. ‖Who is speaking tonight? jyēr-'wǎn-shang 'shéy jyǎng-'yǎn-na? ‖You'll have to speak to the boy about that. nǐ děy bǎ 'nèy-jyàn-shř gěy nèy-ge-'háy-dz 'jyǎng-jyǎng.

Generally speaking. ‖Generally speaking, he is home every evening. yàw-shr bù-jáw-'jēr de-hwà, ké-yi shwō, tā 'méy-tyān-'wǎn-shang dēw dzày-'jyā.

On speaking terms. ‖We're not on speaking terms. *meaning* We don't know each other. wǒ-men 'lyǎ méy-'shwō-gwò- hwà. *or meaning* We aren't friends any longer. wǒ-men 'lyǎ bù-shwō-'hwà-le. *or* wǒ-men 'lya bú-gwò-'hwà.

To speak for (*to represent*) tì (*or* wèy *or* dày-'byǎw) ... shwō; (*to make a bid for*) see RESERVE, SELL, *etc.* ‖I'm speaking for my friend. wǒ shř 'tì-wǒ-'péng-yew 'shwō-ya. ‖We've already spoken for him for our team. *is expressed as* We've already asked him to play on our team. wǒm 'yǐ-jìng 'ywē-hǎw-le 'tā láy rù 'wǒm-jèy-'dwèy-le. ‖Next Saturday is already spoken for. *is expressed as* Next Saturday there won't be any time. 'shyà 'shīng-chī-'lyèw méy-'kùngr-le. ‖Those ticket are already spoken for. *is expressed as* Those tickets have been reserved. nèy-shyē-jang-'pyàw 'yǐ-jìng yěw 'rén 'dìng-le.

To speak of see MENTION. Nothing to speak of 'méy-shéme, bù-lywǔ-'hwèy. ‖Are you hurt? Nothing to speak of. 'pèng-jàw-le-ma? bù-lywǔ-'hwèy.

To speak one's mind shwō ... 'yì-jyàn.

To speak up. ‖Speak up! I can't hear you. 'dà-dyǎr shēngr 'shwō. wǒ 'tīng-bú-'jyàn.

SPECIAL. tè-'byé, tè-'shū. ‖She bought her gown for a special occasion. tā 'mǎy nèy-jyàn-'yī-shang shř 'wèy yěw-shéme-tè-'byé-'shř-ching 'chwān-de. ‖I have a special reason. wǒ 'yěw yí-ge-tè-'byé-de-'lǐ-yéw. ‖Does this book go in any special place? jèy-běr-'shū děy 'gē dzày shéme-tè-'byé-de-'dì-fangr-ma? ‖He's had special training in his field. 'tā dzày nèy-'mén-li shèw-gwò tè-'shū-de-'shywùn-lyàn.

A special train (a train chartered for a particular person or group) 'jwān-chē; (an extra train to take care of an unusually large number of passengers) jyā-'chē. ‖Is there a special train for the weekend? jēw-'mwò yěw °jyā-'chē (°'jwān-chē)-ma?

Special delivery píng-'kwày; or, when the service also includes registering of the mail, 'kwày-shìn. ‖Send the letter special delivery. jèy-fēng-'shìn fā píng-'kwày.

SPEECH. See SPEAK. (To speak) shwō-'hwà, jyǎng-'hwà. ‖Sometimes gestures are more expressive than speech. 'byǎw-shř 'yì-jyàn yěw-de-'shf-hewr 'tày-du bǐ shwō-de-'hwà háy chwán-'shén. ‖He has the speech of an educated person. tā-shwō-'hwà yì-'tīng jyèw-'shř 'shèw-gwò-'jyàw-ywu-de-'rén. ‖He has an impediment in his speech. tā shwō-'hwà 'yěw-dyǎr 'jyē-jye-bā-'bā-de. ‖You can often tell where a person comes from by his speech. 'tīng yí-ge-'rén shwō-'hwà jyèw 'wǎng-wǎng 'jř-daw tā shř 'nǎr-de-'rén. or expressed as Often when you hear a person's accent, you know where he's from. nǐ 'cháng-hwer 'tīng yí-ge-rén-de-'kěw-yīn jyèw 'jř-daw tā shř 'nǎr-de-'rén.

(Address) jyǎng-'yǎn, yǎn-'jyǎng, yǎn-'shwō. ‖That was a very good speech. 'nèy-ge-yǎn-'jyǎng 'jyǎng-de hěn 'hǎw.

To make a speech jyǎng-'yǎn, yǎn-'jyǎng.

SPEED. 'sù-dù (literary). ‖The train is moving at a very slow speed. hwǒ-'chē-shyàn-'dzày-sù-'dù hěn 'màn. ‖Speed limit 30 miles per hour. sù-'dù měy-shyǎw-'shf bù-néng 'chāw-gwò 'sān-shf-lǐ. But ‖Let's put on a little speed. is expressed as Let's hurry. dzám 'kwày-dyǎr-ba. or as Let's step on the gas. dzám jyā-dyǎr 'yéw-ba. ‖We're moving at a good speed now. is expressed as We're going plenty fast now. wǒm shyàn-'dzày 'dzěw-de gèw 'kwày-de-le. ‖Full speed ahead! is expressed as Add horsepower and go ahead. jyā 'dzú-lew 'mǎ-lì wàng-chyán 'dzěw. ‖We are going at top speed. is expressed as We've ádded enough horsepower. wǒ-men jyā 'dzú-le 'mǎ-lì-le. ‖The greatest speed is needed for this job. is expressed as This job needs to be done fast. 'jèy-jyàn-shř 'bì-děy kwày-'kwār-de 'dzwò.

(Gear ratio) já. ‖This car has four speeds forward. jèy-lyàng-'chē wàng-'chyán dzěw yěw 'sż-dàw-já.

(To go fast) pǎw. ‖We were speeding along the highway when we saw the accident. wǒ-men 'shwèn-je dà-'dàw 'pǎw de-'shf-hewr 'kàn-jyàn nèr chū-le-'shř-le.

(To drive too fast) ‖We were arrested for speeding. wǒ-men kāy-'che kāy-de tày 'kwày-le, jyèw bèy 'bǔ-le.

To speed up. ‖Speed up the work. is expressed as Tighten the work. 'jyā-jǐn 'gūng-dzwò. or as You must hurry on that work. jèy-ge-'hwóer děy 'gǎn-yi-gǎn. or as Hurry in doing that. 'kwày-je-dyǎr 'dzwò. ‖Can't you speed things up a little? is expressed as Can't you hurry? nǐ bù-néng °'kwày-dyǎr-ma? (°'gǎn-je-dyǎr-ma?)

SPELL. pīn, or pīn-'dž. ‖He doesn't know how to spell yet. tā háy bú-'hwèy pīn-'dzèr-ne. ‖How do you spell that? dzěm 'pīn nèy-ge-'dž? ‖It's spelled the same, but pronounced differently. 'pīn-fǎr yí-'yàng, bú-gwò 'nyàn-fǎr bù-'túng.

(To relieve) tì. ‖I'll spell you for a while. wǒ 'tì-nǐ hwěr.

(Period of time) jèn, 'jèn-dz. ‖This hot spell won't last long. jèy-jèn-dz-'rè-jyèr 'cháng-bù-lyǎw. ‖He works for short spells now and then. tā dzwò-'shèr nème yí-'jèn-dz-yí-'jen-dz-de. or expressed as Every once in a while he does a few days' work. tā 'yěw-shf-hew dzwò jǐ-tyān shèr. or as Now and then he works a little. tā ěw-'ěr 'dzwò-dyǎr shèr. ‖He had a coughing spell. tā 'ké-sèw-le °'yí-jèn. (°'yì-'hwěr.) ‖Do you have fainting spells? is expressed as Do you sometimes faint? nǐ 'yěw-shf-hewr 'ywūn-gwò-chywù-ma?

(Magical charm) shyé, 'shyé-wán-yèr, 'shyé-mér, 'shyé-jyàw. ‖We don't believe in spells and charms. is expressed as We don't believe in witchcraft. wǒ-men bú-shìn 'shyé. (Figuratively) ‖Have you come under his spell, too? is expressed as Have you let him charm you, too? nǐ shř 'yě 'jyàw-ta gěy 'mí-jù-le-ma?

SPEND (SPENT). (To use up, pay out) hwā, yùng; (to waste) fèy, 'shyāw-hàw. ‖Have you spent your whole salary already? nǐ 'yǐ-jìng bǎ 'shīn-shwěy dēw 'hwā-le-ma? ‖The enemy spent most of its supplies in that one attack. dí-rén yì-dwō-'bàn-de-'jīng-li dēw dzày nèy-tsż-jìn-'gūng de-'shf-hew 'shyāw-hàw-le. ‖My money's all spent. wǒ-de-'chyán dēw 'hwā-le.

(To pay out money) hwā 'chyán, chū 'chyán; to spend a lot chū ('dà-)°'jyàr or °'jyà-chyan; not to spend much 'bù-chū ('dà-)°'jyàr or °'jyà-chyan. ‖I'm willing to spend a lot for a piano. wǒ 'ywàn-yi 'hwā yí-'dà-bǐ-'chyán 'mǎy yí-jyà-gāng-'chín.

(Of time). (To expend for a purpose) yùng, fèy, hwā; (to pass, stay) gwò, dāy. ‖We spent several hours at the museum. wǒm dzày bwó-wù-'ywàn dāy-le 'hǎw-jǐ-ge-'jūng-téw. ‖We spent several hours looking for a suitable gift. wǒm °'yùng-le (°'fèv-le, °'hwā-le) hǎw-jǐ-ge-'jūng-'téw-de-'gūng-fu jǎw yí-jyàn-hé-'shř-de-'lǐ-wù. ‖I want to spend the night here. wǒ yàw dzày-jèr °gwò-'yè. (°'dāy yí-yè.)

SPENT. (*Exhausted*) lèy-'jí-le, jīn-'pí-lì-'jìn. ‖**After the race, the runner was completely spent.** sày 'wán-le yǐ-'hèw, sày-'paw-de-'rén jyàn-'jŕ shŕ jīn-'pí-lì-'jìn.

SPIRIT. (*Mind, soul*) shīn. ‖**The spirit is willing, but the flesh is weak.** shīn yěw-'ywú ér-'lì bù-'dzú. *But* ‖**I'll be with you in spirit.** *is expressed as* **I'll always be thinking of you.** wǒ yí-'dìng lǎw 'dyàn-jì-je 'nǐ.

(*Disposition*) 'jīng-shen. ‖**We were told of the defiant spirit of the conquered people.** wǒm 'tīng-shwō dǎ-'bày-le-de-nàr 'rén-mín-'jīng-shén háy hěn chyáng-hàn. ‖**These tales reveal the spirit of the country.** jèy-shyē-'gù-shr byǎw-shyàn gwó-jyā-de-'jīng-shen. ‖**Well, it's the spirit of the times.** 'nèy-shr jèy-ge-shŕ-'dày-de-'jīng-shen. *or expressed as* **It's the modern trend.** 'nèy-shr jèy-ge-shŕ-'dày-de-'cháw-lyéw.

(*Feeling, emotion*) 'chíng-shywù. ‖**A spirit of revolt was evident among the men.** dzày nèy-chywún-rén-li hěn 'míng-shyǎn-de yěw yì-jǔng-'pàn-byàn-de-'chíng-shywù.

(*Attitude*) 'tày-dù. ‖**You don't go about it in the right spirit.** nǐ-de-'tày-dù bú-'dwèy. ‖**That's the right spirit!** nèy-ge-'tày-dù jyèw 'dwèy-le. *or expressed as* **That's the way!** 'jyèw shŕ nà-'yàngr. ‖**He tries to judge according to the spirit of the law.** *is expressed as* **He tries to judge according to the true meaning of the law.** tā jìn-'lyèr àn-je 'fǎ-lywù-de-jēn-'yì láy 'pàn-dwàn.

(*Liveliness*). (*Of people or horses*) 'jīng-shen; (*of animals; be lively*) 'hwān-shr; (*of animals and children*) 'hwó-pwo. ‖**That kid has a lot of spirit.** nèy-ge-shyǎw-'hár tǐng 'jīng-shen. ‖**You have a horse with a lot of spirit there.** 'nǐ nèr nèy-pǐ-'mǎ hěn yěw 'jīng-shen. ‖**They played the music with spirit.** tā-men dzèw-'ywè 'dzèw-de hěn yěw 'jīng-shen. ‖**That pup has a lot of spirit.** nèy-ge-shyǎw-'gěwr tǐng 'hwān-shr.

(*Supernatural being*) 'jīng-lyengr; (*ghost*) gwěy; (*god*) shén. ‖**The natives say there's a spirit in this tree.** 'tǔ-rén shwō jèy-kē-'shù °nàw 'gwěy (°shŕ kē-'shén-shù).

Spirits 'shīn-chíng, 'jīng-shen. ‖**I hope you're in good spirits.** wǒ 'shī-wàng nǐ shyàn-'dzày 'shīn-chíng bú-'tswò. *or expressed as* **I hope you're happy.** wǒ 'shī-wàng nǐ shyàn-'dzày hěn gāw-'shìng. ‖**I'm in low spirits.** wǒ-'shīn-shywù bù-'jyā.

Spirits of ammonia 'yǎ-mwó-ní-'yǎ.

SPIT. (*To release from the mouth, not vehemently*) tǔ-'tán; (*to spit with gusto*) tswèy; (*to vomit*) tù. ‖**No spitting.** yán-'jìn tǔ-'tán. *or* jìn-'jŕ tǔ-'tán. ‖**Don't spit on the floor.** byé wàng 'dì-shang °tǔ-'tán (°tswèy 'tù-mèy). ‖**He spit blood.** tā tù-'shyě-le. ‖**If it tastes bad, spit it out.** yàw-shr bù-hǎw-'chŕ, °'tswèy-chū-láy. (°'tù-chū-láy.)

(*Skewer*) gwèr. ‖**We can roast the chicken on a spit.** wǒ-men 'ké-yi ná yí-gēn-'gwèr 'chā-shang jèy-jŕ-'jī 'shāw-shaw.

SPLENDID. (*Very good*) 'dzwèy hǎw, 'tày hǎw, 'jēn hǎw, hǎw 'jí-le. ‖**I think what you have done is splendid.** wǒ jywé-de nǐ-'dzwò-de 'tày hǎw-le. ‖**This is splendid weather for swimming.** jèy-jǔng-'tyān-chi fù-'shwéy dzwèy 'hǎw. ‖**Splendid!** myàw 'jí-le.

(*Elaborate*) 'jyǎng-jyew. ‖**Their house is a little too splendid for my taste.** wǒ 'jywé-de tām-de-'fáng-dz 'tày 'jyǎng-jyew.

SPOIL. (*To ruin*) bǎ . . . gěy (*or* nùng) °'hwěy-le (*or* °'hwày-le, *or* °'jyǎw-hwo-le, *or* °'jyǎw-le). ‖**The dinner is already spoiled.** jèy-dwèn-'fàn yǐ-'rán nùng 'hwày-le. ‖**The bad weather spoiled our vacation.** hwày-'tyār bǎ wǒm-de-'jyà gěy °'hwěy-le. *or* °'jyǎw-hwo-le. ‖**Don't spoil my plans by telling anyone what I'm going to do.** byé 'gàw-su 'byé-rén wǒ yàw 'gàn shéme, hwéy-'téw bǎ wǒ-de-'jì-hwà gěy nùng 'hwěy-le.

(*To go bad*) hwày, làn. ‖**These apples are beginning to spoil.** 'jèy-shyē-'píng-gwo yǐ-jīng 'làn-le. ‖**Food spoils quickly in hot weather.** 'rè-tyān-de-'shŕ-hew 'dūng-shi 'dzwèy rúng-yi 'hwày.

(*To overindulge*) bǎ . . . °gwàn-'hwày-le (°'dzùng-'hwày-le, °'fàng-dzùng-'hwày-le). ‖**The little boy is being spoiled by his grandmother.** shyǎw-'hár jyàw tā-dzǔ-'mǔ gěy gwàn-'hwày-le. ‖**He's a spoiled child.** 'tā jèy-ge-'háy-dz gwàn-'hwày-le. ‖**Don't spoil him.** byé 'bǎ-tā gwàn-'hwày-lew.

Spoils 'hǎw-chù. ‖**They got their share of the spoils, you can be sure.** tām yí-'dìng fēn-jaw 'hǎw-chù-le.

SPOKE. (*Of a wheel*) tyáw, chē-'tyáw. ‖**Do you have another bicycle spoke to replace this one?** nǐ 'háy yěw méy-yěw 'byé-de-chē-'tyáw gěy jèy-dz-shíng-'chē 'hwàn yì-'gēr? ‖**This wheel has a broken spoke.** jèy-ge-'lwén-dz 'shé-le yì-gēr-'tyáw.

SPOON. chér, 'chŕ-dz, tyáw-'gēng, sháwr, gēng-'chŕ, sháw-dz. ‖**Do you still feed her with a spoon?** nǐ 'háy-shŕ yùng 'chŕ-dz 'wèy-ta-ma?

To spoon up 'wǎy-chu-láy, 'kwǎy-chū-láy, 'yǎw-chū-láy. ‖**See if you can spoon up the soup that's left in the kettle.** nǐ 'shŕ-shŕ 'néng-bù-néng bǎ 'gwō-li-'shèng-shyà-de nèy-dyǎr-'tāng 'wǎy-chū-láy.

SPORT. (*Exercise, physical games*) 'ywùn-dung; **sports page** 'tǐ-ywù-'lán, 'ywùn-dung-lán. ‖**Do you like sports?** nǐ 'shǐ-hwān 'ywùn-dung-ma? ‖**Swimming is my favorite sport.** yéw-'yǔng shŕ wǒ-dzwèy-'shǐ-hwan-de-'ywùn-dung. ‖**I have to wear sports clothes.** wǒ děy 'chwān-shang 'ywùn-dung-'yī. ‖**I always read the sports page first.** wǒ yǔng-'ywǎn shŕ 'shyān kàn 'tǐ-ywù-lán. *But* ‖**This is fine sport.** *is expressed as* **This is really interesting.** jèy 'jēn yěw 'yì-sz.

(*Of a person*). ‖She's a poor sport. 'tā-rén hěn 'shyǎw-chì. ‖He's a good sport. 'tā-rén hěn °'dà-chì. or °'dà-fāng.

To sport (*something new*) lèw or 'shyàn-bey. ‖Aren't you sporting a new tie today? nǐ jyēr °'lèw-lew (or °shyǎn-bey) shīn-lǐng-'dày-ya? or expressed 'as Isn't the tie you're wearing today new? nǐ-'jīn-tyán-dǎ-de-lǐng-'dày shr̀-bu-shr̀ 'shīn-de-ya?

SPOT. (*Small mark*) dyǎr, 'dyǎn-dz; (*dirty mark, stain*) dzāng-'dyǎr, dzāngr. ‖She had on a white dress with red spots. tā chwān-le yí-jyàn-'báy-de-dày-húng-'dyǎr-de-'yī-shang. ‖Can you get these spots out of my pants? nǐ néng bǎ wǒ-'kù-dz-shang-de 'jèy-jǐ-kwày-'dzāngr 'chywù-le-ma?

(*Place*) 'dì-fangr; (*point*) dyǎn. ‖Show me the exact spot you mean. bǎ nǐ-swǒ-'shwō-de-nèy-yì-'dyǎn 'jř-chū-láy. or bǎ nǐ-swǒ-'shwō-de nèy-ge-'dì-fang 'jř gěy-wǒ 'kàn-kan.

(*Moment*) yì-'hwěr. ‖That was a bright spot in an otherwise dull day. is expressed as Of the whole day only that moment was rather interesting. nèy-yì-jěng-'tyār háy 'jyèw-shř 'nèy-yì-hwěr 'bǐ-jyǎw 'yěw-dyǎr 'yì-sz.

On the spot (*right there*) dzày-'nèr, dzày nèy-ge-'dì-fangr. ‖I was right on the spot when it happened. chū-'shèr de-shř-hew wǒ 'jèng 'dzày-nèr.

On the spot (*immediately*) lì-'kè, lì-'shř, dāng-'shř. ‖They hired him on the spot. tām dāng-'shř jyèw 'bǎ-ta 'gù-le.

To be on the spot dzwò-'là, wéy-'nán. ‖That really put me on the spot. nèy jyǎn-'jř shř 'jyǎw-'wǒ dzwò-'là.

To spot (*stain*) nùng-'hwā. ‖Will water spot this material? 'shwěy něng bǎ jèy-jyàn-'lyàw-dz nùng 'hwā-le-ma?

To spot. See **RECOGNIZE**. ‖I spotted you in the crowd as soon as I saw your hat. is expressed as I saw your hat in the crowd and immediately knew it was you. dzày 'rén-chywún-li wǒ yí 'kàn-jyàn nǐ-de-'màw-dz mǎ-'shàng jyèw 'jř-daw shr̀-'nǐ.

SPREAD. (*To lay out*) 'dǎ-kāy, 'tān-kāy, 'pū-kāy. ‖Spread the rug out and let me look at it. bǎ dì-'tǎn 'tān-kāy jyàw-wǒ 'chyáw-chyaw. ‖He spread the papers out on the table. tā bǎ-'jř 'dǎ-kāy 'pū-dzay 'jwō-dz-shang-le.

{To open} 'dǎ-kāy, 'fēn-kāy. ‖The eagle spread its wings and flew away. nèy-ge-'yīng 'dǎ-kāy chř-'bǎngr jyèw 'fēy-le. ‖Spread your fingers apart. bǎ 'nǐ-de-shěw-'jř-tew 'fēn-kāy.

(*To extend*) jàn; (*to occupy*) 'jàn-chū. ‖The factory spreads over two acres. nèy-ge-gūng-'chǎng 'jàn-le yěw 'lyǎng-mǔ-dì. ‖The farm spreads out for miles. jèy-kwày-'dì 'jàn-chū-le yěw 'hǎw-shyē-lǐ-'dì chywù.

(*To distribute; to throw with the motion of sowing seed, a powdered fertilizer, etc.*) sǎ; (*to spread a thick substance like tar with a shovel or other instrument*) tān, tān-'píng-lew; (*to smear butter, etc.; the same motion as* tān, *only on a much smaller scale*) mwǒ.

‖Spread the fertilizer evenly. (*If it is powder*) bǎ 'féy-lyàw sǎ 'ywún-lew. or (*If it is manure or a thick substance*) bǎ 'féy-lyàw tān 'ywún-lew. ‖Spread the honey on the bread. myàn-'bāw-shang 'mwǒ-dyǎr 'fēng-'mì.

(*Figuratively*). ‖He repaid me in small amounts, spread over several years. is expressed as He divided the money and repaid me a little at a time for several years. tā 'fēn-kay jǐ-'nyán yì-'dyǎr yì-'dyǎr-de bǎ-chyán 'hwán-gey-wǒ-de.

(*To expand*) nàw-chǐ-lay, chwán; (*of fire only*) yán-'shāw; (*of fire or disease*) 'màn-yán; (*of ideas or of disease*) lyéw-'shíng. ‖The rumor spread rapidly. 'yáw-yan chwán-de hěn 'kwày. ‖The fire spread rapidly, once it got started. 'hwǒ yì-'jáw-chǐ-lay 'màn-yán-de tǐng 'kwày. ‖These ideas are spreading everywhere. jèy-shyē-'sz-shyǎng 'dàw-chù lyéw-'shíng. ‖They tried to check the spread of the disease. is expressed as They tried to stop the disease from spreading. tām shyǎng bú-jyàw jèy-bìng 'nàw-chi-lay. But ‖What's the wingspread of that plane? is expressed as How wide is that plane? nèy-ge-fēy-'jī yěw dwó-'kwān?

SPRING (**SPRANG, SPRUNG**). (*To jump*) bèng, tyàw. ‖He sprang to his feet. tā yí 'tyàw jyèw 'jàn-chǐ-lay-le. (*Of animals*) pū. ‖The cat sprang at the mouse. nèy-ge-'māw 'pū nèy-ge-'hàw-dz.

(*To do ... suddenly*) hū-'rán-de ..., lěng-gu-'dīng-de ..., chēw-gu-'lěng-dz .... ‖The teacher sprang that test on us without warning. 'shyān-sheng tū-'rán-de 'kǎw-le wóm yí-'shyàr. ‖What did you spring that question on me for? nǐ chēw-gu-'lěng-dz 'wèn wǒ 'nèm-ge-'wèn-tí gàn-'shéme?

(*To appear suddenly is expressed as* appear, grow, be built, *etc.*). ‖Mushrooms sprang up all along the lake. 'mwó-gu dzày hú-'byār-shang 'jǎng-chǐ-láy-le. ‖Towns sprang up almost overnight. 'hū-rán-jyan 'jèr yí-ge-'chéng 'nàr yí-ge-'jèn-de jyèw dēw 'gày-chǐ-láy-le.

(*To become bent*) 'chyàw-chǐ-láy; (*to hump up in the middle*) 'gǔ-chǐ-láy. ‖The car door has sprung again. nèy-ge-chē-'mér yěw 'chyàw-chǐ-láy-le.

(*To pry open by force*). (*By using an instrument*) 'chyàw-kāy; (*by twisting with the hands or pliers*) 'nǐng-kāy. ‖See if we can spring this lock. 'kàn-kan wǒ-men bǎ jèy-ge-swǒ 'chyàw-kay 'shíng-bù-shíng. ‖When the police arrived, they found that the lock had been sprung. jǐng-'chá 'dàw-le de-shř-hewr jyèw fā-'shyàn 'swǒ shř 'nǐng-kāy-de.

(*Elastic metal device*) hwáng, bēng-'hwáng, lā-'hwáng, tán-'hwáng. ‖The spring seems to be broken. 'hwáng hǎw 'shyàng 'shé-le shr̀-de. ‖This bed has good springs. jèy-ge-'chwáng-de-'hwáng hěn 'hǎw.

(*Water source*) chywán, 'chywán-yǎn; spring water chywán-'shwěy. ‖We filled our cups at the spring. wóm dzày 'chywán-yǎn-nèr bǎ 'bēy-dz 'gwàn-mǎn-le 'shwěy-le. ‖This mountain has three springs. jèy-ge-'shān yěw 'sān-ge-°'chywán. or °'chywán-yan. ‖Let's have a drink of nice cool spring water. dzăm 'hē-dyăr yèw-'lyáng-yèw-'tyán-de-chywán-'shwěy-ba.

(*Season*) 'chwēn-tyan, 'chwēn-jì. ‖We won't be leaving town before spring. 'chwēn-tyan yĭ-'chyán wŏm 'bú-hwèy 'lí-kay jèr. ‖This is beautiful spring weather. jēn-shr̀ 'chwēn-gwāng míng-'mèy.

SQUARE. (*Equilateral rectangle*) (sz̀-)fāng-'kwàr; (*square shaped*) ('sz̀-)fāng. ‖They cut the cake into small squares. tā-men 'bǎ 'nèy-ge-'dyǎn-shin 'chyē-chéng 'shyǎw-sz̀-fāng-'kwàr. ‖I want a square box. wŏ 'yàw yí-ge-'fāng-shyá-dz.

Square unit of measurement fāng; ... square ... jyàn-'fang. ‖How many square feet does the building cover? jèy-dzwò-'láw-de-'dì-jī yěw 'dwō-shaw-fāng-'chr̀? ‖Our back yard is twenty feet square. wŏ-men-hèw-'ywàr shr̀ èr-shr-'chr̀ jyàn-'fāng. or *expressed as* Our back yard is twenty by twenty feet. wŏm hèw-'ywàr-de-cháng-'kwān dēw shì 'èr-shŕ-'chr̀. ‖This scarf is two feet square. jèy-ge-wéy-'bwóer shr̀ 'èr-chr̀-jyàn-'fāng.

(*Carpenter's tool, T square*) 'dīng-dz-'chr̀.

(*Open space in town.*) May be called kùng-'chǎngr or gwǎng-'chǎng.

(*Honest, fair*) 'gūng-dàw, 'chéng-shŕ-de; (*literary*) 'fāng-jèng. ‖He's a pretty square fellow. tā shr̀ ge-'chéng-shŕ-de-'rén. ‖Do you think they gave him a square deal? *is expressed as* Do you think they were fair? nǐ 'jýwé-hu-je 'tā-men 'gūng-dàw-ma? ‖Play square! 'gūng-dàw-dyar!

(*Exactly*) jèng, jěng, jèng-'hǎw. ‖The arrow hit the target square in the middle. jèy yí-'jyàn 'jèng shè-de bǎ dāng-'jyàr. ‖Hit him square between the eyes. yí-'shyàr 'jèng dǎ-de lyǎ-'yǎn dāng-'jyàr. ‖Hit the nail square on the head. bǎ 'dīng-dz dīng 'jèng-lew.

To square. ‖I'll square things with you later. dzám yĭ-'hèw dzǎy swàn-'jàng-ba. ‖My accounts never square at the end of the month. *is expressed as* My accounts are never cleared up at the end of the month. wŏ-de-'jàng 'nǎy-ge-ywè-'dǐ yě 'méy-nùng 'chīng.

STAB. năng, jā, tsz̀. ‖The dead man had been stabbed twice with a dagger. nèy-ge-'sz̀-rén shr̀ ràng-'rén ná 'dāw-dz 'jā-le lyǎng-'shyà-dz. ‖Don't stab yourself with those scissors! byé ràng 'jyǎn-dz jā-jaw. ‖He made a stab at him with a knife. tā ná 'dāw-dz chùng-ta 'bǐ-hwo-le yí-'shyàr. or tā ná 'dāw-dz chùng-ta 'jā-le yí-'shyàr.

To make a stab at (*try*) shr̀. ‖I'm not sure I can solve this problem, but I'll make a stab at it. wŏ bù-gǎn-shwō wŏ néng bǎ jèy-ge-'wèn-tí 'jyě-jywé-le, 'kě-shr wŏ děy 'shr̀ yí-'shyà-dz.

STABLE. (*Steady*) wěn; *in formal and literary usage* 'wěn-dìng. ‖She's a pretty stable person. tā-'jèy-ge-rén hěn 'wěn. ‖They haven't had a stable government

for centuries. jǐ-bǎy-'nyán-le tā-men yě 'méy-yew yí-ge-'wěn-dìng-de-'jèng-fŭ. ‖The situation on the stock market is pretty stable. jyāw-yì-'swŏ 'jyāw-yì-de-'chíng-shíng hěn 'wěn-dìng.

A stable mǎ-'péng, mǎ-'hàw, mǎ-'jywàn. ‖I can smell the stables. wŏ 'wén-jyàn mǎ-jywàn-'wèr-le.

To stable. ‖The horses will be stabled for the night. 'wǎn-shang děy bǎ-'mǎ 'gē-de mǎ-'jywàn-lǐ-tew.

STAIRS. (*Leading to a door, outside a building*) táy-'jyēr; (*the stairs leading from one floor to another*) léw-'tī; one step yì-tséng-°táy-'jyēr or °léw-'tī. ‖Take the stairs to your right. dzěw 'yèw-byār nèy-ge-táy-'jyēr.

STAMP. (*To step on with the foot*) tsǎy. To stamp one's foot dwò-'jyǎw. ‖Stamp on that cigarette butt. bǎ 'nèy-ge-'yān-jywǎr-'téwr 'tsǎy-le. ‖Teach that child not to stamp his foot. 'gàw-su nèy-ge-'háy-dz byé dwò-'jyǎw.

(*To imprint or impress with a mark*) dǎ-'chwōer, gày-(tú-)'jāng; gày-'yìn (*to print*). ‖Please stamp this "Handle with Care." láw-'jyà bǎ jèy-ge "shyǎw-shīn-chīng-'fàng"-de-'chwō-dz gěy 'dǎ-shang. ‖He stamps his name on all his books. tā bǎ tā-'swŏ-yěw-de-'shū dēw 'dǎ-shang tā-de-'míng-dz-le.

(*To put on a postage stamp*) 'tyē yéw-'pyàw. ‖Have you stamped your letter? nǐ-de-'shìn nǐ 'tyē yéw-'pyàw-le-ma? ‖Give me twenty stamped envelopes, please. láw-'jyà gěy-wo 'èr-shŕ-ge-°tyē-yéw-'pyàw-de-shìn-'fēngr. or °dày-yéw-'pyàw-de-shìn-'fēngr.

(*Instrument that stamps or the mark left by it*) 'chwō-dz, 'tú-jāng, yìn. ‖Please buy me a rubber stamp. láw-'jyà, gěy-wo 'mǎy yí-ge-shyàng-pí-'chwō-dz láy. ‖Everything that goes out of the office must have his stamp. tsúng-jèr 'ná-chū-chywu-de-'dūng-shi 'dēw děy 'yěw tā-de-'tú-jāng.

Postage stamp yéw-'pyàw. ‖I want twenty cents' worth of stamps. wŏ yàw 'lyǎng-máw-chyán-de-yéw-'pyàw. ‖Give me an air-mail stamp. gěy-wo yì-jāng-háng-'kūng-yéw-'pyàw.

Tax stamp yìn-'hwā(-shwèy-'pyàw).

STAND. (*To rise to one's feet*) 'jàn-chǐ-láy, 'lì-chǐ-láy. ‖The audience stood when they saw the conductor come in. 'tīng-jùng 'kàn-jyàn jr̀-'dǎw-'ywán 'jìn-lay dēw 'jàn-chǐ-láy-le.

(*To be upright*) jàn, lì. ‖Stand still a minute, will you? hǎw-'hāwr-de 'jàn yì-hwěr 'hǎw-ma? ‖I'm tired of standing here waiting. wŏ 'jàn dzǎy-jèr děng 'lèy-le. ‖Stand where you were. 'jàn-de nǐ ywán-'láy-de-'dì-fangr. ‖The others ran away, but she stood fast. 'byé-rén dēw 'pǎw-le, 'kě-shr 'tā háy 'jàn-je méy-'dùng. ‖He stands six feet two in his stocking feet. *is expressed as* Standing and not wearing shoes, he's six feet two. tā 'jàn-je bù-chwān 'shyé shr̀ 'lyèw-chr̀-'èr. ‖The ladder is standing in the corner. 'tī-dz dzǎy nèy-'jyǎwr-shang 'lì-je-ne.

(*To set upright*) bǎ . . . °lì or °shù. ‖He stood the box on end. tā 'bǎ nèy-ge 'shyāng-dz 'shù-chǐ-láy-le. ‖Stand your umbrella over there. bǎ nǐ-de-'sǎn 'lì-dé nèr.

(*To remain*). ‖The old clock has stood on that shelf for years. *is expressed as* That old clock has been placed on that shelf a good many years. nèy-ge-'jyèw-jūng dzày nèy-ge-'jyà-dz-shang 'gē-le hǎw-jǐ-'nyán-le. ‖Let the milk stand overnight. *is expressed as* Put the milk there overnight. bǎ nyéw-'nǎy 'dzày-nèr 'gē yí-'yè. ‖What I said the other day still stands. *is expressed as* What I said the other day is still effective. wǒ 'nèy-tyān swǒ 'shwō-de-'hwà háy yěw 'shyàw. (*See also* HOLD). ‖That statement is wrong, but let it stand. *is expressed as* That statement is wrong; however, let it be that way. nèy-ge-'hwà bú-'dwèy, dé-le, jyèw 'nème-je-ba.

(*To endure; of people only*) shèw, rěn, 'rěn-shèw; (*of people or things*) jīn-de-'jù. ‖I can't stand your friend. nǐ-nèy-'péng-yěw wǒ 'shèw-bù-'lyǎw. ‖Will you stop that noise? I can't stand it. láw-'jyà byé 'chǎw-le, wǒ 'shèw-bù-'lyǎw-le. ‖This cloth won't stand much washing. jèy-ge-'bù jīn-bù-'jù 'jǐn-dz 'shǐ. ‖Will the car stand the punishment it will get on the trip? jèy-ge-'chē 'dzěw jèy-'tàng jīn-de-'jù-ma?

(*To be*). *See also* BE. ‖In this opinion I do not stand alone. *is expressed as* I am not the only person who expresses this idea. jèy-hwa 'bú-shř gwāng wǒ 'yí-ge-rén dzème 'shwō. ‖He stands in danger of losing his job, *is expressed as* His job may not be secure. tā nèy-'shř-ching pǎ bǎw-bu-jù. ‖How much for it as it stands? *is expressed as* How much do you want for that as it is, not changed? nèy-ge jyèw 'nǎ-yàngr bú-'dùng, yàw 'dwō-shǎw-'chyán? ‖As things stand now, I'll have to leave. *is expressed as* With things going as they are now, I'll have to leave. shyàn-'dzày 'shř-ching chéng-le 'jè-yàngr-le wǒ děy 'dzěw-le. ‖I stand corrected. wǒ 'jyē-shèw jyèw-'jèng.

A stand (*position*) lì-'chǎng. ‖You'll have to take a stand either for or against the idea. *is expressed as* Regarding that idea, whether you approve or oppose it, °you must have a position. *or* °you must stand on one side. nǐ 'dwèy-ywú jèy-ge-'yì-jyàn shř 'dzàn-chéng shř fǎn-dwèy °děy yěw yí-ge-lì-'chǎng. *or* °děy 'jàn yì-'byār.

A stand (*small table*) 'jwō-dz; (*place for a small business*) 'tān-dz, tār. ‖The telephone stand is in the hall. dyàn-hwà-'jwōr dzày dà-'tīng-li-ne. ‖There's a newsstand at the corner. gwǎy-'jyàwr-nèr yěw ge-bàw-'tār.

To make a stand fáng-'shèw. ‖The enemy decided to make a stand outside the city limits. 'dí-rén jywé-'dìng dzày jèy-ge-'chéng-de-jyāw-'wày fáng-'shèw.

To stand a chance. (*Have a chance*) yěw 'jī-hwèy; (*get a chance*) 'dé-jáw 'jī-hwey. ‖I'm afraid you don't stand a chance of getting a job here. wǒ kǔng-'pà nǐ dzày-'jèr 'méy-yew 'jī-hwèy 'jǎw-jáw 'shř-ching. ‖He's entered the contest, but he doesn't stand a chance of

winning. tā jyā-'rù bǐ-'sày láy-je, kě-shř méy-'dé-jaw 'jī-hwey 'yíng. ‖He stands a chance of being promoted. tā yěw 'shěng-shang-chywu-de-'jī-hwey. ‖He stands a chance of being fired. *is expressed as* It may happen that he' will be fired. tā pèng-'chyǎw-le jyèw 'shywǔ bèy 'tsáy.

To stand aside 'dwǒ-kāy. ‖Stand aside a minute. 'dwǒ-kāy yì-'hwěr. ‖Stand out of the way. 'dwǒ-kāy 'dàwr.

To stand back wàng-'hèw °'jàn-jan or °'twèy-twey. ‖Stand back and give her air. wàng-'hèw 'jàn-jan, byé 'chī-hu-je ta.

To stand by (*to be near but not participate in something*) 'jàn dzày yì-'byār; yì-'byār 'jàn-je; *or expressed as* to remain aloof with one's hands in one's sleeves shyèw-'shěw páng-'gwān. ‖He stood by, doing nothing while the men fought. nèy-shyē-'rén dǎ-'jyà de-'shř-hew tā 'dzày-nèr shyèw-'shěw páng-'gwān.

To stand by (*to help*) bāng-'máng. ‖You know that I'll always stand by you in case of trouble. nǐ 'jř-dàw nǐ yěw shéme-'shř de-'shř-hew wǒ 'yǔng-ywǎn bāng-'máng.

To stand by (*to wait*) děng. ‖Stand by for the latest news bulletin. *is expressed as* Wait here to listen to the latest news. 'děng byé 'dùng tīng dzwèy-'hèw-de-shīn-'wén.

To stand by one's word. ‖You can count on him to stand by his word. *is expressed as* You can rest easy, that man always means what he says. nǐ fàng-'shīn-ba, tā nèy-ge-'rén shyàng-'láy shř shwō-'hwà swàn 'hwà.

To stand clear of *something* 'dwǒ-kāy . . .; lí . . . 'ywǎn-dyǎr. ‖Stand clear of the sparks. 'dwǒ-kāy nà-hwǒ-'shyēngr 'dyǎr. or lí hwǒ-'shyēngr ywǎn-dyǎr.

To stand for (*to uphold*) 'dzàn-chéng. ‖That candidate stands for free trade. 'nèy-ge-hèw-shywǎn-'rén dzàn-'chéng dž-'yéw màw-'yì. *See also* ALLOW.

To stand for (*to represent*) dày-'byǎw. ‖In their code each number stands for a letter. 'tā-men-nèy-ge-dyàn-'mǎr 'měy-yí-ge-shù-mù-'dzèr dày-'byǎw 'yí-ge-dž-'mǔ.

To stand in with gēn . . . 'dzěw-de hěn 'jìn-hu. ‖Does he stand in with the boss? tā gēn-'téwr 'dzěw-de hěn 'jìn-hu-ma?

To stand out (*to be noticeable*) shyǎn-'yǎn. ‖Her clothes make her stand out in a crowd. tā-de-'yī-shang dzày 'dà-tíng-gwǎng-'jùng-jr-'shyà hěn shyǎn-'yǎn.

To stand to (*surely*) jwěn; (*probably*) dà-'gày or yì-dwō-'bàr. ‖Now that the race has started, our horse stands to win. shyàn-'dzày jèy-chǎng-sày-'mǎ yǐ-'rán kāy-'shř-le, 'wǒ-men-nèy-pǐ-'mǎ yì-dwō-'bàr 'yíng.

It stands to reason that àn-'lǐ. ‖It stands to reason that she wouldn't do that. àn-lǐ tā bú-'hwèy 'nà-men 'bàn.

To stand trial chř 'gwān-sz.

To stand up (*to fail to meet*). ‖She stood me up. *is expressed as* She let me wait in vain. tā 'ràng-wǒ dzày-'nèr 'báy děng-le. *or as* She cheated me; she said she'd come and she didn't. tā 'pyàn-le wo-le, 'shwō láy bù-'láy.

To stand up to. ‖Why don't you stand up to your father once in a while? *is expressed as* Why don't you sometimes discuss the reason with your father? nǐ wèy-'shéme bù 'yěw-shŕ-hewr yě gén nǐ-'fù-chin 'jyǎng-jyang 'lǐ. *or as* Why do you always listen to your father? nǐ gàn-'má 'lǎw tīng nǐ-'fù-chin-de?

STANDARD. (*Norm*) 'byāw-jwěn. ‖You can't judge him by ordinary standards. nǐ bù-néng ná 'píng-'cháng-de-'byāw-jwěn láy 'pàn-dwàn 'tā. ‖Who sets the standard of work here? jèr shŕ-'shéy 'dìng-de 'gūng-dzwò-'byāw-jwěn-na? ‖The schools have reached a very high standard. shywé-'shyàw-de-'chéng-dù dew hěn 'gāw-le. ‖His work is not up to standard today. 'jīn-tyān tā-de-'gūng-dzwò bú-jì-'gé. ‖This leather is below standard. jèy-ge-'pí-dz 'chéng-shar dī.

Standard of living 'shēng-hwó-'byāw-jwěn.

Gold standard jīn-běn-'wèy.

Silver standard yín-běn-'wèy.

(*Established*) píng-'cháng, pu-'tūng. ‖This is the standard size. jèy-ge shŕ pǔ-'tūng-'hàwr-de.

STAR. (*Heavenly body*) 'shīng(-shing). ‖The sky is full of stars tonight. jyèr-'wǎn-shang 'tyān-shang-de 'shīng-shing dēw 'mǎn-le. *or* jyèr-'wǎn-shang shŕ 'mǎn-tyān 'shīng. ‖Her dress has white stars on a dark background. tā-de-'yī-shang 'dyèr shŕ 'àn-de 'shàng-tew yěw báy-'shīng-shing.

(*In entertainment*) míng-'shīng. ‖There are three stars in that picture. 'nèy-jāng-dyàn-yěngr-'pyān-dz-li yěw 'sān-ge-míng-'shīng.

(*Outstanding*) dé-'yì-de. ‖This is my star pupil. 'jèy-ge shŕ wǒ-dé-'yì-de-'shywé-sheng.

(*To mark with a star*) hwà 'shīng-shing-'jì-hàwr. ‖Omit the starred passages. bǎ hwà-'shīng-shing-'jì-hàwr-de-nèy-jǐ-'dwàr chywǔ-'shyāw.

(*To play the leading role*) dāng 'jǔ-jyǎwr. ‖She's starred in every picture she's been in. tā-'yǎn-de-měy-yí-ge-'pyān-dz dēw-shŕ tā dāng 'jǔ-jyǎwr.

START. (*To begin*) kāy-'shŕ, kāy-'téwr, chǐ-'téwr; *also a verb plus* -chǐ-láy. ‖Has the performance started yet? byāw-'yǎn yǐ-'rán kāy-'shŕ-le-ma? ‖When will we start taking lessons? wǒ-men 'shéme-'shŕ-hew °kāy-'shŕ shàng-'kè? *or* °kāy-'kè? ‖It's starting to rain. 'shyà-chǐ-'ywǔ-láy-le. ‖The joke started us laughing. *is expressed as* The joke made us start laughing. nèy-ge-'shyàw-hwàr jyàw-wǒm 'shyàw-chǐ-láy-le.

(*To set out*) chū-'fā, dzěw, chywù, dùng-'shēn, chǐ-'shēn. ‖When do we start for the country? wǒ-men dàw 'shyāng-shyà chywu shéme-'shŕ-hewr chǐ-'shēn?

(*To set going; of a motor*) bǎ . . . 'kāy-kay; (*of a fire*) lúng; (*of a rumor or an idea*) dzàw. To start

a precedent 'shyān 'chǐ-shŕ; to start a riot chǐ-'shŕ. ‖Start the engine. bǎ 'jī-chi 'kāy-kay. ‖Who started the fire? 'shéy lúng-de 'hwǒ? ‖What started the fire? *is expressed as* How did the fire start? hwǒ 'dzěm 'jáw-chǐ-láy-de? ‖Who started this rumor? 'shéy 'dzàw-de jèy-ge-'yáw-yán? ‖I'll start the ball rolling. *is expressed as* I'll fire the first shot. wǒ láy 'fàng dì-yí-'pàw.

(*Beginning*) téwr, *or expressed verbally*; from start to finish tsúng-'téwr dàw-'lyǎwr. ‖This thing has been wrong from the start. jèy jyàn shŕ yì-kāy-'téwr jyèw 'tswò-le. ‖We got an early start. (*Of work*) wǒ-men chǐ-'téwr chǐ-de 'dzǎw. *or*. (*Of a trip*) wǒ-men 'shēn chǐ-de 'dzǎw. ‖It's important to make a good start. chǐ-'téwr 'chǐ-de 'hǎw shŕ tǐng 'yàw-jǐn-de. ‖He got his start in a small office. tā (°chǐ-'chū *or* °chǐ-'téwr *or*) °chū-'chǐ dzày yí-ge-shyǎw-'jī-gwān-li dzwò-'shŕ.

(*Head*) start. ‖We gave him eight yards' start. *is expressed as* We let him have eight yards. wǒ-men sày-'pǎw 'ràng-tā bā-'mǎ.

(*Shock*). ‖You gave me quite a start. nǐ 'shyà-le wǒ yí-dà-'tyàw. ‖She started with surprise. tā 'shyà-le yí-'tyàw.

STATE. (*Situation*) 'chíng-shing. ‖I'm in a bad state. wǒ-de-'chíng-shing hwày-'tèw-le. ‖Anything is better than the present state of things. 'dzěme-je dēw 'bǐ mù-'chyán-de-'chíng-shing 'chyáng.

(*Nation*) 'gwó-jyā. State Department gwó-wù-bù. ‖The railroads are owned by the State. tyě-'lù shŕ 'gwó-jyā-'bàn-de. ‖All the states of Europe sent delegates to the convention. nèy-ge-hwèy-'yì ēw-jēw-swǒ-'yěw-de-gwó-'jyā dēw 'pày-le dày-'byǎw-le.

(*Unit of a nation*). (*Province used of the Chinese provinces*) shěng; (*one of the states of the United States*) jēw.

To state shwō. ‖State your business. bǎ 'nǐ-de-'shŕ-ching 'shwō-shwo. ‖The facts are as stated. yǐ-jing 'shwō-gwo-de 'dēw 'shŕ-chíng.

STATEMENT. (*Report*) bàw-'gàw; (*bill*) jàng-'dār; (*public bulletin*) tūng-'gàw; (*notice sent to an individual*) tūng-'jŕ. ‖The bank will send you a statement every four months. yín-'háng měy-'sž-ge-'ywè gěy-ni 'sùng yí-'tsž-tūng-'jŕ. ‖Has the store sent a statement of my account? 'nèy-ge-'pù-dz gěy-wo 'sùng jàng-'dār láy-le-ma?

(*Utterance*) hwà. ‖Have you any statement to make? nǐ yàw 'shwō shéme-'hwà-ma? ‖Is that statement true? nèy-jywù-'hwǎ kě-'kàw-ma?

STATION. (*Stop*) jàn; (*railroad station*) chē-'jàn, 'hwǒ-chē-jàn; (*bus station*) gūng 'gùng-'chǐ-chē-'jàn. ‖Get off at the next station. 'shyà-yí-'jàn shyà-'chē. ‖Where is the railroad station? hwǒ-chē-'jàn dzày-'nǎr? ‖I'll meet you at the bus station. gūng-'gùng-'chǐ-chē-'jàn 'jyàn.

(*Broadcasting unit*) dyàn-'táy, wú-shyàn-'dyàn-'táy. ‖**What stations can you get on your radio?** nǐ-de-wú-shyàn-'dyàn néng 'shēw-jew nǎy-jǐ-ge-dyàn-'táy-de? ‖**This is station wàn-'shyáng.** *is expressed as* **This is wàn-'shyáng broadcasting station.** wàn-'shyáng gwǎng-'bwō-dyàn-'táy.

(*Place for research*). (*A field*) 'chǎng; (*an office or building*) -'swǒ; (*a zone*) -'chywū. ‖**There's an agricultural experiment station near here.** jèr fù-'jìn 'yěw yí-ge-'núng-yè-shr̀-yàn-'chǎng.

(*Assigned place*) 'dì-fangr. ‖**You'd better take a station as an outpost.** nǐ dǐng 'hǎw 'jǎw ge-'dì-fangr 'shywún-shywun 'fēng.

Fire station shyāw-fǎng-'dwèy.

Police station jǐng-chá-fēn-'jywú, 'pay-chū-'swǒ, fēn-jù-'swǒ.

(*To assign*) pày; (*to be assigned: one person*) jù-'já; (*to be assigned; a group of people*) jù-'twén, jù-'fáng. ‖**He's stationed abroad.** tā shr̀ 'pày dzày gwó-'wày. ‖**The police stationed a man at the door.** pày-le yí-ge-jǐng-'chá-dzày mén-'kěwr jàn-'gǎng. ‖**Where is your division stationed?** nǐ nèy-'shr̀ dzày-nǎr jù-'fáng?

STAY. (*To remain*) dǎy. ‖**I intend to stay for a week.** wǒ 'dǎ-swàn 'dǎy yì-shǐng-'chī. ‖**Stay a while.** 'dǎy yì-hwěr. ‖**Don't stay up late.** byé 'dǎy tày 'wǎn-le. ‖**They stayed out all night.** tā-men dzày 'wày-tew 'dǎy-le yì-jěng-'yè.

(*To live*) jù. ‖**Where are you staying?** nǐ 'jù-dzày 'nǎr? ‖**I'm staying with friends.** wǒ 'jù-dzày 'péng-yew-jyā. ‖**We had a very pleasant stay at their house.** wǒ-men dzày 'tā-men-jyā 'jù-de hěn 'tùng-kwày.

To stay *plus an adjective is expressed by the appropriate adjective or verb.* ‖**When I fix a thing, it stays fixed.** wǒ 'shēw-shr̀ 'dūng-shi, 'méy ge-'hwày. ‖**See how long you can stay clean.** (*To a child*) dàw 'chyáw-chyaw nǐ néng 'gān-jing dwō-shǎw-'shr̀-hew. ‖**He stayed mad for several hours.** tā yí 'chì 'chì-le 'hǎw-jǐ-ge-jǔng-'téw.

To stay away from ... lí ... 'ywǎn. ‖**Stay away from that place.** lí nèy-ge-'dì-fang 'ywǎn-dyǎr.

STEADY. (*Firm, not shaky*) 'wěn-dang, wěn. ‖**This needs a steady hand.** dzwò 'jèy-ge 'shěw děy 'wěn. ‖**Is the ladder steady enough?** 'tī-dz 'lì 'wěn-dang-le-ma? ‖**Steady now!** 'wěn-je-dyǎr!

To steady *is expressed as* **to make steady.** ‖**Steady the ladder so I won't fall.** bǎ 'tī-dz nùng 'wěn-lew, wǒ 'byé 'dyàw-shyà-láy.

(*Regular*). (*Even*) ywún; (*always*) cháng. ‖**We didn't go fast, but kept up a good steady pace.** wǒ-men 'dzěw-de bú-'kwày, 'kě-shr 'jyàw-bù dzěw-de hěn 'ywún. ‖**He's made steady progress.** tā jìn-'bù-de hěn 'ywún. ‖**I'm a steady customer here.** wǒ shr̀ 'jèr-de-'cháng-jǔ-gu. ‖**He has a steady job now.** shyàn-'dzày tā 'jǎw-jǎw-le yí-ge-'cháng-shr̀.

Other expressions in English. ‖**She has a steady disposition.** tā-de-'pí-chì hèn 'hǎw. ‖**They're going**

steady. *is expressed as* **They're very good friends.** tā-men 'lyǎ 'hǎw-je-ne. *or as* **They're always together.** tā-men 'lyǎ 'lǎw dzày yí-'kwàr. ‖**He just needs to steady down a little.** *is expressed as* **He just needs to subdue his spirits a little.** tā 'jyèw-shr̀ děy 'tā-shyà-dyǎr 'shīn chywù.

STEAL (STOLE, STOLEN). (*To take dishonestly*) tēw. ‖**He'd steal candy from a baby.** jyèw-shr shyǎw-'hár-de 'táng tā yě hwèy 'tēw-de. ‖**He stole my book.** tā 'tēw-rè wǒ-de-'shū-le. ‖**My car has been stolen.** wǒ-de-'chē jyàw-'rén gěy tēw-'dzěw-le. ‖**They made a big steal from the family treasury.** 'tā-men tsúng jàng-'fángr-li 'tēw-le yí-'dà-bǐ-'chyán. ‖**That song hit is a steal from an old folk song.** nèy-ge-'gēer shr̀ tsúng 'jyèw-gēer-li 'tēw-chū-láy-de.

(*To go stealthily*) tēw-'tēwr-de *or* 'tēw-tew-mwō-'mwō-de *plus a verb of motion*. ‖**They stole away through the woods.** tā-men tēw-'tēwr-de dǎ shù-'lín-dz 'pǎw-le. ‖**The children stole into the room on tiptoe.** 'háy-dz-men chyàn-je 'jyǎwr 'tēw-tew-mwō-'mwō-de dàw 'wū-li 'chywù-le.

Stolen goods dzàng-'hwò, dzàng.

To steal the show. ‖**The new actress stole the show.** *is expressed as* **The new actress sang, thereby getting all the attention.** nèy-chū-'shì gěy nèy-ge-shīn-nywǔ-'shì-dz 'chàng-le. *or as* **The new actress suppressed all the other people in the play.** nèy-chū-'shì nèy-ge-'shīn-'kwēn-jywé bǎ 'byé-rén 'dēw gěy 'yā-shyà-chywù-le.

STEAM. (*Vapor, gas; especially as a source of power*) chì; (*vapor*) jēng-'chì; (*hot vapor*) rè-'chì. **Steam (heating)** nwǎn-'chì *or* chì-'lú-dz; **steam radiator** chì-'gwǎn-dz, 'nwǎn-chì-'gwǎn-dz, 'nwǎn-chì-'lú-dz; **steam engine** chì-'jī; **steam roller** chì-'nyǎn-dz; **steamship** chì-'chwán; **steam train** hwǒ-'chē. ‖**Melt the glue with steam.** bǎ nèy-'jyāw gē-de rè-'chì-li 'hwà-hwa. ‖**Does it run by steam or electricity?** nèy-ge 'kǎy-chī-láy shr̀ yùng 'chì háy-shr̀ yùng 'dyàn-na? ‖**Is there steam heat in their new house?** 'tā-men-de-'shīn-'fáng-dz-li yěw 'nwǎn-'chì-ma?

(*To give off steam*) màw-'chì, fàng-'chì, màw-rè-'chì. ‖**The water's steaming.** shwěy 'màw-rè-'chyèr-le. ‖**Your car is steaming.** nǐ-de-'chē jr̀ màw-'chì.

To steam *open* 'shywǔ-shywu. ‖**He steamed open the letter.** tā 'bǎ nèy-fēng-'shìn gē-de 'kǎy-shwěy-shang 'shywū-shywu jyèw 'dǎ-kǎy-le.

(*To cook by steaming*) jēng. ‖**Steam the rice half an hour.** bǎ-'fàn 'jēng 'bàn-dyǎn-jūng.

(*To move by steam*) kāy. ‖**He watched the ship steam out of the harbor.** tā 'kàn-je nèy-tyáw-'chwán 'kāy-chū 'gǎng chywù-le.

To get (*or be*) **steamed up** (*to be covered with steam*) hā-'chì; (*to get excited*) chì-'jìn *or* 'shīng-fen. ‖**The windows are steamed up.** 'chwāng-hu-shang 'dēw-shr̀ hā-'chì. ‖**The mirror's getting steamed up.** 'jìng-dz-shang nùng-le hǎw-'shyē-hā-'chì. ‖**He got all**

steamed up about the idea. tā dwèy-ywu nèy-ge-'yì-jyàn hěn chǐ-'jìn.

To get up steam. (Of a machine) shàng-'jyèr; (of people) shàng-'jyèr, chǐ-'jìn, jyā-'jǐn. ‖The machine is getting up steam. 'jī-chi yǐ-jing shàng-'jyèr-le. ‖We'll have to get up steam and finish this in a hurry. wǒ-men děy 'chǐ-dyǎr 'jìn, 'kwày-dyǎr bǎ-'jèy nùng 'wán-le.

STEEL. gāng, gāng-'tyě. ‖The bridge is all made of steel. jèy-ge-'chyáw 'chywán-shr̀ 'gāng dzwò-de. ‖The bullet bounded off his 'steel helmet. dž-'dàn tsúng tā-gāng-'kwēy-shang 'bèng-shyà-chywù-le. ‖He worked for a while in a steel mill. tā dzày tyě-gūng-'chǎng-li 'dzwò-le yí-jèn-dz-'shr̀.

STEEP. (Of a slope) děw. ‖That slope is steeper than it looks. nèy-ge-'pwōer shr̀-'jì bǐ 'kàn-je 'děw.

(Of a price) gwèy, gāw. ‖That's a pretty steep price for that house. nèy-swǒ-'fáng-dz-de-'jyàer kě 'jēn gèw 'gwèy-de.

To steep mēn, pàw. ‖Let the tea steep a little longer. 'chá dwō 'mēn yì-hwěr

STEP. (Movement of the foot) bù; (more formal, used especially of dancing and marching) 'bù-dz. ‖He took one step forward. tā wàng-'chyán 'mày-le yí-'bù. ‖I don't know the steps of that dance. wǒ 'bú-hwèy 'nèy-jǔng-tyàw-'wǔ-de-'bù-dz.

(Person's way of walking) dzěw-'dàwr-de-yàngr (its appearance); jyǎw-bù-'shēngr (its sound). ‖I thought I heard steps. wó 'jywé-je wǒ 'tīng-jyàn jyǎw-bù-'shēngr-le. ‖I know who it is; I can recognize his step. (If by watching him walk) wǒ kàn dzěw-'dàwr-de-yàngr jyèw 'jr̄-daw shr̀-'shéy. or (If by listening to him walk) wǒ 'tīng jyǎw-bù-'shēngr jyèw 'jr̄-daw shr̀-'shéy.

(Agreeing pace) 'jyǎw-bù, 'bù-dz. ‖Keep in step with me. bǎ 'jyǎw-bù 'gēn-wo 'dzěw yí-'yàng-le. ‖He's out of step. tā-'jyǎw-bù bú-'dwèy. (Figuratively) ‖He's out of step with the times. is expressed as He's out of place in marching. tā lè-'wǔ-le.

(Unit of action) bù, 'bù-dzěw. ‖This is only the first step in the process. 'jèy-ge 'bú-gwò shr̀ dì-'yí-bù-'shěw-shywù. ‖This is a great step forward. 'jèy-ge shr̀ yí-ge-hěn-'dà-de-jìn-'bù.

(On a stairway) yí-dèngr-°táy-'jyèr or °léw-'tī; steps táy-'jyèr, or (a flight of stairs leading from one floor to another) léw-'tī. ‖I stopped and sat on the top step. wǒ 'jàn-jù-le, dzwò-dzày dzwèy-'gāw-de-nèy-dèng-léw-'tī-shang-le. ‖He ran up the steps to the porch. tā 'pǎw-shang táy-'jyēr dàw 'láng-dz-shang chywù-le.

Step by step 'yí-bù-yí-'bù-de, 'yì-dyǎr-yì-'dyǎr-de. ‖We built up our business step by step. wǒ-men-de-'shr̀-yè shr̀ 'yì-dyǎr-yì-'dyǎr-de 'dzwò-chǐ-láy-de.

To take steps shyǎng-'fár. ‖I'll have to take steps to stop the gossip. wǒ děy shyǎng-'fár 'byé ràng tā-men shwō shyán-'hwà-le. ‖If things don't improve, we'll

have to take steps. yàw-shr 'shr̀-ching háy 'méy-yew jìn-'bù, wǒ-men děy shyǎng-'fár 'bàn-ban.

To watch one's step. ‖Watch your step! is expressed as Be careful. lyéw-'shén. or as Be careful of your footing. 'lyéw-shén jyàw 'dǐ-shyà. or as Pay attention. jù-'yì.

To step (to go) 'dzěw; (to put the foot down on) tsǎy; (to reach out with the foot) mày; step over something 'mày-gwò; step up on something 'mày-shàng, step down from something 'mày-shyà; in some combinations expressed as stand. ‖I stepped in a puddle. wǒ 'dzěw-de shwéy-'kēngr-li-le. ‖Don't step on the flowers. byé 'tsǎy-lew 'hwār. ‖Step over the fence. 'mày-gwò nèy-ge-'lí-ba chywù. ‖He just stepped off the train. tā 'gāng 'mày-shyà ,'chē láy. ‖Step lively now! 'kwày dzěw. ‖Step aside. wàng páng-'byār 'jàn-jàn. ‖Step back a little. wàng-hèw °'jàn-dyǎr or °'twèy-twey.

To step in (for a visit). ‖I just stepped in for a moment. is expressed as I just came to see you a moment; then I must go. wǒ 'jyèw-shr̀ láy 'kàn-kan 'nǐ-men yì-'hwěr jyèw děy 'dzěw.

To step in (to intervene) 'chū-lay °'lyǎw or °tyáw-ting or °'shwō-he. ‖He stepped in to stop the fight. tā 'chū-lay 'géy tā-men 'shwō-he 'shwō-he 'bú-ràng tā-men 'dǎ-le.

To step up (to move forward) wàng-'chyán 'dzěw. ‖Step right up for your tickets. wàng-'chyán 'dzěw ná-'pyàw chywù. (To increase) dzēng-'jyā. ‖Try to step up production. 'jìn-'lyàngr dzēng-'jyā shēng-'chǎn.

STICK (STUCK). (To thrust into) chā; (to hook through something) byé; (slip, tuck in) sāy. ‖Stick this pin in your lapel. bǎ jèy-ge-byé-'jēn 'byé-dzay-nǐ-'lǐng-dz-shang. ‖She stuck a flower in her hair. tā dzày 'téw-fa-shang 'chā-le yì-dwǒ-'hwār. ‖Someone stuck a knife in the wall. yěw-'rén dzày 'chyáng-shang 'chā-le yì-bǎ-'dāw. ‖He stuck the paper in his pocket. tā bǎ-'jr̄ 'sāy-de tā-'dēwr-li-le.

(To prick) jā. ‖That pin is sticking me. nèy-ge-'jēn 'jā-le wǒ-le. ‖He stuck her with a pin. tā ná-'jēn 'jā-ta láy-je.

(To fasten with glue) bǎ . . . jān; for thin things like paper bǎ . . . tyē. ‖Stick the stamp on the envelope. bǎ yéw-'pyàw 'tyē-dzay shìn-'fēngr-shang. ‖Stick these pictures in your album. bǎ jèy-shyē-shyàng-'pyār 'tyē-dzay nǐ-de-shyàng-pyār-'běr-shang. ‖Stick it together with glue. ná-'jyāw 'jān-shang.

(To adhere) jān; for thin things like paper tyē. ‖The paper sticks to my fingers. jèy-ge-'jr̄ jān-'shěw. ‖There's a piece of gum stuck on my shoe. yí-kwày-'kěw-shyāng-'táng 'jān-dzay wǒ-'shyé-shang-le. ‖This label won't stick. jèy-ge-'fēng-tyaw tyē-bú-'shàng-le. ‖I tried to tear off the label but it stuck. wǒ 'dǎ-swàn-bǎ nèy-ge-'fēng-tyaw 'jyě-shyà-lay 'kě-shr̀ 'jān-jù-le.

(*To be immovable, blocked in some way*) 'chyá-shang-le, 'chyá-jù-le, *or indirect expressions.* ‖This drawer °sticks. *or* °is stuck. jèy-ge-'chēw-ti 'chyá-shang-le. *or expressed as* This drawer °can't be pulled open. °lā-bu-'kāy-le. *or as* °can't be moved by pulling. °lā-bú-'dùng-le. *or as* °can't be moved by pushing. °twēy-bu-'dùng-le. ‖Our car is stuck in the mud. *is expressed as* Our car is sunk in the mud. wǒ-men-'chē °'shyàn (*or* °'shywàn) dzày 'ní-li-le.

(*To place*) gē, fàng. ‖They stuck a "For Rent" sign in the window. tā-men dzày 'chwāng-hu-ner 'fàng-le yì-jāng-"tsz̆-'fáng-jāw-'dzū"-ć ͺ'tyáwr. ‖Stick it over there. 'shyàn gē-dzày nèy-'byàr-ba.

(*Not to change*) bù-'gǎy; *also other expressions for working, talking, etc.* ‖Stick to the subject. *is expressed as* Don't get off the subject. byé lí 'tí. ‖Stick to the original. 'byé gǎy ywán-'láy-de-'yàngr. ‖He stuck to his story. tā yì-'jŕ-de bù-gǎy 'dzwěy. ‖Pick a good brand and then stick to it. jǎw yí-ge-'hǎw-de jyēw byé"gǎy-le.

To stick out chū; (*especially of an arm, leg, etc.*) shēn, jŕ; to stick out *or* stick up (*visibly*) lèw *or* lèw-chū-lay. ‖He stuck his feet out into the aisle. tā bǎ-'jyǎw 'shēn-daw dzěw-'dàw-shang-le. ‖Your shirt-tail is sticking out. ni-chèn-shān-'hèw-tew 'jŕ-chū-lay-le. ‖Watch out for that pipe sticking up over there. lyéw-'shén 'nèy-byàr-'jŕ-chū-lay-de-nèy-ge-'gwǎn-dz,

To stick it out rěn, rěn-'này. ‖Try to stick it out a little longer. shyǎng-'fár dwō 'rěn yì-'hwěr. ‖He stuck it out to the bitter end. nèy-ge-'shŕ-ching tā rěn-'này-je dzwò-'wán-le.

To stick up for (*be partial to*) shyàng; (*help*) bāng. ‖He always sticks up for you. tā 'lǎw shŕ 'shyàng-je nǐ.

To be stuck (*of a person*). ‖He's stuck on that problem. *is expressed as* He really has no rules to go by on that problem. nèy-ge-'wèn-tí tā 'jyǎn-jŕ shŕ méy-'jé. ‖The train broke down and we were stuck there for hours. *is express 1 as* The train broke down and we were stranded there for hours. hwǒ-'chē 'hwày-le wǒm dzày-ner 'dwēn-le hǎw-jǐ-ge-jūng-!téw.

(*Remain*) ‖His name stuck in my mind. *is expressed as* His name made me remember it. tā-de-'míng-dz ràng-wǒ 'jì-dzày 'shīn-li-le.

‖Don't stick your nose into other people's business. *is expressed as* Don't mind other people's affairs. byé gwǎn 'byé-rén-de-shyán-'shŕ.

A stick (*walking stick*) shěw-'jàng *or* gwǎy-'gwèr *or* gwǎy-'jàng; (*a trimmed branch, smooth stick or stake*) 'gwèn-dz, gwèr; (*twig, branch*) shù-'jēr. ‖He knocked on the door with his stick. tā 'yùng tā-de-shěw-'jàng chyǎw 'mén láy-je. ‖I hit him with a stick. wǒ nǎ 'gwèn-dz 'dǎ tā láy-je. ‖Pick up the sticks in the yard. bǎ 'ywàn-dz-li-de-shù-'jēr 'jyǎn-chǐ-lay.

A stick of. *Various measures including* tyáw *and* r. A stick of gum yí-'kwày-kěw-shyāng-'táng.

STICKY. nyán. ‖My fingers are sticky from the honey. wǒ-shěw-'jŕ-tew nùng-shang 'mì-le, hěn 'nyán.

(*Hot and humid*) nyán, 'mēn-rè. ‖What a sticky day! hǎw-'nyán-de-tyàr! *or* tyàr 'mēn-rè!

STIFF. (*Hard to bend*) yìng, ‖How stiff shall I starch your collars? nǐ-de-'lǐng-dz yǎw 'jyāng 'dwó-yìng-nga? ‖Use a stiff brush. yùng yì-bǎ-'yìng-'shwā-dz. ‖The book is bound in stiff paper. nèy-běr-'shū dīng-le ge-'yìng-pyér.

(*Lame, not supple*) swān. ‖To have a stiff neck 'làw-le 'jěn-le. ‖I'm stiff from that exercise yesterday. dzwóer wǒ 'bèng-de hwén-'shēn fā-'swān.

(*Thick, viscous*) chéw; (*too thick to whip*) chéw-de dǎ bú-'dùng-le. ‖Beat it until it's stiff. bǎ nèy-ge 'dǎ-de 'chéw-de dǎ bú-'dùng-lew. *But* ‖Beat the egg whites until stiff. *is expressed as* Beat up the egg whites. bǎ jī-dàn-'chyēngr 'dǎ-chǐ-lay.

(*Formal*) jyāng, bǎn, 'běng-je. ‖Don't be so stiff. byé 'nème 'běng-je.

Special expressions in English. ‖Is it a stiff examination? *is expressed as* Is the examination difficult? nèy-ge 'kǎw-de 'nán-ma? ‖He charges stiff fees. *is expressed as* The prices he wants are too high. tā-'yàw-de-'jyàr tày °'dà `*or* °'gāw *or* °'dwō. ‖A good stiff breeze sprang up. yí-'jèn shyǎw-'yìng-fēngr 'gwā-de tǐng 'hǎw. ‖Please pour me a stiff drink. *is expressed as* Please give me a strong drink. láw-'jyà gěy-wǒ 'dàw yì-bēy-'chùng-dyàr-de-'jyěw.

STILL. (*Motionless*) jù, wěn; *or expressed as* not to move bú-'dùng. ‖Hold still a minute. byé 'dùng. ‖Keep your feet still. ni-'jyǎw byé 'dùng. ‖Stand still. 'jàn-je byé 'dùng. *or* jàn-'jù-lew. *or* jàn-'wěn-lew. ‖She sat perfectly still. tā 'dzwò nèr yì-'dyàr dēw bú-'dùng.

(*Quiet*) 'ān-jìng. ‖Be still. 'ān-jìng-dyǎr. *or expressed as* Don't make noise. byé 'chǎw. *or as* Don't speak. byé 'yán-ywǔ-le. ‖The whole house was still. jěng-'gèr-de-'fáng-dz-li hěn 'ān-jing. *or expressed as* Throughout the house there wasn't a sound. jěng-'gèr-de-'fáng-dz-li yì-'dyǎr 'shēngr dēw méy-'yěw. ‖Keep still about this. *is expressed as* Don't mention this. 'jèy-ge byé 'gēn-rén 'tí. *or as* Don't say anything about this. 'jèy-ge byé 'shwō-chu-chywu. *or as* Don't talk about this. 'dwèy-ywú 'jèy-ge byé 'yán-ywu tsáy 'hǎw.

(*Calm and quiet; of water*) 'píng-jìng. ‖The lake is still today. 'jyèr hú-li hěn 'píng-jìng. *But* ‖The air is very still. *is expressed as* There's not a bit of wind. yì-dyàr-'fēng dēw méy-'yěw. *or, if the air is both motionless and silent, as* yèw méy-'fēng yèw 'ān-jing.

(*As yet, now as before*) háy, hwán, *or* 'réng-jyèw. ‖I am still waiting to hear from him. wǒ háy dzày 'děng-je 'tīng tā-de-'shyāw-shi-ne. ‖He's still the same. tā 'háy shŕ nà-'yàngr. ‖He built it while his wife was still alive. tā 'gày 'nèy-ge de-'shŕ-hewr tā-'tày-tay háy 'hwó-je-ne. ‖Eat it while it's still hot. chèn-je háy 'rè-ie-ne, 'chŕ-ba. *or* 'chŕ-ba, chèn 'rèr.

(*Even*) (háy . . .) dzày; *with compara es using* gèng, *also* (háy . . .) gèng. ‖He asked for still more books. tā 'háy yàw dzày 'dwō jǎw-dyǎr shū. ‖I want to go still further up the mountain. ney-ge-'shān wǒ yàw 'dzày shàng 'gāw-dyǎr. *or* nèy-ge-'shān wǒ yàw 'gèng shàng 'gāw-dyǎr.

Even so . . . still 'jyèw-shř 'jè-yàng . . . hay: although . . . still 'swéy-rán . . . kě-shr . . . háy. ‖Still, I think you did the right thing. 'jyèw-shř 'jè-yàng, wǒ 'háy 'yǐ-wéy nǐ dzwò 'dwèy-le. ‖Although I don't like him, still I have to admit he's clever. 'swéy-rán wǒ bù-'shǐ-hwan ta, kě-shr wǒ 'háy shwō tā tsung-ming.

STOCK. (*Supply, stored goods*) tswén-'hwò; (*goods*) dǐ-'hwò, hwò A stock yì-'pī-tswén-'hwò. ‖I'll look through my stock and see if I have it. wǒ yàw bá tswén-'hwò 'kàn yí-byàn 'kàn-kan wǒ 'yěw nèy-ge méy-yěw. *But* ‖I want to lay in a stock of soap. *is expressed as* I want to store a supply of soap. wǒ yàw 'tswén yì-'pī-'yí-dz.

(*Subscribed capital*) gǔ-'pyàw. ‖I have several shares of their stock. dzày 'tā-men-de-gǔ-'pyàw-li wǒ yěw jǐ-'gǔr.

Stock market jyāw-yì-'swǒ; to play the stock market dzwò dǎw-'bǎ-de-'shēng-yì; *or expressed as* buy and sell on margin dzwò mǎy-'kūng mày-'kūngr.

(*Livestock*) 'shēng-kew. ‖He keeps all kinds of stock on his farm. tā dzày tā-de-'dì-li yǎng-le 'gè-shr 'gè-yàngr-de-'shēng-kew.

(*Breed*) jǔngr. ‖Are these animals of healthy stock? 'jèy-shyē-'shēng-kew-de-'jǔngr 'hǎw-ma?

In stock. ‖What do you have in stock? *is expressed as* What goods do you have stored? nǐ 'tswén-de yěw 'shéme-'hwò?

Out of stock. ‖That size glove is out of stock. *is expressed as* That size glove is not among the goods. nèy-'hàwr-de-shěw-'tàwr °méy-'hwò-le. *or meaning* sold out °mày-'wán-le.

To put stock in. ‖I don't put much stock in that reporter's stories. *is expressed as* I don't much believe that reporter's news. wǒ bú-dà-'shìn nèy-ge-shīn-wēn-jì-'jě-de-'shyāw-shi.

To take stock. ‖Next week we're taking stock. *is expressed as* Next week we're going to check the whole stock. shyà-shīng-'chī wǒ-men yàw 'chīng-ching hwò-'dǐ-dz-le. ‖Why don't you stop and take stock of the situation? *is expressed as* Why don't you stop and investigate the situation? nǐ wèy-'shéme bù-tíng-shyà-lay °dyàw-cha jèy-ge-'chíng-shing-ne? *or as* Why don't you inspect the situation? °'kǎw-cha jèy-ge-'chíng-shing-ne? *or as* Why don't you study the situation? °'yán-jyew jèy-ge-'chíng-shing-ne?

To stock tswén. ‖Are you stocked up for the winter? 'jīn-nyán-'dūng-tyan-de-'hwò nǐ 'tswén-le-ma? ‖The hotel is well stocked with linen. jèy-ge-lywǔ-'gwǎn 'tswén-le bù-'shǎw-de-chwáng-'dān-dz. ‖We don't stock that brand. wǒ-men bù-'tswén nèy-jǔng-'páy-dz-de.

STOCKING. (*Either short or long stockings*) 'wà-dz; (*long stockings*) 'cháng-tǔngr-'wà-dz *or* gāw-'yàwr-wà-dz. ‖I want three pairs of stockings, size nine and a half. wǒ yàw 'sān-shwāng-'jyěw-hàwr-'bàn-de-'cháng-tǔngr-'wa-dz.

In one's stocking feet. (*without shoes*) 'gwáng-je wà-'dyěr. ‖He walks around the house in his stocking feet. tā 'gwāng-je wà-'dyěr dzày 'fáng-dz-li dzěw-láy dzěw-'chywù.

STOMACH. wèy; (*abdomen*) 'dù-dz; *or expressed as* heart shīn; (*upper and front part of the body*) shīn-'kěw. ‖Rich foods don't set well on my stomach. yěw 'nì-de-'dūng-shi wǒ 'chř-de °'dù-dz-li bù-hǎw 'shèw. *or* °'shīn-li bù hǎw 'gwò. ‖I have a pain in my stomach. (*If in the lower part*) wǒ-'dù-dz 'téng. *or* wǒ-°'wèy (*or* °'wey-chì) 'téng. *or* (*If in the upper part*) wǒ-shīn-'kěw 'téng. ‖Hit him in the stomach. 'dǎ-de tā shīn-'kěw-shang-le.

Empty stomach kùng-'dùr, kūng-je-'wèy. ‖Don't exercise on an empty stomach. kùng-je-'dùr de-'shř-hewr byé 'ywùn-dùng.

To stomach. ‖I can't stomach such rich food. wǒ bù-néng 'chř dzème-yéw-'nì-de-'dūng-shi. ‖He couldn't stomach the insult. nèy-jǔng-de-'wū-rǔ tā shèw-bù-'lyǎw.

STONE. 'shř-tew; (*pebble*) shř-tew-'dzěr. ‖The house is built entirely of stone. jèy-ge-'fáng-dz jěng-'gèr-de shř 'shř-tew-'gày-de. ‖The stones of the wall are cool. 'chyáng-shang-de-'shř-tew lyáng-bu-'jyēr-de. ‖We had a beautiful stone put on his grave. wǒ-men dzày tā-de-'fén-shang 'gē-le yí-kwày-hěn-hǎw-'kàn-de-'shř-tew. ‖It's hard walking on these stones. dzày 'jèy-shyē-'shř-tew-shang hěn 'bù-hǎw 'dzěw. ‖Who threw that stone? nèy-ge-shř-tew-'dzěr shř-'shéy 'rēng-de? ‖Can you lift that stone? nǐ néng 'jywǔ-chǐ nèy-kwày-'shř-tew láy-ma? ‖The kitchen has a stone floor. chú-'fáng-de-dì-'bǎn shř 'shř-tew-de. ‖We decided to put three stone benches in the garden. wǒ-men jywé-'dìng dzày hwā-'ywár-li gē 'sān-ge-'shř-tew-'dèng-dz.

(*Gem*) bǎw-'shř, *or* 'shř-tewr. ‖Have you any precious stones to declare? nǐ yěw 'shéme-bǎw-'shř děy bàw-'shwèy-ma?

(*Pit*) húr, *or* héer. ‖I was eating cherries and throwing the stones out the window. wǒ chř-je 'yīng-taw bǎ-'húr jyèw 'rēng-de 'chwāng-hu-'wày-tew chywù-le.

(*Completely*). Stone-deaf jěng-'gèr-de 'lúng-le, stone-blind jěng-'gèr-de 'shyā-le. ‖I am stone-broke. *is expressed as* I haven't a single copper. wǒ 'chyúng-de yí-ge-'dà yě 'méy-yew-le.

A stone's throw. ‖He lives just a stone's throw from us. *is expressed as* He lives the distance of an arrow from us. tā 'jù-de-dì-fangr lí 'wǒ-men-jèr yě 'jyèw-shř yí-'jyàn 'ywǎn.

STOP. (*To bring to a halt*) ràng (*or* bǎ) . . . 'jàn-ju *or* 'tíng; (*to stop a vehicle*) 'dǎ-jù; (*to stop someone or something from doing something by putting up a barrier, or by using persuasion)* lán, dǎng; 'lán-jù-le, 'dǎng-jù-le. ‖**We were stopped by the police.** shywún-'jīng °ràng 'wǒ-men 'jàn-jù-le. *or* °bǎ wǒ-men 'lán-jù-le. ‖**Stop the car at the next crossing.** 'shyà-yí-ge-'shŕ-dz-'lù-'kěwr bǎ-'chē 'tíng-shyà-ba. ‖**He brought the train to a full stop.** tā bǎ-'chē 'dǎ-jù-le. ‖**He was trying to go out, but I stopped him.** tā shyǎng 'chū-chywù wǒ 'bǎ-ta °'lán-jù-le. *or* °'dǎng-jù-le. *or expressed as* **He wanted to go out but I wouldn't let him go.** tā shyǎng 'chū-chywù kě-shr méy-'jyàw-ta 'chū-chywù. ‖**If anyone tries to stop you, let me know.** 'yàw-shr yěw-'rén 'lán-ni-ya, gàw-su wo.

(To halt) tíng, 'jàn-ju; *(of vehicles especially, and sometimes of people walking or working)* 'dǎ-jù. ‖**He stopped short and turned around.** tā nème yì 'tíng jyèw 'jwàn-gwo-chywù-le. ‖**This car will stop on a dime.** *is expressed as* **The brakes on this car are very good; it stops in an instant.** jèy-ge-'chē 'já hěn 'líng, yí-'shyàr jyèw 'jàn-ju. *or as* **The brakes on this car are very good; you say stop and it stops.** jèy-ge-'chē 'já hěn 'líng, 'shwō dǎ-jù jyèw néng 'dǎ-jù. ‖**When do we stop for lunch?** *(If you're either working or driving)* wǒ-men 'shéme-shŕ-hewr 'dǎ-jù hǎw chŕ-'fàn chywù? ‖**We made several stops before we got here.** wǒ-men 'dàw-'jèr láy dzày 'dàwr-shang 'jàn-ju-le hǎw-jǐ-'tsż. ‖**The passers-by stopped to look.** nèy-ge-gwò-'lù-de-'rén 'jàn-ju-le 'kàn-le-yi-kàn. ‖**My watch just stopped.** wǒ-'byǎw 'gāng 'jàn-ju-le. *or expressed as* ‖**My watch has stopped going.** wǒ-'byǎw gāng bù-'dzěw-le.

(To prevent) lán *(see first paragraph above),* or bú-'ràng; *(to stop pain, bleeding, etc.)* jŕ. ‖**Can't you stop him from talking that way?** nǐ 'kě-yi 'lán-lan tā byé 'ràng-ta nème 'shwō-ma? ‖**You can't stop me from thinking about it.** nǐ 'méy-fǎr bú-ràng-wo 'shyǎng nèy-ge-'shŕ-ching. *or* wǒ 'shyǎng nèy-ge-'shŕ nǐ 'lán-bù-lyǎw. ‖**This medicine ought to stop the pain.** jèy-ge-'yàw yí-'dìng jŕ-'téng. ‖**Stop her from hitting him.** bǎ nèy-ge-'nywǔ-de 'lán-jù, byé ràng-'tā 'dǎ-ta.

(To cease) bù . . . le; *(when asking someone to stop something)* byé *(don't).* ‖**I've stopped worrying about it.** 'nèy-jyàn-'shŕ wǒ yě bù-jāw-'jí-le. ‖**When do you stop work?** nǐ 'shéme-shŕ-hewr jyèw bú-dzwò-'shŕ-le? ‖**Has it stopped raining?** ywǔ bú-'shyà-le-ma? ‖**He stopped in the middle of a sentence.** tā 'shwō-bàn-jywù-'hwà jyèw bù-'shwō-le. ‖**Stop reading a minute.** shyān byé nyàn-ne. *or* 'děng-dengr 'dzày nyàn. ‖**Stop it!** 'dé-le-ba! ‖**I stopped having headaches.** wǒ 'dzày méy téw-'téng-gwo.

(To stay) jù. ‖**We stopped at a farmhouse overnight.** wǒ-men 'dzày yí-ge-'núng-rén-'jyā-li 'jù-le yí-'yè.

To stop off 'tíng-°yi-tíng, °yi-hwěr, °yi-shyàr; *or* 'jàn-°yi-jàn, °yi-hwěr, °yi-shyàr. ‖**Let's stop off at the beach.** 'dzám dzày hǎy-'byǎr-shang 'tíng yí-shyàr.

To stop over *is expressed as* **to stay a couple of days** 'jù lyǎng-tyǎn.

To stop up dǔ, tyán. ‖**This hole should be stopped up.** jèy-ge-'kū-lung děy 'dǔ-shang. *or* jèy-'kēngr děy 'tyán-shang. ‖**My nose is stopped up.** wǒ-de-'bí-dz 'dǔ-jù-le.

(Stopping place) jàn. ‖**Get off the bus at the next stop.** 'shyà-yí-jàn shyà-'chē.

STORE. *(Shop)* dyàn, 'pù-dz, *or* yáng-'háng *(see* SHOP). ‖**I know a store where you can buy that.** wǒ 'jŕ-dàw yěw yí-ge-'pù-dz nǐ néng 'mǎy-jaw 'nèy-ge. ‖**Run down to the grocery store for me.** tì-wo 'pǎw yí-tàng yéw-yán-'dyàn.

(To lay away) tswén, shēw; *also* fàng *or* gē *(to put).* ‖**Where shall I store the potatoes?** wǒ bǎ jèy-shyē-tǔ-'dèwr tswén-'nǎr? ‖**We have a big store of supplies right now.** *is expressed as* **We've stored a lot of things now.** shyàn-'dzày wǒ-men 'tswén-le bù-'shǎw-de-'dūng-shi. ‖**We've canned some vegetables to have in store for the winter.** wǒ-men bǎ-'tsày 'jwāng-le dyǎr-'gwàn-tew 'tswén-chi-lay wèy 'dūng-tyan 'chŕ.

In store for *(the future).* ‖**I wonder what's in store for us?** *is expressed as* **I don't know what the future will be like for us.** wǒ bù-jŕ-'dàw wǒ-men 'jyāng-láy dzěme-'yàng.

STORM. bàw-fēng-'ywǔ *or* dà-'fēng-dà-'ywǔ; *(snowstorm)* bàw-fēng-'shywě *or* dà-'fēng-dà-'shywě. ‖**Do you remember that storm we had last summer?** nǐ háy 'jì-de 'chywù-nyán wǒ-men 'gǎn-shàng-de nèy-'chǎng-bàw-fēng-'ywǔ-ma? ‖**There was a foot of snow after the storm yesterday.** dzwóer nèy-'chǎng-dà-'fēng-dà-'shywě yǐ-'hèw 'shywě yěw 'yì-chŕ 'shēn.

(To attack) 'gūng-jī. ‖**We stormed the enemy positions.** wǒ-men gūng-jī 'dí-rén-de-'jèn-di.

Take by storm. ‖**We took the enemy by storm.** *is expressed as* **We gave the enemy a blow when he wasn't watching.** wǒ-men dzày 'dí-rén méy-lyéw-'shén de-shŕ-hewr gěy-ta 'láy-le yí-shyà-dz.

STORY. *(Narrative)* 'shŕ-ching. ‖**Do you know the story of his life?** nǐ 'jŕ-daw tā nèy-yí-'bèy-dz-de-'shŕ-ching-ma? ‖**The whole story is in the paper.** nèy-jyàn-'shŕ-ching jěng-'gèr-de-jīng-'gwò dēw shàng-le 'bàw-le.

(Short tale) shyǎw-'shwōr. ‖**She wrote a story for the school magazine.** tā gěy shywé-'shyàw-de-'kān-wù 'shyě-le yì-pyān-shyǎw-'shwōr.

(Joke) 'shyǎw-hwar. ‖**Know any new stories?** 'jŕ-dàw shéme-shīn-'shyàw-hwàr-ma?

(Account) hwà, shwō-de-'hwà, *or* 'shwō-de. ‖**Their stories don't agree.** tā-men-de-'hwà bù-yí-'yàng. ‖**That's my story, and I'll stick to it.** 'nà-shŕ wǒ-'shwō-de, wǒ yǔng-'ywǎn nàme 'shwō. ‖**It's a plausible story.** nèy-ge-'hwà hěn hé-'lǐ. ‖**The story goes that he really doesn't know her.** *is expressed as* **They say that he really doesn't know her.** tā-men shwō tā 'shŕ-dzày 'bìng bú-'rèn-shr nèy-ge-'nywǔ-de. ‖**So the story goes.** *is expressed as* **So they say.** 'tām dzème 'shwō-de.

‖It'll be another story tomorrow. *is expressed as* Tomorrow it'll be another way. 'myéngr-ge jyèw 'lìng-yí-ge-'yàngr-le.

(*Floor*) léw *with measure* tséng. ‖She lives on the second story. tā 'jù-dzày 'èr-tséng-'léw. ‖It's a four-story building. 'nèy-ge shř 'yí-ge-'sž-tséng-'léw-de-léw-'fáng.

STOVE. 'lú-dz, dzàw. ‖Put the beans on the stove. bǎ-'dèwr gē-de 'lú-dz-shang. ‖We bought a new electric stove. wǒ-men 'mǎy-le yí-ge-'shīn-dyàn-'lú-dz.

STRAIGHT. jř, jř-lyew; (*in a straight course*) yì-'jř. ‖We need a good straight stick. wǒ-men yàw yì-'gēr-'jř-gwèr. ‖Draw a straight line through it. 'hwà yì-tyáw-'jř-shyàn 'jīng-gwò nèy-ge. ‖The road is straight for five miles on this side of the bridge. *is expressed as* On this side of the bridge the road is straight as a pen for five miles. chyáw 'jèy-byàr yěw 'wǔ-lǐ-cháng-'bì-jř-de-dà-'dàw. ‖Hold your arm out straight. bǎ nǐ-de-'gē-bey shēn 'jř-lew. ‖Look straight down. 'jř-je wàng-shyà 'kàn. ‖Stand up straight. jàn 'jř-lew. ‖Go straight ahead. yì-'jř 'dzěw. ‖Go straight across the square. 'jř-je (*or* yì-'jř-de) wàng-chyán 'dzěw, 'chwān-gwò nèy-ge-'chǎng-dz chywù. ‖He walked straight to the telephone pole. tā-yì-'jř-de 'dzěw-de 'dyàn-shyan-'gān-dz shàng-le.

(*Directly*) yì-'jř-de *or* jř-'jyē-de. ‖Go straight home. yì-'jř-de hwéy-'jyā-ya. ‖Come straight over after the show. kàn-wán 'shì jř-'jyē-de shàng-'jèr láy-ya.

(*Properly*). (*At right angles to something*) jèng; (*right, correct*) 'jèng-dàng *or* dwèy. ‖Is my hat on straight? wǒ-de-'màw-dz dày 'jèng-le-ma? ‖He can't think straight, much less talk straight. tā 'shyǎng-de bú-'jèng-dang, 'shwō-de-'hwà 'gèng bú-'jèng-dang. ‖Try to get the story straight. *is expressed as* Understand the situation clearly. bǎ 'jèy-ge-'shř-ching kàn 'míng-bay-lew. ‖Be sure to get your facts straight before you put them into the report. *is expressed as* Get the real situation clear, then write the report. bǎ 'jēn-shyàng nèng °'chīng-chu-le (*or* °'míng-bay-le) dzày shyě bàw-'gàw.

(*Honest*) 'chéng-shŕ *or* 'chéng-kěn. ‖He's always been straight with me. tā 'dwèy-wo 'lǎw shř 'nàme-'chéng-kěn.

(*Undiluted*). ‖He drank his whisky straight. *is expressed as* He drank his whisky with nothing added to it. tā 'hē wēy-shř-'jì jyěw shéme yě méy-'chān.

. . . straight (*at a stretch*) yí-'shyàr, yì-'jř-de, yí-'chyèr, yí-kěw-'chyèr. ‖We worked for fifteen hours straight. wǒ-men yì-'jř-de 'dzwò-le shŕ-'wǔ-ge-jūng-'téw.

A straight face. ‖I told it with a straight face. wǒ 'běng-je-'lyǎn shwō-de.

STRANGE. (*Unfamiliar*) shēng. ‖It's good to see you among all these strange faces. dzày 'jèy-shyē-'shēng-rén-'lǐ-tew 'kàn-jyàn 'nǐ jēn bú-'tswò. ‖All this is strange to me. wǒ 'jywé-de 'jèy-ge dēw hěn 'shēng.

(*Peculiar*) gwày *or* 'chí-gwày; (*special, unusual*) tè-'byé. ‖There is something strange about this house. jèy-ge-'fáng-dz 'yěw-dyǎr tè-'byé. ‖That's a strange thing to say. 'nème shwō-'hwà hěn 'chí-gwày. ‖He's a strange character. 'tā-nèy-ge-rén jēn 'gwày. ‖It's strange, but true. nèy-ge jēn tè-'byé, 'kě-shr bù-'jyǎ. ‖It feels strange to be doing this kind of work. dzwò 'jèy-jǔng-'shř-ching jywé-de hěn 'gwày. ‖Strange to say, I didn't notice it. 'shwō-chǐ-láy tǐng 'gwày, wǒ méy-jù-'yì.

STRANGER. (*Unknown person*) 'shēng-rén. ‖I had dinner with a total stranger. wǒ gēn yí-ge-'shēng-rén dzày yí-'kwàr chř-'fàn láy-je. ‖He's a complete stranger to me. *is expressed as* I'm not familiar with him. wǒ 'gēn-ta bù-'shú. *or as* I never met him. wǒ méy-'jyàn-gwo ta. *or as* I'm not acquainted with him. wǒ bú-'rèn-shr ta. ‖You're quite a stranger around here. *is expressed as* You're really a guest. nǐ 'jēn shř ge-'shī-kè. ‖I'm a stranger here myself. wǒ dzàv-'ièr 'yě shř hěn 'shēng. *or* wǒ dzày-'jèr 'yě shř bù-'shéw.

STREET. jyē, dà-'jyē, mǎ-'lù, *or* lù; (*small street or alley*) hú-'tùngr; (*lane*) shyàng. ‖Be careful when you cross the street. gwò-'jyē de-'shŕ-hewr lyéw-dyǎr 'shén. ‖What street do I get off at? wǒ dzày 'něy-tyáw-jyē 'shyà-lay? ‖I live at 47 East Chang-an Street. wǒ 'jù-dzày 'dūng-cháng-ān-'jyē 'sž-shŕ-'chí-hàw. ‖The children shouldn't play in the street. 'háy-dz-men yí-'dìng 'bù-néng dzày 'jyē-shang wár. ‖I ran into him on the street the other day. wǒ nèy-'tyān dzày 'jyē-shang 'péng-jyàn 'tā-le.

Dead-end street sž-hú-'tùngr.

STRENGTH. 'lì-lyang, jìn, jyèr, jìn-'téwr. ‖I haven't that much strength. wǒ 'méy-yěw nème-'dà-de-'lì-lyang. ‖I haven't the strength to climb that mountain. wǒ méy-'jyèr pá-'shān-le. ‖Steel has more strength than almost any other metal. 'gāng chà-bù-'dwō bǐ 'shéme-'jīn-shǔ-de-'lì-lyang dēw 'dà. ‖I'm afraid this medicine has lost its strength. wǒ kǔng-'pà jèy-ge-'yàw méy-le 'lì-lyang-le.

(*Strong point in a person's character*) 'cháng-chù. ‖His strength lies in his patience. tā-de-'cháng-chu 'jyèw shř néng 'rěn. *But* ‖He has great strength of character. *is expressed as* His character is very straight. tā-de-rén-'géer hěn 'jeng

(*Military strength*) 'jàn-dèw-'lì, *or* 'lì-lyang. ‖We haven't tried to judge the strength of the enemy. 'wǒ-men 'bìng méy-'gū-jì 'dí-rén-de-'jàn-dèw-'lì.

On the strength of (*because*) 'yīn-wèy. ‖We hired those five men on the strength of your recommendation. wǒ-men 'yùng nèy-wǔ-ge-'rén shř 'yīn-wèy 'nǐ-'jyè-shàw-de.

STRETCH. (*To stretch out*) 'lā-kāy, 'dǎ-kāy, *or* 'ch̄'-kāy; (*to stretch tight*) lā-'jǐn-le, bēng-'jǐn-le.

stretched the clothesline between the trees. tā bǎ
iyàng-'yī-shang-de-'shéng-dz 'lā-kay 'shwān-daw 'shù-
shang-le.

(*To extend*) jàn or 'jàn-chū-chyᴡu (*to occupy*);
'tūng-chū (*to pass through*); 'chū-chywù (*to go*).
‖The wheat fields stretch out for miles. nèy-pyàn-
'mà/y-dz-'dì 'jàn-le yěw 'hǎw-jǐ-lǐ-'dì. ‖How far does
this road stretch? jèy-tyáw-'lù °'tūng-chū (*or* °'chū-
chywù) yěw 'dwō-ywǎn-na?

(*To extend a part of the body*) shēn. ‖It feels good
to stretch my legs after that long ride. pǎw-le dzème-
'ywǎn-yí-'tàng yǐ-'hèw 'shēn-shen 'twěy 'jywé-je tǐng
'shū-fu. ‖Can you get that off the shelf if you stretch
for it? nǐ shēn-chǐ 'gē-be láy néng bǎ 'nèy-ge
tsúng 'jyà-dz-shang 'gèw-shyà-lay-ma? ‖Stop yawn-
ing and stretching. byé dǎ 'hā-chi yě byé shēn 'lǎn-
yāw. (shēn 'lǎn-yāw *means literally to stretch one's
lazy waist; thus to stretch the upper part of your
body the way you do when you yawn.*) *But* ‖He
stretched out on the couch. *is expressed as* He lay out
straight on the couch. tā 'jǐ-jr-lyēw-'lyēwr dzày
'chwáng-shang 'tǎng-je.

(*To become larger*) dà or sūng. ‖Will this sweater
stretch when I wash it? nèy-ge-máw-shyàn-'yī shyà-
'shwěy yǐ-'hèw 'sūng-bù-sūng?

(*To become larger when pulled*) 'lā-de-chū-láy or
'chēn-de-chū-láy. ‖This elastic won't stretch worth two
cents. jèy-ge-sūng-jǐn-'dàr yì-dyǎr dēw 'lā-bù-chū-
'láy. ‖Does that rubber band have much stretch? nèy-
ge-shyàng-pí-'chywǎr háy 'lā-de-chū-'láy-ma?

(*To make larger by pulling*) 'lā-chū-láy *or* 'chēn-
chū-láy. ‖I stretched the sweater. wǒ bǎ nèy-jyàn-
máw-'yī 'chēn-chū-dyǎr láy.

(*To make larger by putting something inside*) chēng;
(*shoes only*) páy or shywàn. ‖Can you stretch my shoes
a little? nǐ néng bǎ wǒ-jèy-shwàng-'shyé 'chēng-chū
yì-dyǎr láy-ma?

(*Extent*) dwàn, dwàr. ‖The next stretch of road is
not bad. 'shyà-byar nèy-dwàn-'lù bú-'hwày. ‖There's
a long stretch of beach at the edge of the town. jèy-
ge-chéng-'byār-shang yěw 'tǐng-'cháng-de-yí-dwàr-
hǎy-'tān.

At a stretch. ‖He worked about two hours at a
stretch. tā yì-kěw-'chyèr 'dzwò-le lyǎ-jūng-'téw.

(*Figuratively*). ‖I think he's stretching the facts a
little. *is expressed as* I think he's adding leaves to the
branches a bit. wǒ 'jywé-hu-je tā bǎ nèy-ge-'shr̀-
ching 'shwō-de yěw dyǎr-yěw-'jēr-tyān-'yèr. ‖Let's
stretch a point and let him go. *is expressed as* Let's
loosen a little and let him go. dzám fàng-°'sūng-
(*or* °'kwān) dyǎr, 'ràng-ta 'dzěw-ba.

STRIKE (STRUCK). (*To hit*) *see* **HIT**; dǎ, azew
(*Peiping*) *or* (*to hit with a hammer or other instrument*) dzáw; (*to collide*) jwàng. ‖She struck him in
the face. tā dǎ-le nèy-ge-'nan-de yı-ge-'dzwěy-ba.
‖He struck at the dog with a stick. tā ná
shěw-'jàng dǎ-le 'nèy-ge-'gěw yí-'shyà-dz. ‖He struck

the rock sharply with a hammer. tā ná 'chwéy-dz
shr̀-jìn 'dzáw-le nèy-ge-'shr̀-téw yí-'shyà-dz. ‖We
struck back at the enemy. wǒ-men yí-'shyà-dz jyèw
bǎ 'dí-rén gěy 'dǎ-hwéy-chywù-le. ‖The ship struck a
rock. chwán 'jwàng-dzày 'shr̀-tew-shang-le.

Special expressions in English. ‖That tree's been
struck by lightning. *is expressed as* That tree has
been split by thunder. nèy-ge-'shù ràng léy 'pī-le.
‖The stone struck bottom. *is expressed as* The stone
got to the bottom. nèy-ge-'shr̀-tew dàw-'dyěr-le.
‖Wait till the light strikes it. *is expressed as* Wait
until the light illumines it. 'děng-je ná 'dēng 'jàw-
daw nàr dzày !shwō.

(*Of a clock*) dǎ. ‖Did the clock strike? jūng 'dǎ-gwò-
le-ma? ‖It just struck seven. gāng 'dǎ-gwò chī-'dyǎn.

Strike a match 'hwá yì-gēn-yáng-'hᴠǒ.

To strike sparks (*by collision*) 'jwàng-(*or* 'pèng)-
chū hwǒ-'shyēngr láy; *or* (*by striking*) 'tsèng-(*or*
'dǎ)-chū hwǒ-'shyēngr láy.

(*To stop work*) bà-'gūng. ‖What are they striking
for? 'tā-men wèy-'shéme bà-'gūng? ‖How long did
the miners' strike last? kwàng-'gūng bà-'gūng bà-le
'dwō-jyěw? ‖They promised not to go on strike during
the conference. tā-men 'dā-ying dzày 'shāng-lyang
de-'shr̀-hewr bú-bà-'gūng.

(*To seem to someone*). ‖How does that suggestion
strike you? *is expressed as* How do you feel about that
suggestion? nèy-ge-'yì-sz nǐ jywé-de 'dzěme-'yàng?
‖The situation struck me funny. *is expressed as* I
thought the situation was funny. nèy-ge-'chíng-shing
wǒ 'jywé-de hěn kě-'shyàw.

(*Make a sudden impression on*). ‖That idea really
struck my fancy. *is expressed as* I thought that idea
was very good. nèy-ge-'yì-jyàn wǒ 'jywé-de jēn 'hǎw.
‖That idea just struck me. *is expressed as* I just had
the idea. wǒ gāng-'tsáy 'hū-rán shyǎng-dàw-de nèm-
ge-'far.

(*To come upon*) 'pèng-jyàn (*meet*); 'jǎw-jaw
(*find*); fā-'shyàn (*discover*). To strike luck *is expressed as* go to good luck dzěw 'ywùn; to strike a
gold mine (*either a real mine or a wonderful source of
income*) *is expressed as* dig a gold mine 'wā-jaw jīn-
'kwàng; to strike it rich fā 'tsáy. ‖Has anyone ever
struck oil around here? yěw 'rén dzày fù-'jìn fā-
'shyàn yéw-'kwàng-le-ma? ‖You're the first man I've
struck who thinks so. wǒ 'pèng-jyàn-de-'rén-lǐ-tew
yěw 'jèy-jǔng-'sz-shyǎng-de 'nǐ shr̀ 'téw-yí-gè.

To strike off (*or* out) chywǔ-'shyāw (*delete*);
(*draw a line through*) 'lá-le-chywù *or* 'hwá-le-chywù.
‖Strike his name off the list. bǎ tā-de-'míng-dz tsúng
míng-'dār-shang 'hwá-le-chywù. ‖Strike out the last
paragraph. bǎ mwò-yí-'dwàr chywù-shyāw.

To strike up. ‖The two of them struck up a friendship very quickly. *is expressed as* The two of them
were familiar after a little while. tām-'lyǎ yì-'hwěr
jyèw 'shéw-le. ‖The band struck up the national anthem. ywè-'dwèy dzèw-chī gwó-'gēer láy-le.

‖We finally struck a bargain. wǒ-men dàw-'lyǎwr
'chéng-le (*or* °'dzwò-le) yí-'hàwr-'mǎy-may.

STRING (STRUNG, STRUNG). (*Thread or fine string*) shyàn *or* shyàr; (*thick string, rope*) shéngr *or* 'shéng-dz. ‖Could you tie this up with string? nǐ 'néng ná 'shéng-dz bǎ 'jèy-ge 'shwān-sha g-ma?

(*Of musical instrument or sports racket*) shyán. ‖Do you have violin strings? nǐ yěw shyǎw-tí-'chín-de-'shyán-ma? ‖My racket needs to be restrung. wǒ-de-chyéwr-'pāy-dz děy 'hwàn 'shyán-le. (*A piano string is* yīn *tone.*) ‖One of the piano strings is out of tune. gāng-'chín-shang yěw yí-ge-'yīn bù-'jwěn-le.

A string of . . . . (*A series of things on ª string*) chwàn; (*a line, column*) chwàn, lyèw. ‖She's wearing a beautiful string of pearls. tā dày-de nèy-chwàn-'jēn-jū 'jēn hǎw-'kàn. (*In the case of a necklace the measure may also be* gwà *something that is hung.*) ‖There's a long string of busses waiting to be filled. yěw yí-dà-'lyèw-kǎ-'chē 'děng-je shàng 'rén-ne.

(*Figurative*). ‖There are no strings attached to the offer. *is expressed as* This affair has no other °trouble. *or* °details. *or* °snags. 'jèy-jyàn-'shr̀-ching 'méy-shéme-lìng-'wày-de-°'má-fan. *or* °'jr̄-jyé. *or* °'jēw-jé.

To pull strings twō rén-'chíng (*get other people to do things for you*). ‖I never was too good at pulling strings. wǒ tsúng-'láy yě bú-'hwèy twō-rén-'chíng.

(*To stretch; see* STRETCH) lā; *or* ān (*to fix, put*). ‖They strung the electric wire from pole to pole. tā-men bǎ dyàn-'shyàn shwèn-je 'dyàn-shyàn-'gān-dz yì-'dwàr-yì-'dwàr-de 'ān-shàng-le.

(*To thread*) chwān. ‖Where can I have my amber beads strung? shéme-'dì-fangr néng bǎ wǒ-de-'hǔpe-'sù-jù gěy 'chwān-shang?

(*To string beans*) 'jáy. ‖Please help me string the beans. láw-'jyà 'bāng-je wǒ 'jáy-jay 'dèwr.

To be strung out *is expressed as* to stand in a line. ‖The policemen were strung out along the sidewalk. jǐng-'chá 'shwèn-je byàn-'dàw jàn-le °yì-'háng. *or* °yì-'páy. *or* °yí-'lyèw.

To string (*someone*) along (*trick*) 'shwǎ; (*cheat*) wān, pyàn, dzwàn. ‖Are you stringing me along? shr̀ 'shwǎ-wo-ne-ma? ‖She's been stringing him along for months. nèy-ge-'nywǔ-de ná-ta 'shwǎ-je wár 'shwǎ-le hǎw-jǐ-ge-'ywè.

STRONG. (*Powerful*) bàng (*colloquial*); yěw-'lì-lyang *or* yěw-'jìn; 'lì-lyang 'dà *or* 'jyèr 'dà; chyáng (*literary*). In special combinations other expressions are used; a strong wind 'yìng-fēng *or* fēng hěn 'c ng. ‖He has strong hands. tā-de-'shěw hěn yěw-'jìn. ‖Are you strong enough to swim that far? nǐ yěw 'nème-dà-de-'lì-lyang fù 'nème-'ywǎn-ma? ‖The current is pretty strong. *is expressed as* The water flows very fast. shwěy 'lyéw-de hěn 'jí. ‖I'm not very strong yet (*after an illness*). *is expressed as* My body is still soft. wǒ-'shēn-dz háy shr̀ 'rwǎn. ‖They are a strong nation. tā-men shr̀ ge-'chyáng-gwó. ‖He believes in a strong navy. *is expressed as* He maintains that one ought to have a large and strong navy. tā 'jǔ-jǎng yīng-'gāy yěw yí-ge-chyáng-'dà-de-hǎy-'jywūn.

(*Firm, solid*) 'jyē-shr. ‖Do you have a good strong rope? nǐ yěw 'jyē-shr-de-'shéng-dz-ma? ‖Is this ladder strong? jèy-ge-'tī-dz 'jyē-shr-ma? ‖Is this ladder strong enough to hold me? *is expressed as* Can this ladder hold me? jèy-ge-'tī-dz 'jīn-de-'jù wǒ-ma?

(*Concentrated*) chùng *or* 'lì-hay. ‖This drink is too strong. jèy-ge-'jyěw tày 'chùng. ‖She likes strong perfume. tā 'shǐ-hwān wèr-'chùng-de-shyāng-'shwěr.

(*Numerically large*). ‖This political party isn't very strong yet. *is expressed as* The influence of this party isn't very great. 'jèy-dǎng-de-'shr̀-lì háy 'bú-swàn 'dà. *or as* There aren't many members of this party. 'jèy-dǎng-de-'dǎng-ywán háy bù-'dwō. (*In Chinese one must distinguish the two meanings, since a large party is not necessarily a strong one.*)

(*Intense*). ‖He showed a strong desire to see it. *is expressed as* He showed that he wanted very much to see it. kàn tā-nèy-'yàng-dz 'hěn shyǎng yàw 'kàn-kan nèy-ge. ‖I have strong feelings on that subject. *is expressed as* My emotions on that subject are very deep. nèy-ge-'wèn-tí wǒ 'gǎn-shyǎng hěn 'shēn. ‖It made a strong impression on me. *is expressed as* It gave me a very deep impression. 'nèy-ge 'gěy-wǒ 'yí-ge-hěn-'shēn-de-'yìn-shyàng.

To be strong-minded (*have made up one's mind what one wants*) yěw 'jú-yì. ‖He's a very strong-minded person. tā 'shr̀ ge-hěn-yěw-'jú-yì-de-'rén.

STUDENT. 'shywé-sheng. ‖He's a student at the university. tā shr̀ nèy-ge-dà-'shywé-li-de-'shywé-sheng. *But* ‖She's a serious student of the subject. *is expressed as* She does research in that field very seriously. 'tā dzày nèy-yì-'mér-li hěn rèn-'jēn-de 'yán-jyew.

STUDY. kàn (*to look at, read*); nyàn (*to read, sometimes to read aloud*); dú (*to read*); 'yán-jyew (*to do research*); shywé (*to learn, to be a student*). ‖I've studied the situation carefully. wǒ bǎ 'nèy-ge-'chíng-shing 'dž-shì-de 'yán-jyew-le-'yán-jyew. ‖We studied the map before we started. wǒ-men chū-'fā yǐ-'chyán bǎ dì-'tú 'yán-jyew-le yí-'shyàr. ‖I've studied all the literature on the subject. wǒ bǎ 'gwān-wú nèy-ge-'tí-mu-de-shū gēn 'wén-jāng dēw °'kàn-le. *or* °'nyàn-le. *or* °'dú-le. ‖He's busy studying. *is expressed as* He's busy reading books. tā jèng 'máng-je nyàn-'shū-ne. ‖This book requires careful study. 'jèy-běr-'shū děy hǎw-'hāwr-de °'kàn-kan. *or* °'nyàn-nyan. *or* °'dú-du. ‖I'll have to make a study of that situation. wǒ děy 'yán-jyew 'yán-jyew 'nèy-ge-'chíng-shing. ‖I'm studying medicine at the university. wǒ dzày dà-'shywé-lì-téw shywé 'yī-shywé. ‖He studied under some famous men. tā 'gēn-je jǐ-ge-'míng-rén °'shywé-de. *or* °'yán-jyew-de. *or* °'nyàn-de. *or* °'dú-de.

(*Problem studied*) mér (*course*); 'yán-jyew (*research problem*). ‖Geometry is his principal study. tā 'yán-jyew-de-'jǔ-yàw-de-yì mér jyèw-shr̀ jǐ-hé. ‖He is doing very well in his studies. *is expressed as* He studies all his books very well. tā-'shū dēw 'nyàn-de bú-'tswò. ‖This batt'e would make a good study for a historian. jèy-yí-jàng hěn 'jŕ-de ràng 'yán-jyew-lì-shŕ-de 'yán-jyew yí-shyàr.

(*Written results of research*). ‖He has published several studies in that field. gwān-ywu nèy-'mér tā fā-'byǎw-gwo °'jǐ-pyān-'dūng-shi. *or* °'jǐ-pyān-'wén-jāng.

(*Private library or reading room*) shū-'fáng. ‖I'll be in the study if you want me. nǐ 'hwéy-téw yàw 'jǎw-wǒ de-'hwà wǒ dzày shū-'fáng.

STUFF. 'dūng-shi. ‖Put some of that stuff on your hand. bǎ nèy-ge-'dūng-shi 'shàng-de nǐ-'shěw-shang ·ɑyǎr. ‖What's that stuff you're eating? nǐ 'chŕ-dę shŕ 'shéme-'dūng-shi? ‖Give me a drink of that stuff, whatever it is. 'bù-gwǎn nèy-ge 'shŕ shéme, 'gěy-wǒ 'hē-dyǎr. ‖Get your stuff out of my room. bǎ 'nǐ-de-'dūng-shi tsúng 'wǒ-de-'wū-dz-li 'ná-chū-chywu. ‖I don't like the stuff he's been writing lately. tā 'jìn-láy 'shyě-de nèy-shyē-'dūng-shi wǒ bù-'shŕ-hwan. ‖Throw that old stuff away. bǎ 'nèy-ge-'jyew-dūng-shi 'rēng-lew-ba.

Special expressions in English. ‖That book is great stuff! *is expressed as* That book's not bad. 'nèy-běr-'shū bú-'tswò. ‖None of that stuff! byé 'nème-je! ‖No rough stuff allowed. bù-'shywǔ yě-'mán.

To stuff jwāng (*pack*); sāy *or* sēy (*cram, squeeze into something*); tyán (*fill*); yē (*tuck in, slip in*); dǔ (*plug up*). ‖She keeps her handbag stuffed full of junk. 'tā-de-pí-'bāw-li jwāng 'mǎn-le lwàn-chi-bā-'dzāw-de-'dūng-shi. ‖Stuff your ears with cotton. bǎ nǐ-'ěr-dwo ná 'myán-hwa °'dǔ-shang. *or* °'sāy-shang. *or* °'tyán-shang. ‖Stuff it down that hole. bǎ 'nèy-ge 'sāy-de nèy-ge-'kū-lung-li. ‖I stuffed the paper under the cushion. wǒ bǎ nèy-jāng-'jŕ 'yē-de 'dyàn-dz 'dǐ-shya-le. ‖He stuffed his things into a suitcase. tā bǎ 'tā-de-'dūng-shi dēw °'tyán-de (*or* °'sāy-de) 'shyāng-dz-li-le. ‖Did you stuff the pepper? nǐ bǎ chín-'jyāw 'jwāng-shang-'shyàr-le-ma?

To stuff oneself *is expressed in terms of eating a lot.* ‖Don't stuff yourself. byé chŕ tày 'dwō-lew. ‖I can't eat any more; I'm stuffed. wǒ tày 'bǎw-le, 'chŕ bú-shyà-'chywù-le.

To be stuffed up. ‖My head is all stuffed up from my cold. *is expressed as* I have a cold and my head is pushing outwards. wǒ jāw-'lyáng-le, 'nǎw-dǎy fā-'jàng.

(*To put filling into something to make it retain its shape*) shywàn. ‖He stuffs animals for the museum. tā·gěy 'bwó-wù-'gwǎn 'shywàn yě-'shèw.

STYLE. (*Fashion*) 'yàng-dz, 'yàng-shŕ, 'shŕ-yàng(r); *also* shŕ-'máwr *or* shŕ-'shīng (*to be fashionable*), *or* mwó-'dēng (*to be modern, up-to-date*). ‖It's the latest style. 'nèy-ge shŕ dzwèy-'shīn-de-'yàng-dz. ‖Is this dress in style? 'jèy-jyàn-'yī-fu shŕ-'shīng-ma? ‖I

don't like the style of that dress. wǒ bù-'shŕ-hwan nèy-jyàn-'yī-fu-de-'yàng-dz. ‖Her clothes haven't any style. 'tā-de-'yī-shang bù-mwó-'dēng. ‖She has a lot of style. tā hěn shŕ-'máwr.

(*Manner of expression*) 'bǐ-fǎ, 'shyě-fǎr (*way of writing*); 'hwà-fǎr (*way of painting*); (*an artist's personal style*) 'tí-tsáy *or* dzwò-'fēng. ‖I don't like that author's style. wǒ bù-'shŕ-hwān nèy-ge-jù-dzwò-'jyā-de-dzwò-'fēng. ‖He writes in the style of the last century. tā shyě 'dūng-shi yùng 'shàng yí-shŕ-'jì-de-'shyě-fǎr. ‖His work is in the style of the modern French painters. tā-de-'hwà-fǎr shŕ fǎng 'jìn-dày-'fà-gwó-pày.

SUBJECT. 'tí-mu (*topic*); mén *or* mér (*field*). ‖Are you familiar with this subject? jèy-ge-'tí-mu nǐ 'shú-shi-ma? *or* nǐ. 'dwèy-ywú 'jèy-yì-'mér 'shú-shi-ma? ‖Don't change the subject. byé 'gǎy 'tí-mu-wa. ‖What was the subject of his lecture? tā-de-jyǎng-'yǎn shŕ 'shéme-'tí-mu? ‖What subject did you study in school last year? 'chywù-nyán nǐ dzày shywé-'shyàw-li nyàn °'nǎy-'mén? *or* (*which course*) °'nǎy-'kē?

‖He's a British subject. tā shŕ 'yīng-gwo-°'de-'shǔ-mín. *or* °'rén.

To be subject to. ‖These rates are subject to change without notice. 'jyà-mù byàn-'gēng 'shù-bù-tūng-'jŕ. (byán-'gēng 'shù-bù-tūng-'jŕ *is a standard phrase corresponding to our* Subject to change without notice.) ‖All my actions are subject to his approval. *is expressed as* All my actions must go through him and be approved. wǒ-de-'shíng-dùng 'dēw děy jīng tā °'túng-'yì. *or* °'shywǔ-'kě. ‖Everyone on board was subject to international law. *is expressed as* Everyone on board had to obey international law. 'měy-yí-ge-'rén dzày 'chwán-shang dēw děy 'fú-tsúng 'gwó-jì-gūng-'fǎ.

SUCCEED. chéng *or* chéng-'gūng (*to be successful*). ‖Don't worry if you don't succeed right away. mǎ-'shàng 'yàw-shŕ bù-'chéng (*or* bù-néng chéng-'gūng) béng jāw-'jí. ‖The plan didn't succeed equally well in all cases. jèy-ge-'fǎr dzày 'gè-júng-'dì-fangr yěw-de 'chéng yěw-de bú-dà 'chéng.

To succeed in (*doing something*) *a verb of action followed by* -hǎw-le, -chéng-le, -jáw-le, -chǐ-láy-le, -wán-le (*see Chinese-English side for each*); to succeed in finding 'jǎw-jáw-le; to succeed in writing 'shyě°-wán-le, °-chéng-le, °-hǎw-le, °-chǐ-láy-le; to succeed in doing 'dzwò°-chéng-le, °-hǎw-le, °-dàw-le, °-chǐ-láy-le, °-wán-le. ‖Did you succeed in getting him on the phone? nǐ dǎ-dyàn-'hwà 'jǎw-ta 'jǎw-jaw-le-ma?

(*To follow, take the place of*) jyē (*literally,* receive). ‖Who succeeded him in office? shéy 'jyē tā-de-'shŕ-ching-le? ‖If he dies, who will succeed him as emperor? 'yàw-shr tā 'sž-lew shéy 'jyē-je dzwò 'hwáng-shang?

SUCCESS. *See also* SUCCEED. ‖He's had a good deal of success in handling such cases. *is expressed as* He's done this sort of thing successfully several times. 'jèy-yàngr-de-'shŕ-ching tā bàn-'chéng-le hǎw-'shyē-hwéy-le. ‖Congratulations on your success. *is expressed as* You've been successful; I must congratulate you. nǐ 'jèy-hwéy chéng-'gūng-le, děy gěy-nǐ dàw-'shǐ-ya. ‖His play was an instant success. *is expressed as* The play was immediately successful. tā nèy-chū-'shì yì-'yǎn 'mǎ-shang jyèw chéng-'gūng-le. ‖Did he make a success of his business? *is expressed as* Was his business successful? tā-de-'mǎy-may °dzwò-'chéng-le-ma *or* °chéng-'gūng-le-ma?

(*Achievement; a literary word*) chéng-'jyèw. ‖He's had several successes in this line. dzày 'jèy-háng-li tā 'yěw-dyǎr 'chéng-jyèw.

SUCH. 'jème, 'jè(me)-yàngr; *or* 'nàme, 'nà(me)-yàngr, *or* 'nèm-yàngr; *or* 'dzème-yàngr; *or* (*thus*) rú-'tsž; *or* (*of one kind*) yí-'lèy-de. ‖All such statements are exaggerated. 'fán shŕ 'jèy-yàngr-de-'hwà 'dēw shŕ 'yán-gwò-chí-'shŕ. *or* jèy-yí-'lèy-de-'hwà dēw yěw-dyǎr 'shwō-de gwò-'hwŏr. ‖We can't examine every such complaint. 'jèy-yàngr-de-'shŕ wǒ-men 'méy-fár gè-'gèr dēw 'chá. ‖She never says such things. tā 'tsúng-láy bù-shwō 'jèy-yàngr-de-'hwà. ‖I never heard of such a thing happening. wǒ 'méy-tīng-'shwō-gwò 'jèy-yàngr-de-'shŕ-ching. ‖Such is life. rú-'tsž rén-'shēng! ‖It must have been some such place where I saw him. wǒ yí-'dìng shŕ dzày shyàng 'jèm-yàngr-de-yí-ge-'dì-fangr 'kàn-jyàn-gwo tā. ‖There's no such person here. jèr 'méy-yěw 'dzème-ge-'rén. ‖I've seldom seen such beauty. wǒ hěn 'shǎw kàn-jyan 'dzème-hǎw-'kàn-de. ‖Nobody wanted to work for him, he was such a slave-driver. tā 'dày-rén nàme 'hěn, 'méy-yěw-rén 'ywàn-yi gēn-'tā dzwò-'shŕ. ‖I've never tasted such food. wǒ tsúng-'láy yě méy-'chŕ-gwo 'jè-yàngr-de-'chŕ-de. ‖Don't be in such a hurry. byé dzèm 'máng-nga. ‖He's just such a man as I imagined he would be. tā 'jèng-shŕ wǒ-'shīn-li 'shyǎng-de 'nèm yí-ge-'rén. ‖He said it in such a way that I couldn't help laughing. tā 'nème yì-'shwō ràng-wǒ bù-'néng bú-'shyàw.

As such. ‖They have no hotels, as such, in this region. *is expressed as* In this region there are no hotel-like hotels. jèy-yí-'dày méy-shyàng-'yàngr-de-lywǔ-'gwǎn. ‖He's acting chairman, and as such should be respected. *is expressed as* He's already chairman, and everyone should respect him. tā jì-'rán shŕ jǔ-'shí; dà-jyā-'hwŏr jyèw yīng-dāng 'dzwēn-jìng tā.

Such as shyàng. ‖Conduct such as this is inexcusable. shyàng 'jèy-yàngr-de-'shíng-wey shŕ 'bù-néng-'ywán-lyàng-de. ‖It's too cold here for some fruit trees, such as the peach. jèr 'tyān-chi dwèy-ywú jǐ-jǔng-gwǒ-dz tày 'lěng, shyàng 'táwr shéme-de.

SUDDEN (SUDDENLY). méy-shyǎng-'dàw *or* shyǎng-bú-'dàw (*unexpected*); 'hū-rán (*suddenly*); lěng-bù-'fáng (*when one's guard was down*); chěw-gu-'lěng-dz, měng-gu-'dīng-de, *or* lěng-gu-'dīng-de (*all of a sudden*); 'yí-bu-lyéw-'shén *or* 'yí-bu-'shyǎw-shīn (*when one wasn't watching*); yí-'shyà-dz *or* 'pā-de yí-'shyà-dz (*at once*.) ‖This is so sudden! 'jèy-ge jēn méy-shyǎng-'dàw. ‖He died a sudden death. tā 'hū-rán jyew 'sž-le. ‖He turned on us in sudden anger. tā 'hū-rán jyew 'gēn wǒ-men 'fā pí-chi. ‖Our army made a sudden attack. wǒ-men-de-jywūn-'dwèy chěw-'lěng-dz jìn-'gūng-le yí-'shyà-dz. ‖All of a sudden (*or* Suddenly) I remembered that I had to mail a letter. wǒ měng-gu-'dīng-de 'shyang-chǐ-láy děy 'fā yì-fēng-'shìn.

SUFFER. shèw-'kǔ (*go through hardship*); shèw-'dzwèy (*go through an ordeal*); nán-'shèw *or* nán-'gwò (*not be feeling well*); bù-'shū-fu (*be ill, uncomfortable, unhappy*); bù-hǎw 'shèw *or* bù-hǎw 'gwò (*be ill*); bú-'tùng-kwày (*feel restrained, unhappy, resentful*). ‖Did you suffer much after your operation? dùng 'shěw-shù yǐ-'hèw nǐ shèw shéme-'dzwèy 'méy-yew? ‖She's suffering from an infected tooth. tā nàw 'yá-ne, tǐng shèw-'dzwèy-de. *But* ‖Are you suffering any pain? nǐ 'jywé-je 'téng-ma?

(*To be injured*) (nùng-) 'hwày-le, (nùng-) 'hwěy-le; shèw 'swěn-shr (*suffer damage—physical, financial*); chŕ-'kwēy (*get the worst of it*). ‖The buildings along the river suffered severely from the flood. yán-je-'hé-de 'nèy-shyē-léw fā-'shwěy de-'shŕ-hewr 'dēw gěy nùng-'hwěy-le. ‖Your reputation will suffer if you do it. nǐ 'yàw-shr nèm 'bàn, nǐ-de-'míng-ywù jyèw 'hwěy-le. ‖The school didn't suffer much from the fire yesterday. dzwóer-ge-jáw-'hwǒ shywé-'shyàw méy-'shèw. shéme-'swěn-shr. ‖You'll certainly suffer if you insist on doing it that way. nǐ 'yàw-shŕ nème 'dzwò yí-'dìng chŕ-'kwēy. ‖Our army has suffered heavy losses. *is expressed as* The losses of our army have been heavy. wǒ-jywūn swěn-'shŕ shèn 'jùng.

SUGAR. táng; (*powdered sugar*) 'báy-táng *or* èr-'gùng-táng; (*granulated sugar*) 'shā-táng; (*lump sugar*) 'fāng-táng; (*light brown sugar*) 'cháw-báy-táng; (*dark brown sugar*) 'hēy-táng *or* 'húng-táng; (*rock candy, used for sweetening in beverages and desserts*) 'bīng-táng. ‖Please pass the sugar. láw-'jyà, bǎ-'táng 'dì-gěy wǒ. ‖She's sugaring the cupcakes. tā wàng nèy-ge-'dyǎn-shīn-shang °jyā-'táng-ne. *or* °gē-'táng-ne. *or* °fàng-'táng-ne.

SUGGEST. shwō (*to say*); tí-'yì (*to propose*). ‖Do you have anyone to suggest for the job? jèy-ge-'shŕ-ching nǐ shwō yùng 'shéy láy 'dzwò? ‖What do you suggest we do tonight? nǐ shwō 'jyèr-'wǎn-shang wǒ-men gàn 'shéme? ‖I suggest that we ask him to come too. 'wǒ shwō dzám 'chǐng-tā yí-'kwàr láy. ‖Are you suggesting that I'm wrong? nǐ shř 'shwō wǒ 'tswò-le-ma?

(*To bring to mind*) ràng . . . 'shyǎng-chǐ-láy (*to remind you of something you'd forgotten*); 'kàn-je shyàng (*to look like*); 'mwō-je shyàng (*to feel like*); 'tīng-je shyàng (*to sound like*); 'cháng-je shyàng (*to taste like*); 'wén-je shyàng (*to smell like*). ‖Does this suggest anything to you? *is expressed as* Does this make you remember anything? jèy-ge 'ràng nǐ 'shyǎng-chǐ-dyǎr 'shéme láy-ma? *or as* Do you think this is like something? 'jèy-ge nǐ 'jywé-je shyàng 'shéme? ‖The shape of the cloud suggests a horse. *is expressed as* The shape of the cloud looks like a horse. jèy-kwày-'ywún-tsay-de-'yàng-dz 'kàn-je 'shyàng yì-pǐ-'mǎ. ‖The shape of the cloud suggests a horse to me. *is expressed as* I think the shape of that cloud is like a horse. jèy-kwày-'ywún-tsay-de-'yàng-dz wǒ 'jywé-je 'shyàng yì-pǐ-'mǎ.

SUIT. (*Clothes*) 'yī-shang, 'yī-fu, *with measure* tàw *or* shēn. ‖This suit doesn't fit him very well. jèy-tàw-'yī-sháng tā 'chwān-je 'bú-dà hé-'shř. ‖How do you like her new suit? nǐ 'shǐ-hwan 'tā-de-nèy-shēn-'shīn-'yī-fu-ma?

(*Legal*) 'àn-dz. ‖Who is the lawyer handling the suit? 'nǎy-ge-lywù-'shř gwǎn 'jèy-ge-'àn-dz?

(*In cards*) mén. ‖Diamonds were his strongest suit. fāng-'kwàr shř tā-'shěw-li dzwèy-'bàng-de-yì-'mén.

(*To satisfy*) mǎn-'yì (*to be satisfied*); *or* 'shǐ-hwan (*to be pleased, to like something*); *or* jywé-je °hǎw *or* °hé-'shř. ‖Does the program suit you? 'jyé-mù jèy-yǎngr °nǐ 'shǐ-hwan-ma. *or* °nǐ mǎn-'yì-ma? ‖This gift ought to suit him. wǒ shyǎng tā hwèy 'shǐ-hwan jèy-jyàn-'lǐ-wu. *or* jèy-jyàn-'lǐ-wu 'wǒ shyǎng tā hwèy mǎn-'yì. ‖Our prices will suit everybody. wǒm-'dìng-de-'jyàer 'jwěn jyàw dà-jyā-'hwǒ 'dēw mǎn-'yì.

(*Be suitable*) hé-'shř; *or* dwèy (*to fit, match*); *or* shyàng-'fú *or* 'fú-hé (*to coincide*). ‖This color doesn't suit you. jèy-ge-'yán-sher nǐ 'chwān-je bù-hé-'shř. *or expressed as* This color isn't becoming for you to wear. jèy-ge-'yán-shǎr nǐ 'chwān-je bù-shř-'yàngr. ‖A three-room apartment suits our family nicely. yì-swǒ-'sān-jyān-'wū-dz-de-'fáng-dz wèy wǒ-men-'jyā hěn hé-'shř. ‖This insurance policy will suit your purpose very well. jèy-jǔng bǎw-'shyǎn wèy-'nǐ tǐng hé-'shř.

To follow suit. ‖I'm out of hearts; I can't follow suit. *is expressed as* I haven't any hearts; I haven't any way to follow. wǒ méy-húng-'táwr-le, wǒ méy-'fár 'gēn-je 'chū. *or as* I haven't any hearts; I have tó fill in one. wǒ méy-húng-'táwr-le, wǒ děy 'dyàn yì-'jāng. ‖If he's going home early, I think I'll follow suit. *is expressed as* If he's going home early, I think I ought to, too. tā 'yàw-shř 'dzǎw hwéy-'jyā-ya, wǒ 'shyǎng wǒ yě děy nème 'bàn.

SUM. (*Amount, figure*) shùr *or* 'shù-mu; (*total gained by adding numbers*) dzǔng-'shù(r); a sum of money yì-bǐ-'chyán; a large sum of money yí-'dà-bǐ-'chyán; a small sum of money hěn-'shyǎw-de-yì-bǐ-'chyán. ‖The sum of all these numbers is 1000. jè-shyē-'shù-mu 'jyā-chǐ-láy-de-dzǔng-'shùr 'děng-ywú yì-'chyān. ‖I want to deposit a large sum of money to my account. wǒ yàw 'dzày wǒ-'jé-dz-shang 'tswén yí-'dà-bǐ-'chyán. ‖Can you pay me a small sum in advance? nǐ shyān 'fù gěy-wǒ °'yí-ge-'shyǎw-shùr (*or* °'yì-'dyǎr *or* °'yì-dyǎr-'chyán) 'shíng-bù-'shíng? ‖It's a small sum. jèy-ge-'shù-mu hěn 'shyǎw. *or* jèy-bǐ-'chyán hěn 'shyǎw.

To sum up 'dzǔng-ér-yán-'jř (*in a word, or in a nutshell*). ‖To sum up, he's not good at all. 'dzǔng-ér-yán-'jř, tā yì-'dyǎr dēw bù-'hǎw.

Special expressions in English. ‖He summed up the situation in a few words. *is expressed as* He used few sentences and made the situation understandable. tā yùng jǐ-'jywù-hwà jyèw bǎ nèy-ge-'chíng-shing shwō 'míng-bay-le.

SUMMER. 'shyà-tyan. ‖Does it rain much here during the summer? jèr 'shyà-tyan 'ywǔ-shwey 'dwō-ma? ‖She invited us to her summer cottage. tā 'chǐng wǒ-men 'dàw tā-'shyà-tyan bì-'shǔ-de-'dì-fangr 'chywù. ‖I need some summer clothes. wǒ 'dwǎn-dvǎr 'shyà-tyan-de-'yī-fu.

SUN. 'tày-yang, (*local*) lǎw-yéer; (*sunlight*) yáng-'gwāng. In the sun 'tày-yang 'dì-li *or* yáng-'gwāng 'dǐ-shya (*under the sun*). ‖The sun just went down. 'tày-yang 'gāng shyà-chywu. ‖I couldn't see you because the sun was in my eyes. 'tày-yang 'hwǎng wǒ-'yǎn-jing láy-je, méy-'kàn-jyan ni. ‖The sun is pretty hot today. *is expressed as* The sun today is really severe. jyēr 'tày-yang jēn 'dú. ‖Stay out of the afternoon sun. 'shyà-wǔ byé dzày 'tày-yang 'dì-li dāy-je. ‖I've been out in the sun all day. wǒ dzày 'wày-tew 'tày-yang 'dì-li dāy-le yì-'jěng-'tyān.

To get sunburned jyàw 'tày-yang 'shày-le (*be overexposed to the sun*), °shày-'húng-le (*get tanned or red*), °shày twō 'pí-le (*get so burned that the skin peels*), °shày 'hēy-le (*be sunburned*); to have a sunstroke *or* be overcome by the sun jyàw 'tày-yang °shày 'ywūn-gwò-chywu-le, °shày 'hwēn-gwò-chywu-le, °shày 'bing-le. °shày 'mí-hu-le, *or* jùng-'shǔ *or* shèw-'shǔ; to drop dead from the heat jùng-'shǔ sž-le.

SUNDAY. shīng-'chī *or* lǐ-'bày; shīng-chī-°'ř, *or* °'tyān; *or* lǐ-bày-°'ř, *or* °'tyān.

SUPPER. wǎn-'fàn. ‖Supper is ready. wǎn-'fàn 'dé-le. ‖We eat supper about six o'clock. wǒ-men dà-'gày 'lyèw-dyǎn-jūng 'chř wǎn-'fàn.

SUPPLY. A supply of yì-pī ... (*a load or shipment of*) ; a larg` supply bù-'shǎw-de-. . .; a small supply méy-dwŏ shǎw . . .; (my) supply of (wǒ-de) . . ., *or* (wǒ) jè`-de . . . . ‖We need a fresh supply of tennis balls. wǒ-men děy 'yàw yì-pī-'shīn-wǎng-'chyéw. ‖I need another supply of carbon paper. *is expressed as* I need some more carbon paper. wǒ 'háy děy 'yàw-dyǎr fù-shyě-'jř. ‖I carried a good supply of reading matter with me. wǒ dày-le bù-'shǎw-de-'shū gēn dzá-'jř shéme-de. ‖We have just a small supply of these on hand. 'jèy-ge wǒ-men 'shěw-li °'méy-dwō-'shǎw. *or* °'jyèw yěw yì-'dyǎr. ‖How large a supply of towels do you have? nǐ 'tswén-le yěw 'dwō-shǎw-tyáw-'shěw-jìn? ‖My supply of paper is running low. wǒ jèr-de-'jř kwày 'yùng-'wán-le.

(*Available amount*). ‖The supply of silk stockings can't begin to meet the demand. *is expressed as* The silk stockings being produced aren't enough to supply the demand. sž-'wà-dz 'chū-de gūng-bú-'shàng 'mày-de. *or as* The silk stockings that have been stored up aren't enough to supply the demand. 'tswén-de-sž-'wà-dz gūng-bú-'shàng 'mày-de. *or as* All the stockings available can't meet the demand. sž-'wà-dz shř 'gūng-bu-yìng-'chyéw.

To supply gūng (*to supply a demand, or to supply money*) ; jyè (*to lend*) ; sùng *or* gěy (*to give*) ; chū (*to give out, produce*). ‖The store has enough shoes on hand to supply any normal demand. jèy-ge-'pù-dz-li 'tswén-de-'shyé jàw píng-'cháng-de-yàngr 'mày, 'dzěm-je yě gūng-de-'shàng. ‖I'll supply the money for you. wǒ 'gūng-ni 'chyán yùng. ‖I'll supply the money for your schooling. wǒ 'gūng-ni shàng-'shywé. ‖You supply the money and I'll do the work. 'nǐ chū-'chyán, 'wǒ chū-'lì. ‖That company supplies us with ice. nèy-ge-gūng-'sž gěy wǒ-men sùng-'bīng. ‖I'll supply anything else you need. nǐ 'háy yàw-'shéme wǒ děw 'kě-yǐ-'gěy-ni.

Supplies 'dūng-shi. ‖We are running out of supplies. wǒm-de-'dūng-shi děw kwày yùng-'wán-le. ‖I'm going to town for groceries and other supplics. wǒ yàw dàw chéng-'lǐ mǎy dyǎr-'tsày gēn líng-'swèy-de-'dūng-shi.

SUPPORT. (*To hold up*) fú (*to keep something standing erect with hand*) ; jř-je (*to support something from underneath by poles*) ; dǐng (*to carry on one's head; also used figuratively of poles*) ; chān (*to support a person by taking his arm lightly*) ; jyà (*to support a person or thing by lifting it up forcibly*) ; *see also* **CARRY;** be able to support jīn-de-'jù. ‖Support the ladder to keep it from falling. 'fú-je nèy-ge-'tī-dz-dyǎr byé 'ràng-ta 'dǎw-lew. ‖The board was supported by the two benches. nèy-kwày-'bǎn-dz chywán 'jàng-je nèy-lyǎng-tyáw-'dèng-dz 'jyà-je-ne. ‖The house is supported on piles. jèy-ge-'fáng-dz děw 'jàng-je nèy-jǐ-gēr-'jù-dz °'jř-je-ne, *or* °'dǐng-je-ne. ‖He put his arm under hers to support her. tā bǎ-shěw 'gē-de nèy-nywǔ-de-gē-bey-'jěwr-nèr 'chān-je tā. ‖That

bridge isn't strong enough to support so much weight. nèy-ge-'chyáw bú-gèw-'jyē-shr jīn-bu-'jù nème-'jùng.

(*To uphold*). ‖I'll support your claims. *is expressed as* I'll help you speak. wǒ 'bāng-je nǐ 'shwō. ‖That supports my argument. *is expressed as* That makes what I say appear more reasonable. nème yì-'láy 'gèng shyǎn-je wǒ yěw 'lǐ-le. ‖Does this paper support his policies? *is expressed as* Does this paper approve of his policies? jèy-ge-'bàw 'dzàn-chéng tā-de-'bàn-fǎ-ma? ‖I've spoken in support of this idea before. *is expressed as* I've spoken before and approved of that idea. wǒ yǐ-'chyán 'shwō-gwo wǒ 'dzàn-chéng nèy-ge-'bàn-fǎ. ‖Can you offer any evidence in support of this statement? *is expressed as* Can you produce any facts to prove that statement? nǐ 'néng ná-chū shř-'shř láy 'jèng-míng nèy-ge-'hwà-ma?

(*To provide maintenance for*) 'yǎng-hwo (*to support anyone*) ; yǎng-'jyā (*to support one's own wife or family*). ‖Are you supporting a family? nǐ děy yǎng-'jyā-ma? ‖Several relatives depend on him for their support. tā yěw hǎw-jǐ-gè-'chīn-chi děw 'jàng-je tā 'yǎng-hwo-je. *But* ‖I'm the main support of my family. *is expressed as* My family mostly depends on me. wǒ-'jyā gwò-'r-dz 'dwō-bàr 'jàng-je 'wǒ.

A support (*pole*) 'jù-dz, (*wall*) chyáng. ‖The supports under the porch don't look very strong to me. nèy-ge-'láng-dz-de-'jù-dz wǒ 'kàn bú-'dà 'jyē-shr.

SUPPOSE. (*To think*) shyǎng, 'yǐ-wéy, 'jywé-de. ‖I suppose so. wǒ 'shyǎng shř 'nà-yàngr. ‖He's all right, I suppose. wǒ 'jywé-de tā bú-'tswò. ‖Do you suppose that this is true? nǐ 'yǐ-wéy nèy shř 'jēn-de-ma? ‖He is generally supposed to be a rich man. *is expressed as* Everyone thinks he's very wealthy. dà-'hwǒr děw 'yǐ-wéy tā 'hěn 'kwò. ‖It's supposed to be true. *is expressed as* Everyone thinks it's that. dà-jyā-'hwǒr děw 'yǐ-wéy shř nèm-hwéy-'shř.

(*Granted*) *various expressions* jyǎ-'shè (*or* 'yàw-shr *or* rú-'gwǒ) . . . dzěme-'yàng; *or* wèy-'shéme bù . . . (*why not* . . .). ‖Suppose he turns up, what then? jyǎ-'shè tā 'láy-le, 'dzěme 'bàn? ‖Suppose we go to the show tonight instead of tomorrow. wǒ-men wèy-'shéme bù-'jyěr-ge kàn dyàn-'yěngr chywù, 'myér-ge 'béng chywù-le. ‖Suppose you wait till tomorrow. nǐ 'yàw-shr 'děng dàw 'myár-ge 'dzěme-yàng-ne? *or* nǐ 'wèy-shéme bù-děng-de 'myár-ge-ne? *or expressed as* Wait until tomorrow—OK? nǐ děng dàw 'myár-ge dzày 'shwō, 'shíng-bù-shíng? ‖Let's suppose, for the sake of argument, that I'm right. *is expressed as* Just assume for now that I'm right. jyèw 'bǐ-fang shwō wǒ 'dwèy-le-ba.

To be supposed to yīng-'dāng *or* yīng-'gāy. ‖I was supposed to go with him. běn-'láy yīng-'dāng shř 'wǒ gēn-ta 'chywù. ‖You're supposed to do it yourself. nǐ 'yīng-gāy 'dž-jǐ 'dzwò. ‖It's supposed to rain today. *is expressed as* Someone said it would rain today. jywù 'shwō jyēr yàw shyà-'ywù.

SURE. To be sure of *something* 'jwĕn 'jŕ-daw (*know for certain*); găn 'shwō (*dare to say*). ‖Are you sure of that? 'nèy-ge nĭ 'jwĕn 'jŕ-daw-ma? oɤ 'nèy-ge nĭ găn 'shwō-ma? or *expressed as* Is that true? nèy-ge shŕ 'jēn-de-ma? ‖What are you going to do? I'm not sure. nĭ 'shyăng gàn 'shéme-ya? wŏ 'háy méy-'jwĕr-nè .(*literally,* I'm not certain yet). or wŏ 'bù-găn shwō. or wŏ háy bù-jŕ-'dàw-ne (*literally,* I don't know yet). ‖I'm sure of one thing, that he dislikes us. yĕw 'yí-yàngr shŕ wŏ găn 'shwō-de, 'jyèw-shŕ tā bù-'shĭ-hwan wŏ-men.

To feel sure that jywé-de ... yí-'dìng. ‖I feel sure that you will be all right. wŏ 'jywé-de nĭ yí-'dìng 'kĕ-yi. ‖I feel sure of success. wŏ 'jywé-de yí-'dìng kĕ-yi 'chéng.

Be sure (*when ordering someone*) 'yí-'dìng (or 'bì-dìng) (dĕy). ‖Be sure and wear your coat. yí-'dìng dĕy 'chŵān-shang-dyăr dà-'yī. ‖Be sure to lock the door before you go to bed. shwèy-'jyàw yĭ-'chyán yí-'dìng yaw 'swŏ-shang 'mén.

To make sure; *see* To be sure of *and* Be sure, *above. When the English means* See to it that, *there are many Chinese expressions, depending on the method of making sure. The following sentences illustrate various ways of expressing the idea.* ‖Make sure you're on time. shyăng-'fár yí-'dìng àn 'shŕ-hew 'láy. ‖I'll make sure we never see him again. wŏ yí-'dìng shyăng-'fár ràng wŏ-men tsúng-'tsž 'dzày yĕ bú-'jyàn-ta-le. ‖Make sure there isn't a single mistake. 'chywè-shŕ dwèy-'hăw-le, 'yí-ge-tswòr dēw 'bù-néng 'yĕw. ‖Make sure the thing works before you buy it. *is expressed as* Try it to see if it's all right, then buy it. shŕ 'hăw-le dzày 'măy.

To be sure to (*to be certain to*) yí-'dìng or jwĕn. ‖He is sure to be back by nine o'clock. tā 'jyĕw-dyăn-jūng yí-'dìng kĕ-yi 'hwéy-laɤ. ‖Whatever he does is sure to be interesting. tā 'nùng-chū 'shéme-lay dēw yí-'dìng yĕw 'yì-sz. ‖I'm sure to forget it if you don't remind me. nĭ 'yàw-shr bù-'tí-wo yì-'shēngr wŏ yí-'dìng jyèw 'wàng-le.

To be sure (*dependable*) jwĕn 'chéng, jwĕn 'shíng (*certainly be accomplished*); kàw-de-'jù (*be dependable*); yĕw 'bă-wù (*be safe*); 'wàn-wú-yì-'shŕ (*never miss*). ‖This method is slow but sure. 'jèy-ge-'fá-dz 'màn, kĕ-shr jwĕn 'shíng. ‖That investment is a sure thing. ná-chū 'chyán-lay dzwò 'nèy-ge-'măy-may hĕn kàw-de-'jù. ‖Our final victory is absolutely sure. wŏ-men-de-dzwèy-'hèw-shèng-'lì shŕ 'jywé-dwèy yĕw 'bă-wu.

Sure *or* surely (*certainly*) jēn. ‖I'd sure like to see them, but I won't have time. wŏ jēn 'ywàn-yi 'kàn-kan tă-men, kĕ-shr wŏ méy 'gūng-fu. ‖You said it would rain, and sure enough it did. nĭ shwō 'tyān yàw shyà-'ywŭ, jyèw jēn 'shyà-le.

As sure as fate bĭ 'shyĕ-shya háy 'jwĕn (*more certain than if it were written down*), or méy 'wèn-tí (*there's no question about it*), or méy-'tswòr (*there's no mistake about it*). ‖As sure as fate he'll be there. tā 'jwĕn 'dzày-nèr yí-'dìng méy-'tswòr.

‖Sure! Surely! (*OK! Of course!*) hăw, āy, dăng-'rán, yí-'dìng.

SURPRISE. (*To startle*) shyà yí-'tyàw, chŕ yì-'jīng; (*to be surprised*) 'jywé-je tè-'byé *or* chí-'gwày (*think it's odd*). or méy-shyăng-'dàw (*not to have expected it*). ‖Are you surprised that I came? wŏ 'láy-le nĭ 'jywé-de hĕn 'gwày-ma? ‖He surprised us by doing such a good job. 'nèy-jyàn-'shŕ tā 'dzwò-de 'nème hăw °jēn 'shyà wŏm yí-'tyàw. or °wŏm 'jēn shŕ méy-shyăng-'dàw. or °jēn jyàw-wŏm jywé-je chí-'gwày. ‖I'm surprised at you. nĭ kĕ 'jēn ràng-wŏ méy-shyăng-'dàw. ‖I got the surprise of my life when I saw him. wŏ yí-'kàn-jyàn tā 'shyà-wŏ yí-dà-'tyàw. or *expressed as* To see him there was the most unexpected thing of my life. wŏ néng dzày-nèr 'kàn-jyàn 'tā jēn shŕ yí-'bèy-dz méy-shyăng-'dàw-de-'shèr. ‖I've got a surprise for you in this package. *is expressed as* You can't guess what's in this package. nĭ yí-'dìng °shyăng-bú-'dàw (or °tsăy-bù-'jáw) jèy-'bāw-li shŕ 'shéme. ‖That was a surprise. *is expressed as* Nobody would have thought of it. 'nèy-ge jēn ràng-rén shyăng-bú-'dàw. ‖They paid us a surprise visit. *is expressed as* They unexpectedly came to see us. méy-shyăng-'dàw 'tā-men láy 'kàn wŏ-men láy-le.

‖Imagine my surprise! *is expressed as* You can think how surprised and bewildered I was. nĭ 'shyăng-shyang wŏ nà-ge-chí-'gwày-ba!

‖I later learned, to my surprise, that he was right. *is expressed as* I later learned that he was actually right. wŏ 'hèw-láy 'tīng-shwō tā 'jywū-rán 'dwèy-le.

SWEET. (*To the taste*) tyán. ‖Is the lemonade sweet enough? nèy-ge-níng-méng-'shwĕy gèw 'tyán-de-le-ma? ‖Do you have any sweet pickles? nĭ yĕw shéme-tyán-pàw-'tsày-ma?

(*Not soured*). ‖Is the milk still sweet? *is expressed as* Hasn't the milk gotten sour? nyéw-'năy háy méy-'swàn-ne-ma?

(*To the smell*) shyāng; 'shyāng-tyán (*smelling so good that it would probably taste good, too*). ‖These flowers smell too sweet. jèy-'shyĕ-'hwār tày 'shyāng-le. ‖What's that sweet smell? nèy-ge-nème-'shyāng-tyán-shyāng-'tyán-de shŕ 'shéme?

(*Nice, pleasant*) hăw. ‖How sweet of you! nĭ jēn 'hăw! ‖She has a very sweet disposition. tā-de-'pí-chi jēn 'hăw. ‖Her voice is very sweet. tā-de-'săng-dz hĕn 'hăw.

Sweeten jyā- (or gē- or fàng-)'táng (*add sugar*). ‖We haven't sweetened the cocoa yet. 'kēw-kew-lì-tew wŏ-men háy méy-jyā-'táng.

SWELL (SWOLLEN). jŭng (*to swell because of infection*); jàng (*to become bigger because of a change in temperature, dampness, etc.: to warp*). ‖My foot is beginning to swell up. wŏ-de-'jyăw 'jŭng-chĭ-láy-le ‖Your ankle looks swollen. nĭ-de-jyăw-'wàn-dz 'kàn je shyàng 'jŭng-le shŕ-de. ‖The hot water has made my hand swell. rè-'shwěy bǎ wǒ-'shěw gěy pàw-'jàng-le. ‖The wood has swelled and the door won't open. 'mù-tew 'jàng-le, 'mén kāy-bu-'kāy-le.

(To increase) dzēng-'jyā. ‖Their numbers are swelling fast. tā-men-de-'rén-shur dzēng-'jyā-de hěn kwày.

(Very good) hǎw-'jí-le, gāw-'jí-le, bàng-'jí-le; hěn (or jēn or tǐng or tày) °'hǎw (or °'gāw or °'bàng). ‖Swell! hǎw-'jí-le! ‖That's a swell idea. nèy-ge-'yì-sz tǐng 'hǎw. ‖She's a swell person. tā nèy-ge-'rén hǎw-'jí-le.

SWIFT. kwày; (of current) jí. ‖Is the current swift? 'shwěy 'lyéw-de 'jí-ma? ‖He kept up a swift pace. tā 'dzěw-de hěn 'kwày. ‖The end was so swift that it took everyone by surprise. nèy-ge 'wán-de tày 'kwày-le, 'shéy dēw méy-shyǎng-'dàw.

SWIM (SWAM, SWUM). fù-'shwěy, yéw-'yǔng, yéw-'shwěy. ‖Do you know how to swim? nǐ hwèy yéw-'yǔng-ma? ‖Let's go swimming this afternoon. jyēr-'shyà-wǔ 'dzám fù-'shwěy chywù-ba. ‖We'll have to swim the river. wǒ-men děy 'fù-gwò jèy-tyáw-'hé chywù. ‖We had a good swim. wǒ-men fù-'shwěy 'wár-de tǐng 'hǎw. ‖I'm going out for a swim. wǒ

yàw 'chywù 'fù-fu 'shwěy. ‖The blow made my head swim. is expressed as The blow made my head dizzy and my eyes see stars. nèy-yí-'shyà-dz 'dǎ-de wǒ-'téw-ywùn-yǎn-'hwā.

SYSTEM. 'shì-tǔng (organic or organized whole), in compounds also shì; 'jř-du (method or policy; of political or social organizations), in compounds also jř. ‖Our railway system isn't very good yet. wǒ-men-de-'tyě-lù-'shì-tǔng háy 'bú-swàn 'hǎw. ‖He's reading about the solar system. tā jèng 'yán-jyew 'tày-yang-'shì-ne. ‖We're proud of our school system. wǒ-men 'jywé-de wǒ-men-de-shywé-'shyàw 'jř-du háy bú-'tswò. ‖We use the metric system here. 'wǒ-men jèr 'yùng 'mǐ-dá-'jř.

(Plan, method) 'fá-dz, 'fāng-fa, 'bàn-fǎ. ‖What is your system for getting things done? nǐ yùng 'shéme-'fá-dz 'dzwò-chu-lay-de? ‖Do you understand the system well enough? 'nèy-ge-fá-dz nǐ 'shéw-bu-shéw?

(Physical tract) is expressed as blood shyě or as body shēn-dz. ‖He hasn't got rid of all the poison in his system yet. tā-shyě-li-de-'dú háy méy-chú-'jìng.

T

TABLE. (Furniture) 'jwō(-dz). ‖Push the table against the wall. bǎ 'jwō-dz 'twěy-de kàw-je 'chyáng. or bǎ 'jwō-dz 'yǐ-dàw 'chyáng-nàr chywù.

To set the table (literally) bǎy-'jwō. ‖She set the table very attractively. tā bǎy-'jwō 'bǎy-de hěn hǎw-'kàn.

To set a table (figuratively). ‖They set a good table. tām 'ywù-bèy-de-'tsày hěn °'hǎw. or °'fēng-fù.

(Array of data) byǎw. Time table shŕ-jyān-'byǎw; table of contents 'mù-lù or mù-lù-'byǎw. ‖The figures are given in the table on page twenty. yàw-jǎw-de-'shùr dzày dì-'èr-shr-'yè-de-'byǎw-shang. ‖He's looking it up in the table of contents. tā jèng dzày 'mù-lù-nèr 'jǎw-ne. or tā jèng dzày chá 'mù-lù-ne.

To turn the tables on 'jř-jř or gěy . . . 'láy yí-shyà-dz. ‖Let's turn the tables on him; we can't always be doing what he says. dzám děy shyǎng-'fár 'jř-jr ta-le, 'bù-néng 'jìng tīng-'tā-de. ‖Let's turn the tables on him; we can't always let him get the best of us. dzám yě gěy-'tā láy yí-'shyà-dz-ba; byé 'jìng jyàw-'tā jàn 'pyán-yi.

To table 'yā-chǐ-láy or gē-dzay yì-'byār. ‖They tabled the motion. tām bǎ yì-'àn 'yā-chi-lay-le. or tām bǎ yì-'àn gē-dzay yì-'byār-le.

TAIL. (Of the body) 'yǐ-ba. ‖The puppy had a clipped tail. shyǎw-'gěwr-de-'yǐ-ba shř 'dwò-le-de.

Tails (side of coin) mèr. ‖Heads or tails? yàw-'dzèr yàw-'mèr.

To tail or to tail behind 'gēn-je (láy or chywù on occasion). ‖We'll tail right behind your car. wǒm jǐn 'gēn-je nǐ-de-'chē.

Tail end (of something that is taking time) mwò-mwo-'lyǎwr or kwày-'wán-le-de-shŕ-hew; (of something that extends in space) jǐn-'hèw-tew-nèy-'dwàr or jǐn-'hèw-tew-nèy-'jyéer. ‖We arrived at the tail end of the first act. wǒm dzày 'téw-yí-'mù-de-mwò-mwo-'lyǎwr 'dàw-de. or wǒm dzày dì-'yí-mù-shì-kwày-'wán-le-de-shŕ-hew 'dàw-de. ‖The tail end of the train was blocking the road. hwǒ-'chē-jǐn-'hèw-tew-nèy-'jyéer 'jèng bǎ-'lù 'dǎng-shang.

Tail light hèw-'dēng or yǐ-ba-'dēng. ‖I'm having the tail light on my car fixed. wǒ jèng 'shēw-shr wǒ-'chē-shang-de-hèw-'dēng.

‖His lecture was so confusing, we couldn't make head or tail of it. tā-de-yǎn-'jyǎng 'lwàn-chi-bā-'dzāw-de, wǒm jyàn-'jř bù-jř-'dàw tā-shwō-de shř-'shéme.

TAILOR. 'tsáy-feng. ‖Where can I find a good tailor? 'nǎr yěw hǎw-'tsáy-feng?

Tailor (shop) tsáy-feng-'pù or shī-fú-'dyàn. ‖Take this suit to the tailor to be fixed. bǎ jèy-tàw-'yī-fu ná-dàw tsáy-feng-'pù chywù 'gǎy yí-shyàr.

To tailor expressed by dzwò to make. ‖This skirt is well tailored. jèy-ge-'chywún-dz dzwò-de hěn 'hǎw. ‖How long will it take to tailor this coat? jèy-jyàn-shàng-'yī 'děy dzwò 'dwō-shaw-shŕ-hew?

TAKE. (*Want or accept*) yàw; (*choose*) tyāw; (*buy*) mǎy; (*rent*) dzū. ‖**Will you take a check for the bill?** jř-'pyàw nǐ 'yàw-bu-yàw? ‖**Which room will you take?** nǐ yàw 'něy-jyān-'wū-dz? *or* nǐ shyǎng 'tyāw 'něy-jyān-'wū-dz? ‖**I'll take the room with bath.** wǒ yàw dày-shǐ-dzǎw-'fáng-de-nèy-jyān-'wū-dz. ‖**I think I'll take the blue hat.** wǒ shyǎng 'mǎy nèy-dǐng-'lán-shǎr-de-'màw-dz. ‖**Let's take a house in the country for the summer.** dzán 'shyà-tyar dzày chéng-'wày-tew dzū swǒr-'fáng jù.

(*Grasp and carry*) bān, 'dī-le, *and various other terms depending on the method of carrying; see* CARRY, BRING. ‖**Here, boy, take my bags!** 'chá-fang, bān 'shíng-li! *or* 'chá-fang, 'dī-le 'shyāng-dz.

(*Call for and carry away for some purpose*) láy chywǔ-'dzěw. ‖**Did the man take my laundry yet?** nèy-ge-'rén láy bǎ wǒ-de-'dzāng-'yī-fu chywǔ-'dzěw-le méy-yew?

(*To appropriate without permission*) jì, dǎ, yùng, ná-'dzěw, chāw-'dzěw, dày-'dzěw. ‖**I wish you wouldn't keep taking my ties!** wǒ 'shī-wang nǐ byé 'lǎw 'jì (*or* 'dǎ) wǒ-de-lǐng-'dày! *or* nǐ bú-'yùng wǒ-de-lǐng-'dày, 'shíng-bu-shíng? ‖**Who took my book?** 'shéy bǎ wǒ-de-'shū ná- (*or* chāw-)'dzěw-le? ‖**Don't take my hat!** byé 'chāw wǒ-de-'màw-dz! *or* byé bǎ wǒ-de-'màw-dz dày-'dzěw. ‖**Who took the papers out of my drawer?** 'shéy bǎ wǒ-'chēw-ti-li-de-wén-'jyàn ná-'dzěw-le. ‖**Has anything been taken from your room?** *is expressed as* **Is your room short anything?** nǐ-'wū-dz-li 'dwǎn-le shéme-'dūng-shi méy-yew?

(*To consider, to bring into the picture*) ná. ‖**Take that man over there, for example.** jyèw ná 'nèr-nèy-ge-'rén dzwò ge-'bǐ-fang.

(*To use*) yùng, *or expressed with a specific verb appropriate to the particular thing used.* ‖**Will you let me take your car?** wǒ 'ké-yi yùng nǐ-de-'chē-ma? ‖**I take cream with my coffee.** *is expressed as* **When I drink coffee I put cream in it.** wǒ hē jyā-'fēy gē nǎy-'yéw.

(*To go by a means of transportation*) kāy *if one operates the vehicle oneself;* dzwò *otherwise.* ‖**I'm glad you took your car.** shìng-'kwēy-le nǐ bǎ-'chē 'kāy-láy-le. ‖**We're taking the train tomorrow.** wǒm 'míng-tyan dzwò hwǒ-'chē dzěw.

(*To capture*) 'gūng-shyà-láy, 'dǎ-shyà-láy, dé-daw 'shěw. ‖**Our troops took the town in two hours.** wǒm-'jywūn-dwèy 'lyǎng-ge-'jūng-tew-de-gūng-fu jyèw bǎ-'chéng 'gūng-shyà-láy-le. *or* 'dǎ-shyà-láy-le. *or* 'dé-daw 'shěw-le.

(*To win*) yíng. ‖**Who do you think will take the tennis match?** nǐ shwō wǎng-'chyéwr-bì-'sày 'shéy hwèy 'yíng?

(*To require personnel*) yěw . . . tsáy; (*to require additional personnel*) háy děy tyān . . . tsáy. ‖**It will take two more men to move this safe.** nwó jèy-ge-bǎw-shyǎn-'shyāng 'dzày yěw 'lyǎng-ge-rén tsáy 'shíng. *or* 'háy děy tyān 'lyǎng-ge-rén tsáy 'shíng.

(*To require time*) yùng, děy yùng, fèy, děy fèy. ‖**How long does the trip take?** yí-'chywù yùng 'dwō-shaw-shf-hew? ‖**It took a long time for me to come here.** wǒ shàng-'jèr-lay yùng-le hǎw-'shyē-'shf-hew. ‖**How long will it take to press my clothes?** bǎ wǒ-'yī-fu 'tàng-yi-tàng děy fèy 'dwō-shaw-shf-hew?

Take advantage of. ‖**Thanks, I'll take advantage of your offer.** 'shyè-shye, wǒ yǐ-'hèw yí-'dìng láy °'má-fan nín. *or* °gēn-nin chǐng 'jyàw. *or* °chǐng-nín bāng-'máng. *or* 'shyè-shye, wǒ yí-'hèw yí-'dìng jàw-'bàn.

Take advice tīng-'hwà. ‖**Take my advice.** tīng wǒ-de-'hwà.

Take *someone's* **arm** chān. ‖**Let me take your arm.** ràng-wo 'chān-je ni 'dzǒw.

Take a bath shǐ-'dzǎw. ‖**I'd like to take a bath now.** wǒ shyǎng shyàn-dzày shǐ-'dzǎw.

Take a beating 'āy yí-dwèn-'dzěw. ‖**He certainly took a whale of a beating.** tā dzú-'dzur-de 'āy-le dwèn-'dzěw. *or, Figuratively, is expressed as* **He's really lost badly.** tā 'shū-de jēn 'tsǎn.

Take the blame (for). ‖**I won't take the blame for his mistake.** 'tā-de-tswòr 'píng-shéme 'wǒ rèn? *or* 'wǒ wèy-shéme gěy-'tā dzwò tì-sž-'gwěy? *or* 'wǒ tsáy bú-tì-'tā rèn-'tswòr-ne. ‖**He took all the blame himself.** tā-'yí-ge-rén bēy 'hēy-gwō.

Take care of *a matter* bàn. ‖**I took care of that matter.** nèy-jyàn-'shèr wǒ 'yǐ-jing 'bàn-le. *For* ‖**Take care of yourself.** *there are set phrases* 'dwō-dwo bǎw-'jùng! *or* 'shyǎw-shīn-dyǎr! *or* dwō 'lyéw-dyǎr 'shén! *or* hǎw-'hāwr-de!

Take charge of *a house or family* kān-'jyā. ‖**Who's taking charge of the house while you're away?** nǐ chū-'mér de-shf-hew 'shéy gěy-ni kān-'jyā?

Take charge of *matters* bàn, gwǎn.

Take a chance on *someone* 'shř-shr. ‖**Let's take a chance on him.** dzám jyèw 'shř-shr ta-ba.

Take it easy. ‖**We ought to take it easy in this weather.** shyàng 'jè-yàng-de-'tyār dzám yīng-dang °màn-'mār láy. *or* °'dzěw-je 'chyáw. *or* °'yēw-je-'jyèr-de dzwò. *or* °'hǎw yì-hwěr. ‖**Take it easy!** 'màn-dyǎr láy! *or* lyéw-'shén! *or* byé jáw-'jí!

Take for granted. ‖**Don't take so many things for granted.** byé 'tày 'dà-yì-le. *or* byé dyǎwr-lāng-'dǎng-de. *or* byé 'jywé-de 'shéme dēw tǐng-'rúng-yì-'shř-de. *or* byé 'yǐ-wéy méy 'wèn-tí-le shř-de.

Take it that . . . jywù . . . 'kàn. ‖**I take it you're in trouble.** jywù wǒ 'kàn, nǐ dà-'gày yew rě-'shř-le.

Take *something* **hard.** ‖**Don't take it so hard.** hé-'bì wǎng 'shīn-li chywù. *or* hé-'bì nème 'dzày-hu. *or* byé shyǎng-bu-'kāy. *or* 'yùng-bu-jáw dzwǎn nyéw-jī-jyaw.

Take hold of; *or* **take** *alone, with this meaning* jyēw, jwā, dzwàn, ná, táy, *and others, depending on the type of holding. See* GRASP, HOLD. ‖**Take hold of this rope and help us pull the boat in.** 'jyēw- (*or* 'jwā- *or* 'dzwàn- *or* 'ná-)jù-le jèy-gēr-'shéng-dz hǎw bāng-je wǒ-men bǎ-'chwán 'lā-jìn-lay. ‖**Will you take the other end of the desk and help me move it?** nǐ 'táy-je jwō-dz-'nèy-téwr 'bāng-je wǒ 'nwó-yi-nwó, hǎw-ma?

Take medicine. (*If in solid form*) chř-'yàw; (*if in liquid form*) hē-'yàw; (*for either*) fú-'yàw. ‖Have you taken your medicine this morning? nǐ jyēr-'dzǎw-chen chř-'yàw-le-ma?

Take a nap 'shyē yì-hwěr, 'shwèy yì-shyǎw-'jyàw, 'mǐ-feng yì-hwěr, dǎ ge-'dwěr. ‖We always take a nap after dinner. wǒm chř wǎn-'fàn yǐ-'hèw 'lǎw 'shyē yì-hwěr.

Take offense 'dzày-yì, 'dzày-hu, shēng-'chì, *and other expressions meaning* to get angry *and the like.* ‖You shouldn't take offense at what was said. gāng-tsáy nèy-jywù-'hwà nǐ 'yùng-bu-jáw 'dzày-yì.

Take pictures *or* **photographs** jàw-'shyàng. ‖Are you allowed to take pictures here? 'jèr shywǔ jàw-'shyàng-ma?

Take place. *Most events which in English are said to take place are expressed by verbs in Chinese;* thus chū-'shř an accident takes place, chū-'bìn a funeral takes place, *and so on; see, therefore, the other English words involved. See* HAPPEN.

Take a seat dzwò. ‖Take a seat, please. chǐng 'dzwò (chǐng 'dzwò). ‖Is this seat taken? 'jèr yěw-'rén 'dzwò-ma? *or expressed as* Does this seat have anyone? jèy-ge-'wèy-dz yěw-'rén-le-ma?

Take sick *or* **be taken sick** bìng, dé-'bìng, shēng-'bìng. ‖When did he take sick? tā 'shéme-shŕ-hew 'bìng-de? ‖I heard she was taken sick in the theater. wǒ 'tīng-shwō tā dzày shì-'ywán-dz-li jyèw 'bìng-le.

Take *someone's* **temperature** shř-'byǎw. ‖Did the doctor take your temperature this morning? 'dày-fu jyēr-'dzǎw-chen gěy-ni shř-'byǎw-le-ma?

Take one's time. ‖Let's take our time about getting there. dzám màn-'mār-de wǎng-nèr 'chywù, hǎw-le. ‖Can I take my time? wǒ màn-'mār-de 'dzwò, 'shíng-ma?

Take the trouble to, *in making a polite request* láw-'jyà. ‖Will you take the trouble to look at this a bit for me? láw-'jyà 'tì-wo 'kàn yí-shvàr. *But, if indicating annoyance or doubt, it is rephrased.* ‖Should I take the trouble to go out there this afternoon? wǒ jyēr-'shyà-wǔ 'yùng-de-jáw 'wǎng-nèr 'pǎw-yí-tàng-ma?

Take a walk 'lyēw-de-lyēw-da, 'dzěw-dzěw, sàn-sàn 'bù. ‖Would you like to take a walk? nǐ shyǎng sàn-sàn 'bù-ma?

Take after (*resemble*) shyàng. ‖Who do you take after, your father or your mother? nǐ-shř 'jǎng-de shyàng nǐ-'fù-chin háy-shr shyàng nǐ-'mǔ-chin?

Take *something* **away;** *expressed as* carry-leave; *see* CARRY *for the possible combinations; the leave part is* dzěw *or* chywù. ‖Have the trunks been taken away yet? 'shāng-dz 'yǐ-jing ná-'dzěw-le-ma?

Take *something* **back;** *the same words for* CARRY *with* hwéy *added.* ‖I won't need your book, so why don't you take it back? wǒ 'yùng-bu-jáw nǐ-de-'shū-le, nǐ 'ná-hwéy-chywù dé-le.

Take *something* **down** (*actual motion*); *the same words for* CARRY *or* GRASP *or* BRING *with* shyà

(-láy) *added.* ‖Take the picture down from the wall. bǎ nèy-jāng-'hwàr tsúng 'chyáng-shang 'jāy-shyà lay

Take *notes or minutes* **down,** *or take with this meaning* jì, 'jì-shyà-lay. ‖Who's taking down the minutes? 'shéy jì jì-'lù-ne? ‖Will you take this down, please. chǐng-ni bǎ 'jèy-ge 'jì-shya-lay. ‖He's taking notes at the conference. tā jèng dzày yì-'shí-shang jì bǐ-'jì-ne.

Take *someone* **down a peg** jyàw . . . shyà-bu-'láy 'táy. ‖She certainly took him down a peg. tā kě 'jēn 'jyàw-ta shyà-bu-'láy 'táy.

Take *someone* **for** *someone* 'yǐ-wéy . . . shř . . . , *or expressed as* to see wrongly kàn-'tswò-le *or* to recognize wrongly rèn-'tswò-le. ‖Sorry, I took you for someone else. dwèy-bu-'jù, wǒ 'yǐ-wéy 'nǐ shř 'lìng-yí-ge-rén-ne. *or* dwèy-bu-'jù, wǒ rèn-'tswò-le rén-le.

Take in (*see or look at*) kàn, chyáw. ‖Let's take in a movie this afteroon. dzám jyēr-'shyà-wǔ chyáw dyán-'yěngr chywù-ba. ‖We haven't enough time to take in all the sights. wǒm méy 'gūng-fu bǎ 'swǒ-yěw-de 'chywán kàn-'dàw-le.

Take in *money* jèng, jìn, jwàn, shēw-'rù. ‖How much do you take in in a month? ní 'yí-ge-ywè jèng 'dwō-shǎw-chyán?

Take in *people, guests* shēw, jù, 'jāw-dày, yěw. ‖Even in the winter this hotel takes in a lot of people. jyèw-shr 'dūng-tyan-de-shŕ-hew jèy-ge-lywǔ-'gwǎn yě 'jāw-dày bù-'shǎw-dc 'kè-rén.

Take *someone* **in** (*deceive*) bǎ . . . gěy hǔ-'jù, bǎ . . . gěy 'mēng jù. ‖He certainly took us in with his stories. tā-'shwō-de jēn bǎ-wǒm gěy mēng-jù-le.

Take *clothes* **in** (*make smaller*) shēw-'jìn, myān-'jìn, chyā-'jìn. ‖Will you take this dress in at the waist? nǐ néng bǎ jèy-jyàn-'yī-fu-de-'yāw-shēn shēw-'jìn yì-dyǎr chywù-ma?

Take *a baby* **in** *one's arms* bàw. ‖Will you take the baby in your arms? nǐ 'bàw-yi-bàw 'háy-dz, hǎw-ma?

Take off (*of a plane*) chǐ-'fēy, kǎy. ‖When does the plane take off? fēy-'jī 'shéme-shŕ-hew chǐ-'fēy?

Take off *clothing;* jāy *for hats, ties, and other clothing that does not have to be worn for modesty;* kwān *for a topcoat;* twǒ *for shoes, coats, trousers, etc.* ‖Take off your hat. jāy-le 'màw-dz.

Take off (*mimic*) shywé. ‖My friend can take off almost any actor you name. bù-gwǎn nǐ tí 'něy-ge-'shì-dz, wǒ-'péng-yew chà-bu-dwō 'dēw néng 'shywé.

Take on (*get emotional*) shyǎng-bu-'kāy, chéw-'méy bù-'jǎn, 'dž-gěr gēn dž-'gěr gwò-bu-'chywù. ‖Don't take on so. byé shyǎng-bu-'kāy!

Take on *personnel* (*hire*) tyān, shēw, gu; jyā (*if personnel is additional*). ‖I hear the factory is taking on some new men. wǒ 'tīng-shwō gūng-'chǎng gù shīn-'rén-le.

Take on *a job* 'kāy-shř 'dzwò, dé, lǎn. ‖We took on a new job yesterday. wǒm 'dzwór-ge kāy-shř dzwò 'shīn-de-'gūng-dzwò. *or* wǒm 'dzwór-ge 'lǎn-le yí-ge-'shīn-de-'chāy-shř.

Take *someone* **on** (*to challenge*). ‖**I'll have to take you on for some tennis.** wǒ děy gēn-ni 'sày-say wǎng-'chyewr.

Take *something* **out of** *a place* ná, jwā, *and other words meaning* GRASP, CARRY, *and so on, plus* chū. ‖**Take the fruit out of the bag.** bǎ 'gwǒ-dz tsúng-'kwāngr-lǐ 'ná-chu-lay.

Take *dirt* **out of** *something* chywù-'dyàw, 'nùng-shyà-chywu. ‖**Can you take the spot out of these pants?** nǐ néng bǎ jèy-tyáw-'kù-dz-shang-de-'dzāngr °'nùng-shyà-chywu-ma? *or* °'chywù-'dyàw-le-ma?

Take *it* **out on** *someone* ná . . . sā-'chì, ná . . . chū-'chì, 'jǎw-shywun, gēn . . . gwò-bu-'chywù. ‖**Well, you don't have to take it out on me!** nǐ 'yùng-bu-jáw ná-'wǒ sā-'chì!

Take to *someone.* ‖**They take to him like their own child.** tām 'ày-ta gēn ày 'dž-jǐ-de-'háy-dz shř-de.

Take to *a place* (*run away to*) 'táw-dàw, 'pǎw-dàw. ‖**When we approached, the enemy took to the woods.** děng-dàw wǒm 'kwày 'dàw-le nèr de-shř-hew, 'dí-rén táw-daw shù-'lín-dz-li chywù-le.

Take *something or someone* **to** *a place: various words listed under* GRASP, CARRY, BRING, SEND (*plus* dàw *or* shàng *or* hwéy). ‖**Who's taking her to the station?** 'shéy sùng-ta 'shàng chē-'jàn-na? ‖**Please take me home now.** chǐng-ni lì-'shř sùng-wo hwéy-'jyā-ba. ‖**When were you taken to the hospital?** tām 'shéme-shř-hew bǎ-ni.sùng-jìn yī-'ywàn-de? ‖**Take this letter to the post office.** bǎ jèy-fēng-'shìn sùng-daw yéw-jèng-'jywú-chywù. ‖**May I take you to dinner?** wǒ chǐng-ni chywù chř-'fàn, hǎw-bu-hǎw?

Take *something or someone* **to** *a place, if said of a route or a vehicle, requires rephrasing.* ‖**The train will take you there in three hours.** *is expressed as* **If you go by train you can get there in three hours.** nǐ dzwò hwǒ-'chē sā-'jūng-téw-yǐ-'nèy jyèw ké-yi 'dàw-nèr. ‖**Where will that road take us?** *is expressed as* **That road goes where?** jèy-tyáw-'dàwr °'tūng-dàw 'nǎr? *or* °'chywù-'nǎr? *or* °'shàng-'nǎr?

Take up (*begin working on*) kāy-shř 'shywé, chǐ-shř 'shywé, kāy-shř 'nyàn, chǐ-shř 'nyàn. ‖**I think I'll take up some language this year.** wǒ shyǎng 'jīn-nyán chǐ-shr 'shywé dyǎr-wày-gwo-'hwà.

Take *something* **up with** *someone* gēn . . . 'shāng-lyang, jǎw . . . , gēn . . . 'dàw-dàw, gēn . . . swàn-'jàng, wèn. ‖**You'll have to take that matter up with someone else.** 'nèy-jyàn-shèr nǐ ¹dzwèy-hǎw chywù gēn 'byé-rén 'shāng-lyang.

Take up (*shorten at bottom*) gǎy 'dwǎn. ‖**Take up the gown a little.** bǎ dà-'gwàr gǎy 'dwǎn yì-dyǎr.

Take *someone* **up on** *something* gàn, gēn . . . láy, chř-'jyàng. ‖**He offered me a bet, but I didn't take him up on it** tā yàw gēn-wo dǎ-'dǔ láy-je, °'wǒ méy-'gàn. *or* °'wǒ méy gēn-ta 'láy. *or* °'wǒ bù-chř-'jyàng.

Take up with *someone* gēn . . . 'wǎng-láy, gēn . . . dǎ 'jyāw-dày. ‖**I wouldn't take up with those people if I were you.** 'wǒ yàw-shr 'nǐ de-hwà, jywé bù gēn 'nèy-bāng-rén 'wǎng-láy.

The take (*amount taken in*) *expressed verbally.* ‖**What was the take this week at the theater?** shì-'ywán-dz 'jèy-yí-ge-lǐ-'bày yí-'gùng 'jìn-le 'dwō-shaw-chyán?

TALK. shwō, shwō-'hwà. ‖**Who's he talking to?** tā 'gēn-shéy shwō-'hwà? ‖**Let's see, what were we just talking about?** dzám 'gāng shwō 'shéme láy-je? ‖**Don't you think she talks too much?** nǐ 'shř-bu-shř 'jywé-de tā °shwō-'hwà tày 'dwō? *or* °'tày hàw shwō-'hwà? *or* °'shwō-'hwà 'tày bù-'shyǎw-shin? ‖**Why don't you talk sense for a change?** nǐ shwō yì-dyǎr-yěw-'yì-sz-de 'shíng-bu-shíng? ‖**Please talk slower.** chǐng 'màn-yi-dyǎr 'shwō.

Talk too much (*be garrulous*) ày dwō 'dzwěy, 'pín-chi, 'pín-dzwěy-gwà-'shé-de; (*gossip*) ày chwán shyán-'hwà, ày ch...án-'shé.

Talk loud (*loudly and angrily*) 'rāng-rang, chǎw, chě-je 'sǎng-dz 'hǎn.

Talk *something* **over** (*discuss*) 'tán-tán; (*figure*) 'dǎ-swàn-dǎ-swan; (*consult*) 'shāng-lyàng-shāng-lyang; (*instead of getting mad*) yěw-'hwà hǎw-'hāwr shwō. ‖**We'll have to talk over our plans for tomorrow.** dzám děy 'tán-yi-tán gwān-ywu 'míng-tyan-de-'jì-hwa. *or* děy 'dǎ-swàn-dǎ-swan 'myéngr-ge 'gàn shéme. ‖**Let's talk this over!** dzám 'shāng-lyàng-shāng-lyang jèy-ge. *or* dzám yěw-'hwà hǎw-'hāwr shwō!

Talk *someone* **into** *something.* ‖**He talked me into coming along.** *is expressed as* **My coming is because he persuaded me.** wǒ 'láy shř 'tā chywàn-de. *or as* **My coming was under his influence.** wǒ 'láy shř shèw 'tā-de-yǐng-'shyǎng.

Talk back **to** dǐng . . . yí-jywù, gēn . . . táy-'gàng, gēn . . . jyàng-'lǐ, gēn . . . bàn-'dzwěy, gēn . . . jēng-'lwèn, gēn . . . fēn-'byàn, gēn . . . fèy 'tù-mey, gēn . . . dèng-'yǎn, bwó, dǐng, gēn . . . yì-bān 'jyàn-shr. ‖**For once he dared to talk back to her.** jèy-hwéy tā kě 'jēn 'dǐng-le ta yí-'jywù. ‖**I wouldn't talk back to them, if I were you.** 'wǒ yàw-shr 'nǐ de-hwà, jyèw bù-'gēn-tam jēng-'lwèn. ‖**There's no use talking back to them.** 'yùng-bu-jáw 'bwó tā-men.

A talk yǎn-'jyǎng, yǎn-'shwō. ‖**His talk was long and dull.** tā-de-yǎn-'jyǎng shwō-de yèw 'cháng yèw méy-'wèr.

Talk (*gossip, empty talk*). ‖**Oh, that's just talk!** 'nà bú-gwò shř °'shwō-shwo ér-'yǐ! *or* °'dàw-'tú chwán-'shwō! *or* °yěw-'rén nème 'shwō ér-'yǐ!

Talk (*malicious gossip*) shyán-'hwà. ‖**Her actions have caused a lot of talk.** tā-de-'shíng-wéy 'jāw-le hěn-'dwō-de-shyán-'hwà.

The talk of the town *is expressed as* **the whole town stormed** mǎn-'chéng fēng-'ywù. ‖**That affair became the talk of the town.** nèy-jyàn-'shèr 'nàw-de mǎn-'chéng fēng-'ywǔ.

TALL. gāw. ‖**How tall are you?** nǐ yěw dwō-'gāw? ‖**Have you ever seen such a tall building?** nǐ 'jyàn-gwo jème-'gāw-de-'léw-ma?

Tall order. ‖That's a pretty tall order, but I'll try to do it. nǐ-jyàw-wo-'bàn-de-jèy-jyàn-'shèr °bú-'dà rúng-yi 'bàn (or °'yé-shywu bù-'shíng), kě-shr wǒ 'dzǔng hwèy shyǎng-fár 'shr̀-shr̀-de.

Tall story. ‖He's really telling tall stories. tā-'shwō-de jēn 'rè-naw. or tā yán-gwò chí-'shr̀.

TASK. shr̀, 'gūng-dzwò, 'léy-jwèy.

Take *someone* to task mà, 'mán-ywàn, swěn. ‖Lots of people are taking him to task because of that incident. hǎw-'shyē-rén wèy 'nèy-jyàn-shèr jr̀ 'mà-ta.

TASTE. 1. (*To the tongue*) wèr (noun) ; cháng (verb); *the five tastes are* **sweet** tyán, **sour** swān, **bitter** kǔ, **hot** (*peppery*) là, *and* **salty** shyán. ‖This meat has a strange taste. jèy-kwày-'rèw-de-'wèr hěn 'tè-byé. or jèy-kwày-'rèw yěw-'wèr-le. ‖I don't like the taste of this milk. wǒ bù-'shǐ-hwan jèy-ge-nyéw-'nǎy-de-'wèr. ‖Just taste this coffee! 'cháng-yi-cháng jèy-jǔng-jyǎ-'fēy! ‖I can't taste a thing with this cold. wǒ shāng-'fēng-le, 'chr̄ shéme dēw méy-'wèr. ‖This soup tastes too much of garlic. jèy-ge-'tāng 'swàn-wèr tày °'dà. or °'chùng. or °'núng. ‖This wine tastes bitter. jèy-ge-'jyěw fā-'kǔ. ‖Give me a taste of that soup. wǒ láy (or ràng-wo) 'cháng-dyǎr nèy-ge-'tāng.

(*Eat a little*). chr̄. ‖She hasn't tasted anything since yesterday. tā tsúng 'dzwór chǐ, 'shéme dēw méy-'chr̄.

2. (*Preference*). ‖Suit your own taste. swéy-'nǐ. or nǐ 'shǐ-hwan dzěme-'yàng jyèw dzěme-'yàng-ba.

(*Ability to choose*). ‖She has good taste in clothes. tā hěn 'hwèy chwān 'yī-fu. or tā 'yī-fu chwān-de hěn 'yǎ.

Poor taste. ‖That remark was in very poor taste. shwō 'nèy-jǔng-hwà hěn 'sú-chi.

TAX. shwèy. **To levy a tax** shàng-'shwèy, jēng-'shwèy, chēw-'shwèy, shēw-'shwèy. ‖How much is the tax on these cigarettes? yān-'jywǎr shàng 'dwō-shaw-shwèy? ‖I think they're taxing us too much on our property. wǒ 'jywé-de tām dzày dzám-de-chǎn-'yè-shang chēw-'shwèy chēw-de tày 'dwō-le.

To pay taxes jyāw-'shwèy, nà-'shwèy, bǎ 'shwèy-chyán-'jyāw-jìn-chywù. ‖I hope I can get my taxes in on time this year. wǒ 'shī-wang wǒ 'jīn-nyán néng bǎ 'shwèy-chyán àn-je 'shŕ-hew 'jyāw-jìn-chywu.

(*Tiring*). ‖Reading this small print is very taxing on the eyes. kàn jème-'dyǎr-de-shyǎw-'dzèr kě 'jēn °fèy-'yǎn. or °lèy-'yǎn. or °shāng-'yǎn. ‖This heat is taxing my strength. tyár 'rè-de wǒ dēw kwày 'tān-le.

TEA. (*Ready to drink*) chá; (*leaves*) chá-'yè. ‖I'll take tea, please. 'shyè-shye wǒ hē-'chá (hǎw-le). ‖I'll have a pound (catty) of tea, please. chǐng-ni gěy-wo yì-jīn-chá-'yè.

To have tea hē-'chá, chr̄-'chá, chr̄ 'chá-dyǎn. ‖Let's invite them over for tea Sunday afternoon. dzám lǐ-bày-'tyān-'shyà-wǔ 'chǐng tā-men 'gwò-lay chr̄ 'chá-dyǎn, hǎw-bu-hǎw?

TEACH. jyāw, 'jyāw-gěy, jyāw-'hwèy; *less formal* 'jyǎng-yi-jyǎng, 'jǐ-dyǎn, 'gàw-sung. ‖Will you teach me your language? nǐ 'jyāw-wo shwō nǐ-de-'hwà, hǎw-ma? ‖Would you teach me something about the customs of your country? nǐ 'ywàn-yi 'jyǎng-yi-jyǎng nǐm-'gwó-li-de-'fēng-sú-ma? ‖You'll have to teach me how to use this machine. nǐ děy 'gàw-sung (or 'jǐ-dyǎn or 'jyāw-gey) wo dzěm 'yùng jèy-ge-'jī-chì. ‖Who taught you how to drive a car? 'shéy jyāw-'hwèy-le ni kāy-'chē-de? ‖Is music taught here? 'jèr jyāw yīn-'ywè-ma? ‖Is that the way you've been taught to handle tools? 'shéy 'jyāw-gey ni 'nème shr̄ 'jyā-hwo-de?

TEACHER. jyāw-'ywán, jyāw-'shū-de; *in addressing a teacher directly usually* 'shyān-sheng.

TEAM. (*Athletic*) dwèy, *with game specified; thus* **basketball team** lán-chyéw-'dwèy; **baseball team** bàng-chyéw-'dwèy; *etc.*

Working as a team dā-'hwǒr, 'hé-chi-lay, hé-dzay yí-'kwàr, yí-'kwàr. ‖They make a very good team for that work. tām-'lyǎ dā-'hwǒr dzwò 'nèy-jyàn-shr̄ jèng 'hǎw.

Team up with *is expressed as* **breathe through the same nose** gēn . . . yí-ge-'bí-dz chū-'chyèr. ‖We'll go places if we team up with them. dzám yàw-shr néng gēn tā-men 'yí-ge-bí-dz chū 'chyèr, 'nà kě 'jyèw jēn 'lyǎw-bu-de-le.

TEAR. (*Something flat and flexible, like paper or cloth*) chě (*if with one motion*); sz̄ (*if into many small scraps*); *either of these with an appropriate post-verb such as* kāy **open** *or* **apart**, pwò **into shreds** *or* **tatters**, *etc.* ‖Be careful not to tear your clothes. 'shyǎw-shīn byé bǎ 'yī-fu 'chě-le. ‖I hope you tore up my last letter. wǒ 'shǐ-wàng nǐ bǎ wǒ-'shàng-yì-fēng-'shìn 'sz̄-le. ‖Who tore this package open? 'shéy bǎ jèy-ge-'bāwr 'chě-kay-le? ‖I tore my pants. wǒ bǎ 'kù-dz 'chě-le. ‖Who tore the label off the bottle? 'shéy bǎ 'pyéngr-shang-de-jr̄'tyáw gěy 'sz̄-shyà-chywu-le? ‖I see a page has been torn out of this book. jèy-běr-'shū jyàw-rén gěy 'chě-le yì-'pyār-chywu.

(*If by catching on something*) gwǎ-'pwò-le. ‖My shirt got torn at the elbow. wǒ chèn-'shār-de-'gē-be-jěwr-nèr gwǎ-'pwò-le.

To tear down *a building*, **to tear up** (*wreck*) *things* chāy. ‖They plan to tear down that dirty old hotel next month. tām 'ywù-bey 'shyà-yí-ge-ywè bǎ nèy-ge-yèw-'pwò-yèw-'lǎw-de-lywǔ-'gwǎn 'chāy-le.

A tear; *expressed with the verbs already given; thus* chě-'pwò-le-de-dì-fang **torn place**, *and the like;* or *one says* 'kěw-dz **hole.** ‖Can this tear be repaired in a hurry? chě-'pwò-le-de-jèy-'kwày néng lì-'shŕ 'bǔ-shang-ma? or nǐ néng bǎ jèy-ge-'kěw-dz gǎn-'jǐn jyèw 'bǔ-shang-ma?

TEARS. yǎn-'lèy or yǎn-'lèr. *Where English has* **tears** *Chinese often has* kū *to cry.* ‖She breaks out into tears at a moment's notice. tā shwō 'kū jyèw 'kū. *or expressed as* Her tears are like tap water. tā yǎn-'lèr gēn dz-láy-'shwěr shr̀-de. ‖Tears won't do you any good. nǐ 'kū yě méy-'yùng.

TELEGRAM, TELEGRAPH. Telegram dyàn-'bàw; to send a telegram *or* to telegraph dǎ dyàn-'bàw; to transmit telegrams fā dyàn-'bàw; to receive telegrams shēw dyàn-'bàw; by telegraph yùng dyàn-'bàw. ‖Telegraph us when you get there. 'dàw-nèr de-shŕ-hew gěy-wǒm °dǎ ge-dyàn-'bàw. *or* °láy ge-dyàn-'bàw. ‖I'm going to telegraph my folks for some money. wǒ yàw gěy 'jyā-li dǎ dyàn-'bàw hǎw yàw dyǎr-'chyán. ‖Can I send a telegram here? *or* Do you take telegrams here? nǐm 'jèr (shēw-) 'fā dyàn-'bàw-ma? ‖Are there any telegrams for me? yěw wǒ-de-dyàn-'bàw-ma? ‖Shall we send the news by telegraph? jèy-ge-'shyāw-shi wǒm 'shr̀-bu-shr̀ yàw yùng dyàn-'bàw 'fā-chu-chywù? ‖I want to send a telegram to . . . wǒ yàw 'dǎ yí-ge-dyàn-'bàw °gěy . . . *(person)*. *or* °dàw . . . *(place)*. *or* wǒ yàw wǎng . . . *(place)* dǎ dyàn-'bàw.
Telegraph office dyàn-bàw-'jywú.

TELEPHONE. dyàn-'hwà; to telephone dǎ dyàn-'hwà. ‖Do you have a telephone? nǐ-nèr yěw dyàn-'hwà-le ma? *or, if asking someone more conversationally whether his house or office is so equipped,* nǐ 'ān dyàn-'hwà-le-ma? ‖Can I use your telephone, please? 'jyè nín-de-dyàn-'hwà 'shr̀-shr, shíng-ma? ‖Did anyone telephone me? yěw wǒ-de-dyàn-'hwà-ma? *or* yěw-'rén gěy-wo dǎ dyàn-'hwà láy-je-ma? ‖Where can I telephone you this evening? jyēr-'wǎn-shang wǒ wàng-'nǎr gěy-ni dǎ dyàn-'hwà?

TELL. *(Give someone information about something)* 'gàw-sung or 'gàw-su, gěy . . . 'jyǎng yí-shyàr, gēn . . . 'tí. ‖Tell him your name. 'gàw-sung ta nǐ 'jyàw shéme. ‖Can you tell me how to get to the station? chǐng-ni 'gàw-sung wo dàw hwǒ-chē-'jàn dzěme chywù. ‖Tell me all about it. 'tùng-tung-kwǎr-'kwǎr-de 'gàw-sung wo. *or* tsúng-'téwr dàw-'lyǎwr gěy-wo 'jyǎng yí-shyàr. ‖Did they tell you anything about their plans for this evening? tām gēn-ni 'tí-le méy-tí jyēr-'wǎn-shang tām-shr̀ 'ywù-bey 'gàn shéme?
(Order someone to do something) jyàw. ‖Tell them not to make so much noise. jyàw-tam byé 'rǎng. ‖Tell the driver to wait for us. jyàw nèy-ge-kāy-'chē-de 'děng-je dzám. ‖I was told to wait here. tām jyàw-wo dzày-'jèr děng.
Tell me *or* Tell us, *as introductory remark to an informal question, is often simply omitted.* ‖Tell me, what are you doing tonight? nǐ jyēr-'wǎn-shang 'gàn shéme?
Don't tell me. ‖Don't tell me I'm too late! *(Because I know it perfectly well already.)* wǒ 'wǎn-le, 'yùng-bu-jáw 'nǐ shwō. *or* wǒ 'jr̄-daw wǒ 'wǎn-le, 'nǐ jyèw

byé 'shwō-le! *or* nǐ kě byé 'shwō wǒ 'láy-de tày 'wǎn-le. ‖Don't tell me I'm too late! *(That can't be!)* mwò-'fēy wǒ 'jēn 'wǎn-le-ma?
Tell the truth shwō shŕ-'hwà. ‖Are you telling the truth? nǐ-shr̀ shwō shŕ-'hwà-ne-ma?
(To know) 'jr̄-dàw. ‖You never can tell what he's going to do next. nǐ 'tsúng-láy jyèw méy-'fár 'jr̄-dàw tā yàw 'gàn shéme.
Tell the difference between 'fēn-chū-láy, 'shwō-chū-láy, 'chyáw-chū-láy. ‖I can't tell the difference between these two materials. wǒ 'fēn-bu-chu-láy (*or* 'shwō-bu-chu-láy *or* 'chyáw-bu-chu-láy) jèy-lyǎng-jǔng-'tsáy-lyàwr yěw shéme-bù-yí-'yàng-de. ‖Even if you'd seen them up close, you couldn't have told them apart. nǐ jyèw-shr jàn-dzay tā-men-gēn-'chyǎr yě 'fēn-bu-chu-láy ta-men. ‖How do you tell one from another? *is expressed as* What's your method of distinguishing? nǐ dzěm 'fēn-fǎr?
Be able to tell time rèn-shr 'jūng. ‖Can your little boy tell time? nǐ-de-shyǎw-'hár rèn-shr 'jūng-le-ma?
Tell *someone* off mà . . . yí-dwèn, 'jyàw-shywun . . . yí-dwèn, 'shwō . . . yí-dwèn. ‖I'm going to tell him off one of these days. 'něy-tyān wǒ fěy-děy hǎw-'hǎwr-de 'mà-ta yí-dwèn.
‖I told you so! wǒ 'dzǎw jyèw gēn-ni 'shwō-gwo! *or* nǐ bù-'tīng °'hǎw-rén 'yán! *or* °'lǎw-rén 'yán!

TEMPERATURE. *(Of a person)* rè-dù, 'tǐ-wēn; *(of a person or the weather)* 'wēn-dù. ‖What's the temperature today? jīn-tyan-de-'wēn-dù shr̀ dwō-shaw? *or* 'jyēr dwō-shaw-'dù? ‖She's been running a high temperature for three days now. 'jèy-sān-tyān tā-de-'rè-dù hěn 'gāw.
To run a temperature fā-'shāw; to run a high temperature fā 'dà-shāw.
To take a temperature shr̀-'byǎw, shr̀ 'rè-dù, shr̀ 'tǐ-wēn, shr̀ 'wēn-dù. ‖You'd better have the nurse take your temperature. nǐ ràng 'kān-hu °'shr̀-shr nǐ-de-'rè-dù-ba. *or* °gěy-ni 'shr̀-shr 'byǎw-ba.

TEN. shŕ. The tenth dì-'shŕ; one tenth 'shŕ-fēn-jr-'yī.

TERM. *(In office)* rèn. ‖Do you think he deserves another term in office? nǐ 'jywé-de tā °gèw (*or* °pèy) 'dz-gé 'dzày dzwò °yí-'rèn-ma? *or* °'lyán-'rèn-ma?
(In school) shywé-'chī, jì. ‖When does the new term at school begin? shywé-'shyàw 'shyà-°'yì-shywé-'chī (*or* °'yí-'jì) 'shéme-shŕ-hew 'kāy-shr̀?
Terms *(conditions)* 'tyáw-jyàn. ‖What are your terms on this automobile? nǐ chū-'mày jèy-lyàng-'chē dēw yěw shéme-'tyáw-jyàn? ‖I think my terms are pretty fair. wǒ 'jywé-de wǒ-de-tyáw-jyàn hěn hé-'lǐ.
(Technical name) *rephrased with* jyàw *is called.* ‖Do you know the term for this part of the machine? nǐ 'jr̄-dàw 'jī-chi-de-'jèy-yí-'bù-fen jyàw 'shéme-ma?
To speak of *someone* in flattering terms 'fèng-cheng, pěng. ‖People are always speaking of him in flattering terms. dà-'jyā lǎw ày 'fèng-cheng ta.

Not be on speaking terms lyán shwō-'hwà děw bù-'shwō-le. ‖We're not even on speaking terms now. wǒm shyàn-dzày lyán shwō-'hwà děw bù-'shwō-le.

Be on good terms with. ‖I've been on very good terms with that man up until lately. wǒ 'jř dàw dzwèy-'jìn gēn 'nèy-ge-rén °'wéy-chŕ-je hěn-hǎw-de-'gwān-shì láy-je. or °'hwèn-de tǐng 'hǎw láy-je.

Bring someone to terms gēn . . . hé-'jyě. ‖Can we bring him to terms, or will we have to go to court? dzám 'shř-bu-shř néng gēn-ta hé-'jyě, háy-shr děy gēn-ta dǎ 'gwān-sz?

(Be called). ‖He is what might be termed a wealthy man. tā dà-'gày °ké-yi 'swàn-shř yí-ge-'kwò-rén. or °ké-yi 'shwō shr yí-ge-'kwò-rén.

TERRIBLE. 'lì-hày, dà, added to intensify the unpleasant nature of something already made clear by other words. ‖Wasn't that a terrible storm last night? dzwór-'yè-li nèy-jèn-bàw-fēng-'ywú 'shř-bu-shř gèw °'lì-hay-de? or °'dà-de? ‖I've got a terrible cold. wǒ jāw-'lyáng jāw-de hěn 'lì-hay.

‖Gee! That's terrible! 'āy-ya! 'nà kě bù-'hǎw.

‖We had a terrible time at their party. wǒm dzày tām-nèr-'wár-de yì-dyǎr yě méy 'yì-sz.

TEST. (Chemically or medically) yàn, hwà-'yàn. ‖I think we'd better test this water before we drink it. wǒ shyǎng 'dǐng hǎw wǒm 'shyān bǎ-'shwéy °'yàn-yàn (or °'hwà yàn) dzày 'hē.

(Physically, mechanically) jyǎn-'yàn, jyǎn-'chá; very general shř. ‖Take the machine back to the shop and have it tested. bǎ 'jī-chì ná-hwéy 'chǎng-li chywù °'shř-yi-shř. or °'jyǎn-'yàn-jyǎn-yàn. or °'jyǎn-'chá.

(Examine a person) kǎw. ‖That teacher gives hard tests. 'nèy-wèy-jyàw-'ywán 'kǎw-de hěn 'nán. ‖You'll have to take a test before you can get your driver's license. nǐ děy 'kǎw yí-shyàr 'tsáy néng ná-je kāy-chē-'jèng.

‖His music will stand the test of time. is expressed as His music certainly isn't capable of being popular for a short while and then being done for. tā de-yīn-'ywè jywé bú-'hwèy húng yí-'jèr jyèw 'wán-le.

THAN. bǐ. ‖Have you something better than this? nǐ yěw bǐ-jèy-ge-'hǎw-dyǎr-de-ma? ‖Can't you work any faster than that? nǐ 'bù-néng dzwò-de bǐ 'nèy-ge dzày 'kwày-dyǎr-ma? ‖He's a foot taller than you. 'tā bǐ-'nǐ yěw yì-chř-'gāw.

Other than . . . , something else than . . . (except). chú-le . . . (yǐ-'wày). ‖We have no dictionary other than an out-dated one. wǒm-jer 'chú-le běr-lǎw-'dž-dyǎn yǐ-'wāy méy-yěw dž-'dyǎn-le. ‖Can't you think of something else than going to the movies? nán-daw-shwō 'chú-le kàn-dyàn-'yěngr nǐ jyèw yěw byé-de-'shèr láy 'gàn-de ma?

‖I'd rather stay home than go to that dull play. is expressed as I much prefer staying home and also don't want to go to that dull play. wǒ chíng-'ywàn dzày 'jyā-li dāy-je, yě bù-'shyǎng chywù kàn nèy-ge-wú-'wèy-de-'shì.

THANK. shyè. ‖Let's send her a letter of thanks. dzám shyè fēng-'shìn 'shyè-shye tā. ‖He thanked me profusely before he left. tā gēn wǒ 'shyè-ie-yèw-shyè tsáy 'dzěw-de. or tā 'chyàn-shyè-wàn-shyè-de 'dzěw-de. ‖Give thanks only where they're due. 'gāy-shyè-de dzày 'shyè. or 'bù-gāy-shyè-de jyèw 'byé shyè.

‖Thanks. or Thank you. 'shyè-shye. or dwō-'shyè. or fèy-'shīn (fèy-shīn). or (for something not yet done, such as a future favor) láw-'jyà láw-jyà. ‖Many thanks. dwō-'shyè (dwō-shyè). or tày fèy-'shīn-le. or 'jēn-shr fèy-'shīn-le. ‖Thanks for the idea. jèy-ge 'yì-sz hěn 'hǎw, dwō 'shyè. ‖Thanks for coming. 'máfan nǐ 'pǎw-ie yí-tàng. or láw-'bù, láw-'bù. ‖Thanks for the flowers. jēn fèy-'shīn-le, háy sùng-'hwäer-lay.

‖No, thanks. (1) (for a thing offered) (cordial) dwō-'shyè, (wǒ) bú-yàw. or (abrupt) bú-'yàw. (2) (for more of something) (dwō-'shyè,) bú-'yàw-le. or 'gèw-le gèw-le. (3) (for a service, as offered by a host) dwō-'shyè, bú-yùng fèy-'shīn-le. or tày 'kè-chi-le, bù-gǎn-'dāng. or (to a servant) 'bú-yùng-le. (4) (for further service offered) bú-yùng dzày fèy-'shīn-le. ‖No, thanks! (sarcastic) hāw-me, 'nà kě bù-'shíng. or wǒ kě bú-'gàn.

‖Thanks to you, I didn't get my furlough. 'dēw-shr 'nǐ-de 'dé-jèng, (or 'dēw-shr 'nǐ-de 'gūng-law,) jyàw-wo méy-gàw-shya-'jyà-lay.

Thanks to 'kwēy-le yěw . . . bāng-'máng, shìng-kwēy yěw . . . bāng-'máng. ‖Thanks to him I was able to get my trunks all right. kwēy-le yěw-'tā bāng-'máng, wǒ tsáy bǎ wǒ-de-'shyāng-dz ná-dàw 'shěw.

‖I have only myself to thank for this mess. 'shi ching dàw 'jèy-jǔng-'dì-bu chywán 'ywàn wǒ-dz-jǐ-'gěr.

THAT (THOSE). (See also THIS.) Not followed by a noun, referring to something made clear by context, that is nèy or nèy-ge or nèy plus some specific measure, except that nèy (alone) occurs only in the first part of the sentence, never after a verb. ‖That's what I want. wǒ-yàw-de shř 'nèy-ge. ‖What does that mean? 'nèy-shř shéme-'yì-sz? ‖How about THAT? 'nèy-ge dzěm-'yàng? ‖How ABOUT that? dzěm-'yàng? ‖That's the book I've been looking for. 'nèy jèng-shř wǒ-'shyǎng-yàw-de-nèy-běr-'shū. ‖I don't see why you have to do that before dinner. wǒ jyèw bù-'míng-bay nǐ 'wèy-shéme děy dzày chř-'fàn-yǐ-'chyán dzwò 'nèy-ge. ‖Give me some of those. gěy-wo dyǎr-'nèy-ge.

Followed by a noun, nèy plus a measure. ‖Who are those people you were talking to? nǐ-gāng-gēn-'tām-shwō-'hwàr-de-'nèy-shyē-rén děw shř-'shéy? ‖Those children are making too much noise! nèy-shyē-'háy-dz tày 'chǎw-le! ‖Just look at that magnificent view, will you! nǐ 'chyáw-chyaw nèy-pyàn-jīng-'jř!

Followed by an adjective, nè-me or nème or nèm. ‖I didn't know the dress was that expensive. wǒ bù-jř-'dàw jèy-jyàn-'yī-fu yěw 'nèm-gwèy. ‖Is it THAT far to your house? dàw nǐ-'jyā yěw 'nème-ywǎn-ma? ‖I don't want that much milk. wǒ bú-'yàw nème-'dwō-de-nyéw-'nǎy.

That way nè-me, nème, nèm. ‖I just can't see it that way. wǒ jyèw-shr bù-néng nèm 'kàn.

That *is sometimes omitted.* ‖How do you know THAT? 'nèy-ge nǐ dzěme 'jř-daw-de? *But* ‖How do you KNOW that? nǐ 'dzěme néng 'jř-dàw-ne?

That *connecting an English noun with a following clause which modifies the noun is not expressed in Chinese; the modifying clause comes before the noun with* de *inserted, or the sentence is otherwise rephrased.* ‖What was that you said a minute ago? nǐ-gāng-tsáy-'shwō-de shř shéme? ‖Show me the best box of candy that you have. gěy-wo 'chyáw-chyáw nǐ-men-dzwèy-'hǎw-de-nèy-héer-'táng. ‖When was the last time that I saw you? wǒ-'shàng-yí-tsz̀ shř 'shéme-shř-hew 'kàn-jyàn ni-de? ‖Have you read the book that everybody's talking about? nǐ 'kàn-gwo dà-'jyā-hwǒr-jř-'shwō-de-nèy-běr-'shū-le-ma? ‖Who's the man that just came in? gāng-'jìn-lay-de-nèy-ge-rén shř-'shéy? ‖Can we find anybody that knows this town? dzám néng 'jǎw-je 'shéw-shi-dì-'myàr-de-'nèm-yí-ge-rén-ma? ‖Let's meet at the same place (that) we met last night. dzám dzày dzwór-'wǎn-shang-jyàn-'myàr-de-nèy-ge-'dì-fang jyàn, hǎw-le.

That *connecting a verb or an adjective* (to hope that, to think that, to be sorry that, etc.) *with a following clause is not expressed in Chinese.* ‖We always knew that he couldn't be trusted. wǒm yí-'shyàng jyèw 'jř-dàw 'tā-nèy-ge-rén bù-kě-'kàw.

So that hǎw. ‖Let's finish this story so that we can start on something else tomorrow. dzám bǎ 'jèy-dwàr-'gù-shr shyě-'wán-le-ba, 'myéngr-ge hǎw shyě 'byé-de.

Not that I care. ‖They've bought a bigger house than ours; not that I care. chí-shř wǒ 'bìng bú-'dzày-hu, bú-gwò tām 'mǎy-le yì-swǒr-'fáng-dz bǐ 'dzám-de 'dà.

THE. *For showing degrees of definiteness English has the choice between* the, this, that, *or no special expression; Chinese has only the last three* (jèy *plus a measure for* this, nèy *plus a measure for* that, *or no special expression*). *Cases which in English have the require in Chinese* jèy, nèy, *or the is often not expressed.* ‖I've been trying to find the hotel all day. wǒ 'jǎw °nèy-ge- (*or* °jèy-ge-)lywǔ-'gwǎn 'jǎw-le yì-'tyān-le. ‖Do you know who runs the store? nǐ 'rèn-shr kāy-°jèy-ge- (*or* °nèy-ge-)'pù-dz-de-rén-ma? ‖Haven't you heard the President speak? nǐ 'tsúng-láy méy-'tīng-jyan-gwo dà-dzǔng-'tǔng yǎn-'jyǎng-ma? ‖The sky is cloudy today. 'jyěr yīn-'tyān.

The (*stressed for emphasis on exclusiveness*), *rephrased in Chinese with* jèng just, just exactly, precisely. ‖He's THE man for the job. tā 'jèng-shř dzwò-nèy-jyàn-'shř-de-rén.

The . . . the . . . ywè . . . ywè . . . . ‖The sooner we get paid, the better. ywè 'dzǎw gěy-wom 'chyán ywè 'hǎw. ‖The cooler it is, the better I can work. wǒ-shř ywè 'lyáng-kway 'dzwò-de ywè 'hǎw. *or* 'tyār ywè 'lyáng-kway, wǒ-'dzwò-de ywè 'hǎw.

The more the . . . ywè 'láy ywè . . . .

THEATER. (*Drama*) shì; (*place for presenting dramas*) shì-'ywán(-dz); (*place for presenting movies*) dyàn-yǐng-'ywàn; to attend the theater kàn-'shì *or* tīng-'shì; theater tickets shì-'pyàw(-dz). ‖Do you like the theater? nǐ 'shì-hwan °kàn- (*or* °tīng) 'shì-ma? ‖Do you like this theater? nǐ 'shì-hwan jèy-ge-shì-'ywán-dz-ma? ‖When does the theater open? shì-'ywán-dz 'shéme-shř-hew 'kāy? ‖Do you have the theater tickets? shì-'pyàw shř nǐ 'ná-je-ne-ma?

THEIR, THEIRS. *See* THEY.

THEM. *See* THEY.

THEN. (*At that time*) 'nèy-ge-shř-hew. ‖I ought to know by then. 'nèy-ge-shř-hew wǒ dà-'gày jyèw ké-yi 'jř-dàw-le.

(*Afterwards, next*) yǐ-'hèw, 'hèw-láy. ‖What do I do then? yǐ-'hèw wǒ 'yěw gāy 'dzěm-yàng-ne? ‖Then what happened? 'hèw-láy-ne? *or* yǐ-'hèw dzěm-'yàng-le? *or* 'hèw-láy 'yěw dzěme-le?

(*Also, in addition*) háy. ‖Then there's the trunk; we must have it taken down to the basement. háy yěw nèy-ge-'shyāng-dz; dzám dzǔng děy ná-daw dì-'yìn-dz-li chywù.

(*In that case*) nà(-me)(-je). ‖Then we can forget all about it. 'nème-je 'bú-yùng gwǎn jèy-ge-'shř.

(*In the light of what you have said*) 'jèm shwō. ‖Then you didn't expect me today? 'jèm shwō nǐ méy-'shyǎng-dàw wǒ 'jyēr-ge hwèy 'láy?

Well then 'hǎw-le. ‖Well then, let's eat. 'hǎw-le; dzám jyèw 'chř-ba.

Now and then 'yěw(-de)-shř-hew, ěw-'ěr. ‖We go to the movies now and then. wǒm 'yěw-shř-hew chywù kàn dyàn-'yěngr. ‖Oh, we see them every now and then. wǒm ěw-'ěr 'kàn-jyàn tam yí-tsz̀.

Then and there jyèw, dāng-'shř jyèw, lì-'kè jyèw. ‖I knew then and there that it was the house to buy. wǒ lì-'kè jyèw kàn 'jùng-le 'nèy-swǒr-fáng-dz-le.

THERE. (*That place*) nàr, nèr, 'nà-li, nèy-ge-'dì-fang. ‖I've never been there. wǒ méy-'dàw-gwo nèr. ‖I was through there yesterday, and the roads are still closed. wǒ 'dzwór 'tsúng-nèr 'gwò de-shř-hew 'lù háy méy-'tūng-ne. ‖Can you get there by car? dzwò-'chē chywù dàw-de-'lyǎw nèr-ma? ‖How did you get over there? nǐ 'dzěme chywù-de 'nèr?

(*In that respect, concerning that point* nèy, 'nèy-ge-dì-fang (*or, with reference to something which has just been said,* 'jèy-ge-dì-fang). ‖You're wrong there! 'nèy nǐ kě bú-'dwèy! *or* 'jèy-ge-dì-fang nǐ kě 'tswò-le!

(*Exclamation; of consolation*) ày; (*of, surprise or anger*) nǐ 'kàn. ‖There, I vouldn't worry so much. 'ày, 'wǒ yàw-shr 'nǐ- 'jywé bú 'nème fă-'chéw. ‖There, now you've done it! nǐ 'kan, nǐ jè bú-shr 'dzwò-chu-lay-le-ma?

Here and there jǐ-'chùr, jǐ-ge-'dì-fang, yěw-de-'dì-fang. ‖Here and there in his book he's got some good ideas. tā nèy-běr-'shū yěw jǐ-'chùr 'shvě-de 'háy swàn bú-tswò.

‖There you are! *meaning* Take a look. nǐ 'kàn! *or meaning* It works! 'shíng-le! *or meaning* It's finished! *or* It's ready! 'dé-le!

Not all there yěw yì-dyǎr °bàn-'fēngr *or* °shǎ. ‖Don't be surprised at the way he acts; he's not all there. nǐ kàn tā-'nèy-ge jyèr byé 'jywé-je chí-'gwày; tā yěw dyǎr-'shǎ.

There is, there are, there were, there was, *with unstressed* there *and the subject following*, yěw. ‖There are few good hotels in town. 'chéng-li méy-yěw 'jǐ-ge-hǎw-lywǔ-'gwǎn. ‖Áre there any vacancies? yěw kūng-'fáng-ma?

THEREFORE. 'swǒ-yǐ. (*See also* SO.) ‖A equals B and B equals C; therefore A equals C. yīn-wèy 'ēy děng-ywu 'bì, 'bì děng-ywu 'shī, 'swǒ-yǐ 'ēy děng-ywu 'shī.

THEY (THEIR, THEIRS, THEM). (*Referring to some definite group of people*) tā-men, tām. ‖Can they stay with us over the weekend? tām 'néng gēn-wom gwò yí-ge-shīng-chī-'wěy-ma? ‖Are they the people you told me about? 'tā-men jyèw-shr nǐ-gēn-wo-'tí-gwo-de-'nèy-shyē-rén-ma? ‖Do you know their address? nǐ 'jŕ-daw tām-de-jù-'jŕ-ma? ‖Are you a friend of theirs? nǐ 'rèn-shr tam-ma? *or* nǐ-shř tā-men-de-'péng-yew-ma?

(*Referring to people in general*) rén. ‖Well, you know what they say. 'ày, 'rén bú-shr cháng 'shwō-ma? ‖They say he's very good. yěw rén 'shwō tā hěn 'hǎw.

(*Referring to persons unknown*). ‖They give concerts here in the summer. 'shyà-tyār-de-shŕ-hew dzày-'jèr yǎn-'dzèw. ‖When do they open the dining room? fàn-'tīng 'shéme-shŕ-hew 'kāy?

(*Referring to things*). *Often omitted, but* jèy-shyē, nèy-shyē, dēw, chywán, *etc. are sometimes used.* ‖Put them on the table. dēw gē-dzày 'jwō-dz-shang.

Themselves. *See* SELF.

THICK. (*In dimension*) hèw. ‖I need a piece of wood about three inches thick. wǒ yàw yí-kwày-'sān-tswèn-'hèw-de-'mù-tew. ‖I want a thick steak. wǒ yàw yí-kwày-hèw-'hēwr-de-rèw-'páy. ‖Is the ice thick enough for skating? jèr-de-'bīng dùng-de 'hèw-de néng 'lyēw-le-ma?

(*In consistency*) chéw, nǔng. ‖I don't like such thick soup. wǒ bù-'shŕ-hwan jème-°'chéw- (*or* °'núng-)de-'tāng.

(*In distribution or density*) yèw 'dwō yèw 'shēn. ‖The weeds are too thick for walking here. jèr-de-'tsǎw yèw 'dwō yèw 'shēn, bù-néng 'dzěw.

(*Of fog*) dà. ‖The fog is getting thick. 'wù ywè 'láy ywè 'dà.

(*Of an accent*) 'lì-hay, jùng. ‖He has a very thick accent. tā-de-wày-gwo-'kěw-yīn hěn °'lì-hay. *or* °'jùng.

Be thick-headed bèn. ‖Can't I get this through your thick head? nǐ 'dzěme jème-'bèn-na, wǒ méy-'fár gēn-ni 'shwō-le.

Through thick and thin. yěw 'hwàn-nàn-de-shŕ-hew. ‖He stuck by us through thick and thin. wǒm yěw 'hwàn-nàn-de-shŕ-hew, tā 'jēn gèw 'péng-yew.

Thick and fast. ‖It's raining thick and fast. 'ywǔ 'shyà-de gèw °'dà-de. *or* °'lì-hay-de.

THIEF. dzéy, shyǎw-'tēwr, 'shyáw-li, tēw-'dūng-shi-de ‖Have they found the thief yet? tām °'jǎw-jáw (*or* °'dēy-jáw *or* °'jwā-jáw) nèy-ge-tēw-'dūng-shi-de-le-ma?

THIN. (*In dimension*) báw. ‖This book is thin enough to slip into your pocket. jèy-běr-'shū 'báw-de kě-yi fàng-dzay 'dēwr-li-tew. ‖The walls of my room are too thin to keep out the noise. wǒ-'wūr-li-de-'chyáng tày 'báw, 'páng-byar °shéme-'shēng-yīn dēw tīng-de-'jyàn. *or* °shéme-'shēngr yě gé-bu-'jù. ‖Cut the bread thin. bǎ myàn-'bāw chyē-'báw yì-dyǎr.

(*Distribution or density*) shī, shǎw. ‖The grass is rather thin this year. jīn-nyan-de-'tsǎw tǐng 'shī. ‖My hair is thinning. wǒ-'téw-fa °ywè 'láy ywè 'shǎw. *or* ·(*Falling out*) °jŕ 'dyàw. *or* °'twō-de hěn 'lì-hay.

(*Lacking fatty tissue*) shèw. ‖You're too thin; you ought to eat more. nǐ tày 'shèw; yīng-dang dwō 'chŕ-dyǎr. ‖I was shocked to see how thin he'd gotten. wǒ 'chyáw-jyàn tā 'shèw-chéng 'nà-yàngr-le shyà-le yí-'tyàw.

(*Of consistency*) shī. ‖This soup is too thin. jèy-ge-'tāng tày 'shī-le.

(*Of a sound or the voice*) shyǎw. ‖His voice was so thin we could hardly hear him. tā-'shēng-yīn 'shyǎw-de wǒ-men jyǎn-'jŕ tīng-bu-'jyàn ta.

That's a pretty thin excuse. jèy-ge-lǐ-'yéw °bù-chūng-'dzú. *or* °bù-dzème-'yàng.

To thin out (*of a crowd*) dzěw-'jìng-le, dzěw-'wán-le, dzěw-'sàn-le. ‖Let's wait until the crowd thins out. dzám 'děng rén °'dzěw-'jìng-le (*or* °'dzěw-'wán-le *or* °'dzěw-'sàn-le) 'dzày shwō-ba.

To thin out (*growing things*) bá-chū jǐ-ge chywù. ‖We'll have to thin out these carrots. jèy-shyē-hú-'lwó-ba jùng-de tày 'mì-le, dzám děy 'bá-chu 'jǐ-gēr-chywu.

THING. (*Indefinite material objects*) 'dūng-shi; *if context defines what type of thing is meant the Chinese may have a more specific word.* ‖What are those things you're carrying? nǐ-'ná-de-nèy-shyē shŕ shéme 'dūng-shi? ‖I've got to go now; did you see where I put my things? wǒ děy 'dzěw₁le; nǐ 'kàn-jyàn wǒ bǎ wǒ-de-'dūng-shi gē-dzay 'năr-le-ma? ‖Have you packed all your things yet? nǐ-de-'dūng-shi (*or your baggage* nǐ-de-'shíng-li) dēw jwāng-'hǎw-le-ma?

(*Indefinite non-material entities*) shr̀, shèr. ‖There've been some funny things going on in that house. tām-'jyā 'jìn-láy jìng-shr lí-'chí gǔ-'gwày-de-shèr. ‖That job's the very thing I want. nèy-jyàn-'chāy-shr̀ 'jèng-shr̀ wǒ-shyǎng-'dzwò-de.

Not a thing (*intensifying the negative*) 'shéme yě bū-, 'shéme yě méy-, yì-'dyǎr-. . . yě °bū- *or* °méy-. ‖I can't see a thing from my seat. wǒ dzwò-dzay 'jèr 'shéme yě chyáw-bu-'jyàn. ‖We haven't done a thing all week. wǒm yí-ge-lǐ-'bày 'shéme yě méy-'gàn. ‖I can't think of a thing. wǒ 'yì-dyǎr-jú-'yì yě 'méy-yew. ‖There's not a thing wrong with me. wǒ shéme-'máw-bìng yě 'méy-yew.

A thing or two. ‖He certainly knows a thing or two about business. yàw shwō dzwò 'mǎy-may 'tā kě 'jēn yěw lyǎng-'shyà-dz.

Poor thing (*person*). ‖When her parents died, the poor thing didn't know what to do. tā-'fù₁mǔ 'gwò-chywu yǐ-'hèw, nèy-ge-kě-lyán-'chúng bù-'jř-dàw 'dzěme-je 'hǎw-le. ‖You poor thing! nǐ 'tày kě-'lyán-le! *or* nǐ 'tày 'tsàn-le! *or* nǐ 'jèy kě-lyán-'jyèr-de!

Of all things jēn chí-'gwày, 'jēn-shr̀ méy-'yěngr-de-'shr̀. ‖Well, of all things, what are you doing here? 'jēn-shr̀ méy-'yěngr-de-'shr̀, nǐ dzày-'jèr gàn-'má-ne?

To see things (*have hallucinations*) 'hú-li-hu-'dū-de, dzěw-'shér, 'hú-sz̀ lwàn-'shyǎng, shyǎng-'rù 'fēy₁fēy. ‖I think you've been seeing things ever since that accident. wǒ 'jywé-de nǐ 'dž-tsúng nèy-tsz̀-chū-'shèr yǐ-'hèw 'cháng yěw-de-'shŕ-hew 'hú-li-hu-'dū-de.

Many English sentences with thing *correspond to Chinese sentences with no equivalent whatsoever. Some typical examples follow.* ‖We've heard a lot of nice things about you. wǒm 'tīng-jyàn bù-'shǎwrén °shwō nǐ 'hǎw. *or* °'kwā-ni. ‖How are things? dzěm-'yàng? ‖Things are pretty tough these days. 'jèy-nyán-téwr gèw 'shyèw-de. ‖Let's sit down and talk things over. dzám 'dzwò-shyà hǎw-'hǎwr de 'tántán. ‖She says she's in love, and I think it's the real thing. tā shwō tā 'ày-shàng-le yí-ge-'rén, 'wǒ-shyǎng 'jèy-hwéy °shr̀ 'jēn-de. *or* °'dà-'gày 'chéng-le. ‖They've certainly made a good thing of that shop. tām nèy-ge-'pù-dz 'mǎy-mày 'dzwò-de kě 'jēn bú-'tswò.

THINK (THOUGHT). (*To use one's brains well*) yùng 'nǎw-dz. ‖He's never really learned how to think. tā 'tsúng-láy jyèw bù-jř-'dàw 'dzěme yùng 'nǎw-dz.

To think (*that or so or not*) shyǎng, 'shyǎng-dàw, 'yǐ-wéy, 'jywé-de, shyǎng-'shìn, kàn. ‖I think so. wǒ shyǎng 'shr̀. *or* wǒ shyǎng 'shr̀ nèy-yàngr. ‖I thought so. . . wǒ 'shyǎng jyèw-shr̀ 'nèy-yàngr. *or* gēn wǒ-'shyǎng-de yí-'yàngr. ‖I didn't think you'd come. wǒ méy-'shyǎng-dàw nǐ hwèy 'láy. *or* wǒ 'shyǎng nǐ bù-'láy-le-ne. *or* wǒ 'yǐ-wéy nǐ bù-'láy-le-ne. ‖I think

you're all wrong on that. wǒ °'jywé-de (*or* shyǎng-'shìn) nǐ wán-'chywán bú-'dwèy. *or* wǒ jywé-de nǐ-'shwō-de 'háw-wú-dàw-'lǐ. ‖I think I'll go now. wǒ 'kàn wǒ shyàn-dzày 'dzěw-ba. ‖I thought you weren't coming along! wǒ 'yǐ-wèy nǐ 'bù-gēn wǒ-men yí-kwàr 'chywù-ne.

To think about shyǎng. ‖Why don't you think about it for a while before you make up your mind? nǐ 'wèy-shéme bù 'shyān 'shyǎng-shyǎng 'dzày dǎ jú-'yì? ‖What're you thinking about? nǐ shyǎng 'shéme-ne?

To think *something* over 'shyǎng-(yi-)shyǎng, kǎw-'lywù. ‖I'll have to think it over. wǒ děy (dwō) °'shyǎng-shyǎng. *or* 'kǎw-'lywù-kǎw-lywù.

To think *something* up (*fictitious*) 'dzēw- (*or* 'byān-)chu-lay; (*worthwhile*) 'shyǎng- (*or* 'dzwó-me-)chu-lay. ‖Who thought this up? 'jèy-ge shr̀-'shéy °'shyǎng-chu-lay-de? *or* °'dzēw-chu-lay-de? ‖You'd better think up a good excuse for being late. nǐ láy 'wǎn-le, chèn-dzǎwr °'dzēw- (*or* °'dzwó-me- *or* °'shyǎng- *or* °'byān-)chu ge-'lǐ-yéw-lay.

To think of (*remember, recall*) 'shyǎng-chǐ-láy. ‖I can't think of his address. wǒ 'shyǎng-bu-chǐ-'láy tā jù-'năr. ‖Can you think of that man's name? nǐ 'shyǎng-de-chǐ-'láy nèy-ge-rén-de-'míng-dz-ma?

To think *what* of kàn, 'jywé-de, shwō. ‖What do you think of going to the movies tonight? dzám jyēr-'wǎn-shang chywù kàn ge-dyàn-'yěngr, nǐ shwō dzěme-'yàng? ‖What do you think of that guy? nǐ °'kàn (*or* °'jywé-de *or* °'shwō), 'nèy₁ge-'rén (*or* °'jyā-hwo *or* °'shyǎw-dz) dzěme-'yàng?

To be well thought of. ‖He's well thought of, don't you think? nǐ 'shr̀-bu-shr̀ 'jywé-de dà-'jyā-hwǒr dēw shyāng-'dāng-de 'dày-jìng ta.

To think twice. ‖I'd think twice about that if I were you. wǒ yàw-shr 'nǐ, wǒ yí-'dìng dzày-'sān-de 'shyǎng-shyǎng.

To think better of. ‖You're taking a big chance, and I'd think better of it if I were you. nǐ yěw dyǎr tày màw-'shyǎn-le, 'wǒ yàw-shr 'nǐ wǒ yí-'dìng hǎw-'hāwr-de 'shyǎng-shyǎng. ‖We think better of him since we've learned the facts. wǒm yì 'míng-bay shr̀ 'dzěme-hwéy-'shr̀ yǐ-'hèw, dwèy-ta 'yìn-shyàng hǎw 'dwō-le.

‖Think nothing of it! 'năr-de-'hwà! *or* méy 'gwānshi! *or* shyǎw-'yì-sz! *or* (*In response to an apology*) byé 'kè-chi!

THIRD. The third dì-'sān; one third 'sān-fēn-jr-'yī.

THIRSTY. kě. ‖I'm very thirsty wǒ kě 'jí-le. ‖This salty food makes me thirsty. chr̀ jèy-ge-'shyán-de-dūng-shi jyàw wo dzwěy 'kě.

THIRTEEN. shŕ-'sān. The thirteenth dì-shŕ-'sān; one thirteenth shŕ-'sān-fēn-jr-'yī.

THIRTY. 'sān-shŕ. The thirtieth dì-'sān-shŕ; one thirtieth 'sān-shr-fēn-jr-'yī.

THIS (THESE). (See also **THAT.**) Not followed by a noun, referring to something made clear by context, this is jèy or jèy-ge or jèy plus some specific measure, except that jêy (alone) occurs only in the first part of the sentence, never after a verb. ‖What's this? 'jèy-shr̀ shéme? ‖This is too much for me! wǒ 'jēn shèw-bu-'lyǎw 'jèy-ge! ‖Is this yours? jèy-shr 'nǐ-de-ma? ‖I'd like a pound of these and half a pound of those. wǒ 'shyǎng láy yí-bàng-'jèy-ge bàn-bàng-'nèy-ge.

Followed by a noun, jèy plus a measure. ‖Do you know this man? nǐ 'rèn-de jèy-ge-'rén-ma? ‖What are we going to do this weekend? dzám jèy-ge-jēw-'mwò gàn-'má? ‖I like this room. wǒ 'shǐ-hwan jèy-jyān-'wū-dz. ‖Have you met all these people? jèy-shyē-'wèy nǐ dēw 'jyàn-gwo-le-ma? ‖Are these bags yours? jèy-shyē-kěw-'dày shr̀ 'nǐ-de-ma? ‖These shoes are too small. jèy-shwāng-'shyé tày 'shyǎw.

Followed by an adjective, jè-me or jème or jèm. ‖I can't eat this much food. wǒ chr̄-bu-'lyǎw 'jème-dwō-de-dūng-shi. ‖As long as we've come this far, we might as well go on. wǒm jì-'rán 'yǐ-jing dzěw-le jème-'ywǎn-le, háy-shr 'jyē-je dzěw-ba.

This minute lì-'shŕ, 'mǎ-shàng or mǎ-'shàng, gǎn-'jǐn, gwāy-'gwār-de. ‖Come here this minute! meaning don't argue about it any more gwāy-'gwār-de gěy-wo 'gwò-lay!

After this tsúng 'jīn yǐ-'hèw. ‖After this I'll be sure to get to the office on time. tsúng 'jīn yǐ-'hèw wǒ yí-'dìng 'jwěn-shŕ shàng-'bān.

This with certain periods of time requires special terms. This week běn-lǐ-'bày or běn-shīng-'chī; this Tuesday meaning Tuesday of this week 'běn-lǐ-bày-'èr or 'běn-shīng-chī-'èr; this month běn-'ywè; this year 'jīn-nyán.

THOROUGH. chè-'dǐ, rèn-'jēn, jèng-'jǐng, shì-'shēn, bù-'má-ma-hu-'hū-de. ‖I'll make a thorough investigation. wǒ yí-'dìng chè-'dǐ-de 'chá yí-shyàr. ‖That fellow is very thorough in everything he does. nèy-ge-'rén bù-'gwǎn dzwò 'shéme dēw hěn °rèn-'jēn. or °chè-'dǐ. or etc.

THOUGH. (But) 'bú-gwò, 'kě-shr, 'dàn-shr. ‖I'll attend, though I may be late. wǒ yí-'dìng 'chywù, °'bú-gwò (or °kě-shr or °dàn-shr) 'yě-shywu děy 'wǎn-yì-dyǎr 'dàw. ‖I think it was his fault, though naturally I'm willing to give him another chance. wǒ 'shyǎw-dé nèy-ge shr̀ tā-dé-'tswòr, dā shr wú-lwèn-rú-'hé wǒ 'ywàn-yi 'dzày gěy-ta yí-ge-'jī-hwèy.

(Even) though 'swéy-rán (or jyèw-shr) . . . °háy-shr or °'yě. ‖I didn't catch my train, though I ran all the way. wǒ 'swéy-rán yí-'lùr 'jīn-je 'pǎw, °háy-shr (or °yě) méy-'gǎn-shàng 'chē. ‖We invited him to our house, even though we don't like him. wǒm 'swéy-rán bù-'shǐ-hwan ta, yě bǎ-ta chǐng dàw 'jyā-li chywù-le. ‖Though I may miss my train, I mean to see you before I go. wǒ jyèw-shr bǎ-'chē dān-wù-le, yě děy dzày méy-'dzěw-yǐ-'chyán 'jyàn-jyan ni.

To seem as though hǎw 'shyàng, 'fǎng-fú. ‖It seems as though I know him. wǒ hǎw °'shyàng (or °'fǎng-fú) 'rèn-shr ta shr̀-de.

To look as though 'chyáw-je (or 'kàn-je) hǎw 'shyàng. ‖It looks as though it may rain. 'chyáw-je hǎw 'shyàng yàw shyà-'ywǔ. ·

THOUGHT. 'gāw-jyàn, 'jyàn-jyě, 'yì-jyàn. ‖Have you any thoughts on the subject? gwān-ywu jèy-gè-'wèn-tí, nǐ yěw shéme-°'gāw-jyàn? or °'jyàn-jyě? or °'yì-jyàn?

Where English uses the noun thought or thoughts Chinese often has a verbal expression such as shyǎng to think. ‖A penny for your thoughts. nǐ shyǎng 'shéme-ne? ‖We'll have to give some thought to this matter. jèy-jyàn-'shèr dzám děy hǎw-'hāwr-de °'shyǎng-shyǎng. or °'yán-jyèw-yán-jyèw, or °kǎw-'lywù-kǎw-lywù. ‖Can't you show a little thought for others? nǐ nán-'dàw jyèw 'bù-néng tì 'byé-rén 'shyǎng-shyǎng-ma? or mwò-'fēy nǐ jyèw bù-'jī-dàw 'gù-je dyǎr 'byé-rén-ma?

THOUSAND. chyān. The thousandth dì-yì-'chyān; one thousandth 'chyān-fēn-jr-'yī; ten thousand wàn; the ten thousandth dì-yí-'wàn; one ten-thousandth 'wàn-fēn-jr-'yī.

THREE. sān; sā (equals sān plus a measure).

THROAT. 'sǎng-dz. ‖I have a sore throat. wǒ 'sǎng-dz téng. or wǒ nàw 'sǎng-dz-ne.

(Figuratively). ‖Every time I see this town, I get a lump in my throat. wǒ yí 'kàn-jyàn jèy-ge-'chéng, °'shīn-li jyèw nán-'shèw? or °'shīn-li jyèw nán-'gwò. or °('shīn-li) jyèw 'dǔ-de hěn. or °jyèw bú-'shèng gǎn-'kǎy. ‖Don't jump down my throat! nǐ 'yùng-bu-jáw gēn-wo °rǎng. or °fā 'pí-chi. ‖He'd cut your throat for a dollar. jàn-le-'chyán, tā jyèw wú-swǒ-bù-'wéy. ‖I tried to apologize, but the words stuck in my throat. wǒ 'běn-láy shyǎng-daw 'chyàn láy-je, kě-shr 'hwà 'méy-néng 'shwō-chu-lay.

THROUGH. (Motion). If attention is centered on a point reached after passing through something, tsúng or dǎ; if attention is centered on the place passed through itself, gwò as postverb with any suitable verb of motion; if one is concerned with the possibility of obstructed passage, tūng to be passable; if specifically passing through a door on one's way in, jìn-'mér. ‖Who's the lady coming through the door? 'jèng-jìn-'mér-de-nèy-wèy-'fù-rén shr̀-'shéy? ‖The rock went through the window. 'shŕ-tew 'chwān-gwò 'chwǎng-hu chywù-le. ‖Can you get through this street? jèy-tyáw-'jyē °dzěw-de-'gwò-chywù-ma? or °'tūng-ma? ‖Which door did he come in through? tā °tsúng (or °dǎ) 'něy-ge-mér 'jìn-lay-de?

With lines of sight, routes, etc., where motion is not present but only theoretically possible, the same terms are used. ‖He looked out through the window. tā tsúng 'chwǎng-hu 'wàng-wày 'kàn.

But sometimes **through** *need not be expressed.* ‖**Can you see it through this fog?** *is expressed as* **In this fog can you see?** dzày 'wù-li nǐ kàn-de-'jyàn-ma? ‖**I can't see anything through this window pane.** *is expressed as* **With this window pane obstructing (the view) I can't see anything.** wǒ °'jyē-je jèy-kwày-'bwō-li (*or* °'gé-je jèy-kwày-'bwō-li *or* °yěw jèy-kwày-'bwō-li dǎng-je) 'shéme dēw kàn-bu-'jyàn.

Through *meaning* **reason** *is expressed with* 'yīn-wèy; *if meaning* **because,** *is followed by a suitable verbal expression.* ‖**Through his negligence the work will have to be held up two weeks.** yīn-wey ͺtā nème-yì-'lǎ-hu jèy-jyàn-'gūng-dzwò děy 'dān-wù 'lyǎ-lǐ-'bày. ‖**He got where he is through lots of hard work.** tā 'jř swǒ-yi néng yěw jīn-'tyān shř 'yīn-wèy tā 'tsúng-chyán kěn 'gàn.

(*Finished*) **wán** *as postverb or alone.* ‖**I think I can get through with this book tonight.** wǒ shyǎng wǒ jyēr-'wǎn-shang ké-yi bǎ jèy-běr-'shū kàn-'wán-le. ‖**Are you through so soon?** nǐ jème-'kwày jyèw 'wán-le? ‖**I'll be through work at five o'clock.** wǒ 'wǔ-dyǎn-jūng °wán-'shèr. *or* (*Quit work*) °'shyà-'bān.

Through and through chè-'dǐ, dàw-'jyā. ‖**He knows his business through and through.** tā dwèy-ywu tā-běn-'háng 'jēn-shř 'jř-dàw-de °hěn chè-'dǐ. *or* °dàw-'jyā-le.

Through train tūng-'chē, jř-dá-°'hwǒ-'chē *or* °kè-'chē *or* °kwày-'chē.

Through street *is expressed verbally.* ‖**Is this a through street?** *is expressed as* **Can you get through on this street?** jèy-tyáw-'jyē °dzěw-de-'gwò-chywù-ma? *or* °'tūng-ma? *or as* **This street isn't a blind alley, is it?** jèy-tyáw-'jyē 'bú-shr sž-hú-'tùngr-ba?

Through ticket tūng-'pyàw.

To see through *someone* kàn-'tèw-le. ‖**Everybody can see through that guy.** 'shéy dēw néng bǎ a kàn-'tèw-le.

THROUGHOUT. (*See also* ALL, WHOLE).

‖**This hotel is famous throughout the world.** jèy-ge-lywǔ-'gwǎn °shř 'míng-byàn chywán-'chyéw. *or* °'shř-'jyè yěw-'míng.

THROW (THREW, THROWN). (*Cast, toss, hurl*)

rēng, rěng, pyě. ‖**Let's see how far you can throw this rock.** 'kàn-kàn nǐ néng bǎ jèy-kwày-'shŕ-tew °rēng (*or* °rěng *or* °pyě) dwō-'ywǎn. ‖**That was some throw!** 'nèy-shyàr 'rēng-de jēn °'bú-tswò! *or* °'ywǎn! *or* 'kě-yǐ!

(*Of a horse*) 'shwāy-shyà-láy. ‖**Be careful your horse doesn't throw you.** lyéw-'shén byé jyàw-'mǎ bǎ-ni gěy 'shwāy-shyà-lay.

To throw *a switch.* (*If closing the circuit*) kāy, 'kāy-kay; (*if opening the circuit*) gwān, 'gwān-shàng. ‖**You'll have to throw that switch to get the machine started.** nǐ děy shyān bǎ dyàn-'mén 'kāy-kay, 'jī-chì tsáy néng 'dùng.

To throw *a light in a direction* wàng . . . (*direction*) 'jàw. ‖**Throw that light this way, please.** bǎ nèy-ge-'dēng wàng 'jèy-byar 'jàw.

Throw oneself at *someone* gēn . . . °'byàw *or* °nème 'chīn-rè, 'yéw-je. ‖**Oh, stop throwing yourself at him!** 'ày, byé °'jìng gēn-ta 'byàw-le! *or* °'jìng 'yéw-je ta! *or* °gēn-ta nème 'chīn-rè!

Throw *something* **away** rēng, rěng, dàw. ‖**Throw the rest of my dinner away.** bǎ wǒ-chŕ-'shèng-shyà-de-°'rēng-le-ba. *or* °'rěng-le-ba. *or* °'dàw-le-ba.

Be thrown into disorder nùng-'lwàn-le, 'nùng-de 'lwàn-chi-bā-'dzāw. ‖**Everything was thrown into disorder.** 'dūng-shi chywán °nùng-'lwàn-le. *or* °'nùng-de 'lwàn-chi-bā-'dzāw-le.

Throw a glance at 'dèng (*or* 'chyáw *or* 'kàn) . . . yì-'yǎn. ‖**She threw a glance at us when we came into the room.** wǒm jìn-'wūr de-shŕ-hew tā °'dèng-le (*or* °'chyáw-le *or* °'kàn-le) wom yì-'yǎn.

Throw *something* **in(to).** (*Pack carelessly*) 'sēy-dàw, 'dwēy-dàw. ‖**Throw my things into a bag; I have to catch my train.** bǎ wǒ-de-'dūng-shi °'sēy-dàw (*or* °'dwēy-dàw) jèy-ge-'bāwr-li; wǒ děy 'gǎn hwǒ-'chē.

Throw in (*add, usually casually*) 'dwō láy, 'dzày gěy. ‖**Throw in an extra loaf of bread.** 'dwō láy yì-tyáwr-myàn-'bāw.

Throw off *an infection* bǎ . . . jŕ-'hǎw-le, bǎ . . . 'chywù-le. ‖**I haven't been able to throw off this cold all winter.** wǒ shāng-'fēng shāng-le yì-'dūng-tyar-le, yě méy-néng °'hǎw. *or* °bǎ-'bìng jŕ-'hǎw-le. *or* °bǎ-'bìng 'chywù-le.

Throw on *an outer garment* 'pēy-shàng. ‖**I'll just throw a coat on and go down to the store.** wǒ 'pēy-shang jyàn-dà-'yī chywù 'pù-dz yí-tàng.

Throw *someone* **out** 'hūng-chu-chywu, 'gǎn-chu-chywu. ‖**We'd better pay our rent soon, or they'll throw us out.** dzán gǎn-'jǐn bǎ 'fáng-chyán 'gěy-le-ba, 'yàw-bu-rán fáng-'dūng jyèw yàw bǎ-dzám °'hūng-chu-chywu-le. *or* °'gǎn-chu-chywu-le. ‖**I've been thrown out of better places than this!** *is expressed as* **You don't think I care about this, do you!** 'jè swàn 'shéme! *or other similar expressions.* ‖**Do you think they'll throw my application out?** *is expressed as* **Do you think they'll give me the brush-off?** nǐ kàn tām hwèy 'bǎ-wo 'shwā-shya-lay-ma?

Throw over *plans* jyǎw, gǎy-'byàn. ‖**His illness made us throw over our plans for the summer.** tā yí 'bìng bǎ wǒm-'shyà-tyar-de-'jì-hwà gěy 'jyǎw-le. *or* wǒm yīn-wey tā 'bìng-le jŕ 'hǎw gǎy-'byàn wǒm-shǔ-'jyà-de-'jì-hwà.

Throw *someone* **over** shwā, shwǎy, rēng, rěng, gēn . . . 'chwēy. ‖**I hear she's throwing him over.** wǒ 'tīng-shwō tā yàw bǎ-ta gěy °'shwā-le. *or* °'shwǎy-le. *or* °'rēng-le. *or* °'rěng-le. *or* wǒ 'tīng-shwō tā yàw gēn-ta 'chwēy.

Throw up (*vomit*) tù. ‖**I throw up every time I ride on the train.** wǒ yí dzwò hwǒ-'chē jyèw 'tù.

Throw up (*abandon*) 'gē-shyà, 'tsź, rēng. ‖**Don't 'et her throw up her job.** byé 'ràng-ta bǎ 'shř-ching °'gē-shyà. *or* °'tsź-le. *or* °'rēng-le.

Throw *something* **up to** *someone* 'twēy-gěy. ‖**That's the second time you've thrown it up to me!** nǐ 'dzěme bǎ nèy-ge 'yèw 'twēy-gey wo-le!

THUMB. dà-me-'jř, dàm-'jř, dà-me-'gē, dàm-'gē. ‖**I burned my thumb with a match.** wǒ yùng yáng-'hwǒr bǎ dà-me-'jř 'shāw-le.

THUNDER. To thunder dǎ-'léy. ‖**It's beginning to thunder.** dǎ-'léy-le. ‖**Don't be afraid of thunder.** byé 'pà dǎ-'léy. ‖**Did you hear all that thunder last night?** nǐ dzwór-'wǎn-shang 'tīng-jyan dǎ-'léy-le-ma?

Figuratively, referring to a loud noise or the making thereof, Chinese uses other devices of intensification. ‖**The speaker couldn't be heard above the thunder of applause.** dà-'jyā-hwǒr pāy-'shěw 'pāy-de tày 'shyǎng-le, yǎn-jyǎng-'ywán-'shwō-de shř 'shéme dēw tīng-bu-'jyàn-le. ‖**You shouldn't let him thunder at you like that.** nǐ bù-'yīng-dang ràng-ta 'nème-yéw-je-'shyèngr-de gēn-ni 'rǎng. ‖**The train thundered over the bridge.** hwǒ-'chē tsúng 'chyáw-shang 'jī-dùng-'gūng-dung-de 'gwò-chywù-le.

THURSDAY. lǐ-bày-'sż, shīng-chī-'sż.

TICKET. pyàw, *with particular purpose specified; thus* ticket for a play shì-'pyàw, movie ticket dyàn-yěngr-'pyàw, boat ticket chwán-'pyàw, plane ticket fēy-jī-'pyàw, train ticket hwǒ-chē-'pyàw, bus ticket *(or for any public vehicular conveyance)* chē-'pyàw, ticket to be taken at a door or gate as one enters mén-'pyàw, season ticket jì-'pyàw, commuter's ticket *(railway, etc.)* cháng-chī-'pyàw, *etc.* ‖**Have you got your tickets yet?** nǐ 'yàw-je 'pyàw-le-ma? *or* nǐ 'mǎy-je mén-'pyàw-le-ma? *or* nǐ dǎ-'pyàw-le-ma? ‖**I want a round-trip ticket for Peiping.** wǒ yàw yì-jāng-shàng-běy-'píng-de-'láy-hwéy-'pyàw.

(List of candidates) 'hèw-shywǎn-rén-míng-'dār. ‖**Are there any women candidates on the ticket?** 'hèw-shywǎn-rén-míng-'dār-shang yěw 'nywǔ-de-ma? ‖**That's the ticket!** 'dwèy! *or* 'shř 'nèy-yangr!

TIE. *(Bind, fasten) a knot or a string* jì; *(to wrap string around)* kwěn; *(to secure something movable to something fixed by fastening each to one end of a string or rope)* shwān; *(to tie a person to something by wrapping rope around both, or to tie a person's wrists or ankles together, or to bandage a person)* bǎng; *(to fasten the ends of two strings or ropes together)* jyē; *(to secure packages or baggage)* dǎ; *where English has* **tie up** *Chinese may add* shàng *or* chǐ-láy *to any of the above.* ‖**Please tie this up for me.** láw-'jyà bǎ 'jèy-ge gěy-wo °'jì-shang. *or* °'kwěn-shang. *or etc.* ‖**Let's tie the boat up and have our lunch.** dzám bǎ-'chwán 'shwān-shang hǎw chř shǎng-'fàn.

(Equal a score or record). (During a particular game or competition) píng; *(match a record previously established)* 'gǎn-shàng. ‖**I don't think we can tie the**

score now. wǒ 'jywé-de shyàn-dzày píng-bu-'lyǎw-le. ‖**Can you tie that record?** nǐ néng 'gǎn-shang nèy-ge-'jì-lù-ma?

Be tied up *or* **down** *(occupied, delayed)* yěw-'shř, kwèn, dwēn. ‖**Are you tied up this evening?** nǐ jyēr-'wǎn-shang yěw-'shř-ma? ‖**I'm afraid we'll be tied down in the city all weekend.** kǔng-'pà jèy-ge-jēw-'mwò dzám yàw °'kwèn-dzày (*or* 'dwēn-dzày) chéng-'lǐ-tew.

(Neckwear) lǐng-'dày; **bow tie** lǐng-'hwār, lǐng-'jyēr. **To tie a tie** 'dǎ(-shàng) lǐng-'dày *or* 'jì(-shàng) lǐng-'dày. ‖**Is my tie straight?** wǒ-de-lǐng-'dày 'jèng-bu-jèng? ‖**Won't you straighten my tie for me, please?** láw-'jyà, bǎ wǒ-lǐng-'dày gěy nèng-'jèng-le.

(In railroad roadbed) jěn-'mù.

(In music) lyán-'hàwr *or* lyán-'fú.

TIGHT. jǐn; *(motionless)* jù; *(too small)* shyǎw; *(airtight)* yán; *(solidly)* 'tsź-shř; *(to bind)* gū; *(to pinch)* chyā. ‖**Shut your eyes tight.** bǎ-'yǎn bì-'jǐn-le. ‖**I have to tie my shoelace tighter.** wǒ děy bǎ shyé-'dàr jì-'jǐn yì-dyǎr. ‖**Pull the rope tight.** bǎ 'shéng-dz lā-'jǐn-le. ‖**This is a tight fit.** *(General)* 'jèy-ge 'jǐn-yì-dyǎr. *(Of clothes)* 'jèy-ge gū-je 'shēn-dz. *or* jèy-shř chyā-'yāw-de-'yī-fu. ‖**This suit is too tight for me.** jèy-shēr-'yī-fu wǒ 'chwān-je °'shyǎw. *or* °tày 'jǐn. *or* °'gū-de-heng. ‖**Hold tight onto the rail or you'll fall.** 'fú-jù-le lán-'gār (*or* 'jyēw-jù-le 'fú-shěwr), bù-rán nǐ jyèw shywǔ 'dyàw-shya-chywu. ‖**Shut the lid tight on the glass jar.** bǎ bwō-li-'píng-dz-shang-de-'gàr nǐng-°'jǐn-le. *or* °'yǎn-le. *or* °'tsź-shr-le. ‖**Sit tight; it'll only take a minute.** 'dzwò-jù-le, 'yì-hwěr jyèw 'wán.

To seal tight. *(To cork up, to seal up)* dǔ *or* sāy, *plus postverb* shàng *(up) or* sž *(dead) or* jù *(motionless)*. ‖**Is this water pipe sealed tight?** jèy-ge-shwěy-'gwǎn-dz shř 'jěng-gèr °'dǔ-shǎng-le-ma? *or* °'sāy-shàng-le-ma? *or* jèy-ge-shwěy-'gwǎn-dz shř °'dǔ-'sž-le-ma? *or* °'dǔ-jù-le-ma? *or* °'sāy-'sž-le-ma? *or* °'sāy-jù-le-ma?

(Drunk) dzwèy. ‖**Boy, was I tight last night after the party!** hǎw-'jyā-hwo, dzwór-'wǎn-shang nèy-ge-'yìng-chew 'wán-le yǐ-'hèw wǒ 'kě jēn 'dzwèy-le!

Sew *a* **deal up tight** jwěn (*or* jēn) 'lā-shàng. ‖**He's got the deal sewed up tight.** nèy-tàng-dz-'mǎy-may tā jwěn 'lā-shang-le.

Be in a tight spot 'ywù-jyàn kwèn-nan, dǎw-'méy, chū 'má-fan. ‖**I've been in tight spots before.** wǒ yǐ-'chyán yě °'ywù-jyàn-gwo 'kwèn-nan. *or* °'dǎw-gwo 'méy. *or* ‘'chū-gwo 'má-fan.

(With money). ‖**He's plenty tight with his money.** tā dzày yùng-'chyán-shang hěn 'shyǎw-chì. *or ex-pressed as* **He's a tightwad.** tā shř ge-chyán-'hěn-dz. *or as* **He's tight-fisted.** tā-de-'shěw hěn 'jǐn.

TILL. *(Up to a time)* dàw; *or* tsáy *(then and not before) in the other part of the sentence; or both.* ‖**Let's work till ten tonight.** dzám jyēr-'wǎn-shang yì-jř 'dzwò-daw 'shŕ-dyǎn-ba. ‖**Wait till I come back.**

dĕng-daw wó 'hwéy-lay 'dzày shwō. ‖We can't begin till he's finished. 'fēy-dĕy 'dĕng tā 'wán-le wŏm 'tsáy néng kāy-'shĭ. ‖I won't be able to see you till next week. ╱wŏ 'bú-dàw 'shyà-yí-ge-lĭ-'bày bù-néng 'jyàn-ni. or wŏ 'dĕy dàw 'shyà-yí-ge-lĭ-'bày tsáy néng 'jyàn-ni.

(To plow, plant, etc.) jùng, páw, gēng, jīng. ‖That soil hasn't been tilled for at least five years. nèy-kwày-'dì yĕw 'wŭ-nyán méy-°'jùng-le. or °'páw-le. or etc.

(Small drawer for money) expressed as drawer 'chēw-tì. ‖How much change is there in the till? 'chēw-tì-li yĕw 'dwō-shaw-'líng-chyán?

TIME. (Most general term) 'shĭ-hew. ‖It's time to leave. dàw gāy-'dzĕw-de-shĭ-hew-le. ‖Where were you at that time? 'nèy-ge-shĭ-hew nĭ dzày-'năr-ne? ‖What time do we eat? dzám 'shéme-shĭ-hew chĭ-'fàn? ‖At times I work twenty-four hours at a stretch. 'yĕw (-de)-shĭ-hew wŏ yí-'shyàr dzwò èr-shr-'sž-ge-jūng-'téw. ‖It'll probably be some time before I can come here again. wŏ 'dà-gày dĕy 'gwò shyē-shĭ-hew tsáy néng láy-jèr. ‖What was the time in the last race? 'shàng-tsž-sày-'păw °'yùng-le 'dwō-shaw-shĭ-hew? or °-de-'jì-lù shĭ 'dwō-shaw shĭ-hew?

(Hour of day) dyăn(-jūng). What time? 'jĭ-dyăn (-jūng) or jĭ-'shĭ. ‖What time do we eat? dzám jĭ-'shĭ chĭ-'fàn? ‖What time is it? jĭ-'dyăn-le?

(Day) r, tyān. ‖Let's make it some other time. dzám găy-°'r (or °'tyān) 'dzày shwō-ba.

(Era, age) shĭ-'dày, 'shĭ-hew. ‖I'd like to know more about those times. wŏ hĕn 'shyăng 'dwō jĭ-daw yì-dyăr °'nèy-yí-ge-shĭ-'dày-de-'shĭ. or °'nèy-shyē-shĭ-hew-de-'shĭ. ‖That was before my time. is expressed as That was at my before. 'nà-shĭ dzày 'wŏ-yĭ-'chyán.

(Occasion) tsž, shyà(r), tàng, hwéy. ‖We'll try to do a little better next time. wŏm 'shyà-yí-tsž shyăng-'fár dzwò 'hăw-yì-dyăr. ‖This is the last time I'll ever come here. 'jèy-shĭ wŏ dzwèy-'hèw-yí-tsž láy-'jèr-le. or expressed as I won't come here again. wŏ 'dzày yĕ bù-láy-'jèr-le.

(Conditions). ‖Times have been tough lately, haven't they? 'jìn-láy °nyán-'jīng (or °shĭ-'ywùn or °'gwāng-'jīng or °'r-dz) 'bú-dà 'hăw(-gwò), 'dwèy-bu-dwèy?

(Leisure, opportunity) 'gūng-fu, kùngr, shyán-'kùngr, 'jī-hwèy. ‖I haven't had a moment's time to myself. wŏ 'yì-dyăr-shyán-'kùngr yĕ 'méy-yew. ‖I wonder if we'll have time to see them before they go. bù-'jĭ-daw dzám 'shĭ-bu-shĭ néng yĕw °'jī-hwèy (or °'kùngr) dzày tām méy-'dzĕw yĭ-'chyán 'kàn-kan tā-men. ‖We've got no time for such nonsense. wŏm méy 'gūng-fu 'nàw-je 'wár.

(The future) 'jyāng-láy. ‖Time will tell whether he can do the job. 'jĭ hăw 'jyāng-láy 'kàn-le.

(Time consumed) 'jūng-dyăr. ‖We'll have to make up our time on Sunday. wŏm dĕy dzày lĭ-bày-'tyān bă 'jūng-dyăr 'bŭ-shàng.

(Pay for time during which work is done) expressed as money chyán. ‖You can get your time at the pay window now. nĭ kĕ-yi dàw lĭng-'shīn-shwĕy-de-'chwāng-hu-kĕwr-nèr ná-'chyán chywù-le.

(Rhythm) 'pāy-dz. ‖That couple isn't keeping time to the music. nèy-yí-'dwèr °'tyàw-de bù-hé 'pāy-dz. or °'bú-àn-je 'pāy-dz 'tyàw.

In time with the music gēn-je yīn-'ywè. ‖He drummed on the table in time with the music. tā 'gēn-je yīn-'ywè dzày 'jwō-dz-shang chyāw-chu 'dyăr-lay.

Work against time pīn-je-'mìng-de 'găn.

Do time or serve time dzwò-'jyān.

From time to time cháng, yĕw 'kùngr (de-shĭ-hew), ĕw-'ĕr, shĭ-'cháng. ‖I'll drop around from time to time. wŏ yĭ-'hèw °cháng 'láy. or °yĕw-'kùngr jyèw 'láy.

A long time hăw 'jyĕw. ‖It's been a long time since I've seen you. hăw 'jyĕw méy-'jyàn-ni-le.

Be behind the times lwò-'wŭ, lwò-'hèw, gwò-'shĭ. ‖His ideas are way behind the times. tā-de-'sž-shyăng tày °lwò-'wŭ-le. or °lwò-'hèw-le. or °gwò-'shĭ-le.

Have a good time wár-de 'hăw. ‖Have a nice time last night? dzwór-'wăn-shang wár-de 'hăw-ma?

Have a tough time. ‖I had a tough time with that exam. wŏ nèy-tsž-'kăw-shĭ shyāng-'dāng fèy-'jìn.

At the same time (concessive) bú-gwò . . . yĕ, kĕ-shr . . . yĕ, dàn-shr . . . yĕ. ‖You're right, but at the same time something can be said for him too. nĭ-shwō-de yĕw-'lĭ, 'bú-gwò nĭ 'yĕ bù-néng 'shwō 'tā wán-'chywán bú-'dwèy.

For the time being 'jàw-shĭ, 'mù-chyán, shyàn-'dzày.

In good time or in due time dàw 'shĭ-hew, àn 'shĭ-hew, kwày, 'yì-hwĕr jyèw. ‖I'll pay you back in good time. wŏ dàw 'shĭ-hewr jwĕn 'hwán-gey ni. ‖Don't worry; I'll be there in good time. byé fā-'chéw; wŏ °'jwĕn àn 'shĭ-hew (or °'kwày or 'yì-hwĕr jyèw) 'dàw-nèr-le.

In no time (at all) lì-'kè, lì-'shĭ, 'mă-shàng or mă-'shàng, shyàn-dzày, shwō-'hwà, all followed by jyèw. ‖We can finish the job in no time at all. wŏm °'lì-'kè (or °lì-'shĭ or °'mă-shàng or etc.) jyèw néng bă nèy-jyàn-'shèr dzwò-'wán-le.

In time (sooner or later) dzăw-'wăn. ‖I'm sure we'll get it finished in time. wŏ 'shyāng-shìn wŏ-men dzăw-'wăn jwĕn néng dzwò-'wán-le.

In time (soon enough) dàw-le 'shĭ-hew. ‖I'm sure we'll get it finished in time. dàw-le 'shĭ-hew yí-'dìng kĕ-yi dzwò-'wán-le. ‖Do you think we'll be in time to catch the train? is expressed as Do you think we can hurry sufficiently to make the train? nĭ shyăng dzám 'néng-gèw 'găn-shàng hwŏ-'chē-ma?

On time (on schedule) àn 'jūng-dyăr. ‖Is the express on time? kwày-'chē àn 'jūng-dyăr dàw-ma?

On time (in easy payments) fēn-'chī. ‖Do you want to pay cash for this radio, or will you take it on time? nĭ măy jèy-ge-wú-shyàn-'dyàn shĭ gĕy 'shyàn-chyán. háy-shr dă-swàn fēn-'chī fù-'kwăn?

Time after time, time and again, time and time again 'dwō-shaw-hwéy, 'dwō-shaw-tsz̀, lywŭ-'tsz̀, 'sān-fān-wŭ-'tsz̀, bù-jr̄-'dàw yěw 'dwō-shaw-'hwéy-le. ‖**Time after time I've told you not to shout at me that way.** wǒ 'gàw-sung-ni 'dwō-shaw-'tsz̀-le nǐ 'byé nème 'dà-shēng 'hǎn-wo. ‖**I've passed that store time and again without realizing you were the owner.** wǒ 'lù-gwò nèy-ge-'pù-dz bù-jr̄-'dàw yěw 'dwō-shaw-hwéy-le, kě-shr 'tsúng-láy méy fā-'shyàn 'nǐ shr̀ 'dūng-jyā.

To time (*keep track of time used*) jì-'shŕ, jì-je 'shŕ-hew, kàn-je 'byǎw. ‖**From now on we'll have to time our work.** tsúng-'jīn yǐ-'hèw dzám dzwò-'shèr děy °jì-je dyǎr 'shŕ-hew-le. or °kàn-je 'byǎw 'dzwò.

To time (*allot amounts of time*) swàn shŕ-'jyān, swàn 'shŕ-hew, àn 'shŕ-hew. ‖**I didn't get to that point because I timed my speech poorly.** wǒ shŕ-'jyān méy-swàn-'hǎw-le, swǒ-yi méy-néng bǎ 'nèy-dyǎn 'shwō-chu-lay. ‖**The show is timed to end by eleven.** yàw-shr àn 'shŕ-hew de-hwà shŕ-'yī-dyǎn sàn-'shì.

To time (*to do at the most suitable moment*). ‖**She timed that entrance beautifully.** *is expressed as* Her entrance was just the time. tā 'jìn-lay-de 'jèng shr̀ 'shŕ-hew. ‖**That speech wasn't very well timed, was it?** *is expressed as* The giving of that speech wasn't the time. 'nèy-ge-yǎn-'jyǎng 'shwō-de 'bú-shr̀ 'shŕ-hew.

Times (*multiplying*) chéng. ‖**Two times two equals four.** 'èr chéng-'èr děng-ywu 'sz̀.

Times (*in the name of a newspaper*) shŕ-'bàw.

TIN. shí. ‖**That candy dish is made of pure tin.** nèy-ge-'táng-dyér shr̀ yùng chwén-'shí dzwò-de.

Tin can. *See* CAN.

TIRE. chē-'dày, pí-'dày, 'gú-lù, lwén-'dày. ‖**One of my tires blew out coming down here.** wǒ wǎng-jèr 'láy de-shŕ-hew yěw yí-ge-chē-'dày fàng-'pàw-le. ‖**I need some air in these tires.** jèy-jǐ-tyáw-chē-'dày děy dǎ-'chì-le. ‖**Check my tires.** 'yàn-yàn wǒ-de-chē-'dày. or 'kàn-kàn (*or* 'chyáw-chyáw) chē-'dày. 'shr̀-bu-shr̀ děy dǎ-'chì-le. ‖**I need a whole new set of tires.** wǒ chē-'dày dēw děy 'hwàn-le.

TIRE (TIRED). (*Be or get fatigued*) lèy, fá, tān, kwèn. ‖**I tire very easily in this hot weather.** shyàng jème-'rè-de-tyār wǒ yì 'láy jyèw °'lèy-le. or °'fá-le. or °'tān-le. ‖**I'm afraid that trip will tire me out too much.** wǒ kǔng-'pà 'chū-chywù 'nème-yí-tàng yí-'dìng hwèy bǎ-wo °'lèy-hwày-le. or °'lèy-je-le. ‖**I'm too tired to go on.** wǒ 'lèy-de bù-néng ('jyē-je or 'dzày) wàng-'shyà dzwò-le. ‖**Are you tired?** nǐ 'lèy-le-ma? ‖**I'm tired and I want to go to sleep.** wǒ yěw 'fá yèw 'kwèn, shyǎng chywù shwèy-'jyàw-le.

(*Be bored*). ‖**I'm tired of this place.** wǒ dzày-'jèr dāy 'nì-le.

Be tiring (*boring*) wú-'lyáw, wú-'wèy, méy-'wèr, jyàw-rén chī-'nì, jyàw-rén méy-'jìn. ‖**His talks are**

always very tiring. tā shwō-'hwà 'lǎw-shr̀ °hěn wú-'lyáw. or °gān-dzàw wú-'wèy. or tā-de-'hwà 'tīng-je °hěn méy-'wèr. or °jyàw-rén chī-'nì.

TITLE. (*Name of a thing*) 'míng-dz, myéngr, or a compound ending in míng or myéngr. **Title of a movie** pyān-'míng; **title of a book** shū-'míng; *etc.* ‖**I wish I could remember the title of that movie.** wǒ mú-'jì-de nèy-ge-dyàn-'yěngr-de-°'míng-dz-le. or °pyān-'míng-le.

(*Official term for a person holding some position*) míng-'yì, míng-'shyán, téw-'shyán, gwān-'shyán. ‖**What's your exact title in this office?** nǐ dzày-'jèr-jēn-'jèng-de-°'míng-'yì (*or* °'míng-'shyán or *etc.*) shr̀ 'shéme?

(*Championship*) (bǐ-'sày-de-)°'téw-yì-míng or °'gwàn-'jywūn or °'jìn-'byǎw. ‖**Who do you think will win the tennis title this year?** nǐ shyǎng 'jīn-nyan 'wǎng-chyéw-bǐ-'sày 'shéy néng dé °'téw-yì-míng? or °'gwàn-'jywūn? or °'jìn-'byǎw?

(*Legal right to property*). ‖**Do you have title to this property?** *is expressed as* Is this property yours? jèy-ge-'chǎn-yè shr̀ 'nǐ-de-ma?

TO. (*Marking place or position reached*) dzày or dàw *as postverb with a verb of motion; often a Chinese verb of motion contains within itself the to idea and no separate word is necessary, thus* to go to shàng. ‖**Nail this announcement to the door.** bǎ jèy-ge-tūng-jr̄ 'dīng-dzày 'mén-shang.

(*Towards, in the direction of*) wǎng, wàng, shyàng. ‖**Take the first turn to your right.** jyàn 'wār jyèw wàng-'yèw gwǎy.

(*In stating distances rather than motion*) lí. *See also* FROM. ‖**How far is it to town?** lí-'chéng yěw dwō-'ywǎn?

(*Time before an hour*). ‖**It's ten minutes to four.** *is expressed as* Lacks ten minutes (not to) four o'clock. chà 'shŕ-fēn (bú-dàw) 'sz̀-dyǎn-le. or, *less often, as* (It's) four o'clock short ten minutes. 'sz̀-dyǎn chyàn 'shŕ-fen. or, *most often, as* It's three-fifty. 'sān-dyǎn 'wǔ-shr-fēn.

(*With reference to, concerning, as regards*) dwèy (*a person*), 'dwèy-ywu, 'gwān-ywu. ‖**You're very kind to me.** nǐ dwèy(-ywu) 'wǒ tày 'hǎw-le. ‖**What do you say to this?** nǐ °'dwèy-ywu (*or* °'gwān-ywu) 'jèy-ge yěw shéme 'shwō-de?

(*Marking resultant state*) de; chéng *as postverb with a verb of action, followed by a nominal expression of the resultant state; or simply a postverb with proper meaning.* ‖**The dog chewed the pillow to pieces.** 'gěw bǎ 'jěn-tew jyáw-'làn-le. or 'jěn-tew ràng-'gěw 'jyáw-°chéng (*or* °de) shī-'làn.

(*Marking a personal recipient or someone consulted with*) gěy, gēn. ‖**Give this to him when he comes in.** tā 'jìn-lay de-shŕ-hew bǎ jèy-ge 'gěy-ta. ‖**Explain that to me.** bǎ nèy-ge gěy-wo 'jyǎng-yi-jyǎng. ‖**Let me put it to you this way.** wo 'jème-yàngr gēn-ni shwō-ba.

(*As compared with*) bǐ. ‖We won six to two. 'lyèw bǐ-'èr, wǒm 'yíng-le.

(*Shut*) shàng *as postverb*. ‖Please pull the door to. chǐng-ni bǎ-'mén 'dày-shang.

⟨*Other uses of* to *are bound up with specific other words, e.g.,* come to, fall to, to go, true to life, *etc., and are treated with those other words.*

TOBACCO. yān-'yè(-dz), yān-'tsǎw.

TODAY. (*Literally*) 'jīn-tyan, 'jyér(-ge). ‖What do you have on the menu today? nǐm °'jīn-tyan ·(*or* °'jyér) yěw shéme-'tsày? ‖Is today payday? 'jīn-tyan (*or* 'jyér) shr̀ fā-'shīn-de-r̀-dz-ma?

(*Modern times*) dāng-'chyán, mù-'chyán, jīn-'r̀, shyàn-'jīn, shyàn-'dzày. ‖Today's main problem is do-ing away with war. dāng-'chyán- (*or* mù-'chyán- *or etc.*) de-'jǔ-yàw-'wèn-tí shr̀ chywǔ-'shyāw jàn-'jēng.

TOE. jyǎw-'jŕ-tew, jyǎw-'jŕ-tew. ‖My toes are frozen. wǒ bǎ jyǎw-'jŕ-tew 'dùng-le.

Toe of a sock *or* stocking wà-dz-'jyār. ‖I've got a hole in the toe of my sock. wǒ wà-dz-'jyār-shang yěw yí-ge-'kū-lung.

Toe of a shoe shyé-'téwr; (*upper part*) shyé-'lyǎr. Toe of a boot shywē-'téwr *or* shywē-'lyǎr *similarly*.

TOGETHER. dzày yí-'kwàr *or* dzày yì-'chǐ, *with* dzày *as coverb or as postverb*. ‖They work together very well. tām dzày yí-'kwàr dzwò-'shr̀ hěn hé-'shěwr. ‖Try to put these newspapers together in the right order. bǎ jèy-shyē-bàw-'jŕ àn-je-'r̀-dz °'mǎ-dzày yí-'kwàr. *or* °'lwò-dzày yí-'kwàr. *or* °'fàng-dzày yí-'kwàr. *or etc., with various other verbs*. ‖Let's call them together for a meeting. bǎ-tām 'jāw-jì-dzày yì-'chǐ kāy yí-tsz̄-'hwèy.

(*With one will, cooperatively*) yì-'túng, yì-'chǐ, túng-'shīn. ‖Let's all push together. dà-'jyā °yì-'túng (*or* °yì-'chǐ) 'gàn.

Where together *might be replaced in English by* up, *Chinese may use* chǐ-láy *as postverb*. ‖Please add these figures together. láw-'jyà bǎ jèy-shyē-'shù-mù 'jyā-chǐ-láy.

To get together (*for fun, talk, etc.*) 'jywù-yi-jywù, 'hwèy-yi-hwèy, 'wár-yi-wár, jyàn-jyan 'myàr, *each with an appropriate plural pronoun or noun expression*. ‖Do you suppose we can get together some evening? nǐ shyǎng dzám 'nǎ-yi-tyān-'wǎn-shang kě-yi °'jywù-yi-jywù-ma? *or* °'hwèy-yi-hwèy-ma? *or etc.*

Together with (*including also*) lyán. ‖The price of this ticket together with tax is fifty-two dollars. jèy-jāng-'pyàw lyán-'shwèy shr̀ 'wǔ-shr-'èr-kwày-chyán.

TOILET. tsè-'swǒ, máw-'fáng, byàn-'swǒ; (*bathroom*) shǐ-lyàn-'fáng, dzǎw-'fáng, ywù-'shr̀; (*washroom, as in a restaurant*) shǐ-shěw-'jyān.

TOMORROW. 'míng-tyan, 'myéngr(-ge), 'myér(-ge). ‖Is tomorrow Wednesday? 'myéngr-ge shr̀ shīng-chī-'sān-ma? ‖I'll see you tomorrow morning. wǒ myéngr-'dzǎw-chen 'jyàn-ni. ‖See you tomorrow! myéngr 'jyàn! ‖I'll be back tomorrow. wǒ 'míng-tyan 'hwéy-lay.

(*Times to come*) míng-'r̀, 'wèy-láy, 'jyāng-láy. Th world of tomorrow 'wèy-láy-shr̀-'jyè.

TONGUE. 'shé-tew. ‖Watch out you don't burn your tongue on this hot soup. lyéw-'shén byé jyàw jèy-ge-rè-'tāng bǎ nǐ-'shé-tew 'tàng-je.

(*Food*) 'shé-tew *or* kěw-'tyáw, *often with source specified, as* beef tongue nyéw-'shé-tew *or* nyéw-kěw-'tyáw. ‖I'd like a plate of sliced tongue. wǒ yàw yì-'pár-kěw-tyáw-'pyàr.

(*Language*) hwà; *in compounds* ywǔ *or* wén. ‖What's your native tongue? nǐ shwō ·'nǎr-de-hwà? *or* (*more formal*) nǐ-de-'běn-gwó-'ywǔ shr̀ 'něy-yí-ge?

On the tip of one's tongue *is expressed as* on the edge of one's mouth dzày 'dzwěy-byār-shang. ‖Just a minute; I have his name on the tip of my tongue. byé 'máng; tā-'míng-dz jyèw dzày wǒ 'dzwěy-byār-shang.

‖Hold your tongue! jù-'dzwěy! *or* byé 'shwō-le! *or* 'dé-le, 'shíng-le!

TONIGHT. 'wǎn-shang *or* jyér-'wǎn-shang, jīn-tyan-'wǎn-shang. ‖See you tonight! 'wǎn-shang 'jyàn! ‖What shall we do tonight? dzǎm jyér-'wǎn-shang gàn-'shéme? ‖Have you seen tonight's paper? nǐ 'kàn-le jyér-'wǎn-shang-de-'bàw-le-ma? *or expressed is* Have you seen today's evening paper? nǐ 'kàn-le jyér-de-wǎn-'bàw-le-ma?

TOO. (*Also*) yě. ‖May I come too? wǒ 'yě chywù, 'shíng-ma? ‖I'd like a half pound of those too. wǒ 'yě shyǎng yàw bàn-bàng-'nèy-yàngr-de.

(*Excessively*) tày. ‖It's too hot. tày 'rè-le. *or* tày 'tàng-le. ‖Am I too late? wǒ tày 'wǎn-le-ma? ‖I think you're asking too much for this hat. jèy-dǐng-'màw-dz nǐ yàw-'jyàr yàw-de tày °'dà-le *or* °'dwō-le. ‖You're going too far! nǐ 'tày gwò-'hwǒr-le! *or* nǐ yě 'tày bù-jyǎng 'myàn-dz-le!

All too tày *with some such expression as* really jēn. ‖Our stay here was all too short. wǒm dzày 'jèr 'dāy de-shf-hew °'jēn-shr̀ (*or* °'gēn-'běn or ·°'jyàn-'jŕ) tày 'dwǎn-le.

‖Too bad! 'jēn dzāw-'gāw! *or* 'jēn chà-'jìn! *or* 'jè-shr̀ dzěm 'shwō-de! *or* (hwó-) 'gāy! *or* 'jēn kě 'shī!

TOOL. 'jyā-hwo. ‖Could I borrow your tools? gěy-wo nǐ-de-'jyā-hwo 'yùng-yi-yùng kě-yǐ-ma? ‖Be careful of those tools. yùng nèy-shyē-'jyā-hwo de-shf-hew 'shyǎw-shīn-dyǎr.

(*Person used by powerful interests*) kwéy-'lěy, shèw-'lì-yùng. ‖The mayor is only a tool of the party. shr̀-'jǎng yě bú-'gwò °shr̀ 'dǎng-de-kwéy-'lěy. *or* °shèw 'dǎng-de-'lì-yùng.

To tool (*leather, designs, etc.*) *various verbs, especially* **to make** dzwò; **to carve** kè; *or* (*using heat, as to apply gold leaf*) tàng. ‖He's been tooling leather for years. tā dzwò 'pí-hwò dwō-'nyán-le.

TOOTH (TEETH). yá. ‖This tooth·hurts. 'jèy-ge-yá 'téng. ‖I think I need to have this tooth filled. wǒ shyǎng wǒ děy bǎ jèy-ge-'yá 'bǔ-shang. ‖This tooth needs to be pulled. jèy-ge-'yá děy 'bá.

(*Of saw or gear wheel*) chř, chěr. ‖This saw has a broken tooth. jèy-ge-'jywù-shang-de-'chěr 'bēn-le yí-ge.

TOP. On (the) top of dzày ... °-shang, °'shàng-byan, °'shàng-byar, °'shàng-myan, °'shàng-myar, °'shàng-tew, °'shàng-tewr. ‖I'm sure my wallet was on top of the dresser. wǒ 'gǎn shwō wǒ-de-chyán-'bāwr shř dzày wǔ-tǔng-'gwèy-shang láy-je.

To come out on top dé dì-'yī, yíng, shèng, chéng-'gūng. ‖I'm glad you came out on top. nǐ dé dì-'yī wǒ hěn 'gāw-shìng.

Top man (*person in charge*) téwr, yěw-'dz̄-ge, dzwèy-'néng-gàn-de-rén.

Mountain top shān-'dǐng, shān-'dyěngr, shān-'jyār, shān-'dyān, shān-'téw; *meaning* **peak** shān-'fēng. ‖How high is the top of the mountain? shān-'dyěngr (*or* shān-'jyār *or etc.*) yěw dwō 'gāw?

Top of an automobile (*solid*) chē-'dyěngr; (*flexible*) chē-'péng(r). ‖Are you going to put down the top? nǐ yàw bǎ chē-'péngr 'lyàw-shya-lay-ma?

From top to bottom lyán-'shàng dày-'shyà, tsúng-'shàng dàw-'shyà, *or expressed as in the following sentence.* ‖We searched the house from top to bottom. wǒm 'léw-shyà léw-'shàng dēw jǎw-'byàn-le.

At the top of one's voice pīn-je-'mìng-de, chě-je-'sǎng-dz, chě-je-'bwó-dz. ‖You don't have to shout at the top of your voice! nǐ 'yùng-bu-jáw pīn-je-'mìng-de 'hǎn!

(*Toy*) twó-'lwó, nyǎn-nyan-'jwàr. ‖The boy got a top for his birthday. shyǎw-'hár 'shēng-r̀ 'dé-le yí-ge twó-'lwó.

To sleep like a top. ‖I slept like a top all last night. wǒ dzwór-'wǎn-shang shwèy-de tǐng 'shyāng.

Tops. ‖You're tops with me. dzǎy 'wǒ kàn nǐ 'jēn °'kě-yi. *or* °'shř dì-'yī-le. *or* wǒ kě 'jēn fú-ni fú-daw 'jyā-le.

To top *a score.* ‖He topped my score by at least ten points. tā chǐ-'mǎ bǐ-'wǒ dwō shǐ-'fēr. *or* tā jř 'shǎw 'yíng-le wǒ shǐ-'fēr.

To top *a story* 'gǎn-gwò-chywù. ‖Can you top that one? nǐ néng 'gǎn-gwò 'nèy-ge chywù-ma?

To top *something* **off.** ‖Let's top off the dinner with some wine. dzám chī-'fàn 'mwò-mwo-lyǎwr děy 'hē dyǎr-'jyěw.

TOTAL. To total up 'jyā-chǐ-láy. ‖Let's total up expenses for the month. dzám bǎ jèy-ge-'ywè-de-'kāy-shyàw 'jyā-chi-lay 'kàn-yi-kàn.

Other expressions in English. ‖What is the total amount of the bill? *is expressed as* The bill altogether is how much? 'jàng yí-'gùng-dzǔng shř 'dwō-shaw? ‖This car is a total loss. *is expressed as* This car is completely ruined. jèy-lyàng-'chē °'wán-'chywán (*or* °'jěng-'gèr) 'hwěy-le. ‖Will you figure out the total for me? *is expressed as* Can you figure out the complete amount for me? nǐ néng bǎ dzǔng-'shùr gěy-wo 'swàn-chu-lay-ma? ‖His income totals two thousand dollars a year. *is expressed as* His one-year's income has two thousand dollars. tā 'yì-nyán-de-shēw-'rù yěw 'lyǎng-chyān-kwày-chyán.

TOUCH. 1. To touch, *in the sense of physical contact,* **a touch,** *in the sense of an act of touching, and* **the touch,** *in the sense of tactile sensation, are all expressed with the following:* **to touch, to stroke lightly,** *or* **to feel by touching, with finger or hand** mwō, 'mwō-swo, *or* 'mā-sa; **to touch·at lightly with a finger or pointed object** dyǎn *or* 'dyǎn-da; **to touch against accidentally** (*may refer to a force ranging from very light to a heavy collision*) pèng *or* 'pèng-jáw; **to be touching very lightly** *or* **to move very close** to āy *or* 'āy-jáw; **to rub against** *or* **scrape against** tsèng *or* 'tsèng-jáw; **to move** *or* **disturb** *something* dùng *or* dùng-'shěw; **to be in contact with** *something, especially water or something sticky* 'jān-jáw; **to hang down so as to reach** 'dā-la-dàw *or* 'dā-la-dzày; (*the same, if the thing hanging down is in motion, as a dress touching the floor as a woman walks along*) 'tū-lu-dàw *or* 'tū-lu-dzày; **to touch with the head** dǐng *or* 'dǐng-jáw.

‖Don't touch that; it breaks easily. byé °'dùng (*or* °'mwō *or* °'mwō-swo *or* °'mā-sa *or* °'dùng-'shěw *or* °'chǔ *or* °'chǔ-da *or* °'dyǎn-da *or* °'āy *or* °'pèng *or* °'tsèng); rúng-yi-'hwày. ‖You may look at it but don't touch (it). shywǔ 'kàn, bù-shywǔ 'mwō. *or* 'kàn shř kě-yi 'kàn, kě byé °'dùng. *or* °'dùng-'shěw. *or etc.* ‖Please don't touch those books. byé 'dùng nèy-shyē-'shū. ‖These pants are much too long; they almost touch the ground. nèy-tyáw-'kù-dz 'cháng-de 'jyǎn-jř yàw °'dā-la-dàw (*or* °'tū-lu) 'dì-shàng-le. *or* °'jān-jáw (*or* °'tsèng-jáw) 'dì-le. ‖His head nearly touched the ceiling. tā 'nǎw-dày 'kwày yàw °'dǐng-jáw (*or* °'tsèng-jáw *or* °'āy-jáw) fáng-'dǐng-dz-le.

‖One touch and it will break. yí °'dùng (*or* °'mwō *or* 'mwō-swo *or etc.*) jyèw °'hwày. *or* °'pwò. *or* °'swèy. *or* °'sǎn. ‖I feel a gentle touch on my shoulder. wǒ 'jywé-de yěw-rén chīng-'chyěngr-de °'tǔng- (*or* °'chǔ- *or* °'mwō- *or* °'dyǎn- *or* °'pèng- *or* °'āy- *or* °'tsèng-) wǒ-jyān-'bǎngr yí-shyàr.

‖That cloth feels nice to the touch. nèy-kwày-'lyàw-dz 'mwō-je tǐng °'rwǎn-hwo. *or* °'hwá-lyew.

2. To touch (*to concern*). ‖I admit it's a pretty bad situation, but it doesn't touch us directly. *is expressed as* ... but it has nothing·to do with us. wǒ 'chéng-rèn 'chíng-shing shř bú-'dà hǎw, °kě-shr gēn 'wǒ-men méy shéme-'gwān-shi. *or as* ... but it doesn't obstruct our work. °kě-shr 'āy-bu-jáw dzám-de-'shř.

3. To touch at *or* on *a port* dzày . . . 'tíng, dzày . . . kàw-'àn. ‖What ports did your boat touch at during your trip? nǐ-dzwò-de-nèy-tyáw-'chwán dēw dzày-'nǎr °'tíng (*or* °kàw-'àn) láy-je?

4. To touch off (*give rise to*) 'yǐn-chǐ-láy. ‖Her remarks touched off a violent argument. tā-de-'hwà 'yǐn-chǐ yì-chǎng-'dà-'chǎw-dz-lay.

5. To touch (on) (*mention*) 'tí(-dàw), 'tán(-dàw), 'lwèn-(dàw), 'shwō(-dàw). ‖What subjects did he touch on in the lecture? tā yǎn-'jyǎng de-shí-hew dēw °'tí- (*or* °'tán- *or* °'lwèn- *or* °'shwō-)dàw 'shéme-le? ‖I wouldn't touch on any of his family problems if I were you. 'wǒ yàw-shr 'nǐ-ya, 'jywé-bù °'shwō (*or* °'lwèn *or* °'tí *or* °'tán) tā-'jyā-li-de-'shèr.

6. To touch up *a photograph* bǎ . . . shyēw-'bǎn; *to touch up* (*take care of minor repairs and decorations*) jyàn-jyan 'shín. ‖My apartment needs touching up. wǒ-'jù-de-dì-fang děy jyàn-jyan 'shín-le.

7. Be touching (*evocative of emotion*) 'dùng-rén, jyàw-rén shèw 'gǎn-dùng. ‖How touching! 'jēn-shr jyàw-rén rèw-'má! *or*, (*sarcastically*) 'dwō rèw-'má! ‖It was a touching scene. (*Of a play or movie*) 'nèy-dwàr hěn °'dùng-rén. *or* °jyàw-rén shèw 'gǎn-dùng. (*Of a happening*) nèy-ge-'chíng-shing hěn °'dùng-rén. *or* °jyàw-rén shèw 'gǎn-dùng.

8. Be (a little) touched yěw dyǎr-'fēng *or* 'fēng-feng-dyan-dyǎn-de *or* yěw shén-jīng-'bìng. ‖Don't mind him; he's a little touched. béng 'lǐ-ta; tā °yěw dyǎr-'fēng. *or* °yěw shén-jīng-'bìng. *or* °'fēng-feng-byan-byǎn-de.

9. Be touchy. ‖He's touchy about his baldness. *is expressed as* He doesn't like people to mention that he's bald. tā °'gè-ying (*or* °'nǐ-wey) rén 'jyǎng tā tū-'téw. ‖Touchy, isn't he! *is expressed as* He really gets mad whether you disturb him or not. tā 'jēn-shr 'dùng-bu-dùngr jyèw 'nǎw.

10. (*Contact through communication*). ‖Keep in touch with me. cháng 'gwān-jàw-wo dyǎr. *or* 'jyē-cháng bú-'dwàn-de gēn-wo 'jyē-jye 'téw. *or* 'cháng gěy-wo láy ge-°'hwàr *or* °shyèr. ‖I've been **out** of touch with things here for several months now. jèr-de-'shèr wǒ yěw 'hǎw-jǐ-ge-'ywè °méy-'tīng-jyan shéme-le. *or* °méy-'gwǎn-le. ‖Have you lost touch with your friends back home? nǐ gēn lǎw-'jyā-de-'péng-yew dēw °méy shéme-láy-'wǎng-le-ma? *or* °bù-tūng-'shìn-le-ma?

11. A touch of dyǎr, shyàr. ‖There was a touch of humor in his speech. tā-de-yǎn-'jyǎng °yěw dyǎr-yěw-'mwò. *or* °'yěw nème-yì-dyǎr-'yěw-mwò. *or* °'yěw nème-yì-dyǎr-yàw-'yǐn-rén-'shyàw-de-yì-sz. ‖This soup needs a touch of salt. jèy-ge-'tāng-li děy °'sǎ (*or* °'jyāʃ dyǎr-'yán. ‖This chair needs a few more touches of paint. jèy-bǎ-'yǐ-dz háy děy °'yéw (*or* °'chī) lyǎng-shyàr. *or* jèy-bǎ-'yǐ-dz yěw 'jǐ-chù-dì-fang háy děy 'yéw-yew.

12. Touch and go 'shywán-hú-je; (*of living conditions*) 'jyèw-hu-je, 'jyāng-jyèw-je. ‖It's been touch and go for a long time. 'shèr nème 'shywán-hú-je yěw 'hǎw-shyē-r̀-dz-le. ‖Things were touch and go for a long time. 'hǎw-shyē-'shí-le nème °'jyèw-hu-je (*or* °'jyāng-jyèw-je) gwò-de.

TOWARD(S). (*Direction*) shyàng, wàng, wǎng. ‖Let's go towards town. dzám wàng 'chéng-li dzěw-ba. ‖He's coming toward us now. tā 'jèng wàng wǒm-'jèr láy-ne.

(*Approximate, in specifying a time*) dǐng. ‖I'll be there towards late afternoon. wǒ dǐng 'hèw-bàn-shǎngr 'dàw-nèr.

(*Concerning*) dwèy, 'dwèy-ywu, 'gwān-ywu. ‖I feel very sympathetic towards you. wǒ dwèy-'nǐ hěn 'byǎw túng-'chíng.

TOWEL. 'shěw-jīn, 'hàn-jīn; bath towel 'dzǎw-jīn, shǐ-dzǎw-'bù, tsā-dzǎw-'bù; turkish towel 'máw-jīn; face towel shǐ-lyǎn-'shěw-jīn.

TOWN. chéng (*particularly one which has a wall*); 'dì-fang (*refers to any size*). *Where* town *means a relatively smaller community, one can say* small city shyǎw-'chéng. ‖How far is the next town? lí 'shyà-yí-ge-'chéng yěw dwō-'ywǎn? ‖I won't be coming into town this weekend. wǒ jèy-ge-jēw-'mwò bú-jìn-'chéng. ‖I'd rather live in a town than a village; but a city is still better. wǒ 'jywé-de jù-dzày 'shyǎw-chéng-li bǐ 'tswēn-dz-li 'hǎw, 'dà-chéng-li gèng 'hǎw.

(*People of a town*) 'chéng-li-de-rén; the whole town (*everyone in town*) 'chywán-chéng-de-rén. ‖The whole town's talking about them. 'chywán-chéng-de-rén dēw dzày 'tán-lwèn tām.

TRACK. Railroad tracks hwǒ-chē-'dàw, chē-'gwěy, tyě-'gwěy; streetcar tracks dyàn-chē-'dàw. ‖Watch out for trains when you cross the tracks. gwò hwǒ-chē-'dàw de-shí-hew lyéw-'shén hwǒ-'chē.

(*Trail left by walking*) jyǎw-'yèr. ‖Let's follow his tracks to see where he went. dzám gēn-je tā-jyǎw-'yèr dzěw, kàn tā chywù-'nǎr-le

(*Horse racing course*) pǎw-mǎ-'chǎng. ‖If we want to see the first race, we've got to be at the track at one-thirty. dzám yàw-shr shyǎng kàn 'téw-yì-chǎng-sày-'mǎ de-hwà, kě 'děy 'yì-dyǎn-'bàn yǐ-'chyán dàw pǎw-mǎ-'chǎng.

(*Running sports*) jìng-'sày; track and field tyán-jìng-'sày. ‖When he was at college, he went out for track. tā dzày 'dà-shywé de-shí-hew, tsān-'jyā gwò 'jìng-sày.

To track down *a fugitive* sēw-'shywún, sēw-'bǔ. ‖The police are trying to track down the escaped convict. jīng-'chá jèng dzày °sēw-'shywún (*or* °sēw-'bǔ) nèy-ge-'táw-fàn.

To track down *a story* 'dyàw-cha. ‖Could you track down that story for me? nǐ néng tì-wo 'dyàw-cha dyàw-cha nèy-jyàn-'shr̀-ma?

To track up (*get dirty marks on*) tsăy-'dzāng, bà-je-'dzāng. ‖Clean off your shoes; you're tracking up the kitchen. bă-'shyé tsèng-'gǎn-jǐng-le; nǐ 'kàn, nǐ bǎ 'chú-fáng-de-'dì dēw °tsǎy-'dzāng-le. or °bà-je-'dzāng-le.

Be off the track bù-tyē-'tí, lí-le běn-'tí-le. ‖What you say is true, but it's off the track. nǐ-'shwō-de dàwshr 'dwèy, kě-shr °bù-tyē-'tí. or °lí-le běn-'tí-le.

‖You're on the right track. nǐ dzèw 'dwèy-le. or nǐ jēn yěw-'mér. or 'shíng. nǐ swàn °yěw-'mér-le. or °mwō-je 'mér-le.

To keep track of. ‖I hope you don't expect me to keep track of all the details. nǐ kě 'byé jǐ-je 'wǒ láy 'gwǎn nèy-shyē-'líng-chi-bā-'swèy-de-'shř.

To lose track of. ‖I'm afraid I've completely lost track of him. *is expressed as* Where he's gone to I just don't know. tā rú-'jīn-dzày 'nǎr, wǒ kě 'jēn-shř bù-jř-'dàw. *or as* I haven't even a little news of him. gwān-ywu-'tā-de-shyāw-shi wǒ-shř 'yì-dyǎr yě 'méy-yew.

To make tracks for gǎn-'jǐn °dzěw (*or* °hwéy *or other verb of going*), kāy-'twěy jyèw 'pǎw, sā-'yā-dz jyèw 'pǎw. ‖It's getting rather late, so we'd better make tracks for home. 'tyān bù-'dzǎw-le; dzám gǎn-'jǐn hwéy-'jyā-ba.

TRADE. (*The carrying on of business*) 'shēng-yì, mǎy-may. ‖Do you have much trade in the summer? 'shyà-tyar °'shēng-yì (*or* °'mǎy-may) °'dwō-ma? *or* °'máng-ma? ‖Is there any trade across the border? 'jèr 'yěw-méy-yew chū-'rù-kěw-de-'mǎy-may?

(*Occupation*). ‖What's your trade? *is expressed as* Where do you prosper? nín dzày-'nǎr fā-'tsáy? *or as* In what occupation do you do business? nín-shř dzày 'něy-yì-háng jīng-'shāng? ‖Why, I'm a butcher by trade, but right now I'm working in a factory. *is expressed as* My original occupation is butcher, ... wǒ-'běn-háng shř tú-dzǎy-'yè, kě-shr shyàn-dzày shř dzày gūng-'chǎng-li dzwò-'shř.

(*Customers*) 'jǔ-gù. ‖I think my product will appeal to your trade. wǒ shyǎng wǒ-jèr-chū-de-'hwò yí-'dìng hwèy 'jyàw nǐ-de-'jǔ-gù 'shǐ-hwan.

To trade jyāw-'hwàn. ‖Let's trade. dzám jyāw-'hwàn-ba

To trade *one thing* in for *another* nà . . . tyē-'hwàn . . . . ‖I want to trade this car in for a new one. wǒ shyǎng ná 'jèy-lyàng-chē tyē-'hwàn yí-lyàng-'shīn-de.

To trade *something* off (*get rid of*) dǎw-chu 'shěw-chywù, 'twēy-chu-chywù, 'mày-chu-chywù. ‖We've got to trade off some of this old merchandise. dzám dzŭng děy shyǎng-'fǎr bǎ jèy-shyē-'jyèw-hwò °dǎw-chu 'shěw-chywù. or °'twēy-chu-chywù. or °'mày-chu-chywù.

To trade on jř-je . . . chř-'rén, jř-je . . . . °jǎw (*or* °jàn) 'pyán-yì. ‖She's been trading on her looks for years. tā jème-shyē-'nyán-le jyèw-shr jř-je 'mú-yàngr jàn 'pyán-yì.

TRAIN. (*Railroad*) hwǒ-'chē, chē. ‖When does the train leave? hwǒ-'chē 'shéme-shř-hew 'kāy? ‖The train is late. hwǒ-'chē wù-'dyǎn-le. ‖I have to catch an early train. wǒ děy 'gǎn yí-tàng-'dzǎw-chē. ‖I'll see you to the train. wǒ 'sùng-ni shàng-'chē.

(*Column of vehicles*) lyèw, dà-'lyèw. A train of trucks yí-dà-'lyèw-de-kǎ-'chē.

To train (*as for athletic events*) lyàn, 'shywùn-lyàn. ‖I hope you've been training for our tennis match next week. dzám 'shyà-lǐ-bày sày wǎng-'chyéwr, wǒ 'shī-wang nǐ jèy-shyē-'ř-dz 'lyàn láy-je.

To be trained in (*to have studied and learned*) 'nyàn-gwo. ‖Have you been trained in law? nǐ 'nyàn-gwo fǎ-'lyùwu-ma?

TRANSLATE. fān, 'fān-yì. ‖How do you translate this? 'jèy-ge nǐ dzěme 'fān? ‖Where can I find someone to translate this letter? dàw-'nǎr-chywù 'jǎw ge-rén bǎ jèy-fēng-'shìn gěy-wo 'fān-chu-lay? ‖That's a difficult expression to translate. 'jèy-jǔng-'shwō-fa hěn nán 'fān. *or expressed as* That expression is hard to say in Chinese (French, German, etc.). 'jèy-jǔng-'shwō-fa hěn 'nán yùng 'jūng-wén 'shwō.

TRAVEL. 'yéw-lì, lywǔ-'shíng. ‖Where are you planning to travel for your spring vacation? nǐ chwēn-'jyà 'dǎ-swàn dàw-'nǎr chywù lywǔ-'shíng?

To travel by *car, train, etc.* dzwò; (*if one is operating the vehicle oneself*) kāy; (*if one sits astride, as on horseback or a bicycle*) chí. ‖Which is the best way to travel? dzwò-'shéme dzwèy 'hǎw?

(*To move fast*) dzěw-de (*or* 'fēy-de *or etc.*) dwō-'kwày. ‖Boy, is this plane traveling! hǎw-'jyā-hwo, jèy-ge-fēy-'jī 'fēy-de dwō-'kwày-ya!

(*Movement of traffic*). ‖Travel on this road is always light. *is expressed as* This road isn't crowded. jèy-tyáw-'lù(-shang) bù-'jǐ.

Traveler lywǔ-'kè.

TREAT. (*Medically*) jř. ‖Has the doctor been treating you long? 'dày-fu gěy-ni 'jř-le yěw shyē-'shř-hew-le-ma?

(*To pay for someone else; the act of paying for someone else*) *usually expressed with* to invite chǐng; *sometimes with* to give gěy *or with* to calculate swàn. ‖How about treating me for a change? 'yě gāy 'chǐng-ching 'wǒ-le. ‖I insist, dinner's my treat. bù-'shíng, 'jèy-dwèn-fàn yí-'dìng děy °swàn 'wǒ-de. or °ràng-'wǒ chǐng. or °ràng-'wǒ gěy. ‖The treat's on you this time. 'jèy-hwéy shř-'nǐ chǐng.

To treat (of) (*be about*) 'yán-jyew, jyǎng, 'gwān ywu, 'tǎw-lwèn. ‖Can you recommend a book that treats (of) current social problems? nǐ néng 'jyè-shaw yì-běr-°'yán-jyew-(or °jyǎng- or etc.) shè-'hwèy-'wèn-tí-de-'shū-ma?

To treat *someone in a specified way* dày, 'dwèy-fu. ‖You're not treating me fairly. nǐ 'dày-wo bù-gūng-'dàw. ‖How would you treat him in a case like this?

shyàng 'jèy-yàngr nǐ 'dzěme 'dwèy-fu ta? ‖How's the **world been treating you?** *is expressed as* **How've you been these days?** 'jìn-láy rú-'hé. *or* 'jìn-láy dzěme-'yàng?

To **treat** *something* as 'yǐ-wéy *or* 'rèn-wey. ‖You **shouldn't treat that as a laughing matter.** nǐ bù-'yǐng-dang °'yǐ-wey (*or* °'rèn-wey) 'nèy-jyàn-shr̀ kě-'shyàw.

A **treat** (*pleasure*) *is expressed in terms of* **be interesting** yěw 'yì-sz *or* láy-'jìn, *or* **be satisfying** gwò-'yǐn. ‖It will be a treat to hear the n w concert. chywù tīng nèy-ge-'shīn-yīn-ywè-'hwèy yí-'dìng hěn °yěw 'yì-sz. *or* °láy-'jìn. *or* °gwò-'yǐn.

TREE. shù. ‖I just missed hitting a tree while driving **over here.** wǒ kāy-'chē wàng-'jèr láy de-shŕ-hew 'chà-dyǎr méy-'jwàng 'shù-shang.

Be up a tree. ‖That problem really has me up a tree. nèy-ge-'wèn-tí 'jēn jyàw-wo °dzwò-'là. *or* °méy-'lùr. *or* °méy-'jé. *or* °wéy-'nán.

TRIAL. (*A test*) *expressed with* **to try** shŕ. ‖Why don't **you give this automobile a trial?** nǐ 'wèy-shéme bú-'shr̀-shr jèy-lyàng-'chē? ‖We'll hire you for a week's **trial.** wǒm 'shyān ràng-ni dzwǒ yí-ge-lǐ-'bày °'shr̀-shr. *or* °shr̀-'gūng. *or* °shr̀-'shěwr.

(*A period of emotional hardship*). *Expressed with* **hard to bear** nán-'shèw. ‖It must have been a great **trial to lose your father.** lìng 'dzwēn chywù-'shr̀ nǐ yí-'dìng hěn nán-'shèw.

(*Legal*). *Expressed with* **be tried** gwò-'tíng *or* kāy-'shěn. ‖Our case comes up for trial next Monday. dzám-de-'àn-dz 'shyà-lǐ-bày-'yī °gwò-'tíng. *or* °kāy-'shěn.

TRICK. (*Knack*) 'mén-daw, chyàwr, 'jywé-jāwr. ‖There's a trick to making a good cake. 'dyǎn-shin yàw snyáng dzwò-'hǎw-le děy 'jŕ-dàw nèy-ge-°'mén-daw. *or* °'chyàwr. *or* bǎ 'dyǎn-shīn dzwò-'hǎw-le, yěw ge-'jywé-jāwr.

(*Mischief*). ‖She's full of tricks, isn't she? tā °shīn-'yǎr jēn 'dwō (*or* °hěn 'hwá-téw *or* °jú-'yì tǐng 'dwō *or* sēw jú-'yì hěn 'dwō), 'shr̀-bu-shr̀?

(*Habit*). ‖She's got a trick of frowning when she's **thinking.** tā yì 'shyǎng shéme jyèw 'jèw méy-'téw-dz.

(*In cards*) yí-fù-'páy, yí-lwòr-'páy. ‖Who took that **last trick?** 'shàng-yí-fù-'páy shr̀-'shéy 'ná-de? ‖All **we need is two more tricks now.** dzám 'dzày ná lyǎng-lwòr-'páy jyèw 'gèw-le.

(*Legerdemain*) wán-'yèr, shì-'fǎr. ‖He knows some **pretty good tricks with cards.** tā hwèy jǐ-'shěwr 'hěn ná-jŕ-'páy-°'wár-de-wán-'yèr. *or* °'byàn-de-shì-'fǎr.

(*Treacherous act*). ‖That's a mean trick to play on **me.** 'nèy-yì-'shěwr gěy-wo-'láy-de kě 'jēn bú-'shàn. *or* nèy-ge-wán-'shyàw gēn-wo-'kāy-de kě 'jēn bù-'shyǎw.

(*Attempts to disrupt or escape*). ‖Don't try any tricks! byé °'tēw-tew-mwō-'mwō-de (*or* °'gwěy-gwey-swèy-'swèy-de) °shwǎ hwā-'jāwr! *or* °shwǎ hwā-'hwó! *or* °shwǎ-'gwěy! *or* °shr̀-'hwày! *or* °chū 'sēw-jú-'yì! *or* shwǎ hwá-'téw!

To **turn the trick** (*accomplish the end in view*) líng, shíng, chéng. ‖Your idea will turn the trick. 'shíng, nǐ nèy-yí-'shyà-dz jwěn °'líng, *or* °'shíng. *or* °'chéng.

To **trick** *someone* pyàn, dzwàn, mēng, ywān, shwǎ, kēng. ‖Just my luck, tricked again! jēn dǎw-'méy, 'yèw jyàw-rén gěy °'pyàn-le! *or* °'dzwàn-le! *etc.* ‖I **had confidence in him, but he tricked me and didn't do as we had agreed he would.** wǒ 'dàw-shr tǐng 'shìn-rèn ta láy-je, kě-shr tā 'pyàn-wo, 'bú-àn-je wǒ-men-de-'yì-sz 'dzwò.

To **trick** *someone into doing something*. ‖Are you **trying to trick me into saying that?** nǐ-shr shyǎng 'tàw wǒ-de-'hwà-ma? *or* nǐ-shr 'byàn-je 'fāngr-de ràng-wo 'shwō-chu-láy-ya?

TRIP. (*Journey*) (yí-tàng-)lywǔ-'shíng, (yí-tàng-) 'dzěw-de; (*for pleasure*) (yí-tàng-)chū-chywu-'wár-de. ‖How was your trip? nǐ-'jèy-tàng-lywǔ-'shíng (*or* nǐ-'jèy-tàng-chū-chywu-'wár-de *or* nǐ-'jèy-tàng-'dzěw-de) dzěme-'yàng? ‖How long a trip is it? jèy-yí-'tàng yěw dwō-'ywǎn?

(*To cause to stumble*) bàn . . . yì-'gēn-dew. ‖If you **don't pull your legs out of the aisle, you're liable to trip someone.** nǐ yàw-shr bù-bǎ-'twěy tsúng dzěw-'dàw-shang 'chè-hwey-lay, hwéy-'téw yí-'shyà-dz 'bàn-rén yì-'gēn-dew.

(*To stumble*) bàn yi-'gēn-dew, bàn-'dǎw-le. ‖He **tripped and fell.** tā 'bàn-le yì-'gēn-dew, bàn-'dǎw-le.

To **trip** *someone* **up** (*figuratively*) dǎw-'lwàn. ‖We **would have finished on time if somebody hadn't tripped us up somewhere.** yàw-shr 'méy-rén gēn-'dzám dǎw-'lwàn de-hwà, dzám bú-'jyèw kě-yi àn 'shŕ-hew dzwò-'wán-le-ma?

TROUBLE. (*Disturbance*) 'lwàn-dz, *or expressed in proper context as* **affair** shr̀. ‖The police are trying to **break up that trouble down the street.** shywún-'jǐng 'jèng shyǎng bǎ 'jyē-nèy-téwr-de-°'nèy-ge-'lwàn-dz (*or* °'nèy-dàng-dz-'shr̀) 'lyǎw-le.

(*Interference or a fight*). ‖Are you asking for trouble? nǐ-shr̀ 'méy-chár jǎw-'chár háy-shr 'dzěme-je? *or* nǐ-shr̀ yàw jǎw 'má-fan-ma? *or* nǐ 'shǎw gwǎn shyán-'shr̀. *or* nǐ jǎw-'dzèw-a?

(*Distress or wrongdoing*). ‖I'm in trouble. wǒ chū-'shèr-le. *or* (*Less empha c*) wǒ chū-le 'má-fan-le. *or* (*Experiencing bad luck*) wǒ dǎw-le 'méy-le. *or* (*Because of one's wrongdoings or mistakes*) wǒ 'tǔng-le 'léw-dz-le. *or* wǒ rě-'hwò-le.

(*Inconvenience or minor interruption*). ‖What's the **trouble?** 'dzěme-le? *or* shéme-'shèr?

To **trouble** (*to make uncomfortable*) ràng . . . bù-'shū-fu. ‖My arm has been troubling me ever since my

Moslem sector of Sian

Watchtowers accent the Great Wall

accident. tsúng wǒ chū-le 'shŕ yǐ-'hèw wǒ-de-'gē-be yì-'jŕ-de ràng-wo bù-'shū-fu.

Trouble *is often used in a sentence of request to make it more polite; Chinese may have* 'má-fan *used in some similar way, or may achieve the polite tone by other means.* ‖May I trouble you for a match? gēn-nín °shín (beg, *or* °jyè borrow) gēr-yáng-'hwǒ. ‖Don't put yourself to any trouble. hé-'bì dz̀-'jǐ jǎw 'má-fan? ‖Thanks for your trouble. 'jēn-shŕ 'má-fan nín-le. *or* jyàw-nín shèw-'lèy. ‖Sorry to trouble you. 'jè-shŕ dzěme-'shwō-de, jyàw-nín shèw-'lèy. ‖(It was) nu trouble at all! 'nǎr-de-'hwà! ‖Would it be any trouble for you to work tonight? jyēr-'wǎn-shang 'má-fan nǐ dwō 'dzwò-hwěr, shíng-ma?

TRUCK. (*Vehicle*) kǎ-'chē, dà-chì-'chē, dzày-jùng-chì-'chē, ywùn-hwǒ-chì-'chē; *when context or situation indicates what type of vehicle is involved one says simply* chē. ‖Where can I park my truck? wǒ néng bǎ-'chē tíng-dzay 'nǎr?

To truck (*transport*) yùng °kǎ-'chē (*or another word for the vehicle*) ywùn; *if context is clear, one says simply to transport* ywùn. ‖It took us two days to truck this furniture across town. wǒm fèy-le 'lyǎng-tyān-de-'gūng-fu tsáy bǎ 'jyā-jywù 'ywùn-daw chéng-'nèy-byar-chywu.

To sell *someone* truck *or give someone* truck (*cheat or kid or tease*) ywān, dzwàn, pyàn. ‖You can't sell me that truck! *or* Don't give me any of that truck! nǐ °'ywān- (*or* °'dzwàn- *or* °'pyàn-)bu-lyǎw wo!

(*Garden produce*) *expressed with* vegetables tsày. ‖The farmer sold all his truck in half a day. 'jwāng-jya-rén bàn-'tyār-de-'gūng-fu jyèw bǎ tā-de-'tsày mày-'gwāng-le.

TRUE. (*Factual*) jēn; (*genuine*) jēn-'jèng; (*accurate*) jēn *or* jèng *in compounds.* True north (*meaning accurate north*) jèng-'běy; (*meaning in contrast to magnetic north; used only by surveyors and the like in China*) jēn-'běy. ‖Is that story true? 'nèy-dwàr-'shèr shŕ 'jēn-de-ma? ‖That picture is a true likeness of you. nèy-jāng-shyàng-'pyār jēn 'shyǎng-ni. ‖He's a true scientist. tā-shŕ yí-ge-jēn-'jèng-de-kē-shywé-'jyā. ‖You'll find him a true friend. nǐ yí-'dìng hwèy fā-'shyàn tā-'nèy-ge-rén shŕ ge-jēn-'jèng-de-'péng-yew. *or expressed as* You'll certainly find him sufficiently a friend. nǐ yí-'dìng hwèy fā-'shyàn tā-'nèy-ge-rén hěn-gèw-'péng-yew. ‖Where's true north from here? jēn-'běy (*or* jèng-'běy) dzày-'nǎr?

Is it true that *is expressed with stressed* shŕ. ‖Is it true that you got a new car? nǐ 'shŕ mǎy-le lyàng-'shīn-'chē-ma?

Be true to one's word shwō-'hwà 'swàn-hwà *or* shwō-'hwà jyèw 'swàn. ‖He's always true to his word. tā 'shyàng-láy shŕ °shwō-'hwà 'swàn-hwà, *or* °shwō-'hwà jyèw 'swàn.

TRUNK. (*Of a tree*) shù(-'gàn), shù(-'běn). ‖Nail the notice on the trunk of that tree. bǎ 'páy-dz dīng-de nèy-ge-shù-shang.

(*For clothes, etc.*) (dà-)'shyāng-dz, dà-'shyāng. ‖I want to send my trunk through on my ticket. wǒ shyǎng bǎ 'shyāng-dz dǎ shíng-li-'pyàw dày-'dzěw.

(*Part of the body*) *expressed as* body 'shēn(-dz), *which may be made to exclude the extremities and head by specific mention, but otherwise includes them.*

Trunks (*short outside trouser-like garment*) kù 'chǎr, dwǎn-'kù-dz. ‖These trunks are too tight. jèy-tyáw-kù-'chǎr tày 'shèw.

Trunk line (*railroad or highway*) jèng-'lù *or* dà-'lù; (*railroad only, but a bit literary*) gàn-'shyàn.

TRUST. To trust *or* to put trust in shìn, 'shìn-rèn. ‖I'm putting my trust in you. wǒ 'shìn-rèn ni. ‖Don't you trust me? nǐ bú-'shìn-rèn wǒ-ma? ‖I guess we've got to take his story on trust. wǒ kàn, dzám jŕ 'hǎw 'shìn-ta-de. ‖You shouldn't trust your memory so much. *is expressed as* Don't expect your memory to be so good. nǐ byé 'yí-wéy nǐ-de-'jì-shìng 'hǎw.

(*To rely on*) kàw. ‖Im looking for a servant that I can trust. wǒ jèng dzày 'jǎw yí-ge-chéng-'shŕ-kě-'kàw-de-'yùng-rén. ‖I don't trust this driver. wǒ 'jywé-hu-je jèy-ge-kāy-'chē-de kàw-bu-'jù.

To trust *something* to *someone* 'jyāw-gěy. ‖They trusted the money to his care. tām bǎ-'chyán jyāw-gey 'tā gwǎn-le.

To hold in trust (*legal*). ‖His father's estate was held in trust for him by his uncle until he was twenty-one. *is expressed as* His uncle took care of his father's property for him until he was twenty-one before it was given to him. tā-de-'shū-shu tì-ta 'gwǎn-je tā-'fù-chin-de-chǎn-'yè, yì-'jŕ dàw tā èr-shŕ-'yī-swèy, tsáy 'jyāw-gey ta.

Of great trust 'dzé-rèn hěn 'dà. ‖He holds a position of great trust. tā-de-'shèr 'dzé-rèn hěn 'dà.

To trust *someone* (*said in asking for a loan*). ‖Can you trust me until payday? *is expressed as* Wait till payday and I'll pay you back, OK? děng wǒ gwān-'shyǎng de-shŕ-hewr dzày 'hwán-ni, 'shíng-ma?

(*In polite greetings or invitations*). *Expressed as* to hope 'shī-wàng, *or unexpressed, a different formula for politeness being used.* ‖I trust you'll be able to come to dinner. wǒ 'shī-wàng nín láy gēn wǒ-men chŕ wǎn-'fàn. ‖I trust you slept well. nǐ shwèy-'hǎw-le-ba!

TRUTH. (*Words which state facts*) shŕ-'hwà. ‖That's the truth. nà-shŕ shŕ-'hwà. ‖Are you telling me the truth? nǐ-shŕ gēn-wo shwō shŕ-'hwà-ne-ma?

(*Element of accuracy*) jēn-'gé-de. ‖Do you think there's any truth in that story? nǐ 'jywé-de tā-shwō-de-'hwà yěw dyǎr-jēn-'gé-dé-ma?

TRY. To try *a key, a pen, etc.* shŕ; to try *a food is expressed with* to cook dzwò *or with* to taste cháng. ‖Did you try the key? 'yàw-shr nǐ 'shŕ-le-ma? ‖Here, try my pen. éy, 'shr̀-shr 'wǒ-de-gāng-'bǐ. ‖I think I'll try some soup. wǒ shyǎng wǒ láy dyǎr-'tāng ᵉ'shr̀-shr. or °'cháng-chang. ‖I've never tried this dish before. wǒ 'tsúng-láy méy-°'dzwò- (or °'cháng-) gwo jèy-jǔng-'tsày.

To try a case (in court, of the judge) shěn. ‖Who's going to try your case? 'shéy láy 'shěn nǐ-jèy-ge-'àn-dz-a?

To try one's patience ràng . . . °'jāw-jí or °'bú-này-'fán. ‖Sometimes you try my patience. yěw-'shŕ-hew nǐ 'jēn ràng-wo °'jāw-jí. or °'bú-này-'fán.

To try clothes on 'shr̀-shr, 'chwā -shang (or 'dày-shang or other word for wear, depending on what type of clothing is involved) . . . 'shr̀-shr. ‖First I'd like to try that suit on again. wǒ 'shyān dzày 'chwān-shang nèy-jyàn-'yī-shang 'shr̀-shr. or wǒ dzày 'shr̀-shr nèy-jyàn-'yī-shang dzày 'shwō.

To try out for a part in a play, radio, football, etc.; expressed in terms of going to see the proper person and taking a try and seeing whether it works 'shr̀-shr kàn 'shíng-bu-shíng.

To try to or and do something shyǎng-'fár; (after the trial) shr̀; often omit ed. ‖Let's try and get there on time. dzǎm shyǎng-'fár àn-je 'shŕ-hew 'dàw-hèr. ‖Try to do better next time. 'shyà-yì-hwéy (shyǎng-'fár) dzwò 'hǎw-dyǎr. ‖We'll try to finish today for sure. wǒ-men shyǎng-'fá-dz jyēr yí-'dìng dzwò-'wán-le. ‖I tried to follow your instructions. wǒ àn-je nǐ-gàw-sung-wo-de-'fá-dz 'shr̀ láy-je.

To have (or make or take) a try (at) shr̀. ‖He made several tries, but failed each time. tā 'shr̀-le hǎw-jǐ-'hwéy, 'měy-hwéy dēw bù-'shíng. ‖Let's take another try at solving the problem. dzǎm 'dzày 'shr̀ yì-hwéy-ba.

Be trying tǎw-'yàn, chyáw, shèw. ‖That noise outside is very trying, especially when you want to work. 'wày-tew-de nèy-ge-'shēng-yin tǐng tǎw-'yàn, nǐ 'ywè yàw dzwò-'shr̀ nèr ywè 'shyǎng. ‖This has been a trying day. 'jèy-yì-tyān jēn gèw °'chyáw-de. or °'shèw-de.

TUESDAY. lǐ-bày-'èr, shīng-chī-'èr.

TURN. 1. (To revolve) jwàn; (of a person, to change position of the body) jwàn-gwò 'shēr (láy, chywù), jwàn-gwò 'lyǎr (láy, chywù), jwǎn-gwò 'shēr (láy, chywù), jwǎn-gwò 'lyǎr (láy, chywù); (of the wind) jwàn. ‖The wheels won't even turn in this mud. 'gū-lu dzày 'ní-li lyán-'jwàn dēw bú-'jwàn. ‖He turned and beckoned to us to follow him. tā °'jwàn-gwo 'shēn-lay (or °'jwàn-gwò 'lyǎr-lay or etc.) gēn wǒ-men dǎ ge-'jāw-hu ràng wǒ-men 'gēn-je ta. ‖Looks like the wind is turning. chyáw 'jèy-ge-yì-sz jwǎn-'fēng-le.

2. To turn a corner gwǎy-'wār. ‖He just turned the corner. tā gāng gwǎy-gwò 'wār-chywu.

(To cause to revolve) jwàn. ‖Try to turn the knob. 'jwàn-jwàn nèy-ge-'bǎ-shew 'shr̀-shr.

(To twist) wǎy, nyěw. ‖She turned her ankle on the edge of the sidewalk. tā dzày mǎ-lù-'yár-nèr bǎ jyǎw-'wàn-dz °'wǎy-le (or °'nyěw-le) yí-shyàr.

To turn someone's head. ‖He's one person who won't let praise turn his head. tū 'nèy-rén dzěme bā-jye, yě bù-gǎy 'jú-yì.

To turn someone's stomach. ‖I'm afraid this food will turn my stomach. kǔng-'pà wǒ yì chr̄ jèy-jǔng-'tsày, 'shīn-li jyèw děy 'nàw-de-heng.

To turn tail nyěw-'téwr. ‖The little boy turned tail and ran, when he saw his father coming. shyǎw-'hár yì 'chyáw-jyàn tā-'bà-ba, nyěw-'téwr jyèw 'pǎw.

To turn the tables on gěy . . . 'láy yí-shyà-dz. ‖Let's turn the tables on them for a change and see how they like it. wǒ-men 'yě gěy 'tā-men 'láy yí-shyà-dz, kàn-kan 'tā-men dzěme-'yàng.

To turn the tide against 'yā-shyà-chywù; to turn the tide for or in favor of 'táy-chǐ-láy; to be turned, (of the tide) 'byàn-le, 'jwǎn-gwò-láy-le. ‖The city vote turned the tide against (or for) our candidate. chéng-'lǐ-tew-'téw-de-'pyàw bǎ wǒ-men-de-hèw-shywǎn-'rén gěy °'yā-shyà-chywù-le. (or °'táy-chǐ-láy-le.) ‖But once he spoke in favor of my proposal the tide was turned. 'tā yì shwō tā 'dzàn-cheng 'wǒ-de-yì-sz, nèy-ge-'shíng-shr̀ jyèw °'byàn-le. or °'jwǎn-gwò-láy-le.

3. To turn white, pale, sour, etc., expressed with to become byàn followed by the adjective, or by the adjective plus le. ‖She turned pale when she heard the news. tā yì 'tīng-jyàn nèy-ge-'shyāw-shì 'lyǎn-shang lì-'shŕ °'byàn-le 'shǎr-le. or °byàn-'báy-le. ‖Don't leave the milk on the table, or it'll turn sour. byé bǎ nyéw-'nǎy 'lyàw-dzày 'jwō-dz shang, 'yàw-bù-rán jyèw 'swān-le.

4. To turn an age, expressed with not to be more than bú-'gwò. ‖She claims she's just turning thirty. jywù tā-'shwō, tā bú-'gwò sān-'shŕ. ‖She's just turning thirty. tā bú-'gwò sān-'shŕ.

5. To turn around (of a person) jwàn-gwò 'lyǎr (láy or chywù), jwàn-gwo 'shēr (láy or chywù), jwǎn-gwò 'lyǎr (láy or chywù), jwǎn-gwò 'shēr (láy or chywù). ‖He turned around and looked at us. tā jwàn-gwò 'lyǎr-lay (or etc.) 'kàn wǒ-men.

To turn something around (physically) 'jwàn-gwò (láy or chywù). ‖Let's turn the table around. bǎ 'jwō-dz 'jwàn-gwo-lay.

To turn something said around (misinterpret) jyě-shǐ 'tswò. ‖You're turning my words around. nǐ bǎ wǒ-de-'hwà jyě-shǐ 'tswò-le.

6. To turn back wàng-'hwéy dzěw. ‖Let's turn back. dzám wàng-'hwéy dzěw-ba.

To turn someone back ràng . . . 'hwéy-chywù. ‖Turn them back; the road's blocked up ahead. ràng tā-men 'hwéy-chywu-ba, 'chyán-byar 'dàwr bù-'tūng.

7 To turn down a road, etc. wàng . . . gwǎy(-'wār). ‖Turn down this road. wàng 'jèy-byar gwǎy-'wār.

To turn something down (fold it back) 'shyān-kāy. ‖Turn down the blanket. bǎ 'bèy-wo 'shyān-kay.

To turn *something* **down** (*reject*) 'jywù-jywé, *or expressed negatively with* not accept bù-jyē-'shèw. ‖My application for a job was turned down for some reason. wǒ-méw-'shr̀-de-chǐng-chyéw-'shū 'yīn-wèy dyǎr-'ywán-gu °bèy 'jywù-jywé-le. *or* °tā-men méy-jyē-'shèw.

8. To turn **in** (*go to bed*) 'shwèy, shwèy-'jyàw. ‖We ought to turn in early tonight. dzám jyēr-'wǎn-shang yīng-dang °'dzǎw shwèy-'jyàw. *or* °'dzǎw-dyǎr 'shwèy.

To turn in *a driveway, road, etc.* 'jìn-chywù. ‖Turn in at the next drive. 'shyà-yí-ge-'kěwr-nèr 'jìn-chywu. ‖Turn in at the next gate. 'shyà-yí-ge-mén-'kěwr-nèr 'jìn-chywù.

To turn *something* **in** hwán. ‖You'll have to turn in your equipment before we can release you. wǒ-men ràng-ni 'dzěw yǐ-'chyán, nǐ děy bǎ 'dūng-shi 'hwán-le.

9. Turn **into** (*become*) °'byàn-chéng. ‖She's turned into an old gossip. tā 'byàn-chéng ge-'swèy-dzwěy-dz-lāw-'dāw-de-lǎw-'tày-tày-le. ‖The discussion turned into a brawl. *is expressed as* As they discussed and discussed they started fighting. 'shāng-lyang-'shāng-lyang-je 'dǎ-chi-láy-le.

Turn *something* **into** *something else* bǎ ... . 'hwàn-chéng. ‖Of course, you can always turn your bonds into cash. 'dāng-rán nǐ 'shéme-shf-hewr dēw néng bǎ gūn_ 'jày 'hwàn-chéng shyàn-'chyán.

10. Turn *something* **off** 'gwān-shàng. ‖Turn off the light, it hurts my eyes. bǎ dyàn-'dēng 'gwān-shàng, 'hwǎng wǒ-'yǎn-jing. ‖I wonder if I forgot to turn off the gas. wa 'shr̀-bu-shr̀ 'wàng-le bǎ °chì-'mén '(*or* °méy-'chì) 'gwān-shàng-le.

11. To turn *something* **on** 'kāy-kay. ‖You'd better turn on the shower (*or* the shower on) while the water's still hot. nǐ chèn-'dzǎwr chèn-je 'shwěy háy 'rè bǎ 'pēn-dz 'kāy-kay. ‖Turn on the lights. bǎ-'dēng 'kāy-kay.

To turn on *something* (*depend on for validity*) kàn. ‖All our plans turn on whether he gets back in time. wǒm-yí-'chyè-de-'jì-hwà děy 'kàn tā 'shr̀-bu-shr̀ néng dàw-'shf-hew 'hwéy-láy. ‖The whole argument turns on that point. 'swǒ-yěw-de-'jēng-lwèn dēw 'kàn 'jèy-yì-dyǎn dzěme-'yàng-le.

To turn on *someone* (*cease to agree with or be pleasant to*) 'hū-rán gēn ... gwò-bu-'chywù, 'jywū-rán gēn ... dàw-'lwàn. ‖Why are you turning on me so? nǐ gàn-'má 'hū-rán gēn-wo jème gwò-bu-'chywù? ‖I didn't expect you'd turn on me too. méy-'shyǎng-dàw 'nǐ 'jywū-rán 'yě hwèy gēn-wo dàw-'lwàn.

To turn on one's heel nyěw-'téwr. ‖She turned on her heel and left. tā nyěw-'téwr jyèw 'dzěw.

12. To turn **out** (*get up*) chǐ(-láy). ‖What time do you turn out every morning? nǐ 'měy-tyān-'dzǎw-chen 'shéme-shf-hew 'chǐ?

To turn out (*assemble*) dàw-'chǎng, chū-'shí, chywù, láy. ‖How many turned out? yěw 'dwō-shaw-rén °dàw-'chǎng-le? *or* °chū-'shí-le? *or* °'chywù-le? *or* °'láy-le? ‖A large crowd turned out for the meeting?

is expressed as The people who came to the meeting were quite numerous. dàw-'hwèy-de-rén hěn 'dwō.

To turn *someone* **out** (*expel*) 'hūng-chu-láy, 'hūng-chu-chywù. ‖I've been turned out. wǒ jyàw-rén gěy 'hūng-chu-láy-le. ‖When I mentioned politics, he nearly turned me out of the house. wǒ yì tí gwó-'shr̀, tā 'chà-dyǎr bǎ-wo 'hūng-chu-chywù.

To turn *something* **out** (*extinguish*) 'gwān-shàng, nùng-'myè-le. ‖Turn out the lights. bǎ-'dēng °'gwān-shàng. *or* °nùng-'myè-le.

To turn *something* **out** (*produce*) chū. ‖That factory turns out a great many guns in one year. nèy-ge-gūng-'chǎng yì-'nyán chū hěn-'dwō-de-chyāng-'pàw. ‖He turns out his books wholesale. tā chū-'shū chū-de yèw 'dwō yèw 'kwày.

To turn out *in a certain way.* ‖How did the party turn out? nèy-ge-'hwèy dzěme-'yàng-le? ‖This turned out very well. *is expressed as* This result is quite good. 'jèy-ge-jyē-'gwǒ hěn 'hǎw.

13. To turn **over** 'fān-gwò-chywù. ‖Watch out! We almost turned over that time. lyéw-'shén! 'nèy-hwéy 'chà-dyǎr (méy-) 'fān-gwò-chywǔ.

To turn *something* **over** 'jē-gwò-láy, 'fān-gwò-láy. ‖Turn that box over. bǎ 'shyāng-dz °'jē-gwò-láy. *or* °'fān-gwò-láy.

To turn over a new leaf 'gǎy-gwò dz̀-'shīn. ‖Do you think he's sincere when he says he's going to turn over a new leaf? tā shwō tā yàw 'gǎy-gwò dz̀-'shīn, nǐ 'jywé-de tā 'jēn-shr̀ 'yàw nà-yàngr-ma?

To turn *something* over to *someone* 'jyāw-gěy. ‖He turned over his business to his son. tā bǎ 'mǎy-may 'jyāw-gey tā-'ér-dz-le.

To turn *something* over in one's mind *or* head *etc.* 'shyǎng-yi-shyáng, dzày °'shīn-li (*or* °'nǎw-dz) °'jwàn-jwàn (*or* °'pán-swan-pán-swan). ‖Turn it over in your mind first, before you give me your answer. nǐ 'shyān dzày 'shīn-li 'jwàn-jwan dzày 'gàw-sung wo. ‖I've been turning this over in my head for months, but I still can't make up my mind. 'jèy-jyàn-shèr dzày wǒ-'nǎw-dz-li 'jwàn-le yěw 'hǎw-jǐ-ge-'ywè-le, 'kě-shr wǒ 'háy-shr ná-bu-'dìng jú-'yì.

14. To turn **to** *a page* 'fān-dàw. ‖You'll find those figures if you turn to page fifty. nǐ 'fān-dàw dì-'wǔ-shr̀-'yè jyèw kě-yi 'kàn-jyàn nèy-shyē-'shùr-le.

To turn to *someone* (*for help*) chyéw, jǎw. ‖You can always turn to him for help. nǐ 'dzǔng kě-yì °chyéw (*or* °jǎw) 'tā bāng-bang 'máng. ‖I have no one to turn to. wǒ 'méy-rén kě-'chyéw.

15. To turn **up** (*arise*) hwèy yěw. ‖Come around next week; maybe some news will have turned up by then. nǐ 'shyà-lǐ-bày 'láy yí-tàng, dàw 'nèy-ge-shf-hew hwǒ-je hwèy yěw dyǎr-'shyāw-shi-shéme-de.

To turn up (*appear unexpectedly, of a person*). ‖He's always turning up where you don't want him. 'nǎr bú-'yàw-ta, tā shàng-'nǎr 'chywù.

To turn up *a driveway, etc.* gwǎy-'wǎr. ‖Blow your horn when you turn up the driveway. gwǎy-'wǎr de shf-hew 'èn-èn 'lǎ-ba.

To turn *something* up (*increase*) kāy 'dà-dyǎr. ‖You'll have to turn the heat up here if you don't want to freeze. nǐ yàw-shr bù-'dǎ-swàn āy-'dùng de-hwà, dzŭng děy bǎ jèr-de-chì-'lú-dz kāy 'dà-dyǎr. ‖Turn the radio up, will you? láw-'jyà, bǎ wú-shyàn-'dyàn kāy 'dà-dyǎr!

To turn *something* up (*fold back*) 'jywǎn-chǐ-láy, 'myān-chǐ-láy, 'wǎn-chǐ-láy. ‖I'll have to turn this cuff up. wǒ děy bǎ jèy-ge-shyèw-'kěwr °'jywǎn-chi dyǎr-láy. *or* °'myān-chi dyǎr-láy. *or etc.*

16. (*A change of direction*) *expressed with verbs in Chinese.* ‖Make a left turn at the next corner. *is expressed as* Turn to the left at the corner. dàw 'chyán-tew-gwǎy-'jyǎwr-nèr wàng-'dzwǒ gwǎy. ‖He was very ill last week, but he's taken a turn for the better *is expressed as* He was very ill last week, but later on he soon got better. tā 'shàng-lǐ-bày bìng-de tǐng 'lì-hay, kě-shr 'hèw-lay jyèw·jyàn 'hǎw-le.

17. (*Place where direction is changed*) gwǎy (*or* jwǎn)-'wǎr-de-dì-fangr; (*time when direction is changed*) gwǎy (*or* jwǎn)-'wǎr-de-shŕ-hewr; *both may be expressed with verbs.* ‖He took the turn at high speed. tā gwǎy-'wǎr gwǎy-de fēy 'kwày. *or* jwǎn-'wǎr-de-shŕ-hewr háy 'kāy-de hěn 'kwày.

18. (*Proper place in rotation*). To take turns lwén-'bār, hwàn, dǎw-'hwàn, lwén-'lyéw. ‖Let's take turns at the wheel. dzám °lwén-'bār-je (*or* °'hwàn-je *or* °'dǎw-'hwàn-je *or* °'lwén-'lyéw-je) 'kāy-ba.

In turn āy-je-'bār-de. ‖They were given their pay in turn. tā-men yí-gèr-yí-'gèr-āy-je-'bār-de dēw 'lǐng-dàw 'chyán-le.

To await *one's* turn děng-je gǎy 'bār. ‖You'll have to wait your turn. nǐ děy 'děng-je gǎy nǐ-de-'bār nǐ dzày 'chywù.

Out of turn. ‖You're talking out of turn. *meaning* You're talking now when it isn't proper for you to. 'háy bù-gāy-'nǐ shwō-'hwà-ne, nǐ jyèw 'shwō-le. *but meaning* You're saying improper things. nǐ 'chě-dàw 'nǎr chywù-le.

19. *Other expressions in English.* ‖Let's take a turn around the park. dzám dàw gūng-'ywán-li °'dzěw-dzew. *or* °'jwàn-jwàn. *or* °'lyèw-lyèw. *or* °'lyēw-da-lyēw-da. *or* °'sàn-san 'bù. ‖I've heard that story before, but you gave it a new turn. nèy-'dwàr wǒ 'tīng-shwō-gwo, 'bú-gwò 'nǐ shwō-de shŕ 'lìng-yí-yàngr. ‖He failed at every turn. tā °'dzǔng (*or* °'dzěme-je yě) shr̀ bù-'shíng.

‖You gave me quite a turn. nǐ 'shyà-le wo yí-'tyàw.
‖This meat is cooked to a turn. jèy-ge-'rèw 'dwèn-de 'hwǒ-hewr jèng 'hǎw.

TWELVE. shŕ-'èr. The twelfth dì-shŕ-'èr; one twelfth shŕ-'èr-fēn-jŕ-'yī.

TWENTY. 'èr-shr. The twentieth dì-'èr-shr; one twentieth 'èr-shr-fēn-jŕ-'yī.

TWICE. (*Two times*) 'lyǎng-tsž. *See also* **Time.** ‖I've been here twice already. wǒ 'yǐ-jīng láy-gwo jèr 'lyǎng-tsž-le. *But* ‖You'd better think it over twice before you come to any decision. (*Twice is here expressed as* again dzày *or as* carefully 'dž-shì *or* hǎw-'hāwr-de.) 'dzwèy-hǎw °'dzày (*or* °'dž-shì, *or* °hǎw-'hāwr-de) shyǎng-yi-shyǎng, rán-'hèw dǎ 'jú-yì.

Twice as . . . *is expressed as* . . . yí-'bèy. ‖That's twice as much as I want. nèy-ge bǐ wǒ-'yàw-de 'dwō yí-bèy.

TWO. èr (*as independent numeral: element in compound numerals: the only form before the measure for an ounce* lyǎng; *may be used with many measures of distance, time, and weight, and before the numerals* hundred bǎy, thousand chyán, *and* ten thousand wàn); lyǎng (*alternates with* èr *before many measures of distance, time, and weight, and before the numerals* hundred, thousand, *and* ten thousand; *the only form before other measures*): lyǎ (*equals* lyǎng *plus a measure, followed directly by a noun*). Twenty-two èr-shr-'èr; two hundred twenty-two 'èr-bǎy èr-shr-'èr *or* 'lyǎng-bǎy èr-shr-'èr. ‖Can you lend me two dollars? nǐ néng jyè-wǒ 'lyǎng-kwày-chyán-ma? ‖I'd say two or three days. wǒ kàn yě jyèw-shr 'lyǎng-sān-tyān-de-'yàng-dz. ‖Let's go by twos. dzám 'lyǎ-rén-lyǎ-'rén-de dzěw.

Put two and two together. ‖I put two and two together and figured he must be sick. wǒ 'gū-me-je tā yí-dìng 'bìng-le.

TYPE. (*Kind; especially of inherent type*) jǔng; (*especially as distinguished by appearance, shape, form, etc.*) yàng *or* yàngr *or* jǔng-'yàngr; (*a class, all the members of which have some common characteristic*) lèy; (*a group that people type by some characteristic*) pày; (*of people characterized · by a way of life or habits*) lù. *See also* **KIND.** ‖What type of shoes do you wear? nǐ chwān 'shéme-yàngr-de-shyé? ‖I don't like that type of girl. wǒ bù-'shǐ-hwān °nèy-jǔng-de-'nywǔ-rén. *or* (*Of physical type*) °nèy-yàngr-de-'nywǔ-rén. *or* (*Of a certain way of life*) °nèy-lù-de-'nywǔ-rén. *or* °nèy-lèy-de-'nywǔ-rén. *or* (*Assuming a bad type*) °nèy-jǔng-'jyèr-de 'nywǔ-rén. *or* °nèy-jǔng- 'shén-chì-de-'nywǔ-rén. *or* °nèy-jǔng-'dé-shìng-de-nywǔ-rén. ‖I can't type him (*tell what type he is*). wǒ 'kàn-bu-chū láy tā shr̀ °'něy-lù-de-rén. *or* °'dzěme-yàng-de-rén. (*Printing*) dzèr. *See also* **PRINT.** ‖The type is too small. dzèr tày 'shyǎw.

(*To write on a typewriter: to engage in the activity of typing*) dǎ-dž; (*make a copy by typing*) 'dǎ-chū-lay. ‖Do you know how to type? nǐ hwèy dǎ-'dž-ma? ‖Will you type these letters for me, please? láw-'jyà bǎ jèy-shyē-'shìn gěy-wǒ 'dǎ-chū-lay.

U

UGLY. (*To the eye*) bù-hǎw-'kàn, nán-'kàn, chěw, chwěn. ‖The picture looks ugly to me. nèy-jāng-'hwàr 'wǒ jywé-de bù-hǎw-'kàn.

(*Of a disposition*) bù-'hǎw, dzàw. ‖That dog has an ugly disposition. nèy-tyáw-'gěw 'shìng-ching bù-'hǎw. ‖I was in an ugly mood when I got up this morning. wǒ jyēr-'dzàw-shang 'chǐ-lay de-shr-hew °'pí-chi hěn 'dzàw. or °'shīn-ching bù-'hǎw.

UMBRELLA. yáng-'sǎn, ywǔ-'sǎn; (*made of oil paper or oilcloth*) yéw-'sǎn; *including also* parasol sǎn. ‖It looks like rain; you'd better take an umbrella. jèy-'tyār shyàng yàw shyà-'ywǔ, nǐ dày-je dyǎr °'sǎn-ba. or °'ywǔ-'sǎn-ba. *etc.*

UNDER. dzày (*or* tsúng *or* dàw) . . .°-'shyà-byar or °'dǐ-shya. ‖Slip the letter under the door. bǎ jèy-fēng-'shìn tsúng 'mén-shyà-byar °'sāy-jìn-chywù. or °'tǔng-jìn-chywù. ‖Can this boat go under the bridge? jèy-ge-'chwán néng-bu-néng tsúng chyáw-'shyà-byar 'dzěw-ne?

Under water *is expressed as* in the water dzày 'shwěy-lǐ ew *or as* under (the surface of) the water dzày 'shwěy-dǐ-shya. To swim under water *also* jā 'měng-dz. ‖I like to swim under water. wǒ 'ywàn-yi dzày °'shwěy-lǐ-tew (*or* 'shwěy-dǐ-shya) yéw-'yǔng. or wǒ 'shǐ-hwan jā 'měng-dz.

(*By the provisions of*) 'gēn-jywù, 'àn-je. ‖Under the new law such actions can be punished by a heavy fine. 'gēn-jywu (*or* 'àn-je) 'shīn-fǎ-'lywù, jèy-jǔng-'shíng-wéy yīng-gay shèw yán-'jùng-chǔ-'fá.

Be under discussion dzày tǎw-'lwèn-jūng. ‖The matter is under discussion. jèy-jyàn-'shǐ-ching jèng dzày tǎw-'lwèn-jūng. or *expressed as* They're just now discussing the matter. 'jèng tǎw-'lwèn jèy-jyàn-'shǐ-ne.

Under the control of gwèy . . . 'gwǎn, yéw . . . 'gwǎn-li. ‖The factory is under military control. nèy-ge-gūng-'chǎng shr °gwēy jywūn-'dwèy 'gwǎn. or °yéw jywūn-'dwèy 'gwǎn-li.

Be under oath chǐ-gwo 'shr. ‖You're under oath to tell the truth. nǐ chǐ-gwo 'shr, děy shwō shŕ-'hwà.

Under the circumstances jì-rán shr 'jè-yàngr-ne. ‖Under the circumstances I'll accept your apology. jì-rán shr 'jè-yàngr-ne, wǒ 'ywán-lyàng ni.

To go under (*to use*) yùng. ‖He goes under an assumed name. tā yùng yí-ge-'jyǎ-míng-dz.

To plow *something* **under** chú-chywu. ‖The weeds have been plowed under. yě-'tsǎw dēw chú-chywu-le.

To be snowed under. ‖He was snowed under in the election. nèy-tsz̀-shywǎn-'jywǔ jyǎn-'jŕ-de méy 'shéme-rén 'shywǎn-ta.

Under side *of anything* . . . 'dǐ-shya, . . .-dyěr. ‖The under side of the boat needs painting. chwán-de-'dǐ-shya (*or* chwán-'dyěr) °děy shàng yéw-'chī-le. or °děy 'yéw-yew-le.

Special expression in English. ‖Is everything under control? 'méy shéme-'shr̀-ba? *or* yí-'chyè dēw °rú-'yì-ma? *or* °'shwèn-'shīn-ma? *or* 'shéme dēw 'ān-pay-'hǎw-le-ma?

UNDERNEATH. (*On the under side of*) . . . 'dǐ-shyà. ‖The garage is underneath the house. chē-'fáng dzày 'wū-dz-dǐ-shya.

(*The under side*) 'dǐ-shyà, 'shyà-byar. ‖These pipes will have to be fixed from underneath. jèy-shyē-'gwǎn-dz děy tsúng 'shyà-byar 'shyēw-li. ‖Is there an opening underneath? 'dǐ-shya (*or* 'shyà-byar) yéw-'kěwr-ma? ‖The box is wooden on top and iron underneath. jèy-ge-'shyāng-dz 'shàng-tew shr̀ 'mù-tew-de, 'shyà-byar shr̀ 'tyě-de.

UNDERSTAND. (*Get the meaning of*) dǔng, 'míng-bay. ‖I don't understand what you mean. wǒ bù-°'dǔng (*or* °'míng-bay) nǐ-de-'yì-sz. ‖He said he didn't understand the instructions. tā shwō tā bù-'míng-bay nèy-ge-shwō-'míng. or tā shwō nèy-bĕn-shwō-míng-'shū tā dēw kàn-bu-'dǔng.

(*Be thoroughly acquainted with*) rèn-shr. ‖It takes a long time to understand these people. rèn-shr 'jèy-yàng-de-rén děy yàw hěn-cháng-de-shŕ-'jyān.

(*To be of the impression that*) jywé-je, 'yǐ-wéy. ‖He understood that you would meet him. tā °'jywé-je (*or* °'yǐ-wéy) nǐ néng chywù jyan ta.

(*To have heard that*) 'tīng-shwō. ‖I understand you're going away. wǒ 'tīng-shwō nǐ yàw 'dzěw.

UNION. (*A uniting*) *expressed with* to unite lyán-'hé. ‖A strong political party was formed by the union of several small groups. nèy-ge-yěw-'lì-lyang-de-'èng-'dǎng shr̀ tsúng jǐ-ge-'shyǎw-dzǔ lyán-'hé-chi-lay-de.

Labor union gūng-'hwèy.

UNITE. (*To form a union*) lyán-'hé-chi-láy, hé-'bìng-chǐ-láy, 'jyē-chǐ-láy; (*to cause to form a union*) bǎ . . . tǔng-'yī. ‖The outbreak of war united the nation. 'jàn-shr̀ yì 'chǐ-lay bǎ gwó-'jyā tǔng-'yī-le. or chywán-'gwó yīn-'wey kàng-'jàn ér-'twán-jyē-chi-lay-le. ‖The two clubs decided to unite. nèy-lyǎng-ge-'hwèy 'jywé-dìng hé-'bìng-chi-lay. ‖The country is united behind the president. jèy-ge-gwó-'jyā dzày dzǔng-'tǔng-lǐng-'dàw-jr-'shyà tǔng-'yī-le.

UNIVERSAL. *Expressed with* the whole world chywán-shr̀-'jyè; everybody 'nán-nywǔ-lǎw-'shàw, *etc.* ‖That movie has a universal appeal. nèy-ge-dyàn-'yěngr 'shéme-rén 'kàn-je dēw néng 'shǐ-hwan. ‖We believe that there is a universal desire for peace. wǒm 'shyāng-shìn chywán-shr̀-'jyè dēw 'shǐ-wàng hé-'píng.

UNIVERSITY. 'dà-shywé, dà-shywé-'shyàw. ‖He graduated from the university at the age of twenty-two. tā èr-shr-'èr-'swèy dzày nèy-ge-'dà-shywé bì-de 'yè. ‖The conference will be held at the university. nèy-ge-'hwèy yàw dzày 'dà-shywé-li 'kāy.

UNLESS. chú-'fēy, or expressed as if not rè-shr (or yàw-shr) ... bū. ‖We'll go on our trip tomorrow unless it rains. chú-'fēy shr̀ shyà-'ywǔ, 'bù-rán 'míng-tyan wǒm yí-'dìng chywù lywǔ-'shíng.

UNTIL. dàw. ‖It rained until four o'clock. 'ywǔ yì-'jŕ shyà-daw 'sz̀-dyǎn-jūng. (tsáy 'jù). ‖He didn't stop work until past midnight. tā yì-'jŕ-méy-'tíng-de dzwò-daw 'hèw-bàn-yè. ‖He won't give his answer until next week. bú-dàw 'shyà-shīng-chī tā bú-hwèy 'dá-fu. ‖He waited until everyone had left the train. tā 'děng-daw 'měy-yí-ge-rén dēw shyà-le 'chē.

Not until sometimes expressed as dzày ... yǐ-'chyán bū. ‖We won't leave until you're ready. dzày nǐ-'ywù-bèy-'hǎw-le yǐ-'chyán wǒm bù-'lí-kay jèr.

To wait until děng, 'děng-dàw. ‖May I wait until he comes back? wǒ 'děng tā 'hwéy-lay, 'hǎw-bu-háw?

UP. 1. Be up (referring to anything that may be happening). ‖What's up? chū-le shéme-'shr̀-le? or 'dzěme-le? or shéme-shr̀? or 'dzěme-hwéy-'shr̀? ‖I knew something was up when I heard the alarm. wǒ 'tīng-jyan nèy-ge-jǐng-'líng jyèw 'jŕ-daw shr̀ 'chū-le shéme-'shr̀-le.

Be up (of a window). If it opens upwards 'kāy-je; If it opens downwards 'gwān-je. ‖Is the window up? meaning Is the window open? nèy-ge-'chwāng-hu 'kāy-je-ne-ma? meaning Is the window closed? nèy-ge-'chwāng-hu 'gwān-je-ne-ma?

Be up (of a person, meaning out of bed in the morning) 'chǐ-láy-le. ‖He wasn't up yet when we called on him. wǒ-men dàw tā-'nèr de-shŕ-hew tā háy méy-'chǐ-lay-ne.

Be up and about (after illness) shyà-'dì-le. ‖He was sick last week, but now he's up and about. tā 'shàng-shīng-chī 'bìng-le, shyàn-dzày yǐ-jing shyà-'dì-le.

Be up against it (in financial straits) chyán hěn 'jǐn, jyǔng. ‖That family has really been up against it lately. nèy-jyār-'rén 'jìn-lay 'chyán hěn 'jǐn. or tām-'jyā 'jìn-lay hěn 'jyǔng.

Be up to someone. ‖It's up to you to decide where we'll go. is expressed as Where we go, is for you to decide. wǒm shàng-'nǎr chywù, yéw-'nǐ láy jywé-'dìng. or as Where shall we go? We'll do what you say. shàng-'nǎr? wǒm tīng-'nǐ-de.

Be up to something. ‖What're you up to now? nǐ shyàn-dzày °gàn (or °dzwò) 'shéme-ne? or meaning What trouble are you making now? nǐ shyàn-dzày °yèw dǎw shéme-'lwàn-ne? or °byé shéme-'hwày-ne? or °chū shéme-sēw-'jú-yì-ne?

2. Specific combinations of up after a verb are to be found generally at the appropriate verb entry. The following selection is only illustrative. Up in such combinations is often equivalent to the Chinese postverbs 'chǐ-láy, shàng, 'chū-lay, kāy, mǎn, wán, gwāng, dàw, or to the verb shàng; in other cases a single Chinese verb is equivalent to the English combination of verb and up.

Examples with 'chǐ-láy. ‖She looked up from her book when she heard the phone. tā kàn-'shū de-shŕ-hew 'tīng-jyan dyàn-'hwà 'shyǎng jyèw 'táy-chi 'téw-lay-le. ‖How fast can he add up a column of figures? tā bǎ yì-háng-'shùr 'jyā-chi-láy dzwèy 'kwày yùng 'dwō-shaw-shŕ-hew?

Example with shàng. ‖Did you lock up the house before we left? wǒ-men 'dzěw de-shŕ-hew, nǐ 'swǒ-shang 'mén-le-ma?

Examples with shàng as verb. ‖He went up the ladder to pick some apples. tā shàng(-daw) 'tī-dz(-shang) (chywù) 'jāy dyǎr-'píng-gwo. ‖He lives on the fifth floor, and we have to walk up. tā 'jù-dzay 'wǔ-tséng-léw; wǒm děy 'dzěw-je 'shàng-chywù. ‖We live up on a hill. is expressed as We live at a hill's topside. wǒ-men jù-dzay 'shān-shang.

Example with 'chū-láy. ‖Who brought up this problem? shéy 'tí-chu-lay-de jèy-ge-'wèn-tí?

Example with choice of kāy, shàng, or 'chǐ-láy (with different main verbs). ‖Put the umbrella up; it's raining. shyà-'ywǔ-le; bǎ-'sǎn °'dǎ-kay-ba. or °'jŕ-shang-ba. or °'jŕ-chi-láy-ba.

Examples with up giving the idea of completion, using wán, dàw, or gwāng, as verbs or postverbs. ‖Your time is up. nǐ-de-shŕ-'jyān °'dàw-le. or °'wán-le. ‖We used up all our money to get here. wǒm dàw-'jèr lay bǎ 'swǒ-yěw-de-'chyán dēw yùng-°'wán-le. or °'gwāng-le. ‖My car burned up last week. shàng-lǐ-bày wǒ-de-chē shāw-'gwāng-le.

Example with up meaning full mǎn. ‖Fill this pail up with water. bǎ jèy-ge-'tǔng-li jwāng-'mǎn-le 'shwěy.

Examples in which a single Chinese verb covers an English expression of verb plus up. ‖Don't forget to call me (up) tonight. jyēr-'wǎn-shang byé 'wàng-le gěy-wo dǎ dyàn-'hwà. ‖They were coming up the street to meet us. is expressed as They walked along on the street to meet us. tām dzày 'jyē-shang 'dzěw-gwò-láy 'jǎw wǒ-men. ‖Prices have gone up a lot in the last year. 'chywù-nyan 'wù-jyà 'jǎng-de hěn 'dwō. ‖The temperature went up to ninety. wēn-'dù 'jǎng-dàw jyěw-shr-'dù-le. ‖Please hang your hat (up) in the hall. 'màw-dz ké-yi 'gwà-dzay dà-'tīng-li. ‖Hurry (up), you're wasting too much time. 'kwày-dyǎr, nǐ 'tày 'dān-wù 'gūng-fu-le. ‖We invited our friends (up) for dinner. wǒm 'chǐng wǒm-de-'péng-yew chŕ-'fàn. ‖It's time to make up your mind. gāy °jywé-'dìng-le. or °'dǎ jú-'yì-le. ‖He ran up against a lot of trouble before he was elected. tā dzày bèy-'shywǎn yǐ-'chyán 'ywù-jyan hěn-'dwō-de-'kwèn-nan. ‖The post sticks up out of the water. is expressed as

The post in the water sticks out a section. nèy-gēr-'jù-dz dzày 'shwěy-lǐ-tew 'lèw-chu-yì-'jyér-lay. ‖We'll take that plan up at the next meeting. 'shyà⸱tsž-hwèy wǒ-men yàw tǎw-'lwèn nèy-ge-'jì-hwa. ‖He walked up the aisle to his seat. *is expressed as* He walked through the aisle to his seat. tā tsúng gwò-'dàwr 'dzěw-daw tā-de-'dzwòr-nèr chywù-le. ‖I don't think he did us justice when he wrote (up) the story. wǒ 'jywé-de tā 'shyě-de nèy-ge-'gù-shř bǎ wǒ-men 'shyě-de bù-gūng-'píng.

3. *To up* prices jyā, jǎng. ‖He's upped his prices since we were here last. tsúng wǒ-men 'shàng-tsž láy-le yǐ-'hèw, tā °jǎng-'jyàr-le. *or* jyā-'jyàr-le.

To up *production* 'dzēng-jyā. ‖They're upping production by leaps and bounds. tām 'jèng dzày 'dà-lyàng 'dzēng-jyā shēng-'chǎn.

4. *To up and* do something 'mǎ-shang jyèw. ‖I told him what you said, and he up and hit me. wǒ bǎ nǐ-de-'hwà 'gàw-su ta-le, tā 'mǎ-shang jyèw 'gěy-le wo yí-'shyà-dz.

5. *Up and coming* yěw 'shī-wang. ‖The new mayor is an up and coming politician. jèy-ge-'shīn-shř-'jǎng dzày 'jèng-jyè hěn yěw 'shī-wang.

UPPER. shàng. ‖I'd just as soon take the upper berth. wǒ kě-yi shwèy 'shàng-pù. ‖The fire started on one of the upper floors of this hotel. 'hwǒ shř tsúng jèy-ge-lywǔ-'gwǎn-léw-'shàng chǐ-de.

URGE. (*To ask earnestly*) chywàn. ‖We urged him to take a vacation. wǒm 'chywàn-ta 'shyēw-shi-shyēw-shi.

To urge *a* horse (*on or* forward) jyàw, *or, if by a specific action, a verb expressing that action; thus if by* kicking tī, *if by* pulling lā, *etc.* ‖He urged his horse forward. tā jyàw-'mǎ wàng-'chyán dzěw. *or* tā tī-je 'mǎ wàng-'chyán dzěw. *etc.*

An urge. ‖He felt a great urge to go back home. *is expressed as* He felt that he absolutely had to go back home. tā 'jywé-de 'fēy-děy hwéy-'jyā bù-'kě.

US. *See* **WE.**

USE. (*Utilization, handling, function*) *usually expressed in terms of* to use yùng; to be of use gàn .   yùng, yěw-'yùng; it's no use *doing so-and-so* méy-'yung *or* 'shéme-de. ‖Are you sure you know the proper use of this machine? nǐ-shr 'jēn 'jř-dàw dzěme yùng jèy-ge-'jī-chi-ma? ‖He's lost the use of his right arm. tā-de-'yèw-gē-be bù-néng 'yùng-le. ‖What possible use can there be for this gadget? jèy-ge-shyàw-'dūng-shi gàn shéme-'yùng-a? ‖What's the use of

arguing? táy-'gàng (*or* bàn-'dzwěy) yěw shéme-'yùng? ‖There's no use hurrying; we've already missed the train. wǒm fǎn-'jèn gǎn-bu-'shàng 'chē-le, ᵓ'máng yě měy-'yùng. *or* °'máng shéme-de?

To have no use for *someone.* ‖I have no use for that sort of person. *meaning* There's no vacancy for such a person here. 'nèy-yàng-de-rén wǒ-'jèr yùng-bu-'jàw. *or meaning* I can't stand to have such a person around. 'nèy-jǔng-rén wǒ °'jàw-bu-de. *or meaning* I can't stand contact with such a person. °'rě-bu-de. *or meaning* I can't stand being close to such a person. °'jìn-bu-de.

To be in use yùng-je, *or some specific verb depending on the object.* ‖You'll have to wait a minute; the telephone's in use now. nǐ 'děng-yi-hwěr-ba; dyàn-'hwà shyàn-dzày °'yùng-je-ne. *or* °yěw-'rén 'dǎ-je-ne. ‖This type of machine has only been in use for a few years. *is expressed as* This machine came out only a few years ago. 'jey-yàng-de-'jī-chi tsáy 'chū-le jǐ-'nyán.

To use yùng, *or some specific verb depending on the thing used.* ‖May I use your telephone? 'yung-yung nín-de-dyàn-'hwà shíng-ma? *or expressed as* May I borrow your telephone and use it? jyè nín-dyàn-'hwà 'shř-shř, 'hǎw-ma? ‖He's using the telephone right now. *is expressed as* He's telephoning right now. tā jèng dzày dǎ dyàn-'hwà-ne.

To use *something* up yùng-'gwāng-le, yùng-'wán-le; (*of money*) hwā-'gwāng-le, hwā-'wán-le. ‖I've used up all my money. wǒ bǎ-'chyán dēw °hwā-'gwāng-le. *or* °hwā-'wán-le. *or* yùng-'gwāng-le. *or* °yùng-'wán-le.

Be used to. ‖I'm not used to doing it this way. 'jème-je wǒ 'jywé-je yěw-dyǎr °bú-gwàn. *or* °bù-shéw.

Used to (*past customary-action*) *expressed with no modification of the verb in Chinese, and the addition of a time phrase such as* formerly tsúng-'chyán, dāng-'chū, yǐ-'chyán, *or at* earlier times yǐ-'chyán-de-shř-hew. ‖I used to eat there every day. wǒ °yǐ-'chyán(-de-shř-hew) (*or* °dāng-'chū) tyān-'tyār dzày-nàr 'chř. ‖I didn't use to like him very well. wǒ tsúng-'chyán 'bù-dzěme 'shǐ-hwan-ta.

USEFUL. yěw-'yùng-de. ‖He gave me some useful information. tā gàw-sung wǒ shyē-ge-yěw-'yùng-de-°'shř-ching. *or* °'shyàw-shi. *or* °'hwà.

USUAL. 'ywán-láy-de, *usually* 'píng-cháng. ‖Let's go home the usual way. wǒ-men háy dzěw 'ywán-láy-de-nèy-ge-'dàwr hwéy-'jyā-ba. *or* wǒ-men háy dzěw 'píng-cháng-dzěw-de-nèy-ge-'dàwr hwéy-'jyā-ba. ‖I had lunch at the usual place. wǒ 'háy dzày 'ywán-láy-nèy-ge-'dì-fang chř-'fàn. *or expressed as* I still ate at that place. wǒ 'háy-shr dzày nèy-ge-'dì-fang chř-de 'fàn.

V

VACATION. To have *or* take a vacation fàng-'jyà, shyēw-'jyà. ‖When's your vacation? nǐ 'shéme-shŕ-hew °fàng-'jyà? *or* °shyēw-'jyà? ‖I'm going to the mountains for my vacation this summer. jīn-nyan 'shyà-tyan wǒ yàw dàw 'shān-shang chywu shyēw-'jyà. *or* jīn-nyan shyēw-'jyà wǒ yàw dàw 'shān-shang chywù.

VALLEY. shān-'gǔ, shān-'gēwr. ‖There's a deep valley between the mountains. shān-'jūng-jyar yěw yí-ge-hěn-'shēn-de-°shān-'gǔ. *or* °shān-'gēwr. ‖The land in the river valley is very fertile. *is expressed as* The land along the river is very fertile. yán-je-'hé-de-dì hěn 'féy.

VALUABLE. yěw-'jyà-jŕ-de. ‖They gave us valuable information. tām 'gàw-sung-le wǒ-men dyǎr-yěw-'jyà-jŕ-de-'shyāw-shi. ‖How valuable are these things? *is expressed as* How about the value of these things? jèy-ge-'dūng-shi-'jyà-jŕ dzéme-'yàng?

Valuables shì-'rwǎn-de-dūng-shi, húng-'hwò, jŕ-'chyán-de-dūng-shi. ‖You'd better put your valuables in the safe. nǐ 'dǐng hǎw bǎ shì-'rwǎn-de-dūng-shi gē-dzay bǎw-shyǎn-'gwèy-li.

VALUE. 'jyà-jr; *often expressed with* to be worth money jŕ-'chyán *or* to be worth it jŕ. ‖What value do you put on this land? 'nǐ kàn, °jèy-kwày-'dì jŕ 'dwōer-chyán? *or* °jèy-kwày-'dì-de-'jyà-jr dzéme-'yàng? ‖Do you think you got good value for your money? nǐ 'jywé-de nǐ-'hwā-de-'chyán 'jŕ-ma?

(*Worth; monetary or non-monetary*) 'jyà-jr; (*only non-monetary*) yùng. ‖This book has no value at all. jèy-běr-'shū 'yì-dyǎr-°'jyà-jr (*or* °'yùng) yě 'méy-yew.

(*Given in another monetary system*) *expressed with* exchanges for *so-much* money hé . . . 'chyán. ‖What's the value of an American dollar in this country? dzày-'jèr 'yí-kwày-měy-'jīn hé 'dwōer-chyán?

To value *something* *at such-and-such an amount* gū-'jì (*or* 'swàn-ji-swàn-ji *or* 'swàn-swàn) . . . jŕ . . . 'chyán. ‖What do you value your property at? nǐ gū-'jì nǐ-de-'tsáy-chǎn jŕ 'dwōer-chyán?

To value *an opinion.* ‖I value his opinion very highly. (*Generally*) wǒ hěn 'jùng-shŕ tā-de-'yì-jyàn. (*Of a specific opinion*) tā-'nèy-ge-'yì-jyan wǒ 'jywé-je hěn 'hǎw.

VARIOUS. shǎw-'shyē, shǎw-'jǐ-ge, shyē, shyē-ge, 'gè-jǔng-bù-'túng-de, 'gè-shŕ-gè-'yàngr-de, 'hǎw-shyē-jǔng-bù-'túng-de, jǐ, hǎw-'shyē, hǎw-'jǐ-ge, gè-fāng-'myàn-de. ‖Various friends of mine have said they

liked him. wǒ-de-gè-fāng-'myàn-de-'péng-yew (*or* wǒ yěw hǎw-'shyē-'péng-yew) 'dēw shwō hěn 'shǐ-hwan tā. ‖He suggested various places they could go. tā shwō yěw °'shǎw-shyē-(*or* °shǎw-jǐ-ge- *or* °shyē- *or* °'shyě-ge-) 'dì-fangr tām néng 'chywù. ‖Various books have been written on that subject. gwān-ywu jèy-ge-'tí-mù yěw °'gè-jǔng-bù-'túng-de- (*or* °'gè-shŕ-gè-'yàngr-de- *or* °'hǎw-'shyē-jǔng-bù-'tǔng-de-) 'shū.

VEGETABLES. (*Type of food*) tsày, chīng-'tsày. ‖What kinds of vegetables do you grow in your garden? nǐ-'ywán-dz-li jùng shéme-'tsày?

(*Member of the vegetable kingdom, plant*) 'jŕ-wù.

VERY. hěn, tǐng, tày, twēy, jēn, (*Peiping*) bèr; *or* (*after the word modified*) 'jí-le, 'hěn, -de-heng, -de-hwang, -de 'lì-hày, -de 'lyǎw-bu-dé. *Modifiers put after the word modified are stronger than those put before.* ‖He's a very easy person to get along with. tā-'jèy-ge-rén °hěn 'rúng-yi shyāng-'chǔ. *or* °hěn hǎw shwō-'hwàr. *or* tā 'pí-chi hěn 'hǎw. ‖I was very pleased to get his letter. wǒ 'shēw-dàw tā-de-'shìn hěn 'gāw-shìng.

Not very bù-hěn, bú-'tày, bù-dzéme, bú-'nème, bú-'dà. ‖The bank isn't very far from here. tsúng-'jèr dàw nèy-ge-yín-'háng °bú-'tày (*or* °bù-hěn) 'ywǎn.

(*Exact, precise*) *expressed with* just precisely jywéw-shr *or* jèng-shr; even including lyán. ‖The very day I arrived war was declared. jyèw shr wǒ-'dàw-de-nèy-tyān, jyèw shywān-'jàn-le. ‖He's the very man you want. 'tā °jyèw-shr (*or* °jèng-shr) nǐ-'yàw-de-nèy-ge-rén. ‖The very thought of leaving is unpleasant to me. lí-kay-nèy-jyàn-'shŕ wǒ lyán 'shyáng dēw bú-'ywàn-yi shyáng.

VICTORY. shèng, shèng-'lì. To win victory dé-'shèng, dé-daw shèng-'lì. ‖The battle ended in a complete victory for our side. jèy-tsž-dzwò-'jàn 'jyē-gwǒ wǒ-men wán-'chywán shèng-'lì.

VIEW. (*Scene*) jǐng-'jŕ, jǐng-'jèr; (*of landscape*) fēng-'jǐng. ‖You get a beautiful view from this window. tsúng jèy-ge-'chwāng-hu 'kàn-chu-chywu, jǐng-'jèr hěn 'hǎw.

(*Attitude, opinion*) 'yì-jyàn, jyàn-'jyě, 'yì-sz, 'kàn-fa. ‖What are your views on the subject? dwèy-ywu jèy-jyàn-'shŕ nǐ-de-'yì-jyan dzéme-'yàng?

Be on view (*of a performance or movie*) yǎn, shàng-'yǎn, kāy-'yǎn. ‖The picture will be on view the end of the month. nèy-ge-dyàn-yěngr-'pyān-dz ywè-'dǐ 'yǎn.

In view of àn-je . . . láy 'kàn. ‖In view of present conditions, all shipping will probably be stopped. àn-je shyàn-'dzày-'shíng-shŕ láy 'kàn, 'swǒ-yěw-de-shāng-'chwān 'dà-gày dēw yàw 'tíng-le.

Be in full view of. ‖He was in full view of the crowd. *is expressed as* The whole crowd could see him. nèy-yì-chywún-'rén dēw kàn-de-'jyàn ta.

With a view to *doing so and so* 'dǎ-swàn. ‖I'm saving money with a view to buying a home of my own some day. wǒ dzǎn-'chyán shr̀ 'dǎ-swàn 'jyāng-láy wèy wǒ-'dz̀-jǐ mǎy swǒr-'fáng-dz.

To view 'rèn-wéy, 'yǐ-wéy, kàn-je, jywé. ‖Most people viewed that possibility with alarm. dà-'dwō-shùr-de-'rén dēw 'rèn-wéy 'nèy-ge-shr̀-ching kě 'pà. ‖The sergeant viewed the recruits with disgust. nèy-ge-jūng-'shr̀ kàn-je nèy-chywún-shīn-'bīng 'shīn-li bù-gāw-'shíng.

VILLAGE. 'tswēn-dz, tswēr. ‖This is a small village of about five hundred people. jè-shr yí-ge-shyǎw-'tswēr, 'dà-gày yěw 'wǔ-bǎy-rén. ‖The village post office is half a mile from here. jèy-ge-'tswēn-dz-li-de-yéw-jèng-'jywú lí-'jèr yěw 'bàn-lǐ-'dì.

(*People of a village*) 'tswēn-dz-li-de-'rén. ‖The whole village gathered to hear the speech. 'tswēn-dz-li 'swǒ-yěw-de-rén dēw láy tīng nèy-ge-yǎn-'jyǎng.

VINE. wàr. Grapevines pú-taw-'shù. ‖What kind of grapes do you get from these vines? jèy-ge-pú-taw-'shù-shàng jyē shéme-'pú-taw?

VIOLENT. měng-'lyè, 'lì-hày, dà, shyūng. ‖There was a violent explosion in the factory yesterday. 'dzwó-tyan gūng-'chǎng-lǐ-tew °měng-'lyè bàw-'jà. *or* °'jà-de hěn 'lì-hay. ‖I've never seen such a violent wind. wǒ 'tsúng-láy méy-'kàn-jyán-gwo jème-°'dà-de-fēng. *or* °'lì-hày-de-'fēng. ‖She had a violent headache and called the doctor. tā 'téw-téng-de hěn 'lì-hay, jǎw 'dày-fu láy 'kàn-yi-kan. ‖We had a violent argument. wǒm táy-'gàng táy-de hěn °'lì-hay. *or* °'shyūng.

Violent death. ‖He met with a violent death. tā-shr hèng-'sz̀-de. *or expressed negatively as* He didn't get to die peacefully. tā méy-'dé °shàn-'jūng. *or* hǎw-'sz̀

VISIT. To visit *or* to pay a visit to láy (*or* chywù) 'kàn, láy (*or* chywù) 'jyàn; (*if very formal*) gěy . . . bày-'fǎng. ‖We planned to visit them during our summer vacation. wǒ-men dǎ-'swàn-je dzày shǔ-'jyà de-shŕ-hew chywù 'kàn ta-men. ‖While we're here, I'd like to pay a visit to some friends. wǒm 'dzày-jèr de-shŕ-hew wǒ shyǎng chywù kàn jǐ-ge-'péng-yew.

(*To or by a doctor*) *expressed by saying the doctor* examines kàn. ‖The doctor charges five dollars for a visit. jèy-ge-'dày-fu kàn yí-'tsz̀ yàw 'wǔ-kwày-chyán.

VOICE. (*In speaking*) 'shēng-yīn. ‖Her voice grates on my ears. tā-de-'shēng-yīn °chǎw (*or* °'jā) 'ěr-dwo.

(*In singing*) sǎng-'yīn *or expressed as* throat 'sǎng-dz. ‖He has a good voice for singing popular music. tā-de-°'sǎng-dz (*or* °sǎng-'yīn) chàng 'pǔ-tung-'gēer hěn 'hǎw.

To lose one's voice shwō-'hwà dēw méy-'shēngr-le, 'sǎng-dz 'yǎ-le. ‖She had a bad cold and lost her voice. tā jāw-'lyáng jāw-de hěn 'lì-hay, °shwō-'hwà dēw méy-'shēngr-le. *or* °'sǎng-dz dēw 'yǎ-le.

(*Right to express oneself*) fā-yán-'chywán. ‖Does he have any voice in the discussion? jèy-ge-tǎw-'lwèn tā yěw fā-yán-'chywán-ma?

To voice fā-'byǎw. ‖Everyone was asked to voice an opinion. tām °chǐng (*or* °ràng) 'měy-yí-ge-rén fā-'byǎw dyǎr-'yì-jyàn.

VOLUME. (*Book*) shū *with measure* běn *or* tsè, *sometimes* běn *or* tsè *alone*, 'běn-dz, 'tsè-dz. ‖How many volumes do you have in your library? nǐ-de-tú-shū-'gwǎn-li yěw 'dwō-shaw-běr-'shū.

(*Space occupied*) rúng-'lyàng. ‖What's the volume of the cold storage room? jèy-ge-lěng-tsáng-'shr̀-de-rúng-'lyàng dwō 'dà?

(*Of sound*). ‖Turn up the volume on the radio, please. *is expressed as* Please turn the radio up bigger. láw-'jvà, bǎ wú-shyàn-'dyàn kāy 'dà-dyǎr.

VOTE. pyàw; (*act of voting*) byǎw-'jywé. ‖He was elected by 2,000 votes. tā dwō 'lyǎng-chyān-'pyàw 'shywǎn-de-'shàng. ‖He'll have to win the labor vote in order to be elected. tā děy 'dé-jáw 'gūng-rén-de-'pyàw, tsáy 'shywán-de-'shàng. ‖The vote proved that the majority of the people were opposed to the law. jèy-ge-byǎw-'jywé jèng-'míng dà-'dwō-shù-de-'rén-mín fǎn-'dwèy jèy-ge-'fǎ-lywù.

To vote for 'shywǎn. ‖We're voting for a new governor next month. wǒm 'shyà-ywè 'shywǎn yí-ge-'shīn-shěng-'jǎng.

To vote *a sum of money, expressed as* to decide to appropriate yì-'jywé 'ná-chu-lay. ‖The board voted five hundred dollars for relief. jèy-ge-'hwèy yì-'jywé ná-chu 'wǔ-bǎy-kwày-'chyán-lay wèy 'jyèw-jì yùng.

To be voted down méy-'tūng-gwò, fěw-'jywé-le. ‖The proposal was voted down. jèy-ge-°'jyàn-yì (*or* °'tí-yì) °méy-'tūng-gwò. *or* °fěw-'jywé-le.

W

WAGE. 'gūng-chyán; (*including also* **salary**) 'bàw-chéw. ‖**Your wages will be thirty-five dollars a week starting tomorrow.** nǐ-de-'gūng-chyán shr̀ 'sān-shr̀-'wǔ-kwày-chyán yì-'shīng-chī; 'míng-tyan kǎy-s̠hr láy 'dzwò. ‖**What's the wage scale here?** *is expressed as* **How's the treatment** (*financial or otherwise*) **here?** jèr-de-'dày-ywù dzěme-'yàng?

To wage war tsúng-'s̠hr̀ jàn-'jēng, jìn-'shíng jàn-'jēng, dǎ-'jàng. ‖**That country isn't capable of waging a long war.** nèy-ge-gwó-'jyā °méy-yew néng-'lì tsúng-'shr̀ (*or* jìn-'shíng) cháng-'chī jàn-'jēng. *or* °jīn-bu-'jù 'lǎw dǎ-'jàng.

WAIST. (*Of the body*) yāw. ‖**She has a very slim waist.** tā-de-'yāw jēn 'shì.

(*Of a garment*) yāw, 'yāw-shen. ‖**This suit is too loose in the waist.** jèy-jyàn-'yī-fu 'yāw-shen tày 'féx.

WAIT. děng. ‖**I'll wait for you until five o'clock.** wǒ 'děng ni dàw 'wǔ-dyǎn-jūng. ‖**I'm sorry to keep you waiting so long.** dwèy-bu-'jù, ràng-nín děng 'bàn-tyān. ‖**We can let that job wait till tomorrow.** 'nèy-jyàn-shr̀ wǒ-men kě-yi děng 'míng-tyan dzày 'dzwò. ‖**My parents waited up for me last night.** dzwóer-'wǎn-shang wǒ-de-fù-'mǔ 'děng-je wo láy-je. ‖**There will be an hour's wait before the train gets in.** *is expressed as* **We have to wait an hour before the train can get in.** wǒm děy 'děng °'yì-dyǎn-jūng (*or* °yì-'shyǎw-shŕ) 'chē tsáy néng 'láy.

(*Postpone*) wàng-'hèw nwó. ‖**We've waited dinner an hour for you.** wèy děng-'nǐ wǒm bǎ chr̀-'fàn-de-shŕ-'jyān wàng-'hèw 'nwó-le 'yì-dyǎn-jūng.

To wait on (*attend to*) 'ts̠z-̀hew, 'fú-shr. ‖**After his leg was broken he had to have someone wait on him.** tsúng tā-'twěy 'hwày-le yǐ-'hèw, 'lǎw děy yěw-'rén °'fú-shr ta. *or* °'ts̠z̀-hew ta. ‖**Where's the girl who's waiting on this table?** ts̠z̀-hew-jèy-ge-'jwō-dz-de-nywǔ-'háy-dz dzày-'nǎr-ne?

To lie in wait for byē-je. ‖**They were lying in wait for us.** tām 'byē-je wǒm láy-je.

WAKE. (*From sleeping*) shíng; **to wake** *someone* **up** (*by calling*) jyàw-'shǐng-le *or* jyàw; (*by pushing*) twēy-'shǐng-le; (*by disturbing*) chǎw-'shǐng-le; *etc.* **with a main verb specifying the means used.** ‖**Please wake me at seven o'clock.** láw-'jyà. 'chī-dyǎn-jūng 'jyàw-wo. ‖**The child woke with a start.** bǎ háy-dz chǎw-'shǐng-le. ‖**Wake me up before you go.** nǐ 'dzěw yǐ-'chyán jyàw-'shǐng wo. ‖**I woke up early this morning.** jyēr-'dzǎw-chen wǒ 'shǐng-de 'dzǎw-dyǎr. ‖**Wake up!** 'shǐng-yi-shǐng!

To wake up to the fact that 'míng-bay-le, 'jŕ-daw-le. ‖**He finally woke up to the fact that the man was his enemy.** tā 'hèw-lay 'jŕ-daw-le, nèy-ge-'rén shr̀ tā-de-'dí-rén.

(*Of a ship*) shwěy-'lyèw. ‖**Our boat was caught in the wake of the steamer.** wǒ-men-de-'chwán dzěw-dàw nèy-ge-'lwén-chwán-de-shwěy-'lyèw-li-le.

WALK. dzěw. ‖**Do you think we can walk it in an hour?** nǐ shyǎng wǒm 'dzěw 'yì-dyǎn-jūng dàw-de-'lyǎw-ma? ‖**It takes him twenty minutes to walk home from the office.** tā tsúng gūng-shr̀-'fáng hwéy-'jyā yàw dzěw 'èr-shr-fēn-'jūng. ‖**It's a long walk from here to the station.** tsúng-'jèr dàw chē-'jàn 'chyě děy dzěw-'hwer-ne.

To take a walk *or* go for a walk 'dzěw-yi-dzěw, sàn-san 'bù, 'lyěw-da-lyěw-da *or* 'lyèw-da-lyèw-da. ‖**Let's go for a walk in the park.** dzám dàw gūng-'ywán chywù sàn-san 'bù.

(*Path*) dàwr, lù, dzěw-'dàwr. ‖**They planted flowers on both sides of the walk.** tām dzày 'dàwr-de-'lyǎng-byār jùng-shang 'hwār-le.

(*Gait*) dzěw-'dàwr-de-'yàng-dz. ‖**You can always tell him by his walk.** nèy-ge-dzěw-'dàwr-de-'yàng-dz nǐ yí 'kàn jyèw 'jŕ-daw shŕ-'tā.

(*To cause to walk*) lyèw; **to walk a dog** lyèw-'gěw. ‖**Walk the horses a while so they won't get overheated.** bǎ-'mǎ 'lyèw-yi-lyèw, hǎw 'shyǎw-shyaw 'hàn.

In all walks of life. ‖**He has friends in all walks of life.** tā-de-'péng-yew gàn-'shéme-de dēw 'yěw.

WALL. chyáng; (*if it makes an enclosure*) wéy-'chyáng. ‖**Hang the picture on this wall.** bǎ-'hwàr gwà-dzay jèy-ge-'chyáng-shang. ‖**He built a high wall around his garden.** tā bǎ tā-de-hwā-'ywán-dz ̀chì-shang ̣gāw-de-wéy-'chyáng-le.

To wall *something* up chì-'chyáng bǎ . . . 'dǔ-shang-le. ‖**They've walled up the entrance to the cave.** tām chì̀le yí-dzwò-'chyáng ̣á nèy-ge-dùng-'mén-kěw 'dǔ-shang-le.

(*Figuratively; a barrier*). ‖**Not even her best friends could break down the wall she built around herself.** jyèw-shr tā-de-'dzwèy-hǎw-de-'péng-yew yě 'bù-néng gēn-ta dzěme 'chīn-jìn.

Backs to the wall. ‖**We have our backs to the wall.** *is expressed as* **We're really where there's no way out.** wǒm shŕ-'dzày shr̀ dzěw-'téw-wú-'lù.

WANT. yàw, shyǎng; **to want** *someone* **to do something** (*when asking that person for the favor*) shyǎng 'twō, 'dǎ-swàn 'chyéw, 'dǎ-swàn 'chǐng. ‖**I want to go swimming.** wǒ yàw fù-'shwěy chywù. ‖**I want you to do me a favor.** wǒ shyǎng 'twō-ni bàn jyàn-'shr̀. *or* wǒ 'dǎ-swan °'chyéw-(*or* °'chǐng-)ni 'bāng shyàr-'máng. ‖**He was wanted by the police for murder.** yīn-wey yí-jyàn-rén-mìng-'àn-dz, shywún-'jīng 'jǎw-ta láy-je. ‖**I want some more tea.** wǒ 'háy shyǎng yàw dyǎr-'chá.

Want *something* **of** (*or* **with**) *someone*. ‖**What do you want with him?** nǐ 'jǎw-ta 'gàn shéme? *or* nǐ 'gēn-ta yěw shéme-'shèr?

To want for (*lack*) 'dwǎn. ‖**He's never wanted for enough to live on.** tā 'tsúng-láy chř-'hē-shang méy-'dwǎn-gwo shéme.

A want of. ‖**There's a great want of affection in that home.** *is expressed as* The people in that family don't have much love for each other. nèy-yì-'jyār-rén bǐ-'tsž 'méy shéme-'gǎn-chíng. ‖**That pole is rotting for want of paint.** *is expressed as* That pole, always having no paint, is rotting. nèy-gēr-'gān-dz lǎw méy-'yéw děw 'làn-le.

To live in want. ‖**After the war many families were living in want.** 'jàng dǎ-'wán-le yǐ-'hèw, yěw 'hàw-shyē-rén-'jyār 'shéme děw 'chywē.

Wants shyǎng-'yàw-de. ‖**My wants are very simple.** wǒ-shyǎng-'yàw-de hěn 'jyǎn-dān.

WAR. jàn, jàn-'jēng; the (First) World War shř-'jyè-dà-'jàn (*sometimes called* the European War ēw-'jàn). ‖**After a long war the country finally gained its independence.** jīng-gwò yí-'tsž-hěn-'cháng-jyěw-de-jàn-'jēng nèy-ge-'gwó tsáy 'swàn-shř dú-'lì-le. ‖**When did the First World War start?.** 'shàng-tsž-shř-'jyè-dà-'jàn shř 'shéme-shf-hew 'chǐ-de?

To make war on 'chīn-fàn, dǎ, shyàng . . . 'tyǎw-shìn; **to be at war** dǎ-'jàng. ‖**They had no excuse for making war on us.** tām méy-yew 'lǐ-yéw láy °'chīn-fàn wǒ-men. *or* °'dǎ wǒ-men. *or* °shyàng wǒ-men 'tyǎw-shìn. ‖**That country has been at war for five years.** nèy-yì-'gwó dǎ-'jàng yǐ-jing 'dǎ-le 'wǔ-nyán-le.

Warship jywūn-'jyàn; **war plane** jywūn-yùng-'jī; *similarly, other compounds which have* **war** *in English often have* **armed forces** jywūn- *in Chinese.* ‖**How many war planes were produced this year?** 'jīn-nyan jywūn-yùng-'jī yí-'gùng chū-le 'dwō-shaw-jyà? ‖**An unidentified warship sank our ship.** yì-tyǎw-'gwó-jì-bù-'míng-de-jywūn-'jyàn bǎ wǒ-men-de-'chwán dǎ-'chén-le.

Warring nations jyāw-jàn-'gwó. ‖**The warring nations finally came to an agreement.** jyāw-jàn-'gwó 'jyē-gwò swàn-shr 'chéng-lì-le yí-ge-shyé-dìng.

WARM. 'nwǎn-he; (*of the sun*) dú; (*hot, used sometimes where English has* **warm**) rè. ‖**It gets very warm here in the afternoon.** shyà-wǔ jèr hěn 'nwǎn-he. ‖**Isn't the sun warm today?** 'jyěr-de-'tày-yang 'dú-bu-dú? ‖**We were uncomfortably warm at the theater.** wǒm dzày shì-'ywán-dz-li de-shf-hew jēn 're-de nán-'shèw. ‖**Put some warm clothes on before you go outside.** 'chwān-shang dyǎr-'nwǎn-he-'yī-shang dzày 'chū-chywu.

(*Affectionate*) chīn-'rè. ‖**She closed her letter with warm greetings to the family.** tā dzày 'shìn-hèw-tew 'jyā-shang-le yì-'bǐ, hěn-chīn-'rè-de 'wèn tām-yì-'jyā-dz 'hǎw.

To warm oneself 'nwǎn-he-nwǎn-he; (*by a fire*) 'kǎw-kaw 'hwǒ. ‖**Come in and warm yourself by the fire!** 'jìn-lay, °'kǎw-kaw 'hwǒ! *or* °'nwǎn-he-nwǎn-he!

To warm someone's heart gěy . . . hěn-'dà-de-'ān-wey. ‖**His kind words warmed our hearts.** tā-de-'hwà gěy wǒ-men hěn-'dà-de-'ān-wey.

(*Of colors*) *expressed by specifying them individually.* ‖**She looks best in warm colors.** *is expressed as* She looks best wearing bright colors like red and yellow. tā chwān 'húng-de-'hwáng-de-'nà-yàngr-'pyàw-lyang-de-'yī-fu hǎw 'kàn.

To be getting warm (*in guessing*) chà-bu-'dwō-le. ‖**That isn't the right answer, but you're getting warm.** nǐ 'dá-de bú-'dwèy, kě-shr chà-bu-'dwō-le.

To warm up rè, nùng-'rè. ‖**We'll have supper as soon as the soup is warmed up.** 'tāng yí 'rè wǒm jyèw chř-'fàn.

To warm up (*before a game*) lyàn-'shí. ‖**The players are warming up before the game.** nèy-shyē-dwèy-'ywán 'dzày-nèr lyàn-'shí-ne, 'háy méy-'sày-ne.

To warm up to *someone* gēn . . . °'shéw-chi-lay *or* °'chīn-jìn-le *or* °'hǎw-le. ‖**He was shy at first, but soon warmed up to us.** tā 'gēn wǒ-men chǐ-'shyān yěw dyǎr-°'shēng-fen (*or* °'wèy-wey-swō-'swō-de), 'méy dwō-shaw-shf-hew jyèw °'shéw-chi-lay-le. *etc.*

WARN. jīng-'gàw. ‖**I've been warned that this road is dangerous.** 'rén-jyǎ jīng-'gàw wo shwō jèy-ge-'lù wéy-'shyǎn.

WASH. shǐ; **to wash one's hands** *or* **to wash up** shǐ-'shěw. ‖**Who's going to wash the dishes?** 'shéy shǐ 'dyé-dz-a? ‖**These shirts need to be washed.** jèy-shyē-chèn-'shān gāy 'shǐ-le. ‖**Wash your hands before dinner.** chř-'fàn yǐ-'chyán 'shǐ-shi 'shěw. ‖**Can this material be washed?** jèy-ge-'lyàw-dz néng 'shǐ-ma? ‖**I always wash on Monday.** wǒ 'yǔng-ywǎn shř shīng-chī-'yī shǐ 'dūng-shi. ‖**Let's wash up before dinner.** dzám chř-'fàn yǐ-'chyán 'shǐ-shi 'shěw.

The wash (*before being washed*) gāy-'shǐ-de-'yī-fu; (*after being washed*) 'shǐ-de-'yī-fu. ‖**The wash hasn't come back from the laundry yet.** shǐ-de-'yī-fu háy méy-tsúng shǐ-yī-'dyàn 'ná-hwéy-láy-ne.

To wash against (*of waves*) dǎ. ‖**Listen to the waves washing against the side of the boat.** tīng 'làng-tew 'dǎ nèy-ge-'chwán-byār-ba.

To wash *something* **away** chūng-'dzěw-le. ‖**Last spring the flood washed away the dam.** jīn-nyan-'chwēn-tyan fā-'shwěy bǎ-'já gěy chūng-'dzěw-le.

To wash *something* **up** 'chūng-dàw . . .-shang. ‖**A lot of shells were washed up on the beach.** hǎw-shyē-gé-lì-bèng-dz 'chūng-daw hǎy-'byār-shang láy-le.

To be all washed up shř-'bày-le. ‖**Our vacation plans are all washed up.** wǒm-'jyà-chǐ-jūng-de-'jì-hwa, wán-'chywan shř-'bày-le.

WASTE. fèy; to waste money 'báy hwā-'chyán. ‖He wastes a lot of time talking. tā 'hĕn-dwō-de-'shŕ-hewr dēw 'fèy-dzay shwō-shyán-'hwà-shang-le. ‖This seems like a waste of money. 'jème-yàngr hăw 'shyàng-shŕ 'báy hwā-'chyán. ‖That process involves too much waste. 'nèy-jŭng-'dzwò-far tày 'fèy.

Waste paper làn-'jŕ, fèy-'jŕ; waste land hwāng-'dì. ‖Put the waste paper in the basket. bă làn-'jŕ rēng-dzay dž-jŕ-'lĕw-dz-li. ‖The plains beyond the mountains are all waste land. 'shān-'nèy-byar-de-píng-'dì dēw-shr hwāng-'dì.

Go to waste 'dzāw-tà, 'hwāng-fèy. ‖The property went to waste because it wasn't taken care of. nèy-dyăr-'chăn-yè méy hăw-'hāwr-de 'gwăn, dēw °'dzāw-tà-le. or °'hwāng-fèy-le.

To waste away shèw, dyàw-'bàng. ‖During his illness he wasted away until he weighed only a hundred pounds. tā 'bìng de-shŕ-hew °shèw-dàw (or °dyàw-'bàng dàw) 'hèw-lay jyéw shèng yì-băy-'bàng-le.

To lay waste jà-'hwĕy-le, dă-'hwày-le, hūng-'píng-le. ‖The army laid waste the entire area. jywūn-'dwèy bă jèy-yí-'dày dēw °jà-'hwèy-le. etc.

WATCH. (Keep looking at) chyáw. ‖We watched the planes landing at the airport. wŏm chyáw fēy-'jī 'lè-dzay fēy-jī-'chăng-shang. ‖I wasn't watching when we passed that sign. dzám 'lù-gwo nèy-ge-'pár de-shŕ-hew wŏ méy wàng 'nèy-byar 'chyáw. ‖Watch your step! 'chyăw-je dyăr 'dàwr (dzĕw)!

Watch out (be careful) lyéw-'shén, 'shyăw-shīn. ‖Watch out when you handle that box of dynamite. nĭ 'dùng nèy-shyāng-dz-jà-'yàw de-shŕ-hew °lyéw-'shén. or °'shyăw-shīn-dyăr.

(Keep an eye on and guard) kān. ‖Watch my car for me, will you please? láw-'jyà 'chāng-ni gĕy-wo 'kān-je-dyăr 'chē.

Watch over shĕw. ‖The dog watched over the child all night. 'gĕw 'shĕw-je shyăw-'hár 'shĕw-le yí-'yè.

Be on watch, stand watch jàn-'gāng. ‖The guards are on watch four hours and rest eight. wèy-'bīng-men shŕ 'jàn-'sž-ge-jūng-'téw-de-'găng, 'rán-hèw 'shyē 'bā-ge-jūng-'téw. ‖Every sailor on this ship has to stand an eight-hour watch. jèy-chwán-shang 'swŏ-yĕw-de-'shwĕy-shĕw 'dēw dĕy 'jàn 'bā-ge-jūng-téw-de-'găng.

Be on the watch for 'fáng-bèy, 'jīng-bèy. ‖The police were warned to be on the watch for trouble. yĕw-rén 'mì-bàw jīng-'chá °'fáng-bèy (or °'jīng-bèy) chŭ-'shèr.

Watch out for someone (guard against) 'dī-fang. ‖Watch out for him; he's a slippery customer. 'dī-fang-je ta dyăr; tā yĕw dyăr-'hwá-téw-hwá-'năw-de.

Watch out for (take care of) 'jàw-ying. ‖Don't worry; he's watching out for his own interests. béng fā-'chéw; tā hwèy 'jàw-ying-je 'dž-jĭ-'gĕr.

(Timepiece) byăw. ‖What time is it by your watch? nĭ-de-'byăw jĭ-'dyăn-le? ‖This is a watch repair shop. 'jèy-shr ge-'shyēw-lı-jūng-'byăw-de-'pù-dz.

WATER. shwĕy. ‖Please give me a glass of water. láw-'jyà, gĕy-wo yì-bēy-'shwĕy. ‖The water's too cold for swimming today. jīn-tyan-de-'shwĕy yéw-'yŭng tày 'lyáng. ‖Our house is near the water. wŏm-de-'fáng-dz °dzày 'shwĕy-byăr-shang. or °kàw-'shwĕy. ‖Do you like water sports? nĭ 'shĭ-hwan 'shwĕy-shang-'ywùn-dùng-ma?

To water animals yìn; plants and gardens jyāw. ‖Don't forget to water the horses before we go. wŏm dzày 'dzĕw yi-'chyán byé 'wàng-le yìn-'mă. ‖When did you last water the flowers? nĭ 'shéme-shŕ-hew jyāw-de 'hwār?

To water (of eyes) lyéw yăn-'lèy; (of mouth) lyéw kĕw-'shwĕy. ‖The smoke from the fire made my eyes water. jèy-ge-'lú-dz-li-de-'yān shywūn-de wo jŕ lyéw yăn-'lèy. ‖That cake makes my mouth water. nèy-kwày-'dyăn-shīn ràng-wo lyéw kĕw-'shwĕy.

To water (dilute) dwèy-'shwĕy. ‖He was put in jail for watering the milk. tā wàng nyéw-'năy-li dwèy-'shwĕy, swŏ-yi shyà-'ywù-le.

By water (of travel) dzwò-'chwán, dzĕw shwĕy-'lù. ‖At this time of the year the only way you can get there is by water. yì-nyán-lĭ-tew-de-'jèy-ge-shŕ-hew, nĭ 'jŕ néng °dzwò-'chwán chywu. or °dzĕw shwĕy-'lù.

To hold water (figuratively) yĕw-'jìn. ‖That argument doesn't hold water. nèy-ge-'hwà shwō-de méy-'jìn.

WAVE. (In water). làng, 'làng-tew. ‖During storms the waves are sometimes twenty feet high here. dà-'fēng dà-'ywŭ de-shŕ-hew jèr jèy-ge-'làng 'yĕw-de-shŕ-hew yĕw 'èr-shr-'chŕ 'gāw.

To wave 'pyāw-yáng, 'pyāw-dàng, 'pyāw-wŭ, 'fēy-wŭ. ‖They watched the flags waving in the breeze. tām kàn-je nèy-shyē-'chí-dz dzày 'fēng-li 'pyāw-yáng.

To wave the hand jāw-'shĕw. ‖We waved our hands to attract his attention. wŏ-men shyàng-ta jāw-'shĕw, yĭn-ta jù-'yì. ‖He waved to the car to stop at the corner. tā shyàng nèy-ge-'chē jāw-'shĕw. ràng-ta dzày nèy-ge-jyē-'jyăwr-nèr 'jàn-je.

(In the hair) 'téw-fa-shang-de-'wār. ‖She was afraid that the rain would spoil her wave. tā kŭng-'pà 'ywŭ bă tā-'téw-fa-shang-de-'wār nùng-'méy-le.

WAY. (Route, path) dàw(r), lù, 'dàw-lù. ‖Is this the right way to town? jèy-tyăw-'dàwr shŕ dàw chéng-'lĭ-tew chywù-de-ma? or shàng chéng-'lĭ-tew chywù dzĕw 'jèy-tyăw-lù 'dwèy-ma? ‖We passed a new restaurant on our way home. hwéy-'jyā de-shŕ-hew wŏm dzày 'dàwr-shang 'lù-gwò yì-jyār-'shīn-fàn-'gwăn-dz.

Across the way dwèy-'mér, dwèy-'gwòr, dwèy-'myàr. ‖His house is just across the way from ours. tā-de-'fáng-dz jyèw dzày 'wŏ-men-dwèy-'mér.

(Figuratively). ‖They let him go his own way. tām °yéw (or °swéy) 'tā chywù-le. or tām bù-'gwăn-ta-le.

(*Distance*) ywǎn. ‖**These students are a long way from home.** jèy-shyē-'shywé-sheng lí-'jyā hěn 'ywǎn. ‖**I see them way off in the distance.** wǒ lǎw-'ywǎn-de 'kàn-jyan tā-men. ‖**The village is still quite a way(s) off.** nèy-ge-'tswēn-dz háy 'ywǎn-je-ne.

By way of (*route*) tsúng, dǎ. ‖**We'll come back by way of the mountains.** wǒm yàw dǎ 'shān-lù 'hwéy-lay. ‖**He went by way of Peiping and came back by way of Tientsin.** tā 'chywù shř tsúng běy-'píng chywù-de, 'hwéy-lay shř tsúng 'tyān-jìn 'hwéy-lay-de.

Make way, get out of the way. (*Literally*) bǎ-'dàwr °'ràng-kay or °'dwǒ-kay. ‖**Get that truck out of the way, will you?** bǎ nèy-ge-kǎ-'chē 'nwó-nwo °'ràng- (or °'dwǒ-)kay 'dàwr, 'hǎw-bu-hǎw? ‖**Traffic was forced to make way for the fire engines.** jyèw-hwǒ-'chē láy-le, 'byé-de-chē dēw bǎ-'dàwr 'ràng-kay-le. (*Figuratively*). ‖**They gave him the money to get him out of the way.** *is expressed as* **They gave him the money so he wouldn't make trouble.** tām gěy-ta nèy-ge-'chyán jyèw 'wèy-de-shř rang-ta bù-dǎw-'lwàn.

Out of the way. ‖**I finally got that back work out of the way.** *is expressed as* **I finally got that back work done.** dàw-'lyǎwr wǒ bǎ 'shèng-shya-de-jèy-dyǎr-'shèr dzwò-'wán-le. ‖**He lives in an out-of-the-way part of the city.** *is expressed as* **The place where he lives is too obscure.** tā-'jù-de-dǐ-fang tày 'bèy.

Be in the way ày-le 'shř-le. ‖**They said we'd just be in the way if we tried to help.** tām shwō wǒm méy-'bāng-lyǎw 'máng, dàw ày-le 'shř-le.

Right of way. ‖**We gave the other car the right of way.** *is expressed as* **We let the other car go by first.** wǒm ràng 'nèy-lyàng-chē 'shyān gwò-chywu.

Get under way (*or weigh*) chū-'fā. ‖**The ship will get under way at noon.** jèy-jř-'chwán 'jūng-wǔ chū-'fā.

Work one's way through. ‖**He's working his way through school.** tā-'dž-jǐ gūng 'dž-jǐ-nyàn-de-'shū.

See one's way clear to jyǎn-'jř-de néng. ‖**I can't see my way clear to take a vacation this month.** 'běn-ywè wǒ jyǎn-'jř-de bù-néng shyēw-'jyà.

Pay one's own way gěy 'dž-jǐ-de-'chyán. ‖**I always pay my own way when I go out with him.** wǒ gēn-'tā yí-'kwàr 'chū-chywu de-shř-hewr 'dzǔng-shř wǒ gěy wǒ-'dž-jǐ-de-'chyán.

Go out of one's way to jìn-'lì, jìn-'lyàngr, shř-'jìn 'fāng-fa, byàn-jr-bǎ-'fāngr-de. ‖**We went out of our way to make him feel at home.** wǒm °'jìn-'lì (or °'jìn-'lyàngr *etc.*) ràng-ta byé 'gǎn-jywé 'jywū-su.

(*Manner*) yàng, yàngr; **way of acting** 'tày-dù, chǔ-'shř-de-'fāng-fa. ‖**I don't like the way he acts.** wǒ bù-'shǐ-hwan tā°-'nà-yàngr. or °'nèy-ge-'tày-dù. or °'chǔ-'shř-de-'fāng-fa. ‖**I never did like his ways.** wǒ 'tsúng-láy yě bú-'shyàng 'tā-nà-yàngr.

This way 'jème-yàngr, jème; **that way** 'nàme-yàngr, nàme. ‖**Do it this way!** 'jème(-yàngr) 'dzwò! or 'dzème-je! or 'jème-yàngr!

(*Means, method*) 'fāng-fa, 'fá-dz; **ways and means** *expressed with the same terms*. ‖**He still hasn't found a way of making a living.** tā 'háy méy-'jǎw-jáw yí-ge-méw-'shēng-de-'fāng-fa-ne. ‖**Can you find a way to get him home?** nǐ yěw 'fá-dz ràng-ta shàng-'jèr láy-ma? ‖**We discussed ways and means of putting the plan into operation.** wǒm tǎw-'lwèn shř-'shíng-nèy-ge-'jì-hwa-de-°'fāng-fa. or °'fá-dz.

Have a way with. ‖**He has a way with women.** *is expressed as* **He knows how to please women.** tā hwèy 'dwèy-fu 'nywǔ-rén.

Be in a bad way yěw dyǎr-°bù-'shū-fu, °bù-hǎw-'shèw, °bù-hǎw-'gwò, °bù-hé-'shř. ‖**He was in a bad way after the party last night.** dzwór-'wǎn-shang yàn-'hwèy 'wán-le yǐ-'hèw tā yěw dyǎr-°bù-'shū-fu. *etc.*

In a way dzày 'yì-fāng-myan shwō. ‖**In a way we're lucky to be here.** dzày 'yì-fāng-myan shwō, wǒm dàw-'jèr shř hěn 'shìng-ywùn.

By the way èy! ‖**By the way, are you coming with us tonight?** 'èy! wǒ 'shwō, nǐ jyēr-'wǎn-shang 'láy-bu-láy-ya?

By way of joking 'bú-gwò shr °nàw-je 'wár or °kāy wán-'shyàw. ‖**He said it only by way of joking.** tā 'shwō nèy-ge 'bú-gwò shř °nàw-je 'wár. *etc.*

In some ways 'yěw-de-dì-fangr. ‖**In some ways this plan is better than the other one.** jèy-ge-'jì-hwà 'yěw-de-dì-fangr bǐ 'nèy-ge 'chyáng.

In the way of shéme-yàngr. ‖**What've you got in the way of portable radios?** nǐ-'jèr yěw shéme-yàngr-shěw-'tí-shř-de-wú-shyàn-'dyàn?

Have one's way. ‖**She thought it was bad for the child to have his own way all the time.** tā shyǎng lǎw 'yéw-je háy-dz-de-'shyèngr shř 'bú-dà. 'hǎw.

To give way (*of a dam or other object*) hwày; (*of a military force*) twèy; **to give way to one's emotions** dùng chíng-'gǎn. ‖**When the dam gave way the river flooded the town.** hé-'bà 'hwày-le, 'shwěy bǎ-'chéng 'yān-le. ‖**When our fresh troops arrived, the enemy was forced to give way.** wǒ-men-de-'shēng-lì-'jywūn yí 'dàw jyèw °bǎ 'dí-rén gěy dǎ-'twèy-le. or °'jyàw 'dí-ren wàng-'hèw 'twèy.

WE (US, OUR, OURS). We *or* us wǒ-men, wǒm; (*informal, and definitely including person or persons spoken to*) 'dzán-men, 'dzám; our *or* ours wǒ-men(-de), wǒm(-de); 'dzán-men(-de), dzám(-de). ‖**We expect to be home this afternoon.** wǒm 'shyǎng jyēr-ge-'shyà-wǔ dzày-'jyā. ‖**My friend has invited both of us to the concert tonight.** wǒ-de-'péng-yew jyēr-'wǎn-shang chǐng wǒ-men-'lyǎ chywù tīng yīn-'ywè. ‖**Let's go together!** dzám yì-'túng 'chywù-ba. ‖**These are ours.** 'jèy-shyē shř °'wǒ-men-de. or °'dzám-de.

In certain formal contexts one says this běn *instead of* our. **Our company** běn-'háng; **our country** 'běn-gwó; *etc.*

For **OURSELVES** *see* **SELF.**

WEAK. (*Not solid, frail*) bù-'jyē-shr. ‖This bridge is too weak to support heavy traffic. jèy-ge-'chyáw tày bù-'jyē-shr, jīn-bu-'jù tày-'dwō-de-chē dzày 'shàng-tew 'dzěw. ‖The cloth will tear at this weak place. jèy-ge-'bù dzày jèy-ge-bù-'jyē-shr-de-dì-fang hwèy 'pwò.

(*Lacking strength*) 'rwǎn, rwǎn-'rwò, réw-'rwò. ‖He felt very weak after the operation. tā dùng-shěw-'shù yì-'hèw jywé-de hěn 'rwǎn. ‖The country has a weak government. jèy-ge-gwó-'jyā-de-'jèng-fǔ hěn rwǎn-'rwò.

(*Low in alcoholic content*) méy 'lì-lyang, bú-'chùng. ‖This drink is too weak. jèy-ge-'jyěw °méy 'lì-lyang. or °bú-'chùng.

(*Inadequate*) bù-'shíng, méy 'lì-lyang. ‖That's a weak argument. nèy-ge-'hwà méy-'jìn. ‖Mathematics is his weakest subject. 'shù-shywé shr̀ tā-dzwèy-bù-'shíng-de-yì-mér-'gūng-kè.

WEALTH. tsáy-'chǎn. ‖He inherited most of his wealth. tā-de-tsáy-'chǎn dà-'bù-fen shr̀ chéng-'shèw láy-de.

WEAR (WORE, WORN). (*For most clothes*) chwān; (*for hats and decorations*) dày; (*for neckties*) jì; *and some others* (*see* put on *under* PUT). Men's wear 'nán-rén-chwān-de-'yī-fu. ‖What are you going to wear to dinner tonight? jyér-'wǎn-shang chr̄-'fàn-chywu nǐ 'dǎ-swan chwān shéme-'yī-shang? ‖A good coat will wear longer than a cheap one. yí-jyàn-'hǎw-yī-shang bǐ 'tsź-de °jìn 'chwān. or ° chwān-de r̀-dz 'dwō. or °'chwān-de cháng-ywan. ‖This dress was worn by my mother at her wedding. jèy-jyàn-'yī-shang shr̀ wǒ-'mǔ-chin jyē-'hwēn de-shf-hew 'chwān-de. ‖Does this store sell men's wear? jèy-ge-'pù-dz mày 'nán-rén-chwān-de-'yī-fu-ma? ‖He wears his shoes out very fast. tā chwān-'shyé chwān-de jēn 'fèy. or *expressed as* His shoes are spoiled very fast. tā-'shyé °'hwày-de (or °'pwò-de) jēn 'kwày. ‖This coat was meant for evening wear. jèy-jyàn-wày-'tàwr shr̀ wèy 'wǎr-shang 'chwān-de. ‖There's still a lot of wear left in these ties. *is expressed as* These ties can still be worn a while. jèy-shyē-tyáw-lǐng-'dày háy chyě néng 'jì yí-chì-ne.

Wear *a hole in something, etc.; expressed with* to scrape tsā *and other such specific verbs.* ‖The constant erasing wore a hole in the paper. 'lǎw dzày-nèr-'tsā, bǎ-jř-(nèr) dēw 'tsā-le yí-ge-'kū-lung. ‖The cuffs on my trousers show signs of wear. wǒ-kù-'jyǎwr-nèr mwó-°'máw-le byàr-le. or °'lyàng-le. or °'má-'hwār-le. or °'hwày-le. or °'tū-lu-le. or °le. ‖The tires got a lot of wear and tear from the rough roads. jèy-jǐ-tyáw-pí-'dày dzày nèy-ge-'hwày-'dàwr-shang °'mwó-de (or °'kěn-de) hěn 'lì-hay.

Wear *something or someone* down mwó; wear smooth mwó-'píng-le, mwó-'gwāng-le; wear out mwó-'hwày-le. ‖We finally wore him down and he did what we

asked. 'jyē-gwǒ wǒm 'mwó-de ta 'ràng-ta gàn-'shéme tā jyèw 'gàn shéme. ‖They finally wore down his resistance. tām dàw-'lyǎwr bǎ-ta 'mwó-de hwéy-'shīn-jwǎn-'yì-le. ‖The record is so worn down we can hardly hear it. jèy-jāng-chàng-'pyār mwó-°'píng-le (or °'gwāng-le or °'hwày-le), wǒm dēw 'tīng-bu-jyàn 'shēngr-le.

Wear off 'gwò-chywù. ‖The effect of the drug will wear off in a few hours. jèy-ge-'yàw-de-'lì-lyàng jǐ-ge-jūng-'téw jyèw 'gwò-chywu-le.

Be completely worn out, be worn to a frazzle (*of a person*) lèy-'jí-le, (pí-)fá 'jí-le, jīn-pí-lì-'jìn, 'yì-dyǎr-'jyèngr dēw 'méy-yew-le. ‖He came home from the factory completely worn out. tā tsúng gūng-chǎng 'hwéy-lay yì-'hèw °lèy-'jí-le. etc.

Tired and worn 'lèy, 'shīn-kǔ, 'fá, 'pí-fá. ‖Her face is tired and worn. tā 'lyǎn-shang 'dày-je hěn-'lèy-de-yàng-dz. ‖He looked tired and worn on Monday morning. shīng-chī-'yī-'dzǎw-chen tā 'kàn-je shyàng hěn °'lèy- (or °'shīn-ku- et:.) de-yàng-dz.

WEATHER. 'tyān-chi, tyār, 'chì-hèw. ‖We've had a lot of rainy weather lately. *is expressed as* Recently the weather is always raining. 'jìn-lay °'tyān-chi (or °'tyār) jìng shyà-'ywǔ.

To weather *a storm* 'jīng-gwò. ‖This old ship has weathered a good many storms. jèy-tyáw-jyèw-'chwán 'jīng-gwo-le bù-'shǎw-de-fēng-'làng.

To be weathered *or* weatherbeaten. 'fēng-chwēy-ywǔ-'dǎ-de. ‖The gravestone was old and weathered. jèy-kwày-shf-'běy 'nyán-dzer 'dwō-le, 'fēng-chwēy-ywǔ-'dǎ-de dēw bù-'chīng-chu-le.

Be under the weather *is expressed with any of a number of terms meaning* not be comfortable, not be well yet, *etc.* ‖He caught a bad cold yesterday and he's still pretty much under the weather. 'dzwór-ge tā jāw-'lyáng jāw-de tǐng 'lì-hay, shyàn-'dzày 'hǎy °bù-'shū-fu-ne. or °bù-hé-'shr̀-ne. or °bù-hǎw-'gwò-ne. or °bù-hǎw-'shèw-ne. or °nán-'gwò-ne. or °nán-'shèw-ne. or °méy-'hǎw-ne.

WEDNESDAY. lǐ-bày-'sān, shīng-chī-'sān.

WEEK. lǐ-'bày, shīng-'chī. This week 'běn-lǐ-'bày, 'běn-shīng-'chī; last week 'shàng-lǐ-'bày, 'shàng-shīng-'chī; next week 'shyà-lǐ-'bày, 'shyà-shīng-'chī. ‖It'll be a week before I see you again. háy děy gwò °'yí-ge-shīng-'chī (or °'yì-shīng-'chī) wǒ 'tsáy néng 'dzày kàn-jyan ni-ne. ‖I'm going to start a new job next week. 'shyà-shīng-'chī (or 'shyà-lǐ-'bày) wǒ yàw 'kāy-shř dzwò yí-ge-'shīn-shr̀-ching-le. ‖This factory is on a six-day week. jèy-ge-gūng-'chǎng shr̀ 'yí-ge-lǐ-'bày dzwò 'lyèw-tyān-'gūng.

WEIGH. To weigh *so much* yěw ... jùng. ‖This piece of meat weighs four pounds. jèy-kwày-'rèw yěw 'sż-bàng 'jùng.

To **weigh (out)** *something* bǎ . . . 'yāw, chēng yāw; **to weigh oneself** *or* **to get weighed** gwò-'bàng. ‖Please weigh this package for me. láw-'jyà, gěy-wo 'yāw-yāw jèy-bāw-'dūng-shi. ‖I was weighed the other day at the doctor's. nèy-tyan wǒ dzày 'dày-fu-nèr 'gwò-le-gwò 'bàng. ‖She asked the storekeeper to weigh out ten pounds of sugar. tā chǐng nèy-ge-jǎng-'gwèy-de gěy-ta 'yāw 'shŕ-bàng-'táng.

To **weigh one's words** kǎw-'lywù. ‖He weighed his words carefully before answering. tā hwéy-'dá yǐ-'chyán, kǎw-'lywù-de hěn dž-'shì.

To **weigh** *something* **down** yā. ‖The canoe is weighed down with supplies. nèy-ge-shyǎw-'chwár jyàw 'dūng-shi 'yā-de chŕ-'shwěy hěn 'shēn.

To **weigh anchor** chǐ-'máw. ‖What time did the ship weigh anchor? jèy-ge-'chwán 'shéne-shf-hew chǐ-'máw.

To **weigh on.** ‖The responsibility of his job doesn't weigh on him very much. *is expressed as* He certainly doesn't consider his job very difficult. tā dwèy nèy-ge-'gūng-dzwò 'bìng bù-'jywé-de wéy-'nán.

WEIGHT. 'jùng-lyàng. ‖The weight of the bridge is supported by cables. jèy-ge-'chyáw-de-'jùng-lyàng dēw jàng-je jèy-shyē-tyě-'shéng-dz 'dyàw-je-ne.

To **gain weight** jǎng (*or* jyā) tǐ-'jùng; to **lose weight** jyǎn tǐ-'jùng, chīng-le. ‖I've gained a lot of weight since I've been here. wǒ 'dàw-jèr yǐ-'hèw, tǐ-'jùng °'jǎng-le (*or* °'jyā-le), bù-'shǎw. ‖I've lost a lot of weight since I've been here. wǒ 'dàw-jèr yǐ-'hèw °'chīng-le hěn 'dwō. *or* °tǐ-'jùng 'jyǎn-le hěn 'dwō.

To **have** *so much* **weight,** to be *so much* **in weight** yěw . . . jùng (*see* WEIGH). ‖The weight of the trunk is two hundred pounds, but the suitcase only weighs fifty. dà-'shyāng-dz yěw 'èr-bǎy-bàng 'jùng, shěw-tí-'shyāng tsáy 'wǔ-shf-bàng.

To **weight** jyā 'fèn-lyang. ‖Make them balance by weighting this side. 'jèy-byār dzày 'jyā dyǎr-'fèn-lyang, jyèw 'píng-le.

(*Piece of metal used to balance*) 'fá-mǎr; (*anything heavy*) jùng-'dūng-shi, chén-'dūng-shi. ‖Another two-pound weight should make the scale balance. dzày 'gē-shang lyǎng-'bàng-de-'fá-mǎr tyān-'píng jyèw 'píng-le. ‖Put a weight on those papers to keep them from blowing away. ná yang-'jùng-dūng-shi bǎ-'jř 'yā-shang.

(*Figuratively*). ‖You've just lifted a weight off my mind. nǐ 'jè tsáy swàn-'chywù-le wǒ-yí-kwày-'shīn-bìng. ‖Don't attach too much weight to what he says. tā-de-'hwà °bú-'bì tày dzày-'yì. *or* °bú-'bì tày wàng-'shīn-li chywù. *or* °bú-'bì tày shyǎng-'shìn. *or* °bú-'dà 'jùng-yàw. ‖This isn't a matter of great weight. 'jèy-jyàn-shŕ bú-'dà °'jùng-yàw. *or* °'yàw-jǐn.

WELCOME. (*Characterizing something one is glad to hear or have*) hǎw. ‖That's the most welcome news I've heard in months. 'nèy-ge shŕ wǒ-'jèy-jǐ-ge-'ywè-'tīng-jyàn-de-dzwèy-'hǎw-de-'shyāw-shi. ‖Welcome home again! 'hwéy-láy-le! hǎw-'jí-le!

To **welcome** *someone* 'hwān-yíng. ‖Welcome to Tientsin! 'láy-le, 'hwān-yíng-hwān-ying! ‖They welcomed us to the club. tām 'hwān-yíng wǒ-men jyā-'rù nèy-ge-'hwèy. ‖They gave us a warm welcome when we came back. wǒm 'hwéy-lay de-shŕ-hewr, tām hěn 'rè-lyè-de 'hwān-yíng wǒ-men láy-je.

(*In answer to thanks offered, or otherwise indicating concession freely given*) *expressed as* **don't, act like a guest** byé 'kè-chi *or* bú-'kè-chi, *or as* **it's nothing** 'méy shéme. ‖You're welcome. byé 'kè-chi. *or* bú-'kè-chi. *or* 'méy shéme. ‖You're welcome to use my car. nín 'dwō-dzen yàw yùng-'chē de-shŕ-hew chǐng byé 'kè-chi.

WELL. (*In a good way*) hǎw, myàw, gǎw, bú-'tswò, bú-'hwày, bú-'lày. ‖They do their work very well. tām dzwò-'shŕ dzwò-de hěn 'hǎw. ‖He's doing very well in his business. tā 'shēng-yı dzwò-de hěn bú-'tswò.

(*Not ill*) hǎw, bú-'bìng. ‖Is your father feeling well these days? jèy-shyē-'r̀-dz nín-làw-tày-'yé ʲhǎw-wa? ‖He doesn't look like a well man to me. tā-de- 'chì-sè (*or* °'yàngr *or* °'shén-chi *or* °'yàng-dz) wǒ kàn-je bú-dà 'hǎw.

Well done (*in cooking*) lǎw(-dyǎr)-de. ‖Do you want your steak well done? nǐ-de-rèw-'páy yàw 'lǎw (-dyǎr)-de-ma?

Well over *an amount* . . .-dwō. ‖The play attracted well over a thousand people. jèy-chū-'shì jyàw-le yěw yì-'chyān-dwō-'dzwòr.

(*Exclamation; of surprise*) 'á, 'hē; (*of concession, or just a filler while thinking of what to say*) *usually omitted.* ‖Well! I wouldn't have thought THAT of her! 'hē! wǒ méy-shyǎng-'dàw tā hwèy 'nà-yàngr! ‖Well what do you know! 'á, 'jywū-rán-rú-'tsž!' *or* 'á, shŕ 'nème-je-ya! ‖Well, OK 'hǎw, jyèw 'nème bàn-ba. *or* 'hǎw, jyèw 'nèm. ɛ-ɐə́. (*In these the* hǎw *means* OK, *and does not translate the* well, *which is implied only by the wording of the whole sentences.*)

Be just as well that. ‖It's just as well that you got here when you did. *is expressed as* Good, you got here just at the right time. hěn 'hǎw, nǐ 'dàw-de 'jèng shŕ 'shŕ-hewr.

Not very well *do so-and-so.* ‖He couldn't very well go by train, because he couldn't get a reservation. tā yīn-wey méy-'dìng-jáw 'dzwòr, swǒ-yi 'méy-fár dzwò hwǒ-'chē 'dzěw.

As well, as well as (*in addition, in addition to*) yěw . . . yěw . . . , yě . . . yě . . . . ‖She sings, and she plays the piano as well. tā 'yěw (*or* °'yě) chàng-'gēer °'yěw (*or* °'yě) tán gāng-'chín. ‖She bought a hat as well as the new dress. tā mǎy-le yì-shēr-shīn-'yī-fu, yèw mǎy-le yì-dǐng-'màw-dz.

Leave well enough alone. ‖I advise you to leave well enough alone. wǒ 'chywàn-ni byé 'dùng-ta-le; hwéy-'téw 'lúng-dz gěy jř 'yǎ-ba-le.

To **think well of.** ‖Do you think well of him? nǐ 'jywé-de tā-'dzwò-de 'hǎw-ma?

Be well off yěw dyǎr-'tsáy-chǎn. ‖He left his wife well off. tā 'sž-le yǐ-'hèw, gěy tā-'tày-tay 'lyéw-shyà-le dyǎr-'tsáy-chǎn.

(*For water*) jǐng; salt well yán-'jǐng, yán-'jyěngr. ‖How deep a well did you have to dig to get water here? jèr-de-'jǐng děy 'wā dwō-'shēn tsáy néng jyàn-'shwěy-ne?

To well up (*of liquid*) mǎn; (*of feelings*) 'gēw-chǐ-láy. ‖The water is welling up where the pipe is broken. 'gwǎn-dz-'hwày-le-de-nèy-ge-'dì-fangr 'shwéy dēw 'mǎn-le. ‖That was the last straw; all his feelings on the matter welled up and he said what he'd been wanting to say for so long. 'nème yì-láy, bǎ tā-de-'shǐn-shř 'gēw-chi-lay-le, tā bǎ yàw-shwō-de-'hwà 'pī-le-pā-'lā-de dēw 'shwō-chu-lay-le.

WEST (WESTERN). shī; (*area*) shī-'bù, 'shī-byar. ‖The road leads to the west. jèy-ge-'lù shř wàng-'shī chywù-de. ‖In the west the mountains are higher than here. shī-'bù-de-'shān bǐ 'jèr-de 'gāw. ‖The little island is three miles west of the big one. nèy-ge-'shyǎw-dǎw dzày 'dà-dǎw-de-'shī-byar 'sān-lǐ-'dì. ‖Go west at the next turn. jyàn-'wǎr wàng-'shī gwǎy. ‖He lives west of the river. tā jù-dzay 'hé-de-'shī-byar. ‖There's a strong west wind blowing up. 'shī-fēng 'gwā-chǐ-láy-le. ‖They live in the western part of the province. tām 'jù-dzay jèy-'shěng-de-shī-'bù.

WET. shř, cháw; (*not dry*) bù-'gān. ‖Keep a wet dressing on your arm. nǐ dzày 'gē-be-shang 'wéy yí-kwày-'shř-'bù.

To get wet nùng-'shř-le, shř-le, to make wet *or* to wet nùng-'shř-le! pwō-'shř-le, *etc.*, *the main verb indicating the method used.* ‖You'll get wet! nǐ hwéy-'téw nùng-'shř-le! ‖They wet the street to keep the dust down. tam bǎ-'jyē pwō-'shř-le, bǎ-'tǔ 'yā-shya-chywu.

Wet Paint! (*literary*) yéw-'chī wey-'gān!

To wet pants (*of a baby*) nyàw 'kù-dz. ‖The baby wet her pants. nèy-ge-'háy-dz nyàw-le 'kù-dz-le.

see DRY.

WHAT. shéme; *sometimes* nǎ *or* něy *plus a measure.* ‖What do you want for supper? nǐ wǎn-'fàn yàw chř 'shéme? ‖What did you say? nǐ gāng shwō 'shéme láy-je? ‖What's left? 'shèng-shya shéme-le? ‖What? 'shéme? ‖What else? 'háy (yěw) shéme? ‖What's missing? chà shéme-'dūng-shi? ‖Do you know what train we're supposed to take? nǐ 'jř-daw wǒm gāy dzwò 'něy-yí-tàng-'chē-ma? ‖He always says what he thinks. tā yǔng-'ywǎn 'shyǎng shéme jyèw 'shwō shéme. ‖We know what ships were in the harbor. wǒm 'jř-daw dēw yěw shéme-'chwán dzày gǎng-'kěw.

What kind of shéme-'yàng-de. ‖What kind of a house are you looking for? nǐ iǎw shéme-'yàng-de-'fáng-dz?

I'll tell you what 'dzěme-je-ba. ‖I'll tell you what; let's go to the movies tonight. 'dzěme-je-ba; wǒm jyěr-'wǎn-shang kàn dyàn-'yěngr chywù-ba.

What a . . . ! ‖What a beautiful flower! jèy-ge-'hwār 'jēn hǎw 'kàn! ‖What a time I had getting home! wǒ hwéy-'jyā de-shí-hewr, 'jèy-yí-tàng-a!

What! (*exclamation*) 'shéme-a! *or* 'dzěme-a! *or* 'á! ‖What! Isn't he here yet? 'shéme-a! (*or* 'dzěme-a!) *etc.*) tā 'háy méy-'láy-ne!

What about dzěme-'yàng. ‖What about your appointment? nǐ-de-ywē-'hwèr dzěme-'yàng?

What if yàw-shr . . . °dzěme-'yàng *or* °dzěme 'bàn. ‖What if the train's late? 'chē yàw-shr wù-'dyǎn-le °dzěme-'yàng? *or* °dzěme 'bàn?

What of it yěw shéme-'gwān-shi-ne? ‖He didn't get here on time, but what of it? tā méy-àn-je 'shř-hew 'dàw, yěw shéme-'gwān-shi-ne?

WHATEVER. sheme . . . dēw, wú-'lwèn : . . shéme; no . . . whatever yì-dyǎr . . . yě bū. ‖Do whatever you like; I don't care. nǐ yàw gàn 'shéme dēw 'shíng; wǒ bú-'dzày-hu. ‖Whatever you do, be sure to tell me about it. nǐ wú-'lwèn gàn 'shéme yí-'dìng děy 'gàw-su wo. ‖He has no money whatever. tā 'yì-dyǎr-chyán yě 'méy-yew. ‖She lost whatever respect she had for him. *is expressed as* Now she doesn't respect him at all. tā shyàn-dzày 'yì-dyǎr dēw chyáw-bu-'chǐ-ta-le.

WHEAT. 'mày-dz. ‖Do you raise wheat on your farm? nǐ-de-'dì-li jùng 'mày-dz-ma? ‖How is the wheat crop this year? jīn-nyán 'mày-dz shēw-cheng dzěme-'yàng?

WHEEL. lwén-dz, lwér; water wheel shwěy-'chēer. ‖The front wheels of the car need to be tightened. 'chē-de-chyán-'lwér děy 'jǐn-jin-le. ‖The water wheel produces all the power we use on this farm. jěng-gèr-núng-'chàng dēw yùng jèy-shwěy-'chēer-fā-de-'dyàn.

To wheel *something, expressed by a verb indicating the specific method of causing the motion, such as to* push twēy, *with some other verb of motion.* ‖They were wheeling the baby carriage through the park. tām dzày gūng-'ywán-li 'twēy-je yáw-'chēer 'lyēw-da láy-je.

To wheel around jwàn-gwo 'shēr-lay. ‖He wheeled around and looked daggers at me. tā jwàn-gwo 'shēr-lay hěn-'hēr-de 'dèng-le wo yì-'yǎn.

WHEN. 'shéme-shř-hew, 'jǐ-shř, 'dwō-dzen; (*what day*) 'něy-yì-tyān; (*what hour*) 'jǐ-dyǎn-jūng. ‖When can I see you again? wǒ °'jǐ-shř (*or* °'dwō-dzen *etc.*) néng dzày 'jyàn-je ni? ‖Tell me when to expect you. 'gàw-sung wo nǐ (dà-'gày) 'shéme-shř-hew °láy. *or* °'dàw.

Introducing an expression which specifies the time at which something else occurs, . . . -de-shř-hew(r). When the work is done, you can go. nǐ bǎ-'shèr dzwò-'wán-le de-shř-hewr, nǐ jyèw kě-yi 'dzěw-le. ‖I wasn't home when he called. tā láy de-shř-hew wǒ méy-dzày-'jyā. ‖I feel very uncomfortable when it's hot. tyǎr 'rè de-shř-hewr wǒ dzǔng 'jywé-de bū-'shū-fu.

There are times when . . . , there are days when . . . 'yěw-de-shŕ-hew. ‖There are times when I prefer to be alone. 'yěw-de-shŕ-hew wǒ 'ywàn-'yì 'yí-ge-rén 'dāy-je. ‖There are days when he's very depressed, and days when he's on top of the world. tā 'yěw-de-shŕ-hew fā-'chéw, 'yěw-de-shŕ-hew 'gāw-shìng-de 'lyǎw-bu-dé.

(*Although*) chí-'shŕ. ‖He gave the boy some money when he should have known better. tā gěy-le nèy-ge-shyǎw-nán-'hár dyǎr-'chyán, chí-'shŕ tā 'yīng-dang 'jŕ-daw bù-'gāy nème 'dzwò.

WHENEVER. shéme-'shŕ-hew, . . . de-shŕ-hew. ‖Come to see us whenever you have time. shéme-'shŕ-hew yěw 'gūng-fu, swéy-'byàn láy. ‖Whenever he visits us I feel funny. tā yì láy 'kàn wǒ-men de-shŕ-hew, wǒ 'dzǔng jywé-de yěw dyǎr-'byè-nyew.

(*Showing surprise*) 'nǎr-láy-de. ‖Whenever did you find time to do all this? nǐ 'nǎr-láy-de nème-shyē-'shŕ-hew dzwò-le jème-shyē-'shèr?

WHERE. nǎr; shéme-'dì-fang. ‖Where's the nearest hotel? lí-jèr dzwèy-'jìn-de-lywǔ-'gwǎn dzày shéme-'dì-fang? ‖Can you tell me where you live? nǐ dzày-'nǎr jù? *or* (*Very polite*) nín 'fǔ-shang shéme-'dì-fang? ‖Where're you going? nǐ shàng-'nǎr chywù? ‖Where does your friend come from? nǐ-de-'péng-yew tsúng-'nǎr láy?

In such expressions as the place where I was born, where *is omitted in Chinese and the description of the place precedes the word for the place.* ‖The house where I used to live is on this street. wǒ-yǐ-'chyán-'jù-gwo-de-nèy-swǒr-'fáng-dz jyèw dzày 'jèy-tyáw-jyē-shang. ‖The restaurant where we wanted to go was closed. wǒ-men-yàw-'chywù-de-nèy-ge-fàn-'gwǎn-dz 'gwān-le. ‖We found him just where he said he would be. wǒm jyèw dzày tā-'shwō-de-nèy-ge-dì-fang bǎ-ta 'jǎw-je-le. ‖The nurses will be sent where they are needed most. yàw bǎ jèy-shyē-'kàn-hu sùng-daw dzwèy-'shywū-yàw-tam-de-'dì-fang chywù.

WHETHER. *Expressed by giving alternatives, sometimes with* háy-shr *between them.* ‖I don't know whether they will come. wǒ bù-jŕ-'dàw tām 'láy 'bù-láy. ‖Do you know whether this story is true or not? nǐ 'jŕ-dàw jèy-ge-'gù-shr shr 'jēn-de háy-shr 'jyǎ-de-ma? ‖We can't tell whether it'll rain or snow, but it looks like it's going to do something. wǒm bù-gǎn 'shwō shr yàw shyà-'ywǔ háy-shr shyà-'shywě, fǎn-'jèng 'kàn-yàng shr yàw nàw-'tyār.

WHICH. 'nǎ(-yī) *or* 'něy(-yī) *plus a measure; referring to people, also expressed as* who shwéy *or* shéy. ‖Which of the men will be better for the job? dzwò nèy-ge-'gūng-dzwò 'něy-yí-ge-rén 'hǎw? ‖Which is the

one you picked out? 'něy-ge shr 'nǐ-'tyāw-chu-ɪay-de? ‖He didn't know which to take. tā bù-jŕ-'dàw ná 'něy-ge 'hǎw. ‖Which book do you want? nǐ yàw ná 'něy-běn-shū? ‖When you look at the twins, it's hard to tell which is which. nǐ 'kàn-jyan nèy-dwèy-'shwàng-shengr de-shŕ-hew, hěn nán 'fēn-chu-lay °'něy-ge shr 'něy-ge. *or* °'shéy shŕ-'shéy.

In expressions like the book which you borrowed, which *is omitted and the limiting phrase is put before the word for the thing.* ‖Please return the book (which) you borrowed. chǐng-ni bǎ nǐ-'jyè-de-'shū 'hwán-le-ba. ‖The double rooms, which are on the second floor, are all taken. 'èr-tséng-'léw-shang-de-'shwàng-rén-'fáng-jyān dēw jù-'mǎn-le.

WHILE. (*During the time that*) . . . de-shŕ-hew, *often with* háy *or* -je *in what precedes.* ‖I want to arrive while it's still light. wǒ shyǎng chèn-je 'tyān 'háy 'lyàng-je de-shŕ-hew 'dàw-nèr.

(*And yet, but, though*) *often omitted.* ‖Some of the students are serious, while others are not. 'yěw-de-shywé-sheng hěn yùng-'gūng, chí-'ywù-de 'bù-dzème-'yàng.

Wait a (little) while 'děng yì-hwěr, shāw 'hèw-yi-hew. ‖You'll have to wait a little while before you can see him. nǐ děy shāw 'hèw-yi-hew tsáy néng 'jyàn-je ta.

Be worth one's while bé-'swàn, shàng-'swàn, 'jŕ-de. ‖It's not worth your while to do this. nǐ dzwò 'jèy-ge bù-°hé-'swàn. *or* °shàng-'swàn. *or* °'jŕ-de.

To while away the time. ‖How can we while away the time until dinner? *is expressed as* We still have to wai: a bit for dinner; shall we do a bit of something? lí chī-'fàn háy děy 'hwěr-ne, dzám 'gàn dyǎr-'már?

WHITE. báy; white color báy-'yán-shǎr. ‖She was dressed in white. tā-'chwān-de shr 'báy-de. ‖This white will glare in the sun. jèy-ge-báy-'yán-shǎr dzày 'tày-yang-dyèr-li hwǎng-'yǎn. ‖Would it be all right to wear white shoes? chwān 'báy-shyé 'shíng-ma? ‖I want the walls painted white and the ceiling blue. 'chyáng wǒ yàw 'báy-de, dǐng-'péng yàw 'lán-de. ‖She went white when she heard the news. tā 'tīng-jyan nèy-ge-'shyāw-shi 'lyǎn dēw 'báy-le. ‖She's able to walk again, but she still looks awfully white. tā néng shyà-'dì-le, kě-shr 'lyǎn-shang 'háy-shr shà-'báy.

(*Part of egg*) dàn-'báy, jī-dàn-'chīng. ‖To make this cake you'll need the whites of four eggs. dzwò jèy-ge-'gāw nǐ děy yùng 'ɪɀ-ge-°jī-dàn-de-dàn-'báy. *or* °jī-dàn-'chīng.

(*Of an eye*) báy-yǎn-'jūr, báy-yǎn-'chyéwr. ‖The whites of her eyes are bloodshot. tā-de-báy-yǎn-'jūr-li yěw shyě-'sēr.

White Christmas *expressed in terms of* snowing shyà-'shywě. ‖Do you think we'll have a white Christmas? nǐ shyǎng jīn-nyán-shèng-dàn-'jyé hwéy shyà-'shywě-ma?

WHO (WHOM, WHOSE). shéy, shwéy. ‖Who told you? shr̀-'shéy 'gàw-su ni-de? ‖Who's that pérson you were just talking with? nǐ-gāng-'gēn-ta-shwō-'hwà-de-nèy-ge-rén shr̀-'shéy? ‖Do you know who was responsible for this? nǐ 'jr̀-daw °'shéy fù jèy-ge-dzé-'rèn-ma? or °'shéy gwǎn 'jèy-ge-ma?

Who's who shéy shr̀ 'dzěme-hwéy-'shr̀. ‖Can you tell me who's who at the university? nǐ 'jr̀-daw jèy-ge-'dà-shywé-li-de-rén 'shéy-shr̀ 'dzěme-hwéy-'shr̀-ma?

In expressions like **the man who just came in,** *the latter part* (**just came in**) *is put before the first part* (**the man**), *with* de *between, and no word for* **who.** ‖The man who just came in is the owner of the store. 'gāng-'jìn-lay-de-nèy-ge-rén shr̀ jèy-ge-'pù-dz-li-de-lǎw-'bǎn.

In expressions like **my children, who are now on vacation,** *where the* **who** *clause is a parenthetical comment, the information which follows* **who** *is in Chinese given as a coordinate expression. Thus* ‖My two children, who are now on vacation, will be back next week. *is expressed as* My two children are now on vacation; next week they're coming back. wǒ-de-nèy-'lyǎng-ge-'háy-dz fàng-'jyà-le, 'shyà-shīng-chī jyèw 'hwéy-lay-le

Whose 'shwéy-de, 'shéy-de. ‖Whose watch is this? jèy-ge-'byǎw shr̀ 'shéy-de? ‖Whose is this? 'jèy-ge shr̀ 'shéy-de? ‖I'd like to know whose car this is. wǒ shyǎng 'jr̀-daw jèy-ge-'chē shr̀ 'shéy-de.

WHOLE. chywán, yì-'jěng, jěng-'gèr. ‖The whole office was dismissed at noon. chywán-gùng-shr̀-'fáng-de-rén 'jèng-wǔ de-shr̀-hew dēw shywǔ 'dzěw-le. ‖Look at the thing as a whole. 'yīng-dang 'gè-'fāng-myàn chywán shyang-'ɑɑw-le. ‖He sat through the whole play. tā 'dzwò-dzay nèr 'kàn-le yì-'jěng-chū-'shì. ‖I intend to stay a (whole) week. wǒ 'dǎ-swàn 'jù ('jěng-)yí-ge-lǐ-'bày.

(*Not in parts*) *expressed as* **not broken,** *etc.* ‖Did the pitcher break when you dropped it, or is it still whole? 'gwàn-dz shwāy-'swèy-le méy-yew?

On the whole dà-'jr̀-shang. ‖On the whole I agree with you. wǒ dà-'jr̀-shang gēn-ni túng-'yì.

A whole lot of, *etc.* hǎw-shyē, dà. ‖I ate a whole lot of cookies. wǒ 'chr̀-le hǎw-shyē-'táng. ‖He caught a whole string of fish. tā 'dyàw-le yí-'dà-chwàr-'ywú. ‖He told a whole pack of lies. tā 'sā-le yí-'dà-pyān-'hwǎng.

WHOLLY. wán-'chywán, jyǎn-'jr̀. ‖The decision is wholly up to you. dzwèy-'hèw-yí-jywù-'hwà wán-'chywán dzày-'nǐ-le. ‖This is wholly out of the question. 'jèy jyǎn-'jr̀ shr̀ bàn-bu-'dàw-de.

WHY. 'wey-shéme; (*in what way, how come that*) 'dzěme. ‖Why's the train so crowded this morning? jèy-ge-'chē jyēr-'dzǎw-chen 'wèy-shéme dzème 'jǐ-ya? ‖Can you tell me why this work isn't done? 'jèy-ge-gūng-dzwo 'dzěmé méy-dzwò-'wán-ne? ‖I can't

imagine any reasons why he shŏuld refuse to come. wǒ 'shyǎng-bu-chu-'láy 'wèy-shéme tā bú-!ywàn-yi láy.

Why not (*making a suggestion*) . . . , 'hǎw-bu-hǎw? or . . . , 'shíng-bu-shíng? *etc.* ‖Why not come along? 'nǐ yě 'láy, 'hǎw-bu-hǎw?

Whys and wherefores, *expressed with* why 'wèy-shéme. ‖They tried to find 'out the whys and where-fores of his absence. tām 'shyǎng 'chá-chu-'láy 'wèy-shéme tā méy-'dàw.

WIDE. kwān. ‖Is this road wide enough for two-way traffic? jèy-tyáw-'lù 'lyǎng-lyàng-chē 'bìng-je dzěw gèw 'kwān-de-ma? ‖The window is three feet wide by six feet high. jèy-ge-'chwāng-hu yěw 'sān-chr̀ kwān, 'lyèw-chr̀ 'gāw. ‖Is the coat wide enough for you through the shoulders? jèy-jyàn-'shàng-yī jyàn-'bǎngr gèw 'kwān-ma?

(*Of great range*) gwǎng, dwō. ‖This newspaper has a wide circulation. jèy-ge-bàw-'jr̀ fā-'shíng-de hěn gwǎng.

(*Fully, particularly fully open*) dà; with wide open eyes dèng-je 'yǎn-jing. ‖Open the window a bit wider. bǎ 'chwāng-hu kāy 'dà-dyǎr. ‖The baby looked at the kitten with eyes wide open. nèy-ge-shyǎw-'hár dèng-je 'yǎn-jing 'kàn nèy-ge-shyǎw-'māwr.

(*Far from the mark*) ywǎn. ‖Your last shot at the target was wide. nǐ dz vèy-'hèw-nèy-yí-'shyà-dz dǎ-de lí 'mù-byāw tày 'ywǎn le. ‖The bullet went wide of its mark. jèy-ge-dž-'dàn dǎ-de lí mù-'byāw tày 'ywǎn-le.

Wide open (*lawless*) wú-'fǎ-wú-'tyān. ‖This is a wide open town. jèy-ge-'chéng wú-'fǎ-wú-'tyān.

Leave oneself wide open. ‖You left yourself wide open. (*for past, present, or future trouble*) nǐ-'dž-jǐ yì-dyǎr-bǎw-'jàng yě 'méy-yew. or (*for results already finished*) nà shr̀ 'lày nǐ-'dž-jǐ bù-'shyǎw-shīn,

WIFE. 'tày-tay (*see also Appendix A*). ‖Where's your wife? nǐ-'tày-tay dzày-'nǎr-ne? ‖Are their wives permitted to see them? 'shywǔ tām-de-'tày-tay 'kàn tā-men-ma?

WILD. Wild animal yě-'shèw; wild country kwàng-'yě; wild idea gwày-'jú-yì; wild storm bàw-fēng-'ywǔ. ‖Is there any danger of wild animals in the woods? jìn shù-'lín-dz-li chywù 'shr̀-bu-shr̀ hwèy yěw 'ywù-jyàn-yě-'shèw-de-'wéy-shyǎn? ‖A hundred years ago this was all wild country. yì-'bǎy-nyán yǐ-'chyán jèr shr̀ kwàng-'yě. ‖I hate to waste time on such a wild idea. wǒ bú-'ywàn-yi dzày nème-ge-gwày-'jú-yì-shang fèy 'gūng-fu. ‖The ship was wrecked during a wild storm at sea. 'chwán-dzay 'hǎy-shang jyàw yí-jèn-bàw-fēng-'ywǔ gěy gwā-'hwày-le.

Make a wild shot (*at tennis etc.*) 'hú-dǎ, 'shyā-dǎ. ‖He'd play a good game of tennis if he didn't make so many wild shots. tā-de-wǎng-'chyéwr yàw-shr̀ bù-°'hú-dǎ (*or* °'shyā-dǎ) 'kě-yǐ dǎ-de tǐng bú-'tswò.

To run wild (*of cattle*) bù-'jywān-je mǎn-'chùr 'pǎw. ‖During the winter the cattle were allowed to run wild. 'dūng-tyār 'nyéw bù-'jywān-je, mǎn-'chùr 'pǎw.

Go wild (*of a shot*) shr̀ fēy-'dàn. ‖The first two shots went wild; the third hit the bull's-eye. 'téw-lyǎng-shyàr shr̀ fēy-'dàn, dì-'sān-shyàr jèng dǎ-je bǎ-'dì.

Have a wild time wár-de kě 'jēn kě-'yǐ-de. ‖We had a wild time at the party last night. wǒm dzwór-'wǎn-shang chywù nèy-ge-'hwèy 'wár-de kě 'jēn kě-'yǐ-de.

Go wild (*as with joy*) 'shǐ-hwan-de 'lyǎw-bu-dé, 'lè-de gēn 'fēng-le shr̀-de. ‖The crowd went wild when the news came out. 'shyāw-shi 'chwán-chu-lay yǐ-'hèw rén °'shǐ-hwan-de 'lyǎw-bu-dé. *or* °'lè-de gēn 'fēng-le shr̀-de.

WILL. (*Indicating future time*). 'hwèy, yàw; (*if in an order*) děy; *often not separately expressed.* ‖They'll be surprised to see you here. tām dzày-jèr 'chyáw-jyàn ni yí-'dìng hwèy 'jywé-de hěn chí-'gwày. ‖The order read: You will proceed at once to the next town. "'mìng-lìng shwō: nǐ lì-'kè jyèw děy dàw 'shyà-yí-ge-'chéng chywù. ‖I'll meet you at the corner at three o'clock. wǒ 'sān-dyǎn dzày gwǎy-'jyǎwr-nèr 'jyàn-ni. ‖Won't you come in for a minute? 'jìn-lay 'dāy-hwěr, dzěme-yàng? ‖I won't be but a minute. wǒ 'yùng-bu-lyǎw 'yì-fēn-jūng. ‖Will you reserve a room for me for tomorrow? nǐ 'míng-tyan gěy-wo 'lyéw jyān-'wū-dz, 'shíng-bu-shíng?

(*Denoting habitual behavior*) néng. ‖He'll go for days without smoking a cigarette; then in two days sometimes he'll smoke half a carton. tā néng 'hǎw-shyē-'r̀-dz lyán 'yì-gēr-yān yě bù-'chēw; kě-shr tā 'yě néng dzày 'lyǎng-tyān-li chēw 'wǔ-bāw-'yān.

(*Denoting capacity or ability*) kě-yi, néng. ‖This theater will hold a thousand people. jèy-ge-shì-'ywán-dz kě-yi dzwò yì-'chyān-rén. ‖This machine won't work. jèy-ge-'jī-chi bù-néng 'yùng-le. *or expressed as* This machine is broken. jèy-ge-'jī-chi 'hwày-le.

As he wills, his will. ‖We'll have to do °as he wills. *or* °his will *is expressed as* We'll have to do as he says. wǒm dzǔng děy jàw tā-'shwō-de 'bàn. *or as* We'll have to do according to his ideas. wǒm dzǔng děy àn-je tā-de-'yì-sz dzwò. *or as* We'll have to listen to him. dzám 'jř̌ hǎw tīng-'tā-de..

Against one's will. ‖He went to school against his will. *is expressed as* He didn't want to go to school but he went anyway. tā 'jř̌ bù-'shyǎng shàng-'shywé chywù, kě-shr 'háy-shr 'chywù-le.

At will swéy-'byàn. ‖The prisoners are free to have visitors at will. 'chyěw-fàn kě-yi swéy-'byàn gēn láy-'kàn-tā-men-de-rén jyàn-'myàr.

With a will 'bàw-je-jywé-'shǐn-de. ‖The men set to work with a will. nèy-shyē-'rén bàw-je-jywé-'shǐn-de chywù 'dzwò-le.

Have a will of one's own 'pí-chi gèw 'nìng-de. ‖That child certainly has a will of his own. nèy-ge-'háy-dz 'pí-chi jēn gèw 'nìng-de.

(*Document*) yí-'jǔ. ‖He died without leaving a will. tā chywù-'shř̌ de-shř̌-hew méy-'lyéw-shyà yí-'jǔ.

To will *something* to yí-'jǔ-shang shyě bǎ ... jywān-gey .... ‖He willed all his property to the city. tā-yí-'jǔ-shang 'shyě-je bǎ tā-'swǒ-yěw-de-'tsáy-chǎn dēw 'jywān-gey dì-'myàr-shang-le.

WIN. yíng. ‖Which team do you think will win? nǐ shyǎng 'nǎ-yí-dwèy 'yíng? ‖I'm going to win this game ıf it's the last thing I do. wǒ °jyèw-shr bù-'hwó-je-le (*or* °'dzěme-je *or* °jyèw-shr 'sž-le) yě děy yàw bǎ jèy-chǎng-'chyéwr,'yíng-le.

(*To attain*) dé. ‖He won first prize in the contest. 'nèy-tsž-bǐ-'sày tā dé-de téw-'jyǎng. ‖His story won everyone's sympathy. *is expressed as* Whoever heard his story was sympathetic. 'shév tīng-jyan tā-de-nèy-dwàr-'gù-shř̌ dēw túng-'chíng.

To win *someone* over 'gǎy-gwò-láy. ‖We finally won him over to our way of thinking. tā-de-'sž-shyǎng dàw-'lyǎwr ràng-wom gěy 'gǎy-gwo-lay-le.

WIND. fēng; be windy gwā-'fēng. ‖There was a violent wind during the storm last night. dzwór-'wǎn-shang-de-dà-'fēng-dà-'ywǔ 'fēng kě ('gwā-de) jēn 'dà. ‖A stiff wind made it difficult for the boat to reach port. nèy-jèn-'fēng jēn 'yìng, 'chwán dēw 'gwā-de bù-'rúng-yi kāy-jìn 'gǎng chywù-le. ‖He flew the plane into the wind. tā 'dǐng-je 'fēngr 'kāy nèy-ge-fēy-'jī.

(*Breathing, need to breathe*) hú-'shī; *or expressed with* to breathe chwǎn. ‖His wind is bad because he smokes too much. tā chēw-'yan chēw-de tày 'dwō, swǒ-yi °cháng ày 'chwǎn. *or* °hú-'shī bù 'hǎw.

To knock the wind out of dǎ-de ... 'chū-bu-láy 'chyěr-le. ‖It knocked the wind out of him. nèy-yí-'shyà-dz 'dǎ-de ta °'chū-bu-láy 'chyěr-le. *or* °'dàw-shī yì-kěw-'chì.

To get winded chwǎn. ‖He's not a good swimmer because he gets winded too easily. tā yéw-'yǔng yéw-de bù-'shíng, 'yéw bú-dà-'hwěr jyèw 'chwǎn-le. ‖That run upstairs winded me. wǒ 'pàw-je shàng-le 'léw, 'pǎw-de wǒ jř̌ 'chwǎn.

(*Empty talk*) 'fèy-hwà. ‖There was nothing but wind in what he said. tā-'shwō-de 'chywán shř̌ 'fèy-hwà.

In the wind. ‖There's a rumor in the wind that we may get the afternoon off. yěw yí-ge-'yáw-yán shwō dzám jyèr-'shyà-wǔ yě-shywǔ fang-'jyà.

To get wind of (*literally*) 'wèn-jvàn; (*figuratively*) 'tīng-jyàn-le dyǎr-'fēngr, 'jř̌-daw-le dyǎr, 'tıng-shwō-le dyǎr. ‖The dogs got wind of the deer. 'gěw 'wèn-jyan 'lù-de-'wèr-le. ‖I got wind of their plans yesterday. wǒ 'dzwór-ge °'jř̌-dàw-le dyǎr (*or* °'tīng-shwō-le dyǎr) tām-de-'jì-hwà. *or* tām-de-'jì-hwa wǒ 'dzwór-ge 'tīng-jyàn-le dyǎr-'fēngr.

Take the wind out of someone's sails. ‖It certainly took the wind out of his sails when he lost his job. tā shř̌-'yè-le yí-'hèw jēn 'shèw-le dyǎr-'dǎ-jī.

WIND (WOUND). (*Tighten; a spring*) shàng. ‖I forgot to wind my watch. wǒ 'wàng-le shàng-'byǎw-le. *or* wǒ-de-'byǎw 'wàng-le shàng-'shyán-le. ‖Did you wind up the clock before you came upstairs? nǐ shàng-'léw yǐ-'chyán °shàng-'jūng-le-ma? *or* °bǎ-'jūng 'shàng-shang-le-ma?

(*To follow a curving course*) ràw, gwǎy. ‖The cows were winding their way home through the pasture. 'nyéw °ràw-je (*or* °gwǎy-je) ('wār) 'dzěw tsúng tsǎw-'dì-nèr 'chwān-gwò-chywù hǎw hwéy-'jyā. ‖The road winds through the old part of town, nèy-tyáw-'dàwr °'gwǎy-de (*or* °'ràw-de) 'lǎw-chéng-li chywù-le.

(*To twist around something*) chán, ràw. ‖Wind the string into a ball. bǎ 'shéng-dz °'chán-chéng (*or* °'ràw-chéng) ge-'chyéwr. ‖Wind the wire up on this spool. bǎ-'shyàn °'chán-dàw (*or* °'ràw-dàw) shyàn-'jéwr-shang. ‖They wound the bandage tightly around his arm. tām bǎ bēng-'dày dzày tā-'gē-be ιang °'ràw-de (*or* °'chán-de) tǐng 'jǐn. ‖The snake wound itself around a tree. 'shé °'ràw-daw (*or* °'chán-dàw *or* °'pán-dàw) 'shù-shang-le.

To wind up *business* 'lyàw-lǐ, bàn-'wán, 'jěng-lǐ, 'jyé-su. ‖He had two weeks to wind up his affairs before entering the army. tā jìn jywūn-'dwey yǐ-'chyán, yěw 'lyǎng-ge-shīng-'chī-de-'shŕ-jyān °'lyàw-lǐ (*or* °'bàn-'wán *etc.*) tā-'dż-jǐ-de-'shŕ-ching.

To wind up *a speech* (*finish*) *expressed as* quickly finish jèng yàw 'wán, jèng dzwò 'jyé-su. ‖He was just starting to wind up his speech when we got there. wǒ-men 'jìn-chywù de-shŕ-hew, tā-de-yǎn-'jyǎng jèng yàw 'wán.

WINDOW. 'chwāng-hu. ‖Which one of you kids broke the window? 'nǐ-men 'něy-ge-háy-dz bǎ 'chwāng-hu dǎ-'pwò-le? ‖These windows need washing. jèy-shyē-'chwāng-hu děy 'tsā-shǐ-tsā-'shǐ-le.

WING. (*Of bird or plane*) 'bǎng-dz, chŕ-'bǎng. ‖The pigeon broke its wing when it hit the window. 'gē-dz jwàng-dzày 'chwāng-hu-shang bǎ °'bǎng-dz (*or* °'chŕ-'bǎng) jwàng-'hwày-le. ‖The new airplanes have a tremendous wing spread. shīn-fēy-'jī-de-'bǎng-dz dà-'jí-le. ‖One wing of the plane was sheared completely off when it hit the ground. fēy-'jī jyàng-'lè de-shŕ-hew yí-ge-'bǎng-dz pèng-de 'dì-shang-le jěng-'gèer-de 'shé-shya-lay-le.

(*Of a house*) shyāng-'fáng. ‖We're planning to build a new wing on the house. wǒm jèng ιdǎ-swan-je bǎ jèy-ge-'fáng-dz 'jyē-chu ge-shyāng-'fáng-lay.

(*Of the stage*) *expressed as* in the curtains dzày táy-'lyár-lì-tew. ‖He stood in the wings waiting for his cue. tā 'jàn-dzày táy-'lyár-lì-tew děng-je shàng-'chǎng-ne.

On the wing (*literally*) *expressed as* while flying 'fēy-je. ‖He was τying to shoot ducks on the wing. tā shyǎng yàw dzày nèy-shyē-'yā-dz 'fēy-je de-shŕ-hew kāy-chyāng láy dǎ. ‖He's such a busy person,

you'll have to catch him on the wing. tā-shŕ ge-'máng-rén, nǐ děy 'jwēy-ya gǎn-de tsáy jǎw-de-'jáw-ta.

Take *someone* under one's wing jàw-gu. ‖She took the newcomer under her wing. tā hěn 'jàw-gu nèy-ge-shīn-'láy-de-rén.

WINTER. 'dūng(-tyan). ‖We usually have a mild winter here. jèr 'píng-cháng 'dūng-tyan bù-'lěng. ‖It's getting cold enough to wear a winter coat. 'jèy-tyār 'lěng-de děy chwān 'dūng-dà-'yī-le.

(*Period of cold weather*) 'lěng-de-shŕ-hew. ‖We're in for a spell of winter. 'dàw-le 'lěng-de-shŕ-hew-le.

To winter gwò 'dūng-tyan. ‖Where did you winter last year? nǐ 'chywù-nyan dzày-'nǎr gwò-de 'dūng-tyan'?

WIRE. (*Electric*) dyàn-'shyàn; (*iron or sometimes other metal, whatever the use*) tyě-'sž. ‖The telephone wires were blown down by the storm. nèy-ge-bàw-fēng-'ywǔ bǎ dyàn-'shyàn gwā-'shé-le. ‖We put up wire screens to keep out the flies. wǒm 'ān-shàng °'tyě-sž-'shā (*or simply* metal screens °'tyě-shā-'chwāng) 'dǎng-dang 'tsāng-ying.

(*To furnish with wires*) 'ān dyàn-'shyàn. ‖Is the house wired for electricity? jèy-ge-'fáng-dz °'ān-le dyàn-'shyàn-le-ma? *or expressed as* Does this house have electricity? °'yěw dyàn-'dēng-ma?

(*A telegram*) dyàn-'bàw; to wire dǎ dyàn-'bàw; to wire *someone* gěy . . . dǎ dyàn-'bàw; to send a message by wire dǎ dyàn-'bàw. ‖He wired me to meet him at the train. tā gěy-wo dǎ-le yí-ge-dyàn-'bàw ràng-wo dàw chē-'jàn chywù 'jyē-ta. ‖I'll wire if I can. yàw 'néng dǎ dyàn-'bàw, wǒ gěy-ni 'dǎ yí-ge. ‖You'll have to send this message to him by wire. jèy-jyàn-'shŕ-ching nǐ děy gěy-ta dǎ ge-dyàn-'bàw. ‖Send him a wire to tell him we're coming. gěy-ta dǎ ge-dyàn-'bàw gàw-sung ta wǒm jyèw yàw 'láy-le.

To pull wires twō (*or* chyéw) 'hǎw-shyē-rén. ‖He had to pull a lot of wires to get that job. tā děy °'twō (*or* °'chyéw)-le 'hǎw-shyē-rén 'tsáy 'dé-jaw nèy-ge-'chāy-shŕ.

WISE. 'tsūng-míng. ‖His decision to remain is very wise. tā jywé-'dìng bù-'dzěw shŕ hěn tsūng-míng-de. ‖He's a pretty wise fellow. tā-'jèy-ge-rén hěn 'tsūng-míng.

To get wise to 'míng-bay. ‖He never got wise to their little scheme. tā yì-'jŕ-de méy-'míng-bay tām-de-bǎ-'shì.

To put *someone* wise 'gàw-su(ng). ‖Don't you think we ought to put him wise? nǐ shyǎng wǒm bù-'yīng-gay 'gàw-sung ta-ma?

WISH. (*To want, to want to*) 'shī-wang, 'ywàn-yi, shyǎng. ‖I wish I could stay here longer. wǒ dàw-shŕ °'shī-wang (*or* °'ywàn-yi) néng dzày-'jèr 'dwō dāy shyē-shŕ. ‖What do you wish for most? nǐ dzwèy °'shī-wang (*or* °shyǎng) yàw 'shéme?

A **wish** 'shī-wang, *or often expressed verbally.* ‖Her wish for a trip abroad came true. tā-yàw-dàw-gwó-'wày-chywù-de-'shī-wàng shŕ-'shyàn-le. *or* tā 'dzǎw jyèw °shyǎng yàw (*or* °'shī-wang) chū-'gwó, jēn 'chéng-le. ‖She expressed a wish to spend the summer at the beach. *is expressed as* She said she wished to spend the summer at the beach. tā shwō tā °yàw (*or* °'shī-wang *or* °shyǎng *or* °'pàn-wàng néng) dàw hǎy-'byār-shang chywù gwò-'shyà.

(*In giving an order*) chǐng. ‖I wish you to finish by twelve o'clock. *or* I wish you would finish by twelve o'clock. chǐng-ni shŕ-'èr-dyǎn-jūng dzwò-'wán.

A **wish** (*in the sense of the power to ask for something and have it granted*). ‖The goblin gave the little girl three wishes. *is expressed as* The goblin told the little girl she could request three things. 'shén-shyān gēn shyǎw-'gū-nyang shwō tā kě-yi 'chyéw sān-jyàn-'shŕ.

(*In leave-takings and greetings*). ‖We wished him luck. wǒm 'jù-ta jū-'shŕ-rú-'yì. ‖We sent him our best wishes for luck in his new job. wǒm jù-ta shīn-'shŕ-yè yì-'fān-fēng-'shwèn. ‖Best wishes! (*at end of letter*) jìng-'hèw dà-'ān! ‖Best wishes on your birthday! gěy-ni bày-'shèw! ‖I've come to wish you good-by. wǒ láy °gēn-nín tsź-'shíng. *or* °gěy-nín sùng 'shíng.

Wish *something* (**off**) on 'jyāw-gey, 'twēy-gey. ‖Who wished this job on me? 'shéy bǎ jèy-ge-'shŕ 'twēy-gey 'wǒ-le? ‖Let's wish this off on someone else. dzám bǎ jèy-jyàn-'shŕ °'jyāw-gey (*or* °'twēy-gey) 'byé-rén-ba.

WITH. (*Accompaniment and closely allied meanings*) gēn, hé, túng. ‖I plan to have lunch with him today. wǒ 'dǎ-swàn gēn-ta yí-'kwàr chŕ wǔ-'fàn. ‖Why did you break up with him? nǐ 'wèy-shéme gēn-ta jywé-'jyāw-le? ‖Rent is rising with the cost of living. fáng-'dzū gēn-je 'shēng-hwó-'fèy-yùng yí-'kwàr wàng 'shàng 'jǎng. ‖Your ideas don't agree with mine. nǐ-de-'yì-jyan gēn 'wǒ-de bù-°'yí-'jŕ. *or* °'yí-'yàng. *or* °shyǎng-'hé. *or* °shyǎng-'túng. ‖I beg to differ with you. wǒ gēn nín-de-'jyàn-jye bù-'yí-'yàng.

With each other bǐ-'tsź. ‖The two countries were at war with each other for many years. jèy-lyǎng-'gwó bǐ-'tsź dǎ-'jàng dǎ-le hǎw-jǐ-'nyán-le.

(*Having*) dày, yěw. ‖I want a room with bath. wǒ yàw yì-jyān-dày-dzǎw-'fáng-de-'wū-dz. ‖Your friend talks with an accent. ɹˇ-de-'péng-yew shwō-'hwà °dày (*or* °yěw) 'kěw-yīn. ‖He took a gun with him for protection. tā dày-je yì-gǎn-'chyáng 'fáng-bèy-fáng-bey.

(*Using as instrument*) ná, yùng, shŕ. ‖He chopped down the tree with an ax. tā °ná (*or* °yùng *etc.*). yì-bǎ-'fǔ-dz bǎ-'shù kǎn-'dǎw-le.

(*Including*) lyán, 'jyā-shang, 'dā-shang.

(*Among*) dzày . . .-li. ‖The candidate is more popular with the farmers than with business men. jèy-ge-hèw-shywǎn-'rén dzày 'núng-rén-li bǐ dzày 'shāng-rén-li 'húng.

(*For the sake of*) wèy. ‖He's done some valuable work with the people in rural communities. tā dzày 'shyāng-shyà wèy 'rén-mín dzwò-le dyǎr-yěw-'yí-chu-de-'shŕ-ching.

(*Because of, after, or both*) *expressed by putting the expression following* **with** *in the first part of the sentence, or* yīn-wey. ‖With that remark he left the room. tā shwō-le nàme-yí-jywú-'hwà jyèw tsúng 'wū-dz-li 'chū-chywu-le. ‖With the hot weather the beaches will be crowded. yīn-wey tyār 'rè hǎy-'byār-shang yí-dìng hěn 'jǐ. ‖I went home with a cold. wǒ 'jāw-le dyǎr-'lyáng jyèw hwéy-'jyā-le. ‖The price of radios went up with the increasing demand. wú-shyàn-'dyàn-de-'jyàr 'jǎng-le, shŕ 'yīn-wey 'mǎy-de-rén 'dwō-le.

(*Despite*) 'swéy-rán. ‖With all the work he's done on it, the book still isn't finished. tā 'swéy-rán shr bǎ 'gūng-fu 'dēw gē-shang-le, kě-shr nèy-běr-'shū háy méy-shyě-'wán.

With . . .'s **permission** 'dé-jáw . . .-de-shywǔ-'kě, . . . túng-'yì-de. ‖I made all my plans with the commanding officer's permission. wǒ yí-'chyè-de-'jì-hwá dēw °'dé-jáw jǔ-'gwǎn-'jǎng-gwān-de-shywǔ-'kě-le. *or* °'shŕ jǎng-'gwān túng-'yì-de.

‖**Handle with care!** 'shyǎw-shīn chīng-'fàng!

Leave . . . **with**. ‖Leave your keys with the hotel clerk. *is expressed as* Leave your keys at the hotel desk. bǎ nǐ-de-'yàw-shr 'tswén-dzày lywǔ-'gwǎn-de-'gwèy-shang.

Be pleased with shǐ-hwan, jywé-de . . . hǎw-'kàn (*or other appropriate adjective*). ‖Are you pleased with the view from your windows? nǐ 'shǐ-hwan nǐ-'chwāng-hu-'wày-tew-de-'jǐng-jŕ-ma? *or* nǐ 'jywé-de nǐ-'chwāng-hu-'wày-tew-de-'jǐng-jŕ hǎw-'kàn-ma?

Other English expressions. ‖The house was built with cheap labor. *is expressed as* The labor that built that house was cheap. jèy-ge-'fáng-dz-'gày-de-'gūng-cheng bù-'shíng. ‖Do you want something to drink with your meal? *is expressed as* In addition to what you eat would you also like something to drink? 'chŕ-de yǐ-'wày nín 'háy yàw dyǎr-'shéme 'hē-de-ma? ‖With him, it's all a matter of money. *is expressed as* As he sees things, it's all a matter of money. dzày 'tā kàn, nà 'wán-chywán shŕ 'chyán-de-gwān-shi.

WITHIN. dzày . . . °lǐ-tew *or* °jŕ-'nèy *or* °yǐ-'nèy. ‖I'll be back within a few hours. wǒ 'jǐ-ge-jūng-'téw-yǐ-'nèy jyèw 'hwéy-lay. ‖Speeding is forbidden within the city limits. dzày chéng-'lǐ-tew bù-'jwěn kāy-de tày 'kwày-le.

Other English expressions. ‖Try to keep within the speed limit. *is expressed as* Don't drive too fast. byé bǎ-'chē 'kāy-de tày 'kwày-le. ‖The letters came within a few days of each other. *is expressed as* In between the time of the arrival of the two letters not many days were skipped. lyǎng-fēng-'shìn-dàw-de-shŕ-hew 'jūng-jyàr méy-'gé jǐ-tyān. ‖Please stay within call. is expressed as Don't go far away, OK? byé shàng 'ywǎn-chù-chywù, 'hǎw-ba? or byé dzěw 'ywǎn-le, 'hǎw-ba? ‖Are we within walking distance of the beach? is expressed as Can we walk from here to the beach? tsúng-'jèr dàw hǎy-'byār-shang 'lyēw-da chywù 'shíng-ma? ‖He doesn't live within his income. tā bú lyàng-'rù-wéy-'chū. or tā 'hwā-de dzǔng bǐ 'jìn-de 'dwō.

WITHOUT. méy, méy-yew. ‖We had to do without a car during the summer. yí-'shyà-tyan wǒm méy-yew 'chē, jyèw nème 'dwèy-fu-je 'gwò-de. ‖It's very inconvenient to do this without a car. dzwò 'jèy-ge 'méy(-yew) 'chē 'jēn bù-'fāng-byan. ‖She passed without seeing us. tā 'lù-gwò méy-'chyáw-jyàn wǒ-men. or tā 'dzěw-gwo-chywu de-shŕ-hew méy-'kàn-jyan wǒ-men. ‖He walked right in, without any fear. tā yì-'jŕ 'dzěw-jìn-chywu-le, 'yì-dyǎr yě méy-hày-'pà. ‖Can I get into the hall without a ticket? wǒ méy-'pyàw néng jìn léw-'lǐ-tew chywù-ma? ‖Can this be done without being detected? is expressed as Can this be done and not let anyone see it? yàw-shr 'nème-je, néng-gew 'bú-jyàw-rén 'kàn-chu-lay-ma?

Without delay 'gǎn-jǐn, 'mǎ-shang. ‖I want this work finished without delay. jèy-jyàn-'shŕ děy °'gǎn-jǐn (or °'mǎ-shang) gěy-wo bàn-'wán-le.

It goes without saying háy yùng 'shwō-ma? or 'yùng-bu-jáw 'shwō-le! ‖It goes without saying that this is an imitation. 'háy yùng 'shwō-r a? (or 'yùng-bu-jáw 'shwō-le!) jèy-shŕ ge-'jyǎ-de.

WOMAN (WOMEN). 'nywǔ-rén; in compounds nywǔ. ‖Who's that pretty woman you were just dancing with? nǐ-'gāng-gēn-ta-'tyàw-wǔ-de-nèy-ge-hǎw-'kàn-de-'nywǔ-rén shŕ-'shéy? ‖Do you want a woman doctor? nǐ yàw 'jǎw yí-ge-'nywǔ-dày-fu-ma? ‖Is he a woman hater? is expressed as Doesn't he like women? tā bù-'shǐ-hwan 'nywǔ-rén-ma? ‖There are more women than men in this office. jèy-ge-gūng-shŕ-'fáng-li 'nywǔ-de bǐ 'nán-de 'dwō. ‖WOMEN. nywǔ.

WONDER. To be a wonder (be strange) ('chí-)gwày; (be a remarkable accomplishment) nán 'dé; to wonder that something should be so 'jywé-de hěn 'chí-gwày, bù-'míng-bay, nà-'mèr; to wonder why the same or bù-jŕ-'dàw, shyǎng. ‖It's a wonder that you got here at all. nǐ dàw-'lyǎwr hwèy dàw-jèr 'láy-le, jēn nán 'dé. ‖I wondered why he didn't apologize. wǒ °'jywé-de hěn 'chí-gwày (or °bù-'míng-bay or °nà-'mèr) tā 'dzěme bú-dàw-'chyàn-ne. ‖They watched the airplane with wonder. tām kàn-je nèy-ge-fēy-'jī °'jywé-de hěn (chí-)'gwày. or °jŕ nà-'mèr. ‖I wonder why he doesn't call me up. wǒ °nà-'mèr (or °bù-jŕ-'dàw) tā 'wèy-shéme bù-gěy-wo dǎ dyàn-'hwà. ‖I was just wondering what you were doing. wǒ jèng jèr °nà-'mèr (or °shyǎng) nǐ-nèr gàn 'shéme-ne.

Not wonder if expressed in terms of **most probably** 'dwō-bàn, or for sure jwěn. ‖I shouldn't wonder if he's had car trouble. tā °'dwō-bàn (or °'jwěn) shŕ 'chē chū-le 'máw-bìng-le.

To work (or do) wonders with or for. ‖The new treatment has worked wonders with the child. nèy-ge-'shīn-'jŕ-far jŕ shyǎw-'hár jēn yěw °'chí-shyàw. or °'shyàw-yàn. ‖A new hat will do wonders for her morale. yì-dǐng-'shīn-'màw-dz néng ràng-ta 'tè-byé gāw-'shìng.

For a wonder jēn 'gwày; no wonder nán-gwày...-a. ‖He's got a clean shirt on today, for a wonder. jēn 'gwày, tā 'jyēr hwèy˘ 'chwān-shang gān-jing-chèn-'shān-le. ‖No wonder it's cold (in here); the window is open. 'nán-gwày dzème 'lěng-nga, 'gǎn-ching nèy-ge-'chwāng-hu 'kāy-je-ne.

(A person) chū-'lèy-bá-'tswèy-de-'rén-wù, 'lyǎw-bu-dé-de-'rén-wù; (in an uncomplimentary sense) 'gwày-wu. ‖She can cook, dance, speak nineteen languages, look pretty without any make-up, please a saint or a sinner—she's really a wonder. tā hwèy dzwò-'fàn, hwèy tyàw-'wǔ, hwèy shwō shŕ-'jyěw-jǔng-ywù-'yán, 'bú-yùng dzème-'dǎ-ban jyèw tǐng 'pyàw-lyàng, háy néng jyàn 'shéme-rén shwō shéme-'hwà—tā 'jēn-shŕ ge-°'chū-'lèy-bá-'tswèy-de-'rén-wù. or °'lyǎw-bu-dé-de-'rén-wù.

WONDERFUL. 'tè-byé-'hǎw. ‖We found a wonderful place to spend the summer. wǒm 'jǎw-jáw-le yí-ge-'tè-byé-'hǎw-de-dì-fang chywù gwò-'shyà. ‖He has a wonderful stamp collection. tā sēw-'jí-le yí-tàw-'tè-byé-'hǎw-de-yéw-'pyàw.

WOOD. 'mù-tew; firewood pǐ-'cháy. ‖This kind of wood makes a very hot fire. 'jèy-jǔng-'mù-tew 'shāw-chi-lay hěn 'nwǎn-he. ‖How much wood will you need to build the porch? gày jèy-ge-'láng-dz děy yùng 'dwō-shaw-mù-tew? ‖Pile the wood up neatly behind the house. bǎ jèy-shyē-'mù-tew dzày 'fáng-dz-hèw-tew dwēy-'jěng-chi-le. ‖Build a wood fire in the stove. dzày 'lú-dz-li 'shāw dyǎr-pǐ-'cháy.

Woods (forest) shù-'lín-dz.

WOOL. yáng-'máw, máw; (of a light, fluffy kind) 'máw-rúng; wool thread 'máw-shyàn; wool cloth or material 'yáng-máw-'lyàw-dz. ‖Is this suit made of pure wool? 'jèy-tàw-'yī-shang-de-'lyàw-dz shŕ 'chwén(-yáng)-máw-de-ma? ‖Extra fine blankets, 100% wool. 'shàng-hǎw máw-'tǎn, 'chwén-yáng-'máw-de. ‖The store is having a sale on wool blankets. jèy-pù-dz-de-°'yáng-'máw- (or °'máw-shyàn-, or °'máw-rúng-, or °'máw-) 'tǎn-dz jèng jyàn-'jyà-ne.

WORD. dż (means word with reference to languages other than Chinese, character with reference to Chinese). ‖How do you write that word (that is, character)? nèy-ge-'dż dzème 'shyě? ‖How do you spell that word (not Chinese, or Chinese written alphabetically) nèy-ge-'dż dzème 'pīn? ‖You're only allowed fifty words in the message. 'shìn-li (or dyàn-'bàw-li) yí-'gùng jř shywǔ shyě 'wǔ-shr-ge-'dż. ‖I remember the tune, but I forget the words. 'dyàw-dz wǒ 'jì-de, °'dż (or °'dzèr) kě dēw 'wàng-le. ‖Not a single word is to be changed. 'yí-ge-dzèr yě bù-néng 'gǎy.

(Meaning phrase or short fragment of speech) yí-jywù-'hwà, sometimes yí-ge-'dzèr. ‖There's not a word of truth in what he says. tā-'shwō-de °'yí-jywù-shŕ-'hwà yě 'méy-yew. or °'yí-ge-'dzèr yě bù-néng 'shìn. or expressed as None of what he says is true. °'yì-dyǎr yě bú-shř 'shŕ-hwà. ‖He said a few words to the police before he left. tā gēn 'jǐng-chá °'shwō-le jí-jywù-'hwà (or °'dāw-daw-le jí-'jywù) tsáy 'dzěw-de. ‖I didn't say a word. wǒ 'yí-jywù-'hwà yě méy-°'shwō. or °'tí. or expressed as I didn't say a sound. wǒ 'yì-shēngr yě méy 'yán-ywu. ‖May I have a word with you? wǒ yěw jywù-'hwà yàw gēn-ni °'tí-ti. or °'shwō-shwo. or °'iyǎng-jyang. or °'shāng-lyang-shāng-lyang. or °'tán-tan.

(Meaning message or speech) hwà, hwàr. ‖Did he leave any word? tā 'lyéw(-shya) 'hwàr-le-ma? ‖He left word that you're to call him at East Exchange 3169. tā 'lyéw-le ge-'hwàr, chǐng-nín gěy-ta dǎ dyàn-'hwà, dǎ-daw 'dūng-jywú 'sān-yī-'lyèw-'jyěw. ‖You should have left word with their maid. nǐ gǎy gēn tām-lǎw-'mār lyéw-ge 'hwàr láy-je. ‖I'll take your word for it then. wǒ jyèw 'shìn nǐ-de-'hwà-le. ‖Don't take my word for it; I'm not sure about it myself. 'wǒ-de-hwà (or 'wǒ-shwō-de) 'bú-jyàn-de jyèw dwèy; wǒ-'dż-jǐ yě 'bú-shr 'jwěn jř-daw shř 'dzěme-hwéy-'shř.

Have words with (argue with) gēn . . . °'chǎw yí-dwèn or °'bàn hwéy-'dzwěy. ‖He had some words with her; that's why he left. tā gēn-ta °'chǎw-le yí-dwèn (or °'bàn-le hwéy-'dzwěy); 'yīn-tsž jyèw 'dzěw-le.

Give one's word 'dā-ying, shwō; (very serious) chǐ-'shř. ‖He gave his word that he would finish the job. tā 'dā-ying-le (or tā 'shwō-le or tā-'shwō-de shř) yí-'dìng bǎ jèy-shèr bàn-'wán-le. ‖I give you my word (of honor) that this is absolutely true. 'jèy-shř 'chyān-jēn-wàn-'chywè-de; wǒ gǎn gēn-ni chǐ-'shř.

Beyond words. ‖She's beautiful beyond words. tā-shr °'shíng-rung-bu-chu-'láy-de (or °'méy-hwà kě-yi 'shíng-rung-de or °'shwō-bu-chu-'láy-ue) 'měy.

(Message other than oral; letter) shìn, shyèr; (orders) 'mìng-lìng. ‖Have you had any word from your son lately? 'jìn-lay lìng-'láng °yěw-'shyèr láy-ma? or °shyě-'shìn láy-le-ma? ‖The word was given that we would attack at dawn. yěw 'mìng-lìng shwō (or mìng-ling 'shyà-lay-le, shwō shř, or 'yǐ-jing 'fèng-daw 'mìng-lìng, shwō shř) yì chīng-'dzǎwr jìn-'gūng.

To word tswò-'tsź, shyě, shwō. ‖How do you want to word this telegram? jèy-fēng-dyàn-'bàw dzěme °'tswò-'tsź-ne? or °'shyě-ne? ‖I think it'd be better if you worded it this way. wǒ 'jywé-je háy-shr 'dzème-je °shyě (or °'shwō or °'tswò-'tsź) 'hǎw-dyǎr.

‖In a word, no! 'jyǎn-dwàn-jyé-'shwō, (jyèw-shr) bù-'shíng! or 'yí-jywù-'hwà, bù-'shíng! or 'jŕ-jyé-lyǎw-'dàng-de shwō-ba, bù-'shíng!

In so many words 'pī-cha-pā-'chā-de; or yě 'méy-shwō 'fèy-hwà, yì-'jŕ-de jyèw; or 'yì-dyǎr méy-ràw-'wār-de; or 'tùng-tung-kwār-'kwār-de. ‖I told him in so many words what I thought of him. wǒ 'pī-cha-pā-'chā-de °'mà-le (or °'shwō-le) ta yí-'dwèn. or wǒ °yě 'méy-shwō 'fèy-hwà, yì-'jŕ-de jyèw (or either of the others) 'mà-le ta yí-'dwèn.

Have the last word. ‖She always has to have the last word in an argument. tā gēn-rén °'byàn (or °'jēng-lwèn), 'fěy °shwō-'yíng-le (or °bǎ-rén 'shwō-de méy-'hwà-le) bù-'jŕ.

Put in a good word. ‖Will you put in a good word for me with the old man? (Not very serious) láw-jyà dzày lǎw-'téwr-nàr gěy-wo °'shwō jywù-hǎw-'hwà-ba. or °'chwēy-shywu-chwēy-shywu-ba. or (Pleading) chyéw-ni dzày lǎw-'téwr-nàr gěy-wo °'shwō jywù-hǎw-'hwà-ba. etc.

WORK. (Physical labor) gūng, 'gūng-dzwò; (general, but especially brain work) shř, shèr; to work (at physical labor) dzwò-'gūng, bàn-'gūng; to work (general or of brain work) dzwò-'shř, dzwò-'shèr; to work (of a carpenter, barber, or tailor, especially of a woman tailor) dzwò-'hwó(r); to work at hard labor dzwò kǔ-'lì, dzwò 'lì-chi-hwór, mày 'lì-chi, dzwò 'lèy-hwór; to do light work dzwò 'chīng-sung-hwór, dzwò 'chīng-sheng-hwór. ‖They work forty hours a week at the mill. tām dzày gūng-'chǎng-li yì-shīng-'chī dzwò 'sž-shr-dyǎn-'jūng-de-'gūng. ‖He goes out and works all day and comes back at night tired to death. tā yì-'jěng-tyār °'chū-chywu °bàn-'gūng (or °dzwò-'gūng or °dzwò-'shèr), yè-li hwéy-'jyā de-shŕ-hew 'lèy-de yàw-'mìng. ‖He works every other day. tā 'gé-yì-tyān dzwò yì-tyān-°'gūng. or °'shèr. ‖I'm not working this summer. 'jin-nyán-'shyà-tyan wǒ bú-dzwò-'shř. ‖What kind of work do you do? nǐ-shyàn-dzày-'dzwò-de shř 'shéme-°'shř? or °'shř-ching? ‖He's doing government work. tā dzày 'jèng-fǔ-jī-'gwān dzwò-'shř. ‖He's been out of work since the factory closed. tsúng nèy-ge-gūng-'chǎng gwān-'mén yǐ-'hèw, tā jyèw méy-°'shř-le. or °dzwò-'shř. ‖It took a lot of work to convince him that we were right. hěn °fèy-le dyǎr-'shř (or °'fèy-le dyǎr-'jēw-jé or °'má-fan-le yí-'jèn-dz) tsáy ràng tā-men 'chéng-rèn wǒ-men 'dwèy-le.

To work someone yùng. ‖He works his employees very hard. tā yùng-'rén yùng-de hěn °'kǔ. or °'kè.

To work oneself. ‖She's working herself to death. tā °'dzwò-'shř dzwò-de (or °'tsàw-láw-de or °'tsāw-law 'shèr) tày 'dwō, kwày bǎ tā-'dż-ǐ 'lèy-sž-le.

To work on a book shyě. ‖He's working on a new book. tā 'jèng-dzày shyě yì-běr-'shū.

To work a typewriter or other apparatus yùng. ‖Do you know how to work a typewriter? nǐ hwèy yùng dǎ-dż-'jī-ma?

To work *a region (as a salesman)* dzày . . . mày. ‖**The other salesman has worked this region pretty thoroughly.** 'nèy-yí-ge-mày-hwò-'shĕw yǐ-jing dzày 'jèy-yí-dày-'dì-fang 'mày-de hĕn 'dwō-le.

To work *something into place, loose, etc.* nwó, twēy, bān. ‖**They finally worked the box into place.** tām dàw-'lyǎwr bǎ nèy-ge-'shyāng-dz °'nwó-dàw (*or* °'twēy-dàw *or* °'bān-dàw) nèr chywù-le.

To work loose sūng. ‖**A screw worked loose.** yĕw yí-ge-'lwó-sz sūng-le.

To work *oneself into a mood.* ‖**He worked himself into an angry mood.** tā-dž-'gĕr ywè-°'shyǎng (*or* °'dzwó-me *or* °'dzā-me) ywè shēng-'chì.

To work *something with the hands* yùng-'shĕw °'chwāy *or* °'réw. ‖**Work the dough thoroughly with your hands.** bǎ-'myàn yùng-'shĕw °'chwāy-'hǎw-le. *or* °'réw-'hǎw-le.

To work *something into a context* yín-dàw, 'jyā-dàw. ‖**Can you work this quotation into your speech?** nǐ néng bǎ nèy-jywù-'hwà °'yín-dàw (*or* °'jyā-dàw) nǐ-de-jyǎng-'yǎn-li-ma?

To work on *someone (try to persuade)* shyǎng-'fár (gēn . . . shwō) ràng. ‖**We're working on him to give us the day off.** wǒm jèng shyǎng-'fár ('gēn-ta shwō) ràng-ta fàng wǒ-men yì-tyān-'jýà.

To work on *something (repair)* 'shyēw-li, 'shŕ-dew, nùng. ‖**The mechanic's at work on your car now.** shyàn-'dzày nèy-ge-jī-chi-'jyàng jèng °'shyēw-li (*or* °'shŕ-dew *or* °'nùng) nǐ-de-'chē-ne.

To work hard *at something* yùng 'gūng-fu, shyà 'gūng-fu. ‖**He really worked hard at your portrait.** tā dzày 'nǐ-nèy-jāng-'shyàng-shang jēn °'yùng-le (*or* °'shyà-le) dyǎr-'gūng-fu.

To work one's way through a crowd. ‖**We worked our way through the crowd.** wǒ-men hǎw-'rúng-yi tsáy tsúng nèy-chywún-'rén-li 'jǐ-gwò-láy.

To work one's way through college 'dž-ji gung 'dž-jǐ shàng dà-'shywé.

To work out *a plan* dzwò. ‖**The captain is working out a plan of attack.** lyán-'jǎng jèng-dzày dzwò jìn-'gūng-de-'jì-hwà.

To work out a solution jyĕ-'jywé, 'nùng-chu ge-'jyĕ-gwǒ-lay. ‖**It took us a long time to work out a solution to the problem.** wǒm yùng-le hĕn-'dwō-de-'shŕ-jyān tsáy bǎ nèy-ge-'wèn-tí °'jyĕ-'jywé-le. *or* °'nùng-chu ge-'jyĕ-gwǒ-lay.

To work over *someone* 'jywē-ba. ‖**The lifeguard worked over him for an hour before he could revive him.** jyèw-hù-'ywán 'jywē-ba-le ta yĕw yí-ge-'jūng-'téw, tā tsáy 'hwǎn-gwò-lay.

To work *something over (rework).* ‖**He worked his paper over half a dozen times before he was satisfied with it.** tā-de-'jywàn-dz dzwò-le yĕw 'lyèw-chī-'hwéy tā tsáy jywé-je 'shíng-le.

To work up an appetite. ‖**I've worked up an awful appetite.** wǒ 'lèy-le yí-jèn, 'è-de 'lì-hay. ‖**All that exercise made me work up an appetite.** nèy-jèn-'ywùn-dùng 'nùng-de wǒ 'è 'jí-le.

To work *(be usable, not be out of order)* shíng, bú-'hwày, dzĕw, chéng, yĕw-'yùng, 'kĕ-yi, 'bàn-de-'tūng, 'shíng-chu-chywù. ‖**The elevator isn't working.** dyàn-'tī 'bù-'shíng-le. *or* °'hwày-le. *or* °bù-'dzĕw-le. ‖**Do you think that plan might work?** nǐ shyǎng nèy-ge-'jì-hwà °'shíng-ma? *or* °'chéng-ma? *or* °yĕw-'yùng-ma? *or* °'kĕ-yi-ma? *or* °bàn-de-'tūng-ma? *or* °'shíng-de-chu-'chywù-ma? ‖**How do you think this idea might work out?** nǐ 'jywé-de jèy-ge-'bàn-fa °'shíng-ma? o °'shíng-bu-shíng?

Works *(any kind)* dzwò-'pǐn, 'dzwò-de(-dūng-shi); *(writings)* shyĕ-de(-dūng-shi); *(paintings)* hwà-de (-'hwàr). ‖**All of his works are very popular.** tā-de-dzwò-'pǐn (*or* tā-dzwò-de-'dūng-shi *etc.*) 'rén-rén dēw 'shǐ-hwan.

A work of art. ‖**That's a work of art.** *(As a simple statement of fact)* 'nà-shŕ yí-jyàn-'yì-shù-'pǐn. *(As an aesthetic comment, the expression depending on the type of work involved)* 'nèy-ge °'dzwò-de (*or, of writing or calligraphy,* °'shyĕ-de, *or, of painting,* °'hwà-de, *or, of carving,* °'kè-de, *or, of architecture or handiwork,* °'dzàw-de) 'jēn °'mĕy. *or* °'hǎw-'kàn. *or* °yĕw 'gūng-fu.

A nice piece of work. ‖**That bridge is a nice piece of work.** nèy-ge-'chyáw°-de-'gūng-cheng (*or* °'dzàw-de *or* ˙'shyēw-de) jēn 'hǎw.

WORLD. *(The earth)* 'shŕ-jyè; *especially in literary or semi-literary language:* *(everything below heaven)* 'tyān-shyà, *(on earth)* 'dì-shang, *(among men)* 'rén-jyān, *(the mortal world)* 'rén-shŕ, *(mankind)* 'rén-lèy; **the whole world** 'chywán-shŕ-jyè, *(the whole globe)* chywán-'chyéw, *(all mankind)* 'shŕ-jyè-shang-'swǒ-yĕw-de-'rén, 'rén-lèy; **world power** 'chyáng-gwó *or* 'dà-chyáng-'gwó; *sometimes not expressed in phrases such as* **nothing in the world, no one in the world, (everyone in) the world; World War I** dì-'yí-tsz̀ (*or* 'shàng-tsz̀)-'shŕ-jyè-dà-'jàn; **World War II** dì-'èr-tsz̀ (*or* 'jèy-tsz̀)-'shŕ-jyè-dà-'jàn. ‖**He's traveled all over the world.** chywán-shŕ-'jyè tā °'nǎr dēw 'dàw-gwo. *or* °dēw dzĕw-'byàn-le. *or* tā 'jēw-yéw-gwo chywán-°'shŕ-'jyè. *or* °'chyéw. ‖**He compiled a chronological chart of world history.** tā byān-le yì-bĕr-'shŕ-jyè-'lì-shŕ-'dà-shŕ-nyán-'byǎw. ‖**He's writing a history of the world.** tā jèng-dzày shyĕ yì-bĕn-'shŕ-jyè-lì-'shŕ. ‖**He's been around the world three times.** tā wéy-je chywán-'chyéw dzĕw-gwo 'sān-dzāwr. *or* tā 'sān-tsz̀ 'jēw-yéw shŕ-'jyè. ‖**He planned to conquer the world.** tā shyǎng 'jēng-fú °'chywán-shŕ-'jyè. *or* °'tyān-'shyà. ‖**What part of the world does this fruit come from?** jèy-shyē-'shwĕy-gwǒ shŕ °'dì-'chyéw-shang (*or* °'shŕ-jyè-shang)-'shéme-dì-fang-'chū-de? *or simply* °'nǎr-láy-de? ‖**He's known throughout the world.** 'chywán-shŕ-ｼ,ｭ dēw jŕ-dàw tā-jèy-ge-rén. *or* tā shŕ 'tyān-shyà-wén-'míng. *or* tā shŕ 'míng-jèn 'chywán-'chyéw. ‖**You can't find another like him in the whole wide world.** shyàng-'tā-jèy-yàngr-de-rén °'dzĕw-byàn 'tyān-shyà (*or, with a lantern,* °dǎ-je 'dēng-lung) yĕ 'jǎw-bu-jáw dì-'èr-ge. *or* (*With a bad* *connotation*) tā shr̀ ge-'rén-jyān-shǎw-'yěw-'dì-shang-wú-'shwāng-de-ge-'bǎw-bey. ‖There's not another pearl like this in the whole world. 'jèy-ge-'jū-dz °chywán-shr̀-'jyè méy-yěw dì-'èr-ge. *or* °chywán-shr̀-'jyè méy-yěw bǐ-de-'shàng-de. *or* °chywán-shr̀-'jyè shr̀ 'dú-yí-'fèr. *or* °shr̀ 'rén-jyān-'jr̀-bǎw. *or* °shr̀ 'tyān-shyà-'jr̀-bǎw. *or* °shr̀ 'dì-shang-'wú-shwāng-jr̀-'bǎw. *or* °shr̀ 'tyān-shang-shǎw-yěw-'dì shyà-wú-'shwāng-de-'bǎw-bey. *or* °shr̀ 'rén-jyān-shǎw-'yěw-dì-shang-wú-'shwāng-de-'bǎw-bey. ‖He's a world champion. tā shr̀ 'tyān-shyà-wú-'dí. ‖He's the world champion (*in boxing*). tā shr̀ 'shr̀-jyè-'chywán-wáng. ‖He's the world champion (*in some aspect of track*). tā shr̀ 'shr̀-jyè-gwàn-'jywūn. ‖The whole world will benefit by this new discovery. 'jèy-jǔng-'fā-míng ywú °chywán-shr̀-'jyè (*or* °'shr̀-jyè-shang-'swǒ-yěw-de-'rén, *or* °'rén-lèy) 'dēw yěw 'hǎw-chù. ‖All the countries in the world are represented here in New York. dzày nyéw-'ywē-jer 'shr̀-jyè-'gè-gwó-de-rén 'dēw-yěw. ‖He predicted that the end of the world would come in the year 2001 A.D. tā 'ywù-yán shwō dzày 'èr-chyán-líng-'yī-nyán shr̀ 'shr̀-jyè-mwò-'r̀. ‖Nothing in the world can compare with this. ('shr̀-jyè-shang) 'dzày yě méy-yěw 'jèm-°'yàngr-de-le. *or* (*Only if it is good*) °'hǎw-de-le. *or* (*Only if it is bad*) °'bù-hǎw-de-le. *or* ('shr̀-jyè-shang) 'shéme yě 'bǐ-bu-shǎng 'jèy-ge. ‖No one in the world can do it. (shr̀-jyè-shang) 'shéy yě gàn-bu-'lyǎw. ‖No one else in the world can do it but you. (shr̀-jyè-shang) chú-le-'nǐ 'dzày yě méy-yěw °'néng-dzwò-'jèy-ge-de-'rén-le. *or* °'byé-rén néng dzwò 'jèy-ge-de-le. ‖He thinks he's always right and the world is always wrong. tā jywé-je 'shéy dēw bú-'dwèy, 'jr̀ yěw tā-dz̀-'gěr 'dwèy. ‖There's nothing in the world I'd like better. 'dzày yě méy-yěw bǐ 'jèy-ge jyàw-wǒ °'shǐ-hwān-de-le. *or* (*to do*) °'ywàn-yi-'gàn-de-le. ‖You have nothing in the world to worry about. nǐ yì-'dyǎr yě yùng-bu-jáw °wéy-'nán. *or* °tsāw-'shīn.

The Western world 'shī-yáng(-de-gwó). ‖The whole Western world was shocked. 'shī-yáng-'gè-gwó chywán-dēw dà-'jīng.

The New World *is expressed as* the New Continent shīn-dà-'lù. ‖"The New World" means North and South America. shīn-dà-'lù shr̀ jr̀-je 'nán-'běy-'měy-jēw shwō-de.

The world to come. ‖He worried himself to death thinking about the world to come. tā 'jìng chéw °'sž-hèw 'hwén-líng dzěm-'yàng-le gěy 'chéw-sž-le. *or* (*as said by Christians and Mohammedans*) °'sž-hèw shr̀ thinking about the world to come. tā 'jìng chéw °'sž-le. *or* (*as said by Buddhists and Taoists*) °'sž-hèw jyàn 'yán-wáng-de-'shèr gěy 'chéw-sž-le.

The animal world 'swǒ-yěw-de-'dùng-wù. ‖He studied all about the animal world. 'swǒ-yěw-de-'dùng-wù tā 'dēw yán-jyew-gwo.

The scholastic world 'shywé-shù-'jyè. ‖He's well known in the scholastic world. tā dzày 'shywé-shù-'jyè 'tǐng yěw 'míng-chi.

(*A creation of fancy*). ‖He built up a queer sort of world about himself. tā-'shīn-sž (*or* tā-'shìng-chíng) °'gǔ-gwày. *or* °'gwày-pì. *or* (*Of insanity*) tā 'fēng-feng-dyān-'dyān-de. *or* tā shr̀ ge-'mwó-jeng. ‖He lives in a little world of his own. tā hěn 'gū-pì. *or* tā 'dzwò-jīng gwān-'tyān. *or* tā 'gū-lèw gwǎ-'wén. *or* tā gēn-rén 'méy-shéme 'láy-wang.

For the world, for all the world, for anything in the world 'jywé-bu-'kěn. ‖I wouldn't hurt him for all the world. wǒ 'jywé-bu-'kěn jyàw-tā °chr̀-'kǔ-de. *or* °shèw-'dzwèy-de. *or* °'shīn-li nán-'shèw-de.

Think the world of *is expressed as* like very much. ‖My father thinks the world of you. wǒ-'fù-chin 'shŕ-fen 'shǐ-hwān nǐ. (*See also* VERY, LIKE, RESPECT, *etc.*).

Do one a world of good. ‖It'll do him a world of good to get away from home. tā yàw-shr 'lí-kāy jyā °'dwèy-ywu tā ·'shŕ-dzay yěw shwō-bu-'jìn-de-'hǎw-chu. *or* °'dwèy-ywu tā 'tǐng yěw 'hǎw-chù. *and similar expressions*.

Where in the world (*location*) dzày-'nǎr; (*motion to*) dàw-'nǎr. ‖Where in the world have you been? nǐ-'jè shr̀-dàw-'nǎr chywu láy-je? ‖Where in the world did you find such a queer thing? nǐ-'jè shr̀ dzày-'nǎr °'shywé-mu (*or* °'nèng)-láy-de, 'dzèm-gwày-de-ge-'dūng-shi.

What in the world shéme. ‖What in the world does he mean? tā-'nà shr̀ 'shwō-de-'shéme-ya? *or* tā-'shwō-de 'dēw shr̀ 'shéme-'yì-sz-a?

On top of the world. ‖He's feeling on top of the world because of his new promotion. tā 'shīn-jìn shēng-'gwān-le (*or* tā 'shīn-jìn 'wèy-jr 'shēng-le), swǒ-yǐ 'měy-de 'lyǎw-bu-dé.

WORRY. jāw-'jí. ‖They worry a lot about their children. tām wèy tā-men-de-'háy-dz hěn jāw-'jí. ‖Your actions worry me a lot. nǐ-de-'shíng-wèy ràng-wo hěn jāw-'jí. ‖We were worried when you didn't get here on time. nǐ méy-àn 'shŕ-hew láy, ràng wǒ-men 'jāw-le yí-jèn-'jí. ‖Most of his worries are about money. tā-jāw-'jí-de dwō-'bàr dēw-shr̀ 'chyán.

WORSE. bǐ . . . (háy) °'hwày *or* °'bù-'hǎw; (*more violent*) bǐ . . . (háy) °'lì-hay; get worse *or* worse and worse ywè 'láy ywè 'hwày. ‖The patient felt worse this morning than he did last night. jèy-ge-'bìng-rén jyēr-'dzǎw-chen bǐ dzwór-'wǎn-shang háy bù-'hǎw. ‖The road got worse as we went along. wǒm 'dzěw-de nèy-ge-'lù ywè 'láy ywè 'hwày-le. ‖Her condition got worse and worse. tā-de-'chíng-shíng ywè 'láy ywè 'hwày. ‖It's snowing worse than ever. 'shywɔ' 'shyà-de bǐ yǐ-'chyán gèng 'lì-hay-le.

None the worse. ‖They don't seem any the worse for having got caught in the storm. *is expressed as* They were caught in the storm for a spell, but it's of no consequence. tām ràng nèy-ge-dà-'fēng-dà 'ywǔ 'lwén-le yí-jèn, 'bìng méy-dzěme-'yàng.

WORST. dzwèy 'hwày, dzwèy 'lì-hay, or dzwèy *followed by some other appropriate adjective meaning* **bad** *or* **serious.** ‖That was the worst accident in the city's history. tsúng 'nèy-hwéy-chū-de-'shr̀ shr̀ jèy-ge-'chéng yěw 'shr̀ yǐ-'láy dzwèy-'lì-hay-de. ‖He felt worst about leaving his children. tā 'lí-kay tā-de-'háy-dz-men 'jywé-de 'dzwèy nán-'shèw-le. ‖But wait; I haven't told you the worst! 'háy yěw-ne; wǒ háy méy-'gàw-su ni nèy-ge-dzwèy-'hwày de-ne. ‖The worst of it is that they aren't insured. dzwèy-dzǎw-'gāw-de shr̀ tām méy-'bǎw-gwo 'shyǎn.

At the worst yàw-shr bù-'hǎw de-hwà. ‖At worst, the storm may last a week. yàw-shr bù-'hǎw de-hwà, jèy-ge-baw-fēng-'ywǔ jyèw-shywǔ néng 'gàn yí-ge-shīng-'chī.

If worst comes to worst jyèw-shr 'hwày dàw-°'jyā *or* °'téwr *or* °'jí-dyǎn *or* °bù-'kě-kāy-'jyāw. ‖If worst comes to worst, we can always sell our property. jyèw-shr 'hwày dàw-'jyā, wǒm 'háy néng byàn-'mày wǒ-men-de·chǎn-'yè-ne.

To think (*or* believe) the worst of shyǎng . . .-de-'hwày-chù. ‖He always thinks the worst of everybody. tā 'lǎ y shyang rén-'jyā-de-'hwày-chù.

WORTH. Be worth *so much* (*of a commodity, etc.; not of a person*) jŕ. ‖That horse is worth five hundred dollars. nèy-pǐ-'mǎ jŕ 'wǔ-bǎy-kwày-chyán. ‖Will the result be worth all this trouble? 'jŕ-de jème-'má-fan-ma?

Be worth *so much* (*of a person*) chèn. ‖He's worth a cool million. tā 'chèn yì-bǎy-'wàn.

So much money's worth *of something* -de-. ‖Give me a dollar's worth of sugar. gěy-wo láy yí-kwày-'chyán-de-'táng.

Get one's money's worth gèw-'běr-le. ‖We certainly got our money's worth out of our car. wǒm-jèy-lyàng-'chē kě 'jēn gèw-'běr-le.

Other English expressions. ‖He was never aware of his secretary's real worth. tā 'tsúng-láy jyèw méy-'jywé-chu-lay tā-de-nywǔ-'shū-jì shr̀ 'dwō-me nán-'dé-de. ‖He hung on to the property for all he was worth. tā ná-'jù-le nèy-dyǎr-'chǎn-yè, shwō 'shéme ye bú-fàng-'shěw.

WORTHY. Be worthy of jŕ-de; (*of a person*) pèy. ‖This plan isn't worthy of further consideration. jèy-ge-'bàn-fa 'bù-'jŕ-de (*or* °'jŕ-bu-de) dzày 'kǎw-lywù-le. ‖I don't feel I'm worthy of all that praise. wǒ 'jywé-de wǒ bú-'pèy ràng 'rén-jyā nème 'kwā-jyǎng.

Worthy charities 'jèng-dàng-de- (*or* °'jēn-bàn-'shr̀-de- *or* °'wú-'dì-fang-shang-'jēn-yěw-'hǎw-chu-de-) 'tsź-shàn-'shr̀-yè.

WOULD. (*Past of* will) yàw, hwèy, néng, *or not expressed.* ‖They hoped their wishes would come true. tām pàn-'wàng-je tām-de-'shī-wang shŕ-'shyàn. ‖I thought that would happen. wǒ jywé-je nèy-ge-'shèr yàw °'láy-le. *or* °fā-'shēng-le. ‖He said he'd go

if I would. tā shwō-le 'wǒ yàw ywàn-yi 'chywù 'tā yě 'chywù. ‖She just wouldn't be comforted. dzěme 'àn-wey-ta, tā yě bù-'tīng.

(*In polite questions*) yàw.

(*Probability or improbability*) ywàn-yi, *or a resultative compound in potential form.* ‖He wouldn't take the job for any amount of money. gěy-ta 'dwō-shaw-chyán tā 'yě bú-'ywàn-yi dzwò 'nèy-ge-shr̀. ‖Do you think this bridge would carry a two-ton truck? nǐ shyǎng jèy-ge-'chyáw 'jīn-de-jù 'lyǎng-dwēn-de-kǎ-'chē-ma?

(*Past habitual action*) *expressed with an adverb like* **often** 'cháng-cháng, **always** 'lǎw(-shr) *or* **customarily in the past** 'tsúng-láy. ‖He would study for hours without stopping. tā 'lǎw-shr yí-'chyèr nyàn 'jǐ-dyǎn-jūng-de-'shū, 'yì-dyǎr yě bù-'shyē.

Would like to shyǎng, (shyǎng) yàw. ‖He'd like to have us consider him a friend. tā 'shyǎng gēn wǒ-men láy-'wǎng. ‖What would you like to drink? nǐ yàw 'hē 'shéme?

WOUND. shāng; to be wounded shèw-'shāng. ‖It'll be a couple of months before the wound in his leg can heal. tā-'twéy-shang-de-nèy-kwày-'shāng háy děy 'lyǎ-ywè tsáy néng 'hǎw-ne. ‖Several men were wounded in the explosion. nèy-tsź-bàw-'jà yěw 'hǎw-jǐ-ge-rén shèw-'shāng-le.

Be *or* feel wounded (*emotionally*) shāng-'shīn. ‖She was wounded by his indifference. nèy-ge-'nán-de dwèy-ywu ta nàme-'lěng-dàn, ràng-ta hěn shāng-'shīn.

WRITE (WROTE, WRITTEN). shyě, shyě-'dz̀; write a book shyě-'shū, dzwò-'shū; write letters shyě 'shìn; (*when filling in a form of some kind*) shyě, tyán; write *something* down 'shyě-shyà-láy, 'jì-shyà-láy; write *something* in 'shyě-shang, 'tyán-jìn-chywù; write *a check or receipt* kāy, 'kāy-chu-láy; (*as a career*) shyě-'dzwò. ‖The children are learning how to read and write. 'háy-dz-men jèng shywé nyàn-'shū shyě-'dz̀-ne. ‖He wrote a book about his experiences in the Army. tā bǎ tā-dzày-jywūn-'dwèy-shang-de-'jīng-yàn °'shyě-le (*or* °'dzwò-le) yì-běr-'shū. ‖Who wrote that book you're reading? nǐ-'nyàn-de-nèy-běr-'shū shr̀-'shéy °'shyě-de? *or* °'dzwò-de? ‖He promised to write once a week while he was away. tā 'dā-ying wo tā 'dzěw-le yì-'hèw yí-ge-shīng-'chī 'shyě yì-fēng-'shìn-lay. ‖Have you written your family yet? nǐ yǐ-jing gěy nǐ-'jyā-li shyě-'shìn-le-ma? ‖Write your name in the space at the bottom of the page. bǎ nǐ-de-'míng-dz °shyě-dzay (*or* °tyán-dzay) jèy-'yè-dǐ-shya-de-'kùngr-nèr. ‖Write down that telephone number before you forget it. bǎ ney-ge-'dyàn-hwà-hàw-'mǎr °'shyě-shyà-lay (*or* °'jì-shyà-lay), byé hwéy-'téw 'wàng-le. ‖My candidate wasn't on the ballot, so

I had to write in his name. wǒ-yàw-'shywǎn-de-nèy-ge-'rén 'pyāw-shang 'méy-yew, swǒ-yi wǒ déy bǎ tā-de-'míng-dz °'tyán-jìn-chywù. *or* °'shyě-shang. ‖Please write out that check for me before I go. láw-'jyà, dzày wǒ 'dzěv yǐ-'chyán, bǎ nèy-ge-jř-'pyàw gěy-wo 'kāy-chu-lay, 'hǎw-ba? ‖He hadn't written out a receipt yet. shēw-'tyáwr tā háy méy-'kēy-chu-lay-ne. ‖When she got through college, she planned to write for a career. tā 'dǎ-swàn nyàn-'wán dà-'shywé yǐ-'hèw jyèw ná shyě-'dzwò dàng tā-de-'shř-yè-le. ‖He wrote up an account of the fire for the local paper. tā bǎ nèy-ge-hwǒ-'jǐng gěy běn-'dì-de-bàw-'jř 'shyě-le yí-dwàr-'shyāw-shi. ‖This pen doesn't write well. jèy-gwǎn-'bǐ bù-hǎw °'shyě. *or expressed as* This pen isn't good to use. °'shř. *or* °'yùng.

Write *something* off gēw. ‖When the company failed, we had to write off its debts. nèy-ge-'mǎy-may 'gwān-le de-shř-hewr, wǒm bù-'dé bù-bǎ tā-de-'jàng (gěy) 'gēw-le.

WRONG. tswò. ‖Did I say the wrong thing? wǒ shwō-'tswò-le-ma? ‖I got lost because I took the wrong road. wǒ dzěw-'dyěw-le, yīn-wey wǒ dzěw-'tswò-le 'dàwr-le. ‖I added these figures wrong. wǒ bǎ jèy-shyē-'shùr jyā-'tswò-le. ‖Did I do wrong to wait so long? wǒ 'děng-le dzème-'jyěw, děng-'tswò-le-ma?

Something wrong (*mechanically*) 'máw-bìng. ‖Something is wrong with the telephone. dyàn-'hwà yěw dyǎr-shéme-'máw-bìng. ‖Something went wrong with the plane, so the pilot decided to land. fēy-'jī chū-le dyǎr-shéme-'máw-bìng, swǒ-yi nèy-ge-fēy-jī-'shř jyèw jywé-'dìng 'lè-shya-lay-le.

To be wronged shèw-'chywū, shèw 'wěy-chywū. ‖They feel that they've been wronged. tām 'jywé-de tām shèw-le °'chywū-le. *or* °'wěy-chywu-le.

To be in the wrong tswò. ‖He admitted he was in the wrong, and paid the fine. tā chéng-'rèn tā 'tswò-le, bìng-chyě 'jyāw-le fá-'jīn-le.

Y

YARD. (*Measure of length*) mǎ. (*See also Appendix B*). ‖How much is this material by the yard? jèy-ge-'lyàw-dz 'dwō-shaw-chyán yì-'mǎ?

(*Ground around a house*) *in China such open space is normally enclosed by the house, and is called a* court *or* courtyard 'ywàn-dz; *sometimes called* empty land kūng-'dì. ‖Does this place have a yard for the children to play in? jèy-ge-'dì-fang 'yěw-méy-yew yí-kwày-kūng-'dì kě-yi ràng 'háy-dz-men 'wár-wár?

Lumber yard mù-'chǎng-dz; railroad yards hwǒ-chē-'chǎng-dz *or* (*specifically for repair*) shyēw-chē-'chǎng.

YEAR. (*Of time*) nyán; this year 'jīn-nyán; last year 'chywù-nyán; next year 'míng-nyán (*sometimes* gwò-'nyán). ‖What was the year of your birth? nǐ-shř 'něy-yì-nyán 'shēng-de? ‖I hope to come back next year. wǒ 'shī-wang 'míng-nyán 'hwéy-lay. ‖How long is the school year here? 'jèr yì-'shywé-nyán yěw dwō-'cháng? ‖I haven't done this for years. wǒ 'yěw °'jǐ-nyán (*or* °'hǎw-'jǐ-nyán *or* °'hǎw-'shyě-nyán) méy 'gàn jèy-ge-le. ‖It will take years to finish this work. bǎ jèy-ge-'shř-ching dzwò-'wán-le, háy děy 'hǎw-jǐ-nyán.

(*Of age*) swèy. ‖He's thirty years old. tā 'sān-shr-swèy.

Year in, year out 'hǎw-jǐ-nyán *or* yì-nyán-yì-'nyán-de 'hǎw-jǐ-nyán. ‖He's been at this job year in, year out. tā dzwò nèy-ge-'shř-ching yì-nyán-yì-'nyán-de 'hǎw-jǐ-nyán-le.

To show one's years jyàn-'lǎw. ‖She's beginning to show her years. tā jyàn-'lǎw-le.

YELLOW. hwáng; yellow color 'hwáng-sè, 'hwáng-shǎr, hwáng-de-'ván-sè. ‖Fill in the background with yellow. bǎ 'dyèr tú-chéng 'hwáng-de. ‖She's wearing a bright yellow dress. tā chwān-le yí-tàw-'é-hwáng-de-'yī-shang.

To (turn) yellow byàn-'hwáng. ‖Her wedding dress has all yellowed with age. tā-de-jyē-'hwēn-lǐ-'fú 'nyán-téwr 'dwō-le dēw byàn-'hwáng-le.

(*Part of an egg*) jī-dàn-'hwángr, dàn-'hwángr. ‖Separate the yellow from the white. bǎ jī-dàn-de-'hwángr gēn 'chyēngr 'fēn-kay. *or* bǎ jī-dàn-'hwángr gēn jī-dàn-'chyēngr 'fēn-kay.

Have a yellow streak dǎr-'shyǎw. ‖He seems to have a yellow streak. tā hǎw 'shyàng tyān-'shēng-de dǎr-'shyǎw.

YES. *The affirmative answer to a question is given by repeating the verb or adjective of the question in affirmative (simple) form; this may be reinforced with* it is so shř. ‖Yes, I'll be glad to go. 'shř, wǒ 'ywàn-yi chywù.

To yes. ‖I'm disgusted with the way he always yesses his boss. *is expressed as* I'm disgusted with the way he always, when the boss says a certain thing, agrees with it. wǒ tǎw-'yàn tā 'nà-yàngr 'lǎw-shř 'téwr shwō shéme 'shř shéme.

YESTERDAY. 'dzwó-tyan, dzwór, 'dzwór-ge. Day before yesterday 'chyán-tyan, chyár, 'chyár-ge; day before day before yesterday dà-'chyán-tyan. ‖I just arrived yesterday. wǒ 'dzwór tsáy 'dàw.

YET. Not yet háy bū-, háy méy-. ‖He hasn't come in yet. tā háy méy-'láy-ne.

Not just yet (*in a suggestion*) shyān. ‖Don't go just yet. 'shyān byé 'dzěw-ne.

(*In questions*) 'yǐ-jing. ‖Has he come yet? tā 'yǐ-jing 'láy-le méy-yew?

(*In negative questions*) háy méy-. ‖**Hasn't he come yet?** tā háy méy-'láy-ne-ma?

(*Sometime in the future*) 'shéme-shŕ-hew; (*sooner or later*) dzăw-'wăn. ‖**I'll get him yet!** wŏ dzăw-wăn yàw 'gěy-ta yí-'shyà-dz-le!

And yet kě-shr. ‖**And yet you promised to help me!** nĭ kě-shr 'dā-ying-gwo wŏ '**bāng**-wo '**máng**-a!

YOU (YOUR, YOURS). (*To one person*) nĭ; (*to several people*) nĭ-men, nĭm; (*with especial politeness to one person*) nín; *often omitted and understood from context*. ‖**What do you want?** (nĭ) yàw 'shéme? *or* (nĭm) yàw 'shéme? ‖**This is for you.** 'jèy-gè shŕ °gěy-'nĭ-de. *or* °gěy 'nĭ-men-de. ‖**I'll help you one after another.** wŏ 'yí-ger-yí-'gèr-de 'bāng-je nĭ-men. ‖**All you people with tickets, this way!** nĭm-'gè-wèy-yěw-'pyàw-de, 'jèr láy! ‖**Is this your seat?** jèy-ge shŕ °'nĭ-de- (*or* °'nín-de-) 'dzwòr-ma? ‖**All of you hold on to your tickets!** nĭm-'gè-wèy dēw bă-'pyàw 'lyéw-je! ‖**This hat is yours.** 'jèy-ge-màw-dz shŕ °'nĭ-de. *or* °'nín-de. ‖**Yours is prettier than hers.** 'nĭ-de bĭ 'tā-de hăw-'kàn.

(*Meaning some indefinite person*) *usually not expressed; sometimes* rén, *occasionally* nĭ. ‖**To get there, you take a bus and then the ferry.** shàng-nèr 'chywù, shyăn dzwò gūng-gùng-chì-'chē, rán-'hèw dzày dzwò **lwén-'dù.** ‖**It makes you sick to hear about it.** 'tīng **nèy**-ge ràng-rén 'nì-de-heng.

Your Honor 'lăw-yé.

Yours truly (*at end of letter*) jĭn-'chĭ. ‖**He signed the letter "Yours truly."** tā dzày shìn-'hèw-tew shyě-le "jĭn-'chĭ"-lyăng-ge-'dzèr.

Yourself, yourselves, *see* SELF.

YOUNG. nyán-'chīng, shyăw. ‖**I never worked very hard in my younger days.** wŏ °nyán-'chīng de-shŕ-hew (*or* ° sh′ w de-shŕ-hew) 'méy dzěme tày nŭ-'lì. ‖**I'm not as young as I used to be.** wŏ 'bú-shr yĭ-'chyán name-nyán-'chīng-le. ‖**You're very young for your age.** nĭ 'kàn-je hěn °shyăw. *or* °nyán-'chīng.

(*Immature animals*) 'dzăy-dz, 'dzăr; shyăw *followed by the word for the adult animal.* ‖**The cat fought to protect her young.** nèy-ge-mŭ-'māw wèy 'hù-je °'dzăy-dz (*or* °shyăw-'māw) dă-'jyà.

(*Not far advanced*) dzăw. ‖**The night is still young.** *is expressed as* The day is still early. 'tyān háy 'dzăw-ne. *or as* It's still early. háy 'dzăw-je-ne.

YOUR, YOURS. *See* YOU.

YOUTH. (*Being young*) 'chīng-nyán; (*time of being young*) 'chíng-nyán-de-shŕ-hew. ‖**He has all the enthusiasm of youth.** tā chūng-'măn-le chīng-'nyán-de-'rè-chíng. ‖**His father tried to convince him that youth is the best time of life.** tā-de-'fù-chin gěy-ta 'jyăng, ràng-ta 'míng-bay 'chīng-nyán-de-shŕ-hew shŕ rén-'shēng-de-dzwèy-'hăw-de-shŕ-hewr.

Z

ZERO. (*The written figure*) líng, líng-'dž; (*if written with the Arabic numeral instead of with the Chinese character*) chywār. ‖**You should have three zeros in the answer.** nĭ-nèy-ge-'dá-shùr děy yěw 'sān-ge-°'líng (*or* °'chywār) tsáy 'dwèy-ne.

(*Point on a scale*) líng-'dù; **above zero** líng-'shàng *or unexpressed;* **below zero** líng-'shyà. ‖**The thermome-** ter is five above zero. nèy-ge-hán-shŭ-'byăw shŕ °'wŭ-dù. *or* °líng-'shàng wŭ-'dù. ‖**Does the temperature ever get below zero here?** 'jèr wēn-'dù 'dàw-gwo líng-'shyà-ma?

Visibility zero. ‖**The pilot reported visibility zero.** *is expressed as* The pilot reported that nothing could be seen. nèy-ge-jyà-shŕ-'ywán bàw-'gàw shwō 'shémè yě kàn-bu-'jyàn.

PART V

APPENDIXES

A. KINSHIP TERMS

Chinese kinship terms ("father, uncle, cousin" and the like) are confusing to speakers of English because in certain cases relative *age* of speaker and person referred to, or of intermediaries in the relationship, is a factor. The following outline will help. Characters equivalent to the elements which occur are listed to the left.

fù 父
chīn 親
bà 爸
dyē 爹
jyā 家
yán 嚴
shyān 先
lìng 令
dzwēn 尊
yé 爺
mǔ 母
mā 媽
nyáng 娘
tsź 慈
táng 堂
shwāng 雙

Parents. "Father" is 'fù-chin; child-words like "papa" are 'bà-ba and dyē. One refers to his own father politely as wǒ-'fù-chin, jyā-'fù, or jyā-'yán; or, if he is deceased, shyān-'fù or shyān-'yán; the father of the person addressed is politely referred to as nǐ-'fù-chin, (nín-de-)lǎw-tày-'yé, or lìng-'dzwēn. "Mother" is 'mǔ-chin; child-words are mā, 'mā-ma, and nyáng. One refers to his own mother politely as wǒ-'mǔ-chin, jyā-'mǔ, or jyā-'tsź, or, if she is deceased, shyān-'mǔ or shyān-'tsź; the mother of the person addressed is politely referred to as nǐ-'mǔ-chin, (nín-de-)lǎw-'tày-tay, or lìng-'táng. The collective terms for parents are fù-'mǔ and (literary) shwāng-'chīn.

shyūng 兄
gē 哥
dì 弟
jyě 姐, 姊
mèy 妹
shè 舍

Brothers and Sisters. The fundamental elements involved are *shyūng or *gē for "brother older than the speaker", *dì for "brother younger than the speaker", *jyě for "sister older than the speaker", and *mèy for "sister younger than the speaker". In referring to a brother or sister one says 'gē-ge, 'dì-di, 'jyě-jye, and 'mèy-mèy. In referring politely to one's own brother or sister, when addressing someone outside the family, one may say rather jyā-'shyūng, shè-'dì, jyā-'jyě, and shè-'mèy. In referring politely to the brother or sister of the one spoken to, one says often lìng-'shyung, lìng-'dì, lìng-'jyě, and lìng-'mèy. Collective terms are 'dì-shyung "brothers" and jyě-'mèy "sisters".

The children in a family are sometimes designated serially: dà-'gē, èr-'gē, sān-'gē and so on for the older brothers, shyǎw-'dì(-di) for the youngest brother (or for oneself); dà-'jyě, èr-'jyě and so on for sisters; shyǎw-'mèy for the youngest little sister; lǎw-'dà, lǎw-'èr, lǎw-'sān (or lǎw-'sār) and so on, either naming just the males in order or naming all the children, male and female, in order. Such terms are used generally within the family. (dà "big"; shyǎw "small"; lǎw "old".)

843

ér	兒	**Children.** Parents address their children by name, and refer to them familiarly as
nywǔ	女	wǒm-(nèy-ge-)lǎw-'dà "our oldest son", wǒm-(nèy-ge-)lǎw-'èr "our second oldest son",
láng	郎	and so on. Other terms used to refer to one's children are (wǒ-de-)'háy-dz "(my)
ày	愛	child", -'ér-dz "(my) son", -'nywǔ-ér "(my) daughter". Very formally, as in corre-

spondence, a parent may refer to sons simply as ér, to daughters simply as nywǔ. The children of the person addressed are formally referred to as lìng-'láng "your son" and lìng-'ày "your daughter"

jàn	丈	**Husband and Wife.** The general rather formal terms are 'jàng-fu and 'chī-dz. At
fū	夫	present reference is often made to any husband or wife with the terms 'shyān-sheng
chī	妻	"mister, sir", and 'tày-tay "Mrs., madam". An older term which one used in referring
fù	婦	to one's own wife when speaking to someone outside the family circle is 'nèy-rén "person

who stays within (the house)". A husband and wife are collectively referred to as fū-'fù, gūng-mu-'lyǎ, gūm-'lyǎ, lyǎng-'kěw-dz, or lyǎng-'kěwr.

yé	爺	**Grandparents.** Paternal grandfather is called 'yé-ye or dzǔ-'fù; paternal grandmother
dzǔ	祖	is called 'nǎy-nay or dzǔ-'mǔ. Maternal grandfather is 'lǎw-yé or wày-dzǔ-'fù; maternal
nǎy	奶	grandmother is 'nǎy-nay or wày-dzǔ-'mǔ. The terms lìng- "your", jyā- "my", and
wày	外	shyān- "my deceased" may be prefixed to dzǔ-'fù and dzǔ-'mǔ. Great-grandfather
dzēng	曾	(father's paternal grandfather) is dzēng-'dzǔ, and his father is sāw-'dzǔ; their wives
gāw	高	are dzēng-dzǔ-'mǔ and gāw-dzǔ-'mǔ. Other relationships than those on the father's

father's side are indirectly expressed as "father's maternal grandfather", "maternal grandmother's father", and so on.

swēn	孫	**Grandchildren.** One's sons' sons are 'swēn-dz; one's sons' daughters are swēn-'nywǔr.
chúng	重	One's daughters' sons are wày-'swēn; one's daughters' daughters are wày-swēn-'nywǔr.
shywán	玄	Great-grandchildren through the male line are 'dzēng-swēn or 'chúng-swēn-dz; their

sons are 'shywán-swēn. Other great-grandchildren than those through the male line are called "daughter's male-line grandchildren", "son's female-line grandchildren", and so on.

bwó	伯	**Uncles and Aunts.** An older brother of one's father is called 'bwó-bwo or bwó-'fù; if
shū	叔	there are several, they are enumerated as dà-'bwó-bwo, èr-'bwó-bwo, and so on. lǎw-'bwó
shěn	嬸	"old uncle" is a term of address to one's father's male friend or the father of one's friend.
gū	姑	An aunt who is the wife of one's father's older brother is called bwó-'mǔ; such aunts
fū.	夫	are likewise numbered, depending not on their own relative age but on the relative age
jyèw	舅	of their husbands. An alternate way of numbering such aunts is with the terms dà-'mā,
yí	姨	èr-dà-'mā, and so on.

A *younger* brother of one's father is called 'shū-shu or shū-'fù, numbered as èr-shū and so on. The numbering is in terms of position among *all* the brothers, not just the younger ones, so that there can be no dà-'shū, no èr-'shū if the father is the second son of his parents, and so on.

An aunt who is the wife of one's father's younger brother is called 'shěn-dz or shěn-'mǔ, similarly numbered on the basis of the relative ages of their husbands.

An aunt who is one's father's sister (any age) is called 'gū-gu, gū-'mā, or gū-'mǔ. numbered dà-, èr-, etc. An uncle who is the husband of such an aunt is called 'gū-fū, numbered on the basis of their wives' relative ages, not their own.

An uncle who is one's mother's brother (any age) is called 'jyèw-jyew or jyèw-'fù, numbered as are the others. The wife of such an uncle is called 'jyèw-mǔ, similarly numbered.

An aunt who is one's mother's sister (any age) is called yér or yí-'mǔ, with similar numbering; the husband of such an aunt is called 'yí-fū.

jŕ	侄 姪	
shēng	甥	

Nephews and Nieces. Your father's brothers and sisters, and your father's brothers' wives, call you 'jŕ(-dz) or 'jŕ-er if you are male ("nephew"), 'jŕ-nywur if you are female ("niece").

Your father's sisters' husbands, however, will prefix those terms with wày-.

Your mother's brothers and sisters, and their wives and husbands, will call you 'wày-sheng if you are male, wày-sheng-'nywŭr if you are female.

Most of these terms can be enumerated when there is more than one: dà-'jŕ-dz, èr-'jŕ-dz, and so on; dà-'wày-sheng, èr-'wày-sheng, and so on.

táng	堂
shū	叔
bwó	伯
byǎw	表

Cousins. The children of two brothers may call each other simply by the various terms for "brother" and "sister" (older and younger in each case). When necessary to specify that the relationship is that of cousins, not of brothers and sisters, the term táng- or 'shū-bwo is prefixed.

The children of two sisters or of a brother and sister, but of the same generation, call each other by the terms byǎw-'gē "male cousin older than oneself", byǎw-'dì "male cousin younger than oneself", byǎw-'jyě "female cousin older than oneself", byǎw-'mèy "female cousin younger than oneself". When talking about these cousins, gū- is prefixed to specify the child of one's father's sister, and yí- is prefixed to specify the child of one's mother's sister. Without one of these prefixes, the terms are assumed to refer to children of one's mother's brother.

ywè	岳
jàng	丈
gūng	公
pwó	婆
shywù	壻，婿
shí	媳
fù	婦
sǎw	嫂
bāy	伯
lyán	聯
jīn	襟

In-Laws. A man calls his father-in-law ywè-'fù, and refers to him when speaking to others as 'jàng-rén; he calls his mother-in-law ywè-'mŭ and refers to her as jàng-'mŭ or jàng-mŭ-'nyáng. A woman calls her father-in-law 'bà-ba and refers to him as 'gūng-gung; she calls her mother-in-law 'mā-ma and refers to her as 'pwó-pwó. Notice that a woman calls her husband's parents by the same names he uses.

A man or woman calls his or her sons-in-law and daughters-in-law by name, but refers to a son-in-law as 'nywŭ-shywù and a daughter-in-law as ér-'shí-fu or ér-'shí-fer.

A sister-in-law who is the wife of an elder brother is called 'sǎw-dz, numbered 'dà-sǎw, 'èr-sǎw, etc.

A sister-in-law who is the wife of a younger brother is called dì-'mèy.

A sister-in-law who is the older sister of one's wife is called dà-'yí-dz; the younger sister of one's wife is shyǎw-'yí-dz. All sisters of one's wife may be numbered as dà-'yí, èr-'yí, etc.

A brother-in-law who is the brother of one's wife is called by name or by the terms the wife uses, but the wife's older brother is referred to as nèy-'shyūng, her younger brother as nèy-'dì.

A brother-in-law who is one's older sister's husband is called 'jyě-fu; a younger sister's husband is 'mèy-fu.

A brother-in-law who is one's wife's sister's husband is referred to as 'lyán-jīn, or, by number, dà-'yí-fu, èr-'yí-fu, etc. He is addressed by personal name.

A wife addresses her husband's brothers and sisters as he does, but older brothers of one's husband may be referred to as 'dà-bāy-dz, and younger brothers as 'shyǎw-shū-oz.

B. WEIGHTS AND MEASURES

The forms treated in this Appendix are all grammatically *Mmeas.* There are three systems in use: the *Old Standard*, adopted in 1914; the *Market Standard*, adopted in 1929 as a step towards clearer correlation with the Metric System; and the *Metric System*, now official for government use but not yet universal. English equivalents are given in what follows when they exist; otherwise the Chinese term is defined in terms of other Chinese terms and by equivalence in English or Metric measure.

Weight

OLD STANDARD

分	fēn	*none*	
錢	chyán	mace = 10 fēn	
兩	lyǎng	tael = 10 chyán = 37.8 grams	
斤	jīn	catty = 16 lyǎng =604.79 grams, or 1.33 pounds	
擔	dàn	picul =100 jīn = 60.479 kilos, or 133.33 pounds	

MARKET STANDARD

The terms are the same as the above, with shr̀ 市 prefixed. The Market Standard lyǎng=31.25 grams, or 1.1 ounces; the Market Standard jīn=500 grams, or 1.1 pounds; the Market Standard dàn=110.23 pounds.

METRIC SYSTEM

The terms, except for metric ton, are made by prefixing gūng 公 to the Old Standard terms:

gūng-'fèn	gram
gūng-'chyán	decagram
gūng-'lyǎng	hectogram
gūng-'jīn	kilogram
gūng-'dwèn	metric ton (100 kilograms)

Capacity

OLD STANDARD

合	hé		
升	shēng =10 hé	=1.09 liquid quarts, or 1.035 liters	
斗	děw =10 shēng		
觚	hú = 5 děw		
石	shŕ = 2 hú		

MARKET STANDARD

Formed from the above by prefixing shr̀ 市 ; hú is omitted. 10 Market Standard hé=1 Market Standard shēng=1 liter; 10 shēng=1 děw; 10 děw=1 shŕ.

METRIC SYSTEM

Formed from the Old Standard terms by prefixing gūng 公 , omitting hú:

gūng-'hé	deciliter
gūng-'shēng	liter
gūng-'děw	decaliter
gūng-'shŕ	hectoliter

Length

OLD STANDARD

分	fēn		
寸	tswèn=	10 fēn	= 1.41 inches
尺	chř =	10 tswèn	=14.1 inches
丈	jàng =	10 chř	=11.75 feet
里	lǐ =	180 jàng	=about ⅓ mile

MARKET STANDARD

Formed from the above by prefixing shř 市 . A Market Standard chř=⅓ meter; the Market Standard lǐ is defined as 150 jàng, thus equaling ½ kilometer or 0.31 mile.

METRIC SYSTEM

Formed from the Old Standard terms by prefixing gūng 公 ; tswèn is omitted:

gūng-'lǐ	millimeter
gūng-'fēn	centimeter
gūng-'chř	meter
gūng-'jàng	decameter
gūng-'lǐ	kilometer

Area

"Square meter, square inch", and so on, are formed by prefixing fāng 方 to the appropriate term of length.

OLD STANDARD

畝	mǔ =	60 fāng-'jàng= ⅛ acre
頃	chǐng	=100 mǔ
方里	fāng-'lǐ	=540 mǔ

MARKET STANDARD

Prefix shř 市 as usual. One shř-'mǔ=0.1647 acre; one shř-'chǐng=16.47 acres, or 100 shř-'mǔ.

METRIC SYSTEM

Prefix gūng 公 as usual. A gūng-'mǔ is an are; a gūng-'chǐng is a hectare.

General

Certain of the most important terms of the English system of weights and measures are formed from the nearest equivalents in the various Chinese systems by prefixing yīng "English". Thus yīng-'mǔ is an acre, yīng-'chř an English foot, yīng-'lǐ an English mile. bàng 磅 "pound" is a word taken from English.

When finer subdivisions of any system of weighing or measuring are needed, there is a series of four terms which are used, each specifying a tenth of the preceding:

分	fēn
釐，厘	lí
毫	háw
絲	sž

The first two of these will be found in the above tables. Thus, referring to length, gūng-'háw is ¹⁄₁₀ millimeter, gūng-'sž ¹⁄₁₀₀ millimeter; in referring to weight the same terms are ¹⁄₁₀ and ¹⁄₁₀₀ gram.

White Bridge, Gweilin